BERND MANTZ

GABRIEL MANTZ

YEARBOOK OF EUROPEAN FOOTBALL

2021-2022

British Library Cataloguing in Publication Data
A catalogue record for this book is available from the British Library

ISBN 978-1-86223-467-3

Copyright © 2021, SOCCER BOOKS LIMITED (01472 696226)
72 St. Peter's Avenue, Cleethorpes, N.E. Lincolnshire, DN35 8HU, England

Web site www.soccer-books.co.uk • e-mail info@soccer-books.co.uk

Printed in the UK by 4edge

Dear Readers

It was hoped that the 2020/2021 season would be the first "after the pandemic", but unfortunately this was not to be the case and European football once again had to deal with the difficulties caused by pandemic conditions. Due to these difficulties, the previous season had been completed much later than usual so most championships did not commence until September 2020 with the associated transfer period also delayed. This led to the requirement of a hectic schedule of games for the season to be completed in time for the postponed Euro 2020 tournament which was rearranged for June and July 2021.

The games for the 2nd UEFA Nations League took place between September and November 2020 with all 55 UEFA countries – spread over 4 leagues – playing in the group stage. In League A, all 4 groups were won by the teams which were among the favourites so there were no real shocks other than some unexpected results such as Spain's 6-0 demolition of Germany! Italy, Belgium, France and Spain qualified for the finals, which will be played during the autumn of 2021. In the other Leagues, Hungary (League B3) won promotion to League A although the three other participants in the group (Serbia, Russia and Turkey) were more highly ranked. In League C1, Luxembourg collected a remarkable 10 points (3 wins against Cyprus, Azerbaijan and Montenegro with the last 2 won away from home!) but their efforts weren't quite enough to win promotion. Albania topped League C4 to win promotion to League B.

During the free dates in the international calendar, some friendlies were played, but more important were the play-offs for Euro 2020 where the final four participants were determined. Iceland won their first match against Romania, but were defeated by Hungary in Budapest, losing to a goal in the final seconds of the game. It seems that the exceptional generation of Icelandic players which has overachieved is slowly becoming too old and the new generation isn't at the same level. Scotland won both of their play-off games on penalties to qualify for their first major tournament since 1998, Slovakia defeated Northern Ireland in Belfast following extra-time and North Macedonia qualified for a major tournament for the first time.

When the original plans for the Euro 2020 tournament were revealed, with the matches to be played in 11 cities across Europe from London to Bakı, not many were as enthusiastic about the idea as Michel Platini, the President of UEFA at the time. The difficulties for fans travelling to watch their team in different countries would always have been a problem and the ongoing pandemic made this even more the case with travel restrictions making it all but impossible to attend some games. Despite the postponement of the tournament for 12 months, it wasn't possible for a return to normality, much as this was desired by all, and the number of spectators allowed in stadia varied dependent on the country-specific COVID-19 measures in place. Only Hungary, with a relatively high vaccination rate, decided to allow normal attendances without any restrictions, but many of the other matches didn't have quite the atmosphere which can be generated by a full stadium. In the event, there were no serious outbreaks of infection within the teams despite a small number of cases and play was able to continue as scheduled.

There were some great games, big surprises and a beautiful, tragic finale. Almost all the favourites prevailed in the group phase, but some big names were eliminated in the Second Round of 16. Chief of these names were the reigning World Champions, a hugely-talented France team, who were guilty of complacency as they squandered a 3-1 lead against Switzerland in the final 15 minutes of regulation time before losing on penalties. Germany had only just managed to survive the group stage following a very lucky 2-2 draw against Hungary but weren't so lucky against a strong England team, a defeat which marked the end of the successful Joachim Löw era. Title-holders Portugal were also eliminated, losing by a single goal to Belgium and not even a Ronaldo in good form was enough to see them through this time. The Netherlands were feeling confident after their impressive attacking play earned 3 wins in the group stage but were shocked by the Czech Republic who won 2-0. Sweden faced the Ukraine who had only just sneaked through the group stage finishing with the worst record of all qualifiers (1 win and 2 defeats). After a tense and hard-fought game, the Ukraine team left it as late as possible to win, scoring in additional time at the end of extra-time! Italy – following a perfect group stage with 3 wins and no goals conceded – found Austria a tough nut to crack but eventually won 2-1 after extra-time. In an exciting game, Spain raced into a 3-1 lead against Croatia only to concede two late goals, the equaliser coming in stoppage time. However, the Spaniards responded well and scored twice in extra-time to seal their place in the quarter-finals. Last, but not least, Denmark proved much too strong for Wales and cantered to a 4-0 victory. Following the shocking events of their first game in the tournament when midfielder Christian Eriksen almost lost his life following a cardiac arrest but was saved by the prompt actions of medical staff, the team's progression without their talisman was well-deserved.

In the quarter-finals, the strongest teams progressed, though some managed it more easily than others. The Spanish team faced an obdurate Swiss side who equalised after conceding an early goal and then held on to take the game to penalties. However, all the hard work by Switzerland was undone following a hopeless performance in the shoot-out where they scored with just 1 of their 4 kicks and so the Spaniards progressed. The toughest match to call was between Italy, who had played some of the best football in the tournament and Belgium, who were the World's number 1 ranked team. Italy edged out the Belgians in a game featuring some excellent play from both sides. In the other two matches, Denmark proved too good for the Czechs and England comfortably eased past a tired-looking Ukraine side.

It is probably fair to say that the semi-finalists were the 4 best teams in the tournament and Italy faced Spain in a close and enthralling semi-final match. Despite dominating possession, the Spaniards' lack of a top-quality striker once again showed as they faced extra-time for the third consecutive game and it was no surprise when Italy won the penalty shoot-out. In the other game, England were the dominant team against Denmark but required extra-time to overcome their determined yet tired-looking opponents and reach their first major final for 55 years. Effectively playing with home advantage in front of large partisan crowd at Wembley following relaxation of Covid restrictions, England looked to be the favourites in the final and took the lead as early as the second minute. However, Gareth Southgate's young team failed to build on the lead, allowing Italy to dominate possession and the second-half equaliser was fully deserved. There were no further goals and it was no surprise when the Italians won the ensuing penalty shoot-out. The England goalkeeper, Pickford, did well to save two penalties but England failed with three, two of which were missed by Rashford and Sancho, players brought on just before the final whistle to take a penalty! The Italians were the best team in the tournament and deserved to win their second European Championship title but Southgate's young team continues to improve and perhaps inch their way towards a much-desired trophy.

At the end of March 2021, the first matches of the 2022 FIFA World Cup Qualifiers also took place in Europe. After just a few games it was too early to conclude what might happen in the competition, but some results were unexpected. Spain only managed to draw 1-1 against Greece despite home advantage, World Champions France also drew 1-1 against Ukraine in Paris, and then the Ukrainians couldn't beat Kazakhstan in Kyiv. Denmark began qualification very well, with three wins including a 4-0 thumping of Austria in Vienna. Turkey also started furiously with a 4-2 victory against the Netherlands and a 3-0 victory against Norway but then couldn't beat Latvia. Most surprisingly, Germany lost 3-2 in Duisburg to North Macedonia! The qualifiers will end in November 2021, with the 10 Group winners automatically qualifying for the 2022 FIFA World Cup Final Tournament and 12 other teams entering play-offs in March 2022 to determine the final 3 European participants.

At club level, the season began with the European Super Cup which was won by FC Bayern München. In the calendar year 2020, this meant that Bayern won practically every competition they entered – the Bundesliga Championship and National Cup followed by the German Super Cup, the Champions League, the European Super Cup and finally the FIFA Club World Cup – an unbelievable winning streak!

The result of the 2020/2021 UEFA Champions League was a little unexpected, but deserved, as an all-English final was won by Chelsea FC who beat Manchester City FC by a single goal. This was the London club's second European title and the result certainly couldn't have been predicted in January 2021 when the team were struggling despite great expenditure on players during the summer. However, a remarkable turnaround in fortunes following the arrival of German coach Thomas Tuchel in late January saw the team galvanised and their victory was fully deserved.

The UEFA Europa League 2020/2021 went back to Spain yet again for the 7th time in a decade. Manchester United FC were favourites with an array of talented attacking players but failed to perform against a well-organised Villarreal CF team and the game finished 1-1 after extra-time. In a remarkable penalty shoot-out, both teams scored all of their first 10 penalties which meant the goalkeepers were required to step up and take their turn. Rulli, the Villarreal keeper, scored his penalty then saved the effort from his counterpart, De Gea, to win the club a first major trophy.

It should be noted that for this season, the inherent scheduling issues caused by the ongoing pandemic meant that the qualifying games for both of the European club trophies were limited to just one game instead of two and the team to play at home in each tie was determined by the drawing of lots.

This fourth edition of the Yearbook of European Football contains complete statistics for the national championships of all European countries with league results and tables. Player appearances and goals scored are presented for all top division clubs from Europe, this year including Kosovo. You will also find national cup competition details including final match statistics and of course there are also complete statistics for national teams and the international players for each country and their clubs. Squads of all 24 teams from the Euro 2020 tournament are also presented.

Great thanks once again to Mr. Dirk Karsdorp for providing full line-ups and complete statistics for both of the major European Club competitions during 2020/2021.

Please enjoy the read!

The Author

FIFA COUNTRY CODES

EUROPE

ALB	Albania	GER	Germany	NIR	Northern Ireland
AND	Andorra	GIB	Gibraltar	NOR	Norway
ARM	Armenia	GRE	Greece	POL	Poland
AUT	Austria	HUN	Hungary	POR	Portugal
AZE	Azerbaijan	ISL	Iceland	IRL	Republic of Ireland
BLR	Belarus	ISR	Israel	ROU	Romania
BEL	Belgium	ITA	Italy	RUS	Russia
BIH	Bosnia-Herzegovina	KAZ	Kazakhstan	SMR	San Marino
BUL	Bulgaria	KVX	Kosovo	SCO	Scotland
CRO	Croatia	LVA	Latvia	SRB	Serbia
CYP	Cyprus	LIE	Liechtenstein	SVK	Slovakia
CZE	Czech Republic	LTU	Lithuania	SVN	Slovenia
DEN	Denmark	LUX	Luxembourg	ESP	Spain
ENG	England	MLT	Malta	SWE	Sweden
EST	Estonia	MDA	Moldova	SUI	Switzerland
FRO	Faroe Islands	MNE	Montenegro	TUR	Turkey
FIN	Finland	NED	Netherlands	UKR	Ukraine
FRA	France	MKD	North Macedonia	WAL	Wales
GEO	Georgia				

ASIA

AFG	Afghanistan
AUS	Australia
BHR	Bahrain
CAM	Cambodia
CHN	China P.R.
TPE	Chinese Taipei
IDN	Indonesia
IRN	Iran
IRQ	Iraq
JPN	Japan
JOR	Jordan
KOR	Korea Republic
KUW	Kuwait
KGZ	Kyrgyzstan
LIB	Lebanon
MAS	Malaysia
MON	Mongolia
PLE	Palestine
PHI	Philippines
KSA	Saudi Arabia
TJK	Tajikistan
TKM	Turkmenistan
UAE	United Arab Emirates
UZB	Uzbekistan

AFRICA

ALG	Algeria
ANG	Angola
BEN	Benin
BFA	Burkina Faso
BDI	Burundi
CMR	Cameroon
CPV	Cape Verde Islands
CTA	Central African Republic
CHA	Chad
COM	Comoros Islands
CGO	Congo
COD	D.R. Congo
EGY	Egypt
EQG	Equatorial Guinea
ERI	Eritrea
GAB	Gabon
GAM	Gambia
GHA	Ghana
GUI	Guinea
GNB	Guinea-Bissau
CIV	Ivory Coast
KEN	Kenya
LBR	Liberia
LBY	Libya
MAD	Madagascar
MWI	Malawi
MLI	Mali
MTN	Mauritania
MRI	Mauritius
MAR	Morocco
MOZ	Mozambique
NAM	Namibia
NIG	Niger
NGA	Nigeria
RWA	Rwanda
STP	São Tome e Principe
SEN	Senegal
SLE	Sierra Leone
RSA	South Africa
TAN	Tanzania
TOG	Togo
TUN	Tunisia
UGA	Uganda
ZAM	Zambia
ZIM	Zimbabwe

NORTH AND CENTRAL AMERICA

ATG	Antigua and Barbuda
BRB	Barbados
CAN	Canada
CRC	Costa Rica
CUB	Cuba
CUW	Curaçao
DOM	Dominican Republic
SLV	El Salvador
GYF	French Guiana
GLP	Guadeloupe
GUA	Guatemala
GUI	Guyana
HAI	Haiti
HON	Honduras
JAM	Jamaica
MTQ	Martinique
MEX	Mexico
NCA	Nicaragua
PAN	Panama
SKN	Saint Kitts and Nevis
SUR	Suriname
TRI	Trinidad and Tobago
USA	United States

SOUTH AMERICA

ARG	Argentina
BOL	Bolivia
BRA	Brazil
CHI	Chile
COL	Colombia
ECU	Ecuador
PAR	Paraguay
PER	Peru
URU	Uruguay
VEN	Venezuela

OCEANIA

NZL	New Zealand
PNG	Papua New Guinea

OTHER ABBREVIATIONS

DOB Date of birth
M Matches played
G Goals
(s) Matches played as a substitute

(F) International friendly matches
(ECQPO) 2020 Euro Championship Play-offs
(EC) 2020 European Championship Finals
(WCQ) 2022 FIFA World Cup Qualifiers
(UNL) 2020-2021 UEFA Nations League
(BC) 2021 Baltic Cup

SUMMARY

COMPETITIONS FOR NATIONAL TEAMS

EUROPEAN CLUB COMPETITIONS

NATIONAL ASSOCIATIONS

COMPETITIONS FOR NATIONAL TEAMS

UEFA EUROPEAN CHAMPIONSHIP 2020

QUALIFYING PLAY-OFFS

Teams that failed to reach the final tournament in the qualifying group stage could still qualify through the play-offs. Each league in the 2018/2019 UEFA Nations League was allocated one of the four remaining final tournament spots. Four teams from each league that had not already qualified for the European Championship finals competed in the play-offs of their league. The play-off berths were first allocated to each Nations League group winner, and if any of the group winners had already qualified for the European Championship finals, then to the next best ranked team of the league.

Path A	08.10.2020	Reykjavík	Iceland - Romania	2-1(2-0)
	08.10.2020	Sofia	Bulgaria - Hungary	1-3(0-1)
	12.11.2020	Budapest	**Hungary** - Iceland	2-1(0-1)

Path B	08.10.2020	Sarajevo	Bosnia and Herzegovina - Northern Ireland	1-1(1-0,1-1,1-1); 3-4 on penalties
	08.10.2020	Bratislava	Slovakia - Republic of Ireland	0-0; 4-2 on penalties
	12.11.2020	Belfast	Northern Ireland - **Slovakia**	1-2(0-1,1-1)

Path C	08.10.2020	Glasgow	Scotland - Israel	0-0; 5-3 on penalties
	08.10.2020	Oslo	Norway - Serbia	1-2(0-0,1-1)
	12.11.2020	Beograd	Serbia - **Scotland**	1-1(0-0,1-1,1-1); 4-5 on penalties

Path D	08.10.2020	Tbilisi	Georgia - Belarus	1-0(1-0)
	08.10.2020	Skopje	North Macedonia - Kosovo	2-1(2-1)
	12.11.2020	Tbilisi	Georgia - **North Macedonia**	0-1(0-0)

Teams in bold were qualified for the final tournament.

FINAL TOURNAMENT

The 2020 UEFA European Football Championship was the 16th UEFA European Championship, the quadrennial international men's football championship of Europe organised by the Union of European Football Associations. To celebrate the 60th anniversary of the European Championship competition, Michel Platini (UEFA president between 2007-2015) declared that the tournament would be hosted in several nations, with 11 cities in 11 UEFA countries each providing venues for the tournament.

Due to the COVID-19 pandemic in Europe during 2020, the tournament was postponed to summer 2021, retaining the name UEFA Euro 2020 and host venues. Initially, 13 venues were chosen for the tournament but two were later dropped (Bruxelles after the building of Eurostadium was abandoned / Dublin because there was no guarantee that spectators could attend). Bilbao (Spain) was changed as a host venue to Sevilla (Spain) to allow for spectators at matches.

The host cities were divided into six pairings, established on the basis of sporting strength (assuming all host teams qualify), geographical considerations and security or political constraints. Each qualified host country played a minimum of two matches at home. The following group venue pairings were announced:

Group A: Roma (Italy) & Bakı (Azerbaijan)
Group B: Saint Petersburg (Russia) & København (Denmark)
Group C: Amsterdam (Netherlands) & Bucureşti (Romania)

Group D: London (England) & Glasgow (Scotland)
Group E: Sevilla (Spain) & Saint Petersburg (Russia)
Group F: München (Germany) & Budapest (Hungary)

The following was the composition of the seeding pots:
Pot 1: Belgium, Italy, England, Germany, Spain, Ukraine.
Pot 2: France, Poland, Switzerland, Croatia, Netherlands, Russia.
Pot 3: Portugal, Turkey, Denmark, Austria, Sweden, Czech Republic.
Pot 4: Wales, Finland, Hungary, Slovakia, Scotland, North Macedonia.

The 24 teams were drawn in following groups:

GROUP A
Turkey
Italy
Wales
Switzerland

GROUP B
Denmark
Finland
Belgium
Russia

GROUP C
Netherlands
Ukraine
Austria
North Macedonia

GROUP D
England
Croatia
Scotland
Czech Republic

GROUP E
Spain
Sweden
Poland
Slovakia

GROUP F
Hungary
Portugal
France
Germany

List of venues:

City	Country	Stadium	Capacity*
Amsterdam	Netherlands	"Johan Cruyff" ArenA	54,990
Bakı	Azerbaijan	Olympic Stadium	68,700
Bucureşti	Romania	Arena Naţională	55,600
Budapest	Hungary	Puskás Aréna	67,215
København	Denmark	Parken Stadium	38,065
Glasgow	Scotland	Hampden Park	51,866
London	England	Wembley Stadium	90,000
München	Germany	Allianz Arena	70,000
Roma	Italy	Stadio Olimpico	70,634
Saint Petersburg	Russia	Krestovsky Stadium	68,134
Sevilla	Spain	Estadio de La Cartuja	60,000

*regardless of capacity, due to the COVID-19 pandemic and the resulting restrictions on public gatherings, many of the venues at the tournament were unable to operate at full capacity. Budapest (Puskás Aréna) was the only stadium operating with full capacity, subject to spectators fulfilling strict stadium entry requirements.

The Denmark - Finland match (Group B) was suspended minutes prior to half-time after Danish midfielder Christian Eriksen collapsed on the pitch due to a sudden cardiac arrest. He was transferred to the hospital and stabilised, with the match resuming later that evening (by the decision of the Danish team).

Title holders Portugal were eliminated in the Second Round of 16 by Belgium, together with France (World Cup winners 2018), Germany and the Netherlands. Italy won their second European Championship title by defeating England on penalties in the final match, following a 1-1 draw after extra time.

GROUP STAGE

Please note: group winners, runners-up, and the best four third-placed teams advanced to the second round of 16.

GROUP A

Results

11.06.2021	Roma	Turkey - Italy	0-3(0-0)
12.06.2021	Bakı	Wales - Switzerland	1-1(0-0)
16.06.2021	Bakı	Turkey - Wales	0-2(0-1)
16.06.2021	Roma	Italy - Switzerland	3-0(1-0)
20.06.2021	Bakı	Switzerland - Turkey	3-1(2-0)
20.06.2021	Roma	Italy - Wales	1-0(1-0)

Final Standings

1.	**Italy**	3	3	0	0	7	-	0	9
2.	**Wales**	3	1	1	1	3	-	2	4
3.	*Switzerland*	3	1	1	1	4	-	5	4
4.	Turkey	3	0	0	3	1	-	8	0

GROUP B

Results

12.06.2021	København	Denmark - Finland	0-1(0-0)
12.06.2021	St. Petersburg	Belgium - Russia	3-0(2-0)
16.06.2021	St. Petersburg	Finland - Russia	0-1(0-1)
17.06.2021	København	Denmark - Belgium	1-2(1-0)
21.06.2021	København	Russia - Denmark	1-4(0-1)
21.06.2021	St. Petersburg	Finland - Belgium	0-2(0-0)

Final Standings

1.	**Belgium**	3	3	0	0	7	-	1	9
2.	**Denmark**	3	1	0	2	5	-	4	3
3.	*Finland*	3	1	0	2	1	-	3	3
4.	Russia	3	1	0	2	2	-	7	3

GROUP C

Results

13.06.2021	Bucureşti	Austria - North Macedonia	3-1(1-1)
13.06.2021	Amsterdam	Netherlands - Ukraine	3-2(0-0)
17.06.2021	Bucureşti	Ukraine - North Macedonia	2-1(2-0)
17.06.2021	Amsterdam	Netherlands - Austria	2-0(1-0)
21.06.2021	Amsterdam	N. Macedonia - Netherlands	0-3(0-1)
21.06.2021	Bucureşti	Ukraine - Austria	0-1(0-1)

Final Standings

1.	**Netherlands**	3	3	0	0	8	-	2	9
2.	**Austria**	3	2	0	1	4	-	3	6
3.	*Ukraine*	3	1	0	2	4	-	5	3
4.	N. Macedonia	3	0	0	3	2	-	8	0

GROUP D

	Results		
13.06.2021	London	England - Croatia	1-0(1-0)
14.06.2021	Glasgow	Scotland - Czech Republic	0-2(0-1)
18.06.2021	Glasgow	Croatia - Czech Republic	1-1(0-1)
18.06.2021	London	England - Scotland	0-0
22.06.2021	Glasgow	Croatia - Scotland	3-1(1-1)
22.06.2021	London	Czech Republic - England	0-1(0-1)

	Final Standings								
1.	England	3	2	1	0	2	-	0	7
2.	Croatia	3	1	1	1	4	-	3	4
3.	Czech Rep.	3	1	1	1	3	-	2	4
4.	Scotland	3	0	1	2	1	-	5	1

GROUP E

	Results		
14.06.2021	Saint Petersburg	Poland - Slovakia	1-2(0-1)
14.06.2021	Sevilla	Spain - Sweden	0-0
18.06.2021	Saint Petersburg	Sweden - Slovakia	1-0(0-0)
19.06.2021	Sevilla	Spain - Poland	1-1(1-0)
23.06.2021	Sevilla	Slovakia - Spain	0-5(0-2)
23.06.2021	Saint Petersburg	Sweden - Poland	3-2(1-0)

	Final Standings								
1.	Sweden	3	2	1	0	4	-	2	7
2.	Spain	3	1	2	0	6	-	1	5
3.	Slovakia	3	1	0	2	2	-	7	3
4.	Poland	3	0	1	2	4	-	6	1

GROUP F

	Results		
15.06.2021	Budapest	Hungary - Portugal	0-3(0-0)
15.06.2021	München	France - Germany	1-0(1-0)
19.06.2021	Budapest	Hungary - France	1-1(1-0)
19.06.2021	München	Portugal - Germany	2-4(1-2)
23.06.2021	Budapest	Portugal - France	2-2(1-1)
23.06.2021	München	Germany - Hungary	2-2(0-1)

	Final Standings								
1.	France	3	1	2	0	4	-	3	5
2.	Germany	3	1	1	1	6	-	5	4
3.	Portugal	3	1	1	1	7	-	6	4
4.	Hungary	3	0	2	1	3	-	6	2

RANKING OF THIRD-PLACED TEAMS

1.	Portugal	3	1	1	1	7	-	6	4
2.	Czech Republic	3	1	1	1	3	-	2	4
3.	Switzerland	3	1	1	1	4	-	5	4
4.	Ukraine	3	1	0	2	4	-	5	3
5.	Finland	3	1	0	2	1	-	3	3
6.	Slovakia	3	1	0	2	2	-	7	3

KNOCKOUT STAGE

SECOND ROUND OF 16

26.06.2021	Amsterdam	Wales - Denmark	0-4(0-1)
26.06.2021	London	Italy - Austria	2-1(0-0,0-0)
27.06.2021	Budapest	Netherlands - Czech Republic	0-2(0-0)
27.06.2021	Sevilla	Belgium - Portugal	1-0(1-0)
28.06.2021	København	Croatia - Spain	3-5(1-1,3-3)
28.06.2021	Bucureşti	France - Switzerland	3-3(0-1,3-3,3-3); 4-5 pen
29.06.2021	London	England - Germany	2-0(0-0)
29.06.2021	Glasgow	Sweden - Ukraine	1-2(1-1,1-1)

QUARTER-FINALS

02.07.2021	Saint Petersburg	Switzerland - Spain	1-1(0-1,1-1,1-1); 1-3 pen
02.07.2021	München	Belgium - Italy	1-2(1-2)
03.07.2021	Bakı	Czech Republic - Denmark	1-2(0-2)
03.07.2021	Roma	Ukraine - England	0-4(0-1)

SEMI-FINALS

06.07.2021	London	Italy - Spain	1-1(0-0,1-1,1-1); 6-7 pen
07.07.2021	London	England - Denmark	2-1(1-1,1-1)

FINAL

11.07.2021; Wembley Stadium, London; Referee: Björn Kuipers (Netherlands); Attendance: 67,173

ITALY - ENGLAND   **1-1(0-1,1-1,1-1); 3-2 on penalties**

ITA: Gianluigi Donnarumma, Giovanni Di Lorenzo, Leonardo Bonucci, Giorgio Chiellini (Cap), Emerson (118.Alessandro Florenzi), Marco Verratti (96.Manuel Locatelli), Jorginho, Nicolò Barella (54.Bryan Cristante), Federico Chiesa (86.Federico Bernardeschi), Ciro Immobile (55.Domenico Berardi), Lorenzo Insigne (91.Andrea Belotti). Trainer: Roberto Mancini.

ENG: Jordan Lee Pickford, Kyle Andrew Walker (120.Jadon Malik Sancho), Kieran John Trippier (70.Bukayo Ayoyinka Saka), Jacob Harry Maguire, John Stones, Luke Paul Hoare Shaw, Mason Tony Mount (99.Jack Peter Grealish), Kalvin Mark Phillips, Declan Rice (74.Jordan Brian Henderson; 120.Marcus Rashford), Raheem Shaquille Sterling, Harry Edward Kane (Cap). Trainer: Gareth Southgate.

Goals: 0-1 Luke Paul Hoare Shaw (2), 1-1 Leonardo Bonucci (67).

Penalties: Domenico Berardi 1-0; Harry Edward Kane 1-1; Andrea Belotti (saved); Jacob Harry Maguire 1-2; Leonardo Bonucci 2-2; Marcus Rashford (missed); Federico Bernardeschi 3-2; Jadon Malik Sancho (saved); Jorginho (saved); Bukayo Ayoyinka Saka (saved).

FINAL TOURNAMENT - SQUADS

AUSTRIA
Trainer: Franco Foda (Germany)

Goalkeepers:
1	Alexander Schlager	01.02.1996
12	Pavao Pervan	13.11.1987
13	Daniel Bachmann	09.07.1994

Defenders:
2	Andreas Ulmer	30.10.1985
3	Aleksandar Dragović	06.03.1991
4	Martin Hinteregger	07.09.1992
5	Stefan Posch	14.05.1997
8	David Olatukunbo Alaba	24.06.1992
15	Philipp Lienhart	11.07.1996
16	Christopher Trimmel	24.02.1987
21	Stefan Lainer	27.08.1992
26	Marco Friedl	16.03.1998

Midfielders:
6	Stefan Ilsanker	18.05.1989
9	Marcel Sabitzer	17.03.1994
10	Florian Grillitsch	07.08.1995
14	Christoph Baumgartner	01.08.1999
17	Louis Schaub	29.12.1994
18	Alessandro André Schöpf	07.02.1994
19	Christoph Baumgartner	01.08.1999
22	Valentin Lando Lazaro	24.03.1996
23	Xaver Schlager	28.09.1997
24	Konrad Laimer	27.05.1997

Forwards:
7	Marko Arnautović	19.04.1989
11	Michael Gregoritsch	18.04.1994
20	Karim Onisiwo	17.03.1992
25	Saša Kalajdžić	07.07.1997

BELGIUM
Trainer: Roberto Martínez Montoliu (Spain)

Goalkeepers:
1	Thibaut Nicolas Marc Courtois	11.05.1992
12	Simon Luc Hildebert Mignolet*	06.03.1988
13	Matz Willy Els Sels	26.02.1992

Defenders:
2	Toby Albertine Maurits Alderweireld	02.03.1989
3	Thomas Vermaelen	14.11.1985
4	Anga Dedryck Boyata	28.11.1990
5	Jan Bert Lieve Vertonghen	24.04.1987
15	Thomas Meunier	12.09.1991
18	Jason Grégory Marianne Denayer	28.06.1995
21	Timothy Castagne	05.12.1995

Midfielders:
6	Axel Tomas Laurent Angel Lambert Witsel	12.01.1989
7	Kevin De Bruyne	28.06.1991
8	Youri Marion Tielemans	07.05.1997
11	Yannick Ferreira Carrasco	04.09.1993
16	Thorgan Ganael Francis Hazard	29.03.1993
17	Hans Vanaken	24.08.1992
19	Leander Dendoncker	15.04.1995
22	Nacer Chadli	02.08.1989
26	Dennis Pierre Jacques Albert Praet	14.05.1994

Forwards:
9	Romelu Menama Lukaku Bolingoli	13.05.1993
10	Eden Michael Hazard	07.01.1991
14	Dries Mertens	06.05.1987
20	Christian Benteke Liolo	03.12.1990
23	Michy Batshuayi-Atunga	02.10.1993
24	Leandro Trossard	04.12.1994
25	Jérémy Doku	27.05.2002

*Thomas Kaminski 23.10.1992 (from 28.06.2021)

CROATIA
Trainer: Zlatko Dalić

Goalkeepers:
1	Dominik Livaković	09.01.1995
12	Lovre Kalinić	03.04.1990
23	Simon Sluga	17.03.1993

Defenders:
2	Šime Vrsaljko	10.01.1992
3	Borna Barišić	10.11.1992
5	Duje Ćaleta-Car	17.09.1996
6	Dejan Lovren	05.07.1989
16	Mile Škorić	19.06.1991
21	Domagoj Vida	29.04.1989
22	Josip Juranović	16.08.1995
24	Domagoj Bradarić	10.12.1999
25	Joško Gvardiol	23.01.2002

Midfielders:
4	Ivan Perišić	02.02.1989
8	Mateo Kovačić	06.05.1994
10	Luka Modrić	09.09.1985
11	Marcelo Brozović	16.11.1992
13	Nikola Vlašić	04.10.1997
15	Mario Pašalić	09.02.1995
19	Milan Badelj	25.02.1989
26	Luka Ivanušec	26.11.1998

Forwards:
7	Josip Brekalo	23.06.1998
9	Andrej Kramarić	19.06.1991
14	Ante Budimir	22.07.1991
17	Ante Rebić	21.09.1993
18	Mislav Oršić	29.12.1992
20	Bruno Petković	16.09.1994

CZECH REPUBLIC
Trainer: Jaroslav Šilhavý

Goalkeepers:
1	Tomáš Vaclík	29.03.1989
16	Aleš Mandous	21.04.1992
23	Tomáš Koubek	26.08.1992

Defenders:
2	Pavel Kadeřábek	25.04.1992
3	Ondřej Čelůstka	18.06.1989
4	Jakub Brabec	06.08.1992
5	Vladimír Coufal	22.08.1992
6	Tomáš Kalas	15.05.1993
9	Tomáš Holeš	31.03.1993
17	David Zima	08.11.2000
18	Jan Bořil	11.01.1991
22	Aleš Matějů	03.06.1996

Midfielders:
7	Antonín Barák	03.12.1994
8	Vladimír Darida	08.08.1990
12	Lukáš Masopust	12.02.1993
13	Petr Ševčík	04.05.1994
14	Jakub Jankto	19.01.1996
15	Tomáš Souček	27.02.1995
21	Alex Král	19.05.1998
25	Jakub Pešek	24.06.1993
26	Michal Sadílek	31.05.1999

Forwards:
10	Patrik Schick	24.01.1996
11	Michael Krmenčík	15.03.1993
19	Adam Hložek	25.07.2002
20	Matěj Vydra	01.05.1992
24	Tomáš Pekhart	26.05.1989

DENMARK

Trainer: Kasper Hjulmand

Goalkeepers:
1	Kasper Peter Schmeichel	05.11.1986
16	Jonas Bybjerg Lössl	01.02.1989
22	Frederik Riis Rønnow	04.08.1992

Defenders:
2	Joachim Christian Andersen	31.05.1996
3	Jannik Vestergaard	03.08.1992
4	Simon Thorup Kjær	26.03.1989
5	Joakim Mæhle Pedersen	20.05.1997
6	Andreas Bødtker Christensen	10.04.1996
13	Mathias Jattah-Njie Jørgensen	23.04.1990
17	Jens Stryger Larsen	21.02.1991
26	Nicolai Møller Boilesen	16.02.1992

Midfielders:
7	Robert Skov	20.05.1996
8	Thomas Joseph Delaney	03.09.1991
10	Christian Dannemann Eriksen	14.02.1992
15	Christian Thers Nørgaard	10.03.1994
18	Daniel Wass	31.05.1989
23	Pierre-Emile Kordt Højbjerg	05.08.1995
24	Mathias Jensen	01.01.1996
25	Anders Bleg Christiansen	08.06.1990

Forwards:
9	Martin Braithwaite Christensen	05.06.1991
11	Andreas Skov Olsen	02.12.1999
12	Kasper Dolberg Rasmussen	06.10.1997
14	Mikkel Krogh Damsgaard	03.07.2000
19	Jonas Older Wind	07.02.1999
20	Yussuf Yurary Poulsen	15.06.1994
21	Andreas Evald Cornelius	16.03.1993

ENGLAND

Trainer: Gareth Southgate

Goalkeepers:
1	Jordan Lee Pickford	07.03.1994
13	Dean Bradley Henderson*	12.03.1997
23	Samuel Luke Johnstone	25.03.1993

Defenders:
2	Kyle Andrew Walker	28.05.1990
3	Luke Paul Hoare Shaw	12.07.1995
5	John Stones	28.05.1994
6	Jacob Harry Maguire	05.03.1993
12	Kieran John Trippier	19.09.1990
15	Tyrone Deon Mings	13.03.1993
16	Conor David Coady	25.02.1993
21	Benjamin James Chilwell	21.12.1996
22	Benjamin William White	08.10.1997
24	Reece James	08.12.1999

Midfielders:
4	Declan Rice	14.01.1999
7	Jack Peter Grealish	10.09.1995
8	Jordan Brian Henderson	17.06.1990
14	Kalvin Mark Phillips	02.12.1995
19	Mason Tony Mount	10.01.1999
20	Philip Walter Foden	28.05.2000
25	Bukayo Ayoyinka Saka	05.09.2001
26	Jude Victor William Bellingham	29.06.2003

Forwards:
9	Harry Edward Kane	28.07.1993
10	Raheem Shaquille Sterling	08.12.1994
11	Marcus Rashford	31.10.1997
17	Jadon Malik Sancho	25.03.2000
18	Dominic Nathaniel Calvert-Lewin	16.03.1997

*Aaron Christopher Ramsdale 14.05.1998 (from 15.06.2021)

FINLAND

Trainer: Markku Kanerva

Goalkeepers:
1	Lukáš Hrádecký	24.11.1989
12	Jesse Pekka Joronen	21.03.1993
23	Anssi Valtteri Jaakkola	13.03.1987

Defenders:
2	Paulus Verneri Arajuuri	15.06.1988
3	Daniel Michael O'Shaughnessy	14.09.1994
4	Joona Marko Aleksi Toivio	10.03.1988
5	Sauli Aapo Kasperi Väisänen	05.06.1994
15	Nicholas Antero Hämäläinen	05.03.1997
17	Nikolai Aleksanteri Alho	12.03.1993
18	Jere Juhani Uronen	13.07.1994
22	Jukka Raitala	15.09.1988
25	Robert Ivanov	19.09.1994

Midfielders:
6	Glen Adjei Kamara	28.10.1995
7	Robert Thomas Taylor	21.10.1994
8	Robin Lod	17.04.1993
9	Hans Fredrik Jensen	09.09.1997
11	Rasmus Schüller	18.06.1991
13	Pyry Henri Hidipo Soiri	22.09.1994
14	Tim Sparv	20.02.1987
16	Thomas Anton Rudolph Lam	18.12.1993
19	Joni Kauko	12.07.1990
24	Onni Valakari	18.08.1999

Forwards:
10	Teemu Eino Antero Pukki	29.03.1990
20	Joel Julius Ilmari Pohjanpalo	13.09.1994
21	Lassi Lappalainen	24.08.1998
26	Marcus Forss	18.06.1999

FRANCE

Trainer: Didier Claude Deschamps

Goalkeepers:
1	Hugo Hadrien Dominique Lloris	26.12.1986
16	Steve Mandanda Mpidi	28.03.1985
23	Mike Maignan	03.07.1995

Defenders:
2	Benjamin Jacques Marcel Pavard	28.03.1996
3	Presnel Kimpembe	13.08.1995
4	Raphaël Xavier Varane	25.04.1993
5	Clément Nicolas Laurent Lenglet	17.06.1995
15	Kurt Happy Zouma	27.10.1994
18	Lucas Digne	20.07.1993
21	Lucas François Bernard Hernández	14.02.1996
24	Léo Michel Joseph Claude Dubois	14.09.1994
25	Jules Olivier Koundé	12.11.1998

Midfielders:
6	Paul Labile Pogba	15.03.1993
8	Thomas Benoît Lemar	12.11.1995
12	Corentin Tolisso	03.08.1994
13	N'Golo Kanté	29.03.1991
14	Adrien Rabiot-Provost	03.04.1995
17	Moussa Sissoko	16.08.1989

Forwards:
7	Antoine Griezmann	21.03.1991
9	Olivier Jonathan Giroud	30.09.1986
10	Kylian Sanmi Mbappé Lottin	20.12.1998
11	Masour Ousmane Dembélé	15.05.1997
19	Karim Mostafa Benzema	19.12.1987
20	Kingsley Junior Coman	13.06.1996
22	Wissam Ben Yedder	12.08.1990
26	Marcus Lilian Thuram-Ulien	06.08.1997

GERMANY

Trainer: Joachim Löw

	Goalkeepers:	
1	Manuel Peter Neuer	27.03.1986
12	Bernd Leno	04.03.1992
22	Kevin Trapp	08.07.1990

	Defenders:	
2	Antonio Rüdiger	03.03.1993
3	Marcel Halstenberg	27.09.1991
4	Matthias Lukas Ginter	19.01.1994
5	Mats Julian Hummels	16.12.1988
15	Niklas Süle	03.09.1995
16	Lukas Manuel Klostermann	03.06.1996
20	Robin Everardus Gosens	05.07.1994
23	Emre Can	12.01.1994
24	Robin Koch	17.07.1996
26	Christian Günter	28.02.1993

	Midfielders:	
6	Joshua Walter Kimmich	08.02.1995
8	Toni Kroos	04.01.1990
13	Jonas Hofmann	14.07.1992
14	Jamal Musiala	26.02.2003
17	Florian Christian Neuhaus	16.03.1997
18	Leon Christoph Goretzka	06.02.1995
19	Leroy Aziz Sané	11.01.1996
21	İlkay Gündoğan	24.10.1990

	Forwards:	
7	Kai Lukas Havertz	11.06.1999
9	Kevin Volland	30.07.1992
10	Serge David Gnabry	14.07.1995
11	Timo Werner	06.03.1996
25	Thomas Müller	13.09.1989

HUNGARY

Trainer: Marco Rossi (Italy)

	Goalkeepers:	
1	Péter Gulácsi	06.05.1990
12	Dénes Dibusz	16.11.1990
22	Ádám Bogdán	27.09.1987

	Defenders:	
2	Ádám Lang	17.01.1993
3	Ákos Kecskés	04.01.1996
4	Attila Árpád Szalai	20.01.1998
5	Attila Fiola	17.02.1990
6	Vilmos Tamás Orbán	03.11.1992
7	Loïc Négo	15.01.1991
14	Gergő Lovrencsics	01.09.1988
21	Endre Botka	25.08.1994
26	Bendegúz Bolla	22.11.1999

	Midfielders:	
8	Ádám Nagy	17.06.1995
10	Tamás Cseri	15.01.1988
13	András Schäfer	13.04.1999
15	László Kleinheisler	08.04.1994
16	Dániel Gazdag	02.03.1996
18	Dávid Miklós Sigér	30.11.1990
19	Kevin Varga	30.03.1996

	Forwards:	
9	Ádám Csaba Szalai	09.12.1987
11	Filip Holender	27.07.1994
17	Roland Varga	23.01.1990
20	Roland Sallai	22.05.1997
23	Nemanja Nikolić	31.12.1987
24	Szabolcs Schön	27.09.2000
25	János Csaba Hahn	15.03.1995

ITALY

Trainer: Roberto Mancini

	Goalkeepers:	
1	Salvatore Sirigu	12.01.1987
21	Gianluigi Donnarumma	25.02.1999
26	Alex Meret	22.03.1997

	Defenders:	
2	Giovanni Di Lorenzo	04.08.1993
3	Giorgio Chiellini	14.08.1984
4	Leonardo Spinazzola	25.03.1993
13	Emerson Palmieri dos Santos	03.08.1994
15	Francesco Acerbi	10.08.1988
19	Leonardo Bonucci	01.05.1987
23	Alessandro Bastoni	13.04.1999
24	Alessandro Florenzi	11.03.1991
25	Rafael Tolói	10.10.1990

	Midfielders:	
5	Manuel Locatelli	08.01.1998
6	Marco Verratti	05.11.1992
7	Gaetano Castrovilli	17.02.1997
8	Jorge Luiz Frello Filho "Jorginho"	20.12.1991
12	Matteo Pessina	21.04.1997
16	Bryan Cristante	03.03.1995
18	Nicolò Barella	07.02.1997
20	Federico Bernardeschi	16.02.1994

	Forwards:	
9	Andrea Belotti	20.12.1993
10	Lorenzo Insigne	04.06.1991
11	Domenico Berardi	01.08.1994
14	Federico Chiesa	25.10.1997
17	Ciro Immobile	20.02.1990
22	Giacomo Raspadori	18.02.2000

NETHERLANDS

Trainer: Franciscus de Boer

	Goalkeepers:	
1	Maarten Stekelenburg	22.09.1982
13	Timothy Michael Krul	03.04.1988
23	Marco Bizot	10.03.1991

	Defenders:	
2	Joël Ivo Veltman	15.01.1992
3	Matthijs de Ligt	12.08.1999
4	Nathan Benjamin Aké	18.02.1995
5	Owen Wijndal	28.11.1999
6	Stefan de Vrij	05.02.1992
12	Patrick John Miguel van Aanholt	29.08.1990
17	Daley Blind	09.03.1990
22	Denzel Justus Morris Dumfries	18.04.1996
25	Jurriën David Norman Timber	17.06.2001

	Midfielders:	
8	Georginio Gregion Emile Wijnaldum	11.11.1990
11	Quincy Anton Promes	04.01.1992
14	Davy Klaassen	21.02.1993
15	Marten Elco de Roon	29.03.1991
16	Ryan Jiro Gravenberch	16.05.2002
20	Donny van de Beek (*injured / not replaced*)	18.04.1997
21	Frenkie de Jong	12.05.1997
24	Teun Koopmeiners	28.02.1998

	Forwards:	
7	Steven Berghuis	19.12.1991
9	Luuk de Jong	27.08.1990
10	Memphis Depay	13.02.1994
18	Donyell Malen	19.01.1999
19	Wout Weghorst	07.08.1992
26	Cody Mathès Gakpo	07.05.1999

NORTH MACEDONIA

Trainer: Igor Angelovski

Goalkeepers:

1	Stole Dimitrievski	25.12.1993
12	Risto Jankov	05.09.1998
22	Damjan Šiškovski	18.03.1995

Defenders:

2	Egzon Bejtulai	07.01.1994
3	Gjoko Zajkov	10.02.1995
4	Kire Ristevski	22.10.1990
6	Visar Musliu	13.11.1994
13	Stefan Ristovski	12.02.1992
14	Darko Velkovski	21.06.1995

Midfielders:

5	Arijan Ademi	29.05.1991
8	Ezgjan Alioski	12.02.1992
11	Ferhan Hasani	18.06.1990
15	Tihomir Kostadinov	04.03.1996
16	Boban Nikolov	28.07.1994
17	Enis Bardi	02.07.1995
20	Stefan Spirovski	23.08.1990
21	Eljif Elmas	27.09.1999
24	Daniel Avramovski	20.02.1995
25	Darko Churlinov	11.07.2000

Forwards:

7	Ivan Tričkovski	18.04.1987
9	Aleksandar Trajkovski	05.09.1992
10	Goran Pandev	27.07.1983
18	Vlatko Stojanovski	23.04.1997
19	Krste Velkoski	20.02.1988
23	Marjan Radeski	10.02.1995
26	Milan Ristovski	08.04.1998

POLAND

Trainer: Paulo Manuel Carvalho Sousa (Portugal)

Goalkeepers:

1	Wojciech Tomasz Szczęsny	18.04.1990
12	Łukasz Skorupski	05.05.1991
22	Łukasz Marek Fabiański	18.04.1985

Defenders:

2	Kamil Piątkowski	21.06.2000
3	Paweł Marek Dawidowicz	20.05.1995
4	Tomasz Karol Kędziora	11.06.1994
5	Jan Kacper Bednarek	12.04.1996
13	Maciej Rybus	19.08.1989
15	Kamil Jacek Glik	03.02.1988
18	Bartosz Bereszyński	12.07.1992
25	Michał Sławomir Helik	09.09.1995
26	Tymoteusz Puchacz	23.01.1999

Midfielders:

6	Kacper Kozłowski	16.10.2003
8	Karol Linetty	02.02.1995
10	Grzegorz Krychowiak	29.01.1990
14	Mateusz Andrzej Klich	13.06.1990
16	Jakub Piotr Moder	07.04.1999
17	Przemysław Płacheta	23.03.1998
19	Przemysław Frankowski	12.04.1995
20	Piotr Sebastian Zieliński	20.05.1994
21	Kamil Jóźwiak	22.04.1998

Forwards:

7	Arkadiusz Krystian Milik (*injured / not replaced*)	28.02.1994
9	Robert Lewandowski	21.08.1988
11	Karol Świderski	23.01.1997
23	Dawid Igor Kownacki	14.03.1997
24	Jakub Świerczok	28.12.1992

PORTUGAL

Trainer: Fernando Manuel Fernandes da Costa Santos

Goalkeepers:

1	Rui Pedro dos Santos Patrício	15.02.1988
12	Anthony Lopes	01.10.1990
22	Rui Tiago Dantas da Silva	07.02.1994

Defenders:

2	Nélson Cabral Semedo "Nelsinho"	16.11.1993
3	Képler Laveran Lima Ferreira "Pepe"	26.02.1983
4	Rúben Santos Gato Alves Dias	14.05.1997
5	Raphaël Adelino José Guerreiro	22.12.1993
6	José Miguel da Rocha Fonte	22.12.1983
20	José Diogo Dalot Teixeira	18.03.1999
25	Nuno Alexandre Tavares Mendes	19.06.2002

Midfielders:

8	João Filipe Iria Santos Moutinho	08.09.1986
10	Bernardo Mota Veiga de Carvalho e Silva	10.08.1994
11	Bruno Miguel Borges Fernandes	08.09.1994
13	Danilo Luís Hélio Pereira	09.09.1991
14	William Silva de Carvalho	07.04.1992
15	Rafael Alexandre Fernandes Ferreira da Silva	17.05.1993
16	Renato Júnior Luz Sanches	18.08.1997
18	Rúben Diogo da Silva Neves	13.03.1997
19	Pedro António Pereira Gonçalves	28.06.1998
24	Sérgio Miguel Relvas de Oliveira	02.06.1992
26	João Maria Lobo Alves Palhinha Gonçalves	09.07.1995

Forwards:

7	Cristiano Ronaldo dos Santos Aveiro	05.02.1985
9	André Miguel Valente Silva	06.11.1995
17	Gonçalo Manuel Ganchinho Guedes	29.11.1996
21	Diogo José Teixeira da Silva "Diogo Jota"	04.12.1996
23	João Félix Sequeira	10.11.1999

RUSSIA

Trainer: Stanislav Cherchesov

Goalkeepers:

1	Anton Shunin	27.01.1987
12	Yuriy Dyupin	17.03.1988
16	Matvei Safonov	25.02.1999

Defenders:

2	Mário Figueira Fernandes	19.09.1990
3	Igor Diveyev	27.09.1999
4	Vyacheslav Karavayev	20.05.1995
5	Andrey Semyonov	24.03.1989
13	Fyodor Kudryashov	05.04.1987
14	Georgiy Dzhikiya	21.11.1993
24	Roman Yevgenyev	23.02.1999

Midfielders:

6	Denis Cheryshev	26.12.1990
7	Magomed Ozdoyev	05.11.1992
8	Dmitriy Barinov	11.09.1996
11	Roman Zobnin	11.02.1994
15	Aleksey Miranchuk	17.10.1995
17	Aleksandr Golovin	30.05.1996
18	Yuriy Zhirkov	20.08.1983
19	Rifat Zhemaletdinov	20.09.1996
20	Aleksey Ionov	18.02.1989
21	Daniil Fomin	02.03.1997
23	Daler Kuzyayev	15.01.1993
25	Denis Makarov	18.02.1998
26	Maksim Mukhin	04.11.2001

Forwards:

9	Aleksandr Sobolev	07.03.1997
10	Anton Zabolotniy	13.06.1991
22	Artyom Dzyuba	22.08.1988

SCOTLAND	
Trainer: Stephen Clarke	

Goalkeepers:		
1	David James Marshall	05.03.1985
12	Craig Sinclair Gordon	31.12.1982
21	Jonathan Peter McLaughlin	09.09.1987

Defenders:		
2	Stephen Gerard O'Donnell	11.05.1992
3	Andrew Henry Robertson	11.03.1994
5	Grant Campbell Hanley	20.11.1991
6	Kieran Tierney	05.06.1997
13	Greg John Taylor	05.11.1997
15	Declan Patrick Gallagher	13.02.1991
16	Liam David Ian Cooper	30.08.1991
22	Nathan Kenneth Patterson	16.10.2001
24	Jack William Hendry	07.05.1995
26	Scott Fraser McKenna	12.11.1996

Midfielders:		
4	Scott Francis McTominay	08.12.1996
7	John McGinn	18.10.1994
8	Callum William McGregor	14.06.1993
11	Ryan Christie	22.02.1995
14	John Alexander Fleck	24.08.1991
17	Stuart Armstrong	30.03.1992
18	David Turnbull	10.07.1999
23	Billy Clifford Gilmour	11.06.2001
25	James Forrest	07.07.1991

Forwards:		
9	Lyndon Dykes	07.10.1995
10	Ché Zach Everton Fred Adams	13.07.1996
19	Kevin Michael Nisbet	08.03.1997
20	Ryan Fraser	24.02.1994

SLOVAKIA	
Trainer: Štefan Tarkovič	

Goalkeepers:		
1	Martin Dúbravka	15.01.1989
12	Dušan Kuciak	21.05.1985
23	Marek Rodák	13.12.1996

Defenders:		
2	Peter Pekarík	30.10.1986
3	Denis Vavro	10.04.1996
4	Martin Valjent	11.12.1995
5	Ľubomír Šatka	02.12.1995
14	Milan Škriniar	11.02.1995
15	Tomáš Hubočan	17.09.1985
16	Dávid Hancko	13.12.1997
24	Martin Koscelník	02.03.1995

Midfielders:		
6	Ján Greguš	29.01.1991
7	Vladimír Weiss	30.11.1989
8	Ondrej Duda	05.12.1994
10	Tomáš Suslov	07.06.2002
11	László Bénes	09.09.1997
13	Patrik Hrošovský	22.04.1992
17	Marek Hamšík	27.07.1987
18	Lukáš Haraslín	26.05.1996
19	Juraj Kucka	26.02.1987
22	Stanislav Lobotka	25.11.1994
25	Jakub Hromada	25.05.1996

Forwards:		
9	Róbert Boženík	18.11.1999
20	Róbert Mak	08.03.1991
21	Michal Ďuriš	01.06.1988
26	Ivan Schranz	13.09.1993

SPAIN	
Trainer: Luis Enrique Martínez García	

Goalkeepers:		
1	David de Gea Quintana	07.11.1990
13	Robert Lynch Sánchez	18.11.1997
23	Unai Simón Mendibil	11.06.1997

Defenders:		
2	César Azpilicueta Tanco	28.08.1989
3	Diego Javier Llorente Ríos	16.08.1993
4	Pau Francisco Torres	16.01.1997
12	Eric García Martret	09.01.2001
14	José Luis Gayà Peña	25.03.1995
18	Jordi Alba Ramos	21.03.1989
24	Aymeric Jean Louis Gérard Alphonse Laporte	27.05.1994

Midfielders:		
5	Sergio Busquets i Burgos	16.07.1988
6	Marcos Llorente Moreno	30.01.1995
8	Joge Resurrección Merodio "Koke"	08.01.1992
10	Thiago Alcântara do Nascimento	11.04.1991
16	Rodrigo Hernández Cascante "Rodri"	22.06.1996
17	Fabián Ruiz Peña	03.04.1996
19	Daniel Olmo Carvajal	07.05.1998
20	Adama Traoré Diarra	25.01.1996
22	Pablo Sarabia García	11.05.1992
26	Pedro González López "Pedri"	25.11.2002

Forwards:		
7	Álvaro Borja Morata Martín	23.10.1992
9	Gerard Moreno Balagueró	07.04.1992
11	Ferran Torres García	29.02.2000
21	Mikel Oyarzabal Ugarte	21.04.1997

Please note: only 24 players nominated

SWEDEN	
Trainer: Jan Olof Andersson	

Goalkeepers:		
1	Robin Patrick Olsen	08.01.1990
12	Karl-Johan Anton Johnsson	28.01.1990
23	Bo Kristoffer Nordfeldt	23.06.1989

Defenders:		
2	Carl Mikael Lustig	13.12.1986
3	Victor Jörgen Nilsson Lindelöf	17.07.1994
4	Andreas Granqvist	16.04.1985
5	Pierre Thomas Robin Bengtsson	12.04.1988
6	Hans Carl Ludwig Augustinsson	21.04.1994
14	Filip Viktor Helander	22.04.1993
16	Emil Henry Kristoffer Krafth	02.08.1994
18	Pontus Sven Gustav Jansson	13.02.1991
24	Marcus Andreas Danielsson	08.04.1989

Midfielders:		
7	Bengt Ulf Sebastian Larsson	06.06.1985
8	Albin Ekdal	28.07.1989
10	Emil Peter Forsberg	23.10.1991
13	Karl Gustav Johan Svensson	07.02.1987
15	Ken Nlata Sema	30.09.1993
17	Viktor Johan Anton Claesson	02.01.1992
19	Mattias Olof Svanberg	05.01.1999
20	Mats Kristoffer Olsson	30.06.1995
26	Jens-Lys Michel Cajuste	10.08.1999

Forwards:		
9	Bengt Eric Marcus Berg	17.08.1986
11	Alexander Isak	21.09.1999
21	Dejan Kuluševski	25.04.2000
22	Robin Kwamina Quaison	09.10.1993
25	Carl Henrik Jordan Larsson	20.06.1997

SWITZERLAND

Trainer: Vladimir Petković (Bosnia and Herzegovina)

Goalkeepers:

1	Yann Sommer	17.12.1988
12	Yvon Landry Mvogo Nganoma	06.06.1994
21	Jonas Omlin*	10.01.1994

Defenders:

2	Melingo Kevin Mbabu	19.04.1995
3	Silvan Dominic Widmer	05.03.1993
4	Nico Elvedi	30.09.1996
5	Manuel Obafemi Akanji	19.07.1995
13	Ricardo Iván Rodríguez Araya	25.08.1992
17	Loris Benito Souto	07.01.1992
22	Fabian Lukas Schär	20.12.1991
24	Becir Omeragić	20.01.2002
25	Eray Ervin Cömert	04.02.1998
26	Mvula Jordan Lotomba	29.09.1998

Midfielders:

6	Denis Lemi Zakaria Lako Lado	20.11.1996
8	Remo Marco Freuler	15.04.1992
10	Granit Xhaka	27.09.1992
11	Rubén Estephan Vargas Martínez	05.08.1998
14	Steven Zuber	17.08.1991
15	Mohameth Djibril Ibrahima Sow	06.02.1997
16	Christian Fassnacht	11.11.1993
20	Edimilson Fernandes Ribeiro	15.04.1996
23	Xherdan Shaqiri	10.10.1991

Forwards:

7	Breel Donald Embolo	14.02.1997
9	Haris Seferović	22.02.1992
18	Admir Mehmedi	16.03.1991
19	Mario Gavranović	24.11.1989

*Gregor Kobel 06.12.1997 (from 13.06.2021)

TURKEY

Trainer: Şenol Güneş

Goalkeepers:

1	Fehmi Mert Günok	01.03.1989
12	Altay Bayındır	14.04.1998
23	Uğurcan Çakır	

Defenders:

2	Mehmet Zeki Çelik	17.02.1997
3	Merih Demiral	05.03.1998
4	Çağlar Söyüncü	23.05.1996
13	Cengiz Umut Meraş	20.12.1995
15	Ozan Muhammed Kabak	25.03.2000
18	Rıdvan Yılmaz	21.05.2001
22	Kaan Ayhan	10.11.1994
25	Mert Müldür	03.04.1999

Midfielders:

5	Okay Yokuşlu	09.03.1994
6	Ozan Tufan	23.03.1995
8	Dorukhan Toköz	21.05.1996
10	Hakan Çalhanoğlu	08.02.1994
11	Yusuf Yazıcı	29.01.1997
14	Taylan Antalyalı	08.01.1995
19	Orkun Kökçü	29.12.2000
20	Abdülkadir Ömür	25.06.1999
21	İrfan Can Kahveci	15.06.1995
24	Kerem Aktürkoğlu	21.10.1998

Forwards:

7	Cengiz Ünder	14.07.1997
9	Kenan Karaman	05.03.1994
16	Enes Ünal	10.05.1997
17	Burak Yılmaz	15.07.1985
26	Halil İbrahi Dervişoğlu	08.12.1999

UKRAINE

Trainer: Andriy Shevchenko

Goalkeepers:

1	Heorhiy Bushchan	31.05.1994
12	Andriy Pyatov	28.06.1984
23	Anatoliy Trubin	01.08.2001

Defenders:

2	Eduard Sobol	20.04.1995
4	Serhiy Kryvtsov	15.03.1991
13	Illya Zabarnyi	01.09.2002
16	Vitaliy Mykolenko	29.05.1999
17	Oleksandr Zinchenko	15.12.1996
21	Oleksandr Karavayev	02.06.1992
22	Mykola Matviyenko	02.05.1996
24	Oleksandr Tymchyk	20.01.1997
25	Denys Popov	17.02.1999

Midfielders:

3	Heorhiy Sudakov	01.09.2002
5	Serhiy Sydorchuk	02.05.1991
6	Taras Stepanenko	08.08.1989
8	Ruslan Malinovskiy	04.05.1993
10	Mykola Shaparenko	04.10.1998
11	Marlos Romero Bonfim	07.06.1988
14	Yevhen Makarenko	21.05.1991
15	Viktor Tsyhankov	15.11.1997
18	Roman Bezus	26.09.1990

Forwards:

7	Andriy Yarmolenko	23.10.1989
9	Roman Yaremchuk	27.11.1995
19	Artem Besyedin	31.03.1996
20	Oleksandr Zubkov	03.08.1996
26	Artem Dovbyk	21.06.1997

WALES

Trainer: Robert John Page

Goalkeepers:

1	Wayne Robert Hennessey	24.01.1987
12	Daniel Ward	22.06.1993
21	Adam Rhys Davies	17.07.1992

Defenders:

2	Christopher Ross Gunter	21.07.1989
3	Neco Shay Williams	13.04.2001
4	Benjamin Thomas Davies	24.04.1993
5	Thomas Alun Lockyer	03.12.1994
6	Joseph Peter Rodon	22.10.1997
14	Connor Richard John Roberts	23.09.1995
15	Ethan Kwame Colm Raymond Ampadu	14.09.2000
17	Rhys Llewelyn Norrington-Davies	22.04.1999
22	Christopher James Mepham	05.10.1997
24	Benjamin Cabango	30.05.2000

Midfielders:

7	Joseph Michael Allen	14.03.1990
8	Harry Wilson	22.03.1997
10	Aaron James Ramsey	26.12.1990
16	Joseff John Morrell	03.01.1997
18	Jonathan Peter Williams	09.10.1993
19	David Robert Brooks	08.07.1997
23	Dylan James Christopher Levitt	17.11.2000
25	Rubin James Colwill	27.04.2002
26	Matthew Robert Smith	22.11.1999

Forwards:

9	Tyler D'Whyte Roberts	12.01.1999
11	Gareth Frank Bale	16.07.1989
13	Kieffer Roberto Francisco Moore	08.08.1992
20	Daniel Owen James	10.11.1997

2020 - 2021 UEFA NATIONS LEAGUE

The 2020-2021 UEFA Nations League is the second edition of the UEFA Nations League, a competition involving the men's national teams of the 55 member associations of UEFA. The competition is being held from September to November 2020 (league phase), October 2021 (Nations League Finals) and March 2022 (relegation play-outs).

All 55 UEFA national teams entered the competition and, due to the format change of the competition, no teams were actually relegated from the 2018-2019 season. In addition to the group winners, the second-placed teams in Leagues C and D, along with the best-ranked third-placed team of League D, were also promoted. In the 2020-2021 access list, UEFA ranked teams based on the 2018-2019 Nations League overall ranking, with a slight modification: teams that were originally relegated in the previous season were ranked immediately below teams promoted prior to the format change.

The 55 UEFA national teams would be divided into the four "Leagues": 16 teams in League A, 16 teams in League B, 16 teams in League C, and 7 teams in League D, according to their UEFA national team coefficients after the conclusion of the 2018 FIFA World Cup qualifiers, with the highest-ranked teams playing in League A. The seeding pots were as follows:

LEAGUE A

Team	Pot
Portugal (title holders) Netherlands England Switzerland	1
Belgium France Spain Italy	2
Bosnia and Herzegovina (P) Ukraine (P) Denmark (P) Sweden (P)	3
Croatia (R) Poland (R) Germany (R) Iceland (R)	4

LEAGUE B

Team	Pot
Russia Austria Wales Czech Republic	1
Scotland (P) Norway (P) Serbia (P) Finland (P)	2
Slovakia (R) Turkey (R) Republic of Ireland (R) Northern Ireland (R)	3
Bulgaria (PF) Israel (PF) Hungary (PF) Romania (PF)	4

LEAGUE C

Team	Pot
Greece Albania Montenegro Georgia (P)	1
North Macedonia (P) Kosovo (P) Belarus (P) Cyprus (R)	2
Estonia (R) Slovenia (R) Lithuania (R) Luxembourg (PF)	3
Armenia (PF) Azerbaijan (PF) Kazakhstan (PF) Moldova (PF)	4

LEAGUE D

Team	Pot
Gibraltar Faroe Islands Latvia Liechtenstein	1
Andorra Malta San Marino	2

(P) = originally promoted in previous season (prior to format change);
(R) = originally relegated in previous season (spared after format change);
(PF) = promoted after format change;

The draw for the league phase took place at the "Beurs van Berlage" Conference Centre in Amsterdam (Netherlands) on 03.03.2020.

LEAGUE A

GROUP A1

Results

04.09.2020	Firenze	Netherlands - Poland	1-0(0-0)
04.09.2020	Amsterdam	Italy - Bosnia and Herzeg.	1-1(0-0)
07.09.2020	Zenica	Netherlands - Italy	0-1(0-1)
07.09.2020	Amsterdam	Bosnia and Herzeg - Poland	1-2(1-1)
11.10.2020	Zenica	Bosnia and H. - Netherlands	0-0
11.10.2020	Gdańsk	Poland - Italy	0-0
14.10.2020	Bergamo	Italy - Netherlands	1-1(1-1)
14.10.2020	Wrocław	Poland - Bosnia and Herzeg	3-0(2-0)
15.11.2020	Amsterdam	Netherlands - Bosnia and H.	3-1(2-0)
15.11.2020	Regg. Emilia	Italy - Poland	2-0(1-0)
18.11.2020	Sarajevo	Bosnia and Herzeg - Italy	0-2(0-1)
18.11.2020	Chorzów	Poland - Netherlands	1-2(1-0)

Final Standings

1.	**Italy**	6	3	3	0	7	-	2	12
2.	Netherlands	6	3	2	1	7	-	4	11
3.	Poland	6	2	1	3	6	-	6	7
4.	Bosnia and H.	6	0	2	4	3	-	11	2

Italy qualified for the Final Tournament
Bosnia and Herzegovina relegated to League B

GROUP A2

Results

05.09.2020	Reykjavík	Iceland - England	0-1(0-0)
05.09.2020	København	Denmark - Belgium	0-2(0-1)
08.09.2020	Bruxelles	Belgium - Iceland	5-1(2-1)
08.09.2020	København	Denmark - England	0-0
11.10.2020	London	England - Belgium	2-1(1-1)
11.10.2020	Reykjavík	Iceland - Denmark	0-3(0-1)
14.10.2020	London	England - Denmark	0-1(0-1)
14.10.2020	Reykjavík	Iceland - Belgium	1-2(1-2)
15.11.2020	Leuven	Belgium - England	2-0(2-0)
15.11.2020	København	Denmark - Iceland	2-1(1-0)
18.11.2020	Leuven	Belgium - Denmark	4-2(1-1)
18.11.2020	London	England - Iceland	4-0(2-0)

Final Standings

1.	**Belgium**	6	5	0	1	16	-	6	15
2.	Denmark	6	3	1	2	8	-	7	10
3.	England	6	3	1	2	7	-	4	10
4.	Iceland	6	0	0	6	3	-	17	0

Belgium qualified for the Final Tournament
Iceland relegated to League B

GROUP A3

Results

05.09.2020	Porto	Portugal - Croatia	4-1(1-0)
05.09.2020	Stockholm	Sweden - France	0-1(0-1)
08.09.2020	Paris	France - Croatia	4-2(2-1)
08.09.2020	Stockholm	Sweden - Portugal	0-2(0-1)
11.10.2020	Zagreb	Croatia - Sweden	2-1(1-0)
11.10.2020	Paris	France - Portugal	0-0
14.10.2020	Zagreb	Croatia - France	1-2(0-1)
14.10.2020	Lisboa	Portugal - Sweden	3-0(2-0)
14.11.2020	Lisboa	Portugal - France	0-1(0-0)
14.11.2020	Stockholm	Sweden - Croatia	2-1(2-0)
17.11.2020	Split	Croatia - Portugal	2-3(1-0)
17.11.2020	Paris	France - Sweden	4-2(2-1)

Final Standings

1.	**France**	6	5	1	0	12	-	5	16
2.	Portugal	6	4	1	1	12	-	4	13
3.	Croatia	6	1	0	5	9	-	16	3
4.	Sweden	6	1	0	5	5	-	13	3

France qualified for the Final Tournament
Sweden relegated to League B

GROUP A4

Results

03.09.2020	Stuttgart	Germany - Spain	1-1(0-0)
03.09.2020	Lviv	Ukraine - Switzerland	2-1(1-1)
06.09.2020	Madrid	Spain - Ukraine	4-0(3-0)
06.09.2020	Basel	Switzerland - Germany	1-1(0-1)
10.10.2020	Madrid	Spain - Switzerland	1-0(1-0)
10.10.2020	Kyiv	Ukraine - Germany	1-2(0-1)
13.10.2020	Köln	Germany - Switzerland	3-3(1-2)
13.10.2020	Kyiv	Ukraine - Spain	1-0(0-0)
14.11.2020	Leipzig	Germany - Ukraine	3-1(2-1)
14.11.2020	Basel	Switzerland - Spain	1-1(1-0)
17.11.2020	Luzern	Switzerland - Ukraine	3-0 *awd*
17.11.2020	Sevilla	Spain - Germany	6-0(3-0)

Final Standings

1.	**Spain**	6	3	2	1	13	-	3	11
2.	Germany	6	2	3	1	10	-	13	9
3.	Switzerland	6	1	3	2	9	-	8	6
4.	Ukraine	6	2	0	4	5	-	13	6

Spain qualified for the Final Tournament
Ukraine relegated to League B

LEAGUE B

GROUP B1

Results

04.09.2020	Oslo	Norway - Austria	1-2(0-1)
04.09.2020	Bucureşti	Romania - Northern Ireland	1-1(1-0)
07.09.2020	Klagenfurt	Austria - Romania	2-3(1-1)
07.09.2020	Belfast	Northern Ireland - Norway	1-5(1-3)
11.10.2020	Oslo	Norway - Romania	4-0(2-0)
11.10.2020	Belfast	Northern Ireland - Austria	0-1(0-1)
14.10.2020	Oslo	Norway - Northern Ireland	1-0(0-0)
14.10.2020	Ploieşti	Romania - Austria	0-1(0-0)
15.11.2020	Bucureşti	Romania - Norway	3-0 awd
15.11.2020	Wien	Austria - Northern Ireland	2-1(0-0)
18.11.2020	Wien	Austria - Norway	1-1(0-0)
18.11.2020	Belfast	Northern Ireland - Romania	1-1(0-0)

Final Standings

1.	**Austria**	6	4	1	1	9 - 6	13
2.	Norway	6	3	1	2	12 - 7	10
3.	Romania	6	2	2	2	8 - 9	8
4.	North. Ireland	6	0	2	4	4 - 11	2

Austria promoted to League A
Northern Ireland relegated to League C

GROUP B2

Results

04.09.2020	Glasgow	Scotland - Israel	1-1(1-0)
04.09.2020	Bratislava	Slovakia - Czech Republic	1-3(0-0)
07.09.2020	Olomouc	Czech Republic - Scotland	1-2(1-1)
07.09.2020	Netanya	Israel - Slovakia	1-1(0-1)
11.10.2020	Haifa	Israel - Czech Republic	1-2(0-1)
11.10.2020	Glasgow	Scotland - Slovakia	1-0(0-0)
14.10.2020	Glasgow	Scotland - Czech Republic	1-0(1-0)
14.10.2020	Trnava	Slovakia - Israel	2-3(2-0)
15.11.2020	Trnava	Slovakia - Scotland	1-0(1-0)
15.11.2020	Plzeň	Czech Republic - Israel	1-0(1-0)
18.11.2020	Plzeň	Czech Republic - Slovakia	2-0(1-0)
18.11.2020	Netanya	Israel - Scotland	1-0(1-0)

Final Standings

1.	**Czech Rep.**	6	4	0	2	9 - 5	12
2.	Scotland	6	3	1	2	5 - 4	10
3.	Israel	6	2	2	2	7 - 7	8
4.	Slovakia	6	1	1	4	5 - 10	4

Czech Republic promoted to League A
Slovakia relegated to League C

GROUP B3

Results

03.09.2020	Moskva	Russia - Serbia	3-1(0-0)
03.09.2020	Sivas	Turkey - Hungary	0-1(0-0)
06.09.2020	Budapest	Hungary - Russia	2-3(0-2)
06.09.2020	Beograd	Serbia - Turkey	0-0
11.10.2020	Moskva	Russia - Turkey	1-1(1-0)
11.10.2020	Beograd	Serbia - Hungary	0-1(0-1)
14.10.2020	Moskva	Russia - Hungary	0-0
14.10.2020	İstanbul	Turkey - Serbia	2-2(0-1)
15.11.2020	İstanbul	Turkey - Russia	3-2(2-1)
15.11.2020	Budapest	Hungary - Serbia	1-1(1-1)
18.11.2020	Budapest	Hungary - Turkey	2-0(0-0)
18.11.2020	Beograd	Serbia - Russia	5-0(4-0)

Final Standings

1.	**Hungary**	6	3	2	1	7 - 4	11
2.	Russia	6	2	2	2	9 - 12	8
3.	Serbia	6	1	3	2	9 - 7	6
4.	Turkey	6	1	3	2	6 - 8	6

Hungary promoted to League A
Turkey relegated to League C

GROUP B4

Results

03.09.2020	Sofia	Bulgaria - Rep. of Ireland	1-1(0-0)
03.09.2020	Helsinki	Finland - Wales	0-1(0-0)
06.09.2020	Cardoff	Wales - Bulgaria	1-0(0-0)
06.09.2020	Dublin	Rep. of Ireland - Finland	0-1(0-0)
11.10.2020	Dublin	Republic of Ireland - Wales	0-0
11.10.2020	Helsinki	Finland - Bulgaria	2-0(0-0)
14.10.2020	Helsinki	Finland - Rep. of Ireland	1-0(0-0)
14.10.2020	Sofia	Bulgaria - Wales	0-1(0-0)
15.11.2020	Sofia	Bulgaria - Finland	1-2(0-2)
15.11.2020	Cardiff	Wales - Republic of Ireland	1-0(0-0)
18.11.2020	Dublin	Rep. of Ireland - Bulgaria	0-0
18.11.2020	Cardiff	Wales - Finland	3-1(1-0)

Final Standings

1.	**Wales**	6	5	1	0	7 - 1	16
2.	Finland	6	4	0	2	7 - 5	12
3.	R. of Ireland	6	0	3	3	1 - 4	3
4.	Bulgaria	6	0	2	4	2 - 7	2

Wales promoted to League A
Bulgaria relegated to League C

LEAGUE C

GROUP C1

Results

05.09.2020	Bakı	Azerbaijan - Luxembourg	1-2(1-0)
05.09.2020	Nicosia	Cyprus - Montenegro	0-2(0-0)
08.09.2020	Nicosia	Cyprus - Azerbaijan	0-1(0-1)
08.09.2020	Lëtzebuerg	Luxembourg - Montenegro	0-1(0-0)
10.10.2020	Lëtzebuerg	Luxembourg - Cyprus	2-0(2-0)
10.10.2020	Podgorica	Montenegro - Azerbaijan	2-0(1-0)
13.10.2020	Elbasan	Azerbaijan - Cyprus	0-0
13.10.2020	Podgorica	Montenegro - Luxembourg	1-2(1-1)
14.11.2020	Zaprešić	Azerbaijan - Montenegro	0-0
14.11.2020	Nicosia	Cyprus - Luxembourg	2-1(1-1)
17.11.2020	Lëtzebuerg	Luxembourg - Azerbaijan	0-0
17.11.2020	Podgorica	Montenegro - Cyprus	4-0(3-0)

Final Standings

1.	**Montenegro**	6	4	1	1	10	-	2	13
2.	Luxembourg	6	3	1	2	7	-	5	10
3.	Azerbaijan	6	1	3	2	2	-	4	6
4.	Cyprus	6	1	1	4	2	-	10	4

Montenegro promoted to League B
Cyprus qualified to relegation play-outs

GROUP C2

Results

05.09.2020	Skopje	North Macedonia - Armenia	2-1(2-0)
05.09.2020	Tallinn	Estonia - Georgia	0-1(0-1)
08.09.2020	Tbilisi	Georgia - North Macedonia	1-1(1-1)
08.09.2020	Yerevan	Armenia - Estonia	2-0(1-0)
11.10.2020	Tychy	Armenia - Georgia	2-2(1-0)
11.10.2020	Tallinn	Estonia - North Macedonia	3-3(1-1)
14.10.2020	Skopje	North Macedonia - Georgia	1-0(0-0)
14.10.2020	Tallinn	Estonia - Armenia	1-1(1-1)
15.11.2020	Skopje	North Macedonia - Estonia	2-1(1-0)
15.11.2020	Tbilisi	Georgia - Armenia	1-2(0-1)
18.11.2020	Nicosia	Armenia - North Macedonia	1-0(0-0)
18.11.2020	Tbilisi	Georgia - Estonia	0-0

Final Standings

1.	**Armenia**	6	3	2	1	9	-	6	11
2.	N.Macedonia	6	2	3	1	9	-	8	9
3.	Georgia	6	1	4	1	6	-	6	7
4.	Estonia	6	0	3	3	5	-	9	3

Armenia promoted to League B
Estonia qualified to relegation play-outs

GROUP C3

Results

03.09.2020	Parma	Moldova - Kosovo	1-1(1-0)
03.09.2020	Ljubljana	Slovenia - Greece	0-0
06.09.2020	Ljubljana	Slovenia - Moldova	1-0(1-0)
06.09.2020	Prishtina	Kosovo - Greece	1-2(0-1)
11.10.2020	Athína	Greece - Moldova	2-0(1-0)
11.10.2020	Prishtina	Kosovo - Slovenia	0-1(0-1)
14.10.2020	Athína	Greece - Kosovo	0-0
14.10.2020	Chişinău	Moldova - Slovenia	0-4(0-3)
15.11.2020	Chişinău	Moldova - Greece	0-2(0-2)
15.11.2020	Ljubljana	Slovenia - Kosovo	2-1(0-0)
18.11.2020	Athína	Greece - Slovenia	0-0
18.11.2020	Prishtina	Kosovo - Moldova	1-0(1-0)

Final Standings

1.	**Slovenia**	6	4	2	0	8	-	1	14
2.	Greece	6	3	3	0	6	-	1	12
3.	Kosovo	6	1	2	3	4	-	6	5
4.	Moldova	6	0	1	5	1	-	11	1

Slovenia promoted to League B
Moldova qualified to relegation play-outs

GROUP C4

Results

04.09.2020	Vilnius	Lithuania - Kazakhstan	0-2(0-1)
04.09.2020	Minsk	Belarus - Albania	0-2(0-1)
07.09.2020	Almaty	Kazakhstan - Belarus	1-2(0-0)
07.09.2020	Tiranë	Albania - Lithuania	0-1(0-0)
11.10.2020	Almaty	Kazakhstan - Albania	0-0
11.10.2020	Vilnius	Lithuania - Belarus	2-2(1-0)
14.10.2020	Vilnius	Lithuania - Albania	0-0
14.10.2020	Minsk	Belarus - Kazakhstan	2-0(1-0)
15.11.2020	Minsk	Belarus - Lithuania	2-0(2-0)
15.11.2020	Tiranë	Albania - Kazakhstan	3-1(2-1)
18.11.2020	Tiranë	Albania - Belarus	3-2(3-1)
18.11.2020	Almaty	Kazakhstan - Lithuania	1-2(1-1)

Final Standings

1.	**Albania**	6	3	2	1	8	-	4	11
2.	Belarus	6	3	1	2	10	-	8	10
3.	Lithuania	6	2	2	2	5	-	7	8
4.	Kazakhstan	6	1	1	4	5	-	9	4

Albania promoted to League B
Kazakhstan qualified to relegation play-outs

LEAGUE D

GROUP D1

Results

03.09.2020	Rīga	Latvia - Andorra	0-0
03.09.2020	Tórshavn	Faroe Islands - Malta	3-2(1-1)
06.09.2020	Andorra la V.	Andorra - Faroe Islands	0-1(0-1)
06.09.2020	Attard	Malta - Latvia	1-1(1-1)
10.10.2020	Tórshavn	Faroe Islands - Latvia	1-1(0-0)
10.10.2020	Andorra la V.	Andorra - Malta	0-0
13.10.2020	Rīga	Latvia - Malta	0-1(0-0)
13.10.2020	Tórshavn	Faroe Islands - Andorra	2-0(2-0)
14.11.2020	Attard	Malta - Andorra	3-1(0-1)
14.11.2020	Rīga	Latvia - Faroe Islands	1-1(0-0)
17.11.2020	Andorra la V.	Andorra - Latvia	0-5(0-1)
17.11.2020	Attard	Malta - Faroe Islands	1-1(0-0)

Final Standings

1.	**Faroe Isl.**	6	3	3	0	9	-	5	12
2.	Malta	6	2	3	1	8	-	6	9
3.	Latvia	6	1	4	1	8	-	4	7
4.	Andorra	6	0	2	4	1	-	11	2

Faroe Islands promoted to League C

GROUP D2

Results

05.09.2020	Gibraltar	Gibraltar - San Marino	1-0(1-0)
08.09.2020	Rimini	San Marino - Liechtenstein	0-2(0-2)
10.10.2020	Vaduz	Liechtenstein - Gibraltar	0-1(0-1)
13.10.2020	Vaduz	Liechtenstein - San Marino	0-0
14.11.2020	Serravalle	San Marino - Gibraltar	0-0
17.11.2020	Gibraltar	Gibraltar - Liechtenstein	1-1(1-1)

Final Standings

1.	**Gibraltar**	4	2	2	0	3	-	1	8
2.	Liechtenstein	4	1	2	1	3	-	2	5
3.	San Marino	4	0	2	2	0	-	3	2

Gibraltar promoted to League C

2022 FIFA WORLD CUP
EUROPEAN QUALIFIERS

The 22nd FIFA World Cup will be hosted by Qatar between 21.11. and 18.12.2022. All 55 FIFA-affiliated national teams from UEFA entered qualification, a total of 13 slots in the final tournament are available for European national teams. The qualification will depend, in part, on results from the 2020-2021 UEFA Nations League.

In the group stage, the 55 teams were drawn in 5 groups of 5 teams and 5 groups of 6 teams (with the 4 teams that make the 2020-2021 UEFA Nations League Finals put into the smaller groups) with group winners qualifying for the World Cup finals. In the Play-off stage: the 10 group runners-up would be joined by the best 2 Nations League group winners, based on the Nations League overall ranking, that finished outside the top two of their qualifying group. These 12 teams will be drawn into three play-off paths, playing two rounds of single-match play-offs (semi-finals and finals, with the home teams to be drawn), with the 3 path winners qualifying for the World Cup final tournament.

The draw for the group stage was held in Zürich (Switzerland), on 07.12.2020. The 55 teams were seeded into six pots based on the FIFA World Rankings of November 2020 (shawn in brackets), as follows:

Pot 1	Pot 2	Pot 3	Pot 4	Pot 5	Pot 6
Belgium (1)	Switzerland (16)	Russia (39)	Bosnia and Herz. (55)	Armenia (99)	Malta (176)
France (2)	Wales (18)	Hungary (40)	Slovenia (62)	Cyprus (100)	Moldova (177)
England (4)	Poland (19)	Repub. of Ireland (42)	Montenegro (63)	Faroe Islands (107)	Liechtenstein (181)
Portugal (5)	Sweden (20)	Czech Republic (42)	North Macedonia (65)	Azerbaijan (109)	Gibraltar (195)
Spain (6)	Austria (23)	Norway (44)	Albania (66)	Estonia (109)	San Marino (210)
Italy (10)	Ukraine (24)	Northern Ireland (45)	Bulgaria (68)	Kosovo (117)	
Croatia (11)	Serbia (30)	Iceland (46)	Israel (87)	Kazakhstan (122)	
Denmark (12)	Turkey (32)	Scotland (48)	Belarus (88)	Lithuania (129)	
Germany (13)	Slovakia (33)	Greece (53)	Georgia (89)	Latvia (136)	
Netherlands (14)	Romania (37)	Finland (54)	Luxembourg (98)	Andorra (151)	

GROUP A

Results

24.03.2021	Torino	Portugal - Azerbaijan	1-0(1-0)
24.03.2021	Beograd	Serbia - Republic of Ireland	3-2(1-1)
27.03.2021	Dublin	R. of Ireland - Luxembourg	0-1(0-0)
27.03.2021	Beograd	Serbia - Portugal	2-2(0-2)
30.03.2021	Bakı	Azerbaijan - Serbia	1-2(0-1)
30.03.2021	Lëtzebuerg	Luxembourg - Portugal	1-3(1-1)

Standings

1.	Portugal	3	2	1	0	6	-	3	7
2.	Serbia	3	2	1	0	7	-	5	7
3.	Luxembourg	2	1	0	1	2	-	3	3
4.	Rep. Ireland	2	0	0	2	2	-	4	0
5.	Azerbaijan	2	0	0	2	1	-	3	0

Next matches:

01.09.2021	Luxembourg - Azerbaijan; Portugal - Republic of Ireland;
04.09.2021	Republic of Ireland - Azerbaijan; Serbia - Luxembourg
07.09.2021	Azerbaijan - Portugal; Republic of Ireland - Serbia
09.10.2021	Azerbaijan - Republic of Ireland; Luxembourg - Serbia
12.10.2021	Portugal - Luxembourg; Serbia - Azerbaijan
11.11.2021	Azerbaijan - Luxembourg; Republic of Ireland - Portugal
14.11.2021	Luxembourg - Republic of Ireland; Portugal - Serbia

GROUP B

Results

25.03.2021	Stockholm	Sweden - Georgia	1-0(1-0)
25.03.2021	Granada	Spain - Greece	1-1(1-0)
28.03.2021	Tbilisi	Georgia - Spain	1-2(1-0)
28.03.2021	Prishtina	Kosovo - Sweden	0-3(0-2)
31.03.2021	Thessaloníki	Greece - Georgia	1-1(0-0)
31.03.2021	Sevilla	Spain - Kosovo	3-1(2-0)

Standings

1.	Spain	3	2	1	0	6	-	3	7
2.	Sweden	2	2	0	0	4	-	0	6
3.	Greece	2	0	2	0	2	-	2	2
4.	Georgia	3	0	1	2	2	-	4	1
5.	Kosovo	2	0	0	2	1	-	6	0

Next matches:

02.09.2021	Georgia - Kosovo; Sweden - Spain
05.09.2021	Kosovo - Greece; Spain - Georgia
08.09.2021	Greece - Sweden; Kosovo - Spain
09.10.2021	Georgia - Greece; Sweden - Kosovo
12.10.2021	Kosovo - Georgia; Sweden - Greece
11.11.2021	Georgia - Sweden; Greece - Spain
14.11.2021	Greece - Kosovo; Spain - Sweden

GROUP C

Results

25.03.2021	Sofia	Bulgaria - Switzerland	1-3(0-3)
25.03.2021	Parma	Italy - Northern Ireland	2-0(2-0)
28.03.2021	Sofia	Bulgaria - Italy	0-2(0-1)
28.03.2021	St. Gallen	Switzerland - Lithuania	1-0(1-0)
31.03.2021	Vilnius	Lithuania - Italy	0-2(0-0)
31.03.2021	Belfast	Northern Ireland - Bulgaria	0-0

Standings

1.	Italy	3	3	0	0	6	-	0	9
2.	Switzerland	2	2	0	0	4	-	1	6
3.	North. Ireland	2	0	1	1	0	-	2	1
4.	Bulgaria	3	0	1	2	1	-	5	1
5.	Lithuania	2	0	0	2	0	-	3	0

Next matches:

02.09.2021	Italy - Bulgaria; Lithuania - Northern Ireland
05.09.2021	Bulgaria - Lithuania; Switzerland - Italy
08.09.2021	Italy - Lithuania; Northern Ireland - Switzerland
09.10.2021	Lithuania - Bulgaria; Switzerland - Northern Ireland
12.10.2021	Bulgaria - Northern Ireland; Lithuania - Switzerland
12.11.2021	Italy - Switzerland; Northern Ireland - Lithuania
15.11.2021	Northern Ireland - Italy; Switzerland - Bulgaria

GROUP D

Results

24.03.2021	Helsinki	Finland - Bosnia and Herz.	2-2(0-0)
24.03.2021	Paris	France - Ukraine	1-1(1-0)
28.03.2021	Nur-Sultan	Kazakhstan - France	0-2(0-2)
28.03.2021	Kyiv	Ukraine - Finland	1-1(0-0)
31.03.2021	Sarajevo	Bosnia and Herz. - France	0-1(0-0)
31.03.2021	Kyiv	Ukraine - Kazakhstan	1-1(1-0)

Standings

1.	France	3	2	1	0	4	-	1	7
2.	Ukraine	3	0	3	0	3	-	3	3
3.	Finland	2	0	2	0	3	-	3	2
4.	Bosnia and H.	2	0	1	1	2	-	3	1
5.	Kazakhstan	2	0	1	1	1	-	3	1

Next matches:

01.09.2021	Kazakhstan - Ukraine; France - Bosnia and Herzegovina
04.09.2021	Finland - Kazakhstan; Ukraine - France
07.09.2021	Bosnia and Herzegovina - Kazakhstan; France - Finland
09.10.2021	Kazakhstan - Bosnia and Herzegovina; Finland - Ukraine
12.10.2021	Kazakhstan - Finland; Ukraine - Bosnia and Herzegovina
13.11.2021	Bosnia and Herzegovina - Finland; France - Kazakhstan
16.11.2021	Bosnia and Herzegovina - Ukraine; Finland - France

GROUP E

Results

24.03.2021	Leuven	Belgium - Wales	3-1(2-1)
24.03.2021	Lublin	Estonia - Czech Republic	2-6(1-4)
27.03.2021	Minsk	Belarus - Estonia	4-2(1-1)
27.03.2021	Praha	Czech Republic - Belgium	1-1(0-0)
30.03.2021	Leuven	Belgium - Belarus	8-0(4-0)
30.03.2021	Cardiff	Wales - Czech Republic	1-0(0-0)

Standings

1.	Belgium	3	2	1	0	12	-	2	7
2.	Czech Rep.	3	1	1	1	7	-	4	4
3.	Wales	2	1	0	1	2	-	3	3
4.	Belarus	2	1	0	1	4	-	10	3
5.	Estonia	2	0	0	2	4	-	10	0

Next matches:

02.09.2021	Estonia - Belgium; Czech Republic - Belarus
05.09.2021	Belarus - Wales; Belgium - Czech Republic
08.09.2021	Belarus - Belgium; Wales - Estonia
08.10.2021	Estonia - Belarus; Czech Republic - Wales
11.10.2021	Belarus - Czech Republic; Estonia - Wales
13.11.2021	Belgium - Estonia; Wales - Belarus
16.11.2021	Czech Republic - Estonia; Wales - Belgium

GROUP F

Results

25.03.2021	Tel Aviv	Israel - Denmark	0-2(0-1)
25.03.2021	Chişinău	Moldova - Faroe Islands	1-1(1-0)
25.03.2021	Glasgow	Scotland - Austria	2-2(0-0)
28.03.2021	Herning	Denmark - Moldova	8-0(5-0)
28.03.2021	Tel Aviv	Israel - Scotland	1-1(1-0)
28.03.2021	Wien	Austria - Faroe Islands	3-1(3-1)
31.03.2021	Chişinău	Moldova - Israel	1-4(1-1)
31.03.2021	Wien	Austria - Denmark	0-4(0-0)
31.03.2021	Glasgow	Scotland - Faroe Islands	4-0(1-0)

Standings

1.	Denmark	3	3	0	0	14	-	0	9
2.	Scotland	3	1	2	0	7	-	3	5
3.	Israel	3	1	1	1	5	-	4	4
4.	Austria	3	1	1	1	5	-	7	4
5.	Faroe Islands	3	0	1	2	2	-	8	1
6.	Moldova	3	0	1	2	2	-	13	1

Next matches:

01.09.2021	Denmark - Scotland; Faroe Islands - Israel; Moldova - Austria
04.09.2021	Faroe Islands - Denmark ; Israel - Austria ; Scotland - Moldova
07.09.2021	Denmark - Israel; Faroe Islands - Moldova; Austria - Scotland
09.10.2021	Scotland - Israel; Faroe Islands - Austria; Moldova - Denmark
12.10.2021	Denmark - Austria; Faroe Islands - Scotland; Israel - Moldova
12.11.2021	Moldova - Scotland; Denmark - Faroe Islands; Austria - Israel
15.11.2021	Israel - Faroe Islands; Austria - Moldova; Scotland - Denmark

GROUP G

Results

24.03.2021	İstanbul	Turkey - Netherlands	4-2(2-0)
24.03.2021	Gibraltar	Gibraltar - Norway	0-3(0-2)
24.03.2021	Rīga	Latvia - Montenegro	1-2(1-1)
27.03.2021	Podgorica	Montenegro - Gibraltar	4-1(2-1)
27.03.2021	Amsterdam	Netherlands - Latvia	2-0(1-0)
27.03.2021	Málaga	Norway - Turkey	0-3(0-2)
30.03.2021	Gibraltar	Gibraltar - Netherlands	0-7(0-1)
30.03.2021	Podgorica	Montenegro - Norway	0-1(0-1)
30.03.2021	İstanbul	Turkey - Latvia	3-3(2-1)

Standings

1.	Turkey	3	2	1	0	10	-	5	7
2.	Netherlands	3	2	0	1	11	-	4	6
3.	Montenegro	3	2	0	1	6	-	3	6
4.	Norway	3	2	0	1	4	-	3	6
5.	Latvia	3	0	1	2	4	-	7	1
6.	Gibraltar	3	0	0	3	1	-	14	0

Next matches:

01.09.2021	Latvia - Gibraltar; Norway - Netherlands; Turkey - Montenegro
04.09.2021	Latvia - Norway; Gibraltar - Turkey; Netherlands - Montenegro
07.09.2021	Montenegro - Latvia; Netherlands - Turkey; Norway - Gibraltar
08.10.2021	Gibraltar - Montenegro; Latvia - Netherlands; Turkey - Norway
11.10.2021	Latvia - Turkey; Netherlands - Gibraltar; Norway - Montenegro
13.11.2021	Norway - Latvia; Turkey - Gibraltar; Montenegro - Netherlands
16.11.2021	Gibraltar - Latvia; Montenegro - Turkey; Netherlands - Norway

GROUP H

Results

24.03.2021	Attard	Malta - Russia	1-3(0-2)
24.03.2021	Ljubljana	Slovenia - Croatia	1-0(1-0)
24.03.2021	Nicosia	Cyprus - Slovakia	0-0
27.03.2021	Sochi	Russia - Slovenia	2-1(2-1)
27.03.2021	Rijeka	Croatia - Cyprus	1-0(1-0)
27.03.2021	Trnava	Slovakia - Malta	2-2(0-2)
30.03.2021	Nicosia	Cyprus - Slovenia	1-0(1-0)
30.03.2021	Rijeka	Croatia - Malta	3-0(0-0)
30.03.2021	Trnava	Slovakia - Russia	2-1(1-0)

Standings

1.	Croatia	3	2	0	1	4	-	1	6
2.	Russia	3	2	0	1	6	-	4	6
3.	Slovakia	3	1	2	0	4	-	3	5
4.	Cyprus	3	1	1	1	1	-	1	4
5.	Slovenia	3	1	0	2	2	-	3	3
6.	Malta	3	0	1	2	3	-	8	1

Next matches:

01.09.2021	Malta - Cyprus; Russia - Croatia; Slovenia - Slovakia
04.09.2021	Slovenia - Malta; Cyprus - Russia; Slovakia - Croatia
07.09.2021	Croatia - Slovenia; Russia - Malta; Slovakia - Cyprus
08.10.2021	Malta - Slovenia; Russia - Slovakia; Cyprus - Croatia
11.10.2021	Cyprus - Malta; Croatia - Slovakia; Slovenia - Russia
11.11.2021	Russia - Cyprus; Malta - Croatia; Slovakia - Slovenia
14.11.2021	Croatia - Russia; Malta - Slovakia; Slovenia - Cyprus

GROUP I

Results

25.03.2021	Andorra la V.	Andorra - Albania	0-1(0-1)
25.03.2021	London	England - San Marino	5-0(3-0)
25.03.2021	Budapest	Hungary - Poland	3-3(1-0)
28.03.2021	Tiranë	Albania - England	0-2(0-1)
28.03.2021	Warszawa	Poland - Andorra	3-0(1-0)
28.03.2021	Serravalle	San Marino - Hungary	0-3(0-1)
31.03.2021	Andorra la V.	Andorra - Hungary	1-4(0-1)
31.03.2021	London	England - Poland	2-1(1-0)
31.03.2021	Serravalle	San Marino - Albania	0-2(0-0)

Standings

1.	England	3	3	0	0	9	-	1	9
2.	Hungary	3	2	1	0	10	-	3	7
3.	Albania	3	2	0	1	3	-	2	6
4.	Poland	3	1	1	1	7	-	5	4
5.	Andorra	3	0	0	3	1	-	8	0
6.	San Marino	3	0	0	3	0	-	10	0

Next matches:

02.09.2021	Andorra - San Marino; Poland - Albania; Hungary - England
05.09.2021	Albania - Hungary; England - Andorra; San Marino - Poland
08.09.2021	Albania - San Marino; Poland - England; Hungary - Andorra
09.10.2021	Andorra - England; Poland - San Marino; Hungary - Albania
12.10.2021	Albania - Poland; England - Hungary; San Marino - Andorra
12.11.2021	Andorra - Poland; England - Albania; Hungary - San Marino
15.11.2021	Albania - Andorra; Poland - Hungary; San Marino - England

GROUP J

Results

25.03.2021	Duisburg	Germany - Iceland	3-0(2-0)
25.03.2021	Vaduz	Liechtenstein - Armenia	0-1(0-0)
25.03.2021	Bucureşti	Romania - No. Macedonia	3-2(1-0)
28.03.2021	Yerevan	Armenia - Iceland	2-0(0-0)
28.03.2021	Skopje	No. Macedonia - Liechtenstein	5-0(1-0)
28.03.2021	Bucureşti	Romania - Germany	0-1(0-1)
31.03.2021	Yerevan	Armenia - Romania	3-2(0-0)
31.03.2021	Duisburg	Germany - No. Macedonia	1-2(0-1)
31.03.2021	Vaduz	Liechtenstein - Iceland	1-4(0-2)

Standings

1.	Armenia	3	3	0	0	6	-	2	9
2.	N. Macedonia	3	2	0	1	9	-	4	6
3.	Germany	3	2	0	1	5	-	2	6
4.	Romania	3	1	0	2	5	-	6	3
5.	Iceland	3	1	0	2	4	-	6	3
6.	Liechtenstein	3	0	0	3	1	-	10	0

Next matches:

02.09.2021	Iceland - Romania; Liechtenstein - Germany; North Macedonia - Armenia
05.09.2021	Iceland - North Macedonia; Germany - Armenia; Romania - Liechtenstein
08.09.2021	Armenia - Liechtenstein; Iceland - Germany; North Macedonia - Romania
08.10.2021	Germany - Romania; Iceland - Armenia; Liechtenstein - North Macedonia
11.10.2021	Iceland - Liechtenstein; North Macedonia - Germany; Romania - Armenia
11.11.2021	Armenia - North Macedonia; Germany - Liechtenstein; Romania - Iceland
14.11.2021	Armenia - Germany; Liechtenstein - Romania; North Macedonia - Iceland

PRELIMINARY ROUND – SEMI-FINALS

08.08.2020; Centre sportif de Colovray, Nyon (Switzerland)
Referee: Balász Berke (Hungary)
SP Tre Fiori – LINFIELD FC BELFAST 0-2(0-0)
SP Tre Fiori: Aldo Sioncini, Alessandro D'Addario, Peda Misimovic, Davide Simoncini (89.Luca Angelini), Angelo Gregorio, Louseny Kalissa (70.Pier Figone), Nicholas Santoni, Francesco Lunardini, Giacomo Pracucci [*sent off 86*], Bojan Gjurchinoski, Joel Hijuelos (76.Adriano Marzeglia). Trainer: Matteo Cechetti (Italy).
Linfield FC: Christopher Johns, Ross Larkin, Jimmy Callacher, Ethan Boyle, Niall Quinn, Navid Nasseri (65.Andrew Waterworth), Daniel Kearns, Jamie Mulgrew, Kirk Millar, Shayne Lavery (65.Bastien Héry), Kyle McClean (65.Christy Manzinga). Trainer: David Healy.
Goals: 71' Bastien Héry 0-1, 83' Christy Manzinga 0-2.

08.08.2020; Centre sportif de Colovray, Nyon (Switzerland)
Referee: Robert Jenkins (Wales)
KF DRITA GJILAN – Inter Club d'Escaldes 2-1(2-1)
Drita Gjilan: Faton Maloku, Ardian Limani, Ardijan Cuculi, Ilir Blakçori, Hamdi Namani, Erjon Vuçaj, Astrit Fazliu (82.Albin Krasniqi), Xhevdet Shabani, Bunjamin Shabani, Almir Ajzeraj (89.Drilon Islami), Kastriot Rexha (73.Betim Haxhimusa). Trainer: Ardijan Nuhiji.
Inter Club d'Escaldes: Josep Gómes, Federico Bessone, Emili García, Óscar Reyes, Toni Lao (61.Ludovic Clemente), Feher, Genís, Bruninho (72.Jordi Betriu), Jordi Roca, Sergi Moreno (90.Andrés Briñez), Bruno Lemiechevsky. Trainer: Adolfo Baines.
Goals: 21' Xhevdet Shabani 1-0, 29' Emili García 1-1, 45+3' Hamdi Namani 2-1.

PRELIMINARY ROUND – FINALS

11.08.2020; Centre sportif de Colovray, Nyon (Switzerland)
Referee: Ioannis Papadopoulos (Greece)
KF Drita Gjilan – LINFIELD FC BELFAST 0-3
Please note: this match could not be played due to two players from KF Drita Gjilan testing positive for COVID-19 and the whole team being put into quarantine by the Swiss authorities. Linfield FC Belfast were subsequently awarded a 3-0 victory by UEFA according to the regulations related to COVID-19.

FIRST QUALIFYING ROUND

18.08.2020; „Tofiq Bahramov" adina Respublika stadionu, Bakı
Referee: Yaroslav Kozyk (Ukraine)
QARABAĞ FK BAKI – FK Sileks Kratovo 4-0(2-0)
Qarabağ FK: Sahrudin Mahammadaliyev, Maksim Medvedev (79.Abbas Hüseynov), Badavi Hüseynov, Kevin Medina, Jaime Romero (83.Elvin Dzhafarquliyev), Uros Matic, Filip Ozobic, Wilde-Donald Guerrier, Abdellah Zoubir (72.Owusu Kwabena), Ismayil Ibrahimli, Mahir Emreli. Trainer: Qurban Qurbanov.
Sileks Kratovo: Daniel Bozinovski, Srdjan Draskovic, Hristijan Grozdanoski, Denis Ristov (59.Milos Zeravica), Angelce Timovski, Burhan Mustafov (84.Bojan Spirkoski), Dejan Tanturovski (74.Kristijan Kostovski), Viktor Serafimovski, Daniel Karceski, Pepi Gorgiev, Ivan Ivanovski. Trainer: Goran Simov. Goals: 11' Jaime Romero 1-0, 40', 51' Wilde-Donald Guerrier 2-0, 3-0, 80' Mahir Emreli 4-0.

18.08.2020; Regional Sport Complex Brestsky, Brest
Referee: Novak Simović (Serbia)
FC Dinamo Brest – ASTANA FC 6-3(4-1)
Dinamo Brest: Sergey Ignatovich, Yevhen Khacheridi, Kirill Pechenin, Gaby Kiki, Sergey Kislyak (73.Sergey Krivets), Roman Yuzepchuk, Pavel Sedko, David Tweh, Artem Milevskiy (86.Artem Bykov), Mikhail Gordeychuk (73.Pavel Savitskiy), Abdoulaye Diallo. Trainer: Sergey Kovalchuk.
Astana FC: Dmytro Nepogodov, Abzal Beysebekov, Uros Radakovic, Luka Simunovic, Marin Tomasov, Dmitriy Shomko, Ivan Maevski, Yuri Pertsukh (34.Tigran Barseghyan), Maks Ebong, Aleksey Shchetkin (34.Dorin Rotariu), Pieros Soteriou. Trainer: Michal Bílek (Czech Republic).
Goals: 16' Mikhail Gordeychuk 1-0, 17' Kirill Pechenin 2-0, 22' Mikhail Gordeychuk 3-0, 37' Pavel Sedko 4-0, 45' Marin Tomasov 4-1, 53' Dorin Rotariu 4-2, 55' Abdoulaye Diallo 5-2, 87' Abzal Beysebekov 5-3, 90' Abdoulaye Diallo 6-3.

18.08.2020; Stadion "Rajko Mitić", Beograd
Referee: Volen Chinkov (Bulgaria)
FK CRVENA ZVEZDA BEOGRAD – Europa FC 5-0(2-0)
Crvena Zvezda: Milan Borjan, Nemanja Milunovic, Milan Rodic (46.Milan Gajic), Milos Degenek, Marko Gobeljic, Aleksandar Katai, Srdjan Spiridonovic (68.Tómané), Sékou Sanogo (74.Milos Vulic), Guélor Kanga, Mirko Ivanic, El Fardou Ben Nabouhane. Trainer: Dejan Stanković.
Europa FC: Javi Muñoz, Olmo González, Jayce Olivero, Juampe Rico, Liam Walker, Willy (64.Polaco), Blas Álvarez (70.Álex Quillo), Marco Rosa, Ale Carrascal, Mohamed Badr Hassan, Adrián Gallardo (60.Manu Dimas). Trainer: Rafael Escobar Obrero (Spain).
Goals: 35', 44', 52' El Fardou Ben Nabouhane 1-0, 2-0, 3-0, 78', 87' Mirko Ivanic 4-0, 5-0.

18.08.2020; Stadion Wojska Polskiego, Warszawa
Referee: Nicolas Laforge (Belgium)
LEGIA WARSZAWA – Linfield FC Belfast 1-0(1-0)
Legia Warszawa: Artur Boruc, Artur Jedrzejczyk, Filip Mladenovic, Mateusz Wieteska, Michal Karbownik, Domagoj Antolic, Pawel Wszolek, Valeriane Gvilia, Bartosz Slisz (46.Maciej Rosolek), Luquinhas, Tomás Pekhart (70.José Kanté). Trainer: Aleksandar Vuković (Serbia).
Linfield FC: Christopher Johns, Matthew Clarke, Mark Stafford, Ross Larkin, Niall Quinn (84.Navid Nasseri), Ethan Boyle, Jamie Mulgrew, Kirk Millar [*sent off 75*], Bastien Héry (79.Conor Pepper), Stephen Fallon, Shayne Lavery (76.Christy Manzinga). Trainer: David Healy.
Goal: 82' José Kanté 1-0.

18.08.2020; Celtic Park, Glasgow
Referee: Sebastian Gishamer (Austria)
CELTIC FC GLASGOW – KR Reykjavík 6-0(3-0)
Celtic: Vassilis Barkas, Hatem Abd Elhamed, Christopher Jullien, Greg Taylor, Scott Brown (62.Olivier Ntcham), Nir Bitton, James Forrest, Callum McGregor, Mohamed Elyounoussi, Ryan Christie (72.Patryk Klimala), Odsonne Édouard (72.Albian Ajeti). Trainer: Neil Francis Lennon (Northern Ireland).
KR Reykjavík: Beitir Ólafsson, Arnór Adalsteinsson, Kristinn Jónsson (46.Atli Sigurjónsson) Finnur Tómas Pálmason, Pálmi Pálmason, Finnur Margeirsson, Arnthór Ingi Kristinsson, Pablo Punyed, Óskar Hauksson (73.Alex Freyr Hilmarsson), Kennie Chopart, Kristján Finnbogason (73.Ægir Jónasson). Trainer: Rúnar Kristinsson.
Goals: 6' Mohamed Elyounoussi 1-0, 17' Arnór Adalsteinsson 2-0 (own goal), 31' Christopher Jullien 3-0, 46' Greg Taylor 4-0, 72' Odsonne Édouard 5-0, 90+1' Mohamed Elyounoussi 6-0.

19.08.2020; Stadion Yerevan Football Academy, Yerevan
Referee: Viktor Shimusik (Belarus)
FC Ararat-Armenia Yerevan – AC OMONIA NICOSIA 0-1(0-0,0-0)
Ararat-Armenia: Stefan Cupic, Alemão (85.Sargis Shahinyan), Sergiy Vakulenko, Ângelo Meneses (111.Aleksandar Damcevski), David Bollo [*sent off 97*], Yoan Gouffran (90+2.Armen Ambartsumyan), Kódjo Alphonse, Furdjel Narsingh, Yusuf Otubanjo (73.Zakaria Sanogo), Louis Ogana, Mailson. Trainer: David Campaña Piquer (Spain).
Omonia Nicosia: Fabiano, Jan Lecjaks, Tomás Hubocan, Michael Lüftner, Ádam Lang, Jordi Gómez, Vítor Gomes (91.Ioannis Kousoulos), Charis Mavrias (81.Loizos Loizou), Michal Djuris (67.Éric Bauthéac), Thiago Santos (103.Marinos Tzionis), Andronikos Kakoullis. Trainer: Henning Stille Berg (Norway).
Goal: 94' Thiago Santos 0-1.

19.08.2020; Aker Stadion, Molde
Referee: Bryn Markham-Jones (Wales)
MOLDE FK – Kuopion Palloseura 5-0(2-0)
Molde FK: Andreas Linde, Kristoffer Haugen, Sheriff Sinyan, Magnus Eikrem (86.Tobias Christensen), Etzaz Hussain, Eirik Hestad, Fredrik Aursnes, Martin Ellingsen, Henry Wingo (74.Marcus Pedersen), Ola Brynhildsen (79.Erling Knudtzon), Ohi Omoijuanfo. Trainer: Erling Moe.
Kuopion PS: Otso Virtanen, Juho Pirttijoki, Nuno Tomás (66.Joel Vartiainen), Luc Tabi Manga, Petteri Pennanen, Bismark Adjei-Boateng, Ilmari Niskanen, Urhu Nissilä, Saku Savolainen, Rangel (74.Aniekpeno Udoh), Usman Sale (74.Ats Purje). Trainer: Arne Erlandsen.
Goals: 26' Eirik Hestad 1-0, 37' Magnus Eikrem 2-0, 69' Ohi Omoijuanfo 3-0, 90+1' Marcus Pedersen 4-0, 90+3' Erling Knudtzon 5-0.

19.08.2020; Groupama Aréna, Budapest
Referee: Fedayi San (Switzerland)
FERENCVÁROSI TC – Djurgårdens IF Stockholm 2-0(1-0)
Ferencvárosi TC: Dénes Dibusz, Endre Botka, Miha Blazic, Adnan Kovacevic, Eldar Civic, Somália, Igor Kharatin, Isael (75.Aïssa Laïdouni), Tokmac Nguen (63.Michal Skvarka), Franck Boli, Myrto Uzuni (84.Roland Varga). Trainer: Serhiy Rebrov (Ukraine).
Djurgårdens IF: Per Bråtveit, Erik Berg, Jacob Une-Larsson, Jesper Nyholm, Aslak Witry, Jonathan Augustinsson, Fredrik Ulvestad, Jesper Karlström, Curtis Edwards (75.Haris Radetinac), Emmanuel Banda (18.Karl Holmberg), Emir Kujovic (46.Edward Chilufya). Trainer: Kim Bergstrand.
Goals: 33', 62' Tokmac Nguen 1-0, 2-0.

19.08.2020; „Boris Paichadze" Dinamo Arena, Tbilisi
Referee: Roomer Tarajev (Estonia)
Dinamo Tbilisi – KF TIRANË 0-2(0-1)
Dinamo Tbilisi: Roin Kvaskhvadze, Nodar Iashvili, Luka Lochoshvili, Davit Kobouri (59.Giorgi Kimadze), Simon Gbegnon, Giorgi Papava, Bakar Kardava (67.Giorgi Kutsia), Akaki Shulaia, Irakli Bugridze (81.Giorgi Gabedava), Tornike Kapanadze, Pernambuco. Trainer: Kakhaber Chkhetiani.
KF Tiranë: Ilion Lika, Kristi Vangjeli, Kristijan Tosevski, Marsel Ismajlgeci, Filip Najdovski, Idriz Batha, Jurgen Çelhaka, Agustin Torassa (83.Gentian Muça), Elton Calé (71.Ardit Toli), Winful Cobbinah, Ernest Muçi (87.Albion Avdijaj). Trainer: Ndubuisi Emmanuel Egbo (Nigeria).
Goals: 45+4' Agustin Torassa 0-1, 86' Marsel Ismajlgeci 0-2.

19.08.2020; Stadionul Sheriff, Tiraspol
Referee: Balász Berke (Hungary)
FC SHERIFF TIRASPOL – CS Fola Esch 2-0(1-0)
FC Sheriff Tiraspol: Dumitru Celeadnic, Andrei Peteleu, Ousmane N'Diaye, Faith Obilor, William Parra (90+3.Max Veloso), Cristiano, Charles Petro, Benedik Mioc, Gabrijel Boban (88.Andriy Bliznichenko), Anatole Abang, Frank Castañeda (67.Andrej Lukic). Trainer: Zoran Zekić (Croatia).
CS Fola Esch: Emmanuel Cabral, Julien Klein, Sylvio Ouassiero (80.Achraf Drif), Cédric Sacras, Rodrigue Dikaba (62.Zachary Hadji), Dejvid Sinani (82.Bruno Freire), Diogo Pimentel, Stefano Bensi, Gauthier Caron, Gilson Delgado, Jules Diallo. Trainer: Sébastian Richard Grandjean.
Goals: 36' Anatole Abang 1-0, 81' Andrej Lukic 2-0.

19.08.2020; Stadion Pod Goricom, Podgorica
Referee: Ferenc Karakó (Hungary)
FK Buducnost Podgorica–PFC LUDOGORETS RAZGRAD 1-3(1-2)
Buducnost Podgorica: Milos Dragojevic, Vladan Adzic, Luka Mirkovic, Igor Cukovic, Nemanja Sekulic, Milos Raickovic (82.Dejan Zarubica), Vasilije Terzic (75.Miomir Djurickovic), Petar Vukcevic, Igor Ivanovic, Panagiotis Moraitis, Ivan Bojovic (76.Aleksandar Vujacic). Trainer: Mladen Milinković.
Ludogorets Razgrad: Renan, Cosmin Moti, Dragos Grigore, Cicinho, Anton Nedyalkov, Mavis Tchibota (65.Dominik Yankov), Stéphane Badji, Cauly, Alex Santana, Higinio Marín (76.Claudiu Keserü), Bernard Tekpetey (85.Jorghinho). Trainer: Pavel Vrba.
Goals: 12' Higinio Marín 0-1, 25' Mavis Tchibota 0-2, 31' Igor Cukovic 1-2, 90+3' Cauly 1-3.

19.08.2020; A. Le Coq Arena, Tallinn
Referee: Nejc Kajtazović (Slovenia)
FC Flora Tallinn – FK SŪDUVA MARIJAMPOLĖ 1-1(0-0,1-1); 2-4 on penalties
FC Flora: Matvei Igonen, Ken Kallaste (106.Henri Järvelaid), Märten Kuusk, Henrik Pürg, Michael Lilander, Konstantin Vassiljev, Martin Miller (62.Rauno Alliku), Markus Soomets, Vladislavs Kreida, Rauno Sappinen, Vlasiy Sinyavskiy (84.Frank Liivak). Trainer: Jürgen Henn.
FK Sūduva: Ivan Kardum, Vaidas Slavickas, Thomas Salamon (120.Valērijs Sabala), Aleksandar Zivanovic, Semir Kerla, Ivan Hladík, Evgen Efremov (72.Andro Svrljuga), Povilas Leimonas (37.Domagoj Pusic), Giedrius Matulevicius (61.Eligijus Jankauskas), Josip Tadic, Mihrit Topcagic. Trainer: Saulius Sirmelis.
Goals: 49' Rauno Sappinen 1-0, 78' Mihret Topcagic 1-1 (penalty).
Penalties: Andro Svrljuga 0-1, Konstantin Vassiljev (missed), Valērijs Sabala 0-2, Rauno Sappinen 1-2, Josip Tadic (missed), Henri Järvelaid 2-2, Domagoj Pusic 2-3, Markus Soomets (missed), Mihrit Topcagic 2-4.

19.08.2020; Bloomfield Stadium, Tel Aviv
Referee: Igor Pajac (Croatia)
MACCABI TEL AVIV FC – Rīga FC 2-0(0-0)
Maccabi Tel Aviv: Daniel Tenenbaum, Sheran Yeini, Eitan Tibi, Saborit, Maor Kandil, Avi Rikan, Dor Peretz (84.Itay Shechter), Dan Glazer, Eduardo Guerrero (46.Dan Bitton), Nick Blackman, Eylon Almog (82.Tal Ben Haim). Trainer: Georgios Donis (Greece).
Riga FC: Roberts Ozols, Herdi Prenga, Antonijs Cernomordijs, Ritvars Rugins, Vyacheslav Sharpar, Jakub Hora (71.Dário Júnior), Felipe Brisola, Stefan Panic, Stênio Júnior (62.Jordan N'Kololo), Vladislavs Fjodorovs, Kule Mbombo (59.Roger). Trainer: Oleg Komonov.
Goals: 58', 88' Nick Blackman 1-0 (penalty), 2-0 (penalty).

19.08.2020; „Szusza Ferenc" Stadion, Budapest (Hungary)
Referee: Vítor Jorge Fernandes Ferreira (Portugal)
NK CELJE – Dundalk FC 3-0(1-0)
NK Celje: Matjaz Rozman, Josip Calusic, Denis Marandici, Advan Kadusic, Zan Zaletel, Matic Vrbanec (86.Nino Pungarsek), Lan Stravs, Mitja Lotric, Dario Vizinger (90+3.Filip Dangubic), Ivan Bozic (82.Jakob Novak), Luka Kerin. Trainer: Dušan Kosič.
Dundalk FC: Gary Rogers, Brian Gartland (76.Nathan Oduwa), Sean Gannon, Sean Hoare, Darragh Leahy, Chris Shields (82.David McMillan), Patrick McEleney, Jordan Flores (69.Sean Murray), Stefan Colovic, Patrick Hoban, Michael Duffy. Trainer: Vinny Perth.
Goals: 43' Luka Kerin 1-0, 89' Dario Vizinger 2-0, 90+5' Filip Dangubic 3-0.

19.08.2020; Cardiff City Stadium, Cardiff
Referee: Jamie Robinson (Northern Ireland)
Connah's Quay Nomads FC – FK SARAJEVO 0-2(0-1)
Connah's Quay Nomads: Lewis Brass, George Horan, Danny Holmes, Callum Roberts, Pristley Parquharson, Danny Harrison (46.Sameron Dool), Aeron Edwards (78.John Disney), Callum Morris, Declan Poole (83.Jamie Insall), Michael Wilde, Craig Curran. Trainer: Andy Morrison.
FK Sarajevo: Vladan Kovacevic, Amer Dupovac, Dusan Hodzic, Andrej Djokanovic, Mirko Oremus, Hrvoje Milicevic, Amar Rahmanovic, Ivan Jukic, Mersudin Ahmetovic (81.Haris Handzic), Benjamin Tatar (71.Krste Velkoski), Djani Salcin (60.Selmir Pidro). Trainer: Vinko Marinović.
Goals: 16', 65' Benjamin Tatar 0-1, 0-2.

19.08.2020; MFA Centenary Stadium, Ta'Qali
Referee: Laurent Kopriwa (Luxembourg)
Floriana FC – FC CFR 1907 CLUJ 0-2(0-0)
Floriana FC: Ini Akpan, Enzo Ruiz, Alex Cini (69.Moustapha Beye), Jurgen Pisani (82.Brandon Paiber), Ryan Camenzuli, Diego Venancio, Nicola Leone, Matías García, Kristian Keqi, Flávio Carioca (67.Marcelo Dias), Tiago Adan. Trainer: Vincenzo Potenza (Italy).
CFR Cluj: Cristian Balgradean, Paulo Vinícius, Camora, Mike Cestor, Andrei Burca, Ciprian Deac, Alexandru Chipciu (89.Catalin Golofca), Ovidiu Hoban, Mickaël Pereira (83.Mateo Susic), Catalin Itu (67.Luís Aurélio), Mário Rondón. Trainer: Dan Vasile Petrescu.
Goals: 53' Mike Cestor 0-1, 90+7' Catalin Golofca 0-2.

21.08.2020; Við Djúpumýrar, Klaksvík
Referee: Kristoffer Hagenes (Norway)
KÍ KLAKSVÍK – ŠK Slovan Bratislava 3-0
Please note: This match was originally scheduled to be played on 19.08.2020, but was postponed to 21.08.2020, due to one staff member from Slovan Bratislava testing positive for COVID-19 and the whole team being put into quarantine by the Faroese authorities. On 21.08.2020 the match could not be played due to one player from Slovan Bratislava testing positive for COVID-19 and the whole second team being put into quarantine by the Faroese authotities. KÍ Klaksvík were subsequently awarded a 3-0 victory by UEFA according to the regulations related to COVID-19.

SECOND QUALIFYING ROUND

CHAMPIONS PATH

25.08.2020; Air Albania Stadium, Tiranë
Referee: Kaspar Sjöberg (Sweden)
KF Tiranë – FK CRVENA ZVEZDA BEOGRAD 0-1(0-0)
KF Tiranë: Ilion Lika, Kristi Vangjeli, Kristijan Tosevski, Erion Hoxhallari (76.Ardit Toli), Filip Najdovski, Idriz Batha, Jurgen Çelhaka, Agustin Torassa, Elton Calé (85.Albion Avdijaj), Winful Cobbinah (73 Jurgen Vrapi), Ernest Muçi. Trainer: Ndubuisi Emmanuel Egbo (Nigeria).
Crvena Zvezda: Milan Borjan, Nemanja Milunovic, Milos Degenek (61.Milan Rodic), Marko Gobeljic, Radovan Pankov, Aleksandar Katai, Srdjan Spiridonovic (46.Mirko Ivanic), Sékou Sanogo, Guélor Kanga (83.Njegos Petrovic), Veljko Nikolic, Tómané. Trainer: Dejan Stanković.
Goal: 62' Tomané 0-1.

26.08.2020; Celtic Park, Glasgow
Referee: Allard Lindhout (Netherlands)
Celtic FC Glasgow – FERENCVÁROSI TC 1-2(0-1)
Celtic: Vassilis Barkas, Hatem Abd Elhamed (78.Jeremie Frimpong), Christopher Jullien, Kristoffer Ajer, Greg Taylor, Scott Brown, James Forrest (78.Albian Ajeti), Callum McGregor, Mohamed Elyounoussi, Olivier Ntcham, Ryan Christie. Trainer: Neil Francis Lennon (Northern Ireland).
Ferencvárosi TC: Dénes Dibusz, Endre Botka, Miha Blazic, Adnan Kovacevic, Eldar Civic, Somália, Dávid Sigér, Igor Kharatin, Isael (71.Franck Boli), Tokmac Nguen (80.Michal Skvarka), Myrto Uzuni (86.Lasha Dvali). Trainer: Serhiy Rebrov (Ukraine).
Goals: 7' Dávid Sigér 0-1, 53' Ryan Christie 1-1, 75' Tokmac Nguen 1-2.

26.08.2020; Stadion Z'dezele, Celje
Referee: Christopher Jäger (Austria)
NK Celje – MOLDE FK 1-2(1-0)
NK Celje: Matjaz Rozman, Josip Calusic, Denis Marandici, Advan Kadusic, Zan Zaletel, Matic Vrbanec, Lan Stravs (70.Nino Pungarsek), Mitja Lotric (84.Jakob Novak), Dario Vizinger, Ivan Bozic (85.Filip Dangubic), Luka Kerin. Trainer: Dušan Kosič.
Molde FK: Andreas Linde, Kristoffer Haugen, Sheriff Sinyan, Marcus Pedersen, Magnus Eikrem (79.Tobias Christensen), Etzaz Hussain, Eirik Hestad (84.Ola Brynhildsen), Fredrik Aursnes, Martin Ellingsen, Erling Knudtzon (56.Ohi Omoijuanfo), Leke James. Trainer: Erling Moe.
Goals: 38' Mitja Lotric 1-0, 57' Etzaz Hussain 1-1, 74' Leke James 1-2.

26.08.2020; Wankdorf Stadion, Bern
Referee: Athanasios Tzilos (Greece)
BSC YOUNG BOYS BERN – KÍ Klaksvík 3-1(0-0)
Young Boys: David von Ballmoos, Fabian Lustenberger, Jordan Lefort, Mohamed Camara, Quentin Maceiras (64.Ulisses Garcia), Miralem Sulejmani (64.Marvin Spielmann), Nicolas Moumi Ngamaleu, Christian Fassnacht, Vincent Sierro, Michel Aebischer (74.Christopher Martins), Jean-Pierre Nsamé. Trainer: Gerardo Seoane Castro.
KÍ Klaksvík: Kristian Joensen, Odmar Færø, Heini Vatnsdal, Jesper Brinck, Deni Pavlovic (77.Jonn Johanssen), Jákup Andreasen, Jóannes Bjartalid (89.Boris Dosljak), Jóannes Danielsen, Páll Klettskard, Patrik Johannesen, Ole Erik Midtskogen (90+2.Steinbjørn Olsen). Trainer: Mikkjal Thomassen (Faroe Islands).
Goals: 51' Jean-Pierre Nsame 1-0, 57' Miralem Sulejmani 2-0, 79' Jonn Johannesen 2-1, 82' Nicolas Moumi Ngamaleu 3-1.

26.08.2020; Regional Sport Complex Brestsky, Brest
Referee: Loukas Soteriou (Cyprus)
FC DINAMO BREST – FK Sarajevo 2-1(1-1)
Dinamo Brest: Sergey Ignatovich, Yevhen Khacheridi, Kirill Pechenin, Gaby Kiki, Sergey Kislyak, Roman Yuzepchuk, Pavel Sedko (79.Pavel Savitskiy), David Tweh, Artem Milevskiy (86.Artem Bykov), Mikhail Gordeychuk (73.Sergey Krivets), Abdoulaye Diallo. Trainer: Sergey Kovalchuk.
FK Sarajevo: Vladan Kovacevic, Amer Dupovac, Dusan Hodzic, Andrej Djokanovic (80.Haris Handzic), Mirko Oremus (90.Tino-Sven Susic), Hrvoje Milicevic, Amar Rahmanovic, Ivan Jukic (66.Matthias Fanimo), Mersudin Ahmetovic, Benjamin Tatar, Djani Salcin. Trainer: Vinko Marinović. Goals: 3' Mikhail Gordeychuk 1-0, 34' Andrej Djokanovic 1-1, 49' Abdoulaye Diallo 2-1.

26.08.2020; Hikvision arena, Marijampolé
Referee: Rade Obrenović (Slovenia)
FK Süduva Marijampolé – MACCABI TEL AVIV FC 0-3(0-1)
FK Süduva: Ivan Kardum, Vaidas Slavickas, Thomas Salamon, Aleksandar Zivanovic, Semir Kerla, Ivan Hladík, Evgen Efremov (46.Andro Svrljuga), Povilas Leimonas (72.Renan Oliveira), Domagoj Pusic, Josip Tadic, Mihrit Topcagic (63 Eligijus Jankauskas). Trainer: Saulius Sirmelis.
Maccabi Tel Aviv: Daniel Tenenbaum, Sheran Yeini, Eitan Tibi, Ofir Davidzada, Saborit (76 Matan Baltaxa), Maor Kandil, Avi Rikan (81.Eylon Almog), Dor Peretz, Dan Glazer, Dan Bitton (88.Ben Bitton), Nick Blackman. Trainer: Georgios Donis (Greece).
Goals: 30' Avi Rikan 0-1, 74' Nick Blackman 0-2, 90+2' Ofir Davidzada 0-3.

26.08.2020; „Tofiq Bahramov" adina Respublika stadionu, Bakı
Referee: Mykola Balakin (Ukraine)
QARABAĞ FK BAKI – FC Sheriff Tiraspol 2-1(1-0)
Qarabağ FK: Sahrudin Mahammadaliyev, Maksim Medvedev, Qara Qarayev, Badavi Hüseynov, Kevin Medina, Jaime Romero (89.Owusu Kwabena), Uros Matic, Filip Ozobic (70.Ismayil Ibrahimli), Wilde-Donald Guerrier (90+4.Abbas Hüseynov), Abdellah Zoubir, Mahir Emreli. Trainer: Qurban Qurbanov.
FC Sheriff Tiraspol: Dumitru Celeadnic, Andrei Peteleu, Ousmane N'Diaye, Faith Obilor (74.Keston Julien), Andrej Lukic, William Parra, Cristiano, Charles Petro, Benedik Mioc (46.Frank Castañeda), Gabrijel Boban (74.Richard Gadze), Anatole Abang [sent off 37]. Trainer: Zoran Zekić (Croatia).
Goals: 22' Uros Matic 1-0 (penalty), 63' Mahir Emreli 2-0, 78' Frank Castañeda 2-1.

26.08.2020; Huvepharma Arena, Razgrad
Referee: Denys Shurman (Ukraine)
PFC Ludogorets Razgrad – FC MIDTJYLLAND HERNING 0-1(0-0)
Ludogorets Razgrad: Renan, Cosmin Moti, Dragos Grigore, Cicinho, Anton Nedyalkov, Anicet Andrianantenaina (55.Bernard Tekpetey), Mavis Tchibota (79.Jorghinho), Stéphane Badji, Cauly, Alex Santana, Claudiu Keserü (54.Higinio Marín). Trainer: Pavel Vrba.
FC Midtjylland: Jesper Hansen, Erik Sviatchenko, Alexander Scholz, Joel Andersson, Paulinho, Awer Mabil, Bozhidar Kraev (65.Júnior Brumado), Anders Dreyer, Frank Onyeka, Jens Cajuste, Sory Kaba (75' Mikael Anderson). Trainer: Brian Priske.
Goal: 78' Júnior Brumado 0-1.

26.08.2020; Stadionul "Dr. Constantin Rădulescu", Cluj-Napoca
Referee: António Emanuel Carvalho Nobre (Portugal)
FC CFR 1907 Cluj – GNK DINAMO ZAGREB 2-2(0-1,2-2); 5-6 on penalties
CFR Cluj: Cristian Balgradean, Paulo Vinícius, Camora, Kévin Boli, Andrei Burca (82.Mateo Susic), Ciprian Deac, Alexandru Chipciu (46.Mário Rondón), Damjan Djokovic, Mickaël Pereira (68.Catalin Golofca), Mihai Bordeianu (113.Catalin Itu), Gabriel Debeljuh. Trainer: Dan Vasile Petrescu.
Dinamo Zagreb: Dominik Livakovic, Marin Leovac, Kévin Théophile-Catherine [sent off 51], Emir Dilaver, Petar Stojanovic, Arijan Ademi, Amer Gojak, Luka Ivanusec (68.Bruno Petkovic), Lovro Majer (54.Lirim Kastrati), Mario Gavranovic (54.Josko Gvardiol), Mislav Orsic (108.Sadegh Moharrami). Trainer: Zoran Mamić.
Goals: 14' Amer Gojak 0-1, 64' Mickaël Pereira 1-1, 78' Lirim Kastrati 1-2, 90+3' Gabriel Debeljuh 2-2.
Penalties: Bruno Petkovic 0-1, Paulo Vinícius 1-1, Marin Leovac 1-2, Damjan Djokovic 2-2, Arijan Ademi 2-3, Mário Rondón 3-3, Petar Stojanovic 3-4, Mateo Susic 4-4, Amer Gojak (missed), Catalin Golofca (missed), Emir Dilaver 4-5, Ciprian Deac 5-5, Josko Gvardiol 5-6, Kévin Boli (missed).

26.08.2020; Stadion Wojska Polskiego, Warszawa
Referee: Nathan Verboomen (Belgium)
Legia Warszawa – AC OMONIA NICOSIA 0-2(0-0,0-0)
Legia Warszawa: Artur Boruc, Artur Jedrzejczyk, Igor Lewczuk [sent off 56], Filip Mladenovic, Michal Karbownik, Domagoj Antolic, Valeriane Gvilia (60.Mateusz Wieteska, 108.André Martins), Luquinhas, Tomás Pekhart (70.José Kanté), Maciej Rosolek (79.Bartosz Kapustka). Trainer: Aleksandar Vuković (Serbia).
Omonia Nicosia: Fabiano, Jan Lecjaks, Michael Lüftner, Ádam Lang, Ioannis Kousoulos, Jordi Gómez, Éric Bauthéac (91.Loizos Loizou), Vítor Gomes (103.Charis Mavrias), Marinos Tzionis (76.Ernest Asante), Michal Djuris, Thiago Santos (112.Kiko). Trainer: Henning Stille Berg (Norway).
Goals: 92' Jordi Gómes 0-1 (penalty), 107' Thiago Santos 0-2.

LEAGUE PATH

25.08.2020; Stádio Toumba, Thessaloníki
Referee: Daniele Doveri (Italy)
PAOK THESSALONÍKI – Beşiktaş JK İstanbul 3-1(3-1)
PAOK: Zivko Zivkovic, Fernando Varela, Sverrir Ingason, Rodrigo Alves (44.Dimitris Limnios), Dimitris Giannoulis, Giannis Michailidis, Omar El Kaddouri, Stefan Schwab, Dimitrios Pelkas (76.Anderson Esiti), Chuba Akpom, Christos Tzolis (84.Léo Jabá). Trainer: Abel Fernando Moreira Ferreira (Portugal).
Beşiktaş: Ersin Destanoglu, Domagoj Vida, Fabrice N'Sakala (82.Umut Nayir), Wellinton Souza, Jeremain Lens, Atiba Hutchinson, Necip Uysal, Georges-Kévin N'Koudou, Bernard Mensah (69.Dorukhan Toköz), Tyler Boyd (46.Oguzhan Özyakup), Cyle Larin. Trainer: Sergen Yalçın.
Goals: 7', 24' Christos Tzolis 1-0, 2-0, 30' Dimitrios Pelkas 3-0, 37' Cyle Larin 3-1.

26.08.2020; AFAS Stadion, Alkmaar
Referee: Luis Miguel Branco Godinho (Portugal)
AZ ALKMAAR – FC Viktoria Plzeň 3-1(0-0,1-1)
AZ Alkmaar: Marco Bizot, Ron Vlaar (76.Ramon Leeuwin), Jonas Svensson, Owen Wijndal, Jordy Clasie (80.Ferdy Druijf), Fredrik Midtsjø, Dani de Wit, Teun Koopmeiners, Oussama Idrissi (93.Yukinari Sugawara), Myron Boadu, Calvin Stengs (64.Albert Gudmundsson). Trainer: Arne Slot.
Viktoria Plzeň: Ales Hruska, David Limberský, Jakub Brabec, Lukás Hejda, Milan Havel, Jan Kopic (87.Jan Kovarík), Ales Cermák, Lukás Kalvach (105.Miroslav Kácer), Ondrej Mihálik (74.Adriel D'Avila Ba Loua), Pavel Bucha, Jean-David Beauguel (90+3.Ludek Pernica). Trainer: Adrián Gula.
Goals: 78' David Limberský 0-1, 90+5' Teun Koopmeiners 1-1 (penalty), 98', 118' Albert Gudmundsson 2-1, 3-1.

28.08.2020; Stadion Kranjčevićeva, Zagreb
Referee: Juan Martínez Munuera (Spain)
NK Lokomotiva Zagreb – SK RAPID WIEN 0-1(0-1)
Lokomotiva Zagreb: Krunoslav Hendija, Denis Kolinger, Stipo Markovic (61.Mario Budimir), Ivan Celikovic, Kemal Osmankovic, Marko Djira, Fran Karacic, Oliver Petrak (72.Sherif Kallaku), Dino Halilovic, Mario Cuze, Indrit Tuci (46.Jorge Sammir). Trainer: Goran Tomić.
Rapid Wien: Richard Strebinger, Filip Stojkovic, Maximilian Hofmann, Maximilian Ullmann, Leo Greiml, Thomas Murg (64.Srdjan Grahovac), Dejan Petrovic, Dejan Ljubicic, Taxiarchis Fountas (86.Koya Kitagawa), Ercan Kara, Kelvin Arase (76.Thorsten Schick). Trainer: Dietmar Kühbauer.
Goal: 32' Ercan Kara 0-1.

THIRD QUALIFYING ROUND

CHAMPIONS PATH

16.09.2020; MCH Arena, Herning
Referee: Georgi Kabakov (Bulgaria)
FC MIDTJYLLAND HERNING – BSC Young Boys Bern 3-0(0-0)
FC Midtjylland: Jesper Hansen, Erik Sviatchenko, Alexander Scholz, Joel Andersson, Paulinho, Awer Mabil, Bozhidar Kraev (62.Pione Sisto), Anders Dreyer (84.Evander), Frank Onyeka, Jens Cajuste, Sory Kaba (78.Júnior Brumado). Trainer: Brian Priske.
Young Boys: David von Ballmoos, Fabian Lustenberger, Jordan Lefort, Silvan Hefti, Mohamed Camara, Miralem Sulejmani (66.Marvin Spielmann), Christopher Martins, Nicolas Moumi Ngamaleu (66.Theoson Siebatcheu), Christian Fassnacht (82.Felix Mambimbi), Michel Aebischer, Jean-Pierre Nsamé. Trainer: Gerardo Seoane Castro.
Goals: 51' Jordan Lefort 1-0 (own goal), 61' Anders Dreyer 2-0, 84' Awer Mabil 3-0.

16.09.2020; AEK Arena – Stádio "Georgios Karapatakis", Larnaca (Cyprus)
Referee: Srđan Jovanović (Serbia)
Qarabağ FK Bakı – MOLDE FK 0-0; 5-6 on penalties
Qarabağ FK: Sahrudin Mahammadaliyev, Maksim Medvedev, Qara Qarayev (77.Ismayil Ibrahimli), Badavi Hüseynov, Kevin Medina, Uros Matic, Filip Ozobic (82.Patrick Andrade), Wilde-Donald Guerrier (114.Elvin Dzhafarquliyev), Abdellah Zoubir, Mahir Emreli (106.Abbas Hüseynov), Owusu Kwabena. Trainer: Qurban Qurbanov.
Molde FK: Andreas Linde, Kristoffer Haugen, Stian Gregersen, Magnus Eikrem (79.Ohi Omoijuanfo), Etzaz Hussain (120.Tobias Christensen), Eirik Hestad, Fredrik Aursnes, Martin Ellingsen, Henry Wingo, Erling Knudtzon (69.Ola Brynhildsen), Leke James (99.Mathis Bolly). Trainer: Erling Moe.
Penalties: Ohi Omoijuanfo 0-1, Uros Matic 1-1, Fredrik Aursnes 1-2, Maksim Medvedev 2-2, Eirik Hestad 2-3, Patrick Andrade 3-3, Tobias Christensen 3-4, Kevin Medina 4-4, Martin Ellingsen 4-5, Sahrudin Mahammadaliyev 5-5, Kristoffer Haugen 5-6, Badavi Hüseynov (missed).

16.09.2020; Bloomfield Stadium, Tel Aviv
Referee: Davide Massa (Italy)
MACCABI TEL AVIV FC – FC Dinamo Brest 1-0(0-0)
Maccabi Tel Aviv: Daniel Tenenbaum, Sheran Yeini, Eitan Tibi, Ofir Davidzada, Saborit, Maor Kandil, Eyal Golasa (65.Avi Rikan), Dor Peretz, Dan Glazer, Dan Bitton (82.Yonathan Cohen), Itay Shechter (57.Nick Blackman). Trainer: Georgios Donis (Greece).
Dinamo Brest: Sergey Ignatovich, Yevhen Khacheridi (62.Aleksandr Pavlovets), Kirill Pechenin, Gaby Kiki, Sergey Kislyak, Roman Yuzepchuk, Pavel Sedko, David Tweh, Artem Milevskiy (86.Artem Bykov), Mikhail Gordeychuk (70.Pavel Savitskiy), Abdoulaye Diallo. Trainer: Sergey Kovalchuk.
Goal: 50' Dan Bitton 1-0 (penalty).

16.09.2020; Groupama Aréna, Budapest
Referee: Tobias Stieler (Germany)
FERENCVÁROSI TC – GNK Dinamo Zagreb 2-1(1-1)
Ferencvárosi TC: Dénes Dibusz, Gergö Lovrencsics (25.Endre Botka), Miha Blazic, Adnan Kovacevic (73.Abraham Frimpong), Eldar Civic, Somália, Dávid Sigér, Igor Kharatin, Tokmac Nguen, Franck Boli (68.Isael), Myrto Uzuni. Trainer: Serhiy Rebrov (Ukraine).
Dinamo Zagreb: Dominik Livakovic, Marin Leovac, Emir Dilaver, Petar Stojanovic, Josko Gvardiol, Arijan Ademi, Amer Gojak (71.Mario Gavranovic), Lovro Majer (60.Kristijan Jakic), Mislav Orsic (72.Luka Ivanusec), Bruno Petkovic, Lirim Kastrati. Trainer: Zoran Mamić.
Goals: 2' Gergö Lovrencsics 1-0, 23' Myrto Uzuni 1-1 (own goal), 65' Myrto Uzuni 2-1.

16.09.2020; Stádio Neo GSP, Nicosia
Referee: Chris Kavanagh (England)
AC OMONIA NICOSIA – FK Crvena Zvezda Beograd 1-1(1-1,1-1); 4-2 on penalties
Omonia Nicosia: Fabiano, Jan Lecjaks, Tomás Hubocan (90+3.Ioannis Kousoulos), Michael Lüftner, Ádam Lang, Jordi Gómez, Éric Bauthéac, Vítor Gomes, Thiago Santos (118.Ernest Asante), Fotis Papoulis (98.Loizos Loizou), Andronikos Kakoullis (65.Kaly Sene). Trainer: Henning Stille Berg (Norway).
Crvena Zvezda: Milan Borjan, Nemanja Milunovic, Milan Rodic (106.Milan Gajic), Milos Degenek, Marko Gobeljic, Aleksandar Katai (101.Zeljko Gavric), Sékou Sanogo, Guélor Kanga, Mirko Ivanic (81.Dusan Jovancic), El Fardou Ben Nabouhane, Aleksa Vukanovic (89.Diego Falcinelli). Trainer: Dejan Stanković.
Goals: 31' Michael Lüftner 1-0, Mirko Ivanic 1-1.
Penalties: Zeljko Gavric 0-1, Jordi Gómez 1-1, El Fardou Ben Nabouhane 1-2, Vítor Gomes 2-2, Diego Falcinelli (missed), Ernest Asante 3-2, Milos Degenek (missed), Jan Lecjaks 4-2.

LEAGUE PATH

15.09.2020; Stádio Toumba, Thessaloníki
Referee: Dr. Felix Brych (Germany)
PAOK THESSALONÍKI – Sport Lisboa e Benfica 2-1(0-0)
PAOK: Zivko Zivkovic, José Ángel Crespo, Fernando Varela, Sverrir Ingason, Dimitris Giannoulis, Giannis Michailidis, Omar El Kaddouri, Stefan Schwab, Dimitrios Pelkas (67.Andrija Zivkovic), Chuba Akpom (70.Karol Swiderski), Christos Tzolis (80.Anderson Esiti). Trainer: Abel Fernando Moreira Ferreira (Portugal).
Benfica: Odisseas Vlachodimos, Jan Vertonghen, André Almeida, Álex Grimaldo, Rúben Dias, Adel Taarabt (76.Rafa Silva), Pizzi, Julian Weigl, Éverton, Pedrinho (65.Darwin Núñez), Haris Seferovic (72.Carlos Vunícius). Trainer: Jorge Fernando Pinheiro de Jesus.
Goals: 64' Dimitris Giannoulis 1-0, 75' Andrija Zivkovic 2-0, 90+4' Rafa Silva 2-1.

15.09.2020; NSC Olimpiyskiy Stadium, Kyiv
Referee: Orel Grinfeld (Israel)
FK DINAMO KYIV – AZ Alkmaar 2-0(0-0)
Dinamo Kyiv: Georgiy Bushchan, Tomasz Kedziora, Oleksandr Karavayev, Vitali Mykolenko, Illia Zabarnyi, Sergiy Sydorchuk, Vitaly Buyalskiy (79.Oleksandr Andrievsky), Carlos de Pena, Mykola Shaparenko (90+1.Bohdan Lyednyev), Gerson Rodrigues, Vladyslav Supriaha (74.Benjamin Verbic). Trainer: Mircea Lucescu (Romania).
AZ Alkmaar: Marco Bizot, Ron Vlaar (80.Yukinari Sugawara), Jonas Svensson, Owen Wijndal, Jordy Clasie, Fredrik Midtsjø (66.Ferdy Druijf), Dani de Wit, Teun Koopmeiners, Albert Gudmundsson (58.Oussama Idrissi), Myron Boadu, Calvin Stengs. Trainer: Arne Slot.
Goals: 49' Gerson Rodrigues 1-0, 86' Mykola Shaparenko 2-0.

15.09.2020; GHELAMCO-arena, Gent
Referee: Andreas Ekberg (Sweden)
KAA GENT – SK Rapid Wien 2-1(1-0)
KAA Gent: Davy Roef, Dino Arslanagic, Michael Ngadeu-Ngadjui, Núrio Fortuna, Alessio Castro-Montes, Sven Kums, Niklas Dorsch (64.Vadis Odjidja-Ofoe), Elisha Owusu, Giorgi Chakvetadze (60.Roman Bezus), Laurent Depoitre, Roman Yaremchuk (89.Tim Kleindienst). Trainer: Wim De Decker.
Rapid Wien: Richard Strebinger, Filip Stojkovic, Maximilian Hofmann, Maximilian Ullmann, Leo Greiml, Thomas Murg, Dejan Petrovic (86.Srdjan Grahovac), Dejan Ljubicic, Taxiarchis Fountas, Ercan Kara (86.Koya Kitagawa), Kelvin Arase (73.Yusuf Demir). Trainer: Dietmar Kühbauer.
Goals: 36' Niklas Dorsch 1-0, 59' Roman Yaremchuk 2-0 (penalty), 90+3' Yusuf Demir 2-1.

CHAMPIONS PATH

22.09.2020; Stadion Sinobo, Praha
Referee: Cüneyt Çakir (Turkey)
SK Slavia Praha – FC Midtjylland Herning 0-0
Slavia Praha: Ondrej Kolár, Jan Boril, Vladimír Coufal, Tomás Holes, David Hovorka, David Zima, Nicolae Stanciu (90+1.Laco Takács), Lukás Masopust (71.Lukás Provod), Petr Sevcík, Peter Olayinka, Stanislav Tecl (59.Petar Musa). Trainer: Jindrich Trpisovský.
FC Midtjylland: Jesper Hansen, Erik Sviatchenko, Alexander Scholz, Joel Andersson, Paulinho, Awer Mabil, Anders Dreyer (67.Pione Sisto), Evander (76.Mikael Anderson), Frank Onyeka, Jens Cajuste, Sory Kaba (89.Júnior Brumado). Trainer: Brian Priske.

22.09.2020; Bloomfield Stadium, Tel Aviv
Referee: Michael Oliver (England)
Maccabi Tel Aviv FC – FC Red Bull Salzburg 1-2(1-0)
Maccabi Tel Aviv: Daniel Tenenbaum, Sheran Yeini, Eitan Tibi, Ofir Davidzada, Ben Bitton, Eyal Golasa, Roslan Barsky (61.Tal Ben Haim), Matan Baltaxa (82.Matan Hozez), Dan Bitton, Eden Karzev (71.Itay Shechter), Eylon Almog. Trainer: Georgios Donis (Greece).
Red Bull Salzburg: Cican Stankovic, Andreas Ulmer, André Ramalho, Max Wöber, Rasmus Kristensen, Masaya Okugawa (76.Noah Okafor), Antoine Bernède, Dominik Szoboszlai (86.Mohamed Camara), Enock Mwepu, Mërgim Berisha (46.Sékou Koïta), Patson Daka. Trainer: Jesse Marsch (United States).
Goals: 9' Dan Bitton 1-0, 49' Dominik Szoboszlai 1-1 (penalty), 57' Masaya Okugawa 1-2.

23.09.2020; Stádio „Giórgos Karaïskáki", Peiraiás
Referee: Danny Desmond Makkelie (Netherlands)
Olympiacos SFP Peiraiás – AC Omonia Nicosia 2-0(0-0)
Olympiacos: José Sá, Rafinha, José Holebas, Rúben Semedo, Ousseynou Ba, Mathieu Valbuena, Kostas Fortounis (59.Youssef El-Arabi), Andreas Bouchalakis, Georgios Masouras (59.Lazar Randjelovic), Mady Camara, Koka (76.Yann M'Vila). Trainer: Pedro Rui da Mota Vieira Martins (Portugal).
Omonia Nicosia: Fabiano, Jan Lecjaks, Tomás Hubocan, Michael Lüftner, Ádam Lang, Jordi Gómez, Éric Bauthéac (87.Loizos Loizou), Vítor Gomes, Thiago Santos, Fotis Papoulis (81.Ernest Asante), Kaly Sene (46.Michal Duris). Trainer: Henning Stille Berg (Norway).
Goals: 69' Mathieu Valbuena 1-0 (penalty), 90+2' Youssef El-Arabi 2-0.

23.09.2020; Aker Stadion, Molde
Referee: Carlos Del Cerro Grande (Spain)
Molde FK – Ferencvárosi TC 3-3(0-1)
Molde FK: Andreas Linde, Kristoffer Haugen, Stian Gregersen, Magnus Eikrem (81 Ohi Omoijuanfo), Etzaz Hussain, Eirik Hestad, Fredrik Aursnes, Martin Ellingsen, Henry Wingo, Erling Knudtzon (57.Ola Brynhildsen), Leke James (89.Mathis Bolly). Trainer: Erling Moe.
Ferencvárosi TC: Dénes Dibusz, Endre Botka, Miha Blazic, Abraham Frimpong, Eldar Civic, Somália (71.Dávid Sigér), Igor Kharatin, Aïssa Laïdouni, Tokmac Nguen (88.Isael), Franck Boli (73.Oleksandr Zubkov), Myrto Uzuni. Trainer: Serhiy Rebrov (Ukraine).
Goals: 7' Franck Boli 0-1, 52' Myrto Uzumi 0-2, 55' Leke James 1-2, 65' Magnus Eikrem 2-2, 83' Martin Ellingsen 3-2, 87' Igor Kharatin 3-3 (penalty).

30.09.2020; MCH Arena, Herning
Referee: Damir Skomina (Slovenia)
FC MIDTJYLLAND HERNING – SK Slavia Praha 4-1(0-1)
FC Midtjylland: Jesper Hansen, Erik Sviatchenko, Alexander Scholz, Joel Andersson, Paulinho, Pione Sisto (58.Anders Dreyer), Awer Mabil (90+2.Mikael Anderson), Evander (58.Bozhidar Kraev), Frank Onyeka, Jens Cajuste, Sory Kaba. Trainer: Brian Priske.
Slavia Praha: Ondrej Kolár, Ondrej Kúdela, Jan Boril, Vladimír Coufal, Tomás Holes, David Hovorka, Nicolae Stanciu (68.Ibrahim Traoré), Lukás Masopust (73.Petar Musa), Petr Sevcík, Peter Olayinka (84.Jan Kuchta), Lukás Provod. Trainer: Jindrich Trpisovský.
Goals: 3' Peter Olayinka 0-1, 65' Sory Kaba 1-1, 84' Alexander Scholz 2-1 (penalty), 88' Frank Onyeka 3-1, 90+1' Andres Dreyer 4-1.

30.09.2020; Red Bull Arena, Wals-Siezenheim
Referee: Dr. Felix Brych (Germany)
FC RED BULL SALZBURG – Maccabi Tel Aviv FC 3-1(2-1)
Red Bull Salzburg: Cican Stankovic, Andreas Ulmer, André Ramalho, Albert Vallci, Max Wöber, Masaya Okugawa (82.Noah Okafor), Dominik Szoboszlai, Enock Mwepu, Mohamed Camara (74.Zlatko Junuzovic), Patson Daka, Sékou Koïta (66.Mërgim Berisha). Trainer: Jesse Marsch (United States).
Maccabi Tel Aviv: Daniel Tenenbaum, Sheran Yeini, Eitan Tibi, Ben Bitton (65.Matan Hozez), Maor Kandil (74.Amit Glazer), Eyal Golasa, Matan Baltaxa, Dan Bitton, Eden Karzev, Itay Shechter, Eylon Almog (75.Ronen Hanzis). Trainer: Georgios Donis (Greece).
Goals: 16' Patson Daka 1-0, 30' Eden Karzev 1-1, 45+4' Dominik Szoboszlai 2-1 (penalty), 68' Patson Daka 3-1.

29.09.2020; Stádio Neo GSP, Nicosia
Referee: Antonio Miguel Mateu Lahoz (Spain)
AC Omonia Nicosia – OLYMPIACOS SFP PEIRAIÁS 0-0
Omonia Nicosia: Fabiano, Jan Lecjaks, Tomás Hubocan, Michael Lüftner, Ádam Lang, Ioannis Kousoulos, Éric Bauthéac, Vítor Gomes, Marinos Tzionis (84.Kaly Sene), Michal Duris (70.Andronikos Kakoullis), Fotis Papoulis (70.Ernest Asante). Trainer: Henning Stille Berg (Norway).
Olympiacos: José Sá, Rafinha, José Holebas, Rúben Semedo, Ousseynou Ba, Mathieu Valbuena (90+2.Kostas Fortounis), Yann M'Vila, Andreas Bouchalakis, Lazar Randjelovic (75.Georgios Masouras), Mady Camara (90+2.Cafú), Youssef El-Arabi. Trainer: Pedro Rui da Mota Vieira Martins (Portugal).

29.09.2020; Groupama Aréna, Budapest
Referee: Björn Kuipers (Netherlands)
FERENCVÁROSI TC – Molde FK 0-0
Ferencvárosi TC: Dénes Dibusz, Gergö Lovrencsics, Marcel Heister, Endre Botka, Miha Blazic, Somália (87.Abraham Frimpong), Dávid Sigér (79.Aïssa Laïdouni), Igor Kharatin, Tokmac Nguen (79.Isael), Oleksandr Zubkov, Myrto Uzuni. Trainer: Serhiy Rebrov (Ukraine).
Molde FK: Andreas Linde, Kristoffer Haugen, Stian Gregersen, Magnus Pedersen, Magnus Eikrem, Etzaz Hussain (83.Ohi Omoijuanfo), Eirik Hestad, Fredrik Aursnes, Martin Ellingsen, Erlind Knudtzon (64.Ola Brynhildsen), Leke James. Trainer: Erling Moe.

LEAGUE PATH

22.09.2020; Krasnodar Stadion, Krasnodar
Referee: Clément Turpin (France)
FK Krasnodar – PAOK Thessaloníki 2-1(1-1)
FK Krasnodar: Matvey Safonov, Sergey Petrov, Cristian Ramírez, Egor Sorokin, Rémy Cabella (81.Daniil Utkin), Victor Claesson, Tonny Vilhena, Kristoffer Olsson, Kaio Pantaleão, Marcus Berg, Wanderson (86.Magomed Suleymanov). Trainer: Murad Musaev.
PAOK: Zivko Zivkovic, José Ángel Crespo, Fernando Varela, Sverrir Ingason, Dimitris Giannoulis, Giannis Michailidis, Omar El Kaddouri, Stefan Schwab, Andrija Zivkovic, Dimitrios Pelkas (79.Diego Biseswar), Christos Tzolis (84.Karol Swiderski). Trainer: Abel Fernando Moreira Ferreira (Portugal).
Goals: 32' Dimitrios Pelkas 0-1, 39' Victor Claesson 1-1 (penalty), 70' Rémy Cabella 2-1.

30.09.2020; Stádio Toumba, Thessaloníki
Referee: Daniele Orsato (Italy)
PAOK Thessaloníki – FK KRASNODAR 1-2(0-0)
PAOK: Zivko Zivkovic, José Ángel Crespo (59.Moussa Wagué), Fernando Varela (76.Karol Swiderski)), Sverrir Ingason, Dimitris Giannoulis, Giannis Michailidis, Omar El Kaddouri, Stefan Schwab, Andrija Zivkovic, Dimitrios Pelkas (59.Antonio Colak), Christos Tzolis. Trainer: Abel Fernando Moreira Ferreira (Portugal).
FK Krasnodar: Matvey Safonov, Aleksandr Martynovich, Sergey Petrov, Cristian Ramírez, Rémy Cabella (85.Magomed Suleymanov), Yuri Gazinskiy (83.Ruslan Kambolov), Victor Claesson, Tonny Vilhena, Kaio Pantaleão, Daniil Utkin (58.Igor Smolnikov), Marcus Berg. Trainer: Murad Musaev.
Goals: 73' Giannis Michailidis 0-1 (own goal), 77' Omar El Kaddouri 1-1, 77' Rémy Cabella 1-2.

23.09.2020; GHELAMCO-arena, Gent
Referee: Ovidiu Alin Haţegan (Romania)
KAA Gent – FK Dinamo Kyiv 1-2(1-1)
KAA Gent: Davy Roef, Igor Plastun, Michael Ngadeu-Ngadjui, Núrio Fortuna, Alessio Castro-Montes, Vadis Odjidja-Ofoe (62.Jordan Botaka), Roman Bezus [*sent off 53*], Niklas Dorsch, Elisha Owusu, Laurent Depoitre (72.Milad Mohammadi), Roman Yaremchuk (23.Tim Kleindienst). Trainer: Wim De Decker.
Dinamo Kyiv: Georgiy Bushchan, Tomasz Kedziora, Oleksandr Karavayev, Vitali Mykolenko, Illia Zabarnyi, Sergiy Sydorchuk, Vitaly Buyalskiy, Carlos de Pena, Mykola Shaparenko (82.Volodymyr Shepelyev), Gerson Rodrigues (59.Viktor Tsygankov), Vladyslav Supriaha (66.Benjamin Verbic). Trainer: Mircea Lucescu (Romania).
Goals: 9' Vladyslav Supriaha 0-1, 41' Tim Kleindienst 1-1, 79' Carlos de Pena 1-2.

29.09.2020; NSC Olimpiyskiy Stadium, Kyiv
Referee: Szymon Marciniak (Poland)
FK DINAMO KYIV – KAA Gent 3-0(2-0)
Dinamo Kyiv: Georgiy Bushchan, Tomasz Kedziora, Oleksandr Karavayev, Vitali Mykolenko, Illia Zabarnyi, Sergiy Sydorchuk, Vitaly Buyalskiy, Carlos de Pena (59.Benjamin Verbic), Mykola Shaparenko (77.Oleksandr Andrievsky), Gerson Rodrigues (60.Viktor Tsygankov), Vladyslav Supriaha. Trainer: Mircea Lucescu (Romania).
KAA Gent: Davy Roef, Igor Plastun, Michael Ngadeu-Ngadjui, Núrio Fortuna, Alessio Castro-Montes (65.Jordan Botaka), Niklas Dorsch, Elisha Owusu (54.Sulayman Marreh), Laurent Depoitre (74.Matisse Samoise), Tim Kleindienst, Anderson Niangbo, Osman Bukari. Trainer: Wim De Decker.
Goals: 9' Vitaly Buyalskiy 1-0, 36' Carlos de Pena 2-0 (penalty), Gerson Rodrigues 3-0 (penalty).

GROUP STAGE								

Please note: Winners and runners-up of each group were qualified for the Round of 16. Teams ranked third were qualified for the UEFA Europa League.

GROUP A									
1.	**FC Bayern München**	6	5	1	0	18	-	5	16
2.	**Club Atlético de Madrid**	6	2	3	1	7	-	8	9
3.	*FC Red Bull Salzburg*	6	1	1	4	10	-	17	4
4.	FK Lokomotiv Moskva	6	0	3	3	5	-	10	3

21.10.2020; Red Bull Arena, Wals-Siezenheim
Referee: Serdar Gözübüyük (Netherlands); Attendance: 3,000
FC Red Bull Salzburg – FK Lokomotiv Moskva 2-2(1-1)
Red Bull Salzburg: Cican Stankovic, Andreas Ulmer, André Ramalho, Albert Vallci, Max Wöber, Zlatko Junuzovic (84.Noah Okafor), Dominik Szoboszlai, Enock Mwepu, Mohamed Camara (73.Masaya Okugawa), Patson Daka, Sékou Koïta (66.Mërgim Berisha). Trainer: Jesse Marsch (United States).
Lokomotiv Moskva: Guilherme, Vedran Corluka, Maciej Rybus, Dmitri Zhivoglyadov, Murilo Cerqueira, Grzegorz Krychowiak, Anton Miranchuk (69.Vitaliy Lisakovich), Daniil Kulikov, Fedor Smolov (62.Dmitry Rybchinsky), Éder (69.Zé Luís), Rifat Zhemaletdinov (63.François Kamano). Trainer: Marko Nikolić (Serbia).
Goals: 19' Éder 0-1, 45' Dominik Szoboszlai 1-1, 50' Zlatko Junuzovic 2-1, 75' Vitaliy Lisakovich 2-2.

21.10.2020; Allianz Arena, München
Referee: Michael Oliver (England)
FC Bayern München – Club Atlético de Madrid 4-0(2-0)
Bayern München: Manuel Neuer, David Alaba, Niklas Süle, Lucas Hernández, Benjamin Pavard (73.Bouna Sarr), Leon Goretzka (83.Javi Martínez), Corentin Tolisso, Joshua Kimmich, Thomas Müller (83.Alphonso Davies), Robert Lewandowski (83.Eric Maxim Choupo-Moting), Kingsley Coman (73.Douglas Costa). Trainer: Hans-Dieter Flick.
Atlético Madrid: Jan Oblak, Stefan Savic, Kieran Trippier, Felipe Monteiro, Renan Lodi, Héctor Herrera, Koke (79.Lucas Torreira), Yannick Carrasco (76.Vitolo), Marcos Llorente (79.Thomas Lemar), Luis Suárez (75.Ángel Correa), João Félix. Trainer: Diego Pablo Simeone (Argentina).
Goals: 28' Kingsley Coman 1-0, 41' Leon Goretzka 2-0, 66' Corentin Tolisso 3-0, 72' Kingsley Coman 4-0.

27.10.2020; RZD Arena, Moskva
Referee: István Kovács (Romania); Attendance: 8,196
FK Lokomotiv Moskva – FC Bayern München 1-2(0-1)
Lokomotiv Moskva: Guilherme, Vedran Corluka (46.Slobodan Rajkovic), Maciej Rybus, Dmitri Zhivoglyadov, Murilo Cerqueira, Vladislav Ignatiev (76.Rifat Zhemaletdinov), Grzegorz Krychowiak, Anton Miranchuk, Daniil Kulikov (89.Vitaliy Lisakovich), Fedor Smolov (75.Dmitry Rybchinsky), Zé Luís. Trainer: Marko Nikolić (Serbia).
Bayern München: Manuel Neuer, David Alaba, Niklas Süle, Lucas Hernández, Benjamin Pavard, Leon Goretzka (46.Javi Martínez), Corentin Tolisso, Joshua Kimmich, Thomas Müller (46.Serge Gnabry), Robert Lewandowski, Kingsley Coman (69.Douglas Costa). Trainer: Hans-Dieter Flick.
Goals: 13' Leon Goretzka 0-1, 70' Anton Miranchuk 1-1, 79' Joshua Kimmich 1-2.

27.10.2020; Estadio Wanda Metropolitano, Madrid
Referee: Ovidiu Alin Haţegan (Romania)
Club Atlético de Madrid – FC Red Bull Salzburg 3-2(1-1)
Atlético Madrid: Jan Oblak, Stefan Savic, Kieran Trippier, Felipe Monteiro, Renan Lodi (82.Mario Hermoso), Héctor Herrera (82.Lucas Torreira), Koke, Marcos Llorente, Luis Suárez (82.Thomas Lemar), Ángel Correa, João Félix. Trainer: Diego Pablo Simeone (Argentina).
Red Bull Salzburg: Cican Stankovic, Andreas Ulmer, André Ramalho, Max Wöber (63.Jérôme Onguéné), Rasmus Kristensen, Zlatko Junuzovic (63.Majeed Ashimeru), Dominik Szoboszlai, Enock Mwepu, Mohamed Camara, Mërgim Berisha, Patson Daka (30.Sékou Koïta, 84.Noah Okafor). Trainer: Jesse Marsch (United States).
Goals: 29' Marcos Llorente 1-0, 40' Dominik Szobolszlai 1-1, 47' Felipe Monteiro 1-2 (own goal), 52', 85' João Félix 2-2, 3-2.

03.11.2020; RZD Arena, Moskva
Referee: Benoît Bastien (France); Attendance: 8,147
FK Lokomotiv Moskva – Club Atlético de Madrid 1-1(1-1)
Lokomotiv Moskva: Guilherme, Slobodan Rajkovic, Maciej Rybus, Dmitri Zhivoglyadov, Murilo Cerqueira, Vladislav Ignatiev, Grzegorz Krychowiak, Anton Miranchuk (89.Dmitry Rybchinsky), Daniil Kulikov, Fedor Smolov (64.Rifat Zhemaletdinov), Zé Luís. Trainer: Marko Nikolić (Serbia).
Atlético Madrid: Jan Oblak, Stefan Savic, Kieran Trippier, José Giménez, Renan Lodi, Héctor Herrera, Saúl (46.Koke), Marcos Llorente (69.Vitolo, 78.Lucas Torreira), Luis Suárez, Ángel Correa, (69.Thomas Lemar) João Félix. Trainer: Diego Pablo Simeone (Argentina).
Goals: 18' José Giménez 0-1, 25' Anton Miranchuk 1-1 (penalty).

03.11.2020; Red Bull Arena, Wals-Siezenheim
Referee: Danny Desmond Makkelie (Netherlands)
FC Red Bull Salzburg – FC Bayern München 2-6(1-2)
Red Bull Salzburg: Cican Stankovic, Andreas Ulmer, André Ramalho, Max Wöber, Rasmus Kristensen, Zlatko Junuzovic (65.Masaya Okugawa), Dominik Szoboszlai, Enock Mwepu, Mohamed Camara, Mërgim Berisha (76.Jérôme Onguéné), Sékou Koïta (65.Noah Okafor). Trainer: Jesse Marsch (United States).
Bayern München: Manuel Neuer, Jérôme Boateng, David Alaba, Lucas Hernández, Benjamin Pavard (74.Bouna Sarr), Corentin Tolisso (74.Javi Martínez), Joshua Kimmich, Thomas Müller (90+1.Jamal Musiala), Robert Lewandowski, Serge Gnaby (90+1.Douglas Costa), Kingsley Coman (74.Leroy Sané). Trainer: Hans-Dieter Flick.
Goals: 4' Mërgim Berisha 1-0, 21' Robert Lewandowski 1-1 (penalty), 44' Rasmus Kristensen 1-2 (own goal), 66' Masaya Okugawa 2-2, 79' Jérôme Boateng 2-3, 83' Leroy Sané 2-4, 88' Robert Lewandowski 2-5, 90+2' Lucas Hernández 2-6.

25.11.2020; Estadio Wanda Metropolitano, Madrid
Referee: Slavko Vinčić (Slovenia)
Club Atlético de Madrid – FK Lokomotiv Moskva 0-0
Atlético Madrid: Jan Oblak, Stefan Savic, Kieran Trippier, José Giménez, Renan Lodi (60.Mario Hermoso), Saúl, Koke, Yannick Carrasco (80.Sergio Camello), Marcos Llorente (60.Thomas Lemar), Ángel Correa, João Félix. Trainer: Diego Pablo Simeone (Argentina).
Lokomotiv Moskva: Guilherme, Vedran Corluka, Maciej Rybus, Dmitri Zhivoglyadov, Murilo Cerqueira, Vladislav Ignatiev, Grzegorz Krychowiak, Anton Miranchuk (76.Stanislav Magkeev), Daniil Kulikov, Zé Luís, François Kamano (76.Dmitry Rybchinsky). Trainer: Marko Nikolić (Serbia).

01.12.2020; RZD Arena, Moskva
Referee: Ali Palabiyik (Turkey); Attendance: 6,759
FK Lokomotiv Moskva – FC Red Bull Salzburg 1-3(0-2)
Lokomotiv Moskva: Guilherme, Vedran Corluka, Slobodan Rajkovic (46.Vladislav Ignatiev), Maciej Rybus, Vitaliy Lystsov (46.Anton Miranchuk), Dmitri Zhivoglyadov (84.Dmitry Rybchinsky), Murilo Cerqueira, Stanislav Magkeev, Éder, Zé Luís (89.François Kamano), Vitaliy Lisakovich (46.Maksim Mukhin). Trainer: Marko Nikolić (Serbia).
Red Bull Salzburg: Cican Stankovic, Andreas Ulmer, André Ramalho, Max Wöber, Rasmus Kristensen, Zlatko Junuzovic, Dominik Szoboszlai (77.Patson Daka), Enock Mwepu, Mohamed Camara (69.Luka Sucic), Mërgim Berisha (90+3.Jérôme Onguéné), Sékou Koïta (70.Karim Adeyemi). Trainer: Jesse Marsch (United States).
Goals: 28', 41' Mërgim Berisha 0-1, 0-2, 79' Anton Miranchuk 1-2 (penalty), 81' Karim Adeyemi 1-3.

09.12.2020; Allianz Arena, München
Referee: Sandro Schärer (Switzerland)
FC Bayern München – FK Lokomotiv Moskva 2-0(0-0)
Bayern München: Manuel Neuer, Jérôme Boateng (69.Chris Richards), Bouna Sarr, Niklas Süle, Alphonso Davies (69.Lucas Hernández), Douglas Costa, Leon Goretzka (61.Jamal Musiala), Marc Roca, Eric Maxim Choupo-Moting, Thomas Müller (46.Serge Gnabry), Leroy Sané (84.Angelo Stiller). Trainer: Hans-Dieter Flick.
Lokomotiv Moskva: Guilherme, Vedran Corluka, Slobodan Rajkovic, Maciej Rybus, Dmitri Zhivoglyadov, Stanislav Magkeev, Vladislav Ignatiev, Anton Miranchuk, Dmitry Rybchinsky (88.Aleksandr Silyanov), Éder, François Kamano (76.Nikita Iosifov). Trainer: Marko Nikolić (Serbia).
Goals: 63' Niklas Süle 1-0, 80' Eric Maxim Choupo-Moting 2-0.

25.11.2020; Allianz Arena, München
Referee: Orel Grinfeld (Israel)
FC Bayern München – FC Red Bull Salzurg 3-1(1-0)
Bayern München: Manuel Neuer, Jérôme Boateng, David Alaba, Benjamin Pavard (63.Lucas Hernández), Chris Richards (79.Javi Martínez), Leon Goretzka, Marc Roca [sent off 66], Thomas Müller, Robert Lewandowski, Serge Gnaby (62.Leroy Sané), Kingsley Coman (78.Douglas Costa). Trainer: Hans-Dieter Flick.
Red Bull Salzburg: Cican Stankovic, Andreas Ulmer, André Ramalho, Max Wöber, Rasmus Kristensen, Zlatko Junuzovic (71.Karim Adeyemi), Dominik Szoboszlai (71.Luka Sucic), Enock Mwepu (72.Majeed Ashimeru), Mohamed Camara, Mërgim Berisha, Sékou Koïta. Trainer: Jesse Marsch (United States).
Goals: 43' Robert Lewandowski 1-0, 52' Kingsley Coman 2-0, 68' Leroy Sané 3-0, 73' Mërgim Berisha 3-1.

01.12.2020; Estadio Wanda Metropolitano, Madrid
Referee: Clément Turpin (France)
Club Atlético de Madrid – FC Bayern München 1-1(1-0)
Atlético Madrid: Jan Oblak, Stefan Savic, Kieran Trippier, José Giménez (68.Felipe Monteiro), Mario Hermoso, Saúl, Koke, Yannick Carrasco (87.Renan Lodi), Marcos Llorente, Ángel Correa (80.Héctor Herrera), João Félix (87.Thomas Lemar). Trainer: Diego Pablo Simeone (Argentina).
Bayern München: Alexander Nübel, David Alaba, Bouna Sarr (62.Chris Richards), Niklas Süle, Lucas Hernández, Bright Arrey-Mbi (61') Serge Gnabry, Javi Martínez (62.Thomas Müller), Douglas Costa (86.Joshua Zirkzee), Jamal Musiala (76.Angelo Stiller), Eric Maxim Choupo-Moting, Leroy Sané. Trainer: Hans-Dieter Flick.
Goals: 26' João Félix 1-0, 86' Thomas Müller 1-1 (penalty).

09.12.2020; Red Bull Arena, Wals-Siezenheim
Referee: Anthony Taylor (England)
FC Red Bull Salzburg – Club Atlético de Madrid 0-2(0-1)
Red Bull Salzburg: Cican Stankovic, Andreas Ulmer, André Ramalho, Max Wöber (89.Jérôme Onguéné), Rasmus Kristensen, Zlatko Junuzovic, Dominik Szoboszlai (89.Masaya Okugawa), Enock Mwepu (89.Luka Sucic), Mërgim Berisha, Patson Daka (73.Noah Okafor), Sékou Koïta (70.Karim Adeyemi). Trainer: Jesse Marsch (United States).
Atlético Madrid: Jan Oblak, Stefan Savic, Kieran Trippier, Felipe Monteiro, Mario Hermoso, Saúl (64.Héctor Herrera), Koke, Yannick Carrasco (89.Thomas Lemar), Marcos Llorente (90+1.Renan Lodi), Luis Suárez (64.Ángel Correa), João Félix (89.Lucas Torreira). Trainer: Diego Pablo Simeone (Argentina).
Goals: 39' Mario Hermoso 0-1, 86' Yannick Carrasco 0-2.

GROUP B								
1. **Real Madrid CF**	6	3	1	2	11	-	9	10
2. **VfL Borussia Mönchengladbach**	6	2	2	2	16	-	9	8
3. *FK Shakhtar Donetsk*	6	2	2	2	5	-	12	8
4. FC Internazionale Milano	6	1	3	2	7	-	9	6

21.10.2020; Estadio „Alfredo Di Stéfano", Madrid
Referee: Srđan Jovanović (Serbia)
Real Madrid CF – FK Shakhtar Donetsk 2-3(0-3)
Real Madrid: Thibaut Courtois, Marcelo, Raphaël Varane, Ferland Mendy, Éder Militão, Luka Modric (70.Toni Kroos), Casemiro, Federico Valverde, Luka Jovic (59.Vinícius Júnior), Marco Asensio, Rodrygo (46.Karim Benzema). Trainer: Zinédine Zidane (France).
Shakhtar Donetsk: Anatolii Trubin, Davit Khocholava, Valeriy Bondar, Dodô, Viktor Kornienko, Dentinho (86.Heorhii Sudakov), Marlos, Manor Solomon (90+2.Vitão), Maycon, Marcos Antônio (90+4.Bogdan Viunnik), Mateus Martins Tetê. Trainer: Luís Manuel Ribeiro Castro (Portugal).
Goals: 29' Mateus Martins Tetê 0-1, 33' Raphaël Varane 0-2 (own goal), 42' Manor Solomon 0-3, 54' Luka Modric 1-3, 59' Vinícius Júnior 2-3.

21.10.2020; Stadio „Giuseppe Meazza", Milano
Referee: Björn Kuipers (Netherlands); Attendance: 1,000
FC Internazionale Milano – Borussia VfL Mönchengladbach 2-2(0-0)
Internazionale: Samir Handanovic, Matteo Darmian, Aleksandar Kolarov, Stefan de Vrij, Danilo D'Ambrosio, Ivan Perisic (79.Alessandro Bastoni), Arturo Vidal, Christian Eriksen (79.Marcelo Brozovic), Nicolò Barella, Alexis Sánchez (46.Lautaro Martínez), Romelu Lukaku. Trainer: Antonio Conte.
Borussia Mönchengladbach: Yann Sommer, Stefan Lainer, Matthias Ginter, Nico Elvedi, Ramy Bensebaini, Christoph Kramer, Jonas Hofmann, Florian Neuhaus (90.Lars Stindl), Breel Embolo (74.Patrick Herrmann), Marcus Thuram (90+5.Hannes Wolf). Trainer: Marco Rose.
Goals: 49' Romelu Lukaku 1-0, 63' Ramy Bensebaini 1-1 (penalty), 84' Janos Hofmann 1-2, 90' Romelu Lukaku 2-2.

27.10.2020; NSC Olimpiyskiy Stadium, Kyiv
Referee: Georgi Kabakov (Bulgaria); Attendance: 10,178
FK Shakhtar Donetsk – FC Internazionale Milano 0-0
Shakhtar Donetsk: Anatolii Trubin, Davit Khocholava (62.Mykola Matvienko), Valeriy Bondar, Dodô, Viktor Kornienko, Dentinho (15.Taison), Marlos (88.Alan Patrick), Manor Solomon, Maycon, Marcos Antônio, Mateus Martins Tetê. Trainer: Luís Manuel Ribeiro Castro (Portugal).
Internazionale: Samir Handanovic, Ashley Young (85.Andrea Pinamonti), Stefan de Vrij, Danilo D'Ambrosio (80.Matteo Darmian), Achraf Hakimi, Alessandro Bastoni, Arturo Vidal (79.Christian Eriksen), Marcelo Brozovic, Nicolò Barella, Romelu Lukaku, Lautaro Martínez (72.Ivan Perisic). Trainer: Antonio Conte.

03.11.2020; NSC Olimpiyskiy Stadium, Kyiv
Referee: Serdar Güzübüyük (Netherlands)
FK Shakhtar Donetsk – Borussia VfL Mönchengladbach 0-6(0-4)
Shakhtar Donetsk: Anatolii Trubin, Davit Khocholava, Valeriy Bondar, Dodô, Viktor Kornienko, Marlos (46.Viktor Kovalenko), Taison (46.Júnior Moraes), Manor Solomon, Maycon (69.Taras Stepanenko), Marcos Antônio (46.Alan Patrick), Mateus Martins Tetê. Trainer: Luís Manuel Ribeiro Castro (Portugal).
Borussia Mönchengladbach: Yann Sommer, Stefan Lainer (82.Michael Lang), Matthias Ginter, Nico Elvedi (82.Tony Jantschke), Ramy Bensebaini, Lars Stindl (69.Hannes Wolf), Christoph Kramer, Jonas Hofmann (75.Valentino Lazaro), Florian Neuhaus, Alassane Pléa (82.Ibrahima Traoré), Marcus Thuram. Trainer: Marco Rose.
Goals: 8' Alassane Pléa 0-1, 17' Valeriy Bondar 0-2 (own goal), 26' Alassane Pléa 0-3, 44' Ramy Bensebaini 0-4, 65' Lars Stindl 0-5, 78' Alassane Pléa 0-6.

25.11.2020; Borussia-Park, Mönchengladbach
Referee: Cüneyt Çakir (Turkey)
Borussia VfL Mönchengladbach – FK Shakhtar Donetsk 4-0(3-0)
Borussia Mönchengladbach: Yann Sommer, Oscar Wendt, Stefan Lainer, Matthias Ginter, Nico Elvedi, Lars Stindl (81.László Bénes), Christoph Kramer, Valentino Lazaro (69.Patrick Herrmann), Florian Neuhaus (69.Denis Zakaria), Breel Embolo (69.Alassane Pléa), Marcus Thuram (84') Ibrahima Traoré. Trainer: Marco Rose.
Shakhtar Donetsk: Andriy Pyatov, Sergiy Kryvtsov, Mykola Matvienko, Valeriy Bondar, Dodô, Marlos (70.Marcos Antônio), Taras Stepanenko, Alan Patrick (81.Maycon), Manor Solomon (59.Fernando), Mateus Martins Tetê, Júnior Moraes. Trainer: Luís Manuel Ribeiro Castro (Portugal).
Goals: 17' Lars Stindl 1-0 (penalty), 34' Nico Elvedi 2-0, 45+1' Breel Embolo 3-0, 77' Oscar Wendt 4-0.

01.12.2020; NSC Olimpiyskiy Stadium, Kyiv
Referee: Ovidiu Alin Haţegan (Romania)
FK Shakhtar Donetsk – Real Madrid CF 2-0(0-0)
Shakhtar Donetsk: Anatolii Trubin, Mykola Matvienko, Valeriy Bondar, Dodô, Vitão, Marlos (73.Maycon), Taras Stepanenko, Taison (74.Manor Solomon), Viktor Kovalenko (85.Alan Patrick), Mateus Martins Tetê, Júnior Moraes (25.Dentinho, 85.Fernando). Trainer: Luís Manuel Ribeiro Castro (Portugal).
Real Madrid: Thibaut Courtois, Nacho, Raphaël Varane, Ferland Mendy, Luka Modric, Toni Kroos, Lucas Vázquez, Martin Ødegaard (77.Isco), Karim Benzema (77.Mariano Díaz), Marco Asensio, Rodrygo (77.Vinícius Júnior). Trainer: Zinédine Zidane (France).
Goals: 57' Dentinho 1-0, 82' Manor Solomon 2-0.

09.12.2020; Estadio „Alfredo Di Stéfano", Madrid
Referee: Björn Kuipers (Netherlands)
Real Madrid CF – Borussia VfL Mönchengladbach 2-0(2-0)
Real Madrid: Thibaut Courtois, Sergio Ramos, Raphaël Varane, Ferland Mendy, Luka Modric, Toni Kroos, Casemiro, Lucas Vázquez, Karim Benzema, Vinícius Júnior (74.Marco Asensio), Rodrygo (74.Sergio Arribas). Trainer: Zinédine Zidane (France).
Borussia Mönchengladbach: Yann Sommer, Oscar Wendt (78.Valentino Lazaro), Stefan Lainer, Matthias Ginter, Nico Elvedi, Lars Stindl (85.Hannes Wolf), Christoph Kramer (85.László Bénes), Florian Neuhaus, Alassane Pléa, Breel Embolo (46.Denis Zakaria), Marcus Thuram (85.Patrick Herrmann). Trainer: Marco Rose.
Goals: 9', 32' Karim Benzema 1-0, 2-0.

27.10.2020; Borussia-Park, Mönchengladbach
Referee: Orel Grinfeld (Israel)
Borussia VfL Mönchengladbach – Real Madrid CF 2-2(1-0)
Borussia Mönchengladbach: Yann Sommer, Stefan Lainer, Matthias Ginter, Nico Elvedi, Ramy Bensebaini, Lars Stindl (79.Hannes Wolf), Christoph Kramer, Jonas Hofmann, Florian Neuhaus, Alassane Pléa (79.Breel Embolo), Marcus Thuram (71.Patrick Herrmann). Trainer: Marco Rose.
Real Madrid: Thibaut Courtois, Sergio Ramos, Raphaël Varane, Ferland Mendy, Toni Kroos (71.Luka Modric), Casemiro, Lucas Vázquez, Federico Valverde, Karim Benzema, Marco Asensio (84.Rodrygo), Vinícius Júnior (70.Eden Hazard). Trainer: Zinédine Zidane (France).
Goals: 33', 58' Marcus Thuram 1-0, 2-0, 87' Karim Benzema 2-1, 90+3' Casemiro 2-2.

03.11.2020; Estadio „Alfredo Di Stéfano", Madrid
Referee: Clément Turpin (France)
Real Madrid CF – FC Internazionale Milano 3-2(2-1)
Real Madrid: Thibaut Courtois, Sergio Ramos, Raphaël Varane, Ferland Mendy, Toni Kroos (78.Luka Modric), Casemiro, Lucas Vázquez, Federico Valverde, Karim Benzema, Eden Hazard (64.Vinícius Júnior), Marco Asensio (64.Rodrygo). Trainer: Zinédine Zidane (France).
Internazionale: Samir Handanovic, Ashley Young, Stefan de Vrij, Danilo D'Ambrosio, Achraf Hakimi, Alessandro Bastoni, Ivan Perisic (78.Alexis Sánchez), Arturo Vidal (87.Radja Nainggolan), Marcelo Brozovic, Nicolò Barella (78.Roberto Gagliardini), Lautaro Martínez. Trainer: Antonio Conte.
Goals: 25' Karim Benzema 1-0, 33' Sergio Ramos 2-0, 35' Lautaro Martínez 2-1, 68' Ivan Perisic 2-2, 80' Rodrygo 3-2.

25.11.2020; Stadio „Giuseppe Meazza", Milano
Referee: Anthony Taylor (England)
FC Internazionale Milano – Real Madrid CF 0-2(0-1)
Internazionale: Samir Handanovic, Ashley Young, Stefan de Vrij, Milan Skriniar, Achraf Hakimi (63.Alexis Sánchez), Alessandro Bastoni (46.Danilo D'Ambrosio), Arturo Vidal [sent off 33], Roberto Gagliardini (78.Stefano Sensi), Nicolò Barella, Romelu Lukaku, Lautaro Martínez (46.Ivan Perisic). Trainer: Antonio Conte.
Real Madrid: Thibaut Courtois, Nacho, Dani Carvajal, Raphaël Varane, Ferland Mendy, Luka Modric, Toni Kroos, Lucas Vázquez, Martin Ødegaard (58.Casemiro), Eden Hazard (78.Vinícius Júnior), Mariano Díaz (58.Rodrygo). Trainer: Zinédine Zidane (France).
Goals: 7' Eden Hazard 0-1 (penalty), 59' Achraf Hakimi 0-2 (own goal).

01.12.2020; Borussia-Park, Mönchengladbach
Referee: Danny Desmond Makkelie (Netherlands)
Borussia VfL Mönchengladbach – FC Internazionale Milano 2-3(1-1)
Borussia Mönchengladbach: Yann Sommer, Oscar Wendt (78.Hannes Wolf), Tony Jantschke (46') Denis Zakaria, Stefan Lainer, Matthias Ginter, Lars Stindl (70.Breel Embolo), Christoph Kramer, Valentino Lazaro, Florian Neuhaus, Alassane Pléa, Marcus Thuram. Trainer: Marco Rose.
Internazionale: Samir Handanovic, Ashley Young (87.Ivan Perisic), Matteo Darmian (60.Achraf Hakimi), Stefan de Vrij, Milan Skriniar, Alessandro Bastoni, Marcelo Brozovic, Roberto Gagliardini, Nicolò Barella, Romelu Lukaku, Lautaro Martínez (71.Alexis Sánchez). Trainer: Antonio Conte.
Goals: 17' Matteo Darmian 0-1, 45+1' Alassane Pléa 1-1, 64', 73' Romelu Lukaku 1-2, 1-3, 76' Alassane Pléa 2-3.

09.12.2020; Stadio „Giuseppe Meazza", Milano
Referee: Slavko Vinčić (Slovenia)
FC Internazionale Milano – FK Shakhtar Donetsk 0-0
Internazionale: Samir Handanovic, Ashley Young (68.Ivan Perisic), Stefan de Vrij, Milan Skriniar, Achraf Hakimi (85.Matteo Darmian), Alessandro Bastoni (85.Danilo D'Ambrosio), Marcelo Brozovic, Roberto Gagliardini (75.Alexis Sánchez), Nicolò Barella, Romelu Lukaku, Lautaro Martínez (85.Christian Eriksen). Trainer: Antonio Conte.
Shakhtar Donetsk: Anatolii Trubin, Mykola Matvienko, Valeriy Bondar, Dodô, Vitão (36.Davit Khocholava), Marlos (64.Alan Patrick), Taras Stepanenko, Taison (86.Dentinho), Viktor Kovalenko, Maycon, Mateus Martins Tetê (65.Manor Solomon). Trainer: Luís Manuel Ribeiro Castro (Portugal).

GROUP C	1.	**Manchester City FC**	6	5	1	0	13	- 1	16
	2.	**FC do Porto**	6	4	1	1	10	- 3	13
	3.	*Olympiacos SFP Peiraiás*	6	1	0	5	2	- 10	3
	4.	Olympique de Marseille	6	1	0	5	2	- 13	3

21.10.2020; Etihad Stadium, Manchester
Referee: Andris Treimanis (Latvia)
Manchester City FC – FC do Porto 3-1(1-1)
Manchester City: Ederson Moraes, Kyle Walker, João Cancelo, Rúben Dias, Eric García, Ilkay Gündogan (68.Phil Foden), Bernardo Silva, Rodri Hernández (85.Fernandinho, 90+4.John Stones), Kun Agüero (68.Ferrán Torres), Riyad Mahrez, Raheem Sterling. Trainer: Josep Guardiola (Spain).
FC Porto: Agustin Marchesín, Pepe, Chancel Mbemba, Malang Sarr (80.Evanilson), Zaidu Sanusi (76.Shoya Nakajima), Sérgio Oliveira, Mateus Uribe, Fábio Vieira (77.Mehdi Taremi), Jesús Corona (77.Nanu), Moussa Marega, Luis Díaz (55.Wilson Manafá). Trainer: Sérgio Paulo Marceneiro da Conceição.
Goals: 14' Luis Díaz 0-1, 20' Kun Agüero 1-1 (penalty), 65' Ilkay Gündogan 2-1, 73' Ferrán Torres 3-1.

27.10.2020; Estádio do Dragão, Porto
Referee: Daniel Siebert (Germany); Attendance: 2,450
FC do Porto – Olympiacos SFP Peiraiás 2-0(1-0)
FC Porto: Agustin Marchesín, Pepe, Chancel Mbemba, Wilson Manafá, Zaidu Sanusi, Sérgio Oliveira (89.Romário Baró), Mateus Uribe, Otávio (70.Marko Grujic), Fábio Vieira (60.Shoya Nakajima), Jesús Corona (69.Evanilson), Moussa Marega. Trainer: Sérgio Paulo Marceneiro da Conceição.
Olympiacos: José Sá, Rafinha, José Holebas (70.Rúben Vinagre), Rúben Semedo, Pape Cissé, Mathieu Valbuena (84.Ahmed Hassan "Koka"), Yann M'Vila, Andreas Bouchalakis (84.Pêpê Rodrigues), Georgios Masouras (53.Kostas Fortounis), Lazar Randjelovic (70.Bruma), Youssef El-Arabi. Trainer: Pedro Rui da Mota Vieira Martins (Portugal).
Goals: 11' Fábio Vieira 1-0, 85' Sérgio Oliveira 2-0.

03.11.2020; Etihad Stadium, Manchester
Referee: Carlos del Cerro Grande (Spain)
Manchester City FC – Olympiacos SFP Peiraiás 3-0(1-0)
Manchester City: Ederson Moraes, Kyle Walker (82.João Cancelo), Nathan Aké, John Stones, Ilkay Gündogan, Kevin De Bruyne (85.Felix Nmecha), Oleksandr Zinchenko, Phil Foden (69.Rodri Hernández), Riyad Mahrez (69.Gabriel Jesus), Raheem Sterling (82.Bernardo Silva), Ferrán Torres. Trainer: Josep Guardiola (Spain).
Olympiacos: José Sá, Rafinha, José Holebas, Rúben Semedo, Pape Cissé, Mathieu Valbuena (85.El Arbi Soudani), Yann M'Vila, Andreas Bouchalakis (46.Pêpê Rodrigues), Lazar Randjelovic (46.Bruma), Mady Camara (73.Georgios Masouras), Youssef El-Arabi (76.Ahmed Hassan "Koka"). Trainer: Pedro Rui da Mota Vieira Martins (Portugal).
Goals: 12' Ferrán Torres 1-0, 81' Gabriel Jesus 2-0, João Cancelo 3-0.

25.11.2020; Stádio „Giórgos Karaïskáki", Peiraiás
Referee: Davide Massa (Italy)
Olympiacos SFP Peiraiás – Manchester City FC 0-1(0-1)
Olympiacos: José Sá, Rafinha, Rúben Semedo, Mohamed Dräger (66.Marios Vrousai), Pape Cissé, Ousseynou Ba, Yann M'Vila, Kostas Fortounis, Pêpê Rodrigues (71.Andreas Bouchalakis), Georgios Masouras (78.El Arbi Soudani), Mady Camara. Trainer: Pedro Rui da Mota Vieira Martins (Portugal).
Manchester City: Ederson Moraes, João Cancelo, Benjamin Mendy (78.Oleksandr Zinchenko), John Stones, Rúben Dias, Ilkay Gündogan (86.Thomas Doyle), Bernardo Silva, Rodri Hernández (76.Fernandinho), Phil Foden, Raheem Sterling (76.Riyad Mahrez), Gabriel Jesus (78.Kun Agüero). Trainer: Josep Guardiola (Spain).
Goal: 36' Phil Foden 0-1.

21.10.2020; Stádio „Giórgos Karaïskáki", Peiraiás
Referee: Daniele Orsato (Italy)
Olympiacos SFP Peiraiás – Olympique de Marseille 1-0(0-0)
Olympiacos: José Sá, Rafinha, José Holebas, Rúben Semedo, Ousseynou Ba, Mathieu Valbuena (90+3.Pape Cissé), Yann M'Vila, Andreas Bouchalakis, Georgios Masouras (84.Ahmed Hassan "Koka"), Lazar Randjelovic (78.Kostas Fortounis), Youssef El-Arabi (90+3.Rúben Vinagre). Trainer: Pedro Rui da Mota Vieira Martins (Portugal).
Olympique Marseille: Steve Mandanda, Hiroki Sakai, Álvaro González, Jordan Amavi, Duje Caleta-Car, Dimitri Payet (76.Nemanja Radonjic), Morgan Sanson (77.Michaël Cuisance), Valentin Rongier, Pape Alassane Gueye (85.Kevin Strootman), Dario Benedetto (77.Luis Henrique), Florian Thauvin (82.Valère Germain). Trainer: Luís André de Pina Cabral e Villas Boas (Portugal).
Goal: 90+1' Ahmed Hassan "Koka" 1-0.

27.10.2020; Stade Vélodrome, Marseille
Referee: Tobias Stieler (Germany)
Olympique de Marseille – Manchester City FC 0-3(0-1)
Olympique Marseille: Steve Mandanda, Hiroki Sakai, Álvaro González, Jordan Amavi, Duje Caleta-Car, Boubacar Kamara, Leonardo Balerdi, Nemanja Radonjic (78.Dario Benedetto), Valentin Rongier (64.Morgan Sanson), Michaël Cuisance (85.Pape Alassane Gueye), Florian Thauvin (78.Dimitri Payet). Trainer: Luís André de Pina Cabral e Villas Boas (Portugal).
Manchester City: Ederson Moraes, Kyle Walker, Aymeric Laporte (77.John Stones), Rúben Dias, Ilkay Gündogan (78.Bernardo Silva), Kevin De Bruyne (82.Cole Palmer), Oleksandr Zinchenko (68.João Cancelo), Rodri Hernández, Phil Foden, Raheem Sterling, Ferrán Torres (77.Riyad Mahrez). Trainer: Josep Guardiola (Spain).
Goals: 18' Ferrán Torres 0-1, 76' Ilkay Gündogan 0-2, 81' Raheem Sterling 0-3.

03.11.2020; Estádio do Dragão, Porto
Referee: Antonio Miguel Mateu Lahoz (Spain)
FC do Porto – Olympique de Marseille 3-0(2-0)
FC Porto: Agustin Marchesín, Chancel Mbemba, Wilson Manafá, Malang Sarr, Zaidu Sanusi, Sérgio Oliveira (89.Marko Grujic), Mateus Uribe, Otávio (88.Mehdi Taremi), Jesús Corona (85.Fábio Vieira), Moussa Marega (88.Romário Baró), Luis Díaz (75.Shoya Nakajima). Trainer: Sérgio Paulo Marceneiro da Conceição.
Olympique Marseille: Steve Mandanda, Hiroki Sakai, Álvaro González, Jordan Amavi, Duje Caleta-Car, Boubacar Kamara (82.Kevin Strootman), Dimitri Payet (65.Luis Henríque), Morgan Sanson (65.Michaël Cuisance), Valentin Rongier, Dario Benedetto (77.Valère Germain), Florian Thauvin (82.Marley Aké). Trainer: Luís André de Pina Cabral e Villas Boas (Portugal).
Goals: 4' Moussa Marega 1-0, 28' Sérgio Oliveira 2-0 (penalty), 69' Luis Díaz 3-0.

25.11.2020; Stade Vélodrome, Marseille
Referee: Andreas Ekberg (Sweden)
Olympique de Marseille – FC do Porto 0-2(0-1)
Olympique Marseille: Steve Mandanda, Hiroki Sakai, Álvaro González, Jordan Amavi, Boubacar Kamara (59.Michaël Cuisance), Leonardo Balerdi [*sent off 70*], Morgan Sanson (77.Yuto Nagatomo), Valentin Rongier, Valère Germain (59.Dario Benedetto), Florian Thauvin (78.Marley Aké), Luis Henríque (59.Dimitri Payet). Trainer: Luís André de Pina Cabral e Villas Boas (Portugal).
FC Porto: Agustin Marchesín, Chancel Mbemba, Wilson Manafá, Malang Sarr, Zaidu Sanusi, Sérgio Oliveira (90.Mamadou Loum N'Diaye), Otávio, Marko Grujic [*sent off 67*], Jesús Corona (78.Mehdi Taremi), Moussa Marega (79.José Mário), Luis Díaz (79.Shoya Nakajima). Trainer: Sérgio Paulo Marceneiro da Conceição.
Goals: 39' Zaidu Sanusi 0-1, 72' Sérgio Oliveira 0-2 (penalty).

01.12.2020; Stade Vélodrome, Marseille
Referee: Jesús Gil Manzano (Spain)
Olympique de Marseille – Olympiacos SFP Peiraiás 2-1(0-1)
Olympique Marseille: Steve Mandanda, Hiroki Sakai, Álvaro González, Jordan Amavi, Duje Caleta-Car, Boubacar Kamara, Dimitri Payet, Valentin Rongier (85.Pape Alassane Gueye), Michaël Cuisance (55.Morgan Sanson), Dario Benedetto (46.Valère Germain), Florian Thauvin (90+5.Marley Aké). Trainer: Luís André de Pina Cabral e Villas Boas (Portugal).
Olympiacos: José Sá, Rafinha, José Holebas, Rúben Semedo, Pape Cissé, Yann M'Vila (79.Georgios Masouras), Kostas Fortounis, Andreas Bouchalakis, Mady Camara, Youssef El-Arabi, Marios Vrousai (90+2.El Arbi Soudani). Trainer: Pedro Rui da Mota Vieira Martins (Portugal).
Goals: 33' Mady Camara 0-1, 55', 75' Dimitri Payet 1-1 (penalty), 2-1 (penalty).

09.12.2020; Etihad Stadium, Manchester
Referee: Halil Umut Meler (Turkey)
Manchester City FC – Olympique de Marseille 3-0(0-0)
Manchester City: Zack Steffen, Kyle Walker, Aymeric Laporte, Nathan Aké, Eric García (28.John Stones), Fernandinho, Ilkay Gündogan (46.Raheem Sterling), Bernardo Silva, Phil Foden, Riyad Mahrez (67.Kun Agüero), Ferrán Torres. Trainer: Josep Guardiola (Spain).
Olympique Marseille: Steve Mandanda, Yuto Nagatomo, Hiroki Sakai, Álvaro González, Boubacar Kamara (66.Valentin Rongier), Leonardo Balerdi, Dimitri Payet (67.Michaël Cuisance), Morgan Sanson, Pape Alassane Gueye (75.Kevin Strootman), Valère Germain (76.Dario Benedetto), Florian Thauvin (75.Marley Aké). Trainer: Luís André de Pina Cabral e Villas Boas (Portugal).
Goals: 48' Ferrán Torres 1-0, 77' Kun Agüero 2-0, 90' Álvaro González 3-0 (own goal).

01.12.2020; Estádio do Dragão, Porto
Referee: Björn Kuipers (Netherlands)
FC do Porto – Manchester City FC 0-0
FC Porto: Agustin Marchesín, Chancel Mbemba, Wilson Manafá (72.Nanu), Malang Sarr, Diogo Leite, Zaidu Sanusi, Sérgio Oliveira, Mateus Uribe, Otávio (87.Fábio Vieira), Jesús Corona (63.Luis Díaz), Moussa Marega (72.Evanilson). Trainer: Sérgio Paulo Marceneiro da Conceição.
Manchester City: Ederson Moraes, João Cancelo, Rúben Dias, Eric García, Fernandinho, Oleksandr Zinchenko, Bernardo Silva, Rodri Hernández, Phil Foden, Raheem Sterling, Ferrán Torres (71.Gabriel Jesus). Trainer: Josep Guardiola (Spain).

09.12.2020; Stádio „Giórgos Karaïskáki", Peiraiás
Referee: Dr. Felix Brych (Germany)
Olympiacos SFP Peiraiás – FC do Porto 0-2(0-1)
Olympiacos: José Sá, Rafinha, José Holebas, Rúben Semedo [*sent off* 79], Pape Cissé, Yann M'Vila, Andreas Bouchalakis, Georgios Masouras (46.Lazar Randjelovic), Mady Camara (35.Kostas Fortounis), Youssef El-Arabi (81.Ousseynou Ba), Marios Vrousai (73.El Arbi Soudani). Trainer: Pedro Rui da Mota Vieira Martins (Portugal).
FC Porto: Diogo Costa, Chancel Mbemba, Nanu, Diogo Leite, Zaidu Sanusi, Otávio (79.Malang Sarr), Marko Grujic, Romário Baró (64.Mateus Uribe), Felipe Anderson (63.Luis Díaz), Toni Martínez (80.Evanilson), João Mário (72.Jesús Corona). Trainer: Sérgio Paulo Marceneiro da Conceição.
Goals: 10' Otávio 0-1 (penalty), 77' Mateus Uribe 0-2.

GROUP D	1.	**Liverpool FC**	6	4	1	1	10 - 3	13
	2.	**Atalanta Bergamasca Calcio**	6	3	2	1	10 - 8	11
	3.	*AFC Ajax Amsterdam*	6	2	1	3	7 - 7	7
	4.	FC Midtjylland Herning	6	0	2	4	4 - 13	2

21.10.2020; „Johan Cruijff" ArenA, Amsterdam
Referee: Dr. Felix Brych (Germany)
AFC Ajax Amsterdam – Liverpool FC 0-1(0-1)
AFC Ajax: André Onana, Daley Blind (83.Klaas Jan Huntelaar), Nicolás Tagliafico, Noussair Mazraoui, Perr Schuurs (84.Lassina Traoré), Lisandro Martínez, Davy Klaassen (74.Jurgen Ekkelenkamp), Ryan Gravenberch, Mohammed Kudus (9.Quincy Promes), Dusan Tadic, David Neres (74.Zakaria Labyad). Trainer: Erik ten Hag.
Liverpool FC: Adrián, Andrew Robertson, Joe Gomez, Trent Alexander-Arnold, James Milner (90+2.Rhys Williams), Georginio Wijnaldum, Fabinho, Curtis Jones (46.Jordan Henderson), Roberto Firmino (60.Diogo Jota), Mohamed Salah (60.Xherdan Shaqiri), Sadio Mané (60.Takumi Minamino). Trainer: Jürgen Klopp (Germany).
Goal: Nicolás Tagliafico 0-1 (own goal).

21.10.2020; MCH Arena, Herning
Referee: Artur Manuel Ribeiro Soares Dias (Portugal); Attendance: 132
FC Midtjylland Herning – Atalanta Bergamasca Calcio 0-4(0-3)
FC Midtjylland: Jesper Hansen, Erik Sviatchenko, Alexander Scholz, Joel Andersson, Paulinho, Pione Sisto (87.Mikael Anderson), Awer Mabil (75.Lasse Vibe), Anders Dreyer, Frank Onyeka (87.Bozhidar Kraev), Jens Cajuste (76.Nicolas Madsen), Sory Kaba (60.Evander). Trainer: Brian Priske.
Atalanta: Marco Sportiello, Rafael Tolói, Berat Djimsiti, Hans Hateboer, Robin Gosens, Cristian Romero (86.José Palomino), Papu Gómez (68.Mario Pasalic), Marten de Roon, Remo Freuler (80.Matteo Pessina), Duván Zapata (80.Aleksey Miranchuk), Luis Muriel (68.Josip Ilicic). Trainer: Gian Piero Gasperini.
Goals: 26' Duván Zapata 0-1, 36' Papu Gómez 0-2, 42' Luis Muriel 0-3, 89' Aleksey Miranchuk 0-4.

27.10.2020; Anfield Road, Liverpool
Referee: Pawel Raczkowski (Poland)
Liverpool FC – FC Midtjylland Herning 2-0(0-0)
Liverpool FC: Alisson, Andrew Robertson, Joe Gomez, Trent Alexander-Arnold, James Milner, Jordan Henderson (46.Georginio Wijnaldum), Xherdan Shaqiri, Fabinho (30.Rhys Williams), Takumi Minamino (61.Mohamed Salah), Divock Origi (60.Sadio Mané), Diogo Jota (81.Roberto Firmino). Trainer: Jürgen Klopp (Germany).
FC Midtjylland: Mikkel Andersen, Erik Sviatchenko, Alexander Scholz, Joel Andersson, Paulinho, Pione Sisto (72.Evander), Awer Mabil (66.Mikael Anderson), Anders Dreyer, Frank Onyeka, Jens Cajuste (81.Bozhidar Kraev), Sory Kaba (81.Luca Pfeiffer). Trainer: Brian Priske.
Goals: 55' Diogo Jota 1-0, 90+3' Mohamed Salah 2-0 (penalty).

27.10.2020; Gewiss Stadium, Bergamo
Referee: Damir Skomina (Slovenia)
Atalanta Bergamasca Calcio – AFC Ajax Amsterdam 2-2(0-2)
Atalanta: Marco Sportiello, Rafael Tolói, Berat Djimsiti, Hans Hateboer, Robin Gosens, Cristian Romero, Papu Gómez (78.Luis Muriel), Josip Ilicic (79.Ruslan Malinovskiy), Remo Freuler, Mario Pasalic, Duván Zapata. Trainer: Gian Piero Gasperini.
AFC Ajax: André Onana, Daley Blind, Nicolás Tagliafico, Noussair Mazraoui (56.Sean Klaiber), Perr Schuurs, Davy Klaassen, Ryan Gravenberch, Dusan Tadic, David Neres (69.Quincy Promes), Lassina Traoré, Antony (90+4.Zakaria Labyad). Trainer: Erik ten Hag.
Goals: 30' Dusan Tadic 0-1 (penalty), 38' Lassina Traoré 0-2, 54', 60' Duván Zapata 2-1, 2-2.

03.11.2020; MCH Arena, Herning
Referee: Robert Madden (Scotland); Attendance: 132
FC Midtjylland Herning – AFC Ajax Amsterdam 1-2(1-2)
FC Midtjylland: Mikkel Andersen, Erik Sviatchenko, Alexander Scholz, Joel Andersson (64.Dion Cools), Paulinho, Pione Sisto, Awer Mabil, Anders Dreyer (75.Bozhidar Kraev), Frank Onyeka, Jens Cajuste (81.Evander), Sory Kaba (81.Lasse Vibe). Trainer: Brian Priske.
AFC Ajax: André Onana, Daley Blind, Nicolás Tagliafico, Noussair Mazraoui (77.Sean Klaiber), Perr Schuurs (60.Edson Álvarez), Lisandro Martínez, Jurgen Ekkelenkamp (46.Davy Klaassen), Ryan Gravenberch, Dusan Tadic, Quincy Promes, Antony (90.Lassina Traoré.) Trainer: Erik ten Hag.
Goals: 1' Antony 0-1, 13' Dusan Tadic 0-2, 18' Anders Dreyer 1-2.

25.11.2020; Anfield Road, Liverpool
Referee: Carlos del Cerro Grande (Spain)
Liverpool FC – Atalanta Bergamasca Calcio 0-2(0-0)
Liverpool FC: Alisson, Joel Matip (84.Takumi Minamino), Kostas Tsimikas (61.Andrew Robertson), Neco Williams, Rhys Williams, James Milner, Georginio Wijnaldum (61.Fabinho), Curtis Jones, Mohamed Salah (61.Roberto Firmino), Sadio Mané, Divock Origi (61.Diogo Jota). Trainer: Jürgen Klopp (Germany).
Atalanta: Pierluigi Gollini, Rafael Tolói, Berat Djimsiti, Hans Hateboer, Robin Gosens (75.Johan Mojica), Cristian Romero, Papu Gómez, Josip Ilicic (70.Duván Zapata), Marten de Roon, Remo Freuler, Matteo Pessina (85.Aleksey Miranchuk). Trainer: Gian Piero Gasperini.
Goals: 60' Josip Ilicic 0-1, 64' Robin Gosens 0-2.

01.12.2020; Anfield Road, Liverpool
Referee: Tobias Stieler (Germany)
Liverpool FC – AFC Ajax Amsterdam 1-0(0-0)
Liverpool FC: Caoimhin Kelleher, Joel Matip, Andrew Robertson, Neco Williams, Georginio Wijnaldum, Jordan Henderson, Fabinho, Curtis Jones, Mohamed Salah (90.Rhys Williams), Sadio Mané, Diogo Jota (68.Roberto Firmino). Trainer: Jürgen Klopp (Germany).
AFC Ajax: André Onana, Daley Blind (86.Lisandro Martínez), Nicolás Tagliafico, Noussair Mazraoui (86.Klaas Jan Huntelaar), Perr Schuurs, Edson Álvarez (69.Zakaria Labyad), Davy Klaassen, Ryan Gravenberch, Dusan Tadic, David Neres (81.Lassina Traoré), Antony. Trainer: Erik ten Hag.
Goal: 58' Curtis Jones 1-0.

09.12.2020; „Johan Cruijff" ArenA, Amsterdam
Referee: Carlos del Cerro Grande (Spain)
AFC Ajax Amsterdam – Atalanta Bergamasca Calcio 0-1(0-0)
AFC Ajax: André Onana, Nicolás Tagliafico (64.Klaas Jan Huntelaar), Noussair Mazraoui, Perr Schuurs, Lisandro Martínez (90+2.Jurriën Timber; 90+6.Edson Álvarez), Zakaria Labyad (63.Jurgen Ekkelenkamp), Davy Klaassen, Ryan Gravenberch [sent off 79], Dusan Tadic, Brian Brobbey (46.Quincy Promes), Antony. Trainer: Erik ten Hag.
Atalanta: Pierluigi Gollini, Rafael Tolói, Berat Djimsiti, Hans Hateboer, Robin Gosens (79.José Palomino), Cristian Romero, Papu Gómez, Marten de Roon, Remo Freuler, Matteo Pessina, Duván Zapata (79.Luis Muriel). Trainer: Gian Piero Gasperini.
Goal: 85' Luis Muriel 0-1.

03.11.2020; Gewiss Stadium, Bergamo
Referee: Ovidiu Alin Haţegan (Romania)
Atalanta Bergamasca Calcio – Liverpool FC 0-5(0-2)
Atalanta: Marco Sportiello, Rafael Tolói, José Palomino (81.Matteo Ruggeri), Berat Djimsiti, Hans Hateboer (81.Fabio Depaoli), Papu Gómez (81.Sam Lammers), Remo Freuler, Mario Pasalic (63.Ruslan Malinovskiy), Duván Zapata, Luis Muriel (53.Matteo Pessina). Trainer: Gian Piero Gasperini.
Liverpool FC: Alisson, Andrew Robertson (66'Naby Keïta), Joe Gomez, Trent Alexander-Arnold (82.Neco Williams), Rhys Williams, Georginio Wijnaldum (82.Kostas Tsimikas), Jordan Henderson (65.James Milner), Curtis Jones, Mohamed Salah, Sadio Mané, Diogo Jota (65.Roberto Firmino). Trainer: Jürgen Klopp (Germany).
Goals: 16', 44' Diogo Jota 0-1, 0-2, 47' Mohamed Salah 0-3, 49' Sadio Mané 0-4, 54' Diogo Jota 0-5.

25.11.2020; „Johan Cruijff" ArenA, Amsterdam
Referee: Sergei Karasov (Russia)
AFC Ajax Amsterdam – FC Midtjylland Herning 3-1(0-0)
AFC Ajax: André Onana, Daley Blind (66.Lisandro Martínez), Nicolás Tagliafico, Noussair Mazraoui (82.Sean Klaiber), Perr Schuurs, Zakaria Labyad (81.Quincy Promes), Davy Klaassen (66.Edson Álvarez), Ryan Gravenberch, Dusan Tadic, David Neres (90+3.Jurgen Ekkelenkamp), Lassina Traoré. Trainer: Erik ten Hag.
FC Midtjylland: Jesper Hansen, Erik Sviatchenko [sent off 90+1], Alexander Scholz, Paulinho (26.Joel Andersson), Dion Cools, Pione Sisto (81.Luka Pfeiffer), Awer Mabil, Anders Dreyer (82.Gustav Isaksen), Frank Onyeka, Nicolas Madsen (69.Mikael Anderson), Sory Kaba (69.Bozhidar Kraev). Trainer: Brian Priske.
Goals: 47' Ryan Gravenberch 1-0, 49' Noussair Mazraoui 2-0, 66' David Neres 3-0, 80' Awer Mabil 3-1 (penalty).

01.12.2020; Gewiss Stadium, Bergamo
Referee: Anastasios Sidiropoulos (Greece)
Atalanta Bergamasca Calcio – FC Midtjylland Herning 1-1(0-1)
Atalanta: Marco Sportiello, José Palomino (68.Rafael Tolói), Berat Djimsiti, Hans Hateboer, Robin Gosens (86.Matteo Ruggeri), Cristian Romero, Papu Gómez (46.Josip Ilicic), Remo Freuler (68.Marten de Roon), Matteo Pessina, Duván Zapata, Luis Muriel (68.Amad Diallo Traoré). Trainer: Gian Piero Gasperini.
FC Midtjylland: Jesper Hansen, Daniel Høegh, Alexander Scholz, Joel Andersson, Manjrekar James, Paulinho, Awer Mabil (67.Lasse Vibe), Anders Dreyer (82.Gustav Isaksen), Mikael Anderson, Frank Onyeka, Sory Kaba (82.Nicolas Madsen). Trainer: Brian Priske.
Goals: 13' Alexander Scholz 0-1, 79' Cristian Romero 1-1.

09.12.2020; MCH Arena, Herning
Referee: François Letexier (France); Attendance: 147
FC Midtjylland Herning – Liverpool FC 1-1(0-1)
FC Midtjylland: Jesper Hansen, Erik Sviatchenko, Alexander Scholz, Paulinho, Dion Cools, Awer Mabil (63.Mikael Anderson), Anders Dreyer (76.Pione Sisto), Evander (90.Nicolas Madsen), Frank Onyeka (63.Gustav Isaksen), Jens Cajuste, Sory Kaba (90.Luca Pfeiffer). Trainer: Brian Priske.
Liverpool FC: Caoimhin Kelleher, Kostas Tsimikas (61.Andrew Robertson), Trent Alexander-Arnold, Rhys Williams, Fabinho (46.Billy Koumetio), Naby Keïta (61.Jordan Henderson), Leighton Clarkson, Mohamed Salah, Takumi Minamino, Divock Origi (71.Roberto Firmino), Diogo Jota (87.Sadio Mané). Trainer: Jürgen Klopp (Germany).
Goals: 1' Mohamed Salah 0-1, 62' Alexander Scholz 1-1 (penalty).

GROUP E	1.	**Chelsea FC London**	6	4	2	0	14	- 2	14
	2.	**Sevilla FC**	6	4	1	1	9	- 8	13
	3.	*FK Krasnodar*	6	1	2	3	6	- 11	5
	4.	Stade Rennais FC	6	0	1	5	3	- 11	1

20.10.2020; Stamford Bridge, London
Referee: Davide Massa (Italy)
Chelsea FC London – Sevilla FC 0-0
Chelsea FC: Edouard Mendy, Thiago Silva, Kurt Zouma, Ben Chilwell, Reece James, Jorginho (65.Mateo Kovacic), N'Golo Kanté, Mason Mount (62.Hakim Ziyech), Christian Pulisic (90+1.Callum Hudson-Odoi), Kai Havertz, Timo Werner (90+1.Tammy Abraham). Trainer: Frank James Lampard
Sevilla FC: Yassine Bounou, Jesús Navas, Sergi Gómez (33.Joan Jordán), Diego Carlos, Ivan Rakitic (80.Franco Vázquez), Fernando, Nemanja Gudelj, Lucas Ocampos, Marcos Acuña, Suso (58.Óliver Torres), Luuk de Jong (80.Youssef En-Nesyri). Trainer: Julen Lopetegui Agote.

28.10.2020; Krasnodar Stadion, Krasnodar
Referee: Ali Palabiyik (Turkey); Attendance: 10,544
FK Krasnodar – Chelsea FC London 0-4(0-1)
FK Krasnodar: Matvey Safonov, Igor Smolnikov, Aleksandr Martynovich, Cristian Ramírez, Evheniy Chernov, Yuri Gazinskiy, Tonny Vilhena, Kristoffer Olsson (82.Eduard Spertsyan), Kaio Pantaleão, Daniil Utkin (74.Magomed Suleymanov), Marcus Berg (87.Leon Sabua). Trainer: Murad Musaev. Chelsea FC: Edouard Mendy, Azpilicueta, Kurt Zouma, Antonio Rüdiger, Ben Chilwell (81.Emerson), Mateo Kovacic (71.N'Golo Kanté), Jorginho (71.Mason Mount), Hakim Ziyech (80.Tammy Abraham), Kai Havertz, Callum Hudson-Odoi (71.Christian Pulisic), Timo Werner. Trainer: Frank James Lampard. Goals: 37' Callum Hudson-Odoi 0-1, 76' Timo Werner 0-2 (penalty), 79' Hakim Ziyech 0-3, 90' Christian Pulisic 0-4.

04.11.2020; Estádio „Ramón Sánchez Pizjuán", Sevilla
Referee: Dr. Felix Brych (Germany)
Sevilla FC – FK Krasnodar 3-2(1-2)
Sevilla FC: Tomás Vaclík, Jesús Navas [*sent off 45+4*], Escudero (34.Marcos Acuña), Diego Carlos, Jules Koundé (34.Óscar Rodríguez), Ivan Rakitic, Nemanja Gudelj, Lucas Ocampos, Joan Jordán (60.Youssef En-Nesyri), Luuk de Jong (83.Karim Rekik), Munir (60.Fernando). Trainer: Julen Lopetegui Agote.
FK Krasnodar: Matvey Safonov, Aleksandr Martynovich, Cristian Ramírez (46.Egor Sorokin), Evheniy Chernov, Yuri Gazinskiy, Kristoffer Olsson, Kaio Pantaleão, Daniil Utkin (75.Wanderson), Leon Sabua (34.Eduard Spertsyan, 66.Victor Claesson), Marcus Berg, Magomed Suleymanov. Trainer: Murad Musaev.
Goals: 17' Magomed Suleymanov 0-1, 21' Marcus Berg 0-2 (penalty), 42' Ivan Rakitic 1-2, 69', 72' Youssef En-Nesyri 2-2, 3-2.

24.11.2020; Krasnodar Stadion, Krasnodar
Referee: Marco Guida (Italy); Attendance: 10,554
FK Krasnodar – Sevilla FC 1-2(0-1)
FK Krasnodar: Evgeniy Gorodov, Igor Smolnikov, Aleksandr Martynovich, Cristian Ramírez, Rémy Cabella (85.Daniil Utkin), Yuri Gazinskiy, Victor Claesson (84.Evheniy Chernov), Kristoffer Olsson (67.Tonny Vilhena, Kaio Pantaleão, Marcus Berg (67.Ari), Magomed Suleymanov (46.Wanderson). Trainer: Murad Musaev.
Sevilla FC: Tomás Vaclík, Escudero (61.Karim Rekik), Diego Carlos, Jules Koundé, Ivan Rakitic (61.Óliver Torres), Fernando, Nemanja Gudelj, Lucas Ocampos (72.Oussama Idrissi), Óscar Rodríguez (53.Joan Jordán), Luuk de Jong (72.Youssef En-Nesyri), Munir. Trainer: Julen Lopetegui Agote.
Goals: 4' Ivan Rakitic 0-1, 56' Wanderson 1-1, 90+5' Munir 1-2.

02.12.2020; Krasnodar Stadion, Krasnodar
Referee: William Collum (Scotland); Attendance: 8,747
FK Krasnodar – Stade Rennais FC 1-0(0-0)
FK Krasnodar: Matvey Safonov, Igor Smolnikov, Aleksandr Martynovich, Cristian Ramírez, Rémy Cabella, Yuri Gazinskiy (87.Ruslan Kambolov), Victor Claesson, Tonny Vilhena, Kaio Pantaleão, Marcus Berg (90+1.Ari), Wanderson (66.Magomed Suleymanov). Trainer: Murad Musaev.
Stade Rennais: Romain Salin, Damien Da Silva, Hamari Traoré, Gerzino Nyamsi, Adrien Truffert, Steven N'Zonzi, Benjamin Bourigeaud (73.Yann Gboho), James Lea Siliki (65.Clément Grenier), Eduardo Camavinga (82.Flavien Tait), Adrien Hunou (65.M'Baye Niang), Jérémy Doku. Trainer: Julien Stéphan.Goal: 71' Marcus Berg 1-0.

20.10.2020; Roazhon Park, Rennes
Referee: Anastasios Sidiropoulos (Greece); Attendance: 4,973
Stade Rennais FC – FK Krasnodar 1-1(0-0)
Stade Rennais: Alfred Gomis, Damien Da Silva, Hamari Traoré, Dalbert Henrique (81.Adrien Truffert), Nayef Aguerd, Steven N'Zonzi, Benjamin Bourigeaud (69.Flavien Tait), Martin Terrier, Eduardo Camavinga (81.Adrien Hunou), Serhou Guirassy, Romain Del Castillo (62.Jérémy Doku). Trainer: Julien Stéphan.
FK Krasnodar: Matvey Safonov, Igor Smolnikov, Sergey Petrov (72.Magomed Suleymanov), Cristian Ramírez, Evheniy Chernov, Egor Sorokin, Tonny Vilhena, Kristoffer Olsson, Kaio Pantaleão, Daniil Utkin (72.Yuri Gazinskiy), Marcus Berg. Trainer: Murad Musaev.
Goals: 56' Serhou Guirassy 1-0 (penalty), 59' Cristian Ramírez 1-1.

28.10.2020; Estádio „Ramón Sánchez Pizjuán", Sevilla
Referee: Cüneyt Çakir (Turkey)
Sevilla FC – Stade Rennais FC 1-0(0-0)
Sevilla FC: Yassine Bounou, Jesús Navas, Diego Carlos, Jules Koundé, Fernando, Lucas Ocampos, Marcos Acuña, Óliver Torres (76.Ivan Rakitic), Joan Jordán (89.Nemanja Gudelj), Luuk de Jong (85.Youssef En-Nesyri), Munir (85.Franco Vázquez). Trainer: Julen Lopetegui Agote.
Stade Rennais: Alfred Gomis, Damien Da Silva, Daniele Rugani (17.Nayef Aguerd), Hamari Traoré, Brandon Soppy (77.Dalbert Henrique), Clément Grenier (77.Romain Del Castillo), Jonas Martin, Benjamin Bourigeaud (49.James Lea Siliki), Martin Terrier, Serhou Guirassy, Jérémy Doku. Trainer: Julien Stéphan.
Goal: 55' Luuk de Jong 1-0.

04.11.2020; Stamford Bridge, London
Referee: Felix Zwayer (Germany)
Chelsea FC London – Stade Rennais FC 3-0(2-0)
Chelsea FC: Edouard Mendy, Thiago Silva (68.Antonio Rüdiger), Kurt Zouma, Ben Chilwell (81.Emerson), Reece James, Jorginho, N'Golo Kanté (62.Mateo Kovacic), Hakim Ziyech (75.Callum Hudson-Odoi), Mason Mount, Timo Werner, Tammy Abraham (63.Olivier Giroud). Trainer: Frank James Lampard.
Stade Rennais: Alfred Gomis, Damien Da Silva, Hamari Traoré, Dalbert Henrique [*sent off 40*], Nayef Aguerd, Steven N'Zonzi (62.Clément Grenier), Benjamin Bourigeaud, James Lea Siliki (46.Adrien Truffert), Martin Terrier (62.Jérémy Doku), Yann Gboho (62.Romain Del Castillo), Serhou Guirassy (76.Adrian Hunou). Trainer: Julien Stéphan.
Goals: 10', 41' Timo Werner 1-0 (penalty), 2-0 (penalty), 50' Tammy Abraham 3-0.

24.11.2020; Roazhon Park, Rennes
Referee: Björn Kuipers (Netherlands)
Stade Rennais FC – Chelsea FC London 1-2(0-1)
Stade Rennais: Alfred Gomis, Damien Da Silva, Hamari Traoré, Gerzino Nyamsi, Adrien Truffert (86.Faitout Maouassa), Steven N'Zonzi, Benjamin Bourigeaud, James Lea Siliki (63.Romain Del Castillo), Eduardo Camavinga (78.Clément Grenier), Serhou Guirassy (86.M'Baye Niang), Jérémy Doku (86.Yann Gboho). Trainer: Julien Stéphan.
Chelsea FC: Edouard Mendy, Thiago Silva, Azpilicueta, Kurt Zouma, Ben Chilwell, Mateo Kovacic (76.Kai Havertz), Jorginho, Mason Mount (68.N'Golo Kanté), Callum Hudson-Odoi (75.Hakim Ziyech), Timo Werner (90+2.Reece James), Tammy Abraham (69.Olivier Giroud). Trainer: Frank James Lampard. Goals: 22' Callum Hudson-Odoi 0-1, 85' Serhou Guirassy 1-1, 90+1' Olivier Giroud 1-2.

02.12.2020; Estádio „Ramón Sánchez Pizjuán", Sevilla
Referee: Artur Manuel Ribeiro Soares Dias (Portugal)
Sevilla FC – Chelsea FC London 0-4(0-1)
Sevilla FC: Alfonso Pastor, Jesús Navas (59.Jules Koundé), Sergi Gómez, Karim Rekik, Diego Carlos, Ivan Rakitic (75.Óliver Torres), Franco Vásquez (66.Munir), Nemanja Gudelj, Óscar Rodríguez (60.Joan Jordán), Oussama Idrissi (59.Lucas Ocampos), Youssef En-Nesyri. Trainer: Julen Lopetegui Agote.
Chelsea FC: Edouard Mendy, Azpilicueta, Emerson, Antonio Rüdiger, Andreas Christensen, Mateo Kovacic (67.Hakim Ziyech), Jorginho (85.Billy Gilmour), Christian Pulisic (67.Mason Mount), Kai Havertz (67.N'Golo Kanté), Callum Hudson-Odoi, Olivier Giroud (84.Timo Werner). Trainer: Frank James Lampard.
Goals: 8', 54', 74', 83' Olivier Giroud 0-1, 0-2, 0-3, 0-4 (penalty).

08.12.2020; Stamford Bridge, London
Referee: Pavel Královec (Czech Republic); Attendance: 2,000
Chelsea FC London – FK Krasnodar 1-1(1-1)
Chelsea FC: Kepa, Azpilicueta, Emerson, Antonio Rüdiger, Andreas Christensen, Mateo Kovacic (74.N'Golo Kanté), Jorginho, Kai Havertz (74.Timo Werner), Billy Gilmour, Faustino Anjorin (80.Olivier Giroud), Tammy Abraham. Trainer: Frank James Lampard.
FK Krasnodar: Evgeniy Gorodov, Igor Smolnikov, Aleksandr Martynovich, Cristian Ramírez, Rémy Cabella (80.Magomed Suleymanov), Victor Claesson, Tonny Vilhena, Kristoffer Olsson (80.Ruslan Kambolov), Kaio Pantaleão (74.Egor Sorokin), Marcus Berg (90.Evgeniy Markov). Wanderson (80.Evgeniy Chernov). Trainer: Murad Musaev.
Goals: 24' Rémy Cabella 0-1, 28' Joginho 1-1 (penalty).

08.12.2020; Roazhon Park, Rennes
Referee: Bartosz Frankowski (Poland)
Stade Rennais FC – Sevilla FC 1-3(0-2)
Stade Rennais: Romain Salin, Damien Da Silva (70.Nayef Aguerd), Hamari Traoré, Dalbert Henrique, Brandon Soppy, Clément Grenier (79.Flavien Tait), Steven N'Zonzi, Faitout Maouassa (79.Adrien Truffert), Eduardo Camavinga, M'Baye Niang (70.Georginio Rutter), Jérémy Doku (79.Yann Gboho). Trainer: Julien Stéphan.
Sevilla FC: Yassine Bounou, Sergi Gómez (76.Fernando), Karim Rekik, Diego Carlos, Jules Koundé, Ivan Rakitic, Nemanja Gudelj, Suso (76.Óscar Rodríguez), Óliver Torres (83.Franco Vásquez), Oussama Idrissi (72.Lucas Ocampos), Youssef En-Nesyri (83.Carlos Fernández). Trainer: Julen Lopetegui Agote.
Goals: 32' Jules Koundé 0-1, 45+2', 81' Youssef En-Nesyri 0-2, 0-3, 86' Georginio Rutter 1-3 (penalty).

GROUP F	1.	**BV 09 Borussia Dortmund**	6	4	1	1	12 - 5	13
	2.	**SS Lazio Roma**	6	2	4	0	11 - 7	10
	3.	*Club Brugge KV*	6	2	2	2	8 - 10	8
	4.	FK Zenit Saint Petersburg	6	0	1	5	4 - 13	1

20.10.2020; Gazprom Arena, Saint Petersburg
Referee: Benoît Bastien (France); Attendance: 16,682
FK Zenit Saint Petersburg – Club Brugge KV 1-2(0-0)
Zenit Saint Petersburg: Mikhail Kerzhakov, Dejan Lovren, Yaroslav Rakitskiy, Vyacheslav Karavaev, Danil Krugovoy, Magomed Ozdoev (88.Aleksandr Erokhin), Wilmar Barrios, Daler Kuzyaev (72.Wendel), Artyom Dzyuba, Sardar Azmoun, Sebastián Driussi (72.Andrey Mostovoy). Trainer: Sergey Semak.
Club Brugge: Ethan Horvath, Eduard Sobol, Clinton Mata, Brandon Mechele, Federico Ricca, Ruud Vormer, Mats Rits, Hans Vanaken, Krépin Diatta (78.Noa Lang), Charles De Ketelaere, Emmanuel Dennis (82.Youssouph Badji). Trainer: Philippe Clement.
Goals: 63' Emmanuel Dennis 0-1, 74' Ethan Horvath 1-1 (own goal), 90+3' Charles De Ketelaere 1-2.

20.10.2020; Stadio Olimpico, Roma
Referee: Clément Turpin (France); Attendance: 1,000
SS Lazio Roma – BV 09 Borussia Dortmund 3-1(2-0)
Lazio Roma: Thomas Strakosha, Francesco Acerbi, Patric, Adam Marusic, Luiz Felipe (51.Wesley Hoedt), Lucas Leiva, Luis Alberto (80.Marco Parolo), Joaquín Correa (67.Vedat Muriqi), Sergej Milinkovic-Savic (67.Jean-Daniel Akpa-Akpro), Mohamed Fares, Ciro Immobile (80.Felipe Caicedo). Trainer: Simone Inzaghi.
Borussia Dortmund: Marwin Hitz, Mats Hummels, Lukasz Piszczek (65.Julian Brandt), Raphaël Guerreiro, Axel Witsel, Thomas Delaney, Thomas Meunier, Jadon Sancho, Jude Bellingham (46.Giovanni Reyna), Marco Reus (78.Reinier), Erling Håland. Trainer: Lucien Favre (Switzerland).
Goals: 6' Ciro Immobile 1-0, 23' Marwin Hitz 2-0 (own goal), 71' Erling Håland 2-1, 76' Jean-Daniel Akpa-Akpro 3-1.

28.10.2020; Signal-Iduna Park, Dortmund
Referee: Björn Kuipers (Netherlands)
BV 09 Borussia Dortmund – FK Zenit Saint Petersburg 2-0(0-0)
Borussia Dortmund: Roman Bürki, Mats Hummels, Raphaël Guerreiro, Manuel Akanji, Axel Witsel, Thomas Meunier, Mahmoud Dahoud (66.Thorgan Hazard), Jadon Sancho (84.Thomas Delaney), Giovanni Reyna (84.Jude Bellingham), Marco Reus (74.Julian Brandt), Erling Håland. Trainer: Lucien Favre (Switzerland).
Zenit Saint Petersburg: Mikhail Kerzhakov, Dejan Lovren, Yaroslav Rakitskiy, Vyacheslav Karavaev, Douglas Santos, Aleksandr Erokhin, Wilmar Barrios (81.Aleksey Sutormin), Daler Kuzyaev (71.Magomed Ozdoev), Wendel, Artyom Dzyuba (46.Andrey Mostovoy), Sebastián Driussi (74.Yuriy Zhirkov). Trainer: Sergey Semak.
Goals: 78' Jadon Sancho 1-0 (penalty), 90+1' Erling Håland 2-0.

28.10.2020; „Jan Breydel" Stadion, Brugge
Referee: Anthony Taylor (England)
Club Brugge KV – SS Lazio Roma 1-1(1-1)
Club Brugge: Simon Mignolet, Eduard Sobol, Clinton Mata, Simon Deli, Odilon Kossounou, Ruud Vormer, Mats Rits, Hans Vanaken, Krépin Diatta, Charles De Ketelaere (84.Noa Lang), Emmanuel Dennis (88.Michael Krmencík). Trainer: Philippe Clement.
Lazio Roma: Pepe Reina, Francesco Acerbi, Patric (46.Andreas Pereira), Adam Marusic, Wesley Hoedt, Marco Parolo, Jean-Daniel Akpa-Akpro, Joaquín Correa, Sergej Milinkovic-Savic, Mohamed Fares (56.Vedat Muriqi), Felipe Caicedo (68.Szymon Czyz). Trainer: Simone Inzaghi.
Goals: 14' Joaquín Correa 0-1, 42' Hans Vanaken 1-1 (penalty).

04.11.2020; Gazprom Arena, Saint Petersburg
Referee: Artur Manuel Ribeiro Soares Dias (Portugal); Attendance: 17,427
FK Zenit Saint Petersburg – SS Lazio Roma 1-1(1-0)
Zenit Saint Petersburg: Mikhail Kerzhakov, Dejan Lovren, Yaroslav Rakitskiy, Vyacheslav Karavaev, Douglas Santos, Yuriy Zhirkov (78.Danil Krugovoy), Aleksandr Erokhin (61.Andrey Mostovoy), Magomed Ozdoev (90+1.Aleksey Sutormin), Wilmar Barrios, Daler Kuzyaev (90+1.Wendel), Artyom Dzyuba. Trainer: Sergey Semak.
Lazio Roma: Pepe Reina, Francesco Acerbi, Patric, Adam Marusic, Wesley Hoedt, Marco Parolo (52.Danilo Cataldi), Jean-Daniel Akpa-Akpro, Joaquín Correa (85.Luiz Felipe), Sergej Milinkovic-Savic, Mohamed Fares (59.Andreas Pereira), Vedat Muriqi (59.Felipe Caicedo). Trainer: Simone Inzaghi.
Goals: 32' Aleksandr Erokhin 1-0, 82' Felipe Caicedo 1-1.

04.11.2020; „Jan Breydel" Stadion, Brugge
Referee: Damir Skomina (Slovenia)
Club Brugge KV – BV 09 Borussia Dortmund 0-3(0-3)
Club Brugge: Simon Mignolet, Eduard Sobol, Clinton Mata, Simon Deli, Odilon Kossounou, Ruud Vormer (71.Éder Balanta), Mats Rits, Hans Vanaken (85.Siebe Schrijvers), Krépin Diatta, Emmanuel Dennis (85.Michael Krmencík), Noa Lang (76.Charles De Ketelaere). Trainer: Philippe Clement.
Borussia Dortmund: Roman Bürki, Raphaël Guerreiro, Manuel Akanji, Axel Witsel, Thomas Delaney (72.Jude Bellingham), Thomas Meunier (84.Mateu Morey), Thorgan Hazard, Julian Brandt (72.Marco Reus), Mahmoud Dahoud, Giovanni Reyna (77.Felix Passlack), Erling Håland (84.Reinier). Trainer: Lucien Favre (Switzerland).
Goals: 14' Thorgan Hazard 0-1, 18', 32' Erling Håland 0-2, 0-3.

24.11.2020; Stadio Olimpico, Roma
Referee: Michael Oliver (England)
SS Lazio Roma – FK Zenit Saint Petersburg 3-1(2-1)
Lazio Roma: Pepe Reina, Francesco Acerbi, Patric (60.Luiz Felipe), Adam Marusic, Wesley Hoedt, Lucas Leiva (68.Danilo Cataldi), Marco Parolo (60.Jean-Daniel Akpa-Akpro), Luis Alberto, Joaquín Correa, Manuel Lazzari (68.Mohamed Fares), Ciro Immobile (81.Vedat Muriqi). Trainer: Simone Inzaghi.
Zenit Saint Petersburg: Mikhail Kerzhakov, Dejan Lovren, Yaroslav Rakitskiy, Douglas Santos (37.Aleksey Sutormin), Yuriy Zhirkov (73.Sardar Azmoun), Aleksandr Erokhin (74.Daniil Shamkin), Wilmar Barrios (59.Sebastián Driussi), Daler Kuzyaev, Andrey Mostovoy (59.Leon Musaev), Artyom Dzyuba, Malcom. Trainer: Sergey Semak.
Goals: 3' Ciro Immobile 1-0, 22' Marco Parolo 2-0, 25' Artyom Dzyuba 2-1, 55' Ciro Immobile 3-1 (penalty).

02.12.2020; Signal-Iduna Park, Dortmund
Referee: Antonio Miguel Mateu Lahoz (Spain)
BV 09 Borussia Dortmund – SS Lazio Roma 1-1(1-0)
Borussia Dortmund: Roman Bürki, Mats Hummels, Lukasz Piszczek, Raphaël Guerreiro (62.Nico Schulz), Manuel Akanji, Mateu Morey, Thomas Delaney, Thorgan Hazard (76.Julian Brandt), Giovanni Reyna, Jude Bellingham (88.Axel Witsel), Marco Reus (76.Jadon Sancho). Trainer: Lucien Favre (Switzerland).
Lazio Roma: Pepe Reina, Francesco Acerbi, Patric, Adam Marusic, Wesley Hoedt, Lucas Leiva (70.Jean-Daniel Akpa-Akpro), Luis Alberto (79.Gonzalo Escalante), Joaquín Correa (70.Andreas Pereira), Sergej Milinkovic-Savic (79.Felipe Caicedo), Mohamed Fares (70.Manuel Lazzari), Ciro Immobile. Trainer: Simone Inzaghi.
Goals: 44' Raphaël Guerreiro 1-0, 67' Ciro Immobile 1-1 (penalty).

08.12.2020; Gazprom Arena, Saint Petersburg
Referee: István Kovács (Romania); Attendance: 10,860
FK Zenit Saint Petersburg – BV 09 Borussia Dortmund 1-2(1-0)
Zenit Saint Petersburg: Mikhail Kerzhakov, Yaroslav Rakitskiy (67.Dejan Lovren), Douglas Santos, Danila Prokhin, Magomed Ozdoev (79.Danil Krugovoy), Wilmar Barrios, Daler Kuzyaev (60.Wendel), Aleksey Sutormin, Sardar Azmoun, Sebastián Driussi (60.Artem Dzyuba), Malcom (79.Vyacheslav Karavaev). Trainer: Sergey Semak.
Borussia Dortmund: Marwin Hitz, Mats Hummels (72.Jadon Sancho), Lukasz Piszczek (72.Dan-Axel Zagadou), Nico Schulz, Axel Witsel, Thorgan Hazard (83.Ansgar Knauff), Emre Can, Julian Brandt (58.Giovanni Reyna), Felix Passlack (58.Youssoufa Moukoko), Jude Bellingham, Marco Reus. Trainer: Lucien Favre (Switzerland).
Goals: 16' Sebastián Driussi 1-0, 68' Felix Passlack 1-1, 78' Axel Witsel 1-2.

24.11.2020; Signal-Iduna Park, Dortmund
Referee: Ivan Kružliak (Slovakia)
BV 09 Borussia Dortmund – Club Brugge KV 3-0(2-0)
Borussia Dortmund: Roman Bürki, Mats Hummels, Raphaël Guerreiro (80.Felix Passlack), Manuel Akanji, Thomas Delaney (72.Emre Can), Thomas Meunier (73.Mateu Morey), Thorgan Hazard, Jadon Sancho, Giovanni Reyna (81.Julian Brandt), Jude Bellingham, Erling Håland (81.Marco Reus). Trainer: Lucien Favre (Switzerland).
Club Brugge: Simon Mignolet, Clinton Mata, Simon Deli, Odilon Kossounou, Ruud Vormer, Hans Vanaken, Éder Balanta (52.Mats Rits), Krépin Diatta (74.David Okereke), Charles De Ketelaere, Michael Krmencík (66.Youssouph Badji), Noa Lang (74.Siebe Schrijvers). Trainer: Philippe Clement.
Goals: 18' Erling Håland 1-0, 45' Jadon Sancho 2-0, 60' Erling Håland 3-0.

02.12.2020; „Jan Breydel" Stadion, Brugge
Referee: Serdar Gözübüyük (Netherlands)
Club Brugge KV – FK Zenit Saint Petersburg 3-0(1-0)
Club Brugge: Simon Mignolet, Clinton Mata (90+1.Thomas Van Den Deybus), Brandon Mechele, Federico Ricca, Odilon Kossounou, Ruud Vormer (88.Siebe Schrijvers), Hans Vanaken (87.Eduard Sobol), Éder Balanta, Charles De Ketelaere, Emmanuel Dennis, Noa Lang (87.David Okereke). Trainer: Philippe Clement.
Zenit Saint Petersburg: Mikhail Kerzhakov, Yaroslav Rakitskiy (46.Danil Krugovoy), Douglas Santos, Danila Prokhin, Aleksandr Erokhin (46.Andrey Mostovoy), Wilmar Barrios, Daler Kuzyaev (65.Leon Musaev), Aleksey Sutormin, Sardar Azmoun, Sebastián Driussi (46.Magomed Ozdoev), Malcom (75.Daniil Shamkin). Trainer: Sergey Semak.
Goals: 33' Charles De Ketelaere 1-0, 58' Hans Vanaken 2-0 (penalty), 73' Noa Lang 3-0.

08.12.2020; Stadio Olimpico, Roma
Referee: Cüneyt Çakir (Turkey)
SS Lazio Roma – Club Brugge KV 2-2(2-1)
Lazio Roma: Pepe Reina, Francesco Acerbi, Adam Marusic, Wesley Hoedt (46.Stefan Radu), Luis Felipe, Lucas Leiva (75.Gonzalo Escalante), Luis Alberto (75.Jean-Daniel Akpa-Akpro), Joaquín Correa (86.Andreas Pereira), Manuel Lazzari, Sergej Milinkovic-Savic, Ciro Immobile (75.Felipe Caicedo). Trainer: Simone Inzaghi.
Club Brugge: Simon Mignolet, Eduard Sobol [sent off 39], Clinton Mata (84.Ignace Van Der Brempt), Federico Ricca, Odilon Kossounou, Ruud Vormer, Hans Vanaken, Éder Balanta (73.Mats Rits), Krépin Diatta (84.David Okereke), Charles De Ketelaere, Noa Lang (42.Simon Deli). Trainer: Philippe Clement.
Goals: 12' Joaquín Correa 1-0, 15' Ruud Vormer 1-1, 27' Ciro Immobile 2-1 (penalty), 76' Hans Vanaken 2-2.

	GROUP G							
1.	**Juventus FC Torino**	6	5	0	1	14 - 4	15
2.	**FC Barcelona**	6	5	0	1	16 - 5	15
3.	*FK Dinamo Kyiv*	6	1	1	4	4 - 13	4
4.	Ferencvárosi TC	6	0	1	5	5 - 17	1

20.10.2020; NSC Olimpiyskiy Stadium, Kyiv
Referee: Ovidiu Alin Haţegan (Romania); Attendance: 14,850
FK Dinamo Kyiv – Juventus FC Torino 0-2(0-0)
Dinamo Kyiv: Georgiy Bushchan, Tomasz Kedziora, Oleksandr Karavayev (70.Denys Popov), Vitali Mykolenko, Illia Zabarnyi, Sergiy Sydorchuk, Vitaliy Buyalskiy (89.Denys Garmash), Carlos de Pena (60.Gerson Rodrigues), Viktor Tsygankov (70.Benjamin Verbic), Mykola Shaparenko, Vladyslav Supriaha. Trainer: Mircea Lucescu (Romania).
Juventus: Wojciech Szczesny, Leonardo Bonucci, Giorgio Chiellini (19.Merih Demiral), Danilo, Juan Cuadrado, Aaron Ramsey (79.Federico Bernardeschi), Adrien Rabiot, Rodrigo Bentancur (79.Arthur), Dejan Kulusevski (56.Paulo Dybala), Morata, Federico Chiesa. Trainer: Andrea Pirlo.
Goals: 46', 84' Morata 0-1, 0-2.

20.10.2020; Estadio Camp Nou, Barcelona
Referee: Sandro Schärer (Switzerland)
FC Barcelona – Ferencvárosi TC 5-1(2-0)
FC Barcelona: Neto, Piqué [sent off 68], Sergi Roberto (62.Junior Firpo), Clément Lenglet, Sergiño Dest, Miralem Pjanic (76.Busquets), Philippe Coutinho (70.Ronald Araújo), Frenkie de Jong, Lionel Messi, Trincão (63.Ousmane Dembélé), Ansu Fati (62.Pedri). Trainer: Ronald Koeman (Netherlands).
Ferencvárosi TC: Dénes Dibusz, Endre Botka (77.Gergő Lovrencsics), Miha Blazic, Adrian Kovacevic, Eldar Civic (63.Marcel Heister), Dávid Sigér, Igor Kharatin, Aïssa Laïdouni (63.Somália), Isael, Tokmac Nguen (71.Franck Boli), Oleksandr Zubkov (71.Róbert Mak). Trainer: Serhiy Rebrov (Ukraine).
Goals: 27' Lionel Messi 1-0 (penalty), 42' Ansu Fati 2-0, 52' Philippe Coutinho 3-0, 70' Igor Kharatin 3-1 (penalty), 82' Pedri 4-1, 89' Ousmane Dembélé 5-1.

28.10.2020; Allianz Stadium, Torino
Referee: Danny Desmond Makkelie (Netherlands)
Juventus FC Torino – FC Barcelona 0-2(0-1)
Juventus: Wojciech Szczesny, Leonardo Bonucci, Danilo, Merih Demiral [*sent off 85*], Juan Cuadrado, Adrien Rabiot (83.Federico Bernardeschi), Rodrigo Bentancur (83.Arthur), Dejan Kulusevski (75.Weston McKennie), Morata, Paulo Dybala, Federico Chiesa. Trainer: Andrea Pirlo.
FC Barcelona: Neto, Jordi Alba, Sergi Roberto, Clément Lenglet, Ronald Araújo (46.Busquets), Miralem Pjanic, Frenkie de Jong, Lionel Messi, Antoine Griezmann (89.Junior Firpo), Ousmane Dembélé (66.Ansu Fati), Pedri (90+2.Martin Braithwaite). Trainer: Ronald Koeman (Netherlands).
Goals: 14' Ousmane Dembélé 0-1, Lionel Messi 0-2 (penalty).

04.11.2020; Estadio Camp Nou, Barcelona
Referee: Michael Oliver (England)
FC Barcelona – FK Dinamo Kyiv 2-1(1-0)
FC Barcelona: Marc-André ter Stegen, Piqué, Jordi Alba, Sergiño Dest, Miralem Pjanic (60.Sergi Roberto), Busquets (74.Clément Lenglet), Frenkie de Jong, Lionel Messi, Antoine Griezmann (60.Ousmane Dembélé), Ansu Fati (74.Trincão), Pedri (83.Carles Aleñá). Trainer: Ronald Koeman (Netherlands).
Dinamo Kyiv: Ruslan Neshcheret, Tomasz Kedziora, Artem Shabanov, Denys Popov, Illia Zabarnyi, Vitaly Buyalskiy (86.Bohdan Lednev), Oleksandr Andrievsky, Viktor Tsygankov, Volodymyr Shepelev, Gerson Rodrigues (71.Carlos de Pena), Vladyslav Supriaha (71.Benjamin Verbic). Trainer: Mircea Lucescu (Romania).
Goals: 5' Lionel Messi 1-0 (penalty), 65' Piqué 2-0, 75' Viktor Tsygankov 2-1.

24.11.2020; NSC Olimpiyskiy Stadium, Kyiv
Referee: Matej Jug (Slovenia)
FK Dinamo Kyiv – FC Barcelona 0-4(0-0)
Dinamo Kyiv: Georgiy Bushchan, Tomasz Kedziora, Oleksandr Karavayev (59.Denys Popov), Vitali Mykolenko, Illia Zabarnyi, Denys Garmash (59.Oleksandr Andrievsky), Vitaly Buyalskiy, Benjamin Verbic, Carlos de Pena (71.Vladyslav Supriaha), Mykola Shaparenko (71.Bohdan Lednev), Volodymyr Shepelev (83.Tudor Baluta). Trainer: Mircea Lucescu (Romania).
FC Barcelona: Marc-André ter Stegen, Clément Lenglet (65.Jordi Alba), Junior Firpo, Óscar Mingueza, Sergiño Dest, Miralem Pjanic (65.Riqui Puig), Philippe Coutinho (65.Antoine Griezmann), Carles Aleñá, Martin Braithwaite, Trincão (83.Konrad de la Fuente), Pedri (73.Matheus Fernandes). Trainer: Ronald Koeman (Netherlands).
Goals: 52' Sergiño Dest 0-1, 57', 70' Martin Braithwaite 0-2, 0-3 (penalty), 90+2' Antoine Griezmann 0-4.

02.12.2020; Allainz Stadium, Torino
Referee: Stéphanie Frappart (France)
Juventus FC Torino – FK Dinamo Kyiv 3-0(1-0)
Juventus: Wojciech Szczesny, Leonardo Bonucci (62.Danilo), Alex Sandro, Merih Demiral (69.Radu Dragusin), Matthijs de Ligt, Aaron Ramsey (62.Federico Bernardeschi), Rodrigo Bentancur (76.Arthur), Weston McKennie, Cristiano Ronaldo, Morata, Federico Chiesa (76.Dejan Kulusevski). Trainer: Andrea Pirlo.
Dinamo Kyiv: Georgiy Bushchan, Tomasz Kedziora, Denys Popov, Vitali Mykolenko (84.Oleksandr Karavayev), Illia Zabarnyi, Sergiy Sydorchuk, Benjamin Verbic (72.Vladyslav Supriaha), Viktor Tsygankov (90+1.Bohdan Lednev), Mykola Shaparenko, Volodymyr Shepelev (72.Denys Garmash), Gerson Rodrigues (72.Carlos de Pena). Trainer: Mircea Lucescu (Romania). Goals: 21' Federico Chiesa 1-0, 57' Cristiano Ronaldo 2-0, 66' Morata 3-0.

08.12.2020; Estadio Camp Nou, Barcelona
Referee: Tobias Stieler (Germany)
FC Barcelona – Juventus FC Torino 0-3(0-2)
FC Barcelona: Marc-André ter Stegen, Jordi Alba (55.Junior Firpo), Clément Lenglet (55.Samuel Umtiti), Ronald Araújo (82.Óscar Mingueza), Sergiño Dest, Miralem Pjanic, Frenkie de Jong, Lionel Messi, Antoine Griezmann, Trincão (46.Martin Braithwaite), Pedri (66.Riqui Puig). Trainer: Ronald Koeman (Netherlands).
Juventus: Gianluigi Buffon, Leonardo Bonucci, Danilo, Alex Sandro, Matthijs de Ligt, Juan Cuadrado (85.Federico Bernardeschi), Aaron Ramsey (71.Adrien Rabiot), Arthur (71.Rodrigo Bentancur), Weston McKennie, Cristiano Ronaldo (90+2.Federico Chiesa), Morata (85.Paulo Dybala). Trainer: Andrea Pirlo.
Goals: 12' Cristiano Ronaldo 0-1 (penalty), 20' Weston McKennie 0-2, 52' Cristiano Ronaldo 0-3 (penalty).

28.10.2020; Groupama Aréna, Budapest
Referee: Ivan Kružliak (Slovakia); Attendance: 6,171
Ferencvárosi TC – FK Dinamo Kyiv 2-2(0-2)
Ferencvárosi TC: Dénes Dibusz, Gergö Lovrencsics (86.Endre Botka), Marcel Heister, Miha Blazic, Adrian Kovacevic (86.Lasha Dvali), Somália, Dávid Sigér (73.Róbert Mak), Igor Kharatin (65.Aïssa Laïdouni), Isael (73 Franck Boli), Tokmac Nguen, Oleksandr Zubkov. Trainer: Serhiy Rebrov (Ukraine).
Dinamo Kyiv: Denis Boyko, Tomasz Kedziora, Oleksandr Karavayev, Denys Popov, Illia Zabarnyi, Sergiy Sydorchuk [*sent off 86*], Vitaly Buyalskiy (82.Denys Garmash), Carlos de Pena, Viktor Tsygankov (90+3.Gerson Rodrigues), Mykola Shaparenko (89.Tudor Baluta), Vladyslav Supriaha (89.Benjamin Verbic). Trainer: Mircea Lucescu (Romania). Goals: 28' Viktor Tsygankov 0-1 (penalty), 41' Carlos de Pena 0-2, 59' Tokmac Nguen 1-2, 90' Franck Boli 2-2.

04.11.2020; Puskás Aréna, Budapest
Referee: Orel Grinfeld (Israel); Attendance: 18,531
Ferencvárosi FC – Juventus FC Torino 1-4(0-1)
Ferencvárosi TC: Dénes Dibusz, Gergö Lovrencsics (68.Marcel Heister), Miha Blazic, Endre Botka, Lasha Dvali, Somália, Dávid Sigér, Igor Kharatin, Isael (73.Franck Boli), Tokmac Nguen (73.Róbert Mak), Oleksandr Zubkov (80.Myrto Uzuni). Trainer: Serhiy Rebrov (Ukraine).
Juventus: Wojciech Szczesny, Leonardo Bonucci, Giorgio Chiellini, Danilo, Juan Cuadrado (76.Gianluca Frabotta), Aaron Ramsey (53.Weston McKennie), Adrien Rabiot, Arthur (46.Rodrigo Bentancur), Cristiano Ronaldo, Morata (67.Paulo Dybala), Federico Chiesa (76.Federico Bernardeschi). Trainer: Andrea Pirlo.
Goals: 7', 60' Morato 0-1, 0-2, 73' Paulo Dybala 0-3, 81' Lasha Dvali 0-4 (own goal), 90' Franck Boli 1-4.

24.11.2020; Allainz Stadium, Torino
Referee: Daniel Siebert (Germany)
Juventus FC Torino – Ferencvárosi TC 2-1(1-1)
Juventus: Wojciech Szczesny, Danilo, Alex Sandro, Matthijs de Ligt, Juan Cuadrado, Arthur (82.Aaron Ramsey), Rodrigo Bentancur (83.Adrien Rabiot), Weston McKennie (62.Dejan Kulusevski), Cristiano Ronaldo, Paulo Dybala (62.Morata), Federico Bernardeschi (62.Federico Chiesa). Trainer: Andrea Pirlo.
Ferencvárosi TC: Dénes Dibusz, Gergö Lovrencsics (75.Endre Botka), Marcel Heister, Miha Blazic, Abraham Frimpong, Lasha Dvali, Somália, Dávid Sigér (75.Aïssa Laïdouni), Tokmac Nguen (70.Franck Boli), Oleksandr Zubkov (70.Isael), Myrto Uzuni. Trainer: Serhiy Rebrov (Ukraine).
Goals: 19' Myrto Uzuni 0-1, 35' Cristiano Ronaldo 1-1, 90+2' Morata 2-1.

02.12.2020; Puskás Aréna, Budapest
Referee: Aleksei Kulbakov (Belarus)
Ferencvárosi TC – FC Barcelona 0-3(0-3)
Ferencvárosi TC: Dénes Dibusz, Marcel Heister (64.Gergö Lovrencsics), Endre Botka, Miha Blazic, Abraham Frimpong, Lasha Dvali, Somália (81.Igor Kharatin), Dávid Sigér (64.Aïssa Laïdouni), Isael, Tokmac Nguen (71.Róbert Mak), Myrto Uzuni (71.Roko Baturina). Trainer: Serhiy Rebrov (Ukraine).
FC Barcelona: Neto, Jordi Alba (46.Junior Firpo), Clément Lenglet (65.Carles Aleñá), Óscar Mingueza, Sergiño Dest, Miralem Pjanic, Busquets (46.Frenkie de Jong), Antoine Griezmann (65.Riqui Puig), Martin Braithwaite (80.Konrad de la Fuente), Ousmane Dembélé, Trincão. Trainer: Ronald Koeman (Netherlands).
Goals: 14' Antoine Griezmann 0-1, 21' Martin Braithwaite 0-2, 28' Ousmane Dembélé 0-3 (penalty).

08.12.2020; NSC Olimpiyskiy Stadium, Kyiv
Referee: Andreas Ekberg (Sweden)
FK Dinamo Kyiv – Ferencvárosi TC 1-0(0-0)
Dinamo Kyiv: Georgiy Bushchan, Tomasz Kedziora, Denys Popov, Vitali Mykolenko, Illia Zabarnyi, Sergiy Sydorchuk (90+2.Oleksandr Andrievsky), Denys Garmash (70.Volodymyr Shepelev), Benjamin Verbic (86.Gerson Rodrigues), Carlos de Pena (70.Vladyslav Supriaha), Viktor Tsygankov (86.Bohdan Lednev), Mykola Shaparenko. Trainer: Mircea Lucescu (Romania).
Ferencvárosi TC: Dénes Dibusz, Gergö Lovrencsics (80.Endre Botka), Marcel Heister, Miha Blazic, Lasha Dvali, Somália, Igor Kharatin (74.Isael), Aïssa Laïdouni, Tokmac Nguen (86.Franck Boli), Oleksandr Zubkov (80.Róbert Mak), Myrto Uzuni (73.Roko Baturina). Trainer: Serhiy Rebrov (Ukraine).
Goal: 60' Denys Popov 1-0.

GROUP H	1. **Paris Saint-Germain FC**	6	4	0	2	13 - 6	12
	2. **RasenBallsport Leipzig**	6	4	0	2	11 - 12	12
	3. *Manchester United FC*	6	3	0	3	15 - 10	9
	4. İstanbul Başakşehir FK	6	1	0	5	7 - 18	3

20.10.2020; Stade Parc des Princes, Paris
Referee: Antonio Miguel Mateu Lahoz (Spain)
Paris Saint-Germain FC – Manchester United FC 1-2(0-1)
Paris Saint-Germain: Keylor Navas, Layvin Kurzawa (86.Mitchel Bakker), Alessandro Florenzi (79.Colin Dagba), Presnel Kimpembe, Abdou Diallo, Ángel Di María (86.Pablo Sarabia), Ander Herrera (78.Rafinha), Idrissa Gueye (46.Moise Kean), Danilo Pereira, Neymar, Kylian Mbappé. Trainer: Thomas Tuchel (Germany).
Manchester United: David de Gea, Alex Telles (67.Paul Pogba), Victor Lindelöf, Luke Shaw, Axel Tuanzebe, Aaron Wan-Bissaka, Fred, Bruno Fernandes (88.Donny van de Beek), Scott McTominay, Anthony Martial (88.Daniel James), Marcus Rashford. Trainer: Ole Gunnar Solskjær (Norway).
Goals: 23' Bruno Fernandes 0-1 (own goal), 55' Anthony Martial 1-1 (own goal), 87' Marcus Rashford 1-2.

28.10.2020; Başakşehir „Fatih Terim" Stadyumu, Istanbul
Referee: Andreas Ekberg (Sweden); Attendance: 350
İstanbul Başakşehir FK – Paris Saint-Germain FC 0-2(0-0)
İstanbul Başakşehir: Mert Günok, Martin Skrtel, Alexandru Epureanu, Rafael, Boli Bolingoli-Mbombo (63.Hasan-Ali Kaldirim), Mehmet Topal (68.Demba Ba), Edin Visca, Irfan Kahveci, Deniz Türüç (81.Danijel Aleksic), Berkay Özcan, Enzo Crivelli (81.Giuliano). Trainer: Okan Buruk.
Paris Saint-Germain: Keylor Navas, Layvin Kurzawa (87.Mitchel Bakker), Marquinhos, Alessandro Florenzi (73.Thilo Kehrer), Presnel Kimpembe, Ángel Di María (73.Rafinha), Ander Herrera (87.Idrissa Gueye), Danilo Pereira, Neymar (26.Pablo Sarabia), Kylian Mbappé, Moise Kean. Trainer: Thomas Tuchel (Germany).
Goals: 64', 79' Moise Kean 0-1, 0-2.

04.11.2020; Başakşehir „Fatih Terim" Stadyumu, Istanbul
Referee: Davide Massa (Italy); Attendance: 350
İstanbul Başakşehir FK – Manchester United FC 2-1(2-1)
İstanbul Başakşehir: Mert Günok, Martin Skrtel, Alexandru Epureanu, Rafael, Boli Bolingoli-Mbombo, Danijel Aleksic, Edin Visca, Irfan Kahveci (90.Ponck), Deniz Türüç, Berkay Özcan (87.Mehmet Topal), Demba Ba (79.Fredrik Gulbrandsen). Trainer: Okan Buruk.
Manchester United: Dean Henderson, Harry Maguire, Luke Shaw, Axel Tuanzebe (46.Scott McTominay), Aaron Wan-Bissaka (76.Timothy Fosu-Mensah), Mata (61.Edinson Cavani), Nemanja Matic, Bruno Fernandes, Donny van de Beek (61.Paul Pogba), Anthony Martial, Marcus Rashford (76.Mason Greenwood). Trainer: Ole Gunnar Solskjær (Norway).
Goals: 13' Demba Ba 1-0, 40' Edin Visca 2-0, 43' Anthony Martial 2-1.

24.11.2020; Old Trafford, Manchester
Referee: Ovidiu Alin Hațegan (Romania); Attendance: 545
Manchester United FC – İstanbul Başakşehir FK 4-1(3-0)
Manchester United: David de Gea, Alex Telles, Victor Lindelöf (46.Axel Tuanzebe), Harry Maguire, Aaron Wan-Bissaka (59.Brandon Williams), Fred, Bruno Fernandes (59.Mason Greenwood), Donny van de Beek, Edinson Cavani, Anthony Martial (82.Nemanja Matic), Marcus Rashford (59.Daniel James). Trainer: Ole Gunnar Solskjær (Norway).
İstanbul Başakşehir: Mert Günok, Martin Skrtel (87.Ponck), Alexandru Epureanu, Rafael, Boli Bolingoli-Mbombo (74.Hasan-Ali Kaldirim), Nacer Chadli (61.Fredrik Gulbrandsen), Edin Visca, Irfan Kahveci (46.Mahmut Tekdemir), Deniz Türüç, Berkay Özcan (74.Giuliano), Demba Ba. Trainer: Okan Buruk.
Goals: 7', 19' Bruno Fernandes 1-0, 2-0, 35' Marcus Rashford 3-0 (penalty), 75' Deniz Türüç 3-1, 90+2' Daniel James 4-1.

20.10.2020; Red Bull Arena, Leipzig
Referee: Jesús Gil Manzano (Spain); Attendance: 999
RasenBallsport Leipzig – İstanbul Başakşehir FK 2-0(2-0)
RB Leipzig: Péter Gulácsi, Marcel Halstenberg, Willi Orban, José Angeliño, Nordi Mukiele, Dayot Upamecano (65.Ibrahima Konaté), Kevin Kampl (58.Tyler Adams), Christopher Nkunku (70.Justin Kluivert), Daniel Olmo (65.Benjamin Henrichs), Emil Forsberg (46.Hwang Hee-Chan), Yussuf Poulsen. Trainer: Julian Nagelsmann.
İstanbul Başakşehir: Mert Günok, Martin Skrtel, Alexandru Epureanu, Rafael, Júnior Caiçara (30.Berkay Özcan), Boli Bolingoli-Mbombo, Mehmet Topal (66.Demba Ba), Edin Visca, Irfan Kahveci (83.Danijel Aleksic), Deniz Türüç (83.Giuliano), Enzo Crivelli. Trainer: Okan Buruk.
Goals: 16', 20' José Angeliño 1-0, 2-0.

28.10.2020; Old Trafford, Manchester
Referee: Matej Jug (Slovenia); Attendance: 577
Manchester United FC – RasenBallsport Leipzig 5-0(1-0)
Manchester United: David de Gea, Victor Lindelöf, Harry Maguire, Luke Shaw, Aaron Wan-Bissaka (81.Axel Tuanzebe), Nemanja Matic (63.Scott McTominay), Paul Pogba (81.Edinson Cavani), Fred, Donny van de Beek (68.Bruno Fernandes), Anthony Martial, Mason Greenwood (63.Marcus Rashford). Trainer: Ole Gunnar Solskjær (Norway).
RB Leipzig: Péter Gulácsi, Marcel Halstenberg, Benjamin Henrichs (63.Marcel Sabitzer), José Angeliño, Dayot Upamecano, Ibrahima Konaté, Kevin Kampl (76.Justin Kluivert), Christopher Nkunku (65.Alexander Sorloth), Daniel Olmo, Emil Forsberg, Yussuf Poulsen. Trainer: Julian Nagelsmann.
Goals: 21' Mason Greenwood 1-0, 74', 78' Marcus Rashford 2-0, 3-0, 87' Anthony Martial
4-0 (penalty), 90+2' Marcus Rashford 5-0.

04.11.2020; Red Bull Arena, Leipzig
Referee: Szymon Marciniak (Poland)
RasenBallsport Leipzig – Paris Saint-Germain FC 2-1(1-1)
RB Leipzig: Péter Gulácsi, Willi Orban, José Angeliño, Nordi Mukiele (64.Benjamin Henrichs), Dayot Upamecano, Ibrahima Konaté, Marcel Sabitzer (90.Kevin Kampl), Christopher Nkunku, Daniel Olmo (64.Yussuf Poulsen), Amadou Haïdara (76.Tyler Adams), Emil Forsberg (76.Justin Kluivert). Trainer: Julian Nagelsmann.
Paris Saint-Germain: Keylor Navas, Layvin Kurzawa (73.Mitchel Bakker), Alessandro Florenzi (84.Rafinha), Presnel Kimpembe [sent off 90+5], Ángel Di María, Ander Herrera, Idrissa Gueye [sent off 69], Pablo Sarabia (73.Thilo Kehrer), Danilo Pereira, Moise Kean. Trainer: Thomas Tuchel (Germany).
Goals: 6' Ángel Di María 0-1, 42' Christopher Nkunku 1-1, 57' Emil Forsberg 2-1 (penalty).

24.11.2020; Stade Parc des Princes, Paris
Referee: Danny Desmond Makkelie (Netherlands)
Paris Saint-Germain FC – RasenBallsport Leipzig 1-0(1-0)
Paris Saint-Germain: Keylor Navas, Marquinhos, Alessandro Florenzi, Abdou Diallo, Mitchel Bakker, Ángel Di María (64.Rafinha), Ander Herrera (83.Marco Verratti), Danilo Pereira, Leandro Paredes, Neymar (90.Pablo Sarabia), Kylian Mbappé (90.Moise Kean). Trainer: Thomas Tuchel (Germany).
RB Leipzig: Péter Gulácsi, José Angeliño, Nordi Mukiele (63.Willi Orban), Dayot Upamecano, Ibrahima Konaté, Marcel Sabitzer, Christopher Nkunku, Daniel Olmo (64.Justin Kluivert), Amadou Haïdara, Emil Forsberg (74.Alexander Sorloth), Yussuf Poulsen. Trainer: Julian Nagelsmann.
Goal: 11' Neymar 1-0 (penalty).

02.12.2020; Başakşehir „Fatih Terim" Stadyumu, Istanbul
Referee: Carlos del Cerro Grande (Spain)
İstanbul Başakşehir FK – RasenBallsport Leipzig 3-4(1-2)
İstanbul Başakşehir: Mert Günok, Martin Skrtel (46.Alexandru Epureanu), Rafael, Boli Bolingoli-Mbombo (36.Nacer Chadli), Ponck, Edin Visca (64.Giuliano), Irfan Kahveci, Deniz Türüç, Berkay Özcan (46.Mahmut Tekdemir), Demba Ba, Fredrik Gulbrandsen (84.Enzo Crivelli). Trainer: Okan Buruk.
RB Leipzig: Péter Gulácsi, José Angeliño, Nordi Mukiele, Dayot Upamecano, Ibrahima Konaté, Kevin Kampl (46.Tyler Adams), Marcel Sabitzer, Daniel Olmo (87.Justin Kluivert), Amadou Haïdara (90+4.Willi Orban), Emil Forsberg (65.Alexander Sorloth), Yussuf Poulsen. Trainer: Julian Nagelsmann.
Goals: 26' Yussuf Poulsen 0-1, 43' Nordi Mukiele 0-2, 45+3' Irfan Kahveci 1-2, 66' Daniel Olmo 1-3, 72', 85' Irfan Kahveci 2-3, 3-3, 90+2' Alexander Sorloth 3-4.

08.12.2020; Red Bull Arena, Leipzig
Referee: Antonio Miguel Mateu Lahoz (Spain)
RasenBallsport Leipzig – Manchester United FC 3-2(2-0)
RB Leipzig: Péter Gulácsi, Willi Orban, José Angeliño (87.Marcel Halstenberg), Nordi Mukiele, Ibrahima Konaté, Kevin Kampl (75.Tyler Adams), Marcel Sabitzer, Christopher Nkunku, Daniel Olmo (56.Justin Kluivert), Amadou Haïdara, Emil Forsberg (56.Yussuf Poulsen). Trainer: Julian Nagelsmann.
Manchester United: David de Gea, Alex Telles (46.Donny van de Beek), Victor Lindelöf (77.Axel Tuanzebe), Harry Maguire, Luke Shaw (61.Brandon Williams), Aaron Wan-Bissaka (77.Timothy Fosu-Mensah), Nemanja Matic (61.Paul Pogba), Bruno Fernandes, Scott McTominay, Marcus Rashford, Mason Greenwood. Trainer: Ole Gunnar Solskjær (Norway).
Goals: 2' José Angeliño 1-0, 13' Amadou Haïdara 2-0, 69' Justin Kluivert 3-0, 80' Bruno Fernandes 3-1 (penalty), 82' Ibrahima Konaté 3-2 (own goal).

02.12.2020; Old Trafford, Manchester
Referee: Daniele Orsato (Italy); Attendance: 638
Manchester United FC – Paris Saint-Germain FC 1-3(1-1)
Manchester United: David de Gea, Alex Telles, Victor Lindelöf, Harry Maguire, Aaron Wan-Bissaka (90.Odion Ighalo), Fred [sent off 70], Bruno Fernandes, Scott McTominay, Edinson Cavani (79.Donny van de Beek), Anthony Martial (79.Mason Greenwood), Marcus Rashford (74.Paul Pogba). Trainer: Ole Gunnar Solskjær (Norway).
Paris Saint-Germain: Keylor Navas, Marquinhos, Alessandro Florenzi (78.Thilo Kehrer), Presnel Kimpembe, Abdou Diallo (90.Idrissa Gueye), Marco Verratti (78.Rafinha), Danilo Pereira, Leandro Paredes (65.Ander Herrera), Neymar, Kylian Mbappé, Moise Kean (65.Mitchel Bakker). Trainer: Thomas Tuchel (Germany).
Goals: 6' Neymar 0-1, 32' Marcus Rashford 1-1, 69' Marquinhos 1-2, 90+1' Neymar 1-3.

09.12.2020; Stade Parc des Princes, Paris
Referee: Ovidiu Alin Haţegan (Romania, on 08.12.2020) & Danny Desmond Makkelie (Netherlands, on 09.12.2020).
Paris Saint-Germain FC – İstanbul Başakşehir FK 5-1(3-0)
Paris Saint-Germain: Keylor Navas, Marquinhos (67.Thilo Kehrer), Alessandro Florenzi (80.Timothée Pembele), Presnel Kimpembe (80.Abdou Diallo), Mitchel Bakker, Marco Verratti (80.Idrissa Gueye), Danilo Pereira, Leandro Paredes, Rafinha (46.Ángel Di María), Neymar, Kylian Mbappé. Trainer: Thomas Tuchel (Germany).
İstanbul Başakşehir: Mert Günok, Hasan-Ali Kaldirim (68.Boli Bolingoli-Mbombo), Rafael (68.Giuliano), Ponck, Mehmet Topal, Mahmut Tekdemir (89.Nacer Chadli), Irfan Kahveci, Deniz Türüç, Berkay Özcan, Fredrik Gulbrandsen (80.Emre Kaplan), Enzo Crivelli (68.Demba Ba). Trainer: Okan Buruk.
Goals: 21', 38' Neymar 1-0, 2-0, 42' Kylian Mbappé 3-0 (penalty), 50' Neymar 4-0, 57' Mehmet Topal 4-1, 62' Kylian Mbappé 5-1.
Please note: On 08.12.2020 the match was suspended after 14 minutes (score 0-0), as both teams left the pitch in protest after an alleged racist indicent by a match official directed at the assistant manager of İstanbul Başakşehir FK. The match was resumed on 09.12.2020, with a new team of match officials.

16.02.2021; Puskás Aréna, Budapest (Hungary)
Referee: Slavko Vinčić (Slovenia)
RasenBallsport Leipzig – Liverpool FC 0-2(0-0)
RB Leipzig: Péter Gulácsi, Lukas Klostermann, José Angeliño, Nordi Mukiele (64.Willi Orban), Dayot Upamecano, Kevin Kampl (73.Hwang Hee-Chan), Marcel Sabitzer, Christopher Nkunku, Daniel Olmo, Tyler Adams, Amadou Haïdara (64.Yussuf Poulsen). Trainer: Julian Nagelsmann.
Liverpool FC: Alisson, Andrew Robertson, Trent Alexander-Arnold, Ozan Kabak, Georginio Wijnaldum, Jordan Henderson, Thiago Alcântara (72.Alex Oxlade-Chamberlain), Curtis Jones, Roberto Firmino (72.Xherdan Shaqiri), Mohamed Salah (90.Neco Williams), Sadio Mané. Trainer: Jürgen Klopp (Germany).
Goals: 53' Mohamed Salah 0-1, 58' Sadio Mané 0-2.

16.02.2021; Estadio Camp Nou, Barcelona
Referee: Björn Kuipers (Netherlands)
FC Barcelona – Paris Saint-Germain FC 1-4(1-1)
FC Barcelona: Marc-André ter Stegen, Piqué (78.Riqui Puig), Jordi Alba, Clément Lenglet, Sergiño Dest (71.Óscar Mingueza), Busquets (79.Miralem Pjanic), Frenkie de Jong, Lionel Messi, Antoine Griezmann (85.Martin Braithwaite), Ousmane Dembélé, Pedri (79.Trincão). Trainer: Ronald Koeman (Netherlands).
Paris Saint-Germain: Keylor Navas, Layvin Kurzawa, Marquinhos, Alessandro Florenzi (89.Thilo Kehrer), Presnel Kimpembe, Marco Verratti (73.Julian Draxler), Idrissa Gueye (46.Ander Herrera), Leandro Paredes, Mauro Icardi, Kylian Mbappé, Moise Kean (85.Danilo Pereira). Trainer: Mauricio Roberto Pochettino Trossero (Argentina).
Goals: 27' Lionel Messi 1-0 (penalty), 32', 65' Kylian Mbappé 1-1, 1-2, 70' Moise Kean 1-3, 85' Kylian Mbappé 1-4.

17.02.2021; Estádio do Dragão, Porto
Referee: Carlos Del Cerro Grande (Spain)
FC do Porto – Juventus FC Torino 2-1(1-0)
FC Porto: Agustín Marchesín, Pepe, Chancel Mbemba, Wilson Manafá, Zaidu Sanusi, Sérgio Oliveira (90+1.Francisco Conceição), Mateus Uribe, Otávio (57.Luis Díaz), Jesús Corona (90+1.Mamadou Loum), Mehdi Taremi, Moussa Marega (66.Marko Grujic). Trainer: Sérgio Paulo Marceneiro da Conceição.
Juventus: Wojciech Szczesny, Giorgio Chiellini (35.Merih Demiral), Danilo, Alex Sandro, Matthijs de Ligt, Adrien Rabiot, Rodrigo Bentancur, Weston McKennie (63.Morata), Dejan Kulusevski (77.Aaron Ramsey), Cristiano Ronaldo, Federico Chiesa. Trainer: Andrea Pirlo.
Goals: 2' Mehdi Taremi 1-0, 46' Moussa Marega 2-0, 82' Federico Chiesa 2-1.

17.02.2021; Estádio „Ramón Sánchez Pizjuán", Sevilla
Referee: Danny Desmond Makkelie (Netherlands)
Sevilla FC – BV 09 Borussia Dortmund 2-3(1-3)
Sevilla FC: Yassine Bounou, Jesús Navas, Escudero, Diego Carlos, Jules Koundé, Ivan Rakitic (46.Nemanja Gudelj), Papu Gómez (60.Óliver Torres), Fernando, Suso (60.Luuk de Jong), Joan Jordán (72.Óscar Rodríguez), Youssef En-Nesyri (60.Munir). Trainer: Julen Lopetegui Agote.
Borussia Dortmund: Marwin Hitz, Mats Hummels, Raphaël Guerreiro (76.Felix Passlack), Manuel Akanji, Mateu Morey, Emre Can, Mahmoud Dahoud (89.Thomas Meunier), Jadon Sancho, Jude Bellingham, Marco Reus (80.Julian Brandt), Erling Håland. Trainer: Edin Terzic.
Goals: 7' Suso 1-0, 19' Mahmoud Dahoud 1-1, 27', 43' Erling Håland 1-2, 1-3, 84' Luuk de Jong 2-3.

23.02.2021; Stadio Olimpico, Roma
Referee: Orel Grinfeld (Israel)
SS Lazio Roma – FC Bayern München 1-4(0-3)
Lazio Roma: Pepe Reina, Mateo Musacchio (31.Senad Lulic), Francesco Acerbi, Patric (53.Wesley Hoedt), Adam Marusic, Lucas Leiva (53.Gonzalo Escalante), Luis Alberto (81.Jean-Daniel Akpa-Akpro), Joaquín Correa, Manuel Lazzari, Sergej Milinkovic-Savic (81.Danilo Cataldi), Ciro Immobile. Trainer: Simone Inzaghi.
Bayern München: Manuel Neuer, Jérôme Boateng, David Alaba, Niklas Süle, Alphonso Davies, Leon Goretzka (63.Javi Martínez), Joshua Kimmich, Jamal Musiala (90.Eric Maxim Choupo-Moting), Robert Lewandowski, Kingsley Coman (75.Lucas Hernández), Leroy Sané (90.Bouna Sarr). Trainer: Hans-Dieter Flick.
Goals: 9' Robert Lewandowski 0-1, 24' Jamal Musiala 0-2, 42' Leroy Sané 0-3, 47' Francesco Acerbi 0-4 (own goal), 49' Joaquín Correa 1-4.

10.03.2021; Puskás Aréna, Budapest (Hungary)
Referee: Clément Turpin (France)
LIVERPOOL FC – RasenBallsport Leipzig 2-0(0-0)
Liverpool FC: Alisson, Andrew Robertson (90.Kostas Tsimikas), Trent Alexander-Arnold, Nathaniel Phillips, Ozan Kabak, Georginio Wijnaldum (82.James Milner), Thiago Alcântara (72.Naby Keïta), Fabinho, Mohamed Salah, Sadio Mané (89.Alex Oxlade-Chamberlain), Diogo Jota (71.Divock Origi). Trainer: Jürgen Klopp (Germany).
RB Leipzig: Péter Gulácsi, Lukas Klostermann, Nordi Mukiele, Dayot Upamecano, Kevin Kampl (46.Alexander Sørloth), Marcel Sabitzer, Christopher Nkunku, Daniel Olmo (72.Amadou Haïdara), Tyler Adams, Emil Forsberg (60.Justin Kluivert), Yussuf Poulsen (60.Hwang Hee-Chan). Trainer: Julian Nagelsmann.
Goals: 70' Mohamed Salah 1-0, 74' Sadio Mané 2-0.

10.03.2021; Stade Parc des Princes, Paris
Referee: Anthony Taylor (England)
PARIS SAINT-GERMAIN FC – FC Barcelona 1-1(1-1)
Paris Saint-Germain: Keylor Navas, Layvin Kurzawa (46.Abdou Diallo), Marquinhos, Alessandro Florenzi (76.Colin Dagba), Presnel Kimpembe, Marco Verratti (84.Rafinha), Idrissa Gueye (60.Danilo Pereira), Leandro Paredes, Julian Draxler (59.Ángel Di María), Mauro Icardi, Kylian Mbappé. Trainer: Mauricio Roberto Pochettino Trossero (Argentina).
FC Barcelona: Marc-André ter Stegen, Jordi Alba, Clément Lenglet, Óscar Mingueza (35.Junior Firpo), Sergiño Dest (66.Trincão), Busquets (79.Ilaix Kourouma), Frenkie de Jong, Lionel Messi, Antoine Griezmann, Ousmane Dembélé (78.Martin Braithwaite), Pedri (78.Miralem Pjanic). Trainer: Ronald Koeman (Netherlands).
Goals: 31' Kylian Mbappé 1-0 (penalty), 37' Lionel Messi 1-1.

09.03.2021; Allianz Stadium, Torino
Referee: Björn Kuipers (Netherlands)
Juventus FC Torino – FC DO PORTO 3-2(0-1,2-1)
Juventus: Wojciech Szczesny, Leonardo Bonucci (75.Matthijs de Ligt), Alex Sandro, Merih Demiral, Juan Cuadrado, Aaron Ramsey (75.Weston McKennie), Adrien Rabiot, Arthur (102.Dejan Kulusevski), Cristiano Ronaldo, Morata, Federico Chiesa (102.Federico Bernardeschi). Trainer: Andrea Pirlo.
FC Porto: Agustín Marchesín, Pepe, Chancel Mbemba, Wilson Manafá, Zaidu Sanusi (71.Luis Díaz), Sérgio Oliveira (118.Mamadou Loum), Mateus Uribe (90.Marko Grujic), Otávio (62.Malang Sarr), Jesús Corona (118.Diogo Leite), Mehdi Taremi [sent off 54], Moussa Marega (106.Toni Martínez). Trainer: Sérgio Paulo Marceneiro da Conceição.
Goals: 19' Sérgio Oliveira 0-1 (penalty), 48', 63' Federico Chiesa 1-1, 2-1, 115' Sérgio Oliveira 2-2, 117' Adrien Rabiot 3-2.

09.03.2021; Signal-Iduna Park, Dortmund
Referee: Cüneyt Çakir (Turkey)
BV 09 BORUSSIA DORTMUND – Sevilla FC 2-2(1-0)
Borussia Dortmund: Marwin Hitz, Mats Hummels, Nico Schulz (89.Dan-Axel Zagadou), Mateu Morey (90+5.Thomas Meunier), Thomas Delaney, Thorgan Hazard (67.Felix Passlack), Emre Can, Mahmoud Dahoud, Jude Bellingham, Marco Reus, Erling Håland. Trainer: Edin Terzic.
Sevilla FC: Yassine Bounou, Jesús Navas, Diego Carlos, Jules Koundé, Fernando (86.Ivan Rakitic), Lucas Ocampos (60.Luuk de Jong), Marcos Acuña, Suso (86.Munir), Joan Jordán (60.Papu Gómez), Óscar Rodríguez (79.Óliver Torres), Youssef En-Nesyri. Trainer: Julen Lopetegui Agote.
Goals: 35', 54' Erling Håland 1-0, 2-0 (penalty), 69', 90+6' Youssef En-Nesyri 2-1 (penalty), 2-2.

17.03.2021; Allianz Arena, München
Referee: István Kovács (Romania)
FC BAYERN MÜNCHEN – SS Lazio Roma 2-1(1-0)
Bayern München: Alexander Nübel, Jérôme Boateng (46.Niklas Süle), David Alaba, Lucas Hernández, Benjamin Pavard, Leon Goretzka (64.Alphonso Davies), Joshua Kimmich (77.Javi Martínez), Thomas Müller (71.Jamal Musiala), Robert Lewandowski (71.Eric Maxim Choupo-Moting), Serge Gnabry, Leroy Sané. Trainer: Hans-Dieter Flick.
Lazio Roma: Pepe Reina, Stefan Radu, Francesco Acerbi, Adam Marusic, Luis Alberto (75.Danilo Cataldi), Joaquín Correa, Gonzalo Escalante (84.Jean-Daniel Akpa-Akpro), Manuel Lazzari (57.Marco Parolo), Sergej Milinkovic-Savic, Mohamed Fares (46.Senad Lulic), Vedat Muriqi (56.Andreas Pereira). Trainer: Simone Inzaghi.
Goals: 33' Robert Lewandowski 1-0 (penalty), 73' Eric Maxim Choupo-Moting 2-0, 82' Marco Parolo 2-1.

23.02.2021; Arena Naţională, Bucureşti (Romania)
Referee: Dr. Felix Brych (Germany)
Club Atlético de Madrid – Chelsea FC London 0-1(0-0)
Atlético Madrid: Jan Oblak, Stefan Savic, Felipe Monteiro, Mario Hermoso (84.Vitolo), Saúl (82.Lucas Torreira), Koke, Thomas Lemar, Marcos Llorente, Luis Suárez, Ángel Correa (82.Moussa Dembélé), João Félix (82.Renan Lodi). Trainer: Diego Pablo Simeone (Argentina).
Chelsea FC: Edouard Mendy, Azpilicueta, Marcos Alonso, Antonio Rüdiger, Andreas Christensen, Mateo Kovacic (74.Hakim Ziyech), Jorginho, Mason Mount (74.N'Golo Kanté), Olivier Giroud (87.Kai Havertz), Timo Werner (87.Christian Pulisic), Callum Hudson-Odoi (80.Reece James). Trainer: Thomas Tuchel (Germany).
Goal: 68' Olivier Giroud 0-1.

24.02.2021; Puskás Aréna, Budapest (Hungary)
Referee: Artur Manuel Ribeiro Soares Dias (Portugal)
Borussia VfL Mönchengladbach – Manchester City FC 0-2(0-1)
Borussia Mönchengladbach: Yann Sommer, Stefan Lainer (63.Valentino Lazaro), Matthias Ginter, Nico Elvedi, Ramy Bensebaini, Lars Stindl (74.Breel Embolo), Christoph Kramer, Jonas Hofmann (87.Hannes Wolf), Florian Neuhaus, Denis Zakaria, Alassane Pléa (63.Marcus Thuram). Trainer: Marco Rose.
Manchester City: Ederson Moraes, Kyle Walker, João Cancelo, Aymeric Laporte, Rúben Dias, Ilkay Gündogan, Bernardo Silva, Rodri, Phil Foden (80.Ferrán Torres), Raheem Sterling (69.Riyad Mahrez), Gabriel Jesus (80.Kun Agüero). Trainer: Josep Guardiola (Spain).
Goals: 29' Bernardo Silva 0-1, 65' Gabriel Jesus 0-2.

24.02.2021; Gewiss Stadium, Bergamo
Referee: Tobias Stieler (Germany)
Atalanta Bergamasca Calcio – Real Madrid CF 0-1(0-0)
Atalanta: Pierluigi Gollini, Rafael Tolói, Berat Djimsiti, Robin Gosens, Cristian Romero, Joakim Mæhle (86.José Palomino), Marten de Roon, Remo Freuler [*sent off 17*], Matteo Pessina, Duván Zapata (30.Mario Pasalic), Luis Muriel (56.Josip Ilicic, 86.Ruslan Malinovskiy). Trainer: Gian Piero Gasperini.
Real Madrid: Thibaut Courtois, Nacho, Raphaël Varane, Ferland Mendy, Luka Modric, Toni Kroos, Casemiro, Isco (76.Hugo Duro), Lucas Vázquez, Marco Asensio (76.Sergio Arribas), Vinícius Júnior (57.Mariano Díaz). Trainer: Zinédine Zidane (France).
Goal: 86' Ferland Mendy 0-1.

17.03.2021; Stamford Bridge, London
Referee: Daniele Orsato (Italy)
CHELSEA FC LONDON – Club Atlético de Madrid 2-0(1-0)
Chelsea FC: Edouard Mendy, Azpilicueta, Marcos Alonso (90+4.Ben Chilwell), Kurt Zouma, Antonio Rüdiger, Reece James, Mateo Kovacic, N'Golo Kanté, Hakim Ziyech (77.Christian Pulisic), Kai Havertz (90+3.Emerson), Timo Werner (83.Callum Hudson-Odoi). Trainer: Thomas Tuchel (Germany).
Atlético Madrid: Jan Oblak, Stefan Savic [*sent off 81*], Kieran Trippier (69.Thomas Lemar), José Giménez, Rena Lodi (46.Mario Hermoso), Saúl, Koke, Yannick Carrasco (53.Moussa Dembélé), Marcos Llorente, Luis Suárez (59.Ángel Correa), João Félix. Trainer: Diego Pablo Simeone (Argentina).
Goals: 34' Hakim Ziyech 1-0, 90+4' Emerson 2-0.

16.03.2021; Puskás Aréna, Budapest (Hungary)
Referee: Sergey Karasev (Russia)
MANCHESTER CITY FC–Borussia VfL Mönchengladbach 2-0(2-0)
Manchester City: Ederson Moraes, Kyle Walker, João Cancelo (64.Oleksandr Zinchenko), John Stones, Rúben Dias (70.Aymeric Laporte), Ilkay Gündogan (70.Raheem Sterling), Kevin De Bruyne, Bernardo Silva (75.Kun Agüero), Rodri (63.Fernandinho), Phil Foden, Riyad Mahrez. Trainer: Josep Guardiola (Spain).
Borussia Mönchengladbach: Yann Sommer, Stefan Lainer, Matthias Ginter, Nico Elvedi (88.Tony Jantschke), Ramy Bensebaini (88.Oscar Wendt), Lars Stindl (80.Ibrahima Traoré), Jonas Hofmann, Florian Neuhaus, Denis Zakaria, Breel Embolo (65.Hannes Wolf), Marcus Thuram (65.Alassane Pléa). Trainer: Marco Rose.
Goals: 12' Kevin De Bruyne 1-0, 18' Ilkay Gündogan 2-0.

16.03.2021; Estadio „Alfredo Di Stéfano", Madrid
Referee: Danny Desmond Makkelie (Netherlands)
REAL MADRID CF – Atalanta Bergamasca Calcio 3-1(1-0)
Real Madrid: Thibaut Courtois, Sergio Ramos (64.Éder Militão), Nacho, Raphaël Varane, Ferland Mendy, Luka Modric, Toni Kroos, Lucas Vázquez, Federico Valverde (82.Marco Asensio), Karim Benzema, Vinícius Júnior (69.Rodrygo). Trainer: Zinédine Zidane (France).
Atalanta: Marco Sportiello, Rafael Tolói (61.José Palomino), Berat Djimsiti, Robin Gosens (57.Josip Ilicic), Cristian Romero, Joakim Mæhle, Marten de Roon, Mario Pasalic (46.Duván Zapata), Ruslan Malinovskiy, Matteo Pessina (84.Mattia Caldara), Luis Muriel (84.Aleksey Miranchuk). Trainer: Gian Piero Gasperini.
Goals: 34' Karim Benzema 1-0, 60' Sergio Ramos 2-0 (penalty), 83' Luis Muriel 2-1, 84' Marco Asensio 3-1.

QUARTER-FINALS

06.04.2021; Etihad Stadium, Manchester
Referee: Ovidiu Alin Haţegan (Romania)
Manchester City FC – BV 09 Borussia Dortmund 2-1(1-0)
Manchester City: Ederson Moraes, Kyle Walker, João Cancelo, John Stones, Rúben Dias, Ilkay Gündogan, Kevin De Bruyne, Bernardo Silva (59.Gabriel Jesus), Rodri, Phil Foden, Riyad Mahrez. Trainer: Josep Guardiola (Spain).
Borussia Dortmund: Marwin Hitz, Mats Hummels, Raphaël Guerreiro, Manuel Akanji, Mateu Morey (81.Thomas Meunier), Emre Can, Mahmoud Dahoud (81.Thomas Delaney), Ansgar Knauff (63.Giovanni Reyna), Jude Bellingham, Marco Reus, Erling Håland. Trainer: Edin Terzic. Goals: 19' Kevin De Bruyne 1-0, 84' Marco Reus 1-1, 90' Phil Foden 2-1.

06.04.2021; Estadio „Alfredo Di Stéfano", Madrid
Referee: Dr. Felix Brych (Germany)
Real Madrid CF – Liverpool FC 3-1(2-0)
Real Madrid: Thibaut Courtois, Nacho, Ferland Mendy, Éder Militão, Luka Modric, Toni Kroos, Casemiro, Lucas Vázquez, Karim Benzema, Marco Asensio (70.Federico Valverde), Vinícius Júnior (85.Rodrygo). Trainer: Zinédine Zidane (France).
Liverpool FC: Alisson, Andrew Robertson, Trent Alexander-Arnold, Nathaniel Phillips, Ozan Kabak (81.Roberto Firmino), Georginio Wijnaldum, Fabinho, Naby Keïta (42.Thiago Alcântara), Mohamed Salah, Sadio Mané, Diogo Jota (81.Xherdan Shaqiri). Trainer: Jürgen Klopp (Germany).
Goals: 27' Vinícius Júnior 1-0, 36' Marco Asension 2-0, 51' Mohamed Salah 2-1, 65' Vinícius Júnior 3-1.

14.04.2021; Signal-Iduna Park, Dortmund
Referee: Carlos del Cerro Grande (Spain)
BV 09 Borussia Dortmund – MANCHESTER CITY FC 1-2(1-0)
Borussia Dortmund: Marwin Hitz, Mats Hummels, Raphaël Guerreiro, Manuel Akanji, Mateu Morey (81.Steffen Tigges), Emre Can, Mahmoud Dahoud (76.Thorgan Hazard), Ansgar Knauff (68.Giovanni Reyna), Jude Bellingham (81.Julian Brandt), Marco Reus, Erling Håland. Trainer: Edin Terzic.
Manchester City: Ederson Moraes, Kyle Walker, John Stones, Rúben Dias, Ilkay Gündogan, Kevin De Bruyne, Oleksandr Zinchenko, Bernardo Silva, Rodri, Phil Foden, Riyad Mahrez (88.Raheem Sterling). Trainer: Josep Guardiola (Spain).
Goals: 15' Jude Bellingham 1-0, 55' Riyad Mahrez 1-1 (penalty), 75' Phil Foden 1-2.

14.04.2021; Anfield Road, Liverpool
Referee: Björn Kuipers (Netherlands)
Liverpool FC – REAL MADRID CF 0-0
Liverpool FC: Alisson, Andrew Robertson, Trent Alexander-Arnold, Nathaniel Phillips, Ozan Kabak (60.Diogo Jota), James Milner (60.Thiago Alcântara), Georginio Wijnaldum, Fabinho, Roberto Firmino (82.Xherdan Shaqiri), Mohamed Salah, Sadio Mané (82.Alex Oxlade-Chamberlain). Trainer: Jürgen Klopp (Germany).
Real Madrid: Thibaut Courtois, Nacho, Ferland Mendy, Éder Militão, Luka Modric, Toni Kroos (72.Odriozola), Casemiro, Federico Valverde, Karim Benzema, Marco Asensio (82.Isco), Vinícius Júnior (72.Rodrygo). Trainer: Zinédine Zidane (France).

07.04.2021; Estádio „Ramón Sánchez Pizjuán", Sevilla (Spain)
Referee: Slavko Vinčić (Slovenia)
FC do Porto – Chelsea FC London 0-2(0-1)
FC Porto: Agustín Marchesín, Pepe, Chancel Mbemba, Wilson Manafá (83.Francisco Conceição), Zaidu Sanusi, Mateus Uribe, Otávio (83.Fábio Vieira), Marko Grujic, Jesús Corona, Moussa Marega (83.Toni Martínez), Luis Díaz. Trainer: Sérgio Paulo Marceneiro da Conceição.
Chelsea FC: Edouard Mendy, Azpilicueta, Antonio Rüdiger, Andreas Christensen, Ben Chilwell, Reece James (80.Thiago Silva), Mateo Kovacic (90+2.Emerson), Jorginho, Mason Mount (80.N'Golo Kanté), Kai Havertz (65.Olivier Giroud), Timo Werner (65.Christian Pulisic). Trainer: Thomas Tuchel (Germany).
Goals: 32' Mason Mount 0-1, 85' Ben Chilwell 0-2.

07.04.2021; Allianz Arena, München
Referee: Antonio Miguel Mateu Lahoz (Spain)
FC Bayern München – Paris Saint-Germain FC 2-3(1-2)
Bayern München: Manuel Neuer, David Alaba, Niklas Süle (42.Jérôme Boateng), Lucas Hernández, Benjamin Pavard, Leon Goretzka (33.Alphonso Davies), Joshua Kimmich, Eric Maxim Choupo-Moting, Thomas Müller, Kingsley Coman, Leroy Sané. Trainer: Hans-Dieter Flick.
Paris Saint-Germain: Keylor Navas, Marquinhos (31'Ander Herrera), Presnel Kimpembe, Abdou Diallo (46.Mitchel Bakker), Colin Dagba, Ángel Di María (71.Moise Kean), Idrissa Gueye, Danilo Pereira, Julian Draxler, Neymar (90.Rafinha), Kylian Mbappé. Trainer: Mauricio Roberto Pochettino Trossero (Argentina).
Goals: 3' Kylian Mbappé 0-1, 28' Marquinhos 0-2, 37' Eric Maxim Choupo-Moting 1-2, 60' Thomas Müller 2-2, 68' Kylian Mbappé 2-3.

13.04.2021; Estádio „Ramón Sánchez Pizjuán", Sevilla (Spain)
Referee: Clément Turpin (France)
CHELSEA FC LONDON – FC do Porto 0-1(0-0)
Chelsea FC: Edouard Mendy, Thiago Silva, Azpilicueta, Antonio Rüdiger, Ben Chilwell, Reece James, Jorginho, N'Golo Kanté, Mason Mount (86.Hakim Ziyech), Christian Pulisic, Kai Havertz (90+2.Olivier Giroud). Trainer: Thomas Tuchel (Germany).
FC Porto: Agustín Marchesín, Pepe, Chancel Mbemba, Wilson Manafá (75.Nanu), Zaidu Sanusi, Sérgio Oliveira (84.Fábio Vieira), Mateus Uribe, Otávio, Marko Grujic (63.Mehdi Taremi), Jesús Corona (75.Luis Díaz), Moussa Marega (75.Evanilson). Trainer: Sérgio Paulo Marceneiro da Conceição.
Goal: 90+4' Mehdi Taremi 0-1.

13.04.2021; Stade Parc des Princes, Paris
Referee: Daniele Orsato (Italy)
PARIS SAINT-GERMAIN FC – FC Bayern München 0-1(0-1)
Paris Saint-Germain: Keylor Navas, Presnel Kimpembe, Abdou Diallo (58.Mitchel Bakker), Colin Dagba, Ángel Di María (88.Ander Herrera), Idrissa Gueye, Danilo Pereira, Leandro Paredes, Julian Draxler (73.Moise Kean), Neymar, Kylian Mbappé. Trainer: Mauricio Roberto Pochettino Trossero (Argentina).
Bayern München: Manuel Neuer, Jérôme Boateng, David Alaba, Lucas Hernández, Benjamin Pavard, Alphonso Davies (71.Jamal Musiala), Joshua Kimmich, Eric Maxim Choupo-Moting (85.Javi Martínez), Thomas Müller, Kingsley Coman, Leroy Sané. Trainer: Hans-Dieter Flick.
Goal: 40' Eric Maxim Choupo-Moting 0-1.

SEMI-FINALS

27.04.2021; Estadio „Alfredo Di Stéfano", Madrid
Referee: Danny Desmond Makkelie (Netherlands)
Real Madrid CF – Chelsea FC London 1-1(1-1)
Real Madrid: Thibaut Courtois, Marcelo (77.Marco Asensio), Nacho, Dani Carvajal (77 Odriozola), Raphaël Varane, Éder Militão, Luka Modric, Toni Kroos, Casemiro, Karim Benzema (90+2.Rodrygo), Vinícius Júnior (66.Eden Hazard). Trainer: Zinédine Zidane (France).
Chelsea FC: Edouard Mendy, Thiago Silva, Azpilicueta (66.Reece James), Antonio Rüdiger, Andreas Christensen, Ben Chilwell, Jorginho, N'Golo Kanté, Mason Mount, Christian Pulisic (66.Hakim Ziyech), Timo Werner (66.Kai Havertz). Trainer: Thomas Tuchel (Germany).
Goals: 14' Christian Pulisic 0-1, 29' Karim Benzema 1-1.

28.04.2021; Stade Parc des Princes, Paris
Referee: Dr. Felix Brych (Germany)
Paris Saint-Germain FC – Manchester City FC 1-2(1-0)
Paris Saint-Germain: Keylor Navas, Marquinhos, Alessandro Florenzi, Presnel Kimpembe, Mitchel Bakker, Ángel Di María (80.Danilo Pereira), Marco Verratti, Idrissa Gueye [sent off 77], Leandro Paredes (83.Ander Herrera), Neymar, Kylian Mbappé. Trainer: Mauricio Roberto Pochettino Trossero (Argentina).
Manchester City: Ederson Moraes, Kyle Walker, João Cancelo (61.Oleksandr Zinchenko), John Stones, Rúben Dias, Ilkay Gündogan, Kevin De Bruyne, Bernardo Silva, Rodri, Phil Foden, Riyad Mahrez. Trainer: Josep Guardiola (Spain).
Goals: 15' Marquinhos 1-0, 64' Kevin De Bruyne 1-1, 71' Riyad Mahrez 1-2.

05.05.2021; Stamford Bridge, London
Referee: Daniele Orsato (Italy)
CHELSEA FC LONDON – Real Madrid CF 2-0(1-0)
Chelsea FC: Edouard Mendy, Thiago Silva, Azpilicueta (88.Reece James), Antonio Rüdiger, Andreas Christensen, Ben Chilwell, Jorginho, N'Golo Kanté, Mason Mount (88.Hakim Ziyech), Kai Havertz (90+4.Olivier Giroud), Timo Werner (67.Christian Pulisic). Trainer: Thomas Tuchel (Germany).
Real Madrid: Thibaut Courtois, Sergio Ramos, Nacho, Ferland Mendy (63.Federico Valverde), Éder Militão, Luka Modric, Toni Kroos, Casemiro (76.Rodrygo), Karim Benzema, Eden Hazard (89.Mariano Díaz), Vinícius Júnior (63.Marco Asensio). Trainer: Zinédine Zidane (France).
Goals: 28' Timo Werner 1-0, 85' Mason Mount 2-0.

04.05.2021; Etihad Stadium, Manchester
Referee: Björn Kuipers (Netherlands)
MANCHESTER CITY FC – Paris Saint-Germain FC 2-0(1-0)
Manchester City: Ederson Moraes, Kyle Walker, John Stones, Rúben Dias, Fernandinho, Ilkay Gündogan, Kevin De Bruyne (82.Gabriel Jesus), Oleksandr Zinchenko, Bernardo Silva (82.Raheem Sterling), Phil Foden (85.Kun Agüero), Riyad Mahrez. Trainer: Josep Guardiola (Spain).
Paris Saint-Germain: Keylor Navas, Marquinhos, Alessandro Florenzi (75.Colin Dagba), Presnel Kimpembe, Abdou Diallo (82.Mitchel Bakker), Ángel Di María [sent off 69], Ander Herrera (62.Julian Draxler), Marco Verratti, Leandro Paredes (75.Danilo Pereira), Neymar, Mauro Icardi (62.Moise Kean). Trainer: Mauricio Roberto Pochettino Trossero (Argentina).
Goals: 11', 63' Riyad Mahrez 1-0, 2-0.

FINAL

29.05.2021; Estádio do Dragão, Porto (Portugal); Referee: Antonio Miguel Mateu Lahoz (Spain); Attendance: 14,110
Manchester City FC – Chelsea FC London 0-1(0-1)
Manchester City: Ederson Moraes, Oleksandr Zinchenko, Rúben Dias, John Stones, Kyle Walker, Phil Foden, Ilkay Gündogan, Bernardo Silva (64.Fernandinho), Raheem Sterling (77.Kun Agüero), Kevin De Bruyne (60.Gabriel Jesus), Riyad Mahrez. Trainer: Josep Guardiola (Spain).
Chelsea FC: Edouard Mendy, Antonio Rüdiger, Thiago Silva (39.Andreas Christensen), Azpilicueta, Ben Chilwell, Jorginho, N'Golo Kanté, Reece James, Mason Mount (80.Mateo Kovacic), Kai Havertz, Timo Werner (66.Christian Pulisic). Trainer: Thomas Tuchel (Germany).
Goal: 42' Kai Havertz 0-1.

UEFA Champions League Winner 2020/2021: **Chelsea FC London** (England)

Best Goalscorer: Erling Braut Haaland (NOR, BV 09 Borussia Dortmund) – 10 goals

EUROPEAN CHAMPION CLUBS' CUP (1955 – 1992)
UEFA CHAMPIONS LEAGUE (1992 – 2021)
TABLE OF HONOURS

1955/1956	Real Madrid CF	*Spain*
1956/1957	Real Madrid CF	*Spain*
1957/1958	Real Madrid CF	*Spain*
1958/1959	Real Madrid CF	*Spain*
1959/1960	Real Madrid CF	*Spain*
1960/1961	Sport Lisboa e Benfica	*Portugal*
1961/1962	Sport Lisboa e Benfica	*Portugal*
1962/1963	AC Milan	*Italy*
1963/1964	FC Internazionale Milano	*Italy*
1964/1965	FC Internazionale Milano	*Italy*
1965/1966	Real Madrid CF	*Spain*
1966/1967	Celtic FC Glasgow	*Scotland*
1967/1968	Manchester United FC	*England*
1968/1969	AC Milan	*Italy*
1969/1970	SC Feijenoord Rotterdam	*Netherlands*
1970/1971	AFC Ajax Amsterdam	*Netherlands*
1971/1972	AFC Ajax Amsterdam	*Netherlands*
1972/1973	AFC Ajax Amsterdam	*Netherlands*
1973/1974	FC Bayern München	*Germany*
1974/1975	FC Bayern München	*Germany*
1975/1976	FC Bayern München	*Germany*
1976/1977	Liverpool FC	*England*
1977/1978	Liverpool FC	*England*
1978/1979	Nottingham Forest FC	*England*
1979/1980	Nottingham Forest FC	*England*
1980/1981	Liverpool FC	*England*
1981/1982	Aston Villa FC Birmingham	*England*
1982/1983	Hamburger SV	*Germany*
1983/1984	Liverpool FC	*England*
1984/1985	Juventus FC Torino	*Italy*
1985/1986	FC Steaua Bucureşti	*Romania*
1986/1987	FC do Porto	*Portugal*
1987/1988	PSV Eindhoven	*Netherlands*
1988/1989	AC Milan	*Italy*
1989/1990	AC Milan	*Italy*
1990/1991	FK Crvena Zvezda Beograd	*Serbia*
1991/1992	FC Barcelona	*Spain*
1992/1993	Olympique de Marseille	*France*
1993/1994	AC Milan	*Italy*
1994/1995	AFC Ajax Amsterdam	*Netherlands*
1995/1996	Juventus FC Torino	*Italy*
1996/1997	BV Borussia 09 Dortmund	*Germany*
1997/1998	Real Madrid CF	*Spain*
1998/1999	Manchester United FC	*England*
1999/2000	Real Madrid CF	*Spain*
2000/2001	FC Bayern München	*Germany*
2001/2002	Real Madrid CF	*Spain*
2002/2003	AC Milan	*Italy*
2003/2004	FC do Porto	*Portugal*
2004/2005	Liverpool FC	*England*
2005/2006	FC Barcelona	*Spain*
2006/2007	AC Milan	*Italy*
2007/2008	Manchester United FC	*England*
2008/2009	FC Barcelona	*Spain*
2009/2010	FC Internazionale Milano	*Italy*
2010/2011	FC Barcelona	*Spain*
2011/2012	Chelsea FC London	*England*
2012/2013	FC Bayern München	*Germany*
2013/2014	Real Madrid CF	*Spain*
2014/2015	FC Barcelona	*Spain*
2015/2016	Real Madrid CF	*Spain*
2016/2017	Real Madrid CF	*Spain*
2017/2018	Real Madrid CF	*Spain*
2018/2019	Liverpool FC	*England*
2019/2020	FC Bayern München	*Germany*
2020/2021	Chelsea FC London	*England*

PRELIMINARY ROUND

18.08.2020; Estadi Comunal, Andorra la Vella
Referee: Juxhin Xhaja (Albania)
UE Engordany – FK ZETA GOLUBOVCI 1-3(0-1)
UE Engordany: Coca, Lucas Sousa, Pedro Muñoz, Matías Rudler, Edson (75.Guillaume Lopez), Mario Spano, Kyllan Ramé (87.João Teixeira), Sébastien Aguéro, Luigi San Nicolas (67.Morgan Lafont), Aaron Sánchez, Sebastián Gómez. Trainer: José Prades.
FK Zeta Golubovci: Zoran Akovic, Aleksandar Milic, Ognjen Djinovic, Zvonko Ceklic, Goran Milojko, Srdjan Krstovic, Lazar Lambulic (89.Ilija Tripunovic), Amel Tuzovic, Mijat Lambulic (81.Matija Lambulic), Vasko Kalezic, Ivan Vuksevic (89.Nemanja Djurovic). Trainer: Dejan Ragonovic.
Goals: 45+1' Ivan Vukcevic 0-1, 54' Mijat Lambulic 0-2, 63' Lazar Lambulic 0-3, 90+4' Sebastián Gómez 1-3 (penalty).

20.08.2020; Svangaskard, Toftir
Referee: Pavel Rejžek (Czech Republic)
NSÍ RUNAVÍK – Barry Town United FC 5-1(0-0)
NSÍ Runavík: Tórdur Thomsen, Oddur Højgaard, Jóhan Davidsen, Rógvi Nielsen, Jesper Christjansen (82.Aron Knudsen), Petur Knudsen, Jann Benjaminsen, Mórits Heini Mortensen, Bárdur Jógvansson-Hansen (60.Pætur Skipanes), Salmundur Bech, Klæmint Olsen (79.Steffan Abrahamsson Løkin). Trainer: Glenn Leif Ståhl.
Barry Town United: Mike Lewis, Chris Hugh, Luke Cooper, Luke Cummings, Robbie Patten (70.Michael George), David Cotterill (70.Jordan Cotterill), Theo Wharton, Clayton Green, Evan Press, Kayne McLaggon, Nathaniel Jarvis (82.Keyon Reffell). Trainer: Gavin Chesterfield.
Goals: 52', 63' Klæmint Olsen 1-0, 2-0, 67' Petur Kundsen 3-0, 74' Klæmint Olsen 4-0, 83' Steffan Abrahamsson Løkin 5-0, 88' Kayne McLaggon 5-1.

20.08.2020; The Oval, Belfast
Referee: Lukas Fähndrich (Switzerland)
GLENTORAN FC BELFAST – HB Tórshavn 1-0(1-0)
Glentoran Belfast: Dayle Coleing, Patrick McClean, Caolan Marron, Keith Cowan, Marcus Kane, Gaël Bigirimana, Chris Gallagher, Seanan Clucas (68.Luke McCullough), Rory Donnelly (83.Cameron Stewart), Robbie McDaid, Paul O'Neill (72.Jamie McDonagh). Trainer: Mick McDermott.
HB Tórshavn: Teitur Gestsson, Jógvan Davidsen (62.René Joensen), Delphin Tshiembe, Daniel Johansen, Bartal Wardum, Hedin Hansen, Dan í Soylu (75.Mads Mikkelsen), Pætur Petersen (46.Adrian Justinussen), Mathias Nygaard, Hilmar Leon Jakobsen, Mikkel Dahl. Trainer: Jens Berthel Askou.
Goal: 42' Robbie McDaid 1-0.

21.08.2020; San Marino Stadium, Serravalle
Referee: Alex Troleis (Faroe Islands)
SP Tre Penne – SC GJILANI 1-3(1-1)
SP Tre Penne: Mattia Migani, Christofer Genestreti, Nicolas Lombardi, Riccardo Mezzadri, Luca Patregnani, Alex Gasperoni (68.Davide Cesarini), Nicola Gai, Michael Battistini, Luca Sorrentino [*sent off 43*], Luca Ceccaroli (50.Enrico Cibelli), Alessandro Chiurato (74.Riccardo Pieri). Trainer: Stefano Ceci.
SC Gjilani: Enea Koliçi, Oltion Rapa, Armend Halili (83.Ylber Kastrati), Erlis Frashëri, Franc Veliu, Ardit Hila, Muhamed Useini, Fiton Hajdari (79.Muhamed Dubova), Fjoart Jonuzi (50.Edvin Kuc), Darko Nikac, Gerhard Progni. Trainer: Gentian Mezani.
Goals: 16' Nicola Gai 1-0, 24' Darko Nikac 1-1, 64' Fiton Hajdari 1-2, 68' Ardir Hila 1-3.

20.08.2020; Victoria Stadium, Gibraltar
Referee: Jasmin Sabotić (Luxembourg)
St. Joseph's FC – B36 TÓRSHAVN 1-2(1-2)
St. Joseph's FC: Mateo, Pecci, Federico Villar, Ezequiel, Carlos Carrasco (77.Ángel Guirado), Nano, Alain Pons (87.Aymen Mouelhi), Juanma González, Domingo Ferrer (61.Pedro Fernández), Boro, Juanfri. Trainer: Raúl Procopio.
B36 Tórshavn: Rói Hentze, Andrias Eriksen, Bjarni Petersen (61.Benjamin Heinesen), Sonni Nattestad, Alex Mellemgaard (79.Erling Jacobsen), Magnus Holm Jacobsen (86.Stefan Radosavljevic), Eli Nielsen, Árni Frederiksberg, Meinhard Olsen, Sebastian Pingel, Michal Przybylski. Trainer: Jákup á Borg.
Goals: 28' Michal Przybylski 0-1, 30' Boro 1-1, 43' Alex Mellemgaard 1-2 (penalty).

20.08.2020; Estadi Comunal, Andorra la Vella
Referee: Keith Kennedy (Northern Ireland)
FC Santa Coloma – FK ISKRA DANILOVGRAD 0-0; 3-4 on penalties
FC Santa Coloma: Casals, Moisés San Nicolas, Juanma Miranda, Álex Sánchez, Aleix Cistero, Txus Rubio, Marc Rebés (116.Javi Camochu), Enric Pi (46.Diego Nájero), Jordi Aláez [*sent off 40*], Luis Blanco (81.Pedro Santos), Alexandre Martínez (90.Hamza Bouharma). Trainer: Albert Jorquera Fortià (Spain).
Iskra Danilovgrad: Srdjan Blazic, Nikola Kumburovic, Luka Malesevic, Milos Drincic, Irfan Sahman, Balsa Boricic, Vladislav Rogosic (89.Bogdan Milic), Miroje Jovanovic (113.Ognjen Obradovic), Aldin Adzovic (68.Milan Djurisic), Sho Yamamoto (81.Bogdan Mandic), Ivan Vukovic. Trainer: Aleksandar Nedovic.
Penalties: Milan Djurisic 0-1, Aleix Cistero 1-1, Ognjen Obradovic 1-2, Juanma Miranda 2-2, Ivan Vukovic 2-3, Hamza Bouharma (missed), Balsa Boricic (missed), Javi Camochu 3-3, Milos Drincic 3-4, Pedro Santos (missed).

20.08.2020; The Showgrounds, Coleraine
Referee: Christian-Petru Ciochirca (Austria)
COLERAINE FC – SP La Fiorita 1-0(0-0)
Coleraine FC: Gareth Deane, Lyndon Kane, Aaron Canning, Ben Doherty, Stephen O'Donnell, Aaron Jarvis, Stephen Lowry, Josh Carson (46.Stewart Nixon), Aaron Traynor, James McLaughlin, Curtis Allen (62.Eoin Bradley). Trainer: Oran Kearney.
SP La Fiorita: Gianluca Vivan, Andrea Brighi, Roberto Di Maio, Andrea Grandoni, Marco Gasperoni, Simone Errico (65.Tommaso Guidi), Simone Loiodice, Armando Amati, Christian Damiano (74.Michele Pieri), Danilo Rinaldi, Lucio Peluso (79.Marcello Mularoni). Trainer: Nicola Berardi.
Goal: 89' James McLaughlin 1-0.

22.08.2020; Victoria Stadium, Gibraltar
Referee: David Munro (Scotland)
LINCOLN RED IMPS FC – KF Prishtina 3-0
Please note: match was re-scheduled from 18.08.2020, as several members from KF Prishtina's delegation testing positive for COVID-19 and the whole team put into quarantine by the Gibraltarian authorities. On 22.08.2020 the match could not be played due to eight players from KF Prishtina testing positive for COVID-19 and the whole second team being put into quarantine by the Gibraltarian authorities. Lincoln Red Imps were subsequently awarded a 3-0 victory by UEFA according to the regulations related to COVID-19.

25.08.2020; LFF stadionas, Vilnius
Referee: Ville Nevalainen (Finland)
FK RITERIAI – Derry City FC 3-2(1-1,2-2)
FK Riteriai: Tadas Simaitis, Akseli Kalermo, Ricardas Sveikauskas, Dominykas Barauskas, Ángel Lezama, Deividas Malzinskas, Mindaugas GRĪgaravicius (116.Bright Godwin), Tomas Dombrauskis (88.Matas Ramanauskas), Lajo Traore (77.Dominyk Kodz), Donatas Kazlauskas, Gytis Paulauskas (101.Rokas Filipavicius). Trainer: Tommi Petteri Pikkarainen (Finland).
Derry City: Peter Cherrie, Ciarán Coll, Darren Cole, Colm Horgan, Eoin Toal, Adam Hammill, Conor McCormack, Joe Thomson (73.Connor Clifford, 112.Gerardo Bruna), Jake Dunwoody (56.Stephen Mallon), James Akintunde, Ibrahim Meité (85.Ciaron Harkin). Trainer: Declan Devine.
Goals: 18' Joe Thomson 0-1, 39', 49' Gytis Paulauskas 1-1, 2-1 , 63' Eoin Toal 2-2, 91' Donatas Kazlauskas 3-2.

27.08.2020; Olimpiska centra Ventspils Stadiona, Ventspils
Referee: Eldorjan Hamiti (Albania)
FK VENTSPILS – FC Dinamo-Auto Tiraspol 2-1(1-1)
FK Ventspils: Dele Alampasu, Giorgi Rekhviashvili, Andriy Sakhnevich, Giorgi Mchedlishvili, Dmitrijs Litvinskis, Guga Palavandishvili [*sent off 90+4*], Giorgi Eristavi, Lucas Villela, Abdulla Genaev (70.Daniils Ulimbasevs), Kaspars Svārups (80.Chris Ondong Mba), Evgeny Kozlov. Trainer: Viorel Frunză (Moldova).
FC Dinamo-Auto: Victor Straistari, Radu Rogac, Oleksandr Masalov, Dmitri Nagiyev (78.Octavian Bulat), Vadim Dijinari, Maxim Mihaliov, Vadim Paireli, Alexandr Belousov, Artiom Bilinschii, Yehor Kondratyuk, Dumitru Rogac. Trainer: Igor Dobrovolskiy (Russia).
Goals: 15' Dumitru Rogac 0-1, 22' Lucas Villela 1-1, 75' Evgeny Kozlov 2-1 (penalty).

27.08.2020; Ortaliq Stadion, Almaty
Referee: Kristoffer Karlsson (Sweden)
FC KAIRAT ALMATY – FC Noah Yerevan 4-1(2-1)
Kairat: Stas Pokatilov, Dino Mikanovic, Rade Dugalic, Nuraly Alip, Kamo Hovhannisyan, Nebojsa Kosovic, Jacek Góralski, Konrad Wrzesinski (59.Aybol Abiken), Gulzhygit Alykulov (74.Daniyar Uzenov), Vágner Love, Abat Aymbetov (79.Aderinsola Eseola). Trainer: Aleksey Shpilevskiy (Belarus).
FC Noah: Valerio Vimercati, Vladislav Kryuchkov, Mikhail Kovalenko (71.Saná Gomes), Soslan Kagermazov, Denis Dedechko, Pavel Deobald (46.Artem Simonyan), Vladimir Azarov (72.Benik Hovhannisyan), Eduards Emsis, Dmitri Lavrishchev, Kirill Bor, Danu Spataru. Trainer: Vladimir Japalau (Moldova).
Goals: 8' Kirill Bor 0-1, 12' Gulzhygit Alykulov 1-1, 35', 70' Vágner Love 2-1, 3-1, 90+4' Aderinsola Eseola 4-1.

27.08.2020; Gradski Stadion, Banja Luka
Referee: Morten Krogh (Denmark)
FK BORAC BANJA LUKA – FK Sutjeska Nikšić 1-0(1-0)
Borac Banja Luka: Bojan Pavlovic, Nemanja Janicic, Marko Jovanovic, Djordje Cosic, Stojan Vranjes, Goran Zakaric, Sinisa Dujakovic (79.Sasa Kajkut), Marko Brtan (63.Aleksandar Vojinovic), Almedin Dino Ziljkic, Vladan Danilovic, Jovo Lukic (72.Aleksandar Radulovic). Trainer: Vlado Jagodic.
Sutjeska Nikšić: Vladan Giljen, Darko Bulatovic, Nikola Stijepovic, Filip Mitrovic, Dragan Grivic, Marko Cetkovic, Damir Kojasevic (10.Milivoje Raicevic), Branislav Jankovic (74.Bozo Markovic), Milutin Osmajic, Balsa Dubljevic (67.Aleksa Marusic), Admir Adrovic. Trainer: Dragan Radojicic.
Goal: 35' Stojan Vranjes 1-0.

27.08.2020; Victoria Stadium, Gilbraltar
Referee: Helgi Mikael Jónasson (Iceland)
LINCOLN RED IMPS FC – Union Titus Pétange 2-0(1-0)
Lincoln Red Imps: Lolo Soler, Scott Wiseman, Bernardo Lopes, Roy Chipolina, Ethan Britto, Mustapha Yahaya, Jack Sergeant, Graeme Torilla, Anthony Hernandez (73.Kyle Casciaro),
Lee Casciaro (78.James Coombes), Kike Gómez (85.Eric Same). Trainer: William.
Union Titus Pétange: Tom Ottele, Alexandre Laurienté, Mike Schneider (75.Joel Rodrigues da Cruz), Mounir Hamzaoui, Allan Hauguel, Yannick Kakoko, Boyou Kodjia, Bilel El Hamzaoui, Abdoul Kabore, Robert Maah (63.Jonathan Nanizayamo), Luca Duriatti (55.Eliot Gashi). Trainer: Ismaël Bouzid (Algeria).
Goals: 36' Lee Casciaro 1-0, 90+5' Mustapha Yahaya 2-0.

26.08.2020; Stade Municipal de Differdange, Differdange
Referee: Rahim Hasanov (Azerbaijan)
FC PROGRÈS NIEDERKORN – FK Zeta Golubovci 3-0(1-0)
Progrès Niederkorn: Sebastian Flauss, Tom Laterza, Adrien Ferino, Metin Karayer, Aldin Skenderovic, Sébastien Thill, Kevin Holtz (67.Belmin Muratovic), Christian Silaj, Ryad Habbas (78.Antonio Luisi), Kempes Tekiela, Irvin Latic (86.Florik Shala). Trainer: Roland Vrabec (Germany).
FK Zeta Golubovci: Zoran Akovic, Aleksandar Milic, Zvonko Ceklic (67.Nemanja Djurovic), Ognjen Djinovic, Alphonse Soppo, Goran Milojko, Vasko Kalezic (62.Elom Nya-Vedji), Amel Tuzovic, Srdjan Krstovic, Ivan Vukcevic, Mijat Lambulic (55.Lazar Lambulic). Trainer: Dejan Roganovic.
Goals: 11', 55' Kempes Tekiela 1-0, 2-0 (penalty), 90+3' Sébastien Thill 3-0.

27.08.2020; Stadion "Qajimuqan Munaytpasov", Shymkent
Referee: Rauf Jabbarov (Azerbaijan)
FK Ordabasy – FC BOTOȘANI 1-2(1-2)
FK Ordabasy: Bekkhan Shayzada, Viktor Dmitrenko (84.Mirzad Mehanovic), Pablo Fontanello, Damir Dautov, João Paulo (76.Toktar Zhangylyshbay), Abdoulaye Diakhaté, May Mahlangu, Ziguy Badibanga, Rúben Brígido, Timur Dosmagambetov, Sergey Khizhnichenko (46.Aleksandar Simcevic). Trainer: Kakhaber Tskhadadze (Georgia).
FC Botoșani: Eduard Pap, Marcel Holzmann, Stefan Ashkovski (89.Alexandru Tiganasu), Alin Seroni, Denis Harut, Andrei Chindris, Bryan Mendoza, Eduard Florescu, Jonathan Rodriguez, Reagy Ofosu (74.Hamidou Keyta), Marko Dugandzic (90+2.Mihai Roman). Trainer: Marius Croitoru.
Goals: 25' Marcel Holzmann 0-1, 31' May Mahlangu 1-1, 33' Marko Dugandzic 1-2.

27.08.2020; Stadiumi „Niko Dovana", Durrës
Referee: Nikolas Neokleous (Cyprus)
KF TEUTA DURRËS – Beitar Jerusalem FC 2-0(1-0)
Teuta Durrës: Stivi Frashëri, Renato Arapi, Blagoja Todorovski, Rustem Hoxha, Alexandros Kouros, Fabjan Beqja (63.Ildi Gruda), Emiljano Vila, Albano Aleksi, Florent Avdyli (90+2.Ledjo Beqja), Blerim Krasniqi (65.Rubin Hebaj), Lorenco Vila. Trainer: Eduard Martini.
Beitar Jerusalem: Itamar Nitzan, Orel Dgani, Diogo Verdasca, Oren Biton (76.Uri Magbo), Shay Konstantini, Ofir Kriaf, Ali Mohamed Muhammad, Liran Rotman (46.Gleofilo Hasselbaink Vlijter), Idan Vered, Eliran Atar (70.Shalom Edri), Shlomi Azulay. Trainer: Roni Levy.
Goals: 6' Blerim Krasniqi 1-0, 87' Rubin Hebaj 2-0.

27.08.2020; Stadion Dynama, Minsk
Referee: Lazar Lukić (Serbia)
FC Dinamo Minsk – GKS PIAST GLIWICE 0-2(0-1)
Dinamo Minsk: Evgeniy Pomazan, Sergey Matveychik, Igor Shitov, Artem Sukhotskyi, Miha Goropevsek, Dominik Dinga, Edgar Olekhnovich (73.Kirill Vergeychik), Vladislav Klimovich, Ivan Bakhar, Silas (59.Mikhail Kozlov), Yevgeniy Shikavka (79.Vladimir Khvashchinskiy). Trainer: Leonid Kuchuk.
Piast Gliwice: Frantisek Plach, Mikkel Kirkeskov, Jakub Czerwinski, Tomás Huk, Martin Konczkowski, Gerard Badía (72.Dominik Steczyk), Patryk Lipski, Patryk Sokolowski, Jakub Swierczok, Krisztófer Vida (82.Sebastian Milewski), Piotr Parzyszek (55.Michal Zyro). Trainer: Waldemar Fornalik.
Goals: 10' Patryk Lipski 0-1, 56' Jakub Swierczok 0-2.

27.08.2020; Bakcell Arena, Bakı
Referee: Aleksandrs Golubevs (Latvia)
NEFTÇİ PFK BAKI – KF Shkupi Čair 2-1(0-0)
Neftçi: Aqil Mammadov, Thallyson (90+2.Vojislav Stankovic), Mamadou Mbodj, Anton Krivotsyuk, Dzhabir Amirli, Steeven Joseph-Monrose (90.Mirabdulla Abbasov), Emin Makhmudov, Namiq Alasgarov, Sabir Bougrine, Mamadou Kane, Yusuf Lawal. Trainer: Fuzuli Mammadov.
KF Shkupi: Kristijan Naumovski, Darko Glisic, Filip Gligorov, Besart Krivanjeva, Bianor, Sabit Bilalli, Besar Iseni (65.Freddy Álvarez), Lamine Diack, Dembo Darboe, Ilirid Ademi (73.Fatjon Jusufi), Oumar Goudiaby [*sent off 70*]. Traineres: Muharem Bajrami & Vladimir Kolev.
Goals: 66' Sabir Bougrine 1-0, 88' Anton Krivotsyuk 2-0, 90+3' Dembo Darboe 2-1.

27.08.2020; Aspmyra Stadion, Bodø
Referee: Kaarlo Oskari Hämäläinen (Finland)
FK BODØ/GLIMT – FK Kauno Žalgiris Kaunas 6-1(2-0)
FK Bodø/Glimt: Nikita Haikin, Marius Høibråten, Marius Lode (59.Ole Amund Sveen), Alfons Sampsted, Fredrik Bjørkan (62.Aleksander Foosnæs), Ulrik Saltnes, Patrick Berg, Jens Hauge, Philip Zinckernagel (77.Sebastian Tounekti), Sondre Fet, Victor Boniface. Trainer: Kjetil Knutsen.
Kauno Žalgiris: Deividas Mikelionis, Steven Trichot, Egidijus Vaitkunas, Martynas Dapkus, Rudinilson Silva, Karolis Silkaitis, Linas Pilibaitis (73.Deividas Sesplaukis), Yuriy Bushman, Simonas Urbys (82.Benas Anisas), Gratas Sirgedas, Emmanuel David (61.Philip Otele). Trainer: Rokas Garastas.
Goals: 27', 36' Philip Zinckernagel 1-0, 2-0, 52', 59' Jens Hauge 3-0, 4-0 (penalty), 78' Philip Otele 4-1, 79' Victor Boniface 5-1, 81' Sebastian Tounekti 6-1.

27.08.2020; „Vazgen Sargsyan" Hanrapetakan Stadium, Yerevan
Referee: Nick Walsh (Scotland)
FC Alashkert Yerevan – KF RENOVA DŽEPČIŠTE 0-1(0-0)
FC Alashkert: Ognjen Cancarevic, Risto Mitrevski, Taron Voskanyan, Igor Gonchar, Bryan Garcia, Tiago Cametá (67.Aghvan Papikyan), Artak Grigoryan (80.Nikita Tankov), Thiago Galvão, Wangu Gome, Perdigão (61.Pape Camara), Aleksandar Glisic. Trainer: Eghishe Melikyan.
KF Renova: Hadis Velii, Nenad Miskovski, Xhelil Abdulla, Bashkim Velija, Argjent Gafuri (86.Artan Veliu), Saimir Fetai, Burim Sadiki, Emran Ramadani (71.Alen Jasaroski), Alush Gavazaj, Remzi Selmani (63.Filip Stojchevski), Shefit Shefiti. Trainer: Bujar Islami.
Goal: 58' Nenad Miskovski 0-1.

27.08.2020; Stadion Stožice, Ljubljana
Referee: Walter Altmann (Austria)
NK OLIMPIJA LJUBLJANA – Víkingur Reykjavík 2-1(0-1,1-1)
Olimpija Ljubljana: Ziga Frelih, Uros Korun, Miral Samardzic, Jan Andrejasic (46.Matic Fink), Enrik Ostrc, Timi Elsnik, Angel Lyaskov (91.Michael Pavlovic), Mihail Caimacov, Ante Vukusic (71.Jucie Lupeta), Drazen Bagaric (58.Jakov Blagaic), Radivoj Bosic. Trainer: Dino Skender.
Víkingur Reykjavík: Ingvar Jónsson, Sölvi Ottesen [sent off 5], Kári Árnason, Halldór Sigurdsson, Atli Barkarson, David Atlason (96.Dofri Snorrason), Július Magnússon (60.Viktor Örlygur Andrason), Erlingur Agnarsson, Nikolaj Hansen (60.Halldór Thórdarson; 110.Helgi Gudjónsson), Óttar Karlsson, Ágúst Edvald Hlynsson. Trainer: Arnar Gunnlaugsson.
Goals: 27' Óttar Karlsson 0-1, 88' Matic Fink 1-1, 106' Radivoj Bosic 2-1.

27.08.2020; LFF stadionas, Vilnius
Referee: Petri Viljanen (Finland)
FK ŽALGIRIS VILNIUS – Paide Linnameeskond 2-0(2-0)
FK Žalgiris: Martin Berkovec, Donovan Slijngard, Ivan Tatomirovic, Nemanja Ljubisavljevic, Saulius Mikoliūnas, Hugo Vidémont (90+1.Francis Kyeremeh), Domantas Simkus, Modestas Vorobjovas, Karlo Kamenar (68.Mantas Kuklys), Andrija Kaludjerovic, Liviu Antal (81.Richie Ennin). Trainer: Aleksei Baga.
Paide Linnameeskond: Mait Toom, Karl Mööl, Martin Kase, Kristjan Pelt, Sander Sinilaid (46.Bruno Caprioli), Sergei Mosnikov, Andre Frolov (76.Deabeas Owusu-Sekyere), Siim Luts (63.Edrisa Lubega), Joseph Saliste, Henri Anier, Edgar Tur. Trainer: Vjatseslav Zahovaiko.
Goals: 9' Andrija Kaludjerovic 1-0, 32' Liviu Antal 2-0.

27.08.2020; Tele2 Arena, Stockholm
Referee: Mario Zebec (Croatia)
HAMMARBY IF STOCKHOLM – Puskás Akadémia FC Felcsút 3-0(2-0)
Hammarby IF: David Ousted, David Fällman, Mads Fenger, Mohanad Jeahze (80.Vladimir Rodic), Imad Khalili, Abdul Khalili (77.Alexander Kacaniklic), Darijan Bojanic, Jeppe Andersen, Tim Söderström, Paulinho, Muamer Tankovic (55.Aron Jóhannsson). Trainer: Stefan Billborn.
Puskás Akadémia FC: Martin Auerbach, Kamen Hadzhiev, Roland Szolnoki, Csaba Spandler, Zsolt Nagy, László Deutsch, Jakub Plsek, Liridon Latifi (61.György Komáromi), Tamás Kiss (81.Benedek Kalmár), Márton Radics, Weslen Júnior (69.Marius Corbu). Trainer: Zsolt Hornyák.
Goals: 14' Abdul Khalili 1-0, 32' Darijan Bojanic 2-0, 84' Paulinho 3-0.

27.08.2020; Stádio Neo GSP, Nicosia
Referee: Adrien Jaccottet (Switzerland)
APOLLON LIMASSOL FC – FC Saburtalo Tbilisi 5-1(2-0)
Apollon Limassol: Joël Mall, Valentin Roberge, Attila Szalai, Ioannis Pittas, Nicolas Diguiny (64.Sasa Markovic), Héctor Yuste, Florentin Matei (75.Petros Psychas), Esteban Sachetti, Djordje Denic (64.Diego Aguirre), Bagaliy Dabo, Giannis Gianniotas. Trainer: Sofronis Avgousti.
FC Saburtalo Tbilisi: Lazare Kupatadze, Levan Kakubava, Tedore GRĭgalashvili, Gagi Margvelashvili, Nikoloz Mali, Olivier Boumal (78.Giorgi Gocholeishvili), Jeroen Lumu (63.Giorgi Guliashvili), Sandro Altunashvili, Alwyn Tera (66.Anri Chichinadze [sent off 81]), Iuri Tabatadze, Beka Kavtaradze. Trainer: Teimuraz Shalamberidze.
Goals: 3', 32' Bagaliy Dabo 1-0, 2-0, 59' Nicolas Diguiny 3-0, 69' Giorgi Guliashvili 3-1, 76' Bagaliy Dabo 4-1, 86' Giannis Gianniotas 5-1.

27.08.2020; Kapital Bank Arena, Sumgayit
Referee: Arman Ismuratov (Kazakhstan)
Sumqayıt FK – KF SHKËNDIJA TETOVO 0-2(0-0)
Sumqayıt FK: Mekhti Dzhenetov, Vurgun Hüseynov, Elvin Badalov, Dzhamaldin Khodzhaniyazov, Tellur Mütallimov [sent off 89], Elvin Mammadov (73.Rüfat Abdullazade), Vüqar Mustafayev, Rahim Sadikhov, Khayal Najafov (63.Sabuhi Abdullazade), Süleyman Ahmadov (62.Adam Hemati), Ali Ghorbani. Trainer: Aykhan Abbasov.
KF Shkëndija: Kostadin Zahov, Mevlan Murati (90+5.Medzit Neziri), Antonio Pavic, Egzon Bejtulai, Ján Krivák, Bruno Dita, Valon Ahmedi, Ennur Totre, Omar Imeri (77.Arbin Zejnullai), Besart Ibraimi, Ljupco Doriev (90+3.Abou Baker Es Sahhal). Trainer: Ernest Gjoka.
Goals: 56' Besart Ibraimi 0-1 (penalty), 89' Ljupco Doriev 0-2 (penalty).

27.08.2020; MOL Aréna Sóstó, Székesfehérvár
Referee: Timotheos Christofi (Cyprus)
FEHÉRVÁR FC SZÉKESFEHÉRVÁR – Bohemians FC Dublin 1-1(1-1,1-1); 4-2 on penalties
Fehérvár FC: Ádám Kovácsik, Attila Fiola, Loïc Négo, Stopira, Adrián Rus, Ivan Petryak (109.Krisztián Géresi), Lyes Houri, Alef (75.Máté Pátkai), Nemanja Nikolic (74.Armin Hodzic), Evandro (101.Boban Nikolov), Funsho Bamgboye. Trainer: Gábor Márton.
Bohemians FC: Stephen McGuinness, Robert Cornwall (71.James Finnerty), Anto Breslin, Dan Casey, Andy Lyons, Keith Ward (83.Dawson Devoy), Keith Buckley (109.Daniel Mandroiu), Kris Twardek, Jonathan Lunney (79.Conor Levingston), Andre Wright, Daniel Grant. Trainer: Keith Long.
Goals: 22' Keith Ward 0-1, 37' Nemanja Nikolic 1-1 (penalty).
Penalties: Armin Hodzic (missed), Daniel Mandroiu 0-1, Nemanja Nikolov 1-1, Conor Levingston 1-2, Krisztián Géresi 2-2, Dan Casey (missed), Stopira 3-2, Kris Twardek (missed), Lyes Houri 4-2.

27.08.2020; Lerkendal Stadion, Trondheim
Referee: Matthew De Gabriele (Malta)
ROSENBORG BK TRONDHEIM – Breiðablik Kópavogur 4-2(4-0)
Rosenborg: Julian Faye Lund, Tore Reginiussen, Even Hovland, Vegar Hedenstad (80.Waren Kamanzi), Erlend Reitan, Gjermund Åsen, Kristoffer Zachariassen, Edvard Tagseth (61.Filip Brattbakk), Torgeir Børven, Dino Islamovic, Carl Holse. Trainer: Trond Henriksen.
Breidablik: Anton Ari Einarsson, Damir Muminovic, Elfar Helgason, Andri Yeoman (39.Oliver Sigurjónsson), Höskuldur Gunnlaugsson, Gísli Eyjólfsson, Viktor Einarsson, Brynjólfur Willumsson, Róbert Thorkelsson (78.Viktor Örn Margeirsson), Thomas Mikkelsen, Alexander Sigurdarson (70.Kristinn Steindórsson). Trainer: Óskar Hrafn Thorvaldsson. Goals: 3' Torgeir Børven 1-0, 17' Tore Reginiussen 2-0, 24' Even Hovland 3-0, 29' Torgeir Børven 4-0, 60' Viktor Einarsson 4-1, 90+1' Thomas Mikkelsen 4-2 (penalty).

27.08.2020; Eleda Stadion, Malmö
Referee: Urs Schnyder (Switzerland)
MALMÖ FF – KS Cracovia Kraków 2-0(2-0)
Malmö FF: Marko Johansson, Eric Larsson, Jonas Knudsen, Franz Brorsson, Anel Ahmedhodzic, Søren Rieks, Anders Christiansen, Oscar Lewicki, Erdal Rakip (75.Arnór Traustason), Jo Inge Berget (67.Amin Sarr), Isaac Kiese Thelin. Trainer: Jon Dahl Tomasson (Denmark).
Cracovia Kraków: Lukás Hrosso, Cornel Rapa, David Jablonský, Michal Helik, Michal Siplak (58.Diego Ferraresso), Sergiu Hanca, Pelle van Amersfoort, Mateusz Wdowiak, Florian Loshaj, Marcos Álvarez (79.Tomás Vestenický), Rivaldinho (46.Milan Dimun). Trainer: Michal Probierz.
Goals: 1' Jo Inge Berget 1-0, 44' Søren Rieks 2-0.

27.08.2020; Ceres Park & Arena, Aarhus
Referee: Ioannis Papadopoulos (Greece)
AGF AARHUS – FC Honka Espoo 5-2(3-1)
Aarhus: William Eskelinen, Casper Højer Nielsen, Alexander Munksgaard, Frederik Tingager, Sebastian Hausner, Nikolai Poulsen, Patrick Olsen, Bror Blume (86.Benjamin Hvidt), Jón Dagur Thorsteinsson (70.Søren Tengstedt), Gift Links (78.Milan Jevtovic), Patrick Mortensen. Trainer: David Nielsen.
FC Honka: Tim Murray, Henri Aalto (69.Macoumba Kandji), Dani Hatakka, Jonas Levänen, Robert Ivanov, Konsta Rasimus, Javi Hervás, Jerry Voutilainen, Lucas Kaufmann, Jean Dongou, Borjas Martín (79.Arlind Sejdiu). Trainer: Vesa Vasara.
Goals: 21' Frederik Tingager 1-0, 29' Patrick Mortensen 2-0, 35' Borjas Martín 2-1, 45+2' Patrick Mortensen 3-1 (penalty), 64' Lucas Kaufmann 3-2, 90+1' Patrick Olsen 4-2, 90+2' Søren Tengstedt 5-2.

27.08.2020; ASK Arena, Bakı
Referee: Georgi Kikacheishvili (Georgia)
Keşla FK – KF LAÇI 0-0; 4-5 on penalties
Keşla FK: Stanislav Namasco, Mijusko Bojovic, Ilkin Qirtimov, Azer Salahli, Shahriyar Aliyev [*sent off 112*], Artur (81.Dzhavid Imamverdiyev), Rahman Hadzhiyev, John Kamara, Dmytro Klyots, Vüsal Isgendarli (119.Tural Akhundov), Alexander Cristovão (64.Sílvio). Trainer: Yunis Hüseynov.
KF Laçi: Alen Sherri, Aleksandar Ignjatovic, Rudolf Turkaj, Adolf Selmani, Ardit Deliu (99.Donald Rapo), Regi Lushkja, Lucas Ramos [*sent off 72*], Albion Marku, Teco (120.Mentor Mazrekaj), Kyrian Nwabueze, Redon Xhixha (105.Klejdi Rapo). Trainer: Armando Cungu.
Penalties: Kyrian Nwabueze 0-1, Dmytro Klyots 1-1, Regi Lushkja 1-2, Silvio 2-2, Donald Rapo 2-3, Tural Akhundov 3-3, Mentor Mazrekaj 3-4, Rahman Hadzhiyev 4-4, Aleksandar Ignjatovic 4-5, Ilkin Qirtimov (missed).

27.08.2020; Stadioni „Mikheil Meskhi", Tbilisi
Referee: Miloš Đorđić (Serbia)
FC LOKOMOTIVI TBILISI – CS Universitatea Craiova 2-1(0-0)
Lokomotivi Tbilisi: Giorgi Mamardashvili, Nika Sandokhnadze (77.Aleksandre Andronikashvili), Giorgi Gabadze, Aleksandre Gureshidze, Daviti Ubilava, Temur Shonia, Davit Samurkasovi (80.Nika Tchanturia), Tornike Kirkitadze, Beka Dartsmelia, Imran Oulad Omar (69.Tornike Dzebniauri), Irakli Sikharulidze. Trainer: Giorgi Chiabrishvili.
Universitatea Craiova: Mirko Pigliacelli, Marius Constantin, Bogdan Vatajelu, Nicusor Bancu, Stephane Acka, Alexandru Mateiu (67.Vladimir Screciu), Dan Nistor (77.Stefan Baiaram), Cristian Barbut (61.Valentin Mihaila), Alexandru Cicâldau, Elvir Koljic, Andrei Ivan. Trainer: Cristiano Bergodi (Italy).
Goals: 57' Irakli Sikharulidze 1-0, 61' Imran Oulad Omar 2-0, 90+4' Stefan Baiaram 2-1.

27.08.2020; Kaplakrikavöllur, Hafnarfjördur
Referee: Jason Lee Barcelo (Gibraltar)
FH Hafnarfjördur – FK DAC DUNAJSKÁ STREDA 0-2(0-1)
FH Hafnarfjördur: Gunnar Nielsen, Pétur Vidarsson, Gudmann Thórisson, Hördur Ingi Gunnarsson, Daníel Hafsteinsson (71.Atli Gudnason), Thórir Jóhann Helgason, Gudmundur Kristjánsson, Eggert Jónsson, Björn Sverrisson (82.Baldur Sigurdsson), Olafur Finsen (58.Jónathan Jónsson), Steven Lennon. Traineres: Eidur Gudjohnsen & Logi Ólafsson.
DAC Dunajská Streda: Martin Jedlicka, Éric Davis, Jannik Müller, Dominik Kruzliak, César Blackman, Zsolt Kalmár, Andrija Balic, Sidney Friede, András Schäfer, Eric Ramírez, Marko Divkovic (71.Andrej Fábry). Trainer: Bernd Storck (Germany).
Goals: 23' Andrija Balic 0-1, 76' Eric Ramírez 0-2.

27.08.2020; Rheinpark Stadion, Vaduz
Referee: Luís Miguel do Nascimento Teixeira (Portugal)
FC Vaduz – HIBERNIANS FC PAOLA 0-2(0-1)
FC Vaduz: Benjamin Büchel, Denis Simani, Pius Dorn (75.Matteo Di Giusto), Yannick Schmid, Cédric Gasser, Sandro Wieser, Gabriel Lüchinger (67.Nicolae Milinceanu), Sebastian Santin (67.Nico Hug), Mohamed Coulibaly, Manuel Sutter, Tunahan Çiçek. Trainer: Mario Frick.
Hibernians FC: Matthew Calleja Cremona, Leandro Almeida, Andrei Agius, Zachary Grech, Gabriel Izquier, Bjorn Kristensen [*sent off 64*], Jake Grech, Wilkson (63.Rundell Winchester), Shola Shodiya (75.Timothy Tabone Desira), Jurgen Degabriele, Ayrton Attard (70.Edafe Uzeh). Trainer: Stefano Sanderra.
Goals: 34', 57' Jurgen Degabriele 0-1, 0-2.

27.08.2020; Stadion Balgarska Armija, Sofia
Referee: Krzysztof Jakubik (Poland)
PFC CSKA SOFIA – Sirens FC San Pawl il-Baħar 2-1(0-0)
CSKA Sofia: Busatto, Jurgen Mattheij, Plamen Galabov, Bradley Mazikou, Valentin Antov, Graham Carey (57.Georgi Yomov), Tiago Rodrigues, Amos Youga (71.Ahmed Ahmedov), Stefano Beltrame (65.Younousse Sankharé), Ali Sowe, Henrique. Trainer: Stamen Belchev.
Sirens FC: David Cassar, Adrian Borg, Ryan Scicluna, Sergio Raphael, Thiaguinho, Manuel Bustos, Romeu (30.Jacob Walker), Terence Agius (82.Ryan Grech), Wilfried Domoraud, Maxuell Samurai, Wellington Petinha (79.Michael Mifsud). Trainer: Stephen D'Amato.
Goals: 69' Maxuell Samurai 0-1, 75' Ahmed Ahmedov 1-1, 90+1' Ali Sowe 2-1.

27.08.2020; Stadiumi „Fadil Vokrri", Prishtina
Referee: Yigal Frid (Israel)
SC Gjilani – APOEL FC NICOSIA 0-2(0-0,0-0)
SC Gjilani: Enea Koliçi, Franc Veliu, Jackson (105.Arbër Prekazi), Oltion Rapa (72.Erlis Frashëri), Ylber Kastrati, Muhamed Useini (77.Edvin Kuc), Ardit Hila (96.Fjoart Jonuzi), Keita Lanzeni Aziz, Gerhard Progni, Darko Nikac, Fiton Hajdari. Trainer: Gentian Mezani.
APOEL Nicosia: Miguel Silva, Giorgios Merkis, Nicholas Ioannou, Rafael Santos, Mike Jensen (117.Christos Shelis), Dragan Mihajlovic, Tomás De Vincenti, Marius Lundemo, Ghayas Zahid (67.Ben Sahar), Moussa Al Taamari (90.Giorgos Efrem), Viktor Klonaridis (79.Dieumerci Ndongala). Trainer: Marinos Ouzounidis.
Goals: 102' Giorgos Efrem 0-1, 116' Dieumerci Ndongala 0-2.

27.08.2020; Stroitel Stadium, Solihorsk
Referee: Dragan Petrović (Bosnia and Herzegovina)
FC Shakhtyor Solihorsk – FC SFÂNTUL GHEORGHE 0-0; 1-4 on penalties
Shakhtyor Solihorsk: Alyaksandr Gutor, Aleksandr Sachivko, Igor Burko, Roman Begunov (105.Viktor Sotnikov), Ruslan Khadarkevich, Yuri Kendysh (68.Július Szöke), Aleksandr Selyava, Igor Ivanovic (46.Sergey Balanovich), Dmitri Podstrelov, Darko Bodul [*sent off 28*], Artem Arkhipov (46.Jasurbek Yakhshiboev). Trainer: Yuriy Vernydub.
FC Sfântul Gheorghe: Nicolae Cebotari, Andrey Novicov, Maxim Focsa, Serghei Svinarenco, Eugeniu Slivca, Petru Ojog, Sidy Sagna (84.Vitalie Plamadeala), Yevhen Smirnov, Dimitrii Mandrîcenco (90+1.Alexandru Suvorov), Rienat Mochulyak (79.Maxim Iurcu), Roman Volkov. Trainer: Sergiu Cebotari. [Maxim Railean *(not used sub, sent off 121*)].
Penalties: Alexandru Suvorov 0-1, Aleksandr Sachivko 1-1, Roman Volkov 1-2, Viktor Sotnikov (missed), Maxim Iurcu 1-3, Jasurbek Yakhshiboev (missed), Eugeniu Slivca 1-4.

27.08.2020; Park Hall Stadium, Oswestry
Referee: Manfredas Lukjančukas (Lithuania)
THE NEW SAINTS FC – MŠK Žilina 3-1(0-0,1-1)
The New Saints: Paul Harrison, Simon Spender (48.Ryan Harrington), Chris Marriott, Blaine Hudson, Ryan Astles, Daniel Redmond (104.Jon Routledge), Ryan Brobbel (81.Leo Smith), Tom Holland, Jamie Mullan, Dean Ebbe, Louis Robles (87.Adrian Cieslewicz). Trainer: Scott Ruscoe.
MŠK Žilina: Samuel Petráš, Jan Minárik, Kristián Vallo, Branislav Sluka [sent off 108], Adam Kopas, Jakub Paur (85.Dawid Kurminowski), Ján Bernát (90+3.Vahan Bichakhchyan), Patrik Myslovic, Miroslav Gono, Dávid Duris (118.Adrián Kaprálik), Patrik Ilko (101.Matúš Rusnák). Trainer: Pavol Stano.
Goals: 56' Louis Robles 1-0, 77' Patrik Myslovic 1-1 (penalty), 100' Leo Smith 2-1, 108' Adrian Cieslewicz 3-1 (penalty).

27.08.2020; Tórsvøllur, Tórshavn
Referee: Donald Robertson (Scotland)
B36 TÓRSHAVN – FCI Levadia Tallinn 4-3(0-0,2-2)
B36 Tórshavn: Rói Hentze, Alex Mellemgaard, Sonni Nattestad, Eli Nielsen (69.Andrass Johansen, 115.Bjarni Petersen), Árni Frederiksberg, Benjamin Heinesen, Andrias Eriksen, Michal Przybylski, Magnus Holm Jacobsen (90+1.Ragnar Samuelsen), Stefan Radosavljevic (60.Hannes Agnarsson), Sebastian Pingel. Trainer: Jákup á Borg.
FCI Levadia Tallinn: Artur Kotenko, Markus Jürgenson, Dmitri Kruglov, Maksim Podholjuzin, Trevor Elhi, Zurab Ochihava, Brent Lepistu, Mark Roosnupp (115.Rasmus Peetson), Elysee Kouadio, Karl Õigus, Artjom Komlov (105.Marko Lipp). Trainer: Vladimir Vassiljev.
Goals: 52' Karl Õigus 0-1, 72', 76' Sebastian Pingel 1-1, 2-1, 80' Trevor Elhi 2-2, 101' Elysee Kouadio 2-3, 107' Ragnar Samuelsen 3-3, 113' Hannes Agnarsson 4-3.

27.08.2020; MFA Centenary Stadium, Ta'Qali
Referee: Luca Barbeno (San Marino)
Valletta FC – BALA TOWN FC 0-1(0-1)
Valletta FC: Henry Bonello, Jonathan Caruana, Mihailo Jovanovic, Jean Borg, Rowen Muscat, Enmy Peña, Shaun Dimech (68.Taisei Marukawa), Santiago Malano, Miguel Alba (46.Kyrian Nwoko), Matteo Piciollo (60.Taylon), Mario Fontanella. Trainer: Jesmond Zerafa.
Bala Town FC: Alex Ramsay, Anthony Stephens, Sean Smith, Jonathan Spittle, Antony Kay, Steven Leslie (69.Kieran Smith), Chris Venables, Will Evans, Oliver Shannon, Lassana Mendes, Raul Correia (79.Henry Jones). Trainer: Colin Caton.
Goal: 38' Chris Venables 0-1.

27.08.2020; Stadionul Zimbru, Chişinău
Referee: Sebastian Colţescu (Romania)
CS Petrocub Hîncesti – FK TSC BAČKA TOPOLA 0-2(0-1)
CS Petrocub Hîncesti: Cristian Avram, Petru Racu, Ion Jardan, Iaser Turcan (68.Victor Bogaciuc), Andrei Cojocari, Artiom Rozgoniuc [sent off 54], Dan Taras (53.Alexandru Bejan), Vladimir Ambros (68.Ilie Damascan), Jacques Onana Ndzomo, Donalio Melachio Douanla, Sergiu Platica. Trainer: Lilian Popescu.
TSC Bačka Topola: Nenad Filipovic, Goran Antonic, Dajan Ponjevic, Filip Babic, Nenad Lukic, Sasa Tomanovic, Boris Varga [sent off 17], Djuro Zec (90+1.Vasilije Djuric), Vladimir Siladji (44.Nemanja Petrovic), Dejan Milicevic, Borko Duronjic (74.Mihajlo Banjac). Trainer: Zoltán Szabó.
Goals: 17' Sasa Tomanovic 0-1, 55' Nenad Lukic 0-2 (penalty).

27.08.2020; Stade de Genève, Genève
Referee: Viktor Kopiievskyi (Ukraine)
SERVETTE FC GENÈVE – MFK Ružomberok 3-0(0-0)
Servette Genève: Jérémy Frick, Anthony Sauthier, Vincent Sasso, Steve Rouiller, Arial Mendy, Miroslav Stevanovic, Gaël Ondoua, Timothé Cognat (87.Andrea Maccoppi), Varol Tasar (69.Alexis Antunes), Kastriot Imeri (76.Boris Cespedes), Grejohn Kyei. Trainer: Alain Geiger.
MFK Ružomberok: Matús Macík, Ján Maslo, Matej Curma, Matej Madlenák, Alexander Mojzis, Matej Kochan, Dalibor Takác (60.Peter Dungel), Marek Zsigmund, Timejj Múdry (65.Adam Brenkus), Stefan Gerec, Ladislav Almási (70.Tomás Bobcek). Trainer: Ján Haspra.
Goals: 54' Miroslav Stevanovic 1-0, 77' Arial Mendy 2-0, 86' Alexis Antunes 3-0.

27.08.2020; HaMoshava Stadium, Petak Tikva
Referee: Aleksandrs Anufrijevs (Latvia)
HAPOEL BE'ER SHEVA FC – FC Dinamo Batumi 3-0(2-0)
Hapoel Be'er Sheva: Ohad Levita, Miguel Vítor (79.Loai Taha), Shir Tzedek, Sean Goldberg, Elton Acolatse, Or Dadya, Sintayehu Sallalich, Josué, Marwan Kabha (62.Tomer Yosefi), David Keltjens, Itamar Shviro (75.Gaëtan Varenne). Trainer: Yossi Abukasis.
Dinamo Batumi: Mikheil Alavidze, Giorgi Navalovski (45.Lasha Chaladze), Mamuka Kobakhidze, Godfrey Oboabona, Jambuli Jighauri, Benjamin Teidi, Vladimer Mamuchashvili, Giuly Mandzgaladze (79.Tornike Gaprindashvili), Giorgi Nikabadze (64.Reynaldo), Vagner Gonçalves, Flamarion. Trainer: George Geguchadze.
Goals: 9' Josué 1-0, 21' Mamuka Kobakhidze 2-0 (own goal), 61' Josué 3-0.

27.08.2020; Stadion pod Bijelim Brijegom, Mostar
Referee: Aristotelis Diamantopoulos (Greece)
HŠK ZRINJSKI MOSTAR – FC Differdange 03 3-0(2-0)
Zrinjski Mostar: Ivan Brkic, Mario Ticinovic, Tomislav Barbaric, Pero Stojkic, Slobodan Jakovljevic, Ognjen Todorovic (82.Miljan Govedarica), Dinko Trebotic, Milos Filipovic (74.Ivan Basic), Ivan Enin, Nemanja Bilbija, Anes Masic (64.Josip Ivancic). Trainer: Mladen Zizovic.
FC Differdange 03: Kevin Strauss, Geoffrey Franzoni, Maxime De Taddeo, Dylan Lempereur, Théo Brusco, Gonçalo Almeida (84.Shean Garlito y Romo), Quentin Leite Pereira (80.Fadel Gobitaka), Mamadou Sanoussy Baldé (46.Hugo Komano), Kilian Gulluni, Aurélien Joachim, Andreas Buch. Trainer: Paolo Amodio.
Goals: 37' Nemanja Bilbija 1-0, 40' Milos Filipovic 2-0, 79' Josip Ivancic 3-0.

27.08.2020; Air Albania Stadium, Tirana
Referee: Arda Kardesler (Turkey)
FK KUKËSI – PFC Slavia Sofia 2-1(0-0)
FK Kukësi: Dashamir Xhika, Kenan Horic, Edis Malikji, Erhun Obanor, Bruno Telushi, Emiljano Musta, Eduart Rroca, Besar Musolli, Enis Gavazaj (46.Albin Gashi), Vesel Limaj (65.Zenel Gavazaj), Patrick Eze (66.Godberg Cooper). Trainer: Skënder Gega.
Slavia Sofia: Antonis Stergiakis, Hristo Popadiyn, Petar Patev, Andrea Hristov, Georgi Valchev (73.Ventsislav Bengyuzov), Milen Gamakov, Emil Stoev (87.Dimitar Stoyanov), Yanis Karabelyov, Filip Krastev, Dimitar Rangelov (62.Ivailo Dimitrov), Kaloyan Krastev. Trainer: Zlatomir Zagorcic.
Goals: 56' Patrick Eze 1-0 (penalty), 81' Kaloyan Krastev 1-1, 85' Godberg Cooper 2-1.

27.08.2020; Stadion Pod Goricom, Podgorica
Referee: Gergő Bogár (Hungary)
FK Iskra Danilovgrad – PFC LOKOMOTIV PLOVDIV 0-1(0-0)
Iskra Danilovgrad: Marko Kordic, Luka Malesevic, Nikola Kumburovic, Milos Drincic, Miroje Jovanovic, Kōhei Katō, Irfan Sahman, Balsa Boricic (82.Milan Djuricic), Ivan Vukovic, Aldin Adzovic (78.Bogdan Milic), Zoran Petrovic (73.Vladislav Rogosic). Trainer: Aleksandar Nedovic.
Lokomotiv Plovdiv: Martin Lukov, Milos Petrovic, Dinis Almeida, Lucas Masoero, Momchil Tsvetanov, Parvizchon Umarbaev (90.Nikolay Nikolaev), Petar Vitanov, Lucas Salinas (65.Christian Ilic), Dimitar Iliev, Birsent Karagaren, Ante Aralica (73.Georgi Minchev). Trainer: Bruno Akrapovic (Bosnia and Herzegovina).
Goal: 75' Dimitar Iliev 0-1 (penalty).

27.08.2020; Arena Naţională, Bucureşti
Referee: Admir Šehović (Bosnia and Herzegovina)
SC FCSB BUCUREŞTI – Shirak SC Gyumri 3-0(1-0)
FCSB: Andrei Vlad, Valentin Cretu, Iulian Cristea, George Andrei Miron, Ionut Pantîru, Ovidiu Popescu, Darius Olaru, Sergiu Bus (46.Alexandru Buziuc), Florin Tanase (86.Ionut Vina), Florinel Coman, Dennis Man (78.Olimpiu Morutan). Trainer: Anton Petrea.
Shirak SC: Vsevolod Ermakov, Hrayr Mkoyan, Aghvan Davoyan, Marko Prijevic, Zhirayr Margaryan, Edgar Malakyan, Davit Manoyan (69.Solomon Udo), Karen Muradyan, Arman Aslanyan (74.Junior Avo Leibe), Urus Nenadovic (74.Artem Gevorkyan), Mory Kone. Trainer: Tigran Davtyan.
Goals: 34' Darius Olaru 1-0, 65' Florin Tanase 2-0 (penalty), 83' Alexandru Buziuc 3-0.

27.08.2020; Ljudski vrt, Maribor
Referee: Kai Erik Steen (Norway)
NK Maribor – COLERAINE FC 1-1(0-0,1-1); 4-5 on penalties
NK Maribor: Azbe Jug, Mitja Viler, Martin Milec, Nemanja Mitrovic, Spiro Pericic, Rok Kronaveter (84.Jan Mlakar), Alexandru Cretu, Aleks Pihler (102.Amir Dervisevic), Martin Kramaric (61.Marcos Tavares), Jasmin Mesanovic, Aljosa Matko (61.Rudi Vancas Pozeg). Trainer: Sergej Jakirovic.
Coleraine FC: Gareth Deane, Aaron Canning, Aaron Traynor (105.Gareth McConaghie), Stephen O'Donnell, Lyndon Kane, Stephen Lowry, Josh Carson, Ben Doherty, Aaron Jarvis (72.Ronan Wilson), James McLaughlin (95.Ian Parkhill), Stewart Nixon (85.Eoin Bradley). Trainer: Oran Kearney.
Goals: 62' James McLaughlin 0-1, 65' Rudi Vancas Pozeg 1-1.
Penalties: Amir Dervesevic 1-0, Ian Parkhill 1-1, Jan Mlakar 2-1, Lyndon Kane 2-2, Marcos Tavares 3-2, Gareth McConaghie 3-3, Jasmin Mesanovic 4-3, Eoin Bradley 4-4, Rudi Vancas Pozeg (missed), Ben Doherty 4-5.

27.08.2020; Fir Park, Motherwell
Referee: Bram Van Driessche (Belgium)
MOTHERWELL FC – Glentoran FC Belfast 5-1(0-0)
Motherwell FC: Trevor Carson, Declan Gallagher, Stephen O'Donnell (82.Harry Robinson), Ricki Lamie, Liam Grimshaw (60.Sherwin Seedorf), Bevis Mugabi, Liam Polworth, Mark O'Hara, Allan Campbell, Chris Long, Callum Lang (70.Tony Watt). Trainer: Stephen Robinson.
Glentoran Belfast: Dayle Coleing, Keith Cowan, Patrick McClean, Caolan Marron, Marcus Kane, Gaël Bigirimana, Seanan Clucas [sent off 52], Chris Gallagher (78.Ciarán O'Connor), Rory Donnelly (73.Cameron Stewart), Robbie McDaid, Paul O'Neill (62.Jamie McDonagh). Trainer: Mick McDermott.
Goals: 58' Callum Lang 1-0, 72' Stephen O'Donnell 2-0, 75' Liam Polworth 3-0, 78' Tony Watt 4-0, 87' Chris Long 5-0, 90' Robbie McDaid 5-1 (penalty).

27.08.2020; Tallaght Stadium, Dublin
Referee: Michal Ocenás (Slovakia)
SHAMROCK ROVERS FC – FC Ilves Tampere 2-2(1-1,2-2); 12-11 on penalties
Shamrock Rovers: Alan Mannus, Joey O'Brien, Roberto Lopes, Liam Scales [sent off 88], Ronan Finn, Aaron McEneff, Jack Byrne, Gary O'Neill, Neil Farrugia (78.Dean Williams), Aaron Greene (105+2.Danny Lafferty), Graham Burke (64.Dylan Watts). Trainer: Stephen Bradley.
Ilves Tampere: Mika Hilander, Felipe Aspegren (111.Doni Arifi), Tatu Miettunen, Diogo Tomas, Mikael Almen, Joona Veteli (83.Tuure Siira), Lauri Ala-Myllymäki, Jair, Naatan Skyttä, Eero Tamminen (102.Eetu Mömmö), Ilari Mettälä (79.Eemeli Raittinen). Trainer: Jarkko Wiss.
Goals: 10' Lauri Ala-Myllymäki 0-1 (penalty), 14' Graham Burke 1-1, 62' Joona Veteli 1-2, 78' Roberto Lopes 2-2.
Penalties: Lauri Ala-Myllymäki 0-1, Jack Byrne (missed), Jair (missed), Joey O'Brien 1-1, Eemeli Raittinen 1-2, Dylan Watts 2-2, Tuure Siira 2-3, Gary O'Neill 3-3, Naatan Skyttä 3-4, Aaron McEneff 4-4, Eetu Mömmö 4-5, Dean Williams 5-5, Diogo Tomas 5-6, Roberto Lopes 6-6, Mikael Almen 6-7, Danny Lafferty 7-7, Tatu Miettunen 7-8, Ronan Finn 8-8, Mika Hilander 8-9, Alan Mannus 9-9, Lauri Ala-Myllymäki 9-10, Dylan Watts 10-10, Jair 10-11, Aaron McEneff 11-11, Eemeli Raittinen (missed), Joey O'Brien 12-11.

27.08.2020; Stadion Miejski, Poznań
Referee: Ondřej Pechanec (Czech Republic)
KKS LECH POZNAŃ – Valmiera FC 3-0(0-0)
Lech Poznań: Filip Bednarek, Lubomir Satka, Djordje Crnomarkovic, Robert Gumny, Tymoteusz Puchacz, Pedro Tiba (80.Filip Marchwinski), Dani Ramírez, Kamil Józwiak, Jakub Moder, Jacub Kaminski (63.Alan Czerwinski), Mikael Ishak (88.Filip Szymczak). Trainer: Dariusz Zuraw.
Valmiera FC: Rūdolfs Soloha, Julien Celestine, Olaide Badmus, Pape Yaré Fall, Kriss Kārklins, Mykola Musolitin, Luka Silagadze (46.Mootez Zaddem), Alvis Jaunzems (83.Daniils Skopenko), Mohamed Victor Diagne, Jorge Teixeira (76.Djibril Gueyé), Toluwalase Arokodare. Trainer: Tamaz Pertia.
Goals: 59', 78' Mikael Ishak 1-0, 2-0, 88' Filip Szymczak 3-0.

27.08.2020; Pittodrie Stadium, Aberdeen
Referee: Ívar Orri Kristjánsson (Iceland)
ABERDEEN FC – NSÍ Runavík 6-0(2-0)
Aberdeen FC: Joe Lewis, Andrew Considine, Scott McKenna, Jonny Hayes, Marley Watkins (73.Bruce Anderson), Matthew Kennedy, Dylan McGeouch, Ross McCrorie, Lewis Ferguson, Curtis Main (46.Ryan Hedges), Scott Wright (82.Niall McGinn). Trainer: Derek McInnes.
NSÍ Runavík: Tórdur Thomsen, Oddur Højgaard, Jóhan Davidsen, Bárdur Jógvansson-Hansen (59.Jákup Jakobsen), Rógvi Nielsen, Jesper Christjansen, Salmundur Bech (88.Aron Knudsen), Petur Knudsen, Mórits Heini Mortensen (70.Steffan Abrahamsson Løkin), Jann Benjaminsen, Klæmint Olsen. Trainer: Glenn Leif Ståhl.
Goals: 37' Lewis Ferguson 1-0, 43' Curtis Main 2-0, 50', 59' Ryan Hedges 3-0, 4-0, 60' Jonny Hayes 5-0, 87' Ryan Hedges 6-0 (penalty).

27.08.2020; „Hidegkuti Nándor" Stadion, Budapest
Referee: Gal Leibovitz (Israel)
BUDAPEST HONVÉD FC – FC Inter Turku 2-1(0-0,1-1)
Budapest Honvéd: Tomás Tujvel, Eke Uzoma, Ivan Lovric, Botond Baráth (46.Mohamed Mezghrani), Bence Batík, Patrik Hidi (107.Djordje Kamber), Barna Kesztyüs, Donát Zsótér, Dániel Gazdag, Roland Ugrai (120.Naser Aliji), Kristóf Tóth-Gábor (72.Boubacar Traoré). Trainer: Tamás Bódog.
FC Inter Turku: Henrik Moisander, Jesper Engström (106.Kevin Kouassivi-Benissan), Juuso Hämäläinen, Rick Ketting, Arttu Hoskonen, Anthony Annan, Álvaro Muñiz (106.Taiki Kagayama), Aleksi Paananen (65.Matias Ojala), Connor Ruane, Timo Furuholm, Benjamin Källman (89.Liliu). Trainer: José Luis Riveiro (Spain).
Goals: 90' Boubacar Traoré 1-0, 90+1' Liliu 1-1, 105' Juuso Hämäläinen 2-1 (own goal).

27.08.2020; Stadion Partizana, Beograd
Referee: Zaven Hovhannisyan (Armenia)
FK PARTIZAN BEOGRAD – FK Rīgas Futbola skola 1-0(0-0)
Partizan Beograd: Vladimir Stojkovic, Uros Vitas, Nemanja Miletic, Macky Frank Bagnack, Slobodan Urosevic, Bibras Natcho (90+2.Milan Smiljanic), Aleksandar Scekic, Sasa Zdjelar, Takuma Asano (90+5.Dennis Stojkovic), Umar Sadiq, Filip Stevanovic (72.Seydouba Soumah). Trainer: Savo Milosevic.
FK Rīgas Futbola skola: Danylo Kucher, Aleksandrs Solovjovs, Vitālijs Jagodinskis, Ziga Lipuscek, Tomás Simkovic (71.Chinonso Nnamdi), Tomislav Saric, Roberts Savalnieks, Jānis Ikaunieks, Leonel Strumia, Darko Lemajic, Alain Cedric Kouadio (70.Baiano). Trainer: Viktors Morozs.
Goal: 52' Bibras Natcho 1-0 (penalty).

09.09.2020; „Sammy Ofer" Stadium, Haifa
Referee: Jørgen Burchardt (Denmark)
MACCABI HAIFA FC – FK Željezničar Sarajevo 3-1(1-1)
Maccabi Haifa: Josh Cohen, Ernest Mabouka, Sun Menachem, Ayed Habashi, Ofri Arad, Tjaronn Chery, Yuval Ashkenazi, Neta Lavi, Mohammad Abu Fani (54.Dolev Haziza), Nikita Rukavytsya (76.Stav Nachmani), Yanic Wildschut (69.Yarden Shua). Trainer: Barak Bakhar.
Željezničar Sarajevo: Irfan Fejzic, Sinisa Stevanovic, Aleksandar Kosoric, Luka Miletic, Mehmed Alispahic (75.Damir Sadikovic), Semir Stilic, Mladen Veselinovic (63.Mustafa Mujezinovic), Haris Hajdarevic, Eldar Sehic (75.Luka Juricic), Ivan Lendric, Ante Blazevic. Trainer: Amar Osim.
Goals: 34' Ivan Lendric 0-1, 38' Tjaronn Chery 1-1, 59' Nikita Rukavytsya 2-1, 66' Yuval Ashkenazi 3-1.

10.09.2020; „Szusza Ferenc" Stadion, Budapest (Hungary)
Referee: Robert Hennessy (Republic of Ireland)
JK Nõmme Kalju – NŠ MURA MURSKA SOBOTA 0-4(0-4)
JK Nõmme Kalju: Marko Meerits, Kirill Aleksandr Antonov (89.Frank Kenneth Liblikmann), Sander Puri, Andreas Raudsepp, Kaspar Paur, Marcus Suurväli, Kaarel Usta, Arthur Jersov (46.Kirill Sustov), Jevgeni Demidov, Alex Matthias Tamm, Kristjan Rattasepp. Trainer: Marko Kristal.
NŠ Mura: Matko Obradovic, Ziga Kous, Klemen Sturm, Jan Gorenc, Zan Kamiczik, Matic Marusko (46.Kai Cipot), Nino Kouter (78.Amadej Marosa), Alen Kozar (66.Marko Brkic), Tomi Horvat, Kevin Zizek, Andrija Filipovic. Trainer: Ante Simundza.
Goals: 17', 27' Kevin Zizek 0-1, 0-2, 32' Ziga Kous 0-3, 36' Alen Kozar 0-4.

SECOND QUALIFYING ROUND

CHAMPIONS PATH

17.09.2020; Ortaliq Stadion, Almaty
Referee: Dumitri Muntean (Moldova)
Astana FC Nur-Sultan – FK BUDUĆNOST PODGORICA 0-1(0-1)
Astana: Nenad Eric, Evgeny Postnikov, Uros Radakovic, Luka Simunovic, Rúnar Sigurjónsson, Dmitriy Shomko (50.Abzal Beysebekov), Ivan Maevski, Maks Ebong (86.Aleksey Shchetkin), Tigran Barseghyan, Pieros Sotiriou, Dorin Rotariu (57.Marin Tomasov). Trainer: Paul Ashworth.
Budućnost Podgorica: Milos Dragojevic, Vladan Adzic, Luka Mirkovic, Igor Cukovic, Nemanja Sekulic, Petar Grbic, Milos Raickovic, Vasilije Terzic (89.Aleksandar Vujacic), Petar Vuksevic (9.Bogdan Milic), Igor Ivanovic, Panagiotis Moraitis (90+5.Miomir Djurickovic). Trainer: Mladen Milinkovic.
Goal: 25' Vasilije Terzic 0-1.

17.09.2020; Savon Sanomat Areena, Kuopio
Referee: Volen Chinkov (Bulgaria)
KUOPION PALLOSEURA – ŠK Slovan Bratislava 1-1(0-0,0-0); 4-3 on penalties
Kuopion PS: Otso Virtanen, Artur Pikk, Juho Pirttijoki (88.Luc Tabi Manga), Nuno Tomás, Petteri Pennanen, Ville Saxman (115.Igors Tarasovs), Bismark Adjei-Boateng, Ilmari Niskanen, Urho Nissilä, Saku Savolainen (115.Usman Sale), Rangel (87.Aniekpeno Udoh). Trainer: Arne Erlandsen (Norway).
Slovan Bratislava: Dominik Greif, Lukás Pauschek, Kenan Bajric, Vernon De Marco, Myenty Abena, Ibrahim Rabiu (69.Nono Delgado), Dávid Holman (103.Dejan Drazic), Joeri de Kamps, Erik Daniel (69.Aleksandar Cavric), Rafael Ratão, Zan Medved (114.Alen Ozbolt). Trainer: Darko Milanic (Slovenia).
Goals: 111' Zan Medved 0-2, 120' Aniekpeno Udoh 1-1.
Penalties: Petteri Pennanen 1-0, Vernon De Marco 1-1, Aniekpeno Udoh 2-1, Alen Ozbolt 2-2, Ilmari Niskanen (missed), Joeri de Kamps 2-3, Nuno Tomás 3-3, Rafael Ratão (missed), Bismark Adjei-Boateng 4-3, Nono Delgado (missed).

17.09.2020; Tele2 Arena, Stockholm
Referee: Stéphanie Frappart (France)
DJURGÅRDENS IF STOCKHOLM – Europa FC 2-1(1-0)
Djurgårdens IF: Per Bråtveit, Elliot Käck, Jacob Une-Larsson, Aslak Witry, Haris Radetinac (84.Jonathan Ring), Magnus Eriksson, Fredrik Ulvestad, Jesper Karlström, Curtis Edwards (64.Jonathan Augustinsson), Karl Holmberg, Edward Chilufya (72.Emir Kujovic). Trainer: Kim Bergstrand.
Europa FC: Javi Muñoz, Olmo González, Ethan Jolley, Jayce Olivero, Álex Quillo [sent off 62], Polaco (85.Mitchell Gibson), Juampe Rico (79.Michael Yome), Liam Walker, Marco Rosa (36.Kwadwo Poku), Ale Carrascal, Adrián Gallardo. Trainer: Rafael Escobar Obrero (Spain).
Goals: 42' Curtis Edwards 1-0, 57' Adrián Gallardo 1-1, 69' Fredrik Ulvestad 2-1 (penalty).

17.09.2020; „Vazgen Sargsyan" Hanrapetakan Stadium, Yerevan
Referee: Enea Jorgji (Albania)
FC ARARAT-ARMENIA YEREVAN – CS Fola Esch 4-3(1-1,3-3)
FC Ararat-Armenia: Stefan Cupic, Alemão, Sergiy Vakulenko, Ângelo Meneses, Alex Christian Júnior [sent off 43], Yoan Gouffran (84.Louis Ogana), Kódjo Alphonse (70.Sargis Shahinyan), Furdjel Narsingh, Yusuf Otubanjo (60.Mailson), Zakaria Sanogo, Jeisson Martínez (96.Armen Ambartsumyan). Trainer: David Campaña.
CS Fola Esch: Thomas Hym, Julien Klein, Jean Sylvio Ouassiero, Cédric Sacras, Rodrigues Dikaba, Bruno Freire (84.Tiago Semedo Monteiro), Diogo Pimentel [sent off 90], Stefano Bensi (87.Billy Bernard), Gilson Delgado, Jules Diallo (70.Achraf Drif), Zachary Hadji (117.Guillaume Mura). Trainer: Sébastian Grandjean.
Goals: 16' Jeisson Martínez 1-0, 19' Diogo Pimentel 1-1, 56' Stefano Bensi 1-2 (penalty), 81' Zachary Hadji 1-3, 90+1', 90+4' Mailson 2-3 (penalty), 3-3 (penalty), 113' Sergiy Vakulenko 4-3.

17.09.2020; A. Le Coq Arena, Tallinn
Referee: Sigurd Smehus Kringstad (Norway)
FC FLORA TALLINN – KR Reykjavík 2-1(2-0)
Flora Tallinn: Matvei Igonen, Märten Kuusk, Henrik Pürg, Marco Lukka, Michael Lilander, Konstantin Vassiljev, Martin Miller (46.Markus Soomets), Vladislavs Kreida, Rauno Alliku (74.Frank Liivak), Rauno Sappinen (81.Mark Lepik), Vlasiy Sinyavskiy. Trainer: Jürgen Henn.
KR Reykjavík: Beitir Ólafsson, Arnór Adalsteinsson, Kristinn Jónsson, Finnur Tómas Pálmason (66.Óskar Hauksson), Pálmi Pálmason, Finnur Margeirsson (6.Pablo Punyed), Atli Sigurjónsson, Stefán Árni Geirsson, Kennie Chopart, Kristján Finnbogason, Ægir Jónasson [sent off 58]. Trainer: Rúnar Kristinsson.
Goals: 7' Rauno Sappinen 1-0, 37' Michael Lilander 2-0, 74' Kristján Finnbogason 2-1.

17.09.2020; Racecourse Ground, Wrexham
Referee: Alain Durieux (Luxembourg)
Connah's Quay Nomads FC – FC DINAMO TBILISI 0-1(0-0)
Connah's Quay Nomads: Lewis Brass, John Disney, Daniel Davies, Kris Owens, Callum Roberts, Priestley Farquharson, Aeron Edwards, Jay Owen, Declan Poole, Sameron Dool, Jamie Insall (87.Aron Williams). Trainer: Andy Morrison.
Dinamo Tbilisi: Roin Kvaskhvadze, Giorgi Kimadze, Nodar Iashvili, Davit Kobouri, Simon Ghegnon, Giorgi Papava, Nodar Kavtaradze (90+5.Rodney Klooster), Bakar Kardava, Giorgi Zaria (80.Tornike Kapanadze), Giorgi Gabedava, Filip Orsula (59.José Vitor Pernambuco). Trainer: Francisco Javier Muñoz Llompart (Spain).
Goal: 90+7' Giorgi Gabedava 0-1 (penalty).

17.09.2020; Estadi Comunal d'Andorra la Vella, Andorra la Vella
Referee: Viktor Shimusik (Belarus)
Inter Club d'Escaldes – DUNDALK FC 0-1(0-1)
Inter Club d'Escaldes: Josep Gómes, Ildefons Lima, Federico Bessone, Jordi Rubio (86.Óscar Reyes), Emili García, Raul Feher, Marc Pujol, Albert Reyes, Sergi Moreno (82.Jordi Roca), Genis Soldevila, Jordi Betriu (78.Bruninho). Trainer: Adolfo Baines.
Dundalk FC: Gary Rogers, Brian Gartland, Andrew Boyle [*sent off 58*], Sean Hoare, Darragh Leahy, Chris Shields, Sean Murray (70.John Mountney), Gregory Sloggett, Stefan Colovic (60.Sean Gannon), David McMillan (71.Patrick Hoban), Michael Duffy. Trainer: Shane Keegan.
Goal: 14' David McMillan 0-1.

17.09.2020; Windsor Park, Belfast
Referee: David Munro (Scotland)
Linfield FC Belfast – FLORIANA FC 0-1(0-1)
Linfield FC: Christopher Johns, Matthew Clarke (62.Andrew Waterworth), Niall Quinn, Ethan Boyle, Jamie Mulgrew, Jimmy Callacher, Bastien Héry (78.Daniel Kearns), Stephen Fallon, Navid Nasseri (61.Christy Manzinga), Shayne Lavery, Ross Larkin [*sent off 74*]. Trainer: David Healy.
Floriana FC: Ini Akpan, Enzo Ruiz, Jurgen Pisani, Ryan Camenzuli, Diego Venancio Silva, Nicola Leone, Brandon Paiber (61.Ulises Arias, 86.Moustapha Beye), Matías García, Kristian Keqi (83.Flávio Carioca), Tiago Adan, Marcelo Dias. Trainer: Vincenzo Potenza (Italy).
Goal: 10' Matías Dias 0-1.

17.09.2020; Nacionalna Arena "Toše Proeski", Skopje
Referee: Andy Madley (England)
FK Sileks Kratovo – KF DRITA GJILAN 0-2(0-0)
Sileks Kratovo: Daniel Bozhinovski, Srdjan Draskovic, Hristijan Grozdanoski [*sent off 78*], Denis Ristov (81.Bojan Spirkoski), Angelce Timovski, Burhan Mustafov, Dejan Tanturovski, Viktor Serafimovski, Daniel Karcheski, Pepi Gorgiev (55.Stefan Djuric), Ivan Ivanovski (46.Kristijan Kostovski). Trainer: Goran Simov.
Drita Gjilan: Faton Maloku, Ardijan Cuculi, Fidan Gërbeshi, Ardian Limani, Ilir Blakçori, Erjon Vucaj (76.Bujar Shabani), Xhevdet Shabani (67.Vladica Brdarovski), Hamdi Namani, Almir Ajzeraj, Astrit Fazliu (88.Ergyn Ahmeti), Betim Haxhimusa. Trainer: Ardijan Nuhiji.
Goals: 48' Fidan Gërbeshi 0-1 (penalty), 81' Ardian Limani 0-2.

17.09.2020; Skonto stadions, Rīga
Referee: Kári Jóannesarson á Høvdanum (Faroe Islands)
RĪGA FC – SP Tre Fiori Fiorentino 1-0(0-0)
Rīga FC: Roberts Ozols, Elvis Stuglis, Herdi Prenga, Vladimirs Kamess, Ritvars Rugins, Felipe Brisola, Pedrinho (85.Vyacheslav Sharpar), Stefan Panic, Jordan N'Kololo, Vladislavs Fjororovs, Stefan Milosevic (78.Kule Mbombo). Trainer: Oleg Kononov (Russia).
SP Tre Fiori: Aldo Simoncini, Davide Simoncini, Giovanni Bonini, Angelo Gregorio, Luca Angelini (83.Pablo Martini), Paolo Vandi (90+1.Lorenzo Perotto), Pier Figone, Lounseny Kalissa, Nicholas Santoni (79.Durell Bilendo Duma), Joel Apezteguía Hijuelos, Bojan Gjurchinoski. Trainer: Matteo Cecchetti.
Goal: 57' Pedrinho 1-0.

LEAGUE PATH

16.09.2020; Stade Parc des Sports, Differdange
Referee: Mykola Balakin (Ukraine)
FC Progrès Niederkorn – WILLEM II TILBURG 0-5(0-3)
Progrès Niederkorn: Sebastian Flauss, Mathias Jänisch (64.Metin Karayer), Adrien Ferino, Aldin Skenderovic, Yannis Dublin, Yannick Bastos, Kevin Holtz (64.Florik Shala), Christian Silaj, Ryad Habbas (46.Antonio Luisi), Kempes Tekiela, Irvin Latic. Trainer: Roland Vrabec (Germany).
Willem II: Robbin Ruiter, Jordens Peters, Miquel Nelom (62.Derrick Köhn), Freek Heerkens (41.Victor van den Bogert), Sebastian Holmén, Pol Llonch (62.Driess Saddiki), Görkem Saglam, Mike Trésor, Vangelis Pavlidis, Mats Köhlert, Ché Nunnely. Trainer: Adrie Koster.
Goals: 20' Vangelis Pavlidis 0-1, 28' Görkem Saglam 0-2, 34' Vangelis Pavlidis 0-3, 46' Ché Nunnely 0-4, 65' Mike Trésor 0-5.

16.09.2020; Tórsvøllur, Tórshavn
Referee: Ian McNabb (Northern Ireland)
B36 TÓRSHAVN – The New Saints FC 2-2(0-0,1-1); 5-4 on penalties
B36 Tórshavn: Rói Hentze, Alex Mellemgaard, Sonni Nattestad, Eli Nielsen, Árni Frederiksberg (68.Hannes Agnarsson), Benjamin Heinesen, Andrias Eriksen (111.Erling Jacobsen), Michal Przybylski, Magnus Holm Jacobsen (113.Andrass Johansen), Ragnar Samuelsen (86.Stefan Radosavljevic), Sebastian Pingel. Trainer: Jákup á Borg.
The New Saints: Paul Harrison, Keston Davies (30.Ben Clark), Ryan Harrington, Jon Routledge (71.Leo Smith), Daniel Redmond, Ryan Brobbel (77.Adrian Cieslewicz), Ryan Astles, Tom Holland, Jamie Mullan, Dean Ebbe, Louis Robles (116.Greg Draper). Trainer: Scott Ruscoe.
Goals: 47' Michal Przybylski 1-0, 80' Leo Smith 1-1, 112' Dean Ebbe 1-2, 120+2' Stefan Radosavljevic 2-2.
Penalties: Sonni Nattestad 1-0, Paul Harrison 1-1, Alex Mellemgaard 2-1, Adrian Cieslewicz 2-2, Benjamin Heinesen 3-2, Greg Draper 3-3, Michal Przybylski (missed), Leo Smith 3-4, Stefan Radosavljevic 4-4, Dean Ebbe (missed), Sebastian Pingel 5-4, Daniel Redmond (missed).

16.09.2020; Tele2 Arena, Stockholm
Referee: Sascha Stegemann (Germany)
Hammarby IF Stockholm – KKS LECH POZNAŃ 0-3(0-0)
Hammarby IF: David Ousted, David Fällman (46.Richárd Magyar), Mads Fenger, Mohanad Jeahze, Kalle Björklund, Serge-Junior Martinsson-Ngouali, Abdul Khalili, Jeppe Andersen [*sent off 63*], Paulinho (77.Alexander Kacaniklic), Aron Jóhannsson, Gustav Ludwigson. Trainer: Stefan Billborn.
Lech Poznań: Filip Bednarek, Lubomir Satka, Alan Czerwinski, Djordje Crnomarkovic, Tymoteusz Puchacz, Jan Sýkora (73.Michal Skóras), Pedro Tiba (84.Filip Marchwinski), Dani Ramírez, Jakub Moder, Jacub Kaminski, Mikael Ishak (90+1.Mohamad Awaed). Trainer: Dariusz Zuraw. Goals: 56' Pedro Tiba 0-1, 89' Jakub Kaminski 0-2, 90+3' Filip Marchwinski 0-3.

17.09.2020; Stadion „Qajimuqan Muñaytpasov", Shymkent
Referee: Jens Maae (Denmark)
FC Kaysar Kyzylorda – APOEL FC NICOSIA 1-4(1-2)
Kaysar Kyzylorda: Aleksandr Zarutskiy, Ilyas Amirseitov (89.Dinmukhamed Kashken), Ivan Graf, Aleksandr Marochkin, Bagdat Kairov, Clarence Bitang, Ashkat Tagybergen (85.Mark Gurman), Duman Narzildaev (58.Aleksandar Stanisavljevic), Aleksandar Kolev, Elguja Lobjanidze, Maksim Fedin. Trainer: Stoicho Mladenov.
APOEL Nicosia: Miguel Silva, Emilio N'Sue, Christos Wheeler, Christos Shelis, Rafael Santos, Tomás De Vincenti, Ghayas Zahid, Anuar Tuhami, Ben Sahar (58.Moussa Al Taamari), Viktor Klonaridis (46.Omer Atzili), Dieumerci Ndongala (85.Atdhe Nuhiu). Trainer: Marinos Ouzounidis.
Goals: 6' Elguja Lobjanidze 1-0, 15' Tomás De Vincenti 1-1, 25' Anuar Tuhami 1-2, 48' Omer Atzili 1-3, 90+4' Tomás De Vincenti 1-4.

17.09.2020; Olimpiskā centra Ventspils Stadionā, Ventspils
Referee: Paul McLaughlin (Republic of Ireland)
FK Ventspils – ROSENBORG BK TRONDHEIM 1-5(1-3)
FK Ventspils: Dele Alampasu, Abdoul Mamah, Giorgi Rekhviashvili, Andriy Sakhnevich, Giorgi Mchedlishvili, Dmitrijs Litvinskis [*sent off 63*], Giorgi Eristavi (53.Dumte Pyagbara), Daniils Ulimbasevs, Lucas Villela, Kaspars Svārups (75.Kazeem Ojo Aderounmu), Evgeny Kozlov (81.Kaspars Kokins). Trainer: Viorel Frunză (Moldova).
Rosenborg: André Hansen, Even Hovland, Vegar Hedenstad, Gustav Valsvik, Erlend Reitan, Per Skjelbred, Anders Konradsen (71.Gjermund Åsen), Kristoffer Zachariassen, Dino Islamovic (90.Torgeir Børven), Samuel Adegbenro (58.Emil Ceïde), Carl Holse. Trainer: Åge Hareide.
Goals: 5' Evgeny Kozlov 1-0, 14' Dino Islamovic 1-1 (penalty), 37' Anders Konradsen 1-2, 45+2' Dino Islamovic 1-3, 64' Carl Holse 1-4, 71' Kristoffer Zachariassen 1-5.

17.09.2020; Trening centar „Petar Miloševski", Skopje
Referee: João Pedro da Silva Pinheiro (Portugal)
KF Renova Džepčište – HNK HAJDUK SPLIT 0-1(0-1)
KF Renova: Hadis Velii, Nenad Miskovski, Xhelil Abdulla, Bashkim Velija, Arbër Shala, Argjent Gafuri, Saimir Fetai (46.Suhejlj Muharem), Burim Sadiki (72.Artan Veliu), Emran Ramadani (77.Alen Jasaroski), Alush Gavazaj, Shefit Shefiti. Trainer: Bujar Islami.
Hajduk Split: Josip Posavec, Darko Todorovic, David Colina, Nihad Mujakic, Mario Vuskovic, Ádám Gyurcsó (65.Ivan Dolcek), Mijo Caktas, Stanko Juric, Darko Nejasmic (77.Jani Atanasov), Jairo (82.Marin Jakolis), Dimitrios Diamantakos. Trainer: Hari Vukas.
Goal: 4' Mijo Caktas 0-1.

17.09.2020; Stadiumi"Niko Dovana", Durrës
Referee: Willy Delajod (France)
KF Teuta Durrës – GRANADA CF 0-4(0-3)
Teuta Durrës: Stivi Frashëri, Renato Arapi, Rustem Hoxha, Alexandros Kouros, Fabjan Beqja [sent off 80], Emiljano Vila, Asion Daja (46.Ildi Gruda), Albano Aleksi, Florent Avdyli (56.Rubin Hebaj), Blerim Krasniqi (68.Ledjo Beqja), Lorenco Vila. Trainer: Eduard Martini.
Granada CF: Rui Silva, Víctor Díaz, Germán Sánchez, Domingos Duarte (46.Jesús Vallejo), Carlos Neva, Montoro (58.Fede Vico), Maxime Gonalons, Antonio Puertas, Kenedy, Yangel Herrera, Soldado (46.Jorge Molina). Trainer: Diego Martínez Penas.
Goals: 5' Soldado 0-1, 10' Kenedy 0-2, 31', 46' Yangel Herrera 0-3, 0-4.

17.09.2020; Stadionul Municipal, Botoşani
Referee: Mohammed Al-Hakim (Sweden)
FC Botoşani – KF SHKËNDIJA TETOVO 0-1(0-1)
FC Botoşani: Eduard Pap, Alexandru Tiganasu, Alin Seroni, Denis Harut, Andrei Chindris, David Babunski (79.Mihai Roman), Eduard Florescu (71.Andrei Patache), Jonathan Rodriguez, Reagy Ofosu, Stefan Ashkovski (46') Hamidou Keyta, Marko Dugandzic. Trainer: Marius Croitoru.
KF Shkëndija: Kostadin Zahov, Mevlan Murati, Antonio Pavic, Egzon Bejtulai, Ján Krivák, Armend Alimi [sent off 67], Bruno Dita, Valon Ahmedi, Ennur Totre (75.Arbin Zejnullai), Besart Ibraimi (88.Zija Merdzhani), Ljupco Doriev (70.Valmir Nafiu). Trainer: Ernest Gjoka.
Goal: 2' Besart Ibraimi 0-1.

17.09.2020; Bakı Olimpiya Stadionu, Bakı
Referee: Kevin Clancy (Scotland)
Neftçi PFK Bakı – GALATASARAY SK ISTANBUL 1-3(0-1)
Neftçi: Aqil Mammadov, Vojislav Stankovic, Mamadou Mbodj, Anton Krivotsyuk, Omar Buludov, Emin Makhmudov, Namiq Alasgarov (65.Thallyson), Saman Nariman Jahan (70.Sabir Bougrine), Mamadou Kane, Yusuf Lawal, Prince Ibara (76.Mirabdulla Abbasov). Trainer: Fuzuli Mammadov.
Galatasaray: Fatih Öztürk, Ömer Bayram, Martin Linnes, Marcão Teixeira, Marcelo Saracchi, Christian Luyindama Nekadio, Younès Belhanda (46.Sofiane Féghouli), Taylan Antalyali, Emre Kilinç (68.Arda Turan), Ryan Babel (83.Jimmy Durmaz), Mbaye Diagne. Trainer: Fatih Terim.
Goals: 19' Mbaye Diagne 0-1, 46' Mamadou Mbodj 1-1, 48' Christian Luyindama Nekadio 1-2, 63' Mbaye Diagne 1-3.

17.09.2020; LFF stadionas, Vilnius
Referee: Espen Eskås (Norway)
FK Riteriai Vilnius – FC SLOVAN LIBEREC 1-5(0-2)
FK Riteriai: Tadas Simaitis, Valdemaras Borovskis (83.Dovydas Virksas), Ricardas Sveikauskas, Dominykas Barauskas, Ángel Lezama, Deividas Malzinskas, Mindaugas Grīgaravicius, Tomas Dombrauskis (62.Rokas Filipavicius), Lajo Traore (40.Matas Ramanauskas), Donatas Kazlauskas, Gytis Paulauskas. Trainer: Tommi Petteri Pikkarainen (Finland).
Slovan Liberec: Filip Nguyen, Taras Kacharaba, Jan Mikula, Martin Koscelník, Mohamed Tijani, Jhon Mosquera, Jakub Hromada (80.Matej Chalus), Jakub Pesek (88.Jan Matousek), Kamso Mara, Michal Beran (63.Michael Rabusic), Abdulla Yusuf Helal. Trainer: Pavel Hoftych.
Goals: 12' Kamso Mara 0-1 (penalty), 20' Jakub Hromada 0-2, 61' Ángel Lezama 1-2, 84' Michael Rabusci 1-3, 89' Abdulla Yusuf Helal 1-4 (penalty), 90+3' Jan Matousek 1-5.

17.09.2020; Stadion Stožice, Ljubljana
Referee: Ricardo De Burgos Bengoetxea (Spain)
NK Olimpija Ljubljana – HŠK ZRINJSKI MOSTAR 2-3(1-0,2-2)
Olimpija Ljubljana: Ziga Frelih, Uros Korun, Miral Samardzic, Matic Fink, Enrik Ostrc (56.Michael Pavlovic), Nik Kapun (105.Gal Kurez), Timi Elsnik, Angel Lyaskov (90.Drazen Bagaric), Mihail Caimacov, Andrés Vombergar (85.Ante Vukusic), Djordje Ivanovic. Trainer: Dino Skender.
Zrinjski Mostar: Ivan Brkic, Mario Ticinovic (78.Josip Corluka), Tomislav Barbaric, Pero Stojkic (73.Luis Ibáñez), Slobodan Jakovljevic, Ognjen Todorovic, Dinko Trebotic (66.Damir Zlomislic), Milos Filipovic, Ivan Enin, Nemanja Bilbija, Josip Ivancic (96.Anes Masic). Trainer: Mladen Zizovic.
Goals: 19' Djordje Ivanovic 1-0, 51' Nemanja Bilbija 1-1, 81' Andrés Vombergar 2-1, 84' Nemanja Bilbija 2-2, 92' Josip Ivancic 2-3.

17.09.2020; Victoria Stadium, Gibraltar
Referee: Iwan Arwel Griffith (Wales)
Lincoln Red Imps FC – RANGERS FC GLASGOW 0-5(0-2)
Lincoln Red Imps: Kyle Goldwin, Scott Wiseman (56.Diego Gámez), Bernardo Lopes, Roy Chipolina, Ethan Britto, Mustapha Yahaya, Jack Sergeant (68.Jesús Toscano), Graeme Torilla, Anthony Hernandez (52.Tjay De Barr), Lee Casciaro, Kike Gómez. Trainer: William.
Rangers FC: Allan McGregor, James Tavernier (46.Alfredo Morelos), Connor Goldson, Borna Barisic, George Edmundson, Scott Arfield, Glen Kamara, Ianis Hagi, Greg Stewart, Kemar Roofe (42.Nathan Patterson), Cedric Itten (66'Jermain Defoe). Trainer: Steven George Gerrard (England).
Goals: 21' James Tavernier 0-1, 45+4' Connor Goldson 0-2, 67' Alfredo Morelos 0-3, 84' Jermain Defoe 0-4, 88' Alfredo Morelos 0-5.

17.09.2020; Stadion Lokomotiv, Plovdiv
Referee: Harm Osmers (Germany)
PFC Lokomotiv Plovdiv – TOTTENHAM HOTSPUR FC LONDON 1-2(0-0)
Lokomotiv Plovdiv: Martin Lukov, Milos Petrovic, Dinis Almeida [sent off 78], Lucas Masoero, Momchil Tsvetanov, Parvizchon Umaraev (68.Georgi Minchev), Petar Vitanov (81.Filip Mihaljevic), Lucas Salinas, Dimitar Iliev, Birsent Karagaren [sent off 79], Ante Aralica (68.Christian Ilic). Trainer: Bruno Akrapovic (Bosnia and Herzegovina).
Tottenham Hotspur: Hugo Lloris, Matt Doherty, Ben Davies, Davinson Sánchez (72.Lucas Moura), Moussa Sissoko (61.Tanguy NDombèlé), Pierre-Emile Højbjerg, Eric Dier, Giovani Lo Celso, Son Heung-Min, Harry Kane, Steven Bergwijn (70.Érik Lamela). Trainer: José Mário dos Santos Félix Mourinho (Portugal).
Goals: 71' Georgi Minchev 1-0, 80' Harry Kane 1-1 (penalty), 84' Tanguy NDombèlé 1-2.

17.09.2020; Ullevi Stadion, Göteborg
Referee: Guillermo Cuadra Fernández (Spain)
IFK Göteborg – FC KØBENHAVN 1-2(0-0)
IFK Göteborg: Giannis Anestis, Mattias Bjärsmyr, André Calisir, Alexander Jallow (87.Hosam Aiesh), Yahya Kalley (69.Emil Holm), Jakob Johansson, Pontus Wernbloom, Tobias Sana, Alexander Farnerud (65.Sargon Abraham), August Erlingmark, Alhassan Yusuf. Trainer: Roland Nilsson.
FC København: Kalle Johnsson, Pierre Bengtsson, Andreas Bjelland (78.Robert Mudrazija), Guillermo Varela, Victor Nelsson, Rasmus Falk, Zeca, Viktor Fischer (78.Mikkel Kaufmann), Jens Stage (78.Pep Biel Mas), Kamil Wilczek, Jonas Wind. Trainer: Ståle Solbakken (Norway).
Goals: 73' Tobias Sana 1-0, 82' Robert Mudrazija 1-1, 85' Jonas Wind 1-2.

17.09.2020; Aspmyra Stadion, Bodø
Referee: Peter Královic (Slovakia)
FK BODØ/GLIMT – FK Žalgiris Vilnius 3-1(2-1)
FK Bodø/Glimt: Nikita Haikin, Marius Høibråten, Marius Lode, Fredrik Bjørkan, Ulrik Saltnes, Morten Konradsen (72.Alfons Sampsted), Patrick Berg, Jens Hauge, Philip Zinckernagel, Sondre Fet (78.Ola Solbakken), Victor Boniface (89.Ole Amund Sveen). Trainer: Kjetil Knutsen.
FK Žalgiris: Martin Berkovec, Saulius Mikoliūnas, Donovan Slijngard, Ivan Tatomirovic, Nemanja Ljubisavljevic, Hugo Vidémont, Domantas Simkus (84.Mantas Kuklys), Modestas Vorobjovas, Andrija Kaludjerovic, Liviu Antal, Francis Kyeremeh (68.Marko Karamarko). Trainer: Aleksei Baga.
Goals: 20' Philip Zinckernagel 1-0, 26' Liviu Antal 1-1, 32' Victor Boniface 2-1, 81' Fredrik Bjørkan 3-1.

17.09.2020; Stadionul Zimbru, Chişinău
Referee: Juri Frischer (Estonia)
FC Sfântul Gheorghe – FK PARTIZAN BEOGRAD 0-1(0-0,0-0)
FC Sfântul Gheorghe: Nicolae Calancea, Andrey Novicov (90.Valerii Stepanenko), Serghei Svinarenko, Eugeniu Slivca, Vitalie Plamadeala, Petru Ojog, Sidy Sagna, Yevhen Smirnov, Dimitrii Mandrîcenco, Rienat Mochulyak (86.Mihail Ghecev), Roman Volkov (57.Sergiu Istrati). Trainer: Sergiu Cebotari.
Partizan Beograd: Vladimir Stojkovic, Aleksandar Miljkovic, Uros Vitas, Bojan Ostojic, Slobodan Urosevic, Bibras Natcho, Seydouba Soumah (110.Aleksandar Scekic), Sasa Zdjelar, Takuma Asano (90.Aleksandar Lutovac), Umar Sadiq (78.Bojan Matic), Filip Stevanovic (63.Lazar Markovic). Trainer: Aleksandar Stanojevic.
Goal: 104' Bibras Natcho 0-1 (penalty).

17.09.2020; Stadioni „Mikheil Meskhi", Tbilisi
Referee: Karim Abed (France)
FC LOKOMOTIVI TBILISI – FK Dinamo Moskva 2-1(0-0)
Lokomotivi Tbilisi: Giorgi Mamardashvili, Nika Sandokhadze, Giorgi Gabadze, Aleksandre Gureshidze, Daviti Ubilava, Temur Shonia, Davit Samurkasovi (62.Tornike Dzebniauri), Tornike Kirkitadze (83.Aleksandr Kobakhidze), Beka Dartsmelia, Imran Oulad Omar (65.Mamia Gavashelushvili), Irakli Sikharulidze. Trainer: Giorgi Chiabrishvili.
Dinamo Moskva: Anton Shunin, Sergey Parshivlyuk, Ivan Ordets, Dmitriy Skopintsev (46.Grigori Morozov), Roman Evgenjev, Charles Kaboré, Maximilian Philipp (69.Sylvester Igboun), Daniil Fomin, Sebastian Szymanski, Clinton N'Jie (61.Daniil Lesovoy), Nikolay Komlichenko. Trainer: Kirill Novikov.
Goals: 54' Irakli Sikharulidze 1-0, 76' Mamia Gavashelishvili 2-0, 90' Nikolay Komlichenko 2-1 (penalty).

17.09.2020; Elbasan Arena, Elbasan
Referee: Jochem Kamphuis (Netherlands)
KF Laçi – HAPOEL BE'ER SHEVA FC 1-2(0-0)
KF Laçi: Alen Sherri, Aleksandar Ignjatovic, Rudolf Turkaj, Adolf Selmani, Ardit Deliu [sent off 86], Regi Lushkja, Juljan Shehu (46.Endrit Marku), Albion Marku (46.Donald Rapo), Teco, Kyrian Nwabueze (89.Renato Malota), Redon Xhixha. Trainer: Armando Cungu.
Hapoel Be'er Sheva: Ohad Levita, Miguel Vítor, Loai Taha, Sean Goldberg, Elton Acolatse, Or Dadya, Sintayehu Sallalich (74.Rotem Hatuel), Josué, Marwan Kabha, Tomer Yosefi (61.Jhonatan Agudelo), Itamar Shviro (61.Gaëtan Varenne). Trainer: Yossi Abukasis.
Goals: 59' Kyrian Nwabueze 1-0, 90' Jhonatan Agudelo 1-1, 90+3' Gaëtan Varenne 1-2.

17.09.2020; Stádio „Theodoros Vardinogiannis", Heraklion
Referee: Fabio Maresca (Italy)
OFI Heraklion – APOLLON LIMASSOL FC 0-1(0-0)
OFI Heraklion: Boy Waterman, Konstantinos Giannoulis (80.Nikos Korovesis), Nikolaos Marinakis (68.Adil Nabi), Praxitelis Vouros, Vahid Selimovic, Abul Rahman Oues, Miguel Mellado, Paschalis Staikos (68.Nazareno Solis), Juan Neira, Adrián Sardinero, João Figueiredo. Trainer: Georgios Simos.
Apollon Limassol: Demetris Demetriou, Valentin Roberge, Attila Szalai, Nicolas Diguiny, Héctor Yuste, Florentin Matei (46.Charlison Benschop), Diego Aguirre, Esteban Sachetti, Djordje Denic, João Pedro (46.Ioannis Pittas), Bagaliy Dabo (79.Giannis Gianniotas). Trainer: Sofronis Avgousti.
Goal: 50' Attila Szalai 0-1.

17.09.2020; Tallaght Stadium, Dublin
Referee: Ádám Farkas (Hungary)
Shamrock Rovers FC – AC MILAN 0-2(0-1)
Shamrock Rovers: Alan Mannus, Joey O'Brien, Roberto Lopes, Lee Grace, Ronan Finn, Aaron McEneff, Jack Byrne, Gary O'Neill (70.Dylan Watts), Neil Farrugia (83.Sean Kavanagh), Aaron Greene (88.Dean Williams), Graham Burke. Trainer: Stephen Bradley.
AC Milan: Gianluigi Donnarumma, Simon Kjær, Davide Calabria, Theo Hernández, Matteo Gabbia, Hakan Çalhanoglu (84.Brahim Díaz), Samu Castillejo, Franck Kessié, Ismaël Bennacar (84.Sandro Tonali), Alexis Saelemaekers (74.Rade Krunic), Zlatan Ibrahimovic. Trainer: Stefano Pioli.
Goals: 23' Zlatan Ibrahimovic 0-1, 67' Hakan Çalhanoglu 0-2.

17.09.2020; Stade „Maurice Dufrasne", Liège
Referee: Trustin Farrugia Cann (Malta)
R STANDARD LIÈGE – Bala Town FC 2-0(2-0)
Standard Liège: Arnaud Bodart, Kostas Laifis, Nicolas Gavory, Collins Fai, Zinho Vanheusden, Mehdi Carcela-González, Gojko Cimirot (72.Merveille Bopé Bokadi), Eden Shamir, Selim Amallah (67.Jackson Muleka), Felipe Avenatti (84.Obbi Oularé), Michel Balikwisha. Trainer: Philippe Montanier (France).
Bala Town FC: Alex Ramsay, Antony Kay (81.Anthony Stephens), Nathan Peate, Sean Smith, Jonathan Spittle, Steven Leslie (81.Henry Jones), Chris Venables, Will Evans, Oliver Shannon, Lassana Mendes, Raul Correia (57.Kieran Smith). Trainer: Colin Caton.
Goals: 19' Felipe Avenatti 1-0 (penalty), 34' Selim Amallah 2-0.

17.09.2020; Stadion Bâlgarska Armija, Sofia
Referee: Horaţiu Feşnic (Romania)
PFC CSKA SOFIA – FC BATE Borisov 2-0(1-0)
CSKA Sofia: Busatto, Jurgen Mattheij, Plamen Galabov, Geferson, Bradley Mazikou, Valentin Antov, Younousse Sankharé (68.Tiago Rodrigues), Amos Youga, Georgi Yomov (73.Jules Keita), Ali Sowe, Henrique (79.Graham Carey). Trainer: Stamen Belchev.
BATE Borisov: Denis Shcherbitskiy, Egor Filipenko, Bojan Nastic, Aleksander Filipovic, Jakov Filipovic, Pavel Nekhaychik, Dmitriy Baga (77.Hervaine Moukam), Evgeni Yablonski (69.Aleksandr Volodko), Willum Thór Willumsson, Nemanja Milic (80.Bojan Dubajic), Maksim Skavysh. Trainer: Kirill Alshevskiy.
Goals: 44' Ali Sowe 1-0, 90+5' Graham Carey 2-0.

17.09.2020; MFA Centenary Stadium, Ta'Qali
Referee: Ivaylo Stoyanov (Bulgaria)
Hibernians FC Paola - FEHÉRVÁR FC SZÉKESFEHÉRVÁR 0-1(0-0)
Hibernians FC: Matthew Calleja Cremona, Leandro Almeida, Andrei Agius, Ferdinando Apap, Zachary Grech (64.Rundell Winchester), Gabriel Izquier, Jake Grech, Wilkson (74.Edafe Uzeh), Shola Shodiya [sent off 90+3], Jurgen Degabriele, Ayrton Attard (83.Dustan Vella). Trainer: Stefano Sanderra.
Fehérvár FC: Ádám Kovácsik, Attila Fiola, Loïc Négo, Stopira, Visar Musliu, Bendegúz Bolla, Ivan Petryak (83.Evandro), Boban Nikolov, Lyes Houri, Alef (51.Máté Pátkai), Budu Zivzivadze (88.Nemanja Nikolic). Trainer: Gábor Márton.
Goals: 61' Boban Nikolov 0-1.

17.09.2020; „Sammy Ofer" Stadium, Haifa
Referee: Mads-Kristoffer Kristoffersen (Denmark)
MACCABI HAIFA FC – FC Kairat Almaty 2-1(1-1)
Maccabi Haifa: Josh Cohen, Ernest Mabouka, Sun Menachem, Ayed Habashi, Ofri Arad, Tjaronn Chery, Yuval Ashkenazi (55.Dolev Haziza), Neta Lavi, Mohammad Abu Fani, Nikita Rukavytsya (84.José Rodríguez), Yanic Wildschut (74.Bogdan Planic). Trainer: Barak Bakhar.
Kairat: Stas Pokatilov, Gafurzhan Suyumbayev, Dino Mikanovic, Rade Dugalic, Nuraly Alip, Nebojsa Kosovic, Jacek Góralski, Aybol Abiken (87.Yerkebulan Tungyshbayev), Gulzhygit Alykulov (81.Konrad Wrzesinski), Vágner Love, Abat Aymbetov (64.Aderinsola Eseola). Trainer: Aleksey Shpilevskiy (Belarus).
Goals: 31' Yuval Ashkenazi 1-0, 45+1' Vágner Love 1-1, 72' Nikita Rukavytsya 2-1.

17.09.2020; Stadion Miejski, Gliwice
Referee: Erik Lambrechts (Belgium)
GKS PIAST GLIWICE – TSV Hartberg 3-2(1-1)
Piast Gliwice: Frantisek Plach, Piotr Malarczyk (89.Bartosz Rymaniak), Mikkel Kirkeskov, Jakub Czerwinski, Tomás Huk, Martin Konczkowski, Tomasz Jodlowiec, Krisztófer Vida (78.Dominik Steczyk), Patryk Lipski, Patryk Sokolowski, Piotr Parzyszek (55.Michal Zyro). Trainer: Waldemar Fornalik.
TSV Hartberg: Rene Swete, Andreas Lienhart (73.Stefan Gölles), Christian Klem, Manfred Gollner (67.Julius Ertlthaler), Thomas Rotter, Tobias Kainz, Felix Luckeneder, Lukas Ried, Samson Tijani (89.Michael Huber), Dario Tadic, Rajko Rep. Trainer: Markus Schopp.
Goals: 10' Martin Konczkowski 1-0, 33' Tobias Kainz 1-1, 62' Patryk Sokolowski 2-1, 75' Lukas Ried 2-2, 84' Michal Zyro 3-2.

17.09.2020; Stádio " Kleanthis Vikelidis", Thessaloníki
Referee: Lionel Tschudi (Switzerland)
Aris Thessaloníki – FK KOLOS KOVALIVKA 1-2(0-0)
Aris Thessaloníki: Julián Cuesta, Lindsay Rose, Toni Datkovic, Cristian Ganea (69.Dimitrios Manos), Bruno Gama, Javier Matilla, Facundo Bertoglio, Ioannis Fetfatzidis, Lucas Sasha (78.Daniel Mancini), James Jeggo, Cristian López. Trainer: Michael Oenning (Germany).
Kolos Kovalivka: Evgen Volynets, Vitaly Gavrish, Evgen Novak, Kyrylo Petrov, Oleksy Zozulya (51.Yevgeniy Morozko), Vladislav Emets, Evgeniy Zadoya, Andriy Bogdanov, Yevgeniy Smyrnyi (88.Denys Kostyshyn), Vladimir Lisenko (64.Yevhen Seleznyov), Denys Antyukh. Trainer: Ruslan Kostyshyn.
Goals: 47' Evgen Novak 0-1, 55' Bruno Gama 1-1, 62' Denys Antyukh 1-2.

17.09.2020; Gradski Stadion, Banja Luka
Referee: Peter Kjærsgaard-Andersen (Denmark)
FK Borac Banja Luka – RIO AVE FC 0-2(-0)
Borac Banja Luka: Bojan Pavlovic, Marko Jovanovic, Djordje Cosic, Djordje Milojevic, Stojan Vranjes, Goran Zakaric, Sinisa Dujakovic (90+5.Boban Georgiev), Marko Brtan (90+1.Aleksandar Vojinovic), Almedin Dino Ziljkic, Vladan Danilovic, Jovo Lukic (87.Sasa Kajkut). Trainer: Vlado Jagodic.
Rio Ave FC: Pawel Kieszek, Ivo Pinto, Aderllan Santos, Matheus Reis, Toni Borevkovic, Tarantini, Filipe Augusto, Francisco "Chico" Geraldes (75.Gelson Dala), Bruno Moreira (90+3.Nikola Jambor), Carlos Mané, Lucas Piazón (90+5.Gabrielzinho). Trainer: Mário Fernando Magalhães da Silva.
Goals: 90' Tarantini 0-1, 90+6' Nikola Jambor 0-2.

17.09.2020; Mestni Stadion Fazanerija, Murska Soboto
Referee: Giorgi Kruashvili (Georgia)
NŠ MURA MURSKA SOBOTA – AGF Aarhus 3-0(1-0)
NŠ Mura: Matko Obradovic, Ziga Kous, Klemen Sturm, Jan Gorenc, Zan Karniczik, Nino Kouter (90+2.Amadej Marosa), Alen Kozar, Luka Bobicanec (82.Dragan Lovric), Kevin Zizek, Andrija Filipovic (69.Tomi Horvat), Kai Cipot. Trainer: Ante Simundza.
Aarhus: William Eskelinen, Niklas Backman, Casper Højer Nielsen, Alexander Munksgaard, Frederik Tingager, Nikolai Poulsen, Patrick Olsen, Bror Blume (73.Nicklas Helenius), Jón Dagur Thorsteinsson (76.Albert Erlykke), Gift Links (30.Søren Tengstedt), Patrick Mortensen. Trainer: David Nielsen.
Goals: 37' Jan Gorenc 1-0, 72' Kevin Zizek 2-0, 90+5' Amadej Marosa 3-0.

17.09.2020; SR-Bank Arena, Stavanger
Referee: Filip Glova (Slovakia)
Viking FK Stavanger – ABERDEEN FC 0-2(0-1)
Viking: Iven Austbø, Rolf Vikstøl, Viljar Vevatne (76.Sondre Bjørshol), Alex Andrésson (76.Tommy Høiland), Henrik Heggheim, Fredrik Torsteinbø, Zymer Bytyqi, Joe Bell, Veton Berisha, Yann-Erik de Lanlay (85.Even Østensen), Yildren Ibrahimaj. Trainer: Bjarne Berntsen.
Aberdeen FC: Joe Lewis, Andrew Considine, Tommie Hoban, Scott McKenna, Jonny Hayes, Marley Watkins (90+1.Curtis Main), Dylan McGeouch (73.Shay Logan), Ryan Hedges, Ross McCrorie, Lewis Ferguson, Scott Wright (72.Funso Ojo). Trainer: Derek McInnes.
Goals: 44' Ross McCrorie 0-1, 78' Ryan Hedges 0-2.

17.09.2020; Stade de Genève, Genève
Referee: Stuart Steven Attwell (England)
Servette FC Genève – STADE DE REIMS 0-1(0-1)
Servette Genève: Jérémy Frick, Anthony Sauthier, Vincent Sasso, Steve Rouiller, Arial Mendy (85.Moussa Diallo), Miroslav Stevanovic, Gaël Ondoua, Timothé Cognat, Varol Tasar (46.Koro Koné), Kastriot Imeri (74.Alex Schalk), Grejohn Kyei. Trainer: Alain Geiger.
Stade de Reims: Predrag Rajkovic, Thomas Foket, Wout Faes, Ghislain Konan, Valon Berisha, Xavier Chavalerin, Dereck Kutesa (65.Kaj Sierhuis), Moreto Cassamá (81.Mathieu Cafaro), Marshall Munetsi, Boulaye Dia (90+2.Arber Zeneli), El Bilal Touré. Trainer: David Guion.
Goal: 4' Valon Berisha 0-1.

17.09.2020; Air Albania Stadium, Tirana
Referee: Duje Strukan (Croatia)
FK Kukësi – VFL WOLFSBURG 0-4(0-2)
FK Kukësi: Entonjo Elezaj, Kenan Horic, Edis Malikji, Erhun Obanor, Besir Demiri, Bruno Telushi, Emiljano Musta (46.Albin Gashi), Eduart Rroca (70.Godberg Cooper), Besar Musolli (60.Zenel Gavazaj), Vesel Limaj, Patrick Eze. Trainer: Skënder Gega.
VfL Wolfsburg: Koen Casteels, Paulo Otávio, Maxence Lacroix, Admir Mehmedi, Josuha Guilavogui, Felix Klaus (68.Jérôme Roussillon), Maximilian Arnold (36.Yannick Gerhardt), Renato Steffen, Xaver Schlager, Josip Brekalo (74.João Victor), Wout Weghorst. Trainer: Oliver Glasner (Austria).
Goals: 21' Wout Weghorst 0-1, 33' Maxence Lacroix 0-2, 74' Wout Weghorst 0-3, 89' Admir Mehmedi 0-4.

17.09.2020; The Snowgrounds, Coleraine
Referee: Antti Mumukka (Finland)
Coleraine FC – MOTHERWELL FC 2-2(0-2,2-2); 0-3 on penalties
Coleraine FC: Gareth Deane, Aaron Traynor (74.Ian Parkhill), Gareth McConaghie, Stephen O'Donnell, Lyndon Kane, Stephen Lowry, Josh Carson, Ben Doherty, Aaron Jarvis (8.Jamie Glackin), James McLaughlin (117.Curtis Allen), Stewart Nixon (52.Eoin Bradley). Trainer: Oran Kearney.
Motherwell FC: Trevor Carson, Declan Gallagher, Stephen O'Donnell, Ricki Lamie, Nathan McGinley (65.Sherwin Seedorf), Bevis Mugabi [sent off 89], Liam Polworth (87.Barry Maguire), Mark O'Hara, Allan Campbell (91.Chris Long), Tony Watt, Callum Lang (87.Jake Hastie). Trainer: Stephen Robinson.
Goals: 16' Callum Lang 0-1, 37' Tony Watt 0-2, 49', 90' Ben Doherty 1-2 (penalty), 2-2 (penalty).
Penalties: Mark O'Hara 0-1, Ian Parkhill (missed), Tony Watt 0-2, Lyndon Kane (missed), Stephen O'Donnell 0-3, Gareth McConaghie (missed).

17.09.2020; MOL Aréna, Dunajská Streda
Referee: Marco Di Bello (Italy)
FK DAC DUNAJSKÁ STREDA – FK Jablonec 5-3(1-1,3-3)
DAC Dunajská Streda: Martin Jedlicka, Éric Davis, Jannik Müller, Dominik Kruzliak, César Blackman, Zsolt Kalmár (120+2.Sainey Njie), Andrija Balic (105.Martin Bednár), Andrej Fábry (78.Ion Nilolaescu), András, Schäfer, Eric Ramírez, Marko Divkovic (113.Danilo Beskorovayniy). Trainer: Bernd Storck (Germany).
FK Jablonec: Jan Hanus, Jakub Prodaný, Jaroslav Zelený (110.Dominik Plestil), Vojtech Kubista, Libor Holík, Jakub Martinec, Tomás Hübschman, Jakub Povazanez (98.Václav Pilar), Tomás Ladra (86.Vladimir Jovovic), Ivan Schranz, Tomás Cvancara (79.Martin Dolezal). Trainer: Petr Rada.
Goals: 6' Marko Divkovic 1-0, 25' Jaroslav Zelený 1-1, 57' Ivan Schranz 1-2, 65' Marko Divkovic 2-2, 71' Ivan Schranz 2-3 (penalty), 85', 96' Ion Nicolaescu 3-3, 4-3, 114' Éric Davis 5-3.

17.09.2020; Stadion Gradski vrt, Osijek
Referee: José Luis Munuera Montero (Spain)
NK Osijek – FC BASEL 1-2(0-2)
NK Osijek: Ivica Ivusic, Mile Skoric, Ante Majstorovic, Igor Carioca, Talys Oliveira, Vedran Jugovic, László Kleinheisler (76.Marin Pilj), Petar Bockaj (81.Alen Grgic), Mihael Zaper, Ante Erceg, Eros Grezda (64.Ramón Miérez). Trainer: Nenad Bjelica.
FC Basel: Djordje Nikolic, Silvan Widmer, Omar Alderete, Eray Cömert, Andrea Padula, Valentin Stocker, Fabian Frei, Samuele Campo (85.Jasper van der Werff), Ricky van Wolfswinkel, Arthur Cabral (63.Kemal Ademi), Afimico Pululu (70.Julian von Moos). Trainer: Ciriaco Sforza.
Goals: 18' Arthur Cabral 0-1, 44' Valentin Stocker 0-2, 84' Ante Majstorovic 1-2.

17.09.2020; Gradski Stadion, Senta
Referee: Dennis Higler (Netherlands)
FK TSC Bačka Topola – SC FCSB BUCUREȘTI 6-6(2-1,4-4); 4-5 on penalties
TSC Bačka Topola: Nenad Filipovic, Goran Antonic, Dajan Ponjevic [*sent off 44*], Filip Babic (64.Mihajlo Banjac), Bojan Balaz, Janko Tumbasevic, Nenad Lukic (75.Vladimir Siladji [*sent off 103*]), Sasa Tomanovic, Djuro Zec, Dejan Milicevic (115.Vasilije Djuric), Borko Duronjic (45+1.Nemanja Petrovic). Trainer: Zoltán Szabó.
FCSB: Razvan Ducan, Valentin Cretu, Marius Briceag, Ionut Pantîru, Grigoras Pantea (21.Adrian Petre), Olimpiu Morutan, Gabriel Simion, Ovidiu Perianu, Alexandru Buziuc (46.Robert Ion), Florinel Coman (73.Ovidiu Horsia), Dennis Man. Trainer: Anton Petrea.
Goals: 11' Dejan Milicevic 1-0, 14' Borko Duronjic 2-0, 25' Florinel Coman 2-1, 50' Dennis Man 2-2, 51' Goran Antonic 3-2, 63' Dennis Man 3-3 (penalty), 90+2' Bojan Balaz 3-4 (own goal), 90+4' Sasa Tomanovic 4-4, 1-5' Dennis Man 4-5, 105+1' Janko Tumbasevic 5-5, 108' Adrian Petre 5-6, 117' Sasa Tomanovic 6-6.
Penalties: Sasa Tomanovic 1-0, Olimpiu Morutan 1-1, Djuro Zec 2-1, Ovidiu Perianu 2-2, Mihajlo Banjac (missed), Ionut Pantîru 2-3, Goran Antonic 3-3, Adrian Petre 3-4, Vasilije Djuric 4-4, Dennis Man 4-5.

17.09.2020; „Hidegkuti Nándor" Stadion, Budapest
Referee: Anastasios Papapetrou (Greece)
Budapest Honvéd FC – MALMÖ FF 0-2(0-1)
Budapest Honvéd: Tomás Tujvel, Botond Baráth, Bence Batík, Naser Aliji, Mohamed Mezghrani, Patrik Hidi, Donát Zsótér (46.Norbert Szendrei), Dániel Gazdag, Bertalan Bocskay (84.Barna Kesztyüs), Roland Ugrai, Norbert Balogh (69.Boubacar Traoré). Trainer: Tamás Bódog.
Malmö FF: Marko Johansson, Eric Larsson, Lasse Nielsen, Jonas Knudsen, Anel Ahmedhodzic, Søren Rieks (79.Arnór Traustason), Oscar Lewicki (90+3.Samuel Adrian), Erdal Rakip, Ola Toivonen, Jo Inge Berget, Amin Sarr (67.Adi Nalic). Trainer: Jon Dahl Tomasson (Denmark).
Goals: 42' Ola Toivonen 0-1, 86' Arnór Traustason 0-2.

THIRD QUALIFYING ROUND

CHAMPIONS PATH

KF TIRANË and **PFC LUDOGORETS RAZGRAD** received a bye.

24.09.2020; FFA Academy Stadium, Yerevan
Referee: John Beaton (Scotland)
FC ARARAT-ARMENIA YEREVAN – NK Celje 1-0(0-0,0-0)
FC Ararat-Armenia: Stefan Cupic, Alemão, Sergiy Vakulenko, Ângelo Meneses, David Humanes (83.Yusuf Otubanjo), Yoan Gouffran (105.Armen Ambartsumyan), Sargis Shahinyan, Furdjel Narsingh, Zakaria Sanogo, Mailson, Jeisson Martínez (120+1.Louis Ogana). Trainer: David Campaña.
NK Celje: Matjaz Rozman, Denis Marandici, Amadej Brecl, Zan Zaletel, Dusan Stojinovic, Matic Vrbanec (91.Nino Pungarsek), Lan Stravs (99.Zan Benedicic), Mitja Lotric, Filip Dangubic, Ivan Bozic (112.Mico Kuzmanovic), Luka Kerin (86.Jakob Novak). Trainer: Dusan Kosic.
Goal: 111' Sergiy Vakalenko 1-0.

24.09.2020; Savon Sanomat Areena, Kuopio
Referee: Manuel Schüttengruber (Austria)
KUOPION PALLOSEURA – FK Sūdova Marijampolé 2-0(1-0)
Kuopion PS: Otso Virtanen, Igors Tarasovs, Artur Pikk, Nuno Tomás, Petteri Pennanen, Bismark Adjei-Boateng, Urho Nissilä, Ats Purje, Saku Savolainen, Rangel (86.Aniekpeno Udoh), Usman Sale. Trainer: Arne Erlandsen (Norway).
FK Sūdova Marijampolé: Ivan Kardum, Vaidas Slavickas, Thomas Salamon, Andro Svrljuga, Aleksandar Zivanovic, Semir Kerla, Ivan Haldík, Nicolás Gorobsov (66.Domagoj Pusic), Giedrius Matulevicius (76.Eligijus Jankauskas), Josip Tadic, Valērijs Sabala (59.Mihret Topcagic). Trainer: Saulius Sirmelis.
Goals: 31' Rangel 1-0, 72' Igors Tarasovs 2-0.

24.09.2020; Skonto stadions, Rīga
Referee: Fábio José Costa Veríssimo (Portugal)
Rīga FC – CELTIC FC GLASGOW 0-1(0-0)
Rīga FC: Roberts Ozols, Armands Pētersons, Elvis Stuglis, Herdi Prenga, Vladimirs Kamess, Ritvars Rugins, Stefan Panic, Marko Djurisic, Roger, Roman Debelko (67.Stefan Milosevic, 90+1.Jordan N'Kololo), Wesley Natã (71.Felipe Brisola). Trainer: Oleg Kononov (Russia).
Celtic: Vassilis Barkas, Shane Duffy, Kristoffer Ajer, Greg Taylor, Scott Brown, Nir Bitton, James Forrest (34.Jeremie Frimpong), Callum McGregor, Olivier Ntcham (72.Albian Ajeti), Ryan Christie, Odsonne Édouard (82.Mohamed Elyounoussi). Trainer: Neil Francis Lennon (Northern Ireland).
Goal: 90' Mohamed Elyounoussi 0-1.

24.09.2020; Tele2 Arena, Stockholm
Referee: Bartosz Frankowski (Poland)
Djurgårdens IF Stockholm – FC CFR 1907 CLUJ-NAPOCA 0-1(0-0)
Djurgårdens IF: Per Bråtveit, Elliot Käck, Jacob Une-Larsson, Aslak Witry, Jonathan Augustinsson, Haris Radetinac, Magnus Eriksson, Fredrik Ulvestad, Jesper Karlström, Curtis Edwards (78.Emir Kujovic), Edward Chilufya (72.Jonathan Ring). Trainer: Kim Bergstrand.
CFR Cluj: Cristian Balgradean, Paulo Vinícius, Mateo Susic, Camora, Andrei Burca, Ciprian Deac, Damjan Djokovic, Mihai Bordeianu, Adrian Paun (89.Michaël Pereira), Mário Rondón (90+3.Ovidiu Hoban), Billel Omrani (86.Gabriel Debeljuh). Trainer: Dan Vasile Petrescu.
Goal: 56' Paulo Vinícius 0-1.

24.09.2020; Ta'Qali National Stadium, Attard
Referee: Irfan Peljto (Bosnia and Herzegovina)
Floriana FC – FC FLORA TALLINN 0-0; 2-4 on penalties
Floriana FC: Ini Akpan, Enzo Ruiz, Jurgen Pisani, Ryan Camenzuli, Diego Venancio Silva, Nicola Leone (118.Jan Busuttil), Brandon Paiber (81.Flávio Carioca), Matías García, Kristian Keqi, Tiago Adan, Marcelo Dias. Trainer: Vincenzo Potenza (Italy).
Flora Tallinn: Matvei Igonen, Märten Kuusk, Henrik Pürg, Marco Lukka, Michael Lilander, Konstantin Vassiljev (90.Markus Poom), Markus Soomets, Vladislavs Kreida, Rauno Alliku (69.Martin Miller), Rauno Sappinen (81.Mark Lepik), Vlasiy Sinyavskiy (106.Frank Liivak). Trainer: Jürgen Henn.
Penalties: Michael Lilander 0-1, Kristian Keqi (missed), Vladislavs Kreida 0-2, Diego Venancio Silva (missed), Markus Poom (missed), Tiago Adan 1-2, Märten Kuusk 1-3, Jan Busuttil 2-3, Frank Liivak 2-4.

24.09.2020; Bolshava Sportivnaya Arena, Tiraspol
Referee: Aleksandar Stavrev (North Macedonia)
FC Sheriff Tiraspol – DUNDALK FC 1-1(1-1,1-1); 3-5 on penalties
FC Sheriff Tiraspol: Zvonimir Mikulic, Veaceslav Posmac, Andrei Peteleu (64.Charles Petro), Ousmane N'Diaye, Faith Obilor, William Parra, Cristiano, Dimitrios Kolovos (88.Dabney dos Santos), Andriy Bliznichenko (46.Rifet Kapic), Benedik Mioc (99.Max Veloso), Frank Castañeda. Trainer: Zoran Zekic.
Dundalk FC: Gary Rogers, Brian Gartland, Sean Gannon (13.John Mountney, 88.Daniel Kelly), Sean Hoare, Daniel Cleary, Darragh Leahy, Chris Shields, Sean Murray (72.Patrick McEleney), Gregory Sloggett, Patrick Hoban, Michael Duffy (102.Stefan Colovic). Trainer: Shane Keegan.
Goals: 8' Veaceslav Posmac 1-0, 45+1' Sean Murray 1-1.
Penalties: Stefan Colovic 0-1, Rifet Kapic 1-1, Patrick Hoban 1-2, Faith Obilor (missed), Sean Hoare 1-3, Max Veloso 2-3, Patrick McEleney 2-4, William Parra 3-4, Chris Shields 3-5.

24.09.2020; Stadion Bilino Polje, Zenica
Referee: José María Sánchez Martínez (Spain)
FK SARAJEVO – FK Budućnost Podgorica 2-1(1-1)
FK Sarajevo: Vladan Kovacevic, Amer Dupovac, Besim Serbecic, Selmir Pidro, Mirko Oremus, Aleksandr Pejovic, Tino-Sven Suric (58.Andrej Djokanovic), Amar Rahmanovic [*sent off 75*], Mersudin Ahmetovic (81.Haris Handzic), Matthias Fanimo (90+1.Krste Velkoski), Benjamin Tatar. Trainer: Vinko Marinovic.
FK Budučnost Podgorica: Milos Dragojevic, Vladan Adzic, Luka Mirkovic, Igor Cukovic, Nemanja Sekulic, Bogdan Milic, Petar Grbic, Milos Raickovic, Vasilije Terzic (85.Aleksandar Vujacic), Igor Ivanovic, Panagiotis Moraitis. Trainer: Mladen Milinkovic.
Goals: 4' Benjamin Tatar 1-0, 44' Panagiotis Moraitis 1-1, 67' Matthias Fanimo 2-1.

24.09.2020; Stadion Wojska Polskiego, Warszawa
Referee: Halis Özkahya (Turkey)
LEGIA WARSZAWA – KF Drita Gjilan 2-0(2-0)
Legia Warszawa: Artur Boruc, Artur Jedrzejczyk, Filip Mladenovic, Mateusz Wieteska, Josip Juranovic, Michal Karbownik, Pawel Wszolek, Bartosz Slisz, Luquinhas (67.Bartosz Kapustka), Tomás Pekhart (72.José Kanté), Joel Valencia (63.Valeriane Gvilia). Trainer: Czeslaw Michniewicz.
Drita Gjilan: Faton Maloku, Ardijan Cuculi, Vladica Brdarovski (66.Erjon Vucaj), Fidan Gërbeshi, Ilir Blakçori, Bujar Shabani, Xhevdet Shabani, Hamdi Namani, Almir Ajzeraj (74.Festim Alidema), Kastriot Rexha (56.Betim Haxhimusa), Astrit Fazliu. Trainer: Ardijan Nuhiji.
Goals: 24' Pawel Wszolek 1-0, 43' Tomás Pekhart 2-0.

24.09.2020; Tórsvøllur, Tórshavn
Referee: Thorvaldur Árnason (Iceland)
KÍ KLAKSVÍK – FC Dinamo Tbilisi 6-1(1-0)
KÍ Klaksvík: Kristian Joensen, Odmar Færø, Heini Vatnsdal, Jesper Brinck, Deni Pavlovic (75.David Skrbec), Jákup Andreasen, Jóannes Bjartalid, Jóannes Danielsen, Páll Klettskard (82.Jonn Johannesen), Patrik Johannesen (89.Boris Dosljak), Ole Erik Midtskogen. Trainer: Mikkjal Thomassen.
Dinamo Tbilisi: Roin Kvaskhvadze, Giorgi Kimadze, Nodar Iashvili, Davit Kobouri (74.Giorgi Kukhianidze), Simon Ghegnon, Giorgi Papava, Nodar Kavtaradze, Bakar Kardava, Giorgi Zaria (61.Giorgi Kutsia), Giorgi Gabedava, Filip Orsula (52.José Vitor Pernambuco). Trainer: Francisco Javier Muñoz Llompart (Spain).
Goals: 22' Deni Pavlovic 1-0, 58' Patrik Johannesen 2-0, 60', 69' Páll Klettskard 3-0, 4-0, 71' José Vitor Pernambuco 4-1, 73' Páll Klettskard 5-1, 85' Jonn Johannesen 6-1.

LEAGUE PATH

23.09.2020; Stádio Neo GSP, Nicosia
Referee: Mattias Gestranius (Finland)
Apollon Limassol FC – KKS LECH POZNAŃ 0-5(0-1)
Apollon Limassol: Demetris Demetriou, Valentin Roberge, Attila Szalai, Ioannis Pittas (46.Daniel Larsson), Nicolas Diguiny, Diego Aguirre, Esteban Sachetti (66.Sasa Markovic), Djordje Denic, Fanos Katelaris, Charlison Benschop, Bagaliy Dabo (14.Giannis Gianniotas).
Trainer: Sofronis Avgousti.
Lech Poznań: Filip Bednarek, Lubomir Satka, Alan Czerwinski, Djordje Crnomarkovic, Tymoteusz Puchacz, Jan Sýkora, Pedro Tiba, Dani Ramírez, Jakub Moder (73.Karlo Muhar), Jakub Kaminski (76.Michal Skóras), Mikael Ishak (67.Nika Kacharava). Trainer: Dariusz Zuraw.
Goals: 42' Pedro Tiba 0-1, 47' Mikael Ishak 0-2, 58' Jakub Kaminski 0-3, 81' Jan Sýkora 0-4, 90+1' Pedro Tiba 0-5.

24.09.2020; Doosan Aréna, Plzen
Referee: Donatas Rumšas (Lithuania)
FC VIKTORIA PLZEŇ – Sønderjysk Elitesport 3-0(2-0)
Viktoria Plzen: Ales Hruska, David Limberský, Jakub Brabec, Lukás Hejda, Milan Havel, Jan Kopic, Ales Cermák (90.Pavel Bucha), Miroslav Kácer, Lukás Kalvach, Adriel D'Avila Ba Loua (71.Joel Kayamba), Zdenek Ondrásek (79.Jean-David Beauguel). Trainer: Adrián Gula.
SønderjyskE: Lawrence Thomas, Pierre Kanstrup, Marc Hende, Patrick Banggaard, Stefan Gartenmann, Mads Albæk (72.Emil Frederiksen), Alexander Bah, Victor Ekani, Johan Absalonsen (74.Haji Wright), Anders Jacobsen, Rilwan Hassan (31.Julius Eskesen). Trainer: Glen Riddersholm.
Goals: 35' Zdenek Ondrásek 1-0 (penalty), 41' Adriel D'Avila Ba Loua 2-0, 51' Miroslav Kácer 3-0.

24.09.2020; Mestni Stadion Fazanerija, Murska Sobota
Referee: Sandro Schärer (Switzerland)
NŠ Mura Murska Sobota – PSV EINDHOVEN 1-5(1-2)
NŠ Mura: Matko Obradovic, Ziga Kous, Klemen Sturm, Jan Gorenc, Zan Karniczik, Nino Kouter, Alen Kozar, Luka Bobicanec, Tomi Horvat (76.Marko Brkic), Kevin Zizek (81.Amadej Marosa), Andrija Filipovic (76.Luka Maric). Trainer: Ante Simundza.
PSV Eindhoven: Yvon Mvogo, Philipp Max, Olivier Boscagli, Denzel Dumfries, Jordan Teze, Ryan Thomas (76.Michal Sadílek), Mauro Júnior, Pablo Rosario, Bruma, Maximiliano Romero (11.Cody Gakpo), Donyell Malen (86.Noni Madueke). Trainer: Roger Schmidt (Germany).
Goals: 17' Donyell Malen 0-1, 21' Nino Kouter 1-1, 28' Mauro Júnior 1-2, 54' Cody Gakpo 1-3, 65' Donyell Malen 14, 90' Cody Gakpo 1-5.

24.09.2020; MOL Aréna Sóstó, Székesfehérvár
Referee: Matej Jug (Slovenia)
FEHÉRVÁR FC SZÉKESFEHÉRVÁR – Stade de Reims 0-0; 4-1 on penalties
Fehérvár FC: Ádam Kovácsik, Attila Fiola, Loïc Négo, Stopira, Visar Musliu, Szilveszter Hangya, Bendegúz Bolla, Ivan Petryak (76.Armin Hodzic), Boban Nikolov, Lyes Houri, Budu Zivzivadze (68.Evandro). Trainer: Gábor Márton.
Stade de Reims: Predrag Rajkovic, Yunis Abdelhamid, Thomas Foket [*sent off 115*], Wout Faes, Ghislain Konan, Valon Berisha (80.El Bilal Touré), Xavier Chavalerin, Dereck Kutesa (69.Anastasios Donis), Marshall Munetsi, Arber Zeneli (63.Kaj Sierhuis), Boulaye Dia. Trainer: David Guion. Penalties: Evandro 1-0, Boulaye Dia (missed), Stopira 2-0, Yunis Abdelhamid (missed), Armin Hodzic 3-0, Ghislain Konan 3-1, Loïc Négo 4-1.

24.09.2020; Rostov Arena, Rostov-na-Donu
Referee: Petr Ardeleánu (Czech Republic)
FK Rostov – MACCABI HAIFA FC 1-2(1-1)
FK Rostov: Sergei Pesyakov, Aleksey Kozlov, Evgeniy Chernov, Maksim Osipenko, Roman Eremenko (64.Kento Hashimoto), Aleksey Ionov, Khoren Bayramyan (64.Dmitriy Poloz), Mathias Normann, Dennis Hadzikadunic, Danil Glebov [*sent off 68*], Eldor Shomurodov (82.David Tosevski). Trainer: Valeriy Karpin.
Maccabi Haifa: Josh Cohen, Ernest Mabouka, Bogdan Planic, Sun Menachem, Ayed Habashi, Ofri Arad, Tjaronn Chery, Neta Lavi, Mohammad Abu Fani (83.José Rodríguez), Nikita Rukavytsya (89.Stav Nachmani), Dolev Haziza (84.Yuval Ashkenazi). Trainer: Barak Bakhar.
Goals: 9' Eldor Shomurodov 1-0, 20' Nikita Rukavytsya 1-1, 60' Mohammad Abu Fani 1-2.

24.09.2020; Stade du Pays de Charleroi, Charleroi
Referee: Robert Adam Madden (Scotland)
R CHARLEROI SC – FK Partizan Beograd 2-1(1-0,1-1)
Charleroi SC: Nicolas Penneteau, Dorian Dessoleil, Steeven Willems, Maxime Busi, Ryota Morioka, Marco Ilaimaharitra, Joris Kayembe (114.Ivan Goranov), Mamadou Fall (109.Ken Nkuba), Ali Gholizadeh (112.Lucas Ribeiro Costa), Kaveh Rezaei (118.Guillaume Gillet), Shamar Nicholson. Trainer: Karim Belhocine (France).
Partizan Beograd: Vladimir Stojkovic, Aleksandar Miljkovic, Uros Vitas (91.Bojan Ostojic),
Macky Bagnack, Slobodan Urosevic, Bibras Natcho (98.Aleksandar Scekic), Lazar Markovic, Sasa Zdjelar, Takuma Asano (111.Dennis Stojkovic), Umar Sadiq, Filip Stevanovic (46.Seydouba Soumah). Trainer: Aleksandar Stanojevic.
Goals: 10' Dorian Dessoleil 1-0, 53' Seydouba Soumah 1-1, 108' Kaveh Rezaei 2-1.

24.09.2020; Eleda Stadion, Malmö
Referee: François Letexier (France)
MALMÖ FF – NK Lokomotiva Zagreb 5-0(3-0)
Malmö FF: Marko Johansson, Eric Larsson, Lasse Nielsen, Jonas Knudsen (46.Behrang Safari), Anel Ahmedhodzic, Søren Rieks (76.Amin Sarr), Oscar Lewicki, Erdal Rakip (63.Bonke Innocent), Adi Nalic, Jo Inge Berget, Isaac Kiese Thelin. Trainer: Jon Dahl Tomasson (Denmark).
Lokomotiva Zagreb: Krunoslav Hendija, Denis Kolinger, Stipo Markovic, Dominik Kovacic, Marko Djira (75.Ivan Celikovic), Fran Karacic, Jon Mersinaj, Jorge Sammir (69.Indrit Tuci), Oliver Petrak, Sherif Kallaku (84.Reuben Acquah), Enis Çokaj. Trainer; Goran Tomic.
Goals: 5', 17' Isaac Kiese Thelin 1-0, 2-0, 31' Adi Nalic 3-0, 52' Eric Larsson 4-0, 72' Søren Rieks 5-0.

24.09.2020; Vodafone Park, Istanbul
Referee: Daniel Siebert (Germany)
Beşiktaş JK İstanbul – RIO AVE FC 1-1(1-0,1-1); 2-4 on penalties
Beşiktaş: Utku Yuvakuran, Welinton Souza, Javi Montero, Ridvan Yilmaz, Jeremain Lens (101.Ajdin Hasic), Adem Ljalic (72.Bernard Mensah), Necip Uysal, Oguzhan Özyakup, Dorukhan Toköz, Tyler Boyd (84.Gökhan Töre), Güven Yalçin (64.Cyle Larin). Trainer: Sergen Yalçin.
Rio Ave FC: Pawel Kieszek, Ivo Pinto (79.Nikola Jambor), Aderllan Santos, Matheus Reis, Toni Borevkovic, Tarantini (79.Ryotaro Meshino), Filipe Augusto, Francisco "Chico" Geraldes (97.Gabrielzinho), Bruno Moreira, Carlos Mané, Lucas Piazón (69.Diego Lopes). Trainer: Mário Fernando Magalhães da Silva.
Goals: 15' Güven Yalçin 1-0, 85' Bruno Moreira 1-1.
Penalties: Bernard Mensah 1-0, Bruno Moreira 1-1, Gökhan Töre 2-1, Aderllan Santos 2-2, Welinton Souza (missed), Nikola Jambor 2-3, Cyle Larin (missed), Matheus Reis 2-4.

24.09.2020; Stadionul „Marin Anastasovici", Giurgiu
Referee: Əliyar Ağayev (Azerbaijan)
SC FCSB Bucureşti – FC SLOVAN LIBEREC 0-2(0-0)
FCSB: Catalin Straton, Aristides Soiledis, Ionut Pantîru, Gabriel Enache, David Caiado, Adrian Sut, Gabriel Simion, Stefan Cana [*sent off 20*], Ovidiu Perianu, Goran Karanovic (10.Octavian Popescu), Adrian Petre (68.Robert Ion). Trainer: Anton Petrea.
Slovan Liberec: Filip Nguyen, Taras Kacharaba, Jan Mikula, Martin Koscelník, Mohamed Tijani, Jhon Mosquera, Jakub Hromada (88.Matej Chalus), Jakub Pesek (84.Jan Matousek), Kamso Mara, Michal Beran (51.Michael Rabusic), Abdulla Yusuf Helal. Trainer: Pavel Hoftych.
Goals: 64' Abdulla Yusuf Helal 0-1, 82' Michael Rabusic 0-2.

24.09.2020; Nacionalna Arena "Toše Proeski", Skopje
Referee: Ali Palabiyik (Turkey)
KF Shkëndija Tetovo – TOTTENHAM HOTSPUR FC LONDON 1-2(0-1)
KF Shkëndija: Kostadin Zahov, Mevlan Murati, Antonio Pavic, Egzon Bejtulai, Ján Krivák, Bruno Dita (77.Arbin Zejnullai), Valon Ahmedi, Ennur Totre, Besart Ibraimi, Valmir Nafiu (85.Florent Ramadani), Ljupco Doriev (85.Zija Merdzhani). Trainer: Ernest Gjoka.
Tottenham Hotspur: Joe Hart, Toby Alderweireld, Serge Aurier, Ben Davies, Davinson Sánchez, Érik Lamela, Dele Alli (60.Harry Kane), Harry Winks (59.Giovani Lo Celso), Tanguy NDombèlé, Son Heung-Min, Steven Bergwijn (65.Lucas Moura). Trainer: José Mário dos Santos Félix Mourinho (Portugal).
Goals: 5' Érik Lamela 0-1, 55' Valmir Nafiu 1-1, 70' Son Heung-Min 1-2, 79' Harry Kane 1-3.

24.09.2020; Stade „Maurice Dufrasne", Liège
Referee: Harald Lechner (Austria)
R STANDARD LIÈGE – FK Vojvodina Novi Sad 2-1(0-0,1-1)
Standard Liège: Arnaud Bodart, Kostas Laifis, Nicolas Gavory, Collins Fai, Zinho Vanheusden, Mehdi Carcela-González (98.Duje Cop), Gojko Cimirot (92.Eden Shamir), Merveille Bopé Bokadi, Selim Amallah, Nicolas Raskin (107.Noë Dussenne), Felipe Avenatti (72.Jackson Muleka). Trainer: Philippe Montanier (France).
Vojvodina Novi Sad: Goran Vuklis, Stefan Djordjevic, Slavko Bralic, Nikola Andric, Sinisa Sanicanin (105.Novica Maksimovic), Arandel Stojkovic (105.Dejan Zukic), Nikola Drincic, Petar Bojic, Miljan Vukadinovic (86.Miodrag Gemovic), Nemanja Covic, Momcilo Mrkaic (59.Ognjen Djuricin). Trainer: Nenad Lalatovic.
Goals: 47' Felipe Avenatti 1-0 (penalty), 75' Petar Bojic 1-1, 91' Selim Amallah 2-1.

24.09.2020; Lerkendal Stadion, Trondheim
Referee: Kristo Tohver (Estonia)
ROSENBORG BK TRONDHEIM – Alanyaspor 1-0(0-0)
Rosenborg: André Hansen, Tore Reginiussen, Hólmar Eyjólfsson, Vegar Hedenstad, Pa Konate, Per Skjelbred, Anders Konradsen [*sent off 66*], Kristoffer Zachariassen, Dino Islamovic, Samuel Adegbenro (71.Edvard Tagseth), Carl Holse (81.Erlend Reitan). Trainer: Åge Hareide.
Alanyaspor: Marafona, Giorgos Tzavellas, Steven Caulker, François Moubandje, Juanfran (85.Onur Bulut), Fatih Aksoy (90+3.Khouma Babacar [*sent off 90+3*]), Efecan Karaca (81.Mustafa Pektemek), Salih Uçan, Anastasios Bakasetas, Davidson, Adam Bareiro. Trainer: Semih Tokatli.
Goal: 59' Anders Konradsen 1-0.

24.09.2020; Stadion Bâlgarska Armija, Sofia
Referee: Tamás Bognár (Hungary)
PFC CSKA SOFIA – B36 Tórshavn 3-1(2-0)
CSKA Sofia: Busatto, Jurgen Mattheij, Plamen Galabov, Geferson (61.Tiago Rodrigues), Bradley Mazikou, Valentin Antov, Younousse Sankharé, Graham Carey (84.Henrique), Amos Youga, Georgi Yomov (69.Jules Keita), Ali Sowe. Trainer: Stamen Belchev.
B36 Tórshavn: Símun Rógvi Hansen, Erling Jacobsen, Alex Mellemgaard, Eli Nielsen (59.Stefan Radosavljevic), Árni Frederiksberg, Benjamin Heinesen, Andrias Eriksen, Michal Przybylski, Magnus Holm Jacobsen (68.Andrass Johansen), Ragnar Samuelsson (59.Hannes Agnarsson), Sebastian Pingel. Trainer: Jákup á Borg.
Goals: 27' Ali Sowe 1-0, 38' Georgi Yomov 2-0, 61' Sebastian Pingel 2-1, 83' Jules Keita 3-1.

24.09.2020; HaMoshava Stadium, Petach-Tikva
Referee: Sergey Boyko (Ukraine)
HAPOEL BE'ER SHEVA FC – Motherwell FC 3-0(1-0)
Hapoel Be'er Sheva: Ohad Levita, Miguel Vítor, Loai Taha, Sean Goldberg, Elton Acolatse (86.Tomer Yosefi), Lucas Bareiro, Or Dadya, Sintayehu Sallalich (86.Marcelo Meli), Josué, Marwan Kabha, Jhonatan Agudelo (59.Gaëtan Varenne). Trainer: Yossi Abukasis.
Motherwell FC: Trevor Carson, Declan Gallagher [*sent off 70*], Stephen O'Donnell, Ricki Lamie, Liam Grimshaw, Nathan McGinley, Liam Polworth (86.Barry Maguire), Mark O'Hara, Allan Campbell, Tony Watt (75.Jordan White), Chris Long (72.Callum Lang). Trainer: Stephen Robinson.
Goals: 43' Miguel Vítor 1-0, 71' Josué 2-0 (penalty), 82' Elton Acolatse 3-0.

24.09.2020; Estadio Nuevo Los Cármenes, Granada
Referee: Serdar Gözübüyük (Netherlands)
GRANADA CF – FC Lokomotivi Tbilisi 2-0(0-0)
Granada CF: Rui Silva, Víctor Díaz, Germán Sánchez, Jesús Vallejo, Carlos Neva, Montoro, Maxime Gonalons, Luis Milla, Kenedy (62.Alberto Soro), Soldado (67.Jorge Molina), Darwin Machís (80.Antonio Puertas). Trainer: Diego Martínez Penas.
Lokomotivi Tbilisi: Giorgi Mamardashvili, Nika Sandokhadze, Giorgi Gabadze [*sent off 59*], Aleksandre Gureshidze, Daviti Ubilava, Temur Shonia, Davit Samurkasovi (60.Rati Mtchedlishvili), Tornike Kirkitadze (75.Mamia Gavashelushvili), Beka Dartsmelia, Imran Oulad Omar (71.Aleksandr Kobakhidze), Irakli Sikharulidze. Trainer: Giorgi Chiabrishvili.
Goals: 48' Darwin Machís 1-0, 90+1' Jorge Molina 2-0.

24.09.2020; Türk Telekom Stadyumu, Istanbul
Referee: Craig Pawson (England)
GALATASARAY SK ISTANBUL – HNK Hajduk Split 2-0(0-0)
Galatasaray: Fatih Öztürk, Ömer Bayram (71.Younès Belhanda), Martin Linnes, Emre Tasdemir (80.Omar Elabdellaoui), Marcão Teixeira, Ryan Donk, Sofiane Féghouli (89.Emre Kilinç), Taylan Antalyali, Oghenekaro Etebo, Ryan Babel, Mbaye Diagne. Trainer: Fatih Terim.
Hajduk Split: Josip Posavec, David Colina, Nihad Mujakic, Mario Vuskovic, Ádám Gyurcsó (84.Leon Krekovic), Mijo Caktas, Bassel Jradi (84.Jani Atanasov), Stanko Juric (74.Darko Nejasmic), Jairo, Dimitrios Diamantakos, Marin Jakolis. Trainer: Hari Vukas.
Goals: 77' Younès Belhanda 1-0, 86' Ryan Babel 2-0.

24.09.2020; Telia Parken, Copenhagen
Referee: Roi Reinshreiber (Israel)
FC KØBENHAVN – GKS Piast Gliwice 3-0(1-0)
FC København: Kalle Johnsson, Pierre Bengtsson, Ragnar Sigurdsson (68.Marios Oikonomou), Guillermo Varela, Victor Nelsson, Rasmus Falk (53.Robert Mudrazija), Zeca, Viktor Fischer (75.Jens Stage), Pep Biel Mas, Kamil Wilczek, Jonas Wind. Trainer: Ståle Solbakken (Norway).
Piast Gliwice: Frantisek Plach, Mikkel Kirkeskov, Jakub Czerwinski, Tomás Huk, Jakub Holúbek, Martin Konczkowski, Tomasz Jodlowiec, Krisztófer Vida, Patryk Lipski (82.Sebastian Milewski), Patryk Sokolowski (62.Michal Zyro), Piotr Parzyszek (89.Dominik Steczyk). Trainer: Waldemar Fornalik.
Goals: 14' Kamil Wilczek 1-0, 58' Jonas Wind 2-0, 90+5' Pep Biel Mas 3-0.

24.09.2020; AOK Stadion, Wolfsburg
Referee: Lawrence Visser (Belgium)
VFL WOLFSBURG – FK Desna Chernihiv 2-0(1-0)
VfL Wolfsburg: Koen Casteels, Jérôme Roussillon, Maxence Lacroix (62.John Anthony Brooks), Admir Mehmedi, Josuha Guilavogui, Maximilian Arnold, Renato Steffen, Xaver Schlager, João Victor, Wout Weghorst (78.Daniel Ginczek), Omar Marmoush (59.Paulo Otávio). Trainer: Oliver Glasner (Austria).
Desna Chernihiv: Evgen Past, Joonas Tamm [sent off 60], Andriy Gitchenko, Andriy Mostovyi, Yukhym Konoplya, Vladislav Ogirya, Vladislav Kalitvintsev, Egor Kartushov (46.Oleksiy Gutsulyak), Andriy Totovytskyi, Andriy Dombrovskyi (65.Vitaliy Ermakov), Pylyp Budkivskyi (84.Ilya Shevtsov). Trainer: Oleksandr Ryabokon.
Goals: 16' Josuha Guilavogui 1-0, 90+2' Daniel Ginczek 2-0.

24.09.2020; Linzer Stadion, Linz
Referee: Jérôme Brisard (France)
LINZER ASK – FK DAC Dunajská Streda 7-0(2-0)
LASK: Alexander Schlager, Petar Filipovic (58.Christian Ramsebner), Gernot Trauner, Reinhold Ranftl, Philipp Wiesinger, James Holland, Peter Michorl, René Renner, Husein Balic (72.Thomas Sabitzer), Andreas Gruber (58.Dominik Reiter), Marko Raguz. Trainer: Dominik Thalhammer.
DAC Dunajská Streda: Martin Jedlicka, Éric Davis, Jannik Müller, Dominik Kruzliak, César Blackman [sent off 48], Zsolt Kalmár, Andrija Balic, Andrej Fábry (36.Danilo Beskorovayniy), András Schäfer, Eric Ramírez (60.Ion Nilolaescu), Marko Divkovic (60.Martin Bednár). Trainer: Bernd Storck (Germany).
Goals: 6', 16' Marko Raguz 1-0, 2-0, 46' Petar Filipovic 3-0, 51' Peter Michori 4-0, 53' Andreas Gruber 5-0, 55' Husein Balic 6-0, 77' Thomas Sabitzer 7-0.

24.09.2020; St. Jakob-Park, Basel
Referee: Radu Marían Petrescu (Romania)
FC BASEL – Anorthosis Famagusta FC 3-2(3-1)
FC Basel: Djordje Nikolic, Silvan Widmer, Omar Alderete, Eray Cömert, Andrea Padula, Valentin Stocker (76.Dimitri Oberlin), Fabian Frei, Samuele Campo (85.Jasper van der Werff), Ricky van Wolfswinkel, Arthur Cabral, Afimico Pululu (60.Julian von Moos [sent off 88]). Trainer: Ciriaco Sforza.
Anorthosis Famagusta: Giorgi Loria, Gordon Schildenfeld, Evgen Selin (78.Georgios Galitsios), Branko Vrgoc, Hovhannes Hambardzumyan, Anderson Correia (46.Dimitris Christofi), Murtaz Daushvili, Renato Margaça (61.Dor Micha), Tornike Okriashvili [sent off 50], Kanagiotis Artymatas, Giorgi Kvilitaia. Trainer: Temur Ketsbaia (Georgia).
Goals: 3' Silvan Widmer 1-0, 12' Samuele Campo 2-0, 21' Hovhannes Hambardzumyan 3-0 (own goal), 45' Branko Vrgoc 3-1, 67' Giorgi Kvilitaia 3-2 (penalty).

24.09.2020; Stádio Neo GSP, Nicosia
Referee: Daniel Stefanski (Poland)
APOEL FC NICOSIA – HŠK Zrinjski Mostar 2-2(2-1,2-2); 4-2 on penalties
APOEL Nicosia: Miguel Silva, Emilio N'Sue, Geraldes, Artur Jorge, Rafael Santos, Tomás De Vincenti, Ghayas Zahid (64.Mike Jensen), Anuar Tuhami (86.Marius Lundemo), Atdhe Nuhiu (98.Ben Sahar), Dieumerci Ndongala (73.Moussa Al Taamari), Omer Atzili. Trainer: Marinos Ouzounidis.
Zrinjski Mostar: Ivan Brkic, Luis Ibáñez, Tomislav Barbaric (57.Almir Bekic), Slobodan Jakovljevic, Ognjen Todorovic, Dinko Trebotic (66.Damir Zlomislic), Milos Filipovic, Josip Corluka (105.Rijad Sadiku), Ivan Enin, Nemanja Bilbija, Josip Ivancic (76.Miljan Govedarica). Trainer: Mladen Zizovic.
Goals: 11' Josip Ivancic 0-1, 14' Omer Atzili 1-1, 26' Atdhe Nuhiu 2-1, 69' Nemanja Bilbija 2-2.
Penalties: Mike Jensen 1-0, Milos Filipovic 1-1, Omer Atzili (missed), Luis Ibáñez (missed), Ben Sahar 2-1, Nemanja Bilbija (missed), Moussa Al Taamari 3-1, Miljan Govedarica 3-2, Tomás De Vincenti 4-2.

24.09.2020; Kybunpark Stadion, St. Gallen
Referee: Alejandro José Hernández Hernández (Spain)
FC St. Gallen – AEK ATHÍNA 0-1(0-0)
FC St. Gallen: Lawrence Ati-Zigi, Miro Muheim, Leonidas Stergiou, Jordi Quintillà, Basil Stillhart (74.André Ribeiro), Kwadwo Duah (62.Florian Kamberi), Alessandro Kräuchi, Betim Fazliji, Lukas Görtler [sent off 90+5], Victor Ruiz (74.Élie Youan), Jérémy Guillemenot. Trainer: Peter Zeidler (Switzerland).
AEK Athína: Panagiotis Tsintotas, Dmytro Chygrynskiy, Emanuel Insúa, Stavros Vasilantonopoulos, Efstratios Svarnas, Nenad Krsticic, Petros Mandalos, André Simões, Karim Ansarifard (68.Levi García), Nélson Oliveira, Marko Livaja (90.Yevhen Shakhov). Trainer: Massimo Carrera (Italy).
Goal: 72' Nélson Oliveira 0-1.

24.09.2020; Stadio „Giuseppe Meazza", Milano
Referee: Fran Jović (Croatia)
AC MILAN – FK Bodø/Glimt 3-2(2-1)
AC Milan: Gianluigi Donnarumma, Simon Kjær, Davide Calabria, Theo Hernández, Matteo Gabbia, Hakan Çalhanoglu, Samu Castillejo (66.Rade Krunic), Franck Kessié, Ismaël Bennacar (80.Sandro Tonali), Alexis Saelemaekers, Lorenzo Colombo (57.Daniel Maldini). Trainer: Stefano Pioli.
FK Bodø/Glimt: Nikita Haikin, Brede Moe, Marius Lode, Alfons Sampsted (83.Ola Solbakken), Fredrik Bjørkan, Ulrik Saltnes, Patrick Berg, Jens Hauge, Kasper Junker (90.Victor Boniface), Philip Zinckernagel, Sondre Fet (65.Morten Konradsen). Trainer: Kjetil Knutsen.
Goals: 15' Kasper Junker 0-1, 16' Hakan Çalhanoglu 1-1, 32' Lorenzo Colombo 2-1, 50' Hakan Çalhanoglu 3-1, 55' Jens Hauge 3-2.

24.09.2020; Stadion HNK Rijeka, Rijeka
Referee: Tiago Bruno Lopes Martins (Portugal)
HNK RIJEKA – FK Kolos Kovalivka 2-0(0-0,0-0)
HNK Rijeka: Ivan Nevistic, Ivan Tomecak (90+1.Momcilo Raspopovic), Darko Velkovski, Daniel Stefulj, Hrvoje Smolcic, Franko Andrijasevic, Domagoj Pavicic (71.Sandro Kulenovic), Luka Capan, Robert Muric, Stjepan Loncar, Adam Gnezda Cerin (99.Ivan Lepinjica). Trainer: Simon Rozman.
Kolos Kovalivka: Evgen Volynets, Vitaly Gavrish, Evgen Novak, Kyrylo Petrov (109.Pavel Orikhovskyi), Vladislav Emets, Evgeniy Zadoya, Andriy Bogdanov, Mykyta Kravchenko, Yevgeniy Smyrnyi (84.Denys Kostyshyn), Vladimir Lisenko (71.Yevhen Seleznyov), Denys Antyukh (90+4.Yevgeniy Morozko). Trainer: Ruslan Kostyshyn.
Goals: 1-2' João Escoval 1-0, 115' Franko Andrijasevic 2-0.

24.09.2020; "Koning Willem II" Stadion, Tilburg
Referee: Maurizio Mariani (Italy)
Willem II Tilburg – RANGERS FC GLASGOW 0-4(0-2)
Willem II: Robbin Ruiter, Jordens Peters (73.Victor van den Bogert), Miquel Nelom, Sebastian Holmén, Derrick Köhn, Pol Llonch, Görkem Saglam, Driess Saddiki (59.John Yeboah), Mike Trésor, Vangelis Pavlidis, Ché Nunnely (60.Mats Köhlert). Trainer: Adrie Koster.
Rangers FC: Allan McGregor, James Tavernier, Connor Goldson, Filip Helander, Borna Barisic (74.Calvin Bassey), Steven Davis, Scott Arfield, Glen Kamara, Ianis Hagi, Alfredo Morelos (79.Cedric Itten), Ryan Kent (72.Jordan Jones). Trainer: Steven George Gerrard (England).
Goals: 22' James Tavernier 0-1 (penalty), 25' Ryan Kent 0-2, 55' Filip Helander 0-3, 71' Connor Goldson 0-4.

24.09.2020; Estádio „José Alvalade", Lisboa
Referee: Nikola Dabanović (Montenegro)
SPORTING CLUBE DE PORTUGAL LISBOA – Aberdeen FC 1-0(1-0)
Sporting: Antonio Adán, Luis Carlos Neto, Sebastián Coates, Zouhair Feddal, Pedro Porro (88.Gonzalo Plata), Nuno Mendes, Wendel (86.Daniel Bragança), Matheus Nunes, Luciano Vietto, Jovane Cabral, Tiago Tomás (77.Andraz Sporar). Trainer: Emanuel José Batista Ferro dos Santos.
Aberdeen FC: Joe Lewis, Andrew Considine, Shay Logan (83.Connor McLennan), Ash Taylor, Tommie Hoban, Jonny Hayes, Marley Watkins (81.Ryan Edmondson), Dylan McGeouch (69.Scott Wright), Ryan Hedges, Ross McCrorie, Lewis Ferguson. Trainer: Derek McInnes.
Goal: 7' Tiago Tomás 1-0.

PLAY-OFFS

CHAMPIONS PATH

01.10.2020; Stadionul „Dr. Constantin Rădulescu", Cluj-Napoca
Referee: Ivan Bebek (Croatia)
FC CFR 1907 CLUJ-NAPOCA – Kuopion Palloseura 3-1(2-0)
CFR Cluj: Cristian Balgradean, Paulo Vinícius, Mateo Susic, Camora, Andrei Burca, Ciprian Deac (78.Michaël Pereira), Damjan Djokovic, Mihai Bordeianu, Adrian Paun (86.Ovidiu Hoban), Mário Rondón, Gabriel Debeljuh (83.Billel Omrani). Trainer: Dan Vasile Petrescu.
Kuopion PS: Otso Virtanen, Igors Tarasovs, Artur Pikk, Nuno Tomás, Petteri Pennanen, Ville Saxman (76.Arttu Heinonen), Bismark Adjei-Boateng, Urho Nissilä (77.Ats Purje), Saku Savolainen, Rangel (82.Aniekpeno Udoh), Usman Sale. Trainer: Arne Erlandsen (Norway).
Goals: 5' Mário Rondón 1-0, 42' Gabriel Debeljuh 2-0, 56' Mário Rondón 3-0, 90+1' Aniekpeno Udoh 3-1.

01.10.2020; Stadion Maksimir, Zagreb
Referee: Ali Palabiyik (Turkey)
GNK DINAMO ZAGREB – FC Flora Tallinn 3-1(2-0)
Dinamo Zagreb: Dominik Livakovic, Marin Leovac, Kévin Théophile-Catherine, Petar Stojanovic, Josko Gvardiol, Arijan Ademi, Kristijan Jakic, Lovro Majer (84.Lirim Kastrati), Mario Gavranovic (65.Luka Ivanusec), Mislav Orsic (68.Amer Gojak), Bruno Petkovic. Trainer: Zoran Mamic.
Flora Tallinn: Matvei Igonen, Märten Kuusk, Henrik Pürg, Marco Lukka, Michael Lilander, Konstantin Vassiljev, Markus Soomets (81.Martin Miller), Vladislavs Kreida (88.Markus Poom), Rauno Alliku, Frank Liivak (76.Mark Lepik), Vlasiy Sinyavskiy. Trainer: Jürgen Henn.
Goals: 11' Mario Gavranovic 1-0, 26' Arijan Ademi 2-0, 65' Vlasiy Sinyavskiy 2-1, 87' Arijan Ademi 3-1.

01.10.2020; Stádio Neo GSP, Nicosia (Cyprus)
Referee: Anasthasios Sidiropoulos (Greece)
FC Ararat-Armenia Yerevan – FK CRVENA ZVEZDA BEOGRAD 1-2(0-1)
FC Ararat-Armenia: Stefan Cupic, Alemão (65.Yusuf Otubanjo), Sergiy Vakulenko, Ângelo Meneses, David Humanes, Yoan Gouffran, Sargis Shahinyan (70.Armen Ambartsumyan), Furdjel Narsingh, Zakaria Sanogo, Mailson, Jeisson Martínez. Trainer: David Campaña.
Crvena Zvezda: Milan Borjan, Milan Rodic, Milos Degenek, Milan Gajic, Radovan Pankov, Aleksandar Katai (77.Zeljko Gavric), Guélor Kanga (65.Njegos Petrovic), Mirko Ivanic, Veljko Nikolic, Diego Falcinelli, El Fardou Ben Nabouhane (81.Marko Gobeljic). Trainer: Dejan Stankovic.
Goals: 45' Aleksandar Katai 0-1, 60' Diego Falcinelli 0-2, 71' Mailson 1-2.

01.10.2020; Stadion Dynama, Minsk
Referee: Slavko Vinčić (Slovenia)
FC Dinamo Brest – PFC LUDOGORETS RAZGRAD 0-2(0-0)
Dinamo Brest: Sergey Ignatovich, Maksim Vitus, Yevhen Khacheridi, Gaby Kiki, Sergey Kislyak, Pavel Savitskiy, Artem Bykov (80.Sergey Krivets), Roman Yuzepchuk (88.Kirill Pechenin), Pavel Sedko, David Tweh, Abdoulaye Diallo (46.Mikhail Gordeychuk). Trainer: Sergey Kovalchuk.
Ludogorets Razgrad: Plamen Iliev, Cosmin Moti, Cicinho, Anton Nedyalkov, Olivier Verdon, Stéphane Badji, Cauly (88.Jordan Ikoko), Alex Santana, Dominik Yankov, Claudiu Keserü (77.Higinio Marín), Bernard Tekpetey (66.Elvis Manu). Trainer: Pavel Vrba.
Goals: 73' Elvis Manu 0-1, 79' Higinio Marín 0-2.

01.10.2020; Stadion Bilino Polje, Zenica
FK Sarajevo – CELTIC FC GLASGOW 0-1(0-0)
Referee: Benoît Bastien (France)
FK Sarajevo: Vladan Kovacevic, Amer Dupovac, Selmir Pidro, Andrej Djokanovic (86.Ivan Jukic), Mirko Oremus, Aleksandr Pejovic, Hrvoje Milicevic, Tino-Sven Suric, Mersudin Ahmetovic (68.Haris Handzic), Matthias Fanimo (86.Krste Velkoski), Benjamin Tatar. Trainer: Vinko Marinovic.
Celtic: Vassilis Barkas, Shane Duffy, Kristoffer Ajer, Greg Taylor, Jeremie Frimpong, Scott Brown, Nir Bitton (11.Hatem Abd Elhamed), Callum McGregor, Mohamed Elyounoussi, Ryan Christie (86.Olivier Ntcham), Odsonne Édouard (78.Patryk Klimala). Trainer: Neil Francis Lennon (Northern Ireland).
Goal: 70' Odsonne Édouard 0-1.

01.10.2020; Stadion Wojska Polskiego, Warszawa
Referee: Tobias Stieler (Germany)
Legia Warszawa – QARABAĞ FK BAKI 0-3(0-0)
Legia Warszawa: Artur Boruc, Artur Jedrzejczyk, Igor Lewczuk, Filip Mladenovic, Josip Juranovic, Domagoj Antolic (63.Luquinhas), Bartosz Kapustka (66.Michal Karbownik), Bartosz Slisz, Tomás Pekhart, Rafael Lopes (56.Pawel Wszolek), Joel Valencia. Trainer: Czeslaw Michniewicz.
Qarabağ FK: Sahrudin Mahammadaliyev, Maksim Medvedev, Qara Qarayev, Badavi Hüseynov, Abbas Hüseynov, Kevin Medina, Uros Matic, Filip Ozobic (75.Jaime Romero), Abdellah Zoubir (63.Mahir Emreli), Patrick Andrade, Owusu Kwabena (84.Elvin Dzhafarquliyev). Trainer: Qurban Qurbanov.
Goals: 50' Patrick Andrade 0-1, 62' Abdellah Zoubir 0-2, 70' Filip Ozobic 0-3.

01.10.2020; Wankdorf Stadion, Bern
Referee: Sergei Karasev (Russia)
BSC YOUNG BOYS BERN – KF Tiranë 3-0(1-0)
Young Boys: David von Ballmoos, Fabian Lustenberger, Jordan Lefort, Ulisses Garcia, Silvan Hefti, Mohamed Camara, Nicolas Moumi Ngamaleu (66.Gianluca Gaudino), Christian Fassnacht (72.Felix Mambimbi), Vincent Sierro, Jean-Pierre Nsamé (73.Theoson Siebatcheu), Meschack Elia. Trainer: Gerardo Seoane.
KF Tiranë: Visar Bekaj, Kristi Vangjeli, Kristijan Tosevski, Marsel Ismajlgeci, Filip Najdovski, Idriz Batha, Jurgen Çelhaka, Agustin Torassa [sent off 67], Elton Calé (89.Grent Halili), Winful Cobbinah (71.Derrick Sasraku), Ernest Muçi (85.Erion Hoxhallari). Trainer: Ndubuisi Egbo.
Goals: 42' Christian Fassnacht 1-0, 52', 64' Jean-Pierre Nsamé 2-0, 3-0.

01.10.2020; Aviva Stadium, Dublin
Referee: Maurizio Mariana (Italy)
DUNDALK FC – KÍ Klaksvík 3-1(1-0)
Dundalk FC: Gary Rogers, Brian Gartland, Sean Hoare, Daniel Cleary, Darragh Leahy, Patrick McEleney (81.John Mountney), Sean Murray, Gregory Sloggett, Stefan Colovic (71.Daniel Kelly), Patrick Hoban (71.David McMillan), Michael Duffy. Trainer: Shane Keegan.
KÍ Klaksvík: Kristian Joensen, Odmar Færø, Heini Vatnsdal, Jesper Brinck, Deni Pavlovic (86.Jonn Johannesen), Jákup Andreasen, Jóannes Bjartalid, Jóannes Danielsen, Páll Klettskard (55.Boris Dosljak), Patrik Johannesen, Ole Erik Midtskogen. Trainer: Mikkjal Thomassen.
Goals: 33' Sean Murray 1-0, 48' Daniel Cleary 2-0, 66' Ole Erik Midtskogen 2-1, 79' Daniel Kelly 3-1.

01.10.2020; Lerkendal Stadion, Trondheim
Referee: Davide Massa (Italy)
Rosenborg BK Trondheim – PSV EINDHOVEN 0-2(0-1)
Rosenborg: André Hansen, Tore Regiuniussen, Hólmar Eyjólfsson, Vegar Hedenstad (77.Erlend Reitan), Pa Konate, Per Skjelbred, Markus Henriksen, Kristoffer Zachariassen, Dino Islamovic, Samuel Adegbenro (65.Pál André Helland), Carl Holse. Trainer: Åge Hareide.
PSV Eindhoven: Yvon Mvogo, Philipp Max (60.Nick Viergever), Olivier Boscagli, Denzel Dumfries, Jordan Teze, Ryan Thomas (21.Jorrit Hendrix), Mauro Júnior, Pablo Rosario, Eran Zahavi (90+3.Noni Madueke), Donyell Malen, Cody Gakpo. Trainer: Roger Schmidt (Germany).
Goals: 22' Eran Zahavi 0-1, 61' Cody Gakpo 0-2.

01.10.2020; Eleda Stadion, Malmö
Referee: Danny Desmond Makkelie (Netherlands)
Malmö FF – GRANADA CF 1-3(1-1)
Malmö FF: Marko Johansson, Eric Larsson, Jonas Knudsen, Franz Brorsson, Anel Ahmedhodzic, Søren Rieks (71.Arnór Traustason), Oscar Lewicki, Erdal Rakip (71.Anders Christiansen), Ola Toivonen, Jo Inge Berget, Isaac Kiese Thelin (77.Adi Nalic). Trainer: Jon Dahl Tomasson (Denmark).
Granada CF: Rui Silva, Víctor Díaz, Germán Sánchez, Domingos Duarte, Carlos Neva, Montoro, Maxime Gonalons, Antonio Puertas (74.Kenedy), Yangel Herrera, Soldado (81.Jorge Molina), Darwin Machís (89.Dimitri Foulquier). Trainer: Diego Martínez Penas.
Goals: 30' Darwin Machís 0-1, 45' Jo Inge Berget 1-1, 58' Antonio Puertas 1-2, 85' Yangel Herrera 1-3.

01.10.2020; HaMoshava Stadium, Petach-Tikva
Referee: Srđan Jovanović (Serbia)
HAPOEL BE'ER SHEVA FC – FC Viktoria Plzeň 1-0(1-0)
Hapoel Be'er Sheva: Ohad Levita, Miguel Vítor, Loai Taha, Sean Goldberg, Elton Acolatse (81.Tomer Yosefi), Lucas Bareiro, Or Dadya, Sintayehu Sallalich (90+1.David Keltjens), Josué, Marwan Kabha, Jhonatan Agudelo (75.Gaëtan Varenne). Trainer: Yossi Abukasis.
Viktoria Plzen: Ales Hruska, David Limberský, Jakub Brabec, Lukás Hejda, Milan Havel, Jan Kopic, Ales Cermák, Lukás Kalvach, Adriel D'Avila Ba Loua (62.Joel Kayamba), Pavel Bucha (89.Ludek Pernica), Zdenek Ondrásek (80.Jean-David Beauguel). Trainer: Adrián Gula.
Goal: 4' Josué 1-0 (penalty).

01.10.2020; Stade „Maurice Dufrasne", Liège
Referee: William Collum (Scotland)
R STANDARD LIÈGE – Fehérvár FC Székesfehérvár 3-1(0-1)
Standard Liège: Arnaud Bodart, Kostas Laifis (59.Noë Dussenne), Nicolas Gavory, Collins Fai, Zinho Vanheusden, Mehdi Carcela-González (82.Eden Shamir), Gojko Cimirot, Merveille Bopé Bokadi (46.Michel Balikwisha), Selim Amallah, Nicolas Raskin, Jackson Muleka. Trainer: Philippe Montanier (France).
Fehérvár FC: Ádam Kovácsik, Attila Fiola, Loïc Négo, Stopira, Visar Musliu, Szilveszter Hangya, Bendegúz Bolla, Ivan Petryak (63.Funsho Bamgboye), Boban Nikolov, Lyes Houri (89.Armin Hodzic), Nemanja Nikolic (65.Budu Zivzivadze). Trainer: Gábor Márton.
Goals: 10' Nemanja Nikoliv 0-1, 50' Nicolas Gavory 1-1, 77', 85' Selim Amallah 2-1 (penalty), 3-1 (penalty).

01.10.2020; Stádio Olympiako „Spiros Louis", Athína
Referee: Artur Manuel Ribeiro Soares Dias (Portugal)
AEK ATHÍNA – VfL Wolfsburg 2-1(0-1)
AEK Athína: Panagiotis Tsintotas, Dmytro Chygrynskiy, Emanuel Insúa, Stavros Vasilantonopoulos, Efstratios Svarnas, Nenad Krsticic, Yevhen Shakhov, Petros Mandalos (63.Marko Livaja), André Simões, Nélson Oliveira (87.Karim Ansarifard), Levi García (81.Theodosis Macheras). Trainer: Massimo Carrera (Italy).
VfL Wolfsburg: Pavao Pervan, Jérôme Roussillon, Paulo Otávio, Maxence Lacroix, Admir Mehmedi, Josuha Guilavogui, Maximilian Arnold, Renato Steffen, Xaver Schlager (61.Yannick Gerhardt), Josip Brekalo (79.Bartosz Bialek), Wout Weghorst. Trainer: Oliver Glasner (Austria).
Goals: 45+1' Admir Mehmedi 0-1, 64' André Simões 1-1, 90+4' Karim Ansarifard 2-1.

01.10.2020; Stade du Pays de Charleroi
Referee: Felix Zwayer (Germany)
R Charleroi SC – KKS LECH POZNAŃ 1-2(0-2)
Charleroi SC: Nicolas Penneteau, Dorian Dessoleil, Steeven Willems (83.David Henen), Maxime Busi (57.Modou Diagne), Ryota Morioka, Marco Ilaimaharitra (89.Lucas Ribeiro Costa), Joris Kayembe, Mamadou Fall, Ali Gholizadeh, Kaveh Rezaei, Shamar Nicholson. Trainer: Karim Belhocine (France).
Lech Poznań: Filip Bednarek, Lubomir Satka [sent off 77], Alan Czerwinski, Vasyl Kravets (71.Michal Skóras), Djordje Crnomarkovic, Tymoteusz Puchacz, Pedro Tiba, Dani Ramírez (79.Thomas Rogne), Jakub Moder, Jakub Kaminski, Mikael Ishak (87.Filip Marchwinski). Trainer: Dariusz Zuraw.
Goals: 33' Dani Ramírez 0-1, 42' Tymoteusz Puchacz 0-2, 56' Mamadou Fall 1-2.

01.10.2020; Stadion u Nisy, Liberec
Referee: Andreas Ekberg (Sweden)
FC SLOVAN LIBEREC – APOEL FC Nicosia 1-0(0-0)
Slovan Liberec: Filip Nguyen, Taras Kacharaba, Jan Mikula, Martin Koscelník, Mohamed Tijani, Jhon Mosquera, Jakub Hromada, Jakub Pesek (80.Jan Matousek), Kamso Mara, Michal Beran (55.Michael Rabusic), Abdulla Yusuf Helal. Trainer: Pavel Hoftych.
APOEL Nicosia: Miguel Silva, Emilio N'Sue, Geraldes, Artur Jorge, Christos Shelis, Tomás De Vincenti, Ghayas Zahid, Anuar Tuhami (90+4.Giorgios Merkis), Atdhe Nuhiu, Dieumerci Ndongala (68.Omer Atzili), Moussa Al Taamari (82.Viktor Klonaridis). Trainer: Marinos Ouzounidis.
Goal: 90+5' Kamso Mara 1-0 (penalty).

01.10.2020; Telia Parken, Copenhagen
Referee: Chris Kavanagh (England)
FC København – HNK RIJEKA 0-1(0-1)
FC København: Kalle Johnsson, Pierre Bengtsson, Ragnar Sigurdsson, Peter Andersen (67.Karlo Bartolec), Victor Nelsson, Zeca, Viktor Fischer (46.Mikkel Kaufmann), Pep Biel Mas, Jens Stage (56.Robert Mudrazija), Kamil Wilczek, Jonas Wind. Trainer: Ståle Solbakken (Norway).
HNK Rijeka: Ivan Nevistic, Ivan Tomecak (90+1.Momcilo Raspopovic), Darko Velkovski, Daniel Stefulj, Hrvoje Smolcic, Franko Andrijasevic, Domagoj Pavicic (76.Ivan Lepinjica), Luka Capan, Stjepan Loncar, Adam Gnezda Cerin, Sandro Kulenovic (83.João Escoval). Trainer: Simon Rozman.
Goal: 20' Peter Ankersen 0-1 (own goal).

01.10.2020; St. Jakob-Park, Basel
Referee: Ivan Kružliak (Slovakia)
FC Basel – PFC CSKA SOFIA 1-3(0-0)
FC Basel: Djordje Nikolic, Silvan Widmer, Omar Alderete, Eray Cömert, Andrea Padula, Valentin Stocker (90+1.Aldo Kalulu), Fabian Frei, Orges Bunjaku (90+1.Samuele Campo), Ricky van Wolfswinkel, Arthur Cabral (77.Edon Zhegrova), Afimico Pululu. Trainer: Ciriaco Sforza.
CSKA Sofia: Busatto, Jurgen Mattheij, Plamen Galabov, Geferson (59.Tiago Rodrigues), Bradley Mazikou, Valentin Antov, Younousse Sankharé (90+1.Ahmed Ahmedov), Amos Youga, Georgi Yomov, Ali Sowe, Jules Keita (60.Henrique). Trainer: Stamen Belchev.
Goals: 54' Arthur Cabral 1-0 (penalty), 72', 88' Tiago Rodrigues 1-1, 1-2, 90+6' Ahmed Ahmedov 1-3.

01.10.2020; Ibrox Stadium, Glasgow
Referee: Andris Treimanis (Latvia)
RANGERS FC GLASGOW – Galatasaray SK Istanbul 2-1(0-0)
Rangers FC: Allan McGregor, James Tavernier, Connor Goldson, Filip Helander, Borna Barisic, Steven Davis, Scott Arfield, Glen Kamara, Ianis Hagi (78.Ryan Jack), Alfredo Morelos (87.Cedric Itten), Ryan Kent. Trainer: Steven George Gerrard (England).
Galatasaray: Fatih Öztürk, Martin Linnes, Omar Elabdellaoui, Marcão Teixeira, Christian Luyindama, Sofiane Féghouli (73.Mbaye Diagne), Younès Belhanda (66.Oghenekaro Etebo), Taylan Antalyali, Emre Kilinç, Ryan Babel (65.Ömer Bayram), Radamel Falcao. Trainer: Fatih Terim.
Goals: 52' Scott Arfield 1-0, 59' James Tavernier 2-0, 87' Marcão Teixeira 2-1.

01.10.2020; Estádio „José Alvalade", Lisboa
Referee: Aleksei Kulbakov (Belarus)
Sporting Clube de Portugal Lisboa – LINZER ASK 1-4(1-1)
Sporting: Antonio Adán, Luis Carlos Neto, Sebastián Coates [*sent off 63*], Zouhair Feddal, Pedro Porro, Nuno Mendes, Wendel, Matheus Nunes (71.Andraz Sporar), Luciano Vietto (67.Pedro Gonçalves), Nuno Santos (78.Antunes), Tiago Tomás. Trainer: Emanuel José Batista Ferro dos Santos.
LASK: Alexander Schlager, Petar Filipovic (78.Andrés Andrade), Gernot Trauner, Reinhold Ranftl, Philipp Wiesinger, James Holland, Peter Michorl (87.Lukas Grgic), René Renner, Husein Balic, Andreas Gruber (74.Patrick Plojer), Marko Raguz. Trainer: Dominik Thalhammer.
Goals: 14' Gernot Trauner 0-1, 42' Tiago Tomás 1-1, 58' Marko Raguz 1-2, 65' Peter Michorl 1-3, 68' Andreas Gruber 1-4.

01.10.2020; Tottenham Hotspur Stadium, London
Referee: Ruddy Buquet (France)
TOTTENHAM HOTSPUR FC LONDON – Maccabi Haifa FC 7-2(4-1)
Tottenham Hotspur: Joe Hart, Toby Alderweireld, Matt Doherty, Ben Davies, Davinson Sánchez, Lucas Moura, Pierre-Emile Højbjerg (63.Moussa Sissoko), Harry Winks, Giovani Lo Celso (46.Dele Alli), Harry Kane (75.Reguilón), Steven Bergwijn. Trainer: José Mário dos Santos Félix Mourinho (Portugal).
Maccabi Haifa: Josh Cohen, Ernest Mabouka, Bogdan Planic, Sun Menachem, Ayed Habashi, Ofri Arad (71.Godsway Donyoh), Tjaronn Chery, Neta Lavi, Mohammad Abu Fani (87.Yuval Ashkenazi), Nikita Rukavytsya, Dolev Haziza (84.José Rodríguez). Trainer: Barak Bakhar.
Goals: 2' Harry Kane 1-0, 17' Tjaronn Chery 1-1, 20' Lucas Moura 2-1, 36', 39' Giovanni Lo Celso 3-1, 4-1, 52' Nikita Rukavytsya 4-2 (penalty), 56', 74' Harry Kane 5-2 (penalty), 6-2, 90+1' Dele Alli 7-2 (penalty).

01.10.2020; Estádio do Rio Ave Futebol Clube, Vila do Conde
Referee: Jesús Gil Manzano (Spain)
Rio Ave FC – AC MILAN 2-2(0-0,1-1); 8-9 on penalties
Rio Ave FC: Pawel Kieszek, Ivo Pinto, Aderllan Santos, Nélson Monte, Toni Borevkovic [*sent off 120*], Tarantini (75.Nikola Jambor), Filipe Augusto, Diego Lopes (66.Francisco "Chico" Geraldes), Bruno Moreira (86.Gelson Dala), Carlos Mané (109.Gabrielzinho), Lucas Piazón. Trainer: Mário Fernando Magalhães da Silva.
AC Milan: Gianluigi Donnarumma, Simon Kjær, Davide Calabria, Theo Hernández, Matteo Gabbia, Hakan Çalhanoglu, Samu Castillejo (46.Brahim Díaz), Franck Kessié (105.Sandro Tonali), Ismaël Bennacer, Alexis Saelemaekers (95.Lorenzo Colombo), Daniel Maldini (67.Rafael Leão). Trainer: Stefano Pioli.
Goals: 51' Alexis Saelemaekers 0-1, 72' Francisco "Chico" Geraldes 1-1, 91' Gelson Dala 2-1, 120+2' Hakan Çalhanoglu 2-2.
Penalties: Ismaël Bennacer 0-1, Francisco "Chico" Geraldes 1-1, Simon Kjær 1-2, Aderllan Santos 2-2, Theo Hernández 2-3, Nikola Jambor 3-3, Brahim Díaz 3-4, Lucas Piazón 4-4, Hakan Çalhanoglu 4-5, Filipe Augusto 5-5, Davide Calabria 5-6, Gelson Dala 6-6, Sandro Tonali 6-7, Gabrielzinho 7-7, Lorenzo Colombo (missed), Nélson Monte (missed), Rafael Leão 7-8, Ivo Pinto 8-8, Gianluigi Donnarumma (missed), Pawel Kieszek (missed), Ismaël Bennacer (missed), Francisco "Chico" Geraldes (missed), Kjær Simon 8-9, Aderllan Santos (missed).

Winners and runners-up of each group were qualified for the Round of 32.

GROUP A	1.	**AS Roma**	6	4	1	1	13 - 5	13
	2.	**BSC Young Boys Bern**	6	3	1	2	9 - 7	10
	3.	FC CFR 1907 Cluj-Napoca	6	1	2	3	4 - 10	5
	4.	PFC CSKA Sofia	6	1	2	3	3 - 7	5

22.10.2020; Wankdorf Stadion, Bern
Referee: Carlos del Cerro Grande (Spain); Attendance: 600
BSC Young Boys Bern – AS Roma 1-2(1-0)
Young Boys: David von Ballmoos, Fabian Lustenberger, Nicolas Bürgy, Cédric Zesiger, Silvan Hefti, Quentin Maceiras, Nicolas Moumi Ngamaleu (65.Felix Mambimbi), Christian Fassnacht (65.Meschack Elia), Vincent Sierro (79.Gianluca Gaudino), Fabian Rieder (70.Michel Aebischer), Jean-Pierre Nsamé (79.Theoson Siebatcheu). Trainer: Gerardo Seoane.
AS Roma: Pau López, Federico Fazio, Bruno Peres, Juan Jesus (69.Lorenzo Pellegrini), Rick Karsdorp (46.Leonardo Spinazzola), Marash Kumbulla, Bryan Cristante, Gonzalo Villar (59.Jordan Veretout), Pedro (59.Henrikh Mkhitaryan), Borja Mayoral (59.Edin Dzeko), Carles Pérez. Trainer: Paulo Alexandre Rodrigues Fonseca (Portugal).
Goals: 14' Jean-Pierre Nsamé 1-0 (penalty), 69' Bruno Peres 1-1, 73' Marash Kumbulla 1-2.

29.10.2020; Stadio Olimpico, Roma
Referee: Aleksei Kulbakov (Belarus)
AS Roma – PFC CSKA Sofia 0-0
AS Roma: Pau López, Federico Fazio, Chris Smalling (56.Juan Jesus), Bruno Peres, Leonardo Spinazzola (46.Rick Karsdorp), Marash Kumbulla, Henrikh Mkhitaryan (46.Pedro), Bryan Cristante, Gonzalo Villar, Borja Mayoral (71.Edin Dzeko), Carles Pérez (75.Lorenzo Pellegrini). Trainer: Paulo Alexandre Rodrigues Fonseca (Portugal).
CSKA Sofia: Busatto, Petar Zanev, Thibaut Vion (89.Ivan Turitsov), Geferson (80.Tiago Rodrigues), Bradley Mazikou, Valentin Antov, Younousse Sankharé (89.Ahmed Ahmedov), Amos Youga (82.Stefano Beltrame), Georgi Yomov, Ali Sowe, Jerome Sinclair (64.Henrique). Trainer: Daniel Alexandre Morales Batagello (Brasil).

05.11.2020; Stadio Olimpico, Roma
Referee: Matej Jug (Slovenia)
AS Roma – FC CFR 1907 Cluj-Napoca 5-0(3-0)
AS Roma: Pau López, Federico Fazio, Bruno Peres, Leonardo Spinazzola (46.Juan Jesus), Marash Kumbulla, Ibañez (61.Chris Smalling), Henrikh Mkhitaryan (46.Lorenzo Pellegrini), Jordan Veretout (46.Pedro), Bryan Cristante (74.Tommaso Milanese), Gonzalo Villar, Borja Mayoral. Trainer: Paulo Alexandre Rodrigues Fonseca (Portugal).
CFR Cluj: Cristian Balgradean, Mateo Susic (78.Iasmin Latovlevici), Camora, Cristian Manea, Denis Ciobotariu, Ciprian Deac (46.Michaël Pereira), Ovidiu Hoban, Damjan Djokovic, Catalin Itu (46.Adrian Paun), Mário Rondón (90.Andrei Joca), Gabriel Debeljuh (67.Nicolae Cârnat). Trainer: Dan Vasile Petrescu.
Goals: 1' Henrikh Mkhitaryan 1-0, 24' Ibañez 2-0, 34', 84' Borja Mayoral 3-0, 4-0, 89' Pedro 5-0.

26.11.2020; Nationalen Stadion "Vasil Levski", Sofia
Referee: Fábio José Costa Veríssimo (Portugal)
PFC CSKA Sofia – BSC Young Boys Bern 0-1(0-1)
CSKA Sofia: Busatto, Petar Zanev, Jurgen Mattheij, Valentin Antov, Ivan Turitsov (59.Jerome Sinclair), Younousse Sankharé (75.Amos Youga), Graham Carey, Tiago Rodrigues (75.Ahmed Ahmedov), Stefano Beltrame (90.Jules Keita), Georgi Yomov (75.Adalberto Peñaranda), Ali Sowe. Trainer: Bruno Akrapovic (Bosnia and Herzegovina).
Young Boys: David von Ballmoos, Fabian Lustenberger (74.Jordan Lefort), Ulisses Garcia, Silvan Hefti, Mohamed Camara, Nicolas Moumi Ngamaleu (87.Nicolas Bürgy), Christian Fassnacht (74.Felix Mambimbi), Vincent Sierro, Fabian Rieder (74.Gianluca Gaudino), Jean-Pierre Nsamé, Meschack Elia (60.Michel Aebischer). Trainer: Gerardo Seoane.
Goal: 34' Jean-Pierre Nsamé 0-1.

22.10.2020; Nationalen Stadion "Vasil Levski", Sofia
Referee: Halil Umut Meler (Turkey); Attendance: 11,958
PFC CSKA Sofia – FC CFR 1907 Cluj-Napoca 0-2(0-0)
CSKA Sofia: Busatto, Jurgen Mattheij, Thibaut Vion, Bradley Mazikou, Valentin Antov, Younousse Sankharé (71.Ahmed Ahmedov), Tiago Rodrigues (81.Stefano Beltrame), Amos Youga, Georgi Yomov (80.Henrique), Ali Sowe, Jerome Sinclair (63.Jules Keita). Trainer: Stamen Belchev.
CFR Cluj: Cristian Balgradean, Paulo Vinícius, Mateo Susic, Camora, Andrei Burca, Ciprian Deac (78.Alexandru Chipciu), Ovidiu Hoban, Damjan Djokovic, Adrian Paun (83.Michaël Pereira), Mário Rondón (87.Nicolae Cârnat), Gabriel Debeljuh (87.Jakub Vojtus). Trainer: Dan Vasile Petrescu.
Goals: 53' Mário Rondón 0-1, 74' Ciprian Deac 0-2 (penalty).

29.10.2020; Stadionul „Dr. Constantin Rădulescu", Cluj-Napoca
Referee: Glenn Nyberg (Sweden)
FC CFR 1907 Cluj-Napoca – BSC Young Boys Bern 1-1(0-0)
CFR Cluj: Cristian Balgradean, Paulo Vinícius (14.Cristian Manea), Mateo Susic, Camora, Andrei Burca, Ciprian Deac (63.Alexandru Chipciu), Ovidiu Hoban (79.Catalin Itu), Damjan Djokovic, Adrian Paun (79.Michaël Pereira), Mário Rondón, Gabriel Debeljuh (46.Billel Omrani). Trainer: Dan Vasile Petrescu.
Young Boys: David von Ballmoos, Fabian Lustenberger, Cédric Zesiger, Silvan Hefti (63.Ulisses Garcia), Mohamed Camara (74.Miralem Sulejmani), Quentin Maceiras, Nicolas Moumi Ngamaleu (74.Theoson Siebatcheu), Christian Fassnacht, Michel Aebischer (75.Vincent Sierro), Jean-Pierre Nsamé, Meschack Elia (63.Gianluca Gaudino). Trainer: Gerardo Seoane.
Goals: 62' Mário Rondón 1-0, 69' Christian Fassnacht 1-1.

05.11.2020; Wankdorf Stadion, Bern
Referee: Lawrence Visser (Belgium)
BSC Young Boys Bern – PFC CSKA Sofia 3-0(3-0)
Young Boys: David von Ballmoos, Fabian Lustenberger, Jordan Lefort, Silvan Hefti, Mohamed Camara (63.Ulisses Garcia), Miralem Sulejmani (70.Gianluca Gaudino), Christian Fassnacht, Vincent Sierro (62.Michel Aebischer), Fabian Rieder, Jean-Pierre Nsamé (69.Theoson Siebatcheu), Felix Mambimbi (70.Meschack Elia). Trainer: Gerardo Seoane.
CSKA Sofia: Busatto, Jurgen Mattheij, Thibaut Vion (87.Ivan Turitsov), Bradley Mazikou, Valentin Antov, Younousse Sankharé (87.Ahmed Ahmedov), Amos Youga, Georgi Yomov (79.Jules Keita), Ali Sowe, Jerome Sinclair (69.Graham Carey), Adalberto Peñaranda (68.Tiago Rodrigues). Trainer: Daniel Alexandre Morales Batagello (Brasil).
Goals: 2' Felix Mambimbi 1-0, 18' Miralem Sulejmani 2-0, 32' Felix Mambimbi 3-0.

26.11.2020; Stadionul „Dr. Constantin Rădulescu", Cluj-Napoca
Referee: Harald Lechner (Austria)
FC CFR 1907 Cluj-Napoca – AS Roma 0-2(0-0)
CFR Cluj: Cristian Balgradean, Mateo Susic, Camora, Andrei Burca, Cristian Manea, Damjan Djokovic, Michaël Pereira, Adrian Paun (71.Nicolae Cârnat), Catalin Itu (51.Alexandru Chipciu), Mário Rondón, Gabriel Debeljuh (70.Jakub Vojtus). Trainer: Dan Vasile Petrescu.
AS Roma: Pau López, Bruno Peres, Juan Jesus, Leonardo Spinazzola (64.Henrikh Mkhitaryan), Riccardo Calafiori, Bryan Cristante, Lorenzo Pellegrini (46.Jordan Veretout), Gonzalo Villar, Amadou Diawara (77.Tommaso Milanese), Borja Mayoral (63.Edin Dzeko), Carles Pérez (84.Filippo Tripi). Trainer: Paulo Alexandre Rodrigues Fonseca (Portugal).
Goals: 49' Gabriel Debeljuh 0-1 (own goal), 67' Jordan Veretout 0-2 (penalty).

03.12.2020; Stadio Olimpico, Roma
Referee: Fran Jović (Croatia)
AS Roma – BSC Young Boys Bern 3-1(1-1)
AS Roma: Pau López, Bruno Peres, Juan Jesus, Ibañez (46.Leonardo Spinazzola), Riccardo Calafiori, Bryan Cristante (65.Federico Fazio), Gonzalo Villar (60.Lorenzo Pellegrini), Amadou Diawara, Pedro (46.Henrikh Mkhitaryan), Borja Mayoral (60.Edin Dzeko), Carles Pérez. Trainer: Paulo Alexandre Rodrigues Fonseca (Portugal).
Young Boys: David von Ballmoos, Jordan Lefort, Ulisses Garcia (68.Meschack Elia), Cédric Zesiger, Silvan Hefti, Mohamed Camara [*sent off 82*], Nicolas Moumi Ngamaleu (76.Felix Mambimbi), Christian Fassnacht, Michel Aebischer (67.Gianluca Gaudino), Fabian Rieder (58.Vincent Sierro), Jean-Pierre Nsamé (76.Theoson Siebatcheu). Trainer: Gerardo Seoane.
Goals: 34' Jean-Pierre Nsamé 0-1, 44' Borja Mayoral 1-1, 59' Riccardo Calafiori 2-1, 81' Edin Dzeko 3-1.

10.12.2020; Wankdorf Stadion, Bern
Referee: Benoît Bastien (France)
BSC Young Boys Bern – FC CFR 1907 Cluj-Napoca 2-1(0-0)
Young Boys: David von Ballmoos, Jordan Lefort, Ulisses Garcia, Nicolas Bürgy (86.Theoson Siebatcheu), Silvan Hefti, Miralem Sulejmani (58.Gianluca Gaudino), Nicolas Moumi Ngamaleu (82.Cédric Zesiger), Michel Aebischer, Fabian Rieder (58.Christopher Martins Pereira), Jean-Pierre Nsamé [*sent off 90+5*], Felix Mambimbi (58.Meschack Elia). Trainer: Gerardo Seoane.
CFR Cluj: Cristian Balgradean [*sent off 90*], Paulo Vinícius, Camora, Andrei Burca, Cristian Manea, Ciprian Deac (90+2.Grzegorz Sandomierski), Ovidiu Hoban, Damjan Djokovic [*sent off 90+7*], Michaël Pereira (88.Mateo Susic), Adrian Paun (74.Gabriel Debeljuh), Mário Rondón. Trainer: Edward Iordanescu.
Goals: 84' Gabriel Debeljuh 0-1, 90+3' Jean-Pierre Nsamé 1-1 (penalty), 90+6' Gianluca Gaudino 2-1.

03.12.2020; Stadionul „Dr. Constantin Rădulescu", Cluj-Napoca
Referee: Amaury Delerue (France)
FC CFR 1907 Cluj-Napoca – PFC CSKA Sofia 0-0
CFR Cluj: Cristian Balgradean, Mateo Susic, Camora, Andrei Burca, Cristian Manea, Alexandru Chipciu [*sent off 85*], Damjan Djokovic, Michaël Pereira (61.Ciprian Deac), Adrian Paun (75.Nicolae Cârnat), Mário Rondón, Gabriel Debeljuh (86.Jakub Vojtus). Trainer: Dan Vasile Petrescu.
CSKA Sofia: Busatto, Petar Zanev, Jurgen Mattheij, Thibaut Vion, Geferson, Valentin Antov, Younousse Sankharé (78.Tiago Rodrigues), Graham Carey, Amos Youga, Georgi Yomov (77.Henrique), Ali Sowe. Trainer: Bruno Akrapovic (Bosnia and Herzegovina).

10.12.2020; Nationalen Stadion "Vasil Levski", Sofia
Referee: Irfan Peljto (Bosnia and Herzegovina)
PFC CSKA Sofia – AS Roma 3-1(2-1)
CSKA Sofia: Busatto, Petar Zanev, Jurgen Mattheij, Geferson, Bradley Mazikou, Valentin Antov, Younousse Sankharé (63.Stefano Beltrame), Tiago Rodrigues (81.Henrique), Amos Youga (74.Plamen Galabov), Georgi Yomov (63.Thibaut Vion), Ali Sowe (74.Ahmed Ahmedov). Trainer: Bruno Akrapovic (Bosnia and Herzegovina).
AS Roma: Pietro Boer, Federico Fazio, Bruno Peres (81.Filippo Tripi), Juan Jesus, Marash Kumbulla (46.Chris Smalling), Amadou Diawara, Tommaso Milanese (62.Gonzalo Villar), Pedro, Borja Mayoral, Carles Pérez, Mory Bamba (62.Rick Karsdorp). Trainer: Paulo Alexandre Rodrigues Fonseca (Portugal).
Goals: 5' Tiago Rodrigues 1-0, 22' Tommaso Milanese 1-1, 34', 55' Ali Sowe 2-1, 3-1.

GROUP B	1. **Arsenal FC London**	6	6	0	0	20 - 5	18
	2. Molde FK	6	3	1	2	9 - 11	10
	3. SK Rapid Wien	6	2	1	3	11 - 13	7
	4. Dundalk FC	6	0	0	6	8 - 19	0

22.10.2020; Tallaght Stadium, Dublin
Referee: Petri Viljanen (Finland)
Dundalk FC – Molde FK 1-2(1-0)
Dundalk FC: Gary Rogers, Brian Gartland, Sean Gannon (77.David McMillan), Daniel Cleary, Darragh Leahy (77.Cameron Dummigan), Chris Shields, Sean Murray (77.Andy Boyle), John Mountney, Gregory Sloggett (64.Patrick McEleney), Patrick Hoban, Michael Duffy (80.Stefan Colovic). Trainer: Shane Keegan.
Molde FK: Andreas Linde, Kristoffer Haugen, Martin Bjørnbak, Stian Gregersen, Marcus Pedersen, Magnus Wolff Eikrem (82.Martin Ellingsen), Etzaz Hussain, Eirik Hestad, Fredrik Aursnes, Mathis Bolly (69.Erling Knudtzon), Ohi Omoijuanfo (90+4.Ola Brynhildsen). Trainer: Erling Moe.
Goals: 35' Sean Murray 1-0, 62' Etzaz Hussain 1-1, 72' Ohi Omoijuanfo 1-2 (penalty).

29.10.2020; Emirates Stadium, London
Referee: Filip Glova (Slovakia)
Arsenal FC London – Dundalk FC 3-0(2-0)
Arsenal FC: Rúnar Alex Rúnarsson, Shkodran Mustafi (61.Dani Ceballos), Cédric Soares, Sead Kolasinac, Granit Xhaka (74.Kieran Tierney), Mohamed Elneny, Ainsley Maitland-Niles, Joseph Willock, Nicolas Pépé (62.Willian), Eddie Nketiah (74.Folarin Balogun), Reiss Nelson. Trainer: Mikel Amatriain Arteta (Spain).
Dundalk FC: Gary Rogers, Brian Gartland, Andy Boyle, Daniel Cleary (53.Sean Hoare), Cameron Dummigan, Chris Shields (62.Sean Gannon), Patrick McEleney (53.Jordan Flores), Sean Murray (46.Gregory Sloggett), John Mountney, Patrick Hoban, Michael Duffy (70.Stefan Colovic). Trainer: Shane Keegan.
Goals: 42' Eddie Nketiah 1-0, 44' Joseph Willock 2-0, 46' Nicolas Pépé 3-0.

22.10.2020; Allianz Stadion, Wien
Referee: Pavel Královec (Czech Republic); Attendance: 3,000
SK Rapid Wien – Arsenal FC London 1-2(0-0)
Rapid Wien: Richard Strebinger, Filip Stojkovic, Maximilian Hofmann, Maximilian Ullmann, Mateo Barac, Marcel Ritzmaier (88.Christoph Knasmüllner), Srdjan Grahovac, Dejan Ljubicic, Taxiarchis Fountas, Ercan Kara (76.Koya Kitagawa), Kelvin Arase (79.Thorsten Schick). Trainer: Dietmar Kühbauer.
Arsenal FC: Bernd Leno, David Luiz, Cédric Soares (61.Héctor Bellerín), Sead Kolasinac, Gabriel Magalhães, Bukayo Saka (84.Kieran Tierney), Mohamed Elneny, Thomas Partey, Alexandre Lacazette (84.Joseph Willock), Nicolas Pépé (90+4.Reiss Nelson), Eddie Nketiah (61.Pierre-Emerick Aubameyang). Trainer: Mikel Amatriain Arteta (Spain).
Goals: 51' Taxiarchis Fountas 1-0, 70' David Luiz 1-1, 74' Pierre-Emerick Aubameyang 1-2.

29.10.2020; Åker Stadion, Molde
Referee: Petr Ardeleánu (Czech Republic); Attendance: 600
Molde FK – SK Rapid Wien 1-0(0-0)
Molde FK: Andreas Linde, Kristoffer Haugen, Martin Bjørnbak, Stian Gregersen, Magnus Wolff Eikrem (83.Leke James), Eirik Hestad (68.Mathis Bolly), Fredrik Aursnes, Martin Ellingsen, Henry Wingo, Ola Brynhildsen (77.Etzaz Hussain), Ohi Omoijuanfo. Trainer: Erling Moe.
Rapid Wien: Paul Gartler, Filip Stojkovic, Maximilian Ullmann, Mateo Barac, Leo Greiml, Thorsten Schick (46.Kelvin Arase), Marcel Ritzmaier, Srdjan Grahovac (77.Melih Ibrahimoglu), Dejan Ljubicic, Koya Kitagawa (59.Christoph Knasmüllner), Ercan Kara. Trainer: Dietmar Kühbauer.
Goal: 65' Ohi Omoijuanfo 1-0.

05.11.2020; Allianz Stadion, Wien
Referee: Trustin Farrugia Cann (Malta)
SK Rapid Wien – Dundalk FC 4-3(1-1)
Rapid Wien: Paul Gartler, Filip Stojkovic, Maximilian Hofmann, Maximilian Ullmann, Mateo Barac (54.Mario Sonnleitner), Christoph Knasmüllner (72.Yusuf Demir), Thorsten Schick, Dejan Petrovic (72.Srdjan Grahovac), Dejan Ljubicic, Ercan Kara, Kelvin Arase. Trainer: Dietmar Kühbauer.
Dundalk FC: Aaron McCarey, Andy Boyle, Sean Gannon (65.John Mountney), Sean Hoare, Daniel Cleary, Darragh Leahy (65.Cameron Dummigan), Chris Shields, Gregory Sloggett, Jordan Flores (76.Sean Murray), Patrick Hoban (76.David McMillan), Michael Duffy (72.Nathan Oduwa). Trainer: Shane Keegan.
Goals: 7' Patrick Hoban 0-1, 22' Dejan Ljubicic 1-1, 79' Kelvin Arase 2-1, 82' David McMillan 2-2 (penalty), 87' Maximilian Hofmann 3-2, 90' Yusuf Demir 4-2, 90+6' David McMillan 4-3 (penalty).

26.11.2020; Åker Stadion, Molde
Referee: Irfan Peljto (Bosnia and Herzegovina); Attendance: 600
Molde FK – Arsenal FC London 0-3(0-0)
Molde FK: Andreas Linde, Stian Gregersen (85.Erling Knudtzon), Birk Risa (82.Marcus Pedersen), Sheriff Sinyan, Magnus Wolff Eikrem (81.Ola Brynhildsen), Etzaz Hussain (61.Mathis Bolly), Eirik Hestad, Fredrik Aursnes, Martin Ellingsen, Henry Wingo, Leke James (61.Ohi Omoijuanfo). Trainer: Erling Moe.
Arsenal FC: Rúnar Alex Rúnarsson, David Luiz (46.Rob Holding), Shkodran Mustafi, Cédric Soares, Granit Xhaka (62.Dani Ceballos), Ainsley Maitland-Niles, Joseph Willock (75.Kieran Tierney), Alexandre Lacazette (75.Emile Smith-Rowe), Nicolas Pépé, Eddie Nketiah (82.Folarin Balogun), Reiss Nelson. Trainer: Mikel Amatriain Arteta (Spain).
Goals: 50' Nicolas Pépé 0-1, 55' Reiss Nelson 0-2, 83' Folarin Balogun 0-3.

03.12.2020; Emirates Stadium, London
Referee: Radu Marian Petrescu (Romania); Attendance: 2,000
Arsenal FC London – SK Rapid Wien 4-1(3-0)
Arsenal FC: Rúnar Alex Rúnarsson, Shkodran Mustafi (70.Calum Chambers), Cédric Soares, Pablo Marí, Sead Kolasinac, Mohamed Elneny (63.Dani Ceballos), Ainsley Maitland-Niles, Alexandre Lacazette (63.Emile Smith-Rowe), Nicolas Pépé, Eddie Nketiah (81.Folarin Balogun), Reiss Nelson (63.Willian). Trainer: Mikel Amatriain Arteta (Spain).
Rapid Wien: Richard Strebinger, Mario Sonnleitner, Maximilian Hofmann (46.Mateo Barac), Maximilian Ullmann (46.Thorsten Schick), Leo Greiml, Marcel Ritzmaier (65.Christoph Knasmüllner), Lion Schuster, Deni Alar (77.Lukas Sulzbacher), Koya Kitagawa (65.Ercan Kara), Kelvin Arase, Yusuf Demir. Trainer: Dietmar Kühbauer.
Goals: 10' Alexandre Lacazette 1-0, 17' Pablo Marí 2-0, 44' Eddie Nketiah 3-0, 47' Koya Kitagawa 3-1, 66' Emile Smith-Rowe 4-1.

10.12.2020; Aviva Stadium, Dublin
Referee: Ivan Bebek (Croatia)
Dundalk FC – Arsenal FC London 2-4(1-2)
Dundalk FC: Gary Rogers, Andy Boyle (46.Brian Gartland), Sean Gannon (54.John Mountney), Sean Hoare, Daniel Cleary, Darragh Leahy, Chris Shields, Patrick McEleney (78.Stefan Colovic), Jordan Flores, David McMillan (53.Daniel Kelly), Michael Duffy (77.Jamie Wynne). Trainer: Shane Keegan.
Arsenal FC: Rúnar Alex Rúnarsson, Shkodran Mustafi, Cédric Soares, Pablo Marí, Calum Chambers, Mohamed Elneny (62.Dani Ceballos), Ainsley Maitland-Niles, Joseph Willock (83.Miguel Azeez), Emile Smith-Rowe (77.Ben Cottrell), Nicolas Pépé, Eddie Nketiah (62.Folarin Balogun). Trainer: Mikel Amatriain Arteta (Spain).
Goals: 12' Eddie Nketiah 0-1, 18' Mohamed Elneny 0-2, 22' Jordan Flores 1-2, 67' Joseph Willock 1-3, 80' Folarin Balogun 1-4, 85' Sean Hoare 2-4.

05.11.2020; Emirates Stadium, London
Referee: Halil Umut Meler (Turkey)
Arsenal FC London – Molde FK 4-1(1-1)
Arsenal FC: Bernd Leno, David Luiz, Shkodran Mustafi, Sead Kolasinac, Granit Xhaka (80.Kieran Tierney), Ainsley Maitland-Niles (63.Cédric Soares), Dani Ceballos (80.Mohamed Elneny), Joseph Willock, Willian (63.Bukayo Saka), Nicolas Pépé, Eddie Nketiah. Trainer: Mikel Amatriain Arteta (Spain).
Molde FK: Andreas Linde, Kristoffer Haugen, Martin Bjørnbak, Stian Gregersen (46.Sheriff Sinyan), Magnus Wolff Eikrem (74.Ola Brynhildsen), Etzaz Hussain, Fredrik Aursnes, Martin Ellingsen (86.Mattias Moström), Henry Wingo, Mathis Bolly (63.Erling Knudtzon), Ohi Omoijuanfo (74.Leke James). Trainer: Erling Moe.
Goals: 22' Martin Ellingsen 0-1, 45+1' Kristoffer Haugen 1-1 (own goal), 62' Sheriff Sinyan 2-1 (own goal), 69' Nicolas Pépé 3-1, 88' Joseph Willock 4-1.

26.11.2020; Aviva Stadium, Dublin
Referee: Tamás Bognár (Hungary)
Dundalk FC – SK Rapid Wien 1-3(0-2)
Dundalk FC: Gary Rogers, Andy Boyle, Sean Gannon, Sean Hoare (46.Daniel Kelly), Daniel Cleary, Cameron Dummigan (81.Darragh Leahy), Chris Shields, Gregory Sloggett (72.Sean Murray), Stefan Colovic (46.Patrick McEleney), David McMillan (46.Nathan Oduwa), Michael Duffy. Trainer: Shane Keegan.
Rapid Wien: Paul Gartler, Filip Stojkovic, Maximilian Hofmann, Maximilian Ullmann, Mateo Barac, Christoph Knasmüllner (81.Yusuf Demir), Thorsten Schick, Srdjan Grahovac, Melih Ibrahimoglu (55.Kelvin Arase), Taxiarchis Fountas (66.Lion Schuster), Ercan Kara (66.Koya Kitagawa). Trainer: Dietmar Kühbauer.
Goals: 11' Christoph Knasmüllner 0-1, 37', 58' Ercan Kara 0-2, 0-3, 63' Chris Shields 1-3 (penalty).

03.12.2020; Åker Stadion, Molde
Referee: Daniel Siebert (Germany); Attendance: 600
Molde FK – Dundalk FC 3-1(2-0)
Molde FK: Andreas Linde, Stian Gregersen (68.Etzaz Hussain), Birk Risa, Sheriff Sinyan, Magnus Wolff Eikrem (78.Leke James), Eirik Hestad (79.Mattias Moström), Fredrik Aursnes (78.Tobias Christensen), Martin Ellingsen, Henry Wingo, Erling Knudtzon, Ohi Omoijuanfo (86.Mathis Bolly). Trainer: Erling Moe.
Dundalk FC: Gary Rogers, Brian Gartland, Andy Boyle (61.Daniel Cleary), Sean Gannon, Sean Hoare, Cameron Dummigan, Chris Shields (68.John Mountney), Gregory Sloggett (61.Patrick McEleney), Jordan Flores, Daniel Kelly (73.David McMillan), Nathan Oduwa (61.Michael Duffy). Trainer: Shane Keegan.
Goals: 30' Magnus Wolff Eikrem 1-0, 41' Ohi Omoijuanfo 2-0, 67' Martin Ellingsen 3-0, 90+4' Jordan Flores 3-1.

10.12.2020; Allianz Stadion, Wien
Referee: Marco Guida (Italy)
SK Rapid Wien – Molde FK 2-2(1-1)
Rapid Wien: Paul Gartler, Filip Stojkovic, Maximilian Hofmann, Maximilian Ullmann, Mateo Barac, Christoph Knasmüllner (46.Taxiarchis Fountas), Thorsten Schick, Marcel Ritzmaier (61.Melih Ibrahimoglu), Srdjan Grahovac, Ercan Kara (75.Koya Kitagawa), Kelvin Arase (46.Yusuf Demir). Trainer: Dietmar Kühbauer.
Molde FK: Andreas Linde, Stian Gregersen, Birk Risa, Sheriff Sinyan, Marcus Pedersen, Magnus Wolff Eikrem (57.Etzaz Hussain), Eirik Hestad (45.Erling Knudtzon), Fredrik Aursnes, Martin Ellingsen, Ola Brynhildsen (56.Ohi Omoijuanfo), Leke James (85.Henry Wingo). Trainer: Erling Moe.
Goals: 12' Magnus Wolff Eikrem 0-1, 43' Marcel Ritzmaier 1-1, 46' Magnus Wolff Eikrem 1-2, 90' Melih Ibrahimoglu 2-2.

1.	**TSV Bayer 04 Leverkusen**	6	5	0	1	21	-	8	15
2.	**SK Slavia Praha**	6	4	0	2	11	-	10	12
3.	Hapoel Be'er Sheva FC	6	2	0	4	7	-	13	6
4.	OGC Nice	6	1	0	5	8	-	16	3

GROUP C

22.10.2020; BayArena, Leverkusen
Referee: Fran Jović (Croatia)
TSV Bayer 04 Leverkusen – OGC Nice 6-2(2-1)
Bayer Leverkusen: Lukás Hrádecký, Sven Bender (81.Jonathan Tah), Lars Bender (82.Aleksandar Dragovic), Wendell, Edmond Tapsoba, Julian Baumgartlinger, Nadiem Amiri, Exequiel Palacios (74.Florian Wirtz), Lucas Alario (74.Karim Bellarabi), Leon Bailey, Moussa Diaby. Trainer: Peter Bosz (Netherlands).
OGC Nice: Walter Benítez, Dante, Jordan Lotomba (79.Youcef Atal), Stanley N'Soki (63.Rony Lopes), Robson Bambu, Morgan Schneiderlin, Hassane Kamara, Pierre Lees-Melou (79.Dan N'Doye), Hichem Boudaoui (63.Alexis Claude-Maurice), Kasper Dolberg (71.Myziane Maolida), Amine Gouiri. Trainer: Patrick Vieira.
Goals: 11' Nadiem Amiri 1-0, 16' Lucas Alario 2-0, 31' Amine Gouiri 2-1, 61' Moussa Diaby 3-1, 79, 83' Karim Bellarabi 4-1, 5-1, 87' Florian Wirtz 6-1, 90' Alexis Claude-Maurice 6-2.

29.10.2020; Stadion Sinobo, Praha
Referee: William Collum (Scotland)
SK Slavia Praha – TSV Bayer 04 Leverkusen 1-0(0-0)
Slavia Praha: Ondrej Kolár, Ondrej Kúdela, Jan Boril, Tomás Holes (61.Nicolae Stanciu), David Zima, Tomás Malinský (71.Abdallah Sima), Lukás Masopust, Petr Sevcík, Lukás Provod (76.Ibrahim Traoré), Ondrej Lingr (46.Petar Musa), Oscar Dorley (61.Peter Olayinka). Trainer: Jindrich Trpisovský.
Bayer Leverkusen: Lukás Hrádecký, Aleksandar Dragovic, Wendell, Tin Jedvaj, Jonathan Tah, Julian Baumgartlinger, Kerem Demirbay, Florian Wirtz (67.Nadiem Amiri), Karim Bellarabi [sent off 22], Lucas Alario (46.Leon Bailey), Moussa Diaby. Trainer: Peter Bosz (Netherlands).
Goal: 80' Peter Olayinka 1-0.

05.11.2020; Stadion Sinobo, Praha
Referee: Jakob Kehlet (Denmark)
SK Slavia Praha – OGC Nice 3-2(2-1)
Slavia Praha: Ondrej Kolár, Tomás Holes, David Hovorka (86.Jakub Kristan), David Zima, Lukás Masopust, Petr Sevcík, Peter Olayinka, Ondrej Lingr (70.Ibrahim Traoré), Oscar Dorley, Jan Kuchta (77.Stanislav Tecl), Abdallah Sima. Trainer: Jindrich Trpisovský.
OGC Nice: Walter Benítez, Jordan Lotomba, Robson Bambu, Andy Pelmard, Flavius Daniliuc, Morgan Schneiderlin, Hassane Kamara (88.Dan N'Doye), Pierre Lees-Melou (65.Alexis Claude-Maurice), Rony Lopes (65.Jeff Reine-Adélaïde), Kasper Dolberg (81.Youcef Atal), Amine Gouiri. Trainer: Patrick Vieira.
Goals: 16' Jan Kuchta 1-0, 33' Amine Gouiri 1-1, 43' Abdallah Sima 2-1, 71' Jan Kuchta 3-1, 90+3' Dan N'Doye 3-2.

26.11.2020; Bay Arena, Leverkusen
Referee: Paweł Gil (Poland)
TSV Bayer 04 Leverkusen – Hapoel Be'er Sheva FC 4-1(1-0)
Bayer Leverkusen: Lukás Hrádecký, Aleksandar Dragovic, Wendell, Tin Jedvaj, Jonathan Tah, Kerem Demirbay, Nadiem Amiri (90+1.Julian Baumgartlinger), Florian Wirtz (80.Daley Sinkgraven), Karim Bellarabi (80.Emrehan Gedikli), Patrik Schick (68.Lucas Alario), Leon Bailey (68.Moussa Diaby). Trainer: Peter Bosz (Netherlands).
Hapoel Be'er Sheva: Ohad Levita, Loai Taha, Sean Goldberg (70.Dudu Twito), Lucas Bareiro, Or Dadya, Sintayehu Sallalich (70.Jhonatan Agudelo, 85.Gaëtan Varenne), Marwan Kabha, César Marcelo Meli (81.Ilay Madmon), David Keltjens, Tomer Yosefi, Itamar Shviro (80.Rotem Hatuel). Trainer: Yossi Abukasis.
Goals: 29' Patrik Schick 1-0, 48' Leon Bailey 2-0, 58' Itamar Shviro 2-1, 76' Kerem Demirbay 3-1, 80' Lucas Alario 4-1.

22.10.2020; HaMoshava Stadium, Petach-Tikva
Referee: Lawrence Visser (Belgium); Attendance: 40
Hapoel Be'er Sheva FC – SK Slavia Praha 3-1(1-0)
Hapoel Be'er Sheva: Ohad Levita, Miguel Vítor, Loai Taha (46.Shir Tzedek), Sean Goldberg, Elton Acolatse (89.Gaëtan Varenne), Lucas Bareiro, Or Dadya, Sintayehu Sallalich (79.Tomer Yosefi), Josué (90.David Keltjens), Marwan Kabha, Jhonatan Agudelo (70.César Marcelo Meli). Trainer: Yossi Abukasis.
Slavia Praha: Ondrej Kolár, Ondrej Kúdela, Jan Boril, David Hovorka, Tomás Malinský (58.Lukás Masopust), Petr Sevcík (75.Ondrej Lingr), Lukás Provod, Ibrahim Traoré (46.Nicolae Stanciu), Oscar Dorley (89.Abdallah Sima), Stanislav Tecl (57.Jan Kuchta), Petar Musa. Trainer: Jindrich Trpisovský.
Goals: 45' Jhonatan Agudelo 1-0, 75' Lukás Provod 1-1, 86', 88' Elton Acolatse 2-1, 3-1.

29.10.2020; Allianz Riviera, Nice
Referee: Chris Kavanagh (England)
OGC Nice – Hapoel Be'er Sheva FC 1-0(1-0)
OGC Nice: Walter Benítez, Dante, Stanley N'Soki (46.Andy Pelmard), Youcef Atal (68.Jordan Lotomba), Robson Bambu, Morgan Schneiderlin, Hassane Kamara, Alexis Claude-Maurice (58.Jeff Reine-Adélaïde), Khéphren Thuram-Ulien, Kasper Dolberg (85.Hichem Boudaoui), Amine Gouiri (69.Myziane Maolida). Trainer: Patrick Vieira.
Hapoel Be'er Sheva: Ohad Levita, Miguel Vítor, Loai Taha, Sean Goldberg (76.Gaëtan Varenne), Elton Acolatse (88.Dudu Twito), Lucas Bareiro (81.Ramzi Safouri), Or Dadya, Sintayehu Sallalich (76.César Marcelo Meli), Josué, Marwan Kabha, Tomer Yosefi (46.Jhonatan Agudelo). Trainer: Yossi Abukasis.
Goal: 23' Amine Gouiri 1-0.

05.11.2020; HaMoshava Stadium, Petach-Tikva
Referee: Radu Marian Petrescu (Romania)
Hapoel Be'er Sheva FC – TSV Bayer 04 Leverkusen 2-4(2-2)
Hapoel Be'er Sheva: Ohad Levita, Miguel Vítor, Loai Taha, Sean Goldberg (84.Ramzi Safouri), Elton Acolatse (89.César Marcelo Meli), Lucas Bareiro, Or Dadya, Sintayehu Sallalich (64.Itamar Shviro), Josué, Marwan Kabha (84.Gaëtan Varenne), Jhonatan Agudelo (64.Tomer Yosefi). Trainer: Yossi Abukasis.
Bayer Leverkusen: Lukás Hrádecký, Aleksandar Dragovic, Wendell, Tin Jedvaj (62.Lars Bender), Jonathan Tah, Kerem Demirbay, Nadiem Amiri, Exequiel Palacios, Florian Wirtz, Lucas Alario (46.Moussa Diaby), Leon Bailey. Trainer: Peter Bosz (Netherlands).
Goals: 5' Leon Bailey 0-1, 11', 25' Elton Acolatse 1-1, 2-1, 39' Or Dadya 2-2 (own goal), 75' Leon Bailey 2-3, 88' Florian Wirtz 2-4.

26.11.2020; Allianz Riviera, Nice
Referee: Glenn Nyberg (Sweden)
OGC Nice – SK Slavia Praha 1-3(0-1)
OGC Nice: Walter Benítez, Jordan Lotomba, Stanley N'Soki, Youcef Atal (66.Dan N'Doye), Robson Bambu, Morgan Schneiderlin, Jeff Reine-Adélaïde, Alexis Claude-Maurice (72.Hichem Boudaoui [sent off 90+1]), Rony Lopes, Myziane Maolida, Amine Gouiri (78.Andy Pelmard). Trainer: Patrick Vieira.
Slavia Praha: Ondrej Kolár, Ondrej Kúdela, Jan Boril, Tomás Holes (87.Ondrej Karafiát), David Zima, Lukás Masopust, Petr Sevcík, Peter Olayinka (88.Tomás Malínský), Ondrej Lingr (63.Ibrahim Traoré), Jan Kuchta (82.Lukás Provod), Abdallah Sima (87.Stanislav Tecl). Trainer: Jindrich Trpisovský.
Goals: 14' Ondrej Lingr 0-1, 61' Amine Gouiri 1-1, 64' Peter Olayinka 1-2, 75' Abdallah Sima 1-3.

03.12.2020; Stadion Sinobo, Praha
Referee: Tamás Bognár (Hungary); Attendance: 600
SK Slavia Praha – Hapoel Be'er Sheva FC 3-0(2-0)
Slavia Praha: Ondrej Kolár, Ondrej Kúdela, Tomás Holes, David Zima, Nicolae Stanciu (64.Ondrej Lingr), Lukás Masopust (81.Lukás Provod), Petr Sevcík (80.Ibrahim Traoré), Peter Olayinka, Oscar Dorley (61.Jan Boril), Jan Kuchta (81.Petar Musa), Abdallah Sima. Trainer: Jindrich Trpisovský.
Hapoel Be'er Sheva: Ohad Levita, Loai Taha (81.Noam Gamon), Shir Tzedek, Lucas Bareiro (46.Ilay Madmon), Dudu Twito, Or Dadya, Sintayehu Sallalich (62.Tomer Yosefi), Josué (76.Rotem Hatuel), Marwan Kabha, David Keltjens, Gaëtan Varenne (61.Itamar Shviro). Trainer: Yossi Abukasis.
Goals: 31' Abdallah Sima 1-0, 36' Nicolae Stanciu 2-0, 85' Dudu Twito 3-0 (own goal).

10.12.2020; BayArena, Leverkusen
Referee: Anastasios Sidiropoulos (Greece)
TSV Bayer 04 Leverkusen – SK Slavia Praha 4-0(2-0)
Bayer Leverkusen: Niklas Lomb, Aleksandar Dragovic, Wendell, Tin Jedvaj, Daley Sinkgraven (62.Samed Onur), Edmond Tapsoba, Julian Baumgartlinger (62.Lars Bender), Nadiem Amiri (74.Cem Türkmen), Karim Bellarabi, Patrik Schick (46.Emrehan Gedikli), Leon Bailey (46.Moussa Diaby). Trainer: Peter Bosz (Netherlands).
Slavia Praha: Ondrej Kolár, Jan Boril, David Zima, Lukás Masopust, Petr Sevcík (19.Nicolae Stanciu), Peter Olayinka, Ibrahim Traoré (82.Ondrej Karafiát), Ondrej Lingr (82.Tomás Rigo), Oscar Dorley, Petar Musa (53.Stanislav Tecl), Abdallah Sima (82.Matej Jarásek). Trainer: Jindrich Trpisovský.
Goals: 8', 32' Leon Bailey 1-0, 2-0, 59' Moussa Diaby 3-0, 90+1' Karim Bellarabi 4-0.

03.12.2020; Allianz Riviera, Nice
Referee: Maurizio Mariani (Italy)
OGC Nice – TSV Bayer 04 Leverkusen 2-3(1-2)
OGC Nice: Walter Benítez, Jordan Lotomba, Stanley N'Soki, Robson Bambu, Flavius Daniliuc, Hassane Kamara (72.Racine Coly), Danilo Barbosa (67.Khéphren Thuram-Ulien), Jeff Reine-Adélaïde, Alexis Claude-Maurice, Myziane Maolida (29.Dan N'Doye), Amine Gouiri (72.Alexis Trouillet). Trainer: Patrick Vieira.
Bayer Leverkusen: Lukás Hrádecký, Lars Bender (46.Edmond Tapsoba), Aleksandar Dragovic, Wendell, Jonathan Tah, Julian Baumgartlinger, Kerem Demirbay (86.Florian Wirtz), Nadiem Amiri (68.Cem Türkmen), Karim Bellarabi, Patrik Schick (46.Leon Bailey), Moussa Diaby (68.Emrehan Gedikli). Trainer: Peter Bosz (Netherlands).
Goals: 22' Moussa Diaby 0-1, 26' Hassane Kamara 1-1, 32' Aleksandar Dragovic 1-2, 47' Dan N'Doye 2-2, 51' Julian Baumgartlinger 2-3.

10.12.2020; HaMoshava Stadium, Petach-Tikva
Referee: Kristo Tohver (Estonia)
Hapoel Be'er Sheva FC – OGC Nice 1-0(0-0)
Hapoel Be'er Sheva: Raz Rahamim, Loai Taha, Shir Tzedek, Noam Gamon, Dudu Twito, Marwan Kabha, David Keltjens, Tomer Yosefi (66.Josué), Ilay Madmon, Gaëtan Varenne (65.Itamar Shviro, 76.Ramzi Safouri), Rotem Hatuel (84.Sintayehu Sallalich). Trainer: Yossi Abukasis.
OGC Nice: Yoan Cardinale, Racine Coly (28.Hicham Mahou), Robson Bambu, Andy Pelmard, Théo Pionnier-Bertrand (82.Noah Crétier), Morgan Schneiderlin (46.Hichem Boudaoui), Alexis Claude-Maurice, Alexis Trouillet, Khéphren Thuram-Ulien, Rony Lopes (46.Selim Ben Seghir), Dan N'Doye. Trainer: Adrian Dante Ursea (Romania).
Goal: 71' Rotem Hatuel 1-0.

GROUP D	1. **Rangers FC Glasgow**	6	4	2	0	13 - 7	14
	2. **Sport Lisboa e Benfica**	6	3	3	0	18 - 9	12
	3. R Standard Liège	6	1	1	4	7 - 14	4
	4. KKS Lech Poznań	6	1	0	5	6 - 14	3

22.10.2020; Stade „Maurice Dufrasne", Liège
Referee: Jakob Kehlet (Denmark); Attendance: 3,139
R Standard Liège – Rangers FC Glasgow 0-2(0-1)
Standard Liège: Arnaud Bodart, Noë Dussenne (78.Laurent Jans), Nicolas Gavory, Collins Fai (63.Mehdi Carcela-González), Zinho Vanheusden, Maxime Lestienne (72.Felipe Avenatti), Gojko Cimirot, Merveille Bopé Bokadi, Samuel Bastien, Selim Amallah (72.Duje Cop), Jackson Muleka (46.Obbi Oularé). Trainer: Philippe Montanier (France).
Rangers FC: Allan McGregor, Leon Balogun, James Tavernier, Connor Goldson, Borna Barisic (43.Calvin Bassey Ughelumba), Scott Arfield, Ryan Jack, Glen Kamara, Ianis Hagi (67.Joe Ayodele-Aribo), Alfredo Morelos (74.Kemar Roofe), Ryan Kent. Trainer: Steven George Gerrard (England).
Goals: 19' James Tavernier 0-1 (penalty), 90+3' Kemar Roofe 0-2.

29.10.2020; Estádio da Luz, Lisboa
Referee: François Letexier (France); Attendance: 4,750
Sport Lisboa e Benfica – R Standard Liège 3-0(0-0)
Benfica: Odisseas Vlachodimos, Jan Vertonghen, Nicolás Otamendi, Nuno Tavares, Pizzi (79.Gonçalo Ramos), Gabriel (72.Julian Weigl), Diogo Gonçalves, Éverton, Pedrinho (46.Rafa Silva), Luca Waldschmidt (68.Adel Taarabt), Darwin Núñez (72.Haris Seferovic). Trainer: Jorge Fernando Pinheiro de Jesus.
Standard Liège: Arnaud Bodart, Noë Dussenne, Nicolas Gavory, Collins Fai, Zinho Vanheusden (76.Kostas Laifis), Mehdi Carcela-González, Gojko Cimirot (75.Joachim Carcela-González), Merveille Bopé Bokadi, Samuel Bastien, Selim Amallah (80.Felipe Avenatti), Obbi Oularé (70.Aleksandar Boljevic). Trainer: Philippe Montanier (France).
Goals: 49' Pizzi 1-0 (penalty), 66' Luca Waldschmidt 2-0 (penalty), 76' Pizzi 3-0.

22.10.2020; Stadion Miejski, Poznań
Referee: Nikola Dabanović (Montenegro)
KKS Lech Poznań – Sport Lisboa e Benfica 2-4(1-2)
Lech Poznań: Filip Bednarek, Alan Czerwinski, Tomasz Dejewski, Djordje Crnomarkovic, Tymoteusz Puchacz (74.Vasyl Kravets), Pedro Tiba, Dani Ramírez (67.Karlo Muhar), Jakub Moder, Michal Skóras (90+1.Mohamed Awaed), Jakub Kaminski (67.Filip Marchwinski), Mikael Ishak (74.Nika Kacharava). Trainer: Dariusz Zuraw.
Benfica: Odisseas Vlachodimos, Jan Vertonghen, Nicolás Otamendi, Gabriel, Álex Grinaldo (67.Nuno Tavares), Adel Taarabt (62.Julian Weigl), Pizzi (46.Rafa Silva), Gabriel, Éverton (87.Jardel), Luca Waldschmidt (62.Pedrinho), Darwin Núñez. Trainer: Jorge Fernando Pinheiro de Jesus.
Goals: 9' Pizzi 0-1 (penalty), 15' Mikael Ishak 1-1, 42' Darwin Núñez 1-2, 48' Mikael Ishak 2-2, 60', 90+3' Darwin Núñez 2-3, 2-4.

29.10.2020; Ibrox Stadium, Glasgow
Referee: Kristo Tohver (Estonia); Attendance: 11
Rangers FC Glasgow – KKS Lech Poznań 1-0(0-0)
Rangers FC: Allan McGregor, Leon Balogun, James Tavernier, Connor Goldson, Borna Barisic, Steven Davis, Scott Arfield (80.Ryan Jack), Glen Kamara, Ianis Hagi (69.Joe Ayodele-Aribo), Kemar Roofe (63.Alfredo Morelos), Ryan Kent (81.Brandon Barker). Trainer: Steven George Gerrard (England).
Lech Poznań: Filip Bednarek, Thomas Rogne, Lubomír Satka, Alan Czerwinski, Vasyl Kravets, Tymoteusz Puchacz, Dani Ramírez (87.Nika Kacharava), Jakub Moder, Michal Skóras (74.Jan Sýkora), Filip Marchwinski (82.Mohamed Awaed), Mikael Ishak. Trainer: Dariusz Zuraw.
Goal: 68' Alfredo Morelos 1-0.

05.11.2020; Estádio da Luz, Lisboa
Referee: Jesús Gil Manzano (Spain)
Sport Lisboa e Benfica – Rangers FC Glasgow 3-3(1-2)
Benfica: Odisseas Vlachodimos, Jan Vertonghen, Nicolás Otamendi [*sent off 19*], Nuno Tavares (46.Álex Grimaldo), Adel Taarabt, Pizzi (21.Jardel), Rafa Silva, Julian Weigl, Diogo Gonçalves (46.Gilberto), Éverton (67.Luca Waldschmidt), Haris Seferovic (60.Darwin Núñez). Trainer: Jorge Fernando Pinheiro de Jesus.
Rangers FC: Allan McGregor, James Tavernier, Connor Goldson, Filip Helander, Borna Barisic, Steven Davis, Ryan Jack, Glen Kamara, Joe Ayodele-Aribo (69.Scott Arfield), Alfredo Morelos, Ryan Kent. Trainer: Steven George Gerrard (England).
Goals: 2' Connor Goldson 1-0 (own goal), 24' Diogo Gonçalves 1-1 (own goal), 25' Glen Kamara 1-2, 51' Alfredo Morelos 1-3, 77' Rafa Silva 2-3, 90+1' Darwin Núñez 3-3.

26.11.2020; Stade „Maurice Dufrasne", Liège
Referee: Petr Ardeleánu (Czech Republic)
R Standard Liège – KKS Lech Poznań 2-1(0-0)
Standard Liège: Arnaud Bodart, Noë Dussenne, Kostas Laifis, Nicolas Gavory (76.Laurent Jans), Collins Fai, Maxime Lestienne (46.Aleksandar Boljevic), Gojko Cimirot, Merveille Bopé Bokadi (46.Abdoul Tapsoba), Nicolas Raskin (76.Samuel Bastien), Obbi Oularé [*sent off 45+2*], Michel Balikwisha (76.Felipe Avenatti). Trainer: Philippe Montanier (France).
Lech Poznań: Filip Bednarek, Thomas Rogne, Bogdan Butko, Djordje Crnomarkovic [*sent off 74*], Tymoteusz Puchacz, Jan Sýkora (64.Vasyl Kravets), Pedro Tiba (78.Filip Marchwinski), Dani Ramírez, Jakub Moder (78.Lubomír Satka), Michal Skóras (64.Alan Czerwinski), Mikael Ishak (83.Nika Kacharava). Trainer: Dariusz Zuraw.
Goals: 61' Mikael Ishak 0-1, 63' Abdoul Tapsoba 1-1, 90+4' Kostas Laifis 2-1.

03.12.2020; Estádio da Luz, Lisboa
Referee: Srđan Jovanović (Serbia)
Sport Lisboa e Benfica – KKS Lech Poznań 4-0(1-0)
Benfica: Odisseas Vlachodimos, Jan Vertonghen, Nicolás Otamendi, Gilberto, Álex Grimaldo, Pizzi (59.Luca Waldschmidt), Gabriel, Rafa Silva (77.Franco Cervi), Éverton (70.Pedrinho), Chiquinho (60.Julian Weigl), Darwin Núñez (60.Haris Seferovic). Trainer: Jorge Fernando Pinheiro de Jesus.
Lech Poznań: Filip Bednarek, Bogdan Butko, Lubomír Satka, Tomasz Dejewski, Tymoteusz Puchacz, Jan Sýkora (63.Vasyl Kravets), Karlo Muhar, Michal Skóras (63.Alan Czerwinski), Filip Marchwinski (82.Jakub Moder), Nika Kacharava (42.Mikael Ishak), Mohamad Awaed (63.Dani Ramírez). Trainer: Dariusz Zuraw.
Goals: 36' Jan Vertonghen 1-0, 57' Darwin Núñez 2-0, 58' Pizzi 3-0, 89' Julian Weigl 4-0.

10.12.2020; Stade „Maurice Dufrasne", Liège
Referee: Aleksei Kulbakov (Belarus)
R Standard Liège – Sport Lisboa e Benfica 2-2(1-1)
Standard Liège: Arnaud Bodart, Laurent Jans, Kostas Laifis, Nicolas Gavory, Gojko Cimirot, Eden Shamir (59.Collins Fai), Merveille Bopé Bokadi, Samuel Bastien, Nicolas Raskin (80.Joachim Carcela-González), Abdoul Tapsoba (72.Obbi Oularé), Michel Balikwisha (59.Jackson Muleka). Trainer: Philippe Montanier (France).
Benfica: Helton Leite, Jan Vertonghen, Jardel, Nuno Tavares (80.Franco Cervi), João Ferreira, Adel Taarabt (83.Haris Seferovic), Julian Weigl (80.Gabriel), Éverton, Pedrinho (64.Rafa Silva), Luca Waldschmidt (64.Pizzi), Darwin Núñez. Trainer: Jorge Fernando Pinheiro de Jesus.
Goals: 12' Nicolas Raskin 1-0, 16' Éverton 1-1, 60' Abdoul Tapsoba 2-1, 67' Pizzi 2-2 (penalty).

05.11.2020; Stadion Miejski, Poznań
Referee: Manuel Schüttengruber (Austria)
KKS Lech Poznań – R Standard Liège 3-1(2-1)
Lech Poznań: Filip Bednarek, Thomas Rogne, Lubomír Satka, Alan Czerwinski, Tymoteusz Puchacz, Pedro Tiba (81.Karlo Muhar), Dani Ramírez (81.Mohamed Awaed), Jakub Moder, Michal Skóras (62.Jan Sýkora), Filip Marchwinski (62.Jakub Kaminski), Mikael Ishak (85.Nika Kacharava). Trainer: Dariusz Zuraw.
Standard Liège: Arnaud Bodart, Noë Dussenne, Laurent Jans, Nicolas Gavory (46.Hugo Siquet), Maxime Lestienne (73.Obbi Oularé), Gojko Cimirot (88.Joachim Carcela-González), Merveille Bopé Bokadi, Samuel Bastien, Selim Amallah (60.Aleksandar Boljevic), Nicolas Raskin (73.Mehdi Carcela-González), Michel Balikwisha. Trainer: Philippe Montanier (France).
Goals: 14' Michal Skóras 1-0, 22' Mikael Ishak 2-0, 29' Maxime Lestienne 2-1, 48' Mikael Ishak 3-1.

26.11.2020; Ibrox Stadium, Glasgow
Referee: Radu Marian Petrescu (Romania)
Rangers FC Glasgow – Sport Lisboa e Benfica 2-2(1-0)
Rangers FC: Allan McGregor, Leon Balogun, James Tavernier, Connor Goldson, Borna Barisic, Steven Davis, Scott Arfield, Glen Kamara, Kemar Roofe, Alfredo Morelos, Ryan Kent. Trainer: Steven George Gerrard (England).
Benfica: Helton Leite, Jan Vertonghen, Jardel, Gilberto (70.Gonçalo Ramos), Álex Grimaldo, Gabriel, Rafa Silva, Éverton, Chiquinho (56.Pizzi), Haris Seferovic (90+3.Ferro), Luca Waldschmidt (56.Diogo Gonçalves). Trainer: Jorge Fernando Pinheiro de Jesus.
Goals: 7' Scott Arfield 1-0, 69' Kemar Roofe 2-0, 78' James Tavernier 2-1 (own goal), 81' Pizzi 2-2.

03.12.2020; Ibrox Stadium, Glasgow
Referee: Bojan Pandzić (Sweden)
Rangers FC Glasgow – R Standard Liège 3-2(2-2)
Rangers FC: Allan McGregor, Leon Balogun, James Tavernier, Connor Goldson, Borna Barisic (89.Calvin Bassey Ughelumba), Steven Davis, Scott Arfield (86.Bongani Zungu), Glen Kamara, Kemar Roofe (89.Cedric Itten), Alfredo Morelos (79.Joe Ayodele-Aribo), Ryan Kent. Trainer: Steven George Gerrard (England).
Standard Liège: Arnaud Bodart, Noë Dussenne, Laurent Jans (86.Nicolas Gavory), Kostas Laifis, Collins Fai, Maxime Lestienne (71.Felipe Avenatti), Eden Shamir (71.Nicolas Raskin), Merveille Bopé Bokadi, Samuel Bastien, Duje Cop (46.Michel Balikwisha), Abdoul Tapsoba. Trainer: Philippe Montanier (France).
Goals: 6' Maxime Lestienne 0-1, 39' Connor Goldson 1-1, 41' Duje Cop 1-2, 45+1' James Tavernier 2-2 (penalty), 63' Scott Arfield 3-2.

10.12.2020; Stadion Miejski, Poznań
Referee: José María Sánchez Martínez (Spain)
KKS Lech Poznań – Rangers FC Glasgow 0-2(0-1)
Lech Poznań: Filip Bednarek, Bogdan Butko, Lubomír Satka, Djordje Crnomarkovic, Tymoteusz Puchacz, Petro Tiba (46.Jakub Moder), Karlo Muhar, Michal Skóras (12.Jan Sýkora, 64.Dani Ramírez), Filip Marchwinski, Jakub Kaminski (46.Vasyl Kravets), Mikael Ishak (64.Mohamad Awaed). Trainer: Dariusz Zuraw.
Rangers FC: Jon McLaughlin, Leon Balogun (80.Calvin Bassey Ughelumba), Connor Goldson, Borna Barisic, Nathan Patterson (66.James Tavernier), Scott Arfield, Bongani Zungu (76.Brandon Barker), Glen Kamara, Joe Ayodele-Aribo, Ianis Hagi (77.Ryan Kent), Cedric Itten (80.Alfredo Morelos). Trainer: Steven George Gerrard (England).
Goals: 31' Cedric Itten 0-1, 72' Ianis Hagi 0-2.

<table>
<tr><td rowspan="4">**GROUP E**</td><td>1. **PSV Eindhoven**</td><td>6</td><td>4</td><td>0</td><td>2</td><td>12 - 9</td><td>12</td></tr>
<tr><td>2. **Granada CF**</td><td>6</td><td>3</td><td>2</td><td>1</td><td>6 - 3</td><td>11</td></tr>
<tr><td>3. PAOK Thessaloníki</td><td>6</td><td>1</td><td>3</td><td>2</td><td>8 - 7</td><td>6</td></tr>
<tr><td>4. AC Omonia Nicosia</td><td>6</td><td>1</td><td>1</td><td>4</td><td>5 - 12</td><td>4</td></tr>
</table>

22.10.2020; Philips Stadion, Eindhoven
Referee: Felix Zwayer (Germany)
PSV Eindhoven – Granada CF 1-2(1-0)
PSV Eindhoven: Yvon Mvogo, Philipp Max, Timo Baumgartl, Olivier Boscagli, Denzel Dumfries, Mario Götze (46.Nick Viergever), Jorrit Hendrix, Mauro Júnior (73.Noni Madueke), Ibrahim Sangaré, Mohamed Ihattaren, Donyell Malen. Trainer: Roger Schmidt (Germany).
Granada CF: Rui Silva, Germán Sánchez, Dimitri Foulquier, Jesús Vallejo, Carlos Neva, Maxime Gonalons (35.Montero), Antonio Puertas, Luis Milla (81.Yan Eteki), Yangel Herrera, Jorge Molina (69.Luis Suárez), Darwin Machís (81.Alberto Soro). Trainer: Diego Martínez Penas.
Goals: 45+1' Mario Götze 1-0, 57' Jorge Molina 1-1, 66' Darwin Machís 1-2.

29.10.2020; Stádio Neo GSP, Nicosia
Referee: Donatas Rumšas (Lithuania)
AC Omonia Nicosia – PSV Eindhoven 1-2(1-1)
Omonia Nicosia: Fabiano, Jan Lecjaks, Tomás Hubocan, Michael Lüftner, Ádám Lang, Jordi Gómez, Éric Bauthéac (90+3.Ioannis Kousoulos), Vítor Gomes, Marinos Tzionis, Michal Duris (81.Andronikos Kakoullis), Fotis Papoulis (81.Ernest Asante). Trainer: Henning Stille Berg (Norway).
PSV Eindhoven: Yvon Mvogo, Philipp Max, Olivier Boscagli, Jordan Teze, Mario Götze, Ryan Thomas, Jorrit Hendrix, Ibrahim Sangaré, Mohamed Ihattaren, Donyell Malen, Noni Madueke (83.Adrian Fein). Trainer: Roger Schmidt (Germany).
Goals: 29' Jordi Gómez 1-0, 40', 90+3' Donyell Malen 1-1, 1-2.

05.11.2020; Stádio Toumbas, Thessaloníki
Referee: Daniel Stefanski (Poland)
PAOK Thessaloníki – PSV Eindhoven 4-1(0-1)
PAOK: Zivko Zivkovic, José Ángel Crespo, Fernando Varela, Rodrigo Alves, Dimitris Giannoulis (71.Lefteris Lyratzis), Diego Biseswar (46.Christos Tzolis), Omar El Kaddouri (81.Theocharis Tsiggaras), Stefan Schwab, Andrija Zivkovic (84.Thomas Murg), Douglas Augusto, Antonio Colak (46.Karol Swiderski). Trainer: Pablo Gabriel García Pérez (Uruguay).
PSV Eindhoven: Yvon Mvogo, Philipp Max, Olivier Boscagli, Jordan Teze, Mario Götze (83.Ismael Saibari), Ryan Thomas (58.Noni Madueke), Ibrahim Sangaré (83.Richie Ledezma), Pablo Rosario (46.Adrian Fein), Mohamed Ihattaren (58.Mauro Júnior), Eran Zahavi, Donyell Malen. Trainer: Roger Schmidt (Germany).
Goals: 20' Eran Zahavi 0-1 (penalty), 47' Stefan Schwab 1-1, 56' Andrija Zivkovic 2-1, 58' Christos Tzolis 3-1, 66' Andrija Zivkovic 4-1.

26.11.2020; Philips Stadion, Eindhoven
Referee: Andris Treimanis (Latvia)
PSV Eindhoven – PAOK Thessaloníki 3-2(1-2)
PSV Eindhoven: Yvon Mvogo, Philipp Max, Olivier Boscagli, Denzel Dumfries, Jordan Teze, Ibrahim Sangaré, Pablo Rosario, Eran Zahavi (71.Jorrit Hendrix), Donyell Malen (90+2.Richie Ledezma), Cody Gakpo, Noni Madueke (78.Mauro Júnior). Trainer: Roger Schmidt (Germany).
PAOK: Zivko Zivkovic, José Ángel Crespo (86.Moussa Wagué), Fernando Varela, Sverrir Ingason, Rodrigo Alves, Omar El Kaddouri (85.Diego Biseswar), Stefan Schwab, Andrija Zivkovic, Theocharis Tsiggaras (69.Douglas Augusto), Antonio Colak (69.Karol Swiderski), Christos Tzolis (58.Thomas Murg). Trainer: Pablo Gabriel García Pérez (Uruguay).
Goals: 4' Fernando Varela 0-1, 13' Christos Tzolis 0-2, 20' Cody Gakpo 1-2, 51' Noni Madueke 2-2, 53' Donyell Malen 3-2.

22.10.2020; Stádio Toumbas, Thessaloníki
Referee: Robert Adam Madden (Scotland)
PAOK Thessaloníki – AC Omonia Nicosia 1-1(0-1)
PAOK: Zivko Zivkovic, Léo Matos (61.Rodrigo Alves), Fernando Varela, Sverrir Ingason, Dimitris Giannoulis, Giannis Michailidis, Stefan Schwab, Thomas Murg (73.Diego Biseswar), Andrija Zivkovic (73.Christos Tzolis), Anderson Esiti (46.Douglas Augusto), Antonio Colak (61.Karol Swiderski). Trainer: Abel Fernando Moreira Ferreira (Portugal).
Omonia Nicosia: Fabiano, Jan Lecjaks, Tomás Hubocan, Michael Lüftner, Ádám Lang, Jordi Gómez (74.Ioannis Kousoulos), Éric Bauthéac (90+2.Loizos Loizou), Vítor Gomes, Marinos Tzionis, Michal Duris (76.Andronikos Kakoullis), Fotis Papoulis (75.Ernest Asante). Trainer: Henning Stille Berg (Norway).
Goals: 16' Éric Bauthéac 0-1, 56' Thomas Murg 1-1.

29.10.2020; Estadio Nuevo Los Cármenes, Granada
Referee: Tiago Bruno Lopes Martins (Portugal)
Granada CF – PAOK Thessaloníki 0-0
Granada CF: Rui Silva, Germán Sánchez, Jesús Vallejo, Carlos Neva, Maxime Gonalons (90.Yan Eteki), Antonio Puertas, Luis Milla, Kenedy (73.Montoro), Yangel Herrera (59.Jorge Molina), Darwin Machís (90.Domingos Duarte), Luis Suárez (73.Alberto Soro). Trainer: Diego Martínez Penas.
PAOK: Zivko Zivkovic, José Ángel Crespo, Fernando Varela, Sverrir Ingason, Rodrigo Alves (74.Moussa Wagué), Dimitris Giannoulis, Stefan Schwab, Thomas Murg (70.Omar El Kaddouri), Andrija Zivkovic, Douglas Augusto, Antonio Colak (69.Karol Swiderski). Trainer: Abel Fernando Moreira Ferreira (Portugal).

05.11.2020; Stádio Neo GSP, Nicosia
Referee: Ivan Bebek (Croatia)
AC Omonia Nicosia – Granada CF 0-2(0-1)
Omonia Nicosia: Fabiano, Jan Lecjaks, Tomás Hubocan, Michael Lüftner, Ádám Lang, Jordi Gómez (46.Abdullahi Shehu), Éric Bauthéac (46.Ernest Asante), Vítor Gomes, Marinos Tzionis (72.Thiago Santos), Michal Duris [sent off 41], Fotis Papoulis (46.Ioannis Kousoulos). Trainer: Henning Stille Berg (Norway).
Granada CF: Rui Silva, Germán Sánchez, Domingos Duarte, Carlos Neva, Pepe Sánchez (89.Nehuén Pérez), Montoro (46.Luis Milla), Maxime Gonalons, Kenedy (76.Alberto Soro), Yangel Herrera (90.Yan Eteki), Darwin Machís, Luis Suárez (75.Jorge Molina). Trainer: Diego Martínez Penas.
Goals: 4' Yangel Herrera 0-1, 63' Luis Suárez 0-2.

26.11.2020; Estadio Nuevo Los Cármenes, Granada
Referee: Stéphanie Frappart (France)
Granada CF – AC Omonia Nicosia 2-1(1-0)
Granada CF: Rui Silva, Jesús Vallejo, Domingos Duarte, Carlos Neva, Nehuén Pérez (66.Dimitri Foulquier), Maxime Gonalons (66.Darwin Machís), Luis Milla, Yangel Herrera, Alberto Soro (79.Antonio Puertas), Soldado (79.Jorge Molina), Luis Suárez (79.Yan Eteki). Trainer: Diego Martínez Penas.
Omonia Nicosia: Fabiano, Tomás Hubocan, Michael Lüftner, Ádám Lang, Kiko (59.Jan Lecjaks), Ioannis Kousoulos, Éric Bauthéac (36.Ernest Asante), Charis Mavrias, Abdullahi Shehu (58.Jordi Gómez), Marinos Tzionis (59.Thiago Santos), Andronikos Kakoullis (74.Mamadou Kaly Sene). Trainer: Henning Stille Berg (Norway).
Goals: 8' Luis Suárez 1-0, 60' Ernest Asante 1-1, 73' Alberto Soro 2-1.

03.12.2020; Estadio Nuevo Los Cármenes, Granada
Referee: Roi Reinshreiber (Israel)
Granada CF – PSV Eindhoven 0-1(0-1)
Granada CF: Rui Silva, Germán Sánchez (56.Dimitri Foulquier), Jesús Vallejo, Domingos Duarte, Carlos Neva, Maxime Gonalons, Luis Milla (76.Jorge Molina), Yangel Herrera, Alberto Soro (56.Luis Suárez), Soldado (83.Antonio Puertas), Darwin Machís. Trainer: Diego Martínez Penas.
PSV Eindhoven: Yvon Mvogo, Philipp Max, Olivier Boscagli, Denzel Dumfries (71.Timo Baumgartl), Jordan Teze, Mario Götze, Ibrahim Sangaré, Pablo Rosario, Donyell Malen, Cody Gakpo, Noni Madueke (38.Eran Zahavi, 88.Jorrit Hendrix). Trainer: Roger Schmidt (Germany).
Goal: 38' Donyell Malen 0-1.

10.12.2020; Philips Stadion, Eindhoven
Referee: Kevin Clancy (Scotland)
PSV Eindhoven – AC Omonia Nicosia 4-0(1-0)
PSV Eindhoven: Yvon Mvogo, Nick Viergever, Philipp Max (46.Olivier Boscagli), Timo Baumgartl, Denzel Dumfries (81.Jordan Teze), Jorrit Hendrix, Pablo Rosario (46.Ibrahim Sangaré), Richie Ledezma (17.Adrian Fein), Mohamed Ihattaren, Donyell Malen (46.Cody Gakpo), Joël Piroe. Trainer: Roger Schmidt (Germany).
Omonia Nicosia: Fabiano, Michael Lüftner, Ádám Lang, Kiko (60.Jan Lecjaks), Ioannis Kousoulos (60.Jordi Gómez), Vítor Gomes, Abdullahi Shehu, Marinos Tzionis, Thiago Santos, Mamadou Kaly Sene (61.Michal Duris), Loizos Loizou. Trainer: Henning Stille Berg (Norway).
Goals: 35' Donyell Malen 1-0, 63' Denzel Dumfries 2-0 (penalty), 90+1', 90+3' Joël Piroe 3-0, 4-0.

03.12.2020; Stádio Neo GSP, Nicosia
Referee: Craig Pawson (England)
AC Omonia Nicosia – PAOK Thessaloníki 2-1(1-1)
Omonia Nicosia: Fabiano, Tomás Hubocan, Michael Lüftner, Ádám Lang, Kiko (59.Jan Lecjaks), Ioannis Kousoulos (60.Jordi Gómez), Vítor Gomes, Marinos Tzionis, Andronikos Kakoullis (21.Abdullahi Shehu), Mamadou Kaly Sene (59.Michal Duris), Loizos Loizou (85.Ernest Asante). Trainer: Henning Stille Berg (Norway).
PAOK: Zivko Zivkovic, José Ángel Crespo, Fernando Varela, Rodrigo Alves, Moussa Wagué (46.Dimitris Giannoulis), Omar El Kaddouri, Stefan Schwab (46.Thomas Murg), Andrija Zivkovic, Theocharis Tsiggaras (79.Diego Biseswar), Karol Swiderski, Christos Tzolis. Trainer: Pablo Gabriel García Pérez (Uruguay).
Goals: 9' Andronikos Kakoullis 1-0, 39' Christos Tzolis 1-1, 84' Jordi Gómez 2-1 (penalty).

10.12.2020; Stádio Toumbas, Thessaloníki
Referee: John Beaton (Scotland)
PAOK Thessaloníki – Granada CF 0-0
PAOK: Alexandros Paschalakis, José Ángel Crespo, Fernando Varela, Sverrir Ingason, Lefteris Lyratzis (63.Moussa Wagué), Omar El Kaddouri, Thomas Murg, Anderson Esiti (63.Douglas Augusto), Antonio Colak (81.Karol Swiderski), Christos Tzolis (46.Andrija Zivkovic), Giorgios Koutsias (46.Theocharis Tsiggaras). Trainer: Pablo Gabriel García Pérez (Uruguay).
Granada CF: Aarón Escandell, Germán Sánchez, Dimitri Foulquier, Nehuén Pérez, Pepe Sánchez (66.Carlos Neva), Antonio Puertas, Luis Milla (75.Maxime Gonalons), Kenedy (67.Luis Suárez), Yan Eteki (85.Soldado), Alberto Soro (75.Darwin Machís), Jorge Molina. Trainer: Diego Martínez Penas.

GROUP F	1. **SSC Napoli**	6	3	2	1	7	-	4	11
	2. **Real Sociedad de Fútbol San Sebastián**	6	2	3	1	5	-	4	9
	3. AZ Almaar	6	2	2	2	7	-	5	8
	4. HNK Rijeka	6	1	1	4	6	-	12	4

22.10.2020; Stadio San Paolo, Napoli
Referee: Daniel Stefanski (Poland); Attendance: 494
SSC Napoli – AZ Alkmaar 0-1(0-0)
SSC Napoli: Alex Meret, Nikola Maksimovic, Kalidou Koulibaly, Elseid Hysaj (59.Mário Rui), Giovanni Di Lorenzo, Stanislav Lobotka (66.Diego Demme), Fabián Ruiz, Dries Mertens, Matteo Politano (83.Tiemoué Bakayoko), Hirving Lozano (59.Lorenzo Insigne), Victor Osimhen (66.Andrea Petagna). Trainer: Gennaro Gattuso.
AZ Alkmaar: Marco Bizot, Bruno Martins Indi, Jonas Svensson, Pantelis Hatzidiakos, Owen Wijndal, Yukinari Sugawara, Fredrik Midtsjø (88.Ramon Leeuwin), Dani de Wit, Teun Koopmeiners, Jesper Karlsson (88.Albert Gudmundsson), Calvin Tengs. Trainer: Arne Slot.
Goal: 57' Dani de Wit 0-1.

29.10.2020; Reale Arena, San Sebastián
Referee: Craig Pawson (England)
Real Sociedad de Fútbol San Sebastián – SSC Napoli 0-1(0-0)
Real Sociedad: Álex Remiro, Nacho Monreal, Andoni Gorosabel (79.Ander Barrenetxea), Robin Le Normand, Modibo Sagnan, David Silva, Mikel Merino (79.Martín Zubimendi), Guevara, Portu (67.Jon Bautista), Mikel Oyarzabal (86.Jon Guridi), Alexander Isak (67.Willian José). Trainer: Imanol Alguacil Barrenetxea.
SSC Napoli: David Ospina, Nikola Maksimovic, Mário Rui, Kalidou Koulibaly, Elseid Hysaj, Diego Demme (89.Fabián Ruiz), Tiemoué Bakayoko, Stanislav Lobotka (61.Dries Mertens), Lorenzo Insigne (22.Hirving Lozano), Matteo Politano (61.Giovanni Di Lorenzo), Andrea Petagna (61.Victor Osimhen [*sent off 90+2*]). Trainer: Gennaro Gattuso.
Goal: 56' Matteo Politano 0-1.

22.10.2020; Stadion Rujevica, Rijeka
Referee: Bartosz Frankowski (Poland); Attendance: 2,089
HNK Rijeka – Real Sociedad de Fútbol San Sebastián 0-1(0-0)
HNK Rijeka: Ivan Nevistic, Ivan Tomecak, Darko Velkovski, João Escoval, Daniel Stefulj, Hrvoje Smolcic, Franko Andrijasevic (63.Sterling Yatéké), Domagoj Pavicic, Stjepan Loncar (87.Luka Capan), Adam Gnezda Cerin, Sandro Kulenovic (77.Ivan Lepinjica). Trainer: Simon Rozman.
Real Sociedad: Álex Remiro, Nacho Monreal, Aritz Elustondo, Andoni Gorosabel, Robin Le Normand, David Silva, Mikel Merino, Martín Zubimendi, Portu (89.Adnan Januzaj), Mikel Oyarzabal (85.Jon Bautista), Alexander Isak (72.Willian José). Trainer: Imanol Alguacil Barrenetxea.
Goal: 90+3' Jon Bautista 0-1.

29.10.2020; AFAS Stadion, Alkmaar
Referee: Sergey Ivanov (Russia)
AZ Alkmaar – HNK Rijeka 4-1(2-0)
AZ Alkmaar: Marco Bizot, Bruno Martins Indi (90.Maxim Gullit), Jonas Svensson, Pantelis Hatzidiakos (60.Ramon Leeuwin), Owen Wijndal, Fredrik Midtsjø, Dani de Wit, Teun Koopmeiners, Albert Gudmundsson (90.Yusuf Barasi), Jesper Karlsson (67.Håkon Evjen), Calvin Tengs (66.Zakaria Aboukhlal). Trainer: Arne Slot.
HNK Rijeka: Ivan Nevistic, Ivan Tomecak (80.Momcilo Raspopovic), Darko Velkovski (65.Ivan Lepinjica), João Escoval (80.Armando Anastasio), Hrvoje Smolcic, Franko Andrijasevic (64.Tibor Halilovic), Domagoj Pavicic, Stjepan Loncar, Luka Menalo (64.Sterling Yatéké), Sandro Kulenovic. Trainer: Simon Rozman.
Goals: 6' Teun Koopmeiners 1-0 (penalty), 20' Albert Gudmundsson 2-0, 51' Jesper Karlsson 3-0, 60' Albert Gudmundsson 4-0, 72' Sandro Kulenovic 4-1.

05.11.2020; Reale Arena, San Sebastián
Referee: John Beaton (Scotland)
Real Sociedad de Fútbol San Sebastián – AZ Alkmaar 1-0(0-0)
Real Sociedad: Moyà, Nacho Monreal, Aritz Elustondo, Robin Le Normand, Modibo Sagnan, David Silva, Mikel Merino (76.Martín Zubimendi), Guevara, Portu (76.Adnan Januzaj), Mikel Oyarzabal (89.Ander Barrenetxea), Alexander Isak (62.Willian José). Trainer: Imanol Alguacil Barrenetxea.
AZ Alkmaar: Marco Bizot, Jonas Svensson, Pantelis Hatzidiakos (70.Timo Letschert), Owen Wijndal, Fredrik Midtsjø, Dani de Wit, Teun Koopmeiners, Albert Gudmundsson (63.Zakaria Aboukhlal), Jesper Karlsson (63.Ferdy Druijf), Myron Boadu (62.Håkon Evjen), Calvin Tengs (70.Tijs Velthuis). Trainer: Arne Slot.
Goal: 58' Portu 1-0.

26.11.2020; Stadio San Paolo, Napoli
Referee: Halis Özkahya (Turkey)
SSC Napoli – HNK Rijeka 2-0(1-0)
SSC Napoli: Alex Meret, Nikola Maksimovic, Kalidou Koulibaly, Faouzi Ghoulam, Giovanni Di Lorenzo, Diego Demme (69.Stanislav Lobotka), Piotr Zielinski (64.Lorenzo Insigne), Tiemoué Bakayoko, Eljif Elmas (69.Dries Mertens), Matteo Politano (64.Hirving Lozano), Andrea Petagna (81.Fabián Ruiz). Trainer: Gennaro Gattuso.
HNK Rijeka: Ivan Nevistic, Ivan Tomecak, Darko Velkovski, Nino Galovic, Armando Anastasio (80.Filip Braut), Daniel Stefulj, Hrvoje Smolcic, Franko Andrijasevic (87.Matija GRīgan), Robert Muric (78.Sterling Yatéké), Stjepan Loncar, Adam Gnezda Cerin (87.Veldin Hodza). Trainer: Simon Rozman.
Goals: 41' Matteo Politano 1-0, 75' Hiring Lozano 2-0.

03.12.2020; AFAS Stadion, Alkmaar
Referee: Ruddy Buquet (France)
AZ Alkmaar – SSC Napoli 1-1(0-1)
AZ Alkmaar: Marco Bizot, Bruno Martins Indi, Pantelis Hatzidiakos, Owen Wijndal, Yukinari Sugawara, Fredrik Midtsjø, Dani de Wit, Teun Koopmeiners, Albert Gudmundsson (70.Myron Boadu), Calvin Tengs, Zakaria Aboukhlal (82.Jesper Karlsson). Trainer: Arne Slot.
SSC Napoli: David Ospina, Nikola Maksimovic, Kalidou Koulibaly, Faouzi Ghoulam (66.Mário Rui), Giovanni Di Lorenzo, Piotr Zielinski (61.Andrea Petagna), Tiemoué Bakayoko, Fabián Ruiz (57.Eljif Elmas), Dries Mertens (66.Diego Demme), Lorenzo Insigne, Matteo Politano (61.Hirving Lozano). Trainer: Gennaro Gattuso.
Goals: 6' Dries Mertens 0-1, 54' Bruno Martins Indi 1-1.

10.12.2020; Stadio „Diego Armando Maradona", Napoli
Referee: Orel Grinfeld (Israel)
SSC Napoli – Real Sociedad de Fútbol San Sebastián 1-1(1-0)
SSC Napoli: David Ospina, Nikola Maksimovic, Mário Rui (82.Faouzi Ghoulam), Kalidou Koulibaly, Giovanni Di Lorenzo, Piotr Zielinski (74.Eljif Elmas), Tiemoué Bakayoko (70.Diego Demme), Fabián Ruiz, Dries Mertens (70.Andrea Petagna), Lorenzo Insigne, Hirving Lozano (70.Matteo Politano). Trainer: Gennaro Gattuso.
Real Sociedad: Álex Remiro, Nacho Monreal (78.Aihen Muñoz), Joseba Zaldúa (46.Andoni Gorosabel), Robin Le Normand (78.Alexander Isak), Adnan Januzaj, Mikel Merino, Zubeldía, Guevara (78.Modibo Sagnan), Martín Zubimendi, Willian José, Portu (56.Ander Barrenetxea). Trainer: Imanol Alguacil Barrenetxea.
Goals: 35' Piotr Zielinski 1-0, 90+2' Willian José 1-1.

05.11.2020; Stadion Rujevica, Rijeka
Referee: Mattias Gestranius (Finland)
HNK Rijeka – SSC Napoli 1-2(1-1)
HNK Rijeka: Ivan Nevistic, Ivan Tomecak, Darko Velkovski, João Escoval, Filip Braut (64.Daniel Stefulj), Hrvoje Smolcic, Robert Muric (24.Sterling Yatéké, 64.Momcilo Raspopovic), Stjepan Loncar, Adam Gnezda Cerin, Luka Menalo, Sandro Kulenovic. Trainer: Simon Rozman.
SSC Napoli: Alex Meret, Nikola Maksimovic, Mário Rui (80.Piotr Zielinski), Kalidou Koulibaly, Giovanni Di Lorenzo, Diego Demme, Stanislav Lobotka (59.Lorenzo Insigne), Eljif Elmas (59.Fabián Ruiz), Dries Mertens, Matteo Politano (69.Hirving Lozano), Andrea Petagna (80.Faouzi Ghoulam). Trainer: Gennaro Gattuso.
Goals: 13' Robert Muric 1-0, 43' Diego Demme 1-1, 62' Filip Braut 1-2 (own goal).

26.11.2020; AFAS Stadion, Alkmaar:
Referee: Aleksandar Stavrev (North Macedonia)
AZ Alkmaar – Real Sociedad de Fútbol San Sebastián 0-0
AZ Alkmaar: Marco Bizot, Bruno Martins Indi, Jonas Svensson, Pantelis Hatzidiakos, Owen Wijndal, Fredrik Midtsjø, Dani de Wit, Teun Koopmeiners, Albert Gudmundsson (71.Myron Boadu), Jesper Karlsson (71.Zakaria Aboukhlal), Calvin Tengs. Trainer: Arne Slot.
Real Sociedad: Álex Remiro, Nacho Monreal, Joseba Zaldúa, Aritz Elustondo, Robin Le Normand, Adnan Januzaj (73.Roberto López), Mikel Merino, Martín Zubimendi, Portu (82.Ander Barrenetxea), Mikel Oyarzabal (86.Martín Merquelanz), Alexander Isak (73.Willian José). Trainer: Imanol Alguacil Barrenetxea.

03.12.2020; Reale Arena, San Sebastián
Referee: João Pedro da Silva Pinheiro (Portugal)
Real Sociedad de Fútbol San Sebastián – HNK Rijeka 2-2(0-1)
Real Sociedad: Álex Remiro, Nacho Monreal, Joseba Zaldúa (67.Andoni Gorosabel), Robin Le Normand, David Silva (68.Willian José), Adnan Januzaj (80.Portu), Mikel Merino, Zubeldía, Martín Zubimendi, Mikel Oyarzabal (80.Roberto López), Alexander Isak (58.Jon Bautista). Trainer: Imanol Alguacil Barrenetxea.
HNK Rijeka: Ivan Nevistic, Ivan Tomecak, Darko Velkovski (86.João Escoval), Nino Galovic, Daniel Stefulj, Franko Andrijasevic (86.Sterling Yatéké), Luka Capan, Robert Muric (75.Domagoj Pavicic), Tibor Halilovic, Stjepan Loncar, Luka Menalo (80.Armando Anastasio). Trainer: Simon Rozman.
Goals: 38' Darko Velkovski 0-1, 69' Jon Bautista 1-1, 73' Stjepan Loncar 1-2, 79' Nacho Monreal 2-2.

10.12.2020; Stadion Rujevica, Rijeka
Referee: Sergei Karasev (Russia)
HNK Rijeka – AZ Alkmaar 2-1(0-0)
HNK Rijeka: Ivan Nevistic, Ivan Tomecak, Nino Galovic, Daniel Stefulj, Hrvoje Smolcic, Franko Andrijasevic, Luka Capan, Robert Muric (71.Sandro Kulenovic), Tibor Halilovic, Stjepan Loncar, Luka Menalo (71.Domagoj Pavicic). Trainer: Simon Rozman.
AZ Alkmaar: Marco Bizot, Bruno Martins Indi (18.Timo Letschert), Pantelis Hatzidiakos, Owen Wijndal, Yukinari Sugawara, Fredrik Midtsjø, Teun Koopmeiners, Albert Gudmundsson (71.Zakaria Aboukhlal), Jesper Karlsson [sent off 80], Myron Boadu (89.Ferdy Druijf), Calvin Tengs. Trainer: Pascal Jansen.
Goals: 52' Luka Menalo 1-0, 57' Owen Wijndal 1-1, 90+3' Ivan Tomecak 2-1.

GROUP G	1. **Leicester City FC**	6	4	1	1	14 - 5	13
	2. **Sporting Clube de Braga**	6	4	1	1	14 - 10	13
	3. FK Zorya Luhansk	6	2	0	4	6 - 11	6
	4. AEK Athína	6	1	0	5	7 - 15	3

22.10.2020; Estádio Municipal de Braga, Braga
Referee: Ruddy Buquet (France); Attendance: 2,196
Sporting Clube de Braga – AEK Athína 3-0(1-0)
Sporting Braga: Matheus Magalhães, Ricardo Esgaio, Nuno Sequeira, Bruno Viana, David Carmo, Andre Castro (90+2.Guilherme Schettine), Fransérgio (84.Francisco Moura), Iuri Medeiros (59.André Horta), Paulinho, Ricardo Horta (90+2.João Novais), Galeno (84.Almoatasembellah Ali Al Musrati). Trainer: Carlos Augusto Soares da Costa Faria Carvalhal.
AEK Athína: Panagiotis Tsintotas, Dmytro Chygrynskiy (61.Marko Livaja, 89.Theodosis Macheras), Hélder Lopes, Stavros Vasilantonopoulos, Ionut Nedelcearu, Efstratios Svarnas, Nenad Krsticic, Yevhen Shakhov, Petros Mandalos, Karim Ansarifard (62.Muamer Tankovic), Nélson Oliveira. Trainer: Massimo Carrera (Italy).
Goals: 44' Galeno 1-0, 78' Paulinho 2-0, 88' Ricardo Horta 3-0.

29.10.2020; Stádio Olympiako „Spiros Louis", Athína
Referee: Harald Lechner (Austria)
AEK Athína – Leicester City FC 1-2(0-2)
AEK Athína: Panagiotis Tsintotas, Michalis Bakakis (86.Stavros Vasilantonopoulos), Hélder Lopes, Emanuel Insúa (87.Theodosis Macheras), Ionut Nedelcearu, Efstratios Svarnas, Nenad Krsticic, Yevhen Shakhov (86.Anel Sabanadzovic), Petros Mandalos, Karim Ansarifard (46.Nélson Oliveira), Marko Livaja (46.Muamer Tankovic). Trainer: Massimo Carrera (Italy).
Leicester City: Kasper Schmeichel, Christian Fuchs (46.Luke Thomas), Wes Morgan, James Justin, Wesley Fofana, Marc Albrighton, Youri Tielemans, James Maddison (74.Harvey Barnes), Cengiz Ünder (66.Dennis Praet), Hamza Choudhury (66.Nampalys Mendy), Jamie Vardy (71.Kelechi Iheanacho). Trainer: Brendan Rodgers (Northern Ireland).
Goals: 18' Jamie Vardy 0-1 (penalty), 39' Hamza Choudhury 0-2, 49' Muamer Tankovic 1-2.

05.11.2020; King Power Stadium, Leicester
Referee: Hendrikus Sebastiaan Hermanus „Bas" Nijhuis (Netherlands)
Leicester City FC – Sporting Clube de Braga 4-0(1-0)
Leicester City: Kasper Schmeichel, Christian Fuchs, James Justin, Luke Thomas, Wesley Fofana, Marc Albrighton (62.Wes Morgan), Youri Tielemans (72.Harvey Barnes), James Maddison, Cengiz Ünder (62.Dennis Praet), Hamza Choudhury, Kelechi Iheanacho (72.Ayoze Pérez). Trainer: Brendan Rodgers (Northern Ireland).
Sporting Braga: Matheus Magalhães, Raúl Silva, Ricardo Esgaio, Bruno Viana, David Carmo, João Novais, Almoatasembellah Ali Al Musrati (71.Andre Castro), André Horta (62.Iuri Medeiros), Paulinho (72.Nicolás Gaitán), Galeno (71.Francisco Moura), Abel Ruiz (62.Guilherme Schettine). Trainer: Carlos Augusto Soares da Costa Faria Carvalhal.
Goals: 21', 48' Kelechi Iheanacho 1-0, 2-0, 67' Dennis Praet 3-0, 78' James Maddison 4-0.

26.11.2020; Estádio Municipal de Braga, Braga
Referee: Daniele Orsato (Italy)
Sporting Clube de Braga – Leicester City FC 3-3(2-1)
Sporting Braga: Matheus Magalhães, Ricardo Esgaio, Nuno Sequeira, Bruno Viana, Vítor Tormena, Andre Castro (87.André Horta), Almoatasembellah Ali Al Musrati, Iuri Medeiros (77.Fransérgio), Paulinho (87.Guilherme Schettine), Ricardo Horta (69.Raúl Silva), Galeno.
Trainer: Carlos Augusto Soares da Costa Faria Carvalhal.
Leicester City: Kasper Schmeichel, Christian Fuchs (46.Wesley Fofana), Jonny Evans, James Justin, Luke Thomas, Marc Albrighton, Dennis Praet (46.Youri Tielemans), Cengiz Ünder (62.Jamie Vardy), Hamza Choudhury, Harvey Barnes (62.James Maddison), Kelechi Iheanacho (68.Ayoze Pérez). Trainer: Brendan Rodgers (Northern Ireland).
Goals: 4' Almoatasembellah Ali Al Musrati 1-0, 9' Harvey Barnes 1-1, 24' Paulinho 2-1, 79' Luke Thomas 2-2, 90+1' Fransérgio 3-2, 90+5' Jamie Vardy 3-3.

22.10.2020; King Power Stadium, Leicester
Referee: Stéphanie Frappart (France)
Leicester City FC – FK Zorya Luhansk 3-0(2-0)
Leicester City: Kasper Schmeichel, Christian Fuchs, Jonny Evans (82.Wes Morgan), Timothy Castagne (82.James Justin), Wesley Fofana, Nampalys Mendy, Dennis Praet, Youri Tielemans (71.Hamza Choudhury), James Maddison (65.Cengiz Ünder), Harvey Barnes, Kelechi Iheanacho (72.Ayoze Pérez). Trainer: Brendan Rodgers (Northern Ireland).
Zorya Luhansk: Mykyta Shevchenko, Vitaliy Vernydub, Dmitriy Ivanisenya, Denis Favorov (76.Agron Rufati), Dmytro Khomchenovsky (76.Andrejs Ciganiks), Vladlen Yurchenko, Lovro Cvek, Vladyslav Kochergin (85.Sergiy Gryn), Egor Nazaryna, Vladyslav Kabayev (64.Mihailo Perovic), Maksym Lunev (65.Oleksandr Gladkyi). Trainer: Viktor Skripnik.
Goals: 29' James Maddison 1-0, 45' Harvey Barnes 2-0, 67' Kelechi Iheanacho 3-0.

29.10.2020; Slavutych-Arena, Zaporizhia
Referee: Giorgi Kruashvili (Georgia); Attendance: 853
FK Zorya Luhansk – Sporting Clube de Braga 1-2(0-2)
Zorya Luhansk: Nikola Vasilj, Vitaliy Vernydub, Dmitriy Ivanisenya, Denis Favorov (87.Joel Abu Hanna), Dmytro Khomchenovsky, Vladlen Yurchenko (87.Mihailo Perovic), Lovro Cvek, Vladyslav Kochergin, Egor Nazaryna, Vladyslav Kabayev (81.Allahyar Sayyadmanesh), Maksym Lunev (62.Oleksandr Gladkyi). Trainer: Viktor Skripnik.
Sporting Braga: Matheus Magalhães, Raúl Silva, Ricardo Esgaio (90+1.Vítor Tormena), Bruno Viana, Francisco Moura, David Carmo, Andre Castro (79.Almoatasembellah Ali Al Musrati), Nicolás Gaitán (66.Iuri Medeiros), Fransérgio, Paulinho (79.Guilherme Schettine), Ricardo Horta (66.André Horta). Trainer: Carlos Augusto Soares da Costa Faria Carvalhal.
Goals: 4' Paulinho 0-1, 11' Nicolás Gaitán 0-2, 90+6' Dmitriy Ivanisenya 1-2.

05.11.2020; Slavutych-Arena, Zaporizhia
Referee: William Collum (Scotland)
FK Zorya Luhansk – AEK Athína 1-4(0-2)
Zorya Luhansk: Mykyta Shevchenko, Vitaliy Vernydub, Dmitriy Ivanisenya, Joel Abu Hanna, Artem Gromov (46.Allahyar Sayyadmanesh), Dmytro Khomchenovsky (59.Denis Favorov), Vladlen Yurchenko, Andrejs Ciganiks, Vladyslav Kochergin, Vladyslav Kabayev (59.Oleksandr Gladkyi), Maksym Lunev (46.Egor Nazaryna). Trainer: Viktor Skripnik.
AEK Athína: Panagiotis Tsintotas, Dmitro Chygrynskiy, Emanuel Insúa, Stavros Vasilantonopoulos, Ionut Nedelcearu, Efstratios Svarnas, Nenad Krsticic (85.Konstantinos Galanopoulos), Yevhen Shakhov (70.Anel Sabanadzovic), Petros Mandalos (85.Giannis-Fivos Botos), Marko Livaja, Muamer Tankovic (75.Karim Ansarifard). Trainer: Massimo Carrera (Italy).
Goals: 7' Muamer Tankovic 0-1, 34' Petros Mandalos 0-2, 54' Marko Livaja 0-3, 81' Vladyslav Kochergin 1-3, 81' Marko Livaja 1-4.

26.11.2020; Stádio Olympiako „Spiros Louis", Athína
Referee: Əliyar Ağayev (Azerbaijan)
AEK Athína – FK Zorya Luhansk 0-3(0-0)
AEK Athína: Georgios Athanasiadis, Dmitro Chygrynskiy, Michalis Bakakis (65.Konstantinos Galanopoulos), Emanuel Insúa, Ionut Nedelcearu, Efstratios Svarnas (82.Stavros Vasilantonopoulos), Nenad Krsticic, Yevhen Shakhov [sent off 48], André Simões (87.Theodosis Macheras), Marko Livaja, Muamer Tankovic (75.Karim Ansarifard). Trainer: Massimo Carrera (Italy).
Zorya Luhansk: Mykyta Shevchenko, Vitaliy Vernydub, Dmitriy Ivanisenya, Denis Favorov, Joel Abu Hanna, Artem Gromov (87.Sergiy Gryn), Vladlen Yurchenko (87.Mihailo Perovic), Andrejs Ciganiks, Vladyslav Kochergin (82.Maksym Lunev), Oleksandr Gladkyi (63.Egor Nazaryna), Vladyslav Kabayev (87.Allahyar Sayyadmanesh). Trainer: Viktor Skripnik.
Goals: 61' Artem Gromov 0-1, 76' Vladyslav Kabayev 0-2, 86' Vladlen Yurchenko 0-3 (penalty).

03.12.2020; Stádio Olympiako „Spiros Louis", Athína
Referee: Georgi Kabakov (Bulgaria)
AEK Athína – Sporting Clube de Braga 2-4(1-3)
AEK Athína: Panagiotis Tsintotas, Michalis Bakakis (46.Stavros Vasilantonopoulos), Emanuel Insúa, Ionut Nedelcearu, Nassim Hnid, Petros Mandalos (74.Levi García), André Simões, Konstantinos Galanopoulos, Nélson Oliveira (60.Karim Ansarifard), Marko Livaja, Christos Albanis (60.Muamer Tankovic). Trainer: Massimo Carrera (Italy).
Sporting Braga: Matheus Magalhães, Ricardo Esgaio, Nuno Sequeira, Bruno Viana (46.David Carmo), Vítor Tormena, Andre Castro (78.João Novais), Almoatasembellah Ali Al Musrati (57.Fransérgio), Iuri Medeiros (57.André Horta), Paulinho (71.Guilherme Schettine), Ricardo Horta, Galeno. Trainer: Carlos Augusto Soares da Costa Faria Carvalhal.
Goals: 8' Vítor Tormena 0-1, 10' Ricardo Esgaio 0-2, 31' Nélson Oliveira 1-2, 45' Ricardo Horta 1-3, 83' Galeno 1-4, 89' Stavros Vasilantonopoulos 2-4.

10.12.2020; Estádio Municipal de Braga, Braga
Sporting Clube de Braga – FK Zorya Luhansk 2-0(0-0)
Referee: Daniel Stefanski (Poland)
Sporting Braga: Tiago Sá, Raúl Silva, Vítor Tormena, Zé Carlos (73.Bruno Viana), David Carmo, Fransérgio, João Novais (77.Almoatasembellah Ali Al Musrati), André Horta (67.Iuri Medeiros), Guilherme Schettine (68.Paulinho), Galeno, Abel Ruiz (68.Ricardo Horta). Trainer: Carlos Augusto Soares da Costa Faria Carvalhal.
Zorya Luhansk: Mykyta Shevchenko, Dmitriy Ivanisenya, Denis Favorov (87.Dmytro Khomchenovsky), Joel Abu Hanna, Artem Gromov (77.Sergiy Gryn), Vladlen Yurchenko, Andrejs Ciganiks, Vladyslav Kochergin (87.Dmytro Piddubnyi), Egor Nazaryna, Oleksandr Gladkyi (77.Mihailo Perovic), Vladyslav Kabayev (77.Maksym Lunev). Trainer: Viktor Skripnik.
Goals: 61' Joel Abu Hanna 1-0 (own goal), 68' Ricardo Horta 2-0.

03.12.2020; Slavutych-Arena, Zaporizhia
Referee: Espen Eskås (Norway)
FK Zorya Luhansk – Leicester City FC 1-0(0-0)
Zorya Luhansk: Nikola Vasilj, Dmitriy Ivanisenya, Denis Favorov, Joel Abu Hanna, Artem Gromov (90+3.Mihailo Perovic), Vladlen Yurchenko, Andrejs Ciganiks, Vladyslav Kochergin, Egor Nazaryna, Oleksandr Gladkyi (81.Allahyar Sayyadmanesh), Vladyslav Kabayev. Trainer: Viktor Skripnik.
Leicester City: Danny Ward, Wes Morgan (56.Christian Fuchs), Ricardo Pereira (46.Luke Thomas), Çaglar Söyüncü (17.Wesley Fofana), James Justin, Dennis Praet (77.James Maddison), Wilfred Ndidi (56.Nampalys Mendy), Cengiz Ünder, Hamza Choudhury, Harvey Barnes, Kelechi Iheanacho. Trainer: Brendan Rodgers (Northern Ireland).
Goal: 84' Allahyar Sayyadmanesh 1-0.

10.12.2020; King Power Stadium, Leicester
Referee: Lawrence Visser (Belgium)
Leicester City FC – AEK Athína 2-0(2-0)
Leicester City: Danny Ward, Jonny Evans, James Justin, Luke Thomas, Wesley Fofana (81.Wes Morgan), Dennis Praet, Youri Tielemans (82.Hamza Choudhury), Wilfred Ndidi (63.Nampalys Mendy), Cengiz Ünder, Harvey Barnes, Kelechi Iheanacho (67.Ayoze Pérez). Trainer: Brendan Rodgers (Northern Ireland).
AEK Athína: Panagiotis Tsintotas, Stavros Vasilantonopoulos, Ionut Nedelcearu, Efstratios Svarnas (56.Yevhen Shakhov), Nassim Hnid, Nenad Krsticic, Petros Mandalos (66.Christos Albanis), André Simões (81.Konstantinos Galanopoulos), Mario Mitaj, Karim Ansarifard (66.Nélson Oliveira), Levi García (55.Theodosis Macheras). Trainer: Massimo Carrera (Italy).
Goals: 12' Cengiz Ünder 1-0, 14' Harvey Barnes 2-0.

GROUP H	1. **AC Milan**	6	4	1	1	12 - 7	13
	2. **Lille OSC**	6	3	2	1	14 - 8	11
	3. AC Sparta Praha	6	2	0	4	10 - 12	6
	4. Celtic FC Glasgow	6	1	1	4	10 - 19	4

22.10.2020; Celtic Park, Glasgow
Referee: Matej Jug (Slovenia); Attendance: 316
Celtic FC Glasgow – AC Milan 1-3(0-2)
Celtic: Vassilis Barkas, Shane Duffy, Diego Laxalt (77.Greg Taylor), Kristoffer Ajer, Stephen Welsh (46.Mohamed Elyounoussi), Jeremie Frimpong, Scott Brown (64.Tom Rogic), Callum McGregor, Olivier Ntcham, Leigh Griffiths (46.Ryan Christie), Albian Ajeti (77.Patryk Klimala). Trainer: Neil Francis Lennon (Northern Ireland).
AC Milan: Gianluigi Donnarumma, Simon Kjær, Alessio Romagnoli, Theo Hernández, Diogo Dalot, Samu Castillejo (79.Alexis Saelemaekers), Rade Krunic, Franck Kessié (66.Ismaël Bennacar), Sandro Tonali, Zlatan Ibrahimovic (66.Rafael Leão), Brahim Díaz (79.Jens Hauge). Trainer: Stefano Pioli.
Goals: 14' Rade Krunic 0-1, 42' Brahim Díaz 0-2, 76' Mohamed Elyounoussi 1-2, 90+2' Jens Hauge 1-3.

29.10.2020; Stadio „Giuseppe Meazza", Milano
Referee: Halis Özkahya (Turkey)
AC Milan – AC Sparta Praha 3-0(1-0)
AC Milan: Ciprian Tatarusanu, Simon Kjær, Alessio Romagnoli (80.Léo Duarte), Davide Calabria (68.Andrea Conti), Diogo Dalot, Samu Castillejo, Rade Krunic (88.Daniel Maldini), Ismaël Bennacar (81.Franck Kessié), Sandro Tonali, Zlatan Ibrahimovic (46.Rafael Leão), Brahim Díaz. Trainer: Stefano Pioli.
Sparta Praha: Milan Heca, Ondrej Celustka, Andreas Vindheim, Matej Hanousek, David Lischka (80.Dominik Plechatý), Borek Dockal (90.Vojtech Patrák), David Pavelka, Ladislav Krejci (I) (63.David Moberg-Karlsson), Michal Trávník (80.Adam Karabec), Michal Sácek, Lukás Julis (63.Libor Kozák). Trainer: Václav Kotal.
Goals: 24' Brahim Díaz 1-0, 57' Rafael Leão 2-0, 67' Diogo Dalot 3-0.

22.10.2020; Generali Arena, Praha
Referee: Duje Strukan (Croatia)
AC Sparta Praha – Lille OSC 1-4(0-1)
Sparta Praha: Milan Heca, Andreas Vindheim, Matej Hanousek (90+1.Martin Minchev), David Lischka, Borek Dockal, David Pavelka, Michal Trávník (78.Adam Karabec), David Moberg-Karlsson (74.Matej Polidar), Michal Sácek (90+1.Martin Vitík), Ladislav Krejci (II) [sent off 23], Lukás Julis (46.Adam Hlozek). Trainer: Václav Kotal.
Lille OSC: Mike Maignan, José Fonte, Jérémy Pied, Sven Botman (78.Adama Soumaoro), Domagoj Bradaric (63.Reinildo), Xeka, Jonathan Ikoné, Boubakary Soumaré, Yusuf Yazici (80.Timothy Weah), Jonathan Bamba (78.Luiz Araujo), Jonathan David (63.Burak Yilmaz). Trainer: Christophe Galtier.
Goals: 45+1' Yusuf Yazici 0-1, 47' Borek Dockal 1-1, 60' Yusuf Yazici 1-2, 66' Jonathan Ikoné 1-3, 75' Yusuf Yazici 1-4.

29.10.2020; Stade „Pierre-Mauroy", Villeneuve-d'Ascq
Referee: Aleksandar Stavrev (North Macedonia)
Lille OSC – Celtic FC Glasgow 2-2(0-2)
Lille OSC: Mike Maignan, Adama Soumaoro, Mehmet Zeki Çelik, Sven Botman, Domagoj Bradaric, Benjamin André (63.Renato Sanches), Jonathan Ikoné, Boubakary Soumaré, Yusuf Yazici (82.Timothy Weah), Jonathan Bamba (63.Luiz Araujo), Jonathan David (64.Burak Yilmaz). Trainer: Christophe Galtier.
Celtic: Scott Bain, Shane Duffy, Diego Laxalt, Kristoffer Ajer (53.Nir Bitton), Jeremie Frimpong, Scott Brown (81.Ismaila Soro), Callum McGregor, Mohamed Elyounoussi, Olivier Ntcham (82.Stephen Welsh), Ryan Christie (81.Tom Rogic), Albian Ajeti (64.Odsonne Édouard). Trainer: Neil Francis Lennon (Northern Ireland).
Goals: 28', 33' Mohamed Elyounoussi 0-1, 0-2, 67' Mehmet Zeki Çelik 1-2, 75' Jonathan Ikoné 2-2.

05.11.2020; Celtic Park, Glasgow
Referee: István Kovács (Romania); Attendance: 397
Celtic FC Glasgow – AC Sparta Praha 1-4(0-2)
Celtic: Scott Bain, Shane Duffy, Diego Laxalt (80.Olivier Ntcham), Jeremie Frimpong, Scott Brown (60.Hatem Abd Elhamed), Nir Bitton, Callum McGregor, Mohamed Elyounoussi (59.Leigh Griffiths), Tom Rogic, Ryan Christie, Odsonne Édouard (80.Albian Ajeti). Trainer: Neil Francis Lennon (Northern Ireland).
Sparta Praha: Florin Nita, Andreas Vindheim, Dávid Hancko (73.David Lischka), Dominik Plechatý, David Pavelka, David Moberg-Karlsson (88.Srdjan Plavsic), Matej Polidar (79.Ladislav Krejci (I)), Michal Sácek (88.Borek Dockal), Ladislav Krejci (II), Adam Karabec (74.Michal Trávník), Lukás Julis. Trainer: Václav Kotal.
Goals: 26', 45' Lukás Julis 0-1, 0-2, 65' Leigh Griffiths 1-2, 77' Lukás Julis 1-3, 90' Ladislav Krejci (I) 1-4.

26.11.2020; Generali Arena, Praha
Referee: Tobias Stieler (Germany)
AC Sparta Praha – Celtic FC Glasgow 4-1(2-1)
Sparta Praha: Florin Nita, Andreas Vindheim, Matej Hanousek, Dávid Hancko (67.Filip Soucek), Dominik Plechatý, Borek Dockal, David Pavelka, Michal Trávník (76.Ladislav Krejci (I)), David Moberg-Karlsson (86.Srdjan Plavsic), Ladislav Krejci (II), Lukás Julis (86.Martin Minchev). Trainer: Václav Kotal.
Celtic: Scott Bain, Hatem Abd Elhamed, Christopher Jullien, Diego Laxalt, Kristoffer Ajer, Scott Brown (66.Tom Rogic), Callum McGregor, Mohamed Elyounoussi, Olivier Ntcham, Ryan Christie, Odsonne Édouard (82.Patryk Klimala). Trainer: Neil Francis Lennon (Northern Ireland).
Goals: 15' Odsonne Édouard 0-1, 26' Dávid Hancko 1-1, 38', 80' Lukás Julis 2-1, 3-1, 90+4' Srdjan Plavsic 4-1.

03.12.2020; Stadio „Giuseppe Meazza", Milano
Referee: Ricardo de Burgos Bengoetxea (Spain)
AC Milan – Celtic FC Glasgow 4-2(2-2)
AC Milan: Gianluigi Donnarumma, Simon Kjær (11.Alessio Romagnoli), Theo Hernández, Diogo Dalot, Matteo Gabbia, Hakan Çalhanoglu (61.Brahim Díaz), Samu Castillejo, Rade Krunic (46.Sandro Tonali), Franck Kessié (62.Ismaël Bennacar), Jens Hauge, Ante Rebic (83.Lorenzo Colombo). Trainer: Stefano Pioli.
Celtic: Vassilis Barkas, Hatem Abd Elhamed, Diego Laxalt, Kristoffer Ajer, Jeremie Frimpong, Scott Brown (78.Ismaila Soro), Nir Bitton, Callum McGregor, Tom Rogic (67.Olivier Ntcham), Ryan Christie (86.Patryk Klimala), Odsonne Édouard. Trainer: Neil Francis Lennon (Northern Ireland).
Goals: 7' Tom Rogic 0-1, 14' Odsonne Édouard 0-2, 24' Hakan Çalhanoglu 1-2, 26' Samu Castillejo 2-2, 50' Jens Hauge 3-2, 82' Brahim Díaz 4-2.

10.12.2020; Celtic Park, Glasgow
Referee: Fábio José Costa Veríssimo (Portugal); Attendance: 300
Celtic FC Glasgow – Lille OSC 3-2(2-1)
Celtic: Conor Hazard, Shane Duffy, Christopher Jullien, Diego Laxalt, Kristoffer Ajer (87.Stephen Welsh), Jeremie Frimpong (30.Ewan Henderson), Callum McGregor, Mohamed Elyounoussi, David Turnbull (87.Tom Rogic), Ismaila Soro, Patryk Klimala (78.Albian Ajeti). Trainer: Neil Francis Lennon (Northern Ireland).
Lille OSC: Mike Maignan, José Fonte (46.Sven Botman), Tiago Djaló, Domagoj Bradaric, Xeka, Jonathan Ikoné (66.Isaac Lihadji), Boubakary Soumaré (66.Benjamin André), Yusuf Yazici, Cheikh Niasse (71.Jonathan Bamba), Timothy Weah (78.Reinildo), Jonathan David. Trainer: Christophe Galtier.
Goals: 21' Christopher Jullien 1-0, 24' Jonathan Ikoné 1-1, 28' Callum McGregor 2-1 (penalty), 71' Timothy Weah 2-2, 75' David Turnbull 3-2.

05.11.2020; Stadio „Giuseppe Meazza", Milano
Referee: Bartosz Frankowski (Poland)
AC Milan – Lille OSC 0-3(0-1)
AC Milan: Gianluigi Donnarumma, Simon Kjær, Alessio Romagnoli, Theo Hernández, Diogo Dalot, Samu Castillejo (46.Rafael Leão), Rade Krunic (46.Hakan Çalhanoglu), Franck Kessié, Sandro Tonali (61.Ismaël Bennacar), Zlatan Ibrahimovic (61.Ante Rebic), Brahim Díaz (78.Jens Hauge). Trainer: Stefano Pioli.
Lille OSC: Mike Maignan, José Fonte, Mehmet Zeki Çelik, Sven Botman, Domagoj Bradaric, Renato Sanches (80.Boubakary Soumaré), Xeka (65.Benjamin André), Jonathan Ikoné (65.Isaac Lihadji), Yusuf Yazici (80.Burak Yilmaz), Jonathan Bamba (84.Reinildo), Jonathan David. Trainer: Christophe Galtier.
Goals: 22', 55', 58' Yusuf Yazici 0-1 (penalty), 0-2, 0-3.

26.11.2020; Stade „Pierre-Mauroy", Villeneuve-d'Ascq
Referee: Craig Pawson (England)
Lille OSC – AC Milan 1-1(0-0)
Lille OSC: Mike Maignan, José Fonte, Jérémy Pied (79.Tiago Djaló), Reinildo, Sven Botman, Benjamin André, Xeka (63.Boubakary Soumaré), Yusuf Yazici (63.Jonathan Ikoné), Isaac Lihadji, Jonathan Bamba, Jonathan David. Trainer: Christophe Galtier.
AC Milan: Gianluigi Donnarumma, Simon Kjær, Theo Hernández, Diogo Dalot, Matteo Gabbia, Hakan Çalhanoglu (61.Brahim Díaz), Samu Castillejo, Ismaël Bennacar, Jens Hauge (77.Rade Krunic), Sandro Tonali, Ante Rebic (61.Lorenzo Colombo). Trainer: Stefano Pioli.
Goals: 46' Samu Castillejo 0-1, 65' Jonathan Bamba 1-1.

03.12.2020; Stade „Pierre-Mauroy", Villeneuve-d'Ascq
Referee: Xavier Estrada Fernández (Spain)
Lille OSC – AC Sparta Praha 2-1(0-0)
Lille OSC: Mike Maignan, José Fonte, Tiago Djaló (77.Timothy Weah), Sven Botman, Domagoj Bradaric (85.Reinildo), Benjamin André (85.Boubakary Soumaré), Xeka, Yusuf Yazici (77.Burak Yilmaz), Luiz Araujo (68.Jonathan Ikoné), Jonathan Bamba, Jonathan David. Trainer: Christophe Galtier.
Sparta Praha: Florin Nita, Ondrej Celustka [sent off 64], Andreas Vindheim, Dominik Plechatý, Borek Dockal (89.Adam Karabec), David Pavelka, Ladislav Krejci (I) (89.Martin Minchev), David Moberg-Karlsson (46.Srdjan Plavsic), Ladislav Krejci (II), Filip Soucek (81.Michal Trávník), Lukás Julis (81.Matej Hanousek). Trainer: Václav Kotal.
Goals: 71' Ladislav Krejci (II) 0-1, 80', 84' Burak Yilmaz 1-1, 2-1.

10.12.2020; Generali Arena, Praha
Referee: Daniel Siebert (Germany)
AC Sparta Praha – AC Milan 0-1(0-1)
Sparta Praha: Milan Heca, David Lischka, Tomás Wiesner, Dominik Plechatý [sent off 77], Martin Vitík, Srdjan Plavsic (65.David Moberg-Karlsson), Matej Polidar, Michal Sácek (82.Ladislav Krejci (I)), Martin Minchev (65.Lukás Julis), Filip Soucek, Adam Karabec (45.Ladislav Krejci (II)). Trainer: Václav Kotal.
AC Milan: Ciprian Tatarusanu, Andrea Conti, Diogo Dalot, Léo Duarte, Pierre Kalulu, Samu Castillejo, Rade Krunic, Jens Hauge (90.Brahim Díaz), Sandro Tonali, Lorenzo Colombo (67.Rafael Leão), Daniel Maldini (78.Franck Kessié). Trainer: Stefano Pioli.
Goal: 23' Jens Hauge 0-1.

GROUP I	1. **Villarreal CF**	6	5	1	0	17 - 5	16
	2. **Maccabi Tel Aviv FC**	6	3	2	1	6 - 7	11
	3. Sivasspor Kulübü	6	2	0	4	9 - 11	6
	4. Qarabağ FK Bakı	6	0	1	5	4 - 13	1

22.10.2020; Estadio de la Cerámica, Villarreal
Referee: Pawel Raczkowski (Poland)
Villarreal CF – Sivasspor Kulübü 5-3(2-2)
Villarreal: Gerónimo Rulli, Raúl Albiol, Jaume Costa (70.Alfonso Pedraza), Juan Foyth, Francis Coquelin (79.Yeremi Pino), Manu Trigueros (58.Moi Gómez), Rubén Peña, Samuel Chukwueze, Takefusa Kubo, Álex Baena (46.Iborra), Carlos Bacca (70.Paco Alcácer). Trainer: Unai Emery Etxegoien (Spain).
Sivasspor: Mamadou Samassa, Caner Osmanpasa, Ugur Çiftçi, Samba Camara (79.Claudemir), Hakan Arslan, Fayçal Fajr, Isaac Cofie, Robin Yalçın, Mustapha Yatabaré, Max Gradel (82.Yasin Öztekin), Olarenwaju Kayode (82.Arouna Koné). Trainer: Riza Çalimbary.
Goals: 12' Takefusa Kubo 1-0, 20' Carlos Bacca 2-0, 33' Olarenwaju Kayode 2-1, 43' Mustapha Yatabaré 2-2, 57' Juan Foyth 3-2, 64' Max Gradel 3-3, 74', 78' Paco Alcácer 4-3, 5-3.

29.10.2020; Başaksehir "Fatih Terim" Stadyumu, Istanbul (Turkey)
Referee: Pavel Orel (Czech Republic)
Qarabağ FK Bakı – Villarreal CF 1-3(0-0)
Qarabağ FK: Sahrudin Mahammadaliyev, Qara Qarayev, Abbas Hüseynov, Kevin Medina, Rahil Mammadov, Jaime Romero (61.Uros Matic), Filip Ozobic (61.Mahir Emreli), Wilde-Donald Guerrier, Abdellah Zoubir (82.Elvin Dzhafarquliyev), Patrick Andrade (90+2.Ismayil Ibrahimli), Owusu Kwabena (90+2.Tural Bayramov). Trainer: Qurban Qurbanov.
Villarreal: Gerónimo Rulli, Jaume Costa (74.Moi Gómez), Pau Torres, Juan Foyth (90+2.Ramiro Funes Mori), Iborra, Manu Trigueros, Rubén Peña, Alfonso Pedraza, Samuel Chukwueze (86.Álex Baena), Takefusa Kubo (74.Paco Alcácer), Carlos Bacca (74.Yeremi Pino). Trainer: Unai Emery Etxegoien (Spain).
Goals: 78' Owusu Kwabena 1-0, 80' Yeremi Pino 1-1, 84', 90+6' Paco Alcácer 1-2, 1-3 (penalty).

05.11.2020; Yeni Sivas 4 Eylül Stadyumu, Sivas
Referee: Sandro Schärer (Switzerland); Attendance: 296
Sivasspor Kulübü – Qarabağ FK Bakı 2-0(1-0)
Sivasspor: Mamadou Samassa, Caner Osmanpasa, Ugur Çiftçi, Marcelo Goiano, Claudemir (90+1.Isaac Cofie), Hakan Arslan, Fayçal Fajr, Robin Yalçın, Erdogan Yesilyurt (59.Max Gradel), Mustapha Yatabaré (59.Olarenwaju Kayode), Casimir Ninga (67.Yasin Öztekin). Trainer: Riza Çalimbary.
Qarabağ FK: Sahrudin Mahammadaliyev, Maksim Medvedev (85.Rahil Mammadov), Qara Qarayev, Badavi Hüseynov (61.Abbas Hüseynov), Kevin Medina, Uros Matic (84.Ismayil Ibrahimli), Filip Ozobic (62.Jaime Romero), Wilde-Donald Guerrier, Abdellah Zoubir, Patrick Andrade (46.Mahir Emreli), Owusu Kwabena. Trainer: Qurban Qurbanov.
Goals: 11' Caner Osmanpasa 1-0, 88' Olarenwaju Kayode 2-0.

26.11.2020; Bloomfield Stadium, Tel Aviv
Referee: Tiago Bruno Lopes Martins (Portugal)
Maccabi Tel Aviv FC – Villarreal CF 1-1(0-1)
Maccabi Tel Aviv: Daniel Tenenbaum, Eitan Tibi, Luis Hernández, Saborit [sent off 89], Maor Kandil, Eyal Golasa (90+2.Ofir Davidzada), Dor Peretz, Dan Glazer (54.Nick Blackman), Dan Biton (85.Sheran Yeini), Aleksandar Pesic (85.Avi Rikan), Yonatan Cohen (90+2.Eden Karzev). Trainer: Georgios Donis (Greece).
Villarreal: Gerónimo Rulli, Ramiro Funes Mori, Juan Foyth, Francis Coquelin, Manu Trigueros (63.Yeremi Pino), Rubén Peña, Alfonso Pedraza, Samuel Chukwueze (63.Dani Parejo), Takefusa Kubo (63.Gerard Moreno), Álex Baena (75.Iborra), Carlos Bacca (63.Fer Niño). Trainer: Unai Emery Etxegoien (Spain).
Goals: 44' Álex Baena 0-1, 47' Aleksandar Pesic 1-1.

22.10.2020; Bloomfield Stadium, Tel Aviv
Referee: John Beaton (Scotland)
Maccabi Tel Aviv FC – Qarabağ FK Bakı 1-0(1-0)
Maccabi Tel Aviv: Daniel Tenenbaum, Sheran Yeini, Eitan Tibi, Ofir Davidzada (46.Ben Bitton), Saborit (84.Luis Hernández), Maor Kandil, Eyal Golasa (78.Tal Ben Haim), Dor Peretz, Dan Glazer, Itay Shechter (46.Eduardo Guerrero), Yonatan Cohen (69.Avi Rikan). Trainer: Georgios Donis (Greece).
Qarabağ FK: Sahrudin Mahammadaliyev, Maksim Medvedev, Qara Qarayev (81.Ismayil Ibrahimli), Abbas Hüseynov, Kevin Medina, Jaime Romero (86.Musa Qurbanly), Uros Matic (60.Owusu Kwabena), Filip Ozobic (80.Elvin Dzhafarquliyev), Wilde-Donald Guerrier, Abdellah Zoubir (86.Tural Bayramov), Patrick Andrade. Trainer: Qurban Qurbanov.
Goal: 10' Yonatan Cohen 1-0.

29.10.2020; Yeni Sivas 4 Eylül Stadyumu, Sivas
Referee: Irfan Peljto (Bosnia and Herzegovina); Attendance: 348
Sivasspor Kulübü – Maccabi Tel Aviv FC 1-2(0-0)
Sivasspor: Mamadou Samassa, Caner Osmanpasa, Ugur Çiftçi, Samba Camara [sent off 67], Claudemir (81.Arouna Koné), Hakan Arslan, Fayçal Fajr, Robin Yalçın, Mustapha Yatabaré (78.Casimir Ninga), Olarenwaju Kayode (75.Isaac Cofie). Trainer: Riza Çalimbary.
Maccabi Tel Aviv: Daniel Tenenbaum, Sheran Yeini, Eitan Tibi, Ofir Davidzada, Luis Hernández, Maor Kandil (65.Eyal Golasa), Avi Rikan (88.Eden Karzev), Dor Peretz (90+1.Saborit), Dan Glazer, Dan Biton (88.Yonatan Cohen), Itay Shechter (65.Aleksandar Pesic). Trainer: Georgios Donis (Greece).
Goals: 55' Olarenwaju Kayode 1-0, 69' Dan Biton 1-1 (penalty), 74' Dor Petetz 1-2.

05.11.2020; Estadio de la Cerámica, Villarreal
Referee: Nikola Dabanović (Montenegro)
Villarreal CF – Maccabi Tel Aviv FC 4-0(1-0)
Villarreal: Gerónimo Rulli, Raúl Albiol, Jaume Costa (65.Moi Gómez), Ramiro Funes Mori, Iborra (59.Manu Trigueros), Dani Parejo (59.Pervis Estupiñán), Rubén Peña, Takefusa Kubo, Álex Baena (74.Gerard Moreno), Yeremi Pino, Carlos Bacca (74.Fer Niño). Trainer: Unai Emery Etxegoien (Spain).
Maccabi Tel Aviv: Daniel Tenenbaum, Eitan Tibi, Ben Biton, Luis Hernández, Saborit, Tal Ben Haim (61.Dan Biton), Dan Glazer (68.Dor Peretz), Matan Baltaxa, Eden Karzev (61.Eyal Golasa), Nick Blackman (51.Aleksandar Pesic), Yonatan Cohen (68.Itay Shechter). Trainer: Georgios Donis (Greece).
Goals: 4', 52' Carlos Bacca 1-0, 2-0, 71' Álex Baena 3-0, 81' Fer Niño 4-0.

26.11.2020; Başaksehir "Fatih Terim" Stadyumu, Istanbul (Turkey)
Referee: Jakob Kehlet (Denmark)
Qarabağ FK Bakı – Sivasspor Kulübü 2-3(1-1)
Qarabağ FK: Sahrudin Mahammadaliyev, Qara Qarayev, Kevin Medina, Uros Matic, Wilde-Donald Guerrier, Abdellah Zoubir, Ismayil Ibrahimli, Tural Bayramov (66.Jaime Romero), Elvin Dzhafarquliyev, Mahir Emreli, Owusu Kwabena. Trainer: Qurban Qurbanov.
Sivasspor: Mamadou Samassa, Caner Osmanpasa, Ugur Çiftçi, Marcelo Goiano, Aaron Appindangoyé, Claudemir, Yasin Öztekin (90+3.Samba Camara), Robin Yalçın (20.Isaac Cofie), Arouna Koné, Max Gradel, Casimir Ninga (57.Olarenwaju Kayode). Trainer: Riza Çalimbary.
Goals: 8' Abdellah Zoubir 1-0, 40' Arouna Koné 1-1 (penalty), 51' Uros Matic 2-1, 58' Olarenwaju Kayode 2-2, 79' Arouna Koné 2-3.

03.12.2020; Başakşehir "Fatih Terim" Stadyumu, Istanbul (Turkey)
Referee: Robert Hennessy (Republic of Ireland)
Qarabağ FK Bakı – Maccabi Tel Aviv FC 1-1(1-1)
Qarabağ FK: Sahrudin Mahammadaliyev, Qara Qarayev, Kevin Medina, Jaime Romero (72.Tural Bayramov), Uros Matic, Filip Ozobic (83.Rahil Mammadov), Wilde-Donald Guerrier, Abdellah Zoubir, Ismayil Ibrahimli, Elvin Dzhafarquliyev, Owusu Kwabena. Trainer: Qurban Qurbanov.
Maccabi Tel Aviv: Daniel Tenenbaum, Sheran Yeini, Eitan Tibi, Ofir Davidzada, Luis Hernández, Maor Kandil (69.Dan Glazer), Eyal Golasa (83.Itay Shechter), Dor Peretz (83.Tal Ben Haim), Dan Biton, Nick Blackman (65.Eduardo Guerrero), Yonatan Cohen. Trainer: Georgios Donis (Greece).
Goals: 22' Yonatan Cohen 0-1 (penalty), 37' Jaime Romero 1-1.

10.12.2020; Estadio de la Cerámica, Villarreal:
Referee: Mykola Balakin (Ukraine)
Villarreal CF – Qarabağ FK Bakı 3-0(awarded)

Match was cancelled and awarded as a 3-0 win to Villarreal CF after several players of the Qarabağ FK Bakı squad were tested positive for the COVID-19.

03.12.2020; Yeni Sivas 4 Eylül Stadyumu, Sivas
Referee: Duje Strukan (Croatia)
Sivasspor Kulübü – Villarreal CF 0-1(0-0)
Sivasspor: Mamadou Samassa, Caner Osmanpasa, Ziya Erdal, Samba Camara, Aaron Appindangoyé, Yasin Öztekin, Fayçal Fajr, Isaac Cofie (82.Claudemir), Robin Yalçin (77.Arouna Koné), Mustapha Yatabaré (80.Casimir Ninga), Max Gradel. Trainer: Riza Çalimbary.
Villarreal: Gerónimo Rulli, Jaume Costa (77.Pervis Estupiñán), Ramiro Funes Mori, Juan Foyth, Iborra, Francis Coquelin (68.Manu Trigueros), Rubén Peña, Samuel Chukwueze (76.Gerard Moreno), Takefusa Kubo (58.Yeremi Pino), Álex Baena (68.Dani Parejo), Fer Niño. Trainer: Unai Emery Etxegoien (Spain).
Goal: 75' Samuel Chukwueze 0-1.

10.12.2020; Bloomfield Stadium, Tel Aviv
Referee: Andris Treimanis (Latvia)
Maccabi Tel Aviv FC – Sivasspor Kulübü 1-0(0-0)
Maccabi Tel Aviv: Daniel Tenenbaum, Eitan Tibi, Luis Hernández, Saborit (85.Sheran Yeini), Maor Kandil, Eyal Golasa (74.Tal Ben Haim), Dor Peretz, Dan Glazer, Dan Biton (63.Ofir Davidzada), Aleksandar Pesic (85.Nick Blackman), Yonatan Cohen (74.Avi Rikan). Trainer: Georgios Donis (Greece).
Sivasspor: Mamadou Samassa, Caner Osmanpasa, Samba Camara, Aaron Appindangoyé, Claudemir (63.Arouna Koné), Hakan Arslan, Fayçal Fajr, Robin Yalçin, Mustapha Yatabaré, Max Gradel, Olarenwaju Kayode. Trainer: Riza Çalimbary.
Goal: 66' Saborit 1-0.

GROUP J									
1. **Tottenham Hotspur FC London**	6	4	1	1	15	-	5	13
2. **Royal Antwerp FC**	6	4	0	2	8	-	5	12
3. Linzer ASK	6	3	1	2	11	-	12	10
4. PFC Ludogorets Razgrad	6	0	0	6	7	-	19	0

22.10.2020; Tottenham Hotspur Stadium, London
Referee: Mohammed Al-Hakim (Sweden)
Tottenham Hotspur FC London – Linzer ASK 3-0(2-0)
Tottenham Hotspur: Joe Hart, Matt Doherty, Ben Davies, Davinson Sánchez, Reguilón, Érik Lamela (62.Dele Alli), Lucas Moura (78.Giovani Lo Celso), Pierre-Emile Højbjerg (62.Moussa Sissoko), Harry Winks, Gareth Bale (62.Son Heung-Min), Carlos Vinícius (86.Jack Clarke). Trainer: José Mário dos Santos Félix Mourinho (Portugal).
LASK: Alexander Schlager, Gernot Trauner, Reinhold Ranftl, Philipp Wiesinger, James Holland (5.Lukas Grgic), Peter Michorl, René Renner (39.Petar Filipovic), Husein Balic (78.Thomas Goiginger), Andrés Andrade (46.Marvin Potzmann), Andreas Gruber (46.Johannes Eggestein), Marko Raguz. Trainer: Dominik Thalhammer.
Goals: 18' Lucas Moura 1-0, 27' Andrés Andrade 2-0 (own goal), 84' Son Heung-Min 3-0.

29.11.2020; Linzer Stadion, Linz
Referee: Xavier Estrada Fernández (Spain); Attendance: 1,487
Linzer ASK – PFC Ludogorets Razgrad 4-3(3-1)
LASK: Alexander Schlager, Petar Filipovic, Gernot Trauner, Reinhold Ranftl, Philipp Wiesinger, Peter Michorl, Lukas Grgic [sent off 73], Husein Balic (63.Johannes Eggestein), Andrés Andrade, Andreas Gruber (63.Thomas Goiginger), Marko Raguz. Trainer: Dominik Thalhammer.
Ludogorets Razgrad: Plamen Iliev, Cosmin Moti, Cicinho, Anton Nedyalkov, Olivier Verdon, Anicet Andrianantenaina, Stéphane Badji (53.Cauly), Alex Santana, Dominik Yankov (80.Mavis Tchibota), Elvis Manu, Bernard Tekpetey (88.Jordan Ikoko). Trainer: Stanislav Genchev.
Goals: 2' Husein Balic 1-0, 11' Andreas Gruber 2-0, 15' Elvis Manu 2-1, 35' Marko Raguz 3-1, 56' Olivier Verdon 4-1 (own goal), 67', 73' Elvis Manu 4-2, 4-3 (penalty).

22.10.2020; Huvepharma Arena, Razgrad
Referee: Roi Reinshreiber (Israel); Attendance: 2,321
PFC Ludogorest Razgrad – Royal Antwerp FC 1-2(0-0)
Ludogorets Razgrad: Plamen Iliev, Cicinho, Georgi Terziev, Anton Nedyalkov, Olivier Verdon, Stéphane Badji (83.Anicet Andrianantenaina), Cauly (78.Claudiu Kerserü), Alex Santana, Dominik Yankov (77.Bernard Tekpetey), Kiril Despodov (45+1.Elvis Manu), Higinio Marín. Trainer: Pavel Vrba.
Antwerp FC: Jean Butez, Ritchie De Laet, Simen Juklerød, Dylan Batubinsika, Jérémy Gelin, Faris Haroun, Lior Refaelov (72.Buta), Cristián Benavente (59.Nana Ampomah), Pieter Gerkens, Koji Miyoshi, Martin Hongla Yma (80.Birger Verstraete). Trainer: Ivan Leko (Croatia).
Goals: 46' Higinio Marín 1-0, 63' Pieter Gerkens 1-1, 70' Lior Refaelov 1-2.

29.10.2020; Bosuilstadion, Antwerp
Referee: Maurizio Mariana (Italy)
Royal Antwerp FC – Tottenham Hotspur FC London 1-0(1-0)
Antwerp FC: Jean Butez, Ritchie De Laet, Simen Juklerød, Jérémy Gelin, Abdoulaye Seck, Faris Haroun, Lior Refaelov (88.Cristián Benavente), Pieter Gerkens, Koji Miyoshi (58.Buta), Martin Hongla Yma (70.Birger Verstraete), Dieumerci Mbokani. Trainer: Ivan Leko (Croatia).
Tottenham Hotspur: Hugo Lloris, Serge Aurier, Ben Davies, Davinson Sánchez, Reguilón, Dele Alli (46.Érik Lamela), Harry Winks, Giovani Lo Celso (46.Pierre-Emile Højbjerg), Gareth Bale (58.Harry Kane), Steven Bergwijn (46.Lucas Moura), Carlos Vinícius (46.Son Heung-Min). Trainer: José Mário dos Santos Félix Mourinho (Portugal).
Goal: 29' Lior Refaelov 1-0.

05.11.2020; Huvepharma Arena, Razgrad
Referee: Fran Jović (Croatia)
PFC Ludogorets Razgrad – Tottenham Hotspur FC London 1-3(0-2)
Ludogorets Razgrad: Plamen Iliev, Georgi Terziev, Jordan Ikoko, Anton Nedyalkov, Olivier Verdon, Anicet Andrianantenaina (59.Alex Santana), Stéphane Badji (90+2.Ivan Yordanov), Cauly, Dominik Yankov (80.Mavis Tchibota), Claudiu Keserü (59.Dimitar Mitkov), Elvis Manu (46.Bernard Tekpetey). Trainer: Stanislav Genchev.
Tottenham Hotspur: Joe Hart, Toby Alderweireld, Matt Doherty, Ben Davies, Moussa Sissoko (46.Pierre-Emile Højbjerg), Lucas Moura (61.Son Heung-Min), Eric Dier, Harry Winks, Giovani Lo Celso (72.Tanguy NDombélé), Gareth Bale (65.Steven Bergwijn), Harry Kane (46.Carlos Vinícius). Trainer: José Mário dos Santos Félix Mourinho (Portugal).
Goals: 13' Harry Kane 0-1, 32' Lucas Moura 0-2, 50' Claudiu Keserü 1-2, 62' Giovani Lo Celso 1-3.

26.11.2020; Linzer Stadion, Linz
Referee: Donatas Rumšas (Lithuania)
Linzer ASK – Royal Antwerp FC 0-2(0-0)
LASK: Alexander Schlager, Petar Filipovic (73.Marvin Potzmann), Gernot Trauner [*sent off 50*], Reinhold Ranftl, Philipp Wiesinger, Peter Michorl, René Renner, Husein Balic, Mads Madsen (53.Andrés Andrade), Andreas Gruber (60.Thomas Goiginger), Johannes Eggestein. Trainer: Dominik Thalhammer.
Antwerp FC: Jean Butez, Ritchie De Laet, Simen Juklerød (81.Buta), Dylan Batubinsika, Abdoulaye Seck, Faris Haroun, Lior Refaelov (88.Manuel Benson), Cristián Benavente (67.Nana Ampomah), Pieter Gerkens, Koji Miyoshi (81.Jordan Lukaku), Martin Hongla Yma. Trainer: Ivan Leko (Croatia).
Goals: 52' Lior Refaelov 0-1, 83' Pieter Gerkens 0-2.

03.12.2020; Linzer Stadion, Linz
Referee: Pawel Raczkowski (Poland)
Linzer ASK – Tottenham Hotspur FC London 3-3(1-1)
LASK: Alexander Schlager, Reinhold Ranftl, Philipp Wiesinger, James Holland, Peter Michorl, René Renner, Andrés Andrade, Mads Madsen, Thomas Goiginger (69.Mamoudou Karamoko), Andreas Gruber (69.Dominik Reiter), Johannes Eggestein. Trainer: Dominik Thalhammer.
Tottenham Hotspur: Joe Hart, Matt Doherty, Ben Davies, Davinson Sánchez, Japhet Tanganga, Lucas Moura (65.Moussa Sissoko), Pierre-Emile Højbjerg, Tanguy NDombélé (65.Steven Bergwijn), Giovani Lo Celso (71.Eric Dier), Gareth Bale (82.Serge Aurier), Son Heung-Min (82.Dele Alli). Trainer: José Mário dos Santos Félix Mourinho (Portugal).
Goals: 42' Peter Michorl 1-0, 45+2' Gareth Bale 1-1 (penalty), 56' Son Heung-Min 1-2, 84' Johannes Eggestein 2-2, 87' Dele Alli 2-3 (penalty), 90+3' Mamoudou Karamoko 3-3.

10.12.2020; Tottenham Hotspur Stadium, London
Referee: Jesús Gil Manzano (Spain); Attendance: 2,000
Tottenham Hotspur FC London – Royal Antwerp 2-0(0-0)
Tottenham Hotspur: Joe Hart, Matt Doherty, Ben Davies, Davinson Sánchez, Reguilón (47.Steven Bergwijn), Japhet Tanganga, Lucas Moura (68.Moussa Sissoko), Harry Winks (59.Tanguy NDombélé), Giovani Lo Celso, Gareth Bale (58.Son Heung-Min), Carlos Vinícius (59.Harry Kane). Trainer: José Mário dos Santos Félix Mourinho (Portugal).
Antwerp FC: Alireza Beiranvand, Jordan Lukaku (61.Simen Juklerød), Dylan Batubinsika, Buta, Jérémy Gelin, Abdoulaye Seck (72.Birger Verstraete), Faris Haroun, Lior Refaelov (46.Nana Ampomah), Cristián Benavente, Martin Hongla Yma (61.Frank Boya), Manuel Benson (72.Koji Miyoshi). Trainer: Ivan Leko (Croatia).
Goals: 57' Carlos Vinícius 1-0, 71' Giovani Lo Celso 2-0.

05.11.2020; Bosuilstadion, Antwerp
Referee: Yevhen Aranovskiy (Ukraine)
Royal Antwerp FC – Linzer ASK 0-1(0-0)
Antwerp FC: Jean Butez, Ritchie De Laet, Simen Juklerød (75.Cristián Benavente), Abdoulaye Seck, Faris Haroun (87.Frank Boya), Lior Refaelov (87.Jordan Lukaku), Pieter Gerkens, Birger Verstraete (64.Nana Ampomah), Koji Miyoshi (64.Buta), Martin Hongla Yma, Dieumerci Mbokani. Trainer: Ivan Leko (Croatia).
LASK: Alexander Schlager, Petar Filipovic, Gernot Trauner, Reinhold Ranftl, Philipp Wiesinger, James Holland [*sent off 68*], Peter Michorl, René Renner, Husein Balic, Andreas Gruber (66.Thomas Goiginger), Marko Raguz (40.Johannes Eggestein). Trainer: Dominik Thalhammer.
Goal: 54' Johannes Eggestein 0-1.

26.11.2020; Tottenham Hotspur Stadium, London
Referee: Giorgi Kruashvili (Georgia)
Tottenham Hotspur FC London – PFC Ludogorets Razgrad 4-0(2-0)
Tottenham Hotspur: Joe Hart (82.Alfie Whiteman), Matt Doherty, Ben Davies, Davinson Sánchez, Japhet Tanganga, Lucas Moura (82.Dane Scarlett), Dele Alli (82.Harvey White), Harry Winks, Tanguy NDombélé (61.Pierre-Emile Højbjerg), Gareth Bale (68.Jack Clarke), Carlos Vinícius. Trainer: José Mário dos Santos Félix Mourinho (Portugal).
Ludogorets Razgrad: Plamen Iliev, Cosmin Moti, Dragos Grigore, Jordan Ikoko, Anton Nedyalkov, Olivier Verdon, Anicet Andrianantenaina (68.Cauly), Stéphane Badji (89.Ivan Yordanov), Dominik Yankov (90.Dimitar Mitkov), Claudiu Keserü (68.Mavis Tchibota), Kiril Despodov (64.Bernard Tekpetey). Trainer: Stanislav Genchev.
Goals: 16', 34' Carlos Vinícius 1-0, 2-0, 63' Harry Winks 3-0, 73' Lucas Moura 4-0.

03.12.2020; Bosuilstadion, Antwerp
Referee: Pavel Orel (Czech Republic)
Royal Antwerp FC – PFC Ludogorets Razgrad 3-1(1-0)
Antwerp FC: Jean Butez, Ritchie De Laet, Simen Juklerød (64.Manuel Benson), Jérémy Gelin, Abdoulaye Seck, Faris Haroun, Lior Refaelov (77.Buta), Cristián Benavente (64.Nana Ampomah), Pieter Gerkens (84.Dieumerci Mbokani), Koji Miyoshi, Martin Hongla Yma (77.Frank Boya). Trainer: Ivan Leko (Croatia).
Ludogorets Razgrad: Vladislav Stoyanov, Dragos Grigore [*sent off 90*], Jordan Ikoko (44.Georgi Terziev), Anton Nedyalkov, Olivier Verdon, Anicet Andrianantenaina, Mavis Tchibota (67.Bernard Tekpetey), Stéphane Badji (83.Alex Santana), Cauly, Claudiu Keserü (67.Elvis Manu), Kiril Despodov (83.Dimitar Mitkov). Trainer: Stanislav Genchev.
Goals: 19' Martin Hongla Yma 1-0, 53' Kiril Despodov 1-1, 72' Ritchie De Laet 2-1, 87' Manuel Benson 3-1.

10.12.2020; Huvepharma Arena, Razgrad
Referee: Vitali Meshkov (Russia)
PFC Ludogorets Razgrad – Linzer ASK 1-3(0-0)
Ludogorets Razgrad: Plamen Iliev, Cicinho, Josué Sá, Jordan Ikoko (70.Georgi Terziev), Olivier Verdon, Mavis Tchibota (46.Elvis Manu), Stéphane Badji (77.Anicet Andrianantenaina), Cauly (77.Dominik Yankov), Alex Santana [*sent off 61*], Claudiu Keserü (77.Bernard Tekpetey), Kiril Despodov. Trainer: Stanislav Genchev.
LASK: Alexander Schlager, Reinhold Ranftl (74.Marvin Potzmann), Philipp Wiesinger (86.Christian Ramsebner), Yevgen Cheberko, James Holland, René Renner, Andrés Andrade, Dominik Reiter (63.Andreas Gruber), Mads Madsen, Thomas Goiginger (62.Husein Balic), Johannes Eggestein (73.Patrick Plojer). Trainer: Dominik Thalhammer.
Goals: 46' Elvis Manu 1-0, 56' Philipp Wiesinger 1-1, 61' René Renner 1-2 (penalty), 67' Mads Madsen 1-3.

1.	GNK Dinamo Zagreb	6	4	2	0	9	-	1	14
2.	Wolfsberger AC	6	3	1	2	7	-	6	10
3.	Feyenoord Rotterdam	6	1	2	3	4	-	8	5
4.	FK CSKA Moskva	6	0	3	3	3	-	8	3

22.10.2020; Stadion Maksimir, Zagreb
Referee: Mattias Gestranius (Finland); Attendance: 1,271
GNK Dinamo Zagreb – Feyenoord Rotterdam 0-0
Dinamo Zagreb: Dominik Livakovic, Kévin Théophile-Catherine, Petar Stojanovic, Rasmus Lauritsen, Josko Gvardiol, Arijan Ademi, Kristijan Jakic (71.Bartol Franjic), Lovro Majer, Mario Gavranovic (54.Bruno Petkovic), Mislav Orsic, Lirim Kastrati (I) (54.Luka Ivanusec). Trainer: Zoran Mamic.
Feyenoord: Justin Bijlow, Uros Spajic, Ridgeciano Haps, Bart Nieuwkoop, Marcos Senesi [*sent off 73*], Jens Toornstra, João Carlos Teixeira, Mark Diemers (81.Nicolai Jørgensen), Orkun Kökçü (74.Eric Botteghin), Bryan Linssen, Steven Berghuis. Trainer: Dick Advocaat.

29.10.2020; VEB Arena, Moskva
Referee: Radu Marian Petrescu (Romania); Attendance: 6,411
FK CSKA Moskva – GNK Dinamo Zagreb 0-0
CSKA Moskva: Igor Akinfeev, Mário Fernandes (84.Kristijan Bistrovic), Hördur Magnússon, Igor Diveev, Nikola Vlasic, Baktiyor Zaynutdinov, Konstantin Kuchaev (81.Ilzat Akhmetov), Ivan Oblyakov (80.Alan Dzagoev), Konstantin Maradishvili, Fedor Chalov (74.Adolfo Gaich), Chidera Ejuke (75.Arnór Sigurdsson). Trainer: Victor Goncharenko (Belarus).
Dinamo Zagreb: Dominik Livakovic, Petar Stojanovic, Dino Peric (81.Lirim Kastrati (I)), Rasmus Lauritsen, Josko Gvardiol, Arijan Ademi, Luka Ivanusec (66.Kristijan Jakic), Lovro Majer, Bartol Franjic, Mislav Orsic (90+3.Sadegh Moharrami), Bruno Petkovic (65.Mario Gavranovic). Trainer: Zoran Mamic.

05.11.2020; Stadion Maksimir, Zagreb
Referee: Jérôme Brisard (France)
GNK Dinamo Zagreb – Wolfsberger AC 1-0(0-0)
Dinamo Zagreb: Danijel Zagorac, Dino Peric (15.Marin Leovac), Sadegh Moharrami (74.Iyayi Atiemwen), Rasmus Lauritsen, Josko Gvardiol, Arijan Ademi, Kristijan Jakic (46.Lirim Kastrati (I)), Lovro Majer, Bartol Franjic, Mario Gavranovic (90+2.Robbie Burton), Mislav Orsic. Trainer: Zoran Mamic.
Wolfsberger AC: Alexander Kofler, Michael Novak, Mario Pavelic (81.Amar Hodzic), Dominik Baumgartner, Luka Lochoshvili, Christopher Wernitznig, Eliel Peretz (80.Marc Andre Schmerböck), Matthäus Taferner [*sent off 45*], Kai Stratznig, Cheikhou Dieng (54.Dario Vizinger), Dejan Joveljic (46.Stefan Peric). Trainer: Ferdinand Feldhofer.
Goal: 76' Iyayi Atiemwen 1-0.

26.11.2020; VEB Arena, Moskva
Referee: Kristo Tohver (Estonia); Attendance: 5,407
FK CSKA Moskva – Feyenoord Rotterdam 0-0
CSKA Moskva: Igor Akinfeev, Georgiy Shchennikov (64.Ilzat Akhmetov), Hördur Magnússon, Igor Diveev, Nikola Vlasic, Baktiyor Zaynutdinov, Arnór Sigurdsson (63.Ilya Shkurin), Ivan Oblyakov (71.Kristijan Bistrovic), Konstantin Maradishvili, Fedor Chalov (80.Nayair Tiknizyan), Chidera Ejuke (81.Adolfo Gaich). Trainer: Victor Goncharenko (Belarus).
Feyenoord: Nick Marsman, Uros Spajic, Bart Nieuwkoop, Marcos Senesi, Lutsharel Geertruida, Jens Toornstra (71.Jordy Wehrmann), Mark Diemers, Orkun Kökçü, Bryan Linssen, Nicolai Jørgensen [*sent off 48*], Steven Berghuis (82.Eric Botteghin). Trainer: Dick Advocaat.

22.10.2020; Wörthersee Stadion, Klagenfurt
Referee: Sascha Stegemann (Germany); Attendance: 3,000
Wolfsberger AC – FK CSKA Moskva 1-1(1-1)
Wolfsberger AC: Alexander Kofler, Michael Novak, Jonathan Scherzer (84.Mario Pavelic), Dominik Baumgartner, Luka Lochoshvili, Michael Liendl, Mario Leitgeb, Christopher Wernitznig (73.Eliel Peretz), Matthäus Taferner, Cheikhou Dieng (78.Marc Andre Schmerböck), Dejan Joveljic. Trainer: Ferdinand Feldhofer.
CSKA Moskva: Igor Akinfeev, Viktor Vasin (46.Alan Dzagoev), Hördur Magnússon, Igor Diveev, Nikola Vlasic (86.Kristijan Bistrovic), Baktiyor Zaynutdinov, Konstantin Kuchaev (76.Ilzat Akhmetov), Ivan Oblyakov, Nayair Tiknizyan (46.Chidera Ejuke), Konstantin Maradishvili, Adolfo Gaich (61.Fedor Chalov). Trainer: Victor Goncharenko (Belarus).
Goals: 5' Adolfo Gaich 0-1, 42' Michael Liendl 1-1 (penalty).

29.10.2020; Stadion Feijenoord, Rotterdam
Referee: Srđan Jovanović (Serbia)
Feyenoord Rotterdam – Wolfsberger AC 1-4(0-2)
Feyenoord: Justin Bijlow, Eric Botteghin, Uros Spajic, Ridgeciano Haps, Bart Nieuwkoop (46.Luciano Narsingh), Lutsharel Geertruida, Jens Toornstra, Mark Diemers, Orkun Kökçü, Bryan Linssen (76.Naoufal Bannis), Steven Berghuis. Trainer: Dick Advocaat.
Wolfsberger AC: Alexander Kofler, Michael Novak, Jonathan Scherzer, Dominik Baumgartner, Luka Lochoshvili, Michael Liendl, Mario Leitgeb, Christopher Wernitznig (82.Eliel Peretz), Matthäus Taferner (60.Kai Stratznig), Cheikhou Dieng (82.Dario Vizinger), Dejan Joveljic (67.Nemanja Rnic). Trainer: Ferdinand Feldhofer.
Goals: 4', 13' Michael Liendl 0-1 (penalty), 0-2 (penalty), 53' Steven Berghuis 1-2, 60' Michael Liendl 1-3, 66' Dejan Joveljic 1-4 (penalty).

05.11.2020; Stadion Feijenoord, Rotterdam
Referee: Roi Reinshreiber (Israel)
Feyenoord Rotterdam – FK CSKA Moskva 3-1(0-0)
Feyenoord: Justin Bijlow, Uros Spajic, Ridgeciano Haps, Tyrell Malacia, Marcos Senesi, Lutsharel Geertruida, Jens Toornstra, Mark Diemers, Orkun Kökçü (76.João Carlos Teixeira), Bryan Linssen, Steven Berghuis. Trainer: Dick Advocaat.
CSKA Moskva: Igor Akinfeev, Mário Fernandes (31.Alan Dzagoev), Hördur Magnússon (77.Viktor Vasin), Igor Diveev, Nikola Vlasic, Baktiyor Zaynutdinov, Arnór Sigurdsson, Konstantin Kuchaev (68.Fedor Chalov), Ivan Oblyakov (77.Kristijan Bistrovic), Konstantin Maradishvili, Chidera Ejuke (76.Nayair Tiknizyan). Trainer: Victor Goncharenko (Belarus).
Goals: 63' Ridgeciano Haps 1-0, 71' Orkun Kökçü 2-0, 72' Lutsharel Geertruida 3-0, 79' Marcos Senesi 3-1 (own goal).

26.11.2020; Wörthersee Stadion, Klagenfurt
Referee: Serhiy Boyko (Ukraine)
Wolfsberger AC – GNK Dinamo Zagreb 0-3(0-0)
Wolfsberger AC: Manuel Kuttin, Michael Novak, Jonathan Scherzer (82.Guram Giorbelidze), Dominik Baumgartner (46.Nemanja Rnic), Luka Lochoshvili, Michael Liendl, Mario Leitgeb, Christopher Wernitznig (66.Dejan Joveljic), Eliel Peretz, Kai Stratznig (72.Sven Sprangler), Dario Vizinger (82.Marc Andre Schmerböck). Trainer: Ferdinand Feldhofer.
Dinamo Zagreb: Dominik Livakovic, Kévin Théophile-Catherine, Sadegh Moharrami, Rasmus Lauritsen, Josko Gvardiol, Arijan Ademi (90+2.Robbie Burton), Kristijan Jakic (83.Marko Tolic), Lovro Majer (74.Bartol Franjic), Mislav Orsic (74.Luka Ivanusec), Bruno Petkovic, Lirim Kastrati (I). Trainer: Zoran Mamic.
Goals: 60' Lovro Majer 0-1, 75' Bruno Petkovic 0-2, 90+1' Luka Ivanusec 0-3.

03.12.2020; VEB Arena, Moskva
Referee: Nikola Dabanović (Montenegro); Attendance: 4,321
FK CSKA Moskva – Wolfsberger AC 0-1(0-1)
CSKA Moskva: Igor Akinfeev, Georgiy Shchennikov (63.Nayair Tiknizyan), Hördur Magnússon, Igor Diveev, Nikola Vlasic, Ilzat Akhmetov (64.Kristijan Bistrovic), Baktiyor Zaynutdinov, Konstantin Kuchaev (46.Chidera Ejuke), Ivan Oblyakov (76.Arnór Sigurdsson), Konstantin Maradishvili, Fedor Chalov (46.Adolfo Gaich). Trainer: Victor Goncharenko (Belarus).
Wolfsberger AC: Alexander Kofler, Michael Novak, Jonathan Scherzer, Dominik Baumgartner, Luka Lochoshvili, Michael Liendl (81.Christopher Wernitznig), Mario Leitgeb, Sven Sprangler (82.Nemanja Rnic), Eliel Peretz, Matthäus Taferner (61.Kai Stratznig), Dario Vizinger (70.Dejan Joveljic). Trainer: Ferdinand Feldhofer.
Goal: 22' Dario Vizinger 0-1.

10.12.2020; Stadion Maksimir, Zagreb
Referee: Tiago Bruno Lopes Martins (Portugal)
GNK Dinamo Zagreb – FK CSKA Moskva 3-1(2-0)
Dinamo Zagreb: Dominik Livakovic, Martin Leovac (20.Dino Peric), Kévin Théophile-Catherine, Sadegh Moharrami, Josko Gvardiol, Arijan Ademi (35.Bartol Franjic), Kristijan Jakic, Lovro Majer (78.Marko Tolic), Mario Gavranovic (78.Iyayi Atiemwen), Mislav Orsic (78.Mario Cuze), Lirim Kastrati (I). Trainer: Zoran Mamic.
CSKA Moskva: Igor Akinfeev, Viktor Vasin, Georgiy Shchennikov (71.Adolfo Gaich), Igor Diveev (78.Vadim Karpov), Ilzat Akhmetov (63.Nayair Tiknizyan), Baktiyor Zaynutdinov, Kristijan Bistrovic, Arnór Sigurdsson, Ivan Oblyakov, Konstantin Maradishvili, Ilya Shkurin (63.Fedor Chalov). Trainer: Victor Goncharenko (Belarus).
Goals: 28' Josko Gvardiol 1-0, 41' Mislav Orsic 2-0, 75' Lirim Kastrati (I) 3-0, 76' Kristijan Bistrovic 3-1.

03.12.2020; Stadion Feijenoord, Rotterdam
Referee: Chris Kavanagh (England)
Feyenoord Rotterdam – GNK Dinamo Zagreb 0-2(0-1)
Feyenoord: Nick Marsman, Uros Spajic (46.Eric Botteghin), Tyrell Malacia, Marcos Senesi, Lutsharel Geertruida, Jens Toornstra, Mark Diemers (69.João Carlos Teixeira), Orkun Kökçü, Bryan Linssen (36.Naoufal Bannis), Luciano Narsingh, Steven Berghuis. Trainer: Dick Advocaat.
Dinamo Zagreb: Dominik Livakovic, Kévin Théophile-Catherine, Sadegh Moharrami, Rasmus Lauritsen, Josko Gvardiol, Arijan Ademi, Kristijan Jakic, Luka Ivanusec (72.Mislav Orsic), Lovro Majer (65.Bartol Franjic), Bruno Petkovic (88.Marko Tolic), Lirim Kastrati (I) (88.Dino Peric). Trainer: Zoran Mamic.
Goals: 45+5' Bruno Petkovic 0-1 (penalty), 53' Lovro Majer 0-2.

10.12.2020; Wörthersee Stadion, Klagenfurt
Referee: Pawel Raczkowski (Poland)
Wolfsberger AC – Feyenoord Rotterdam 1-0(1-0)
Wolfsberger AC: Alexander Kofler, Michael Novak, Jonathan Scherzer, Dominik Baumgartner, Luka Lochoshvili, Michael Liendl, Mario Leitgeb, Sven Sprangler, Matthäus Taferner (68.Nemanja Rnic), Dario Vizinger (83.Kai Stratznig), Dejan Joveljic (56.Eliel Peretz). Trainer: Ferdinand Feldhofer.
Feyenoord: Nick Marsman, Uros Spajic (72.João Carlos Teixeira), Tyrell Malacia (79.Naoufal Bannis), Marcos Senesi, Lutsharel Geertruida, Jens Toornstra, Mark Diemers, Orkun Kökçü, Bryan Linssen (72.Luis Sinisterra), Nicolai Jørgensen, Steven Berghuis. Trainer: Dick Advocaat
Goal: 31' Dejan Joveljic 1-0.

GROUP L	1.	**TSG 1899 Hoffenheim**	6	5	1	0	17 - 2	16
	2.	**FK Crvena Zvezda Beograd**	6	3	2	1	9 - 4	11
	3.	FC Slovan Liberec	6	2	1	3	4 - 13	7
	4.	KAA Gent	6	0	0	6	4 - 15	0

22.10.2020; PreZero Arena, Sinsheim
Referee: Alejandro José Hernández Hernández (Spain)
TSG 1899 Hoffenheim – FK Crvena Zvezda Beograd 2-0(0-0)
Hoffenheim: Oliver Baumann, Kevin Vogt, Kevin Akpoguma, Stefan Posch, Sebastian Rudy, Florian Grillitsch (46.Diadié Samassekou), Mijat Gacinovic (46.Dennis Geiger), Christoph Baumgartner (78.Ihlas Bebou), Ryan Sessegnon (90.Robert Skov), Ishak Belfodil (78.Jacob Bruun Larsen), Munas Dabour. Trainer: Sebastian Hoeneß.
Crvena Zvezda: Milan Borjan, Nemanja Milunovic, Milan Rodic, Milos Degenek, Milan Gajic (85.Veljko Simic), Strahinja Erakovic, Aleksandar Katai (75.Aleksa Vukanovic), Srdjan Spiridonovic (76.El Fardou Ben Nabouhane), Sékou Sanogo (76.Njegos Petrovic), Veljko Nikolic, Diego Falcinelli (85.Milan Pavkov). Trainer: Dejan Stankovic [sent off 65].
Goals: 64' Christoph Baumgartner 1-0, 90+3' Munas Dabour 2-0.

29.10.2020; GHELAMCO-arena, Gent
Referee: Sandro Schärer (Switzerland)
KAA Gent – TSG 1899 Hoffenheim 1-4(0-1)
KAA Gent: Davy Roef, Michael Ngadeu-Ngadjui, Núrio Fortuna, Andreas Hanche-Olsen, Milad Mohammadi, Alessio Castro-Montes (77.Sulayman Marreh), Sven Kums (69.Tim Kleindienst), Roman Bezus (56.Vadis Odjidja-Ofoe), Niklas Dorsch (77.Jordan Botaka), Roman Yaremchuk (69.Anderson Niangbo), Osman Bukari. Trainer: Wim De Decker.
Hoffenheim: Oliver Baumann, Kevin Vogt, Kevin Akpoguma, Stefan Posch (82.Munas Dabour), Sebastian Rudy (67.Mijat Gacinovic), Florian Grillitsch (77.Christoph Baumgartner), Diadié Samassekou, Ryan Sessegnon, Ishak Belfodil (77.Klauss), Ihlas Bebou (67.Sargis Adamyan), Robert Skov. Trainer: Sebastian Hoeneß.
Goals: 35' Ishak Belfodil 0-1 (penalty), 52' Florian Grillitsch 0-2, 73' Mijat Gacinovic 0-3, 90+3' Tim Kleindienst 1-3, 90+4' Munas Dabour 1-4.

22.10.2020; Stadion u Nisy, Liberec
Referee: Manuel Schüttengruber (Austria)
FC Slovan Liberec – KAA Gent 1-0(1-0)
Slovan Liberec: Filip Nguyen, Jakub Jugas, Jan Mikula, Martin Koscelník, Mohamed Tijani, Jhon Mosquera, Jakub Hromada (79.Matej Chalus), Jakub Pesek (68.Jan Matousek), Kamso Mara, Michal Beran (57.Michal Sadílek), Abdulla Yusuf Helal (58.Michael Rabusic). Trainer: Pavel Hoftych.
KAA Gent: Davy Roef, Jordan Botaka (77.Anderson Niangbo), Michael Ngadeu-Ngadjui, Núrio Fortuna (87.Igor Plastun), Andreas Hanche-Olsen, Alessio Castro-Montes, Sven Kums, Sulayman Marreh, Roman Yaremchuk, Tim Kleindienst (76.Laurent Depoitre), Osman Bukari. Trainer: Wim De Decker.
Goal: 29' Abdulla Yusuf Helal 1-0.

29.10.2020; Stadion "Rajko Mitić", Beograd
Referee: Fábio José Costa Veríssimo (Portugal)
FK Crvena Zvezda Beograd – FC Slovan Liberec 5-1(2-1)
Crvena Zvezda: Milan Borjan, Nemanja Milunovic, Milan Rodic (75.Marko Gobeljic), Milos Degenek, Milan Gajic, Aleksandar Katai (88.Aleksa Vukanovic), Sékou Sanogo, Mirko Ivanic (83.Zeljko Gavric), Veljko Nikolic, Diego Falcinelli (88.Radovan Pankov), El Fardou Ben Nabouhane (83.Njegos Petrovic). Trainer: Dejan Stankovic.
Slovan Liberec: Filip Nguyen, Jan Mikula, Martin Koscelník, Matej Chalus, Mohamed Tijani, Jhon Mosquera (90.Michal Fukala), Jakub Hromada (86.Jan Sulc), Michal Sadílek, Jan Matousek (75.Michal Beran), Kamso Mara (90+1.Jakub Barac), Abdulla Yusuf Helal (75.Michael Rabusic). Trainer: Pavel Hoftych.
Goals: 7', 22' El Fardou Ben Nabouhane 1-0, 2-0, 41' Jan Matousek 2-1, 50' Milan Gajic 3-1, 67' Aleksandar Katai 4-1, 69' Diego Falcinelli 5-1.

05.11.2020; Stadion "Rajko Mitić", Beograd
Referee: Michael Fabbri (Italy)
FK Crvena Zvezda Beograd – KAA Gent 2-1(1-1)
Crvena Zvezda: Milan Borjan, Nemanja Milunovic, Milos Degenek, Marko Gobeljic, Milan Gajic, Aleksandar Katai (90+1.Veljko Nikolic), Sékou Sanogo, Guélor Kanga (83.Radovan Pankov), Mirko Ivanic (64.Njegos Petrovic), Diego Falcinelli, El Fardou Ben Nabouhane (90+1.Srdjan Spiridonovic). Trainer: Dejan Stankovic.
KAA Gent: Colin Coosemans, Jordan Botaka (63.Anderson Niangbo), Andreas Hanche-Olsen, Milad Mohammadi, Alessio Castro-Montes, Vadis Odjidja-Ofoe (80.Tim Kleindienst), Sulayman Marreh, Niklas Dorsch, Elisha Owusu (75.Sven Kums), Roman Yaremchuk, Osman Bukari. Trainer: Wim De Decker.
Goals: 12' Guélor Kanga 1-0, 31' Vadis Odjidja-Ofoe 1-1, 59' Aleksandar Katai 2-1.

26.11.2020; GHELAMCO-arena, Gent
Referee: Filip Glova (Slovakia)
KAA Gent – FK Crvena Zvezda Beograd 0-2(0-1)
KAA Gent: Sinan Bolat, Jordan Botaka (46.Alessio Castro-Montes), Michael Ngadeu-Ngadjui, Núrio Fortuna, Andreas Hanche-Olsen, Milad Mohammadi, Sven Kums (84.Wouter George), Roman Bezus, Niklas Dorsch, Elisha Owusu (58.Vadis Odjidja-Ofoe), Osman Bukari (66.Anderson Niangbo). Trainer: Wim De Decker.
Crvena Zvezda: Milan Borjan, Nemanja Milunovic, Milos Degenek, Milan Gajic, Radovan Pankov, Mirko Ivanic, Njegos Petrovic (72.Strahinja Erakovic), Veljko Nikolic, Diego Falcinelli (87.Richmond Boakye), El Fardou Ben Nabouhane (72.Srdjan Spiridonovic), Aleksa Vukanovic (87.Andrija Radulovic). Trainer: Dejan Stankovic.
Goals: 1' Njegos Petrovic 0-1, 58' Nemanja Milunovic 0-1.

03.12.2020; GHELAMCO-arena, Gent
Referee: Kateryna Monzul (Ukraine)
KAA Gent – FC Slovan Liberec 1-2(0-1)
KAA Gent: Sinan Bolat, Dino Arslanagic, Núrio Fortuna, Andreas Hanche-Olsen, Milad Mohammadi, Alessio Castro-Montes (56.Tim Kleindienst), Sven Kums, Niklas Dorsch, Elisha Owusu (62.Roman Bezus), Roman Yaremchuk, Osman Bukari. Trainer: Wim De Decker.
Slovan Liberec: Filip Nguyen, Jakub Jugas, Taras Kacharaba, Jan Mikula, Martin Koscelník, Jhon Mosquera, Jakub Pesek (75.Jan Matousek), Michal Sadílek, Kamso Mara, Michal Beran (68.Jakub Hromada), Abdulla Yusuf Helal (70.Michael Rabusic). Trainer: Pavel Hoftych.
Goals: 32' Kamso Mara 0-1, 55' Taras Kacharaba 0-2, 59' Roman Yaremchuk 1-2.

10.12.2020; PreZero Arena, Sinsheim
Referee: Anastasios Papapetrou (Greece)
TSG 1899 Hoffenheim – KAA Gent 4-1(2-0)
Hoffenheim: Philipp Pentke, Kevin Akpoguma, Stefan Posch (46.Håvard Nordtveit), Kasim Adams Nuhu, Mijat Gacinovic, Dennis Geiger (75.Alfons Amade), Marco John, Munas Dabour, Robert Skov (61.Ishak Belfodil), Klauss (62.Andrej Kramaric), Maximilian Beier (75.Christoph Baumgartner). Trainer: Sebastian Hoeneß.
KAA Gent: Dany Roef, Igor Plastun, Dino Arslanagic, Michel Ngadeu-Ngadjui, Milad Mohammadi (46.Núrio Fortuna), Alessio Castro-Montes (76.Jordan Botaka), Roman Bezus, Niklas Dorsch (56.Sven Kums), Elisha Owusu (56.Vadis Odjidja-Ofoe), Tim Kleindienst, Osman Bukari (56.Roman Yaremchuk). Trainer: Hein Vanhaezebrouck.
Goals: 21' Maximilian Beier 1-0, 26' Robert Skov 2-0, 49' Maximilian Beier 3-0, 64' Andrej Kramaric 4-0, 81' Núrio Fortuna 4-1.

05.11.2020; PreZero Arena, Sinsheim
Referee: Sergei Karasev (Russia)
TSG 1899 Hoffenheim – FC Slovan Liberec 5-0(2-0)
Hoffenheim: Oliver Baumann, Kevin Vogt (46.Florian Grillitsch), Kevin Akpoguma (60.Håvard Nordtveit), Melayro Bogarde, Sebastian Rudy (46.Diadié Samassekou), Mijat Gacinovic, Christoph Baumgartner (73.Ishak Belfodil), Munas Dabour (61.Sargis Adamyan), Ihlas Bebou, Robert Skov, Klauss. Trainer: Sebastian Hoeneß.
Slovan Liberec: Lukás Hasalík, Taras Kacharaba, Jan Mikula, Martin Koscelník, Daniel Kosek (90+1.Matyás Kazda), Marios Pourzitidis, David Cancola (90+1.Miroslav Dvorák), Jakub Hromada (77.Kristian Michal), Ales Nesický (90+1.Radim Cernický), Kamso Mara, Imad Rondic (67.Lukás Csáno). Trainer: Pavel Hoftych.
Goals: 22', 29' Munas Dabour 1-0, 2-0, 59' Florian Grillitsch 3-0, 71', 76' Sargis Adamyan 4-0, 5-0.

26.11.2020; Stadion u Nisy, Liberec
Referee: Jérôme Brisard (France)
FC Slovan Liberec – TSG 1899 Hoffenheim 0-2(0-0)
Slovan Liberec: Filip Nguyen, Jakub Jugas, Taras Kacharaba, Jan Mikula, Martin Koscelník, Matej Chalus (83.Imad Rondic), Jhon Mosquera, Jakub Pesek (83.Jan Matousek), Michal Sadílek (89.Michal Beran), Abdulla Yusuf Helal (70.Michael Rabusic). Trainer: Pavel Hoftych.
Hoffenheim: Oliver Baumann, Håvard Nordtveit, Kasim Adams Nuhu, Melayro Bogarde, Sebastian Rudy (61.Ihlas Bebou), Florian Grillitsch (78.Diadié Samassekou), Mijat Gacinovic, Christoph Baumgartner (78.Dennis Geiger), Ryan Sessegnon (46.Robert Skov), Klauss, Maximilian Beier (60.Andrej Kramaric). Trainer: Sebastian Hoeneß.
Goals: 77' Christoph Baumgartner 0-1, 89' Andrej Kramaric 0-2 (penalty).

03.12.2020; Stadion "Rajko Mitić", Beograd
Referee: Robert Adam Madden (Scotland)
FK Crvena Zvezda Beograd – TSG 1899 Hoffenheim 0-0
Crvena Zvezda: Milan Borjan, Nemanja Milunovic, Milos Degenek, Milan Gajic, Radovan Pankov, Srdjan Spiridonovic (46.Aleksa Vukanovic), Sékou Sanogo, Guélor Kanga (81.Veljko Nikolic), Njegos Petrovic, Diego Falcinelli (89.Richmond Boakye), El Fardou Ben Nabouhane (81.Strahinja Erakovic). Trainer: Dejan Stankovic.
Hoffenheim: Oliver Baumann, Håvard Nordtveit, Kevin Vogt, Melayro Bogarde, Sebastian Rudy (72.Kasim Adams Nuhu), Mijat Gacinovic (72.Christoph Baumgartner), Dennis Geiger (58.Florian Grillitsch), Marco John, Munas Dabour (46.Andrej Kramaric), Robert Skov (89.Ryan Sessegnon), Klauss. Trainer: Sebastian Hoeneß.

10.12.2020; Stadion u Nisy, Liberec
Referee: Mattias Gestranius (Finland)
FC Slovan Liberec – FK Crvena Zvezda Beograd 0-0
Slovan Liberec: Milan Knobloch, Jakub Jugas, Taras Kacharaba, Jan Mikula, Martin Koscelník, Jhon Mosquera (89.Michal Fukala), Jakub Pesek (68.Jan Matousek), Michal Sadílek, Kamso Mara, Michal Beran (68.Jakub Hromada), Abdulla Yusuf Helal (75.Michael Rabusic). Trainer: Pavel Hoftych.
Crvena Zvezda: Milan Borjan, Nemanja Milunovic, Milan Rodic (71.Marko Gobeljic), Milos Degenek (80.Radovan Pankov), Milan Gajic, Sékou Sanogo, Guélor Kanga (53.Veljko Nikolic), Mirko Ivanic (71.Richmond Boakye), Njegos Petrovic, Diego Falcinelli, El Fardou Ben Nabouhane (81.Strahinja Erakovic). Trainer: Dejan Stankovic.

Please note: Manchester United FC, Club Brugge KV, FK Shakhtar Donetsk, AFC Ajax Amsterdam, FK Krasnodar, FC Red Bull Salzburg, FK Dinamo Kyiv and Olympiacos SFP Peiraiás entered the UEFA Europa League as the group stage third-placed teams from the UEFA Champions League.

18.02.2021; NSC Olimpiyskiy Stadium, Kyiv
Referee: Mattias Gestranius (Finland); Attendance: 3,284
FK Dinamo Kyiv – Club Brugge KV 1-1(0-0)
Dynamo Kyiv: Georgiy Bushchan, Tomasz Kedziora (81.Oleksandr Karavayev), Denys Popov, Vitali Mykolenko, Illia Zabarnyi, Sergiy Sydorchuk, Vitaliy Buyalskyi, Carlos de Pena (72.Gerson Rodrigues), Viktor Tsygankov, Mykola Shaparenko (73.Volodymyr Shepelyev), Artem Besedin (81.Vladyslav Supryaga). Trainer: Mircea Lucescu (Romania).
Club Brugge: Simon Mignolet, Clinton Mata, Brandon Mechele, Federico Ricca, Odilon Kossounou, Ruud Vormer, Nabil Dirar (70.Ignace Van Der Brempt), Éder Balanta, Charles De Ketelaere, Bas Dost (90+2.Maxim De Cuyper), David Okereke (69.Youssouph Badji). Trainer: Philippe Clement.
Goals: 62' Vitaliy Buyalskyi 1-0, 67' Brandon Mechele 1-1.

18.02.2021; Puskás Aréna, Budapest (Hungary)
Referee: Ali Palabiyik (Turkey)
Wolfsberger AC – Tottenham Hotspur FC London 1-4(0-3)
Wolfsberger AC: Alexander Kofler, Michael Novak (81.Mario Pavelic), Jonathan Scherzer, Dominik Baumgartner, Luka Lochoshvili, Michael Liendl, Christopher Wernitznig, Sven Sprangler (65.Guram Giorbelidze), Matthäus Taferner (46.Gustav Henriksson), Dario Vizinger (46.Kai Stratznig), Dejan Joveljic (65.Cheikhou Dieng). Trainer: Ferdinand Feldhofer.
Tottenham Hotspur: Hugo Lloris, Toby Alderweireld, Matt Doherty, Ben Davies, Moussa Sissoko (78.Pierre-Emile Højbjerg), Lucas Moura (64.Steven Bergwijn), Dele Alli (78.Tanguy NDombèlé), Eric Dier, Harry Winks, Gareth Bale (64.Érik Lamela), Son Heung-Min (46.Carlos Vinícius). Trainer: José Mário dos Santos Félix Mourinho (Portugal).
Goals: 13' Son Heung-Min 0-1, 28' Gareth Bale 0-2, 34' Lucas Moura 0-3, 55' Michael Liendl 1-3 (penalty), 88' Calos Vinícius 1-4.

18.02.2021; Allianz Stadium, Torino (Italy)
Referee: Sandro Schärer (Switzerland)
Real Sociedad de Fútbol San Sebastián – Manchester United FC 0-4(0-1)
Real Sociedad: Álex Remiro, Nacho Monreal, Joseba Zaldúa (73.Andoni Gorosabel), Robin Le Normand, David Silva, Illarramendi (73.Guevara), Adnan Januzaj (79.Portu), Mikel Merino, Zubeldía, Mikel Oyarzabal (86.Jon Bautista), Alexander Isak (80.Ander Barrenetxea). Trainer: Imanol Alguacil Barrenetxea.
Manchester United: Dean Henderson, Alex Telles, Harry Maguire, Eric Bailly, Aaron Wan-Bissaka, Fred, Bruno Fernandes (83.Mata), Daniel James, Scott McTominay (60.Nemanja Matic), Marcus Rashford (68.Anthony Martial), Mason Greenwood (83.Amad Diallo). Trainer: Ole Gunnar Solskjær (Norway).
Goals: 27', 57' Bruno Fernandes 0-1, 0-2, 64' Marcus Rashford 0-3, 90' Daniel James 0-4.

18.02.2021; Stadion "Rajko Mitić", Beograd
Referee: Anastasios Sidiropoulos (Greece)
FK Crvena Zvezda Beograd – AC Milan 2-2(0-1)
Crvena Zvezda: Milan Borjan, Nemanja Milunovic, Milan Rodic [sent off 77], Milos Degenek, Marko Gobeljic (74.Milan Gajic), Radovan Pankov, Guélor Kanga, Mirko Ivanic (80.Axel Bakayoko), Njegos Petrovic (81.Sékou Sanogo), Diego Falcinelli (80.Milan Pavkov), Fardou Ben Nabouhane (62.Filippo Falco). Trainer: Dejan Stankovic.
AC Milan: Gianluigi Donnarumma, Alessio Romagnoli, Fikayo Tomori, Theo Hernández (78.Diogo Dalot), Pierre Kalulu, Soualiho Meïté, Samu Castillejo, Rade Krunic, Ismaël Bennacer (39.Sandro Tonali), Mario Mandzukic (82.Hakan Çalhanoglu), Ante Rebic (46.Rafael Leão). Trainer: Stefano Pioli.
Goals: 42' Radovan Pankov 0-1 (own goal), 52' Guélor Kanga 1-1 (penalty), 61' Theo Hernández 1-2 (penalty), 90+3' Milan Pavkov 2-2.

25.02.2021; „Jan Breydel" Stadion, Brugge
Referee: Srđan Jovanović (Serbia)
Club Brugge KV – FK DINAMO KYIV 0-1(0-0)
Club Brugge: Simon Mignolet, Eduard Sobol (84.Maxim De Cuyper), Clinton Mata, Brandon Mechele, Federico Ricca, Odilon Kossounou, Ruud Vormer, Nabil Dirar (84.David Okereke), Éder Balanta, Thomas Van Den Keybus (46.Ignace Van Der Brempt), Bas Dost (58.Youssouph Badji). Trainer: Philippe Clement.
Dynamo Kyiv: Georgiy Bushchan, Tomasz Kedziora (77.Oleksandr Karavayev), Vitali Mykolenko, Oleksandr Syrota, Illia Zabarnyi, Sergiy Sydorchuk, Vitaliy Buyalskyi (86.Oleksandr Andrievsky), Viktor Tsygankov, Volodymyr Shepelyev (68.Mykola Shaparenko), Gerson Rodrigues, Artem Besedin. Trainer: Mircea Lucescu (Romania).
Goal: 83' Vitaliy Buyalskyi 0-1.

24.02.2021; Tottenham Hotspur Stadium, London
Referee: Matej Jug (Slovenia)
TOTTENHAM HOTSPUR FC LONDON – Wolfsberger AC 4-0(1-0)
Tottenham Hotspur: Joe Hart, Toby Alderweireld, Matt Doherty (74.Marcel Lavinier), Ben Davies, Moussa Sissoko (81.Nile John), Érik Lamela (68.Gareth Bale), Dele Alli (81.Dane Scarlett), Eric Dier, Harry Winks, Steven Bergwijn (69.Lucas Moura), Carlos Vinícius. Trainer: José Mário dos Santos Félix Mourinho (Portugal).
Wolfsberger AC: Manuel Kuttin, Michael Novak (46.Mario Pavelic), Jonathan Scherzer (65.Stefan Peric), Dominik Baumgartner (65.Guram Giorbelidze), Luka Lochoshvili, Gustav Henriksson, Michael Liendl, Christopher Wernitznig, Kai Stratznig (79.Nemanja Rnic), Cheikhou Dieng, Dario Vizinger (46.Dejan Joveljic). Trainer: Ferdinand Feldhofer.
Goals: 11' Dele Alli 1-0, 50' Carlos Vinícius 2-0, 73' Gareth Bale 3-0, 83' Carlos Vinícius 4-0.

25.02.2021; Old Trafford, Manchester
Referee: Lawrence Visser (Belgium)
MANCHESTER UNITED FC – Real Sociedad de Fútbol San Sebastián 0-0
Manchester United: Dean Henderson, Alex Telles, Victor Lindelöf, Eric Bailly, Aaron Wan-Bissaka (46.Brandon Williams), Nemanja Matic, Fred (46.Axel Tuanzebe), Bruno Fernandes (46.Marcus Rashford), Daniel James (59.Amad Diallo), Anthony Martial, Mason Greenwood (76.Shola Shoretire). Trainer: Ole Gunnar Solskjær (Norway).
Real Sociedad: Álex Remiro, Andoni Gorosabel (46.Jon Bautista), Modibo Sagnan, Aihen Muñoz, Adnan Januzaj (66.Martín Merquelanz), Mikel Merino, Zubeldía, Guevara (72.Jon Guridi), Martín Zubimendi, Mikel Oyarzabal (46.Ander Barrenetxea), Alexander Isak (46.Portu). Trainer: Imanol Alguacil Barrenetxea.

25.02.2021; Stadio „Giuseppe Meazza", Milano
Referee: Jesús Gil Manzano (Spain)
AC MILAN – FK Crvena Zvezda Beograd 1-1(1-1)
AC Milan: Gianluigi Donnarumma, Alessio Romagnoli, Davide Calabria (66.Theo Hernández), Fikayo Tomori, Diogo Dalot, Hakan Çalhanoglu, Soualiho Meïté, Samu Castillejo (66.Alexis Saelemaekers), Rade Krunic (46.Ante Rebic), Franck Kessié, Rafael Leão (46.Zlatan Ibrahimovic). Trainer: Stefano Pioli.
Crvena Zvezda: Milan Borjan, Milos Degenek, Marko Gobeljic [sent off 70], Milan Gajic, Radovan Pankov, Slavoljub Srnic (46.Njegos Petrovic), Sékou Sanogo, Guélor Kanga (69.Aleksandar Katai), Mirko Ivanic (84.Veljko Nikolic), Diego Falcinelli (72.Milan Pavkov), Fardou Ben Nabouhane (69.Filippo Falco). Trainer: Dejan Stankovic.
Goals: 9' Franck Kessié 1-0 (penalty), 24' Fardou Ben Nabouhane 1-1.

18.02.2021; Stadion Sinobo, Praha
Referee: Marco Guida (Italy); Attendance: 600
SK Slavia Praha – Leicester City FC 0-0
Slavia Praha: Ondrej Kolár, Ondrej Kúdela, Jan Boril, Tomás Holes (30.Jakub Hromada), Alexander Bah, David Zima, Nicolae Stanciu (73.Ibrahim Traoré), Lukás Provod (90+1.Ondrej Lingr), Peter Olayinka, Jan Kuchta (73.Lukás Masopust), Abdallah Sima. Trainer: Jindrich Trpisovský.
Leicester City: Kasper Schmeichel, Jonny Evans, Daniel Amartey, Çaglar Söyüncü, Luke Thomas, Marc Albrighton (64.Cengiz Ünder), Youri Tielemans, Wilfred Ndidi, James Maddison (76.Hamza Choudhury), Harvey Barnes, Jamie Vardy (64.Kelechi Iheanacho). Trainer: Brendan Rodgers (Northern Ireland).

18.02.2021; Estádio Municipal de Braga, Braga
Referee: István Kovács (Romania)
Sporting Clube de Braga – AS Roma 0-2(0-1)
Sporting Braga: Matheus Magalhães, Raúl Silva, Ricardo Esgaio [*sent off 54*], Nuno Sequeira, Vítor Tormena, Nicolás Gaitán (57.Zé Carlos), Fransérgio (69.André Horta), Ali Al Musrati, Andraz Sporar (62.Abel Ruiz), Ricardo Horta (62.Lucas Piazón), Galeno (70.Cristian Borja). Trainer: Carlos Augusto Soares da Costa Faria Carvalhal.
AS Roma: Pau López, Leonardo Spinazzola, Rick Karsdorp, Gianluca Mancini, Ibañez (53.Gonzalo Villar), Henrikh Mkhitaryan, Jordan Veretout, Bryan Cristante (7.Bruno Peres), Amadou Diawara, Edin Dzeko (70.Borja Mayoral), Pedro (71.Stephan El Shaarawy). Trainer: Paulo Alexandre Rodrigues Fonseca (Portugal).
Goals: 5' Edin Dzeko 0-1, 86' Borja Mayoral 0-2.

18.02.2021; Krasnodar Stadium, Krasnodar
Referee: Bartosz Frankowski (Poland); Attendance: 9,897
FK Krasnodar – GNK Dinamo Zagreb 2-3(1-1)
FK Krasnodar: Evgeniy Gorodov, Igor Smolnikov, Aleksandr Martynovich, Evgeniy Chernov (80.Aleksey Ionov), Rémy Cabella, Victor Claesson, Tonny Vilhena, Kristoffer Olsson (62.Yuri Gazinskiy), Kaio Pantaleão, Marcus Berg, Magomed Suleymanov (46.Wanderson). Trainer: Murad Musaev.
Dinamo Zagreb: Dominik Livakovic, Kévin Théophile-Catherine, Stefan Ristovski, Rasmus Lauritsen, Josko Gvardiol, Arijan Ademi, Kristijan Jakic, Luka Ivanusec (78.Bartol Franjic), Lovro Majer (64.Iyayi Atiemwen), Mislav Orsic (90+4.Josip Misic), Bruno Petkovic. Trainer: Zoran Mamic. Goals: 15' Bruno Petkovic 0-1, 28' Marcus Berg 1-1, 54' Bruno Petkovic 1-2, 69' Victor Claesson 2-2, 75' Iyayi Atiemwen 1-2.

18.02.2021; Wankdorf Stadion, Bern
Referee: Antonio Miguel Mateu Lahoz (Spain)
BSC Young Boys Bern – TSV Bayer 04 Leverkusen 4-3(3-0)
Young Boys: David von Ballmoos, Fabian Lustenberger, Jordan Lefort (74.Miralem Sulejmani), Cédric Zesiger, Silvan Hefti, Nicolas Moumi Ngamaleu (58.Ulisses Garcia), Christian Fassnacht (80.Gianluca Gaudino), Sandro Lauper (81.Fabian Rieder), Michel Aebischer, Theoson Siebatcheu, Meschack Elia (74.Felix Mambimbi). Trainer: Gerardo Seoane.
Bayer Leverkusen: Niklas Lomb, Aleksandar Dragovic, Jonathan Tah, Daley Sinkgraven, Jeremie Frimpong, Kerem Demirbay, Nadiem Amiri (46.Edmond Tapsoba), Demarai Gray, Florian Wirtz, Patrik Schick, Leon Bailey (65.Moussa Diaby). Trainer: Peter Bosz (Netherlands).
Goals: 3' Christian Fassnacht 1-0, 19' Theoson Siebatcheu 2-0, 44' Meschack Elia 3-0, 49', 52' Patrik Schick 3-1, 3-2, 68' Moussa Diaby 3-3, 89' Theoson Siebatcheu 4-3.

18.02.2021; Stádio „Giórgos Karaïskáki", Peiraiás
Referee: Andreas Ekberg (Sweden)
Olympiacos SFP Peiraiás – PSV Eindhoven 4-2(3-2)
Olympiacos: José Sá, Sokratis Papastathopoulos, Kenny Lala (80.Athanasios Androutsos), Oleg Reabciuk, Ousseynou Ba, Mathieu Valbuena (68.Georgios Masouras), Yann M'Vila (80.Marios Vrousai), Andreas Bouchalakis, Mohamed Camara, Youssef El-Arabi (75.Kostas Fortounis), Bruma (80.Koka). Trainer: Pedro Rui da Mota Vieira Martins (Portugal).
PSV Eindhoven: Yvon Mvogo, Philipp Max, Olivier Boscagli (38.Timo Baumgartl), Denzel Dumfries, Jordan Teze, Mario Götze (70.Mauro Júnior), Ryan Thomas (85.Marco van Ginkel), Ibrahim Sangaré (71.Yorbe Vertessen), Pablo Rosario, Eran Zahavi (85.Érick Gutiérrez), Donyell Malen. Trainer: Roger Schmidt (Germany).
Goals: 9' Andreas Bouchalakis 1-0, 14' Eran Zahavi 1-1, 37' Yann M'Vila 2-1, 39' Eran Zahavi 2-2, 45+2' Youssef El-Arabi 3-2, 83' Georgios Masouras 4-2.

25.02.2021; King Power Stadium, Leicester
Referee: Serdar Gözübüyük (Netherlands)
Leicester City FC – SK SLAVIA PRAHA 0-2(0-0)
Leicester City: Kasper Schmeichel, Jonny Evans, Daniel Amartey (61.Ricardo Pereira), Çaglar Söyüncü, Luke Thomas, Marc Albrighton (61.Timothy Castagne), Youri Tielemans, Wilfred Ndidi (80.Sidnei Tavares), Hamza Choudhury (61.Harvey Barnes), Jamie Vardy. Trainer: Brendan Rodgers (Northern Ireland).
Slavia Praha: Ondrej Kolár, Ondrej Kúdela, Jan Boril, Alexander Bah, David Zima, Nicolae Stanciu (69.Oscar Dorley), Lukás Provod, Jakub Hromada (75.Ondrej Lingr), Peter Olayinka, Jan Kuchta (84.Lukás Masopust), Abdallah Sima. Trainer: Jindrich Trpisovský.
Goals: 49' Lukás Provod 0-1, 79' Abdallah Sima 0-2.

25.02.2021; Stadio Olimpico, Roma
Referee: Andreas Ekberg (Sweden)
AS ROMA – Sporting Clube de Braga 3-1(1-0)
AS Roma: Pau López, Bruno Peres, Rick Karsdorp, Gianluca Mancini, Jordan Veretout (59.Leonardo Spinazzola), Bryan Cristante, Gonzalo Villar, Amadou Diawara, Edin Dzeko (67.Borja Mayoral), Pedro (77.Henrikh Mkhitaryan), Stephan El Shaarawy (59.Carles Pérez). Trainer: Paulo Alexandre Rodrigues Fonseca (Portugal).
Sporting Braga: Tiago Sá, Rolando, Nuno Sequeira (70.Cristian Borja), Vítor Tormena, Zé Carlos, Nicolás Gaitán (60.Ricardo Horta), João Novais, André Horta, Lucas Piazón (60.Fransérgio), Andraz Sporar (60.Abel Ruiz), Galeno (77.Hernâni Infande Silva). Trainer: Carlos Augusto Soares da Costa Faria Carvalhal.
Goals: 24' Edin Dzeko 1-0, 75' Carles Pérez 2-0, 88' Bryan Cristante 2-1 (own goal), 90+1' Borja Mayoral 3-1.

25.02.2021; Stadion Maksimir, Zagreb
Referee: Halil Umut Meler (Turkey)
GNK DINAMO ZAGREB – FK Krasnodar 1-0(1-0)
Dinamo Zagreb: Dominik Livakovic, Kévin Théophile-Catherine, Stefan Ristovski, Rasmus Lauritsen, Josko Gvardiol, Arijan Ademi, Kristijan Jakic, Luka Ivanusec (83.Iyayi Atiemwen), Lovro Majer (69.Josip Misic), Mislav Orsic, Bruno Petkovic (87.Mario Gavranovic). Trainer: Zoran Mamic.
FK Krasnodar: Stanislav Agkatsev, Igor Smolnikov (70.Magomed Suleymanov), Aleksandr Martynovich, Evgeniy Chernov, Aleksey Ionov, Rémy Cabella, Yuri Gazinskiy (69.Ari), Victor Claesson, Tonny Vilhena (60.Kristoffer Olsson), Kaio Pantaleão, Wanderson. Trainer: Murad Musaev.
Goal: 31' Mislav Orsic 1-0.

25.02.2021; BayArena, Leverkusen
Referee: Davide Massa (Italy)
TSV Bayer 04 Leverkusen – BSC YOUNG BOYS BERN 0-2(0-0)
Bayer Leverkusen: Niklas Lomb, Aleksandar Dragovic (63.Demarai Gray), Jonathan Tah, Daley Sinkgraven, Jeremie Frimpong (78.Nadiem Amiri), Edmond Tapsoba, Charles Aránguiz, Florian Wirtz, Patrik Schick, Leon Bailey (63.Lucas Alario), Moussa Diaby. Trainer: Peter Bosz (Netherlands).
Young Boys: David von Ballmoos, Fabian Lustenberger, Jordan Lefort, Cédric Zesiger, Silvan Hefti, Nicolas Moumi Ngamaleu (69.Fabian Rieder), Christian Fassnacht (87.Gianluca Gaudino), Sandro Lauper, Michel Aebischer (87.Vincent Sierro), Theoson Siebatcheu (78.Marvin Spielmann), Meschack Elia (78.Felix Mambimbi). Trainer: Gerardo Seoane.
Goals: 48' Theoson Siebatcheu 0-1, 86' Christian Fassnacht 0-2.

25.02.2021; Philips Stadion, Eindhoven
Referee: Clément Turpin (France)
PSV Eindhoven – OLYMPIACOS SFP PEIRAIÁS 2-1(2-0)
PSV Eindhoven: Yvon Mvogo, Nick Viergever, Philipp Max, Olivier Boscagli, Denzel Dumfries, Jordan Teze, Mario Götze (89.Yorbe Vertessen), Ryan Thomas (90.Mauro Júnior), Pablo Rosario, Eran Zahavi, Donyell Malen. Trainer: Roger Schmidt (Germany).
Olympiacos: José Sá, Kenny Lala (79.Athanasios Androutsos), Rúben Semedo, Oleg Reabciuk, Ousseynou Ba, Mathieu Valbuena (46.Georgios Masouras), Yann M'Vila, Andreas Bouchalakis (46.Kostas Fortounis), Mohamed Camara, Youssef El-Arabi (90.Sokratis Papastathopoulos), Bruma (79.Koka). Trainer: Pedro Rui da Mota Vieira Martins (Portugal).
Goals: 23', 44' Eran Zahavi 1-0, 2-0, 88' Koka 2-1.

18.02.2021; Stadio Olimpico, Roma (Italy)
Referee: Cüneyt Çakir (Turkey)
Sport Lisboa e Benfica – Arsenal FC London 1-1(0-0)
Benfica: Helton Leite, Jan Vertonghen, Nicolás Otamendi, Álex Grimaldo, Lucas Veríssimo (85.Chiquinho), Adel Taarabt (77.Gabriel), Pizzi (64.Éverton), Julian Weigl, Diogo Gonçalves, Luca Waldschmidt (46.Rafa Silva), Darwin Núñez (64.Haris Seferovic). Trainer: Jorge Fernando Pinheiro de Jesus.
Arsenal FC: Bernd Leno, David Luiz, Cédric Soares (64.Kieran Tierney), Héctor Bellerín, Gabriel Magalhães, Granit Xhaka, Martin Ødegaard (90.Willian), Dani Ceballos (90.Mohamed Elneny), Emile Smith-Rowe (77.Gabriel Martinelli), Bukayo Saka, Pierre-Emerick Aubameyang (77.Nicolas Pépé). Trainer: Mikel Amatriain Arteta (Spain).
Goals: 55' Pizzi 1-0 (penalty), 57' Bukayo Saka 1-1.

18.02.2021; Bosuilstadion, Antwerp
Referee: Georgi Kabakov (Bulgaria)
Royal Antwerp FC – Rangers FC Glasgow 3-4(2-1)
Antwerp FC: Alireza Beiranvand (77.Ortwin De Wolf), Ritchie De Laet, Maxime Le Marchand, Jordan Lukaku, Buta, Abdoulaye Seck [sent off 88], Lior Refaelov (90+2.Nana Ampomah), Pieter Gerkens (90+2.Koji Miyoshi), Frank Boya (69.Birger Verstraete), Martin Hongla Yma (90+1.Jérémy Gelin), Felipe Avenatti. Trainer: Frank Vercauteren.
Rangers FC: Allan McGregor, James Tavernier (24.Leon Balogun), Connor Goldson, Filip Helander, Borna Barisic, Steven Davis, Scott Arfield (74.Ryan Jack), Glen Kamara (74.Ianis Hagi), Joe Ayodele-Aribo, Kemar Roofe (45+5.Ryan Kent), Alfredo Morelos. Trainer: Steven George Gerrard (England).
Goals: 39' Joe Ayodele-Aribo 0-1, 45' Felipe Avenatti 1-1, 45+8' Lior Refaelov 2-1 (penalty), 59' Borna Barisic 2-2 (penalty), 67' Martin Hongla Yma 3-2, 83' Ryan Kent 3-3, 90' Borna Barisic 3-4 (penalty).

18.02.2021; Red Bull Arena, Wals-Siezenheim
Referee: Andris Treimanis (Latvia)
FC Red Bull Salzburg – Villarreal CF 0-2(0-1)
Red Bull Salzburg: Cican Stankovic, Andreas Ulmer, Albert Vallçi, Rasmus Kristensen, Oumar Solet, Zlatko Junuzovic (74.Antoine Bernède), Enock Mwepu, Brenden Aaronson (61.Karim Adeyemi), Luka Sucic (61.Noah Okafor), Mërgim Berisha, Patson Daka. Trainer: Jesse Marsch (United States).
Villarreal: Gerónimo Rulli, Raúl Albiol, Pervis Estupiñán, Pau Torres, Étienne Capoue (74.Jaume Costa), Dani Parejo, Moi Gómez (60.Pedraza), Manu Trigueros, Rubén Peña (46.Juan Foyth), Paco Alcácer (60.Fer Niño), Gerard Moreno (83.Yeremi Pino). Trainer: Unai Emery Etxegoien (Spain).
Goals: 41' Paco Alcácer 0-1, 71' Fer Niño 0-2.

18.02.2021; Estadio de la Cerámica, Villarreal (Spain)
Referee: Stéphanie Frappart (France)
Molde FK – TSG 1899 Hoffenheim 3-3(1-3)
Molde FK: Andreas Linde, Kristoffer Haugen, Martin Bjørnbak, Stian Gregersen, Marcus Pedersen, Magnus Wolff Eikrem, Eirik Andersen (86.Tobias Christensen), Fredrik Aursnes, Martin Ellingsen, Björn Sigurdarson (64.David Fofana), Mathis Bolly (64.Erling Knudtzon). Trainer: Erling Moe.
Hoffenheim: Oliver Baumann, Kevin Vogt, Kasim Adams Nuhu (83.Melayro Bogarde), Chris Richards, Sebastian Rudy, Mijat Gacinovic (26.Pavel Kaderábek), Diadié Samassékou (62.Florian Grillitsch), Christoph Baumgartner, Marco John, Munas Dabour (83.Georginio Rutter), Ihlas Bebou (62.Sargis Adamyan). Trainer: Sebastian Hoeneß.
Goals: 8', 28' Munas Dabour 0-1, 0-2, 41' Martin Ellingsen 1-2, 45+3' Christoph Baumgartner 1-3, 70' Eirik Andersen 2-3, 74' David Fofana 3-3.

18.02.2021; Estadio Nuevo Los Cármenes, Granada
Referee: Sergei Karasev (Russia)
Granada CF – SSC Napoli 2-0(2-0)
Granada CF: Rui Silva, Dimitri Foulquier, Jesús Vallejo (23.Germán Sánchez), Domingos Duarte, Carlos Neva (78.Víctor Díaz), Montoro, Maxime Gonalons (78.Yan Eteki), Kenedy (70.Alberto Soro), Yangel Herrera, Jorge Molina, Darwin Machís (70.Antonio Puertas). Trainer: Diego Martínez Penas.
SSC Napoli: Alex Meret, Nikola Maksimovic, Mário Rui, Giovanni Di Lorenzo, Amir Rrahmani, Stanislav Lobotka (64.Tiemoué Bakayoko), Fabián Ruiz, Eljif Elmas, Lorenzo Insigne, Matteo Politano (46.Piotr Zielinski), Victor Osimhen. Trainer: Gennaro Gattuso.
Goals: 19' Yangel Herrera 1-0, 21' Kenedy 2-0.

25.02.2021; Stádio „Giórgos Karaïskáki", Peiraiás (Greece)
Referee: Björn Kuipers (Netherlands)
ARSENAL FC LONDON – Sport Lisboa e Benfica 3-2(1-1)
Arsenal FC: Bernd Leno, David Luiz, Héctor Bellerín (78.Alexandre Lacazette), Kieran Tierney, Gabriel Magalhães, Granit Xhaka, Martin Ødegaard (90.Mohamed Elneny), Dani Ceballos (63.Thomas Partey), Emile Smith-Rowe (63.Willian), Bukayo Saka (90.Calum Chambers), Pierre-Emerick Aubameyang. Trainer: Mikel Amatriain Arteta (Spain).
Benfica: Helton Leite, Jan Vertonghen, Nicolás Otamendi, Álex Grimaldo (85.Nuno Tavares), Lucas Veríssimo, Adel Taarabt (58.Gabriel), Pizzi (58.Éverton), Rafa Silva, Julian Weigl (90.Luca Waldschmidt), Diogo Gonçalves, Haris Seferovic (57.Darwin Núñez). Trainer: Jorge Fernando Pinheiro de Jesus.
Goals: 21' Pierre-Emerick Aubameyang 1-0, 43' Diogo Gonçalves 1-1, 61' Rafa Silva 1-2, 67' Kieran Tierney 2-2, 87' Pierre-Emerick Aubameyang 3-2.

25.02.2021; Ibrox Stadium, Glasgow
Referee: Pawel Raczkowski (Poland)
RANGERS FC GLASGOW – Royal Antwerp FC 5-2(1-1)
Rangers FC: Allan McGregor, Leon Balogun (46.Nathan Patterson), Connor Goldson, Filip Helander, Borna Barisic, Steven Davis (82.Bongani Zungu), Glen Kamara, Joe Ayodele-Aribo, Ianis Hagi (71.Scott Arfield), Alfredo Morelos (85.Cedric Itten), Ryan Kent (82.Scott Wright). Trainer: Steven George Gerrard (England).
Antwerp FC: Ortwin De Wolf, Ritchie De Laet, Maxime Le Marchand, Jordan Lukaku (75.Nana Ampomah), Buta, Jérémy Gelin (46.Frank Boya), Lior Refaelov, Pieter Gerkens (75.Felipe Avenatti), Birger Verstraete, Martin Hongla Yma (82.Koji Miyoshi), Didier Lamkel Zé. Trainer: Frank Vercauteren.
Goals: 9' Alfredo Morelos 1-0, 32' Lior Refaelov 1-1, 46' Nathan Patterson 2-1, 55' Ryan Kent 3-1, 57' Didier Lamkel Zé 3-2, 79' Borna Barisic 4-2 (penalty), 90+2' Cedric Itten 5-2 (penalty).

25.02.2021; Estadio de la Cerámica, Villarreal
Referee: Felix Zwayer (Germany)
VILLARREAL CF – FC Red Bull Salzburg 2-1(1-1)
Villarreal: Gerónimo Rulli, Raúl Albiol, Jaume Costa (82.Juan Foyth), Pervis Estupiñán, Pau Torres, Étienne Capoue, Dani Parejo (90.Álex Baena), Manu Trigueros, Pedraza (66.Moi Gómez), Paco Alcácer (66.Samuel Chukwueze), Gerard Moreno (90.Fer Niño). Trainer: Unai Emery Etxegoien (Spain).
Red Bull Salzburg: Cican Stankovic, Andreas Ulmer, André Ramalho, Albert Vallçi (46.Max Wöber), Rasmus Kristensen (90+2.Oumar Solet), Zlatko Junuzovic, Antoine Bernède (60.Karim Adeyemi), Enock Mwepu, Brenden Aaronson (60.Luka Sucic), Mërgim Berisha, Patson Daka (90+2.Antonín Svoboda). Trainer: Jesse Marsch (United States).
Goals: 17' Mërgim Berisha 0-1, 40', 89' Gerard Moreno 1-1, 2-1 (penalty).

25.02.2021; PreZero Arena, Sinsheim
Referee: Aleksey Kulbakov (Belarus)
TSG 1899 Hoffenheim – MOLDE FK 0-2(0-1)
Hoffenheim: Oliver Baumann, Kevin Vogt, Pavel Kaderábek (70.Sargis Adamyan), Chris Richards, Sebastian Rudy, Florian Grillitsch, Diadié Samassékou (83.Georginio Rutter), Christoph Baumgartner (56.Andrej Kramaric), Marco John (70.Ryan Sessegnon), Munas Dabour, Ihlas Bebou. Trainer: Sebastian Hoeneß.
Molde FK: Andreas Linde, Kristoffer Haugen, Birk Risa, Sheriff Sinyan, Marcus Pedersen, Magnus Wolff Eikrem, Eirik Andersen, Fredrik Aursnes, Martin Ellingsen, Björn Sigurdarson (63.Mathis Bolly), Erling Knudtzon (79.Eirik Hestad). Trainer: Erling Moe.
Goals: 19', 90+4' Eirik Andersen 0-1, 0-2.

25.02.2021; Stadio „Diego Armando Maradona", Napoli
Referee: Daniel Siebert (Germany)
SSC Napoli – GRANADA CF 2-1(1-1)
SSC Napoli: Alex Meret, Nikola Maksimovic (46.Faouzi Ghoulam), Kalidou Koulibaly, Giovanni Di Lorenzo, Amir Rrahmani, Piotr Zielinski, Tiemoué Bakayoko, Fabián Ruiz, Eljif Elmas (60.Dries Mertens), Lorenzo Insigne, Matteo Politano. Trainer: Gennaro Gattuso.
Granada CF: Rui Silva, Germán Sánchez (56.Yangel Herrera), Dimitri Foulquier, Domingos Duarte, Carlos Neva (46.Nehuén Pérez), Montoro (83.Jesús Vallejo), Maxime Gonalons (45+2.Víctor Díaz), Antonio Puertas, Kenedy, Yan Eteki, Jorge Molina (84.Soldado). Trainer: Diego Martínez Penas.
Goals: 3' Piotr Zielinksi 1-0, 25' Montoro 1-1, 59' Fabián Ruiz 2-1.

18.02.2021; Bloomfield Stadium, Tel Aviv
Referee: François Letexier (France)
Maccabi Tel Aviv FC – FK Shakhtar Donetsk 0-2(0-1)
Maccabi Tel Aviv: Daniel Tenenbaum, Eitan Tibi, Luis Hernández, Saborit, Geraldes, Avi Rikan (63.Eyal Golasa), Dor Peretz, Dan Glazer, Dan Biton (46.Matan Hozez), Tal Ben Haim (63.Nick Blackman), Aleksandar Pesic (84.Eduardo Guerrero). Trainer: Patrick van Leeuwen (Netherlands).
Shakhtar Donetsk: Anatolii Trubin, Sergiy Kryvtsov, Mykola Matviienko, Dodô, Vitão, Marlos (77.Maycon), Taras Stepanenko, Taison (77.Yevhen Konoplyanka), Alan Patrick (88.Marcos Antônio), Manor Solomon (73.Mateus Martins Tetê), Júnior Moraes (89.Fernando). Trainer: Luís Manuel Ribeiro Castro (Portugal).
<u>Goals</u>: 31' Alan Patrick 0-1, 90+3' Mateus Martins Tetê 0-2.

18.02.2021; Stade „Pierre-Mauroy", Villeneuve-d'Ascq
Referee: Ivan Kružliak (Slovakia)
Lille OSC – AFC Ajax Amsterdam 1-2(0-0)
Lille OSC: Mike Maignan, José Fonte, Reinildo (82.Domagoj Bradaric), Zeki Çelik, Sven Botman, Renato Sanches, Boubakary Soumaré, Yusuf Yazici (62.Luiz Araujo), Jonathan Bamba, Timothy Weah, Jonathan David (78.Jonathan Ikoné). Trainer: Christophe Galtier.
AFC Ajax: Maarten Stekelenburg, Daley Blind, Nicolás Tagliafico, Edson Álvarez, Lisandro Martínez, Jurriën Timber, Devyne Rensch (82.Perr Schuurs), Davy Klaassen, Dusan Tadic, David Neres (74.Brian Brobbey), Antony (82.Oussama Idrissi). Trainer: Erik ten Hag.
<u>Goals</u>: 72' Timothy Weah 1-0, 87' Dusan Tadic 1-1 (penalty), 89' Brian Brobbey 1-2.

25.02.2021; NSC Olimpiyskiy Stadium, Kyiv
Referee: José María Sánchez Martínez (Spain); Attendance: 10,217
FK SHAKHTAR DONETSK – Maccabi Tel Aviv FC 1-0(0-0)
Shakhtar Donetsk: Anatolii Trubin, Sergiy Kryvtsov, Mykola Matviienko, Dodô, Vitão (78.Viktor Kornienko), Marlos (46.Marcos Antônio), Taison (78.Yevhen Konoplyanka), Alan Patrick, Manor Solomon (46.Mateus Martins Tetê), Maycon, Júnior Moraes (78.Fernando). Trainer: Luís Manuel Ribeiro Castro (Portugal).
Maccabi Tel Aviv: Daniel Tenenbaum, Eitan Tibi, Luis Hernández, Saborit, Geraldes, Eyal Golasa (77.Avi Rikan), Dor Peretz, Dan Glazer, Tal Ben Haim (68.Eduardo Guerrero), Aleksandar Pesic (68.Nick Blackman), Matan Hozez (77.Dan Biton). Trainer: Patrick van Leeuwen (Netherlands).
<u>Goal</u>: 67' Júnior Moraes 1-0 (penalty).

25.02.2021; „Johan Cruijff" ArenA, Amsterdam
Referee: William Collum (Scotland)
AFC AJAX AMSTERDAM – Lille OSC 2-1(1-0)
AFC Ajax: Maarten Stekelenburg, Daley Blind, Edson Álvarez, Lisandro Martínez, Jurriën Timber, Devyne Rensch, Davy Klaassen, Ryan Gravenberch (90.Mohammed Kudus), Dusan Tadic, David Neres (89.Oussama Idrissi), Antony (55.Brian Brobbey). Trainer: Erik ten Hag.
Lille OSC: Mike Maignan, Zeki Çelik (62.Jérémy Pied), Tiago Djaló, Sven Botman, Domagoj Bradaric, Renato Sanches, Xeka (70.Boubakary Soumaré), Jonathan Ikoné (62.Luiz Araujo), Yusuf Yazici, Jonathan Bamba (62.Jonathan David), Timothy Weah (78.Isaac Lihadji). Trainer: Christophe Galtier.
<u>Goals</u>: 15' Davy Klaassen 1-0, 78' Yusuf Yazici 1-1 (penalty), 88' David Neres 2-1.

ROUND OF 16

11.03.2021; „Johan Cruijff" ArenA, Amsterdam
Referee: Marco Guida (Italy)
AFC Ajax Amsterdam – BSC Young Boys Bern 3-0(0-0)
AFC Ajax: Maarten Stekelenburg, Nicolás Tagliafico, Edson Álvarez, Lisandro Martínez, Jurriën Timber, Devyne Rensch (67.Perr Schuurs), Davy Klaassen, Ryan Gravenberch, Dusan Tadic, David Neres (83.Brian Brobbey), Antony (68.Oussama Idrissi). Trainer: Erik ten Hag.
Young Boys: Guillaume Faivre, Fabian Lustenberger, Jordan Lefort, Silvan Hefti, Mohamed Ali Camara (34.Cédric Zesiger), Miralem Sulejmani (46.Nicolas Moumi Ngamaleu), Christian Fassnacht (84.Theoson Siebatcheu), Sandro Lauper (71.Vincent Sierro), Michel Aebischer, Jean-Pierre Nsame, Meschack Elia (71.Felix Mambimbi). Trainer: Gerardo Seoane.
<u>Goals</u>: 62' Davy Klaassen 1-0, 82' Dusan Tadic 2-0, 90+2' Brian Brobbey 3-0.

11.03.2021; NSC Olimpiyskiy Stadium, Kyiv
FK Dinamo Kyiv – Villarreal CF 0-2(0-1)
Referee: Michael Oliver (England); Attendance: 12,751
Dynamo Kyiv: Georgiy Bushchan, Tomasz Kedziora (84.Oleksandr Karavayev), Vitali Mykolenko, Oleksandr Syrota, Illia Zabarnyi, Sergiy Sydorchuk (68.Oleksandr Andrievsky), Vitaliy Buyalskyi, Viktor Tsygankov, Mykola Shaparenko (68.Volodymyr Shepelyev), Gerson Rodrigues, Artem Besedin. Trainer: Mircea Lucescu (Romania).
Villarreal: Gerónimo Rulli, Raúl Albiol, Pau Torres (46.Ramiro Funes Mori), Juan Foyth, Étienne Capoue, Dani Parejo, Manu Trigueros (85.Moi Gómez), Pedraza, Samuel Chukwueze (84.Jaume Costa), Paco Alcácer (63.Carlos Bacca), Gerard Moreno (90.Álex Baena). Trainer: Unai Emery Etxegoien (Spain).
<u>Goals</u>: 30' Pau Torres 0-1, 52' Raúl Albiol 0-2.

11.03.2021; Old Trafford, Manchester
Referee: Slavko Vinčić (Slovenia)
Manchester United FC – AC Milan 1-1(0-0)
Manchester United: Dean Henderson, Alex Telles, Harry Maguire, Eric Bailly, Aaron Wan-Bissaka (74.Brandon Williams), Nemanja Matic, Bruno Fernandes (74.Fred), Daniel James (74.Luke Shaw), Scott McTominay, Anthony Martial (46.Amad Diallo), Mason Greenwood. Trainer: Ole Gunnar Solskjær (Norway).
AC Milan: Gianluigi Donnarumma, Simon Kjær, Davide Calabria (74.Pierre Kalulu), Fikayo Tomori, Diogo Dalot, Soualiho Meïté, Rade Krunic, Franck Kessié, Alexis Saelemaekers (69.Samu Castillejo), Rafael Leão, Brahim Díaz (69.Sandro Tonali). Trainer: Stefano Pioli.
<u>Goals</u>: 50' Amad Diallo 1-0, 90+2' Simon Kjær 1-1.

18.03.2021; Wankdorf Stadion, Bern
BSC Young Boys Bern – AFC AJAX AMSTERDAM 0-2(0-1)
Referee: Robert Madden (Scotland)
Young Boys: Guillaume Faivre, Fabian Lustenberger, Jordan Lefort (46.Quentin Maceiras), Silvan Hefti, Mohamed Ali Camara (65.Fabian Rieder), Miralem Sulejmani (71.Marvin Spielmann), Christian Fassnacht (71.Gianluca Gaudino), Vincent Sierro, Sandro Lauper, Jean-Pierre Nsame, Meschack Elia (65.Felix Mambimbi). Trainer: Gerardo Seoane.
AFC Ajax: Maarten Stekelenburg, Daley Blind (65.Mohammed Kudus), Nicolás Tagliafico (74.Sean Klaiber), Edson Álvarez, Lisandro Martínez, Devyne Rensch (80.Perr Schuurs), Davy Klaassen, Ryan Gravenberch, Dusan Tadic, David Neres (65.Oussama Idrissi), Antony (81.Brian Brobbey). Trainer: Erik ten Hag.
<u>Goals</u>: 21' David Neres 0-1, 49' Dusan Tadic 0-2 (penalty).

18.03.2021; Estadio de la Cerámica, Villarreal
Referee: Andreas Ekberg (Sweden)
VILLARREAL CF – FK Dinamo Kyiv 2-0(2-0)
Villarreal: Asenjo, Raúl Albiol, Ramiro Funes Mori, Juan Foyth (63.Mario Gaspar), Étienne Capoue, Dani Parejo, Manu Trigueros (79.Jaume Costa), Pedraza, Samuel Chukwueze (71.Álex Baena), Carlos Bacca (63.Yeremi Pino), Gerard Moreno (79.Dani Raba). Trainer: Unai Emery Etxegoien (Spain).
Dynamo Kyiv: Georgiy Bushchan, Tomasz Kedziora, Vitali Mykolenko (83.Sidcley), Oleksandr Syrota (83.Denys Popov), Illia Zabarnyi, Sergiy Sydorchuk, Vitaliy Buyalskyi, Oleksandr Andrievsky (65.Volodymyr Shepelyev), Carlos de Pena, Viktor Tsygankov (46.Vladyslav Supryaha), Gerson Rodrigues (65.Bohdan Lednev). Trainer: Mircea Lucescu (Romania).
<u>Goals</u>: 13', 36' Gerard Moreno 1-0, 2-0.

18.03.2021; Stadio „Giuseppe Meazza", Milano
Referee: Dr. Felix Brych (Germany)
AC Milan – MANCHESTER UNITED FC 0-1(0-0)
AC Milan: Gianluigi Donnarumma, Simon Kjær, Fikayo Tomori, Theo Hernández, Pierre Kalulu (65.Diogo Dalot), Hakan Çalhanoglu, Soualiho Meïté, Samu Castillejo (65.Zlatan Ibrahimovic), Rade Krunic (72.Brahim Díaz), Franck Kessié, Alexis Saelemaekers. Trainer: Stefano Pioli.
Manchester United: Dean Henderson, Victor Lindelöf, Harry Maguire, Luke Shaw, Aaron Wan-Bissaka, Fred, Bruno Fernandes, Daniel James, Scott McTominay, Marcus Rashford (46.Paul Pogba), Mason Greenwood. Trainer: Ole Gunnar Solskjær (Norway).
<u>Goal</u>: 49' Paul Pogba 0-1.

11.03.2021; Stadion Sinobo, Praha
Referee: Ovidiu Alin Haţegan (Romania); Attendance: 300
SK Slavia Praha – Rangers FC Glasgow 1-1(1-1)
Slavia Praha: Ondřej Kolář, Ondřej Kúdela, Jan Boril, Tomás Holeš, Alexander Bah, David Zima, Nicolae Stanciu (76.Ondrej Lingr), Lukás Provod, Peter Olayinka (46.Lukás Masopust), Jan Kuchta (71.Oscar Dorley), Abdallah Sima. Trainer: Jindrich Trpisovský.
Rangers FC: Allan McGregor, Connor Goldson, Filip Helander, Borna Barisic, Nathan Patterson, Steven Davis, Glen Kamara (88.Bongani Zungu), Joe Ayodele-Aribo (81.Kemar Roofe), Ianis Hagi (63.Scott Arfield), Alfredo Morelos, Ryan Kent. Trainer: Steven George Gerrard (England).
Goals: 7' Nicolae Stanciu 1-0, 36' Filip Helander 1-1.

11.03.2021; Stadio Olimpico, Roma
Referee: Artur Manuel Ribeiro Soares Dias (Portugal)
AS Roma – FK Shakhtar Donetsk 3-0(1-0)
AS Roma: Pau López, Leonardo Spinazzola (78.Bruno Peres), Rick Karsdorp, Gianluca Mancini, Marash Kumbulla, Henrikh Mkhitaryan (35.Borja Mayoral), Bryan Cristante, Lorenzo Pellegrini (78.Carles Pérez), Gonzalo Villar, Amadou Diawara (79.Ibañez), Pedro (62.Stephan El Shaarawy). Trainer: Paulo Alexandre Rodrigues Fonseca (Portugal).
Shakhtar Donetsk: Anatolii Trubin, Ismaily, Mykola Matvienko, Dodô, Vitão, Marlos (88.Marcos Antônio), Taison (79.Manor Solomon), Alan Patrick (79.Heorhii Sudakov), Maycon, Mateus Martins Tetê (87.Yevhen Konoplyanka), Júnior Moraes (76.Dentinho). Trainer: Luís Manuel Ribeiro Castro (Portugal).
Goals: 23' Lorenzo Pellegrini 1-0, 73' Stephan El Shaarawy 2-0, 77' Gianluca Mancini 3-0.

11.03.2021; Stádio „Giórgos Karaïskáki", Peiraiás
Referee: Daniel Siebert (Germany)
Olympiacos SFP Peiraiás – Arsenal FC London 1-3(0-1)
Olympiacos: José Sá, Sokratis Papastathopoulos, Kenny Lala, Oleg Reabciuk (46.José Holebas), Mathieu Valbuena (46.Kostas Fortounis), Yann M'Vila, Andreas Bouchalakis, Georgios Masouras (86.Athanasios Androutsos), Mohamed Camara, Youssef El-Arabi (77.Koka), Bruma (59.Lazar Randjelovic). Trainer: Pedro Rui da Mota Vieira Martins (Portugal).
Arsenal FC: Bernd Leno, David Luiz, Héctor Bellerín, Kieran Tierney, Gabriel Magalhães, Granit Xhaka, Thomas Partey (55.Dani Ceballos), Martin Ødegaard (82.Emile Smith-Rowe), Bukayo Saka (82.Nicolas Pépé), Willian (82.Mohamed Elneny), Pierre-Emerick Aubameyang (88.Alexandre Lacazette). Trainer: Mikel Amatriain Arteta (Spain).
Goals: 34' Martin Ødegaard 0-1, 58' Youssef El-Arabi 1-1, 80' Gabriel Magalhães 1-2, 85' Mohamed Elneny 1-3.

11.03.2021; Tottenham Hotspur Stadium, London
Referee: Serder Gözübüyük (Netherlands)
Tottenham Hotspur FC London – GNK Dinamo Zagreb 2-0(1-0)
Tottenham Hotspur: Hugo Lloris, Serge Aurier, Ben Davies, Davinson Sánchez, Moussa Sissoko, Érik Lamela (64.Gareth Bale), Dele Alli (64.Steven Bergwijn), Eric Dier, Tanguy NDombèlé (72.Pierre-Emile Højbjerg), Son Heung-Min (64.Lucas Moura), Harry Kane (84.Carlos Vinícius). Trainer: José Mário dos Santos Félix Mourinho (Portugal).
Dinamo Zagreb: Dominik Livakovic, Marin Leovac, Kévin Théophile-Catherine, Stefan Ristovski, Rasmus Lauritsen, Arijan Ademi (90.Bartol Franjic), Kristijan Jakic, Luka Ivanusec, Lovro Majer (64.Lirim Kastrati), Mislav Orsic (64.Iyayi Atiemwen), Bruno Petkovic (78.Mario Gavranovic). Trainer: Zoran Mamic.
Goals: 25', 70' Harry Kane 1-0, 2-0.

11.03.2021; Estadio Nuevo Los Cármenes, Granada
Referee: Pawel Raczkowski (Poland)
Granada CF – Molde FK 2-0(1-0)
Granada CF: Rui Silva, Víctor Díaz, Dimitri Foulquier, Domingos Duarte, Nehuén Pérez, Maxime Gonalons, Antonio Puertas (90+1.Jesús Vallejo), Kenedy, Yan Eteki, Soldado (81.Ismael Ruiz), Jorge Molina. Trainer: Diego Martínez Penas.
Molde FK: Andreas Linde, Kristoffer Haugen, Stian Gregersen, Sheriff Sinyan, Marcus Pedersen, Magnus Wolff Eikrem, Eirik Andersen (86.Mathis Bolly), Eirik Hestad (65.Erling Knudtzon), Fredrik Aursnes, Martin Ellingsen [sent off 71], Björn Sigurdarson (73.David Fofana). Trainer: Erling Moe.
Goals: 26' Jorge Molina 1-0, 76' Soldado 2-0.

18.03.2021; Ibrox Stadium, Glasgow
Referee: Orel Grinfeld (Israel)
Rangers FC Glasgow – SK SLAVIA PRAHA 0-2(0-1)
Rangers FC: Allan McGregor, Leon Balogun [sent off 73], Connor Goldson, Borna Barisic, Nathan Patterson (78.Jack Simpson), Steven Davis (83.Cedric Itten), Scott Arfield (55.Kemar Roofe [sent off 61]), Glen Kamara, Joe Ayodele-Aribo, Alfredo Morelos (83.Scott Wright), Ryan Kent (82.Bongani Zungu). Trainer: Steven George Gerrard (England).
Slavia Praha: Ondrej Kolár (65.Matyás Vágner), Ondrej Kúdela, Jan Boril, Simon Deli, Alexander Bah, Nicolae Stanciu (90.Ondrej Lingr), Lukás Provod, Jakub Hromada (58.Tomás Holes), Oscar Dorley (58.Jan Kuchta), Peter Olayinka (58.Lukás Masopust), Abdallah Sima. Trainer: Jindrich Trpisovský.
Goals: 14' Peter Olayinka 0-1, 74' Nicolae Stanciu 0-2.

18.03.2021; NSC Olimpiyskiy Stadium, Kyiv
Referee: Antonio Miguel Mateu Lahoz (Spain)
FK Shakhtar Donetsk – AS ROMA 1-2(0-0)
Shakhtar Donetsk: Anatolii Trubin, Sergiy Kryvtsov, Mykola Matvienko, Dodô (82.Sergiy Bolbat), Vitão, Alan Patrick (60.Yevhen Konoplyanka), Manor Solomon (77.Heorhii Sudakov), Maycon, Marcos Antônio, Mateus Martins Tetê (60.Marlos), Júnior Moraes (76.Dentinho). Trainer: Luís Manuel Ribeiro Castro (Portugal).
AS Roma: Pau López, Leonardo Spinazzola (58.Riccardo Calafiori), Rick Karsdorp (58.Bruno Peres), Marash Kumbulla, Ibañez (46.Gianluca Mancini), Bryan Cristante, Gonzalo Villar, Amadou Diawara (59.Lorenzo Pellegrini), Pedro (75.Stephan El Shaarawy), Borja Mayoral, Carles Pérez. Trainer: Paulo Alexandre Rodrigues Fonseca (Portugal).
Goals: 48' Borja Mayoral 0-1, 59' Júnior Moraes 1-1, 72' Borja Mayoral 1-2.

18.03.2021; Emirates Stadium, London
Referee: Carlos del Cerro Grande (Spain)
ARSENAL FC LONDON – Olympiakos Pireus 0-1(0-0)
Arsenal FC: Bernd Leno, David Luiz, Héctor Bellerín (82.Calum Chambers), Kieran Tierney, Gabriel Magalhães, Granit Xhaka, Mohamed Elneny (57.Thomas Partey), Dani Ceballos (57.Martin Ødegaard), Emile Smith-Rowe (81.Gabriel Martinelli), Pierre-Emerick Aubameyang, Nicolas Pépé. Trainer: Mikel Amatriain Arteta (Spain).
Olympiacos: José Sá, José Holebas, Sokratis Papastathopoulos, Oleg Reabciuk (84.Kenny Lala), Ousseynou Ba [sent off 83], Yann M'Vila, Kostas Fortounis (84.Andreas Bouchalakis), Georgios Masouras (63.Bruma), Athanasios Androutsos (62.Lazar Randjelovic), Mohamed Camara, Youssef El-Arabi. Trainer: Pedro Rui da Mota Vieira Martins (Portugal).
Goal: 51' Youssef El-Arabi 0-1.

18.03.2021; Stadion Maksimir, Zagreb
Referee: Davide Massa (Italy)
GNK DINAMO ZAGREB – Tottenham Hotspur FC London 3-0(0-0,2-0)
Dinamo Zagreb: Dominik Livakovic, Kévin Théophile-Catherine, Stefan Ristovski (90.Petar Stojanovic), Rasmus Lauritsen, Arijan Ademi (118.Dino Peric), Kristijan Jakic (75.Iyayi Atiemwen), Luka Ivanusec, Lovro Majer (81.Mario Gavranovic), Bartol Franjic (81.Marin Leovac), Mislav Orsic, Bruno Petkovic (90.Josip Misic). Trainer: Damir Krznar.
Tottenham Hotspur: Hugo Lloris, Serge Aurier (108.Steven Bergwijn), Ben Davies (90.Reguilón), Davinson Sánchez, Moussa Sissoko, Érik Lamela (60.Gareth Bale), Lucas Moura (85.Carlos Vinícius), Dele Alli (68.Giovani Lo Celso), Eric Dier, Harry Winks (68.Tanguy NDombèlé), Harry Kane. Trainer: José Mário dos Santos Félix Mourinho (Portugal).
Goals: 62,' 83', 106' Mislav Orsic 1-0, 2-0, 3-0.

18.03.2021; Puskás Aréna, Budapest (Hungary)
Referee: Srđan Jovanović (Serbia)
Molde FK – GRANADA CF 2-1(1-0)
Molde FK: Andreas Linde, Martin Bjørnbak, Stian Gregersen (46.Sheriff Sinyan), Birk Risa (77.Kristoffer Haugen), Emil Breivik (82.Etzaz Hussain), Marcus Pedersen, Magnus Wolff Eikrem, Eirik Andersen (77.Erling Knudtzon), Eirik Hestad, Fredrik Aursnes, Björn Sigurdarson (63.David Fofana). Trainer: Erling Moe.
Granada CF: Rui Silva, Víctor Díaz, Germán Sánchez, Jesús Vallejo (83.Nehuén Pérez), Domingos Duarte, Montoro (83.Darwin Machís), Maxime Gonalons (76.Yan Eteki), Antonio Puertas, Kenedy, Yangel Herrera, Jorge Molina (64.Soldado). Trainer: Diego Martínez Penas.
Goals: 29' Jesús Vallejo 1-0 (own goal), 72' Soldado 1-1, 90' Eirik Hestad 2-1 (penalty).

08.04.2021; Estadio Nuevo Los Cármenes, Granada
Referee: Artur Manuel Ribeiro Soares Dias (Portugal)
Granada CF – Manchester United FC 0-2(0-1)
Granada CF: Rui Silva, Víctor Díaz, Jesús Vallejo, Domingos Duarte (54.Germán Sánchez), Carlos Neva (74.Dimitri Foulquier), Montoro, Maxime Gonalons (86.Yan Eteki), Antonio Puertas, Kenedy (75.Darwin Machís), Yangel Herrera, Soldado (87.Luis Suárez). Trainer: Diego Martínez Penas.
Manchester United: David de Gea, Victor Lindelöf, Harry Maguire, Luke Shaw (46.Alex Telles), Aaron Wan-Bissaka, Paul Pogba (74.Nemanja Matic), Bruno Fernandes, Daniel James, Scott McTominay, Marcus Rashford (66.Edinson Cavani), Mason Greenwood (85.Donny van de Beek). Trainer: Ole Gunnar Solskjær (Norway).
Goals: 31' Marcus Rashford 0-1, 90' Bruno Fernandes 0-2 (penalty).

08.04.2021; Emirates Stadium, London
Referee: Andreas Ekberg (Sweden)
Arsenal FC London – SK Slavia Praha 1-1(0-0)
Arsenal FC: Bernd Leno, Cédric Soares, Héctor Bellerín, Rob Holding, Gabriel Magalhães, Granit Xhaka, Thomas Partey (78.Mohamed Elneny), Emile Smith-Rowe (88.Dani Ceballos), Bukayo Saka (78.Nicolas Pépé), Willian (73.Gabriel Martinelli), Alexandre Lacazette (78.Pierre-Emerick Aubameyang). Trainer: Mikel Amatriain Arteta (Spain).
Slavia Praha: Ondrej Kolár, Jan Boril, Tomás Holes, Alexander Bah, David Zima, Nicolae Stanciu (84.Lukás Masopust), Lukás Provod, Jakub Hromada (46.Petr Sevcík), Oscar Dorley (69.Ondrej Lingr), Peter Olayinka (85.Ibrahim Traoré), Abdallah Sima (69.Jan Kuchta). Trainer: Jindrich Trpisovský.
Goals: 86' Nicolas Pépé 1-0, 90+4' Tomás Holes 1-1.

08.04.2021; „Johan Cruijff" ArenA, Amsterdam
Referee: Sergey Karasev (Russia)
AFC Ajax Amsterdam – AS Roma 1-2(1-0)
AFC Ajax: Kjell Scherpen, Nicolás Tagliafico, Edson Álvarez, Lisandro Martínez, Jurriën Timber, Devyne Rensch (78.Sean Klaiber), Davy Klaassen, Ryan Gravenberch, Dusan Tadic, David Neres (64.Brian Brobbey), Antony (88.Oussama Idrissi). Trainer: Erik ten Hag.
AS Roma: Pau López, Bruno Peres, Leonardo Spinazzola (29.Riccardo Calafiori), Gianluca Mancini, Ibañez, Jordan Veretout (77.Gonzalo Villar), Bryan Cristante, Lorenzo Pellegrini, Amadou Diawara, Edin Dzeko (77.Borja Mayoral), Pedro (89.Carles Pérez). Trainer: Paulo Alexandre Rodrigues Fonseca (Portugal).
Goals: 39' Davy Klaassen 1-0, 57' Lorenzo Pellegrini 1-1, 87' Ibañez 1-2.

08.04.2021; Stadion Maksimir, Zagreb
Referee: Daniel Siebert (Germany)
GNK Dinamo Zagreb – Villarreal CF 0-1(0-1)
Dinamo Zagreb: Dominik Livakovic, Kévin Théophile-Catherine, Stefan Ristovski, Rasmus Lauritsen, Josko Gvardiol (71.Marin Leovac), Arijan Ademi, Kristijan Jakic (61.Lirim Kastrati), Luka Ivanusec, Iyayi Atiemwen (61.Bruno Petkovic), Lovro Majer (82.Bartol Franjic), Mislav Orsic (82.Marko Tolic). Trainer: Damir Krznar.
Villarreal: Gerónimo Rulli, Raúl Albiol, Pau Torres, Juan Foyth, Étienne Capoue, Dani Parejo, Manu Trigueros (86.Rubén Peña), Pedraza, Samuel Chukwueze (69.Moi Gómez), Carlos Bacca (46.Paco Alcácer), Gerard Moreno. Trainer: Unai Emery Etxegoien (Spain).
Goal: 44' Gerard Moreno 0-1 (penalty).

15.04.2021; Old Trafford, Manchester
Referee: István Kovács (Romania)
MANCHESTER UNITED FC – Granada CF 2-0(1-0)
Manchester United: David de Gea, Alex Telles, Victor Lindelöf, Axel Tuanzebe, Aaron Wan-Bissaka (82.Brandon Williams), Nemanja Matic, Paul Pogba (46.Donny van de Beek), Fred, Bruno Fernandes (73.Mata), Edinson Cavani (60.Daniel James), Mason Greenwood (82.Amad Diallo). Trainer: Ole Gunnar Solskjær (Norway).
Granada CF: Rui Silva, Germán Sánchez (82.Nehuén Pérez), Dimitri Foulquier, Jesús Vallejo, Carlos Neva (74.Víctor Díaz), Montoro, Maxime Gonalons (32.Jorge Molina), Kenedy (46.Antonio Puertas), Yangel Herrera, Soldado (46.Luis Suárez), Darwin Machís. Trainer: Diego Martínez Penas.
Goals: 6' Edinson Cavani 1-0, 90' Jesús Vallejo 2-0 (own goal).

15.04.2021; Stadion Sinobo, Praha
Referee: Cüneyt Çakir (Turkey); Attendance: 750
SK Slavia Praha – ARSENAL FC LONDON 0-4(0-3)
Slavia Praha: Ondrej Kolár, Jan Boril (46.Oscar Dorley), Tomás Holes, Alexander Bah (46.Denis Visinský), David Zima, Nicolae Stanciu (46.Ondrej Lingr), Petr Sevcík, Lukás Provod, Jakub Hromada (46.Lukás Masopust), Peter Olayinka, Jan Kuchta (71.Stanislav Tecl). Trainer: Jindrich Trpisovský.
Arsenal FC: Bernd Leno, Pablo Marí, Calum Chambers, Rob Holding, Granit Xhaka, Thomas Partey (79.Cédric Soares), Dani Ceballos, Emile Smith-Rowe (67.Mohamed Elneny), Bukayo Saka (79.Gabriel Martinelli), Alexandre Lacazette (79.Eddie Nketiah), Nicolas Pépé (88.Folarin Balogun). Trainer: Mikel Amatriain Arteta (Spain).
Goals: 18' Nicolas Pépé 0-1, 21' Alexandre Lacazette 0-2 (penalty), 24' Bukayo Saka 0-3, 77' Alexandre Lacazette 0-4.

15.04.2021; Stadio Olimpico, Roma
Referee: Anthony Taylor (England)
AS ROMA – AFC Ajax Amsterdam 1-1(0-0)
AS Roma: Pau López, Rick Karsdorp, Gianluca Mancini, Ibañez, Riccardo Calafiori (81.Gonzalo Villar), Henrikh Mkhitaryan (87.Pedro), Jordan Veretout, Bryan Cristante, Lorenzo Pellegrini, Amadou Diawara, Edin Dzeko (80.Borja Mayoral). Trainer: Paulo Alexandre Rodrigues Fonseca (Portugal).
AFC Ajax: Maarten Stekelenburg, Nicolás Tagliafico, Sean Klaiber (22.Perr Schuurs, 83.Oussama Idrissi), Edson Álvarez (69.Mohammed Kudus), Lisandro Martínez, Jurriën Timber, Davy Klaassen, Ryan Gravenberch, Dusan Tadic, David Neres (83.Lassina Traoré), Antony (46.Brian Brobbey). Trainer: Erik ten Hag.
Goals: 49' Brain Brobbey 0-1, 72' Edin Dzeko 1-1.

15.04.2021; Estadio de la Cerámica, Villarreal
Referee: Danny Desmond Makkelie (Netherlands)
VILLARREAL CF – GNK Dinamo Zagreb 2-1(2-0)
Villarreal: Gerónimo Rulli, Raúl Albiol, Pau Torres, Juan Foyth, Étienne Capoue, Dani Parejo (84.Francis Coquelin), Manu Trigueros (63.Moi Gómez), Pedraza (90.Alberto Moreno), Samuel Chukwueze (90.Rubén Peña), Paco Alcácer (90.Álex Baena), Gerard Moreno. Trainer: Unai Emery Etxegoien (Spain).
Dinamo Zagreb: Dominik Livakovic, Kévin Théophile-Catherine (82.Dino Peric), Stefan Ristovski (62.Petar Stojanovic), Rasmus Lauritsen, Josko Gvardiol, Arijan Ademi (82.Josip Misic), Kristijan Jakic, Luka Ivanusec (76.Iyayi Atiemwen), Lovro Majer (62.Bartol Franjic), Mislav Orsic, Bruno Petkovic. Trainer: Damir Krznar.
Goals: 36' Paco Alcácer 1-0, 43' Gerard Moreno 2-0, 74' Mislav Orsic 2-1.

29.04.2021; Old Trafford, Manchester
Referee: Carlos del Cerro Grande (Spain)
Manchester United FC – AS Roma 6-2(1-2)
Manchester United: David de Gea, Victor Lindelöf, Harry Maguire, Luke Shaw, Aaron Wan-Bissaka, Paul Pogba, Fred (83.Nemanja Matic), Bruno Fernandes (89.Mata), Scott McTominay, Edinson Cavani, Marcus Rashford (76.Mason Greenwood). Trainer: Ole Gunnar Solskjær (Norway).
AS Roma: Pau López (27.Antonio Mirante), Chris Smalling, Leonardo Spinazzola (37.Bruno Peres), Rick Karsdorp, Ibañez, Henrikh Mkhitaryan, Jordan Veretout (5.Gonzalo Villar), Bryan Cristante, Lorenzo Pellegrini, Amadou Diawara, Edin Dzeko. Trainer: Paulo Alexandre Rodrigues Fonseca (Portugal).
Goals: 9' Bruno Fernandes 1-0, 15' Lorenzo Pellegrini 1-1 (penalty), 34' Edin Dzeko 1-2, 48', 64' Edinson Cavani 2-2, 3-2, 71' Bruno Fernandes 4-2 (penalty), 75' Paul Pogba 5-2, 86' Mason Greenwood 6-2.

29.04.2021; Estadio de la Cerámica, Villarreal
Referee: Artur Manuel Ribeiro Soares Dias (Portugal)
Villarreal CF – Arsenal FC London 2-1(2-0)
Villarreal: Gerónimo Rulli, Raúl Albiol, Pau Torres, Juan Foyth (70.Mario Gaspar), Étienne Capoue [sent off 80], Dani Parejo, Manu Trigueros (80.Moi Gómez), Pedraza (81.Alberto Moreno), Samuel Chukwueze, Paco Alcácer (46.Francis Coquelin), Gerard Moreno. Trainer: Unai Emery Etxegoien (Spain).
Arsenal FC: Bernd Leno, Pablo Marí, Calum Chambers, Rob Holding, Granit Xhaka, Thomas Partey, Martin Ødegaard (63.Gabriel Martinelli), Dani Ceballos [sent off 57], Emile Smith-Rowe (90+5.Mohamed Elneny), Bukayo Saka (85.Pierre-Emerick Aubameyang), Nicolas Pépé (90+5.Willian). Trainer: Mikel Amatriain Arteta (Spain).
Goals: 5' Manu Trigueros 1-0, 29' Raúl Albiol 2-0, 73' Nicolas Pépé 2-1 (penalty).

06.05.2021; Stadio Olimpico, Roma
Referee: Dr. Felix Brych (Germany)
AS Roma – MANCHESTER UNITED FC 3-2(0-1)
AS Roma: Antonio Mirante, Chris Smalling (30.Ebrima Darboe), Bruno Peres (69.Davide Santon), Rick Karsdorp, Gianluca Mancini, Ibañez, Henrikh Mkhitaryan, Bryan Cristante, Lorenzo Pellegrini, Edin Dzeko (76.Borja Mayoral), Pedro (76.Nicola Zalewski). Trainer: Paulo Alexandre Rodrigues Fonseca (Portugal).
Manchester United: David de Gea, Harry Maguire, Luke Shaw (46.Alex Telles), Eric Bailly, Aaron Wan-Bissaka (46.Brandon Williams), Paul Pogba (64.Nemanja Matic), Fred, Bruno Fernandes (84.Mata), Donny van de Beek, Edinson Cavani (73.Marcus Rashford), Mason Greenwood. Trainer: Ole Gunnar Solskjær (Norway).
Goals: 39' Edinson Cavani 0-1, 57' Edin Dzeko 1-1, 60' Bryan Cristante 2-1, 68' Edinson Cavani 2-2, 83' Alex Telles 3-2 (own goal).

06.05.2021; Emirates Stadium, London
Referee: Slavko Vinčić (Slovenia)
Arsenal FC London – VILLARREAL CF 0-0
Arsenal FC: Bernd Leno, Pablo Marí, Héctor Bellerín (90+1.Eddie Nketiah), Kieran Tierney (80.Willian), Rob Holding, Thomas Partey, Martin Ødegaard (66.Gabriel Martinelli), Emile Smith-Rowe, Bukayo Saka, Pierre-Emerick Aubameyang (79.Alexandre Lacazette), Nicolas Pépé. Trainer: Mikel Amatriain Arteta (Spain).
Villarreal: Gerónimo Rulli, Raúl Albiol, Mario Gaspar, Pau Torres, Dani Parejo, Francis Coquelin, Manu Trigueros, Pedraza (90+1.Alberto Moreno), Samuel Chukwueze (29.Yeremi Pino, 90+1.Moi Gómez), Paco Alcácer (72.Carlos Bacca), Gerard Moreno. Trainer: Unai Emery Etxegoien (Spain).

26.05.2021; Polsat Plus Arena, Gdansk (Poland); Referee: Clément Turpin (France); Attendance: 9,412
Villarreal CF – Manchester United FC 1-1(1-0,1-1); 11-10 on penalties
Villarreal: Gerónimo Rulli, Raúl Albiol, Pau Torres, Juan Foyth (88.Mario Gaspar), Étienne Capoue (120+3.Dani Raba), Dani Parejo, Manu Trigueros (77.Moi Gómez), Pedraza (88.Alberto Moreno), Yeremi Pino (77.Paco Alcácer), Carlos Bacca (60.Francis Coquelin), Gerard Moreno. Trainer: Unai Emery Etxegoien (Spain).
Manchester United: David de Gea, Victor Lindelöf, Luke Shaw, Eric Bailly (116.Axel Tuanzebe), Aaron Wan-Bissaka (120+3.Mata), Paul Pogba (115.Daniel James), Bruno Fernandes, Scott McTominay (120+3.Alex Telles), Edinson Cavani, Marcus Rashford, Mason Greenwood (100.Fred). Trainer: Ole Gunnar Solskjær (Norway).
Goals: 29' Gerard Moreno 1-0, 55' Edinson Cavani 1-1.
Penalties: Gerard Moreno 1-0, Mata 1-1, Dani Raba 2-1, Alex Telles 2-2, Paco Alcácer 3-2, Bruno Fernandes 3-3, Alberto Moreno 4-3, Marcus Rashford 4-4, Dani Parejo 5-4, Edinson Cavani 5-5, Moi Gómez 6-5, Fred 6-6, Raúl Albiol 7-6, Daniel James 7-7, Francis Coquelin 8-7, Luke Shaw 8-8, Mario Gaspar 9-8, Axel Tuanzebe 9-9, Pau Torres 10-9, Victor Lindelöf 10-10, Gerónimo Rulli 11-10, David de Gea (missed).

UEFA Europa League Winner 2020/2021: **Villarreal CF** (Spain)

Best Goalscorers:
Luis Miguel Afonso Fernandes "Pizzi" (Sport Lisboa e Benfica),
Borja Mayoral Moya (ESP, AS Roma),
Gerardo Moreno Balagueró (Villarreal CF),
Yusuf Yazıcı (TUR, Lille OSC) – 7 goals each

FAIRS CUP (1958-1971)
UEFA CUP (1972-2009)
UEFA EUROPA LEAGUE (2010-2021)
TABLE OF HONOURS

1955/1958	FC Barcelona	Spain
1958/1960	FC Barcelona	Spain
1960/1961	AS Roma	Italy
1961/1962	Valencia CF	Spain
1962/1963	Valencia CF	Spain
1963/1964	Real Zaragoza	Spain
1964/1965	Ferencvárosi TC	Hungary
1965/1966	FC Barcelona	Spain
1966/1967	GNK Dinamo Zagreb	Croatia
1967/1968	Leeds United FC	England
1968/1969	Newcastle United FC	England
1969/1970	Arsenal FC London	England
1970/1971	Leeds United FC	England
1971/1972	Tottenham Hotspur FC London	England
1972/1973	Liverpool FC	England
1973/1974	Feyenoord Rotterdam	Netherlands
1974/1975	Borussia VfL Mönchengladbach	Germany
1975/1976	Liverpool FC	England
1976/1977	Juventus FC Torino	Italy
1977/1978	PSV Eindhoven	Netherlands
1978/1979	Borussia VfL Mönchengladbach	Germany
1979/1980	Eintracht Frankfurt	Germany
1980/1981	Ipswich Town FC	England
1981/1982	IFK Göteborg	Sweden
1982/1983	RSC Anderlecht Bruxelles	Belgium
1983/1984	Tottenham Hotspur FC London	England
1984/1985	Real Madrid CF	Spain
1985/1986	Real Madrid CF	Spain
1986/1987	IFK Göteborg	Sweden
1987/1988	TSV Bayer 04 Leverkusen	Germany
1988/1989	SSC Napoli	Italy
1989/1990	Juventus FC Torino	Italy
1990/1991	FC Internazionale Milano	Italy
1991/1992	AFC Ajax Amsterdam	Netherlands
1992/1993	Juventus FC Torino	Italy
1993/1994	FC Internazionale Milano	Italy
1994/1995	Parma AC	Italy
1995/1996	FC Bayern München	Germany
1996/1997	FC Schalke 04 Gelsenkirchen	Germany
1997/1998	FC Internazionale Milano	Italy
1998/1999	Parma AC	Italy
1999/2000	Galatasaray SK İstanbul	Turkey
2000/2001	Liverpool FC	England
2001/2002	Feyenoord Rotterdam	Netherlands
2002/2003	FC do Porto	Portugal
2003/2004	Valencia CF	Spain
2004/2005	FK CSKA Moskva	Russia
2005/2006	Sevilla FC	Spain
2006/2007	Sevilla FC	Spain
2007/2008	FK Zenit Saint Petersburg	Russia
2008/2009	FK Shakhtar Donetsk	Ukraine
2009/2010	Club Atlético de Madrid	Spain
2010/2011	FC do Porto	Portugal
2011/2012	Club Atlético de Madrid	Spain
2012/2013	Chelsea FC London	England
2013/2014	Sevilla FC	Spain
2014/2015	Sevilla FC	Spain
2015/2016	Sevilla FC	Spain
2016/2017	Manchester United FC	England
2017/2018	Club Atlético de Madrid	Spain
2018/2019	Chelsea FC London	England
2019/2020	Sevilla FC	Spain
2020/2021	Villarreal CF	Spain

UEFA SUPERCUP 2020

The 2020 UEFA Super Cup was the 45th edition of the UEFA Super Cup, an annual football match organised by UEFA and contested by the winners of the two main European club competitions, the UEFA Champions League and the UEFA Europa League. The 2020 final match featured FC Bayern München (winners of the 2019/2020 UEFA Champions League) and Sevilla FC (the winners of the 2019/2020 UEFA Europa League).

24.09.2020; Puskás Aréna, Budapest (Hungary); Referee: Anthony Taylor (England); Attendance: 15,180

FC Bayern München – Sevilla FC 2-1(0-1,1-1)

Bayern München: Manuel Peter Neuer (Cap), Benjamin Jacques Marcel Pavard, Niklas Süle, David Olatukunbo Alaba (112.Jérôme Agyenim Boateng), Lucas François Bernard Hernández (99.Alphonso Boyle Davies), Joshua Walter Kimmich, Leon Christoph Goretzka (99.Javier Martínez Aginaga „Javi Martínez"), Leroy Aziz Sané (70.Corentin Tolisso), Thomas Müller, Serge David Gnabry, Robert Lewandowski. Trainer: Hans-Dieter Flick.

Sevilla FC: Yassine Bounou, Jesús Navas González (Cap), Diego Carlos Santos Silva, Jules Koundé, Sergio Escudero Palomo, Joan Jordán Moreno (94.Franco Damián Vázquez), Fernando Francisco Reges, Ivan Rakitić (56.Óliver Torres Muñoz), Jesús Joaquín Fernández Sáez de la Torre „Suso" (73.Nemanja Gudelj), Luuk de Jong (56.Óliver Torres Muñoz), Lucas Ariel Ocampos. Trainer: Julen Lopetegui Agote.

Goals: 0-1 Lucas Ariel Ocampos (13 (penalty)), 1-1 Leon Christoph Goretzka (34), 2-1 Javier Martínez Aginaga „Javi Martínez" (104).

UEFA Supercup Winner 2020: **FC Bayern München** (Germany)

UEFA SUPER CUP (SINCE 1972)
TABLE OF HONOURS

1972	AFC Ajax Amsterdam (not official)	*Netherlands*
1973	AFC Ajax Amsterdam	*Netherlands*
1974	*Not played*	
1975	FK Dinamo Kyiv	*Soviet Union*
1976	RSC Anderlecht Bruxelles	*Belgium*
1977	Liverpool FC	*England*
1978	RSC Anderlecht Bruxelles	*Belgium*
1979	Nottingham Forest FC	*England*
1980	CF Valencia	*Spain*
1981	*Not played*	
1982	Aston Villa FC Birmingham	*England*
1983	Aberdeen FC	*Scotland*
1984	Juventus FC Torino	*Italy*
1985	*Not played*	
1986	FC Steaua Bucureşti	*Romania*
1987	FC do Porto	*Portugal*
1988	KV Mechelen	*Belgium*
1989	AC Milan	*Italy*
1990	AC Milan	*Italy*
1991	Manchester United FC	*England*
1992	FC Barcelona	*Spain*
1993	Parma AC	*Italy*
1994	AC Milan	*Italy*
1995	AFC Ajax Amsterdam	*Netherlands*
1996	Juventus FC Torino	*Italy*
1997	FC Barcelona	*Spain*
1998	Chelsea FC London	*England*
1999	SS Lazio Roma	*Italy*
2000	Galatasaray SK İstanbul	*Turkey*
2001	Liverpool FC	*England*
2002	Real Madrid CF	*Spain*
2003	AC Milan	*Italy*
2004	Valencia CF	*Spain*
2005	Liverpool FC	*England*
2006	Sevilla FC	*Spain*
2007	AC Milan	*Italy*
2008	FK Zenit Saint Petersburg	*Russia*
2009	FC Barcelona	*Spain*
2010	Club Atlético de Madrid	*Spain*
2011	FC Barcelona	*Spain*
2012	Club Atlético de Madrid	*Spain*
2013	FC Bayern München	*Germany*
2014	Real Madrid CF	*Spain*
2015	FC Barcelona	*Spain*
2016	Real Madrid CF	*Spain*
2017	Real Madrid CF	*Spain*
2018	Club Atlético de Madrid	*Spain*
2019	Liverpool FC	*England*
2020	FC Bayern München	*Germany*

ALBANIA

The Country:
Republic of Albania (Republika e Shqipërisë)
Capital: Tiranë
Surface: 28,748 km²
Inhabitants: 2,845,955 [2020]
Time: UTC+1

The FA:
Federata Shqiptare e Futbollit
Rr. Liman Kaba Nd5, 1019 Tiranë
Tel: +355 42 346 605
Foundation date: 06.06.1930
Member of FIFA since: 12.06.1932
Member of UEFA since: 1954
Website: www.fshf.org

NATIONAL TEAM RECORDS

RECORDS		
First international match:	07.10.1946, Tiranë:	Albania – Yugoslavia 2-3
Most international caps:	Lorik Cana	- 93 caps (2003-2016)
Most international goals:	Erjon Bogdani	- 18 goal / 74 caps (1996-2013)

UEFA EUROPEAN CHAMPIONSHIP	
1960	Qualifiers
1964	Qualifiers
1968	Qualifiers
1972	Qualifiers
1976	Did not enter
1980	Did not enter
1984	Qualifiers
1988	Qualifiers
1992	Qualifiers
1996	Qualifiers
2000	Qualifiers
2004	Qualifiers
2008	Qualifiers
2012	Qualifiers
2016	Final Tournament (Group Stage)
2020	Qualifiers

FIFA WORLD CUP	
1930	Did not enter
1934	Did not enter
1938	Did not enter
1950	Did not enter
1954	Did not enter
1958	Did not enter
1962	Did not enter
1966	Qualifiers
1970	*Entry not accepted by FIFA*
1974	Qualifiers
1978	Did not enter
1982	Qualifiers
1986	Qualifiers
1990	Qualifiers
1994	Qualifiers
1998	Qualifiers
2002	Qualifiers
2006	Qualifiers
2010	Qualifiers
2014	Qualifiers
2018	Qualifiers

OLYMPIC TOURNAMENTS	
1908	-
1912	-
1920	-
1924	-
1928	-
1936	-
1948	-
1952	-
1956	-
1960	-
1964	-
1968	-
1972	-
1976	-
1980	-
1984	*Withdrew*
1988	-
1992	*Withdrew*
1996	-
2000	Qualifiers
2004	Qualifiers
2008	Qualifiers
2012	Qualifiers
2016	Qualifiers

UEFA NATIONS LEAGUE	
2018/2019	League C
2020/2021	League C (promoted to League B)

FIFA CONFEDERATIONS CUP 1992-2017
None

ALBANIAN CLUB HONOURS IN EUROPEAN CLUB COMPETITIONS:

European Champion Clubs' Cup (1956-1992) / UEFA Champions League (1993-2021)
None

Fairs Cup (1858-1971) / UEFA Cup (1972-2009) / UEFA Europa League (2010-2021)
None

UEFA Super Cup (1972-2020)
None

*European Cup Winners' Cup 1961-1999**
None

*defunct competition

NATIONAL COMPETITIONS
TABLE OF HONOURS

	CHAMPIONS	CUP WINNERS	BEST GOALSCORERS	
1930	SK Tiranë	-	-	
1931	SK Tiranë	-	Teli Samsuri (Skënderbeu Korçë)	9
1932	SK Tiranë	-	-	
1933	Skënderbeu Korçë	-	Servet Tefik Agai (Skënderbeu Korçë)	7
1934	SK Tiranë	-	Mark Gurashi (SK Tiranë)	12
1935	*No Competition*	-	*No Competition*	
1936	SK Tiranë	-	Riza Lushta (SK Tiranë)	11
1937	SK Tiranë	-	Riza Lushta (SK Tiranë)	25
1938	*No Competition*	-	*No Competition*	
1939	SK Tiranë (*unofficial*)	SK Tiranë	-	
1940	Vllaznia Shkodër (*unofficial*)	*No Competition*	-	
1941	*No Competition*	*No Competition*	*No Competition*	
1942	SK Tiranë (*unofficial*)	*No Competition*	-	
1943	*No Competition*	*No Competition*	*No Competition*	
1944	*No Competition*	*No Competition*	*No Competition*	
1945	Vllaznia Shkodër	*No Competition*	Loro Boriçi (Vllaznia Shkodër)	11
1946	Vllaznia Shkodër	*No Competition*	Xhevdet Shaqiri (Vllaznia Shkodër)	11
1947	Partizani Tiranë	*No Competition*	Hamdi Bakalli (Partizani Tiranë)	7
1948	Partizani Tiranë	Partizani Tiranë	Tish Daija (Flamurtari Vlorë) Zihni Gjinali (Partizani Tiranë)	11
1949	Partizani Tiranë	Partizani Tiranë	Zihni Gjinali (Partizani Tiranë)	14
1950	Dinamo Tiranë	Dinamo Tiranë	Refik Resmja (Partizani Tiranë)	?
1951	Dinamo Tiranë	Dinamo Tiranë	Refik Resmja (Partizani Tiranë)	59
1952	Dinamo Tiranë	Dinamo Tiranë	Refik Resmja (Partizani Tiranë)	17
1953	Dinamo Tiranë	Dinamo Tiranë	Refik Resmja (Partizani Tiranë)	9
1954	Partizani Tiranë	Dinamo Tiranë	Refik Resmja (Partizani Tiranë)	13
1955	Dinamo Tiranë	*No Competition*	Refik Resmja (Partizani Tiranë) Skënder Jareci (Dinamo Tiranë)	23
1956	Dinamo Tiranë	*No Competition*	Refik Resmja (Partizani Tiranë)	17
1957	Partizani Tiranë	Partizani Tiranë	Niko Bespalla (Teuta)	15
1958	Partizani Tiranë	Partizani Tiranë	Skënder Jareci (Dinamo Tiranë)	14
1959	Partizani Tiranë	*No Competition*	Stavri Lubonja (Dinamo Tiranë)	11
1960	Dinamo Tiranë	Dinamo Tiranë	Skënder Jareci (Dinamo Tiranë)	16
1961	Partizani Tiranë	Partizani Tiranë	Panajot Pano (Partizani Tiranë)	17
1962/1963	Partizani Tiranë	*No Competition*	Robert Jashari (Partizani Tiranë)	18
1963/1964	Partizani Tiranë	17 Nëntori Tiranë	Robert Jashari (Partizani Tiranë)	9
1964/1965	17 Nëntori Tiranë	Partizani Tiranë	Robert Jashari (Partizani Tiranë)	14
1965/1966	17 Nëntori Tiranë	Vllaznia Shkodër	Sajmir Dauti (Dinamo Tiranë)	13
1966/1967	Dinamo Tiranë	Partizani Tiranë	Medin Zhega (Dinamo Tiranë)	19
1968	17 Nëntori Tiranë	Partizani Tiranë	Skënder Hyka (17 Nëntori Tiranë)	19
1969/1970	17 Nëntori Tiranë	Partizani Tiranë	Panajot Pano (Partizani Tiranë)	17
1970/1971	Partizani Tiranë	Dinamo Tiranë	Ilir Përnaska (Dinamo Tiranë)	19
1971/1972	Vllaznia Shkodër	Vllaznia Shkodër	Ilir Përnaska (Dinamo Tiranë)	17
1972/1973	Dinamo Tiranë	Partizani Tiranë	Ilir Përnaska (Dinamo Tiranë)	12
1973/1974	Vllaznia Shkodër	Dinamo Tiranë	Ilir Përnaska (Dinamo Tiranë)	19
1974/1975	Dinamo Tiranë	Elbasani	Ilir Përnaska (Dinamo Tiranë)	17
1975/1976	Dinamo Tiranë	17 Nëntori Tiranë	Ilir Përnaska (Dinamo Tiranë)	18
1976/1977	Dinamo Tiranë	17 Nëntori Tiranë	Agim Murati (Partizani Tiranë)	12
1977/1978	Vllaznia Shkodër	Dinamo Tiranë	Agim Murati (Partizani Tiranë)	14
1978/1979	Partizani Tiranë	Vllaznia Shkodër	Agim Murati (Partizani Tiranë) Petrit Dibra (17 Nëntori Tiranë)	14
1979/1980	Dinamo Tiranë	Partizani Tiranë	Përparim Kovaçi (Tomori Berat)	18
1980/1981	Partizani Tiranë	Vllaznia Shkodër	Dashnor Bajaziti (Besa Kavajë)	12
1981/1982	KF Tiranë	Dinamo Tiranë	Vasil Ruci (Flamurtari Vlorë)	12
1982/1983	Vllaznia Shkodër	17 Nëntori Tiranë	Dashnor Bajaziti (Besa Kavajë)	16
1983/1984	Elbasani	17 Nëntori Tiranë	Vasil Ruci (Flamurtari Vlorë)	12
1984/1985	17 Nëntori Tiranë	Flamurtari Vlorë	Faslli Fakja (Vllaznia Shkodër) Arben Minga (17 Nëntori Tiranë)	13
1985/1986	Dinamo Tiranë	17 Nëntori Tiranë	Kujtim Majaci (Apolonia Fier)	20
1986/1987	Partizani Tiranë	Vllaznia Shkodër	Arben Arbëri (Tomori Berat)	14
1987/1988	17 Nëntori Tiranë	Flamurtari Vlorë	Agustin Kola (17 Nëntori Tiranë)	18
1988/1989	17 Nëntori Tiranë	Dinamo Tiranë	Agustin Kola (17 Nëntori Tiranë)	19
1989/1990	Dinamo Tiranë	Dinamo Tiranë	Kujtim Majaci (Apolonia Fier)	19
1990/1991	KS Flamurtari Vlorë	FK Partizani Tiranë	Kliton Bozgo (FK Tomori Berat)	29
1991/1992	KF Vllaznia Shkodër	KF Elbasani	Edmir Bilali (KF Vllaznia Shkodër)	21
1992/1993	FK Partizani Tiranë	Partizani Tiranë	Edmond Dosti (FK Partizani Tiranë)	20
1993/1994	KF Teuta Durrës	KF Tiranë	Edi Martini (KF Vllaznia Shkodër)	14
1994/1995	KF Tiranë	KF Teuta Durrës	Arben Shehu (Luftëtari Gjirokastër FC)	21
1995/1996	KF Tiranë	KF Tiranë	Altin Çuko (FK Tomori Berat & KF Laçi)	21
1996/1997	KF Tiranë	FK Partizani Tiranë	Viktor Paço (KS Flamurtari Vlorë)	14
1997/1998	KF Vllaznia Shkodër	KF Apolonia Fier	Dorian Bubeqi (KS Shkumbini Peqin)	26
1998/1999	KF Tiranë	KF Tiranë	Artan Bano (KS Lushnja)	22

1999/2000	KF Tiranë	KF Teuta Durrës	Klodian Arbëri (FK Tomori Berat)	18
2000/2001	KF Vllaznia Shkodër	KF Tiranë	Indrit Fortuzi (KF Tiranë)	31
2001/2002	FK Dinamo Tiranë	KF Tiranë	Indrit Fortuzi (KF Tiranë)	24
2002/2003	KF Tiranë	FK Dinamo Tiranë	Mahir Halili (KF Tiranë)	20
2003/2004	KF Tiranë	FK Partizani Tiranë	Vioresin Sinani (KF Vllaznia Shkodër)	36
2004/2005	KF Tiranë	KF Teuta Durrës	Dorian Bylykbashi (FK Partizani Tiranë)	24
2005/2006	KF Elbasani	KF Tiranë	Hamdi Salihi (KF Tiranë)	29
2006/2007	KF Tiranë	KS Besa Kavajë	Vioresin Sinani (KF Tiranë)	23
2007/2008	FK Dinamo Tiranë	KF Vllaznia Shkodër	Vioresin Sinani (KF Vllaznia Shkodër)	20
2008/2009	KF Tiranë	KS Flamurtari Vlorë	Migen Memelli (KF Tiranë)	23
2009/2010	FK Dinamo Tiranë	KS Besa Kavajë	Daniel Xhafa (KS Besa Kavajë)	18
2010/2011	KF Skënderbeu Korçë	KF Tiranë	Daniel Xhafa (KS Flamurtari Vlorë)	19
2011/2012	KF Skënderbeu Korçë	KF Tiranë	Roland Dervishi (KS Shkumbini Peqin)	20
2012/2013	KF Skënderbeu Korçë	KF Laçi	Migen Memelli (KS Flamurtari Vlorë)	19
2013/2014	KF Skënderbeu Korçë	KS Flamurtari Vlorë	Pero Pejić (CRO, KF Skënderbeu Korçë)	20
2014/2015	KF Skënderbeu Korçë	KF Laçi	Pero Pejić (CRO, FK Kukësi)	31
2015/2016	KF Skënderbeu Korçë	FK Kukësi	Hamdi Salihi (KF Skënderbeu Korçë)	27
2016/2017	FK Kukësi	KF Tiranë	Pero Pejić (CRO, FK Kukësi)	28
2017/2018	KF Skënderbeu Korçë	KF Skënderbeu Korçë	Ali Sowe (GAM, KF Skënderbeu Korçë)	21
2018/2019	FK Partizani Tiranë	FK Kukësi	Reginaldo Artur Faife (MOZ, FK Kukësi)	13
2019/2020	KF Tiranë	KF Teuta Durrës	Kyrian Chinazorm Nwabueze (NGA, KF Laçi)	24
2020/2021	KF Teuta Durrës	KF Vllaznia Shkodër	Dejvi Bregu (KF Teuta Durrës)	16

NATIONAL CHAMPIONSHIP
Albanian Superliga / Kategoria Superiore 2020/2021
(04.11.2020 – 26.05.2021)

Results

Round 1 [04.11.2020]
KS Kastrioti - FK Partizani 2-1(1-0)
KF Tiranë - FK Kukësi 2-0(2-0)
Bylis Ballsh - KF Laçi 1-1(1-0)
Teuta Durrës - Skënderbeu Korçë 1-1(1-1)
FK Vllaznia - Apolonia Fier 2-0(0-0)

Round 2 [08.11.2020]
Apolonia Fier - Bylis Ballsh 2-2(2-1)
FK Kukësi - FK Partizani 0-2(0-0)
KF Laçi - KS Kastrioti 1-1(0-0)
KF Tiranë - Teuta Durrës 0-1(0-1)
Skënderbeu Korçë - FK Vllaznia 0-2(0-2)

Round 3 [21.11.2020]
KS Kastrioti - Apolonia Fier 1-1(0-0)
Bylis Ballsh - Skënderbeu Korçë 0-2(0-0)
FK Partizani - KF Laçi 0-0
Teuta Durrës - FK Kukësi 0-0
FK Vllaznia - KF Tiranë 3-2(1-0)

Round 4 [25.11.2020]
Apolonia Fier - FK Partizani 0-3(0-1)
KF Tiranë - Bylis Ballsh 0-0
Skënderbeu Korçë - KS Kastrioti 1-2(0-1)
FK Kukësi - KF Laçi 1-0(1-0)
Teuta Durrës - FK Vllaznia 0-0

Round 5 [29.11.2020]
KS Kastrioti - KF Tiranë 1-1(1-1)
KF Laçi - Apolonia Fier 6-1(2-1)
Bylis Ballsh - Teuta Durrës 0-0
FK Partizani - Skënderbeu Korçë 4-0(3-0)
FK Vllaznia - FK Kukësi 2-4(1-2)

Round 6 [04-05.12.2020]
KF Tiranë - FK Partizani 0-0
Skënderbeu Korçë - KF Laçi 1-1(0-0)
FK Vllaznia - Bylis Ballsh 1-0(0-0)
FK Kukësi - Apolonia Fier 1-0(0-0)
Teuta Durrës - KS Kastrioti 1-1(0-0)

Round 7 [09.12.2020]
Apolonia Fier - Skënderbeu Korçë 1-0(0-0)
KS Kastrioti - FK Vllaznia 0-3(0-3)
KF Laçi - KF Tiranë 0-1(0-1)
Bylis Ballsh - FK Kukësi 0-3(0-2)
FK Partizani - Teuta Durrës 0-0

Round 8 [13.12.2020]
KF Tiranë - Apolonia Fier 3-0(0-0)
Bylis Ballsh - KS Kastrioti 2-1(2-1)
FK Kukësi - Skënderbeu Korçë 3-1(1-0)
Teuta Durrës - KF Laçi 1-1(1-1)
FK Vllaznia - FK Partizani 1-0(0-0)

Round 9 [19.12.2020]
Apolonia Fier - Teuta Durrës 0-1(0-1)
KS Kastrioti - FK Kukësi 1-0(1-0)
KF Laçi - FK Vllaznia 1-0(0-0)
Skënderbeu Korçë - KF Tiranë 1-1(1-0)
FK Partizani - Bylis Ballsh 0-0

Round 10 [23.12.2020]
Apolonia Fier - FK Vllaznia 0-1(0-1)
KF Laçi - Bylis Ballsh 2-0(1-0)
FK Partizani - KS Kastrioti 2-0(0-0)
Skënderbeu Korçë - Teuta Durrës 1-3(0-1)
FK Kukësi - KF Tiranë 0-0

Round 11 [27.12.2020]
KS Kastrioti - KF Laçi 1-0(1-0)
Bylis Ballsh - Apolonia Fier 3-1(1-0)
FK Vllaznia - Skënderbeu Korçë 5-1(3-0)
FK Partizani - FK Kukësi 4-1(1-0)
Teuta Durrës - KF Tiranë 1-1(0-1)

Round 12 [30.12.2020]
Apolonia Fier - KS Kastrioti 2-1(1-1)
KF Laçi - FK Partizani 3-2(1-1)
KF Tiranë - FK Vllaznia 1-0(1-0)
Skënderbeu Korçë - Bylis Ballsh 4-3(2-1)
FK Kukësi - Teuta Durrës 0-3(0-0)

Round 13 [08-09.01.2021]
FK Vllaznia - Teuta Durrës 1-0(0-0)
KS Kastrioti - Skënderbeu Korçë 2-2(1-0)
KF Laçi - FK Kukësi 3-2(2-0)
Bylis Ballsh - KF Tiranë 0-0
FK Partizani - Apolonia Fier 1-1(0-0)

Round 14 [15-16.01.2021]
FK Kukësi - FK Vllaznia 0-1(0-0)
Teuta Durrës - Bylis Ballsh 2-0(1-0)
Apolonia Fier - KF Laçi 1-0(1-0)
KF Tiranë - KS Kastrioti 2-1(1-1)
Skënderbeu Korçë - FK Partizani 1-2(0-2)

Round 15 [20-21.01.2021]
Apolonia Fier - FK Kukësi 1-3(0-1)
KS Kastrioti - Teuta Durrës 0-1(0-0)
KF Laçi - Skënderbeu Korçë 1-1(0-1)
Bylis Ballsh - FK Vllaznia 0-1(0-0)
FK Partizani - KF Tiranë 1-0(0-0)

Round 16 [24-25.01.2021]
FK Kukësi - Bylis Ballsh 2-1(1-1)
Skënderbeu Korçë - Apolonia Fier 1-1(0-0)
FK Vllaznia - KS Kastrioti 0-0
KF Tiranë - KF Laçi 0-1(0-0)
Teuta Durrës - FK Partizani 1-1(1-1)

Round 17 [30-31.01.2021]
KS Kastrioti - Bylis Ballsh 1-0(0-0)
Skënderbeu Korçë - FK Kukësi 0-4(0-3)
Apolonia Fier - KF Tiranë 0-1(0-0)
KF Laçi - Teuta Durrës 1-0(1-0)
FK Partizani - FK Vllaznia 0-0

Round 18 [05-07.02.2021]
FK Vllaznia - KF Laçi 1-2(0-0)
KF Tiranë - Skënderbeu Korçë 2-0(2-0)
Bylis Ballsh - FK Partizani 1-2(0-0)
Teuta Durrës - Apolonia Fier 1-0(0-0)
FK Kukësi - KS Kastrioti 0-1(0-1)

Round 19 [12-13.02.2021]
Teuta Durrës - Skënderbeu Korçë 2-0(1-0)
KS Kastrioti - FK Partizani 0-3(0-0)
KF Tiranë - FK Kukësi 0-2(0-1)
Bylis Ballsh - KF Laçi 0-1(0-0)
FK Vllaznia - Apolonia Fier 1-0(0-0)

Round 20 [20-21.02.2021]
Apolonia Fier - Bylis Ballsh 0-1(0-0)
KF Laçi - KS Kastrioti 1-0(1-0)
KF Tiranë - Teuta Durrës 0-1(0-1)
Skënderbeu Korçë - FK Vllaznia 1-1(1-0)
FK Kukësi - FK Partizani 1-2(0-0)

Round 21 [26-27.02.2021]
Teuta Durrës - FK Kukësi 2-2(1-0)
KS Kastrioti - Apolonia Fier 0-0
Bylis Ballsh - Skënderbeu Korçë 1-0(0-0)
FK Vllaznia - KF Tiranë 1-2(1-1)
FK Partizani - KF Laçi 1-1(1-0)

Round 22 [03.03.2021]
Apolonia Fier - FK Partizani 1-1(1-0)
KF Tiranë - Bylis Ballsh 2-0(1-0)
Skënderbeu Korçë - KS Kastrioti 0-1(0-0)
FK Kukësi - KF Laçi 1-2(0-1)
Teuta Durrës - FK Vllaznia 1-0(1-0)

Round 23 [07-08.03.2021]
KS Kastrioti - KF Tiranë 1-2(0-1)
Bylis Ballsh - Teuta Durrës 1-1(1-1)
FK Partizani - Skënderbeu Korçë 0-1(0-0)
KF Laçi - Apolonia Fier 1-1(0-0)
FK Vllaznia - FK Kukësi 0-0

Round 24 [12-13.03.2021]
FK Kukësi - Apolonia Fier 1-1(1-0)
FK Vllaznia - Bylis Ballsh 1-2(1-0)
KF Tiranë - FK Partizani 1-2(1-1)
Skënderbeu Korçë - KF Laçi 0-2(0-0)
Teuta Durrës - KS Kastrioti 0-0

Round 25 [21.03.2021]
Apolonia Fier - Skënderbeu Korçë 1-2(0-1)
KS Kastrioti - FK Vllaznia 0-1(0-0)
KF Laçi - KF Tiranë 1-2(1-1)
Bylis Ballsh - FK Kukësi 2-1(2-0)
FK Partizani - Teuta Durrës 0-0

Round 26 [03-04.04.2021]
Teuta Durrës - KF Laçi 1-0(0-0)
FK Vllaznia - FK Partizani 0-0
Bylis Ballsh - KS Kastrioti 1-1(1-1)
FK Kukësi - Skënderbeu Korçë 0-1(0-0)
KF Tiranë - Apolonia Fier 5-2(1-2)

Round 27 [10-11.04.2021]
KS Kastrioti - FK Kukësi 0-3(0-0)
Skënderbeu Korçë - KF Tiranë 0-0
Apolonia Fier - Teuta Durrës 0-2(0-1)
KF Laçi - FK Vllaznia 0-0
FK Partizani - Bylis Ballsh 3-0(1-0)

Round 28 [17-18.04.2021]
FK Kukësi - KF Tiranë 2-2(1-0)
FK Partizani - KS Kastrioti 3-1(1-1)
Apolonia Fier - FK Vllaznia 0-6(0-3)
KF Laçi - Bylis Ballsh 2-1(0-0)
Skënderbeu Korçë - Teuta Durrës 0-1(0-1)

Round 29 [24.04.2021]
KS Kastrioti - KF Laçi 0-0
Bylis Ballsh - Apolonia Fier 1-0(0-0)
FK Vllaznia - Skënderbeu Korçë 2-1(1-1)
FK Partizani - FK Kukësi 4-0(2-0)
Teuta Durrës - KF Tiranë 0-2(0-0)

Round 30 [28.04.2021]
Apolonia Fier - KS Kastrioti 2-1(2-0)
Skënderbeu Korçë - Bylis Ballsh 2-1(2-1)
FK Kukësi - Teuta Durrës 0-2(0-1)
KF Laçi - FK Partizani 2-2(1-1)
KF Tiranë - FK Vllaznia 1-0(0-0)

Round 31 [02-03.05.2021]
KS Kastrioti - Skënderbeu Korçë 0-2(0-0)
Bylis Ballsh - KF Tiranë 0-0
KF Laçi - FK Kukësi 2-0(2-0)
FK Partizani - Apolonia Fier 1-0(0-0)
FK Vllaznia - Teuta Durrës 0-0

Round 32 [07-08.05.2021]
FK Kukësi - FK Vllaznia 3-1(2-0)
Apolonia Fier - KF Laçi 0-1(0-0)
KF Tiranë - KS Kastrioti 1-0(0-0)
Skënderbeu Korçë - FK Partizani 1-1(0-1)
Teuta Durrës - Bylis Ballsh 4-0(2-0)

Round 33 [13.05.2021]
Apolonia Fier - FK Kukësi 0-3(0-1)
KS Kastrioti - Teuta Durrës 1-2(0-1)
KF Laçi - Skënderbeu Korçë 0-0
Bylis Ballsh - FK Vllaznia 0-1(0-1)
FK Partizani - KF Tiranë 0-0

Round 34 [17.05.2021]
FK Kukësi - Bylis Ballsh 2-1(0-1)
KF Tiranë - KF Laçi 0-1(0-0)
Skënderbeu Korçë - Apolonia Fier 2-0(2-0)
Teuta Durrës - FK Partizani 0-1(0-1)
FK Vllaznia - KS Kastrioti 1-0(0-0)

Round 35 [21.05.2021]
Apolonia Fier - KF Tiranë 1-1(0-1)
KS Kastrioti - Bylis Ballsh 1-1(0-1)
KF Laçi - Teuta Durrës 0-0
FK Partizani - FK Vllaznia 0-1(0-0)
Skënderbeu Korçë - FK Kukësi 2-1(2-0)

Round 36 [26.05.2021]
FK Kukësi - KS Kastrioti 1-2(0-1)
KF Tiranë - Skënderbeu Korçë 3-1(2-1)
Bylis Ballsh - FK Partizani 2-4(1-1)
Teuta Durrës - Apolonia Fier 6-1(2-1)
FK Vllaznia - KF Laçi 2-0(1-0)

Final Standings

		Total					Home					Away				
1.	**KF Teuta Durrës**	36	17	15	4	42 - 16	66	7	9	2	24 - 11	10	6	2	18 - 5
2.	KF Vllaznia Shkodër	36	19	9	8	44 - 22	66	10	4	4	24 - 14	9	5	4	20 - 8
3.	Alban Bekim Hoxha	36	17	14	5	53 - 23	65	8	8	2	24 - 6	9	6	3	29 - 17
4.	KF Laçi	36	16	13	7	41 - 26	61	9	7	2	27 - 14	7	6	5	14 - 12
5.	KF Tiranë	36	15	13	8	41 - 26	58	9	3	6	23 - 13	6	10	2	18 - 13
6.	FK Kukësi	36	13	6	17	47 - 48	45	6	3	9	18 - 23	7	3	8	29 - 25
7.	KF Skënderbeu Korçë	36	9	10	17	34 - 55	37	4	6	8	18 - 27	5	4	9	16 - 28
8.	KS Kastrioti Krujë (*Relegation Play-off*)	36	8	11	17	26 - 44	35	4	6	8	12 - 23	4	5	9	14 - 21
9.	KF Bylis Ballsh (*Relegated*)	36	7	10	19	28 - 51	31	5	6	7	15 - 20	2	4	12	13 - 31
10.	KF Apolonia Fier (*Relegated*)	36	4	9	23	22 - 67	21	4	3	11	12 - 30	0	6	12	10 - 37

Top goalscorers:

16	**Dejvi Bregu**	***KF Teuta Durrës***
15	Patrick Friday Eze (NGA)	*FK Kukësi*
15	Agim Ibraimi (MKD)	*FK Kukësi*
12	Ardit Hoxhaj	*KF Vllaznia Shkodër*
11	Haris Dilaver (BIH)	*KF Vllaznia Shkodër*

Relegation Play-off [30.05.2021]

KS Kastrioti Krujë – KF Tomori Berat   2-1(1-0)

KS Kastrioti Krujë remains at First Level for 2021/2022.

NATIONAL CUP
Kupa e Shqipërisë 2020/2021

First Round [01.11.2020]

KF Tiranë - KF Shkumbini	4-1	
KF Laçi - KF Vora	3-0	
KF Teuta Durrës - KF Tërbuni Pukë	4-0	
KF Bylis Ballsh - KF Veleçiku Koplik	2-1	
Flamurtari FC Vlorë - FK Dinamo Tiranë	1-2	
KS Kastrioti Krujë - KF Burreli	2-1	
KF Besëlidhja Lezhë - KF Egnatia Rrogozhinë	3-4 pen	
KS Korabi Peshkopi - KF Erzeni Shijak	2-0	
KF Skënderbeu Korçë - FK Tomori Berat	1-0	
FK Partizani Tiranë - KF Iliria Fushë-Krujë	5-0	
KF Vllaznia Shkodër - KF Devolli	7-0	
KF Luftëtari Gjirokastër - KF Elbasani	0-3	*awarded*
KF Apolonia Fier - KF Turbina Cërrik	4-1	
KS Pogradeci - KF Oriku	9-1	
KF Lushnjë - KF Besa Kavajë	0-1 aet	
FK Kukësi - KF Maliqi	5-0	

1/8-Finals [12-14.11.2020]

KF Tiranë - KS Korabi Peshkopi	0-1 aet	
KF Teuta Durrës - KS Kastrioti Krujë	5-0	
KF Bylis Ballsh - FK Dinamo Tiranë	1-2 aet	
FK Kukësi - KF Besa Kavajë	2-1	
KF Skënderbeu Korçë - KS Pogradeci	3-0	
FK Partizani Tiranë - KF Apolonia Fier	1-0	
KF Vllaznia Shkodër - KF Elbasani	8-0	
KF Laçi - KF Egnatia Rrogozhinë	3-1 aet	

Quarter-Finals [17.03.2021]

KF Laçi - FK Partizani Tiranë	4-3 pen	
FK Dinamo Tiranë - KF Skënderbeu Korçë	1-3	
KF Vllaznia Shkodër - KS Korabi Peshkopi	1-0	
KF Teuta Durrës - FK Kukësi	1-0	

Semi-Finals [14.04.2021]

KF Vllaznia Shkodër - KF Laçi	1-0	
KF Teuta Durrës - KF Skënderbeu Korçë	0-2	

Final

31.05.2021; Arena Kombëtare, Tiranë; Referee: Juxhin Xhaja; Attendance: 1,000
KF Vllaznia Shkodër - KF Skënderbeu Korçë   **1-0 (1-0)**

Vllaznia Shkodër: Bojan Zogovič, Mevlan Adili, Eni Imami, Erdenis Gurishta, Aleksandar Isaevski, Victor Matheus Da Silva Matos (87.Miloš Kalezić), Herald Marku, Ardit Krymi, Arsid Kruja (70.Albion Avdijaj), Fjoart Jonuzi, Haris Dilaver (70.Ardit Hoxhaj). Trainer: Thomas Brdarić (Germany).

Skënderbeu Korçë: Bekim Redjepi, Vangjel Zguro [*sent off 86*], Leard Sadriu, Leonat Vitija, Kosta Vangjeli (75.Melos Bajrami), Jorgo Meksi, Jean Victor Gonçalves (82.Dennis Dowouna), Randy Dwumfour, Ščiprim Taipi, Uerdi Mara (64.Belajdi Pusi), Alfred Mensah. Trainer: Migen Memelli.

Goal: 1-0 Victor Matheus Da Silva Matos (39).

THE CLUBS 2020/2021

Klubi i Futbollit Apolonia Fier

Founded:	17.06.1925	
Stadium:	Stadiumi „Loni Papuçiu", Fier (6,800)	
Trainer:	Giovanni Colella (ITA)	10.08.1966
[30.11.2020]	Nikolin Çoçlli	17.10.1968
[16.12.2020]	Bledar Borova	27.10.1983
[01.01.2021]	Fabrizio Cammarata (ITA)	30.08.1975

Goalkeepers:	DOB	M	(s)	G
Endrit Çako	20.03.1992	2		
Romeo Harizaj	26.09.1998	34		
Defenders:	**DOB**	**M**	**(s)**	**G**
Benjamin Agyare (GHA)	08.05.1994	32		
Ersildjo Asllanaj	11.10.2001	6	(6)	
Drago Bumbar	10.11.1997	7		
Benito Çulli	10.04.2000		(2)	
Ismaila Diop (SEN)	19.12.1999	10		1
Denis Duda	14.02.1996		(1)	
Arlind Kurti	24.01.2005		(1)	
Serjan Repaj	05.09.2000	18	(3)	
Elion Sota	24.05.1998	36		
Midfielders:	**DOB**	**M**	**(s)**	**G**
Dejan Andoni	23.06.1995		(1)	
Eljo Gjata	01.07.2003		(1)	
Sali Kumani	29.01.2000	8	(2)	
Skerdilajd Levendi	01.10.2001	15	(7)	2
Ksement Mehmeti	31.10.1998	13	(6)	
Glejdis Ndraxhi	08.05.1998		(5)	

	DOB	M	(s)	G
Stefano Omeri	11.07.1999	14	(8)	1
Kristian Papa (GRE)	21.03.2002		(1)	
Mateo Shanaj	06.09.2001	12	(4)	
Erisildo Smaçi	15.07.1998	31	(3)	1
Kofi Yeboah (GHA)	14.05.1995	22	(5)	
Alexandros Zaimaj	19.01.1998	9	(9)	1
Rubin Zijaj	11.03.2002		(2)	
Forwards:	**DOB**	**M**	**(s)**	**G**
Bernard Arthur (GHA)	25.12.1996	4	(1)	
Effiong Eyoh (NGA)	12.07.1996	9	(9)	
Mario Gjata	06.07.2000	25	(10)	8
Rimal Haxhiu	04.03.1999	24	(4)	1
Rubin Hebeja	21.06.2001	2	(7)	
Jeton Krasniqi	16.01.2001	5	(7)	
Redon Mihana	28.06.1999	34		4
Mariel Sota	21.01.2001		(14)	
Enea Topi	07.01.2004		(1)	
Mario Vasilj (SVN)	25.01.1995	8	(7)	1
Krisild Zoga	26.10.2000	16	(10)	

Klubi i Futbollit Bylis Ballsh

Founded:	1972		
Stadium:	Stadiumi „Adush Muça", Ballsh (5,200)		
Trainer:	Veljko Dovedan (SRB)		01.06.1954

Goalkeepers:	DOB	M	(s)	G
Hektor Mali	07.09.1995	1		
Pano Qirko	16.06.1999	35		
Defenders:	**DOB**	**M**	**(s)**	**G**
Alan Henrique Ferreira Bastos Soares (BRA)	19.06.1991	12		
Klaus Alinani	03.03.2002		(1)	
Dojran Bajrami	02.03.1996	1	(1)	
Andi Hadroj	22.02.1999	33	(1)	2
Stivian Janku	23.06.1997	21		
Lorran de Oliveira Quintanilha (BRA)	08.01.1996	22	(1)	
Ariel Muçollari	19.04.2001	1	(3)	
Edison Ndreca	05.07.1994	32		6
Marcelino Preka	02.08.2003	8	(3)	
Miloš Stojanović (SRB)	18.01.1997	30		1
Franc Ymeralilaj	14.01.1995	30	(2)	
Midfielders:	**DOB**	**M**	**(s)**	**G**
Alexandre Cardoso Garcia (BRA)	30.04.1992	17	(2)	
Aleksandar Desančić (SRB)	20.02.1996	10	(1)	1
Jurgen Dushkaj	09.06.1995	2	(3)	
Alessio Hyseni	04.01.1997	1		
Xhoeli Maçolli	23.09.2001	1	(1)	

Marco Antonio Morgon Filho „Marquinho" (BRA)	24.02.1988		(8)	
Donald Mëllugja	31.05.1995	7	(5)	
Valentino Murataj	15.08.1996	12		1
Kreshnik Nebihu (KVX)	18.06.1997	9	(4)	
Neto Marcolino Silva Lima de Sá (BRA)	17.05.1996		(1)	
Odirah Franklin Ntephe (NGA)	26.09.1993	17	(8)	2
Eridon Qardaku	10.08.2000	9	(13)	
Flamur Ruçi	19.01.2002	1	(1)	
Serxho Ujka	27.08.1998	9	(20)	
Forwards:	**DOB**	**M**	**(s)**	**G**
Amos Beji Anthony (NGA)	04.01.1999	28	(6)	10
Xhoi Carkanji	31.08.1994	12	(10)	1
Serxhio Emini	03.12.2002		(1)	
Haris Harba (BIH)	14.07.1988	1	(10)	
Nemanja Kojić (SRB)	03.02.1990	9	(9)	
Qudus Lawal (NGA)	04.09.1995	3	(4)	
Gresild Lika	02.11.1997		(5)	
Arber Mehmetllari	19.04.2000	18	(6)	1
Renato Spahiu (GRE)	14.12.1998	2	(12)	2
Aleksandër Trumci	31.12.2000	2	(7)	

Klubi Sportiv Kastrioti Krujë

Founded:	1926		
Stadium:	Stadiumi Kamëz, Kamëz (5,500)		
Trainer:	Ramadan Ndreu		30.03.1966

Goalkeepers:	DOB	M	(s)	G
Isli Hidi	15.10.1980	36		
Defenders:	**DOB**	**M**	**(s)**	**G**
Amer Duka	21.01.1999		(1)	
Lukman Hussein (NGA)	28.08.1996	16	(1)	
Edward Nicolas M'Boyom (CMR)	12.12.1988	15	(3)	
Sokol Neziri	30.06.1996	21	(7)	
Indrit Prodani	20.05.1998	29	(1)	2
Armando Rami	24.07.1997	21	(9)	
Silvester Shkalla	10.08.1995	21	(7)	1
Realf Zhivanaj	15.03.1998	9	(4)	
Midfielders:	**DOB**	**M**	**(s)**	**G**
Arbër Basha	13.01.1998		(7)	
Emiliano Çela	21.07.1985	30	(1)	
Fjoralb Deliaj	04.04.1997	11	(13)	

Abaz Karakaçi	25.08.1992		(2)	
Xhuljo Mehmeti	29.12.1993	31	(2)	1
Rei Nuriu	16.10.1998	14	(3)	
Henry Chimuchem Okebugwu (NGA)	19.06.1998	19	(9)	2
Laurenc Xheka	07.08.2000		(5)	
Forwards:	**DOB**	**M**	**(s)**	**G**
Agnaldo Pinto de Moraes Júnior (BRA)	11.03.1994	29	(4)	
Spartak Ajazi	03.07.1994		(5)	
Patrik Bardhi	21.05.1998	32		1
Joan Çela	06.01.2000		(6)	
Klejdi Daci	22.04.1999	5	(18)	5
Devid de Santana Silva (BRA)	28.03.1996	28	(1)	10
Sebino Plaku	20.05.1985	4	(6)	2
Ermir Rezi	12.05.1994	24	(7)	2
Silvio Vokrri	25.05.2001	1	(11)	

Futboll Klub Kukësi

Founded:	04.03.1930		
Stadium:	Elbasan Arena, Elbasan (12,800)		
Trainer:	Skënder Gega		14.11.1963
[27.12.2020]	Rrahman Hallaçi		12.11.1983
[25.01.2021]	Mirel Josa		01.06.1963

Goalkeepers:	DOB	M	(s)	G
Angelo Tafas	05.07.2000	18		
Dashamir Xhika	23.05.1989	18		
Defenders:	**DOB**	**M**	**(s)**	**G**
Rolandas Baravykas (LTU)	23.08.1995	7	(10)	
Altin Bytyçi (KVX)	14.01.2001	24	(1)	
Besir Demiri	01.08.1994	33		
Redon Dragoshi	18.03.2000	24	(5)	1
Mehdi Hetemaj (AUT)	07.05.1997	3	(5)	
Kenan Horić (BIH)	13.09.1990	7		
Blerim Kotobelli	10.08.1992	25	(5)	
Numan Kurdić (BIH)	01.07.1999	14		1
Bruno Lulaj	02.04.1995	26	(1)	1
Midfielders:	**DOB**	**M**	**(s)**	**G**
Albin Gashi (AUT)	25.01.1997	18	(9)	

Xhoi Hajdëraj	07.05.2000		(1)	
Vesel Limaj (GER)	01.12.1996	22	(9)	8
Xheron Osma	20.08.2002		(1)	
Gjelbrim Taipi (KVX)	13.12.1992	36		2
Mate Tsintsadze (GEO)	07.01.1995	14	(1)	1
Ersil Ymeraj	06.07.1994	6	(9)	
Forwards:	**DOB**	**M**	**(s)**	**G**
Godberg Cooper (ITA)	20.08.1997		(7)	
Fluturim Domi	14.10.2000	1	(9)	
Patrick Friday Eze (NGA)	22.12.1992	30	(3)	15
Zenel Gavazaj	02.05.2000	2	(11)	1
Agim Ibraimi (MKD)	29.08.1988	35		15
Matheus Leiria Dos Santos (BRA)	22.01.1995	22	(1)	1
Ergys Peposhi	26.08.2000	10	(9)	1
Serxhio Tabaku	15.05.2000	1		

Klubi i Futbollit Laçi

Founded: 1960
Stadium: Stadiumi Laçi, Laçi (2,300)
Trainer: Armando Cungu — 23.04.1973
[26.11.2020] Stavri Nica — 08.07.1954
[05.12.2020] Klevis Hima
[12.12.2020] Shpëtim Duro — 24.12.1959

Goalkeepers:	DOB	M	(s)	G
Edmir Sali	07.08.1997	2		
Alen Sherri	15.12.1997	34	(1)	
Defenders:	DOB	M	(s)	G
Arbër Deliu	01.04.2000		(4)	
Aleksandar Ignjatović (SRB)	11.04.1988	29	(2)	
Dorian Kërçiku	30.08.1993	4	(10)	
Renato Malota	24.06.1989	20	(2)	1
Albion Marku	14.10.2000	30	(1)	1
Emiljano Musta	31.01.1992	32		5
Erhun Obanor (NGA)	05.09.1995	25	(2)	
Donald Rapo	04.10.1990	2	(5)	
Adolf Selmani	26.06.2000	20		
Henri Sulovari	12.09.2002		(3)	
Rudolf Turkaj	03.02.1995	6	(10)	

Midfielders:	DOB	M	(s)	G
Arbër Bytyqi	16.10.2003	1	(6)	
Ardit Deliu	26.10.1997	33		1
Lucas Ramos de Oliveira (BRA)	18.01.1995	6	(9)	
Regi Lushkja	17.05.1996	32	(1)	5
Klejdi Rapo	18.06.1994	2	(2)	
Bryan Rodriguez (USA)	09.09.1997		(1)	
Juljan Shehu	06.09.1998	32		3
Forwards:	DOB	M	(s)	G
Van-Dave Harmon (LBR)	22.09.1995	22	(9)	5
Mentor Mazrekaj	08.02.1989	16	(13)	6
Kyrian Chinazorm Nwabueze (NGA)	11.12.1992	11	(4)	7
Fatmir Prengaj	01.05.2001	3	(11)	1
Teldiano Guimaraes Franca Junior „Teco" (BRA)	26.06.1995	6	(2)	
Redon Xhixha	14.07.1998	23	(8)	5
Iljasa Zulfiji (SRB)	27.03.1998	5	(4)	

Futboll Klub Partizani Tiranë

Founded: 04.02.1946
Stadium: Elbasan Arena, Elbasan (12,800)
Trainer: Ilir Daja — 20.10.1966

Goalkeepers:	DOB	M	(s)	G
Alban Bekim Hoxha	23.11.1987	34		
Aldo Teqja	04.05.1995	2		
Defenders:	DOB	M	(s)	G
Egzon Belica (MKD)	03.09.1990	32		1
Eneo Bitri	26.08.1996	35		2
Loti Celina (KVX)	05.06.2000		(1)	
Agim Dajçi	27.07.2000		(4)	
Roberto Carlos Domínguez Fuentes (SLV)	09.05.1997	1	(1)	
Ersin Hakaj	06.12.1996	35		1
Hektor Idrizaj	15.04.1989	22	(6)	1
Midfielders:	DOB	M	(s)	G
Denis Balla	28.08.1998		(4)	
Jurgen Bardhi	06.11.1997	32	(2)	5
Rron Broja (KVX)	09.04.1996	30	(2)	
Besnik Ferati (MKD)	19.04.2000		(2)	
Gehard Hasa	23.02.1997		(2)	

	DOB	M	(s)	G
Ferhan Hasani (MKD)	18.06.1990	1	(11)	
Alessio Hyseni	04.01.1997	2	(7)	1
Eneid Kodra	04.11.1999		(4)	
Kristi Kote	26.09.1998	13	(10)	
Esat Mala	18.10.1998	34	(1)	4
Donald Mëllugja	31.05.1995		(2)	
Valentino Murataj	15.08.1996	20		1
Geri Selita	08.03.2001		(1)	1
Forwards:	DOB	M	(s)	G
Jasir Asani	19.05.1995	25	(5)	9
Tedi Cara	15.04.2000	5	(29)	5
Eraldo Cinari	11.10.1996	20	(2)	8
Kevi Llanaj	09.04.1999		(2)	
Lucas Ferreira Cardoso (BRA)	07.04.1994	16	(11)	5
Theophilus Solomon (NGA)	18.01.1996	15		3
Stênio Marcos da Fonseca Salazar Júnior (BRA)	10.06.1991	10	(6)	6
William Cordeiro Melo (BRA)	15.07.1993	12	(6)	

Klubi Futbollistik Skënderbeu Korçë

Founded: 1925
Stadium: Stadiumi Skënderbeu, Korçë (12,343)
Trainer: Julian Ahmataj — 24.05.1979
[03.02.2021] Migen Memelli — 25.04.1980

Goalkeepers:	DOB	M	(s)	G
Mario Dajsinani	23.12.1998	30		
Bekim Redjepi (MKD)	27.10.1996	6		
Defenders:	DOB	M	(s)	G
Abbey Agbodzie (GHA)	25.12.1999	2	(2)	
Melos Bajrami (KVX)	29.09.2001	14	(3)	
Ditmar Bicaj	26.02.1989	10		
Amer Duka	21.01.1999	1	(2)	
Drin Govori (KVX)	17.05.1999	4	(1)	
Jorgo Meksi	21.03.1995	33		5
Fallou Njie (GAM)	05.01.1999	1	(1)	
Harallamb Qaqi	17.09.1993	12	(1)	1
Leard Sadriu (KVX)	22.04.2001	18		1
Kosta Vangjeli	21.07.2000	15	(8)	3
Leonat Vitija (KVX)	22.08.2000	24	(4)	
Vangjel Zguro	04.03.1993	20		
Midfielders:	DOB	M	(s)	G
Dennis Dowouna (GHA)	18.05.2000	22	(9)	1
Randy Dwumfour (GHA)	23.11.2000	25	(3)	

	DOB	M	(s)	G
Jean Victor Gonçalves (BRA)	21.03.1995	17	(2)	3
Uerdi Mara	30.01.1999	25	(7)	3
Rei Pecani	08.05.2002		(1)	
Arinaldo Rrapaj	09.08.2001	12	(18)	
Alban Shabani (KVX)	18.05.2000	1	(11)	
Šćiprim Taipi	19.02.1997	27	(1)	1
Vasil Tuni	10.10.2002	1		
Forwards:	DOB	M	(s)	G
Alexandros Abdel Rahim (GRE)	23.02.1993	1	(1)	
Samuel Armah (GHA)	01.05.2000	1	(6)	1
Elvi Berisha	02.03.1999	21	(9)	3
Joan Çela	06.01.2000	1	(5)	
Redi Kaçanolli	01.05.2004	1	(2)	
Krisi Kaso	06.02.2001	1	(1)	
Alfred Mensah (GHA)	08.08.1999	31	(1)	7
Belajdi Pusi	23.01.1998	16	(14)	4
Alexandros Tereziou (GRE)	01.03.2000	3	(10)	1
Skerdi Xhixho	15.01.2005		(1)	

Klubi Futbollit Teuta Durrës

Founded:	1920		
Stadium:	Stadiumi"Niko Dovana", Durrës (12,040)		
Trainer:	Eduard Martini		02.01.1975

Goalkeepers:	DOB	M	(s)	G
Stivi Frashëri	29.08.1990	36		
Defenders:	**DOB**	**M**	**(s)**	**G**
Renato Arapi	28.09.1986	33		1
Rustem Hoxha	04.07.1991	34		2
Jackson Ferreira Silvério (BRA)	12.04.1991	12	(4)	
Alexandros Kouros (GRE)	21.08.1993	25	(4)	
Denis Pjeshka	28.05.1995	3	(2)	
Blagoja Todorovski (MKD)	11.06.1985	34		
Midfielders:	**DOB**	**M**	**(s)**	**G**
Albano Aleksi	10.10.1992	33		1
Florent Avdyli (KVX)	10.07.1993	15	(9)	
Fabjan Beqja	15.02.1994	1	(3)	
Ledjo Beqja	18.06.2001		(5)	
Asion Daja	14.03.1990	15	(11)	
Iran da Conceição Gonçalves Júnior (BRA)	10.10.1995	2	(8)	
Erando Karabeci	06.09.1988	13	(10)	1
Emiljano Vila	12.03.1988	36		2
Silvio Zogaj	25.07.1997		(9)	
Forwards:	**DOB**	**M**	**(s)**	**G**
Dejvi Bregu	24.10.1995	36		16
Ildi Gruda	13.02.1999	4	(21)	1
Rubin Hebaj	30.07.1998	5	(6)	1
Dejvid Kapllani	03.06.2001		(10)	1
Blerim Krasniqi	05.07.1996	27	(7)	4
Sebino Plaku	20.05.1985	2	(7)	1
Lorenco Vila	14.12.1998	30	(3)	10

Klubi i Futbollit Tirana

Founded:	15.08.1920 (as Shoqata Sportive Agimi)		
Stadium:	Stadiumi"Selman Stërmasi", Tiranë (9,600)		
Trainer:	Ndubuisi Emmanuel Egbo (NGA)		25.07.1973
[13.11.2020]	Nevil Dede		10.01.1975
[25.01.2021]	Tefik Osmani		08.06.1985
[27.01.2021]	Orges Shehi		25.09.1977

Goalkeepers:	DOB	M	(s)	G
Visar Bekaj (KVX)	24.05.1997	35		
Ilion Lika	17.05.1980	1		
Defenders:	**DOB**	**M**	**(s)**	**G**
Jocelin Behiratche (CIV)	08.05.2000	8	(7)	1
Erion Hoxhallari	15.10.1995	33		5
Marsel Ismajlgeci	14.03.2000	31	(2)	4
Omar Musaj	15.04.2002		(4)	
Filip Najdovski (MKD)	13.09.1992	29	(1)	2
Marlind Nuriu	05.07.1997	3	(10)	
Ardit Toli	12.07.1997	24	(4)	
Kristijan Toševski (MKD)	06.05.1994	27	(2)	
Kristi Vangjeli	05.09.1985	19	(3)	
Midfielders:	**DOB**	**M**	**(s)**	**G**
Idriz Batha	28.03.1992	30		9
Luis Birçaj	19.05.2003		(2)	
Winful Cobbinah (GHA)	06.09.1991	2		
Jurgen Çelhaka	06.12.2000	15	(1)	1
Isaac Gyamfi (GHA)	09.09.2000	10	(12)	
Grent Halili	24.05.1998	22	(8)	1
Enes Kuka	14.01.2002	3	(4)	
Klevi Qefalija	12.12.2003		(1)	
Andri Stafa	14.02.2002	1	(1)	
Ibrahim Sulley (GHA)	06.07.2001	1	(1)	
Jurgen Vrapi	14.11.1998	8	(11)	
Forwards:	**DOB**	**M**	**(s)**	**G**
Mario Beshiraj	29.10.1999		(1)	
Élton Pereira Gomes „Calé" (BRA)	12.07.1988	8	(10)	3
Richard Danso (GHA)	16.09.2000	14	(7)	
Aldi Gjumsi	15.03.2002	1	(3)	1
Eldis Kraja	22.03.2000		(1)	
Ernest Muçi	19.03.2001	20		5
Derrick Sasraku (GHA)	12.04.1994	6	(4)	1
Taulant Fatmir Seferi	15.11.1996	22	(1)	7
Agustín Gonzalo Torassa (ARG)	20.10.1988	21	(4)	1
Tim Väyrynen (FIN)	30.03.1993	2	(12)	

Klubi I Futbollit Vllaznia Shkodër

Founded:	16.02.1919 (as Shoqëria Sportive Vllaznia)		
Stadium:	Stadiumi "Loro Boriçi", Shkodër (16,022)		
Trainer:	Thomas Brdarić (GER)		23.01.1975

Goalkeepers:	DOB	M	(s)	G
Kristi Qarri	13.12.2000		(1)	
Bojan Zogovič (MNE)	16.02.1989	36		
Defenders:	**DOB**	**M**	**(s)**	**G**
Mevlan Adili (MKD)	30.03.1994	33		
Tim Brdarić (GER)	04.07.2000		(1)	1
Erdenis Gurishta	24.04.1995	34		
Nertil Hoxhaj	21.05.1997	1	(1)	
Eni Imami	19.12.1992	25		1
Aleksandar Isaevski (MKD)	19.05.1995	29		
Elmir Lekaj	18.01.2000		(1)	
Dajan Shehi	19.03.1997	16	(5)	2
Midfielders:	**DOB**	**M**	**(s)**	**G**
Fjoart Jonuzi	09.07.1996	27	(6)	
Miloš Kalezić (MNE)	09.08.1993	2	(9)	
Arsid Kruja	08.06.1993	18	(14)	
Ardit Krymi	02.05.1996	31	(1)	
Herald Marku	18.05.1996	30		4
Elom Nya-Vedji (TOG)	24.11.1997	2	(11)	
Behar Ramadani	06.04.1990		(6)	
Victor Matheus Da Silva Matos (BRA)	04.01.1995	16	(8)	3
Forwards:	**DOB**	**M**	**(s)**	**G**
Albion Avdijaj	12.01.1994	4	(8)	1
Salim Cissé (GUI)	24.12.1992	2	(13)	
Mehdi Çoba	09.03.2000		(4)	
Haris Dilaver (BIH)	06.02.1990	28	(6)	11
Ismael Salim Dunga (KEN)	24.02.1993	3	(4)	4
Ardit Hoxhaj	20.07.1994	26	(8)	12
Demir Imeri (MKD)	27.10.1995	30	(3)	4
Arlind Kalaja	27.12.1995	3	(22)	1

Group A

1.	KF Burreli	16	10	4	2	26	-	10	34
2.	KS Korabi Peshkopi	16	10	3	3	17	-	8	33
3.	FK Dinamo Tiranë	16	10	2	4	23	-	9	32
4.	KF Vorë	16	6	3	7	10	-	18	21
5.	KF Besëlidhja Lezhë	16	5	5	6	19	-	17	20
6.	KF Erzeni Shijak	16	5	4	7	15	-	13	19
7.	FK Partizani Tiranë "B"	16	3	6	7	14	-	25	15
8.	KF Oriku	16	4	3	9	7	-	15	15
9.	KF Veleçiku Koplik	16	2	4	10	10	-	26	10

Group B

1.	KF Egnatia Rrogozhinë	14	9	4	1	25	-	5	31
2.	KF Tomori Berat	14	9	2	3	23	-	11	29
3.	KS Pogradeci	14	9	1	4	24	-	14	28
4.	KF Besa Kavajë	14	6	3	5	19	-	13	21
5.	KF Lushnja	14	5	4	5	16	-	20	19
6.	KF Turbina Cërrik	14	4	6	4	14	-	16	18
7.	Flamurtari FC Vlorë	14	3	1	10	7	-	20	10
8.	KF Elbasani	14	0	1	13	5	-	34	1
9.	KF Luftëtari Gjirokastër (*Dissolved*)								

Top-4 of each group were qualified for the Promotion Round, while teams ranked 5-9 qualified for the Relegation Round.

Relegation Round

Group A

5.	KF Besëlidhja Lezhë	24	10	6	8	32	-	26	36
6.	KF Erzeni Shijak	24	9	7	8	29	-	22	34
7.	KF Oriku (*Relegation Play-out*)	24	9	4	11	18	-	21	31
8.	FK Partizani Tiranë "B" (*Relegated*)	24	6	6	12	26	-	38	24
9.	KF Veleçiku Koplik (*Relegated*)	24	2	5	17	17	-	46	11

Please note: KF Tërbuni Pukë were excluded from the league and relegated due to violent incidents during their match in Round 22.

Group B

5.	KF Lushnja	20	7	7	6	21	-	25	28
6.	KF Turbina Cërrik	20	6	7	7	23	-	24	25
7.	Flamurtari FC Vlorë (*Relegation Play-out*)	20	5	2	13	14	-	30	14
8.	KF Elbasani (*Relegated*)	20	3	2	15	13	-	40	11

Relegation Play-out [05-06.06.2021]

KF Oriku - KF Butrinti Sarandë	0-1(0-1)
Flamurtari FC Vlorë - KF Tërbuni Pukë	0-0; 4-5 on penalties

Both KF Butrinti Sarandë and KF Tërbuni Pukë will play next season at Second Level, while both KF Oriku and Flamurtari FC Vlorë were relegated to Kategoria e Dytë (Third Level).

Promotion Round

Group A

1.	FK Dinamo Tiranë (*Promoted*)	22	15	2	5	32	-	13	47
2.	KF Burreli (*Promotion Play-off*)	22	13	5	4	35	-	15	44
3.	KS Korabi Peshkopi	22	13	4	5	28	-	14	43
4.	KF Vorë	22	6	3	13	14	-	36	21

Group B

1.	KF Egnatia Rrogozhinë (*Promoted*)	20	14	4	2	36	-	10	46
2.	KF Tomori Berat (*Promotion Play-off*)	20	12	4	4	36	-	20	40
3.	KS Pogradeci	20	10	3	7	32	-	26	33
4.	KF Besa Kavajë	20	7	3	10	26	-	26	24

Promotion Play-off [26.05.2021, Elbasan]

KF Burreli - KF Tomori Berat	1-2(0-1)

First Division Final [22.05.2021, Elbasan]

FK Dinamo Tiranë - KF Egnatia Rrogozhinë	0-1(0-0)

First Division Champions 2020/2021: **KF Egnatia Rrogozhinë**

INTERNATIONAL MATCHES
(16.07.2020 – 15.07.2021)

04.09.2020	Minsk	Belarus - Albania	0-2(0-1)	(UNL)
07.09.2020	Tiranë	Albania - Lithuania	0-1(0-0)	(UNL)
11.10.2020	Almaty	Kazakhstan - Albania	0-0	(UNL)
14.10.2020	Vilnius	Lithuania - Albania	0-0	(UNL)
11.11.2020	Elbasan	Albania - Kosovo	2-1(1-0)	(F)
15.11.2020	Tiranë	Albania - Kazakhstan	3-1(2-1)	(UNL)
18.11.2020	Tiranë	Albania - Belarus	3-2(3-1)	(UNL)
25.03.2021	Andorra la Vella	Andorra - Albania	0-1(0-1)	(WCQ)
28.03.2021	Tiranë	Albania - England	0-2(0-1)	(WCQ)
31.03.2021	Serravalle	San Marino - Albania	0-2(0-0)	(WCQ)
05.06.2021	Cardiff	Wales - Albania	0-0	(F)
08.06.2021	Praha	Czech Republic - Albania	3-1(1-1)	(F)

04.09.2020   BELARUS - ALBANIA   **0-2(0-1)**   2nd UEFA Nations League C, Group 4
Stadion Dynama, Minsk; Referee: Kristoffer Karlsson (Sweden); Attendance: 0
ALB: Thomas Strakosha, Frédéric Shtjefan Veseli, Elseid Gëzim Hysaj (Cap), Berat Ridvan Gjimshiti, Kastriot Luan Dermaku, Lorenc Trashi (68.Odise Roshi), Amir Malush Abrashi, Klaus Fatmir Gjasula, Keidi Bare, Sokol Çikalleshi (72.Bekim Abdyl Balaj), Rey Aldo Manaj (90.Enea Mihaj). Trainer: Edoardo Reja (Italy).
Goals: Sokol Çikalleshi (23), Keidi Bare (78).

07.09.2020   ALBANIA - LITHUANIA   **0-1(0-0)**   2nd UEFA Nations League C, Group 4
Air Albania Stadium, Tiranë; Referee: Serhiy Boyko (Ukraine); Attendance: 0
ALB: Thomas Strakosha, Elseid Gëzim Hysaj (Cap) [*sent off 87*], Berat Ridvan Gjimshiti, Kastriot Luan Dermaku, Lorenc Trashi (60.Odise Roshi; 75.Armando Broja), Enea Mihaj, Amir Malush Abrashi, Klaus Fatmir Gjasula (60.Myrto Artan Uzuni), Qazim Laçi, Armando Durim Sadiku, Rey Aldo Manaj. Trainer: Edoardo Reja (Italy).

11.10.2020   KAZAKHSTAN - ALBANIA   **0-0**   2nd UEFA Nations League C, Group 4
Central Stadium, Almaty; Referee: Dumitru Muntean (Moldova); Attendance: 0
ALB: Etrit Fadil Berisha (Cap), Frédéric Shtjefan Veseli, Berat Ridvan Gjimshiti, Kastriot Luan Dermaku, Lorenc Trashi (82.Hysen Memolla), Marash Kumbulla, Amir Malush Abrashi (86.Qazim Laçi), Keidi Bare, Sherif Kallaku, Rey Aldo Manaj (82.Taulant Fatmir Seferi), Armando Broja. Trainer: Edoardo Reja (Italy).

14.10.2020   LITHUANIA - ALBANIA   **0-0**   2nd UEFA Nations League C, Group 4
LFF stadionas, Vilnius; Referee: Karim Abed (France); Attendance: 696
ALB: Etrit Fadil Berisha (Cap), Ermir Limon Lenjani (46.Lorenc Trashi), Frédéric Shtjefan Veseli, Berat Ridvan Gjimshiti, Kastriot Luan Dermaku, Marash Kumbulla (57.Enea Mihaj), Amir Malush Abrashi, Qazim Laçi (63.Endri Çekiçi), Keidi Bare, Taulant Fatmir Seferi (78.Rey Aldo Manaj), Armando Broja (57.Giacomo Vrioni). Trainer: Edoardo Reja (Italy).

11.11.2020   ALBANIA - KOSOVO   **2-1(1-0)**   Friendly International
Elbasan Arena, Elbasan; Referee: Hüseyin Göçek (Turkey); Attendance: 0
ALB: Etrit Fadil Berisha (Cap) (46.Alban Bekim Hoxha), Erion Hoxhallari (46.Frédéric Shtjefan Veseli), Ardian Ilmi Ismajli, Albi Doka, Ramën Çepele, Qazim Laçi, Ylber Latif Ramadani, Lindon Selahi (65.Sherif Kallaku), Bekim Abdyl Balaj (46.Elseid Gëzim Hysaj), Taulant Fatmir Seferi (46.Rey Aldo Manaj), Myrto Artan Uzuni (85.Marsel Ismailgeci). Trainer: Edoardo Reja (Italy).
Goals: Bekim Abdyl Balaj (31), Myrto Artan Uzuni (65).

15.11.2020   ALBANIA - KAZAKHSTAN   **3-1(2-1)**   2nd UEFA Nations League C, Group 4
Arena Kombëtare, Tiranë; Referee: Xavier Estrada Fernández (Spain); Attendance: 0
ALB: Etrit Fadil Berisha (Cap), Frédéric Shtjefan Veseli, Elseid Gëzim Hysaj, Berat Ridvan Gjimshiti, Ardian Ilmi Ismajli, Amir Malush Abrashi, Ledian Memushaj (87.Lindon Selahi), Sherif Kallaku (54.Klaus Fatmir Gjasula), Sokol Çikalleshi (86.Taulant Fatmir Seferi), Myrto Artan Uzuni (67.Albi Doka), Rey Aldo Manaj (86.Bekim Abdyl Balaj). Trainer: Edoardo Reja (Italy).
Goals: Sokol Çikalleshi (16), Ardian Ilmi Ismajli (23), Rey Aldo Manaj (63 penalty).

18.11.2020   ALBANIA - BELARUS   **3-2(3-1)**   2nd UEFA Nations League C, Group 4
Arena Kombëtare, Tiranë; Referee: Radu Marian Petrescu (Romania); Attendance: 0
ALB: Etrit Fadil Berisha (Cap), Frédéric Shtjefan Veseli, Berat Ridvan Gjimshiti, Hysen Memolla, Ardian Ilmi Ismajli, Albi Doka, Ledian Memushaj (64.Lindon Selahi), Klaus Fatmir Gjasula, Qazim Laçi (90+2.Ylber Latif Ramadani), Sokol Çikalleshi (64.Bekim Abdyl Balaj), Rey Aldo Manaj (71.Myrto Artan Uzuni). Trainer: Edoardo Reja (Italy).
Goals: Sokol Çikalleshi (20, 27 penalty), Rey Aldo Manaj (44).

25.03.2021   ANDORRA - ALBANIA   **0-1(0-1)**   22nd FIFA WC. Qualifiers
Estadi Nacional, Andorra la Vella; Referee: Volen Chinkov (Bulgaria); Attendance: 285
ALB: Etrit Fadil Berisha (Cap), Ermir Limon Lenjani (81.Odise Roshi), Elseid Gëzim Hysaj, Berat Ridvan Gjimshiti, Marash Kumbulla, Ardian Ilmi Ismajli, Ledian Memushaj (62.Qazim Laçi), Klaus Fatmir Gjasula, Keidi Bare, Sokol Çikalleshi (81.Armando Broja), Rey Aldo Manaj (62.Myrto Artan Uzuni). Trainer: Edoardo Reja (Italy).
Goal: Ermir Limon Lenjani (41).

28.03.2021   ALBANIA - ENGLAND   **0-2(0-1)**   22nd FIFA WC. Qualifiers
Arena Kombëtare, Tiranë; Referee: Orel Grinfeld (Israel); Attendance: 200
ALB: Etrit Fadil Berisha (Cap), Frédéric Shtjefan Veseli, Elseid Gëzim Hysaj, Berat Ridvan Gjimshiti, Hysen Memolla (59.Klaus Fatmir Gjasula), Ardian Ilmi Ismajli, Qazim Laçi (89.Ylber Latif Ramadani), Keidi Bare (71.Ledian Memushaj), Sokol Çikalleshi (59.Rey Aldo Manaj), Myrto Artan Uzuni, Armando Broja (59.Ermir Limon Lenjani). Trainer: Edoardo Reja (Italy).

31.03.2021   **SAN MARINO - ALBANIA**   **0-2(0-0)**   22nd FIFA WC. Qualifiers
San Marino Stadium, Serravalle; Referee: Kai Erik Steen (Norway); Attendance: 0
ALB: Thomas Strakosha, Ermir Limon Lenjani (88.Mario Mitaj), Frédéric Shtjefan Veseli, Elseid Gëzim Hysaj (Cap), Berat Ridvan Gjimshiti, Arlind Ajeti, Qazim Laçi (46.Myrto Artan Uzuni), Keidi Bare, Ylber Latif Ramadani, Rey Aldo Manaj (87.Sokol Çikalleshi), Armando Broja (46.Odise Roshi). Trainer: Edoardo Reja (Italy).
Goals: Rey Aldo Manaj (63), Myrto Artan Uzuni (85).

05.06.2021   **WALES - ALBANIA**   **0-0**   Friendly International
Cardiff City Stadium, Cardiff; Referee: Neil Anthony Doyle (Republic of Ireland); Attendance: 6,500
ALB: Gentian Selmani, Ermir Limon Lenjani (61.Lorenc Trashi), Berat Ridvan Gjimshiti, Marash Kumbulla, Ardian Ilmi Ismajli, Albi Doka (46.Frédéric Shtjefan Veseli), Amir Malush Abrashi (Cap), Endri Çekiçi (76.Sherif Kallaku), Keidi Bare (76.Qazim Laçi), Bekim Abdyl Balaj (60.Sokol Çikalleshi), Rey Aldo Manaj (77.Taulant Fatmir Seferi). Trainer: Edoardo Reja (Italy).

08.06.2021   **CZECH REPUBLIC - ALBANIA**   **3-1(1-1)**   Friendly International
Generali Arena, Praha; Referee: Peter Kralović (Slovakia); Attendance: 1,351
ALB: Gentian Selmani, Frédéric Shtjefan Veseli (71.Albi Doka), Berat Ridvan Gjimshiti, Lorenc Trashi (71.Ermir Limon Lenjani), Marash Kumbulla, Ardian Ilmi Ismajli, Amir Malush Abrashi (Cap) (81.Qazim Laçi), Keidi Bare, Sherif Kallaku (54.Endri Çekiçi), Sokol Çikalleshi (81.Taulant Fatmir Seferi), Rey Aldo Manaj (81.Bekim Abdyl Balaj). Trainer: Edoardo Reja (Italy).
Goal: Sokol Çikalleshi (42).

NATIONAL TEAM PLAYERS
(16.07.2020 – 15.07.2021)

Name	DOB	Caps	Goals	2020/2021:	*Club*
Goalkeepers					
Etrit Fadil BERISHA	10.03.1989	66	0	2020/2021:	*SPAL Ferrara (ITA)*
Alban Bekim HOXHA	23.11.1987	4	0	2020:	*FK Partizani Tiranë*
Gentian SELMANI	09.03.1998	2	0	2021:	*Boluspor Kulübü (TUR)*
Thomas STRAKOSHA	19.03.1995	15	0	2020/2021:	*SS Lazio Roma (ITA)*
Defenders					
Arlind Afrim AJETI	25.09.1993	21	1	2021:	*AC Reggiana 1919 (ITA)*
Ramën ÇEPELE	21.03.2003	1	0	2020:	*SV Hannover 96 (GER)*
Kastriot Luan DERMAKU	15.01.1992	11	1	2020:	*Parma Calcio 1913 (ITA)*
				05.10.2020->	*US Lecce (ITA)*
Albi DOKA	26.06.1977	5	0	2020/2021:	*HNK Gorica (CRO)*
Berat Ridvan GJIMSHITI	19.02.1993	40	1	2020/2021:	*Atalanta Bergamasca Calcio (ITA)*
Erion HOXHALLARI	15.10.1995	1	0	2020:	*KF Tiranë*
Elseid Gëzim HYSAJ	02.02.1994	59	1	2020/2021:	*SSC Napoli (ITA)*
Marsel ISMAILGECI	14.03.2000	1	0	2020:	*KF Tiranë*
Ardian Ilmi ISMAJLI	30.09.1996	18	0	2020/2021:	*Spezia Calcio (ITA)*
Marash KUMBULLA	08.02.2000	6	0	2020/2021:	*AS Roma (ITA)*
Ermir Limon LENJANI	05.08.1989	39	4	2020/2021:	*Grasshopper Club Zürich (SUI)*
Hysen MEMOLLA	03.07.1992	6	0	2020/2021:	*Diósgyőri VTK (HUN)*
Enea MIHAJ	05.07.1998	5	0	2020:	*PAOK Thessaloníki (GRE)*
Mario MITAJ	06.08.2003	1	0	2021:	*AEK Athína (GRE)*
Lorenc TRASHI	19.05.1992	9	1	2020/2021:	*Al Qadisia SC Kuwait City (KUW)*
Frédéric Shtjefan VESELI	20.11.1992	36	0	2020/2021:	*US Salernitana 1919 (ITA)*
Midfielders					
Amir Malush ABRASHI	27.03.1990	42	1	2020:	*SC Freiburg (GER)*
				27.01.2021->	*FC Basel (SUI)*
Keidi BARE	28.08.1997	15	2	2020:	*Málaga CF (ESP)*
				22.09.2020->	*RCD Espanyol Barcelona (ESP)*
Endri ÇEKIÇI	23.11.1996	3	0	2020/2021:	*MKE Ankaragücü SK (TUR)*
Klaus Fatmir GJASULA	14.12.1989	11	0	2020/2021:	*Hamburger SV (GER)*
Sherif KALLAKU	01.03.1998	5	0	2020/2021:	*NK Lokomotiva Zagreb (CRO)*
Qazim LAÇI	19.01.1996	10	0	2020/2021:	*AC Ajaccio (FRA)*
Ledian MEMUSHAJ	07.12.1986	44	1	2020/2021:	*Delfino Pescara 1936 (ITA)*
Ylber Latif RAMADANI	12.04.1996	11	1	2020/2021:	*Vejle BK (DEN)*
Odise ROSHI	22.05.1991	61	5	2020:	*FK Akhmat Grozny (RUS)*
				15.02.2021->	*Diósgyőri VTK (HUN)*
Lindon SELAHI	26.02.1999	4	0	2020:	*FC Twente Enschede (NED)*

				Forwards	
Bekim Abdyl BALAJ	11.01.1991	43	8	2020/2021:	*SK Sturm Graz (AUT)*
Armando BROJA	10.09.2001	6	0	2020/2021:	*SBV Vitesse Arnhem (NED)*
Sokol ÇIKALLESHI	27.07.1990	42	11	2020:	*Akhisar Belediye Gençlik ve Spor Kulübü (TUR)*
				11.09.2020->	*Konyaspor Kulübü (TUR)*
Rey Aldo MANAJ	24.02.1997	25	6	2020/2021:	*FC Barcelona (ESP)*
Armando Durim SADIKU	27.05.1991	38	12	2020:	*Büyükşehir Belediye Erzurumspor (TUR)*
Taulant Fatmir SEFERI	15.11.1996	1	0	2020:	*BSC Young Boys Bern (SUI)*
				04.01.2021->	*KF Tiranë*
Myrto Artan UZUNI	31.05.1995	8	0	2020/2021:	*Ferencvárosi TC (HUN)*
Giacomo VRIONI	15.10.1998	2	0	2020:	*Juventus FC Torino (ITA)*

	Trainer	
Edoardo REJA (Italy) [from 17.04.2019]	10.10.1945	20 M; 9 W; 4 D; 7 L; 27-22

ANDORRA

The Country:
Principality of Andorra (Principat d'Andorra)
Capital: Andorra la Vella
Surface: 467,63 km²
Inhabitants: 77,543 [2020]
Time: UTC+1

The FA:
Federació Andorrana de Futbol
c/ Batlle Tomàs, 4 Baixos, AD700 Escaldes-Engordany
Tel: +376 805 830
Foundation date: 1994
Member of FIFA since: 1996
Member of UEFA since: 1996
Website: www.faf.ad

NATIONAL TEAM RECORDS

RECORDS
First international match:	13.11.1996, Andorra la Vella: Andorra – Estonia 1-6
Most international caps:	Ildefons Lima Solà - 130 caps (1997-2019)
Most international goals:	Ildefons Lima Solà - 11 goal / 130 caps (1997-2019)

UEFA EUROPEAN CHAMPIONSHIP
1960	-
1964	-
1968	-
1972	-
1976	-
1980	-
1984	-
1988	-
1992	-
1996	Did not enter
2000	Qualifiers
2004	Qualifiers
2008	Qualifiers
2012	Qualifiers
2016	Qualifiers
2020	Qualifiers

FIFA WORLD CUP
1930	-
1934	-
1938	-
1950	-
1954	-
1958	-
1962	-
1966	-
1970	-
1974	-
1978	-
1982	-
1986	-
1990	-
1994	Did not enter
1998	Did not enter
2002	Qualifiers
2006	Qualifiers
2010	Qualifiers
2014	Qualifiers
2018	Qualifiers

OLYMPIC TOURNAMENTS
1908	-
1912	-
1920	-
1924	-
1928	-
1936	-
1948	-
1952	-
1956	-
1960	-
1964	-
1968	-
1972	-
1976	-
1980	-
1984	*Withdrew*
1988	-
1992	*Withdrew*
1996	-
2000	Qualifiers
2004	Qualifiers
2008	Did not enter
2012	Qualifiers
2016	Qualifiers

UEFA NATIONS LEAGUE
2018/2019	League D
2020/2021	League D

FIFA CONFEDERATIONS CUP 1992-2017
None

ANDORRAN CLUB HONOURS IN EUROPEAN CLUB COMPETITIONS:

European Champion Clubs.Cup (1956-1992) / UEFA Champions League (1993-2021)
None

Fairs Cup (1858-1971) / UEFA Cup (1972-2009) / UEFA Europa League (2010-2021)
None

UEFA Super Cup (1972-2020)
None

European Cup Winners.Cup 1961-1999*
None

*defunct competition

	CHAMPIONS	CUP WINNERS	BEST GOALSCORERS	
1990/1991	-	FC Santa Coloma	-	
1991/1992	-	*No competition*	-	
1992/1993	-	*No competition*	-	
1993/1994	-	CE Principat Andorra La Vella	-	
1994/1995	FC Santa Colomaa	CE Principat Andorra La Vella	-	
1995/1996	FC Encamp	CE Principat Andorra La Vella	-	
1996/1997	CE Principat Andorra La Vella	CE Principat Andorra La Vella	Patricio González Fernández (CE Principat Andorra La Vella)	25
1997/1998	CE Principat Andorra La Vella	CE Principat Andorra La Vella	Rafael Sánchez Pedrosa (ESP, FC Santa Coloma)	36
1998/1999	CE Principat Andorra La Vella	CE Principat Andorra La Vella	-	
1999/2000	Constel·lació Esportiva Andorra La Vella	Constel·lació Esportiva Andorra La Vella	-	
2000/2001	FC Santa Coloma	FC Santa Coloma	-	
2001/2002	FC Encamp	FC Lusitanos Andorra La Vella	-	
2002/2003	FC Santa Coloma	FC Santa Coloma	-	
2003/2004	FC Santa Coloma	FC Santa Coloma	Jorge Filipe Sa Silva Carneiro (POR, UE Sant Julià)	16
2004/2005	UE Sant Julià	FC Santa Coloma	-	
2005/2006	FC Rànger's Andorra La Vella	FC Santa Coloma	-	
2006/2007	FC Rànger's Andorra La Vella	FC Santa Coloma	Norberto Urbani (ARG, FC Rànger's Andorra La Vella) Joan Carles Toscano Beltrán (FC Santa Coloma)	14
2007/2008	FC Santa Coloma	UE Sant Julià	-	-
2008/2009	UE Sant Julià	FC Santa Coloma	Norberto Urbani (ARG, FC Rànger's Andorra La Vella)	22
2009/2010	FC Santa Coloma	UE Sant Julià	Gabriel Riera Lancha (UE Sant Julià)	19
2010/2011	FC Santa Coloma	UE Sant Julià	Victor Bernat Cuadros (ESP, UE Santa Coloma)	16
2011/2012	FC Lusitanos Andorra La Vella	FC Santa Coloma	Victor Bernat Cuadros (ESP, UE Santa Coloma)	14
2012/2013	FC Lusitanos Andorra La Vella	UE Santa Coloma	Bruno Filipe Raposo Fernandes "Bruninho" (POR, FC Lusitanos Andorra La Vella)	17
2013/2014	FC Santa Coloma	UE Sant Julià	Luis Miguel dos Reis (POR, FC Lusitanos Andorra La Vella)	13
2014/2015	FC Santa Coloma	UE Sant Julià	Cristian Martínez Alejo (FC Santa Coloma)	22
2015/2016	FC Santa Coloma	UE Santa Coloma	Victor Bernat Cuadros (ESP, UE Santa Coloma)	12
2016/2017	FC Santa Coloma	UE Santa Coloma	Victor Bernat Cuadros (ESP, UE Santa Coloma)	18
2017/2018	FC Santa Coloma	FC Santa Coloma	Jesús David Sosa Sebastiá "Chus Sosa" (ESP, FC Santa Coloma)	14
2018/2019	FC Santa Coloma	UE Engordany	Nicolás Estebán Medina Ríos (CHI, FC Lusitanos Andorra La Vella) Joel Méndez del Río (ESP, UE Sant Julià) Enric Pi Solá (ESP, UE Sant Julià) Genís Soldevila Soldurga (ESP, Inter Club d'Escaldes)	10
2019/2020	Inter Club d'Escaldes	Inter Club d'Escaldes	Genís Soldevila Soldurga (ESP, Inter Club d'Escaldes)	15
2020/2021	Inter Club d'Escaldes	UE Sant Julià	Guillaume Silvain Lopez (FRA, UE Engordany)	16

NATIONAL CHAMPIONSHIP
Primera Divisió 2020/2021
(29.11.2020 – 23.05.2021)

Regular Season - Results

Round 1 [29.11.2020]
FC Santa Coloma - UE Engordany 2-2
Inter Club d'Escaldes - UE Sant Julià 3-1
CE Carroi - FC Penya 0-3 *awarded*
AC d'Escaldes-UE Santa Coloma 0-0 [09.12.]

Round 2 [06.12.2020]
FC Penya - Inter Club d'Escaldes 0-1
UE Santa Coloma - CE Carroi 1-0
UE Engordany-AC d'Escaldes 1-1 [17.01.21]
UE Sant Julià-FC Santa Coloma 1-1[17.01.21]

Round 3 [13.12.2020]
AC d'Escaldes - CE Carroi 2-1
FC Santa Coloma - FC Penya 3-0
Inter Club d'Escaldes - UE Santa Coloma 0-0
UE Engordany-UE Sant Julià 3-0 [21.01.2021]

Round 4 [16-17.12.2020]
UE Sant Julià - AC d'Escaldes 2-1
FC Penya - UE Engordany 1-1
UE Santa Coloma - FC Santa Coloma 0-1
CE Carroi - Inter Club d'Escaldes 2-0

Round 5 [20.12.2020]
UE Engordany - UE Santa Coloma 2-0
FC Santa Coloma - CE Carroi 1-2
AC d'Escaldes - Inter Club d'Escaldes 2-1
UE Sant Julià - FC Penya 6-2

Round 6 [24.01.2021]
UE Santa Coloma - UE Sant Julià 1-2
AC d'Escaldes - FC Penya 3-0
CE Carroi - UE Engordany 0-2
Inter Club d'Escaldes - FC Santa Coloma 1-1

Round 7 [31.01.2021]
FC Penya - UE Santa Coloma 1-2
UE Sant Julià - CE Carroi 2-1
FC Santa Coloma - AC d'Escaldes 0-2
UE Engordany - Inter Club d'Escaldes 0-2

Round 8 [07.02.2021]
UE Engordany - FC Santa Coloma 2-2
UE Sant Julià - Inter Club d'Escaldes 0-2
FC Penya - CE Carroi 3-0
UE Santa Coloma - AC d'Escaldes 1-0

Round 9 [14.02.2021]
AC d'Escaldes - UE Engordany 3-3
Inter Club d'Escaldes - FC Penya 6-0
FC Santa Coloma - UE Sant Julià 2-2
CE Carroi - UE Santa Coloma 1-3

Round 10 [21.02.2021]
CE Carroi - AC d'Escaldes 0-2
UE Santa Coloma - Inter Club d'Escaldes 0-3
FC Penya - FC Santa Coloma 0-2
UE Sant Julià - UE Engordany 1-2

Round 11 [28.02.2021]
UE Engordany - FC Penya 5-0
Inter Club d'Escaldes - CE Carroi 2-0
AC d'Escaldes - UE Sant Julià 1-1
FC Santa Coloma - UE Santa Coloma 1-0

Round 12 [07.03.2021]
UE Santa Coloma - UE Engordany 3-1
FC Penya - UE Sant Julià 0-3
CE Carroi - FC Santa Coloma 0-3
Inter Club d'Escaldes - AC d'Escaldes 0-0

Round 13 [14.03.2021]	Round 14 [11.04.2021]
UE Sant Julià - UE Santa Coloma 3-1	CE Carroi - UE Sant Julià 0-3
FC Santa Coloma - Inter Club d'Escaldes 1-1	AC d'Escaldes - FC Santa Coloma 0-2
UE Engordany - CE Carroi 1-1	Inter Club d'Escaldes - UE Engordany 0-0
FC Penya - AC d'Escaldes 0-8	UE Santa Coloma - FC Penya 7-0 [18.04.]

Regular Season - League table

					Total			Home			Away	
1. Inter Club d'Escaldes	14	7	5	2	22 - 7	26	3 4 0	12 - 2		4 1 2	10 - 5	
2. FC Santa Coloma	14	6	6	2	22 - 13	24	2 3 2	10 - 9		4 3 0	12 - 4	
3. UE Sant Julià	14	7	3	4	27 - 20	24	4 1 2	15 - 10		3 2 2	12 - 10	
4. Atlètic Club d'Escaldes Escaldes-Engordany	14	6	5	3	25 - 12	23	3 3 1	11 - 8		3 2 2	14 - 4	
5. UE Engordany	14	5	7	2	25 - 16	22	3 3 1	14 - 6		2 4 1	11 - 10	
6. UE Santa Coloma	14	6	2	6	19 - 15	20	4 0 3	13 - 7		2 2 3	6 - 8	
7. FC Penya d'Andorra	14	2	1	11	10 - 47	7	1 1 5	5 - 17		1 0 6	5 - 30	
8. CE Carroi	14	2	1	11	8 - 28	7	1 0 6	3 - 16		1 1 5	5 - 12	

Top-4 teams were qualified for the Championship Play-offs, while teams ranked 5-8 were qualified for the Relegation Play-offs.

Relegation Play-offs - Results

Round 15 [21-22.04.2021]	Round 16 [25.04.2021]	Round 17 [02.05.2021]
FC Penya - UE Engordany 0-4	CE Carroi - UE Engordany 1-1	UE Engordany - UE Santa Coloma 2-5
UE Santa Coloma - CE Carroi 1-1	UE Santa Coloma - FC Penya 9-0	FC Penya - CE Carroi 1-3

Round 18 [09.05.2021]	Round 19 [16.05.2021]	Round 20 [21-22.05.2021]
UE Engordany - FC Penya 4-3	UE Engordany - CE Carroi 1-1	CE Carroi - FC Penya 3-0
CE Carroi - UE Santa Coloma 3-2	FC Penya - UE Santa Coloma 0-4	UE Santa Coloma - UE Engordany 4-6

Final Standings

					Total			Home			Away	
5. UE Engordany	20	8	9	3	43 - 30	33	4 4 2	21 - 15		4 5 1	22 - 15	
6. UE Santa Coloma	20	9	3	8	44 - 27	30	5 1 4	27 - 14		4 2 4	17 - 13	
7. CE Carroi (Relegation Play-off)	20	5	4	11	20 - 33	19	3 1 6	10 - 19		2 3 5	10 - 14	
8. FC Penya d'Andorra (Relegated)	20	2	1	17	13 - 74	7	1 1 8	5 - 28		1 0 9	8 - 46	

Championship Play-offs - Results

Round 15 [18.04.2021]	Round 16 [25.04.2021]	Round 17 [02.05.2021]
UE Sant Julià - AC d'Escaldes 2-2	AC d'Escaldes - Inter Club d'Escaldes 1-4	FC Santa Coloma - AC d'Escaldes 0-0
FC Santa Coloma - Inter Club d'Escaldes 1-2	UE Sant Julià - FC Santa Coloma 2-0	Inter Club d'Escal. - UE Sant Julià 1-0 [12.05.]

Round 18 [09.05.2021]	Round 19 [16.05.2021]	Round 20 [23.05.2021]
Inter Club d'Escaldes - FC Santa Coloma 1-1	Inter Club d'Escaldes - AC d'Escaldes 4-0	UE Sant Julià - Inter Club d'Escaldes 1-0
AC d'Escaldes - UE Sant Julià 0-1	FC Santa Coloma - UE Sant Julià 1-0	AC d'Escaldes - FC Santa Coloma 1-3

Final Standings

					Total			Home			Away	
1. Inter Club d'Escaldes	20	11	6	3	34 - 11	39	5 5 0	18 - 3		6 1 3	16 - 8	
2. UE Sant Julià	20	10	4	6	33 - 24	34	6 2 2	20 - 12		4 2 4	13 - 12	
3. FC Santa Coloma	20	8	8	4	28 - 19	32	3 4 3	12 - 11		5 4 1	16 - 8	
4. Atlètic Club d'Escaldes Escaldes-Engordany	20	6	7	7	29 - 26	25	3 3 4	13 - 16		3 4 3	16 - 10	

Top goalscorers:	
16 Guillaume Silvain Lopez (FRA)	UE Engordany
15 Youssef Ezzejjari Lhasnaoui (ESP)	CE Carroi
15 Joel Paredes Leonés (ESP)	UE Santa Coloma
13 Genís Soldevila Soldúga (ESP)	Inter Club d'Escaldes
12 Victor Bernat Cuadros (ESP)	UE Santa Coloma

Relegation Play-offs

FS La Massana - CE Carroi   0-2   1-3
CE Carroi remains at first level for 2021/2022.

NATIONAL CUP
Copa Constitució Final 2020/2021

First Round [17-18.02.2021]				
CE Carroi - CF Atlètic Amèrica	2-0	FC Santa Coloma - FC Encamp	7-0
FC Penya d'Andorra – FC Ordino	2-1	UE Santa Coloma - FS La Massana	4-0

Quarter-Finals [03-04.03.2021]				
Inter Club d'Escaldes - CE Carroi	2-0	UE Engordany - FC Santa Coloma	0-1
UE Sant Julià - FC Penya d'Andorra	4-1	Atlètic Club d'Escaldes - UE Santa Coloma	3-0

Semi-Finals [14-15.04.2021]				
Inter Club d'Escaldes - UE Sant Julià	1-2	FC Santa Coloma - Atlètic Club d'Escaldes	1-2

Final

30.05.2021; Estadi Nacional, Andorra la Vella; Referee: Rui Miquel Maciel De Queiros; Attendance: 0
UE Sant Julià - Atlètic Club d'Escaldes Escaldes-Engordany   **2-1(1-1)**

UE Sant Julià: Ismael Gúzman Gómez, Miguel Ruiz Enamorado [*sent off 87*], Xavier „Xavi" Carmona Velasco (46.Pedro Muñoz Fontalba), Lambilate Jordan Tawaba Tawaba, Rui Filipe Figueiras de Beja, Matías Nicolás Vaamonde (67.Frédéric Koutou Nimani Ngalou), Sebastià Bertrán Suárez (82.Valentín Rizzo), Óscar García González, François David Gomis Mendy, David Virgili Fernández, Bubacar Njie Kambi „Bácari". Trainer: Fernando Néstor Ochoaizpur Iturain (Bolivia).

AC d'Escaldes: Alejandro „Álex" Ruiz Campagne, Matías Rudler, Adrián Rodrigues Gonçalves [*sent off 52*], Moisés San Nicolás Schellens, Rafael Amaral Santos Brito, Xavier Vieira de Vasconcelos, Nikola Žugić (67.Jaime Andrés Grondona Bobadilla), Jesús Álvarez Marín, Luigi San Nicolas Schellens (62.Gilson Correia), Fabio Felipe Serra Alves, Borja Pimentel (83.Gastón Rodrigo Machado López). Trainer: Luis Blanco Torrado (Spain).

Goals: 0-1 Nikola Žugić (37), 1-1 Bubacar Njie Kambi „Bácari" (42), 2-1 Rafael Amaral Santos Brito (90+2 own goal).

THE CLUBS 2020/2021

Please note: number of matches, substitutes and goals includes statistics of both regular season and Play-offs (Championship & Relegation Play-offs).

Atlètic Club d'Escaldes Escaldes-Engordany

Founded: 2002
Stadium: Camp de Fútbol d'Aixovall (1,000)
Trainer: Luis Blanco Torrado (ESP)   27.12.1959

Goalkeepers:	DOB	M	(s)	G
Alejandro „Álex" Ruiz Campagne (FRA)	03.09.1991	20		
Defenders:	**DOB**	**M**	**(s)**	**G**
Rafael Amaral Santos Brito (POR)	06.07.1986	14		2
Gilson Correia (GNB)	05.04.1997	6	(4)	
David Maneiro Ton	16.02.1989		(4)	
Christián Alexander Paredes Ponce (PER)	16.04.1987		(3)	
Adrián Rodrigues Gonçalves	14.08.1988	19		2
Jesús Rubio Gómez	09.09.1994	4	(3)	
Matías Rudler (ARG)	25.04.1988	18		
Moisés San Nicolás Schellens	17.09.1993	18		
Midfielders:	**DOB**	**M**	**(s)**	**G**
Jesús Álvarez Marín (ESP)	01.04.1993	9	(3)	
Felipe Xavier Vasconcelos (BRA)	19.01.1999		(4)	

	DOB	M	(s)	G
Gastón Rodrigo Machado López (URU)	19.01.1986	7	(8)	5
Nicolas Mariano Minutella (ARG)	23.03.1995	10	(5)	1
José María Ramírez Gutiérrez (MEX)	21.01.1999	2	(4)	
Gemelson Nayry Fay Bill Vieira (GNB)	04.08.1992	13	(3)	3
Xavier Vieira de Vasconcelos	14.01.1992	14	(5)	4
Nikola Žugić (SRB)	30.01.1990	17		2
Forwards:	**DOB**	**M**	**(s)**	**G**
Fabio Felipe Serra Alves (POR)	24.08.1984	17		
Jaime Andrés Grondona Bobadilla (CHI)	15.04.1987	13	(4)	3
Dylan Hernández Orribo (ESP)	20.04.1996	1	(3)	1
Borja Pimentel		7	(10)	4
Daniel Alberto Rojas Gómez (COL)	09.07.1996		(3)	
Luigi San Nicolas Schellens	28.06.1992	11	(5)	2

Club Esportiu Carroi

Founded: 2014
Stadium: Camp de Fútbol d'Aixovall (1,000)
Trainer: Francisco „Paco" Muñoz Montesinos   22.11.1983

Goalkeepers:	DOB	M	(s)	G
Matías Basterrechea (ARG)	02.01.1994	13	(1)	
José Carlos Cortaberría Gasso (URU)	30.08.1990	7	(1)	
Defenders:	**DOB**	**M**	**(s)**	**G**
Armando Avelar Castañeda	17.08.1991	2	(2)	
Ahmed Chelli (TUN)	16.03.1980	1	(3)	
Renzo Alejandro Dezotti (ARG)	17.11.1990		(3)	
Quentin Laffont (FRA)	17.01.1996	10	(1)	
Alfredo Martins (POR)	01.01.1997	12	(4)	
Jorge Miquel Pinto Pedro	15.05.1994	16	(1)	
Rui Filipe Barroso Ribeiro (POR)	13.09.1997	8	(8)	
Souleymane Sylla (ESP)	27.06.1995	1	(3)	
Rodrigo Varela (ARG)	12.04.1991	6	(5)	
Xabier Zaldua Marcen (ESP)	19.07.2001	17		

Midfielders:	DOB	M	(s)	G
Abdelghani El Bachir (NED)	24.06.2000	4	(3)	
Gianni Giglio (FRA)	03.02.1995	5	(4)	1
Gustavo Giordani (BRA)	08.12.1993	9	(4)	
Hélder Jesus Teixeira (POR)	10.04.1996	8	(8)	
Alfonso Alejandro Huerta (MEX)	19.11.1990	16	(2)	1
Amin Kechout (FRA)	11.01.1999	12		
José Rafael Martins Alves	07.11.1991	8	(4)	2
Víctor Hugo Pérez Reyes (MEX)	12.11.1990	16	(1)	
Mohamed Sow (SEN)	24.01.2000	20		
Forwards:	**DOB**	**M**	**(s)**	**G**
Youssef Ezzejjari Lhasnaoui (ESP)	10.05.1993	18	(2)	15
Daniel Alberto Rojas Gómez (COL)	09.07.1996	2	(2)	
Bryan Estefano Orbegozo Chang Kau (PER)	10.07.1995	7	(3)	
Cristian Alexander Ruiz (COL)	11.04.1997	2	(11)	1

Unió Esportiva Engordany

Founded: 1980
Stadium: Estadi Comunal d'Andorra la Vella (1,300)
Trainer: José Luis Mengual Prades   16.03.1963
[01.11.2020] Emiliano González Arquez (ESP)   20.09.1969

Goalkeepers:	DOB	M	(s)	G
Jesús Coca Noguerol (ESP)	22.05.1989	11		
Sebastián Obregón Valencia (COL)	16.01.1995	1		
Francisco Manuel Pires Costa „Xisco"	25.01.1998	8		
Defenders:	**DOB**	**M**	**(s)**	**G**
Sébastien Jacques Manuel Aguero (FRA)	17.08.1993	20		
Marvin Assane (FRA)	30.07.1993	10	(3)	1
Denzel Budde (NED)	08.04.1997	7		
Sergio Peris Martínez (ESP)	04.08.1994	16	(1)	
Lucas Maciel Sousa (POR)	06.03.1991	11	(3)	1
Antonio "Toni" Jesús Escobedo Luna (ESP)	29.11.1996	6	(2)	
Midfielders:	**DOB**	**M**	**(s)**	**G**
Amath Diedhiou (SEN)	19.11.1989	11	(7)	4
Edson da Silva Oliveira (POR)	15.12.1998	1		
Steven Leblanc (GYF)	24.09.2001	2	(5)	

	DOB	M	(s)	G
Kalvin Paul (FRA)	02.07.2001	11	(6)	1
Kyllan Ramé (FRA)	25.07.1997	11	(1)	1
Mario Valentín Spano (URU)	07.02.1986	9	(2)	1
João Pedro da Silva Teixeira (POR)	17.07.1996	15	(2)	
Forwards:	**DOB**	**M**	**(s)**	**G**
Brice Boufrizi (FRA)	22.02.1998	4	(4)	
Elías Iñarra Portilla (ESP)	1995		(1)	
Sebastián Gómez Pérez	01.11.1983	14	(2)	3
Morgan Lafont (FRA)	22.11.1996	17	(3)	5
Guillaume Silvain Lopez (FRA)	30.01.1999	18		16
Agustín Gustavo Márquez Cancela (URU)	18.06.1985	3	(10)	
Cristian Manuel Millán Pichel	02.06.2003		(1)	
Aarón Sánchez Alburquerque	05.06.1996	11	(6)	8
William Da Silva Oliveira (BRA)	21.02.1995	3	(9)	1

Inter Club d'Escaldes

Founded: 1991
Stadium: Estadi Comunal d'Andorra la Vella (1,300)
Trainer: Antonio Rodríguez Sarabia "Rodri"(ESP)   28.01.1971

Goalkeepers:	DOB	M	(s)	G
Josep Antoni Gomes Moreira	03.12.1985	18	(1)	
Jordi Ribó Puig (ESP)	1993	1		
Gerardo José Rubio Ortuna (ESP)	17.05.1987	1		
Defenders:	**DOB**	**M**	**(s)**	**G**
Federico Bessone Luna (ARG)	23.01.1984	2	(2)	
Pau Bosch Hueso (ESP)	30.03.1988	15		2
Iván De Nova Ruiz (ESP)	22.09.1996	12		1
Josep Maria Cabanes Foix	02.04.1996		(2)	
Adrià Gallego Arias (ESP)	09.04.1990	5	(5)	
Emili Josep García Miramontes	11.01.1989	14	(3)	
Ildefons Lima Solà	10.12.1979	8	(2)	1
Xavier Moreno Marín	03.12.1990		(2)	
Óscar Reyes Sánchez (ESP)	12.03.1988	2	(1)	
José Antonio Rodríguez Munera (ESP)	01.07.1985	14		
Jordi Rubio Gómez	01.11.1987	12	(2)	
Rui Filipe Figueiras de Beja (POR)	14.04.1993		(1)	

Midfielders:	DOB	M	(s)	G
Andrés Briñez Aranda (COL)	1996	2	(2)	
Ludovic Clemente Garcés	09.06.1987	4	(6)	
Marc Pujol Pons	21.08.1982	13		5
Jordi Roca Grau	23.08.1989	9	(5)	
Antonio Lao Dona „Toni Lao" (ESP)	17.01.1984	6	(11)	
Forwards:	**DOB**	**M**	**(s)**	**G**
Gerard Artigas Fonullet (ESP)	10.01.1995	13	(2)	7
Jordi Betriu Armengol (ESP)	29.06.1995	15	(5)	2
Bruno Filipe Raposo Fernandes "Bruninho" (POR)	11.01.1986	7	(11)	1
Bruno Mauricio Lemiechevsky Melessi (URU)	03.03.1994	2	(3)	
Cristian Martínez Alejo	16.10.1989	5	(9)	1
Nicolás Esteban Medina Ríos (CHI)	28.03.1987	3	(5)	1
Sergio Moreno Marín	25.11.1987	17	(2)	
Julià Sánchez Soto	20.06.1978		(1)	
Genís Soldevila Solduga (ESP)	03.03.1987	20		13

Fútbol Club Penya d'Andorra

Founded: 2009
Stadium: Centre d'Entrenament de la FAF, Andorra la Vella (300)
Trainer: Albert Jansà Girona

Goalkeepers:	DOB	M	(s)	G
David Emanuel Martins Gonçalves		2		
Jordi Rodríguez Bertran	01.12.1993	17		
Defenders:	**DOB**	**M**	**(s)**	**G**
Alexandre Correia Alfaiate (POR)	17.08.1995	19		2
Miguel Ángel Braz Vieira	01.10.1997	1	(2)	
David Sebastián Cortez Lillo	1993	4	(1)	
Francesc Estragues Valor (ESP)	17.04.1990	12	(2)	
Hugo Micael Costa Gonçalves (POR)		10	(3)	
Rui Filipe Gonçalves Pinheiro	17.08.1991	1	(1)	
Aarón Martínez Jiménez	24.05.2000	7	(6)	
Jaime Alberto Ruiz Córdoba (COL)*	11.04.1997	9	(4)	
Jaime Andrés Ruiz Córdoba (COL)	20.11.1994	14	(5)	
Midfielders:	**DOB**	**M**	**(s)**	**G**
Jules Bidau (FRA)	30.07.1996	10	(1)	
Tom Issac Robin Bondon (FRA)	15.03.1997	17	(2)	1
Iván Prada Panizo (ESP)	06.03.1998	8	(3)	

	DOB	M	(s)	G
Mohamed Kara (FRA)	16.08.1999	2	(5)	
Manuel „Manu" Jiménez Pesquer (ESP)	16.12.1996	5		1
Diego Rafael Marinho Leite	16.06.1992	3	(2)	
Dominic Pereira Cunha	04.05.1994	12		
Rui Manuel Sampaio Vilela	08.07.2000	1		
Forwards:	**DOB**	**M**	**(s)**	**G**
Raúl Ahibar Torres (ESP)	03.05.1991	3	(1)	1
Narcis Barrera Vilert (ESP)	28.10.1988		(1)	
Lucas Emanuel Galvez (ARG)	05.04.1992	5	(1)	
Carlos Manuel Gomes Do Nascimento	18.10.1993	11	(2)	3
Gabriel Marcel Leighton Mateos	16.10.2000	9	(9)	
Lluis Martins Batista (BRA)	1998	13	(4)	2
Karim Nlamu (FRA)	28.02.2000	4	(3)	
Joan Palomino Abril (ESP)	2001	2		
Rafael Pereira Lameiro	1998		(1)	
Brian Pubill dos Santos	26.07.2000	10	(3)	1
Sergio Urbano López (ESP)	08.12.1986	9	(3)	

played 1 match as goalkeeper (Relegation Round, Round 20: CE Carroi - FC Penya 3-0).

Unió Esportiva Sant Julià de Lòria

Founded: 1982
Stadium: Estadi Comunal d'Andorra la Vella (1,300)
Trainer: Claudio David Festa Celiz (ARG)
[03.03.2021] Fernando Néstor Ochoaizpur Iturain (BOL)   18.03.1971

Goalkeepers:	DOB	M	(s)	G
Fermín Holgado Guerediaga (ARG)	17.05.1994	18		
Iván Periáñez Meca	25.01.1982	2	(1)	
Defenders:	**DOB**	**M**	**(s)**	**G**
Rui Filipe Figueiras de Beja (POR)	14.04.1993	12		
Marco Adrián Colono Limia (ARG)	03.03.1995	11	(1)	1
Guillem Joan Laporta Echevarría (ESP)	20.03.1997	2	(3)	
Hernán Festa Sáez (ESP)	23.08.2000		(4)	
Leandro González Andrada (ESP)	14.10.1999	2	(2)	
Pedro Muñoz Fontalba (ESP)	09.01.1988	13	(1)	
Miguel Ruiz Enamorado (ESP)	16.07.1982	17	(1)	1
Lambilate Jordan Tawaba Tawaba (FRA)	22.05.1994	9	(1)	
Matías Nicolás Vaamonde (ARG)	30.11.1989	13	(4)	1
Xavier „Xavi" Carmona Velasco (ESP)	21.01.1993	16	(2)	2
Midfielders:	**DOB**	**M**	**(s)**	**G**
Sebastià Bertrán Suárez	10.12.1992	16	(4)	3

	DOB	M	(s)	G
Álvaro Luis Correa Gómez	08.11.1996	1	(6)	1
Óscar García González (ESP)	08.11.1996	3	(7)	2
François David Gomis Mendy (ESP)	29.12.1997	18		1
Carlos Eduardo Peppe Britos	28.01.1983	1	(3)	
Monsif Khttar El Yousfi (MAR)	09.07.1999	4	(1)	2
Forwards:	**DOB**	**M**	**(s)**	**G**
Bubacar Njie Kambi „Bácari" (GAM)	14.03.1988	16		10
Jean Marc Christopher Deroches (FRA)	20.02.1997		(1)	
José Antonio Aguilar Gómez „Josele" (ESP)	11.10.1999	7	(3)	2
Carlos Junior Pérez Díaz (ESP)	19.03.2001	2	(14)	
Milosz Juan Pablo Fernández Kepka (USA)	10.01.2001		(2)	
Frédéric Koutou Nimani NGalou (CTA)	08.10.1988	2	(4)	
Valentín Rizzo (ARG)	10.02.1998	11	(1)	
Alberto Molina Rodríguez (ESP)	21.04.1988	4		1
David Virgili Fernández (ESP)	30.09.1988	20		6

<table>
<tr><td>

Fútbol Club Santa Coloma

</td><td>

Founded: 1986
Stadium: Estadi Comunal d'Andorra la Vella (1,300)
Trainer: Albert Jorquera Fortià (ESP) 03.03.1979

</td></tr>
</table>

Goalkeepers:	DOB	M	(s)	G		DOB	M	(s)	G
Andrés Fabián Benítez Ruiz Díaz (PAR)	11.01.1983	6	(2)		Miguel Ángel Laborda Gil (ESP)	18.02.1995		(1)	
Miguel Ángel Ramos Prada (ESP)	05.10.1986	14			Ferrán Muxella Cervós	27.07.2003		(2)	
Defenders:	**DOB**	**M**	**(s)**	**G**	David Rodríguez López	02.07.1999	12	(1)	
Aleix Cístero Serna (ESP)	25.06.1994	13		2	Hamza Ryahi Bouharma (ESP)	11.03.1994	16	(1)	2
Eric de Pablos Solà	08.03.1999	8	(4)		Pedro Santos Escolano (ESP)	01.06.1993	18	(1)	
Juan Manuel Miranda Rodríguez „Juanma" (ESP)	01.03.1994	16	(1)		**Forwards:**	**DOB**	**M**	**(s)**	**G**
Enric Pi Sola (ESP)	20.05.1983	1	(6)		Baba Draman Konaré Diarra (MLI)	27.06.1995	1	(7)	1
Robert Ramos Isus (ESP)	11.12.1992	11	(4)	2	Alexandre Martínez Palau	10.10.1998	17		5
Andreu Ramos Isus (ESP)	19.01.1989	8	(3)		Diego Alejandro Nájera Quintero (MEX)	11.12.1994	9	(8)	3
Marc Rebés Ruíz	03.07.1994	14	(1)	1	Jesús "Chus" David Sosa Sebastiá (ESP)	05.01.1994	4	(9)	2
Álex Sánchez Rodríguez (ESP)	19.01.1991	16			Josep María Tizón Fernández	03.10.1997	1	(4)	
Midfielders:	**DOB**	**M**	**(s)**	**G**	Juan Manuel Torres Tena „Juanma Torres" (ESP)	23.02.1990	17	(1)	5
Luis Emilio Blanco Coto	15.01.1990	10	(8)	2	Xavier „Xavi" Puerto Bellart (ESP)	12.09.1991	8	(2)	2

<table>
<tr><td>

Unió Esportiva Santa Coloma

</td><td>

Founded: 1986
Stadium: Estadi Comunal d'Andorra la Vella (1,300)
Trainer: Vicente Muñoz Castellanos 02.06.1981

</td></tr>
</table>

Goalkeepers:	DOB	M	(s)	G		DOB	M	(s)	G
Ricard Fernández Lizarte (ESP)	26.05.1975	4			Andrés Briñez Aranda (COL)	24.07.1996	9	(2)	
Ferran Pol Pérez	28.02.1983	16	(1)		Marc Ferré Nazzaro	11.01.1994	19		
Defenders:	**DOB**	**M**	**(s)**	**G**	Albert Reyes Roig	24.03.1996	9	(2)	
Sergio dos Santos Alvarelhos	15.12.1996	2			Brian Andre Teixeira Filipe	26.06.1995		(2)	
Walid Bousenine Nafae	07.04.1993	9	(5)		**Forwards:**	**DOB**	**M**	**(s)**	**G**
Miguel Del Castillo Somoza	30.09.1999	3	(10)		Gerard Aloy Soler	17.04.1989	14	(1)	
Leandro Filipe Fernandes Gomes (POR)	06.11.1998	2	(5)		Victor Bernat Cuadros (ESP)	17.05.1987	13	(2)	12
Francisco Javier López Martín „Javi López" (ESP)	21.04.1990	9	(2)	1	Boris Antón Codina	27.02.1987	12	(6)	3
Alexandre Martínez Gutiérrez	04.03.1987	12	(1)	1	David Corominas Saura (ESP)	29.09.1985	9		2
João Pedro Ferreira Monteiro (POR)	11.12.1995	3			Andreu Matos Muñoz	01.12.1995	3	(12)	
Joel Martínez Palau	01.08.2000	1	(3)		Joel Paredes Leonés (ESP)	03.05.1995	10	(2)	15
Óscar Reyes Sánchez (ESP)	12.03.1988	11			Roberto Carlos Gomes Rebelo	21.10.1999	16	(2)	2
Midfielders:	**DOB**	**M**	**(s)**	**G**	Arturo Riestra Torrejón (ESP)	18.10.1999		(5)	
Joel Agraz Llaves (ESP)	2000	4	(3)		Sergi Suárez Otal	02.07.1998	7	(5)	
Sergio Crespo Alonso	29.09.1992	15	(3)	1	Alberto López Medel "Tete" (ESP)	21.11.1998	5	(6)	3
					Rodrigo Armando Vergara Brango (COL)	13.06.1995	3	(4)	2

SECOND LEVEL
Segona Divisió 2020/2021

Regular Season - League table

1.	FS La Massana	14	11	2	1	29	-	9	35
2.	FC Ordino	14	11	2	1	42	-	10	35
3.	FC Encamp	14	8	2	4	24	-	15	26
4.	CE Jenlai Escaldes-Endorgany	14	6	0	8	27	-	30	18
5.	CF Atlètic Amèrica	14	5	1	8	11	-	19	16
6.	UE Santa Coloma "B"	14	4	2	8	18	-	35	14
7.	UE Endorgany "B"	14	3	1	10	15	-	36	10
8.	FC Ránger's Andorra la Vella	14	2	2	10	19	-	31	8

Top-4 teams were qualified for the Play-off Round.

Play-off Round

1.	FC Ordino (*Promoted*)	20	15	4	1	57	-	15	49
2.	FS La Massana (*Promotion Play-offs*)	20	15	3	2	42	-	14	48
3.	FC Encamp	20	10	2	8	32	-	26	32
4.	CE Jenlai Escaldes-Endorgany	20	6	1	13	33	-	51	19

INTERNATIONAL MATCHES
(16.07.2020 – 15.07.2021)

03.09.2020	Rīga	Latvia - Andorra	0-0	(UNL)
06.09.2020	Andorra la Vella	Andorra - Faroe Islands	0-1(0-1)	(UNL)
07.10.2020	Andorra la Vella	Andorra - Cape Verde	1-2(1-1)	(F)
10.10.2020	Andorra la Vella	Andorra - Malta	0-0	(UNL)
13.10.2020	Tórshavn	Faroe Islands - Andorra	2-0(2-0)	(UNL)
11.11.2020	Lisboa	Portugal - Andorra	7-0(2-0)	(F)
14.11.2020	Attard	Malta - Andorra	3-1(0-1)	(UNL)
17.11.2020	Andorra la Vella	Andorra - Latvia	0-5(0-1)	(UNL)
25.03.2021	Andorra la Vella	Andorra - Albania	0-1(0-1)	(WCQ)
28.03.2021	Warszawa	Poland - Andorra	3-0(1-0)	(WCQ)
31.03.2021	Andorra la Vella	Andorra - Hungary	1-4(0-1)	(WCQ)
03.06.2021	Andorra la Vella	Andorra - Republic of Ireland	1-4(0-0)	(F)
07.06.2021	Andorra la Vella	Andorra - Gibraltar	0-0	(F)

03.09.2020   LATVIA - ANDORRA   0-0   2nd UEFA Nations League D, Group 1
Daugavas Stadions, Rīga; Referee: Timotheos Hristofi (Cyprus); Attendance: 0
AND: Josep Antoni Gómes Moreira, Emili Josep García Miramontes, Marc Vales González, Moisés San Nicolás Schellens, Marc Rebés Ruiz, Jesús Rubio Gómez, Max Llovera González-Adrio, Márcio Vieira de Vasconcelos (75.Aarón Sánchez Alburquerque), Marc Pujol Pons (Cap), Cristian Martínez Alejo (84.Ludovic Clemente Garcés), Àlexandre Martínez Palau (90+2.Jordi Aláez Peña). Trainer: Jesús Luis Álvarez de Eulate Güergue "Koldo".

06.09.2020   ANDORRA - FAROE ISLANDS   0-1(0-1)   2nd UEFA Nations League D, Group 1
Estadi Nacional, Andorra la Vella; Referee: Harald Lechner (Austria); Attendance: 0
AND: Josep Antoni Gómes Moreira, Emili Josep García Miramontes, Moisés San Nicolás Schellens, Marc Rebés Ruiz (69.Victor Bernat Cuadros), Jesús Rubio Gómez (88.Luis Emilio Blanco Coto), Márcio Vieira de Vasconcelos, Marc Pujol Pons (Cap), Max Llovera González-Adrio, Ludovic Clemente Garcés (24.Àlexandre Martínez Palau), Jordi Aláez Peña, Cristian Martínez Alejo. Trainer: Jesús Luis Álvarez de Eulate Güergue "Koldo".

07.10.2020   ANDORRA - CAPE VERDE   1-2(1-1)   Friendly International
Estadi Nacional, Andorra la Vella; Referee: José Luis Munuera Montero (Spain); Attendance: 0
AND: Josep Antoni Gómes Moreira (64.Francisco Manuel Pires Costa), Jordi Rubio Gómez, Emili Josep García Miramontes, Adrián Rodrígues Gonçalves, Moisés San Nicolás Schellens, Marc García Renom, Marc Rebés Ruiz (82.Albert Reyes Roig), Sergio Moreno Marín (Cap) (75.Marc Pujol Pons), Victor Bernat Cuadros (39.Cristian Martínez Alejo), Luigi San Nicolás Schellens (65.Márcio Vieira de Vasconcelos), Aarón Sánchez Alburquerque (74.Marc Ferré Nazzaro). Trainer: Jesús Luis Álvarez de Eulate Güergue "Koldo".
Goal: Carlos dos Santos Rodrigues (17 own goal).

10.10.2020   ANDORRA - MALTA   0-0   2nd UEFA Nations League D, Group 1
Estadi Nacional, Andorra la Vella; Referee: Alain Durieux (Luxembourg); Attendance: 0
AND: Josep Antoni Gómes Moreira, Jordi Rubio Gómez, Emili Josep García Miramontes, Marc Vales González, Joan Cervós Moro, Márcio Vieira de Vasconcelos, Marc Pujol Pons (Cap), Cristian Martínez Alejo (85.Marc García Renom), Aarón Sánchez Alburquerque (85.Luigi San Nicolás Schellens), Àlexandre Martínez Palau (90+4.Victor Bernat Cuadros), Ricard Fernández Betriu (70.Jordi Aláez Peña). Trainer: Jesús Luis Álvarez de Eulate Güergue "Koldo".

13.10.2020   FAROE ISLANDS - ANDORRA   2-0(2-0)   2nd UEFA Nations League D, Group 1
Tórsvøllur, Tórshavn; Referee: Antti Munukka (Finland); Attendance: 0
AND: Josep Antoni Gómes Moreira, Emili Josep García Miramontes, Moisés San Nicolás Schellens, Marc Rebés Ruiz (88.Sergio Moreno Marín), Joan Cervós Moro, Albert Alavedra Jiménez, Márcio Vieira de Vasconcelos (62.Cristian Martínez Alejo), Marc Pujol Pons (Cap), Jordi Aláez Peña (89.Victor Bernat Cuadros), Àlexandre Martínez Palau (71.Jordi Rubio Gómez), Ricard Fernández Betriu (71.Aarón Sánchez Alburquerque). Trainer: Jesús Luis Álvarez de Eulate Güergue "Koldo".

11.11.2020   PORTUGAL - ANDORRA   7-0(2-0)   Friendly International
Estádio da Luz, Lisboa; Referee: Alain Bieri (Switzerland); Attendance: 0
AND: Josep Antoni Gómes Moreira, Jordi Rubio Gómez, Emili Josep García Miramontes, Adrián Rodrígues Gonçalves, Marc García Renom (46.Moisés San Nicolás Schellens), Marc Rebés Ruiz (59.Albert Alavedra Jiménez), Joan Cervós Moro (69.Àlexandre Martínez Palau), Márcio Vieira de Vasconcelos (59.Jordi Aláez Peña), Marc Pujol Pons (Cap) (80.Sergio Moreno Marín), Cristian Martínez Alejo (69.Ludovic Clemente Garcés), Aarón Sánchez Alburquerque. Trainer: Jesús Luis Álvarez de Eulate Güergue "Koldo".

14.11.2020   MALTA - ANDORRA   3-1(0-1)   2nd UEFA Nations League D, Group 1
Ta`Qali National Stadium, Attard; Referee: Peter Kralović (Slovakia); Attendance: 0
AND: Josep Antoni Gómes Moreira, Emili Josep García Miramontes, Moisés San Nicolás Schellens, Marc Rebés Ruiz (77.Luis Emilio Blanco Coto), Joan Cervós Moro, Albert Alavedra Jiménez, Márcio Vieira de Vasconcelos (Cap), Jordi Aláez Peña, Cristian Martínez Alejo (77.Victor Bernat Cuadros), Àlexandre Martínez Palau (69.Luigi San Nicolás Schellens), Ricard Fernández Betriu (69.Aarón Sánchez Alburquerque). Trainer: Jesús Luis Álvarez de Eulate Güergue "Koldo".
Goal: Marc Rebés Ruiz (3).

17.11.2020   ANDORRA - LATVIA   0-5(0-1)   2nd UEFA Nations League D, Group 1
Estadi Nacional, Andorra la Vella; Referee: Dimitar Meckarovski (North Macedonia); Attendance: 0
AND: Josep Antoni Gómes Moreira, Jordi Rubio Gómez (66.Àlexandre Martínez Palau), Emili Josep García Miramontes, Moisés San Nicolás Schellens, Marc Rebés Ruiz, Joan Cervós Moro, Christian García González [*sent off 90*], Márcio Vieira de Vasconcelos (Cap) (66.Jordi Aláez Peña), Marc Pujol Pons (85.Sergio Moreno Marín), Cristian Martínez Alejo (84.Ludovic Clemente Garcés), Ricard Fernández Betriu (78.Aarón Sánchez Alburquerque). Trainer: Jesús Luis Álvarez de Eulate Güergue "Koldo".

25.03.2021   **ANDORRA - ALBANIA**   **0-1(0-1)**   22nd FIFA WC. Qualifiers
Estadi Nacional, Andorra la Vella; Referee: Volen Chinkov (Bulgaria); Attendance: 285
AND: Josep Antoni Gómes Moreira, Marc Vales González, Moisés San Nicolás Schellens, Marc Rebés Ruiz (79.Sergio Moreno Marín), Jesús Rubio Gómez (56.Albert Alavedra Jiménez), Max Llovera González-Adrio, Joan Cervós Moro, Márcio Vieira de Vasconcelos (Cap) (79.Marc Pujol Pons), Jordi Aláez Peña, Àlexandre Martínez Palau (70.Aarón Sánchez Alburquerque), Ricard Fernández Betriu (70.Cristian Martínez Alejo). Trainer: Jesús Luis Álvarez de Eulate Güergue "Koldo".

28.03.2021   **POLAND - ANDORRA**   **3-0(1-0)**   22nd FIFA WC. Qualifiers
Stadion Wojska Polskiego, Warszawa; Referee: Erik Lambrechts (Belgium); Attendance: 0
AND: Iker Álvarez de Eulate Molné, Emili Josep García Miramontes, Marc Vales González, Marc García Renom (58.Joan Cervós Moro), Moisés San Nicolás Schellens, Marc Rebés Ruiz (87.Márcio Vieira de Vasconcelos), Christian García González, Albert Alavedra Jiménez, Marc Pujol Pons (Cap) (58.Jordi Aláez Peña), Cristian Martínez Alejo (74.Àlexandre Martínez Palau), Aarón Sánchez Alburquerque (87.Luigi San Nicolás Schellens). Trainer: Jesús Luis Álvarez de Eulate Güergue "Koldo".

31.03.2021   **ANDORRA - HUNGARY**   **1-4(0-1)**   22nd FIFA WC. Qualifiers
Estadi Nacional, Andorra la Vella; Referee: Vilhjálmur Alvar Þórarinsson (Iceland); Attendance: 338
AND: Josep Antoni Gómes Moreira, Emili Josep García Miramontes, Marc Vales González, Moisés San Nicolás Schellens (61.Jesús Rubio Gómez), Max Llovera González-Adrio, Joan Cervós Moro, Albert Alavedra Jiménez (77.Marc Rebés Ruiz), Márcio Vieira de Vasconcelos (Cap) (77.Marc Pujol Pons), Jordi Aláez Peña, Àlexandre Martínez Palau (62.Cristian Martínez Alejo), Ricard Fernández Betriu (82.Aarón Sánchez Alburquerque). Trainer: Jesús Luis Álvarez de Eulate Güergue "Koldo".
Goal: Marc Pujol Pons (90+2 penalty).

03.06.2021   **ANDORRA - REPUBLIC OF IRELAND**   **1-4(0-0)**   Friendly International
Estadi Nacional, Andorra la Vella; Referee: Xavier Estrada Fernández (Spain); Attendance: 320
AND: Iker Álvarez de Eulate Molné (77.Francisco Manuel Pires Costa), Marc Vales González, Max Llovera González-Adrio, Joan Cervós Moro, Marc Rebés Ruiz (72.Christian Garcia González), Moisés San Nicolás Schellens (73.Eric de Pablos Solà), Márcio Vieira de Vasconcelos (Cap), Àlexandre Martínez Palau (76.Ildefons Lima Solà), Jordi Aláez Peña, Ludovic Clemente Garcés (60.Cristian Martínez Alejo), Ricard Fernández Betriu (59.Aarón Sánchez Alburquerque). Trainer: Jesús Luis Álvarez de Eulate Güergue "Koldo".
Goal: Marc Vales González (54).

07.06.2021   **ANDORRA - GIBRALTAR**   **0-0**   Friendly International
Estadi Nacional, Andorra la Vella; Referee: Philip Farrugia (Malta); Attendance: 0
AND: Josep Antoni Gómes Moreira, Marc Vales González, Marc Pujol Pons (Cap), Max Llovera González-Adrio, Albert Alavedra Jiménez (86.Ildefons Lima Solà), Marc García Renom, Moisés San Nicolás Schellens, Cristian Martínez Alejo (65.Jordi Aláez Peña), Sergio Moreno Marín (76.Xavier Vieira de Vasconcelos), Àlexandre Martínez Palau (77.Victor Bernat Cuadros), Aarón Sánchez Alburquerque (65.Ricard Fernández Betriu). Trainer: Jesús Luis Álvarez de Eulate Güergue "Koldo".

NATIONAL TEAM PLAYERS
(16.07.2020 – 15.07.2021)

Name	DOB	Caps	Goals	2020/2021:	Club
Goalkeepers					
Iker ÁLVAREZ de Eulate Molné	25.07.2001	2	0	2021:	Villarreal CF "C" (ESP)
Josep Antoni GÓMES Moreira	03.12.1985	74	0	2020/2021:	Inter Club d'Escaldes
Francisco Manuel "Xisco" PIRES Costa	25.01.1998	2	0	2020/2021:	UE Engordany
Defenders					
Albert ALAVEDRA Jiménez	26.02.1999	7	0	2020:	CD Calahorra (ESP)
				28.01.2021->	CF Pobla de Mafumet (ESP)
Joan CERVÓS Moro	24.02.1998	26	0	2020:	Colorado Springs Switchbacks FC (USA)
				31.01.2021->	AE Prat (ESP)
Eric DE PABLOS Solà	08.03.1999	1	0	2021:	FC Santa Coloma
Christian GARCÍA González	04.02.1999	3	0	2020/2021:	AD Alcorcón "B" (ESP)
Emili Josep GARCÍA Miramontes	11.01.1989	56	1	2020/2021:	Inter Club d'Escaldes
Ildefons LIMA Solà	10.12.1979	130	11	2021:	Inter Club d'Escaldes
Max LLOVERA González-Adrio	08.01.1997	42	0	2020/2021:	EC Granollers (ESP)
Marc PUJOL Pons	21.08.1982	94	9	2020/2021:	Inter Club d'Escaldes
Marc REBÉS Ruiz	03.07.1994	41	3	2020/2021:	FC Santa Coloma
Adrián "Adri" RODRÍGUES Gonçalves	14.08.1988	18	0	2020:	Atlètic Club d'Escaldes Escaldes-Engordany
Jesús "Txus" RUBIO Gómez	09.09.1994	29	0	2020/2021:	Atlètic Club d'Escaldes Escaldes-Engordany
Jordi RUBIO Gómez	01.11.1987	51	0	2020:	Inter Club d'Escaldes
Marc VALES González	04.04.1990	74	2	2020/2021:	Sandefjord Fotball (NOR)
Midfielders					
Jordi ALÁEZ Peña	23.01.1998	39	1	2020:	FC Santa Coloma
				22.09.2020->	PAE GS Diagóras Rhodos (GRE)
Luis Emilio BLANCO Coto	15.01.1990	2	0	2020:	FC Santa Coloma
Marc FERRÉ Nazzaro	11.01.1994	3	0	2020:	unattached
Marc GARCÍA Renom „Chiqui"	21.03.1988	49	0	2020/2021:	CF Montañesa Barcelona (ESP)
Cristian MARTÍNEZ Alejo	16.10.1989	72	5	2020/2021:	Inter Club d'Escaldes
Albert REYES Roig	24.03.1996	1	0	2020:	Inter Club d'Escaldes
Moisés SAN NICOLÁS Schellens	17.09.1993	60	0	2020/2021:	Atlètic Club d'Escaldes Escaldes-Engordany
Márcio VIEIRA de Vasconcelos	10.10.1984	104	0	2020/2021:	CF Atlético de Monzón (ESP)
Xavier VIEIRA de Vasconcelos	14.01.1992	3	0	2021:	Atlètic Club d'Escaldes Escaldes-Engordany
Forwards					
Victor BERNAT Cuadros	17.05.1987	6	0	2020/2021:	UE Santa Coloma
Ludovic CLEMENTE Garcés	09.05.1986	41	0	2020:	Inter Club d'Escaldes
Ricard FERNÁNDEZ Betriu	19.03.1999	15	0	2020/2021:	SD Formentera San Francesc Xavier (ESP)
Àlexandre MARTÍNEZ Palau	10.10.1998	34	1	2020/2021:	FC Santa Coloma
Sergio MORENO Marín	25.11.1987	72	0	2020/2021:	Inter Club d'Escaldes
Luigi SAN NICOLÁS Schellens	28.06.1992	5	0	2020:	UE Engordany
				12.10.2020->	Atlètic Club d'Escaldes Escaldes-Engordany
Aarón SÁNCHEZ Alburquerque	05.06.1996	24	0	2020/2021:	UE Engordany
Trainer					
Jesús Luis Álvarez de Eulate „KOLDO" [from 02.02.2010]	04.09.1970	90 M; 4 W; 14 D; 72 L; 21-201			

ARMENIA

The Country:
Republic of Armenia (Hayastani Hanrapetut'yun)
Capital: Yerevan
Surface: 29,743 km²
Inhabitants: 2,967,900 [2020]
Time: UTC+4

The FA:
Football Federation of Armenia
Khanjyan Street 27, 0010 Yerevan
Tel: +374 11 888 808
Foundation date: 18.01.1992
Member of FIFA since: 1992
Member of UEFA since: 1993
Website: www.ffa.am

NATIONAL TEAM RECORDS

RECORDS		
First international match:	14.10.1992, Yerevan	Armenia – Moldova 0-0
Most international caps:	Sargis Hovsepyan	- 132 caps (1992-2012)
Most international goals:	Henrikh Mkhitaryan	- 30 goals / 88 caps (since 2007)

UEFA EUROPEAN CHAMPIONSHIP		FIFA WORLD CUP		OLYMPIC TOURNAMENTS	
1960	-	1930	-	1908	-
1964	-	1934	-	1912	-
1968	-	1938	-	1920	-
1972	-	1950	-	1924	-
1976	-	1954	-	1928	-
1980	-	1958	-	1936	-
1984	-	1962	-	1948	-
1988	-	1966	-	1952	-
1992	Did not enter	1970	-	1956	-
1996	Qualifiers	1974	-	1960	-
2000	Qualifiers	1978	-	1964	-
2004	Qualifiers	1982	-	1968	-
2008	Qualifiers	1986	-	1972	-
2012	Qualifiers	1990	-	1976	-
2016	Qualifiers	1994	Did not enter	1980	-
2020	Qualifiers	1998	Qualifiers	1984	-
		2002	Qualifiers	1988	-
		2006	Qualifiers	1992	Did not enter
		2010	Qualifiers	1996	Did not enter
		2014	Qualifiers	2000	Qualifiers
		2018	Qualifiers	2004	Qualifiers
				2008	Qualifiers
				2012	Qualifiers
				2016	Qualifiers

UEFA NATIONS LEAGUE

2018/2019	League D
2020/2021	League C (promoted to League B)

FIFA CONFEDERATIONS CUP 1992-2017

None

ARMENIAN CLUB HONOURS IN EUROPEAN CLUB COMPETITIONS:

European Champion Clubs.Cup (1956-1992) / UEFA Champions League (1993-2021)
None

Fairs Cup (1858-1971) / UEFA Cup (1972-2009) / UEFA Europa League (2010-2021)
None

UEFA Super Cup (1972-2020)
None

European Cup Winners.Cup 1961-1999
None

*defunct competition

NATIONAL COMPETITIONS
TABLE OF HONOURS

ARMENIAN SSR (SOVIET ERA) CHAMPIONS

Year	Champion	Year	Champion	Year	Champion
1936	Dinamo Yerevan	1955	Khimik Kirovakan	1971	FIMA Yerevan
1937	Dinamo Yerevan	1956	FIMA Yerevan	1972	Zvezda Yerevan
1938	Spartak Yerevan	1957	Karmir Drosh Leninakan	1973	Kotayk Abovyan
1939	Spartak Yerevan	1958	FIMA Yerevan	1974	FIMA Yerevan
1940	Spartak Yerevan	1959	FIMA Yerevan	1975	Kotayk Abovyan
1941-44	*No competition*	1960	Tekstilshchik Leninakan	1976	Kotayk Abovyan
1945	Spartak Yerevan	1961	Tekstilshchik Leninakan	1977	Araks Yerevan
1946	Dinamo Yerevan	1962	Tekstilshchik Leninakan	1978	Kanaz Yerevan
1947	Dinamo Yerevan	1963	Lokomotiv Yerevan	1979	Aragats Leninakan
1948	Dinamo Yerevan	1964	Khimik Kirovakan	1980	Aragats Leninakan
1949	Dinamo Yerevan	1965	Araks Yerevan	1981–86	*No competition*
1950	Urozhai Yerevan	1966	Elektrotekhnik Yerevan	1987	Aragats Leninakan
1951	Shinarar Yerevan	1967	Kotayk Abovyan	1988	Elektrotekhnik Yerevan
1952	Spartak Yerevan	1968	Araks Yerevan	1989	FC Kapan
1953	Karmir Drosh Leninakan	1969	Araks Yerevan	1990	Ararat-2 Yerevan
1954	Spartak Yerevan	1970	Motor Yerevan	1991	Syunik Kapan

	CHAMPIONS	CUP WINNERS	BEST GOALSCORERS	
1992	Shirak SC Gyumri / Homenetmen Yerevan (shared)	FC Banants Yerevan	Vahe Yaghmuryan (FC Ararat Yerevan)	38
1993	FC Ararat Yerevan	FC Ararat Yerevan	Andranik Hovsepyan (Banants) / Gegham Hovhannisyan (Homenetmen Yerevan)	26
1994	Shirak SC Gyumri	FC Ararat Yerevan	Arsen Avetisyan (Homenetmen Yerevan)	39
1995	*Transitional Season (No Winner)*	FC Ararat Yerevan	-	
1995/1996	FC Pyunik Yerevan	FC Pyunik Yerevan	Arayik Adamyan (Shirak SC Gyumri)	28
1996/1997	FC Pyunik Yerevan	FC Ararat Yerevan	Arsen Avetisyan (FC Pyunik Yerevan)	24
1997	FC Yerevan	-	Artur Petrosyan (Shirak SC Gyumri)	18
1998	FC Tsement Ararat	FC Tsement Ararat	Ara Hakobyan (Dvin Artashat)	20
1999	Shirak SC Gyumri	FC Tsement Ararat	Shirak SC Gyumri Sarikyan (FC Tsement Ararat)	21
2000	Araks Ararat FC	FC Mika Yerevan	Ara Hakobyan (Araks Ararat FC)	21
2001	FC Pyunik Yerevan	FC Mika Yerevan	Arman Karamyan (FC Pyunik Yerevan)	21
2002	FC Pyunik Yerevan	FC Pyunik Yerevan	Arman Karamyan (FC Pyunik Yerevan)	36
2003	FC Pyunik Yerevan	FC Mika Yerevan	Ara Hakobyan (FC Banants Yerevan)	45
2004	FC Pyunik Yerevan	FC Pyunik Yerevan	Edgar Manucharyan (FC Pyunik Yerevan) / Galust Petrosyan (FC Pyunik Yerevan)	21
2005	FC Pyunik Yerevan	FC Mika Yerevan	Nshan Erzrumyan (Kilikia FC Yerevan)	18
2006	FC Pyunik Yerevan	FC Mika Yerevan	Aram Hakobyan (FC Banants Yerevan)	25
2007	FC Pyunik Yerevan	FC Banants Yerevan	Marcos Pinheiro Pizzelli (Ararat Yerevan)	22
2008	FC Pyunik Yerevan	FC Ararat Yerevan	Marcos Pinheiro Pizzelli (Ararat Yerevan)	17
2009	FC Pyunik Yerevan	FC Pyunik Yerevan	Artur Kocharyan (Ulisses FC Yerevan)	15
2010	FC Pyunik Yerevan	FC Pyunik Yerevan	Marcos Pinheiro Pizzelli (FC Pyunik Yerevan) / Gevorg Ghazaryan (FC Pyunik Yerevan)	16
2011	Ulisses FC Yerevan	FC Mika Yerevan	Bruno César Correa (BRA, FC Banants Yerevan)	16
2011/2012	*Transitional Season (No winner)*	Shirak SC Gyumri	-	
2012/2013	Shirak SC Gyumri	FC Pyunik Yerevan	Norayr Gyozalyan (Impuls FC Dilijan)	21
2013/2014	FC Banants Yerevan	FC Pyunik Yerevan	Mihran Manasyan (FC Alashkert Yerevan)	17
2014/2015	FC Pyunik Yerevan	FC Pyunik Yerevan	César Romero Zamora (USA, FC Pyunik Yerevan) / Jean-Jacques Bougouhi (CIV, Shirak SC Gyumri)	21
2015/2016	FC Alashkert Yerevan	FC Banants Yerevan	Héber Araujo dos Santos (BRA, FC Alashkert Yerevan); / Mihran Manasyan (FC Alashkert Yerevan)	16
2016/2017	FC Alashkert Yerevan	Shirak SC Gyumri	Artak Yedigaryan (FC Alashkert Yerevan) / Mihran Manasyan (FC Alashkert Yerevan)	13
2017/2018	FC Alashkert Yerevan	FC Gandzasar Kapan	Artak Yedigaryan (FC Alashkert Yerevan) / Gegham Harutyunyan (FC Gandzasar Kapan)	12
2018/2019	FC Ararat-Armenia Yerevan	FC Alashkert Yerevan	Jonel Désiré (HAI, Lori FC Vanadzor)	17
2019/2020	FC Ararat-Armenia Yerevan	FC Noah Yerevan	Mory Koné (CIV, Shirak SC Gyumri)	23
2020/2021	FC Alashkert Yerevan	FC Ararat Yerevan	Yusuf Olaitan Otubanjo (NGA, FC Ararat-Armenia Yerevan)	10

Please note: Homenetmen Yerevan became FC Pyunik Yerevan (1995); Tsement Ararat changed its name to Araks Ararat FC (2000).

NATIONAL CHAMPIONSHIP
Armenian Premier League / Bardsragujn chumb 2020/2021
(14.08.2020 – 30.05.2021)

Results

Round 1 [14-17.08.2020]
FC Alashkert - FC Ararat-Armenia 0-0
FC Van - Gandzasar Kapan *annulled*
FC Noah - Shirak SC 2-2
FC Ararat - FC Pyunik 1-0
FC Urartu - Lori FC 3-0 *awarded*

Round 2 [21-23.08.2020]
FC Alashkert - FC Noah 1-0
FC Ararat-Armenia - Gandzasar Kap. *annulled*
FC Pyunik - FC Urartu 0-0
Lori FC - FC Van 0-1 [15.09.]
Shirak SC - FC Ararat 0-3 [26.09.]

Round 3 [29.08.2020]
Gandzasar Kapan - Lori FC *not played*
FC Van - FC Pyunik 1-0
FC Noah - FC Ararat-Armenia 0-0 [08.11.20]
FC Urartu - Shirak SC 1-0 [01.05.2021]
FC Ararat - FC Alashkert 0-1 [25.05.2021]

Round 4 [11-13.09.2020]
FC Noah - FC Ararat 2-1
FC Ararat-Armenia - Lori FC 1-2
FC Pyunik - Gandzasar Kapan *annulled*
FC Alashkert - FC Urartu 1-2
Shirak SC - FC Van 0-0 [24.02.2021]

Round 5 [22-24.09.2020]
FC Urartu - FC Noah 0-3
Gandzasar Kapan - Shirak SC *annulled*
Lori FC - FC Pyunik 1-0
FC Van - FC Alashkert 0-1
FC Ararat - FC Ararat-Armenia 1-0 [25.02.21]

Round 6 [29.09.2020]
FC Alashkert - Gandzasar Kapan *not played*
FC Noah - FC Van 4-0 [19.02.2021]
Shirak SC - Lori FC 0-1 [20.02.2021]
FC Ararat - FC Urartu 2-0 [21.02.2021]
Ararat-Armenia - FC Pyunik 2-1 [21.02.21]

Round 7 [03.10.2020]
Gandzasar Kapan - FC Noah *not played*
FC Van - FC Ararat 0-1 [10.12.2020]
FC Pyunik - Shirak SC 0-2 [12.12.2020]
Lori FC - FC Alashkert 0-1 [24.02.2021]
FC Urartu - Ararat-Armenia 1-2 [15.05.2021]

Round 8 [17-19.10.2020]
FC Ararat-Armenia - Shirak SC 7-0
FC Alashkert - FC Pyunik 0-0
FC Ararat - Gandzasar Kapan *annulled*
FC Urartu - FC Van 2-0
FC Noah - Lori FC 3-1 [08.03.2021]

Round 9 [25-26.10.2020]
FC Van - FC Ararat-Armenia 0-1
Lori FC - FC Ararat 1-0
Shirak SC - FC Alashkert 1-1
Gandzasar Kapan - FC Urartu *annulled*
FC Pyunik - FC Noah 0-1 [15.05.2021]

Round 10 [29-31.10.2020]
Lori FC - FC Urartu 1-1
Shirak SC - FC Noah 0-3
Gandzasar Kapan - FC Van *annulled*
FC Pyunik - FC Ararat 1-1
Ararat-Armenia - FC Alashkert 1-2 [22.05.21]

Round 11 [02-04.11.2020]
FC Noah - FC Alashkert 1-2
Gandzasar K. - FC Ararat-Armenia *not played*
FC Ararat - Shirak SC 4-0
FC Van - Lori FC 1-2
FC Urartu - FC Pyunik 0-1 [19.04.2021]

Round 12 [21-23.11.2020]
Lori FC - Gandzasar Kapan *not played*
FC Alashkert - FC Ararat 1-2
FC Pyunik - FC Van 0-0
Shirak SC - FC Urartu 0-3
FC Ararat-Armenia - FC Noah 3-1

Round 13 [25-28.11.2020]
Gandzasar Kapan - FC Pyunik *not played*
FC Van - Shirak SC 3-1
FC Urartu - FC Alashkert 1-2
FC Ararat - FC Noah 1-1
Lori FC - FC Ararat-Armenia 0-1

Round 14 [29.11.-02.12.2020]
Shirak SC - Gandzasar Kapan *not played*
FC Alashkert - FC Van 2-1
FC Noah - FC Urartu 1-1
FC Ararat-Armenia - FC Ararat 0-0
FC Pyunik - Lori FC 1-1

Round 15 [05-08.12.2020]
Gandzasar Kapan - FC Alashkert *not played*
FC Van - FC Noah 0-1
FC Pyunik - FC Ararat-Armenia 0-1
Lori FC - Shirak SC 3-2
FC Urartu - FC Ararat 2-0 [22.05.2021]

Round 16 [28.02.-02.03.2021]
FC Noah - Gandzasar Kapan *not played*
FC Alashkert - Lori FC 2-1
FC Ararat - FC Van 0-0
Shirak SC - FC Pyunik 0-2
FC Ararat-Armenia - FC Urartu 0-1

Round 17 [04-07.03.2021]
Lori FC - FC Noah 2-0
Gandzasar Kapan - FC Ararat *not played*
FC Pyunik - FC Alashkert 1-1
FC Van - FC Urartu 3-1
Shirak SC - FC Ararat-Armenia 2-2

Round 18 [16-18.03.2021]
FC Ararat - Lori FC 3-0 *awarded*
FC Urartu - Gandzasar Kapan *not played*
FC Noah - FC Pyunik 0-1
FC Alashkert - Shirak SC 0-0
FC Ararat-Armenia - FC Van 3-0

Round 19 [07-11.04.2021]
FC Urartu - FC Ararat 1-0
FC Ararat-Armenia - FC Van 2-3
FC Noah - FC Pyunik 1-0
Shirak SC - FC Alashkert 0-0

Round 20 [13-15.04.2021]
Lori FC - FC Ararat-Armenia 0-3 *awarded*
FC Van - FC Pyunik 0-3
FC Alashkert - FC Urartu 1-0
FC Ararat-Armenia - Shirak SC 2-1
FC Ararat - FC Noah 2-3

Round 21 [23-26.04.2021]
Shirak SC - Lori FC 3-0 *awarded*
Shirak SC - FC Van 1-2
FC Pyunik - FC Ararat 1-2
FC Urartu - FC Ararat-Armenia 0-0
FC Noah - FC Alashkert 1-0

Round 22 [02-07.05.2021]
Lori FC - FC Urartu 0-3 *awarded*
FC Van - FC Ararat 1-1
FC Alashkert - FC Pyunik 1-0
FC Ararat-Armenia - FC Noah 0-0
Shirak SC - FC Urartu 1-1

Round 23 [10-11.05.2021]
FC Ararat - FC Alashkert 0-0
FC Noah - Lori FC 3-0 *awarded*
FC Noah - Shirak SC 3-0
FC Urartu - FC Van 2-1
FC Pyunik - FC Ararat-Armenia 0-0

Round 24 [19-20.05.2021]
Lori FC - FC Pyunik 0-3 *awarded*
FC Van - FC Alashkert 3-1
FC Ararat-Armenia - FC Ararat 1-1
FC Urartu - FC Noah 1-0
Shirak SC - FC Pyunik 1-5

Round 25 [28.05.2021]
FC Ararat - Lori FC 3-0 *awarded*
FC Noah - FC Van 1-2
FC Pyunik - FC Urartu 0-1
FC Ararat - Shirak SC 5-2
FC Alashkert - FC Ararat-Armenia 1-0

Round 26 [23.05.2021]
Lori FC - FC Alashkert 0-3 *awarded*

Round 27 [30.05.2021]
FC Van - Lori FC 3-0 *awarded*

Please note:
1. FC Gandzasar Kapan were excluded from the league (03.11.2020), as they announced that they were withdrawing from the League and Armenian Cup due to the ongoing financial constraints relating to the COVID-19 pandemic in Armenia and the 2020 Nagorno-Karabakh conflict. All matches played were annulled and declared as 0-3 forfeits.

2. All matches from Round 19-27 involving Lori FC Vanadzor were declared 0-3 forfeits.

Final Standings

				Total					**Home**					**Away**			
1. **FC Alashkert Yerevan**	24	13	7	4	25 - 15	46	6	3	2	10 - 6	7	4	2	15 - 9
2. FC Noah Yerevan	24	12	5	7	35 - 20	41	7	3	3	22 - 10	5	2	4	13 - 10
3. FC Urartu Yerevan	24	12	5	7	28 - 19	41	8	1	4	17 - 9	4	4	3	11 - 10
4. FC Ararat Yerevan	24	11	7	6	34 - 18	40	6	3	2	19 - 7	5	4	4	15 - 11
5. FC Ararat -Armenia Yerevan	24	10	8	6	32 - 17	38	6	3	4	25 - 12	4	5	2	7 - 5
6. FC Van Charentsavan	24	9	4	11	25 - 30	31	4	1	6	12 - 13	5	3	5	13 - 17
7. FC Pyunik Yerevan	24	6	7	11	20 - 18	25	0	6	5	4 - 10	6	1	6	16 - 8
8. Lori FC Vanadzor	24	2	7	15	19 - 53	23	1	5	7	9 - 23	1	2	8	10 - 30
9. Shirak SC Gyumri (*Relegated*)	24	7	2	15	16 - 44	13	4	1	7	8 - 18	3	1	8	8 - 26
10. FC Gandzasar Kapan (*Dissolved*)	0	0	0	0	0 - 0									

Top goalscorers:

10	Yusuf Olaitan Otubanjo (NGA)	*FC Ararat-Armenia Yerevan*
8	Jonel Désiré (HAI)	*FC Urartu Yerevan*
8	Wilfried Kwassi Eza (CIV)	*FC Van Charentsavan*

NATIONAL CUP
Armenian Cup 2020/2021

First Round [18-19.09./07-09./22.11.2020/25.02.2021]

First Leg			Second Leg	
FC West Armenia Yerevan - FC Gandzasar Kapan	3-2		FC Gandzasar Kapan - FC West Armenia Yerevan	0-3 *awarded*
FC Van Charentsavan - Noravank Sport Club	0-0		Noravank Sport Club - FC Van Charentsavan	0-2
FC Urartu Yerevan - FC Pyunik Yerevan	2-1		FC Pyunik Yerevan - FC Urartu Yerevan	0-0
BKMA Yerevan - Lori FC Vanadzor	0-0		Lori FC Vanadzor - BKMA Yerevan	2-2
Shirak SC Gyumri - FC Alashkert Yerevan	1-2		FC Alashkert Yerevan - Shirak SC Gyumri	1-0
FC Ararat Yerevan - FC Sevan	3-0		FC Sevan - FC Ararat Yerevan	1-3

Quarter-Finals [11-12.03./03-05.04.2021]

First Leg			Second Leg	
FC West Armenia Yerevan - FC Ararat Yerevan	2-0		FC Ararat Yerevan - FC West Armenia Yerevan	5-1
FC Alashkert Yerevan - BKMA Yerevan	4-0		BKMA Yerevan - FC Alashkert Yerevan	1-2
FC Van Charentsavan - FC Ararat -Armenia Yerevan	0-1		FC Ararat -Armenia Yerevan - FC Van Charentsavan	0-1 aet
FC Urartu Yerevan - FC Noah Yerevan	0-2		FC Noah Yerevan - FC Urartu Yerevan	2-2

Semi-Finals [20.04./30.04.-01.05.2021]

First Leg			Second Leg	
FC Alashkert Yerevan - FC Noah Yerevan	1-1		FC Noah Yerevan - FC Alashkert Yerevan	1-3
FC Ararat Yerevan - FC Ararat -Armenia Yerevan	2-0		FC Ararat -Armenia Yerevan - FC Ararat Yerevan	2-1

Final

15.05.2021; „Vazgen Sargsyan" Hanrapetakan Stadium, Yerevan; Referee: Benoît Millot (France); Attendance: 4,000

FC Alashkert Yerevan - FC Ararat Yerevan   **1-3(0-2)**

Alashkert: David Yurchenko, Dejan Boljević, Didier Kadio, Taron Voskanyan, Tiago Coelho Andrade "Tiago Cametá", Mihailo Jovanović (28.David Davidyan), Artak Grigoryan, Vincent Bezecourt (62.Mihran Manasyan), Rumyan Hovsepyan [*sent off 90*], Branko Mihajlović (62.Grigor Aghekyan), Aleksandar Glišić (71.Sunday Umaru Ngbede). Trainer: Abraham Khashmanyan.

Ararat Yerevan: Vsevolod Ermakov, Juan David Bravo Padilla, Marko Prljević, Zhirayr Margaryan, Christián Jiménez, Edgar Malakyan (84.Artur Danielyan), David Manoyan (72.Dimitrije Pobulić), Aghvan Papikyan (46.Maksym Zaderaka), Karen Muradyan, David Khurtsidze, Mory Kone (62.Uroš Nenadović). Trainer: Vardan Bichakhchyan.

Goals: 0-1 Aghvan Papikyan (12), 0-2 Mory Kone (19), 0-3 Mory Kone (55), 1-3 Mihran Manasyan (85).

Football Club Alashkert Yerevan

Founded:	1990		
Stadium:	Alashkert Stadium, Yerevan (6,850)		
Trainer:	Yegishe Melikyan		13.08.1979
[07.01.2021]	Abraham Khashmanyan		11.11.1967
[28.05.2021]	Aleksandr Grigoryan		28.09.1966

Goalkeepers:	DOB	M	(s)	G
Ognjen Čančarević (SRB)	25.09.1989	18		
David Yurchenko	27.03.1986	5		
Defenders:	**DOB**	**M**	**(s)**	**G**
Dejan Boljević (MNE)	30.05.1990	11	(2)	1
Bryan Silva Garcia (BRA)	28.03.1992	9		
Tiago Coelho Andrade "Tiago Cametá" (BRA)	05.05.1992	20	(1)	
Gagik Dagbashyan	19.10.1990	7	(4)	
Igor Gonchar (UKR)	10.01.1993	7	(1)	
Mihailo Jovanović (SRB)	15.02.1989	5	(2)	
Didier Kadio (CIV)	05.04.1990	13		
Vaspurak Minasyan	29.06.1994	7	(1)	
Risto Mitrevski (MKD)	05.10.1991	4		
Marko Tomić (SRB)	28.10.1991	4	(2)	
Taron Voskanyan	22.02.1993	20		2
Midfielders:	**DOB**	**M**	**(s)**	**G**
Vincent Bezecourt (FRA)	10.06.1993	3	(5)	1
Pape Abdou Camara (SEN)	24.09.1991	5	(10)	
Wangu Batista Gome (NAM)	13.02.1993	18	(2)	3

Artak Grigoryan	19.10.1987	19	(1)	1
Vahagn Hayrapetyan	14.06.1997		(1)	
Rumyan Hovsepyan	13.11.1991	11	(8)	1
Davit Minasyan	09.03.1993		(2)	
Erik Soghomonyan	02.04.2000		(4)	
Tiago Galvão da Silva (BRA)	24.08.1989	15	(1)	2
Forwards:	**DOB**	**M**	**(s)**	**G**
Grigor Aghekyan	06.04.1996	2	(10)	
David Davidyan	14.12.1997	15	(4)	5
Hayk Galstyan	23.03.1998		(1)	
Aleksandar Glišić (BIH)	03.09.1992	15	(1)	3
Mihran Manasyan	13.01.1989	1	(2)	
Branko Mihajlović (SRB)	20.02.1991	5	(7)	1
Sunday Umaru Ngbede (NGA)	23.04.1998	4	(5)	
Aghvan Papikyan	08.02.1994		(1)	
Jeferson Fernandes Macedo „Perdigão"	17.07.1991	3	(2)	
Ghukas Poghosyan	06.02.1994		(3)	
Nikita Tankov (RUS)	29.09.1996	7	(12)	2

Football Club Ararat Yerevan

Founded:	10.05.1935		
Stadium:	„Vazgen Sargsyan" Stadium, Yerevan (14,403)		
Trainer:	Vardan Bichakhchyan		09.10.1977

Goalkeepers:	DOB	M	(s)	G
Poghos Ayvazyan	09.06.1995	1		
Vsevolod Ermakov (RUS)	06.01.1996	22		
Defenders:	**DOB**	**M**	**(s)**	**G**
Juan David Bravo Padilla (COL)	01.04.1990	17	(2)	2
Artur Danielyan	09.02.1998	3	(2)	
Christián Jiménez (ESP)	04.07.1996	6	(3)	
Yuri Maghakyan	22.06.2000		(1)	
Zhirayr Margaryan	13.09.1997	19	(1)	
Hrar Mkoyan	02.09.1986	18	(1)	
Vahe Muradyan	28.01.1998		(1)	
Marko Prljević (SRB)	02.08.1988	18	(2)	
Aleksandre Saganelidze (GEO)	09.08.1999		(1)	
Ivan Spychka (UKR)	18.01.1991	8	(1)	
Midfielders:	**DOB**	**M**	**(s)**	**G**
Zaven Badoyan	22.12.1989	1	(14)	1
Serob Galstyan	23.09.2002		(1)	

David Khurtsidze (RUS)	04.07.1993	20	(2)	2
Edgar Malakyan	22.09.1990	10	(3)	1
David Manoyan	05.07.1990	14	(7)	1
Karen Muradyan	01.11.1992	22		
Dimitrije Pobulić (SRB)	10.05.1994	5	(7)	3
Seroj Titizian	01.02.2000	1	(3)	
Solomon Ime Udo (NGA)	15.07.1995	4	(5)	
Artak Yedigaryan	18.03.1990	7	(10)	
Forwards:	**DOB**	**M**	**(s)**	**G**
Razmik Hakobyan	09.02.1996	1	(4)	
Mory Kone (CIV)	13.07.1995	16	(6)	7
Grigor Muradyan	06.08.2002		(1)	
Uroš Nenadović (SRB)	28.01.1994	16	(2)	6
Aghvan Papikyan	08.02.1994	15	(3)	1
Igor Stanojević (SRB)	24.10.1991	4	(4)	1
Maksym Zaderaka (UKR)	07.09.1994	5	(5)	3

Football Club Ararat-Armenia Yerevan

Founded:	2017		
Stadium:	Yerevan Football Academy Stadium, Yerevan (1,428)		
Trainer:	David Campaña Piquer (ESP)		23.05.1974
[05.03.2021]	Armen Adamyan		14.10.1967
[24.03.3021]	Anatoliy Baydachniy (RUS)		01.10.1952

Goalkeepers:	DOB	M	(s)	G
Dmitri Abakumov (RUS)	08.07.1989	15		
Stefan Čupić (SRB)	07.05.1994	6		
Nikola Petrić (SRB)	11.05.1991	3	(1)	
Defenders:	**DOB**	**M**	**(s)**	**G**
Guilherme António de Souza "Alemão" (BRA)	07.12.1992	9	(5)	
Ângelo Rafael Teixeira Alpoim Meneses(POR)	03.07.1993	10	(2)	
Aleksandar Damčevski (MKD)	21.11.1992	1		
Artur Danielyan	09.02.1998	2	(2)	
José Junior Julio Bueno (COL)	03.09.1996	8	(1)	1
David Humanes Muñoz "David Bollo" (ESP)	13.11.1996	14	(1)	2
Alex Júnior Christian (HAI)	12.05.1993	2	(2)	
Albert Khachumyan	23.06.1999	10	(4)	
Yegor Klymenchuk (UKR)	11.11.1997	3	(1)	
David Terteryan	17.12.1997	10	(3)	
Serhiy Vakulenko (UKR)	07.09.1993	15		1
Midfielders:	**DOB**	**M**	**(s)**	**G**
Kódjo Kassé Alphonse (CIV)	28.05.1993	3		

Armen Ambartsumyan	11.04.1994	18	(4)	
Wbeymar Angulo Mosquera	06.03.1992	9	(2)	1
Yoan Gouffran (FRA)	25.05.1986	20	(3)	
Hovhannes Harutyunyan	25.05.1991	1	(2)	
Mailson Lima Duarte Lopes (CPV)	29.05.1994	8	(2)	4
Armen Nahapetyan	24.07.1999		(2)	
Heradi Rashidi (COD)	24.07.1994	1	(5)	
Sargis Shahinyan	10.09.1995	9	(12)	1
Forwards:	**DOB**	**M**	**(s)**	**G**
Armen Hovhannisyan	07.03.2000		(4)	
Aleksandr Karapetyan	23.12.1987	10	(2)	4
Ogana Louis Ugochukwu (NGA)	29.12.1995	6	(3)	2
Jeisson Enrique Martínez Aranibar (PER)	28.12.1994	6	(7)	2
Furdjel Narsingh (NED)	13.03.1988	18	(2)	
Yusuf Olaitan Otubanjo (NGA)	12.09.1992	17	(4)	10
Zakaria Sanogo (BFA)	11.12.1996	21	(2)	1
Artur Serobyan	02.07.2003	4	(9)	
Dan Spătaru (MDA)	24.05.1994	5	(3)	

Football Club Gandzasar Kapan

Founded: 2004
Stadium: Yerevan Football Academy Stadium, Yerevan (1,428)
Trainer: Armen Petrosyan   06.09.1985

Goalkeepers:	DOB	M	(s)	G
Grigor Meliksetyan	18.08.1986	8		
Defenders:	**DOB**	**M**	**(s)**	**G**
Diogo Manuel Gonçalves Coelho (POR)	08.07.1992	4		
Hakob Hambardzumyan	26.05.1997		(3)	
Alexander Hovhannisyan	20.07.1996	4	(1)	
Hayk Ishkhanyan	24.06.1989	8		
Vaspurak Minasyan	29.06.1994	8		
Gevorg Nranyan	09.03.1986	4	(1)	
David Terteryan	17.12.1997	6	(1)	
Midfielders:	**DOB**	**M**	**(s)**	**G**
Ashot Adamyan	15.06.1997		(2)	
Wbeymar Angulo Mosquera	06.03.1992	8		3

	DOB	M	(s)	G
Narek Aslanyan	04.06.1996	1	(3)	
Edvard Avagyan	21.03.1996		(3)	
Davit Minasyan	09.03.1993	5	(1)	
Abdoul Karim Zoko (BFA)	27.07.1993	8		
Forwards:	**DOB**	**M**	**(s)**	**G**
Joseph Oma Adah (NGA)	08.06.1999	8		1
Gegham Harutyunyan	23.08.1990	3		2
Armen Hovhannisyan	07.03.2000	1	(3)	
Israel Roberto Ferreira Junior (BRA)	07.10.1998		(4)	
Andranik Kocharyan	29.01.1994	8		
Ashot Kocharyan	13.07.1999		(5)	
Rokas Krusnauskas	04.11.1995	4	(3)	3

Lori Football Club Vanadzor

Founded: 1936
Stadium: Vanadzor Football Academy Stadium, Vanadzot (880)
Trainer: Albert Solomonov (RUS)   25.09.1973

Goalkeepers:	DOB	M	(s)	G
Artem Gomelko (BLR)	08.12.1989	13		
Nemanja Šćekić (MNE)	17.12.1991	2		
Defenders:	**DOB**	**M**	**(s)**	**G**
Nana Antwi (GHA)	10.08.2000	14	(1)	
Arthur Avagyan	04.07.1987	9		
Ivan Božović (SRB)	29.05.1990	9	(3)	
Deou Dosa Olatunji (NGA)	29.07.1998		(4)	
Yevgeniy Kirisov (RUS)	14.02.1994	1	(1)	
Luiz Matheus Servo de Carvalho (BRA)	10.01.1993		(2)	
Timur Rudoselskiy (KAZ)	21.12.1994	12		1
Aleksandr Stepanov (RUS)	05.06.1996	15		
Arsen Yeghiazaryan	15.01.2000	1	(1)	
Midfielders:	**DOB**	**M**	**(s)**	**G**
Naor Aboudi (ISR)	17.07.1993	5	(3)	1
Djimy Alexis (HAI)	08.10.1997	12	(1)	2
Aram Kocharyan	05.03.1996	11	(2)	1
André Luiz Leão Lima „André Mensalão" (BRA)	21.06.1990	3	(1)	2

	DOB	M	(s)	G
Almog Ohayon (ISR)	05.08.1994	6	(2)	2
Pavel Osipov (RUS)	28.01.1996	7	(6)	1
David Paremuzyan	02.03.2000	1	(9)	
Yevgeniy Skoblikov	10.07.1990	11	(4)	1
Manuel Alexander Vargas Moreno (PAN)	19.01.1991		(1)	
Victor César Santos da Conceição "Vitinho" (BRA)	27.07.1999		(6)	
Forwards:	**DOB**	**M**	**(s)**	**G**
Vardan Bakalyan	04.04.1995	2	(3)	
Claudir Marini Junior (BRA)	06.08.1992	12	(1)	3
Fernando Camões de Araújo „Fernandinho" (POR)	21.02.1997	8	(3)	
Pavel Kudryashov (RUS)	27.11.1996		(3)	
Karapet Manukyan	25.07.1992	3		
Robert Minasyan	08.04.1997	3	(3)	
Anicet Oura (CIV)	07.12.1999	2	(1)	
Ghukas Poghosyan	06.02.1994	1	(3)	1
Nikola Popović (SRB)	31.05.1994		(1)	
Nikola Tripković (SRB)	28.01.1998	2	(3)	1

Football Club Noah Yerevan

Founded: 2017
Stadium: Alashkert Stadium, Yerevan (6,850)
Trainer: Igor Picusceac (MDA)   27.10.1983
[05.11.2020] Dmitriy Gunko (RUS)   01.03.1976

Goalkeepers:	DOB	M	(s)	G
Maksim Shvagirev (RUS)	12.08.1994	2		
Valerio Vimercati (ITA)	04.03.1995	21		
Defenders:	**DOB**	**M**	**(s)**	**G**
Jordy João Monroy Ararat	03.01.1996	23		1
Saná Gomes (GNB)	10.10.1999	15	(3)	2
Jefferson Alves Oliveira (BRA)	25.02.1990	5	(1)	
Soslan Kagermazov (RUS)	20.08.1996		(2)	
Mikhail Kovalenko (RUS)	25.01.1995	14	(2)	
Vladislav Kryuchkov (RUS)	24.08.1989	16		
Arman Mkrtchyan	09.07.1999		(3)	
Alan Tataev (RUS)	03.08.1995	6		
Midfielders:	**DOB**	**M**	**(s)**	**G**
Ashot Adamyan	15.06.1997		(1)	
Alexandre Miguel Simões Oliveira (POR)	29.08.2000	8	(12)	3
Petros Avetisyan	07.01.1996	10		5
Vladimir Azarov (RUS)	19.03.1994	14	(2)	6
Maksim Danilin (RUS)	13.09.2001	2	(2)	
Denys Dedechko (UKR)	02.07.1987	18		

	DOB	M	(s)	G
Pavel Deobald (RUS)	25.06.1990	3	(5)	
Nikita Dubchak (RUS)	12.08.1993	2		
Eduards Emsis (LVA)	23.02.1996	15	(2)	1
Yuri Gareginyan	03.02.1994	6	(7)	
Benik Hovhannisyan	01.05.1993	15	(7)	2
Helistano Ciro Manga (GNB)	20.05.1999	9	(6)	
Yaroslav Matvienko (URS)	22.03.1998		(1)	
Artem Simonyan	20.02.1995	7	(2)	3
Forwards:	**DOB**	**M**	**(s)**	**G**
Kirill Bor (RUS)	09.11.1998	5	(4)	
Raymond Gyasi (GHA)	05.08.1994	7	(2)	
Gegham Harutyunyan	23.08.1990		(5)	
Pavel Kireenko (RUS)	14.06.1994	8	(3)	3
Dmitriy Lavrishchev (RUS)	23.12.1998	2	(8)	
Maksim Mayrovich (RUS)	06.02.1996	6	(1)	2
Vadim Paireli (MDA)	08.11.1995	4	(2)	1
Dan Spătaru (MDA)	24.05.1994	9	(1)	2
Andrey Titov (RUS)	05.03.1996	1	(7)	
Dobrivoje Velemir (SRB)	14.03.1997		(5)	

Football Club Pyunik Yerevan

Founded: 1992 (*as Homenetmen Yerevan*)
Stadium: „Vazgen Sargsyan" Stadium, Yerevan (14,403)
Trainer: Artak Oseyan — 16.05.1987
[07.01.2021] Eghishe Melikyan — 13.08.1979

Goalkeepers:	DOB	M	(s)	G
Stanislav Buchnev (RUS)	17.07.1990	19		
Herman Penkov (UKR)	26.05.1994	5	(2)	
Defenders:	**DOB**	**M**	**(s)**	**G**
Artak Asatryan	25.01.2001		(1)	
Valeriy Boldenkov (UKR)	08.09.1994	5	(2)	
Anton Bratkov (UKR)	14.05.1993	9		
Igor Gonchar (UKR)	10.01.1993	12	(1)	
Serob Grigoryan	04.02.1995	19	(1)	1
Robert Hakobyan	22.10.1996	5	(2)	
Arman Hovhannisyan	07.07.1993	8		
Rommell Jhoan Ibarra Hernández (VEN)	24.03.2000	5	(1)	
Artur Kartashyan	08.01.1997	6	(4)	
Magomed Musalov (RUS)	09.02.1994	3	(1)	
Salomon Nirisarike (RWA)	23.11.1993	9		
Alexandre Yeoulé (CIV)	23.12.1995	11		
Midfielders:	**DOB**	**M**	**(s)**	**G**
Alik Arakelyan	21.05.1996	22	(1)	1
Erik Azizyan	04.03.2000		(9)	
José Enrique Caraballo Rosal (VEN)	21.02.1996	12		3
Artur Grigoryan	10.07.1993	8	(11)	
Artem Habelok (UKR)	02.01.1995	6	(1)	
Hovhannes Harutyunyan	25.05.1999	4	(7)	1
Higor Barbosa Rodrigues Leite (BRA)	02.06.1993	5	(3)	2
Muhammad Yusuf Ladan (NGA)	18.01.2000	5	(2)	
Gor Malakyan	12.06.1994	8	(2)	
Armen Nahapetyan	24.07.1999		(5)	1
Dramane Salou (BFA)	22.05.1998	18	(2)	
Mykyta Tatarkov (UKR)	04.01.1995	12		2
Julius David Ufuoma (NGA)	14.02.2000	5	(4)	
Forwards:	**DOB**	**M**	**(s)**	**G**
Steven Alfred (NGA)	11.10.1997	3	(5)	1
Artyom Avanesyan	17.07.1999	12	(9)	2
José Manuel Balza Liscano (VEN)	15.06.1997	4	(1)	1
Yevhen Budnik (UKR)	04.09.1990	2	(6)	
Vrezh Chiloyan	06.04.2002		(2)	1
Anton Kobyalko	14.05.1986	9	(7)	1
Oleh Kozhushko (UKR)	17.02.1998	5	(8)	2
Aras Özbiliz	09.03.1990	6		
Levon Vardanyan	02.11.2003	2	(7)	

Shirak Sports Club Gyumri

Founded: 1958
Stadium: Gyumri City Stadium, Gyumri (4,000)
Trainer: Tigran Davtyan — 10.06.1978

Goalkeepers:	DOB	M	(s)	G
Sokrat Hovhannisyan	05.04.1996	5	(1)	
Lyova Karapetyan	01.03.2001		(1)	
Gevorg Kasparov	25.07.1980	7		
Spasoje Stefanović (SRB)	12.10.1992	12		
Defenders:	**DOB**	**M**	**(s)**	**G**
Vardan Arzoyan	30.04.1995	13	(4)	
Aghvan Davoyan	21.03.1990	16	(3)	
Hrachya Geghamyan	02.12.1999	4	(1)	
Robert Hakobyan	22.10.1996	5	(4)	1
Hayk Ishkhanyan	24.06.1989	11		
Artyom Mikaelyan	12.07.1991	16		2
Hovhannes Nazaryan	11.03.1998	16	(5)	
Arsen Sadoyan	16.03.1999	8	(3)	
Seryozha Urushanyan	01.08.1997	14	(2)	
Hakob Vardanyan	01.06.1999	1	(3)	
Midfielders:	**DOB**	**M**	**(s)**	**G**
Petros Afajanyan	31.10.1998	10	(3)	
Arman Aslanyan	30.01.1994	16	(4)	2
Levon Darbinyan	24.01.2002	3		
Tidiane Amédé Diomandé (CIV)	14.03.1999	1	(4)	
Sergey Manukyan	03.04.2004		(1)	
Rafik Misakyan	02.01.2000		(1)	
Rudik Mkrtchyan	26.10.1998	18	(2)	1
Erik Vardanyan	08.03.1999	12	(5)	
Forwards:	**DOB**	**M**	**(s)**	**G**
Leibe Junior Avo (CIV)	20.12.1997	14	(3)	1
Vardan Bakalyan	04.04.1995	4	(5)	
Artem Gevorkyan (RUS)	21.05.1993	17	(3)	1
Martin Grigoryan	25.09.2000	4	(12)	
Mory Kone (CIV)	13.07.1995	1		
Lyova Mryan	11.05.2000	2	(18)	1
Aram Muradyan	14.04.1995	12	(9)	1
Dognimani Yacouba Silue (CIV)	01.01.2002	10	(3)	1
Igor Stanojević (SRB)	24.10.1991	10	(2)	2
Arlen Tsaturyan	05.01.1999		(2)	
Emil Yeghiazaryan	03.11.1997	2	(5)	

Football Club Urartu Yerevan

Founded: 20.01.1992 (*as FC Banants Yerevan*)
Stadium: Banants Stadium, Yerevan (4,860)
Trainer: Aleksandr Grigoryan — 28.09.1966
[09.03.2021] Tigran Yesayan — 02.06.1972

Goalkeepers:	DOB	M	(s)	G
Anatoly Ayvazov	08.06.1996	4		
Arsen Beglaryan	18.02.1993	18		
Grigori Matevosyan	09.06.1999	1		
Defenders:	**DOB**	**M**	**(s)**	**G**
Khariton Ayvazyan	08.11.2003	3	(5)	
Robert Darbinyan	04.10.1995	4		
Edgar Grigoryan	25.08.1998	13	(2)	
Dmitry Guz (RUS)	15.05.1988	9		
Annan Mensah (GHA)	06.07.1996	10	(1)	
Salomon Nirisarike (RWA)	23.03.1993	11	(1)	
Yevgeniy Osipov (RUS)	29.10.1986	9		
Vadym Paramonov	18.03.1991	12		1
Narek Petrosyan	25.01.1996		(1)	
Erik Piloyan	29.01.2001		(1)	
Eric Simonyan	12.07.2003	3		
Pyotr Ten (RUS)	12.07.1992	12	(1)	
Midfielders:	**DOB**	**M**	**(s)**	**G**
Isah Aliyu (NGA)	08.08.1999	3	(10)	1
Tigran Ayunts	15.03.2000		(1)	
Robert Baghramyan	29.06.2002	2	(1)	
Hakob Hakobyan	29.03.1997	19	(2)	
Uguchukwu Christus Iwu (NGA)	28.10.1999	21		2
James Santos das Neves (BRA)	15.07.1995	9	(7)	
Gor Lulukyan	02.01.2003	2	(3)	
Maksim Mashnev (RUS)	12.01.1993	2	(4)	
Karen Melkonyan	25.03.1999	11	(7)	
Peter Mutumosi Zilu (COD)	25.05.1998	7	(8)	1
Oleg Polyakov (RUS)	29.11.1990	15	(2)	2
Víctor Hugo Coelho Vieira „Vitinho" (BRA)	08.09.1997	18	(4)	1
Forwards:	**DOB**	**M**	**(s)**	**G**
Jonel Désiré (HAI)	12.02.1997	16	(1)	8
Yevgeniy Kobzar (RUS)	09.08.1992	4	(11)	2
Artur Miranyan	27.12.1995	8	(2)	3
Igor Paderin (RUS)	24.11.1989	2	(6)	1
Abraham Portugalyan	08.01.1999		(1)	
Aleksandr Radchenko (RUS)	14.09.1993	4	(2)	1
Gevorg Tarakhchyan	13.05.2002	1	(14)	

Football Club Van Charentsavan

Founded:	2019	
Stadium:	Charentsavan City Stadium, Charentsavan (5,000)	
Trainer:	Sevada Arzumanyan	24.05.1969
[09.02.2021]	Artur Asoyan	03.12.1970

Goalkeepers:	DOB	M	(s)	G
Samur Agamagomedov	30.11.1998	15	(1)	
Henri Avagyan	16.01.1996	10		
Defenders:	**DOB**	**M**	**(s)**	**G**
Vahagn Ayvazyan	16.04.1992	17	(4)	2
Deou Dosa Olatunji (NGA)	29.07.1998	9	(1)	1
Ebert Cardoso da Silva (BRA)	25.05.1993	12	(1)	
Josué Gaba (CIV)	12.01.2002	10	(2)	
Michael Gnolou (CIV)	05.01.1998		(1)	
Alexander Hovhannisyan	20.07.1996	7	(2)	
Rustam Isaev	02.06.1998	6	(1)	
Arman Khachatryan	09.06.1997		(1)	
Pavel Korkin (RUS)	24.01.2000		(1)	
Argishti Petrosyan	16.10.1992	22		
Aleksandr Tenyaev	11.03.1996	20	(2)	2
Andranik Voskanyan	11.04.1990	24	(1)	
Midfielders:	**DOB**	**M**	**(s)**	**G**
Davit Ayvazyan	12.08.1999		(1)	
Muslim Bammatgereev	15.01.1996	13		1
Essien Edem Ededem (NGA)	14.04.1998	24	(1)	

	DOB	M	(s)	G
Stanislav Efimov	09.08.1993	5	(7)	1
Garegin Kirakosyan	26.11.1995	4	(13)	1
Media Ladji Traoré (CIV)	01.01.2002		(3)	
Davit Nalbandyan	09.08.1999		(4)	
Lie Pato Ngavouka-Tseke (CGO)	15.01.1991	6	(2)	
Vladislav Vasiljev (RUS)	27.07.1999	11	(1)	
Maks Zhestarev	01.08.2002		(1)	
Forwards:	**DOB**	**M**	**(s)**	**G**
Stéphane Adjoumani (CIV)	18.11.1998	11	(3)	3
Viulen Ayvazyan	01.01.1995	3	(3)	
Wilfried Kwassi Eza (CIV)	28.12.1996	19	(3)	8
David Ghandilyan	04.06.1993		(7)	
Orbeli Hambardzumyan	26.03.1996		(1)	
Emmanuel Mireku Attah (GHA)	25.12.1997	2	(4)	
Aleksandr Maksimenko	22.03.1996	2	(7)	
Mihran Manasyan	13.01.1989	3	(6)	2
Edgar Movsesyan	09.09.1998	11	(14)	4
Mihran Petrosyan	19.09.1999	2	(7)	1
Aleksey Shishkin (RUS)	29.11.1997	7	(3)	

SECOND LEVEL
Armenian First League 2020/2021

1.	FC Sevan (*Promoted*)	27	22	2	3	75 - 23	68
2.	BKMA Yerevan	27	21	2	4	84 - 22	65
3.	Noravank SC Vayk	27	16	2	9	45 - 31	50
4.	FC West Armenia Yerevan	27	16	2	9	71 - 36	50
5.	Lernayin Artsakh FC Stepanakert	27	12	2	13	37 - 50	38
6.	FC Urartu-2 Yerevan	27	10	5	12	43 - 53	35
7.	FC Ararat-2 Yerevan	27	10	2	15	44 - 56	32
8.	FC Pyunik-2 Yerevan	27	6	2	19	25 - 72	20
9.	Shirak SC-2 Gyumri	27	5	2	20	21 - 68	17
10.	FC Ararat-Armenia-2 Yerevan	27	4	5	18	28 - 62	17

05.09.2020	Skopje	North Macedonia - Armenia	2-1(2-0)	(UNL)
08.09.2020	Yerevan	Armenia - Estonia	2-0(1-0)	(UNL)
11.10.2020	Tychy	Armenia - Georgia	2-2(1-0)	(UNL)
14.10.2020	Tallinn	Estonia - Armenia	1-1(1-1)	(UNL)
15.11.2020	Tbilisi	Georgia - Armenia	1-2(0-1)	(UNL)
18.11.2020	Nicosia	Armenia - North Macedonia	1-0(0-0)	(UNL)
25.03.2021	Vaduz	Liechtenstein - Armenia	0-1(0-0)	(WCQ)
28.03.2021	Yerevan	Armenia - Iceland	2-0(0-0)	(WCQ)
31.03.2021	Yerevan	Armenia - Romania	3-2(0-0)	(WCQ)
01.06.2021	Velika Gorica	Croatia - Armenia	1-1(1-0)	(F)
05.06.2021	Stockholm	Sweden - Armenia	3-1(2-0)	(F)

05.09.2020   **NORTH MACEDONIA - ARMENIA**   **2-1(2-0)**   2nd UEFA Nations League C, Group 2
"Toše Proeski" Arena, Skopje; Referee: Irfan Peljto (Bosnia and Herzegovina); Attendance: 0
ARM: David Yurchenko, Hovhannes Hambartsumyan, André Jack Calisir, Varazdat Haroyan (Cap), Serob Grigoryan (46.Edgar Babayan), Kamo Hovhannisyan, Artak Grigoryan, Wbeymar Angulo Mosquera, Khoren Bayramyan (46.Tigran Barseghyan), Arshak Koryan, Aleksandr Karapetyan (76.Norberto Alejandro Briasco Balekian). Trainer: Joaquín de Jesús Caparrós Camino (Spain).
Goal: Tigran Barseghyan (90+4 penalty).

08.09.2020   **ARMENIA - ESTONIA**   **2-0(1-0)**   2nd UEFA Nations League C, Group 2
„Vazgen Sargsyan" Hanrapetakan Stadium, Yerevan; Referee: David Coote (England); Attendance: 0
ARM: David Yurchenko, Hovhannes Hambartsumyan, André Jack Calisir (46.Taron Voskanyan), Varazdat Haroyan (Cap), Arman Hovhannisyan, Artak Grigoryan, Gegam Kadimyan (73.Khoren Bayramyan), Wbeymar Angulo Mosquera, Arshak Koryan (64.Vahan Bichakhchyan), Aleksandr Karapetyan, Tigran Barseghyan. Trainer: Joaquín de Jesús Caparrós Camino (Spain).
Goals: Aleksandr Karapetyan (43), Wbeymar Angulo Mosquera (65).

11.10.2020   **ARMENIA - GEORGIA**   **2-2(1-0)**   2nd UEFA Nations League C, Group 2
Stadion Miejski, Tichy (Poland); Referee: Ivan Bebek (Croatia); Attendance: 0
ARM: David Yurchenko, André Jack Calisir, Varazdat Haroyan, Arman Hovhannisyan, Henrikh Mkhitaryan (Cap), Kamo Hovhannisyan (81.Gegam Kadimyan), Artak Grigoryan, Wbeymar Angulo Mosquera (67.Yuri Gareginyan), Khoren Bayramyan, Aleksandr Karapetyan (67.Edgar Babayan), Tigran Barseghyan (90.Vahan Bichakhchyan). Trainer: Joaquín de Jesús Caparrós Camino (Spain).
Goals: Khoren Bayramyan (6), Henrikh Mkhitaryan (89 penalty).

14.10.2020   **ESTONIA - ARMENIA**   **1-1(1-1)**   2nd UEFA Nations League C, Group 2
A. Le Coq Arena, Tallinn; Referee: Luis Miguel Branco Godinho (Portugal); Attendance: 1,007
ARM: David Yurchenko, André Jack Calisir, Taron Voskanyan, Arman Hovhannisyan (46.Serob Grigoryan), Henrikh Mkhitaryan (Cap), Kamo Hovhannisyan, Artak Grigoryan (42.Solomon Ime Udo), Wbeymar Angulo Mosquera, Edgar Babayan (57.Gevorg Ghazaryan), Aleksandr Karapetyan (83.Gegam Kadimyan), Tigran Barseghyan (83.Vahan Bichakhchyan). Trainer: Joaquín de Jesús Caparrós Camino (Spain).
Goal: Kamo Hovhannisyan (8).

15.11.2020   **GEORGIA - ARMENIA**   **1-2(0-1)**   2nd UEFA Nations League C, Group 2
„Boris Paichadze" Dinamo Arena, Tbilisi; Referee: Marco Guida (Italy); Attendance: 0
ARM: David Yurchenko, Hovhannes Hambartsumyan, André Jack Calisir, Varazdat Haroyan, Arman Hovhannisyan (69.Serob Grigoryan), Artak Grigoryan, Solomon Ime Udo (77.Karen Muradyan), Gevorg Ghazaryan (Cap) (77.Vahan Bichakhchyan), Aleksandr Karapetyan (77.Arshak Koryan), Tigran Barseghyan, Sargis Adamyan (89.Taron Voskanyan). Trainer: Joaquín de Jesús Caparrós Camino (Spain).
Goals: Gevorg Ghazaryan (33), Sargis Adamyan (86).

18.11.2020   **ARMENIA - NORTH MACEDONIA**   **1-0(0-0)**   2nd UEFA Nations League C, Group 2
Stádio GSP, Nicosia (Cyprus); Referee: Robert Adam Madden (Scotland); Attendance: 0
ARM: David Yurchenko, Hovhannes Hambartsumyan, Varazdat Haroyan (Cap), Taron Voskanyan, Kamo Hovhannisyan, Artak Grigoryan, Arshak Koryan (65.Serob Grigoryan), Solomon Ime Udo (46.Wbeymar Angulo Mosquera), Hakob Hakobyan (70.Karen Muradyan), Aleksandr Karapetyan (46.Vahan Bichakhchyan), Tigran Barseghyan (90+1.Hayk Ishkhanyan). Trainer: Joaquín de Jesús Caparrós Camino (Spain).
Goal: Hovhannes Hambartsumyan (55).

25.03.2021   **LIECHTENSTEIN - ARMENIA**   **0-1(0-0)**   22nd FIFA WC. Qualifiers
Rheinpark Stadion, Vaduz; Referee: Julian Weinberger (Austria); Attendance: 0
ARM: David Yurchenko, Hovhannes Hambartsumyan, André Jack Calisir, Varazdat Haroyan (Cap), Kamo Hovhannisyan, Artak Grigoryan (46.Aleksandr Karapetyan), Khoren Bayramyan (75.Edgar Babayan), Solomon Ime Udo, Tigran Barseghyan (90+2.Vahan Bichakhchyan), Sargis Adamyan, Norberto Alejandro Briasco Balekian (64.Artur Miranyan). Trainer: Joaquín de Jesús Caparrós Camino (Spain).
Goal: Noah Frommelt (83 own goal).

28.03.2021   **ARMENIA - ICELAND**   **2-0(0-0)**   22nd FIFA WC. Qualifiers
„Vazgen Sargsyan" Hanrapetakan Stadium, Yerevan; Referee: Enea Jorgji (Albania); Attendance: 4,300
ARM: David Yurchenko, Hovhannes Hambartsumyan, Varazdat Haroyan (Cap), Taron Voskanyan, Kamo Hovhannisyan, Artak Grigoryan, Solomon Ime Udo (81.Karen Muradyan), Hakob Hakobyan (56.Khoren Bayramyan), Tigran Barseghyan, Sargis Adamyan (81.Zhirayr Shaghoyan), Norberto Alejandro Briasco Balekian (64.Aleksandr Karapetyan). Trainer: Joaquín de Jesús Caparrós Camino (Spain).
Goals: Tigran Barseghyan (53), Khoren Bayramyan (74).

31.03.2021   **ARMENIA - ROMANIA**   **3-2(0-0)**   22nd FIFA WC. Qualifiers
„Vazgen Sargsyan" Hanrapetakan Stadium, Yerevan; Referee: Andris Treimanis (Latvia); Attendance: 4,300
ARM: David Yurchenko, André Jack Calisir, Hovhannes Hambartsumyan, Varazdat Haroyan (Cap), Kamo Hovhannisyan, Artak Grigoryan, Khoren Bayramyan, Karen Muradyan (46.Eduard Spertsyan), Aleksandr Karapetyan (46.Zhirayr Shaghoyan), Tigran Barseghyan (90+2.Solomon Ime Udo), Norberto Alejandro Briasco Balekian (46.Sargis Adamyan). Trainer: Joaquín de Jesús Caparrós Camino (Spain).
Goals: Eduard Spertsyan (56), Varazdat Haroyan (87), Tigran Barseghyan (89 penalty).

01.06.2021   **CROATIA - ARMENIA**   **1-1(1-0)**   Friendly International

Stadion Radnik, Velika Gorica; Referee: Luka Bilbija (Bosnia and Herzegovina); Attendance: 0
ARM: David Yurchenko, André Jack Calisir, Taron Voskanyan, David Terteryan (62.Jordy Ararat), Kamo Hovhannisyan (Cap), Khoren Bayramyan (62.Zhirayr Shaghoyan), Artak Grigoryan (79.Karen Muradyan), Edgar Babayan (46.Karen Melkonyan), Eduard Spertsyan (46.Wbeymar Angulo Mosquera), Tigran Barseghyan, Sargis Adamyan (46.Vahan Bichakhchyan). Trainer: Joaquín de Jesús Caparrós Camino (Spain).
Goal: Wbeymar Angulo Mosquera (72).

05.06.2021   **SWEDEN - ARMENIA**   **3-1(2-0)**   Friendly International

Friends Arena, Stockholm; Referee: Mattias Gestranius (Finland); Attendance: 500
ARM: David Yurchenko, André Jack Calisir (72.Albert Khachumyan), Taron Voskanyan, Jordy Ararat, Kamo Hovhannisyan (Cap), Wbeymar Angulo Mosquera (46.Khoren Bayramyan), Hakob Hakobyan (46.Karen Muradyan), Vahan Bichakhchyan, Artur Miranyan (46.Tigran Barseghyan), Eduard Spertsyan (46.Artak Grigoryan), Sargis Adamyan (82.Zhirayr Shaghoyan). Trainer: Joaquín de Jesús Caparrós Camino (Spain).
Goal: Vahan Bichakhchyan (64).

NATIONAL TEAM PLAYERS
(16.07.2020 – 15.07.2021)

Name	DOB	Caps	Goals	2020/2021:	Club
Goalkeepers					
David YURCHENKO	27.03.1986	11	0	2020:	FC Shakhter Karagandy (KAZ)
				15.01.2021->	FC Alashkert Yerevan
Defenders					
Jordy João Monroy ARARAT	03.01.1996	4	0	2020/2021:	FC Noah Yerevan
André Jack CALISIR	13.06.1990	17	0	2020:	IFK Göteborg (SWE)
				01.01.2021->	GS Apollon Smyrna (GRE)
Serob GRIGORYAN	04.02.1995	4	0	2020:	FC Pyunik Yerevan
Hakob HAKOBYAN	29.03.1997	3	0	2020/2021:	FC Urartu Yerevan
Hovhannes HAMBARTSUMYAN	04.10.1990	42	4	2020/2021:	Anorthosis Famagusta FC (CYP)
Varazdat HAROYAN	24.08.1992	58	3	2020:	FK Tambov (RUS)
				15.02.2021->	Astana FC (KAZ)
Arman HOVHANNISYAN	07.07.1993	7	0	2020:	FC Tobol Kostanay (KAZ)
Kamo HOVHANNISYAN	05.10.1990	59	1	2020/2021:	FC Kairat Almaty (KAZ)
Hayk ISHKHANYAN	24.06.1989	13	1	2020/2021:	FC Gandzasar Kapan
Albert KHACHUMYAN	23.06.1999	1	0	2021:	FC Ararat -Armenia Yerevan
David TERTERYAN	17.12.1997	1	0	2021:	FC Ararat -Armenia Yerevan
Taron VOSKANYAN	22.02.1993	34	0	2020/2021:	FC Alashkert Yerevan
Midfielders					
Wbeymar ANGULO Mosquera	06.03.1992	7	2	2020:	FC Gandzasar Kapan
				01.01.2021->	FC Ararat -Armenia Yerevan
Edgar BABAYAN	28.10.1995	13	1	2020:	Hobro IK (DEN)
				15.02.2021->	Rīga FC (LVA)
Khoren BAYRAMYAN	07.01.1992	8	2	2020/2021:	FK Rostov (RUS)
Vahan BICHAKHCHYAN	09.07.1999	8	1	2020/2021:	MŠK Žilina (SVK)
Yuri GAREGINYAN	03.02.1994	1	0	2020:	FC Noah Yerevan
Gevorg GHAZARYAN	05.04.1988	73	14	2020:	AEL Limassol (CYP)
Artak GRIGORYAN	19.10.1987	37	1	2020/2021:	FC Alashkert Yerevan
Henrikh MKHITARYAN	21.01.1989	88	30	2020:	AS Roma (ITA)
Karen MURADYAN	01.11.1992	10	0	2020/2021:	FC Ararat Yerevan
Zhirayr SHAGHOYAN	10.04.2001	4	0	2021:	BKMA Yerevan
Eduard SPERTSYAN	07.06.2000	3	1	2021:	FK Krasnodar (RUS)
Solomon Ime UDO	15.07.1995	6	0	2020:	FC Ararat Yerevan
				22.02.2021->	FC Shakhter Karagandy (KAZ)
Forwards					
Sargis ADAMYAN	23.05.1993	24	2	2020/2021:	TSG 1899 Hoffenheim (GER)
Tigran BARSEGHYAN	22.09.1993	39	8	2020/2021:	Astana FC (KAZ)
Norberto Alejandro BRIASCO Balekian	29.02.1996	8	0	2020/2021:	CA Huracán Buenos Aires (ARG)
Gegam KADIMYAN	19.10.1992	13	2	2020:	FC Neman Grodno (BLR)
Aleksandr KARAPETYAN	23.12.1987	22	6	2020:	FK Tambov (RUS)
				09.02.2021>	FC Ararat -Armenia Yerevan
Arshak KORYAN	17.06.1995	4	0	2020:	FK Khimki (RUS)
Karen MELKONYAN	25.03.1999	1	0	2021:	FC Urartu Yerevan
Artur MIRANYAN	27.12.1995	3	0	2021:	FC Urartu Yerevan
Trainer					
Joaquín de Jesús CAPARRÓS Camino (ESP) [from 10.03.2020]	15.10.1955			11 M; 6 W; 3 D; 2 L; 17-12	

AUSTRIA

The Country:
Republic of Austria (Republik Österreich)
Capital: Vienna
Surface: 83,879 km²
Inhabitants: 8,935,112 [2020]
Time: UTC+1

The FA:
Österreichischer Fußball-Bund
Ernst-Happel-Stadion - Sektor A/F, Meiereistrasse 7, 1021 Wien
Tel: +43 1 727 180
Foundation date: 1904
Member of FIFA since: 1905
Member of UEFA since: 1954
Website: www.oefb.at

NATIONAL TEAM RECORDS

RECORDS

First international match:	12.10.1902, Wien: Austria – Hungary 5-0	
Most international caps:	Andreas Herzog	- 103 caps (1988-2003)
Most international goals:	Anton Polster	- 44 goals / 95 caps (1982-2000)

UEFA EUROPEAN CHAMPIONSHIP

1960	Qualifiers
1964	Qualifiers
1968	Qualifiers
1972	Qualifiers
1976	Qualifiers
1980	Qualifiers
1984	Qualifiers
1988	Qualifiers
1992	Qualifiers
1996	Qualifiers
2000	Qualifiers
2004	Qualifiers
2008	Final Tournament (Group Stage)
2012	Qualifiers
2016	Final Tournament (Group Stage)
2020	Final Tournament (2nd Round of 16)

FIFA WORLD CUP

1930	*Did not enter*
1934	Final Tournament (4th Place)
1938	*Withdrew*
1950	*Withdrew*
1954	Final Tournament (3rd Place)
1958	Final Tournament (Group Stage)
1962	*Withdrew*
1966	Qualifiers
1970	Qualifiers
1974	Qualifiers
1978	Final Tournament (2nd Round)
1982	Final Tournament (2nd Round)
1986	Qualifiers
1990	Final Tournament (Group Stage)
1994	Qualifiers
1998	Final Tournament (Group Stage)
2002	Qualifiers
2006	Qualifiers
2010	Qualifiers
2014	Qualifiers
2018	Qualifiers

OLYMPIC TOURNAMENTS

1908	-
1912	FT/ Quarter-Finals
1920	*Did not enter*
1924	*Did not enter*
1928	*Did not enter*
1936	FT/ Runners-up
1948	FT/ 1/8-Finals
1952	FT/ Quarter-Finals
1956	*Did not enter*
1960	Qualifiers
1964	Qualifiers
1968	Qualifiers
1972	Qualifiers
1976	Qualifiers
1980	Qualifiers
1984	*Did not enter*
1988	Qualifiers
1992	Qualifiers
1996	Qualifiers
2000	Qualifiers
2004	Qualifiers
2008	Qualifiers
2012	Qualifiers
2016	Qualifiers

UEFA NATIONS LEAGUE

2018/2019	League B
2020/2021	League B (Promoted to League A)

FIFA CONFEDERATIONS CUP 1992-2017

None

AUSTRIAN CLUB HONOURS IN EUROPEAN CLUB COMPETITIONS:

European Champion Clubs.Cup (1956-1992) / UEFA Champions League (1993-2021)
None
Fairs Cup (1858-1971) / UEFA Cup (1972-2009) / UEFA Europa League (2010-2021)
None
UEFA Super Cup (1972-2020)
None
European Cup Winners.Cup 1961-1999*
None

*defunct competition

NATIONAL COMPETITIONS
TABLE OF HONOURS

	CHAMPIONS	CUP WINNERS	BEST GOALSCORERS	
1911/1912	SK Rapid Wien	-	Johann Schwarz II (First Vienna FC 1894 Wien)	22
1912/1913	SK Rapid Wien	-	Richard Kuthan (SK Rapid Wien)	16
1913/1914	Wiener AF	-	Johann Neumann (Wiener AC)	25
1914/1915	Wiener AC	-	Leopold Deutsch (Floridsdorfer AC & Wiener AC)	12
1915/1916	SK Rapid Wien	-	Richard Kuthan (SK Rapid Wien)	24
1916/1917	SK Rapid Wien	-	Eduard Bauer (SK Rapid Wien) Leopold Neubauer (Wiener AF)	21
1917/1918	Floridsdorfer AC	-	Eduard Bauer (SK Rapid Wien)	21
1918/1919	SK Rapid Wien	SK Rapid Wien	Josef Uridil (SK Rapid Wien)	16
1919/1920	SK Rapid Wien	SK Rapid Wien	Josef Uridil (SK Rapid Wien) Ernst Winkler (SpC Rudolfshügel)	21
1920/1921	SK Rapid Wien	Wiener SV Amateure	Josef Uridil (SK Rapid Wien)	35
1921/1922	Wiener Sport-Club	Wiener AF	Richard Kuthan (SK Rapid Wien)	20
1922/1923	SK Rapid Wien	Wiener Sport-Club	Ferdinand Swatosch (Wiener SV Amateure)	22
1923/1924	Wiener SV Amateure	Wiener SV Amateure	Gustav Wieser (Wiener SV Amateure)	16
1924/1925	SC Hakoah Wien	Wiener SV Amateure	Gustav Wieser (Wiener SV Amateure)	19
1925/1926	Wiener SV Amateure	Wiener SV Amateure	Gustav Wieser (Wiener SV Amateure)	25
1926/1927	SK Admira Wien	SK Rapid Wien	Anton Schall (SK Admira Wien)	27
1927/1928	SK Admira Wien	SK Admira Wien	Anton Schall (SK Admira Wien)	36
1928/1929	SK Rapid Wien	First Vienna FC 1894 Wien	Anton Schall (SK Admira Wien)	21
1929/1930	SK Rapid Wien	First Vienna FC 1894 Wien	Franz Weselik (SK Rapid Wien)	24
1930/1931	First Vienna FC 1894 Wien	Wiener AC	Anton Schall (SK Admira Wien)	25
1931/1932	SK Admira Wien	SK Admira Wien	Anton Schall (SK Admira Wien)	22
1932/1933	First Vienna FC 1894 Wien	FK Austria Wien	Franz Binder (SK Rapid Wien)	25
1933/1934	SK Admira Wien	SK Admira Wien	Josef Bican (SK Rapid Wien)	29
1934/1935	SK Rapid Wien	FK Austria Wien	Matthias Kaburek (SK Rapid Wien)	29
1935/1936	SK Admira Wien	FK Austria Wien	Wilhelm Hahnemann (SK Admira Wien)	23
1936/1937	SK Admira Wien	First Vienna FC 1894 Wien	Franz Binder (SK Rapid Wien)	29
1937/1938	SK Rapid Wien	Wiener AC – Schwarz-Rot Wien	Franz Binder (SK Rapid Wien)	22
1938/1939	SK Admira Wien	-	Franz Binder (SK Rapid Wien)	27
1939/1940	SK Rapid Wien	-	Franz Binder (SK Rapid Wien)	18
1940/1941	SK Rapid Wien	-	Franz Binder (SK Rapid Wien)	27
1941/1942	Vienna FC Wien	-	Ernst Reitermaier (SC Wacker Wien)	20
1942/1943	Vienna FC Wien	-	Karl Kerbach (Floridsdorfer AC)	31
1943/1944	Vienna FC Wien	-	Karl Decker (First Vienna FC 1894 Wien)	32
1944/1945	SK Rapid Wien	-	Richard Fischer (First Vienna FC 1894 Wien)	15
1945/1946	SK Rapid Wien	SK Rapid Wien	Ernst Stojaspal I (FK Austria Wien)	34
1946/1947	SC Wacker Wien	SC Wacker Wien	Ernst Stojaspal I (FK Austria Wien)	18
1947/1948	SK Rapid Wien	FK Austria Wien	Ernst Stojaspal I (FK Austria Wien)	24
1948/1949	FK Austria Wien	FK Austria Wien	Erich Habitzl (SK Admira Wien)	23
1949/1950	FK Austria Wien	-	Karl Decker (First Vienna FC 1894 Wien)	23
1950/1951	SK Rapid Wien	-	Robert Dienst (SK Rapid Wien)	32
1951/1952	SK Rapid Wien	-	Ernst Stojaspal I (FK Austria Wien)	31
1952/1953	FK Austria Wien	-	Ernst Stojaspal I (FK Austria Wien) Robert Dienst (SK Rapid Wien)	30
1953/1954	SK Rapid Wien	-	Robert Dienst (SK Rapid Wien)	25
1954/1955	First Vienna FC 1894 Wien	-	Richard Brousek (SC Wacker Wien)	31
1955/1956	SK Rapid Wien	-	Johann Buzek (First Vienna FC 1894 Wien)	33
1956/1957	SK Rapid Wien	-	Robert Dienst (SK Rapid Wien)	32
1957/1958	Wiener Sport-Club	-	Walter Horak (Wiener Sport-Club)	33
1958/1959	Wiener Sport-Club	Wiener AC	Erich Hof (Wiener Sport-Club)	32
1959/1960	SK Rapid Wien	FK Austria Wien	Friedrich Cejka (Wiener Sport-Club)	28
1960/1961	FK Austria Wien	SK Rapid Wien	Horst Nemec (FK Austria Wien)	31
1961/1962	FK Austria Wien	FK Austria Wien	Horst Nemec (FK Austria Wien)	24
1962/1963	FK Austria Wien	FK Austria Wien	Erich Hof (Wiener Sport-Club)	21
1963/1964	SK Rapid Wien	ESV Admira Energie Wien	Horst Nemec (FK Austria Wien)	21
1964/1965	Linzer ASK	Linzer ASK	Wolfgang Gayer (Wiener Sport-Club)	18
1965/1966	ESV Admira Energie Wien	ESV Admira Energie Wien	Johann Buzek (FK Austria Wien)	18
1966/1967	SK Rapid Wien	FK Austria Wien	August Starek (SK Rapid Wien)	21
1967/1968	SK Rapid Wien	SK Rapid Wien	Jørn Bjerregaard (DEN, SK Rapid Wien)	23
1968/1969	FK Austria Wien	SK Rapid Wien	Helmut Köglberger (FK Austria Wien)	31
1969/1970	FK Austria Wien	FC Wacker Innsbruck	Günter Kaltenbrunner (Wiener Sport-Club)	22
1970/1971	FC Wacker Innsbruck	FK Austria Wien	Wilhelm Kreuz (ESV Admira Energie Wien)	26
1971/1972	SSW Innsbruck	Wiener Sport-Club	Alfred Riedl (FK Austria Wien)	16
1972/1973	SSW Innsbruck	SSW Innsbruck	Wolfgang Breuer (SSW Innsbruck)	22
1973/1974	SK VÖEST Linz	FK Austria Wien	Johann Krankl (SK Rapid Wien)	36
1974/1975	SSW Innsbruck	SSW Innsbruck	Helmut Köglberger (FK Austria/WAC Wien - Linzer ASK)	22
1975/1976	FK Austria/WAC Wien	SK Rapid Wien	Hans Pirkner (FK Austria/WAC Wien)	21
1976/1977	SSW Innsbruck	FK Austria Wien	Johann Krankl (SK Rapid Wien)	32
1977/1978	FK Austria Wien	SSW Innsbruck	Johann Krankl (SK Rapid Wien)	32

Season	Champion		Top Scorer	Goals
1978/1979	FK Austria Wien	SSW Innsbruck	Walter Schachner (FK Austria Wien)	24
1979/1980	FK Austria Wien	FK Austria Wien	Walter Schachner (FK Austria Wien)	34
1980/1981	FK Austria Wien	Grazer AK	Gernot Jurtin (SK Sturm Graz)	20
1981/1982	SK Rapid Wien	FK Austria Wien	Božo Bakota (YUG, SK Sturm Graz)	24
1982/1983	SK Rapid Wien	SK Rapid Wien	Johann Krankl (SK Rapid Wien)	23
1983/1984	FK Austria Wien	SK Rapid Wien	Tibor Nyilasi (HUN, FK Austria Wien)	26
1984/1985	FK Austria Wien	SK Rapid Wien	Anton Polster (FK Austria Wien)	24
1985/1986	FK Austria Wien	FK Austria Wien	Anton Polster (FK Austria Wien)	33
1986/1987	SK Rapid Wien	SK Rapid Wien	Anton Polster (FK Austria Wien)	39
1987/1988	SK Rapid Wien	Kremser SC	Zoran Stojadinović (YUG, SK Rapid Wien)	27
1988/1989	FC Swarovski Tirol Innsbruck	FC Swarovski Tirol Innsbruck	Peter Pacult (FC Swarovski Tirol)	26
1989/1990	FC Swarovski Tirol Innsbruck	FK Austria Wien	Gerhard Rodax (FC Admira/Wacker Wien)	35
1990/1991	FK Austria Wien	SV Stockerau	Václav Daněk (TCH, FC Swarovski Tirol)	29
1991/1992	FK Austria Wien	FK Austria Wien	Christoph Westerthaler (FC Swarovski Tirol)	17
1992/1993	FK Austria Wien	FC Wacker Innsbruck	Václav Daněk (TCH, FC Wacker Tirol)	24
1993/1994	SV Austria Salzburg	FK Austria Wien	Nikola Jurčević (CRO, SV Austria Salzburg) Heimo Pfeifenberger (SV Austria Salzburg)	14
1994/1995	SV Austria Salzburg	SK Rapid Wien	Souleyman Sané (SEN, FC Tirol Innsbruck)	20
1995/1996	SK Rapid Wien	SK Sturm Graz	Ivica Vastic (SK Sturm Graz)	20
1996/1997	SV Austria Salzburg	SK Sturm Graz	René Wagner (CZE, SK Rapid Wien)	28
1997/1998	SK Sturm Graz	SV Ried im Innkreis	Geir Frigård (NOR, LASK Linz)	23
1998/1999	SK Sturm Graz	SK Sturm Graz	Eduard Glieder (SV Austria Salzburg)	22
1999/2000	FC Tirol Innsbruck	Grazer AK	Ivica Vastic (SK Sturm Graz)	32
2000/2001	FC Tirol Innsbruck	FC Kärnten	Radosław Gilewicz (POL, FC Tirol Innsbruck)	22
2001/2002	FC Tirol Innsbruck	Grazer AK	Ronald Brunmayr (Grazer AK)	27
2002/2003	FK Austria Wien	FK Austria Wien	Axel Lawarée (BEL, SC Schwarz-Weiß Bregenz)	21
2003/2004	Grazer AK	Grazer AK	Roland Kollmann (Grazer AK)	24
2004/2005	SK Rapid Wien	FK Austria Wien	Christian Mayrleb (Grazer AK)	27
2005/2006	FK Austria Wien	FK Austria Wien	Sanel Kuljic (SV Ried) Roland Linz (FK Austria Wien)	15
2006/2007	FC Red Bull Salzburg	FK Austria Wien	Alexander Zickler (GER, FC Red Bull Salzburg)	22
2007/2008	SK Rapid Wien	-	Alexander Zickler (GER, FC Red Bull Salzburg)	16
2008/2009	FC Red Bull Salzburg	FK Austria Wien	Marc Janko (FC Red Bull Salzburg)	39
2009/2010	FC Red Bull Salzburg	SK Sturm Graz	Steffen Hofmann (GER, SK Rapid Wien)	20
2010/2011	SK Sturm Graz	SV Ried im Innkreis	Roland Linz (FK Austria Wien) Roman Kienast (SK Sturm Graz)	21
2011/2012	FC Red Bull Salzburg	FC Red Bull Salzburg	Jakob Jantscher (FC Red Bull Salzburg) Stefan Maierhofer (FC Red Bull Salzburg)	14
2012/2013	FK Austria Wien	FC Pasching	Philipp Hosiner (FK Austria Wien)	32
2013/2014	FC Red Bull Salzburg	FC Red Bull Salzburg	Jonathan Soriano Casas (ESP, FC Red Bull Salzburg)	31
2014/2015	FC Red Bull Salzburg	FC Red Bull Salzburg	Jonathan Soriano Casas (ESP, FC Red Bull Salzburg)	31
2015/2016	FC Red Bull Salzburg	FC Red Bull Salzburg	Jonathan Soriano Casas (ESP, FC Red Bull Salzburg)	21
2016/2017	FC Red Bull Salzburg	FC Red Bull Salzburg	Olarenwaju Ayobami Kayode (NGA, FK Austria Wien)	17
2017/2018	FC Red Bull Salzburg	SK Sturm Graz	Moanes Dabour (ISR, FC Red Bull Salzburg)	22
2018/2019	FC Red Bull Salzburg	FC Red Bull Salzburg	Moanes Dabour (ISR, FC Red Bull Salzburg)	20
2019/2020	FC Red Bull Salzburg	FC Red Bull Salzburg	Shon Zalman Weissman (ISR, Wolfsberger AC)	30
2020/2021	FC Red Bull Salzburg	FC Red Bull Salzburg	Patson Daka (ZAM, FC Red Bull Salzburg)	27

NATIONAL CHAMPIONSHIP
Österreichische Fußballmeisterschaft – Bundesliga 2020/2021
(11.09.2020 – 22.05.2021)

Regular Season - Results

Round 1 [11-13.09.2020]
Rapid Wien - Admira Wacker 4-1(2-0)
Linzer ASK - Austria Wien 1-0(1-0)
SCR Altach - TSV Hartberg 1-1(1-0)
SV Ried - WSG Tirol 3-2(1-2)
SKN St. Pölten - Sturm Graz 0-0
Wolfsberger AC - RB Salzburg 1-3(0-2)

Round 2 [19-20.09.2020]
RB Salzburg - SCR Altach 4-1(2-1)
WSG Tirol - Linzer ASK 1-1(1-1)
Sturm Graz - Rapid Wien 1-1(0-1)
TSV Hartberg - Wolfsberger AC 0-2(0-0)
Admira Wacker - SKN St. Pölten 0-5(0-4)
Austria Wien - SV Ried 2-1(1-0)

Round 3 [26-27.09.2020]
SCR Altach - WSG Tirol 0-2(0-1)
SKN St. Pölten - Rapid Wien 1-2(1-2)
SV Ried - RB Salzburg 1-3(0-1)
Austria Wien - Admira Wacker 2-2(1-1)
TSV Hartberg - Sturm Graz 1-1(0-1)
Linzer ASK - Wolfsberger AC 3-1(1-0)

Round 4 [03-04.10.2020]
Admira Wacker - SV Ried 3-1(2-0)
WSG Tirol - Austria Wien 0-2(0-0)
Wolfsberger AC - SKN St. Pölten 2-4(1-3)
Sturm Graz - SCR Altach 4-0(3-0)
RB Salzburg - TSV Hartberg 7-1(2-0)
Rapid Wien - Linzer ASK 3-0(2-0)

Round 5 [24-25.10.2020]
Austria Wien - RB Salzburg 0-2(0-0)
SCR Altach - Admira Wacker 4-2(2-1)
SV Ried - Sturm Graz 0-2(0-1)
Linzer ASK - SKN St. Pölten 4-0(1-0)
WSG Tirol - TSV Hartberg 1-1(1-0)
Wolfsberger AC - Rapid Wien 3-4(0-2)

Round 6 [31.10.-01.11.2020]
RB Salzburg - WSG Tirol 5-0(2-0)
TSV Hartberg - Austria Wien 2-1(1-1)
SKN St. Pölten - SV Ried 4-0(2-0)
Rapid Wien - SCR Altach 3-1(1-0)
Admira Wacker - Wolfsberger AC 1-3(0-3)
Sturm Graz - Linzer ASK 0-2(0-1)

Round 7 [07-08.11.2020]
SCR Altach - Austria Wien 0-0
SKN St. Pölten - WSG Tirol 0-1(0-1)
SV Ried - TSV Hartberg 2-0(1-0)
Linzer ASK - Admira Wacker 4-0(1-0)
Rapid Wien - RB Salzburg 1-1(0-1)
Wolfsberger AC - Sturm Graz 0-0 [17.01.21]

Round 8 [21-22.11.2020]
RB Salzburg - Sturm Graz 1-3(0-0)
TSV Hartberg - Linzer ASK 1-1(0-1)
SCR Altach - Wolfsberger AC 0-2(0-0)
Austria Wien - SKN St. Pölten 1-1(0-1)
WSG Tirol - Admira Wacker 3-0(2-0)
SV Ried - Rapid Wien 4-3(2-1)

Round 9 [28-29.11.2020]
Sturm Graz - WSG Tirol 1-0(0-0)
SKN St. Pölten - RB Salzburg 2-8(1-4)
Admira Wacker - TSV Hartberg 2-3(2-1)
Wolfsberger AC - SV Ried 1-1(0-0)
Linzer ASK - SCR Altach 3-0(0-0)
Rapid Wien - Austria Wien 1-1(1-1)

Round 10 [05-06.12.2020]
Austria Wien - Sturm Graz 0-4(0-1)
SCR Altach - SKN St. Pölten 0-4(0-1)
Admira Wacker - RB Salzburg 1-0(0-0)
TSV Hartberg - Rapid Wien 1-3(0-2)
WSG Tirol - Wolfsberger AC 4-1(2-0)
Linzer ASK - SV Ried 3-0(2-0)

Round 11 [12-13.12.2020]
Sturm Graz - Admira Wacker 3-0(1-0)
SKN St. Pölten - TSV Hartberg 2-2(2-1)
SV Ried - SCR Altach 1-4(1-1)
Rapid Wien - WSG Tirol 0-3(0-2)
Wolfsberger AC - Austria Wien 3-2(1-1)
RB Salzburg - Linzer ASK 3-1(0-1)

Round 12 [19-20.12.2020]
TSV Hartberg - SCR Altach 1-0(0-0)
Admira Wacker - Rapid Wien 0-1(0-1)
Sturm Graz - SKN St. Pölten 3-0(1-0)
WSG Tirol - SV Ried 1-3(1-0)
RB Salzburg - Wolfsberger AC 2-3(0-0)
Austria Wien - Linzer ASK 1-1(1-1)

Round 13 [22-24.01.2021]
Rapid Wien - Sturm Graz 4-1(2-1)
Wolfsberger AC - TSV Hartberg 0-0
SKN St. Pölten - Admira Wacker 2-2(2-1)
SV Ried - Austria Wien 0-1(0-1)
SCR Altach - RB Salzburg 0-2(0-0)
Linzer ASK - WSG Tirol 2-4(2-3)

Round 14 [26-27.01.2021]
Admira Wacker - Austria Wien 0-4(0-0)
Sturm Graz - TSV Hartberg 2-1(2-0)
WSG Tirol - SCR Altach 3-1(3-1)
Rapid Wien - SKN St. Pölten 2-1(1-1)
RB Salzburg - SV Ried 3-0(3-0)
Wolfsberger AC - Linzer ASK 0-3(0-0)

Round 15 [30-31.01.2021]
SV Ried - Admira Wacker 0-0
SCR Altach - Sturm Graz 2-1(2-1)
TSV Hartberg - RB Salzburg 0-3(0-2)
Austria Wien - WSG Tirol 2-2(1-0)
SKN St. Pölten - Wolfsberger AC 0-2(0-1)
Linzer ASK - Rapid Wien 1-2(1-2)

Round 16 [09-10.02.2021]
Sturm Graz - SV Ried 2-1(1-0)
Rapid Wien - Wolfsberger AC 1-0(1-0)
SKN St. Pölten - Linzer ASK 1-3(0-2)
Admira Wacker - SCR Altach 3-1(1-0)
RB Salzburg - Austria Wien 3-1(0-0)
TSV Hartberg - WSG Tirol 1-0(0-0) [23.02.]

Round 17 [13-14.02.2021]
WSG Tirol - RB Salzburg 2-4(1-1)
SCR Altach - Rapid Wien 0-0
Wolfsberger AC - Admira Wacker 2-1(1-1)
Austria Wien - TSV Hartberg 0-1(0-1)
SV Ried - SKN St. Pölten 1-1(1-0)
Linzer ASK - Sturm Graz 2-0(1-0)

Round 18 [20-21.02.2021]
Austria Wien - SCR Altach 5-1(0-1)
WSG Tirol - SKN St. Pölten 0-1(0-0)
TSV Hartberg - SV Ried 1-1(1-1)
Sturm Graz - Wolfsberger AC 1-2(1-1)
Admira Wacker - Linzer ASK 1-2(0-1)
RB Salzburg - Rapid Wien 4-2(1-0)

Round 19 [27-28.02.2021]
Linzer ASK - TSV Hartberg 1-2(1-2)
Admira Wacker - WSG Tirol 1-1(1-0)
Rapid Wien - SV Ried 1-0(0-0)
SKN St. Pölten - Austria Wien 0-2(0-2)
Wolfsberger AC - SCR Altach 0-1(0-0)
Sturm Graz - RB Salzburg 2-1(2-0)

Round 20 [06-07.03.2021]
SCR Altach - Linzer ASK 0-1(0-1)
WSG Tirol - Sturm Graz 1-1(0-0)
TSV Hartberg - Admira Wacker 2-1(1-1)
SV Ried - Wolfsberger AC 0-4(0-2)
RB Salzburg - SKN St. Pölten 4-1(2-1)
Austria Wien - Rapid Wien 0-0

Round 21 [13-14.03.2021]
RB Salzburg - Admira Wacker 3-1(3-0)
Rapid Wien - TSV Hartberg 4-0(1-0)
Sturm Graz - Austria Wien 2-1(0-0)
SKN St. Pölten - SCR Altach 0-1(0-0)
Wolfsberger AC - WSG Tirol 3-5(1-3)
SV Ried - Linzer ASK 0-3(0-1)

Round 22 [20-21.03.2021]
Linzer ASK - RB Salzburg 0-1(0-1)
WSG Tirol - Rapid Wien 1-1(0-0)
Austria Wien - Wolfsberger AC 3-5(1-3)
Admira Wacker - Sturm Graz 0-0
TSV Hartberg - SKN St. Pölten 3-3(0-1)
SCR Altach - SV Ried 2-1(0-1)

Final Standings

1.	FC Red Bull Salzburg	22	17	1	4	67	-	24	52
2.	SK Rapid Wien	22	13	6	3	43	-	25	45
3.	Linzer ASK	22	13	3	6	42	-	21	42
4.	SK Sturm Graz	22	11	6	5	34	-	20	39
5.	Wolfsberger AC	22	10	3	9	40	-	39	33
6.	WSG Swarovski Tirol Wattens	22	8	6	8	37	-	34	30
7.	TSV Hartberg	22	7	8	7	25	-	38	29
8.	FK Austria Wien	22	6	7	9	31	-	32	25
9.	SKN St. Pölten	22	5	6	11	33	-	43	21
10.	SC Rheindorf Altach	22	6	3	13	20	-	43	21
11.	SV Ried im Innkreis	22	4	4	14	21	-	46	16
12.	FC Admira Wacker Mödling	22	3	5	14	22	-	50	14

Teams ranked 1-6 were qualified for the Championship Round, while teams ranked 7-12 were qualified for the Relegation Round.
The points obtained during the regular season were halved (and rounded down) before the start of the play-offs.
As a result, the teams started with the following points:
Championship Round: FC Red Bull Salzburg 26, SK Rapid Wien 22, Linzer ASK 21 points, SK Sturm Graz 19, Wolfsberger AC 16, WSG Swarovski Tirol Wattens 15.
Relegation Round: TSV Hartberg 14, FK Austria Wien 12, SKN St. Pölten 10, SC Rheindorf Altach 10, SV Ried im Innkreis 8, FC Admira Wacker Mödling 7.

Championship Round

Results

Round 23 [04.04.2021]
Wolfsberger AC - Rapid Wien 1-8(1-2)
WSG Tirol - Linzer ASK 2-0(0-0)
RB Salzburg - Sturm Graz 3-1(3-1)

Round 24 [11.04.2021]
Linzer ASK - Wolfsberger AC 2-1(1-0)
Sturm Graz - WSG Tirol 3-2(3-1)
Rapid Wien - RB Salzburg 0-3(0-1)

Round 25 [18.04.2021]
RB Salzburg - Linzer ASK 2-0(0-0)
Wolfsberger AC - WSG Tirol 2-0(1-0)
Rapid Wien - Sturm Graz 0-0

Round 26 [21.04.2021]
Sturm Graz - Wolfsberger AC 0-1(0-0)
WSG Tirol - RB Salzburg 3-2(1-1)
Linzer ASK - Rapid Wien 1-1(0-0)

Round 27 [25.04.2021]
Rapid Wien - WSG Tirol 4-0(1-0)
Wolfsberger AC - RB Salzburg 1-2(1-1)
Sturm Graz - Linzer ASK 3-1(2-0)

Round 28 [28.04.2021]
WSG Tirol - Rapid Wien 2-3(0-1)
RB Salzburg - Wolfsberger AC 1-1(0-0)
Linzer ASK - Sturm Graz 0-0

Round 29 [09.05.2021]
Linzer ASK - WSG Tirol 3-3(1-1)
Sturm Graz - RB Salzburg 1-3(0-1)
Rapid Wien - Wolfsberger AC 1-2(0-0)

Round 30 [12.05.2021]
Wolfsberger AC - Linzer ASK 0-4(0-2)
WSG Tirol - Sturm Graz 2-3(1-2)
RB Salzburg - Rapid Wien 2-0(1-0)

Round 31 [16.05.2021]
Linzer ASK - RB Salzburg 2-5(1-3)
WSG Tirol - Wolfsberger AC 2-2(1-0)
Sturm Graz - Rapid Wien 4-1(0-1)

Round 32 [22.05.2021]
Wolfsberger AC - Sturm Graz 1-3(1-0)
RB Salzburg - WSG Tirol 4-0(3-0)
Rapid Wien - Linzer ASK 3-0(0-0)

Final Standings

					Total			Home					Away			
1. **FC Red Bull Salzburg**	32	25	2	5	94 - 33	51	13	1	2	51 - 16	12	1	3	43 - 17
2. SK Rapid Wien	32	17	8	7	64 - 40	36	10	3	3	32 - 14	7	5	4	32 - 26
3. SK Sturm Graz	32	16	8	8	52 - 34	36	11	1	4	32 - 17	5	7	4	20 - 17
4. Linzer ASK	32	15	6	11	55 - 41	30	8	3	5	32 - 20	7	3	6	23 - 21
5. Wolfsberger AC	32	13	5	14	52 - 62	27	3	3	10	20 - 41	10	2	4	32 - 21
6. WSG Swarovski Tirol Wattens	32	10	8	14	53 - 60	23	5	5	6	28 - 26	5	3	8	25 - 34

Wolfsberger AC were qualified for the Europa Conference League Play-offs Final.

Relegation Round

Results

Round 23 [03.04.2021]
Austria Wien - SCR Altach 2-0(0-0)
SKN St. Pölten - Admira Wacker 0-1(0-1)
SV Ried - TSV Hartberg 3-2(1-2)

Round 24 [10.04.2021]
TSV Hartberg - Austria Wien 1-0(0-0)
SCR Altach - SKN St. Pölten 1-0(0-0)
Admira Wacker - SV Ried 0-2(0-0)

Round 25 [17.04.2021]
SKN St. Pölten - Austria Wien 1-2(1-1)
SV Ried - SCR Altach 0-0
Admira Wacker - TSV Hartberg 0-1(0-0)

Round 26 [20.04.2021]
TSV Hartberg - SKN St. Pölten 0-0
SCR Altach - Admira Wacker 0-1(0-0)
Austria Wien - SV Ried 2-2(1-1)

Round 27 [24.04.2021]
SV Ried - SKN St. Pölten 2-1(0-0)
SCR Altach - TSV Hartberg 2-2(2-1)
Admira Wacker - Austria Wien 0-2(0-1)

Round 28 [27.04.2021]
SKN St. Pölten - SV Ried 0-0
TSV Hartberg - SCR Altach 2-1(1-1)
Austria Wien - Admira Wacker 0-0

Round 29 [08.05.2021]
SCR Altach - Austria Wien 2-1(2-0)
Admira Wacker - SKN St. Pölten 2-0(1-0)
TSV Hartberg - SV Ried 1-1(0-0)

Round 30 [11.05.2021]
SV Ried - Admira Wacker 0-0
SKN St. Pölten - SCR Altach 3-3(2-0)
Austria Wien - TSV Hartberg 3-1(2-0)

Round 31 [15.05.2021]
Austria Wien - SKN St. Pölten 2-1(1-1)
SCR Altach - SV Ried 3-0(1-0)
TSV Hartberg - Admira Wacker 2-0(1-0)

Round 32 [21.05.2021]
SKN St. Pölten - TSV Hartberg 0-1(0-1)
Admira Wacker - SCR Altach 1-1(0-0)
SV Ried - Austria Wien 3-2(0-1)

Final Standings

					Total			Home					Away			
1. TSV Hartberg	32	12	11	9	38 - 48	32	7	6	3	19 - 18	5	5	6	19 - 30
2. FK Austria Wien	32	11	9	12	47 - 43	29	5	7	4	25 - 24	6	2	8	22 - 19
3. SV Ried im Innkreis	32	8	9	15	34 - 57	25	6	4	6	20 - 28	2	5	9	14 - 29
4. SC Rheindorf Altach	32	9	7	16	33 - 55	23	6	4	6	17 - 20	3	3	10	16 - 35
5. FC Admira Wacker Mödling	32	6	8	18	27 - 58	19	4	3	9	15 - 27	2	5	9	12 - 31
6. SKN St. Pölten (*Relegation Play-offs*)	32	5	9	18	39 - 57	13	1	5	10	16 - 30	4	4	8	23 - 27

TSV Hartberg and FK Austria Wien were qualified for the Europa Conference League Play-offs Semi-Final.

Top goalscorers:

27	**Patson Daka (ZAM)**	*FC Red Bull Salzburg*
18	Nikolai Baden Frederiksen (DEN)	*WSG Swarovski Tirol Wattens*
17	Dejan Joveljić (SRB)	*Wolfsberger AC*
15	Ercan Kara	*SK Rapid Wien*
14	Mërgim Berisha (GER)	*FC Red Bull Salzburg*
14	Sékou Koïta (MLI)	*FC Red Bull Salzburg*
13	Alexander Schmidt	*SKN St. Pölten*
12	Johannes Eggestein (GER)	*Linzer ASK*
12	Christoph Knasmüllner	*SK Rapid Wien*

TSV Hartberg - FK Austria Wien	0-3(0-1)

FK Austria Wien - Wolfsberger AC	3-0(1-0)	2-1(1-1)

Relegation Play-offs [26-29.05.2021]

As the top two teams of the Second Austrian Level did not receive a license for the 2021/2022 Bundesliga season, relegation play-offs were played between the last ranked team from the 2020/2021 Bundesliga and the best-placed team with a license from Second Level.

SK Austria Klagenfurt - SKN St. Pölten	4-0(2-0)	1-0(0-0)

SK Austria Klagenfurt promoted for the next season's Bundesliga.

NATIONAL CUP
ÖFB Cup 2020/2021

First Round [28-30.08./08-09/12/16/22/30.09.2020]

Wolfsberger AC - SC Neusiedl am See 1919	5-2(1-0, 2-2)		WSG Swarovski Tirol Wattens - USV St. Anna	3-1(0-1)
WSC Hertha Wels - FC Admira Wacker Mödling	0-3(0-2)		ASV Siegendorf - Linzer ASK	0-3(0-0)
SK Austria Klagenfurt - ATSV Stadl-Paura	7-1(2-0)		Dornbirner SV - TSV Hartberg	0-7(0-3)
SV Grödig - SKU Amstetten	1-2(0-1)		FK Austria Wien - SC Retz	5-0(1-0)
SK Treibach - SV Horn	1-2(0-2)		SK Rapid Wien - TSV St. Johann	5-0(2-0)
FC Gleisdorf 09 - SV Ried im Innkreis	1-1 aet; 3-5 pen		Grazer AK - SV Seekirchen	0-1(0-1)
First Vienna FC - FC Marchfeld Donauauen	4-0(2-0)		FC Blau Weiß Linz - SC Team Wiener Linien	5-1(3-0)
SV Wörgl - Union Vöcklamarkt	4-2(2-2)		FC Deutschkreutz - 1. Wiener Neustädter SC	0-3(0-0)
Kapfenberger SV - USK Maximarkt Anif	5-1(5-1)		Wiener Sport-Club - SV St. Jakob/Rosental	5-0(2-0)
SK Sturm Graz - SV Innsbruck	8-0(5-0)		SK Vorwärts Steyr - ASK-BSC Bruck/Leitha	1-0(1-0)
ATSV Wolfsberg - SKN St. Pölten	1-3(0-2)		Schwarz-Weiß Bregenz - FC Red Bull Salzburg	0-10(0-8)
FC Dornbirn 1913 - USV Allerheiligen	1-3(0-3)		SV Wallern - SVG Reichenau	0-1(0-0)
Floridsdorfer AC Wien - ASV Draßburg	3-0(1-0)		Union Gurten - SCR Altach	1-3(0-0)
ASV Schrems - FC Wacker Innsbruck	1-3(1-3)		SC Weiz - AS Koma Elektra	0-1(0-1)
SC Austria Lustenau - SV Stripfing/Weiden	1-2(0-0)		SC Schwaz - VfB Hohenems	1-3(1-3)
TuS Bad Gleichenberg - SV Lafnitz	0-1(0-0,0-0)			

Second Round [16-18.10./14.11.2020]

FC Admira Wacker Mödling - Kapfenberger SV	2-2 aet; 3-4 pen		FC Wacker Innsbruck - SV Stripfing/Weiden	1-0(0-0)
WSG Swarovski Tirol Wattens - Floridsdorfer AC	0-1(0-1)		SCR Altach - SV Seekirchen	7-0(3-0)
SV Lafnitz - SK Austria Klagenfurt	2-4(0-3)		1. Wiener Neustädter SC - SK Rapid Wien	1-5(1-3)
SV Horn - AS Koma Elektra	0-3(0-0)		Linzer ASK - SV Wörgl	3-0(1-0)
Wiener Sport-Club - FK Austria Wien	1-3(0-1)		First Vienna FC - SK Vorwärts Steyr	3-2(2-0)
SKN St. Pölten - FC Red Bull Salzburg	0-3(0-1)		Wolfsberger AC - SV Ried im Innkreis	2-2 aet; 4-3 pen
ASKÖ Gmünd - TSV Hartberg	3-4(2-1,3-3)		USV Allerheiligen - SKU Amstetten	0-1(0-0,0-0)
VfB Hohenems - SK Sturm Graz	1-2(0-1)		SVG Reichenau - FC Blau Weiß Linz	0-3(0-2)

1/8-Finals [14/24-25.11./15-16.12.2020]

Floridsdorfer AC Wien - SK Austria Klagenfurt	1-3(0-0,1-1)		Kapfenberger SV - FC Blau Weiß Linz	2-0(0-0)
SK Sturm Graz - FC Wacker Innsbruck	1-0(0-0)		Wolfsberger AC - SKU Amstetten	2-0(1-0)
FK Austria Wien - TSV Hartberg	5-3(3-0)		Linzer ASK - AS Koma Elektra	3-0(3-0)
First Vienna FC - SCR Altach	2-1(1-1)		FC Red Bull Salzburg- SK Rapid Wien	6-2(3-1)

Quarter-Finals [05-07.02.2021]

Kapfenberger SV - Wolfsberger AC	1-2(1-1,1-1)		FC Red Bull Salzburg- FK Austria Wien	2-0(1-0)
SK Sturm Graz - First Vienna FC	1-0(0-0)		Linzer ASK - SK Austria Klagenfurt	5-3(0-1,2-2)

Semi-Finals [03.03.2021]

Wolfsberger AC - Linzer ASK	0-1(0-0,0-0)		SK Sturm Graz - FC Red Bull Salzburg	0-4(0-1)

Final

01.05.2021; Wörthersee Stadion, Klagenfurt; Referee: Walter Altmann; Attendance: 0
Linzer ASK - FC Red Bull Salzburg	**0-3(0-1)**

LASK: Alexander Schlager, Petar Filipović, Gernot Trauner, Reinhold Ranftl, Andrés Alberto Andrade Cedeño, René Renner, Peter Michorl (63.Lukas Grgić), James Robert Holland, Johannes Eggestein (80.Metehan Altunbaş), Thomas Goiginger (63.Dominik Reiter), Husein Balić. Trainer: Dominik Thalhammer.

RB Salzburg: Cican Stanković, André Ramalho da Silva, Andreas Ulmer, Max Wöber, Rasmus Kristensen, Brenden Aaronson (88.Nicolas Seiwald), Zlatko Junuzović (76.Bernardo Fernandes da Silva Junior), Antoine Bernède (88.Luka Sučić), Enock Mwepu (88.Noah Okafor), Mërgim Berisha, Patson Daka (72.Karim Adeyemi). Trainer: Jesse Alan Marsch (United States).

Goals: 0-1 Mërgim Berisha (45), 0-2 Brenden Aaronson (67), 0-3 Enock Mwepu (88).

Please note: appearances and goals includes statistics of both regular season and play-offs (Championship Round & Relegation Round).

Fußballclub Admira Wacker Mödling

Founded:	1905	
Stadium:	BSFZ-Arena, Maria Enzersdorf – Südstadt (10,600)	
Trainer:	Zvonimir Soldo (CRO)	02.11.1967
[13.09.2020]	Patrick Helmes (GER)	01.03.1984
[22.09.2020]	Damir Burić (CRO)	07.07.1964
[25.02.2021]	Klaus Schmidt	21.10.1967

Goalkeepers:	DOB	M	(s)	G
Andreas Leitner	25.03.1994	32		
Defenders:	DOB	M	(s)	G
Emanuel Aiwu	25.12.2000	28		1
Stephan Auer	11.01.1991	19	(3)	
Sebastian Bauer	07.11.1992	20		1
Julian Buchta	11.07.2000	1	(1)	
Niko Datković (CRO)	21.04.1993	13	(1)	1
Paul-Friedrich Koller	22.02.2002	1		
Leonardo Lukačević	21.01.1999	6	(2)	
Lukas Malicsek	06.06.1999	12	(8)	
Phoenix Missi Tomp (CMR)	08.08.1999		(2)	
Matthias Ostrzolek (GER)	05.06.1990	11	(4)	
Pascal Petlach	18.01.1999	4	(1)	
Lukas Rath	18.01.1992	10		
Christoph Schösswendter	16.07.1988	1	(1)	
Miloš Spasić (SRB)	29.01.1998	4	(2)	
Julian Turi	03.07.2001		(1)	
Wilhelm Vorsager	29.06.1997	13	(5)	
Midfielders:	DOB	M	(s)	G
Onurhan Babuscu	05.09.2003		(2)	
Joseph Ganda (ISR)	10.03.1997	6	(5)	
Christian Gartner	03.04.1994	4	(3)	

Morten Hjulmand (DEN)	25.06.1999	8	(1)	
Marco Kadlec	28.02.2000	6	(3)	
Daniel Kalajdžić	24.11.2000		(1)	
Roman Kerschbaum	19.01.1994	29		6
Marcus Maier	18.12.1995	15	(4)	
Felix Kekoh Ndifor II (CMR)	02.03.2001		(3)	
Muhammed-Cham Saracevic	26.09.2000	1	(1)	
Tomislav Tomić (BIH)	16.11.1990	13	(1)	1
Nicolas Zdichynec	28.01.2002		(1)	
Forwards:	DOB	M	(s)	G
David Atanga (GHA)	25.12.1996	15		2
Mamina Badji (SEN)	23.08.2002		(1)	
Maximilian Breunig (GER)	14.08.2000	14	(9)	5
Aleksandar Ćirković (SRB)	21.09.2001	3		
Angelo Gattermayer	06.06.2002		(1)	
Marco Hausjell	06.06.1999	9	(11)	1
Erwin Hoffer	14.04.1987	12	(8)	2
Luca Kronberger	15.02.2002	10	(13)	1
Stefan Maierhofer	16.08.1982	1	(6)	
Maximilian Sax	22.11.1992		(4)	
Dominik Starkl	06.11.1993	17	(4)	1
Andrew Wooten (USA)	30.09.1989	14	(5)	3

Fußballklub Austria Wien

Founded:	15.03.1911	
Stadium:	Generali Arena, Wien (17,500)	
Trainer:	Peter Stöger	11.04.1966

Goalkeepers:	DOB	M	(s)	G
Patrick Pentz	02.01.1997	32		
Defenders:	DOB	M	(s)	G
Johannes Handl	07.05.1998	16	(6)	3
Maudo Lamine Jarjué (GAM)	30.09.1997	2	(2)	
Michael Madl	21.03.1988	7	(4)	
Christoph Martschinko	13.02.1994	1		
Erik Palmer-Brown (USA)	24.04.1997	24		
Andreas Poulsen (DEN)	13.10.1999	10	(1)	
Christoph Schösswendter	16.07.1988	15	(2)	1
Markus Suttner	16.04.1987	16	(2)	
Georg Teigl	09.02.1991	24	(5)	2
Stephan Zwierschitz	17.09.1990	22	(6)	
Midfielders:	DOB	M	(s)	G
Matthias Braunöder	27.03.2002		(1)	
Vesel Demaku	05.02.2000	10	(2)	1
Thomas Ebner	22.02.1992	18	(7)	

Dominik Fitz	16.06.1999	19	(5)	5
Alexander Grünwald	01.05.1989	8	(11)	3
Niels Hahn	24.05.2001	2	(2)	
Aleksandar Jukić	26.07.2000	11	(12)	2
Eric Martel (GER)	29.04.2002	17	(1)	1
Patrick Wimmer	30.05.2001	22	(9)	5
Forwards:	DOB	M	(s)	G
Marco Djuricin	12.12.1992	8	(6)	4
Bright Osagie Edomwonyi (NGA)	24.07.1994	1	(4)	
Muharem Huskovic	05.03.2003		(1)	
Christoph Monschein	22.10.1992	16	(8)	5
Benedikt Pichler	20.07.1997	19	(3)	6
Manprit Sarkaria	26.08.1996	28	(2)	6
Maximilian Sax	22.11.1992	2	(4)	
Alon Turgeman (ISR)	09.06.1991	1	(1)	1
Agim Zeka (ALB)	06.09.1998	1	(9)	1

Linzer Athletik-Sport-Klub

Founded:	07.08.1908	
Stadium:	Raiffeisen-Arena [Waldstadion], Pasching (7,870)	
Trainer:	Dominik Thalhammer	02.10.1970

Goalkeepers:	DOB	M	(s)	G
Tobias Lawal	07.06.2000	2		
Alexander Schlager	01.02.1996	30		
Defenders:	DOB	M	(s)	G
Andrés Alberto Andrade Cedeño (PAN)	16.10.1998	21	(11)	
Yevgen Cheberko (UKR)	23.01.1998	2	(3)	
Petar Filipović (CRO)	14.09.1990	15	(3)	1
Christian Ramsebner	26.03.1989	2	(3)	
Gernot Trauner	25.03.1992	29		4
Philipp Wiesinger	23.05.1994	26		2
Midfielders:	DOB	M	(s)	G
Lukas Grgic	17.08.1995	9	(6)	2
Stefan Haudum	27.11.1994		(1)	
James Robert Holland (AUS)	15.05.1989	23	(4)	3
Mads Emil Madsen (DEN)	14.01.1998	9	(15)	
Peter Michorl	09.05.1995	29	(2)	3

Marvin Potzmann	07.12.1993	6	(9)	1
Reinhold Ranftl	24.01.1992	31	(1)	4
René Renner	29.11.1993	26	(3)	2
Forwards:	DOB	M	(s)	G
Metehan Altunbaş (TUR)	07.01.2003		(3)	
Husein Balić (BIH)	15.02.1996	20	(9)	3
Johannes Eggestein (GER)	08.05.1998	26	(2)	12
Thomas Goiginger	15.03.1993	22	(6)	6
Adam Gríger (SVK)	16.03.2004		(4)	
Andreas Gruber	29.06.1995	16	(1)	5
Mamoudou Karamoko (FRA)	08.09.1999		(2)	1
Patrick Plojer	26.03.2001		(7)	
Marko Raguž	10.06.1998	5	(1)	2
Dominik Reiter	04.01.1998	3	(19)	3
Thomas Sabitzer	12.10.2000		(4)	

Sportklub Rapid Wien

Founded:	1899		
Stadium:	Allianz Stadion, Wien (28,000)		
Trainer:	Dietmar Kühbauer	04.04.1971	

Goalkeepers:	DOB	M	(s)	G
Paul Gartler	10.03.1997	7		
Richard Strebinger	14.02.1993	25		
Defenders:	**DOB**	**M**	**(s)**	**G**
Mateo Barać (CRO)	20.07.1994	25	(2)	
Leo Greiml	03.07.2001	15	(6)	
Maximilian Hofmann	07.08.1993	22		
Mario Sonnleitner	08.10.1986	1	(6)	
Filip Stojković (MNE)	22.01.1993	27	(2)	
Lukas Sulzbacher	06.04.2000		(1)	
Maximilian Ullmann	17.06.1996	32		1
Midfielders:	**DOB**	**M**	**(s)**	**G**
Yusuf Demir	02.06.2003	6	(19)	6
Srđan Grahovac (BIH)	19.09.1992	11	(16)	1
Christoph Knasmüllner	30.04.1992	16	(11)	12
Melih İbrahimoğlu	17.07.2000	1	(1)	
Dejan Ljubicic	08.10.1997	23	(1)	
Thomas Murg	14.11.1994	4		2
Dejan Petrovič (SVN)	12.01.1998	24		
Marcel Ritzmaier	22.04.1993	18	(6)	2
Thorsten Schick	19.05.1990	24	(5)	3
Lion Schuster	09.08.2000	5	(5)	1
Forwards:	**DOB**	**M**	**(s)**	**G**
Deni Alar	18.01.1990		(4)	1
Kelvin Arase	15.01.1999	13	(11)	4
Taxiarchis Fountas (GRE)	04.09.1995	20	(4)	9
Ercan Kara	03.01.1996	28	(4)	15
Koya Kitagawa (JPN)	26.07.1996	5	(13)	3
Dragoljub Savić (SRB)	25.04.2001		(1)	

Football Club Red Bull Salzburg

Founded:	13.09.1933 (as SV Austria Salzburg)		
Stadium:	Red Bull Arena, Wals-Siezenheim (30,188)		
Trainer:	Jesse Alan Marsch (USA)	08.11.1973	

Goalkeepers:	DOB	M	(s)	G
Carlos Miguel Coronel (BRA)	29.12.1996	1		
Nico Mantl (GER)	06.02.2000	2		
Cican Stanković	04.11.1992	29		
Defenders:	**DOB**	**M**	**(s)**	**G**
David Affengruber	19.03.2001	1	(4)	
André Ramalho da Silva (BRA)	16.02.1992	26	(2)	1
Bernardo Fernandes da Silva Junior (BRA)	14.05.1995	5	(9)	1
Patrick Farkas	09.09.1992	4	(7)	
Rasmus Kristensen (DEN)	11.07.1997	25	(6)	3
Jérôme Junior Onguéné (FRA)	22.12.1997	6	(3)	1
Oumar Solet (FRA)	07.02.2000	7	(3)	
Andreas Ulmer	30.10.1985	24	(6)	
Albert Vallci	02.07.1995	13	(4)	1
Maximilian Wöber	04.02.1998	19	(1)	
Midfielders:	**DOB**	**M**	**(s)**	**G**
Brenden Aaronson (USA)	22.10.2000	15	(5)	5
Majeed Ashimeru (GHA)	10.10.1997	5	(4)	
Antoine Bernède (FRA)	26.05.1999	17	(2)	1
Mohamed Camara (MLI)	06.01.2000	9	(6)	
Zlatko Junuzović	26.09.1987	19	(6)	1
Maurits Kjærgaard (DEN)	26.06.2003		(1)	
Enock Mwepu (ZAM)	01.01.1998	22	(7)	5
Masaya Okugawa (JPN)	14.04.1996	3	(4)	
Nicolas Seiwald	04.05.2001	5	(10)	
Luka Sučić (CRO)	08.09.2002	8	(9)	1
Dominik Szoboszlai (HUN)	25.10.2000	11	(1)	4
Forwards:	**DOB**	**M**	**(s)**	**G**
Karim Adeyemi (GER)	18.01.2002	11	(18)	7
Mërgim Berisha (GER)	11.05.1998	24	(4)	14
Patson Daka (ZAM)	09.10.1998	21	(7)	27
Sékou Koïta (MLI)	28.11.1999	8	(9)	14
Noah Okafor (SUI)	24.05.2000	12	(6)	6
Benjamin Šeško (SVN)	31.05.2003		(1)	

Sportclub Rheindorf Altach

Founded:	26.12.1929		
Stadium:	Stadion Schnabelholz, Altach (8,500)		
Trainer:	Alexander Anton Aiko Pastoor (NED)	26.10.1966	
[24.02.2021]	Damir Canadi	06.05.1970	

Goalkeepers:	DOB	M	(s)	G
Tino Casali	14.11.1995	5		
Martin Kobras	19.06.1986	27		
Defenders:	**DOB**	**M**	**(s)**	**G**
Anderson dos Santos Gomes (BRA)	03.01.1998	9	(6)	
David Bumberger	05.02.1999	11	(4)	
Berkay Dabanlı (GER)	27.06.1990	22		
Nosa Iyobosa Edokpolor (NGA)	22.09.1996	17	(3)	
Emir Karic	09.06.1997	18	(5)	
Philipp Netzer	02.10.1985	11	(7)	1
Philipp Schmiedl	23.07.1997		(1)	
Neven Subotić (SRB)	10.12.1988	10		
Manuel Thurnwald	16.07.1998	22	(2)	2
Jan Zwischenbrugger	16.06.1990	23	(3)	
Midfielders:	**DOB**	**M**	**(s)**	**G**
Aljaz Casar (SVN)	17.09.2000	10	(11)	1
Manfred Fischer	06.08.1995	25	(6)	7
Samuel Yves Oum Gouet (CMR)	14.12.1997	23	(7)	1
Stefan Haudum	27.11.1994	17	(2)	1
Marco Meilinger	03.08.1991	16	(7)	1
Emanuel Schreiner	02.02.1989	12	(7)	4
Johannes Tartarotti	02.08.1999	6	(7)	1
Alain Wiss (SUI)	21.08.1990	10	(5)	
Forwards:	**DOB**	**M**	**(s)**	**G**
Nana Kofi Babil (GHA)	04.01.2002		(2)	
Csaba Bukta (HUN)	25.07.2001	4	(13)	
Danilo Ezequiel Carando (ARG)	05.08.1988		(3)	2
Daniel Maderner	12.10.1995	17	(14)	5
Daniel Nussbaumer	29.11.1999	17	(9)	3
Chinedu Obasi Ogbuke (NGA)	01.06.1986	14	(10)	2
Mario Stefel	08.02.1996	6	(12)	2

Sportklub Niederösterreich St. Pölten

Founded:	2000		
Stadium:	NV Arena, Sankt Pölten (8,000)		
Trainer:	Robert Ibertsberger	20.01.1977	
[06.04.2021]	Georg Zellhofer	25.08.1960	
[28.04.2021]	Gerald Baumgartner	14.11.1964	

Goalkeepers:	DOB	M	(s)	G
Armin Gremsl	18.08.1994	2		
Christoph Riegler	30.03.1992	30		
Defenders:	**DOB**	**M**	**(s)**	**G**
Michael Blauensteiner	11.02.1995	27	(1)	
Daniel Drescher	07.10.1989	10	(6)	
Luan Leite Da Silva (BRA)	31.05.1996	11		2
Martin Majnovics (HUN)	26.10.2000		(5)	
Manuel Maranda	09.07.1997	13	(3)	
Ahmet Muhamedbegovic	30.10.1998	27	(1)	2
Kofi Schulz (GER)	21.07.1989	30	(1)	3
Michael Steinwender	04.05.2000	18	(8)	
Midfielders:	**DOB**	**M**	**(s)**	**G**
Reza Asadi (IRN)	17.01.1996	1	(5)	
Taylor Anthony Booth (USA)	31.05.2001	9	(6)	3
George Davies (SLE)	16.11.1996	18	(10)	
Christoph Halper	21.05.1998	6	(12)	1
Robert Ljubičić (CRO)	14.07.1999	25	(5)	2
Daniel Luxbacher	13.03.1992	13	(8)	
Emilian Metu	18.04.2003		(3)	
Peter Pokorný (SVK)	08.08.2001	26	(3)	
Daniel Schütz	19.06.1991	9	(12)	
Brandon Iván Servania (USA)	12.03.1999	7	(3)	
Lukas Tursch	29.03.1996	4		
Forwards:	**DOB**	**M**	**(s)**	**G**
Lukas Grozurek	22.12.1991	2	(7)	1
Dor Hugi (ISR)	10.07.1995	27	(4)	8
Nicolas Meister	28.09.1999	2	(10)	2
Alexander Schmidt	19.01.1988	24	(4)	13
Marcel Tanzmayr	13.01.2002	2	(8)	1
Samuel Tetteh (GHA)	28.07.1996	9	(8)	1

Sportklub Sturm Graz

Founded:	1909		
Stadium:	Merkur-Arena, Graz (14,364)		
Trainer:	Christian Ilzer		21.10.1977

Goalkeepers:	DOB	M	(s)	G
Tobias Schützenauer	19.05.1997	1	(1)	
Jörg Siebenhandl	18.01.1990	31		
Defenders:	**DOB**	**M**	**(s)**	**G**
Amadou Dante (MLI)	07.10.2000	30	(1)	1
Jusuf Gazibegović (BIH)	11.03.2000	15	(10)	1
Niklas Geyrhofer	11.02.2000	7	(3)	
Sandro Ingolitsch	18.04.1997	16		
Paul Komposch	13.05.2001		(2)	
David Nemeth	18.03.2001	28		2
Gregory Wüthrich (SUI)	04.12.1994	20	(3)	1
Midfielders:	**DOB**	**M**	**(s)**	**G**
Stefan Hierländer	03.02.1991	31	(1)	3
Philipp Huspek	05.02.1991		(15)	
Lukas Jäger	12.02.1994	6	(16)	1
Otar Kiteishvili (GEO)	26.03.1996	23	(3)	7
Tobias Koch	06.04.2001		(1)	
Andreas Kuen	24.03.1995	27	(4)	2
Ivan Ljubić	07.07.1996	23	(9)	7
Sandro Schendl	19.03.2003		(1)	
Dardan Shabanhaxhaj	23.04.2001		(15)	
Jon Gorenc Stanković (SVN)	14.01.1996	29	(1)	3
Samuel Stückler	14.02.2001		(1)	
Sebastian Zettl	01.07.2001		(3)	
Forwards:	**DOB**	**M**	**(s)**	**G**
Bekim Balaj (ALB)	11.01.1991	4	(25)	3
Kevin Friesenbichler	06.05.1994	18	(6)	4
Jakob Jantscher	08.01.1989	31		9
Francisco Mwepu (ZAM)	29.02.2000		(8)	
Kelvin Kwarteng Yeboah (GHA)	06.05.2000	12	(4)	6

Sportvereinigung Ried von 1912

Founded:	1912		
Stadium:	Keine Sorgen Arena, Ried im Innkreis (7,680)		
Trainer:	Gerald Baumgartner	14.11.1964
[15.12.2020]	Gerhard Schweitzer	28.06.1963
[01.01.2021]	Miron Muslić	14.09.1982
[25.03.2021]	Andreas Heraf	10.09.1967

Goalkeepers:	DOB	M	(s)	G
Daniel-Edward Daniliuc	16.11.1999	4		
Lukas Gütlbauer	06.12.2000	1		
Samuel Şahin-Radlinger	07.11.1992	27		
Defenders:	**DOB**	**M**	**(s)**	**G**
Kennedy Boateng (GHA)	29.11.1996	20	(4)	
Manuel Haas	07.05.1996	2	(3)	
Manuel Kerhe	03.06.1987	8	(6)	1
Michael Lercher	04.01.1996	26		
Luca Meisl	04.03.1999	20	(5)	
Thomas Reifeltshammer	03.07.1988	27	(5)	
Constantin Reiner	11.07.1997	16	(7)	2
Felix Seiwald	20.08.2000		(1)	
Balakiyem Takougnadi (TOG)	16.11.1992	8	(2)	
Midfielders:	**DOB**	**M**	**(s)**	**G**
Ante Bajic	22.08.1995	20	(5)	5
Marcel Canadi	27.10.1997	2	(12)	
Matthias Gragger	03.11.2001	4	(4)	
Valentin Grubeck	26.02.1995	2	(4)	1
Markus Lackner	05.04.1991	12	(10)	
Patrick Möschl	06.03.1993	4	(5)	
Stefan Nutz	15.02.1992	25	(5)	2
Daniel Offenbacher	18.02.1992	18	(7)	
Murat Satin	30.08.1996	2	(12)	
Nikola Stošić (SRB)	29.01.2000	2	(2)	
Julian Wießmeier (GER)	04.11.1992	14	(14)	4
Marcel Ziegl	20.12.1992	30	(1)	2
Forwards:	**DOB**	**M**	**(s)**	**G**
Filip Borsos (HUN)	22.06.2000	2		
Marco Grüll	06.07.1998	28	(3)	11
Bernd Gschweidl	08.09.1995	14	(8)	2
Seth Paintsil (GHA)	20.05.1996	4	(7)	1
Patrick Schmidt	22.07.1998	7	(3)	1
Sadam Sulley (GHA)	16.10.1996	3	(1)	

Turn- und Sportverein Hartberg

Founded:	29.04.1946		
Stadium:	Profertil Arena, Hartberg (4,635)		
Trainer:	Markus Schopp		22.02.1974

Goalkeepers:	DOB	M	(s)	G
Raphael Sallinger	08.12.1995	1		
Rene Swete	01.06.1990	31		
Defenders:	**DOB**	**M**	**(s)**	**G**
Stefan Gölles	04.10.1991	4	(7)	
Manfred Gollner	22.12.1990	24	(4)	2
Michael Huber	14.01.1990	1	(1)	
Christian Klem	21.04.1991	26	(2)	
Andreas Lienhart	28.01.1986	17	(5)	
Felix Luckeneder	21.03.1994	31		1
Thomas Rotter	27.01.1992	15	(8)	3
Midfielders:	**DOB**	**M**	**(s)**	**G**
Julius Ertlthaler	25.04.1997	8	(17)	1
Florian Flecker	29.10.1995	14		3
Lukas Gabbichler	12.05.1998		(2)	
Jürgen Heil	04.04.1997	17	(9)	
Matija Horvat (CRO)	07.05.1999	11	(5)	
Sascha Horvath	22.08.1996	21	(3)	2
Tobias Kainz	31.10.1992	28	(1)	2
Bakary Nimaga (MLI)	06.12.1994	21		2
Stefan Rakowitz	03.04.1990	2	(12)	3
Rajko Rep (SVN)	20.06.1990	24	(4)	6
Lukas Ried	10.10.1995	12	(11)	1
Philipp Sturm	23.02.1999	3	(2)	1
Samson Okikiola Tijani (NGA)	17.05.2002	7	(7)	
Abdoul Said Razack Yoda (BFA)	20.12.2000	3	(2)	
Forwards:	**DOB**	**M**	**(s)**	**G**
Seifedin Chabbi	04.07.1993	5	(18)	5
Kelvin Emmanuel Igbonekwu	16.01.2002		(1)	
Marc Andre Schmerböck	01.04.1994	4	(3)	
Dario Tadić	11.05.1990	22	(9)	6

Wolfsberger Athletik Club

Founded: 1931
Stadium: Lavanttal-Arena, Wolfsberg (7,300)
Trainer: Ferdinand Feldhofer   23.10.1979
[04.03.2021]   Roman Stary   18.12.1973

Goalkeepers:	DOB	M	(s)	G
Alexander Kofler	06.11.1986	18		
Manuel Kuttin	17.12.1993	14	(1)	
Marko Soldo	13.06.1996		(1)	
Defenders:	**DOB**	**M**	**(s)**	**G**
Dominik Baumgartner	20.07.1996	28		4
Guram Giorbelidze (GEO)	25.02.1996	10	(5)	
Gustav Henriksson (SWE)	03.02.1998	9	(2)	1
Luka Lochoshvili (GEO)	29.05.1998	17	(4)	1
Tarik Muharemović (BIH)	28.02.2003	4	(1)	
Michael Novak	30.12.1990	28		
Mario Pavelić	19.09.1993	6	(4)	
Stefan Perić	13.02.1997	5	(1)	
Nemanja Rnić (SRB)	30.09.1984	4	(6)	
Jonathan Scherzer	22.07.1995	21	(4)	1
Midfielders:	**DOB**	**M**	**(s)**	**G**
Adis Jasic	12.02.2003		(6)	
Mario Leitgeb	30.06.1988	20	(3)	
Michael Liendl	25.10.1985	28	(4)	8
Eliel Peretz (ISR)	18.11.1996	7	(8)	4
Lukas Schöfl	11.02.2001	4	(2)	
Sven Sprangler	27.03.1995	13		
Kai Stratznig	15.04.2002	10	(13)	
Matthäus Taferner	30.01.2001	25	(4)	1
Leo Vielgut	23.02.2001		(1)	
Christopher Wernitznig	24.02.1990	16	(12)	1
Forwards:	**DOB**	**M**	**(s)**	**G**
Cheikhou Dieng (SEN)	23.11.1993	5	(16)	3
Amar Hodzic	12.07.1999		(1)	
Dejan Joveljić (SRB)	07.08.1999	26	(6)	17
Thorsten Röcher	11.06.1991	13	(8)	4
Marc Andre Schmerböck	01.04.1994	2	(3)	
Dario Vizinger (CRO)	06.06.1998	19	(12)	6

Wattener Sportgemeinschaft Tirol Swarovski Innsbruck

Founded: 1930
Stadium: Tivoli-Neu Stadion, Innsbruck (16,008)
Trainer: Thomas Silberberger   03.06.1973

Goalkeepers:	DOB	M	(s)	G
Ferdinand Oswald (GER)	05.10.1990	28		
Benjamin Ožegović	09.08.1999	4		
Defenders:	**DOB**	**M**	**(s)**	**G**
Raffael Behounek	16.04.1997	29		1
Bruno Gabriel Soares (BRA)	21.08.1988	1	(9)	
Florian Buchacher	28.09.1987	3	(10)	
Julian Gölles	22.09.1999	2	(7)	
David Gugganig	10.02.1997	31		2
Stefan Hager	25.01.1995	3	(10)	
Fabian Koch	24.06.1989	28		1
David Schnegg	29.09.1998	28	(1)	2
Midfielders:	**DOB**	**M**	**(s)**	**G**
Tobias Anselm	24.02.2000	8	(18)	6
Nemanja Celic	26.04.1999	29		1
Johannes Naschberger	25.01.2000	7	(21)	
Thanos Petsos (GRE)	05.06.1991	29		1
Benjamin Pranter	22.09.1989	9	(19)	1
Florian Rieder	16.05.1996	23	(9)	3
Žan Rogelj (SVN)	25.11.1999	28		3
Renny Smith	03.10.1996	3	(20)	3
Florian Toplitsch	07.09.1991		(8)	
Forwards:	**DOB**	**M**	**(s)**	**G**
Zlatko Dedič (SVN)	05.10.1984	17	(7)	5
Nikolai Baden Frederiksen (DEN)	18.05.2000	28	(3)	18
Stefan Lauf	22.01.2002		(1)	
Kelvin Kwarteng Yeboah (GHA)	06.05.2000	14	(1)	4

SECOND LEVEL
2. Liga 2020/2021

1.	FC Blau-Weiß Linz	30	20	3	7	70 - 31	63
2.	FC Liefering	30	19	6	5	69 - 31	63
3.	SK Austria Klagenfurt (*Promotion Play-offs*)	30	17	8	5	64 - 32	59
4.	FC Wacker Innsbruck	30	17	6	7	50 - 33	57
5.	SV Lafnitz	30	17	4	9	56 - 35	55
6.	Grazer AK	30	13	7	10	46 - 42	46
7.	FC Dornbirn 1913	30	11	5	14	40 - 53	38
8.	FC Juniors OÖ Pasching	30	10	7	13	38 - 49	37
9.	Floridsdorfer AC Wien	30	10	6	14	39 - 41	36
10.	Kapfenberger SV	30	9	6	15	34 - 51	33
11.	FK Austria Wien II	30	8	8	14	41 - 52	32
12.	SKU Amstetten	30	8	7	15	38 - 61	31
13.	SC Austria Lustenau	30	8	6	16	44 - 55	30
14.	SK Rapid Wien II	30	8	6	16	37 - 53	30
15.	SK Vorwärts Steyr	30	7	9	14	30 - 55	30
16.	SV Horn	30	8	6	16	40 - 62	30

<u>Please note</u>: FC Blau-Weiß Linz is not eligible for promotion as they did not apply for a First Level license; FC Liefering (as feeder club for FC Red Bull Salzburg) were not eligible for promotion.

INTERNATIONAL MATCHES
(16.07.2020 – 15.07.2021)

Date	City	Match	Result	Type
04.09.2020	Oslo	Norway - Austria	1-2(0-1)	(UNL)
07.09.2020	Klagenfurt	Austria - Romania	2-3(1-1)	(UNL)
07.10.2020	Klagenfurt	Austria - Greece	2-1(0-0)	(F)
11.10.2020	Belfast	Northern Ireland - Austria	0-1(0-1)	(UNL)
14.10.2020	Ploieşti	Romania - Austria	0-1(0-0)	(UNL)
11.11.2020	Lëtzebuerg	Luxembourg - Austria	0-3(0-0)	(F)
15.11.2020	Wien	Austria - Northern Ireland	2-1(0-0)	(UNL)
18.11.2020	Wien	Austria - Norway	1-1(0-0)	(UNL)
25.03.2021	Glasgow	Scotland - Austria	2-2(0-0)	(WCQ)
28.03.2021	Wien	Austria - Faroe Islands	3-1(3-1)	(WCQ)
31.03.2021	Wien	Austria - Denmark	0-4(0-0)	(WCQ)
02.06.2021	Middlesbrough	England - Austria	1-0(0-0)	(F)
06.06.2021	Wien	Austria - Slovakia	0-0	(F)
13.06.2021	Bucureşti	Austria - North Macedonia	3-1(1-1)	(EC)
17.06.2021	Amsterdam	Netherlands - Austria	2-0(1-0)	(EC)
21.06.2021	Bucureşti	Ukraine - Austria	0-1(0-1)	(EC)
26.06.2021	London	Italy - Austria	2-1(0-0,0-0)	(EC)

04.09.2020   NORWAY - AUSTRIA   1-2(0-1)   2nd UEFA Nations League B, Group 1
Ullevaal Stadion, Oslo; Referee: Mattias Gestranius (Finland); Attendance: 0
AUT: Alexander Schlager, Andreas Ulmer, Stefan Lainer, Martin Hinteregger (Cap) (40.Aleksandar Dragović), Stefan Posch, Stefan Ilsanker, Xaver Schlager, Christoph Baumgartner, Michael Gregoritsch (79.Adrian Grbić), Marcel Sabitzer, Karim Onisiwo (86.Julian Baumgartlinger). Trainer: Franco Foda (Germany).
Goals: Michael Gregoritsch (35), Marcel Sabitzer (54 penalty).

07.09.2020   AUSTRIA - ROMANIA   2-3(1-1)   2nd UEFA Nations League B, Group 1
Wörthersee Stadion, Klagenfurt; Referee: Glenn Nyberg (Sweden); Attendance: 0
AUT: Alexander Schlager, Andreas Ulmer, Stefan Lainer, Martin Hinteregger, Xaver Schlager, Stefan Posch, Julian Baumgartlinger (Cap) (59.Karim Onisiwo), Florian Grillitsch (81.Christoph Monschein), Michael Gregoritsch (73.Adrian Grbić), Marcel Sabitzer, Christoph Baumgartner. Trainer: Franco Foda (Germany).
Goals: Christoph Baumgartner (17), Karim Onisiwo (81).

07.10.2020   AUSTRIA - GREECE   2-1(0-0)   Friendly International
Wörthersee Stadion, Klagenfurt; Referee: Matej Jug (Slovenia); Attendance: 1,500
AUT: Pavao Pervan, Aleksandar Dragović, Christopher Trimmel (46.Christoph Baumgartner), Martin Hinteregger (46.Stefan Posch), Marco Friedl, Julian Baumgartlinger (Cap) 46.46.Stefan Lainer), Stefan Ilsanker, Alessandro André Schöpf (46.Florian Grillitsch), Raphael Holzhauser (66.Michael Gregoritsch), Adrian Grbić, Karim Onisiwo (76.Louis Schaub). Trainer: Franco Foda (Germany).
Goals: Adrian Grbić (77), Christoph Baumgartner (80).

11.10.2020   NORTHERN IRELAND - AUSTRIA   0-1(0-1)   2nd UEFA Nations League B, Group 1
Windsor Park, Belfast; Referee: Petr Ardeleánu (Czech Republic); Attendance: 600
AUT: Pavao Pervan, Reinhold Ranftl (73.Christopher Trimmel), Aleksandar Dragović, Martin Hinteregger, David Olatukunbo Alaba, Stefan Lainer, Julian Baumgartlinger (Cap), Stefan Ilsanker, Xaver Schlager, Michael Gregoritsch (80.Adrian Grbić), Christoph Baumgartner. Trainer: Franco Foda (Germany).
Goal: Michael Gregoritsch (42).

14.10.2020   ROMANIA - AUSTRIA   0-1(0-0)   2nd UEFA Nations League B, Group 1
Stadionul "Ilie Oană", Ploieşti; Referee: Daniel Stefański (Poland); Attendance: 0
AUT: Pavao Pervan, Aleksandar Dragović, Martin Hinteregger (53.Stefan Posch), David Olatukunbo Alaba, Stefan Lainer, Julian Baumgartlinger (Cap) (76.Florian Grillitsch), Stefan Ilsanker, Alessandro André Schöpf (76.Reinhold Ranftl), Xaver Schlager, Michael Gregoritsch (90.Saša Kalajdžić), Christoph Baumgartner. Trainer: Franco Foda (Germany).
Goal: Alessandro André Schöpf (76).

11.11.2020   LUXEMBOURG - AUSTRIA   0-3(0-0)   Friendly International
Stade "Josy Barthel", Lëtzebuerg; Referee: Amaury Delerue (France); Attendance: 0
AUT: Pavao Pervan, Christopher Trimmel, Martin Hinteregger (Cap) (46.Aleksandar Dragović), Gernot Trauner, Philipp Wiesinger, Philipp Lienhart, Raphael Holzhauser (81.Julian Baumgartlinger), Peter Žulj, Valentin Lando Lazaro (58.Husein Balić), Louis Schaub (58.Reinhold Ranftl; 88.Karim Onisiwo), Saša Kalajdžić (46.Adrian Grbić). Trainer: Franco Foda (Germany).
Goals: Gernot Trauer (61), Adrian Grbić (83), Philipp Wiesinger (90+3).

15.11.2020   AUSTRIA - NORTHERN IRELAND   2-1(0-0)   2nd UEFA Nations League B, Group 1
"Ernst Happel Stadion", Wien; Referee: Maurizio Mariani (Italy); Attendance: 0
AUT: Pavao Pervan, Andreas Ulmer (78.Adrian Grbić), Aleksandar Dragović (46.Reinhold Ranftl), Martin Hinteregger, David Olatukunbo Alaba, Stefan Lainer, Julian Baumgartlinger (Cap) (78.Louis Schaub), Stefan Ilsanker, Marcel Sabitzer, Xaver Schlager, Michael Gregoritsch (63.Marko Arnautović). Trainer: Franco Foda (Germany).
Goals: Louis Schaub (81), Adrian Grbić (87).

18.11.2020   AUSTRIA - NORWAY   1-1(0-0)   2nd UEFA Nations League B, Group 1
"Ernst Happel Stadion", Wien; Referee: Benoît Bastien (France); Attendance: 0
AUT: Pavao Pervan, Andreas Ulmer, Martin Hinteregger, David Olatukunbo Alaba, Stefan Lainer, Reinhold Ranftl, Julian Baumgartlinger (Cap), Stefan Ilsanker (81.Gernot Trauner), Marcel Sabitzer, Xaver Schlager (65.Adrian Grbić), Marko Arnautović. Trainer: Franco Foda (Germany).
Goal: Adrian Grbić (90+4).

25.03.2021   SCOTLAND - AUSTRIA   2-2(0-0)   22nd FIFA WC. Qualifiers
Hampden Park, Glasgow; Referee: Carlos del Cerro Grande (Spain); Attendance: 0
AUT: Alexander Schlager, Aleksandar Dragović, David Olatukunbo Alaba (Cap), Stefan Lainer, Philipp Lienhart, Stefan Ilsanker, Florian Grillitsch, Xaver Schlager, Christoph Baumgartner, Adrian Grbić (68.Louis Schaub), Saša Kalajdžić. Trainer: Franco Foda (Germany).
Goals: Saša Kalajdžić (55, 80).

28.03.2021   AUSTRIA - FAROE ISLANDS   3-1(3-1)   22nd FIFA WC. Qualifiers
"Ernst Happel Stadion", Wien; Referee: Kateryna Monzul (Ukraine); Attendance: 0
AUT: Alexander Schlager, Andreas Ulmer, Aleksandar Dragović, David Olatukunbo Alaba (Cap) (64.Alessandro André Schöpf), Stefan Lainer (76.Christopher Trimmel), Gernot Trauner, Marcel Sabitzer, Louis Schaub (85.Yusuf Demir), Florian Grillitsch, Christoph Baumgartner (76.Karim Onisiwo), Saša Kalajdžić (63.Michael Gregoritsch). Trainer: Franco Foda (Germany).
Goals: Aleksandar Dragović (30), Julian Baumgartlinger (37), Saša Kalajdžić (44).

31.03.2021   AUSTRIA - DENMARK   0-4(0-0)   22nd FIFA WC. Qualifiers
"Ernst Happel" Stadion, Wien; Referee: Artur Manuel Ribeiro Soares Dias (Portugal); Attendance: 0
AUT: Alexander Schlager, Andreas Ulmer (82.Marco Friedl), Aleksandar Dragović, David Olatukunbo Alaba (Cap), Stefan Lainer, Gernot Trauner (82.Stefan Posch), Stefan Ilsanker (65.Valentin Lando Lazaro), Xaver Schlager (74.Ercan Kara), Marcel Sabitzer, Christoph Baumgartner, Saša Kalajdžić (82.Adrian Grbić). Trainer: Franco Foda (Germany).

02.06.2021   ENGLAND - AUSTRIA   1-0(0-0)   Friendly International
Riverside Stadium, Middlesbrough; Referee: Lawrence Visser (Belgium); Attendance: 6,606
AUT: Daniel Bachmann, Marco Friedl, Aleksandar Dragović, Martin Hinteregger, David Olatukunbo Alaba (Cap) (72.Alessandro André Schöpf), Stefan Lainer (81.Christopher Trimmel), Christoph Baumgartner (62.Louis Schaub), Xaver Schlager (81.Julian Baumgartlinger), Marcel Sabitzer, Konrad Laimer (62.Florian Grillitsch), Saša Kalajdžić (71.Michael Gregoritsch). Trainer: Franco Foda (Germany).

06.06.2021   AUSTRIA - SLOVAKIA   0-0   Friendly International
"Ernst Happel Stadion", Wien; Referee: Urs Schnyder (Switzerland); Attendance: 3,000
AUT: Daniel Bachmann, Christopher Trimmel (78.Stefan Posch), Philipp Lienhart, Martin Hinteregger, David Olatukunbo Alaba (Cap) (46.Konrad Laimer), Andreas Ulmer, Marcel Sabitzer (46.Louis Schaub), Florian Grillitsch, Valentin Lando Lazaro (78.Michael Gregoritsch), Christoph Baumgartner (54.Stefan Ilsanker), Saša Kalajdžić (63.Marko Arnautović). Trainer: Franco Foda (Germany).

13.06.2021   AUSTRIA - NORTH MACEDONIA   3-1(1-1)   16th EC. Group Stage.
Arena Naţională, Bucureşti (Romania); Referee: Andreas Ekberg (Sweden); Attendance: 9,082
AUT: Daniel Bachmann, Aleksandar Dragović (46.Philipp Lienhart), Martin Hinteregger, David Olatukunbo Alaba (Cap), Andreas Ulmer, Stefan Lainer, Marcel Sabitzer, Xaver Schlager (90+4.Stefan Ilsanker), Konrad Laimer (90+3.Julian Baumgartlinger), Christoph Baumgartner (58.Michael Gregoritsch), Saša Kalajdžić (59.Marko Arnautović). Trainer: Franco Foda (Germany).
Goals: Stefan Lainer (18), Michael Gregoritsch (78), Marko Arnautović (89).

17.06.2021   NETHERLANDS - AUSTRIA   2-0(1-0)   16th EC. Group Stage.
"Johan Cruyff" Arena, Amsterdam; Referee: Orel Grinfeld (Israel); Attendance: 15,243
AUT: Daniel Bachmann, Aleksandar Dragović (84.Philipp Lienhart), Martin Hinteregger, David Olatukunbo Alaba (Cap), Andreas Ulmer, Stefan Lainer, Xaver Schlager (84.Karim Onisiwo), Marcel Sabitzer, Konrad Laimer (61.Florian Grillitsch), Michael Gregoritsch (62.Saša Kalajdžić), Christoph Baumgartner (70.Valentin Lando Lazaro). Trainer: Franco Foda (Germany).

21.06.2021   UKRAINE - AUSTRIA   0-1(0-1)   16th EC. Group Stage.
Arena Naţională, Bucureşti (Romania); Referee: Cüneyt Çakır (Turkey); Attendance: 10,472
AUT: Daniel Bachmann, Stefan Lainer, Aleksandar Dragović, Martin Hinteregger, David Olatukunbo Alaba (Cap), Marcel Sabitzer, Florian Grillitsch, Konrad Laimer (72.Stefan Ilsanker), Xaver Schlager, Christoph Baumgartner (32.Alessandro André Schöpf), Marko Arnautović (90.Saša Kalajdžić). Trainer: Franco Foda (Germany).
Goal: Christoph Baumgartner (21).

26.06.2021   ITALY - AUSTRIA   2-1(0-0,0-0)   16th EC. 2nd Round of 16.
Wembley Stadium, London (England); Referee: Anthony Taylor (England); Attendance: 18,910
AUT: Daniel Bachmann, Stefan Lainer (114.Christopher Trimmel), Aleksandar Dragović, Martin Hinteregger, David Olatukunbo Alaba (Cap), Marcel Sabitzer, Florian Grillitsch (106.Louis Schaub), Konrad Laimer (114.Stefan Ilsanker), Christoph Baumgartner (90.Alessandro André Schöpf), Xaver Schlager (106.Michael Gregoritsch), Marko Arnautović (97.Saša Kalajdžić). Trainer: Franco Foda (Germany).
Goal: Saša Kalajdžić (114).

NATIONAL TEAM PLAYERS
(16.07.2020 – 15.07.2021)

Name	DOB	Caps	Goals	2020/2021:	Club
Goalkeepers					
Daniel BACHMANN	09.07.1994	6	0	2021:	*Watford FC (ENG)*
Pavao PERVAN	13.11.1987	7	0	2020:	*VfL Wolfsburg (GER)*
Alexander SCHLAGER	01.02.1996	6	0	2020/2021:	*Linzer ASK*
Defenders					
David Olatukunbo ALABA	24.06.1992	85	14	2020/2021:	*FC Bayern München (GER)*
Aleksandar DRAGOVIĆ	06.03.1991	94	2	2020/2021:	*TSV Bayer 04 Leverkusen (GER)*
Marco FRIEDL	16.03.1998	3	0	2020/2021:	*SV Werder Bremen (GER)*
Martin HINTEREGGER	07.09.1992	59	4	2020/2021:	*Eintracht Frankfurt (GER)*
Stefan LAINER	27.08.1992	33	2	2020/2021:	*Borussia VfL Mönchengladbach (GER)*
Philipp LIENHART	11.07.1996	6	0	2020/2021:	*SC Freiburg (GER)*
Stefan POSCH	14.05.1997	11	1	2020/2021:	*TSG 1899 Hoffenheim (GER)*
Gernot TRAUNER	25.03.1992	5	1	2020/2021:	*Linzer ASK*
Christopher TRIMMEL	24.02.1987	14	0	2020/2021:	*1. FC Union Berlin (GER)*
Andreas ULMER	30.10.1985	26	0	2020/2021:	*FC Red Bull Salzburg*
Philipp WIESINGER	23.05.1994	1	1	2020:	*Linzer ASK*
Midfielders					
Husein BALIĆ	15.02.1996	1	0	2020:	*Linzer ASK*
Julian BAUMGARTLINGER	02.01.1988	84	1	2020/2021:	*TSV Bayer 04 Leverkusen (GER)*
Christoph BAUMGARTNER	01.08.1999	14	4	2020/2021:	*TSG 1899 Hoffenheim (GER)*
Yusuf DEMIR	02.06.2003	1	0	2021:	*SK Rapid Wien*
Florian GRILLITSCH	07.08.1995	26	1	2020/2021:	*TSG 1899 Hoffenheim (GER)*
Raphael HOLZHAUSER	16.02.1993	2	0	2020:	*K Beerschot VAC (BEL)*
Stefan ILSANKER	18.05.1989	54	0	2020/2021:	*Eintracht Frankfurt (GER)*
Konrad LAIMER	27.05.1997	13	1	2021:	*RasenBallsport Leipzig (GER)*
Valentin Lando LAZARO	24.03.1996	32	3	2020/2021:	*Borussia VfL Mönchengladbach (GER)*
Reinhold RANFTL	24.01.1992	6	0	2020/2021:	*Linzer ASK*
Louis SCHAUB	29.12.1994	22	6	2020/2021:	*FC Luzern (SUI)*
Xaver SCHLAGER	28.09.1997	24	1	2020/2021:	*VfL Wolfsburg (GER)*
Alessandro André SCHÖPF	07.02.1994	28	5	2020/2021:	*FC Schalke 04 Gelsenkirchen (GER)*
Peter ŽULJ	09.06.1993	11	0	2020:	*RSC Anderlecht Bruxelles (BEL)*
Forwards					
Marko ARNAUTOVIĆ	19.04.1989	91	27	2020/2021:	*Shanghai SIPG FC (CHN)*
Adrian GRBIĆ	04.08.1996	9	4	2020/2021:	*FC Lorient-Bretagne Sud (FRA)*
Michael GREGORITSCH	18.04.1994	29	5	2020/2021:	*FC Augsburg (GER)*
Saša KALAJDŽIĆ	07.07.1997	11	4	2020/2021:	*VfB Stuttgart (GER)*
Ercan KARA	03.01.1996	1	0	2021:	*SK Rapid Wien*
Christoph MONSCHEIN	22.10.1992	1	0	2020:	*FK Austria Wien*
Karim ONISIWO	17.03.1992	12	1	2020/2021:	*1.FSV Mainz 05 (GER)*
Marcel SABITZER	17.03.1994	54	8	2020/2021:	*RasenBallsport Leipzig (GER)*
Trainer					
Franco FODA (Germany) [from 14.11.2017]		23.04.1966		39 M; 23 W; 5 D; 11 L; 60-38	

AZERBAIJAN

AFFA
Azərbaycan Futbol
Federasiyaları Assosiasiyası

The Country:
Republic of Azerbaijan (Azərbaycan Respublikası)
Capital: Bakı
Surface: 86,600 km²
Inhabitants: 10,130,100 [2021]
Time: UTC+4

The FA:
Azərbaycan Futbol Federasiyaları Assosiasiyası
2208 Nobel prospekti 1025, Bakı
Tel: +994 12 404 27 77
Foundation date: 1992
Member of FIFA since: 1994
Member of UEFA since: 1994
Website: www.affa.az

NATIONAL TEAM RECORDS

RECORDS

First international match:	17.09.1992, Gurdzhaani:	Georgia – Azerbaijan 6-3
Most international caps:	Rəşad Ferhad Sadıqov	- 111 caps (2001-2017)
Most international goals:	Qurban Osman Qurbanov	- 12 goals / 65 caps (1992-2005)

UEFA EUROPEAN CHAMPIONSHIP		FIFA WORLD CUP		OLYMPIC TOURNAMENTS	
1960	-	1930	-	1908	-
1964	-	1934	-	1912	-
1968	-	1938	-	1920	-
1972	-	1950	-	1924	-
1976	-	1954	-	1928	-
1980	-	1958	-	1936	-
1984	-	1962	-	1948	-
1988	-	1966	-	1952	-
1992	-	1970	-	1956	-
1996	Qualifiers	1974	-	1960	-
2000	Qualifiers	1978	-	1964	-
2004	Qualifiers	1982	-	1968	-
2008	Qualifiers	1986	-	1972	-
2012	Qualifiers	1990	-	1976	-
2016	Qualifiers	1994	*Did not enter*	1980	-
2020	Qualifiers	1998	Qualifiers	1984	-
		2002	Qualifiers	1988	-
		2006	Qualifiers	1992	-
		2010	Qualifiers	1996	Qualifiers
		2014	Qualifiers	2000	Qualifiers
		2018	Qualifiers	2004	Qualifiers
				2008	Qualifiers
				2012	Qualifiers
				2016	Qualifiers

UEFA NATIONS LEAGUE

2018/2019	League D
2020/2021	League C

FIFA CONFEDERATIONS CUP 1992-2017

None

AZERBAIJAN CLUB HONOURS IN EUROPEAN CLUB COMPETITIONS:

European Champion Clubs.Cup (1956-1992) / UEFA Champions League (1993-2021)
None

Fairs Cup (1858-1971) / UEFA Cup (1972-2009) / UEFA Europa League (2010-2021)
None

UEFA Super Cup (1972-2020)
None

*European Cup Winners.Cup 1961-1999**
None

*defunct competition

NATIONAL COMPETITIONS
TABLE OF HONOURS

AZERBAIJAN SSR (SOVIET ERA) CHAMPIONS

Year	Champion	Year	Champion	Year	Champion
1928	Progress-2 Baku	1954	Zavod S.M. Budennogo Baku	1973	Araz Baku
1929–33	*Not known*	1955	Ordjonikidzeneft Baku	1974	Araz Baku
1934	Profsoyuz Baku	1956	NPU Ordgonikidzeneft Baku	1975	Araz Baku
1935	Stroitel Yuga Baku	1957	NPU Ordgonikidzeneft Baku	1976	Araz Baku
1936	Stroitel Yuga Baku	1958	NPU Ordgonikidzeneft Baku	1977	Karabakh Khankendi
1937	Lokomotiv Baku	1959	Baku Teams (Spartakiada)	1978	SKIF Baku
1938	Lokomotiv Baku	1960	SKA Baku	1979	SKA Baku
1939	Lokomotiv Baku	1961	Spartak Guba	1980	Energetik Ali-Bayramly
1940	Lokomotiv Baku	1962	SKA Baku	1981	Gandjlik Baku
1941–43	*Not known*	1963	Araz Baku	1982	Tokhudju Baku
1944	Dinamo Baku	1964	Polad Sumgait	1983	Termist Baku
1945	*No competition*	1965	Vostok Baku	1984	Termist Baku
1946	Lokomotiv Baku	1966	Vostok Baku	1985	Khazar Sumgayit
1947	Trudovye Rezervy Baku	1967	Araz Baku	1986	Göyəzən
1948	KKF Baku	1968	SKA Baku	1987	Araz Naxçıvan
1949	KKF Baku	1969	Araz Baku	1988	Qarabağ Ağdam
1950	Iskra Baku	1970	SKA Baku	1989	Stroitel Sabirabad
1951	Ordjonikidzeneft Baku	1971	Khimik Salyany	1990	Qarabağ Ağdam
1952	Ordjonikidzeneft Baku	1972	Surahanets Baku	1991	Khazar Sumgayit
1953	Ordjonikidzeneft Baku				

	CHAMPIONS	CUP WINNERS	BEST GOALSCORERS	
1992	Neftçi PFK Bakı	İnşaatçı Bakı FK	Nazim Aliyev (FK Xəzər Lənkəran Sumqayit)	39
1993	Qarabağ FK Ağdam	Qarabağ FK Ağdam	Samir Alakbarov (Neftçi PFK Bakı)	16
1993/1994	FK Turan Tovuz	Kəpəz FK Gəncə	Musa Gurbanov (FK Turan Tovuz)	35
1994/1995	Kəpəz FK Gəncə	Neftçi PFK Bakı	Nazim Aliyev (Neftçi PFK Bakı)	26
1995/1996	Neftçi PFK Bakı	Neftçi PFK Bakı	Fazil Parvarov (Kəpəz FK Gəncə) Rovshan Ahmadov (Kəpəz FK Gəncə)	23
1996/1997	Neftçi PFK Bakı	Kəpəz FK Gəncə	Gurban Gurbanov (Neftçi PFK Bakı)	34
1997/1998	Kəpəz FK Gəncə	Kəpəz FK Gəncə	Nazim Aliyev (Bakı FK)	23
1998/1999	Kəpəz FK Gəncə	Neftçi PFK Bakı	Alay Bahramov (FK Viləş Masallı)	24
1999/2000	FK Şəmkir	Kəpəz FK Gəncə	Badri Kvaratskhelia (FK Şəmkir)	16
2000/2001	FK Şəmkir	Şəfa Bakı FK	Pasha Aliyev (Bakılı PFK Bakı)	12
2001/2002	*Championship abandoned*	Neftçi PFK Bakı	-	
2002/2003	*No competition*	*No competition*	-	
2003/2004	Neftçi PFK Bakı	Neftçi PFK Bakı	Samir Musayev (Qarabağ FK Ağdam)	20
2004/2005	Neftçi PFK Bakı	Bakı FK	Zaur Ramazanov (Karvan FK)	21
2005/2006	Bakı FK	Qarabağ FK Bakı	Yacouba Bamba (CIV, Karvan FK)	16
2006/2007	Xəzər Lənkəran FK	Xəzər Lənkəran FK	Zaur Ramazanov (Xəzər Lənkəran FK)	20
2007/2008	İnter PİK Bakı	Xəzər Lənkəran FK	Khagani Mammadov (İnter PİK Bakı)	19
2008/2009	Bakı FK	Qarabağ FK Bakı	Walter Guglielmone Gómez (URU, İnter PİK Bakı)	17
2009/2010	İnter PİK Bakı	Bakı FK	Farid Guliyev (Standard FK Sumqayit)	16
2010/2011	Neftçi PFK Bakı	Xəzər Lənkəran FK	Georgi Adamia (GEO, Qarabağ FK Bakı)	18
2011/2012	Neftçi PFK Bakı	Bakı FK	Bahodir Nasimov (UZB, Neftçi PFK Bakı)	16
2012/2013	Neftçi PFK Bakı	Neftçi PFK Bakı	Nicolás Sebastián Canales Calas (CHI, Neftçi PFK Bakı)	26
2013/2014	Qarabağ FK Bakı	Neftçi PFK Bakı	Reynaldo dos Santos Silva (Qarabağ FK Bakı)	22
2014/2015	Qarabağ FK Bakı	Qarabağ FK Bakı	Nurlan Novruzov (Bakı FK)	15
2015/2016	Qarabağ FK Bakı	Qarabağ FK Bakı	Daniel Quintana Sosa "Dani Quintana" (ESP, Qarabağ FK Bakı)	15
2016/2017	Qarabağ FK Bakı	Qarabağ FK Bakı	Filip Ozobić (CRO, Qəbələ FK) Rauf Aliyev (İnter PİK Bakı)	11
2017/2018	Qarabağ FK Bakı	Keşlə FK Bakı	Bagaliy Dabo (FRA, Qəbələ FK)	13
2018/2019	Qarabağ FK Bakı	Qəbələ FK	Mahir Anar Mədətov (Qarabağ FK Bakı)	16
2019/2020	Qarabağ FK Bakı	*Competition cancelled*	Peyman Babaei (IRN, Sumqayıt FK) Steeven Joseph-Monrose (FRA, Neftçi PFK Bakı) Bagaliy Dabo (FRA, Neftçi PFK Bakı) Mahir Anar Emreli (Qarabağ FK Bakı)	7
2020/2021	Neftçi PFK Bakı	Keşlə FK Bakı	Namiq Ələsgərov (Neftçi PFK Bakı)	19

Please note: Qarabağ FK moved 1993 from Ağdam to Bakı.

NATIONAL CHAMPIONSHIP
Azerbaijan Premier League – Azərbaycan Premyer Liqası 2020/2021
(21.08.2020 – 19.05.2021)

Results

Round 1 [21-23.08.2020]
Sumqayıt FK - Keşlə FK Bakı 0-1(0-0)
Neftçi PFK Bakı - Səbail FK Bakı 2-1(1-0)
Qarabağ FK - Sabah FK 2-0(1-0)
Qəbələ FK - Zira FK 1-1(1-1)

Round 2 [11-13.09.2020]
Neftçi PFK Bakı - Sumqayıt FK 0-2(0-1)
Keşlə FK Bakı - Qarabağ FK 0-0
Səbail FK Bakı - Zira FK 1-2(0-0)
Sabah FK - Qəbələ FK 3-0(2-0)

Round 3 [19-20.09.2020]
Qəbələ FK - Keşlə FK Bakı 0-0
Sumqayıt FK - Səbail FK Bakı 2-1(2-1)
Zira FK - Sabah FK 0-2(0-0)
Qarabağ FK - Neftçi PFK Bakı 1-2(1-1)

Round 4 [25-27.09.2020]
Sumqayıt FK - Qarabağ FK 2-2(0-0)
Səbail FK Bakı - Sabah FK 2-1(0-1)
Keşlə FK Bakı - Zira FK 2-3(1-1)
Neftçi PFK Bakı - Qəbələ FK 1-1(0-1)

Round 5 [02-03.10.2020]
Sabah FK - Keşlə FK Bakı 0-2(0-0)
Qəbələ FK - Sumqayıt FK 1-1(1-1)
Zira FK - Neftçi PFK Bakı 1-0(0-0)
Qarabağ FK - Səbail FK 4-0(2-0) [28.01.2021]

Round 6 [17-18.10.2020]
Səbail FK Bakı - Keşlə FK Bakı 1-1(0-0)
Qarabağ FK - Qəbələ FK 3-0(1-0)
Neftçi PFK Bakı - Sabah FK 1-0(1-0)
Sumqayıt FK - Zira FK 2-1(1-1)

Round 7 [24-25.10.2020]
Qəbələ FK - Səbail FK Bakı 1-1(1-1)
Keşlə FK Bakı - Neftçi PFK Bakı 0-1(0-0)
Sabah FK - Sumqayıt FK 1-2(0-1)
Zira FK - Qarabağ FK 0-0

Round 8 [31.10.-01.11.2020]
Qəbələ FK - Sabah FK 2-1(1-0)
Zira FK - Səbail FK Bakı 0-0
Sumqayıt FK - Neftçi PFK Bakı 0-0
Qarabağ FK - Keşlə FK Bakı 6-1(3-1)

Round 9 [07-08.11.2020]
Keşlə FK Bakı - Qəbələ FK 3-1(1-1)
Səbail FK Bakı - Sumqayıt FK 2-1(1-0)
Neftçi PFK Bakı - Qarabağ FK 0-6(0-3)
Sabah FK - Zira FK 0-1(0-0)

Round 10 [21-23.11.2020]
Qarabağ FK - Sumqayıt FK 6-1(3-0)
Qəbələ FK - Neftçi PFK Bakı 1-4(0-1)
Zira FK - Keşlə FK Bakı 3-1(1-0)
Sabah FK - Səbail FK Bakı 2-1(2-0)

Round 11 [28-30.11.2020]
Neftçi PFK Bakı - Zira FK 0-0
Keşlə FK Bakı - Sabah FK 1-1(0-0)
Səbail FK Bakı - Qarabağ FK 1-1(0-0)
Sumqayıt FK - Qəbələ FK 0-1(0-1)

Round 12 [20.12.2020]
Qəbələ FK - Qarabağ FK 1-1(0-0)
Keşlə FK Bakı - Səbail FK Bakı 0-2(0-2)
Zira FK - Sumqayıt FK 2-2(0-1)
Sabah FK - Neftçi PFK Bakı 0-2(0-1)

Round 13 [24.12.2020]
Səbail FK Bakı - Qəbələ FK 1-3(0-2)
Sumqayıt FK - Sabah FK 1-2(1-1)
Qarabağ FK - Zira FK 3-2(0-1)
Neftçi PFK Bakı - Keşlə FK Bakı 2-1(0-0)

Round 14 [21-22.01.2021]
Səbail FK Bakı - Neftçi PFK Bakı 1-3(1-1)
Zira FK - Qəbələ FK 2-0(1-0)
Sabah FK - Qarabağ FK 1-2(0-1)
Keşlə FK Bakı - Sumqayıt FK 0-1(0-1)

Round 15 [13-14.02.2021]
Sumqayıt FK - Səbail FK Bakı 3-0(2-0)
Qarabağ FK - Neftçi PFK Bakı 1-2(0-1)
Qəbələ FK - Keşlə FK Bakı 2-0(0-0)
Zira FK - Sabah FK 2-2(0-1)

Round 16 [19-20.02.2021]
Səbail FK Bakı - Sabah FK 2-0(1-0)
Sumqayıt FK - Qarabağ FK 0-0
Keşlə FK Bakı - Zira FK 2-2(2-1)
Neftçi PFK Bakı - Qəbələ FK 1-0(0-0)

Round 17 [25.02.2021]
Qəbələ FK - Sumqayıt FK 1-0(0-0)
Zira FK - Neftçi PFK Bakı 1-0(0-0)
Sabah FK - Keşlə FK Bakı 1-1(0-0)
Qarabağ FK - Səbail FK Bakı 1-0(0-0)

Round 18 [02-03.03.2021]
Səbail FK Bakı - Keşlə FK Bakı 1-1(0-0)
Qarabağ FK - Qəbələ FK 3-0(3-0)
Sumqayıt FK - Zira FK 0-0
Neftçi PFK Bakı - Sabah FK 2-1(1-0)

Round 19 [08-09.03.2021]
Sabah FK - Sumqayıt FK 1-1(1-0)
Neftçi PFK Bakı - Keşlə FK Bakı 3-1(2-0)
Qəbələ FK - Səbail FK Bakı 1-1(0-0)
Zira FK - Qarabağ FK 0-2(0-2)

Round 20 [13-14.03.2021]
Qarabağ FK - Sabah FK 2-0(1-0)
Sumqayıt FK - Keşlə FK Bakı 2-2(0-1)
Qəbələ FK - Zira FK 1-1(1-0)
Neftçi PFK Bakı - Səbail FK Bakı 4-0(1-0)

Round 21 [03-04.04.2021]
Səbail FK Bakı - Zira FK 0-0
Neftçi PFK Bakı - Sumqayıt FK 0-2(0-2)
Sabah FK - Qəbələ FK 1-0(1-0)
Keşlə FK Bakı - Qarabağ FK 1-1(1-0)

Round 22 [10-11.04.2021]
Qəbələ FK - Neftçi PFK Bakı 2-2(0-0)
Sabah FK - Səbail FK Bakı 0-0
Zira FK - Keşlə FK Bakı 0-0
Qarabağ FK - Sumqayıt FK 4-1(1-0)

Round 23 [16-17.04.2021]
Səbail FK Bakı - Qarabağ FK 1-1(1-1)
Sumqayıt FK - Qəbələ FK 2-0(0-0)
Keşlə FK Bakı - Sabah FK 0-0
Neftçi PFK Bakı - Zira FK 4-0(0-0)

Round 24 [25.04.2021]
Qəbələ FK - Qarabağ FK 0-5(0-0)
Keşlə FK Bakı - Səbail FK Bakı 1-0(0-0)
Sabah FK - Neftçi PFK Bakı 2-2(2-1)
Zira FK - Sumqayıt FK 0-0

Round 25 [03-04.05.2021]
Neftçi PFK Bakı - Keşlə FK Bakı 3-0(1-0)
Səbail FK Bakı - Qəbələ FK 1-0(0-0)
Qarabağ FK - Zira FK 1-1(1-1)
Sumqayıt FK - Sabah FK 0-2(0-1)

Round 26 [08-09.05.2021]
Keşlə FK Bakı - Sumqayıt FK 0-1(0-0)
Səbail FK Bakı - Neftçi PFK Bakı 0-4(0-1)
Zira FK - Qəbələ FK 0-0
Sabah FK - Qarabağ FK 0-4(0-4)

Round 27 [14.05.2021]
Qəbələ FK - Sabah FK 2-2(0-1)
Qarabağ FK - Keşlə FK Bakı 2-0(0-0)
Sumqayıt FK - Neftçi PFK Bakı 0-1(0-1)
Zira FK - Səbail FK Bakı 2-0(0-0)

Round 28 [19.05.2021]
Keşlə FK Bakı - Qəbələ FK 3-1(2-1)
Sabah FK - Zira FK 2-1(1-0)
Səbail FK Bakı - Sumqayıt FK 0-1(0-1)
Neftçi PFK Bakı - Qarabağ FK 1-0(0-0)

Final Standings

		Total						Home				Away		
1. **Neftçi PFK Bakı**	28	18	5	5	47 - 25	59	9	2	3	21 - 15	9	3	2	26 - 10
2. Qarabağ FK Bakı	28	16	9	3	64 - 18	57	11	1	2	39 - 10	5	8	1	25 - 8
3. Sumqayıt FK	28	10	9	9	30 - 31	39	4	5	5	14 - 13	6	4	4	16 - 18
4. Zirə FK Bakı	28	8	14	6	28 - 28	38	5	7	2	13 - 9	3	7	4	15 - 19
5. Sabah FC Bakı	28	7	8	13	28 - 38	29	4	4	6	14 - 19	3	4	7	14 - 19
6. Keşlə FK Bakı	28	5	11	12	25 - 40	26	3	5	6	13 - 17	2	6	6	12 - 23
7. Qəbələ FK	28	5	11	12	23 - 44	26	3	9	2	16 - 20	2	2	10	7 - 24
8. Səbail FK Bakı	28	5	9	14	21 - 42	24	4	5	5	14 - 19	1	4	9	7 - 23

Top goalscorers:

19	**Namiq Ələsgərov**	*Neftçi PFK Bakı*
18	Mahir Emreli	*Qarabağ FK Bakı*
11	Filip Ozobić (CRO)	*Qarabağ FK Bakı*
9	Ali Ghorbani	*Sumqayıt FK*

NATIONAL CUP
Azərbaycan Kuboku 2020/2021

First Round [24-25.01.2021]

Səbail FK Bakı - Zaqatala PFK	3-2	Qaradağ Lökbatan FK - Zirə FK Bakı	0-4
Turan Tovuz IK - Qəbələ FK	0-2	Sabah FC Bakı - Kəpəz FK Gəncə	1-2

Quarter-Finals [01-02/06-07.02.2021]

First Leg		Second Leg	
Sumqayıt FK - Səbail FK Bakı	0-1	Səbail FK Bakı - Sumqayıt FK	1-2
Qarabağ FK Bakı - Qəbələ FK	3-1	Qəbələ FK - Qarabağ FK Bakı	0-3
Keşlə FK Bakı - Kəpəz FK Gəncə	1-0	Kəpəz FK Gəncə - Keşlə FK Bakı	0-2
Neftçi PFK Bakı - Zirə FK Bakı	0-1	Zirə FK Bakı - Neftçi PFK Bakı	0-0

Semi-Finals [21/29.04.2021]

First Leg		Second Leg	
Keşlə FK Bakı - Zirə FK Bakı	1-2	Zirə FK Bakı - Keşlə FK Bakı	2-3 aet
Sumqayıt FK - Qarabağ FK Bakı	0-0	Qarabağ FK Bakı - Sumqayıt FK	0-0

Final

24.05.2021; Bank Resoublika Arena, Masazır; Referee: Əliyar Ağayev; Attendance: n/a
Keşlə FK Bakı - Sumqayıt FK   **2-1(1-1)**

Keşlə FK: Stanislav Namaşco, Mijuško Bojović, Tural Axundov, Azər Salahlı, Şəhriyar Əliyev, Rahman Hacıyev, Sadio Tounkara, Rafael Məhərrəmli (90+1.İikin Qırtımov), César Daniel Meza Colli, Sílvio Rodrigues Pereira Júnior (46.Turan Vəlizadə), Anatole Bertrand Abang. Trainer: Sanan Qurbanov.

Sumqayıt FK: Aydin Bayramov, Elvin Bədəlov, Dzhamaldin Khodzhaniyazov, Höccət Haqqverdi, Tellur Mütəllimov (82.Rüfat Abdullazadə), Süleyman Əhmədov, Vüqar Mustafayev, Ragim Sadikhov, Xəyal Nəcəfov (77.Mehdi Sharifi), Murad Xaçayev (77.Elvin Məmmədov), Ali Ghorbani. Trainer: Ayxan Abbasov.

Goals: 0-1 Mijuško Bojović (3 own goal), 1-1 Şəhriyar Əliyev (37), 2-1 Mijuško Bojović (57).

THE CLUBS 2020/2021

Keşlə Futbol Klubu Bakı

Founded:	1997	
Stadium:	ASK Arena, Keşlə (8,125)	
Trainer:	Yunis Hüseynov	01.02.1965
[25.01.2021]	Sanan Qurbanov	04.08.1980

Goalkeepers:	DOB	M	(s)	G
Kamal Bayramov	19.08.1985	5		
Stanislav Namaşco (MDA)	10.11.1986	23		
Defenders:	**DOB**	**M**	**(s)**	**G**
Artur Sérgio Batista de Souza (BRA)	05.08.1994	7	(2)	
Tural Axundov	01.08.1988	16	(2)	1
Mijuško Bojović (MNE)	09.08.1988	13	(1)	
Şəhriyar Əliyev	25.12.1992	25		2
Ruslan Əmircanov	01.02.1985	1	(1)	
İikin Qırtımov	04.11.1990	12		
Rail Məlikov	18.12.1985	1		
Elçin Mustafayev	05.07.2000	1		
Tərlan Quliyev	19.04.1992	16	(2)	
Azər Salahlı	11.04.1994	25		4
Midfielders:	**DOB**	**M**	**(s)**	**G**
Alvaro Luis Tavares Vieira (BRA)	10.03.1995	1	(5)	
Parviz Azadov	19.10.2000	2	(1)	
Eugeniu Cociuc (MDA)	11.05.1993	5		

	DOB	M	(s)	G
Rahman Hacıyev	25.07.1993	16	(4)	4
Cavid İmamverdiyev	08.01.1990		(1)	
John Bankolé Kamara (SLE)	05.12.1988	22	(1)	
Dmytro Klyots (UKR)	15.04.1996	12	(1)	1
César Daniel Meza Colli (PAR)	05.10.1991	16	(3)	2
Rafael Məhərrəmli	01.10.1999	16	(4)	
Turan Vəlizadə	01.01.2001	9	(7)	
Forwards:	**DOB**	**M**	**(s)**	**G**
Anatole Bertrand Abang (CMR)	06.07.1996	11	(2)	
Alexander Domingos Christovão M'Futila (ANG)	14.03.1993	1		
Shokhrukh Gadoev (UZB)	31.12.1991	1		
Bahadur Həziyev	26.03.1999		(5)	
Vüsal İsgəndərli	03.11.1995	21	(5)	3
Nicat Qurbanov	17.02.1992	6	(5)	1
Xəzər Mahmudov	23.11.2000	1	(1)	
Sílvio Rodrigues Pereira Júnior (BRA)	04.05.1994	17	(10)	4
Sadio Tounkara (MLI)	27.04.1992	6	(6)	1

Neftçi Peşəkar Futbol Klubu Bakı

	Founded:	18.03.1937	
	Stadium:	Bakcell Arena, Bakı (10,200)	
	Trainer:	Fuzuli Mammadov	08.09.1977
	[11.11.2020]	Samir Abbasov	01.02.1978

Goalkeepers:	DOB	M	(s)	G
Sələhət Ağayev	04.01.1991	1		
Aqil Məmmədov	01.05.1989	27		
Defenders:	DOB	M	(s)	G
Ömər Buludov	15.12.1998	20	(3)	1
Mert Çelik	10.06.2000	10	(2)	1
Elton Əlibəyli	04.02.2000		(1)	
Cabir Əmirli	06.01.1997	2	(2)	
Anton Krivotsyuk	20.08.1998	21		2
Pape Mamadou Mbodj (SEN)	12.03.1993	21	(2)	
Vojislav Stanković (SRB)	22.09.1987	25	(2)	3
Thallyson Augusto Tavares Dias (BRA)	01.12.1991	16	(2)	
İsmayıl Zülfüqarlı	16.04.2001		(2)	
Midfielders:	DOB	M	(s)	G
Sabir Bougrine (FRA)	10.07.1996	21	(4)	3
Namiq Ələsgərov	03.02.1995	26		19
Asim Əlizadə	05.02.2000		(1)	
Vusal Əsgərov	23.08.2001		(1)	
Keisuke Honda (JPN)	13.06.1986	6	(1)	2
Mamadou Kane (GUI)	22.01.1997	25		
Emin Mahmudov	27.04.1992	23		4
Bruno Telushi (ALB)	14.11.1990	6	(3)	
Farid Yusifli	20.02.2002		(1)	
Emin Zamanov	26.12.1997		(2)	
Forwards:	DOB	M	(s)	G
Mirabdulla Abassov	27.04.1995	14	(9)	6
Ahmed Ahmedov (BUL)	04.03.1995	2	(7)	1
Prince Vinny Ibara Doniama (CGO)	07.02.1996	2	(5)	1
Yusuf Lawal (NGA)	23.03.1998	23	(1)	2
Steeven Joseph-Monrose (FRA)	20.07.1990	8	(7)	2
Fahmin Muradbəyli	16.03.1996	5	(7)	
Saman Nariman Jahan (IRN)	18.04.1991	4	(9)	

Qarabağ Futbol Klubu Bakı

	Founded:	1951	
	Stadium:	Azersun Arena, Bakı (5,200)	
	Trainer:	Qurban Qurbanov	13.04.1992

Goalkeepers:	DOB	M	(s)	G
Emil Balayev	17.04.1994	10	(2)	
Şahrudin Məhəmmədəliyev	12.06.1994	18		
Defenders:	DOB	M	(s)	G
Elvin Cəfərquliyev	26.10.2000	21	(1)	
Abbas Hüseynov	13.06.1995	14	(4)	
Bədavi Hüseynov	11.07.1991	21	(1)	1
Wilde-Donald Guerrier (HAI)	31.03.1989	7	(1)	4
Kevin David Medina Rentería (COL)	09.03.1993	20		
Maksim Medvedev	20.09.1989	20	(3)	1
Rahil Məmmədov	24.11.1995	8	(2)	1
Midfielders:	DOB	M	(s)	G
Cavid Bayramov	27.02.1998		(4)	
Qara Qarayev	12.10.1992	21	(4)	1
İsmayıl İbrahimli	13.02.1998	20	(5)	
Uroš Matić (SRB)	23.05.1990	11	(7)	1
Filip Ozobić (CRO)	08.04.1991	16	(4)	11
Erickson Patrick Correia Andrade (CPV)	09.02.1993	21	(2)	4
Forwards:	DOB	M	(s)	G
Toral Bayramov	23.02.2001	10	(8)	2
Mahir Emreli	01.07.1997	18	(4)	18
Owusu Kwabena (GHA)	18.06.1997	18	(8)	7
Musa Qurbanlı	13.04.2002	1	(4)	1
Jaime Romero Gómez (ESP)	31.07.1990	13	(7)	4
Abdellah Zoubir (FRA)	05.12.1991	20	(6)	7

Qəbələ Futbol Klubu

	Founded:	01.09.1955	
	Stadium:	Qabala City Stadium, Qabala (4,500)	
	Trainer:	Elmar Baxşiyev	03.08.1980

Goalkeepers:	DOB	M	(s)	G
Tarlan Əhmədli	21.11.1994	6	(1)	
Anar Nəzirov	08.09.1985	22		
Defenders:	DOB	M	(s)	G
Rufat Əhmədov	22.09.2002	17		
Jurgen Goxha (ALB)	29.12.1992	23	(1)	2
Faiq Hacıyev	22.05.1999	2		
Vinko Medimorec (CRO)	01.06.1996	23		1
Murad Musayev	13.06.1994	16	(2)	
Yusif Nəbiyev	03.09.1997	6	(8)	2
Sadiq Quliyev	09.03.1995		(1)	
Midfielders:	DOB	M	(s)	G
Yaovi Akakpo (TOG)	03.11.1999		(1)	
Qismat Alıyev	24.10.1996	5		
Merab Gigauri (GEO)	05.06.1993	21	(1)	1
Roman Hüseynov	26.12.1997		(6)	
Cavid Hüseynov	09.03.1988	7	(13)	
İdris İnqilablı	06.10.2001	13	(2)	
Asif Məmmədov	05.08.1986	23	(2)	2
Kamal Mirzəyev	14.09.1994	2	(2)	
Stefan Vukčević (MNE)	11.04.1997	21	(4)	1
Forwards:	DOB	M	(s)	G
Segun James Adeniyi (NGA)	20.12.1992	17	(6)	4
Raphael Schorr Utzig „Raphael Alemão" (BRA)	08.08.1996	25		5
Rodrigo Pablo Gattas Bertoni (CHI)	02.12.1991	2		
Ülvi İsgəndərov	17.04.1998	5	(13)	1
Rövlan Muradov	28.03.1998	15	(6)	1
Nicolas Rajsel (SVN)	31.05.1993	26		3
Ehtiram Şahverdiyev	01.10.1996	11	(5)	

Sabah Football Club Bakı

	Founded:	2016	
	Stadium:	Bank Respublika Arena, Masazır (13,000)	
	Trainer:	Vicente Gómez Fernández (ESP)	09.09.1971
	[11.03.2021]	Ramin Quliyev	22.06.1981

Goalkeepers:	DOB	M	(s)	G
Nicat Mehbalıyev	11.09.2000	2		
Sasa Stamenković (SRB)	05.01.1985	18		
Álvaro Villete Melgar (URU)	01.07.1991	8		
Defenders:	DOB	M	(s)	G
Ruslan Abışov	10.10.1987	4	(1)	
Arsen Ağcabəyov	11.09.2000		(1)	
Slavik Alxasov	06.02.2003	17	(2)	2
Bəxtiyar Həsənalızadə	29.12.1992	8		
Filip Ivanović (SRB)	13.02.1992	16	(1)	
Mahammad Mirzəbəyov	16.11.1990	3	(6)	
Bəhlul Mustafazadə	27.02.1997	17		1
Zurab Ochihava (UKR)	18.05.1995	10		
Amin Seydiyev	15.11.1998	21	(3)	1
Nikola Vujadinović (MNE)	31.07.1986	8		
Midfielders:	DOB	M	(s)	G
Elşən Abdullayev	05.02.1994		(1)	
Eugeniu Cociuc (MDA)	11.05.1993	5	(3)	
Coşqun Diniyev	13.09.1995	16	(6)	1
Aleksey Isayev	09.11.1995	16	(4)	1
Dmytro Klyots (UKR)	15.04.1996	4	(2)	
Mario Marina (CRO)	03.08.1989	23		1
Ceyhun Nuriyev	30.03.2001	3	(2)	
Veysal Rzayev	24.10.2002	9	(3)	
Şakir Seyidov	31.12.2000	11	(3)	
Abdulax Xaybulayev	19.08.2001		(1)	
Forwards:	DOB	M	(s)	G
Camal Cəfərov	25.02.2002	1	(3)	
Amadou Diallo (FRA)	21.06.1994	7	(7)	1
Ulysse Diallo (MLI)	26.10.1992	1		
Tiemoko Fofana (CIV)	22.10.1999	11	(1)	2
Ozan Kökcü	18.08.1998	11	(1)	
Kévin Koubemba (CGO)	23.03.1993	14	(8)	5
Julio César Rodríguez Giménez (PAR)	05.12.1990	17	(8)	3
Ramil Şeydayev	15.03.1996	15	(10)	6
Təmkin Xəlilzadə	06.08.1993	12	(4)	3

Səbail Futbol Klubu Bakı

Founded: 2016
Stadium: Bayil Arena, Bakı (5,000)
Trainer: Aftandil Hacıyev   13.08.1981

Goalkeepers:	DOB	M	(s)	G
Kamran Ağayev	09.02.1986	1		
Elxan Əhmədov	02.07.1993	1		
Nicholas George Hagen Godoy (GUA)	02.08.1996	26		
Defenders:	**DOB**	**M**	**(s)**	**G**
Ürfan Abbasov	14.10.1992	27		2
Arsen Ağcabəyov	11.09.2000		(1)	
Məqsəd İsayev	07.06.1994	13	(7)	
Peyman Keshavarz (IRN)	03.03.1996	14	(1)	2
Turan Manafov	19.09.1998	28		1
Adil Nağıyev	11.09.1995	24		1
Kamal Qurbanov	06.05.1994		(2)	
Mohamed Alie Sesay (SLE)	02.08.1994	13		
Midfielders:	**DOB**	**M**	**(s)**	**G**
Vüqar Bəybalayev	05.08.1993	7	(2)	
Hendrick Ekstein (RSA)	01.01.1991	20		1

	DOB	M	(s)	G
Rahid Əmirquliyev	01.09.1989	26		
Ruslan Hacıyev	26.03.1998	2	(13)	
Chikito Lema Mabidi (COD)	11.06.1993	4		
Milovan Petrovikj (MKD)	23.01.1990	13		
Ədilkhan Qarəhmədov	05.06.2001	3	(11)	
Bakhtiar Rahmani (IRN)	23.09.1991	3		
Elçin Rəhimli	17.06.1991	5	(10)	
Forwards:	**DOB**	**M**	**(s)**	**G**
Mirsahib Abbasov	19.01.1993	2	(8)	
Rauf Əliyev	12.02.1989	15	(8)	4
Bahadur Həziyev	26.03.1999	6	(3)	1
Luka Imnadze (GEO)	26.08.1997	9	(4)	
Əfran İsmayılov	08.10.1988	18	(4)	3
Florian Kadriu (MKD)	30.09.1995	16	(2)	
Elgün Nəbiyev	04.01.1996		(2)	
Amil Yunanov	06.01.1993	12	(5)	6

Sumqayıt Futbol Klubu

Founded: 1961 (*as Metallurg Sumqayit*)
Stadium: Kapital Bank Arena, Sumqayit (1,400)
Trainer: Ayxan Abbasov   25.08.1981

Goalkeepers:	DOB	M	(s)	G
Aydin Bayramov	18.02.1996	10	(1)	
Mehdi Cənnətov	26.01.1992	18		
Defenders:	**DOB**	**M**	**(s)**	**G**
Rüfat Abdullazadə	17.01.2001	3	(11)	
Elvin Bədəlov	14.06.1995	24	(1)	
Nicat Əliyev	24.09.2001		(1)	
Cabir Əmirli	06.01.1997	3	(4)	
Höccət Haqqverdi	03.02.1993	15		
Vurğun Hüseynov	25.04.1988	16	(2)	
Dzhamaldin Khodzhaniyazov (RUS)	18.07.1996	23		3
Dmitri Nağıyev	27.11.1995	6	(1)	
Karam Sultanov	15.04.1996	2	(5)	
Midfielders:	**DOB**	**M**	**(s)**	**G**
Sabuhi Abdullazadə	18.12.2001	5	(9)	1
Sanan Ağayev	16.06.1994		(1)	

	DOB	M	(s)	G
Süleyman Əhmədov	25.11.1999	14	(3)	1
Adam Hemati (IRN)	22.01.1995	8	(4)	
Cavid İmamverdiyev	08.01.1990	4	(9)	
Nabi Məmmədov	20.08.1999		(1)	
Vüqar Mustafayev	05.08.1994	25		
Tellur Mütəllimov	08.04.1995	24	(1)	3
Xəyal Nəcəfov	19.12.1997	24	(2)	1
Ragim Sadikhov	18.07.1996	25	(2)	8
Eltun Turabov	18.02.1997	9	(5)	
Murad Xaçayev	14.04.1998	22	(1)	3
Forwards:	**DOB**	**M**	**(s)**	**G**
Ali Ghorbani	18.09.1990	17	(2)	9
Nurlan Quliyev	16.02.1998		(1)	
Elvin Məmmədov	18.07.1988	5	(13)	
Mehdi Sharifi (IRN)	16.08.1992	6	(4)	

Zirə Futbol Klubu Bakı

Founded: 28.07.2014
Stadium: Zirə Olympic Spot Complex Stadium, Bakı (1,300)
Trainer: Rəşad Sadıqov   16.06.1982

Goalkeepers:	DOB	M	(s)	G
Matheus Albino Carneiro (BRA)	04.02.1995	26		
Rəşad Əzizli	01.01.1994	2		
Defenders:	**DOB**	**M**	**(s)**	**G**
Nemanja Anđelković (SRB)	26.04.1997	14		1
Dimitrios Chantakias (GRE)	04.01.1995	22	(1)	1
Karim Diniyev	05.09.1993		(2)	
Lazar Đorđević (SRB)	14.07.1992	16	(2)	1
Calal Hüseynov	02.01.2003	5	(4)	
Şəhriyar Rəhimov	06.04.1989	6	(3)	
Mohamed Alie Sesay (SLE)	02.08.1994	2	(1)	
Sertan Taşqın	08.10.1997	22	(2)	
Midfielders:	**DOB**	**M**	**(s)**	**G**
Qismat Alıyev	24.10.1996	22		2
Richard Almeida de Oliveira	20.03.1989	19	(1)	
Tural Bayramlı	07.01.1998	7	(9)	

	DOB	M	(s)	G
Elvin Camalov	04.02.1995	21	(4)	
Hacıağa Hacılı	30.01.1998	19	(5)	
İlkin Muradov	05.03.1996	23	(4)	
Əli Şirinov	09.08.1998		(2)	
Forwards:	**DOB**	**M**	**(s)**	**G**
Louis Marie Rodrigue Bongongui Assougou (CMR)	07.02.1993	5	(5)	
Caio Rangel da Silva (BRA)	16.01.1996	1	(2)	
Clésio Palmirim David Baúque (MOZ)	11.10.1994	25	(3)	5
Rəşad Əyyubov	03.12.1992	1	(2)	
Filipe Pachtmann (BRA)	11.04.2000		(1)	
Facundo Emmanuel Melivilo (ARG)	12.08.1992	2	(2)	2
Musa Qurbanlı	13.04.2002	3	(6)	1
Ruslan Qurbanov	12.09.1991	4	(11)	1
Aghabala Ramazanov	20.01.1993	20	(2)	6
Davit Volkovi (GEO)	03.06.1995	21	(3)	8

SECOND LEVEL
First Division - Azərbaycan Birinci Divizionu 2020/2021

1.	Neftçi PFK-2 Bakı	27	20	4	3	64	-	17	64
2.	Zaqatala PFK	27	18	2	7	54	-	34	56
3.	Turan Tovuz IK	27	14	9	4	41	-	22	51
4.	Sabah FC-2 Bakı	27	14	3	10	47	-	37	45
5.	Qarabağ FK-2 Bakı	27	10	4	13	30	-	28	34
6.	Keşla FK-2 Bakı	27	9	4	14	32	-	54	31
7.	Qaradağ Lökbatan FK	27	8	5	14	29	-	41	29
8.	Kəpəz FK Gəncə	27	7	7	13	30	-	38	28
9.	Sumqayıt FK-2	27	5	7	15	26	-	49	22
10.	MOIK Bakı	27	5	5	17	30	-	63	20

INTERNATIONAL MATCHES
(16.07.2020 – 15.07.2021)

05.09.2020	Bakı	Azerbaijan - Luxembourg	1-2(1-0)	(UNL)
08.09.2020	Nicosia	Cyprus - Azerbaijan	0-1(0-1)	(UNL)
10.10.2020	Podgorica	Montenegro - Azerbaijan	2-0(1-0)	(UNL)
13.10.2020	Elbasan	Azerbaijan - Cyprus	0-0	(UNL)
11.11.2020	Ljubljana	Slovenia - Azerbaijan	0-0	(F)
14.11.2020	Zaprešić	Azerbaijan - Montenegro	0-0	(UNL)
17.11.2020	Lëtzebuerg	Luxembourg - Azerbaijan	0-0	(UNL)
24.03.2021	Torino	Portugal - Azerbaijan	1-0(1-0)	(WCQ)
27.03.2021	Debrecen	Qatar - Azerbaijan	2-1(0-1)	(WCQ)
30.03.2021	Bakı	Azerbaijan - Serbia	1-2(0-1)	(WCQ)
27.05.2021	Alanya	Turkey - Azerbaijan	2-1(2-1)	(F)
02.06.2021	Minsk	Belarus - Azerbaijan	1-2(0-0)	(F)
06.06.2021	Chişinău	Moldova - Azerbaijan	1-0(1-0)	(F)

05.09.2020   AZERBAIJAN - LUXEMBOURG   1-2(1-0)   2nd UEFA Nations League C, Group 1
Bakı Olimpiya Stadionu, Bakı; Referee: Chris Kavanagh (England); Attendance: 0
AZE: Emil Balayev, Maksim Medvedev (Cap), Qara Qarayev, Badavi Hüseynov, Təmkin Xəlilzadə (77.Araz Abdullayev), Bəhlul Mustafazadə, Anton Krivotsyuk, Namiq Ələsgərov (67.Adil Nağıyev), Elvin Camalov, Ramil Şeydayev (58.Renat Dadaşov), Mahir Emreli [*sent off 26*]. Trainer: Giovanni Girolamo De Biasi (Italy).
Goal: Ramil Şeydayev (43).

08.09.2020   CYPRUS - AZERBAIJAN   0-1(0-1)   2nd UEFA Nations League C, Group 1
Stádio GSP, Nicosia; Referee: Filip Glova (Slovakia); Attendance: 0
AZE: Emil Balayev, Maksim Medvedev (Cap), Qara Qarayev, Badavi Hüseynov, Təmkin Xəlilzadə (64.Araz Abdullayev), Bəhlul Mustafazadə, Abbas Hüseynov, Anton Krivotsyuk, Elvin Camalov (59.Coşğun Diniyev), Rəhim Sadıxov (77.Namiq Ələsgərov), Ramil Şeydayev. Trainer: Giovanni Girolamo De Biasi (Italy).
Goal: Maksim Medvedev (29).

10.10.2020   MONTENEGRO - AZERBAIJAN   2-0(1-0)   2nd UEFA Nations League C, Group 1
Stadion pod Goricom, Podgorica; Referee: Ricardo de Burgos Bengoetxea (Spain); Attendance: 0
AZE: Emil Balayev, Bəhlul Mustafazadə, Maksim Medvedev (Cap) (46.Azər Salahlı), Badavi Hüseynov, Qara Qarayev (60.Coşğun Diniyev), Abbas Hüseynov, Anton Krivotsyuk, Namiq Ələsgərov (79.Mirabdulla Abbasov), Elvin Camalov, Rəhim Sadıxov (61.Rəhman Hacıyev), Əli Qurbani (60.Ramil Şeydayev). Trainer: Giovanni Girolamo De Biasi (Italy).

13.10.2020   AZERBAIJAN - CYPRUS   0-0   2nd UEFA Nations League C, Group 1
Elbasan Arena, Elbasan (Albania); Referee: Fran Jović (Croatia); Attendance: 0
AZE: Şahruddin Məhəmmədəliyev, Qara Qarayev (Cap), Azər Salahlı (57.Namiq Ələsgərov), Elvin Bədəlov, Bəhlul Mustafazadə (71.Amin Seydiyev), Abbas Hüseynov, Anton Krivotsyuk, Vüqar Mustafayev, Rəhim Sadıxov (71.Rəhman Hacıyev), Ismayıl İbrahimli (57.Coşğun Diniyev), Ramil Şeydayev (81.Əli Qurbani). Trainer: Giovanni Girolamo De Biasi (Italy).

11.11.2020   SLOVENIA - AZERBAIJAN   0-0   Friendly International
Stadion Stožice, Ljubljana; Referee: Ferenc Karakó (Hungary); Attendance: 0
AZE: Emil Balayev, Maksim Medvedev (Cap) (46.Elvin Bədəlov), Badavi Hüseynov (46.Rahil Məmmədov), Azər Salahlı, Təmkin Xəlilzadə (56.Vüsal İsgəndərli), Amin Seydiyev, Tellur Mütəllimov (71.Abbas Hüseynov), Anton Krivotsyuk, Vüqar Mustafayev (46.Elvin Camalov), Ismayıl İbrahimli, Mahir Emreli (56.Musa Qurbanlı). Trainer: Giovanni Girolamo De Biasi (Italy).

14.11.2020   AZERBAIJAN - MONTENEGRO   0-0   2nd UEFA Nations League C, Group 1
Stadion "Ivan Laljak-Ivić", Zaprešić (Croatia); Referee: Sergei Ivanov (Russia); Attendance: 0
AZE: Şahruddin Məhəmmədəliyev, Maksim Medvedev (Cap), Qara Qarayev, Badavi Hüseynov, Azər Salahlı, Elvin Bədəlov (67.Vüsal İsgəndərli), Abbas Hüseynov (43.Amin Seydiyev), Vüqar Mustafayev (46.Elvin Camalov), Rəhim Sadıxov (46.Ramil Şeydayev), Mahir Emreli, Tellur Mütəllimov (81.Xəyal Nəcəfov). Trainer: Giovanni Girolamo De Biasi (Italy).

17.11.2020   LUXEMBOURG - AZERBAIJAN   0-0   2nd UEFA Nations League C, Group 1
Stade "Josy Barthel", Lëtzebuerg; Referee: Felix Zwayer (Germany); Attendance: 100
AZE: Şahruddin Məhəmmədəliyev, Qara Qarayev (Cap), Badavi Hüseynov (43.Şəhriyar Əliyev), Azər Salahlı, Elvin Bədəlov, Amin Seydiyev, Tellur Mütəllimov (69.Vüqar Mustafayev), Anton Krivotsyuk, Ismayıl İbrahimli (85.Xəyal Nəcəfov), Ramil Şeydayev, Mahir Emreli (85.Rəhim Sadıxov). Trainer: Giovanni Girolamo De Biasi (Italy).

24.03.2021   PORTUGAL - AZERBAIJAN   1-0(1-0)   22nd FIFA WC. Qualifiers
Juventus Stadium, Turin (Italy); Referee: Daniel Siebert (Germany); Attendance: 0
AZE: Şahruddin Məhəmmədəliyev, Maksim Medvedev (Cap), Badavi Hüseynov, Azər Salahlı, Elvin Bədəlov, Abbas Hüseynov (46.Anatoli Nuriyev), Anton Krivotsyuk, Emin Mahmudov (85.Aleksey Isayev), Vüqar Mustafayev (46.Ismayıl İbrahimli), Mahir Emreli (85.Namiq Ələsgərov, Əli Qurbani (85.Ramil Şeydayev). Trainer: Giovanni Girolamo De Biasi (Italy).

27.03.2021   QATAR - AZERBAIJAN   2-1(0-1)   Friendly International
Nagyerdei Stadion, Debrecen (Hungary); Referee: Ivan Kružliak (Slovakia); Attendance: 0
AZE: Emil Balayev (Cap), Şəhriyar Əliyev, Təmkin Xəlilzadə, Sertan Taşkın, Bəhlul Mustafazadə (78.Amin Seydiyev), Tellur Mütəllimov (74.Abbas Hüseynov), Aleksey Isayev (57.Rəhim Sadıxov), Ismayıl İbrahimli (75.Amil Yunanov), Ramil Şeydayev, Mahir Emreli (56.Namiq Ələsgərov), Anatoli Nuriyev (56.Vüqar Mustafayev). Trainer: Giovanni Girolamo De Biasi (Italy).
Goal: Ramil Şeydayev (16 penalty).

30.03.2021   AZERBAIJAN - SERBIA   1-2(0-1)   22nd FIFA WC. Qualifiers

Bakı Olimpiya Stadionu, Bakı; Referee: Roi Reinshreiber (Israel); Attendance: 0

AZE: Şahruddin Məhəmmədəliyev, Maksim Medvedev (Cap), Badavi Hüseynov, Azər Salahlı (72.Təmkin Xəlilzadə), Elvin Bədəlov, Abbas Hüseynov, Anton Krivotsyuk, Emin Mahmudov, Ismayıl İbrahimli, Əli Qurbani (69.Ramil Şeydayev), Anatoli Nuriyev (69.Mahir Emreli; 79.Elvin Cəfərquliyev). Trainer: Giovanni Girolamo De Biasi (Italy).

Goal: Emin Mahmudov (59 penalty).

27.05.2021   TURKEY - AZERBAIJAN   2-1(2-1)   Friendly International

Bahçeşehir Okulları Stadyumu, Alanya; Referee: Genc Nuza (Kosovo); Attendance: 400

AZE: Emil Balayev, Maksim Medvedev (Cap), Qara Qarayev, Badavi Hüseynov, Abbas Hüseynov (72.Toral Bayramov), Anton Krivotsyuk, Emin Mahmudov (79.Vüqar Mustafayev), Namiq Ələsgərov (79.Təmkin Xəlilzadə), Ismayıl İbrahimli (63.Murad Xaçayev), Elvin Cəfərquliyev (63.Azər Salahlı), Ramil Şeydayev (63.Əli Qurbani). Trainer: Giovanni Girolamo De Biasi (Italy).

Goal: Emin Mahmudov (28).

02.06.2021   BELARUS - AZERBAIJAN   1-2(0-0)   Friendly International

Stadion Dynama, Minsk; Referee: Dumitru Muntean (Moldova); Attendance: 4,120

AZE: Emil Balayev, Maksim Medvedev (Cap), Qara Qarayev (76.Vüqar Mustafayev), Badavi Hüseynov, Azər Salahlı, Hoccət Haqqverdi, Anton Krivotsyuk (68.Rüstəm Əhmədzadə), Emin Mahmudov (75.Aleksey Isayev), Namiq Ələsgərov (68.Elvin Cəfərquliyev), Toral Bayramov (76.Anatoli Nuriyev), Əli Qurbani (68.Ramil Şeydayev). Trainer: Giovanni Girolamo De Biasi (Italy).

Goals: Bədavi Hüseynov (73), Ramil Şeydayev (90+1).

06.06.2021   MOLDOVA - AZERBAIJAN   1-0(1-0)   Friendly International

Stadionul Zimbru, Chişinău; Referee: Marian Alexandru Barbu (Romania); Attendance: 2,130

AZE: Mehdi Cənnətov, Maksim Medvedev (Cap) (52.Şəhriyar Əliyev), Qara Qarayev, Badavi Hüseynov, Azər Salahlı (76.Elvin Cəfərquliyev), Hoccət Haqqverdi (46.Sertan Taşkın), Anton Krivotsyuk (46.Rüstəm Əhmədzadə), Emin Mahmudov (65.Anatoli Nuriyev), Namiq Ələsgərov (46.Toral Bayramov), Aleksey Isayev, Ramil Şeydayev. Trainer: Giovanni Girolamo De Biasi (Italy).

NATIONAL TEAM PLAYERS
(16.07.2020 – 15.07.2021)

Name	DOB	Caps	Goals	2020/2021:	Club
Goalkeepers					
Emil BALAYEV	17.04.1994	12	0	2020/2021:	*Qarabağ FK Bakı*
Mehdi CƏNNƏTOV	26.01.1992	1	0	2021:	*Sumqayıt FK*
Şahruddin MƏHƏMMƏDƏLIYEV	12.06.1994	5	0	2020/2021:	*Qarabağ FK Bakı*
Defenders					
Elvin BƏDƏLOV	14.06.1995	6	0	2020/2021:	*Sumqayıt FK*
Şəhriyar ƏLIYEV	25.12.1992	3	0	2020/2021:	*Keşlə FK Bakı*
Hoccət HAQQVERDI	03.02.1993	2	0	2021:	*Sumqayıt FK*
Abbas HÜSEYNOV	13.06.1995	12	0	2020/2021:	*Qarabağ FK Bakı*
Bədavi HÜSEYNOV	11.07.1991	60	1	2020/2021:	*Qarabağ FK Bakı*
Anton KRIVOTSYUK	20.08.1998	18	0	2020/2021:	*Neftçi PFK Bakı*
Maksim MEDVEDEV	29.05.1989	70	4	2020/2021:	*Qarabağ FK Bakı*
Bəhlul MUSTAFAZADƏ	27.02.1997	11	0	2020/2021:	*Sabah FC Bakı*
Rahil MƏMMƏDOV	24.11.1995	10	0	2020:	*Qarabağ FK Bakı*
Adil NAĞIYEV	11.09.1995	2	0	2020:	*Səbail FK Bakı*
Azər SALAHLI	11.04.1994	10	0	2020/2021:	*Keşlə FK Bakı*
Amin SEYDIYEV	15.11.1998	5	0	2020/2021:	*Sabah FC Bakı*
Sertan TAŞKIN	08.10.1997	2	0	2021:	*Zirə FK Bakı*
Təmkin XƏLILZADƏ	06.08.1993	23	3	2020/2021:	*Sabah FC Bakı*
Midfielders					
Araz ABDULLAYEV	18.04.1992	40	3	2020/2021:	*Qarabağ FK Bakı*
Toral BAYRAMOV	23.02.2001	3	0	2021:	*Qarabağ FK Bakı*
Elvin CAMALOV	04.02.1995	6	0	2020:	*Zirə FK Bakı*
Elvin CƏFƏRQULIYEV	26.10.2000	4	0	2021:	*Qarabağ FK Bakı*
Coşğun DINIYEV	13.09.1995	11	0	2020:	*Sabah FC Bakı*
Namiq ƏLƏSGƏROV	03.02.1995	25	0	2020/2021:	*Neftçi PFK Bakı*
Rəhman HACIYEV	25.07.1993	9	0	2020:	*Keşlə FK Bakı*
Ismayıl İBRAHIMLI	13.02.1998	7	0	2020/2021:	*Qarabağ FK Bakı*
Vüsal İSGƏNDƏRLI	03.11.1995	3	0	2020:	*Keşlə FK Bakı*
Aleksey ISAYEV	09.11.1995	4	0	2021:	*Sabah FC Bakı*
Qara QARAYEV	12.10.1992	66	0	2020/2021:	*Qarabağ FK Bakı*
Emin MAHMUDOV	27.04.1992	19	3	2021:	*Neftçi PFK Bakı*
Vüqar MUSTAFAYEV	05.08.1994	9	0	2020/2021:	*Sumqayıt FK*
Tellur MÜTƏLLIMOV	08.04.1995	5	0	2020/2021:	*Sumqayıt FK*
Xəyal NƏCƏFOV	19.12.1997	2	0	2020:	*Sumqayıt FK*
Rəhim SADIXOV	18.07.1996	6	0	2020/2021:	*Sumqayıt FK*
Murad XAÇAYEV	14.04.1998	1	0	2021:	*Sumqayıt FK*
Forwards					
Mirabdulla ABBASOV	27.04.1995	4	0	2020:	*Neftçi PFK Bakı*
Renat DADAŞOV	17.05.1999	7	0	2020/2021:	*Grasshopper Club Zürich (SUI)*
Mahir EMRELI	01.07.1997	26	4	2020/2021:	*Qarabağ FK Bakı*
Rüstəm ƏHMƏDZADƏ	25.12.2000	2	0	2021:	*FK Mynai (UKR)*
Əli QURBANI	18.09.1990	6	0	2020/2021:	*Sumqayıt FK*
Musa QURBANLI	13.04.2002	1	0	2020:	*Qarabağ FK Bakı*
Anatoli NURIYEV	20.05.1996	5	0	2021:	*FK Mynai (UKR)*
Ramil ŞEYDAYEV	15.03.1996	38	7	2020/2021:	*Sabah FC Bakı*
Amil YUNANOV	06.01.1993	5	0	2021:	*Səbail FK Bakı*
Trainer					
Giovanni Girolamo DE BIASI (ITA) [from 11.07.2020]	16.06.1956			13 M; 2 W; 4 D; 7 L; 7-13	

BELARUS

АБФФ

The Country:
Рэспубліка Беларусь (Republic of Belarus)
Capital: Minsk
Surface: 207,595 km^2
Inhabitants: 9,349,645 [2021]
Time: UTC+3

The FA:
Belaruskaya Federatiya Futbola
Prospekt Pobeditelei, 20/3 220020, Minsk
Tel: +375 17 254 56 00
Foundation date: 1889
Member of FIFA since: 1992
Member of UEFA since: 1993
Website: www.bff.by

NATIONAL TEAM RECORDS

RECORDS
First international match:	28.10.1992, Minsk:	Belarus – Ukraine 1-1
Most international caps:	Alyaksandr Kulchy	- 102 caps (1996-2012)
Most international goals:	Maxym Romashchenko	- 20 goal / 64 caps (1998-2008)

UEFA EUROPEAN CHAMPIONSHIP		FIFA WORLD CUP		OLYMPIC TOURNAMENTS	
1960	-	1930	-	1908	-
1964	-	1934	-	1912	-
1968	-	1938	-	1920	-
1972	-	1950	-	1924	-
1976	-	1954	-	1928	-
1980	-	1958	-	1936	-
1984	-	1962	-	1948	-
1988	-	1966	-	1952	-
1992	-	1970	-	1956	-
1996	Qualifiers	1974	-	1960	-
2000	Qualifiers	1978	-	1964	-
2004	Qualifiers	1982	-	1968	-
2008	Qualifiers	1986	-	1972	-
2012	Qualifiers	1990	-	1976	-
2016	Qualifiers	1994	*Did not enter*	1980	-
2020	Qualifiers	1998	Qualifiers	1984	-
		2002	Qualifiers	1988	-
		2006	Qualifiers	1992	-
		2010	Qualifiers	1996	Qualifiers
		2014	Qualifiers	2000	Qualifiers
		2018	Qualifiers	2004	Qualifiers
				2008	Qualifiers
				2012	Final Tournament (Group Stage)
				2016	Qualifiers

<u>Please note</u>: *was part of Soviet Union until 1990.*

UEFA NATIONS LEAGUE
2018/2019	League D (promoted to League C)
2020/2021	League C

FIFA CONFEDERATIONS CUP 1992-2017
None

BELARUSIAN CLUB HONOURS IN EUROPEAN CLUB COMPETITIONS:

European Champion Clubs.Cup (1956-1992) / UEFA Champions League (1993-2021)
None

Fairs Cup (1858-1971) / UEFA Cup (1972-2009) / UEFA Europa League (2010-2021)
None

UEFA Super Cup (1972-2020)
None

*European Cup Winners.Cup 1961-1999**
None

*defunct competition

NATIONAL COMPETITIONS
TABLE OF HONOURS

BELARUS SSR (SOVIET ERA) CHAMPIONS

Year	Champion	Year	Champion	Year	Champion
1922	Minsk (city team)	1949	Traktor MTZ Minsk	1970	Torpedo Zhodino
1923	*Not known*	1950	ODO Minsk	1971	Torpedo Zhodino
1924	Minsk (city team)	1951	Dinamo Minsk	1972	Stroitel.Bobruisk
1925	*Not known*	1952	ODO Minsk	1973	Stroitel.Bobruisk
1926	Bobruisk (city team)	1953	Spartak Minsk	1974	BATE Borisov
1927	Unknown	1954	ODO Minsk	1975	Dinamo Minsk
1928	Gomel (city team)	1955	FSM Minsk	1976	BATE Borisov
1929–32	*Not known*	1956	Spartak Minsk	1977	Sputnik Minsk
1933	Gomel (city team)	1957	Sputnik Minsk	1978	Shinnik Bobruisk
1934	BVO Minsk	1958	Spartak Bobruisk	1979	BATE Borisov
1935	BVO Minsk	1959	Minsk (city team)	1980	Torpedo Zhodino
1936	BVO Minsk	1960	Sputnik Minsk	1981	Torpedo Zhodino
1937	Dinamo Minsk	1961	Volna Pinsk	1982	Torpedo Mogilev
1938	Dinamo Minsk	1962	Torpedo Minsk	1983	Obuvschik Lida
1939	Dinamo Minsk	1963	Naroch.Molodechno	1984	Orbita Minsk
1940	DKA Minsk	1964	SKA Minsk	1985	Obuvschik Lida
1941–44	*Not known*	1965	SKA Minsk	1986	Obuvschik Lida
1945	Dinamo Minsk	1966	Torpedo Minsk	1987	Shinnik Bobruisk
1946	ODO Minsk	1967	Torpedo Minsk	1988	Sputnik Minsk
1947	Torpedo Minsk	1968	Sputnik Minsk	1989	Obuvschik Lida
1948	Traktor MTZ Minsk	1969	Torpedo Minsk	1990	Sputnik Minsk
				1991	Metallurg Molodechno

	CHAMPIONS	CUP WINNERS	BEST GOALSCORERS	
1992	FC Dinamo Minsk	FC Dinamo Minsk	Andrey Skorobogatko (FC Dnepr Mogilev)	11
1992/1993	FC Dinamo Minsk	FC Neman Grodno	Syarhey Baranovsky (FC Dinamo Minsk) Miroslav Romaschenko (FC Vedrich Rechitsa / FC Dnepr Mogilev)	19
1993/1994	FC Dinamo Minsk	FC Dinamo Minsk	Pyotr Kachuro (FC Dinamo-93 Minsk / FC Dinamo Minsk)	21
1994/1995	FC Dinamo Minsk	-	Pavel Shavrov (FC Dinamo-93 Minsk)	19
1995	FC Dinamo Minsk	FC Dinamo-93 Minsk	Syarhey Yaromko (MPKC Mozyr)	16
1996	MPKC Mozyr	MPKC Mozyr	Andrey Khlebasolaw (FC Belshina Bobruisk)	34
1997	FC Dinamo Minsk	FC Belshina Bobruisk	Andrey Khlebasolaw (FC Belshina Bobruisk)	19
1998	FC Dnepr Mogilev	FC Lokomotiv-96 Vitebsk	Syarhey Yaromko (FC Torpedo Minsk)	19
1999	FC BATE Borisov	FC Belshina Bobruisk	Valery Strypeykis (FC Slavia Mozyr)	21
2000	FC Slavia Mozyr	FC Slavia Mozyr	Raman Vasilyuk (FC Slavia Mozyr)	31
2001	FC Belshina Bobruisk	FC Belshina Bobruisk	Sergei Davydov (RUS, FC Neman Grodno)	25
2002	FC BATE Borisov	FC Gomel	Valery Strypeykis (FC Belshina Bobruisk)	18
2003	FC Gomel	FC Dinamo Minsk	Gennadi Bliznyuk (FC Gomel)	18
2004	FC Dinamo Minsk	FC Shakhtyor Solihorsk	Valery Strypeykis (Naftan Novopolotsk)	18
2005	FC Shakhtyor Solihorsk	MTZ-RIPO Minsk	Valery Strypeykis (Naftan Novopolotsk)	16
2006	FC BATE Borisov	FC BATE Borisov	Alyaksandr Klimenka (FC Shakhtyor Solihorsk)	17
2007	FC BATE Borisov	FC Dynamo Brest	Raman Vasilyuk (FC Gomel)	24
2008	FC BATE Borisov	MTZ-RIPO Minsk	Gennadi Bliznyuk (FC BATE Borisov) Vitali Rodionov (FC BATE Borisov)	16
2009	FC BATE Borisov	FC Naftan Novopolotsk	Maycon Rogério Silva Calijuri (BRA, FC Gomel)	15
2010	FC BATE Borisov	FC BATE Borisov	Renan Bardini Bressan (BRA, FC BATE Borisov)	15
2011	FC BATE Borisov	FC Gomel	Renan Bardini Bressan (BRA, FC BATE Borisov)	13
2012	FC BATE Borisov	FC Naftan Novopolotsk	Dzmitry Asipenka (FC Shakhtyor Solihorsk)	14
2013	FC BATE Borisov	FC Minsk	Vitali Rodionov (FC BATE Borisov)	14
2014	FC BATE Borisov	FC Shakhtyor Solihorsk	Mikalay Yanush (FC Shakhtyor Solihorsk)	15
2015	FC BATE Borisov	FC BATE Borisov	Mikalay Yanush (FC Shakhtyor Solihorsk)	15
2016	FC BATE Borisov	FC Torpedo-BelAZ Zhodino	Vitali Rodionov (FC BATE Borisov) Mikhayl Gordeichuk (FC BATE Borisov)	16
2017	FC BATE Borisov	FC Dinamo Brest	Mikhayl Gordeichuk (FC BATE Borisov)	18
2018	FC BATE Borisov	FC Dinamo Brest	Pavel Savitski (FC Dinamo Brest)	15
2019	FC Dinamo Brest	FC Shakhtyor Solihorsk	Ilya Shkurin (FC Energetik-BGU Minsk)	19
2020	FC Shakhtyor Solihorsk	FC BATE Borisov	Maksim Skavysh (FC BATE Borisov)	19

NATIONAL CHAMPIONSHIP
Belarusian Premier League 2020
(19.03.2020 – 28.11.2020)

Results

Round 1 [19-22.03.2020]
Energetik-BGU - BATE Borisov 3-1(2-0)
Shakhtyor Solih. - Torpedo-BelAZ 0-1(0-0)
Dinamo Brest - FC Smolevichi 1-1(0-0)
Dinamo Minsk - Rukh Brest 0-1(0-1)
FC Vitebsk - FC Gorodeya 1-0(1-0)
Isloch Minsk - Neman Grodno 1-0(0-0)
FC Slutsk - FC Slaviya Mozyr 3-1(1-1)
FC Belshina - FC Minsk 1-3(1-0)

Round 2 [27-29.03.2020]
Torpedo-BelAZ - FC Belshina 1-0(0-0)
Rukh Brest - Energetik-BGU 0-1(0-1)
FC Slutsk - Dinamo Brest 0-1(0-1)
FC Slaviya Mozyr - BATE Borisov 2-1(1-1)
FC Minsk - Dinamo Minsk 3-2(3-0)
FC Gorodeya - Shakhtyor Solihorsk 0-2(0-0)
Isloch Minsk - FC Smolevichi 1-0(1-0)
Neman Grodno - FC Vitebsk 2-0(0-0)

Round 3 [03-05.04.2020]
FC Belshina - FC Gorodeya 0-1(0-0)
Dinamo Minsk - Torpedo-BelAZ 2-0(2-0)
Shakhtyor Solihorsk - Neman Grodno 0-0
BATE Borisov - Rukh Brest 1-0(1-0)
Dinamo Brest - FC Slaviya Mozyr 1-2(0-0)
Energetik-BGU - FC Minsk 2-0(1-0)
FC Smolevichi - FC Vitebsk 0-1(0-1)
Isloch Minsk - FC Slutsk 2-3(0-1)

Round 4 [10-13.04.2020]
Neman Grodno - FC Belshina 1-1(1-0)
FC Slutsk - FC Vitebsk 1-1(0-1)
Torpedo-BelAZ - Energetik-BGU 2-0(0-0)
FC Gorodeya - Dinamo Minsk 1-0(1-0)
FC Minsk - BATE Borisov 0-3(0-2)
FC Smolevichi - Shakhtyor Solihorsk 0-0
Dinamo Brest - Isloch Minsk 3-1(1-1)
FC Slaviya Mozyr - Rukh Brest 0-0

Round 5 [16-18.04.2020]
Energetik-BGU - FC Gorodeya 0-1(0-1)
Dinamo Minsk - Neman Grodno 2-0(0-0)
FC Belshina - FC Smolevichi 1-1(0-0)
Shakhtyor Solihorsk - FC Slutsk 1-2(0-2)
Isloch Minsk - FC Slaviya Mozyr 2-1(0-0)
Rukh Brest - FC Minsk 1-0(0-0)
FC Vitebsk - Dinamo Brest 1-0(0-0)
BATE Borisov - Torpedo-BelAZ 0-0

Round 6 [24-26.04.2020]
FC Smolevichi - Dinamo Minsk 1-3(0-2)
Neman Grodno - Energetik-BGU 3-0(0-0)
FC Slaviya Mozyr - FC Minsk 1-3(0-1)
FC Gorodeya - BATE Borisov 0-2(0-0)
Dinamo Brest - Shakhtyor Solihorsk 0-2(0-1)
FC Slutsk - FC Belshina 3-2(2-1)
Torpedo-BelAZ - Rukh Brest 0-0
Isloch Minsk - FC Vitebsk 2-0(1-0)

Round 7 [01-03.05.2020]
FC Smolevichi - Energetik-BGU 0-2(0-1)
FC Minsk - Torpedo-BelAZ 2-5(1-4)
Rukh Brest - FC Gorodeya 1-1(0-0)
Dinamo Minsk - FC Slutsk 1-2(0-1)
FC Belshina - Dinamo Brest 0-3(0-1)
FC Vitebsk - FC Slaviya Mozyr 2-3(0-1)
BATE Borisov - Neman Grodno 3-1(2-1)
Shakhtyor Solihorsk - Isloch Minsk 4-0(1-0)

Round 8 [08-10.05.2020]
FC Slutsk - Energetik-BGU 1-2(1-2)
FC Gorodeya - FC Minsk 1-1(1-1)
FC Slaviya Mozyr - Torpedo-BelAZ 0-0
Neman Grodno - Rukh Brest 2-4(0-2)
Isloch Minsk - FC Belshina 2-1(1-0)
FC Vitebsk - Shakhtyor Solihorsk 0-0
FC Smolevichi - BATE Borisov 3-5(1-3)
Dinamo Brest - Dinamo Minsk 2-1(1-1)

Round 9 [15-17.05.2020]
Torpedo-BelAZ - FC Gorodeya 3-1(1-0)
Energetik-BGU - Dinamo Brest 2-1(1-0)
Shakhtyor Solihorsk - Slaviya Mozyr 2-0(1-0)
BATE Borisov - FC Slutsk 3-0(2-0)
FC Belshina - FC Vitebsk 1-1(0-0)
Dinamo Minsk - Isloch Minsk 1-0(0-0)
Rukh Brest - FC Smolevichi 0-0
FC Minsk - Neman Grodno 4-3(3-1) [29.08.]

Round 10 [20-23.05.2020]
Dinamo Brest - BATE Borisov 1-3(1-1)
Neman Grodno - Torpedo-BelAZ 3-1(1-1)
FC Slaviya Mozyr - FC Gorodeya 1-0(0-1)
Shakhtyor Solihorsk - FC Belshina 4-0(1-0)
FC Slutsk - Rukh Brest 1-1(0-0)
Isloch Minsk - Energetik-BGU 1-2(1-1)
FC Vitebsk - Dinamo Minsk 1-1(1-1)
FC Smolevichi - FC Minsk 0-4(0-1) [23.09.]

Round 11 [29.05.-01.06.2020]
Torpedo-BelAZ - FC Smolevichi 2-1(1-1)
FC Gorodeya - Neman Grodno 0-2(0-0)
FC Belshina - FC Slaviya Mozyr 2-3(2-1)
Dinamo Minsk - Shakhtyor Solihorsk 0-1(0-0)
Energetik-BGU - FC Vitebsk 3-3(3-2)
BATE Borisov - Isloch Minsk 1-0(1-0)
Rukh Brest - Dinamo Brest 1-4(1-1)
FC Minsk - FC Slutsk 1-0(1-0)

Round 12 [05-07.06.2020]
FC Smolevichi - FC Gorodeya 4-1(2-0)
FC Slutsk - Torpedo-BelAZ 1-1(0-0)
Isloch Minsk - Rukh Brest 1-1(0-0)
FC Slaviya Mozyr - Neman Grodno 1-3(1-1)
Dinamo Brest - FC Minsk 6-1(1-1)
FC Vitebsk - BATE Borisov 2-2(0-1)
FC Belshina - Dinamo Minsk 0-4(0-2)
Shakhtyor Solih. - Energetik-BGU 1-0(1-0)

Round 13 [12-14.06.2020]
FC Minsk - Isloch Minsk 0-1(0-0)
FC Gorodeya - FC Slutsk 3-0(1-0)
Neman Grodno - FC Smolevichi 2-0(0-0)
Torpedo-BelAZ - Dinamo Brest 0-2(0-2)
Dinamo Minsk - FC Slaviya Mozyr 1-0(1-0)
Energetik-BGU - FC Belshina 0-1(0-0)
Rukh Brest - FC Vitebsk 0-1(0-1)
BATE Borisov - Shakhtyor Solihorsk 2-2(0-1)

Round 14 [19-21.06.2020]
FC Slaviya Mozyr - FC Smolevichi 2-1(0-0)
FC Slutsk - Neman Grodno 0-1(0-1)
Isloch Minsk - Torpedo-BelAZ 2-2(0-1)
Dinamo Brest - FC Gorodeya 3-1(1-1)
Dinamo Minsk - Energetik-BGU 0-0
FC Belshina - BATE Borisov 0-2(0-1)
FC Vitebsk - FC Minsk 1-0(1-0)
Shakhtyor Solihorsk - Rukh Brest 1-1(0-0)

Round 15 [26-28.06.2020]
Energetik-BGU - FC Slaviya Mozyr 5-0(1-0)
FC Smolevichi - FC Slutsk 2-1(1-1)
FC Minsk - Shakhtyor Solihorsk 1-1(0-0)
Neman Grodno - Dinamo Brest 1-0(1-0)
BATE Borisov - Dinamo Minsk 0-2(0-0)
Torpedo-BelAZ - FC Vitebsk 1-0(0-0)
Rukh Brest - FC Belshina 3-0(3-0)
FC Gorodeya - Isloch Minsk 0-2(0-1)

Round 16 [03-05.07.2020]
FC Slaviya Mozyr - FC Slutsk 3-1(2-1)
FC Smolevichi - Dinamo Brest 3-3(0-2)
BATE Borisov - Energetik-BGU 0-1(0-1)
FC Gorodeya - FC Vitebsk 2-2(1-1)
Neman Grodno - Isloch Minsk 1-0(0-0)
FC Minsk - FC Belshina 2-2(1-1)
Torpedo-BelAZ - Shakhtyor Solih. 1-4(0-1)
Rukh Brest - Dinamo Minsk 1-0(1-0)

Round 17 [10-12.07.2020]
FC Smolevichi - Isloch Minsk 3-1(2-0)
FC Belshina - Torpedo-BelAZ 2-1(1-1)
BATE Borisov - FC Slaviya Mozyr 1-1(0-0)
Shakhtyor Solihorsk - FC Gorodeya 4-1(3-0)
Energetik-BGU - Rukh Brest 1-8(0-4)
Dinamo Minsk - FC Minsk 1-0(1-0)
FC Vitebsk - Neman Grodno 0-0
Dinamo Brest - FC Slutsk 3-1(1-1) [22.10.]

Round 18 [17-19.07.2020]
FC Slutsk - Isloch Minsk 2-1(0-1)
FC Gorodeya - FC Belshina 2-1(0-0)
FC Vitebsk - FC Smolevichi 1-0(0-0)
Rukh Brest - BATE Borisov 0-3(0-3)
FC Minsk - Energetik-BGU 2-1(1-1)
Neman Grodno - Shakhtyor Solihorsk 0-0
Torpedo-BelAZ - Dinamo Minsk 0-0
Slaviya Moz. - Dinamo Brest 1-1(0-0) [31.10.]

Round 19 [24-26.07.2020]
Rukh Brest - FC Slaviya Mozyr 3-3(1-0)
FC Vitebsk - FC Slutsk 2-0(1-0)
Isloch Minsk - Dinamo Brest 2-0(1-0)
FC Belshina - Neman Grodno 0-1(0-1)
Dinamo Minsk - FC Gorodeya 1-0(0-0)
Energetik-BGU - Torpedo-BelAZ 1-4(1-1)
BATE Borisov - FC Minsk 6-0(2-0)
Shakhtyor Solihorsk - FC Smolevichi 4-0(1-0)

Round 20 [31.07.-02.08.2020]
FC Slutsk - Shakhtyor Solihorsk 0-2(0-1)
Dinamo Brest - FC Vitebsk 1-0(1-0)
FC Smolevichi - FC Belshina 0-3(0-1)
FC Slaviya Mozyr - Isloch Minsk 2-4(1-2)
Neman Grodno - Dinamo Minsk 1-0(0-0)
Torpedo-BelAZ - BATE Borisov 3-2(1-2)
FC Minsk - Rukh Brest 0-1(0-1)
FC Gorodeya - Energetik-BGU 1-1(0-0)

Round 21 [06-08.08.2020]
FC Belshina - FC Slutsk 4-2(3-0)
Shakhtyor Solihorsk - Dinamo Brest 1-0(0-0)
FC Vitebsk - Isloch Minsk 2-3(1-1)
Energetik-BGU - Neman Grodno 1-1(1-0)
Rukh Brest - Torpedo-BelAZ 3-3(1-1)
BATE Borisov - FC Gorodeya 1-0(1-0)
Dinamo Minsk - Smolevichi 2-1(2-0) [02.10.]
FC Minsk - Slaviya Mozyr 2-1(1-0) [21.10.]

Round 22 [21-23.08.2020]
FC Slutsk - Dinamo Minsk 1-2(1-1)
Isloch Minsk - Shakhtyor Solihorsk 4-2(1-0)
Dinamo Brest - FC Belshina 1-2(0-1)
Energetik-BGU - FC Smolevichi 4-1(2-0)
FC Gorodeya - Rukh Brest 1-3(0-2)
FC Slaviya Mozyr - FC Vitebsk 1-1(1-1)
Torpedo-BelAZ - FC Minsk 1-1(1-0)
Neman Grodno - BATE Borisov 0-2(0-1)

Round 23 [11-13.09.2020]
FC Minsk - FC Gorodeya 3-0(1-0)
Rukh Brest - Neman Grodno 2-3(0-2)
BATE Borisov - FC Smolevichi 5-2(2-0)
Shakhtyor Solihorsk - FC Vitebsk 5-0(2-0)
Dinamo Minsk - Dinamo Brest 2-4(1-0)
FC Belshina - Isloch Minsk 2-3(1-1)
Torpedo-BelAZ - FC Slaviya Mozyr 4-2(2-1)
Energetik-BGU - FC Slutsk 0-2(0-0) [01.11.]

Round 24 [18-20.09.2020]
FC Smolevichi - Rukh Brest 0-6(0-2)
Neman Grodno - FC Minsk 2-0(2-0)
FC Vitebsk - FC Belshina 1-1(0-0)
Dinamo Brest - Energetik-BGU 2-1(2-1)
FC Gorodeya - Torpedo-BelAZ 1-3(0-2)
Isloch Minsk - Dinamo Minsk 2-1(1-0)
FC Slutsk - BATE Borisov 1-3(1-2)
Slaviya Mozyr - Shakhtyor Solihorsk 1-0(0-0)

Round 25 [26-28.09.2020]
Energetik-BGU - Isloch Minsk 1-1(1-0)
FC Gorodeya - FC Slaviya Mozyr 1-1(0-0)
Torpedo-BelAZ - Neman Grodno 0-1(0-1)
BATE Borisov - Dinamo Brest 2-4(0-1)
Dinamo Minsk - FC Vitebsk 1-0(0-0)
Rukh Brest - FC Slutsk 5-0(2-0)
FC Minsk - FC Smolevichi 2-1(0-1)
FC Belshina - Shakhtyor Sol. 1-5(0-0) [31.10.]

Round 26 [16-18.10.2020]
FC Slutsk - FC Minsk 2-1(1-0)
FC Vitebsk - Energetik-BGU 1-0(0-0)
Neman Grodno - FC Gorodeya 0-1(0-0)
FC Smolevichi - Torpedo-BelAZ 1-4(1-1)
Isloch Minsk - BATE Borisov 2-2(1-1)
Shakhtyor Solihorsk - Dinamo Minsk 0-1(0-0)
Dinamo Brest - Rukh Brest 5-2(1-2)
Slaviya Mozyr - FC Belshina 1-1(1-0) [04.11.]

Round 27 [24-26.10.2020]
FC Gorodeya - FC Smolevichi 4-0(1-0)
BATE Borisov - FC Vitebsk 3-1(1-0)
Dinamo Minsk - FC Belshina 3-1(1-1)
Neman Grodno - FC Slaviya Mozyr 1-2(0-2)
Energetik-BGU - Shakhtyor Solih. 1-2(0-2)
Rukh Brest - Isloch Minsk 1-1(1-0)
FC Minsk - Dinamo Brest 1-2(1-1)
Torpedo-BelAZ - FC Slutsk 4-1(3-1)

Round 28 [06-08.11.2020]
Isloch Minsk - FC Minsk 3-4(2-1)
FC Vitebsk - Rukh Brest 0-0
FC Smolevichi - Neman Grodno 1-4(0-3)
FC Slutsk - FC Gorodeya 0-1(0-1)
Dinamo Brest - Torpedo-BelAZ 2-3(1-0)
Shakhtyor Solihorsk - BATE Borisov 1-1(0-1)
FC Belshina - Energetik-BGU 1-5(0-2)
FC Slaviya Mozyr - Dinamo Minsk 0-1(0-0)

Round 29 [22.11.2020]
FC Smolevichi - FC Slaviya Mozyr 0-3(0-1)
Neman Grodno - FC Slutsk 1-0(1-0)
FC Gorodeya - Dinamo Brest 1-4(0-0)
Torpedo-BelAZ - Isloch Minsk 2-0(1-0)
FC Minsk - FC Vitebsk 2-2(2-1)
Rukh Brest - Shakhtyor Solihorsk 1-2(1-2)
BATE Borisov - FC Belshina 5-0(1-0)
Energetik-BGU - Dinamo Minsk 2-3(1-3)

Round 30 [28.11.2020]
FC Slutsk - FC Smolevichi *not played*
FC Slaviya Mozyr - Energetik-BGU 2-1(0-0)
Dinamo Minsk - BATE Borisov 0-0
FC Belshina - Rukh Brest 3-7(1-4)
Shakhtyor Solihorsk - FC Minsk 4-2(1-1)
FC Vitebsk - Torpedo-BelAZ 2-3(1-1)
Isloch Minsk - FC Gorodeya 2-2(1-2)
Dinamo Brest - Neman Grodno 3-1(1-1)

Final Standings

									Total				Home					Away		
1.	**FC Shakhtyor Solihorsk**	30	17	8	5	57	-	21	59	9	3	3	32	-	9	8	5	2	25	-	12
2.	FC BATE Borisov	30	17	7	6	65	-	32	58	9	3	3	33	-	14	8	4	3	32	-	18
3.	FC Torpedo-BelAZ Zhodino	30	16	8	6	55	-	37	56	9	3	3	24	-	15	7	5	3	31	-	22
4.	FC Dinamo Brest	30	17	3	10	63	-	40	54	9	1	5	34	-	22	8	2	5	29	-	18
5.	FC Neman Grodno	30	16	5	9	41	-	29	53	9	2	4	20	-	11	7	3	5	21	-	18
6.	FC Dinamo Minsk	30	16	4	10	38	-	25	52	9	2	4	17	-	10	7	2	6	21	-	15
7.	FC Isloch Minsk Raion	30	13	6	11	47	-	46	45	8	4	3	29	-	21	5	2	8	18	-	25
8.	FC Rukh Brest	30	11	11	8	57	-	38	44	4	5	6	22	-	22	7	6	2	35	-	16
9.	FC Slavia Mozyr	30	10	9	11	41	-	49	39	5	6	4	18	-	19	5	3	7	23	-	30
10.	FC Energetik-BGU Minsk	30	11	5	14	43	-	46	38	5	3	7	26	-	29	6	2	7	17	-	17
11.	FC Minsk	30	11	5	14	45	-	57	38	7	3	5	25	-	25	4	2	9	20	-	32
12.	FC Vitebsk	30	8	12	10	30	-	38	36	6	6	3	17	-	13	2	6	7	13	-	25
13.	FC Gorodeya	30	8	7	15	30	-	48	31	4	4	7	18	-	24	4	3	8	12	-	24
14.	FC Slutsk (*Relegation Play-offs*)	29	8	3	18	31	-	55	27	4	3	7	16	-	20	4	0	11	15	-	35
15.	FC Belshina Bobruisk (*Relegated*)	30	5	6	19	34	-	71	21	2	2	11	18	-	42	3	4	8	16	-	29
16.	FC Smolevichi (*Relegated*)	29	3	5	21	27	-	72	14	3	2	10	18	-	41	0	3	11	9	-	31

Top goalscorers:

19	**Maksim Skavysh**	*FC BATE Borisov*
16	Jasurbek Yakhshiboev (UZB)	*FC Energetik-BGU Minsk / FC Shakhtyor Solihorsk*
12	Gegam Kadimyan (ARM)	*FC Neman Grodno*
12	Pavel Nyakhaychyk	*FC BATE Borisov*
11	Gabriel Ramos da Penha (BRA)	*Torpedo-BelAZ Zhodino*
11	Dzyanis Laptev	*FC Dinamo Brest*
11	Yevgeniy Shikavka	*FC Dinamo Minsk*

Relegation Play-offs

NFC Krumkachy Minsk - FC Slutsk   0-2(0-1)   1-2(0-2)

FC Slutsk remains at first level.

NATIONAL CUP
Kubak Belarusi 2019/2020

First Round [22.05.2019]

Servolyuks Mogilev Region - FC Ivatsevichi	2-6(2-2)	FC Alfa Minsk - Victoria Maryina Gorka	0-5(0-2)
Montazhnik Mozyr - Dyush-3 Stenles Pinsk	3-1(1-1)	Dush Pinsk Region - FK Čisť	1-3(1-1)
FC Detskoselskiy - FC Smolevichi	0-0 aet; 7-8 pen	PK Kremko Kvasovka - FC Energetik-BGATU Minsk	2-1(2-0)

Second Round [12.06.2019]

FC Victoria Maryina Gorka - FC Sputnik Rechitsa	2-3(0-1)	FC Oshmyany - FC Khimik Svetlogorsk	2-1(2-0)
FC Montazhnik Mozyr - FC Naftan Novopolotsk	0-1(0-1)	FC SMlautotrans Smolevichi - FC Smorgon	0-6(0-3)
FC UAS Zhitkovichi - NFC Krumkachy Minsk	0-3 awarded	FC Molodechno - FC Arsenal Dzerzhinsk	0-5(0-2)
FC Kletsk - FC Orsha	2-2 aet; 5-4 pen	FC Uzda - FC Belshina Bobruisk	1-2(0-1)
FC Osipovichi - FC Smolevichi	0-1(0-0)	PK Kremko Kvasovka - FC Slonim-2017	0-2(0-2)
FC Čisť - FC Lida	1-3(0-1)	FC Gorki - FC Volna Pinsk	0-3(0-2)
FC Ivatsevichi - FC Rukh Brest	2-3(1-1,2-2)	FC Neman-Agro Stolbtsy - FC Baranovichi	1-2(1-0)

Third Round [26.06./24.07./27-28.07.2019]

FC Slonim-2017 - FC Vitebsk	1-3(0-2)	NFC Krumkachy Minsk - FC Slaviya Mozyr	1-3(0-0,1-1)
FC Smolevichi - FC Shakhtyor Solihorsk	0-2(0-1)	FC Volna Pinsk - FC Dnyapro Mogilev	1-3(0-0)
FC Sputnik Rechitsa - FC BATE Borisov	2-5(0-4)	FC Rukh Brest - FC Dinamo Brest	0-1(0-1)
FC Granit Mikashevichi - FC Dinamo Minsk	0-2(0-0)	FC Arsenal Dzerzhinsk - FC Energetik-BGU Minsk	0-6(0-2)
FC Baranovichi - FC Torpedo-BelAZ Zhodino	1-7(1-3)	FC Oshmyany - FC Isloch Minsk Raion	1-3(1-0)
FC Naftan Novopolotsk - FC Neman Grodno	2-1(0-1,1-1)	FC Belshina Bobruisk - FC Minsk	1-3(0-2)
FC Smorgon - FC Gomel	1-4(0-3)	FC Lida - FC Slutsk	3-3 aet; 3-4 pen
FC Lokomotiv Gomel - FC Gorodeya	3-0(2-0)	FC Kletsk - FC Torpedo Minsk	2-7(0-1)

1/8-Finals [03-04.08.2019]

FC Energetik-BGU Minsk - FC Isloch Minsk Raion	2-3(0-2)	Naftan Novopolotsk - FC Torpedo-BelAZ Zhodino	1-4(1-2)
FC Dinamo Minsk - FC Gomel	3-1(1-0,1-1)	FC Dnyapro Mogilev - FC Slutsk	2-1(1-0)
FC BATE Borisov - FC Torpedo Minsk	8-1(4-1)	FC Slaviya Mozyr - FC Vitebsk	3-1(2-1)
FC Dinamo Brest - FC Minsk	3-1(0-1)	FC Lokomotiv Gomel - FC Shakhtyor Solihorsk	1-2(0-2)

Quarter-Finals [09-10/14-15.03.2020]

First Leg		Second Leg	
FC Dnyapro Mogilev - FC Slaviya Mozyr	*not played*	FC Slaviya Mozyr - FC Dnyapro Mogilev	*not played*
Torpedo-BelAZ Zhodino - FC Shakhtyor Solihorsk	0-1(0-1)	FC Shakhtyor Solihorsk - Torpedo-BelAZ Zhodino	2-0(0-0)
FC Dinamo Minsk - FC BATE Borisov	1-2(1-1)	FC BATE Borisov - FC Dinamo Minsk	3-2(2-2)
FC Dinamo Brest - FC Isloch Minsk Raion	0-0	FC Isloch Minsk Raion - FC Dinamo Brest	0-0 aet; 3-5 pen

Semi-Finals [08/29.04.2020]

First Leg		Second Leg	
FC Slaviya Mozyr - FC BATE Borisov	1-0(1-0)	FC BATE Borisov - FC Slaviya Mozyr	2-0(2-0)
FC Dinamo Brest - FC Shakhtyor Solihorsk	2-0(2-0)	FC Shakhtyor Solihorsk - FC Dinamo Brest	4-2(0-2)

Final

24.05.2020; Stadion Dynama, Minsk; Referee: Amin Kurgheli; Attendance: 5,700
FC BATE Borisov - FC Dinamo Brest　　　　　　　　　　　　　**1-0(0-0,0-0)**

BATE Borisov: Anton Chichkan, Aleksander Filipović, Zakhar Volkov, Ihar Filipenko (42.Boris Kopitović), Bojan Nastić, Dzmitry Baha (101.Willum Thór Willumsson), Yawhen Yablonski, Stanislaw Drahun, Ihar Stasevich (Cap), Maksim Skavysh, Pavel Nyakhaychyk (65.Nemanja Milić). Trainer: Kirill Alshevsky.

Dinamo Brest: Syarhey Ignatovich, Raman Yuzapchuk, Alyaksandar Pawlavets, Gaby Kiki, Maksim Vitus (105.Aleh Veratsila), Syarhey Kislyak (Cap), Oleksandr Noyok, Artem Bykov, Pavel Savitski, Mikhail Gordeychuk (70.Dzyanis Laptsew), Artem Milevskiy (106.Syarhey Krivets). Trainer: Syarhey Kovalchuk.

Goal: 1-0 Zakhar Volkov (120+1).

THE CLUBS 2020

Football Club BATE Borisov

Founded:	1996		
Stadium:	Borisov Arena, Borisov (13,126)		
Trainer:	Kirill Alshevskiy		27.01.1982
(23.09.2020)	Alyaksandr Lisovskiy		29.04.1975

Goalkeepers:	DOB	M	(s)	G
Anton Chichkan	10.07.1995	16		
Dzyanis Scherbitski	14.04.1996	14		
Defenders:	**DOB**	**M**	**(s)**	**G**
Ihar Filipenko	10.04.1988	24		1
Aleksander Filipović (SRB)	20.12.1994	26	(1)	
Jakov Filipović (CRO)	17.10.1992	20		1
Boris Kopitović (MNE)	17.09.1994	3	(3)	
Bojan Nastić (SRB)	06.07.1994	26		1
Zakhar Volkov	12.08.1997	16		
Midfielders:	**DOB**	**M**	**(s)**	**G**
Dzmitry Baga	04.01.1990	22	(3)	2
Yawhen Berezkin	05.07.1996	1	(5)	
Dzmitry Bessmertny	03.01.1997	8	(12)	

	DOB	M	(s)	G
Stanislav Dragun	04.06.1988	24	(1)	6
Ihar Stasevich	21.10.1985	22	(2)	6
Alyaksandr Volodjko	18.06.1986	2	(2)	
Willum Þór Willumsson (ISL)	23.10.1998	12	(6)	3
Evgeni Yablonski	10.05.1995	25	(2)	1
Forwards:	**DOB**	**M**	**(s)**	**G**
Bojan Dubajić (SRB)	01.09.1990	2	(6)	1
Nemanja Milić (SRB)	25.05.1990	15	(9)	8
Hervaine Moukam (FRA)	24.05.1994	4	(9)	1
Pavel Nekhaychik	17.05.1988	23	(5)	12
Anton Saroka	05.03.1992	4	(2)	2
Mikalay Signevich	20.02.1992		(4)	
Maksim Skavysh	13.11.1989	21	(8)	19

Football Club Belshina Bobruisk

Founded: 1976
Stadium: Spartak Stadium, Bobruisk (3,700)
Trainer: Eduard Gradoboev — 28.09.1971
(07.05.2020) Dmitri Migas — 25.02.1980
(21.05.2020) Eduard Gradoboev — 28.09.1971
(02.07.2020) Dmitri Migas — 25.02.1980

Goalkeepers:	DOB	M	(s)	G
Alyaksey Kharitonovich	30.04.1995	20		
Pavel Okhremchuk	18.06.1993	1		
Syarhey Turanok	29.03.1986	9		
Defenders:	**DOB**	**M**	**(s)**	**G**
Maksim Grek (KAZ)	26.03.1993	8	(2)	
Evgeniy Kirisov (RUS)	14.02.1994	14	(1)	
Dzyanis Kovalevski	02.05.1992	8		
Konstantin Kuchinski	15.07.1998	19	(5)	
Kirill Malyarov (RUS)	07.03.1997	8	(2)	
Danila Nechaev	30.10.1999	17	(2)	1
Samuel Odeoyobo	28.09.1993	28		
Mykhailo Pysko (UKR)	19.03.1993	1		
Nikita Rochev	06.11.1992	8		
Stanislav Sazonovich	06.03.1992	6		1
Vladislav Yasyukevich	30.05.1994	25	(2)	
Midfielders:	**DOB**	**M**	**(s)**	**G**
Mikhail Bashilov (RUS)	12.01.1993	13		1
Andrey Bezhonov (RUS)	06.04.1993	2	(6)	
Pavel Bordukov	10.04.1993	16	(4)	1
Evgeniy Butakov (RUS)	24.07.1998		(4)	
Syarhey Glebko	23.08.1992	21	(4)	4
Dzmitry Lebedev	13.05.1986		(7)	1
Dzmitry Rekish	14.09.1988	17	(7)	6
Vladislav Shpitalnyi (RUS)	05.09.1996	1	(1)	
Evgeni Skoblikov	10.07.1990	6	(3)	
Vladislav Solanovich	26.05.1999	19	(6)	1
Roman Vorobei (UKR)	22.02.1994		(1)	
Forwards:	**DOB**	**M**	**(s)**	**G**
German Barkovskiy	25.06.2002		(5)	
Egor Chernyshev (RUS)	10.07.1998		(1)	
Leonid Kovel	29.07.1986	29	(1)	8
Pavel Kudryashov (RUS)	27.11.1996		(2)	
Dzyanis Levitskiy	05.02.1997	10	(2)	4
Nivaldo Rodriguez Ferreira (BRA)	22.06.1988	3	(13)	1
Anton Novik	23.07.1998		(2)	
Roman Salimov (RUS)	24.03.1995	21	(3)	4

Football Club Dinamo Brest

Founded: 1960
Stadium: Regional Sport Complex Brestsky (10,600)
Trainer: Syarhey Kovalchuk — 16.12.1973

Goalkeepers:	DOB	M	(s)	G
Syarhey Ignatovich	29.06.1992	17	(1)	
Pavel Pawlyuchenka	01.01.1998	13		
Defenders:	**DOB**	**M**	**(s)**	**G**
Yevhen Khacheridi (UKR)	28.07.1987	16		
Gaby Kiki (CMR)	15.02.1995	23		3
Alyaksandar Pawlavets	13.08.1996	18	(2)	1
Kiryl Pyachenin	18.03.1997	21	(2)	1
Aleh Veretilo	10.07.1988	18	(3)	
Maksim Vitus	11.02.1989	7	(8)	
Raman Yuzapchuk	24.07.1997	20	(4)	1
Midfielders:	**DOB**	**M**	**(s)**	**G**
Artsyom Bykaw	19.10.1992	14	(9)	1
Syarhey Kislyak	06.08.1987	24		4
Syarhey Krivets	08.06.1986	11	(8)	4
Oleksandr Noyok (UKR)	15.05.1992	21	(1)	2
Pavel Syadzko	03.04.1998	5	(7)	1
David Tweh (USA)	25.12.1998	12		1
Forwards:	**DOB**	**M**	**(s)**	**G**
Elis Bakaj (ALB)	25.06.1987	3	(1)	
Abdoulaye Diallo (SEN)	15.01.1996	3	(3)	3
Mikhail Gordeychuk	23.10.1989	27	(2)	10
Dzyanis Laptsew	01.08.1991	20	(6)	11
Artem Milevskiy (UKR)	12.01.1985	18	(9)	6
Vsevolod Sadovskiy	04.10.1996	2	(7)	
Pavel Savitskiy	12.07.1994	15	(7)	10
Evgeni Shevchenko	06.06.1996	2	(5)	

Football Club Dinamo Minsk

Founded: 18.06.1927
Stadium: Dinamo National Olympic Stadium, Minsk (22,246)
Trainer: Sergei Gurenko — 30.09.1972
(22.04.2020) Leonid Kuchuk — 27.08.1959

Goalkeepers:	DOB	M	(s)	G
Maksim Plotnikaw	29.01.1998	14		
Evgeniy Pomazan (RUS)	31.01.1989	13		
Konstantin Rudenok	15.12.1990	1		
Daniil Shapko	29.04.2001	2		
Defenders:	**DOB**	**M**	**(s)**	**G**
Andriy Batsula	06.02.1992	13		
Karlo Bručić (CRO)	17.04.1992	11	(1)	2
Alyaksandr Chyzh	10.02.1997	1		
Dominik Dinga (SRB)	07.04.1994	24	(1)	1
Miha Goropevšek (SVN)	12.03.1991	19	(3)	2
Syarhey Matvejchik	05.06.1988	10	(2)	
Alyaksey Rios	14.05.1987	23	(2)	
Ihar Shitov	24.10.1986	17	(2)	1
Maksim Shvyatsow	02.04.1998	21	(2)	
Artem Sukhotskiy (UKR)	06.12.1992	24	(1)	
Midfielders:	**DOB**	**M**	**(s)**	**G**
Dmitri Borodin	19.07.1999		(5)	
Alyaksey Butarevich	12.01.1997	2	(2)	
Richard Danilo Maciel Sousa Campos (BEL)	13.01.1990	8	(3)	2
Raman Davyskiba	31.03.2001	1	(2)	
Mikhail Kozlov	12.02.1990	16	(5)	2
Edgar Olekhnovich	17.05.1987	23	(2)	
Marko Pavlovski (SRB)	07.02.1994	9	(4)	
Gleb Rovdo	04.06.2002		(1)	
Silas Araújo da Silva (BRA)	30.05.1996	2	(5)	
Forwards:	**DOB**	**M**	**(s)**	**G**
Ivan Bakhar	10.07.1998	22	(7)	7
Dmytro Bilonoh (UKR)	26.05.1995		(6)	
Vladimir Khvashchinskiy	10.05.1990	5	(5)	3
Kim Jun-young (KOR)	31.05.1999		(2)	
Vladislav Klimovich	12.06.1996	27	(2)	6
Vladislav Lozhkin	25.03.2002		(2)	
Yawhen Shikavka	15.10.1992	19	(9)	11
Kirill Vergeychik	23.08.1991	3	(9)	1

Football Club Energetik-BGU Minsk

Founded: 1996
Stadium: RCOP BGU Stadium, Minsk (1,500)
Trainer: Vladimir Belyavskiy   27.06.1962

Goalkeepers:	DOB	M	(s)	G
Vladislav Bakonin (RUS)	01.08.2001	1		
Artur Lesko	25.04.1984	11	(1)	
Artem Makavchik	04.07.2000	6		
Dzyanis Sadovskiy	11.08.1997	12		
Defenders:	**DOB**	**M**	**(s)**	**G**
Dmitri Girs	11.06.1997	14	(11)	2
Daniil Miroshnikov	01.11.2000	20	(3)	1
German Osnov	07.05.2001	3		
Artyom Shkurdyuk	20.08.1998	23	(2)	
Pavel Shorats	30.01.1998		(1)	
Artem Sokol	30.03.1994	22		
Yawhen Yudchits	25.11.1996	23	(1)	5
Midfielders:	**DOB**	**M**	**(s)**	**G**
Mikhail Bashilov	12.01.1993	12		
Khumoyunmirzo Iminov (UZB)	15.01.2000	6	(2)	
Arnaud Dje Mani Bi (CIV)	17.12.2001	1	(1)	
Jérémy Mawatu (FRA)	12.08.1997	25	(3)	1
Alyaksey Nosko	15.08.1996	28		1
Andrey Rylach	05.06.2002	1	(2)	
Aleh Skvyra	23.06.2000		(1)	
Vasili Sovpel	23.03.1999	5	(20)	3
Aliaksandr Svirepa	24.08.1999	23	(1)	1
David Tweh (LBR)	25.12.1998	15		3
Wictor Diaz (BRA)	23.08.2000		(3)	
Forwards:	**DOB**	**M**	**(s)**	**G**
Junior Atemengue (CMR)	01.07.1995	8	(6)	
Dušan Bakić (MNE)	23.02.1999	18	(6)	8
Vladislav Mukhamedov	04.01.1998		(3)	1
Aik Musahagian	20.03.1998	18	(6)	3
Shakhboz Umarov (UZB)	09.03.1999	21	(9)	4
Jasurbek Yakhshiboev (UZB)	24.06.1997	14		9

Football Club Gorodeya

Founded: 2004
Stadium: Gorodeya Stadium, Gorodeya (2,100)
Trainer: Aleh Radushko   10.01.1967

Goalkeepers:	DOB	M	(s)	G
Syarhey Chernik	20.07.1988	5		
Igor Dovgyallo	17.07.1985	23		
Andrey Sakovich	15.04.1992	2	(1)	
Artem Zakharov	12.07.2002		(1)	
Defenders:	**DOB**	**M**	**(s)**	**G**
Ilariya Baglay	21.04.1998	4	(2)	
Dmitri Bayduk	03.08.1996	18	(7)	
Albert Gabaraev (RUS)	28.09.1997	10	(2)	1
Dzmitry Ignatenko	01.02.1995	19	(3)	1
Milan Joksimović (SRB)	09.02.1990	18		1
Illia Lukashevich	01.08.1998	1	(1)	
Kirill Pavlyuchek	27.06.1984	16		1
Pavel Pashevich	04.06.2001		(2)	
Alexandr Poznyak	23.07.1994	24		1
Syarhey Pushnyakov	08.02.1993	16	(4)	
Stanislav Sazonovich	06.03.1992	12	(4)	
Semen Shestilovsky	30.05.1994	15	(4)	
Maksim Smirnov	14.02.2000	5	(1)	
Syarhey Usenya	04.03.1988	7		
Midfielders:	**DOB**	**M**	**(s)**	**G**
Alexander Bulychev	19.11.1999	1	(2)	
Didine Djouhary (FRAU)	08.02.1999	5		2
Dzmitry Lebedev	13.05.1986		(2)	
Yanis Linda	01.03.1994	4		
Yan Senkevich	18.02.1995	3	(4)	2
Mikhail Shibun	01.01.1996	10	(15)	1
Artem Solovey	01.11.1990	6	(1)	
Andrey Sorokin (RUS)	28.03.1996	16	(4)	2
Artem Volovich	15.03.1999	2	(6)	
Yuri Volovik	19.06.1993	13	(7)	
Dzyanis Yaskovich	30.08.1995	19	(3)	1
Forwards:	**DOB**	**M**	**(s)**	**G**
Artem Arkhipov (RUS)	15.12.1996	2		
Sergey Arkhipov (RUS)	15.12.1996	17	(5)	7
Dzhamal Dibirgadzhiev (RUS)	02.08.1996	4		1
Yevgeni Kozel	22.02.2001	4	(2)	
Lazar Sajčić (SRB)	24.09.1996	27	(1)	8
Rostislav Shavel	02.04.2001	2	(3)	

Football Club Isloch Minsk Raion

Founded: 2007
Stadium: FC Minsk Stadium, Minsk (3,000)
Trainer: Vitali Zhukovski   17.05.1984

Goalkeepers:	DOB	M	(s)	G
Yahor Hatkevich	09.07.1988	29		
Vladislav Vasilyuchek	28.03.1994	1		
Defenders:	**DOB**	**M**	**(s)**	**G**
Oluwaseun Adegbola (NGA)	23.09.1999		(4)	
Vladislav Glinskiy	29.05.2000	1	(2)	
Syarhey Karpovich	29.03.1994	29	(1)	1
Syarhey Kontsevoy	21.06.1986	26	(1)	
Igor Kuzmenok	06.07.1990	14		3
Semen Lazarchik	03.09.2000	1	(1)	
Alexey Orlovich	22.08.2002		(1)	
Oleksandr Papush (UKR)	14.01.1985	14	(11)	
Pavel Rybak	11.09.1983	13	(1)	1
Godfrey Bitok Stephen (NGA)	22.08.2002	27		2
Raman Vegerya	14.07.2000	1		
Alyaksey Yanushkevich	15.01.1986	15	(2)	1
Midfielders:	**DOB**	**M**	**(s)**	**G**
Dmitri Borodin	19.07.1999	5	(1)	
Alyaksandr Bychenok	30.05.1985	5	(10)	
Klimentiy Gavrilov	09.08.2002		(2)	
Yawhen Krasnov	09.02.1998	1	(3)	
Raman Lisovskiy	22.11.2001	1	(5)	
Vadim Melnik	28.01.2001	5	(2)	
Mohamed Katana Nyanje (KEN)	24.12.1999		(1)	
Aleh Patotskiy	24.06.1991	27	(1)	
Sandro Tsveiba (RUS)	05.09.1993	16	(1)	
Abdulrazak Yusuf (NGA)	10.01.2000	1		
Forwards:	**DOB**	**M**	**(s)**	**G**
Dzyanis Firago	20.11.2000		(1)	
Alyaksandr Kholodinsky	16.10.1991	4	(6)	
Dzmitry Komarovskiy	10.10.1986	28		7
Alyaksandr Makas	08.10.1991	19	(6)	9
Dzmitry Nekrashevich	26.08.2001		(2)	
Nivaldo Rodriguez Ferreira (BRA)	22.06.1988		(3)	
Momo Yansane (GUI)	29.07.1997	20	(3)	8
Nikolai Yanush	09.09.1984	15	(5)	9
Dmytro Yusov	11.05.1993	12	(1)	6

Football Club Minsk

Founded: 2006
Stadium: FC Minsk Stadium, Minsk (3,000)
Trainer: Andrey Razin — 12.08.1979
(05.08.2020) Vadim Skripchenko — 26.11.1975

Goalkeepers:	DOB	M	(s)	G
Artyom Leonov (RUS)	28.06.1994	23		
Pavel Prishivalko	25.07.1999	1		
Syarhey Veremko	16.10.1982	6		
Defenders:	**DOB**	**M**	**(s)**	**G**
Yevgeniy Chagovets (UKR)	24.03.1998	23	(1)	1
Hleb Gurban	15.05.2001	1	(1)	
Alyaksey Ivanov	19.02.1997	5	(3)	
Dmitry Klimovich	09.02.1984	8	(1)	
Alyaksey Lavrik	07.08.2000	1		
Yuriy Ostroukh	21.01.1988	16	(2)	
Dmitry Pryshchepa	21.06.2001	20	(2)	
Dmytro Ryzhuk (UKR)	05.04.1992	23		1
Pyotr Ten	12.07.1992	8		
Alyaksey Zaleskiy	07.10.1994	25		1
Dmitri Zinovich	29.03.1995	4	(5)	
Midfielders:	**DOB**	**M**	**(s)**	**G**
Ilya Aleksievich	10.02.1991	2	(3)	
Alyaksandr Anufriev	21.07.1995	6	(4)	4

Aleh Evdokimov	25.02.1994	22	(1)	3
Evgeni Malashevich	10.12.2002		(1)	
Vladislav Nasibulin (UKR)	06.07.1989	16	(3)	2
Semen Penchuk	17.01.2001		(3)	1
Syarhey Sazonchik	20.10.2000	9	(4)	
Oleksandr Vasyliev (UKR)	27.04.1994	22	(1)	9
Yaroslav Yarotski	28.03.1996	14	(9)	2
Kamil Zakirov	15.11.1998	1	(1)	
Kirill Zinovich	05.03.2003	4	(4)	1
Forwards:	**DOB**	**M**	**(s)**	**G**
Pavel Gorbach	13.03.2000	6	(4)	
Raman Gribovskiy	17.07.1995	23	(4)	6
Vladimir Khvashchinskiy	10.05.1990	13		5
Ognjen Rolović (MNE)	25.08.1993	1	(8)	1
Andrey Shemruk	27.04.1994	5	(2)	
Anton Shramchenko	12.02.1993	21	(5)	4
Artem Vasilyev	23.01.1997		(14)	2
Gleb Zherdev	18.05.2000	1	(2)	1

Football Club Neman Grodno

Founded: 1964
Stadium: Neman Stadium, Grodno (8,479)
Trainer: Ihar Kovalevich — 03.02.1968

Goalkeepers:	DOB	M	(s)	G
Dmitri Dudar	08.11.1991	19		
Syarhey Kurganski	15.05.1986	11	(1)	
Defenders:	**DOB**	**M**	**(s)**	**G**
Giorgi Kantaria (GEO)	27.04.1997	10	(14)	1
Yahor Khvalko	18.02.1997	1		
Yawhen Leshko	24.06.1996	8	(5)	
Oleg Murachev (RUS)	22.02.1995	4	(3)	
Artur Slabashevich	09.02.1989	23	(1)	
Danijel Stojković (SRB)	14.08.1990	29		1
Andrey Vasilyev (RUS)	11.02.1992	29		
Raman Vyahera	14.07.2000		(6)	
Midfielders:	**DOB**	**M**	**(s)**	**G**
Alyaksey Legchilin	11.04.1992	25		
Zoran Marušić (SRB)	29.11.1993	25	(2)	10

Emir Shigaybaev (KGZ)	12.08.2001		(1)	
Anton Suchkov	29.05.2002		(2)	
Maksim Yablonski	15.08.1996	4	(13)	2
Andrey Yakimov	17.11.1989	30		
Vladislav Yatskevich	29.09.1998	2	(4)	
Pavel Zabelin	30.06.1995	27	(1)	7
Valeriy Zhukovskiy	21.05.1984	19	(4)	6
Forwards:	**DOB**	**M**	**(s)**	**G**
Dmitry Ivanov	21.02.1997		(9)	
Gegam Kadimyan (ARM)	19.10.1992	29		12
Volodymir Koval (UKR)	06.03.1992	6	(5)	
Raman Pasevich	28.11.1999	2	(2)	
Jean-Morel Poé (CMR)	15.12.1996	14		
Gleb Rassadkin	05.04.1995	13	(6)	1

Football Club Rukh Brest

Founded: 2016
Stadium: Yunost Stadium, Brest (2,310)
Trainer: Alyaksandr Sednev — 16.08.1973

Goalkeepers:	DOB	M	(s)	G
Artem Denisenko	12.04.1999	2		
Alyaksandr Nechaev	21.04.1994	13		
Raman Stepanov	06.08.1991	15		
Defenders:	**DOB**	**M**	**(s)**	**G**
Vitaly Gayduchik	12.07.1989	21		
Illya Kolpachuk	09.10.1990	15	(5)	1
Oleksiy Kovtun (UKR)	05.02.1995	17		1
Artem Rakhmanov	10.07.1990	25		2
João William Alves de Jesus (BRA)	11.06.1996	16		
Midfielders:	**DOB**	**M**	**(s)**	**G**
Gheorghe Andronic (MDA)	25.09.1991	8		1
Alyaksey Antilevski	02.02.2002	2	(2)	2
Maksim Chyzh	08.10.1993	5	(5)	
Dzyanis Grechikho	22.05.1999	26		6
Artem Kontsevoy	26.08.1999	23	(2)	5
Oleksandr Mihunov (UKR)	13.04.1994	25	(2)	1

Chukwuemeka Nwafor (NGA)	10.01.2002	2	(4)	
Yaroslav Oreshkevich	08.09.2000	4	(7)	1
Chidi Ema Osuchukwu (NGA)	11.10.1993	11		
Bogdan Sadovskiy	01.08.1999	4	(6)	
Pavel Sedko	03.04.1998	9	(2)	2
Dimitri Sibilev	23.07.2000		(1)	
Syarhey Tikhonovskiy	26.06.1991	11	(7)	
Vladislav Vasiliev (KAZ)	10.04.1997	25	(1)	8
Forwards:	**DOB**	**M**	**(s)**	**G**
Ihar Bogomolskiy	03.06.2000	11	(12)	3
Abdoulaye Diallo (SEN)	15.01.1996	10	(4)	4
Vladislav Morozov	12.10.2000		(7)	
Aleh Nikiforenko	17.03.2001	5	(11)	5
Artyom Petrenko	01.03.2000	5	(6)	1
Vsevolod Sadovskiy	04.10.1996	5	(4)	9
Evgeni Shevchenko	06.06.1996	15		5
Kirill Tsepenkov	08.07.2004		(2)	

Football Club Shakhtyor Solihorsk

Founded: 1961
Stadium: Stroitel Stadium, Solihorsk (4,200)
Trainer: Yuriy Vernydub — 22.01.1966
(05.09.2020) Roman Grygorchuk (UKR) — 22.03.1965

Goalkeepers:	DOB	M	(s)	G
Pavel Chesnovskiy	04.03.1986	2		
Alyaksandr Hutar	18.04.1989	28		
Defenders:	**DOB**	**M**	**(s)**	**G**
Nikola Antić (SRB)	04.01.1994	25		4
Raman Begunov	22.03.1993	12	(1)	3
Igor Burko	08.09.1988	11	(8)	1
Ruslan Hadarkevich	18.06.1993	25		
Zarija Lambulić (SRB)	25.05.1998	1	(1)	
Syarhey Matvejchik	05.06.1988	3		
Syarhey Politevich	09.04.1990	5		
Alyaksandr Sachywka	05.01.1986	23	(1)	
Midfielders:	**DOB**	**M**	**(s)**	**G**
Syarhey Balanovich	29.08.1987	16	(7)	1
Alexander Bulychev	19.11.1999		(3)	
Giorgi Diasamidze (GEO)	08.05.1992	8	(2)	2
Igor Ivanović (SRB)	28.07.1997	26	(2)	4
Yuri Kendysh	10.06.1990	23	(1)	4
Nikita Korzun	06.03.1995	1		
Makar Litskevich	03.03.2002		(1)	
Alyaksandr Selyava	17.05.1992	20	(2)	
Viktor Sotnikov	27.07.2001	1	(2)	
Július Szöke (SVK)	01.08.1995	24		2
Forwards:	**DOB**	**M**	**(s)**	**G**
Artem Arkhipov		8	(6)	7
Darko Bodul (CRO)	11.01.1989	6	(19)	3
Diego Silva Nascimento Santos „Carioca" (BRA)	06.02.1998	2	(2)	
Junior Kabananga Kalonji (COD)	04.04.1989	4	(1)	
Vitaliy Lisakovich	08.02.1998	13	(4)	9
Azdren Llullaku (ALB)	15.02.1988	2	(5)	
Dmitri Podstrelov	06.09.1998	18	(12)	8
Lasha Shindagoridze (GEO)	30.01.1993	2	(1)	
Tin Vukmanić (CRO)	17.04.1999	10		
Jasurbek Yakhshiboev (UZB)	24.06.1997	11	(2)	7

Football Club Slavia Mozyr

Founded: 1987
Stadium: Yunost [Junactva] Stadium, Mozyr (5,300)
Trainer: Mikhail Martinovich — 14.09.1979

Goalkeepers:	DOB	M	(s)	G
Mikhail Baranovskiy (RUS)	04.01.1983	21		
Nikolai Romanyuk	02.06.1984	9		
Defenders:	**DOB**	**M**	**(s)**	**G**
Andrey Chukhley	02.10.1987	17	(3)	4
Dzyanis Kovalevski	02.05.1992	5	(2)	
Vladislav Malkevich	09.12.1999	13	(4)	2
Victor Mudrac	03.03.1994	7		
Yuri Nedashkovskiy (RUS)	11.04.1986	19	(1)	1
Yurii Pantia (UKR)	05.04.1990	22	(2)	
Kirill Pavlyuchek	27.06.1984	4		
Egor Potapov (RUS)	21.09.1993	19		
Alyaksandr Raevskiy	19.06.1988	13		
Hleb Shawchenka	17.02.1999	19	(4)	2
Semen Shestilovski	30.05.1994	5		1
Igor Tymonyuk	31.03.1994	19	(1)	
Midfielders:	**DOB**	**M**	**(s)**	**G**
Alyaksandr Anufriev	21.07.1995		(1)	
Igor Costrov (MDA)	03.08.1987	16	(5)	
Alyaksandr Kotlyarov	30.01.1993	17	(2)	1
Dmitri Krivosheev	19.09.1998		(2)	
Maksim Myakish	03.03.2000	1	(2)	
Guido Marcelo Ratto Canziani (ARG)	08.06.1999	1		
Valery Senko	07.04.1998	2	(6)	
Marko Stojanović (SRB)	01.02.1998	2	(1)	
Vladislav Zhuk	11.06.1994	22	(4)	4
Forwards:	**DOB**	**M**	**(s)**	**G**
Evgeni Barsukov	05.07.1990	11	(1)	
Nikita Melnikov (RUS)	28.02.1997	12	(9)	3
Francis Narh (GHA)	18.04.1994	28	(1)	6
Maksim Sliusar (UKR)	01.07.1997	5	(14)	7
Dennis Tetteh (GHA)	06.03.1997	14	(8)	4
Islam Tlupov	23.03.1994	4	(5)	3
Ilya Vasilevich	14.04.2000	3	(7)	

Football Club Slutsk

Founded: 1998
Stadium: City Stadium, Slutsk (2,150)
Trainer: Vitaly Pavlov — 21.08.1965
(01.07.2020) Alyaksandr Konchits — 27.08.1965
(06.10.2020) Alyaksandr Brazevich — 01.06.1973

Goalkeepers:	DOB	M	(s)	G
Ilya Branovets	16.04.1990	9		
Boris Pankratov	30.12.1982	20		
Defenders:	**DOB**	**M**	**(s)**	**G**
Kirill Aloyan	22.01.1999		(2)	
Alyaksandr Anyukevich	10.04.1992	18	(3)	
Sergiy Chebotaev (UKR)	07.03.1988	15		
Souleymane Koanda (BFA)	21.09.1992	25	(1)	3
Raman Krivulkin	18.02.1996	17		
Dzyanis Obrazov	24.04.1988	14		
Artem Ponikarov	05.01.1997	7		
Ilya Raschenya	27.05.1997	5		
Andrei Rum	19.01.2002		(1)	
Soslan Takulov (RUS)	28.04.1995	15		1
Vitaliy Trubilo	07.01.1985	13	(5)	
Vitali Zaprudskikh	01.01.1991		(1)	
Midfielders:	**DOB**	**M**	**(s)**	**G**
Ihar Bobko	09.09.1985	5	(3)	
Marat Buraev (RUS)	22.10.1995	12	(3)	1
Yuri Kozlov	21.05.1991	21		3
Andrey Kren	11.11.2003		(1)	
Syarhey Rusak	03.09.1993	5		
Mikhail Sachkovsky	21.11.2002	1		
Dramane Salou (BFA)	22.05.1998	11	(2)	1
Dzmitry Sasin	21.08.1996	8		2
Ihar Semenov	06.01.1988	24	(2)	4
Vladislav Sychev	26.01.2002	1	(2)	
Yuriy Teterenko (UKR)	22.01.1997	10	(7)	
Mohammed Umar Bala (NGA)	07.03.1998	14	(11)	4
Forwards:	**DOB**	**M**	**(s)**	**G**
Evgeni Apanasovich	18.07.2002	1	(2)	
Abdoul Gafar (BFA)	30.12.1998	20	(4)	6
Alan Koroev (RUS)	19.04.1998	2	(9)	
Artem Serdyuk (RUS)	22.01.1990	9	(16)	5
Evgeni Veljko	23.02.1997	16	(3)	
Pavel Zuevich	12.07.1997	1	(3)	

Football Club Smolevichi

Founded: 2009
Stadium: Ozorny Stadium, Smolevichi (1,600)
Trainer: Alyaksandr Brazevich — 01.06.1973
(08.07.2020) Alyaksey Mikhailov — 05.03.1987

Goalkeepers:	DOB	M	(s)	G
Alyaksandr Filtsov	02.01.1990	6		
Artem Gomelko	08.12.1989	12		
Djemal Kurshubadze	22.04.1997	5		
Nikita Lazovskiy	16.08.1999	6		
Defenders:	DOB	M	(s)	G
Mutalip Alibekov (RUS)	18.06.1997	22	(2)	
Arseni Bondarenko	09.10.1995	8	(2)	
Hleb Gurban	15.05.2001	2	(2)	
Nikita Khalimonchik	03.01.2000	9		
Maxim Kovel	12.01.1999	7		
Yaroslav Makushinskiy	05.03.1998	2	(4)	
Ilya Raschenya	27.05.1997	11		
Kirill Rodionov	09.05.2000	6	(1)	
Ilyaz Safi	21.01.1999	1	(1)	
Maksim Savostikov	13.08.1998	3	(3)	
Ivan Shavel	13.07.2001	3		
Ivan Vasilyonok	17.05.1989	7		
Alyaksey Vakulich	24.06.1998	10	(3)	3
Eduard Zhevnerov	01.11.1987	25		

Midfielders:	DOB	M	(s)	G
Alyaksandr Aleksandrovich	06.07.1997	6	(13)	
Valery Bocherov	10.08.2000	7		
Alyaksey Butarevich	12.01.1997	15		1
Nikita Demchenko	06.09.2002	9	(3)	
Alyaksandr Dzhigero	15.04.1996	22	(2)	5
Konstantin Kotov (RUS)	25.06.1998	11	(1)	
Anatoli Makarov	10.04.1996	26	(1)	3
Andrey Potapenko	09.02.2000	6	(2)	
Syarhey Rusak	03.09.1993		(4)	
Pavel Sadovskiy	17.02.1999		(1)	
Dzmitry Shegrikovich	07.12.1983	11	(6)	1
Forwards:	DOB	M	(s)	G
Evgeni Barsukov	05.07.1990	11		3
Vladislav Lozhkin	25.03.2002	10		3
Vladislav Mukhamedov	04.01.1998	11	(4)	2
Jean-Morel Poé (CIV)	15.12.1996	13	(1)	1
Aleksey Turik (RUS)	25.04.1995	3	(5)	
Ivan Veras	22.04.1997	6	(6)	
Leonid Khankevich	21.08.1995	5	(9)	3
Anton Bogdanov	27.04.2001	2	(2)	
Alexander Chizh	08.03.2002		(2)	

Football Club Torpedo-BelAZ Zhodino

Founded: 1961
Stadium: Torpedo Stadium, Zhodino (6,524)
Trainer: Yuri Puntus — 08.10.1960

Goalkeepers:	DOB	M	(s)	G
Vladimir Bushma	24.11.1983	16		
Aleksey Kozlov (RUS)	23.01.1999	9		
Rodion Syamuk	11.03.1989	5		
Defenders:	DOB	M	(s)	G
Dzmitry Aliseyko	28.08.1992	5	(1)	
Alan Aussi (UKR)	30.06.2001	5	(1)	
Maksim Bordachev	18.05.1986	25		2
Yuriy Gabovda	06.05.1989	9	(1)	6
Vladimir Shcherbo	01.04.1986	13	(2)	
Nikita Stepanov	06.04.1996	8	(2)	
Vitali Ustinov (RUS)	03.05.1991	29		
Artem Vyatkin	05.03.1996	2		
Dmitriy Yashin (RUS)	25.04.1993	29		1
Midfielders:	DOB	M	(s)	G
Mikhail Afanasjev	04.11.1986	6	(15)	1

	DOB	M	(s)	G
Nikita Kaplenko	18.09.1995	16	(1)	1
Andrey Khachaturyan	02.09.1987	26		5
Ilya Kukharchyk	10.03.1997	2		
Luis Felipe Veloso Santos (BRA)	07.04.1997	22	(5)	6
Matheus Celestino Moresche Rodrigues (BRA)	24.06.1998	4	(3)	
Nikita Nikolaevich	11.09.1997	3	(24)	2
Yuri Pavlyukovets	24.06.1994	9	(5)	
Kirill Premudrov	11.06.1992	18	(3)	6
Forwards:	DOB	M	(s)	G
Dzmitry Antsilewski	12.06.1997	20	(5)	7
Gabriel Ramos da Penha (BRA)	20.03.1996	28		11
Valery Gorbachik	19.01.1995	14	(2)	5
Kirill Leonovich	21.04.1998		(4)	
Dzyanis Levitskiy	05.02.1997		(3)	
Dmytro Yusov (UKR)	11.05.1993	6	(6)	1
Vasili Zhurnevich	21.02.1995	1	(4)	

Football Club Vitebsk

Founded: 1960
Stadium: Vitebsky Central Sport Complex, Vitebsk (8,100)
Trainer: Syarhey Yasinsky — 07.01.1965

Goalkeepers:	DOB	M	(s)	G
Dmitri Gushchenko	12.05.1988	11		
Artem Soroko	01.04.1992	19		
Defenders:	DOB	M	(s)	G
Daniil Chalov (RUS)	17.06.1994	28		1
Júlio César Basílio da Silva (BRA)	06.12.1996	15	(4)	3
Oleh Karamushka (UKR)	30.04.1984	3		
Artur Kats	26.12.1994	1	(5)	
Evgeni Klopotskiy	12.08.1993	22	(1)	2
Nikita Kostomarov	29.06.1999	1		
Pavel Nazarenko	20.01.1995	25	(3)	1
Artem Skitov	21.01.1991	27		
Midfielders:	DOB	M	(s)	G
Maksim Drobysh	30.01.2001	1	(2)	
Maksym Kalenchuk (UKR)	05.12.1989	28		

	DOB	M	(s)	G
Yawhen Krasnov	09.02.1998	2	(2)	
Alyaksandr Ksenofontov	05.05.1999	4	(6)	1
Yan Skibski	25.12.2002	2		
Ilya Vasiljev (RUS)	24.04.1997		(14)	
Syarhey Volkaw	27.01.1999	23	(3)	2
Wanderson Calvacante Melo (BRA)	27.06.1994	19	(5)	1
Forwards:	DOB	M	(s)	G
Diego Silva Nascimento Santos „Carioca" (BRA)	06.02.1998	19	(3)	4
Zakhar Chervyakov	30.08.2002		(2)	2
Vladislav Fedosov	05.05.1998	2	(7)	
Artem Gurenko	18.06.1994	25	(3)	1
Anton Matveenko	03.09.1986	26	(1)	2
Ion Nicolăescu (MDA)	07.09.1998	17	(1)	9
Ruslan Teverov	01.05.1994	5	(18)	
Kirill Vergeychik	23.08.1991	5		

1.	FC Sputnik Rechitsa (*Promoted*)	26	19	4	3	50 - 18	61
2.	FC Gomel[1] (*Promoted*)	26	18	5	3	60 - 20	54
3.	NFC Krumkachy Minsk (*Promotion Play-offs*)	26	16	4	6	46 - 28	52
4.	FC Arsenal Dzerzhinsk	26	13	7	6	41 - 28	46
5.	FC Lokomotiv Gomel	26	13	6	7	56 - 38	45
6.	FC Smorgon	26	10	6	10	29 - 26	36
7.	FC Lida[2]	26	9	7	10	37 - 42	31
8.	FC Slonim-2017	26	8	6	12	22 - 32	30
9.	FC Volna Pinsk	26	7	6	13	41 - 52	27
10.	FC Oshmyany	26	6	8	12	35 - 43	26
11.	FC Orsha[2]	26	7	6	13	30 - 42	24
12.	FC Naftan Novopolotsk[3]	26	10	6	10	36 - 43	21
13.	FC Granit Mikashevichi	26	4	5	17	21 - 52	17
14.	FC Khimik Svetlogorsk[4] (*Relegated*)	26	2	4	20	12 - 52	1

[1] *5 points deducted as a result of match-fixing investigation in the previous season.*
[2] *3 points deducted as a result of match-fixing investigation in the previous season.*
[3] *15 points deducted as a result of match-fixing investigation in the previous season.*
[4] *9 points deducted as a result of match-fixing investigation in the previous season.*

NATIONAL TEAM

INTERNATIONAL MATCHES
(16.07.2020 – 15.07.2021)

04.09.2020	Minsk	Belarus - Albania	0-2(0-1)	(UNL)
07.09.2020	Almaty	Kazakhstan - Belarus	1-2(0-0)	(UNL)
08.10.2020	Tbilisi	Georgia - Belarus	1-0(1-0)	(ECQPO)
11.10.2020	Vilnius	Lithuania - Belarus	2-2(1-0)	(UNL)
14.10.2020	Minsk	Belarus - Kazakhstan	2-0(1-0)	(UNL)
11.11.2020	Ploieşti	Romania - Belarus	5-3(4-0)	(F)
15.11.2020	Minsk	Belarus - Lithuania	2-0(2-0)	(UNL)
18.11.2020	Tiranë	Albania - Belarus	3-2(3-1)	(UNL)
24.03.2021	Zhodino	Belarus - Honduras	1-1(1-1)	(F)
27.03.2021	Minsk	Belarus - Estonia	4-2(1-1)	(WCQ)
30.03.2021	Leuven	Belgium - Belarus	8-0(4-0)	(WCQ)
02.06.2021	Minsk	Belarus - Azerbaijan	1-2(0-0)	(F)

04.09.2020 BELARUS - ALBANIA   0-2(0-1)   2nd UEFA Nations League C, Group 4
Stadion Dynama, Minsk; Referee: Kristoffer Karlsson (Sweden); Attendance: 0
BLR: Alyaksandr Hutar, Maksim Bardachow, Alyaksandr Martynovich (Cap), Mikita Navumaw, Mikalay Zolataw (76.Maksim Skavysh), Pavel Nyakhaychyk, Ihar Stasevich, Stanislaw Drahun, Alyaksandr Syalyava (46.Andrey Khachaturan), Yawhen Yablonski (86.Ivan Bakhar), Vital Lisakovich. Trainer: Mikhail Markhel.

07.09.2020 KAZAKHSTAN - BELARUS   1-2(0-0)   2nd UEFA Nations League C, Group 4
Central Stadium, Almaty; Referee: Giorgi Kruashvili (Georgia); Attendance: 0
BLR: Alyaksandr Hutar, Maksim Bardachow, Alyaksandr Martynovich (Cap), Mikita Navumaw, Mikalay Zolataw, Pavel Nyakhaychyk (80.Dzmitry Padstrelaw), Ihar Stasevich, Stanislaw Drahun, Yawhen Yablonski, Afrid Max Ebong Ngome (85.Andrey Khachaturan), Maksim Skavysh (56.Vital Lisakovich). Trainer: Mikhail Markhel.
Goals: Maksim Bardachow (53), Vital Lisakovich (86).

08.10.2020 GEORGIA - BELARUS   1-0(1-0)   16th EC. Qualifiers Play-offs, Semi-Finals
„Boris Paichadze" Dinamo Arena, Tbilisi; Referee: Cüneyt Çakır (Turkey); Attendance: 0
BLR: Yahor Hatkevich, Maksim Bardachow (73.Kiryl Pyachenin), Alyaksandr Martynovich (Cap), Mikita Navumaw, Mikalay Zolataw, Pavel Nyakhaychyk, Andrey Khachaturan (46.Ivan Maewski), Ivan Bakhar (63.Dzmitry Padstrelaw), Afrid Max Ebong Ngome, Yawhen Yablonski (63.Maksim Skavysh), Vital Lisakovich (70.Dzyanis Laptsew). Trainer: Mikhail Markhel.

11.10.2020 LITHUANIA - BELARUS   2-2(1-0)   2nd UEFA Nations League C, Group 4
LFF stadionas, Vilnius; Referee: Julian Weinberger (Austria); Attendance: 963
BLR: Yahor Hatkevich, Alyaksandr Martynovich (Cap), Alyaksandr Sachywka, Mikalay Zolataw, Kiryl Pyachenin, Ihar Stasevich (80.Ivan Bakhar), Ivan Maewski, Valeryi Hramyka (57.Vital Lisakovich), Raman Yuzapchuk (69.Dzmitry Padstrelaw), Afrid Max Ebong Ngome (80.Andrey Khachaturan), Maksim Skavysh (57.Dzyanis Laptsew). Trainer: Mikhail Markhel.
Goals: Vital Lisakovich (59 penalty), Alyaksandr Sachywka (66).

14.10.2020 BELARUS - KAZAKHSTAN   2-0(1-0)   2nd UEFA Nations League C, Group 4
Stadion Dynama, Minsk; Referee: Chris Kavanagh (England); Attendance: 1,985
BLR: Alyaksandr Hutar, Dzyanis Palyakow, Alyaksandr Sachywka (42.Maksim Bardachow), Mikita Navumaw, Kiryl Pyachenin (66.Mikalay Zolataw), Ihar Stasevich (Cap) (66.Uladislaw Klimovich), Ivan Maewski (47.Andrey Khachaturan), Yawhen Yablonski, Raman Yuzapchuk, Maksim Skavysh, Vital Lisakovich (66.Ivan Bakhar). Trainer: Mikhail Markhel.
Goals: Yawhen Yablonski (36), Raman Yuzapchuk (90+3).

11.11.2020   **ROMANIA - BELARUS**   **5-3(4-0)**   Friendly International
Stadionul "Ilie Oană", Ploieşti; Referee: Georgi Kabakov (Bulgaria); Attendance: 0
BLR: Anton Chychkan, Dzyanis Palyakow, Maksim Bardachow, Mikita Navumaw (46.Raman Yuzapchuk), Kiryl Pyachenin, Andrey Khachaturan (70.Uladislaw Klimovich), Ivan Maewski (Cap) (62.Yawhen Yablonski), Yury Kendysh, Ivan Bakhar, Afrid Max Ebong Ngome (62.Ihar Stasevich), Dzyanis Laptsew (62.Maksim Skavysh). Trainer: Mikhail Markhel.
Goals: Yury Kendysh (63), Ivan Bakhar (80), Uladislaw Klimovich (90+2).

15.11.2020   **BELARUS - LITHUANIA**   **2-0(2-0)**   2nd UEFA Nations League C, Group 4
Stadion Dynama, Minsk; Referee: Chris Kavanagh (England); Attendance: 1,985
BLR: Yahor Hatkevich, Dzyanis Palyakow, Maksim Bardachow, Alyaksandr Sachywka, Yury Kendysh (58.Ivan Maewski), Yawhen Yablonski, Ihar Stasevich (Cap) (82.Dzmitry Antsilewski), Raman Yuzapchuk, Afrid Max Ebong Ngome, Maksim Skavysh (82.Uladislaw Klimovich), Vital Lisakovich (72.Ivan Bakhar). Trainer: Mikhail Markhel.
Goals: Yawhen Yablonski (5), Afrid Max Ebong Ngome (20).

18.11.2020   **ALBANIA - BELARUS**   **3-2(3-1)**   2nd UEFA Nations League C, Group 4
Arena Kombëtare, Tiranë; Referee: Radu Marian Petrescu (Romania); Attendance: 0
BLR: Yahor Hatkevich, Dzyanis Palyakow, Maksim Bardachow (46.Kiryl Pyachenin), Alyaksandr Sachywka, Ihar Stasevich (Cap), Ivan Maewski (77.Dzmitry Antsilewski), Yawhen Yablonski (63.Yury Kendysh), Raman Yuzapchuk, Afrid Max Ebong Ngome, Maksim Skavysh (86.Uladislaw Klimovich), Vital Lisakovich (77.Dzyanis Laptsew). Trainer: Mikhail Markhel.
Goals: Maksim Skavysh (35), Afrid Max Ebong Ngome (80).

24.03.2021   **BELARUS - HONDURAS**   **1-1(1-1)**   Friendly International
Torpedo Stadium, Zhodino; Referee: Aleksey Matyunin (Russia); Attendance: 425
BLR: Pavel Pawlyuchenka, Dzyanis Palyakow, Alyaksandar Pawlavets, Maksim Shvyatsow, Raman Yuzapchuk (46.Danila Nyachayew), Syarhey Kislyak (Cap) (46.Uladislaw Klimovich), Ivan Maewski (73.Yury Kendysh), Pavel Savitski (62.Dzmitry Antsilewski), Afrid Max Ebong Ngome (46.Ivan Bakhar), Dzyanis Laptsew [sent off 55], Mikalay Signevich (82.Dzmitry Padstrelaw). Trainer: Mikhail Markhel.
Goals: Pavel Savitski (22).

27.03.2021   **BELARUS - ESTONIA**   **4-2(1-1)**   22nd FIFA WC.Qualifiers
Stadion Dynama, Minsk; Referee: Robert Hennessy (Republic of Ireland); Attendance: 3,611
BLR: Alyaksandr Hutar, Maksim Bardachow, Mikita Navumaw, Mikalay Zolataw, Raman Yuzapchuk, Ihar Stasevich (Cap), Yury Kendysh (87.Uladislaw Klimovich), Yawhen Yablonski (58.Mikalay Signevich), Afrid Max Ebong Ngome (58.Pavel Savitski), Dzyanis Laptsew (46.Syarhey Kislyak), Vital Lisakovich (85.Ivan Bakhar). Trainer: Mikhail Markhel.
Goals: Vital Lisakovich (45 penalty), Yury Kendysh (64), Pavel Savitski (81), Vital Lisakovich (83).

30.03.2021   **BELGIUM - BELARUS**   **8-0(4-0)**   22nd FIFA WC.Qualifiers
Stadion Den Dreef, Leuven; Referee: Donatas Rumšas (Lithuania); Attendance: 0
BLR: Alyaksandr Hutar, Dzyanis Palyakow, Mikita Navumaw, Alyaksandar Pawlavets, Raman Yuzapchuk, Ihar Stasevich (Cap), Syarhey Kislyak (61.Ivan Maewski), Yury Kendysh (87.Ivan Bakhar), Dzmitry Padstrelaw (46.Mikalay Signevich), Afrid Max Ebong Ngome (46.Pavel Savitski), Vital Lisakovich (74.Uladislaw Klimovich). Trainer: Mikhail Markhel.

02.06.2021   **BELARUS - AZERBAIJAN**   **1-2(0-0)**   Friendly International
Stadion Dynama, Minsk; Referee: Dumitru Muntean (Moldova); Attendance: 4,120
BLR: Pavel Pawlyuchenka, Maksim Shvyatsow, Ruslan Hadarkevich, Maksim Valadzko, Yawhen Yablonski, Mikalay Zolataw (76.Hleb Shawchenka), Artsyom Bykaw (70.Uladislaw Klimovich), Kiryl Pyachenin (46.Raman Yuzapchuk), Afrid Max Ebong Ngome (84.Pavel Syadzko), Dzmitry Antsilewski (77.Dzmitry Padstrelaw), Maksim Skavysh (Cap) (83.Andrey Salavey). Trainer: Heorhiy Kandratsyew.
Goal: Maksim Skavysh (56).

NATIONAL TEAM PLAYERS (16.07.2020 – 15.07.2021)					
Name	**DOB**	**Caps**	**Goals**	**2020/2021:**	*Club*
Goalkeepers					
Anton CHYCHKAN	10.07.1995	1	0	2020:	*FC BATE Borisov*
Yahor HATKEVICH	09.07.1988	5	0	2020/2021:	*FC Isloch Minsk Raion*
Alyaksandr HUTAR	18.04.1989	21	0	2020/2021:	*FC Shakhtyor Solihorsk*
Pavel PAWLYUCHENKA	01.01.1998	4	0	2021:	*FC Rukh Brest*
Defenders					
Maksim BARDACHOW	18.06.1986	52	3	2020/2021:	*FC Torpedo-BelAZ Zhodino*
Ruslan HADARKEVICH	18.06.1993	1	0	2021:	*FC Shakhtyor Solihorsk*
Alyaksandr MARTYNOVICH	26.08.1987	75	2	2020:	*FK Krasnodar (RUS)*
Mikita NAVUMAW	15.11.1989	13	1	2020: 19.01.2021->	*FC Zhetisu Taldiqorghan (KAZ) FC Dinamo Minsk*
Danila NYACHAYEW	30.10.1999	1	0	2021:	*FC BATE Borisov*
Dzyanis PALYAKOW	17.04.1991	48	1	2020/2021:	*FK Kairat Almaty (KAZ)*
Alyaksandar PAWLAVETS	13.08.1996	8	0	2021:	*FK Rostov-na-Donu (RUS)*
Kiryl PYACHENIN	18.03.1997	8	0	2020: 13.02.2021->	*FC Dinamo Brest FC Rukh Brest*
Alyaksandr SACHYWKA	05.01.1986	9	1	2020:	*FC Shakhtyor Solihorsk*

Hleb SHAWCHENKA	17.02.1999	1	0	2021:	FC Shakhtyor Solihorsk
Maksim SHVYATSOW	02.04.1998	4	0	2021:	FC Dinamo Minsk
Maksim VALADZKO	10.11.1992	33	2	2021:	FC BATE Borisov
Mikalay ZOLATAW	11.11.1994	9	0	2020:	FK Ural Yekaterinburg (RUS)
				06.02.2021->	FK Kolos Kovalivka

Midfielders

Ivan BAKHAR	10.07.1998	13	1	2020/2021:	FC Dinamo Brest
Artsyom BYKAW	19.10.1992	10	0	2021:	FC Dinamo Minsk
Stanislaw DRAHUN	04.06.1988	68	11	2020/2021:	FC BATE Borisov
Afrid Max EBONG Ngome	26.08.1999	12	2	2020/2021:	Astana FC (KAZ)
Valeryi HRAMYKA	23.01.1997	2	0	2020:	FK Arsenal Tula (RUS)
Yury KENDYSH	10.06.1990	15	2	2020/2021:	FC Shakhtyor Solihorsk
Andrey KHACHATURAN	02.09.1987	8	0	2020:	FC Torpedo-BelAZ Zhodino
Syarhey KISLYAK	06.08.1987	74	9	2021:	FC Dinamo Minsk
Uladislaw KLIMOVICH	12.06.1996	12	1	2020/2021:	FC Dinamo Minsk
Ivan MAEWSKI	05.05.1988	42	0	2020:	Astana FC (KAZ)
				13.01.2021->	FK Rotor Volgograd (RUS)
Pavel NYAKHAYCHYK	15.07.1988	37	3	2020/2021:	FC BATE Borisov
Pavel SAVITSKI	12.07.1994	22	6	2021:	FC Rukh Brest
Ihar STASEVICH	21.10.1985	63	5	2020:	FC BATE Borisov
				09.01.2021->	FC Shakhtyor Solihorsk
Pavel SYADZKO	03.04.1998	2	0	2021:	FC Dinamo Brest
Alyaksandr SYALYAVA	17.05.1992	1	0	2020:	FC Shakhtyor Solihorsk
Yawhen YABLONSKI	10.05.1995	15	2	2020/2021:	FC BATE Borisov
Raman YUZAPCHUK	24.07.1997	10	1	2020:	FC Dinamo Brest
				26.01.2021->	FC Rukh Brest

Forwards

Dzmitry ANTSILEWSKI	12.06.1997	4	0	2020/2021:	FC Torpedo-BelAZ Zhodino
Dzyanis LAPTSEW	01.08.1991	30	0	2020:	FC Dinamo Brest
				06.01.2021->	FC Rukh Brest
Vital LISAKOVICH	08.02.1998	14	4	2020/2021:	FK Lokomotiv Moskva (RUS)
Dzmitry PADSTRELAW	06.09.1998	8	1	2020/2021:	FC Shakhtyor Solihorsk
Andrey SALAVEY	13.12.1994	1	0	2021:	FC Gomel
Mikalay SIGNEVICH	20.02.1992	21	1	2021:	FC BATE Borisov
Maksim SKAVYSH	13.11.1989	28	4	2020/2021:	FC BATE Borisov

Trainer

Mikhail MARKHEL [20.06.2019 – 05.04.2021]	10.03.1966	19 M; 7 W; 3 D; 9 L; 23-35
Heorhiy KANDRATSYEW [from 06.04.2021]	07.01.1960	1 M; 0 W; 0 D; 1 L; 1-2
		Complete record as trainer of Belarus:
		29 M; 9 W; 8 D; 12 L; 38-37
		(29.02.2012 – 12.10.2014) & (from 06.04.2021)

BELGIUM

ROYAL BELGIAN FA·1895

The Country:
Royaume de Belgique / Koninkrijk België (Kingdom of Belgium)
Capital: Bruxelles
Surface: 30,528 km²
Inhabitants: 11,492,641 [2020]
Time: UTC+1

The FA:
Union royale belge des sociétés de football association / Koninklijke Belgische Voetbalbond
145, Avenue Houba de Strooper, 1020 Bruxelles
Tel: +32 2 477 1211
Foundation date: 1895
Member of FIFA since: 1904
Member of UEFA since: 1954
Website: www.belgianfootball.be

NATIONAL TEAM RECORDS

RECORDS
First international match:	01.05.1994, Bruxelles: Belgium – France 3-3
Most international caps:	Jan Bert Lieve Vertonghen – 131 caps (since 2007)
Most international goals:	Romelu Menama Lukaku Bolingoli – 62 goals / 98 caps (since 2010)

UEFA EUROPEAN CHAMPIONSHIP
1960	*Did not enter*
1964	Qualifiers
1968	Qualifiers
1972	Final Tournament (3rd Place)
1976	Qualifiers
1980	Final Tournament (Runners-up)
1984	Final Tournament (Group Stage)
1988	Qualifiers
1992	Qualifiers
1996	Qualifiers
2000	Final Tournament (Group Stage)
2004	Qualifiers
2008	Qualifiers
2012	Qualifiers
2016	Final Tournament (Quarter-Finals)
2020	Final Tournament (Quarter-Finals)

FIFA WORLD CUP
1930	Final Tournament (Group Stage)
1934	Final Tournament (1st Round)
1938	Final Tournament (1st Round)
1950	*Withdrew*
1954	Final Tournament (Group Stage)
1958	Qualifiers
1962	Qualifiers
1966	Qualifiers
1970	Final Tournament (Group Stage)
1974	Qualifiers
1978	Qualifiers
1982	Final Tournament (2nd Round)
1986	Final Tournament (4th Place)
1990	Final Tournament (2nd Round of 16)
1994	Final Tournament (2nd Round of 16)
1998	Final Tournament (Group Stage)
2002	Final Tournament (2nd Round of 16)
2006	Qualifiers
2010	Qualifiers
2014	Final Tournament (Quarter-Finals)
2018	Final Tournament (3rd Place)

OLYMPIC TOURNAMENTS
1908	-
1912	-
1920	**Winners**
1924	Final Tournament (1/8-Finals)
1928	Quarter-Finals
1936	*Did not enter*
1948	*Did not enter*
1952	*Did not enter*
1956	*Did not enter*
1960	*Did not enter*
1964	*Did not enter*
1968	*Did not enter*
1972	*Did not enter*
1976	*Did not enter*
1980	Qualifiers
1984	Qualifiers
1988	Qualifiers
1992	Qualifiers
1996	Qualifiers
2000	Qualifiers
2004	Qualifiers
2008	Final Tournament (4th Place)
2012	Qualifiers
2016	Qualifiers

UEFA NATIONS LEAGUE
2018/2019	League A
2020/2021	League A (Qualified for the Final Tournament)

FIFA CONFEDERATIONS CUP 1992-2017
None

BELGIAN CLUB HONOURS IN EUROPEAN CLUB COMPETITIONS:

European Champion Clubs' Cup (1956-1992) / UEFA Champions League (1993-2021)
None

Fairs Cup (1858-1971) / UEFA Cup (1972-2009) / UEFA Europa League (2010-2021)
RSC Anderlecht Bruxelles	1	1982/1983

UEFA Super Cup (1972-2020)
RSC Anderlecht Bruxelles	2	1976, 1978
KV Mechelen	1	1988

*European Cup Winners' Cup 1961-1999**
RSC Anderlecht Bruxelles	2	1975/1976, 1977/1978
KV Mechelen	1	1987/1988

*defunct competition

NATIONAL COMPETITIONS
TABLE OF HONOURS

	CHAMPIONS	CUP WINNERS	BEST GOALSCORERS	
1895/1896	FC Liégeois	-	Samuel Hickson (ENG, FC Liégeois)	?
1896/1897	Racing Club de Bruxelles	-	Samuel Hickson (ENG, FC Liégeois)	?
1897/1898	FC Liégeois	-	Franz König (SUI, Racing Club de Bruxelles)	?
1898/1899	FC Liégeois	-	Franz König (SUI, Racing Club de Bruxelles)	?
1899/1900	Racing Club de Bruxelles	-	Charles Richard Atkinson-Grimshaw (ENG, Racing Club de Bruxelles)	?
1900/1901	Racing Club de Bruxelles	-	Herbert Alfred Potts (ENG, K Beerschot VAC)	26
1901/1902	Racing Club de Bruxelles	-	Herbert Alfred Potts (ENG, K Beerschot VAC)	16
1902/1903	Racing Club de Bruxelles	-	Gustave Vanderstappen (Royale Union Saint-Gilloise)	?
1903/1904	Royale Union Saint-Gilloise	-	Gustave Vanderstappen (Royale Union Saint-Gilloise)	30
1904/1905	Royale Union Saint-Gilloise	-	Robert De Veen (FC Brugeois)	?
1905/1906	Royale Union Saint-Gilloise	-	Robert De Veen (FC Brugeois)	26
1906/1907	Royale Union Saint-Gilloise	-	Maurice Vertongen (Racing Club de Bruxelles)	29
1907/1908	Racing Club de Bruxelles	-	Maurice Vertongen (Racing Club de Bruxelles)	23
1908/1909	Royale Union Saint-Gilloise	-	Vahram Kevorkian (RUS, Racing Club de Bruxelles)	30
1909/1910	Royale Union Saint-Gilloise	-	Maurice Vertongen (Royale Union Saint-Gilloise)	36
1910/1911	CS Brugeois	-	Alphonse Six (CS Brugeois)	40
1911/1912	Daring Club de Bruxelles	Racing Club de Bruxelles	Maurice Taylor Bunyan (ENG, Racing Club de Bruxelles)	35
1912/1913	Royale Union Saint-Gilloise	Royale Union Saint-Gilloise	Sylva Brébart (Daring Club de Bruxelles)	31
1913/1914	Daring Club de Bruxelles	Royale Union Saint-Gilloise	Maurice Bunyan (ENG, Racing Club de Bruxelles)	28
1915-1919	*No competition*	*No competition*	-	
1919/1920	FC Brugeois	*No competition*	Honoré Vlamynck (Daring Club de Bruxelles)	26
1920/1921	Daring Club de Bruxelles	*No competition*	Ivan Thys (K Beerschot VAC)	23
1921/1922	K Beerschot VAC	*No competition*	Ivan Thys (K Beerschot VAC)	21
1922/1923	Royale Union Saint-Gilloise	*No competition*	Achille Meyskens (Royale Union Saint-Gilloise)	24
1923/1924	K Beerschot VAC	*No competition*	Charles Jooris (Racing Club de Bruxelles)	18
1924/1925	K Beerschot VAC	*No competition*	Joseph Taeymans (K Berchem Sport)	20
1925/1926	K Beerschot VAC	*No competition*	Laurent Grimmonprez (RC Gent)	28
1926/1927	RCS Brugeois	RCS Brugeois	Lucien Fabry (R Standard Liège)	28
1927/1928	K Beerschot VAC	*No competition*	Raymond Braine (K Beerschot VAC)	35
1928/1929	R Antwerp FC	*No competition*	Raymond Braine (K Beerschot VAC)	30
1929/1930	RCS Brugeois	*No competition*	Pierre De Vidts (Daring Club de Bruxelles)	26
1930/1931	R Antwerp FC	*No competition*	Jacques Secretin (RCFC Montegnée) Joseph Van Beeck (R Antwerp FC	21
1931/1932	K Lierse SK	*No competition*	Bernard Delmez (K Lierse SK)	26
1932/1933	Royale Union Saint-Gilloise	*No competition*	Willy Ulens (R Antwerp FC)	26
1933/1934	Royale Union Saint-Gilloise	*No competition*	Vital Van Landeghem (Royale Union Saint-Gilloise)	29
1934/1935	Royale Union Saint-Gilloise	Daring Club de Bruxelles	Marius Mondelé (Daring Club de Bruxelles)	28
1935/1936	Daring Club de Bruxelles SR	*No competition*	Flor Lambrechts (R Antwerp FC)	37
1936/1937	Daring Club de Bruxelles SR	*No competition*	Jean Collet (White Star WAC Bruxelles)	22
1937/1938	R Beerschot AC Antwerp	*No competition*	Marius Mondelé (Daring Club de Bruxelles)	32
1938/1939	R Beerschot AC Antwerp	*No competition*	Jozef Wagner (R Antwerp FC)	31
1939-1941	*No competition*	*No competition*	-	
1941/1942	K Liersche SK	*No competition*	Bert De Cleyn (R Antwerp FC)	34
1942/1943	RFC Malinois	*No competition*	Arthur Ceuleers (K Beerschot VAC) Jules Van Craen (K Lierse SK)	41
1943/1944	R Antwerp FC	*No competition*	Jan Goossens (ROC Charleroi)	34
1944/1945	*No competition*	*No competition*	-	
1945/1946	RFC Malinois	*No competition*	-	
1946/1947	RSC Anderlecht Bruxelles	*No competition*	Jef Mermans (RSC Anderlecht Bruxelles)	39
1947/1948	RFC Malinois	*No competition*	Jef Mermans (RSC Anderlecht Bruxelles)	23
1948/1949	RSC Anderlecht Bruxelles	*No competition*	René Thirifays (R Charleroi SC)	26
1949/1950	RSC Anderlecht Bruxelles	*No competition*	Jef Mermans (RSC Anderlecht Bruxelles)	37
1950/1951	RSC Anderlecht Bruxelles	*No competition*	Albert Dehert (K Berchem Sport)	27
1951/1952	RFC Liégeois	*No competition*	Jozef Mannaerts (KRC Mechelen)	25
1952/1953	RFC Liégeois	*No competition*	Rik Coppens (K Beerschot VAC)	35
1953/1954	RSC Anderlecht Bruxelles	R Standard Liège	Hippolyte Van Den Bosch (RSC Anderlecht Bruxelles)	29
1954/1955	RSC Anderlecht Bruxelles	R Antwerp FC	Rik Coppens (K Beerschot VAC)	35
1955/1956	RSC Anderlecht Bruxelles	RRC Tournaisien	Jean Mathonet (R Standard Liège)	26
1956/1957	R Antwerp FC	*No competition*	Maurice Willems (KAA Gent)	35
1957/1958	R Standard Liège	*No competition*	Jef Vliers (K Beerschot VAC)	25
1958/1959	RSC Anderlecht Bruxelles	*No competition*	Victor Wegria (RFC Liégeois)	26
1959/1960	K Lierse SK	*No competition*	Victor Wegria (RFC Liégeois)	21
1960/1961	R Standard Liège	*No competition*	Victor Wegria (RFC Liégeois)	23
1961/1962	RSC Anderlecht Bruxelles	*No competition*	Jacky Stockman (RSC Anderlecht Bruxelles)	29
1962/1963	R Standard Liège	*No competition*	Victor Wegria (RFC Liégeois)	29
1963/1964	RSC Anderlecht Bruxelles	ARA La Gantoise	Paul Van Himst (RSC Anderlecht Bruxelles)	26
1964/1965	RSC Anderlecht Bruxelles	RSC Anderlecht Bruxelles	Jean-Paul Colonval (RFC Tilleur Saint-Nicolas)	25

1965/1966	RSC Anderlecht Bruxelles	R Standard Liège	Paul Van Himst (RSC Anderlecht Bruxelles)	25
1966/1967	RSC Anderlecht Bruxelles	R Standard Liège	Johan Mulder (NED, RSC Anderlecht Bruxelles)	20
1967/1968	RSC Anderlecht Bruxelles	Club Brugge KV	Roger Claessen (R Standard Liège Liège) Paul Van Himst (RSC Anderlecht Bruxelles)	20
1968/1969	R Standard Liège	K Lierse SK	Antal Nagy (HUN, R Standard Liège Liège)	20
1969/1970	R Standard Liège	Club Brugge KV	Lothar Emmerich (GER, K Beerschot VAC)	29
1970/1971	R Standard Liège	K Beerschot VAV	Erwin Kostedde (GER, R Standard Liège Liège)	26
1971/1972	RSC Anderlecht Bruxelles	RSC Anderlecht Bruxelles	Raoul Lambert (Club Brugge KV)	17
1972/1973	Club Brugge KV	RSC Anderlecht Bruxelles	Pieter Robert Rensenbrink (NED, RSC Anderlecht Bruxelles) Alfred Riedl (AUT, K Sint-Truidense VV)	16
1973/1974	RSC Anderlecht Bruxelles	KSV Waregem	Attila Ladynski (HUN, RSC Anderlecht Bruxelles)	22
1974/1975	R White Daring Molenbeek	RSC Anderlecht Bruxelles	Alfred Riedl (AUT, R Antwerp FC)	28
1975/1976	Club Brugge KV	RSC Anderlecht Bruxelles	Hans Posthumus (K Lierse SK)	26
1976/1977	Club Brugge KV	Club Brugge KV	François Van Der Elst (RSC Anderlecht Bruxelles)	21
1977/1978	Club Brugge KV	KSK Beveren	Harald Nickel (R Standard Liège Liège)	22
1978/1979	KSK Beveren	K Beerschot VAV	Erwin Albert (KSK Beveren)	28
1979/1980	Club Brugge KV	K Waterschei SV Thor Genk	Erwin Vandenbergh (K Lierse SK)	39
1980/1981	RSC Anderlecht Bruxelles	R Standard Liège	Erwin Vandenbergh (K Lierse SK)	24
1981/1982	R Standard Liège	K Waterschei SV Thor Genk	Erwin Vandenbergh (K Lierse SK)	25
1982/1983	R Standard Liège	KSK Beveren	Erwin Vandenbergh (RSC Anderlecht Bruxelles)	20
1983/1984	KSK Beveren	KAA Gent	Nicolaas Pieter Claesen (RFC Seraing)	27
1984/1985	RSC Anderlecht Bruxelles	Cercle Brugge KSV	Ronny Martens (KAA Gent)	23
1985/1986	RSC Anderlecht Bruxelles	Club Brugge KV	Erwin Vandenbergh (RSC Anderlecht Bruxelles)	27
1986/1987	RSC Anderlecht Bruxelles	KV Mechelen	Arnór Guðjohnsen (ISL, RSC Anderlecht Bruxelles)	19
1987/1988	Club Brugge KV	RSC Anderlecht Bruxelles	Francis Severeyns (R Antwerp FC)	24
1988/1989	KV Mechelen	RSC Anderlecht Bruxelles	Edward Krncevic (AUS, RSC Anderlecht Bruxelles)	23
1989/1990	Club Brugge KV	RFC Liégeois	Frank Farina (AUS, Club Brugge KV)	24
1990/1991	RSC Anderlecht Bruxelles	Club Brugge KV	Erwin Vandenbergh (KAA Gent)	23
1991/1992	Club Brugge KV	Royal Antwerp F.C.	Josip Weber (CRO, Cercle Brugge KSV)	26
1992/1993	RSC Anderlecht Bruxelles	R Standard Liège	Josip Weber (CRO, Cercle Brugge KSV)	31
1993/1994	RSC Anderlecht Bruxelles	RSC Anderlecht Bruxelles	Josip Weber (Cercle Brugge KSV)	31
1994/1995	RSC Anderlecht Bruxelles	Club Brugge KV	Aurelio Vidmar (AUS, R Standard Liège Liège)	22
1995/1996	Club Brugge KV	Club Brugge KV	Mario Stanić (CRO, Club Brugge KV)	20
1996/1997	K Lierse SK	KFC Germinal Ekeren	Robert Špehar (CRO, Club Brugge KV)	26
1997/1998	Club Brugge KV	KRC Genk	Branko Strupar (KRC Genk)	22
1998/1999	KRC Genk	Lierse S.K.	Jan Koller (CZE, Lokeren)	24
1999/2000	RSC Anderlecht Bruxelles	KRC Genk	Ole Martin Årst (NOR, KAA Gent) Antonio Brogno (KVC Westerlo)	30
2000/2001	RSC Anderlecht Bruxelles	KVC Westerlo	Tomasz Radzinski (CAN, RSC Anderlecht Bruxelles)	23
2001/2002	KRC Genk	Club Brugge KV	Wesley Sonck (KRC Genk)	30
2002/2003	Club Brugge KV	RAA La Louvière	Cédric Roussel (RAEC Mons) Wesley Sonck (KRC Genk)	22
2003/2004	RSC Anderlecht Bruxelles	Club Brugge KV	Luigi Pieroni (Mouscron)	28
2004/2005	Club Brugge KV	KFC Germinal Beerschot	Nenad Jestrović (SRB, RSC Anderlecht Bruxelles)	18
2005/2006	RSC Anderlecht Bruxelles	SV Zulte-Waregem	Tosin Dosunmu (NGA, KFC Germinal Beerschot Antwerpen)	18
2006/2007	RSC Anderlecht Bruxelles	Club Brugge KV	François Sterchele (KFC Germinal Beerschot Antwerpen)	21
2007/2008	R Standard Liège	RSC Anderlecht Bruxelles	Joseph Eneojo Akpala (NGA, R Charleroi SC)	18
2008/2009	R Standard Liège	KRC Genk	Jaime Alfonso Ruiz (COL, KVC Westerlo)	18
2009/2010	RSC Anderlecht Bruxelles	KAA Gent	Romelu Menama Lukaku Bolingoli (RSC Anderlecht Bruxelles)	15
2010/2011	KRC Genk	R Standard Liège	Ivan Perišić (CRO, Club Brugge KV)	22
2011/2012	RSC Anderlecht Bruxelles	KSC Lokeren	Jérémy Perbet (FRA, RAEC Mons)	25
2012/2013	RSC Anderlecht Bruxelles	KRC Genk	Carlos Arturo Bacca Ahumada (COL, Club Brugge KV)	25
2013/2014	RSC Anderlecht Bruxelles	KSC Lokeren	Hamdi Harbaoui (TUN, KSC Lokeren Oost-Vlaanderen)	22
2014/2015	KAA Gent	Club Brugge KV	Aleksandar Mitrović (SRB, RSC Anderlecht Bruxelles)	20
2015/2016	Club Brugge KV	R Standard Liège	Jérémy Perbet (FRA, R Charleroi SC)	22
2016/2017	RSC Anderlecht Bruxelles	SV Zulte Waregem	Łukasz Teodorczyk (POL, RSC Anderlecht Bruxelles)	22
2017/2018	Club Brugge KV	R Standard Liège	Hamdi Harbaoui (TUN, SV Zulte Waregem)	22
2018/2019	KRC Genk	KV Mechelen	Hamdi Harbaoui (TUN, SV Zulte Waregem)	25
2019/2020	Club Brugge KV	Royal Antwerp FC	Dieudonné Mbokani Bezua (COD, R Antwerp FC) Jonathan Christian David (CAN, KAA Gent)	18
2020/2021	Club Brugge KV	KRC Genk	Ebere Paul Onuachu (NGA, KRC Genk)	33

NATIONAL CHAMPIONSHIP
Eerste Divisie / Jupiler Pro League - 2020/2021
(08.08.2020 – 23.05.2021)

Regular Season - Results

Round 1 [08-10.08.2020]
Club Brugge - Charleroi 0-1(0-0)
Antwerp FC - Excel Mouscron 1-1(0-0)
Standard Liège - Cercle Brugge 1-0(0-0)
Sint-Truidense VV - KAA Gent 2-1(1-1)
SV Zulte Waregem - KRC Genk 1-2(1-0)
KV Mechelen - Anderlecht 2-2(0-0)
KV Kortrijk - Waasland-Beveren 1-3(0-1)
KV Oostende - Beerschot 1-2(0-1)
Oud-Heverlee - KKAS Eupen 1-1(0-0)

Round 2 [14-17.08.2020]
Excel Mouscron - KV Mechelen 0-1(0-1)
KRC Genk - Oud-Heverlee 1-1(0-0)
KAA Gent - KV Kortrijk 1-2(0-1)
Charleroi - KV Oostende 1-0(0-0)
Cercle Brugge - Antwerp FC 2-1(0-1)
Beerschot - SV Zulte Waregem 3-1(1-0)
KAS Eupen - Club Brugge 0-4(0-1)
Anderlecht - Sint-Truidense VV 3-1(1-0)
Waasland-Beveren - Standard Liège 1-2(0-0)

Round 3 [21-24.08.2020]
KV Kortrijk - KAS Eupen 0-0
Zulte Waregem - Waasland-Beveren 4-1(1-0)
KV Mechelen - Cercle Brugge 2-3(1-0)
Oud-Heverlee - Charleroi 1-3(1-1)
Antwerp FC - KAA Gent 1-0(1-0)
Standard Liège - KRC Genk 0-0
Club Brugge - Beerschot 0-1(0-1)
Anderlecht - Excel Mouscron 1-1(0-0)
Sint-Truidense VV - KV Oostende 0-0

Round 4 [28-30.08.2020]
KV Oostende - Anderlecht 2-2(2-1)
KAS Eupen - Sint-Truidense VV 1-1(1-0)
Cercle Brugge - KV Kortrijk 0-1(0-0)
Waasland-Beveren - Oud-Heverlee 1-3(0-1)
Excel Mouscron - SV Zulte Waregem 0-1(0-0)
KRC Genk - Club Brugge 1-2(0-1)
Beerschot - Standard Liège 0-3(0-1)
Charleroi - Antwerp FC 2-0(1-0)
KAA Gent - KV Mechelen 1-0(1-0)

Round 5 [11-14.09.2020]
KAS Eupen - KAA Gent 2-1(1-0)
KV Mechelen - KV Oostende 0-1(0-0)
Oud-Heverlee - Standard Liège 1-0(0-0)
Club Brugge - Waasland-Beveren 4-1(2-1)
Anderlecht - Cercle Brugge 2-0(1-0)
Sint-Truidense VV - Antwerp FC 2-3(2-2)
SV Zulte Waregem - Charleroi 0-2(0-0)
KV Kortrijk - Excel Mouscron 3-0(0-0)
Beerschot - KRC Genk 5-2(1-1)

Round 6 [18-21.09.2020]
Charleroi - Beerschot 3-1(1-0)
KV Oostende - Oud-Heverlee 3-1(1-0)
Excel Mouscron - KAA Gent 0-1(0-1)
Waasland-Beveren - Anderlecht 2-4(0-2)
SV Zulte Waregem - Club Brugge 0-6(0-4)
Standard Liège - KV Kortrijk 2-1(2-1)
KRC Genk - KV Mechelen 3-1(1-1)
Antwerp FC - KAS Eupen 2-2(0-1)
Cercle Brugge - Sint-Truidense VV 3-0(2-0)

Round 7 [25-28.09.2020]
KV Kortrijk - Antwerp FC 1-3(1-0)
Beerschot - Waasland-Beveren 3-2(1-2)
KV Mechelen - Sint-Truidense VV 2-0(0-0)
KAA Gent - Oud-Heverlee 2-3(0-2)
Standard Liège - SV Zulte Waregem 2-2(0-1)
Anderlecht - KAS Eupen 1-1(0-0)
Club Brugge - Cercle Brugge 2-1(1-0)
Excel Mouscron - Charleroi 1-1(1-1)
KRC Genk - KV Oostende 2-2(1-1)

Round 8 [02-04.10.2020]
Antwerp FC - KV Mechelen 4-1(3-0)
Waasland-Beveren - KRC Genk 1-1(0-0)
KAS Eupen - Cercle Brugge 1-2(1-1)
Oud-Heverlee - SV Zulte Waregem 2-1(1-0)
Sint-Truidense VV - KV Kortrijk 0-0
Club Brugge - Anderlecht 3-0(1-0)
KAA Gent - Beerschot 5-1(3-0)
Charleroi - Standard Liège 1-2(0-0)
KV Oostende - Excel Mouscron 3-0(0-0)

Round 9 [17-18.10.2020]
Cercle Brugge - KAA Gent 5-2(2-1)
Beerschot - Sint-Truidense VV 6-3(5-1)
KV Mechelen - KV Kortrijk 1-2(0-0)
Standard Liège - Club Brugge 1-1(0-1)
SV Zulte Waregem - Antwerp FC 1-3(1-0)
Excel Mouscron - KAS Eupen 0-2(0-0)
KRC Genk - Charleroi 2-1(1-0)
Anderlecht - Oud-Heverlee 2-2(0-0)
Waasland-B. - KV Oostende 2-0(0-0) [24.11.]

Round 10 [23-26.10.2020]
KV Kortrijk - Anderlecht 1-3(0-2)
Oud-Heverlee - Club Brugge 2-1(1-1)
Antwerp FC - Beerschot 3-2(2-1)
KV Oostende - SV Zulte Waregem 3-0(3-0)
Sint-Truidense VV - Standard Liège 2-0(1-0)
KAA Gent - KRC Genk 1-2(1-1)
Cercle Brugge - Mouscron 1-2(0-0) [25.11.]
Charleroi - Waasland-Bev. 0-2(0-1) [02.12.]
KAS Eupen - KV Mechelen 1-1(1-0) [03.12.]

Round 11 [30.10.-02.11.2020]
KRC Genk - KAS Eupen 4-0(1-0)
Beerschot - Oud-Heverlee 4-2(2-1)
Charleroi - Cercle Brugge 3-0(0-0)
Club Brugge - KV Mechelen 2-2(2-1)
Anderlecht - Antwerp FC 1-0(0-0)
Standard Liège - KV Oostende 1-0(0-0)
Waasland-Beveren - KAA Gent 1-4(0-4)
SV Zulte Waregem - KV Kortrijk 1-1(0-0)
Mouscron - Sint-Truidense 3-2(1-0) [01.12.]

Round 12 [06-08.11.2020]
KV Mechelen - Charleroi 3-3(2-1)
KV Kortrijk - Beerschot 5-5(2-1)
KAS Eupen - Waasland-Beveren 1-1(0-1)
Sint-Truidense VV - KRC Genk 1-2(1-2)
Antwerp FC - Standard Liège 1-1(1-0)
KV Oostende - Club Brugge 1-3(1-1)
KAA Gent - Anderlecht 1-1(0-1)
Cercle Brugge - SV Zulte Waregem 1-3(0-2)
Oud-Heverlee - Mouscron 2-0(0-0) [08.12.]

Round 13 [21-23.11.2020]
Standard Liège - KAS Eupen 2-2(1-1)
KV Oostende - Antwerp FC 1-1(0-0)
Waasland-Beveren - Cercle Brugge 0-2(0-1)
Club Brugge - KV Kortrijk 1-0(0-0)
Beerschot - Anderlecht 2-1(1-0)
SV Zulte Waregem - KV Mechelen 1-2(0-1)
Charleroi - KAA Gent 0-1(0-1)
KRC Genk - Excel Mouscron 4-1(1-1)
Oud-Heverlee - Sint-Truidense VV 2-2(1-1)

Round 14 [27-30.11.2020]
KAS Eupen - Charleroi 3-1(1-0)
Sint-Truidense - Waasland-Beveren 1-1(1-0)
Cercle Brugge - KRC Genk 1-5(0-4)
Excel Mouscron - Club Brugge 0-0
KV Mechelen - Beerschot 2-3(2-1)
KAA Gent - SV Zulte Waregem 0-3(0-2)
Anderlecht - Standard Liège 0-0
KV Kortrijk - KV Oostende 3-1(1-1)
Antwerp FC - Oud-Heverlee 3-2(2-2)

Round 15 [04-07.12.2020]
SV Zulte Waregem - Anderlecht 2-2(1-1)
Waasland-Beveren - Excel Mouscron 2-0(0-0)
Oud-Heverlee - Cercle Brugge 2-1(1-0)
Club Brugge - Sint-Truidense VV 1-0(0-0)
KRC Genk - Antwerp FC 4-2(2-1)
Beerschot - KAS Eupen 0-1(0-1)
Standard Liège - KV Mechelen 2-2(1-0)
KV Oostende - KAA Gent 2-1(0-1)
Charleroi - KV Kortrijk 0-0

Round 16 [11-13.12.2020]
Anderlecht - KRC Genk 1-0(0-0)
Excel Mouscron - Beerschot 3-1(1-0)
Cercle Brugge - KV Oostende 0-1(0-1)
KV Kortrijk - Oud-Heverlee 0-3(0-0)
Sint-Truidense VV - Charleroi 1-2(1-1)
Antwerp FC - Club Brugge 0-2(0-1)
KAA Gent - Standard Liège 2-1(1-1)
KV Mechelen - Waasland-Beveren 2-3(1-0)
KAS Eupen - Zulte Waregem 2-3(1-0)[29.12.]

Round 17 [18-20.12.2020]
Charleroi - Anderlecht 1-0(0-0)
SV Zulte Waregem - Sint-Truidense 0-2(0-0)
KRC Genk - KV Kortrijk 2-0(1-0)
Club Brugge - KAA Gent 0-1(0-0)
Oud-Heverlee - KV Mechelen 1-2(0-2)
Standard Liège - Excel Mouscron 0-1(0-1)
Waasland-Beveren - Antwerp FC 0-3(0-3)
Oostende - KAS Eupen 1-1(0-0) [12.01.21]
Beerschot - Cercle Brugge 1-1(1-0) [13.01.21]

Round 18 [15-17.12.2020]
Cercle Brugge - Charleroi 3-4(2-0)
Excel Mouscron - Oud-Heverlee 2-2(0-1)
Anderlecht - KV Oostende 2-1(1-0)
Antwerp FC - SV Zulte Waregem 0-1(0-1)
KAA Gent - Waasland-Beveren 3-0(1-0)
KV Kortrijk - Standard Liège 2-1(2-0)
KV Mechelen - Club Brugge 0-3(0-0)
Sint-Truidense - Beerschot 1-0(1-0) [30.12.]
KAS Eupen - KRC Genk 1-4(1-2) [06.01.21]

Round 19 [26-27.12.2020]
Club Brugge - KAS Eupen 3-0(0-0)
SV Zulte Waregem - Cercle Brugge 1-0(0-0)
Oud-Heverlee - KV Oostende 1-2(1-0)
KV Kortrijk - KAA Gent 1-0(0-0)
Standard Liège - Sint-Truidense VV 1-2(0-2)
Antwerp FC - Charleroi 2-1(0-0)
KRC Genk - Waasland-Beveren 1-1(1-1)
Anderlecht - Beerschot 2-0(1-0)
KV Mechelen - Excel Mouscron 2-1(1-0)

Round 20 [15-17.01.2021]
KAS Eupen - Anderlecht 2-0(0-0)
KV Oostende - KV Kortrijk 2-1(1-0)
Excel Mouscron - KRC Genk 2-0(1-0)
Waasland-Beveren - Zulte Waregem 1-5(0-2)
Charleroi - KV Mechelen 0-1(0-0)
KAA Gent - Antwerp FC 0-1(0-0)
Cercle Brugge - Standard Liège 0-1(0-1)
Beerschot - Club Brugge 0-3(0-2)
Sint-Truidense VV - Oud-Heverlee 3-1(2-1)

Round 21 [22-24.01.2021]
Anderlecht - Waasland-Beveren 0-0
KV Mechelen - KAS Eupen 3-0(1-0)
KV Kortrijk - Cercle Brugge 1-2(1-2)
Sint-Truidense VV - Excel Mouscron 0-2(0-1)
Antwerp FC - KV Oostende 1-2(1-1)
Club Brugge - KRC Genk 3-2(1-2)
SV Zulte Waregem - Beerschot 0-3(0-0)
Standard Liège - Charleroi 3-2(2-1)
Oud-Heverlee - KAA Gent 0-3(0-1)

Round 22 [26-28.01.2021]
KAS Eupen - Antwerp FC 0-2(0-2)
Waasland-Beveren - KV Mechelen 2-3(0-2)
Excel Mouscron - Anderlecht 1-1(1-0)
Beerschot - KV Kortrijk 0-0
KRC Genk - SV Zulte Waregem 3-2(1-0)
KAA Gent - Sint-Truidense VV 1-1(0-1)
Charleroi - Oud-Heverlee 1-1(0-1)
Cercle Brugge - Club Brugge 1-2(1-1)
KV Oostende - Standard Liège 2-2(1-0)

Round 23 [29-31.01.2021]
Antwerp FC - Waasland-Beveren 3-2(1-1)
KV Mechelen - KRC Genk 0-0
KAS Eupen - Excel Mouscron 1-1(1-0)
Oud-Heverlee - Beerschot 0-1(0-0)
KV Kortrijk - Charleroi 1-3(0-1)
Club Brugge - Standard Liège 3-1(2-1)
SV Zulte Waregem - KV Oostende 2-1(1-1)
Anderlecht - KAA Gent 0-0
Sint-Truidense VV - Cercle Brugge 3-0(1-0)

Round 24 [05-07.02.2021]
Excel Mouscron - KV Kortrijk 0-3(0-2)
KV Oostende - Sint-Truidense VV 3-1(1-0)
Cercle Brugge - KV Mechelen 0-1(0-0)
Waasland-Beveren - Club Brugge 0-2(0-1)
Standard Liège - Oud-Heverlee 1-1(0-0)
Beerschot - Antwerp FC 1-2(0-0)
Charleroi - SV Zulte Waregem 1-1(1-0)
KRC Genk - Anderlecht 1-2(1-2)
KAA Gent - KAS Eupen 2-2(2-1)

Round 25 [19-21.01.2021]
Excel Mouscron - Waasland-Beveren 1-1(0-0)
Anderlecht - Charleroi 3-0(2-0)
KV Kortrijk - Sint-Truidense VV 0-2(0-2)
KAS Eupen - Beerschot 3-1(2-1)
KV Mechelen - Standard Liège 0-4(0-1)
Antwerp FC - Cercle Brugge 1-0(0-0)
Club Brugge - KV Oostende 2-1(1-1)
SV Zulte Waregem - Oud-Heverlee 2-3(2-1)
KRC Genk - KAA Gent 1-1(1-1)

Round 26 [12-17.02.2021]
Oud-Heverlee - KV Kortrijk 3-1(3-0)
Sint-Truidense VV - Zulte Waregem 1-2(0-0)
Standard Liège - Antwerp FC 1-1(1-1)
Beerschot - KV Mechelen 1-2(0-0)
Cercle Brugge - Anderlecht 0-0
KAA Gent - Excel Mouscron 4-0(1-0)
Waasland-Beveren - KAS Eupen 1-0(1-0)
KV Oostende - KRC Genk 3-1(2-1)
Charleroi - Club Brugge 1-1(0-1) [12.03.]

Round 27 [19-22.02.2021]
KV Mechelen - KAA Gent 1-1(1-1)
KAS Eupen - KV Oostende 1-1(0-0)
Excel Mouscron - Cercle Brugge 1-2(0-1)
Waasland-Beveren - Charleroi 1-1(0-0)
Anderlecht - KV Kortrijk 0-2(0-1)
SV Zulte Waregem - Standard Liège 3-2(1-1)
KRC Genk - Beerschot 1-2(0-0)
Antwerp FC - Sint-Truidense VV 0-0
Club Brugge - Oud-Heverlee 3-0(2-0)

Round 28 [26.02.-01.03.2021]
Charleroi - KRC Genk 1-2(0-1)
Cercle Brugge - Waasland-Beveren 2-0(1-0)
KV Oostende - KV Mechelen 2-0(1-0)
KV Kortrijk - SV Zulte Waregem 1-2(1-1)
Standard Liège - Anderlecht 1-3(0-1)
Beerschot - Excel Mouscron 2-2(0-1)
Sint-Truidense VV - KAS Eupen 0-2(0-1)
Oud-Heverlee - Antwerp FC 2-0(2-0)
KAA Gent - Club Brugge 0-4(0-0) [15.03.]

Round 29 [05-08.03.2021]
Charleroi - Sint-Truidense VV 0-0
KAS Eupen - Oud-Heverlee 3-3(2-2)
Waasland-Beveren - Beerschot 1-2(1-1)
Antwerp FC - KV Kortrijk 4-2(1-0)
Excel Mouscron - Standard Liège 1-0(1-0)
Club Brugge - SV Zulte Waregem 3-0(2-0)
Anderlecht - KV Mechelen 1-1(1-0)
KRC Genk - Cercle Brugge 2-0(2-0)
KAA Gent - KV Oostende 1-0(1-0)

Round 30 [09-11.01.2021]
SV Zulte Waregem - Excel Mouscron 1-0(1-0)
Cercle Brugge - KAS Eupen 1-2(0-0)
KV Kortrijk - KRC Genk 2-1(1-1)
KV Oostende - Charleroi 3-2(1-1)
KV Mechelen - Antwerp FC 3-0(0-0)
Beerschot - KAA Gent 1-1(1-1)
Oud-Heverlee - Anderlecht 1-0(0-0)
Sint-Truidense VV - Club Brugge 1-2(0-2)
Standard Liège - Waasland-Beveren 3-1(1-0)

Round 31 [19-21.03.2021]
KRC Genk - Standard Liège 2-2(0-0)
Excel Mouscron - KV Oostende 0-1(0-0)
KAS Eupen - KV Kortrijk 2-0(0-0)
Club Brugge - Antwerp FC 0-2(0-2)
KV Mechelen - Oud-Heverlee 2-2(1-1)
Anderlecht - SV Zulte Waregem 4-1(2-1)
KAA Gent - Cercle Brugge 1-0(0-0)
Waasland-B. - Sint-Truidense 2-4(1-1)[06.04.]
Beerschot - Charleroi 2-1(1-0) [07.04.]

Round 32 [03-05.04.2021]
KV Oostende - Waasland-Beveren 0-2(0-2)
Sint-Truidense VV - KV Mechelen 2-1(2-0)
KV Kortrijk - Club Brugge 1-2(1-1)
Cercle Brugge - Beerschot 2-1(2-0)
Standard Liège - KAA Gent 2-1(0-1)
Charleroi - Excel Mouscron 1-0(0-0)
Oud-Heverlee - KRC Genk 2-3(0-1)
SV Zulte Waregem - KAS Eupen 2-1(0-1)
Antwerp FC - Anderlecht 1-4(0-0)

Round 33 [09-12.04.2021]
KAS Eupen - Standard Liège 0-4(0-1)
Cercle Brugge - Oud-Heverlee 3-0(1-0)
KV Mechelen - SV Zulte Waregem 4-2(2-0)
KAA Gent - Charleroi 4-0(2-0)
KRC Genk - Sint-Truidense VV 4-0(3-0)
Waasland-Beveren - KV Kortrijk 3-4(2-1)
Anderlecht - Club Brugge 2-1(0-0)
Beerschot - KV Oostende 1-2(1-0)
Excel Mouscron - Antwerp FC 2-3(0-1)

Round 34 [17-18.04.2021]
Charleroi - KAS Eupen 2-3(1-3)
Antwerp FC - KRC Genk 3-2(0-1)
Club Brugge - Excel Mouscron 4-2(0-0)
KV Kortrijk - KV Mechelen 1-4(1-2)
KV Oostende - Cercle Brugge 1-1(0-0)
Oud-Heverlee - Waasland-Beveren 1-2(0-1)
Standard Liège - Beerschot 3-0(1-0)
SV Zulte Waregem - KAA Gent 2-7(0-3)
Sint-Truidense VV - Anderlecht 0-1(0-0)

								Home					Away				
1. Club Brugge KV	34	24	4	6	73 - 26	76	12	1	4	34 - 15		12	3	2	39 - 11
2. Antwerp FC	34	18	6	10	57 - 48	60	9	4	4	30 - 25		9	2	6	27 - 23
3. RSC Anderlecht Bruxelles	34	15	13	6	51 - 34	58	9	7	1	25 - 11		6	6	5	26 - 23
4. KRC Genk	34	16	8	10	67 - 48	56	9	5	3	38 - 20		7	3	7	29 - 28
5. KV Oostende	34	15	8	11	49 - 41	53	9	5	3	33 - 21		6	3	8	16 - 20
6. R Standard Liège	34	13	11	10	52 - 41	50	7	7	3	26 - 20		6	4	7	26 - 21
7. KAA Gent	34	14	7	13	55 - 42	49	8	3	6	29 - 21		6	4	7	26 - 21
8. KV Mechelen	34	13	9	12	54 - 54	48	5	5	7	29 - 30		8	4	5	25 - 24
9. K Beerschot VA	34	14	5	15	58 - 64	47	7	4	6	32 - 29		7	1	9	26 - 35
10. SV Zulte Waregem	34	14	4	16	53 - 69	46	6	2	9	23 - 38		8	2	7	30 - 31
11. Oud-Heverle Leuven	34	12	9	13	54 - 59	45	8	2	7	24 - 23		4	7	6	30 - 36
12. KAS Eupen	34	10	13	11	44 - 55	43	5	6	6	24 - 30		5	7	5	20 - 25
13. R Charleroi SC	34	11	9	14	46 - 49	42	5	6	6	18 - 16		6	3	8	28 - 33
14. KV Kortrijk	34	11	6	17	44 - 57	39	5	2	10	24 - 35		6	4	7	20 - 22
15. Sint-Truidense VV	34	10	8	16	41 - 52	38	6	3	8	20 - 20		4	5	8	21 - 32
16. Cercle Brugge KSV	34	11	3	20	40 - 51	36	6	1	10	25 - 26		5	2	10	15 - 25
17. KVRS Waasland-Beveren (*Relegation Play-offs*)	34	8	7	19	44 - 70	31	3	2	12	21 - 40		5	5	7	23 - 30
18. Royal Excel Mouscron (*Relegated*)	34	7	10	17	32 - 54	31	4	5	8	17 - 22		3	5	9	15 - 32

Teams ranked 1-4 were qualified for the Play-Off I (Championship), while teams ranked 5-8 were qualified for the Play-Off II (Europe).

Play-Off I

Please note: the points obtained during the regular season were halved (and rounded up) before the start of the playoff. As a result, the teams started with the following points before the playoff: Club Brugge KV 38, Antwerp FC 30, RSC Anderlecht Bruxelles 29, KRC Genk 28.

Round 1 [30.04.-02.05.2021]
Antwerp FC - KRC Genk 2-3(0-1)
Club Brugge - Anderlecht 2-2(0-0)

Round 2 [07-08.05.2021]
KRC Genk - Club Brugge 3-0(0-0)
Anderlecht - Antwerp FC 2-2(0-0)

Round 3 [12-13.05.2021]
KRC Genk - Anderlecht 1-1(0-1)
Antwerp FC - Club Brugge 0-0

Round 4 [15-16.05.2021]
Anderlecht - KRC Genk 1-2(1-1)
Club Brugge - Antwerp FC 2-1(0-0)

Round 5 [20.05.2021]
KRC Genk - Antwerp FC 4-0(1-0)
Anderlecht - Club Brugge 3-3(1-1)

Round 6 [23.05.2021]
Antwerp FC - Anderlecht 1-0(0-0)
Club Brugge - KRC Genk 1-2(0-0)

Final Standings

								Home					Away			
1. **Club Brugge KV**	6	1	3	2	8 - 11	44	1	1	1	5 - 5	0	2	1	3 - 6
2. KRC Genk	6	5	1	0	15 - 5	44	2	1	0	8 - 1	3	0	0	7 - 4
3. Antwerp FC	6	1	2	3	6 - 11	35	1	1	1	3 - 3	0	1	2	3 - 8
4. RSC Anderlecht Bruxelles	6	0	4	2	9 - 11	33	0	2	1	6 - 7	0	2	1	3 - 4

Play-Off II

Please note: the points obtained during the regular season were halved (and rounded up) before the start of the playoff. As a result, the teams started with the following points before the playoff: KV Oostende 27, R Standard Liège 25, KAA Gent 25, KV Mechelen 24.

Round 1 [01-02.05.2021]
KV Oostende - Standard Liège 6-2(3-2)
KAA Gent - KV Mechelen 2-2(0-2)

Round 2 [08-09.05.2021]
Standard Liège - KAA Gent 2-1(0-1)
KV Mechelen - KV Oostende 5-3(2-2)

Round 3 [13.05.2021]
KAA Gent - KV Oostende 2-1(1-0)
Standard Liège - KV Mechelen 1-2(0-1)

Round 4 [16.05.2021]
KV Oostende - KAA Gent 0-4(0-2)
KV Mechelen - Standard Liège 3-1(1-0)

Round 5 [19.05.2021]
KV Oostende - KV Mechelen 2-2(2-0)
KAA Gent - Standard Liège 2-0(1-0)

Round 6 [22.05.2021]
KV Mechelen - KAA Gent 1-2(0-0)
Standard Liège - KV Oostende 1-3(1-1)

Final Standings

								Home					Away			
5. KAA Gent	6	4	1	1	13 - 6	38	2	1	0	6 - 3	2	0	1	7 - 3
6. KV Mechelen	6	3	2	1	15 - 11	35	2	0	1	9 - 6	1	2	0	6 - 5
7. KV Oostende	6	2	1	3	15 - 16	34	1	1	1	8 - 8	1	0	2	7 - 8
8. R Standard Liège	6	1	0	5	7 - 17	28	1	0	2	4 - 6	0	0	3	3 - 11

KAA Gent were qualified for the Europa Conference League (second qualifying Round) 2021/2022.

Top goalscorers:		
33 **Ebere Paul Onuachu (NGA)**	*KRC Genk*
21 Thomas Henry (FRA)	*Oud-Heverle Leuven*
20 Gianni Bruno	*SV Zulte Waregem*
20 Roman Yaremchuk (UKR)	*KAA Gent*
18 Lukas Nmecha (GER)	*RSC Anderlecht Bruxelles*
17 Yuma Suzuki (JPN)	*Sint-Truidense VV*

Relegation Play-offs [01-08.05.2021]

RFC Seraing - KVRS Waasland-Beveren	1-1(0-0)	5-2(2-1)

RFC Seraing promoted to Jupiler Pro League 2021/2022.

NATIONAL CUP
Coupe de Belgique / Beker van België Final 2020/2021

Fifth Round [10-11.10.2020]

Waasland-Beveren - KFC Sparta Petegem	3-0(1-0)	Royale Union Saint-Gilloise - KSK Heist	4-0(1-0)
KVV THES Sport Tessenderlo - SK Deinze	3-1(1-0,1-1)	KVC Westerlo - RC Hades	5-1(3-0)
City Pirates Merksem - K Rupel Boom FC	1-2(1-1)	Olsa Brakel - FCV Dender EH	2-0(0-0)
VC Jong Lede - KSC Lokeren-Temse	0-2(0-1)	RFC Seraing - KSC Blankenberge	6-1(4-0)
R Olympic Charleroi CF - SC Eendracht Aalst	2-1(1-1,1-1)	RFC Warnant - RFC de Liège	0-1(0-1)
URSL Visé - KFC Dessel Sport	1-2(1-1,1-1)	RAA La Louviéroise - RSD Jette	2-0(1-0)
KSK Tongeren - Union St.-Ghislain Tertre-Hautrage	3-0(1-0)	Royal Knokke FC - Oud-Heverlee Leuven	0-2(0-1)
Lommel SK - KVV Zelzate	3-2(1-1)	RJ Rochefortoise FC - RWD Molenbeek	1-8(0-4)

Sixth Round [02-03.02.2021]

K Rupel Boom FC - KAS Eupen	0-5 *awarded*	KAA Gent - KSK Tongeren	5-0(2-0)
KVV THES Sport Tessenderlo - KRC Genk	0-5 *awarded*	Oud-Heverlee Leuven - Cercle Brugge KSV	2-3(1-2)
KFC Dessel Sport - K Beerschot VA	0-5 *awarded*	RFC Seraing - R Standard Liège	1-4(0-2)
Antwerp FC - RAA La Louviéroise	2-1(1-0)	Club Brugge KV - Olsa Brakel	6-1(2-1)
Royale Union Saint-Gilloise - Royal Excel Mouscron	2-1(0-1)	KSC Lokeren-Temse - Sint-Truidense VV	0-2(0-1)
Lommel SK - KV Kortrijk	1-3(0-1)	Waasland-Beveren - KV Oostende	2-3(1-1)
KV Mechelen - RWD Molenbeek	2-0(1-0)	R Olympic Charleroi CF - SV Zulte Waregem	1-0(0-0)
R Charleroi SC - KVC Westerlo	1-0(0-0)	RFC de Liège - RSC Anderlecht Bruxelles	0-2(0-1)

1/8-Finals [09-11.02.2021]

Cercle Brugge KSV - KV Oostende	3-1(1-1)	Club Brugge KV - Antwerp FC	3-1(0-0)
KV Kortrijk - R Standard Liège	1-1 aet; 5-6 pen	K Beerschot VA - KV Mechelen	0-1(0-1)
KAS Eupen - R Olympic Charleroi CF	5-1(1-1)	KAA Gent - R Charleroi SC	3-1(0-1)
KRC Genk - Sint-Truidense VV	1-0(0-0)	Royale Union S.Gilloise - RSC Anderlecht Bruxelles	0-5(0-1)

Quarter-Finals [03-04.03.2021]

KAS Eupen - KAA Gent	1-0(0-0)	KRC Genk - KV Mechelen	4-1(2-0)
RSC Anderlecht Bruxelles - Cercle Brugge KSV	1-0(1-0)	R Standard Liège - Club Brugge KV	1-0(0-0)

Semi-Finals [13-14.03.2021]

KAS Eupen - R Standard Liège	0-1(0-0)	RSC Anderlecht Bruxelles - KRC Genk	1-2(0-1)

Final

25.04.2021; Stade "Roi Baudouin", Bruxelles; Referee: Bram Van Driessche; Attendance: 0
KRC Genk - R Standard Liège   **2-1(0-0)**

Genk: Maarten Vandevoordt, Daniel Muñoz Mejia, Carlos Eccohomo Cuesta Figueroa, Jhon Janer Lucumi Bonilla, Gerardo Daniel Arteaga Zamora, Junya Ito, Patrik Hrošovský, Kristian Thorstvedt (87.Mark Alexander McKenzie), Bryan Heynen, Théo Bongonda, Ebere Paul Onuachu. Trainer: Joseph Antonius van den Brom (Netherlands).

Standard Liège: Arnaud Bodart, Hugo Siquet, Moussa Sissako [*sent off 90+2*], Konstantinos Laifis, Nicolas Gavory, Selim Amallah, Samuel Bastien (75.Maxime Lestienne), Gojko Cimirot (66.Mehdi Carcela-González), Nicolas Raskin, João Klauss de Mello, Michel Balikwisha (57.Jackson Muleka Kyanvubu). Trainer: Mbaye Leye (Senegal).

Goals: 1-0 Junya Ito (48), 2-0 Théo Bongonda (80), 2-1 Jackson Muleka Kyanvubu (83).

Royal Sporting Club Anderlecht Bruxelles

Founded: 27.05.1908
Stadium: Lotto Park [Stade "Constant Vanden Stock"], Bruxelles (21,500)
Trainer: François Vercauteren   28.10.1956
[17.08.2021]   Vincent Jean Mpoy Kompany   10.04.1986

Goalkeepers:	DOB	M	(s)	G
Hendrik Van Crombrugge	30.04.1993	12		
Bart Verbruggen (NED)	18.08.2002	6		
Timon Wellenreuther (GER)	03.12.1995	22	(1)	
Defenders:	**DOB**	**M**	**(s)**	**G**
Elias Cobbaut	24.11.1997	11	(2)	
Zeno Debast	24.10.2003		(2)	
Hannes Delcroix	28.02.1999	23		
Kemar Michael Lawrence (JAM)	17.09.1992	14	(1)	1
Lucas Lissens	25.07.2001	2		
Derrick Luckassen (NED)	03.07.1995	7	(1)	
Matthew Miazga (USA)	19.07.1995	30		1
Michael Murillo (PAN)	11.02.1996	33	(3)	4
Bogdan Mykhaylychenko (UKR)	21.03.1997	23		1
Killian Sardella	02.05.2002	13	(3)	
Ognjen Vranješ (BIH)	24.10.1989	4		
Midfielders:	**DOB**	**M**	**(s)**	**G**
Anouar Ait El Hadj	20.04.2002	22	(6)	4
Kristian Arnstad (NOR)	07.09.2003	1	(1)	
Majeed Ashimeru (GHA)	10.10.1997	9	(2)	1
Josh Cullen (IRL)	07.04.1996	20	(7)	
Marco Kana	08.08.2002	4	(4)	
Edo Kayembe (COD)	03.06.1998		(2)	
Albert Sambi Lokonga	22.10.1999	33		3
Mario Stroeykens	29.09.2004		(3)	
Percy Muzi Tau (RSA)	13.05.1994	12	(2)	4
Adrien Trebel (FRA)	03.03.1991	11	(7)	2
Yari Verschaeren	12.07.2001	18	(4)	6
Michel Vlap (NED)	02.06.1997	8	(3)	1
Peter Žulj (AUT)	09.06.1993	7	(1)	
Forwards:	**DOB**	**M**	**(s)**	**G**
Francis Amuzu	23.08.1999	18	(17)	2
Zakaria Bakkali	26.01.1996	2		
Jacob Bruun Larsen (DEN)	19.09.1998	5	(10)	2
Mustapha Bundu (SLE)	28.02.1997	5	(4)	
Antoine Colassin	26.02.2001	1	(6)	
Mohammed Dauda (GHA)	20.02.1998		(17)	1
Abdoulay Diaby (MLI)	21.05.1991	2	(7)	1
Landry Nany Dimata	01.09.1997	4	(10)	2
Jérémy Doku	27.05.2002	7		2
Paul Omo Mukairu (NGA)	18.01.2000	15	(10)	2
Lukas Nmecha (GER)	14.12.1998	36	(1)	18

Royal Antwerp Football Club

Founded: 1880
Stadium: Bosuilstadion, Antwerp (12,975)
Trainer: Ivan Leko (CRO)   07.02.1978
[04.01.2021]   François Vercauteren   28.10.1956

Goalkeepers:	DOB	M	(s)	G
Alireza Beiranvand (IRN)	21.09.1992	10		
Jean Butez (FRA)	08.06.1995	24		
Ortwin De Wolf	23.04.1997	6	(1)	
Defenders:	**DOB**	**M**	**(s)**	**G**
Dylan Batubinsika (FRA)	15.02.1996	22	(4)	3
Aurélio Gabriel Ulineia Buta (POR)	10.02.1997	16	(9)	
Ritchie De Laet	28.11.1988	39		
Jérémy Gelin (FRA)	24.04.1997	10	(2)	
Simen Juklerød (NOR)	18.05.1994	12	(7)	3
Maxime Le Marchand (FRA)	11.10.1989	13		3
Jordan Lukaku	25.07.1994	20	(2)	
Júnior Udeme Pius (NGA)	20.12.1995	4	(2)	2
Abdoulaye Seck (SEN)	04.06.1992	37		4
Midfielders:	**DOB**	**M**	**(s)**	**G**
Cristián Benavente Bristol (PER)	19.05.1994	1	(8)	2
Frank Thierry Boya (CMR)	01.07.1996	6	(6)	
Alexis De Sart	12.11.1996	3	(5)	
Pieter Gerkens	17.02.1995	31	(6)	3
Faris Haroun	22.09.1985	21	(1)	1
Martin Hongla Yma (CMR)	16.03.1998	32	(2)	3
Koji Miyoshi (JPN)	26.03.1997	14	(9)	3
Lior Refaelov (ISR)	26.04.1986	32	(1)	9
Birger Verstraete	16.04.1994	18	(5)	1
Louis Verstraete	04.05.1999	1	(2)	
Forwards:	**DOB**	**M**	**(s)**	**G**
Nana Opoku Ampomah (GHA)	02.01.1996	4	(11)	1
Felipe Nicolás Avenatti Dovillabichus (URU)	26.04.1993		(4)	
Manuel Benson	28.03.1997	1	(4)	
Jonathan Bolingi Mpangi Merikani (COD)	30.06.1994		(1)	
Nill De Pauw	06.01.1990	14	(10)	1
Didier Lamkel Zé (CMR)	17.09.1996	19	(2)	8
Guy Carel Mbenza Kamboleke (CGO)	01.04.2000		(1)	
Dieudonné Mbokani Bezua (COD)	22.11.1985	29	(3)	14
Bruny Nsimba	05.04.2000	1	(4)	

Koninklijke Beerschot Voetbalclub Antwerpen

Founded: 1921
Stadium: Olympisch Stadion, Antwerp (12,771)
Trainer: Hernán Pablo Losada (ARG)   09.05.1982
[19.01.2021]   William Still   14.10.1992

Goalkeepers:	DOB	M	(s)	G
Mike Vanhamel	16.11.1989	34		
Defenders:	**DOB**	**M**	**(s)**	**G**
Pierre Bourdin (FRA)	06.01.1994	22	(9)	3
Joren Dom	29.11.1989	25	(2)	2
Frédéric Frans	03.01.1989	31		2
Grégory Grisez	17.08.1989		(2)	
Mohamed Halaïmia (ALG)	28.08.1996	8	(8)	
Ayrton Mboko	23.10.1997	3	(1)	
Denys Prychynenko (UKR)	17.02.1992	11	(5)	1
Stipe Radić (CRO)	10.06.2000	9		1
Jan Van den Bergh	02.10.1994	27	(1)	4
Dario Van Den Buijs	12.09.1995	7	(11)	
Yan Vorogovskiy (KAZ)	07.08.1996	16	(5)	1
Midfielders:	**DOB**	**M**	**(s)**	**G**
George Broadbent (ENG)	30.09.2000		(2)	
Ismaila Coulibaly (MLI)	25.12.2000	17	(5)	5
Raphael Holzhauser (AUT)	16.02.1993	34		16
Alexander Maes	26.03.1992		(1)	
Tom Pietermaat	06.09.1992	29	(1)	
Ryan Sanusi	05.01.1992	32		1
Forwards:	**DOB**	**M**	**(s)**	**G**
Zakaria Bakkali	26.01.1996	1	(3)	
Loris Brogno	18.09.1992	9	(7)	3
Blessing Chibuike Eleke (NGA)	05.03.1996	5	(15)	1
David Mukuna-Trouet	02.10.2001		(7)	
Marius Noubissi (CMR)	28.11.1996	9	(7)	4
Euloge Mêmê Placca Fessou (TOG)	31.12.1994		(1)	
Abdoulie Sanyang (GAM)	08.05.1999	7	(12)	
Musashi Suzuki (JPN)	11.02.1994	22	(4)	6
Tarik Tissoudali (MAR)	02.04.1993	16	(3)	8

Cercle Brugge Koninklijke Sportvereniging

Founded: 1899
Stadium: "Jan Breydel" Stadium, Brugge (29,042)
Trainer: Paul Clement (ENG) — 08.01.1972
[03.02.2021] Yves Vanderhaeghe — 30.01.1970

Goalkeepers:	DOB	M	(s)	G
Sébastien Bruzzese	01.03.1989	1		
Thomas Didillon (FRA)	28.11.1995	30		
Warleson Stellion Lisboa Oliveira (BRA)	31.08.1996	3		
Defenders:	**DOB**	**M**	**(s)**	**G**
David Robert Bates (SCO)	05.10.1996	19		
Giulian Biancone (FRA)	31.03.2000	17	(1)	1
Arne Cassaert	20.11.2000	1	(1)	
Alexander Corryn	03.01.1994	6	(10)	
Robbe Decostere	08.05.1998	15	(1)	
Jean Marcelin (FRA)	12.02.2000	20		1
Strahinja Pavlović (SRB)	24.05.2001	11		1
Philippe Raux-Yao (FRA)	30.05.1999	1	(1)	
Jérémy Taravel (FRA)	17.04.1987	18		1
Naomichi Ueda (JPN)	24.10.1994	7	(1)	
Dimitar Velkovski (BUL)	22.01.1995	13	(2)	
Victor Alexander da Silva „Vitinho" (BRA)	23.07.1999	21	(7)	1

Midfielders:	DOB	M	(s)	G
Calvin Dekuyper	24.02.2000		(2)	
Olivier Deman	06.04.2000	8	(1)	
Aldom Deuro (MLI)	20.12.2000		(1)	
Kévin Hoggas (FRA)	16.11.1991	28	(4)	1
Franck Kanouté (SEN)	13.12.1998	13	(3)	1
Leonardo Adelino da Silva Lopes (POR)	30.11.1998	11	(8)	1
Johanna Ochieng Omolo (KEN)	31.07.1989	6	(4)	
Hannes Van der Bruggen	01.04.1993	5	(5)	
Charles Vanhoutte	16.09.1998	19	(9)	
Forwards:	**DOB**	**M**	**(s)**	**G**
Kevin Denkey (TOG)	30.11.2000	1	(12)	2
Alimani Gory (FRA)	30.08.1996		(2)	
Kylian Hazard	05.08.1995	15	(3)	1
Dino Hotič (BIH)	26.07.1995	26	(6)	4
Guy Carel Mbenza Kamboleke (CGO)	01.04.2000	2		2
Anthony Musaba (NED)	06.12.2000	23	(6)	6
Thibo Somers	16.03.1999	2	(19)	1
Iké Dominique Ugbo (ENG)	21.09.1998	32		16

Royal Charleroi Sporting Club

Founded: 01.01.1904
Stadium: Stade du Pays de Charleroi, Charleroi (14,000)
Trainer: Karim Belhocine (FRA) — 02.04.1978

Goalkeepers:	DOB	M	(s)	G
Rémy Descamps (FRA)	25.06.1996	14		
Nicolas Penneteau (FRA)	28.02.1981	20		
Defenders:	**DOB**	**M**	**(s)**	**G**
Reda Akbib	29.01.2001		(1)	
Maxime Busi	14.10.1999	7		
Dorian Dessoleil	07.08.1992	34		2
Modou Diagne (SEN)	03.01.1994	7	(2)	
Ivan Goranov (BUL)	10.06.1992		(2)	
Joris Kayembe Ditu	08.08.1994	34		1
Cédric Kipré (FRA)	09.12.1996	5		
Levi Malungu	12.06.2002		(1)	
Jules van Cleemput	11.04.1997	16	(2)	
Ognjen Vranješ (BIH)	24.10.1989	9		
Steeven Willems (FRA)	31.08.1990	18		
Midfielders:	**DOB**	**M**	**(s)**	**G**
Cristián Benavente Bristol (PER)	19.05.1994	1	(2)	
Amine Benchaib	18.06.1998	7	(10)	1
Christophe Diandy (SEN)	25.11.1990		(1)	

Guillaume Gillet	09.03.1984	29	(3)	
Gaëtan Hendrickx	30.03.1995		(4)	
David Henen	19.04.1996		(2)	
Marco Ilaimaharitra (MAD)	26.07.1995	22	(5)	1
Lucas Ribeiro Costa (BRA)	09.10.1998	1	(7)	
Ryota Morioka (JPN)	12.04.1991	28		2
Forwards:	**DOB**	**M**	**(s)**	**G**
Saido Berahino (BDI)	04.08.1993	5	(11)	2
Jordan Botaka (COD)	24.06.1993	9	(1)	
Massimo Bruno	17.09.1993	6	(12)	2
Anthony Descotte	03.08.2003		(1)	
Mamadou Fall (SEN)	31.12.1991	28	(1)	9
Ali Gholizadeh (IRN)	10.03.1996	32	(2)	8
Shamar Nicholson (JAM)	16.03.1997	23	(10)	9
Ken Nkuba	21.01.2002	1	(10)	
Kaveh Rezaei (IRN)	05.04.1992	18	(7)	7
Łukasz Teodorczyk (POL)	03.06.1991		(15)	
Frank Tsadjout (ITA)	28.07.1999		(3)	

Club Brugge Koninklijke Voetbalvereniging

Founded: 13.11.1891
Stadium: "Jan Breydel" Stadium, Brugge (29,042)
Trainer: Philippe Clement — 22.03.1974

Goalkeepers:	DOB	M	(s)	G
Ethan Horvath (USA)	09.06.1995	2		
Simon Luc Hildebert Mignolet	06.03.1988	38		
Defenders:	**DOB**	**M**	**(s)**	**G**
Clinton Mata Pedro Lourenço (ANG)	07.11.1992	36	(3)	1
Simon Deli (CIV)	27.10.1991	11	(2)	1
Stefano Denswil (NED)	07.05.1993	5	(7)	
Odilon Kossounou (CIV)	04.01.2001	30	(3)	1
Noah Mbamba-Muanda	05.01.2005	1		
Brandon Mechele	28.01.1993	35		2
Matej Mitrović (CRO)	10.11.1993	4	(2)	
Federico Ricca Rostagnol (URU)	01.12.1994	9	(5)	
Eduard Sobol (UKR)	20.04.1995	26	(4)	2
Ignace Van Der Brempt	01.04.2002	4	(5)	1
Midfielders:	**DOB**	**M**	**(s)**	**G**
Éder Fabián Álvarez Balanta (COL)	28.02.1993	13	(12)	1
Charles De Ketelaere	10.03.2001	26	(12)	4

Mats Rits	18.07.1993	32	(5)	2
Thomas Van Den Keybus	25.04.2001		(2)	
Hans Vanaken	24.08.1992	34	(2)	11
Ruud Vormer (NED)	11.05.1988	36	(1)	6
Forwards:	**DOB**	**M**	**(s)**	**G**
Youssouph Badji (SEN)	20.12.2001	12	(14)	4
Tahith Chong (NED)	04.12.1999	5	(5)	
Emmanuel Dennis Bonaventure (NGA)	15.11.1997	6	(3)	
Krépin Diatta (SEN)	25.02.1999	17	(2)	10
Nabil Dirar (MAR)	25.02.1986		(2)	
Bas Dost (NED)	31.05.1989	17	(2)	9
Michal Krmenčík (CZE)	15.03.1993	5	(4)	3
Noa Lang (NED)	17.06.1999	26	(3)	16
David Chidozie Okereke (NGA)	29.08.1997	7	(21)	4
Daniel Alejandro Pérez Córdova (VEN)	17.01.2002		(7)	1
Siebe Schrijvers	18.07.1996	3	(7)	

Königliche Allgemeine Sportvereinigung Eupen

Founded:	1945	
Stadium:	Kehrwegstadion, Eupen (8,363)	
Trainer:	Beñat San José Gil (ESP)	24.09.1979

Goalkeepers:	DOB	M	(s)	G
Théo Defourny	25.04.1992	20	(1)	
Ortwin De Wolf	23.04.1997	12		
Robin Himmelmann (GER)	05.02.1989	1		
Abdul Nurudeen (GHA)	08.02.1999	1		
Defenders:	**DOB**	**M**	**(s)**	**G**
Emmanuel Adjei (GHA)	16.01.1998		(2)	
Adriano Correia Claro (BRA)	26.10.1984	22	(2)	
Emmanuel Agbadou (CIV)	17.06.1997	23		1
Andreas Beck (GER)	13.03.1987	1	(18)	
Rocky Bushiri	30.11.1999	1		
Jonathan Heris	03.09.1990	19	(7)	2
Menno Robert Maria Koch (NED)	02.07.1994	9	(8)	2
Jordi Amat Maas (ESP)	21.03.1992	26	(3)	
Gary Magnée	12.10.1999	1	(1)	
Senna Miangue (CGO)	05.02.1997	22	(2)	
Benoît Poulain (FRA)	27.07.1987	15	(2)	

Midfielders:	DOB	M	(s)	G
Carlos Apna Embalo (GNB)	25.11.1994	3	(5)	
Marciano Aziz	13.07.2001		(1)	
Jens Cools	16.10.1990	19	(4)	1
Edo Kayembe (COD)	03.06.1998	19	(4)	
Isaac Nuhu (GHA)	22.06.2002	5	(2)	1
Stef Peeters	09.02.1992	33		3
Nils Schouterden	14.12.1988	8	(2)	
Víctor Vázquez Solsona (ESP)	20.01.1987		(1)	
Forwards:	**DOB**	**M**	**(s)**	**G**
Amara Baby (SEN)	23.02.1989	12	(12)	2
Aleksandar Boljević (MNE)	12.12.1995	6	(1)	
Mamadou Koné (CIV)	25.12.1991	7	(7)	
Knowledge Musona (ZIM)	21.06.1990	22	(2)	7
Konan N'Dri (CIV)	27.10.2000	22	(11)	1
Julien N'Goy	02.11.1997	22	(10)	5
Smail Prevljak (BIH)	10.05.1995	23	(4)	16

Koninklijke Racing Club Genk

Founded:	1988	
Stadium:	Luminus Arena, Genk (24,956)	
Trainer:	Hannes Wolf (GER)	15.04.1981
[15.09.2020]	Domenico Olivieri (ITA)	16.01.1968
[24.09.2020]	Jess Christian Thorup (DEN)	21.02.1970
[08.11.2020]	Joseph Antonius van den Brom (NED)	04.10.1966

Goalkeepers:	DOB	M	(s)	G
Maarten Vandevoordt	26.02.2002	16		
Danny Vuković (AUS)	27.03.1985	24		
Defenders:	**DOB**	**M**	**(s)**	**G**
Gerardo Daniel Arteaga Zamora (MEX)	07.09.1998	21	(4)	1
Carlos Eccohomo Cuesta Figueroa (COL)	09.03.1999	34		
Jhon Janer Lucumi Bonilla (COL)	26.06.1998	36	(2)	
Joakim Mæhle (DEN)	20.05.1997	16		1
Mark Alexander McKenzie (USA)	25.02.1999	8	(5)	
Daniel Muñoz Mejia (COL)	25.05.1996	37	(3)	
Mats Møller Dæhli (NOR)	02.03.1995	3	(2)	
Ángelo Smit Preciado Quiñónez (ECU)	18.02.1998	7	(3)	
Jere Uronen (FIN)	13.07.1994	21	(1)	
Dries Wouters	28.01.1997	4	(4)	

Midfielders:	DOB	M	(s)	G
Pierre Dwomoh	21.06.2004		(2)	
Kouassi Eboue (CIV)	13.12.1997	7	(11)	
Bryan Heynen	06.02.1997	27	(2)	2
Patrik Hrošovský (SVK)	22.04.1992	27	(3)	2
Luca Oyen	14.03.2003	4	(16)	
Elias Sierra-Cappelleti	25.08.2001		(1)	
Kristian Thorstvedt (NOR)	13.03.1999	22	(8)	7
Bastien Toma (SUI)	24.06.1999	12	(7)	2
Forwards:	**DOB**	**M**	**(s)**	**G**
Théo Bongonda	20.11.1995	34	(1)	16
Cyriel Dessers (NGA)	08.12.1994	5	(26)	7
Junya Ito (JPN)	09.03.1993	37	(1)	11
Bryan Limbombe	14.05.2001		(4)	
Benjamin Nygren (SWE)	08.07.2001	1	(2)	
Ebere Paul Onuachu (NGA)	28.05.1994	37	(2)	33

Koninklijke Atletiek Associatie Gent

Founded:	1900	
Stadium:	Ghelamco Arena, Gent (20,000)	
Trainer:	Jess Christian Thorup (DEN)	21.02.1970
[20.08.2020]	László Bölöni (ROU)	11.03.1953
[14.09.2020]	Wim De Decker	06.04.1982
[04.12.2020]	Hein Vanhaezebrouck	16.02.1964

Goalkeepers:	DOB	M	(s)	G
Sinan Bolat (TUR)	03.09.1988	33		
Thomas Kaminski	23.10.1992	1		
Davy Roef	06.02.1994	6		
Defenders:	**DOB**	**M**	**(s)**	**G**
Dino Arslanagić	24.04.1993	12	(4)	
Alessio Castro-Montes	17.05.1997	37		7
Bruno Godeau	10.05.1992	13	(4)	1
Andreas Hanche-Olsen (NOR)	17.01.1997	31		1
Milad Mohammadi (IRN)	29.09.1993	27	(5)	1
Michael Ngadeu-Ngadjui (CMR)	23.11.1990	26	(1)	1
Núrio Domingos Matias Fortuna (ANG)	24.03.1995	24	(2)	1
Igor Plastun (UKR)	20.08.1990	9	(5)	2
Midfielders:	**DOB**	**M**	**(s)**	**G**
Roman Bezus (UKR)	26.09.1990	20	(8)	6
Giorgi Chakvetadze (GEO)	29.08.1999	2	(1)	
Alexandre De Bruyn	04.06.1994		(5)	2
Brecht Dejaegere	29.05.1991		(1)	
Niklas Dorsch (GER)	15.01.1998	23	(10)	3

	DOB	M	(s)	G
Wouter George	03.03.2002		(1)	
Sven Kums	26.02.1988	32	(4)	3
Sulayman Marreh (GAM)	15.01.1996	9	(5)	
Vadis Odjidja-Ofoe	21.02.1989	19	(6)	2
Adewale Oladoye (NGA)	25.08.2001		(1)	
Elisha Owusu (FRA)	07.11.1997	19	(6)	
Mathéo Parmentier	31.10.2002		(1)	
Matisse Samoise	21.11.2001	4	(5)	1
Forwards:	**DOB**	**M**	**(s)**	**G**
Jordan Rolly Botaka (COD)	24.06.1993	4	(4)	
Osman Bukari (GHA)	13.12.1998	18	(8)	4
Laurent Depoitre	07.12.1988	11	(12)	2
Chinonso Emeka (NGA)	30.08.2001		(1)	
Tim Kleindienst (GER)	31.08.1995	4	(11)	1
Yonas Malede (ISR)	14.11.1999	4	(7)	1
Dylan Mbayo	11.10.2001		(4)	
Anderson Niangbo (CIV)	06.10.1999	11	(7)	1
Tarik Tissoudali (MAR)	02.04.1993	7	(7)	5
Roman Yaremchuk (UKR)	27.11.1995	34		20

Koninklijke Voetbalclub Kortrijk

Founded: 1901
Stadium: Guldensporen Stadion, Kortrijk (9,399)
Trainer: Yves Vanderhaeghe   30.01.1970
[31.01.2021] Luka Elsner (SVN)   02.08.1982

Goalkeepers:	DOB	M	(s)	G
Marko Ilić (SRB)	03.02.1998	22		
Adam Jakubech (SVK)	02.01.1997	12		
Defenders:	**DOB**	**M**	**(s)**	**G**
Kristof D'Haene	06.06.1990	7	(1)	
Timothy Derijck	25.05.1987	32	(1)	1
Gilles Dewaele	13.02.1996	29	(1)	3
Petar Golubović (SRB)	13.07.1994	24	(3)	
Brendan Hines-Ike (USA)	07.04.1994	8		
Aleksandar Radovanović (SRB)	11.11.1993	7		
Lucas Rougeaux (FRA)	10.03.1994	14	(2)	
Trent Lucas Sainsbury (AUS)	05.01.1992	15	(2)	2
Midfielders:	**DOB**	**M**	**(s)**	**G**
Abdul Jeleel Ajagun (NGA)	10.02.1993		(3)	
Julien De Sart	23.12.1994	23	(1)	1
Gaëtan Hendrickx	30.03.1995	3	(3)	
Michiel Jonckheere	03.01.1990	13	(11)	2
Christophe Lepoint	24.10.1984	3	(4)	

	DOB	M	(s)	G
Evgeniy Makarenko (UKR)	21.05.1991	24	(4)	3
Ante Palaversa (CRO)	06.04.2000	6	(3)	2
Loïc Ritière	25.07.2001	1		
Sambou Sissoko (MLI)	29.06.2000	3		
Jovan Stojanović (SRB)	21.04.1992	1	(20)	
Hannes Van der Bruggen	01.04.1993	14	(3)	1
Forwards:	**DOB**	**M**	**(s)**	**G**
Muhammed Badamosi (GAM)	27.12.1997		(10)	
Teddy Chevalier (FRA)	28.06.1987	9	(5)	
Zinho Gano	13.10.1993	9	(2)	6
Pape Gueye (SEN)	20.09.1999	21	(10)	5
Ilombe M'Boyo	22.04.1987	19		8
Teremas Igobor Moffi (NGA)	25.05.1999	2		1
Eric Ocansey (GHA)	22.08.1997	29	(2)	1
Faïz Selemani (COM)	14.11.1993	23	(7)	8
Luqman Shamsudin (MAS)	05.03.2002	1	(1)	
Yani van den Bossche	01.06.2001		(8)	

Koninklijke Voetbalclub Mechelen

Founded: 1904
Stadium: AFAS-stadion Achter de Kazerne, Mechelen (1904)
Trainer: Wouter Vrancken   03.02.1979

Goalkeepers:	DOB	M	(s)	G
Gaëtan Coucke	03.11.1998	16		
Yannick Thoelen	18.07.1990	24		
Defenders:	**DOB**	**M**	**(s)**	**G**
Sheldon Michael Louis Bateau (TRI)	29.01.1991	9	(3)	1
Lucas Bijker (NED)	04.03.1993	32		
Rocky Bushiri Kisonga	30.11.1999	6		
Issa Kaboré (BFA)	12.05.2001	15	(12)	
Thibault Peyre (FRA)	03.10.1992	31	(2)	
Jules van Cleemput	04.02.1997		(1)	
Jordi Vanlerberghe	27.06.1996	27	(4)	2
Siemen Voet	03.02.2000	8	(1)	1
Sandy Walsh (NED)	14.03.1995	29	(1)	3
Victor Wernersson (SWE)	06.07.1995	7	(1)	

Midfielders:	DOB	M	(s)	G
Steven Arnold Defour	15.04.1988	9	(7)	
Geoffry Hairemans	21.10.1991	36	(3)	8
Onur Kaya	20.04.1986	3	(26)	
Kerim Mrabti (SWE)	20.05.1994	35		7
Rob Schoofs	23.03.1994	38	(2)	6
Joachim Van Damme	23.07.1991	23		2
Aster Vranckx	04.10.2002	21	(13)	4
Forwards:	**DOB**	**M**	**(s)**	**G**
Igor de Camargo	12.05.1983	15	(18)	9
Ferdy Druijf (NED)	12.02.1998	11	(9)	6
Gustav Engvall (SWE)	29.04.1996	7	(6)	
Marian Shved (UKR)	16.07.1997	9	(13)	4
Nikola Storm	30.09.1994	23	(11)	11
William Togui (CIV)	07.08.1996	6	(8)	1

Royal Excel Mouscron

Founded: 1922 (*as RRC Péruwelz*)
Stadium: Stade Le Canonnier, Mouscron (10,571)
Trainer: Fernando Da Cruz   25.10.1972
[20.10.2020] António Jorge Rocha Simão (POR)   12.08.1976

Goalkeepers:	DOB	M	(s)	G
Hervé Koffi (BFA)	16.10.1996	34		
Defenders:	**DOB**	**M**	**(s)**	**G**
Saad Agouzoul (MAR)	10.08.1997	33		1
Nemanja Antonov (SRB)	06.05.1995	2		
Eric Bocat (FRA)	16.07.1999	8		
Alessandro Ciranni	28.06.1996	31		1
Kouadio-Yves Dabila (CIV)	01.01.1997	6	(1)	
El Hadji Gueye (SEN)	20.08.1999	2	(1)	
Robbe Quirynen	03.11.2001	7	(3)	
Matías Agustín Silvestre (ARG)	25.09.1984	24		3
Midfielders:	**DOB**	**M**	**(s)**	**G**
Marko Bakić (MNE)	01.11.1993	17	(5)	2
Bruno Alexandre Vieira Almeida „Bruno Xadas“ (POR)	02.12.1997	20	(5)	2
Deni Hočko (MNE)	22.04.1994	24	(5)	
Christophe Lepoint	24.10.1984	8	(3)	1
Dimitri Mohamed (FRA)	11.06.1989	20		2

	DOB	M	(s)	G
Darly N'Landu (FRA)	14.07.2000	5	(6)	
Jean Emile Junior Onana Onana (CMR)	08.01.2000	26	(2)	2
Enes Sağlık	08.07.1991		(2)	
Benjamin Van Durmen	20.03.1997	4	(3)	
Forwards:	**DOB**	**M**	**(s)**	**G**
Béni Badibanga	19.02.1996	11	(15)	
Charles-Andreas Brym (CAN)	08.08.1998	2	(5)	
Osvaldo Pedro Capemba „Capita“ (ANG)	10.01.2002		(3)	
Imad Faraj (FRA)	11.02.1999	11	(16)	1
Harlem Gnohéré (FRA)	21.02.1988	8	(13)	2
Hamdi Harbaoui (TUN)	05.01.1985	3	(7)	2
Nuno Miguel da Costa Jóia (CPV)	10.02.1991	24	(1)	6
Fabrice Olinga Essono (CMR)	12.05.1996	19	(5)	2
Omo Cedric Omoigui Olague (NGA)	11.11.1994		(1)	
Virgiliu Postolachi (FRA)	17.03.2000	4	(2)	
Serge Tabekou Ouambe (CMR)	15.10.1996	21	(9)	4

Koninklijke Voetbalclub Oostende

Founded: 1904
Stadium: Versluys Arena, Ostend (8,432)
Trainer: Alexander Blessin (GER)   28.05.1973

Goalkeepers:	DOB	M	(s)	G
Bram Castro	30.09.1982	3	(1)	
Guillaume Hubert	11.01.1994	37		
Defenders:	**DOB**	**M**	**(s)**	**G**
Jelle Bataille	20.05.1999	34	(3)	1
Brecht Capon	24.04.1988	9	(3)	1
Robbie D'Haese	25.02.1999	21	(7)	1
Jack Hendry (SCO)	07.05.1995	29	(1)	2
Frederik Jäkel (GER)	07.03.2001	14	(2)	
Théo Matam (FRA)	20.04.2000	9	(13)	1
Manuel Osifo	31.07.2003		(1)	
Ari Skúlason (ISL)	14.05.1987	15	(5)	
Anton Tanghe	28.01.1999	31		1
Arthur Theate	25.05.2000	35		5

Midfielders:	DOB	M	(s)	G
Nick Bätzner (GER)	15.03.2000	13	(11)	1
Indy Boonen	04.01.1999	5	(11)	2
Maxime D'Arpino (FRA)	17.06.1996	39		1
Andrew Hjulsager (DEN)	15.01.1995	36	(1)	6
François Marquet	17.04.1995	3	(11)	
Cameron McGeehan (NIR)	06.04.1995	8	(12)	3
Evangelos Patoulidis	24.09.2001	1	(3)	
Kévin Vandendriessche (FRA)	07.08.1989	27	(7)	5
Forwards:	**DOB**	**M**	**(s)**	**G**
Makhtar Gueye (SEN)	04.12.1997	27	(6)	11
Sindrit Guri (ALB)	23.10.1993		(3)	
Marko Kvasina (AUT)	20.12.1996	11	(22)	5
Fashion Sakala (ZAM)	14.03.1997	31	(2)	16
Mamadou Thiam (SEN)	20.03.1995	2	(19)	

Oud-Heverlee Leuven

Founded:	2002	
Stadium:	Stadion Den Dreef, Leuven (10,000)	
Trainer:	Marc Brys	10.05.1962

Goalkeepers:	DOB	M	(s)	G
Daniel Lønne Iversen (DEN)	19.07.1997	5		
Darren Keet (RSA)	05.08.1989	1		
Rafael Enrique Romo Pérez (VEN)	25.02.1990	28	(1)	
Kawin Thamsatchanan (THA)	26.01.1990		(1)	
Defenders:	**DOB**	**M**	**(s)**	**G**
Filip Benković (CRO)	13.07.1997	1		
Barnabás Bese (HUN)	06.05.1994	7	(5)	
Casper De Norre	07.02.1997	23		1
Frédéric Duplus (FRA)	07.04.1990	6		1
Václav Jemelka (CZE)	23.06.1995	21	(2)	
Sascha Kotysch (GER)	02.10.1988	19	(1)	1
Pierre-Yves Ngawa	09.02.1992	22	(5)	1
Dylan Ouédraogo (BFA)	22.07.1998	8	(1)	
Louis Patris	07.06.2001	2		
Toon Raemaekers	09.09.2000	7	(3)	
Kenneth Schuermans	25.05.1991	1		
Derrick Tshimanga	06.11.1988	6	(4)	
Midfielders:	**DOB**	**M**	**(s)**	**G**
Isaac Asante	29.08.2002	3	(2)	
David Hubert	12.02.1988	30	(1)	1
Aboubakar Keita (CIV)	05.11.1997		(3)	
Mandela Keita	10.05.2002	1		
Andrew Philip King (WAL)	29.10.1988		(1)	
Mathieu Maertens	27.03.1995	17	(1)	3
Kristiyan Malinov (BUL)	30.03.1994	25	(2)	2
Xavier Mercier (FRA)	25.07.1989	34		10
Kamal Sowah (GHA)	09.01.2000	34		8
Tom Van Hyfte	28.04.1986		(1)	
Forwards:	**DOB**	**M**	**(s)**	**G**
Yannick Aguemon (BEN)	11.02.1992	2	(4)	
Musa Suleiman Al Tamari (JOR)	10.06.1997	11	(11)	1
Arthur Allemeersch	27.07.2001	1	(1)	
Yohan Croizet (FRA)	15.02.1992	2	(3)	
Joshua Eppiah	11.10.1998		(11)	1
Thomas Henry (FRA)	20.09.1994	31		21
Olivier Myny	10.11.1994	2	(14)	
Jérémy Perbet (FRA)	12.12.1984		(2)	
Siebe Schrijvers	18.07.1996	5	(7)	2
Milan Tučić (SVN)	15.08.1996		(1)	
Daan Vekemans	22.02.2000	2	(12)	
Thibault Vlietinck	19.08.1997	17	(2)	1

Koninklijke Sint-Truidense Voetbalvereniging

Founded:	1924	
Stadium:	Stayen Stadium, Sint-Truiden (14,600)	
Trainer:	Kevin Vincent Muscat (AUS)	07.08.1973
[01.12.2020]	Stef Van Winckel	06.04.1967
[08.12.2020]	Peter Maes	01.06.1964

Goalkeepers:	DOB	M	(s)	G
Daniel Schmidt (JPN)	03.02.1992	24		
Kenny Steppe	14.11.1988	10		
Defenders:	**DOB**	**M**	**(s)**	**G**
Jonathan Buatu (ANG)	27.09.1993	26	(3)	1
Liberato Cacace (NZL)	27.09.2000	27		
Maximiliano Caufriez	16.02.1997	18	(1)	1
Daiki Hashioka (JPN)	17.05.1999	5	(1)	
Wolke Janssens	11.01.1995	5	(4)	
Avelino Jorge Filipe Teixeira (POR)	27.08.1986	20		1
Pol García Tena (ESP)	18.02.1995	15	(1)	1
Júnior Udeme Pius (NGA)	20.12.1995	4		
Dimitri Lavalée	13.01.1997	11		
Ko Matsubara (JPN)	30.08.1996	5	(2)	
Samy Mmaee	08.09.1996	9	(2)	
Ibrahima Sankhon (GUI)	01.01.1996	12	(4)	
Midfielders:	**DOB**	**M**	**(s)**	**G**
Samuel Asamoah (GHA)	23.03.1994	14	(4)	
Christian Brüls	30.09.1988	12	(2)	1
Santiago Colombatto (ARG)	17.01.1997	10	(1)	
Steve De Ridder	25.02.1987	25		1
Chris Durkin (USA)	08.02.2000	20	(8)	1
Jhonny Lucas Flora Barbosa (BRA)	21.02.2000	1	(2)	
Mory Konaté (GUI)	15.11.1993	8	(7)	
Jarne Steuckers	04.02.2002	1	(5)	
Stan Van Dessel	24.07.2001	2	(4)	
Forwards:	**DOB**	**M**	**(s)**	**G**
Nelson Balongo (COD)	15.04.1999		(7)	1
Facundo Colidio (ARG)	04.01.2000	17	(14)	2
Oleksandr Filippov (UKR)	23.10.1992	7	(8)	1
Tatsuya Ito (JPN)	26.06.1997		(7)	
Lee Seung-woo (KOR)	06.01.1998	7	(6)	2
Ilombe M'Boyo	22.04.1987	14	(1)	4
Keito Nakamura (JPN)	28.07.2000	2	(3)	1
Duckens Moses Nazon (HAI)	07.04.1994	9	(13)	6
Yuma Suzuki (JPN)	26.04.1996	34		17

Royal Standard de Liège

Founded:	1898	
Stadium:	Stade "Maurice Dufrasne", Liège (30,023)	
Trainer:	Philippe Jacques William Montanier (FRA)	15.11.1964
[30.12.2020]	Mbaye Leye (SEN)	01.12.1982

Goalkeepers:	DOB	M	(s)	G
Arnaud Bodart	11.03.1998	37		1
Jean-François Gillet	31.05.1979	2	(1)	
Laurent Henkinet	14.09.1992	1		
Defenders:	**DOB**	**M**	**(s)**	**G**
Bopé Bokadi (COD)	21.05.1996	27	(4)	4
Allan Delferriere	03.03.2002	4	(1)	
Noë Dussenne	07.04.1992	19	(4)	2
Collins Fai (CMR)	13.08.1992	16	(3)	
Nicolas Gavory (FRA)	16.02.1995	36	(1)	1
Laurent Jans (LUX)	05.08.1992	6	(7)	
Konstantinos Laifis (CYP)	19.05.1993	27	(4)	1
Nathan Ngoy	10.06.2003	1		
Hugo Siquet	09.07.2002	18	(2)	
Moussa Sissako (MLI)	10.11.2000	7	(1)	
Zinho Vanheusden	29.07.1999	9	(3)	
Mërgim Vojvoda (KVX)	01.02.1995	3		
Midfielders:	**DOB**	**M**	**(s)**	**G**
Selim Amallah (MAR)	15.11.1996	24	(3)	10
Samuel Bastien	26.09.1996	27	(2)	4
Alexandro Calut	22.04.2003	2	(1)	
Gojko Cimirot (BIH)	19.12.1992	21	(4)	
Damjan Pavlović	09.07.2001	3	(6)	
Nicolas Raskin	23.02.2001	29	(3)	2
Eden Shamir (ISR)	25.06.1995	7	(9)	
Forwards:	**DOB**	**M**	**(s)**	**G**
Felipe Nicolás Avenatti Dovillabichus (URU)	26.04.1993	5	(5)	1
Michel Balikwisha	10.05.2001	23	(7)	9
William Balikwisha	12.05.1999	1	(4)	
Aleksandar Boljević (MNE)	12.12.1995	3	(3)	
Mehdi Carcela-González (MAR)	01.07.1989	12	(15)	2
Duje Čop (CRO)	01.02.1990	5	(5)	
João Klauss de Mello (BRA)	01.03.1997	16	(3)	5
Maxime Lestienne	17.06.1992	24	(9)	5
Jackson Muleka Kyanvubu (COD)	04.10.1999	14	(9)	9
Obbi Oularé	08.01.1996	5	(7)	2
Eddy Sylvestre (FRA)	29.08.1999	1		
Abdoul Tapsoba (BFA)	23.08.2001	5	(18)	

Koninklijke Voetbalclub Red Star Waasland-Sportkring-Beveren

Founded:	2010 (*merged with KSK Beveren*)	
Stadium:	Freethiel Stadion, Beveren (8,190)	
Trainer:	Nicky Hayen	16.08.1980

Goalkeepers:	DOB	M	(s)	G
Brent Gabriël	27.01.1999	2		
Nordin Jackers	05.09.1997	28		
Lucas Pirard	10.03.1995	4		

Defenders:	DOB	M	(s)	G
Felix Bastians (GER)	09.05.1988	9		
Maximiliano Caufriez	16.02.1997	4		
Daam Foulon	23.03.1999		(1)	
Alexis Yohaslin Gamboa Rojas (CRC)	20.03.1999	7	(1)	
Amine Khammas (MAR)	06.04.1999	12		
Serge Sedoine Tchaha Leuko (CMR)	04.08.1993	11	(3)	
Jenthe Mertens	18.10.1999	6	(8)	
Luís Miguel Vieira Silva (POR)	08.10.1990	6		
Brendan Schoonbaert	09.05.2000	22	(5)	
Jur Schryvers	11.03.1997	18	(7)	1
Andrija Vukčević (MNE)	11.10.1996	7	(2)	
Aleksandar Vukotić (SRB)	22.07.1995	24	(2)	2
Andreas Wiegel (GER)	21.07.1991	13	(1)	
Dries Wuytens	18.03.1991	22	(2)	1

Midfielders:	DOB	M	(s)	G
Leonardo Bertone (SUI)	14.03.1994	28		1
Djihad Bizimana (RWA)	12.12.1996	3	(3)	
Daan Heymans	15.06.1999	25	(5)	8
Denzel Jubitana	06.05.1999		(5)	
Yuki Kobayashi (JPN)	24.04.1992	1		
Georges Constant Mandjeck (CMR)	09.12.1988	16		
Sivert Heltne Nilsen (NOR)	02.10.1991	8	(1)	
Matthias Verreth	20.02.1998	2	(2)	
Louis Verstraete	04.05.1999	5		3

Forwards:	DOB	M	(s)	G
Alessandro Albanese	12.01.2000	16	(7)	1
Jeremy Cijntje (CUW)	08.01.1998		(4)	
Joseph Isiah Efford (USA)	29.08.1996	12	(14)	2
Jordan Faucher (FRA)	06.11.1991	5	(11)	2
Michael Frey (SUI)	19.07.1994	27		12
Aboubakary Koita	20.09.1998	20	(7)	7
Stefan Milošević (MNE)	23.06.1996	1	(2)	
Tom Reyners	20.04.2000		(1)	
Danel Sinani (LUX)	05.04.1997	10	(8)	3
Din Sula (ALB)	02.03.1998		(6)	1

Sportvereniging Zulte Waregem

Founded:	01.07.2001	
Stadium:	Regenboogstadion, Waregem (12,500)	
Trainer:	Francky Dury	11.10.1957

Goalkeepers:	DOB	M	(s)	G
Eike Bansen (GER)	21.02.1998	6		
Louis Bostyn	04.10.1993	28		

Defenders:	DOB	M	(s)	G
William Bianda (FRA)	30.04.2000	6	(1)	
Laurens De Bock	07.11.1992	30	(1)	2
Olivier Deschacht	16.02.1981	33		2
Cameron Humphreys Grant (ENG)	22.08.1998	25	(1)	
Nikolaos Kainourgios (GRE)	08.09.1998	9	(6)	2
Dan Opare (GHA)	18.10.1990	27	(2)	
Ewoud Pletinckx	10.10.2000	12	(11)	2

Midfielders:	DOB	M	(s)	G
Mathieu De Smet	27.04.2000	3	(5)	1
Omar Nicolás Govea García (MEX)	18.01.1996	27	(1)	2
Damien Marcq (FRA)	08.12.1988	26	(1)	
Ibrahima Seck (SEN)	10.08.1989	30	(1)	2
Abdoulaye Sissako (FRA)	26.05.1998	7	(13)	
Jannes Van Hecke	15.01.2002	9	(3)	

Forwards:	DOB	M	(s)	G
Panagiotis Armenakas (AUS)	05.08.1998	2	(7)	2
Saido Berahino (BDI)	04.08.1993	6	(2)	2
Gianni Bruno	19.08.1991	33	(1)	20
Tomáš Chorý (CZE)	26.01.1995	9	(7)	4
Antoine Benjamin Colassin	26.02.2001		(10)	
Jean-Luc Dompé (FRA)	12.08.1995	14	(13)	6
Mikael Soisalo (FIN)	24.04.1998	1	(1)	
Bassem Srarfi (TUN)	25.06.1997	8	(10)	
Idrissa Sylla (GUI)	03.12.1990		(2)	
Youssuf Sylla	19.12.2002	1	(2)	
Jelle Vossen	22.03.1989	22	(7)	6

SECOND LEVEL
First Division B 2020/2021

1.	Royale Union Saint-Gilloise (*Promoted*)	28	22	4	2	69 - 24	70
2.	RFC Seraing (*Promotion Play-offs*)	28	16	4	8	54 - 37	52
3.	Lommel SK	28	13	4	11	49 - 47	43
4.	KVC Westerlo	28	10	13	5	41 - 30	43
5.	KMSK Deinze	28	10	9	9	45 - 46	39
6.	RWD Molenbeek	28	10	5	13	44 - 48	35
7.	Lierse Kempenzonen	28	4	4	20	25 - 54	16
8.	Club NXT Brugge	28	2	7	19	23 - 64	13

Please note: Club NXT Brugge was not eligible for promotion or relegation, being disbanded after the season.

BELGIUM NATIONAL TEAM

INTERNATIONAL MATCHES
(16.07.2020 – 15.07.2021)

05.09.2020	København	Denmark - Belgium	0-2(0-1)	(UNL)
08.09.2020	Bruxelles	Belgium - Iceland	5-1(2-1)	(UNL)
08.10.2020	Bruxelles	Belgium - Ivory Coast	1-1(0-0)	(F)
11.10.2020	London	England - Belgium	2-1(1-1)	(UNL)
14.10.2020	Reykjavík	Iceland - Belgium	1-2(1-2)	(UNL)
11.11.2020	Leuven	Belgium - Switzerland	2-1(0-1)	(F)
15.11.2020	Leuven	Belgium - England	2-0(2-0)	(UNL)
18.11.2020	Leuven	Belgium - Denmark	4-2(1-1)	(UNL)
24.03.2021	Leuven	Belgium - Wales	3-1(2-1)	(WCQ)
27.03.2021	Praha	Czech Republic - Belgium	1-1(0-0)	(WCQ)
30.03.2021	Leuven	Belgium - Belarus	8-0(4-0)	(WCQ)
03.06.2021	Bruxelles	Belgium - Greece	1-1(1-0)	(F)
06.06.2021	Bruxelles	Belgium - Croatia	1-0(1-0)	(F)
12.06.2021	Saint Petersburg	Belgium - Russia	3-0(2-0)	(EC)
17.06.2021	København	Denmark - Belgium	1-2(1-0)	(EC)
21.06.2021	Saint Petersburg	Finland - Belgium	0-2(0-0)	(EC)
27.06.2021	Sevilla	Belgium - Portugal	1-0(1-0)	(EC)
02.07.2021	München	Belgium - Italy	1-2(1-2)	(EC)

05.09.2020   DENMARK - BELGIUM   0-2(0-1)   2nd UEFA Nations League A, Group 2
Parken Stadium, City; Referee: Sandro Schärer (Switzerland); Attendance: 0
BEL: Simon Luc Hildebert Mignolet, Jan Bert Lieve Vertonghen (Cap), Toby Albertine Maurits Alderweireld, Timothy Castagne, Jason Grégory Marianne Denayer, Axel Tomas Laurent Angel Lambert Witsel, Yannick Ferreira Carrasco (57.Dennis Pierre Jacques Albert Praet), Thorgan Ganael Francis Hazard, Youri Marion Tielemans (87.Jeremy Doku), Dries Mertens (80.Leandro Trossard), Romelu Menama Lukaku Bolingoli. Trainer: Roberto Martínez Montoliu (Spain).
Goals: Jason Grégory Marianne Denayer (9), Dries Mertens (77).

08.09.2020   BELGIUM - ICELAND   5-1(2-1)   2nd UEFA Nations League A, Group 2
Stade "Roi Baudouin", Bruxelles; Referee: Paweł Raczkowski (Poland); Attendance: 0
BEL: Koen Casteels (55.Simon Luc Hildebert Mignolet), Thomas Meunier, Jan Bert Lieve Vertonghen, Toby Albertine Maurits Alderweireld (Cap), Jason Grégory Marianne Denayer, Axel Tomas Laurent Angel Lambert Witsel, Kevin De Bruyne (80.Hans Vanaken), Thorgan Ganael Francis Hazard (65.Yari Verschaeren), Dries Mertens, Michy Batshuayi-Atunga, Jeremy Doku. Trainer: Roberto Martínez Montoliu (Spain).
Goals: Axel Tomas Laurent Angel Lambert Witsel (13), Michy Batshuayi-Atunga-Atunga (17), Dries Mertens (50), Michy Batshuayi-Atunga-Atunga (69), Jeremy Doku (80).

08.10.2020   BELGIUM - IVORY COAST   1-1(0-0)   Friendly International
Stade "Roi Baudouin", Bruxelles; Referee: Serdar Gözübüyük (Netherlands); Attendance: 7,000
BEL: Simon Luc Hildebert Mignolet (Cap), (77.Hendrik Van Crombrugge), Anga Dedryck Boyata, Leander Dendoncker, Brandon Mechele, Timothy Castagne (90.Joris Kayembe Ditu), Zinho Vanheusden (77.Sebastiaan Bornauw), Hans Vanaken, Alexis Jesse Saelemaekers, Leandro Trossard (68.Yari Verschaeren), Michy Batshuayi-Atunga (68.Christian Benteke Liolo), Jeremy Doku (68.Divock Okoth Origi). Trainer: Roberto Martínez Montoliu (Spain).
Goal: Michy Batshuayi-Atunga-Atunga (54).

11.10.2020   ENGLAND - BELGIUM   2-1(1-1)   2nd UEFA Nations League A, Group 2
Wembley Stadium, London; Referee: Tobias Stieler (Germany); Attendance: 0
BEL: Simon Luc Hildebert Mignolet, Thomas Meunier, Toby Albertine Maurits Alderweireld, Anga Dedryck Boyata, Timothy Castagne, Jason Grégory Marianne Denayer, Axel Tomas Laurent Angel Lambert Witsel, Kevin De Bruyne (Cap) (73.Yari Verschaeren), Yannick Ferreira Carrasco (83.Jeremy Doku), Youri Marion Tielemans, Romelu Menama Lukaku Bolingoli. Trainer: Roberto Martínez Montoliu (Spain).
Goal: Romelu Menama Lukaku Bolingoli (16 penalty).

14.10.2020   ICELAND - BELGIUM   1-2(1-2)   2nd UEFA Nations League A, Group 2
Laugardalsvöllur, Reykjavík; Referee: Andris Treimanis (Latvia); Attendance: 59
BEL: Simon Luc Hildebert Mignolet, Thomas Meunier, Toby Albertine Maurits Alderweireld, Anga Dedryck Boyata, Jason Grégory Marianne Denayer, Axel Tomas Laurent Angel Lambert Witsel, Leandro Trossard (61.Hans Vanaken), Yannick Ferreira Carrasco, Youri Marion Tielemans, Romelu Menama Lukaku Bolingoli (Cap), Jeremy Doku (68.Timothy Castagne). Trainer: Roberto Martínez Montoliu (Spain).
Goals: Romelu Menama Lukaku Bolingoli (9, 38 penalty).

11.11.2020   BELGIUM - SWITZERLAND   2-1(0-1)   Friendly International
Den Dreef Stadion, Leuven; Referee: Jérôme Brissard (France); Attendance: 0
BEL: Simon Luc Hildebert Mignolet, Jan Bert Lieve Vertonghen (Cap), (58.Hannes Delcroix), Brandon Mechele, Hans Vanaken, Dennis Pierre Jacques Albert Praet, Sebastiaan Bornauw (90+2.Jason Grégory Marianne Denayer), Thorgan Ganael Francis Hazard (90+1.Charles De Ketelaere), Leander Dendoncker (46.Youri Marion Tielemans), Michy Batshuayi-Atunga, Dodi Lukébakio Ngandoli (83.Joris Kayembe Ditu). Trainer: Roberto Martínez Montoliu (Spain).
Goals: Michy Batshuayi-Atunga (49, 70).

15.11.2020   BELGIUM - ENGLAND   2-0(2-0)   2nd UEFA Nations League A, Group 2
Den Dreef Stadion, Leuven; Referee: Referee: Danny Desmond Makkelie (Netherlands); Attendance: 0
BEL: Thibaut Nicolas Marc Courtois, Thomas Meunier, Jan Bert Lieve Vertonghen (Cap), Toby Albertine Maurits Alderweireld, Jason Grégory Marianne Denayer, Axel Tomas Laurent Angel Lambert Witsel, Youri Marion Tielemans, Kevin De Bruyne, Thorgan Ganael Francis Hazard, Dries Mertens (83.Dennis Pierre Jacques Albert Praet), Romelu Menama Lukaku Bolingoli. Trainer: Roberto Martínez Montoliu (Spain).
Goals: Youri Marion Tielemans (10), Dries Mertens (23).

18.11.2020   **BELGIUM - DENMARK**   **4-2(1-1)**   2nd UEFA Nations League A, Group 2
Den Dreef Stadion, Leuven; Referee: Slavko Vinčić (Slovenia); Attendance: 0
BEL: Thibaut Nicolas Marc Courtois, Jan Bert Lieve Vertonghen (Cap) (90+2.Anga Dedryck Boyata), Toby Albertine Maurits Alderweireld, Jason Grégory Marianne Denayer, Leander Dendoncker, Nacer Chadli, Kevin De Bruyne, Thorgan Ganael Francis Hazard (77.Thomas Foket), Youri Marion Tielemans, Dries Mertens, Romelu Menama Lukaku Bolingoli. Trainer: Roberto Martínez Montoliu (Spain).
Goals: Youri Marion Tielemans (3), Romelu Menama Lukaku Bolingoli (57, 69), Kevin De Bruyne (87).

24.03.2021   **BELGIUM - WALES**   **3-1(2-1)**   22nd FIFA WC. Qualifiers
Den Dreef Stadion, Leuven; Referee: Cüneyt Çakır (Turkey); Attendance: 0
BEL: Thibaut Nicolas Marc Courtois, Thomas Meunier, Thomas Vermaelen (46.Jason Grégory Marianne Denayer), Jan Bert Lieve Vertonghen (Cap), Toby Albertine Maurits Alderweireld, Kevin De Bruyne, Thorgan Ganael Francis Hazard (83.Timothy Castagne), Leander Dendoncker, Youri Marion Tielemans, Dries Mertens (90+3.Leandro Trossard), Romelu Menama Lukaku Bolingoli. Trainer: Roberto Martínez Montoliu (Spain).
Goals: Kevin De Bruyne (22), Thorgan Ganael Francis Hazard (28), Romelu Menama Lukaku Bolingoli (73 penalty).

27.03.2021   **CZECH REPUBLIC - BELGIUM**   **1-1(0-0)**   22nd FIFA WC. Qualifiers
Eden Arena, Praha; Referee: William Collum (Scotland); Attendance: 0
BEL: Thibaut Nicolas Marc Courtois, Jan Bert Lieve Vertonghen (Cap), Toby Albertine Maurits Alderweireld, Timothy Castagne, Jason Grégory Marianne Denayer, Nacer Chadli (56.Thomas Foket), Kevin De Bruyne, Leander Dendoncker, Youri Marion Tielemans, Dries Mertens (56.Leandro Trossard), Romelu Menama Lukaku Bolingoli. Trainer: Roberto Martínez Montoliu (Spain).
Goal: Romelu Menama Lukaku Bolingoli (60).

30.03.2021   **BELGIUM - BELARUS**   **8-0(4-0)**   22nd FIFA WC. Qualifiers
Den Dreef Stadion, Leuven; Referee: Donatas Rumšas (Lithuania); Attendance: 0
BEL: Simon Luc Hildebert Mignolet, Thomas Meunier, Jan Bert Lieve Vertonghen (Cap) (64.Leander Dendoncker), Toby Albertine Maurits Alderweireld, Jason Grégory Marianne Denayer (46.Anga Dedryck Boyata), Hans Vanaken, Dennis Pierre Jacques Albert Praet (71.Youri Marion Tielemans), Thorgan Ganael Francis Hazard, Leandro Trossard, Michy Batshuayi-Atunga (64.Christian Benteke Liolo), Jeremy Doku (77.Adnan Januzaj). Trainer: Roberto Martínez Montoliu (Spain).
Goals: Michy Batshuayi-Atunga (14), Hans Vanaken (17), Leandro Trossard (38), Jeremy Doku (42), Dennis Pierre Jacques Albert Praet (49), Christian Benteke Liolo (70), Leandro Trossard (75), Hans Vanaken (89).

03.06.2021   **BELGIUM - GREECE**   **1-1(1-0)**   Friendly International
Stade "Roi Baudouin", Bruxelles; Referee: Robert Hennessy (Republic of Ireland); Attendance: 0
BEL: Simon Luc Hildebert Mignolet (90+1.Matz Willy Els Sels), Thomas Meunier, Toby Albertine Maurits Alderweireld (82.Youri Marion Tielemans), Anga Dedryck Boyata, Leander Dendoncker, Jason Grégory Marianne Denayer, Dennis Pierre Jacques Albert Praet, Thorgan Ganael Francis Hazard (74.Nacer Chadli), Yannick Ferreira Carrasco (74.Leandro Trossard), Romelu Menama Lukaku Bolingoli (Cap) (46.Michy Batshuayi-Atunga), Jeremy Doku (46.Dries Mertens). Trainer: Roberto Martínez Montoliu (Spain).
Goal: Thorgan Ganael Francis Hazard (20).

06.06.2021   **BELGIUM - CROATIA**   **1-0(1-0)**   Friendly International
Stade "Roi Baudouin", Bruxelles; Referee: Deniz Aytekin (Germany); Attendance: 50
BEL: Thibaut Nicolas Marc Courtois, Jan Bert Lieve Vertonghen (Cap) (46.Thomas Vermaelen), Toby Albertine Maurits Alderweireld, Leander Dendoncker (81.Eden Michael Hazard), Timothy Castagne, Jason Grégory Marianne Denayer, Nacer Chadli (71.Thorgan Ganael Francis Hazard), Youri Marion Tielemans, Yannick Ferreira Carrasco (81.Jeremy Doku), Dries Mertens (68.Hans Vanaken), Romelu Menama Lukaku Bolingoli. Trainer: Roberto Martínez Montoliu (Spain).
Goal: Romelu Menama Lukaku Bolingoli (38).

12.06.2021   **BELGIUM - RUSSIA**   **3-0(2-0)**   16th EC. Group Stage.
Gazprom Arena, Saint Petersburg; Referee: Antonio Miguel Mateu Lahoz (Spain); Attendance: 26,264
BEL: Thibaut Nicolas Marc Courtois, Jan Bert Lieve Vertonghen (Cap) (77.Thomas Vermaelen), Toby Albertine Maurits Alderweireld, Anga Dedryck Boyata, Leander Dendoncker, Timothy Castagne (27.Thomas Meunier), Thorgan Ganael Francis Hazard, Yannick Ferreira Carrasco (77.Dennis Pierre Jacques Albert Praet), Youri Marion Tielemans, Dries Mertens (72.Eden Michael Hazard), Romelu Menama Lukaku Bolingoli. Trainer: Roberto Martínez Montoliu (Spain).
Goals: Romelu Menama Lukaku Bolingoli (10), Thomas Meunier (34), Romelu Menama Lukaku Bolingoli (88).

17.06.2021   **DENMARK - BELGIUM**   **1-2(1-0)**   16th EC. Group Stage.
Parken Stadium, København; Referee: Björn Kuipers (Netherlands); Attendance: 23,395
BEL: Thibaut Nicolas Marc Courtois, Thomas Meunier, Jan Bert Lieve Vertonghen (Cap), Toby Albertine Maurits Alderweireld, Leander Dendoncker (59.Axel Tomas Laurent Angel Lambert Witsel), Jason Grégory Marianne Denayer, Dries Mertens (46.Kevin De Bruyne), Yannick Ferreira Carrasco (59.Eden Michael Hazard), Youri Marion Tielemans, Romelu Menama Lukaku Bolingoli, Thorgan Ganael Francis Hazard (90+4.Thomas Vermaelen). Trainer: Roberto Martínez Montoliu (Spain).
Goals: Thorgan Ganael Francis Hazard (55), Kevin De Bruyne (70).

21.06.2021   **FINLAND - BELGIUM**   **0-2(0-0)**   16th EC. Group Stage.
Krestovsky Stadium, Saint Petersburg (Russia); Referee: Dr. Felix Brych (Germany); Attendance: 18,545
BEL: Thibaut Nicolas Marc Courtois, Thomas Vermaelen, Anga Dedryck Boyata, Jason Grégory Marianne Denayer, Axel Tomas Laurent Angel Lambert Witsel, Nacer Chadli, Kevin De Bruyne (90+1.Hans Vanaken), Eden Michael Hazard (Cap), Leandro Trossard (75.Thomas Meunier), Romelu Menama Lukaku Bolingoli (84.Christian Benteke Liolo), Jeremy Doku (76.Michy Batshuayi-Atunga). Trainer: Roberto Martínez Montoliu (Spain).
Goals: Lukáš Hrádecký (74 own goal), Romelu Menama Lukaku Bolingoli (81).

27.06.2021   **BELGIUM - PORTUGAL**   **1-0(1-0)**   16th EC. 2nd Round of 16.
Estadio La Cartuja, Sevilla (Spain); Referee: Dr. Felix Brych (Germany); Attendance: 11,504
BEL: Thibaut Nicolas Marc Courtois, Thomas Meunier, Thomas Vermaelen, Jan Bert Lieve Vertonghen, Toby Albertine Maurits Alderweireld, Axel Tomas Laurent Angel Lambert Witsel, Kevin De Bruyne (48.Dries Mertens), Eden Michael Hazard (Cap) (87.Yannick Ferreira Carrasco), Thorgan Ganael Francis Hazard (90+5.Leander Dendoncker), Youri Marion Tielemans, Romelu Menama Lukaku Bolingoli. Trainer: Roberto Martínez Montoliu (Spain).
Goal: Thorgan Ganael Francis Hazard (42).

Football Arena (Allianz), München (Germany); Referee: Slavko Vinčić (Slovenia); Attendance: 12,984

BEL: Thibaut Nicolas Marc Courtois, Thomas Meunier (69.Nacer Chadli; 73.Dennis Pierre Jacques Albert Praet), Thomas Vermaelen, Jan Bert Lieve Vertonghen (Cap), Toby Albertine Maurits Alderweireld, Axel Tomas Laurent Angel Lambert Witsel, Kevin De Bruyne, Youri Marion Tielemans (69.Dries Mertens), Thorgan Ganael Francis Hazard, Romelu Menama Lukaku Bolingoli, Jeremy Doku. Trainer: Roberto Martínez Montoliu (Spain).

Goal: Romelu Menama Lukaku Bolingoli (45+2 penalty).

NATIONAL TEAM PLAYERS
(16.07.2020 – 15.07.2021)

Name	DOB	Caps	Goals	2020/2021:	Club
Goalkeepers					
Koen CASTEELS	25.06.1992	1	0	2020:	VfL Wolfsburg (GER)
Thibaut Nicolas Marc COURTOIS	11.05.1992	89	0	2020/2021:	Real Madrid CF (ESP)
Simon Luc Hildebert MIGNOLET	06.03.1988	31	0	2020/2021:	Club Brugge KV
Matz Willy Els SELS	26.02.1992	1	0	2021:	Racing Club de Strasbourg (FRA)
Hendrik VAN CROMBRUGGE	30.04.1993	1	0	2020:	RSC Anderlecht Bruxelles
Defenders					
Toby Albertine Maurits ALDERWEIRELD	02.03.1989	113	5	2020/2021:	Tottenham Hotspur FC London (ENG)
Sebastiaan BORNAUW	22.03.1999	2	0	2020:	1.FC Köln (GER)
Anga Dedryck BOYATA	28.11.1990	25	0	2020/2021:	Hertha BSC Berlin (GER)
Timothy CASTAGNE	05.12.1995	15	2	2020/2021:	Leicester City FC (ENG)
Hannes DELCROIX	28.02.1999	1	0	2020:	RSC Anderlecht Bruxelles
Jason Grégory Marianne DENAYER	28.06.1995	27	1	2020/2021:	Olympique Lyonnais (FRA)
Leander DENDONCKER	15.04.1995	20	0	2020/2021:	Wolverhampton Wanderers FC (ENG)
Brandon MECHELE	28.01.1993	3	0	2020/2021:	Club Brugge KV
Thomas MEUNIER	12.09.1991	52	8	2020/2021:	BV Borussia 09 Dortmund (GER)
Zinho VANHEUSDEN	29.07.1999	1	0	2020:	R Standard Liège
Thomas VERMAELEN	14.11.1985	85	2	2020/2021:	Vissel Kobe (JPN)
Jan Bert Lieve VERTONGHEN	24.04.1987	131	9	2020/2021:	Sport Lisboa e Benfica (POR)
Midfielders					
Yannick Ferreira CARRASCO	04.09.1993	49	6	2020:	Dalian Professional FC (CHN)
				08.09.2020->	Club Atlético de Madrid (ESP)
Nacer CHADLI	02.08.1989	66	8	2020/2021:	İstanbul Başakşehir FK (TUR)
Kevin DE BRUYNE	28.06.1991	84	22	2020/2021:	Manchester City FC (ENG)
Thomas FOKET	25.09.1994	5	0	2020/2021:	Stade de Reims (FRA)
Adnan JANUZAJ	05.02.1995	13	1	2021:	Real Sociedad San Sebastián (ESP)
Joris KAYEMBE Ditu	08.08.1994	2	0	2020:	R Charleroi SC
Dennis Pierre Jacques Albert PRAET	14.05.1994	13	1	2020/2021:	Leicester City FC (ENG)
Alexis Jesse SAELEMAEKERS	27.06.1999	1	0	2020:	AC Milan (ITA)
Youri Marion TIELEMANS	07.05.1997	43	4	2020/2021:	Leicester City FC (ENG)
Leandro TROSSARD	04.12.1994	8	2	2020/2021:	Brighton & Hove Albion FC (ENG)
Hans VANAKEN	24.08.1992	11	2	2020/2021:	Club Brugge KV
Yari VERSCHAEREN	12.07.2001	6	1	2020/2021:	RSC Anderlecht Bruxelles
Axel Tomas Laurent Angel Lambert WITSEL	12.01.1989	114	10	2020/2021:	BV Borussia 09 Dortmund (GER)
Forwards					
Michy BATSHUAYI-ATUNGA	02.10.1993	35	22	2020:	Chelsea FC London (ENG)
				10.09.2020->	Crystal Palace FC London (ENG)
Christian BENTEKE Liolo	03.12.1990	40	16	2020/2021:	Crystal Palace FC London (ENG)
Charles DE KETELAERE	10.03.2001	1	0	2020:	Club Brugge KV
Jérémy DOKU	27.05.2002	10	2	2020/2021:	Stade Rennais FC (FRA)
Eden Michael HAZARD	07.01.1991	111	32	2020/2021:	Real Madrid CF (ESP)
Thorgan Ganael Francis HAZARD	29.03.1993	39	8	2020/2021:	BV Borussia 09 Dortmund (GER)
Romelu Menama LUKAKU Bolingoli	13.05.1993	98	62	2020/2021:	FC Internazionale Milano (ITA)
Dodi LUKÉBAKIO Ngandoli	24.09.1997	1	0	2020:	Hertha BSC Berlin (GER)
Dries MERTENS	06.05.1987	102	21	2020/2021:	SSC Napoli (ITA)
Divock Okoth ORIGI	18.04.1995	29	3	2020/2021:	Liverpool FC (ENG)

National team coach

Roberto MARTÍNEZ Montoliu (Spain) [from 03.06.2016]	13.07.1973	61 M; 47 W; 9 D; 5 L; 176-47	

BOSNIA AND HERZEGOVINA

The Country:
Bosnia and Herzegovina (Bosna i Hercegovina / Босна и Херцеговина)
Capital: Sarajevo
Surface: 51,197 km²
Inhabitants: 3,824,782 [2021]
Time: UTC+1

The FA:
Nogometni/Fudbalski Savez Bosne i Hercegovine
Bulevar Meše Selimovica 95, 71000 Sarajevo
Tel: +387 33 276 676
Foundation date: 1920 / 1992
Member of FIFA since: 1996
Member of UEFA since: 1998
Website: www.nfsbih.ba

NATIONAL TEAM RECORDS

RECORDS
First international match:	30.11.1995, Tiranë Albania - Bosnia and Herzegovina 2-0
Most international caps:	Edin Džeko - 114 caps (since 2007)
Most international goals:	Edin Džeko - 59 goals / 107 caps (since 2007)

UEFA EUROPEAN CHAMPIONSHIP
1960	-
1964	-
1968	-
1972	-
1976	-
1980	-
1984	-
1988	-
1992	-
1996	Did not enter
2000	Qualifiers
2004	Qualifiers
2008	Qualifiers
2012	Qualifiers
2016	Qualifiers
2020	Qualifiers

was part of Yugoslavia until 01.03.1992

FIFA WORLD CUP
1930	-
1934	-
1938	-
1950	-
1954	-
1958	-
1962	-
1966	-
1970	-
1974	-
1978	-
1982	-
1986	-
1990	-
1994	-
1998	Qualifiers
2002	Qualifiers
2006	Qualifiers
2010	Qualifiers
2014	Final Tournament (Group Stage)
2018	Qualifiers

OLYMPIC TOURNAMENTS
1908	-
1912	-
1920	-
1924	-
1928	-
1936	-
1948	-
1952	-
1956	-
1960	-
1964	-
1968	-
1972	-
1976	-
1980	-
1984	-
1988	-
1992	-
1996	-
2000	Qualifiers
2004	Qualifiers
2008	-
2012	Qualifiers
2016	Qualifiers

UEFA NATIONS LEAGUE
2018/2019	League B (promoted to League A)
2020/2021	League A (relegated to League B)

FIFA CONFEDERATIONS CUP 1992-2017
None

BOSNIAN CLUB HONOURS IN EUROPEAN CLUB COMPETITIONS:

European Champion Clubs' Cup (1956-1992) / UEFA Champions League (1993-2021)
None

Fairs Cup (1858-1971) / UEFA Cup (1972-2009) / UEFA Europa League (2010-2021)
None

UEFA Super Cup (1972-2020)
None

*European Cup Winners' Cup 1961-1999**
None

defunct competition

NATIONAL COMPETITIONS
TABLE OF HONOURS

FIRST LEAGUE OF BOSNIA AND HERZEGOVINA CHAMPIONS	
1994/1995	NK Čelik Zenica
1995/1996	NK Čelik Zenica
1996/1997	NK Čelik Zenica
1997/1998	NK Bosna Visoko
1998/1999	FK Sarajevo
1999/2000	NK Jedinstvo Bihać

FIRST LEAGUE OF HERZEG-BOSNIA CHAMPIONS	
1993/1994	NK Široki Brijeg
1994/1995	NK Široki Brijeg
1995/1996	NK Široki Brijeg
1996/1997	NK Široki Brijeg
1997/1998	NK Široki Brijeg
1998/1999	NK Posušje
1999/2000	NK Posušje

FIRST LEAGUE OF THE REPUBLIKA SRPSKA CHAMPIONS	
1995/1996	FK Boksit Milići
1996/1997	FK Rudar Ugljevik
1997/1998	FK Rudar Ugljevik
1998/1999	FK Radnik Bijeljina
1999/2000	FK Boksit Milići
2000/2001	FK Borac Banja Luka
2001/2002	FK Leotar Trebinje

BOSNIA AND HERZEGOVINA CUP WINNERS	
1994/1995	NK Čelik Zenica
1995/1996	NK Čelik Zenica
1996/1997	FK Sarajevo
1997/1998	FK Sarajevo
1998/1999	NK Bosna Visoko

HERZEG-BOSNIA CUP WINNERS	
1994/1995	NK Bigeste Ljubuški
1995/1996	NK Bigeste Ljubuški
1996/1997	NK Troglav 1918 Livno
1997/1998	HNK Orašje
1998/1999	NK Brotnjo
1999/2000	HNK Orašje

REPUBLIKA SRPSKA CUP WINNERS	
1993/1994	FK Kozara Gradiška
1994/1995	FK Borac Banja Luka
1995/1996	FK Borac Banja Luka
1996/1997	FK Sloga Trn
1997/1998	FK Rudar Ugljevik
1998/1999	FK Rudar Ugljevik
1999/2000	FK Kozara Gradiška

	PLAYOFF CHAMPIONS	CUP WINNERS	BEST GOALSCORERS	
1997/1998	FK Željezničar Sarajevo	FK Sarajevo	Stanko Bubalo (CRO, NK Široki Brijeg) Hadis Zubanović (FK Željezničar Sarajevo)	3
1998/1999	FK Sarajevo (Regional NK Posušje winners FK Radnik Bijeljina shared)	No competition	-	
1999/2000	NK Brotnjo	FK Željezničar Sarajevo	Zikret Kuljaninović (FK Budućnost Banovići) Alen Škoro (FK Sarajevo) Halim Stupac (NK Jedinstvo Bihać)	5
	PREMIER LEAGUE			
2000/2001	FK Željezničar Sarajevo	FK Željezničar Sarajevo	Dželaludin Muharemović (FK Željezničar Sarajevo)	31
2001/2002	FK Željezničar Sarajevo	FK Sarajevo	Ivica Huljev (FK Željezničar Sarajevo)	15
2002/2003	FK Leotar Trebinje	FK Željezničar Sarajevo	Emir Obuća (FK Sarajevo)	24
2003/2004	NK Široki Brijeg	FK Modriča	Alen Škoro (FK Sarajevo)	20
2004/2005	HŠK Zrinjski Mostar	FK Sarajevo	Zoran Rajović (SRB, HŠK Zrinjski Mostar)	17
2005/2006	NK Široki Brijeg	HNK Orašje	Petar Jelić (FK Modriča)	19
2006/2007	FK Sarajevo	NK Široki Brijeg	Stevo Nikolić (FK Modriča) Dragan Benić (FK Borac Banja Luka)	19
2007/2008	FK Modriča	HŠK Zrinjski Mostar	Darko Spalević (SRB, FK Slavija Sarajevo)	18
2008/2009	HŠK Zrinjski Mostar	FK Slavija Sarajevo	Darko Spalević (SRB, FK Slavija Sarajevo)	17
2009/2010	FK Željezničar Sarajevo	FK Borac Banja Luka	Feđa Dudić (NK Travnik)	16
2010/2011	FK Borac Banja Luka	FK Željezničar Sarajevo	Ivan Lendrić (CRO, HŠK Zrinjski Mostar)	16
2011/2012	FK Željezničar Sarajevo	FK Željezničar Sarajevo	Eldin Adilović (FK Željezničar Sarajevo)	19
2012/2013	FK Željezničar Sarajevo	NK Široki Brijeg	Emir Hadžić (FK Sarajevo)	20
2013/2014	HŠK Zrinjski Mostar	FK Sarajevo	Wagner Santos Lago (BRA, NK Široki Brijeg)	18
2014/2015	FK Sarajevo	FK Olimpik Sarajevo	Riad Bajić (FK Željezničar Sarajevo)	15
2015/2016	HŠK Zrinjski Mostar	FK Radnik Bijeljina	Leon Benko (CRO, FK Sarajevo)	17
2016/2017	HŠK Zrinjski Mostar	NK Široki Brijeg	Ivan Lendrić (CRO, FK Željezničar Sarajevo)	19
2017/2018	HŠK Zrinjski Mostar	FK Željezničar Sarajevo	Miloš Filipović (SRB, HŠK Zrinjski Mostar)	16
2018/2019	FK Sarajevo	FK Sarajevo	Sulejman Krpić (FK Sarajevo)	16
2019/2020	FK Sarajevo	*Competition cancelled*	Mersudin Ahmetović (FK Sarajevo)	13
2020/2021	FK Borac Banja Luka	FK Sarajevo	Nemanja Bilbija (HŠK Zrinjski Mostar)	17

NATIONAL CHAMPIONSHIP
M:tel Premijer Liga 2020/2021
(01.08.2020 – 30.05.2021)

Results

Round 1 [01-02.08.2020]
Sloboda Tuzla - Radnik Bijeljina 1-1(0-1)
Borac Banja Luka - FK Mladost 6-0(4-0)
Zrinjski Mostar - Olimpik Sarajevo 1-0(0-0)
FK Željezničar - Velež Mostar 3-0(3-0)
FK Krupa - FK Sarajevo 0-2(0-0)
Široki Brijeg - FK Tuzla City 1-0(1-0)

Round 2 [07-08.08.2020]
Radnik Bijeljina - FK Željezničar 0-2(0-1)
Borac Banja Luka - Sloboda Tuzla 2-0(0-0)
FK Mladost - FK Sarajevo 2-2(0-0)
Olimpik Sarajevo - Široki Brijeg 1-2(0-1)
Velež Mostar - Zrinjski Mostar 2-0(1-0)
FK Tuzla City - FK Krupa 1-0(0-0)

Round 3 [11-12.08.2020]
FK Željezničar - Borac Banja Luka 2-1(0-0)
Široki Brijeg - Velež Mostar 2-2(2-1)
FK Sarajevo - FK Tuzla City 1-0(1-0)
FK Krupa - Olimpik Sarajevo 1-0(0-0)
Sloboda Tuzla - FK Mladost 3-0(1-0)
Zrinjski Mostar - Radnik Bijeljina 0-0

Round 4 [15-16.08.2020]
FK Mladost - FK Tuzla City 2-5(0-3)
Sloboda Tuzla - FK Željezničar 0-2(0-1)
Velež Mostar - FK Krupa 2-0(0-0)
Borac Banja Luka - Zrinjski Mostar 1-0(1-0)
Radnik Bijeljina - Široki Brijeg 1-1(0-0)
Olimpik Sar. - FK Sarajevo 1-3(0-1) [16.09.]

Round 5 [21-23.08.2020]
FK Željezničar - FK Mladost 0-1(0-1)
Široki Brijeg - Borac Banja Luka 3-0(2-0)
Zrinjski Mostar - Sloboda Tuzla 1-0(1-0)
FK Krupa - Radnik Bijeljina 1-1(0-0)
FK Tuzla City - Olimpik Sarajevo 3-2(2-1)
FK Sarajevo - Velež Mostar 1-1(0-1)

Round 6 [29-31.08.2020]
FK Mladost - Olimpik Sarajevo 1-0(1-0)
Velež Mostar - FK Tuzla City 1-1(1-0)
Sloboda Tuzla - Široki Brijeg 3-0(2-0)
Radnik Bijeljina - FK Sarajevo 0-2(0-2)
Borac Banja Luka - FK Krupa 3-1(1-0)
Željezničar - Zrinjski Mostar 1-0(0-0) [28.10.]

Round 7 [11-13.09.2020]
FK Sarajevo - Borac Banja Luka 4-2(2-1)
Olimpik Sarajevo - Velež Mostar 2-1(0-0)
Zrinjski Mostar - FK Mladost 2-0(1-0)
FK Krupa - Sloboda Tuzla 2-3(0-0)
Široki Brijeg - FK Željezničar 0-1(0-0)
FK Tuzla City - Radnik Bijeljina 1-0(0-0)

Round 8 [19-21.09.2020]
FK Mladost - Velež Mostar 1-2(0-1)
Radnik Bijeljina - Olimpik Sarajevo 4-0(1-0)
FK Željezničar - FK Krupa 0-1(0-1)
Sloboda Tuzla - FK Sarajevo 2-3(1-2)
Borac Banja Luka - FK Tuzla City 2-0(0-0)
Zrinjski Most. - Široki Brijeg 2-1(2-0) [04.11.]

Round 9 [26-28.09.2020]
Olimpik Sarajevo - Borac Banja Luka 1-4(0-1)
Velež Mostar - Radnik Bijeljina 2-1(1-1)
FK Tuzla City - Sloboda Tuzla 2-1(1-0)
Široki Brijeg - FK Mladost 2-1(1-1)
FK Krupa - Zrinjski Mostar 0-3(0-2)
FK Sarajevo - Željezničar 1-1(1-0) [04.11.]

Round 10 [03-05.10.2020]
FK Mladost - Radnik Bijeljina 3-2(1-1)
Sloboda Tuzla - Olimpik Sarajevo 2-0(2-0)
Borac Banja Luka - Velež Mostar 2-0(0-0)
Široki Brijeg - FK Krupa 1-0(1-0)
Zrinjski Mostar - FK Sarajevo 2-3(1-1)
FK Željezničar - FK Tuzla City 1-0(0-0)

Round 11 [16-17.10.2020]
FK Tuzla City - Zrinjski Mostar 0-4(0-3)
Radnik Bijeljina - Borac Banja Luka 1-0(0-0)
Velež Mostar - Sloboda Tuzla 3-0(1-0)
FK Krupa - FK Mladost 0-1(0-0)
Olimpik Sarajevo - FK Željezničar 0-3(0-1)
FK Sarajevo - Široki Brijeg 2-0(1-0)

Round 12 [24-25.10.2020]
Olimpik Sarajevo - Zrinjski Mostar 3-0(0-0)
FK Tuzla City - Široki Brijeg 1-1(0-0)
Velež Mostar - FK Željezničar 1-1(1-0)
FK Mladost - Borac Banja Luka 0-2(0-0)
FK Sarajevo - FK Krupa 3-0(2-0)
Radnik Bijeljina - Sloboda Tuzla 1-1(0-0)

Round 13 [30.10.-01.11.2020]
FK Sarajevo - FK Mladost 5-1(3-0)
FK Krupa - FK Tuzla City 0-1(0-0)
Široki Brijeg - Olimpik Sarajevo 1-0(0-0)
Zrinjski Mostar - Velež Mostar 3-1(1-0)
FK Željezničar - Radnik Bijeljina 3-1(2-1)
Sloboda Tuzla - Borac Banja Luka 1-0(1-0)

Round 14 [07-09.11.2020]
FK Mladost - Sloboda Tuzla 2-0(1-0)
Olimpik Sarajevo - FK Krupa 1-1(0-0)
FK Tuzla City - FK Sarajevo 0-0
Velež Mostar - Široki Brijeg 2-1(0-0)
Radnik Bijeljina - Zrinjski Mostar 0-2(0-0)
Borac Banja Luka - FK Željezničar 4-3(3-2)

Round 15 [21-22.11.2020]
FK Tuzla City - FK Mladost 1-0(1-0)
FK Željezničar - Sloboda Tuzla 2-2(1-1)
Zrinjski Mostar - Borac Banja Luka 2-1(2-1)
FK Krupa - Velež Mostar 1-1(0-0)
FK Sarajevo - Olimpik Sarajevo 2-0(1-0)
Široki Brijeg - Radnik Bijeljina 5-0(3-0)

Round 16 [27-29.11.2020]
FK Mladost - FK Željezničar 0-4(0-1)
Olimpik Sarajevo - FK Tuzla City 3-2(1-1)
Sloboda Tuzla - Zrinjski Mostar 0-0
Velež Mostar - FK Sarajevo 0-0
Borac Banja Luka - Široki Brijeg 1-1(1-0)
Radnik Bijeljina - FK Krupa 1-1(0-1)

Round 17 [01-02.12.2020]
FK Tuzla City - Velež Mostar 1-3(1-1)
Široki Brijeg - Sloboda Tuzla 3-0(3-0)
FK Krupa - Borac Banja Luka 1-3(0-1)
Olimpik Sarajevo - FK Mladost 0-2(0-1)
Zrinjski Mostar - FK Željezničar 1-2(1-0)
FK Sarajevo - Radnik Bijeljina 2-1(0-0)

Round 18 [05-06.12.2020]
Radnik Bijeljina - FK Tuzla City 2-1(1-1)
Velež Mostar - Olimpik Sarajevo 2-0(1-0)
FK Mladost - Zrinjski Mostar 0-1(0-1)
Sloboda Tuzla - FK Krupa 2-0(0-0)
FK Željezničar - Široki Brijeg 2-3(0-1)
Borac Banja Luka - FK Sarajevo 2-2(1-0)

Round 19 [12-13.12.2020]
FK Krupa - FK Željezničar 2-1(1-0)
Olimpik Sarajevo - Radnik Bijeljina 1-0(1-0)
FK Sarajevo - Sloboda Tuzla 2-1(2-0)
FK Tuzla City - Borac Banja Luka 2-0(1-0)
Velež Mostar - FK Mladost 4-0(2-0)
Široki Brijeg - Zrinjski Mostar 2-1(1-0)

Round 20 [27.02.-01.03.2021]
Radnik Bijeljina - Velež Mostar 0-0
Borac Banja Luka - Olimpik Sarajevo 2-0(0-0)
Zrinjski Mostar - FK Krupa 1-0(1-0)
FK Mladost - Široki Brijeg 0-1(0-0)
Sloboda Tuzla - FK Tuzla City 0-2(0-0)
FK Željezničar - FK Sarajevo 0-0

Round 21 [05-08.03.2021]
Velež Mostar - Borac Banja Luka 2-0(1-0)
FK Krupa - Široki Brijeg 1-1(0-0)
FK Tuzla City - FK Željezničar 2-0(1-0)
FK Sarajevo - Zrinjski Mostar 0-1(0-1)
Radnik Bijeljina - FK Mladost 3-1(2-0)
Olimpik Sarajevo - Sloboda Tuzla 2-0(1-0)

Round 22 [13-15.03.2021]
FK Mladost - FK Krupa 1-0(1-0)
Sloboda Tuzla - Velež Mostar 1-2(1-1)
Zrinjski Mostar - FK Tuzla City 1-2(1-1)
Široki Brijeg - FK Sarajevo 1-0(0-0)
FK Željezničar - Olimpik Sarajevo 0-1(0-0)
Borac Banja Luka - Radnik Bijeljina 2-0(2-0)

Round 23 [20-21.03.2021]
Borac Banja Luka - FK Mladost 1-0(0-0)
Velež Mostar - Radnik Bijeljina 2-2(1-1)
Zrinjski Mostar - Sloboda Tuzla 3-1(3-0)
FK Sarajevo - FK Krupa 1-0(0-0)
Široki Brijeg - Olimpik Sarajevo 3-0(1-0)
FK Željezničar - FK Tuzla City 0-0

Round 24 [02-05.04.2021]
FK Mladost - Zrinjski Mostar 1-1(1-1)
Radnik Bijeljina - Borac Banja Luka 1-3(0-1)
Sloboda Tuzla - FK Željezničar 1-0(0-0)
FK Krupa - FK Tuzla City 1-1(0-0)
FK Sarajevo - Široki Brijeg 1-0(1-0)
Olimpik Sarajevo - Velež Mostar 1-1(0-0)

Round 25 [10-12.04.2021]
FK Željezničar - FK Mladost 4-4(1-3)
Zrinjski Mostar - Radnik Bijeljina 3-0(1-0)
FK Tuzla City - Sloboda Tuzla 1-0(0-0)
Široki Brijeg - FK Krupa 2-2(1-1)
Borac Banja Luka - Olimpik Sarajevo 3-0(1-0)
Velež Mostar - FK Sarajevo 1-0(1-0)

Round 26 [17-18.04.2021]
FK Mladost - FK Tuzla City 2-0(1-0)
FK Krupa - Sloboda Tuzla 1-0(1-0)
FK Sarajevo - Borac Banja Luka 0-2(0-1)
Olimpik Sarajevo - Zrinjski Mostar 0-3(0-1)
Radnik Bijeljina - FK Željezničar 1-1(0-1)
Široki Brijeg - Velež Mostar 0-2(0-1)

Round 27 [24-25.04.2021]
Sloboda Tuzla - FK Mladost 1-0(1-0)
Velež Mostar - FK Krupa 2-1(1-0)
Zrinjski Mostar - FK Sarajevo 1-0(1-0)
FK Tuzla City - Radnik Bijeljina 2-0(1-0)
FK Željezničar - Olimpik Sarajevo 1-2(1-1)
Borac Banja Luka - Široki Brijeg 2-1(1-0)

Round 28 [30.04.-03.05.2021]
Radnik Bijeljina - Sloboda Tuzla 1-2(1-0)
Velež Mostar - Borac Banja Luka 1-1(0-0)
FK Krupa - FK Mladost 3-0(2-0)
FK Sarajevo - FK Željezničar 3-1(2-0)
Široki Brijeg - Zrinjski Mostar 1-0(0-0)
Olimpik Sarajevo - FK Tuzla City 1-1(0-1)

Round 29 [07-08.05.2021]
FK Tuzla City - FK Sarajevo 1-1(1-1)
FK Željezničar - Široki Brijeg 1-3(0-0)
FK Mladost - Radnik Bijeljina 0-0
Sloboda Tuzla - Olimpik Sarajevo 2-0(1-0)
Borac Banja Luka - FK Krupa 1-0(1-0)
Zrinjski Mostar - Velež Mostar 1-1(0-1)

Round 30 [11-12.05.2021]
FK Sarajevo - Sloboda Tuzla 0-0
Borac Banja Luka - Zrinjski Mostar 2-1(2-1)
FK Krupa - Radnik Bijeljina 1-0(0-0)
Olimpik Sarajevo - FK Mladost 0-0
Široki Brijeg - FK Tuzla City 0-0
Velež Mostar - FK Željezničar 2-2(1-2)

Round 31 [16.05.2021]
Sloboda Tuzla - Široki Brijeg 1-1(1-1)
FK Tuzla City - Velež Mostar 1-1(0-1)
FK Željezničar - Borac Banja Luka 1-2(0-0)
Radnik Bijeljina - Olimpik Sarajevo 1-0(1-0)
FK Mladost - FK Sarajevo 0-0
Zrinjski Mostar - FK Krupa 3-1(2-1)

Round 32 [23.05.2021]
FK Krupa - Olimpik Sarajevo 3-0 awarded
Velež Mostar - Sloboda Tuzla 2-0(0-0)
Široki Brijeg - FK Mladost 1-0(1-0)
FK Sarajevo - Radnik Bijeljina 3-0(0-0)
Zrinjski Mostar - FK Željezničar 4-2(2-1)
Borac Banja Luka - FK Tuzla City 2-0(1-0)

Round 33 [30.05.2021]
Olimpik Sarajevo - FK Sarajevo 0-3 awarded
FK Mladost - Velež Mostar 0-1(0-1)
FK Tuzla City - Zrinjski Mostar 1-2(0-2)
Radnik Bijeljina - Široki Brijeg 0-2(0-1)
Sloboda Tuzla - Borac Banja Luka 0-0
FK Željezničar - FK Krupa 3-0(2-0)

Please note: FK Olimpik Sarajevo withdrew from the league before round 32 and have both their remaining matches awarded 0-3 against them.

Final Standings

								Home						Away				
1. **FK Borac Banja Luka**	33	21	4	8	59 - 31	67	15	2	0	38 - 9		6	2	8	21 - 22
2. FK Sarajevo	33	18	11	4	53 - 24	65	12	3	2	31 - 11		6	8	2	22 - 13
3. FK Velež Mostar	33	16	13	4	50 - 30	61	11	6	0	31 - 10		5	7	4	19 - 20
4. NK Široki Brijeg	33	17	8	8	47 - 30	59	12	3	2	28 - 9		5	5	6	19 - 21
5. HŠK Zrinjski Mostar	33	18	5	10	50 - 30	59	11	3	3	31 - 16		7	2	7	19 - 14
6. FK Tuzla City	33	13	9	11	36 - 35	48	9	4	3	20 - 15		4	5	8	16 - 20
7. FK Željezničar Sarajevo	33	12	8	13	50 - 43	44	6	4	7	24 - 21		6	4	6	26 - 22
8. FK Sloboda Tuzla	33	10	7	16	31 - 41	37	8	4	4	20 - 11		2	3	12	11 - 30
9. FK Mladost Doboj Kakanj (Relegated)*	33	8	6	19	26 - 57	30	5	4	7	15 - 21		3	2	12	11 - 36
10. FK Krupa na Vrbasu (Relegated)*	33	7	7	19	26 - 46	28	6	4	6	18 - 18		1	3	13	8 - 28
11. FK Radnik Bijeljina	33	5	10	18	26 - 51	25	5	5	6	17 - 19		0	5	12	9 - 32
12. FK Olimpik Sarajevo (Relegated)	33	7	4	22	22 - 58	25	5	4	7	17 - 26		2	0	15	5 - 32

*both FK Mladost Doboj Kakanj and FK Krupa na Vrbasu were relegated due to failing to obtain a license for the 2021/2022 Premijer Liga.

Top goalscorers:	
17 **Nemanja Bilbija**	**HŠK Zrinjski Mostar**
15 Stojan Vranješ	FK Borac Banja Luka
12 Goran Zakarić	FK Borac Banja Luka
11 Obren Cvijanović	FK Velež Mostar
10 Matthias Olubori Ayodluwa Fanimo (ENG)	FK Sarajevo
10 Benjamin Tatar	FK Sarajevo

NATIONAL CUP
Kup Bosne i Hercegovine u nogometu 2020/2021

First Round [30.09./13.10.2020]

NK Travnik - FK Borac Banja Luka	0-4(0-2)	NK GOŠK Gabela - NK Široki Brijeg	0-1(0-0)
FK Rudar Prijador - FK Olimpik Sarajevo	4-0(0-0)	NK Zvijezda Gradačac - FK Radnik Bijeljina	0-1(0-0)
FK Goražde - FK Sloboda Tuzla	2-2 aet; 5-4 pen	FK Zvijezda 09 Bijeljina - FK Modriča	2-1(1-1)
FK Sloboda Novi Grad - FK Tuzla City	0-2(0-0)	FK Klis - FK UNIS Vogošća	6-2(4-1)
FK Budućnost Banovići - FK Željezničar Sarajevo	1-2(0-2)	FK Velež Nevesinje - FK Igman Konjic	2-1(1-0)
FK Tekstilac Derventa - HŠK Zrinjski Mostar	1-7(0-3)	NK Fortuna Zenica - FK Rudar Kakanj	0-1(0-0)
FK Dizdaruša Brčko - FK Velež Mostar	0-3(0-3)	FK Leotar Trebinje - FK Krupa na Vrbasu	0-4(0-3)
FK Slavija Sarajevo - FK Mladost Doboj Kakanj	2-2 aet; 8-7 pen	FK Radnički Lukavac - FK Sarajevo	0-4(0-4)

1/8-Finals [21.10./14.11.2020]

FK Tuzla City - FK Radnik Bijeljina	3-1(1-0)	FK Rudar Kakanj - FK Borac Banja Luka	1-6(0-2)
FK Željezničar Sarajevo - FK Goražde	3-0(0-0)	FK Velež Nevesinje - FK Klis	0-2(0-1)
FK Rudar Prijador - FK Zvijezda 09 Bijeljina	0-0 aet; 3-4 pen	HŠK Zrinjski Mostar - FK Slavija Sarajevo	4-0(0-0)
FK Krupa na Vrbasu - FK Sarajevo	2-4(0-3)	FK Velež Mostar - NK Široki Brijeg	0-1(0-1)

Quarter-Finals [10.03.2021]

FK Tuzla City - FK Željezničar Sarajevo	1-1 aet; 3-2 pen	NK Široki Brijeg - FK Borac Banja Luka	0-2(0-2)
FK Klis - Zvijezda 09 Bijeljina	1-0(1-0)	FK Sarajevo - HŠK Zrinjski Mostar	1-0(1-0)

Semi-Finals [07/21.04.2021]

First Leg		Second Leg	
FK Tuzla City - FK Sarajevo	0-1(0-0)	FK Sarajevo - FK Tuzla City	3-1(0-0)
FK Borac Banja Luka - FK Klis	4-1(1-0)	FK Klis - FK Borac Banja Luka	1-2(1-2)

26.05.2021; Nogometni/Fudbalski Savez Bosne i Hercegovine Training Centre, Zenica; Referee: Irfan Peljto; Attendance: 0
FK Sarajevo - FK Borac Banja Luka **0-0; 4-1 on penalties**

FK Sarajevo: Vladan Kovačević, Hrvoje Miličević, Amer Dupovac, Mirko Oremuš, Anel Hebibović (85.Zinedin Mustedanagić), Ivan Jukić (64.Haris Handžić), Andrej Đokanović (77.Slobodan Milanović), Matthias Olubori Ayodluwa Fanimo, Joachim Adukor, Jasmin Mešanović, Krste Velkoski. Trainer: Dženan Uščuplić.

Borac Banja Luka: Nikola Lakić, Dejan Uzelac, Đorđe Ćosić, Siniša Dujaković, Aleksandar Vojinović, Aleksandar Subić (90.Dejan Bosančić), Marko Brtan (90.Amar Tahrić), David Čavić, Stojan Vranješ (64.Panagiotis Moraitis), Dejan Meleg (77.Đorđe Milojević), Elvis Mehanović. Trainer: Marko Maksimović.

Penalties: Hrvoje Miličević 1-0; David Čavić (missed); Krste Velkoski 2-0; Amar Tahrić (saved); Zinedin Mustedanagić 3-0; Dejan Uzelac 3-1; Haris Handžić 4-1.

THE CLUBS 2020/2021

Fudbalski klub Borac Banja Luka

Founded:	04.07.1926		
Stadium:	Gradski stadion Banja Luka, Banja Luka (10,030)		
Trainer:	Vlado Jagodić		22.03.1964
[26.12.2020]	Marko Maksimović		20.08.1984

Goalkeepers:	DOB	M	(s)	G
Nikola Lakić	01.10.1995	4	(1)	
Bojan Pavlović (SRB)	08.11.1986	29		
Defenders:	**DOB**	**M**	**(s)**	**G**
Miloš Borovčanin	26.12.2000	4	(6)	
Dino Ćorić	30.06.1990	11	(1)	
Đorđe Ćosić	11.09.1995	21	(4)	1
Douglas Nanato Oliveira Cruz (BRA)	04.09.1998	5	(5)	1
Siniša Dujaković	22.11.1991	19	(9)	
Nemanja Janičić (SRB)	13.07.1986	2		
Marko Jovanović (SRB)	26.03.1988	17		
Marko Kujundić	14.10.2002	4	(10)	
Đorđe Milojević	10.05.2001	17	(1)	
Aleksandar Subić	27.09.1993	19	(5)	1
Dejan Uzelac	29.11.1993	11		1
Midfielders:	**DOB**	**M**	**(s)**	**G**
Luka Bobić	08.02.2002		(1)	
Dejan Bosančić	02.06.1998	3	(9)	
Marko Brtan (CRO)	07.04.1991	26	(1)	
Vladan Danilović	27.07.1999	7		2
Boban Georgiev (MKD)	26.01.1997	2	(11)	
Dino Kalesić	06.12.1997	2	(2)	

Dejan Meleg (SRB)	01.10.1994	13	(7)	4
Donald Molls Ntchamda (CMR)	14.07.1998	5	(5)	
Aleksandar Radulović	09.02.1987	1	(10)	
Amar Tahrić	04.05.2002	1		
Aleksandar Vojinović	03.10.1996	24	(6)	
Stojan Vranješ	11.10.1986	25		15
Forwards:	**DOB**	**M**	**(s)**	**G**
Ivan Crnov (CRO)	01.02.1990		(5)	
David Čavić	21.11.2002	2	(10)	
Boro Erić	21.01.2003		(1)	
Momodou Jallow (USA)	17.09.1996		(3)	
Dejan Javorac	15.07.2002		(1)	
Saša Kajkut	07.07.1984	3	(11)	
Jovo Lukić	28.11.1998	16	(1)	8
Bojan Marković	13.11.1999	2	(5)	
Elvis Mehanović	10.04.2000	8	(5)	1
Panagiotis Moraitis (GRE)	01.02.1997	3	(7)	2
Milan Šikanjić	03.01.2000	1	(3)	
David Vuković	21.12.2003		(1)	
Goran Zakarić	07.11.1992	30		12
Almedin Dino Ziljkić	25.02.1996	26	(2)	7

Fudbalski klub Krupa na Vrbasu

Founded:	1983		
Stadium:	Stadion Gradski, Krupa na Vrbasu (3,500)		
Trainer:	Zoran Marić (SRB)		21.02.1960
[15.09.2020]	Velimir Stojnić		29.10.1962
[30.10.2020]	Vladimir Ilić		20.07.1998

Goalkeepers:	DOB	M	(s)	G
Tarik Abdulahović	18.04.1998	5		
Vasilije Kolak	08.03.1995	27		
Defenders:	**DOB**	**M**	**(s)**	**G**
Muharem Čivić	04.01.1993	11		
Miladin Filipović	02.09.1995	8	(3)	
Marin Galić	21.09.1995	23		
Miloš Karišik (SRB)	07.10.1988	25		
Igor Makitan	12.10.1994	22	(3)	1
Stojan Maksimović (SRB)	06.01.1996	13	(8)	
Stefan Nikolić (SRB)	14.03.1994	1		
Jovan Pavlović	11.02.2000	11	(3)	
Bojan Puzigača	10.05.1985	7	(9)	
Miloš Simonović	28.05.1990	3	(3)	
Nemanja Vidović	25.09.1993	1	(4)	
Midfielders:	**DOB**	**M**	**(s)**	**G**
Emanullah Blažević	22.07.1999		(9)	
Nikola Dujaković	27.06.1996	27	(3)	6
Milivoj Krmar (SRB)	01.04.1997		(2)	

Nikola Mandić (CRO)	19.03.1995	24	(4)	3
Sanin Muminovič	02.11.1990	12		
Lazar Nikolić	30.04.1999	8	(14)	2
Đorđe Nišić	24.01.2002		(1)	
Kerim Palić	24.01.1997	24	(4)	1
Ajdin Redžić	25.01.1997	25	(6)	
Muamer Svraka	14.02.1988	3	(6)	
Nemanja Vukmanović (SRB)	06.02.1999	13	(5)	1
Forwards:	**DOB**	**M**	**(s)**	**G**
Milos Ačimovič (SRB)	06.07.1997	3	(15)	4
Aleksa Andrejić (SRB)	24.01.1993	12	(2)	
Aleksandar Erak (SRB)	19.05.1996	1	(9)	
Dejan Glišić	15.02.1997	1	(3)	
Marko Golubović (SRB)	20.09.1995	5	(6)	
Toni Jović (CRO)	02.09.1992	11		1
Mihael Modić	14.01.1998	10	(9)	
Stefan Nikolić (MNE)	16.04.1990	12	(1)	4
Aleksandar Rakić (SRB)	17.01.1987	4	(3)	

Fudbalski klub Mladost Doboj Kakanj

Founded:	25.05.1959	
Stadium:	MGM Farm Arena, Doboj (3,000)	
Trainer:	Fahrudin Solbić	23.10.1958
[08.08.2020]	Elvedin Beganović	07.11.1971
[24.08.2020]	Nemanja Miljanović (SWE)	04.08.1971

Goalkeepers:	DOB	M	(s)	G
Semir Bukvić	21.05.1991	20		
Emil Velić (SVN)	06.02.1995	13		
Defenders:	**DOB**	**M**	**(s)**	**G**
Enes Alić	03.09.1999	28		4
Benaris Duraković	16.03.2001	2		
Anđelo Guzijan	12.08.2000	2	(5)	
Hasan Jahić	30.07.2001	6	(1)	
Faruk Jusić	13.08.1999	2		
Marko Klisura (SRB)	15.10.1992	2	(1)	
Milan Lalić (SRB)	25.07.1995	15		
Azur Mahmić	06.05.2003	27	(1)	
Daniel Miljanović (SWE)	11.04.2001	5	(5)	
Miloš Nikolić (SRB)	03.10.1994	16		2
Rijad Sadiku	18.01.2000	10		
Halid Šabanović	22.08.1999	11		
Anes Vehab	28.09.1996		(2)	
Midfielders:	**DOB**	**M**	**(s)**	**G**
Amar Begić	07.08.2000	25	(5)	
Edin Biber	06.01.1999	10	(4)	
Karlo Buhač (CRO)	19.08.1998		(2)	
Anel Dedić	02.05.1991	24		2
Kenan Handžić	23.01.1991	8	(5)	
Amer Hiroš	10.06.1996	23	(1)	7
Aleksandar Mirkov (SRB)	08.01.1996	2	(4)	
Aldin Šišić	29.09.1990	4	(7)	
Anes Vazda	24.07.1997	19	(5)	
Demirel Veladžić	15.05.1999	1	(4)	
Marko Žulj	14.05.1996	18	(2)	
Forwards:	**DOB**	**M**	**(s)**	**G**
Safet Čago	26.08.2002	1	(5)	
Armin Ćerimagić	14.01.1994	7	(7)	
Alen Dejanović	19.01.2000	19	(7)	1
Harun Goralija	02.06.2002		(1)	
Nedim Hadžić	19.03.1994	26		9
Anes Hrustanović	13.03.2002	2	(16)	
Fahrudin Kovač	23.04.1996	2	(13)	
Nikola Marić (CRO)	04.08.1997	2	(2)	
Amir Mašić	14.02.1998		(7)	
Kemal Mujarić	12.09.1999	2	(2)	
Kenan Šarić	18.12.1997	4	(7)	
Predrag Vladić	04.02.1999	5	(6)	1

Fudbalski klub Olimpik Sarajevo

Founded:	03.10.1993	
Stadium:	Stadion Okota, Sarajevo (3,000)	
Trainer:	Darko Vojvodić	08.05.1970
[05.09.2020]	Esad Selimović	06.08.1969
[12.12.2020]	Slavko Petrović (SRB)	10.08.1958

Goalkeepers:	DOB	M	(s)	G
Adnan Hadžić	15.01.1988	28		
Luka Kačavenda	01.11.2001	2		
Marko Sušac	23.10.1988	1		
Defenders:	**DOB**	**M**	**(s)**	**G**
Muamer Adžem	01.11.1992	7		1
Amar Beširević	08.08.1999	3	(2)	
Ivan Dujmović	19.04.1998	14	(5)	
Kenan Horić	13.09.1990	12		1
Armin Imamović	17.02.2000	7	(10)	
Tarik Isić	08.10.1994	10		
Nemanja Lekanič (SRB)	10.01.1990	24	(5)	3
Đoko Milović	16.09.1992	15	(6)	1
Branko Ojdanić	21.06.1990	14	(2)	
Sedin Ramić	28.11.2000		(2)	
Midfielders:	**DOB**	**M**	**(s)**	**G**
Semir Bajraktarević	14.10.1987	16	(7)	
Ivan Ćurjurić (CRO)	29.09.1989	11		
Nebojša Gavrić (SRB)	27.08.1991	9	(1)	1
Adis Hadžanović	02.01.1993	20	(6)	
Faris Handžić	27.05.1995	10	(13)	1
Kenan Handžić	23.01.1991	17		1
Eldar Hasanović	12.01.1990	3	(1)	
Mahir Karić	05.03.1992	11	(9)	
Dženan Kišić	30.04.1999		(3)	
Nikola Mojović	21.12.1991		(3)	
Milan Muminović	02.10.1983	9	(6)	
Marko Perišić	25.01.1991	19	(1)	
Zajko Zeba	22.05.1983	5	(1)	
Forwards:	**DOB**	**M**	**(s)**	**G**
Ahmed Hasanović	06.07.2000	2	(6)	2
Meldin Jusufi	30.12.1998	1	(5)	
Adnan Osmanović	20.03.1997	29		7
Ermin Mahmutović	12.05.2001	1	(7)	
Slobodan Milanović	27.08.1992	11		1
Nathan Crepaldi da Cruz (BRA)	28.05.1999	11	(5)	
Aladin Šišic	28.09.1991	19	(8)	3
Aid Tabaković	17.09.2002		(9)	

Fudbalski klub Radnik Bijeljina

Founded:	14.06.1945	
Stadium:	Stadion Gradski, Bijeljina (6,000)	
Trainer:	Slavko Petrović (SRB)	10.08.1958
[24.11.2020]	Darko Nestorović	04.04.1965
[17.01.2021]	Jovo Borković	17.03.1963
[21.04.2021]	Vlado Jagodić	22.03.1964

Goalkeepers:	DOB	M	(s)	G
Luka Bilobrk	08.12.1985	11		
Dalibor Kozić	10.02.1988	22		
Defenders:	**DOB**	**M**	**(s)**	**G**
Miladin Filipović (SRB)	02.09.1995	10	(3)	
Dejan Koraksić (SRB)	31.12.1991	16		
Nenad Nikić	08.07.2001	7	(11)	
Saša Novaković (CRO)	27.05.1991	22		1
Marko Savinović (SRB)	13.01.1991		(1)	
Miloš Simonović (SRB)	28.05.1990	14		
Pavle Sušić	15.04.1988	18	(6)	
Ivan Šubert (SRB)	14.10.1993	27	(1)	
Mustafa Šukilović	01.01.2003		(1)	
Aleksandar Vasić	21.05.1991	17	(3)	
Luka Vinski	12.02.1999		(1)	
Uroš Zupur	08.07.2002		(1)	
Midfielders:	**DOB**	**M**	**(s)**	**G**
Velibor Đurić	05.05.1982	15	(7)	1
Faruk Gogić	04.10.1999	13	(13)	1
Vladimir Grahovac	12.01.1995		(5)	
Stefan Janjić	11.02.1996	14	(9)	1
Milivoje Lazić	19.09.1992	1	(14)	1
Nedim Mekić	15.04.1995	23	(2)	2
Marko Milenković (SRB)	19.07.1991	11	(2)	
Nikola Popara	08.03.1992	22	(5)	1
Forwards:	**DOB**	**M**	**(s)**	**G**
Vladimir Bradonjić	11.12.1999	15	(1)	5
Ermin Huseinbašić	11.07.1993	19	(3)	3
Matej Jelić (CRO)	05.11.1990	6	(4)	2
Mahir Karić	14.12.1986	22	(3)	1
Bojan Mitrović	02.02.1999		(1)	
Jovan Motika	11.09.1998	11	(12)	
Kenan Sarić	18.12.1997	6	(8)	2
Milan Vušurović (MNE)	18.04.1995	18	(2)	4
Seid Zukić	09.04.1994	3	(13)	1

Fudbalski klub Sarajevo

Founded: 24.10.1946
Stadium: Stadion "Asim Ferhatović Hase", Sarajevo (34,500)
Trainer: Vinko Marinović   03.02.1971
[13.05.2021]   Dženan Uščuplić   18.08.1975

Goalkeepers:	DOB	M	(s)	G
Belmin Dizdarević	09.08.2001	1		
Elvis Džafić (SVN)	19.12.1990	2		
Vladan Kovačević	11.04.1998	29		
Defenders:	**DOB**	**M**	**(s)**	**G**
Hamza Bešić	27.09.2000	1		
Amer Dupovac	29.05.1991	27	(1)	1
Dušan Hodžić	31.10.1993	11	(10)	
Dino Islamović	23.01.2001		(1)	
Hrvoje Miličević (CRO)	20.04.1993	26		
Selmir Pidro	03.03.1998	26	(3)	
Besim Šerbečić	01.05.1998	7	(2)	
Midfielders:	**DOB**	**M**	**(s)**	**G**
Joachim Adukor (GHA)	02.05.1993	10	(5)	
Andrej Đokanović	01.03.2001	23	(7)	
Faruk Hodžić	04.08.2003		(1)	
Zinedin Mustedanagić	01.08.1998	5	(8)	2
Mirko Oremuš (CRO)	06.09.1988	23		
Aleksandr Pejović (SRB)	28.12.1990	21	(2)	
Amar Rahmanović	13.05.1994	13	(1)	6
Đani Salčin	19.03.2000	4	(6)	
Tino-Sven Sušić	13.02.1992	12	(8)	1
Dal Varešanović	23.05.2001	1		1
Forwards:	**DOB**	**M**	**(s)**	**G**
Mersudin Ahmetović	19.03.1985	5	(5)	3
Boris Cmiljanić (MNE)	17.03.1996		(2)	
Kenan Dervišagić	29.07.2000		(1)	
Matthias Olubori Ayodluwa Fanimo (ENG)	28.01.1994	21	(9)	10
Haris Handžić	20.06.1990	17	(13)	5
Anel Hebibović	07.07.1990	8	(11)	2
Ivan Jukić	21.06.1996	8	(16)	2
Jasmin Mešanović	06.01.1992	12		2
Slobodan Milanović	27.08.1992	5	(4)	
Benjamin Tatar	18.05.1994	17		10
Krste Velkoski (MKD)	20.02.1988	17	(9)	3

Fudbalski Klub Sloboda Tuzla

Founded: 10.10.1919
Stadium: Stadion Tušanj, Tuzla (7,200)
Trainer: Gradimir Crnogorac   14.11.1982
[16.03.2021]   Mladen Žižović   27.12.1980

Goalkeepers:	DOB	M	(s)	G
Adnan Golubovič (SVN)	22.07.1995	28		
Luka Kukić (CRO)	16.05.1996	5		
Defenders:	**DOB**	**M**	**(s)**	**G**
Nedim Avdić	03.02.2003	4		
Amar Beganović	25.11.1999	26		2
Kenin Devedzić	01.01.2000	13	(6)	
Nemanja Ilić (SRB)	27.08.1992	9		
Adnan Islamović (SRB)	06.04.1997	4	(1)	
Emir Jusić	13.06.1986	28	(1)	2
Edvin Kovačević	06.07.2002		(1)	
Adnan Mujkić	27.10.1995	4	(1)	
Jasmin Osmic	13.07.2001	21	(6)	1
Adnan Salihović	18.10.1992	3	(3)	
Nemanja Tomašević	09.08.1999	19		1
Dejan Uzelac (SRB)	29.11.1993	10	(1)	
Midfielders:	**DOB**	**M**	**(s)**	**G**
Josip Balić (CRO)	08.07.1993	7		1
Bojan Đorđić (SRB)	26.05.1994		(6)	
Elvedin Herić	09.02.1997	4	(2)	
Said Husejinović	17.05.1988	27	(1)	4
Ermin Kadrić	29.11.2001	3	(10)	
Alen Kurtalić	28.10.1999	22	(6)	2
Nikola Leko	30.09.1996	2	(6)	
Saša Maksimović	18.12.1999	25	(5)	3
Vanja Marković	20.06.1994	1	(2)	
Eldar Mehmedović	10.04.2003		(3)	
Robert Mišković (CRO)	20.10.1999	8	(5)	2
Semir Pezer	18.08.1992	5		
Fedor Predragović	08.04.1995	28	(1)	2
Tarik Saletović	20.10.2002	1		
Denis Žerić	21.03.1998		(3)	
Forwards:	**DOB**	**M**	**(s)**	**G**
Adi Alić	05.03.2002	3	(16)	1
Dženis Beganović	23.03.1996	27		5
Mirza Halvadžić	15.02.1996		(1)	
Esmir Hasukić	22.09.2001		(7)	
Anel Husić	12.12.1994	3	(1)	
Abid Mujagič	05.08.1993	21	(9)	3
Nail Omerović	20.10.2002		(3)	
Ševkija Resić	04.12.1999		(4)	
Dušan Ristić (SRB)	24.09.1997	2	(14)	1

Nogometni klub Široki Brijeg

Founded: 1948
Stadium: Stadion Pecara, Široki Brijeg (5,628)
Trainer: Toni Karačić   06.12.1974

Goalkeepers:	DOB	M	(s)	G
Dario Miškić (CRO)	18.04.1996	20	(1)	
Martin Zlomislić	16.08.1998	13		
Defenders:	**DOB**	**M**	**(s)**	**G**
Filip Brekalo (CRO)	09.06.2002		(9)	
Branimir Cipetić (CRO)	24.05.1995	13	(2)	
Dino Ćorić	30.06.1990	16	(1)	3
Tomislav Čuljak (CRO)	25.05.1987	19		
Gabrijel Drmač	11.01.2003	1		
Teo Herceg	01.09.2000	1	(1)	
Ante Hrkać	11.03.1992		(1)	
Marko Jurić (CRO)	07.10.1994	21	(4)	
Mate Lasić	29.03.2002	1		
Bernardo Matić (CRO)	27.07.1994	3		
Kristijan Medić	17.03.2000	15	(1)	1
Božo Musa (CRO)	15.09.1988	9		
Ivan Mustapić	27.02.2002		(1)	
Jure Obšivač (CRO)	28.05.1990	16	(2)	1
Stjepan Radeljić	05.09.1997	15		1
Petar Raguž (CRO)	05.10.1996	1	(4)	
Midfielders:	**DOB**	**M**	**(s)**	**G**
Franjo Baketarić	10.05.2003		(1)	
Zvonimir Begić	22.09.1990	25	(1)	1
Ivan Grgić	02.02.2003	2	(8)	
Luka Knežević	14.03.1999	1	(4)	
Mateo Marić	18.03.1998	19		1
David Martić	10.04.2002	1		
Ilija Mašić	08.04.1999	3	(14)	
Marko Pervan (CRO)	04.04.1996	14	(2)	2
Mato Stanić	11.01.1998	27	(4)	2
Mijo Šabić (CRO)	08.10.1994	4	(7)	
Bože Vukoja	03.04.1998	19	(9)	
Forwards:	**DOB**	**M**	**(s)**	**G**
Viktor Angelov (MKD)	27.03.1994	6	(6)	4
Ivan Ikić (CRO)	13.09.1999	19	(6)	5
Toni Jović (CRO)	02.09.1992	10	(6)	5
Stipe Jurić	19.11.1998	12	(17)	10
Alen Jurilj	07.03.1996	26	(5)	7
Josip Maganjić (CRO)	06.01.1999	1	(3)	
Josip Majić (CRO)	05.07.1994	1	(6)	
Karlo Marić	27.01.2002		(1)	
Luka Miletić	12.03.2002	1		
Josip Planinić	07.07.2003	1		
Stipe Tokić	14.01.2002	1		
Mateusz Zachara (POL)	27.03.1990	6	(3)	1

Fudbalski klub Tuzla City

Founded: 1955 (*as FK Sloga Simin Han*)
Stadium: Stadion Tušanj, Tuzla (7,200)
Trainer: Zlatan Nalić — 23.01.1969
[19.10.2020] Nermin Bašić — 24.11.1983
[15.01.2021] Husref Musemić — 04.07.1961

Goalkeepers:	DOB	M	(s)	G
Nevres Fejzić	04.11.1990	20		
Azir Muminović	18.04.1997	13	(1)	
Defenders:	**DOB**	**M**	**(s)**	**G**
Hrvoje Barišić (CRO)	03.02.1991	25	(1)	1
Elvir Duraković	07.02.2000	2	(7)	
Boban Đerić	20.08.1993	13	(7)	
Jovo Kojić	08.04.1988	11		
Ivan Kostić (SRB)	24.06.1989	6	(2)	
Luka Lučić (CRO)	02.01.1995	9	(1)	1
Damir Mehidić	07.01.1992	9	(3)	
Darrick-Kobie Morris (CRO)	15.07.1995	22	(8)	
Dario Rugašević	29.01.1991	18		
Midfielders:	**DOB**	**M**	**(s)**	**G**
Goran Brkić (SRB)	28.04.1991	8		4
Haris Džaferović	17.02.1999		(2)	
Adnan Džafić	10.05.1990	20	(7)	3

	DOB	M	(s)	G
Nermin Hodžić	13.07.1994		(4)	
Huso Karjašević	10.07.1997	29	(1)	1
Dejan Maksimović	11.10.1995	17	(8)	3
Belmin Mešinović	06.12.2001	3	(11)	
Petar Mišić (CRO)	24.07.1994	12		3
Nemanja Nikolić (MNE)	01.01.1988	11	(2)	
Ajdin Nukić	26.11.1997	29		1
Edin Rustemović	06.01.1993	14	(3)	1
Forwards:	**DOB**	**M**	**(s)**	**G**
Badara Badji (SEN)	24.02.1994	13	(13)	4
Dženis Beganović	23.03.1996	1	(1)	
Nermin Crnkić	31.08.1992	15	(10)	5
Agustin Doffo (ARG)	25.05.1995	15	(3)	
Vedin Kulović	12.12.1995		(1)	
Mirsad Ramić	06.12.1992	8	(20)	2
Vojo Ubiparip (SRB)	10.05.1988	20	(9)	7

Fudbalski klub Velež Mostar

Founded: 26.06.1922
Stadium: Stadion Rođeni, Mostar (7,000)
Trainer: Feđa Dudić — 01.02.1983

Goalkeepers:	DOB	M	(s)	G
Adnan Bobić	04.02.1987	14		
Slaviša Bogdanović	11.10.1993	15	(1)	
Vedran Kjosevski	22.05.1995	4		
Defenders:	**DOB**	**M**	**(s)**	**G**
Nermin Alagić	03.05.2001		(4)	
Faruk Bihorać (SRB)	12.05.1996	7	(4)	
Konstantin Cheshmedijev (MKD)	29.01.1996	12	(4)	
Muharem Čivić	04.01.1993	7	(10)	1
Mehmed Ćosić	25.06.1997	28	(3)	2
Fernando Darío Ferreyra	19.01.1997	20	(5)	1
Slaviša Radović (SRB)	08.10.1993	14	(6)	
Samir Zeljković	04.09.1997	27	(1)	1
Denis Zvonić	08.02.1992	20	(8)	3
Midfielders:	**DOB**	**M**	**(s)**	**G**
Seid Behram	12.07.1998		(6)	1

	DOB	M	(s)	G
Dino Hasanović	21.01.1996	9	(2)	
Melvin Osmić	16.02.1999	10	(20)	
Haris Ovcina	24.10.1996	10	(22)	2
Omar Pršeš	07.05.1997	17	(13)	
Samir Radovac	25.01.1996	30		6
Forwards:	**DOB**	**M**	**(s)**	**G**
Nemanja Anđušić	17.10.1996	14	(6)	4
Ubiratan Brandao de Souza (BRA)	01.11.1995	27	(3)	2
Obren Cvijanović	30.08.1994	23	(3)	11
Berin Ćatić	30.01.2000		(4)	
Dejan Georgijević (SRB)	19.01.1994	14		4
Dženit Hajdarević	15.05.2003		(2)	
Fejsal Mulić	03.10.1994	16	(3)	9
Dževad Sijamija	18.02.2002		(3)	
Edo Vehabović	01.05.1995	25	(6)	2
Faris Zubanović	12.06.2000		(6)	

Hrvatski športski klub Zrinjski Mostar

Founded: 1905
Stadium: Stadion pod Bijelim Brijegom, Mostar (9,000)
Trainer: Mladen Žižović — 27.12.1980
[28.12.2020] Sergej Jakirović — 23.12.1976

Goalkeepers:	DOB	M	(s)	G
Ivan Brkić (CRO)	29.06.1995	13		
Dinko Horkaš (CRO)	10.03.1999	5		
Antonio Soldo	12.01.1988	2	(1)	
Miro Varvodić (CRO)	15.05.1989	13		
Defenders:	**DOB**	**M**	**(s)**	**G**
Tomislav Barbarić (CRO)	29.03.1989	12		
Almir Bekić	01.06.1989	23	(4)	
Josip Čorluka (CRO)	03.03.1995	27	(1)	1
Luis Ezequiel Ibáñez (ARG)	15.07.1988	4	(4)	
Slobodan Jakovljević (SRB)	26.05.1989	30		1
Ivor Krešić	14.03.2001	1	(1)	
Zarija Lambulić	25.05.1998	1		
Marin Magdić (CRO)	13.04.1999	12		1
Rijad Sadiku	18.01.2001	1	(1)	
Pero Stojkić	09.12.1986	6	(8)	
Mario Tičinović (CRO)	20.08.1991	17	(8)	1
Midfielders:	**DOB**	**M**	**(s)**	**G**
Filip Arežina	08.11.1992	3	(5)	
Ivan Bašić	30.04.2002	6	(7)	2
Blaž Bošković	15.12.2001		(4)	

	DOB	M	(s)	G
Mateo Božić	08.11.2000		(1)	
Ivan Enin (RUS)	06.02.1994	24	(4)	1
Miloš Filipović (SRB)	09.05.1990	20	(4)	5
Dragan Juranović (CRO)	10.02.1994	14		4
Juraj Ljubić (CRO)	26.05.2000	2	(6)	
Domagoj Pušić (CRO)	24.10.1991	4	(3)	
Ognjen Todorović	24.03.1989	16	(16)	2
Dinko Trebotić (CRO)	30.07.1990	14	(9)	2
Zvonimir Vukoja (CRO)	29.07.1997	1	(3)	
Damir Zlomislić	20.07.1991	29		2
Forwards:	**DOB**	**M**	**(s)**	**G**
Nemanja Bilbija	02.11.1990	28		17
Miljan Govedarica	26.05.1994	7	(10)	1
Josip Ivančić	29.03.1991	12	(7)	5
Petar Kunić	15.07.1993	3	(6)	
Domagoj Marušić	19.03.2000	1	(5)	
Anes Masić	08.02.2000	11	(14)	4
Suad Sahiti	06.02.1995		(5)	
Miljan Škrbić (SRB)	18.09.1995	1	(5)	
Asim Zec	23.01.1994		(2)	

Fudbalski klub Željezničar Sarajevo

Founded:	19.09.1921		
Stadium:	Stadion Grbavica, Sarajevo (13,146)		
Trainer:	Amar Osim		18.07.1967
[15.04.2021]	Blaž Slišković		30.05.1959

Goalkeepers:	DOB	M	(s)	G
Josip Bender (CRO)	01.03.1995	4		
Filip Erić (SRB)	10.10.1994	19		
Irfan Fejzić	01.07.1986	8		
Vedad Muftić	25.10.2001	2		
Defenders:	**DOB**	**M**	**(s)**	**G**
Ante Blažević (CRO)	05.05.1996	13	(5)	
Amar Drina	30.05.2002		(1)	
Frane Ikić (CRO)	19.06.1994	25		2
Aleksandar Kosorić	30.01.1987	23	(1)	
Luka Miletić	04.10.1994	13	(5)	1
Ivan Miličević	16.07.1998	17	(4)	2
Siniša Stevanović (SRB)	12.01.1989	20		1
Eldar Šehić	28.04.2000	16	(2)	
Vedran Vrhovac	20.11.1998	5	(4)	
Midfielders:	**DOB**	**M**	**(s)**	**G**
Mehmed Alispahić	24.11.1987	25	(4)	2
Omar Beca	01.01.2002	1	(3)	
Samir Bekrić	20.10.1984	13	(17)	4
Petar Bojo	08.01.1998	13	(7)	2

	DOB	M	(s)	G
Jasmin Čeliković	07.01.1999	12	(1)	
Faruk Duraković	05.09.2002	1	(2)	1
Haris Hajdarević	07.10.1998	16		
Nermin Jamak	25.08.1986		(2)	
Mustafa Mujezinović	06.05.1993	23	(9)	5
Sinan Ramović	13.10.1992	3	(1)	
Damir Sadiković	07.04.1995	6		
Sedad Subašić	16.02.2001	6	(11)	
Anel Šabanadžović	24.05.1999		(2)	
Semir Štilić	08.10.1987	19	(7)	8
Forwards:	**DOB**	**M**	**(s)**	**G**
Hamza Gasal	16.12.2002	6	(2)	1
Anel Hajrič	04.03.1996		(7)	
Damir Hrelja	13.10.2001		(4)	
Luka Juričić	25.11.1996	18	(7)	8
Ivan Lendrić (CRO)	08.08.1991	14	(10)	6
Salko Nargalić	16.07.2001		(1)	
Asim Zec	23.01.1994	1	(3)	
Ermin Zec	18.02.1988	10	(8)	5
Mladen Veselinović	04.01.1993	11	(12)	2

SECOND LEVEL
First League – m:tel Prva liga 2020/2021

First League of the Federation of Bosnia and Herzegovina

1.	HŠK Posušje (*Promoted*)	30	18	7	5	49	-	15	61
2.	NK TOŠK Tešanj	30	16	6	8	48	-	28	54
3.	FK Rudar Kakanj	30	15	5	10	43	-	31	50
4.	FK Goražde	30	14	7	9	43	-	37	49
5.	NK Zvijezda Gradačac	30	14	6	10	44	-	31	48
6.	NK Bratstvo Gračanica	30	14	6	10	43	-	30	48
7.	NK GOŠK Gabela	30	12	7	11	38	-	27	43
8.	NK Jedinstvo Bihać	30	13	4	13	26	-	36	43
9.	FK Radnik Hadžići	30	11	7	12	32	-	36	40
10.	FK Budućnost Banovići	30	12	4	14	38	-	49	40
11.	NK Vis Simm Bau	30	11	6	13	42	-	37	39
12.	NK Travnik	30	10	9	11	31	-	37	39
13.	FK Igman Konjic	30	10	7	13	38	-	35	37
14.	HNK Orašje (*Relegated*)	30	10	6	14	43	-	51	36
15.	HNK Čapljina (*Relegated*)	30	10	6	14	38	-	49	36
16.	NK Slaven Živinice (*Relegated*)	30	1	5	24	17	-	84	8

First League of of the Republika Srpska

1.	FK Rudar Prijedor (*Promoted*)	30	19	6	5	51	-	20	63
2.	FK Leotar Trebinje (*Promoted*)	30	14	12	4	47	-	27	54
3.	FK Zvijezda 09 Dvorovi	30	15	8	7	50	-	33	53
4.	FK Željezničar Banja Luka	30	12	10	8	46	-	37	46
5.	FK Tekstilac Derventa	30	13	6	11	35	-	36	45
6.	FK Sloboda Novi Grad	30	12	8	10	25	-	27	44
7.	FK Alfa Modriča	30	12	7	11	52	-	37	43
8.	FK Kozara Gradiška	30	11	9	10	34	-	28	42
9.	FK Slavija Sarajevo	30	10	11	9	30	-	33	41
10.	FK Borac Kozarska Dubica	30	11	6	13	35	-	38	39
11.	FK Sloga Doboj	30	9	11	10	34	-	29	38
12.	FK Ljubić Prnjavor	30	11	5	14	45	-	45	38
13.	FK Drina Zvornik	30	10	8	12	39	-	50	38
14.	FK Sutjeska Foča	30	10	5	15	39	-	40	35
15.	FK Podrinje Janja	30	5	6	19	17	-	56	21
16.	FK Jedinstvo Brčko (*Relegated*)	30	4	6	20	29	-	72	18

INTERNATIONAL MATCHES
(16.07.2020 – 15.07.2021)

Date	Venue	Match	Result	Comp
04.09.2020	Firenze	Italy - Bosnia and Herzegovina	1-1(0-0)	(UNL)
07.09.2020	Zenica	Bosnia and Herzegovina - Poland	1-2(1-1)	(UNL)
08.10.2020	Sarajevo	Bosnia and Herzegovina - Northern Ireland	1-1(1-0,1-1,1-1); 3-4 on penalties	(ECQPO)
11.10.2020	Zenica	Bosnia and Herzegovina - Netherlands	0-0	(UNL)
14.10.2020	Wrocław	Poland - Bosnia and Herzegovina	3-0(2-0)	(UNL)
12.11.2020	Sarajevo	Bosnia and Herzegovina - Iran	0-2(0-0)	(F)
15.11.2020	Amsterdam	Netherlands - Bosnia and Herzegovina	3-1(2-0)	(UNL)
18.11.2020	Sarajevo	Bosnia and Herzegovina - Italy	0-2(0-1)	(UNL)
24.03.2021	Helsinki	Finland - Bosnia and Herzegovina	2-2(0-0)	(WCQ)
27.03.2021	Zenica	Bosnia and Herzegovina - Costa Rica	0-0	(F)
31.03.2021	Sarajevo	Bosnia and Herzegovina - France	0-1(0-0)	(WCQ)
02.06.2021	Sarajevo	Bosnia and Herzegovina - Montenegro	0-0	(F)
06.06.2021	Brøndby	Denmark - Bosnia and Herzegovina	2-0(1-0)	(F)

04.09.2020   ITALY - BOSNIA AND HERZEGOVINA   1-1(0-0)   2nd UEFA Nations League A, Group 1
Stadio "Artemio Franchi", Firenze; Referee: Anastasios Sidiropoulos (Greece); Attendance: 0
BIH: Ibrahim Šehić, Toni Šunjić, Siniša Saničanin, Branimir Cipetić, Sead Kolašinac (83.Eldar Ćivić), Edin Višća (86.Deni Milošević), Gojko Cimirot, Amir Hadžiahmetović, Amer Gojak, Edin Džeko (Cap), Armin Hodžić (77.Muhamed Bešić). Trainer: Dušan Bajević.
Goal: Edin Džeko (57).

07.09.2020   BOSNIA AND HERZEGOVINA - POLAND   1-2(1-1)   2nd UEFA Nations League A, Group 1
Stadion Bilino Polje, Zenica; Referee: Cüneyt Çakır (Turkey); Attendance: 0
BIH: Asmir Begović (Cap), Ermin Bičakčić, Eldar Ćivić (82.Deni Milošević), Siniša Saničanin, Zoran Kvržić, Muhamed Bešić (60.Edin Džeko), Haris Hajradinović, Amir Hadžiahmetović, Amer Gojak (46.Edin Višća), Armin Hodžić, Elvir Koljić. Trainer: Dušan Bajević.
Goal: Haris Hajradinović (24 penalty).

08.10.2020   BOSNIA AND HERZEGOVINA - NORTHERN IRELAND   1-1 aet; 3-4 pen.   16th EC. Qualifiers Play-offs, Semi-Finals
Stadion Grbavica, Sarajevo; Referee: Antonio Miguel Mateu Lahoz (Spain); Attendance: 1,800
BIH: Ibrahim Šehić, Siniša Saničanin, Anel Ahmedhodžić, Branimir Cipetić, Sead Kolašinac (118.Haris Hajradinović), Miralem Pjanić, Edin Višća, Gojko Cimirot (106.Stjepan Lončar), Amir Hadžiahmetović(83.Amer Gojak), Edin Džeko (Cap), Rade Krunić (88.Dino Hotič). Trainer: Dušan Bajević.
Goal: Rade Krunić (14).
Penalties: Miralem Pjanić, Haris Hajradinović (saved), Edin Višća (missed), Dino Hotič, Edin Džeko.

11.10.2020   BOSNIA AND HERZEGOVINA - NETHERLANDS   0-0   2nd UEFA Nations League A, Group 1
Stadion Bilino Polje, Zenica; Referee: István Kovács (Romania); Attendance: 1,600
BIH: Ibrahim Šehić, Siniša Saničanin, Darko Todorović, Advan Kadušić (46.Sead Kolašinac), Miralem Pjanić (Cap) (75.Stjepan Lončar), Gojko Cimirot, Rade Krunić (75.Armin Hodžić), Amer Gojak, Dennis Hadžikadunić, Milan Đurić (61.Edin Džeko), Benjamin Tatar (54.Amir Hadžiahmetović). Trainer: Dušan Bajević.

14.10.2020   POLAND - BOSNIA AND HERZEGOVINA   3-0(2-0)   2nd UEFA Nations League A, Group 1
Stadion Miejski, Wrocław; Referee: Craig Pawson (England); Attendance: 8,152
BIH: Ibrahim Šehić, Siniša Saničanin, Anel Ahmedhodžić [sent off 15], Branimir Cipetić, Sead Kolašinac, Miralem Pjanić (33.Dennis Hadžikadunić), Edin Višća (58.Amer Gojak), Gojko Cimirot, Amir Hadžiahmetović (74.Haris Hajradinović), Edin Džeko (Cap) (58.Smail Prevljak), Rade Krunić (74.Deni Milošević). Trainer: Dušan Bajević.

12.11.2020   BOSNIA AND HERZEGOVINA - IRAN   0-2(0-0)   Friendly International
Stadion "Asim Ferhatović Hase", Sarajevo; Referee: Mkilovan Milačić (Montenegro); Attendance: 0
BIH: Jasmin Burić (22.Kenan Pirić), Josip Ćorluka, Adnan Kovačević, Siniša Saničanin, Bojan Nastić (58.Advan Kadušić), Stjepan Lončar, Miralem Pjanić (Cap) (46.Gojko Cimirot), Amar Rahmanović (81.Deni Milošević), Irfan Hadžić (58.Smail Prevljak), Amer Gojak (46.Armin Hodžić), Benjamin Tatar. Trainer: Dušan Bajević.

15.11.2020   NETHERLANDS - BOSNIA AND HERZEGOVINA   3-1(2-0)   2nd UEFA Nations League A, Group 1
"Johan Cruyff" Arena, Amsterdam; Referee: François Letexier (France); Attendance: 0
BIH: Ibrahim Šehić, Siniša Saničanin, Darko Todorović, Edin Višća (78.Benjamin Tatar), Sead Kolašinac, Gojko Cimirot, Rade Krunić (78.Amar Rahmanović), Dennis Hadžikadunić, Miralem Pjanić (Cap) (89.Almedin Ziljkić), Amer Gojak (61.Vladan Danilović), Armin Hodžić (61.Smail Prevljak). Trainer: Dušan Bajević.
Goal: Smail Prevljak (63).

18.11.2020   BOSNIA AND HERZEGOVINA - ITALY   0-2(0-1)   2nd UEFA Nations League A, Group 1
Stadion Grbavica, Sarajevo; Referee: Artur Manuel Ribeiro Soares Dias (Portugal); Attendance: 0
BIH: Kenan Pirić, Josip Ćorluka, Siniša Saničanin, Advan Kadušić (79.Darko Todorović), Miralem Pjanić (Cap) (76.Vladan Danilović), Gojko Cimirot, Rade Krunić (71.Stjepan Lončar), Amer Gojak, Dennis Hadžikadunić, Benjamin Tatar (79.Amar Rahmanović), Smail Prevljak (79.Irfan Hadžić). Trainer: Dušan Bajević.

24.03.2021   FINLAND - BOSNIA AND HERZEGOVINA   2-2(0-0)   22nd FIFA WC. Qualifiers
Olympiastadion, Helsinki; Referee: Anastasios Sidiropoulos (Greece); Attendance: 0
BIH: Ibrahim Šehić, Eldar Ćivić, Siniša Saničanin, Darko Todorović, Miroslav Stevanović (89.Sead Kolašinac), Miralem Pjanić, Gojko Cimirot (85.Ermedin Demirović), Amer Gojak (64.Haris Duljević), Dennis Hadžikadunić, Rade Krunić, Edin Džeko (Cap). Trainer: Ivaylo Petev (Bulgaria).
Goals: Miralem Pjanić (55), Miroslav Stevanović (84).

27.03.2021　　**BOSNIA AND HERZEGOVINA - COSTA RICA**　　　　**0-0**　　　　　　　Friendly International
Stadion Bilino Polje, Zenica; Referee: Nejc Kajtazovič (Slovenia); Attendance: 0
BIH: Nikola Vasilj (58.Kenan Pirić), Anel Ahmedhodžić, Branimir Cipetić, Sead Kolašinac (Cap) (80.Selmir Pidro), Amar Rahmanović (46.Smail Prevljak), Amir Hadžiahmetović, Marko Mihojević (76.Dennis Hadžikadunić), Haris Duljević (58.Amer Gojak), Ermedin Demirović, Luka Menalo (80.Obren Cvijanović), Stjepan Lončar. Trainer: Ivaylo Petev (Bulgaria).

31.03.2021　　**BOSNIA AND HERZEGOVINA - FRANCE**　　　　**0-1(0-0)**　　　　　22nd FIFA WC. Qualifiers
Stadion Grbavica, Sarajevo; Referee: Daniele Orsato (Italy); Attendance: 0
BIH: Ibrahim Šehić, Siniša Saničanin, Darko Todorović (77.Miroslav Stevanović), Anel Ahmedhodžić, Sead Kolašinac, Miralem Pjanić, Gojko Cimirot (86.Amer Gojak), Amir Hadžiahmetović, Dennis Hadžikadunić, Edin Džeko (Cap), Rade Krunić (86.Smail Prevljak). Trainer: Ivaylo Petev (Bulgaria).

02.06.2021　　**BOSNIA AND HERZEGOVINA - MONTENEGRO**　　　**0-0**　　　　　　　Friendly International
Stadion Grbavica, Sarajevo; Referee: Novak Simović (Serbia); Attendance: 0
BIH: Ibrahim Šehić (Cap), Aleksandar Jovičić, Anel Ahmedhodžić (84.Vladan Danilović), Dennis Hadžikadunić, Darko Todorović (64.Jusuf Gazibegović), Rade Krunić, Amir Hadžiahmetović, Dino Beširević (54.Damir Sadiković), Eldar Ćivić, Adi Nalić (84.Luka Menalo), Ermedin Demirović (65.Smail Prevljak). Trainer: Ivaylo Petev (Bulgaria).

06.06.2021　　**DENMARK - BOSNIA AND HERZEGOVINA**　　　**2-0(1-0)**　　　　　　Friendly International
Brøndby Stadium, Brøndby; Referee: Petri Viljanen (Finland); Attendance: 7,459
BIH: Nikola Vasilj (78.Kenan Pirić), Eldar Ćivić (61.Branimir Cipetić), Siniša Saničanin (Cap), Anel Ahmedhodžić, Jusuf Gazibegović, Andrej Đokanović (78.Ajdin Nukić), Amir Hadžiahmetović, Dennis Hadžikadunić, Vladan Danilović (61.Dino Beširević), Adi Nalić (53.Smail Prevljak), Ermedin Demirović (78.Almedin Ziljkić). Trainer: Ivaylo Petev (Bulgaria).

NATIONAL TEAM PLAYERS
(16.07.2020 – 15.07.2021)

Name	DOB	Caps	Goals	2020/2021:	Club
Goalkeepers					
Asmir BEGOVIĆ	20.06.1987	63	0	2020:	*AFC Bournemouth (ENG)*
Jasmin BURIĆ	18.02.1987	3	0	2021:	*Hapoel Haifa FC (ISR)*
Kenan PIRIĆ	07.07.1994	6	0	2020/2021:	*NK Maribor (SVN)*
Ibrahim ŠEHIĆ	02.09.1988	35	0	2020/2021:	*Konyaspor Kulübü (TUR)*
Nikola VASILJ	02.12.1995	2	0	2021:	*FK Zorya Luhansk (UKR)*
Defenders					
Anel AHMEDHODŽIĆ	26.03.1999	6	0	2020/2021:	*Malmö FF (SWE)*
Ermin BIČAKČIĆ	24.01.1990	35	3	2020:	*TSG 1899 Hoffenheim (GER)*
Branimir CIPETIĆ	24.05.1995	5	0	2020: 20.01.2021->	*NK Široki Brijeg NK Lokomotiva Zagreb (CRO)*
Eldar ČIVIĆ	28.05.1996	14	1	2020/2021:	*Ferencvárosi TC (HUN)*
Josip ĆORLUKA	03.03.1995	2	0	2020:	*HŠK Zrinjski Mostar*
Jusuf GAZIBEGOVIĆ	11.03.2000	2	0	2021:	*SK Sturm Graz (AUT)*
Dennis HADŽIKADUNIĆ	09.07.1998	9	0	2020/2021:	*FK Rostov (RUS)*
Aleksandar JOVIČIĆ	18.01.1995	1	0	2021:	*HNK Gorica (CRO)*
Advan KADUŠIĆ	14.10.1997	3	0	2020:	*NK Celje (SVN)*
Sead KOLAŠINAC	20.06.1993	38	0	2020: 04.01.2021->	*Arsenal FC London (GER) FC Schalke 04 Gelsenkirchen (GER)*
Adnan KOVAČEVIĆ	09.09.1993	4	0	2020:	*Ferencvárosi TC (HUN)*
Zoran KVRŽIĆ	07.08.1988	7	0	2020:	*Kayserispor Kulübü (TUR)*
Marko MIHOJEVIĆ	21.04.1996	4	0	2021:	*Göztepe SK İzmir (TUR)*
Bojan NASTIĆ	06.07.1994	5	0	2020:	*FC BATE Borisov (BLR)*
Selmir PIDRO	03.03.1998	1	0	2021:	*FK Sarajevo*
Siniša SANIČANIN	24.04.1995	11	0	2020/2021:	*FK Vojvodina Novi Sad (SRB)*
Toni ŠUNJIĆ	15.12.1988	41	1	2020:	*FK Dinamo Moskva (RUS)*
Darko TODOROVIĆ	05.05.1997	16	0	2020/2021:	*HNK Hajduk Split (CRO)*

Midfielders

Muhamed BEŠIĆ	10.09.1992	45	0	2020:	Everton FC Liverpool (ENG)
Dino BEŠIROVIĆ	31.01.1994	4	0	2021:	Mezőkövesdi SE (HUN)
Gojko CIMIROT	19.12.1992	31	0	2020/2021:	R Standard Liège (BEL)
Vladan DANILOVIĆ	27.07.1999	4	0	2020/2021:	CD Nacional Funchal (POR)
Haris DULJEVIĆ	16.11.1993	25	1	2021:	Nîmes Olympique FC (FRA)
Andrej ĐOKANOVIĆ	01.03.2001	1	0	2021:	FK Sarajevo
Amer GOJAK	13.02.1997	21	4	2020:	GNK Dinamo Zagreb (CRO)
				05.10.2020->	Torino FC (ITA)
Amir HADŽIAHMETOVIĆ	08.03.1997	9	0	2020/2021:	Konyaspor Kulübü (TUR)
Haris HAJRADINOVIĆ	18.02.1994	4	1	2020:	Kasımpaşa Spor Kulübü (TUR)
Dino HOTIČ	26.07.1995	2	0	2020:	Cercle Brugge KSV (BEL)
Rade KRUNIĆ	07.10.1993	21	2	2020/2021:	AC Milan (ITA)
Stjepan LONČAR	10.11.1996	9	0	2020/2021:	HNK Rijeka (CRO)
Luka MENALO	22.07.1996	4	0	2021:	HNK Rijeka (CRO)
Adi NALIĆ	01.12.1997	2	0	2021:	Malmö FF (SWE)
Ajdin NUKIĆ	26.11.1997	1	0	2021:	FK Tuzla City
Amar RAHMANOVIĆ	13.05.1994	4	0	2020/2021:	FK Sarajevo
Damir SADIKOVIĆ	07.04.1995	1	0	2021:	KS Cracovia Kraków (POL)
Benjamin TATAR	18.05.1994	4	0	2020:	FK Sarajevo
Miroslav STEVANOVIĆ	29.07.1990	15	2	2021:	Servette FC Genève (SUI)
Almedin ZILJKIĆ	25.02.1996	2	0	2020/2021:	FK Borac Banja Luka

Forwards

Obren CVIJANOVIĆ	30.09.1994	1	0	2021:	FK Velež Mostar
Ermedin DEMIROVIĆ	25.03.1998	4	0	2021:	SC Freiburg (GER)
Edin DŽEKO	17.03.1986	114	59	2020/2021:	AS Roma (ITA)
Milan ĐURIĆ	22.05.1990	15	7	2020:	US Salernitana 1919 (ITA)
Irfan HADŽIĆ	15.06.1993	2	0	2020:	Ahkisar SK (TUR)
Armin HODŽIĆ	17.11.1994	14	3	2020:	Kasımpaşa Spor Kulübü (TUR)
Elvir KOLJIĆ	08.07.1995	4	0	2020:	CS Universitatea Craiova (ROU)
Deni MILOŠEVIĆ	09.03.1995	11	1	2020:	Konyaspor Kulübü (TUR)
Miralem PJANIĆ	02.04.1990	100	16	2020/2021:	FC Barcelona (ESP)
Smail PREVLJAK	10.05.1995	9	1	2020/2021:	KAS Eupen (BEL)
Edin VIŠĆA	17.02.1990	55	10	2020:	İstanbul Başakşehir FK (TUR)

Trainer

Dušan BAJEVIĆ [21.12.2019 – 01.12.2020]	10.12.1948	8 M; 0 W; 3 D; 5 L; 4-14
Ivaylo PETEV (Bulgaria) [from 27.01.2021]	09.07.1975	5 M; 0 W; 3 D; 2 L; 2-5

BULGARIA

The Country:
Република България (Republic of Bulgaria)
Capital: Sofia
Surface: 110,994 km^2
Inhabitants: 6,951,482 [2019]
Time: UTC+2

The FA:
Български футболен съюз (Bulgarian Football Union)
18 Vitoshko lale Str. BG - 1616, Sofia
Tel: +359 2 9426 202
Foundation date: 1923
Member of FIFA since: 1924
Member of UEFA since: 1954
Website: www.bfunion.bg

NATIONAL TEAM RECORDS

RECORDS
First international match:	21.05.1924, Wien: Austria – Bulgaria 6-0
Most international caps:	Stilian Petrov - 105 caps (1998-2011)
Most international goals:	Dimitar Berbatov - 48 goals / 78 caps (1999-2010)

UEFA EUROPEAN CHAMPIONSHIP
1960	Qualifiers
1964	Qualifiers
1968	Qualifiers
1972	Qualifiers
1976	Qualifiers
1980	Qualifiers
1984	Qualifiers
1988	Qualifiers
1992	Qualifiers
1996	Final Tournament (Group Stage)
2000	Qualifiers
2004	Final Tournament (Group Stage)
2008	Qualifiers
2012	Qualifiers
2016	Qualifiers
2020	Qualifiers

FIFA WORLD CUP
1930	Did not enter
1934	Qualifiers
1938	Qualifiers
1950	Did not enter
1954	Qualifiers
1958	Qualifiers
1962	Final Tournament (Group Stage)
1966	Final Tournament (Group Stage)
1970	Final Tournament (Group Stage)
1974	Final Tournament (Group Stage)
1978	Qualifiers
1982	Qualifiers
1986	Final Tournament (2nd Round of 16)
1990	Qualifiers
1994	Final Tournament (4th Place)
1998	Final Tournament (Group Stage)
2002	Qualifiers
2006	Qualifiers
2010	Qualifiers
2014	Qualifiers
2018	Qualifiers

OLYMPIC TOURNAMENTS
1908	*Did not enter*
1912	*Did not enter*
1920	*Did not enter*
1924	1st Round
1928	*Did not enter*
1936	*Did not enter*
1948	*Did not enter*
1952	1st Round
1956	Semi-Finals
1960	Group Stage
1964	Qualifiers
1968	Runners-up
1972	Qualifiers
1976	Qualifiers
1980	Qualifiers
1984	Qualifiers
1988	Qualifiers
1992	Qualifiers
1996	Qualifiers
2000	Qualifiers
2004	Qualifiers
2008	Qualifiers
2012	Qualifiers
2016	Qualifiers

UEFA NATIONS LEAGUE
2018/2019	League C (promoted to League B)
2020/2021	League B (relegated to League C)

FIFA CONFEDERATIONS CUP 1992-2017
None

BULGARIAN CLUB HONOURS IN EUROPEAN CLUB COMPETITIONS:

European Champion Clubs' Cup (1956-1992) / UEFA Champions League (1993-2021)
None

Fairs Cup (1858-1971) / UEFA Cup (1972-2009) / UEFA Europa League (2010-2021)
None

UEFA Super Cup (1972-2020)
None

*European Cup Winners' Cup 1961-1999**
None

*defunct competition

NATIONAL COMPETITIONS
TABLE OF HONOURS

	STATE CHAMPIONSHIPS CHAMPIONS	CUP WINNERS*	BEST GOALSCORERS	
1924	*Not finished*	-	-	
1925	Vladislav Varna	-	-	
1926	Vladislav Varna	-	-	
1927	*No competition*	-	-	
1928	Slavia Sofia	-	-	
1929	Botev Plovdiv	-	-	
1930	SK Slavia Sofia	-	-	
1931	AS 23 Sofia	-	-	
1932	Spartak Varna	-	-	
1933	SK Levski Sofia	-	-	
1934	Vladislav Varna	-	-	
1935	Sportklub Sofia	-	-	
1936	SK Slavia Sofia	-	-	
1937	SK Levski Sofia	-	-	
1937/1938	Ticha Varna	FC 13 Sofia	Krum Milev (Slavia Sofia)	12
1938/1939	SK Slavia Sofia	Shipka Sofia	Georgi Pachedzhiev (AS 23 Sofia)	14
1939/1940	Lokomotiv Sofia	FC 13 Sofia	-	
1941	SK Slavia Sofia	AS 23 Sofia	-	
1942	SK Levski Sofia	Levski Sofia	-	
1943	Slavia Sofia	-	-	
1944	*Not finished*	-	-	

*called between 1938-1942 Tsar's Cup.

	REPUBLIC CHAMPIONSHIPS CHAMPIONS	CUP WINNERS**	BEST GOALSCORERS
1945	Lokomotiv Sofia	-	-
1946	SK Levski Sofia	SK Levski Sofia	-
1947	SK Levski Sofia	SK Levski Sofia	-
1948	CDNV Sofia	Lokomotiv Sofia	-

	„A" GROUP CHAMPIONS	CUP WINNERS**	BEST GOALSCORERS	
1948/1949	SK Levski Sofia	SK Levski Sofia	Dimitar Milanov (CSKA Sofia) Nedko Nedev (Cherno More Varna)	11
1950	SK Levski Sofia	SK Levski Sofia	Lyubomir Hranov (SK Levski Sofia)	13
1951	CDNA Sofia	CDNA Sofia	Dimitar Milanov (CDNA Sofia)	14
1952	CDNA Sofia	GUTP-DSO Udarnik Sofia	Dimitar Isakov (GUTP-DSO Udarnik Sofia) Dobromir Tashkov (Spartak Sofia)	10
1953	SK Levski Sofia	Lokomotiv Sofia	Dimitar Minchev (Spartak Pleven / VVS Sofia)	15
1954	CDNA Sofia	CDNA Sofia	Dobromir Tashkov (GUTP-DSO Udarnik Sofia)	25
1955	CDNA Sofia	CDNA Sofia	Todor Diev (Spartak Plovdiv)	13
1956	CDNA Sofia	SK Levski Sofia	Pavel Vladimirov (Minyor Pernik)	16
1957	CDNA Sofia	SK Levski Sofia	Hristo Iliev (SK Levski Sofia) Dimitar Milanov (CDNA Sofia)	14
1958	CDNA Sofia	Spartak Plovdiv	Dobromir Tashkov (FD Slavia Sofia) Georgi Arnaudov (Spartak Varna)	9
1958/1959	CDNA Sofia	SK Levski Sofia	Aleksandar Vasilev (FD Slavia Sofia)	13
1959/1960	CDNA Sofia	Septemvri Sofia	Dimitar Yordanov (SK Levski Sofia) Lyuben Kostov (Spartak Varna)	12
1960/1961	CDNA Sofia	CDNA Sofia	Ivan Sotirov (Botev Plovdiv)	20
1961/1962	CDNA Sofia	Botev Plovdiv	Nikola Yordanov (Dunav Ruse) Todor Diev (Spartak Plovdiv)	23
1962/1963	Spartak Plovdiv	FD Slavia Sofia	Todor Diev (Spartak Plovdiv)	26
1963/1964	Lokomotiv Sofia	FD Slavia Sofia	Nikola Tsanev (CDNA Sofia)	26
1964/1965	SK Levski Sofia	CSKA Cerveno Zname Sofia	Georgi Asparuhov (SK Levski Sofia)	27
1965/1966	CSKA Cerveno Zname Sofia	FD Slavia Sofia	Traycho Spasov (Marek Dupnitsa)	21
1966/1967	Botev Plovdiv	SK Levski Sofia	Petar Zhekov (Beroe Stara Zagora)	21
1967/1968	SK Levski Sofia	Spartak Sofia	Petar Zhekov (Beroe Stara Zagora)	31
1968/1969	CSKA Septemvrijsko Zname Sofia	CSKA Septemvrijsko Zname Sofia	Petar Zhekov (CSKA Septemvrijsko Zname Sofia)	36
1969/1970	DFS Levski-Spartak Sofia	DFS Levski-Spartak Sofia	Petar Zhekov (CSKA Septemvrijsko Zname Sofia)	31
1970/1971	CSKA Septemvrijsko Zname Sofia	DFS Levski-Spartak Sofia	Dimitar Yakimov (CSKA Septemvrijsko Zname Sofia)	26
1971/1972	CSKA Septemvrijsko Zname Sofia	CSKA Septemvrijsko Zname Sofia	Petar Zhekov (CSKA Septemvrijsko Zname Sofia)	27
1972/1973	CSKA Septemvrijsko Zname Sofia	CSKA Septemvrijsko Zname Sofia	Petar Zhekov (CSKA Septemvrijsko Zname Sofia)	29
1973/1974	DFS Levski-Spartak Sofia	CSKA Septemvrijsko Zname Sofia	Petko Petkov (Beroe Stara Zagora) Kiril Milanov (DFS Levski-Spartak Sofia)	19
1974/1975	CSKA Septemvrijsko Zname Sofia	DFS Slavia Sofia	Ivan Pritargov (Botev Plovdiv)	20
1975/1976	CSKA Septemvrijsko Zname Sofia	DFS Levski-Spartak Sofia	Petko Petkov (Beroe Stara Zagora) Pavel Panov (DFS Levski-Spartak Sofia)	18
1976/1977	DFS Levski-Spartak Sofia	DFS Levski-Spartak Sofia	Pavel Panov (DFS Levski-Spartak Sofia)	20
1977/1978	Lokomotiv Sofia	Marek Dupnitsa	Stoycho Mladenov (Beroe Stara Zagora)	21
1978/1979	DFS Levski-Spartak Sofia	DFS Levski-Spartak Sofia	Rusi Gochev	

			(Chernomorets Burgas / DFS Levski-Spartak Sofia)	19
1979/1980	CSKA Septemvrijsko Zname Sofia	DFS Slavia Sofia	Spas Dzhevizov (CSKA Sofia)	23
1980/1981	CSKA Septemvrijsko Zname Sofia	Botev Plovdiv	Georgi Slavkov (Botev Plovdiv)	31
1981/1982	CSKA Septemvrijsko Zname Sofia	Lokomotiv Sofia	Mihail Valchev (DFS Levski-Spartak Sofia)	24
1982/1983	CSKA Septemvrijsko Zname Sofia	CSKA Septemvrijsko Zname Sofia	Antim Pehlivanov (Botev Plovdiv)	20
1983/1984	DFS Levski-Spartak Sofia	DFS Levski-Spartak Sofia	Eduard Eranosyan (Lokomotiv Plovdiv) Emil Spasov (DFS Levski-Spartak Sofia)	19
1984/1985	DFS Levski-Spartak Sofia	CSKA Septemvrijsko Zname Sofia	Plamen Getov (Spartak Pleven)	26
1985/1986	Beroe Stara Zagora	FK Vitosha Sofia	Atanas Pashev (Botev Plovdiv)	30
1986/1987	FK Sredets Sofia	FK Sredets Sofia	Nasko Sirakov (FK Vitosha Sofia)	36
1987/1988	FK Vitosha Sofia	FK Sredets Sofia	Nasko Sirakov (FK Vitosha Sofia)	28
1988/1989	CFKA Sredets Sofia	FK Sredets Sofia	Hristo Stoichkov (CFKA Sredets Sofia)	23
1989/1990	CFKA Sofia	FC Sliven	Hristo Stoichkov (CFKA Sofia)	38
1990/1991	FC Etar Veliko Tarnovo	PFC Levski Sofia	Ivaylo Yordanov (FC Lokomotiv Gorna Oryahovitsa)	21
1991/1992	PFC CSKA Sofia	PFC Levski Sofia	Nasko Sirakov (PFC Levski Sofia)	26
1992/1993	PFC Levski Sofia	PFC CSKA Sofia	Plamen Getov (PFC Levski Sofia)	26
1993/1994	PFC Levski Sofia	PFC Levski Sofia	Nasko Sirakov (PFC Levski Sofia)	30
1994/1995	PFC Levski Sofia	PFC Lokomotiv Sofia	Petar Mihtarski (PFC CSKA Sofia)	24
1995/1996	PFC Slavia Sofia	PFC Slavia Sofia	Ivo Georgiev (FC Spartak Varna)	21
1996/1997	PFC CSKA Sofia	PFC CSKA Sofia	Todor Pramatarov (PFC Slavia Sofia)	26
1997/1998	PFC Litex Lovech	PFC Levski Sofia	Anton Spasov (PFC Naftex Burgas) Bontcho Guentchev (PFC CSKA Sofia)	17
1998/1999	PFC Litex Lovech	PFC CSKA Sofia	Dimcho Belyakov (PFC Litex Lovech)	21
1999/2000	PFC Levski Sofia	PFC Levski Sofia	Mihail Mihaylov (FC Velbazhd Kyustendil)	20
2000/2001	PFC Levski Sofia	PFC Litex Lovech	Georgi Ivanov (PFC Levski Sofia)	22
2001/2002	PFC Levski Sofia	PFC Levski Sofia	Vladimir Manchev (PFC CSKA Sofia)	21
2002/2003	PFC CSKA Sofia	PFC Levski Sofia	Georgi Chilikov (PFC Levski Sofia)	23
2003/2004	PFC Lokomotiv Plovdiv	PFC Litex Lovech	Martin Kamburov (PFC Lokomotiv Plovdiv)	25
2004/2005	PFC CSKA Sofia	PFC Levski Sofia	Martin Kamburov (PFC Lokomotiv Plovdiv)	27
2005/2006	PFC Levski Sofia	PFC CSKA Sofia	Milivoje Novaković (SVN, Litex Lovech) José Emílio Robalo Furtado (CPV, OFC Vihren Sandanski / PFC CSKA Sofia)	16
2006/2007	PFC Levski Sofia	PFC Levski Sofia	Tsvetan Genkov (PFC Lokomotiv Sofia)	27
2007/2008	PFC CSKA Sofia	PFC Litex Lovech	Georgi Hristov (PFC Botev Plovdiv)	19
2008/2009	PFC Levski Sofia	PFC Litex Lovech	Martin Kamburov (PFC Lokomotiv Sofia)	17
2009/2010	PFC Litex Lovech	PFC Beroe Stara Zagora	Wilfried Niflore (FRA, PFC Litex Lovech)	19
2010/2011	PFC Litex Lovech	PFC CSKA Sofia	Garra Dembélé (MLI, PFC Levski Sofia)	26
2011/2012	PFC Ludogorets Razgrad	PFC Ludogorets Razgrad	Ivan Stoyanov (PFC Ludogorets Razgrad) Aluísio Chaves Ribeiro Moraes Júnior (BRA, PFC CSKA Sofia)	16
2012/2013	PFC Ludogorets Razgrad	PFC Beroe Stara Zagora	Basile Salomon Pereira de Carvalho (GNB, PFC Levski Sofia)	19
2013/2014	PFC Ludogorets Razgrad	PFC Ludogorets Razgrad	Wilmar Jordán Gil (COL, PFC Litex Lovech) Martin Kamburov (PFC Lokomotiv Plovdiv)	20
2014/2015	PFC Ludogorets Razgrad	PFC Cherno More Varna	Antonio Salas Quinta „Añete" (ESP, PFC Levski Sofia)	14
2015/2016	PFC Ludogorets Razgrad	PFC CSKA Sofia	Martin Kamburov (PFC Lokomotiv Plovdiv)	18
2016/2017	PFC Ludogorets Razgrad	PFC Botev Plovdiv	Claudiu Andrei Keşerü (ROU, PFC Ludogorets Razgrad)	22
2017/2018	PFC Ludogorets Razgrad	PFC Slavia Sofia	Claudiu Andrei Keşerü (ROU, PFC Ludogorets Razgrad)	26
2018/2019	PFC Ludogorets Razgrad	PFC Lokomotiv Plovdiv	Stanislav Kostov (PFC Levski Sofia)	24
2019/2020	PFC Ludogorets Razgrad	PFC Lokomotiv Plovdiv	Martin Kamburov (PFC Beroe Stara Zagora)	18
2020/2021	PFC Ludogorets Razgrad	PFC CSKA Sofia	Claudiu Andrei Keşerü (ROU, PFC Ludogorets Razgrad)	18

**called "Cup of the Soviet Army" (between 1945 - 1982) and Bulgarian Cup (from 1982 until today).

Please note:

FC CSKA Sofia changed several times its name as following: 1948 CDNV Sofia, 1949 NV Sofia, 1950 NA Sofia, 1951 CDNA Sofia, 1953 Sofijski Garnizon Sofia, 1953 CDNA Sofia, 1964 CSKA Cerveno Zname Sofia, 1968 CSKA Septemvrijsko Zname Sofia, 1985 FK Sredets Sofia, 1987 CFKA Sredets Sofia, November 1989 CFKA Sofia, 1st january 1990 PFC CSKA Sofia.

FC Levski Sofia changed several times its name as following: 1914 CS Levski Sofia, SK Levski Sofia, 1949 Dinamo Sofia, 1957 FD Levski Sofia, 1969 DFS Levski-Spartak Sofia, 1985 FK Vitosha Sofia, 1990 FK Levski-1914 Sofia, 1998 PFC Levski Sofia.

FC Slavia Sofia changed several times its name as following: 1913 Botev Sofia, 1915 SK Slavia Sofia, 1945 NFD Slavia Sofia, 1949 DSO Strojtel Sofia, 1951 USS-DSO Udarnik Sofia, 1952 GUTP-DSO Udarnik Sofia, 1957 FD Slavia Sofia, 1969 ZSK Slavia Sofia, 1971 DFS Slavia Sofia, 1986 FC Slavia Sofia; 1990 PFC Slavia Sofia.

NATIONAL CHAMPIONSHIP
First Professional Football League – Efbet League 2020/2021
(07.08.2020 – 26.05.2021)

Regular Season - Results

Round 1 [07-11.08.2020]
CSKA 1948 Sofia - CSKA Sofia 2-2(2-1)
FC Montana - Arda Kardzhali 3-3(0-2)
Botev Vratsa - PFC Ludogorets 3-1(1-0)
Botev Plovdiv - Lokomotiv Plovdiv 2-0(1-0)
Slavia Sofia - Cherno More Varna 1-1(1-0)
Levski Sofia - Beroe Stara Zagora 0-2(0-2)
Tsarsko Selo - Etar V. Tarnovo 3-0(1-0)

Round 2 [14-17.08.2020]
PFC Ludogorets - Slavia Sofia 3-0(1-0)
Lokomotiv Plovdiv - Botev Vratsa 2-1(1-1)
Arda Kardzhali - Levski Sofia 1-1(1-0)
Etar V. Tarnovo - Cherno More 0-4(0-2)
CSKA Sofia - Botev Plovdiv 2-1(1-0)
Tsarsko Selo - FC Montana 0-0
Beroe Stara Zagora - CSKA 1948 Sofia 0-0

Round 3 [21-24.08.2020]
Slavia Sofia - Lokomotiv Plovdiv 0-2(0-1)
Botev Vratsa - CSKA Sofia 1-2(1-1)
Cherno More - PFC Ludogorets 1-4(1-2)
Levski Sofia - Tsarsko Selo 0-1(0-1)
Botev Plovdiv - Beroe Stara Zagora 3-3(0-2)
FC Montana - Etar V. Tarnovo 1-0(0-0)
CSKA 1948 Sofia - Arda Kardzhali 0-2(0-1)

Round 4 [28-30.08.2020]
Tsarsko Selo - CSKA 1948 Sofia 0-0
Beroe Stara Zagora - Botev Vratsa 6-0(3-0)
Arda Kardzhali - Botev Plovdiv 3-2(1-2)
FC Montana - Levski Sofia 0-4(0-2)
Etar V. Tarnovo - PFC Ludogorets 0-2(0-0)
Lokomotiv Plovdiv - Cherno More 2-1(1-1)
CSKA Sofia - Slavia Sofia 1-0(0-0)

Round 5 [11-14.09.2020]
Botev Vratsa - Arda Kardzhali 0-0
Botev Plovdiv - Tsarsko Selo 0-0
Cherno More Varna - CSKA Sofia 1-1(1-0)
PFC Ludogorets - Lokomotiv Plovdiv 3-1(0-0)
CSKA 1948 Sofia - FC Montana 2-0(1-0)
Levski Sofia - Etar V. Tarnovo 2-1(1-1)
Slavia Sofia - Beroe Stara Zagora 0-2(0-1)

Round 6 [18-21.09.2020]
Tsarsko Selo - Botev Vratsa 1-2(0-1)
FC Montana - Botev Plovdiv 3-1(2-1)
Beroe Stara Zagora - Cherno More 4-0(1-0)
Levski Sofia - CSKA 1948 Sofia 3-0(1-0)
Etar V. Tarnovo - Lokomotiv Plovdiv 1-3(1-2)
CSKA Sofia - PFC Ludogorets 2-2(0-1)
Arda Kardzhali - Slavia Sofia 2-1(0-1)

Round 7 [25-28.09.2020]
Botev Vratsa - FC Montana 2-0(1-0)
CSKA 1948 Sofia - Etar V. Tarnovo 5-1(3-1)
PFC Ludogorets - Beroe Stara Zagora 2-0(2-0)
Botev Plovdiv - Levski Sofia 2-1(2-1)
Cherno More Varna - Arda Kardzhali 2-0(1-0)
Lokomotiv Plovdiv - CSKA Sofia 2-1(2-0)
Slavia Sofia - Tsarsko Selo 1-0(0-0)

Round 8 [02-04.10.2020]
Tsarsko Selo - Cherno More Varna 1-0(0-0)
CSKA 1948 Sofia - Botev Plovdiv 5-0(2-0)
FC Montana - Slavia Sofia 2-1(2-1)
Levski Sofia - Botev Vratsa 1-0(0-0)
Beroe Stara Zagora – Lokom.Plovdiv 1-3(1-1)
Etar V. Tarnovo - CSKA Sofia 2-2(2-0)
Arda Kardzhali - Ludogorets 2-2(1-1) [17.12.]

Round 9 [17-20.10.2020]
PFC Ludogorets - Tsarsko Selo 1-1(1-0)
CSKA Sofia - Beroe Stara Zagora 1-1(0-0)
Botev Vratsa - CSKA 1948 Sofia 0-0
Cherno More Varna - FC Montana 3-0(2-0)
Slavia Sofia - Levski Sofia 1-0(1-0)
Botev Plovdiv - Etar V. Tarnovo 1-1(1-0)
Lokomotiv Plovdiv - Arda Kardzhali 0-0

Round 10 [24-26.10.2020]
Tsarsko Selo - Lokomotiv Plovdiv 0-3(0-0)
Levski Sofia - Cherno More Varna 1-2(1-0)
CSKA 1948 Sofia - Slavia Sofia 5-1(2-0)
Arda Kardzhali - CSKA Sofia 1-0(0-0)
FC Montana - PFC Ludogorets 1-3(1-1)
Botev Plovdiv - Botev Vratsa 2-0(0-0)
Etar V. Tarnovo - Beroe Stara Zagora 2-3(0-1)

Round 11 [30.10.-02.11.2020]
Cherno More - CSKA 1948 Sofia 1-2(1-1)
Lokomotiv Plovdiv - FC Montana 2-2(2-2)
Beroe Stara Zagora - Arda Kardzhali 0-1(0-0)
CSKA Sofia - Tsarsko Selo 1-0(0-0)
PFC Ludogorets - Levski Sofia 1-0(0-0)
Botev Vratsa - Etar V. Tarnovo 5-1(2-0)
Slavia Sofia - Botev Plovdiv 0-0 [02.12.]

Round 12 [07-08.11.2020]
Botev Plovdiv - Cherno More Varna 0-0
Etar V. Tarnovo - Arda Kardzhali 0-0
FC Montana - Levski Sofia 1-2(0-1)
CSKA 1948 Sofia - PFC Ludogorets 0-3(0-1)
Levski Sofia - Lok. Plovdiv 1-0(1-0) [02.12.]
Botev Vratsa - Slavia Sofia 1-2(0-1) [10.12.]
Tsarsko Selo - Beroe St. Zag. 0-2(0-1) [16.12.]

Round 13 [21-23.11.2020]
Slavia Sofia - Etar V. Tarnovo 0-0
Cherno More Varna - Botev Vratsa 2-1(1-1)
Lokomotiv Plovdiv - CSKA 1948 1-1(1-1)
Arda Kardzhali - Tsarsko Selo 2-0(2-0)
CSKA Sofia - Levski Sofia 1-0(1-0) [18.12.]
Beroe Stara Zagora - FC Montana 0-0 [19.12.
Ludogorets - Botev Plovdiv 2-1(1-0) [20.12.]

Round 14 [27-29.11.2020]
Cherno More Varna - Slavia Sofia 3-2(1-1)
Arda Kardzhali - FC Montana 3-0(1-0)
Lokomotiv Plovdiv - Botev Plovdiv 6-0(4-0)
PFC Ludogorets - Botev Vratsa 2-1(2-1)
CSKA Sofia - CSKA 1948 Sofia 2-0(1-0)
Etar Tarnovo - Tsarsko Selo 1-0(1-0) [01.12.]
Beroe St. Z. - Levski Sofia 2-1(1-1) [09.12.]

Round 15 [04-07.12.2020]
Cherno More - Etar V. Tarnovo 0-1(0-1)
CSKA 1948 - Beroe Stara Zagora 1-0(0-0)
Levski Sofia - Arda Kardzhali 1-2(0-1)
Botev Vratsa - Lokomotiv Plovdiv 0-1(0-1)
Botev Plovdiv - CSKA Sofia 0-3(0-1)
Slavia Sofia - PFC Ludogorets 0-2(0-0)
FC Montana - Tsarsko Selo 3-4(0-2)

Round 16 [11-15.12.2020]
Arda Kardzhali - CSKA 1948 Sofia 1-1(0-0)
Beroe Stara Zagora - Botev Plovdiv 3-0(1-0)
Tsarsko Selo - Levski Sofia 2-2(1-2)
CSKA Sofia - Botev Vratsa 3-1(1-0)
PFC Ludogorets - Cherno More 1-0(1-0)
Lokomotiv Plovdiv - Slavia Sofia 2-0(1-0)
Etar V. Tarnovo - FC Montana 0-0

Round 17 [12-15.02.2021]
Botev Plovdiv - Arda Kardzhali 0-2(0-1)
Botev Vratsa - Beroe Stara Zagora 1-2(1-1)
Cherno More Varna - Lokomotiv Plovdiv 0-0
Slavia Sofia - CSKA Sofia 0-1(0-1)
CSKA 1948 Sofia - Tsarsko Selo 2-1(1-0)
Levski Sofia - FC Montana 2-0(1-0)
PFC Ludogorets - Etar V. Tarnovo 6-0(4-0)

Round 18 [19-22.02.2021]
FC Montana - CSKA 1948 Sofia 1-0(1-0)
Arda Kardzhali - Botev Vratsa 3-2(2-0)
Lokomotiv Plovdiv - PFC Ludogorets 3-2(2-1)
CSKA Sofia - Cherno More Varna 1-0(0-0)
Beroe Stara Zagora - Slavia Sofia 1-1(1-0)
Etar V. Tarnovo - Levski Sofia 0-0
Tsarsko Selo - Botev Plovdiv 2-2(1-0)

Round 19 [26-28.02.2021]
Lokomotiv Plovdiv - Etar V. Tarnovo 1-1(1-0)
Slavia Sofia - Arda Kardzhali 3-2(1-2)
PFC Ludogorets - CSKA Sofia 1-0(1-0)
Cherno More - Beroe Stara Zagora 2-1(1-0)
Botev Vratsa - Tsarsko Selo 0-3(0-2)
Botev Plovdiv - FC Montana 1-1(0-0)
CSKA 1948 Sofia - Levski Sofia 0-0

Round 20 [06-09.03.2021]
Arda Kardzhali - Cherno More Varna 1-0(1-0)
CSKA Sofia - Lokomotiv Plovdiv 0-0
Etar V. Tarnovo - CSKA 1948 Sofia 3-1(1-1)
Beroe Stara Zagora - PFC Ludogorets 1-4(0-1)
Levski Sofia - Botev Plovdiv 2-2(2-2)
Tsarsko Selo - Slavia Sofia 2-0(1-0)
FC Montana - Botev Vratsa 0-1(0-0)

Round 21 [12-15.03.2021]
PFC Ludogorets - Arda Kardzhali 1-0(0-0)
Lokom. Plovdiv - Beroe Stara Zagora 1-1(0-1)
Slavia Sofia - FC Montana 2-1(2-1)
Botev Plovdiv - CSKA 1948 Sofia 3-2(2-0)
Botev Vratsa - Levski Sofia 1-3(1-0)
CSKA Sofia - Etar V. Tarnovo 1-0(0-0)
Cherno More Varna - Tsarsko Selo 1-0(1-0)

Round 22 [19-21.03.2021]
Etar V. Tarnovo - Botev Plovdiv 0-0
FC Montana - Cherno More Varna 1-1(0-0)
Arda Kardzhali - Lokomotiv Plovdiv 0-2(0-0)
Tsarsko Selo - PFC Ludogorets 1-1(0-0)
CSKA 1948 Sofia - Botev Vratsa 0-0(0-0)
Beroe Stara Zagora - CSKA Sofia 1-0(0-0)
Levski Sofia - Slavia Sofia 1-0(0-0)

Round 23 [08-12.04.2021]
Botev Vratsa - Botev Plovdiv 1-2(1-1)
Lokomotiv Plovdiv - Tsarsko Selo 2-0(1-0)
Slavia Sofia - CSKA 1948 Sofia 1-3(0-0)
PFC Ludogorets - FC Montana 1-0(0-0)
CSKA Sofia - Arda Kardzhali 1-1(0-0)
Cherno More Varna - Levski Sofia 0-0
Beroe Stara Zagora - Etar V. Tarnovo 1-2(0-1)

Round 24 [15-18.04.2021]
FC Montana - Lokomotiv Plovdiv 0-1(0-0)
Etar V. Tarnovo - Botev Vratsa 0-0
CSKA 1948 Sofia - Cherno More Varna 0-0
Botev Plovdiv - Slavia Sofia 0-1(0-1)
Arda Kardzhali - Beroe Stara Zagora 1-0(0-0)
Tsarsko Selo - CSKA Sofia 2-1(1-0)
Levski Sofia - PFC Ludogorets 0-3(0-2)

Round 25 [20-22.04.2021]
Slavia Sofia - Botev Vratsa 0-2(0-2)
Arda Kardzhali - Etar V. Tarnovo 3-2(1-1)
Cherno More Varna - Botev Plovdiv 1-0(1-0)
Beroe Stara Zagora - Tsarsko Selo 0-1(0-0)
CSKA Sofia - FC Montana 6-0(2-0)
Lokomotiv Plovdiv - Levski Sofia 1-0(0-0)
PFC Ludogorets - CSKA 1948 Sofia 4-0(3-0)

Round 26 [23-26.04.2021]
Botev Vratsa - Cherno More Varna 0-1(0-0)
Etar V. Tarnovo - Slavia Sofia 1-1(0-0)
FC Montana - Beroe Stara Zagora 1-1(0-1)
Levski Sofia - CSKA Sofia 0-2(0-2)
Tsarsko Selo - Arda Kardzhali 4-0(3-0)
CSKA 1948 - Lokomotiv Plovdiv 1-0(0-0)
Botev Plovdiv - PFC Ludogorets 0-2(0-0)

Final Standings

1.	PFC Ludogorets Razgrad	26	20	4	2	59	-	18	64
2.	PFC Lokomotiv Plovdiv	26	15	7	4	41	-	19	52
3.	PFC CSKA Sofia	26	14	8	4	39	-	20	50
4.	FC Arda 1924 Kardzhali	26	12	9	5	36	-	29	45
5.	FC CSKA 1948 Sofia	26	10	8	8	34	-	30	38
6.	PFC Beroe Stara Zagora	26	10	7	9	38	-	28	37
7.	PFC Cherno More Varna	26	10	7	9	27	-	25	37
8.	FC Tsarsko Selo Sofia	26	9	7	10	29	-	27	34
9.	PFC Levski Sofia	26	7	7	12	25	-	27	28
10.	PFC Botev Plovdiv	26	5	9	12	25	-	46	24
11.	PFC Slavia Sofia	26	6	5	15	19	-	40	23
12.	POFC Botev Vratsa	26	6	4	16	26	-	39	22
13.	SFC Etar Veliko Tarnovo	26	4	10	12	20	-	45	22
14.	FC Montana	26	4	8	14	21	-	46	20

Teams ranked 1-6 were qualified for the Championship Round, teams ranked 7-10 were qualified for the Europa Conference League Round, while teams ranked 11-14 were qualified for the Relegation Round.

Relegation Round

Results

Round 27 [03.05.2021]
Botev Vratsa - Etar V. Tarnovo 2-0(0-0)
Slavia Sofia - FC Montana 1-1(1-1)

Round 28 [06.05.2021]
FC Montana - Etar V. Tarnovo 1-0(0-0)
Slavia Sofia - Botev Vratsa 2-0(1-0)

Round 29 [10.05.2021]
Botev Vratsa - FC Montana 1-0(0-0)
Etar V. Tarnovo - Slavia Sofia 0-3(0-0)

Round 30 [14.05.2021]
Etar V. Tarnovo - Botev Vratsa 2-0(1-0)
FC Montana - Slavia Sofia 0-2(0-1)

Round 31 [18.05.2021]
Etar V. Tarnovo - FC Montana 1-2(1-1)
Botev Vratsa - Slavia Sofia 1-1(1-1)

Round 32 [21.05.2021]
FC Montana - Botev Vratsa 1-1(1-1)
Slavia Sofia - Etar V. Tarnovo 0-2(0-1)

Final Standings

										Home						Away					
1.	PFC Slavia Sofia	32	9	7	16	28	-	44	34	5	4	7	12	-	19	4	3	9	16	-	25
2.	POFC Botev Vratsa (*Relegation Play-offs*)	32	8	6	18	31	-	45	30	5	3	8	19	-	19	3	3	10	12	-	26
3.	FC Montana (*Relegated*)	32	6	10	16	26	-	52	28	5	4	7	19	-	25	1	6	9	7	-	27
4.	SFC Etar Veliko Tarnovo (*Relegated*)	32	6	10	16	25	-	53	28	3	7	6	13	-	21	3	3	10	12	-	32

Relegation Play-offs [28.05.2021]

POFC Botev Vratsa - PFC Septemvri Sofia   1-0(0-0)
POFC Botev Vratsa remains at first level for 2021/2022.

Europa Conference League Round

Results

Round 27 [05.05.2021]
Cherno More Varna - Botev Plovdiv 3-1(3-1)
Tsarsko Selo - Levski Sofia 0-2(0-1)

Round 28 [09.05.2021]
Cherno More Varna - Tsarsko Selo 3-3(3-1)
Botev Plovdiv - Levski Sofia 0-1(0-1)

Round 29 [13.05.2021]
Tsarsko Selo - Botev Plovdiv 0-0
Levski Sofia - Cherno More Varna 2-1(1-1)

Round 30 [17.05.2021]
Botev Plovdiv - Cherno More Varna 1-1(0-1)
Levski Sofia - Tsarsko Selo 1-1(0-0)

Round 31 [20.05.2021]
Tsarsko Selo - Cherno More Varna 0-1(0-0)
Levski Sofia - Botev Plovdiv 1-2(1-0)

Round 32 [23.05.2021]
Botev Plovdiv - Tsarsko Selo 5-0(1-0)
Cherno More Varna - Levski Sofia 1-2(1-0)

Final Standings

										Home						Away					
1.	PFC Cherno More Varna	32	12	9	11	37	-	34	45	8	4	4	24	-	18	4	5	7	13	-	16
2.	PFC Levski Sofia	32	11	8	13	34	-	32	41	6	3	7	17	-	19	5	5	6	17	-	13
3.	FC Tsarsko Selo Sofia	32	9	10	13	33	-	39	37	5	6	5	18	-	16	4	4	8	15	-	23
4.	PFC Botev Plovdiv	32	7	11	14	34	-	52	32	5	6	5	20	-	18	2	5	9	14	-	34

PFC Cherno More Varna were qualified for the Europa Conference League Play-off Final.

Results

Round 27 [03-04.05.2021]
CSKA Sofia - Arda Kardzhali 1-0(0-0)
PFC Ludogorets - Beroe Stara Zagora 3-1(1-1)
Lokomotiv Plovdiv - CSKA 1948 Sofia 0-0 [19.05.]

Round 28 [07-08.05.2021]
Beroe Stara Zagora - Arda Kardzhali 0-2(0-1)
PFC Ludogorets - Lokomotiv Plovdiv 1-2(1-2)
CSKA 1948 - CSKA Sofia 1-0(0-0) [22.05.]

Round 29 [11-12.05.2021]
Lokomotiv Plovdiv - Beroe Stara Zagora 0-0
Arda Kardzhali - CSKA 1948 Sofia 0-0
CSKA Sofia - PFC Ludogorets 4-1(1-0)

Round 30 [15-16.05.2021]
PFC Ludogorets - Arda Kardzhali 4-1(2-1)
Lokomotiv Plovdiv - CSKA Sofia 2-0(0-0)
Beroe Stara Zagora - CSKA 1948 3-3(0-1)

Round 31 [26.05.2021]
CSKA Sofia - Beroe Stara Zagora 2-0(1-0)
Arda Kardzhali - Lokomotiv Plovdiv 3-3(2-1)
CSKA 1948 Sofia - PFC Ludogorets 3-1(2-0)

Final Standings

		Total					Home					Away				
1. **PFC Ludogorets Razgrad**	31	22	4	5	69 - 29	70	14	1	1	36 - 8	8	3	4	33 - 21
2. PFC Lokomotiv Plovdiv	31	17	10	4	48 - 23	61	9	7	0	27 - 10	8	3	4	21 - 13
3. PFC CSKA Sofia	31	17	8	6	46 - 24	59	12	4	0	28 - 7	5	4	6	18 - 17
4. FC Arda 1924 Kardzhali	31	13	11	7	42 - 37	50	8	6	1	26 - 17	5	5	6	16 - 20
5. FC CSKA 1948 Sofia	31	12	11	8	41 - 34	47	10	3	2	28 - 11	2	8	6	13 - 23
6. PFC Beroe Stara Zagora	31	10	9	12	42 - 38	39	5	4	6	23 - 18	5	5	6	19 - 20

FC Arda 1924 Kardzhali were qualified for the Europa Conference League Play-off Final.

Europa Conference League Play-offs [30.05.2021]

FC Arda 1924 Kardzhali - PFC Cherno More Varna   1-0(1-0)

Top goalscorers:

18	**Claudiu Andrei Keşerü (ROU)**	*PFC Ludogorets Razgrad*
16	Atanas Iliev	*PFC Botev Plovdiv*
15	Mathias Coureur (MTQ)	*PFC Cherno More Varna*
14	Martin Kamburov	*FC CSKA 1948 Sofia / PFC Beroe Stara Zagora*
13	Dimitar Iliev	*PFC Lokomotiv Plovdiv*
12	Preslav Borukov	*SFC Etar Veliko Tarnovo*

NATIONAL CUP
Bulgarian Cup 2020/2021

First Round [20-22.10./03-04.11./14.11.2020/11.02.2021]

FC Kariana Erden - FC Tsarsko Selo Sofia	0-1(0-0)	FK Nadezhda Dobroslavtsi - POFC Botev Vratsa	0-2(0-2)
FC Partizan Cherven Bryag - PFC Levski Sofia	1-4(1-2)	FC Oborishte Panagyurishte - PFC Botev Plovdiv	0-4(0-2)
FC Sevlievo - PFC Slavia Sofia	1-5(1-1)	FC Sozopol - SFC Etar Veliko Tarnovo	0-0 aet; 2-4 pen
FC Izvor Gorski Izvor - FC Montana	1-2(0-0)	FC Zagorets Nova Zagora - PFC Lokomotiv Plovdiv	3-4(1-2,2-2)
FC Yantra Gabrovo - Cherno More Varna	1-6(1-2)	FC Spartak Varna - FC Arda 1924 Kardzhali	1-2(0-1)
FK Drenovets - FC CSKA 1948 Sofia	0-6(0-5)	OFC Botev Ihtiman - PFC CSKA Sofia	0-5(0-1)
OFC Pirin Blagoevgrad - PFC Beroe Stara Zagora	3-4(2-1)	FK Sportist Svoge - PFC Ludogorets Razgrad	1-3(0-1)
FC Chernomorets Balchik - PFC Septemvri Sofia	1-0(1-0)		

1/8-Finals [01-04.03.2021]

PFC Lokomotiv Plovdiv - Belasitsa Petrich	2-1(0-0)	FC Tsarsko Selo Sofia - PFC Ludogorets Razgrad	1-2(0-2)
SFC Etar Veliko Tarnovo - FC Arda 1924 Kardzhali	0-1(0-1)	PFC Levski Sofia - PFC Beroe Stara Zagora	3-1(1-1)
PFC CSKA Sofia - Cherno More Varna	3-1(2-0)	POFC Botev Vratsa - FC Chernomorets Balchik	3-0(0-0)
PFC Botev Plovdiv - FC CSKA 1948 Sofia	1-2(0-1,1-1)	PFC Slavia Sofia - FC Montana	1-1 aet; 5-3 pen

Quarter-Finals [16-18.03.2021]

PFC Ludogorets Razgrad - PFC Lokomotiv Plovdiv	2-1(0-0,1-1)	PFC Slavia Sofia - PFC Levski Sofia	2-1(0-0)
FC CSKA 1948 Sofia - FC Arda 1924 Kardzhali	0-1(0-0)	PFC CSKA Sofia - POFC Botev Vratsa	4-0(2-0)

Semi-Finals [06-07.04./13-14.04.2021]

First Leg		Second Leg	
FC Arda 1924 Kardzhali - PFC Slavia Sofia	0-0	PFC Slavia Sofia - FC Arda 1924 Kardzhali	0-1(0-1)
PFC CSKA Sofia - PFC Ludogorets Razgrad	1-1(0-0)	PFC Ludogorets Razgrad - PFC CSKA Sofia	1-2(0-2)

19.05.2021; Nationalen Stadion "Vasil Levski", Sofia; Referee: Volen Chinkov; Attendance: 22,000
PFC CSKA Sofia - FC Arda 1924 Kardzhali   **1-0(0-0)**

CSKA Sofia: Gustavo Busatto, Ivan Turitsov, Jurgen Mattheij, Menno Koch, Bradley Mazikou, Amos Youga, Graham Carey (72.Henrique Roberto Rafael), Tiago Filipe Sousa Nóbrega Rodrigues (Cap), Federico Nicolás Varela (46.Thibaut Vion), Jerome Terence Sinclair (61.Georgi Yomov), Jordy Josué Caicedo Medina (61.Bismark Charles). Trainer: Lyuboslav Penev.

Arda Kardzhali: Ivan Karadzhov, Deyan Lozev, Alex Petkov, Plamen Krumov (Cap), Milen Zhelev, Emil Martinov, Lachezar Kotev, Ivan Kokonov, Ivan Tilev, Spas Delev (73.Rumen Rumenov), Tonislav Yordanov (83.Edimar Ribeiro da Costa „Juninho"). Trainer: Nikolai Kirov.

Goal: 1-0 Bismark Charles (85).

THE CLUBS 2020/2021

Please note: appearances and goals are including statistics of regular season and play-offs (Championship, Europa Conference League and Relegation Round).

Professional Football Club Arda 1924 Kardzhali

Founded:	10.08.1924	
Stadium:	Arena Arda, Arda (15,000)	
Trainer:	Nikolai Kirov	12.06.1975

Goalkeepers:	DOB	M	(s)	G
Ivan Karadzhov	12.07.1989	21		
Vasil Simeonov	04.02.1998	10		
Defenders:	**DOB**	**M**	**(s)**	**G**
Petko Ganev	17.09.1996	11		
Aleksandar Georgiev	10.10.1997	18	(3)	
Martin Kostadinov	13.05.1996	2	(8)	
Plamen Krumov	04.11.1985	15	(1)	1
Deyan Lozev	26.10.1993	24	(1)	
Matheus Izidorio Leoni (BRA)	20.09.1991	15		1
Alex Petkov	25.07.1999	9	(1)	
Rebin Ghareeb Solaka Adhamat (IRQ)	12.04.1992	11	(1)	
Milen Stoev	29.09.1999	20	(3)	
Nicolas Taravel (FRA)	13.10.1994	8		
Radoslav Uzunov	25.03.2006		(2)	
Milen Zhelev	17.07.1993	19	(6)	2

Midfielders:	DOB	M	(s)	G
Andrija Bubnjar (CRO)	29.06.1997		(3)	
Moussa Haddad (FRA)	15.05.1998		(3)	
Lachezar Kotev	05.01.1998	21	(3)	
Emil Martinov	18.03.1992	28		
Rumen Rumenov	07.06.1993	18	(8)	3
Forwards:	**DOB**	**M**	**(s)**	**G**
Mihail Aleksandrov	11.06.1989		(9)	
Georgi Atanasov (CAN)	06.03.2004	3	(6)	
Spas Delev	22.09.1989	22	(3)	8
Edimar Ribeiro da Costa „Juninho" (BRA)	26.02.1999	2	(8)	4
Lovre Knežević (CRO)	22.07.1998		(8)	
Ivan Kokonov	17.08.1991	23	(3)	8
Svetoslav Kovachev	14.03.1998	14	(1)	3
Ivan Tilev	05.01.1999	12	(16)	2
Radoslav Vasilev	12.10.1990	3	(1)	1
Tonislav Yordanov	27.11.1998	12	(3)	8

Professional Football Club Beroe Stara Zagora

Founded:	06.05.1916	
Stadium:	Stadion Beroe, Stara Zagora (12,128)	
Trainer:	Dimitar Dimitrov	09.06.1959
[22.04.2021]	Petar Kolev	25.11.1974

Goalkeepers:	DOB	M	(s)	G
Gennady Ganev (UKR)	15.05.1990	17		
Dušan Perniš (SVK)	28.11.1984	4		
Hristiyan Vasilev	05.12.1997	10		
Defenders:	**DOB**	**M**	**(s)**	**G**
Dzhuneyt Ali	05.09.1994	4	(7)	
Georgi Angelov	12.11.1990	30		1
Georgi Dinkov	20.05.1991	1		
Steeve Furtado (CPV)	22.11.1994	25		
Ilias Hassani (ALG)	08.11.1995	16	(6)	
Teddy Mézague (FRA)	27.05.1990	30		
Krum Stoyanov	01.08.1991	16	(4)	
Aleksandar Vasilev	27.04.1995	15	(8)	
Midfielders:	**DOB**	**M**	**(s)**	**G**
Radoslav Apostolov	07.06.1997		(2)	
Ibrahima Sory Conté I (GUI)	03.04.1991	13	(4)	3

Gaïus Makouta (CGO)	25.07.1997	26		7
Ivan Minchev	28.05.1991	17	(8)	5
Octávio Merlo Manteca (BRA)	29.12.1993	13	(11)	3
Carlos Ohene (GHA)	21.07.1993	3	(2)	
Bozhidar Penchev	17.03.2002		(1)	
Iliyan Stefanov	20.09.1998	5	(2)	
Aleksandar Tsvetkov	31.08.1990	28	(1)	
Forwards:	**DOB**	**M**	**(s)**	**G**
Attila Ahmed	22.04.2002		(1)	
Dimo Bakalov	19.12.1988	3	(12)	
Erivaldo Jorge Paulo Ferreira (ANG)	08.02.1994	14	(7)	2
Alioune Fall (SEN)	24.12.1994	25	(3)	10
Martin Kamburov	13.10.1980	11	(3)	5
Erson Stiven Dias Costa „Kukula" (CPV)	22.01.1993	5	(17)	3
Keelan Lebon (FRA)	04.07.1997	10	(9)	1

Professional Football Club Botev Plovdiv

Founded: 12.03.1912
Stadium: Futbolen kompleks Botev 1912, Plovdiv (4,000)
Trainer: Ferario Spasov 20.02.1962
[16.10.2020] Petar Penchev 12.08.1969
[07.12.2020] Stefan Stoyanov 24.01.1979
[06.01.2021] Azrudin Valentić (BIH) 21.07.1970

Goalkeepers:	DOB	M	(s)	G
Georgi Argilashki	13.06.1991	25	(1)	
Yanko Georgiev	22.10.1988	7		
Hristiyan Slavkov	26.02.2003		(1)	
Defenders:	**DOB**	**M**	**(s)**	**G**
Ivan Bandalovski	23.11.1986	6		
Ventsislav Bogdanov	29.03.2002		(1)	
Atanas Chernev	25.03.2002	4	(2)	
Mite Cikarski (MKD)	06.01.1993	18	(8)	1
Anwar Elyounoussi (NOR)	29.03.1999		(1)	
Filip Filipov	02.08.1988	24	(2)	
Viktor Genev	27.10.1988	28	(1)	
Kevin Höög Jansson (SWE)	29.09.2000	7	(2)	
Johnathan Carlos Pereira (BRA)	04.04.1995	16	(2)	2
Pa Konaté (GUI)	25.04.1994	13	(2)	1
Marcos Garbelotto "Marquinhos Pedroso" (BRA)	04.10.1993	11		
Mario Mladenovski (MKD)	16.09.2000	9	(2)	
Stanislav Rabotov	14.06.2002	22	(5)	
Midfielders:	**DOB**	**M**	**(s)**	**G**
Lachezar Baltanov	11.07.1988	2	(4)	
Biser Bonev	04.06.2003	2	(8)	
Blagovest Danchev	25.06.2001		(1)	
Michel Espinosa (FRA)	15.09.1993	20	(5)	3
Petar Itov	12.02.2002		(1)	
Dimitar Proychev	10.09.2001	1	(2)	
Réda Rabeï (ALG)	12.07.1994	14	(1)	1
Martin Rusev	01.03.2002		(1)	
Slavcho Shokolarov	20.08.1989	26	(6)	
Stanislav Shopov	23.02.2002	2	(5)	
Emmanuel Tokú (GHA)	10.07.2000	16		3
Dimitar Tonev	15.10.2001	12	(5)	1
Antonio Vutov	06.06.1996	3	(1)	
Forwards:	**DOB**	**M**	**(s)**	**G**
Fáider Fabio Burbano Castillo (COL)	12.06.1992		(1)	
Salif Cissé (FRA)	12.07.1992	5	(13)	2
Kristian Dobrev	27.04.2001	7	(11)	
Atanas Iliev	09.10.1994	27	(1)	16
José Marcos Costa Martins „Marquinhos" (BRA)	23.10.1999	10		
Todor Nedelev	07.02.1992	12		3
Stefan Popov	06.08.2002		(1)	
Georgi Trifonov	13.02.2002	1	(2)	
Ivan Vasilev	16.05.2001	2	(6)	

Professional Football Club Botev Vratsa

Founded: 1921
Stadium: Stadion "Hristo Botev", Vratsa (12,000)
Trainer: Antoni Zdravkov 20.08.1964
[15.03.2021] Veselin Velikov 19.03.1977

Goalkeepers:	DOB	M	(s)	G
Damyan Damyanov	29.06.2000	2		
Dar Korolev (RUS)	27.11.1995		(1)	
Krasimir Kostov	11.02.1995	29		
Hristo Mitov	24.01.1985	1		
Defenders:	**DOB**	**M**	**(s)**	**G**
Dimitar Burov	31.08.1997	14	(6)	2
Vasil Dobrev	05.01.1998	3	(3)	
Petar Genchev	29.03.1998	2	(2)	
Ventsislav Kerchev	02.06.1997	29		1
Martin Kostadinov	13.05.1996	6	(1)	
Iliya Milanov	19.02.1992	28		
Kostadin Nichev	22.07.1987	7	(5)	1
Martin Nikolov	01.01.1993	15		1
Angel Tsolov	10.10.1990		(1)	
Atanas Zehirov	13.02.1989	30		
Midfielders:	**DOB**	**M**	**(s)**	**G**
Samir Ahmed Ayass (LIB)	24.12.1990	3	(5)	
Daniel Gadzhev	21.06.1985	14	(6)	
Chavdar Ivaylov	09.07.1996	11	(10)	3
Nikola Kolev	06.06.1995	3	(7)	
Ivaylo Mihaylov	18.01.1991	2	(7)	
Alassane N'Diaye (FRA)	25.02.1990	24	(1)	1
Pedro Manuel Grácio Lagoa (POR)	21.08.1997	10	(7)	2
Wellington Brito da Silva "Tom" (BRA)	23.07.1995	8	(9)	
Vladislav Uzunov	25.05.1991	5	(7)	
Hristo Zlatinski	22.01.1985	21	(4)	1
Forwards:	**DOB**	**M**	**(s)**	**G**
Petar Atanasov	13.10.1990	24	(7)	2
Dorian Babunski (MKD)	29.08.1996	9	(7)	3
Valeri Domovchiyski	05.10.1986	11	(8)	4
Daniel Genov	19.05.1989	30	(1)	8
Miroslav Marinov	07.03.2004		(2)	
Yulian Nenov	17.11.1994	11	(17)	2
Jordan Zhelev	26.07.2004		(1)	

Professional Football Club Cherno More Varna

Founded: 03.03.1913
Stadium: Stadion Ticha, Varna (8,250)
Trainer: Ilian Iliev 02.07.1968

Goalkeepers:	DOB	M	(s)	G
Ivan Dichevski	24.04.2001	3		
Ivan Dyulgerov	15.07.1999	14		
Georgi Georgiev	12.10.1988	15		
Defenders:	**DOB**	**M**	**(s)**	**G**
Martin Dichev	22.08.2000	3	(9)	
Daniel Dimov	21.01.1989	24	(2)	
Vlatko Drobarov (MKD)	02.11.1992	17		1
Miroslav Enchev	08.08.1991	5	(1)	
Tsvetomir Panov	17.04.1989	30	(1)	
Viktor Popov	05.03.2000	31		
Stefan Stanchev	26.04.1989	13	(1)	1
Emil Yanchev	08.02.1999	6	(1)	
Midfielders:	**DOB**	**M**	**(s)**	**G**
Mehdi Boukassi (ALG)	15.06.1996		(5)	
Pavel Georgiev	25.10.2001		(10)	
Ilian Iliev	20.08.1999	26		2
Dani Ayman Kiki	08.01.1988	1	(2)	
Leandro Livramento Andrade (POR)	24.09.1999	14	(10)	
Pablo Álvarez García (ESP)	23.04.1997	10	(4)	2
Vasil Panayotov	16.07.1990	29		4
Erickson Patrick Correia Andrade (CPV)	09.02.1993	1	(1)	
Stefan Velev	02.05.1989	24	(3)	3
Forwards:	**DOB**	**M**	**(s)**	**G**
Denislav Angelov	05.01.2001	1	(11)	1
Georgi Bozhilov	12.02.1987	9	(2)	
Mathias Coureur (MTQ)	22.03.1988	15		15
Ismail Issa	26.06.1989	16	(10)	
Faysel Kasmi (BEL)	31.10.1995	15	(9)	2
Rodrigo Henrique Santana da Silva (BRA)	02.07.1993	20	(4)	3
Rodrigo Abreu de Sá Vilela (POR)	15.03.1995	5	(13)	
Velislav Vasilev	08.05.2001	1	(12)	
José Gomes „Zé Gomes" (POR)	08.04.1999	13	(1)	3

Professional Football Club
Centralen Sporten Klub na Armiyata (CSKA) Sofia

Founded:	05.05.1948	
Stadium:	Balgarska Armiya Stadion, Sofia (22,995)	
Trainer:	Stamen Belchev	07.05.1969
[26.10.2020]	Daniel Alexandre Morales Batagello (BRA)	06.12.1975
[11.11.2020]	Bruno Akrapović (BIH)	26.09.1967
[28.03.2021]	Lyuboslav Penev	31.08.1966

Goalkeepers:	DOB	M	(s)	G
Gustavo Busatto (BRA)	23.10.1990	26		
Dimitar Evtimov	07.09.1993	5	(1)	
Defenders:	**DOB**	**M**	**(s)**	**G**
Valentin Antov	09.11.2000	14	(2)	2
Asen Donchev	22.10.2001	1	(1)	
Plamen Plamen Galabov	02.11.1995	12	(7)	
Geferson Cerqueira Teles (BRA)	13.05.1994	12	(3)	
Menno Koch (NED)	02.07.1994	12	(1)	2
Jurgen Mattheij (NED)	01.04.1993	25		3
Bradley Mazikou (CGO)	02.06.1996	22	(3)	1
Ivan Turitsov	18.07.1999	13	(6)	
Thibaut Vion (FRA)	11.12.1993	18	(1)	2
Petar Zanev	18.10.1985	16	(3)	
Midfielders:	**DOB**	**M**	**(s)**	**G**
Stefano Beltrame (ITA)	08.02.1993	2	(12)	1
Kristiyan Malinov	30.03.1994		(1)	
Younousse Sankharé (SEN)	10.09.1989	10	(2)	3
Martin Smolenski	08.03.2003	1	(6)	
Tiago Filipe Sousa Nóbrega Rodrigues (POR)	29.01.1992	21	(6)	4
Federico Nicolás Varela (ARG)	18.04.1997	7	(3)	
Amos Youga (CTA)	08.12.1992	25	(4)	
Forwards:	**DOB**	**M**	**(s)**	**G**
Ahmed Ahmedov	04.03.1995	2	(9)	1
Jordy Josué Caicedo Medina (ECU)	18.11.1997	11	(3)	6
Graham Carey (IRL)	20.05.1989	13	(11)	1
Bismark Charles (GHA)	26.05.2001	5	(7)	2
Henrique Roberto Rafael (BRA)	23.08.1993	13	(9)	2
Tomislav Jurić (AUS)	22.07.1991	1	(2)	1
Jules Keita (GUI)	20.07.1998	9	(5)	2
Adalberto Peñaranda Maestre (VEN)	31.05.1997	5		
Mitko Mitkov	28.08.2000		(4)	
Jerome Terence Sinclair (ENG)	20.09.1996	10	(8)	1
Ali Sowe (GAM)	14.06.1994	15	(1)	8
Georgi Yomov	06.07.1997	15	(11)	
Tonislav Yordanov	27.11.1998		(1)	

Football Club Central Sports Club of the Army 1948 Sofia

Founded:	19.07.2016	
Stadium:	Nationalen Stadion "Vasil Levski", Sofia (44,000)	
Trainer:	Krasimir Balakov	29.03.1966
[23.03.2021]	Rosen Kirilov	04.01.1973
[24.04.2021]	Todor Kiselichkov	04.09.1975

Goalkeepers:	DOB	M	(s)	G
Daniel Naumov	29.03.1998	30		
Nikola Videnov	22.03.2002	1		
Defenders:	**DOB**	**M**	**(s)**	**G**
Sasho Aleksandrov	30.07.1986	25		
Dimo Atanasov	24.10.1985	3		
Aleksandar Georgiev	28.05.2003		(1)	
Angel Lyaskov	16.03.1998	10	(1)	
Lazar Marin	09.02.1994	22	(3)	
Mihail Minkov	06.02.1993	4	(9)	
Mihael Orachev	03.10.1995	1	(2)	
Simeon Petrov	12.01.2000	15	(3)	
Dimitar Pirgov	23.10.1989	22	(2)	
Dimitar Savov	09.09.1998	4	(1)	
Ventsislav Vasilev	08.07.1988	18	(4)	
Midfielders:	**DOB**	**M**	**(s)**	**G**
Ivaylo Chochev	18.02.1993	13	(3)	3
Georgi Gospodinov	08.03.2002	2		
Martin Haydarov	22.01.2003	4	(5)	
Galin Ivanov	15.04.1988	19	(2)	9
Georgi Ivanov	25.07.1993	1	(1)	
Ivaylo Klimentov	03.02.1998	7	(8)	
Emmanuel Lichev	17.04.2000	2	(4)	
Kristiyan Nikolov	18.12.2003		(1)	
Vasil Shopov	09.11.1991	19	(3)	3
Tsvetomir Todorov	31.03.1991		(1)	
Mario Topuzov	25.07.1999	14	(11)	1
Serkan Yusein	31.03.1996	18		
Forwards:	**DOB**	**M**	**(s)**	**G**
Denislav Aleksandrov	19.07.1997	20	(3)	3
Angel Bastunov	18.05.1999	15	(14)	4
Borislav Damyanov	01.01.1998	3	(4)	
Nikolay Ganchev	16.10.1999		(4)	
Andon Gushterov	16.02.1990	4	(7)	
Martin Kamburov	13.10.1980	14	(1)	9
Dimitar Mitkov	27.01.2000	5	(5)	
Daniel Mladenov	25.05.1987	6	(8)	1
Georgi Rusev	02.07.1998	20	(4)	6

Sports Football Club Etar Veliko Tarnovo

Founded:	17.07.2013	
Stadium:	Stadion Ivaylo, Veliko Tarnovo (15,000)	
Trainer:	Petko Petkov	29.03.1968
[10.12.2020]	Kaloyan Chakarov	17.02.1971
[19.11.2020]	Aleksandar Tomash	02.09.1978

Goalkeepers:	DOB	M	(s)	G
Anatoli Gospodinov	21.03.1994	9	(1)	
Hristo Ivanov	06.04.1982	23		
Defenders:	**DOB**	**M**	**(s)**	**G**
Erol Alkan (TUR)	16.02.1994	1		
José Ángel Córdoba Chambers (PAN)	06.03.2001	5	(5)	
Mark Edur (EST)	11.12.1998	1	(1)	
Venelin Filipov	20.08.1990	5	(2)	
Hristofor Hubchev	24.11.1995	16	(4)	
Zdravko Iliev	19.10.1984	22		
Mariyan Ivanov	10.07.1990	25	(1)	
Plamen Krachunov	11.01.1989	25		1
Francisco Puertas Trujillano „Paco Puertas" (ESP)	07.11.1995	1	(2)	
Yulian Raykov	03.02.2002		(1)	
Ivan Skerlev	28.01.1986	4	(1)	
Kolyo Stanev	10.10.2001	14	(13)	1
Midfielders:	**DOB**	**M**	**(s)**	**G**
Aldaír Caputo Ferreira (ANG)	26.03.1998	19	(5)	1
Stelian Dobrev	13.09.2002	9	(3)	1
Nicolás Federico Femia (ARG)	08.08.1996	1	(5)	
Bozhidar Katsarov	30.12.1993	26		
Nikola Kolev	06.06.1995	5		
Georgi Kupenov	24.02.1997	13	(2)	
Simeon Mechev	16.03.1990	15	(1)	
Ivan Mihaylov	30.09.1998	1	(5)	
Kaloyan Mitev	02.12.2002		(1)	
Daniel Pehlivanov	01.07.1994	8	(4)	
Yani Pehlivanov	14.07.1988	14	(7)	
Svilen Shterev	14.12.1992	3	(7)	1
Forwards:	**DOB**	**M**	**(s)**	**G**
Milcho Angelov	02.01.1995	21	(10)	3
Preslav Borukov	23.04.2000	25	(5)	12
Romeesh Nathaniel Ivey Belgrave (PAN)	14.07.1994	5	(4)	
Lovre Knežević (CRO)	22.07.1998	11	(4)	1
Borislav Markov	11.02.2002		(1)	
Hristo Markov	16.02.2003		(1)	
Gaëtan Missi Mezu (GAB)	04.05.1996	11	(3)	3
Daniel Mladenov	25.05.1987	5	(6)	1
Anton Ognyanov	30.06.1988	8	(1)	
Ivan Petkov	22.01.1982		(6)	
Valentin Yoskov	05.06.1998	1	(6)	

Professional Football Club Levski Sofia

	Founded:	24.05.1914	
	Stadium:	Stadion Vivacom Arena „Georgi Asparuhov", Sofia (25,000)	
	Trainer:	Georgi Todorov	13.06.1956
	[10.11.2020]	Slaviša Stojanović (SVN)	06.12.1969

Goalkeepers:	DOB	M	(s)	G
Plamen Andreev	15.12.2004		(1)	
Nikolay Krastev	06.12.1996	1		
Nikolay Mihaylov	28.06.1988	18		
Zvonimir Mikulić (CRO)	05.02.1990	13		
Defenders:	**DOB**	**M**	**(s)**	**G**
Georgi Aleksandrov	21.05.2001	8	(2)	
Zhivko Atanasov	03.02.1991	28		4
Thomas Dasquet (FRA)	03.06.1994	21	(3)	
Deyan Ivanov	12.04.1996		(4)	
Dragan Mihajlović (SUI)	22.08.1991	13		
Ignacio Monsalve Vicente „Nacho Monsalve" (ESP)	27.04.1994	9	(2)	1
Ivaylo Naydenov	22.03.1998	27		1
Alex Petkov	25.07.1999	12		
Faycal Rherras (MAR)	07.04.1993	6	(1)	
Rebin Ghareeb Solaka Adhamat (IRQ)	12.04.1992	4		
Mateo Stamatov	22.03.1999	10	(2)	
Orlin Starokin	08.01.1987	8	(3)	
Midfielders:	**DOB**	**M**	**(s)**	**G**
Adrian Kraev	14.02.1999	11	(2)	
Asen Mitkov	17.02.2005	1		
Martin Raynov	25.04.1992	22		1
Simeon Slavchev	25.09.1993	2	(5)	
Stijn Spierings (NED)	12.03.1996	7		2
Borislav Tsonev	29.04.1995	4	(6)	6
Radoslav Tsonev	29.04.1995	2	(4)	1
Iliya Yurukov	22.09.1999	14	(5)	
Forwards:	**DOB**	**M**	**(s)**	**G**
Bilal Bari (MAR)	19.01.1998	6	(9)	
Valeri Bojinov	15.02.1986		(10)	1
Zdravko Dimitrov	24.08.1998	21	(6)	1
Iliya Dimitrov	10.07.1996	1	(6)	
Patrick-Gabriel Galchev	14.04.2001	12	(4)	
Stanislav Ivanov	16.04.1999	8	(4)	1
Nasiru Mohammed (GHA)	06.06.1994	9	(9)	1
Paulo Victor de Menezes Melo „Paulinho" (BRA)	29.05.1993	13	(1)	4
Marin Petkov	02.10.2003	7	(9)	2
Martin Petkov	15.08.2002	13	(7)	1
Steven Petkov	07.05.1995	3	(11)	1
Nigel Robertha (CUW)	13.02.1998	18	(1)	6

Professional Football Club Lokomotiv Plovdiv

	Founded:	25.07.1926	
	Stadium:	Stadion Lokomotiv, Plovdiv (13,220)	
	Trainer:	Bruno Akrapović (BIH)	26.09.1967
	[11.11.2020]	Aleksandar Tunchev	10.07.1981

Goalkeepers:	DOB	M	(s)	G
Martin Lukov	05.07.1993	19		
Ilko Pirgov	23.05.1986	11	(1)	
Kristian Tomov	23.06.1905	1		
Defenders:	**DOB**	**M**	**(s)**	**G**
Dinis Costa Lima Almeida (POR)	28.05.1995	30		4
Christian Gomis (SEN)	25.08.1998	10	(11)	1
David Zeferino Malembana (MOZ)	11.10.1995	11	(5)	
Lucas Gabriel Masoero Masi (ARG)	01.02.1995	28		1
Nikolay Nikolaev	01.10.1992	4	(19)	1
Miloš Petrović (SRB)	05.05.1990	15		
Connor Ruane (ENG)	15.11.1993	2	(8)	
Josip Tomašević (CRO)	04.03.1994	2		
Midfielders:	**DOB**	**M**	**(s)**	**G**
Ivan Aramazov	07.01.2003		(2)	
Cristopher Paolo César Hurtado Huertas (PER)	27.07.1990		(1)	
Christian Ilić (CRO)	22.07.1996	19	(7)	4
Daniel Ivanov		1	(2)	
Aleksandar Kolev	03.04.2002	1	(2)	1
Lucas Spinola Salinas (BRA)	14.10.1995	15	(4)	2
Ivan Mikhailov (RUS)	25.01.2002		(1)	
Valentino Pugliese (SUI)	18.07.1997		(3)	
Vidol Seimenski	11.04.2003		(1)	
Parvizchon Umarbaev (TJK)	01.11.1994	28	(3)	1
Petar Vitanov	10.03.1995	27	(3)	
Forwards:	**DOB**	**M**	**(s)**	**G**
Ante Aralica (CRO)	23.07.1996	6	(4)	1
Daniel Dimitrov	20.07.2002		(2)	
Dimitar Iliev	25.09.1988	30		13
Aleksandar Ivanov	29.09.1999	1	(2)	1
Bircent Hamdi Karagaren	06.12.1992	29	(2)	4
Georgi Mavrodiev	20.09.2003		(6)	
Filip Mihaljević (CRO)	14.11.2000		(3)	
Georgi Minchev	20.04.1995	23	(7)	9
Kenan Muslimović (AUT)	13.02.1997	1	(9)	
Momchil Tsvetanov	03.12.1990	27	(3)	4

Professional Football Club Ludogorets Razgrad

	Founded:	1945	
	Stadium:	Ludogorets Arena, Razgrad (10,442)	
	Trainer:	Pavel Vrba (CZE)	06.12.1963
	[25.10.2020]	Stanislav Genchev	20.03.1981
	[03.01.2021]	Valdas Dambrauskas (LTU)	07.01.1977

Goalkeepers:	DOB	M	(s)	G
Damyan Hristov	10.11.2002	1		
Plamen Iliev	30.11.1991	9		
Kristijan Kahlina (CRO)	24.07.1992	9		
Renan dos Santos (BRA)	18.05.1989	7		
Vladislav Stoyanov	08.06.1987	5	(1)	
Defenders:	**DOB**	**M**	**(s)**	**G**
Ilker Budinov	11.08.2000	1		
Neuciano de Jesus Gusmão „Cicinho"	26.12.1988	22	(1)	3
Tihomir Dimitrov	04.02.2000	1		
Aleksandar Ganchev	09.07.2001	1		
Dragoş Grigore (ROU)	07.09.1986	9	(1)	1
Jordan Ikoko (COD)	03.02.1994	12	(6)	
Josué Humberto Gonçalves Leal Sá (POR)	17.06.1992	17		2
Aleks Lukanov	22.02.2002		(1)	
Cosmin Iosif Moţi (ROU)	03.12.1984	8	(1)	1
Anton Anton Nedyalkov	30.04.1993	20	(2)	
Taleb Tawatha (ISR)	21.06.1992	1		
Georgi Terziev	18.04.1992	11	(4)	
Valentin Tsvetanov	08.04.2002		(1)	
Olivier Verdon (BEN)	05.10.1995	18	(1)	
Midfielders:	**DOB**	**M**	**(s)**	**G**
Alex Paulo Menezes Santana (BRA)	13.05.1995	17	(6)	5
Anicet Andrianantenaina Abel (MAD)	13.03.1990	12	(7)	1
Stéphane Badji (SEN)	18.01.1990	14	(5)	
Cauly Oliveira-Souza (BRA)	15.09.1995	25	(2)	6
Svetoslav Dyakov	31.05.1984	12	(8)	
Petar Georgiev	10.05.2002		(1)	
Tsvetoslav Petrov	29.05.1999	1		
Dominik Yankov	28.07.2000	16	(12)	5
Ivan Yordanov	07.11.2000	2	(1)	
Forwards:	**DOB**	**M**	**(s)**	**G**
Georgi Chukalov	25.02.1998		(1)	
Kiril Despodov	11.11.1996	18	(2)	5
Higinio Marín Escavy (ESP)	19.10.1993	4	(4)	4
Hyusein Kelyovluev	11.05.2000	1		
Jorge Fernando Barbosa Intima „Jorghinho"(GNB)	21.09.1995	3	(5)	1
Claudiu Andrei Keşerü (ROU)	02.12.1986	22	(5)	18
Branimir Kostadinov	04.03.1989	1		
Elvis Manu (GHA)	13.08.1993	9	(13)	4
Dimitar Mitkov	27.01.2000	2	(2)	
Vladislav Naydenov	29.11.2001		(1)	
Pieros Sotiriou (CYP)	13.01.1993		(9)	1
Jakub Świerczok (POL)	28.12.1992	1		
Mavis Tchibota Dufounou (CGO)	07.05.1996	7	(10)	3
Bernard Tekpetey (GHA)	03.09.1997	17	(7)	2
Wanderson Cristaldo Farias (BRA)	02.01.1988	5	(3)	3

Football Club Montana

Founded: 20.03.1921 (*as SC Hristo Mihaylov*)
Stadium: Stadion Ogosta, Montana (6,000)
Trainer: Nikola Spasov (†**23.11.2020**) — 15.12.1958
[24.11.2020] Svetlan Kondev — 23.01.1976
[01.12.2020] Atanas Atanasov — 17.03.1969
[15.05.2021] Svetlan Kondev — 23.01.1976

Goalkeepers:	DOB	M	(s)	G
Mario Kirev	15.08.1989	2		
Blagoy Makendzhiev	11.07.1988	22		
Marin Orlinov	30.10.1994	8		
Defenders:	**DOB**	**M**	**(s)**	**G**
Vladimir Aytov	12.04.1996	16	(7)	3
Aleksandar Bashliev	16.11.1989	29	(1)	
Valeri Hristov	10.03.1998	5	(7)	
Enagnon David Kiki (BEN)	25.11.1993	22	(1)	1
Ivan Mihov	08.06.1991	23		
Mihael Orachev	03.10.1995		(3)	
Preslav Petrov	01.05.1995	2	(2)	1
Preslav I. Petrov	14.02.1997	2	(1)	
Stoyan Predev	19.08.1993	3	(3)	
Rayan Senhadji (FRA)	13.06.1997	11	(3)	1
Radoslav Terziev	06.08.1994	10	(3)	
Stefan Tsonkov	24.01.1995	24	(2)	1

Midfielders:	DOB	M	(s)	G
Yanko Angelov	29.06.1993	26	(3)	1
Borislav Baldzhiyski	12.10.1990	8	(2)	1
Adam Boujamaa (FRA)	24.10.1998		(4)	
Dimitar Iliev	27.07.1986	14		
Ivelin Iliev	08.08.1997		(5)	
Stefan Kamenov	13.03.2001	13	(6)	
Nikolay Tsvetkov	10.08.1987	7	(5)	
Yordan Yordanov	20.04.1992	13	(13)	
Forwards:	**DOB**	**M**	**(s)**	**G**
Bilal Bari	19.01.1998	11	(1)	3
Sergey Georgiev	05.05.1992	17	(9)	1
Rosen Krastev	18.03.1998	7	(10)	1
Nikolay Minkov	13.08.1997	30	(1)	4
Toni Tasev	25.03.1994	27		5
Dimitar Zakonov	30.06.1999		(6)	

Professional Football Club Slavia Sofia

Founded: 10.04.1913
Stadium: Stadion Slavia, Sofia (25,556)
Trainer: Zlatomir Zagorčić — 15.06.1971
[07.09.2020] Martin Kushev — 25.08.1973
[17.09.2020] Aleksandr Tarkhanov — 06.09.1954
[12.04.2021] Zlatomir Zagorčić — 15.06.1971

Goalkeepers:	DOB	M	(s)	G
Georgi Petkov	14.03.1976	4		
Antonis Stergiakis (GRE)	16.03.1999	7		
Svetoslav Vutsov	09.07.2002	21	(1)	
Defenders:	**DOB**	**M**	**(s)**	**G**
Filip Antovski (MKD)	24.11.2000	23	(1)	
Venelin Filipov	20.08.1990	1		
Nader Ghandri (TUN)	18.02.1995	13		
Andrea Hristov	01.03.1999	26		1
Petar Patev	21.05.1993	10	(1)	
Radoslav Terziev	06.08.1994	9		
Ertan Tombak	30.05.1999	12	(3)	
Kostadin Velkov	26.03.1989		(2)	
Emil Viyachki	18.05.1990	16	(3)	
Midfielders:	**DOB**	**M**	**(s)**	**G**
Martin Atanasov	19.01.2002		(4)	
Ventsislav Bengyuzov	22.01.1991	7	(4)	
Erol Dost	29.05.1999	9	(2)	1
Milen Gamakov	12.04.1994	12	(1)	
Yanis Karabelyov	23.01.1996	12		
Filip Krastev	15.10.2001	13	(1)	1

	DOB	M	(s)	G
Peter Makrillos (AUS)	04.09.1995	15		7
Hristo Popadiyn	06.01.1994	10	(1)	
Emil Stoev	17.01.1996	22	(3)	1
Dimitar Stoyanov	14.04.2001		(4)	
Darko Tasevski (MKD)	20.05.1984	1	(12)	
Vladislav Uzunov	25.05.1991	3	(4)	
Georgi Valchev	07.03.1991	22	(6)	3
Petar Vutsov	07.08.2000		(1)	
Aleksandar Zlatkov	31.01.1999	1		
Forwards:	**DOB**	**M**	**(s)**	**G**
Mihail Aleksandrov	11.06.1989	8	(6)	
Tsvetelin Chunchukov	26.12.1994		(1)	
Ivaylo Dimitrov	26.03.1989	7	(9)	2
Dragoş Petruţ Firtulescu (ROU)	15.05.1989	2	(1)	
Ventsislav Hristov	09.11.1988		(1)	
Atanas Kabov	11.04.1999	2	(5)	
Radoslav Kirilov	29.06.1992	28	(1)	6
Kaloyan Krastev	24.01.1999	17	(11)	3
Dimitar Rangelov	09.02.1983	15	(10)	3
Martin Sorakov	23.10.2003	2	(9)	
Georgi Yomov	06.07.1997	2		

Football Club Tsarko Selo Sofia

Founded: 01.07.2015
Stadium: Arena Tsarko Selo, Sofia (1,550)
Trainer: Lyuboslav Penev — 31.08.1966
[29.03.2021] Antoni Zdravkov — 20.08.1964

Goalkeepers:	DOB	M	(s)	G
Mihail Ivanov	07.08.1989	4		
Johny Placide (HAI)	29.01.1988	28		
Defenders:	**DOB**	**M**	**(s)**	**G**
Ivan Bandalovski	23.11.1986	20		
Vasil Bozhinov	08.12.1996	1	(1)	
Reyan Daskalov	10.02.1995	24	(1)	2
Dobrin Denev	20.01.2002		(1)	
Dilyan Georgiev	23.06.1905	3	(3)	
Julio César Rodríguez López (ESP)	07.12.1995	6		
Martin Kavdanski	13.02.1987	19	(6)	4
Luis Pedro da Silva Ferreira (ANG)	06.01.1992	16	(5)	
Ivaylo Markov	05.06.1997	23	(1)	
Louis Nganioni (FRA)	03.06.1995	6	(3)	
Bozhidar Tomovski	21.08.2004		(2)	
Bozhidar Vasev	14.03.1993	11	(1)	1
Midfielders:	**DOB**	**M**	**(s)**	**G**
Lachezar Baltanov	11.07.1988	17	(3)	2
Hritiyan Chipev	23.07.2001	1	(2)	
Hari Denkov	23.05.2002	2	(2)	
Boris Galchev	31.10.1983	12		

	DOB	M	(s)	G
Antonio Georgiev	26.10.1997	21	(5)	1
Giannis Gerolemou (CYP)	27.01.2000	1	(5)	
Dimitar Kostadinov	14.08.1999	13	(1)	5
Alex Lyubenov		1		
Simeon Mechev	16.03.1990	1	(4)	
Dylan Mertens (NED)	20.07.1995	20	(5)	1
Hristo Popadiyn	06.01.1994	9	(3)	
Kristiyan Todorov			(2)	
Wesley Natã Wachholz (BRA)	18.04.1995	2		
Forwards:	**DOB**	**M**	**(s)**	**G**
Anderson Cordeiro Costa (BRA)	10.10.1998	22	(6)	7
Mohamed Amine Brahimi (FRA)	17.09.1998		(3)	
Miroslav Budinov	23.01.1996	9	(4)	1
Salif Cissé (FRA)	12.07.1992	6		
Lesly de Sa (NED)	02.04.1993	2	(10)	
Stefan Hristov	28.08.1989	17	(8)	2
Panagiotis Louka (CYP)	08.09.2000	12	(9)	1
Emanuil Manev	19.04.1992	17	(12)	4
Karim Rossi (SUI)	01.05.1994	4	(9)	
Alen Stevanović (SRB)	07.01.1991	2	(2)	
Toma Ushagelov	17.04.2001		(4)	

SECOND LEVEL
Second Professional Football League 2020/2021

1.	OFC Pirin Blagoevgrad (*Promoted*)	30	20	5	5	66	-	26	65
2.	FC Lokomotiv 1929 Sofia (*Promoted*)	30	19	5	6	65	-	30	62
3.	PFC Septemvri Sofia (*Promotion Play-offs*)	30	17	5	8	54	-	29	56
4.	PFC Ludogorets Razgrad II	30	14	8	8	56	-	38	50
5.	FC Sportist Svoge	30	14	7	9	43	-	36	49
6.	FC Hebar Pazardzhik	30	13	9	8	50	-	36	48
7.	PFC Litex Lovech	30	9	12	9	36	-	31	39
8.	FC Sozopol	30	10	9	11	35	-	40	39
9.	FC Minyor Pernik	30	10	9	11	30	-	37	39
10.	FC Strumska Slava Radomir	30	8	10	12	31	-	37	34
11.	FC Yantra Gabrovo	30	10	4	16	30	-	47	34
12.	FC Septemvri Simitli	30	9	6	15	34	-	42	33
13.	FC Dobrudzha Dobrich	30	7	9	14	28	-	46	30
14.	PFC Neftochimic Burgas	30	7	6	17	27	-	61	27
15.	FC Lokomotiv Gorna Oryahovitsa (*Relegated*)	30	5	10	15	24	-	43	25
16.	FC Kariana Erden (*Dissolved*)	30	9	4	17	29	-	59	31
17.	FC Vitosha Bistritsa (*Dissolved*)	0	0	0	0	0	-	0	0

Please note: both FC Vitosha Bistritsa (28.09.2020) and FC Kariana Erden (19.01.2021) retired voluntarily from the league due to financial reasons. All remaining results (FC Kariana Erden) were awarded as 3-0 for the opposing teams, while all remaining fixtures involving FC Vitosha Bistritsa were cancelled. Both clubs were dissolved at end of the season.

NATIONAL TEAM

INTERNATIONAL MATCHES
(16.07.2020 – 15.07.2021)

03.09.2020	Sofia	Bulgaria - Republic of Ireland	1-1(0-0)	(UNL)
06.09.2020	Cardiff	Wales - Bulgaria	1-0(0-0)	(UNL)
08.10.2020	Sofia	Bulgaria - Hungary	1-3(0-1)	(ECQPO)
11.10.2020	Helsinki	Finland - Bulgaria	2-0(0-0)	(UNL)
14.10.2020	Sofia	Bulgaria - Wales	0-1(0-0)	(UNL)
11.11.2020	Sofia	Bulgaria - Gibraltar	3-0(3-0)	(F)
15.11.2020	Sofia	Bulgaria - Finland	1-2(0-2)	(UNL)
18.11.2020	Dublin	Republic of Ireland - Bulgaria	0-0	(UNL)
25.03.2021	Sofia	Bulgaria - Switzerland	1-3(0-3)	(WCQ)
28.03.2021	Sofia	Bulgaria - Italy	0-2(0-1)	(WCQ)
31.03.2021	Belfast	Northern Ireland - Bulgaria	0-0	(WCQ)
01.06.2021	Ried im Innkreis	Slovakia - Bulgaria	1-1(1-1)	(F)
05.06.2021	Moskva	Russia - Bulgaria	1-0(0-0)	(F)
08.06.2021	Paris	France - Bulgaria	3-0(1-0)	(F)

03.09.2020   BULGARIA - REPUBLIC OF IRELAND   1-1(0-0)   2nd UEFA Nations League B, Group 4
Nationalen Stadion "Vasil Levski", Sofia; Referee: Manuel Schüttengruber (Austria); Attendance: 0
BUL: Georgi Georgiev, Petar Zanev (Cap) (79.Plamen Galabov), Anton Nedyalkov, Strahil Popov, Kristian Dimitrov, Galin Ivanov, Georgi Kostadinov, Kristiyan Malinov, Todor Nedelev (83.Aleksandar Tsvetkov), Bozhidar Kraev, Spas Delev (76.Bircent Hamdi Karagaren). Trainer: Georgi Dermendzhiev.
Goal: Bozhidar Kraev (57).

06.09.2020   WALES - BULGARIA   1-0(0-0)   2nd UEFA Nations League B, Group 4
Cardiff City Stadium, Cardiff; Referee: Fábio José Costa Veríssimo (Portugal); Attendance: 0
BUL: Georgi Georgiev, Neuciano de Jesus Gusmão „Cicinho", Ivan Goranov, Anton Nedyalkov, Kristian Dimitrov, Galin Ivanov (70.Spas Delev), Georgi Kostadinov (Cap), Todor Nedelev (82.Filip Krastev), Yanis Karabelyov, Bozhidar Kraev (61.Dimitar Iliev), Bircent Hamdi Karagaren. Trainer: Georgi Dermendzhiev.

08.10.2020   BULGARIA - HUNGARY   1-3(0-1)   16th EC. Qualifiers Play-offs, Semi-Finals
Nationalen Stadion "Vasil Levski", Sofia; Referee: Szymon Marciniak (Poland); Attendance: 1,929
BUL: Plamen Iliev, Neuciano de Jesus Gusmão „Cicinho", Vasil Bozhikov (Cap), Georgi Terziev, Anton Nedyalkov, Galin Ivanov (31.Georgi Yomov), Kristiyan Malinov, Todor Nedelev (80.Dominik Yankov), Yanis Karabelyov, Bozhidar Kraev (79.Ismail Isa Mustafa), Bircent Hamdi Karagaren (58.Kiril Despodov). Trainer: Georgi Dermendzhiev.
Goal: Georgi Yomov (89).

11.10.2020   FINLAND - BULGARIA   2-0(0-0)   2nd UEFA Nations League B, Group 4
Olympiastadion, Helsinki; Referee: Erik Lambrechts (Belgium); Attendance: 6,587
BUL: Martin Lukov, Strahil Popov, Vasil Bozhikov (Cap), Anton Nedyalkov (60.Dimitar Velkovski), Kristian Dimitrov, Aleksandar Tsvetkov (75.Yanis Karabelyov), Kristiyan Malinov, Georgi Yomov, Ismail Isa Mustafa (60.Bozhidar Kraev), Dimitar Iliev (75.Todor Nedelev), Kiril Despodov. Trainer: Georgi Dermendzhiev.

14.10.2020   BULGARIA - WALES   0-1(0-0)   2nd UEFA Nations League B, Group 4
Nationalen Stadion "Vasil Levski", Sofia; Referee: Əliyar Ağayev (Azerbaijan); Attendance: 478
BUL: Njikolay Mihaylov (Cap), Neuciano de Jesus Gusmão „Cicinho", Georgi Terziev, Anton Nedyalkov, Kristian Dimitrov, Kristiyan Malinov (46.Aleksandar Tsvetkov), Todor Nedelev, Yanis Karabelyov, Bozhidar Kraev (75.Ismail Isa Mustafa), Georgi Yomov, Kiril Despodov (84.Bircent Hamdi Karagaren). Trainer: Georgi Dermendzhiev.

11.11.2020　　**BULGARIA - GIBRALTAR**　　　　　　　**3-0(3-0)**　　　　　　　　Friendly International
Nationalen Stadion "Vasil Levski", Sofia; Referee: Constantin Sebastian Colţescu (Romania); Attendance: 0
BUL: Martin Lukov, Neuciano de Jesus Gusmão „Cicinho" (65.Dimitar Velkovski), Strahil Popov (78.Viktor Popov), Vasil Bozhikov (Cap), Valentin Antov, Galin Ivanov (65.Svetoslav Kovachev), Aleksandar Tsvetkov, Kristiyan Malinov, Georgi Yomov (78.Zdravko Dimitrov), Dominik Yankov (80.Bozhidar Kraev), Dimitar Iliev. Trainer: Georgi Dermendzhiev.
Goals: Aleksandar Tsvetkov (6), Georgi Yomov (15), Dimitar Iliev (45).

15.11.2020　　**BULGARIA - FINLAND**　　　　　　　**1-2(0-2)**　　　　　2nd UEFA Nations League B, Group 4
Nationalen Stadion "Vasil Levski", Sofia; Referee: Donatas Rumšas (Lithuania); Attendance: 0
BUL: Martin Lukov, Strahil Popov, Vasil Bozhikov (Cap), Dimitar Velkovski, Kristian Dimitrov, Galin Ivanov (78.Bircent Hamdi Karagaren), Kristiyan Malinov, Yanis Karabelyov (85.Aleksandar Tsvetkov), Bozhidar Kraev, Dominik Yankov (65.Dimitar Iliev), Spas Delev (78.Svetoslav Kovachev). Trainer: Georgi Dermendzhiev.
Goal: Dimitar Iliev (68 penalty).

18.11.2020　　**REPUBLIC OF IRELAND - BULGARIA**　　　　**0-0**　　　　2nd UEFA Nations League B, Group 4
Aviva Stadium, Dublin; Referee: Lawrence Visser (Belgium); Attendance: 0
BUL: Martin Lukov, Neuciano de Jesus Gusmão „Cicinho" (60.Aleksandar Vasilev), Strahil Popov (Cap), Kristian Dimitrov, Galin Ivanov (60.Bircent Hamdi Karagaren), Georgi Angelov, Aleksandar Tsvetkov, Kristiyan Malinov, Bozhidar Kraev, Dimitar Iliev (81.Denislav Aleksandrov), Spas Delev (61.Svetoslav Kovachev). Trainer: Georgi Dermendzhiev.

25.03.2021　　**BULGARIA - SWITZERLAND**　　　　　　**1-3(0-3)**　　　　　　22nd FIFA WC. Qualifiers
Nationalen Stadion "Vasil Levski", Sofia; Referee: Nikola Dabanović (Montenegro); Attendance: 0
BUL: Plamen Iliev, Daniel Dimov, Petar Zanev, Neuciano de Jesus Gusmão „Cicinho" (72.Momchil Tsvetanov), Strahil Popov, Vasil Bozhikov, Georgi Kostadinov (Cap), Kristiyan Malinov (71.Ivaylo Chochev), Dimitar Iliev (46.Atanas Iliev), Kiril Despodov (48.Spas Delev), Georgi Yomov (70.Ilian Iliev). Trainer: Yasen Petrov.
Goal: Kiril Despodov (46).

28.03.2021　　**BULGARIA - ITALY**　　　　　　　　**0-2(0-1)**　　　　　　　22nd FIFA WC. Qualifiers
Nationalen Stadion "Vasil Levski", Sofia; Referee: Slavko Vinčić (Slovenia); Attendance: 0
BUL: Plamen Iliev, Daniel Dimov, Neuciano de Jesus Gusmão „Cicinho" (46.Bircent Hamdi Karagaren), Vasil Bozhikov, Valentin Antov, Momchil Tsvetanov, Georgi Kostadinov (Cap) (62.Kristiyan Malinov), Ivaylo Chochev, Vitanov (88.Martin Raynov), Spas Delev (76.Atanas Iliev), Andrey Galabinov. Trainer: Yasen Petrov.

31.03.2021　　**NORTHERN IRELAND - BULGARIA**　　　　**0-0**　　　　　　22nd FIFA WC. Qualifiers
Windsor Park, Belfast; Referee: Yigal Frid (Israel); Attendance: 0
BUL: Daniel Naumov, Petko Hristov, Valentin Antov, Andrea Hristov, Momchil Tsvetanov (73.Petar Zanev), Georgi Kostadinov (Cap) (43.Petar Vitanov), Ivaylo Chochev, Antonio Vutov (46.Dimitar Iliev), Andrey Galabinov (73.Atanas Iliev), Kiril Despodov, Georgi Yomov (72.Bircent Hamdi Karagaren). Trainer: Yasen Petrov.

01.06.2021　　**SLOVAKIA - BULGARIA**　　　　　　　**1-1(1-1)**　　　　　　　Friendly International
Keine Sorgen Stadion, Ried im Innkreis (Austria); Referee: Walter Altmann (Austria); Attendance: 0
BUL: Daniel Naumov (46.Nikolay Mihaylov), Vasil Bozhikov (Cap), Petko Hristov, Valentin Antov, Ivan Turitsov, Momchil Tsvetanov (46.Dominik Yankov), Ivaylo Chochev, Bozhidar Kraev (46.Dimitar Iliev), Atanas Iliev (60.Georgi Minchev), Kiril Despodov (82.Bircent Hamdi Karagaren), Petar Vitanov (69.Kristiyan Malinov). Trainer: Yasen Petrov.
Goal: Atanas Iliev (9).

05.06.2021　　**RUSSIA - BULGARIA**　　　　　　　　**1-0(0-0)**　　　　　　　Friendly International
VTB Arena, Moskva; Referee: Aleksei Kulbakov (Belarus); Attendance: 11,100
BUL: Ivan Karadzhov (46.Georgi Georgiev), Petko Hristov, Valentin Antov, Andrea Hristov, Momchil Tsvetanov, Ivaylo Chochev (88.Georgi Minchev), Kristiyan Malinov (9.Petar Vitanov), Dominik Yankov (62.Antonio Vutov), Kiril Despodov (Cap), Bircent Hamdi Karagaren (78.Ivan Turitsov), Andrey Galabinov (58.Atanas Iliev). Trainer: Yasen Petrov.

08.06.2021　　**FRANCE - BULGARIA**　　　　　　　　**3-0(1-0)**　　　　　　　Friendly International
Stade de France, Saint-Denis, Paris; Referee: Anastasios Sidiropoulos (Greece); Attendance: 5,000
BUL: Daniel Naumov, Vasil Bozhikov (Cap), Petko Hristov, Valentin Antov, Ivan Turitsov (71.Bircent Hamdi Karagaren), Ivaylo Chochev (52.Petar Vitanov), Bozhidar Kraev (58.Momchil Tsvetanov), Ilian Iliev, Dominik Yankov (70.Andrea Hristov), Kiril Despodov (58.Dimitar Iliev), Atanas Iliev (58.Georgi Minchev). Trainer: Yasen Petrov.

NATIONAL TEAM PLAYERS (16.07.2020 – 15.07.2021)					
Name	**DOB**	**Caps**	**Goals**	**2020/2021:**	*Club*
Goalkeepers					
Georgi GEORGIEV	12.10.1988	6	0	2020/2021:	*PFC Cherno More Varna*
Plamen ILIEV	30.11.1991	19	0	2020/2021:	*PFC Ludogorets Razgrad*
Ivan KARADZHOV	12.07.1989	1	0	2021:	*FC Arda Kardzhali*
Martin LUKOV	05.07.1993	4	0	2020:	*PFC Lokomotiv Plovdiv*
Nikolay MIHAYLOV	28.06.1988	39	0	2020/2021:	*PFC Levski Sofia*
Daniel NAUMOV	29.03.1998	3	0	2021:	*FC CSKA 1948 Sofia*

Defenders

Name	Date of Birth	Apps	Goals	Year	Club
Georgi ANGELOV	12.11.1990	1	0	2020:	*PFC Beroe Stara Zagora*
Valentin ANTOV	09.11.2000	8	0	2020:	*PFC CSKA Sofia*
				01.02.2021->	*Bologna FC 1909 (ITA)*
Vasil BOZHIKOV	02.06.1988	34	2	2020/2021:	*ŠK Slovan Bratislava (SVK)*
Neuciano de Jesus Gusmão „CICINHO"	26.12.1988	7	0	2020/2021:	*PFC Ludogorets Razgrad*
Kristian DIMITROV	27.02.1997	12	1	2020:	*HNK Hajduk Split (CRO)*
Daniel DIMOV	21.01.1989	2	0	2021:	*PFC Cherno More Varna*
Plamen GALABOV	02.11.1995	1	0	2020:	*PFC CSKA Sofia*
Ivan GORANOV	10.06.1992	7	0	2020:	*R Charleroi SC (BEL)*
Andrea HRISTOV	01.03.1999	3	0	2021:	*PFC Slavia Sofia*
Petko HRISTOV	01.03.1999	4	0	2021:	*FC Pro Vercelli 1892 (ITA)*
Anton NEDYALKOV	30.04.1993	19	0	2020:	*PFC Ludogorets Razgrad*
Strahil POPOV	31.08.1990	35	0	2020/2021:	*Hatayspor Antakya (TUR)*
Viktor POPOV	05.03.2000	3	0	2020:	*PFC Cherno More Varna*
Georgi TERZIEV	18.04.1992	16	0	2020:	*PFC Ludogorets Razgrad*
Ivan TURITSOV	18.07.1999	4	0	2021:	*PFC CSKA Sofia*
Aleksandar VASILEV	27.04.1995	1	0	2020:	*PFC Beroe Stara Zagora*
Dimitar VELKOVSKI	22.01.1995	3	0	2020:	*Cercle Brugge KSV (BEL)*
Petar ZANEV	18.10.1985	46	0	2020/2021:	*PFC CSKA Sofia*

Midfielders

Name	Date of Birth	Apps	Goals	Year	Club
Ivaylo CHOCHEV	18.02.1993	24	3	2020/2021:	*FC CSKA 1948 Sofia*
Dimitar ILIEV	25.09.1988	10	2	2020/2021:	*PFC Lokomotiv Plovdiv*
Ilian ILIEV	20.08.1999	2	0	2021:	*PFC Cherno More Varna*
Galin IVANOV	15.04.1988	16	1	2020:	*FC CSKA 1948 Sofia*
Yanis KARABELYOV	23.01.1996	6	0	2020:	*PFC Slavia Sofia*
Georgi KOSTADINOV	07.09.1990	28	3	2020/2021:	*FK Arsenal Tula (RUS)*
Bozhidar KRAEV	23.06.1997	24	3	2020:	*FC Midtjylland Herning (DEN)*
				11.01.2021->	*FC Famalicão (POR)*
Filip KRASTEV	15.10.2001	1	0	2020:	*PFC Slavia Sofia*
Kristiyan MALINOV	30.03.1994	23	0	2020/2021:	*Oud-Heverlee Leuven (BEL)*
Todor NEDELEV	07.02.1993	33	2	2020:	*PFC Botev Plovdiv*
Martin RAYNOV	25.04.1992	8	0	2021:	*PFC Levski Sofia*
Momchil TSVETANOV	03.12.1990	6	0	2021:	*PFC Lokomotiv Plovdiv*
Aleksandar TSVETKOV	31.08.1990	11	1	2020:	*PFC Beroe Stara Zagora*
Petar VITANOV	10.03.1995	5	0	2021:	*PFC Lokomotiv Plovdiv*
Antonio VUTOV	06.06.1996	2	0	2021:	*Mezőkövesdi SE (HUN)*
Dominik YANKOV	28.07.2000	6	0	2020/2021:	*PFC Ludogorets Razgrad*

Forwards

Name	Date of Birth	Apps	Goals	Year	Club
Denislav ALEKSANDROV	19.07.1997	1	0	2020:	*FC CSKA 1948 Sofia*
Spas DELEV	22.09.1989	31	2	2020/2021:	*FC Arda Kardzhali*
Kiril DESPODOV	11.08.1996	20	2	2020/2021:	*PFC Ludogorets Razgrad*
Zdravko DIMITROV	24.08.1998	1	0	2020:	*PFC Levski Sofia*
Andrey GALABINOV	27.11.1988	14	2	2020/2021:	*Spezia Calcio (ITA)*
Atanas ILIEV	09.10.1994	6	1	2021:	*PFC Botev Plovdiv*
Ismail ISA Mustafa	26.06.1989	8	1	2020:	*PFC Cherno More Varna*
Bircent Hamdi KARAGAREN	06.12.1992	12	0	2020/2021:	*PFC Lokomotiv Plovdiv*
Svetoslav KOVACHEV	14.03.1998	4	0	2020:	*FC Arda Kardzhali*
Georgi MINCHEV	20.04.1995	3	0	2021:	*PFC Lokomotiv Plovdiv*
Georgi YOMOV	06.07.1997	6	2	2020/2021:	*PFC CSKA Sofia*

Trainer

Name	Date of Birth	Record
Georgi DERMENDZHIEV [28.10.2019 – 01.01.2021]	04.01.1955	11 M; 2 W; 2 D; 7 L; 7-12
Yasen PETROV [from 14.01.2021]	23.06.1968	6 M; 0 W; 2 D; 4 L; 2-10

CROATIA

The Country:
Republika Hrvatska (Republic of Croatia)
Capital: Zagreb
Surface: 56,594 km²
Inhabitants: 4,076,246 [2019]
Time: UTC+1

The FA:
Hrvatski nogometni savez
Vukovarska 269A, 10000 Zagreb
Tel: +385 1 2361 555
Foundation date: 16.07.1941 (as Independent State of Croatia); 03.07.1992 (as Croatia)
Member of FIFA since: 1992
Member of UEFA since: 1993
Website: www.hns-cff.hr

NATIONAL TEAM RECORDS

RECORDS		
First international match:	02.04.1940, Zagreb:	Croatia – Switzerland 4-0
Most international caps:	Luka Modrić	- 142 caps (2006-2021)
Most international goals:	Davor Šuker	- 45 goals / 69 caps (1990-2002)

UEFA EUROPEAN CHAMPIONSHIP	
1960	-
1964	-
1968	-
1972	-
1976	-
1980	-
1984	-
1988	-
1992	-
1996	Final Tournament (Quarter-Finals)
2000	Qualifiers
2004	Final Tournament (Group Stage)
2008	Final Tournament (Quarter-Finals)
2012	Final Tournament (Group Stage)
2016	Final Tournament (Group Stage)
2020	Final Tournament (2nd Round of 16)

FIFA WORLD CUP	
1930	-
1934	-
1938	-
1950	-
1954	-
1958	-
1962	-
1966	-
1970	-
1974	-
1978	-
1982	-
1986	-
1990	-
1994	Did not enter
1998	Final Tournament (3rd Place)
2002	Final Tournament (Group Stage)
2006	Final Tournament (Group Stage)
2010	Qualifiers
2014	Final Tournament (Group Stage)
2018	Final Tournament (Runners-up)

OLYMPIC TOURNAMENTS	
1908	-
1912	-
1920	-
1924	-
1928	-
1936	-
1948	-
1952	-
1956	-
1960	-
1964	-
1968	-
1972	-
1976	-
1980	-
1984	-
1988	-
1992	-
1996	Qualifiers
2000	Qualifiers
2004	Qualifiers
2008	Qualifiers
2012	Qualifiers
2016	Qualifiers

UEFA NATIONS LEAGUE	
2018/2019	League A
2020/2021	League A

FIFA CONFEDERATIONS CUP 1992-2017
None

CROATIAN CLUB HONOURS IN EUROPEAN CLUB COMPETITIONS:

European Champion Clubs' Cup (1956-1992) / UEFA Champions League (1993-2021)		
None		
Fairs Cup (1858-1971) / UEFA Cup (1972-2009) / UEFA Europa League (2010-2021)		
GNK Dinamo Zagreb*	1	1966/1967
*represented Yugoslavia		
UEFA Super Cup (1972-2020)		
None		
European Cup Winners' Cup 1961-1999*		
None		

*defunct competition

NATIONAL COMPETITIONS
TABLE OF HONOURS

	CHAMPIONS	CUP WINNERS	BEST GOALSCORERS	
1992	HNK Hajduk Split	NK Inter Zaprešić	Ardian Kozniku (HNK Hajduk Split)	12
1992/1993	NK Croatia Zagreb	HNK Hajduk Split	Goran Vlaović (NK Croatia Zagreb)	23
1993/1994	HNK Hajduk Split	NK Croatia Zagreb	Goran Vlaović (NK Croatia Zagreb)	29
1994/1995	HNK Hajduk Split	HNK Hajduk Split	Robert Špehar (NK Osijek)	23
1995/1996	NK Croatia Zagreb	NK Croatia Zagreb	Igor Cvitanović (NK Croatia Zagreb)	19
1996/1997	NK Croatia Zagreb	NK Croatia Zagreb	Igor Cvitanović (NK Croatia Zagreb)	20
1997/1998	NK Croatia Zagreb	NK Croatia Zagreb	Mate Baturina (NK Zagreb)	18
1998/1999	NK Croatia Zagreb	NK Osijek	Joško Popović (HNK Šibenik)	21
1999/2000	GNK Dinamo Zagreb	HNK Hajduk Split	Tomo Šokota (GNK Dinamo Zagreb)	21
2000/2001	HNK Hajduk Split	GNK Dinamo Zagreb	Tomo Šokota (GNK Dinamo Zagreb)	20
2001/2002	NK Zagreb	GNK Dinamo Zagreb	Ivica Olić (NK Zagreb)	21
2002/2003	GNK Dinamo Zagreb	HNK Hajduk Split	Ivica Olić (GNK Dinamo Zagreb)	16
2003/2004	HNK Hajduk Split	GNK Dinamo Zagreb	Robert Špehar (NK Osijek)	18
2004/2005	HNK Hajduk Split	HNK Rijeka	Tomislav Erceg (HNK Rijeka)	17
2005/2006	GNK Dinamo Zagreb	HNK Rijeka	Ivan Bošnjak (GNK Dinamo Zagreb)	22
2006/2007	GNK Dinamo Zagreb	GNK Dinamo Zagreb	Eduardo (GNK Dinamo Zagreb)	34
2007/2008	GNK Dinamo Zagreb	GNK Dinamo Zagreb	Želimir Terkeš (BIH, NK Zadar)	21
2008/2009	GNK Dinamo Zagreb	GNK Dinamo Zagreb	Mario Mandžukić (GNK Dinamo Zagreb)	16
2009/2010	GNK Dinamo Zagreb	HNK Hajduk Split	Davor Vugrinec (NK Zagreb)	18
2010/2011	GNK Dinamo Zagreb	GNK Dinamo Zagreb	Ivan Krstanović (BIH, NK Zagreb)	19
2011/2012	GNK Dinamo Zagreb	GNK Dinamo Zagreb	Fatos Bećiraj (MNE, GNK Dinamo Zagreb)	15
2012/2013	GNK Dinamo Zagreb	HNK Hajduk Split	Leon Benko (HNK Rijeka)	19
2013/2014	GNK Dinamo Zagreb	HNK Rijeka	Duje Čop (GNK Dinamo Zagreb)	22
2014/2015	GNK Dinamo Zagreb	GNK Dinamo Zagreb	Andrej Kramarić (HNK Rijeka)	21
2015/2016	GNK Dinamo Zagreb	GNK Dinamo Zagreb	Ilija Nestorovski (MKD, NK Inter Zaprešić)	25
2016/2017	HNK Rijeka	HNK Rijeka	Márkó Futács (HUN, HNK Hajduk Split)	18
2017/2018	GNK Dinamo Zagreb	GNK Dinamo Zagreb	El Arabi Hillel Soudani (ALG, GNK Dinamo Zagreb)	17
2018/2019	GNK Dinamo Zagreb	HNK Rijeka	Mijo Caktaš (HNK Hajduk Split)	19
2019/2020	GNK Dinamo Zagreb	HNK Rijeka	Antonio Čolak (HNK Rijeka) Mijo Caktaš (HNK Hajduk Split) Mirko Marić (NK Osijek)	20
2020/2021	GNK Dinamo Zagreb	GNK Dinamo Zagreb	Ramón Nazareno Miérez (ARG, NK Osijek)	22

Please note: GNK Dinamo Zagreb were called NK Croatia Zagreb between 1993 and 2000.

NATIONAL CHAMPIONSHIP
Hrvatski Telekom Prva liga 2020/2021
(14.08.2020 – 22.05.2021)

Results

Round 1 [14-16.08.2020]
NK Varaždin - HNK Gorica 1-5(0-1)
HNK Rijeka - HNK Šibenik 2-1(0-1)
NK Osijek - Slaven Belupo 0-0
Hajduk Split - NK Istra 1961 2-0(0-0)
Dinamo Zagreb - Lokomotiva Zagreb 6-0(2-0)

Round 2 [21-23.08.2020]
Lokomotiva Zagreb - HNK Rijeka 1-0(0-0)
NK Istra 1961 - Dinamo Zagreb 0-1(0-0)
Slaven Belupo - HNK Gorica 1-2(1-0)
HNK Šibenik - NK Varaždin 0-1(0-0)
NK Osijek - Hajduk Split 1-2(1-2)

Round 3 [28-30.08.2020]
HNK Gorica - HNK Šibenik 3-2(1-0)
HNK Rijeka - NK Istra 1961 2-1(1-0)
Hajduk Split - Slaven Belupo 2-2(0-1)
NK Varaždin - Lokomotiva Zagreb 1-1(1-0)
Dinamo Zagreb - NK Osijek 4-1(1-0)

Round 4 [11-13.09.2020]
Slaven Belupo - HNK Šibenik 0-0
NK Osijek - HNK Rijeka 3-0(2-0)
Hajduk Split - Dinamo Zagreb 1-2(0-1)
NK Istra 1961 - NK Varaždin 0-1(0-1)
Lokomotiva Zagreb - HNK Gorica 1-2(0-1)

Round 5 [18-20.09.2020]
HNK Šibenik - Lokomotiva Zagreb 3-2(2-1)
HNK Gorica - NK Istra 1961 2-2(1-1)
Dinamo Zagreb - Slaven Belupo 3-3(2-2)
NK Varaždin - NK Osijek 0-1(0-1)
Rijeka - Hajduk Split 0-1(0-0) [10.02.2021]

Round 6 [26-27.09.2020]
NK Istra 1961 - HNK Šibenik 1-0(1-0)
NK Osijek - HNK Gorica 2-1(1-0)
Hajduk Split - NK Varaždin 2-0(1-0)
Slaven Belupo - Lokomotiva 0-0 [28.10.2020]
Dinamo Zagreb - Rijeka 0-2(0-0) [19.01.2021]

Round 7 [02-04.10.2020]
Lokomotiva Zagreb - NK Istra 1961 0-0
HNK Šibenik - NK Osijek 0-2(0-0)
HNK Gorica - Hajduk Split 2-1(0-1)
NK Varaždin - Dinamo Zagreb 1-2(1-1)
HNK Rijeka - Slaven Belupo 2-0(0-0)

Round 8 [16-18.10.2020]
Slaven Belupo - NK Istra 1961 5-1(2-0)
Dinamo Zagreb - HNK Gorica 3-2(2-0)
HNK Rijeka - NK Varaždin 2-1(2-1)
Hajduk Split - HNK Šibenik 0-1(0-1)
Osijek - Lokomotiva Z. 2-1(2-0) [04.11.2020]

Round 9 [23-25.10.2020]
NK Varaždin - Slaven Belupo 1-2(0-1)
HNK Šibenik - Dinamo Zagreb 0-2(0-0)
Lokomotiva - Hajduk Split 1-2(0-1) [24.11.20]
NK Istra 1961 - Osijek 1-4(1-2) [25.11.2020]
HNK Gorica - HNK Rijeka 0-0 [17.02.2021]

Round 10 [31.10.-01.11.2020]
Slaven Belupo - NK Osijek 0-1(0-0)
NK Istra 1961 - Hajduk Split 1-0(0-0)
HNK Šibenik - HNK Rijeka 2-0(1-0)
Lokomotiva Zagreb - Dinamo Zagreb 1-1(1-1)
HNK Gorica - Varaždin 1-0(1-0) [23.11.2020]

Round 11 [07-08.11.2020]
NK Varaždin - HNK Šibenik 1-3(0-2)
Hajduk Split - NK Osijek 1-1(0-1)
Dinamo Zagreb - NK Istra 1961 5-0(2-0)
HNK Rijeka - Lokomotiva Zagreb 1-0(1-0)
Gorica - Slaven Belupo 0-1(0-0) [02.12.2020]

Round 12 [20-21.11.2020]
Lokomotiva Zagreb - NK Varaždin 2-2(1-1)
HNK Šibenik - HNK Gorica 1-3(1-0)
NK Osijek - Dinamo Zagreb 2-0(0-0)
Slaven Belupo - Hajduk Split 0-2(0-1)
NK Istra 1961 - Rijeka 1-2(1-1) [27.01.2021]

Round 13 [27-29.11.2020]	Round 14 [05-06.12.2020]	Round 15 [12-13.12.2020]
HNK Šibenik - Slaven Belupo 0-3(0-2)	NK Osijek - NK Varaždin 1-0(0-0)	HNK Gorica - NK Osijek 4-1(1-0)
NK Varaždin - NK Istra 1961 1-1(0-0)	Slaven Belupo - Dinamo Zagreb 1-5(0-2)	NK Varaždin - Hajduk Split 4-2(2-0)
HNK Gorica - Lokomotiva Zagreb 1-1(1-0)	Hajduk Split - HNK Rijeka 1-2(1-1)	Lokomotiva Zagreb - Slaven Belupo 2-1(0-1)
HNK Rijeka - NK Osijek 1-1(0-0)	Istra 1961 - HNK Gorica 1-1(0-0) [19.01.21]	HNK Rijeka - Dinamo Zagreb 2-2(2-1)
Dinamo Z. - Hajduk Split 3-1(2-1) [27.01.21]	Lokomotiva - Šibenik 0-4(0-2) [26.01.21]	Šibenik - NK Istra 1961 1-0(0-0) [10.02.2021]

Round 16 [19-20.12.2020]	Round 17 [22-24.01.2021]	Round 18 [29-31.01.2021]
NK Osijek - HNK Šibenik 1-0(1-0)	Lokomotiva Zagreb - NK Osijek 0-3(0-2)	Slaven Belupo - NK Varaždin 2-0(2-0)
Dinamo Zagreb - NK Varaždin 4-0(2-0)	HNK Šibenik - Hajduk Split 0-1(0-0)	NK Osijek - NK Istra 1961 1-0(1-0)
Hajduk Split - HNK Gorica 2-4(1-1)	NK Varaždin - HNK Rijeka 2-1(2-0)	Dinamo Zagreb - HNK Šibenik 1-2(1-1)
NK Istra - Lokomotiva 3-1(2-1) [10.03.2021]	HNK Gorica - Dinamo Zagreb 3-4(2-2)	Hajduk Split - Lokomotiva Zagreb 0-1(0-1)
Slaven Belupo - Rijeka 1-3(1-0) [17.03.2021]	NK Istra 1961 - Slaven Belupo 2-1(0-1)	HNK Rijeka - HNK Gorica 0-2(0-2)

Round 19 [02-03.02.2021]	Round 20 [06-08.02.2021]	Round 21 [12-14.02.2021]
NK Osijek - Slaven Belupo 3-0(1-0)	NK Osijek - Hajduk Split 2-0(0-0)	NK Varaždin - Lokomotiva Zagreb 0-1(0-1)
Dinamo Zagreb - Lokomotiva Zagreb 2-0(1-0)	Lokomotiva Zagreb - HNK Rijeka 2-3(1-0)	HNK Gorica - HNK Šibenik 1-0(0-0)
NK Varaždin - HNK Gorica 2-1(0-1)	HNK Šibenik - NK Varaždin 0-0	Dinamo Zagreb - NK Osijek 1-0(1-0)
HNK Rijeka - HNK Šibenik 2-2(1-2)	NK Istra 1961 - Dinamo Zagreb 0-1(0-1)	HNK Rijeka - NK Istra 1961 1-1(1-1)
Hajduk Split - NK Istra 1961 1-0(1-0)	Slaven Belupo - HNK Gorica 0-1(0-0)	Hajduk S. - Slaven Belupo 2-2(1-0) [07.04.21]

Round 22 [19-21.02.2021]	Round 23 [26-28.02.2021]	Round 24 [05-07.03.2021]
Slaven Belupo - HNK Šibenik 2-2(2-2)	NK Varaždin - NK Osijek 2-3(2-0)	NK Istra 1961 - HNK Šibenik 3-2(0-1)
NK Istra 1961 - NK Varaždin 0-1(0-0)	HNK Šibenik - Lokomotiva Zagreb 0-0	Slaven Belupo - Lokomotiva Zagreb 0-0
Lokomotiva Zagreb - HNK Gorica 0-3(0-1)	HNK Rijeka - Hajduk Split 0-1(0-0)	Hajduk Split - NK Varaždin 2-0(2-0)
NK Osijek - HNK Rijeka 2-0(1-0)	HNK Gorica - NK Istra 1961 2-1(0-1)	NK Osijek - HNK Gorica 1-1(0-0)
Hajduk Split - Dinamo Z. 1-1(1-1) [05.05.21]	Dinamo Zagreb - Slaven Belupo 3-0(0-0)	Dinamo Zagreb - HNK Rijeka 2-0(1-0)

Round 25 [12-14.03.2021]	Round 26 [19-21.03.2021]	Round 27 [02-03.04.2021]
HNK Rijeka - Slaven Belupo 1-1(0-0)	NK Osijek - Lokomotiva Zagreb 2-0(1-0)	NK Varaždin - Slaven Belupo 1-1(1-0)
Lokomotiva Zagreb - NK Istra 1961 0-1(0-1)	Slaven Belupo - NK Istra 1961 1-1(1-1)	Lokomotiva Zagreb - Hajduk Split 0-2(0-1)
HNK Gorica - Hajduk Split 1-1(1-1)	Hajduk Split - HNK Šibenik 1-0(0-0)	NK Istra 1961 - NK Osijek 0-2(0-1)
NK Varaždin - Dinamo Zagreb 0-5(0-3)	HNK Rijeka - NK Varaždin 2-0(2-0)	HNK Šibenik - Dinamo Zagreb 1-1(0-0)
HNK Šibenik - NK Osijek 0-4(0-1)	Dinamo Zagreb - HNK Gorica 1-0(0-0)	HNK Gorica - HNK Rijeka 3-4(0-2)

Round 28 [10-11.04.2021]	Round 29 [16-18.04.2021]	Round 30 [20-21.04.2021]
HNK Gorica - NK Varaždin 0-0	NK Varaždin - HNK Šibenik 1-1(1-0)	HNK Šibenik - HNK Gorica 1-1(1-0)
HNK Šibenik - HNK Rijeka 0-1(0-0)	HNK Gorica - Slaven Belupo 0-1(0-1)	Slaven Belupo - Hajduk Split 1-1(0-1)
Slaven Belupo - NK Osijek 2-2(1-1)	Hajduk Split - NK Osijek 0-1(0-0)	Lokomotiva Zagreb - NK Varaždin 4-0(2-0)
NK Istra 1961 - Hajduk Split 0-1(0-0)	HNK Rijeka - Lokomotiva Zagreb 3-0(3-0)	NK Istra 1961 - HNK Rijeka 1-2(1-2)
Lokomotiva Zagreb - Dinamo Zagreb 0-2(0-1)	Dinamo Zagreb - NK Istra 1961 1-0(1-0)	NK Osijek - Dinamo Zagreb 1-1(0-1)

Round 31 [24-26.04.2021]	Round 32 [30.04.-02.05.2021]	Round 33 [07-09.05.2021]
HNK Šibenik - Slaven Belupo 2-0(2-0)	Lokomotiva Zagreb - HNK Šibenik 1-0(0-0)	Lokomotiva Zagreb - Slaven Belupo 3-1(1-1)
HNK Gorica - Lokomotiva Zagreb 4-2(2-1)	Slaven Belupo - Dinamo Zagreb 0-2(0-0)	HNK Šibenik - NK Istra 1961 1-0(0-0)
HNK Rijeka - NK Osijek 0-0	Hajduk Split - HNK Rijeka 3-2(2-1)	HNK Gorica - NK Osijek 1-0(0-0)
Dinamo Zagreb - Hajduk Split 2-0(2-0)	NK Istra 1961 - HNK Gorica 0-2(0-1)	NK Varaždin - Hajduk Split 0-1(0-0)
NK Varaždin - NK Istra 1961 1-1(1-1)	NK Osijek - NK Varaždin 1-1(0-0)	HNK Rijeka - Dinamo Zagreb 1-5(1-1)

Round 34 [11-12.05.2021]	Round 35 [15-16.05.2021]	Round 36 [22.05.2021]
NK Istra 1961 - Lokomotiva Zagreb 1-1(1-1)	NK Istra 1961 - Slaven Belupo 1-0(0-0)	Hajduk Split - Lokomotiva Zagreb 2-0(1-0)
NK Osijek - HNK Šibenik 3-0(0-0)	Lokomotiva Zagreb - NK Osijek 0-2(0-0)	HNK Rijeka - HNK Gorica 2-1(1-1)
Slaven Belupo - HNK Rijeka 0-2(0-1)	NK Varaždin - HNK Rijeka 2-3(1-0)	NK Osijek - NK Istra 1961 2-1(1-1)
Dinamo Zagreb - NK Varaždin 2-2(2-1)	HNK Šibenik - Hajduk Split 0-2(0-0)	Slaven Belupo - NK Varaždin 1-0(0-0)
Hajduk Split - HNK Gorica 4-0(4-0)	HNK Gorica - Dinamo Zagreb 0-3(0-2)	Dinamo Zagreb - HNK Šibenik 1-0(0-0)

Final Standings

					Total			Home					Away			
1. **GNK Dinamo Zagreb**	36	26	7	3	84 - 28	85	14	2	2	44 - 13	12	5	1	40 - 15
2. NK Osijek	36	23	8	5	59 - 25	77	13	4	1	30 - 8	10	4	4	29 - 17
3. HNK Rijeka	36	18	7	11	51 - 46	61	8	6	4	24 - 20	10	1	7	27 - 26
4. HNK Hajduk Split	36	18	6	12	48 - 37	60	8	4	6	27 - 19	10	2	6	21 - 18
5. HNK Gorica	36	17	8	11	60 - 47	59	8	5	5	28 - 24	9	3	6	32 - 23
6. HNK Šibenik	36	9	8	19	32 - 47	35	5	4	9	12 - 23	4	4	10	20 - 24
7. NK Slaven Belupo Koprivnica	36	7	13	16	36 - 53	34	3	7	8	17 - 25	4	6	8	19 - 28
8. NK Lokomotiva Zagreb	36	7	9	20	29 - 60	30	5	3	10	18 - 29	2	6	10	11 - 31
9. NK Istra 1961 Pula	36	7	8	21	27 - 52	29	6	2	10	16 - 23	1	6	11	11 - 29
10. NK Varaždin (*Relegated*)	36	6	10	20	30 - 61	28	3	5	10	21 - 35	3	5	10	9 - 26

Top goalscorers:		
22 **Ramón Nazareno Miérez (ARG)**		*NK Osijek*
17 Mario Gavranović (SUI)		*GNK Dinamo Zagreb*
16 Mislav Oršić		*GNK Dinamo Zagreb*
15 Kristijan Lovrić		*HNK Gorica*
13 Franko Andrijašević		*HNK Rijeka*

NATIONAL CUP
Hrvatski nogometni kup 2020/2021

First Round [26-29-30.09./06-07-10-20.10.2020]

NK Ferdinandovac - GNK Dinamo Zagreb	1-7(1-2)		NK Polet Sveti Martin na Muri - NK Istra 1961 Pula	0-2(0-0)
NK Rudar M. Središće - NK Slaven Belupo	0-9(0-2)		NK Croatia Zmijavci - HNK Šibenik	0-2(0-0,0-0)
NK Kurilovec - NK Vinogradar Lokošin Dol	6-0(5-0)		NK Oriolik - Radnicki NK Split	1-0(1-0)
NK Graničar Županja - HNK Hajduk Split	1-2(1-1)		NK Mladost Ždralovi - NK Zagreb	0-1(0-0,0-0)
NK Crikvenica - NK Osijek	1-5(0-4)		NK Sesvete Zagreb - HNK Gorica	3-4(2-4)
NK GOŠK Dubrovnik 1919 - NK Zadar	3-0 *awarded*		NK Novigrad - NK Rudeš	1-3(1-2)
NK Dilj Vinkovci - HNK Rijeka	0-6(0-3)		NK Varaždin - HNK Cibalia Vinkovci	2-0(0-0)
NK Gaj Mace - NK Lokomotiva Zagreb	2-3(0-0,2-2)		NK Rudar Labin - NK Inter Zaprešić	2-0(0-0)

1/8-Finals [14.11./07.12./16.12.2020/23-24.02./28.02./02.03.2021]

NK Kurilovec Velika Gorica - NK Osijek	0-4(0-1)		NK GOŠK Dubrovnik 1919 - NK Slaven Belupo	1-4(1-1)
HNK Gorica - NK Lokomotiva Zagreb	3-1(1-0)		HNK Šibenik - NK Istra 1961 Pula	0-2(0-0)
NK Rudeš - GNK Dinamo Zagreb	0-2(0-0)		NK Oriolik - NK Rudar Labin	1-0(0-0,0-0)
NK Varaždin - HNK Rijeka	1-2(1-0)		NK Zagreb - HNK Hajduk Split	0-3(0-0)

Quarter-Finals [03.03./16.03.2021]

NK Osijek - HNK Rijeka	1-2(1-1)		NK Oriolik - NK Istra 1961 Pula	0-3(0-0)
GNK Dinamo Zagreb - NK Slaven Belupo	2-0(0-0)		HNK Gorica - HNK Hajduk Split	3-0(1-0)

Semi-Finals [14.04./28.04.2021]

NK Istra 1961 Pula - HNK Rijeka	3-2(3-0)		GNK Dinamo Zagreb - HNK Gorica	4-1(0-1,1-1)

Final

19.05.2021; Stadion Gradski, Velika Gorica; Referee: Duje Strukan; Attendance: 0

GNK Dinamo Zagreb - NK Istra 1961 Pula   **6-3(3-0)**

Dinamo Zagreb: Danijel Zagorac, Stefan Ristovski, Rasmus Lauritsen, Kévin Théophile-Catherine, Joško Gvardiol, Arijan Ademi (Cap), Kristijan Jakić (62.Josip Mišić), Luka Ivanušec (73.Marko Tolić), Lovro Majer (85.Bartol Franjić), Mislav Oršić (85.Lirim Kastrati), Bruno Petković (62.Mario Gavranović). Trainer: Damir Krznar.

Istra Pula: Ivan Lučić, Luka Hujber, Josip Šutalo, Josip Tomašević, Sergio González Testón „Sergi", Einar Galilea Azaceta (64.Antonio Perera Calderón), Dino Halilović (Cap) (64.Slavko Blagojević), Šime Gržan (85.Josip Špoljarić), Antonio Ivančić (70.Hassane Bandé), Matej Vuk (85.Mateo Lisica), Taichi Hara. Trainer: Danijel Jumić.

Goals: 1-0 Mislav Oršić (5), 2-0 Arijan Ademi (9), 3-0 Lovro Majer (33), 3-1 Taichi Hara (52), 3-2 Taichi Hara (53), 4-2 Josip Šutalo (59 own goal), 4-3 Šime Gržan (64 penalty), 5-3 Mislav Oršić (74), 6-3 Mario Gavranović (84).

THE CLUBS 2020/2021

Građanski nogometni klub Dinamo Zagreb

Founded:	09.06.1945
Stadium:	Stadion Maksimir, Zagreb (35,123)
Trainer:	Zoran Mamić	30.09.1971
[18.03.2021]	Damir Krznar	10.07.1972

Goalkeepers:	DOB	M	(s)	G
Renato Josipović	12.06.2001		(1)	
Dominik Livaković	09.01.1995	33		
Danijel Zagorac	07.02.1987	3		
Defenders:	**DOB**	**M**	**(s)**	**G**
Marijan Čabraja	25.02.1997	3	(5)	
Damjan Daničić	24.01.2000	3		
Emir Dilaver (AUT)	07.05.1991	3		
Joško Gvardiol	23.01.2002	21	(4)	2
Rasmus Lauritsen (DEN)	27.02.1996	24		1
Marin Leovac	07.08.1988	11	(1)	
Stefan Milić (MNE)	06.07.2000	2	(1)	1
Sadegh Moharrami (IRN)	01.03.1996	12		
Dino Perić	12.07.1994	13	(4)	1
Stefan Ristovski (MKD)	12.02.1992	6	(2)	
Petar Stojanović (SVN)	07.10.1995	18	(5)	
Josip Šutalo	28.02.2000	1	(2)	
Kévin Théophile-Catherine (FRA)	28.10.1989	24	(3)	1
Midfielders:	**DOB**	**M**	**(s)**	**G**
Arijan Ademi (MKD)	29.05.1991	19	(8)	1
Martin Baturina	16.02.2003	1	(1)	

	DOB	M	(s)	G
Robbie Burton (WAL)	26.12.1999	7	(6)	
Bartol Franjić	14.01.2000	11	(11)	
Amer Gojak (BIH)	13.02.1997	2	(3)	
Niko Janković	25.08.2001		(1)	
Kristijan Jakić	14.05.1997	22	(7)	1
Lovro Majer	17.01.1998	27	(4)	7
Josip Mišić	28.06.1994	10	(6)	2
Ivan Šaranić	12.05.2003		(3)	
Marko Tolić	05.07.1996	5	(16)	4
Forwards:	**DOB**	**M**	**(s)**	**G**
Komnen Andrić (SRB)	01.07.1995		(3)	2
Iyayi Believe Atiemwen (NGA)	24.01.1996	7	(11)	5
Mario Gavranović (SUI)	24.11.1989	21	(6)	17
Izet Hajrović (BIH)	04.08.1991	3	(10)	2
Luka Ivanušec	26.11.1998	23	(7)	7
Lirim Kastrati (KVX)	16.01.1999	13	(14)	2
Sandro Kulenović	04.12.1999	1	(1)	
Luka Menalo (BIH)	22.07.1996		(1)	
Mislav Oršić	29.12.1992	29	(3)	16
Bruno Petković	16.09.1994	18	(7)	9
Jakov-Anton Vasilj	02.06.2002		(1)	

Hrvatski Nogometni Klub Gorica

Founded:	16.07.2009 (*as merger of NK Radnik Velika Gorica and NK Polet Buševec*)			
Stadium:	Stadion Gradski, Velika Gorica (5,000)			
Trainer:	Valdas Dambrauskas (LTU)			07.01.1977
[03.01.2021]	Siniša Oreščanin			30.07.1972

Goalkeepers:	DOB	M	(s)	G
Ivan Banić	18.07.1994	22		
Kristijan Kahlina (SVN)	24.07.1992	14		
Defenders:	**DOB**	**M**	**(s)**	**G**
Marijan Čabraja	25.02.1997	17		1
Albi Doka (ALB)	26.06.1997	19	(4)	1
Aleksandar Jovičić (BIH)	18.07.1995	28		2
Cheick Keita (MLI)	16.04.1996	5	(4)	
Krešimir Krizmanić	03.07.2000	24	(4)	
Nasiru Moro (GHA)	24.09.1996	8	(5)	1
Musa Muhammed Shehu (NGA)	31.10.1996	18	(5)	
Matthew Steenvoorden (NED)	09.01.1993	27		1
Midfielders:	**DOB**	**M**	**(s)**	**G**
Hrvoje Babec	28.07.1999	32	(1)	3
Dario Čanađija	17.04.1994	5	(2)	1
Paulius Golubickas (LTU)	19.08.1999	2	(10)	

	DOB	M	(s)	G
Jiloan Hamad (SWE)	06.11.1990	16	(11)	3
Anthony Kalik (AUS)	05.11.1997	18	(3)	2
Serge-Junior Martinsson Ngouali (GAB)	23.01.1992	6	(5)	
Jurica Pršir	29.05.2000	3	(10)	
Joey Suk (NED)	08.07.1989	19	(2)	1
Forwards:	**DOB**	**M**	**(s)**	**G**
Younes Delfi (IRN)	02.10.2000	1	(4)	2
Matar Dièye (SEN)	10.01.1998	22	(8)	5
Matija Dvorneković	01.01.1989	9	(24)	
Kristijan Lovrić	01.12.1995	24	(5)	15
Josip Mitrović	11.06.2000	9	(17)	4
Ognjen Mudrinski (SRB)	15.11.1991	11	(16)	9
Cherif Ndiaye (SEN)	23.01.1996	2		
Sylvanus Nimely (LBR)	04.09.1998	5	(4)	
Dario Špikić	22.03.1999	30	(4)	6

Hrvatski nogometni klub Hajduk Split

Founded:	13.02.1911		
Stadium:	Stadion Poljud, Split (34,198)		
Trainer:	Igor Tudor	16.04.1978	
[08.09.2020]	Hari Vukas	06.10.1972	
[04.11.2020]	Boro Primorac	05.12.1954	
[27.11.2020]	Toni Golem	14.01.1982	
[18.01.2021]	Paolo Tramezzani (ITA)	30.07.1970	

Goalkeepers:	DOB	M	(s)	G
Lovre Kalinić	03.04.1990	21		
Marin Ljubić	18.10.1997	1		
Josip Posavec	10.03.1996	14		
Defenders:	**DOB**	**M**	**(s)**	**G**
Branimir Barišić	31.05.1998		(1)	
David Čolina	19.07.2000	29		2
Kristian Dimitrov (BUL)	27.02.1997	16	(4)	2
Ardian Ismajli (ALB)	30.09.1996	2	(1)	
Nihad Mujakić (BIH)	15.04.1998	13	(4)	
Vicko Ševelj	19.09.2000	1	(2)	
Stefan Simič (CZE)	20.01.1995	24		1
Darko Todorović (BIH)	05.05.1997	23	(3)	
Mario Vušković	16.11.2001	28	(1)	2
Midfielders:	**DOB**	**M**	**(s)**	**G**
Jani Atanasov (MKD)	31.10.1999	11	(12)	2
Mijo Caktaš	08.05.1992	16	(1)	9
Mario Čuić	22.04.2001	4	(3)	
Marco Fossati (ITA)	05.10.1992	13		

	DOB	M	(s)	G
Bassel Jradi (LIB)	06.07.1993	14	(1)	
Stanko Jurić	16.08.1996	32	(1)	1
Alexander Kačaniklić (SWE)	13.08.1991	12	(2)	2
Darko Nejašmić	25.01.1999	8	(9)	
Dino Skorup	04.10.1999	1		
Tonio Teklić	09.09.1999	5	(8)	1
Forwards:	**DOB**	**M**	**(s)**	**G**
Stipe Biuk	26.12.2002	8	(1)	3
Ivan Brnić	23.08.2001	2	(3)	
Dimitrios Diamantakos (GRE)	05.03.1993	9	(10)	2
Ivan Dolček	24.04.2000	6	(10)	
Ádám Gyurcsó (HUN)	06.03.1991	14	(2)	3
Jairo De Macedo Da Silva (BRA)	06.05.1992	17	(7)	1
Marin Jakoliš	26.12.1996	15	(13)	1
Leon Kreković	07.05.2000		(3)	
Marko Livaja	26.08.1993	15		6
Marin Ljubičić	28.02.2002	2	(5)	1
Umut Nayir (TUR)	28.06.1993	20	(5)	6
Francesco Tahiraj (ALB)	21.09.1996		(1)	

Nogometni Klub Istra 1961 Pula

Founded:	1948		
Stadium:	Stadion "Aldo Drosina", Pula (9,800)		
Trainer:	Danijel Jumić	27.06.1986	
[26.08.2020]	Fausto Budicin	01.05.1981	
[11.02.2021]	Danijel Jumić	27.06.1986	

Goalkeepers:	DOB	M	(s)	G
Lovro Jurić	01.09.1996	5		
Ivan Lučić (AUT)	23.03.1995	23		
Lovro Majkić	08.10.1999	8		
Defenders:	**DOB**	**M**	**(s)**	**G**
Petar Bosančić	19.04.1996	19	(1)	
Einar Galilea Azaceta (ESP)	22.05.1994	25		1
Luka Hujber	16.06.1999	17	(5)	
João Pedro Eira Antunes Silva (POR)	14.01.1999	6	(4)	
Kim Hyun-woo (KOR)	07.03.1999	1	(4)	
Mauro Perković	22.03.2003	4	(2)	
Rafael „Rafa" Jesús Navarro Mazuelos (ESP)	24.02.1994	15	(2)	1
Rafa Páez Cardona (ESP)	10.08.1994	7	(2)	
Agron Rufati (MKD)	06.04.1999		(1)	
Sergio González Testón „Sergi" (ESP)	26.05.1995	22	(2)	1
Josip Šutalo	28.02.2000	22		
Josip Tomašević	26.09.1993	19	(1)	
Mario Vojković (AUT)	11.01.1995	2	(1)	
Midfielders:	**DOB**	**M**	**(s)**	**G**
Antonio Perera Calderón (ESP)	08.06.1997	8	(6)	
Slavko Blagojević	21.03.1987	28	(1)	

	DOB	M	(s)	G
Dino Halilović	08.02.1998	6	(11)	
Antonio Ivančić	25.05.1995	20	(7)	5
Kim Kyu-hyeong (KOR)	29.03.1999	1	(3)	
Dylan Levitt (WAL)	17.11.2000	2	(5)	
Stefan Lončar (MNE)	19.02.1996	12	(13)	
Regan Obeng (GHA)	15.08.1994	2		
Octavio Andrés Páez Gil (VEN)	28.02.2000		(2)	
Forwards:	**DOB**	**M**	**(s)**	**G**
Adrián Fuentes González (ESP)	17.07.1996	4	(7)	
Hassane Bandé (BFA)	30.10.1998	10	(6)	1
Marko Bibić	12.01.2001		(1)	
Šime Gržan	06.04.1994	32	(1)	5
Gedeon Guzina (BIH)	26.12.1993	12	(14)	1
Taichi Hara (JPN)	05.05.1999	14		2
Mateo Lisica	09.07.2003	7	(10)	
Robert Perić-Komšić	30.03.1999		(1)	
Drilon Sadiku (BEL)	27.05.2000		(2)	
Arona Sané (SEN)	21.06.1995	5	(9)	
Leon Šipoš	28.02.2000	2	(7)	
Josip Špoljarić	05.01.1997	15	(10)	4
Matej Vuk	10.06.2000	21	(5)	6

Nogometni klub Lokomotiva Zagreb

Founded: 01.05.1914 (*as ŽSK Victoria Zagreb*)
Stadium: Stadion u Kranjčevićevoj ulici, Zagreb (5,350)
Trainer: Goran Tomić — 18.03.1977
[09.01.2021] Jerko Leko — 09.04.1980
[14.03.2021] Samir Toplak — 23.04.1970

Goalkeepers:	DOB	M	(s)	G
Alexandre Dos Santos Ferreira (BRA)	15.01.1999	2		
Krunoslav Hendija	19.03.1989	17		
Krševan Santini	11.04.1987	17		
Defenders:	**DOB**	**M**	**(s)**	**G**
Ivan Čeliković	10.04.1989	13	(10)	
Branimir Cipetić (BIH)	24.05.1995	14	(6)	
Petar Gluhaković (AUT)	25.03.1996	4	(1)	
Luka Hujber	16.06.1999		(1)	
Fran Karačić (AUS)	12.05.1996	12		1
Denis Kolinger	14.01.1994	12		
Dominik Kovačić	05.01.1994	9	(2)	
Marko Lešković	27.04.1991	17		1
Edis Malikji (MKD)	04.05.1995	4		
Stipo Marković (BIH)	03.12.1993	14	(5)	
Jon Mersinaj (ALB)	08.02.1999	3		
Mario Musa	06.07.1990	2	(2)	
Kemal Osmanković (BIH)	04.03.1997	7	(8)	
Kyriakos Papadopoulos (GRE)	23.02.1992	24		2
Josip Pivarić	30.01.1989	20	(3)	6
Hajdin Salihu (KVX)	18.01.2002	3		
Midfielders:	**DOB**	**M**	**(s)**	**G**
Reuben Acquah (GHA)	03.11.1996	2	(1)	
Enis Çokaj (ALB)	23.02.1999	19	(9)	
Marko Dira	05.05.1999	17	(5)	
Dino Halilović	08.02.1998	1	(1)	1
Lukas Kačavenda	02.03.2003	8	(2)	1
Sherif Kallaku (ALB)	01.03.1998	17	(9)	2
Kim Jeong-hyun (KOR)	09.06.2000	1		
Mate Maleš	11.03.1989	9	(1)	1
Mateo Marić (BIH)	18.03.1998	17	(2)	
Oliver Petrak	06.02.1991	20	(6)	1
Jorge Sammir Cruz Campos	23.04.1987	5	(4)	1
Luka Stojković	28.10.2003	1	(4)	
Frane Vojković	20.12.1996	1	(2)	
Forwards:	**DOB**	**M**	**(s)**	**G**
Ibrahim Aliyu (NGA)	16.01.2002	14	(5)	2
Alan Leonel Bonansea (ARG)	06.05.1996		(4)	
Mario Budimir	12.02.1986	1	(3)	
Moutir Chajia (BEL)	04.06.1998	15	(12)	2
Mario Čuže	24.04.1999	4	(2)	
Emerson Santana Deocleciano (BRA)	27.07.1999	2	(1)	
Irfan Hadžić (BIH)	15.06.1993	9	(2)	1
Nikica Jelavić		1	(3)	
Krešimir Kovačević	07.08.1994		(2)	
Josip Majić	05.07.1994	1	(1)	
Antonio Marin	09.01.2001	6	(9)	
Roko Šimić	10.09.2003	15	(10)	3
Francesco Tahiraj (ALB)	21.09.1996	4	(6)	
Indrit Tuci (ALB)	14.09.2000	12	(2)	3
Bruno Zdunić	06.02.2001		(1)	

Nogometni klub Osijek

Founded: 27.02.1947
Stadium: Stadion Gradski vrt, Osijek (18,856)
Trainer: Ivica Kulešević — 31.10.1969
[05.09.2020] Nenad Bjelica — 20.08.1971

Goalkeepers:	DOB	M	(s)	G
Ivica Ivušić	01.02.1995	36		
Defenders:	**DOB**	**M**	**(s)**	**G**
Adrian Barišić (BIH)	19.07.2001	2	(1)	
José Antonio Caro Martínez (ESP)	08.03.1993	3	(2)	
Yevgen Cheberko (UKR)	23.01.1998	12	(1)	
Alen Grgić	10.08.1994		(4)	1
Gutieri Tomelin „Guti" (BRA)	29.06.1991	7	(8)	
Igor Silva de Almeida „Igor Carioca" (BRA)	21.08.1996	29	(2)	
Mario Jurčević (SVN)	01.06.1995	18	(5)	
Danijel Lončar	26.06.1997	15	(5)	
Ante Majstorović	06.11.1993	14		
Filip Mekić	13.09.2002		(3)	
Mato Miloš	30.06.1993	10	(3)	
Mile Škorić	19.06.1991	30		1
Talys Alves Pereira Oliveira (BRA)	10.02.1999	5	(3)	
Todor Todoroski (MKD)	26.02.1999		(2)	
Midfielders:	**DOB**	**M**	**(s)**	**G**
Domagoj Babin	03.06.2000		(1)	
Petar Brlek	29.01.1994	4	(2)	1
Vedran Jugović	31.07.1989	16	(7)	2
László Kleinheisler (HUN)	08.04.1994	22	(9)	6
Juraj Ljubić	26.05.2000	1	(1)	
Dmytro Lyopa (UKR)	23.11.1988	5	(10)	
Šimun Mikolčić	21.01.2004		(1)	
Robert Mišković	20.10.1999		(3)	
Marin Pilj	03.12.1996	21	(9)	2
Dario Pudić	27.01.2001		(1)	
Josip Vuković	02.05.1992	10	(10)	
Mihael Žaper	11.08.1998	30		5
Forwards:	**DOB**	**M**	**(s)**	**G**
Dion Drena Beljo	01.03.2002	1	(8)	1
Petar Bočkaj	23.07.1996	22	(7)	2
Damjan Bohar (SVN)	18.10.1991	25	(6)	7
Luka Branšteter	19.06.2002		(1)	
Ante Erceg	12.12.1989	9	(18)	4
Eros Grezda (ALB)	15.04.1995	3	(1)	1
Ádám Gyurcsó (HUN)	06.03.1991	2	(2)	1
Ramón Nazareno Miérez (ARG)	13.05.1997	30	(1)	22
Merveil Valthy Streeker Ndockyt (CGO)	20.07.1998	7	(5)	
Josip Špoljarić	05.01.1997	1	(2)	
Ivan Santini	21.05.1989	6	(6)	3
Martin Sekulić	04.01.1999		(1)	

Hrvatski Nogometni Klub Rijeka

Founded: 29.07.1946 (*as Sportsko Društvo Kvarner*)
Stadium: Stadion Rujevica, Rijeka (8,279)
Trainer: Simon Rožman (SVN) — 06.04.1983
[01.03.2021] Goran Tomić — 18.03.1977

Goalkeepers:	DOB	M	(s)	G
Ivan Nevistić	31.07.1998	33		
Ivor Pandur	25.03.2000	2		
Andrej Prskalo	01.05.1987	1		
Defenders:	**DOB**	**M**	**(s)**	**G**
Armando Anastasio (ITA)	24.07.1996	1		
Zoran Arsenić	02.06.1994	7	(2)	
Filip Braut	05.06.2002	4	(3)	
Luka Capan	06.04.1995	23		1
Niko Galešić	26.03.2001	6	(2)	
Nino Galović	06.07.1992	31		4
João Rodrigo Pereira Escoval (POR)	08.05.1997	14	(5)	
Roko Jurišić	28.09.2001	1	(1)	
Momcilo Raspopović (MNE)	18.03.1994	1	(4)	
Hrvoje Smolčić	17.08.2000	15	(1)	
Daniel Štefulj	08.11.1999	23	(9)	
Ivan Tomečak	07.12.1989	30	(2)	
Darko Velkovski (MKD)	21.06.1995	7	(1)	
Andrija Vukčević (MNE)	11.10.1996	9	(4)	
Midfielders:	**DOB**	**M**	**(s)**	**G**
Franko Andrijašević	22.06.1991	30		13
Adam Gnezda Čerin (SVN)	16.07.1999	26	(2)	1
Daniel „Dani" Iglesias Gago (ESP)	18.08.1995		(2)	
Tibor Halilović	18.03.1995	5		
Ivan Lepinjica	09.07.1999	4	(11)	
Adrian Liber	09.01.2001		(6)	
Stjepan Lončar (BIH)	10.11.1996	29	(2)	2
Robert Mudražija	05.05.1997	8	(9)	
Domagoj Pavičić	09.03.1994	14	(15)	1
Forwards:	**DOB**	**M**	**(s)**	**G**
Antonio Čolak	17.09.1993	4		
Josip Drmić (SUI)	08.08.1992	11	(5)	6
Sandro Kulenović	04.12.1999	16	(13)	7
Luka Menalo (BIH)	22.07.1996	20	(8)	6
Robert Murić	12.03.1996	18	(12)	8
Milan Ristovski (MKD)	08.04.1998		(3)	
Tomislav Turčin	31.05.1997		(1)	
Sterling Yatéké (CTA)	15.09.1999	3	(15)	1

Nogometni klub Slaven Belupo Koprivnica

Founded:	1907		
Stadium:	Gradski Stadion "Ivan Kušek Apaš", Koprivnica (3,205)		
Trainer:	Tomislav Stipić		01.08.1979

Goalkeepers:	DOB	M	(s)	G
Ivan Čović	17.09.1990	1		
Ivan Filipović	13.11.1994	35		
Defenders:	**DOB**	**M**	**(s)**	**G**
Mitch Apau (NED)	27.04.1990	4	(1)	
Antonio Bosec	28.08.1997	9	(4)	
Tomislav Božić	01.11.1987	31	(1)	2
Gonzalo Julian Gamarra Leyton (ARG)	02.07.1999	7	(4)	
Bruno Goda	17.04.1998	28	(1)	
Kim Hyun-woo (KOR)	07.03.1999	6	(3)	
Frane Maglica	02.07.1997		(2)	
Tin Petričič	18.03.2004		(1)	
Franjo Prce	07.01.1996	16	(4)	1
Vinko Soldo	15.02.1998	14		1
Damian van Bruggen (NED)	18.03.1996	15	(13)	1
Matko Zirdum	21.07.1998		(4)	
Midfielders:	**DOB**	**M**	**(s)**	**G**
Stipe Bačelić-Grgić	16.02.1988	17	(4)	2
Arijan Brković	03.02.2001	1	(3)	
Nemanja Glavčić (SRB)	19.02.1997	33	(2)	5
Niko Janković	25.08.2001		(2)	
Matej Jukić	07.04.1997		(1)	
Edin Julardžija	21.01.2001	1	(7)	
Kim Kyu-hyeong (KOR)	29.03.1999		(1)	
Luka Liklin	21.02.2001	1	(3)	
Karlo Lulić	10.05.1996	34		1
Frano Mlinar	30.03.1992	17	(8)	
Allen Njie (LBR)	26.07.1999	1		
Goran Paracki	21.01.1987	31		
Nikola Turanjanin (BIH)	12.04.2001		(2)	
Matija Vuić	11.03.2001		(1)	
Lovro Zvonarek	08.05.2005		(2)	1
Forwards:	**DOB**	**M**	**(s)**	**G**
Martin Boakye (ITA)	10.02.1995	4	(6)	1
Bruno Bogojević	29.06.1998	23	(5)	1
Ivan Delić	29.09.1998		(13)	1
Franck M'bia Etoundi (CMR)	30.08.1990	10	(10)	2
Miroslav Iličić	17.04.1998	9	(10)	2
Törles Knöll (GER)	13.09.1997	25	(10)	7
Ivan Krstanović (BIH)	05.01.1983	21	(8)	8
Jeffrén Isaac Suárez Bermúdez (VEN)	20.01.1988	2	(6)	

Hrvatski nogometni klub Šibenik

Founded:	01.12.1932		
Stadium:	Stadion Šubićevac, Šibenik (3,412)		
Trainer:	Krunoslav Rendulić		26.09.1973
[31.03.2021]	Sergio Escobar Cabus (ESP)		13.04.1975

Goalkeepers:	DOB	M	(s)	G
Nediljko Labrović	10.10.1999	26		
Lovre Rogić (GER)	27.08.1995	10		
Defenders:	**DOB**	**M**	**(s)**	**G**
Silvio Anočić	10.09.1997	4		1
Ivica Batarelo	12.05.1998	15	(3)	
Karlo Bilić	06.09.1993	29	(2)	1
Doni Grdić (AUS)	22.01.2002		(2)	
Josip Kvesić (BIH)	21.09.1990	29	(4)	
Juan Camilo Mesa Antúnez (COL)	23.02.1998	21	(1)	1
Marcos David Mina Lucumí (COL)	12.04.1999	3	(7)	
Arian Mršulja	11.02.1998		(2)	
Martin Pajić	11.11.1999	30	(3)	
Boris Pandža (BIH)	15.12.1986	10	(1)	
Gordon Schildenfeld	18.03.1985	21		
Todor Todoroski (MKD)	26.02.1999	5	(13)	
Midfielders:	**DOB**	**M**	**(s)**	**G**
Isnik Alimi (ALB)	02.02.1994	10	(14)	
Marko Bulat	26.09.2001	31		3
Luka Čelić	13.10.1997	1	(5)	
Mario Ćurić	28.09.1998	33	(2)	1
Keres Masangu (BEL)	07.03.2000		(1)	
Ivan Močinić	30.04.1993		(1)	
Niko Rak	26.07.2003		(4)	
Toni Španja	21.08.1992	1	(6)	
Forwards:	**DOB**	**M**	**(s)**	**G**
Álvaro Martín De Frías (ESP)	15.01.2001	9	(14)	
Prince Ampem (GHA)	13.04.1998	24	(6)	4
Ignacio Daniel Bailone (ARG)	20.01.1994	2	(8)	
Yeferson Andrés Contreras Villamizar (COL)	10.08.1999	2	(4)	
Deni Jurić (AUS)	03.09.1997	29	(3)	11
Ivan Laća	15.02.2003	1	(16)	
Nikola Rak	29.08.1987	13	(12)	1
Emir Sahiti (ALB)	29.11.1998	29	(4)	7
Suad Sahiti (KVX)	06.02.1995	7	(6)	2
Carlos Eduardo Torres Góngora (COL)	20.10.2002	1	(2)	

Nogometni klub Varaždin

Founded:	01.07.2012		
Stadium:	Stadion „Anđelko Herjavec", Varaždin (8,850)		
Trainer:	Samir Toplak		23.04.1970
[08.12.2020]	Zoran Kastel		22.10.1972

Goalkeepers:	DOB	M	(s)	G
Dinko Horkaš	10.03.1999	22		
Oliver Zelenika	14.05.1993	14	(2)	
Defenders:	**DOB**	**M**	**(s)**	**G**
Maks Juraj Čelić	08.03.1996	11	(3)	
Fran Cerovčec	06.02.2001		(1)	
Damjan Daničić	24.01.2000	3	(2)	
Kerim Memija (BIH)	06.01.1996	20	(4)	
Stefan Milić	06.07.2000	5	(1)	
Ivan Novoselec	19.06.1995	7	(3)	1
Jorgo Pëllumbi (ALB)	15.07.2000	24		
Matej Rodin	13.02.1996	2		
Marko Stolnik	08.07.1996	22	(3)	
Nikola Tkalčić	03.12.1989	18	(3)	
Itsuki Urata (JPN)	29.01.1997	20	(3)	1
Midfielders:	**DOB**	**M**	**(s)**	**G**
Neven Đurasek	15.08.1998	32		3
Agon Elezi (MKD)	01.03.2001	10	(6)	1
Jurica Grgec	01.09.1992	9	(11)	1
Jessie Jensen Guera Djou (CMR)	03.05.1997	5	(3)	
Matija Kolarić	14.04.1996	6	(12)	
Karlo Lusavec	30.10.2003		(2)	
Luka Mezga	29.01.2001		(1)	
Igor Postonjski	04.02.1995	18	(2)	
Matej Senić	21.02.1995	26	(4)	3
Dino Skorup	04.10.1994	2	(6)	
Mijo Šabić	08.10.1994	1	(1)	
Forwards:	**DOB**	**M**	**(s)**	**G**
Leon Benko	11.11.1983	6	(23)	2
Gabrijel Boban	23.07.1989	6	(5)	1
Ivan Delić	29.09.1998	6	(7)	1
Domagoj Drožđek	20.03.1996	12	(1)	1
Dominik Glavina	06.12.1992	1	(3)	
Andris Jesús Herrera Palomino (VEN)	20.10.1996	9	(6)	2
Mehdi Mehdikhani	28.07.1997	5	(1)	1
Jorge Leonardo Obregón Rojas (COL)	29.03.1997	32	(2)	7
Demir Peco (BIH)	31.07.1996	13	(5)	1
Vinko Petković	01.10.1995	8	(12)	1
Borna Petrović	16.10.1997		(5)	
Ivan Posavec	05.07.1998	16	(10)	2
Leonard Vuk	23.05.1995	5	(5)	

1. NK Hrvatski Dragovoljac Zagreb (*Promoted*)	34	16	11	7	49	-	39	59
2. NK Rudeš	34	15	12	7	52	-	41	57
3. NK BSK Bijelo Brdo	34	14	13	7	52	-	40	55
4. HNK Cibalia Vinkovci	34	15	6	13	50	-	43	51
5. NK Kustošija	34	12	15	7	43	-	38	51
6. NK Sesvete	34	15	6	13	62	-	59	51
7. NK Opatija	34	12	14	8	42	-	41	50
8. NK Dugopolje	34	13	9	12	49	-	45	48
9. NK Dubrava Zagreb	34	13	7	14	45	-	46	46
10. NK Inker Zaprešić	34	12	9	13	49	-	41	45
11. HNK Orijent 1919 Sušak	34	12	9	13	52	-	49	45
12. NK Croatia Zmijavci	34	13	5	16	52	-	53	44
13. GNK Dinamo Zagreb II*	34	12	7	15	45	-	41	43
14. NK Osijek II*	34	11	9	14	42	-	42	42
15. HNK Hajduk Split II* (*Dissolved at end of the season*)	34	11	8	15	58	-	60	41
16. NK Solin	34	10	8	16	45	-	56	38
17. NK Junak Sinj (*Relegated*)	34	7	13	14	46	-	58	34
18. NK Međimurje Čakovec (*Relegated*)	34	9	7	18	44	-	85	34

*Please note: reserve teams are ineligible for promotion to the Croatian First Football League!

NATIONAL TEAM

INTERNATIONAL MATCHES
(16.07.2020 – 15.07.2021)

05.09.2020	Porto	Portugal - Croatia	4-1(1-0)		(UNL)
08.09.2020	Paris	France - Croatia	4-2(2-1)		(UNL)
07.10.2020	St. Gallen	Switzerland - Croatia	1-2(1-1)		(F)
11.10.2020	Zagreb	Croatia - Sweden	2-1(1-0)		(UNL)
14.10.2020	Zagreb	Croatia - France	1-2(0-1)		(UNL)
11.11.2020	İstanbul	Turkey - Croatia	3-3(2-1)		(F)
14.11.2020	Stockholm	Sweden - Croatia	2-1(2-0)		(UNL)
17.11.2020	Split	Croatia - Portugal	2-3(1-0)		(UNL)
24.03.2021	Ljubljana	Slovenia - Croatia	1-0(1-0)		(WCQ)
27.03.2021	Rijeka	Croatia - Cyprus	1-0(1-0)		(WCQ)
30.03.2021	Rijeka	Croatia - Malta	3-0(0-0)		(WCQ)
01.06.2021	Velika Gorica	Croatia - Armenia	1-1(1-0)		(F)
06.06.2021	Bruxelles	Belgium - Croatia	1-0(1-0)		(F)
13.06.2021	London	England - Croatia	1-0(0-0)		(EC)
18.06.2021	Glasgow	Croatia - Czech Republic	1-1(0-1)		(EC)
22.06.2021	Glasgow	Croatia - Scotland	3-1(1-1)		(EC)
28.06.2021	København	Croatia - Spain	3-5(1-1,3-3)		(EC)

05.09.2020   PORTUGAL - CROATIA   **4-1(1-0)**   2nd UEFA Nations League A, Group 3
Estádio do Dragão, Porto; Referee: Davide Massa (Italy); Attendance: 0
CRO: Dominik Livaković, Dejan Lovren, Tin Jedvaj, Domagoj Vida (Cap), Borna Barišić, Mateo Kovačić, Mario Pašalić (61.Marcelo Brozović), Nikola Vlašić, Josip Brekalo (61.Ivan Perišić), Andrej Kramarić (74.Bruno Petković), Ante Rebić. Trainer: Zlatko Dalić.
Goal: Bruno Petković (90+1).

08.09.2020   FRANCE - CROATIA   **4-2(2-1)**   2nd UEFA Nations League A, Group 3
Stade de France, Saint-Denis, Paris; Referee: Ovidiu Alin Haţegan (Romania); Attendance: 0
CRO: Dominik Livaković, Duje Ćaleta-Car, Dejan Lovren, Dario Melnjak, Filip Uremović (57.Domagoj Vida), Marcelo Brozović, Mateo Kovačić, Nikola Vlašić, Ivan Perišić (Cap) (66.Mario Pašalić), Andrej Kramarić, Ante Rebić (46.Josip Brekalo). Trainer: Zlatko Dalić.
Goals: Dejan Lovren (17), Josip Brekalo (55).

07.10.2020   SWITZERLAND - CROATIA   **1-2(1-1)**   Friendly International
Kybunpark, St. Gallen; Referee: Tiago Bruno Lopes Martins (Portugal); Attendance: 4,500
CRO: Dominik Livaković, Duje Ćaleta-Car, Dario Melnjak, Domagoj Vida (Cap), Filip Uremović (62.Tin Jedvaj), Domagoj Bradarić, Milan Badelj (46.Marcelo Brozović), Mateo Kovačić (57.Marko Rog), Mario Pašalić (75.Luka Modrić), Bruno Petković (57.Ante Budimir), Josip Brekalo (75.Ivan Perišić). Trainer: Zlatko Dalić.
Goals: Josip Brekalo (42), Mario Pašalić (67).

11.10.2020   CROATIA - SWEDEN   **2-1(1-0)**   2nd UEFA Nations League A, Group 3
Stadion Maksimir, Zagreb; Referee: John William Beaton (Scotland); Attendance: 2,020
CRO: Dominik Livaković, Duje Ćaleta-Car, Dejan Lovren, Dario Melnjak (75.Andrej Kramarić), Filip Uremović, Marcelo Brozović, Luka Modrić (Cap), Mateo Kovačić (61.Mario Pašalić), Nikola Vlašić, Ivan Perišić (85.Bruno Petković), Josip Brekalo (74.Domagoj Bradarić). Trainer: Zlatko Dalić.
Goals: Nikola Vlašić (32), Andrej Kramarić (84).

14.10.2020   CROATIA - FRANCE   **1-2(0-1)**   2nd UEFA Nations League A, Group 3
Stadion Maksimir, Zagreb; Referee: Björn Kuipers (Netherlands); Attendance: 6,266
CRO: Dominik Livaković, Dejan Lovren, Domagoj Vida, Borna Barišić, Filip Uremović, Milan Badelj (46.Mateo Kovačić), Luka Modrić (Cap), Mario Pašalić (46.Josip Brekalo), Nikola Vlašić (80.Andrej Kramarić), Ivan Perišić (78.Domagoj Bradarić), Bruno Petković (61.Ante Budimir). Trainer: Zlatko Dalić.
Goal: Nikola Vlašić (65).

11.11.2020   TURKEY - CROATIA   **3-3(2-1)**   Friendly International
Vodafone Park, İstanbul; Referee: Slavko Vinčić (Slovenia); Attendance: 0
CRO: Simon Sluga, Domagoj Vida (Cap) (46.Filip Uremović), Dario Melnjak, Josip Juranović, Marin Pongračić (61.Duje Ćaleta-Car), Milan Badelj (60.Toma Bašić), Mario Pašalić (77.Luka Modrić), Marko Rog, Ante Budimir (66.Antonio-Mirko Čolak), Josip Brekalo (60.Ivan Perišić), Mislav Oršić. Trainer: Zlatko Dalić.
Goals: Ante Budimir (32), Mario Pašalić (53), Josip Brekalo (56).

14.11.2020   SWEDEN - CROATIA   **2-1(2-0)**   2nd UEFA Nations League A, Group 3
Friends Arena, Stockholm; Referee: Daniel Siebert (Germany); Attendance: 0
CRO: Dominik Livaković, Duje Ćaleta-Car, Borna Barišić, Filip Uremović (41.Josip Juranović), Marin Pongračić (77.Dario Melnjak), Mateo Kovačić (77.Marko Rog), Luka Modrić (Cap), Nikola Vlašić, Ivan Perišić, Ante Budimir (63.Mario Pašalić), Josip Brekalo (77.Bruno Petković). Trainer: Zlatko Dalić.
Goals: Marcus Andreas Danielson (82 own goal).

17.11.2020   CROATIA - PORTUGAL   **2-3(1-0)**   2nd UEFA Nations League A, Group 3
Stadion Poljud, Split; Referee: Michael Oliver (England); Attendance: 0
CRO: Dominik Livaković, Dejan Lovren, Mile Škorić, Josip Juranović, Domagoj Bradarić, Mateo Kovačić (90+1.Toma Bašić), Luka Modrić (Cap), Mario Pašalić (64.Josip Brekalo), Marko Rog[*sent off 51*], Nikola Vlašić (83.Mislav Oršić), Ivan Perišić. Trainer: Zlatko Dalić.
Goals: Mateo Kovačić (29, 65).

24.03.2021   SLOVENIA - CROATIA   **1-0(1-0)**   22nd FIFA WC. Qualifiers
Stadion Stožice, Ljubljana; Referee: Antonio Miguel Mateu Lahoz (Spain); Attendance: 0
CRO: Dominik Livaković, Šime Vrsaljko, Dejan Lovren, Domagoj Vida, Borna Barišić (46.Mislav Oršić), Marcelo Brozović, Mateo Kovačić (83.Mario Pašalić), Luka Modrić (Cap), Nikola Vlašić (69.Ante Budimir), Ivan Perišić, Andrej Kramarić (64.Josip Brekalo). Trainer: Zlatko Dalić.

27.03.2021   CROATIA - CYPRUS   **1-0(1-0)**   22nd FIFA WC. Qualifiers
Stadion Rujevica, Rijeka; Referee: Kristo Tohver (Estonia); Attendance: 0
CRO: Dominik Livaković, Šime Vrsaljko (46.Josip Juranović), Duje Ćaleta-Car, Dejan Lovren, Borna Barišić, Marcelo Brozović, Luka Modrić (Cap), Mario Pašalić (66.Mislav Oršić), Ivan Perišić (76.Mateo Kovačić), Josip Brekalo (66.Nikola Vlašić), Ante Budimir (57.Andrej Kramarić). Trainer: Zlatko Dalić.
Goal: Mario Pašalić (40).

30.03.2021   CROATIA - MALTA   **3-0(0-0)**   22nd FIFA WC. Qualifiers
Stadion Rujevica, Rijeka; Referee: Lionel Tschudi (Switzerland); Attendance: 0
CRO: Dominik Livaković, Duje Ćaleta-Car, Dario Melnjak (57.Borna Barišić), Domagoj Vida (Cap), Josip Juranović, Milan Badelj (54.Luka Modrić), Mateo Kovačić, Mario Pašalić (54.Josip Brekalo), Nikola Vlašić, Ante Budimir (54.Ivan Perišić), Mislav Oršić (78.Kristijan Lovrić). Trainer: Zlatko Dalić.
Goals: Ivan Perišić (62), Luka Modrić (76 penalty), Josip Brekalo (90).

01.06.2021   CROATIA - ARMENIA   **1-1(1-0)**   Friendly International
Stadion Radnik, Velika Gorica; Referee: Luka Bilbija (Bosnia and Herzegovina); Attendance: 0
CRO: Dominik Livaković, Šime Vrsaljko (46.Josip Juranović), Duje Ćaleta-Car, Domagoj Vida (46.Mile Škorić), Borna Barišić, Marcelo Brozović, Luka Modrić (Cap) (46.Ante Rebić), Nikola Vlašić (46.Bruno Petković), Ivan Perišić (61.Milan Badelj), Josip Brekalo (26.Mario Pašalić), Andrej Kramarić. Trainer: Zlatko Dalić.
Goal: Ivan Perišić (24).

06.06.2021   BELGIUM - CROATIA   **1-0(1-0)**   Friendly International
Stade "Roi Baudouin", Bruxelles; Referee: Deniz Aytekin (Germany); Attendance: 50
CRO: Dominik Livaković, Šime Vrsaljko, Duje Ćaleta-Car, Domagoj Vida, Borna Barišić (46.Joško Gvardiol), Marcelo Brozović, Luka Modrić (Cap) (61.Mario Pašalić), Mateo Kovačić (62.Nikola Vlašić), Ivan Perišić (80.Mislav Oršić), Bruno Petković (70.Josip Brekalo), Ante Rebić (62.Andrej Kramarić). Trainer: Zlatko Dalić.

13.06.2021   ENGLAND - CROATIA   **1-0(0-0)**   16th EC. Group Stage.
Wembley Stadium, London; Referee: Daniele Orsato (Italy); Attendance: 18,497
CRO: Dominik Livaković, Šime Vrsaljko, Duje Ćaleta-Car, Domagoj Vida, Joško Gvardiol, Luka Modrić (Cap), Ivan Perišić, Marcelo Brozović (70.Nikola Vlašić), Mateo Kovačić (85.85.Mario Pašalić), Andrej Kramarić (70.Josip Brekalo), Ante Rebić (78.Bruno Petković). Trainer: Zlatko Dalić.

18.06.2021   CROATIA - CZECH REPUBLIC   **1-1(0-1)**   16th EC. Group Stage.
Hampden Park, Glasgow (Scotland); Referee: Carlos del Cerro Grande (Spain); Attendance: 5,607
CRO: Dominik Livaković, Šime Vrsaljko, Dejan Lovren, Domagoj Vida, Joško Gvardiol, Mateo Kovačić (87.Marcelo Brozović), Luka Modrić (Cap), Ivan Perišić, Josip Brekalo (46.Luka Ivanušec), Andrej Kramarić (62.Nikola Vlašić), Ante Rebić (46.Bruno Petković). Trainer: Zlatko Dalić.
Goal: Ivan Perišić (47).

22.06.2021   CROATIA - SCOTLAND   **3-1(1-1)**   16th EC. Group Stage.
Hampden Park, Glasgow; Referee: Fernando Andrés Rapallini (Argentina); Attendance: 9,896
CRO: Dominik Livaković, Josip Juranović, Dejan Lovren, Domagoj Vida, Joško Gvardiol (71.Borna Barišić), Marcelo Brozović, Luka Modrić (Cap), Mateo Kovačić, Ivan Perišić (81.Ante Rebić), Nikola Vlašić (76.Luka Ivanušec), Bruno Petković (71.Andrej Kramarić). Trainer: Zlatko Dalić.
Goals: Nikola Vlašić (17), Luka Modrić (62), Ivan Perišić (77).

28.06.2021   **CROATIA - SPAIN**   **3-5(1-1,3-3)**   16th EC. 2nd Round of 16.

Parken Stadium, København (Denmark); Referee: Cüneyt Çakır (Turkey); Attendance: 22,771

CRO: Dominik Livaković, Duje Ćaleta-Car, Josip Juranović (74.Josip Brekalo), Domagoj Vida, Joško Gvardiol, Luka Modrić (Cap) (114.Luka Ivanušec), Marcelo Brozović, Mateo Kovačić (79.Ante Budimir), Bruno Petković (46.Andrej Kramarić), Nikola Vlašić (79.Mario Pašalić), Ante Rebić (67.Mislav Oršić). Trainer: Zlatko Dalić.

Goals: Pedro González López "Pedri" (20 own goal), Mislav Oršić (85), Mario Pašalić (90+2).

NATIONAL TEAM PLAYERS
(16.07.2020 – 15.07.2021)

Name	DOB	Caps	Goals	2020/2021:	Club
Goalkeepers					
Dominik LIVAKOVIĆ	09.01.1995	25	0	2020/2021:	GNK Dinamo Zagreb
Simon SLUGA	17.03.1993	3	0	2020:	Luton Town FC (ENG)
Defenders					
Borna BARIŠIĆ	10.11.1992	21	1	2020/2021:	Rangers FC Glasgow (SCO)
Domagoj BRADARIĆ	10.12.1999	4	0	2020:	Lille OSC (FRA)
Duje ĆALETA-CAR	17.09.1996	16	0	2020/2021:	Olympique de Marseille (FRA)
Joško GVARDIOL	23.01.2002	5	0	2021:	GNK Dinamo Zagreb
Tin JEDVAJ	28.11.1995	26	2	2020:	TSV Bayer 04 Leverkusen (GER)
Josip JURANOVIĆ	16.08.1995	10	0	2020/2021:	Legia Warszawa (POL)
Dejan LOVREN	05.07.1989	66	4	2020/2021:	FK Zenit Saint Petersburg (RUS)
Marin PONGRAČIĆ	11.09.1997	2	0	2020:	VfL Wolfsburg (GER)
Mile ŠKORIĆ	19.06.1991	5	0	2020/2021:	NK Osijek
Filip UREMOVIĆ	11.02.1997	6	0	2020:	FK Rubin Kazan (RUS)
Domagoj VIDA	29.04.1989	92	4	2020/2021:	Beşiktaş JK Istanbul (TUR)
Šime VRSALJKO	10.01.1992	51	0	2021:	Club Atlético de Madrid (ESP)
Midfielders					
Milan BADELJ	25.02.1989	55	2	2020/2021:	Genoa C&FC (ITA)
Toma BAŠIĆ	25.11.1996	2	0	2020:	FC Girondins de Bordeaux (FRA)
Marcelo BROZOVIĆ	16.11.1992	63	6	2020/2021:	FC Internazionale Milano (ITA)
Luka IVANUŠEC	26.11.1998	5	1	2021:	GNK Dinamo Zagreb
Mateo KOVAČIĆ	06.05.1994	71	3	2020/2021:	Chelsea FC London (ENG)
Luka MODRIĆ	09.09.1985	142	18	2020/2021:	Real Madrid CF (ESP)
Mario PAŠALIĆ	09.02.1995	27	4	2020/2021:	Atalanta Bergamasca Calcio (ITA)
Ivan PERIŠIĆ	02.02.1989	104	30	2020/2021:	FC Internazionale Milano (ITA)
Marko ROG	19.07.1995	21	0	2020:	Cagliari Calcio (ITA)
Nikola VLAŠIĆ	04.10.1997	26	6	2020/2021:	FK CSKA Moskva (RUS)
Forwards					
Josip BREKALO	23.06.1998	27	4	2020/2021:	VfL Wolfsburg (GER)
Ante BUDIMIR	22.07.1991	8	1	2020/2021:	CA Osasuna Pamplona (ESP)
Antonio-Mirko ČOLAK	11.11.2020	1	0	2020:	PAOK Thessaloníki (GRE)
Andrej KRAMARIĆ	19.06.1991	58	14	2020/2021:	TSG 1899 Hoffenheim (GER)
Kristijan LOVRIĆ	01.12.1995	1	0	2021:	HNK Gorica
Dario MELNJAK	31.10.1992	8	0	2020/2021:	Çaykur Rizespor Kulübü (TUR)
Mislav ORŠIĆ	29.12.1992	10	1	2020/2021:	GNK Dinamo Zagreb
Bruno PETKOVIĆ	16.09.1994	19	6	2020/2021:	GNK Dinamo Zagreb
Ante REBIĆ	21.09.1993	42	3	2020/2021:	AC Milan (ITA)
Trainer					
Zlatko DALIĆ [from 07.10.2017]	26.10.1966	47 M; 21 W; 10 D; 16 L; 76-68			

CYPRUS

The Country:
Κυπριακή Δημοκρατία (Republic of Cyprus)
Capital: Nicosia
Surface: 9,251 km²
Inhabitants: 1,189,265 [2019]
Time: UTC+2

The FA:
Cyprus Football Association
10 Achaion Street 2413 Engomi, PO Box 25071, 1306 Nicosia
Tel: +357 22 352 341
Foundation date: 23.09.1934
Member of FIFA since: 1948
Member of UEFA since: 1962
Website: www.cfa.com.cy

NATIONAL TEAM RECORDS

RECORDS

First international match:	13.11.1960, Nicosia: Cyprus – Israel 1-1
Most international caps:	Yiannakis Okkas - 103 caps (1997-2011)
Most international goals:	Michalis Konstantinou - 32 goals / 84 caps (1997-2012)

UEFA EUROPEAN CHAMPIONSHIP

1960	Did not enter
1964	Did not enter
1968	Qualifiers
1972	Qualifiers
1976	Qualifiers
1980	Qualifiers
1984	Qualifiers
1988	Qualifiers
1992	Qualifiers
1996	Qualifiers
2000	Qualifiers
2004	Qualifiers
2008	Qualifiers
2012	Qualifiers
2016	Qualifiers
2020	Qualifiers

FIFA WORLD CUP

1930	Did not enter
1934	Did not enter
1938	Did not enter
1950	Did not enter
1954	Did not enter
1958	Did not enter
1962	Qualifiers
1966	Qualifiers
1970	Qualifiers
1974	Qualifiers
1978	Qualifiers
1982	Qualifiers
1986	Qualifiers
1990	Qualifiers
1994	Qualifiers
1998	Qualifiers
2002	Qualifiers
2006	Qualifiers
2010	Qualifiers
2014	Qualifiers
2018	Qualifiers

OLYMPIC TOURNAMENTS

1908	-
1912	-
1920	-
1924	-
1928	-
1936	-
1948	-
1952	-
1956	-
1960	-
1964	-
1968	-
1972	-
1976	-
1980	-
1984	-
1988	-
1992	Qualifiers
1996	Qualifiers
2000	Qualifiers
2004	Qualifiers
2008	Qualifiers
2012	Qualifiers
2016	Qualifiers

UEFA NATIONS LEAGUE

2018/2019	League C
2020/2021	League C (qualified for the Relegation Play-outs)

FIFA CONFEDERATIONS CUP 1992-2017

None

CYPRIOT CLUB HONOURS IN EUROPEAN CLUB COMPETITIONS:

European Champion Clubs' Cup (1956-1992) / UEFA Champions League (1993-2021)
None

Fairs Cup (1858-1971) / UEFA Cup (1972-2009) / UEFA Europa League (2010-2021)
None

UEFA Super Cup (1972-2020)
None

*European Cup Winners' Cup 1961-1999**
None

defunct competition

NATIONAL COMPETITIONS
TABLE OF HONOURS

	CHAMPIONS	CUP WINNERS	BEST GOALSCORERS	
1934/1935	Enosis Neon Trust Nicosia	Enosis Neon Trust Nicosia	-	
1935/1936	APOEL FC Nicosia	Enosis Neon Trust Nicosia	-	
1936/1937	APOEL FC Nicosia	APOEL FC Nicosia	-	
1937/1938	APOEL FC Nicosia	Enosis Neon Trust Nicosia	-	
1938/1939	APOEL FC Nicosia	AEL Limassol	-	
1939/1940	APOEL FC Nicosia	AEL Limassol	-	
1940/1941	AEL Limassol	APOEL FC Nicosia	-	
1941-1944	*No competition*	*No competition*	-	
1944/1945	EPA Larnaca FC	EPA Larnaca FC	-	
1945/1946	EPA Larnaca FC	EPA Larnaca FC	-	
1946/1947	APOEL FC Nicosia	APOEL FC Nicosia	-	
1947/1948	APOEL FC Nicosia	AEL Limassol	-	
1948/1949	APOEL FC Nicosia	Anorthosis Famagusta FC	-	
1949/1950	Anorthosis Famagusta FC	EPA Larnaca FC	-	
1950/1951	Çetinkaya Türk Spor Kulübü	APOEL FC Nicosia	-	
1951/1952	APOEL FC Nicosia	Çetinkaya Türk Spor Kulübü	-	
1952/1953	AEL Limassol	EPA Larnaca FC	-	
1953/1954	Pezoporikos Larnaca FC	Çetinkaya Türk Spor Kulübü	-	
1954/1955	AEL Limassol	EPA Larnaca FC	-	
1955/1956	AEL Limassol	*No competition*	-	
1956/1957	Anorthosis Famagusta FC	*No competition*	-	
1957/1958	Anorthosis Famagusta FC	*No competition*	-	
1958/1959	*No competition*	Anorthosis Famagusta FC	-	
1959/1960	Anorthosis Famagusta FC	*No competition*	-	
1960/1961	AC Omonia Nicosia	*No competition*	Panikos Krystallis (Apollon Limassol FC)	26
1961/1962	Anorthosis Famagusta FC	Anorthosis Famagusta FC	Michalis Shialis (Anorthosis Famagusta FC)	22
1962/1963	Anorthosis Famagusta FC	APOEL FC Nicosia	Panikos Papadopoulos (AEL Limassol)	24
1963/1964	*Championship Abandoned*	Anorthosis Famagusta FC	*Championship abandoned*	
1964/1965	APOEL FC Nicosia	AC Omonia Nicosia	Kostakis Pieridis (Olympiakos Nicosia FC)	21
1965/1966	AC Omonia Nicosia	Apollon Limassol FC	Panikos Efthymiades (Olympiakos Nicosia FC)	20
1966/1967	Olympiakos Nicosia FC	Apollon Limassol FC	Andreas Stylianou (APOEL FC Nicosia)	29
1967/1968	AEL Limassol	APOEL FC Nicosia	Charalambos Papadopoulos (AEL Limassol)	31
1968/1969	Olympiakos Nicosia FC	APOEL FC Nicosia	Panikos Efthymiades (Olympiakos Nicosia FC)	17
1969/1970	EPA Larnaca FC	Pezoporikos Larnaca FC	Tasos Constantinou (EPA Larnaca FC)	24
1970/1971	Olympiakos Nicosia FC	Anorthosis Famagusta FC	Andreas Stylianou (APOEL FC Nicosia) Kostas Vasiliades (Apollon Limassol FC) Panikos Efthymiades (Olympiakos Nicosia FC)	11
1971/1972	AC Omonia Nicosia	AC Omonia Nicosia	Sotiris Kaiafas (AC Omonia Nicosia)	24
1972/1973	APOEL FC Nicosia	APOEL FC Nicosia	Lakis Theodorou (EPA Larnaca FC)	17
1973/1974	AC Omonia Nicosia	AC Omonia Nicosia	Sotiris Kaiafas (AC Omonia Nicosia)	20
1974/1975	AC Omonia Nicosia	Anorthosis Famagusta FC	Andros Savva (AC Omonia Nicosia)	21
1975/1976	AC Omonia Nicosia	APOEL FC Nicosia	Sotiris Kaiafas (AC Omonia Nicosia)	39
1976/1977	AC Omonia Nicosia	Olympiakos Nicosia FC	Sotiris Kaiafas (AC Omonia Nicosia)	44
1977/1978	AC Omonia Nicosia	APOEL FC Nicosia	Andreas Kanaris (AC Omonia Nicosia)	20
1978/1979	AC Omonia Nicosia	APOEL FC Nicosia	Sotiris Kaiafas (AC Omonia Nicosia)	28
1979/1980	APOEL FC Nicosia	AC Omonia Nicosia	Sotiris Kaiafas (AC Omonia Nicosia)	23
1980/1981	AC Omonia Nicosia	AC Omonia Nicosia	Sotiris Kaiafas (AC Omonia Nicosia)	14
1981/1982	AC Omonia Nicosia	AC Omonia Nicosia	Sotiris Kaiafas (AC Omonia Nicosia)	19
1982/1983	AC Omonia Nicosia	AC Omonia Nicosia	Panikos Hatziloizou (Aris Limassol FC)	17
1983/1984	AC Omonia Nicosia	APOEL FC Nicosia	Sylvester Vernon (Pezoporikos Larnaca FC) Lenos Kittos (Ermis Aradippou FC)	14
1984/1985	AC Omonia Nicosia	AEL Limassol	Giorgos Savvidis (AC Omonia Nicosia)	24
1985/1986	APOEL FC Nicosia	Apollon Limassol FC	Yiannos Ioannou (APOEL FC Nicosia)	22
1986/1987	AC Omonia Nicosia	AEL Limassol	Spas Dzhevizov (BUL, AC Omonia Nicosia)	32
1987/1988	Pezoporikos Larnaca FC	AC Omonia Nicosia	Tasos Zouvanis (Enosis Neon Paralimni FC)	23
1988/1989	AC Omonia Nicosia	AEL Limassol	Nigel McNeal (ENG, Nea Salamis Famagusta FC)	19
1989/1990	APOEL FC Nicosia	Nea Salamis Famagusta FC	Siniša Gogić (YUG, APOEL FC Nicosia)	19
1990/1991	Apollon Limassol FC	AC Omonia Nicosia	Suad Beširević (YUG, Apollon Limassol FC) Panikos Xiourouppas (AC Omonia Nicosia)	19
1991/1992	APOEL FC Nicosia	Apollon Limassol FC	József Dzurják (HUN, AC Omonia Nicosia)	21
1992/1993	AC Omonia Nicosia	APOEL FC Nicosia	Slađan Šćepović (YUG, Apollon Limassol FC)	25
1993/1994	Apollon Limassol FC	AC Omonia Nicosia	Siniša Gogić (YUG, Anorthosis Famagusta FC)	26
1994/1995	Anorthosis Famagusta FC	APOEL FC Nicosia	Pambis Andreou (Nea Salamis Famagusta FC)	25
1995/1996	APOEL FC Nicosia	APOEL FC Nicosia	József Kiprich (HUN, APOEL FC Nicosia)	25
1996/1997	Anorthosis Famagusta FC	APOEL FC Nicosia	Michalis Konstantinou (Enosis Neon Paralimni FC)	17
1997/1998	Anorthosis Famagusta FC	Anorthosis Famagusta FC	Rainer Rauffmann (GER, AC Omonia Nicosia)	42
1998/1999	Anorthosis Famagusta FC	APOEL FC Nicosia	Rainer Rauffmann (GER, AC Omonia Nicosia)	35
1999/2000	Anorthosis Famagusta FC	AC Omonia Nicosia	Rainer Rauffmann (GER, AC Omonia Nicosia)	34
2000/2001	AC Omonia Nicosia	Apollon Limassol FC	Rainer Rauffmann (GER, AC Omonia Nicosia)	30
2001/2002	APOEL FC Nicosia	Anorthosis Famagusta FC	Wojciech Kowalczyk (POL, Anorthosis Famagusta FC)	22
2002/2003	AC Omonia Nicosia	Anorthosis Famagusta FC	Marios Neophytou (Anorthosis Famagusta FC)	33
2003/2004	APOEL FC Nicosia	AEK Larnaca FC	Łukasz Sosin (POL, Apollon Limassol FC)	

			Jozef Kožlej (SVK, AC Omonia Nicosia)	21
2004/2005	Anorthosis Famagusta FC	AC Omonia Nicosia	Łukasz Sosin (POL, Apollon Limassol FC)	21
2005/2006	Apollon Limassol FC	APOEL FC Nicosia	Łukasz Sosin (POL, Apollon Limassol FC)	28
2006/2007	APOEL FC Nicosia	Anorthosis Famagusta FC	Esteban Andrés Solari Poggio (ARG, APOEL FC Nicosia)	20
2007/2008	Anorthosis Famagusta FC	APOEL FC Nicosia	David Pereira da Costa (BRA, Doxa Katokopias FC) Łukasz Sosin (POL, Anorthosis Famagusta FC)	16
2008/2009	APOEL FC Nicosia	APOP Kinyras Peyias FC	Sérgio Luis Gardino da Silva "Serjão" (BRA, Doxa Katokopias FC)	24
2009/2010	AC Omonia Nicosia	Apollon Limassol FC	Joeano Pinto Chaves (BRA, Ermis Aradippou FC) José Filipe CorreiaSemedo (CPV, APOP Kinyras)	22
2010/2011	APOEL FC Nicosia	AC Omonia Nicosia	Miljan Mrdaković (SRB, Apollon Limassol FC)	21
2011/2012	AEL Limassol	AC Omonia Nicosia	Frederico Castro Roque dos Santos "Freddy" (ANG, AC Omonia Nicosia)	17
2012/2013	APOEL FC Nicosia	Apollon Limassol FC	Bernardo Lino Castro Paes Vasconcelos (POR, Alki Larnaca FC)	18
2013/2014	APOEL FC Nicosia	APOEL FC Nicosia	Gastón Maximiliano Sangoy (ARG, Apollon Limassol FC) Marco Tagbajumi (NGA, Ermis Aradippou FC) Jorge Filipe Monteiro dos Santos Lourenço (POR, AEL Limassol)	18
2014/2015	APOEL FC Nicosia	APOEL FC Nicosia	Mickaël Poté (BEN, AC Omonia Nicosia)	17
2015/2016	APOEL FC Nicosia	Apollon Limassol FC	Fernando Ezequiel Cavenaghi (ARG, APOEL FC Nicosia) André Alves dos Santos (BRA, AEK Larnaca FC) Dimitar Makriev (BUL, Nea Salamis Famagusta FC)	19
2016/2017	APOEL FC Nicosia	Apollon Limassol FC	Matthew Anthony Derbyshire (ENG, AC Omonia Nicosia)	24
2017/2018	APOEL FC Nicosia	AEK Larnaca FC	Matthew Anthony Derbyshire (ENG, AC Omonia Nicosia)	23
2018/2019	APOEL FC Nicosia	AEL Limassol	Adam Nemec (SVK, Pafos FC Paphos)	16
2019/2020	*Championship abandoned*	*Competition abandoned*	-	
2020/2021	AC Omonia Nicosia	Anorthosis Famagusta FC	Berat Sadik (FIN, Doxa Katokopias FC)	18

NATIONAL CHAMPIONSHIP
Cypriot First Division 2020/2021
(21.08.2020 – 29.05.2021)

Regular Season - Results

Round 1 [21-26.08.2020]
APOEL Nicosia - Karmiotissa 2-2(1-1)
Pafos FC - AC Omonia 2-2(1-0)
Apollon Limassol - Doxa Katokopias 1-1(0-1)
Olympiakos - AEL Limassol 1-2(0-1)
Anorthosis - Ermis Aradippou 3-1(1-1)
Nea Salamina - AEK Larnaca 1-2(0-1)
Ethnikos Achna - Neon Paralimni 2-0(1-0)

Round 2 [28-30.08.2020]
Pafos FC - Anorthosis 0-1(0-0)
AEL Limassol - Nea Salamina 2-1(1-1)
Doxa Katokopias - Ethnikos Achna 2-1(1-1)
Neon Paralimni - Olympiakos 1-2(0-1)
AC Omonia - Karmiotissa 1-0(0-0)
Ermis Aradippou - Apollon Limassol 0-6(0-3)
AEK Larnaca - APOEL Nicosia 3-0(1-0)

Round 3 [12-14.09.2020]
APOEL Nicosia - AEL Limassol 1-0(0-0)
Apollon Limassol - Pafos FC 1-0(0-0)
Anorthosis - AC Omonia 1-1(1-1)
Nea Salamina - Neon Paralimni 2-0(0-0)
Karmiotissa - AEK Larnaca 0-0
Olympiakos - Doxa Katokopias 1-2(1-1)
Ethnikos Achna - Ermis Aradippou 0-2(0-0)

Round 4 [18-20.09.2020]
Ermis Aradippou - Olympiakos 0-1(0-0)
Pafos FC - Ethnikos Achna 2-2(1-1)
AEL Limassol - Karmiotissa 3-1(1-1)
AC Omonia - AEK Larnaca 2-1(1-0)
Neon Paralimni - APOEL Nicosia 0-2(0-1)
Anorthosis - Apollon Limassol 1-3(1-2)
Doxa Katok. - Nea Salamina 2-0(0-0) [21.10.]

Round 5 [25-28.09.2020]
Karmiotissa - Neon Paralimni 2-1(0-1)
AEK Larnaca - AEL Limassol 2-1(1-1)
Olympiakos - Pafos FC 2-1(0-0)
Nea Salamina - Ermis Ar. 0-1(0-0) [28.10.20]
Ethnikos A. - Anorthosis 0-1(0-0) [28.10.20]
APOEL - Doxa Katokop. 2-0(0-0) [25.11.20]
Apollon Lim. - AC Omonia 0-0 [13.01.21]

Round 6 [02-04.10.2020]
Neon Paralimni - AEK Larnaca 2-1(0-1)
Doxa Katokopias - Karmiotissa 3-3(0-1)
Anorthosis - Olympiakos 2-0(1-0)
Apollon Limassol - Ethnikos Achna 2-1(2-1)
Pafos FC - Nea Salamina 1-0(0-0)
AC Omonia - AEL Limassol 3-0(0-0)
Ermis Aradippou - APOEL Nicosia 0-0

Round 7 [17-19.10.2020]
AEK Larnaca - Doxa Katokopias 2-0(1-0)
Nea Salamina - Anorthosis 1-4(1-2)
Karmiotissa - Ermis Aradippou 0-1(0-0)
Ethnikos Achna - AC Omonia 1-2(0-2)
APOEL Nicosia - Pafos FC 0-1(0-0)
Olympiakos - Apollon Limassol 0-1(0-0)
AEL Limassol - Neon Paralimni 4-1(3-1)

Round 8 [23-26.10.2020]
Pafos FC - Karmiotissa 3-0(2-0)
Apollon Limassol - Nea Salamina 3-0(2-0)
Ermis Aradippou - AEK Larnaca 0-2(0-1)
Anorthosis - APOEL Nicosia 2-0(1-0)
AC Omonia - Neon Paralimni 2-0(1-0)
Ethnikos Achna - Olympiakos 1-3(1-0)
Doxa Katokopias - AEL Limassol 1-2(1-1)

Round 9 [30.10.-02.11.2020]
Neon Paralimni - Doxa Katokopias 0-0
AEL Limassol - Ermis Aradippou 2-1(1-0)
APOEL Nicosia - Apollon Limassol 1-1(0-0)
Olympiakos - AC Omonia 1-0(0-0)
Karmiotissa - Anorthosis 1-1(0-0)
Nea Salamina - Ethnikos Achna 1-1(1-0)
AEK Larnaca - Pafos FC 0-0 [09.12.]

Round 10 [06-08.11.2020]
Apollon Limassol - Karmiotissa 1-2(1-1)
Pafos FC - AEL Limassol 1-0(1-0)
Ermis Aradippou - Neon Paralimni 1-1(0-0)
Ethnikos Achna - APOEL Nicosia 0-0
Olympiakos - Nea Salamina 0-0
Anorthosis - AEK Larnaca 1-0(1-0)
AC Omonia - Doxa Katokopias 0-0

Round 11 [21-23.11.2020]
Doxa Katokopias - Ermis Aradippou 0-0
APOEL Nicosia - Olympiakos 0-1(0-1)
Nea Salamina - AC Omonia 2-1(1-1)
AEL Limassol - Anorthosis 1-0(0-0)
AEK Larnaca - Apollon Limassol 1-2(0-1)
Karmiotissa - Ethnikos Achna 1-1(1-0)
Neon Paralimni - Pafos FC 0-0

Round 12 [27-30.11.2020]
Olympiakos - Karmiotissa 3-2(1-1)
Anorthosis - Neon Paralimni 4-2(1-0)
Nea Salamina - APOEL Nicosia 0-3(0-1)
Pafos FC - Doxa Katokopias 2-0(0-0)
Apollon Limassol - AEL Limassol 1-2(0-1)
AC Omonia - Ermis Aradippou 0-0
Ethnikos Achna - AEK Larnaca 0-3(0-1)

Round 13 [04-07.12.2020]
Doxa Katokopias - Anorthosis 2-1(1-0)
Karmiotissa - Nea Salamina 0-1(0-1)
AEL Limassol - Ethnikos Achna 5-0(4-0)
AEK Larnaca - Olympiakos 4-0(2-0)
Neon Paralimni - Apollon Limassol 1-5(0-2)
Ermis Aradippou - Pafos FC 1-1(0-1)
APOEL Nicosia - AC Omonia 0-3(0-1)

Round 14 [11-14.12.2020]
Doxa Katokopias - Apollon Limassol 0-1(0-0)
Ermis Aradippou - Anorthosis 1-1(1-0)
AEK Larnaca - Nea Salamina 1-0(0-0)
Neon Paralimni - Ethnikos Achna 0-0
AC Omonia - Pafos FC 2-1(1-1)
Karmiotissa - APOEL 1-0(1-0) [28.12.]
AEL Limassol - Olympiakos 3-0(1-0) [28.12.]

Round 15 [18-20.12.2020]
Anorthosis - Pafos FC 1-0(0-0)
Karmiotissa - AC Omonia 1-5(0-2)
Nea Salamina - AEL Limassol 1-1(0-1)
Apollon Limassol - Ermis Aradippou 4-0(2-0)
Ethnikos Achna - Doxa Katokopias 0-1(0-1)
APOEL - AEK Larnaca 1-1(0-0) [13.01.2021]
Olympiakos - Neon Par. 0-1(0-0) [20.01.2021]

Round 16 [22-24.12.2020]
Neon Paralimni - Nea Salamina 1-3(0-1)
AC Omonia - Anorthosis 3-0(2-0)
Pafos FC - Apollon Limassol 1-1(0-1)
AEK Larnaca - Karmiotissa 1-0(0-0)
Doxa Katokopias - Olympiakos 1-1(0-0)
Ermis Aradippou - Ethnikos Achna 0-0
AEL Limassol - APOEL 2-0(1-0) [03.02.21]

Round 17 [02-03.01.2021]
Olympiakos - Ermis Aradippou 0-0
Karmiotissa - AEL Limassol 0-1(0-1)
Nea Salamina - Doxa Katokopias 4-3(2-1)
APOEL Nicosia - Neon Paralimni 0-2(0-1)
Ethnikos Achna - Pafos FC 2-1(1-1)
AEK Larnaca - AC Omonia 0-3(0-3)
Apollon Limassol - Anorthosis 3-2(0-2)

Round 18 [05-07.01.2021]
Neon Paralimni - Karmiotissa 2-2(1-1)
Ermis Aradippou - Nea Salamina 1-2(1-0)
Doxa Katokopias - APOEL Nicosia 2-1(1-1)
Anorthosis - Ethnikos Achna 1-0(1-0)
AC Omonia - Apollon Limassol 2-1(1-1)
AEL Limassol - AEK Larnaca 3-1(1-1)
Pafos FC - Olympiakos 5-0(2-0)

Round 19 [09-11.01.2021]
AEL Limassol - AC Omonia 1-1(0-1)
Ethnikos Achna - Apollon Limassol 1-4(0-1)
APOEL Nicosia - Ermis Aradippou 3-0(1-0)
Karmiotissa - Doxa Katokopias 1-1(1-0)
AEK Larnaca - Neon Paralimni 1-2(0-1)
Olympiakos - Anorthosis 0-3(0-2)
Nea Salamina - Pafos FC 2-0(2-0)

Round 20 [15-18.01.2021]
Neon Paralimni - AEL Limassol 1-0(0-0)
Ermis Aradippou - Karmiotissa 2-0(0-0)
AC Omonia - Ethnikos Achna 2-0(1-0)
Anorthosis - Nea Salamina 2-0(1-0)
Pafos FC - APOEL Nicosia 2-3(1-1)
Apollon Limassol - Olympiakos 2-1(1-0)
Doxa Katokopias - AEK Larnaca 0-0

Round 21 [22-25.01.2021]
AEL Limassol - Doxa Katokopias 3-1(2-1)
AEK Larnaca - Ermis Aradippou 3-1(3-1)
Olympiakos - Ethnikos Achna 1-2(0-0)
Neon Paralimni - AC Omonia 0-1(0-0)
APOEL Nicosia - Anorthosis 0-0
Nea Salamina - Apollon Limassol 1-1(0-1)
Karmiotissa - Pafos FC 0-0

Round 22 [29.01.-01.02.2021]
AC Omonia - Olympiakos 1-1(1-1)
Ermis Aradippou - AEL Limassol 2-2(0-1)
Doxa Katokopias - Neon Paralimni 1-0(1-0)
Apollon Limassol - APOEL Nicosia 1-0(0-0)
Pafos FC - AEK Larnaca 1-4(0-1)
Ethnikos Achna - Nea Salamina 1-1(0-0)
Anorthosis - Karmiotissa 2-1(2-0)

Round 23 [04-07.02.2021]
Neon Paralimni - Ermis Aradippou 1-0(1-0)
Doxa Katokopias - AC Omonia 0-3(0-1)
Nea Salamina - Olympiakos 1-2(1-1)
AEK Larnaca - Anorthosis 0-0
Karmiotissa - Apollon Limassol 1-1(0-0)
APOEL Nicosia - Ethnikos Achna 2-3(1-2)
AEL Limassol - Pafos FC 1-0(0-0)

Round 24 [08-11.02.2021]
Ermis Aradippou - Doxa Katokopias 2-1(0-0)
AC Omonia - Nea Salamina 2-0(2-0)
Apollon Limassol - AEK Larnaca 3-0(1-0)
Olympiakos - APOEL Nicosia 2-3(0-1)
Anorthosis - AEL Limassol 0-0
Ethnikos Achna - Karmiotissa 2-1(1-0)
Pafos FC - Neon Paralimni 2-1(1-0)

Round 25 [13-16.02.2021]
Ermis Aradippou - AC Omonia 0-2(0-2)
Karmiotissa - Olympiakos 0-3(0-1)
APOEL Nicosia - Nea Salamina 3-1(2-0)
AEK Larnaca - Ethnikos Achna 3-1(1-1)
AEL Limassol - Apollon Limassol 2-1(1-0)
Doxa Katokopias - Pafos FC 0-0
Neon Paralimni - Anorthosis 1-2(1-1)

Round 26 [19-22.02.2021]
Nea Salamina - Karmiotissa 4-0(1-0)
Olympiakos - AEK Larnaca 1-0(1-0)
Anorthosis - Doxa Katokopias 1-0(1-0)
AC Omonia - APOEL Nicosia 1-0(1-0)
Ethnikos Achna - AEL Limassol 1-2(0-1)
Apollon Limassol - Neon Paralimni 2-1(0-0)
Pafos FC - Ermis Aradippou 3-1(1-1)

Final Standings

1.	AC Omonia Nicosia	26	16	8	2	43 - 13	56
2.	AEL Limassol	26	17	4	5	45 - 23	55
3.	Apollon Limassol FC	26	16	6	4	52 - 22	54
4.	Anorthosis Famagusta FC	26	15	6	5	37 - 21	51
5.	AEK Larnaca FC	26	12	5	9	36 - 25	41
6.	Olympiakos Nicosia FC	26	10	4	12	27 - 38	34
7.	Pafos FC Paphos	26	8	8	10	30 - 27	32
8.	APOEL FC Nicosia	26	8	6	12	27 - 31	30
9.	Doxa Katokopias FC	26	7	9	10	24 - 32	30
10.	Nea Salamis Famagusta FC	26	8	5	13	29 - 38	29
11.	Enosis Neon Paralimni FC	26	6	6	14	22 - 39	24
12.	Ermis Aradippou FC	26	5	9	12	18 - 38	24
13.	Ethnikos Achna FC	26	5	7	14	23 - 43	22
14.	Karmiotissa Pano Polemidia FC	26	3	9	14	22 - 45	18

Teams ranked 1-6 were qualified for the Championship Round, while teams ranked 7-14 were qualified for the Relegation Round.

Relegation Round

Results

Round 27 [27.02.-01.03.2021]
Nea Salamina - Neon Paralimni 1-2(1-0)
Doxa Katokopias - Ermis Aradippou 1-1(0-0)
APOEL Nicosia - Ethnikos Achna 2-0(1-0)
Pafos FC - Karmiotissa 2-1(2-0)

Round 28 [05-08.03.2021]
Karmiotissa - Neon Paralimni 4-2(2-1)
Pafos FC - APOEL Nicosia 1-1(0-0)
Ermis Aradippou - Nea Salamina 1-2(0-0)
Ethnikos Achna - Doxa Katokopias 2-1(1-0)

Round 29 [12-15.03.2021]
Doxa Katokopias - Pafos FC 1-0(0-0)
Nea Salamina - Ethnikos Achna 0-2(0-1)
Neon Paralimni - Ermis Aradippou 0-1(0-0)
APOEL Nicosia - Karmiotissa 2-0(0-0)

Round 30 [19-20.03.2021]
Karmiotissa - Ermis Aradippou 2-2(1-2)
APOEL Nicosia - Doxa Katokopias 1-0(0-0)
Pafos FC - Nea Salamina 3-0(2-0)
Ethnikos Achna - Neon Paralimni 1-0(0-0)

Round 31 [04-06.04.2021]
Nea Salamina - APOEL Nicosia 1-2(0-1)
Ermis Aradippou - Ethnikos Achna 1-2(1-2)
Neon Paralimni - Pafos FC 2-1(1-1) [28.04.]
Doxa Katok. - Karmiotissa 6-1(2-1) [28.04.]

Round 32 [09-13.04.2021]
Doxa Katokopias - Nea Salamina 0-0
APOEL Nicosia - Neon Paralimni 1-0(1-0)
Pafos FC - Ermis Aradippou 3-1(2-0)
Karmiotissa - Ethnikos Achna 2-4(1-1)

Round 33 [16-19.04.2021]
Neon Paralimni - Doxa Katokopias 0-0
Ermis Aradippou - APOEL Nicosia 2-0(1-0)
Ethnikos Achna - Pafos FC 0-2(0-0)
Nea Salamina - Karmiotissa 1-1(1-1)

Round 34 [23-25.04.2021]
Ermis Aradippou - Doxa Katokopias 0-1(0-0)
Karmiotissa - Pafos FC 0-6(0-2)
Neon Paralimni - Nea Salamina 3-3(0-3)
Ethnikos Achna - APOEL Nicosia 1-1(1-1)

Round 35 [05-07.05.2021]
APOEL Nicosia - Pafos FC 0-1(0-1)
Neon Paralimni - Karmiotissa 1-1(0-1)
Nea Salamina - Ermis Aradippou 3-1(2-1)
Doxa Katokopias - Ethnikos Achna 0-1(0-0)

Round 36 [10-12.05.2021]
Karmiotissa - APOEL Nicosia 1-6(0-2)
Ermis Aradippou - Neon Paralimni 4-2(1-1)
Pafos FC - Doxa Katokopias 2-1(1-1)
Ethnikos Achna - Nea Salamina 2-2(2-0)

Round 37 [16-17.05.2021]
Nea Salamina - Pafos FC 1-2(1-0)
Neon Paralimni - Ethnikos Achna 1-1(0-0)
Ermis Aradippou - Karmiotissa 7-1(2-0)
Doxa Katokopias - APOEL Nicosia 1-2(0-0)

Round 38 [20-21.05.2021]
Pafos FC - Neon Paralimni 2-0(2-0)
APOEL Nicosia - Nea Salamina 0-0
Karmiotissa - Doxa Katokopias 0-5(0-4)
Ethnikos Achna - Ermis Aradippou 2-0(0-0)

Round 39 [24-25.05.2021]
Ermis Aradippou - Pafos FC 1-2(0-1)
Neon Paralimni - APOEL Nicosia 0-1(0-1)
Ethnikos Achna - Karmiotissa 5-0(3-0)
Nea Salamina - Doxa Katokopias 1-4(0-2)

Round 40 [28-29.05.2021]
Karmiotissa - Nea Salamina 0-4(0-2)
APOEL Nicosia - Ermis Aradippou 2-0(1-0)
Doxa Katokopias - Neon Paralimni 1-0(0-0)
Pafos FC - Ethnikos Achna 1-2(0-1)

Standings

			Total					Home					Away		
7.	Pafos FC Paphos	40	18	9	13	58 - 38	63	12	4	4	39 - 21	6	5	9	19 - 17
8.	APOEL FC Nicosia	40	17	9	14	48 - 39	60	9	5	6	23 - 16	8	4	8	25 - 23
9.	Ethnikos Achna FC	40	14	10	16	48 - 56	52	7	4	9	24 - 27	7	6	7	24 - 29
10.	Doxa Katokopias FC	40	13	12	15	46 - 43	51	8	7	5	24 - 18	5	5	10	22 - 25
11.	Nea Salamis Famagusta FC (*Relegated*)	40	11	10	19	48 - 61	43	6	4	10	28 - 33	5	6	9	20 - 28
12.	Ermis Aradippou FC (*Relegated*)	40	9	11	20	40 - 61	38	5	6	9	26 - 29	4	5	11	14 - 32
13.	Enosis Neon Paralimni FC (*Relegated*)	40	8	10	22	35 - 61	34	4	8	8	17 - 26	4	2	14	18 - 35
14.	Karmiotissa Pano Polemidia FC (*Relegated*)	40	4	12	24	36 - 98	24	3	7	10	17 - 45	1	5	14	19 - 53

Championship Round

Results

Round 27 [26.02.-01.03.2021]
AEL Limassol - AEK Larnaca 3-0(2-0)
Olympiakos - AC Omonia 0-1(0-0)
Anorthosis - Apollon Limassol 2-2(0-1)

Round 28 [06-08.03.2021]
AC Omonia - Anorthosis 0-0
AEK Larnaca - Olympiakos 2-1(2-0)
Apollon Limassol - AEL Limassol 0-0

Round 29 [12-14.03.2021]
AEK Larnaca - Apollon Limassol 0-2(0-1)
AEL Limassol - AC Omonia 1-2(1-2)
Olympiakos - Anorthosis 2-0(1-0)

Round 30 [18-21.03.2021]
AC Omonia - AEK Larnaca 1-0(0-0)
Olympiakos - Apollon Limassol 0-2(0-1)
Anorthosis - AEL Limassol 1-2(1-2)

Round 31 [05-06.04.2021]
AEK Larnaca - Anorthosis 2-1(0-1)
Apollon Limassol - AC Omonia 1-0(0-0)
AEL Limassol - Olympiakos 2-0(1-0)

Round 32 [10-11.04.2021]
Apollon Limassol - Anorthosis 1-1(0-0)
AEK Larnaca - AEL Limassol 0-1(0-0)
AC Omonia - Olympiakos 2-0(1-0)

Round 33 [17-18.04.2021]
Anorthosis - AC Omonia 0-2(0-1)
AEL Limassol - Apollon Limassol 1-2(0-1)
Olympiakos - AEK Larnaca 2-1(0-1)

Round 34 [25-26.04.2021]
Apollon Limassol - AEK Larnaca 3-1(1-0)
Anorthosis - Olympiakos 0-2(0-1)
AC Omonia - AEL Limassol 2-1(0-1)

Round 35 [04-05.05.2021]
Apollon Limassol - Olympiakos 2-2(0-0)
AEK Larnaca - AC Omonia 0-1(0-0)
AEL Limassol - Anorthosis 1-2(1-1)

Round 36 [09-10.05.2021]
Anorthosis - AEK Larnaca 0-2(0-0)
Olympiakos - AEL Limassol 2-1(2-0)
AC Omonia - Apollon Limassol 1-1(0-0)

Standings

		Total						Home					Away			
1. **AC Omonia Nicosia**	36	23	10	3	55 - 17	79	12	6	0	25 - 6	11	4	3	30 - 11
2. Apollon Limassol FC	36	21	11	4	68 - 30	74	11	5	2	31 - 14	10	6	2	37 - 16
3. AEL Limassol	36	21	5	10	58 - 34	68	14	1	3	40 - 14	7	4	7	18 - 20
4. Anorthosis Famagusta FC	36	16	9	11	44 - 37	57	10	3	5	24 - 18	6	6	6	20 - 19
5. AEK Larnaca FC	36	15	5	16	44 - 40	50	10	2	6	25 - 16	5	3	10	19 - 24
6. Olympiakos Nicosia FC	36	14	5	17	38 - 51	47	7	2	9	18 - 22	7	3	8	20 - 29

Top goalscorers:

18	**Berat Sadik (FIN)**	*Doxa Katokopias FC*
17	Nicolas Diguiny (FRA)	*Apollon Limassol FC*
17	Onisiforos Roushias	*Ermis Aradippou FC*
17	Tomáš Wágner (CZE)	*Nea Salamis Famagusta FC*
16	Ivan Tričkovski (MKD)	*AEK Larnaca FC*

NATIONAL CUP
Kypello Kyprou 2020/2021

First Round [16.09./23.09./08.10./21.10.2020]

AEL Limassol - Omonoia Psevda FD	5-0	Olympiakos Nicosia - Podosfairikos O.X. 2006	4-0
Athlitikos Omilos Ayia Napa FC - Pafos FC Paphos	1-5	Alki Oroklini FC - Ypsonas FC	4-0
Karmiotissa P. Polemidia FC - EN THOI Lakatamia	4-0	Digenis Akritas Morphou FC - Onisilos Sotira 2014	1-3
Nea Salamis Famagusta FC - Achyronas Liopetri	4-1	Aris Limassol FC - Ethnikos Achna FC	1-4
PAEEK Kyrenia - Doxa Katokopias FC	2-1	**Intermediate Round [28.10.2020]**	
Ermis Aradippou FC - Akritas Chlorakas FC	3-0	PAEEK Kyrenia - APOEL FC Nicosia	0-4
Kouris Erimis - AEK Larnaca FC	0-11		

1/8-Finals [28.10./04.11./25.11./16.12.2020 & 20.01.2021]

Onisilos Sotira 2014 - Karmiotissa P. Polemidia FC	0-2	Ermis Aradippou FC - Nea Salamis Famagusta FC	1-2
Enosis Neon Paralimni FC - Olympiakos Nicosia FC	0-2	Alki Oroklini FC - Ethnikos Achna FC	1-2
Anorthosis Famagusta FC - Pafos FC Paphos	1-0	APOEL Nicosia - Apollon Limassol FC	2-1
AEK Larnaca FC - AEL Limassol	0-2	AC Omonia Nicosia received a bye.	

Quarter-Finals [24.02.-03.03.2021/10-17.03.2021]

First Leg		Second Leg	
Karmiotissa P. Pol. FC - Anorthosis Famagusta FC	1-2(0-1)	Anorthosis Famagusta FC - Karmiotissa P. Pol. FC	5-1(3-0)
APOEL Nicosia - AC Omonia Nicosia	1-1(0-0)	AC Omonia Nicosia - APOEL Nicosia	0-1(0-0)
AEL Limassol - Nea Salamis Famagusta FC	2-0(0-0)	Nea Salamis Famagusta FC - AEL Limassol	1-0(0-0)
Ethnikos Achna FC - Olympiakos Nicosia FC	1-1(0-1)	Olympiakos Nicosia FC - Ethnikos Achna FC	1-0(0-0)

Semi-Finals [14.04./21.04.2021]

First Leg		Second Leg	
Anorthosis Famagusta FC - APOEL Nicosia	1-0(1-0)	APOEL Nicosia - Anorthosis Famagusta FC	1-3(1-2)
Olympiakos Nicosia FC - AEL Limassol	4-2(3-1)	AEL Limassol - Olympiakos Nicosia FC	0-1(0-1)

Final

15.05.2021; Stádio GSP, Nicosia; Referee: Ovidiu Alin Haţegan (Romania); Attendance: n/a
Anorthosis Famagusta FC - Olympiakos Nicosia FC   **2-1(0-0,1-1)**

Anorthosis: Giorgi Loria, Branko Vrgoč, Anderson Correia de Barros (105.Charles Bertrand Etoundi Eloundou), Spyros Risvanis (85.Georgios Galitsios), Pavlos Korrea, Murtaz Daushvili (46.Josef Hušbauer), Tornike Okriashvili, Panagiotis Artymatas, Dor Mikha (64.Renato João Inacio Margaça), Nikolaos Kaltsas (91.Dimitris Christofi), Giorgi Kvilitaia. Trainer: Temur Ketsbaia (Georgia).

Olympiakos: Neofytos Michail, Mamadu Samba Candé „Sambinha" (90+1.Stelios Andreou), Konstantinos Sotiriou, Paris Psaltis, Evangelos Kyriakou, Omar Santana Cabrera (100.Iraklis Garoufalias), Nanísio Justino Mendes Soares, Kingsley Sarfo (106.Gustavo Nascimento da Costa), Pangiotis Zachariou (81.Fabrice Kah Nkwoh), Edgar Nicaise Constant Salli, Vasilios Mantzis (106.Stanislav Kostov). Trainer: Čedomir Janevski (North Macedonia).

Goals: 1-0 Panagiotis Artymatas (59), 1-1 Kingsley Sarfo (61), 2-1 Charles Bertrand Etoundi Eloundou (110).

Please note: appearances and goals are including statistics of both regular season and play-offs (Championship and Relegation Round).

Athlletiki Enosi Kition Larnakas (AEK Larnaca)

	Founded:	18.07.1994	
	Stadium:	AEK Arena, Larnaca (7,400)	
	Trainer:	David Caneda Pérez (ESP)	30.01.1970
[21.09.2020]		Joan Antoni Carrillo Milán (ESP)	08.09.1968
[24.11.2020]		Sofronis Avgousti	09.03.1977
[20.04.2021]		Panagiotis Giannou	

Goalkeepers:	DOB	M	(s)	G
Andreas Christodoulou	26.03.1997	1		
Joël Mall (SUI)	05.04.1991	16		
Jens Teunckens (BEL)	30.01.1998	9		
Antonio Ramírez Martínez „Toño" (ESP)	23.11.1986	10		
Defenders:	DOB	M	(s)	G
Henry Andreou	02.04.2001	1		
Marios Antoniades	14.05.1990	20		
José Manuel Fernández Reyes (ESP)	18.11.1989	26	(4)	
Héctor Martínez Torres (ESP)	01.01.1995	2	(4)	
Thomas Ioannou	19.07.1995	27	(3)	
Kevin Pierre Lafrance (HAI)	13.01.1990	2	(2)	
Mikel González de Martín Martínez (ESP)	24.09.1985	31		
Daniel Mojsov (MKD)	25.12.1987	16	(3)	
Simranjit Singh Thandi (ENG)	11.10.1999	11	(6)	1
Joan Guillem Truyols Mascaró (ESP)	11.11.1989	22		1
Midfielders:	DOB	M	(s)	G
Abraham González Casanova (ESP)	16.07.1985	9	(1)	2

	DOB	M	(s)	G
Thomas Nathan Hateley (ENG)	12.09.1989	27	(5)	1
Fredrik Haugen (NOR)	13.06.1992		(9)	
Giorgos Naoum	21.02.2001	5	(3)	
Iakovos Savvidis	05.10.2001		(2)	
Nils Schouterden (BEL)	14.12.1988	4	(4)	
Stefan Spirovski (MKD)	23.08.1990	23	(7)	1
Matija Špoljarić (SRB)	02.04.1997	15	(11)	
Forwards:	DOB	M	(s)	G
Acorán Barrera Reyes (ESP)	31.01.1983	26	(7)	5
Konstantinos Anastasiou	05.07.1999	1	(3)	
Konstantinos Konstantinou	08.10.1999	1	(6)	
Andreas Makris	27.11.1995	19	(8)	4
José Manuel García Naranjo (ESP)	28.07.1994	19	(11)	6
Fernando „Nando" García Puchades (ESP)	13.06.1994	15	(16)	2
Orthodoxos Orthodoxou	17.04.2004		(1)	
Thierry Alain Florian Taulemesse (FRA)	31.01.1986	12	(15)	5
Ivan Tričkovski (MKD)	18.04.1987	26	(4)	16

Athlitiki Enosi Lemesou (AEL Limassol)

	Founded:	04.10.1930	
	Stadium:	Stádio Tsirion, Limassol (13,331)	
	Trainer:	Dušan Kerkez (BIH)	01.05.1976

Goalkeepers:	DOB	M	(s)	G
Antreas Keravnos	05.05.1999	2		
Josimar Diaz Vózinha (CPV)	03.06.1986	34		
Defenders:	DOB	M	(s)	G
André Ferreira Teixeira (POR)	14.08.1993	31	(1)	2
Bruno Araújo Dos Santos (BRA)	07.02.1993	24	(4)	1
Gordan Bunoza (BIH)	05.02.1988	8	(1)	1
Christos Efstathiou	12.03.2003		(1)	
Elosman Euller Silva Cavalcanti (BRA)	04.01.1995	8	(6)	1
Strahinja Kerkez	13.12.2002	8	(4)	
Charalambos Kyriakou	15.10.1989	18	(5)	
Kypros Neofytou	13.08.2002		(1)	
Aleksandar Pantić (SRB)	11.04.1992	8	(2)	
Christophe Charles Steven René Psyché (FRA)	28.07.1988	3	(2)	
Momčilo Rašo (MNE)	06.02.1997	13	(2)	
Midfielders:	DOB	M	(s)	G
Marko Adamović (SRB)	11.03.1991	10	(15)	2
Minas Antoniou	22.02.1994	22	(6)	2
Andreas Avraam	06.06.1987	13	(6)	2

	DOB	M	(s)	G
Dimitris Avraam	28.01.2001	3	(7)	
Richard Danilo Maciel Sousa Campos (BEL)	13.01.1990	23	(4)	6
Andreas Georgiou	02.01.2003		(1)	
Anthony Georgiou	24.02.1997	10	(3)	2
Michalis Konstantinidis	25.08.2001	1	(5)	
Konstantinos Marneros	01.09.2003		(1)	
Slobodan Medojević (SRB)	20.11.1990	22	(2)	1
Charalampos Melanakitis	21.01.2002		(3)	
Vasilios Papafotis	10.08.1995	16	(3)	2
Llorenc Riera Ortega „Sito Riera" (ESP)	05.01.1987	25	(5)	6
Davor Zdravkovski (MKD)	20.03.1998	23	(5)	1
Forwards:	DOB	M	(s)	G
Donis Avdijaj (KVX)	25.08.1996	2	(7)	
Matko Babić (CRO)	28.07.1998	12	(16)	7
Gevorg Ghazaryan (ARM)	05.04.1988	2	(4)	1
Andrija Majdevac (SRB)	07.08.1997	1	(7)	1
Manuel Torres Jiménez (ESP)	05.01.1991	31	(1)	5
Ryan Mmaee (MAR)	01.11.1997	23	(7)	14
Adonis Nikolettidis	16.03.2003		(1)	1

Anorthosis Famagusta Football Club

	Founded:	30.01.1911	
	Stadium:	Stádio "Antonis Papadopoulos", Larnaca (10,230)	
	Trainer:	Temur Ketsbaia (GEO)	18.03.1968

Goalkeepers:	DOB	M	(s)	G
Giorgi Loria (GEO)	27.01.1986	34		
Assaf Tzur (ISR)	28.08.1998	2		
Defenders:	DOB	M	(s)	G
Anderson Correia de Barros (BRA)	06.05.1991	31	(3)	
Panagiotis Artymatas	12.11.1998	1		
Georgios Galitsios (GRE)	06.07.1986	19	(6)	2
Hovhannes Hambardzumyan (ARM)	04.10.1990	17	(4)	2
Pavlos Korrea	14.07.1998	6	(5)	1
Kostas Pileas	11.12.1998	1	(6)	
Spyros Risvanis (GRE)	03.01.1994	16		
Gordon Schildenfeld (CRO)	18.03.1985	16		
Yevgen Selin (UKR)	09.05.1988	9	(2)	1
Branko Vrgoč (CRO)	18.12.1989	29		2

Midfielders:	DOB	M	(s)	G
Kostakis Artymatas	15.04.1993	30	(3)	1
Azer Bušuladžić (BIH)	12.11.1991	7	(3)	
Murtaz Daushvili (GEO)	01.05.1989	29	(2)	
Josef Hušbauer (CZE)	16.03.1990	19	(12)	1
Renato João Inacio Margaça	17.07.1985	13	(13)	1
Nikolaos Kaltsas (GRE)	03.05.1990	26	(5)	4
Dor Mikha (ISR)	02.03.1992	23	(5)	1
Forwards:	DOB	M	(s)	G
Dimitris Christofi	28.09.1988	10	(20)	
Charles Bertrand Etoundi Eloundou (CMR)	04.12.1994	6	(18)	1
Nika Kacharava (GEO)	13.01.1994	2		
Giorgi Kvilitaia (GEO)	01.10.1993	28	(3)	14
Michalis Manias (GRE)	20.02.1990	5	(22)	4
Tornike Okriashvili (GEO)	12.02.1992	17	(3)	9

Athletikos Podosferikos Omilos Ellinon Lefkosias (APOEL Football Club Nicosia)

Founded: 08.11.1926
Stadium: Stádio GSP, Nicosia (22,859)
Trainer: Marinos Ouzounidis — 10.10.1968
[26.10.2020] Loukas Chatziloukas — 06.06.1967
[02.11.2020] Michael Joseph McCarthy (IRL) — 07.02.1959
[06.01.2021] Savvas Poursaitidis — 23.06.1976

Goalkeepers:	DOB	M	(s)	G
João Miguel Macedo Silva (POR)	07.04.1995	21		
Dimitrios Priniotaki	11.03.1999	1		
Francis Odinaka Uzoho (NGA)	28.10.1998	18		
Defenders:	**DOB**	**M**	**(s)**	**G**
Kostas Apostolakis (GRE)	28.05.1999	6	(1)	
Artur Jorge Marques Amorim (POR)	14.08.1994	18	(1)	
André Geraldes de Barros (POR)	02.05.1991	7	(2)	
Nikolas Ioannou	10.11.1995	2		
Giorgios Merkis	30.07.1984	18	(4)	1
Dragan Mihajlović (SUI)	22.08.1991	2		
Emilio N'Sue López (EQG)	30.09.1989	22	(5)	3
Rafael Santos de Sousa (BRA)	02.02.1998	18	(1)	1
Christos Sielis	02.02.2000	21	(5)	
Paulo Vinicius Souza Dos Santos (HUN)	21.02.1990	12		1
Christos Wheeler	29.06.1997	19	(11)	
Facundo Gabriel Zabala (ARG)	02.01.1999	12	(3)	1
Midfielders:	**DOB**	**M**	**(s)**	**G**
Jack Byrne (IRL)	24.04.1996	2	(3)	
Carlos Eduardo Oliveira Dias (BRA)	23.01.2000	4	(4)	
Tomás Sebastián De Vincenti (ARG)	09.02.1989	23	(5)	2
Stavros Gavriel	29.01.2002	8	(9)	1
Mike Jensen (DEN)	19.02.1988	10		

	DOB	M	(s)	G
Marios Kokkinoftas	15.03.2003	1		
Marius Lundemo (NOR)	11.04.1994	15	(12)	1
Giannis Satsias	28.12.2002	6	(11)	1
Iasonas Toumazos	24.04.2003		(1)	
Ioannis Tsoutsouki	14.04.2004	2		
Anuar Tuhami (MAR)	15.01.1995	22	(2)	1
Stylianos Vrontis	05.11.2004	3	(2)	
Ghayas Zahid (NOR)	08.09.1994	29	(5)	3
Forwards:	**DOB**	**M**	**(s)**	**G**
Musa Suliman Al Taamari (JOR)	10.06.1997	3	(1)	
Omar Hani Ismail Al Zebdieh (JOR)	27.06.1999		(1)	
Omer Atzili (ISR)	27.07.1993	7	(4)	
Nikolas Dimitriou	22.04.2002		(2)	
Giorgos Efrem	05.07.1989	10	(7)	1
Joseph Alan Garner (ENG)	12.04.1988	9	(2)	8
Stavros Georgiou	19.10.2004	2	(3)	1
Andreas Katsantonis	16.02.2000	16	(7)	3
Viktor Klonaridis (BEL)	28.07.1992	26	(6)	6
Nicolas Koutsakos	14.11.2003	6	(4)	3
Dieumerci Ndongala (COD)	14.06.1991	13	(12)	2
Atdhe Nuhiu (KVX)	29.07.1989	10	(13)	
Ben Sahar (ISR)	10.08.1989	16	(16)	6

Apollon Lemesou (Apollon Football Club Limassol)

Founded: 14.04.1954
Stadium: Stádio Tsirion, Limassol (13,331)
Trainer: Sofronis Avgousti — 09.03.1977
[18.11.2020] Giannis Petrakis (GRE) — 20.05.1959

Goalkeepers:	DOB	M	(s)	G
Dimitris Dimitriou	15.01.1999	22	(1)	
Aleksandar Jovanović (SRB)	06.12.1992	11		
Joël Mall (SUI)	05.04.1991	3		
Defenders:	**DOB**	**M**	**(s)**	**G**
Wilde-Donald Guerrier (HAI)	31.03.1989	8	(1)	4
Héctor Yuste Canton (ESP)	12.01.1988	32		
João Pedro Guerra Cunha (POR)	04.05.1986	30	(2)	1
Fanos Katelaris	26.08.1996	7	(5)	
Giorgos Malekkidis	14.07.1997	3	(3)	
Andreas Panayiotou Filiotis	31.05.1995	7	(8)	1
Valentin Sébastien Roger Roberge (FRA)	09.06.1987	27		
Attila Árpád Szalai (HUN)	20.01.1998	11	(5)	2
Giorgos Vasiliou	12.06.1984	11	(6)	
Midfielders:	**DOB**	**M**	**(s)**	**G**
Diego Marvin Biseswar (SUR)	08.03.1988	13	(2)	3
Đorđe Denić (SRB)	01.04.1996	25	(8)	1

	DOB	M	(s)	G
Chambos Kyriakou	09.02.1995	23	(8)	
Saša Marković (SRB)	13.03.1991	14	(10)	1
Florentin Matei (ROU)	15.04.1993	16	(12)	7
Esteban Fernando Sachetti (ARG)	21.11.1985	10	(8)	
Forwards:	**DOB**	**M**	**(s)**	**G**
Charalambos Antoniou	01.07.2005		(1)	
Charlison Benschop (CUW)	21.08.1989	11	(17)	7
Bagaliy Dabo (FRA)	27.07.1988	16	(9)	6
Diego Aguirre Parra (ESP)	17.10.1990	7		
Nicolas Diguiny (FRA)	31.05.1988	27	(5)	17
Serge Gakpé (TOG)	07.05.1987	2	(5)	
Giannis Gianniotas (GRE)	29.04.1993	19	(8)	3
Daniel Larsson (SWE)	25.01.1987	2	(2)	1
Giorgi Papunashvili (GEO)	02.09.1995	4	(4)	
Ioannis Pittas	10.07.1996	30	(4)	13
Petros Psychas	28.08.1998	5	(7)	

Doxa Katokopias Football Club

Founded: 1954
Stadium: Stádio "Makario", Nicosia (16,000)
Trainer: Kostas Sakkas — 1973
[09.03.2021] Marinos Satsias — 24.05.1978
[18.05.2021] Angelos Efthymiou — 18.01.1984

Goalkeepers:	DOB	M	(s)	G
Freiderikos Konstantinou	31.12.2002		(1)	
Andreas Paraskevas	15.09.1998	6		
Damjan Siskovski (MKD)	18.03.1995	34		
Defenders:	**DOB**	**M**	**(s)**	**G**
Zacharias Adoni	13.07.1999	15	(7)	
Martinos Christofi	26.07.1993	21	(7)	1
Nikos Englezou	11.07.1993	34		2
Darko Glisić (MKD)	23.09.1991	2	(11)	
Konstantinos Mintikkis	14.07.1989	17	(2)	
Stephanos Mouktaris	10.07.1994	32	(1)	2
Aleksandar Pantić (SRB)	11.04.1992	13	(3)	
Román Golobart Benet (ESP)	21.03.1992	13	(2)	1
Midfielders:	**DOB**	**M**	**(s)**	**G**
Benjamin Asamoah (GHA)	04.01.1994	20	(7)	3
Vladimir Boljević (MNE)	17.01.1988	35	(2)	1
Alexandros Fasouliotis	20.01.2003	1	(1)	
Marios Fasouliotis	26.05.2005	1	(4)	1

	DOB	M	(s)	G
Gilson Sequeira Costa (POR)	24.09.1996	3	(15)	
Bilal Hamdi (ALG)	01.05.1991	4	(11)	1
Kévin Renato Fortes Oliveira (CPV)	08.06.1996	17	(12)	
Konstantinos Michailidis	03.09.2003	1	(1)	
Giorgos Oikonomides	10.04.1990	27	(6)	1
Duško Trajčevski (MKD)	01.11.1990	30	(3)	2
Forwards:	**DOB**	**M**	**(s)**	**G**
Frédéric Bulot (GAB)	27.09.1990		(5)	
Carlos Miguel Tavares de Oliveira „Carlitos" (POR)	09.03.1993	15	(9)	4
Kyriakos Chrysomilis	04.01.2004		(1)	
Hugo Filipe Pinto Servulo Firmino (POR)	22.12.1988	4	(8)	
João Diogo Alves Rodrigues „Kikas" (POR)	17.09.1998	23	(7)	6
Aboubakar Karamoko (CIV)	15.10.1999	1	(3)	
Andreas Komodikis	02.06.1997	1	(7)	
Luís Carlos Eneas da Conceição Lima (BRA)	15.06.1987	14	(14)	1
Buomesca Tue Na Bangna „Mesca" (GNB)	06.05.1993	19	(2)	1
Berat Sadik (FIN)	14.09.1986	37		18

Enosi Neon Paralimniou
(Enosis Neon Paralimni Football Club)

Founded:	1936		
Stadium:	Stádio "Tasos Markou", Paralimni (5,800)		
Trainer:	Marios Karas		24.10.1974
[22.09.2020]	Carlos Alós Ferrer (ESP)		21.07.1975
[26.03.2021]	Eleftherakis Eleftheriou		12.06.1974
[12.04.2021]	Sotiris Antoniou (GRE)		10.09.1975

Goalkeepers:	DOB	M	(s)	G
Filip Gačevski (MKD)	17.08.1990	29		
Theodoros Koutsou	19.04.2004		(1)	
Konstantinos Petrou	23.09.1997	11		
Defenders:	DOB	M	(s)	G
Gregor Balažic (SVN)	12.02.1988	36		1
Diego Martín Barboza González (URU)	09.01.1991	34	(2)	1
Kelly Irep (GPE)	01.09.1995	13	(9)	
Andreas Kyriakou	05.02.1994	27	(1)	1
Demetris Moulazimis	15.01.1992	6	(17)	
Omiros Tikkis	22.02.2005		(1)	
Midfielders:	DOB	M	(s)	G
Junes Barny (SWE)	04.11.1989	16		1
Mauro Benildo Bellone (ARG)	03.07.1990	19	(5)	
Juan Felipe Alves Ribeiro (BRA)	05.12.1987	35	(2)	8
Loizos Kosmas	25.01.1995	13	(11)	
Fotis Kotsonis	10.02.2003	7	(5)	
Óscar Adrián Lucero (ARG)	16.08.1985	38	(1)	
Irakli Maisuradze (GEO)	22.08.1988	11	(13)	1

Dimitris Mavroudis	03.05.2002	4	(5)	
Kyriakos Panagi	22.04.1996		(3)	
Mickaël Panos (FRA)	10.02.1997	8		1
Marcos Stylianides	27.05.1999	2	(1)	
Pele van Anholt (NED)	23.04.1991	10	(3)	
Konstantinos Xiouros	10.08.2000		(1)	
Forwards:	DOB	M	(s)	G
Shaloze Chigozie Udoji (NGA)	16.07.1986	9	(18)	2
Fernando Emanuel Dening (ARG)	04.07.1988	29	(5)	5
Aimé Marcelin Gando Biala (CMR)	27.02.1997	4	(7)	1
Dimitris Flouris	23.07.2002	1	(1)	
Pantelis Gavriel	07.01.2004		(2)	
Jonathan Boareto Dos Reis „Jonathan Balotelli" (BRA)	02.04.1989	9	(5)	3
Theodoros Kolokoudias	06.07.1994	4	(1)	
Panagiotis Kynigopoulos (GRE)	24.09.1996	2		
Ilya Markovskyy (UKR)	06.06.1997	19	(18)	2
Michael Ayodeji Ngoo (ENG)	22.10.1992	9	(8)	
Christoforos Stavrou	08.03.2002		(1)	
Dimitris Theodorou	10.09.1997	35	(3)	6

Ermis Aradippou Football Club

Founded:	1958		
Stadium:	Stádio Ammochostos, Larnaca (5,500)		
Trainer:	Nicos Panayiotou		16.12.1970
[02.09.2020]	Nikos Andronikou		09.11.1961
[02.11.2020]	Marinos Satsias		24.05.1978
[08.02.2021]	Nikolas Martides		15.02.1981
[09.03.2021]	Siniša Dobrašinović		17.02.1977
[13.04.2021]	Demetris Daskalakis		18.11.1977

Goalkeepers:	DOB	M	(s)	G
Alexandros Antoniou	03.09.1999	1	(2)	
Caique Luiz Santos da Purificação (BRA)	31.07.1997	30		
Giannis Firinidis (GRE)	01.07.1983	9	(2)	
Defenders:	DOB	M	(s)	G
Saado Abdelsalam Fouflia (GRE)	23.11.1997	12	(3)	
Aristos Christodoulou	03.09.2003	1	(3)	
Stelios Dimitriou	04.10.1990	33	(1)	3
Christoforos Gavriil	28.10.1990	30	(2)	1
Eleftherios Hatziantonis	10.01.2004		(2)	
Kevin Holt (SCO)	25.01.1993	27		2
Pavlos Kyriakidis (GRE)	03.09.1991	32	(1)	
Pedro Jorge Pires Fernandes Lemos (POR)	17.03.1993	11	(4)	
Roberto Dias Correia Filho (BRA)	08.08.1988	32	(2)	
Mohamadou Sissoko (FRA)	08.08.1988	2		
Vasilios Vallianos (GRE)	11.09.1988	1	(5)	
Midfielders:	DOB	M	(s)	G
Petros Adamou	07.04.2000		(2)	
Aírton Ribeiro Santos (BRA)	21.02.1990	1	(1)	
Theocharis Chari	04.08.2003	1	(1)	
Miltiadis Erotokritou	20.04.2003		(1)	
Zdeněk Folprecht (CZE)	01.07.1991	17	(2)	2
Nikola Gatarić (CRO)	09.03.1992	11	(6)	2
Iakovos Kaiserlidis	01.07.1998	5	(9)	1

Vasilis Karagounis (GRE)	18.01.1994	24	(7)	
Marcio Andre Meira Fernandes (POR)	09.01.1994	33	(4)	1
Di Giovanni Nouma Oum (FRA)	01.01.1997	1	(1)	
Ejike Okoh (NGA)	26.01.1999		(1)	
Stylianos Panteli	07.08.1999	7	(13)	1
Magomed Paragulgov (KAZ)	26.03.1994	2	(5)	
Lancinet Sidibe (GUI)	01.01.1997	25	(4)	
Wesley Dias Claudino (BRA)	22.06.1995	2		
Curtis Yebli (FRA)	30.03.1997	2		
Kiriakos Zavos	15.01.2004	1	(2)	
Forwards:	DOB	M	(s)	G
Lefteris Alambritis	26.09.1996	2	(4)	
Ilias Georgiou	24.07.1997	6	(6)	1
Hugo da Silva Cabral (BRA)	06.09.1988	1	(2)	
Jonatan Ferreira Reis (BRA)	30.06.1989	1		
Brahima Bruno Koné (CIV)	30.03.1995	11	(4)	1
Stavrinos Konstantinou	19.03.1997		(3)	
Krešimir Kovačević (CRO)	07.08.1994	10	(6)	3
Theodosis Kyprou	24.02.1992	9	(17)	2
Andreas Papathanasiou	03.10.1983	1	(22)	
Rafael Gomes de Oliveira „Rafinha" (BRA)	26.04.1990	4	(4)	1
Onisiforos Roushias	15.07.1992	32	(5)	17
Arsenio Valpoort (NED)	05.08.1992	10	(5)	2

Ethnikos Achnas Football Club

Founded:	1968		
Stadium:	Stádio Dasaki, Achna (7,000)		
Trainer:	Dean Klafurić (CRO)		26.07.1972
[27.10.2020]	Bojan Markoski (MKD)		08.08.1983
[17.11.2020]	Apostolos Makrides		12.02.1968
[08.12.2020]	Elias Charalambous		25.09.1980

Goalkeepers:	DOB	M	(s)	G
Martin Bogatinov (MKD)	26.04.1986	32		
Giorgos Christodoulou	26.01.2002		(1)	
Alexander Kavaleouski	26.12.2004	1		
Kyriakos Stratilatis (GRE)	05.01.1988	7	(1)	
Defenders:	DOB	M	(s)	G
Deyvison Denílson de Sousa Bessas (BRA)	18.10.1988	26	(4)	
Toni Gorupec (CRO)	04.07.1993	26	(4)	1
Petros Ioannou	10.01.1999	6	(2)	
Dimitris Kyprianou	02.02.1993	20	(10)	
Marios Peratikos	08.09.1999	31	(3)	
Josip Projić (SRB)	23.08.1987	5		
Milan Savić (SRB)	04.04.1994	15	(2)	
Igors Tarasovs (LVA)	16.10.1988	12	(4)	
Midfielders:	DOB	M	(s)	G
Dimitris Charalambous	09.04.1997	5	(14)	
Christoforos Christofi	23.03.1991	25	(6)	
Gonçalo José Gonçalves dos Santos (POR)	15.11.1986	8		1

Konstantinos Ilia	25.10.2000	14	(8)	
Igor Khudobyak (UKR)	20.02.1985	34	(2)	3
Petros Kkolos	04.07.2003	1	(1)	2
Antonis Koumis	11.02.1997	6	(7)	
Giorgos Kousiappa	27.09.1998	6	(2)	
Luís Miguel Teixeira Ribeiro „Miguelito" (POR)	09.03.1990	18	(11)	3
Paraskevas Moiseos	05.05.2001	3	(1)	
Giorgos Papageorgiou	07.06.1997	25	(10)	4
Forwards:	DOB	M	(s)	G
Jan Doležal (CRO)	12.02.1993	18	(11)	3
Andreas Elia	09.08.1997		(1)	
Marios Elia	19.05.1996	20	(15)	10
Ibrahim Koneh (CMR)	09.09.1994	9	(6)	
Jovan Kostovski (MKD)	19.04.1987	7	(14)	1
Andrija Majdevac (SRB)	07.08.1997	12	(3)	6
Idir Ouali (FRA)	21.05.1988	16	(3)	3
Hélios Sessolo (SUI)	26.05.1993		(1)	
Goba Elysée Zakpa (POR)	17.08.1992	32	(5)	7

Karmiotissa Pano polemidion Football Club

Founded:	1979	
Stadium:	Stádio „Stelios Kyriakides", Paphos (9,394)	
Trainer:	Chrysis Mihail	26.05.1977
[12.02.2021]	Filippos Filippou	24.06.1975
[16.02.2021]	Yiannakis Pontikos	09.10.1973

Goalkeepers:	DOB	M	(s)	G
Charalambos Kairinos	06.06.1982	4		
Stefanos Kittos	23.02.2002	9	(1)	
Dimitrios Kyriakidis (GRE)	24.09.1986	13		
Efstathios Paplomatas	06.01.2002	5		
Ioakeim Toumpas	19.02.1994	9	(1)	
Defenders:	**DOB**	**M**	**(s)**	**G**
Nikita Baranov (EST)	19.08.1992	22	(1)	
Alkiviades Christofi	20.01.1992	31	(2)	1
Yiannis Efstathiou	14.02.1993	21	(6)	
Konstantinos Eleftheriou	30.07.2003		(3)	
Vangelis Ikonomou (GRE)	18.07.1987	7		
Charis Kapsos	27.02.2001	8	(3)	
Alexandros Michail	28.01.2000	5	(1)	
Yarin Perez (ISR)	17.07.1998	25	(1)	
Giannis Savva	18.08.1991	6	(7)	
Marios Stylianou	23.09.1993	7	(2)	
Giannis Tsaparillas	14.04.2004		(1)	
Midfielders:	**DOB**	**M**	**(s)**	**G**
Nikolas Charalambous	19.12.2004	1	(1)	
Anastasios Charalampous	15.10.2002		(1)	
Andreas Christou	12.03.1994	29	(4)	1
Duarte Urtigueira Gouveia Beirao Valente (POR)	02.11.1999	3	(9)	
Eduardo Pincelli (BRA)	23.04.1983		(1)	
Kiriakos Genethliou	31.10.2002	3	(3)	

	DOB	M	(s)	G
Marios Georgiou	16.01.1996		(3)	
Eden Hershkovitz (ISR)	23.08.1997	7	(6)	
Antonakis Liasidis	04.10.2004	1	(4)	
Andreas Neophytou	07.07.1998	19	(6)	
Adamos Orfanidis	23.05.2003	3	(4)	
Andreas Pachipis	16.12.1994	10	(12)	
Agathoklis Polyzos (GRE)	05.02.1999	2	(3)	
Alasdair David Reynolds (SCO)	02.09.1996	30	(2)	
Mohamed Sassi (TUN)	10.12.1987	24	(5)	2
Charalampos Statiotis	16.03.2003	2		
Forwards:	**DOB**	**M**	**(s)**	**G**
Alexandros Achilleos	17.05.2004		(2)	
Kenan Bargan (GRE)	25.10.1988	10	(9)	2
Ioannis Chatzivasilis	26.04.1990	27	(7)	7
Andreas Chrysostomou	27.01.2003	2		
Rois Chrysostomou	09.08.2002		(2)	
Andreas Dimitriou	08.10.2003	5	(3)	
Stefanos Georgiou	10.04.2003	1	(4)	
Andreas Frangos	14.07.1997	1	(4)	
Chrysovalantis Kapartis	26.10.1991	3	(15)	1
Andreas Komodikis	02.06.1997	2	(8)	
Giorgos Malekkidis	14.07.1997	13	(5)	1
José Rafael Romo Pérez (VEN)	06.12.1993	34	(2)	11
Ismaïl Sassi (TUN)	24.12.1991	30	(1)	10
Boubakari Soumbounou (FRA)	15.03.1999	6	(7)	

Nea Salamis Famagusta Football Club

Founded:	07.03.1948	
Stadium:	Stádio Ammochostos, Larnaca (5,500)	
Trainer:	Pambos Christodoulou	17.10.1967
[30.10.2020]	Savvas Damianou	22.05.1979
[15.03.2021]	Chrysis Mihail	26.05.1977
[20.04.2021]	Konstantinos Mina	01.05.1974

Goalkeepers:	DOB	M	(s)	G
Tasos Kissas	18.01.1988	7		
Kypros Onisiforou	07.11.1993	1		
Robert Veselovsky (SVK)	02.09.1985	32		
Defenders:	**DOB**	**M**	**(s)**	**G**
Rolandas Baravykas (LTU)	23.08.1995	5		
Breno Lorran da Silva Talvares (BRA)	06.03.1993	14	(15)	1
Daniel Christofi	16.05.2003	1		
Kypros Christoforou	23.04.1993	35		1
Pavel Čmovš (CZE)	29.06.1990	16		
Mamadou Kamissoko (FRA)	15.04.1993	20		2
Antonis Kyriakou	24.09.2003	1		
Thomas Nikolaou	22.10.2001	23	(5)	1
Timotheus Pavlou	08.09.1994	6	(11)	
Konstantinos Sergiou	02.10.2000	29	(2)	
Midfielders:	**DOB**	**M**	**(s)**	**G**
Adamos Andreou	18.12.1994	16	(8)	
Hervé William Bodiong Andiolo (CMR)	17.06.1997	6	(3)	
Aloïs Confais (FRA)	07.09.1996	33	(2)	
Cristian Montes López „Cris Montes" (ESP)	10.08.1997	1	(4)	

	DOB	M	(s)	G
Loukas Kalogirou	21.02.2002	1	(1)	
Andreas Lemesios	24.09.1997	1	(6)	
Soni Mustivar (HAI)	12.02.1990	11	(4)	
Barnes Osei (GHA)	08.01.1995	32	(2)	3
Filippos Papouis	27.08.2003		(2)	
Baïssama Sankoh (GUI)	20.03.1992	16	(6)	
Theodosis Siathas	16.12.1998	9	(15)	2
Stavros Tsoukalas (GRE)	28.05.1988	17	(4)	2
Vinicius Oliveira Franco (BRA)	16.05.1986	8	(3)	
Forwards:	**DOB**	**M**	**(s)**	**G**
Theodoros Chatziantonis	30.11.2003	1	(1)	
Francisco Gonçalves Sacalumbo „Chico Banza"(ANG)	17.12.1998		(4)	
Andreas Christou	13.03.2003	1	(1)	1
Demetris Chrysostomou	20.12.2002	1		
Vincent Créhin (FRA)	21.01.1989	12	(12)	2
Danilo Cirino de Oliveira (BRA)	11.11.1996	31	(2)	13
Dylan Duventru (MTQ)	03.01.1989	11	(7)	
Iasonas Pikis	11.11.2000	3	(10)	
Nicolás Varela Batista (URU)	19.01.1991	15	(11)	2
Tomáš Wágner (CZE)	06.03.1990	24	(6)	17

Olympiakos Nicosia Football Club

Founded:	1931	
Stadium:	Stádio Makario, Nicosia (16,000)	
Trainer:	Giannis Petrakis (GRE)	20.05.1959
[18.11.2020]	Kostas Seraphim	
[31.12.2020]	Leonidas Vokolos (GRE)	31.08.1970
[28.01.2021]	Čedomir Janevski (MKD)	03.07.1961

Goalkeepers:	DOB	M	(s)	G
Michalis Agrimakis (GRE)	29.07.1992	2		
Stefan Čupić (SRB)	07.05.1994	3		
Christos Karadais (GRE)	26.01.1999	5		
Neofytos Michail	16.12.1993	26	(1)	
Defenders:	**DOB**	**M**	**(s)**	**G**
Stelios Andreou	24.07.2002	31	(1)	1
Dimitrios Konstantinidis (GRE)	02.06.1994	6	(1)	
Christian Manrique Díaz (ESP)	02.10.1998	26	(5)	1
Nemanja Miletić (SRB)	26.07.1991	6	(6)	
Paris Psaltis	12.11.1996	24	(6)	
Mamadu Samba Candé „Sambinha" (POR)	23.09.1992	15	(2)	
Konstantinos Sotiriou	21.06.1996	21	(2)	1
Midfielders:	**DOB**	**M**	**(s)**	**G**
Stefanos Charalampous	03.09.1999	2	(6)	1
Filippos Eftychidis	26.02.2002	2	(4)	
Iraklis Garoufalias (GRE)	01.05.1993	10	(11)	

	DOB	M	(s)	G
Gustavo Nascimento da Costa (BRA)	20.03.1995	28	(4)	4
Evangelos Kyriakou	03.02.1994	14	(7)	
Nanísio Justino Mendes Soares (GNB)	17.09.1991	30	(3)	
Omar Santana Cabrera (ESP)	14.04.1991	16	(8)	1
Kingsley Sarfo (GHA)	13.02.1995	16	(6)	1
Forwards:	**DOB**	**M**	**(s)**	**G**
Omar Hani Ismail Al Zebdieh (JOR)	27.06.1999	6	(12)	
Loukas Andreou	17.01.2002	2	(1)	
Kiprianos Irakleous	06.02.2002		(1)	
Fabrice Kah Nkwoh (CMR)	09.03.1996	11	(12)	2
Stanislav Kostov (BUL)	02.10.1991	7	(13)	1
Vasilios Mantzis (GRE)	04.12.1991	26	(4)	11
Marios Pechlivanis	23.05.1995	15	(6)	1
Edgar Nicaise Constant Salli (CMR)	17.08.1992	19	(11)	4
Gino Ronald van Kessel (CUW)	09.03.1993	11	(9)	3
Christos Venizelos	08.02.2002		(1)	
Pangiotis Zachariou	26.02.1996	16	(4)	4

Athlitikos Sillogos Omonia Lefkosias
(Athletic Club Omonia Nicosia)

Founded: 04.06.1948
Stadium: Stádio GSP, Nicosia (22,859)
Trainer: Henning Stille Berg (NOR)   01.09.1969

Goalkeepers:	DOB	M	(s)	G
Fabiano Ribeiro de Freitas (BRA)	29.02.1988	32		
Charalambos Kyriakides	30.11.1998	1		
Kostas Panayi	08.10.1994	3		
Defenders:	**DOB**	**M**	**(s)**	**G**
Tomáš Hubočan (SVK)	17.09.1985	21	(3)	
Francisco Manuel Geraldo Rosa „Kiko" (POR)	20.01.1993	6	(1)	1
Ádám Lang (HUN)	17.01.1993	21	(5)	
Jan Lecjaks (CZE)	09.08.1990	30		
Michael Lüftner (CZE)	14.03.1994	29		1
Charis Mavrias (GRE)	21.02.1994	5	(2)	
Nikos Panagiotou	12.05.2000	3	(2)	
Midfielders:	**DOB**	**M**	**(s)**	**G**
Charalampos Charalampous	04.04.2002	2		
Jordi Gómez García-Penche (ESP)	24.05.1985	30	(1)	

	DOB	M	(s)	G
Ioannis Kousoulos	14.06.1996	30	(5)	4
Fotis Papoulis (GRE)	22.01.1985	18	(11)	8
Abdullahi Shehu (NGA)	12.03.1993	28	(2)	
Konstantinos Venizelos	05.07.2004	2		
Vítor Hugo Gomes da Silva (POR)	25.12.1987	8	(6)	
Forwards:	**DOB**	**M**	**(s)**	**G**
Ernest Asante (GHA)	06.11.1988	26	(4)	8
Éric Bauthéac (FRA)	24.08.1987	11	(11)	5
Michal Ďuriš (SVK)	01.06.1988	9	(15)	2
Andronikos Kakouli	03.05.2001	3	(12)	2
Loizos Loizou	18.07.2003	17	(10)	2
Mamadou Kaly Sene (SEN)	28.05.2001	4	(6)	1
Marko Šćepović (SRB)	23.05.1991	14	(2)	8
Thiago Ferreira Dos Santos (BRA)	12.07.1987	26	(3)	3
Marinos Tzionis	16.07.2001	17	(15)	7

Pafos Football Club Paphos

Founded: 10.06.2014 (*after the merger of AEK Kouklia and AEP Paphos*)
Stadium: Stádio „Stelios Kyriakides", Paphos (9,394)
Trainer: Jon Cameron Toshack (WAL)   07.03.1970
[20.10.2020] Dmitro Mikhaylenko (UKR)   13.07.1973
[04.02.2021] Stephen Phillip Constantine (ENG)   16.10.1962

Goalkeepers:	DOB	M	(s)	G
Evgenios Petrou	06.09.1997	2		
Artur Rudko (UKR)	07.05.1992	38		
Defenders:	**DOB**	**M**	**(s)**	**G**
Kyriakos Antoniou	03.05.2001	7	(5)	
Paulus Arajuuri (FIN)	15.06.1988	28		1
João Miguel Coimbra Aurélio (POR)	17.08.1988	36	(1)	1
Josef Kvída (CZE)	23.01.1997	27	(1)	1
Juan Camillo Saiz Ortegón (COL)	01.03.1992	35	(1)	2
Georgios Valerianos (GRE)	13.02.1992	15	(3)	
Joaquin Varela Romero (URU)	27.06.1998	5	(4)	
Víctor Guillermo Álvarez Delgado (ESP)	14.03.1993	4		
Midfielders:	**DOB**	**M**	**(s)**	**G**
Brayan Angulo Mosquera (COL)	19.07.1993	10	(4)	1
Jack Marcus Evans (WAL)	25.04.1998	1	(1)	
Navarone Foor (NED)	04.02.1992	32	(2)	1
Gerasimos Fylaktou	24.07.1991	11	(8)	
Samuel Edward Hutchinson (ENG)	03.08.1989	5		

	DOB	M	(s)	G
Pavel Lelyukhin (RUS)	23.04.1998	2	(5)	
Stefan Panić (SRB)	20.09.1992	20	(2)	1
Mickaël Panos (FRA)	10.02.1997	3	(1)	
Jason Puncheon (ENG)	26.06.1986	27	(2)	4
Alexandros Spontas	27.11.2002		(4)	
Onni Valakari (FIN)	18.08.1999	36		13
Danila Yanov (RUS)	27.01.2000	1	(2)	
Forwards:	**DOB**	**M**	**(s)**	**G**
Mukwelle Akale (USA)	18.01.1997		(6)	
Kévin Bérigaud (FRA)	09.05.1988	30	(4)	13
Jerson Cabral (CPV)	03.01.1991	9	(9)	1
Rushian Hepburn-Murphy (ENG)	28.08.1998	11	(12)	5
Orest Kuzyk (UKR)	17.05.1995	7	(5)	1
Lysandros Papastylianou	29.11.2005		(1)	
Deniss Rakels (LVA)	20.08.1992	5	(19)	1
Marcelo Luis Torres (ARG)	06.11.1997	15	(15)	7
Vladimiro Etson António Félix „Vá" (ANG)	24.04.1998	18	(5)	3

SECOND LEVEL
Cypriot Second Division 2020/2021

1.	PAEEK Kyrenia (*Promoted*)	34	21	7	6	68	-	28	70
2.	Aris Limassol FC (*Promoted*)	34	21	10	3	50	-	22	70
3.	AC Othellos Athienou	34	20	9	5	55	-	32	69
4.	Athlitikos Omilos Ayia Napa FC	34	16	12	6	51	-	36	60
5.	Alki Oroklini FC	34	13	14	7	56	-	38	53
6.	Omonia Aradippou FC	34	15	6	13	55	-	49	51
7.	Onisilos Sotira 2014	34	13	12	9	61	-	51	48
8.	ASIL Lysi	34	13	7	14	34	-	34	46
9.	Enosis Neon Ahironas Liopetriou FC	34	12	9	13	43	-	43	45
10.	Anagennisi Deryneia FC	34	12	8	14	50	-	50	44
11.	Akritas Chlorakas FC	34	11	10	13	41	-	47	43
12.	Podosfairikos Omilos Xylotymbou 2006	34	10	11	13	42	-	45	41
13.	AME Kouris Erimi (*Relegated*)	34	10	9	15	50	-	56	39
14.	Digenis Akritas Morphou FC (*Relegated*)	34	9	10	15	43	-	53	37
15.	Athletic Union of Zakaki (*Relegated*)	34	8	10	16	32	-	51	34
16.	Omonia Psevda FD (*Relegated*)	34	9	7	18	44	-	62	28
17.	EN THOI Lakatamia (*Relegated*)	34	5	8	21	35	-	68	20
18.	Ypsonas FC (*Relegated*)	34	5	7	22	32	-	77	19

INTERNATIONAL MATCHES
(16.07.2020 – 15.07.2021)

05.09.2020	Nicosia	Cyprus - Montenegro	0-2(0-0)	(UNL)
08.09.2020	Nicosia	Cyprus - Azerbaijan	0-1(0-1)	(UNL)
07.10.2020	Larnaca	Cyprus - Czech Republic	1-2(1-2)	(F)
10.10.2020	Lëtzebuerg	Luxembourg - Cyprus	2-0(2-0)	(UNL)
13.10.2020	Elbasan	Azerbaijan - Cyprus	0-0	(UNL)
11.11.2020	Athína	Greece - Cyprus	2-1(2-0)	(F)
14.11.2020	Nicosia	Cyprus - Luxembourg	2-1(1-1)	(UNL)
17.11.2020	Podgorica	Montenegro - Cyprus	4-0(3-0)	(UNL)
24.03.2021	Nicosia	Cyprus - Slovakia	0-0	(WCQ)
27.03.2021	Rijeka	Croatia - Cyprus	1-0(1-0)	(WCQ)
30.03.2021	Nicosia	Cyprus - Slovenia	1-0(1-0)	(WCQ)
04.06.2021	Budapest	Hungary - Cyprus	1-0(1-0)	(F)
07.06.2021	Kharkiv	Ukraine - Cyprus	4-0(2-0)	(F)

05.09.2020   CYPRUS - MONTENEGRO   0-2(0-0)   2nd UEFA Nations League C, Group 1
Stádio GSP, Nicosia; Referee: Harm Osmers (Germany); Attendance: 0
CYP: Charalambos Kyriakidis, Konstantinos Laifis, Andreas Karo, Hristos Wheeler, Ioannis Kousoulos, Dimitris Christofi (Cap) (63.Loizos Loizou), Grigoris Kastanos, Marinos Tzionis (85.Andreas Avraam), Minas Antoniou, Marios Ilia (78.Pieros Sotiriou), Ioannis Pittas. Trainer: Johan Walem (Belgium).

08.09.2020   CYPRUS - AZERBAIJAN   0-1(0-1)   2nd UEFA Nations League C, Group 1
Stádio GSP, Nicosia; Referee: Filip Glova (Slovakia); Attendance: 0
CYP: Charalambos Kyriakidis, Valentinos Sielis, Konstantinos Laifis, Andreas Karo, Ioannis Kousoulos (57.Charalambos Kyriakou), Dimitris Christofi (Cap) (57.Loizos Loizou), Charalambos "Haris" Kyriakou, Grigoris Kastanos (76.Matija Špoljarić), Marinos Tzionis, Pieros Sotiriou, Ioannis Pittas. Trainer: Johan Walem (Belgium).

07.10.2020   CYPRUS - CZECH REPUBLIC   1-2(1-2)   Friendly International
AEK Arena "Georgios Karapatakis", Larnaca; Referee: Lionel Tschudi (Switzerland); Attendance: 0
CYP: Charalambos Kyriakidis, Thomas Ioannou, Andreas Karo (64.Matija Špoljarić), Ioannis Kosti (46.Kostakis Artymatas), Christos Sielis, Alexandros Gogić (46.Charalambos Kyriakou), Grigoris Kastanos (Cap) (46.Fanos Katelaris), Panayiotis Zachariou (73.Dimitris Christofi), Minas Antoniou, Andronikos Kakoullis (73.Ioannis Pittas), Loizos Loizou. Trainer: Johan Walem (Belgium).
Goal: Loizos Loizou (32).

10.10.2020   LUXEMBOURG - CYPRUS   2-0(2-0)   2nd UEFA Nations League C, Group 1
Stade "Josy Barthel", Lëtzebuerg; Referee: Donald Robertson (Scotland); Attendance: 1,334
CYP: Charalambos Kyriakidis, Konstantinos Laifis, Andreas Karo (61.Alexandros Gogić), Hristos Wheeler (53.Thomas Ioannou), Ioannis Kousoulos, Dimitris Christofi (Cap), Kostakis Artymatas (75.Charalambos Kyriakou), Grigoris Kastanos, Marinos Tzionis (46.Minas Antoniou), Pieros Sotiriou, Ioannis Pittas (75.Loizos Loizou). Trainer: Johan Walem (Belgium).

13.10.2020   AZERBAIJAN - CYPRUS   0-0   2nd UEFA Nations League C, Group 1
Elbasan Arena, Elbasan (Albania); Referee: Fran Jović (Croatia); Attendance: 0
CYP: Dimitris Dimitriou, Konstantinos Laifis, Charalambos Kyriakou (46.Panayiotis Zachariou), Andreas Karo, Hristos Wheeler, Dimitris Christofi (Cap) (69.Loizos Loizou), Kostakis Artymatas, Grigoris Kastanos, Marinos Tzionis (81.Ioannis Kousoulos), Pieros Sotiriou (19.Ioannis Pittas), Minas Antoniou. Trainer: Johan Walem (Belgium).

11.11.2020   GREECE - CYPRUS   2-1(2-0)   Friendly International
Stádio "Georgios Kamaras", Athína; Referee: Harm Osmers (Germany); Attendance: 0
CYP: Dimitris Dimitriou, Charalambos Kyriakou , Nicholas Ioannou (62.Thomas Ioannou), Christos Sielis (75.Vasilios Papafotis), Charalambos "Haris" Kyriakou (62.Ioannis Kousoulos), Kostakis Artymatas (Cap), Alexandros Gogić (46.Grigoris Kastanos), Fanos Katelaris (46.Andreas Karo), Minas Antoniou, Marios Ilia (86.Marinos Tzionis), Ioannis Pittas. Trainer: Johan Walem (Belgium).
Goal: Marios Ilia (58).

14.11.2020   CYPRUS - LUXEMBOURG   2-1(1-1)   2nd UEFA Nations League C, Group 1
Stádio GSP, Nicosia; Referee: Referee: Mattias Gestranius (Finland); Attendance: 0
CYP: Dimitris Dimitriou, Konstantinos Laifis, Nicholas Ioannou, Ioannis Kousoulos (62.Charalambos Kyriakou), Christos Sielis, Kostakis Artymatas (Cap), Grigoris Kastanos (82.Vasilios Papafotis), Marinos Tzionis (62.Thomas Ioannou), Minas Antoniou (82.Charalambos "Haris" Kyriakou), Marios Ilia, Ioannis Pittas. Trainer: Johan Walem (Belgium).
Goals: Grigoris Kastanos (34 penalty, 71).

17.11.2020   MONTENEGRO - CYPRUS   4-0(3-0)   2nd UEFA Nations League C, Group 1
Stadion pod Goricom, Gorica; Referee: Eitan Shemeulevitch (Israel); Attendance: 0
CYP: Dimitris Dimitriou, Konstantinos Laifis, Thomas Ioannou (66.Loizos Loizou), Nicholas Ioannou, Ioannis Kousoulos (65.Alexandros Gogić), Christos Sielis, Charalambos "Haris" Kyriakou, Kostakis Artymatas (Cap) (46.Charalambos Kyriakou), Grigoris Kastanos (85.Andreas Makris), Ioannis Pittas, Andronikos Kakoullis (65.Marinos Tzionis). Trainer: Johan Walem (Belgium).

24.03.2021   CYPRUS - SLOVAKIA   0-0   22nd FIFA WC. Qualifiers
Stádio GSP, Nicosia; Referee: Aleksandar Stavrev (North Macedonia); Attendance: 0
CYP: Dimitris Dimitriou, Konstantinos Laifis, Konstantinos Sotiriou, Nicholas Ioannou, Ioannis Kousoulos, Kostakis Artymatas (Cap), Grigoris Kastanos (66.Charalambos Kyriakou), Fotios Papoulis (72.Loizos Loizou), Pieros Sotiriou (90+2.Marios Ilia), Minas Antoniou, Ioannis Pittas. Trainer: Nikolaos Kostenoglou (Greece).

27.03.2021   **CROATIA - CYPRUS**   **1-0(1-0)**   22nd FIFA WC. Qualifiers

Stadion Rujevica, Rijeka; Referee: Kristo Tohver (Estonia); Attendance: 0
CYP: Dimitris Dimitriou (39.Neofytos Michael), Konstantinos Laifis (82.Stelios Andreou), Charalambos Kyriakou , Konstantinos Sotiriou, Nicholas Ioannou, Ioannis Kousoulos, Paris Psaltis, Kostakis Artymatas (Cap) (67.Grigoris Kastanos), Marinos Tzionis (67.Fotios Papoulis), Marios Ilia (46.Pieros Sotiriou), Ioannis Pittas. Trainer: Nikolaos Kostenoglou (Greece).

30.03.2021   **CYPRUS - SLOVENIA**   **1-0(1-0)**   22nd FIFA WC. Qualifiers

Stádio GSP, Nicosia; Referee: Andreas Ekberg (Sweden); Attendance: 0
CYP: Neofytos Michael, Konstantinos Laifis, Konstantinos Sotiriou, Nicholas Ioannou, Ioannis Kousoulos, Kostakis Artymatas (90+2.Alexandros Gogić), Grigoris Kastanos (60.Charalambos Kyriakou), Fotios Papoulis (82.Loizos Loizou), Pieros Sotiriou (Cap) (90+2.Marios Ilia), Minas Antoniou, Ioannis Pittas. Trainer: Nikolaos Kostenoglou (Greece).
Goal: Ioannis Pittas (42).

04.06.2021   **HUNGARY - CYPRUS**   **1-0(1-0)**   Friendly International

"Szusza Ferenc" Stadion, Budapest; Referee: Matej Jug (Slovenia); Attendance: 7,500
CYP: Neofytos Michael, Andreas Karo (78.Stelios Andreou), Konstantinos Sotiriou, Nicholas Ioannou, Paris Psaltis (71.Andreas Panayiotou Filiotis), Dimitris Christofi (Cap) (63.Marios Ilia), Andreas Avraam, Kostakis Artymatas (71.Alexandros Gogić), Grigoris Kastanos (64.Charalambos Kyriakou), Fotios Papoulis (71.Loizos Loizou), Ioannis Pittas. Trainer: Nikolaos Kostenoglou (Greece).

07.06.2021   **UKRAINE - CYPRUS**   **4-0(2-0)**   Friendly International

Metalist Oblast Sports Complex, Kharkiv; Referee: Vitālijs Spasjoņņikovs (Latvia); Attendance: 18,000
CYP: Constantinos Panayi, Charalambos Kyriakou (69.Panayiotis Zachariou), Andreas Karo, Konstantinos Sotiriou, Nicholas Ioannou, Andreas Avraam (46.Ioannis Kousoulos), Kostakis Artymatas (Cap) (78.Alexandros Gogić), Fotios Papoulis (61.Grigoris Kastanos), Andreas Panayiotou Filiotis [*sent off 36*], Marios Ilia (46.Dimitris Christofi), Ioannis Pittas (85.Loizos Loizou). Trainer: Nikolaos Kostenoglou (Greece).

NATIONAL TEAM PLAYERS
(16.07.2020 – 15.07.2021)

Name	DOB	Caps	Goals	2020/2021:	Club
Goalkeepers					
Dimitris DIMITRIOU	15.01.1999	6	0	2020/2021:	Apollon Limassol FC
Charalambos KYRIAKIDIS	30.11.1998	4	0	2020:	AC Omonia Nicosia
Neofytos MICHAEL	16.12.1993	4	0	2021:	Olympiakos Nicosia FC
Constantinos PANAYI	08.10.1994	23	0	2021:	AC Omonia Nicosia
Defenders					
Stelios ANDREOU	24.07.2002	2	0	2021:	Olympiakos Nicosia FC
Nicholas IOANNOU	10.11.1995	27	2	2020:	Nottingham Forest FC (ENG)
				08.01.2021->	Aris Thessaloníki (GRE)
Thomas IOANNOU	19.07.1995	5	0	2020:	AEK Larnaca FC
Andreas KARO	09.09.1996	9	0	2020:	US Salernitana 1919 (ITA)
				30.01.2021->	CS Marítimo Funchal (POR)
Ioannis KOUSOULOS	14.06.1996	29	4	2020/2021:	AC Omonia Nicosia
Charalambos "Haris" KYRIAKOU	15.10.1989	12	0	2020:	AEL Limassol
Konstantinos LAIFIS	19.04.1993	43	3	2020/2021:	R Standard Liège (BEL)
Andreas PANAYIOTOU Filiotis	31.05.1995	3	0	2021:	Apollon Limassol FC
Paris PSALTIS	12.11.1996	2	0	2021:	Olympiakos Nicosia FC
Christos SIELIS	02.02.2000	4	0	2020:	APOEL FC Nicosia
Valentinos SIELIS	01.03.1990	17	1	2020:	Jeju United FC (KOR)
Konstantinos SOTIRIOU	21.06.1996	5	0	2021:	Olympiakos Nicosia FC
Hristos WHEELER	29.06.1997	4	0	2020:	APOEL FC Nicosia
Midfielders					
Minas ANTONIOU	22.02.1994	10	0	2020/2021:	AEL Limassol
Kostakis ARTYMATAS	15.04.1993	49	1	2020/2021:	Anorthosis Famagusta FC
Andreas AVRAAM	06.06.1987	44	5	2020/2021:	AEL Limassol
Alexandros GOGIĆ	13.04.1994	7	0	2020/2021:	Hibernian FC Edinburgh (SCO)
Grigoris KASTANOS	30.01.1998	36	3	2020:	Juventus FC Torino (ITA)
				12.09.2020->	Frosinone Calcio (ITA)
Fanos KATELARIS	20.08.1996	10	1	2020:	Apollon Limassol FC
Ioannis KOSTI	17.03.2000	9	0	2020/2021:	AE Lárissa (GRE)
Charalambos KYRIAKOU	09.02.1995	38	0	2020/2021:	Apollon Limassol FC
Loizos LOIZOU	18.07.2003	10	1	2020/2021:	AC Omonia Nicosia
Andreas MAKRIS	27.09.1995	24	0	2020:	AEK Larnaca FC
Vasilios PAPAFOTIS	10.08.1995	4	0	2020:	AEL Limassol
Fotios PAPOULIS	22.01.1985	17	2	2021:	AC Omonia Nicosia
Ioannis PITTAS	10.07.1996	17	1	2020/2021:	Apollon Limassol FC
Matija ŠPOLJARIĆ	02.04.1997	11	0	2020:	AEK Larnaca FC
Marinos TZIONIS	17.07.2001	8	0	2020/2021:	AC Omonia Nicosia
Forwards					
Dimitris CHRISTOFI	28.09.1988	59	8	2020/2021:	Anorthosis Famagusta FC
Marios ILIA	19.05.1996	9	1	2020/2021:	Ethnikos Achna FC
Andronikos KAKOULLIS	03.05.2001	2	0	2020:	AC Omonia Nicosia
Pieros SOTIRIOU	13.01.1993	47	10	2020:	Astana FC Nur-Sultan (KAZ)
				05.02.2021->	PFC Ludogorets Razgrad (BUL)
Panayiotis ZACHARIOU	26.02.1996	7	1	2020/2021:	Olympiakos Nicosia FC
Trainer					
Johan WALEM (Belgium) [25.01.2020 – 17.02.2021]	01.02.1972	8 M; 1 W; 1 D; 6 L; 4-14			
Nikolaos KOSTENOGLOU (Greece) [from 18.02.2021]	03.10.1970	5 M; 1 W; 1 D; 3 L; 1-6			

CZECH REPUBLIC

The Country:
Česká republika (Czech Republic)
Capital: Praha
Surface: 78,866 km^2
Inhabitants: 10,701,777 [2021]
Time: UTC+1

The FA:
Fotbalová asociace České republiky
Atletická 2474/8 169 00, Praha
Tel: +420 233 029 111
Foundation date: 1901 (as Bohemia)
Member of FIFA since: 1907 (as Bohemia)
Member of UEFA since: 1954 (as Czechoslovakia)
Website: www.fotbal.cz

NATIONAL TEAM RECORDS

RECORDS		
First international match:	28.08.1920, Antwerpen: Czechoslovakia - Yugoslavia 7-0	
Most international caps:	Petr Čech	- 124 caps (2002-2016)
Most international goals:	Jan Koller	- 55 goals / 91 caps (1999-2009)

UEFA EUROPEAN CHAMPIONSHIP	
1960	Final Tournament (3rd Place)
1964	Qualifiers
1968	Qualifiers
1972	Qualifiers
1976	**Final Tournament (Winners)**
1980	Final Tournament (3rd Place)
1984	Qualifiers
1988	Qualifiers
1992	Qualifiers
1996	Final Tournament (Runners-up)
2000	Final Tournament (Group Stage)
2004	Final Tournament (Semi-Finals)
2008	Final Tournament (Group Stage)
2012	Final Tournament (Quarter-Finals)
2016	Final Tournament (Qualified)
2020	Final Tournament (Quarter-Finals)

FIFA WORLD CUP	
1930	Did not enter
1934	Final Tournament (Runners-up)
1938	Final Tournament (Quarter-Finals)
1950	Did not enter
1954	Final Tournament (Group Stage)
1958	Final Tournament (Group Stage)
1962	Final Tournament (Runners-up)
1966	Qualifiers
1970	Final Tournament (Group Stage)
1974	Qualifiers
1978	Qualifiers
1982	Final Tournament (Group Stage)
1986	Qualifiers
1990	Final Tournament (Quarter-Finals)
1994	Qualifiers
1998	Qualifiers
2002	Qualifiers
2006	Final Tournament (Group Stage)
2010	Qualifiers
2014	Qualifiers
2018	Qualifiers

OLYMPIC TOURNAMENTS	
1908	-
1912	-
1920	Runners-up
1924	1/8 Finals
1928	Did not enter
1936	Did not enter
1948	Did not enter
1952	Did not enter
1956	Did not enter
1960	Qualifiers
1964	Runners-up
1968	Group Stage
1972	Did not enter
1976	Qualifiers
1980	**Winners**
1984	Did not enter
1988	Qualifiers
1992	Qualifiers
1996	Qualifiers
2000	Group Stage
2004	Qualifiers
2008	Qualifiers
2012	Qualifiers
2016	Qualifiers

UEFA NATIONS LEAGUE	
2018/2019	League B
2020/2021	League B (promoted to League A)

FIFA CONFEDERATIONS CUP 1992-2017
1997 (3rd Place)

CZECH CLUB HONOURS IN EUROPEAN CLUB COMPETITIONS:

European Champion Clubs' Cup (1956-1992) / UEFA Champions League (1993-2021)
None

Fairs Cup (1858-1971) / UEFA Cup (1972-2009) / UEFA Europa League (2010-2021)
None

UEFA Super Cup (1972-2020)
None

*European Cup Winners' Cup 1961-1999**
None

*defunct competition

NATIONAL COMPETITIONS
TABLE OF HONOURS

CZECHOSLOVAKIA 1925-1938 / BOHEMIA-MORAVIA 1938-1944 / CZECHOSLOVAKIA 1945-1993

	CHAMPIONS	CUP WINNERS	BEST GOALSCORERS	
1925	SK Slavia Praha	-	Jan Vaník (SK Slavia Praha)	13
1925/1926	AC Sparta Praha	-	Jan Dvořáček (AC Sparta Praha)	32
1927	AC Sparta Praha	-	Antonín Puč (SK Slavia Praha) Josef Šíma (AC Sparta Praha)	13
1927/1928	SK Viktoria Žižkov	-	Karel Meduna (SK Viktoria Žižkov)	12
1928/1929	SK Slavia Praha	-	Antonín Puč (SK Slavia Praha)	13
1929/1930	SK Slavia Praha	-	František Kloz (SK Kladno)	15
1930/1931	SK Slavia Praha	-	Josef Silný (AC Sparta Praha)	18
1931/1932	AC Sparta Praha	-	Raymond Braine (AC Sparta Praha)	16
1932/1933	SK Slavia Praha	-	Gejza Kocsis (Teplitzer FK / Bohemians AFK Vršovice)	23
1933/1934	SK Slavia Praha	-	Raymond Braine (AC Sparta Praha) Jiří Sobotka (SK Slavia Praha)	18
1934/1935	SK Slavia Praha	-	František Svoboda (SK Slavia Praha)	27
1935/1936	AC Sparta Praha	-	Vojtěch Bradáč (SK Slavia Praha)	42
1936/1937	SK Slavia Praha	-	František Kloz (SK Kladno)	28
1937/1938	AC Sparta Praha	-	Josef Bican (SK Slavia Praha)	22
1938/1939	AC Sparta Praha	-	Josef Bican (SK Slavia Praha)	29
1939/1940	SK Slavia Praha	-	Josef Bican (SK Slavia Praha)	50
1940/1941	SK Slavia Praha	-	Josef Bican (SK Slavia Praha)	38
1941/1942	SK Slavia Praha	-	Josef Bican (SK Slavia Praha)	45
1942/1943	SK Slavia Praha	-	Josef Bican (SK Slavia Praha)	39
1943/1944	AC Sparta Praha	-	Josef Bican (SK Slavia Praha)	57
1944/1945	*No competition*	-	-	
1945/1946	AC Sparta Praha	-	Josef Bican (SK Slavia Praha)	31
1946/1947	SK Slavia Praha	-	Josef Bican (SK Slavia Praha)	43
1947/1948	AC Sparta Praha	-	Jaroslav Cejp (AC Sparta Praha)	21
1948	*Championship abandoned*	-	Josef Bican (Sokol Slavia Praha)	21
1949	ŠK NV Bratislava	-	Ladislav Hlaváček (ZSJ Dynamo Slavia Praha)	28
1950	ŠK NV Bratislava	-	Josef Bican (Sokol Vítkovice Železárny)	22
1951	ŠK NV Bratislava	-	Alois Jaroš (ZSJ Vodotechna Teplice)	16
1952	Sparta ČKD Sokolovo	-	Miroslav Wiecek (OKD Ostrava)	20
1953	ÚDA Praha	-	Josef Majer (DSO Baník Kladno)	13
1954	TJ Spartak Praha Sokolovo	-	Jiří Pešek (TJ Spartak Praha Sokolovo)	13
1955	ŠK Slovan Bratislava	-	Emil Pažický (ÚNV Slovan Bratislava / Jiskra Slovena Žilina)	9
1956	AS Dukla Praha	-	Milan Dvořák (AS Dukla Praha) Miroslav Wiecek (DSO Baník Ostrava)	15
1957/1958	AS Dukla Praha	-	Miroslav Wiecek (DSO Baník Ostrava)	25
1958/1959	ČH Bratislava	-	Miroslav Wiecek (DSO Baník Ostrava)	20
1959/1960	DSO Spartak Hradec Králové	-	Michal Pucher (TJ Slovan Nitra)	18
1960/1961	AS Dukla Praha	AS Dukla Praha	Rudolf Kučera (AS Dukla Praha) Ladislav Pavlovič (TJ Tatran Prešov)	17
1961/1962	AS Dukla Praha	Slovan CHZJD Bratislava	Adolf Scherer (TJ Červená Hviezda Bratislava)	24
1962/1963	AS Dukla Praha	Slovan CHZJD Bratislava	Karel Petroš (TJ Tatran Prešov)	19
1963/1964	AS Dukla Praha	Spartak Praha Sokolovo	Ladislav Pavlovič (TJ Tatran Prešov)	21
1964/1965	TJ Spartak Praha Sokolovo	AS Dukla Praha	Pavol Bencz (Jednota Trenčín)	21
1965/1966	AS Dukla Praha	AS Dukla Praha	Ladislav Michalík (TJ Baník Ostrava)	15
1966/1967	TJ Sparta ČKD Praha	Spartak Trnava	Jozef Adamec (Spartak Trnava)	21
1967/1968	Spartak TAZ Trnava	Slovan CHZJD Bratislava	Jozef Adamec (Spartak TAZ Trnava)	18
1968/1969	Spartak TAZ Trnava	AS Dukla Praha	Ladislav Petráš (AS Dukla Banská Bystrica)	20
1969/1970	Slovan CHZJD Bratislava	TJ Gottwaldov	Jozef Adamec (Spartak TAZ Trnava)	18
1970/1971	Spartak TAZ Trnava	Spartak TAZ Trnava	Jozef Adamec (Spartak TAZ Trnava) Zdeněk Nehoda (TJ Gottwaldov)	16
1971/1972	Spartak TAZ Trnava	TJ Sparta ČKD Praha	Ján Čapkovič (Slovan CHZJD Bratislava)	19
1972/1973	Spartak TAZ Trnava	TJ Baník Ostrava OKD	Ladislav Józsa (TJ Lokomotíva Košice)	21
1973/1974	Slovan CHZJD Bratislava	Slovan CHZJD Bratislava	Ladislav Józsa (TJ Lokomotíva Košice) Přemysl Bičovský (TJ Sklo Union Teplice)	17
1974/1975	Slovan CHZJD Bratislava	Spartak TAZ Trnava	Ladislav Petráš (TJ Internacionál Slovnaft Bratislava)	20
1975/1976	TJ Baník Ostrava OKD	TJ Sparta ČKD Praha	Dušan Galis (TJ VSS Košice)	21
1976/1977	ASVS Dukla Praha	TJ Lokomotíva Košice	Ladislav Józsa (TJ Lokomotíva Košice)	18
1977/1978	Zbrojovka Brno	TJ Baník Ostrava OKD	Karel Kroupa (Zbrojovka Brno)	20
1978/1979	ASVS Dukla Praha	TJ Lokomotíva Košice	Karel Kroupa (Zbrojovka Brno) Zdeněk Nehoda (ASVS Dukla Praha)	17
1979/1980	TJ Baník Ostrava OKD	TJ Sparta ČKD Praha	Werner Lička (TJ Baník Ostrava OKD)	18
1980/1981	TJ Baník Ostrava OKD	ASVS Dukla Praha	Marián Masný (Slovan CHZJD Bratislava)	16
1981/1982	ASVS Dukla Praha	Slovan CHZJD Bratislava	Peter Herda (SK Slavia IPS Praha) Ladislav Vízek (ASVS Dukla Praha)	15
1982/1983	Bohemians ČKD Praha	ASVS Dukla Praha	Pavel Chaloupka (Bohemians ČKD Praha)	17
1983/1984	TJ Sparta ČKD Praha	AC Sparta Praha	Werner Lička (TJ Baník Ostrava OKD)	20

1984/1985	TJ Sparta ČKD Praha	ASVS Dukla Praha	Ivo Knoflíček (SK Slavia IPS Praha)	21
1985/1986	TJ Vítkovice	Spartak TAZ Trnava	Stanislav Griga (TJ Sparta ČKD Praha)	19
1986/1987	TJ Sparta ČKD Praha	DAC Dunajská Streda	Václav Daněk (TJ Baník Ostrava OKD)	24
1987/1988	TJ Sparta ČKD Praha	TJ Sparta ČKD Praha	Milan Luhový (ASVS Dukla Praha)	24
1988/1989	TJ Sparta ČKD Praha	TJ Sparta ČKD Praha	Milan Luhový (ASVS Dukla Praha)	25
1989/1990	TJ Sparta ČKD Praha	ASVS Dukla Praha	Ľubomír Luhový (TJ Internacionál Slovnaft ZŤS Bratislava)	20
1990/1991	TJ Sparta Praha	FC Baník Ostrava	Roman Kukleta (TJ Sparta Praha)	17
1991/1992	ŠK Slovan Bratislava	AC Sparta Praha	Peter Dubovský (ŠK Slovan Bratislava)	27
1992/1993	AC Sparta Praha	1. FC Košice	Peter Dubovský (ŠK Slovan Bratislava)	24

CZECH REPUBLIC (Since 1993)

1993/1994	AC Sparta Praha	FK Viktoria Žižkov	Horst Siegl (AC Sparta Praha)	20
1994/1995	AC Sparta Praha	SK Hradec Králové	Radek Drulák (FK Drnovice)	15
1995/1996	SK Slavia Praha	AC Sparta Praha	Radek Drulák (FK Drnovice)	22
1996/1997	AC Sparta Praha	SK Slavia Praha	Horst Siegl (AC Sparta Praha)	19
1997/1998	AC Sparta Praha	FK Jablonec 97	Horst Siegl (AC Sparta Praha)	13
1998/1999	AC Sparta Praha	SK Slavia Praha	Horst Siegl (AC Sparta Praha)	18
1999/2000	AC Sparta Praha	FC Slovan Liberec	Vratislav Lokvenc (AC Sparta Praha)	22
2000/2001	AC Sparta Praha	FK Viktoria Žižkov	Vítězslav Tuma (FK Drnovice)	15
2001/2002	FC Slovan Liberec	SK Slavia Praha	Jiří Štajner (FC Slovan Liberec)	15
2002/2003	AC Sparta Praha	FK Teplice	Jiří Kowalík (1. FC Synot Uherské Hradiště)	16
2003/2004	FC Baník Ostrava	AC Sparta Praha	Marek Heinz (FC Baník Ostrava)	19
2004/2005	AC Sparta Praha	FC Baník Ostrava	Tomáš Jun (AC Sparta Praha)	14
2005/2006	FC Slovan Liberec	AC Sparta Praha	Milan Ivana (FC Slovácko Uherské Hradiště)	11
2006/2007	AC Sparta Praha	AC Sparta Praha	Luboš Pecka (FK Mladá Boleslav)	16
2007/2008	SK Slavia Praha	AC Sparta Praha	Václav Svěrkoš (FC Baník Ostrava)	15
2008/2009	SK Slavia Praha	FK Teplice	Andrej Kerić (FC Slovan Liberec)	15
2009/2010	AC Sparta Praha	FC Viktoria Plzeň	Michal Ordoš (Sigma Olomouc)	12
2010/2011	FC Viktoria Plzeň	FK Mladá Boleslav	David Lafata (FK Baumit Jablonec)	19
2011/2012	FC Slovan Liberec	SK Sigma Olomouc	David Lafata (FK Baumit Jablonec)	25
2012/2013	FC Viktoria Plzeň	FK Baumit Jablonec	David Lafata (FK Baumit Jablonec / AC Sparta Praha)	20
2013/2014	AC Sparta Praha	AC Sparta Praha	Josef Hušbauer (AC Sparta Praha)	18
2014/2015	FC Viktoria Plzeň	FC Slovan Liberec	David Lafata (AC Sparta Praha)	20
2015/2016	FC Viktoria Plzeň	FK Mladá Boleslav	David Lafata (AC Sparta Praha)	20
2016/2017	SK Slavia Praha	FC Fastav Zlín	Milan Škoda (SK Slavia Praha) David Lafata (AC Sparta Praha)	15
2017/2018	FC Viktoria Plzeň	SK Slavia Praha	Michael Krmenčík (FC Viktoria Plzeň)	16
2018/2019	SK Slavia Praha	SK Slavia Praha	Nikolay Komlichenko (RUS, FK Mladá Boleslav)	29
2019/2020	SK Slavia Praha	AC Sparta Praha	Petar Musa (CRO, FC Slovan Liberec / SK Slavia Praha) Libor Kozák (AC Sparta Praha)	14
2020/2021	SK Slavia Praha	SK Slavia Praha	Jan Kuchta (SK Slavia Praha) Adam Hložek (AC Sparta Praha)	15

Name changements for most important Czech clubs:

AC Sparta Praha:
1893 - Athletic Club Královské Vinohrady; 1894 - Athletic Club Sparta Praha; 1948 - Athletic Club Sparta Bubeneč; 1949 - Sokol Bratrství Sparta Praha; 1951 - Sparta ČKD Sokolovo Praha; 1953 - TJ Spartak Praha Sokolovo; 1965 - TJ Sparta ČKD Praha; 1990 - TJ Sparta Praha; 1991 - AC Sparta Praha; 1993 - AC Sparta Praha fotbal, a.s.

SK Slavia Praha:
1892 - SK ACOS Praha (Sportovní klub Akademický cyklistický odbor Slavia Praha); 1893 - SK Slavia Praha (Sportovní klub Slavia Praha); 1948 - Sokol Slavia Praha; 1949 - ZSJ Dynamo Slavia Praha (Základní sportovní jednota Dynamo Slavia Praha); 1953 - DSO Dynamo Praha (Dobrovolná sportovní organizace Dynamo Praha); 1954 - TJ Dynamo Praha (Tělovýchovná jednota Dynamo Praha); 1965 - SK Slavia Praha (Sportovní klub Slavia Praha); 1973 - TJ Slavia Praha (Tělovýchovná jednota Slavia Praha); 1977 - TJ Slavia IPS Praha (Tělovýchovná jednota Slavia Inženýrské průmyslové stavby Praha); 1978 - SK Slavia IPS Praha (Sportovní klub Slavia Inženýrské průmyslové stavby Praha); 1991 - SK Slavia Praha (Sportovní klub Slavia Praha - fotbal, a.s.)

FK Viktoria Žižkov:
1903 - Sportovní kroužek Viktoria Žižkov; 1904 - SK Viktoria Žižkov; 1950 - Sokol Viktoria Žižkov; 1951 - Sokol ČSAD Žižkov; 1952 - TJ Slavoj Žižkov (after merger with Avia Čakovice); 1965 - TJ Viktoria Žižkov; 1973 - TJ Viktoria Žižkov Strojimport; 1982 - TJ Viktoria Žižkov PSO; 1992 - FK Viktoria Žižkov.

MFK Vítkovice:
1919 - SK Slavoj Vítkovice; 1922 - SK Vítkovice; 1923 - SSK Vítkovice; 1937 - SK Železárny Vítkovice; 1939 - ČSK Vítkovice; 1945 - SK Vítkovice Železárny; 1948 - Sokol Vítkovice Železárny; 1953 - Baník Vítkovice; 1957 - TJ VŽKG Ostrava; 1979 - TJ Vítkovice; 1993 - FC Vítkovice Kovkor; 1994 - FC Karviná-Vítkovice (after merger with Kovona Karviná); 1995 - FC Vítkovice (after spliting); 2012 - MFK Vítkovice.

FK Teplice:
1945 - SK Teplice-Šanov (Sportovní klub Teplice-Šanov); 1948 - Sokol Teplice; 1949 - ZSJ Technomat Teplice (Základní sportovní jednota Technomat Teplice); 1951 - ZSJ Vodotechna Teplice; 1952 - ZSJ Ingstav Teplice; 1953 - DSO Tatran Teplice (Dobrovolná sportovní organizace Tatran Teplice); 1960 - TJ Slovan Teplice (Tělovýchovná jednota Slovan Teplice); 1966 - TJ Sklo Union Teplice; 1991 - TFK VTJ Teplice (Tělovýchovný fotbalový klub Vojenská tělovýchovná jednota Teplice); 1993 - FK Frydrych Teplice (Fotbalový klub Frydrych Teplice); 1994 - FK Teplice (Fotbalový klub Teplice, a.s.).

FK Dukla Praha:
1948 - ATK Praha (Armádní tělovýchovný klub Praha); 1953 - ÚDA Praha (Ústřední dům armády Praha); 1956 - AS Dukla Praha (Armádní středisko Dukla Praha); 1976 - ASVS Dukla Praha (Armádní středisko vrcholového sportu Dukla Praha); 1991 - FC Dukla Praha (Football Club Dukla Praha); 1994 - FK Dukla Praha (Fotbalový klub Dukla Praha); 1996 - FK Marila Příbram (after merger between FC Příbram and FC Dukla Praha); 1998 - FK Dukla Praha, o.s. (Fotbalový klub Dukla Praha, občanské sdružení); 2007 - FK Dukla Praha, a.s. (Fotbalový klub Dukla Praha, akciová společnost).

FC Baník Ostrava:
1922 - SK Slezská Ostrava (Sportovní klub Slezská Ostrava); 1945 - SK Ostrava; 1948 - Sokol Trojice Ostrava; 1951 - Sokol OKD Ostrava (Sokol Ostravsko-karvinské doly Ostrava); 1952 - DSO Baník Ostrava (Dobrovolná sportovní organizace Baník Ostrava); 1961 - TJ Baník Ostrava (Tělovýchovná jednota Baník Ostrava); 1970 - TJ Baník Ostrava OKD; 1990 - FC Baník Ostrava (Football Club Baník Ostrava, a.s.).

FC Zbrojovka Brno:
1913 - SK Židenice; 1951 - Zbrojovka Brno; 1956 - Spartak ZJŠ Brno; 1968 - Zbrojovka Brno; 1992 - Boby Brno; 2000 - Stavo Artikel Brno; 2002 - 1.FC Brno; 2010 - FC Zbrojovka Brno.

Bohemians Praha 1905:
1905 - AFK Vršovice; 1927 - Bohemians AFK Vršovice; 1941 - Bohemia AFK Vršovice; 1945 - Bohemians AFK Vršovice; 1948 - Sokol Vršovice Bohemians; 1949 - Sokol Železničáři Bohemians Praha; 1950 - Sokol Železničáři Praha; 1951 - Sokol ČKD Stalingrad Praha; 1953 - Spartak Praha Stalingrad; 1962 - ČKD Praha; 1965 - Bohemians ČKD Praha; 1993 - Bohemians Praha; 1999 - CU Bohemians Praha; 2001 - FC Bohemians Praha; 2005 - Bohemians 1905; 2013 - Bohemians Praha 1905.

Name changements for most important Slovak clubs:

FK Inter Bratislava:
1940 - ŠK Apollo Bratislava; 1945 - TKNB Bratislava; 1948 - Sokol SNB Bratislava; 1952 - TJ Červená Hviezda Bratislava; 1962 - TJ Iskra Slovnaft Bratislava; 1965 - TJ Internacionál Slovnaft Bratislava; 1986 - TJ Internacionál Slovnaft ZŤS Bratislava (after merge with TJ ZŤS Petržalka); 1991 - AŠK Inter Slovnaft Bratislava; 2004 - FK Inter Bratislava; 2009 - Sold club license to FK Senica; 2009 - Inter Bratislava; 2014 - FK Inter Bratislava a.s.

ŠK Slovan Bratislava:
1919 - 1. ČsŠK Bratislava; 1939 - ŠK Bratislava; 1948 - Sokol ŠK NV Bratislava; 1953 - ÚNV Slovan Bratislava; 1961 - Slovan CHZJD Bratislava; 1990 - ŠK Slovan Bratislava.

FC Lokomotíva Košice:
1946 - ŠK Železničiari Košice; 1946 - ŠK Železničiari Sparta Košice (Merge with ŠK Sparta Košice); 1949 - ZSJ Dynamo ČSD Košice (Merge with Sokol Jednota Dynamo Košice); 1952 - TJ Lokomotíva Košice; 1965 - TJ Lokomotíva VSŽ Košice (Merge with TJ VSŽ Košice); 1967 - TJ Lokomotíva Košice (End of merge with TJ VSŽ Košice); 1990 - FK Lokomotíva Košice; 1994 - FK Lokomotíva Energogas Košice; 1999 - FK Lokomotíva PČSP Košice; 2003 - FC Lokomotíva Košice.

FC Spartak Trnava:
1923 - ŠK Rapid Trnava; 1939 - TSS Trnava; 1948 - Sokol NV Trnava; 1949 - ZTJ Kovosmalt Trnava; 1953 - Spartak Trnava; 1967 - Spartak TAZ Trnava; 1988 - Spartak ZTS Trnava; 1993 - FC Spartak Trnava.

NATIONAL CHAMPIONSHIP
Czech First League / Fortuna Liga 2020/2021
(21.08.2020 - 29.05.2021)

Round 1 [21-23.08.2020]
Viktoria Plzeň - SFC Opava 3-1(1-1)
FC Fastav Zlín - 1. FC Slovácko 1-2(0-0)
1. FK Příbram - FK Teplice 1-3(0-1)
Sigma Olomouc - Slovan Liberec 1-0(1-0)
Zbrojovka Brno - Sparta Praha 1-4(0-4)
SK Dynamo - Slavia Praha 0-6(0-3)
FK Jablonec - FK Pardubice 1-0(0-0)
MFK Karviná - Baník Ostrava 0-0
Bohemians 1905 - Mladá Boleslav 4-0(2-0)

Round 2 [28-30.08.2020]
Baník Ostrava - SK Dynamo 2-2(1-2)
1. FC Slovácko - FK Jablonec 1-1(0-0)
Mladá Boleslav - FC Fastav Zlín 1-3(1-1)
SFC Opava - MFK Karviná 1-2(0-0)
Slavia Praha - 1. FK Příbram 3-0(2-0)
Zbrojovka Brno - Bohemians 1905 0-0
FK Pardubice - FK Teplice 2-1(1-0)
Slovan Liberec - Viktoria Plzeň 4-1(3-1)
Sparta Praha - Sigma Olomouc 3-0(2-0)

Round 3 [11-13.09.2020]
Sigma Olomouc - Bohemians 1905 3-0(1-0)
SK Dynamo - Slovan Liberec 0-2(0-1)
FK Jablonec - Baník Ostrava 2-0(0-0)
1. FK Příbram - SFC Opava 1-1(0-0)
FK Teplice - 1. FC Slovácko 0-2(0-0)
FK Pardubice - Slavia Praha 1-1(1-0)
FC Fastav Zlín - Zbrojovka Brno 3-1(1-1)
MFK Karviná - Sparta Praha 2-5(2-2)
Viktoria Plzeň - Mladá Boleslav 2-1(1-1)

Round 4 [18-21.09.2020]
Slavia Praha - FK Teplice 5-1(3-0)
Baník Ostrava - FK Pardubice 3-0(1-0)
SFC Opava - SK Dynamo 0-0
Bohemians 1905 - Viktoria Plzeň 1-4(0-2)
Zbrojovka Brno - Sigma Olomouc 2-4(1-1)
Slovan Liberec - MFK Karviná 1-1(0-0)
Sparta Praha - FC Fastav Zlín 3-1(0-1)
Mladá Boleslav - FK Jablonec 2-0(1-0)
FC Slovácko - 1. FK Příbram 5-1(1-0) [14.11.]

Round 5 [26-27.09.2020]
FC Fastav Zlín - Sigma Olomouc 0-1(0-0)
FK Teplice - Baník Ostrava 2-1(0-0)
MFK Karviná - Mladá Boleslav 0-0
Slavia Praha - 1. FC Slovácko 3-0(2-0)
FK Jablonec - SFC Opava 4-1(2-1)
FK Pardubice - Slovan Liberec 3-0(2-0)
Viktoria Plzeň - Zbrojovka Brno 4-1(2-0)
1. FK Příbram - Sparta Praha 1-3(1-2)
SK Dynamo - Bohemians 2-1(2-0) [25.11.]

Round 6 [02-04.10.2020]
1. FC Slovácko - FK Pardubice 0-1(0-0)
Zbrojovka Brno - MFK Karviná 0-2(0-0)
Mladá Boleslav - SK Dynamo 2-2(2-1)
SFC Opava - FK Teplice 2-1(1-1)
Sparta Praha - FK Jablonec 2-1(2-0)
Bohemians 1905 - FC Fastav Zlín 2-0(1-0)
Sigma Olomouc - Viktoria Plzeň 2-2(1-1)
Slovan Liberec - 1. FK Příbram 3-0(0-0)
Baník Ostrava - Slavia Praha 0-1(0-0)

Round 7 [06-08.11.2020]
FK Jablonec - Zbrojovka Brno 0-1(0-0)
FK Pardubice - SFC Opava 1-0(0-0)
1. FC Slovácko - Sigma Olomouc 0-0
SK Dynamo - FC Fastav Zlín 1-2(1-0)
1. FK Příbram - Baník Ostrava 0-4(0-0)
FK Teplice - Slovan Liberec 1-2(1-2)
MFK Karviná - Bohemians 1905 2-1(1-0)
Slavia Praha - Mladá Boleslav 1-0(1-0)
Viktoria Plzeň - Sparta Praha 3-1(3-0)

Round 8 [20-22.11.2020]
Slovan Liberec - FK Jablonec 1-3(1-1)
Mladá Boleslav - FK Pardubice 4-1(3-0)
Bohemians 1905 - FK Teplice 2-0(1-0)
Sigma Olomouc - MFK Karviná 3-0(1-0)
SFC Opava - Slavia Praha 0-6(0-1)
Zbrojovka Brno - 1. FK Příbram 1-1(1-0)
FC Fastav Zlín - Viktoria Plzeň 1-0(1-0)
Sparta Praha - SK Dynamo 2-4(1-1)
Baník Ostr. - FC Slovácko 1-2(0-0) [20.01.21]

Round 9 [27-29.11.2020]
FK Pardubice - Sigma Olomouc 1-1(0-0)
1. FK Příbram - Mladá Boleslav 2-1(0-1)
1. FC Slovácko - SFC Opava 3-1(3-1)
MFK Karviná - FC Fastav Zlín 0-2(0-2)
SK Dynamo - Viktoria Plzeň 0-0
FK Teplice - Sparta Praha 0-1(0-0)
Slavia Praha - Zbrojovka Brno 1-1(0-0)
Jablonec - Bohemians 2-1(1-0) [08.12.2020]
Baník Ostr.-Slovan Lib. 1-0(1-0) [27.01.2021]

Round 10 [04-07.12.2020]
FC Fastav Zlín - FK Jablonec 0-2(0-0)
Bohemians 1905 - FK Pardubice 1-1(1-0)
SFC Opava - Baník Ostrava 1-2(0-0)
Sigma Olomouc - 1. FK Příbram 1-1(1-0)
Viktoria Plzeň - MFK Karviná 0-1(0-1)
Zbrojovka Brno - SK Dynamo 1-3(0-2)
Mladá Boleslav - FK Teplice 0-2(0-1)
Sparta Praha - Slavia Praha 0-3(0-2)
Slovan Liberec - 1. FC Slovácko 1-1(1-0)

Round 11 [11-13.12.2020]
Baník Ostrava - Bohemians 1905 1-0(1-0)
SK Dynamo - MFK Karviná 1-1(0-1)
1. FK Příbram - FC Fastav Zlín 1-0(0-0)
SFC Opava - Mladá Boleslav 2-2(2-1)
FK Pardubice - Zbrojovka Brno 2-1(0-0)
FK Teplice - Sigma Olomouc 1-1(0-1)
FK Jablonec - Viktoria Plzeň 3-2(0-2)
1. FC Slovácko - Sparta Praha 1-2(1-1)
Slavia Praha - Slovan Liberec 3-0(2-0)

Round 12 [15-16.12.2020]
Mladá Boleslav - Baník Ostrava 1-3(0-2)
MFK Karviná - FK Jablonec 2-2(0-1)
Bohemians 1905 - 1. FK Příbram 2-1(1-1)
Sigma Olomouc - SK Dynamo 1-1(1-0)
Viktoria Plzeň - FK Teplice 7-0(3-0)
Zbrojovka Brno - 1. FC Slovácko 2-1(0-0)
Slovan Liberec - SFC Opava 2-0(2-0)
Sparta Praha - FK Pardubice 2-0(1-0)
Fastav Zlín - Slavia Praha 2-6(0-5) [27.01.21]

Round 13 [18-20.12.2020]
Baník Ostrava - Sigma Olomouc 1-1(0-0)
FK Jablonec - SK Dynamo 2-1(1-0)
1. FK Příbram - MFK Karviná 0-1(0-1)
Slovan Liberec - Mladá Boleslav 3-0(2-0)
FK Pardubice - FC Fastav Zlín 0-0
FK Teplice - Zbrojovka Brno 1-0(0-0)
1. FC Slovácko - Viktoria Plzeň 4-0(1-0)
Slavia Praha - Bohemians 1905 2-1(1-0)
SFC Opava - Sparta Praha 0-3(0-1) [20.01.21]

Round 14 [22-23.12.2020]
Sigma Olomouc - FK Jablonec 1-3(1-1)
Sparta Praha - Slovan Liberec 1-1(0-1)
Zbrojovka Brno - Baník Ostrava 0-1(0-1)
FC Fastav Zlín - FK Teplice 2-3(1-2)
Mladá Boleslav - 1. FC Slovácko 2-3(1-1)
MFK Karviná - FK Pardubice 0-2(0-1)
Viktoria Plzeň - Slavia Praha 0-1(0-1)
SK Dynamo - FK Příbram 2-1(0-1) [20.01.21]
Bohemians - SFC Opava 0-0 [27.01.2021]

Round 15 [15-17.01.2021]
FK Teplice - FK Jablonec 0-5(0-3)
Mladá Boleslav - Zbrojovka Brno 1-1(0-1)
SFC Opava - FC Fastav Zlín 0-0
1. FC Slovácko - MFK Karviná 2-0(0-0)
Slovan Liberec - Bohemians 1905 1-1(1-0)
Slavia Praha - Sigma Olomouc 3-1(2-1)
FK Pardubice - SK Dynamo 0-2(0-0)
1. FK Příbram - Viktoria Plzeň 0-0
Baník Ostrava - Sparta Praha 0-0

Round 16 [22-24.01.2021]
Zbrojovka Brno - Slovan Liberec 0-3(0-2)
Sigma Olomouc - SFC Opava 4-1(2-0)
Bohemians 1905 - 1. FC Slovácko 1-3(0-3)
FC Fastav Zlín - Baník Ostrava 1-1(1-1)
MFK Karviná - Slavia Praha 1-3(0-0)
SK Dynamo - FK Teplice 2-0(1-0)
FK Jablonec - 1. FK Příbram 2-1(0-0)
Viktoria Plzeň - FK Pardubice 2-0(0-0)
Sparta Praha - Mladá Boleslav 1-0(0-0)

Round 17 [30.01.-02.02.2021]
FK Teplice - MFK Karviná 2-2(2-0)
1. FC Slovácko - SK Dynamo 0-0
FK Pardubice - 1. FK Příbram 1-0(0-0)
Sparta Praha - Bohemians 1905 0-1(0-1)
SFC Opava - Zbrojovka Brno 0-2(0-1)
Baník Ostrava - Viktoria Plzeň 0-2(0-0)
Slavia Praha - FK Jablonec 3-0(2-0)
Mladá Boleslav - Sigma Olomouc 1-1(1-0)
Slovan Liber. - Fastav Zlín 1-0(0-0) [17.02.21]

Round 18 [05-07.02.2021]
SK Dynamo - Baník Ostrava 1-0(0-0)
Bohemians 1905 - Zbrojovka Brno 2-1(2-1)
MFK Karviná - SFC Opava 3-1(0-0)
Viktoria Plzeň - Slovan Liberec 0-2(0-0)
FK Teplice - FK Pardubice 0-1(0-0)
1. FK Příbram - Slavia Praha 3-3(2-1)
Sigma Olomouc - Sparta Praha 2-3(1-0)
Jablonec - 1. FC Slovácko 0-3(0-1) [24.02.]
Fastav Zlín - Mladá Boleslav 2-1(0-0) [24.02.]

Round 19 [12-14.02.2021]
1. FC Slovácko - FK Teplice 2-0(1-0)
Zbrojovka Brno - FC Fastav Zlín 0-0
SFC Opava - 1. FK Příbram 0-0
Slavia Praha - FK Pardubice 3-0(2-0)
Baník Ostrava - FK Jablonec 2-1(2-1)
Bohemians 1905 - Sigma Olomouc 0-0
Mladá Boleslav - Viktoria Plzeň 2-2(1-1)
Slovan Liberec - SK Dynamo 0-0
Sparta Praha - MFK Karviná 4-3(3-2)

Round 20 [19-21.02.2021]
FK Jablonec - Mladá Boleslav 1-1(1-1)
FK Pardubice - Baník Ostrava 3-2(1-0)
1. FK Příbram - 1. FC Slovácko 1-4(0-2)
Sigma Olomouc - Zbrojovka Brno 1-0(0-0)
FC Fastav Zlín - Sparta Praha 0-3(0-2)
SK Dynamo - SFC Opava 0-1(0-0)
MFK Karviná - Slovan Liberec 1-1(0-0)
Viktoria Plzeň - Bohemians 1905 3-1(1-0)
FK Teplice - Slavia Praha 1-1(0-1)

Round 21 [26-28.02.2021]
Slovan Liberec - FK Pardubice 4-1(4-0)
SFC Opava - FK Jablonec 0-1(0-0)
Baník Ostrava - FK Teplice 1-1(0-0)
Bohemians 1905 - SK Dynamo 1-1(0-0)
Zbrojovka Brno - Viktoria Plzeň 0-1(0-0)
Mladá Boleslav - MFK Karviná 2-0(2-0)
Sigma Olomouc - FC Fastav Zlín 0-1(0-1)
1. FC Slovácko - Slavia Praha 2-3(2-1)
Sparta Praha - 1. FK Příbram 4-0(2-0) [09.03.]

Round 22 [06-07.03.2021]
1. FK Příbram - Slovan Liberec 0-2(0-0)
FC Fastav Zlín - Bohemians 1905 0-0
FK Teplice - SFC Opava 3-1(1-1)
Viktoria Plzeň - Sigma Olomouc 1-0(0-0)
SK Dynamo - Mladá Boleslav 1-3(0-1)
MFK Karviná - Zbrojovka Brno 1-1(1-0)
Slavia Praha - Baník Ostrava 2-1(2-1)
Pardubice - 1. FC Slovácko 3-1(2-1) [13.04.]
FK Jablonec - Sparta Praha 1-0(0-0) [14.04.]

Round 23 [12-14.03.2021]
Slovan Liberec - FK Teplice 2-1(0-1)
SFC Opava - FK Pardubice 1-0(1-0)
Baník Ostrava - 1. FK Příbram 5-0(2-0)
FC Fastav Zlín - SK Dynamo 3-0(1-0)
Bohemians 1905 - MFK Karviná 2-0(1-0)
Zbrojovka Brno - FK Jablonec 1-2(0-1)
Mladá Boleslav - Slavia Praha 0-3(0-2)
Sigma Olomouc - 1. FC Slovácko 0-0 [06.04.
Sparta Praha - Viktoria Plzeň 3-1(0-1) [12.05.]

Round 24 [19-21.03.2021]
FK Pardubice - Mladá Boleslav 2-2(1-0)
1. FK Příbram - Zbrojovka Brno 1-1(0-1)
MFK Karviná - Sigma Olomouc 0-1(0-0)
FK Jablonec - Slovan Liberec 2-1(1-0)
1. FC Slovácko - Baník Ostrava 2-1(2-0)
FK Teplice - Bohemians 1905 1-1(0-0)
SK Dynamo - Sparta Praha 0-0
Slavia Praha - SFC Opava 4-0(1-0)
Viktoria Plzeň - Fastav Zlín 2-0(1-0) [14.04.]

Round 25 [02-04.04.2021]
Bohemians 1905 - FK Jablonec 0-0
Sigma Olomouc - FK Pardubice 0-1(0-0)
SFC Opava - 1. FC Slovácko 1-2(0-0)
Slovan Liberec - Baník Ostrava 0-0
Sparta Praha - FK Teplice 7-2(4-1)
FC Fastav Zlín - MFK Karviná 1-2(1-1)
Mladá Boleslav - 1. FK Příbram 0-0
Viktoria Plzeň - SK Dynamo 2-1(1-1)
Zbrojovka Brno - Slavia Praha 0-0

Round 26 [09-11.04.2021]
FK Pardubice - Bohemians 1905 0-2(0-1)
FK Jablonec - FC Fastav Zlín 3-1(0-0)
1. FK Příbram - Sigma Olomouc 0-2(0-0)
MFK Karviná - Viktoria Plzeň 1-1(1-0)
Baník Ostrava - SFC Opava 3-0(2-0)
1. FC Slovácko - Slovan Liberec 1-0(0-0)
SK Dynamo - Zbrojovka Brno 0-2(0-0)
FK Teplice - Mladá Boleslav 1-3(1-1)
Slavia Praha - Sparta Praha 2-0(1-0)

Round 27 [16-18.04.2021]
Bohemians 1905 - Baník Ostrava 1-1(0-0)
Mladá Boleslav - SFC Opava 2-0(0-0)
MFK Karviná - SK Dynamo 3-0(2-0)
Sigma Olomouc - FK Teplice 1-1(1-0)
Viktoria Plzeň - FK Jablonec 1-1(1-0)
Zbrojovka Brno - FK Pardubice 1-2(0-1)
FC Fastav Zlín - 1. FK Příbram 0-1(0-0)
Slovan Liberec - Slavia Praha 0-1(0-0)
Sparta Praha - 1. FC Slovácko 1-0(0-0)

Round 28 [20-21.04.2021]
Baník Ostrava - Mladá Boleslav 2-1(0-1)
SK Dynamo - Sigma Olomouc 2-2(2-0)
FK Jablonec - MFK Karviná 3-0(3-0)
1. FC Slovácko - Zbrojovka Brno 4-2(2-1)
1. FK Příbram - Bohemians 1905 1-4(0-0)
FK Teplice - Viktoria Plzeň 0-1(0-0)
SFC Opava - Slovan Liberec 0-2(0-2)
FK Pardubice - Sparta Praha 2-2(0-2)
Slavia Praha - FC Fastav Zlín 2-1(1-1)

Round 29 [24-25.04.2021]
SK Dynamo - FK Jablonec 0-2(0-2)
Sigma Olomouc - Baník Ostrava 0-2(0-1)
Mladá Boleslav - Slovan Liberec 0-1(0-1)
Viktoria Plzeň - 1. FC Slovácko 2-1(1-1)
Zbrojovka Brno - FK Teplice 0-0
FC Fastav Zlín - FK Pardubice 0-4(0-2)
MFK Karviná - 1. FK Příbram 0-1(0-1)
Sparta Praha - SFC Opava 4-2(2-0)
Bohemians 1905 - Slavia Praha 0-0

Round 30 [01-02.05.2021]
1. FK Příbram - SK Dynamo 0-1(0-1)
SFC Opava - Bohemians 1905 1-1(1-0)
1. FC Slovácko - Mladá Boleslav 0-1(0-1)
Baník Ostrava - Zbrojovka Brno 1-0(0-0)
FK Jablonec - Sigma Olomouc 3-1(1-0)
FK Pardubice - MFK Karviná 2-2(1-1)
FK Teplice - FC Fastav Zlín 0-0
Slovan Liberec - Sparta Praha 2-2(1-0)
Slavia Praha - Viktoria Plzeň 5-1(2-0)

Round 31 [07-09.05.2021]
FK Jablonec - FK Teplice 4-1(2-0)
FC Fastav Zlín - SFC Opava 1-0(0-1)
Zbrojovka Brno - Mladá Boleslav 2-3(0-2)
Viktoria Plzeň - 1. FK Příbram 3-3(1-2)
Bohemians 1905 - Slovan Liberec 3-0(0-0)
SK Dynamo - FK Pardubice 2-0(1-0)
MFK Karviná - 1. FC Slovácko 0-2(0-1)
Sigma Olomouc - Slavia Praha 0-1(0-0)
Sparta Praha - Baník Ostrava 3-1(1-0)

Round 32 [14-16.05.2021]
Slovan Liberec - Zbrojovka Brno 1-1(0-0)
SFC Opava - Sigma Olomouc 1-2(0-0)
Baník Ostrava - FC Fastav Zlín 4-2(2-0)
1. FK Příbram - FK Jablonec 1-0(0-0)
1. FC Slovácko - Bohemians 1905 1-1(1-0)
FK Pardubice - Viktoria Plzeň 3-0(1-0)
FK Teplice - SK Dynamo 2-0(0-0)
Mladá Boleslav - Sparta Praha 4-5(2-2)
Slavia Praha - MFK Karviná 1-1(1-0)

Round 33 [23.05.2021]
Zbrojovka Brno - SFC Opava 4-1(2-0)
Bohemians 1905 - Sparta Praha 1-2(1-1)
SK Dynamo - 1. FC Slovácko 0-1(0-1)
FC Fastav Zlín - Slovan Liberec 0-0
FK Jablonec - Slavia Praha 1-1(1-1)
1. FK Příbram - FK Pardubice 0-1(0-1)
MFK Karviná - FK Teplice 2-0(1-0)
Sigma Olomouc - Mladá Boleslav 0-3(0-1)
Viktoria Plzeň - Baník Ostrava 4-0(1-0)

Final Standings

								Total						Home						Away		
1.	**SK Slavia Praha**	34	26	8	0	85	-	20	86	15	2	0	45	-	9	11	6	0	40	-	11
2.	AC Sparta Praha	34	23	5	6	82	-	43	74	13	1	3	46	-	21	10	4	3	36	-	22
3.	FK Jablonec	34	21	6	7	59	-	33	69	13	2	2	34	-	16	8	4	5	25	-	17
4.	1. FC Slovácko Uherské Hradiště	34	19	6	9	58	-	33	63	9	4	4	30	-	14	10	2	5	28	-	19
5.	FC Viktoria Plzeň	34	17	7	10	60	-	45	58	12	2	3	39	-	15	5	5	7	21	-	30
6.	FC Slovan Liberec	34	14	10	10	44	-	32	52	7	7	3	27	-	15	7	3	7	17	-	17
7.	FK Pardubice	34	15	7	12	41	-	42	52	8	6	3	26	-	18	7	1	9	15	-	24
8.	FC Baník Ostrava	34	13	10	11	48	-	38	49	8	6	3	28	-	15	5	4	8	20	-	23
9.	SK Sigma Olomouc	34	11	12	11	40	-	40	45	5	5	7	20	-	20	6	7	4	20	-	20
10.	Bohemians Praha 1905	34	10	13	11	40	-	37	43	7	7	3	23	-	14	3	6	8	17	-	23
11.	FK Mladá Boleslav	34	10	9	15	49	-	54	39	5	5	7	27	-	28	5	4	8	22	-	26
12.	MFK Karviná	34	9	12	13	37	-	49	39	4	6	7	18	-	23	5	6	6	19	-	26
13.	SK Dynamo České Budějovice	34	9	11	14	33	-	47	38	5	4	8	14	-	24	4	7	6	19	-	23
14.	FC Fastav Zlín	34	8	8	18	30	-	50	32	4	4	9	17	-	28	4	4	9	13	-	22
15.	FK Teplice	34	7	9	18	34	-	66	30	4	6	7	17	-	24	3	3	11	17	-	42
16.	FC Zbrojovka Brno (Relegated)	34	5	11	18	33	-	57	26	2	5	10	15	-	28	3	6	8	18	-	29
17.	1. FK Příbram (Relegated)	34	5	10	19	26	-	65	25	3	4	10	13	-	31	2	6	9	13	-	34
18.	Slezský FC Opava (Relegated)	34	3	8	23	23	-	71	17	2	5	10	11	-	29	1	3	13	12	-	42

	Top goalscorers:	
15	Jan Kuchta	*SK Slavia Praha*
15	Adam Hložek	*AC Sparta Praha*
14	Martin Doležal	*FK Jablonec*
13	Ivan Schranz (SVK)	*FK Jablonec*

NATIONAL CUP
Pohár Českomoravského fotbalového svazu / MOL Cup 2020/2021

Please note: a lot of teams decided not to follow the required COVID-19 testing protocols. Their matches were awarded as a 3-0 win for the opponents.

Second Round [13.09./15-16.09./22-23.09.2020]

SFK Vrchovina - FC Vysočina Jihlava	1-2		TJ Unie Hlubina - MFK Karviná	0-6
FK Frýdek-Místek - FK Blansko	0-3 *awarded*		FC Odra Petřkovice - SK Sigma Olomouc	0-3 *awarded*
FK Olympie Březová - FC Hradec Králové	0-3 *awarded*		TJ Jiskra Ústí nad Orlicí - FC Fastav Zlín	1-0
SK Benešov - FK Teplice	0-3		FC Velké Meziříčí - 1. SK Prostějov	0-3 *awarded*
SK Hanácká Slávia Kroměříž - Slezský FC Opava	0-3 *awarded*		Sokol Hostouň - FK Mladá Boleslav	0-1
SK Český Brod - FK Chlumec nad Cidlinou	0-3 *awarded*		FK Loko Vltavín - 1. FK Příbram	0-3 *awarded*
TJ Jiskra Domažlice - FK Ústí nad Labem	2-0		FC Slovan Velvary - Bohemians Praha 1905	0-2
SK Vysoké Mýto - FK Přepeře	1-2		TJ Sokol Srbice - FC Sellier & Bellot Vlašim	0-3 *awarded*
Povltavská FA - FK MAS Táborsko	0-3 *awarded*		SK Motorlet Praha - MFK Chrudim	0-3 *awarded*
1. SC Znojmo - SK Líšeň	0-3 *awarded*		SK Aritma Praha - FK Dukla Praha	0-3 *awarded*
FC Hlučín - FK Fotbal Třinec	0-3 *awarded*		FK Baník Most - Souš - SK Dynamo Če. Budějovice	0-3
MFK Vyškov - 1. FC Slovácko Uherské Hradiště	0-3 *awarded*		FK Kolín - FK Viktoria Žižkov	0-3 *awarded*
SK Beskyd Frenstat - FC Baník Ostrava	0-4		FC Slavia Karlovy Vary - FC Slavoj Vyšehrad	3-0 *awarded*
FC Slovan Rosice - FC Zbrojovka Brno	0-3 *awarded*			

Third Round [30.09. & 06-09.10.2020/09-11.02. & 23.02.2021]

FK Chlumec nad Cidlinou - FK Teplice	1-3(0-3)		FC Hradec Králové - 1. FK Příbram	2-1(0-0,1-1)
MFK Karviná - FC Sellier & Bellot Vlašim	1-3(0-2)		SK Slavia Praha - FK Dukla Praha	4-1(3-0)
FK MAS Táborsko - Bohemians Praha 1905	0-3(0-0)		FC Slavia Karlovy Vary - Slezský FC Opava	3-0(1-0)
AC Sparta Praha - FK Blansko	2-0(0-0)		FK Jablonec - SK Líšeň	3-0 *awarded*
1. FC Slovácko Uherské Hradiště - 1. SK Prostějov	6-0(4-0)		SK Sigma Olomouc - TJ Jiskra Domažlice	3-1(1-1)
TJ Jiskra Ústí nad Orlicí - SK Dynamo Č. Budějovice	0-3 *awarded*		FC Viktoria Plzeň - FK Přepeře	7-0(5-0)
FC Zbrojovka Brno - FC Vysočina Jihlava	1-0(0-0)		FC Slovan Liberec - FK Viktoria Žižkov	3-1(1-0,1-1)
MFK Chrudim - FK Mladá Boleslav	1-1 aet; 6-7 pen		FC Baník Ostrava - FK Fotbal Třinec	2-0(0-0)

1/8-Finals [02-03.03./09.03./17.03./26-27.03.2021]				
FC Viktoria Plzeň - FC Hradec Králové	3-1(2-0)		Bohemians Praha 1905 - SK Sigma Olomouc	0-2(0-1)
FK Teplice - FC Zbrojovka Brno	2-0(0-0)		AC Sparta Praha - FC Baník Ostrava	1-0(0-0)
FC Slovan Liberec - SK Dynamo České Budějovice	1-0(0-0)		FK Mladá Boleslav - 1. FC Slovácko Uh. Hradiště	4-2(0-1,2-2)
SK Slavia Praha - FC Slavia Karlovy Vary	10-3(6-1)		FC Sellier & Bellot Vlašim - FK Jablonec	2-3(0-1)

Quarter-Finals [07.04./28.04.2021]				
FK Teplice - FK Mladá Boleslav	2-1(1-0)		FC Viktoria Plzeň - FC Slovan Liberec	1-0(0-0)
AC Sparta Praha - FK Jablonec	4-1(0-0)		SK Sigma Olomouc - SK Slavia Praha	0-3(0-1)

Semi-Finals [28.04./05.05.2021]				
FC Viktoria Plzeň - FK Teplice	1-0(0-0)		AC Sparta Praha - SK Slavia Praha	0-3(0-2)

Final

20.05.2021; Doosan Arena, Plzeň; Referee: Roman Hrubeš; Attendance: 0
FC Viktoria Plzeň - SK Slavia Praha   0-1(0-0)

Viktoria Plzeň: Jindřich Staněk, Lukáš Hejda, Matěj Hybš, Jakub Brabec, Milan Havel [*sent off 54*], Pavel Bucha (84.Ondřej Mihálik), Šimon Falta, Lukáš Kalvach, Aleš Čermák (89.Zdeněk Ondrášek), Pavel Šulc (74.Joel Kayamba), Jean-David Beauguel (84.Adriel Ba Loua). Trainer: Michal Bílek.

Slavia Praha: Ondřej Kolář, Simon Deli (80.David Zima), Alexander Bah, Ondřej Kúdela, Jan Bořil, Nicolae Claudiu Stanciu (80.Ondřej Lingr), Lukáš Masopust (60.Ibrahim Traoré), Oscar Dorley, Petr Ševčík, Jakub Hromada (60.Abdallah Sima), Jan Kuchta (80.Mick van Buren). Trainer: Jindřich Trpišovský.

Goal: 0-1 Abdallah Sima (73)

THE CLUBS 2020/2021

Football Club Baník Ostrava

Founded:	1922 (*as SK Slezská Ostrava*)	
Stadium:	Městský stadion, Ostrava (15,123)	
Trainer:	Luboš Kozel	16.03.1971
[27.02.2021]	Ondřej Smetana	04.09.1982

Goalkeepers:	DOB	M	(s)	G
Viktor Budinský (SVK)	09.05.1993	1		
Jan Laštůvka	07.07.1982	32		
Radovan Murin	03.06.1999	1		
Defenders:	DOB	M	(s)	G
Oleksandr Azatskyi (UKR)	13.01.1994		(3)	
Jiří Fleišman	02.10.1984	23	(2)	
Jan Juroška	02.03.1993	7	(2)	
Gigli Ndefe (NED)	02.03.1994	15	(6)	1
Jakub Pokorný	11.09.1996	21	(9)	1
Muhammed Sanneh (GAM)	19.02.2000	5		
Patrizio Stronati	17.11.1994	30		2
Jaroslav Svozil	09.09.1993	18	(7)	1
Midfielders:	DOB	M	(s)	G
David Buchta	27.06.1999	9	(13)	6
Jakub Drozd	13.06.2003		(1)	
Martin Fillo	07.02.1986	22	(10)	
Daniel Holzer	18.08.1995	20	(7)	1

Adam Jánoš	20.07.1992	30	(1)	1
Milan Jirásek	14.05.1992	2	(4)	
Filip Kaloč	27.02.2000	19	(5)	1
Nemanja Kuzmanović (SRB)	27.05.1989	14	(13)	1
José Mena Rodríguez „Pepe Mena" (ESP)	15.05.1998	4	(6)	
Rudolf Reiter	28.09.1994	1	(2)	
Daniel Tetour	17.07.1994	31	(2)	5
Forwards:	DOB	M	(s)	G
Dyjan Carlos De Azevedo (BRA)	23.06.1991	22	(5)	11
Ondřej Chvěja	17.07.1998		(3)	1
Milan Lalkovič (SVK)	09.12.1992	1	(1)	
Roman Potočný	25.04.1991	9	(7)	3
Ondřej Šašinka	21.03.1998	12	(15)	1
Daniel Šmiga	02.01.2004	1	(3)	
Yira Sor (NGA)	24.07.2000	1	(8)	
Muhamed Tijani (NGA)	26.07.2000	3	(8)	1
Tomáš Zajíc	12.08.1996	20	(10)	8

Bohemians Praha 1905

Founded:	1905	
Stadium:	Stadion Ďolíček, Praha (5,000)	
Trainer:	Luděk Klusáček	09.02.1967

Goalkeepers:	DOB	M	(s)	G
Hugo Bačkovský	10.10.1999	5		
Marek Kouba	01.11.1998	2		
Patrik Lé Giang (SVK)	08.09.1992	27		
Defenders:	DOB	M	(s)	G
Jiří Bederka	18.02.1995	24	(3)	
Martin Dostál	23.09.1989	25	(3)	1
Lukáš Hůlka	31.03.1995	20		2
Adam Kadlec	06.07.2003		(2)	
Daniel Kosek	19.05.2001	1	(9)	
Daniel Köstl	23.05.1998	19	(1)	
Daniel Krch	20.03.1992	16	(2)	
Lukáš Pokorný	05.07.1993		(1)	
Till Schumacher (GER)	10.12.1997	15	(5)	1
Jan Vondra	13.09.1995	25	(3)	1
Midfielders:	DOB	M	(s)	G
David Bartek	13.02.1988	5	(5)	3

Filip Hašek	20.03.1997	1	(2)	
Petr Hronek	04.07.1993	28	(3)	4
Josef Jindřišek	14.02.1981	16	(5)	1
Roman Květ	17.12.1997	24	(7)	2
Vladislav Levin (RUS)	28.03.1995	26	(1)	1
Lukáš Musil	05.03.2001		(1)	
Vojtěch Novák	20.01.2002	7	(15)	3
Kamil Vacek	18.05.1987	10	(8)	1
Antonín Vaníček	22.04.1998	21	(6)	1
Jan Vodháněl	25.04.1997	1	(5)	
Forwards:	DOB	M	(s)	G
Ibrahim Keïta (FRA)	18.01.1996	4	(19)	3
Tomáš Necid	13.08.1989	18	(9)	5
Jakub Nečas	26.01.1995		(10)	
Pavel Osmančík	26.02.2000	3	(14)	1
Matěj Pulkrab	23.05.1997	14	(6)	5
David Puškáč	14.05.1993	17	(7)	5

Sportovní klub Dynamo České Budějovice

Founded: 1905
Stadium: Stadion Střelecký ostrov, České Budějovice (6,681)
Trainer: David Horejš · 19.05.1977

Goalkeepers:	DOB	M	(s)	G
Jaroslav Drobný	18.10.1979	22		
Vojtěch Vorel	18.06.1996	12		
Defenders:	**DOB**	**M**	**(s)**	**G**
Benjamin Čolić (BIH)	23.07.1991	26	(1)	8
Lukáš Havel	06.06.1996	15	(8)	1
Jiří Kladrubský	19.11.1985	4	(3)	
Martin Králik (SVK)	03.04.1995	31		
Pavel Novák	30.11.1989	21	(5)	1
Lukáš Skovajsa (SVK)	27.03.1994	17	(3)	1
Maksym Taloverov (UKR)	28.06.2000	24	(2)	1
Midfielders:	**DOB**	**M**	**(s)**	**G**
Marko Alvir (CRO)	19.04.1994	16	(2)	2
Patrik Čavoš	07.01.1995	30	(2)	1
Filip Havelka	21.01.1998	20	(1)	
Petr Javorek	09.02.1986	29	(1)	2
Jakub Kousal	06.09.2002		(1)	
Matej Mršić (CRO)	13.01.1994	24	(10)	2
Pavel Šulc	29.12.2000	4		1
Jonáš Vais	24.11.1999	4	(7)	
Matej Valenta	09.02.2000	6	(13)	1
Forwards:	**DOB**	**M**	**(s)**	**G**
Fortune Akpan Bassey (NGA)	06.10.1998	1	(5)	
Patrik Brandner	04.01.1994	30	(4)	6
Dame Diop (SEN)	15.02.1993	4	(8)	
Ubong Moses Ekpai (NGA)	17.10.1995	4	(6)	
Lukáš Jánošík (SVK)	05.03.1994	1	(11)	2
David Ledecký	24.07.1993	2	(7)	
Lukáš Matějka	20.12.1997	5	(2)	1
Karol Mészáros (SVK)	25.07.1993	14	(11)	2
Mick van Buren (NED)	24.08.1992	8		1
Jan Vitovec	17.08.2002		(1)	

Fotbalový Klub Jablonec

Founded: 1945
Stadium: Stadion Střelnice, Jablonec nad Nisou (6,108)
Trainer: Petr Rada · 21.08.1958

Goalkeepers:	DOB	M	(s)	G
Jan Hanuš	28.04.1988	26		
Vlastimil Hrubý	21.02.1985	8		
Defenders:	**DOB**	**M**	**(s)**	**G**
Patrik Haitl	01.03.1998	5	(6)	
Libor Holík	12.05.1998	20		
Michal Jeřábek	10.09.1993		(2)	
Jan Krob	27.04.1987	24	(3)	1
Jakub Martinec	13.03.1998	21	(1)	
Jakub Podaný	15.06.1987	12	(12)	
David Štěpánek	30.03.1997	14	(2)	
Jaroslav Zelený	20.08.1992	30	(2)	3
Midfielders:	**DOB**	**M**	**(s)**	**G**
Robert Hrubý	27.04.1994	7	(19)	3
Tomáš Hübschman	04.09.1981	18	(11)	1
Miloš Kratochvíl	26.04.1996	20		4
Vojtěch Kubista	19.03.1993	26	(1)	5
Václav Pilař	13.10.1988	17	(5)	2
Dominik Pleštil	09.08.1999	15	(14)	2
Jakub Považanec (SVK)	31.01.1991	33		3
Tomáš Smejkal	07.07.1998	1	(10)	
Forwards:	**DOB**	**M**	**(s)**	**G**
Jan Chramosta	12.10.1990		(9)	1
Tomáš Čvančara	13.08.2000	3	(6)	1
Martin Doležal	03.05.1990	23	(8)	14
Vladimir Jovović (MNE)	26.10.1994	16	(11)	2
Tomáš Ladra	24.04.1997	8	(5)	2
Ivan Schranz (SVK)	13.09.1993	27	(1)	13
Oliver Velich	12.06.2001		(1)	

Městský fotbalový klub Karviná

Founded: 2003
Stadium: Stadion Městský, Karviná (4,833)
Trainer: Juraj Jarábek (SVK) · 03.10.1962
[16.03.2021] Petr Maslej · 18.01.1970
[23.03.2021] Jozef Weber (SVK) · 25.12.1970

Goalkeepers:	DOB	M	(s)	G
Petr Bolek	13.06.1984	15		
Jiří Ciupa	07.05.1998	10		
Vladimir Neuman	10.02.2000	9		
Defenders:	**DOB**	**M**	**(s)**	**G**
Lukáš Bartošák	03.07.1990	31	(1)	3
Soufiane Dramé (FRA)	27.02.1996	15	(9)	
Eduardo Gonzaga Mendes Santos (BRA)	28.11.1997	30	(1)	2
Stelios Kokovas (GRE)	06.07.2001	1	(2)	
Leonardo Pereira dos Santos „Léo Pereira" (BRA)	20.01.1998	2	(1)	
Róbert Mazáň (SVK)	09.02.1994	8	(1)	
Gigli Ndefe (NED)	03.02.1994	14		
Martin Šindelář	22.01.1991	29	(3)	
Filip Twardzik	10.02.1993	10	(1)	
Midfielders:	**DOB**	**M**	**(s)**	**G**
Marek Hanousek	06.08.1991	3	(3)	
Christián Herc (SVK)	30.09.1998	28	(3)	6
Marek Janečka (SVK)	09.06.1983	1	(15)	
Jean Mangabeira da Silva (BRA)	10.03.1997	21	(6)	
Tomáš Jursa	09.03.1989	8	(13)	
Rajmund Mikuš (SVK)	29.11.1995	19	(11)	1
Tomáš Ostrák	05.02.2000	21	(5)	1
Kristi Qose (ALB)	10.06.1995	25	(3)	7
Vojtěch Smrž	20.01.1997	16	(10)	
Martin Vlachovský	28.11.2000		(1)	
Forwards:	**DOB**	**M**	**(s)**	**G**
Lukáš Čmelík (SVK)	13.04.1996	15	(7)	2
Dávid Guba (SVK)	29.06.1991		(7)	
Roman Haša	15.02.1993	2	(23)	2
Michal Papadopulos	14.04.1985	30	(1)	8
Rafael Tavares Dos Santos (BRA)	26.06.2000	8	(9)	3
Vlasiy Sinyavskiy (EST)	27.11.1996	3	(8)	1
Kacper Zych (POL)	05.12.2002		(3)	

Fotbalový klub Mladá Boleslav

Founded: 1902
Stadium: Lokotrans Arena, Mladá Boleslav (5,000)
Trainer: Jozef Weber (SVK)   25.12.1970
[08.12.2020]   Karel Jarolím   23.08.1956

Goalkeepers:	DOB	M	(s)	G
Jakub Diviš	27.07.1986	7		
Jakub Markovič	13.07.2001	1		
Petr Mikulec	05.04.1999	13		
Jan Šeda	17.12.1985	13	(1)	
Defenders:	**DOB**	**M**	**(s)**	**G**
Šimon Gabriel	28.05.2001	1	(3)	
Jakub Klíma	28.08.1998	18	(7)	
Antonín Křapka	22.01.1994	21		
Marco Tulio De Paula Medeiros (BRA)	31.05.1998	12	(1)	1
Petr Mareš	17.01.1991	2		
Róbert Mazáň (SVK)	09.02.1994	13		
Ondřej Mazuch	15.03.1989	2		
Dominik Preisler	20.09.1995	18	(1)	
Radim Řezník	20.01.1989	6	(2)	1
David Šimek	15.02.1998	15	(3)	2
Aleksey Tataev (RUS)	08.10.1998	14		2
Midfielders:	**DOB**	**M**	**(s)**	**G**
Lukáš Budínský	27.03.1992	19	(7)	2
Samuel Dancák (SVK)	06.03.1998	18		
David Douděra	31.05.1998	23	(8)	2
Dominik Janošek	13.06.1998	8	(3)	

	DOB	M	(s)	G
Milan Jirásek	14.05.1992	2	(4)	
Jiří Kulhánek	08.03.1996	2	(4)	
Daniel Langhamer	20.03.2003		(1)	
Tomáš Malínský	25.08.1991	8	(5)	
Dominik Mašek	10.07.1995	7	(6)	3
Marek Matějovský	20.12.1981	12	(4)	1
David Pech	22.02.2002	2		
Laco Takács	15.07.1996	10	(1)	2
Ondřej Zahustel	18.06.1991	13		2
Jaromír Zmrhal	02.08.1993	17	(1)	4
Forwards:	**DOB**	**M**	**(s)**	**G**
Václav Drchal	25.07.1999	8	(17)	6
Ladislav Dufek	23.12.2002		(2)	
Jakub Fulnek	26.04.1994	11	(6)	
Martin Graiciar	11.04.1999	3	(3)	
Dāvis Ikaunieks (LVA)	07.01.1994		(10)	
Jiří Klíma	05.01.1997	14	(4)	7
Tomáš Ladra	24.04.1997	14	(2)	4
Lukáš Mašek	05.08.2004	1	(4)	
Jiří Skalák	12.03.1992	5	(11)	
Michal Škoda	01.03.1988	21	(8)	10

Slezský fotbalový club Opava

Founded: 1907
Stadium: Stadion v Městských sadech, Opava (7,758)
Trainer: Radoslav Kováč   27.11.1979

Goalkeepers:	DOB	M	(s)	G
Tomáš Digaňa (SVK)	14.05.1997	10		
Vilém Fendrich	22.01.1991	20		
Mikulas Kubny	12.09.2004	1		
Kryštof Lasák	25.08.1996	2		
Vojtěch Šrom	03.05.1988	1		
Defenders:	**DOB**	**M**	**(s)**	**G**
Jaromír Blažej	13.03.2003	1		
David Březina	16.02.1997	10	(1)	1
Joss Didiba Moudoumbou (CMR)	07.11.1997	27		
Štěpán Harazim	13.07.2000	8	(9)	1
Matěj Helešic	12.11.1996	25	(6)	4
Matěj Hrabina	29.04.1993	17	(6)	
Tomáš Koschatzký	31.05.2000		(2)	
Adam Rychlý	25.09.1998	1	(4)	
Dalibor Večerka	12.03.2003	16	(7)	
Jakub Vrana	25.01.2001		(1)	
Jan Žídek	04.07.1985	23		3
Midfielders:	**DOB**	**M**	**(s)**	**G**
Denis Darmovzal	17.07.2000	2	(4)	
Bojan Đorđić (SRB)	26.05.1994	9	(2)	
Adam Gorčica	26.05.2001		(2)	
Patrik Hellebrand	16.05.1999	13	(4)	

	DOB	M	(s)	G
Josef Hnaníček	28.12.1986	7	(1)	
Lukáš Kania	19.04.1997	9	(8)	1
Jiří Kulhánek	08.03.1996	15	(1)	
Aleš Nešický	01.06.1992	21		5
Bartosz Pikul (POL)	02.11.1997	1	(5)	1
Jan Řezníček	22.11.1992	8	(7)	
Jan Schaffartzik	15.12.1987	5	(3)	
Adam Ščudla	28.12.2001		(5)	
David Smilek	29.04.2002		(1)	
Jiří Texl	03.01.1993	9		
Christ Joël Tiehi (CIV)	16.06.1998	18	(1)	
Nataniel Wybraniec	26.12.2000		(1)	
Pavel Zavadil	30.04.1978	8		
Forwards:	**DOB**	**M**	**(s)**	**G**
Tomáš Čvančara	13.08.2000	9	(1)	
René Dedič (SVK)	07.08.1993	7	(12)	1
Lukáš Holík	23.08.1992	22	(3)	2
Teodor Janjus	05.04.2001		(2)	
Václav Juřena	02.02.1991	10	(13)	
Denis Kramar	08.08.2003	1	(4)	
Karol Mondek (SVK)	02.06.1991	25	(5)	2
Tomáš Rataj	21.03.2003	5	(12)	1
Tomáš Smola	19.01.1989	8	(6)	1

Fotbalový klub Pardubice

Founded: 2008
Stadium: Stadion Ďolíček, Pardubice (5,000)
Trainer: Jiří Krejčí   22.03.1986

Goalkeepers:	DOB	M	(s)	G
Marek Boháč	31.10.1988	22		
Štěpán Hrnčíř	08.05.1997	1		
Jiří Letáček	09.01.1999	11	(1)	
Defenders:	**DOB**	**M**	**(s)**	**G**
Tomáš Čelůstka	19.07.1991	27	(1)	1
Filip Čihák	10.07.1999	16	(3)	1
Lukáš Hušek	25.10.2000		(3)	
Petr Kůrka	04.07.2002		(1)	
Jan Prosek	23.01.1995	14	(2)	
Martin Šejvl	18.02.1992	22	(3)	
Jiří Sláma	08.01.1999	1	(24)	
Michal Surzyn	10.09.1997	22	(3)	3
Martin Toml	25.03.1996	34		2
Midfielders:	**DOB**	**M**	**(s)**	**G**
Carlos Eduardo Lopes Cruz „Cadu" (BRA)	08.08.1997	24	(5)	7

	DOB	M	(s)	G
Michal Hlavatý	17.06.1998	21	(2)	1
Jan Jeřábek	12.02.1984	24	(3)	2
Lee Sang-hyuk (KOR)	19.01.2000		(8)	
Samuel Šimek	12.04.2002	1	(2)	
Tomáš Solil	01.02.2000	26	(3)	
Vojtěch Sychra	30.11.2001		(1)	
Emil Tischler	13.03.1998	30		5
Matěj Vít	22.07.2001	1		
Forwards:	**DOB**	**M**	**(s)**	**G**
Pavel Černý	28.01.1985	28	(2)	2
Ewerton Paixao da Silva (BRA)	28.12.1996	17	(11)	3
David Huf	23.01.1999	7	(23)	9
Dominik Kostka	04.05.1996	14	(4)	1
Pieter Langedijk (NED)	10.02.1994		(2)	
Michal Petráň	26.06.1992	1	(13)	1
Lukáš Pfeifer	24.06.1999	10	(12)	1

1. Fotbalový Klub Příbram

Founded:	1928	
Stadium:	Stadion Na Litavce, Příbram (9,100)	
Trainer:	Pavel Horváth	22.04.1975
[15.03.2021]	Jozef Valachovič (SVK)	12.07.1975

Goalkeepers:	DOB	M	(s)	G
Ondřej Kočí	07.04.1995	14		
Martin Melichár	06.07.2000	7		
Jakub Šiman	07.01.1995	13		
Defenders:	**DOB**	**M**	**(s)**	**G**
Mihailo Cmiljanović (SRB)	15.06.1994	22	(4)	
Idrissa Diarra (MLI)	03.02.1998	3		
Juan Olivier Simo Kingue (CMR)	20.02.1996	17	(1)	
Steve Kingue (CMR)	23.01.2000	8	(1)	
Peter Kleščík (SVK)	18.09.1988	6	(1)	
Jan Kvída	17.01.1991	7	(12)	
Jiří Mezera	21.07.2000	12	(1)	1
Martin Nový	23.06.1993	29		2
Václav Svoboda	16.09.1999	10	(6)	
Jaroslav Tregler	20.01.1995	24	(2)	1
Stefan Vilotić (SRB)	16.10.1999	8	(4)	
Midfielders:	**DOB**	**M**	**(s)**	**G**
Emmanuel Antwi (GHA)	05.05.1996	9	(15)	2
Zdeněk Folprecht	01.07.1991	10		1
Pavel Hájek	03.08.2001	6	(9)	
Jiří Januška	11.10.1997	1	(7)	
Josef Obdržal	27.07.2001	3	(3)	
Adam Petrák	20.08.1999	2		
Tomáš Pilík	20.12.1988	26	(7)	4
Karel Soldát	07.11.1993	21	(3)	1
Jonáš Vais	24.11.1999	6	(7)	
Filip Zorvan	07.04.1996	28	(1)	2
Forwards:	**DOB**	**M**	**(s)**	**G**
František Belej	29.02.2000	1	(3)	
Isaac Boakye (GHA)	20.03.1997		(6)	
Denis Budínský	22.01.2002		(3)	
Christopher Cortez (USA)	24.07.1988		(3)	
Tomáš Dočekal	24.05.1989		(9)	
Stanislav Gabriel	18.02.2002		(1)	
Milan Lalkovič (SVK)	09.12.1992	7	(1)	
Denis Laňka	13.05.1997	8		
Edrisa Lubega (UGA)	17.04.1998	8	(1)	2
Dušan Pinc	01.05.1998	2	(5)	
Jan Rezek	05.05.1982	21	(4)	1
Stanislav Vávra	20.07.1993	17	(14)	2
Radek Voltr	28.11.1991	18	(7)	5

Sportovní Klub Sigma Olomouc

Founded:	1919 (*as FK Hejčín Olomouc*)	
Stadium:	Stadion Andrův, Olomouc (12,483)	
Trainer:	Radoslav Látal	06.01.1970

Goalkeepers:	DOB	M	(s)	G
Matúš Macík (SVK)	19.05.1993	3		
Aleš Mandous	21.04.1992	30		
Michal Reichl	14.09.1992	1		
Defenders:	**DOB**	**M**	**(s)**	**G**
Vít Beneš	12.08.1988	18	(3)	
Roman Hubník	06.06.1984	25	(1)	
Václav Jemelka	23.06.1995	6		
Milan Kerbr	10.09.1989		(1)	1
Martin Sladký	01.03.1992	13	(7)	
Jan Štěrba	08.07.1994	2	(4)	
Michal Vepřek	17.06.1985	11	(1)	
Midfielders:	**DOB**	**M**	**(s)**	**G**
Radim Breite	10.08.1989	29	(3)	1
Kryštof Daněk	05.01.2003	13	(10)	3
Šimon Falta	23.04.1993	11	(3)	2
Jan Fiala	04.05.2001		(2)	
Lukáš Greššák (SVK)	23.01.1989	15	(1)	1
Martin Hála	24.03.1992	22	(6)	2
Ondřej Hapal	10.05.2001		(2)	
David Houska	29.06.1993	27		5
Radek Látal	16.12.1997	16	(12)	1
Jaroslav Mihalík (SVK)	27.07.1994	2	(8)	
Florent Poulolo (MTQ)	02.01.1997	20	(5)	
Patrik Slaměna	07.07.2000	2	(4)	
Filip Uriča	10.09.2003		(1)	
Tomáš Zahradníček	11.08.1993	10	(13)	
Ondřej Zmrzlý	22.04.1999	21	(3)	2
Forwards:	**DOB**	**M**	**(s)**	**G**
Jean Luc Assoubre (CIV)	08.08.1992		(2)	
Mojmír Chytil	29.04.1999	18	(13)	4
Matěj Hadaš	25.11.2003		(1)	
Martin Nešpor	05.06.1990	19	(7)	3
Pablo González Juárez (ESP)	12.05.1993	28	(2)	7
Dominik Radić (CRO)	26.07.1996		(3)	
Jáchym Šíp	22.01.2003		(6)	
Jakub Yunis	25.03.1996	7	(6)	2
Pavel Zifčak	02.03.1999	5	(15)	3

Sportovní klub Slavia Praha

Founded:	02.11.1902 (*as Akademický cyklistický odbor Slavia*)	
Stadium:	Stadion Sinobo, Praha (19,370)	
Trainer:	Jindřich Trpišovský	27.02.1976

Goalkeepers:	DOB	M	(s)	G
Ondřej Kolář	17.10.1994	31		1
Přemysl Kovář	14.10.1985		(1)	
Jan Stejskal	14.02.1997	1		
Matyáš Vágner	05.02.2003	2		
Defenders:	**DOB**	**M**	**(s)**	**G**
Alexander Bah (DEN)	09.12.1997	14	(3)	1
Jan Bořil	11.01.1991	25	(2)	3
Vladimír Coufal	22.08.1992	4	(1)	
Simon Deli (CIV)	27.10.1991	9	(3)	
Oscar Dorley (LBR)	19.07.1998	19	(7)	2
David Hovorka	07.08.1993	7	(1)	
Taras Kacharaba (UKR)	07.01.1995	7	(3)	
Ondřej Karafiát	01.12.1994	2	(3)	
Ondřej Kúdela	26.03.1987	26	(3)	6
David Zima	08.11.2000	19	(2)	
Midfielders:	**DOB**	**M**	**(s)**	**G**
Michal Beran	22.08.2000	3	(3)	
Tomáš Holeš	31.03.1993	17	(7)	6
Jakub Hromada (SVK)	25.05.1996	7	(7)	
Ondřej Lingr	07.10.1998	11	(16)	4
Tomáš Malínský	25.08.1991	1	(3)	
Lukáš Masopust	12.02.1993	20	(6)	2
Tomáš Rigo (SVK)	03.07.2002		(1)	
Daniel Samek	19.02.2004	2		
Nicolae Claudiu Stanciu (ROU)	07.05.1993	27	(3)	12
Petr Ševčík	04.05.1994	10	(5)	
Laco Takács	15.07.1996	2	(4)	1
Ibrahim Traoré (CIV)	16.09.1988	9	(16)	
Denis Višinský	21.03.2003		(2)	
Forwards:	**DOB**	**M**	**(s)**	**G**
Abdulla Yusuf Abdulrahim Mohamed Helal BHR	12.06.1993	1	(7)	
Matěj Jurásek	30.08.2003	1	(1)	
Jan Kuchta	08.01.1997	22	(5)	15
Petar Musa (CRO)	04.03.1998	4	(10)	4
Peter Oladeji Olayinka (NGA)	16.11.1995	17	(7)	6
Lukáš Provod	23.10.1996	23	(5)	3
Abdallah Sima (SEN)	17.06.2001	17	(4)	11
Stanislav Tecl	01.09.1990	7	(15)	4
Mick van Buren (NED)	24.08.1992	7	(5)	1

1. Fudbalový Klub Slovácko Uherské Hradiště

Founded: 1927 (*as SK Staré Město*)
Stadium: Městský fotbalový stadion "Miroslava Valenty", Uherské Hradiště (8,000)
Trainer: Martin Svědík   27.06.1974

Goalkeepers:	DOB	M	(s)	G
Pavol Bajza (SVK)	04.09.1991	11		
Vít Nemrava	09.01.1996	23		
Defenders:	**DOB**	**M**	**(s)**	**G**
Josef Divíšek	24.09.1990	7	(7)	
Stanislav Hofmann	17.06.1990	31		4
Michal Kadlec	13.12.1984	32		1
Petr Reinberk	23.05.1989	24	(4)	1
Patrik Šimko (SVK)	08.07.1991	12	(14)	
Jaromír Srubek	21.09.2000	1	(7)	1
Michal Tomič (SVK)	30.03.1999	4	(9)	
Midfielders:	**DOB**	**M**	**(s)**	**G**
Vlastimil Daníček	15.07.1991	23	(2)	9
Marek Havlík	08.07.1995	31		2
Patrik Hellebrand	16.05.1999	3	(4)	
Michal Kohút	04.06.2000	15	(14)	2
Daniel Mareček	30.05.1998	4	(3)	
Jan Navrátil	13.04.1990	21	(4)	2
Milan Petržela	19.06.1983	29	(4)	5
Marek Polášek	18.05.2001	1		
Lukáš Sadílek	23.05.1996	33	(1)	6
Forwards:	**DOB**	**M**	**(s)**	**G**
Rigino Cicilia (CUW)	23.09.1994	7	(11)	3
Václav Jurečka	26.06.1994	14	(13)	7
Jan Kalabiška	22.12.1986	18	(7)	4
Jan Kliment	01.09.1993	24	(7)	10
Filip Kubala	02.09.1999	4	(17)	1
Timur Melekestsev (RUS)	03.07.2001		(2)	
Jakub Rezek	29.05.1998	2	(9)	

Football Club Slovan Liberec

Founded: 1958
Stadium: Stadion u Nisy, Liberec (9,900)
Trainer: Pavel Hoftych   09.05.1967

Goalkeepers:	DOB	M	(s)	G
Milan Knobloch	23.08.1992	18	(1)	
Filip Nguyen	14.09.1992	16		
Defenders:	**DOB**	**M**	**(s)**	**G**
Jakub Barac	04.08.1996	1	(2)	
Matěj Chaluš	02.02.1998	23	(3)	
Miroslav Dvořák	18.12.1998		(1)	
Michal Fukala	22.10.2000	17	(10)	
Jakub Jugas	05.05.1992	22	(1)	
Taras Kacharaba (UKR)	07.01.1995	10		2
Ondřej Karafiát	01.12.1994	17	(1)	2
Martin Koscelník (SVK)	02.03.1995	25	(3)	
Daniel Kosek	19.05.2001	1		
Jan Mikula	05.01.1992	31		
Marios Pourzitidis (GRE)	08.05.1999	11	(3)	
Mohamed Tijani (CIV)	10.07.1997	8		
Midfielders:	**DOB**	**M**	**(s)**	**G**
Michal Beran	22.08.2000	7	(3)	
David Cancola (AUT)	23.10.1996	1	(3)	
Radim Černický	18.02.2001		(1)	
Michal Faško (SVK)	24.08.1994	7	(11)	
Jakub Hromada (SVK)	25.05.1996	8	(1)	2
Kamso Mara (GUI)	24.12.1994	26	(4)	2
Jan Matoušek	09.05.1998	12	(7)	
Kristian Michal	26.11.2000	1	(7)	
Aleš Nešický	01.06.1992	2	(3)	
Michal Sadílek	31.05.1999	21	(3)	6
Jan Šulc	02.06.1998		(3)	
Forwards:	**DOB**	**M**	**(s)**	**G**
Lukáš Csáno (SVK)	11.07.2001	1	(1)	
Adama Diamé (FRA)	19.07.2000		(1)	
Dominik Gembický	26.07.1999		(1)	
Abdulla Yusuf Abdulrahim Mohamed Helal(BHR)	12.06.1993	5	(4)	1
Jhon Édison Mosquera Rebolledo (COL)	08.05.1990	25	(4)	7
Jakub Nečas	26.01.1995		(12)	
Jakub Pešek	24.06.1993	27	(4)	6
Michael Rabušic	17.09.1989	18	(11)	9
Imad Rondić (BIH)	16.02.1999	13	(17)	6

Athletic Club Sparta Praha

Founded: 16.11.1893
Stadium: Generali Arena, Praha (18,887)
Trainer: Václav Kotal   02.10.1952
[03.02.2021]   Pavel Vrba   06.12.1963

Goalkeepers:	DOB	M	(s)	G
Milan Heča	23.03.1991	8		
Florin Constantin Niţă (ROU)	03.07.1987	26		
Defenders:	**DOB**	**M**	**(s)**	**G**
Ondřej Čelůstka	18.06.1989	28		1
Dávid Hancko (SVK)	13.12.1997	24		5
Matěj Hanousek	02.06.1993	18	(7)	
David Lischka	15.08.1997	5		
Dominik Plechatý	18.04.1999	8	(1)	
Lukáš Štetina (SVK)	28.07.1991	2		
Andreas Vindheim (NOR)	04.08.1995	14	(3)	1
Martin Vitík	21.01.2003	16	(1)	
Tomáš Wiesner	17.07.1997	13	(1)	4
Midfielders:	**DOB**	**M**	**(s)**	**G**
Bořek Dočkal	30.09.1988	31	(2)	4
Jan Fortelný	19.01.1999		(1)	
Adam Karabec	02.07.2003	6	(17)	3
Ladislav Krejčí I	05.07.1992	16	(5)	3
Ladislav Krejčí II	20.04.1999	20		8
David Pavelka	18.05.1991	24	(1)	2
Matěj Polidar	20.12.1999	7	(7)	3
Michal Sáček	19.09.1996	25	(2)	
Filip Souček	18.09.2000	7	(11)	
Michal Trávník	17.05.1994	4	(14)	
Forwards:	**DOB**	**M**	**(s)**	**G**
Adam Hložek	25.07.2002	18	(1)	15
Lukáš Juliš	02.12.1994	22	(3)	12
Libor Kozák	30.05.1989	4	(9)	4
Martin Minchev (BUL)	22.04.2001	1	(13)	
David Moberg-Karlsson (SWE)	20.03.1994	16	(10)	10
Ondřej Novotný	05.02.1998		(3)	
Srđan Plavšić (SRB)	03.12.1995	11	(11)	2

Fotbalový klub Teplice

Founded:	1945		
Stadium:	Stadion Na Stínadlech, Teplice (18,221)		
Trainer:	Stanislav Hejkal	03.01.1970	
[30.11.2020]	Radim Kučera	01.03.1974	

Goalkeepers:	DOB	M	(s)	G
Jan Čtvrtečka	14.08.1998	10		
Jakub Diviš	27.07.1986	2		
Tomáš Grigar	01.02.1983	16	(1)	
Luděk Němeček	04.01.1999	6		
Defenders:	**DOB**	**M**	**(s)**	**G**
Ruben Droehnle (FRA)	11.07.1998	6	(4)	
Šimon Gabriel	28.05.2001	12	(2)	
David Heidenreich	24.06.2000	9		1
Jan Hošek	01.04.1989	1	(2)	
Alois Hyčka	22.07.1990	13	(6)	
Jan Knapík	11.12.2000	11	(6)	
Ondřej Mazuch	15.03.1989	15	(1)	
Evgeniy Nazarov (RUS)	07.04.1997	2		1
Igor Paradin (RUS)	10.09.1998	1	(1)	
Tomáš Vondrášek	26.10.1987	22	(4)	
Midfielders:	**DOB**	**M**	**(s)**	**G**
Jan Fortelný	19.01.1999	15	(4)	
Robert Jukl	28.10.1998	25	(1)	2
Ladislav Kodad	23.04.1998	9	(6)	2

	DOB	M	(s)	G
Petr Kodeš	31.01.1996		(2)	
Daniel Kováč	03.03.2000		(3)	
Tomáš Kučera	20.07.1991	22	(4)	1
Admir Ljevakovič (BIH)	07.08.1984	5	(11)	
Lukáš Mareček	17.04.1990	18	(2)	2
Matěj Radosta	10.05.2001	7	(15)	1
Jan Shejbal	20.04.1994	5	(3)	
Daniel Trubač	17.07.1997	21	(8)	2
Patrik Žitný	21.01.1999	18	(7)	3
Forwards:	**DOB**	**M**	**(s)**	**G**
David Černý	10.12.1995	23	(7)	
Matyáš Kozák	04.05.2001		(2)	
Martin Macej	15.04.1997	4	(9)	1
Jakub Mareš	26.01.1987	21	(6)	9
Pavel Moulis	07.04.1991	30	(2)	4
Jakub Řezníček	26.05.1988	11	(7)	1
Dominik Šup	28.01.1997		(1)	
Tadeáš Vachoušek	11.01.2004		(1)	
Vukadin Vukadinovič (SRB)	14.12.1990	14	(9)	1

Football Club Viktoria Plzeň

Founded:	11.06.1911		
Stadium:	Doosan Arena, Plzeň (11,700)		
Trainer:	Adrián Guľa (SVK)	29.06.1975	
[10.05.2021]	Michal Bílek	13.04.1965	

Goalkeepers:	DOB	M	(s)	G
Aleš Hruška	23.11.1985	15		
Jindřich Staněk	27.04.1996	19		
Defenders:	**DOB**	**M**	**(s)**	**G**
Jakub Brabec	06.08.1992	31		3
Milan Havel	07.08.1994	25	(1)	2
Lukáš Hejda	09.03.1990	18	(2)	3
Robin Hranáč	29.01.2000		(1)	
Matěj Hybš	03.01.1993	5	(1)	
Filip Kaša	01.01.1994	16	(2)	1
David Limberský	06.10.1983	23		1
Václav Míka	01.06.2000	1	(1)	
Luděk Pernica	16.06.1990	4		
Radim Řezník	20.01.1989	6	(1)	
Midfielders:	**DOB**	**M**	**(s)**	**G**
Marko Alvir (CRO)	19.04.1994		(9)	
Pavel Bucha	11.03.1998	23	(3)	7

	DOB	M	(s)	G
Aleš Čermák	01.10.1994	22	(3)	7
Šimon Falta	23.04.1993	17	(2)	1
Tomáš Hořava	29.05.1988	1	(8)	1
Miroslav Káčer (SVK)	02.02.1996	10	(14)	1
Lukáš Kalvach	19.07.1995	33		2
Jan Kopic	04.06.1990	12	(4)	2
Jan Kovařík	19.06.1988	7	(9)	
Pavel Šulc	29.12.2000	16	(4)	1
Forwards:	**DOB**	**M**	**(s)**	**G**
Adriel Ba Loua (CIV)	25.07.1996	21	(10)	7
Jean-David Beauguel (FRA)	21.03.1992	17	(13)	12
Tomáš Chorý	26.01.1995	1	(1)	
Joel Kayamba (COD)	17.04.1992	13	(8)	1
Lukáš Matějka	20.12.1997		(8)	1
Ondřej Mihálik	02.04.1997	3	(19)	
Zdeněk Ondrášek	22.12.1988	15	(16)	6

Football Club Zbrojovka Brno

Founded:	1913 (*as SK Židenice*)		
Stadium:	Stadion Srbská, Brno (12,550)		
Trainer:	Miloslav Machálek	20.07.1961	
[15.12.2020]	Richard Dostálek	26.04.1974	

Goalkeepers:	DOB	M	(s)	G
Martin Berkovec	12.02.1989	11		
Jiří Floder	03.01.1997	13		
Martin Šustr	03.10.1990	10		
Defenders:	**DOB**	**M**	**(s)**	**G**
Jakub Černín	08.02.1999	3	(2)	
Pavel Dreksa	17.09.1989	21	(2)	
Lukáš Endl	17.06.2003	2	(5)	
Zoran Gajić (SRB)	18.05.1990	9	(3)	
Jan Hlavica	17.07.1994	14	(3)	
Juraj Kotula (SVK)	30.09.1995	6	(1)	
Lukáš Kryštůfek	15.08.1992		(1)	
Luděk Pernica	16.06.1990	19		4
Jakub Šural	01.07.1996	17	(2)	1
Timotej Zahumenský (SVK)	17.07.1995	5	(2)	
Midfielders:	**DOB**	**M**	**(s)**	**G**
Damián Bariš (SVK)	09.12.1994	15	(6)	
Adrián Čermák (SVK)	01.07.1993	15	(3)	
Adam Fousek	08.03.1994	15	(9)	2

	DOB	M	(s)	G
David Jambor	31.03.2003	1	(6)	
Jan Moravec	13.07.1987	24	(4)	
Ondřej Pachlopník	14.02.2000	23	(8)	1
Rudolf Reiter	28.09.1994	9	(6)	
Jan Sedlák	25.10.1994	25	(4)	
Michal Ševčík	13.08.2002		(1)	
Vojtěch Šmíd	16.02.2001		(1)	
Peter Štepanovský (SVK)	12.01.1988	26	(4)	4
Šimon Šumbera	05.01.1991	9	(7)	
Jiří Texl	03.01.1993	9	(5)	2
Ondřej Vaněk	25.07.1990	12	(4)	1
Forwards:	**DOB**	**M**	**(s)**	**G**
Daniel Fila	21.08.2002	4	(17)	1
Jan Hladík	21.09.1993	19	(13)	6
Jan Koudelka	12.03.1992	1	(6)	
Claude Lhotecký	22.02.2001		(1)	
Jakub Přichystal	25.10.1995	13	(12)	4
Antonín Růsek	22.03.1999	24	(6)	7
Marek Vintr	01.08.1997		(6)	

Football Club Fastav Zlín

Founded: 1919
Stadium: Stadion Letná, Zlín (5,783)
Trainer: Bohumil Pánik — 31.12.1956
[10.05.2021] Jan Jelínek — 22.03.1982

Goalkeepers:	DOB	M	(s)	G
Stanislav Dostál	20.06.1991	33	(1)	
Matej Rakovan (SVK)	14.03.1990	1	(1)	
Defenders:	**DOB**	**M**	**(s)**	**G**
Petr Buchta	15.07.1992	31		2
Martin Cedidla	22.11.2001	16	(11)	1
Jakub Kolar	16.01.2000	6	(2)	
Róbert Matejov (SVK)	05.07.1988	11	(7)	
Václav Procházka	08.05.1984	26	(4)	1
Dominik Simerský	29.09.1992	26	(2)	1
Tobiáš Slovák	25.11.2001	1		
David Tkáč	06.07.2002		(2)	
Lukáš Vraštil	10.03.1994	10	(3)	
Midfielders:	**DOB**	**M**	**(s)**	**G**
Vakhtang Chanturishvili (GEO)	05.08.1993	15	(8)	

	DOB	M	(s)	G
Cheick Conde (GUI)	26.07.2000	20		
Youba Dramé (FRA)	16.01.1998	22	(12)	5
Antonín Fantiš	15.04.1992	24	(5)	1
Marek Hlinka (SVK)	04.10.1990	25	(3)	1
Jakub Janetzký	12.06.1997	18	(13)	3
Dominik Janošek	13.06.1998	10	(3)	
Petr Jiráček	02.03.1986	12	(3)	1
Pedro Martínez García (ESP)	09.02.1996	4	(13)	1
Patrik Slaměna	07.07.2000	1	(4)	
Forwards:	**DOB**	**M**	**(s)**	**G**
Šimon Chwaszcz	28.05.1996		(1)	
Lamin Jawo (GAM)	15.03.1995	17	(11)	1
Roman Potočný	25.04.1991	14	(2)	3
Tomáš Poznar	27.09.1988	31		9
Martins Daniel Toutou Mpondo (FRA)	13.03.1996		(7)	

SECOND LEVEL
Czech National Football League 2020/2021

1.	FC Hradec Králové (*Promoted*)	26	17	7	2	51	-	22	58
2.	SK Líšeň Brno	26	13	11	2	43	-	24	50
3.	1. SK Prostějov	26	12	7	7	40	-	35	43
4.	FK Viktoria Žižkov	26	13	3	10	42	-	38	42
5.	FK Ústí nad Labem	26	12	5	9	24	-	29	41
6.	FC Sellier & Bellot Vlašim	26	10	7	9	38	-	33	37
7.	FC Vysočina Jihlava	26	9	8	9	44	-	44	35
8.	FK Dukla Praha	26	9	7	10	36	-	30	34
9.	FK Fotbal Třinec	26	9	6	11	32	-	33	33
10.	MFK Chrudim	26	9	4	13	33	-	36	31
11.	FC MAS Táborsko	26	8	7	11	25	-	28	31
12.	FK Varnsdorf	26	6	12	8	20	-	27	30
13.	FK Blansko (*Relegated*)	26	7	6	13	30	-	34	27
14.	FC Slavoj Vyšehrad (*Relegated*)	26	1	4	21	15	-	60	7

INTERNATIONAL MATCHES
(16.07.2020 – 15.07.2021)

04.09.2020	Bratislava	Slovakia - Czech Republic	1-3(0-0)	(UNL)
07.09.2020	Olomouc	Czech Republic - Scotland	1-2(1-1)	(UNL)
07.10.2020	Larnaca	Cyprus - Czech Republic	1-2(1-2)	(F)
11.10.2020	Haifa	Israel - Czech Republic	1-2(0-1)	(UNL)
14.10.2020	Glasgow	Scotland - Czech Republic	1-0(1-0)	(UNL)
11.11.2020	Leipzig	Germany - Czech Republic	1-0(1-0)	(F)
15.11.2020	Plzeň	Czech Republic - Israel	1-0(1-0)	(UNL)
18.11.2020	Plzeň	Czech Republic - Slovakia	2-0(1-0)	(UNL)
24.03.2021	Lublin	Estonia - Czech Republic	2-6(1-4)	(WCQ)
27.03.2021	Praha	Czech Republic - Belgium	1-1(0-0)	(WCQ)
30.03.2021	Cardiff	Wales - Czech Republic	1-0(0-0)	(WCQ)
04.06.2021	Bologna	Italy - Czech Republic	4-0(2-0)	(F)
08.06.2021	Praha	Czech Republic - Albania	3-1(1-1)	(F)
14.06.2021	Glasgow	Scotland - Czech Republic	0-2(0-1)	(EC)
18.06.2021	Glasgow	Croatia - Czech Republic	1-1(0-1)	(EC)
22.06.2021	London	Czech Republic - England	0-1(0-1)	(EC)
27.06.2021	Budapest	Netherlands - Czech Republic	0-2(0-0)	(EC)
03.07.2021	Bakı	Czech Republic - Denmark	1-2(0-2)	(EC)

04.09.2020 SLOVAKIA - CZECH REPUBLIC 1-3(0-0) 2nd UEFA Nations League B, Group 2
Štadión Tehelné pole, Bratislava; Referee: Andris Treimanis (Latvia); Attendance: 0
CZE: Tomáš Vaclík, Ondřej Čelůstka, Jan Bořil, Vladimír Coufal, Tomáš Kalas, Bořek Dočkal (Cap), Vladimír Darida, Lukáš Masopust (86.Petr Ševčík), Alex Král, Jakub Jankto (68.Lukáš Provod), Adam Hložek (72.Michael Krmenčík). Trainer: Jaroslav Šilhavý.
Goals: Vladimír Coufal (48), Bořek Dočkal (53 penalty), Michael Krmenčík (86).

07.09.2020 CZECH REPUBLIC - SCOTLAND 1-2(1-1) 2nd UEFA Nations League B, Group 2
Andrův stadion, Olomouc; Referee: Serdar Gözübüyük (Netherlands); Attendance: 0
CZE: Aleš Mandous, Roman Hubník (Cap), Jaroslav Zelený, Tomáš Holeš, Adam Jánoš, Václav Jemelka, Marek Havlík (81.Antonín Růsek), Lukáš Budínský (55.Radim Breite), Tomáš Malinský, Jakub Pešek (76.Roman Potočný), Stanislav Tecl. Trainer: Jaroslav Šilhavý.
Goal: Jakub Pešek (12).

07.10.2020 CYPRUS - CZECH REPUBLIC 1-2(1-2) Friendly International
AEK Arena "Georgios Karapatakis", Larnaca; Referee: Lionel Tschudi (Switzerland); Attendance: 0
CZE: Tomáš Koubek, Filip Novák (62.Alex Král), Pavel Kadeřábek, Tomáš Holeš (62.Aleš Matějů), Tomáš Petrášek, David Hovorka, Vladimír Darida (Cap) (71.Bořek Dočkal), Petr Ševčík (70.Lukáš Masopust), Antonín Barák, Lukáš Provod, Matěj Vydra (62.Adam Hložek). Trainer: Jaroslav Šilhavý.
Goals: Tomáš Holeš (13), Vladimír Darida (43 penalty).

11.10.2020 ISRAEL - CZECH REPUBLIC 1-2(0-1) 2nd UEFA Nations League B, Group 2
"Sammy Ofer" Stadium, Haifa; Referee: Tiago Bruno Lopes Martins (Portugal); Attendance: 0
CZE: Tomáš Vaclík, Ondřej Kúdela, Ondřej Čelůstka, Jan Bořil, Vladimír Coufal, Vladimír Darida (Cap) (88.Tomáš Holeš), Lukáš Masopust (68.Pavel Kadeřábek), Lukáš Provod (90+3.Tomáš Petrášek), Tomáš Souček, Alex Král, Matěj Vydra (68.Petr Ševčík). Trainer: Jaroslav Šilhavý.
Goals: Joel Abu Hanna (14 own goal), Matěj Vydra (48).

14.10.2020 SCOTLAND - CZECH REPUBLIC 1-0(1-0) 2nd UEFA Nations League B, Group 2
Hampden Park, Glasgow; Referee: Felix Zwayer (Germany); Attendance: 299
CZE: Tomáš Vaclík, Ondřej Kúdela, Ondřej Čelůstka (20.David Hovorka), Jan Bořil, Vladimír Coufal, Vladimír Darida (Cap), Lukáš Masopust (65.Tomáš Poznar), Lukáš Provod (65.Petr Ševčík), Tomáš Souček, Matěj Vydra (77.Michael Rabušic), Alex Král (77.Pavel Kadeřábek). Trainer: Jaroslav Šilhavý.

11.11.2020 GERMANY - CZECH REPUBLIC 1-0(1-0) Friendly International
Red Bull Arena, Leipzig; Referee: Andris Treimanis (Latvia); Attendance: 0
CZE: Jiří Pavlenka, Filip Novák (46.Tomáš Souček), Jakub Brabec, Aleš Matějů, Václav Jemelka, Bořek Dočkal (Cap) (69.Vladimír Darida), Jan Kopic (78.Zdenek Ondrášek), Tomáš Holeš, Antonín Barák (46.Alex Král), Michael Krmenčík (46.Matěj Vydra), Václav Černý (46.Jakub Jankto). Trainer: Jaroslav Šilhavý.

15.11.2020 CZECH REPUBLIC - ISRAEL 1-0(1-0) 2nd UEFA Nations League B, Group 2
Doosan Arena, Plzeň; Referee: Srđan Jovanović (Serbia); Attendance: 0
CZE: Tomáš Vaclík, Jakub Brabec, Vladimír Coufal, Tomáš Kalas, Aleš Matějů, Vladimír Darida (Cap) (89.Bořek Dočkal), Lukáš Masopust (62.Jan Kopic), Tomáš Souček, Alex Král, Jakub Jankto (82.Matěj Vydra), Zdenek Ondrášek (62.Michael Krmenčík). Trainer: Jaroslav Šilhavý.
Goal: Vladimír Darida (7).

18.11.2020 CZECH REPUBLIC - SLOVAKIA 2-0(1-0) 2nd UEFA Nations League B, Group 2
Doosan Arena, Plzeň; Referee: Cüneyt Çakır (Turkey); Attendance: 0
CZE: Tomáš Vaclík (46.Tomáš Koubek), Jakub Brabec, Vladimír Coufal, Tomáš Kalas, Aleš Matějů, Vladimír Darida (Cap) (88.Antonín Barák), Lukáš Masopust (46.Václav Černý), Tomáš Souček, Alex Král, Jakub Jankto (74.Jan Kopic), Zdenek Ondrášek (66.Matěj Vydra). Trainer: Jaroslav Šilhavý.
Goals: Tomáš Souček (17), Zdenek Ondrášek (55).

24.03.2021 ESTONIA - CZECH REPUBLIC 2-6(1-4) 22nd FIFA WC. Qualifiers
Arena Lublin, Lublin (Poland); Referee: Anastasios Papapetrou (Greece); Attendance: 0
CZE: Jiří Pavlenka, Ondřej Kúdela, Ondřej Čelůstka (85.David Zima), Jan Bořil, Pavel Kadeřábek, Vladimír Darida (Cap), Antonín Barák (65.Tomáš Pekhart), Lukáš Provod (65.Matěj Vydra), Tomáš Souček, Jakub Jankto (65.Lukáš Masopust), Patrik Schick (79.Tomáš Holeš). Trainer: Jaroslav Šilhavý.
Goals: Patrik Schick (18), Antonín Barák (27), Tomáš Souček (32, 43, 48), Jakub Jankto (56).

27.03.2021   **CZECH REPUBLIC - BELGIUM**   1-1(0-0)   22nd FIFA WC. Qualifiers
Eden Arena, Praha; Referee: William Collum (Scotland); Attendance: 0
CZE: Tomáš Vaclík, Ondřej Kúdela, Ondřej Čelůstka, Jan Bořil, Vladimír Coufal, Tomáš Holeš, Antonín Barák (78.David Pavelka), Tomáš Souček (Cap), Jakub Jankto (61.Lukáš Masopust), Michael Krmenčík (78.Matěj Vydra), Lukáš Provod (90+4.Tomáš Pekhart). Trainer: Jaroslav Šilhavý.
Goal: Lukáš Provod (50).

30.03.2021   **WALES - CZECH REPUBLIC**   1-0(0-0)   22nd FIFA WC. Qualifiers
Cardiff City Stadium, Cardiff; Referee: Ovidiu Alin Haţegan (Romania); Attendance: 0
CZE: Tomáš Vaclík, Ondřej Kúdela (87.Antonín Barák), Ondřej Čelůstka, Vladimír Coufal (87.Matěj Vydra), Jan Bořil, Tomáš Holeš (53.Michael Krmenčík), Vladimír Darida (Cap), Lukáš Provod (82.Pavel Kadeřábek), Tomáš Souček, Jakub Jankto (82.Lukáš Masopust), Patrik Schick [*sent off 49*]. Trainer: Jaroslav Šilhavý.

04.06.2021   **ITALY - CZECH REPUBLIC**   4-0(2-0)   Friendly International
Stadio "Renato Dall'Ara", Bologna; Referee: Lionel Tschudi (Switzerland); Attendance: 0
CZE: Jiří Pavlenka, Ondřej Čelůstka (46.David Zima), Jakub Brabec, Jan Bořil, Vladimír Coufal, Vladimír Darida (Cap) (81.Michal Sadílek), Lukáš Masopust (61.Petr Ševčík), Antonín Barák (46.Tomáš Souček), Alex Král, Michael Krmenčík (46.Patrik Schick), Jakub Jankto (61.Matěj Vydra). Trainer: Jaroslav Šilhavý.

08.06.2021   **CZECH REPUBLIC - ALBANIA**   3-1(1-1)   Friendly International
Generali Arena, Praha; Referee: Peter Kralović (Slovakia); Attendance: 1,351
CZE: Tomáš Vaclík, Ondřej Čelůstka, Jan Bořil, Vladimír Coufal, Tomáš Kalas, Vladimír Darida (Cap) (74.Antonín Barák), Lukáš Masopust (74.Jakub Pešek), Tomáš Souček, Jakub Jankto (64.Adam Hložek), Patrik Schick (64.Tomáš Pekhart), Alex Král (64.Tomáš Holeš). Trainer: Jaroslav Šilhavý.
Goals: Patrik Schick (18), Lukáš Masopust (68), Ondřej Čelůstka (89).

14.06.2021   **SCOTLAND - CZECH REPUBLIC**   0-2(0-1)   16th EC. Group Stage.
Hampden Park, Glasgow; Referee: Daniel Siebert (Germany); Attendance: 9,847
CZE: Tomáš Vaclík, Ondřej Čelůstka, Jan Bořil, Vladimír Coufal, Tomáš Kalas, Vladimír Darida (Cap) (87.Petr Ševčík), Lukáš Masopust (72.Matěj Vydra), Tomáš Souček, Alex Král (67.Tomáš Holeš), Jakub Jankto (72.Adam Hložek), Patrik Schick (87.Michael Krmenčík). Trainer: Jaroslav Šilhavý.
Goals: Patrik Schick (42, 52).

18.06.2021   **CROATIA - CZECH REPUBLIC**   1-1(0-1)   16th EC. Group Stage.
Hampden Park, Glasgow (Scotland); Referee: Carlos del Cerro Grande (Spain); Attendance: 5,607
CZE: Tomáš Vaclík, Ondřej Čelůstka, Jan Bořil, Vladimír Coufal, Tomáš Kalas, Tomáš Holeš (63.Alex Král), Lukáš Masopust (63.Adam Hložek), Vladimír Darida (Cap) (87.Antonín Barák), Tomáš Souček, Jakub Jankto (74.Petr Ševčík), Patrik Schick (74.Michael Krmenčík). Trainer: Jaroslav Šilhavý.
Goal: Patrik Schick (37 penalty).

22.06.2021   **CZECH REPUBLIC - ENGLAND**   0-1(0-1)   16th EC. Group Stage.
Wembley Stadium, London; Referee: Artur Manuel Ribeiro Soares Dias (Portugal); Attendance: 19,104
CZE: Tomáš Vaclík, Ondřej Čelůstka, Jan Bořil, Vladimír Coufal, Tomáš Kalas, Tomáš Holeš (84.Matěj Vydra), Vladimír Darida (Cap) (64.Alex Král), Lukáš Masopust (64.Adam Hložek), Tomáš Souček, Jakub Jankto (46.Petr Ševčík), Patrik Schick (75.Tomáš Pekhart). Trainer: Jaroslav Šilhavý.

27.06.2021   **NETHERLANDS - CZECH REPUBLIC**   0-2(0-0)   16th EC. 2nd Round of 16.
Puskás Aréna, Budapest (Hungary); Referee: Sergei Karasev (Russia); Attendance: 52,834
CZE: Tomáš Vaclík, Ondřej Čelůstka, Pavel Kadeřábek, Vladimír Coufal, Tomáš Kalas, Tomáš Holeš (85.Alex Král), Lukáš Masopust (79.Jakub Jankto), Petr Ševčík (85.Adam Hložek), Tomáš Souček (Cap), Antonín Barák (90+2.Michal Sadílek), Patrik Schick (90+2.Michael Krmenčík). Trainer: Jaroslav Šilhavý.
Goals: Tomáš Holeš (68), Patrik Schick (80).

03.07.2021   **CZECH REPUBLIC - DENMARK**   1-2(0-2)   16th EC. Quarter-Finals.
Bakı Olimpiya Stadionu, Bakı (Azerbaijan); Referee: Björn Kuipers (Netherlands); Attendance: 16,306
CZE: Tomáš Vaclík, Ondřej Čelůstka (65.Jakub Brabec), Jan Bořil, Vladimír Coufal, Tomáš Kalas, Tomáš Holeš (46.Jakub Jankto), Lukáš Masopust (46.Michael Krmenčík), Petr Ševčík (80.Vladimír Darida), Antonín Barák, Tomáš Souček (Cap), Patrik Schick (79.Matěj Vydra). Trainer: Jaroslav Šilhavý.
Goal: Patrik Schick (49).

NATIONAL TEAM PLAYERS (16.07.2020 – 15.07.2021)					
Name	**DOB**	**Caps**	**Goals**	**2020/2021:**	*Club*
Goalkeepers					
Tomáš KOUBEK	26.08.1992	11	0	2020:	*FC Augsburg (GER)*
Aleš MANDOUS	21.04.1992	1	0	2020:	*SK Sigma Olomouc*
Jiří PAVLENKA	14.04.1992	14	0	2020/2021:	*SV Werder Bremen (GER)*
Tomáš VACLÍK	29.03.1989	42	0	2020/2021:	*Sevilla FC (ESP)*

Defenders

Name	DOB	Caps	Goals	Season	Club
Jan BOŘIL	11.01.1991	27	0	2020/2021:	*SK Slavia Praha*
Jakub BRABEC	06.08.1992	22	1	2020/2021:	*FC Viktoria Plzeň*
Vladimír COUFAL	22.08.1992	21	1	2020:	*SK Slavia Praha*
				02.10.2020->	*West Ham United FC London (ENG)*
Ondřej ČELŮSTKA	18.06.1989	31	3	2020/2021:	*AC Sparta Praha*
Tomáš HOLEŠ	31.03.1993	13	2	2020/2021:	*SK Slavia Praha*
David HOVORKA	07.08.1993	2	0	2020:	*SK Slavia Praha*
Roman HUBNÍK	06.06.1984	30	3	2020:	*SK Sigma Olomouc*
Václav JEMELKA	23.06.1996	2	0	2020:	*Oud-Heverle Leuven (BEL)*
Pavel KADEŘÁBEK	25.04.1992	48	3	2020/2021:	*TSG 1899 Hoffenheim (GER)*
Tomáš KALAS	15.05.1993	28	2	2020/2021:	*Bristol City FC (ENG)*
Ondřej KÚDELA	26.03.1987	8	0	2020/2021:	*SK Slavia Praha*
Aleš MATĚJŮ	03.06.1996	4	0	2020:	*Brescia Calcio (ITA)*
Filip NOVÁK	26.06.1990	25	1	2020:	*Fenerbahçe SK İstanbul (TUR)*
Tomáš PETRÁŠEK	02.03.1992	2	0	2020:	*RKS Raków Częstochowa (POL)*
Jaroslav ZELENÝ	20.08.1992	1	0	2020:	*FK Jablonec*
David ZIMA	08.11.2000	2	0	2021:	*SK Slavia Praha*

Midfielders

Name	DOB	Caps	Goals	Season	Club
Antonín BARÁK	03.12.1994	23	6	2020/2021:	*Hellas Verona FC (ITA)*
Radim BREITE	10.08.1989	1	0	2020:	*SK Sigma Olomouc*
Lukáš BUDÍNSKÝ	27.03.1992	1	0	2020:	*FK Mladá Boleslav*
Václav ČERNÝ	17.10.1997	2	0	2020:	*FC Twente Enschede (NED)*
Vladimír DARIDA	08.08.1990	76	8	2020/2021:	*Hertha BSC Berlin (GER)*
Bořek DOČKAL	30.09.1988	43	7	2020:	*AC Sparta Praha*
Marek HAVLÍK	08.07.1995	1	0	2020:	*1. FC Slovácko Uherské Hradiště*
Jakub JANKTO	19.01.1996	40	4	2020/2021:	*UC Sampdoria Genova (ITA)*
Adam JÁNOŠ	20.07.1992	1	0	2020:	*FC Baník Ostrava*
Jan KOPIC	04.06.1990	22	3	2020:	*FC Viktoria Plzeň*
Alex KRÁL	19.05.1998	22	2	2020/2021:	*FK Spartak Moskva (RUS)*
Tomáš MALINSKÝ	25.08.1991	1	0	2020:	*SK Slavia Praha*
Lukáš MASOPUST	12.02.1993	27	2	2020/2021:	*SK Slavia Praha*
David PAVELKA	18.05.1991	23	1	2021:	*AC Sparta Praha*
Jakub PEŠEK	24.06.1993	2	1	2020/2021:	*FC Slovan Liberec*
Roman POTOČNÝ	25.04.1991	1	0	2020:	*FC Baník Ostrava*
Lukáš PROVOD	23.10.1996	7	1	2020/2021:	*SK Slavia Praha*
Michal SADÍLEK	31.05.1999	2	0	2021:	*FC Slovan Liberec*
Tomáš SOUČEK	27.02.1995	40	7	2020/2021:	*West Ham United FC London (ENG)*
Petr ŠEVČÍK	04.05.1994	12	0	2020/2021:	*SK Slavia Praha*

Forwards

Name	DOB	Caps	Goals	Season	Club
Adam HLOŽEK	25.07.2002	7	0	2020/2021:	*AC Sparta Praha*
Michael KRMENČÍK	15.03.1993	33	9	2020:	*Club Brügge KV (BEL)*
				04.01.2021->	*PAOK Thessaloníki (GRE)*
Zdenek ONDRÁŠEK	22.12.1988	7	2	2020:	*FC Viktoria Plzeň*
Tomáš PEKHART	26.05.1989	23	2	2021:	*Legia Warszawa (POL)*
Tomáš POZNAR	27.09.1988	1	0	2020:	*FC Fastav Zlín*
Michael RABUŠIC	17.09.1989	4	0	2020:	*FC Slovan Liberec*
Antonín RŮSEK	22.03.1999	1	0	2020:	*FC Zbrojovka Brno*
Patrik SCHICK	24.01.1996	31	16	2021:	*TSV Bayer 04 Leverkusen (GER)*
Stanislav TECL	01.09.1990	6	0	2020:	*SK Slavia Praha*
Matěj VYDRA	01.05.1992	39	6	2020/2021:	*FC Burnley (ENG)*

Trainer

Name	DOB	Record
Jaroslav ŠILHAVÝ [from 18.09.2019]	03.11.1961	32 M; 17 W; 2 D; 13 L; 47-39

DENMARK

The Country:
Kongeriget Danmark (Kingdom of Denmark)
Capital: København
Surface: 42,925 km^2
Inhabitants: 5,850,189 [2021]
Time: UTC+1

The FA:
Dansk Boldspil-Union
House of Football, DBU Allé 1, 2605 Brøndby
Tel: +45 43 262 222
Foundation date: 18.05.1889
Member of FIFA since: 1904
Member of UEFA since: 1954
Website: www.dbu.dk

NATIONAL TEAM RECORDS

RECORDS		
First international match:	19.10.1908, London:	France – Denmark 0-9 (5th OG. 1st Round)
Most international caps:	Peter Schmeichel	- 129 caps (1987-2001)
Most international goals:	Jon Dahl Tomasson	- 52 goals / 112 caps (1997-2008)
	Poul "Tist" Nielsen	- 52 goals / 38 caps (1910-1925)

UEFA EUROPEAN CHAMPIONSHIP	
1960	Qualifiers
1964	Final Tournament (4th Place)
1968	Qualifiers
1972	Qualifiers
1976	Qualifiers
1980	Qualifiers
1984	Final Tournament (Semi-Finals)
1988	Final Tournament (Group Stage)
1992	**Final Tournament (Winners)**
1996	Final Tournament (Group Stage)
2000	Final Tournament (Group Stage)
2004	Final Tournament (Quarter-Finals)
2008	Qualifiers
2012	Final Tournament (Group Stage)
2016	Qualifiers
2020	Final Tournament (Semi-Finals)

FIFA WORLD CUP	
1930	Did not enter
1934	Did not enter
1938	Did not enter
1950	Did not enter
1954	Did not enter
1958	Qualifiers
1962	Did not enter
1966	Qualifiers
1970	Qualifiers
1974	Qualifiers
1978	Qualifiers
1982	Qualifiers
1986	Final Tournament (2nd Round of 16)
1990	Qualifiers
1994	Qualifiers
1998	Final Tournament (Quarter-Finals)
2002	Final Tournament (2nd Round of 16)
2006	Qualifiers
2010	Final Tournament (Group Stage)
2014	Qualifiers
2018	Final Tournament (2nd Round of 16)

OLYMPIC TOURNAMENTS	
1908	Runners-up
1912	Runners-up
1920	First Round
1924	Did not enter
1928	Did not enter
1936	Did not enter
1948	3rd Place
1952	Quarter-Finals
1956	Did not enter
1960	Runners-up
1964	Qualifiers
1968	Did not enter
1972	Second Round
1976	Qualifiers
1980	Qualifiers
1984	Qualifiers
1988	Qualifiers
1992	Group Stage
1996	Qualifiers
2000	Qualifiers
2004	Qualifiers
2008	Qualifiers
2012	Qualifiers
2016	Quarter-Finals

UEFA NATIONS LEAGUE

2018/2019	League B (promoted to League A)
2020/2021	League A

FIFA CONFEDERATIONS CUP 1992-2017

1995 (Winners)

DANISH CLUB HONOURS IN EUROPEAN CLUB COMPETITIONS:

European Champion Clubs' Cup (1956-1992) / UEFA Champions League (1993-2021)
None

Fairs Cup (1858-1971) / UEFA Cup (1972-2009) / UEFA Europa League (2010-2021)
None

UEFA Super Cup (1972-2020)
None

*European Cup Winners' Cup 1961-1999**
None

*defunct competition

	CHAMPIONS	CUP WINNERS*	BEST GOALSCORERS	
1912/1913	Kjøbenhavns Boldklub	-	-	
1913/1914	Kjøbenhavns Boldklub	-	-	
1914/1915	*No competition*	-	-	
1915/1916	B 93 København	-	-	
1916/1917	Kjøbenhavns Boldklub	-	-	
1917/1918	Kjøbenhavns Boldklub	-	-	
1918/1919	Akademisk BK København	-	-	
1919/1920	B 1903 København	-	-	
1920/1921	Akademisk BK København	-	-	
1921/1922	Kjøbenhavns Boldklub	-	-	
1922/1923	BK Frem København	-	-	
1923/1924	B 1903 København	-	-	
1924/1925	Kjøbenhavns Boldklub	-	-	
1925/1926	B 1903 København	-	-	
1926/1927	B 93 København	-	-	
1927/1928	*No competition*	-		
1928/1929	B 93 København	-	*Not available*	
1929/1930	B 93 København	-	*Not available*	
1930/1931	BK Frem København	-	*Not available*	
1931/1932	Kjøbenhavns Boldklub	-	*Not available*	
1932/1933	BK Frem København	-	*Not available*	
1933/1934	B 93 København	-	*Not available*	
1934/1935	B 93 København	-	*Not available*	
1935/1936	BK Frem København	-	*Not available*	
1936/1937	Akademisk BK København	-	Pauli Jørgensen (BK Frem København)	19
1937/1938	B 1903 København	-	Knud Andersen (B 1903 København)	23
1938/1939	B 93 København	-	Erik Petersen (B 93 København)	27
1939/1940	Kjøbenhavns Boldklub	-	Frede Jensen (Køge BK) Kaj Hansen (B 93 København)	12
1940/1941	BK Frem København	-	-	
1941/1942	B 93 København	-	-	
1942/1943	Akademisk BK København	-	-	
1943/1944	BK Frem København	-	-	
1944/1945	Akademisk BK København	-	-	
1945/1946	B 93 København	-	Jørgen Leschly Sørensen (B 93 København)	16
1946/1947	Akademisk BK København	-	Helge Broneé (Østerbros Boldklub)	21
1947/1948	Kjøbenhavns Boldklub	-	John Hansen (BK Frem København)	20
1948/1949	Kjøbenhavns Boldklub	-	Jørgen Leschly Sørensen (Odense Boldklub)	16
1949/1950	Kjøbenhavns Boldklub	-	James Rønvang (Akademisk BK København)	15
1950/1951	Akademisk BK København	-	James Rønvang (Akademisk BK København) Henning Bjerregaard (B 93 København) Jens Peter Hansen (Esbjerg fB)	11
1951/1952	Akademisk BK København	-	Valdemar Kendzior (Skovshoved IF) Poul Erik Petersen (Køge BK)	13
1952/1953	Kjøbenhavns Boldklub	-	Valdemar Kendzior (Skovshoved IF)	17
1953/1954	Køge BK	-	Jens-Carl Kristensen (Akademisk BK København)	12
1954/1955	AGF Aarhus	AGF Aarhus	Henning Jensen (BK Frem København)	17
1955/1956	AGF Aarhus	BK Frem København	Gunnar Kjeldberg (AGF Aarhus)	18
1956/1957	AGF Aarhus	AGF Aarhus	Søren Andersen (BK Frem København)	27
1958	Vejle Boldklub	Vejle Boldklub	Henning Enoksen (Vejle Boldklub)	27
1959	B 1909 Odense	Vejle Boldklub	Per Jensen (Kjøbenhavns Boldklub)	20
1960	AGF Aarhus	AGF Aarhus	Harald Nielsen (Frederikshavn fI)	19
1961	Esbjerg fB	AGF Aarhus	Jørgen Ravn (Kjøbenhavns Boldklub)	26
1962	Esbjerg fB	B 1909 Odense	Henning Enoksen (AGF Aarhus) Carl Emil Christiansen (Esbjerg fB)	24
1963	Esbjerg fB	B 1913 Odense	Mogens Haastrup (B 1909 Odense)	21
1964	B 1909 Odense	Esbjerg fB	Jørgen Ravn (Kjøbenhavns Boldklub)	21
1965	Esbjerg fB	AGF Aarhus	Per Petersen (B 1903 København)	18
1966	Hvidovre IF	Aalborg BK	Henning Enoksen (AGF Aarhus)	16
1967	Akademisk BK København	Randers Freja	Leif Nielsen (BK Frem København)	15
1968	Kjøbenhavns Boldklub	Randers Freja	Niels-Christian Holmstrøm (Kjøbenhavns Boldklub)	23
1969	B 1903 København	Kjøbenhavns Boldklub	Steen Rømer Larsen (B 1903 København)	15
1970	B 1903 København	Aalborg BK	Ole Forsing (B 1903 København)	18
1971	Vejle Boldklub	B 1909 Odense	Uffe Brage (Kjøbenhavns Boldklub) John Nielsen (B 1901 Nykøbing)	19
1972	Vejle Boldklub	Vejle Boldklub	Karsten Lund (Vejle Boldklub) John Nielsen (B 1901 Nykøbing)	16
1973	Hvidovre IF	Randers Freja	Hans Aabech (Hvidovre IF)	28
1974	Kjøbenhavns Boldklub	Vanløse IF	Niels-Christian Holmstrøm (Kjøbenhavns Boldklub)	24
1975	Køge BK	Vejle Boldklub	Bjarne Petersen (Kjøbenhavns Boldklub)	25
1976	B 1903 København	Esbjerg fB	Mogens Jespersen (Aalborg BK)	22
1977	Odense Boldklub	Vejle Boldklub	Allan Hansen (Odense Boldklub)	23

1978	Vejle Boldklub	BK Frem København	John Eriksen (Odense Boldklub)	22
1979	Esbjerg fB	B 1903 København	John Eriksen (Odense Boldklub)	20
1980	Kjøbenhavns Boldklub	Hvidovre IF	Hans Aabech (Kjøbenhavns Boldklub)	19
1981	Hvidovre IF	Vejle Boldklub	Allan Hansen (Odense Boldklub)	28
1982	Odense Boldklub	B 93 København	Ib Jacquet (Vejle Boldklub)	20
1983	Lyngby Boldklub	Odense Boldklub	Vilhelm Munk Nielsen (Odense Boldklub)	20
1984	Vejle Boldklub	Lyngby Boldklub	Steen Thychosen (Vejle Boldklub)	24
1985	Brøndby IF	Lyngby Boldklub	Lars Bastrup (Ikast FS)	20
1986	AGF Aarhus	B 1903 København	Claus Nielsen (Brøndby IF)	16
1987	Brøndby IF	AGF Aarhus	Claus Nielsen (Brøndby IF)	20
1988	Brøndby IF	AGF Aarhus	Bent Christensen (Brøndby IF)	21
1989	Odense Boldklub	Brøndby IF	Miklos Molnar (BK Frem København) Flemming Christensen (Lyngby Boldklub) Lars Jakobsen (Odense Boldklub)	14
1990	Brøndby IF	Lyngby Boldklub	Bent Christensen (Brøndby IF)	17
1991	Brøndby IF	Odense Boldklub	Bent Christensen (Brøndby IF)	11
1991/1992	Lyngby Boldklub	AGF Aarhus	Peter Møller (Aalborg BK)	17
1992/1993	FC København	Odense Boldklub	Peter Møller (Aalborg BK)	22
1993/1994	Silkeborg IF	Brøndby IF	Søren Frederiksen (Silkeborg IF)	18
1994/1995	Aalborg BK	FC København	Erik Bo Andersen (Aalborg BK)	24
1995/1996	Brøndby IF	AGF Aarhus	Thomas Thorninger (AGF Aarhus)	20
1996/1997	Brøndby IF	FC København	Miklos Molnar (Lyngby Boldklub)	26
1997/1998	Brøndby IF	Brøndby IF	Ebbe Sand (Brøndby IF)	28
1998/1999	Aalborg BK	Akademisk BK København	Heine Fernandez (Viborg FF)	23
1999/2000	Herfølge BK	Viborg FF	Peter Lassen (Silkeborg IF)	16
2000/2001	FC København	Silkeborg IF	Peter Graulund (Brøndby IF)	21
2001/2002	Brøndby IF	Odense Boldklub	Peter Madsen (Brøndby IF) Kaspar Dalgas (Odense Boldklub)	22
2002/2003	FC København	Brøndby IF	Søren Frederiksen (Viborg FF) Jan Kristiansen (Esbjerg fB)	18
2003/2004	FC København	FC København	Steffen Højer (Odense Boldklub) Mohamed Zidan (EGY, FC Midtjylland Herning) Tommy Bechmann (Esbjerg fB) Mwape Miti (ZAM, Odense Boldklub)	19
2004/2005	Brøndby IF	Brøndby IF	Steffen Højer (Odense Boldklub)	20
2005/2006	FC København	Randers FC	Steffen Højer (Viborg FF)	16
2006/2007	FC København	Odense Boldklub	Rade Prica (SWE, Aalborg BK)	19
2007/2008	Aalborg BK	Brøndby IF	Jeppe Lund Curth (Aalborg BK)	17
2008/2009	FC København	FC København	Morten Nordstrand (FC København) Marc Nygaard (Randers FC)	16
2009/2010	FC København	FC Nordsjælland Farum	Peter Maduabuchi Utaka (NGA, Odense Boldklub)	18
2010/2011	FC København	FC Nordsjælland Farum	Dame N'Doye (SEN, FC København)	25
2011/2012	FC Nordsjælland Farum	FC København	Dame N'Doye (SEN, FC København)	18
2012/2013	FC København	Esbjerg fB	Andreas Evald Cornelius (FC København)	18
2013/2014	Aalborg BK	Aalborg BK	Thomas Dalgaard (Viborg FF)	18
2014/2015	FC Midtjylland Herning	FC København	Martin Pušić (AUT, Esbjerg fB / FC Midtjylland Herning)	17
2015/2016	FC København	FC København	Lukas Spalvis (LTU, Aalborg BK)	18
2016/2017	FC København	FC København	Marcus Ingvartsen (FC Nordsjælland Farum)	23
2017/2018	FC Midtjylland Herning	Brøndby IF	Pål Alexander Kirkevold (NOR, Hobro IK)	22
2018/2019	FC København	FC Midtjylland Herning	Robert Skov (FC København)	29
2019/2020	FC Midtjylland Herning	Sønderjysk Elitesport	Ronnie Schwartz (Silkeborg IF / FC Midtjylland Herning)	18
2020/2021	Brøndby IF	Randers FC	Mikael Uhre (Brøndby IF)	19

*Cup competition called Landspokalturneringen (1954-1989), Giro Cup (1898-1996), Compaq Cup (1996-1999), DONG Cup (1999-2004), Landspokalturneringen (2004-2008), Ekstra Bladet Cup (2008-2011) and DBU Pokalen (since 2011).

NATIONAL CHAMPIONSHIP
Alka Superligaen 2020/2021
(11.09.2020 – 24.05.2021)

Regular Season - Results

Round 1 [11-14.09.2020]
SønderjyskE - FC Midtjylland 2-0(0-0)
AC Horsens - Randers FC 0-3(0-0)
Lyngby BK - Aalborg BK 0-0
Brøndby IF - FC Nordsjælland 3-2(0-2)
Odense BK - FC København 3-2(3-0)
AGF Aarhus - Vejle BK 4-2(2-0)

Round 2 [19-21.09.2020]
FC Midtjylland - Lyngby BK 1-0(1-0)
FC København - Brøndby IF 1-2(1-1)
Odense BK - FC Nordsjælland 1-1(0-0)
Randers FC - AGF Aarhus 1-1(0-0)
Vejle BK - SønderjyskE 4-1(1-0)
Aalborg BK - AC Horsens 1-0(0-0)

Round 3 [26-28.09.2020]
FC Midtjylland - Randers FC 1-0(1-0)
AGF Aarhus - Odense BK 4-2(2-1)
SønderjyskE - Aalborg BK 3-1(1-0)
Brøndby IF - AC Horsens 2-1(2-0)
Vejle BK - FC København 2-2(0-1)
FC Nordsjælland - Lyngby BK 4-1(0-1)

Round 4 [02-04.10.2020]
Randers FC - Brøndby IF 1-2(0-1)
Lyngby BK - SønderjyskE 2-2(1-1)
Odense BK - Vejle BK 0-1(0-0)
Aalborg BK - AGF Aarhus 1-1(0-1)
AC Horsens - FC Midtjylland 2-2(2-2)
FC København - FC Nordsjælland 3-2(2-1)

Round 5 [17-19.10.2020]
FC Midtjylland - Odense BK 3-1(0-1)
AGF Aarhus - AC Horsens 3-0(1-0)
Vejle BK - Lyngby BK 3-2(1-1)
SønderjyskE - Brøndby IF 2-0(0-0)
FC København - Aalborg BK 1-2(0-2)
FC Nordsjælland - Randers FC 1-0(0-0)

Round 6 [23-26.10.2020]
Lyngby BK - Odense BK 0-3(0-2)
Brøndby IF - FC Midtjylland 2-3(1-0)
AC Horsens - FC Nordsjælland 1-1(1-0)
Randers FC - SønderjyskE 1-2(1-2)
AGF Aarhus - FC København 0-1(0-1)
Aalborg BK - Vejle BK 1-3(1-1)

Round 7 [30.10.-02.11.2020]
Vejle BK - Randers FC 0-3(0-0)
FC Nordsjælland - FC Midtjylland 4-1(2-1)
Odense BK - AC Horsens 1-0(1-0)
FC København - Lyngby BK 4-2(2-0)
Aalborg BK - Brøndby IF 2-1(1-1)
SønderjyskE - AGF Aarhus 1-1(1-1)

Round 8 [06-08.11.2020]
Randers FC - Aalborg BK 1-2(0-1)
FC Nordsjælland - Vejle BK 1-1(1-1)
Lyngby BK - AGF Aarhus 1-2(1-0)
Brøndby IF - Odense BK 3-1(1-0)
FC Midtjylland - FC København 4-0(2-0)
AC Horsens - SønderjyskE 0-3(0-1)

Round 9 [20-23.11.2020]
Lyngby BK - AC Horsens 1-1(1-1)
Aalborg BK - FC Nordsjælland 1-1(0-1)
Odense BK - SønderjyskE 1-1(0-0)
AGF Aarhus - FC Midtjylland 1-2(0-2)
Vejle BK - Brøndby IF 0-2(0-1)
FC København - Randers FC 1-2(0-1)

Round 10 [27-30.11.2020]
Randers FC - Odense BK 2-1(1-0)
FC Midtjylland - Aalborg BK 0-0
AC Horsens - Vejle BK 3-1(2-0)
SønderjyskE - FC København 1-3(0-2)
FC Nordsjælland - AGF Aarhus 3-1(2-1)
Brøndby IF - Lyngby BK 4-1(1-0)

Round 11 [04-07.12.2020]
Odense BK - Aalborg BK 2-1(0-1)
Vejle BK - FC Midtjylland 0-2(0-1)
SønderjyskE - FC Nordsjælland 2-1(1-0)
FC København - AC Horsens 2-0(2-0)
Lyngby BK - Randers FC 0-3(0-0)
AGF Aarhus - Brøndby IF 3-1(1-1)

Round 12 [11-14.12.2020]
Randers FC - Vejle BK 3-1(0-1)
Aalborg BK - Lyngby BK 3-2(2-2)
AC Horsens - AGF Aarhus 1-2(0-1)
FC Nordsjælland - FC København 0-1(0-0)
Brøndby IF - SønderjyskE 2-1(1-1)
Odense BK - FC Midtjylland 1-1(1-0)

Round 13 [20-21.12.2020]
Lyngby BK - Vejle BK 0-0
SønderjyskE - Randers FC 0-1(0-0)
AGF Aarhus - Aalborg BK 3-0(3-0)
FC København - Odense BK 1-1(1-0)
AC Horsens - Brøndby IF 1-2(0-1)
FC Midtjylland - FC Nordsjælland 3-1(2-1)

Round 14 [02-04.02.2021]
Randers FC - AC Horsens 3-0(2-0)
Vejle BK - AGF Aarhus 0-0
Odense BK - Lyngby BK 0-1(0-0)
Aalborg BK - FC København 2-3(2-0)
FC Midtjylland - SønderjyskE 1-2(0-1)
FC Nordsjælland - Brøndby IF 0-1(0-1)

Round 15 [07-08.02.2021]
FC Nordsjælland - Odense BK 0-2(0-1)
SønderjyskE - Vejle BK 0-1(0-0)
AC Horsens - FC København 0-2(0-2)
AGF Aarhus - Lyngby BK 1-0(0-0)
Brøndby IF - Aalborg BK 1-1(0-0)
Randers FC - FC Midtjylland 1-2(0-0)

Round 16 [14-15.02.2021]
Aalborg BK - Randers FC 0-0
Vejle BK - FC Nordsjælland 2-2(1-0)
Lyngby BK - Brøndby IF 0-4(0-2)
FC Midtjylland - AC Horsens 1-0(0-0)
Odense BK - AGF Aarhus 0-0
FC København - SønderjyskE 3-2(1-1)

Round 17 [19-22.02.2021]
Aalborg BK - FC Midtjylland 0-2(0-1)
AC Horsens - Odense BK 0-0
Randers FC - FC Nordsjælland 1-1(1-0)
AGF Aarhus - SønderjyskE 2-0(0-0)
Brøndby IF - Vejle BK 2-1(1-0)
Lyngby BK - FC København 2-2(0-1)

Round 18 [26.02.-01.03.2021]
Vejle BK - AC Horsens 0-0
FC Nordsjælland - Aalborg BK 2-2(1-1)
Odense BK - Randers FC 2-1(1-1)
FC København - AGF Aarhus 3-3(1-3)
FC Midtjylland - Brøndby IF 1-0(0-0)
SønderjyskE - Lyngby BK 1-4(0-2)

Round 19 [03-04.03.2021]
AGF Aarhus - FC Nordsjælland 0-1(0-1)
AC Horsens - Aalborg BK 2-1(1-0)
FC København - Vejle BK 2-1(1-0)
Lyngby BK - FC Midtjylland 2-0(1-0)
SønderjyskE - Odense BK 1-1(0-0)
Brøndby IF - Randers FC 0-0

Round 20 [07-08.03.2021]
Randers FC - Lyngby BK 1-2(1-0)
Brøndby IF - FC København 2-1(0-0)
FC Midtjylland - AGF Aarhus 0-1(0-1)
FC Nordsjælland - AC Horsens 2-2(1-1)
Vejle BK - Odense BK 2-0(0-0)
Aalborg BK - SønderjyskE 1-0(0-0)

Round 21 [12-15.03.2021]
Lyngby BK - FC Nordsjælland 0-3(0-1)
SønderjyskE - AC Horsens 2-0(2-0)
Vejle BK - Aalborg BK 0-2(0-1)
Odense BK - Brøndby IF 0-3(0-3)
FC København - FC Midtjylland 0-0
AGF Aarhus - Randers FC 1-1(1-0)

Round 22 [21.03.2021]
Aalborg BK - Odense BK 0-2(0-1)
AC Horsens - Lyngby BK 1-2(0-2)
Brøndby IF - AGF Aarhus 1-1(1-1)
FC Midtjylland - Vejle BK 5-0(2-0)
FC Nordsjælland - SønderjyskE 2-1(2-0)
Randers FC - FC København 2-1(1-1)

1. Brøndby IF	22	14	3	5	40 - 24	45
2. FC Midtjylland Herning	22	13	4	5	35 - 20	43
3. AGF Aarhus	22	10	8	4	35 - 22	38
4. FC København	22	10	5	7	39 - 35	35
5. Randers FC	22	9	5	8	31 - 21	32
6. FC Nordsjælland Farum	22	7	8	7	35 - 30	29
7. Sønderjysk Elitesport	22	8	4	10	30 - 32	28
8. Odense Boldklub	22	7	7	8	25 - 28	28
9. Aalborg BK	22	7	7	8	24 - 30	28
10. Vejle Boldklub	22	6	6	10	25 - 37	24
11. Lyngby Boldklub	22	5	5	12	25 - 43	20
12. AC Horsens	22	2	6	14	15 - 37	12

Teams ranked 1-6 were qualified for the Championship Round, while teams ranked 7-12 were qualified for the Relegation Round.

Relegation Round

Results

Round 23 [04-06.04.2021]
AC Horsens - Odense BK 1-1(1-0)
Aalborg BK - SønderjyskE 3-2(1-1)
Lyngby BK - Vejle BK 0-0

Round 24 [09-12.04.2021]
Odense BK - Vejle BK 0-1(0-0)
SønderjyskE - AC Horsens 2-3(2-0)
Lyngby BK - Aalborg BK 2-2(0-0)

Round 25 [16-18.04.2021]
Vejle BK - Aalborg BK 1-1(0-1)
AC Horsens - Lyngby BK 1-3(0-1)
Odense BK - SønderjyskE 1-1(1-0)

Round 26 [21-22.04.2021]
Lyngby BK - SønderjyskE 0-1(0-1)
Aalborg BK - Odense BK 3-2(1-0)
Vejle BK - AC Horsens 3-0(2-0)

Round 27 [25.04.2021]
AC Horsens - Aalborg BK 1-0(0-0)
SønderjyskE - Vejle BK 1-0(0-0)
Odense BK - Lyngby BK 2-0(2-0)

Round 28 [30.04.-02.05.2021]
AC Horsens - Vejle BK 3-3(2-0)
Aalborg BK - Lyngby BK 4-0(2-0)
SønderjyskE - Odense BK 2-0(0-0)

Round 29 [07-09.05.2021]
Odense BK - Aalborg BK 1-0(1-0)
Lyngby BK - AC Horsens 3-4(0-2)
Vejle BK - SønderjyskE 4-2(1-0)

Round 30 [14-17.05.2021]
Vejle BK - Odense BK 2-2(2-1)
Aalborg BK - AC Horsens 1-1(0-1)
SønderjyskE - Lyngby BK 2-0(1-0)

Round 31 [19-20.05.2021]
Aalborg BK - Vejle BK 2-1(0-1)
AC Horsens - SønderjyskE 1-2(1-0)
Lyngby BK - Odense BK 1-2(0-1)

Round 32 [24.05.2021]
SønderjyskE - Aalborg BK 0-4(0-2)
Vejle BK - Lyngby BK 2-2(1-2)
Odense BK - AC Horsens 4-0(2-0)

Final Standings

							Total			Home					Away			
1. Aalborg BK	32	12	10	10	44 - 41	46	8	4	4	25 - 21	4	6	6	19 - 20				
2. Sønderjysk Elitesport	32	13	5	14	45 - 48	44	8	2	6	22 - 20	5	3	8	23 - 28				
3. Odense Boldklub	32	11	10	11	40 - 39	43	7	5	4	19 - 14	4	5	7	21 - 25				
4. Vejle Boldklub	32	9	11	12	42 - 50	38	5	7	4	25 - 23	4	4	8	17 - 27				
5. Lyngby Boldklub (Relegated)	32	6	8	18	36 - 63	26	1	7	8	14 - 29	5	1	10	22 - 34				
6. AC Horsens (Relegated)	32	5	9	18	30 - 59	24	3	5	8	18 - 28	2	4	10	12 - 31				

Please note: Aalborg BK were qualified for the Europa Conference League Play-offs.

Championship Round

Results

Round 23 [04-05.04.2021]
FC Nordsjælland - AGF Aarhus 2-0(1-0)
FC København - Randers FC 2-1(2-1)
FC Midtjylland - Brøndby IF 1-0(1-0)

Round 24 [11.04.2021]
Randers FC - FC Nordsjælland 3-4(1-3)
Brøndby IF - FC København 1-3(0-1)
AGF Aarhus - FC Midtjylland 1-4(0-1)

Round 25 [18-19.04.2021]
FC København - FC Nordsjælland 2-2(1-1)
Brøndby IF - AGF Aarhus 2-2(1-2)
Randers FC - FC Midtjylland 0-0

Round 26 [21-22.04.2021]
FC Nordsjælland - Brøndby IF 0-3(0-1)
AGF Aarhus - Randers FC 2-0(1-0)
FC Midtjylland - FC København 4-1(1-0)

Round 27 [25-26.04.2021]
Brøndby IF - Randers FC 2-0(1-0)
AGF Aarhus - FC København 1-2(1-0)
FC Nordsjælland - FC Midtjylland 3-2(1-1)

Round 28 [02-03.05.2021]
Randers FC - Brøndby IF 4-2(1-1)
FC Midtjylland - FC Nordsjælland 3-0(2-0)
FC København - AGF Aarhus 3-2(3-0)

Round 29 [09-10.05.2021]
Randers FC - AGF Aarhus 0-1(0-1)
Brøndby IF - FC Midtjylland 3-1(1-1)
FC Nordsjælland - FC København 2-2(0-0)

Round 30 [16.05.2021]
FC Midtjylland - Randers FC 1-1(0-1)
FC København - Brøndby IF 2-1(1-1)
AGF Aarhus - FC Nordsjælland 3-1(2-1)

Round 31 [19-20.05.2021]
FC Nordsjælland - Randers FC 2-1(2-1)
FC København - FC Midtjylland 4-2(2-2)
AGF Aarhus - Brøndby IF 1-2(1-1)

Round 32 [24.05.2021]
Brøndby IF - FC Nordsjælland 2-0(1-0)
FC Midtjylland - AGF Aarhus 4-0(2-0)
Randers FC - FC København 2-1(0-0)

Final Standings

		Total							Home							Away			
1. **Brøndby IF**	32	19	4	9	58	-	38	61	10	4	2	32	-	19	9	0	7	26	-	19
2. Brøndby IF	32	18	6	8	57	-	33	60	12	2	2	33	-	7	6	4	6	24	-	26
3. FC København	32	16	7	9	61	-	53	55	9	4	3	34	-	25	7	3	6	27	-	28
4. AGF Aarhus	32	13	9	10	48	-	42	48	9	1	6	30	-	19	4	8	4	18	-	23
5. FC Nordsjælland Farum	32	11	10	11	51	-	51	43	8	4	4	28	-	21	3	6	7	23	-	30
6. Randers FC	32	11	7	14	43	-	38	40	6	3	7	26	-	23	5	4	7	17	-	15

<u>Please note</u>: AGF Aarhus were qualified for the Europa Conference League Play-offs.

Top goalscorers:

19	**Mikael Uhre**	***Brøndby IF***
15	Patrick Mortensen	*AGF Aarhus*
15	Jonas Older Wind	*FC København*
11	Sory Kaba (GUI)	*FC Midtjylland Herning*
11	Haji Amir Wright (USA)	*Sønderjysk Elitesport*

Europa Conference League Play-off [28.05.2021]

AGF Aarhus - Aalborg BK 2-2(1-0,1-1,2-2); 3-1 on penalties

NATIONAL CUP
DBU Pokalen / Sydbank Pokalen 2020/2021

First Round [01-03.09./08.09./23.09.2020]

Glamsbjerg IF - Esbjerg fB	0-8	Brønshøj BK - BK Frem København	2-1
Ringsted IF - Vordingborg IK	3-0	Gentofte-Vangede IF - BK Avarta	1-2 aet
Frederikssund IK - Næstved BK	1-4	ASA Aarhus - Aalborg Chang	4-0
Ishöj BK - AB Gladsaxe	1-2 aet	Rønne IK - B 93 København	0-3 *awarded*
BK Skjold - KFUMs BK København	1-1 aet; 5-6 pen	IF Lyseng - Hobro IK	0-7
Vanløse IF - Hillerød GI	1-2 aet	Bispebjerg BK - FC Helsingør	3-2
B 1908 Amager - BK Fremad Amager	1-3	FC ESPM - Solrød FC	2-5
FC Sydvest 05 - FC Fredericia	2-0	BK Rødovre - FC Græsrødderne	2-4
Aalborg Freja - VSK Aarhus	0-4	Fjordager IF - Hedensted IF	1-2
Brønderslev IF - Brabrand IF	0-4	Kjellerup IF - Thisted FC	3-0
Skjold Birkerød - Avedøre IF	1-0	Glostrup FK - Hvidovre IF	0-2
Allerød FK - BK Union København	3-1	Løjt IF - Grindsted GIF	0-2
FK Utopia - Bogense G & IF	1-1 aet; 6-5 pen	Otterup B&IK - Middelfart Boldklub	2-3
Frem Sakskøbing - FC Roskilde	1-6	FIUK Odense - Næsby BK	0-6
Nordfalsters FB - Ledøje-Smørum Fodbold	1-3	FC Skanderborg – OKS	1-1 aet; 2-4 pen
Egebjerg Fodbold - Kolding IF	0-2	Helsted Fremad IF - Holstebro BK	0-1
Sædding/Guldager - Kolding Boldklub	0-1	Slagelse B&I - Dalum IF	2-1 aet
Højslev IF - Viby IF	0-4	Suså IF - Holbæk B&I	1-2
FC Djursland - Skive IK	0-7	St. Restrup IF - Silkeborg IF	0-5
Morsø FC - Viborg FF	0-9	Hundested IK - Ballerup-Skovlunde	0-3
Ringkøbing IF - Vendsyssel FF Hjørring	0-2	Vejgaard BK - Jammerbugt FC	0-2
Nakskov BK - Nykøbing FC	0-3	Vatanspor Braband - Aarhus Fremad	1-5
Skovshoved IF - Hellerup IK	0-0 aet; 5-4 pen	FA 2000 Frederiksberg - HB Køge	0-3

Second Round [06-08.10./13.10.2020]

Solrød FC - B 93 København	0-3(0-1)	OKS - VSK Aarhus	1-2(1-0)
Kjellerup IF - Brabrand IF	2-4(0-2)	KFUMs BK København - Hvidovre IF	0-2(0-0)
Hedensted IF - Viborg FF	3-1(1-0,1-0)	Aarhus Fremad - Vendsyssel FF Hjørring	5-0(1-0)
Ledøje-Smørum Fodbold - FC Roskilde	2-1(0-1)	Allerød FK - AB Gladsaxe	1-2(0-0,0-0)
Ringsted IF - BK Avarta	2-3(0-1,1-1)	Næsby BK - AC Horsens	0-3(0-1)
Skjold Birkerød - Nykøbing FC	0-6(0-4)	Hillerød GI - Odense BK	1-2(1-2)
Bispebjerg BK - HB Køge	0-4(0-3)	Slagelse B&I - Skovshoved IF	2-0(0-0)
FC Sydvest 05 - Randers FC	1-4(1-2)	Holbæk B&I - BK Fremad Amager	0-3(0-0)
Viby IF - Skive IK	1-2(1-0)	Brønshøj BK - Lyngby BK	4-5(2-3,4-4)
Jammerbugt FC - Middelfart Boldklub	2-1(0-1)	Hobro IK - Vejle BK	0-3(0-1)
FK Utopia - Kolding IF	0-5(0-2)	FC Græsrødderne - FC Nordsjælland Farum	1-5(1-3)
Grindsted GIF - ASA Aarhus	1-2(0-2)	Esbjerg fB - Silkeborg IF	2-1(1-1)
Kolding Boldklub - Holstebro BK	0-4(0-3)	Ballerup-Skovlunde - Næstved BK	0-0 aet; 4-3 pen

Third Round [04-05.11./10-12.10./02.12.2020]

BK Avarta - FC København	1-2(1-1)	AB Gladsaxe - Aalborg BK	1-2(1-2)
Ledøje-Smørum Fodbold - Brøndby IF	0-1(0-1)	Brabrand IF - Vejle BK	2-2 aet; 2-4 pen
Aarhus Fremad - Randers FC	1-3(1-1)	Slagelse B&I - Lyngby BK	0-9(0-4)
ASA Aarhus - B 93 København	1-4(1-1)	VSK Aarhus - AC Horsens	2-4(1-2)
Skive IK - Sønderjysk Elitesport	0-1(0-1)	Nykøbing FC - Esbjerg fB	1-0(0-0)
Hedensted IF - BK Fremad Amager	1-5(0-1)	Kolding IF - AGF Aarhus	3-3 aet; 3-4 pen
Ballerup-Skovlunde - Odense BK	0-3(0-2)	Hvidovre IF - FC Nordsjælland Farum	2-0(2-0)
HB Køge - FC Midtjylland Herning	0-1(0-1)	Jammerbugt FC - Holstebro BK	3-4(2-1)

1/8-Finals [08-09.12./15-17.12.2020]				
B 93 København - Aalborg BK	1-0(1-0)	Sønderjysk Elitesport - Lyngby BK	2-1(1-1,1-1)
Nykøbing FC - Odense BK	0-3(0-2)	AGF Aarhus - AC Horsens	1-0(0-0)
Hvidovre IF - Vejle BK	2-3(1-0)	BK Fremad Amager - Brøndby IF	2-1(1-1,1-1)
Holstebro BK - Randers FC	1-3(0-1)	FC København - FC Midtjylland Herning	1-1 aet; 5-6 pen

Quarter-Finals [10-11.02./10-11.03.2021]				
First Leg		**Second Leg**	
BK Fremad Amager - Sønderjysk Elitesport	1-2(0-1)	Sønderjysk Elitesport - BK Fremad Amager	4-1(2-0)
AGF Aarhus - B 93 København	3-1(1-0)	B 93 København - AGF Aarhus	2-1(1-0)
Odense BK - FC Midtjylland Herning	1-2(1-1)	FC Midtjylland Herning - Odense BK	3-0(1-0)
Vejle BK - Randers FC	0-0	Randers FC - Vejle BK	3-1(3-1)

Semi-Finals [08/15.04.2021]				
First Leg		**Second Leg**	
FC Midtjylland Herning - Sønderjysk Elitesport	1-0(0-0)	Sønderjysk Elitesport - FC Midtjylland Herning	3-1(0-0)
AGF Aarhus - Randers FC	0-2(0-0)	Randers FC - AGF Aarhus	1-1(1-1)

Final

13.05.2021; Ceres Park, Aarhus; Referee: Morten Krogh; Attendance: 7,981
Randers FC - Sønderjysk Elitesport   **4-0(2-0)**

Randers FC: Patrik Carlgren, Mikkel Kallesøe Andreasen (80.Jesper Lauridsen), Simon Piesinger, Erik Marxen, Björn Kopplin, Lasse Berg Johnsen (89.Mathias Aaris Kragh Nielsen), Vito Hammershøy-Mistrati (80.Simon Graves Jensen), Kehinde Oluwatosin (70.Tobias Klysner), Frederik Lauenborg, Mathias Peter Greve Petersen (88.Nikola Mileusnić), Marvin Egho. Trainer: Thomas Thomasberg.

Sønderjysk Elitesport: Lawrence Andrew Kingsley Thomas, Stefan Gartenmann, Marc Dal Hende, Pierre Kanstrup, Patrick Banggaard Jensen (46.Emil Frederiksen), Jeppe Friborg Simonsen, Victor Sylvestre Mpindi Ekani (74.Bård Finne), Julius Eskesen (46.Emil Holm), Rilwan Olanrewaju Hassan (65.Mads Albæk), Anders Kvindebjerg Jacobsen, Haji Amir Wright (74.Peter Christiansen). Trainer: Glen Riddersholm.

Goals: 1-0 Erik Marxen (2), 2-0 Mathias Peter Greve Petersen (7), 3-0 Simon Piesinger (52), 4-0 Mathias Peter Greve Petersen (81).

THE CLUBS 2020/2021

Please note: appearances and goals includes statistics of both regular season and play-offs (Championship Round & Relegation Round).

Aalborg Boldspilklub

Founded:	13.05.1985	
Stadium:	Aalborg Portland Park (13,797)	
Trainer:	Jacob Friis	11.12.1976
[29.10.2020]	Peter Feher	07.05.1974
[01.01.2021]	Martí Cifuentes Corvillo (ESP)	07.07.1982

Goalkeepers:	DOB	M	(s)	G
Andreas Hansen	11.08.1995	1	(1)	
Jacob Rinne (SWE)	20.06.1993	31		
Defenders:	**DOB**	**M**	**(s)**	**G**
Jakob Ahlmann Nielsen	18.01.1991	28		3
Thomas Christiansen	19.04.2001		(1)	
Daniel Granli (NOR)	01.05.1994	22	(4)	
Lukas Klitten	01.05.2000	5	(9)	
Tetchi Jores Charlemagne Ulrich Okore	11.08.1992	12	(1)	1
Kristoffer Pallesen	30.04.1990	27	(4)	
Kasper Pedersen	13.01.1991	1		
Mathias Ross	15.01.2001	20	(5)	2
Rasmus Thelander	09.07.1991	26		1
Midfielders:	**DOB**	**M**	**(s)**	**G**
Frederik Børsting	13.02.1995	16	(13)	2
Magnus Christensen	20.08.1997	8	(6)	

	DOB	M	(s)	G
Iver Fossum (NOR)	15.07.1996	30	(1)	9
Marcus Hannesbo	11.05.2002	9	(7)	2
Oscar Karl Niclas Hiljemark (SWE)	28.06.1992	5	(5)	1
Malthe Højholt	16.04.2001	7	(4)	
Robert Kakeeto (UGA)	19.05.1995	4	(4)	
Pedro Miguel Dinis Ferreira (POR)	05.01.1998	25	(3)	
Forwards:	**DOB**	**M**	**(s)**	**G**
Lucas Qvistorff Andersen	13.09.1994	13	(5)	1
Oliver Klitten	01.05.2000		(2)	
Kasper Kusk	10.11.1991	21	(9)	3
Timothé Nkada Zogo (FRA)	20.07.1999		(11)	
Tim Prica (SWE)	23.04.2002	8	(17)	5
Rubén Herráiz Alcaraz „Rufo" (ESP)	13.01.1993	5	(10)	3
Martin Samuelsen (NOR)	17.04.1997	10	(3)	
Tom van Weert (NED)	07.06.1990	18	(13)	8

Aarhus Gymnastikforening

Founded:	1880	
Stadium:	Ceres Park, Aarhus (20,032)	
Trainer:	David Nielsen	01.12.1976

Goalkeepers:	DOB	M	(s)	G
William Eskelinen (SWE)	03.09.1996	4		
Kamil Grabara (POL)	08.01.1999	28		
Defenders:	**DOB**	**M**	**(s)**	**G**
Jacob Andersen	26.01.2004		(1)	
Niklas Backman (SWE)	13.11.1988		(4)	
Kevin Diks (NED)	06.10.1996	20	(4)	7
Alexander Joseph Gersbach (AUS)	08.05.1997	1	(2)	
Sebastian Hausner	11.04.2000	27		
Casper Højer Nielsen	20.11.1994	28		3
Jesper Juelsgård	26.01.1989	19	(5)	
Mikkel Møller Lassen	19.06.2001		(1)	
Alexander Munksgaard	13.12.1997	15	(12)	
Bubacarr Sanneh (GAM)	14.11.1994	5	(3)	
Thomas Thiesson Kristensen	17.01.2002	1	(1)	
Frederik Tingager	22.02.1993	13		1

Midfielders:	DOB	M	(s)	G
Bror Blume	22.01.1992	24	(6)	2
Zachary Duncan (AUS)	31.05.2000	1	(2)	
Albert Grønbæk Erlykke	23.05.2001	21	(10)	5
Benjamin Hvidt	12.03.2000	9	(14)	1
Patrick Olsen	23.04.1994	30		3
Nikolai Poulsen	15.08.1993	23	(1)	
Mathias Sauer	02.04.2004		(1)	
Forwards:	**DOB**	**M**	**(s)**	**G**
Alexander Ammitzbøll	17.02.1999	3	(10)	1
Daniel Arzani (AUS)	04.01.1999	1	(2)	
Nicklas Helenius	08.05.1991		(10)	
Milan Jevtović (SRB)	13.06.1993	1	(13)	
Mathias Jørgensen	20.09.2000		(1)	
Neo Gift Links (RSA)	02.10.1994	21	(7)	4
Patrick Mortensen	13.07.1989	29		15
Søren Tengstedt	30.06.2000	1	(8)	
Jón Dagur Þorsteinsson (ISL)	26.11.1998	27	(4)	6

Brøndbyernes Idrætsforening

Founded: 03.12.1964
Stadium: Brøndby Stadion, Brøndby (29,000)
Trainer: Niels Frederiksen   11.09.1968

Goalkeepers:	DOB	M	(s)	G
Marvin Schwäbe (GER)	25.04.1995	32		
Defenders:	**DOB**	**M**	**(s)**	**G**
Peter Bjur	02.02.2000	18	(3)	
Tobias Borchgrevink Børkeeiet (NOR)	18.04.1999	1	(20)	
Andreas Bruus	16.01.1999	20	(8)	1
Hjörtur Hermannsson (ISL)	08.02.1995	19	(6)	1
Anthony Jung (GER)	03.11.1991	31		
Michael Lumb	09.01.1988	1	(1)	
Andreas Beyer Maxsø	18.03.1994	30		2
Kevin Mensah	15.05.1991	21	(2)	1
Blas Miguel Riveros Galeano (PAR)	03.02.1998	1		1
Sigurd Rosted (NOR)	22.07.1994	16	(7)	3

Midfielders:	DOB	M	(s)	G
Anis Ben Slimane (TUN)	16.03.2001	4	(23)	3
Rezan Corlu	07.08.1997	1	(9)	
Morten Frendrup	07.04.2001	30	(1)	
Jesper Grænge Lindstrøm	29.02.2000	28	(1)	10
Josip Radošević (CRO)	03.04.1994	25	(6)	
Lasse Vigen	15.08.1994	10	(17)	4
Forwards:	**DOB**	**M**	**(s)**	**G**
Oskar Fallenius (SWE)	01.11.2001		(5)	
Simon Hedlund (SWE)	11.03.1993	25	(6)	8
Mathias Kvistgaarden	15.04.2002		(2)	
Andrija Pavlović (SRB)	16.11.1993	7	(13)	4
Mikkel Uhre	30.09.1994	32		19

Alliance Club Horsens

Founded: 1994
Stadium: CASA Arena, Horsens (10,400)
Trainer: Bo Henriksen   07.02.1975
[24.08.2020]   Jonas Dal   07.07.1976
[09.12.2020]   Mads Lyng   23.04.1983
[17.01.2021]   Jens Berthel Askou   19.08.1982

Goalkeepers:	DOB	M	(s)	G
Matej Delač (CRO)	20.08.1992	31		
Aleksander Stanković	25.05.1995	1		
Defenders:	**DOB**	**M**	**(s)**	**G**
Jacob Buus Jacobsen	07.03.1997	18	(9)	2
Nikolas Dyhr	18.06.2001	14	(3)	
Rune Frantsen	15.10.1991	10	(5)	
James Gomez (GAM)	14.11.2001	10	(3)	1
Magnus Jensen	27.10.1996		(9)	
Malte Kiilerich	16.10.1995	29	(2)	
Thor Søndergaard Lange	04.08.1993	2	(4)	
Alexander Ludwig	30.06.1993	29	(1)	1
Michael Lumb	09.01.1988	8		1
Peter Nymann	22.08.1982	16	(10)	
Søren Reese	29.07.1993	15	(1)	
Lukas Wagner			(1)	
Midfielders:	**DOB**	**M**	**(s)**	**G**
Asbjørn Gaarde Agergaard	2003		(1)	

Jonas Gemmer	31.01.1996	14	(12)	
Hallur Hansson (FRO)	08.07.1992	27	(4)	2
Ágúst Eðvald Hlynsson (ISL)	28.03.2000	1	(6)	
Bjarke Jacobsen	21.08.1993	25	(1)	1
David Kruse	15.05.2002	1	(4)	
Angelo Nehme	23.01.2004	1		
Peter Therkildsen	13.06.1998		(1)	
Jonas Thorsen	19.04.1990	11	(8)	1
Forwards:	**DOB**	**M**	**(s)**	**G**
Muamer Brajanac	15.02.2001	10	(14)	1
Nicolai Brock-Madsen	09.01.1993	12	(8)	2
Kjartan Henry Finnbogason (ISL)	09.07.1986	6	(1)	2
Joachim Nielsen			(1)	
Jannik Pohl	06.04.1996	8	(3)	3
Louka Prip	29.06.1997	31	(1)	7
Lirim Qamili	04.06.1998	12	(13)	2
Casper Tengstedt	01.06.2000	10	(14)	3

Football Club København

Founded: 01.07.1992
Stadium: Telia Parken, København (38,065)
Trainer: Ståle Solbakken (NOR)   27.02.1968
[10.10.2020]   Hjalte Bo Nörregaard   08.04.1981
[02.11.2020]   Jess Thorup   21.02.1970

Goalkeepers:	DOB	M	(s)	G
Sten Grytebust (NOR)	25.10.1989	9		
Karl-Johan Johnsson (SWE)	28.01.1990	23		
Defenders:	**DOB**	**M**	**(s)**	**G**
Peter Ankersen	22.09.1990	21		2
Karlo Bartolec (CRO)	20.04.1995	10	(7)	1
Pierre Bengtsson (SWE)	12.04.1988	4	(4)	
Andreas Bjelland	11.07.1988	3		
Nicolai Møller Boilesen	16.02.1992	26		1
Mathias Jattah-Njie Jørgensen	23.04.1990	24	(2)	1
Victor Kristiansen	16.12.2002	8	(7)	
Victor Enok Nelsson	14.10.1998	26	(1)	1
Marios Oikonomou (GRE)	06.10.1992		(8)	
Bryan Josué Oviedo Jiménez (CRC)	18.02.1990	5	(2)	
Ragnar Sigurðsson (ISL)	19.06.1986	2		
Guillermo Varela Olivera (URU)	24.03.1993	1		

Midfielders:	DOB	M	(s)	G
Rasmus Falk Jensen	15.01.1992	27	(1)	4
Lukas Lerager	12.07.1993	14	(3)	4
Robert Mudražija (CRO)	05.05.1997	1	(7)	
Pep Biel Mas Jaume (ESP)	05.09.1996	14	(13)	2
Jens Stage	08.11.1996	18	(5)	5
Marko Stamenić (NZL)	19.02.2002	1		
Nicolaj Thomsen	08.05.1993		(6)	
José Carlos Gonçalves Rodrigues Zeca"(GRE)	31.08.1988	28		2
Forwards:	**DOB**	**M**	**(s)**	**G**
William Bøving	01.03.2003		(1)	
Mustapha Bundu (SLE)	28.02.1997	3	(11)	1
Mohammed Daramy	07.01.2002	16	(12)	5
Viktor Fischer	09.06.1994	19	(8)	4
Rasmus Højlund	04.02.2003	1	(3)	
Mikkel Kaufmann	03.01.2001	3	(12)	1
Kamil Wilczek (POL)	14.01.1988	17	(10)	10
Jonas Older Wind	07.02.1999	28		15

Lyngby Boldklub

Founded: 30.03.1921
Stadium: Lyngby Stadion, Lyngby (8,000)
Trainer: Christian Nielsen 09.01.1974
[21.12.2020] Carit Falch 16.12.1976

Goalkeepers:	DOB	M	(s)	G
Thomas Mikkelsen	27.08.1983	30		
Frederik Schram (ISL)	19.01.1995	2		
Defenders:	**DOB**	**M**	**(s)**	**G**
Svenn Crone	20.05.1995	10	(3)	
Kasper Enghardt	27.05.1992	25	(4)	
Lasse Fosgaard	06.09.1986	19	(11)	1
Jens Martin Gammelby	05.02.1995	21	(5)	4
Nicolai Geertsen	19.06.1991	10	(2)	1
Pascal Gregor	18.02.1994	6	(6)	
Brian Hämäläinen	29.05.1989	13		
Thor Høholt	22.02.2001		(1)	
Kasper Jørgensen	07.11.1999	14	(6)	1
Gustav Mortensen	19.03.2004		(1)	
Kevin Tshiembe	31.03.1997	22	(2)	1
Frederik Winther	04.01.2001	11	(6)	1
Midfielders:	**DOB**	**M**	**(s)**	**G**
Mathias Hebo Rasmussen	02.08.1995	30	(1)	7
Lucas Hey	13.04.2003		(1)	
Emil Kornvig	28.04.2000	16	(6)	
Marcel Rømer	08.08.1991	23	(3)	
Lauge Sandgrav	16.09.2004		(1)	
Victor Torp	30.07.1999	24	(6)	4
Casper Winther	11.02.2003		(6)	
Forwards:	**DOB**	**M**	**(s)**	**G**
Willads Delvin	02.05.2001		(3)	
Frederik Gytkjær	16.03.1993	3	(3)	
Christian Jakobsen	27.03.1993	20	(10)	4
Magnus Kaastrup	28.12.2000	8	(9)	2
Gustav Marcussen	12.06.1998		(2)	
Emil Nielsen	08.11.1993	18	(7)	5
Lucas Ørneborg	25.07.2002		(4)	
Alexander Petræus	29.06.2002		(2)	
André Riel	21.10.1989	3	(2)	
Justin Shaibu	28.10.1997		(6)	
Ertuğrul Tekşen (TUR)	25.04.2000		(2)	
Rasmus Thellufsen	09.01.1997	10	(7)	
Magnus Warming	08.06.2000	14	(16)	4

Football Club Midtjylland Herning

Founded: 02.02.1999
Stadium: MCH Arena, Herning (11,800)
Trainer: Brian Priske 14.05.1977

Goalkeepers:	DOB	M	(s)	G
Mikkel Andersen	17.12.1988	1	(1)	
Jesper Hansen	31.03.1985	18		
Jonas Lössl	01.02.1989	13		
Defenders:	**DOB**	**M**	**(s)**	**G**
Ailton Ferreira Silva (BRA)	16.03.1995	3	(5)	
Joel Andersson (SWE)	11.11.1996	13		
Dion Johan Chai Cools (MAS)	04.06.1996	17	(4)	1
Nikolas Dyhr	18.06.2001	2	(1)	
Daniel Høegh	06.01.1991	2	(2)	
Manjrekar James (CAN)	05.08.1993	4		
Kristoffer Lund	14.05.2002	1		
Paulo Victor da Silva „Paulinho" (BRA)	03.01.1995	25		
Kristian Dirk Riis	17.02.1997		(1)	
Alexander Scholz	24.10.1992	31		7
Japhet Sery	10.04.2000	2	(2)	
Erik Sviatchenko	04.10.1991	28		3
Midfielders:	**DOB**	**M**	**(s)**	**G**
Jens-Lys Cajuste (SWE)	10.08.1999	23	(4)	1
Evander Da Silva Ferreira (BRA)	09.06.1998	26	(2)	6
Bozhidar Kraev (BUL)	23.06.1997	6	(3)	1
Nicolas Madsen	17.03.2000	4	(13)	
Frank Ogochukwu Onyeka (NGA)	01.01.1998	26	(1)	3
Forwards:	**DOB**	**M**	**(s)**	**G**
Mikael Anderson (ISL)	01.07.1998	10	(16)	1
José Francisco dos Santos Júnior „Brumado" (BRA)	15.05.1999	4	(8)	2
Anders Dreyer	02.05.1998	27	(4)	8
Gustav Isaksen	19.04.2001	6	(16)	1
Sory Kaba (GUI)	28.07.1995	23	(4)	11
Awer Mabil (AUS)	15.09.1995	10	(19)	1
Luca Pfeiffer (GER)	20.08.1996	4	(7)	1
Pione Sisto Ifolo Emirmija	04.02.1995	23	(7)	8
Lasse Vibe	22.02.1987		(7)	1

Football Club Nordsjælland Farum

Founded: 01.07.2003
Stadium: Right to Dream Park, Farum (9,900)
Trainer: Flemming Pedersen 30.06.1963

Goalkeepers:	DOB	M	(s)	G
Martin Vantruba (SVK)	07.02.1998	1		
Peter Vindahl Jensen	16.02.1998	31		
Defenders:	**DOB**	**M**	**(s)**	**G**
Johan Danon Djourou-Gbadjere (SUI)	18.01.1987	10	(1)	
Martin Frese	04.01.1998	13	(2)	3
Kian Hansen	03.03.1989	15		
Jonas Jensen-Abbew	20.04.2002		(1)	
Ulrik Jenssen (NOR)	17.07.1996	26	(2)	3
Lucas Lykkegaard	05.04.2002		(2)	
Ivan Mesík (SVK)	01.06.2001	13	(14)	
Adamo Nagalo (CIV)	22.09.2002	4	(2)	
Daniel Svensson (SWE)	12.02.2002	16	(6)	
Mads Thychosen	27.06.1997	25	(1)	
Oliver Villadsen	16.11.2001	16	(7)	
Maxwell Woledzi (GHA)	02.07.2001	8	(2)	1
Midfielders:	**DOB**	**M**	**(s)**	**G**
Francis Abu (GHA)	27.04.2001	7	(12)	5
Oliver Antman (FIN)	15.08.2001	6	(13)	1
Tochi Chukwuani	24.03.2003	8	(18)	2
Mohammed Diomande (CIV)	30.10.2001	11		3
Victor Jensen	08.02.2000	12	(6)	3
Magnus Kofod Andersen	10.05.1999	31	(1)	4
Mikkel Rygaard	25.12.1990	10	(3)	3
Andreas Schjelderup (NOR)	01.06.2004	12	(4)	3
Jacob Steen Christensen	25.06.2001	27	(2)	
Forwards:	**DOB**	**M**	**(s)**	**G**
Simon Adingra (CIV)	01.01.2002	1	(6)	2
Jonathan Amon (USA)	30.04.1999		(1)	1
Isaac Atanga (GHA)	29.07.2000	10	(9)	4
Andreas Bredahl	13.03.2003		(2)	
Emeka Nnamani	04.11.2001	2	(6)	
Joachim Rothmann	29.06.2000	2	(12)	
Ibrahim Sadiq (GHA)	07.05.2000	6	(13)	2
Kamaldeen Sulemana (GHA)	15.02.2002	29		10

Odense Boldklub

Founded: 12.07.1887
Stadium: Nature Energy Park, Odense (15,633)
Trainer: Jakob Michelsen — 30.09.1980
[16.03.2021] Michael Hemmingsen — 02.10.1967

Goalkeepers:	DOB	M	(s)	G
Hans Christian Bernat	13.11.2000	2	(1)	
Oliver Christensen	22.03.1999	25		
Sayouba Mandé (CIV)	15.06.1993	5	(2)	
Defenders:	**DOB**	**M**	**(s)**	**G**
Alexander Juel Andersen	29.01.1991	14	(4)	1
Kasper Larsen	25.01.1993	21	(1)	
Ryan Johnson Laursen	14.04.1992	16	(2)	
Marco Lund	30.06.1996	6	(5)	
Oliver Lund	21.08.1990	20	(1)	1
Robin Østrøm	09.08.2002	9	(3)	
Jørgen Skjelvik (NOR)	05.07.1991	18		1
Jeppe Tverskov	12.03.1993	28	(1)	3
Christian Vestergaard	26.04.2001		(1)	
Midfielders:	**DOB**	**M**	**(s)**	**G**
Janus Drachmann	11.05.1988	10	(6)	
Mads Frøkjær-Jensen	29.07.1999	13	(6)	
Tarik Ibrahimagić	23.01.2001		(2)	
Troels Kløve	23.10.1990	25	(1)	1
Ayo Simon Okosun	21.07.1993	18	(8)	2
Moses Opondo (UGA)	28.10.1997	15	(10)	1
Jens Thomasen	25.06.1996	24	(3)	2
Aron Elís Þrándarson (ISL)	10.11.1994	11	(15)	1
Forwards:	**DOB**	**M**	**(s)**	**G**
Max Fenger	07.08.2001	6	(11)	1
Sveinn Aron Guðjohnsen (ISL)	12.05.1998		(13)	1
Mikkel Hyllegaard	03.04.1999	2	(20)	2
Issam Jebali (TUN)	25.12.1991	30		10
Bashkim Kadrii	09.07.1991	9	(5)	6
Mart Lieder (NED)	01.05.1990	5	(6)	1
Emmanuel Sabbi (USA)	24.12.1997	20	(9)	5
Sander Svendsen (NOR)	06.08.1997		(2)	

Randers Football Club

Founded: 01.01.2003
Stadium: Cepheus Park, Randers (12,000)
Trainer: Thomas Thomasberg — 15.10.1974

Goalkeepers:	DOB	M	(s)	G
Patrik Carlgren (SWE)	08.01.1992	31		
Jonas Dakir	18.04.1997	1		
Defenders:	**DOB**	**M**	**(s)**	**G**
Mikkel Brund	06.03.2003		(1)	
Oliver Bundgaard Kristensen	15.01.2001	8	(4)	
Simon Graves Jensen	22.03.1999	23	(2)	
Mikkel Kallesøe Andreasen	20.04.1997	15	(7)	
Björn Kopplin (GER)	07.01.1989	23	(3)	
Jesper Lauridsen	27.03.1991	14	(8)	
Erik Marxen	02.12.1990	22	(1)	
Mathias Aaris Kragh Nielsen	02.03.1991	12	(11)	
Simon Piesinger (AUT)	13.05.1992	17	(8)	1
Midfielders:	**DOB**	**M**	**(s)**	**G**
Lasse Berg Johnsen (NOR)	18.08.1999	12	(4)	1
Filip Bundgaard Kristensen	03.07.2004		(9)	
Mathias Peter Greve Petersen	11.02.1995	30	(1)	5
Vito Hammershøy-Mistrati	15.06.1992	25	(5)	9
Frederik Lauenborg	18.05.1997	19	(9)	1
André Rømer	18.07.1993	15		4
Forwards:	**DOB**	**M**	**(s)**	**G**
Marvin Egho (AUT)	09.05.1994	27	(4)	5
Kasper Høgh	06.12.2000		(4)	
Emil Riis Jakobsen	24.06.1998	3		2
Alhaji Kamara (SLE)	16.04.1994	14	(5)	9
Tobias Klysner	03.07.2001	11	(20)	2
Karl Leth	22.08.2002		(1)	
Nikola Mileusnić (AUS)	17.07.1993	7	(9)	
Kehinde Oluwatosin (NGA)	18.06.1998	19	(7)	2
Bassala Sambou (ENG)	15.10.1997	4	(19)	2

Silkeborg Idrætsforening

Founded: 26.04.1917
Stadium: Haderslev Football Stadion, Haderslev (10,000)
Trainer: Glen Riddersholm — 24.04.1972

Goalkeepers:	DOB	M	(s)	G
Lawrence Andrew Kingsley Thomas (AUS)	09.05.1992	32		
Defenders:	**DOB**	**M**	**(s)**	**G**
Alexander Hartmann Bah	09.12.1997	12		4
Patrick Banggaard Jensen	04.04.1994	27		1
Marc Dal Hende	06.11.1990	30		4
Stefan Gartenmann	02.02.1997	30		1
Emil Holm (SWE)	13.05.2000	10	(4)	3
Pierre Kanstrup	21.02.1989	21	(6)	
Ísak Óli Ólafsson (ISL)	30.06.2000		(2)	
Philipp Schmiedl (AUT)	23.07.1997	10	(8)	
Jeppe Friborg Simonsen (HAI)	21.11.1995	21	(8)	2
Mads Winther	20.10.2001		(1)	
Midfielders:	**DOB**	**M**	**(s)**	**G**
Mads Albæk	14.01.1990	26		2
Julius Beck	27.04.2005		(3)	
Emil Frederiksen	05.09.2000	7	(18)	1
Adama Guira (BFA)	24.04.1988		(4)	
Mads Hansen	10.04.2001		(1)	
Victor Sylvestre Mpindi Ekani (CMR)	27.02.1997	26	(2)	1
Ogenyi Eddy Onazi (NGA)	25.12.1992		(2)	
Rasmus Vinderslev	12.08.1997	15	(9)	
Forwards:	**DOB**	**M**	**(s)**	**G**
Johan Absalonsen	16.09.1985	1	(4)	1
Peter Christiansen	02.12.1999	3	(19)	
Julius Eskesen	16.03.1999	18	(14)	
Bård Finne (NOR)	13.02.1995	3	(13)	
Rilwan Olanrewaju Hassan (NGA)	09.02.1991	8	(13)	2
Anders Kvindebjerg Jacobsen	27.10.1989	30	(1)	10
Jannick Liburd	26.09.2001		(1)	
Haji Amir Wright (USA)	27.03.1998	22	(7)	11

Vejle Boldklub

Founded: 03.05.1891
Stadium: Vejle Stadion, Vejle (10,418)
Trainer: Constantin Gâlcă (ROU) — 08.03.1972

Goalkeepers:	DOB	M	(s)	G
Alexander Brunst (GER)	07.07.1995	19		
Indy Groothuizen (NED)	22.07.1996	13		
Defenders:	**DOB**	**M**	**(s)**	**G**
Malte Meineche Amundsen	11.02.1998	13	(1)	1
Pierre Bengtsson (SWE)	12.04.1988	13	(1)	
Matthew Anthony Briggs (GUY)	06.03.1991		(3)	
Viljormur í Heiðunum Davidsen (FRO)	19.07.1991	6	(7)	
Mads Greve	12.09.1989	14		1
Thomas Gundelund	06.11.2001	7	(4)	
Denis Kolinger (CRO)	14.01.1994	18		1
Dominik Kovačić (CRO)	05.01.1994	6	(9)	
Goran Alexander Sjöström Milošević (SWE)	30.01.1992	7	(3)	
Tobias Mølgaard	22.07.1996	19	(3)	
Juhani Lauri Henrik Ojala (FIN)	19.06.1989	19	(4)	1
Arthur Kevin Yamga Tientcheu (FRA)	07.09.1996	11	(9)	
Midfielders:	**DOB**	**M**	**(s)**	**G**
Lukas Engel	14.12.1998	12	(5)	2
Saeid Ezatolahi (IRN)	01.10.1996	29		4
Lundrim Hetemi	18.02.2000	12	(7)	
Diego Montiel (SWE)	26.04.1995	3	(9)	
Ylber Ramadani (ALB)	12.04.1996	21	(8)	1
Ivan Repyakh (RUS)	18.10.2001		(1)	
Jacob Schoop	23.12.1988	18	(2)	1
Forwards:	**DOB**	**M**	**(s)**	**G**
Allan Gonçalves Sousa (BRA)	27.01.1997	29	(1)	10
Raphael Vani Dwamena (GHA)	12.09.1995	3	(2)	2
Hugo Ekitike (FRA)	20.06.2002	7	(4)	3
Wahid Faghir	29.07.2003	21	(5)	6
Adama Fofana (CIV)	04.01.2001	1	(1)	
Kjartan Henry Finnbogason (ISL)	09.07.1986		(1)	
Serhiy Gryn (UKR)	06.06.1994	1		
Lucas Jensen	08.10.1994	4	(13)	
Luis Henrique Farinhas Taffner (BRA)	17.03.1998		(5)	
Leonel Dahl Montano	02.10.1999		(6)	
Arbnor Mucolli (ALB)	15.09.1999	21	(5)	4
German Onugkha (RUS)	06.07.1996	5	(12)	5

Regular Season

1.	Viborg FF	22	17	5	0	45 - 14	56
2.	Silkeborg IF	22	16	1	5	53 - 19	49
3.	Esbjerg fB	22	15	3	4	33 - 20	48
4.	FC Helsingør	22	11	3	8	31 - 27	36
5.	FC Fredericia	22	9	5	8	29 - 27	32
6.	HB Køge	22	8	6	8	23 - 25	30
7.	BK Fremad Amager	22	8	4	10	40 - 29	28
8.	Hobro IK	22	6	6	10	30 - 40	24
9.	Hvidovre IF	22	7	2	13	23 - 38	23
10.	Vendsyssel FF Hjørring	22	4	4	14	19 - 40	16
11.	Kolding IF	22	2	8	12	19 - 40	14
12.	Skive IK	22	3	5	14	19 - 45	14

Team ranked 1-6 were qualified for the Promotion Group, while teams ranked 7-12 were qualified for the Relegation Group.

Promotion Group

1.	Viborg FF (*Promoted*)	32	23	7	2	71 - 24	76
2.	Silkeborg IF (*Promoted*)	32	23	4	5	76 - 28	73
3.	Esbjerg fB	32	18	5	9	43 - 38	59
4.	FC Helsingør	32	16	5	11	50 - 41	53
5.	FC Fredericia	32	13	5	14	42 - 44	44
6.	HB Køge	32	8	7	17	28 - 53	31

Relegation Group

7.	Hvidovre IF	32	11	6	15	40 - 47	39
8.	BK Fremad Amager	32	10	5	17	47 - 41	35
9.	Hobro IK	32	8	10	14	38 - 51	34
10.	Vendsyssel FF Hjørring	32	8	8	16	33 - 51	32
11.	Kolding IF (*Relegated*)	32	7	11	14	31 - 49	32
12.	Skive IK (*Relegated*)	32	7	7	18	28 - 60	28

NATIONAL TEAM

INTERNATIONAL MATCHES
(16.07.2020 – 15.07.2021)

05.09.2020	København	Denmark - Belgium	0-2(0-1)	(UNL)
08.09.2020	København	Denmark - England	0-0	(UNL)
07.10.2020	Herning	Denmark - Faroe Islands	4-0(4-0)	(F)
11.10.2020	Reykjavík	Iceland - Denmark	0-3(0-1)	(UNL)
14.10.2020	London	England - Denmark	0-1(0-1)	(UNL)
11.11.2020	Brøndby	Denmark - Sweden	2-0(0-0)	(F)
15.11.2020	København	Denmark - Iceland	2-1(1-0)	(UNL)
18.11.2020	Leuven	Belgium - Denmark	4-2(1-1)	(UNL)
25.03.2021	Tel Aviv	Israel - Denmark	0-2(0-1)	(WCQ)
28.03.2021	Herning	Denmark - Moldova	8-0(5-0)	(WCQ)
31.03.2021	Wien	Austria - Denmark	0-4(0-0)	(WCQ)
02.06.2021	Innsbruck	Germany - Denmark	1-1(0-0)	(F)
06.06.2021	Brøndby	Denmark - Bosnia and Herzegovina	2-0(1-0)	(F)
12.06.2021	København	Denmark - Finland	0-1(0-0)	(EC)
17.06.2021	København	Denmark - Belgium	1-2(1-0)	(EC)
21.06.2021	København	Russia - Denmark	1-4(0-1)	(EC)
26.06.2021	Amsterdam	Wales - Denmark	0-4(0-1)	(EC)
03.07.2021	Bakı	Czech Republic - Denmark	1-2(0-2)	(EC)
07.07.2021	London	England - Denmark	2-1(1-1,1-1)	(EC)

05.09.2020   **DENMARK - BELGIUM**   **0-2(0-1)**   2nd UEFA Nations League A, Group 2

Parken Stadium, City; Referee: Sandro Schärer (Switzerland); Attendance: 0
DEN: Kasper Peter Schmeichel, Simon Thorup Kjær (Cap), Andreas Bødtker Christensen, Daniel Wass (83.Mathias Jattah-Njie Jørgensen), Thomas Joseph Delaney, Christian Dannemann Eriksen, Pierre-Emile Kordt Højbjerg, Robert Skov, Martin Braithwaite Christensen (72.Joakim Mæhle Pedersen), Yussuf Yurary Poulsen, Kasper Dolberg Rasmussen (83.Andreas Evald Cornelius). Trainer: Kasper Hjulmand.

08.09.2020   **DENMARK - ENGLAND**   **0-0**   2nd UEFA Nations League A, Group 2

Parken Stadium, København; Referee: István Kovács (Romania); Attendance: 0
DEN: Kasper Peter Schmeichel (Cap), Andreas Bødtker Christensen, Daniel Wass, Thomas Joseph Delaney, Christian Dannemann Eriksen, Christian Thers Nørgaard (73.Pierre-Emile Kordt Højbjerg), Robert Skov, Mathias Jattah-Njie Jørgensen, Martin Braithwaite Christensen (82.Simon Thorup Kjær), Kasper Dolberg Rasmussen (76.Rasmus Falk Jensen), Yussuf Yurary Poulsen. Trainer: Kasper Hjulmand.

07.10.2020   **DENMARK - FAROE ISLANDS**   **4-0(4-0)**   Friendly International
Messecenter Herning Arena, Herning; Referee: Glenn Nyberg (Sweden); Attendance: 207
DEN: Kasper Peter Schmeichel (Cap), Joakim Mæhle Pedersen, Henrik Dalsgaard (46.Kristian Majdahl Pedersen), Jannik Vestergaard, Mathias Jattah-Njie Jørgensen (82.Simon Thorup Kjær), Mathias Jensen, Philip Anyanwu Billing (72.Andreas Bødtker Christensen), Christian Dannemann Eriksen (72.Jonas Older Wind), Andreas Skov Olsen (62.Yussuf Yurary Poulsen), Martin Braithwaite Christensen, Andreas Evald Cornelius (46.Pione Sisto Ifolo Emirmija). Trainer: Kasper Hjulmand.
Goals: Andreas Skov Olsen (22), Christian Dannemann Eriksen (27 penalty), Joakim Mæhle Pedersen (32), Andreas Evald Cornelius (45).

11.10.2020   **ICELAND - DENMARK**   **0-3(0-1)**   2nd UEFA Nations League A, Group 2
Laugardalsvöllur, Reykjavík; Referee: Bojan Pandžić (Sweden); Attendance: 60
DEN: Kasper Peter Schmeichel, Simon Thorup Kjær (Cap), Andreas Bødtker Christensen, Daniel Wass, Thomas Joseph Delaney, Christian Dannemann Eriksen, Pierre-Emile Kordt Højbjerg, Robert Skov (79.Joakim Mæhle Pedersen), Martin Braithwaite Christensen (87.Mathias Jattah-Njie Jørgensen), Yussuf Yurary Poulsen (66.Andreas Skov Olsen), Kasper Dolberg Rasmussen (79.Pione Sisto Ifolo Emirmija). Trainer: Kasper Hjulmand.
Goals: Rúnar Már Sigurlaugarson Sigurjónsson (45 own goal), Christian Dannemann Eriksen (46), Robert Skov (61).

14.10.2020   **ENGLAND - DENMARK**   **0-1(0-1)**   2nd UEFA Nations League A, Group 2
Wembley Stadium, London; Referee: Jesús Gil Manzano (Spain); Attendance: 0
DEN: Kasper Peter Schmeichel, Simon Thorup Kjær (Cap), Andreas Bødtker Christensen (46.Mathias Jattah-Njie Jørgensen), Daniel Wass, Pierre-Emile Kordt Højbjerg (88.Mathias Jensen), Thomas Joseph Delaney, Christian Dannemann Eriksen, Martin Braithwaite Christensen (73.Jannik Vestergaard), Robert Skov (46.Joakim Mæhle Pedersen), Yussuf Yurary Poulsen, Kasper Dolberg Rasmussen (37.Pione Sisto Ifolo Emirmija). Trainer: Kasper Hjulmand.
Goal: Christian Dannemann Eriksen (35 penalty).

11.11.2020   **DENMARK - SWEDEN**   **2-0(0-0)**   Friendly International
Brøndby Stadion, Brøndby; Referee: Espen Eskas (Norway); Attendance: 141
DEN: Oliver Christensen, Jens Stryger Larsen (46.Andreas Beyer Maxsø), Joakim Mæhle Pedersen (81.Jakob Ahlmann Nielsen), Victor Enok Nelsson, Mathias Jattah-Njie Jørgensen, Thomas Joseph Delaney (60.Oliver Abildgaard Nielsen), Christian Dannemann Eriksen (Cap) (46.Alexander Hartmann Bah), Lucas Qvistorff Andersen (86.Jesper Grænge Lindstrøm), Jens Jønsson, Mikkel Krogh Damsgaard, Kasper Dolberg Rasmussen (46.Jonas Older Wind). Trainer: Kasper Hjulmand.
Goals: Jonas Older Wind (61), Alexander Hartmann Bah (74).

15.11.2020   **DENMARK - ICELAND**   **2-1(1-0)**   2nd UEFA Nations League A, Group 2
Parken Stadium, København; Referee: Halil Umut Meler (Turkey); Attendance: 141
DEN: Kasper Peter Schmeichel (46.Frederik Riis Rønnow), Simon Thorup Kjær (Cap), Jens Stryger Larsen, Jannik Vestergaard (90.Jonas Older Wind), Andreas Bødtker Christensen, Daniel Wass, Thomas Joseph Delaney, Christian Dannemann Eriksen, Mathias Jensen (68.Jens Jønsson), Yussuf Yurary Poulsen, Martin Braithwaite Christensen (76.Lucas Qvistorff Andersen). Trainer: Kasper Hjulmand.
Goals: Christian Dannemann Eriksen (12 penalty, 90+2 penalty).

18.11.2020   **BELGIUM - DENMARK**   **4-2(1-1)**   2nd UEFA Nations League A, Group 2
Den Dreef Stadion, Leuven; Referee: Slavko Vinčić (Slovenia); Attendance: 0
DEN: Kasper Peter Schmeichel, Simon Thorup Kjær (Cap), Joakim Mæhle Pedersen, Daniel Wass, Andreas Bødtker Christensen, Pierre-Emile Kordt Højbjerg, Thomas Joseph Delaney (70.Mathias Jensen), Christian Dannemann Eriksen, Martin Braithwaite Christensen, Yussuf Yurary Poulsen (76.Lucas Qvistorff Andersen), Jonas Older Wind (88.Pione Sisto Ifolo Emirmija). Trainer: Kasper Hjulmand.
Goals: Jonas Older Wind (17), Nacer Chadli (86 own goal).

25.03.2021   **ISRAEL - DENMARK**   **0-2(0-1)**   22nd FIFA WC. Qualifiers
Bloomfield Stadium, Tel Aviv; Referee: Craig Pawson (England); Attendance: 5,000
DEN: Kasper Peter Schmeichel, Simon Thorup Kjær (Cap), Andreas Bødtker Christensen, Joakim Mæhle Pedersen (86.Jens Stryger Larsen), Daniel Wass, Pierre-Emile Kordt Højbjerg, Thomas Joseph Delaney (88.Christian Thers Nørgaard), Christian Dannemann Eriksen, Martin Braithwaite Christensen, Yussuf Yurary Poulsen (77.Andreas Skov Olsen), Jonas Older Wind (77.Joachim Christian Andersen). Trainer: Kasper Hjulmand.
Goals: Martin Braithwaite Christensen (13), Jonas Older Wind (67).

28.03.2021   **DENMARK - MOLDOVA**   **8-0(5-0)**   22nd FIFA WC. Qualifiers
Messecenter Herning Arena, Herning; Referee: Əliyar Ağayev (Azerbaijan); Attendance: 0
DEN: Kasper Peter Schmeichel (Cap), Jens Stryger Larsen (77.Simon Thorup Kjær), Nicolai Møller Boilesen, Jannik Vestergaard, Joachim Christian Andersen, Lasse Schøne (77.Christian Dannemann Eriksen), Christian Thers Nørgaard (64.Jens Jønsson), Mathias Jensen (77.Marcus Ingvartsen), Mikkel Krogh Damsgaard, Kasper Dolberg Rasmussen, Andreas Skov Olsen (46.Robert Skov). Trainer: Kasper Hjulmand.
Goals: Kasper Dolberg Rasmussen (19 penalty), Mikkel Krogh Damsgaard (21, 29), Jens Stryger Larsen (35), Mathias Jensen (39), Kasper Dolberg Rasmussen (48), Robert Skov (81), Marcus Ingvartsen (89).

31.03.2021   **AUSTRIA - DENMARK**   **0-4(0-0)**   22nd FIFA WC. Qualifiers
"Ernst Happel" Stadion, Wien; Referee: Artur Manuel Ribeiro Soares Dias (Portugal); Attendance: 0
DEN: Kasper Peter Schmeichel, Simon Thorup Kjær (Cap), Andreas Bødtker Christensen, Joakim Mæhle Pedersen, Daniel Wass (77.Jens Stryger Larsen), Pierre-Emile Kordt Højbjerg, Thomas Joseph Delaney (77.Christian Thers Nørgaard), Christian Dannemann Eriksen, Martin Braithwaite Christensen (77.Kasper Dolberg Rasmussen), Yussuf Yurary Poulsen (55.Andreas Skov Olsen), Jonas Older Wind (65.Joachim Christian Andersen). Trainer: Kasper Hjulmand.
Goals: Andreas Skov Olsen (58), Joakim Mæhle Pedersen (63), Pierre-Emile Kordt Højbjerg (67), Andreas Skov Olsen (74)

02.06.2021   **GERMANY - DENMARK**   **1-1(0-0)**   Friendly International
Tivoli Stadion Tirol, Innsbruck (Austria); Referee: Julian Weinberger (Austria); Attendance: 0
DEN: Kasper Peter Schmeichel, Joakim Mæhle Pedersen, Simon Thorup Kjær (Cap) (80.Mathias Jattah-Njie Jørgensen), Jannik Vestergaard, Thomas Joseph Delaney, Daniel Wass (85.Anders Bleg Christiansen), Pierre-Emile Kordt Højbjerg (68.Jens Stryger Larsen), Christian Dannemann Eriksen, Andreas Skov Olsen (46.Kasper Dolberg Rasmussen), Yussuf Yurary Poulsen (80.Mikkel Krogh Damsgaard), Martin Braithwaite Christensen (80.Nicolai Møller Boilesen). Trainer: Kasper Hjulmand.
Goal: Yussuf Yurary Poulsen (71).

06.06.2021   **DENMARK - BOSNIA AND HERZEGOVINA**   **2-0(1-0)**   Friendly International

Brøndby Stadium, Brøndby; Referee: Petri Viljanen (Finland); Attendance: 7,459

DEN: Kasper Peter Schmeichel, Simon Thorup Kjær (Cap) (46.Joachim Christian Andersen), Jens Stryger Larsen, Nicolai Møller Boilesen, Andreas Bødtker Christensen, Daniel Wass (71.Andreas Evald Cornelius), Robert Skov (70.Joakim Mæhle Pedersen), Christian Dannemann Eriksen (59.Thomas Joseph Delaney), Mathias Jensen, Martin Braithwaite Christensen (46.Yussuf Yurary Poulsen), Kasper Dolberg Rasmussen (46.Jonas Older Wind). Trainer: Kasper Hjulmand.

Goals: Martin Braithwaite Christensen (18), Andreas Evald Cornelius (73).

12.06.2021   **DENMARK - FINLAND**   **0-1(0-0)**   16th EC. Group Stage.

Parken Stadium, København; Referee: Anthony Taylor (England); Attendance: 15,200

DEN: Kasper Peter Schmeichel, Simon Thorup Kjær (Cap) (83.Jannik Vestergaard), Andreas Bødtker Christensen, Joakim Mæhle Pedersen, Daniel Wass (75.Jens Stryger Larsen), Thomas Joseph Delaney (75.Andreas Evald Cornelius), Christian Dannemann Eriksen (43.Mathias Jensen), Pierre-Emile Kordt Højbjerg, Martin Braithwaite Christensen, Yussuf Yurary Poulsen, Jonas Older Wind (63.Andreas Skov Olsen). Trainer: Kasper Hjulmand.

Please note: In the 43rd minute, the match was suspended for two hours after Danish midfielder Christian Dannemann Eriksen collapsed on the pitch.

17.06.2021   **DENMARK - BELGIUM**   **1-2(1-0)**   16th EC. Group Stage.

Parken Stadium, København; Referee: Björn Kuipers (Netherlands); Attendance: 23,395

DEN: Kasper Peter Schmeichel, Simon Thorup Kjær (Cap), Jannik Vestergaard (84.Andreas Skov Olsen), Andreas Bødtker Christensen, Joakim Mæhle Pedersen, Daniel Wass (61.Jens Stryger Larsen), Thomas Joseph Delaney (72.Mathias Jensen), Pierre-Emile Kordt Højbjerg, Mikkel Krogh Damsgaard (72.Andreas Evald Cornelius), Martin Braithwaite Christensen, Yussuf Yurary Poulsen (61.Christian Thers Nørgaard). Trainer: Kasper Hjulmand.

Goal: Yussuf Yurary Poulsen (2).

21.06.2021   **RUSSIA - DENMARK**   **1-4(0-1)**   16th EC. Group Stage.

Parken Stadium, København; Referee: Clément Turpin (France); Attendance: 23,644

DEN: Kasper Peter Schmeichel, Simon Thorup Kjær (Cap), Jannik Vestergaard, Andreas Bødtker Christensen, Joakim Mæhle Pedersen, Daniel Wass (60.Jens Stryger Larsen), Thomas Joseph Delaney (86.Mathias Jensen), Pierre-Emile Kordt Højbjerg, Mikkel Krogh Damsgaard (72.Christian Thers Nørgaard), Yussuf Yurary Poulsen (60.Kasper Dolberg Rasmussen), Martin Braithwaite Christensen (85.Andreas Evald Cornelius). Trainer: Kasper Hjulmand.

Goals: Mikkel Krogh Damsgaard (38), Yussuf Yurary Poulsen (59), Andreas Bødtker Christensen (79), Joakim Mæhle Pedersen (82).

26.06.2021   **WALES - DENMARK**   **0-4(0-1)**   16th EC. 2nd Round of 16.

"Johan Cruyff" Arena, Amsterdam (Netherlands); Referee: Daniel Siebert (Germany); Attendance: 14,645

DEN: Kasper Peter Schmeichel, Simon Thorup Kjær (Cap) (77.Joachim Christian Andersen), Jens Stryger Larsen (77.Nicolai Møller Boilesen), Andreas Bødtker Christensen, Jannik Vestergaard, Joakim Mæhle Pedersen, Thomas Joseph Delaney (60.Mathias Jensen), Pierre-Emile Kordt Højbjerg, Mikkel Krogh Damsgaard (60.Christian Thers Nørgaard), Martin Braithwaite Christensen, Kasper Dolberg Rasmussen (69.Andreas Evald Cornelius). Trainer: Kasper Hjulmand.

Goals: Kasper Dolberg Rasmussen (27, 48), Joakim Mæhle Pedersen (88), Martin Braithwaite Christensen (90+4).

03.07.2021   **CZECH REPUBLIC - DENMARK**   **1-2(0-2)**   16th EC. Quarter-Finals.

Bakı Olimpiya Stadionu, Bakı (Azerbaijan); Referee: Björn Kuipers (Netherlands); Attendance: 16,306

DEN: Kasper Peter Schmeichel, Simon Thorup Kjær (Cap), Jens Stryger Larsen (71.Daniel Wass), Jannik Vestergaard, Andreas Bødtker Christensen (81.Joachim Christian Andersen), Joakim Mæhle Pedersen, Thomas Joseph Delaney (81.Mathias Jensen), Pierre-Emile Kordt Højbjerg, Mikkel Krogh Damsgaard (60.Christian Thers Nørgaard), Martin Braithwaite Christensen, Kasper Dolberg Rasmussen (59.Yussuf Yurary Poulsen). Trainer: Kasper Hjulmand.

Goals: Thomas Joseph Delaney (5), Kasper Dolberg Rasmussen (42).

07.07.2021   **ENGLAND - DENMARK**   **2-1(1-1,1-1)**   16th EC. Semi-Finals.

Wembley Stadium, London; Referee: Danny Desmond Makkelie (Netherlands); Attendance: 64,950

DEN: Kasper Peter Schmeichel, Simon Thorup Kjær (Cap), Jens Stryger Larsen (67.Daniel Wass), Jannik Vestergaard (105.Jonas Older Wind), Andreas Bødtker Christensen (79.Joachim Christian Andersen), Thomas Joseph Delaney (88.Mathias Jensen), Pierre-Emile Kordt Højbjerg, Mikkel Krogh Damsgaard (67.Yussuf Yurary Poulsen), Joakim Mæhle Pedersen, Kasper Dolberg Rasmussen (67.Christian Thers Nørgaard), Martin Braithwaite Christensen. Trainer: Kasper Hjulmand.

Goal: Mikkel Krogh Damsgaard (30).

Name	DOB	Caps	Goals	2020/2021:	Club
Goalkeepers					
Oliver CHRISTENSEN	22.03.1999	1	0	2020:	Odense Boldklub
Frederik Riis RØNNOW	04.08.1992	8	0	2020:	FC Schalke 04 Gelsenkirchen (GER)
Kasper Peter SCHMEICHEL	05.11.1986	71	0	2020/2021:	Leicester City FC (ENG)
Defenders					
Joachim Christian ANDERSEN	31.05.1996	8	0	2021:	Fulham FC London (ENG)
Alexander Hartmann BAH	09.12.1997	1	0	2020:	Sønderjysk Elitesport
Nicolai Møller BOILESEN	16.02.1992	21	1	2021:	FC København
Andreas Bødtker CHRISTENSEN	10.04.1996	47	2	2020/2021:	Chelsea FC London (ENG)
Henrik DALSGAARD	27.07.1989	26	1	2020:	Brentford FC London (ENG)
Mathias Jattah-Njie JØRGENSEN	23.04.1990	35	2	2020: 05.10.2020->	Fenerbahçe SK İstanbul (TUR) FC København
Simon Thorup KJÆR	26.03.1989	113	3	2020/2021:	AC Milan (ITA)
Andreas Beyer MAXSØ	18.03.1994	1	0	2020:	Brøndby IF
Joakim MÆHLE Pedersen	20.05.1997	16	4	2020: 04.01.2021->	KRC Genk (BEL) Atalanta Bergamasca Calcio (ITA)
Victor Enok NELSSON	14.10.1998	1	0	2020:	FC København
Kristian Majdahl PEDERSEN	04.08.1994	1	0	2020:	Birmingham City FC (ENG)
Jens STRYGER Larsen	21.02.1991	42	2	2020/2021:	Udinese Calcio (ITA)
Jannik VESTERGAARD	03.08.1992	28	1	2020/2021:	Southampton FC (ENG)
Midfielders					
Oliver ABILDGAARD Nielsen	10.06.1996	1	0	2020:	FK Rubin Kazan (RUS)
Jakob AHLMANN Nielsen	18.01.1991	3	0	2020:	Aalborg BK
Philip Anyanwu BILLING	11.06.1996	1	0	2020:	AFC Bournemouth (ENG)
Anders Bleg CHRISTIANSEN	08.06.1990	4	0	2021:	Malmö FF (SWE)
Thomas Joseph DELANEY	03.09.1991	60	6	2020/2021:	BV Borussia 09 Dortmund (GER)
Christian Dannemann ERIKSEN	14.02.1992	109	36	2020/2021:	FC Internazionale Milano (ITA)
Rasmus FALK Jensen	15.01.1992	2	0	2020:	FC København
Pierre-Emile Kordt HØJBJERG	05.08.1995	47	4	2020/2021:	Tottenham Hotspur FC London (ENG)
Mathias JENSEN	01.01.1996	12	1	2020/2021:	Brentford FC London (ENG)
Jens JØNSSON	10.01.1993	3	0	2020/2021:	Cádiz CF (ESP)
Jesper Grænge LINDSTRØM	29.02.2000	1	0	2020:	Brøndby IF
Christian Thers NØRGAARD	10.03.1994	9	0	2020/2021:	Brentford FC London (ENG)
Lasse SCHØNE	27.05.1986	51	3	2020/2021:	SC Heerenveen (NED)
Daniel WASS	31.05.1989	35	0	2020/2021:	Valencia CF (ESP)
Forwards					
Lucas Qvistorff ANDERSEN	13.09.1994	7	0	2020:	Aalborg BK
Martin BRAITHWAITE Christensen	05.06.1991	56	10	2020/2021:	FC Barcelona (ESP)
Andreas Evald CORNELIUS	16.03.1993	32	6	2020/2021:	Parma Calcio 1913 (ITA)
Mikkel Krogh DAMSGAARD	03.07.2000	8	4	2020/2021:	UC Sampdoria Genova (ITA)
Kasper DOLBERG Rasmussen	06.10.1997	30	10	2020/2021:	OGC Nice (FRA)
Marcus INGVARTSEN	04.01.1996	1	1	2021:	1.FC Union Berlin (GER)
Andreas Skov OLSEN	02.12.1999	8	3	2020/2021:	Bologna FC 1909 (ITA)
Yussuf Yurary POULSEN	15.06.1994	59	10	2020/2021:	RasenBallsport Leipzig (GER)
Pione SISTO Ifolo Emirmija	04.02.1995	25	1	2020:	FC Midtjylland Herning
Robert SKOV	20.05.1996	10	5	2020/2021:	TSG 1899 Hoffenheim (GER)
Jonas Older WIND	07.02.1999	9	3	2020/2021:	FC København

Trainer			
Kasper HJULMAND [from 01.08.2020]	09.04.1972	19 M; 12 W; 2 D; 5 L; 43-15	

ENGLAND

The Country:
England
Capital: London
Surface: 130,279 km^2
Inhabitants: 56,286,961 [2019]
Time: UTC

The FA:
The Football Association
Wembley Stadium, P.O. Box 1966, SWIP 9EQ, London
Tel: +44 844 980 8200
Foundation date: 1863
Member of FIFA: 1905-1918, 1924-1928, since 1946
Member of UEFA since: 1954
Website: www.thefa.com

NATIONAL TEAM RECORDS

RECORDS
First international match:	30.11.1872, Glasgow:	Scotland – England 0-0
Most international caps:	Peter Leslie Shilton	- 125 caps (1970-1990)
Most international goals:	Wayne Mark Rooney	- 53 goals / 120 caps (2003-2018)

UEFA EUROPEAN CHAMPIONSHIP
1960	Did not enter
1964	Qualifiers
1968	Final Tournament (3rd Place)
1972	Qualifiers
1976	Qualifiers
1980	Final Tournament (Group Stage)
1984	Qualifiers
1988	Final Tournament (Group Stage)
1992	Final Tournament (Group Stage)
1996	Final Tournament (Semi-Finals)
2000	Final Tournament (Group Stage)
2004	Final Tournament (Quarter-Finals)
2008	Qualifiers
2012	Final Tournament (Quarter-Finals)
2016	Final Tournament (2nd Round of 16)
2020	Final Tournament (Runners-up)

FIFA WORLD CUP
1930	Did not enter
1934	Did not enter
1938	Did not enter
1950	Final Tournament (Group Stage)
1954	Final Tournament (Quarter-Finals)
1958	Final Tournament (Group Stage)
1962	Final Tournament (Quarter-Finals)
1966	**Final Tournament (Winners)**
1970	Final Tournament (Quarter-Finals)
1974	Qualifiers
1978	Qualifiers
1982	Final Tournament (2nd Round)
1986	Final Tournament (Quarter-Finals)
1990	Final Tournament (4th Place)
1994	Qualifiers
1998	Final Tournament (2nd Round of 16)
2002	Final Tournament (Quarter-Finals)
2006	Final Tournament (Quarter-Finals)
2010	Final Tournament (2nd Round of 16)
2014	Final Tournament (Group Stage)
2018	Final Tournament (4th Place)

OLYMPIC TOURNAMENTS
1908	-
1912	-
1920	-
1924	-
1928	-
1936	-
1948	-
1952	-
1956	-
1960	-
1964	-
1968	-
1972	-
1976	-
1980	-
1984	-
1988	-
1992	-
1996	-
2000	-
2004	-
2008	-
2012	-
2016	-

UEFA NATIONS LEAGUE
2018/2019	League A (Final Tournament – 3rd Place)
2020/2021	League A

FIFA CONFEDERATIONS CUP 1992-2017
None

ENGLISH CLUB HONOURS IN EUROPEAN CLUB COMPETITIONS:

European Champion Clubs' Cup (1956-1992) / UEFA Champions League (1993-2021)		
Liverpool FC	6	1976/1977, 1977/1978, 1980/1981, 1983/1984, 2004/2005, 2018/2019
Manchester United FC	3	1967/1968, 1998/1999, 2007/2008
Notthingam Forest FC	2	1978/1979, 1979/1980
Chelsea FC London	2	2011/2012, 2020/2021
Aston Villa FC Birmingham	1	1981/1982
Fairs Cup (1858-1971) / UEFA Cup (1972-2009) / UEFA Europa League (2010-2021)		
Liverpool FC	3	1972/1973, 1975/1976, 2000/2001
Leeds United FC	2	1967/1968, 1970/1971
Tottenham Hotspur FC London	2	1971/1972, 1983/1984
Chelsea FC London	2	2012/2013, 2018/2019

Newcastle United FC	1	1968/1969	
Arsenal FC London	1	1969/1970	
Ipswich Town FC	1	1980/1981	
Manchester United FC	1	2016/2017	
UEFA Super Cup (1972-2020)			
Liverpool FC	4	1977, 2001, 2005, 2019	
Notthingam Forest FC	1	1979	
Aston Villa FC Birmingham	1	1982	
Manchester United FC	1	1991	
Chelsea FC London	1	1998	
*European Cup Winners' Cup 1961-1999**			
Chelsea FC London	2	1970/1971, 1997/1998	
Tottenham Hotspur FC London	1	1962/1963	
West Ham United FC London	1	1964/1965	
Manchester City FC	1	1969/1970	
Everton FC Liverpool	1	1984/1985	
Manchester United FC	1	1990/1991	
Arsenal FC London	1	1993/1994	

defunct competition

NATIONAL COMPETITIONS
TABLE OF HONOURS

	CHAMPIONS	CUP WINNERS	BEST GOALSCORERS	
1871/1872	-	Wanderers FC London	-	
1872/1873	-	Wanderers FC London	-	
1873/1874	-	Oxford University AFC	-	
1874/1875	-	Royal Engineers AFC	-	
1875/1876	-	Wanderers FC London	-	
1876/1877	-	Wanderers FC London	-	
1877/1878	-	Wanderers FC London	-	
1878/1879	-	Old Etonians AFC	-	
1879/1880	-	Clapham Rovers FC	-	
1880/1881	-	Old Carthusians FC	-	
1881/1882	-	Old Etonians AFC	-	
1882/1883	-	Blackburn Olympic FC	-	
1883/1884	-	Blackburn Rovers FC	-	
1884/1885	-	Blackburn Rovers FC	-	
1885/1886	-	Blackburn Rovers FC	-	
1886/1887	-	Aston Villa FC Birmingham	-	
1887/1888	-	West Bromwich Albion FC	-	
1888/1889	Preston North End FC	Preston North End FC	John Goodall (Preston North End FC)	21
1889/1890	Preston North End FC	Blackburn Rovers FC	Jimmy Ross (SCO, Preston North End FC)	24
1890/1891	Everton FC Liverpool	Blackburn Rovers FC	Jack Southworth (Blackburn Rovers FC)	26
1891/1892	Sunderland AFC	West Bromwich Albion FC	John Campbell (SCO, Sunderland AFC)	32
1892/1893	Sunderland AFC	Wolverhampton Wanderers FC	John Campbell (SCO, Sunderland AFC)	31
1893/1894	Aston Villa FC Birmingham	Notts County FC	Jack Southworth (Everton FC Liverpool)	27
1894/1895	Sunderland AFC	Aston Villa FC Birmingham	John Campbell (SCO, Sunderland AFC)	22
1895/1896	Aston Villa FC Birmingham	The Wednesday Sheffield FC	John James Campbell (SCO, Aston Villa FC Birmingham) Stephen Bloomer (Derby County FC)	20
1896/1897	Aston Villa FC Birmingham	Aston Villa FC Birmingham	Stephen Bloomer (Derby County FC)	22
1897/1898	Sheffield United FC	Nottingham Forest FC	Fred Wheldon (Aston Villa FC Birmingham)	21
1898/1899	Aston Villa FC Birmingham	Sheffield United FC	Stephen Bloomer (Derby County FC)	23
1899/1900	Aston Villa FC Birmingham	Bury FC	Billy Garraty (Aston Villa FC Birmingham)	27
1900/1901	Liverpool FC	Tottenham Hotspur FC London	Stephen Bloomer (Derby County FC)	23
1901/1902	Sunderland AFC	Sheffield United FC	Jimmy Settle (Everton FC Liverpool)	18
1902/1903	The Wednesday Sheffield FC	Bury FC	Sam Raybould (Liverpool FC)	31
1903/1904	The Wednesday Sheffield FC	Manchester City FC	Stephen Bloomer (Derby County FC)	20
1904/1905	Newcastle United FC	Aston Villa FC Birmingham	Arthur Brown (Sheffield United FC)	22
1905/1906	Liverpool FC	Everton FC Liverpool	Albert Shepherd (Bolton Wanderers FC)	26
1906/1907	Newcastle United FC	The Wednesday Sheffield FC	Alex Young (SCO, Everton FC Liverpool)	30
1907/1908	Manchester United FC	Wolverhampton Wanderers FC	Enoch West (Nottingham Forest FC)	27
1908/1909	Newcastle United FC	Manchester United FC	Bert Freeman (Everton FC Liverpool)	38
1909/1910	Aston Villa FC Birmingham	Newcastle United FC	Jack Parkinson (Liverpool FC)	30
1910/1911	Manchester United FC	Bradford City AFC	Albert Shepherd (Newcastle United FC)	25
1911/1912	Blackburn Rovers FC	Barnsley FC	Harry Hampton (Aston Villa FC Birmingham) George Holley (Sunderland AFC) David McLean (The Wednesday Sheffield FC)	25
1912/1913	Sunderland AFC	Aston Villa FC Birmingham	David McLean (SCO, The Wednesday Sheffield FC)	30
1913/1914	Blackburn Rovers FC	Burnley FC	George Elliot (Middlesbrough FC)	32
1914/1915	Everton FC Liverpool	Sheffield United FC	Bobby Parker (SCO, Everton FC Liverpool)	35
1915-1919	*No competition*	*No competition*	-	
1919/1920	West Bromwich Albion FC	Aston Villa FC Birmingham	Fred Morris (West Bromwich Albion FC)	37
1920/1921	Burnley FC	Tottenham Hotspur FC London	Joe Smith (Bolton Wanderers FC)	38
1921/1922	Liverpool FC	Huddersfield Town AFC	Andy Wilson (SCO, Middlesbrough FC)	31

1922/1923	Liverpool FC	Bolton Wanderers FC	Charles Murray Buchan (SCO, Sunderland AFC)	30
1923/1924	Huddersfield Town AFC	Newcastle United FC	Wilf Chadwick (Everton FC Liverpool)	28
1924/1925	Huddersfield Town AFC	Sheffield United FC	Frank Roberts (Manchester City FC)	31
1925/1926	Huddersfield Town AFC	Bolton Wanderers FC	Ted Harper (Blackburn Rovers FC)	43
1926/1927	Newcastle United FC	Cardiff City FC (WAL)	Jimmy Trotter (The Wednesday Sheffield FC)	37
1927/1928	Everton FC Liverpool	Blackburn Rovers FC	William Ralph Dean (Everton FC Liverpool)	60
1928/1929	The Wednesday Sheffield FC	Bolton Wanderers FC	Dave Halliday (SCO, Sunderland AFC)	43
1929/1930	Sheffield Wednesday FC	Arsenal FC London	Victor Martin Watson (West Ham United FC)	41
1930/1931	Arsenal FC London	West Bromwich Albion FC	Thomas Waring (Aston Villa FC Birmingham)	49
1931/1932	Everton FC Liverpool	Newcastle United FC	William Ralph Dean (Everton FC Liverpool)	44
1932/1933	Arsenal FC London	Everton FC Liverpool	John William Anslow Bowers (Derby County FC)	35
1933/1934	Arsenal FC London	Manchester City FC	John William Anslow Bowers (Derby County FC)	34
1934/1935	Arsenal FC London	Sheffield Wednesday FC	Edward Joseph Drake (Arsenal FC London)	42
1935/1936	Sunderland AFC	Arsenal FC London	William "Ginger" Richardson (West Bromwich Albion FC)	39
1936/1937	Manchester City FC	Sunderland AFC	Frederick Charles Steele (Stoke City FC)	33
1937/1938	Arsenal FC London	Preston North End FC	Thomas Lawton (Everton FC Liverpool)	28
1938/1939	Everton FC Liverpool	Portsmouth FC	Thomas Lawton (Everton FC Liverpool)	35
1939-1945	*No competition*	*No competition*	-
1945/1946	*No competition*	Derby County FC	-
1946/1947	Liverpool FC	Charlton Athletic FC	Dennis Westcott (Wolverhampton Wanderers FC)	37
1947/1948	Arsenal FC London	Manchester United FC	Ronald Leslie Rooke (Arsenal FC London)	33
1948/1949	Portsmouth FC	Wolverhampton Wanderers FC	William Moir (SCO, Bolton Wanderers FC)	25
1949/1950	Portsmouth FC	Arsenal FC London	Richard Daniel Davis (Sunderland AFC)	25
1950/1951	Tottenham Hotspur FC London	Newcastle United FC	Stanley Harding Mortensen (Blackpool FC)	30
1951/1952	Manchester United FC	Newcastle United FC	Jorge Robledo Oliver (CHI, Newcastle United FC)	33
1952/1953	Arsenal FC London	Blackpool FC	Charles Wayman (Preston North End FC)	24
1953/1954	Wolverhampton Wanderers FC	West Bromwich Albion FC	Jimmy Glazzard (Huddersfield Town AFC)	29
1954/1955	Chelsea FC London	Newcastle United FC	Ronald Allen (West Bromwich Albion FC)	27
1955/1956	Manchester United FC	Manchester City FC	Nathaniel Lofthouse (Bolton Wanderers FC)	33
1956/1957	Manchester United FC	Aston Villa FC Birmingham	William John Charles (WAL, Leeds United FC)	38
1957/1958	Wolverhampton Wanderers FC	Bolton Wanderers FC	Robert Alfred Smith (Tottenham Hotspur FC)	36
1958/1959	Wolverhampton Wanderers FC	Nottingham Forest FC	James Peter Greaves (Chelsea FC London)	33
1959/1960	Burnley FC	Wolverhampton Wanderers FC	Dennis Sydney Viollet (Manchester United FC)	32
1960/1961	Tottenham Hotspur FC London	Tottenham Hotspur FC London	James Peter Greaves (Chelsea FC London)	41
1961/1962	Ipswich Town FC	Tottenham Hotspur FC London	Raymond Crawford (Ipswich Town FC) Derek Tennyson Kevan (West Bromwich Albion FC)	33
1962/1963	Everton FC Liverpool	Manchester United FC	James Peter Greaves (Tottenham Hotspur FC)	37
1963/1964	Liverpool FC	West Ham United FC London	James Peter Greaves (Tottenham Hotspur FC)	35
1964/1965	Manchester United FC	Liverpool FC	Andrew McEvoy (IRL, Blackburn Rovers FC) James Peter Greaves (Tottenham Hotspur FC)	29
1965/1966	Liverpool FC	Everton FC Liverpool	William John Irvine (NIR, Burnley FC)	29
1966/1967	Manchester United FC	Tottenham Hotspur FC London	Ron Davies (WAL, Southampton FC)	37
1967/1968	Manchester City FC	West Bromwich Albion FC	George Best (NIR, Manchester United FC) Ronald Tudor Davies (WAL, Southampton FC)	28
1968/1969	Leeds United FC	Manchester City FC	James Peter Greaves (Tottenham Hotspur FC)	27
1969/1970	Everton FC Liverpool	Chelsea FC London	Jeffrey Astle (West Bromwich Albion FC)	25
1970/1971	Arsenal FC London	Arsenal FC London	Anthony Brown (West Bromwich Albion FC)	28
1971/1972	Derby County FC	Leeds United FC	Francis Henry Lee (Manchester City FC)	33
1972/1973	Liverpool FC	Sunderland AFC	Bryan Stanley Robson (West Ham United FC)	28
1973/1974	Leeds United FC	Liverpool FC	Michael Roger Channon (Southampton FC)	21
1974/1975	Derby County FC	West Ham United FC London	Malcolm Ian Macdonald (Newcastle United FC)	21
1975/1976	Liverpool FC	Southampton FC	Edward John MacDougall (SCO, Norwich City FC)	23
1976/1977	Liverpool FC	Manchester United FC	Malcolm Ian Macdonald (Arsenal FC London) Andrew Mullen Gray (SCO, Aston Villa FC)	25
1977/1978	Nottingham Forest FC	Ipswich Town FC	Robert Dennis Latchford (Everton FC Liverpool)	30
1978/1979	Liverpool FC	Arsenal FC London	Frank Stewart Worthington (Bolton Wanderers FC)	24
1979/1980	Liverpool FC	West Ham United FC London	Philip John Boyer (Southampton FC)	23
1980/1981	Aston Villa FC Birmingham	Tottenham Hotspur FC London	Peter Withe (Aston Villa FC Birmingham) Steven Archibald (SCO, Tottenham Hotspur FC)	20
1981/1982	Liverpool FC	Tottenham Hotspur FC London	Joseph Kevin Keegan (Southampton FC)	26
1982/1983	Liverpool FC	Manchester United FC	Luther Loide Blissett (Watford FC)	27
1983/1984	Liverpool FC	Everton FC Liverpool	Ian James Rush (WAL, Liverpool FC)	32
1984/1985	Everton FC Liverpool	Manchester United FC	Kerry Michael Dixon (Chelsea FC London) Gary Winston Lineker (Leicester City FC)	24
1985/1986	Liverpool FC	Liverpool FC	Gary Winston Lineker (Everton FC Liverpool)	30
1986/1987	Everton FC Liverpool	Coventry City FC	Clive Darren Allen (Tottenham Hotspur FC London)	33
1987/1988	Liverpool FC	Wimbledon	John William Aldridge (IRL, Liverpool FC)	26
1988/1989	Arsenal FC London	Liverpool FC	Alan Martin Smith (Arsenal FC London)	23
1989/1990	Liverpool FC	Manchester United FC	Gary Winston Lineker (Tottenham Hotspur FC)	24
1990/1991	Arsenal FC London	Tottenham Hotspur FC London	Alan Martin Smith (Arsenal FC London)	22
1991/1992	Leeds United FC	Liverpool FC	Ian Edward Wright (Crystal Palace FC London/Arsenal FC London)	29
1992/1993	Manchester United FC	Arsenal FC London	Edward Paul Sheringham (Nottingham Forest FC/Tottenham Hotspur FC London)	22
1993/1994	Manchester United FC	Manchester United FC	Andrew Alexander Cole (Newcastle United FC)	34
1994/1995	Blackburn Rovers FC	Everton FC Liverpool	Alan Shearer (Blackburn Rovers FC)	34

1995/1996	Manchester United FC	Manchester United FC	Alan Shearer (Blackburn Rovers FC)	31
1996/1997	Manchester United FC	Chelsea FC London	Alan Shearer (Newcastle United FC)	25
1997/1998	Arsenal FC London	Arsenal FC London	Christopher Roy Sutton (Blackburn Rovers FC) Dion Dublin (Coventry City FC) Michael James Owen (Liverpool FC)	18
1998/1999	Manchester United FC	Manchester United FC	Jimmy Floyd Hasselbaink (NED, Leeds United FC) Michael James Owen (Liverpool FC) Dwight Eversley Yorke (TRI, Manchester United)	18
1999/2000	Manchester United FC	Chelsea FC London	Kevin Mark Phillips (Sunderland AFC)	30
2000/2001	Manchester United FC	Liverpool FC	Jimmy Floyd Hasselbaink (NED, Chelsea FC London)	23
2001/2002	Arsenal FC London	Arsenal FC London	Thierry Daniel Henry (FRA, Arsenal FC London)	24
2002/2003	Manchester United FC	Arsenal FC London	Rutgerus Johannes Martinus "Ruud" van Nistelrooy (NED, Manchester United FC)	25
2003/2004	Arsenal FC London	Manchester United FC	Thierry Daniel Henry (FRA, Arsenal FC London)	30
2004/2005	Chelsea FC London	Arsenal FC London	Thierry Daniel Henry (FRA, Arsenal FC London)	25
2005/2006	Chelsea FC London	Liverpool FC	Thierry Daniel Henry (FRA, Arsenal FC London)	27
2006/2007	Manchester United FC	Chelsea FC London	Didier Yves Drogba Tébily (CIV, Chelsea FC London)	20
2007/2008	Manchester United FC	Portsmouth FC	Cristiano Ronaldo dos Santos Aveiro (POR, Manchester United FC)	31
2008/2009	Manchester United FC	Chelsea FC London	Nicolas Sébastien Anelka (FRA, Chelsea FC London)	19
2009/2010	Chelsea FC London	Chelsea FC London	Didier Yves Drogba Tébily (CIV, Chelsea FC London)	29
2010/2011	Manchester United FC	Manchester City FC	Dimitar Berbatov (BUL, Manchester United FC) Carlos Alberto Martínez Tevez (ARG, Manchester City FC)	20
2011/2012	Manchester City FC	Chelsea FC London	Robin van Persie (NED, Arsenal FC London)	30
2012/2013	Manchester United FC	Wigan Athletic FC	Robin van Persie (NED, Manchester United FC)	26
2013/2014	Manchester City FC	Arsenal FC London	Luis Alberto Suárez Díaz (URU, Liverpool FC)	31
2014/2015	Chelsea FC London	Arsenal FC London	Sergio Leonel Agüero del Castillo (ARG, Manchester City FC)	26
2015/2016	Leicester City FC	Manchester United FC	Harry Edward Kane (Tottenham Hotspur FC)	25
2016/2017	Chelsea FC London	Arsenal FC London	Harry Edward Kane (Tottenham Hotspur FC)	29
2017/2018	Manchester City FC	Chelsea FC London	Mohamed Salah Ghaly (EGY, Liverpool FC)	32
2018/2019	Manchester City FC	Manchester City FC	Pierre-Emerick Emiliano François Aubameyang (GAB, Arsenal FC London) Sadio Mané (SEN, Liverpool FC) Mohamed Salah Ghaly (EGY, Liverpool FC)	22
2019/2020	Liverpool FC	Arsenal FC London	Jamie Richard Vardy (Leicester City FC)	23
2020/2021	Manchester City FC	Leicester City FC	Harry Edward Kane (Tottenham Hotspur FC)	23

Please note: the championship was called Football League (1888–1892), Football League First Division (1892–1992) and Premier League (1992–present).

EFL (LEAGUE) CUP WINNERS

1960/1961	Aston Villa FC Birmingham	1981/1982	Liverpool FC	2001/2002	Blackburn Rovers FC
1961/1962	Norwich City FC	1982/1983	Liverpool FC	2002/2003	Liverpool FC
1962/1963	Birmingham City FC	1983/1984	Liverpool FC	2003/2004	Middlesbrough FC
1963/1964	Leicester City FC	1984/1985	Norwich City FC	2004/2005	Chelsea FC London
1964/1965	Chelsea FC London	1985/1986	Oxford United FC	2005/2006	Manchester United FC
1965/1966	West Bromwich Albion FC	1986/1987	Arsenal FC London	2006/2007	Chelsea FC London
1966/1967	Queens Park Rangers FC	1987/1988	Luton Town FC	2007/2008	Tottenham Hotspur FC London
1967/1968	Leeds United FC	1988/1989	Nottingham Forest FC	2008/2009	Manchester United FC
1968/1969	Swindon Town FC	1989/1990	Nottingham Forest FC	2009/2010	Manchester United FC
1969/1970	Manchester City FC	1990/1991	Sheffield Wednesday FC	2010/2011	Birmingham City FC
1970/1971	Tottenham Hotspur FC London	1991/1992	Manchester United FC	2011/2012	Liverpool FC
1971/1972	Stoke City FC	1992/1993	Arsenal FC London	2012/2013	Swansea City AFC
1972/1973	Tottenham Hotspur FC London	1993/1994	Aston Villa FC Birmingham	2013/2014	Manchester City FC
1973/1974	Wolverhampton Wanderers FC	1994/1995	Liverpool FC	2014/2015	Chelsea FC London
1974/1975	Aston Villa FC Birmingham	1995/1996	Aston Villa FC Birmingham	2015/2016	Manchester City FC
1975/1976	Manchester City FC	1996/1997	Leicester City FC	2016/2017	Manchester United FC
1976/1977	Aston Villa FC Birmingham	1997/1998	Chelsea FC London	2017/2018	Manchester City FC
1977/1978	Nottingham Forest FC	1998/1999	Tottenham Hotspur FC London	2018/2019	Manchester City FC
1978/1979	Nottingham Forest FC	1999/2000	Leicester City FC	2019/2020	Manchester City FC
1979/1980	Wolverhampton Wanderers FC	2000/2001	Liverpool FC	2020/2021	Manchester City FC
1980/1981	Liverpool FC				

NATIONAL CHAMPIONSHIP
Premier League 2020/2021
(12.09.2020 – 23.05.2021)

Results

Round 1 [12-14.09.2020]
Fulham - Arsenal 0-3(0-1)
Crystal Palace - Southampton 1-0(1-0)
Liverpool FC - Leeds United 4-3(3-2)
West Ham United - Newcastle United 0-2(0-0)
WB Albion - Leicester City 0-3(0-0)
Tottenham Hotspur - Everton 0-1(0-0)
Sheffield United - Wolverhampton 0-2(0-2)
Brighton & Hove - Chelsea 1-3(0-1)
Burnley - Manchester U. 0-1(0-0)[12.01.2021]
Manch. City-Aston Villa 2-0(0-0)[20.01.2021]

Round 2 [19-21.09.2020]
Everton - West Bromwich Albion 5-2(2-1)
Leeds United - Fulham 4-3(2-1)
Manchester United - Crystal Palace 1-3(0-1)
Arsenal - West Ham United 2-1(1-1)
Southampton - Tottenham Hotspur 2-5(1-1)
Newcastle United - Brighton & Hove 0-3(0-2)
Chelsea - Liverpool FC 0-2(0-0)
Leicester City - Burnley 4-2(1-1)
Aston Villa - Sheffield United 1-0(0-0)
Wolverhampton - Manchester City 1-3(0-2)

Round 3 26-28.09.2020 [ ]
Brighton&Hove - Manchester United 2-3(1-1)
Crystal Palace - Everton 1-2(1-2)
West Bromwich Albion - Chelsea 3-3(3-0)
Burnley - Southampton 0-1(0-1)
Sheffield United - Leeds United 0-1(0-0)
Tottenham Hots. - Newcastle United 1-1(1-0)
Manchester City - Leicester City 2-5(1-1)
West Ham United - Wolverhampton 4-0(1-0)
Fulham - Aston Villa 0-3(0-2)
Liverpool FC - Arsenal 3-1(2-1)

Round 4 [03-04.10.2020]
Chelsea - Crystal Palace 4-0(0-0)
Everton - Brighton & Hove 4-2(2-1)
Leeds United - Manchester City 1-1(0-1)
Newcastle United - Burnley 3-1(1-0)
Leicester City - West Ham United 0-3(0-2)
Southampton - WB Albion 2-0(1-0)
Arsenal - Sheffield United 2-1(0-0)
Wolverhampton - Fulham 1-0(0-0)
Manchester Un. - Tottenham Hotspur 1-6(1-4)
Aston Villa - Liverpool FC 7-2(4-1)

Round 5 [17-19.10.2020]
Everton - Liverpool FC 2-2(1-1)
Chelsea - Southampton 3-3(2-1)
Manchester City - Arsenal 1-0(1-0)
Newcastle United - Manchester Unit. 1-4(1-1)
Sheffield United - Fulham 1-1(0-0)
Crystal Palace - Brighton & Hove 1-1(1-0)
Tottenham Hotspur - West Ham Unit. 3-3(3-0)
Leicester City - Aston Villa 0-1(0-0)
West Bromwich Albion - Burnley 0-0
Leeds United - Wolverhampton 0-1(0-0)

Round 6 [23-26.10.2020]
Aston Villa - Leeds United 0-3(0-0)
West Ham United - Manchester City 1-1(1-0)
Fulham - Crystal Palace 1-2(0-1)
Manchester United - Chelsea 0-0
Liverpool FC - Sheffield United 2-1(1-1)
Southampton - Everton 2-0(2-0)
Wolverhampton - Newcastle United 1-1(0-0)
Arsenal - Leicester City 0-1(0-0)
Brighton & Hove - WB Albion 1-1(1-0)
Burnley - Tottenham Hotspur 0-1(0-0)

Round 7 [30.10.-02.11.2020]
Wolverhampton - Crystal Palace 2-0(2-0)
Sheffield United - Manchester City 0-1(0-1)
Burnley - Chelsea 0-3(0-1)
Liverpool FC - West Ham United 2-1(1-1)
Aston Villa - Southampton 3-4(0-3)
Newcastle United - Everton 2-1(0-0)
Manchester United - Arsenal 0-1(0-0)
Tottenham Hotspur - Brighton&Hove 2-1(1-0)
Fulham - West Bromwich Albion 2-0(2-0)
Leeds United - Leicester City 1-4(0-2)

Round 8 [06-08.11.2020]
Brighton & Hove - Burnley 0-0
Southampton - Newcastle United 2-0(1-0)
Everton - Manchester United 1-3(1-2)
Crystal Palace - Leeds United 4-1(3-1)
Chelsea - Sheffield United 4-1(2-1)
West Ham United - Fulham 1-0(0-0)
WB Albion - Tottenham Hotspur 0-1(0-0)
Leicester City - Wolverhampton 1-0(1-0)
Manchester City - Liverpool FC 1-1(1-1)
Arsenal - Aston Villa 0-3(0-1)

Round 9 [21-23.11.2020]
Newcastle United - Chelsea 0-2(0-1)
Aston Villa - Brighton & Hove 1-2(0-1)
Tottenham Hots. - Manchester City 2-0(1-0)
Manchester United - WB Albion 1-0(0-0)
Fulham - Everton 2-3(1-3)
Sheffield United - West Ham United 0-1(0-0)
Leeds United - Arsenal 0-0
Liverpool FC - Leicester City 3-0(2-0)
Burnley - Crystal Palace 1-0(1-0)
Wolverhampton - Southampton 1-1(0-0)

Round 10 [27-30.11.2020]
Crystal Palace - Newcastle United 0-2(0-0)
Brighton & Hove - Liverpool FC 1-1(0-0)
Manchester City - Burnley 5-0(3-0)
Everton - Leeds United 0-1(0-0)
WB Albion - Sheffield United 1-0(1-0)
Southampton - Manchester United 2-3(2-0)
Chelsea - Tottenham Hotspur 0-0
Arsenal - Wolverhampton 1-2(1-2)
Leicester City - Fulham 1-2(0-2)
West Ham United - Aston Villa 2-1(1-1)

Round 11 [05-07.12.2020]
Burnley - Everton 1-1(1-1)
Manchester City - Fulham 2-0(2-0)
West Ham Unit. - Manchester United 1-3(1-0)
Chelsea - Leeds United 3-1(1-1)
WB Albion - Crystal Palace 1-5(1-1)
Sheffield United - Leicester City 1-2(1-1)
Tottenham Hotspur - Arsenal 2-0(2-0)
Liverpool FC - Wolverhampton 4-0(1-0)
Brighton & Hove - Southampton 1-2(1-1)
Aston Villa - Newcastle 2-0(2-0) [23.01.2021]

Round 12 [11-13.12.2020]
Leeds United - West Ham United 1-2(1-1)
Wolverhampton - Aston Villa 0-1(0-0)
Newcastle - West Bromwich Albion 2-1(1-0)
Manchester United - Manchester City 0-0
Everton - Chelsea 1-0(1-0)
Southampton - Sheffield United 3-0(1-0)
Crystal Palace - Tottenham Hotspur 1-1(0-1)
Fulham - Liverpool FC 1-1(1-0)
Arsenal - Burnley 0-1(0-0)
Leicester City - Brighton & Hove 3-0(3-0)

Round 13 [15-17.12.2020]
Wolverhampton - Chelsea 2-1(0-0)
Manchester City - WB Albion 1-1(1-1)
Arsenal - Southampton 1-1(0-1)
Leeds United - Newcastle United 5-2(1-1)
Leicester City - Everton 0-2(0-1)
Fulham - Brighton & Hove 0-0
West Ham United - Crystal Palace 1-1(0-1)
Liverpool FC - Tottenham Hotspur 2-1(1-1)
Aston Villa - Burnley 0-0
Sheffield United - Manchester United 2-3(1-2)

Round 14 [19-21.12.2020]
Crystal Palace - Liverpool FC 0-7(0-3)
Southampton - Manchester City 0-1(0-1)
Everton - Arsenal 2-1(2-1)
Newcastle United - Fulham 1-1(0-1)
Brighton & Hove - Sheffield United 1-1(0-0)
Tottenham Hotspur - Leicester City 0-2(0-1)
Manchester United - Leeds United 6-2(4-1)
West Bromwich Albion - Aston Villa 0-3(0-1)
Burnley - Wolverhampton 2-1(1-0)
Chelsea - West Ham United 3-0(1-0)

Round 15 [26-27.12.2020]
Leicester City - Manchester United 2-2(1-1)
Aston Villa - Crystal Palace 3-0(1-0)
Fulham - Southampton 0-0
Arsenal - Chelsea 3-1(2-0)
Manchester City - Newcastle United 2-0(1-0)
Sheffield United - Everton 0-1(0-0)
Leeds United - Burnley 1-0(1-0)
West Ham United - Brighton & Hove 2-2(0-1)
Liverpool FC - WB Albion 1-1(1-0)
Wolverhampton - Tottenham Hotspur 1-1(0-1)

Round 16 [28-30.12.2020]
Crystal Palace - Leicester City 1-1(0-0)
Chelsea - Aston Villa 1-1(1-0)
Brighton & Hove - Arsenal 0-1(0-0)
Burnley - Sheffield United 1-0(1-0)
Southampton - West Ham United 0-0
WB Albion - Leeds United 0-5(0-4)
Manchester United - Wolverhampton 1-0(0-0)
Newcastle United - Liverpool FC 0-0
Tottenham - Fulham 1-1(1-0) [13.01.2021]
Everton - Manchester C. 1-3(1-1) [17.02.2021]

Round 17 [01-04.01.2021]
Everton - West Ham United 0-1(0-0)
Manchester United - Aston Villa 2-1(1-0)
Tottenham Hotspur - Leeds United 3-0(2-0)
Crystal Palace - Sheffield United 2-0(2-0)
Brighton & Hove - Wolverhampton 3-3(1-3)
West Bromwich Albion - Arsenal 0-4(0-2)
Newcastle United - Leicester City 1-2(0-0)
Chelsea - Manchester City 1-3(0-3)
Southampton - Liverpool FC 1-0(1-0)
Burnley - Fulham 1-1(0-0) [17.02.2021]

Round 18 [12-14.01.2021]
Sheffield United - Newcastle United 1-0(0-0)
Wolverhampton - Everton 1-2(1-1)
Manchester City - Brighton & Hove 1-0(1-0)
Arsenal - Crystal Palace 0-0
West Ham - WB Albion 2-1(1-0) [19.01.]
Leicester City - Chelsea 2-0(2-0) [19.01.]
Fulham - Manchester United 1-2(1-1) [20.01.]
Liverpool FC - Burnley 0-1(0-0) [21.01.]
Leeds United - Southampton 3-0(0-0) [23.02.]
Aston Villa - Tottenham H. 0-2(0-1) [21.03.]

Round 19 [16-18.01.2021]
Wolverhampton - WB Albion 2-3(2-1)
Leeds United - Brighton & Hove 0-1(0-1)
West Ham United - Burnley 1-0(1-0)
Fulham - Chelsea 0-1(0-0)
Leicester City - Southampton 2-0(1-0)
Sheffield Unit. - Tottenham Hotspur 1-3(0-2)
Liverpool FC - Manchester United 0-0
Manchester City - Crystal Palace 4-0(1-0)
Arsenal - Newcastle United 3-0(0-0)
Aston Villa - Everton 0-0 [13.05.]

Round 20 [26-28.01.2021]
Newcastle United - Leeds United 1-2(0-1)
Crystal Palace - West Ham United 2-3(1-2)
WB Albion - Manchester City 0-5(0-4)
Southampton - Arsenal 1-3(1-2)
Burnley - Aston Villa 3-2(0-1)
Chelsea - Wolverhampton 0-0
Brighton & Hove - Fulham 0-0
Everton - Leicester City 1-1(1-0)
Manchester United - Sheffield United 1-2(0-1)
Tottenham Hotspur - Liverpool FC 1-3(0-1)

Round 21 [30-31.01.2021]
Everton - Newcastle United 0-2(0-0)
Crystal Palace - Wolverhampton 1-0(0-0)
Manchester City - Sheffield United 1-0(1-0)
West Bromwich Albion - Fulham 2-2(0-1)
Arsenal - Manchester United 0-0
Southampton - Aston Villa 0-1(0-1)
Chelsea - Burnley 2-0(1-0)
Leicester City - Leeds United 1-3(1-1)
West Ham United - Liverpool FC 1-3(0-0)
Brighton&Hove - Tottenham Hotspur 1-0(1-0)

Round 22 [02-04.02.2021]
Sheffield United - WB Albion 2-1(0-1)
Wolverhampton - Arsenal 2-1(1-1)
Manchester United - Southampton 9-0(4-0)
Newcastle United - Crystal Palace 1-2(1-2)
Burnley - Manchester City 0-2(0-2)
Fulham - Leicester City 0-2(0-2)
Leeds United - Everton 1-2(0-2)
Aston Villa - West Ham United 1-3(0-0)
Liverpool FC - Brighton & Hove 0-1(0-0)
Tottenham Hotspur - Chelsea 0-1(0-1)

Round 23 [06-08.02.2021]
Aston Villa - Arsenal 1-0(1-0)
Burnley - Brighton & Hove 1-1(0-1)
Newcastle United - Southampton 3-2(3-1)
Fulham - West Ham United 0-0
Manchester United - Everton 3-3(2-0)
Tottenham Hotspur - WB Albion 2-0(0-0)
Wolverhampton - Leicester City 0-0
Liverpool FC - Manchester City 1-4(0-0)
Sheffield United - Chelsea 1-2(0-1)
Leeds United - Crystal Palace 2-0(1-0)

Round 24 [13-15.02.2021]
Leicester City - Liverpool FC 3-1(0-0)
Crystal Palace - Burnley 0-3(0-2)
Manchester City - Tottenham 3-0(1-0)
Brighton & Hove - Aston Villa 0-0
Southampton - Wolverhampton 1-2(1-0)
WB Albion - Manchester United 1-1(1-1)
Arsenal - Leeds United 4-2(3-0)
Everton - Fulham 0-2(0-0)
West Ham United - Sheffield United 3-0(1-0)
Chelsea - Newcastle United 2-0(2-0)

Round 25 [19-22.02.2021]
Wolverhampton - Leeds United 1-0(0-0)
Southampton - Chelsea 1-1(1-0)
Burnley - West Bromwich Albion 0-0
Liverpool FC - Everton 0-2(0-1)
Fulham - Sheffield United 1-0(0-0)
West Ham - Tottenham Hotspur 2-1(1-0)
Aston Villa - Leicester City 1-2(0-2)
Arsenal - Manchester City 0-1(0-1)
Manchester United - Newcastle 3-1(1-1)
Brighton & Hove - Crystal Palace 1-2(0-1)

Round 26 [27.02.-01.03.2021]
Manchester City - West Ham United 2-1(1-1)
WB Albion - Brighton & Hove 1-0(1-0)
Leeds United - Aston Villa 0-1(0-1)
Newcastle United - Wolverhampton 1-1(0-0)
Crystal Palace - Fulham 0-0
Leicester City - Arsenal 1-3(1-2)
Tottenham Hotspur - Burnley 4-0(3-0)
Chelsea - Manchester United 0-0
Sheffield United - Liverpool FC 0-2(0-0)
Everton - Southampton 1-0(1-0)

Round 27 [06-08.03.2021]
Burnley - Arsenal 1-1(1-1)
Sheffield United - Southampton 0-2(0-1)
Aston Villa - Wolverhampton 0-0
Brighton & Hove - Leicester City 1-2(1-0)
WB Albion - Newcastle United 0-0
Liverpool FC - Fulham 0-1(0-1)
Manchester City - Manchester United 0-2(0-1)
Tottenham Hotspur - Crystal Palace 4-1(1-1)
Chelsea - Everton 2-0(1-0)
West Ham United - Leeds United 2-0(2-0)

Round 28 [12-15.03.2021]
Newcastle United - Aston Villa 1-1(0-0)
Leeds United - Chelsea 0-0
Crystal Palace - WB Albion 1-0(1-0)
Everton - Burnley 1-2(1-2)
Fulham - Manchester City 0-3(0-0)
Southampton - Brighton & Hove 1-2(1-1)
Leicester City - Sheffield United 5-0(1-0)
Arsenal - Tottenham Hotspur 2-1(1-1)
Manchester United - West Ham 1-0(0-0)
Wolverhampton - Liverpool FC 0-1(0-1)

Round 29 [02-04.03.2021]
Manchester City - Wolverhampton 4-1(1-0)
Burnley - Leicester City 1-1(1-1)
Sheffield United - Aston Villa 1-0(1-0)
Crystal Palace - Manchester United 0-0
West Bromwich Albion - Everton 0-1(0-0)
Liverpool FC - Chelsea 0-1(0-1)
Fulham - Leeds United 1-2(1-1) [19.03.]
Brighton&Hove - Newcastle 3-0(1-0) [20.03.]
West Ham United - Arsenal 3-3(3-1) [21.03.]
Tottenham - Southampton 2-1(0-1) [21.04.]

Round 30 [03-05.04.2021]
Chelsea - West Bromwich Albion 2-5(1-2)
Leeds United - Sheffield United 2-1(1-1)
Leicester City - Manchester City 0-2(0-0)
Arsenal - Liverpool FC 0-3(0-0)
Southampton - Burnley 3-2(2-2)
Newcastle United - Tottenham 2-2(1-2)
Aston Villa - Fulham 3-1(0-0)
Manchester United - Brighton&Hove 2-1(0-1)
Everton - Crystal Palace 1-1(0-0)
Wolverhampton - West Ham United 2-3(1-3)

Round 31 [09-12.04.2021]
Fulham - Wolverhampton 0-1(0-0)
Manchester City - Leeds United 1-2(0-1)
Liverpool FC - Aston Villa 2-1(0-1)
Crystal Palace - Chelsea 1-4(0-3)
Burnley - Newcastle United 1-2(1-0)
West Ham United - Leicester City 3-2(2-0)
Tottenham - Manchester United 1-3(1-0)
Sheffield United - Arsenal 0-3(0-1)
WB Albion - Southampton 3-0(2-0)
Brighton & Hove - Everton 0-0

Round 32 [16-22.04.2021]
Everton - Tottenham Hotspur 2-2(1-1)
Newcastle United - West Ham United 3-2(2-0)
Wolverhampton - Sheffield United 1-0(0-0)
Arsenal - Fulham 1-1(0-0)
Manchester United - Burnley 3-1(0-0)
Leeds United - Liverpool FC 1-1(0-1)
Chelsea - Brighton & Hove 0-0
Aston Villa - Manchester City 1-2(1-2)
Leicester City - WB Albion 3-0(3-0)
Southampton - Crystal Palace 3-1(1-1)[11.05.]

Round 33 [23-26.04.2021]
Fulham - Tottenham Hotspur 0-1(0-1) [04.03.]
Manchester C.-Southampton 5-2(3-1) [10.03.]
Arsenal - Everton 0-1(0-0)
Liverpool FC - Newcastle United 1-1(1-0)
West Ham United - Chelsea 0-1(0-1)
Sheffield United - Brighton & Hove 1-0(1-0)
Wolverhampton - Burnley 0-4(0-3)
Leeds United - Manchester United 0-0
Aston Villa - West Bromwich Albion 2-2(1-1)
Leicester City - Crystal Palace 2-1(0-1)

Round 34 [30.04.-03.05.2021]
Southampton - Leicester City 1-1(0-0)
Crystal Palace - Manchester City 0-2(0-0)
Brighton & Hove - Leeds United 2-0(1-0)
Chelsea - Fulham 2-0(1-0)
Everton - Aston Villa 1-2(1-1)
Newcastle United - Arsenal 0-2(0-1)
Tottenham - Sheffield United 4-0(1-0)
WB Albion - Wolverhampton 1-0(0-1)
Burnley - West Ham United 1-2(1-2)
Manchester Unit. - Liverpool 2-4(1-2) [13.05.]

Round 35 [07-10.05.2021]
Leicester City - Newcastle United 2-4(0-2)
Leeds United - Tottenham Hotspur 3-1(2-1)
Sheffield United - Crystal Palace 0-2(0-1)
Manchester City - Chelsea 1-2(1-0)
Liverpool FC - Southampton 2-0(1-0)
Wolverhampton - Brighton & Hove 2-1(0-1)
Aston Villa - Manchester United 1-3(1-0)
West Ham United - Everton 0-1(0-1)
Arsenal - West Bromwich Albion 3-1(2-0)
Fulham - Burnley 0-2(0-2)

Round 36 [11-16.05.2021]
Manchester United - Leicester City 1-2(1-1)
Chelsea - Arsenal 0-1(0-1)
Newcastle United - Manchester City 3-4(2-2)
Burnley - Leeds United 0-4(0-1)
Southampton - Fulham 3-1(1-0)
Brighton & Hove - West Ham United 1-1(0-0)
Crystal Palace - Aston Villa 3-2(1-2)
Tottenham Hotspur - Wolverhampton 2-0(1-0)
WB Albion - Liverpool FC 1-2(1-1)
Everton - Sheffield United 0-1(0-1)

Round 37 [18-19.05.2021]
Manchester United - Fulham 1-1(1-0)
Southampton - Leeds United 0-2(0-0)
Brighton & Hove - Manchester City 3-2(0-1)
Chelsea - Leicester City 2-1(0-0)
Everton - Wolverhampton 1-0(0-0)
Newcastle United - Sheffield United 1-0(1-0)
Tottenham Hotspur - Aston Villa 1-2(1-2)
Crystal Palace - Arsenal 1-3(0-1)
Burnley - Liverpool FC 0-3(0-1)
WB Albion - West Ham United 1-3(1-1)

Round 38 [23.05.2021]
Arsenal - Brighton & Hove 2-0(0-0)
Aston Villa - Chelsea 2-1(1-0)
Fulham - Newcastle United 0-2(0-1)
Leeds United - WB Albion 3-1(2-0)
Leicester City - Tottenham Hotspur 2-4(1-1)
Liverpool FC - Crystal Palace 2-0(1-0)
Manchester City - Everton 5-0(2-0)
Sheffield United - Burnley 1-0(1-0)
West Ham United - Southampton 3-0(2-0)
Wolverhampton - Manchester United 1-2(1-2)

Final Standings

									Total			Home						Away					
1.	**Manchester City FC**	38	27	5	6	83	-	32	86	13	2	4	43	-	17	14	3	2	40	-	15
2.	Manchester United FC	38	21	11	6	73	-	44	74	9	4	6	38	-	28	12	7	0	35	-	16
3.	Liverpool FC	38	20	9	9	68	-	42	69	10	3	6	29	-	20	10	6	3	39	-	22
4.	Chelsea FC London	38	19	10	9	58	-	36	67	9	6	4	31	-	18	10	4	5	27	-	18
5.	Leicester City FC	38	20	6	12	68	-	50	66	9	1	9	34	-	30	11	5	3	34	-	20
6.	West Ham United FC London	38	19	8	11	62	-	47	65	10	4	5	32	-	22	9	4	6	30	-	25
7.	Tottenham Hotspur FC London	38	18	8	12	68	-	45	62	10	3	6	35	-	20	8	5	6	33	-	25
8.	Arsenal FC London	38	18	7	13	55	-	39	61	8	4	7	24	-	21	10	3	6	31	-	18
9.	Leeds United FC	38	18	5	15	62	-	54	59	8	5	6	28	-	21	10	0	9	34	-	33
10.	Everton FC Liverpool	38	17	8	13	47	-	48	59	6	4	9	24	-	28	11	4	4	23	-	20
11.	Aston Villa FC Birmingham	38	16	7	15	55	-	46	55	7	4	8	29	-	27	9	3	7	26	-	19
12.	Newcastle United FC	38	12	9	17	46	-	62	45	6	5	8	26	-	33	6	4	9	20	-	29
13.	Wolverhampton Wanderers FC	38	12	9	17	36	-	52	45	7	4	8	21	-	25	5	5	9	15	-	27
14.	Crystal Palace FC London	38	12	8	18	41	-	66	44	6	5	8	20	-	32	6	3	10	21	-	34
15.	Southampton FC	38	12	7	19	47	-	68	43	8	3	8	28	-	25	4	4	11	19	-	43
16.	Brighton & Hove Albion FC	38	9	14	15	40	-	46	41	4	9	6	22	-	22	5	5	9	18	-	24
17.	Burnley FC	38	10	9	19	33	-	55	39	4	6	9	14	-	27	6	3	10	19	-	28
18.	Fulham FC London (*Relegated*)	38	5	13	20	27	-	53	28	2	4	13	9	-	28	3	9	7	18	-	25
19.	West Bromwich Albion FC (*Relegated*)	38	5	11	22	35	-	76	26	3	6	10	15	-	39	2	5	12	20	-	37
20.	Sheffield United FC (*Relegated*)	38	7	2	29	20	-	63	23	5	1	13	12	-	27	2	1	16	8	-	36

	Top goalscorers:	
23	**Harry Edward Kane**	***Tottenham Hotspur FC London***
22	Mohamed Salah Ghaly (EGY)	*Liverpool FC*
18	Bruno Miguel Borges Fernandes (POR)	*Manchester United FC*
17	Patrick James Bamford	*Leeds United FC*
17	Son Heung-min (KOR)	*Tottenham Hotspur FC London*
16	Dominic Nathaniel Calvert-Lewin	*Everton FC Liverpool*

EFL (League) Cup Final 2020/2021

25.04.2021; Wembley Stadium, London; Referee: Paul Tierney; Attendance: 7,773
Manchester City FC - Tottenham Hotspur FC London   **2-0(1-0)**

Manchester City: Zackary Thomas Steffen, Kyle Andrew Walker, Rubén dos Santos Gato Alves Dias, Aymeric Jean Louis Gerard Alphonse Laporte, João Pedro Cavaco Cancelo, Kevin De Bruyne (87.Bernardo Mota Veiga de Carvalho e Silva), Fernando Luiz Roza „Fernandinho" (Cap) (84.Rodrigo Hernández Cascante „Rodri"),İlkay Gündoğan, Riyad Karim Mahrez, Raheem Shaquille Sterling, Philip Walter Foden. Trainer: Josep "Pep" Guardiola Sala (Spain).

Tottenham Hotspur: Hugo Lloris (Cap), Serge Alain Stephane Aurier (90.Steven Charles Bergwijn), Tobias Albertine Maurits Alderweireld, Eric Jeremy Edgar Dier, Sergio Reguilón Rodríguez, Harry Billy Winks, Pierre-Emile Kordt Højbjerg (84.Bamidele Jermaine Alli), Lucas Rodrigues Moura da Silva (67.Moussa Sissoko), Giovani Lo Celso (67.Gareth Frank Bale), Son Heung-min, Harry Edward Kane. Trainer: Ryan Glen Mason.

Goal: 1-0 Aymeric Jean Louis Gerard Alphonse Laporte (82).

Second Round [27-30.11.2020]

Tranmere Rovers FC - Brackley Town FC	1-0(0-0)		Stevenage FC - Hull City AFC	1-1 aet; 6-5 pen
Morecambe FC - Solihull Moors FC	4-2(0-1,2-2)		AFC Wimbledon - Crawley Town FC	1-2(1-1)
Newport County AFC - Salford City FC	3-0(0-0)		Stockport County FC - Yeovil Town FC	3-2(1-1,2-2)
Gillingham FC - Exeter City FC	2-3(1-3)		Shrewsbury Town FC - Oxford City FC	1-0(0-0,0-0)
Harrogate Town AFC - Blackpool FC	0-4(0-0)		Mansfield Town FC - Dagenham & Redbridge FC	2-1(1-1,1-1)
Plymouth Argyle FC - Lincoln City FC	2-0(1-0)		Carlisle United FC - Doncaster Rovers FC	1-2(0-2)
Portsmouth FC - King's Lynn Town FC	6-1(2-0)		Barnet FC - Milton Keynes Dons FC	0-1(0-0)
Cheltenham Town FC - Crewe Alexandra FC	2-1(1-0,1-1)		Bristol Rovers FC - Darlington FC	6-0(4-0)
Bradford City AFC - Oldham Athletic AFC	1-2(1-1)		Marine AFC Crosby - Havant & Waterlooville FC	1-0(0-0,0-0)
Peterborough United FC - Chorley FC	1-2(1-0)		Canvey Island FC - Boreham Wood FC	0-3(0-2)

Third Round [08-11/19.01.2021]

Wolverhampton Wanderers FC - Crystal Palace FC	1-0(1-0)		Exeter City FC - Sheffield Wednesday	0-2(0-1)
Aston Villa FC Birmingham - Liverpool FC	1-4(1-1)		Blackpool FC - West Bromwich Albion FC	2-2 aet; 3-2 pen
Everton FC Liverpool - Rotherham United FC	2-1(1-0,1-1)		Arsenal FC London - Newcastle United FC	2-0(0-0,0-0)
Nottingham Forest FC - Cardiff City FC	1-0(1-0)		Huddersfield Town AFC - Plymouth Argyle FC	2-3(2-2)
Boreham Wood FC - Millwall FC London	0-2(0-1)		Brentford FC - Middlesbrough FC	2-1(1-0)
Luton Town FC - Reading FC	1-0(1-0)		Manchester United FC - Watford FC	1-0(1-0)
Norwich City FC - Coventry City FC	2-0(2-0)		Barnsley FC - Tranmere Rovers FC	2-0(0-0)
Chorley FC - Derby County FC	2-0(1-0)		Crawley Town FC - Leeds United FC	3-0(0-0)
AFC Bournemouth - Oldham Athletic AFC	4-1(1-1)		Bristol City FC - Portsmouth FC	2-1(1-1)
Stevenage FC - Swansea City AFC	0-2(0-1)		Manchester City FC - Birmingham City FC	3-0(3-0)
Bristol Rovers FC - Sheffield United FC	2-3(1-1)		Chelsea FC London - Morecambe FC	4-0(2-0)
Blackburn Rovers FC - Doncaster Rovers FC	0-1(0-1)		Cheltenham Town FC - Mansfield Town FC	2-1(0-1,1-1)
Stoke City FC - Leicester City FC	0-4(0-1)		Marine AFC Crosby - Tottenham Hotspur FC	0-5(0-4)
Wycombe Wanderers FC - Preston North End FC	4-1(3-1)		Newport County AFC - Brighton & Hove Albion FC	1-1 aet; 3-4 pen
Burnley FC - Milton Keynes Dons FC	1-1 aet; 4-3 pen		Stockport County FC - West Ham United FC London	0-1(0-0)
Queens Park Rangers FC - Fulham FC London	0-2(0-0,0-0)		Southampton FC - Shrewsbury Town FC	2-0(1-0)

Fourth Round [22-26.01.2021]

Chorley FC - Wolverhampton Wanderers FC	0-1(0-1)		Cheltenham Town FC - Manchester City FC	1-3(0-0)
Southampton FC - Arsenal FC London	1-0(1-0)		Chelsea FC London - Luton Town FC	3-1(2-1)
Swansea City AFC - Nottingham Forest FC	5-1(2-0)		Fulham FC London - Burnley FC	0-3(0-1)
Barnsley FC - Norwich City FC	1-0(0-0)		Brentford FC - Leicester City FC	1-3(1-0)
Millwall FC London - Bristol City FC	0-3(0-1)		Manchester United FC - Liverpool FC	3-2(1-1)
Brighton & Hove Albion FC - Blackpool FC	2-1(1-1)		Everton FC Liverpool - Sheffield Wednesday	3-0(1-0)
Sheffield United FC - Plymouth Argyle FC	2-1(1-0)		Wycombe Wanderers FC - Tottenham Hotspur FC	1-4(1-1)
West Ham United FC London - Doncaster Rovers FC	4-0(2-0)		AFC Bournemouth - Crawley Town FC	2-1(1-0)

1/8-Finals [09-11.02.2021]

Burnley FC - AFC Bournemouth	0-2(0-1)		Leicester City FC - Brighton & Hove Albion FC	1-0(0-0)
Manchester United FC - West Ham United FC	1-0(0-0,0-0)		Everton FC Liverpool - Tottenham Hotspur FC	5-4(3-2,4-4)
Swansea City AFC - Manchester City FC	1-3(0-1)		Wolverhampton Wanderers FC - Southampton FC	0-2(0-0)
Sheffield United FC - Bristol City FC	1-0(0-0)		Barnsley FC - Chelsea FC London	0-1(0-0)

Quarter-Finals [20-21.03.2021]

AFC Bournemouth - Southampton FC	0-3(0-2)		Chelsea FC London - Sheffield United FC	2-0(1-0)
Everton FC Liverpool - Manchester City FC	0-2(0-0)		Leicester City FC - Manchester United FC	3-1(1-1)

Semi-Finals [17-18.04.2021]

Chelsea FC London - Manchester City FC	1-0(0-0)		Leicester City FC - Southampton FC	1-0(0-0)

Final

15.05.2021; Wembley Stadium, London; Referee: Michael Oliver; Attendance: 20,000

Chelsea FC London - Leicester City FC   0-1(0-0)

Chelsea: Kepa Arrizabalaga Revuelta, César Azpilicueta Tanco (Cap) (76.Callum James Hudson-Odoi), Thiago Emiliano da Silva, Antonio Rüdiger, Reece James, N'Golo Kanté, Filho Jorge Luiz Frello „Jorginho" (75.Kai Lukas Havertz), Marcos Alonso Mendoza (68.Benjamin James Chilwell), Hakim Ziyech (68.Christian Pulišić), Mason Tony Mount, Timo Werner (82.Olivier Giroud). Trainer: Thomas Tuchel (Germany).

Leicester City: Kasper Peter Schmeichel (Cap), Wesley Fofana, Jonathan Grant Evans (34.Marc Kevin Albrighton), Çağlar Söyüncü, Timothy Castagne, Youri Marion Tielemans, Onyinye Wilfred Ndidi, Luke Johnathan Thomas (82.Westley Nathan Morgan), Ayoze Pérez Gutiérrez (82.Hamza Dewan Choudhury), Kelechi Promise Iheanacho (67.James Daniel Maddison), Jamie Richard Vardy. Trainer: Brendan Rogers (Northern Ireland).

Goal: 0-1 Youri Marion Tielemans (63).

THE CLUBS 2020/2021

Arsenal Football Club London

Founded: 1886
Stadium: Emirates Stadium, London (60,704)
Trainer: Mikel Amatriain Arteta (ESP) 26.03.1982

Goalkeepers:	DOB	M	(s)	G
Bernd Leno (GER)	04.03.1992	35		
Alex Rúnarsson (ISL)	18.02.1995		(1)	
Mathew David Ryan (AUS)	08.04.1992	3		
Defenders:	**DOB**	**M**	**(s)**	**G**
Cédric Ricardo Alves Soares (POR)	31.08.1991	8	(2)	
Calum Chambers	20.01.1995	8	(2)	
David Luiz Moreira Marinho (BRA)	22.04.1987	17	(3)	1
Gabriel dos Santos Magalhaes (BRA)	19.12.1997	22	(1)	2
Héctor Bellerín Moruno (ESP)	19.03.1995	24	(1)	1
Robert Samuel Holding	20.09.1995	28	(2)	
Sead Kolašinac (BIH)	20.06.1993	1		
Shkodran Mustafi (GER)	17.04.1992		(3)	
Pablo Marí Villar (ESP)	31.08.1993	10		
Kieran Tierney (SCO)	05.06.1997	26	(1)	1
Midfielders:	**DOB**	**M**	**(s)**	**G**
Daniel „Dani" Ceballos Fernández (ESP)	07.08.1996	17	(8)	
Mohamed Naser Elsayed Elneny (EGY)	11.07.1992	17	(6)	1
Ainsley Cory Maitland-Niles	29.08.1997	5	(6)	
Martin Ødegaard (NOR)	17.12.1998	9	(5)	1
Thomas Partey (GHA)	13.06.1993	18	(6)	
Emile Smith Rowe	28.07.2000	18	(2)	2
Joseph George Willock	20.08.1999	2	(5)	
Granit Xhaka (SUI)	27.09.1992	29	(2)	1
Forwards:	**DOB**	**M**	**(s)**	**G**
Pierre Emerick François Aubameyang (GAB)	18.06.1989	26	(3)	10
Gabriel Teodoro Martinelli Silva (BRA)	18.06.2001	7	(7)	2
Alexandre Lacazette (FRA)	28.05.1991	22	(9)	13
Reiss Nelson	10.12.1999		(2)	
Edward Keddar Nketiah	30.05.1999	4	(13)	2
Nicolas Pépé (CIV)	29.05.1995	16	(13)	10
Bukayo Ayoyinka Saka	05.09.2001	30	(2)	5
Willian Borges da Silva (BRA)	09.08.1988	16	(9)	1

Aston Villa Football Club Birmingham

Founded: 21.11.1874
Stadium: Villa Park, Birmingham (42,682)
Trainer: Dean Smith 19.03.1971

Goalkeepers:	DOB	M	(s)	G
Damián Emiliano Martínez Romero (ARG)	02.09.1992	38		
Defenders:	**DOB**	**M**	**(s)**	**G**
Matthew Cash	07.08.1997	28		
Ahmed Eissa Elmohamady Abdel Fattah(EGY)	09.09.1987	8	(6)	
Kortney Paul Duncan Hause	16.07.1995	7		1
Ezri Konsa Ngoyo	23.10.1997	35	(1)	2
Tyrone Deon Mings	13.03.1993	36		2
Matthew Robert Targett	18.09.1995	38		
Neil John Taylor (WAL)	07.02.1989		(1)	
Midfielders:	**DOB**	**M**	**(s)**	**G**
Ross Barkley	05.12.1993	18	(6)	3
Carney Chukwuemeka	20.10.2003		(2)	
Douglas Luiz Soares de Paulo (BRA)	09.05.1998	32	(1)	
Conor Hourihane (IRL)	02.02.1991	3	(1)	1
John McGinn (SCO)	18.10.1994	37		3
Marvelous Nakamba (ZIM)	19.01.1994	9	(4)	
Jacob Ramsey	28.05.2001	6	(16)	
Morgan Sanson (FRA)	18.08.1994	3	(6)	
Forwards:	**DOB**	**M**	**(s)**	**G**
Keinan Vincent Joseph Davis	13.02.1998	1	(14)	1
Anwar El Ghazi (NED)	03.05.1995	17	(11)	10
Jack Peter Grealish	10.09.1995	24	(2)	6
Jaden Philogene-Bidace	18.05.2002		(1)	
Bertrand Traoré (BFA)	06.09.1995	29	(7)	7
Mahmoud Ahmed Ibrahim Hassan (EGY)	01.10.1994	12	(9)	2
Oliver George Arthur Watkins	30.12.1995	37		14
Wesley Moraes Ferreira da Silva (BRA)	26.11.1996		(3)	

Brighton & Hove Albion Football Club

Founded: 24.06.1901
Stadium: Falmer Stadium, Brighton and Hove (30,750)
Trainer: Graham Stephen Potter 20.05.1975

Goalkeepers:	DOB	M	(s)	G
Mathew David Ryan (AUS)	08.04.1992	11		
Robert Lynch Sánchez (ESP)	18.11.1997	27		
Defenders:	**DOB**	**M**	**(s)**	**G**
Bernardo Fernandes da Silva Junior (BRA)	14.05.1995	2	(1)	
Daniel Johnson Burn	09.05.1992	23	(4)	1
Lewis Carl Dunk	21.11.1991	33		5
Tariq Kwame Nii-Lante Lamptey	30.09.2000	11		1
Joël Ivo Veltman (NED)	15.01.1992	25	(3)	1
Adam Harry Webster	04.01.1995	29		1
Benjamin William White	08.10.1997	36		
Midfielders:	**DOB**	**M**	**(s)**	**G**
Steven Alzate (COL)	08.09.1998	10	(5)	1
Yves Bissouma (MLI)	30.08.1996	35	(1)	1
Pascal Groß (GER)	15.06.1991	27	(7)	3
Adam David Lallana	10.05.1988	16	(14)	1
Alexis Mac Allister (ARG)	24.12.1998	13	(8)	1
Solomon Benjamin March	20.07.1994	19	(2)	2
Jakub Moder (POL)	07.04.1999	7	(5)	
Jayson Patrick Molumby (IRL)	06.08.1999		(1)	
David Petrus Wenceslaus Henri Pröpper(NED)	02.09.1991	2	(5)	
Percy Muzi Tau (RSA)	13.05.1994	1	(2)	
Forwards:	**DOB**	**M**	**(s)**	**G**
Aaron Anthony Connolly (IRL)	28.01.2000	9	(8)	2
José Heriberto Izquierdo Jero (COL)	07.07.1992		(1)	
Alireza Jahanbakhsh (IRN)	11.08.1993	6	(15)	
Reda Khadra (GER)	04.07.2001		(1)	
Neal Maupay (FRA)	14.08.1996	29	(4)	8
Leandro Trossard (BEL)	04.12.1994	30	(5)	5
Daniel Nii Tackie Mensah Welbeck	26.11.1990	17	(7)	6
Andi Zeqiri (SUI)	22.06.1999		(9)	

Burnley Football Club

Founded: 18.05.1882
Stadium: Turf Moor, Burnley (21,944)
Trainer: Sean Mark Dyche 28.06.1971

Goalkeepers:	DOB	M	(s)	G
William James Norris	12.08.1993	2		
Bailey Peacock-Farrell (NIR)	29.10.1996	4		
Nicholas David Pope	19.04.1992	32		
Defenders:	**DOB**	**M**	**(s)**	**G**
Phillip Anthony Bardsley (SCO)	28.06.1985	3	(1)	
James Gerard Dunne (IRL)	19.10.1997	3		1
Kevin Finbarr Long (IRL)	18.08.1990	7	(1)	
Matthew John Lowton	09.06.1989	34		1
Benjamin Mee	21.09.1989	30		2
Erik Pieters (NED)	07.08.1988	13	(7)	
James Alan Tarkowski	19.11.1992	36		1
Charles James Taylor	18.09.1993	28	(1)	
Midfielders:	**DOB**	**M**	**(s)**	**G**
Josh Benson	05.12.1999	2	(4)	
Robert Brady (IRL)	14.01.1992	12	(7)	1
Joshua Brownhill	19.12.1995	32	(1)	
Jack Frank Porteous Cork	25.06.1989	15	(1)	
Dale Christopher Stephens	12.06.1989	3	(4)	
Ashley Roy Westwood	01.04.1990	38		3
Forwards:	**DOB**	**M**	**(s)**	**G**
Ashley Luke Barnes	30.10.1989	15	(7)	3
Jóhann Berg Guðmundsson (ISL)	27.10.1990	16	(6)	2
Dwight James Matthew McNeil	22.11.1999	34	(2)	2
Joel Mumbongo (SWE)	09.01.1999		(4)	
Lewis Richardson	07.02.2003		(2)	
Jay Enrique Rodríguez	29.07.1989	12	(19)	1
Matěj Vydra (CZE)	01.05.1992	15	(13)	3
Christopher Grant Wood (NZL)	07.12.1991	32	(1)	12

Chelsea Football Club London

Founded: 10.03.1905
Stadium: Stamford Bridge, London (40,834)
Trainer: Frank James Lampard Junior   20.06.1978
[26.01.2021] Thomas Tuchel (GER)   29.08.1973

Goalkeepers:	DOB	M	(s)	G
Wilfredo Daniel Caballero Lazcano (ARG)	28.09.1981	1		
Kepa Arrizabalaga Revuelta (ESP)	03.10.1994	6	(1)	
Edouard Mendy (SEN)	01.03.1992	31		
Defenders:	**DOB**	**M**	**(s)**	**G**
César Azpilicueta Tanco (ESP)	28.08.1989	24	(2)	1
Benjamin James Chilwell	21.12.1996	27		3
Andreas Bødtker Christensen (DEN)	10.04.1996	15	(2)	
Emerson Palmieri dos Santos (ITA)	03.08.1994		(2)	
Reece James	08.12.1999	25	(7)	1
Marcos Alonso Mendoza (ESP)	28.12.1990	11	(2)	2
Antonio Rüdiger (GER)	03.03.1993	19		1
Thiago Emiliano Silva (BRA)	22.09.1984	23		2
Oluwafikayomi Oluwadamilola Tomori	19.12.1997		(1)	
Kurt Happy Zouma (FRA)	27.10.1994	22	(2)	5

Midfielders:	DOB	M	(s)	G
Ross Barkley	05.12.1993		(2)	
Billy Clifford Gilmour (SCO)	11.06.2001	3	(2)	
Kai Havertz (GER)	11.06.1999	18	(9)	4
Filho Jorge Luiz Frello „Jorginho" (ITA)	20.12.1991	23	(5)	7
N'Golo Kanté (FRA)	29.03.1991	24	(6)	
Mateo Kovačić (CRO)	06.05.1994	21	(6)	
Ruben Ira Loftus-Cheek	23.01.1996	1		
Mason Tony Mount	10.01.1999	32	(4)	6
Hakim Ziyech (MAR)	19.03.1993	15	(8)	2
Forwards:	**DOB**	**M**	**(s)**	**G**
Kevin Oghenetega Tamaraebi Bakumo-Abraham	02.10.1997	12	(10)	6
Olivier Jonathan Giroud (FRA)	30.09.1986	8	(9)	4
Callum James Hudson-Odoi	07.11.2000	10	(13)	2
Christian Pulišić (USA)	18.09.1998	18	(9)	4
Timo Werner (GER)	06.03.1996	29	(6)	6

Crystal Palace Football Club London

Founded: 10.09.1905
Stadium: Selhurst Park, London (25,486)
Trainer: Roy Hodgson   09.08.1947

Goalkeepers:	DOB	M	(s)	G
Jack Butland	10.03.1993	1		
Vicente Guaita Panadero (ESP)	10.01.1987	37		
Defenders:	**DOB**	**M**	**(s)**	**G**
Gary James Cahill	19.12.1985	20		1
Nathaniel Edwin Clyne	05.04.1991	13		
Scott Dann	14.02.1987	15		1
Martin Ronald Kelly	27.04.1990		(1)	
Cheikhou Kouyaté (SEN)	21.12.1989	35	(1)	1
Tyrick Mitchell	01.09.1999	19		1
Mamadou Sakho (FRA)	13.02.1990	3	(1)	
James Oliver Charles Tomkins	29.03.1989	6	(2)	
Patrick John Miguel van Aanholt (NED)	29.08.1990	20	(2)	
Joel Edward Philip Ward	29.10.1989	25	(1)	

Midfielders:	DOB	M	(s)	G
Eberechi Oluchi Eze	29.06.1998	29	(5)	4
James McFarlane McArthur (SCO)	07.10.1987	17	(1)	
James Patrick McCarthy (IRL)	12.11.1990	10	(6)	
Luka Milivojević (SRB)	07.04.1991	27	(4)	1
Jaïro Jocquim Riedewald (NED)	09.09.1996	19	(14)	2
Jeffrey Schlupp (GHA)	23.12.1992	15	(12)	2
Forwards:	**DOB**	**M**	**(s)**	**G**
Jordan Pierre Ayew (GHA)	11.09.1991	23	(10)	1
Michy Batshuayi Atunga (BEL)	02.10.1993	7	(11)	2
Christian Benteke Liolo (BEL)	03.12.1990	21	(9)	10
Jean-Philippe Mateta (FRA)	28.06.1997	2	(5)	1
Andros Darryl Townsend	16.07.1991	25	(9)	1
Dazet Wilfried Armel Zaha (CIV)	10.11.1992	29	(1)	11

Everton Football Club Liverpool

Founded: 1878
Stadium: Goodison Park, Liverpool (39,414)
Trainer: Carlo Ancelotti (ITA)   10.06.1959

Goalkeepers:	DOB	M	(s)	G
João Manuel Neves Virgínia (POR)	10.10.1999		(1)	
Robin Patrick Olsen (SWE)	08.01.1990	7		
Jordan Lee Pickford	07.03.1994	31		
Defenders:	**DOB**	**M**	**(s)**	**G**
Séamus Coleman (IRL)	11.10.1988	18	(7)	
Lucas Digne (FRA)	20.07.1993	30		
Benjamin Matthew Godfrey	15.01.1998	29	(2)	
Mason Anthony Holgate	22.10.1996	26	(2)	1
Michael Vincent Keane	11.01.1993	33	(2)	3
Jonjoe Kenny	15.03.1997	1	(3)	
Yerry Fernando Mina González (COL)	23.09.1994	23	(1)	2
Niels Nkounkou (FRA)	01.11.2000	1	(1)	
Midfielders:	**DOB**	**M**	**(s)**	**G**
Allan Marques Loureiro (BRA)	08.01.1991	23	(1)	
André Filipe Tavares Gomes (POR)	30.07.1993	17	(11)	
Thomas Davies	30.06.1998	17	(8)	

	DOB	M	(s)	G
Fabian Delph	21.11.1989	2	(6)	
Abdoulaye Doucouré (FRA)	01.01.1993	29		2
Jean-Philippe Gbamin (CIV)	25.09.1995		(1)	
James David Rodríguez Rubio (COL)	12.07.1991	21	(2)	6
Gylfi Sigurðsson (ISL)	08.09.1989	24	(12)	6
Forwards:	**DOB**	**M**	**(s)**	**G**
Bernard Anício Caldeira Duarte (BRA)	08.09.1992	3	(9)	1
Nathan Broadhead (WAL)	05.04.1998		(1)	
Dominic Nathaniel Calvert-Lewin	16.03.1997	32	(1)	16
Anthony Michael Gordon	24.02.2001	1	(2)	
Alexander Chuka Iwobi (NGA)	03.05.1996	17	(13)	1
Bioty Moise Kean (ITA)	28.02.2000		(2)	
Joshua Christian Kojo King (NOR)	15.01.1992		(11)	
Richarlison de Andrade (BRA)	10.05.1997	33	(1)	7
Cenk Tosun (TUR)	07.06.1991		(5)	
Theo James Walcott	16.03.1989		(1)	

Fulham Football Club London

Founded: 1879
Stadium: Craven Cottage, London (19,359)
Trainer: Scott Matthew Parker   13.10.1980

Goalkeepers:	DOB	M	(s)	G
Alphonse Aréola (FRA)	27.02.1993	36		
Marek Rodák (SVK)	13.12.1996	2		
Defenders:	**DOB**	**M**	**(s)**	**G**
Abdul-Nasir Oluwatosin Adarabioyo	24.09.1997	33		
Temitayo Olufisayo Olaoluwa Aina (NGA)	08.10.1996	31		2
Joachim Christian Andersen (DEN)	31.05.1996	30	(1)	1
Joseph Edward Bryan	17.09.1993	7	(9)	1
Michael Anthony James Hector (JAM)	19.07.1992	3	(1)	
Terence Kongolo (NED)	14.02.1994	1		
Maxime Le Marchand (FRA)	11.10.1989	1	(1)	
Denis Frimpong Odoi (BEL)	27.05.1988	3		
Timothy Michael Ream (USA)	05.10.1987	7		
Antonee Robinson (USA)	08.08.1997	24	(4)	
Kenny Joelle Tete (NED)	09.10.1995	18	(4)	

Midfielders:	DOB	M	(s)	G
André-Frank Zambo Anguissa (CMR)	16.11.1995	29	(7)	
Thomas Cairney	20.01.1991	9	(1)	1
Fabio Carvalho	30.08.2002	3	(1)	1
Tyrese Jay Francois (AUS)	16.07.2000		(1)	
Neeskens Kebano (COD)	10.03.1992	1	(4)	
Mario Lemina (GAB)	01.09.1993	19	(9)	1
Ruben Ira Loftus-Cheek	23.01.1996	21	(9)	1
Joshua Oghenetega Peter Onomah	27.04.1997	4	(7)	
Harrison James Reed	27.01.1995	26	(5)	
Bobby Armani Decordova-Reid (JAM)	02.02.1993	28	(5)	5
Forwards:	**DOB**	**M**	**(s)**	**G**
Ivan Ricardo Neves Abreu Cavaleiro (POR)	18.10.1993	27	(9)	3
Aboubakar Kamara (FRA)	07.03.1995	2	(9)	
Ademola Lookman Olajide Alade Aylola Lookman	20.10.1997	31	(3)	4
Joshua Erowoli Orisunmihare Oluwaseun Maja (NGA)	27.12.1998	9	(6)	3
Aleksandar Mitrović (SRB)	16.09.1994	13	(14)	3

Leeds United Football Club

Founded: 17.10.1919
Stadium: Elland Road, Leeds (37,792)
Trainer: Marcelo Alberto Bielsa (ARG) 21.07.1955

Goalkeepers:	DOB	M	(s)	G
Francisco Casilla Cortés „Kiko Casilla" (ESP)	02.10.1986	3		
Illan Stéphane Meslier (FRA)	02.03.2000	35		
Defenders:	**DOB**	**M**	**(s)**	**G**
Ezgjan Alioski (MKD)	12.02.1992	29	(7)	2
Luke Ayling	25.08.1991	38		
Gaetano Berardi (SUI)	21.08.1988	1	(1)	
Liam David Ian Cooper (SCO)	30.08.1991	25		1
Stuart Alan Dallas (NIR)	19.04.1991	38		8
Leif Davis	31.12.1999		(2)	
Niall Huggins (WAL)	18.12.2000		(1)	
Robin Koch (GER)	17.07.1996	13	(4)	
Diego Javier Llorente Ríos (ESP)	16.08.1993	14	(1)	1
Pascal Struijk (NED)	11.08.1999	22	(5)	1

Midfielders:	DOB	M	(s)	G
Mateusz Klich (POL)	13.06.1990	28	(7)	4
Pablo Hernández Domínguez (ESP)	11.04.1985	3	(13)	
Kalvin Mark Phillips	02.12.1995	28	(1)	1
Jamie Stuart Shackleton	08.10.1999	3	(10)	
Forwards:	**DOB**	**M**	**(s)**	**G**
Patrick James Bamford	05.09.1993	37	(1)	17
Jack David Harrison	20.11.1996	34	(2)	8
Hélder Wander Sousa de Azevedo (POR)	12.01.1994	13	(9)	3
Ian Carlo Poveda-Ocampo	09.02.2000		(14)	
Raphael Dias Belloli „Raphinha" (BRA)	14.12.1996	26	(4)	6
Tyler D´Whyte Roberts (WAL)	12.01.1999	14	(13)	1
Rodrigo Moreno Machado (ESP)	06.03.1991	14	(12)	7

Leicester City Football Club

Founded: 1884
Stadium: King Power Stadium, Leicester (32,261)
Trainer: Brendan Rodgers (NIR) 26.01.1973

Goalkeepers:	DOB	M	(s)	G
Kasper Peter Schmeichel (DEN)	05.11.1986	38		
Defenders:	**DOB**	**M**	**(s)**	**G**
Timothy Castagne (BEL)	05.12.1995	27		2
Jonathan Grant Evans (NIR)	03.01.1988	28		2
Wesley Fofana (FRA)	17.12.2000	27	(1)	
Christian Fuchs (AUT)	07.04.1986	8	(1)	
James Michael Justin	23.02.1998	23		2
Westley Nathan Morgan (JAM)	21.01.1984		(3)	
Ricardo Domingos Barbosa Pereira (POR)	06.10.1993	10	(5)	
Çağlar Söyüncü (TUR)	23.05.1996	19	(4)	1
Luke Jonathan Thomas	10.06.2001	12	(2)	1
Midfielders:	**DOB**	**M**	**(s)**	**G**
Marc Kevin Albrighton	18.11.1989	17	(14)	1
Daniel Amartey (GHA)	21.12.1994	8	(4)	1
Harvey Lewis Barnes	09.12.1997	22	(3)	9

Hamza Dewan Choudhury	01.10.1997	4	(6)	
Thakgalo Khanya Leshabela (RSA)	18.09.1999		(1)	
James Daniel Maddison	23.11.1996	24	(7)	8
Nampalys Mendy (FRA)	23.06.1992	15	(8)	
Onyinye Wilfred Ndidi (NGA)	16.12.1996	25	(1)	1
Dennis Praet (BEL)	14.05.1994	10	(5)	1
Sidnei Wilson Vieira David Tavares	29.09.2001	1	(1)	
Youri Marion Tielemans (BEL)	07.05.1997	37	(1)	6
Forwards:	**DOB**	**M**	**(s)**	**G**
Ayoze Pérez Gutiérrez (ESP)	29.07.1993	15	(10)	2
Demarai Remelle Gray	28.06.1996		(1)	
Kelechi Promise Iheanacho (NGA)	03.10.1996	16	(9)	12
Islam Slimani (ALG)	18.06.1988		(1)	
Cengiz Ünder (TUR)	14.07.1997	1	(8)	
Jamie Richard Vardy	11.01.1987	31	(3)	15

Liverpool Football Club

Founded: 03.06.1892
Stadium: Anfield Road, Liverpool (53,394)
Trainer: Jürgen Norbert Klopp (GER) 16.06.1967

Goalkeepers:	DOB	M	(s)	G
Adrián San Miguel del Castillo (ESP)	03.01.1987	3		
Alisson Ramses Becker (BRA)	02.10.1992	33		1
Caoimhin Odhran Kelleher (IRL)	23.11.1998	2		
Defenders:	**DOB**	**M**	**(s)**	**G**
Trent John Alexander-Arnold	07.10.1998	34	(2)	2
Joseph Dave Gomez	23.05.1997	6	(1)	
Ozan Kabak (TUR)	25.03.2000	9		
Job Joël André Matip (CMR)	08.08.1991	9	(1)	1
Nathaniel Harry Phillips	21.03.1997	15	(2)	1
Andrew Robertson (SCO)	11.03.1994	38		1
Konstantinos Tsimikas (GRE)	12.05.1996		(2)	
Virgil van Dijk (NED)	08.07.1991	5		1
Neco Shay Williams (WAL)	13.04.2001	3	(3)	
Rhys Williams	03.02.2001	7	(2)	

Midfielders:	DOB	M	(s)	G
Fabio Henrique Tavares "Fabinho" (BRA)	23.10.1993	28	(2)	
Jordan Brian Henderson	17.06.1990	20	(1)	1
Curtis Julian Jones	30.01.2001	13	(11)	1
Naby Keïta (GUI)	10.02.1995	7	(3)	
James Philip Milner	04.01.1986	11	(15)	
Alexander Mark David Oxlade-Chamberlain	15.08.1993	2	(11)	1
Thiago Alcântara do Nascimento (ESP)	11.04.1991	20	(4)	1
Georginio Gregion Emile Wijnaldum (NED)	11.11.1990	34	(4)	2
Forwards:	**DOB**	**M**	**(s)**	**G**
Diogo José Teixeira da Silva (POR)	04.12.1996	12	(7)	9
Sadio Mané (SEN)	10.04.1992	31	(4)	11
Takumi Minamino (JPN)	16.01.1995	2	(7)	1
Divock Okoth Origi (BEL)	18.04.1995	2	(7)	
Roberto Firmino Barbosa de Oliveira (BRA)	02.10.1991	33	(3)	9
Mohamed Salah Ghaly (EGY)	15.06.1992	34	(3)	22
Xherdan Shaqiri (SUI)	10.10.1991	5	(9)	

Manchester City Football Club

Founded: 1880
Stadium: Etihad (City of Manchester) Stadium, Manchester (55,017)
Trainer: Josep "Pep" Guardiola Sala (ESP) 18.01.1971

Goalkeepers:	DOB	M	(s)	G
Scott Paul Carson	03.09.1985	1		
Ederson Santana de Moraes (BRA)	17.08.1993	36		
Zackary Thomas Steffen (USA)	02.04.1995	1		
Defenders:	**DOB**	**M**	**(s)**	**G**
Nathan Benjamin Aké (NED)	18.02.1995	9	(1)	1
Eric García Martret (ESP)	09.01.2001	3	(3)	
João Pedro Cavaco Cancelo (POR)	27.05.1994	27	(1)	2
Aymeric Jean Louis Gerard Alphonse Laporte (FRA)	27.05.1994	14	(2)	
Benjamin Mendy (FRA)	17.07.1994	11	(2)	2
Rúben Santos Gato Alves Dias (POR)	14.05.1997	32		1
John Stones	28.05.1994	22		4
Kyle Andrew Walker	28.05.1990	22	(2)	1
Oleksandr Zinchenko (UKR)	15.12.1996	15	(5)	

Midfielders:	DOB	M	(s)	G
Bernardo Mota Veiga de Carvalho e Silva (POR)	10.08.1994	24	(2)	2
Kevin De Bruyne (BEL)	28.06.1991	23	(2)	6
Fernando Luiz Roza „Fernandinho" (BRA)	04.05.1985	12	(9)	
İlkay Gündoğan (GER)	24.10.1990	23	(5)	13
Rodrigo Hernández Cascante „Rodri" (ESP)	22.06.1996	31	(3)	2
Forwards:	**DOB**	**M**	**(s)**	**G**
Sergio Leonel Agüero del Castillo (ARG)	02.06.1988	7	(5)	4
Liam Rory Delap	08.02.2003		(1)	
Ferrán Torres García (ESP)	29.02.2000	15	(9)	7
Philip Walter Foden	28.05.2000	17	(11)	9
Gabriel Fernando de Jesus (BRA)	03.04.1997	22	(7)	9
Riyad Karim Mahrez (ALG)	21.02.1991	23	(4)	9
Raheem Shaquille Sterling	08.12.1994	28	(3)	10

Manchester United Football Club

Goalkeepers:	DOB	M	(s)	G
David de Gea Quintana (ESP)	07.11.1990	26		
Dean Bradley Henderson	12.03.1997	12	(1)	
Defenders:	DOB	M	(s)	G
Alex Nicolao Telles (BRA)	15.12.1992	8	(1)	
Eric Bertrand Bailly (CIV)	12.04.1994	10	(2)	
William Thomas Fish	17.02.2003		(1)	
Evans Timothy Fosu Fosu-Mensah (NED)	02.01.1998	1		
Victor Jörgen Nilsson Lindelöf (SWE)	17.07.1994	29		1
Jacob Harry Maguire	05.03.1993	34		2
Luke Paul Hoare Shaw	12.07.1995	30	(2)	1
Axel Tuanzebe	14.11.1997	4	(5)	
Aaron Wan-Bissaka	26.11.1997	34		2
Brandon Paul Brian Williams	03.09.2000	2	(2)	
Midfielders:	DOB	M	(s)	G
Bruno Miguel Borges Fernandes (POR)	08.09.1994	35	(2)	18
Frederico Rodrigues de Paula Santos "Fred"(BRA)	05.03.1993	27	(3)	1

Founded: 1878
Stadium: Old Trafford, Manchester (74,140)
Trainer: Ole Gunnar Solskjær (NOR) 26.02.1973

	DOB	M	(s)	G
Juan Manuel Mata García (ESP)	28.04.1988	6	(3)	1
Nemanja Matić (SRB)	01.08.1988	12	(8)	
Scott Francis McTominay (SCO)	08.12.1996	24	(8)	4
Hannibal Mejbri (FRA)	21.01.2003		(1)	
Paul Labile Pogba (FRA)	15.03.1993	21	(5)	3
Donny van de Beek (NED)	18.04.1997	4	(15)	1
Forwards:	DOB	M	(s)	G
Edinson Roberto Gómez Cavani (URU)	14.02.1987	13	(13)	10
Amad Diallo (CIV)	11.07.2002	2	(1)	
Anthony David Junior Elanga (SWE)	27.04.2002	2		1
Mason Will John Greenwood	01.10.2001	21	(10)	7
Odion Jude Ighalo (NGA)	16.06.1989		(1)	
Daniel Owen James (WAL)	10.11.1997	11	(4)	3
Anthony Joran Martial (FRA)	05.12.1995	17	(5)	4
Marcus Rashford	31.10.1997	33	(4)	11
Shola Shoretire (NGA)	02.02.2004		(2)	

Newcastle United Football Club

Goalkeepers:	DOB	M	(s)	G
Karl Darlow	08.10.1990	25		
Martin Dúbravka (SVK)	15.01.1989	13		
Defenders:	DOB	M	(s)	G
Ciaran Clark (IRL)	26.09.1989	21	(1)	1
Paul Dummett (WAL)	26.09.1991	14	(1)	1
Federico Fernández (ARG)	21.02.1989	24		
Emil Henry Kristoffer Krafth (SWE)	02.08.1994	14	(2)	1
Jamaal Lascelles	11.11.1993	19		2
Jamal Piaras Lewis (NIR)	25.01.1998	20	(4)	
Javier Manquillo Gaitán (ESP)	05.05.1994	10	(3)	
Matthew Thomas Ritchie (SCO)	10.09.1989	15	(3)	
Fabian Schär (SUI)	20.12.1991	13	(5)	1
DeAndre Roselle Yedlin (USA)	09.07.1993	5	(1)	
Midfielders:	DOB	M	(s)	G
Miguel Ángel Almiron Rejala (PAR)	10.02.1994	28	(6)	4

Founded: 09.12.1892
Stadium: St James' Park, Newcastle upon Tyne (52,305)
Trainer: Stephen Roger Bruce 31.12.1960

	DOB	M	(s)	G
Elliot Anderson	06.11.2002		(1)	
Isaac Scot Hayden	22.03.1995	22	(2)	
Jeffrey Patrick Hendrick (IRL)	31.01.1992	17	(5)	2
Matthew Longstaff	21.03.2000	4	(1)	
Sean David Longstaff	30.10.1997	15	(7)	
Jonjo Shelvey	27.02.1992	29	(1)	1
Joseph George Willock	20.08.1999	11	(3)	8
Forwards:	DOB	M	(s)	G
Andrew Thomas Carroll	06.01.1989	4	(14)	1
Ryan Fraser (SCO)	24.02.1994	9	(9)	
Dwight Devon Boyd Gayle	17.10.1990	4	(14)	1
Joelinton Cássio Apolinário de Lira (BRA)	14.08.1996	23	(8)	4
Jacob Kai Murphy	24.02.1995	17	(9)	2
Allan Irénée Saint-Maximin (FRA)	12.03.1997	19	(6)	3
Callum Eddie Graham Wilson	27.02.1992	23	(3)	12

Sheffield United Football Club

Goalkeepers:	DOB	M	(s)	G
Aaron Christopher Ramsdale	14.05.1998	38		
Defenders:	DOB	M	(s)	G
Ethan Kwame Colm Raymond Ampadu(WAL)	14.09.2000	23	(2)	
George Henry Ivor Baldock	09.03.1993	32		
Christopher Paul Basham	20.07.1988	31		
Jayden Ian Bogle	27.07.2000	12	(4)	2
Kean Shay Bryan	01.11.1996	12	(1)	1
John Egan (IRL)	20.10.1992	30	(1)	
Philip Nikodem Jagielka	17.08.1982	6	(4)	
Max Josef Lowe	11.05.1997	7	(1)	
Jack William O'Connell	29.03.1994	2		
Jack Robinson	01.09.1993	9	(2)	
Enda John Stevens (IRL)	09.07.1990	30		
Midfielders:	DOB	M	(s)	G
Sander Gard Bolin Berge (NOR)	14.02.1998	13	(2)	1

Founded: 22.03.1889
Stadium: Bramall Lane, Sheffield (32,050)
Trainer: Christopher John Wilder 23.09.1967
[13.03.2021] Paul Heckingbottom 17.07.1977

	DOB	M	(s)	G
John Alexander Fleck (SCO)	24.08.1991	29	(2)	
John David Lundstram	18.02.1994	23	(5)	
Iliman Ndiaye (FRA)	06.03.2000		(1)	
Oliver James Norwood (NIR)	12.04.1991	26	(6)	
Benjamin Jarrod Osborn	05.08.1994	17	(7)	1
Femi Seriki	28.04.2002		(1)	
Forwards:	DOB	M	(s)	G
Rhian Joel Brewster	01.04.2000	12	(15)	
Oliver Jasen Burke (SCO)	07.04.1997	14	(11)	1
Antwoine Hackford	20.03.2004		(1)	
Daniel Jebbison	11.07.2003	3	(1)	1
Oliver Robert McBurnie (SCO)	04.06.1996	12	(11)	1
David James McGoldrick (IRL)	29.11.1987	28	(7)	8
Lys Émilien Mousset (FRA)	08.02.1996	2	(9)	
Billy Louis Sharp	05.02.1986	7	(9)	3

Southampton Football Club

Goalkeepers:	DOB	M	(s)	G
Fraser Gerard Forster	17.03.1988	8		
Alex Simon McCarthy	03.12.1989	30		
Defenders:	DOB	M	(s)	G
Jan Bednarek (POL)	12.04.1996	36		1
Ryan Dominic Bertrand	05.08.1989	29		
Kayne Ramsay	10.10.2000	1		
Karim Salisú (GHA)	17.04.1999	8	(4)	
Jack Stephens	27.01.1994	17	(1)	
Allan Tchaptchet (FRA)	21.12.2001		(1)	
Yan Valery (FRA)	22.02.1999	1	(2)	
Jannik Vestergaard (DEN)	03.08.1992	29	(1)	3
Jake Vokins	17.03.2000	1		
Kyle Leonardus Walker-Peters	13.04.1997	30		
Midfielders:	DOB	M	(s)	G
Stuart Armstrong (SCO)	30.03.1992	32	(1)	4
Ibrahima Diallo (FRA)	08.03.1999	10	(12)	

Founded: 21.11.1885
Stadium: St. Mary's Stadium, Southampton (32,384)
Trainer: Ralph Hasenhüttl (AUT) 09.08.1967

	DOB	M	(s)	G
Alexandre Jankewitz (SUI)	25.12.2001	1	(1)	
Oriol Romeu Vidal (ESP)	24.09.1991	20	(1)	1
William Anthony Patrick Smallbone (IRL)	21.02.2000	2	(1)	
James Michael Edward Ward-Prowse	01.11.1994	38		8
Caleb Cassius Watts (AUS)	16.01.2002		(3)	
Forwards:	DOB	M	(s)	G
Ché Zach Everton Fred Adams (SCO)	13.07.1996	30	(6)	9
Moussa Djénépo (MLI)	15.06.1998	15	(12)	1
Daniel William John Ings	23.07.1992	26	(3)	12
Shane Patrick Long (IRL)	22.01.1987	1	(10)	
Takumi Minamino (JPN)	16.01.1995	9	(1)	2
Daniel N'Lundulu	05.02.1999		(13)	
Michael Oluwadurotimi Obafemi (IRL)	06.07.2000		(4)	
Nathan Daniel Jerome Redmond	06.03.1994	17	(12)	2
Nathan Adewale Temitayo Tella	05.07.1999	7	(11)	1
Theodore James Walcott	16.03.1989	20	(1)	3

Tottenham Hotspur Football Club London

Founded: 05.09.1882
Stadium: Tottenham Hotspur Stadium, London (62,303)
Trainer: José Mário dos Santos Mourinho Félix (POR) 26.01.1963
[19.04.2021] Christopher George Robin Powell 08.09.1969

Goalkeepers:	DOB	M	(s)	G
Hugo Hadrien Dominique Lloris (FRA)	26.12.1986	38		
Defenders:	**DOB**	**M**	**(s)**	**G**
Tobias Albertine Maurits Alderweireld (BEL)	02.03.1989	25		1
Serge Alain Stephane Aurier (CIV)	24.12.1992	19		2
Benjamin Thomas Davies (WAL)	24.04.1993	14	(6)	
Eric Jeremy Edgar Dier	15.01.1994	28		
Matthew James Doherty (IRL)	16.01.1992	13	(4)	
Sergio Reguilón Rodríguez (ESP)	16.12.1996	26	(1)	
Joseph Peter Rodon (WAL)	22.10.1997	8	(4)	
Dávinson Sánchez Mina (COL)	12.06.1996	17	(1)	
Japhet Manzambi Tanganga	31.03.1999	6		
Midfielders:	**DOB**	**M**	**(s)**	**G**
Bamidele Jermaine "Dele" Alli	11.04.1996	7	(8)	
Pierre-Emile Kordt Højbjerg (DEN)	05.08.1995	38		2
Giovani Lo Celso (ARG)	09.04.1996	11	(7)	1
Tanguy Ndombèlè Alvaro (FRA)	28.12.1996	28	(5)	3
Moussa Sissoko (FRA)	16.08.1989	15	(10)	
Harry Billy Winks	02.02.1996	9	(6)	
Forwards:	**DOB**	**M**	**(s)**	**G**
Gareth Frank Bale (WAL)	16.07.1989	10	(10)	11
Steven Charles Bergwijn (NED)	08.10.1997	13	(8)	1
Carlos Vinícius Alves Morais (BRA)	22.03.1995	3	(6)	1
Harry Edward Kane	28.07.1993	35		23
Érik Manuel Lamela (ARG)	04.03.1992	5	(18)	1
Lucas Rodrigues Moura da Silva (BRA)	13.08.1992	14	(16)	3
Dane Scarlett	24.03.2004		(1)	
Son Heung-min (KOR)	08.07.1992	36	(1)	17

West Bromwich Albion Football Club

Founded: 1878
Stadium: The Hawthorns, West Bromwich (26,688)
Trainer: Slaven Bilić (CRO) 11.09.1968
[16.12.2020] Samuel Allardyce 19.10.1954

Goalkeepers:	DOB	M	(s)	G
David Robert Edmund Button	27.02.1989	1		
Samuel Luke Johnstone	25.03.1993	37		
Defenders:	**DOB**	**M**	**(s)**	**G**
Oluwasemilogo Adesewo Ibidapo Ajayi(NGA)	09.11.1993	31	(2)	2
Kyle Louis Bartley	22.05.1991	28	(2)	3
Darnell Anthony Furlong	31.10.1995	32	(3)	1
Kieran James Ricardo Gibbs	26.09.1989	9	(1)	
Ahmed El-Sayed Hegazy (EGY)	25.01.1991	1		
Branislav Ivanović (SRB)	22.02.1984	8	(5)	
Dara O'Shea (IRL)	04.03.1999	25	(3)	
Lee Anthony Peltier	11.12.1986	3	(1)	
Conor Stephen Townsend	04.03.1993	25		
Midfielders:	**DOB**	**M**	**(s)**	**G**
Kyle Hakeem Edwards	17.02.1998	1	(4)	
Samuel Edward Field	08.05.1998		(3)	
Conor Gallagher	06.02.2000	28	(2)	2
Rekeem Jordan Harper	08.03.2000		(2)	
Filip Krovinović (CRO)	29.08.1995	5	(6)	
Jake Cyril Livermore	14.11.1989	15	(3)	
Ainsley Cory Maitland-Niles	29.08.1997	14	(1)	
Romaine Theodore Sawyers (SKN)	02.11.1991	17	(2)	
Okay Yokuşlu (TUR)	09.03.1994	15	(1)	
Forwards:	**DOB**	**M**	**(s)**	**G**
Karlan Laughton Ahearne-Grant	18.09.1997	14	(7)	1
Charles Austin	05.07.1989		(5)	
Mbaye Diagne (SEN)	28.10.1991	14	(2)	3
Grady George Diangana	19.04.1998	15	(5)	1
Kamil Grosicki (POL)	08.06.1988	2	(1)	
Matheus Fellipe Costa Pereira (BRA)	05.05.1996	30	(3)	11
Matthew Phillips (SCO)	13.03.1991	20	(13)	2
Callum Jack Robinson (IRL)	02.02.1995	20	(8)	5
Thomas Henry Alex Robson-Kanu (WAL)	21.05.1989	2	(17)	2
Robert Snodgrass (SCO)	07.09.1987	6	(2)	

West Ham United Football Club London

Founded: 29.06.1895
Stadium: London Stadium, London (60,000)
Trainer: David William Moyes (SCO) 25.04.1963

Goalkeepers:	DOB	M	(s)	G
Łukasz Fabiański (POL)	18.04.1985	35		
Darren Edward Andrew Randolph (IRL)	12.05.1987	3		
Defenders:	**DOB**	**M**	**(s)**	**G**
Fabián Cornelio Balbuena González (PAR)	23.08.1991	13	(1)	1
Vladimír Coufal (CZE)	22.08.1992	34		
Aaron William Cresswell	15.12.1989	36		
Craig Dawson	06.05.1990	22		3
Issa Diop (FRA)	09.01.1997	15	(3)	2
Ryan Marlow Fredericks	10.10.1992	6	(8)	1
Benjamin Anthony Johnson	24.01.2000	5	(9)	1
Fuka-Arthur Masuaku Kawela (COD)	07.11.1993	12		
Obinze Angelo Ogbonna (ITA)	23.05.1988	28		3
Midfielders:	**DOB**	**M**	**(s)**	**G**
Felipe Anderson Pereira Gomes (BRA)	15.04.1993		(2)	
Manuel Lanzini (ARG)	15.02.1993	5	(12)	1
Jesse Ellis Lingard	15.12.1992	16		9
Mark James Noble	08.05.1987	8	(13)	
Pablo Fornals Malla (ESP)	22.02.1996	31	(2)	5
Declan Rice	14.01.1999	32		2
Tomáš Souček (CZE)	27.02.1995	38		10
Forwards:	**DOB**	**M**	**(s)**	**G**
Michail Gregory Antonio (JAM)	28.03.1990	24	(2)	10
Saïd Benrahma (ALG)	10.08.1995	14	(16)	1
Jarrod Bowen	20.12.1996	30	(8)	8
Sébastien Romain Teddy Haller (FRA)	22.06.1994	10	(6)	3
Robert Snodgrass (SCO)	07.09.1987		(3)	
Andrey Yarmolenko (UKR)	23.10.1989	1	(14)	

Wolverhampton Wanderers Football Club

Founded: 1877 (*as St. Luke's FC*)
Stadium: Molineux Stadium, Wolverhampton (32,050)
Trainer: Nuno Herlander Simões do Espírito Santo (POR) 25.01.1974

Goalkeepers:	DOB	M	(s)	G
John Thomas Gordon Ruddy	24.10.1986	1	(1)	
Rui Pedro dos Santos Patrício (POR)	15.02.1988	37		
Defenders:	**DOB**	**M**	**(s)**	**G**
Rayan Aït Nouri (FRA)	06.06.2001	16	(5)	1
Willy Arnaud Zobo Boly (FRA)	03.02.1991	21		1
Oskar Buur Rasmussen (DEN)	31.03.1998		(1)	
Conor David Coady	25.02.1993	37		1
Ki-Jana Delano Hoever (NED)	18.01.2002	5	(7)	
Jonathan Castro Otto "Jonny" (ESP)	03.03.1994	7		
Maximilian William Kilman	23.05.1997	14	(4)	
Fernando Marçal de Oliveira (BRA)	19.02.1989	7	(6)	
Nélson Cabral Semedo (POR)	16.11.1993	34		1
Rúben Gonçalo Silva Nascimento Vinagre (POR)	09.04.1999	1	(1)	
Romain Saïss (MAR)	26.03.1990	27		3
Midfielders:	**DOB**	**M**	**(s)**	**G**
Leander Dendoncker (BEL)	15.04.1995	28	(5)	1
Morgan Anthony Gibbs-White	27.01.2000	4	(7)	1
João Filipe Iria Santos Moutinho (POR)	08.09.1986	28	(5)	1
Owen Otasowie (USA)	06.01.2001	2	(4)	
Rúben Diogo da Silva Neves (POR)	13.03.1997	31	(5)	5
Vítor Machado Ferreira „Vitinha" (POR)	13.02.2000	5	(14)	
Forwards:	**DOB**	**M**	**(s)**	**G**
Adama Traoré Diarra (ESP)	25.01.1996	28	(9)	2
Theodor Alexander Corbeanu (CAN)	17.05.2002		(1)	
Patrick Cutrone (ITA)	03.01.1998		(2)	
Daniel Castelo Podence (POR)	21.10.1995	22	(2)	3
Fábio Daniel Soares Silva (POR)	19.07.2002	11	(21)	4
Raúl Alonso Jiménez Rodríguez (MEX)	05.05.1991	10		4
Pedro Lomba Neto (POR)	09.03.2000	30	(1)	5
Willian José da Silva (BRA)	23.11.1991	12	(5)	1

1.	Norwich City FC (*Promoted*)	46	29	10	7	75	-	36	97
2.	Watford FC (*Promoted*)	46	27	10	9	63	-	30	91
3.	Brentford FC	46	24	15	7	79	-	42	87
4.	Swansea City AFC	46	23	11	12	56	-	39	80
5.	Barnsley FC	46	23	9	14	58	-	50	78
6.	AFC Bournemouth	46	22	11	13	73	-	46	77
7.	Reading FC	46	19	13	14	62	-	54	70
8.	Cardiff City FC	46	18	14	14	66	-	49	68
9.	Queens Park Rangers FC London	46	19	11	16	57	-	55	68
10.	Middlesbrough FC	46	18	10	18	55	-	53	64
11.	Millwall FC London	46	15	17	14	47	-	52	62
12.	Luton Town FC	46	17	11	18	41	-	52	62
13.	Preston North End FC	46	18	7	21	49	-	56	61
14.	Stoke City FC	46	15	15	16	50	-	52	60
15.	Blackburn Rovers FC	46	15	12	19	65	-	54	57
16.	Coventry City FC	46	14	13	19	49	-	61	55
17.	Nottingham Forest FC	46	12	16	18	37	-	45	52
18.	Birmingham City FC	46	13	13	20	37	-	61	52
19.	Bristol City FC	46	15	6	25	46	-	68	51
20.	Huddersfield Town AFC	46	12	13	21	50	-	71	49
21.	Derby County FC	46	11	11	24	36	-	58	44
22.	Wycombe Wanderers FC (*Relegated*)	46	11	10	25	39	-	69	43
23.	Rotherham United FC (*Relegated*)	46	11	9	26	44	-	60	42
24.	Sheffield Wednesday FC (*Relegated*)	46	12	11	23	40	-	61	41

Clubs ranked 3-6 were qualified for the Promotion Play-offs.

Promotion Play-offs [17-29.05.2021]

Play-off Semi-Finals	AFC Bournemouth - Brentford FC	1-0(0-0)	1-3(1-1)
	Barnsley FC - Swansea City AFC	0-1(0-1)	1-1(0-1)

Play-off Finals	Brentford FC - Swansea City AFC	2-0(2-0)	

Brentford FC promoted to the 2021/2022 Premier League.

INTERNATIONAL MATCHES
(16.07.2020 – 15.07.2021)

05.09.2020	Reykjavík	Iceland - England	0-1(0-0)	(UNL)
08.09.2020	København	Denmark - England	0-0	(UNL)
08.10.2020	London	England - Wales	3-0(1-0)	(F)
11.10.2020	London	England - Belgium	2-1(1-1)	(UNL)
14.10.2020	London	England - Denmark	0-1(0-1)	(UNL)
12.11.2020	London	England - Republic of Ireland	3-0(2-0)	(F)
15.11.2020	Leuven	Belgium - England	2-0(2-0)	(UNL)
18.11.2020	London	England - Iceland	4-0(2-0)	(UNL)
25.03.2021	London	England - San Marino	5-0(3-0)	(WCQ)
28.03.2021	Tiranë	Albania - England	0-2(0-1)	(WCQ)
31.03.2021	London	England - Poland	2-1(1-0)	(WCQ)
02.06.2021	Middlesbrough	England - Austria	1-0(0-0)	(F)
06.06.2021	Middlesbrough	England - Romania	1-0(0-0)	(F)
13.06.2021	London	England - Croatia	1-0(0-0)	(EC)
18.06.2021	London	England - Scotland	0-0	(EC)
22.06.2021	London	Czech Republic - England	0-1(0-1)	(EC)
29.06.2021	London	England - Germany	2-0(0-0)	(EC)
03.07.2021	Roma	Ukraine - England	0-4(0-1)	(EC)
07.07.2021	London	England - Denmark	2-1(1-1,1-1)	(EC)
11.07.2021	London	Italy - England	1-1(0-1,1-1,1-1); 3-2 on penalties	(EC)

05.09.2020 ICELAND - ENGLAND   **0-1(0-0)**   2nd UEFA Nations League A, Group 2
Laugardalsvöllur, Reykjavík; Referee: Srđan Jovanović (Serbia); Attendance: 0
ENG: Jordan Lee Pickford, Kyle Andrew Walker [*sent off 71*], Kieran John Trippier, Joseph Dave Gomez, James Michael Edward Ward-Prowse, Eric Jeremy Edgar Dier, Declan Rice, Philip Walter Foden (68.Danny William John Ings), Jadon Malik Sancho (73.Trent John Alexander-Arnold), Harry Edward Kane (Cap) (78.Mason Will John Greenwood), Raheem Shaquille Sterling. Trainer: Gareth Southgate.
Goal: Raheem Shaquille Sterling (90+1 penalty).

08.09.2020 DENMARK - ENGLAND   **0-0**   2nd UEFA Nations League A, Group 2
Parken Stadium, København; Referee: István Kovács (Romania); Attendance: 0
ENG: Jordan Lee Pickford, Eric Jeremy Edgar Dier, Kieran John Trippier, Conor David Coady, Joseph Dave Gomez, Declan Rice, Trent John Alexander-Arnold (86.Ainsley Cory Maitland-Niles), Kalvin Mark Phillips (76.Jack Peter Grealish), Jadon Malik Sancho (60.Mason Tony Mount), Harry Edward Kane (Cap), Raheem Shaquille Sterling. Trainer: Gareth Southgate.

08.10.2020 ENGLAND - WALES   **3-0(1-0)**   Friendly International
Wembley Stadium, London; Referee: Robert Adam Madden (Scotland); Attendance: 0
ENG: Nicholas David Pope, Kieran John Trippier (Cap) (58.Reece James), Conor David Coady, Michael Vincent Keane, Joseph Dave Gomez (58.Tyrone Deon Mings), Jack Peter Grealish (75.Harvey Lewis Barnes), Harry Billy Winks (75.James Michael Edward Ward-Prowse), Bukayo Ayoyinka Saka (76.Ainsley Cory Maitland-Niles), Danny William John Ings, Dominic Nathaniel Calvert-Lewin (58.Mason Tony Mount), Kalvin Mark Phillips. Trainer: Gareth Southgate.
Goals: Dominic Nathaniel Calvert-Lewin (26), Conor David Coady (53), Daniel William John Ings (63).

11.10.2020 ENGLAND - BELGIUM   **2-1(1-1)**   2nd UEFA Nations League A, Group 2
Wembley Stadium, London; Referee: Tobias Stieler (Germany); Attendance: 0
ENG: Jordan Lee Pickford, Kyle Andrew Walker, Kieran John Trippier, Jacob Harry Maguire, Trent John Alexander-Arnold (79.Reece James), Jordan Brian Henderson (Cap) (65.Kalvin Mark Phillips), Eric Jeremy Edgar Dier, Declan Rice, Mason Tony Mount (89.Jadon Malik Sancho), Dominic Nathaniel Calvert-Lewin (65.Harry Edward Kane), Marcus Rashford. Trainer: Gareth Southgate.
Goals: Marcus Rashford (39 penalty), Mason Tony Mount (64).

14.10.2020 ENGLAND - DENMARK   **0-1(0-1)**   2nd UEFA Nations League A, Group 2
Wembley Stadium, London; Referee: Jesús Gil Manzano (Spain); Attendance: 0
ENG: Jordan Lee Pickford, Kyle Andrew Walker, Conor David Coady, Jacob Harry Maguire [*sent off 32*], Reece James[*sent off 90+4*], Ainsley Cory Maitland-Niles (36.Tyrone Deon Mings), Kalvin Mark Phillips, Declan Rice (76.Jordan Brian Henderson), Mason Tony Mount (73.Jadon Malik Sancho), Harry Edward Kane (Cap), Marcus Rashford (72.Dominic Nathaniel Calvert-Lewin). Trainer: Gareth Southgate.

12.11.2020 ENGLAND - REPUBLIC OF IRELAND   **3-0(2-0)**   Friendly International
Wembley Stadium, London; Referee: Carlos del Cerro Grande (Spain); Attendance: 0
ENG: Nicholas David Pope (46.Dean Bradley Henderson), Jacob Harry Maguire (Cap), Michael Vincent Keane, Tyrone Deon Mings (64.Ainsley Cory Maitland-Niles), Reece James, Jack Peter Grealish (62.Philip Walter Foden), Harry Billy Winks, Mason Tony Mount (73.Jude Victor William Bellingham), Jadon Malik Sancho, Bukayo Ayoyinka Saka, Dominic Nathaniel Calvert-Lewin (63.Kevin Oghenetega Tamaraebi Bakumo Abraham). Trainer: Gareth Southgate.
Goals: Jacob Harry Maguire (18), Jadon Malik Sancho (31), Dominic Nathaniel Calvert-Lewin (56 penalty).

15.11.2020 BELGIUM - ENGLAND   **2-0(2-0)**   2nd UEFA Nations League A, Group 2
Den Dreef Stadion, Leuven; Referee: Referee: Danny Desmond Makkelie (Netherlands); Attendance: 0
ENG: Jordan Lee Pickford, Kyle Andrew Walker, Kieran John Trippier (70.Jadon Malik Sancho), Tyrone Deon Mings, Benjamin James Chilwell (38.Bukayo Ayoyinka Saka), Jordan Brian Henderson (46.Harry Billy Winks), Jack Peter Grealish, Declan Rice, Eric Jeremy Edgar Dier, Mason Tony Mount (69.Dominic Nathaniel Calvert-Lewin), Harry Edward Kane (Cap). Trainer: Gareth Southgate.

18.11.2020 ENGLAND - ICELAND   **4-0(2-0)**   2nd UEFA Nations League A, Group 2
Wembley Stadium, London; Referee: Fábio José Costa Veríssimo (Portugal); Attendance: 0
ENG: Jordan Lee Pickford, Jacob Harry Maguire, Kyle Andrew Walker (64.Tyrone Deon Mings), Kieran John Trippier (85.Ainsley Cory Maitland-Niles), Jack Peter Grealish (76.Jadon Malik Sancho), Eric Jeremy Edgar Dier, Mason Tony Mount (64.Harry Billy Winks), Declan Rice, Philip Walter Foden, Bukayo Ayoyinka Saka, Harry Edward Kane (Cap) (76.Kevin Oghenetega Tamaraebi Bakumo Abraham). Trainer: Gareth Southgate.
Goals: Declan Rice (20), Mason Tony Mount (24), Philip Walter Foden (80, 84).

25.03.2021 ENGLAND - SAN MARINO   5-0(3-0)   22nd FIFA WC. Qualifiers

Wembley Stadium, London; Referee: Kirill Levnikov (Russia); Attendance: 0

ENG: Nicholas David Pope, Conor David Coady, John Stones (46.Tyrone Deon Mings), Benjamin James Chilwell, Reece James (46.Kieran John Trippier), James Michael Edward Ward-Prowse, Jesse Ellis Lingard, Mason Tony Mount (46.Jude Victor William Bellingham), Kalvin Mark Phillips, Raheem Shaquille Sterling (Cap) (46.Philip Walter Foden), Dominic Nathaniel Calvert-Lewin (63.Oliver George Arthur Watkins). Trainer: Gareth Southgate.

Goals: James Michael Edward Ward-Prowse (14), Dominic Nathaniel Calvert-Lewin (21), Raheem Shaquille Sterling (31), Dominic Nathaniel Calvert-Lewin (53), Oliver George Arthur Watkins (83).

28.03.2021 ALBANIA - ENGLAND   0-2(0-1)   22nd FIFA WC. Qualifiers

Arena Kombëtare, Tiranë; Referee: Orel Grinfeld (Israel); Attendance: 200

ENG: Nicholas David Pope, Kyle Andrew Walker, Jacob Harry Maguire, John Stones, Luke Paul Hoare Shaw, Mason Tony Mount, Kalvin Mark Phillips (71.James Michael Edward Ward-Prowse), Declan Rice, Philip Walter Foden (81.Jesse Ellis Lingard), Harry Edward Kane (Cap), Raheem Shaquille Sterling. Trainer: Gareth Southgate.

Goals: Harry Edward Kane (38), Mason Tony Mount (63).

31.03.2021 ENGLAND - POLAND   2-1(1-0)   22nd FIFA WC. Qualifiers

Wembley Stadium, London; Referee: Björn Kuipers (Netherlands); Attendance: 0

ENG: Nicholas David Pope, Kyle Andrew Walker, Jacob Harry Maguire, John Stones, Benjamin James Chilwell, Mason Tony Mount, Kalvin Mark Phillips, Declan Rice, Raheem Shaquille Sterling (90.Jesse Ellis Lingard), Harry Edward Kane (Cap) (89.Dominic Nathaniel Calvert-Lewin), Philip Walter Foden (86.Reece James). Trainer: Gareth Southgate.

Goals: Harry Edward Kane (19 penalty), Jacob Harry Maguire (85).

02.06.2021 ENGLAND - AUSTRIA   1-0(0-0)   Friendly International

Riverside Stadium, Middlesbrough; Referee: Lawrence Visser (Belgium); Attendance: 6,606

ENG: Jordan Lee Pickford, Trent John Alexander-Arnold, Conor David Coady, Kieran John Trippier, Tyrone Deon Mings (62.Benjamin Matthew Godfrey), Jack Peter Grealish (71.Benjamin William White), Declan Rice (62.James Michael Edward Ward-Prowse), Jude Victor William Bellingham, Jesse Ellis Lingard (61.Oliver George Arthur Watkins), Harry Edward Kane (Cap) (61.Dominic Nathaniel Calvert-Lewin), Bukayo Ayoyinka Saka. Trainer: Gareth Southgate.

Goal: Bukayo Ayoyinka Saka (56).

06.06.2021 ENGLAND - ROMANIA   1-0(0-0)   Friendly International

Riverside Stadium, Middlesbrough; Referee: Tiago Bruno Lopes Martins (Portugal); Attendance: 6,952

ENG: Samuel Luke Johnstone, Benjamin Matthew Godfrey, Luke Paul Hoare Shaw (75.Kieran John Trippier), Tyrone Deon Mings, Benjamin William White, James Michael Edward Ward-Prowse (65.Declan Rice), Jack Peter Grealish, Kalvin Mark Phillips (46.Jordan Brian Henderson), Jadon Malik Sancho (65.Jude Victor William Bellingham), Marcus Rashford (Cap) (75.Jesse Ellis Lingard), Dominic Nathaniel Calvert-Lewin (82.Oliver George Arthur Watkins). Trainer: Gareth Southgate.

Goal: Marcus Rashford (68 penalty).

13.06.2021 ENGLAND - CROATIA   1-0(0-0)   16th EC. Group Stage.

Wembley Stadium, London; Referee: Daniele Orsato (Italy); Attendance: 18,497

ENG: Jordan Lee Pickford, Kyle Andrew Walker, Kieran John Trippier, John Stones, Tyrone Deon Mings, Mason Tony Mount, Kalvin Mark Phillips, Declan Rice, Philip Walter Foden (71.Marcus Rashford), Harry Edward Kane (Cap) (82.Jude Victor William Bellingham), Raheem Shaquille Sterling (90+2.Dominic Nathaniel Calvert-Lewin). Trainer: Gareth Southgate.

Goal: Raheem Shaquille Sterling (57).

18.06.2021 ENGLAND - SCOTLAND   0-0   16th EC. Group Stage.

Wembley Stadium, London; Referee: Antonio Miguel Mateu Lahoz (Spain); Attendance: 20,306

ENG: Jordan Lee Pickford, John Stones, Tyrone Deon Mings, Luke Paul Hoare Shaw, Reece James, Mason Tony Mount, Kalvin Mark Phillips, Declan Rice, Philip Walter Foden (63.Jack Peter Grealish), Harry Edward Kane (Cap) (74.Marcus Rashford), Raheem Shaquille Sterling. Trainer: Gareth Southgate.

22.06.2021 CZECH REPUBLIC - ENGLAND   0-1(0-1)   16th EC. Group Stage.

Wembley Stadium, London; Referee: Artur Manuel Ribeiro Soares Dias (Portugal); Attendance: 19,104

ENG: Jordan Lee Pickford, Kyle Andrew Walker, Jacob Harry Maguire, John Stones (79.Tyrone Deon Mings), Luke Paul Hoare Shaw, Jack Peter Grealish (68.Jude Victor William Bellingham), Kalvin Mark Phillips, Declan Rice (46.Jordan Brian Henderson), Bukayo Ayoyinka Saka (84.Jadon Malik Sancho), Harry Edward Kane (Cap), Raheem Shaquille Sterling (67.Marcus Rashford). Trainer: Gareth Southgate.

Goal: Raheem Shaquille Sterling (12).

29.06.2021 ENGLAND - GERMANY   2-0(0-0)   16th EC. 2nd Round of 16.

Wembley Stadium, London; Referee: Danny Desmond Makkelie (Netherlands); Attendance: 41,973

ENG: Jordan Lee Pickford, Kyle Andrew Walker, Kieran John Trippier, Jacob Harry Maguire, John Stones, Luke Paul Hoare Shaw, Kalvin Mark Phillips, Declan Rice (88.Jordan Brian Henderson), Bukayo Ayoyinka Saka (69.Jack Peter Grealish), Harry Edward Kane (Cap), Raheem Shaquille Sterling. Trainer: Gareth Southgate.

Goals: Raheem Shaquille Sterling (75), Harry Edward Kane (86).

03.07.2021 UKRAINE - ENGLAND   0-4(0-1)   16th EC. Quarter-Finals.

Stadio Olimpico, Rome (Italy); Referee: Dr. Felix Brych (Germany); Attendance: 11,880

ENG: Jordan Lee Pickford, Kyle Andrew Walker, Jacob Harry Maguire, Mason Tony Mount, John Stones, Luke Paul Hoare Shaw (65.Kieran John Trippier), Kalvin Mark Phillips (65.Jude Victor William Bellingham), Declan Rice (57.Jordan Brian Henderson), Jadon Malik Sancho, Harry Edward Kane (Cap) (73.Dominic Nathaniel Calvert-Lewin), Raheem Shaquille Sterling (65.Marcus Rashford). Trainer: Gareth Southgate.

Goals: Harry Edward Kane (4), Jacob Harry Maguire (46), Harry Edward Kane (50), Jordan Brian Henderson (63).

07.07.2021 ENGLAND - DENMARK   2-1(1-1,1-1)   16th EC. Semi-Finals.

Wembley Stadium, London; Referee: Danny Desmond Makkelie (Netherlands); Attendance: 64,950

ENG: Jordan Lee Pickford, Kyle Andrew Walker, Jacob Harry Maguire, John Stones, Luke Paul Hoare Shaw, Mason Tony Mount (95.Philip Walter Foden), Kalvin Mark Phillips, Declan Rice (95.Jordan Brian Henderson), Bukayo Ayoyinka Saka (69.Jack Peter Grealish; 106.Kieran John Trippier), Harry Edward Kane (Cap), Raheem Shaquille Sterling. Trainer: Gareth Southgate.

Goals: Simon Thorup Kjær (39 own goal), Harry Edward Kane (104).

11.07.2021   **ITALY - ENGLAND**   **1-1(0-1,1-1,1-1); 3-2 on penalties**   16th EC. Final.

Wembley Stadium, London; Referee: Björn Kuipers (Netherlands); Attendance: 67,173

ENG: Jordan Lee Pickford, Kyle Andrew Walker (120.Jadon Malik Sancho), Kieran John Trippier (70.Bukayo Ayoyinka Saka), Jacob Harry Maguire, John Stones, Luke Paul Hoare Shaw, Mason Tony Mount (99.Jack Peter Grealish), Kalvin Mark Phillips, Declan Rice (74.Jordan Brian Henderson; 120.Marcus Rashford), Raheem Shaquille Sterling, Harry Edward Kane (Cap). Trainer: Gareth Southgate.

Goal: Luke Paul Hoare Shaw (2).

Penalties: Harry Edward Kane, Jacob Harry Maguire, Marcus Rashford (missed), Jadon Malik Sancho (saved), Bukayo Ayoyinka Saka (saved).

NATIONAL TEAM PLAYERS
(16.07.2020 – 15.07.2021)

Name	DOB	Caps	Goals	2020/2021:	Club
Goalkeepers					
Dean Bradley HENDERSON	12.03.1997	1	0	2020:	Manchester United FC
Samuel Luke JOHNSTONE	25.03.1993	1	0	2021:	West Bromwich Albion FC
Jordan Lee PICKFORD	07.03.1994	38	0	2020/2021:	Everton FC Liverpool
Nicholas David POPE	19.04.1992	7	0	2020/2021:	Burnley FC
Defenders					
Trent John ALEXANDER-ARNOLD	07.10.1998	13	1	2020/2021:	Liverpool FC
Benjamin James CHILWELL	21.12.1996	14	0	2020/2021:	Chelsea FC London
Conor David COADY	25.02.1993	5	1	2020/2021:	Wolverhampton Wanderers FC
Eric Jeremy Edgar DIER	15.01.1994	45	3	2020:	Tottenham Hotspur FC London
Benjamin Matthew GODFREY	15.01.1998	2	0	2021:	Everton FC Liverpool
Joseph Dave GOMEZ	23.05.1997	11	0	2020:	Liverpool FC
Reece JAMES	08.12.1999	7	0	2020/2021:	Chelsea FC London
Michael Vincent KEANE	11.01.1993	12	1	2020/2021:	Everton FC Liverpool
Jacob Harry MAGUIRE	05.03.1993	37	4	2020/2021:	Manchester United FC
Ainsley Cory MAITLAND-NILES	29.08.1997	5	0	2020:	Arsenal FC London
Tyrone Deon MINGS	13.03.1993	13	0	2020/2021:	Aston Villa FC Birmingham
Luke Paul Hoare SHAW	12.07.1995	16	1	2021:	Manchester United FC
John STONES	28.05.1994	49	2	2020/2021:	Manchester City FC
Kieran John TRIPPIER	19.09.1990	33	1	2020/2021:	Club Atlético de Madrid (ESP)
Kyle Andrew WALKER	28.05.1990	61	0	2020/2021:	Manchester City FC
Benjamin William WHITE	08.10.1997	2	0	2021:	Brighton & Hove Albion FC
Midfielders					
Jude Victor William BELLINGHAM	29.06.2003	7	0	2020/2021:	BV Borussia Dortmund (GER)
Philip Walter FODEN	28.05.2000	9	2	2020/2021:	Manchester City FC
Jordan Brian HENDERSON	17.06.1990	64	1	2020/2021:	Liverpool FC
Jesse Ellis LINGARD	15.12.1992	29	4	2020/2021:	West Ham United FC London
Mason Tony MOUNT	10.01.1999	21	4	2020/2021:	Chelsea FC London
Kalvin Mark PHILLIPS	02.12.1995	15	0	2020/2021:	Leeds United FC
Declan RICE	14.01.1999	27	1	2020/2021:	West Ham United FC London
James Michael Edward WARD-PROWSE	01.11.1994	8	1	2020/2021:	Southampton FC
Harry Billy WINKS	02.02.1996	10	1	2020:	Tottenham Hotspur FC London
Forwards					
Kevin Oghenetega Tamaraebi Bakumo ABRAHAM	02.10.1997	6	1	2020:	Chelsea FC London
Harvey Lewis BARNES	09.12.1997	1	0	2020:	Leicester City FC
Dominic Nathaniel CALVERT-LEWIN	16.03.1997	11	4	2020/2021:	Everton FC Liverpool
Jack Peter GREALISH	10.09.1995	12	0	2020/2021:	Aston Villa FC Birmingham
Mason Will John GREENWOOD	01.10.2001	1	0	2020:	Manchester United FC
Danny William John INGS	23.07.1992	3	1	2020:	Southampton FC
Harry Edward KANE	28.07.1993	61	38	2020/2021:	Tottenham Hotspur FC London
Marcus RASHFORD	31.10.1997	46	12	2020/2021:	Manchester United FC
Bukayo Ayoyinka SAKA	05.09.2001	9	1	2020/2021:	Arsenal FC London
Jadon Malik SANCHO	25.03.2000	22	3	2020/2021:	BV Borussia 09 Dortmund (GER)
Raheem Shaquille STERLING	08.12.1994	68	17	2020/2021:	Manchester City FC
Oliver George Arthur WATKINS	30.12.1995	3	0	2021:	Aston Villa FC Birmingham
National team coach					
Gareth SOUTHGATE [from 30.11.2016]		03.09.1970		61 M; 39 W; 12 D; 10 L; 122-40	

ESTONIA

The Country:
Eesti Vabariik (Republic of Estonia)
Capital: Tallinn
Surface: 45,339 km²
Inhabitants: 1,330,068 [2021]
Time: UTC+2

The FA:
Eesti Jalgpalli Liit
A. Le Coq Arena, Asula 4c, 11312 Tallinn
Tel: +372 627 9960
Foundation date: 14.12.1921
Member of FIFA since: 1923
Member of UEFA since: 1992
Website: www.jalgpall.ee

NATIONAL TEAM RECORDS

First international match:	20.10.1920, Helsinki:	Finland – Estonia 6-0
Most international caps:	Martin Reim	- 157 caps (1991-2009)
Most international goals:	Andres Oper	- 38 goals / 134 caps (1995-2014)

UEFA EUROPEAN CHAMPIONSHIP		FIFA WORLD CUP		OLYMPIC TOURNAMENTS	
1960	-	1930	-	1908	-
1964	-	1934	Qualifiers	1912	-
1968	-	1938	Qualifiers	1920	-
1972	-	1950	-	1924	-
1976	-	1954	-	1928	-
1980	-	1958	-	1936	-
1984	-	1962	-	1948	-
1988	-	1966	-	1952	-
1992	-	1970	-	1956	-
1996	Qualifiers	1974	-	1960	-
2000	Qualifiers	1978	-	1964	-
2004	Qualifiers	1982	-	1968	-
2008	Qualifiers	1986	-	1972	-
2012	Qualifiers	1990	-	1976	-
2016	Qualifiers	1994	Qualifiers	1980	-
2020	Qualifiers	1998	Qualifiers	1984	-
		2002	Qualifiers	1988	-
		2006	Qualifiers	1992	-
		2010	Qualifiers	1996	Qualifiers
		2014	Qualifiers	2000	Qualifiers
		2018	Qualifiers	2004	Qualifiers
				2008	Qualifiers
				2012	Qualifiers
				2016	Qualifiers

<u>Please note</u>: *was part of Soviet Union from 1945 to 1991.*

UEFA NATIONS LEAGUE

2018/2019	League C
2020/2021	League C

FIFA CONFEDERATIONS CUP 1992-2017

None

ESTONIAN CLUB HONOURS IN EUROPEAN CLUB COMPETITIONS:

European Champion Clubs' Cup (1956-1992) / UEFA Champions League (1993-2021)
None

Fairs Cup (1858-1971) / UEFA Cup (1972-2009) / UEFA Europa League (2010-2021)
None

UEFA Super Cup (1972-2020)
None

European Cup Winners' Cup 1961-1999*
None

*defunct competition

NATIONAL COMPETITIONS
TABLE OF HONOURS

ESTONIAN SSR (SOVIET ERA) CHAMPIONS

Year	Champion	Year	Champion	Year	Champion
1945	Dünamo Tallinn	1961	Kalev Kopli	1977	Baltika Narva
1946	BL Tallinn	1962	Kalev Ülemiste	1978	Dünamo Tallinn
1947	Dünamo Tallinn	1963	Tempo Tallinn	1979	Norma Tallinn
1948	Balti Laevastik Tallinn	1964	Norma Tallinn	1980	Dünamo Tallinn
1949	Dünamo Tallinn	1965	Balti Laevastik Tallinn	1981	Dünamo Tallinn
1950	Dünamo Tallinn	1966	Balti Laevastik Tallinn	1982	Tempo Tallinn
1951	Balti Laevastik Tallinn	1967	Norma Tallinn	1983	Dünamo Tallinn
1952	Balti Laevastik Tallinn	1968	Balti Laevastik Tallinn	1984	Estonia Jõhvi
1953	Dünamo Tallinn	1969	Dvigatel Tallinn	1985	Kalakombinaat/MEK Pärnu
1954	Dünamo Tallinn	1970	Norma Tallinn	1986	Zvezda Tallinn
1955	Kalev Tallinn	1971	Tempo Tallinn	1987	Tempo Tallinn
1956	Balti Laevastik Tallinn	1972	Balti Laevastik Tallinn	1988	Norma Tallinn
1957	Kalev Ülemiste	1973	Kreenholm Narva	1989	Zvezda Tallinn
1958	Kalev Ülemiste	1974	Baltika Narva	1990	Tallinna VMK
1959	Kalev Ülemiste	1975	Baltika Narva	1991	Tallinna VMK
1960	Balti Laevastik Tallinn	1976	Dvigatel Tallinn		

Year	CHAMPIONS	CUP WINNERS	BEST GOALSCORERS	
1921	Sport Tallinn	-	-	
1922	Sport Tallinn	-	-	
1923	Kalev Tallinn	-	-	
1924	Sport Tallinn	-	-	
1925	Sport Tallinn	-	-	
1926	Jalgpalliklubi Tallinn	-	-	
1927	Sport Tallinn	-	-	
1928	Jalgpalliklubi Tallinn	-	-	
1929	Sport Tallinn	-	-	
1930	Kalev Tallinn	-	-	
1931	Sport Tallinn	-	-	
1932	Sport Tallinn	-	-	
1933	Sport Tallinn	-	-	
1934	Tallinn	-	-	
1935	Tallinn	-	-	
1936	Tallinn	-	-	
1937/1938	Tallinn	SK Tallinna Sport	-	
1938/1939	Tallinn	Jalgpalliklubi Tallinn	-	
1939/1940	Olümpia Tartu	-	-	
1941	Championship not finished	-	-	
1942	PSR Tartu (unofficial)	-	-	
1943	Tallinn (unofficial)	-	-	
1944	Championship not finished	-	-	
1992	FC Norma Tallinn	-	Sergei Bragin (FC Norma Tallinn)	18
1992/1993	FC Norma Tallinn	FC Nikol Tallinn	Sergei Bragin (FC Norma Tallinn)	27
1993/1994	FC Flora Tallinn	FC Norma Tallinn	Maksim Gruznov (JK Narva Trans/Tevalte Tallinn)	21
1994/1995	FC Flora Tallinn	FC Flora Tallinn	Serhiy Morozov (UKR, FC Lantana Tallinn)	25
1995/1996	FC Lantana Tallinn	JK Tallinna Sadam	Lembit Rajala (FC Flora Tallinn)	16
1996/1997	FC Lantana Tallinn	JK Tallinna Sadam	Sergei Bragin (FC Lantana Tallinn)	18
1997/1998	FC Flora Tallinn	-	Konstantin Kolbassenko (JK Tallinna Sadam)	18
1998	FC Flora Tallinn	FC Flora Tallinn	Konstantin Kolbassenko (JK Tallinna Sadam)	13
1999	FC Levadia Maardu	FC Levadia Maardu	Toomas Krõm (FC Levadia Maardu)	19
2000	FC Levadia Maardu	FC Levadia Maardu	Egidijus Juška (LTU, FC Tallinna VMK) Toomas Krõm (FC Levadia Maardu)	24
2001	FC Flora Tallinn	JK Narva Trans	Maksim Gruznov (JK Narva Trans)	37
2002	FC Flora Tallinn	FC Levadia Maardu	Andrei Krõlov (FC Tallinna VMK)	37
2003	FC Flora Tallinn	FC Tallinna VMK	Tor Henning Hamre (NOR, FC Flora Tallinn)	39
2004	FC Levadia Maardu	FC Levadia Maardu	Vjatšeslav Zahovaiko (FC Flora Tallinn)	28
2005	FC Tallinna VMK	FC Levadia Tallinn	Tarmo Neemelo (FC Tallinna VMK)	41
2006	FC Levadia Tallinn	FC Tallinna VMK	Maksim Gruznov (JK Narva Trans)	31
2007	FC Levadia Tallinn	FC Levadia Tallinn	Russia Dmitri Lipartov (JK Narva Trans)	30
2008	FC Levadia Tallinn	FC Flora Tallinn	Ingemar Teever (Nõmme Kalju FC Tallinn)	23
2009	FC Levadia Tallinn	FC Flora Tallinn	Vitali Gussev (FC Levadia Tallinn)	26
2010	FC Flora Tallinn	FC Levadia Tallinn	Sander Post (FC Flora Tallinn)	24
2011	FC Flora Tallinn	FC Flora Tallinn	Latvia Aleksandrs Čekulajevs (JK Narva Trans)	46
2012	Nõmme Kalju FC Tallinn	FC Levadia Tallinn	Vladislav Ivanov (RUS, JK Sillamäe Kalev / JK Narva Trans)	23
2013	FC Levadia Tallinn	FC Flora Tallinn	Vladimir Voskoboinikov (Nõmme Kalju FC Tallinn)	23
2014	FC Levadia Tallinn	FC Levadia Tallinn	Russia Yevgeni Kabaev (JK Sillamäe Kalev)	36
2015	FC Flora Tallinn	Nõmme Kalju FC Tallinn	Ingemar Teever (FC Levadia Tallinn)	24

2016	FC Infonet Tallinn	FC Flora Tallinn	Russia Yevgeni Kabaev (JK Sillamäe Kalev)	25
2017	FC Flora Tallinn	FC Infonet Tallinn	Albert Prosa (FC Infonet Tallinn) Rauno Sappinen (FC Flora Tallinn)	27
2018	Nõmme Kalju FC Tallinn	FCI Levadia Tallinn	Ellinton Antonio Costa Morais "Liliu" (BRA, Nõmme Kalju FC Tallinn)	31
2019	FC Flora Tallinn	JK Narva Trans	Erik Sorga (FC Flora Tallinn)	31
2020	FC Flora Tallinn	FC Flora Tallinn	Rauno Sappinen (FC Flora Tallinn)	26

NATIONAL CHAMPIONSHIP
Meistriliiga 2020
(06.03.2020 – 12.12.2020)

Results

Round 1 [06-08.03.2020]
FC Flora - Tallinna Legion 3-1(2-1)
Narva Trans - Nõmme Kalju 0-1(0-1)
FCI Levadia - FC Kuressaare 1-0(1-0)
Tallinna Kalev - Linnameeskond 1-8(0-3)
JK Tammeka - Viljandi Tulevik 2-1(0-1)

Round 2 [19-20.05.2020]
Tallinna Legion - FCI Levadia 0-2(0-1)
FC Kuressaare - Nõmme Kalju 0-2(0-2)
Linnameeskond - Viljandi Tulevik 1-2(0-1)
Tallinna Kalev - Narva Trans 1-1(0-1)
FC Flora - JK Tammeka 0-0

Round 3 [23-24.05.2020]
Linnameeskond - FC Kuressaare 2-0(1-0)
Nõmme Kalju - Tallinna Legion 1-2(0-1)
JK Tammeka - Tallinna Kalev 0-2(0-0)
Narva Trans - FC Flora 2-3(1-1)
Viljandi Tulevik - FCI Levadia 1-3(1-0)

Round 4 [30-31.05.2020]
FC Flora - Tallinna Kalev 3-0(1-0)
FC Kuressaare - Narva Trans 3-2(1-2)
Tallinna Legion - JK Tammeka 0-1(0-1)
Viljandi Tulevik - Nõmme Kalju 0-6(0-3)
FCI Levadia - Linnameeskond 4-1(1-0)

Round 5 [02-03.06.2020]
Tallinna Kalev - Tallinna Legion 1-0(0-0)
JK Tammeka - FC Kuressaare 1-2(0-1)
Nõmme Kalju - FCI Levadia 2-0(1-0)
Narva Trans - Viljandi Tulevik 0-2(0-1)
Linnameeskond - FC Flora 1-3(1-1)

Round 6 [06-07.06.2020]
FCI Levadia - Tallinna Kalev 4-0(2-0)
Tallinna Legion - Narva Trans 0-0
Viljandi Tulevik - FC Kuressaare 5-0(1-0)
Nõmme Kalju - FC Flora 1-2(1-0)
JK Tammeka - Linnameeskond 0-2(0-2)

Round 7 [12-14.06.2020]
FC Flora - Viljandi Tulevik 3-0(1-0)
FCI Levadia - JK Tammeka 2-2(1-1)
FC Kuressaare - Tallinna Legion 0-0
Tallinna Kalev - Nõmme Kalju 0-4(0-2)
Linnameeskond - Narva Trans 2-1(1-1)

Round 8 [16-17.06.2020]
Tallinna Legion - Viljandi Tulevik 0-2(0-1)
Narva Trans - JK Tammeka 0-1(0-0)
Tallinna Kalev - FC Kuressaare 0-2(0-1)
Nõmme Kalju - Linnameeskond 0-1(0-1)
FC Flora - FCI Levadia 4-0(2-0)

Round 9 [26-27.06.2020]
JK Tammeka - Nõmme Kalju 0-2(0-0)
FC Kuressaare - FC Flora 0-4(0-2)
Viljandi Tulevik - Tallinna Kalev 2-1(1-1)
Narva Trans - FCI Levadia 4-4(3-2)
Linnameeskond - Tallinna Legion 2-0(1-0)

Round 10 [30.06.-01.07.2020]
Tallinna Legion - Tallinna Kalev 0-0
FC Flora - Narva Trans 3-1(1-0)
FC Kuressaare - Viljandi Tulevik 3-0(2-0)
Linnameeskond - JK Tammeka 3-0(0-0)
FCI Levadia - Nõmme Kalju 1-1(1-0)

Round 11 [07-08.07.2020]
Nõmme Kalju - FC Kuressaare 1-0(1-0)
Tallinna Kalev - FCI Levadia 0-4(0-2)
Viljandi Tulevik - FC Flora 2-1(1-1)
JK Tammeka - Tallinna Legion 1-3(0-1)
Narva Trans - Linnameeskond 1-0(1-0)

Round 12 [11-12.07.2020]
Viljandi Tulevik - Narva Trans 0-1(0-0)
FC Flora - Linnameeskond 3-1(0-0)
FC Kuressaare - JK Tammeka 2-4(2-3)
Nõmme Kalju - Tallinna Kalev 2-0(2-0)
FCI Levadia - Tallinna Legion 4-0(2-0)

Round 13 [17-18.07.2020]
Tallinna Legion - FC Kuressaare 1-1(0-0)
Linnameeskond - Nõmme Kalju 1-3(1-1)
Tallinna Kalev - Viljandi Tulevik 0-2(0-1)
FCI Levadia - FC Flora 1-3(1-1)
JK Tammeka - Narva Trans 2-2(1-2)

Round 14 [24-27.07.2020]
Viljandi Tulevik - JK Tammeka 2-0(1-0)
FC Flora - Nõmme Kalju 2-1(1-1)
Linnameeskond - FCI Levadia 4-2(2-2)
Narva Trans - Tallinna Legion 2-0(0-0)
FC Kuressaare - Tallinna Kalev 2-2(2-2)

Round 15 [31.07.-02.08.2020]
Tallinna Kalev - FC Flora 0-3(0-2)
Nõmme Kalju - JK Tammeka 1-1(1-0)
Tallinna Legion - Linnameeskond 0-3(0-3)
Narva Trans - FC Kuressaare 1-0(0-0)
FCI Levadia - Viljandi Tulevik 5-1(3-0)

Round 16 [07-09.08.2020]
FC Flora - FC Kuressaare 3-0(1-0)
Viljandi Tulevik - Tallinna Legion 0-2(0-2)
Linnameeskond - Tallinna Kalev 4-0(3-0)
Nõmme Kalju - Narva Trans 3-0(0-0)
JK Tammeka - FCI Levadia 1-1(0-1)

Round 17 [14-16.08.2020]
FC Kuressaare - FCI Levadia 2-2(1-0)
JK Tammeka - FC Flora 1-3(1-1)
Tallinna Legion - Nõmme Kalju 0-6(0-5)
Viljandi Tulevik - Linnameeskond 1-3(0-3)
Narva Trans - Tallinna Kalev 1-0(1-0)

Round 18 [21-23.08.2020]
FCI Levadia - Narva Trans 3-0(1-0)
Nõmme Kalju - Viljandi Tulevik 1-0(0-0)
Tallinna Kalev - JK Tammeka 0-2(0-1)
FC Kuressaare - Linnameeskond 0-4(0-0)
Tallinna Legion - FC Flora 1-3(1-1)

Round 19 [30.08.2020]
Narva Trans - FC Kuressaare 0-0
Linnameeskond - JK Tammeka 3-1(3-1)
FCI Levadia - Tallinna Kalev 3-0(2-0)
Nõmme Kalju – Tall. Legion 1-1(0-0) [04.10.]
FC Flora - Viljandi Tulevik 2-1(1-0) [04.10.]

Round 20 [12-13.09.2020]
Tallinna Kalev - FC Flora 1-4(1-0)
Viljandi Tulevik - Linnameeskond 1-4(1-1)
Tallinna Legion - Narva Trans 2-1(0-1)
FC Kuressaare - FCI Levadia 1-5(0-2)
JK Tammeka - Nõmme Kalju 0-0 [23.09.]

Round 21 [19-20.09.2020]
Narva Trans - Viljandi Tulevik 0-1(0-0)
Tallinna Kalev - JK Tammeka 1-2(1-1)
FC Kuressaare - Tallinna Legion 2-2(2-0)
FCI Levadia - Nõmme Kalju 2-1(1-1)
FC Flora - Linnameeskond 1-0(1-0) [28.10.]

Round 22 [26-27.09.2020]
Viljandi Tulevik - FC Kuressaare 1-1(1-0)
Linnameeskond - Tallinna Kalev 4-1(2-1)
Tallinna Legion - JK Tammeka 3-1(1-0)
Nõmme Kalju - Narva Trans 2-1(2-0)
FCI Levadia - FC Flora 0-2(0-0) [02.12.]

Round 23 [29-30.08.2020]
FC Flora - Tallinna Legion 1-0(1-0)
Nõmme Kalju - Viljandi Tulevik 0-0
JK Tammeka - Narva Trans 0-0 [03.10.]
Kuressaare - Tallinna Kalev 0-1(0-1) [03.10.]
Linnameesk. - FCI Levadia 1-0(0-0) [04.10.]

Round 24 [17-21.10.2020]
FCI Levadia - Viljandi Tulevik 2-0(2-0)
Tallinna Kalev - Nõmme Kalju 1-4(0-4)
JK Tammeka - FC Kuressaare 4-2(1-2)
Tallinna Legion - Linnameeskond 0-2(0-0)
Narva Trans - FC Flora 1-2(0-1)

Round 25 [24-25.10.2020]
Viljandi Tulevik - JK Tammeka 0-1(0-0)
Tallinna Legion - Tallinna Kalev 2-0(1-0)
Narva Trans - FCI Levadia 1-2(0-0)
FC Kuressaare - FC Flora 0-4(0-1)
Nõmme Kalju - Linnameeskond 1-3(1-3)

Round 26 [31.10.-01.11.2020]
Tallinna Kalev - Narva Trans 4-1(1-1)
Viljandi Tulevik - Tallinna Legion 0-0
FCI Levadia - JK Tammeka 3-2(1-0)
Linnameeskond - FC Kuressaare 6-2(2-0)
FC Flora - Nõmme Kalju 0-0

Round 27 [07-08.11.2020]
FC Kuressaare - Nõmme Kalju 1-1(1-0)
Linnameeskond - Narva Trans 4-2(2-1)
Tallinna Kalev - Viljandi Tulevik 1-0(0-0)
JK Tammeka - FC Flora 0-1(0-0)
Tallin, Legion - FCI Levadia 1-2(0-2) [14.11.]

Please note: On 07.11.2020, due to the second wave of COVID-19, the season was shortened with the league splitted into three sections:
a) Top 4; b) 5th and 6th ; c) bottom 4 (with each team playing each other in that section=.

Top 4

Round 28 [22.11.2020]
Nõmme Kalju - FC Flora 0-3(0-2)
FCI Levadia - Linnameeskond 2-2(1-2)

Round 29 [29.11.2020]
Linnameeskond - FC Flora 1-7(1-2)
Nõmme Kalju - FCI Levadia 0-2(0-0)

Round 30 [06.12.2020]
Linnameeskond - Nõmme Kalju 7-4(3-2)
FC Flora - FCI Levadia *cancelled*

Place 5-6 Play-off

Round 28 [22.11.2020]
JK Tammeka - Viljandi Tulevik 3-3(2-1)

Bottom 4

Round 28 [21.11.2020]
Tallinna Kalev - Tallinna Legion 0-2(0-2)
FC Kuressaare - Narva Trans 0-3(0-2)

Round 29 [24.11.2020]
Tallinna Legion - FC Kuressaare 0-1(0-1)
Narva Trans - Tallinna Kalev 1-1(0-1)

Round 30 [28.11.2020]
Narva Trans - Tallinna Legion 1-3(0-2)
Tallinna Kalev - FC Kuressaare 1-1(0-0)

Final Standings

									Total					Home					Away		
1.	**FC Flora Tallinn**	29	26	2	1	76	-	17	80	11	2	0	28	-	5	15	0	1	48	-	12
2.	Paide Linnameeskond	30	21	1	8	80	-	43	64	12	0	4	46	-	28	9	1	4	34	-	15
3.	FCI Levadia Tallinn	29	17	6	6	66	-	37	57	10	3	2	37	-	15	7	3	4	29	-	22
4.	Nõmme Kalju FC Tallinn	30	14	7	9	52	-	31	49	5	3	6	15	-	16	9	4	3	37	-	15
5.	Tartu JK Tammeka	28	8	8	12	33	-	44	32	2	5	7	15	-	24	6	3	5	18	-	20
6.	Viljandi JK Tulevik	28	9	4	15	30	-	46	31	4	2	8	15	-	24	5	2	7	15	-	22
7.	Tallinna JK Legion	30	8	7	15	26	-	44	31	3	3	9	10	-	25	5	4	6	16	-	19
8.	JK Narva Trans	30	6	7	17	31	-	49	25	4	3	8	15	-	20	2	4	9	16	-	29
9.	FC Kuressaare (*Relegation Play-offs*)	30	5	9	16	28	-	63	24	2	5	8	16	-	36	3	4	8	12	-	27
10.	JK Tallinna Kalev (*Relegated*)	30	5	5	20	20	-	68	20	3	2	11	12	-	40	2	3	9	8	-	28

Top goalscorers:

26	**Rauno Sappinen**	*FC Flora Tallinn*
14	Edrisa Lubega (UGA)	*Paide Linnameeskond*
12	Tristan Koskor	*Tartu JK Tammeka*
11	Aimé Marcelin Gando Biala (CMR)	*FCI Levadia Tallinn*

Relegation Play-offs [10-13.12.2020]

Maardu Linnameeskond - FC Kuressaare   3-5(2-2)   2-4(1-1)
FC Kuressaare remains at first level.

NATIONAL CUP
Eesti Karikas 2019/2020

First Round [04/08/12-13/19/20-21/26-27.06.2019 & 09/13/15/24.07.2019]

Paide Linnameeskond III - JK Mauruse Saurused	13-2	JK Püsivus Kohila - JK Pärnu Sadam	0-5
Tartu FC Helios - Rumori Calcio II	5-1	FC Flora Tallinn III - Pärnu JK Poseidon II	10-0
Tartu JK Tammeka IV - JK Tallinna Kalev III	0-4	Jõgeva SK Noorus - FC Otepää	2-4 aet
Tallinna FC Zapoos - Tallinna FC Zenit	w/o	Tallinna FC Olympic - Paide Linnameeskond	1-9
FC Mulgi - FC Tallinna Wolves	0-1	Maardu Linnameeskond - Valga FC Warrior	12-0
Kohtla-Järve JK II - JK 32. keskkool	w/o	Põhja-Sakala - Pärnu JK	5-2 aet
Viimsi JK II - Maarjamäe FC Igiliikur	1-2	Rakvere JK Tarvas - Kohtla-Järve JK	0-3
Tallinna FC Eston Villa - JK Metsis	15-0	JK Narva Trans – FC Maardu Aliens	w/o
FC Lelle - FC TransferWise	2-1	Viljandi JK Tulevik - Kadrina SK Moe	w/o
Märjamaa Kompanii - FC Sssolutions	6-2	Põhja-Tallinna JK Volta – Vikings FC	18-0
JK Kernu Kadakas - FC Maksatransport	3-1	Tartu JK Tammeka - FCI Tallinn	8-1
Tallinna FC Soccernet - FC Vastseliina	1-3	FC Elva - EMÜ SK	3-0
Tallinna JK Piraaja - Tallinna JK Legion II	1-3		

Second Round [25/27-29/31.07.2019 & 01-02/06-07/11-14/20-21.08.2019]

Tallinna Jalgpalliselts - FC Tarvastu ja JK Törva ÜM	2-7	Tallinna JK Legion - JK Narva Trans	0-7
FC Tallinna Wolves - FC Vastseliina	5-1	FCI Levadia Tallinn - Tallinna FC Zenit	7-0
FC Kuressaare - JK Kernu Kadakas	12-1	FC Puhkus Mehhikos - Kohtla-Järve JK II	0-6
Põhja-Sakala - Tartu FC Helios	5-1	Kristiine JK - Paide Linnameeskond	0-10
Tallinna JK Legion II - FC Jõgeva Wolves II	9-0	FC Elbato - Maardu Linnameeskond	0-3
Team Helm JK - Rumori Calcio	3-2	FC Hell Hunt - JK Tallinna Kalev	0-1
FC Teleios - Põhja-Tallinna JK Volta	2-4	Maarjamäe FC Igiliikur - Viljandi JK Tulevik	1-7
Läänemaa JK Haapsalu - FC Flora Tallinn II	1-5	Anija JK - Märjamaa Kompanii	2-1
Kohtla-Järve JK - Võru Tartu FC Helios	0-1	FC Elva - Viimsi Lõvid	7-0
JK Loo - Tallinna FC Eston Villa II	0-1	FC Lelle - Tabasalu JK	0-1
FC Järva-Jaani - Tartu JK Welco	1-10	FC NPM Silmet - FC Flora Tallinn III	5-2
Põhja-Tallinna JK Volta II - FC Jõgeva Wolves	6-0	FC Kose - Paide Linnameeskond III	0-5
SC ReUnited - Pärnu JK Poseidon	5-1	JK Pärnu Sadam - FC Otepää	0-0 aet; 4-5 pen
Viimsi JK - Raplamaa JK	2-0	Rasmus Värki Jalgpallikool - Tallinna FC Eston Villa	2-2 aet; 5-3 pen
Pärnu JK Vaprus - JK Tallinna Kalev III	2-3	FC Flora Tallinn - Kohtla-Nõmme	12-0
JK FC Nõmme United - Tartu JK Tammeka	1-3	Nõmme Kalju FC Tallinn - Keila JK	2-0

Third Round [20/24/27.08.2019 & 04-05/07/11/25.09.2019 & 09/12/23/29.10.2019]

FC Tarvastu ja JK Törva ÜM - FC Elva	1-4	Team Helm JK - FCI Levadia Tallinn	1-21
Põhja-Sakala - JK Tallinna Kalev	0-3	Võru Tartu FC Helios - Tartu JK Welco	2-1
SC ReUnited - FC Npm Silmet	5-2	Kohtla-Järve JK II - JK Tallinna Kalev III	0-0aet; 10-9pen
Rasmus Värki Jalgpallikool - Anija JK	3-0	FC Kuressaare - JK Narva Trans	1-3
Paide Linnameeskond - Põhja-Tallinna JK Volta	13-0	Tallinna FC Eston Villa II - FC Otepää	3-0
Viljandi JK Tulevik - FC Tallinna Wolves	11-0	Paide Linnameeskond III - Nõmme Kalju FC Tallinn	0-3 aet
Tallinna JK Legion II - Tartu JK Tammeka	0-1	Maardu Linnameeskond - FC Flora Tallinn	0-7
Põhja-Tallinna JK Volta II - Viimsi JK	2-0	Tabasalu JK - FC Flora Tallinn II	2-1

1/8-Finals [25.09.2019 & 13/22-23/30.10.2019 & 06.11.2019]

SC ReUnited - Kohtla-Järve JK II	1-2	FCI Levadia Tallinn - Nõmme Kalju FC Tallinn	1-2
Rasmus Värki Jalgpallikool - Võru Tartu FC Helios	0-1	Viljandi JK Tulevik - Tartu JK Tammeka	0-1
JK Narva Trans - Tallinna FC Eston Villa II	21-0	Paide Linnameeskond - FC Flora Tallinn	1-3
JK Tallinna Kalev - Põhja-Tallinna JK Volta II	7-0	FC Elva - Tabasalu JK	2-0

Quarter-Finals [10-11.03.2020]

FC Elva - Kohtla-Järve JK II	3-1	Võru Tartu FC Helios - JK Tallinna Kalev	0-6
Nõmme Kalju FC Tallinn - JK Narva Trans	1-2	Tartu JK Tammeka - FC Flora Tallinn	0-3

Semi-Finals [20.06.2020]

FC Elva - FC Flora Tallinn	2-4	JK Narva Trans - JK Tallinna Kalev	4-1

Final

04.07.2020; A. Le Coq Arena, Tallinn; Referee: Joonas Jaanovits; Attendance: 0

FC Flora Tallinn - JK Narva Trans　　　　　　　　　　　**2-1(1-1)**

Flora Tallinn: Ingmar Paplavskis, Märten Kuusk, Henrik Pürg, Michael Lilander, Vladislavs Kreida, Rauno Sappinen, Konstantin Vassiljev, Markus Soomets (71.Mihkel Ainsalu), Henri Järvelaid, Vlasiy Sinyavskiy (58.Martin Miller), Frank Liivak (79.Rauno Alliku). Trainer: Jürgen Henn.

Narva Trans: Aleksei Matrossov, Roman Nesterovski (90.Sergei Kondrattsev), Michael Ofosu-Appiah, Martin Käos, Aleksandr Ivanjušin, Sadio Tounkara, Aleksandr Zakarlyuka (80.Viktor Plotnikov), Elysée Irié Bi Séhi, Nikita Mihhailov (70.Nurlan Novruzov), Roman Sobtšenko, Chinedu Charles Geoffrey. Trainer: Cenk Özcan (Turkey).

Goals: 1-0 Konstantin Vassiljev (18), 1-1 Sadio Tounkara (28), 2-1 Henrik Pürg (73).

Football Club Flora Tallinn

Founded: 10.03.1990
Stadium: A. Le Coq Arena, Tallinn (14,336)
Trainer: Jürgen Henn   02.06.1987

Goalkeepers:	DOB	M	(s)	G
Richard Aland	15.03.1994	1		
Matvei Igonen	02.10.1996	11		
Kristen Lapa	11.02.2000	3	(1)	
Ingmar Paplavskis	17.05.1999	13		
Stiven Raider	04.12.2001	1		
Defenders:	**DOB**	**M**	**(s)**	**G**
Enar Jääger	18.11.1984	5		
Henri Järvelaid	11.12.1998	16		3
Ken Kallaste	31.08.1988	3		
Märten Kuusk	05.04.1996	26		6
Michael Lilander	10.06.1997	26		1
Marco Lukka	04.12.1996	9	(1)	
Henrik Pürg	03.06.1996	23		
Markkus Seppik	16.04.2001	4		
Midfielders:	**DOB**	**M**	**(s)**	**G**
Mihkel Ainsalu	08.03.1996	2	(1)	
Kristo Hussar	28.06.2002	1	(2)	
Vladislavs Kreida	25.09.1999	23	(1)	3
Martin Miller	25.09.1997	19	(3)	5
Markus Poom	27.02.1999	17	(3)	2
Rocco Robert Shein	14.07.2003		(1)	
Markus Soomets	02.03.2000	16	(2)	
Henri Välja	04.11.2001	5	(4)	2
Konstantin Vassiljev	16.08.1984	22	(3)	10
Forwards:	**DOB**	**M**	**(s)**	**G**
Rauno Alliku	02.03.1990	13	(13)	4
Leonid Arhipov	12.03.2002		(1)	
Danil Kuraksin	04.04.2003		(1)	
Mark Anders Lepik	10.09.2000	1	(15)	3
Frank Liivak	07.07.1996	10	(16)	3
Rauno Sappinen	23.01.1996	27	(1)	26
Vlasiy Sinyavskiy	27.11.1996	22	(5)	5
Andreas Kiivit	05.07.2003		(1)	

FCI Levadia Tallinn

Founded: 22.10.1998
Stadium: A. Le Coq Arena, Tallinn (14,336)
Trainer: Vladimir Vassiljev   13.02.1988

Goalkeepers:	DOB	M	(s)	G
Richard Aland	15.03.1994	1		
Artur Kotenko	20.08.1981	27		
Sergei Lepmets	05.04.1987	1		
Defenders:	**DOB**	**M**	**(s)**	**G**
Trevor Elhi	11.04.1993	19	(4)	1
Markus Jürgenson	09.09.1987	20	(4)	3
Dmitri Kruglov	24.05.1984	21	(1)	3
Nemanja Lakić-Pešić	22.09.1991	8		
Marko Lipp	19.03.1999	8	(1)	1
Zurab Ochihava (UKR)	18.05.1995	16	(2)	2
Maksim Podholjuzin	13.11.1992	26	(1)	
Oleksandr Safronov (UKR)	11.06.1999	7	(1)	2
Midfielders:	**DOB**	**M**	**(s)**	**G**
Artjom Komlov	09.09.2002	2	(5)	
Anton Krutogolov	05.04.2001		(2)	
Brent Lepistu	26.03.1993	24	(3)	1
Karl Rudolf Õigus	05.11.1998	13	(9)	3
Rasmus Peetson	03.05.1995	8	(6)	2
Daniil Petrunin	22.03.2001		(1)	
Yuriy Tkachuk (UKR)	18.04.1995	1		
Igor Zhurakhovskyi (UKR)	19.09.1994		(10)	1
Forwards:	**DOB**	**M**	**(s)**	**G**
Aimé Marcelin Gando Biala (CMR)	27.02.1997	22	(6)	11
Robert Kirss	03.09.1994	15	(7)	7
Yuriy Kolomoyets (UKR)	22.03.1990	21	(3)	9
Elysee Kouadio (CIV)	03.10.1990	10	(9)	6
Mark Oliver Roosnupp	12.05.1997	23	(4)	5
Bogdan Vaštšuk	04.10.1995	26	(1)	7

Football Club Kuressaare

Founded: 14.03.1997
Stadium: Kuressaare linnastaadion, Kuressaare (1,000)
Trainer: Roman Kozhukhovskyi (UKR)   24.01.1979

Goalkeepers:	DOB	M	(s)	G
Magnus Karofeld	20.08.1996	29		
Roland Kütt	22.04.1987	1		
Defenders:	**DOB**	**M**	**(s)**	**G**
Ranon Kriisa	28.01.1996	29		2
Marco Lukka	04.12.1996	15		
Mairo Miil	15.02.2000	22	(1)	
Tanel Neubauer	22.02.2000		(3)	
Märten Pajunurm	29.04.1993	25	(1)	4
Rasmus Saar	02.03.2000	17	(5)	2
Michael Schjønning-Larsen	02.02.2001	8	(8)	
Elari Valmas	02.07.1988	1	(19)	
Midfielders:	**DOB**	**M**	**(s)**	**G**
Sören Kaldma	03.07.1996	14		
Silver Alex Kelder	22.10.1995	22	(3)	2
Nevil Krimm	10.12.2001	1	(3)	
Märten Opp	15.09.1999	3	(2)	
Oliver Rass	25.05.2000	24	(3)	
Sander Seeman	12.09.1992	25	(1)	
Daniel Tuhkanen	26.02.2001	9	(10)	
Rauno Tutk	10.04.1988	23	(4)	3
Forwards:	**DOB**	**M**	**(s)**	**G**
Sander Laht	26.09.1991	28		6
Otto-Robert Lipp	02.12.2000	2	(3)	2
Mattias Männilaan	08.09.2001	13	(1)	4
Sten Penzev	13.12.2001		(1)	
Joonas Soomre	17.05.2000	19	(1)	2

Tallinna Jalgpalli Klubi Legion

Founded: 04.01.2007
Stadium: Kadriord staadion, Tallinn (5,000)
Trainer: Denis Belov   01.04.1977

Goalkeepers:	DOB	M	(s)	G
Artem Levizi (RUS)	02.03.1993	1		
Pavel Londak	14.05.1980	29		
Defenders:	**DOB**	**M**	**(s)**	**G**
Artjom Artjunin	24.01.1990	20	(3)	1
Jevgeni Baranov	16.08.2000		(2)	
Dmitri Kovtunovitš	11.05.1991	18	(3)	2
Aleksandr Nikolajev	23.06.2003		(2)	
Danil Pankov	04.11.2002	18	(3)	
Andrei Sidorenkov	12.02.1984	23	(1)	
Artur Šarnin	19.07.2000	16	(2)	
German Ussov	26.08.1997	15	(1)	
Aleksandr Volodin	29.03.1988	23	(2)	
Midfielders:	**DOB**	**M**	**(s)**	**G**
Aleksandr Dmitrijev	18.02.1982	13		
Giorgi Ghvinashvili (GEO)	02.08.1997	3	(9)	1
Nikita Ivanov	16.08.2003	1	(1)	
Nikolai Mašitšev (RUS)	05.12.1988	23	(2)	1
Kirill Nesterov (RUS)	21.07.1989	15	(1)	
Andrei Smirnov	28.06.2003		(1)	
German Šlein	28.03.1996	21	(4)	1
Kirill Vinogradov	05.06.1992	1	(6)	
Denis Vnukov	01.11.1991	21	(2)	3
Vsevolod Zassuhhin	16.01.1999		(3)	
Forwards:	**DOB**	**M**	**(s)**	**G**
Rejal Alijev	14.06.1989	1	(1)	
Nikita Andreev	22.09.1988	13	(1)	10
Leonid Arhipov	12.03.2002	6	(2)	1
Semen Belyakov (RUS)	19.01.1999	2	(5)	
Maksim Gussev	20.07.1994	3	(3)	1
Maksim Lipin	17.03.1992	11	(3)	
Albert Prosa	01.10.1990	3	(10)	
Marek Satov	10.07.1993	14	(10)	5
Stefan Tšendei	13.05.1994	16	(2)	

Jalgpalliklubi Narva Trans

Founded: 1979 (*as Avtomobilist Narva*)
Stadium: Narva Kreenholm staadion, Narva (1,065)
Trainer: Cenk Özcan (TUR)   25.04.1974
(19.06.2020)   Oleg Kurotskin   11.05.1971

Goalkeepers:	DOB	M	(s)	G
Aleksei Matrossov	06.04.1991	22		
Andreas Vaikla (CAN)	19.02.1997	8		
Defenders:	**DOB**	**M**	**(s)**	**G**
Aleksandr Ivanjušin (RUS)	07.09.1995	28		
Martin Käos	18.06.1998	21	(2)	
Sergei Kondrattsev	23.09.2001	3	(6)	
Roman Nesterovski	09.06.1989	18	(2)	1
Michael Ofosu-Appiah (GHA)	29.12.1989	21		1
Nikita Savenkov	28.07.1998	7	(3)	
Artjom Škinjov	30.01.1996	23	(1)	1
Maksim Tšerezov	26.03.2001	8	(5)	

Midfielders:	DOB	M	(s)	G
Elysée Irié Bi Séhi (CIV)	13.09.1989	25		1
Arseni Kovaltšuk	07.01.2001	7	(13)	3
Nikita Mihhailov	20.06.2002	22	(3)	2
Denis Polyakov (RUS)	21.02.1992	2		
Roman Sobtšenko	25.01.1994	21	(1)	3
Aleksandr Zakarlyuka (RUS)	24.06.1995	27		8
Forwards:	**DOB**	**M**	**(s)**	**G**
Chinedu Charles Geoffrey (NGA)	01.10.1997	27	(2)	7
Nurlan Novruzov (AZE)	03.03.1993	13	(9)	1
Viktor Plotnikov	14.07.1989	7	(14)	
Raivo Saar	11.07.2000		(7)	
Sadio Tounkara (MLI)	27.04.1992	20	(1)	2

Nõmme Kalju Football Club Tallinn

Founded: 1923 (Re-established in 1997)
Stadium: Hiiu staadion, Tallinn (650)
Trainer: Marko Kristal   02.06.1973
(07.12.2020)   Sergey Frantsev (RUS)   17.03.1959

Goalkeepers:	DOB	M	(s)	G
Marko Meerits	26.04.1992	28		
Henri Perk	14.10.1999	2		
Defenders:	**DOB**	**M**	**(s)**	**G**
Kirill Aleksandr Antonov	11.04.2004		(4)	
Vladimir Avilov	10.03.1995	10	(1)	
Aleksandr Kulinitš	24.05.1992	19	(6)	1
Ivan Lobay (UKR)	21.05.1996	14	(2)	2
Andriy Markovych (UKR)	25.06.1995	28		
Andreas Raudsepp	13.12.1993	9	(3)	
Mikk Reintam	22.05.1990	10	(6)	
Vladislav Veremeyev (UKR)	25.09.1998	11		
Pedro Victor Calil Sandoval (BRA)	21.03.1993	22	(1)	4
Midfielders:	**DOB**	**M**	**(s)**	**G**
Arthur Jeršov	18.06.2002		(1)	

	DOB	M	(s)	G
Vladyslav Khomutov (UKR)	04.06.1998	21	(6)	9
Amir Natkho (RUS)	09.07.1996	25	(1)	3
Sander Puri	07.05.1988	15	(5)	4
Kristjan Rattasepp	30.04.2002		(1)	
Igor Subbotin	26.06.1990	23	(4)	5
Lauri Suup	11.02.2004	1		
Deniss Tjapkin	30.01.1991	19	(9)	
Forwards:	**DOB**	**M**	**(s)**	**G**
Jevgeni Demidov	11.02.2000	3	(5)	
Peeter Klein	28.01.1997	1	(4)	
Odilávio José da Silva Albuquerque (BRA)	23.07.1996	3	(4)	
Kaspar Paur	16.02.1995	29		7
Alex Tamm	24.07.2001	2	(4)	1
Kaarel Usta	03.11.1999	22	(3)	3
Aleksandr Volkov	11.10.1994	13	(15)	9

Paide Linnameeskond

Founded: 2004
Stadium: Paide linnastaadion, Paide (268)
Trainer: Vjatšeslav Zahovaiko   29.12.1981

Goalkeepers:	DOB	M	(s)	G
Mattias Sapp	08.01.2001	3	(1)	
Mait Toom	07.05.1990	27		
Defenders:	**DOB**	**M**	**(s)**	**G**
Mikel Gurrutxaga Barruetabeña (ESP)	22.08.1996	14	(1)	
Martin Kase	02.09.1993	20		
Karl Mööl	04.03.1992	25		4
Kristjan Pelt	12.07.2001	16	(1)	
Joseph Saliste	10.04.1995	25	(4)	3
Muhammed Sanneh (GAM)	07.11.2000	22	(1)	
Abdul Yusif (GHA)	09.08.2001	10		1
Midfielders:	**DOB**	**M**	**(s)**	**G**
Siim Aer	22.07.2001		(3)	
Bruno Souza Caprioli (BRA)	21.02.1996	6	(2)	
Andre Frolov	18.04.1988	25	(4)	2

	DOB	M	(s)	G
Joel Kokla	20.06.2001	1		
Siim Luts	12.03.1989	15	(5)	9
Sergei Mošnikov	07.01.1988	26	(4)	5
Kevor Palumets	21.11.2002	2	(4)	
Sander Sinilaid	07.10.1990	13	(6)	1
Edgar Tur	28.12.1996	23	(1)	9
Forwards:	**DOB**	**M**	**(s)**	**G**
Henri Anier	17.12.1990	5	(6)	10
Hadji Dramé (MLI)	10.09.2000	2	(2)	1
Kevin Kauber	23.03.1995	9	(13)	3
Edrisa Lubega (UGA)	17.04.1998	17	(9)	14
Jaagup Luts	20.03.2002		(1)	
Deabeas Owusu-Sekyere (NED)	04.11.1999	11	(2)	10
Kristofer Piht	24.04.2001	13	(2)	6
Ander Ott Valge	20.10.1998		(4)	1

Jalgpalliklubi Tallinna Kalev Tallinn

Founded: 1909 (*as Meteor Tallinn*); Re-established on 01.09.2002
Stadium: Kalev Keskstaadion, Tallinn (11,500)
Trainer: Aleksandr Dmitrijev   18.02.1982
(18.03.2020)   Liivo Leetma   20.01.1977
(31.08.2020)   Dmitrijs Kalašnikovs   11.12.1983

Goalkeepers:	DOB	M	(s)	G
Daniil Koroljov	11.12.1999	1		
Karl Andre Vallner	28.02.1998	29		
Defenders:	**DOB**	**M**	**(s)**	**G**
Markus Allast	05.09.2000	24	(1)	
Brandon Bachmann	28.02.2000		(1)	
Alger Džumadil	29.07.1996	22	(7)	
Dominik Ivkič (SVN)	31.07.1997	14		
Taavi Kala	27.05.2003		(1)	
Hugo Palutaja	02.03.2004	5	(6)	
Ralf-Sander Suvinomm	29.10.2001	6		
Daniil Sõtšugov	15.01.2003	26	(4)	
Jakob Tamberg	16.06.2003	7	(1)	
Tanel Tamberg	06.06.1992	28		1
Midfielders:	**DOB**	**M**	**(s)**	**G**
Pavel Dõmov	31.12.1993	12		1

	DOB	M	(s)	G
Sören Kaldma	03.07.1996	10		
Marek Kaljumäe	18.02.1991	29		5
Reinhard Reimaa	12.11.1998	29	(1)	
Tristan Teeväli	19.05.2003	7	(3)	
Martin Vetkal	21.02.2004	9	(2)	
Forwards:	**DOB**	**M**	**(s)**	**G**
Hannes Anier	16.01.1993	25	(1)	9
Selim El Aabchi (MAR)	23.03.1993	2	(7)	
Sandor Dino Franch	29.09.2002	1	(2)	
Eduard Golovljov	25.01.1997	7	(14)	2
Romet Kaupmees	08.03.2004	7	(9)	
Mark Petrov	03.04.2002	2		
Ramol Sillamaa	17.10.2004		(6)	
Markus Vaherna	27.01.1999	12	(5)	
Murad Velijev		16		1

Jalgpallikool Tammeka Tartu

Founded:	13.06.1989	
Stadium:	Tartu Tamme staadion, Tartu (1,500)	
Trainer:	Kaido Koppel	09.05.1988

Goalkeepers:	DOB	M	(s)	G
Carl Kiidjärv	05.12.2001	7	(1)	
Karl Pechter	02.03.1996	21		
Defenders:	**DOB**	**M**	**(s)**	**G**
Kevin Aloe	07.05.1995	27		
Kevin Anderson	10.11.1993	11	(3)	
Igor Dudarev (RUS)	12.08.1993	21		1
Daaniel Maanas	05.01.2000	15	(3)	1
Mikhail Slashchyov (RUS)	21.06.1997	26		3
Alfred Tammiksaar	09.11.2002	5	(2)	
Ats Toomsalu	17.08.2002	7	(1)	
Midfielders:	**DOB**	**M**	**(s)**	**G**
Mikhel Järviste	28.05.2000	26		
Joonas Kartsep	13.11.1997	3	(2)	
Reio Laabus	14.03.1990	21	(3)	
Dominic Laaneots	16.06.2001	1	(14)	
Andre Paju	05.01.1995	22	(3)	6
Tanel Tammik	14.06.2002	2	(3)	
Tauno Tekko	14.12.1994	11	(5)	2
Artur Uljanov	25.03.1999	10	(9)	
Forwards:	**DOB**	**M**	**(s)**	**G**
Martin Jõgi	05.01.1995		(1)	
Tristan Koskor	28.11.1995	26	(2)	12
Erki Mõttus	15.01.1997		(4)	
Mart Preiman	01.05.1997	4	(8)	1
Sten Reinkort	29.04.1998	23	(4)	2
Patrik Veelma	15.04.2002	19	(7)	4

Viljandi Jalgpalliklubi Tulevik

Founded:	1912	
Stadium:	Viljandi linnastaadion, Viljandi (1,084)	
Trainer:	Sander Post	10.09.1984

Goalkeepers:	DOB	M	(s)	G
Kaupo Kruusmäe	12.01.2004	1		
Karl-Romet Nõmm	04.01.1998	27		
Defenders:	**DOB**	**M**	**(s)**	**G**
Martin Allik	13.08.1994	24		1
Marco Budic (AUT)	20.02.2000	13	(4)	
Jeremiah Dabrowski (FRA)	26.09.1995	2	(2)	
Mark Edur	11.12.1998	16		
Gerdo Juhkam	19.06.1994	27		
Alex Roosalu	04.05.1999	14	(3)	
Gustav-Hendrik Seeder	29.11.2000	7		
Midfielders:	**DOB**	**M**	**(s)**	**G**
Jude Barrow (CAN)	11.12.2000	6	(6)	
Kristjan Kask	05.07.1999	23	(1)	4
Nikita Komissarov	25.04.2000	22	(5)	2
Tanel Lang	15.08.1995	23		1
Forwards:	**DOB**	**M**	**(s)**	**G**
Sander Kapper	08.12.1994	26		3
Pavel Marin	14.06.1995	26		11
Rainer Peips	11.08.1990	3	(3)	
Herol Riiberg	14.04.1997	24	(1)	4
Kaimar Saag	05.08.1988	20	(6)	3
Jonas Tossou	14.02.2002	4	(17)	1

SECOND LEVEL
Esiliiga 2020

1.	Pärnu JK Vaprus (*Promoted*)	30	18	8	4	67 - 27	62
2.	Maardu Linnameeskond (*Promotion Play-offs*)	30	19	3	8	64 - 42	60
3.	JK FC Nõmme United	30	15	7	8	74 - 39	52
4.	FC Flora U-21 Tallinn*	30	14	6	10	57 - 40	48
5.	FC Elva	30	13	7	10	49 - 48	46
6.	Tartu JK Tammeka U-21*	30	12	2	16	44 - 62	38
7.	FCI Levadia U-21 Tallinn*	30	12	5	13	42 - 41	41
8.	Pärnu JK (*Relegation Play-offs*)	30	11	7	12	61 - 56	40
9.	JK Vaprus Vändra (*Relegated*)	30	10	2	18	47 - 72	32
10.	Kothla-Järve JK (*Relegated*)	30	1	3	26	13 - 91	3

*as reserve team, not eligible for promotion.

Relegation Play-offs (2nd/3rd Level) [17-23.11.2020]

Pärnu Jalgpalliklubi - JK Tallinna Kalev U-21*
*Cancelled as JK Tallinna Kalev were relegated to Esiliiga 2021.

NATIONAL TEAM

INTERNATIONAL MATCHES
(16.07.2020 – 15.07.2021)

05.09.2020	Tallinn	Estonia - Georgia	0-1(0-1)	(UNL)
08.09.2020	Yerevan	Armenia - Estonia	2-0(1-0)	(UNL)
07.10.2020	Tallinn	Estonia - Lithuania	1-3(0-2)	(F)
11.10.2020	Tallinn	Estonia - North Macedonia	3-3(1-1)	(UNL)
14.10.2020	Tallinn	Estonia - Armenia	1-1(1-1)	(UNL)
11.11.2020	Firenze	Italy - Estonia	4-0(2-0)	(F)
15.11.2020	Skopje	North Macedonia - Estonia	2-1(1-0)	(UNL)
18.11.2020	Tbilisi	Georgia - Estonia	0-0	(UNL)
24.03.2021	Lublin	Estonia - Czech Republic	2-6(1-4)	(WCQ)
27.03.2021	Minsk	Belarus - Estonia	4-2(1-1)	(WCQ)
30.03.2021	Stockholm	Sweden - Estonia	1-0(1-0)	(F)
01.06.2021	Vilnius	Lithuania - Estonia	0-1(0-0)	(BC)
04.06.2021	Helsinki	Finland - Estonia	0-1(0-0)	(F)
10.06.2021	Tallinn	Estonia - Latvia	2-1(2-0)	(BC)

05.09.2020   ESTONIA - GEORGIA   0-1(0-1)   2nd UEFA Nations League C, Group 2
A. Le Coq Arena, Tallinn; Referee: Donatas Rumšas (Lithuania); Attendance: 0
EST: Karl Jakob Hein, Taijo Teniste, Joonas Tamm, Karol Mets, Henri Järvelaid, Konstantin Vassiljev (Cap) (86.Mihkel Ainsalu), Henrik Ojamaa, Mattias Käit, Vladislav Kreida, Georgi Tunjov (71.Frank Liivak), Sergei Zenjov (71.Henri Anier). Trainer: Karel Voolaid.

08.09.2020   ARMENIA - ESTONIA   2-0(1-0)   2nd UEFA Nations League C, Group 2
„Vazgen Sargsyan" Hanrapetakan Stadium, Yerevan; Referee: David Coote (England); Attendance: 0
EST: Karl Jakob Hein, Ken Kallaste (30.Henri Järvelaid), Nikita Baranov, Karol Mets (Cap), Ilja Antonov (66.Konstantin Vassiljev), Mihkel Ainsalu, Mark Oliver Roosnupp, Mattias Käit, Georgi Tunjov (63.Henri Anier), Rauno Sappinen, Vlasiy Sinyavskiy. Trainer: Karel Voolaid.

07.10.2020   ESTONIA - LITHUANIA   1-3(0-2)   Friendly International
A. Le Coq Arena, Tallinn; Referee: Antti Munukka (Finland); Attendance: 718
EST: Matvei Igonen, Taijo Teniste, Nikita Baranov, Märten Kuusk (Cap) (58.Henrik Pürg), Henri Järvelaid (58.Michael Lilander), Pavel Marin, Mihkel Ainsalu (75.Vladislav Kreida), Mattias Käit, Georgi Tunjov (58.Siim Luts), Frank Liivak (65.Edgar Tur), Mark Anders Lepik (65.Rauno Sappinen). Trainer: Karel Voolaid.
Goal: Pavel Marin (58).

11.10.2020   ESTONIA - NORTH MACEDONIA   3-3(1-1)   2nd UEFA Nations League C, Group 2
A. Le Coq Arena, Tallinn; Referee: Mohammed Al Hakim (Sweden); Attendance: 908
EST: Karl Jakob Hein, Taijo Teniste, Nikita Baranov, Artur Pikk, Märten Kuusk, Konstantin Vassiljev (Cap) (70.Frank Liivak), Siim Luts (33.Pavel Marin), Mattias Käit (85.Mihkel Ainsalu), Vladislav Kreida, Rauno Sappinen (70.Mark Anders Lepik), Vlasiy Sinyavskiy (85.Michael Lilander). Trainer: Karel Voolaid.
Goals: Rauno Sappinen (33, 61), Frank Liivak (78 penalty).

14.10.2020   ESTONIA - ARMENIA   1-1(1-1)   2nd UEFA Nations League C, Group 2
A. Le Coq Arena, Tallinn; Referee: Luis Miguel Branco Godinho (Portugal); Attendance: 1,007
EST: Karl Jakob Hein, Taijo Teniste (46.Michael Lilander), Nikita Baranov, Artur Pikk, Märten Kuusk, Konstantin Vassiljev (Cap) (72.Georgi Tunjov), Mattias Käit, Vladislav Kreida, Rauno Sappinen (66.Mark Anders Lepik), Frank Liivak (85.Martin Miller), Vlasiy Sinyavskiy (66.Pavel Marin). Trainer: Karel Voolaid.
Goal: Rauno Sappinen (14).

11.11.2020   ITALY - ESTONIA   4-0(2-0)   Friendly International
Stadio "Artemio Franchi", Firenze; Referee: Rade Obrenović (Slovenia); Attendance: 0
EST: Marko Meerits, Taijo Teniste (46.Michael Lilander), Nikita Baranov, Karol Mets (Cap), Artur Pikk (78.Henri Järvelaid), Pavel Marin (46.Edgar Tur), Mihkel Ainsalu (46.Georgi Tunjov), Martin Miller (58.Erik Sorga), Markus Soomets, Rauno Sappinen (59.Mark Anders Lepik), Frank Liivak. Trainer: Karel Voolaid.

15.11.2020   NORTH MACEDONIA - ESTONIA   2-1(1-0)   2nd UEFA Nations League C, Group 2
"Toše Proeski" National Arena, Skopje; Referee: Ionuţ Marius Avram (Romania); Attendance: 0
EST: Karl Jakob Hein, Taijo Teniste, Joonas Tamm, Karol Mets, Artur Pikk, Konstantin Vassiljev (Cap) (55.Erik Sorga), Mihkel Ainsalu (79.Georgi Tunjov), Vladislav Kreida, Sergei Zenjov (63.Frank Liivak), Rauno Sappinen (63.Henri Anier), Vlasiy Sinyavskiy (79.Martin Miller). Trainer: Karel Voolaid.
Goal: Rauno Sappinen (52).

18.11.2020   GEORGIA - ESTONIA   0-0   2nd UEFA Nations League C, Group 2
„Boris Paichadze" Dinamo Arena, Tbilisi; Referee: Irfan Peljto (Bosnia and Herzegovina); Attendance: 0
EST: Karl Jakob Hein, Taijo Teniste (81.Michael Lilander), Joonas Tamm, Artur Pikk, Märten Kuusk, Konstantin Vassiljev (Cap), Markus Soomets (79.Martin Miller), Vladislav Kreida, Sergei Zenjov (79.Pavel Marin), Rauno Sappinen (86.Henri Anier), Vlasiy Sinyavskiy (86.Frank Liivak). Trainer: Karel Voolaid.

24.03.2021   ESTONIA - CZECH REPUBLIC   2-6(1-4)   22nd FIFA WC.Qualifiers
Arena Lublin, Lublin (Poland); Referee: Anastasios Papapetrou (Greece); Attendance: 0
EST: Mihkel Aksalu, Henrik Pürg, Michael Lilander, Maksim Paskotši, Konstantin Vassiljev (Cap) (73.Henri Anier), Ilja Antonov (75.Sander Puri), Markus Poom, Rauno Alliku (73.Robert Kirss), Bogdan Vaštšuk (82.Andre Frolov), Rauno Sappinen (88.Mark Oliver Roosnupp), Karl Rudolf Õigus. Trainer: Thomas Häberli (Switzerland).
Goals: Rauno Sappinen (12), Henri Anier (86).

27.03.2021   **BELARUS - ESTONIA**   **4-2(1-1)**   22nd FIFA WC.Qualifiers

Stadion Dynama, Minsk; Referee: Robert Hennessy (Republic of Ireland); Attendance: 3,611

EST: Matvei Igonen, Märten Kuusk, Henrik Pürg, Michael Lilander, Maksim Paskotši (87.Robert Kirss), Konstantin Vassiljev (Cap), Markus Poom, Henri Anier, Rauno Alliku (62.Karl Rudolf Õigus [*sent off 77*]), Bogdan Vaštšuk, Rauno Sappinen (79.Sander Puri). Trainer: Thomas Häberli (Switzerland).

Goals: Henri Anier (31, 55).

30.03.2021   **SWEDEN - ESTONIA**   **1-0(1-0)**   Friendly International

Friends Arena, Stockholm; Referee: Marco Fritz (Germany); Attendance: 0

EST: Matvei Igonen, Märten Kuusk, Henrik Pürg, Michael Lilander (88.Karl Rudolf Õigus), Maksim Paskotši, Sander Puri, Konstantin Vassiljev (Cap), Markus Poom (88.Mark Oliver Roosnupp), Henri Anier, Bogdan Vaštšuk (88.Andre Frolov), Robert Kirss (77.Rauno Sappinen). Trainer: Thomas Häberli (Switzerland).

01.06.2021   **LITHUANIA - ESTONIA**   **0-1(0-0)**   19th Baltic Cup

LFF stadionas, Vilnius; Referee: Aleksandrs Anufrijevs (Latvia); Attendance: 0

EST: Matvei Igonen, Joonas Tamm, Artur Pikk, Märten Kuusk, Maksim Paskotši (68.Karol Mets), Konstantin Vassiljev (Cap), Vlasiy Sinyavskiy (56.Sander Puri), Mattias Käit, Vladislav Kreida (68.Markus Soomets), Henri Anier (87.Robert Kirss), Rauno Sappinen (87.Bogdan Vaštšuk). Trainer: Thomas Häberli (Switzerland).

Goal: Henri Anier (59).

04.06.2021   **FINLAND - ESTONIA**   **0-1(0-0)**   Friendly International

Olympiastadion, Helsinki; Referee: Jørgen Burchardt (Denmark); Attendance: 0

EST: Karl Jakob Hein, Taijo Teniste (52.Artur Pikk), Joonas Tamm, Karol Mets, Märten Kuusk, Sander Puri, Konstantin Vassiljev (Cap), Henrik Ojamaa (65.Bogdan Vaštšuk), Mattias Käit (90+1.Markus Poom), Vladislav Kreida (65.Markus Soomets), Rauno Sappinen (65.Henri Anier). Trainer: Thomas Häberli (Switzerland).

Goal: Rauno Sappinen (59 penalty).

10.06.2021   **ESTONIA - LATVIA**   **2-1(2-0)**   19th Baltic Cup

A. Le Coq Arena, Tallinn; Referee: Robertas Valikonis (Lithuania); Attendance: 740

EST: Karl Jakob Hein, Joonas Tamm, Karol Mets, Artur Pikk, Märten Kuusk (27.Maksim Paskotš), Sander Puri (85.Henrik Pürg), Konstantin Vassiljev (Cap) (49.Bogdan Vaštšuk), Mattias Käit (49.Markus Poom), Vladislav Kreida, Henri Anier, Rauno Sappinen (85.Henrik Ojamaa). Trainer: Thomas Häberli (Switzerland).

Goals: Mattias Käit (5, 40).

NATIONAL TEAM PLAYERS
(16.07.2020 – 15.07.2021)

Name	DOB	Caps	Goals	2020/2021:	Club
Goalkeepers					
Mihkel AKSALU	07.11.1984	46	0	2021:	*Paide Linnameeskond*
Karl Jakob HEIN	13.04.2002	8	0	2020/2021:	*Arsenal FC London (ENG)*
Matvei IGONEN	02.10.1996	7	0	2020/2021:	*FC Flora Tallinn*
Marko MEERITS	26.04.1992	13	0	2020:	*Nõmme Kalju FC Tallinn*
Defenders					
Nikita BARANOV	19.08.1992	43	0	2020/2021:	*Karmiotissa Pano Polemidia FC (CYP)*
Henri JÄRVELAID	11.12.1998	4	0	2020:	*Vendsyssel FF Hjørring (DEN)*
Ken KALLASTE	31.08.1988	46	0	2020:	*FC Flora Tallinn*
Märten KUUSK	05.04.1996	11	0	2020/2021:	*FC Flora Tallinn*
Michael LILANDER	20.06.1997	10	0	2020/2021:	*FC Flora Tallinn*
Karol METS	16.05.1993	68	0	2020:	*AIK Stockholm (SWE)*
				11.10.2020->	*Al-Ettifaq FC Dammam (KSA)*
Maksim PASKOTŠI	19.01.2003	5	0	2021:	*Tottenham Hotspur FC London (ENG)*
Artur PIKK	05.03.1993	44	1	2020:	*Kuopion Palloseura (FIN)*
				15.01.2021->	*Diósgyőri VTK (HUN)*
Sander PURI	07.05.1988	84	4	2021:	*Tallinna JK Legion*
Henrik PÜRG	03.06.1996	7	0	2020/2021:	*FC Flora Tallinn*
Joonas TAMM	02.02.1992	41	3	2020/2021:	*FK Desna Chernihiv (UKR)*
Taijo TENISTE	31.01.1988	85	0	2020/2021:	*SK Brann Bergen (NOR)*
Midfielders					
Mihkel AINSALU	08.03.1996	13	0	2020:	*FK Lviv (UKR)*
Ilja ANTONOV	05.12.1992	52	2	2020:	*FC Ararat-Armenia Yerevan (ARM)*
				04.02.2021->	*FCI Levadia Tallinn*
Andre FROLOV	18.04.1988	6	0	2021:	*Paide Linnameeskond*
Vladislav KREIDA	25.09.1999	12	0	2020:	*FC Flora Tallinn*
				17.01.2021->	*Helsingborgs IF (SWE)*
Mattias KÄIT	29.06.1998	34	7	2020/2021:	*NK Domžale (SVN)*
Siim LUTS	12.03.1989	43	4	2020:	*Paide Linnameeskond*
Pavel MARIN	14.06.1995	14	2	2020:	*Viljandi JK Tulevik*
Martin MILLER	25.09.1997	13	1	2020:	*FC Flora Tallinn*
Markus POOM	27.02.1999	7	0	2021:	*FC Flora Tallinn*
Mark Oliver ROOSNUPP	12.05.1997	10	0	2020/2021:	*FCI Levadia Tallinn*
Markus SOOMETS	02.03.2000	4	0	2020/2021:	*FC Flora Tallinn*
Georgi TUNJOV	17.04.2001	6	0	2020:	*SPAL Ferrara (ITA)*
Edgar TUR	28.12.1996	2	0	2020:	*Paide Linnameeskond*
Konstantin VASSILJEV	16.08.1984	131	25	2020/2021:	*FC Flora Tallinn*
Bogdan VAŠTŠUK	04.10.1995	6	0	2021:	*FCI Levadia Tallinn*
Forwards					
Rauno ALLIKU	02.03.1990	10	0	2021:	*FC Flora Tallinn*
Henri ANIER	17.12.1990	71	17	2020/2021:	*Paide Linnameeskond*
Robert KIRSS	03.09.1994	5	0	2021:	*FCI Levadia Tallinn*
Mark Anders LEPIK	10.09.2000	4	0	2020:	*FC Flora Tallinn*
Frank LIIVAK	07.07.1996	24	3	2020:	*FC Flora Tallinn*
Henrik OJAMAA	20.05.1991	46	1	2020:	*RTS Widzew Łódź (POL)*
				07.01.2021->	*FC Flora Tallinn*
Rauno SAPPINEN	23.01.1996	38	8	2020/2021:	*FC Flora Tallinn*
Vlasiy SINYAVSKIY	27.11.1996	8	0	2020/2021:	*MFK Karviná (CZE)*
Erik SORGA	08.07.1999	8	1	2020:	*DC United Washington (USA)*
Sergei ZENJOV	20.04.1989	87	13	2020:	*FC Shakhter Karagandy (KAZ)*
Karl Rudolf ÕIGUS	05.11.1998	3	0	2021:	*FCI Levadia Tallinn*

Trainer

Karel VOOLAID [03.07.2019 – 31.12.2020]	04.07.1977	14 M; 0 W; 4 D; 10 L; 7-31
Thomas HÄBERLI (Switzerland) [from 05.01.2021]	11.04.1974	6 M; 3 W; 0 D; 3 L; 8-12

FAROE ISLANDS

The Country:
Faroe Islands (Føroyar)
Capital: Tórshavn
Surface: 1,399 km²
Inhabitants: 53,358 [2021]
Time: UTC

The FA:
Fótbóltssamband Føroya
Gundadalur P.O. Box 3028, 110 Tórshavn
Tel: +298 351 979
Foundation date: 1979
Member of FIFA since: 1988
Member of UEFA since: 1990
Website: www.football.fo

NATIONAL TEAM RECORDS

RECORDS		
First international match:	24.08.1988, Akranes:	Iceland – Faroe Islands 1-0
Most international caps:	Fróði Benjaminsen	- 95 caps (1999-2017)
Most international goals:	Rógvi Jacobsen	- 10 goals / 53 caps (1999-2009)

UEFA EUROPEAN CHAMPIONSHIP	
1960	-
1964	-
1968	-
1972	-
1976	-
1980	-
1984	-
1988	-
1992	Qualifiers
1996	Qualifiers
2000	Qualifiers
2004	Qualifiers
2008	Qualifiers
2012	Qualifiers
2016	Qualifiers
2020	Qualifiers

FIFA WORLD CUP	
1930	-
1934	-
1938	-
1950	-
1954	-
1958	-
1962	-
1966	-
1970	-
1974	-
1978	-
1982	Did not enter
1986	Did not enter
1990	Did not enter
1994	Qualifiers
1998	Qualifiers
2002	Qualifiers
2006	Qualifiers
2010	Qualifiers
2014	Qualifiers
2018	Qualifiers

OLYMPIC TOURNAMENTS	
1908	-
1912	-
1920	-
1924	-
1928	-
1936	-
1948	-
1952	-
1956	-
1960	-
1964	-
1968	-
1972	-
1976	-
1980	-
1984	Did not enter
1988	Did not enter
1992	Did not enter
1996	Did not enter
2000	Did not enter
2004	Did not enter
2008	Did not enter
2012	Qualifiers
2016	Qualifiers

UEFA NATIONS LEAGUE

2018/2019	League D
2020/2021	League D (Promoted to League C)

FIFA CONFEDERATIONS CUP 1992-2017

None

FAROE ISLANDS CLUB HONOURS IN EUROPEAN CLUB COMPETITIONS:

European Champion Clubs' Cup (1956-1992) / UEFA Champions League (1993-2021)
None

Fairs Cup (1858-1971) / UEFA Cup (1972-2009) / UEFA Europa League (2010-2021)
None

UEFA Super Cup (1972-2020)
None

European Cup Winners' Cup 1961-1999*
None

*defunct competition

NATIONAL COMPETITIONS
TABLE OF HONOURS

	CHAMPIONS	CUP WINNERS	BEST GOALSCORERS	
1942	KÍ Klaksvík	-	-	
1943	TB Tvøroyri	-	-	
1944	*No competition*	-	-	
1945	KÍ Klaksvík	-	-	
1946	B36 Tórshavn	-	-	
1947	SÍ Sørvágur	-	-	
1948	B36 Tórshavn	-	-	
1949	TB Tvøroyri	-	-	
1950	B36 Tórshavn	-	-	
1951	TB Tvøroyri	-	-	
1952	KÍ Klaksvík	-	-	
1953	KÍ Klaksvík	-	-	
1954	KÍ Klaksvík	-	-	
1955	HB Tórshavn	HB Tórshavn	-	
1956	KÍ Klaksvík	TB Tvøroyri	-	
1957	KÍ Klaksvík	HB Tórshavn	-	
1958	KÍ Klaksvík	TB Tvøroyri	-	
1959	B36 Tórshavn	HB Tórshavn	-	
1960	HB Tórshavn	TB Tvøroyri	-	
1961	KÍ Klaksvík	TB Tvøroyri	-	
1962	B36 Tórshavn	HB Tórshavn	-	
1963	HB Tórshavn	HB Tórshavn	-	
1964	HB Tórshavn	HB Tórshavn	-	
1965	HB Tórshavn	B36 Tórshavn	-	
1966	KÍ Klaksvík	KÍ Klaksvík	-	
1967	KÍ Klaksvík	KÍ Klaksvík	-	
1968	KÍ Klaksvík	HB Tórshavn	-	
1969	KÍ Klaksvík	HB Tórshavn	-	
1970	KÍ Klaksvík	*Cup Final not played*	-	
1971	HB Tórshavn	HB Tórshavn	-	
1972	KÍ Klaksvík	HB Tórshavn	-	
1973	HB Tórshavn	HB Tórshavn	-	
1974	HB Tórshavn	VB Vágur	-	
1975	HB Tórshavn	HB Tórshavn	-	
1976	TB Tvøroyri	HB Tórshavn	-	
1977	TB Tvøroyri	TB Tvøroyri	-	
1978	HB Tórshavn	HB Tórshavn	-	
1979	ÍF Fuglafjørður	HB Tórshavn	-	
1980	TB Tvøroyri	HB Tórshavn	Jóan Petur Olgarsson (TB Tvøroyri)	18
1981	HB Tórshavn	HB Tórshavn	Jóannes Jakobsen (HB Tórshavn)	14
1982	HB Tórshavn	HB Tórshavn	Jóannes Jakobsen (HB Tórshavn)	9
1983	Gøtu Ítróttarfelag	Gøtu Ítróttarfelag	Petur Hans Hansen (B68 Toftir) Hans Leo í Bartalsstovu (Gøtu Ítróttarfelag)	10
1984	B68 Toftir	HB Tórshavn	Aksel Højgaard (B68 Toftir) Erling Jacobsen (HB Tórshavn)	10
1985	B68 Toftir	Gøtu Ítróttarfelag	Símun Petur Justinussen (Gøtu Ítróttarfelag)	10
1986	Gøtu Ítróttarfelag	NSÍ Runavík	Jesper Wiemer (DEN, B68 Toftir) Símun Petur Justinussen (Gøtu Ítróttarfelag)	13
1987	TB Tvøroyri	HB Tórshavn	Símun Petur Justinussen (Gøtu Ítróttarfelag)	10
1988	HB Tórshavn	HB Tórshavn	Jógvan Petersen (B68 Toftir)	9
1989	B71 Sandoy	HB Tórshavn	Egill Steinþórsson (ISL, VB Vágur)	16
1990	HB Tórshavn	KÍ Klaksvík	Gunnar Mohr (HB Tórshavn) Jens Erik Rasmussen (MB Miðvágur)	10
1991	Klaksvíkar Ítróttarfelag	B36 Tórshavn	Símun Petur Justinussen (Gøtu Ítróttarfelag)	15
1992	B68 Toftir	HB Tórshavn	Símun Petur Justinussen (Gøtu Ítróttarfelag)	14
1993	Gøtu Ítróttarfelag	B71 Sandur	Uni Arge (HB Tórshavn)	11
1994	Gøtu Ítróttarfelag	KÍ Klaksvík	John Petersen (Gøtu Ítróttarfelag)	21
1995	Gøtu Ítróttarfelag	HB Tórshavn	Súni Fríði Johannesen (B68 Toftir)	24
1996	Gøtu Ítróttarfelag	Gøtu Ítróttarfelag	Kurt Mørkøre (KÍ Klaksvík)	20
1997	B36 Tórshavn	Gøtu Ítróttarfelag	Uni Arge (HB Tórshavn)	24
1998	HB Tórshavn	HB Tórshavn	Jákup á Borg (B36 Tórshavn)	20
1999	Klaksvíkar Ítróttarfelag	KÍ Klaksvík	Jákup á Borg (B36 Tórshavn)	17
2000	VB Vágur	Gøtu Ítróttarfelag	Súni Fríði Johannesen (B36 Tórshavn)	16
2001	B36 Tórshavn	B36 Tórshavn	Helgi L. Petersen (Gøtu Ítróttarfelag)	19
2002	HB Tórshavn	NSÍ Runavík	Andrew av Fløtum (HB Tórshavn)	18
2003	HB Tórshavn	B36 Tórshavn	Hjalgrím Elttør (KÍ Klaksvík)	13
2004	HB Tórshavn	HB Tórshavn	Sonni L. Petersen (EB/Streymur)	13
2005	B36 Tórshavn	Gøtu Ítróttarfelag	Christian Høgni Jacobsen (NSÍ Runavík)	18
2006	HB Tórshavn	B36 Tórshavn	Christian Høgni Jacobsen (NSÍ Runavík)	18
2007	NSÍ Runavík	EB/Streymur	Amed Davy Sylla (FRA, B36 Tórshavn)	18
2008	EB/Streymur	EB/Streymur	Arnbjørn Hansen (EB/Streymur)	20
2009	HB Tórshavn	Víkingur Gøta	Finnur Justinussen (Víkingur Gøta)	19

2010	HB Tórshavn	EB/Streymur	Arnbjørn Hansen (EB/Streymur)	
			Christian Høgni Jacobsen (NSÍ Runavík)	22
2011	B36 Tórshavn	EB/Streymur	Finnur Justinussen (Víkingur Gøta)	21
2012	EB/Streymur	Víkingur Gøta	Clayton Soares do Nascimento (BRA, ÍF Fuglafjørður)	22
			Páll Klettskarð (KÍ Klaksvík)	
2013	HB Tórshavn	Víkingur Gøta	Klæmint Andrasson Olsen (NSÍ Runavík)	21
2014	B36 Tórshavn	Víkingur Gøta	Klæmint Andrasson Olsen (NSÍ Runavík)	22
2015	B36 Tórshavn	Víkingur Gøta	Klæmint Andrasson Olsen (NSÍ Runavík)	21
2016	Víkingur Gøta	KÍ Klaksvík	Klæmint Andrasson Olsen (NSÍ Runavík)	23
2017	Víkingur Gøta	NSÍ Runavík	Adeshina Abayomi Lawal (NGA, (Víkingur Gøta)	17
2018	HB Tórshavn	B36 Tórshavn	Adrian Justinussen (HB Tórshavn)	20
2019	KÍ Klaksvík	HB Tórshavn	Klæmint Andrasson Olsen (NSÍ Runavík)	26
2020	HB Tórshavn	HB Tórshavn	Klæmint Andrasson Olsen (NSÍ Runavík)	
			Uroš Stojanov (SRB, ÍF Fuglafjarðar)	17

NATIONAL CHAMPIONSHIP
Faroe Islands Premier League - Betri deildin 2020
(09.05.2020 – 07.11.2020)

Results

Round 1 [09.05.2020]
NSÍ Runavík - TB Tvøroyri 3-1(2-0)
HB Tórshavn - EB/Streymur 1-0(1-0)
Skála ÍF - ÍF Fuglafjørður 1-2(0-1)
KÍ Klaksvík - B36 Tórshavn 0-2(0-0)
AB Argir - Víkingur Gøta 0-0

Round 2 [16-17.05.2020]
TB Tvøroyri - KÍ Klaksvík 1-2(0-1)
B36 Tórshavn - AB Argir 3-0(2-0)
Víkingur Gøta - Skála ÍF 5-2(1-1)
ÍF Fuglafjørður - HB Tórshavn 1-3(0-3)
EB/Streymur - NSÍ Runavík 0-3(0-2)

Round 3 [22-24.05.2020]
Víkingur Gøta - NSÍ Runavík 1-0(1-0)
B36 Tórshavn - Skála ÍF 6-2(4-1)
ÍF Fuglafjørður - KÍ Klaksvík 1-4(1-2)
EB/Streymur - TB Tvøroyri 2-0(2-0)
AB Argir - HB Tórshavn 0-5(0-5)

Round 4 [27-28.05.2020]
TB Tvøroyri - B36 Tórshavn 1-3(1-2)
NSÍ Runavík - ÍF Fuglafjørður 5-0(1-0)
HB Tórshavn - Víkingur Gøta 3-0(2-0)
KÍ Klaksvík - EB/Streymur 3-0(2-0)
Skála ÍF - AB Argir 1-1(0-1)

Round 5 [01-02.06.2020]
B36 Tórshavn - HB Tórshavn 2-4(1-1)
Víkingur Gøta - TB Tvøroyri 0-0
Skála ÍF - NSÍ Runavík 0-4(0-4)
AB Argir - KÍ Klaksvík 0-6(0-3)
ÍF Fuglafjørður - EB/Streymur 2-1(1-0)

Round 6 [06-07.06.2020]
TB Tvøroyri - HB Tórshavn 0-1(0-1)
EB/Streymur - Skála ÍF 1-0(1-0)
ÍF Fuglafjørður - AB Argir 4-2(2-2)
KÍ Klaksvík - NSÍ Runavík 1-1(0-0)
Víkingur Gøta - B36 Tórshavn 4-2(2-1)

Round 7 [12-13.06.2020]
NSÍ Runavík - AB Argir 3-0(2-0)
B36 Tórshavn - EB/Streymur 4-1(2-0)
TB Tvøroyri - ÍF Fuglafjørður 0-0
HB Tórshavn - Skála ÍF 3-0(0-0)
KÍ Klaksvík - Víkingur Gøta 4-1(2-1)

Round 8 [16-17.06.2020]
AB Argir - EB/Streymur 1-1(1-0)
B36 Tórshavn - NSÍ Runavík 1-1(0-0)
Skála ÍF - TB Tvøroyri 0-2(0-0)
HB Tórshavn - KÍ Klaksvík 3-3(1-2)
Víkingur Gøta - ÍF Fuglafjørður 1-2(0-0)

Round 9 [21-22.06.2020]
ÍF Fuglafjørður - B36 Tórshavn 0-3(0-1)
TB Tvøroyri - AB Argir 1-1(1-1)
KÍ Klaksvík - Skála ÍF 3-0(2-0)
EB/Streymur - Víkingur Gøta 0-2(0-0)
NSÍ Runavík - HB Tórshavn 2-0(2-0)

Round 10 [26-28.06.2020]
EB/Streymur - B36 Tórshavn 0-3(0-1)
ÍF Fuglafjørður - TB Tvøroyri 1-0(0-0)
Víkingur Gøta - KÍ Klaksvík 1-2(1-0)
Skála ÍF - HB Tórshavn 1-3(1-0)
AB Argir - NSÍ Runavík 2-3(1-1)

Round 11 [04.07.2020]
ÍF Fuglafjørður - HB Tórshavn 1-2(1-1)
AB Argir - B36 Tórshavn 0-4(0-1)
Skála ÍF - Víkingur Gøta 0-4(0-4)
KÍ Klaksvík - TB Tvøroyri 2-1(0-1)
NSÍ Runavík - EB/Streymur 1-0(1-0)

Round 12 [12.07.2020]
B36 Tórshavn - KÍ Klaksvík 6-2(3-1)
TB Tvøroyri - NSÍ Runavík 0-1(0-1)
ÍF Fuglafjørður - Skála ÍF 3-0(0-0)
Víkingur Gøta - AB Argir 2-1(1-0)
EB/Streymur - HB Tórshavn 0-2(0-2)

Round 13 [27-29.07.2020]
NSÍ Runavík - KÍ Klaksvík 0-2(0-1)
Skála ÍF - EB/Streymur 1-3(1-1)
AB Argir - ÍF Fuglafjørður 2-2(1-1)
HB Tórshavn - TB Tvøroyri 4-1(0-0)
B36 Tórshavn - Víkingur Gøta 4-2(2-2)

Round 14 [02.08.2020]
Víkingur Gøta - EB/Streymur 6-0(5-0)
Skála ÍF - KÍ Klaksvík 0-6(0-3)
HB Tórshavn - NSÍ Runavík 2-0(1-0)
AB Argir - TB Tvøroyri 0-0
B36 Tórshavn - ÍF Fuglafjørður 2-0(0-0)

Round 15 [06-07.08.2020]
B36 Tórshavn - TB Tvøroyri 4-1(1-1)
ÍF Fuglafjørður - NSÍ Runavík 0-1(0-1)
EB/Streymur - KÍ Klaksvík 0-7(0-3)
Víkingur Gøta - HB Tórshavn 1-3(0-1)
AB Argir - Skála ÍF 1-1(0-1)

Round 16 [11-16.08.2020]
KÍ Klaksvík - ÍF Fuglafjørður 6-0(4-0)
HB Tórshavn - AB Argir 11-0(5-0)
NSÍ Runavík - Víkingur Gøta 1-2(0-1)
TB Tvøroyri - EB/Streymur 0-1(0-1)
Skála ÍF - B36 Tórshavn 1-3(1-0) [01.10.]

Round 17 [23.08.2020]
TB Tvøroyri - Skála ÍF 1-0(0-0)
EB/Streymur - AB Argir 3-1(2-0)
ÍF Fuglafjørður - Víkingur Gøta 1-2(0-2)
KÍ Klaksvík - HB Tórshavn 2-1(0-0) [12.09.]
NSÍ Runavík - B36 Tórshavn 4-2(3-0) [12.09.]

Round 18 [28.08.2020]
NSÍ Runavík - Skála ÍF 1-0(0-0) [22.07.]
KÍ Klaksvík - AB Argir 2-0(2-0) [22.07.]
HB Tórshavn - B36 Tórshavn 2-0(0-0)[23.07.]
TB Tvøroyri - Víkingur Gøta 1-2(1-0)
EB/Streymur - ÍF Fuglafjørður 1-0(0-0)

Round 19 [13-15.09.2020]
EB/Streymur - Víkingur Gøta 2-3(1-0)
AB Argir - TB Tvøroyri 0-3(0-2)
Skála ÍF - KÍ Klaksvík 0-1(0-0)
HB Tórshavn - NSÍ Runavík 2-2(0-1) [28.10.]
Fuglafjørður - B36 Tórshavn 1-2(0-0) [28.10.]

Round 20 [19-20.09.2020]
TB Tvøroyri - KÍ Klaksvík 0-0
NSÍ Runavík - EB/Streymur 4-1(2-1)
B36 Tórshavn - AB Argir 3-0(1-0)
Víkingur Gøta - Skála ÍF 2-1(1-0)
HB Tórshavn - ÍF Fuglafjørður 4-2(3-2)

Round 21 [23.09.2020]
TB Tvøroyri - NSÍ Runavík 0-1(0-0)
EB/Streymur - HB Tórshavn 1-5(1-2)
Skála ÍF - ÍF Fuglafjørður 4-4(2-2)
Víkingur Gøta - AB Argir 4-1(3-0) [30.09.]
KÍ Klaksvík - B36 Tórshavn 1-1(0-0) [21.10.]

Round 22 [27-28.09.2020]
NSÍ Runavík - Skála ÍF 4-1(2-0)
TB Tvøroyri - Víkingur Gøta 0-2(0-2)
ÍF Fuglafjørður - EB/Streymur 1-1(1-0)
B36 Tórshavn - HB Tórshavn 1-2(1-1)
KÍ Klaksvík - AB Argir 3-1(1-1) [04.11.]

Round 23 [03-04.10.2020]
TB Tvøroyri - ÍF Fuglafjørður 1-1(0-0)
HB Tórshavn - Skála ÍF 3-0(1-0)
AB Argir - NSÍ Runavík 1-2(0-2)
EB/Streymur - B36 Tórshavn 2-6(1-5)
Víkingur Gøta - KÍ Klaksvík 1-3(1-1) [28.10.]

Round 24 [17-18.10.2020]
B36 Tórshavn - TB Tvøroyri 2-0(1-0)
KÍ Klaksvík - EB/Streymur 2-1(1-0)
ÍF Fuglafjørður - NSÍ Runavík 2-3(1-0)
HB Tórshavn - Víkingur Gøta 4-0(3-0)
Skála ÍF - AB Argir 2-0(1-0)

Round 25 [24-25.10.2020]		Round 26 [01.11.2020]		Round 27 [07.11.2020]
AB Argir - HB Tórshavn 2-3(0-2)		ÍF Fuglafjørður - AB Argir 1-0(0-0)		B36 Tórshavn - NSÍ Runavík 3-4(1-3)
NSÍ Runavík - Víkingur Gøta 3-2(1-0)		Víkingur Gøta - B36 Tórshavn 1-3(1-0)		KÍ Klaksvík - HB Tórshavn 1-1(0-0)
EB/Streymur - TB Tvøroyri 3-2(2-1)		HB Tórshavn - TB Tvøroyri 4-0(2-0)		TB Tvøroyri - Skála ÍF 3-2(0-0)
Skála ÍF - B36 Tórshavn 1-2(1-1)		NSÍ Runavík - KÍ Klaksvík 1-0(1-0)		AB Argir - EB/Streymur 4-0(2-0)
KÍ Klaksvík - ÍF Fuglafjørður 4-1(0-1)		EB/Streymur - Skála ÍF 1-1(0-0)		Víkingur Gøta - ÍF Fuglafjørður 4-1(2-0)

Final Standings

					Total					Home					Away		
1.	**HB Tórshavn**	27	22	3	2	81	-	23	69	11	2	0	46	- 8	11	1	2	35 - 15
2.	NSÍ Runavík	27	20	3	4	58	-	26	63	11	0	2	32	- 11	9	3	2	26 - 15
3.	KÍ Klaksvík	27	19	5	3	72	-	25	62	10	3	1	34	- 11	9	2	2	38 - 14
4.	B36 Tórshavn	27	19	2	6	77	-	37	59	9	1	3	41	- 19	10	1	3	36 - 18
5.	Víkingur Gøta	27	15	2	10	55	-	44	47	8	1	5	33	- 21	7	1	5	22 - 23
6.	ÍF Fuglafjarðar	27	7	5	15	34	-	59	26	5	1	8	19	- 24	2	4	7	15 - 35
7.	EB/Streymur	27	7	3	17	26	-	65	24	5	1	8	16	- 35	2	2	9	10 - 30
8.	TB Tvøroyri	27	4	6	17	20	-	42	18	2	4	8	9	- 17	2	2	9	11 - 25
9.	AB Argir	27	1	7	19	21	-	73	10	1	5	7	13	- 30	0	2	12	8 - 43
10.	Skála ÍF (*Relegated*)	27	1	4	22	22	-	72	7	1	2	10	12	- 35	0	2	12	10 - 37

Please note: only one team was relegated as only one club from the second level is eligible for promotion.

Top goalscorers:	
17 **Klæmint Andrasson Olsen**	*NSÍ Runavík*
17 **Uroš Stojanov (SRB)**	*ÍF Fuglafjarðar*
16 Petur Knudsen	*NSÍ Runavík*
15 Jóannes Bjartalíð	*KÍ Klaksvík*
14 Mikkel Dahl (DEN)	*HB Tórshavn*

NATIONAL CUP
Løgmanssteypið 2020

First Round [27.06.2020]			
FC Suðuroy - Royn Hvalba	9-1(4-1)	MB Miðvágur - Undrið FF	2-6(2-4)

1/8-Finals [08.07.2020]			
TB Tvøroyri - ÍF Fuglafjørður	1-0(1-0)	B68 Toftir - Víkingur Gøta	0-2(0-1)
07 Vestur Sørvágur - FC Suðuroy	3-1(1-1)	Skála ÍF - FC Hoyvík	4-3(1-0)
KÍ Klaksvík - HB Tórshavn	1-1 aet; 4-5 pen	AB Argir - Undrið FF	4-1(1-0)
EB/Streymur - NSÍ Runavík	1-1 aet; 3-5 pen	B71 Sandoy - B36 Tórshavn	2-7(1-2)

Quarter-Finals [25.11.2020]			
Víkingur Gøta - TB Tvøroyri	1-0(0-0)	NSÍ Runavík - Skála ÍF	1-0(0-0)
B36 Tórshavn - AB Argir	3-0(3-0)	07 Vestur Sørvágur - HB Tórshavn	1-1 aet; 4-5 pen

Semi-Finals [28-29.11.2020]			
Víkingur Gøta - B36 Tórshavn	2-1(1-1)	NSÍ Runavík - HB Tórshavn	1-3(0-2)

Final

05.12.2020; Tórsvøllur, Tórshavn; Referee: Jóhan Hendrik Ellefsen; Attendance: 1,100
HB Tórshavn - Víkingur Gøta   **2-0(1-0)**

HB Tórshavn: Teitur Matras Gestsson (Cap), Heri Mohr, Delphin Tshiembe, Hørður Heðinsson Askham, Daniel Johansen (46.Jógvan Davidsen), Mathias Nygaard, Heðin Hansen, Dan Berg Í Soylu, Adrian Justinussen, Hilmar Leon Jakobsen (46.Mads Mikkelsen), Mikkel Dahl (77.Pætur Petersen). Trainer: Jens Berthel Askou (Denmark).

Víkingur Gøta: Elias Fagrá, Ari Olsen, Gunnar Vatnhamar, Atli Gregersen (Cap), Bergur Gregersen, Bogi Reinert-Petersen (56.Géza David Túri), Noah Mneney (82.Martin Klein), Arnbjørn Svensson (70.Olaf Bárðarson), Jákup Johansen, Sølvi Vatnhamar, Finnur Justinussen. Trainer: Jóhan Poulsen.

Goals: 1-0 Gunnar Vatnhamar (24 own goal), 2-0 Mads Mikkelsen (56).

THE CLUBS 2020

Argja Bóltfelag Argir

Founded: 15.08.1973
Stadium: Skansi Arena, Argir (2,000)
Trainer: Símun Samuelsen   21.05.1985
          Tonny Brimsvík   14.11.1975

Goalkeepers:	DOB	M	(s)	G
Silas Eyðsteinsson	13.02.1998	18		
Bjarti Mørk	07.06.2001	9		
Defenders:	**DOB**	**M**	**(s)**	**G**
Tróndur á Høvdanum	19.08.1995	10		
Ári Arge	02.05.2002	8	(4)	
Jákup Pauli Breckmann	16.04.1998	17	(3)	
Ásbjørn Héðinsson	19.12.2000	23	(1)	
Sørin Samuelsen	29.04.1992	25	(1)	1
Jónas Stenberg	07.04.1987	2	(7)	
Midfielders:	**DOB**	**M**	**(s)**	**G**
Tóki á Lofti	06.12.1993	14	(3)	2
Eli Christiansson	12.04.1998	9	(1)	
Hannes Deboes (BEL)	26.01.1994	1	(1)	
Gert Drangastein	25.08.1994	8		
Jobin Drangastein	01.11.1990	1		
Leivur Fossdal Guttesen	17.01.2002	2	(4)	1

	DOB	M	(s)	G
Mikkjal Hentze	08.12.1986	5	(1)	
Bartal Petersen	22.11.2000	12	(5)	2
Rógvi Poulsen	31.10.1989	14	(3)	
Dánjal Reginsson	17.12.2001	12	(2)	
Gilli Róason	03.04.2002	8	(1)	1
Janus Samuelsen	27.09.1998	11	(6)	1
Bjarni Skála	14.11.1997	18	(4)	
Rógvi Skála	05.09.2000		(1)	
Rói Klakkstein Vilhelm	05.01.2001		(1)	
Forwards:	**DOB**	**M**	**(s)**	**G**
Hans Jákup Annfinsson	19.03.1999	3	(4)	1
Adeshina Lawal (NGA)	17.10.1984	15	(11)	2
Bjarki Nielsen	02.11.1998	27		7
Jón Krosslá Poulsen	17.02.1988	1	(4)	
Ragnar Rasmussen	13.07.2000	1	(6)	
Jasper Van der Heyden (BEL)	03.07.1995	23		2

Bóltfelagið 1936 Tórshavn

Founded: 28.03.1936
Stadium: Gundadalur, Tórshavn (5,000)
Trainer: Jákup á Borg   26.10.1979

Goalkeepers:	DOB	M	(s)	G
Símun Rógvi Hansen	10.04.1987	12	(1)	
Rói Hentze	22.09.1999	14		
Mattias Lamhauge	02.08.1999	1		
Defenders:	**DOB**	**M**	**(s)**	**G**
Martin Agnarsson	07.12.2003		(5)	
Andrias Eriksen	22.02.1994	14		
Erling Jacobsen	14.02.1990	10	(1)	1
Mattias Joensen	15.02.2003		(2)	
Erlendur Magnussen	02.07.1998	10	(2)	
Alex Mellemgaard	27.11.1991	20		6
Sonni Ragnar Nattestad	05.08.1994	22		3
Bjarni Petersen	12.08.1998	4		
Andreas Thomsen	04.10.2001	7	(3)	1

Midfielders:	DOB	M	(s)	G
Hannes Agnarsson	26.02.1999	8	(8)	3
Árni Frederiksberg	13.06.1992	25		7
Benjamin Heinesen	26.03.1996	22	(4)	1
Brian Jacobsen	04.11.1991	1	(10)	1
Magnus Holm Jacobsen	23.05.2000	11	(8)	2
Eli Nielsen	23.09.1992	21	(3)	4
Hugin Samuelsen	12.02.1999	2	(2)	
Ragnar Samuelsen	23.08.1999	11	(7)	3
Forwards:	**DOB**	**M**	**(s)**	**G**
Jóhann Hansson Joensen	17.08.2001		(4)	1
Andrass Johansen	16.11.2001	2	(10)	4
Meinhard Egilsson Olsen	10.04.1997	16		10
Sebastian Pingel (DEN)	11.05.1993	23	(2)	13
Michał Przybylski (POL)	29.12.1997	22	(1)	9
Stefan Radosavljević	08.09.2000	19	(5)	5

Eiðis Bóltfelag / Streymur

Founded: 1993
Stadium: Við Margáir, Streymnes (2,000)
Trainer: Jákup Joensen   07.05.1976

Goalkeepers:	DOB	M	(s)	G
Rói Zachariasen	12.10.1998	27		
Defenders:	**DOB**	**M**	**(s)**	**G**
Gestur Dam	17.09.1994	11		3
Ragnar Danielsen	24.02.1992	24		
Hjalti Djurhuus	14.07.1998	21	(1)	
Magnus Heinason	18.12.1999	1	(11)	
Mikkjal Hellisá	18.02.2002	17	(2)	
Andras Olsen	24.10.1995	22	(3)	1
Poul Olsen	30.09.1991	2		
Rói Olsen	03.03.1997	10	(8)	1
Teitur Olsen	04.02.1992	7	(6)	
Bjarni Petersen	12.08.1998	5		
Bjarki Lindberg Zachariasen (DEN)	23.09.1999	2	(6)	
Petur Zachariassen	19.04.1995	15	(1)	1

Midfielders:	DOB	M	(s)	G
Gutti Dahl-Olsen	19.01.2002	16	(7)	2
Jákup Hummeland	10.12.2003		(1)	
Magnus Jarnskor	14.12.1995	7	(3)	
Tóki Johannesen	17.03.1997	18	(2)	2
Sverri Mariusarson	02.08.2004		(1)	
Árni Olsen	13.09.1993	23		
Bárður Olsen	05.12.1985	14	(1)	3
Fannhard Skoradal	23.08.1998	6	(1)	
Símun Sólheim	25.02.2001	24	(3)	3
Forwards:	**DOB**	**M**	**(s)**	**G**
Arnbjørn Hansen	27.02.1986	4	(13)	3
Høgni Hummeland	14.07.1996		(4)	
Niklas Kruse	11.05.1999	21	(3)	5

Havnar Bóltfelag Tórshavn

Founded: 04.10.1904
Stadium: Gundadalur, Tórshavn (5,000)
Trainer: Jens Berthel Askou (DEN)   19.08.1982

Goalkeepers:	DOB	M	(s)	G
Teitur Matras Gestsson	19.08.1992	27		
Jákup Højgaard	06.02.1994		(1)	
Defenders:	**DOB**	**M**	**(s)**	**G**
Samuel Chukwudi	25.06.2003	12	(6)	
Jógvan Davidsen	09.10.1991	13	(3)	1
Daniel Johansen	09.07.1998	26		4
Delphin Tshiembe (COD)	17.07.1991	9	(1)	1
Bartal Wardum	03.05.1997	23	(2)	3
Midfielders:	**DOB**	**M**	**(s)**	**G**
Hørður Heðinsson Askham	22.09.1994	3	(5)	1
Ási Dam	18.12.2002	1	(6)	
Mikkel Frankoch (DEN)	14.01.1996	15	(2)	
Heðin Hansen	30.07.1993	19	(3)	2
Tróndur Jensen	06.02.1993	3	(3)	

	DOB	M	(s)	G
René Joensen	08.02.1993	15	(2)	6
Mads Mikkelsen (DEN)	11.12.1999	2	(1)	
Heri Mohr	13.05.1997	18	(1)	
Mathias Nygaard (DEN)	07.04.1995	26		7
Pætur Petersen	29.03.1998	15	(8)	5
Dánjal Reginsson	17.12.2001		(1)	
Kevin Schindler (GER)	21.05.1988	1	(2)	
Forwards:	**DOB**	**M**	**(s)**	**G**
Mikkel Dahl (DEN)	22.06.1993	12	(1)	14
Øssur Dalbúð	28.03.1989	6	(13)	5
Dan Berg Í Soylu	09.07.1996	26	(1)	6
Hilmar Leon Jakobsen	02.08.1997	11	(6)	12
Adrian Justinussen	21.07.1998	14	(1)	12
Aki Samuelsen	17.04.2004		(4)	

Ítróttarfelag Fuglafjarðar

Founded: 25.03.1946
Stadium: Í Fløtugerði, Fuglafjørður (3,000)
Trainer: Hans Jørgen Djurhuus   29.11.1978

Goalkeepers:	DOB	M	(s)	G
Miloš Budaković (SRB)	10.07.1991	8		
Jákup Nolsøe Olsen	03.01.1999	19	(1)	
Defenders:	**DOB**	**M**	**(s)**	**G**
Hákun Edmundsson	21.03.1996	24	(1)	
Jan Ellingsgaard	26.06.1990	18	(1)	3
Jákup í Lambanum	08.01.2004		(1)	
Jens Joensen	17.05.1989	22		
Sjúrður Nielsen	18.04.2000	26		1
Gundur Petersen	15.02.2001	15	(10)	2
Midfielders:	**DOB**	**M**	**(s)**	**G**
Dánjal á Lakjuni	22.09.1990	9	(7)	
Ari Ellingsgaard	03.02.1993	16	(3)	1
Bjarti J. Højbro	13.06.2003		(3)	

	DOB	M	(s)	G
Sámal Joensen	15.09.1997	9	(9)	1
Hans Jákup Lervig	26.02.1997	17	(1)	2
Bogi Løkin	22.10.1988	7	(8)	
Karl Løkin	19.04.1991	24		1
Pól Jákup Lundsbjerg	22.12.2000	5	(4)	
Jóhan Petersen	13.08.1998	1	(5)	
Rói Róin	31.10.2001			
Forwards:	**DOB**	**M**	**(s)**	**G**
Filip Đorđević (SRB)	07.03.1994	18	(1)	4
Petur Meinhard Lundsbjerg	13.06.2004		(2)	
Andy Olsen	03.12.1984	24	(3)	2
Tóri Olsen	24.10.2001	9	(2)	
Uroš Stojanov (SRB)	05.01.1989	26		17

Klaksvíkar Ítróttarfelag

Founded: 24.08.1904
Stadium: Við Djúpumýrar, Klaksvík (4,000)
Trainer: Mikkjal Thomassen   12.01.1976

Goalkeepers:	DOB	M	(s)	G
Łukasz Jarosiński (POL)	07.10.1988	7		
Kristian Joensen	21.12.1992	20		
Defenders:	**DOB**	**M**	**(s)**	**G**
Jesper Brinck (DEN)	22.03.1989	21	(2)	
Odmar Færø	01.11.1989	24	(1)	3
Ólavur Niclasen	07.07.1998	4	(6)	
Børge Petersen	24.04.2002	1	(2)	
Ísak Simonsen	12.10.1993	14	(3)	2
Midfielders:	**DOB**	**M**	**(s)**	**G**
Jákup Biskopstø Andreasen	31.05.1998	23	(1)	4
Jóannes Danielsen	10.09.1997	26	(1)	5
Boris Došljak (MNE)	04.06.1989	9	(14)	3
Alessio Hyseni (ALB)	04.01.1997	8	(1)	1

	DOB	M	(s)	G
Jonn Johannesen	30.12.2001	15	(12)	8
Dávid Langgaard	30.03.1995	2	(3)	
Steinbjørn Olsen	11.09.1996	4	(7)	
Deni Pavlović (SRB)	01.09.1993	22	(3)	4
David Škrbec (SVN)	29.01.1997	1	(3)	
Heini Vatnsdal	18.10.1991	10		1
Forwards:	**DOB**	**M**	**(s)**	**G**
Jóannes Bjartalíð	10.07.1996	26	(1)	15
Abubakar Aliyu Ibrahim (NGA)	18.11.1994	1	(1)	
Gulak Jacobsen	09.06.2002		(1)	
Patrik Johannesen	07.09.1995	23	(2)	4
Páll Klettskarð	17.05.1990	15	(12)	12
Ole Erik Midtskogen (NOR)	12.04.1995	21	(4)	8

Nes Sóknar Ítróttarfelag Runavík

Founded: 1957
Stadium: Við Løkin, Runavík (2,000)
Trainer: Glenn Stahl (SWE)   25.08.1971
[01.10.2020] Jens Martin Knudsen   11.06.1967
[26.10.2020] Allan Jepsen (DEN)   04.07.1977

Goalkeepers:	DOB	M	(s)	G
Karstin Hansen	05.10.1997	3	(1)	
Tórður Thomsen	11.06.1986	24		
Defenders:	**DOB**	**M**	**(s)**	**G**
Jóhan Davidsen	31.01.1988	17	(1)	1
Pætur Hentze	06.11.1999	3	(6)	
Oddur Højgaard	12.09.1989	22		1
Jákup Jakobsen	22.11.1992	23		
Rógvi Nielsen	07.12.1992	27		1
Midfielders:	**DOB**	**M**	**(s)**	**G**
Salmundur Bech	10.01.1996	11	(7)	1
Jann Benjaminsen	02.03.1997	27		1
Jesper Christjansen (DEN)	29.12.1987	13		4

	DOB	M	(s)	G
Bárður Hansen	13.03.1992	10	(2)	2
Betuel Hansen	14.03.1997	20	(3)	2
Aron Knudsen	05.11.1999	10	(7)	3
Petur Knudsen	21.04.1998	20	(1)	16
Jann Mortensen	18.07.1989	1	(6)	
Mórits Heini Mortensen	25.03.1999	13	(5)	4
Pætur Skipanes	20.10.2000	9	(5)	2
Forwards:	**DOB**	**M**	**(s)**	**G**
Hans Marius Davidsen	12.05.1998		(3)	
Búi Egilsson	04.01.1996	10	(14)	1
Steffan Abrahamsson Løkin	13.11.2000	8	(8)	1
Jørgin Nielsen	30.11.2003	1	(2)	
Klæmint Andrasson Olsen	17.07.1990	25		17

Skála Ítróttarfelag

Founded: 1965
Stadium: Undir Mýruhjalla, Skála (1,500)
Trainer: William McLeod Jacobsen   30.11.1974
[01.08.2020] Sorin Vasile Anghel Olaru (ROU)   16.07.1979

Goalkeepers:	DOB	M	(s)	G
Bárður á Reynatrøð	08.01.2000	27		
Defenders:	**DOB**	**M**	**(s)**	**G**
Mikal á Reynatrøð	15.05.1999	8	(3)	
Erland Danielsen	16.05.1990	2	(4)	
Jóhan Høgnesen	20.06.1998	10	(1)	
Kristian Martin Jakobsen	10.11.1996	19	(2)	2
Karl Martin Johansen	17.08.1999	6	(3)	
Poul Kallsberg	04.02.2003	20	(7)	2
Hanus Mikkelsen	28.11.2002		(3)	
Petur Mikkelsen	20.06.1990	6		
Djóni Petersen	09.10.1990	10	(2)	
Teitur Poulsen	22.07.2000	4	(3)	
Midfielders:	**DOB**	**M**	**(s)**	**G**
Aksel Danielsen	03.04.1999	7	(12)	2

	DOB	M	(s)	G
Niels Pauli Danielsen	18.01.1989	23	(3)	4
Jan Hansen	08.10.1997	18	(3)	5
Haraldur Højgaard	21.03.1995	9	(2)	
Pætur Jacobsen	05.12.1982	24	(1)	
Jákup Joensen	27.02.2000	1	(4)	
Teitur Joensen	10.11.1986	20		
Dávid Johansen	08.02.1997	1	(3)	
Heðin Klakstein	30.04.1992	19	(4)	
Hjalti Strømsten	21.01.1997	13		
Forwards:	**DOB**	**M**	**(s)**	**G**
Jónhard Frederiksberg	27.08.1980	11	(1)	
Andreas Jacobsen	25.11.1999	14	(2)	2
Jóhan Johansen	11.06.1993	1	(10)	2
Ronny Møller-Iversen (DEN)	17.07.1994	23	(1)	2
Rói Olsen	28.04.2001	1	(3)	

Tvøroyrar Bóltfelag

Founded:	13.05.1892		
Stadium:	Við Stórá Stadium, Trongisvágur (4,000)		
Trainer:	Michael Winter (GER)		27.12.1979

Goalkeepers:	DOB	M	(s)	G
Mads Altschuler (DEN)	25.06.2000	2	(1)	
John Jacobsen	15.04.1993	1		
Meinhardt Pállsson Joensen	27.11.1979	5		
Frederik Mehder (DEN)	20.11.1994	19		
Defenders:	**DOB**	**M**	**(s)**	**G**
Musah Armah (GHA)	01.05.1999	7	(4)	
Eirikur Ellendersen	05.03.1994	11	(2)	
Dánjal Godtfred	07.03.1996	25		
Sebastian Kroner (DEN)	04.08.2000	24	(1)	2
Rasmus Møller (DEN)	03.05.2000	25	(2)	
Teitur Olsen	10.05.1995	2	(1)	
Midfielders:	**DOB**	**M**	**(s)**	**G**
Hávar Albinus	19.02.1998		(2)	
Jens Bruhn	12.05.2002	17	(6)	
Bárður Dimon	09.07.1983		(1)	

	DOB	M	(s)	G
Ndende Adama Guéye (SEN)	05.01.1983	25		3
Rógvi Joensen	14.07.1993	19	(1)	2
Nikolei Johannesen	15.05.2001	13	(9)	1
Mark Kongstedt (DEN)	08.07.1995	11		2
John Villi Leo	13.08.1997	14	(1)	1
Andreas Midjord	11.02.2004	1	(7)	
Jóhan Thomsen	14.05.2002		(2)	
Einar Thorsteinsson	07.10.2000	20	(7)	
Forwards:	**DOB**	**M**	**(s)**	**G**
Ken Fagerberg (SWE)	09.01.1989		(4)	
Poul Ingason	28.09.1995	20	(2)	4
Samudeen Musah (GHA)	24.04.2001	20	(4)	1
Filip Obadović (SRB)	19.08.1997	9	(3)	4
Mads Raben (DEN)	08.02.1996	6	(3)	
Aron Sørensen	22.11.1988	1		

Víkingur Gøta Norðragøta

Founded:	14.01.2008 (*after the merger of GÍ Gøta and Leirvík ÍF*)		
Stadium:	Sarpugerði, Norðragøta (3,000)		
Trainer:	Eyðun Klakstein		28.11.1972
[01.09.2020]	Jóhan Poulsen		08.05.1986

Goalkeepers:	DOB	M	(s)	G
Elias Fagrá	13.05.1996	27		
Defenders:	**DOB**	**M**	**(s)**	**G**
Olaf Bárðarson	20.10.2003	4	(4)	1
Atli Gregersen	15.06.1982	26		1
Bergur Gregersen	11.09.1994	15	(2)	
Noah Mneney	06.12.2002	11	(8)	1
Vukašin Tomić (SRB)	08.04.1987	16	(2)	1
Gunnar Vatnhamar	29.03.1995	25		5
Midfielders:	**DOB**	**M**	**(s)**	**G**
Aron Ellingsgaard	16.09.2002		(2)	
Elias Jóhannesson Lervig	26.02.1997	8	(6)	

	DOB	M	(s)	G
Hans Jákup Jóhannesson Lervig	26.02.1997		(2)	
Ari Olsen	09.09.1998	26		5
Bogi Reinert-Petersen	20.02.1993	22		2
Arnbjørn Svensson	01.07.1999	11	(9)	
Géza David Túri (HUN)	06.10.2001	7	(7)	
Sølvi Vatnhamar	05.05.1986	25		12
Forwards:	**DOB**	**M**	**(s)**	**G**
Łukasz Cieślewicz (POL)	15.11.1987	16	(2)	3
Jákup Johansen	27.04.1993	24	(2)	6
Ingi Jonhardsson	11.09.2001	1	(4)	
Finnur Justinussen	30.03.1989	24	(3)	13
Andreas Lava Olsen	09.10.1987	9	(13)	2

SECOND LEVEL
1.deild 2020

1.	Víkingur Gøta II	27	17	7	3	73 - 36	58
2.	07 Vestur Sørvágur (*Promoted*)	27	16	6	5	60 - 33	54
3.	NSÍ Runavík II	27	15	7	5	80 - 42	52
4.	B68 Toftir	27	14	4	9	56 - 34	46
5.	KÍ Klaksvík II	27	11	5	11	56 - 54	38
6.	B36 Tórshavn II	27	10	4	13	43 - 53	34
7.	HB Tórshavn II	27	10	3	14	53 - 79	33
8.	B71 Sandoy	27	9	5	13	53 - 52	32
9.	AB Argir II (*Relegated*)	27	6	5	16	35 - 58	23
10.	FC Hoyvík (*Relegated*)	27	2	4	21	29 - 97	10

INTERNATIONAL MATCHES
(16.07.2020 – 15.07.2021)

03.09.2020	Tórshavn	Faroe Islands - Malta	3-2(1-1)	(UNL)
06.09.2020	Andorra la Vella	Andorra - Faroe Islands	0-1(0-1)	(UNL)
07.10.2020	Herning	Denmark - Faroe Islands	4-0(4-0)	(F)
10.10.2020	Tórshavn	Faroe Islands - Latvia	1-1(1-1)	(UNL)
13.10.2020	Tórshavn	Faroe Islands - Andorra	2-0(2-0)	(UNL)
11.11.2020	Vilnius	Lithuania - Faroe Islands	2-1(2-0)	(F)
14.11.2020	Rīga	Latvia - Faroe Islands	1-1(0-0)	(UNL)
17.11.2020	Attard	Malta - Faroe Islands	1-1(0-0)	(UNL)
25.03.2021	Chişinău	Moldova - Faroe Islands	1-1(1-0)	(WCQ)
28.03.2021	Wien	Austria - Faroe Islands	3-1(3-1)	(WCQ)
31.03.2021	Glasgow	Scotland - Faroe Islands	4-0(1-0)	(WCQ)
04.06.2021	Tórshavn	Faroe Islands - Iceland	0-1(0-0)	(F)
07.06.2021	Tórshavn	Faroe Islands - Liechtenstein	5-1(3-1)	(F)

03.09.2020   FAROE ISLANDS - MALTA   3-2(1-1)   2nd UEFA Nations League D, Group 1
Tórsvøllur, Tórshavn; Referee: Ádám Farkas (Hungary); Attendance: 0
FRO: Gunnar Nielsen, Heini Vatnsdal, Viljormur í Heiðunum Davidsen, Sonni Ragnar Nattestad, Jóannes Danielsen, Sølvi Vatnhamar, Hallur Hansson (Cap), Brandur Hendriksson Olsen, Meinhard Egilsson Olsen (65.Dan Berg Í Soylu), Jóannes Bjartalíð (79.Patrik Johannesen), Klæmint Andrasson Olsen (71.Andreas Lava Olsen). Trainer: Håkan Ericson (Sweden).
Goals: Klæmint Andrasson Olsen (25), Andreas Lava Olsen (87), Brandur Hendriksson Olsen (90+1).

06.09.2020   ANDORRA - FAROE ISLANDS   0-1(0-1)   2nd UEFA Nations League D, Group 1
Estadi Nacional, Andorra la Vella; Referee: Harald Lechner (Austria); Attendance: 0
FRO: Teitur Matras Gestsson, Heini Vatnsdal, Viljormur í Heiðunum Davidsen, Sonni Ragnar Nattestad, Jóannes Danielsen, Hallur Hansson (Cap), Brandur Hendriksson Olsen, Patrik Johannesen (58.Andreas Lava Olsen), Sølvi Vatnhamar, Jóannes Bjartalíð (72.Meinhard Egilsson Olsen), Klæmint Andrasson Olsen (87.Jákup Biskopstø Andreasen). Trainer: Håkan Ericson (Sweden).
Goal: Klæmint Andrasson Olsen (31).

07.10.2020   DENMARK - FAROE ISLANDS   4-0(4-0)   Friendly International
Messecenter Herning Arena, Herning; Referee: Glenn Nyberg (Sweden); Attendance: 207
FRO: Teitur Matras Gestsson, Heini Vatnsdal (62.Odmar Færø), Viljormur í Heiðunum Davidsen, Sonni Ragnar Nattestad (72.Heðin Hansen), Sølvi Vatnhamar, Jóannes Danielsen (73.Gilli Rólantsson Sørensen), Hallur Hansson (Cap) (83.Dan Berg Í Soylu), Brandur Hendriksson Olsen, Jóannes Bjartalíð (62.Gunnar Vatnhamar), Andreas Lava Olsen (62.Jóan Símun Edmundsson), Patrik Johannesen. Trainer: Håkan Ericson (Sweden).

10.10.2020   FAROE ISLANDS - LATVIA   1-1(1-1)   2nd UEFA Nations League D, Group 1
Tórsvøllur, Tórshavn; Referee: Ivaylo Stoyanov (Bulgaria); Attendance: 447
FRO: Teitur Matras Gestsson, Odmar Færø, Viljormur í Heiðunum Davidsen, Sonni Ragnar Nattestad, Sølvi Vatnhamar (65.Rógvi Asmundur Baldvinsson), Hallur Hansson (Cap), Brandur Hendriksson Olsen (11.Gunnar Vatnhamar), Andreas Lava Olsen (65.Jóan Símun Edmundsson), Jóannes Bjartalíð (82.Patrik Johannesen), Klæmint Andrasson Olsen, Gilli Rólantsson Sørensen (82.Jóannes Danielsen). Trainer: Håkan Ericson (Sweden).
Goal: Odmar Færø (28).

13.10.2020   FAROE ISLANDS - ANDORRA   2-0(2-0)   2nd UEFA Nations League D, Group 1
Tórsvøllur, Tórshavn; Referee: Antti Munukka (Finland); Attendance: 412
FRO: Teitur Matras Gestsson, Odmar Færø, Viljormur í Heiðunum Davidsen, Sonni Ragnar Nattestad (90+2.Heðin Hansen), Sølvi Vatnhamar (72.Andreas Lava Olsen), Hallur Hansson (Cap), Brandur Hendriksson Olsen, Meinhard Egilsson Olsen (55.Jóan Símun Edmundsson), Jóannes Bjartalíð, Jóannes Danielsen (72.Gilli Rólantsson Sørensen), Klæmint Andrasson Olsen. Trainer: Håkan Ericson (Sweden).
Goals: Klæmint Andrasson Olsen (19, 33).

11.11.2020   LITHUANIA - FAROE ISLANDS   2-1(2-0)   Friendly International
LFF stadionas, Vilnius; Referee: Aleksandrs Anufrijevs (Latvia); Attendance: 0
FRO: Gunnar Nielsen, Kaj Leo í Bartalsstovu, Viljormur í Heiðunum Davidsen (Cap) (46.Ári Mohr Jónsson), Heðin Hansen, Bartal Wardum, Gilli Rólantsson Sørensen (61.Jóannes Danielsen), Rógvi Asmundur Baldvinsson (61.Hallur Hansson), Magnus Holm Jacobsen (57.Brandur Hendriksson Olsen), Sølvi Vatnhamar (46.Gunnar Vatnhamar), Hilmar Leon Jakobsen, Meinhard Egilsson Olsen (46.Dan Berg Í Soylu). Trainer: Håkan Ericson (Sweden).
Goal: Gunnar Vatnhamar (90+2).

14.11.2020   LATVIA - FAROE ISLANDS   1-1(0-0)   2nd UEFA Nations League D, Group 1
Daugava stadions, Rīga; Referee: Nikola Dabanović (Montenegro); Attendance: 0
FRO: Teitur Matras Gestsson, Odmar Færø, Viljormur í Heiðunum Davidsen (Cap), Rógvi Asmundur Baldvinsson (68.Ári Mohr Jónsson), Sonni Ragnar Nattestad, Sølvi Vatnhamar, Meinhard Egilsson Olsen (83.Hilmar Leon Jakobsen), Gunnar Vatnhamar, Jóannes Bjartalíð, Gilli Rólantsson Sørensen, Klæmint Andrasson Olsen. Trainer: Håkan Ericson (Sweden).
Goal: Gunnar Vatnhamar (60).

17.11.2020   MALTA - FAROE ISLANDS   1-1(0-0)   2nd UEFA Nations League D, Group 1
Ta.Qali National Stadium, Attard; Referee: Kristo Tohver (Estonia); Attendance: 0
FRO: Teitur Matras Gestsson, Odmar Færø, Viljormur í Heiðunum Davidsen, Sølvi Vatnhamar, Hallur Hansson (Cap) (87.Bartal Wardum), Brandur Hendriksson Olsen, Meinhard Egilsson Olsen (88.Heðin Hansen), Gunnar Vatnhamar, Jóannes Bjartalíð (61.Ári Mohr Jónsson), Gilli Rólantsson Sørensen, Klæmint Andrasson Olsen (81.Hilmar Leon Jakobsen). Trainer: Håkan Ericson (Sweden).
Goal: Ári Mohr Jónsson (70).

25.03.2021   MOLDOVA - FAROE ISLANDS   1-1(1-0)   22nd FIFA WC.Qualifiers

Stadionul Zimbru, Chişinău; Referee: Iwan Arwel Griffith (Wales); Attendance: 0

FRO: Gunnar Nielsen, Odmar Færø (40.Heini Vatnsdal), Viljormur í Heiðunum Davidsen, Sonni Ragnar Nattestad, Jóan Símun Edmundsson (78.Meinhard Egilsson Olsen), Hallur Hansson (Cap) (69.Jóannes Bjartalíð, Brandur Hendriksson Olsen, Gunnar Vatnhamar, Klæmint Andrasson Olsen, Gilli Rólantsson Sørensen, Sølvi Vatnhamar (78.Ári Mohr Jónsson). Trainer: Håkan Ericson (Sweden).

Goal: Meinhard Egilsson Olsen (83).

28.03.2021   AUSTRIA - FAROE ISLANDS   3-1(3-1)   22nd FIFA WC.Qualifiers

"Ernst Happel Stadion", Wien; Referee: Kateryna Monzul (Ukraine); Attendance: 0

FRO: Gunnar Nielsen, Heini Vatnsdal (59.Jákup Biskopstø Andreasen), Viljormur í Heiðunum Davidsen, Sonni Ragnar Nattestad, Sølvi Vatnhamar (58.Jóannes Bjartalíð), Hallur Hansson (Cap) (80.Klæmint Andrasson Olsen), Brandur Hendriksson Olsen, Meinhard Egilsson Olsen (58.Patrik Johannesen), Gunnar Vatnhamar, Gilli Rólantsson Sørensen, Jóan Símun Edmundsson (74.Petur Knudsen). Trainer: Håkan Ericson (Sweden).

Goal: Sonni Ragnar Nattestad (19).

31.03.2021   SCOTLAND - FAROE ISLANDS   4-0(1-0)   22nd FIFA WC.Qualifiers

Hampden Park, Glasgow; Referee: Trustin Farrugia Cann (Malta); Attendance: 0

FRO: Gunnar Nielsen, Sonni Ragnar Nattestad (76.Rógvi Asmundur Baldvinsson), Viljormur í Heiðunum Davidsen, Jóan Símun Edmundsson (76.Heini Vatnsdal), Sølvi Vatnhamar (69.Patrik Johannesen), Hallur Hansson (Cap), Brandur Hendriksson Olsen, Meinhard Egilsson Olsen (58.Ári Mohr Jónsson), Gunnar Vatnhamar, Jákup Biskopstø Andreasen (69.Klæmint Andrasson Olsen), Gilli Rólantsson Sørensen. Trainer: Håkan Ericson (Sweden).

04.06.2021   FAROE ISLANDS - ICELAND   0-1(0-0)   Friendly International

Tórsvøllur, Tórshavn; Referee: Kristo Tohver (Estonia); Attendance: 0

FRO: Teitur Matras Gestsson, Odmar Færø, Heini Vatnsdal, Sølvi Vatnhamar (84.Jákup Johansen), Jóan Símun Edmundsson (66.Andreas Lava Olsen), Viljormur í Heiðunum Davidsen, Hallur Hansson (Cap), Brandur Hendriksson Olsen, Meinhard Egilsson Olsen (84.Petur Knudsen), Jákup Biskopstø Andreasen (78.Klæmint Andrasson Olsen), Gilli Rólantsson Sørensen (66.Jóannes Danielsen). Trainer: Håkan Ericson (Sweden).

07.06.2021   FAROE ISLANDS - LIECHTENSTEIN   5-1(3-1)   Friendly International

Tórsvøllur, Tórshavn; Referee: Ívar Orri Kristjánsson (Iceland); Attendance: 0

FRO: Tórður Thomsen (11.Teitur Matras Gestsson), Jóannes Danielsen, Hørður Heðinsson Askham (46.Hallur Hansson), Heini Vatnsdal (46.Odmar Færø), Viljormur í Heiðunum Davidsen (Cap), Jóan Símun Edmundsson (46.Petur Knudsen), Sølvi Vatnhamar, Heðin Hansen, Brandur Hendriksson Olsen (60.Andreas Lava Olsen), Meinhard Egilsson Olsen (61.Tróndur Jensen), Klæmint Andrasson Olsen. Trainer: Håkan Ericson (Sweden).

Goals: Klæmint Andrasson Olsen (23), Brandur Hendriksson Olsen (38, 41), Klæmint Andrasson Olsen (65), Viljormur í Heiðunum Davidsen (79 penalty).

NATIONAL TEAM PLAYERS
(16.07.2020 – 15.07.2021)

Name	DOB	Caps	Goals	2020/2021:	Club
Goalkeepers					
Teitur Matras GESTSSON	19.08.1992	13	0	2020/2021:	HB Tórshavn
Gunnar Nielsen	07.10.1986	63	0	2020/2021:	FH Hafnarfjarðar (ISL)
Tórður THOMSEN	06.11.1986	3	0	2021:	NSÍ Runavík
Defenders					
Hørður Heðinsson ASKHAM	22.09.1994	2	0	2021:	HB Tórshavn
Rógvi Asmundur BALDVINSSON	06.12.1989	49	4	2020/2021:	Bryne FK (NOR)
Viljormur í Heiðunum DAVIDSEN	19.07.1991	51	2	2020/2021:	Vejle BK (DEN)
Odmar FÆRØ	01.11.1989	37	1	2020/2021:	KÍ Klaksvík
Sonni Ragnar NATTESTAD	05.08.1994	34	3	2020:	B36 Tórshavn
				10.01.2021->	Dundalk FC (IRL)
Gunnar VATNHAMAR	29.03.1995	12	2	2020/2021:	Víkingur Gøta
Heini VATNSDAL	18.10.1991	27	0	2020/2021:	KÍ Klaksvík
Bartal WARDUM	03.05.1997	2	0	2020:	HB Tórshavn
Midfielders					
Jákup Biskopstø ANDREASEN	31.05.1998	4	0	2020/2021:	KÍ Klaksvík
Kaj Leo í BARTALSSTOVU	23.06.1991	28	1	2020:	Valur Reykjavík (ISL)
Jóannes BJARTALÍÐ	10.07.1996	15	0	2020/2021:	KÍ Klaksvík
Jóannes DANIELSEN	10.09.1997	9	0	2020/2021:	KÍ Klaksvík
Heðin HANSEN	30.07.1993	5	0	2020/2021:	HB Tórshavn
Hallur HANSSON	08.07.1992	59	5	2020/2021:	AC Horsens (DEN)
Brandur HENDRIKSSON Olsen	19.12.1995	44	6	2020/2021:	Helsingborgs IF (SWE)
Tróndur JENSEN	06.02.1993	3	0	2021:	NSÍ Runavík
Patrik JOHANNESEN	07.09.1995	12	0	2020/2021:	Egersunds IK (NOR)
Jákup JOHANSEN	27.04.1993	1	0	2021:	Víkingur Gøta
Ári Mohr JÓNSSON	22.07.1994	9	1	2020/2021:	Sandnes Ulf (NOR)
Gilli RÓLANTSSON Sørensen	11.08.1992	46	1	2020:	SK Brann Bergen (NOR)
				10.02.2021->	Odds BK Skien (NOR)
Dan Berg Í SOYLU	09.07.1996	3	0	2020:	HB Tórshavn
Sølvi VATNHAMAR	05.05.1986	50	1	2020/2021:	Víkingur Gøta
Forwards					
Jóan Símun EDMUNDSSON	26.07.1991	66	7	2020/2021:	DSC Arminia Bielefeld (GER)
Magnus Holm JACOBSEN	23.05.2000	1	0	2020:	B36 Tórshavn
Hilmar Leon JAKOBSEN	02.08.1997	3	0	2020:	HB Tórshavn
Petur KNUDSEN	21.04.1998	3	0	2021:	NSÍ Runavík
Andreas Lava OLSEN	09.10.1987	17	2	2020/2021:	Víkingur Gøta
Klæmint Andrasson OLSEN	17.07.1990	39	7	2020/2021:	NSÍ Runavík
Meinhard Egilsson OLSEN	10.04.1997	13	1	2020:	GAIS Göteborg (SWE)
				03.02.2021->	Bryne FK (NOR)
Trainer					
Håkan ERICSON (Sweden) [since 16.12.2019]	29.05.1960			13 M; 4 W; 4 D; 5 L; 17-21	

FINLAND

The Country:
Suomen tasavalta (Republic of Finland)
Capital: Helsinki
Surface: 338,424 km^2
Inhabitants: 5,536,146 [2020]
Time: UTC+2

The FA:
Suomen Palloliitto
Urheilukatu 1 PO Box 191, 00251 Helsinki
Tel: +358 9 7421 51
Foundation date: 1907
Member of FIFA since: 1908
Member of UEFA since: 1954
Website:

NATIONAL TEAM RECORDS

RECORDS		
First international match:	22.10.1911, Helsinki:	Finland – Sweden 2-5
Most international caps:	Jari Olavi Litmanen	- 137 caps (1989-2010)
Most international goals:	Jari Olavi Litmanen	- 32 goals / 137 caps (1989-2010)

UEFA EUROPEAN CHAMPIONSHIP	
1960	Did not enter
1964	Did not enter
1968	Qualifiers
1972	Qualifiers
1976	Qualifiers
1980	Qualifiers
1984	Qualifiers
1988	Qualifiers
1992	Qualifiers
1996	Qualifiers
2000	Qualifiers
2004	Qualifiers
2008	Qualifiers
2012	Qualifiers
2016	Qualifiers
2020	Final Tournament (Group Stage)

FIFA WORLD CUP	
1930	Did not enter
1934	Did not enter
1938	Qualifiers
1950	*Withdrew*
1954	Qualifiers
1958	Qualifiers
1962	Qualifiers
1966	Qualifiers
1970	Qualifiers
1974	Qualifiers
1978	Qualifiers
1982	Qualifiers
1986	Qualifiers
1990	Qualifiers
1994	Qualifiers
1998	Qualifiers
2002	Qualifiers
2006	Qualifiers
2010	Qualifiers
2014	Qualifiers
2018	Qualifiers

OLYMPIC TOURNAMENTS	
1908	-
1912	-
1920	-
1924	-
1928	-
1936	Qualifiers
1948	-
1952	Round 1
1956	-
1960	Qualifiers
1964	Qualifiers
1968	Qualifiers
1972	*Withdrew*
1976	Qualifiers
1980	Group Stage
1984	Qualifiers
1988	Qualifiers
1992	Qualifiers
1996	Qualifiers
2000	Qualifiers
2004	Qualifiers
2008	Qualifiers
2012	Qualifiers
2016	Qualifiers

UEFA NATIONS LEAGUE	
2018/2019	League C (promoted to League B)
2020/2021	League B

FIFA CONFEDERATIONS CUP 1992-2017
None

FINNISH CLUB HONOURS IN EUROPEAN CLUB COMPETITIONS:

European Champion Clubs.Cup (1956-1992) / UEFA Champions League (1993-2021)
None

Fairs Cup (1858-1971) / UEFA Cup (1972-2009) / UEFA Europa League (2010-2021)
None

UEFA Super Cup (1972-2020)
None

*European Cup Winners.Cup 1961-1999**
None

*defunct competition

NATIONAL COMPETITIONS
TABLE OF HONOURS

	CHAMPIONS	CUP WINNERS	BEST GOALSCORERS	
1908	Unitas Helsinki	-	-	
1909	PUS Helsinki	-	-	
1910	Åbo IFK Turku	-	-	
1911	HJK Helsinki	-	-	
1912	HJK Helsinki	-	-	
1913	KIF Helsinki	-	-	
1914	*No competition*	-	-	
1915	KIF Helsinki	-	-	
1916	KIF Helsinki	-	-	
1917	HJK Helsinki	-	-	
1918	HJK Helsinki	-	-	
1919	HJK Helsinki	-	-	
1920	Åbo IFK Turku	-	-	
1921	Helsingin Palloseura	-	-	
1922	Helsingin Palloseura	-	-	
1923	HJK Helsinki	-	-	
1924	Åbo IFK Turku	-	-	
1925	HJK Helsinki	-	-	
1926	Helsingin Palloseura	-	-	
1927	Helsingin Palloseura	-	-	
1928	TPS Turku	-	-	
1929	Helsingin Palloseura	-	-	
1930	IFK Helsingfors	-	Holger Salin (IFK Helsingfors) Olof Strömsten (KIF Helsinki)	9
1931	IFK Helsingfors	-	Holger Salin (IFK Helsingfors)	11
1932	Helsingin Palloseura	-	Lauri Lehtinen (TPS Turku)	13
1933	IFK Helsingfors	-	Olof Strömsten (IFK Helsingfors)	18
1934	Helsingin Palloseura	-	Olof Strömsten (IFK Helsingfors)	15
1935	Helsingin Palloseura	-	Aatos Lehtonen (HJK Helsinki) Nuutti Lintamo (VPS Vaasa)	13
1936	HJK Helsinki	-	Aatos Lehtonen (HJK Helsinki)	14
1937	IFK Helsingfors	-	Aatos Lehtonen (HJK Helsinki)	25
1938	HJK Helsinki	-	Aatos Lehtonen (HJK Helsinki)	14
1939	TPS Turku	-	Aatos Lehtonen (HJK Helsinki)	15
1940	Sudet Viipuri	-	*Not known*	
1941	TPS Turku	-	Jussi Valtonen (TPS Turku)	14
1942	HT Helsinki	-	*Not known*	
1943	*No competition*	-	-	
1944	VIFK Vaasa	-	Urho Teräs (TPS Turku) Leo Turunen (Sudet Viipuri)	9
1945	VPS Vaasa	-	*Not known*	
1946	VIFK Vaasa	-	*Not known*	
1947	IFK Helsingfors	-	*Not known*	
1948	VPS Vaasa	-	Stig-Göran Myntti (VIFK Vaasa)	15
1949	TPS Turku	-	Yrjö Asikainen (Ilves-Kissat Tampere) Kaimo Lintamo (VPS Vaasa)	20
1950	Ilves-Kissat Tampere	-	Yrjö Asikainen (Ilves-Kissat Tampere) Jorma Saarinen (VPS Vaasa)	15
1951	KTP Kotka	-	Åke Forsberg (KIF Helsinki)	16
1952	KTP Kotka	-	Mauri Vanhanen (KTP Kotka)	16
1953	VIFK Vaasa	-	Rainer Forss (Pyrkivä Turku)	15
1954	Pyrkivä Turku	-	Eino Koskinen (TuTo Turku)	16
1955	KIF Helsinki	FC Haka Valkeakoski	Yrjö Asikainen (KIF Helsinki)	12
1956	KuPS Kuopio	PPojat Helsinki	Pentti Styck (HJK Helsinki)	20
1957	Helsingin Palloseura	Drott Pietarsaari	Matti Sundelin (TPS Turku)	21
1958	KuPS Kuopio	KTP Kotka	Kalevi Lehtovirta (TPS Turku) Kai Pahlman (Helsingin Palloseura)	17
1959	IFK Helsingfors	FC Haka Valkeakoski	Matti Sundelin (TPS Turku)	21
1960	FC Haka Valkeakoski	FC Haka Valkeakoski	Matti Sundelin (TPS Turku)	30
1961	IFK Helsingfors	KTP Kotka	Kai Pahlman (Helsingin Palloseura)	20
1962	FC Haka Valkeakoski	Helsingin Palloseura	Tor Österlund (HIK Hanko)	22
1963	Reipas Lahti	FC Haka Valkeakoski	Juha Lyytikäinen (IFK Helsingfors)	16
1964	HJK Helsinki	Reipas Lahti	Arto Tolsa (KTP Kotka)	26
1965	FC Haka Valkeakoski	Åbo IFK Turku	Kai Pahlman (HJK Helsinki)	22
1966	KuPS Kuopio	HJK Helsinki	Markku Hyvärinen (KuPS Kuopio)	16
1967	Reipas Lahti	KTP Kotka	Tommy Lindholm (TPS Turku)	22
1968	TPS Turku	KuPS Kuopio	Tommy Lindholm (TPS Turku)	23
1969	KPV Kokkola	FC Haka Valkeakoski	Hannu Lamberg (KPV Kokkola) Pekka Talaslahti (HJK Helsinki)	18
1970	Reipas Lahti	MP Mikkeli	Matti Paatelainen (IFK Helsingfors)	20
1971	TPS Turku	MP Mikkeli	Pentti Toivola (MP Mikkeli)	17
1972	TPS Turku	Reipas Lahti	Matti Paatelainen (IFK Helsingfors)	

			Heikki Suhonen (TPS Turku)	16
1973	HJK Helsinki	Reipas Lahti	Hannu Lamberg (KPV Kokkola)	13
1974	KuPS Kuopio	Reipas Lahti	Erkki Salo (TPS Turku)	17
1975	TPS Turku	Reipas Lahti	Reijo Rantanen (MiPK Mikkeli)	16
1976	KuPS Kuopio	Reipas Lahti	Matti Paatelainen (FC Haka Valkeakoski)	17
1977	FC Haka Valkeakoski	FC Haka Valkeakoski	Matti Paatelainen (FC Haka Valkeakoski)	20
1978	HJK Helsinki	Reipas Lahti	Atik Ismail (HJK Helsinki)	20
1979	OPS Oulu	FC Ilves Tampere	Atik Ismail (HJK Helsinki) Heikki Suhonen (TPS Turku)	15
1980	OPS Oulu	KTP Kotka	Hannu Rajaniemi (Sepsi-78 Seinäjoki)	19
1981	HJK Helsinki	HJK Helsinki	Juhani Himanka (OPS Oulu)	22
1982	FC Kuusysi Lahti	FC Haka Valkeakoski	Atik Ismail (HJK Helsinki)	19
1983	FC Ilves Tampere	FC Kuusysi Lahti	Mika Lipponen (TPS Turku)	22
1984	FC Kuusysi Lahti	HJK Helsinki	Mika Lipponen (TPS Turku)	25
1985	HJK Helsinki	FC Haka Valkeakoski	Ismo Lius (FC Kuusysi Lahti)	19
1986	FC Kuusysi Lahti	RoPS Rovaniemi	Ismo Lius (FC Kuusysi Lahti) Jari Niinimäki (FC Ilves Tampere)	13
1987	HJK Helsinki	FC Kuusysi Lahti	Ari Hjelm (FC Ilves Tampere)	20
1988	HJK Helsinki	FC Haka Valkeakoski	Ismo Lius (FC Kuusysi Lahti)	22
1989	FC Kuusysi Lahti	KuPS Kuopio	Ismo Lius (FC Kuusysi Lahti)	15
1990	HJK Helsinki	FC Ilves Tampere	Marek Czakon (POL, FC Ilves Tampere) Kimmo Tarkkio (HJK Helsinki)	16
1991	FC Kuusysi Lahti	TPS Turku	Kimmo Tarkkio (FC Haka Valkeakoski)	23
1992	HJK Helsinki	MyPa Myllykoski	Luiz Antônio Moraes (BRA, FC Jazz Pori)	21
1993	FC Jazz Pori	HJK Helsinki	Antti Sumiala (FC Jazz Pori)	20
1994	TPV Tampere	TPS Turku	Dionísio Domingos Rangel (BRA, TPV Tampere)	17
1995	FC Haka Valkeakoski	MyPa Myllykoski	Valeri Popovitch (RUS, FC Haka Valkeakoski)	21
1996	FC Jazz Pori	HJK Helsinki	Luiz Antônio Moraes (BRA, FC Jazz Pori)	17
1997	HJK Helsinki	FC Haka Valkeakoski	Rafael Pires Vieira (BRA, HJK Helsinki)	11
1998	FC Haka Valkeakoski	HJK Helsinki	Matti Hiukka (RoPS Rovaniemi)	11
1999	FC Haka Valkeakoski	Jokerit Helsinki	Valeri Popovitch (FC Haka Valkeakoski)	23
2000	FC Haka Valkeakoski	HJK Helsinki	Shefki Kuqi (Jokerit Helsinki)	19
2001	TamU Tampere	Atlantis Helsinki	Paulus Roiha (HJK Helsinki)	22
2002	HJK Helsinki	FC Haka Valkeakoski	Mika Kottila (HJK Helsinki)	18
2003	HJK Helsinki	HJK Helsinki	Saku Puhakainen (MyPa Myllykoski)	14
2004	FC Haka Valkeakoski	MyPa Myllykoski	Antti Pohja (TamU Tampere)	16
2005	MyPa Myllykoski	FC Haka Valkeakoski	Juho Mäkelä (HJK Helsinki)	16
2006	TamU Tampere	HJK Helsinki	Hermanni Vuorinen (FC Honka Espoo)	16
2007	TamU Tampere	TamU Tampere	Rafael Pires Vieira (BRA, FC Lahti)	14
2008	FC Inter Turku	HJK Helsinki	Aleksandr Kokko (FC Honka Espoo) Henri Myntti (TamU Tampere)	13
2009	HJK Helsinki	FC Inter Turku	Hermanni Vuorinen (FC Honka Espoo)	16
2010	HJK Helsinki	TPS Turku	Juho Mäkelä (HJK Helsinki)	16
2011	HJK Helsinki	HJK Helsinki	Timo Furuholm (FC Inter Turku)	22
2012	HJK Helsinki	FC Honka Espoo	Irakli Sirbiladze (GEO, FC Inter Turku)	17
2013	HJK Helsinki	RoPS Rovaniemi	Tim Väyrynen (FC Honka Espoo)	17
2014	HJK Helsinki	HJK Helsinki	Jonas Emet (FF Jaro Pietarsaari) Luis Emilio Solignac (ARG, IFK Mariehamn)	14
2015	SJK Seinäjoki	IFK Mariehamn	Aleksandr Kokko (RoPS Rovaniemi)	17
2016	IFK Mariehamn	SJK Seinäjoki	Roope Vilhelmi Riski (SJK Seinäjoki)	17
2017	HJK Helsinki	HJK Helsinki	Aleksei Kangaskolkka (IFK Mariehamn)	16
2018	HJK Helsinki	FC Inter Turku	João Klauss De Mello (BRA, HJK Helsinki)	21
2019	Kuopion Palloseura	FC Ilves Tampere	Filip Valenčić (SVN, FC Inter Turku)	17
2020	HJK Helsinki	HJK Helsinki	Roope Vilhelmi Riski (HJK Helsinki)	16

NATIONAL CHAMPIONSHIP
Veikkausliiga 2020
(01.07.2020 – 04.11.2020)

Results

Round 1 [01-02.07.2020]
Haka Valkeakoski - FC Honka 1-1(1-0)
FC Lahti - HJK Helsinki 0-4(0-2)
Helsingfors IFK - Kuopion PS 0-3(0-3)
FC Ilves Tampere - IFK Mariehamn 4-3(0-1)
SJK Seinäjoki - TPS Turku 1-0(1-0)
FC Inter Turku - Rovaniemi PS 3-1(1-0)

Round 2 [07-08.07.2020]
Kuopion PS - FC Inter Turku 1-0(0-0)
TPS Turku - FC Ilves Tampere 0-1(0-0)
FC Lahti - SJK Seinäjoki 0-0
HJK Helsinki - Haka Valkeakoski 3-1(1-0)
IFK Mariehamn - FC Honka 0-0
Rovaniemi PS - Helsingfors IFK 0-1(0-0)

Round 3 [17-18.07.2020]
FC Inter Turku - HJK Helsinki 1-0(0-0)
FC Ilves Tampere - Kuopion PS 0-0
Rovaniemi PS - Haka Valkeakoski 2-2(2-1)
SJK Seinäjoki - IFK Mariehamn 1-2(0-1)
FC Honka - TPS Turku 3-1(0-0)
Helsingfors IFK - FC Lahti 0-3(0-2)

Round 4 [21-22.07.2020]
Rovaniemi PS - FC Ilves Tampere 1-1(0-0)
FC Honka - FC Inter Turku 1-1(0-0)
Helsingfors IFK - SJK Seinäjoki 2-1(1-0)
IFK Mariehamn - Haka Valkeakoski 2-2(1-1)
Kuopion PS - FC Lahti 3-0(2-0)
TPS Turku - HJK Helsinki 0-2(0-1)

Round 5 [25-26.07.2020]
TPS Turku - FC Lahti 1-3(0-1)
HJK Helsinki - FC Ilves Tampere 2-0(1-0)
FC Honka - Rovaniemi PS 1-0(1-0)
Haka Valkeakoski - FC Inter Turku 0-2(0-1)
IFK Mariehamn - Helsingfors IFK 0-3(0-1)
Kuopion PS - SJK Seinäjoki 2-1(2-0)

Round 6 [01-03.08.2020]
FC Inter Turku - IFK Mariehamn 2-1(1-0)
HJK Helsinki - Kuopion PS 2-2(0-1)
FC Ilves Tampere - Helsingfors IFK 2-2(2-1)
Rovaniemi PS - TPS Turku 2-3(1-1)
SJK Seinäjoki - Haka Valkeakoski 1-1(0-0)
FC Lahti - FC Honka 0-0

Round 7 [05-06.08.2020]
Haka Valkeakoski - Helsingfors IFK 0-2(0-0)
IFK Mariehamn - FC Inter Turku 2-0(1-0)
FC Ilves Tampere - Rovaniemi PS 1-0(0-0)
SJK Seinäjoki - Kuopion PS 1-1(0-0)
HJK Helsinki - FC Lahti 1-1(1-0)
TPS Turku - FC Honka 0-2(0-0)

Round 8 [09-10.08.2020]
Rovaniemi PS - IFK Mariehamn 2-3(1-1)
FC Inter Turku - Haka Valkeakoski 2-0(1-0)
FC Lahti - FC Ilves Tampere 3-2(2-0)
Kuopion PS - HJK Helsinki 0-3(0-1)
FC Honka - SJK Seinäjoki 0-0
Helsingfors IFK - TPS Turku 2-0(0-0)

Round 9 [14-16.08.2020]
Haka Valkeakoski - Kuopion PS 2-4(1-1)
FC Lahti - Rovaniemi PS 3-0(1-0)
FC Inter Turku - Helsingfors IFK 3-2(1-1)
HJK Helsinki - FC Honka 1-1(0-1)
FC Ilves Tampere - SJK Seinäjoki 0-0
IFK Mariehamn - TPS Turku 1-0(1-0)

Round 10 [21-23.08.2020]
SJK Seinäjoki - FC Honka 0-2(0-0)
TPS Turku - FC Inter Turku 1-0(1-0)
FC Ilves Tampere - FC Lahti 3-1(1-1)
Kuopion PS - IFK Mariehamn 2-1(1-0)
Rovaniemi PS - HJK Helsinki 0-1(0-0)
Helsingfors IFK - Haka Valkeakoski 0-1(0-1)

Round 11 [26.08.2020]
Inter Turku - Ilves Tampere 5-1(3-0) [11.07.]
FC Honka - Kuopion PS 1-1(0-1) [12.07.]
Haka Valkeakoski - FC Lahti 2-2(1-1)
HJK Helsinki - SJK Seinäjoki 2-0(1-0)
IFK Mariehamn - Rovaniemi PS 4-0(2-0)
TPS Turku - Helsingfors IFK 1-0(0-0)

Round 12 [29.08.-01.09.2020]
SJK Seinäjoki - Rovaniemi PS 2-1(1-0)
Kuopion PS - TPS Turku 3-1(3-1)
HJK Helsinki - IFK Mariehamn 6-1(4-1)
FC Lahti - FC Inter Turku 2-2(2-0)
FC Honka - Helsingfors IFK 0-1(0-1)
Haka Valkeakoski - Ilves Tampere 0-2(0-1)

Round 13 [09-10.09.2020]
FC Honka - FC Ilves Tampere 3-2(1-1)
IFK Mariehamn - FC Lahti 2-2(0-1)
Kuopion PS - Rovaniemi PS 3-0(2-0)
SJK Seinäjoki - FC Inter Turku 3-2(2-1)
TPS Turku - Haka Valkeakoski 2-3(1-2)
Helsingfors IFK - HJK Helsinki 4-3(3-1)

Round 14 [12-14.09.2020]
Haka Valkeakoski - SJK Seinäjoki 1-4(0-2)
Rovaniemi PS - FC Honka 1-3(0-2)
FC Ilves Tampere - HJK Helsinki 1-2(0-1)
TPS Turku - IFK Mariehamn 1-1(0-0)
FC Lahti - Kuopion PS 1-2(1-0)
Helsingfors IFK - FC Inter Turku 0-0

Round 15 [17-20.09.2020]
FC Lahti - TPS Turku 1-1(0-0)
FC Inter Turku - SJK Seinäjoki 0-1(0-1)
Helsingfors IFK - IFK Mariehamn 2-2(2-0)
Ilves Tampere - Haka Valkeakoski 1-1(1-0)
FC Honka - HJK Helsinki 0-0
Rovaniemi PS - Kuopion PS 0-2(0-2)

Round 16 [23-24.09.2020]
Haka Valkeakoski - Rovaniemi PS 0-2(0-0)
FC Inter Turku - FC Honka 0-0
IFK Mariehamn - FC Ilves Tampere 0-2(0-0)
SJK Seinäjoki - FC Lahti 0-1(0-0)
HJK Helsinki - TPS Turku 2-2(0-0)
Kuopion - Helsingfors IFK 3-2(2-0) [08.10.]

Round 17 [27-28.09.2020]
FC Honka - Haka Valkeakoski 1-2(1-1)
IFK Mariehamn - Kuopion PS 0-2(0-1)
FC Ilves Tampere - TPS Turku 4-0(2-0)
HJK Helsinki - Rovaniemi PS 4-0(3-0)
FC Inter Turku - FC Lahti 3-0(1-0)
SJK Seinäjoki - Helsingfors IFK 3-2(2-0)

Round 18 [02-05.10.2020]
Haka Valk. - HJK Helsinki 1-4(0-0) [18.08.]
Rovaniemi - FC Inter Turku 0-2(0-0) [18.08.]
FC Lahti - IFK Mariehamn 3-1(0-1)
Helsingfors IFK - FC Honka 1-1(1-0)
Kuopion PS - FC Ilves Tampere 1-1(0-0)
TPS Turku - SJK Seinäjoki 1-0(0-0) [31.10.]

Round 19 [15-16.10.2020]
Rovaniemi PS - FC Lahti 0-4(0-1)
FC Honka - IFK Mariehamn 1-0(1-0)
FC Inter Turku - Kuopion PS 2-0(1-0)
Helsingfors IFK - FC Ilves Tampere 1-2(0-0)
SJK Seinäjoki - HJK Helsinki 1-2(1-1)
Haka Valkeakoski - TPS Turku 2-1(1-0)

Round 20 [18-19.10.2020]
HJK Helsinki - Helsingfors IFK 3-0(0-0)
IFK Mariehamn - SJK Seinäjoki 2-3(0-1)
FC Ilves Tampere - FC Inter Turku 0-2(0-0)
Kuopion PS - FC Honka 0-2(0-1)
FC Lahti - Haka Valkeakoski 0-0
TPS Turku - Rovaniemi PS 4-1(3-0)

Round 21 [22.10.2020]
Helsingfors IFK - Rovaniemi PS 1-0(0-0)
FC Honka - FC Lahti 2-1(2-0)
FC Inter Turku - TPS Turku 3-0(3-0)
Kuopion PS - Haka Valkeakoski 2-3(1-0)
SJK Seinäjoki - FC Ilves Tampere 1-3(1-3)
Mariehamn - HJK Helsinki 0-5(0-3) [01.11.]

Round 22 [04.11.2020]
Haka Valkeakoski - IFK Mariehamn 0-1(0-1)
FC Lahti - Helsingfors IFK 2-1(0-0)
HJK Helsinki - FC Inter Turku 1-1(0-0)
FC Ilves Tampere - FC Honka 4-1(2-1)
Rovaniemi PS - SJK Seinäjoki 2-3(0-0)
TPS Turku - Kuopion PS 3-2(1-1)

Please note: on 28.10.2020, it was decided to cancel the championship and relegation round due to the COVID-19 pandemic, and the regular season standings after 22 rounds would be considered final.

Final Standings

			Total						Home						Away					
1. **HJK Helsinki**	22	14	6	2	53	-	17	48	6	5	0	27	-	9	8	1	2	26	-	8
2. FC Inter Turku	22	12	5	5	36	-	17	41	9	1	1	24	-	6	3	4	4	12	-	11
3. Kuopion Palloseura	22	12	5	5	39	-	26	41	7	1	3	20	-	14	5	4	2	19	-	12
4. FC Honka Espoo	22	9	10	3	26	-	17	37	5	4	2	13	-	9	4	6	1	13	-	8
5. FC Ilves Tampere	22	10	6	6	37	-	29	36	5	4	2	20	-	12	5	2	4	17	-	17
6. FC Lahti	22	8	8	6	33	-	30	32	4	5	2	15	-	13	4	3	4	18	-	17
7. SJK Seinäjoki	22	8	5	9	27	-	29	29	4	2	5	14	-	17	4	3	4	13	-	12
8. IFK Helsingfors	22	8	4	10	29	-	33	28	4	3	4	13	-	16	4	1	6	16	-	17
9. IFK Mariehamn	22	6	5	11	29	-	43	23	3	3	5	13	-	19	3	2	6	16	-	24
10. FC Haka Valkeakoski	22	5	7	10	25	-	41	22	1	2	8	9	-	25	4	5	2	16	-	16
11. Turun Palloseura Turku	22	6	3	13	23	-	39	21	5	1	5	14	-	15	1	2	8	9	-	24
(Relegation Play-offs)																				
12. Rovaniemen Palloseura *(Relegated)*	22	1	2	19	15	-	51	5	0	2	9	10	-	25	1	0	10	5	-	26

Top goalscorers:	
16 **Roope Vilhelmi Riski**	*HJK Helsinki*
14 Albion Ademi	*IFK Mariehamn*
10 Timo Furuholm	*FC Inter Turku*
9 Jasin-Amin Assehnoun	*FC Lahti*
9 Tim Väyrynen	*HJK Helsinki*

Relegation Play-offs [11-14.11.2020]

Kotkan Työväen Palloilijat - Turun Palloseura Turku	0-0	1-1(0-0)

Kotkan Työväen Palloilijat promoted for the 2021 Veikkausliiga.

NATIONAL CUP
Suomen cup 2020

Group Stage [25.01.-29.02.2020]

Group A
HJK Helsinki - Turun Palloseura Turku	3-0
FC Inter Turku - IFK Mariehamn	3-0
FC Honka Espoo - IFK Helsingfors	1-1
FC Inter Turku - FC Honka Espoo	1-0
IFK Helsingfors - HJK Helsinki	1-2
IFK Mariehamn - Turun Palloseura Turku	1-1
Turun Palloseura Turku - IFK Helsingfors	1-0
FC Honka Espoo - IFK Mariehamn	2-1
HJK Helsinki - FC Inter Turku	1-0
IFK Helsingfors - FC Inter Turku	1-1
Turun Palloseura Turku - FC Honka Espoo	0-0
HJK Helsinki - IFK Mariehamn	3-1
FC Honka Espoo - HJK Helsinki	1-1
FC Inter Turku - Turun Palloseura Turku	1-0
IFK Mariehamn - IFK Helsingfors	2-2

Qualified: HJK Helsinki, FC Inter Turku, FC Honka Espoo, Turun Palloseura Turku

Group B
FC Lahti - FC Ilves Tampere	1-2
Rovaniemen Palloseura - SJK Seinäjoki	1-1
FC Haka Valkeakoski - Kuopion Palloseura	1-1
Kuopion Palloseura - FC Lahti	1-0
SJK Seinäjoki - FC Haka Valkeakoski	1-3
FC Ilves Tampere - Rovaniemen Palloseura	3-1
SJK Seinäjoki - FC Lahti	2-3
FC Ilves Tampere - Kuopion Palloseura	1-1
Rovaniemen Palloseura - FC Haka Valkeakoski	0-1
Kuopion Palloseura - SJK Seinäjoki	1-0
FC Lahti - Rovaniemen Palloseura	2-1
FC Haka Valkeakoski - FC Ilves Tampere	1-1
FC Lahti - FC Haka Valkeakoski	0-1
FC Ilves Tampere - SJK Seinäjoki	3-0
Kuopion Palloseura - Rovaniemen Palloseura	4-0

Qualified: FC Ilves Tampere, Kuopion Palloseura, FC Haka Valkeakoski, FC Ilves Tampere

Group C
Ekenäs IF - IF Gnistan Helsinki	0-4
Mikkelin Palloilijat - Myllykosken Pallo−47	5-1
Musan Salama Pori - Kotkan Työväen Palloilijat	1-2
Kotkan Työväen Palloilijat - Ekenäs IF	2-1
IF Gnistan Helsinki - Mikkelin Palloilijat	1-2
Myllykosken Pallo−47 - Musan Salama Pori	1-2
Musan Salama Pori - Mikkelin Palloilijat	0-3
Kotkan Työväen Palloilijat - IF Gnistan Helsinki	0-0
Ekenäs IF - Myllykosken Pallo−47	2-0
Musan Salama Pori - IF Gnistan Helsinki	1-1
Mikkelin Palloilijat - Ekenäs IF	0-2
Myllykosken Pallo−47 - Kotkan Työväen Palloilijat	0-1
IF Gnistan Helsinki - Myllykosken Pallo−47	2-5
Ekenäs IF - Musan Salama Pori	2-2
Kotkan Työväen Palloilijat - Mikkelin Palloilijat	4-1

Qualified: Kotkan Työväen Palloilijat, Mikkelin Palloilijat

Group D
Kokkolan Palloveikot - AC Oulu	1-1
FF Jaro Jakobstad - AC Kajaani	1-2
Vaasan PS - SJK Akatemia Seinäjoki	0-1
SJK Akatemia Seinäjoki - FF Jaro Jakobstad	2-2
AC Oulu - AC Kajaani	3-1
Kokkolan Palloveikot - Vaasan PS	1-2
FF Jaro Jakobstad - Kokkolan Palloveikot	0-2
Vaasan PS - AC Oulu	2-2
AC Kajaani - SJK Akatemia Seinäjoki	1-0
SJK Akatemia Seinäjoki - Kokkolan Palloveikot	0-6
FF Jaro Jakobstad - AC Oulu	2-3
AC Kajaani - Vaasan PS	1-3
Vaasan PS - FF Jaro Jakobstad	0-2
AC Oulu - SJK Akatemia Seinäjoki	4-0
Kokkolan Palloveikot - AC Kajaani	0-0

Qualified: AC Oulu, Kokkolan Palloveikot

1/8-Finals [16-17.06.2020]				
Kokkolan Palloveikot - HJK Helsinki	0-2(0-1)	KaaPo Kaarina - Kuopion Palloseura	0-2(0-1)
Tikkuliran Palloseura - Turun Palloseura Turku	0-6(0-2)	Jippo Joensuu - FC Inter Turku	0-1(0-1)
Kotkan Työväen Palloilijat - FC Ilves Tampere	0-4(0-2)	PeKa Peli-Karhut - FC Lahti	0-8(0-5)
Mikkelin Palloilijat - FC Haka Valkeakoski	1-3(0-1)	AC Oulu - FC Honka Espoo	0-1(0-1)

Quarter-Finals [23-24.06.2020]			
FC Ilves Tampere - FC Haka Valkeakoski	0-1(0-1)	FC Inter Turku - Kuopion Palloseura	4-4 aet; 4-2 pen
Turun Palloseura Turku - HJK Helsinki	0-1(0-0)	FC Honka Espoo - FC Lahti	0-1(0-1)

Semi-Finals [27-28.06.2020]			
FC Haka Valkeakoski - HJK Helsinki	2-3(1-2)	FC Inter Turku - FC Lahti	5-0(1-0)

Final

03.10.2020; Veritas Stadion, Turku; Referee: Petri Viljanen; Attendance: 2,500
HJK Helsinki - FC Inter Turku   **2-0(1-0)**

HJK Helsinki: Antonio Reguero Chapinal, Luis Carlos Murillo, Miro Tenho, Valtteri Moren (11.Daniel Michael O'Shaughnessy), Bubacar Boi Djaló (46.Markus Halsti), Riku Riski, Lucas Lingman, Rasmus Schüller, Atomu Tanaka (85.David Eric Browne), Roope Vilhelmi Riski (77.Tim Väyrynen), Nikolai Aleksanteri Alho. Trainer: Toni Koskela.

FC Inter Turku: Henrik Moisander, Jesper Engström (63.Noah Nurmi), Rick Ketting, Arttu Hoskonen, Martti Haukioja (63.Matias Ojala), Connor James Ruane, Filip Valenčič, Álvaro Muñiz Cegarra (77.Elias Mastokangas), Aleksi Paananen (75.Anthony Annan), Timo Furuholm, Taiki Kagayama (62.Benjamin Källman). Trainer: José Riveiro (Spain).

Goals: 1-0 Roope Vilhelmi Riski (3), 2-0 Roope Vilhelmi Riski (54).

THE CLUBS 2020

Football Club Valkeakosken Haka

Founded:	1934		
Stadium:	Tehtaan kenttä, Valkeakoski (3,516)		
Trainer:	Teemu Tainio		27.11.1979

Goalkeepers:	DOB	M	(s)	G
Michael Hartmann (USA)	13.06.1994	10		
Joonas Immonen	05.09.1997	1		
Jakob Tånnander (SWE)	10.08.2000	11		
Defenders:	**DOB**	**M**	**(s)**	**G**
Luiyi Ramón de Lucas Pérez (DOM)	31.08.1994	8	(1)	1
Niklas Friberg	14.03.1996	19		1
Jonas Häkkinen (CAN)	21.03.1999	14	(3)	
Jami Kyöstilä	02.03.1996	19	(2)	
Johannes Kytilä	19.01.2000	1		
Seth Saarinen	05.05.2001	6	(5)	
Ville-Valtteri Starck	03.02.1995	3	(1)	
Midfielders:	**DOB**	**M**	**(s)**	**G**
Leevi Antinaho	27.08.2002		(2)	
Jacob Bushue (USA)	15.05.1992	18	(2)	
Henri Malundama	08.06.1995	19	(3)	1
Mohamed Kamara „Medo" (SLE)	16.11.1987	14	(4)	1
Anton Popovitch	11.07.1996	18	(2)	2
Tino Purme	14.03.1998	7	(14)	1
Maximus Tainio	24.05.2001	6	(7)	
Forwards:	**DOB**	**M**	**(s)**	**G**
Samuel Chidi (NGA)	26.09.1990	18	(1)	3
Antto Hilska	22.09.1993	11	(7)	2
Saibou Keïta (NOR)	22.10.1997	6	(3)	2
Akseli Lehtojuuri	24.06.2001		(3)	
Eero Markkanen	03.07.1991	15	(5)	4
Salomo Ojala	17.04.1997	16	(4)	6
Jonni Thusberg	28.02.1997	2	(12)	

Football Club Honka Espoo

Founded:	1957		
Stadium:	Tapiolan Urheilupuisto, Espoo (6,000)		
Trainer:	Vesa Vasara		16.08.1976

Goalkeepers:	DOB	M	(s)	G
Tim Murray (USA)	30.07.1987	16		
Markus Uusitalo	15.05.1997	6		
Defenders:	**DOB**	**M**	**(s)**	**G**
Henri Aalto	20.04.1989	12	(2)	
Edmund Arko-Mensah (GHA)	09.09.2001	2	(15)	
Nasiru Banahene (HUN)	08.07.2000	7	(1)	1
Dani Hatakka	12.03.1994	12	(4)	
Tapio Heikkilä	08.04.1990	15		1
Robert Ivanov	19.09.1994	9	(1)	
Ville Koski	27.01.2002		(1)	
Rui Manuel Muati Modesto (POR)	07.10.1999		(3)	
Midfielders:	**DOB**	**M**	**(s)**	**G**
Duarte Cartaxo-Tammilehto	15.02.1990	10	(11)	
Javier Hervás Salmoral „Javi Hervás" (ESP)	09.06.1989	20	(2)	1
Jonas Levänen	12.01.1994	17	(2)	
Lucas Paz Kaufmann (BRA)	26.03.1991	19	(3)	2
Roope Pyyskänen	08.04.2002		(1)	
Konsta Rasimus	15.12.1990	19	(1)	1
Niilo Saarikivi	06.06.2003		(2)	
Arlind Sejdiu	11.08.2001	2	(7)	
Jerry Voutilainen	29.03.1995	14	(7)	
Forwards:	**DOB**	**M**	**(s)**	**G**
Juan Diego Alegría Arango (COL)	06.06.2002		(6)	
Robbie Azodo	23.04.2001		(1)	
Borjas Martín González (ESP)	28.06.1987	21	(1)	4
Jean Marie Dongou Tsafack (CMR)	20.04.1995	10	(3)	8
Elmo Heinonen	02.04.1997		(7)	
Macoumba Kandji (SEN)	02.08.1985	13	(4)	4
Demba Savage (GAM)	17.06.1988	18	(2)	2

Football Club International Turku

Founded: 1990
Stadium: Veritas Stadion, Turku (10,000)
Trainer: José Riveiro (ESP)　　　15.09.1975

Goalkeepers:	DOB	M	(s)	G
Aati Marttinen	26.12.1997	5		
Henrik Moisander	29.09.1985	17		
Defenders:	**DOB**	**M**	**(s)**	**G**
Jesper Engström	24.04.1992	9	(6)	1
Juuso Hämäläinen	30.11.1992	11	(3)	
Martti Haukioja	06.10.1999	10	(5)	
Arttu Hoskonen	16.04.1997	16	(1)	1
Rick Ketting (NED)	15.01.1996	21		2
Noah Nurmi	06.02.2001	9	(5)	
Connor James Ruane (ENG)	15.11.1993	19	(2)	3

Midfielders:	DOB	M	(s)	G
Álvaro Muñiz Cegarra (ESP)	07.09.1988	20	(1)	
Anthony Gildas Kofi Annan (GHA)	21.07.1986	9	(7)	1
Kevin Kouassivi-Benissan	25.01.1999	12	(7)	1
Elias Mastokangas	01.02.2001	12	(7)	2
Matias Ojala	28.02.1995	6	(8)	1
Aleksi Paananen	25.01.1993	18	(3)	3
Filip Valenčič (SVN)	07.01.1992	7		2
Forwards:	**DOB**	**M**	**(s)**	**G**
Timo Furuholm	11.10.1987	19	(2)	10
Taiki Kagayama (JPN)	14.05.1996	12	(10)	4
Benjamin Källman	17.06.1998	7	(3)	4
Ellinton Antonio Costa Morais „Liliu" (BRA)	30.03.1990	3	(14)	1

Football Club Lahti

Founded: 1996
Stadium: Lahden Stadion, Lahti (15,000)
Trainer: Ilir Zeneli　　　15.01.1984

Goalkeepers:	DOB	M	(s)	G
Patrick Rakovsky (CZE)	02.06.1993	18		
Joona Tiainen	07.05.2000	4		
Defenders:	**DOB**	**M**	**(s)**	**G**
Kari Arkivuo	23.06.1983	19	(2)	1
Jean-Christophe Coubronne (FRA)	30.07.1989	18		1
Lassi Forss	15.01.2002	2	(2)	
Viljami Isotalo	04.06.1998	3	(10)	
Timi Lahti	28.06.1990	20	(1)	1
Mikko Viitikko	18.04.1995	21		1
Midfielders:	**DOB**	**M**	**(s)**	**G**
Arttu Auranen	02.09.1999		(2)	1
Akoete Eninful (TOG)	21.07.1992	21		

	DOB	M	(s)	G
Teemu Jäntti	02.03.2000	8	(6)	1
Matti Klinga	10.12.1994	12	(4)	
Mikko Kuningas	30.07.1997	20	(2)	3
Valdrin Rashica (ALB)	14.12.1992	6	(13)	
Arlind Sejdiu	11.08.2001	2	(2)	
Eemeli Virta	28.09.2000	9	(7)	1
Forwards:	**DOB**	**M**	**(s)**	**G**
Jasin Assehnoun	26.12.1998	20	(2)	9
Vahid Hambo	03.02.1995	11	(6)	3
Dimitry Imbongo Boele (FRA)	28.03.1990	15	(3)	6
Pyry Lampinen	07.03.2002	3	(11)	2
Altin Zeqiri	01.03.2000	10	(10)	2

Idrottsföreningen Kamraterna Helsingfors

Founded: 1897
Stadium: Bolt Arena, Helsinki (10,770)
Trainer: Tor Thodesen (NOR)　　　03.03.1966
(21.07.2020)　Teemu Kankkunen　　　13.01.1980

Goalkeepers:	DOB	M	(s)	G
Otto Huuhtanen	28.02.2000	1		
Arnold Origi Otieno (KEN)	15.11.1983	21		
Defenders:	**DOB**	**M**	**(s)**	**G**
Tuukka Andberg	01.05.1998	6	(1)	
Eero-Matti Auvinen	05.03.1996	15		1
Sakari Mattila	14.07.1989	16	(1)	4
Joel Mero	07.02.1995	10	(1)	
Tino Palmasto	09.10.1998	1	(1)	
Hannu Patronen	23.05.1984	17		1
Midfielders:	**DOB**	**M**	**(s)**	**G**
Jani Bäckman	20.03.1988	13	(3)	2
Adama Fofana (CIV)	04.01.2001	14	(5)	1
Jukka Halme	30.11.1984	11	(4)	

	DOB	M	(s)	G
Matias Hänninen	15.03.1991	5	(4)	
Riku Selander	22.11.1994	16	(3)	
Moshtagh Yaghoubi	08.11.1994	15	(2)	1
Forwards:	**DOB**	**M**	**(s)**	**G**
John Fagerström	27.07.1998	7	(8)	1
Kevin Larsson	15.09.2001	3	(6)	
Luis Henrique Farinhas Taffner (BRA)	17.03.1998	7	(5)	4
Foday Manneh (GAM)	14.01.2000		(7)	1
Joel Mattsson	17.03.1999	19	(2)	1
Nikolas Saira	11.02.1999		(1)	
Jabar Sharza (AFG)	06.04.1994	8	(7)	2
Erikson Carlos Batista dos Santos „Tiquinho" (BRA)	26.02.1995	7	(1)	1
Sakari Tukiainen	02.10.1991	17	(3)	5
João Victor Souza dos Santos „Vitinho" (BRA)	08.09.1998	13	(3)	4

Helsingin Jalkapalloklubi

Founded: 19.06.1907
Stadium: Bolt Arena, Helsinki (10,770)
Trainer: Toni Koskela　　　16.02.1983

Goalkeepers:	DOB	M	(s)	G
Hugo Keto	09.02.1998	7		
Antonio Reguero Chapinal (ESP)	04.07.1982	15		
Defenders:	**DOB**	**M**	**(s)**	**G**
Rico Finnäs	14.10.2000		(1)	
Markus Olof Halsti	19.03.1984	4	(2)	1
Valtteri Moren	15.06.1991	9	(1)	
Luis Carlos Murillo (COL)	16.10.1990	19	(1)	
Daniel Michael O'Shaughnessy	14.09.1994	16	(5)	
Ivan Ostojić (SRB)	26.06.1989	7	(6)	
Miro Tenho	02.04.1995	14		1
Henri Toivomäki	21.02.1991	5	(6)	
Midfielders:	**DOB**	**M**	**(s)**	**G**
Bubacar Boi Djaló (POR)	02.02.1997	12	(5)	
Pyry Petteri Hannola	21.10.2001	1	(5)	

	DOB	M	(s)	G
Ferhan Hasani (MKD)	18.06.1990	7	(2)	5
Lucas Lingman	25.01.1998	18	(2)	2
Riku Riski	16.08.1989	19	(2)	4
Rasmus Schüller	18.06.1991	15	(2)	3
Atomu Tanaka (JPN)	04.10.1987	14	(5)	5
Santeri Väänänen	01.01.2002	3	(5)	
Joonas Vahtera	06.01.1996		(3)	
Eetu Vertainen	11.05.1999	4	(8)	2
Forwards:	**DOB**	**M**	**(s)**	**G**
Nikolai Aleksanteri Alho	12.03.1993	18	(3)	
David Eric Browne (PNG)	27.12.1995	7	(7)	2
Kai Meriluoto	02.01.2003		(3)	1
Roope Vilhelmi Riski	16.08.1991	17	(3)	16
Casper Terho	24.06.2003		(3)	
Tim Väyrynen	30.03.1993	11	(10)	9

Idrottsföreningen Kamraterna Mariehamn

Founded: 1919
Stadium: Wiklöf Holding Arena, Mariehamn (4,000)
Trainer: Lukas Syberyjski (SWE) 02.07.1981

Goalkeepers:	DOB	M	(s)	G
Oskari Forsman	28.01.1988	22		
Defenders:	DOB	M	(s)	G
Robin Buwalda (NED)	17.08.1994	10	(1)	
Frans Grönlund	26.03.2000		(3)	1
Tarik Hamza (SWE)	23.02.1997	1	(8)	
Lassi Järvenpää	28.10.1996	11	(9)	
Aapo Mäenpää	14.01.1998	15	(3)	
Chinaecherem Frankline Okoye (NGA)	06.05.1999	6	(9)	
Mikko Sumusalo	12.03.1990	20		
Kalle Taimi	27.01.1992	22		
Midfielders:	DOB	M	(s)	G
Gustaf Backaliden (SWE)	15.09.1997	21		3
Yanga Baliso (RSA)	27.03.1997	1	(2)	

Dmytro Bilonoh (UKR)	26.05.1995	5	(5)	1
Joel Karlstrom	17.05.2001	4	(7)	1
Vesa Johannes Laaksonen	13.12.1990		(9)	
Niilo Mäenpää	14.01.1998	19	(2)	
Peter Makrillos (AUS)	04.09.1995	16	(2)	4
Saku Ylätupa	04.08.1999	5	(3)	
Forwards:	DOB	M	(s)	G
Albion Ademi (ALB)	19.02.1999	22		14
Alain Richard Ebwelle (CMR)	28.09.1995		(5)	
Akseli Pelvas	08.02.1989	16	(4)	3
Riku Sjöroos	10.03.1995	18	(1)	1
Maximo Tolonen	04.03.2001	6	(14)	
Ivan Yagan (ARM)	11.10.1989	2	(2)	

Tampereen Ilves

Founded: 1931
Stadium: Tammelan Stadion, Tampere (5,040)
Trainer: Jarkko Wiss 17.04.1972

Goalkeepers:	DOB	M	(s)	G
Mika Hilander	17.08.1983	15		
Eetu Huuhtanen	31.01.2003	1		
Matias Riikonen	24.02.2002	6		
Defenders:	DOB	M	(s)	G
Mikael Almen	08.03.2000	16	(3)	2
Felipe Aspegren	12.02.1994	16	(4)	
Tuure Mäntynen	17.01.2000	5	(5)	
Baba Mensah (GHA)	20.08.1994	6	(1)	
Tatu Miettunen	24.04.1995	17	(1)	
Juho Pietola	06.04.2002	2	(2)	
Miska Rautiola	20.06.1998	9	(1)	
Janne Saksela	14.03.1993	5	(3)	
Diogo Tomas	31.07.1997	19	(1)	3
Midfielders:	DOB	M	(s)	G
Lauri Ala-Myllymäki	04.06.1997	18	(3)	7
Doni Arifi	11.04.2002	5	(4)	
Jair Tavares da Silva (BRA)	03.08.1994	20		3

Iiro Järvinen	03.11.1996	9	(8)	
Oiva Jukkola	21.05.2002		(2)	
Janne-Pekka Laine	25.01.2001	2	(6)	
Yussif Daouda Moussa (NIG)	04.09.1998		(1)	
Tuure Siira	25.10.1994	7	(13)	
Naatan Skyttä	07.05.2002	13	(3)	7
Maksim Stjopin	08.04.2003	1	(2)	2
Emile Tendeng (SEN)	09.03.1992	4	(5)	
Joona Veteli	21.04.1995	10	(1)	3
Forwards:	DOB	M	(s)	G
Tiémoko Fofana (CIV)	22.10.1999	10	(7)	2
Ilari Mettälä	26.04.1994	4	(4)	5
Gaëtan Missi Mezu Kouakou (GAB)	04.05.1996	7	(2)	1
Eetu Mömmö	04.05.2002	7	(11)	1
Eemeli Raittinen	03.02.2000	3	(5)	
Stênio Garcia Dutra (BRA)	29.06.1994	1	(4)	
Eero Tamminen	19.05.1995	4	(5)	1

Kuopion Palloseura

Founded: 1923
Stadium: Savon Sanomat Areena, Kuopio (5,000)
Trainer: Arne Erlandsen (NOR) 20.12.1959

Goalkeepers:	DOB	M	(s)	G
Otso Virtanen	03.04.1994	22		
Defenders:	DOB	M	(s)	G
Mats Haakenstad (NOR)	14.11.1993		(2)	
Luc Landry Tabi Manga (CMR)	17.11.1994	17	(1)	2
Jiri Nissinen	30.05.1997	7	(5)	1
Nuno Miguel Adro Tomás (POR)	15.09.1995	17		
Juho Pirttijoki	30.07.1996	14		1
Saku Savolainen	13.08.1996	21	(1)	1
Igors Tarasovs (LVA)	16.10.1988	3	(5)	
Midfielders:	DOB	M	(s)	G
Bismark Adjei-Boateng (GHA)	10.05.1994	18	(1)	2
Arttu Heinonen	22.04.1999	2	(5)	
Tommi Jyry	16.08.1999	1		

Urho Nissilä	04.04.1996	20		5
Petteri Pennanen	19.09.1990	15	(3)	3
Artur Pikk (EST)	05.03.1993	8		
Ville Saxman	15.11.1989	20	(1)	2
Joel Vartiainen	14.03.1994	4	(4)	
Forwards:	DOB	M	(s)	G
Bruno Miguel Braz Rodrigues (POR)	03.10.1996	1	(4)	
Ilmari Niskanen	27.10.1997	12	(1)	6
Pedro Vitor Ferreira da Silva (BRA)	20.03.1998		(4)	
Ats Purje (EST)	03.08.1985	3	(11)	1
Lucas Rangel Nunes Gonvalves (BRA)	29.12.1994	11	(2)	4
Usman Sani Hassan Sale (NGA)	27.08.1995	18	(1)	2
Aniekpeno Christopher Udoh (NGA)	11.11.1996	8	(13)	7

Rovaniemen Palloseura

Founded: 1950
Stadium: Rovaniemen keskuskenttä, Rovaniemi (4,000)
Trainer: Vesa Tauriainen 16.12.1967
(16.09.2020) Mikko Mannila 02.03.1975

Goalkeepers:	DOB	M	(s)	G
Martin Kompalla (GER)	26.08.1992	6		
Sammy N'Djock (CMR)	25.02.1990	4		
Matias Niemelä	15.03.2002	11		
Mikko Rantala	21.01.1994	1		
Defenders:	DOB	M	(s)	G
Juho Hyvärinen	27.03.2000	22		1
Eerik Kantola	09.03.2000	5	(2)	
Kalle Katz	04.01.2000	17		
Simo Majander	02.08.1996	7	(3)	
Jussi Niska	15.08.2002	16	(4)	
Samuel Olawunmi Olabisi (NGA)	17.11.1993	3	(5)	
Atte Sihvonen	18.02.1996	17		
Zurab Tsiskaridze (GEO)	08.12.1986	14	(1)	1
Midfielders:	DOB	M	(s)	G
Kirill Bullat	08.06.2003		(1)	

Rasmus Degerman	23.04.2001	3	(17)	
Tommi Jäntti	07.03.2000	3	(3)	
Tuomas Kaukua	13.10.2000	13	(5)	2
Obed Malolo	18.04.1997	19		
Eetu Muinonen	05.04.1986	13		1
Veka Pyyny	04.01.2000	3	(12)	
Joonas Vahtera	06.01.1996	13		2
Forwards:	DOB	M	(s)	G
Sampo Ala	18.01.2002	3	(9)	
Enoch Banza	04.02.2000	12	(4)	2
Daniel Clive Carr (TRI)	29.05.1994	7		
Raymond Gyasi (NED)	05.08.1994	3		
Aleksandr Kokko	04.06.1987	6	(1)	1
Jarkko Luiro	22.03.1998		(2)	
Youness Rahimi	13.02.1995	8	(1)	1
Matias Tamminen	21.11.2001	13	(8)	3

Seinäjoen Jalkapallokerho

Founded:	05.11.2007	
Stadium:	OmaSP Stadion, Seinäjoki (6,000)	
Trainer:	Jani Honkavaara	02.02.1976

Goalkeepers:	DOB	M	(s)	G
Jesse Öst	20.10.1990	14		
Walter Viitala	09.01.1992	8		
Defenders:	**DOB**	**M**	**(s)**	**G**
Nikko Boxall (NZL)	24.02.1992	17		
Dárvin Francisco Chávez Ramírez (MEX)	21.11.1989	2	(2)	
Tero Mäntylä	18.04.1991	19	(1)	
Niko Markkula	27.06.1990	12	(2)	1
Murilo Henrique de Araujo Santos (BRA)	02.12.1995	10		1
Joonas Sundman	20.01.1998		(5)	
Ville Tikkanen	08.08.1999	14		
Midfielders:	**DOB**	**M**	**(s)**	**G**
Jude Arthur (GHA)	08.06.1999	6	(7)	
Mehmet Hetemaj	08.12.1987	11	(6)	4
Matej Hradecký	17.04.1995	19		2
Keaton Isaksson	21.04.1994	5	(9)	
Emmanuel Jorge Ledesma (ARG)	24.05.1988	11		5
Anel Raskaj (SWE)	19.08.1989	8	(5)	
Robin Sid	21.09.1994	9	(5)	
Matias Vainionpää	02.10.2001	14	(1)	
Forwards:	**DOB**	**M**	**(s)**	**G**
Serge Atakayi	30.01.1999	15	(3)	1
Daniel Håkans	26.10.2000	6	(5)	
William Greenwell Ions (ENG)	11.03.1994	3	(6)	
Jake Mario Jervis (ENG)	17.09.1991	7	(2)	3
Jyri Kiuru	09.02.2000		(1)	
Joonas Lepistö	22.06.1998	7	(7)	4
Ariel Thierry Ngueukam (CMR)	15.11.1988	14	(4)	4
Denys Oliynyk (UKR)	16.06.1987	11	(9)	2
Jeremiah Streng	08.11.2001		(1)	

Turun Palloseura Turku

Founded:	1922	
Stadium:	Veritas Stadion, Turku (10,000)	
Trainer:	Tommi Pikkarainen	06.12.1969
(27.07.2020)	Jonatan Lillebror Johansson (SWE)	16.08.1975

Goalkeepers:	DOB	M	(s)	G
Jere Koponen	23.05.1992	22		
Defenders:	**DOB**	**M**	**(s)**	**G**
Aldayr Hernández Basanta (COL)	04.08.1995	21		2
Jean Carlos de Brito (BRA)	09.06.1995	7	(3)	1
Juri Kinnunen	09.03.1990	1	(5)	
Juhani Pikkarainen	30.07.1998	7	(3)	1
Sami Rähmönen	19.04.1987	12	(2)	
Tatu Varmanen	09.07.1998	18	(2)	
Midfielders:	**DOB**	**M**	**(s)**	**G**
Masahudu Alhassan (GHA)	01.12.1992	17		1
Rasmus Holma	13.09.1992	18	(1)	3
Jesper Karlsson	07.02.2000	3	(1)	
Juho Lähde	11.02.1991	7	(4)	
Joakim Latonen	24.02.1998	9	(7)	1
Alim Moundi (CMR)	03.02.1995	18	(3)	
Jonni Peräaho	05.02.1994	5	(6)	1
Santeri Pohjolainen	05.08.2002		(1)	
Niklas Pyyhtiä	25.09.2003	8	(8)	1
Jami Siirtola	09.10.1996		(2)	
Rodney Strasser (SLE)	30.03.1990	5	(2)	
Forwards:	**DOB**	**M**	**(s)**	**G**
Mika Ääritalo	25.07.1985	12	(5)	4
Babacar Diop (SEN)	21.10.1993	3	(7)	
Eliécer Espinosa Calvo (COL)	12.03.1996		(1)	
Santeri Haarala	17.12.1999	12	(1)	4
Elmo Heinonen	02.04.1997		(3)	
Oskari Jakonen	22.04.1997	11	(8)	
Albijon Muzaci	06.11.1996	14	(5)	1
Onnipekka Pajula	23.06.2003		(2)	
Olawale Tehe (CIV)	20.02.1999	12	(9)	3

SECOND LEVEL
Ykkönen 2020

1.	AC Oulu (*Promoted*)	22	15	5	2	38	-	16	50
2.	Kotkan Työväen Palloilijat (*Promotion Play-offs*)	22	14	5	3	51	-	23	47
3.	FF Jaro Jakobstad	22	12	5	5	50	-	31	41
4.	Ekenäs IF	22	10	6	6	45	-	25	36
5.	Musan Salama Pori	22	10	4	8	38	-	38	34
6.	Vaasan Palloseura	22	9	6	7	37	-	36	33
7.	Mikkelin Palloilijat	22	8	5	9	29	-	35	29
8.	Kokkolan Palloveikot	22	8	4	10	38	-	34	28
9.	IF Gnistan Helsinki	22	7	4	11	38	-	49	25
10.	AC Kajaani (*Relegated*)	22	5	8	9	35	-	37	23
11.	SJK Akatemia Seinäjoki (*Relegated*)	22	4	3	15	22	-	49	15
12.	Myllykosken Pallo−47 (*Relegated*)	22	1	3	18	21	-	69	6

INTERNATIONAL MATCHES
(16.07.2020 – 15.07.2021)

Date	Venue	Match	Result	Comp
03.09.2020	Helsinki	Finland - Wales	0-1(0-0)	(UNL)
06.09.2020	Dublin	Republic of Ireland - Finland	0-1(0-0)	(UNL)
07.10.2020	Gdańsk	Poland - Finland	5-1(3-0)	(F)
11.10.2020	Helsinki	Finland - Bulgaria	2-0(0-0)	(UNL)
14.10.2020	Helsinki	Finland - Republic of Ireland	1-0(0-0)	(UNL)
11.11.2020	Paris	France - Finland	0-2(0-2)	(F)
15.11.2020	Sofia	Bulgaria - Finland	1-2(0-2)	(UNL)
18.11.2020	Cardiff	Wales - Finland	3-1(1-0)	(UNL)
24.03.2021	Helsinki	Finland - Bosnia and Herzegovina	2-2(0-0)	(WCQ)
28.03.2021	Kyiv	Ukraine - Finland	1-1(0-0)	(WCQ)
31.03.2021	St. Gallen	Switzerland - Finland	3-2(1-2)	(F)
29.05.2021	Stockholm	Sweden - Finland	2-0(1-0)	(F)
04.06.2021	Helsinki	Finland - Estonia	0-1(0-0)	(F)
12.06.2021	København	Denmark - Finland	0-1(0-0)	(EC)
16.06.2021	Saint Petersburg	Finland - Russia	0-1(0-1)	(EC)
21.06.2021	Saint Petersburg	Finland - Belgium	0-2(0-0)	(EC)

03.09.2020 FINLAND - WALES 0-1(0-0) 2nd UEFA Nations League B, Group 4
Olympiastadion, Helsinki; Referee: Daniel Siebert (Germany); Attendance: 0
FIN: Lukáš Hrádecký, Juhani Lauri Henrik Ojala, Jere Juhani Uronen, Daniel Michael O'Shaughnessy, Leo Väisänen, Tim Sparv (Cap) (76.Thomas Anton Rudolph Lam), Joni Kauko (71.Hans Fredrik Jensen), Glen Adjei Kamara, Ilmari Niskanen (86.Pyry Henri Hidipo Soiri), Teemu Eino Antero Pukki, Joel Julius Ilmari Pohjanpalo. Trainer: Markku Kanerva.

06.09.2020 REPUBLIC OF IRELAND - FINLAND 0-1(0-0) 2nd UEFA Nations League B, Group 4
Aviva Stadium, Dublin; Referee: Fabio Maresca (Italy); Attendance: 0
FIN: Lukáš Hrádecký, Juhani Lauri Henrik Ojala, Nikolai Aleksanteri Alho, Daniel Michael O'Shaughnessy, Leo Väisänen, Nicholas Antero Hämäläinen (79.Jere Juhani Uronen), Tim Sparv (Cap), Robert Thomas Taylor, Glen Adjei Kamara, Teemu Eino Antero Pukki (90+1.Rasmus Joonatan Karjalainen), Joel Julius Ilmari Pohjanpalo (63.Hans Fredrik Jensen). Trainer: Markku Kanerva.
Goal: Hans Fredrik Jensen (64).

07.10.2020 POLAND - FINLAND 5-1(3-0) Friendly International
Stadion Energa, Gdańsk; Referee: Michal Očenáš (Slovakia); Attendance: 3,000
FIN: Jesse Pekka Joronen, Juha Markus Pirinen (46.Robert Thomas Taylor), Juhani Lauri Henrik Ojala, Nikolai Aleksanteri Alho, Daniel Michael O'Shaughnessy (46.Jere Juhani Uronen), Thomas Anton Rudolph Lam (46.Ilmari Niskanen), Leo Väisänen, Rasmus Schüller (Cap), Joni Kauko (62.Glen Adjei Kamara), Joel Julius Ilmari Pohjanpalo (62.Rasmus Joonatan Karjalainen), Hans Fredrik Jensen (82.Pyry Henri Hidipo Soiri). Trainer: Markku Kanerva.
Goal: Ilmari Niskanen (68).

11.10.2020 FINLAND - BULGARIA 2-0(0-0) 2nd UEFA Nations League B, Group 4
Olympiastadion, Helsinki; Referee: Erik Lambrechts (Belgium); Attendance: 6,587
FIN: Lukáš Hrádecký, Jukka Raitala, Paulus Verneri Arajuuri, Joona Marko Aleksi Toivio, Jere Juhani Uronen, Tim Sparv (Cap), Robert Thomas Taylor (74.Pyry Henri Hidipo Soiri), Glen Adjei Kamara, Ilmari Niskanen (87.Nikolai Aleksanteri Alho), Joel Julius Ilmari Pohjanpalo (65.Hans Fredrik Jensen), Teemu Eino Antero Pukki (87.Rasmus Joonatan Karjalainen). Trainer: Markku Kanerva.
Goals: Robert Thomas Taylor (52), Hans Fredrik Jensen (67).

14.10.2020 FINLAND - REPUBLIC OF IRELAND 1-0(0-0) 2nd UEFA Nations League B, Group 4
Olympiastadion, Helsinki; Referee: Lionel Tschudi (Switzerland); Attendance: 7,900
FIN: Lukáš Hrádecký, Paulus Verneri Arajuuri, Joona Marko Aleksi Toivio, Albin Granlund (86.Jukka Raitala), Jere Juhani Uronen, Tim Sparv (Cap), Robert Thomas Taylor, Pyry Henri Hidipo Soiri (46.Ilmari Niskanen), Glen Adjei Kamara (75.Rasmus Schüller), Teemu Eino Antero Pukki (81.Joel Julius Ilmari Pohjanpalo), Hans Fredrik Jensen (86.Joni Kauko). Trainer: Markku Kanerva.
Goal: Hans Fredrik Jensen (66).

11.11.2020 FRANCE - FINLAND 0-2(0-2) Friendly International
Stade de France, Saint-Denis, Paris; Referee: Nikola Popov (Bulgaria); Attendance: 0
FIN: Jesse Pekka Joronen, Juhani Lauri Henrik Ojala (66.Joona Marko Aleksi Toivio), Daniel Michael O'Shaughnessy, Leo Väisänen (75.Paulus Verneri Arajuuri), Nicholas Antero Hämäläinen, Rasmus Schüller (Cap) (80.Teemu Eino Antero Pukki), Joni Kauko, Onni Valakari (75.Robert Thomas Taylor), Rasmus Joonatan Karjalainen (67.Glen Adjei Kamara), Ilmari Niskanen (67.Nikolai Aleksanteri Alho), Marcus Forss. Trainer: Markku Kanerva.
Goals: Marcus Forss (28), Onni Valakari (31).

15.11.2020 BULGARIA - FINLAND 1-2(0-2) 2nd UEFA Nations League B, Group 4
Nationalen Stadion "Vasil Levski", Sofia; Referee: Donatas Rumšas (Lithuania); Attendance: 0
FIN: Lukáš Hrádecký, Paulus Verneri Arajuuri, Joona Marko Aleksi Toivio, Nikolai Aleksanteri Alho, Jere Juhani Uronen, Tim Sparv (Cap) (68.Rasmus Schüller), Robert Thomas Taylor (68.Pyry Henri Hidipo Soiri), Robin Lod, Glen Adjei Kamara, Joel Julius Ilmari Pohjanpalo (35.Marcus Forss), Teemu Eino Antero Pukki (89.Ilmari Niskanen). Trainer: Markku Kanerva.
Goals: Teemu Eino Antero Pukki (7), Robin Lod (45+1).

18.11.2020 WALES - FINLAND 3-1(1-0) 2nd UEFA Nations League B, Group 4
Cardiff City Stadium, Cardiff; Referee: Jesús Gil Manzano (Spain); Attendance: 0
FIN: Lukáš Hrádecký, Paulus Verneri Arajuuri (Cap), Joona Marko Aleksi Toivio, Nikolai Aleksanteri Alho, Jere Juhani Uronen, Daniel Michael O'Shaughnessy (61.Nicholas Antero Hämäläinen), Robert Thomas Taylor (61.Pyry Henri Hidipo Soiri), Robin Lod, Glen Adjei Kamara, Rasmus Schüller (73.Onni Valakari), Teemu Eino Antero Pukki (89.Marcus Forss). Trainer: Markku Kanerva.
Goal: Teemu Eino Antero Pukki (63).

24.03.2021   FINLAND - BOSNIA AND HERZEGOVINA   2-2(0-0)   22nd FIFA WC.Qualifiers
Olympiastadion, Helsinki; Referee: Anastasios Sidiropoulos (Greece); Attendance: 0
FIN: Jesse Pekka Joronen, Jukka Raitala, Paulus Verneri Arajuuri (Cap), Joona Marko Aleksi Toivio, Nikolai Aleksanteri Alho, Nicholas Antero Hämäläinen, Joni Kauko (82.Tim Sparv), Robin Lod (77.Joel Julius Ilmari Pohjanpalo), Glen Adjei Kamara, Onni Valakari (46.Rasmus Schüller), Teemu Eino Antero Pukki. Trainer: Markku Kanerva.
Goals: Teemu Eino Antero Pukki (58, 77).

28.03.2021   UKRAINE - FINLAND   1-1(0-0)   22nd FIFA WC.Qualifiers
NSC Olimpiyskiy Stadium, Kyiv; Referee: István Kovács (Romania); Attendance: 0
FIN: Jesse Pekka Joronen, Jukka Raitala (76.Nicholas Antero Hämäläinen), Paulus Verneri Arajuuri (Cap), Joona Marko Aleksi Toivio, Albin Granlund (17.Nikolai Aleksanteri Alho), Daniel Michael O'Shaughnessy, Rasmus Schüller (76.Robert Thomas Taylor), Joni Kauko (68.Joel Julius Ilmari Pohjanpalo), Robin Lod, Glen Adjei Kamara, Teemu Eino Antero Pukki. Trainer: Markku Kanerva.
Goal: Teemu Eino Antero Pukki (89 penalty).

31.03.2021   SWITZERLAND - FINLAND   3-2(1-2)   Friendly International
Kybunpark, St. Gallen; Referee: Manuel Schüttengruber (Austria); Attendance: 0
FIN: Jesse Pekka Joronen (46.Niki Emil Antonio Mäenpää), Juha Markus Pirinen, Juhani Lauri Henrik Ojala (Cap), Daniel Michael O'Shaughnessy, Robert Ivanov, Robert Thomas Taylor, Pyry Henri Hidipo Soiri (77.Nikolai Aleksanteri Alho), Thomas Anton Rudolph Lam (65.Glen Adjei Kamara), Onni Valakari (77.Rasmus Schüller), Joel Julius Ilmari Pohjanpalo (77.Teemu Eino Antero Pukki), Marcus Forss (65.Robin Lod). Trainer: Markku Kanerva.
Goals: Joel Julius Ilmari Pohjanpalo (30, 40 penalty).

29.05.2021   SWEDEN - FINLAND   2-0(1-0)   Friendly International
Friends Arena, Stockholm; Referee: Jakob Kehlet (Denmark); Attendance: 0
FIN: Jesse Pekka Joronen, Juhani Lauri Henrik Ojala (62.Leo Väisänen), Nikolai Aleksanteri Alho (69.Pyry Henri Hidipo Soiri), Jere Juhani Uronen (87.Nicholas Antero Hämäläinen), Sauli Aapo Kasperi Väisänen, Robert Ivanov, Tim Sparv (Cap) (46.Thomas Anton Rudolph Lam), Onni Valakari, Jasin-Amin Assehnoun (46.Joni Kauko), Roope Vilhelmi Riski (62.Hans Fredrik Jensen), Lassi Lappalainen. Trainer: Markku Kanerva.

04.06.2021   FINLAND - ESTONIA   0-1(0-0)   Friendly International
Olympiastadion, Helsinki; Referee: Jørgen Burchardt (Denmark); Attendance: 0
FIN: Lukáš Hrádecký (Cap), Jukka Raitala, Paulus Verneri Arajuuri, Joona Marko Aleksi Toivio (46.Daniel Michael O'Shaughnessy), Leo Väisänen (62.Jere Juhani Uronen), Rasmus Schüller (62.Robert Thomas Taylor), Robin Lod, Pyry Henri Hidipo Soiri (82.Nikolai Aleksanteri Alho), Glen Adjei Kamara, Joel Julius Ilmari Pohjanpalo (61.Teemu Eino Antero Pukki), Marcus Forss (46.Hans Fredrik Jensen). Trainer: Markku Kanerva.

12.06.2021   DENMARK - FINLAND   0-1(0-0)   16th EC. Group Stage.
Parken Stadium, København; Referee: Anthony Taylor (England); Attendance: 15,200
FIN: Lukáš Hrádecký, Jukka Raitala (90.Leo Väisänen), Paulus Verneri Arajuuri, Joona Marko Aleksi Toivio, Jere Juhani Uronen, Daniel Michael O'Shaughnessy, Tim Sparv (Cap) (76.Rasmus Schüller), Robin Lod, Glen Adjei Kamara, Teemu Eino Antero Pukki (76.Joni Kauko), Joel Julius Ilmari Pohjanpalo (84.Marcus Forss). Trainer: Markku Kanerva.
Goal: Joel Julius Ilmari Pohjanpalo (60).
<u>Please note</u>: In the 43rd minute, the match was suspended for two hours after Danish midfielder Christian Eriksen collapsed on the pitch.

16.06.2021   FINLAND - RUSSIA   0-1(0-1)   16th EC. Group Stage.
Krestovsky Stadium, Saint Petersburg; Referee: Danny Desmond Makkelie (Netherlands); Attendance: 24,540
FIN: Lukáš Hrádecký, Jukka Raitala (75.Pyry Henri Hidipo Soiri), Paulus Verneri Arajuuri (Cap), Joona Marko Aleksi Toivio (85.Hans Fredrik Jensen), Jere Juhani Uronen, Daniel Michael O'Shaughnessy, Rasmus Schüller (67.Joni Kauko), Robin Lod, Glen Adjei Kamara, Teemu Eino Antero Pukki (75.Lassi Lappalainen), Joel Julius Ilmari Pohjanpalo. Trainer: Markku Kanerva.

21.06.2021   FINLAND - BELGIUM   0-2(0-0)   16th EC. Group Stage.
Krestovsky Stadium, Saint Petersburg (Russia); Referee: Dr. Felix Brych (Germany); Attendance: 18,545
FIN: Lukáš Hrádecký, Jukka Raitala, Paulus Verneri Arajuuri, Joona Marko Aleksi Toivio, Jere Juhani Uronen (70.Nikolai Aleksanteri Alho), Daniel Michael O'Shaughnessy, Tim Sparv (Cap) (59.Rasmus Schüller), Robin Lod (90+1.Marcus Forss), Glen Adjei Kamara, Joel Julius Ilmari Pohjanpalo (70.Joni Kauko), Teemu Eino Antero Pukki (90+1.Hans Fredrik Jensen). Trainer: Markku Kanerva.

NATIONAL TEAM PLAYERS
(16.07.2020 – 15.07.2021)

Name	DOB	Caps	Goals	2020/2021:	Club
Goalkeepers					
Lukáš HRÁDECKÝ	24.11.1989	68	0	2020/2021:	TSV Bayer 04 Leverkusen (GER)
Jesse Pekka JORONEN	21.03.1993	14	0	2020/2021:	Brescia Calcio (ITA)
Niki Emil Antonio MÄENPÄÄ	23.01.1985	27	0	2021:	Venezia FC (ITA)
Defenders					
Nikolai Aleksanteri ALHO	12.03.1993	13	0	2021:	HJK Helsinki
				15.01.2021->	MTK Budapest FC (HUN)
Paulus Verneri ARAJUURI	15.06.1988	54	3	2020/2021:	Pafos FC Paphos (CYP)
Albin GRANLUND	01.09.1989	19	0	2020:	Örebro SK (SWE)
				07.01.2021->	FKS Stal Mielec (POL)
Nicholas Antero HÄMÄLÄINEN	05.03.1997	7	0	2020/2021:	Queens Park Rangers FC London (ENG)
Robert IVANOV	19.09.1994	4	0	2021:	KS Warta Poznań (POL)
Daniel Michael O'SHAUGHNESSY	14.09.1994	14	0	2020/2021:	HJK Helsinki
Juhani Lauri Henrik OJALA	19.06.1989	32	1	2020/2021:	Vejle BK (DEN)
Juha Markus PIRINEN	22.10.1991	20	0	2020/2021:	AS Trenčín (SVK)
Jukka RAITALA	15.09.1988	59	0	2020:	CF Montréal (CAN)
				28.01.2021->	Minnesota United FC (USA)
Joona Marko Aleksi TOIVIO	10.03.1988	76	3	2020/2021:	BK Häcken Göteborg (SWE)
Jere Juhani URONEN	13.07.1994	52	1	2020/2021:	KRC Genk (BEL)
Leo VÄISÄNEN	23.07.1997	9	0	2020/2021:	IF Elfsborg Borås (SWE)
Sauli Aapo Kasperi VÄISÄNEN	05.06.1994	20	0	2020/2021:	AC Chievo Verona (ITA)
Midfielders					
Jasin-Amin ASSEHNOUN	26.12.1998	1	0	2021:	FC Lahti
Hans Fredrik JENSEN	09.09.1997	20	7	2020/2021:	FC Augsburg (GER)
Glen Adjei KAMARA	28.10.1995	34	1	2020/2021:	Rangers FC Glasgow (SCO)
Joni KAUKO	12.07.1990	28	0	2020/2021:	Esbjerg fB (DEN)
Thomas Anton Rudolph LAM	18.12.1993	26	0	2020/2021:	PEC Zwolle (NED)
Robin LOD	17.04.1993	48	4	2020/2021:	Minnesota United FC (USA)
Ilmari NISKANEN	27.10.1997	6	1	2020:	FC Ingolstadt 04 (GER)
Rasmus SCHÜLLER	18.06.1991	52	0	2020:	HJK Helsinki
				01.01.2021->	Djurgårdens IF Stockholm (SWE)
Pyry Henri Hidipo SOIRI	22.09.1994	32	5	2020/2021:	Esbjerg fB (DEN)
Tim SPARV	20.02.1987	83	1	2020/2021:	AE Lárissa (GRE)
Robert Thomas TAYLOR	21.10.1994	20	1	2020/2021:	SK Brann Bergen (NOR)
Onni VALAKARI	18.08.1999	5	1	2020/2021:	Pafos FC Paphos (CYP)
Forwards					
Marcus FORSS	18.06.1999	7	1	2020/2021:	Brentford FC London (ENG)
Rasmus Joonatan KARJALAINEN	04.04.1996	13	1	2020/2021:	Örebro SK (SWE)
Lassi LAPPALAINEN	24.08.1998	9	0	2021:	CF Montréal (CAN)
Joel Julius Ilmari POHJANPALO	13.09.1994	45	10	2020:	TSV Bayer 04 Leverkusen (GER)
				30.09.2020->	1.FC Union Berlin (GER, on loan)
Teemu Eino Antero PUKKI	29.03.1990	94	30	2020/2021:	Norwich City FC (ENG)
Roope Vilhelmi RISKI	16.08.1991	6	1	2021:	HJK Helsinki
Trainer					
Markku KANERVA [from 12.12.2016]	24.05.1964			50 M; 24 W; 7 D; 19 L; 60-51 Complete record as trainer of Finland: 56 M; 26 W; 10 D; 20 L; 65-56 (09.02.2011 – 29.03.2011) & (04.09.2015 – 11.10.2015) & (09.01.2017 – 21.06.2021)	

FRANCE

F F F

The Country:
French Republic (République française)
Capital: Paris
Surface: 643,801 km²
Inhabitants: 67,413,000 [2021]
Time: UTC+1

The FA:
Fédération Française de Football
87, Boulevard de Grenelle, 75738 Paris Cedex 15
Tel: +33 1 4431 3173 00
Foundation date: 07.04.1919
Member of FIFA since: 1907
Member of UEFA since: 1954
Website: www.fff.fr

NATIONAL TEAM RECORDS

RECORDS
First international match:	01.05.1994, Bruxelles:	Belgium – France 3-3
Most international caps:	Lilian Thuram	- 142 caps (1994-2008)
Most international goals:	Thierry Daniel Henry	- 51 goals / 123 caps (1997-2010)

UEFA EUROPEAN CHAMPIONSHIP
1960	Final Tournament (4th Place)
1964	Qualifiers
1968	Qualifiers
1972	Qualifiers
1976	Qualifiers
1980	Qualifiers
1984	**Final Tournament (Winners)**
1988	Qualifiers
1992	Final Tournament (Group Stage)
1996	Final Tournament (Semi-Finals)
2000	**Final Tournament (Winners)**
2004	Final Tournament (Quarter-Finals)
2008	Final Tournament (Group Stage)
2012	Final Tournament (Quarter-Finals)
2016	Final Tournament (Runners-up)
2020	Final Tournament (2nd Round of 16)

FIFA WORLD CUP
1930	Final Tournament (Group Stage)
1934	Final Tournament (1st Round)
1938	Final Tournament (Quarter-Finals)
1950	*Withdrew*
1954	Final Tournament (Group Stage)
1958	Final Tournament (3rd Place)
1962	Qualifiers
1966	Final Tournament (Group Stage)
1970	Qualifiers
1974	Qualifiers
1978	Final Tournament (Group Stage)
1982	Final Tournament (4th Place)
1986	Final Tournament (3rd Place)
1990	Qualifiers
1994	Qualifiers
1998	**Final Tournament (Winners)**
2002	Final Tournament (Group Stage)
2006	Final Tournament (Runners-up)
2010	Final Tournament (Group Stage)
2014	Final Tournament (Quarter-Finals)
2018	**Final Tournament (Winners)**

OLYMPIC TOURNAMENTS
1908	Final Tournament
1912	-
1920	Semi-Finals
1924	Quarter-Finals
1928	1/8-Finals
1936	-
1948	Quarter-Finals
1952	Qualifiers
1956	-
1960	Group Stage
1964	Qualifiers
1968	Quarter-Finals
1972	Qualifiers
1976	Quarter-Finals
1980	Qualifiers
1984	**Winners**
1988	Qualifiers
1992	Qualifiers
1996	Quarter-Finals
2000	Qualifiers
2004	Qualifiers
2008	Qualifiers
2012	Qualifiers
2016	Qualifiers

UEFA NATIONS LEAGUE
2018/2019	League A
2020/2021	League A (Qualified for the Final Tournament)

FIFA CONFEDERATIONS CUP 1992-2017
2001 (Winners), 2003 (Winners)

FRENCH CLUB HONOURS IN EUROPEAN CLUB COMPETITIONS:

European Champion Clubs' Cup (1956-1992) / UEFA Champions League (1993-2021)		
Olympique de Marseille	1	1992/1993
Fairs Cup (1858-1971) / UEFA Cup (1972-2009) / UEFA Europa League (2010-2021)		
None		
UEFA Super Cup (1972-2020)		
None		
European Cup Winners' Cup 1961-1999		
Paris Saint-Germain FC	1	1995/1996

*defunct competition

NATIONAL COMPETITIONS
TABLE OF HONOURS

		CHAMPIONS	CUP WINNERS	BEST GOALSCORERS	
1893/1894		Standard Athletic Club Paris	-	-	
1894/1895		Standard Athletic Club Paris	-	-	
1895/1896		Club Français Paris	-	-	
1896/1897		Standard Athletic Club Paris	-	-	
1897/1898		Standard Athletic Club Paris	-	-	
1898/1899		Le Havre AC	-	-	
1899/1900		Le Havre AC	-	-	
1900/1901		Standard Athletic Club Paris	-	-	
1901/1902		Racing Club de Roubaix	-	-	
1902/1903		Racing Club de Roubaix	-	-	
1903/1904		Racing Club de Roubaix	-	-	
1904/1905		Gallia Club Paris	-	-	
1905/1906		Racing Club de Roubaix	-	-	
1906/1907		Racing Club de France Paris	-	-	
1907/1908		Racing Club de Roubaix	-	-	
1908/1909		Stade Helvétique de Marseille	-	-	
1909/1910		US Tourcoing	-	-	
1910/1911		Stade Helvétique de Marseille	-	-	
1911/1912		Stade Saint-Raphaëlois	-	-	
1912/1913		Stade Helvétique de Marseille	-	-	
1913/1914		Olympique Lillois	-	-	
1914/1915		*No competition*	-	-	
1915/1916		*No competition*	-	-	
1916/1917		*No competition*	-	-	
1917/1918		*No competition*	Olympique de Pantin	-	
1918/1919		Le Havre AC	CASG Paris	-	
1919/1920		*No competition*	Cercle Athlétique de Paris	-	
1920/1921		*No competition*	Red Star FC Paris	-	
1921/1922		*No competition*	Red Star FC Paris	-	
1922/1923		*No competition*	Red Star FC Paris	-	
1923/1924		*No competition*	Olympique de Marseille	-	
1924/1925		*No competition*	CASG Paris	-	
1925/1926		*No competition*	Olympique de Marseille	-	
1926/1927		Cercle Athlétique de Paris	Olympique de Marseille	-	
1927/1928		Stade Français Paris	Red Star FC Paris	-	
1928/1929		Olympique de Marseille	Montpellier Hérault Sport Club	-	
1929/1930		*No competition*	FC Sète	-	
1930/1931		*No competition*	Club Français Paris	-	
1931/1932		*No competition*	AS Cannes	-	
1932/1933		Olympique Lillois	Excelsior Athlétic Club de Roubaix	Walter Kaiser (GER, Stade Rennais FC) Robert Mercier (Club Français Paris)	15
1933/1934		FC Sète	FC Sète	István Lukács (HUN, FC Sète)	28
1934/1935		Sochaux	Olympique de Marseille	André Abegglen (SUI, FC Sochaux-Montbéliard)	30
1935/1936		Racing Club de France Paris	RC Paris	Roger Courtois (FC Sochaux-Montbéliard)	34
1936/1937		Olympique de Marseille	FC FC Sochaux-Montbéliard	Oskar Rohr (GER, Racing Club de Strasbourg)	30
1937/1938		FC Sochaux-Montbéliard	Olympique de Marseille	Jean Nicolas (FC Rouen)	26
1938/1939		FC Sète	Racing Club de France Paris	Roger Courtois (FC Sochaux-Montbéliard) Désiré Koranyi (FC Sète)	27
1939/1940		*No competition*	Racing Club de France Paris	-	
1940/1941		*No competition*	FC Girondins de Bordeaux	-	
1941/1942		*No competition*	Red Star FC Paris	-	
1942/1943		*No competition*	Olympique de Marseille	-	
1943/1944		*No competition*	Équipe fédérale Nancy-Lorraine	-	
1944/1945		*No competition*	Racing Club de France Paris	-	
1945/1946		Lille OSC	Lille OSC	René Bihel (Lille OSC)	28
1946/1947		Racing Club de Roubaix–Tourcoing	Lille OSC	Pierre Sinibaldi (Stade de Reims)	33
1947/1948		Olympique de Marseille	Lille OSC	Jean Baratte (Lille OSC)	31
1948/1949		Stade de Reims	Racing Club de France Paris	Jean Baratte (Lille OSC) Josef Humpál (CZE, FC Sochaux-Montbéliard)	26
1949/1950		FC Girondins de Bordeaux	Stade de Reims	Jean Grumellon (Stade Rennais FC)	25
1950/1951		OGC Nice	Racing Club de Strasbourg	Roger Piantoni (AS Nancy-Lorraine) Jean Courteaux (OGC Nice)	27
1951/1952		OGC Nice	OGC Nice	Gunnar Andersson (SWE, Olympique de Marseille)	31
1952/1953		Stade de Reims	Lille OSC	Gunnar Andersson (SWE, Olympique de Marseille)	35
1953/1954		Lille OSC	OGC Nice	Édouard Kargu (FC Girondins de Bordeaux)	27
1954/1955		Stade de Reims	Lille OSC	René Bliard (Stade de Reims)	30
1955/1956		OGC Nice	CS Sedan	Thadée Cisowski (Racing Club de France Paris)	31
1956/1957		AS Saint-Étienne	Toulouse FC	Thadée Cisowski (Racing Club de France Paris)	33
1957/1958		Stade de Reims	Stade de Reims	Just Fontaine (Stade de Reims)	34
1958/1959		OGC Nice	Le Havre AC	Thadée Cisowski (Racing Club de France Paris)	30
1959/1960		Stade de Reims	AS Monaco FC	Just Fontaine (Stade de Reims)	28
1960/1961		AS Monaco FC	CS Sedan	Roger Piantoni (Stade de Reims)	28

1961/1962	Stade de Reims	AS Saint-Étienne	Sékou Touré (CIV, Montpellier Hérault Sport Club)	25
1962/1963	AS Monaco FC	AS Monaco FC	Serge Masnaghetti (USVA Valenciennes)	35
1963/1964	AS Saint-Étienne	Olympique Lyonnais	Ahmed Oudjani (ALG, Racing Club de Lens)	30
1964/1965	FC Nantes	Stade Rennais FC	Jacques Simon (FC Nantes)	24
1965/1966	FC Nantes	Racing Club de Strasbourg	Philippe Gondet (FC Nantes)	36
1966/1967	AS Saint-Étienne	Olympique Lyonnais	Hervé Revelli (AS Saint-Étienne)	31
1967/1968	AS Saint-Étienne	AS Saint-Étienne	Étienne Sansonetti (AC Ajaccio)	26
1968/1969	AS Saint-Étienne	Olympique de Marseille	André Guy (Olympique Lyonnais)	25
1969/1970	AS Saint-Étienne	AS Saint-Étienne	Hervé Revelli (AS Saint-Étienne)	28
1970/1971	Olympique de Marseille	Stade Rennais FC	Josip Skoblar (YUG, Olympique de Marseille)	44
1971/1972	Olympique de Marseille	Olympique de Marseille	Josip Skoblar (YUG, Olympique de Marseille)	30
1972/1973	FC Nantes	Olympique Lyonnais	Josip Skoblar (YUG, Olympique de Marseille)	26
1973/1974	AS Saint-Étienne	AS Saint-Étienne	Carlos Arcecio Bianchi (ARG, Stade de Reims)	30
1974/1975	AS Saint-Étienne	AS Saint-Étienne	Delio Onnis (ARG, AS Monaco FC)	30
1975/1976	AS Saint-Étienne	Olympique de Marseille	Carlos Arcecio Bianchi (ARG, Stade de Reims)	34
1976/1977	FC Nantes	AS Saint-Étienne	Carlos Arcecio Bianchi (ARG, Stade de Reims)	28
1977/1978	AS Monaco FC	AS Nancy-Lorraine	Carlos Arcecio Bianchi (ARG, Paris Saint-Germain FC)	37
1978/1979	Racing Club de Strasbourg	FC Nantes	Carlos Arcecio Bianchi (ARG, Paris Saint-Germain FC)	27
1979/1980	FC Nantes	AS Monaco FC	Erwin Kostedde (GER, Stade Lavallois) Delio Onnis (ARG, AS Monaco FC)	21
1980/1981	AS Saint-Étienne	SC Bastia	Delio Onnis (ARG, Tours FC)	24
1981/1982	AS Monaco FC	Paris Saint-Germain FC	Delio Onnis (ARG, Tours FC)	29
1982/1983	FC Nantes	Paris Saint-Germain FC	Vahid Halilhodžić (YUG, FC Nantes)	27
1983/1984	FC Girondins de Bordeaux	FC Metz	Patrice Garande (AJ Auxerre) Delio Onnis (ARG, Sporting Club Toulon)	21
1984/1985	FC Girondins de Bordeaux	AS Monaco FC	Vahid Halilhodžić (YUG, FC Nantes)	28
1985/1986	Paris Saint-Germain FC	FC Girondins de Bordeaux	Jules François Bocandé (SEN, FC Metz)	23
1986/1987	FC Girondins de Bordeaux	FC Girondins de Bordeaux	Bernard Zénier (FC Metz)	18
1987/1988	AS Monaco FC	FC Metz	Jean-Pierre Papin (Olympique de Marseille)	19
1988/1989	Olympique de Marseille	Olympique de Marseille	Jean-Pierre Papin (Olympique de Marseille)	22
1989/1990	Olympique de Marseille	Montpellier Hérault Sport Club	Jean-Pierre Papin (Olympique de Marseille)	30
1990/1991	Olympique de Marseille	AS Monaco FC	Jean-Pierre Papin (Olympique de Marseille)	23
1991/1992	Olympique de Marseille	*Not played to end*	Jean-Pierre Papin (Olympique de Marseille)	27
1992/1993	*No winner was declared by FFF*	Paris Saint-Germain FC	Alen Bokšić (CRO, Olympique de Marseille)	22
1993/1994	Paris Saint-Germain FC	AJ Auxerre	Roger Zokou Boli (Racing Club de Lens) Youri Djorkaeff (AS Monaco FC) Nicolas Pierre Ouédec (FC Nantes)	20
1994/1995	FC Nantes	Paris Saint-Germain FC	Patrice Loko (FC Nantes)	22
1995/1996	AJ Auxerre	AJ Auxerre	Anderson da Silva (BRA, AS Monaco FC)	21
1996/1997	AS Monaco FC	OGC Nice	Stéphane Pierre Yves Guivarc'h (Stade Rennais FC)	21
1997/1998	Racing Club de Lens	Paris Saint-Germain FC	Stéphane Pierre Yves Guivarc'h (AJ Auxerre)	21
1998/1999	FC Girondins de Bordeaux	FC Nantes	Sylvain Wiltord (FC Girondins de Bordeaux)	22
1999/2000	AS Monaco FC	FC Nantes	Anderson da Silva (BRA, Olympique Lyonnais)	23
2000/2001	FC Nantes	Racing Club de Strasbourg	Anderson da Silva (BRA, Olympique Lyonnais)	22
2001/2002	Olympique Lyonnais	FC Lorient	Djibril Cissé (AJ Auxerre) Pedro Miguel Carreiro Resendes "Pauleta" (POR, FC Girondins de Bordeaux)	22
2002/2003	Olympique Lyonnais	AJ Auxerre	Shabani Christophe Nonda (COD, AS Monaco FC)	26
2003/2004	Olympique Lyonnais	Paris Saint-Germain FC	Djibril Cissé (AJ Auxerre)	26
2004/2005	Olympique Lyonnais	AJ Auxerre	Alexander Frei (SUI, Stade Rennais FC)	20
2005/2006	Olympique Lyonnais	Paris Saint-Germain FC	Pedro Miguel Carreiro Resendes "Pauleta" (POR, Paris Saint-Germain FC)	21
2006/2007	Olympique Lyonnais	FC Sochaux-Montbéliard	Pedro Miguel Carreiro Resendes "Pauleta" (POR, Paris Saint-Germain FC)	15
2007/2008	Olympique Lyonnais	Olympique Lyonnais	Karim Mostafa Benzema (Olympique Lyonnais)	20
2008/2009	FC Girondins de Bordeaux	En Avant de Guingamp	André-Pierre Christian Gignac (Toulouse FC)	24
2009/2010	Olympique de Marseille	Paris Saint-Germain FC	Mamadou Hamidou Niang (SEN, Olympique de Marseille)	18
2010/2011	Lille OSC	Lille OSC	Moussa Sow (SEN, Lille OSC)	25
2011/2012	Montpellier Hérault Sport Club	Olympique Lyonnais	Olivier Jonathan Giroud (Montpellier Hérault SC) Anderson Luiz de Carvalho "Nenê" (BRA, Paris Saint-Germain FC)	21
2012/2013	Paris Saint-Germain FC	FC Girondins de Bordeaux	Zlatan Ibrahimović (SWE, Paris Saint-Germain FC)	30
2013/2014	Paris Saint-Germain FC	En Avant de Guingamp	Zlatan Ibrahimović (SWE, Paris Saint-Germain FC)	26
2014/2015	Paris Saint-Germain FC	Paris Saint-Germain FC	Alexandre Lacazette (Olympique Lyonnais)	27
2015/2016	Paris Saint-Germain FC	Paris Saint-Germain FC	Zlatan Ibrahimović (SWE, Paris Saint-Germain FC)	38
2016/2017	AS Monaco FC	Paris Saint-Germain FC	Edinson Roberto Cavani Gómez (URU, Paris Saint-Germain FC)	35
2017/2018	Paris Saint-Germain FC	Paris Saint-Germain FC	Edinson Roberto Cavani Gómez (URU, Paris Saint-Germain FC)	28
2018/2019	Paris Saint-Germain FC	Stade Rennais FC	Kylian Sanmi Mbappé Lottin (Paris Saint-Germain FC)	33
2019/2020	Paris Saint-Germain FC	Paris Saint-Germain FC	Wissam Ben Yedder (AS Monaco FC) Kylian Sanmi Mbappé Lottin (Paris Saint-Germain FC)	18
2020/2021	Lille OSC	Paris Saint-Germain FC	Kylian Sanmi Mbappé Lottin (Paris Saint-Germain FC)	27

COUPE DE LA LIGUE* WINNERS

1963/1964	Racing Club de Strasbourg	1998/1999	Racing Club de Lens	2009/2010	Olympique de Marseille
1964/1965	FC Nantes	1999/2000	FC Gueugnon	2010/2011	Olympique de Marseille
1981/1982	Stade Lavallois	2000/2001	Olympique Lyonnais	2011/2012	Olympique de Marseille
1983/1984	Stade Lavallois	2001/2002	FC Girondins de Bordeaux	2012/2013	AS Saint-Étienne
1985/1986	FC Metz	2002/2003	AS Monaco FC	2013/2014	Paris Saint-Germain FC
1990/1991	Stade de Reims	2003/2004	FC Sochaux-Montbéliard	2014/2015	Paris Saint-Germain FC
1991/1992	Montpellier Hérault Sport Club	2004/2005	Racing Club de Strasbourg	2015/2016	Paris Saint-Germain FC
1993/1994	Racing Club de Lens	2005/2006	AS Nancy-Lorraine	2016/2017	Paris Saint-Germain FC
1994/1995	Paris Saint-Germain FC	2006/2007	FC Girondins de Bordeaux	2017/2018	Paris Saint-Germain FC
1995/1996	FC Metz	2007/2008	Paris Saint-Germain FC	2018/2019	Racing Club de Strasbourg
1996/1997	Racing Club de Strasbourg	2008/2009	FC Girondins de Bordeaux	2019/2020	Paris Saint-Germain FC
1997/1998	Paris Saint-Germain FC				

*Competition called: Coupe de la Ligue (1963–1965), Coupe d'Été/Coupe de la Ligue (1982–1994) and Coupe de la Ligue (since 1994).

NATIONAL CHAMPIONSHIP
Ligue 1 2020/2021
(23.08.2020 – 23.05.2021)

Results

Round 1 [21-23.08.2020]
Bordeaux - FC Nantes 0-0
Dijon - Angers 0-1(0-1)
Lille OSC - Stade Rennais 1-1(1-0)
AS Monaco - Stade Reims 2-2(1-2)
FC Lorient - RC Strasbourg 3-1(0-1)
Nîmes Olympique - Stade Brestois 4-0(2-0)
OGC Nice - RC Lens 2-1(1-1)
Montpellier - Olymp. Lyon 2-1(1-0) [15.09.]
Paris St-Germain - FC Metz 1-0(0-0) [16.09.]
Ol. Marseille - Saint-Étienne 0-2(0-1) [17.09.]

Round 2 [28-30.08.2020]
Olympique Lyon - Dijon 4-1(3-1)
Stade Rennais - Montpellier 2-1(1-0)
RC Strasbourg - OGC Nice 0-2(0-1)
Stade Reims - Lille OSC 0-1(0-1)
Angers - Bordeaux 0-2(0-2)
FC Metz - AS Monaco 0-1(0-1)
FC Nantes - Nîmes Olympique 2-1(2-0)
Saint-Étienne - FC Lorient 2-0(1-0)
Stade Brestois - Olympique Marseille 2-3(1-2)
RC Lens - Paris St-Germain 1-0(0-0) [10.09.]

Round 3 [11-13.09.2020]
Bordeaux - Olympique Lyon 0-0
Montpellier - OGC Nice 3-1(1-0)
Saint-Étienne - RC Strasbourg 2-0(0-0)
Lille OSC - FC Metz 1-0(0-0)
Angers - Stade Reims 1-0(0-0)
Dijon - Stade Brestois 0-2(0-1)
FC Lorient - RC Lens 2-3(1-2)
Nîmes Olympique - Stade Rennais 2-4(1-2)
AS Monaco - FC Nantes 2-1(1-0)
Paris Saint-Germain - Ol. Marseille 0-1(0-1)

Round 4 [18-20.09.2020]
Olympique Lyon - Nîmes Olympique 0-0
RC Lens - Bordeaux 2-1(0-0)
Stade Rennais - AS Monaco 2-1(0-1)
OGC Nice - Paris Saint-Germain 0-3(0-2)
Stade Brestois - FC Lorient 3-2(2-1)
FC Metz - Stade Reims 2-1(1-1)
Montpellier - Angers 4-1(2-1)
RC Strasbourg - Dijon 1-0(0-0)
FC Nantes - Saint-Étienne 2-2(0-1)
Olympique Marseille - Lille OSC 1-1(0-0)

Round 5 [25-27.09.2020]
Lille OSC - FC Nantes 2-0(1-0)
Saint-Étienne - Stade Rennais 0-3(0-1)
Olympique Marseille - FC Metz 1-1(0-0)
Bordeaux - OGC Nice 0-0
Angers - Stade Brestois 3-2(1-2)
Dijon - Montpellier 2-2(1-0)
AS Monaco - RC Strasbourg 3-2(2-0)
Nîmes Olympique - RC Lens 1-1(0-1)
FC Lorient - Olympique Lyon 1-1(0-0)
Stade Reims - Paris Saint-Germain 0-2(0-1)

Round 6 [02-04.10.2020]
Paris Saint-Germain - Angers 6-1(2-0)
RC Lens - Saint-Étienne 2-0(1-0)
OGC Nice - FC Nantes 2-1(1-1)
Montpellier - Nîmes Olympique 0-1(0-0)
Bordeaux - Dijon 3-0(2-0)
Stade Brestois - AS Monaco 1-0(1-0)
FC Metz - FC Lorient 3-1(1-1)
RC Strasbourg - Lille OSC 0-3(0-1)
Stade Rennais - Stade Reims 2-2(2-1)
Olympique Lyon - Olymp. Marseille 1-1(1-1)

Round 7 [16-18.10.2020]
Dijon - Stade Rennais 1-1(0-1)
Nîmes Olympique - Paris St-Germain 0-4(0-1)
Stade Reims - FC Lorient 1-3(1-0)
Olympique Marseille - Bordeaux 3-1(1-0)
RC Strasbourg - Olympique Lyon 2-3(1-3)
Angers - FC Metz 1-1(1-1)
AS Monaco - Montpellier 1-1(0-0)
FC Nantes - Stade Brestois 3-1(2-0)
Saint-Étienne - OGC Nice 1-3(0-2)
Lille OSC - RC Lens 4-0(1-0)

Round 8 [23-25.10.2020]
Stade Rennais - Angers 1-2(1-1)
FC Lorient - Olympique Marseille 0-1(0-0)
Paris Saint-Germain - Dijon 4-0(2-0)
Bordeaux - Nîmes Olympique 2-0(0-0)
Stade Brestois - RC Strasbourg 0-3(0-2)
FC Metz - Saint-Étienne 2-0(1-0)
Montpellier - Stade Reims 0-4(0-3)
OGC Nice - Lille OSC 1-1(0-0)
Olympique Lyon - AS Monaco 4-1(4-0)
RC Lens - FC Nantes 1-1(1-0) [25.11.]

Round 9 [31.10.-01.11.2020]
Stade Rennais - Stade Brestois 2-1(0-0)
FC Nantes - Paris Saint-Germain 0-3(0-0)
Saint-Étienne - Montpellier 0-1(0-1)
Angers - OGC Nice 0-3(0-2)
Dijon - FC Lorient 0-0
Nîmes Olympique - FC Metz 0-1(0-1)
Stade Reims - RC Strasbourg 2-1(2-1)
AS Monaco - Bordeaux 4-0(3-0)
Lille OSC - Olympique Lyon 1-1(1-0)
Ol. Marseille - RC Lens 0-1(0-0) [20.01.2021]

Round 10 [06-08.11.2020]
RC Strasbourg - Ol. Marseille 0-1(0-0)
Bordeaux - Montpellier 0-2(0-0)
Paris Saint-Germain - Stade Rennais 3-0(2-0)
Stade Brestois - Lille OSC 3-2(3-1)
RC Lens - Stade Reims 4-4(1-0)
FC Lorient - FC Nantes 0-2(0-0)
FC Metz - Dijon 1-1(1-1)
Nîmes Olympique - Angers 1-5(0-2)
OGC Nice - AS Monaco 1-2(0-1)
Olympique Lyon - Saint-Étienne 2-1(0-1)

Round 11 [20-22.11.2020]
Stade Rennais - Bordeaux 0-1(0-1)
AS Monaco - Paris Saint-Germain 3-2(0-2)
Stade Brestois - Saint-Étienne 4-1(4-1)
FC Nantes - FC Metz 1-1(1-1)
Dijon - RC Lens 0-1(0-1)
Montpellier - RC Strasbourg 4-3(3-3)
Stade Reims - Nîmes Olympique 0-1(0-0)
Angers - Olympique Lyon 0-1(0-0)
Lille OSC - FC Lorient 4-0(1-0)
Marseille - OGC Nice 3-2(2-0) [17.02.2021]

Round 12 [27-29.11.2020]
RC Strasbourg - Stade Rennais 1-1(1-0)
Olympique Marseille - FC Nantes 3-1(2-0)
Paris Saint-Germain - Bordeaux 2-2(2-1)
Olympique Lyon - Stade Reims 3-0(1-0)
RC Lens - Angers 1-3(1-1)
FC Lorient - Montpellier 0-1(0-0)
FC Metz - Stade Brestois 0-2(0-1)
AS Monaco - Nîmes Olympique 3-0(1-0)
OGC Nice - Dijon 1-3(0-2)
Saint-Étienne - Lille OSC 1-1(1-0)

Round 13 [04-06.12.2020]
Nîmes Olympique - Marseille 0-2(0-0)
Stade Rennais - RC Lens 0-2(0-1)
Montpellier - Paris Saint-Germain 1-3(1-1)
Lille OSC - AS Monaco 2-1(0-0)
Angers - FC Lorient 2-0(1-0)
Bordeaux - Stade Brestois 1-0(0-0)
Dijon - Saint-Étienne 0-0
FC Nantes - RC Strasbourg 0-4(0-2)
Stade Reims - OGC Nice 0-0
FC Metz - Olympique Lyon 1-3(0-1)

Round 14 [11-13.12.2020]
Saint-Étienne - Angers 0-0
Olympique Marseille - AS Monaco 2-1(2-0)
RC Lens - Montpellier 2-3(1-2)
OGC Nice - Stade Rennais 0-1(0-1)
Stade Brestois - Stade Reims 2-1(1-0)
FC Lorient - Nîmes Olympique 3-0(2-0)
FC Nantes - Dijon 1-1(1-0)
RC Strasbourg - FC Metz 2-2(0-1)
Lille OSC - Bordeaux 2-1(2-1)
Paris St-Germain - Olympique Lyon 0-1(0-1)

Round 15 [16.12.2020]
Angers - RC Strasbourg 0-2(0-0)
Dijon - Lille OSC 0-2(0-1)
Montpellier - FC Metz 0-2(0-0)
Nîmes Olympique - OGC Nice 0-2(0-0)
Stade Reims - FC Nantes 3-2(0-1)
Bordeaux - Saint-Étienne 1-2(1-1)
Olympique Lyon - Stade Brestois 2-2(0-1)
AS Monaco - RC Lens 0-3(0-3)
Paris Saint-Germain - FC Lorient 2-0(0-0)
Stade Rennais - Olympique Marseille 2-1(0-1)

Round 16 [19-20.12.2020]
FC Metz - RC Lens 2-0(1-0)
Olympique Marseille - Stade Reims 1-1(1-1)
OGC Nice - Olympique Lyon 1-4(1-2)
Stade Brestois - Montpellier 2-2(0-1)
Dijon - AS Monaco 0-1(0-1)
FC Nantes - Angers 1-1(0-1)
Saint-Étienne - Nîmes Olympique 2-2(1-1)
RC Strasbourg - Bordeaux 0-2(0-1)
FC Lorient - Stade Rennais 0-3(0-1)
Lille OSC - Paris Saint-Germain 0-0

Round 17 [23.12.2020]
Bordeaux - Stade Reims 1-3(0-2)
RC Lens - Stade Brestois 2-1(2-0)
OGC Nice - FC Lorient 2-2(2-0)
Nîmes Olympique - Dijon 1-3(1-0)
Stade Rennais - FC Metz 1-0(0-0)
Angers - Olympique Marseille 2-1(2-0)
Olympique Lyon - FC Nantes 3-0(3-0)
AS Monaco - Saint-Étienne 2-2(1-2)
Montpellier - Lille OSC 2-3(0-1)
Paris Saint-Germain - RC Strasbourg 4-0(1-0)

Round 18 [06.01.2021]
Stade Brestois - OGC Nice 2-0(2-0)
FC Lorient - AS Monaco 2-5(1-1)
FC Metz - Bordeaux 0-0
FC Nantes - Stade Rennais 0-0
RC Strasbourg - Nîmes Olympique 5-0(3-0)
Lille OSC - Angers 1-2(1-2)
Olympique Lyon - RC Lens 3-2(1-0)
Olympique Marseille - Montpellier 3-1(1-0)
Stade Reims - Dijon 0-0
Saint-Étienne - Paris Saint-Germain 1-1(1-1)

Round 19 [09.01.2021]
Bordeaux - FC Lorient 2-1(2-1)
Dijon - Olympique Marseille 0-0
RC Lens - RC Strasbourg 0-1(0-1)
FC Metz - OGC Nice 1-1(0-1)
AS Monaco - Angers 3-0(1-0)
Montpellier - FC Nantes 1-1(1-0)
Nîmes Olympique - Lille OSC 0-1(0-1)
Paris Saint-Germain - Stade Brestois 3-0(1-0)
Stade Reims - Saint-Étienne 3-1(2-0)
Stade Rennais - Olympique Lyon 2-2(1-0)

Round 20 [15-17.01.2021]
Montpellier - AS Monaco 2-3(0-2)
Ol. Marseille - Nîmes Olympique 1-2(0-0)
Angers - Paris Saint-Germain 0-1(0-0)
Stade Brestois - Stade Rennais 1-2(1-1)
FC Nantes - RC Lens 1-1(1-0)
OGC Nice - Bordeaux 0-3(0-0)
RC Strasbourg - Saint-Étienne 1-0(1-0)
Lille OSC - Stade Reims 2-1(0-1)
Olympique Lyon - FC Metz 0-1(0-0)
FC Lorient - Dijon 3-2(1-2) [27.01.]

Round 21 [22-24.01.2021]
Paris Saint-Germain - Montpellier 4-0(1-0)
RC Lens - OGC Nice 0-1(0-0)
AS Monaco - Olympique Marseille 3-1(0-1)
Bordeaux - Angers 2-1(2-1)
Dijon - RC Strasbourg 1-1(0-0)
FC Metz - FC Nantes 2-0(1-0)
Stade Reims - Stade Brestois 1-0(1-0)
Stade Rennais - Lille OSC 0-1(0-1)
Saint-Étienne - Olympique Lyon 0-5(0-2)
Nîmes Olymp. - FC Lorient 1-0(0-0) [24.02.]

Round 22 [29-31.01.2021]
Olympique Lyon - Bordeaux 2-1(1-0)
Montpellier - RC Lens 1-2(0-1)
OGC Nice - Saint-Étienne 0-1(0-0)
Angers - Nîmes Olympique 3-1(2-1)
Stade Brestois - FC Metz 2-4(1-1)
FC Lorient - Paris Saint-Germain 3-2(1-1)
RC Strasbourg - Stade Reims 0-1(0-0)
Lille OSC - Dijon 1-0(1-0)
FC Nantes - AS Monaco 1-2(0-1)
Ol. Marseille - Stade Rennais 1-0(0-0) [10.03.]

Round 23 [03.02.2021]
Bordeaux - Lille OSC 0-3(0-0)
FC Metz - Montpellier 1-1(0-0)
Stade Reims - Angers 0-0
Stade Rennais - FC Lorient 1-1(1-0)
RC Strasbourg - Stade Brestois 2-2(1-0)
Dijon - Olympique Lyon 0-1(0-1)
RC Lens - Olympique Marseille 2-2(0-2)
Paris St-Germain - Nîmes Olympique 3-0(2-0)
Saint-Étienne - FC Nantes 1-1(0-1)
AS Monaco - OGC Nice 2-1(1-0)

Round 24 [06-07.02.2021]
FC Lorient - Stade Reims 1-0(0-0)
Olympique Lyon - RC Strasbourg 3-0(2-0)
RC Lens - Stade Rennais 0-0
Stade Brestois - Bordeaux 2-1(0-0)
Montpellier - Dijon 4-2(0-1)
OGC Nice - Angers 3-0(2-0)
Nîmes Olympique - AS Monaco 3-4(2-2)
Saint-Étienne - FC Metz 1-0(1-0)
FC Nantes - Lille OSC 0-2(0-1)
Ol. Marseille - Paris Saint-Germain 0-2(0-2)

Round 25 [13-14.02.2021]
Paris Saint-Germain - OGC Nice 2-1(1-0)
Stade Reims - RC Lens 1-1(1-0)
Olympique Lyon - Montpellier 1-2(1-1)
AS Monaco - FC Lorient 2-2(0-1)
Angers - FC Nantes 1-3(1-2)
Dijon - Nîmes Olympique 0-2(0-0)
FC Metz - RC Strasbourg 1-2(1-1)
Stade Rennais - Saint-Étienne 0-2(0-1)
Lille OSC - Stade Brestois 0-0
Bordeaux - Olympique Marseille 0-0

Round 26 [19-21.02.2021]
Stade Brestois - Olympique Lyon 2-3(0-3)
Saint-Étienne - Stade Reims 1-1(0-0)
FC Nantes - Olympique Marseille 1-1(0-0)
Montpellier - Stade Rennais 2-1(2-0)
RC Lens - Dijon 2-1(1-0)
OGC Nice - FC Metz 1-2(0-2)
Nîmes Olympique - Bordeaux 2-0(1-0)
RC Strasbourg - Angers 0-0
FC Lorient - Lille OSC 1-4(1-2)
Paris Saint-Germain - AS Monaco 0-2(0-1)

Round 27 [26-28.02.2021]
Stade Rennais - OGC Nice 1-2(1-1)
Bordeaux - FC Metz 1-2(1-0)
Dijon - Paris Saint-Germain 0-4(0-2)
AS Monaco - Stade Brestois 2-0(0-0)
Angers - RC Lens 2-2(2-1)
FC Lorient - Saint-Étienne 2-1(0-1)
Nîmes Olympique - FC Nantes 1-1(0-1)
Stade Reims - Montpellier 0-0
Lille OSC - RC Strasbourg 1-1(0-1)
Ol. Marseille - Olympique Lyon 1-1(1-1)

Round 28 [03.03.2021]
Stade Brestois - Dijon 3-1(3-1)
Olympique Lyon - Stade Rennais 1-0(0-0)
FC Metz - Angers 0-1(0-1)
OGC Nice - Nîmes Olympique 2-1(1-0)
Saint-Étienne - RC Lens 2-3(1-2)
Bordeaux - Paris Saint-Germain 0-1(0-1)
Lille OSC - Olympique Marseille 2-0(0-0)
Montpellier - FC Lorient 1-1(1-1)
FC Nantes - Stade Reims 1-2(1-1)
RC Strasbourg - AS Monaco 1-0(0-0)

Round 29 [12-14.03.2021]
Stade Reims - Olympique Lyon 1-1(1-0)
Angers - Saint-Étienne 0-1(0-0)
Olympique Marseille - Stade Brestois 3-1(1-0)
Nîmes Olympique - Montpellier 1-1(0-0)
Dijon - Bordeaux 1-3(0-2)
RC Lens - FC Metz 2-2(2-1)
FC Lorient - OGC Nice 1-1(0-0)
Stade Rennais - RC Strasbourg 1-0(1-0)
AS Monaco - Lille OSC 0-0
Paris Saint-Germain - FC Nantes 1-2(1-0)

Round 30 [19-21.03.2021]
Saint-Étienne - AS Monaco 0-4(0-1)
FC Metz - Stade Rennais 1-3(0-2)
OGC Nice - Olympique Marseille 3-0(1-0)
RC Strasbourg - RC Lens 1-2(1-2)
Stade Brestois - Angers 0-0
Dijon - Stade Reims 0-1(0-0)
Montpellier - Bordeaux 3-1(1-0)
FC Nantes - FC Lorient 1-1(1-0)
Lille OSC - Nîmes Olympique 1-2(1-2)
Olympique Lyon - Paris St-Germain 2-4(0-2)

AS Monaco - FC Metz 4-0(0-0)
Paris Saint-Germain - Lille OSC 0-1(0-1)
RC Lens - Olympique Lyon 1-1(0-0)
Angers - Montpellier 1-1(0-0)
Bordeaux - RC Strasbourg 2-3(2-3)
FC Lorient - Stade Brestois 1-0(1-0)
FC Nantes - OGC Nice 1-2(1-2)
Stade Reims - Stade Rennais 2-2(0-0)
Nîmes Olympique - Saint-Étienne 0-2(0-1)
Olympique Marseille - Dijon 2-0(1-0)

Round 32 [09-11.04.2021]
FC Metz - Lille OSC 0-2(0-0)
RC Strasbourg - Paris Saint-Germain 1-4(0-3)
Montpellier - Olympique Marseille 3-3(1-2)
Stade Rennais - FC Nantes 1-0(0-0)
Stade Brestois - Nîmes Olympique 1-1(1-1)
RC Lens - FC Lorient 4-1(2-1)
OGC Nice - Stade Reims 2-0(1-0)
Saint-Étienne - Bordeaux 4-1(2-1)
AS Monaco - Dijon 3-0(0-0)
Olympique Lyon - Angers 3-0(2-0)

Round 33 [16-18.04.2021]
Lille OSC - Montpellier 1-1(0-1)
Angers - Stade Rennais 0-3(0-1)
Olympique Marseille - FC Lorient 3-2(0-1)
Paris Saint-Germain - Saint-Étienne 3-2(0-0)
Stade Brestois - RC Lens 1-1(1-0)
Dijon - OGC Nice 2-0(0-0)
Nîmes Olympique - RC Strasbourg 1-1(0-0)
Stade Reims - FC Metz 0-0
Bordeaux - AS Monaco 0-3(0-1)
FC Nantes - Olympique Lyon 1-2(0-2)

Round 34 [23-25.04.2021]
Stade Reims - Olympique Marseille 1-3(1-2)
Saint-Étienne - Stade Brestois 1-2(1-0)
FC Metz - Paris Saint-Germain 1-3(0-1)
OGC Nice - Montpellier 3-1(3-1)
RC Lens - Nîmes Olympique 2-1(1-0)
FC Lorient - Bordeaux 4-1(3-0)
Stade Rennais - Dijon 5-1(1-1)
RC Strasbourg - FC Nantes 1-2(1-0)
Angers - AS Monaco 0-1(0-0)
Olympique Lyon - Lille OSC 2-3(2-1)

Round 35 [30.04.-02.05.2021]
Ol. Marseille - RC Strasbourg 1-1(0-0)
Paris Saint-Germain - RC Lens 2-1(1-0)
Lille OSC - OGC Nice 2-0(1-0)
Bordeaux - Stade Rennais 1-0(1-0)
Stade Brestois - FC Nantes 1-4(0-2)
Dijon - FC Metz 1-5(0-2)
FC Lorient - Angers 2-0(1-0)
Nîmes Olympique - Stade Reims 2-2(0-1)
Montpellier - Saint-Étienne 1-2(1-1)
AS Monaco - Olympique Lyon 2-3(1-0)

Round 36 [07-09.05.2021]
RC Lens - Lille OSC 0-3(0-2)
FC Nantes - Bordeaux 3-0(1-0)
Olympique Lyon - FC Lorient 4-1(0-0)
Saint-Étienne - Olympique Marseille 1-0(1-0)
Angers - Dijon 3-0(1-0)
FC Metz - Nîmes Olympique 0-3(0-0)
OGC Nice - Stade Brestois 3-2(1-2)
RC Strasbourg - Montpellier 2-3(0-1)
Stade Reims - AS Monaco 0-1(0-1)
Stade Rennais - Paris Saint-Germain 1-1(0-1)

Round 37 [16.05.2021]
Bordeaux - RC Lens 3-0(1-0)
Dijon - FC Nantes 0-4(0-2)
Lille OSC - Saint-Étienne 0-0
FC Lorient - FC Metz 2-1(1-0)
Olympique Marseille - Angers 3-2(1-0)
AS Monaco - Stade Rennais 2-1(2-0)
Montpellier - Stade Brestois 0-0
OGC Nice - RC Strasbourg 0-2(0-1)
Nîmes Olympique - Olympique Lyon 2-5(1-3)
Paris Saint-Germain - Stade Reims 4-0(2-0)

Round 38 [23.05.2021]
Angers - Lille OSC 1-2(0-2)
Stade Brestois - Paris Saint-Germain 0-2(0-1)
RC Lens - AS Monaco 0-0
Olympique Lyon - OGC Nice 2-3(2-1)
FC Metz - Olympique Marseille 1-1(0-0)
FC Nantes - Montpellier 1-2(1-1)
Stade Reims - Bordeaux 1-2(1-1)
Stade Rennais - Nîmes Olympique 2-0(1-0)
Saint-Étienne - Dijon 0-1(0-1)
RC Strasbourg - FC Lorient 1-1(1-0)

Final Standings

						Total					Home					Away		
1.	Lille OSC	38	24	11	3	64 - 23	83	10	7	2	28 - 11	14	4	1	36 - 12
2.	Paris Saint-Germain FC	38	26	4	8	86 - 28	82	13	1	5	44 - 14	13	3	3	42 - 14
3.	AS Monaco FC	38	24	6	8	76 - 42	78	12	5	2	43 - 21	12	1	6	33 - 21
4.	Olympique Lyonnais	38	22	10	6	81 - 43	76	11	3	5	42 - 23	11	7	1	39 - 20
5.	Olympique de Marseille	38	16	12	10	54 - 47	60	10	5	4	32 - 23	6	7	6	22 - 24
6.	Stade Rennais FC	38	16	10	12	52 - 40	58	9	4	6	26 - 21	7	6	6	26 - 19
7.	Racing Club de Lens	38	15	12	11	55 - 54	57	7	7	5	28 - 26	8	5	6	27 - 28
8.	Montpellier Hérault SC	38	14	12	12	60 - 62	54	7	4	8	34 - 35	7	8	4	26 - 27
9.	OGC Nice	38	15	7	16	50 - 53	52	7	3	9	25 - 30	8	4	7	25 - 23
10.	FC Metz	38	12	11	15	44 - 48	47	5	5	9	19 - 26	7	6	6	25 - 22
11.	AS Saint-Étienne	38	12	10	16	42 - 54	46	5	6	8	20 - 29	7	4	8	22 - 25
12.	FC Girondins de Bordeaux	38	13	6	19	42 - 56	45	7	4	8	19 - 21	6	2	11	23 - 35
13.	Angers SCO	38	12	8	18	40 - 58	44	6	3	10	20 - 27	6	5	8	20 - 31
14.	Stade de Reims	38	9	15	14	42 - 50	42	4	8	7	16 - 21	5	7	7	26 - 29
15.	Racing Club de Strasbourg	38	11	9	18	49 - 58	42	4	5	10	21 - 29	7	4	8	28 - 29
16.	FC Lorient-Bretagne Sud	38	11	9	18	50 - 68	42	10	2	7	31 - 29	1	7	11	19 - 39
17.	Stade Brestois 29	38	11	8	19	50 - 66	41	8	4	7	32 - 33	3	4	12	18 - 33
18.	FC Nantes (*Relegation Play-offs*)	38	9	13	16	47 - 55	40	3	8	8	21 - 29	6	5	8	26 - 26
19.	Nîmes Olympique (*Relegated*)	38	9	8	21	40 - 71	35	3	5	11	22 - 39	6	3	10	18 - 32
20.	Dijon FCO (*Relegated*)	38	4	9	25	25 - 73	21	1	6	12	8 - 31	3	3	13	17 - 42

Top goalscorers:

27	**Kylian Sanmi Mbappé Lottin**	*Paris Saint-Germain FC*
20	Wissam Ben Yedder	*AS Monaco FC*
20	Memphis Depay (NED)	*Olympique Lyonnais*
16	Ludovic Ajorque	*Racing Club de Strasbourg*
16	Gaëtan Laborde	*Montpellier Hérault SC*
16	Kevin Volland (GER)	*AS Monaco FC*
16	Burak Yılmaz (TUR)	*Lille OSC*

Relegation Play-offs [27-30.05.2021]

Toulouse FC - FC Nantes   1-2(1-2)   1-0(0-0)
FC Nantes remains at first level for 2021/2022.

NATIONAL CUP
Coupe de France 2020/2021

Round of 64 [30.01./09-11.02./20-21.02./25.02.2021]

US Sinnamary - Club Franciscain Le François	1-1 aet; 1-3 pen		FC Fleury 91 - FC Annecy	1-1 aet; 4-5 pen
Stade de Reims - Valenciennes FC	3-4(1-1)		US Montagnarde - Stade Briochin	1-1 aet; 3-2 pen
FC Lorient-Bretagne Sud - Paris FC	2-1(0-1)		Loon-Plage FC - US Boulogne-sur-Mer Côte d'Opale	0-3(0-1)
Olympique Lyonnais - AC Ajaccio	5-1(4-0)		Red Star FC Paris - US Quevilly-Rouen	2-1(1-1)
FC Girondins de Bordeaux - Toulouse FC	0-2(0-1)		Aubagne FC - US Lège-Cap-Ferret	2-2 aet; 4-2 pen
Grenoble Foot 38 - AS Monaco FC	0-1(0-1)		GFA Rumilly-Vallières - AS Prix-lès-Mézières	0-0 aet; 4-2 pen
Racing Club de Strasbourg - Montpellier Hérault SC	0-2(0-1)		FC Guichen - Olympique Saumur FC	0-1(0-0)
AJ Auxerre - Olympique de Marseille	0-2(0-0)		OS Aire-sur-la-Lys - AS Beauvais Oise	1-4(1-2)
FC Nantes - Racing Club de Lens	2-4(1-3)		Olympique Alès - AS Fabrègues	2-0(1-0)
Amiens SC - FC Metz	1-2(0-1)		Le Puy Foot 43 - FC Chamalières	0-0 aet; 5-4 pen
Stade Brestois 29- Rodez Aveyron Football	2-1(2-1)		Canet Roussillon FC - Stade Poitevin FC	1-1 aet; 4-2 pen
Nîmes Olympique - OGC Nice	1-3(1-2)		SC Schiltigheim - CS Sedan Ardennes	0-4(0-3)
Dijon FCO - Lille OSC	0-1(0-1)		Les Herbiers Vendée - Voltigeurs de Châteaubriant	0-1(0-0)
Stade Malherbe Caen - Paris Saint-Germain FC	0-1(0-0)		Saint Brice FC - Gazélec FC Ajaccio	0-1(0-1)
FC Sochaux-Montbéliard - AS Saint-Étienne	1-0(1-0)		UF Mâconnais - FC Saint-Louis Neuweg	0-0 aet; 2-4 pen
Angers SCO - Stade Rennais FC	2-1(2-0)		Sologne Olympique Romorantin - FC Mtsapéré	2-0(2-0)

Round of 32 [05-08.03.2021]

AS Beauvais Oise - US Boulogne-sur-Mer	0-2(0-1)		Olympique Saumur FC - US Montagnarde	3-3 aet; 4-3 pen
Aubagne FC - Toulouse FC	0-2(0-1)		Olympique Lyonnais - FC Sochaux-Montbéliard	5-2(3-1)
Red Star FC Paris - Racing Club de Lens	3-2(1-1)		Stade Brestois 29- Paris Saint-Germain FC	0-3(0-2)
GFA Rumilly-Vallières - FC Annecy	1-1 aet; 6-5 pen		Gazélec FC Ajaccio - Lille OSC	1-3(0-1)
FC Saint-Louis Neuweg - CS Sedan Ardennes	0-2(0-0)		Angers SCO - Club Franciscain	5-0(2-0)
Olympique Alès - Montpellier Hérault SC	1-2(1-1)		SO Romorantin - Voltigeurs de Châteaubriant	1-3(0-2)
Valenciennes FC - FC Metz	0-4(0-2)		Canet Roussillon FC - Olympique de Marseille	2-1(1-1)
Le Puy Foot 43 - FC Lorient-Bretagne Sud	1-0(0-0)		OGC Nice - AS Monaco FC	0-2(0-1)

Round of 16 [17.03./06-08.04.2021]

Paris Saint-Germain FC - Lille OSC	3-0(2-0)		Olympique Saumur FC - Toulouse FC	1-2(1-1)
AS Monaco FC - FC Metz	0-0 aet; 5-4 pen		Canet Roussillon FC - US Boulogne-sur-Mer	1-0(1-0)
GFA Rumilly-Vallières - Le Puy Foot 43	4-0(1-0)		Voltigeurs de Châteaubriant-Montpellier Hérault SC	0-1(0-0)
CS Sedan Ardennes - Angers SCO	0-1(0-1)		Red Star FC Paris - Olympique Lyonnais	2-2 aet; 4-5 pen

Quarter-Finals [20-21.04.2021]

GFA Rumilly-Vallières - Toulouse FC	2-0(1-0)		Paris Saint-Germain FC - Angers SCO	5-0(2-0)
Canet Roussillon FC - Montpellier Hérault SC	1-2(1-0)		Olympique Lyonnais - AS Monaco FC	0-2(0-0)

Semi-Finals [12-13.05.2021]

Montpellier Hérault SC - Paris Saint-Germain FC	2-2 aet; 5-6 pen		GFA Rumilly-Vallières - AS Monaco FC	1-5(1-2)

Final

19.05.2021; Stade de France, Saint-Denis, Paris; Referee: François Letexier; Attendance: 0,000

Paris Saint-Germain FC - AS Monaco FC   **2-0(1-0)**

Paris Saint-Germain: Keilor Antonio Navas Gamboa, Jan Thilo Kehrer, Alessandro Florenzi (68.Colin Dagba), Marcos Aoás Corrêa „Marquinhos" (Cap), Abdou Diallo, Leandro Daniel Paredes (79.Ander Herrera Agüera), Danilo Luís Hélio Pereira, Idrissa Gana Gueye, Ángel Fabián Di María Hernández (90.Pablo Sarabia García), Mauro Icardi (79.Bioty Moise Kean), Kylian Sanmi Mbappé Lottin. Trainer: Mauricio Roberto Pochettino Trossero (Argentina).

AS Monaco: Radosław Majecki, Djibril Sidibé, Ruben Aguilar (46.Krépin Diatta), Axel Disasi (74.Benoît Badiashile), Guillermo Alfonso Maripán Loayza, Caio Henrique Oliveira Silva, Aurélien Tchouaméni, Aleksandr Golovin, Youssouf Fofana (60.Gelson Dany Batalha Martins), Kevin Volland (74.Francesc „Cesc" Fàbregas Soler), Wissam Ben Yedder (Cap) (60.Stevan Jovetić). Trainer: Niko Kovač (Croatia).

Goals: 1-0 Mauro Icardi (19), 2-0 Kylian Sanmi Mbappé Lottin (81).

Angers Sporting Club de l'Ouest

Founded: 1919
Stadium: Stade "Raymond Kopa", Angers (18,752)
Trainer: Stéphane Moulin   04.08.1967

Goalkeepers:	DOB	M	(s)	G
Paul Bernardoni	18.04.1997	38		
Defenders:	**DOB**	**M**	**(s)**	**G**
Rayan Aït Nouri	06.06.2001	2	(1)	
Abdoulaye Bamba (CIV)	25.04.1990	16		
Souleyman Doumbia (CIV)	24.09.1996	24	(3)	
Enzo Ebosse	11.03.1999	3	(3)	
Vincent Manceau	10.07.1989	25	(2)	
Mateo Pavlović (CRO)	09.06.1990	12	(2)	
Romain Thomas	12.06.1988	34		4
Ismaël Traoré (CIV)	18.08.1986	34		3
Midfielders:	**DOB**	**M**	**(s)**	**G**
Ibrahim Amadou	06.04.1993	20	(4)	
Antonin Bobichon	14.09.1995	10	(13)	
Sofiane Boufal (MAR)	17.09.1993	9	(5)	1
Pierrick Capelle	15.04.1987	24	(11)	3
Lassana Coulibaly (MLI)	10.04.1996	18	(11)	1
Angelo Fulgini	20.08.1996	33		7

	DOB	M	(s)	G
Thomas Mangani	29.04.1987	32	(3)	3
Zinédine Ould Khaled	14.01.2000		(3)	
Mathias Pereira Lage (POR)	30.11.1996	16	(12)	4
Baptiste Santamaría	09.03.1995	3		
Waniss Taïbi	07.03.2002		(2)	
Forwards:	**DOB**	**M**	**(s)**	**G**
Rachid Alioui (MAR)	18.06.1992		(1)	
Stéphane Bahoken	28.05.1992	18	(12)	6
Jimmy Cabot	18.04.1994	8	(14)	1
Mohamed-Ali Cho	19.01.2004	1	(20)	
Loïs Diony	20.12.1992	20	(16)	5
Farid El Melali (ALG)	05.05.1997	4	(13)	1
Noah Fatar	15.02.2002		(2)	
Yassin Fortuné	30.01.1999		(1)	
Wilfried Kanga Aka	21.02.1998	2		
Casimir Ninga (CHA)	17.05.1993		(1)	
Sada Thioub	01.06.1995	12	(15)	1

Football Club des Girondins de Bordeaux

Founded: 1881
Stadium: Matmut Atlantique, Bordeaux (42,115)
Trainer: Paulo Manuel Carvalho Sousa (POR)   30.08.1970
[10.08.2020] Jean-Louis Gasset   09.12.1953

Goalkeepers:	DOB	M	(s)	G
Benoît Costil	03.07.1987	38		
Defenders:	**DOB**	**M**	**(s)**	**G**
Paul Baysse	18.05.1988	29	(2)	2
Loris Benito (SUI)	07.01.1992	30	(1)	
Loïc Bessilé	19.02.1999	1		
Laurent Koscielny	10.09.1985	25	(1)	
Enock Kwateng	09.04.1997	12	(6)	1
Edson André Sitoe „Mexer" (MOZ)	08.09.1988	8	(1)	
Pablo Nascimento Castro (BRA)	21.06.1991	12	(1)	1
Maxime Poundjé	16.08.1992	4	(10)	
Youssouf Sabaly (SEN)	05.03.1993	33		1
Midfielders:	**DOB**	**M**	**(s)**	**G**
Yacine Adli	29.07.2000	25	(10)	2
Toma Bašić (CRO)	25.11.1996	32	(2)	4
Hatem Ben Arfa	07.03.1987	19	(5)	2

	DOB	M	(s)	G
Tom Lacoux	25.01.2002	6	(7)	
Otávio Henrique Passos Santos (BRA)	04.05.1994	18		1
Rubén Pardo Gutiérrez (ESP)	22.10.1992		(2)	
Jean Michaël Seri (CIV)	19.07.1991	9	(3)	
Issouf Sissokho (MLI)	30.01.2002		(6)	1
Forwards:	**DOB**	**M**	**(s)**	**G**
Dilane Bakwa	26.08.2002		(7)	
Jimmy Briand	02.08.1985	1	(23)	1
Nicolas de Préville	08.01.1991	15	(18)	1
Hwang Ui-jo (KOR)	28.08.1992	32	(4)	12
Samuel Kalu Ojim (NGA)	26.08.1997	14	(6)	4
Joshua Erowoli Orisunmihare Oluwaseun Maja (NGA)	27.12.1998	11	(6)	2
Sékou Mara	30.07.2002	2	(6)	1
Rémi Oudin	18.11.1996	27	(11)	4
Amadou Traoré	07.03.2002		(19)	
Mehdi Zerkane (ALG)	15.07.1999	15	(12)	1

Stade Brestois 29

Founded: 1950
Stadium: Stade „Francis-Le Blé", Brest (15,931)
Trainer: Olivier Dall'Oglio   16.05.1964

Goalkeepers:	DOB	M	(s)	G
Sébastien Cibois	02.03.1998	3		
Gautier Larsonneur	23.02.1997	35		
Defenders:	**DOB**	**M**	**(s)**	**G**
Ludovic Baal (GYF)	24.05.1986	3	(4)	
Lilian Brassier	02.11.1999	11		1
Brendan Chardonnet	22.12.1994	30	(3)	3
Jean-Kevin Duverne	12.07.1997	22	(5)	1
Julien Faussurier	14.01.1987	9	(8)	
Christophe Hérelle	22.08.1992	15	(1)	
Romain Perraud	22.09.1997	35		3
Ronaël Pierre-Gabriel	13.06.1998	28	(1)	1
Midfielders:	**DOB**	**M**	**(s)**	**G**
Cristian Battocchio (ITA)	10.02.1992	2	(13)	
Haris Belkebla (ALG)	28.01.1994	33	(2)	

	DOB	M	(s)	G
Ibrahima Diallo	08.03.1999	5		
Bandiougou Fadiga	15.01.2001		(4)	
Romain Faivre	14.07.1998	33	(3)	6
Jean Lucas de Souza Oliveira (BRA)	22.06.1998	11	(5)	
Paul Lasne	16.01.1989	19	(3)	
Hugo Magnetti	30.05.1998	7	(6)	
Hiang'a Mbock	28.12.1999	4	(8)	
Forwards:	**DOB**	**M**	**(s)**	**G**
Irvin Cardona	08.08.1997	22	(14)	8
Gaëtan Charbonnier	27.12.1988	17	(19)	6
Heriberto Moreno Borges Tavares (POR)	19.02.1997		(4)	
Franck Honorat	11.08.1996	28	(8)	8
Jérémy Le Douaron	21.04.1998	7	(21)	1
Steve Mounié (BEN)	29.09.1994	31	(4)	9
Romain Philippoteaux	02.03.1988	8	(9)	1

Dijon Football Côte d'Or

Founded:	1998		
Stadium:	Stade „Gaston Gérard", Dijon (15,995)		
Trainer:	Stéphane Jobard	21.02.1971	
[06.11.2020]	David Linarès	05.10.1975	

Goalkeepers:	DOB	M	(s)	G
Saturnin Allagbe (BEN)	22.11.1993	12		
Amigo Alfred Junior Gomis (SEN)	05.09.1993	5		
Anthony Racioppi (SUI)	31.12.1998	21		
Defenders:	**DOB**	**M**	**(s)**	**G**
Sacha Boey	13.09.2000	21	(3)	
Fouad Chafik (MAR)	16.10.1986	18	(5)	1
Aníbal Hernán Chalá Ayoví (ECU)	09.05.1996	9	(4)	
Senou Coulibaly	04.09.1994	22		2
Bruno Écuélé Manga (GAB)	16.07.1988	38		2
Wesley Lautoa	25.08.1987	19	(6)	
Glody Ngonda Muzinga (COD)	31.12.1994	25	(5)	2
Ahmad Toure Ngouyamsa Nounchil (CMR)	21.12.2000	2	(1)	
Jonathan Panzo (ENG)	25.10.2000	21	(1)	
Arthur Zagre	04.10.2001	1	(2)	
Midfielders:	**DOB**	**M**	**(s)**	**G**
Romain Amalfitano	27.08.1989	1	(1)	
Yassine Benzia (ALG)	08.09.1994	5	(2)	2
Bersant Celina (KVX)	09.09.1996	25	(7)	

Éric Junior Dina Ebimbe	21.11.2000	25	(5)	1
Pape Cheikh Diop Gueye (ESP)	08.08.1997	13	(8)	
Jordan Marié	29.09.1991	16	(8)	
Didier Ndong (GAB)	17.06.1994	29		
Frédéric Sammaritano	23.03.1986	10	(20)	
Wilitty Younoussa (CMR)	09.09.2001	1	(2)	
Forwards:	**DOB**	**M**	**(s)**	**G**
Roger Assalé (CIV)	13.11.1993	11	(6)	1
Mama Samba Baldé (GNB)	06.11.1995	24	(5)	7
Erwan Belhadji	22.06.2001		(1)	
Mounir Chouiar	23.01.1999	14	(9)	
Charles Costes	16.09.2002		(1)	
Mihai-Alexandru Dobre (ROU)	30.08.1998	4	(18)	
Aboubakar Kamara	07.03.1995	7	(3)	1
Moussa Konaté (SEN)	03.04.1993	13	(14)	5
Rayan Philippe	23.10.2000	1	(3)	
Aurélien Scheidler	04.06.1998	3	(7)	1
Jacques-Julien Siwe	29.07.2001	2	(3)	

Racing Club de Lens

Founded:	1906	
Stadium:	Stade „Bollaert-Delelis", Lens (37,705)	
Trainer:	Franck Haise	15.04.1971

Goalkeepers:	DOB	M	(s)	G
Wuilker Faríñez Aray (VEN)	15.02.1998	1	(2)	
Jean-Louis Leca	21.09.1985	37		
Defenders:	**DOB**	**M**	**(s)**	**G**
Loïc Badé	11.04.2000	29	(2)	
Ismaël Boura	14.08.2000	8	(12)	
Jonathan Clauss	25.09.1992	30	(3)	3
Steven Fortès (CPV)	17.04.1992	16	(2)	
Jonathan Gradit	24.11.1992	33		
Massadio Haïdara	02.12.1992	24	(1)	2
Adrien Louveau	01.02.2000		(1)	
Facundo Axel Medina (ARG)	28.05.1999	23	(1)	2
Clément Michelin	11.05.1997	13	(13)	
Aleksandar Radovanović (SRB)	11.11.1993	1		
Issiaga Sylla (GUI)	01.01.1994	13	(7)	1
Cheick Traoré	31.03.1995		(2)	

Midfielders:	DOB	M	(s)	G
Yannick Cahuzac	18.01.1985	26	(4)	1
David Pereira Da Costa (POR)	05.01.2001	1	(6)	1
Cheick Doucouré (MLI)	08.01.2000	30	(3)	2
Seko Fofana (CIV)	07.05.1995	25	(5)	2
Gaël Romeo Kakuta Mabenga (COD)	21.06.1991	30	(5)	11
Tony Mauricio	22.03.1994	2	(24)	
Manuel Perez	11.05.1991	1	(3)	
Forwards:	**DOB**	**M**	**(s)**	**G**
Simon Banza	13.08.1996	12	(22)	5
Ignatius Kpene Ganago (CMR)	16.02.1999	16	(8)	7
Corentin Jean	15.07.1995	6	(17)	1
Arnaud Kalimuendo	20.01.2002	13	(15)	7
Florian Sotoca	25.10.1990	28	(5)	8
Ansou Sow (SEN)	09.05.2000		(1)	

Lille Olympique Sporting Club

Founded:	23.09.1944	
Stadium:	Stade "Pierre Mauroy", Villeneuve-d'Ascq (50,186)	
Trainer:	Christophe Galtier	26.08.1966

Goalkeepers:	DOB	M	(s)	G
Mike Maignan	03.07.1995	38		
Defenders:	**DOB**	**M**	**(s)**	**G**
Sven Botman (NED)	12.01.2000	37		
Domagoj Bradarić (CRO)	10.12.1999	14	(12)	1
Zeki Çelik (TUR)	17.02.1997	28	(1)	3
José Miguel da Rocha Fonte (POR)	22.12.1983	36		3
Jérémy Pied	23.02.1989	4	(2)	
Reinildo Isnard Mandava (MOZ)	21.01.1994	24	(5)	
Adama Soumaoro	18.06.1992	1	(2)	
Tiago Emanuel Embaló Djaló (POR)	09.04.2000	8	(9)	
Midfielders:	**DOB**	**M**	**(s)**	**G**
Benjamin André	03.08.1990	35		

Renato Júnior Luz Sanches (POR)	18.08.1997	14	(9)	1
Boubakary Soumaré	27.02.1999	21	(11)	
Miguel Ângelo da Silva Rocha „Xeka" (POR)	10.11.1994	11	(22)	1
Yusuf Yazıcı (TUR)	29.01.1997	10	(22)	7
Forwards:	**DOB**	**M**	**(s)**	**G**
Jonathan Bamba	26.03.1996	34	(4)	6
Jonathan Christian David (CAN)	14.01.2000	29	(8)	13
Jonathan Ikoné	02.05.1998	26	(11)	4
Isaac Lihadji	10.04.2002	1	(14)	
Luiz Araujo Guimarães Neto (BRA)	02.06.1996	17	(11)	4
Timothy Tarpeh Weah (USA)	22.02.2000	7	(21)	3
Burak Yılmaz (TUR)	15.07.1985	23	(5)	16

Football Club Lorient-Bretagne Sud

Founded:	1926	
Stadium:	Stade du Moustoir, Lorient (18,890)	
Trainer:	Christophe Pélissier	05.10.1965

Goalkeepers:	DOB	M	(s)	G
Matthieu Dreyer	20.03.1989	15		
Paul Nardi	18.05.1994	23		
Defenders:	**DOB**	**M**	**(s)**	**G**
Trevoh Chalobah (ENG)	05.07.1999	24	(5)	2
Yoann Etienne	19.05.1997	1		
Thomas Fontaine (MAD)	08.05.1991	4		
Andreaw Gravillon (GPE)	08.02.1998	26		1
Jérôme Hergault	05.04.1986	19	(3)	2
Julien Laporte	04.11.1993	30		
Vincent Le Goff	15.10.1989	26		
Houboulang Mendes	04.05.1998	15	(2)	
Jérémy Morel (MAD)	02.04.1984	28		
Loris Mouyokolo	22.05.2001		(1)	
Midfielders:	**DOB**	**M**	**(s)**	**G**
Laurent Abergel	01.02.1993	32	(6)	3

Quentin Boisgard	17.03.1997	17	(7)	2
Jonathan Delaplace	20.03.1986	9	(9)	
Enzo Le Fée	03.02.2000	21	(15)	
Fabien Lemoine	16.03.1987	24	(6)	1
Sylvain Marveaux	15.04.1986	2	(7)	
Thomas Monconduit	10.02.1991	12	(15)	2
Franklin Wadja (CMR)	01.05.1995		(4)	
Forwards:	**DOB**	**M**	**(s)**	**G**
Umut Dilan Bozok (TUR)	19.09.1996		(5)	
Stéphane Diarra (CIV)	09.12.1998	2	(11)	
Adrian Grbić (AUT)	04.08.1996	9	(24)	4
Pierre-Yves Hamel	19.03.1994	7	(16)	4
Armand Laurienté	04.12.1998	16	(13)	3
Terem Igobor Moffi (NGA)	25.05.1999	26	(6)	14
Yoane Wissa	03.09.1996	30	(8)	10

Olympique Lyonnais

Founded: 1950
Stadium: Groupama Stadium, Décines-Charpieu, Lyon (59,186)
Trainer: Rudi García   20.02.1964

Goalkeepers:	DOB	M	(s)	G
Anthony Lopes (POR)	01.10.1990	38		

Defenders:	DOB	M	(s)	G
Joachim Andersen (DEN)	31.05.1996	2	(1)	
Melvin Bard	06.11.2000	4	(10)	
Djamel Eddine Benlamri (ALG)	25.12.1989		(6)	
Maxwel Cornet (CIV)	27.09.1996	29	(7)	2
Mattia De Sciglio (ITA)	20.10.1992	14	(15)	
Jason Denayer (BEL)	28.06.1995	31		1
Sinaly Diomandé (CIV)	09.04.2001	10	(17)	
Léo Michel Joseph Claude Dubois	14.09.1994	35	(2)	2
Malo Gusto	19.05.2003		(2)	
Marcelo Antônio Guedes Filho (BRA)	20.05.1987	34		3
Fernando Marçal de Oliveira (BRA)	19.02.1989	1		
Kenny Joelle Tete (NED)	09.10.1995		(1)	

Midfielders:	DOB	M	(s)	G
Houssem Aouar	30.06.1998	23	(7)	7
Bruno Guimarães Rodriguez Moura (BRA)	16.11.1997	21	(12)	3
Maxence Caqueret	15.02.2000	19	(10)	
Rayan Cherki	17.08.2003	5	(22)	1
Florent Da Silva	02.04.2003		(1)	
Jean Lucas de Souza Oliveira (BRA)	22.06.1998	1	(7)	
Habib Keita (MLI)	05.02.2002		(1)	
Lucas Tolentino Coelho de Lima „Paquetá" (BRA)	27.08.1997	27	(3)	9
Jeff Reine-Adélaïde	17.01.1998		(1)	
Thiago Henrique Mendes Ribeiro (BRA)	15.03.1992	23	(9)	

Forwards:	DOB	M	(s)	G
Moussa Dembélé	12.07.1996	6	(10)	
Memphis Depay (NED)	13.02.1994	33	(4)	20
Tino Kadewere (ZIM)	05.01.1996	24	(9)	10
Islam Slimani (ALG)	18.06.1988	4	(14)	3
Yaya Soumaré	23.06.2000		(3)	
Karl Toko Ekambi (CMR)	14.09.1992	34	(1)	14

Olympique de Marseille

Founded: 31.08.1899
Stadium: Stade Orange Vélodrome, Marseille (67,394)
Trainer: Luís André de Pina Cabral e Villas-Boas   17.10.1977
[03.02.2021] Nasser Larguet (MAR)   06.11.1958
[26.02.2021] Jorge Luis Sampaoli Moya (ARG)   13.03.1960

Goalkeepers:	DOB	M	(s)	G
Steve Mandanda Mpidi	28.03.1985	37		
Yohann Pelé	04.11.1982	1		

Defenders:	DOB	M	(s)	G
Álvaro González Soberón (ESP)	08.01.1990	32		2
Jordan Amavi	09.03.1994	10	(3)	1
Leonardo Julián Balerdi Rosa (ARG)	26.01.1999	19	(2)	2
Duje Ćaleta-Car (CRO)	17.09.1996	32	(1)	2
Pol Mikel Lirola Kosok (ESP)	13.08.1997	17	(2)	2
Yuto Nagatomo (JPN)	12.09.1986	20	(5)	
Lucas Perrin	19.11.1998	3	(4)	1
Christopher Rocchia	01.02.1998		(2)	
Hiroki Sakai (JPN)	12.04.1990	26	(3)	
Bouna Sarr (GUI)	31.01.1992		(2)	

Midfielders:	DOB	M	(s)	G
Mickaël Bruno Dominique Cuisance	16.08.1999	11	(12)	2
Pape Alassane Gueye	24.01.1999	22	(10)	2
Boubacar Kamara	23.11.1999	35		
Saîf-Eddine Khaoui (TUN)	27.04.1995	5	(12)	2
Maxime López	04.12.1997	2	(2)	
Olivier Ntcham	09.02.1996	2	(2)	
Dimitri Payet	29.03.1987	28	(5)	7
Valentin Rongier	07.12.1994	21	(5)	1
Morgan Sanson	18.08.1994	10	(2)	2
Cheick Souaré	03.09.2002		(1)	
Kevin Strootman (NED)	13.02.1990	1	(10)	

Forwards:	DOB	M	(s)	G
Marley Aké	05.01.2001		(9)	
Darío Ismael Benedetto (ARG)	17.05.1990	19	(13)	5
Cheikh Bamba Dieng (SEN)	23.03.2000	2	(3)	
Valère Germain	17.04.1990	6	(18)	3
Luis Henrique Tomaz de Lima (BRA)	14.12.2001	6	(13)	
Arkadiusz Milik (POL)	28.02.1994	14	(1)	9
Nemanja Radonjić (SRB)	15.02.1996	4	(8)	2
Florian Thauvin	26.01.1993	33	(3)	8

Football Club de Metz

Founded: 1932
Stadium: Stade Municipal Saint-Symphorien, Metz (25,636)
Trainer: Vincent Hognon   16.08.1974
[13.10.2020] Frédéric Antonetti   19.08.1961

Goalkeepers:	DOB	M	(s)	G
Marc-Aurèle Caillard	12.05.1994	4	(1)	
Alexandre Oukidja (ALG)	19.07.1988	34		

Defenders:	DOB	M	(s)	G
John Boye (GHA)	23.04.1987	35		1
Dylan Bronn (TUN)	19.06.1995	38		2
Fabien Centonze	16.01.1996	36		1
Thomas Delaine	24.03.1992	19	(5)	3
Mamadou Fofana (MLI)	21.01.1998	11	(5)	
Boubakar Kouyaté (MLI)	15.04.1997	21	(4)	1
Matthieu Udol	20.03.1996	19	(6)	

Midfielders:	DOB	M	(s)	G
Victorien Angban (CIV)	29.09.1996	21	(5)	
Farid Boulaya (ALG)	25.02.1993	32	(1)	6
Habib Maïga (CIV)	01.01.1996	31		1
Youssef Maziz	24.06.1998	2	(9)	
Kévin N'Doram	22.01.1996	4	(2)	
Vincent Pajot	19.08.1990	11	(1)	
Pape Sarr (SEN)	14.09.2002	18	(4)	3
Warren Tchimbembé	21.04.1998	4	(11)	
Boubacar Traoré (MLI)	20.08.2001		(2)	1

Forwards:	DOB	M	(s)	G
Thierry Ambrose	28.03.1997	5	(18)	
Habibou Mouhamadou Diallo (SEN)	18.06.1995	1	(3)	
Lamine Mamadou Gueye (SEN)	13.03.1998	19	(7)	3
Aaron Leya Iseka (BEL)	15.11.1997	12	(9)	4
Opa Nguette	08.07.1994	13	(3)	3
Ibrahima Niane (SEN)	11.03.1999	9	(1)	6
Cheikh Tidiane Sabaly (SEN)	04.03.1999		(1)	
Vagner José Dias Gonçalves (CPV)	10.01.1996	10	(16)	4
Papa Ndiaga Yade (SEN)	05.01.2000	9	(19)	3

Association Sportive de Monaco Football Club

Founded: 23.08.1924
Stadium: Stade „Louis II", Monaco (18,523)
Trainer: Niko Kovač (CRO) 15.10.1971

Goalkeepers:	DOB	M	(s)	G
Benjamin Lecomte	26.04.1991	28		
Radosław Majecki (POL)	16.11.1999	1		
Vito Mannone (ITA)	02.03.1988	9		
Defenders:	**DOB**	**M**	**(s)**	**G**
Ruben Aguilar	26.04.1993	27	(6)	1
Benoît Badiashile	26.03.2001	32	(3)	2
Fodé Ballo-Touré	03.01.1997	6	(18)	
Giulian Biancone	31.03.2000	1	(1)	
Caio Henrique Oliveira Silva (BRA)	31.07.1997	26	(5)	
Axel Disasi	11.03.1998	24	(5)	3
Guillermo Alfonso Maripán Loayza (CHI)	06.05.1994	22	(6)	5
Chrislain Matsima	15.05.2002	3	(6)	
Strahinja Pavlović (SRB)	24.05.2001		(1)	
Djibril Sidibé	29.07.1992	21	(9)	
Midfielders:	**DOB**	**M**	**(s)**	**G**
Jean-Eudes Pascal Aholou (CIV)	20.03.1994		(2)	
Francesc „Cesc" Fàbregas Soler (ESP)	04.05.1987	7	(14)	2
Sofiane Diop	09.06.2000	24	(8)	7
Florentino Ibrain Morris Luís (POR)	19.08.1999	2	(7)	
Youssouf Fofana	10.01.1999	35		
Aleksandr Golovin (RUS)	30.05.1996	12	(9)	5
Eliot Matazo (BEL)	15.02.2002	3	(7)	1
Enzo Millot	17.07.2002		(2)	
Aurélien Tchouaméni	27.01.2000	36		2
Forwards:	**DOB**	**M**	**(s)**	**G**
Wissam Ben Yedder	12.08.1990	32	(5)	20
Krépin Diatta (SEN)	25.02.1999	3	(9)	1
Gelson Dany Batalha Martins (POR)	11.05.1995	20	(3)	3
Willem Geubbels	16.08.2001	2	(12)	1
Stevan Jovetić (MNE)	02.11.1989	6	(23)	6
Henry Chukwuemeka Onyekuru (NGA)	05.06.1997	2	(2)	
Pietro Pellegri (ITA)	17.03.2001		(16)	1
Kevin Volland (GER)	30.07.1992	34	(1)	16

Montpellier Hérault Sport Club

Founded: 1919
Stadium: Stade de la Mosson, Montpellier (32,939)
Trainer: Michel Der Zakarian 18.02.1963

Goalkeepers:	DOB	M	(s)	G
Dimitry Bertaud	06.06.1998	7	(2)	
Jonas Omlin (SUI)	10.01.1994	31		
Defenders:	**DOB**	**M**	**(s)**	**G**
Daniel Congré	05.04.1985	38		2
Nicolas Cozza	08.01.1999	15	(5)	
Vitorino Hilton de Silva (BRA)	13.09.1977	24	(5)	
Ambroise Oyongo Bitolo (CMR)	22.06.1991	5	(8)	1
Pedro Filipe Teodosio Mendes (POR)	01.10.1990	19	(3)	2
Junior Sambia	07.09.1996	26	(10)	1
Arnaud Souquet	12.02.1992	14	(9)	1
Clément Vidal	18.06.2000	1	(1)	
Midfielders:	**DOB**	**M**	**(s)**	**G**
Samy Benchama	25.06.2000		(5)	
Joris Chotard	24.09.2001	11	(18)	
Sacha Delaye	23.04.2002		(1)	
Jordan Ferri	12.03.1992	31	(3)	
Damien Le Tallec	19.04.1990	13	(10)	
Florent Mollet	19.11.1991	30	(4)	3
Mihailo Ristić (SRB)	31.10.1995	26	(8)	
Téji Savanier	22.12.1991	26	(1)	5
Forwards:	**DOB**	**M**	**(s)**	**G**
Andy Delort (ALG)	09.10.1991	30		15
Keagan Larenzo Dolly (RSA)	22.01.1993	3	(15)	
Gaëtan Laborde	03.05.1994	38		16
Stephy Mavididi (ENG)	31.05.1998	23	(12)	9
Petar Škuletić (SRB)	29.06.1990	1	(18)	2
Elye Wahi	02.01.2003	3	(15)	3
Yun Il-lok (KOR)	07.03.1992	3	(9)	

Football Club de Nantes

Founded: 1943
Stadium: Stade de la Beaujoire, Nantes (35,322)
Trainer: Christian Jean Gourcuff 05.04.1955
[26.12.2020] Raymond Domenech 24.01.1952
[11.02.2021] Antoine Krilone Kombouaré 16.11.1963

Goalkeepers:	DOB	M	(s)	G
Alban Lafont	23.01.1999	38		
Defenders:	**DOB**	**M**	**(s)**	**G**
Andrei Girotto (BRA)	17.02.1992	29	(5)	1
Dennis Appiah	09.06.1992	16	(6)	
Jean-Charles Castelletto (CMR)	26.01.1995	22	(2)	1
Sébastien Corchia	01.11.1990	23	(2)	
Fábio Pereira da Silva (BRA)	09.07.1990	19	(3)	
Nicolas Pallois	19.09.1987	31	(1)	2
Abdoulaye Sylla (GUI)	10.04.2000		(2)	
Charles Traoré (MLI)	01.01.1992	19	(3)	1
Midfielders:	**DOB**	**M**	**(s)**	**G**
Mehdi Abeid	06.08.1992	15	(3)	
Ludovic Blas	31.12.1997	32	(4)	10
Imrân Louza (MAR)	01.05.1999	28	(5)	7
Batista Mendy	12.01.2000		(2)	
Samuel Moutoussamy	12.08.1996	1		
Pedro Chirivella Burgos (ESP)	23.05.1997	26	(6)	
Roli Pereira de Sa	10.12.1996		(6)	
Abdoulaye Touré	03.03.1994	20	(9)	2
Forwards:	**DOB**	**M**	**(s)**	**G**
Jean-Kévin Augustin	16.06.1997		(3)	
Abdoul Kader Bamba	25.05.1994	6	(23)	3
Marcus Coco	24.06.1996	16	(16)	
Kalifa Coulibaly (MLI)	21.08.1991	11	(6)	3
Renaud Emond (BEL)	05.12.1991	3	(19)	2
Randal Kolo Muani (COD)	05.12.1998	35	(2)	9
Bridge Ndilu	21.07.2000		(6)	
Moses Daddy-Ayala Simon (NGA)	12.07.1995	28	(5)	6

Olympique Gymnaste Club Nice Côte d'Azur

Founded: 09.07.1904 (*as Le Gymnaste Club de Nice*)
Stadium: Allianz Riviera, Nice (35,624)
Trainer: Patrick Vieira 23.06.1976
[04.12.2020] Adrian Ursea (ROU) 14.09.1967

Goalkeepers:	DOB	M	(s)	G
Walter Daniel Benítez (ARG)	19.01.1993	38		
Defenders:	**DOB**	**M**	**(s)**	**G**
Youcef Atal (ALG)	17.05.1996	13	(5)	1
Patrick Burner	11.04.1996		(1)	
Flavius Daniliuc (AUT)	27.04.2001	15	(8)	1
Bonfim Costa Santos Dante (BRA)	18.10.1983	9		2
Racine Coly (SEN)	08.12.1995		(1)	
Hassane Kamara (CIV)	05.03.1994	34	(2)	2
Jordan Lotomba (SUI)	29.09.1998	24	(6)	1
Stanley N'Soki	09.04.1999	13	(5)	
Andy Pelmard	12.03.2000	12	(7)	
Robson Alves de Barros „Robson Bambu" (BRA)	12.11.1997	12	(3)	
William Saliba	24.03.2001	20		1
Jean-Clair Todibo	30.12.1999	15		1
Midfielders:	**DOB**	**M**	**(s)**	**G**
Hichem Boudaoui (ALG)	23.09.1999	22	(3)	3
Alexis Claude-Maurice	06.06.1998	21	(9)	4
Pierre Lees-Melou	25.05.1993	23	(6)	4
Jeff Reine-Adélaïde	17.01.1998	12	(2)	1
Danilo Barbosa da Silva (BRA)	28.02.1996	3	(1)	
Morgan Schneiderlin	08.11.1989	24	(4)	
Khéphren Thuram	26.03.2001	17	(12)	2
Alexis Trouillet	23.12.2000	1	(4)	
Forwards:	**DOB**	**M**	**(s)**	**G**
Salim Ben Seghir	24.02.2003		(1)	
Kasper Dolberg Rasmussen (DEN)	06.10.1997	21	(4)	6
Amine Gouiri	16.02.2000	31	(3)	12
Evann Guessand	01.07.2001		(3)	
Hicham Mahou	02.07.1999		(2)	
Myziane Maolida	14.02.1999	11	(8)	3
Dan Assane N'Doye (SUI)	25.10.2000	3	(25)	1
Marcos Paulo Mesquita Lopes „Rony Lopes" (POR)	28.12.1995	23	(5)	3
Malik Sellouki	21.03.2000		(4)	1
Eddy Sylvestre	29.08.1999	1	(3)	

Nîmes Olympique

Founded:	10.04.1937	
Stadium:	Stade des Costières, Nîmes (18,482)	
Trainer:	Jérôme Arpinon	16.08.1957
[05.02.2021]	Pascal Plancque	20.08.1963

Goalkeepers:	DOB	M	(s)	G
Baptiste Reynet	28.10.1990	38		
Defenders:	**DOB**	**M**	**(s)**	**G**
Sofiane Alakouch	29.07.1998	17	(5)	
Anthony Briançon	28.11.1994	14	(2)	
Patrick Burner	11.04.1996	14	(8)	
Kelyan Guessoum	05.02.1999	11	(4)	
Loïck Landré	05.05.1992	20		1
Pablo Martinez	21.02.1989	6	(1)	
Birger Meling (NOR)	17.12.1994	26		2
Florian Miguel	01.09.1996	18	(3)	
Gaëtan Paquiez	15.02.1994	11	(5)	
Naomichi Ueda (JPN)	24.10.1994	8	(1)	
Midfielders:	**DOB**	**M**	**(s)**	**G**
Mattéo Ahlinvi	02.07.1999	10	(10)	2
Yassine Benrahou	24.01.1999	15	(8)	
Lucas Buades	28.12.1997		(2)	
Adrián Andrés Cubas (ARG)	22.05.1996	27		1
Lucas Deaux	26.12.1988	19	(6)	1
Haris Duljević (BIH)	16.11.1993	8	(12)	
Niclas Eliasson (SWE)	07.12.1995	19	(11)	4
Zinedine Ferhat (ALG)	01.03.1993	33		6
Lamine Fomba	26.01.1998	24	(8)	1
Adilson Malanda	29.10.2001		(1)	
Renaud Ripart	14.03.1993	35	(3)	11
Sidy Sarr (SEN)	05.06.1996	6	(3)	
Antoine Valério	11.12.1999	1		
Forwards:	**DOB**	**M**	**(s)**	**G**
Karim Aribi (ALG)	24.06.1994	2	(11)	
Sami Ben Amar (MAR)	02.03.1998		(1)	
Nassim Chadli	28.07.2001		(3)	
Clément Depres	25.11.1994		(1)	
Kevin Denkey (TOG)	30.11.2000	6	(4)	1
Mahamadou Doucouré	22.05.2000		(1)	
Moussa Koné (SEN)	30.12.1996	21	(12)	9
Marco Majouga	09.05.2001		(7)	
Romain Philippoteaux	02.03.1988	3		1
Nolan Roux	01.03.1988	6	(13)	

Paris Saint-Germain Football Club

Founded:	12.08.1970	
Stadium:	Stade Parc des Princes, Paris (48,583)	
Trainer:	Thomas Tuchel (GER)	29.08.1973
[02.01.2021]	Mauricio Roberto Pochettino Trossero (ARG)	02.03.1972

Goalkeepers:	DOB	M	(s)	G
Marcin Bułka (POL)	04.10.1999	1		
Keilor Antonio Navas Gamboa (CRC)	15.12.1986	29		
Sergio Rico González (ESP)	01.09.1993	8	(2)	
Defenders:	**DOB**	**M**	**(s)**	**G**
Mitchel Bakker (NED)	20.06.2000	18	(8)	
Colin Dagba	09.09.1998	15	(10)	1
Abdou Diallo (SEN)	04.05.1996	17	(5)	
Alessandro Florenzi (ITA)	11.03.1991	18	(3)	2
Juan Bernat Velasco (ESP)	01.03.1993	2	(1)	
Jan Thilo Kehrer (GER)	21.09.1996	16	(8)	
Presnel Kimpembe	13.08.1995	26	(2)	
Layvin Kurzawa	04.09.1992	15	(4)	1
Marcos Aoás Corrêa „Marquinhos" (BRA)	14.05.1994	24	(1)	3
Timothée Pembélé	09.09.2002	3	(3)	1
Midfielders:	**DOB**	**M**	**(s)**	**G**
Ander Herrera Agüera (ESP)	14.08.1989	18	(13)	1
Bandiougou Fadiga	15.01.2001		(6)	
Idrissa Gana Gueye (SEN)	26.09.1989	20	(8)	2
Édouard Michut	04.03.2003		(1)	
Leandro Daniel Paredes (ARG)	29.06.1994	16	(5)	1
Danilo Luís Hélio Pereira (POR)	09.09.1991	16	(7)	2
Rafael Alcántara do Nascimento „Rafinha" (BRA)	12.02.1993	15	(8)	
Kays Ruiz-Atil	26.08.2002	1	(6)	
Xavi Quentin Shay Simons (NED)	21.04.2003		(1)	
Marco Verratti (ITA)	05.11.1992	16	(5)	
Forwards:	**DOB**	**M**	**(s)**	**G**
Ángel Fabián Di María Hernández (ARG)	14.02.1988	23	(4)	5
Julian Draxler (GER)	20.09.1993	12	(12)	4
Mauro Icardi (ARG)	19.02.1993	11	(9)	7
Jesé Rodríguez Ruíz (ESP)	26.02.1993		(2)	
Arnaud Kalimuendo Muinga	20.01.2002	1		
Bioty Moise Kean (ITA)	28.02.2000	22	(4)	13
Kylian Sanmi Mbappé Lottin	20.12.1998	27	(4)	27
Kenny Nagera	21.02.2002		(1)	
Neymar da Silva Santos Júnior (BRA)	05.02.1992	15	(3)	9
Pablo Sarabia García (ESP)	11.05.1992	13	(14)	6

Stade de Reims

Founded:	1931 (*as Société Sportive du Parc Pommery*)	
Stadium:	Stade „Auguste Delaune", Reims (21,684)	
Trainer:	David Guion	30.09.1967

Goalkeepers:	DOB	M	(s)	G
Yehvann Diouf	16.11.1999	1	(1)	
Predrag Rajković (SRB)	31.10.1995	37		
Defenders:	**DOB**	**M**	**(s)**	**G**
Yunis Abdelhamid (MAR)	28.09.1987	33		3
Thibault De Smet (BEL)	05.06.1998	6	(2)	
Fodé Doucouré (MLI)	03.02.2001	3	(4)	
Wout Faes (BEL)	03.04.1998	33		1
Thomas Foket (BEL)	25.09.1994	37		
Ghislain Konan (CIV)	27.12.1995	29	(2)	2
Dario Maresić (AUT)	29.09.1999	5	(3)	
Midfielders:	**DOB**	**M**	**(s)**	**G**
Valon Berisha (KVX)	07.02.1993	17	(7)	
Mathieu Cafaro	25.03.1997	27	(4)	4
Xavier Chavalerin	07.03.1991	29	(1)	
Tristan Dingomé	17.02.1991		(1)	
Mouhamadou Drammeh	15.05.1999	1	(5)	
Dion Lopy (SEN)	02.02.2002	3	(1)	
Moreto Cassamá (GNB)	16.02.1998	26	(3)	1
Marshall Munetsi (ZIM)	22.06.1996	21	(6)	1
Moïse Sakava Sangola (CMR)	26.12.2000		(1)	
Forwards:	**DOB**	**M**	**(s)**	**G**
Boulaye Dia	16.11.1996	35	(1)	14
Anastasios Donis (GRE)	29.08.1996	1	(2)	
Moussa Doumbia (MLI)	15.08.1994	9	(14)	
Hugo Ekitike	20.06.2002		(2)	
Alexis Flips	18.01.2000		(2)	1
Fraser Hornby (SCO)	13.09.1999		(3)	
Dereck Kutesa (SUI)	06.12.1997	6	(22)	1
Nathanaël Mbuku	16.03.2002	28	(4)	4
Kaj Sierhuis (NED)	27.04.1998	6	(18)	
El Bilal Touré (MLI)	03.10.2001	11	(22)	4
Arbër Zeneli (KVX)	25.02.1995	14	(14)	3

Stade Rennais Football Club

Founded: 10.03.1901
Stadium: Roazhon Park, Rennes (29,778)
Trainer: Julien Stéphan 18.09.1980
[04.03.2021] Bruno Génésio 01.09.1966

Goalkeepers:	DOB	M	(s)	G
Alfred Gomis (SEN)	05.09.1993	22		
Edouard Mendy	01.03.1992	1		
Romain Salin	29.07.1984	15		
Defenders:	**DOB**	**M**	**(s)**	**G**
Nayef Aguerd (MAR)	30.03.1996	35		3
Sacha Boey	13.09.2000	2		
Damien Da Silva	17.05.1988	30		4
Dalbert Henrique Chagas Estevão (BRA)	08.09.1993	3	(10)	
Faitout Maouassa	06.07.1998	13	(10)	
Gerzino Nyamsi	22.01.1997	10	(4)	1
Daniele Rugani (ITA)	29.07.1994	1		
Brandon Soppy	21.02.2002	5	(5)	
Hamari Traoré (MLI)	27.01.1992	34	(1)	1
Adrien Truffert	20.11.2001	23	(6)	1
Midfielders:	**DOB**	**M**	**(s)**	**G**
Benjamin Bourigeaud	14.01.1994	29	(8)	6
Eduardo Celmi Camavinga	10.11.2002	28	(7)	1
Clément Grenier	07.01.1991	12	(11)	4
James Léa Siliki	12.06.1996	3	(4)	
Jonas Martin	09.04.1990	6	(6)	
Steven Nkemboanza Mike Christopher Nzonzi	15.12.1988	33	(1)	1
Flavien Tait	02.02.1993	16	(7)	1
Chimuanya Ugochukwu	26.03.2004	1	(2)	
Forwards:	**DOB**	**M**	**(s)**	**G**
Matthis Abline	28.03.2003		(1)	
Romain Del Castillo	29.03.1996	5	(21)	
Andy Diouf	17.05.2003		(1)	
Jérémy Doku (BEL)	27.05.2002	26	(4)	2
Yann Gboho	14.01.2001	2	(8)	
Serhou Guirassy	12.03.1996	19	(8)	10
Adrien Hunou	19.01.1994	5	(15)	4
M'Baye Niang (SEN)	19.12.1994	4	(5)	1
Raphael Dias Belloli „Raphinha" (BRA)	14.12.1996	5	(1)	1
Georginio Rutter	20.04.2002		(4)	
Martin Terrier	04.03.1997	30	(4)	9

Association Sportive de Saint-Étienne Loire

Founded: 1919
Stadium: Stade „Geoffroy Guichard", Saint-Étienne (41,965)
Trainer: Claude Jacques Puel 02.09.1961

Goalkeepers:	DOB	M	(s)	G
Stefan Bajić	23.12.2001	1		
Etienne Green	19.07.2000	8		
Jessy Moulin	13.01.1986	29		
Defenders:	**DOB**	**M**	**(s)**	**G**
Pape Abou Cissé (SEN)	14.09.1995	14		
Mathieu Debuchy	28.07.1985	25	(1)	2
Wesley Fofana	17.12.2000	3	(1)	
Gabriel Moisés Antunes da Silva (BRA)	13.05.1991	4		
Timothée Kolodziejczak	01.10.1991	23	(1)	
Yvann Maçon	01.10.1996	6		1
Harold Moukoudi (CMR)	27.11.1997	26		3
Panagiotis Retsos (GRE)	09.08.1998	4		
Alpha Sissoko	07.03.1997	6	(3)	
Rayan Souici	28.02.1998		(1)	
Saïdou Sow (GUI)	04.07.2002	10	(5)	
Miguel Angel Trauco Saavedra (PER)	25.08.1992	22	(4)	
Marvin Tshibuabua	08.01.2002		(1)	
Midfielders:	**DOB**	**M**	**(s)**	**G**
Adil Aouchiche	15.07.2002	21	(13)	2
Bilal Benkhedim	20.04.2001	1	(2)	
Ryad Boudebouz (ALG)	19.02.1990	7	(7)	
Mahdi Camara	30.06.1998	37		3
Assane Dioussé El Hadji (SEN)	20.09.1997		(1)	
Baptiste Gabard	28.01.2000	2		
Lucas Gourna-Douath	05.08.2003	13	(17)	
Aimen Moueffek	09.04.2001	6	(13)	
Yann Gérard M'Vila	29.06.1990		(1)	
Yvan Neyou Noupa (CMR)	03.01.1997	29	(2)	1
Zaydou Youssouf	11.07.1999	14	(15)	1
Forwards:	**DOB**	**M**	**(s)**	**G**
Charles Abi	12.04.2000	9	(15)	3
Denis Bouanga (GAB)	11.11.1994	30	(6)	7
Romain Hamouma	29.03.1987	19	(10)	6
Wahbi Khazri (TUN)	08.02.1991	16	(6)	7
Jean-Philippe Krasso (CIV)	17.07.1997	2	(4)	
Yanis Lhéry	07.05.2003		(1)	
Anthony Modeste	14.04.1988	3	(4)	
Kévin Monnet-Paquet	19.08.1988	7	(9)	
Arnaud Nordin	17.06.1998	20	(12)	4
Maxence Rivera	30.05.2002	1	(16)	
Mathys Saban	15.05.2002		(1)	
Abdoulaye Sidibé	09.02.2002		(1)	
Tyrone Tormin	29.06.2001		(3)	

Racing Club de Strasbourg Alsace

Founded: 1906
Stadium: Stade de la Meinau, Strasbourg (29,230)
Trainer: Thierry Laurey 14.02.1964

Goalkeepers:	DOB	M	(s)	G
Bingourou Kamara	21.10.1996	8		
Eiji Kawashima (JPN)	20.03.1983	24		
Matz Sels (BEL)	26.02.1992	6		
Defenders:	**DOB**	**M**	**(s)**	**G**
Ismaël Aaneba	29.05.1999		(2)	
Anthony Caci	01.07.1997	32	(1)	
Lionel Carole	12.04.1991	14	(13)	
Alexander Djiku (GHA)	09.08.1994	29	(1)	
Frédéric Guilbert	24.12.1994	13		1
Lamine Koné (CIV)	01.02.1989	12	(3)	1
Kenny Lala	03.10.1991	21		3
Stefan Mitrović (SRB)	22.05.1990	31	(1)	2
Mohamed Simakan	03.05.2000	19		1
Midfielders:	**DOB**	**M**	**(s)**	**G**
Jean-Eudes Aholou (CIV)	20.03.1994	26	(1)	2
Jean-Ricner Bellegarde	27.06.1998	25	(11)	1
Dimitri Liénard	13.02.1988	19	(15)	2
Sanjin Prcić (BIH)	20.11.1993	3	(11)	
Mahamé Siby	07.07.1996		(7)	
Ibrahima Sissoko	27.10.1997	29	(7)	
Adrien Thomasson	10.12.1993	31	(6)	5
Forwards:	**DOB**	**M**	**(s)**	**G**
Ludovic Ajorque	25.02.1994	34	(1)	16
Mehdi Chahiri	25.07.1996	8	(15)	2
Habib Diallo (SEN)	18.06.1995	27	(5)	9
Idriss Saâdi (ALG)	08.02.1992		(7)	
Moïse Sahi Dion (CIV)	20.12.2001		(6)	1
Majeed Waris (GHA)	19.09.1991	5	(10)	1
Kévin Lucien Zohi (MLI)	19.12.1996	2	(21)	2

SECOND LEVEL
Ligue 2 2020/2021

1.	ES Troyes Aube Champagne (*Promoted*)	38	23	8	7	60	-	36	77
2.	Clermont Foot 63 (*Promoted*)	38	21	9	8	61	-	25	72
3.	Toulouse FC	38	20	10	8	71	-	42	70
4.	Grenoble Foot 38	38	18	11	9	51	-	35	65
5.	Paris FC	38	17	13	8	53	-	37	64
6.	AJ Auxerre	38	16	14	8	64	-	43	62
7.	FC Sochaux-Montbéliard	38	12	15	11	45	-	37	51
8.	AS Nancy-Lorraine	38	11	14	13	53	-	53	47
9.	En Avant de Guingamp	38	10	17	11	41	-	43	47
10.	Amiens SC	38	11	14	13	34	-	40	47
11.	Valenciennes FC	38	12	11	15	50	-	59	47
12.	Le Havre AC	38	11	14	13	38	-	48	47
13.	AC Ajaccio	38	11	13	14	34	-	43	46
14.	Pau FC	38	11	11	16	42	-	49	44
15.	Rodez Aveyron Football	38	8	19	11	38	-	44	43
16.	USL Dunkerque	38	10	11	17	34	-	47	41
17.	Stade Malherbe Caen	38	9	14	15	34	-	49	41
18.	Chamois Niortais FC (*Relegation Play-offs*)	38	9	14	15	34	-	58	41
19.	FC Chambly Oise (*Relegated*)	38	9	11	18	41	-	64	38
20.	La Berrichonne de Châteauroux (*Relegated*)	38	4	11	23	32	-	58	23

Teams ranked 3-5 were qualified for the Promotion Play-offs.

Promotion Play-offs

Grenoble Foot 38 - Paris FC	2-0(1-0)
Toulouse FC - Grenoble Foot 38	3-0(2-0)

Toulouse FC qualified for the Promotion/Relegation Play-offs (1st / 2nd Level).

Relegation Play-offs (2nd / 3rd Level)

FC Villefranche Beaujolais - Chamois Niortais FC	3-1(0-1)	0-2(0-0)

Chamois Niortais FC remains at second level for 2021/2022.

INTERNATIONAL MATCHES
(16.07.2020 – 15.07.2021)

Date	City	Match	Score	Type
05.09.2020	Stockholm	Sweden - France	0-1(0-1)	(UNL)
08.09.2020	Paris	France - Croatia	4-2(2-1)	(UNL)
07.10.2020	Paris	France - Ukraine	7-1(4-0)	(F)
11.10.2020	Paris	France - Portugal	0-0	(UNL)
14.10.2020	Zagreb	Croatia - France	1-2(0-1)	(UNL)
11.11.2020	Paris	France - Finland	0-2(0-2)	(F)
14.11.2020	Lisboa	Portugal - France	0-1(0-0)	(UNL)
17.11.2020	Paris	France - Sweden	4-2(2-1)	(UNL)
24.03.2021	Paris	France - Ukraine	1-1(1-0)	(WCQ)
28.03.2021	Nur-Sultan	Kazakhstan - France	0-2(0-2)	(WCQ)
31.03.2021	Sarajevo	Bosnia and Herzegovina - France	0-1(0-0)	(WCQ)
02.06.2021	Nice	France - Wales	3-0(1-0)	(F)
08.06.2021	Paris	France - Bulgaria	3-0(1-0)	(F)
15.06.2021	München	France - Germany	1-0(1-0)	(EC)
19.06.2021	Budapest	Hungary - France	1-1(1-0)	(EC)
23.06.2021	Budapest	Portugal - France	2-2(1-1)	(EC)
28.06.2021	Bucureşti	France - Switzerland	3-3(0-1,3-3,3-3); 4-5 on penalties	(EC)

05.09.2020 SWEDEN - FRANCE   **0-1(0-1)**   2nd UEFA Nations League A, Group 3
Friends Arena, Stockholm; Referee: Szymon Marciniak (Poland); Attendance: 0
FRA: Hugo Hadrien Dominique Lloris (Cap), Raphaël Xavier Varane, Presnel Kimpembe, Léo Michel Joseph Claude Dubois (88.Ferland Sinna Mendy), Lucas Digne, Dayotchanculle Oswald Upamecano, N'Golo Kanté, Adrien Rabiot-Provost, Olivier Jonathan Giroud (90+2.Steven Nkemboanza Mike Christopher Nzonzi), Antoine Griezmann, Kylian Sanmi Mbappé Lottin (77.Anthony Jordan Martial). Trainer: Didier Claude Deschamps.
Goal: Kylian Sanmi Mbappé Lottin (41).

08.09.2020 FRANCE - CROATIA   **4-2(2-1)**   2nd UEFA Nations League A, Group 3
Stade de France, Saint-Denis, Paris; Referee: Ovidiu Alin Haţegan (Romania); Attendance: 0
FRA: Hugo Hadrien Dominique Lloris (Cap), Clément Nicolas Laurent Lenglet, Ferland Sinna Mendy, Dayotchanculle Oswald Upamecano, Lucas François Bernard Hernández, Moussa Sissoko, Steven Nkemboanza Mike Christopher Nzonzi, N'Golo Kanté (63.Eduardo Celmi Camavinga), Wissam Ben Yedder (63.Olivier Jonathan Giroud), Anthony Jordan Martial, Antoine Griezmann (78.Nabil Fekir). Trainer: Didier Claude Deschamps.
Goals: Antoine Griezmann (43), Dominik Livaković (45+1 own goal), Dayotchanculle Oswald Upamecano (65), Olivier Jonathan Giroud (77 penalty).

07.10.2020 FRANCE - UKRAINE   **7-1(4-0)**   Friendly International
Stade de France, Saint-Denis, Paris; Referee: Andris Treimanis (Latvia); Attendance: 1,000
FRA: Steve Mandanda Mpidi (46.Mike Maignan), Clément Nicolas Laurent Lenglet, Benjamin Jacques Marcel Pavard, Dayotchanculle Oswald Upamecano (46.Raphaël Xavier Varane), Lucas Digne, Steven Nkemboanza Mike Christopher Nzonzi, Corentin Tolisso, Houssem Aouar (59.Antoine Griezmann), Eduardo Celmi Camavinga (59.Paul Labile Pogba), Olivier Jonathan Giroud (Cap) (73.Wissam Ben Yedder), Anthony Jordan Martial (46.Kylian Sanmi Mbappé Lottin). Trainer: Didier Claude Deschamps.
Goals: Eduardo Celmi Camavinga (9), Olivier Jonathan Giroud (24, 34), Vitaliy Mykolenko (39 own goal), Corentin Tolisso (65), Kylian Sanmi Mbappé Lottin (82), Antoine Griezmann (89).

11.10.2020 FRANCE - PORTUGAL   **0-0**   2nd UEFA Nations League A, Group 3
Stade de France, Saint-Denis, Paris; Referee: Carlos del Cerro Grande (Spain); Attendance: 1,000
FRA: Hugo Hadrien Dominique Lloris (Cap), Benjamin Jacques Marcel Pavard, Raphaël Xavier Varane, Presnel Kimpembe, Lucas François Bernard Hernández, Paul Labile Pogba, N'Golo Kanté, Adrien Rabiot-Provost, Olivier Jonathan Giroud (74.Anthony Jordan Martial), Antoine Griezmann, Kylian Sanmi Mbappé Lottin (84.Kingsley Junior Coman). Trainer: Didier Claude Deschamps.

14.10.2020 CROATIA - FRANCE   **1-2(0-1)**   2nd UEFA Nations League A, Group 3
Stadion Maksimir, Zagreb; Referee: Björn Kuipers (Netherlands); Attendance: 6,266
FRA: Hugo Hadrien Dominique Lloris (Cap), Raphaël Xavier Varane, Clément Nicolas Laurent Lenglet, Lucas Digne (83.Lucas François Bernard Hernández), Ferland Sinna Mendy, Steven Nkemboanza Mike Christopher Nzonzi, Adrien Rabiot-Provost (74.Paul Labile Pogba), Anthony Jordan Martial (62.Kingsley Junior Coman), Corentin Tolisso (63.Eduardo Celmi Camavinga), Antoine Griezmann (83.Olivier Jonathan Giroud), Kylian Sanmi Mbappé Lottin. Trainer: Didier Claude Deschamps.
Goals: Antoine Griezmann (8), Kylian Sanmi Mbappé Lottin (79).

11.11.2020 FRANCE - FINLAND   **0-2(0-2)**   Friendly International
Stade de France, Saint-Denis, Paris; Referee: Nikola Popov (Bulgaria); Attendance: 0
FRA: Steve Mandanda Mpidi (Cap), Kurt Happy Zouma, Clément Nicolas Laurent Lenglet (80.Raphaël Xavier Varane), Léo Michel Joseph Claude Dubois (71.Ruben Aguilar), Lucas Digne, Moussa Sissoko, Steven Nkemboanza Mike Christopher Nzonzi, Paul Labile Pogba (57.N'Golo Kanté), Olivier Jonathan Giroud (57.Anthony Jordan Martial), Wissam Ben Yedder (57.Antoine Griezmann), Marcus Lilian Thuram-Ulien. Trainer: Didier Claude Deschamps.

14.11.2020 PORTUGAL - FRANCE   **0-1(0-0)**   2nd UEFA Nations League A, Group 3
Estádio da Luz, Lisboa; Referee: Tobias Stieler (Germany); Attendance: 0
FRA: Hugo Hadrien Dominique Lloris (Cap), Benjamin Jacques Marcel Pavard, Raphaël Xavier Varane, Presnel Kimpembe, Lucas François Bernard Hernández, Paul Labile Pogba, N'Golo Kanté, Adrien Rabiot-Provost, Antoine Griezmann, Anthony Jordan Martial (78.Olivier Jonathan Giroud), Kingsley Junior Coman (59.Marcus Lilian Thuram-Ulien). Trainer: Didier Claude Deschamps.
Goal: N'Golo Kanté (54).

17.11.2020 **FRANCE - SWEDEN** 4-2(2-1) 2nd UEFA Nations League A, Group 3

Stade de France, Saint-Denis, Paris; Referee: Aleksei Kulbakov (Belarus); Attendance: 0

FRA: Hugo Hadrien Dominique Lloris (Cap), Benjamin Jacques Marcel Pavard, Raphaël Xavier Varane (46.Kurt Happy Zouma), Presnel Kimpembe, Lucas François Bernard Hernández (46.Lucas Digne), Moussa Sissoko, Paul Labile Pogba, Adrien Rabiot-Provost (78.Steven Nkemboanza Mike Christopher Nzonzi), Olivier Jonathan Giroud (84.Kingsley Junior Coman), Marcus Lilian Thuram-Ulien (57.Kylian Sanmi Mbappé Lottin), Antoine Griezmann. Trainer: Didier Claude Deschamps.

Goals: Olivier Jonathan Giroud (16), Benjamin Jacques Marcel Pavard (36), Olivier Jonathan Giroud (59), Kingsley Junior Coman (90+5).

24.03.2021 **FRANCE - UKRAINE** 1-1(1-0) 22nd FIFA WC. Qualifiers

Stade de France, Saint-Denis, Paris; Referee: Tobias Stieler (Germany); Attendance: 0

FRA: Hugo Hadrien Dominique Lloris (Cap), Benjamin Jacques Marcel Pavard, Raphaël Xavier Varane, Presnel Kimpembe, Lucas François Bernard Hernández, N'Golo Kanté, Adrien Rabiot-Provost, Olivier Jonathan Giroud (63.Paul Labile Pogba), Antoine Griezmann, Kingsley Junior Coman (63.Masour Ousmane Dembélé), Kylian Sanmi Mbappé Lottin (77.Anthony Jordan Martial). Trainer: Didier Claude Deschamps.

Goal: Antoine Griezmann (19).

28.03.2021 **KAZAKHSTAN - FRANCE** 0-2(0-2) 22nd FIFA WC. Qualifiers

Astana Arena, Nur-Sultan; Referee: Aleksei Kulbakov (Belarus); Attendance: 0

FRA: Hugo Hadrien Dominique Lloris (Cap), Kurt Happy Zouma, Clément Nicolas Laurent Lenglet, Léo Michel Joseph Claude Dubois, Lucas Digne, Paul Labile Pogba (60.Adrien Rabiot-Provost), Thomas Benoît Lemar, Tanguy Ndombele Alvaro (82.Moussa Sissoko), Antoine Griezmann (59.Wissam Ben Yedder), Masour Ousmane Dembélé (90.Kingsley Junior Coman), Anthony Jordan Martial (59.Kylian Sanmi Mbappé Lottin). Trainer: Didier Claude Deschamps.

Goals: Masour Ousmane Dembélé (19), Serhiy Malyi (44 own goal).

31.03.2021 **BOSNIA AND HERZEGOVINA - FRANCE** 0-1(0-0) 22nd FIFA WC. Qualifiers

Stadion Grbavica, Sarajevo; Referee: Daniele Orsato (Italy); Attendance: 0

FRA: Hugo Hadrien Dominique Lloris (Cap), Benjamin Jacques Marcel Pavard, Raphaël Xavier Varane, Presnel Kimpembe, Lucas François Bernard Hernández, Paul Labile Pogba, Thomas Benoît Lemar (90.Moussa Sissoko), Adrien Rabiot-Provost, Kingsley Junior Coman (59.Olivier Jonathan Giroud), Antoine Griezmann, Kylian Sanmi Mbappé Lottin. Trainer: Didier Claude Deschamps.

Goal: Antoine Griezmann (60).

02.06.2021 **FRANCE - WALES** 3-0(1-0) Friendly International

Allianz Riviera, Nice; Referee: Luis Miguel Branco Godinho (Portugal); Attendance: 0

FRA: Hugo Hadrien Dominique Lloris (Cap), Benjamin Jacques Marcel Pavard (46.Jules Olivier Koundé), Raphaël Xavier Varane, Presnel Kimpembe, Lucas François Bernard Hernández (46.Lucas Digne), Corentin Tolisso (64.Moussa Sissoko), Adrien Rabiot-Provost, Paul Labile Pogba (63.Kingsley Junior Coman), Antoine Griezmann (84.Wissam Ben Yedder), Karim Mostafa Benzema, Kylian Sanmi Mbappé Lottin (73.Masour Ousmane Dembélé). Trainer: Didier Claude Deschamps.

Goals: Kylian Sanmi Mbappé Lottin (35), Antoine Griezmann (48), Masour Ousmane Dembélé (79).

08.06.2021 **FRANCE - BULGARIA** 3-0(1-0) Friendly International

Stade de France, Saint-Denis, Paris; Referee: Anastasios Sidiropoulos (Greece); Attendance: 5,000

FRA: Hugo Hadrien Dominique Lloris (Cap), Benjamin Jacques Marcel Pavard, Raphaël Xavier Varane, Presnel Kimpembe, Lucas François Bernard Hernández (46.Lucas Digne), Corentin Tolisso (84.Moussa Sissoko), N'Golo Kanté (65.Thomas Benoît Lemar), Paul Labile Pogba, Karim Mostafa Benzema (41.Olivier Jonathan Giroud), Antoine Griezmann (65.Masour Ousmane Dembélé), Kylian Sanmi Mbappé Lottin (84.Wissam Ben Yedder). Trainer: Didier Claude Deschamps.

Goals: Antoine Griezmann (29), Olivier Jonathan Giroud (83, 90).

15.06.2021 **FRANCE - GERMANY** 1-0(1-0) 16th EC. Group Stage.

Football Arena (Allianz), München; Referee: Carlos del Cerro Grande (Spain); Attendance: 13,000

FRA: Hugo Hadrien Dominique Lloris (Cap), Benjamin Jacques Marcel Pavard, Raphaël Xavier Varane, Presnel Kimpembe, Lucas François Bernard Hernández, Paul Labile Pogba, N'Golo Kanté, Adrien Rabiot-Provost (90+4.Masour Ousmane Dembélé), Karim Mostafa Benzema (88.Corentin Tolisso), Antoine Griezmann, Kylian Sanmi Mbappé Lottin. Trainer: Didier Claude Deschamps.

Goal: Mats Julian Hummels (20 own goal).

19.06.2021 **HUNGARY - FRANCE** 1-1(1-0) 16th EC. Group Stage.

Puskás Aréna, Budapest; Referee: Michael Oliver (England); Attendance: 55,998

FRA: Hugo Hadrien Dominique Lloris (Cap), Benjamin Jacques Marcel Pavard, Raphaël Xavier Varane, Presnel Kimpembe, Lucas Digne, Paul Labile Pogba (76.Corentin Tolisso), N'Golo Kanté, Adrien Rabiot-Provost (57.Masour Ousmane Dembélé; 87.Thomas Benoît Lemar), Antoine Griezmann, Karim Mostafa Benzema (76.Olivier Jonathan Giroud), Kylian Sanmi Mbappé Lottin. Trainer: Didier Claude Deschamps.

Goal: Antoine Griezmann (66).

23.06.2021 **PORTUGAL - FRANCE** 2-2(1-1) 16th EC. Group Stage.

Puskás Aréna, Budapest (Hungary); Referee: Antonio Miguel Mateu Lahoz (Spain); Attendance: 54,886

FRA: Hugo Hadrien Dominique Lloris (Cap), Jules Olivier Koundé, Raphaël Xavier Varane, Presnel Kimpembe, Lucas François Bernard Hernández (46.Lucas Digne; 52.Adrien Rabiot-Provost), Paul Labile Pogba, N'Golo Kanté, Corentin Tolisso (66.Kingsley Junior Coman), Antoine Griezmann (86.Moussa Sissoko), Karim Mostafa Benzema, Kylian Sanmi Mbappé Lottin. Trainer: Didier Claude Deschamps.

Goals: Karim Mostafa Benzema (45 penalty, 47).

28.06.2021 **FRANCE - SWITZERLAND** 3-3(0-1,3-3,3-3); 4-5 on penalties 16th EC. 2nd Round of 16.

Arena Naţională, Bucureşti (Romania); Referee: Fernando Andrés Rapallini (Argentina); Attendance: 22,642

FRA: Hugo Hadrien Dominique Lloris (Cap), Benjamin Jacques Marcel Pavard, Raphaël Xavier Varane, Presnel Kimpembe, Clément Nicolas Laurent Lenglet (46.Kingsley Junior Coman; 111.Marcus Lilian Thuram-Ulien), Paul Labile Pogba, N'Golo Kanté, Adrien Rabiot-Provost, Karim Mostafa Benzema (94.Olivier Jonathan Giroud), Antoine Griezmann (88.Moussa Sissoko), Kylian Sanmi Mbappé Lottin. Trainer: Didier Claude Deschamps.

Goals: Karim Mostafa Benzema (57, 59), Paul Labile Pogba (75).

Penalties: Paul Labile Pogba, Olivier Jonathan Giroud, Marcus Lilian Thuram-Ulien, Presnel Kimpembe, Kylian Sanmi Mbappé Lottin (saved).

NATIONAL TEAM PLAYERS
(16.07.2020 – 15.07.2021)

Name	DOB	Caps	Goals	2020/2021:	Club
Goalkeepers					
Hugo Hadrien Dominique LLORIS	26.12.1986	129	0	2020/2021:	*Tottenham Hotspur FC London (ENG)*
Mike MAIGNAN	03.07.1995	1	0	2020:	*Lille OSC*
Steve MANDANDA Mpidi	28.03.1985	34	0	2020:	*Olympique de Marseille*
Defenders					
Ruben AGUILAR	26.04.1993	1	0	2020:	*AS Monaco FC*
Lucas DIGNE	20.07.1993	40	0	2020/2021:	*Everton FC Liverpool (ENG)*
Léo Michel Joseph Claude DUBOIS	14.09.1994	7	0	2020/2021:	*Olympique Lyonnais*
Lucas François Bernard HERNÁNDEZ	14.02.1996	28	0	2020/2021:	*FC Bayern München (GER)*
Presnel KIMPEMBE	13.08.1995	21	0	2020/2021:	*Paris Saint-Germain FC*
Jules Olivier KOUNDÉ	12.11.1998	2	0	2021:	*Sevilla FC (ESP)*
Clément Nicolas Laurent LENGLET	17.06.1995	13	1	2020/2021:	*FC Barcelona (ESP)*
Ferland Sinna MENDY	08.06.1995	7	0	2020:	*Real Madrid CF (ESP)*
Benjamin Jacques Marcel PAVARD	28.03.1996	38	2	2020/2021:	*FC Bayern München (GER)*
Dayotchanculle Oswald UPAMECANO	27.10.1998	3	1	2020:	*RasenBallsport Leipzig (GER)*
Raphaël Xavier VARANE	25.04.1993	79	5	2020/2021:	*Real Madrid CF (ESP)*
Kurt Happy ZOUMA	27.10.1994	8	1	2020/2021:	*Chelsea FC London (ENG)*
Midfielders					
Houssem AOUAR	30.06.1998	1	0	2020:	*Olympique Lyonnais*
Eduardo Celmi CAMAVINGA	10.11.2002	3	1	2020:	*Stade Rennais FC*
N'Golo KANTÉ	29.03.1991	50	2	2020/2021:	*Chelsea FC London (ENG)*
Thomas Benoît LEMAR	12.11.1995	26	4	2021:	*Club Atlético de Madrid (ESP)*
Tanguy NDOMBELE Alvaro	28.12.1996	7	0	2021:	*Olympique Lyonnais*
Steven Nkemboanza Mike Christopher NZONZI	15.12.1988	20	0	2020:	*Stade Rennais FC*
Paul Labile POGBA	15.03.1993	84	11	2020/2021:	*Manchester United FC (ENG)*
Adrien RABIOT-PROVOST	03.04.1995	19	0	2020/2021:	*Juventus FC Torino (ITA)*
Moussa SISSOKO	16.08.1989	71	2	2020/2021:	*Tottenham Hotspur FC London (ENG)*
Corentin TOLISSO	03.08.1994	28	2	2020/2021:	*FC Bayern München (GER)*
Forwards					
Wissam BEN YEDDER	12.08.1990	14	2	2020/2021:	*AS Monaco FC*
Karim Mostafa BENZEMA	19.12.1987	87	31	2021:	*Real Madrid CF (ESP)*
Kingsley Junior COMAN	13.06.1996	32	5	2020/2021:	*FC Bayern München (GER)*
Masour Ousmane DEMBÉLÉ	15.05.1997	27	4	2021:	*FC Barcelona (ESP)*
Nabil FEKIR	18.07.1993	25	2	2020:	*Real Betis Balompié Sevilla (ESP)*
Olivier Jonathan GIROUD	30.09.1986	110	46	2020/2021:	*Chelsea FC London (ENG)*
Antoine GRIEZMANN	21.03.1991	95	38	2020/2021:	*FC Barcelona (ESP)*
Anthony Jordan MARTIAL	05.12.1995	27	1	2020/2021:	*Manchester United FC (ENG)*
Kylian Sanmi MBAPPÉ Lottin	20.12.1998	48	17	2020/2021:	*Paris Saint-Germain FC*
Marcus Lilian THURAM-ULIEN	06.08.1997	4	0	2020/2021:	*Borussia VfL Mönchengladbach (GER)*
Trainer					
Didier Claude DESCHAMPS [from 08.07.2012]	15.10.1968			117 M; 76 W; 23 D; 18 L; 232-98	

GEORGIA

The Country:
Georgia (საქართველო)
Capital: Tbilisi
Surface: 69,700 km²
Inhabitants: 3,728,573 [2021]
Time: UTC+4

The FA:
Georgian Football Federation
76a Chavchavadze Avenue, 0162 Tbilisi
Tel: +995 32 912 680
Founded: 1936/re-founded 1990
Member of FIFA since: 1992
Member of UEFA since: 1992
Website: www.gff.ge

NATIONAL TEAM RECORDS

RECORDS

First international match:	27.05.1990, Tbilisi:	Georgia – Lithuania 2-2
Most international caps:	Levan Kobiashvili	- 100 caps (1996-2011)
Most international goals:	Shota Arveladze	- 26 goals / 61 caps (1992-2007)

UEFA EUROPEAN CHAMPIONSHIP		FIFA WORLD CUP		OLYMPIC TOURNAMENTS	
1960	-	1930	-	1908	-
1964	-	1934	-	1912	-
1968	-	1938	-	1920	-
1972	-	1950	-	1924	-
1976	-	1954	-	1928	-
1980	-	1958	-	1936	-
1984	-	1962	-	1948	-
1988	-	1966	-	1952	-
1992	-	1970	-	1956	-
1996	Qualifiers	1974	-	1960	-
2000	Qualifiers	1978	-	1964	-
2004	Qualifiers	1982	-	1968	-
2008	Qualifiers	1986	-	1972	-
2012	Qualifiers	1990	-	1976	-
2016	Qualifiers	1994	Did not enter	1980	-
2020	Qualifiers	1998	Qualifiers	1984	-
		2002	Qualifiers	1988	-
		2006	Qualifiers	1992	-
		2010	Qualifiers	1996	Qualifiers
		2014	Qualifiers	2000	Qualifiers
		2018	Qualifiers	2004	Qualifiers
				2008	Qualifiers
				2012	Qualifiers
				2016	Qualifiers

*was part of Soviet Union between 1930-1990

UEFA NATIONS LEAGUE

2018/2019	League D (promoted to League C)
2020/2021	League C

FIFA CONFEDERATIONS CUP 1992-2017

None

GEORGIAN CLUB HONOURS IN EUROPEAN CLUB COMPETITIONS:

European Champion Clubs.Cup (1956-1992) / UEFA Champions League (1993-2021)		
None		
Fairs Cup (1858-1971) / UEFA Cup (1972-2009) / UEFA Europa League (2010-2021)		
None		
UEFA Super Cup (1972-2020)		
None		
*European Cup Winners.Cup 1961-1999**		
FC Dinamo Tbilisi*	1	1980/1981
*represented the Soviet Union		

*defunct competition

NATIONAL COMPETITIONS
TABLE OF HONOURS

GEORGIAN SSR (SOVIET ERA) CHAMPIONS

1927	Batumi XI	1953	TTU Tbilisi	1972	Lokomotivi FC Samtredia
1928	Tbilisi XI	1954	TTU Tbilisi	1973	Dinamo Zugdidi
1929-1935	*No competition*	1955	Dinamo Kutaisi	1974	Metallurg Rustavi
1936	ZII Tbilisi	1956	FC FC Lokomotivi Tbilisi	1975	Magaroeli Chiatura
1937	FC FC Lokomotivi Tbilisi	1957	TTU Tbilisi	1976	SKIF Tbilisi
1938	FC FC Dinamo Batumi	1958	TTU Tbilisi	1977	Mziuri Gali
1939	Nauka Tbilisi	1959	Metallurg Rustavi	1978	Kolheti Poti
1940	FC FC Dinamo Batumi	1960	Imereti Kutaisi	1979	Metallurg Rustavi
1941-1942	*No competition*	1961	FC Guria Lanchkhuti	1980	Meshakhte Tkibuli
1943	ODKA Tbilisi	1962	Imereti Kutaisi	1981	Meshakhte Tkibuli
1944	*No competition*	1963	Imereti Kutaisi	1982	Mertskhali Makharadze
1945	FC FC Lokomotivi Tbilisi	1964	IngurGES Zugdidi	1983	Samgulari Tskhaltubo
1946	Dinamo Kutaisi	1965	Tolia Tbilisi	1984	Metallurg Rustavi
1947	FC Dinamo Sokhumi	1966	FC Guria Lanchkhuti	1985	Shadrevani-83 Tskhaltubo
1948	FC Dinamo Sokhumi	1967	Mertskhali Makharadze	1986	Shevardeni-1906 Tbilisi
1949	FC FC Torpedo Kutaisi	1968	SKA Tbilisi	1987	Mertskhali Makharadze
1950	TODO Tbilisi	1969	Sulori Vani	1988	Kolheti Poti
1951	TODO Tbilisi	1970	SKIF Tbilisi	1989	Shadrevani-83 Tskhaltubo
1952	TTU Tbilisi	1971	FC Guria Lanchkhuti		

	CHAMPIONS	CUP WINNERS	BEST GOALSCORERS	
1990	FC Iberia Tbilisi	FC Guria Lanchkhuti	Gia Guruli (FC Iberia Tbilisi)	
			Mamuka Pantsulaia (FC Gorda Rustavi)	23
1991	FC Iberia Tbilisi	FC Dinamo Tbilisi	Otar Korgalidze (FC Guria Lanchkhuti)	14
1991/1992	FC Dinamo Tbilisi	FC Dinamo Tbilisi	Otar Korgalidze (FC Guria Lanchkhuti)	40
1992/1993	FC Dinamo Tbilisi	FC Dinamo Tbilisi	Merab Megreladze (Samgurali Tskhaltubo)	41
1993/1994	FC Dinamo Tbilisi	FC Dinamo Tbilisi	Merab Megreladze (FC Margveti Zestafoni)	31
1994/1995	FC Dinamo Tbilisi	FC Dinamo Tbilisi	Giorgi Daraselia (FC Kolkheti-1913 Poti)	26
1995/1996	FC Dinamo Tbilisi	FC Dinamo Tbilisi	Zviad Endeladze (FC Margveti Zestafoni)	40
1996/1997	FC Dinamo Tbilisi	FC Dinamo Batumi	Giorgi Demetradze (FC Dinamo Tbilisi)	
			David Ujmajuridze (FC Dinamo Batumi)	26
1997/1998	FC Dinamo Tbilisi	FC Torpedo Kutaisi	Levan Khomeriki (FC Dinamo Tbilisi)	23
1998/1999	FC Dinamo Tbilisi	FC Lokomotivi Tbilisi	Mikheil Ashvetia (FC Dinamo Tbilisi)	26
1999/2000	FC Torpedo Kutaisi	FC Torpedo Kutaisi	Zurab Ionanidze (FC Torpedo Kutaisi)	24
2000/2001	FC Torpedo Kutaisi	FC Lokomotivi Tbilisi	Zaza Zirakishvili (FC Dinamo Tbilisi)	21
2001/2002	FC Torpedo Kutaisi	FC Dinamo Tbilisi	Suliko Davitashvili	
			(FC Lokomotivi Tbilisi / FC Merani Tbilisi)	18
2002/2003	FC Dinamo Tbilisi	FC Dinamo Tbilisi	Zurab Ionanidze (FC Torpedo Kutaisi)	26
2003/2004	FC WIT Georgia Tbilisi	FC Lokomotivi Tbilisi	Suliko Davitashvili (FC Torpedo Kutaisi)	20
2004/2005	FC Dinamo Tbilisi	FC Ameri Tbilisi	Levani Melkadze (FC Dinamo Tbilisi)	27
2005/2006	FC Sioni Bolnisi	FC Ameri Tbilisi	Jaba Dvali (FC Dinamo Tbilisi)	21
2006/2007	FC Olimpi Rustavi	FC Zestafoni	Sandro Iashvili (FC Dinamo Tbilisi)	27
2007/2008	FC Dinamo Tbilisi	FC Dinamo Tbilisi	Mikheil Khutsishvili (FC Dinamo Tbilisi)	16
2008/2009	FC WIT Georgia Tbilisi	FC WIT Georgia Tbilisi	Nikoloz Gelashvili (FC Zestafoni)	20
2009/2010	FC Olimpi Rustavi	FC Gagra	Brazil Anderson Aquino (FC Metalurgi Rustavi)	26
2010/2011	FC Zestafoni	FC Dila Gori	Nikoloz Gelashvili (FC Zestafoni)	18
2011/2012	FC Zestafoni	FC Dinamo Tbilisi	Jaba Dvali (FC Zestafoni)	20
2012/2013	FC Dinamo Tbilisi	FC Dinamo Tbilisi	Spain Xisco (FC Dinamo Tbilisi)	24
2013/2014	FC Dinamo Tbilisi	FC Dinamo Tbilisi	Spain Xisco (FC Dinamo Tbilisi)	19
2014/2015	FC Dila Gori	FC Dinamo Tbilisi	Irakli Modebadze (FC Dila Gori)	16
2015/2016	FC Dinamo Tbilisi	FC Torpedo Kutaisi	Giorgi Kvilitaia (FC Dinamo Tbilisi)	24
2016	FC Samtredia	FC Chikhura Sachkhere	Budu Zivzivadze (FC Samtredia)	11
2017	FC Torpedo Kutaisi	FC Guria Lanchkhuti	Irakli Sikharulidze (FC Lokomotivi Tbilisi)	25
2018	FC Saburtalo Tbilisi	FC Torpedo Kutaisi	Giorgi Gabedava (FC Chikhura Sachkhere)	
			Budu Zivzivadze (FC Dinamo Tbilisi)	22
2019	FC Dinamo Tbilisi	FC Saburtalo Tbilisi	Levan Kutalia (FC Dinamo Tbilisi)	20
2020	FC Dinamo Tbilisi	FC Gagra	Mykola Kovtalyuk (UKR, FC Dila Gori)	10

<u>Please note</u>: FC Dinamo Tbilisi changed its name to FC Iberia Tbilisi between 1990-1992; FC Olimpi Rustavi became FC Metalurgi Rustavi (2011-2015) and later FC Rustavi (since 2011).

NATIONAL CHAMPIONSHIP
Erovnuli Liga 2020
(29.02.2020 – 10.12.2020)

Results

Round 1 [29.02.-01.03.2020]
Dinamo Tbilisi - FC Telavi 0-0
Dinamo Batumi - Merani Tbilisi 0-0
FC Saburtalo - Chikhura Sachkhere 2-1(1-1)
Torpedo Kutaisi - Dila Gori 0-2(0-1)
Lokomotivi Tbilisi - FC Samtredia 3-1(3-1)

Round 2 [07-08.03.2020]
Chikhura Sachk. - Lokomotivi Tbilisi 1-3(1-1)
FC Samtredia - Torpedo Kutaisi 1-0(1-0)
Merani Tbilisi - FC Saburtalo 0-0
FC Telavi - Dila Gori 1-1(1-0)
Dinamo Tbilisi - Dinamo Batumi 1-1(0-0)

Round 3 [25-28.06.2020]
FC Saburtalo - Dinamo Tbilisi 0-3(0-1)
Dinamo Batumi - FC Telavi 1-1(1-0)
Lokomotivi Tbilisi - Merani Tbilisi 1-1(0-0)
Dila Gori - FC Samtredia 1-1(1-1)
Torpedo Kutaisi - Chikhura Sachkh. 2-2(0-1)

Round 4 [02-05.07.2020]
Dinamo Batumi - FC Saburtalo 1-1(0-0)
Dinamo Tbilisi - Lokomotivi Tbilisi 4-0(0-0)
Chikhura Sachkhere - Dila Gori 0-2(0-2)
FC Telavi - FC Samtredia 3-1(2-1)
Merani Tbilisi - Torpedo Kutaisi 0-2(0-1)

Round 5 [09-12.07.2020]
FC Samtredia - Chikhura Sachkhere 0-0
Lokomotivi Tbilisi - Dinamo Batumi 1-4(0-3)
FC Saburtalo - FC Telavi 1-0(0-0)
Dila Gori - Merani Tbilisi 4-0(0-0)
Torpedo Kutaisi - Dinamo Tbilisi 0-0

Round 6 [16-19.07.2020]
FC Telavi - Chikhura Sachkhere 2-0(1-0)
Merani Tbilisi - FC Samtredia 1-2(1-0)
FC Saburtalo - Lokomotivi Tbilisi 0-0
Dinamo Batumi - Torpedo Kutaisi 2-0(1-0)
Dinamo Tbilisi - Dila Gori 1-2(0-1)

Round 7 [23-26.07.2020]
Chikhura Sachkhere - Merani Tbilisi 3-0(0-0)
Torpedo Kutaisi - FC Saburtalo 0-4(0-3)
FC Samtredia - Dinamo Tbilisi 0-4(0-3)
Lokomotivi Tbilisi - FC Telavi 1-1(0-0)
Dila Gori - Dinamo Batumi 1-1(1-1)

Round 8 [31.07.-02.08.2020]
FC Telavi - Merani Tbilisi 0-0
Dinamo Tbilisi - Chikhura Sachkhere 1-0(0-0)
Lokomotivi Tbilisi - Torpedo Kutaisi 1-2(0-1)
FC Saburtalo - Dila Gori 1-1(1-0)
Dinamo Batumi - FC Samtredia 2-0(1-0)

Round 9 [06-11.08.2020]
Torpedo Kutaisi - FC Telavi 1-1(1-0)
Merani Tbilisi - Dinamo Batumi 1-2(0-1)
Chikhura Sachk. - Dinamo Batumi 0-4(0-3)
Dila Gori - Lokomotivi Tbilisi 0-1(0-0)
FC Samtredia - FC Saburtalo 1-2(1-0)

Round 10 [16-19.08.2020]
FC Telavi - Dinamo Tbilisi 0-0 [12.08]
Merani Tbilisi - Dinamo Batumi 1-2(0-0)
FC Samtredia - Lokomotivi Tbilisi 0-0
Chikhura Sachkhere - FC Saburtalo 2-8(1-6)
Dila Gori - Torpedo Kutaisi 3-1(1-1)

Round 11 [09-13.09.2020]
Lokomotivi Tbilisi - Chikhura Sach. 4-1(1-1)
Dinamo Batumi - Dila Gori 1-3(0-2)
FC Saburtalo - Merani Tbilisi 0-0
Dila Gori - FC Telavi 0-0
Torpedo Kutaisi - FC Samtredia 2-1(0-0)

Round 12 [02-04.10.2020]
FC Telavi - Dinamo Batumi 1-3(0-0)
FC Samtredia - Dila Gori 1-0(0-0)
Merani Tbilisi - Lokomotivi Tbilisi 0-4(0-3)
Chikhura Sachkh. - Torpedo Kutaisi 2-2(2-2)
Dinamo Tbilisi - Saburtalo 3-1(3-0) [23.10.]

Round 13 [17-18.10.2020]
FC Samtredia - FC Telavi 0-0
Dila Gori - Chikhura Sachkhere 6-1(2-0)
Torpedo Kutaisi - Merani Tbilisi 1-0(0-0)
FC Saburtalo - Dinamo Batumi 0-1(0-0)
Lokomotivi - Dinamo Tbilisi 0-2(0-0) [08.11.]

Round 14 [25-28.10.2020]
Chikhura Sachkhere - FC Samtredia 0-1(0-0)
Merani Tbilisi - Dila Gori 0-0
FC Telavi - FC Saburtalo 1-1(1-1)
Dinamo Tbilisi - Torpedo Ku. 2-1(0-0)[26.11.]
Dinamo Batumi - Lokomotivi 1-2(0-0)[26.11.]

Round 15 [03-04.11.2020]
Chikhura Sachkhere - FC Telavi 1-2(0-1)
Dila Gori - Dinamo Batumi 0-3(0-2)
Lokomotivi Tbilisi - FC Saburtalo 2-1(1-0)
FC Samtredia - Merani Tbilisi 2-0(2-0)
Torpedo K. - Dinamo Batumi 1-2(1-2)[05.12.]

Round 16 [21-22.11.2020]
FC Saburtalo - Torpedo Kutaisi 1-0(0-0)
FC Telavi - Lokomotivi Tbilisi 1-1(0-1)
Dinamo Batumi - Dila Gori 1-0(0-0)
Merani Tbilisi - Chikhura Sachkhere 1-2(1-0)
Dinamo Tbilisi - Samtredia 1-0(1-0) [05.12.]

Round 17 [30.11.-02.12.2020]
FC Samtredia - Dinamo Batumi 1-2(1-0)
Chikhura Sachkhere - Dinamo Tbilisi 2-0(1-0)
Dila Gori - FC Saburtalo 4-3(1-2)
Torpedo Kutaisi - Lokomotivi Tbilisi 1-5(1-2)
Merani Tbilisi - FC Telavi 1-6(1-4)

Round 18 10.12.2020 [ ]
FC Saburtalo - FC Samtredia 2-1(0-1)
FC Telavi - Torpedo Kutaisi 1-1(0-1)
Dinamo Tbilisi - Merani Tbilisi 3-0(2-0)
Dinamo Batumi - Chikhura Sachkhere 0-0
Lokomotivi Tbilisi - Dila Gori 1-2(0-1)

Final Standings

								Home				Away		
1. **FC Dinamo Tbilisi**	18	12	4	2	33 - 9	40	6	2	1	16 - 5	6	2	1	17 - 4
2. FC Dinamo Batumi	18	10	6	2	29 - 14	36	3	4	2	9 - 7	7	2	0	20 - 7
3. FC Dila Gori	18	8	6	4	29 - 17	30	4	3	2	19 - 11	4	3	2	10 - 6
4. FC Lokomotivi Tbilisi	18	8	5	5	30 - 23	29	3	2	4	14 - 15	5	3	1	16 - 8
5. FC Saburtalo Tbilisi	18	7	6	5	28 - 21	27	4	3	2	7 - 7	3	3	3	21 - 14
6. FC Telavi	18	4	12	2	21 - 14	24	2	6	1	10 - 8	2	6	1	11 - 6
7. FC Samtredia	18	5	4	9	14 - 23	19	3	3	3	6 - 8	2	1	6	8 - 15
8. FC Torpedo Kutaisi (*Relegation Play-offs*)	18	4	5	9	17 - 30	17	2	3	4	8 - 17	2	2	5	9 - 13
9. FC Chikhura Sachkhere (*Relegation Play-offs*)	18	3	4	11	18 - 40	13	2	1	6	11 - 22	1	3	5	7 - 18
10. FC Merani Tbilisi (*Relegated*)	18	0	6	12	6 - 34	6	0	2	7	5 - 20	0	4	5	1 - 14

Top goalscorers:

10	Mykola Kovtalyuk (UKR)	*FC Dila Gori*
9	Irakli Sikharulidze	*FC Lokomotivi Tbilisi*
8	Jambul Jighauri	*FC Dinamo Batumi*
8	Nodar Kavtaradze (RUS)	*FC Dinamo Tbilisi*

Relegation Play-offs [15-19.12.2020]

FC Gagra - **FC Torpedo Kutaisi**	0-2(0-1)	1-1(0-1)
FC Chikhura Sachkhere - **FC Samgurali Tskhaltubo**	0-2(0-0)	0-1(0-0)

FC Torpedo Kutaisi and FC Samgurali Tskhaltubo promoted for the Erovnuli Liga 2021.

NATIONAL CUP
David Kipiani Cup - Sakartvelos tasi 2020

Second Round [24/27/29-30.08.2020]				
FC Bakhmaro Chokhatauri - FC Telavi	0-2		FC Samgurali Tskhaltubo - FC WIT Georgia Tbilisi	3-0
FC Dinamo Zugdidi - FC Chikhura Sachkhere	2-4		Tbilisi City - FC Kobuleti	1-0
FC Khobi - FC Torpedo Kutaisi	0-2		Spaeri FC - FC Metalurgi Rustavi	1-0
FK Imereti Khoni - FC Dila Gori	1-2		FC Betlemi Keda - FC Gori	2-2 aet; 4-3 pen
Varketili FK - FC Samtredia	0-2		FC Gareji Sagarejo - FC Merani Martvili	1-0 aet
FC Sioni Bolnisi - FC Merani Tbilisi	1-4		FC Kolkheti-1913 Poti - FC Gagra	0-4

1/8-Finals [17/19-21.09.2020]				
FC Gareji Sagarejo - FC Samgurali Tskhaltubo	0-2		Tbilisi City - FC Samtredia	3-2
FC Gagra - Dinamo Batumi	1-0		FC Telavi - FC Merani Tbilisi	2-0
Spaeri FC - FC Dila Gori	0-2		FC Saburtalo - Dinamo Tbilisi	1-0
FC Betlemi Keda - FC Torpedo Kutaisi	1-4		FC Chikhura Sachkhere - Lokomotivi Tbilisi	2-1

Quarter-Finals [26-27.09.2020]				
FC Samgurali Tskhaltubo - FC Telavi	2-0		FC Gagra - FC Dila Gori	0-0 aet; 5-3 pen
Tbilisi City - FC Chikhura Sachkhere	2-5		FC Saburtalo - FC Torpedo Kutaisi	2-0

Semi-Finals [08.11.2020]				
FC Gagra - FC Saburtalo	0-0 aet; 4-2 pen		FC Samgurali Tskhaltubo - FC Chikhura Sachkhere	2-0

Final

04.12.2020; Stadioni „Tengiz Burjanadze", Gori; Referee: Giorgi Kruashvili; Attendance: 0
FC Gagra - FC Samgurali Tskhaltubo   **0-0; 5-3 on penalties**

FC Gagra: Davit Kereselidze, Gia Chaduneli, Luka Nozadze, Vasil Khositashvili, Erekle Sultanishvili (106.Lasha Managadze), Ivane Khabelashvili (106.Rati Kakiashvili), Giorgi Kobuladze, Bakar Laghadze (84.Ivane Okropiridze), Giorgi Vekua, Tamaz Makatsaria, Giorgi Ivaniadze (84.Mikheil Ergemlidze). Trainer: Gaga Kirkitadze.

Samgurali Tskhaltubo: Kakhaber Meshveliani, Levan Kurdadze, Omar Patarkatsishvili, Ushangi Bandzeladze, Shalva Burjanadze, Grigol Dolidze (72.Demur Chikhladze), Papuna Poniava, Gaga Gazdeliani, Tedo Kikabidze [*sent off 55*], Yusuf Touré, Sergo Kukhianidze. Trainer: Ucha Sosiashvili.

Penalties: Vasil Khositashvili 1-0; Omar Patarkatsishvili 1-1; Rati Kakiashvili 2-1; Levan Kurdadze 2-2; Gia Chaduneli 3-2; Yusuf Touré (missed); Giorgi Vekua 4-2; Shalva Burjanadze 4-3; Mikheil Ergemlidze 5-3.

THE CLUBS 2020

Football Club Chikhura Sachkhere

Founded: 1938
Stadium: Stadioni „Ramaz Shengelia", Kutaisi (19,400)
Trainer: Vakhtang Turmanidze   19.01.1973

Goalkeepers:	DOB	M	(s)	G
Giorgi Begashvili	12.02.1991	14		
Dino Hamzić (BIH)	22.01.1988	2		
Avto Kapanadze	16.05.2002		(1)	
Tornike Zarkua	01.09.1990	2		
Defenders:	**DOB**	**M**	**(s)**	**G**
Nikita Bastron (RUS)	18.09.1995	2		
Lasha Chikvaidze	04.10.1989	13	(1)	1
Zurab Japiashvili	26.05.1996	9	(2)	
Otar Javashvili	17.08.1993	15	(2)	
Irakli Kamladze	18.02.1997	7		
Shota Kashia	22.10.1984	15		
Giorgi Koripadze	03.10.1989	12		2
Goderdzi Machaidze	17.07.1992	15		
Midfielders:	**DOB**	**M**	**(s)**	**G**
Georgi Berezov (RUS)	31.03.1995	7		
Rezo Gavtadze	11.07.1995	1	(7)	

	DOB	M	(s)	G
Shota Gvazava	26.10.1992	15	(1)	1
Luka Kikabidze	21.01.1995	11	(6)	4
Irakli Levtadze	30.08.1991		(1)	
Oleg Mamasakhlisi	25.11.1995	2		
Levan Nonikashvili	05.04.1995	2		
Ivane Potskhveria	24.07.2002	1	(3)	
Vano Sharvadze	27.05.2002		(1)	
Tengiz Tsikaridze	21.12.1995	11	(1)	2
Forwards:	**DOB**	**M**	**(s)**	**G**
Giorgi Bukhaidze	09.12.1991	12	(3)	3
Beso Dekanoidze	01.03.1992	9	(7)	1
Roman Dzhigkaev (RUS)	29.11.1993	2	(2)	
Vili Isiani	22.03.1991		(1)	
Kakha Kakhabrishvili	08.07.1993	15	(1)	3
Alan Mistulov (RUS)	21.05.1997	2		
David Mujiri	28.01.1999	2	(11)	1
Aleksandre Tepnadze	08.04.2002		(2)	

Football Club Dila Gori

Founded: 1949
Stadium: Stadioni „Tengiz Burjanadze", Gori (8,230)
Trainer: Giorgi Nemsadze   10.05.1972

Goalkeepers:	DOB	M	(s)	G
Giorgi Chochishvili	07.05.1998	2		
Luka Gugeshashvili	29.04.1999	16		
Defenders:	**DOB**	**M**	**(s)**	**G**
Alef Santos de Araujo (BRA)	06.11.1996	8	(5)	
Revaz Chiteishvili	30.01.1994	5	(3)	
Ramaric Presley Etou Thomaso (CGO)	25.01.1995	16		1
Guram Giorbelidze	25.02.1996	4		
Davit Khurtsilava	09.03.1988	15		
Giorgi Latsabidze	15.05.1995	10	(2)	1
Davit Maisashvili	18.02.1989	15		1
Wanderson Henrique do Nascimento Silva (BRA)	13.09.1991	4	(1)	
Balgou Yendountie (TOG)	24.12.1999	13	(2)	

Midfielders:	DOB	M	(s)	G
Irakli Bidzinashvili	27.02.1997	3	(2)	
Nika Gagnidze	20.03.2001	13		3
Tornike Gorgiashvili	27.04.1988	4	(3)	
Irakli Lekvtadze	30.08.1991	10	(6)	2
Francisco Madinga (MWI)	11.02.2000	6	(5)	2
Teimuraz Markozashvili	09.08.1994	11	(2)	1
Amos Nondi Obiero (KEN)	10.02.1999	14		
Giorgi Shalikashvili	03.05.2002		(2)	
Tamaz Tsetskhladze	08.12.1996	1	(1)	
Forwards:	**DOB**	**M**	**(s)**	**G**
Roman Chanturia	09.02.1996		(2)	1
Lidor Cohen (ISR)	16.12.1992	3	(4)	1
Mykola Kovtalyuk (UKR)	26.04.1995	16		10
Nugzar Spanderashvili	16.01.1999	9	(9)	6

Football Club Dinamo Batumi

Founded: 1923
Stadium: Batumi Stadium, Batumi (20,000)
Trainer: Georgi Geguchadze   20.06.1965

Goalkeepers:	DOB	M	(s)	G
Mikheil Alavidze	05.11.1987	16		
Igor Levchenko (UKR)	23.02.1991	2		
Defenders:	**DOB**	**M**	**(s)**	**G**
Lasha Chaladze	11.05.1987	3	(5)	
Malkhaz Gagoshidze	20.02.1993	11	(2)	1
Levan Gegetchkori	05.06.1994	5		
Mamuka Kobakhidze	23.08.1992	15		1
Kichi Meliava	14.04.1992	9		
Giorgi Navalovski	28.06.1986	13		
Godfrey Oboabona (NGA)	16.09.1990	10	(1)	2
Lasha Shergelashvili	17.01.1992	3	(2)	
Midfielders:	**DOB**	**M**	**(s)**	**G**
Tornike Gaprindashvili	20.07.1997	5	(8)	1

	DOB	M	(s)	G
Vladimer Mamuchashvili	28.08.1997	18		
Giuli Manjgaladze	09.09.1992	14	(2)	1
Benjamin Teidi (NGA)	07.05.1994	10	(4)	
Valerian Tevdoradze	11.10.1993		(10)	1
Mate Tsintsadze	07.01.1995	7	(2)	1
Forwards:	**DOB**	**M**	**(s)**	**G**
Vladimer Dvalishvili	20.04.1986	4	(5)	1
Flamarion Jovinho Filho (BRA)	30.07.1996	8		4
Vagner Gonçalves Nogueira de Souza (FRA)	27.04.1996	12	(2)	1
Jambul Jighauri	08.07.1992	18		8
Giorgi Nikabadze	10.01.1991	13	(2)	5
Reynaldo dos Santos Silva (BRA)	24.08.1989	2	(4)	1
Nikoloz Sabanadze	02.05.1991		(2)	

Football Club Dinamo Tbilisi

Founded: 1925
Stadium: „Boris Paichadze" Dinamo Arena, Tbilisi (54,549)
Trainer: Kakhaber Chkhetiani   24.02.1978
(24.08.2020)   Francisco Javier Muñoz Llompart „Xisco" (ESP)   05.09.1980

Goalkeepers:	DOB	M	(s)	G
Roin Kvaskhvadze	31.05.1989	18		
Defenders:	**DOB**	**M**	**(s)**	**G**
Simon Gbegnon (TOG)	27.10.1992	14		1
Nodar Iashvili	24.01.1993	12	(3)	1
Giorgi Kimadze	11.02.1992	12		
Rodney Klooster (NED)	26.11.1996	3		
Davit Kobouri	24.01.1998	18		2
Luka Lochosvili	29.05.1998	10		
Víctor Mongil Adeva (ESP)	21.07.1992	4		
Ivan Trubochkin (UKR)	17.03.1993	4	(1)	
Midfielders:	**DOB**	**M**	**(s)**	**G**
Irakli Azarovi	21.01.2002	1	(4)	
Luka Gagnidze	28.02.2003		(2)	
Bakar Kardava	04.10.1994	9	(1)	1
Nodar Kavtaradze	02.01.1993	12	(2)	8

	DOB	M	(s)	G
Giorgi Kukhianidze	01.07.1992	5	(5)	1
Giorgi Kutsia	27.10.1999	10	(3)	2
Anzor Mekvabishvili	05.06.2001	8	(2)	
Nikoloz Ninua	22.06.1999	1	(1)	1
Giorgi Papava	16.02.1993	16		1
Akaki Shulaia	06.09.1996	2	(5)	
Giorgi Zaria	14.07.1997	1	(5)	1
Forwards:	**DOB**	**M**	**(s)**	**G**
Tornike Akhvlediani	24.07.1999	1	(1)	
Irakli Bugridze	03.01.1998	6	(4)	1
Arfang Daffé (SEN)	24.06.1991		(2)	
Giorgi Gabedava	03.10.1989	5	(4)	4
Tornike Kapanadze	04.06.1992	6	(4)	3
Filip Oršula (SVK)	25.02.1993	4	(2)	
José Vitor Rodrigues da Silva dos Santos (BRA)	28.04.1998	12	(2)	2
Davit Skhirtladze	16.03.1993	4	(1)	3

Football Club Lokomotivi Tbilisi

Founded: 1936
Stadium: Stadioni „Mikheil Meskhi", Tbilisi (27,223)
Trainer: Levan Korgalidze   21.02.1980
(06.07.2020)   Giorgi Chiabrishvili   07.10.1979

Goalkeepers:	DOB	M	(s)	G
Giorgi Mamardashvili	29.09.2000	11		
Luka Sherozia	11.08.1997	7		
Defenders:	**DOB**	**M**	**(s)**	**G**
Aleksandre Andronikashvili	09.04.1999	7	(2)	
Nika Chanturia	19.01.1995	6		
Giorgi Gabadze	02.03.1995	12	(1)	1
Aleksandre Gureshidze	23.04.1995	15		1
Jemali-Jorji Jinjolava	28.06.2000	1	(1)	
Tsotne Kapanadze	30.08.2001	4	(3)	
Giorgi Kveladze	14.12.2001	1	(3)	
Rati Mchedlishvili	17.06.2002	3	(4)	
Nika Sandokhadze	20.02.1994	8		2
Davit Ubilava	27.01.1994	16		1
Midfielders:	**DOB**	**M**	**(s)**	**G**
Irakli Chiabrishvili	02.09.2001		(1)	

	DOB	M	(s)	G
Beka Dartsmelia	21.03.2000	15		
Tornike Dzebniauri	27.11.1999	6	(4)	
Davit Kirkitadze	03.09.1992	5	(5)	2
Tornike Kirkitadze	23.07.1996	11	(3)	
Aleksandre Kobakhidze	11.02.1987	4	(4)	
Imran Oulad Omar (MAR)	11.12.1997	10	(1)	3
Davit Samurkasovi	05.02.1998	10		
Temuri Shonia	28.05.1990	16		2
Forwards:	**DOB**	**M**	**(s)**	**G**
Vato Arveladze	04.03.1998	3	(2)	
Mamia Gavashelishvili	08.01.1995	6	(9)	5
Giorgi Iakobidze	27.02.2001	2	(4)	2
Revaz Injgia	31.12.2000		(2)	
Shota Shekiladze	15.02.2000	1	(5)	
Irakli Sikharulidze	18.07.1990	18		9

Football Club Merani Tbilisi

Founded: 1995
Stadium: Stadioni Sinatle, Tbilisi (2,500)
Trainer: Giorgi Daraselia   16.09.1968

Goalkeepers:	DOB	M	(s)	G
Revaz Tevdoradze	14.02.1988	17		
Beka Shekriladze	28.11.1983	1		
Defenders:	**DOB**	**M**	**(s)**	**G**
Beka Gabiskiria	13.07.1996	8	(3)	
Giorgi Gaprindashvili	06.05.1995	17		
Giorgi Kakhelishvili	22.05.1987	14		
Givi Karkuzashvili	20.09.1986	3		
Moris Nusuev (RUS)	28.06.1997	6	(1)	
Dachi Popkhadze	27.01.1984	15		1
Zurab Tevzadze	28.08.1994	15		
Saba Tolordava	11.06.2000		(2)	
Midfielders:	**DOB**	**M**	**(s)**	**G**
Arsen Avsajanashvili	30.07.1996		(1)	
David Bolkvadze	05.06.1980	2	(5)	1
Giorgi Datunaishvili	09.02.1985	14	(1)	
Iago Deisadze	10.02.1988	9	(1)	1
Revaz Getsadze	11.01.1985	8	(3)	1
Kakhaber Kakashvili	26.06.1993	7	(1)	
Giorgi Mikaberidze	17.02.1988	2	(2)	
Mishiko Sardalishvili	17.09.1992	13	(2)	
Levan Sharikadze	16.07.1989	8		
Giorgi Vasadze	14.06.1989	12	(2)	
Forwards:	**DOB**	**M**	**(s)**	**G**
Cotne Chikovani	20.12.2000	2	(1)	
Giorgi Gogolashvili	02.08.1997	5	(5)	1
Giorgi Khabuliani	25.03.2004	5	(5)	
Bidzina Makharoblidze	10.10.1992	7	(3)	
Davit Natchkebia	21.06.2000	2		
Giorgi Nikabadze	10.01.1991		(1)	
Gogi Pipia	04.02.1985	4	(6)	
Vano Shengelidze	30.03.1996	2	(5)	1

Football Club Saburtalo Tbilisi

Founded: 20.08.1999
Stadium: Stadioni „Mikheil Meskhi", Tbilisi (27,223)
Trainer: Temur Shalamberidze   08.12.1969
(18.09.2020)   Levan Korgalidze   21.02.1980

Goalkeepers:	DOB	M	(s)	G
Davit Kupatadze	06.06.1991	1	(1)	
Lazare Kupatadze	08.02.1996	16		
Tornike Megrelishvili	08.05.1999	1		
Defenders:	**DOB**	**M**	**(s)**	**G**
Sandro Chanturishvili	20.03.1999		(1)	
Anri Chichinadze	05.10.1997	10	(2)	
Tedore Grigalashvili	12.05.1993	11	(1)	1
Levan Kakubava	15.10.1990	14		
Luka Lakvekheliani	20.10.1998	4		
Nikoloz Mali	27.01.1999	12	(1)	1
Gagi Margvelashvili	30.10.1996	17		3
Jardel Rodrigues Afonso Nazaré (STP)	16.05.1995	1	(3)	
Iuri Tabatadze	29.11.1999	11	(3)	2
Midfielders:	**DOB**	**M**	**(s)**	**G**
Sandro Altunashvili	19.05.1997	18		
Oleksandr Belyayev (UKR)	04.10.1999	2	(4)	
Gegi Geguchadze	30.12.2003		(1)	
Levan Kenia	18.10.1990	1	(1)	
Gizo Mamageishvili	15.01.2003		(2)	
Levan Macharashvili	24.03.1997	7	(4)	
Levan Nonikashvili	05.04.1995	3	(2)	1
Shota Nonikashvili	10.01.2001	1		
Alwyn Tera (KEN)	18.01.1997	17		4
Dachi Tsnobiladze	28.01.1994	9	(6)	1
Forwards:	**DOB**	**M**	**(s)**	**G**
Olivier Junior Boumal (CMR)	17.09.1989	7	(1)	
Giorgi Gabedava	03.10.1989	2		1
Teimuraz Gabunia	10.02.2000		(1)	
Giorgi Gocholeishvili	14.02.2001		(5)	
Guram Goshteliani	05.01.1997	1	(1)	
Giorgi Guliashvili	05.09.2001	8	(6)	4
Beka Kavtaradze	15.06.1999	14	(4)	7
Giorgi Kokhreidze	18.11.1998	6		1
Jeroen Lumu (NED)	27.05.1995	4	(3)	1

Football Club Samtredia

Founded: 1936
Stadium: Stadioni „Erosi Manjgaladze", Tbilisi (5,000)
Trainer: Kakhaber Kacharava   19.09.1966
(24.09.2020)   Giorgi Mikadze   21.03.1980

Goalkeepers:	DOB	M	(s)	G
Giorgi Kulua	19.07.1997	2		
Konstantine Sepiashvili	19.03.1986	14		
Stefan Sicaci (MDA)	08.09.1988	2		
Defenders:	**DOB**	**M**	**(s)**	**G**
Giorgi Akhaladze	26.07.1997	13	(1)	1
Aliko Chakvetadze	28.03.1995	2	(1)	
Samuel Inkoom (GHA)	01.06.1989	11	(3)	1
Giorgi Jgerenaia	28.12.1993	9		
Varlam Kilasonia	09.01.1993	16		
Ricardo Miguel Ferreira Guedes Pinheiro (POR)	05.05.1997	2	(1)	
Guja Rukhaia	22.07.1987	14	(1)	
Davit Sajaia	23.08.1993	1		
Kabba Sambou (GAM)	20.04.1996	12	(1)	
Lasha Totadze	24.08.1988	8		2
Midfielders:	**DOB**	**M**	**(s)**	**G**
Diego Diz Martínez (ESP)	12.11.1991	13	(2)	2
Shota Kerdzevadze	20.03.1993	7	(3)	1
Lasha Kochladze	22.08.1995	6	(6)	
Guram Lukava	14.04.1995	1	(3)	
Anatoli Mesiachenko	21.04.2001	6	(5)	
Strahinja Pavišić (SRB)	29.05.1996	14	(1)	1
David Targamadze	22.08.1989	5	(2)	1
Forwards:	**DOB**	**M**	**(s)**	**G**
Arfang Daffé (SEN)	24.06.1991	3	(3)	
Zurab Ghirdaladze	09.06.1994	1		
Giorgi Iluridze	20.02.1992	2	(2)	1
Luka Imnadze	26.08.1997	14	(2)	
Mate Kvirkvia	14.06.1996	8	(7)	
Nathan Júnior Soares de Carvalho (BRA)	10.03.1989	4	(3)	
Nidzhat Qurbanov (AZE)	17.02.1992	8	(2)	4

Football Club Telavi

Founded: 2016
Stadium: Stadioni „Givi Chokheli", Telavi (12,000)
Trainer: Revaz Gotsiridze   17.01.1981

Goalkeepers:	DOB	M	(s)	G
Oto Goshadze	13.10.1997	4		
Luka Sanikidze	19.11.1998	12		
Levan Tandilashvili	27.02.2003	2	(1)	
Defenders:	**DOB**	**M**	**(s)**	**G**
Vaso Bachiashvili	04.11.1992	6		
Ilia Beriashvili	09.07.1998	14		1
Grigol Chabradze	20.04.1996	15		
Ukwubile Raphael Chukwurah (NGA)	17.05.1992	12	(1)	2
Vladimir Dimitrovski (MKD)	30.11.1988	11		1
Tornike Dzotsenidze	07.11.1999	13	(1)	1
Mirian Jikia	14.10.1990	3	(2)	1
Piruz Marakvelidze	21.05.1995	6	(1)	1
Anton Tolordava	02.08.1996	12	(1)	
Midfielders:	**DOB**	**M**	**(s)**	**G**
Mikheil Basheleishvili	21.06.1997	12	(2)	3
Nikoloz Basheleishvili	21.06.1997	12	(3)	1
Aleksandre Koshkadze	04.12.1981		(1)	
Giorgi Moistsrapishvili	29.09.2001	3	(7)	1
Tsotne Mosiashvili	14.02.1995	16	(1)	1
Hovhannes Poghosyan (ARM)	17.12.1997	3		
Irakli Rukhadze	28.10.1996	11	(5)	5
Guram Samushia	05.09.1994	6	(9)	
Beka Varshanidze	01.11.1993	5	(3)	
Forwards:	**DOB**	**M**	**(s)**	**G**
Giorgi Kandelaki	28.09.2001	1	(3)	
Lasha Kokhreidze	18.11.1998	9	(3)	1
Yaroslav Kvasov (UKR)	05.03.1992	10	(5)	2

<table>
<tr><td colspan="3">Football Club Torpedo Kutaisi</td></tr>
</table>

Founded: 1946
Stadium: Stadioni „Ramaz Shengelia", Kutaisi (19,400)
Trainer: Mikhail Ashvetia   10.11.1977

Goalkeepers:	DOB	M	(s)	G
Demetre Buliskeria	09.01.2000	6		
Levan Shovnadze	19.11.1997	12		
Defenders:	**DOB**	**M**	**(s)**	**G**
Guram Adamadze	21.08.1988	10	(4)	1
Vakhtang Botchorishvili	21.08.2001	1		
Andro Giorgadze	03.05.1996	5		
Tornike Grigalashvili	28.01.1993	8	(2)	
Luka Kapianidze	10.01.1999	3	(1)	1
Lasha Kasradze	28.07.1989	11		1
Bakar Mirtskhulava	24.05.1992	9	(4)	
Tsotne Nadaraia	21.02.1997	16		
Vazha Tabatadze	01.02.1991	15		
Midfielders:	**DOB**	**M**	**(s)**	**G**
Mate Abuladze	30.06.2000		(2)	
Ivan Bobko (UKR)	10.12.1990	10		2

	DOB	M	(s)	G
Irakli Dzaria	01.12.1988	6		
Zaur Goguadze	12.08.1996	1	(1)	
Giorgi Ivanishvili	18.10.1989	12	(2)	1
Giorgi Janelidze	25.09.1989	14	(1)	
Oleg Mamasakhlisi	25.11.1995	8		1
Vanja Marković (SRB)	20.06.1994	6	(5)	
Shalva Purtskhvanidze	22.09.1997	2	(1)	
Tamaz Sharvashidze	06.12.2000	1	10)	
Zaza Tsitskishvili	04.07.1995	16	(1)	1
Forwards:	**DOB**	**M**	**(s)**	**G**
Davit Ionanidze	05.08.1998	2	(3)	
Otar Kvernadze	10.09.1993	1	(6)	
Giorgi Pantsulaia	06.01.1994	16	(1)	7
Vitaliy Ponomar (UKR)	31.05.1990	6	(1)	2
Beka Tugushi	24.01.1989	1	(6)	

SECOND LEVEL
Erovnuli Liga 2 2020

1.	FC Shukura Kobuleti (*Promoted*)	18	9	4	5	32 - 14	31
2.	FC Samgurali Tskhaltubo (*Promotion Play-offs*)	18	8	6	4	23 - 12	30
3.	FC Gagra (*Promotion Play-offs*)	18	7	8	3	24 - 10	29
4.	FC Rustavi	18	7	5	6	35 - 27	26
5.	FC Dinamo Zugdidi	18	7	4	7	27 - 31	25
6.	FC Shevardeni-1906 Tbilisi	18	8	1	9	28 - 38	25
7.	FC Sioni Bolnisi	18	5	9	4	23 - 16	24
8.	FC Merani Martvili (*Relegation Play-offs*)	18	6	6	6	23 - 20	24
9.	FC WIT Georgia Tbilisi (*Relegation Play-offs*)	18	5	6	7	17 - 25	21
10.	FC Aragvi Dusheti (*Relegated*)	18	1	5	12	10 - 49	8

Relegation Play-offs (2nd / 3rd Level)

FC Gori - **FC Merani Martvili**	0-0	1-3(0-1)
FC WIT Georgia Tbilisi - FC Kolkheti-1913 Poti	1-0(1-0)	0-1 aet; 4-3 pen

NATIONAL TEAM

INTERNATIONAL MATCHES
(16.07.2020 – 15.07.2021)

05.09.2020	Tallinn	Estonia - Georgia	0-1(0-1)	(UNL)
08.09.2020	Tbilisi	Georgia - North Macedonia	1-1(1-1)	(UNL)
08.10.2020	Tbilisi	Georgia - Belarus	1-0(1-0)	(ECQPO)
11.10.2020	Tychy	Armenia - Georgia	2-2(1-0)	(UNL)
14.10.2020	Skopje	North Macedonia - Georgia	1-1(0-0)	(UNL)
12.11.2020	Tbilisi	Georgia - North Macedonia	0-1(0-0)	(ECQPO)
15.11.2020	Tbilisi	Georgia - Armenia	1-2(0-1)	(UNL)
18.11.2020	Tbilisi	Georgia - Estonia	0-0	(UNL)
25.03.2021	Stockholm	Sweden - Georgia	1-0(1-0)	(WCQ)
28.03.2021	Tbilisi	Georgia - Spain	1-2(1-0)	(WCQ)
31.03.2021	Thessaloníki	Greece - Georgia	1-1(0-0)	(WCQ)
02.06.2021	Ploieşti	Romania - Georgia	1-2(0-1)	(F)
06.06.2021	Enschede	Netherlands - Georgia	3-0(1-0)	(F)

05.09.2020   ESTONIA - GEORGIA   0-1(0-1)   2nd UEFA Nations League C, Group 2
A. Le Coq Arena, Tallinn; Referee: Donatas Rumšas (Lithuania); Attendance: 0
GEO: Giorgi Loria, Solomon Kvirkvelia, Davit Khocholava, Otar Kakabadze, Jaba Kankava (Cap), Nika Kvekveskiri, Tornike Okriashvili, Jambul Jighauri, Giorgi Chakvetadze (78.Giorgi Kvilitaia), Khvicha Kvaratskhelia (90+2.Giorgi Aburjania), Nika Kacharava (68.Saba Lobjanidze). Trainer: Vladimír Weiss (Slovakia).
Goal: Nika Kacharava (32).

08.09.2020   GEORGIA - NORTH MACEDONIA   1-1(1-1)   2nd UEFA Nations League C, Group 2
„Boris Paichadze" Dinamo Arena, Tbilisi; Referee: Peter Kjærsgaard-Andersen (Denmark); Attendance: 0
GEO: Giorgi Loria, Solomon Kvirkvelia, Davit Khocholava, Otar Kakabadze, Nikoloz Mali (75.Levan Shengelia), Jaba Kankava (Cap), Nika Kvekveskiri (85.Nika Kacharava), Tornike Okriashvili, Zuriko Davitashvili, Khvicha Kvaratskhelia, Giorgi Kvilitaia (62.Giorgi Chakvetadze). Trainer: Vladimír Weiss (Slovakia).
Goal: Tornike Okriashvili (13 penalty).

08.10.2020   **GEORGIA - BELARUS**   **1-0(1-0)**   16th EC. Qualifiers Play-offs, Semi-Finals
„Boris Paichadze" Dinamo Arena, Tbilisi; Referee: Cüneyt Çakır (Turkey); Attendance: 0
GEO: Giorgi Loria, Guram Kashia, Solomon Kvirkvelia, Otar Kakabadze (82.Jemal Tabidze), Lasha Dvali, Jaba Kankava (Cap), Nika Kvekveskiri, Tornike Okriashvili (89.Giorgi Kvilitaia), Otar Kiteishvili (65.Valerian Gvilia), Khvicha Kvaratskhelia (90.Elguja Lobjanidze), Valeri Qazaishvili (81.Levan Shengelia). Trainer: Vladimír Weiss (Slovakia).
Goal: Tornike Okriashvili (7 penalty).

11.10.2020   **ARMENIA - GEORGIA**   **2-2(1-0)**   2nd UEFA Nations League C, Group 2
Stadion Miejski, Tichy (Poland); Referee: Ivan Bebek (Croatia); Attendance: 0
GEO: Giorgi Makaridze, Giorgi Navalovski, Gia Grigalava, Mamuka Kobakhidze, Jaba Kankava (Cap) (76.Nika Kvekveskiri), Giorgi Aburjania (76.Murtaz Daushvili), Jambul Jighauri, Levan Shengelia (80.Saba Lobjanidze), Valerian Gvilia (61.Tornike Okriashvili), Valeri Qazaishvili, Nika Kacharava (80.Elguja Lobjanidze). Trainer: Vladimír Weiss (Slovakia).
Goals: Nika Kacharava (46), Tornike Okriashvili (74).

14.10.2020   **NORTH MACEDONIA - GEORGIA**   **1-1(0-0)**   2nd UEFA Nations League C, Group 2
"Toše Proeski" National Arena, Skopje; Referee: Bartosz Frankowski (Poland); Attendance: 0
GEO: Giorgi Loria (Cap), Solomon Kvirkvelia, Lasha Dvali (90+1.Giorgi Navalovski), Jemal Tabidze, Murtaz Daushvili (71.Khvicha Kvaratskhelia), Nika Kvekveskiri, Jambul Jighauri, Otar Kiteishvili (7.Saba Lobjanidze), Valerian Gvilia, Valeri Qazaishvili (90.Mamuka Kobakhidze), Giorgi Kvilitaia (71.Nika Kacharava). Trainer: Vladimír Weiss (Slovakia).
Goal: Khvicha Kvaratskhelia (74).

12.11.2020   **GEORGIA - NORTH MACEDONIA**   **0-1(0-0)**   16th EC. Qualifiers Play-offs, Finals
„Boris Paichadze" Dinamo Arena, Tbilisi; Referee: Anthony Taylor (England); Attendance: 0
GEO: Giorgi Loria, Guram Kashia (88.Jambul Jighauri), Solomon Kvirkvelia, Otar Kakabadze, Lasha Dvali (90+2.Zuriko Davitashvili), Jaba Kankava (Cap), Nika Kvekveskiri, Tornike Okriashvili, Valerian Gvilia (80.Giorgi Papunashvili), Valeri Qazaishvili (90+3.Davit Khocholava), Nika Kacharava (80.Elguja Lobjanidze). Trainer: Vladimír Weiss (Slovakia).

15.11.2020   **GEORGIA - ARMENIA**   **1-2(0-1)**   2nd UEFA Nations League C, Group 2
„Boris Paichadze" Dinamo Arena, Tbilisi; Referee: Marco Guida (Italy); Attendance: 0
GEO: Giorgi Makaridze, Giorgi Navalovski, Gia Grigalava, Davit Khocholava, Jaba Kankava (Cap), Giorgi Aburjania (80.Nika Kvekveskiri), Jambul Jighauri, Saba Lobjanidze (80.Giorgi Papunashvili), Zuriko Davitashvili (56.Valeri Qazaishvili), Valerian Gvilia (80.Beka Mikeltadze), Elguja Lobjanidze (68.Nika Kacharava). Trainer: Vladimír Weiss (Slovakia).
Goal: Valeri Qazaishvili (65 penalty).

18.11.2020   **GEORGIA - ESTONIA**   **0-0**   2nd UEFA Nations League C, Group 2
„Boris Paichadze" Dinamo Arena, Tbilisi; Referee: Irfan Peljto (Bosnia and Herzegovina); Attendance: 0
GEO: Giorgi Loria, Guram Kashia, Davit Khocholava (46.Gia Grigalava), Otar Kakabadze, Jemal Tabidze, Jaba Kankava (Cap), Nika Kvekveskiri, Saba Lobjanidze (85.Beka Mikeltadze), Zuriko Davitashvili (66.Giorgi Papunashvili), Valeri Qazaishvili, Nika Kacharava (79.Elguja Lobjanidze). Trainer: Ramaz Svanadze.

25.03.2021   **SWEDEN - GEORGIA**   **1-0(1-0)**   22nd FIFA WC.Qualifiers
Friends Arena, Tockholm; Referee: Benoît Bastien (France); Attendance: 0
GEO: Giorgi Loria, Guram Kashia, Lasha Dvali, Grigol Chabradze, Guram Giorbelidze, Jaba Kankava (Cap) (60.Valerian Gvilia), Nika Kvekveskiri (60.Levan Shengelia), Giorgi Aburjania, Khvicha Kvaratskhelia (46.Otar Kiteishvili), Saba Lobjanidze (78.Giorgi Beridze), Giorgi Kvilitaia (84.Georges Mikautadze). Trainer: Willy David Frédéric Sagnol (France).

28.03.2021   **GEORGIA - SPAIN**   **1-2(1-0)**   22nd FIFA WC.Qualifiers
„Boris Paichadze" Dinamo Arena, Tbilisi; Referee: Radu Marian Petrescu (Romania); Attendance: 16,500
GEO: Giorgi Loria, Guram Kashia, Otar Kakabadze (79.Grigol Chabradze), Lasha Dvali, Guram Giorbelidze, Jaba Kankava (Cap), Otar Kiteishvili (70.Giorgi Beridze), Valerian Gvilia, Khvicha Kvaratskhelia (79.Nika Kvekveskiri [*sent off 90+4*]), Budu Zivzivadze (62.Giorgi Kvilitaia), Saba Lobjanidze (70.Levan Shengelia). Trainer: Willy David Frédéric Sagnol (France).
Goal: Khvicha Kvaratskhelia (44).

31.03.2021   **GREECE - GEORGIA**   **1-1(0-0)**   22nd FIFA WC.Qualifiers
Stádio Toumba, Thessaloníki; Referee: Szymon Marciniak (Poland); Attendance: 0
GEO: Giorgi Loria, Guram Kashia, Otar Kakabadze, Lasha Dvali, Guram Giorbelidze, Jaba Kankava (Cap), Giorgi Aburjania (74.Valerian Gvilia), Otar Kiteishvili (84.Nika Kvekveskiri), Khvicha Kvaratskhelia, Budu Zivzivadze (63.Giorgi Kvilitaia), Saba Lobjanidze (84.Jambul Jighauri). Trainer: Willy David Frédéric Sagnol (France).
Goal: Khvicha Kvaratskhelia (78).

02.06.2021   **ROMANIA - GEORGIA**   **1-2(0-1)**   Friendly International
Stadionul „Ilie Oană", Ploieşti; Referee: Anastasios Sidiropoulos (Greece); Attendance: 1,000
GEO: Lazare Kupatadze, Solomon Kvirkvelia [*sent off 64*], Davit Khocholava, Grigol Chabradze, Irakli Azarovi, Murtaz Daushvili, Nika Kvekveskiri (57.Otar Kiteishvili), Tornike Okriashvili (Cap) 66.66.Guram Kashia, Giorgi Aburjania (80.Valerian Gvilia), Levan Shengelia (57.Saba Lobjanidze), Georges Mikautadze (81.Budu Zivzivadze). Trainer: Willy David Frédéric Sagnol (France).
Goals: Georges Mikautadze (61), Giorgi Aburjania (71).

06.06.2021   **NETHERLANDS - GEORGIA**   **3-0(1-0)**   Friendly International
De Grolsch Veste, Enschede; Referee: Erik Lambrechts (Belgium); Attendance: 7,600
GEO: Giorgi Loria, Guram Kashia (Cap), Davit Khocholava (66.Jambul Jighauri), Otar Kakabadze, Lasha Dvali, Guram Giorbelidze, Giorgi Aburjania (78.Murtaz Daushvili), Saba Lobjanidze (46.Zuriko Davitashvili), Otar Kiteishvili (88.Sergo Kukhianidze), Valerian Gvilia (78.Nika Kvekveskiri), Budu Zivzivadze (65.Georges Mikautadze). Trainer: Willy David Frédéric Sagnol (France).

Name	DOB	Caps	Goals	2020/2021:	Club
Goalkeepers					
Lazare KUPATADZE	08.02.1996	1	0	2021:	FC Dinamo Batumi
Giorgi LORIA	27.01.1986	66	0	2020/2021:	Anorthosis Famagusta FC (CYP)
Giorgi MAKARIDZE	31.03.1990	17	0	2020:	UD Almería (ESP)
Defenders					
Irakli AZAROVI	21.01.2002	1	0	2021:	FC Dinamo Batumi
Grigol CHABRADZE	20.04.1996	3	0	2021:	FC Dinamo Batumi
Lasha DVALI	14.05.1995	20	1	2020/2021:	Ferencvárosi TC (HUN)
Guram GIORBELIDZE	25.02.1996	4	0	2021:	Wolfsberger AC (AUT)
Gia GRIGALAVA	05.08.1989	34	0	2020/2021:	FK Arsenal Tula (RUS)
Otar KAKABADZE	27.06.1995	41	0	2020: 25.09.2020->	FC Luzern (SUI) CD Tenerife (ESP)
Guram KASHIA	04.07.1987	87	2	2020/2021:	FC Lokomotivi Tbilisi
Davit KHOCHOLAVA	08.02.1993	28	0	2020/2021:	FK Shakhtar Donetsk (UKR)
Mamuka KOBAKHIDZE	23.08.1992	2	0	2020:	FC Dinamo Batumi
Solomon KVIRKVELIA	06.02.1992	42	0	2020/2021:	FK Rotor Volgograd (RUS)
Nikoloz MALI	27.01.1999	1	0	2020:	FC Saburtalo Tbilisi
Giorgi NAVALOVSKI	28.06.1986	41	0	2020:	FC Dinamo Batumi
Jemal TABIDZE	18.03.1996	14	1	2020:	FK Ufa (RUS)
Midfielders					
Giorgi ABURJANIA	02.01.1995	23	1	2020: 20.09.2020-> 28.01.2021->	FC Twente Enschede (NED, on loan) Real Oviedo (ESP) FC Cartagena (ESP)
Giorgi CHAKVETADZE	29.08.1999	9	5	2020:	KAA Gent (BEL)
Murtaz DAUSHVILI	01.05.1989	40	0	2020/2021:	Anorthosis Famagusta FC (CYP)
Zuriko DAVITASHVILI	15.02.2001	7	0	2020/2021:	FK Rotor Volgograd (RUS)
Valerian GVILIA	24.05.1994	37	3	2020/2021:	Legia Warszawa (POL)
Jambul „Jaba" JIGHAURI	08.07.1992	21	0	2020/2021:	FC Dinamo Batumi
Jaba KANKAVA	18.03.1986	96	10	2020: 16.01.2021->	FC Tobol Kostanay (KAZ) Valenciennes FC (FRA)
Otar KITEISHVILI	26.03.1996	23	0	2020/2021:	SK Sturm Graz (AUT)
Khvicha KVARATSKHELIA	12.02.2001	8	3	2020/2021:	FK Rubin Kazan (RUS)
Nika KVEKVESKIRI	29.05.1992	38	0	2020/2021:	KKS Lech Poznań (POL)
Saba LOBJANIDZE	18.12.1994	18	2	2020/2021:	MKE Ankaragücü (TUR)
Tornike OKRIASHVILI	12.02.1992	46	12	2020/2021:	Anorthosis Famagusta FC (CYP)
Giorgi PAPUNASHVILI	02.09.1995	17	3	2020:	Real Zaragoza (ESP)
Valeri QAZAISHVILI	29.01.1993	53	11	2020:	San Jose Earthquakes (USA)
Levan SHENGELIA	27.10.1995	10	0	2020/2021:	Konyaspor Kulübü (TUR)
Forwards					
Giorgi BERIDZE	12.05.1997	4	0	2021:	Újpest FC (HUN)
Nika KACHARAVA	13.01.1994	24	3	2020: 11.09.2020->	Anorthosis Famagusta FC (CYP) KKS Lech Poznań (POL, on loan)
Sergo KUKHIANIDZE	23.04.1999	1	0	2021:	FC Samgurali Tskhaltubo
Giorgi KVILITAIA	01.10.1993	23	6	2020: 17.09.2020->	KAA Gent (BEL) Anorthosis Famagusta FC (CYP, on loan)
Elguja LOBJANIDZE	17.09.1992	11	0	2020:	FC Kaysar Kyzylorda (KAZ)
Georges MIKAUTADZE	31.10.2000	3	1	2021:	RFC Seraing (BEL)
Beka MIKELTADZE	26.11.1997	2	0	2020:	FK Rotor Volgograd (RUS)
Budu ZIVZIVADZE	10.03.1994	8	0	2021:	Fehérvár FC Székesfehérvár (HUN)

Trainer			
Vladimír WEISS (Slovakia) [14.03.2016 – 16.11.2020]	22.09.1964	47 M; 16 W; 15 D; 16 L; 61-53	
Ramaz SVANADZE [16.11.-20.11.2020]	02.03.1981	1 M; 0 W; 1 D; 0 L; 0-0	
Willy David Frédéric SAGNOL (France) [from 15.02.1977]	18.03.1977	6 M; 1 W; 1 D; 4 L; 4-9	

GERMANY

The Country:
Bundesrepublik Deutschland (Federal Republic of Germany)
Capital: Berlin
Surface: 357,168 km²
Inhabitants: 83,190,556 [2020]
Time: UTC+1

The FA:
Deutscher Fußball-Bund
Otto-Fleck-Schneise 6, Postfach 710265, 60492 Frankfurt am Main
Tel: +49 69 678 80
Foundation date: 28.01.1900
Member of FIFA since: 1904
Member of UEFA since: 1954
Website: www.dfb.de

NATIONAL TEAM RECORDS

RECORDS

First international match:	05.04.1908, Basel:	Switzerland – Germany 5-3
Most international caps:	Lothar Herbert Matthäus	- 150 caps (1980-2000)
Most international goals:	Miroslav Klose	- 71 goals / 137 caps (2001-2014)

UEFA EUROPEAN CHAMPIONSHIP

1960	Did not enter
1964	Did not enter
1968	Qualifiers
1972	**Final Tournament (Winners)**
1976	Final Tournament (Runners-up)
1980	**Final Tournament (Winners)**
1984	Final Tournament (Group Stage)
1988	Final Tournament (Semi-Finals)
1992	Final Tournament (Runners-up)
1996	**Final Tournament (Winners)**
2000	Final Tournament (Group Stage)
2004	Final Tournament (Group Stage)
2008	Final Tournament (Runners-up)
2012	Final Tournament (Semi-Finals)
2016	Final Tournament (Semi-Finals)
2020	Final Tournament (2nd Round of 16)

FIFA WORLD CUP

1930	Did not enter
1934	Final Tournament (3rd Place)
1938	Final Tournament (1st Round)
1950	*Banned*
1954	**Final Tournament (Winners)**
1958	Final Tournament (3rd Place)
1962	Final Tournament (Quarter-Finals)
1966	Final Tournament (Runners-up)
1970	Final Tournament (3rd Place)
1974	**Final Tournament (Winners)**
1978	Final Tournament (Second Round)
1982	Final Tournament (Runners-up)
1986	Final Tournament (Runners-up)
1990	**Final Tournament (Winners)**
1994	Final Tournament (Quarter-Finals)
1998	Final Tournament (Quarter-Finals)
2002	Final Tournament (Runners-up)
2006	Final Tournament (3rd Place)
2010	Final Tournament (3rd Place)
2014	**Final Tournament (Winners)**
2018	Final Tournament (Group Stage)

OLYMPIC TOURNAMENTS

1908	-
1912	1st Round
1920	-
1924	-
1928	Quarter-Finals
1936	Quarter-Finals
1948	-
1952	4th Place
1956	1st Round
1960	Qualifiers
1964	Qualifiers
1968	-
1972	Second Round
1976	Qualifiers
1980	Qualifiers
1984	Quarter-Finals
1988	3rd Place
1992	Qualifiers
1996	Qualifiers
2000	Qualifiers
2004	Qualifiers
2008	Qualifiers
2012	Qualifiers
2016	Runners-up

UEFA NATIONS LEAGUE

2018/2019	League A
2020/2021	League A

FIFA CONFEDERATIONS CUP 1992-2017

1999 (Group Stage), 2005 (3rd Place), **2017 (Winners)**

GERMAN CLUB HONOURS IN EUROPEAN CLUB COMPETITIONS:

European Champion Clubs' Cup (1956-1992) / UEFA Champions League (1993-2021)		
FC Bayern München	6	1973/1974, 1974/1975, 1975/1976, 2000/2001, 2012/2013, 2019/2020
Hamburger SV	1	1982/1983
BV Borussia Dortmund	1	1996/1997
Fairs Cup (1858-1971) / UEFA Cup (1972-2009) / UEFA Europa League (2010-2021)		
Borussia VfL Mönchengladbach	2	1974/1975, 1978/1979
Eintracht Frankfurt	1	1979/1980
TSV Bayer 04 Leverkusen	1	1987/1988
FC Bayern München	1	1995/1996
FC Schalke 04 Gelsenkirchen	1	1996/1997

UEFA Super Cup (1972-2020)				
FC Bayern München		2	2013, 2020	
European Cup Winners' Cup 1961-1999				
BV Borussia Dortmund		1	1965/1966	
Hamburger SV		1	1976/1977	
FC Bayern München		1	1966/1967	
SV Werder Bremen		1	1991/1992	

defunct competition

NATIONAL COMPETITIONS
TABLE OF HONOURS

	CHAMPIONS	CUP WINNERS	BEST GOALSCORERS	
1902/1903	VfB Leipzig	-	-	
1903/1904	*No champions (final not played)*	-	-	
1904/1905	Berliner TuFC Union 1892	-	-	
1905/1906	VfB Leipzig	-	-	
1906/1907	Freiburger FC	-	-	
1907/1908	Berliner TuFC Viktoria 1889	-	-	
1908/1909	FC Phönix Karlsruhe	-	-	
1909/1910	Karlsruher FV	-	-	
1910/1911	Berliner TuFC Viktoria 1889	-	-	
1911/1912	Holstein Kiel	-	-	
1912/1913	VfB Leipzig	-	-	
1913/1914	SpVgg Fürth	-	-	
1914-1919	*No competition*	-	-	
1919/1920	1. FC Nürnberg	-	-	
1920/1921	1. FC Nürnberg	-	-	
1921/1922	*No champions (title declined by DFB)*	-	-	
1922/1923	Hamburger SV	-	-	
1923/1924	1. FC Nürnberg	-	-	
1924/1925	1. FC Nürnberg	-	-	
1925/1926	SpVgg Fürth	-	-	
1926/1927	1. FC Nürnberg	-	-	
1927/1928	Hamburger SV	-	-	
1928/1929	SpVgg Fürth	-	-	
1929/1930	Hertha BSC Berlin	-	-	
1930/1931	Hertha BSC Berlin	-	-	
1931/1932	FC Bayern München	-	-	
1932/1933	TSV Fortuna Düsseldorf	-	-	
1933/1934	FC Schalke 04 Gelsenkirchen	-	-	
1934/1935	FC Schalke 04 Gelsenkirchen	1. FC Nürnberg	-	
1935/1936	1. FC Nürnberg	VfB Leipzig	-	
1936/1937	FC Schalke 04 Gelsenkirchen	FC Schalke 04 Gelsenkirchen	-	
1937/1938	SV Hannover 96	SK Rapid Wien	-	
1938/1939	FC Schalke 04 Gelsenkirchen	1. FC Nürnberg	-	
1939/1940	FC Schalke 04 Gelsenkirchen	Dresdner SC	-	
1940/1941	SK Rapid Wien	Dresdner SC	-	
1941/1942	FC Schalke 04 Gelsenkirchen	TSV 1860 München	-	
1942/1943	Dresdner SC	1894 First Vienna FC	-	
1943/1944	Dresdner SC	*No competition*	-	
1944/1945	*No competition*	*No competition*	-	
1945/1946	VfB Stuttgart	*No competition*	-	
1946/1947	1. FC Nürnberg	*No competition*	-	
1947/1948	1. FC Nürnberg	*No competition*	-	
1948/1949	VfR Mannheim	*No competition*	-	
1949/1950	VfB Stuttgart	*No competition*	-	
1950/1951	1. FC Kaiserslautern	*No competition*	-	
1951/1952	VfB Stuttgart	*No competition*	-	
1952/1953	1. FC Kaiserslautern	Rot-Weiss Essen	-	
1953/1954	SV Hannover 96	VfB Stuttgart	-	
1954/1955	Rot-Weiss Essen	Karlsruher SC	-	
1955/1956	BV Borussia 09 Dortmund	Karlsruher SC	-	
1956/1957	BV Borussia 09 Dortmund	FC Bayern München	-	
1957/1958	FC Schalke 04 Gelsenkirchen	VfB Stuttgart	-	
1958/1959	Eintracht Frankfurt	TB Schwarz-Weiß Essen	-	
1959/1960	Hamburger SV	Borussia VfL Mönchengladbach	-	
1960/1961	1. FC Nürnberg	SV Werder Bremen	-	
1961/1962	1. FC Köln	1. FC Nürnberg	-	
1962/1963	BV Borussia 09 Dortmund	Hamburger SV	-	
1963/1964	1. FC Köln	TSV 1860 München	Uwe Seeler (Hamburger SV)	30
1964/1965	SV Werder Bremen	BV Borussia 09 Dortmund	Rudolf Brunnenmeier (TSV 1860 München)	24
1965/1966	TSV 1860 München	FC Bayern München	Lothar Emmerich (BV Borussia 09 Dortmund)	31
1966/1967	TSV Eintracht Braunschweig	FC Bayern München	Lothar Emmerich (BV Borussia 09 Dortmund) Gerhard Müller (FC Bayern München)	28
1967/1968	1. FC Nürnberg	1. FC Köln 1. FC Köln	Johannes Löhr (1. FC Köln)	27

1968/1969	FC Bayern München	FC Bayern München	Gerhard Müller (FC Bayern München)	30
1969/1970	Borussia VfL Mönchengladbach	Kickers Offenbach FC	Gerhard Müller (FC Bayern München)	38
1970/1971	Borussia VfL Mönchengladbach	FC Bayern München	Lothar Kobluhn (SC Rot-Weiß Oberhausen)	24
1971/1972	FC Bayern München	FC Schalke 04 Gelsenkirchen	Gerhard Müller (FC Bayern München)	40
1972/1973	FC Bayern München	Borussia VfL Mönchengladbach	Gerhard Müller (FC Bayern München)	36
1973/1974	FC Bayern München	Eintracht Frankfurt	Gerhard Müller (FC Bayern München) Josef Heynckes (Borussia VfL Mönchengladbach)	30
1974/1975	Borussia VfL Mönchengladbach	Eintracht Frankfurt	Josef Heynckes (Borussia VfL Mönchengladbach)	27
1975/1976	Borussia VfL Mönchengladbach	Hamburger SV	Klaus Fischer (FC Schalke 04 Gelsenkirchen)	29
1976/1977	Borussia VfL Mönchengladbach	1. FC Köln	Dieter Müller (1. FC Köln)	34
1977/1978	1. FC Köln	1. FC Köln	Dieter Müller (1. FC Köln) Gerhard Müller (FC Bayern München)	24
1978/1979	Hamburger SV	TSV Fortuna Düsseldorf	Klaus Allofs (TSV TSV Fortuna Düsseldorf)	22
1979/1980	FC Bayern München	TSV Fortuna Düsseldorf	Karl-Heinz Rummenigge (FC Bayern München)	26
1980/1981	FC Bayern München	Eintracht Frankfurt	Karl-Heinz Rummenigge (FC Bayern München)	29
1981/1982	Hamburger SV	FC Bayern München	Horst Hrubesch (Hamburger SV)	27
1982/1983	Hamburger SV	1. FC Köln	Rudolf Völler (SV Werder Bremen)	23
1983/1984	VfB Stuttgart	FC Bayern München	Karl-Heinz Rummenigge (FC Bayern München)	26
1984/1985	FC Bayern München	FC Bayer 05 Uerdingen	Klaus Allofs (1. FC Köln)	26
1985/1986	FC Bayern München	FC Bayern München	Stefan Kuntz (VfL Bochum)	22
1986/1987	FC Bayern München	Hamburger SV	Uwe Rahn (Borussia VfL Mönchengladbach)	24
1987/1988	SV Werder Bremen	Eintracht Frankfurt	Jürgen Klinsmann (VfB Stuttgart)	19
1988/1989	FC Bayern München	BV Borussia 09 Dortmund	Thomas Allofs (1. FC Köln) Roland Wohlfarth (FC Bayern München)	17
1989/1990	FC Bayern München	1. FC Kaiserslautern	Jørn Andersen (NOR, Eintracht Frankfurt)	18
1990/1991	1. FC Kaiserslautern	SV Werder Bremen	Roland Wohlfarth (FC Bayern München)	21
1991/1992	VfB Stuttgart	SV Hannover 96	Fritz Walter (VfB Stuttgart)	22
1992/1993	SV Werder Bremen	TSV Bayer 04 Leverkusen	Ulf Kirsten (TSV Bayer 04 Leverkusen) Anthony Yeboah (GHA, Eintracht Frankfurt)	20
1993/1994	FC Bayern München	SV Werder Bremen	Stefan Kuntz (1. FC Kaiserslautern) Anthony Yeboah (GHA, Eintracht Frankfurt)	18
1994/1995	BV Borussia 09 Dortmund	Borussia VfL Mönchengladbach	Mario Basler (SV Werder Bremen) Heiko Herrlich (Borussia VfL Mönchengladbach)	20
1995/1996	BV Borussia 09 Dortmund	1. FC Kaiserslautern	Fredi Bobič (VfB Stuttgart)	17
1996/1997	FC Bayern München	VfB Stuttgart	Ulf Kirsten (TSV Bayer 04 Leverkusen)	22
1997/1998	1. FC Kaiserslautern	FC Bayern München	Ulf Kirsten (TSV Bayer 04 Leverkusen)	22
1998/1999	FC Bayern München	SV Werder Bremen	Michael Preetz (Hertha BSC Berlin)	23
1999/2000	FC Bayern München	FC Bayern München	Martin Max (TSV 1860 München)	19
2000/2001	FC Bayern München	FC Schalke 04 Gelsenkirchen	Sergej Barbarez (BIH, Hamburger SV) Ebbe Sand (DEN, FC Schalke 04 Gelsenkirchen)	22
2001/2002	BV Borussia 09 Dortmund	FC Schalke 04 Gelsenkirchen	Márcio Amoroso dos Santos (BRA, BV Borussia 09 Dortmund) Martin Max (TSV 1860 München)	18
2002/2003	FC Bayern München	FC Bayern München	Thomas Christiansen Tarín (DEN, VfL Bochum) Giovane Élber de Souza (BRA, FC Bayern München)	21
2003/2004	SV Werder Bremen	SV Werder Bremen	Aílton Gonçalves da Silva (BRA, SV Werder Bremen)	28
2004/2005	FC Bayern München	FC Bayern München	Marek Mintál (SVK, 1. FC Nürnberg)	24
2005/2006	FC Bayern München	FC Bayern München	Miroslav Klose (SV Werder Bremen)	25
2006/2007	VfB Stuttgart	1. FC Nürnberg	Theofanis Gekas (GRE, VfL Bochum)	20
2007/2008	FC Bayern München	FC Bayern München	Luca Toni Varchetta (ITA, FC Bayern München)	24
2008/2009	VfL Wolfsburg	SV Werder Bremen	Edinaldo Batista Libânio "Grafite" (BRA, VfL Wolfsburg)	28
2009/2010	FC Bayern München	FC Bayern München	Edin Džeko (BIH, VfL Wolfsburg)	22
2010/2011	BV Borussia 09 Dortmund	FC Schalke 04 Gelsenkirchen	Mario Gómez García (FC Bayern München)	28
2011/2012	BV Borussia 09 Dortmund	BV Borussia 09 Dortmund	Dirk Jan Klaas Huntelaar (NED, FC Schalke 04 Gelsenkirchen)	29
2012/2013	FC Bayern München	FC Bayern München	Stefan Kießling (TSV Bayer 04 Leverkusen)	25
2013/2014	FC Bayern München	FC Bayern München	Robert Lewandowski (POL, BV Borussia 09 Dortmund)	20
2014/2015	FC Bayern München	VfL Wolfsburg	Alexander Meier (Eintracht Frankfurt)	19
2015/2016	FC Bayern München	FC Bayern München	Robert Lewandowski (POL, FC Bayern München)	30
2016/2017	FC Bayern München	BV Borussia 09 Dortmund	Pierre-Emerick Emiliano François Aubameyang (GAB, BV Borussia 09 Dortmund)	31
2017/2018	FC Bayern München	Eintracht Frankfurt	Robert Lewandowski (POL, FC Bayern München)	29
2018/2019	FC Bayern München	FC Bayern München	Robert Lewandowski (POL, FC Bayern München)	22
2019/2020	FC Bayern München	FC Bayern München	Robert Lewandowski (POL, FC Bayern München)	34
2020/2021	FC Bayern München	BV Borussia 09 Dortmund	Robert Lewandowski (POL, FC Bayern München)	41

Please note: the Bundesliga was introduced at the start of the 1963/1964 season.

NATIONAL CHAMPIONSHIP
Bundesliga 2020/2021
(18.09.2020 – 22.05.2021)

Results

Round 1 [18-20.09.2020]
Bayern München - Schalke 04 8-0(3-0)
Eintracht Frank. - Arminia Bielefeld 1-1(0-0)
Union Berlin - FC Augsburg 1-3(0-1)
FC Köln - Hoffenheim 2-3(1-2)
Werder Bremen - Hertha BSC 1-4(0-2)
VfB Stuttgart - SC Freiburg 2-3(0-2)
Borussia D. - Mönchengladbach 3-0(1-0)
RB Leipzig - FSV Mainz 05 3-1(2-0)
VfL Wolfsburg - Bayer Leverkusen 0-0

Round 2 [25-27.09.2020]
Hertha BSC - Eintracht Frankfurt 1-3(0-2)
Mönchengladbach - Union Berlin 1-1(0-0)
Bayer Leverkusen - RB Leipzig 1-1(1-1)
FSV Mainz 05 - VfB Stuttgart 1-4(1-1)
FC Augsburg - Borussia Dortmund 2-0(1-0)
Arminia Bielefeld - FC Köln 1-0(0-0)
Schalke 04 - Werder Bremen 1-3(0-2)
Hoffenheim - Bayern München 4-1(2-1)
SC Freiburg - VfL Wolfsburg 1-1(1-1)

Round 3 [02-04.10.2020]
Union Berlin - FSV Mainz 05 4-0(1-0)
Borussia Dortmund - SC Freiburg 4-0(1-0)
Eintracht Frankfurt - Hoffenheim 2-1(0-1)
FC Köln - Mönchengladbach 1-3(0-2)
Werder Bremen - Arminia Bielefeld 1-0(1-0)
VfB Stuttgart - Bayer Leverkusen 1-1(0-1)
RB Leipzig - Schalke 04 4-0(3-0)
VfL Wolfsburg - FC Augsburg 0-0
Bayern München - Hertha BSC 4-3(1-0)

Round 4 [17-18.10.2020]
Hoffenheim - Borussia Dortmund 0-1(0-0)
SC Freiburg - Werder Bremen 1-1(1-1)
Hertha BSC - VfB Stuttgart 0-2(0-1)
FSV Mainz 05 - Bayer Leverkusen 0-1(0-1)
FC Augsburg - RB Leipzig 0-2(0-1)
Arminia Bielefeld - Bayern München 1-4(0-3)
Mönchengladbach - VfL Wolfsburg 1-1(0-0)
FC Köln - Eintracht Frankfurt 1-1(0-1)
Schalke 04 - Union Berlin 1-1(0-0)

Round 5 [23-26.10.2020]
VfB Stuttgart - FC Köln 1-1(1-1)
Bayern München - Eintracht Fr. 5-0(2-0)
RB Leipzig - Hertha BSC 2-1(1-1)
Union Berlin - SC Freiburg 1-1(1-1)
FSV Mainz 05 - Mönchengladbach 2-3(2-1)
Borussia Dortmund - Schalke 04 3-0(0-0)
VfL Wolfsburg - Arminia Bielefeld 2-1(2-0)
Werder Bremen - Hoffenheim 1-1(1-1)
Bayer Leverkusen - FC Augsburg 3-1(1-0)

Round 6 [30.10.-02.11.2020]
Schalke 04 - VfB Stuttgart 1-1(1-0)
Eintracht Frankfurt - Werder Bremen 1-1(0-0)
FC Köln - Bayern München 1-2(0-2)
FC Augsburg - FSV Mainz 05 3-1(1-0)
Arminia Bielefeld - Borussia Dort. 0-2(0-0)
Mönchengladbach - RB Leipzig 1-0(0-0)
SC Freiburg - Bayer Leverkusen 2-4(1-2)
Hertha BSC - VfL Wolfsburg 1-1(1-1)
Hoffenheim - Union Berlin 1-3(0-0)

Round 7 [06-08.11.2020]
Werder Bremen - FC Köln 1-1(0-0)
RB Leipzig - SC Freiburg 3-0(1-0)
Union Berlin - Arminia Bielefeld 5-0(3-0)
FSV Mainz 05 - Schalke 04 2-2(2-1)
FC Augsburg - Hertha BSC 0-3(0-1)
VfB Stuttgart - Eintracht Frankfurt 2-2(2-0)
Borussia Dortm. - Bayern München 2-3(1-1)
VfL Wolfsburg - Hoffenheim 2-1(2-0)
Bayer Leverkus. - Mönchengladbach 4-3(2-2)

Round 8 [21-22.11.2020]
Bayern München - Werder Bremen 1-1(0-1)
Mönchengladbach - FC Augsburg 1-1(1-0)
Hoffenheim - VfB Stuttgart 3-3(1-2)
Schalke 04 - VfL Wolfsburg 0-2(0-2)
Arminia Bielefeld - Bayer Leverk. 1-2(0-1)
Eintracht Frankfurt - RB Leipzig 1-2(1-0)
Hertha BSC - Borussia Dortmund 2-5(1-0)
SC Freiburg - FSV Mainz 05 1-3(0-3)
FC Köln - Union Berlin 1-2(1-1)

Round 9 [27-29.11.2020]
VfL Wolfsburg - Werder Bremen 5-3(3-2)
Borussia Dortmund - FC Köln 1-2(0-1)
RB Leipzig - Arminia Bielefeld 2-1(1-0)
Union Berlin - Eintracht Frankfurt 3-3(2-2)
FC Augsburg - SC Freiburg 1-1(0-0)
VfB Stuttgart - Bayern München 1-3(1-2)
Mönchengladbach - Schalke 04 4-1(2-1)
Bayer Leverkusen - Hertha BSC 0-0
FSV Mainz 05 - Hoffenheim 1-1(1-0)

Round 10 [04-07.12.2020]
Hertha BSC - Union Berlin 3-1(0-1)
SC Freiburg - Mönchengladbach 2-2(1-1)
Eintracht Frank. - Borussia Dortmund 1-1(1-0)
FC Köln - VfL Wolfsburg 2-2(2-1)
Arminia Bielefeld - FSV Mainz 05 2-1(2-0)
Bayern München - RB Leipzig 3-3(2-2)
Werder Bremen - VfB Stuttgart 1-2(0-1)
Schalke 04 - Bayer Leverkusen 0-3(0-1)
Hoffenheim - FC Augsburg 3-1(1-1)

Round 11 [11-13.12.2020]
VfL Wolfsburg - Eintracht Frankfurt 2-1(0-0)
Borussia Dortmund - VfB Stuttgart 1-5(1-1)
RB Leipzig - Werder Bremen 2-0(2-0)
Mönchengladbach - Hertha BSC 1-0(0-0)
SC Freiburg - Arminia Bielefeld 2-0(0-0)
FSV Mainz 05 - FC Köln 0-1(0-0)
Union Berlin - Bayern München 1-1(1-0)
FC Augsburg - Schalke 04 2-2(1-0)
Bayer Leverkusen - Hoffenheim 4-1(2-0)

Round 12 [15-16.12.2020]
Eintracht Frankf. - Mönchengladbach 3-3(3-1)
Hertha BSC - FSV Mainz 05 0-0
Werder Bremen - Borussia Dortmund 1-2(1-1)
VfB Stuttgart - Union Berlin 2-2(0-1)
Schalke 04 - SC Freiburg 0-2(0-0)
Bayern München - VfL Wolfsburg 2-1(1-1)
Hoffenheim - RB Leipzig 0-1(0-0)
FC Köln - Bayer Leverkusen 0-4(0-2)
Arminia Bielefeld - FC Augsburg 0-1(0-0)

Round 13 [18-20.12.2020]
Union Berlin - Borussia Dortmund 2-1(0-0)
RB Leipzig - FC Köln 0-0
Mönchengladbach - Hoffenheim 1-2(1-0)
Schalke 04 - Arminia Bielefeld 0-1(0-0)
FSV Mainz 05 - Werder Bremen 0-1(0-0)
FC Augsburg - Eintracht Frankfurt 0-2(0-0)
Bayer Leverkusen - Bayern München 1-2(1-1)
SC Freiburg - Hertha BSC 4-1(1-0)
VfL Wolfsburg - VfB Stuttgart 1-0(0-0)

Round 14 [02-03.01.2021]
Hoffenheim - SC Freiburg 1-3(0-3)
Eintracht Frankf. - Bayer Leverkusen 2-1(1-1)
FC Köln - FC Augsburg 0-1(0-0)
Werder Bremen - Union Berlin 0-2(0-2)
Arminia Bielef. - Mönchengladbach 0-1(0-0)
Hertha BSC - Schalke 04 3-0(1-0)
VfB Stuttgart - RB Leipzig 0-1(0-0)
Borussia Dortmund - VfL Wolfsburg 2-0(0-0)
Bayern München - FSV Mainz 05 5-2(0-2)

Round 15 [08-10.01.2021]
Mönchengladbach - Bayern München 3-2(2-2)
Bayer Leverkusen - Werder Bremen 1-1(0-0)
SC Freiburg - FC Köln 5-0(2-0)
Union Berlin - VfL Wolfsburg 2-2(1-1)
Schalke 04 - Hoffenheim 4-0(1-0)
FSV Mainz 05 - Eintracht Frankfurt 0-2(0-1)
RB Leipzig - Borussia Dortmund 1-3(0-0)
FC Augsburg - VfB Stuttgart 1-4(0-2)
Arminia Bielefeld - Hertha BSC 1-0(0-0)

Round 16 [15-17.01.2021]
Union Berlin - Bayer Leverkusen 1-0(0-0)
Borussia Dortmund - FSV Mainz 05 1-1(0-0)
Hoffenheim - Arminia Bielefeld 0-0
VfL Wolfsburg - RB Leipzig 2-2(2-1)
FC Köln - Hertha BSC 0-0
Werder Bremen - FC Augsburg 2-0(0-0)
VfB Stuttgart - Mönchengladbach 2-2(0-1)
Bayern München - SC Freiburg 2-1(1-0)
Eintracht Frankfurt - Schalke 04 3-1(1-1)

Round 17 [19-20.01.2021]
Mönchengladbach - Werder Bremen 1-0(0-0)
Bayer Leverk. - Borussia Dortmund 2-1(1-0)
Hertha BSC - Hoffenheim 0-3(0-1)
FSV Mainz 05 - VfL Wolfsburg 0-2(0-0)
Schalke 04 - FC Köln 1-2(0-1)
RB Leipzig - Union Berlin 1-0(0-0)
SC Freiburg - Eintracht Frankfurt 2-2(1-1)
FC Augsburg - Bayern München 0-1(0-1)
Arminia Bielefeld - VfB Stuttgart 3-0(1-0)

Round 18 [22-24.01.2021]
Mönchengladbach - Borussia Dortm. 4-2(2-2)
FSV Mainz 05 - RB Leipzig 3-2(2-2)
Bayer Leverkusen - VfL Wolfsburg 0-1(0-1)
Arminia Bielefeld - Eintracht Frankf. 1-5(1-3)
FC Augsburg - Union Berlin 2-1(1-1)
SC Freiburg - VfB Stuttgart 2-1(2-1)
Hertha BSC - Werder Bremen 1-4(1-2)
Schalke 04 - Bayern München 0-4(0-1)
Hoffenheim - FC Köln 3-0(2-0)

Round 19 [29-31.01.2021]
VfB Stuttgart - FSV Mainz 05 2-0(0-0)
Union Berlin - Mönchengladbach 1-1(1-0)
Bayern München - Hoffenheim 4-1(2-1)
Eintracht Frankfurt - Hertha BSC 3-1(0-0)
Werder Bremen - Schalke 04 1-1(0-1)
Borussia Dortmund - FC Augsburg 3-1(1-1)
RB Leipzig - Bayer Leverkusen 1-0(0-0)
FC Köln - Arminia Bielefeld 3-1(2-0)
VfL Wolfsburg - SC Freiburg 3-0(2-0)

Round 20 [05-07.02.2021]
Hertha BSC - Bayern München 0-1(0-1)
SC Freiburg - Borussia Dortmund 2-1(0-0)
Schalke 04 - RB Leipzig 0-3(0-1)
FC Augsburg - VfL Wolfsburg 0-2(0-1)
FSV Mainz 05 - Union Berlin 1-0(1-0)
Bayer Leverkusen - VfB Stuttgart 5-2(2-0)
Mönchengladbach - FC Köln 1-2(1-1)
Hoffenheim - Eintracht Frankfurt 1-3(0-1)
Arminia Biel. - Werder Br. 0-2(0-0) [10.03.]

Round 21 [12-15.02.2021]
RB Leipzig - FC Augsburg 2-1(2-0)
Borussia Dortmund - Hoffenheim 2-2(1-1)
Werder Bremen - SC Freiburg 0-0
VfB Stuttgart - Hertha BSC 1-1(1-0)
Bayer Leverkusen - FSV Mainz 05 2-2(1-0)
Union Berlin - Schalke 04 0-0
Eintracht Frankfurt - FC Köln 2-0(0-0)
VfL Wolfsburg - Mönchengladbach 0-0
Bayern München - Arminia Bielefeld 3-3(0-2)

Round 22 [19-21.02.2021]
Arminia Bielefeld - VfL Wolfsburg 0-3(0-1)
Eintracht Frankf. - Bayern München 2-1(2-0)
SC Freiburg - Union Berlin 0-1(0-0)
Mönchengladbach - FSV Mainz 05 1-2(1-1)
FC Köln - VfB Stuttgart 0-1(0-0)
Schalke 04 - Borussia Dortmund 0-4(0-2)
FC Augsburg - Bayer Leverkusen 1-1(1-0)
Hertha BSC - RB Leipzig 0-3(0-1)
Hoffenheim - Werder Bremen 4-0(2-0)

Round 23 [26-28.02.2021]
Werder Bremen - Eintracht Frankfurt 2-1(0-1)
VfL Wolfsburg - Hertha BSC 2-0(1-0)
VfB Stuttgart - Schalke 04 5-1(3-1)
Bayern München - FC Köln 5-1(2-0)
Borussia Dortm. - Arminia Bielefeld 3-0(0-0)
RB Leipzig - Mönchengladbach 3-2(0-2)
Union Berlin - Hoffenheim 1-1(1-1)
FSV Mainz 05 - FC Augsburg 0-1(0-1)
Bayer Leverkusen - SC Freiburg 1-2(0-0)

Round 24 [05-07.03.2021]
Schalke 04 - FSV Mainz 05 0-0
SC Freiburg - RB Leipzig 0-3(0-1)
Mönchengladbach - Bayer Leverk. 0-1(0-0)
Hoffenheim - VfL Wolfsburg 2-1(2-1)
Hertha BSC - FC Augsburg 2-1(0-1)
Eintracht Frankfurt - VfB Stuttgart 1-1(0-0)
Bayern München - Borussia Dortm. 4-2(2-2)
FC Köln - Werder Bremen 1-1(0-0)
Arminia Bielefeld - Union Berlin 0-0

Round 25 [12-14.03.2021]
FC Augsburg - Mönchengladbach 3-1(0-0)
Werder Bremen - Bayern München 1-3(0-2)
FSV Mainz 05 - SC Freiburg 1-0(0-0)
VfL Wolfsburg - Schalke 04 5-0(1-0)
Union Berlin - FC Köln 2-1(0-1)
Borussia Dortmund - Hertha BSC 2-0(0-0)
Bayer Leverk. - Arminia Bielefeld 1-2(0-1)
RB Leipzig - Eintracht Frankfurt 1-1(0-0)
VfB Stuttgart - Hoffenheim 2-0(1-0)

Round 26 [19-21.03.2021]
Arminia Bielefeld - RB Leipzig 0-1(0-0)
FC Köln - Borussia Dortmund 2-2(1-1)
Werder Bremen - VfL Wolfsburg 1-2(1-2)
Eintracht Frankfurt - Union Berlin 5-2(4-2)
Bayern München - VfB Stuttgart 4-0(4-0)
Schalke 04 - Mönchengladbach 0-3(0-1)
Hoffenheim - FSV Mainz 05 1-2(1-2)
Hertha BSC - Bayer Leverkusen 3-0(3-0)
SC Freiburg - FC Augsburg 2-0(0-0)

Round 27 [03-04.04.2021]
FC Augsburg - Hoffenheim 2-1(2-0)
Borussia Dortm. - Eintracht Frankf. 1-2(1-1)
Bayer Leverkusen - Schalke 04 2-1(1-0)
VfL Wolfsburg - FC Köln 1-0(0-0)
FSV Mainz 05 - Arminia Bielefeld 1-1(0-0)
RB Leipzig - Bayern München 0-1(0-1)
Mönchengladbach - SC Freiburg 2-1(0-1)
VfB Stuttgart - Werder Bremen 1-0(0-0)
Union Berlin - Hertha BSC 1-1(1-1)

Round 28 [09-12.04.2021]
Arminia Bielefeld - SC Freiburg 1-0(0-0)
Werder Bremen - RB Leipzig 1-4(0-3)
Hertha BSC - Mönchengladbach 2-2(1-2)
Eintracht Frankfurt - VfL Wolfsburg 4-3(2-1)
Bayern München - Union Berlin 1-1(0-0)
VfB Stuttgart - Borussia Dortmund 2-3(1-0)
Schalke 04 - FC Augsburg 1-0(1-0)
FC Köln - FSV Mainz 05 2-3(1-1)
Hoffenheim - Bayer Leverkusen 0-0

Round 29 [16-18.04.2021]
RB Leipzig - Hoffenheim 0-0
VfL Wolfsburg - Bayern München 2-3(1-3)
Mönchengladbach - Eintracht Frankf. 4-0(1-0)
SC Freiburg - Schalke 04 4-0(2-0)
FC Augsburg - Arminia Bielefeld 0-0
Union Berlin - VfB Stuttgart 2-1(2-0)
Bayer Leverkusen - FC Köln 3-0(1-0)
Borussia Dortmund - Werder Bremen 4-1(3-1)
FSV Mainz 05 - Hertha BSC 1-1(1-1) [03.05.]

Round 30 [20-21.04.2021]
FC Köln - RB Leipzig 2-1(0-0)
Bayern München - Bayer Leverkusen 2-0(2-0)
Arminia Bielefeld - Schalke 04 1-0(0-0)
Eintracht Frankfurt - FC Augsburg 2-0(1-0)
Hoffenheim - Mönchengladbach 3-2(0-2)
VfB Stuttgart - VfL Wolfsburg 1-3(0-2)
Borussia Dortmund - Union Berlin 2-0(1-0)
Werder Bremen - FSV Mainz 05 0-1(0-1)
Hertha BSC - SC Freiburg 3-0(2-0) [06.05.]

Round 31 [23-25.04.2021]
FC Augsburg - FC Köln 2-3(0-3)
FSV Mainz 05 - Bayern München 2-1(2-0)
VfL Wolfsburg - Borussia Dortmund 0-2(0-1)
SC Freiburg - Hoffenheim 1-1(0-1)
Union Berlin - Werder Bremen 3-1(0-0)
Bayer Leverkusen - Eintracht Frankf. 3-1(0-0)
RB Leipzig - VfB Stuttgart 2-0(0-0)
Mönchengladbach - Arminia Bielef. 5-0(3-0)
Schalke 04 - Hertha BSC 1-2(1-1) [12.05.]

Round 32 [07-09.05.2021]
VfB Stuttgart - FC Augsburg 2-1(1-0)
Borussia Dortmund - RB Leipzig 3-2(1-0)
Werder Bremen - Bayer Leverkusen 0-0
VfL Wolfsburg - Union Berlin 3-0(1-0)
Hoffenheim - Schalke 04 4-2(0-2)
Bayern München - Mönchengladbach 6-0(4-0)
FC Köln - SC Freiburg 1-4(0-2)
Eintracht Frankfurt - FSV Mainz 05 1-1(0-1)
Hertha BSC - Arminia Bielefeld 0-0

Round 33 [15-16.05.2021]
SC Freiburg - Bayern München 2-2(1-1)
Arminia Bielefeld - Hoffenheim 1-1(1-1)
Schalke 04 - Eintracht Frankfurt 4-3(1-1)
Bayer Leverkusen - Union Berlin 1-1(1-0)
Hertha BSC - FC Köln 0-0
FC Augsburg - Werder Bremen 2-0(0-0)
Mönchengladbach - VfB Stuttgart 1-2(1-0)
FSV Mainz 05 - Borussia Dortmund 1-3(0-2)
RB Leipzig - VfL Wolfsburg 2-2(0-2)

Round 34 [22.05.2021]
Union Berlin - RB Leipzig 2-1(0-0)
Werder Bremen - Mönchengladbach 2-4(0-1)
Borussia Dortmund - Bayer Leverk. 3-1(1-0)
Eintracht Frankfurt - SC Freiburg 3-1(0-0)
Hoffenheim - Hertha BSC 2-1(0-1)
FC Köln - Schalke 04 1-0(0-0)
VfL Wolfsburg - FSV Mainz 05 2-3(0-1)
Bayern München - FC Augsburg 5-2(4-0)
VfB Stuttgart - Arminia Bielefeld 0-2(0-0)

		Total							Home						Away				
1. **FC Bayern München**	34	24	6	4	99	-	44	78	13	4	0	64	-	21	11	2	4	35	-	23
2. RasenBallsport Leipzig	34	19	8	7	60	-	32	65	11	4	2	29	-	13	8	4	5	31	-	19
3. BV Borussia 09 Dortmund	34	20	4	10	75	-	46	64	11	2	4	40	-	20	9	2	6	35	-	26
4. VfL Wolfsburg	34	17	10	7	61	-	37	61	10	4	3	32	-	16	7	6	4	29	-	21
5. Eintracht Frankfurt	34	16	12	6	69	-	53	60	10	7	0	37	-	20	6	5	6	32	-	33
6. TSV Bayer 04 Leverkusen	34	14	10	10	53	-	39	52	8	5	4	34	-	22	6	5	6	19	-	17
7. 1. FC Union Berlin	34	12	14	8	50	-	43	50	8	8	1	32	-	18	4	6	7	18	-	25
8. Borussia VfL Mönchengladbach	34	13	10	11	64	-	56	49	8	4	5	32	-	19	5	6	6	32	-	37
9. VfB Stuttgart	34	12	9	13	56	-	55	45	5	6	6	27	-	26	7	3	7	29	-	29
10. SC Freiburg	34	12	9	13	52	-	52	45	7	6	4	33	-	23	5	3	9	19	-	29
11. TSG 1899 Hoffenheim	34	11	10	13	52	-	54	43	8	3	6	32	-	24	3	7	7	20	-	30
12. 1. FSV Mainz 05	34	10	9	15	39	-	56	39	4	4	9	16	-	26	6	5	6	23	-	30
13. FC Augsburg	34	10	6	18	36	-	54	36	6	4	7	21	-	25	4	2	11	15	-	29
14. Hertha BSC Berlin	34	8	11	15	41	-	52	35	5	5	7	21	-	26	3	6	8	20	-	26
15. DSC Arminia Bielefeld	34	9	8	17	26	-	52	35	6	2	9	13	-	23	3	6	8	13	-	29
16. 1. FC Köln (*Relegation Play-offs*)	34	8	9	17	34	-	60	33	3	5	9	20	-	31	5	4	8	14	-	29
17. SV Werder Bremen (*Relegated*)	34	7	10	17	36	-	57	31	3	5	9	16	-	28	4	5	8	20	-	29
18. FC Schalke 04 Gelsenkirchen (*Relegated*)	34	3	7	24	25	-	86	16	3	3	11	14	-	34	0	4	13	11	-	52

Top goalscorers:	
41 **Robert Lewandowski (POL)**	**FC Bayern München**
28 André Miguel Valente da Silva (POR)	*Eintracht Frankfurt*
27 Erling Braut Håland (NOR)	*BV Borussia 09 Dortmund*
20 Andrej Kramarić (CRO)	*TSG 1899 Hoffenheim*
20 Wout Weghorst (NED)	*VfL Wolfsburg*
16 Saša Kalajdžić (AUT)	*VfB Stuttgart*

Relegation Play-offs (26-29.05.2021)

1. FC Köln - SV Holstein Kiel	0-1(0-0)	5-1(4-1)

1. FC Köln remains at first level for 2021/2022.

NATIONAL CUP
DFB Pokal 2020/2021

First Round [11-14.09./15.10./03.11.2020]

TSV Havelse - 1. FSV Mainz 05	1-5(1-0)		1. FC Rielasingen-Arlen - SV Holstein Kiel	1-7(1-5)
TSV Eintracht Braunschweig - Hertha BSC Berlin	5-4(3-2)		FC Hansa Rostock - VfB Stuttgart	0-1(0-1)
1. FC Nürnberg - RasenBallsport Leipzig	0-3(0-1)		TSV Steinbach Haiger - SV Sandhausen	1-2(1-2)
SV Todesfelde - VfL Osnabrück	0-1(0-0)		SpVgg 07 Elversberg - FC St. Pauli Hamburg	4-2(2-1)
TSV 1860 München - Eintracht Frankfurt	1-2(0-0)		FC Eintracht Norderstedt 03 - Bayer 04 Leverkusen	0-7(0-6)
MTV Eintracht Celle - FC Augsburg	0-7(0-2)		1. FC Kaiserslautern - SSV Jahn Regensburg	1-1 aet; 3-4 pen
FV Engers 07 - VfL Bochum	0-3(0-1)		SC Wiedenbrück - SC Paderborn 07	0-5(0-3)
Union Fürstenwalde - VfL Wolfsburg	1-4(1-2)		SV Wehen Wiesbaden - 1. FC Heidenheim 1846	1-0(0-0)
FC Oberneuland - Borussia VfL Mönchengladbach	0-8(0-5)		SV Waldhof Mannheim - SC Freiburg	1-2(0-1)
RSV Meinerzhagen - SpVgg Greuther Fürth	1-6(0-0,1-1)		1. FC Magdeburg - SV Darmstadt 98	2-3(2-0,2-2)
VSG Altglienicke - 1. FC Köln	0-6(0-3)		SG Dynamo Dresden - Hamburger SV	4-1(2-0)
SSV Ulm 1846 - FC Erzgebirge Aue	2-0(1-0)		Würzburger Kickers - Hannover 96	2-3(0-1)
FC Ingolstadt 04 - TSV Fortuna Düsseldorf	0-1(0-0)		Rot-Weiss Essen - DSC Arminia Bielefeld	1-0(1-0)
Karlsruher SC - 1. FC Union Berlin	0-1(0-0,0-0)		MSV Duisburg - BV Borussia 09 Dortmund	0-5(0-3)
FC Carl Zeiss Jena - SV Werder Bremen	0-2(0-0)		1. FC Düren - FC Bayern München	0-3(0-2)
Chemnitzer FC - TSG 1899 Hoffenheim	2-2 aet; 2-3 pen		1. FC Schweinfurt 05 - FC Schalke 04 Gelsenkirchen	1-4(1-2)

Second Round [22-23.12.2020/12-13.01.2021]

SSV Ulm 1846 - FC Schalke 04 Gelsenkirchen	1-3(0-1)		Rot-Weiss Essen - TSV Fortuna Düsseldorf	3-2(2-1)
1. FC Köln - VfL Osnabrück	1-0(1-0)		VfL Wolfsburg - SV Sandhausen	4-0(3-0)
FC Augsburg - RasenBallsport Leipzig	0-3(0-1)		SV Wehen Wiesbaden - SSV Jahn Regensburg	0-0 aet; 2-4 pen
TSG 1899 Hoffenheim - SpVgg Greuther Fürth	2-2 aet; 6-7 pen		VfB Stuttgart - SC Freiburg	1-0(1-0)
Eintracht Braunschweig - BV Borussia 09 Dortmund	0-2(0-1)		Hannover 96 - SV Werder Bremen	0-3(0-2)
SpVgg 07 Elversberg - Borussia Mönchengladbach	0-5(0-3)		1. FSV Mainz 05 - VfL Bochum	2-2 aet; 0-3 pen
SG Dynamo Dresden - SV Darmstadt 98	0-3(0-1)		Bayer 04 Leverkusen - Eintracht Frankfurt	4-1(1-1)
1. FC Union Berlin - SC Paderborn 07	2-3(1-3)		SV Holstein Kiel - FC Bayern München	2-2 aet; 6-5 pen

Third Round [02-03.02.2021]

Rot-Weiss Essen - Bayer 04 Leverkusen	2-1(0-0,0-0)		VfL Wolfsburg - FC Schalke 04 Gelsenkirchen	1-0(1-0)
SV Holstein Kiel - SV Darmstadt 98	2-2 aet; 7-6 pen		RasenBallsport Leipzig - VfL Bochum	4-0(2-0)
SV Werder Bremen - SpVgg Greuther Fürth	2-0(1-0)		SSV Jahn Regensburg - 1. FC Köln	2-2 aet; 4-3 pen
BV Borussia 09 Dortmund - SC Paderborn 07	3-2(2-0,2-2)		VfB Stuttgart - Borussia VfL Mönchengladbach	1-2(1-1)

Quarter-Finals [02-03.03./07.04.2021]				
Borussia Mönchengladbach - BV Borussia Dortmund	0-1(0-0)		RasenBallsport Leipzig - VfL Wolfsburg	2-0(0-0)
Rot-Weiss Essen - SV Holstein Kiel	0-3(0-2)		SSV Jahn Regensburg - SV Werder Bremen	0-1(0-0)

Semi-Finals [30.04.-01.05.2021]				
SV Werder Bremen - RasenBallsport Leipzig	1-2(0-0,0-0)		BV Borussia 09 Dortmund - SV Holstein Kiel	5-0(5-0)

Final

13.05.2021; Olympiastadion, Berlin; Referee: Dr. Felix Brych; Attendance: 0
RasenBallsport Leipzig - BV Borussia 09 Dortmund   1-4(0-3)

RB Leipzig: Péter Gulácsi, Lukas Manuel Klostermann, Dayotchanculle Upamecano, Marcel Halstenberg, Kevin Kampl (62.Emil Forsberg), Nordi Mukiele Mulere (62.Konrad Laimer), Daniel Olmo Carvajal „Dani Olmo", Marcel Sabitzer (Cap), Amadou Haïdara (70.Benjamin Paa Kwesi Henrichs), Alexander Sørloth (46.Christopher Nkunku), Hwang Hee-chan (46.Yussuf Yurary Poulsen). Trainer: Julian Nagelsmann.

Borussia Dortmund: Roman Bürki, Łukasz Piszczek, Manuel Akanji, Mats Julian Hummels, Raphaël Adelino José Guerreiro, Emre Can, Jude Victor William Bellingham (46.Thorgan Hazard), Mahmoud Dahoud (74.Thomas Joseph Delaney), Jadon Malik Sancho (89.Thomas Meunier), Erling Braut Håland (90+2.Julian Brandt), Marco Reus (Cap) (90+2.Giovanni Alejandro Reyna). Trainer: Edin Terzić.

Goals: 0-1 Jadon Malik Sancho (5), 0-2 Erling Braut Håland (28), 0-3 Jadon Malik Sancho (45+1), 1-3 Daniel Olmo Carvajal „Dani Olmo" (71), 1-4 Erling Braut Håland (87).

THE CLUBS 2020/2021

Deutscher Sport-Club Arminia Bielefeld

Founded:	03.05.1905	
Stadium:	Schüco-Arena, Bielefeld (27,300)	
Trainer:	Uwe Neuhaus	26.11.1959
[02.03.2021]	Frank Kramer	03.05.1972

Goalkeepers:	DOB	M	(s)	G		DOB	M	(s)	G
Stefan Ortega Moreno	06.11.1992	34			Arne Maier	08.01.1999	13	(3)	
Defenders:	**DOB**	**M**	**(s)**	**G**	Masaya Okugawa (JPN)	14.04.1996	11	(2)	1
Brian Behrendt	24.10.1991		(3)		Manuel Prietl (AUT)	03.08.1991	28		1
Cédric Brunner (SUI)	17.02.1994	30	(1)		Nils Seufert	03.02.1997	2	(11)	
Nathan De Medina (BEL)	08.10.1997	7	(9)		Michel Vlap (NED)	02.06.1997	5	(2)	1
Jacob Barrett Laursen (DEN)	17.11.1994	13	(3)		Reinhold Yabo	10.02.1992	8	(5)	1
Anderson-Lenda Lucoqui (ANG)	06.07.1997	18	(3)		**Forwards:**	**DOB**	**M**	**(s)**	**G**
Joakim Nilsson (SWE)	06.02.1994	24	(1)		Sergio Duvan Cordóva Lezama (VEN)	09.08.1997	13	(10)	2
Amos Pieper	17.01.1998	30		1	Ritsu Doan (JPN)	16.06.1998	33	(1)	5
Mike van der Hoorn (NED)	15.10.1992	15	(7)		Christian Gebauer (AUT)	20.12.1993	5	(18)	1
Midfielders:	**DOB**	**M**	**(s)**	**G**	Fabian Klos	02.12.1987	32	(2)	5
Jóan Símun Edmundsson (FRO)	26.07.1991		(5)	1	Sebastian Müller	23.01.2001		(2)	
Marcel Hartel	19.01.1996	20	(2)		Sven Schipplock	08.11.1988	5	(27)	1
Fabian Kunze	14.06.1998	12	(14)		Cebio Soukou (BEN)	02.10.1992	5	(9)	1
					Andreas Voglsammer	09.01.1992	11	(7)	2

Fußball-Club Augsburg 1907

Founded:	08.08.1907	
Stadium:	WWK Arena, Augsburg (30,660)	
Trainer:	Heiko Herrlich	03.12.1971
[26.04.2021]	Markus Weinzierl	28.12.1974

Goalkeepers:	DOB	M	(s)	G		DOB	M	(s)	G
Rafał Gikiewicz (POL)	26.10.1987	34			Carlos Armando Gruezo Arboleda (ECU)	19.04.1995	23	(5)	
Defenders:	**DOB**	**M**	**(s)**	**G**	Fredrik Jensen (FIN)	09.09.1997	1	(12)	
Raphael Framberger	06.09.1995	19	(2)		Rani Khedira	27.01.1994	23	(4)	1
Jeffrey Gouweleeuw (NED)	10.07.1991	32		1	Jan Morávek (CZE)	01.11.1989	3	(2)	
Robert Gumny (POL)	04.06.1998	14	(10)	1	Lukas Petkov	01.11.2000		(1)	
Iago Amaral Borduchi (BRA)	23.03.1997	18		1	Tobias Strobl	12.05.1990	21	(8)	
Reece Joel Oxford (ENG)	16.12.1998	13	(11)		**Forwards:**	**DOB**	**M**	**(s)**	**G**
Mads Giersing Valentin Pedersen (DEN)	01.09.1996	9	(6)		Alfreð Finnbogason (ISL)	01.02.1989	4	(13)	
Marek Suchý (CZE)	29.03.1988	3	(2)		Michael Gregoritsch (AUT)	18.04.1994	9	(15)	1
Ohis Felix Uduokhai	09.09.1997	29		1	André Hahn	13.08.1990	24	(5)	8
Midfielders:	**DOB**	**M**	**(s)**	**G**	Florian Niederlechner	24.10.1990	21	(7)	5
László Bénes (SVK)	09.09.1997	9	(3)	1	Marco Richter	24.11.1997	16	(13)	3
Daniel Caligiuri	15.01.1988	31	(2)	6	Noah Joel Sarenren Bazee (NGA)	21.08.1996		(5)	
Tim Civeja	04.01.2002		(3)		Rubén Estephan Vargas Martínez (SUI)	05.08.1998	18	(12)	6

Bayer 04 Leverkusen Fußball GmbH

Founded: 01.07.1904
Stadium: BayArena, Leverkusen (30,210)
Trainer: Peter Sylvester Bosz (NED) 21.11.1963
[23.03.2021] Hannes Wolf 15.03.1981

Goalkeepers:	DOB	M	(s)	G
Lennart Grill	25.01.1999	4		
Lukáš Hrádecký (FIN)	24.11.1989	29		
Niklas Lomb	28.07.1993	1	(1)	
Defenders:	**DOB**	**M**	**(s)**	**G**
Santiago Arias Naranjo (COL)	13.01.1992			
Lars Bender	27.04.1989	12	(2)	1
Sven Bender	27.04.1989	14	(4)	
Aleksandar Dragović (AUT)	06.03.1991	11	(7)	1
Timothy Fosu-Mensah (NED)	02.01.1998	5	(1)	
Jeremie Frimpong (NED)	10.12.2000	4	(6)	
Tin Jedvaj (CRO)	28.11.1995	2	(1)	
Daley Sinkgraven (NED)	04.07.1995	19	(3)	
Jonathan Glao Tah	11.02.1996	24	(3)	1
Edmond Tapsoba (BFA)	02.02.1999	29	(2)	1
Mitchell Weiser	21.04.1994	2	(3)	1
Wendell Nascimento Borges (BRA)	20.07.1993	15	(7)	

Midfielders:	DOB	M	(s)	G
Nadiem Amiri	27.10.1996	20	(9)	2
Charles Mariano Aránguiz Sandoval (CHI)	17.04.1989	20	(1)	
Julian Baumgartlinger (AUT)	02.01.1988	12	(5)	2
Kerem Demirbay	03.07.1993	20	(9)	4
Exequiel Alejandro Palacios (ARG)	05.10.1998	7	(2)	
Florian Richard Wirtz	03.05.2003	25	(4)	5
Forwards:	**DOB**	**M**	**(s)**	**G**
Lucas Nicolás Alario (ARG)	08.10.1992	12	(13)	11
Leon Bailey Butler (JAM)	09.08.1997	25	(5)	9
Karim Bellarabi	08.04.1990	7	(15)	
Moussa Diaby (FRA)	07.07.1999	28	(4)	4
Emrehan Gedikli	25.04.2003		(1)	
Demarai Gray (ENG)	28.06.1996	5	(5)	1
Paulo Henrique Sampaio Filho „Paulinho" (BRA)	15.07.2000	1		
Joel Pohjanpalo (FIN)	13.09.1994		(1)	
Patrik Schick (CZE)	24.01.1996	20	(9)	9

Fußball-Club Bayern München

Founded: 27.02.1900
Stadium: Allianz Arena, München (75,000)
Trainer: Hans-Dieter Flick 24.02.1965

Goalkeepers:	DOB	M	(s)	G
Manuel Peter Neuer	27.03.1986	33		
Alexander Nübel	30.09.1996	1		
Defenders:	**DOB**	**M**	**(s)**	**G**
David Olatukunbo Alaba (AUT)	24.06.1992	30	(2)	2
Jérôme Agyenim Boateng	03.09.1988	29		1
Alphonso Boyle Davies (CAN)	02.11.2000	22	(1)	1
Lucas François Bernard Hernández (FRA)	14.02.1996	18	(5)	
Tanguy Nianzou Kouassi (FRA)	07.06.2002		(6)	
Benjamin Jacques Marcel Pavard (FRA)	28.03.1996	22	(2)	
Christopher Jeffrey Richards (USA)	28.03.2000	1	(2)	
Bouna Sarr (FRA)	31.01.1992	5	(3)	
Josip Stanišić	02.04.2000	1		
Niklas Süle	03.09.1995	16	(4)	1
Midfielders:	**DOB**	**M**	**(s)**	**G**
Mickaël Cuisance (FRA)	16.08.1999		(1)	
Leon Christoph Goretzka	06.02.1995	18	(6)	5
Javier Martínez Aginaga „Javi Martínez"(ESP)	02.09.1988	4	(15)	
Joshua Walter Kimmich	08.02.1995	25	(2)	4
Marc Roca Junqué (ESP)	26.11.1996	2	(4)	
Jamal Musiala	26.02.2003	7	(19)	6
Christopher Gavin Scott	07.06.2002		(2)	
Tiago Filipe Oliveira Dantas (POR)	24.12.2000	1	(1)	
Corentin Tolisso (FRA)	03.08.1994	7	(9)	1
Forwards:	**DOB**	**M**	**(s)**	**G**
Jean-Eric Maxim Choupo-Moting (CMR)	23.03.1989	8	(14)	3
Douglas Costa de Souza (BRA)	14.09.1990	3	(8)	1
Kingsley Junior Coman (FRA)	13.06.1996	23	(6)	5
Serge David Gnabry	14.07.1995	20	(7)	10
Robert Lewandowski (POL)	21.08.1988	28	(1)	41
Thomas Müller	13.09.1989	31	(1)	11
Leroy Aziz Sané	11.01.1996	18	(14)	6
Joshua Orobosa Zirkzee (NED)	22.05.2001	1	(2)	

Ballspielverein Borussia 09 Dortmund

Founded: 19.12.1909
Stadium: Signal Iduna Park, Dortmund (81,365)
Trainer: Lucien Favre (SUI) 02.11.1957
[13.12.2020] Edin Terzić 30.10.1982

Goalkeepers:	DOB	M	(s)	G
Roman Bürki (SUI)	14.11.1990	18	(1)	
Marwin Hitz (SUI)	18.09.1987	16		
Defenders:	**DOB**	**M**	**(s)**	**G**
Manuel Akanji (SUI)	19.07.1995	26	(2)	2
Raphaël Adelino José Guerreiro (POR)	22.12.1993	25	(2)	5
Mats Julian Hummels	16.12.1988	32	(1)	5
Mateu Jaume Morey Bauzà (ESP)	02.03.2000	10	(3)	
Thomas Meunier (BEL)	12.09.1991	17	(4)	1
Felix Passlack	29.05.1998	3	(4)	1
Łukasz Piszczek (POL)	03.06.1985	5	(6)	
Nico Schulz	01.04.1993	6	(7)	
Dan-Axel Zagadou (FRA)	03.06.1999	3	(6)	
Midfielders:	**DOB**	**M**	**(s)**	**G**
Jude Victor William Bellingham (ENG)	29.06.2003	19	(10)	1
Julian Brandt	02.05.1996	17	(14)	3
Emre Can	12.01.1994	23	(5)	1
Mahmoud Dahoud	01.01.1996	15	(6)	1
Thomas Joseph Delaney (DEN)	03.09.1991	14	(6)	1
Reinier Jesus Carvalho (BRA)	19.01.2002	1	(13)	1
Marco Reus	31.05.1989	27	(5)	8
Giovanni Alejandro Reyna (USA)	13.11.2002	23	(9)	4
Axel Laurent Angel Lambert Witsel (BEL)	12.01.1989	13	(2)	
Forwards:	**DOB**	**M**	**(s)**	**G**
Thorgan Hazard (BEL)	29.03.1993	8	(8)	1
Erling Braut Håland (NOR)	21.07.2000	27	(1)	27
Ansgar Knauff	10.01.2002		(4)	1
Youssoufa Moukoko	20.11.2004	2	(12)	3
Jadon Malik Sancho (ENG)	25.03.2000	24	(2)	8
Steffen Tigges	31.07.1998		(6)	

Borussia Verein für Leibesübungen 1900 Mönchengladbach

Founded: 01.08.1900
Stadium: Borussia-Park, Mönchengladbach (54,057)
Trainer: Marco Rose 11.09.1976

Goalkeepers:	DOB	M	(s)	G
Tobias Sippel	22.03.1988	3	(1)	
Yann Sommer (SUI)	17.12.1988	31		
Defenders:	**DOB**	**M**	**(s)**	**G**
Ramy Bensebaini (ALG)	16.04.1995	20	(5)	4
Jordan Beyer	19.05.2000	2	(2)	
Nico Elvedi (SUI)	30.09.1996	29		3
Matthias Lukas Ginter	19.01.1994	34		2
Tony Jantschke	07.04.1990	3	(5)	
Stefan Lainer (AUT)	27.08.1992	31	(2)	2
Oscar Wendt (SWE)	24.10.1985	15	(7)	1
Midfielders:	**DOB**	**M**	**(s)**	**G**
László Bénes (SVK)	09.09.1997	1	(6)	
Jonas Hofmann	14.07.1992	21	(3)	6
Christoph Kramer	19.02.1991	23	(5)	
Valentino Lando Lazaro (AUT)	24.03.1996	13	(9)	2
Florian Christian Neuhaus	16.03.1997	30	(3)	6
Rocco Reitz	29.05.2002	1	(1)	
Hannes Wolf (AUT)	16.04.1999	14	(18)	3
Denis Zakaria (SUI)	20.11.1996	15	(10)	1
Forwards:	**DOB**	**M**	**(s)**	**G**
Breel-Donald Embolo (SUI)	14.02.1997	16	(15)	5
Patrick Herrmann	12.02.1991	9	(18)	
Alassane Pléa (FRA)	10.03.1993	19	(10)	6
Lars Stindl	26.08.1988	23	(7)	14
Marcus Lilian Thuram-Ulien (FRA)	06.08.1997	20	(9)	8
Ibrahima Traoré (GUI)	21.04.1988	1	(6)	

Eintracht Frankfurt

Founded:	08.03.1899			
Stadium:	Deutsche Bank-Park (Waldstadion), Frankfurt (51,500)			
Trainer:	Adolf Hütter (AUT)			11.02.1970

Goalkeepers:	DOB	M	(s)	G
Elias Bördner	18.02.2002	1		
Kevin Trapp	08.07.1990	33		
Defenders:	**DOB**	**M**	**(s)**	**G**
David Ángel Abraham (ARG)	15.07.1986	14		1
Timothy Chandler (USA)	29.03.1990	3	(12)	1
Danny da Costa	13.07.1993	1	(5)	
Erik Durm	12.05.1992	19	(2)	1
Martin Hinteregger (AUT)	07.09.1992	29		2
Evan N'Dicka (FRA)	20.08.1999	23		3
Almamy Touré (FRA)	28.04.1996	8	(9)	1
Lucas Silva Melo „Tuta" (BRA)	04.07.1999	16	(3)	
Midfielders:	**DOB**	**M**	**(s)**	**G**
Aymane Barkok (MAR)	21.05.1998	9	(17)	2
Makoto Hasebe (JPN)	18.01.1984	26	(3)	
Ajdin Hrustić (AUS)	05.07.1996	1	(10)	1
Stefan Ilsanker (AUT)	18.05.1989	17	(10)	1
Daichi Kamada (JPN)	05.08.1996	28	(4)	5
Dominik Kohr	31.01.1994	2	(5)	
Filip Kostić (SRB)	01.11.1992	29	(1)	4
Sebastian Rode	11.10.1990	19	(8)	1
Djibril Sow (SUI)	06.02.1997	25	(3)	
Amin Younes	06.08.1993	16	(10)	3
Steven Zuber (SUI)	17.08.1991	6	(14)	
Forwards:	**DOB**	**M**	**(s)**	**G**
Ragnar Ache	28.07.1998		(7)	1
André Miguel Valente da Silva (POR)	06.11.1995	32		28
Bas Dost (NED)	31.05.1989	9	(3)	4
Luka Jović (SRB)	23.12.1997	8	(10)	4

Sport-Club Freiburg

Founded:	1904			
Stadium:	Schwarzwald-Stadion, Freiburg (24,000)			
Trainer:	Christian Streich			11.06.1965

Goalkeepers:	DOB	M	(s)	G
Mark Flekken (NED)	13.06.1993	3		
Florian Müller	13.11.1997	31		
Defenders:	**DOB**	**M**	**(s)**	**G**
Manuel Gulde	12.02.1991	22	(5)	2
Christian Günter	28.02.1993	34		3
Dominique Heintz	15.08.1993	14	(7)	
Lukas Kübler	30.08.1992	11	(8)	
Philipp Lienhart (AUT)	11.07.1996	34		4
Keven Schlotterbeck	28.04.1997	18	(6)	
Jonathan Schmid (FRA)	26.06.1990	27	(4)	2
Midfielders:	**DOB**	**M**	**(s)**	**G**
Amir Abrashi (ALB)	27.03.1990		(5)	
Vincenzo Grifo (ITA)	07.04.1993	27	(4)	9
Janik Haberer	02.04.1994	5	(9)	
Nicolas Höfler	09.03.1990	30	(1)	1
Yannik Keitel	15.02.2000	4	(8)	
Kwon Chang-hoon (KOR)	30.06.1994	1	(11)	
Baptiste Santamaría (FRA)	09.03.1995	28	(2)	1
Lino Tempelmann	02.02.1999	2	(8)	
Guus Til (NED)	22.12.1997	1	(6)	
Forwards:	**DOB**	**M**	**(s)**	**G**
Nishan Burkart (SUI)	31.01.2000		(1)	
Ermedin Demirović (BIH)	25.03.1998	19	(11)	5
Lucas Höler	10.07.1994	22	(11)	4
Jeong Woo-yeong (KOR)	20.09.1999	7	(19)	4
Nils Petersen	06.12.1988	12	(20)	8
Roland Sallai (HUN)	22.05.1997	22	(6)	8

Hertha Berliner Sport-Club

Founded:	25.07.1892			
Stadium:	Olympiastadion, Berlin (74,649)			
Trainer:	Bruno Labbadia			08.02.1966
[25.01.2021]	Pál Dárdai (HUN)			16.03.1976

Goalkeepers:	DOB	M	(s)	G
Rune Jarstein (NOR)	29.09.1984	8		
Alexander Schwolow	02.06.1992	26		
Defenders:	**DOB**	**M**	**(s)**	**G**
Omar Federico Alderete Fernández (PAR)	26.12.1996	14	(3)	
Dedryck Boyata (BEL)	28.11.1990	17	(2)	1
Márton Dárdai	12.02.2002	9	(3)	
Lukas Klünter	26.05.1996	11		
Maximilian Mittelstädt	18.03.1997	22	(5)	
Luca Netz	15.05.2003	2	(9)	1
Peter Pekarík (SVK)	30.10.1986	22	(1)	3
Marvin Plattenhardt	26.01.1992	12	(4)	
Niklas Stark	14.04.1995	31	(2)	
Jordan Torunarigha	07.08.1997	11	(3)	
Deyovaisio Zeefuik (NED)	11.03.1998	10	(12)	1
Midfielders:	**DOB**	**M**	**(s)**	**G**
Santiago Lionel Ascacíbar (ARG)	25.02.1997	8	(5)	1
Vladimír Darida (CZE)	08.08.1990	24	(3)	1
Jonas Dirkner	15.07.2002		(1)	
Mattéo Guendouzi (FRA)	14.04.1999	19	(5)	2
Sami Khedira	04.04.1987	4	(5)	
Eduard Löwen	28.01.1997	1	(6)	
Arne Maier	08.01.1999		(2)	
Jonas Michelbrink	23.06.2001		(2)	
Lucas Tousart (FRA)	29.04.1997	25	(1)	1
Forwards:	**DOB**	**M**	**(s)**	**G**
Jhon Andrés Córdoba Copete (COL)	11.05.1993	17	(4)	7
Javairô Dilrosun (NED)	22.06.1998	5	(7)	
Mathew Allan Leckie (AUS)	04.02.1991	5	(12)	
Dodi Lukebakio Ngandoli (BEL)	24.09.1997	21	(8)	5
Matheus Santos Carneiro da Cunha (BRA)	27.05.1999	25	(2)	7
Jessic Ngankam	20.07.2000	2	(13)	2
Krzysztof Piątek (POL)	01.07.1995	18	(14)	7
Nemanja Radonjić (SRB)	15.02.1996	5	(7)	1
Daishawn Orpheo Marvin Redan (DEN)	02.02.2001		(7)	
Marten Winkler	31.10.2002		(1)	

Turn- und Sportgemeinschaft 1899 Hoffenheim

Founded:	01.07.1899			
Stadium:	PreZero Arena, Sinsheim (30,150)			
Trainer:	Sebastian Hoeneß			12.05.1982

Goalkeepers:	DOB	M	(s)	G
Oliver Baumann	02.06.1990	31		
Philipp Pentke	01.05.1985	3		
Defenders:	**DOB**	**M**	**(s)**	**G**
Kasim Adams (GHA)	22.06.1995	11	(1)	
Kevin Akpoguma (NGA)	19.04.1995	14	(2)	1
Ermin Bičakčić (BIH)	24.01.1990	2		1
Melayro Bogarde (NED)	28.05.2002	2	(7)	
Joshua Brenet (NED)	20.03.1994		(1)	
Pavel Kadeřábek (CZE)	25.04.1992	17	(3)	
Håvard Nordtveit (NOR)	21.06.1990	6	(6)	
Stefan Posch (AUT)	14.05.1997	25	(1)	
Christopher Jeffrey Richards (USA)	28.03.2000	11		
Ryan Sessegnon (ENG)	18.05.2000	17	(6)	2
Kevin Vogt	23.09.1991	20	(4)	
Midfielders:	**DOB**	**M**	**(s)**	**G**
Christoph Baumgartner (AUT)	01.08.1999	28	(3)	6
Mijat Gaćinović (SRB)	08.02.1995	7	(16)	
Dennis Geiger	10.06.1998	9		1
Florian Grillitsch (AUT)	07.08.1995	22	(4)	2
Marco John	02.04.2002	12	(2)	
Sebastian Rudy	28.02.1990	21	(4)	1
Diadié Samassékou (MLI)	11.01.1996	31		
Forwards:	**DOB**	**M**	**(s)**	**G**
Sargis Adamyan (ARM)	23.05.1993	3	(15)	2
Ihlas Bebou (TOG)	23.04.1994	23	(9)	9
Maximilian Beier	17.10.2002		(3)	
Ishak Belfodil (ALG)	15.01.1992	7	(7)	
Munas Dabbur (ISR)	14.05.1992	11	(11)	4
João Klauss de Mello (BRA)	01.03.1997		(4)	
Andrej Kramarić (CRO)	19.06.1991	26	(2)	20
Jacob Bruun Larsen (DEN)	19.09.1998	1	(1)	
Georginio Rutter (FRA)	20.04.2002	2	(7)	1
Robert Skov (DEN)	20.05.1996	12	(11)	1

1. Fußball-Club Köln 01/07

Founded:	13.02.1948	
Stadium:	RheinEnergieStadion, Köln (49,698)	
Trainer:	Markus Gisdol (NED)	17.08.1969
[12.04.2021]	Friedhelm Funkel	10.12.1953

Goalkeepers:	DOB	M	(s)	G
Timo Horn	12.05.1993	34		
Ron-Robert Zieler	12.02.1989		(1)	
Defenders:	**DOB**	**M**	**(s)**	**G**
Sebastiaan Bornauw (BEL)	22.03.1999	23	(1)	1
Sava-Arandjel Čestić (SRB)	19.02.2001	11		
Rafael Czichos	14.05.1990	26	(2)	1
Kingsley Ehizibue (NGA)	25.05.1995	15	(6)	
Jannes Horn	06.02.1997	20	(9)	
Jorge Meré Pérez (ESP)	17.04.1997	14	(2)	
Noah Katterbach	13.04.2001	12	(9)	
Benno Schmitz	17.11.1994	4	(8)	
Frederik Hillesborg Sørensen	14.04.1992	1	(2)	
Midfielders:	**DOB**	**M**	**(s)**	**G**
Dominick Drexler	26.05.1990	11	(16)	2
Ondrej Duda (SVK)	05.12.1994	32		7
Jonas Hector	27.05.1990	15	(4)	3
Marco Höger	16.09.1989	1	(2)	
Max Meyer	18.09.1995	3	(7)	
Salih Özcan	11.01.1998	15	(13)	
Elvis Rexhbeçaj	01.11.1997	20	(10)	5
Ellyes Skhiri (TUN)	10.05.1995	32		5
Marius Wolf	27.05.1995	29	(2)	2
Forwards:	**DOB**	**M**	**(s)**	**G**
Sebastian Andersson (SWE)	15.07.1991	14	(2)	3
Toluwalase Emmanuel Arokodare (NGA)	23.11.2000		(10)	
Emmanuel Bonaventure Dennis (NGA)	15.11.1997	6	(3)	
Ismail Jakobs	17.08.1999	18	(5)	1
Florian Kainz (AUT)	24.10.1992	6	(2)	1
Dimitris Limnios (GRE)	27.05.1998	2	(10)	
Anthony Mbu Agogo Modeste (FRA)	14.04.1988	1	(7)	
Jan Thielmann	26.05.2002	9	(15)	2

RasenBallsport Leipzig

Founded:	19.05.2009	
Stadium:	Red Bull Arena, Leipzig (42,558)	
Trainer:	Julian Nagelsmann	23.07.1987

Goalkeepers:	DOB	M	(s)	G
Péter Gulácsi (HUN)	06.05.1990	33		
Josep Martínez Riera (ESP)	27.05.1998	1		
Defenders:	**DOB**	**M**	**(s)**	**G**
Marcel Halstenberg	27.09.1991	19	(5)	2
Benjamin Paa Kwesi Henrichs	23.02.1997	5	(8)	
Lukas Manuel Klostermann	03.06.1996	15	(8)	1
Ibrahima Konaté (FRA)	25.05.1999	8	(6)	1
Nordi Mukiele Mulere (FRA)	01.11.1997	21	(7)	3
Vilmos Tamás „Willi" Orbán (HUN)	03.11.1992	25	(4)	4
Dayotchanculle Upamecano (FRA)	27.10.1998	27	(2)	1
Midfielders:	**DOB**	**M**	**(s)**	**G**
Tyler Shaan Adams (USA)	14.02.1999	21	(6)	1
José Ángel Esmorís Tasende „Angeliño" (ESP)	04.01.1997	24	(2)	4
Daniel Olmo Carvajal „Dani Olmo" (ESP)	07.05.1998	26	(6)	5
Emil Forsberg (SWE)	23.10.1991	20	(9)	7
Amadou Haïdara (MLI)	31.01.1998	21	(10)	3
Kevin Kampl (SVN)	09.10.1990	24	(3)	
Konrad Laimer (AUT)	27.05.1997	1	(2)	
Christopher Nkunku (FRA)	14.11.1997	19	(9)	6
Marcel Sabitzer (AUT)	17.03.1994	24	(3)	8
Lazar Samardžić	24.02.2002	2	(5)	
Joscha Wosz	20.07.2002		(2)	
Forwards:	**DOB**	**M**	**(s)**	**G**
Dennis Borkowski	26.01.2002		(2)	
Hwang Hee-chan (KOR)	26.01.1996	3	(15)	
Justin Kluivert (NED)	05.05.1999	8	(11)	3
Yussuf Yurary Poulsen (DEN)	15.06.1994	14	(13)	5
Alexander Sørloth (NOR)	05.12.1995	13	(16)	5

1. Fußball- und Sportverein Mainz 05

Founded:	16.03.1905	
Stadium:	Opel Arena, Mainz (34,000)	
Trainer:	Achim Beierlorzer	20.11.1967
[28.09.2020]	Jan-Moritz Lichte	12.01.1980
[28.12.2020]	Jan Siewert	23.08.1982
[04.01.2021]	Bo Svensson (DEN)	04.08.1979

Goalkeepers:	DOB	M	(s)	G
Finn Dahmen	27.03.1998	3		
Robin Zentner	28.10.1994	31		
Defenders:	**DOB**	**M**	**(s)**	**G**
Aarón Martín Caricol (ESP)	22.04.1997	3	(2)	
Bote Ridle Nzuzi Baku	08.04.1998	2		
Stefan Bell	24.08.1991	16		1
Daniel Brosinski	17.07.1988	16	(5)	2
Danny da Costa	13.07.1993	15	(1)	
Alexander Hack	08.09.1993	14	(7)	1
Luca Kilian	01.09.1999	4	(2)	
Phillipp Mwene (AUT)	29.01.1994	19	(1)	1
Moussa Niakhaté (FRA)	08.03.1996	32		3
Jerry St. Juste (NED)	19.10.1996	32		
Midfielders:	**DOB**	**M**	**(s)**	**G**
Leandro Barreiro (LUX)	03.01.2000	27	(2)	2
Jean-Paul Boëtius (NED)	22.03.1994	23	(8)	2
Edimilson Fernandes Ribeiro (SUI)	15.04.1996	9	(5)	
Dominik Kohr	31.01.1994	14	(3)	1
Danny Latza	07.12.1989	21	(8)	
Pierre Kunde Malong (CMR)	26.07.1995	6	(5)	
Levin Öztunali	15.03.1996	7	(10)	1
Matondo-Merveille Papela	18.01.2001		(1)	
Kevin Stöger (AUT)	27.08.1993	4	(15)	3
Niklas Tauer	17.02.2001		(5)	
Forwards:	**DOB**	**M**	**(s)**	**G**
Issah Abass (GHA)	26.09.1998		(2)	
Jonathan Burkardt	11.07.2000	16	(13)	2
Robert Glatzel	08.01.1994	3	(10)	2
Ji Dong-won (KOR)	28.05.1991		(6)	
Jean-Philippe Mateta (FRA)	28.06.1997	12	(3)	7
Paul Nebel	10.10.2002		(4)	
Karim Onisiwo (AUT)	17.03.1992	19	(12)	4
Robin Kwamina Quaison (SWE)	09.10.1993	18	(10)	6
Ádám Csaba Szalai (HUN)	09.12.1987	8	(10)	1

Fußballclub Gelsenkirchen-Schalke 04

Founded:	04.05.1904		
Stadium:	Veltins-Arena, Gelsenkirchen (62,271)		
Trainer:	David Wagner (USA)		19.10.1971
[30.09.2020]	Manuel Baum		30.08.1979
[18.12.2020]	Hubertus Jozef Margaretha Stevens (NED)		29.11.1953
[27.12.2020]	Christian Gross (SUI)		14.08.1954
[02.03.2021]	Dimitrios Grammozis (GRE)		08.07.1978

Goalkeepers:	DOB	M	(s)	G
Ralf Fährmann	27.09.1988	22		
Michael Langer (AUT)	06.01.1985	2	(1)	
Frederik Rønnow (DEN)	04.08.1992	10	(1)	
Defenders:	**DOB**	**M**	**(s)**	**G**
Timo Becker	25.03.1997	18	(2)	
Ozan Kabak (TUR)	25.03.2000	14		
Sead Kolašinac (BIH)	20.06.1993	16	(1)	1
Kilian Ludewig	05.03.2000	6		
Henning Matriciani	14.03.2000		(1)	
Hamza Mendyl (MAR)	21.10.1997	1	(2)	
Shkodran Mustafi	17.04.1992	11	(2)	1
Matija Nastasić (SRB)	28.03.1993	14	(1)	
Bastian Oczipka	12.01.1989	20	(7)	
Vasilios Pavlidis (GRE)	04.09.2002		(1)	
Salif Sané (SEN)	25.08.1990	11	(3)	
Malick Thiaw	08.08.2001	15	(4)	1
William de Asevedo Furtado (BRA)	03.04.1995	7	(1)	
Midfielders:	**DOB**	**M**	**(s)**	**G**
Nabil Bentaleb (ALG)	24.11.1994	6	(3)	
Nassim Boujellab (MAR)	20.06.1999	6	(6)	1
Can Bozdoğan	05.04.2001	5	(9)	
Kerim Çalhanoğlu	26.08.2002	4		

	DOB	M	(s)	G
Florian Flick	01.05.2000	4		1
Amine Harit (MAR)	18.06.1997	25	(3)	2
Blendi Idrizi (KVX)	02.05.1998	3		1
Jimmy Kaparos (NED)	25.12.2001		(1)	
Mikail Maden (NOR)	17.01.2002		(1)	
Omar Mascarell González (ESP)	02.02.1993	21	(3)	1
Levent Mercan	10.12.2000		(1)	
Sebastian Rudy	28.02.1990	2		
Alessandro Schöpf (AUT)	07.02.1994	10	(9)	
Benjamin Stambouli (FRA)	13.08.1990	22	(2)	
Suat Serdar	11.04.1997	24	(1)	1
Forwards:	**DOB**	**M**	**(s)**	**G**
Mehmet-Can Aydın	09.02.2002	6		
Gonçalo Mendes Paciência (POR)	01.08.1994	9	(6)	1
Matthew Hoppe (USA)	13.03.2001	15	(7)	6
Dirk Jan Klaas Huntelaar (NED)	12.08.1983	7	(2)	2
Vedad Ibišević (BIH)	06.08.1984	1	(3)	
Ahmed Kutucu (TUR)	01.03.2000		(7)	
Rabbi Matondo (WAL)	09.09.2000	3		
Benito Raman (BEL)	07.11.1994	13	(12)	2
Luca Schuler	22.03.1999		(2)	
Steven Skrzybski	18.11.1992	3	(10)	
Mark Uth	24.08.1991	18	(2)	3

Verein für Bewegungsspiele Stuttgart 1893

Founded:	09.09.1893	
Stadium:	Mercedes-Benz Arena, Stuttgart (60,449)	
Trainer:	Pellegrino Matarazzo (USA)	28.11.1977

Goalkeepers:	DOB	M	(s)	G
Fabian Bredlow	02.03.1995	1		
Gregor Kobel (SUI)	06.12.1997	33		
Defenders:	**DOB**	**M**	**(s)**	**G**
Waldemar Anton	20.07.1996	30	(1)	
Marcin Kamiński (POL)	15.01.1992	2	(3)	
Atakan Karazor	13.10.1996	10	(9)	
Marc Oliver Kempf	28.01.1995	32		2
Konstantinos Mavropanos (GRE)	11.12.1997	19	(2)	
Borna Sosa (CRO)	21.01.1998	25	(1)	
Pascal Stenzel	20.03.1996	14	(9)	
Midfielders:	**DOB**	**M**	**(s)**	**G**
Naouirou Ahamada (FRA)	29.03.2002	3	(3)	
Gonzalo Castro	11.06.1987	23	(3)	4
Daniel Didavi	21.02.1990	10	(13)	4
Lilian Egloff	20.08.2002		(2)	
Wataru Endo (JPN)	09.02.1993	33		3

	DOB	M	(s)	G
Philipp Förster	04.02.1995	17	(8)	3
Philipp Klement	09.09.1992	2	(16)	1
Mateo Klimowicz	06.07.2000	12	(13)	1
Luca Mack	25.05.2000		(1)	
Orel Johnson Mangala (BEL)	18.03.1998	24		1
Roberto Massimo (ITA)	12.10.2000	7	(11)	
Erik Thommy	20.08.1994	3	(5)	
Forwards:	**DOB**	**M**	**(s)**	**G**
Hamadi Al Ghaddioui (MAR)	22.09.1990		(6)	
Darko Churlinov (MKD)	11.07.2000		(14)	
Momo Cissé (GUI)	17.10.2002		(5)	
Tanguy Coulibaly (FRA)	18.02.2001	17	(14)	2
Nicolás Iván González (ARG)	06.04.1998	10	(5)	6
Saša Kalajdžić (AUT)	07.07.1997	23	(10)	16
Mohamed Sankoh (NED)	16.10.2003		(1)	
Silas Wamangituka Fundu (COD)	06.10.1999	24	(1)	11

1. Fußballclub Union Berlin

Founded:	20.01.1966	
Stadium:	Stadion An der Alten Försterei, Berlin (22,012)	
Trainer:	Urs Fischer (SUI)	20.02.1966

Goalkeepers:	DOB	M	(s)	G
Loris Karius	22.06.1993	3	(1)	
Andreas Luthe	10.03.1987	31		
Defenders:	**DOB**	**M**	**(s)**	**G**
Marvin Friedrich	13.12.1995	34		5
Niko Gießelmann	26.09.1991	4	(9)	
Florian Hübner	01.03.1991	6		
Robin Knoche	22.05.1992	34		1
Christopher Lenz	22.09.1994	27		
Julian Ryerson (NOR)	17.11.1997	10	(14)	
Nico Schlotterbeck	01.12.1999	15	(1)	1
Christopher Trimmel (AUT)	24.02.1987	30	(1)	1
Midfielders:	**DOB**	**M**	**(s)**	**G**
Robert Andrich	22.09.1994	29		5
Christian Gentner	14.08.1985	13	(9)	
Akaki Gogia	18.01.1992		(7)	

	DOB	M	(s)	G
Sebastian Griesbeck	03.10.1990	8	(16)	
Marcus Ingvartsen (DEN)	04.01.1996	24	(6)	3
Grischa Prömel	09.01.1995	21	(3)	3
Forwards:	**DOB**	**M**	**(s)**	**G**
Taiwo Michael Awoniyi (NGA)	12.08.1997	16	(5)	5
Sheraldo Becker (SUR)	09.02.1995	15	(3)	3
Marius Bülter	29.03.1993	8	(18)	1
Leon Dajaku	12.04.2001		(2)	
Keita Endo (JPN)	22.11.1997	4	(12)	1
Max Kruse	19.03.1988	19	(3)	11
Tim Luis Maciejewski	05.03.2001		(1)	
Joshua Mees	15.04.1996		(1)	
Petar Musa (CRO)	04.03.1998	8	(6)	1
Joel Pohjanpalo (FIN)	13.09.1994	10	(9)	6
Cedric Teuchert	14.01.1997	5	(19)	3

Sportverein Werder Bremen von 1899

Founded:	04.02.1899		
Stadium:	Wohninvest Weser-Stadion, Bremen (42,100)		
Trainer:	Florian Kohfeldt		05.10.1982
[16.05.2021]	Thomas Schaaf		30.04.1961

Goalkeepers:	DOB	M	(s)	G
Jiří Pavlenka (CZE)	14.04.1992	34		
Defenders:	**DOB**	**M**	**(s)**	**G**
Felix Agu	27.09.1999	8	(7)	1
Hans Carl Ludwig Augustinsson (SWE)	21.04.1994	21	(2)	
Marco Friedl (AUT)	16.03.1998	31	(1)	
Theodor Gebre Selassie (CZE)	24.12.1986	34		3
Niklas Moisander (FIN)	29.09.1985	12	(6)	
Ömer Toprak (TUR)	21.07.1989	24	(2)	2
Miloš Veljković (SRB)	26.09.1995	19	(4)	
Midfielders:	**DOB**	**M**	**(s)**	**G**
Philipp Bargfrede	03.03.1989		(1)	
Leonardo Jesus Loureiro Bittencourt	19.12.1993	19	(8)	4
Maximilian Eggestein	08.12.1996	33		2
Patrick Erras	21.01.1995		(4)	
Christian Groß	08.02.1989	17	(6)	
Ilia Gruev (BUL)	06.05.2000		(1)	
Davy Klaassen (NED)	21.02.1993	3		
Jean-Manuel Mbom	24.02.2000	15	(6)	
Kevin Möhwald	03.07.1993	17	(10)	5
Romano Schmid (AUT)	27.01.2000	13	(9)	
Forwards:	**DOB**	**M**	**(s)**	**G**
Tahith José Chong (NED)	04.12.1999	4	(9)	
Eren Dinkçi	13.12.2001	1	(7)	1
Johannes Eggestein	08.05.1998		(2)	
Niclas Füllkrug	09.02.1993	10	(9)	6
Yuya Osako (JPN)	18.05.1990	7	(17)	
Milot Nexhmedin Rashica (KVX)	28.06.1996	14	(10)	3
Joshua Thomas Sargent (USA)	20.02.2000	30	(2)	5
Davie Selke	20.01.1995	7	(16)	3
Nick Woltemade	14.02.2002	1	(5)	

Verein für Leibesübungen Wolfsburg

Founded:	12.09.1945		
Stadium:	Volkswagen Arena, Wolfsburg (30,000)		
Trainer:	Oliver Glasner (AUT)		28.08.1974

Goalkeepers:	DOB	M	(s)	G
Koen Casteels (BEL)	25.06.1992	32		
Pavao Pervan (AUT)	13.11.1987	2		
Defenders:	**DOB**	**M**	**(s)**	**G**
Bote Ridle Nzuzi Baku	08.04.1998	31	(1)	6
John Anthony Brooks (USA)	28.01.1993	31	(1)	2
Maxence Lacroix (FRA)	06.04.2000	29	(1)	1
Melingo Kevin Mbabu (SUI)	19.04.1995	19	(3)	
Paulo Otávio Rosa da Silva (BRA)	23.11.1994	19	(4)	
Marin Pongračić (CRO)	11.09.1997	7	(3)	
Jérôme Roussillon (FRA)	06.01.1993	14	(6)	
Tim Siersleben	09.03.2000		(1)	
William de Asevedo Furtado (BRA)	03.04.1995		(2)	
Midfielders:	**DOB**	**M**	**(s)**	**G**
Maximilian Arnold	27.05.1994	30		3
Yannick Gerhardt	13.03.1994	21	(8)	2
Josuha Guilavogui (FRA)	19.09.1990	7	(13)	
João Victor Santos Sá (BRA)	27.03.1994	3	(18)	1
Felix Klaus	13.09.1992	1	(5)	
Yunus Mallı	24.02.1992	1		
Xaver Schlager (AUT)	28.09.1997	30	(2)	2
Renato Steffen (SUI)	03.11.1991	19	(2)	5
Forwards:	**DOB**	**M**	**(s)**	**G**
Bartosz Białek (POL)	11.11.2001	1	(18)	2
Josip Brekalo (CRO)	23.06.1998	22	(7)	7
Daniel Ginczek	13.04.1991	1	(10)	
Omar Marmoush (EGY)	07.02.1999		(1)	
Admir Mehmedi (SUI)	16.03.1991	8	(10)	
Maximilian Philipp	01.03.1994	13	(11)	6
Wout Weghorst (NED)	07.08.1992	33	(1)	20

SECOND LEVEL
2. Bundesliga 2020/2021

1.	VfL Bochum (*Promoted*)	34	21	4	9	66 - 39	67
2.	SpVgg Greuther Fürth (*Promoted*)	34	18	10	6	69 - 44	64
3.	SV Holstein Kiel (*Promotion Play-offs*)	34	18	8	8	57 - 35	62
4.	Hamburger SV	34	16	10	8	71 - 44	58
5.	TSV Fortuna Düsseldorf	34	16	8	10	55 - 46	56
6.	Karlsruher SC	34	14	10	10	51 - 44	52
7.	SV Darmstadt 98	34	15	6	13	63 - 55	51
8.	1. FC Heidenheim	34	15	6	13	49 - 49	51
9.	SC Paderborn 07	34	12	11	11	53 - 45	47
10.	FC St. Pauli Hamburg	34	13	8	13	51 - 56	47
11.	1. FC Nürnberg	34	11	11	12	46 - 51	44
12.	FC Erzgebirge Aue	34	12	8	14	44 - 53	44
13.	SV Hannover 96	34	12	6	16	53 - 51	42
14.	SSV Jahn Regensburg	34	9	11	14	37 - 50	38
15.	SV Sandhausen	34	10	4	20	41 - 60	34
16.	VfL Osnabrück (*Relegation Play-offs*)	34	9	6	19	35 - 58	33
17.	TSV Eintracht Braunschweig (*Relegated*)	34	7	10	17	30 - 59	31
18.	Würzburger Kickers (*Relegated*)	34	6	7	21	37 - 69	25

Relegation Play-offs (27-30.05.2021)

FC Ingolstadt 04 - VfL Osnabrück   3-0(2-0)   1-3(1-2)

INTERNATIONAL MATCHES
(16.07.2020 – 15.07.2021)

03.09.2020	Stuttgart	Germany - Spain	1-1(0-0)	(UNL)
06.09.2020	Basel	Switzerland - Germany	1-1(0-1)	(UNL)
07.10.2020	Köln	Germany - Turkey	3-3(1-0)	(F)
10.10.2020	Kyiv	Ukraine - Germany	1-2(0-1)	(UNL)
13.10.2020	Köln	Germany - Switzerland	3-3(1-2)	(UNL)
11.11.2020	Leipzig	Germany - Czech Republic	1-0(1-0)	(F)
14.11.2020	Leipzig	Germany - Ukraine	3-1(2-1)	(UNL)
17.11.2020	Sevilla	Spain - Germany	6-0(3-0)	(UNL)
25.03.2021	Duisburg	Germany - Iceland	3-0(2-0)	(WCQ)
28.03.2021	Bucureşti	Romania - Germany	0-1(0-1)	(WCQ)
31.03.2021	Duisburg	Germany - North Macedonia	1-2(0-1)	(WCQ)
02.06.2021	Innsbruck	Germany - Denmark	1-1(0-0)	(F)
07.06.2021	Düsseldorf	Germany - Latvia	7-1(5-0)	(F)
15.06.2021	München	France - Germany	1-0(1-0)	(EC)
19.06.2021	München	Portugal - Germany	2-4(1-2)	(EC)
23.06.2021	München	Germany - Hungary	2-2(0-1)	(EC)
29.06.2021	London	England - Germany	2-0(0-0)	(EC)

03.09.2020   **GERMANY - SPAIN**   1-1(0-0)   2nd UEFA Nations League A, Group 4
Mercedes-Benz Arena, Stuttgart; Referee: Daniele Orsato (Italy); Attendance: 0
GER: Kevin Trapp, Jan Thilo Kehrer, Antonio Rüdiger, Niklas Süle, Robin Everardus Gosens, Toni Kroos (Cap), İlkay Gündoğan (74.Suat Serdar), Emre Can, Julian Draxler, Leroy Aziz Sané (62.Matthias Lukas Ginter), Timo Werner (90+1.Robin Koch). Trainer: Joachim Löw.
Goal: Timo Werner (51).

06.09.2020   **SWITZERLAND - GERMANY**   1-1(0-1)   2nd UEFA Nations League A, Group 4
St. Jakob-Park, Basel; Referee: Michael Oliver (England); Attendance: 0
GER: Bernd Leno, Matthias Lukas Ginter, Antonio Rüdiger, Niklas Süle (62.Jonathan Glao Tah), Robin Everardus Gosens (78.Emre Can), Jan Thilo Kehrer, Toni Kroos (Cap), İlkay Gündoğan, Julian Draxler, Leroy Aziz Sané (46.Julian Brandt), Timo Werner. Trainer: Joachim Löw.
Goal: İlkay Gündoğan (14).

07.10.2020   **GERMANY - TURKEY**   3-3(1-0)   Friendly International
RheinEnergie Stadion, Köln; Referee: Benoît Bastien (France); Attendance: 0
GER: Bernd Leno, Benjamin Paa Kwesi Henrichs, Antonio Rüdiger (59.Jonathan Glao Tah), Robin Koch, Nico Schulz (70.Robin Everardus Gosens), Emre Can, Julian Draxler (Cap) (59.Jonas Hofmann), Julian Brandt (85.Niklas Stark), Kai Lukas Havertz (90.Nadiem Amiri), Florian Christian Neuhaus (79.Mahmoud Dahoud), Gian-Luca Waldschmidt. Trainer: Joachim Löw.
Goals: Julian Draxler (45+1), Florian Christian Neuhaus (58), Gian-Luca Waldschmidt (81).

10.10.2020   **UKRAINE - GERMANY**   1-2(0-1)   2nd UEFA Nations League A, Group 4
NSC Olimpiyskiy Stadium, Kyiv; Referee: Orel Grinfeld (Israel); Attendance: 17,573
GER: Manuel Peter Neuer (Cap), Marcel Halstenberg, Matthias Lukas Ginter, Antonio Rüdiger, Niklas Süle, Lukas Manuel Klostermann (90.Emre Can), Joshua Walter Kimmich, Toni Kroos, Julian Draxler (80.Timo Werner), Leon Christoph Goretzka, Serge David Gnabry (90+3.Kai Lukas Havertz). Trainer: Joachim Löw.
Goals: Matthias Lukas Ginter (20), Leon Christoph Goretzka (49).

13.10.2020   **GERMANY - SWITZERLAND**   3-3(1-2)   2nd UEFA Nations League A, Group 4
RheinEnergie Stadion, Köln; Referee: Ruddy Buquet (France); Attendance: 0
GER: Manuel Peter Neuer (Cap), Antonio Rüdiger, Matthias Lukas Ginter (77.Emre Can), Lukas Manuel Klostermann, Robin Everardus Gosens (57.Marcel Halstenberg), Joshua Walter Kimmich, Toni Kroos, Leon Christoph Goretzka, Kai Lukas Havertz (77.Julian Draxler), Serge David Gnabry, Timo Werner. Trainer: Joachim Löw.
Goals: Timo Werner (28), Kai Lukas Havertz (55), Serge David Gnabry (60).

11.11.2020   **GERMANY - CZECH REPUBLIC**   1-0(1-0)   Friendly International
Stadium, City; Referee: Andris Leimanis (Latvia); Attendance: 0
GER: Kevin Trapp, Bote Ridle Nzuzi Baku, Antonio Rüdiger, Jonathan Glao Tah, Robin Koch, Philipp Martin Max (69.Nico Schulz), İlkay Gündoğan (Cap) (46.Mahmoud Dahoud), Jonas Hofmann (20.Nadiem Amiri), Florian Christian Neuhaus, Julian Brandt, Gian-Luca Waldschmidt. Trainer: Joachim Löw.
Goal: Gian-Luca Waldschmidt (13).

14.11.2020   **GERMANY - UKRAINE**   3-1(2-1)   2nd UEFA Nations League A, Group 4
Red Bull Arena, Leipzig; Referee: Ovidiu Alin Haţegan (Romania); Attendance: 0
GER: Manuel Peter Neuer (Cap), Matthias Lukas Ginter, Antonio Rüdiger, Robin Koch, Niklas Süle, Philipp Martin Max, İlkay Gündoğan, Leon Christoph Goretzka, Serge David Gnabry, Leroy Aziz Sané (86.Gian-Luca Waldschmidt), Timo Werner (76.Julian Brandt). Trainer: Joachim Löw.
Goals: Leroy Aziz Sané (23), Timo Werner (33, 64).

17.11.2020   **SPAIN - GERMANY**   6-0(3-0)   2nd UEFA Nations League A, Group 4
Estadio La Cartuja, Sevilla; Referee: Andreas Ekberg (Sweden); Attendance: 0
GER: Manuel Peter Neuer (Cap), Matthias Lukas Ginter, Robin Koch, Niklas Süle (46.Jonathan Glao Tah), Philipp Martin Max, Toni Kroos, İlkay Gündoğan, Leon Christoph Goretzka (61.Florian Christian Neuhaus), Serge David Gnabry, Leroy Aziz Sané (61.Gian-Luca Waldschmidt), Timo Werner (76.Benjamin Paa Kwesi Henrichs). Trainer: Joachim Löw.

25.03.2021   **GERMANY - ICELAND**   3-0(2-0)   22nd FIFA WC.Qualifiers
MSV-Arena, Duisburg; Referee: Srđan Jovanović (Serbia); Attendance: 0
GER: Manuel Peter Neuer (Cap), Antonio Rüdiger, Matthias Lukas Ginter, Lukas Manuel Klostermann, İlkay Gündoğan, Emre Can, Joshua Walter Kimmich, Leon Christoph Goretzka (71.Florian Christian Neuhaus), Kai Lukas Havertz (78.Jamal Musiala), Leroy Aziz Sané 78.78.Timo Werner), Serge David Gnabry (86.Amin Younes). Trainer: Joachim Löw.
Goals: Leon Christoph Goretzka (3), Kai Lukas Havertz (7), İlkay Gündoğan (56).

28.03.2021   **ROMANIA - GERMANY**   0-1(0-1)   22nd FIFA WC.Qualifiers
Arena Naţională, Bucureşti; Referee: Clément Turpin (France); Attendance: 0
GER: Manuel Peter Neuer (Cap), Antonio Rüdiger, Matthias Lukas Ginter, Lukas Manuel Klostermann, İlkay Gündoğan, Emre Can, Joshua Walter Kimmich, Leon Christoph Goretzka, Kai Lukas Havertz (77.Timo Werner), Serge David Gnabry (90+2.Florian Christian Neuhaus), Leroy Aziz Sané (90+4.Amin Younes). Trainer: Joachim Löw.
Goal: Serge David Gnabry (17).

31.03.2021   **GERMANY - NORTH MACEDONIA**   1-2(0-1)   22nd FIFA WC.Qualifiers
MSV-Arena, Duisburg; Referee: Sergei Karasev (Russia); Attendance: 0
GER: Marc-André ter Stegen, Matthias Lukas Ginter (88.Jamal Musiala), Antonio Rüdiger, Robin Everardus Gosens (56.Amin Younes), Emre Can, Joshua Walter Kimmich, İlkay Gündoğan (Cap), Leon Christoph Goretzka, Kai Lukas Havertz (56.Timo Werner), Serge David Gnabry, Leroy Aziz Sané. Trainer: Joachim Löw.
Goal: İlkay Gündoğan (63 penalty).

02.06.2021   **GERMANY - DENMARK**   1-1(0-0)   Friendly International
Tivoli Stadion Tirol, Innsbruck (Austria); Referee: Julian Weinberger (Austria); Attendance: 0
GER: Manuel Peter Neuer (Cap), Matthias Lukas Ginter, Niklas Süle, Mats Julian Hummels, Robin Everardus Gosens (79.Christian Günter), Lukas Manuel Klostermann (59.Robin Koch), Joshua Walter Kimmich, Florian Christian Neuhaus, Thomas Müller, Serge David Gnabry (79.Kevin Volland), Leroy Aziz Sané (86.Jonas Hofmann). Trainer: Joachim Löw.
Goal: Florian Christian Neuhaus (48).

07.06.2021   **GERMANY - LATVIA**   7-1(5-0)   Friendly International
Merkur Spiel-Arena, Düsseldorf; Referee: Nikola Dabanović (Montenegro); Attendance: 1,000
GER: Manuel Peter Neuer (Cap), Matthias Lukas Ginter, Antonio Rüdiger (61.Niklas Süle), Mats Julian Hummels, Robin Everardus Gosens (61.Christian Günter), Joshua Walter Kimmich, İlkay Gündoğan (61.Emre Can), Toni Kroos, Thomas Müller (76.Jamal Musiala), Kai Lukas Havertz (46.Timo Werner), Serge David Gnabry (46.Leroy Aziz Sané). Trainer: Joachim Löw.
Goals: Robin Everardus Gosens (19), İlkay Gündoğan (21), Thomas Müller (27), Roberts Ozols (39 own goal), Serge David Gnabry (45), Timo Werner (50), Leroy Aziz Sané (76).

15.06.2021   **FRANCE - GERMANY**   1-0(1-0)   16th EC. Group Stage.
Football Arena (Allianz), München; Referee: Carlos del Cerro Grande (Spain); Attendance: 13,000
GER: Manuel Peter Neuer (Cap), Matthias Lukas Ginter (88.Emre Can), Antonio Rüdiger, Mats Julian Hummels, Robin Everardus Gosens (88.Kevin Volland), Joshua Walter Kimmich, İlkay Gündoğan, Toni Kroos, Thomas Müller, Kai Lukas Havertz (74.Leroy Aziz Sané), Serge David Gnabry (74.Timo Werner). Trainer: Joachim Löw.

19.06.2021   **PORTUGAL - GERMANY**   2-4(1-2)   16th EC. Group Stage.
Football Arena (Allianz), München; Referee: Anthony Taylor (England); Attendance: 12,926
GER: Manuel Peter Neuer (Cap), Matthias Lukas Ginter, Antonio Rüdiger, Mats Julian Hummels (62.Emre Can), Robin Everardus Gosens (62.Marcel Halstenberg), Joshua Walter Kimmich, İlkay Gündoğan (73.Niklas Süle), Toni Kroos, Thomas Müller, Kai Lukas Havertz (73.Leon Christoph Goretzka), Serge David Gnabry (87.Leroy Aziz Sané). Trainer: Joachim Löw.
Goals: Rúben dos Santos Gato Alves Dias (35 own goal), Raphaël Adelino José Guerreiro (39 own goal), Kai Lukas Havertz (51), Robin Everardus Gosens (60).

23.06.2021   **GERMANY - HUNGARY**   2-2(0-1)   16th EC. Group Stage.
Football Arena (Allianz), München; Referee: Sergey Karasev (Russia); Attendance: 12,413
GER: Manuel Peter Neuer (Cap), Matthias Lukas Ginter (82.Kevin Volland), Antonio Rüdiger, Mats Julian Hummels, Robin Everardus Gosens (82.Jamal Musiala), Joshua Walter Kimmich, İlkay Gündoğan (58.Leon Christoph Goretzka), Toni Kroos, Serge David Gnabry (68.Thomas Müller), Kai Lukas Havertz (68.Timo Werner), Leroy Aziz Sané. Trainer: Joachim Löw.
Goals: Kai Lukas Havertz (66), Leon Christoph Goretzka (84).

29.06.2021   **ENGLAND - GERMANY**   2-0(0-0)   16th EC. 2nd Round of 16.
Wembley Stadium, London; Referee: Danny Desmond Makkelie (Netherlands); Attendance: 41,973
GER: Manuel Peter Neuer (Cap), Matthias Lukas Ginter (87.Emre Can), Antonio Rüdiger, Mats Julian Hummels, Robin Everardus Gosens (88.Leroy Aziz Sané), Toni Kroos, Leon Christoph Goretzka, Joshua Walter Kimmich, Thomas Müller (90+2.Jamal Musiala), Kai Lukas Havertz, Timo Werner (69.Serge David Gnabry). Trainer: Joachim Löw.

NATIONAL TEAM PLAYERS
(16.07.2020 – 15.07.2021)

Name	DOB	Caps	Goals	2020/2021:	Club
Goalkeepers					
Bernd LENO	04.03.1992	8	0	2020:	Arsenal FC London (ENG)
Manuel Peter NEUER	27.03.1986	104	0	2020/2021:	FC Bayern München
Marc-André TER STEGEN	30.04.1992	25	0	2021:	FC Barcelona (ESP)
Kevin TRAPP	08.07.1990	5	0	2020:	Eintracht Frankfurt
Defenders					
Bote Ridle Nzuzi BAKU	08.04.1998	1	0	2020:	VfL Wolfsburg
Emre CAN	12.01.1994	37	1	2020/2021:	BV Borussia 09 Dortmund
Matthias Lukas GINTER	19.01.1994	44	2	2020/2021:	Borussia VfL Mönchengladbach
Robin Everardus GOSENS	05.07.1994	11	2	2020/2021:	Atalanta Bergamasca Calcio (ITA)
Christian GÜNTER	28.02.1993	3	0	2021:	SC Freiburg
Marcel HALSTENBERG	27.09.1991	9	1	2020/2021:	RasenBallsport Leipzig
Benjamin Paa Kwesi HENRICHS	23.02.1997	5	0	2020:	RasenBallsport Leipzig
Mats Julian HUMMELS	16.12.1988	76	5	2020/2021:	BV Borussia 09 Dortmund
Jan Thilo KEHRER	21.09.1996	9	0	2020:	Paris Saint-Germain FC (FRA)
Lukas Manuel KLOSTERMANN	03.06.1996	13	0	2020/2021:	RasenBallsport Leipzig
Robin KOCH	17.07.1996	8	0	2020/2021:	Leeds United FC (ENG)
Philipp Martin MAX	30.09.1993	3	0	2020:	PSV Eindhoven (NED)
Antonio RÜDIGER	03.03.1993	45	1	2020/2021:	Chelsea FC London (ENG)
Nico SCHULZ	01.04.1993	12	2	2020:	BV Borussia 09 Dortmund
Niklas STARK	14.04.1995	2	0	2020:	Hertha BSC Berlin
Niklas SÜLE	03.09.1995	32	1	2020/2021:	FC Bayern München
Jonathan Glao TAH	11.02.1996	13	0	2020:	TSV Bayer 04 Leverkusen
Midfielders					
Nadiem AMIRI	27.10.1996	5	0	2020:	TSV Bayer 04 Leverkusen
Julian BRANDT	02.05.1996	35	3	2020:	BV Borussia 09 Dortmund
Mahmoud DAHOUD	01.01.1996	2	0	2020:	BV Borussia 09 Dortmund
Julian DRAXLER	20.09.1993	56	7	2020:	Paris Saint-Germain FC (FRA)
Leon Christoph GORETZKA	06.02.1995	35	14	2020/2021:	FC Bayern München
İlkay GÜNDOĞAN	24.10.1990	49	11	2020/2021:	Manchester City FC (ENG)
Kai Lukas HAVERTZ	11.06.1999	18	5	2020/2021:	Chelsea FC London (ENG)
Jonas HOFMANN	14.07.1992	3	0	2020/2021:	Borussia VfL Mönchengladbach
Joshua Walter KIMMICH	08.02.1995	59	3	2020/2021:	FC Bayern München
Toni KROOS	04.01.1990	106	17	2020/2021:	Real Madrid CF (ESP)
Jamal MUSIALA	26.02.2003	5	0	2021:	FC Bayern München
Thomas MÜLLER	13.09.1989	106	39	2021:	FC Bayern München
Florian Christian NEUHAUS	16.03.1997	6	2	2020/2021:	Borussia VfL Mönchengladbach
Suat SERDAR	11.04.1997	4	0	2020:	FC Schalke 04 Gelsenkirchen
Forwards					
Serge David GNABRY	14.07.1995	26	16	2020/2021:	FC Bayern München
Leroy Aziz SANÉ	11.01.1996	34	7	2020/2021:	FC Bayern München
Kevin VOLLAND	30.07.1992	13	1	2021:	AS Monaco FC (FRA)
Gian-Luca WALDSCHMIDT	19.05.1996	7	2	2020/2021:	Sport Lisboa e Benfica (POR)
Timo WERNER	06.03.1996	42	16	2020/2021:	Chelsea FC London (ENG)
Amin YOUNES	06.08.1993	8	2	2021:	Eintracht Frankfurt
National team coach					
Joachim LÖW [from 12.07.2006]	03.02.1960			198 M; 124 W; 40 D; 34 L; 467-200	

GIBRALTAR

The Country:
Gibraltar [*British Overseas Territory*]
Capital: Gibraltar
Surface: 6,8 km²
Inhabitants: 34,003 [2020]
Time: UTC+1

The FA:
Gibraltar Football Association
7.01b World Trade Center 11, 1AA Gibraltar
Tel: +350 200 42 941
Foundation date: 1895
Member of FIFA since: 13.05.2016
Member of UEFA since: 24.05.2013
Website: www.gibraltarfa.com

NATIONAL TEAM RECORDS

RECORDS

First international match:	19.11.2013, Faro/Loulé (POR): Gibraltar – Slovakia 0-0
Most international caps:	Liam Walker - 53 caps (since 2013)
Most international goals:	Lee Henry Casciaro - 3 goals / 39 caps (since 2014)

UEFA EUROPEAN CHAMPIONSHIP		FIFA WORLD CUP		OLYMPIC TOURNAMENTS	
1960	Not member of UEFA	1930	Not member of FIFA	1908	Not member of FIFA
1964	Not member of UEFA	1934	Not member of FIFA	1912	Not member of FIFA
1968	Not member of UEFA	1938	Not member of FIFA	1920	Not member of FIFA
1972	Not member of UEFA	1950	Not member of FIFA	1924	Not member of FIFA
1976	Not member of UEFA	1954	Not member of FIFA	1928	Not member of FIFA
1980	Not member of UEFA	1958	Not member of FIFA	1936	Not member of FIFA
1984	Not member of UEFA	1962	Not member of FIFA	1948	Not member of FIFA
1988	Not member of UEFA	1966	Not member of FIFA	1952	Not member of FIFA
1992	Not member of UEFA	1970	Not member of FIFA	1956	Not member of FIFA
1996	Not member of UEFA	1974	Not member of FIFA	1960	Not member of FIFA
2000	Not member of UEFA	1978	Not member of FIFA	1964	Not member of FIFA
2004	Not member of UEFA	1982	Not member of FIFA	1968	Not member of FIFA
2008	Not member of UEFA	1986	Not member of FIFA	1972	Not member of FIFA
2012	Not member of UEFA	1990	Not member of FIFA	1976	Not member of FIFA
2016	Qualifiers	1994	Not member of FIFA	1980	Not member of FIFA
2020	Qualifiers	1998	Not member of FIFA	1984	Not member of FIFA
		2002	Not member of FIFA	1988	Not member of FIFA
		2006	Not member of FIFA	1992	Not member of FIFA
		2010	Not member of FIFA	1996	Not member of FIFA
		2014	Not member of FIFA	2000	Not member of FIFA
		2018	Qualifiers	2004	Not member of FIFA
				2008	Not member of FIFA
				2012	Not member of FIFA
				2016	Not member of FIFA

UEFA NATIONS LEAGUE

2018/2019	League D
2020/2021	League D (promoted to League C)

FIFA CONFEDERATIONS CUP 1992-2017

None

GIBRALTARIAN CLUB HONOURS IN EUROPEAN CLUB COMPETITIONS:

European Champion Clubs' Cup (1956-1992) / UEFA Champions League (1993-2021)
None

Fairs Cup (1858-1971) / UEFA Cup (1972-2009) / UEFA Europa League (2010-2021)
None

UEFA Super Cup (1972-2020)
None

*European Cup Winners' Cup 1961-1999**
None

*defunct competition

NATIONAL COMPETITIONS
TABLE OF HONOURS

	CHAMPIONS	CUP WINNERS
1894/1895	-	Gibraltar FC
1895/1896	Gibraltar FC	*Not known*
1896/1897	Jubilee FC	*Not known*
1897/1898	Jubilee FC	*Not known*
1898/1899	Albion FC	*Not known*
1899/1900	Exiles FC	*Not known*
1900/1901	Prince of Wales FC	*Not known*
1901/1902	Exiles FC	*Not known*
1902/1903	Prince of Wales FC	*Not known*
1903/1904	Prince of Wales FC	*Not known*
1904/1905	Athletic FC	*Not known*
1905/1906	Prince of Wales FC	*Not known*
1906/1907	*No competition*	*Not known*
1907/1908	FC Britannia XI	*Not known*
1908/1909	Prince of Wales FC	*Not known*
1909/1910	South United FC	*Not known*
1910/1911	South United FC	*Not known*
1911/1912	FC Britannia XI	*Not known*
1912/1913	FC Britannia XI	*Not known*
1913/1914	Prince of Wales FC	*Not known*
1914/1915	Royal Sovereign	*Not known*
1915/1916	*No competition*	*Not known*
1916/1917	Prince of Wales FC	*Not known*
1917/1918	FC Britannia XI	*Not known*
1918/1919	Prince of Wales FC	*Not known*
1919/1920	FC Britannia XI	*Not known*
1920/1921	Prince of Wales FC	*Not known*
1921/1922	Prince of Wales FC	*Not known*
1922/1923	Prince of Wales FC	*Not known*
1923/1924	Gibraltar FC	*Not known*
1924/1925	Prince of Wales FC	*Not known*
1925/1926	Prince of Wales FC	*Not known*
1926/1927	Prince of Wales FC	*Not known*
1927/1928	Prince of Wales FC	*Not known*
1928/1929	Europa FC	*Not known*
1929/1930	Europa FC	*Not known*
1930/1931	Prince of Wales FC	*Not known*
1931/1932	Europa FC	*Not known*
1932/1933	Europa FC	*Not known*
1933/1934	Commander of the Yard FC	*Not known*
1934/1935	Chief Construction FC	*Not known*
1935/1936	Chief Constructor FC	HMS Hood
1936/1937	FC Britannia XI	FC Britannia XI
1937/1938	Europa FC	Europa FC
1938/1939	Prince of Wales FC	2nd Battalion The King's Regiment
1939/1940	Prince of Wales FC	FC Britannia XI
1940/1941	FC Britannia XI	*No competition*
1941/1942	*No competition*	A.A.R.A.
1942/1943	*No competition*	Royal Air Force New Camp
1943/1944	*No competition*	4th Btallion Royal Scott
1944/1945	*No competition*	*No competition*
1945/1946	*No competition*	Europa FC
1946/1947	Gibraltar United FC	Gibraltar United FC
1947/1948	Gibraltar United FC	FC Britannia XI
1948/1949	Gibraltar United FC	Prince of Wales FC
1949/1950	Gibraltar United FC	Europa FC
1950/1951	Gibraltar United FC	Europa FC
1951/1952	Europa FC	Europa FC
1952/1953	Prince of Wales FC	*Not known*
1953/1954	Gibraltar United FC	*Not known*
1954/1955	FC Britannia XI	*Not known*
1955/1956	FC Britannia XI	*Not known*
1956/1957	FC Britannia XI	*Not known*
1957/1958	FC Britannia XI	*Not known*
1958/1959	FC Britannia XI	*Not known*
1959/1960	Gibraltar United FC	*Not known*
1960/1961	FC Britannia XI	*Not known*
1961/1962	Gibraltar United FC	*Not known*
1962/1963	FC Britannia XI	*Not known*
1963/1964	Gibraltar United FC	*Not known*
1964/1965	Gibraltar United FC	*Not known*

1965/1966	Glacis United FC	*Not known*
1966/1967	Glacis United FC	*Not known*
1967/1968	Glacis United FC	*Not known*
1968/1969	Glacis United FC	*Not known*
1969/1970	Glacis United FC	*Not known*
1970/1971	Glacis United FC	*Not known*
1971/1972	Glacis United FC	*Not known*
1972/1973	Glacis United FC	*Not known*
1973/1974	Glacis United FC	Manchester United FC
1974/1975	Manchester United FC	Glacis United FC
1975/1976	Glacis United FC	2nd Battalion Royal Green Jackets
1976/1977	Manchester United FC	Manchester United FC
1977/1978	*No competition*	*Not known*
1978/1979	Manchester United FC	St Joseph's FC
1979/1980	Manchester United FC	Manchester United FC
1980/1981	Glacis United FC	Glacis United FC
1981/1982	Glacis United FC	Glacis United FC
1982/1983	Glacis United FC	St Joseph's FC
1983/1984	Manchester United FC	St Joseph's FC
1984/1985	Glacis United FC & Lincoln Red Imps FC	St Joseph's FC
1985/1986	Lincoln Red Imps FC	Lincoln Red Imps FC
1986/1987	St Theresa's FC	St Joseph's FC
1987/1988	St Theresa's FC	Royal Air Force Gibraltar
1988/1989	Glacis United FC	Lincoln Red Imps FC
1989/1990	Lincoln Red Imps FC	Lincoln Red Imps FC
1990/1991	Lincoln Red Imps FC	*Not known*
1991/1992	Lincoln Red Imps FC	St Joseph's FC
1992/1993	Lincoln Red Imps FC	Lincoln Red Imps FC
1993/1994	Lincoln Red Imps FC	Lincoln Red Imps FC
1994/1995	Manchester United FC	St Theresa's FC
1995/1996	St Joseph's FC	St Joseph's FC
1996/1997	Glacis United FC	Manchester United FC
1997/1998	St Theresa's FC	Glacis United FC
1998/1999	Manchester United FC	Gibraltar United FC
1999/2000	Glacis United FC	Gibraltar United FC
2000/2001	Lincoln Red Imps FC	Gibraltar United FC
2001/2002	Gibraltar United FC	Lincoln Red Imps FC
2002/2003	Lincoln Red Imps FC	Manchester United FC
2003/2004	Lincoln Red Imps FC	Newcastle FC
2004/2005	Lincoln Red Imps FC	Newcastle FC
2005/2006	Lincoln Red Imps FC	Newcastle FC
2006/2007	Lincoln Red Imps FC	Newcastle FC
2007/2008	Lincoln Red Imps FC	Lincoln Red Imps FC
2008/2009	Lincoln Red Imps FC	Lincoln Red Imps FC
2009/2010	Lincoln Red Imps FC	Lincoln Red Imps FC
2010/2011	Lincoln Red Imps FC	Lincoln Red Imps FC
2011/2012	Lincoln Red Imps FC	St Joseph's FC
2012/2013	Lincoln Red Imps FC	St Joseph's FC
2013/2014	Lincoln Red Imps FC	Lincoln Red Imps FC
2014/2015	Lincoln Red Imps FC	Lincoln Red Imps FC
2015/2016	Lincoln Red Imps FC	Lincoln Red Imps FC
2016/2017	Europa FC	Europa FC
2017/2018	Lincoln Red Imps FC	Europa FC
2018/2019	Lincoln Red Imps FC	Europa FC
2019/2020	*Championship cancelled*	*Competition cancelled*
2020/2021	Lincoln Red Imps FC	Lincoln Red Imps FC

Please note: Manchester United FC changed its name to Manchester 62 FC (2013); Newcastle FC was a temporary name for Lincoln Red Imps FC.

NATIONAL CHAMPIONSHIP
Gibraltar National League 2020/2021
(16.10.2020 – 16.05.2021)

Please note: FC Boca Juniors Gibraltar was refused domestic licence and they was expelled from the league on 09.12.2020. All their results were annulled.

Regular Stage - Results

Round 1 [16-19.10.2020]
Glacis United FC - Mons Calpe SC 0-1
Manchester 62 FC - Lions Gibraltar FC 0-4
Lynx FC - Europa Point FC 3-0
St. Joseph's FC - FC Boca Juniors *annulled*
FCB Magpies - Europa FC 1-3
College 1975 FC - Lincoln Red Imps 0-8

Round 2 [24-27.10.2020]
Mons Calpe SC - St. Joseph's FC 0-5
Lions Gibraltar FC - Glacis United FC 3-0
Europa Point FC - Europa FC 0-9
FC Boca Juniors - College 1975 FC *annulled*
Lincoln Red Imps - FCB Magpies 3-0
Lynx FC - Manchester 62 FC 5-0

Round 3 [30.10.-02.11.2020]
St. Joseph's FC - Lions Gibraltar FC 1-1
Europa FC - Lincoln Red Imps 2-2
FCB Magpies - FC Boca Juniors 3-0 *awarded*
Glacis United FC - Lynx FC 0-3 *awarded*
Manchester 62 FC - Europa Point FC 3-1
College 1975 FC - Mons Calpe SC 0-6

Round 4
Manchester - Glacis United 0-2 [25.11.2020]
Europa Point - Lincoln R. I. 1-6 [02.12.2020]
FC Boca Juniors - Europa FC *not played*
Lynx FC - St. Joseph's FC 1-4 [16.12.2020]
Lions Gibraltar - College 1975 3-2 [22.02.21]
Mons Calpe - FCB Magpies 4-1 [23.02.2021]

Round 5 [20-23.11.2020]
FCB Magpies - Lions Gibraltar FC 0-0
Glacis United - Europa Point FC 3-0 *awarded*
St. Joseph's FC - Manchester 62 FC 11-0
Europa FC - Mons Calpe SC 3-0
Lincoln Red Imps - FC Boca Juniors *annulled*
College 1975 FC - Lynx FC 1-7

Round 6 [27-30.11.2020]
Lions Gibraltar - Europa FC 0-1
Europa Point - FC Boca Juniors 3-0 *awarded*
Mons Calpe SC - Lincoln Red Imps 0-2
Lynx FC - FCB Magpies 1-1
Glacis United - St. Joseph's FC 0-5
Manchester 62 FC - College 1975 FC 3-2

Round 7 [04-07.12.2020]
Europa FC - Lynx FC 3-1
FC Boca Juniors - Mons Calpe SC *annulled*
College 1975 FC - Glacis United FC 1-5
Lincoln Red Imps - Lions Gibraltar FC 3-0
St. Joseph's FC - Europa Point FC 4-0
FCB Magpies - Manchester 62 FC 3-2

Round 8 [11-14.12.2020]
Lynx FC - Lincoln Red Imps 2-0
St. Joseph's FC - College 1975 FC 13-1
Glacis United FC - FCB Magpies 0-1
Lions Gibraltar - FC Boca Juniors *not played*
Manchester 62 FC - Europa FC 0-9
Europa Point FC - Mons Calpe SC 2-4

Round 9 [18-21.12.2020]
Europa FC - Glacis United FC 1-0
College 1975 FC - Europa Point FC 1-3
Lincoln Red Imps - Manchester 62 FC 2-0
Mons Calpe SC - Lions Gibraltar FC 0-0
FCB Magpies - St. Joseph's FC 0-3
FC Boca Juniors - Lynx FC *not played*

Round 10 [24-27.02.2021]
St. Joseph's FC - Europa FC 1-4
Glacis United FC - Lincoln Red Imps 0-3
Europa Point - Lions Gibraltar FC 0-1
College 1975 FC - FCB Magpies 0-3
Lynx FC - Mons Calpe SC 0-1

Round 11 [02-06.03.2021]
Europa FC - College 1975 FC 9-0
Lions Gibraltar FC - Lynx FC 0-3
Lincoln Red Imps - St. Joseph's FC 4-2
Mons Calpe SC - Manchester 62 FC 5-0
FCB Magpies - Europa Point FC 4-0

Final Standings

1. Europa FC	10	9	1	0	44	-	5	28
2. Lincoln Red Imps FC	10	8	1	1	33	-	7	25
3. St. Joseph's FC	10	7	1	2	49	-	11	22
4. Lynx FC	10	6	1	3	26	-	10	19
5. Mons Calpe SC	10	6	1	3	21	-	13	19
6. Lions Gibraltar FC	10	4	3	3	12	-	10	15
7. FC Bruno's Magpies	10	4	2	4	14	-	16	14
8. Glacis United FC	10	3	0	7	10	-	18	9
9. Manchester 62 FC	10	2	0	8	8	-	44	6
10. Europa Point FC	10	1	0	9	7	-	38	3
11. College 1975 FC	10	0	0	10	8	-	60	0
12. FC Boca Juniors Gibraltar (*Dissolved*)								

Teams ranked 1-6 were qualified for the Championship Round, while teams ranked 7-12 were qualified for the Challenge (Relegation) Round.

Challenge Round

Results

Round 1 [11-12.03.2021]
Manchester 62 FC - FCB Magpies 1-4
College 1975 FC - Europa Point FC 4-1

Round 2 [20.03.2021]
Glacis United FC - College 1975 FC 4-1
Europa Point FC - Manchester 62 FC 1-4

Round 3 [25-26.03.2021]
Europa Point FC - FCB Magpies 0-4
Glacis United FC - Manchester 62 FC 4-1

Round 4 [03.04.2021]
Manchester 62 FC - College 1975 FC 3-3
FCB Magpies - Glacis United FC 1-5

Round 5 [09-11.04.2021]
College 1975 FC - FCB Magpies 1-8
Glacis United FC - Europa Point FC 3-1

Round 6 [16-18.04.2021]
FCB Magpies - Manchester 62 FC 4-0
Europa Point FC - College 1975 FC 0-6

Round 7 [25.04.2021]
College 1975 FC - Glacis United FC 0-2
Manchester 62 FC - Europa Point FC 4-0

Round 8 [29-30.04.2021]
Manchester 62 FC - Glacis United FC 4-0
FCB Magpies - Europa Point FC 7-0

Round 9 [02-07.05.2021]
College 1975 FC - Manchester 62 FC 0-0
Glacis United FC - FCB Magpies 4-1

Round 10 [22.04./10.05.2021]
FCB Magpies - College 1975 FC 3-0
Europa Point FC - Glacis United FC 0-3

Final Standings

		Total						Home					Away			
7. FC Bruno's Magpies	18	10	2	6	46	-	27	32	5	1	3	23	-	13	5	1	3	23 - 14
8. Glacis United FC	18	10	0	8	35	-	27	30	5	0	5	18	-	17	5	0	3	17 - 10
9. Manchester 62 FC	18	5	2	11	25	-	60	17	4	1	4	18	-	25	1	1	7	7 - 35
10. College 1975 FC	18	2	2	14	23	-	81	8	1	1	8	8	-	43	1	1	6	15 - 38
11. Europa Point FC	18	1	0	17	10	-	73	3	0	0	8	4	-	37	1	0	9	6 - 36

Championship Round

Results

Round 1 [08-10.03.2021]
Lions Gibraltar FC - Lynx FC 0-1
Mons Calpe SC - St. Joseph's FC 0-4
Europa FC - Lincoln Red Imps 0-3

Round 2 [10-11.04.2021]
St. Joseph's FC - Europa FC 1-1
Lynx FC - Lincoln Red Imps 0-7
Lions Gibraltar FC - Mons Calpe SC 0-4

Round 3 [17.04.2021]
Europa FC - Lynx FC 3-0
St. Joseph's FC - Lions Gibraltar FC 1-0
Lincoln Red Imps - Mons Calpe SC 5-1

Round 4 [23-24.04.2021]
Mons Calpe SC - Lynx FC 3-1 [04.04.]
Lions Gibraltar FC - Europa FC 0-2
Lincoln Red Imps - St. Joseph's FC 0-1

Round 5 [26-27.04.2021]
Europa FC - Mons Calpe SC 2-0
Lynx FC - St. Joseph's FC 0-5
Lions Gibraltar FC - Lincoln Red Imps 1-1

Round 6 [01-02.05.2021]
Lincoln Red Imps - Europa FC 3-1
St. Joseph's FC - Mons Calpe SC 1-4
Lynx FC - Lions Gibraltar FC 4-0

Round 7 [04-05.05.2021]
Europa FC - St. Joseph's FC 0-2
Mons Calpe SC - Lions Gibraltar FC 1-0
Lincoln Red Imps - Lynx FC 1-0

Round 8 [08-09.05.2021]
Lynx FC - Europa FC 0-6
Lions Gibraltar FC - St. Joseph's FC 0-2
Mons Calpe SC - Lincoln Red Imps 0-4

Round 9 [11-13.05.2021]
Europa FC - Lions Gibraltar FC 4-0 (0-0)
Lynx FC - Mons Calpe SC 2-2
St. Joseph's FC - Lincoln Red Imps 2-2

Round 10 [15-16.05.2021]
Mons Calpe SC - Europa FC 0-3
St. Joseph's FC - Lynx FC 3-2
Lincoln Red Imps - Lions Gibraltar FC 3-0

Final Standings

		Total						Home					Away			
1. **Lincoln Red Imps FC**	20	15	3	2	62	-	13	48	8	0	1	24	-	5	7	3	1	38 - 8
2. Europa FC	20	15	2	3	66	-	14	47	7	1	2	27	-	8	8	1	1	39 - 6
3. St. Joseph's FC	20	14	3	3	71	-	20	45	5	3	2	38	-	15	9	0	1	33 - 5
4. Mons Calpe SC	20	10	2	8	36	-	35	32	4	1	5	13	-	20	6	1	3	23 - 15
5. Lynx FC	20	8	2	10	36	-	40	26	4	2	5	18	-	26	4	0	5	18 - 14
6. Lions Gibraltar FC	20	4	4	12	13	-	33	16	2	1	6	7	-	16	2	3	6	6 - 17

Top goalscorers:

24	**Enrique "Kike" Gómez Bernal (PHI)**	**Lincoln Red Imps FC**
22	Juan Francisco García Peña "Juanfri" (ESP)	*St. Joseph's FC*
19	Rubén Blanco Rodríguez (ESP)	*FC Bruno's Magpies*
14	Adrián Gallardo Valdés (ESP)	*Europa FC*

NATIONAL CUP
Rock Cup 2020/2021

First Round [06-07.04.2021]

FC Bruno's Magpies - St. Joseph's FC	1-2	Glacis United FC - FC Hound Dogs	6-1
Europa FC - Europa Point FC	10-0	Lincoln Red Imps FC - Lions Gibraltar FC	6-0

Quarter-Finals [13-14.04.2021]

Europa FC - St. Joseph's FC	3-0	Lincoln Red Imps FC - Lynx FC	2-1
Manchester 62 FC - College 1975 FC	1-1 aet; 5-4 pen	Glacis United FC - Mons Calpe SC	1-1 aet; 4-2 pen

Semi-Finals [20-21.04.2021]

Lincoln Red Imps FC - Europa FC	3-0	Manchester 62 FC - Glacis United FC	0-1

19.05.2021; Victoria Stadium, Gibraltar; Referee: Patrick Canepa; Attendance: 0
Lincoln Red Imps FC - Glacis United FC   **2-0(2-0)**

Lincoln Red Imps FC: Manuel Soler Ortuño, Kian Ronan (65.Andre Tjay De Barr), Scott Nigel Kenneth Wiseman, John Iain Stephen Sergeant, Bernardo Morgado Gaspar Lopes, Lee Henry Casciaro (Cap) (80.George Cabrera), Jesús Toscano Serrano (59.Ethan Britto), Fernando Miguel Carralero García, Carlos Leopoldo Martínez Garrido (80.Luke Wall), Enrique "Kike" Gómez Bernal (59.Alejandro "Álex" José Moreno Cerrillo), Graeme Lee Torrilla. Trainer: Michael McElwee (England).

Glacis United FC: Marcos Raúl Zappacosta, Job Derksen, Niall Serra, Miguel Londero (Cap) (86.Pamilerin Olugbogi Aaron), Jamie Bosio (77.Kivan Ramos), Hatim Smith, Samson Bolaji Ajayi, Nicholas Castle, Wessel Witbreuk (46.Alessandro Borghi), Craig Galliano (64.Stefan Moreno), Chibuike Darlington Nwosu. Trainer: Francisco Javier Sánchez Alfaro (Spain).

Goals: 1-0 Enrique "Kike" Gómez Bernal (4), 2-0 Fernando Miguel Carralero García (19).

THE CLUBS 2020/2021

Please note: appearances and goals are including statistics of both regular season and play-offs (Championship and Relegation Round).

Football Club Boca Juniors Gibraltar

Founded:	2012 – Dissolved 2020	
Stadium:	Victoria Stadium, Gibraltar (2,800)	
Trainer:	Aaron Edwards	1979

Football Club Bruno's Magpies

Founded:	2013	
Stadium:	Victoria Stadium, Gibraltar (2,800)	
Trainer:	José Jonathan Parrado Palma "Johny" (ESP)	26.04.1979

Goalkeepers:	DOB	M	(s)	G
Kean Galia	08.10.2003		(1)	
Alan Andrew Martin (SCO)	01.01.1989	8		
Jordan López Pérez	13.11.1986	5		
David Rodríguez Zamora (ESP)	06.03.1986	5		
Defenders:	**DOB**	**M**	**(s)**	**G**
Daniel Bent (ENG)	10.01.1996	12	(1)	
Jaydan Catania	06.03.1993	2		
Lee Coombes	20.06.1998	7		
Javier "Javi" Gallardo (ESP)	30.09.1988	13	(2)	3
Jean-Carlos Anthony Garcia	05.07.1992	15		1
Leeroy Marquez	05.07.2003		(2)	
Rubén Díaz Menacho (ESP)	10.06.1989	13	(2)	1
Francisco Javier Gil Zúñiga (MEX)	22.12.1990	13		3
Midfielders:	**DOB**	**M**	**(s)**	**G**
Federico Cataruozzolo (ARG)	08.09.1987	8	(5)	
Jayce Consigliero	03.08.1997	5	(3)	1
Evan De Haro	28.09.2002	6	(2)	1

	DOB	M	(s)	G
Edilson Oliveira Do Sousa (BRA)	15.02.1995		(1)	
Shay Jones	24.02.2002	4	(5)	1
Kye William Livingstone	09.03.2003	1	(6)	
Jeremy Lopez	09.07.1989	9	(2)	1
Christian Mason	20.09.1998		(2)	
Matheus Barreira Assumpção (BRA)	26.06.1995	5	(5)	
Luis Ignacio "Nacho" Fernández Ríos (ESP)	28.01.1988	5	(6)	
Brian Perez	16.09.1986		(2)	
Tyson Ruiz	10.03.1988	6		
Etien Victory	21.09.1999		(1)	
Jaron Vinet	12.12.1997	11	(1)	2
Forwards:	**DOB**	**M**	**(s)**	**G**
Francisco Javier "Javi" Casares García (ESP)	13.06.1984	8	(1)	5
Kelvin Morgan	14.11.1997	6	(6)	7
Tristan Olivares	25.03.2002		(1)	
Alan Parker	15.05.1996	10	(5)	1
Rubén Blanco Rodríguez "Rubo" (ESP)	15.06.1993	18		19
Steven Soussi	30.07.1992	3	(1)	

College 1975 Football Club

Founded:	1975	
Stadium:	Victoria Stadium, Gibraltar (2,800)	
Trainer:	Ángel Espinosa Domínguez (ESP)	16.12.1991

Goalkeepers:	DOB	M	(s)	G
Eduardo Oliva Ruiz "Edu Oliva" (ESP)	29.03.1994	6		
Kaydon Migge	16.08.2002	5	(1)	
Mark Warwick	21.04.2003	7	(2)	
Defenders:	**DOB**	**M**	**(s)**	**G**
Angel Field	19.08.2002		(3)	
Joanthan Field	25.06.1989	4		
Javier Antonio Galán Cervino (ESP)	2001		(4)	
Shaun Gonzalez	08.11.1993	1	(1)	
Carlos Méndez	23.06.1987	6		
Christopher Parkinson	20.11.1998	1	(5)	
Guillermo Pérez Sánchez (ESP)	12.07.1989	11		1
Jonatan Rodríguez Parragues (ESP)	18.03.1997	10	(2)	1
Stefan Thorne	28.03.2003	6	(5)	
Midfielders:	**DOB**	**M**	**(s)**	**G**
Antonio Bermúdez Sánchez (ESP)	30.09.1999	4	(3)	
Dylan Borrell	23.03.1998		(2)	
Christian Pacheco López (ESP)	19.11.1998	10	(6)	1
Kaylan Franco	13.08.2001	18		1
Johnny Gingell	28.09.2001	2		
Christian Gonzalez	22.10.1992		(1)	

	DOB	M	(s)	G
Nazim Hughes	08.10.1992	11	(3)	
Jemar Matto	19.01.2001	15	(1)	
Estiven Jesús Molina Ortiz (ESP)	11.06.2001	11		
Nacho Callejón Lucena (ESP)	26.07.1997	2	(1)	
Sean Negrette	17.06.2001		(1)	
Antonio Jiménez Ramos "Ñito" (ESP)	07.05.1996	2		
Pablo Ruiz López (ESP)	09.02.1998	5	(8)	
Mattia Ramundo (ITA)	19.11.1993	8		
Alejandro Carlos Valero González (ESP)	1997		(5)	
Daylian Victor	18.01.1996	1	(1)	
Etien Victory	21.09.1999	9	(1)	
Forwards:	**DOB**	**M**	**(s)**	**G**
Zayne Da Costa	15.11.2001	2	(1)	1
Yuri Ruh Dos Santos (POR)	07.02.1998	6	(7)	
Luis Manuel Gallardo Monje (ESP)	20.07.1992	16		8
Adam Gracia	28.05.2001	9	(1)	7
Juan Francisco Ruiz Rincón „Juanfri" (ESP)	01.05.1998	1	(1)	
James Marrache	03.04.2002		(1)	
José María Marín Criado (ESP)	17.01.2001	3	(3)	2
Antonio Jesús Urenda Aranda (ESP)	27.12.1995	6		
Johan Wahnon	05.06.1998		(1)	

Europa Football Club

Founded: 1925
Stadium: Victoria Stadium, Gibraltar (2,800)
Trainer: Rafael Escobar Obrero (ESP) 12.08.1969

Goalkeepers:	DOB	M	(s)	G
Peter Cabezutto	10.05.2004		(1)	
Christian Lopez	10.02.2001	16	(2)	
Jesús Romero Correa (ESP)	17.01.1990	4	(1)	
Defenders:	**DOB**	**M**	**(s)**	**G**
Ibrahim Ayew (GHA)	16.04.1988	9		1
Julian Britto	28.06.2004		(1)	
Liam Crisp	23.09.1999	3		
Ethan Terence Jolley	29.03.1997	14		
Jayce Lee Mascarenhas-Olivero	02.07.1998	11		
Stefan Moreno	23.09.1994		(1)	
Olmo González Casado (ESP)	15.06.1987	8	(3)	
Sergio Jiménez Sánchez (ESP)	22.08.1987	8	(1)	1
Midfielders:	**DOB**	**M**	**(s)**	**G**
Alejandro Rodríguez Rivas "Álex Quillo" (ESP)	07.10.1986	4	(7)	2
Blas Álvarez Cortés (ESP)	19.07.1995	6	(11)	3
Mohamed Badr Hassan	18.11.1989	10	(1)	
Luke Bautista	09.11.2001		(3)	
Jack Breed	18.06.1999	8		
Alejandro Carrascal Avilés (ESP)	24.04.1995	19		4
Leon Clinton	19.07.1998	2	(5)	1
Evan De Haro	28.09.2002		(1)	
Mitch Gibson	08.10.2001	2	(9)	
Kwadwo Poku (GHA)	19.02.1992	1	(3)	
David Álvarez Vázquez "Polaco" (ESP)	19.02.1990	8	(1)	
Marco Rosa Blanco (ESP)	30.11.1995	11	(4)	3
Liam Walker	13.04.1988	12		9
Forwards:	**DOB**	**M**	**(s)**	**G**
Dylan Borge	15.10.2003	8	(12)	11
José Antonio Díaz Verde „Chico Díaz" (ESP)	09.05.1986		(8)	5
Adrián Gallardo Valdés (ESP)	20.11.1987	11	(6)	14
Juan Pedro Rico Domínguez "Juanpe" (ESP)	24.05.1984	20		7
Kyle Rodriguez	19.12.2004		(1)	
Juan Luis Becerra Gallego „Willy" (ESP)	08.09.1989	10	(5)	4
Michael Thomas Yome	29.08.1994	15	(2)	

Europa Point Football Club

Founded: 2014
Stadium: Victoria Stadium, Gibraltar (2,800)
Trainer: Daniel "Dani" Rodríguez Amaya (ESP) 07.03.1975
[02.11.2020] Steve Cummings
[19.03.2021] Craig Cowell (ENG) 04.03.1970

Goalkeepers:	DOB	M	(s)	G
San Mustafa (SWE)	24.03.2001	1		
Daniel Tudela Barreira (ESP)	09.03.1993	15	(1)	
Jake Victor	18.06.1998	2	(1)	
Defenders:	**DOB**	**M**	**(s)**	**G**
Haytham Acharki	2002	2	(2)	
James Castle	13.06.1997	1		
James Chiles-Cowell	14.02.2003	8	(3)	
Tarik Chrayeh	05.11.1986	4	(1)	
Luke Evans	23.10.1999	1	(1)	
Dion Hammond	18.08.1994	4		
Elias Juel-Saleh	06.05.2003	4	(4)	
Jamie-Luke McCarthy	21.07.1992	16		
Antony Moulds	04.02.1988	7		2
Kalian Perez	22.08.1988	2		
Carlos Pomares Pérez (ESP)	19.10.1994	6		
John Andrew Stewart (SCO)	16.05.1999	11	(1)	3
Dayan Torrilla	12.08.2001	2	(3)	1
Midfielders:	**DOB**	**M**	**(s)**	**G**
Pablo Arjona Ramos (ESP)	18.06.1998	5	(1)	
Julio Bado	03.06.1983	8		
Jayan Brennan	26.05.1995	1		
Omar El Yettefti	23.11.2002	11	(6)	
Bradley Hockin (ENG)	26.06.1993	2		
Andrew Lopez	15.04.1984	3		
Davan Martin	29.01.2003	9		1
Mario Iván Martínez Velazco (ESP)	13.09.1997	9	(5)	
Kiri McGrail	22.04.2003	6	(4)	
Louis Parral	13.03.2002	8	(2)	
Cristian Ramirez Cortés (ESP)	08.02.1990	4		
Jacob Webber (ENG)	11.03.2001	9	(4)	
Josef Webber (ENG)	12.08.2002	13	(1)	
Ellis Wilson	11.09.2003	8	(2)	
Forwards:	**DOB**	**M**	**(s)**	**G**
James Adams (FRA)	05.01.1998	1	(2)	
Correro Álvaro Caravante (ESP)	10.03.1994	1	(1)	
Benjamin Dixon (ENG)	21.06.1998	4	(1)	
Dylan Hayes	19.05.1985	3		
Luis Miguel Pérez Lobato (ESP)	05.02.1992	2	(1)	
Paul Podesta	24.07.1990	2		
Alejandro Serralvo Gómez (ESP)	16.05.1999	3	(3)	2

Glacis United Football Club

Founded: 1965
Stadium: Victoria Stadium, Gibraltar (2,800)
Trainer: Paul Aigbogun (NGA) 1972
[25.10.2020] Francisco Javier Sánchez Alfaro (ESP) 18.02.1975

Goalkeepers:	DOB	M	(s)	G
Rubén Fluxá Cano (ESP)	04.01.1995	2	(1)	
Marcos Raúl Zappacosta (ARG)	17.04.1995	16		
Defenders:	**DOB**	**M**	**(s)**	**G**
Marouan Akhrif	2002		(1)	
Loris Andrulli	18.12.1999	4	(1)	
Julian Brinkman	02.01.2003	8	(1)	
Kaydan Byrne	13.10.1998	5	(3)	
James Castle	13.06.1997	5	(2)	
Kivan Castle	21.02.1990	6	(2)	
James Currer	29.06.1992		(1)	
Job Derksen	19.09.1995	14		1
Luke Evans	23.10.1999	3	(2)	
Jarrett Flores	08.06.2000	1	(3)	
Ethan Llambias	23.11.2000	5		
Miguel Londero (ARG)	03.01.1989	11		1
Stefan Moreno	23.09.1994	4		
Jesse Peralta	19.08.2001	1		
Nicholas Perera	17.08.2001		(1)	
Kivan Ramos	29.01.2003	4	(3)	
Niall Serra	03.05.2001	3	(1)	1
Sam Yeo	27.12.2002	6	(1)	
Midfielders:	**DOB**	**M**	**(s)**	**G**
Samson Bolaji Ajayi (NGA)	03.03.1999	6		2
Jamie Bosio	24.09.1991	4		1
Nicholas Castle	18.01.1994	9	(2)	1
Craig Galliano	23.04.2002	6	(2)	5
Quentin Kaleba (FRA)	03.09.1997	6	(3)	
Joshua Kozuh	02.08.1999	4	(1)	
Duncan Lamont (SCO)	20.05.1996		(3)	
Matthew McGowan	24.03.2001		(1)	
Jonathan Moreno	06.07.1995		(1)	
Chibuike Darlington Nwosu (NGA)	02.01.2001	6	(1)	6
Pamilerin Olugbogi Aaron (NGA)	02.06.2001	2	(2)	1
Kevin Poggio	15.11.2000		(3)	
Hatim Smith	25.12.2000	14	(1)	1
Wessel Witbreuk (NED)	30.07.1998	14	(2)	6
Forwards:	**DOB**	**M**	**(s)**	**G**
Alessandro Borghi (ITA)	10.06.2000	4	(3)	2
Stefano Borghi (ITA)	10.03.1996	9		1
Michele Di Piedi (ITA)	04.12.1980		(3)	
Salvatore Gallo (ITA)	19.08.2001	9	(5)	4
Julian Lopez	14.09.1991	1	(2)	
Lython Marquez	06.02.1995	4	(1)	1
Kaydan Peacock			(2)	
Daniel Pratts	06.06.1998	2	(1)	

Lincoln Red Imps Football Club

	Founded:	1976		
	Stadium:	Victoria Stadium, Gibraltar (2,800)		
	Trainer:	Michael McElwee (ENG)		27.06.1961

Goalkeepers:	DOB	M	(s)	G
Kyle Albert Goldwin	24.04.1985	6		
Manuel Soler Ortuño (ESP)	17.09.1986	14		
Defenders:	**DOB**	**M**	**(s)**	**G**
Bernardo Morgado Gaspar Lopes (POR)	30.07.1993	20		6
Ethan Britto	30.11.2000	4	(7)	1
Roy Alan Chipolina	20.01.1983	12		
Kian Ronan	09.03.2001	12	(7)	1
John Iain Stephen Sergeant	27.02.1995	4	(5)	
Jesús Toscano Serrano (ESP)	13.12.1990	17	(2)	
Scott Nigel Kenneth Wiseman	09.10.1985	17		1
Midfielders:	**DOB**	**M**	**(s)**	**G**
Ryan Azopardi	05.05.2003		(2)	
Kyle Casciaro	02.12.1987	5	(2)	2
Kyle Clinton	18.03.2004		(4)	
Diego Antonio Gámiz Maroto (ESP)	07.06.1992	6	(6)	1

Anthony Alland Hernandez	03.02.1995	1	(2)	
Alejandro "Álex" José Moreno Cerrillo (ESP)	09.07.1992	7	(6)	1
Graeme Lee Torrilla	03.09.1997	11	(4)	1
Julian John Valarino	23.06.2000		(6)	
Mustapha Yahaya (GHA)	09.01.1994	12	(2)	5
Forwards:	**DOB**	**M**	**(s)**	**G**
George Cabrera	14.12.1988		(4)	
Fernando Miguel Carralero García (ESP)	16.05.1986	12		5
Lee Henry Casciaro	29.09.1981	5	(3)	1
Finlay Cawthorn	15.03.2004		(1)	1
James Timothy Barry Coombes	27.05.1996	7	(1)	
Andre Tjay De Barr	13.03.2000	19	(1)	3
Enrique "Kike" Gómez Bernal (PHI)	04.05.1994	19	(1)	24
Carlos Leopoldo Martínez Garrido (ESP)	12.02.1989	5	(2)	5
Sunny Ogbemudia Omoregie (NGA)	02.01.1989	1	(4)	1
Luke Wall	11.11.1996	4	(2)	1

Lions Gibraltar Football Club

	Founded:	1966		
	Stadium:	Victoria Stadium, Gibraltar (2,800)		
	Trainer:	Albert Ferri Sola (ESP)		24.02.1970

Goalkeepers:	DOB	M	(s)	G
Borja Valadés González (ESP)	30.06.1988	19		1
Lewis Victor		1		
Defenders:	**DOB**	**M**	**(s)**	**G**
James Bosio	27.03.1991	20		
Craig Bossano-Anes	22.10.2002	5	(4)	
Shea Breakspear	22.11.1991	18		
Jared Buhagiar	20.10.1992	14	(3)	
Thomas Hastings	23.09.1992	19		
Guillermo Jiménez Zorrilla (ESP)	22.03.1991	8	(3)	
Kaylan Alfred Rumbo	12.12.1990	11	(4)	
Stefan Thorne	28.03.2003		(1)	
Adrián Vera Tovar (ESP)	21.02.1990	19		1
Midfielders:	**DOB**	**M**	**(s)**	**G**
Antonio Cintas Sánchez (ESP)	11.05.1995	16		1
Leigh Dobinson	2003		(1)	

Nikolaj Forrester	04.09.2003		(1)	
John Charles Gaivizo	27.07.1993		(3)	
Aiman Mkerreff	11.12.1996		(1)	
Francisco Luis Morales Sánchez (ESP)	07.01.1994	6	(3)	
Iván Ruiz Pecino (ESP)	16.09.1990	13	(4)	1
Cecil Prescott	10.05.1999	3	(8)	
Kadrian Verjaque	25.09.2003	11	(7)	1
Forwards:	**DOB**	**M**	**(s)**	**G**
Michael Alexander Borja Sánchez (ESP)			(6)	
Alberto Caravaca (ESP)	23.03.1990	6		5
Germán Cortés Narváez (ESP)	03.02.1994	15	(4)	2
Ethan Dobinson	16.03.2000	1	(8)	
Byron Espinosa	15.03.1999		(1)	
Dylan Peacock	24.08.2001	10	(1)	
Abraham Pomares Fernández (ESP)	13.09.1992	5	(5)	1

Lynx Football Club

	Founded:	2007		
	Stadium:	Victoria Stadium, Gibraltar (2,800)		
	Trainer:	Albert Parody		30.08.1968

Goalkeepers:	DOB	M	(s)	G
Bradley Avellano	01.11.2002	3	(1)	
Bradley James Banda	20.01.1998	17		
Ayden Vinales	13.02.1998		(1)	
Defenders:	**DOB**	**M**	**(s)**	**G**
Tyronne Avellano	01.05.2000	1	(1)	
David Alberto Bautista Martos „Bauti" (ESP)	27.02.1992	13		2
Germán Damiá Fernández (ESP)	18.01.1990	6		
Gabriel González (ARG)	16.07.1991	11	(2)	
Shaylon Hanglin	24.04.2002		(3)	
Alejandro "Álex" Espinosa Oñate (ESP)	1997	16		
James Parkinson	21.05.2000	2	(5)	
Javan Parody	06.04.1988		(4)	
Brad Philip Power	29.10.1992	18		
Mario Ruesca Torres (ESP)	17.11.1993	7	(4)	2
Thomas Fabrice Som (ITA)	05.08.1988	10		
Midfielders:	**DOB**	**M**	**(s)**	**G**
Estivien Morente Vélez „Estiven" (ESP)	16.02.1991	6	(9)	1
Antonio González García (ESP)	06.05.1996	15	(3)	2

Niels Hartman (NED)	17.01.2001	2		
Francis Huart	11.05.2004		(11)	
Soumaila Konaré (MLI)	22.07.1991	2	(2)	
Jaydan Parody	08.05.1998	8	(3)	1
David Rico Pérez (ESP)	12.03.1999	2		
Ian Rodríguez	20.07.1988		(3)	
Aidan Serra	28.12.1994	13	(3)	
Julian John Valarino	23.06.2000	9	(1)	1
Jesse Victory	02.04.1996	14	(1)	2
Forwards:	**DOB**	**M**	**(s)**	**G**
Cristóbal Atienza Martos (ESP)	13.05.1993		(2)	
Alberto Caravaca Castro (ESP)	23.03.1990	11	(1)	
Juan España Otero (ESP)	14.02.2001	1		
Michael Gracia	25.11.1992	3	(2)	
Aritz Hernández Durán (ESP)	22.10.1997	12	(5)	11
Dylan Hernández Orribo (ESP)	20.04.1996	7		5
Pedro Henrique Santos Pereira Rodrigues (POR)	14.09.2001	2	(7)	1
Michael Ruiz	07.12.2000	3	(11)	2
José Alberto Mateos Valdivia (ESP)	18.01.1996	6	(4)	2

Manchester 62 Football Club

Founded: 1962
Stadium: Victoria Stadium, Gibraltar (2,800)
Trainer: David Wilson (SCO) 22.02.1974

Goalkeepers:	DOB	M	(s)	G
Juan Carlos Bedmar El Abd (ESP)	15.09.1998	7		
Mikey Borge	17.12.2001	2	(2)	
Ayden Vinales	13.02.1998	8		
Frank Warwick	15.03.1994	1		
Defenders:	**DOB**	**M**	**(s)**	**G**
Liam Asquez	02.04.2003		(3)	
Jesse Ballester	30.06.1993	2	(2)	
Ryan Casciaro	11.05.1984	4		
Matthew Clenahan (ENG)	11.02.1996	14	(1)	2
Mark Edzes	14.08.1991	17		1
Tom Farmer (WAL)	11.12.1996	10	(1)	
Jamie Fortuna	07.07.1995	3		
James Holland (ENG)	13.11.1992	1	(3)	
Ryan McCarthy (IRL)	20.08.1995	2	(2)	
Patrick McElwee	08.03.1998	1	(1)	
Daniel Sanchez	11.11.1997	12	(2)	
Peter Sardena	03.03.1996	12	(2)	
Carl Thomas	06.07.1988	9	(2)	

Midfielders:	DOB	M	(s)	G
Scott Ballantine	12.04.1996	15	(1)	3
Dylan De Los Santos	27.06.2002	6	(1)	4
Shaun De Los Santos	26.01.1998	5	(3)	
Carl De Torres	26.02.2005		(1)	
Tito De Torres	27.11.1997	1	(3)	
Kieron Garcia	04.08.1998	13	(4)	1
Robert Guiling	14.10.1980	4		3
Sachin Gupta			(1)	
Dion Mifsud	02.01.1998	3	(8)	
David Moir (SCO)	06.03.2003	1	(4)	
Michael Negrette	14.09.1998	14	(2)	1
Mariano Nicolás Pereira (ARG)	27.03.1990	16	(1)	5
Jyron Zammitt	04.11.2004		(6)	
Forwards:	**DOB**	**M**	**(s)**	**G**
Mark Chichon	24.12.1994	1	(3)	1
Gerson Aldair Mancilla Pacheco (COL)	22.11.1994		(1)	
Robert Montovio	03.08.1984	12	(4)	2
Charles Sardena	21.06.1983		(3)	1
Theo Pizarro	10.07.1998	1	(2)	
Liam Thorne	13.01.1998	1	(3)	1

Mons Calpe Sports Club

Founded: 2013
Stadium: Victoria Stadium, Gibraltar (2,800)
Trainer: César Javier Vega Perrone (URU) 02.09.1959

Goalkeepers:	DOB	M	(s)	G
Christian Hernán Fraiz García (ARG)	22.02.1988	19		
Marco Antonio Montaño Moreno (ESP)	17.07.1994	1		
Jordan Perez	13.11.1986		(1)	
Defenders:	**DOB**	**M**	**(s)**	**G**
André Luiz Dos Santos (BRA)	19.02.1992	15	(4)	3
Mark Ballester	19.03.1995	15	(4)	2
Ayman Boulaich	02.02.1994	1	(1)	
Diego Martín Caballero Manzanares (URU)	13.06.1991	16	(1)	
Emanuel Alejandro Ojeda (BRA)	25.11.1990	18	(2)	
Renan Bernardes Alt (BRA)	21.03.1992	7	(7)	
Ethan James Santos	22.12.1998	18		
Midfielders:	**DOB**	**M**	**(s)**	**G**
Shaun De Los Santos	26.01.1998		(4)	
Mohamed El Andaloussi	28.06.2001		(3)	

	DOB	M	(s)	G
Naoufal El Andaloussi	07.03.1991	9	(6)	3
Ayoub El Hmidi	30.09.2000	18	(1)	6
Ilyias El Ouahabi	20.06.1999		(1)	
Maximiliano Javier Mallemaci (ARG)	29.04.1989	10	(7)	2
Francisco Javier "Javi" Moreno Arjona (ESP)	18.01.1999	2	(5)	1
Karim Dechraqui Piñero (ESP)	30.04.1992		(4)	
Ashley Rodriguez	13.11.1989	17	(2)	
Nahuel Martín Sendín Saldaña (ARG)	12.01.1993	7		
Forwards:	**DOB**	**M**	**(s)**	**G**
Diego Sebastian Díaz (ARG)	01.12.1991	18		11
Lee Muscat	23.09.1988	2	(2)	1
Elyakim Musoni (BEL)	13.12.1994	7	(6)	5
Kevagn Ronco	20.04.1998	13		
Nathan Santos	11.10.1988	7	(4)	
Liam Thorne	13.01.1998		(2)	

St. Joseph's Football Club

Founded: 1912
Stadium: Victoria Stadium, Gibraltar (2,800)
Trainer: Raúl Procopio Baizán (ESP) 10.07.1968

Goalkeepers:	DOB	M	(s)	G
John Paul Hernandez	08.03.2002	1		
Jamie Kevagn Robba	26.10.1991	16		
Francisco Javier Mateo Vera (ESP)	14.08.1990	3		
Harry Victor	29.01.2004		(1)	
Defenders:	**DOB**	**M**	**(s)**	**G**
Erin Anthony Barnett	02.09.1996	16		1
Francisco José Cano Hernández (ESP)	01.03.1991	2	(1)	
Ryan Casciaro	11.05.1984		(1)	
Kenneth Chipolina	08.04.1994	8	(1)	1
Aymen Mouelhi	14.09.1986	16	(1)	
Antony Moulds	04.02.1988	5	(1)	
Mariano González Maroto "Nano" (ESP)	27.10.1984	16		5
Ezequiel Rojas Piñer (ESP)	22.06.1990	5	(6)	2
Jaime Serra	30.10.1998	3	(4)	
Federico Martín Villar (ARG)	24.11.1985	11	(3)	1

Midfielders:	DOB	M	(s)	G
James Caetano	27.09.2004		(1)	
Carlos Carrasco Llorens (ESP)	05.01.1993	5	(8)	1
Domingo Jesús Ferrer López (ESP)	10.04.1989	9	(5)	4
Sykes Garro	26.02.1993	12	(3)	3
Andrew Hernandez	10.01.1999	6	(8)	
Juan Manuel Gonzáles Pérez "Juanma" (ESP)	02.05.1991	12	(4)	2
Cristian Pecci Macías (ESP)	10.05.1988	14	(1)	1
Alain Anthony Pons	16.09.1995	17	(2)	1
Kevagn Robba	20.09.1994		(1)	
Forwards:	**DOB**	**M**	**(s)**	**G**
Stefano Borghi (ITA)	10.03.1996	6	(6)	3
Salvador Manuel Alegre Delgado "Boro"(ESP)	04.05.1991	12	(3)	13
Pedro Jesús Fernández Martínez (ESP)	23.08.1994	4	(4)	6
Ángel Guirado Aldeguer (PHI)	09.12.1984	2	(5)	1
Juan Francisco García Peña "Juanfri" (ESP)	01.10.1989	19	(1)	21

INTERNATIONAL MATCHES
(16.07.2020 – 15.07.2021)

05.09.2020	Gibraltar	Gibraltar - San Marino	1-0(1-0)	(UNL)
07.10.2020	Attard	Malta - Gibraltar	2-0(1-0)	(F)
10.10.2020	Vaduz	Liechtenstein - Gibraltar	0-1(0-1)	(UNL)
11.11.2020	Sofia	Bulgaria - Gibraltar	3-0(3-0)	(F)
14.11.2020	Serravalle	San Marino - Gibraltar	0-0	(UNL)
17.11.2020	Gibraltar	Gibraltar - Liechtenstein	1-1(1-1)	(UNL)
24.03.2021	Gibraltar	Gibraltar - Norway	0-3(0-2)	(WCQ)
27.03.2021	Podgorica	Montenegro - Gibraltar	4-1(2-1)	(WCQ)
30.03.2021	Gibraltar	Gibraltar - Netherlands	0-7(0-1)	(WCQ)
04.06.2021	Koper	Slovenia - Gibraltar	6-0(4-0)	(F)
07.06.2021	Andorra la Vella	Andorra - Gibraltar	0-0	(F)

05.09.2020 GIBRALTAR - SAN MARINO 1-0(1-0) 2nd UEFA Nations League D, Group 2
Victoria Stadium, Gibraltar; Referee: Aleksandrs Anufrijevs (Latvia); Attendance: 0
GIB: Dayle Edward Coleing, Scott Nigel Kenneth Wiseman, Aymen Mouelhi, Jayce Lee Mascarenhas-Olivero, Roy Alan Chipolina (Cap), Ethan Britto, Louie John Annesley (83.Kian Ronan), Liam Walker, Graeme Lee Torrilla (81.John Iain Stephen Sergeant), Anthony Alland Hernandez, Lee Henry Casciaro (77.Mohamed Badr Hassan). Trainer: Julio César Ribas Vlacovich (Uruguay).
Goal: Graeme Lee Torrilla (42).

07.10.2020 MALTA - GIBRALTAR 2-0(1-0) Friendly International
Ta`Qali National Stadium, Attard; Referee: Nikola Popov (Bulgaria); Attendance: 0
GIB: Kyle Albert Goldwin, Scott Nigel Kenneth Wiseman, Aymen Mouelhi, Erin Anthony Barnett (46.Louie John Annesley), John Iain Stephen Sergeant, Ethan Terence Jolley (49.Mohamed Badr Hassan), Jayce Lee Mascarenhas-Olivero (Cap), Alain Anthony Pons (63.Lee Henry Casciaro), Kian Ronan (46.Liam Walker), Reece Styche (50.Andre Tjay De Barr), James Timothy Barry Coombes (46.Graeme Lee Torrilla). Trainer: Julio César Ribas Vlacovich (Uruguay).

10.10.2020 LIECHTENSTEIN - GIBRALTAR 0-1(0-1) 2nd UEFA Nations League D, Group 2
Rheinpark Stadion, Vaduz; Referee: Kirill Levnikov (Russia); Attendance: 178
GIB: Kyle Albert Goldwin, Scott Nigel Kenneth Wiseman, Aymen Mouelhi, Jayce Lee Mascarenhas-Olivero, Louie John Annesley, Liam Walker, John Iain Stephen Sergeant, Graeme Lee Torrilla, Mohamed Badr Hassan (87.Alain Anthony Pons), Andre Tjay De Barr (72.Reece Styche), Lee Henry Casciaro (Cap) (75.Ethan Terence Jolley). Trainer: Julio César Ribas Vlacovich (Uruguay).
Goal: Andre Tjay De Barr (10).

11.11.2020 BULGARIA - GIBRALTAR 3-0(3-0) Friendly International
Nationalen Stadion "Vasil Levski", Sofia; Referee: Constantin Sebastian Colțescu (Romania); Attendance: 0
GIB: Kyle Albert Goldwin, Scott Nigel Kenneth Wiseman (46.Louie John Annesley), Aymen Mouelhi (46.Jayce Lee Mascarenhas-Olivero), Erin Anthony Barnett, Ethan Terence Jolley, Roy Alan Chipolina (Cap) (46.John Iain Stephen Sergeant), Liam Walker (50.James Timothy Barry Coombes), Alain Anthony Pons, Graeme Lee Torrilla (50.Kyle Casciaro), Kian Ronan, Mohamed Badr Hassan (49.Reece Styche). Trainer: Julio César Ribas Vlacovich (Uruguay).

14.11.2020 SAN MARINO - GIBRALTAR 0-0 2nd UEFA Nations League D, Group 2
San Marino Stadium, Serravalle; Referee: Kateryna Monzul (Ukraine); Attendance: 0
GIB: Dayle Edward Coleing, Scott Nigel Kenneth Wiseman, Aymen Mouelhi (66.Reece Styche), Jayce Lee Mascarenhas-Olivero, Roy Alan Chipolina (Cap), Louie John Annesley, Liam Walker, John Iain Stephen Sergeant, Graeme Lee Torrilla (77.Adam James Priestley), Lee Henry Casciaro (54.Kyle Casciaro), Andre Tjay De Barr. Trainer: Julio César Ribas Vlacovich (Uruguay).

17.11.2020 GIBRALTAR - LIECHTENSTEIN 1-1(1-1) 2nd UEFA Nations League D, Group 2
Victoria Stadium, Gibraltar; Referee: Trustin Farrugia Cann (Malta); Attendance: 0
GIB: Dayle Edward Coleing, Scott Nigel Kenneth Wiseman, Aymen Mouelhi, Jayce Lee Mascarenhas-Olivero, Roy Alan Chipolina (Cap), Louie John Annesley, Liam Walker, John Iain Stephen Sergeant, Kian Ronan (87.Erin Anthony Barnett), Mohamed Badr Hassan (70.Ethan Terence Jolley), Andre Tjay De Barr (90+1.Reece Styche). Trainer: Julio César Ribas Vlacovich (Uruguay).
Goal: Noah Frommelt (17 own goal).

24.03.2021 GIBRALTAR - NORWAY 0-3(0-2) 22nd FIFA WC. Qualifiers
Victoria Stadium, Gibraltar; Referee: Duje Strukan (Croatia); Attendance: 0
GIB: Dayle Edward Coleing, Scott Nigel Kenneth Wiseman, Aymen Mouelhi, Jayce Lee Mascarenhas-Olivero, Roy Alan Chipolina (Cap), Louie John Annesley (72.Erin Anthony Barnett), Liam Walker, John Iain Stephen Sergeant, Kian Ronan (67.James Ralph Bosio), Lee Henry Casciaro (78.Julian John Valarino), Andre Tjay De Barr. Trainer: Julio César Ribas Vlacovich (Uruguay).

27.03.2021 MONTENEGRO - GIBRALTAR 4-1(2-1) 22nd FIFA WC. Qualifiers
Stadion pod Goricom, Podgorica; Referee: Manuel Schüttengruber (Austria); Attendance: 0
GIB: Kyle Albert Goldwin, Erin Anthony Barnett, Ethan Terence Jolley, Julian John Valarino (81.Scott Nigel Kenneth Wiseman), Antony James Moulds, James Ralph Bosio (51.Andrew Albert Hernandez), John Iain Stephen Sergeant (Cap), Ethan James Santos, Mohamed Badr Hassan (46.James Timothy Barry Coombes), Alain Anthony Pons (65.Liam Walker), Reece Styche (65.Dylan Borge). Trainer: Julio César Ribas Vlacovich (Uruguay).
Goal: Reece Styche (30 penalty).

30.03.2021 GIBRALTAR - NETHERLANDS 0-7(0-1) 22nd FIFA WC. Qualifiers
Victoria Stadium, Gibraltar; Referee: João Pedro da Silva Pinheiro (Portugal); Attendance: 335
GIB: Dayle Edward Coleing (74.Kyle Albert Goldwin), Scott Nigel Kenneth Wiseman, Aymen Mouelhi, Ethan Terence Jolley (82.Antony James Moulds), Roy Alan Chipolina (Cap), Louie John Annesley (74.Graeme Lee Torrilla), Liam Walker, John Iain Stephen Sergeant, Kian Ronan (41.Erin Anthony Barnett), Lee Henry Casciaro (82.Julian John Valarino), Andre Tjay De Barr. Trainer: Julio César Ribas Vlacovich (Uruguay).

04.06.2021   **SLOVENIA - GIBRALTAR**   6-0(4-0)   Friendly International

Stadion Bonifika, Koper; Referee: Haris Kaljanac (Bosnia and Herzegovina); Attendance: 1,035

GIB: Dayle Edward Coleing, Scott Nigel Kenneth Wiseman, Aymen Mouelhi (68.Ethan James Santos), Roy Alan Chipolina (Cap), Ethan Britto (37.Julian John Valarino), Kenneth George Chipolina (38.Alain Anthony Pons), Louie John Annesley, James Ralph Bosio, Graeme Lee Torrilla, Kian Ronan (68.Mohamed Badr Hassan), Andre Tjay De Barr (69.Kelvin John Morgan). Trainer: Julio César Ribas Vlacovich (Uruguay).

07.06.2021   **ANDORRA - GIBRALTAR**   0-0   Friendly International

Estadi Nacional, Andorra la Vella; Referee: Philip Farrugia (Malta); Attendance: 0

GIB: Dayle Edward Coleing, Scott Nigel Kenneth Wiseman, Aymen Mouelhi, Roy Alan Chipolina (Cap), Ethan Britto (80.Julian John Valarino), Kenneth George Chipolina, Louie John Annesley (80.Reece Styche), James Ralph Bosio, Graeme Lee Torrilla, Kian Ronan, Andre Tjay De Barr (90+1.Ethan James Santos). Trainer: Julio César Ribas Vlacovich (Uruguay).

NATIONAL TEAM PLAYERS
(16.07.2020 – 15.07.2021)

Name	DOB	Caps	Goals	2020/2021:	Club
Goalkeepers					
Dayle Edward COLEING	23.10.1996	11	0	2020/2021:	Glentoran FC Belfast (NIR)
Kyle Albert GOLDWIN	24.04.1985	19	0	2020/2021:	Lincoln Red Imps FC
Defenders					
Erin Anthony BARNETT	02.09.1996	25	0	2020/2021:	St. Joseph's FC
James Ralph BOSIO	27.03.1991	4	0	2021:	Lions Gibraltar FC
Ethan BRITTO	30.11.2000	11	0	2020/2021:	Lincoln Red Imps FC
Kenneth George CHIPOLINA	08.04.1994	3	0	2021:	St. Joseph's FC
Roy Alan CHIPOLINA	20.01.1983	50	2	2020/2021:	Lincoln Red Imps FC
Ethan Terence JOLLEY	29.03.1997	10	0	2020/2021:	Europa FC
Jayce Lee MASCARENHAS-OLIVERO	02.07.1998	34	0	2020/2021:	Europa FC
Aymen MOUELHI	14.09.1986	17	0	2020/2021:	St. Joseph's FC
Antony James MOULDS	04.02.1988	2	0	2021:	St. Joseph's FC
Ethan James SANTOS	22.12.1998	3	0	2021:	Mons Calpe SC
John Iain Stephen SERGEANT	27.02.1995	37	0	2020/2021:	Lincoln Red Imps FC
Scott Nigel Kenneth WISEMAN	09.10.1985	21	0	2020/2021:	Lincoln Red Imps FC
Midfielders					
Louie John ANNESLEY	03.05.2000	19	0	2020/2021:	Blackburn Rovers FC (ENG)
Mohamed BADR Hassan	25.11.1989	11	0	2020/2021:	Europa FC
Kyle CASCIARO	02.12.1987	26	1	2020:	Lincoln Red Imps FC
Andrew Albert HERNANDEZ	10.01.1999	11	0	2021:	St. Joseph's FC
Anthony Alland HERNANDEZ	03.02.1995	24	1	2020:	Lincoln Red Imps FC
Alain Anthony PONS	16.09.1995	23	0	2020/2021:	St. Joseph's FC
Kian RONAN	09.03.2001	8	0	2020/2021:	Lincoln Red Imps FC
Reece STYCHE	03.05.1989	14	2	2020/2021:	Buxton FC (ENG)
Graeme Lee TORRILLA	03.09.1997	8	1	2020/2021:	Lincoln Red Imps FC
Julian John VALARINO	23.06.2000	5	0	2021:	Lynx FC
Liam WALKER	13.04.1988	53	2	2020/2021:	Europa FC
Forwards					
Dylan BORGE	15.10.2003	1	0	2021:	Europa FC
Lee Henry CASCIARO	29.09.1981	39	3	2020/2021:	Lincoln Red Imps FC
James Timothy Barry COOMBES	27.05.1996	19	0	2020/2021:	Lincoln Red Imps FC
Andre Tjay DE BARR	13.03.2000	24	2	2020/2021:	Lincoln Red Imps FC
Kelvin John MORGAN	14.11.1997	1	0	2021:	FC Bruno's Magpies
Adam James PRIESTLEY	14.08.1990	18	1	2020:	Yorkshire Amateur AFC Leeds (ENG)
Trainer					
Julio César RIBAS Vlacovich (Uruguay) [from 01.07.2020/2021]	08.01.1957	27 M; 2 W; 0 D; 14 L; 8-48			

GREECE

The Country:
Ελληνική Δημοκρατία (Hellenic Republic)
Capital: Athína
Surface: 131,957 km²
Inhabitants: 10,718,565 [2020]
Time: UTC+2

The FA:
Hellenic Football Federation
Goudi Park P.O. Box 14161, 11510 Athens
Tel: +30 210 930 6000
Foundation date: 1926
Member of FIFA since: 1927
Member of UEFA since: 1954
Website: www.epo.gr

NATIONAL TEAM RECORDS

RECORDS
First international match:	07.04.1929, Athína:	Greece – Italy "B" 1-4
Most international caps:	Georgios Karagoúnis	- 139 caps (1999-2014)
Most international goals:	Nikolaos Anastopoulos	- 29 goals / 74 caps (1977-1988)

UEFA EUROPEAN CHAMPIONSHIP
1960	Qualifiers
1964	Did not enter
1968	Qualifiers
1972	Qualifiers
1976	Qualifiers
1980	Final Tournament (Group Stage)
1984	Qualifiers
1988	Qualifiers
1992	Qualifiers
1996	Qualifiers
2000	Qualifiers
2004	**Final Tournament (Winners)**
2008	Final Tournament (Group Stage)
2012	Final Tournament (Quarter-Finals)
2016	Qualifiers
2020	Qualifiers

FIFA WORLD CUP
1930	Did not enter
1934	Qualifiers
1938	Qualifiers
1950	Did not enter
1954	Qualifiers
1958	Qualifiers
1962	Qualifiers
1966	Qualifiers
1970	Qualifiers
1974	Qualifiers
1978	Qualifiers
1982	Qualifiers
1986	Qualifiers
1990	Qualifiers
1994	Final Tournament (Group Stage)
1998	Qualifiers
2002	Qualifiers
2006	Qualifiers
2010	Final Tournament (Group Stage)
2014	Final Tournament (2nd Round of 16)
2018	Qualifiers

OLYMPIC TOURNAMENTS
1908	-
1912	-
1920	Quarter-Finals
1924	-
1928	-
1936	-
1948	-
1952	Preliminary Round
1956	-
1960	Qualifiers
1964	Qualifiers
1968	Qualifiers
1972	Qualifiers
1976	Qualifiers
1980	Group Stage
1984	Qualifiers
1988	Qualifiers
1992	Qualifiers
1996	Qualifiers
2000	Qualifiers
2004	Group Stage
2008	Qualifiers
2012	Qualifiers
2016	Qualifiers

UEFA NATIONS LEAGUE
2018/2019	League C
2020/2021	League C

FIFA CONFEDERATIONS CUP 1992-2017
2005 (Group Stage)

GREEK CLUB HONOURS IN EUROPEAN CLUB COMPETITIONS:

European Champion Clubs' Cup (1956-1992) / UEFA Champions League (1993-2021)
None

Fairs Cup (1858-1971) / UEFA Cup (1972-2009) / UEFA Europa League (2010-2021)
None

UEFA Super Cup (1972-2020)
None

*European Cup Winners' Cup 1961-1999**
None

*defunct competition

NATIONAL COMPETITIONS
TABLE OF HONOURS

	CHAMPIONS	CUP WINNERS	BEST GOALSCORERS	
1905/1906	Ethnikos GS Athína	-	-	
1906/1907	Ethnikos GS Athína	-	-	
1907/1908	FC Goudi Athína	-	-	
1908/1909	Peiraikos Syndesmos	-	-	
1909/1910	FC Goudi Athína	-	-	
1910/1911	Podosferikos Omilos Athinon	-	-	
1911/1912	FC Goudi Athína	-	-	
1912/1913	*No competition*	-	-	
1913/1914	*No competition*	-	-	
1914/1915	*No competition*	-	-	
1915/1916	*No competition*	-	-	
1916/1917	*Championship not finished*	-	-	
1917/1918	*No competition*	-	-	
1918/1919	*No competition*	-	-	
1919/1920	*No competition*	-	-	
1920/1921	*No competition*	-	-	
1921/1922	Panellinios Podosferikos Omilos	-	-	
1922/1923	Peiraikos Syndesmos	-	-	
1923/1924	Apollonas Athína (Athína champions) APS Peiraiás (Athína/Peiraiás champions) Aris Thessaloníki (Thessaloníki champions)	-	-	
1924/1925	PAE Panathinaïkos Athína (Athína champions) Olympiacos SFP Peiraiás (Athína/Peiraiás champions)	-	-	
1925/1926	PAE Panathinaïkos Athína (Athína champions) Olympiacos SFP Peiraiás (Athína/Peiraiás champions) Aris Thessaloníki (Thessaloníki champions)	-	-	
1926/1927	PAE Panathinaïkos Athína (Athína champions) Olympiacos SFP Peiraiás (Athína/Peiraiás champions) Iraklis Thessaloníki (Thessaloníki champions)	-	-	
1927/1928	Aris Thessaloníki	-	-	
1928/1929	*No competition*	-	-	
1929/1930	PAE Panathinaïkos Athína	-	-	
1930/1931	Olympiacos SFP Peiraiás	-	-	
1931/1932	Aris Thessaloníki	AEK Athína	-	
1932/1933	Olympiacos SFP Peiraiás	Ethnikos Peiraiás	-	
1933/1934	Olympiacos SFP Peiraiás	*No competition*	-	
1934/1935	*Championship not finished*	*No competition*	-	
1935/1936	Olympiacos SFP Peiraiás	*No competition*	-	
1936/1937	Olympiacos SFP Peiraiás	*No competition*	-	
1937/1938	Olympiacos SFP Peiraiás	*No competition*	-	
1938/1939	AEK Athína	AEK Athína	-	
1939/1940	AEK Athína	PAE Panathinaïkos Athína	-	
1940/1941	*Championship not finished*	*No competition*	-	
1941/1942	*No competition*	*No competition*	-	
1942/1943	*Championship not finished*	*No competition*	-	
1943/1944	*No competition*	*No competition*	-	
1944/1945	*No competition*	*No competition*	-	
1945/1946	Aris Thessaloníki	*No competition*	-	
1946/1947	Olympiacos SFP Peiraiás	Olympiacos SFP Peiraiás	-	
1947/1948	Olympiacos SFP Peiraiás	PAE Panathinaïkos Athína	-	
1948/1949	PAE Panathinaïkos Athína	AEK Athína	-	
1949/1950	*No competition*	AEK Athína	-	
1950/1951	Olympiacos SFP Peiraiás	Olympiacos SFP Peiraiás	-	
1951/1952	*No competition*	Olympiacos SFP Peiraiás	-	
1952/1953	PAE Panathinaïkos Athína	Olympiacos SFP Peiraiás	-	
1953/1954	Olympiacos SFP Peiraiás	Olympiacos SFP Peiraiás	-	
1954/1955	Olympiacos SFP Peiraiás	PAE Panathinaïkos Athína	-	
1955/1956	Olympiacos SFP Peiraiás	AEK Athína	-	
1956/1957	Olympiacos SFP Peiraiás	Olympiacos SFP Peiraiás	-	
1957/1958	Olympiacos SFP Peiraiás	Olympiacos SFP Peiraiás	-	
1958/1959	Olympiacos SFP Peiraiás	Olympiacos SFP Peiraiás	-	
1959/1960	PAE Panathinaïkos Athína	Olympiacos SFP Peiraiás	Konstantinos Nestoridis (AEK Athína)	30
1960/1961	PAE Panathinaïkos Athína	Olympiacos SFP Peiraiás	Konstantinos Nestoridis (AEK Athína)	27
1961/1962	PAE Panathinaïkos Athína	*Final abandoned, no winner*	Konstantinos Nestoridis (AEK Athína)	29
1962/1963	AEK Athína	Olympiacos SFP Peiraiás	Konstantinos Nestoridis (AEK Athína)	23
1963/1964	PAE Panathinaïkos Athína	AEK Athína	Dimitrios Papaioannou (AEK Athína)	29
1964/1965	PAE Panathinaïkos Athína	Olympiacos SFP Peiraiás	Giorgos Sideris (Olympiacos SFP Peiraiás)	29
1965/1966	Olympiacos SFP Peiraiás	AEK Athína	Dimitrios Papaioannou (AEK Athína)	23
1966/1967	Olympiacos SFP Peiraiás	PAE Panathinaïkos Athína	Giorgos Sideris (Olympiacos SFP Peiraiás)	24

1967/1968	AEK Athína	Olympiacos SFP Peiraiás	Thanasis Intzoglou (Panionios GSS Athína)	24
1968/1969	PAE Panathinaïkos Athína	PAE Panathinaïkos Athína	Giorgos Sideris (Olympiacos SFP Peiraiás)	35
1969/1970	PAE Panathinaïkos Athína	Aris Thessaloníki	Antonis Antoniadis (PAE Panathinaïkos Athína)	25
1970/1971	AEK Athína	Olympiacos SFP Peiraiás	Giorgos Dedes (Panionios GSS Athína)	28
1971/1972	PAE Panathinaïkos Athína	PAOK Thessaloníki	Antonis Antoniadis (PAE Panathinaïkos Athína)	39
1972/1973	Olympiacos SFP Peiraiás	Olympiacos SFP Peiraiás	Antonis Antoniadis (PAE Panathinaïkos Athína)	22
1973/1974	Olympiacos SFP Peiraiás	PAOK Thessaloníki	Antonis Antoniadis (PAE Panathinaïkos Athína)	26
1974/1975	Olympiacos SFP Peiraiás	Olympiacos SFP Peiraiás	Antonis Antoniadis (PAE Panathinaïkos Athína) Roberto Calcadera (URU, Ethnikos Peiraiás)	20
1975/1976	PAOK Thessaloníki	Iraklis Thessaloníki	Giorgos Dedes (AEK Athína)	15
1976/1977	PAE Panathinaïkos Athína	PAE Panathinaïkos Athína	Thanasis Intzoglou (Ethnikos Peiraiás) Dimitrios Papadopoulos (OFI Heraklion)	22
1977/1978	AEK Athína	AEK Athína	Thomas Mavros (AEK Athína)	22
1978/1979	AEK Athína	Panionios GSS Athína	Thomas Mavros (AEK Athína)	31
1979/1980	Olympiacos SFP Peiraiás	AGSK Kastoria	Dušan Bajević (YUG, AEK Athína)	25
1980/1981	Olympiacos SFP Peiraiás	Olympiacos SFP Peiraiás	Dinos Kouis (Aris Thessaloníki)	21
1981/1982	Olympiacos SFP Peiraiás	PAE Panathinaïkos Athína	Grigoris Charalampidis (PAE Panathinaïkos Athína)	21
1982/1983	Olympiacos SFP Peiraiás	AEK Athína	Nikolaos Anastopoulos (Olympiacos SFP Peiraiás)	29
1983/1984	PAE Panathinaïkos Athína	PAE Panathinaïkos Athína	Nikolaos Anastopoulos (Olympiacos SFP Peiraiás)	18
1984/1985	PAOK Thessaloníki	AE Lárissa	Thomas Mavros (AEK Athína)	27
1985/1986	PAE Panathinaïkos Athína	PAE Panathinaïkos Athína	Nikolaos Anastopoulos (Olympiacos SFP Peiraiás)	19
1986/1987	Olympiacos SFP Peiraiás	OFI Heraklion	Nikolaos Anastopoulos (Olympiacos SFP Peiraiás)	16
1987/1988	AE Lárissa	PAE Panathinaïkos Athína	Henrik Nielsen (DEN, AEK Athína)	20
1988/1989	AEK Athína	PAE Panathinaïkos Athína	Imre Boda (HUN, Olympiakos Vólos)	20
1989/1990	PAE Panathinaïkos Athína	Olympiacos SFP Peiraiás	Thomas Mavros (Panionios GSS Athína)	22
1990/1991	PAE Panathinaïkos Athína	PAE Panathinaïkos Athína	Dimitrios Saravakos (PAE Panathinaïkos Athína)	23
1991/1992	AEK Athína	Olympiacos SFP Peiraiás	Vasilios Dimitriadis (AEK Athína)	28
1992/1993	AEK Athína	PAE Panathinaïkos Athína	Vasilios Dimitriadis (AEK Athína)	33
1993/1994	AEK Athína	PAE Panathinaïkos Athína	Alexandros Alexandris (AEK Athína) Krzysztof Warzycha (POL, PAE Panathinaïkos Athína)	24
1994/1995	PAE Panathinaïkos Athína	PAE Panathinaïkos Athína	Krzysztof Warzycha (POL, PAE Panathinaïkos Athína)	29
1995/1996	PAE Panathinaïkos Athína	AEK Athína	Vassilis Tsiartas (AEK Athína)	26
1996/1997	Olympiacos SFP Peiraiás	AEK Athína	Alexandros Alexandris (Olympiacos SFP Peiraiás)	23
1997/1998	Olympiacos SFP Peiraiás	Panionios GSS Athína	Krzysztof Warzycha (POL, PAE Panathinaïkos Athína)	32
1998/1999	Olympiacos SFP Peiraiás	Olympiacos SFP Peiraiás	Themistoklis Nikolaidis (AEK Athína)	22
1999/2000	Olympiacos SFP Peiraiás	AEK Athína	Dimitrios Nalitzis (Panionios, PAOK Thessaloníki)	24
2000/2001	Olympiacos SFP Peiraiás	PAOK Thessaloníki	Alexandros Alexandris (Olympiacos SFP Peiraiás)	19
2001/2002	Olympiacos SFP Peiraiás	AEK Athína	Alexandros Alexandris (Olympiacos SFP Peiraiás)	19
2002/2003	Olympiacos SFP Peiraiás	PAOK Thessaloníki	Nikolaos Liberopoulos (PAE Panathinaïkos Athína)	16
2003/2004	PAE Panathinaïkos Athína	PAE Panathinaïkos Athína	Giovanni Silva de Oliveira (BRA, Olympiacos SFP Peiraiás)	21
2004/2005	Olympiacos SFP Peiraiás	Olympiacos SFP Peiraiás	Theofanis Gekas (PAE Panathinaïkos Athína)	18
2005/2006	Olympiacos SFP Peiraiás	Olympiacos SFP Peiraiás	Dimitrios Salpingidis (PAOK Thessaloníki)	17
2006/2007	Olympiacos SFP Peiraiás	AE Lárissa	Nikolaos Liberopoulos (AEK Athína)	18
2007/2008	Olympiacos SFP Peiraiás	Olympiacos SFP Peiraiás	Ismael Alfonso Blanco (ARG, AEK Athína)	19
2008/2009	Olympiacos SFP Peiraiás	Olympiacos SFP Peiraiás	Ismael Alfonso Blanco (ARG, AEK Athína) Luciano Martín Galletti (ARG, Olympiacos SFP Peiraiás)	14
2009/2010	PAE Panathinaïkos Athína	PAE Panathinaïkos Athína	Djibril Cissé (FRA, PAE Panathinaïkos Athína)	23
2010/2011	Olympiacos SFP Peiraiás	AEK Athína	Djibril Cissé (FRA, PAE Panathinaïkos Athína)	20
2011/2012	Olympiacos SFP Peiraiás	Olympiacos SFP Peiraiás	Kevin Antonio Joel Gislain Mirallas y Castillo (BEL, Olympiacos SFP Peiraiás)	22
2012/2013	Olympiacos SFP Peiraiás	Olympiacos SFP Peiraiás	Rafik Djebbour (ALG, Olympiacos SFP Peiraiás)	20
2013/2014	Olympiacos SFP Peiraiás	PAE Panathinaïkos Athína	Esteban Andrés Solari Poggio (ARG, Skoda Xanthi AC)	16
2014/2015	Olympiacos SFP Peiraiás	Olympiacos SFP Peiraiás	Jerónimo Barrales (ARG, AGS Asteras Tripoli)	17
2015/2016	Olympiacos SFP Peiraiás	AEK Athína	Konstantinos Fortounis (Olympiacos SFP Peiraiás)	18
2016/2017	Olympiacos SFP Peiraiás	PAOK Thessaloníki	Bengt Erik Markus Berg (SWE, PAE Panathinaïkos Athína)	22
2017/2018	AEK Athína	PAOK Thessaloníki	Aleksandar Prijović (SRB, PAOK Thessaloníki)	19
2018/2019	PAOK Thessaloníki	PAOK Thessaloníki	Efthymis Koulouris (APS Atromitos Athína)	19
2019/2020	Olympiacos SFP Peiraiás	Olympiacos SFP Peiraiás	Youssef El-Arabi (MAR, Olympiacos SFP Peiraiás)	20
2020/2021	Olympiacos SFP Peiraiás	PAOK Thessaloníki	Youssef El-Arabi (MAR, Olympiacos SFP Peiraiás)	22

Results

Round 1 [11-13.09.2020]
Aris Thessaloníki - Lamia 3-1(0-1)
PAOK Thessaloníki - AE Lárissa 1-0(1-0)
OFI Heraklion - Panetolikos 1-1(0-1)
Atromitos - Vólos 0-2(0-0)
Asteras Tripolis - Panathinaïkos 1-0(0-0)
Ap. Smyrnis - PAS Giannina 1-2(0-2) [21.10.]
AEK Athína - Olympiacos P. 1-1(0-0) [16.12.]

Round 2 [18-20.09.2020]
PAOK Thessaloníki - Atromitos 1-1(0-0)
Olympiacos P. - Asteras Tripolis 3-0(0-0)
Panetolikos - AEK Athína 0-2(0-0)
Lamia - OFI Heraklion 1-2(0-1)
Vólos - Aris Thessaloníki 0-1(0-1)
Panathinaïkos – Ap. Smyrnis 1-0(1-0) [03.11.]
PAS Giannina - AE Lárissa 1-2(0-0) [04.11.]

Round 3 [26-28.09.2020]
Vólos - PAOK Thessaloníki 0-0
Olympiacos Peiraiás - Panetolikos 2-0(0-0)
Aris Thessaloníki - PAS Giannina 2-2(0-2)
OFI Heraklion - Atromitos 2-2(0-1)
AEK Athína - Lamia 3-0(1-0)
AE Lárissa - Panathinaïkos 1-1(0-1)
Asteras Tripolis - Ap. Smyrnis 0-0 [25.11.]

Round 4 [03-05.10.2020]
Panetolikos - Asteras Tripolis 1-1(0-1)
Panathinaïkos - Aris Thessaloníki 0-1(0-1)
Apollon Smyrnis - AE Lárissa 1-0(0-0)
PAOK Thessaloníki - OFI Heraklion 3-0(1-0)
PAS Giannina - Olympiacos Peiraiás 1-1(1-0)
Atromitos - AEK Athína 1-0(1-0)
Lamia - Vólos 1-2(0-1)

Round 5 [17-19.10.2020]
Vólos - PAS Giannina 2-1(0-1)
Aris Thessaloníki - Apollon Smyrnis 1-0(1-0)
Olympiacos Peiraiás - Atromitos 4-0(0-0)
OFI Heraklion - Panathinaïkos 2-2(0-1)
AE Lárissa - Asteras Tripolis 1-3(0-1)
AEK Athína - PAOK Thessaloníki 1-1(1-0)
Lamia - Panetolikos 0-0

Round 6 [24-26.10.2020]
Panathinaïkos - Vólos 1-1(0-0)
Asteras Tripolis - OFI Heraklion 1-0(0-0)
PAS Giannina - AEK Athína 0-1(0-1)
Atromitos - Panetolikos 2-0(1-0)
Lárissa - Aris Thessaloníki 0-3(0-1) [02.12.20]
PAOK Th. - Olympiacos P 1-1(0-0) [13.01.21]
Apollon Smyrnis - Lamia 0-1(0-1) [18.02.21]

Round 7 [31.10.-01.11.2020]
Olympiacos P. - Apollon Smyrnis 2-0(0-0)
Atromitos - PAS Giannina 0-2(0-1)
Vólos - AE Lárissa 1-1(0-0)
Lamia - Panathinaïkos 0-2(0-1)
Aris Thessaloníki - Asteras Tripolis 1-0(0-0)
Panetolikos - PAOK Thessaloníki 1-3(0-1)
AEK Athína - OFI Heraklion 2-1(1-1)

Round 8 [07-08.11.2020]
PAS Giannina - Panetolikos 0-0
Panathinaïkos - Atromitos 0-1(0-0)
OFI Heraklion - Olympiacos Peiraiás 0-2(0-0)
Apoll. Smyrnis - PAOK Thessaloníki 1-3(0-1)
Asteras Tripolis - Vólos 1-1(1-0) [09.12.2020]
Aris Th. - AEK Athína 0-1(0-0) [14.01.2021]
AE Lárissa - Lamia 0-1(0-1) [24.02.2021]

Round 9 [21-23.11.2020]
Lamia - Asteras Tripolis 2-2(0-1)
Atromitos - Apollon Smyrnis 2-2(1-1)
Olympiacos Peiraiás - Panathinaïkos 1-0(1-0)
AEK Athína - AE Lárissa 4-1(0-0)
Panetolikos - Aris Thessaloníki 0-1(0-1)
PAOK Thessaloníki - PAS Giannina 2-1(0-1)
Vólos - OFI Heraklion 1-4(0-1)

Round 10 [28-30.11.2020]
AE Lárissa - Atromitos 0-0
Aris Thessaloníki - Olympiacos P. 1-2(0-1)
Panathinaïkos - Panetolikos 2-1(2-0)
OFI Heraklion - PAS Giannina 2-1(1-1)
Lamia - PAOK Thessaloníki 0-2(0-1)
Asteras Tripolis - AEK Athína 1-2(1-1)
Apollon Smyrnis - Vólos 3-3(1-0)

Round 11 [05-07.12.2020]
Atromitos - Aris Thessaloníki 2-2(1-0)
Olympiacos Peiraiás - Vólos 4-1(1-1)
OFI Heraklion - Apollon Smyrnis 0-2(0-1)
PAOK Thessal. - Asteras Tripolis 2-0(0-0)
PAS Giannina - Lamia 2-0(1-0)
AEK Athína - Panathinaïkos 1-2(0-2)
Panetolikos - AE Lárissa 2-1(1-0)

Round 12 [12-14.12.2020]
AE Lárissa - OFI Heraklion 0-1(0-0)
Panathinaïkos - PAS Giannina 2-0(1-0)
Lamia - Olympiacos Peiraiás 0-6(0-3)
Apollon Smyrnis - AEK Athína 3-4(1-3)
Vólos - Panetolikos 0-0
Aris Thessaloníki - PAOK Thess. 1-0(1-0)
Asteras Tripolis - Atromitos 2-0(1-0)

Round 13 [19-21.12.2020]
Panetolikos - Apollon Smyrnis 0-1(0-1)
OFI Heraklion - Aris Thessaloníki 0-3(0-2)
Olympiacos Peiraiás - AE Lárissa 5-1(2-1)
PAOK Thessaloníki - Panathinaïkos 2-1(1-1)
PAS Giannina - Asteras Tripolis 2-2(1-1)
AEK Athína - Vólos 2-2(1-2)
Atromitos - Lamia 2-1(1-1) [14.01.2021]

Round 14 [03-04.01.2021]
Panathinaïkos - Asteras Tripolis 0-0
Panetolikos - OFI Heraklion 2-1(0-0)
AE Lárissa - PAOK Thessaloníki 1-1(1-0)
PAS Giannina - Apollon Smyrnis 1-3(1-1)
Olympiacos Peiraiás - AEK Athína 3-0(1-0)
Vólos - Atromitos 1-0(1-0)
Lamia - Aris Thessaloníki 2-0(2-0)

Round 15 [06-07.01.2021]
Apollon Smyrnis - Panathinaïkos 0-1(0-1)
AEK Athína - Panetolikos 1-0(1-0)
AE Lárissa - PAS Giannina 0-0
Asteras Tripolis - Olympiacos P. 0-4(0-2)
Aris Thessaloníki - Vólos 2-0(1-0)
OFI Heraklion - Lamia 2-0(1-0)
Atromitos - PAOK Thessaloníki 3-2(0-1)

Round 16 [09-11.01.2021]
Panetolikos - Olympiacos Peiraiás 1-2(0-1)
PAOK Thessaloníki - Vólos 3-1(1-1)
Apollon Smyrnis - Asteras Tripolis 0-1(0-1)
Atromitos - OFI Heraklion 0-0
Panathinaïkos - AE Lárissa 2-0(1-0)
PAS Giannina - Aris Thessaloníki 0-0
Lamia - AEK Athína 0-1(0-1)

Round 17 [16-17.01.2021]
Asteras Tripolis - Panetolikos 2-0(1-0)
AE Lárissa - Apollon Smyrnis 0-1(0-0)
Olympiacos Peiraiás - PAS Giannina 1-0(0-0)
Vólos - Lamia 1-1(0-0)
OFI Heraklion - PAOK Thessaloníki 0-3(0-0)
Aris Thessaloníki - Panathinaïkos 0-1(0-1)
AEK Athína - Atromitos 2-1(0-0)

Round 18 [23-24.01.2021]
Asteras Tripolis - AE Lárissa 1-0(0-0)
Apollon Smyrnis - Aris Thessaloníki 0-1(0-1)
Panathinaïkos - OFI Heraklion 2-0(1-0)
Atromitos - Olympiacos Peiraiás 0-1(0-1)
Panetolikos - Lamia 0-0
PAS Giannina - Vólos 0-1(0-1)
PAOK Thessaloníki - AEK Athína 2-2(1-1)

Round 19 [26-28.01.2021]
OFI Heraklion - Asteras Tripolis 0-1(0-1)
Aris Thessaloníki - AE Lárissa 1-0(1-0)
Vólos - Panathinaïkos 0-2(0-1)
AEK Athína - PAS Giannina 0-2(0-1)
Lamia - Apollon Smyrnis 1-0(1-0)
Olympiacos P. - PAOK Thessaloníki 3-0(0-0)
Panetolikos - Atromitos 1-1(0-0)

Round 20 [30-31.01.2021]
AE Lárissa - Vólos 0-0
Asteras Tripolis - Aris Thessaloníki 2-1(0-1)
Panathinaïkos - Lamia 0-0
OFI Heraklion - AEK Athína 0-2(0-1)
PAOK Thessaloníki - Panetolikos 5-0(1-0)
PAS Giannina - Atromitos 0-1(0-1)
Apollon Smyrnis - Olympiacos P. 1-3(0-1)

Round 21 [06-08.02.2021]
Atromitos - Panathinaïkos 2-3(1-1)
PAOK Thess. - Apollon Smyrnis 2-2(1-0)
Vólos - Asteras Tripolis 0-1(0-1)
Olympiacos Peiraiás - OFI Heraklion 3-0(2-0)
AEK Athína - Aris Thessaloníki 0-2(0-1)
Panetolikos - PAS Giannina 1-2(1-0)
Lamia - AE Lárissa 2-1(1-1) [10.03.]

Round 22 [13-15.02.2021]
Asteras Tripolis - Lamia 0-0
Apollon Smyrnis - Atromitos 2-1(1-0)
Aris Thessaloníki - Panetolikos 0-0
OFI Heraklion - Vólos 1-2(0-2)
Panathinaïkos - Olympiacos Peiraiás 2-1(1-0)
AE Lárissa - AEK Athína 2-4(0-2)
PAS Giannina - PAOK Thessaloníki 0-2(0-0)

Round 23 [20-22.02.2021]
Atromitos - AE Lárissa 1-1(0-1)
AEK Athína - Asteras Tripolis 2-2(1-2)
Vólos - Apollon Smyrnis 2-0(1-0)
PAOK Thessaloníki - Lamia 4-0(1-0)
PAS Giannina - OFI Heraklion 1-0(1-0)
Olympiacos P. - Aris Thessaloníki 1-1(1-0)
Panetolikos - Panathinaïkos 1-0(1-0)

Round 24 [27.02.-01.03.2021]
Apollon Smyrnis - OFI Heraklion 2-1(1-1)
Asteras Tripolis - PAOK Thess. 2-1(1-0)
Aris Thessaloníki - Atromitos 3-0(1-0)
AE Lárissa - Panetolikos 1-0(1-0)
Lamia - PAS Giannina 0-0
Panathinaïkos - AEK Athína 1-1(0-0)
Vólos - Olympiacos Peiraiás 1-2(1-1)

Round 25 [06-08.03.2021]
OFI Heraklion - AE Lárissa 2-3(1-1)
Atromitos - Asteras Tripolis 1-1(1-0)
PAS Giannina - Panathinaïkos 1-0(1-0)
Olympiacos Peiraiás - Lamia 3-0(3-0)
Panetolikos - Vólos 1-0(0-0)
PAOK Thess. - Aris Thessaloníki 2-2(0-1)
AEK Athína - Apollon Smyrnis 2-0(2-0)

Round 26 [14.03.2021]
AE Lárissa - Olympiacos Peiraiás 1-3(0-1)
Apollon Smyrnis - Panetolikos 1-0(0-0)
Aris Thessaloníki - OFI Heraklion 1-0(1-0)
Asteras Tripolis - PAS Giannina 0-1(0-0)
Vólos - AEK Athína 1-0(1-0)
Panathinaïkos - PAOK Thessaloníki 2-1(1-0)
Lamia - Atromitos 0-0

Final Standings

1.	Olympiacos SFP Peiraiás	26	21	4	1	64	-	13	67
2.	Aris Thessaloníki	26	15	6	5	34	-	16	51
3.	AEK Athína	26	14	6	6	41	-	29	48
4.	PAOK Thessaloníki	26	13	8	5	49	-	26	47
5.	PAE Panathinaïkos Athína	26	13	6	7	30	-	19	45
6.	AGS Asteras Tripolis	26	11	9	6	27	-	25	42
7.	Vólos NPS	26	8	9	9	26	-	32	33
8.	PAS Giannina	26	8	7	11	23	-	26	31
9.	GS Apollon Smyrnis	26	8	4	14	26	-	35	28
10.	APS Atromitos Athína	26	6	10	10	24	-	35	28
11.	PAS Lamia	26	5	8	13	14	-	38	23
12.	Panetolikos GPS Agrinio	26	4	8	14	13	-	32	20
13.	OFI Heraklion	26	5	4	17	22	-	43	19
14.	AE Lárissa	26	3	7	16	18	-	42	16

Teams ranked 1-6 were qualified for the Championship Round, while teams ranked 7-14 were qualified for the Relegation Round.

Relegation Round

Results

Round 27 [20.03.2021]
Apollon Smyrnis - AE Lárissa 0-2(0-0)
Vólos - OFI Heraklion 0-0
PAS Giannina - Atromitos 1-0(1-0)
Panetolikos - Lamia 0-3(0-3)

Round 28 [03.04.2021]
Atromitos - Apollon Smyrnis 1-1(0-0)
OFI Heraklion - PAS Giannina 2-1(0-1)
AE Lárissa - Panetolikos 1-1(1-0)
Lamia - Vólos 1-1(0-0)

Round 29 [10-12.04.2021]
Vólos - Panetolikos 3-1(3-1)
Apollon Smyrnis - OFI Heraklion 0-0
Atromitos - AE Lárissa 0-1(0-1)
PAS Giannina - Lamia 1-2(1-0)

Round 30 [17-19.04.2021]
OFI Heraklion - Atromitos 1-1(0-0)
Panetolikos - Apollon Smyrnis 1-0(0-0)
Vólos - PAS Giannina 1-1(1-1)
Lamia - AE Lárissa 0-0

Round 31 [24-26.04.2021]
PAS Giannina - Panetolikos 0-1(0-1)
AE Lárissa - OFI Heraklion 0-1(0-1)
Atromitos - Lamia 0-0
Apollon Smyrnis - Vólos 0-0

Round 32 [08.05.2021]
Panetolikos - Atromitos 1-3(0-2)
Lamia - OFI Heraklion 0-2(0-1)
Vólos - AE Lárissa 3-1(2-0)
PAS Giannina - Ap. Smyrnis 0-2(0-1) [19.05.]

Round 33 [15.05.2021]
OFI Heraklion - Panetolikos 2-2(1-0)
AE Lárissa - PAS Giannina 2-0(2-0)
Apollon Smyrnis - Lamia 0-1(0-1)
Atromitos - Vólos 1-0(0-0)

Final Standings

		Total								Home							Away					
7.	Vólos NPS	33	10	13	10	34	-	37	43	6	6	5	17	-	16	4	7	5	17	-	21
8.	APS Atromitos Athína	33	8	13	12	30	-	40	37	5	7	5	18	-	19	3	6	7	12	-	21
9.	PAS Giannina	33	9	8	16	27	-	36	35	4	4	9	11	-	18	5	4	7	16	-	18
10.	PAS Lamia	33	8	11	14	21	-	42	35	3	6	7	10	-	21	5	5	7	11	-	21
11.	GS Apollon Smyrnis	33	9	7	17	29	-	40	34	4	3	10	15	-	24	5	4	7	14	-	16
12.	OFI Heraklion	33	8	8	17	30	-	47	32	3	5	8	17	-	28	5	3	9	13	-	19
13.	Panetolikos GPS Agrinio (Relegation Play-offs)	33	6	10	17	20	-	44	28	5	3	8	13	-	21	1	7	9	7	-	23
14.	AE Lárissa (Relegated)	33	6	9	18	25	-	47	27	2	6	8	10	-	20	4	3	10	15	-	27

Results

Round 27 [21.03.2021]
Asteras Tripolis - Panathinaïkos 2-2(0-0)
Olympiacos P. - Aris Thessaloníki 1-0(1-0)
PAOK Thessaloníki - AEK Athína 3-1(1-1)

Round 28 [04.04.2021]
Panathinaïkos - PAOK Thessaloníki 3-0(1-0)
Aris Thessaloníki - Asteras Tripolis 2-0(0-0)
AEK Athína - Olympiacos Peiraiás 1-5(0-4)

Round 29 [11.04.2021]
Aris Thessaloníki - AEK Athína 1-3(0-3)
Asteras Tripolis - PAOK Thess. 1-1(0-0)
Olympiacos Peiraiás - Panathinaïkos 3-1(1-1)

Round 30 [18.04.2021]
Panathinaïkos - Aris Thessaloníki 1-2(1-0)
AEK Athína - Asteras Tripolis 3-1(1-1)
PAOK Thessaloníki - Olympiacos P. 2-0(0-0)

Round 31 [21.04.2021]
Olympiacos P. - Asteras Tripolis 1-0(0-0)
Aris Thessaloníki - PAOK Thess. 0-1(0-1)
AEK Athína - Panathinaïkos 1-1(0-1)

Round 32 [25.04.2021]
PAOK Thessaloníki - Panathinaïkos 0-0
Asteras Tripolis - Aris Thessaloníki 1-1(0-0)
Olympiacos Peiraiás - AEK Athína 2-0(0-0)

Round 33 [05.05.2021]
Aris Thessaloníki - Olympiacos P. 1-1(1-0)
Panathinaïkos - Asteras Tripolis 2-2(1-2)
AEK Athína - PAOK Thessaloníki 1-2(0-0)

Round 34 [09.05.2021]
PAOK Thess. - Aris Thessaloníki 2-0(0-0)
Asteras Tripolis - Olympiacos Peiraiás 0-0
Panathinaïkos - AEK Athína 0-1(0-0)

Round 35 [12.05.2021]
Aris Thessaloníki - Panathinaïkos 0-0
Asteras Tripolis - AEK Athína 1-1(0-0)
Olympiacos P. - PAOK Thessaloníki 1-0(1-0)

Round 36 [16.05.2021]
AEK Athína - Aris Thessaloníki 0-0
Panathinaïkos - Olympiacos Peiraiás 1-4(0-3)
PAOK Thess. - Asteras Tripolis 0-1(0-1)

Final Standings

						Total			Home					Away		
1.	**Olympiacos SFP Peiraiás**	36	28	6	2	82 - 19	90	17	1	0	43 - 4	11	5	2	39 - 15
2.	PAOK Thessaloníki	36	18	10	8	60 - 34	64	11	6	1	37 - 13	7	4	7	23 - 21
3.	Aris Thessaloníki	36	17	10	9	41 - 26	61	9	4	5	20 - 12	8	6	4	21 - 14
4.	AEK Athína	36	17	9	10	53 - 45	60	7	6	5	27 - 24	10	3	5	26 - 21
5.	PAE Panathinaïkos Athína	36	14	11	11	41 - 34	53	8	5	5	22 - 16	6	6	6	19 - 18
6.	AGS Asteras Tripolis	36	12	15	9	36 - 38	51	7	8	3	18 - 15	5	7	6	18 - 23

Top goalscorers:

22	**Youssef El-Arabi (MAR)**	*Olympiacos SFP Peiraiás)*
13	Giorgos Masouras	*Olympiacos SFP Peiraiás*
13	Karim Ansarifard (IRN)	*AEK Athína*
11	Karol Świderski (POL)	*PAOK Thessaloníki*
11	Anastasios Douvikas	*Vólos NPS*
11	Jerónimo Barrales (ARG)	*AGS Asteras Tripolis*

Relegation Play-offs [26-30.05.2021]

AO Xanthi - Panetolikos GPS Agrinio   2-1(0-1)   0-1(0-0)

Panetolikos GPS Agrinio remains at first level for 2021/2022.

NATIONAL CUP
Greek Football Cup - Kypello Elladas 2020/2021

Third Round [20-21.01./03-04.02.2021]

First Leg		Second Leg	
Vólos NPS - OFI Heraklion	2-0(0-0)	OFI Heraklion - Vólos NPS	1-1(1-1)
Aris Thessaloníki - AGS Asteras Tripolis	2-0(0-0)	AGS Asteras Tripolis - Aris Thessaloníki	0-2(0-1)
PAOK Thessaloníki - AE Lárissa	5-0(2-0)	AE Lárissa - PAOK Thessaloníki	1-2(1-2)
Panetolikos GPS Agrinio - Olympiacos SFP Peiraiás	0-3(0-1)	Olympiacos SFP Peiraiás - Panetolikos GPS Agrinio	3-0(2-0)
AEK Athína - GS Apollon Smyrnis	2-0(1-0)	GS Apollon Smyrnis - AEK Athína	2-1(2-1)
PAS Giannina - APS Atromitos Athína	2-2(1-2)	APS Atromitos Athína - PAS Giannina	2-3(1-3)

Quarter-Finals [10/18.02./03-04.03.2021]

First Leg		Second Leg	
AEK Athína - Vólos NPS	4-2(4-1)	Vólos NPS - AEK Athína	1-0(1-0)
PAOK Thessaloníki - PAS Lamia	5-2(2-2)	PAS Lamia - PAOK Thessaloníki	1-1(0-1)
Olympiacos SFP Peiraiás - Aris Thessaloníki	2-1(2-1)	Aris Thessaloníki - Olympiacos SFP Peiraiás	1-1(0-0)
PAS Giannina - PAE Panathinaïkos Athína	2-1(1-1)	PAE Panathinaïkos Athína - PAS Giannina	1-2(0-2)

Semi-Finals [07/28-29.04.2021]				

First Leg			Second Leg	
PAS Giannina - Olympiacos SFP Peiraiás	1-1(1-0)		Olympiacos SFP Peiraiás - PAS Giannina	3-1(2-0)
AEK Athína - PAOK Thessaloníki	0-1(0-0)		PAOK Thessaloníki - AEK Athína	2-1(0-0)

Final

22.05.2021; Stádio Olympiako „Spiros Louis", Athína; Referee: Danny Desmond Makkelie (Netherlands); Attendance: 0
PAOK Thessaloníki - Olympiacos SFP Peiraiás   **2-1(1-0)**

PAOK: Alexandros Paschalakis, Adelino André Vieira de Freitas „Vieirinha" (Cap), Fernando Lopes dos Santos Varela, José Ángel Crespo Rincón, Rodrigo Alves Soares, Abdul Rahman Baba (90+5.Enea Mihaj), Stefan Schwab, Douglas Augusto Soares Gomes, Andrija Živković, Amr Warda (80.Michael Krmenčík), Karol Świderski (80.Theocharis Tsingaras). Trainer: Pablo Gabriel García Pére (Uruguay).

Olympiacos: José Pedro Malheiro de Sá, Rúben Afonso Borges Semedo, Sokratis Papastathopoulos (25.Oleg Reabciuk), Athanasios Androutsos, José Cholevas, Yann Gérard M'Vila, Mady Camara (90+1.Mathieu Valbuena), Andreas Bouchalakis (Cap), Armindo Tué Na Bangna „Bruma" (46.Konstantinos Fortounis), Georgios Masouras (46.Ahmed Hassan Mahgoub Abdelmoneim), Youssef El-Arabi. Trainer: Pedro Rui da Mota Vieira Martins (Portugal).

Goals: 1-0 (36 penalty), 1-1 Yann Gérard M'Vila (50), 2-1 (90).

THE CLUBS 2020/2021

Please note: appearances and goals are including statistics of both regular season and play-offs (Championship and Relegation Round).

Athlitikí Énosis Konstantinoupóleos Athína

Founded:	13.04.1924			
Stadium:	Stádio Olympiako „Spiros Louis", Athína (69,618)			
Trainer:	Massimo Carrera (ITA)		22.04.1964	
[27.12.2020]	Manuel "Manolo" Jiménez Jiménez(ESP)		26.01.1964	

Goalkeepers:	DOB	M	(s)	G
Georgios Athanasiadis	07.04.1993	19		
Panagiotis Tsintotas	04.07.1993	17		
Defenders:	**DOB**	**M**	**(s)**	**G**
Michalis Bakakis	18.03.1991	14	(1)	
Dmitro Chigrinskiy (UKR)	07.11.1986	15	(1)	
Oleg Danchenko (UKR)	01.08.1994	4	(3)	
Hélder Filipe Oliveira Lopes (POR)	04.01.1989	23	(6)	1
Nassim Hnid (TUN)	12.03.1997	7	(3)	
Emanuel Mariano Insúa Zapata (ARG)	10.04.1991	6	(7)	
Žiga Laci (SVN)	20.07.2002	10	(1)	
Mario Mitaj (ALB)	06.08.2003	7	(3)	
Ionuț Nedelcearu (ROU)	25.04.1996	20	(5)	1
Paulo Sérgio Mota „Paulinho" (POR)	13.07.1991	8	(2)	
Vedad Radonja (BIH)	06.09.2001	1		
Efstratios Svarnas	11.11.1997	26	(4)	
Stavros Vasilantonopoulos	28.01.1992	10	(3)	1
Midfielders:	**DOB**	**M**	**(s)**	**G**
André Luis Gomes Simões (POR)	16.12.1989	13	(5)	2

Giannis-Fivos Botos	20.12.2000		(1)	
Konstantinos Galanopoulos	28.12.1997	11	(8)	4
Nenad Krstičić (SRB)	03.07.1990	18	(7)	1
Petros Mantalos	31.08.1991	27	(6)	2
Giannis Sardelis	03.11.2000		(1)	
Yevhen Shakhov (UKR)	30.11.1990	18	(7)	3
Damian Szymański (POL)	16.06.1995	17	(4)	3
Anel Šabanadžović (BIH)	24.05.1999		(2)	
Forwards:	**DOB**	**M**	**(s)**	**G**
Christos Albanis	05.11.1994	10	(12)	2
Karim Ansarifard (IRN)	03.04.1990	28	(6)	13
Efthymios Christopoulos	20.09.2000		(3)	
Bright Enobakhare (NGA)	08.02.1998		(1)	1
Levi Samuel García (TRI)	20.11.1997	23	(3)	5
Michalis Kosidis	09.02.2002		(6)	
Marko Livaja (CRO)	26.08.1993	10	(7)	3
Theodosis Macheras	09.05.2000	5	(11)	1
Nélson Miguel Castro Oliveira (POR)	08.08.1991	12	(14)	6
Muamer Tanković (SWE)	22.02.1995	17	(10)	4

Athlitiki Enosi Lárissa

Founded:	17.05.1964			
Stadium:	Stádio Alcazar, Larissa (13,108)			
Trainer:	Michalis Grigoriou		19.12.1973	
[23.11.2020]	Giannis Tatsis		15.08.1972	
[21.01.2021]	Gianluca Festa (ITA)		16.03.1969	
[10.05.2021]	Michalis Ziogas		27.06.1962	

Goalkeepers:	DOB	M	(s)	G
Vladimir Bajić (SRB)	28.11.1987	7		
Gergely Nagy (HUN)	27.05.1994	25		
Stefanos Souloukos	04.01.2001	1		
Defenders:	**DOB**	**M**	**(s)**	**G**
Manolis Bertos	13.05.1989	25	(2)	
Uroš Ćosić (SRB)	24.10.1992	9	(1)	
Steliano Filip (ROU)	15.05.1994	15		
Nikolaos Gotzamanidis	25.01.2001	1	(2)	
Dinu Graur (MDA)	27.12.1994	5	(3)	
Orestis Grigoropoulos	04.07.2000	1	(7)	
Theocharis Iliadis	05.09.1996	18	(4)	
Adrián Johnny Jusino Cerruto (BOL)	09.07.1992	5	(2)	
Nikolaos Karanikas	04.03.1992	3	(4)	
Georgios Maidanos	12.04.1998	1	(4)	
Maksym Maksymenko (UKR)	28.05.1990	13		
Alexandros Michail	18.08.1986	17	(1)	
Mateo Mužek (CRO)	29.04.1995	6	(3)	1
Nikola Žižić (CRO)	23.01.1988	19	(2)	
Midfielders:	**DOB**	**M**	**(s)**	**G**
Änis Ben-Hatira (TUN)	18.07.1988	8	(3)	
Alexandros Chalatsis	16.06.2000	1	(2)	
Adrián Nicolás Colombino Rodríguez (URU)	12.10.1993	18	(1)	1

Georgios Daktylas	22.09.2001		(1)	
Nikola Jakimovski (MKD)	26.02.1990	12		
Ioannis Kosti (CYP)	17.03.2000	1	(2)	
Radomir Milosavljević (SRB)	28.07.1992	17	(8)	
Aly Ahmed Aly Mohamed (EGY)	01.02.1992		(4)	
Alexandros Nikolias	23.07.1994	17	(4)	1
Tim Sparv (FIN)	20.02.1987	16	(3)	1
Manuel Stiefler (GER)	25.07.1988	11	(1)	1
Adnan Šećerović (BIH)	01.12.1991	4	(1)	
Forwards:	**DOB**	**M**	**(s)**	**G**
Mathías Alexander Acuña Maciel (URU)	28.11.1992	15	(2)	4
Fiorin Durmishaj (ALB)	14.11.1996	22	(5)	5
Spyros Glynos	02.12.1997	2	(9)	
Apostolos Kotsianoulis	29.01.2001		(1)	
Benjamin Moukandjo Bile (CMR)	12.11.1988	4	(6)	
Marko Nunič (SVN)	16.03.1993	1	(11)	2
Dimitrios Pinakas	01.09.2001	21	(8)	7
Vangelis Platellas	01.12.1988	9	(4)	
Gabriel Andrei Torje (ROU)	22.11.1989	4	(4)	
Nikola Trujić (SRB)	14.04.1992	7	(9)	
Hamza Younès (TUN)	16.04.1986	2	(5)	1
Georgios Zacharakis	02.01.2001		(3)	

Gymnastics Club Apollon of Smyrna

Founded: 1891
Stadium: Stádio „Georgios Kamaras", Athína (14,200)
Trainer: Georgios Paraschos   23.08.1952
[17.03.2021] Makis Chavos   05.09.1969

Goalkeepers:	DOB	M	(s)	G
Konstantinos Kotsaris	25.07.1996	3		
Davino Verhulst (BEL)	25.11.1987	30	(1)	
Defenders:	**DOB**	**M**	**(s)**	**G**
Dimosthenis Baxevanidis	14.04.1988	31	(1)	1
Karlo Bručić (CRO)	17.04.1992	20	(3)	
André Calisir (ARM)	13.06.1990	5	(3)	
Diamantis Chouchoumis	17.07.1994	20	(5)	
Luiz Gustavo Domingues (BRA)	28.09.1988	32	(1)	1
Christos Lisgaras	12.02.1986	28		
Adil Rhaili (MAR)	25.04.1991	1		
Antonis Rigopoulos	10.06.2004		(1)	
Savvas Tsabouris	16.07.1986	8	(12)	2
Vasilios Vitlis	28.10.1993	4	(5)	
Midfielders:	**DOB**	**M**	**(s)**	**G**
Fatjon Andoni (ALB)	19.06.1991	26	(2)	5
Israel Coll Emanuel (ARG)	22.07.1993	24	(6)	
Ritchie Kitoko (BEL)	11.06.1988	1	(8)	
Manolis Kragiopoulos	29.05.1998		(1)	
Anastasios Lagos	12.04.1992	3	(11)	
Leonidas Rossi (ALB)	19.04.1999	1	(4)	
Vykintas Slivka (LTU)	29.04.1995	24	(2)	1
Forwards:	**DOB**	**M**	**(s)**	**G**
Abiola Adedeji Dauda (NGA)	03.02.1988	13	(15)	5
Nikolaos Ioannidis	26.04.1994	20	(10)	4
Thanasis Karagounis	25.09.1991		(2)	
Marc Fernández Gràcia (ESP)	29.04.1990	18	(11)	4
Anthony Mounier (FRA)	27.09.1987	4	(20)	
Thomás Jaguaribe Bedinelli (BRA)	24.02.1993	27	(3)	2
Sotiris Tsiloulis	14.02.1995	20	(5)	4
Giannis Varkas	27.03.1998		(5)	

Aris Thessaloníki

Founded: 25.03.1914
Stadium: Stádio " Kleanthis Vikelidis", Thessaloníki (22,800)
Trainer: Michael Oenning (GER)   27.09.1965
[18.09.2020] Apostolos Terzis   13.03.1971
[21.09.2020] Apostolos Mantzios   21.10.1969

Goalkeepers:	DOB	M	(s)	G
Zacharie Boucher (FRA)	07.03.1992	9		
Julián Cuesta Díaz (ESP)	28.03.1991	18		
Marios Siabanis	28.09.1999	9		
Defenders:	**DOB**	**M**	**(s)**	**G**
Petros Bagalianis	06.02.2001		(8)	
Yohan Benalouane (TUN)	28.03.1987	14	(2)	
Toni Datković (CRO)	06.11.1993	3		
Georgios Delizisis	01.12.1987	23		
Cristian George Ganea (ROU)	24.05.1992	17	(5)	1
Nikolas Ioannou (CYP)	10.11.1995	5	(4)	1
Lindsay Rose (MRI)	08.02.1992	33	(1)	2
Emanuel Sakić (AUT)	25.01.1991	24	(7)	
Daniel Sundgren (SWE)	22.11.1990	26	(5)	
Panagiotis Tsagalidis	05.03.2001		(1)	
Midfielders:	**DOB**	**M**	**(s)**	**G**
Petros Bakoutsis	29.06.2001		(1)	
Facundo Daniel Bertoglio (ARG)	30.06.1990	26	(6)	6
Javier Magro Matilla (ESP)	01.01.1988	19	(8)	2
James Alexander Jeggo (AUS)	12.02.1992	23	(7)	
Ergys Kaçe (ALB)	08.07.1993	1	(11)	1
Lucas Pacheco Affini „Sasha" (BRA)	01.03.1990	31	(4)	3
Forwards:	**DOB**	**M**	**(s)**	**G**
Bruno Felipe Souza da Silva (BRA)	26.05.1994	4	(8)	
Bruno Alexandre Vilela Gama (POR)	15.11.1987	31	(2)	5
Konstantinos Chatzipirpiridis	01.05.2001		(1)	
Cristian López Santamaría (ESP)	27.04.1989	5	(13)	1
Ioannis Fetfatzidis	21.12.1990	3		1
Mateo Ezequiel García (ARG)	10.09.1996	20	(9)	1
Daniel Mancini (ARG)	11.11.1996	19	(13)	3
Dimitrios Manos	16.09.1994	19	(16)	7
Konstantinos Mitroglou	12.03.1988	3	(6)	2
Alexandre Nascimento Costa Silva „Xande Silva" (POR)	16.03.1997	11	(18)	4

Athletic Gymnastics Society Asteras Tripolis

Founded: 26.03.1931
Stadium: Stádio "Theodoros Kolokotronis", Tripolis (7,442)
Trainer: Milan Rastavac   01.11.1973

Goalkeepers:	DOB	M	(s)	G
Nikolaos Papadopoulos	11.04.1990	21		1
Antonis Tsiftsis	21.07.1999	15	(1)	
Defenders:	**DOB**	**M**	**(s)**	**G**
Federico Hernán Álvarez (ARG)	07.08.1994	23	(4)	
Georgios Antzoulas	04.02.2000	1		
Giannis Christopoulos	22.07.2000	7	(3)	
Daniel „Dani" Suárez García-Osorio (ESP)	05.07.1990	31		2
Alexandros Kardaris	14.01.2001		(1)	
Giannis Kotsiras	16.12.1992	28	(3)	1
Triantafyllos Pasalidis	19.07.1996	9	(4)	
José Castaño Muñoz „Pepe Castaño" (ESP)	10.12.1998	24	(1)	
Rubén García Canales (ESP)	23.10.1998	8	(6)	
Christos Tasoulis	03.05.1991	13	(4)	
Midfielders:	**DOB**	**M**	**(s)**	**G**
Franco Bellocq (ARG)	15.10.1993	7	(6)	
Borja Fernández Fernández (ESP)	16.08.1995	3	(10)	
Eneko Capilla González (ESP)	13.06.1995	1	(8)	
Walter Matías Iglesias (ARG)	18.04.1985	5	(19)	
José Luis Valiente Giménez (ESP)	18.05.1991	28	(4)	
Georgios Kanellopoulos	29.01.2000	1	(4)	
Juan Manuel Munafo Horta (ARG)	20.03.1988	27	(1)	3
Brian Ezequiel Orosco (ARG)	28.02.1998		(2)	
Panagiotis Tzimas	12.03.2001	3	(7)	1
Forwards:	**DOB**	**M**	**(s)**	**G**
Adrián Riera Torrecillas (ESP)	19.04.1996	19	(12)	4
Sudais Ali Baba (NGA)	25.08.2000	6	(16)	1
Jerónimo Barrales (ARG)	28.01.1986	29		11
Francesc "Xesc" Regis Crespi (ESP)	30.09.1996	24	(11)	2
Rodrigo Manuel Gómez (ARG)	02.01.1993	6	(10)	
Leonardo Costa Silva „Léo Tilica" (BRA)	20.04.1995	14	(18)	
Luis Fernández Teijeiro (ESP)	23.09.1993	12	(8)	7
Andrés Pascual Santoja „Sito" (ESP)	18.11.1996	31	(2)	1

PAE APS Atromitos Athinon Football Club

Founded: 30.04.1923
Stadium: Stádio Peristeri, Athína (10,005)
Trainer: Damir Canadi (AUT) 06.05.1970
[05.02.2021] Savvas Pantelidis 07.04.1965

Goalkeepers:	DOB	M	(s)	G
Andreas Gianniotis	18.12.1992	18		
Christos Mandas	17.09.2001	12	(2)	
Giannis Saltas	05.03.2002		(1)	
Christos Theodorakis	17.09.1996	3	(2)	
Defenders:	**DOB**	**M**	**(s)**	**G**
Nikolaos Athanasiou	16.03.2001	1		
Dimitrios Goutas	04.04.1994	31	(1)	3
Kyriakos Kivrakidis	21.07.1992	19	(3)	
Lucas Galvão da Costa Souza (BRA)	22.06.1991	21	(3)	
Theofanis Mavrommatis	16.01.1997	8	(1)	1
Spyros Natsos	09.06.1998	14	(9)	1
Spyros Risvanis	03.01.1994	6	(3)	
Rodrigo Galo Brito (BRA)	19.09.1986	29	(1)	
Stefanos Stroungis	09.10.1997	12	(4)	
Josip Tomašević (CRO)	04.03.1994	14	(5)	
Midfielders:	**DOB**	**M**	**(s)**	**G**
Azer Bušuladžić (BIH)	12.11.1991	3	(4)	

	DOB	M	(s)	G
Charilaos Charisis	12.01.1995	23	(4)	1
Giannis Ikonomidis	03.01.1998		(3)	
Juan Muñiz Gallego (ESP)	14.03.1992	14	(12)	3
Bryan Martín Rabello Mella (CHI)	16.05.1994	11	(8)	1
Patrick Salomon (AUT)	10.06.1988	26	(3)	1
Javier Horacio Umbides (ARG)	09.02.1982	10	(16)	1
Forwards:	**DOB**	**M**	**(s)**	**G**
Amir Agayev (AZE)	10.02.1992	10	(9)	3
Lazaros Christodoulopoulos	19.12.1986	11	(15)	4
Georgios Daviotis	29.06.1998	6	(4)	
Bright Osagie Edomwonyi (NGA)	24.07.1994	2	(7)	
Petros Giakoumakis	03.07.1992	6	(6)	
Konstantinos Kotsopoulos	17.02.1997	11	(13)	1
Georgios Manousos	03.12.1987	24	(4)	8
Bojan Matić (SRB)	22.12.1991	7	(10)	
Clarck N'Sikulu (COD)	10.07.1992	11	(6)	1
Antonis Trimmatis	29.04.1999		(1)	

PAS Lamia 1964 Football Club

Founded: 01.06.1964
Stadium: Stádio Dimotiko, Lamia (6,000)
Trainer: Georgios Petrakis 08.02.1988
[08.10.2020] Babis Tennes 17.11.1953
[15.12.2020] Michalis Grigoriou 19.12.1973

Goalkeepers:	DOB	M	(s)	G
Devis Epassy (FRA)	02.02.1993	27		
Panagiotis Katsikas	10.03.1999	1		
Konstantinos Theodoropoulos	27.03.1990	5		
Defenders:	**DOB**	**M**	**(s)**	**G**
Daniel Adejo (NGA)	07.08.1989	31		1
Ángel Martínez Ortega (ESP)	15.05.1991	16		
Mark Asigba (GHA)	07.07.1990	6		
Patrick Bahanack (CMR)	03.08.1997	5		
Manjrekar James (CAN)	05.08.1993	2	(5)	
Konstantinos Provydakis	21.05.1996	10	(7)	
Giorgos Saramantas	29.01.1992	9	(5)	
Giannis Skondras	21.02.1990	24	(1)	
Kontantinos Stamoulis	29.10.2000		(1)	
Adam Tzanetopoulos	10.02.1995	23	(2)	1
Valentinos Vlachos	14.02.1992	5	(6)	
Loukas Vyntra	05.02.1981	12		
Angelos Zioulis	01.02.1995	1		
Midfielders:	**DOB**	**M**	**(s)**	**G**
Danny Bryan Bejarano Yañez (BOL)	03.01.1994	26	(1)	
Elmar Bjarnason (ISL)	04.03.1987	7	(10)	
Konstantinos Bouloulis	07.12.1993	6	(5)	

	DOB	M	(s)	G
Zisis Chatzistravos	16.12.1999	2	(6)	
Ibrahima Niasse (SEN)	18.04.1988	3		
Konstantinos Nikolopoulos	13.07.2002		(2)	
Guga Palavandishvili (GEO)	14.08.1993	5	(9)	
Francisco Medina Luna „Piti" (ESP)	26.05.1981	3	(6)	
Tyronne Gustavo del Pino Ramos (ESP)	27.01.1991	7	(3)	
Theofanis Tzandaris	13.06.1993	20	(1)	
Theodoros Vasilakakis	20.07.1988	7	(14)	1
Leonardo Enrique Villalba (ARG)	29.09.1994	2	(2)	
Forwards:	**DOB**	**M**	**(s)**	**G**
Bachana Arabuli (GEO)	05.01.1994	12	(9)	4
Adama Bâ (MTN)	27.08.1993	3	(5)	
Miloš Deletić (SRB)	14.10.1993	23	(3)	6
Gevorg Ghazaryan (ARM)	05.04.1988	2	(3)	
Anastasios Karamanos	21.09.1990	26	(4)	2
Vasilios Kostikas	04.09.1999		(3)	
Miguel Antonio Bianconi Kohl (BRA)	14.05.1992	1	(5)	1
Lazar Romanić (SRB)	23.03.1998	26	(2)	4
Nikolaos Tsoukalos	23.03.1992	1	(5)	1
Andreas Vasilogiannis	21.02.1991	4	(3)	
Anestis Vlachomitros	06.11.2001		(2)	

Ómilos Filáthlon Heraklíou

Founded: 1925
Stadium: Stádio „Theodoros Vardinogiannis", Heraklion (9,088)
Trainer: Georgios Simos 29.03.1978
[08.03.2021] Nikolaos Nioplias 17.01.1965

Goalkeepers:	DOB	M	(s)	G
Dimitrios Sotiriou	13.09.1987	11	(1)	
Boy Waterman (NED)	24.01.1984	22		
Defenders:	**DOB**	**M**	**(s)**	**G**
Apostolos Diamantis	20.05.2000	30		
Konstantinos Giannoulis	09.12.1987	18	(2)	
Nikolaos Korovesis	10.08.1991	27	(3)	
Odysseas Lymperakis	05.06.1998	10	(14)	
Nikolaos Marinakis	12.09.1993	10	(1)	
Vahid Selimović (LUX)	03.04.1997	11	(1)	
Nikolaos Vafeas	21.02.1997	8	(6)	1
Praxitelis Vouros	05.05.1995	16	(4)	
Abdul Rahman Weiss (SYR)	14.06.1998	24	(7)	
Midfielders:	**DOB**	**M**	**(s)**	**G**
Konstantinos Balogiannis	08.02.1999	7	(9)	
Jonathan Alexander de Guzmán (NED)	13.09.1987	11	(6)	5
Frixos Grivas	23.09.2000	10	(13)	
Miguel Alberto Mellado (ARG)	18.03.1993	26	(2)	1

	DOB	M	(s)	G
Theodoros Mingos	06.02.1998		(2)	
Adil Nabi (ENG)	28.02.1994	5		
Juan Ángel Neira (ARG)	21.02.1989	15	(4)	3
Vajebah Sakor (NOR)	24.04.1996	13	(4)	1
Georgios Sournakis	07.11.1999		(2)	
Paschalis Staikos	08.02.1996	20	(3)	3
Forwards:	**DOB**	**M**	**(s)**	**G**
Luc Castaignos (NED)	27.09.1992	4	(4)	1
Fábio Miguel dos Santos Sturgeon (POR)	04.02.1994	25	(6)	6
Felipe Souza Ferreyra (BRA)	21.05.1998		(4)	
Alexandros Gargkalatzidis	12.04.2000	2	(7)	
Apostolos Giannou (AUS)	25.01.1990	7	(8)	
João Vitor Brandão Figueiredo (BRA)	27.05.1996	1		
Vangelis Nikokyrakis	04.10.2001		(3)	
Ricardo Alvares Guedes Vaz (POR)	26.11.1994	1		
Adrián Sardinero Corpa (ESP)	13.10.1990	25	(4)	6
Nazareno Damián Solís (ARG)	22.04.1994	4	(6)	1
Kosmas Tsilianidis	09.05.1994		(5)	

Olympiakós Sýndesmos Filáthlon Peiraiós

Founded: 10.03.1925
Stadium: Stádio „Giórgos Karaïskáki", Peiraiás (32,115)
Trainer: Pedro Rui da Mota Vieira Martins (POR) 17.07.1970

Goalkeepers:	DOB	M	(s)	G
José Pedro Malheiro de Sá (POR)	17.01.1993	29		
Ilias Karargyris	29.06.2002		(1)	
Ögmundur Kristinsson (ISL)	19.06.1989	2		
Konstantinos Tzolakis	08.11.2002	5		
Defenders:	**DOB**	**M**	**(s)**	**G**
Athanasios Georgios Androutsos	06.05.1997	13	(6)	1
Ousseynou Ba (SEN)	11.11.1995	18	(1)	1
José Cholevas	27.06.1984	20	(2)	
Pape Abou Cissé (SEN)	14.09.1995	9	(3)	
Mohamed Dräger (TUN)	25.06.1996	6	(2)	
Alexios Kalogeropoulos	26.07.2004	2	(1)	
Kenny Lala (FRA)	03.10.1991	4	(1)	
Avraam Papadopoulos	03.12.1984	3	(2)	
Sokratis Papastathopoulos	09.06.1988	11	(3)	1
Márcio Rafael Ferreira de Souza „Rafinha" (BRA)	07.09.1985	13	(1)	
Oleg Reabciuk (MDA)	16.01.1998	17	(3)	
Rúben Afonso Borges Semedo (POR)	04.04.1994	29	(1)	1
Rúben Gonçalo Silva Nascimento Vinagre (POR)	09.04.1999	2		

Midfielders:	DOB	M	(s)	G
Andreas Bouchalakis	05.04.1993	23	(7)	3
Carlos Miguel Ribeiro Dias „Cafú" (POR)	26.02.1993		(2)	1
Mady Camara (GUI)	28.02.1997	24	(7)	3
Konstantinos Fortounis	16.10.1992	18	(13)	9
Maximiliano Alberto Lovera (ARG)	09.03.1999	2	(2)	
Yann Gérard M'Vila (FRA)	29.06.1990	28	(5)	4
Pedro Filipe Figueiredo Rodrigues „Pêpê" (POR)	20.05.1997	1	(8)	
Vasilios Sourlis	16.11.2002	2	(1)	
Tiago Rafael Maia Silva (POR)	02.06.1993	7	(9)	
Mathieu Valbuena (FRA)	28.09.1984	13	(13)	1
Forwards:	**DOB**	**M**	**(s)**	**G**
Armindo Tué Na Bangna „Bruma" (POR)	24.10.1994	18	(4)	7
Bruno Felipe Souza da Silva (BRA)	26.05.1994	1	(2)	
Hugo Cuypers (BEL)	07.02.1997	4	(6)	1
Youssef El-Arabi (MAR)	03.02.1987	24	(9)	22
Ahmed Hassan Mahgoub Abdelmoneim (EGY)	05.03.1993	11	(14)	10
Giorgos Masouras	01.01.1994	19	(12)	13
Lazar Ranđelović (SRB)	05.08.1997	7	(16)	
El Arbi Hilel Soudani (ALG)	25.11.1987	1	(4)	2
Marios Vrousai	02.07.1998	10	(4)	2

Panathinaïkós Athlitikós Ómilos Athína

Founded: 03.02.1908
Stadium: Stádio Olympiako „Spiros Louis", Athína (69,618)
Trainer: Daniel "Dani" Poyatos Algaba (ESP) 23.06.1978
[12.10.2020] Sotiris Silaidopoulos 08.02.1979
[19.10.2020] László Bölöni (ROU) 11.03.1953
[11.05.2021] Sotiris Silaidopoulos 08.02.1979

Goalkeepers:	DOB	M	(s)	G
Nikolaos Christogeorgos	03.01.2000	1		
Sokratis Dioudis	03.02.1993	34		
Vasilios Xenopoulos	20.05.1998	1		
Defenders:	**DOB**	**M**	**(s)**	**G**
Ilias Chatzitheodoridis	05.11.1997	4	(2)	
Francisco "Fran" Manuel Vélez Jiménez (ESP)	23.06.1991	25		2
Juan Carlos Pérez López „Juankar" (ESP)	30.03.1990	23	(1)	
Dimitrios Karagiannis	27.02.2001	2	(2)	
Theofanis Mavrommatis	16.01.1997	1	(1)	
Achilleas Poungouras	13.12.1995	24	(3)	
Facundo Sánchez (ARG)	07.03.1990	16	(5)	
Bart Schenkeveld (NED)	28.08.1991	27		1
Vasilios Zagaritis	04.05.2001	11	(1)	
Midfielders:	**DOB**	**M**	**(s)**	**G**
Sotirios Polykarpos Alexandropoulos	26.11.2001	22	(6)	
Andreas Athanasakopoulos	27.11.2001	2	(3)	
Yassin Ayoub (MAR)	06.03.1994	4	(5)	
Giannis Bouzoukis	27.03.1998	5	(8)	

Dimitrios Kourbelis	02.11.1993	10		1
Maurício José Da Silveira Junior (BRA)	21.10.1988	24	(1)	2
Cheikh Niasse (SEN)	19.01.2000	11	(2)	
Younousse Sankharé (SEN)	10.09.1989	7	(3)	3
Dimitrios Serpezis	14.03.2001	1	(7)	
Lucas Martín Villafáñez (ARG)	04.10.1991	20	(6)	2
Forwards:	**DOB**	**M**	**(s)**	**G**
Aitor Cantalapiedra Fernández (ESP)	10.02.1996	11	(11)	3
António Manuel Pereira Xavier (POR)	06.07.1992	4	(3)	
Carlos Daniel López Huesca „Carlitos" (ESP)	12.06.1990	15	(17)	6
Dimitrios Emmanouilidis	24.10.2000	2	(5)	1
Anastasios Hatzigiovanis	31.05.1997	20	(9)	3
Fotis Ioannidis	10.01.2000	13	(10)	4
Anargyros Kampetsis	06.05.1999	10	(9)	3
Federico Macheda (ITA)	22.08.1991	23	(8)	9
Yohan Albert Pierre Stéphane Mollo (FRA)	18.07.1989	19	(5)	
Yeni Atito N'Gbakoto (FRA)	23.01.1992	4	(10)	
Spyros Tzavidas	21.08.2001		(2)	

Panaetolikos Gymnastikos Philekpaideutikos Syllogos Agrinio

Founded: 09.03.1926
Stadium: Stádio Panetolikos, Agrinio (7,321)
Trainer: Makis Chavos 05.09.1969
[28.10.2020] Luciano de Souza (BRA) 21.08.1972
[10.11.2020] Traianos Dellas 31.01.1976

Goalkeepers:	DOB	M	(s)	G
Christopher Knett (AUT)	01.08.1990	27		
Nikolaos Melissas	24.02.1993	6	(2)	
Defenders:	**DOB**	**M**	**(s)**	**G**
Edin Cocalić (BIH)	05.12.1987	12		
Aristotelis Karasalidis	03.05.1991	13	(1)	
Apostolos Konstantopoulos	02.08.2002	23	(1)	
Georgios Liavas	12.02.2001	17	(2)	1
Alexandros Malis	19.03.1997	6	(6)	
Paolo Medina Etienne (MEX)	28.05.1999	9	(7)	
Elías Iván Pereyra (ARG)	15.02.1999	16	(5)	
Manolis Tzanakakis	30.04.1992	12	(4)	
Vanderson Scardovelli (BRA)	27.09.1984	15	(1)	
Midfielders:	**DOB**	**M**	**(s)**	**G**
Joaquín Arzura (ARG)	18.05.1993	5	(4)	
Euciodálcio Gomes „Dálcio" (POR)	22.05.1996	22	(9)	
Antonio Jakoliš (CRO)	28.02.1992	7	(9)	

Franco Eduardo Mazurek (ARG)	24.09.1993	17	(6)	1
Delvin Chanel N'Dinga (CGO)	14.03.1988	11	(1)	1
Aymen Tahar (ALG)	02.10.1989	17	(11)	2
Angelos Tsingaras	24.07.1999	17	(10)	
Forwards:	**DOB**	**M**	**(s)**	**G**
Juan Ignacio Álvarez Morinigo (ARG)	27.10.1997		(3)	
Gboly Ariyibi (USA)	18.01.1995	22	(5)	4
Mohammadreza Azadi (IRN)	07.12.1999	3	(8)	
Jorge Luis Díaz Gutiérrez (URU)	28.06.1989	32		
Frederico Fonseca Pires de Almeida Duarte (POR)	30.03.1999	5	(10)	
Hélder Jorge Leal Rodrigues Barbosa (POR)	25.05.1987	8	(1)	2
Nikolaos Karelis	24.02.1992	7	(5)	
Georgios Manthatis	11.05.1997	5	(5)	
Nicolás Mario Mazzola (ARG)	28.01.1990	6	(6)	1
Javier Osvaldo Mendoza (ARG)	02.09.1992	9	(14)	1
Nikolaos Vergos	13.01.1996	14	(15)	5

Panthessaloníkios Athlitikós Ómilos Konstantinoupolitón

Founded: 20.04.1926
Stadium: Stádio Toumba, Thessaloníki (28,703)
Trainer: Abel Fernando Moreira Ferreira (POR)   22.12.1978
[31.10.2020]   Pablo Gabriel García Pére (URU)   11.05.1977

Goalkeepers:	DOB	M	(s)	G
Alexandros Paschalakis	28.07.1989	18		
Živko Živković (SRB)	14.04.1989	18		
Defenders:	**DOB**	**M**	**(s)**	**G**
José Ángel Crespo Rincón (ESP)	09.02.1987	14	(7)	1
Abdul Rahman Baba (GHA)	02.07.1994	11	(2)	1
Fernando Lopes dos Santos Varela (CPV)	26.11.1987	20	(3)	1
Dimitrios Hristos Giannoulis	17.10.1995	11	(1)	
Sverrir Ingi Ingason (ISL)	05.08.1993	25	(1)	5
Leonardo de Matos Cruz "Léo Matos" (BRA)	02.04.1986	2		
Lefteris Lyratzis	22.02.2000	4	(3)	
Giannis Michailidis	18.02.2000	16	(3)	
Enea Mihaj (ALB)	05.07.1998	3	(2)	
Adrian Nilsen Pereira (NOR)	31.08.1999	9	(1)	
Rodrigo Alves Soares (BRA)	26.12.1992	17	(5)	
Adelino André Vieira de Freitas „Vieirinha"(POR)	24.01.1986	19	(2)	4
Moussa Wagué (SEN)	04.10.1998	4	(3)	
Midfielders:	**DOB**	**M**	**(s)**	**G**
Diego Marvin Biseswar (SUR)	08.03.1988	2	(3)	
Douglas Augusto Soares Gomes (BRA)	13.01.1997	18	(3)	1
Omar El Kaddouri (MAR)	21.08.1990	18	(8)	2

	DOB	M	(s)	G
Anderson Esiti (NGA)	24.05.1994	5	(4)	
Shinji Kagawa (JPN)	17.03.1989	1	(4)	
Giannis Konstantelias	10.05.2003	1	(2)	
Nikoloz Ninua (GEO)	22.06.1999	2	(7)	1
Dimitrios Pelkas	26.10.1993	3	(1)	
Stefan Schwab (AUT)	27.09.1990	28	(5)	7
Theocharis Tsingaras	20.08.2000	9	(7)	
Georgios Vrakas	28.04.2001	1	(1)	
Forwards:	**DOB**	**M**	**(s)**	**G**
Chuba Amechi Akpom (ENG)	09.10.1995	1		
Antonio-Mirko Čolak (CRO)	17.09.1993	3	(7)	1
Georgios Koutsias	08.02.2004		(2)	
Michael Krmenčík (CZE)	15.03.1993	11	(11)	4
Lazaros Lamprou	19.12.1997	1	(8)	
Leonardo Rodrigues Lima "Léo Jabá" (BRA)	02.08.1998		(1)	
Thomas Murg (AUT)	14.11.1994	14	(10)	2
Karol Świderski (POL)	23.01.1997	21	(14)	11
Christos Tzolis	30.01.2002	25	(8)	6
Amr Warda (EGY)	17.09.1993	14	(7)	3
Andrija Živković (SRB)	11.07.1996	27	(6)	10

Panepirotikos Athlitikos Syllogos Giannina

Founded: 08.07.1966
Stadium: Stádio Zosimades, , Giannina (7,652)
Trainer: Argirios Giannikis   09.07.1980

Goalkeepers:	DOB	M	(s)	G
Vasilios Athanasiou	24.07.1999		(2)	
Eleftherios Choutesiotis	20.07.1994	20		
Yuri Lodygin (RUS)	26.05.1990	13		
Defenders:	**DOB**	**M**	**(s)**	**G**
Rodrigo Nahuel Erramuspe (ARG)	03.05.1990	22	(3)	2
Antonios Ikonomopoulos	09.05.1998	9	(3)	
Giannis Kargas	09.12.1994	22	(1)	2
Pantelis Panourgias	13.04.1998	3	(2)	
Epaminondas Pantelakis	10.02.1995	26	(5)	1
Marvin Peersman (BEL)	10.02.1991	30		
Stavros Pilios	10.12.2000	5	(2)	
Manolis Saliakas	12.09.1996	25	(6)	
Midfielders:	**DOB**	**M**	**(s)**	**G**
Edwin Fabry Castro Barros (COL)	21.02.1992	21	(2)	
Pavlos Grosdanis	03.04.2002	1	(3)	

	DOB	M	(s)	G
Juan Domínguez Lamas (ESP)	08.01.1990	19	(7)	
Alexandros Kartalis	29.01.1995	22	(7)	
Angelos Liasos	26.05.2000	7	(16)	1
Vladyslav Naumets (UKR)	07.03.1999	6	(11)	1
Stefanos Siontis	04.09.1987	15	(2)	
Alexis Triadis	16.05.1997		(2)	
Forwards:	**DOB**	**M**	**(s)**	**G**
Fabricio Brener (ARG)	26.05.1998	12	(10)	2
Georgios Doumtsis	04.03.2000		(6)	
Christos Eleftheriadis	30.09.1991	20	(9)	4
Sandi Križman (CRO)	17.08.1989	17	(4)	3
Jean-Baptiste Léo (FRA)	03.05.1996	14	(6)	2
Alexandros Lolis	05.09.2002	3	(7)	
Nicolae Milinceanu (MDA)	01.08.1992	3	(7)	1
Giorgos Pamlidis	13.11.1993	28	(5)	7

Vólos Néos Podosfairikós Sýllogos

Founded: 02.06.2017
Stadium: Stádio Panthessaliko, Vólos (22,700)
Trainer: Miguel Ángel López Pérez (ESP)   05.04.1983
[19.04.2021]   Konstantinos Bratsos   26.04.1977

Goalkeepers:	DOB	M	(s)	G
Athanasios Garavelis	06.08.1992	12		
Boris Klaiman (ISR)	26.10.1990	20		
Symeon Papadopoulos	18.04.2000	1		
Defenders:	**DOB**	**M**	**(s)**	**G**
Rodrigo Jesús Colombo (ARG)	19.11.1992	12	(2)	1
Antonis Dentakis	13.03.1995	12	(5)	
Stergios Dimopoulos	25.05.1990	1	(3)	1
Franco Ferrari (ARG)	09.05.1992	31		1
Lautaro Fausto Grillo (ARG)	20.02.1993	16	(2)	1
Ioannis Kiakos	14.02.1998	4	(17)	1
Pavlos Logaras	18.06.2002	1	(1)	
Gerasimos Mitoglou	20.10.1999	21	(1)	1
Salvador Sánchez (ARG)	31.07.1995	20	(6)	1
Sergio Blázquez Sánchez „Tekio" (ESP)	30.07.1990	14	(3)	
Midfielders:	**DOB**	**M**	**(s)**	**G**
Georgios Ballas	07.04.2001		(2)	

	DOB	M	(s)	G
Jean Pierre Barrientos (URU)	16.09.1990	20	(2)	3
Nicolás Martínez (ARG)	25.09.1987	23	(6)	
Dardo Federico Miloc (ARG)	16.10.1990		(1)	
Sotiris Ninis	03.04.1990	14	(7)	
Daan Rienstra (NED)	06.10.1992	28	(3)	2
Anastasios Tsokanis	02.05.1991	17	(1)	
Forwards:	**DOB**	**M**	**(s)**	**G**
Julián Bartolo (ARG)	15.04.1996	20	(9)	3
Alberto Bueno Calvo (ESP)	20.03.1988	4	(5)	2
Anastasios Douvikas	02.08.1999	29	(1)	11
Iker Guarrotxena Vallejo (ESP)	06.12.1992	3	(4)	
Erik Jendrišek (SVK)	26.10.1986		(4)	
Tasos Kritikos	25.01.1995	3	(7)	1
Juan José Perea Mendoza (COL)	23.02.2000	20	(7)	3
Renato João Saleiro Santos (POR)	05.10.1991	7	(6)	
Amr Warda (EGY)	17.09.1993	10		2

SECOND LEVEL
Super League 2 2020/2021

Regular Season

1.	PAE Ionikos Nikaia	22	14	5	3	35	-	19	47
2.	AO Xanthi	22	11	8	3	24	-	10	41
3.	APO Levadiakos	22	11	8	3	32	-	12	41
4.	GS Ergotelis Heraklion	22	11	3	8	29	-	15	36
5.	AO Chania Kissamikos PAE	22	9	8	5	18	-	13	35
6.	PAE FS Diagóras Rhodes	22	8	6	8	18	-	23	30
7.	Panachaiki 1891 FC Patras	22	7	8	7	19	-	20	29
8.	AO Trikala	22	5	9	8	16	-	20	24
9.	PAE Apollon Lárissa	22	6	6	10	13	-	19	24
10.	GS Doxa Drama	22	6	3	13	17	-	37	21
11.	AE Karaiskakis Arta	22	3	7	12	14	-	32	16
12.	OF Ierapetra	22	2	7	13	17	-	32	13

Team ranked 1-6 were qualified for the Play-off Round, while teams ranked 7-12 were qualified for the Play-out Round.

Play-off Round

1.	PAE Ionikos Nikaia (*Promoted*)	27	16	5	6	44	-	29	53
2.	AO Xanthi (*Promotion Play-offs*)	27	14	9	4	29	-	12	51
3.	APO Levadiakos	27	14	8	5	42	-	16	50
4.	GS Ergotelis Heraklion	27	15	3	9	37	-	18	48
5.	AO Chania Kissamikos PAE	27	11	9	7	22	-	19	42
6.	PAE FS Diagóras Rhodes	27	8	6	13	22	-	38	30

Play-out Round

7.	Panachaiki 1891 FC Patras (*Relegated*)	27	9	10	8	29	-	29	37
8.	AO Trikala	27	6	11	10	21	-	25	29
9.	PAE Apollon Lárissa	27	7	8	12	19	-	27	29
10.	GS Doxa Drama	27	8	4	15	24	-	47	28
11.	AE Karaiskakis Arta	27	5	9	13	24	-	42	24
12.	OF Ierapetra	27	4	8	15	25	-	36	20

NATIONAL TEAM

INTERNATIONAL MATCHES
(16.07.2020 – 15.07.2021)

03.09.2020	Ljubljana	Slovenia - Greece	0-0	(UNL)
06.09.2020	Prishtina	Kosovo - Greece	1-2(0-1)	(UNL)
07.10.2020	Klagenfurt	Austria - Greece	2-1(0-0)	(F)
11.10.2020	Athína	Greece - Moldova	2-0(1-0)	(UNL)
14.10.2020	Athína	Greece - Kosovo	0-0	(UNL)
11.11.2020	Athína	Greece - Cyprus	2-1(2-0)	(F)
15.11.2020	Chişinău	Moldova - Greece	0-2(0-2)	(UNL)
18.11.2020	Athína	Greece - Slovenia	0-0	(UNL)
25.03.2021	Granada	Spain - Greece	1-1(1-0)	(WCQ)
28.03.2021	Thessaloníki	Greece - Honduras	2-1(1-1)	(F)
31.03.2021	Thessaloníki	Greece - Georgia	1-1(0-0)	(WCQ)
03.06.2021	Bruxelles	Belgium - Greece	1-1(1-0)	(F)
06.06.2021	Málaga	Norway - Greece	1-2(0-2)	(F)

03.09.2020   **SLOVENIA - GREECE**   **0-0**   2nd UEFA Nations League C, Group 3
Stadion Stožice, Ljubljana; Referee: Robert Adam Madden (Scotland); Attendance: 0
GRE: Vasilios Barkas, Dimitrios Siovas, Michalis Bakakis, Dimitrios Hristos Giannoulis, Efstratios Svarnas, Petros Mantalos (87.Giorgos Masouras), José Carlos Gonçalves Rodrigues „Zeca", Dimitrios Kourbelis, Anastasios Bakasetas (Cap), Vangelis Pavlidis (76.Taxiarchis Fountas), Dimitrios Limnios. Trainer: Johannes Nicolaas van 't Schip (Netherlands).

06.09.2020   **KOSOVO - GREECE**   **1-2(0-1)**   2nd UEFA Nations League C, Group 3
Stadiumi „Fadil Vokrri", Prishtina; Referee: Pavel Královec (Czech Republic); Attendance: 0
GRE: Vasilios Barkas, Michalis Bakakis, Konstantinos Stafylidis (Cap) (40.Dimitrios Siovas), Dimitrios Hristos Giannoulis, Efstratios Svarnas, Konstantinos Fortounis (60.Giorgos Masouras), José Carlos Gonçalves Rodrigues „Zeca", Dimitrios Kourbelis, Anastasios Bakasetas, Efthimis Koulouris (83.Petros Mantalos), Dimitrios Limnios. Trainer: Johannes Nicolaas van 't Schip (Netherlands).
Goals: Dimitrios Limnios (2), Dimitrios Siovas (51).

07.10.2020   **AUSTRIA - GREECE**   **2-1(0-0)**   Friendly International
Wörthersee Stadion, Klagenfurt; Referee: Matej Jug (Slovenia); Attendance: 1,500
GRE: Sokratis Dioudis, Giorgos Tzavelas, Vasilios Konstantinos Lambropoulos, Giorgos Kyriakopoulos, Efstratios Svarnas (46.Haralambos Lykogiannis; 63.Anastasios Bakasetas), Petros Mantalos (Cap) (46.José Carlos Gonçalves Rodrigues „Zeca"), Konstantinos Fortounis, Andreas Bouchalakis, Dimitrios Kourbelis (46.Giannis Michailidis), Taxiarchis Fountas (67.Efthimis Koulouris), Dimitrios Limnios (81.Hristos Tzolis). Trainer: Johannes Nicolaas van 't Schip (Netherlands).
Goal: Konstantinos Fortounis (63).

11.10.2020   **GREECE - MOLDOVA**   **2-0(1-0)**   2nd UEFA Nations League C, Group 3
Stádio Olympiako „Spiros Louis", Athína; Referee: Dennis Higler (Netherlands); Attendance: 0
GRE: Odisseas Vlachodimos, Giorgos Tzavelas, Dimitrios Hristos Giannoulis, Pantelis Hatzidiakos (69.Lazaros Rota), Efstratios Svarnas, Petros Mantalos (70.Konstantinos Fortounis), José Carlos Gonçalves Rodrigues „Zeca", Dimitrios Kourbelis (83.Andreas Bouchalakis), Anastasios Bakasetas (Cap), Vangelis Pavlidis (83.Taxiarchis Fountas), Dimitrios Limnios (76.Dimitrios Pelkas). Trainer: Johannes Nicolaas van 't Schip (Netherlands).
Goals: Anastasios Bakasetas (45+3 penalty), Petros Mantalos (50).

14.10.2020   **GREECE - KOSOVO**   **0-0**   2nd UEFA Nations League C, Group 3
Stádio Olympiako „Spiros Louis", Athína; Referee: Roi Reinshreiber (Israel); Attendance: 0
GRE: Odisseas Vlachodimos, Giorgos Tzavelas, Dimitrios Hristos Giannoulis, Efstratios Svarnas, Pantelis Hatzidiakos (85.Vasilios Konstantinos Lambropoulos), Petros Mantalos (63.Taxiarchis Fountas), Dimitrios Kourbelis, José Carlos Gonçalves Rodrigues „Zeca" (62.Andreas Bouchalakis), Anastasios Bakasetas (Cap) (73.Konstantinos Fortounis), Vangelis Pavlidis, Dimitrios Limnios (73.Dimitrios Pelkas). Trainer: Johannes Nicolaas van 't Schip (Netherlands).

11.11.2020   **GREECE - CYPRUS**   **2-1(2-0)**   Friendly International
Stádio "Georgios Kamaras", Athína; Referee: Harm Osmers (Germany); Attendance: 0
GRE: Vasilios Barkas, Konstantinos Tsimikas (46.Haralambos Lykogiannis), Giannis Michailidis, Konstantinos Fortounis (46.Andreas Bouchalakis), José Carlos Gonçalves Rodrigues „Zeca" (46.Vasilios Konstantinos Lambropoulos), Dimitrios Kourbelis, Haralampos Mavrias (68.Lazaros Rota), Anastasios Hatzigiovanis, Anastasios Bakasetas (Cap) (46.Dimitrios Pelkas), Giorgos Giakoumakis, Hristos Tzolis (46.Dimitrios Limnios). Trainer: Johannes Nicolaas van 't Schip (Netherlands).
Goals: Hristos Tzolis (8), Giorgos Giakoumakis (17).

15.11.2020   **MOLDOVA - GREECE**   **0-2(0-2)**   2nd UEFA Nations League C, Group 3
Stadionul Zimbru, Chişinău; Referee: Fran Jović (Croatia); Attendance: 0
GRE: Odisseas Vlachodimos, Giorgos Tzavelas, Pantelis Hatzidiakos, Konstantinos Tsimikas (62.Giorgos Kyriakopoulos), Konstantinos Fortounis (65.Hristos Tzolis), José Carlos Gonçalves Rodrigues „Zeca", Andreas Bouchalakis, Haralampos Mavrias, Anastasios Bakasetas (Cap), Vangelis Pavlidis (79.Giorgos Giakoumakis), Dimitrios Limnios (79.Anastasios Hatzigiovanis). Trainer: Johannes Nicolaas van 't Schip (Netherlands).
Goals: Konstantinos Fortounis (32), Anastasios Bakasetas (41).

18.11.2020   **GREECE - SLOVENIA**   **0-0**   2nd UEFA Nations League C, Group 3
Stádio "Georgios Kamaras", Athína; Referee: Carlos del Cerro Grande (Spain); Attendance: 0
GRE: Odisseas Vlachodimos, Giorgos Tzavelas (79.Giorgos Masouras), Pantelis Hatzidiakos [*sent off 90*], Konstantinos Tsimikas (90.Giorgos Kyriakopoulos), Konstantinos Fortounis, José Carlos Gonçalves Rodrigues „Zeca" (67.Hristos Tzolis), Dimitrios Kourbelis, Haralampos Mavrias, Anastasios Bakasetas (Cap), Giorgos Giakoumakis (46.Vangelis Pavlidis), Dimitrios Limnios. Trainer: Johannes Nicolaas van 't Schip (Netherlands).

25.03.2021   **SPAIN - GREECE**   **1-1(1-0)**   22nd FIFA WC. Qualifiers
Estadio Nuevo Los Cármenes, Granada; Referee: Marco Guida (Italy); Attendance: 0
GRE: Odisseas Vlachodimos, Giorgos Tzavelas, Kyriakos Papadopoulos, Michalis Bakakis, Petros Mantalos (46.Hristos Tzolis), José Carlos Gonçalves Rodrigues „Zeca", Konstantinos Tsimikas (80.Giorgos Kyriakopoulos), Giorgos Masouras (65.Konstantinos Fortounis), Andreas Bouchalakis, Anastasios Bakasetas (Cap) (78.Giorgos Giakoumakis), Dimitrios Limnios (46.Emmanouil Siopis). Trainer: Johannes Nicolaas van 't Schip (Netherlands).
Goal: Anastasios Bakasetas (57 penalty).

28.03.2021   **GREECE - HONDURAS**   **2-1(1-1)**   Friendly International
Stádio Toumba, Thessaloníki; Referee: Urs Schnyder (Switzerland); Attendance: 0
GRE: Sokratis Dioudis, Giorgos Kyriakopoulos (77.Sotirios Polykarpos Alexandropoulos), Efstratios Svarnas, Konstantinos Mavropanos, Petros Mantalos (Cap) (83.Anastasios Bakasetas), Konstantinos Fortounis (46.Dimitrios Limnios), Emmanouil Siopis, Haralampos Mavrias, Giorgos Giakoumakis (46.Giorgos Masouras), Vangelis Pavlidis (62.Dimitrios Hristos Giannoulis), Hristos Tzolis (46.Anastasios Douvikas). Trainer: Johannes Nicolaas van 't Schip (Netherlands).
Goals: Vangelis Pavlidis (14, 59).

31.03.2021   **GREECE - GEORGIA**   **1-1(0-0)**   22nd FIFA WC. Qualifiers
Stádio Toumba, Thessaloníki; Referee: Szymon Marciniak (Poland); Attendance: 0
GRE: Odisseas Vlachodimos, Giorgos Tzavelas, Kyriakos Papadopoulos, Michalis Bakakis (42.Haralampos Mavrias), Dimitrios Hristos Giannoulis, Konstantinos Fortounis, José Carlos Gonçalves Rodrigues „Zeca", Andreas Bouchalakis (87.Emmanouil Siopis), Anastasios Bakasetas (Cap) (70.Giorgos Masouras), Hristos Tzolis (46.Dimitrios Limnios), Vangelis Pavlidis (70.Giorgos Giakoumakis). Trainer: Johannes Nicolaas van 't Schip (Netherlands).
Goal: Otar Kakabadze (76 own goal).

03.06.2021   **BELGIUM - GREECE**   **1-1(1-0)**   Friendly International
Stade "Roi Baudouin", Bruxelles; Referee: Robert Hennessy (Republic of Ireland); Attendance: 0
GRE: Odisseas Vlachodimos, Giorgos Tzavelas, Kyriakos Papadopoulos, Dimitrios Hristos Giannoulis, Konstantinos Tsimikas (59.Dimitrios Pelkas), Andreas Bouchalakis (69.Emmanouil Siopis), Giorgos Masouras, Athanasios Georgios Androutsos (80.Manolis Saliakas), Konstantinos Galanopoulos (69.José Carlos Gonçalves Rodrigues „Zeca"), Anastasios Bakasetas (Cap) (80.Petros Mantalos), Vangelis Pavlidis (58.Leonardo Koutris). Trainer: Johannes Nicolaas van 't Schip (Netherlands).
Goal: Giorgos Tzavelas (66).

06.06.2021   **NORWAY - GREECE**   **1-2(0-2)**   Friendly International
Estadio La Rosaleda, Málaga (Spain); Referee: Jakob Kehlet (Denmark); Attendance: 0
GRE: Odisseas Vlachodimos, Giorgos Tzavelas, Kyriakos Papadopoulos, Konstantinos Tsimikas, Konstantinos Mavropanos, Petros Mantalos (Cap) (57.Anastasios Bakasetas), Andreas Bouchalakis (75.Emmanouil Siopis), Dimitrios Pelkas (75.Vangelis Pavlidis), Giorgos Masouras (57.Hristos Tzolis), Athanasios Georgios Androutsos (90+3.Michalis Bakakis), Konstantinos Galanopoulos (57.José Carlos Gonçalves Rodrigues „Zeca"). Trainer: Johannes Nicolaas van 't Schip (Netherlands).
Goals: Giorgos Masouras (13), Athanasios Georgios Androutsos (21).

NATIONAL TEAM PLAYERS
(16.07.2020 – 15.07.2021)

Name	DOB	Caps	Goals	2020/2021:	Club
Goalkeepers					
Vasilios BARKAS	30.05.1994	10	0	2020:	Celtic FC Glasgow (SCO)
Sokratis DIOUDIS	03.02.1993	2	0	2020/2021:	PAE Panathinaïkos Athína
Odisseas VLACHODIMOS	26.04.1994	14	0	2020/2021:	Sport Lisboa e Benfica (POR)
Defenders					
Michalis BAKAKIS	18.04.1991	20	0	2020/2021:	AEK Athína
Dimitrios Hristos GIANNOULIS	17.10.1995	14	0	2020/2021: 19.01.2021->	PAOK Thessaloníki Norwich City FC (ENG, on loan)
Pantelis HATZIDIAKOS	18.01.1997	8	0	2020:	AZ Alkmaar (NED)
Leonardo KOUTRIS	23.07.1995	6	0	2021:	TSV Fortuna Düsseldorf (GER)
Giorgos KYRIAKOPOULOS	05.02.1996	5	0	2020/2021:	US Sassuolo Calcio (ITA)
Vasilios Konstantinos LAMBROPOULOS	31.03.1990	5	0	2020:	VfL Bochum (GER)
Haralambos LYKOGIANNIS	22.10.1993	6	0	2020:	Cagliari Calcio (ITA)
Konstantinos MAVROPANOS	11.12.1997	2	0	2021:	VfB Stuttgart (GER)
Giannis MICHAILIDIS	18.02.2000	2	0	2020:	PAOK Thessaloníki
Kyriakos PAPADOPOULOS	23.02.1992	33	4	2021:	NK Lokomotiva Zagreb (CRO)
Lazaros ROTA	23.08.1997	2	0	2020:	Fortuna Sittard (NED)
Manolis SALIAKAS	12.09.1996	1	0	2021:	PAS Giannina
Dimitrios SIOVAS	16.09.1988	20	0	2020:	CD Leganés (ESP)
Konstantinos STAFYLIDIS	02.12.1993	32	2	2020:	TSG Hoffenheim 1899 (GER)
Efstratios SVARNAS	11.11.1997	6	0	2020/2021:	AEK Athína
Konstantinos TSIMIKAS	12.05.1996	9	0	2020/2021:	Liverpool FC (ENG)
Giorgos TZAVELAS	26.11.1987	40	3	2020/2021:	Alanyaspor (TUR)
Midfielders					
Sotirios Polykarpos ALEXANDROPOULOS	26.11.2001	1	0	2021:	PAE Panathinaïkos Athína
Athanasios Georgios ANDROUTSOS	06.05.1997	3	0	2021:	Olympiacos SFP Peiraiás
Andreas BOUCHALAKIS	05.04.1993	19	0	2020/2021:	Olympiacos SFP Peiraiás
Konstantinos FORTOUNIS	16.10.1992	54	9	2020/2021:	Olympiacos SFP Peiraiás
Konstantinos GALANOPOULOS	28.12.1997	6	1	2021:	AEK Athína
Dimitrios KOURBELIS	02.11.1993	23	1	2020/2021:	PAE Panathinaïkos Athína
Petros MANTALOS	31.08.1991	36	4	2020/2021:	AEK Athína
Haralampos MAVRIAS	21.02.1994	13	0	2020/2021:	AC Omonia Nicosia (CYP)
Dimitrios PELKAS	26.10.1993	20	0	2020/2021:	Fenerbahçe SK İstanbul (TUR)
Emmanouil SIOPIS	14.05.1994	8	0	2021:	Alanyaspor (TUR)
José Carlos Gonçalves Rodrigues "ZECA"	31.08.1988	31	2	2020/2021:	FC København (DEN)
Forwards					
Anastasios BAKASETAS	28.06.1993	38	3	2020: 30.01.2021->	Alanyaspor (TUR) Trabzonspor Kulübü (TUR)
Anastasios DOUVIKAS	02.08.1999	1	0	2021:	Vólos NPS
Taxiarchis FOUNTAS	04.09.1995	7	0	2020:	SK Rapid Wien (AUT)
Giorgos GIAKOUMAKIS	09.12.1994	6	1	2020/2021:	VVV-Venlo (NED)
Anastasios HATZIGIOVANIS	31.05.1997	2	0	2020:	PAE Panathinaïkos Athína
Efthimis KOULOURIS	06.03.1996	17	0	2020/2021:	Toulouse FC (FRA)
Dimitrios LIMNIOS	27.05.1998	16	2	2020/2021:	PAOK Thessaloníki
Giorgos MASOURAS	01.01.1994	19	2	2020/2021:	Olympiacos SFP Peiraiás
Vangelis PAVLIDIS	21.11.1998	14	3	2020/2021:	AZ Alkmaar (NED)
Hristos TZOLIS	30.01.2002	8	1	2020/2021:	PAOK Thessaloníki
Trainer					

Johannes Nicolaas "John" van 't SCHIP (Netherlands)   30.12.1963   19 M; 9 W; 7 D; 3 L; 22-15
[from 31.07.2019]

HUNGARY

The Country:
Magyarország (Hungary)
Capital: Budapest
Surface: 93,030 km²
Inhabitants: 9,730,000 [2021]
Time: UTC+1

The FA:
Magyar Labdarúgó Szövetség
1112 Budapest, Kánai út 2.D
Tel: +36 1 577 9500
Foundation date: 00.00.1900
Member of FIFA since: 1901
Member of UEFA since: 1954
Website: www.mlsz.hu

NATIONAL TEAM RECORDS

RECORDS

First international match:	12.10.1902, Wien: Austria – Hungary 5-0	
Most international caps:	Gábor Király	- 108 caps (1998-2016)
	Balázs Dzsudzsák	- 108 caps (since 2007)
Most international goals:	Ferenc Puskás	- 84 goals / 85 caps (1945-1956)

UEFA EUROPEAN CHAMPIONSHIP

1960	Qualifiers
1964	Final Tournament (3rd Place)
1968	Qualifiers
1972	Final Tournament (4th Place)
1976	Qualifiers
1980	Qualifiers
1984	Qualifiers
1988	Qualifiers
1992	Qualifiers
1996	Qualifiers
2000	Qualifiers
2004	Qualifiers
2008	Qualifiers
2012	Qualifiers
2016	Final Tournament (2nd Round of 16)
2020	Final Tournament (Group Stage)

FIFA WORLD CUP

1930	Did not enter
1934	Final Tournament (Quarter-Finals)
1938	Final Tournament (Runners-up)
1950	Did not enter
1954	Final Tournament (Runners-up)
1958	Final Tournament (Group Stage)
1962	Final Tournament (Quarter-Finals)
1966	Final Tournament (Quarter-Finals)
1970	Qualifiers
1974	Qualifiers
1978	Final Tournament (Group Stage)
1982	Final Tournament (Group Stage)
1986	Final Tournament (Group Stage)
1990	Qualifiers
1994	Qualifiers
1998	Qualifiers
2002	Qualifiers
2006	Qualifiers
2010	Qualifiers
2014	Qualifiers
2018	Qualifiers

OLYMPIC TOURNAMENTS

1908	Did not enter
1912	Quarter-Finals
1920	Did not enter
1924	1/8-Finals
1928	Did not enter
1936	1/8-Finals
1948	Did not enter
1952	**Winners**
1956	Did not enter
1960	3rd Place
1964	**Winners**
1968	**Winners**
1972	Runners-up
1976	Qualifiers
1980	Qualifiers
1984	Qualifiers
1988	Qualifiers
1992	Qualifiers
1996	Group Stage
2000	Qualifiers
2004	Qualifiers
2008	Qualifiers
2012	Qualifiers
2016	Qualifiers

UEFA NATIONS LEAGUE

2018/2019	League C (promoted to League B)
2020/2021	League B (promoted to League A)

FIFA CONFEDERATIONS CUP 1992-2017

None

HUNGARIAN CLUB HONOURS IN EUROPEAN CLUB COMPETITIONS:

European Champion Clubs' Cup (1956-1992) / UEFA Champions League (1993-2021)		
None		
Fairs Cup (1858-1971) / UEFA Cup (1972-2009) / UEFA Europa League (2010-2021)		
Ferencvárosi FC	1	1964/1965
UEFA Super Cup (1972-2020)		
None		
European Cup Winners' Cup 1961-1999*		
None		

*defunct competition

NATIONAL COMPETITIONS
TABLE OF HONOURS

	CHAMPIONS	CUP WINNERS	BEST GOALSCORERS	
1901	Budapesti Torna Club	-	Miltiades Manno (Budapesti Torna Club)	17
1902	Budapesti Torna Club	-	Miltiades Manno (Budapesti Torna Club)	10
1903	Ferencvárosi TC	-	Jenő Károly (MTK Budapest)	15
1904	MTK Budapest	-	József Pokorny (Ferencvárosi TC)	12
1905	Ferencvárosi TC	-	Jenő Károly (MTK Budapest)	13
1906/1907	Ferencvárosi TC	-	Béla Kelemen (Magyar Atlétikai Club)	21
1907/1908	MTK Budapest	-	Gyula Vangel (Magyar Atlétikai Club)	21
1908/1909	Ferencvárosi TC	-	Imre Schlosser (Ferencvárosi TC)	30
1909/1910	Ferencvárosi TC	MTK Budapest	Imre Schlosser (Ferencvárosi TC)	18
1910/1911	Ferencvárosi TC	MTK Budapest	Imre Schlosser (Ferencvárosi TC)	38
1911/1912	Ferencvárosi TC	MTK Budapest	Imre Schlosser (Ferencvárosi TC)	34
1912/1913	Ferencvárosi TC	Ferencvárosi TC	Imre Schlosser (Ferencvárosi TC)	33
1913/1914	MTK Budapest	MTK Budapest	Imre Schlosser (Ferencvárosi TC)	21
1914/1915	*No competition*	*No competition*	-	
1915/1916	*No competition*	*No competition*		
1916/1917	MTK Budapest	*No competition*	Imre Schlosser (MTK Budapest)	38
1917/1918	MTK Budapest	*No competition*	Alfréd Schaffer (MTK Budapest)	46
1918/1919	MTK Budapest	*No competition*	Alfréd Schaffer (MTK Budapest)	41
1919/1920	MTK Budapest	*No competition*	György Orth (MTK Budapest)	28
1920/1921	MTK Budapest	*No competition*	György Orth (MTK Budapest)	21
1921/1922	MTK Budapest	Ferencvárosi TC	György Orth (MTK Budapest)	26
1922/1923	MTK Budapest	MTK Budapest	István Priboj (Újpesti TE)	25
1923/1924	MTK Budapest	*No competition*	József Jeszmás (Újpesti TE)	15
1924/1925	MTK Budapest	MTK Budapest	György Molnár (MTK Budapest)	21
1925/1926	Ferencvárosi TC	Kispest AC	József Takács (Vasas SC Budapest)	29
1926/1927	Ferencvárosi TC	Ferencvárosi TC	László Horváth (Ferencvárosi TC)	14
1927/1928	Ferencvárosi TC	Ferencvárosi TC	József Takács (Ferencvárosi TC)	31
1928/1929	Hungária MTK FC Budapest	*No competition*	József Takács (Ferencvárosi TC)	41
1929/1930	Újpesti TE	Debreceni Bocskai FC	József Takács (Ferencvárosi TC)	40
1930/1931	Újpesti TE	III. Kerületi TVE	Jenő Vincze (Debreceni Bocskai FC)	20
1931/1932	Ferencvárosi TC	Hungária MTK FC Budapest	József Takács (Ferencvárosi TC)	42
1932/1933	Újpesti TE	Ferencvárosi TC	Pál Jávor (Újpesti TE)	31
1933/1934	Ferencvárosi TC	Soroksár FC	Géza Toldi (Ferencvárosi TC)	27
1934/1935	Újpesti TE	Ferencvárosi TC	László Cseh II (MTK Budapest)	23
1935/1936	Hungária MTK FC Budapest	*No competition*	György Sárosi dr. (Ferencvárosi TC)	36
1936/1937	Hungária MTK FC Budapest	*No competition*	László Cseh II (MTK Budapest)	36
1937/1938	Ferencvárosi TC	*No competition*	Gyula Zsengellér (Újpesti TE)	31
1938/1939	Újpesti TE	*No competition*	Gyula Zsengellér (Újpesti TE)	56
1939/1940	Ferencvárosi TC	*No competition*	György Sárosi dr. (Ferencvárosi TC)	23
1940/1941	Ferencvárosi TC	Szolnoki MÁV SE	György Sárosi dr. (Ferencvárosi TC)	29
1941/1942	Csepel SC Budapest	Ferencvárosi TC	György Kalmár (Szegedi AK)	35
1942/1943	Csepel SC Budapest	Ferencvárosi TC	Gyula Zsengellér (Újpesti TE) Jenő Jenőfi (Vasas SC Budapest)	26
1943/1944	Nagyváradi AC	Ferencvárosi TC	Gyula Zsengellér (Újpesti TE)	33
1945	Újpesti TE	*No competition*	Gyula Zsengellér (Újpesti TE)	36
1945/1946	Újpesti TE	*No competition*	Ferenc Deák (Szentlőrinci AC)	66
1946/1947	Újpesti TE	*No competition*	Ferenc Deák (Szentlőrinci AC)	48
1947/1948	Csepel SC Budapest	*No competition*	Ferenc Puskás (Budapest Honvéd SE)	50
1948/1949	Ferencvárosi TC	*No competition*	Ferenc Deák (Ferencvárosi TC)	59
1949/1950	Budapest Honvéd SE	*No competition*	Ferenc Puskás (Budapest Honvéd SE)	31
1950	Budapest Honvéd SE	*No competition*	Ferenc Puskás (Budapest Honvéd SE)	25
1951	Budapesti Textiles SE	*No competition*	Sándor Kocsis (Budapest Honvéd SE)	30
1952	Budapest Honvéd SE	Budapesti Bástya SE	Sándor Kocsis (Budapest Honvéd SE)	36
1953	Budapesti Vörös Lobogó SE	*No competition*	Ferenc Puskás (Budapest Honvéd SE)	27
1954	Budapest Honvéd SE	*No competition*	Sándor Kocsis (Budapest Honvéd SE)	33
1955	Budapest Honvéd SE	Vasas SC Budapest	Zoltán Czibor (Budapest Honvéd SE) Ferenc Machos (Budapest Honvéd SE)	20
1956	*No competition*	*No competition*	-	
1957	Vasas SC Budapest	*No competition*	Gyula Szilágyi (Vasas SC Budapest)	17
1957/1958	MTK Budapest	Ferencvárosi TC	Zoltán Friedmanszky (Ferencvárosi TC) János Molnár (MTK Budapest)	16
1958/1959	Csepel SC Budapest	*No competition*	Róbert Kisuczky (Csepel) Tivadar Monostori (Dorog) Lajos Tichy (Honvéd)	15
1959/1960	Újpesti Dózsa SC	*No competition*	Flórián Albert (Ferencvárosi TC)	27
1960/1961	Vasas SC Budapest	*No competition*	Flórián Albert (Ferencvárosi TC) Lajos Tichy (Budapest Honvéd SE)	21
1961/1962	Vasas SC Budapest	*No competition*	Lajos Tichy (Budapest Honvéd SE)	23
1962/1963	Ferencvárosi TC	*No competition*	Ferenc Bene (Újpesti Dózsa SC)	23
1963	Győri Vasas ETO	*No competition*	Lajos Tichy (Budapest Honvéd SE)	13
1964	Ferencvárosi TC	Budapest Honvéd SE	Lajos Tichy (Budapest Honvéd SE)	28
1965	Vasas SC Budapest	Rába Vasas ETO Győr	Flórián Albert (Ferencvárosi TC)	27

Year	Champion	Cup Winner	Top Scorer	
1966	Vasas SC Budapest	Rába Vasas ETO Győr	János Farkas (Vasas SC Budapest)	25
1967	Ferencvárosi TC	Rába Vasas ETO Győr	Antal Dunai II (Újpesti Dózsa SC)	36
1968	Ferencvárosi TC	MTK Budapest	Antal Dunai II (Újpesti Dózsa SC)	31
1969	Újpesti Dózsa SC	Újpesti Dózsa SC	Ferenc Bene (Újpesti Dózsa SC)	27
1970	Újpesti Dózsa SC	Újpesti Dózsa SC	Antal Dunai II (Újpesti Dózsa SC)	14
1970/1971	Újpesti Dózsa SC	*No competition*	Mihály Kozma (Budapest Honvéd SE)	25
1971/1972	Újpesti Dózsa SC	Ferencvárosi TC	Ferenc Bene (Újpesti Dózsa SC)	29
1972/1973	Újpesti Dózsa SC	Vasas Budapest SC	Ferenc Bene (Újpesti Dózsa SC)	23
1973/1974	Újpesti Dózsa SC	Ferencvárosi TC	Mihály Kozma (Budapest Honvéd SE)	27
1974/1975	Újpesti Dózsa SC	Újpesti Dózsa SC	Mihály Kozma (Budapest Honvéd SE) Ferenc Bene (Újpesti Dózsa SC)	20
1975/1976	Ferencvárosi TC	Ferencvárosi TC	László Fazekas (Újpesti Dózsa SC)	19
1976/1977	Vasas SC Budapest	Diósgyőri VTK	Béla Várady (Vasas SC Budapest)	36
1977/1978	Újpesti Dózsa SC	Ferencvárosi TC	László Fazekas (Újpesti Dózsa SC)	24
1978/1979	Újpesti Dózsa SC	Rába Vasas ETO Győr	László Fekete (Újpesti Dózsa SC)	31
1979/1980	Budapest Honvéd SE	Diósgyőri VTK	László Fekete (Újpesti Dózsa SC)	36
1980/1981	Ferencvárosi TC	Vasas Budapest SC	Tibor Nyilasi (Ferencvárosi TC)	30
1981/1982	Rába Vasas ETO Győr	Újpesti Dózsa SC	Péter Hannich (Rába Vasas ETO Győr)	22
1982/1983	Rába Vasas ETO Győr	Újpesti Dózsa SC	Lajos Dobány (Pécsi MSC / Szombathely)	23
1983/1984	Budapest Honvéd SE	Siófoki Bányász SK	József Szabó (Videoton SC Székesfehérvár)	19
1984/1985	Budapest Honvéd SE	Budapest Honvéd SE	Lajos Détári (Budapest Honvéd SE) József Kiprich (Tatabányai Bányász)	18
1985/1986	Budapest Honvéd SE	Vasas Budapest SC	Lajos Détári (Budapest Honvéd SE)	27
1986/1987	MTK-VM Budapest	Újpesti Dózsa SC	Lajos Détári (Budapest Honvéd SE)	19
1987/1988	Budapest Honvéd SE	Békéscsabai Előre SSC	Béla Melis (Debreceni VSC)	19
1988/1989	Budapest Honvéd SE	Budapest Honvéd SE	Tamás Petres (Videoton SC Székesfehérvár)	19
1989/1990	Újpesti TE	Pécsi MSC	József Dzurják (Ferencvárosi TC)	18
1990/1991	Budapest Honvéd SE	Ferencvárosi TC	József Gregor (Budapest Honvéd SE)	19
1991/1992	Ferencvárosi TC	Újpesti TE	Pál Fischer (Siófoki Bányász SK) Ferenc Orosz (Vác FC)	16
1992/1993	Kispest Honvéd FC	Ferencvárosi TC	László Répási (Vác FC)	16
1993/1994	Vác FC	Ferencvárosi TC	Béla Illés (Kispest Honvéd FC)	17
1994/1995	Ferencvárosi TC	Ferencvárosi TC	Sándor Preisinger (Zalaegerszeg)	21
1995/1996	Ferencvárosi TC	Kispest Honvéd FC	Ihor Nichenko (UKR, Stadler FC / Ferencvárosi TC)	18
1996/1997	MTK Budapest FC	MTK Budapest FC	Béla Illés (MTK Budapest FC)	23
1997/1998	Újpesti TE	MTK Budapest FC	Krisztián Tiber (Gázszer FC Gárdony)	20
1998/1999	MTK Hungária FC Budapest	Debreceni VSC	Béla Illés (MTK Hungária FC Budapest)	22
1999/2000	Dunaferr SE Dunaújváros	MTK Hungária FC Budapest	Attila Tököli (Dunaferr SE Dunaújváros)	22
2000/2001	Ferencvárosi TC	Debreceni VSC	Péter Kabát (Vasas SC Budapest)	24
2001/2002	Zalaegerszegi TE FC	Újpesti TE	Attila Tököli (Dunaferr SE Dunaújváros)	28
2002/2003	MTK Hungária FC Budapest	Ferencvárosi TC	Krisztián Kenesei (Zalaegerszegi TE FC)	23
2003/2004	Ferencvárosi TC	Ferencvárosi TC	Mihály Tóth (Soproni VSE)	17
2004/2005	Debreceni VSC	Sopron FC	Tomáš Medveď (SVK, Pápai FC)	18
2005/2006	Debreceni VSC	FC Fehérvár Székesfehérvár	Péter Rajczi (Újpest FC)	23
2006/2007	Debreceni VSC	Budapest Honvéd FC	Ibrahim Sidibe (SEN, Debreceni VSC) Péter Bajzát (Győri ETO FC)	18
2007/2008	MTK Budapest FC	Debreceni VSC	Róbert Waltner (Zalaegerszegi TE FC)	18
2008/2009	Debreceni VSC	Budapest Honvéd FC	Péter Bajzát (Győri ETO FC)	20
2009/2010	Debreceni VSC	Debreceni VSC	Nemanja Nikolić (SRB, Videoton FC Székesfehérvár)	18
2010/2011	Videoton FC Székesfehérvár	Kecskeméti TE	André Alves dos Santos (BRA, Videoton FC Székesfehérvár)	24
2011/2012	Debreceni VSC	Debreceni VSC	Adamo Coulibaly (FRA, Debreceni VSC)	20
2012/2013	Győri ETO FC	Debreceni VSC	Adamo Coulibaly (FRA, Debreceni VSC)	18
2013/2014	Debreceni VSC	Újpest FC	Nemanja Nikolić (Videoton FC Székesfehérvár) Attila Simon (Paksi FC)	21
2014/2015	Videoton FC Székesfehérvár	Ferencvárosi TC	Nemanja Nikolić (Videoton FC Székesfehérvár)	21
2015/2016	Ferencvárosi TC	Ferencvárosi TC	Dániel Böde (Ferencvárosi TC)	17
2016/2017	Budapest Honvéd FC	Ferencvárosi TC	Márton Eppel (Budapest Honvéd FC)	16
2017/2018	Videoton FC Székesfehérvár	Újpest FC	Davide Lanzafame (ITA, Budapest Honvéd FC)	18
2018/2019	Ferencvárosi TC	MOL Vidi FC Székesfehérvár	Davide Lanzafame (ITA, Budapest Honvéd FC) Filip Holender (Budapest Honvéd FC)	16
2019/2020	Ferencvárosi TC	Budapest Honvéd FC	András Radó (Zalaegerszegi TE FC)	13
2020/2021	Ferencvárosi TC	Újpest FC	János Hahn (Paksi FC)	22

NATIONAL CHAMPIONSHIP
Nemzeti Bajnokság I 2020/2021
(14.08.2020 – 09.05.2021)

Results

Round 1 [14-17.08.2020]
MTK Budapest - Ferencvárosi TC 1-1(1-0)
Paksi FC - Újpest FC 1-2(0-1)
Zalaegerszeg - Fehérvár FC 3-3(2-2)
Diósgyöri VTK - Mezőkövesd 2-1(2-1)
Budafoki MTE - Kisvárda FC 2-1(1-1)
Puskás Ak. - Budap. Honvéd 1-0(0-0) [04.11.]

Round 2 [21-23.08.2020]
Mezőkövesd - Zalaegerszeg 1-1(0-1)
MTK Budapest - Budapest Honvéd 3-1(1-1)
Fehérvár FC - Paksi FC 1-1(0-0)
Újpest FC - Budafoki MTE 1-1(1-0)
Kisvárda - Puskás Akadémia 0-3(0-1) [04.09.]
Ferencváros - Diósgyör 0-1(0-0) [20.01.2021]

Round 3 [28-30.08.2020]
Diósgyöri VTK - MTK Budapest 1-1(1-0)
Paksi FC - Mezőkövesd 1-2(0-2)
Budafoki MTE - Fehérvár FC 1-4(0-1)
Zalaegerszeg - Ferencvárosi TC 1-2(0-1)
Puskás Akadémia - Újpest FC 3-2(1-1)
Budapest Honvéd - Kisvárda FC 1-2(1-2)

Round 4 [11-13.09.2020]
Ferencvárosi TC - Paksi FC 5-0(3-0)
Mezőkövesd - Budafoki MTE 1-0(0-0)
Diósgyöri VTK - Budapest Honvéd 2-4(2-2)
Fehérvár FC - Puskás Akadémia 3-1(1-0)
Újpest FC - Kisvárda FC 2-4(2-2)
MTK Budapest - Zalaegerszeg 0-3(0-1)

Round 5 [25-27.09.2020]
Puskás Akadémia - Mezőkövesd 1-0(0-0)
Paksi FC - MTK Budapest 4-0(1-0)
Zalaegerszeg - Diósgyöri VTK 3-1(2-1)
Budapest Honvéd - Újpest FC 1-2(1-0)
Kisvárda - Fehérvár FC 2-1(1-1) [27.01.2021]
Budafok - Ferencváros 0-3(0-1) [27.01.2021]

Round 6 [02-04.10.2020]
MTK Budapest - Budafoki MTE 1-2(0-1)
Mezőkövesd - Kisvárda FC 1-2(0-2)
Diósgyöri VTK - Paksi FC 1-2(0-1)
Zalaegerszeg - Budapest Honvéd 2-4(0-2)
Ferencvárosi TC - Puskás Akadémia 2-1(1-1)
Fehérvár FC - Újpest FC 5-1(0-0)

Round 7 [16-18.10.2020]
Kisvárda FC - Ferencvárosi TC 0-2(0-0)
Budafoki MTE - Diósgyöri VTK 2-1(1-0)
Újpest FC - Mezőkövesd 1-0(0-0)
Puskás Akadémia - MTK Budapest 0-3(0-2)
Paksi FC - Zalaegerszeg 3-1(1-1)
Budapest Honvéd - Fehérvár FC 2-2(1-0)

Round 8 [24-25.10.2020]
MTK Budapest - Kisvárda FC 1-1(1-0)
Paksi FC - Budapest Honvéd 0-0
Ferencvárosi TC - Újpest FC 2-0(1-0)
Zalaegerszeg - Budafoki MTE 1-3(1-2)
Mezőkövesd - Fehérvár FC 1-2(0-1)
Diósgyöri VTK - Puskás Akadémia 3-0(3-0)

Round 9 [31.10.-01.11.2020]
Puskás Akadémia - Zalaegerszeg 1-2(1-1)
Budapest Honvéd - Mezőkövesd 1-1(0-0)
Fehérvár FC - Ferencvárosi TC 1-1(0-1)
Budafoki MTE - Paksi FC 2-3(2-3)
Újpest FC - MTK Budapest 0-4(0-3)
Kisvárda FC - Diósgyöri VTK 1-0(0-0)

Round 10 [06-08.11.2020]
Diósgyöri VTK - Újpest FC 3-0 *awarded*
Paksi FC - Puskás Akadémia 6-2(3-1)
MTK Budapest - Fehérvár FC 3-1(1-0)
Zalaegerszeg - Kisvárda FC 1-2(0-1)
Ferencvárosi TC - Mezőkövesd 3-0(3-0)
Budafok - Budapest Honvéd 1-2(1-1) [23.11.]

Round 11 [20-22.11.2020]
Kisvárda FC - Paksi FC 3-1(2-1)
Puskás Akadémia - Budafoki MTE 3-0(1-0)
Mezőkövesd - MTK Budapest 0-1(0-1)
Budapest Honvéd - Ferencvárosi TC 0-1(0-1)
Fehérvár FC - Diósgyöri VTK 3-0(1-0)
Újpest FC - Zalaegerszeg 3-2(1-1) [23.12.]

Round 12 [27-29.11.2020]
Újpest FC - Paksi FC 1-1(0-0)
Kisvárda FC - Budafoki MTE 0-0
Fehérvár FC - Zalaegerszeg 2-0(2-0)
Ferencvárosi TC - MTK Budapest 2-0(1-0)
Mezőkövesd - Diósgyöri VTK 2-1(1-0)
Budapest Honvéd - Puskás Akadémia 0-1(0-0)

Round 13 [04-06.12.2020]
Budafoki MTE - Újpest FC 1-1(0-0)
Zalaegerszeg - Mezőkövesd 3-0(2-0)
Diósgyöri VTK - Ferencvárosi TC 1-3(1-2)
Puskás Akadémia - Kisvárda FC 0-0
Budapest Honvéd - MTK Budapest 2-2(2-0)
Paksi FC - Fehérvár FC 1-0(0-0)

Round 14 [11-13.12.2020]
Újpest FC - Puskás Akadémia 1-2(0-0)
Kisvárda FC - Budapest Honvéd 0-0
Ferencvárosi TC - Zalaegerszeg 2-0(0-0)
Fehérvár FC - Budafoki MTE 4-1(3-0)
Mezőkövesd - Paksi FC 4-3(2-1)
MTK Budapest - Diósgyöri VTK 1-0(0-0)

Round 15 [15-16.12.2020]
Kisvárda FC - Újpest FC 1-1(0-0)
Fehérvár FC - Puskás Akadémia 1-1(0-1)
Budapest Honvéd - Diósgyöri VTK 5-1(2-0)
Zalaegerszeg - MTK Budapest 2-0(2-0)
Paksi FC - Ferencvárosi TC 1-3(1-1)
Budafoki MTE - Mezőkövesd 0-1(0-0)

Round 16 [18-20.12.2020]
Fehérvár FC - Kisvárda FC 3-0(1-0)
MTK Budapest - Paksi FC 3-1(0-0)
Diósgyöri VTK - Zalaegerszeg 1-3(0-2)
Ferencvárosi TC - Budafoki MTE 2-1(0-0)
Mezőkövesd - Puskás Akadémia 1-0(1-0)
Újpest FC - Budapest Honvéd 2-1(0-0)

Round 17 [23-24.01.2021]
Kisvárda FC - Mezőkövesd 0-0
Puskás Akadémia - Ferencvárosi TC 1-1(1-0)
Újpest FC - Fehérvár FC 0-5(0-2)
Budafoki MTE - MTK Budapest 2-2(1-2)
Paksi FC - Diósgyöri VTK 2-1(2-0)
Budapest Honvéd - Zalaegerszeg 2-2(1-0)

Round 18 [30-31.01.2021]
MTK Budapest - Puskás Akadémia 0-1(0-0)
Mezőkövesd - Újpest FC 3-2(1-0)
Ferencvárosi TC - Kisvárda FC 1-1(0-1)
Fehérvár FC - Budapest Honvéd 1-2(1-1)
Zalaegerszeg - Paksi FC 4-4(1-2)
Diósgyöri VTK - Budafoki MTE 1-1(1-0)

Round 19 [02-03.02.2021]
Kisvárda FC - MTK Budapest 0-2(0-1)
Fehérvár FC - Mezőkövesd 0-0
Puskás Akadémia - Diósgyöri VTK 2-0(1-0)
Budapest Honvéd - Paksi FC 1-1(0-0)
Budafoki MTE - Zalaegerszeg 3-1(1-0)
Újpest FC - Ferencvárosi TC 0-4(0-1)

Round 20 [06-07.02.2021]
Diósgyöri VTK - Kisvárda FC 2-0(2-0)
Mezőkövesd - Budapest Honvéd 2-0(1-0)
MTK Budapest - Újpest FC 1-3(1-3)
Paksi FC - Budafoki MTE 4-1(2-0)
Zalaegerszeg - Puskás Akadémia 1-2(0-0)
Ferencvárosi TC - Fehérvár FC 2-0(1-0)

Round 21 [12-14.02.2021]
Újpest FC - Diósgyöri VTK 1-0(0-0)
Puskás Akadémia - Paksi FC 3-2(2-0)
Kisvárda FC - Zalaegerszeg 2-1(1-0)
Budapest Honvéd - Budafoki MTE 2-3(2-1)
Mezőkövesd - Ferencvárosi TC 2-2(0-1)
Fehérvár FC - MTK Budapest 1-2(1-0)

Round 22 [19-21.02.2021]
MTK Budapest - Mezőkövesd 0-0
Zalaegerszeg - Újpest FC 3-0(1-0)
Fehérvár FC - Diósgyöri VTK 1-3(1-0)
Ferencvárosi TC - Budapest Honvéd 1-0(0-0)
Budafoki MTE - Puskás Akadémia 0-3(0-1)
Paksi FC - Kisvárda FC 3-0(2-0)

Round 23 [26-28.02.2021]
Diósgyöri VTK - Mezőkövesd 2-2(1-1)
Budafoki MTE - Kisvárda FC 2-0(0-0)
Puskás Akadémia - Budapest Honvéd 1-2(1-1)
MTK Budapest - Ferencvárosi TC 2-2(0-2)
Paksi FC - Újpest FC 1-3(1-0)
Zalaegerszeg - Fehérvár FC 0-2(0-0)

Round 24 [02-03.03.2021]
Kisvárda FC - Puskás Akadémia 0-1(0-1)
Budapest Honvéd - MTK Budapest 3-2(1-2)
Ferencvárosi TC - Diósgyöri VTK 1-0(0-0)
Mezőkövesd - Zalaegerszeg 2-0(2-0)
Újpest FC - Budafoki MTE 2-0(0-0)
Fehérvár FC - Paksi FC 2-2(1-0)

Round 25 [05-07.03.2021]
Diósgyöri VTK - MTK Budapest 0-0
Paksi FC - Mezőkövesd 2-2(0-1)
Puskás Akadémia - Újpest FC 2-1(1-1)
Budapest Honvéd - Kisvárda FC 0-1(0-0)
Zalaegerszeg - Ferencvárosi TC 2-2(1-0)
Budafoki MTE - Fehérvár FC 1-2(1-1)

Round 26 [13-14.03.2021]
Újpest FC - Kisvárda FC 3-0(3-0)
MTK Budapest - Zalaegerszeg 3-0(0-0)
Diósgyöri VTK - Budapest Honvéd 0-0
Mezőkövesd - Budafoki MTE 2-1(1-1)
Ferencvárosi TC - Paksi FC 5-2(1-1)
Puskás Akadémia - Fehérvár FC 1-0(0-0)

Round 27 [03-04.04.2021]
Paksi FC - MTK Budapest 3-1(2-0)
Zalaegerszeg - Diósgyöri VTK 2-0(1-0)
Budapest Honvéd - Újpest FC 2-2(2-2)
Kisvárda FC - Fehérvár FC 0-0
Budafoki MTE - Ferencvárosi TC 0-4(0-0)
Puskás Akadémia - Mezőkövesd 2-0(1-0)

Round 28 [09-11.04.2021]		Round 29 [16-18.04.2021]		Round 30 [20-21.04.2021]

Round 28 [09-11.04.2021]
Mezőkövesd - Kisvárda FC 0-1(0-1)
MTK Budapest - Budafoki MTE 0-0
Fehérvár FC - Újpest FC 4-0(2-0)
Ferencvárosi TC - Puskás Akadémia 1-1(0-1)
Diósgyőri VTK - Paksi FC 1-4(0-2)
Zalaegerszeg - Budapest Honvéd 0-1(0-0)

Round 29 [16-18.04.2021]
Budafoki MTE - Diósgyőri VTK 1-2(0-1)
Újpest FC - Mezőkövesd 3-0(2-0)
Kisvárda FC - Ferencvárosi TC 0-0
Paksi FC - Zalaegerszeg 1-1(0-1)
Puskás Akadémia - MTK Budapest 3-0(2-0)
Budapest Honvéd - Fehérvár FC 2-3(2-1)

Round 30 [20-21.04.2021]
Zalaegerszeg - Budafoki MTE 5-0(2-0)
Ferencvárosi TC - Újpest FC 3-0(2-0)
MTK Budapest - Kisvárda FC 0-1(0-1)
Diósgyőri VTK - Puskás Akadémia 2-1(1-0)
Mezőkövesd - Fehérvár FC 1-3(1-0)
Paksi FC - Budapest Honvéd 2-0(2-0)

Round 31 [24-25.04.2021]
Puskás Akadémia - Zalaegerszeg 1-4(1-1)
Kisvárda FC - Diósgyőri VTK 0-1(0-0)
Újpest FC - MTK Budapest 1-3(1-1)
Budafoki MTE - Paksi FC 2-9(2-4)
Fehérvár FC - Ferencvárosi TC 1-2(0-1)
Budapest Honvéd - Mezőkövesd 2-2(0-1)

Round 32 [29.04.-02.05.2021]
Diósgyőri VTK - Újpest FC 0-0
MTK Budapest - Fehérvár FC 1-3(0-1)
Paksi FC - Puskás Akadémia 4-2(0-1)
Zalaegerszeg - Kisvárda FC 0-0
Ferencvárosi TC - Mezőkövesd 2-1(1-0)
Budafoki MTE - Budapest Honvéd 0-1(0-0)

Round 33 [07-09.05.2021]
Mezőkövesd - MTK Budapest 5-1(2-0)
Budapest Honvéd - Ferencvárosi TC 1-2(1-0)
Újpest FC - Zalaegerszeg 5-4(3-1)
Puskás Akadémia - Budafoki MTE 5-0(4-0)
Diósgyőri VTK - Fehérvár FC 0-4(0-1)
Kisvárda FC - Paksi FC 5-1(4-0)

Final Standings

									Total		Home						Away				
1.	**Ferencvárosi TC**	33	23	9	1	69	-	22	78	13	2	1	34	-	8	10	7	0	35	-	14
2.	Puskás Ferenc Labdarugó Akadémia Felcsút	33	18	4	11	52	-	42	58	11	2	4	30	-	17	7	2	7	22	-	25
3.	Fehérvár FC Székesfehérvár	33	16	8	9	68	-	38	56	7	5	4	33	-	17	9	3	5	35	-	21
4.	Paksi FC	33	14	8	11	76	-	64	50	10	3	4	39	-	21	4	5	7	37	-	43
5.	Kisvárda FC	33	12	10	11	30	-	36	46	5	6	5	14	-	14	7	4	6	16	-	22
6.	Újpest FC	33	12	6	15	46	-	67	42	8	2	6	26	-	31	4	4	9	20	-	36
7.	MTK Budapest FC	33	11	9	13	44	-	49	42	5	5	6	20	-	20	6	4	7	24	-	29
8.	Mezőkövesdi SE	33	11	9	13	40	-	46	42	9	2	5	28	-	21	2	7	8	12	-	25
9.	Zalaegerszegi TE FC	33	10	7	16	58	-	58	37	6	4	7	33	-	26	4	3	9	25	-	32
10.	Budapest Honvéd FC	33	9	10	14	46	-	48	37	2	7	8	27	-	30	7	3	6	19	-	18
11.	Diósgyőri VTK (*Relegated*)	33	9	6	18	34	-	53	33	5	6	6	22	-	26	4	0	12	12	-	27
12.	Budafoki MTE (*Relegated*)	33	7	6	20	34	-	74	27	4	2	11	20	-	40	3	4	9	14	-	34

Please note: Diósgyőri VTK - Újpest FC (Round 10) was not played, as several players from Újpest TE were infected with COVID. The match was declared won by Diósgyőri VTK 3–0, without a game.

Top goalscorers:	
22 János Hahn	*Paksi FC*
15 Nemanja Nikolić	*Fehérvár FC Székesfehérvár*
13 Dániel Gazdag	*Budapest Honvéd FC*
12 Myrto Uzuni (ALB)	*Ferencvárosi TC*
12 Ivan Petryak (UKR)	*Fehérvár FC Székesfehérvár*
11 Dávid Kovács	*Budafoki MTE*
11 Tokmac Chol Nguen (NOR)	*Ferencvárosi TC*

NATIONAL CUP
Magyar Kupa 2020/2021

Seventh Round [21/28-29.10./11/13-14.11.2020]

Budaörsi SC - Aqvital FC Csákvár	1-3	Érdi Városi SE - Kazincbarcikai SC	0-3 *awarded*
Csácsbozsok-Nemesapáti - Budapest Honvéd FC	0-2	Taksony SE - Kozármisleny SE	2-0
Dabas-Gyón FC - Budafoki MTE	2-3	Tarpa SC - BTE Felsőzsolca	4-1
Szentlőrinc SE - Puskás Ferenc L. Akadémia Felcsút	0-4	Budapesti VSC - Debreceni VSC	0-2
Zsámbéki SK - Tállya KSE	1-3	Egri FC - Budapesti Vasas SC	0-2
Kiskunfelegyhazi HTK - Dorogi FC	1-5	Nagykanizsa FC - Debreceni EAC	1-2
Kabai Meteorit SE - Fémalk-Dunavarsány	0-2	Monori SE - Bodajk FC Siófok	2-2 aet; 4-5 pen
Salgotarjáni BTC - Pécsi MFC	1-3	Soroksár SC - Győri ETO FC	3-2
Cso-Ki Sport - Hódmezővásárhelyi FC	0-1	ASR Gázgyár - Kaposvári Rákóczi FC	1-5
Gárdony Városi SC - Fehérvár FC Székesfehérvár	1-4	Kecskeméti TE - Kisvárda FC	0-1
Lipót Pékség SE - Zalaegerszegi TE	1-3	Dunaújváros PASE - Újpest FC	0-6
Gyöngyösi AK-YTONG - Mezőkövesdi SE	1-4	Nyíregyháza Spartacus - Paksi FC	1-2(0-0,1-1)
Bátaszék SE - MTK Budapest FC	1-7	Békéscsaba 1912 Előre SE - Diósgyőri VTK	0-3
III. Kerületi TVE - Szeged-Csanád Grosics Akadémia	2-1	Ménfőcsanaki SE Győr - Szombathelyi Haladás	0-3
Zalaszentgróti VFC - Tiszafured VSE	0-1	Szolnoki MÁV FC - Gyirmót SE Győr	1-0
Ceglédi VSE - FC Ajka	0-1	Bicskei TC - Ferencvárosi TC	0-5

Eighth Round [09-11.02.2021]

Tarpa SC - Diósgyőri VTK	0-3	Fémalk-Dunavarsány - Budafoki MTE	0-11
Szolnoki MÁV FC - Újpest FC	0-2	Tállya KSE - Kaposvári Rákóczi FC	5-3
Dorogi FC - Ferencvárosi TC	1-2	Taksony SE - Bodajk FC Siófok	1-4
III. Kerületi TVE - Budapest Honvéd FC	1-3	Debreceni EAC - Debreceni VSC	1-2
Aqvital FC Csákvár - Paksi FC	2-3	Pécsi MFC - Szombathelyi Haladás	0-1
Hódmezővásárhelyi FC - Puskás Ferenc L. A. Felcsút	0-3	FC Ajka - Mezőkövesdi SE	1-2
Soroksár SC - Kisvárda FC	1-2	Budapesti Vasas SC - Fehérvár FC Székesfehérvár	1-2
Kazincbarcikai SC - MTK Budapest FC	1-4	Tiszafuredi VSE - Zalaegerszegi TE	1-2

Mezőkövesdi SE - Diósgyöri VTK	2-0(2-0)	Puskás Ferenc L. Akadémia Felcsút - Újpest FC	1-2(0-1)
Paksi FC - Budafoki MTE	2-4(2-3)	Debreceni VSC - Bodajk FC Siófok	2-1(1-0,1-1)
Tállya KSE - MTK Budapest FC	1-4(0-2)	Szombathelyi Haladás - Kisvárda FC	0-1(0-1)
Zalaegerszegi TE - Budapest Honvéd FC	2-1(0-1,1-1)	Ferencvárosi TC - Fehérvár FC Székesfehérvár	1-2(1-2)

Quarter-Finals [09-10.03.2021]

Újpest FC - Mezőkövesdi SE	1-1 aet; 5-4 pen	Kisvárda FC - Zalaegerszegi TE	6-1(2-0)
Fehérvár FC Székesfehérvár - Budafoki MTE	2-0(0-0)	Debreceni VSC - MTK Budapest FC	1-2(0-1)

Semi-Finals [14-15.04.2021]

Kisvárda FC - Újpest FC	0-1(0-0)	MTK Budapest FC - Fehérvár FC Székesfehérvár	1-2(1-1)

Final

03.05.2021, Puskás Aréna, Budapest; Referee: Gergő Bogár; Attendance: 4,500
Fehérvár FC Székesfehérvár - Újpest FC   **0-1(0-0,0-0)**

Fehérvár FC: Dániel Kovács, Adrián Rus [*sent off 90*], Visar Musliu, Loïc Négo, Ianique dos Santos Tavares „Stopira",Bendegúz Bolla (62.Attila Fiola), Rúben Rafael Melo Silva Pinto, Funsho Ibrahim Bamgboye (90.Alef dos Santos Saldanha [*sent off 97*]), Ivan Petryak, Budu Zivzivadze, Nemanja Nikolić (77.Lyes Houri). Trainer: Imre Szabics.

Újpest FC: Filip Pajović, Kire Ristevski, Georgios Koutroumpis (102.Péter Szakály), Nemanja Antonov, Branko Pauljević (118.Zsolt Máté), Lirim Kastrati, Nikola Mitrović, Vincent Onovo, Gadji Celi Carmel Junior Tallo (114.Krisztián Simon), Giorgi Beridze (114.Antonio Perošević), Yohan Croizet. Trainer: Michael Oenning (Hungary).

Goal: 0-1 Lirim Kastrati (101).

THE CLUBS 2020/2021

Budafoki Munkás Testedző Egyesület

Founded:	1912
Stadium:	Promontor utcai stadion, Budafok (4,000)
Trainer:	Csaba Czizmadia · 30.05.1985
[27.04.2021]	Bálint Pacsi · 08.11.1974

Goalkeepers:	DOB	M	(s)	G
Balázs Bese	22.01.1999	8		
Zoltán Kovács	29.10.1984	2		
Dániel Póser	12.01.1990	23		
Defenders:	**DOB**	**M**	**(s)**	**G**
András Huszti	29.01.2001	18	(7)	
Marko Iharoš (CRO)	23.06.1996	2	(3)	
Márk Jagodics	10.04.1992	14		
Kornél Khiesz	19.10.1992		(1)	
Henrik Kirják	12.07.1999	1		
Andor Margitics	03.01.1991	15	(5)	
Sinan Medgyes (SVK)	30.06.1993	21	(6)	1
Marko Nikolić (SRB)	31.03.1998	16		
Danijel Romić (CRO)	19.03.1993	17	(2)	
Gergő Vaszicsku	30.06.1991	9	(1)	1
Zsolt Venczel	25.11.2001		(1)	
Márió Zeke	01.09.2000	11	(2)	

Midfielders:	DOB	M	(s)	G
András Csonka	01.05.2000	15	(3)	1
Máté Fekete	22.08.1995		(4)	
Attila Filkor	12.07.1988	17	(1)	
Sebestyén Ihrig-Farkas	28.01.1994	15	(13)	5
Kornél Kulcsár	11.11.1991	13	(17)	2
Attila Lőrinczy	08.04.1994	8	(11)	
Miklós Micsinai	11.01.1998	15	(7)	
Bálint Oláh	02.12.1984	32		1
István Soltész	29.11.2000	1	(4)	
Forwards:	**DOB**	**M**	**(s)**	**G**
Dávid Kovács	18.06.1991	32	(1)	11
Bence Mervó	05.03.1995		(3)	
Alen Skribek	11.04.2001	16	(10)	6
Máté Szabó	26.01.1999	18	(12)	
Ronald Takács	26.01.1998	12	(9)	2
Dániel Zsóri	14.10.2000	12	(9)	3

Budapest Honvéd Football Club

Founded:	03.08.1909
Stadium:	"Hidegkuti Nándor" Stadion, Budapest (5,014)
Trainer:	Tamás Bódog · 27.09.1970
[15.02.2021]	Ferenc Horváth · 06.05.1973

Goalkeepers:	DOB	M	(s)	G
Tomáš Tujvel (SVK)	19.09.1983	33		
Defenders:	**DOB**	**M**	**(s)**	**G**
Naser Aliji (SUI)	27.12.1993	7	(5)	
Botond Baráth	21.04.1992	12	(2)	
Nir Bardea (ISR)	25.01.1996	4	(1)	
Bence Batik	08.11.1993	25		2
Artur Crăciun (MDA)	29.06.1998		(2)	
Đorđe Kamber (BIH)	20.11.1983	13	(7)	
Łukasz Klemenz (POL)	24.09.1995	5	(1)	
Ivan Lovrić (CRO)	11.07.1985	26		1
Alex Szabó	15.05.2002	1		
Krisztián Tamás	18.04.1995	22		2
Eke Uzoma (NGA)	11.08.1989	6	(2)	
Midfielders:	**DOB**	**M**	**(s)**	**G**
Bertalan Bocskay	02.03.2002	7	(7)	
Dániel Gazdag	02.03.1996	30		13
Patrik Hidi	27.11.1990	30		4
Noel Keresztes	16.09.2004		(1)	

	DOB	M	(s)	G
Barna Kesztyűs	04.09.1993	5	(10)	
Dominik Kocsis	01.08.2002	1	(8)	
Mohamed Mezghrani (BEL)	02.06.1994	25		1
Gergő Nagy	07.01.1993	7	(4)	
Norbert Szendrei	27.03.2000	20	(6)	2
Donát Zsótér	06.01.1996	21	(6)	2
Forwards:	**DOB**	**M**	**(s)**	**G**
Norbert Balogh	21.02.1996	21	(5)	10
Lukács Bőle	27.03.1990	6	(5)	1
Dominik Cipf	31.01.2001	1	(1)	
Márton Eppel	26.10.1991	7	(5)	1
Thierry Gale (BRB)	01.05.2002		(9)	1
Zalán Kerezsi	17.07.2003	1		
Dávid László	25.04.2002	4	(3)	
Dominik Nagy	08.05.1995	12	(4)	2
Dániel Németh	10.09.2003		(2)	
Kristóf Tóth-Gábor	11.09.2001	3	(3)	
Boubacar Traoré (MLI)	14.12.1999	4	(14)	2
Roland Ugrai	13.11.1992	5	(3)	1

Diósgyőr-Vasgyári Testgyakorlók Köre

Founded:	06.02.1910	
Stadium:	Diósgyőri Stadion, Miskolc (15,325)	
Trainer:	Tamás Feczkó	08.09.1977
[08.12.2020]	Gergely Geri (SVK)	19.01.1977
[07.01.2021]	Zoran Zekić (CRO)	29.04.1974

Goalkeepers:	DOB	M	(s)	G
Botond Antal	22.08.1991	13		
Branislav Danilović (SRB)	24.06.1988	5		
Marko Malenica (CRO)	08.02.1994	14		
Defenders:	DOB	M	(s)	G
Alen Grgić (CRO)	10.08.1994	18		
János Hegedűs	04.10.1996	23	(2)	2
Dejan Karan (SRB)	25.08.1988	8	(4)	
Luka Marin (CRO)	16.03.1998	9	(2)	
Hysen Memolla (ALB)	03.07.1992	13	(1)	
Goran Milović (CRO)	29.01.1989	17		1
Donát Orosz	28.07.2002		(1)	
Artur Pikk (EST)	05.03.1993	6	(1)	
Kristóf Polgár	28.11.1996	16		
Vinko Soldo (CRO)	15.02.1998	15		
Kornél Szűcs	24.09.2001	9	(6)	
András Vági	25.12.1988	1	(4)	

Midfielders:	DOB	M	(s)	G
Florent Hasani (KVX)	30.03.1997	9	(6)	
Bence Iszlai	29.05.1990	9	(8)	2
Dávid Márkvárt	20.09.1994	24	(6)	
Augusto Max (ARG)	10.08.1992	22	(4)	
Sergiy Shestakov (UKR)	12.04.1990	15	(4)	
Asmir Suljić (BIH)	11.09.1991	12	(5)	3
Diego Živulić (CRO)	23.03.1992	5	(5)	
Forwards:	DOB	M	(s)	G
Stefan Dražić (SRB)	14.08.1992	22	(7)	4
Gheorghe-Teodor Grozav (ROU)	29.09.1990	27	(2)	8
Mirko Ivanovski (MKD)	31.10.1989	11	(16)	3
Kristof Korbely	26.05.2000		(5)	
Gábor Makrai	26.06.1996		(7)	
Gábor Molnár	16.05.1994	7	(6)	5
Odise Roshi (ALB)	22.05.1991	6	(5)	
Rui Pedro Couto Ramalho (POR)	02.07.1988	6	(9)	1
David Vaněček (CZE)	09.03.1991	10	(4)	2

Fehérvár Football Club Székesfehérvár

Founded:	1941	
Stadium:	MOL Aréna Sóstó, Székesfehérvár (14,144)	
Trainer:	Gábor Márton	15.10.1966
[17.02.2021]	Tamás Szalai	10.01.1980
[01.04.2021]	Imre Szabics	22.03.1981

Goalkeepers:	DOB	M	(s)	G
Dániel Kovács	16.01.1994	12		
Adam Kovacsik	04.04.1991	4		
Emil Rockov (SRB)	27.01.1995	17	(1)	
Defenders:	DOB	M	(s)	G
Bendegúz Bolla	22.11.1999	24	(3)	
Attila Fiola	17.02.1990	26	(2)	1
Szilveszter Hangya	02.01.1994	16	(9)	1
Visar Musliu (MKD)	13.11.1994	26		
Loïc Négo (FRA)	15.01.1991	27	(1)	6
Adrián Rus (ROU)	18.03.1996	14	(6)	1
Ianique dos Santos Tavares „Stopira" (CPV)	20.05.1988	31		3
Márió Zeke	01.09.2000		(1)	
Midfielders:	DOB	M	(s)	G
Alef dos Santos Saldanha (BRA)	28.01.1995	13	(9)	1
Samy Bourard (BEL)	10.07.1996		(5)	

	DOB	M	(s)	G
Lyes Houri (FRA)	19.01.1996	26	(6)	4
István Kovács	27.03.1992	1	(2)	
Boban Nikolov (MKD)	28.07.1994	7	(2)	1
Patrik Nyári	09.04.2001	1	(1)	
Máté Pátkai	06.03.1988	2		
Rúben Rafael Melo Silva Pinto (POR)	24.04.1992	14	(4)	
Forwards:	DOB	M	(s)	G
Funsho Ibrahim Bamgboye (NGA)	09.01.1999	22	(9)	7
Palko Dárdai	24.04.1999	9	(5)	2
Evandro da Silva (BRA)	14.01.1997	6	(1)	1
Krisztián Géresi	14.06.1994		(6)	
Armin Hodžić (BIH)	17.11.1994	2	(2)	1
Nemanja Nikolić	31.12.1987	20	(11)	15
Ivan Petryak (UKR)	13.03.1994	21	(12)	12
Levente Szabó	06.06.1999	2	(11)	1
Budu Zivzivadze (GEO)	10.03.1994	20	(11)	9

Ferencvárosi Torna Club

Founded:	03.05.1899	
Stadium:	Groupama Aréna, Budapest (22,043)	
Trainer:	Serhiy Rebrov (UKR)	03.06.1974

Goalkeepers:	DOB	M	(s)	G
Ádám Bogdán	27.09.1987	5		
Dénes Dibusz	16.11.1990	28		
Defenders:	DOB	M	(s)	G
Miha Blažić (SVN)	08.05.1993	24		
Endre Botka	25.08.1994	17	(2)	
Dominik Csontos	08.11.2002		(1)	1
Eldar Čivić (BIH)	28.05.1996	11	(7)	1
Lasha Dvali (GEO)	14.05.1995	17	(4)	
Abraham Frimpong (GHA)	06.04.1993	6	(1)	1
Marcel Heister (GER)	29.07.1992	22	(1)	1
Adnan Kovačević (BIH)	09.09.1993	4	(2)	
Gergő Lovrencsics	01.09.1988	19	(3)	1
Samy Mmaee (MAR)	08.09.1996	8	(1)	
Midfielders:	DOB	M	(s)	G
Isael da Silva Barbosa (BRA)	13.05.1988	19	(9)	6
Igor Kharatin (UKR)	02.02.1995	20	(5)	4

	DOB	M	(s)	G
Aïssa Laïdouni (FRA)	13.12.1996	23	(4)	3
Dávid Miklós Sigér	30.11.1990	11	(13)	1
Michal Škvarka (SVK)	19.08.1992	2	(9)	
Wergiton do Rosario Calmon „Somália"(BRA)	28.09.1988	17	(7)	3
Bálint Vécsei	13.07.1993	1	(13)	1
Henry Wingo (USA)	04.10.1995	5	(7)	
Forwards:	DOB	M	(s)	G
Roko Baturina (CRO)	20.06.2000	4	(16)	4
Bi Sylvestre Franck Fortune Boli (CIV)	07.12.1993	25	(3)	10
Dániel Gera	29.08.1995		(7)	
Giorgi Kharaishvili (GEO)	29.07.1996	2	(2)	1
Róbert Mak (SVK)	08.03.1991	7	(12)	1
Tokmac Chol Nguen (NOR)	20.10.1993	26	(6)	11
Damir Redzic	23.03.2003		(2)	
Myrto Uzuni (ALB)	31.05.1995	23	(3)	12
Roland Varga	23.01.1990	1	(3)	
Oleksandr Zubkov (UKR)	03.08.1996	16	(9)	5

Kisvárda Futball Club

Founded: 1911
Stadium: Várkerti Stadion, Kisvárda (2,993)
Trainer: Attila Supka — 19.09.1962

Goalkeepers:	DOB	M	(s)	G
Dávid Dombó	26.02.1993	30		
Mihai Mincă (ROU)	08.10.1984	3		
Artem Odintsov (UKR)	09.11.2000		(1)	
Defenders:	**DOB**	**M**	**(s)**	**G**
Ádám Baranyai	05.03.1993	2		
Lazar Ćirković (SRB)	22.08.1992	14	(1)	1
Niko Datković (CRO)	21.04.1993	7		1
Cornel Ene (ROU)	21.07.1993	16	(1)	
Viktor Hei (UKR)	02.02.1996	29		
Anton Kravchenko (UKR)	23.03.1991	5	(2)	
Tonći Kukoč-Petraello (CRO)	25.09.1990		(2)	
Matheus Izidorio Leoni (BRA)	20.09.1991	16	(1)	1
Bogdan Melnyk (UKR)	04.01.1997	26	(3)	1
Herdi Prenga (ALB)	31.08.1994	7	(3)	
Tamás Rubus	13.07.1989	14		1
Midfielders:	**DOB**	**M**	**(s)**	**G**
Claudiu Vasile Bumba (ROU)	05.01.1994	28	(3)	4

	DOB	M	(s)	G
Yanis Karabelyov (BUL)	23.01.1996	14	(3)	
Roman Karasyuk (UKR)	27.03.1991	1	(8)	
Lucas Marcolini Dantas Bertucci (BRA)	06.05.1989	19		
Bence Ötvös	13.03.1998	11	(3)	1
Slobodan Simović (SRB)	22.05.1989	17	(2)	3
Levente Szőr	14.01.2001		(1)	
Stavros Tsoukalas (GRE)	28.05.1988	9	(4)	1
Lazar Zličić (SRB)	07.02.1997	6	(14)	
Forwards:	**DOB**	**M**	**(s)**	**G**
Driton Camaj (MNE)	07.03.1997	14	(8)	1
Fernando Viana Jardim Silva (BRA)	20.02.1992	21	(6)	4
Lászó Himics	17.05.2001	1		
Zoltán Horváth	30.07.1989	2	(17)	1
Richárd Jelena	08.01.1998	1	(14)	3
Márk Kovácsréti	01.09.2000	6	(20)	1
Jaroslav Navrátil (CZE)	30.12.1991	20	(8)	4
Jefferson Gomes de Oliveira „Sassá" (BRA)	26.01.1988	24	(8)	2

Mezőkövesdi Sport Egyesület

Founded: 31.01.1975
Stadium: Városi Stadion, Mezőkövesd (4,183)
Trainer: Attila Kuttor — 29.05.1970
[11.11.2020] Attila Pintér — 07.05.1966

Goalkeepers:	DOB	M	(s)	G
Danylo Ryabenko (UKR)	09.10.1998	2		
Péter Szappanos	14.11.1990	31	(1)	
Defenders:	**DOB**	**M**	**(s)**	**G**
Konstantinos Dimitriou (GRE)	30.06.1999	1		
Gábor Eperjesi	12.01.1994	6	(4)	
Danijel Farkaš (SRB)	13.01.1993	27	(1)	1
Richárd Guzmics	16.04.1987	2	(1)	
Márk Jagodics	10.04.1992	4		
Matija Katanec (CRO)	04.05.1990	24		1
Luka Lakvekheliani (GEO)	20.10.1998	7	(2)	
Andriy Nesterov (UKR)	02.07.1990	16	(1)	
Róbert Pillár (SVK)	27.05.1991	12		1
Dániel Vadnai	19.02.1988	20	(2)	1
Midfielders:	**DOB**	**M**	**(s)**	**G**
Dávid Barczi	01.02.1989		(2)	
Zsombor Berecz	13.12.1995	21		4
Dino Beširović (BIH)	31.01.1994	29	(1)	6
Martin Chrien (SVK)	08.09.1995	8	(8)	1

	DOB	M	(s)	G
Karlo Kamenar (CRO)	15.03.1994		(3)	
Aleksandr Karnitskiy (BLR)	14.02.1989	21	(3)	1
Nodar Kavtaradze (RUS)	02.01.1993		(6)	
Manuel Martić (AUT)	15.08.1995	10	(7)	
Mykhailo Meskhi (UKR)	26.02.1997	4	(6)	
Dániel Nagy	15.03.1991	15	(10)	1
Rui Pedro Couto Ramalho (POR)	02.07.1988	2	(8)	
Tamás Szeles	07.12.1993	12	(1)	
Sándor Vajda	14.12.1991	6	(16)	1
Antonio Vutov (BUL)	06.06.1996	21	(6)	5
Forwards:	**DOB**	**M**	**(s)**	**G**
Márk Bencze	30.01.2000		(1)	
Andriy Boryachuk (UKR)	23.04.1996		(6)	
Tamás Cseri	15.01.1988	32		6
Ulysse Diallo (MLI)	26.10.1992		(3)	
Marin Jurina (BIH)	26.11.1993	19	(13)	6
Serder Serderov (RUS)	10.03.1994	9	(4)	2
Jakub Vojtuš (SVK)	22.10.1993	2	(13)	1

Magyar Testgyakorlók Köre Futball Club

Founded: 16.11.1888
Stadium: "Hidegkuti Nándor" Stadion, Budapest (5,014)
Trainer: Michael Boris (GER) — 03.06.1975

Goalkeepers:	DOB	M	(s)	G
Milan Mijatović (MNE)	26.07.1987	32		
Bence Somodi	25.11.1988	1	(1)	
Defenders:	**DOB**	**M**	**(s)**	**G**
Nikolai Alho (FIN)	12.03.1993	9	(4)	
Filip Antonijević (SRB)	24.07.2000		(2)	
Ákos Baki	24.08.1994	5	(1)	
Benjámin Balázs	26.04.1990	10	(6)	
Szabolcs Barna	27.04.1996	1	(5)	
Sebastián Herrera Cardona (COL)	23.01.1995	26		1
Patrick Ikenne-King (NGA)	29.10.1991	16	(10)	1
Zsombor Nagy	21.03.1998	27		1
Marko Perković (CRO)	30.08.1991	11	(2)	
Ádám Pintér	12.06.1988	6	(1)	
Tiago Emanuel Canelas Almeida Ferreira (POR)	10.07.1993	15	(1)	1
Benedek Varju	21.05.2001	13	(5)	
Midfielders:	**DOB**	**M**	**(s)**	**G**
Barnabás Biben	19.11.2003	2	(9)	
Benjámin Cseke	22.07.1994	21	(8)	2

	DOB	M	(s)	G
Srđan Dimitrov (SRB)	28.07.1992	18	(2)	1
József Kanta	24.03.1984	2	(3)	
Mihály Kata	13.04.2002	20	(4)	1
Máté Katona	22.06.1997	4		1
Szabolcs Mezei	18.10.2000	21	(5)	
Martin Palincsar	03.01.1999	5	(14)	
Forwards:	**DOB**	**M**	**(s)**	**G**
Bence Bíró	14.07.1998	3	(13)	
Andrija Drljo (BIH)	06.09.2002		(3)	
Dániel Richárd Gera	29.08.1995	12	(1)	4
László Lencse	02.07.1988	2	(5)	
Bojan Miovski (MKD)	24.06.1999	21	(5)	7
Myke Bouard Ramos (BRA)	30.10.1992	3		
Clinton Osei (GHA)	17.03.2002		(3)	
Dániel Prosser	15.06.1994	15	(13)	4
Szabolcs Gergő Schön	27.09.2000	24	(3)	9
Zalán Vancsa	27.10.2004	1	(2)	
Roland Varga	23.01.1990	17		9

Paksi Futball Club

Founded: 28.11.1952
Stadium: Fehérvári úti Stadion, Paks (6,150)
Trainer: Gábor Osztermajer   12.03.1978
[22.09.2020]   György Bognár   05.11.1961

Goalkeepers:	DOB	M	(s)	G
Lajos Hegedüs	19.12.1987	19		
Ádám Holczer	28.03.1988	5	(1)	
Gergő Rácz	20.11.1995	9		
Defenders:	**DOB**	**M**	**(s)**	**G**
Dávid Bognár	16.08.1997		(3)	
Zsolt Gévay	19.11.1987	13	(2)	2
Dávid Kulcsár	25.02.1988	8	(12)	
Bence Lenzsér	09.04.1996	19	(2)	
Márton Lorentz	01.02.1995	13	(5)	
Attila Osváth	10.12.1995	20	(5)	
János Szabó	11.07.1989	29	(1)	3
Norbert Szélpál	03.03.1996	9	(2)	1
Olivér Tamás	14.04.2001	14		
András Vági	25.12.1988	1	(2)	
Midfielders:	**DOB**	**M**	**(s)**	**G**
Balász Balogh	11.06.1990	21	(1)	2
Lajos Bertus	26.09.1990	24	(5)	

	DOB	M	(s)	G
István Bognár	05.05.1991	29	(1)	10
Richárd Csősz	22.04.1997	1	(5)	
Gergo Gorog	19.02.2002		(1)	
Richárd Nagy	08.04.1994	5	(20)	3
Kristóf Papp	14.05.1993	13	(3)	3
Zoltán Sipos	07.03.2001		(2)	
Bálint Szabó	18.01.2001	3	(3)	
Dénes Szakály	15.03.1988	5	(14)	3
Gábor Vas	29.08.2003	1	(4)	
József Windecker	02.12.1992	8		1
Forwards:	**DOB**	**M**	**(s)**	**G**
Martin Ádám	06.11.1994	13	(15)	8
Dániel Böde	24.10.1986	24	(1)	4
Ákos Debreceni	24.03.2003		(1)	
János Hahn	15.05.1995	25	(3)	22
Zsolt Haraszti	04.11.1991	13	(9)	4
Máté Sajbán	19.12.1995	19	(12)	3
Ákos Szendrei	23.01.2003		(6)	2

Puskás Ferenc Labdarugó Akadémia Felcsút

Founded: 2005
Stadium: Pancho Aréna, Felcsút (3,816)
Trainer: Zsolt Hornyák (SVK)   01.05.1973

Goalkeepers:	DOB	M	(s)	G
Martin Auerbach	03.11.2002	3		
Balázs Tóth	04.09.1997	30		
Defenders:	**DOB**	**M**	**(s)**	**G**
László Deutsch	09.03.1999	18	(4)	
Kamen Hadzhiev (BUL)	22.09.1991	5	(1)	
João Aniceto Grandela Nunes (POR)	19.11.1995	19	(3)	2
Thomas Meißner (GER)	26.03.1991	18	(3)	1
Zsolt Nagy	25.05.1993	26	(1)	3
Csaba Spandler	07.03.1996	25		1
Roland Szolnoki	21.01.1992	23		1
Midfielders:	**DOB**	**M**	**(s)**	**G**
Marius Corbu (ROU)	07.05.2002	9	(11)	
Ganbayar Ganbold (MNG)	03.09.2000	2	(1)	
Josip Knežević (CRO)	03.10.1988	25	(4)	9
Gergő Ominger	25.09.2002	1	(1)	

	DOB	M	(s)	G
Jakub Plšek (CZE)	13.12.1993	19	(10)	7
Márton Radics	02.12.2001	5		
Gábor Sipos	01.11.2002		(1)	
Jozef Urblík (SVK)	22.08.1996	16	(6)	1
Yoëll van Nieff (NED)	17.06.1993	17	(7)	
Forwards:	**DOB**	**M**	**(s)**	**G**
Alexandru Mihail Băluță (ROU)	13.09.1993	15	(10)	4
Krisztián Géresi	14.06.1994	6	(6)	3
Tamás Kiss	24.11.2000	29	(3)	3
György Komáromi	19.01.2002	10	(6)	4
Antonio Mance (CRO)	07.08.1995	16	(10)	7
Luciano Slagveer (NED)	05.10.1993	23	(5)	4
Nandor Támas (ROU)	24.10.2000	2	(6)	
Lázló Vizler	13.10.2002		(2)	
David Vaněček (CZE)	09.03.1991	1	(6)	1
Weslen Junior Faustino Froes de Melo (BRA)	12.11.1999		(9)	

Újpest Football Club

Founded: 16.06.1885
Stadium: "Szusza Ferenc" Stadion, Budapest (12,670)
Trainer: Predrag Rogan (SRB)   02.08.1974
[23.12.2020]   Michael Oenning (GER)   27.09.1965

Goalkeepers:	DOB	M	(s)	G
Dávid Banai	09.05.1994	25		
Márk Németh	20.04.2002	1		
Filip Pajović (SRB)	30.07.1993	6	(1)	
Defenders:	**DOB**	**M**	**(s)**	**G**
Nemanja Antonov (SRB)	06.05.1995	27		4
Jovan Baošić (MNE)	07.07.1995	10	(2)	
Dženan Bureković (BIH)	29.05.1995	3		
Patrik Eckl	21.09.2002		(1)	
Csanád Fehér	13.06.2002	1		
Lirim Kastrati (KVX)	02.02.1999	22	(1)	1
Georgios Koutroumpis (GRE)	10.02.1991	18		
Zsolt Máté	14.09.1997	9	(3)	1
Mauro Rafael Geral Cerqueira (POR)	20.08.1992	2	(3)	1
Branko Pauljević (SRB)	12.06.1989	28	(1)	1
Kire Ristevski (MKD)	22.10.1990	18	(3)	1
Midfielders:	**DOB**	**M**	**(s)**	**G**
Miroslav Bjeloš (SRB)	29.10.1990	1	(7)	
Aron Csongvai	31.10.2000	20	(8)	2
Petar Gigić (SRB)	07.03.1997	2	(6)	
Péter Hajdi	10.09.2003	1		

	DOB	M	(s)	G
Mátyás Katona	30.12.1999	2	(5)	
Nikola Mitrović (SRB)	02.01.1987	29	(1)	4
Obinna Nwobodo (NGA)	29.11.1996	4		
Vincent Onovo (NGA)	10.12.1995	29		1
Péter Szakály	17.08.1986	5	(21)	2
Áron Szűcs	21.04.2003		(1)	
György Varga	23.10.2003		(1)	
Forwards:	**DOB**	**M**	**(s)**	**G**
Patrik Bacsa	03.06.1992	4	(18)	
Giorgi Beridze (GEO)	12.05.1997	15	(10)	10
Dániel Büki	19.08.2004		(1)	
Yohan Croizet (FRA)	15.02.1992	6	(2)	1
Yassine El Ghanassi (BEL)	12.07.1990		(1)	
Levente Laczik	03.06.2003		(1)	
Márk Mucsányi	16.11.2001		(5)	
Zsolt Nagy	26.03.2002	1		
Antonio Perošević (CRO)	06.03.1992	13	(6)	4
Krisztián Simon	10.06.1991	20	(6)	6
Zoltán Stieber	16.10.1988	10	(5)	1
Gadji Celi Carmel Junior Tallo (CIV)	21.12.1992	20	(1)	6

Zalaegerszegi Torna Egylet Football Club

Founded:	1920	
Stadium:	ZTE Aréna, Zalaegerszeg (11,200)	
Trainer:	Gábor Boér	19.12.1982
[15.03.2021]	Róbert Waltner	20.09.1977

Goalkeepers:	DOB	M	(s)	G
Patrik Demjén	22.03.1998	29		
Márton Gyurján	01.12.1995	4		
Defenders:	**DOB**	**M**	**(s)**	**G**
Dávid Bobál	31.08.1995	32		
Bence Gergényi	16.03.1998	20	(7)	1
Dávid Kálnoki-Kis	06.08.1991	10	(1)	
Zoran Lesjak (CRO)	01.02.1988	27		3
Erik Németh	01.06.2000	4	(6)	
László Papp	09.01.2001		(2)	
Dániel Szalai	05.09.1996	7	(3)	1
János Szépe (SVK)	15.03.1996	19	(1)	4
Aleksandar Tanasin (SRB)	15.11.1991	7	(7)	
Žiga Živko (SVN)	21.07.1995	2	(2)	
Midfielders:	**DOB**	**M**	**(s)**	**G**
Bence Bedi	14.11.1996	28		1
Dominik Csoka	29.03.2004		(1)	

	DOB	M	(s)	G
Artem Favorov (UKR)	19.03.1994	24	(4)	8
Barnabás Kovács	14.11.2002	3	(9)	
Bertalan Kun	06.05.1999		(1)	
Sandro Emanuel Gonçalves Reis Pires Semedo (POR)	03.12.1996		(1)	
Bojan Sanković (CRO)	21.11.1993	32		
Mátyás Tajti	02.06.1998	11	(12)	1
Patrik Vass	17.01.1993	12	(10)	1
Forwards:	**DOB**	**M**	**(s)**	**G**
Benjamin Babati	29.11.1995	14	(13)	4
Dávid Filip Dragóner	12.03.1998	2	(5)	
Márkó Futács	22.02.1990	8	(8)	4
Norbert Könyves	10.06.1989	21	(3)	6
Márk Koszta	26.09.1996	13	(15)	9
Dániel Németh	10.09.2003		(2)	
Szabolcs Szalay	17.02.2002		(2)	
Regő Szánthó	22.11.2000	22	(5)	10
Dávid Zimonyi	24.12.1997	12	(13)	4

SECOND LEVEL
Nemzeti Bajnokság II 2020/2021

1.	Debreceni VSC (*Promoted*)	38	24	8	6	89	-	40	80
2.	Gyirmót FC Győr (*Promoted*)	38	24	6	8	60	-	31	78
3.	Vasas FC Budapest	38	23	9	6	65	-	35	78
4.	Pécsi Mecsek FC	38	17	13	8	51	-	33	64
5.	FC Ajka	38	19	5	14	65	-	47	62
6.	Budaörsi SC	38	18	5	15	62	-	59	59
7.	Nyíregyháza Spartacus FC	38	16	9	13	40	-	31	57
8.	Soroksár SC	38	16	9	13	51	-	44	57
9.	Szolnoki MÁV FC	38	15	12	11	43	-	40	57
10.	Szeged-Csanád Grosics Akadémia	38	16	8	14	46	-	54	56
11.	Szombathelyi Haladás	38	14	12	12	50	-	42	54
12.	Győri ETO FC	38	12	10	16	53	-	48	46
13.	BFC Siófok	38	13	6	19	49	-	58	45
14.	Dorogi FC	38	11	11	16	34	-	50	44
15.	Békéscsaba 1912 Előre SE	38	11	11	16	43	-	60	44
16.	Szentlőrinc SE	38	11	9	18	32	-	52	42
17.	Csákvári TK	38	9	11	18	54	-	66	38
18.	Kazincbarcikai SC (*Relegated*)	38	8	9	21	32	-	61	33
19.	Kaposvári Rákóczi FC (*Relegated*)	38	7	12	19	33	-	65	33
20.	Debreceni EAC (*Relegated*)	38	6	5	27	32	-	68	23

INTERNATIONAL MATCHES
(16.07.2020 – 15.07.2021)

03.09.2020	Sivas	Turkey - Hungary	0-1(0-0)	(UNL)
06.09.2020	Budapest	Hungary - Russia	2-3(0-1)	(UNL)
08.10.2020	Sofia	Bulgaria - Hungary	1-3(0-1)	(ECQPO)
11.10.2020	Beograd	Serbia - Hungary	0-1(0-1)	(UNL)
14.10.2020	Moskva	Russia - Hungary	0-0	(UNL)
12.11.2020	Budapest	Hungary - Iceland	2-1(0-1)	(ECQPO)
15.11.2020	Budapest	Hungary - Serbia	1-1(1-1)	(UNL)
18.11.2020	Budapest	Hungary - Turkey	2-0(0-0)	(UNL)
25.03.2021	Budapest	Hungary - Poland	3-3(1-0)	(WCQ)
28.03.2021	Serravalle	San Marino - Hungary	0-3(0-1)	(WCQ)
31.03.2021	Andora la Vella	Andorra - Hungary	1-4(0-1)	(WCQ)
04.06.2021	Budapest	Hungary - Cyprus	1-0(1-0)	(F)
08.06.2021	Budapest	Hungary - Republic of Ireland	0-0	(F)
15.06.2021	Budapest	Hungary - Portugal	0-3(0-0)	(EC)
19.06.2021	Budapest	Hungary - France	1-1(1-0)	(EC)
23.06.2021	München	Germany - Hungary	2-2(0-1)	(EC)

03.09.2020   TURKEY - HUNGARY   **0-1(0-0)**   2nd UEFA Nations League B, Group 3
Yeni 4 Eylül Stadyumu, Sivas; Referee: Artur Manuel Soares Dias (Portugal); Attendance: 0
HUN: Péter Gulácsi, Attila Fiola, Ádám Lang, Vilmos Tamás Orbán, Attila Árpád Szalai, Dávid Miklós Sigér (60.András Schäfer), Ádám Nagy, Dominik Szoboszlai, Filip Holender, Ádám Szalai (Cap) (71.Nemanja Nikolić), Roland Sallai (81.Zsolt Kalmár). Trainer: Marco Rossi (Italy).
Goal: Dominik Szoboszlai (80).

06.09.2020   HUNGARY - RUSSIA   **2-3(0-1)**   2nd UEFA Nations League B, Group 3
Puskás Aréna, Budapest; Referee: Maurizio Mariani (Italy); Attendance: 0
HUN: Péter Gulácsi, Barnabás Bese, Ádám Lang, Vilmos Tamás Orbán, Attila Árpád Szalai, Dávid Miklós Sigér (46.Zsolt Kalmár), Ádám Nagy, Dominik Szoboszlai (82.Tamás Cseri), Filip Holender, Ádám Szalai (Cap) (67.Nemanja Nikolić), Roland Sallai. Trainer: Marco Rossi (Italy).
Goals: Roland Sallai (62), Nemanja Nikolić (70).

08.10.2020   BULGARIA - HUNGARY   **1-3(0-1)**   16th EC. Qualifiers Play-offs, Semi-Finals
Nationalen Stadion "Vasil Levski", Sofia; Referee: Szymon Marciniak (Poland); Attendance: 0
HUN: Péter Gulácsi, Attila Fiola (82.Endre Botka), Ádám Lang, Vilmos Tamás Orbán, Attila Árpád Szalai, Dávid Miklós Sigér, Ádám Nagy (82.Dániel Gazdag), Zsolt Kalmár (70.Szilveszter Hangya), Filip Holender (70.Loïc Négo), Ádám Szalai (Cap) (59.Nemanja Nikolić), Roland Sallai. Trainer: Marco Rossi (Italy).
Goals: Vilmos Tamás Orbán (17), Zsolt Kalmár (47), Nemanja Nikolić (75).

11.10.2020   SERBIA - HUNGARY   **0-1(0-1)**   2nd UEFA Nations League B, Group 3
Stadion "Rajko Mitić", Beograd; Referee: Sandro Schärer (Switzerland); Attendance: 0
HUN: Péter Gulácsi (Cap), Endre Botka, Barnabás Bese (56.Vilmos Tamás Orbán), Ádám Lang, Attila Árpád Szalai, Ádám Nagy, Zsolt Kalmár, Dániel Gazdag (77.András Schäfer), Szilveszter Hangya (46.Filip Holender), Nemanja Nikolić (76.Loïc Négo), Norbert Könyves (63.Ádám Szalai). Trainer: Marco Rossi (Italy).
Goal: Norbert Könyves (20).

14.10.2020   RUSSIA - HUNGARY   **0-0**   2nd UEFA Nations League B, Group 3
VTB Arena, Moskva; Referee: Michael Oliver (England); Attendance: 0
HUN: Dénes Dibusz, Loïc Négo, Endre Botka, Vilmos Tamás Orbán, Attila Árpád Szalai, Zsolt Kalmár (77.András Schäfer), Dávid Miklós Sigér, Dániel Gazdag (46.Ádám Nagy), Filip Holender (46.Attila Fiola), Ádám Szalai (Cap) (83.Norbert Könyves), Nemanja Nikolić (61.Kevin Varga). Trainer: Marco Rossi (Italy).

12.11.2020   HUNGARY - ICELAND   **2-1(0-1)**   16th EC. Qualifiers Play-offs, Finals
Puskás Aréna, Budapest; Referee: Björn Kuipers (Netherlands); Attendance: 0
HUN: Péter Gulácsi, Attila Fiola (61.Gergő Lovrencsics), Endre Botka, Vilmos Tamás Orbán, Attila Árpád Szalai, Zsolt Kalmár (61.Dávid Miklós Sigér), Ádám Nagy (84.Loïc Négo), Dominik Szoboszlai, Filip Holender (72.Nemanja Nikolić), Ádám Szalai (Cap) (84.Norbert Könyves), Roland Sallai. Trainer: Marco Rossi (Italy).
Goals: Loïc Négo (88), Dominik Szoboszlai (90+2).

15.11.2020   HUNGARY - SERBIA   **1-1(1-1)**   2nd UEFA Nations League B, Group 3
Puskás Aréna, Budapest; Referee: Glenn Nyberg (Sweden); Attendance: 0
HUN: Dénes Dibusz, Endre Botka, Barnabás Bese (78.Ádám Gyurcsó, Ádám Lang, Ákos Kecskés, Zsolt Kalmár, Ádám Nagy, Dávid Miklós Sigér (57.Loïc Négo), Dominik Szoboszlai (78.András Schäfer), Filip Holender (68.Szilveszter Hangya), Nemanja Nikolić (Cap) (57.Norbert Könyves). Trainer: Marco Rossi (Italy).
Goal: Zsolt Kalmár (39).

18.11.2020   HUNGARY - TURKEY   **2-0(0-0)**   2nd UEFA Nations League B, Group 3
Puskás Aréna, Budapest; Referee: Ivan Kružliak (Slovakia); Attendance: 0
HUN: Dénes Dibusz, Attila Fiola, Loïc Négo (89.Endre Botka), Ádám Lang, Attila Árpád Szalai, Ádám Nagy, Dávid Miklós Sigér, Zsolt Kalmár (46.Tamás Cseri), Szilveszter Hangya (74.Filip Holender), Norbert Könyves (46.Kevin Varga), Nemanja Nikolić (Cap) (64.Ádám Gyurcsó). Trainer: Marco Rossi (Italy).
Goals: Dávid Miklós Sigér (57), Kevin Varga (90+5).

25.03.2021   **HUNGARY - POLAND**   **3-3(1-0)**   22nd FIFA WC. Qualifiers

Puskás Aréna, Budapest; Referee: Dr. Felix Brych (Germany); Attendance: 0
HUN: Péter Gulácsi, Gergő Lovrencsics (66.Loïc Négo), Attila Fiola [*sent off 90+5*], Vilmos Tamás Orbán, Attila Árpád Szalai, Szilveszter Hangya (66.Ádám Lang), Ádám Nagy, László Kleinheisler, Zsolt Kalmár (81.Dávid Miklós Sigér), Ádám Szalai (Cap), Roland Sallai (72.Kevin Varga). Trainer: Marco Rossi (Italy).
Goals: Roland Sallai (6), Ádám Csaba Szalai (53), Vilmos Tamás Orbán (78).

28.03.2021   **SAN MARINO - HUNGARY**   **0-3(0-1)**   22nd FIFA WC. Qualifiers

San Marino Stadium, Serravalle; Referee: Nicholas Walsh (Scotland); Attendance: 0
HUN: Dénes Dibusz, Endre Botka, Loïc Négo (46.Zsolt Kalmár), Vilmos Tamás Orbán, Attila Árpád Szalai, Tamás Cseri (46.Nemanja Nikolić), Dávid Miklós Sigér, Dániel Gazdag (62.László Kleinheisler), Roland Sallai, Ádám Szalai (Cap) (85.Krisztián Géresi), Kevin Varga (72.Roland Varga). Trainer: Marco Rossi (Italy).
Goals: Ádám Csaba Szalai (13 penalty), Roland Sallai (71), Nemanja Nikolić (88 penalty).

31.03.2021   **ANDORRA - HUNGARY**   **1-4(0-1)**   22nd FIFA WC. Qualifiers

Estadi Nacional, Andorra la Vella; Referee: Vilhjálmur Alvar Þórarinsson (Iceland); Attendance: 338
HUN: Dénes Dibusz, Attila Fiola, Ádám Lang, Attila Árpád Szalai, Szilveszter Hangya, Gergő Lovrencsics (83.Kevin Varga), Ádám Nagy (61.Dávid Miklós Sigér), Zsolt Kalmár (29.Dániel Gazdag), László Kleinheisler (83.Loïc Négo), Ádám Szalai (Cap), Nemanja Nikolić (61.Roland Varga). Trainer: Marco Rossi (Italy).
Goals: Attila Csaba Fiola (45+2), Dániel Gazdag (51), László Kleinheisler (58), Loïc Négo (90).

04.06.2021   **HUNGARY - CYPRUS**   **1-0(1-0)**   Friendly International

"Szusza Ferenc" Stadion, Budapest; Referee: Matej Jug (Slovenia); Attendance: 7,500
HUN: Péter Gulácsi (Cap) (46.Dénes Dibusz), Gergő Lovrencsics (61.Bendegúz Bolla), Endre Botka, Ádám Lang (60.Vilmos Tamás Orbán), Dávid Miklós Sigér (79.Ádám Nagy), László Kleinheisler (48.Loïc Négo), Kevin Varga, András Schäfer, Attila Árpád Szalai, János Csaba Hahn (61.Nemanja Nikolić), Filip Holender. Trainer: Marco Rossi (Italy).
Goal: András Schäfer (36).

08.06.2021   **HUNGARY - REPUBLIC OF IRELAND**   **0-0**   Friendly International

"Szusza Ferenc" Stadion, Budapest; Referee: Daniel Stefański (Poland); Attendance: 7,396
HUN: Péter Gulácsi (63.Ádám Bogdán), Attila Fiola (79.János Csaba Hahn), Ákos Kecskés, Vilmos Tamás Orbán, Attila Árpád Szalai, Bendegúz Bolla (46.Gergő Lovrencsics), László Kleinheisler (63.Loïc Négo), Ádám Nagy, András Schäfer, Ádám Szalai (Cap) (89.Szabolcs Schön), Roland Varga (46.Kevin Varga). Trainer: Marco Rossi (Italy).

15.06.2021   **HUNGARY - PORTUGAL**   **0-3(0-0)**   16th EC. Group Stage.

Puskás Aréna, Budapest; Referee: Cüneyt Çakir (Turkey); Attendance: 55,662
HUN: Péter Gulácsi, Endre Botka, Vilmos Tamás Orbán, Attila Árpád Szalai, Gergő Lovrencsics, László Kleinheisler (78.Dávid Miklós Sigér), Ádám Nagy (90+5.Roland Varga), András Schäfer (65.Loïc Négo), Attila Fiola (88.Kevin Varga), Ádám Szalai (Cap), Roland Sallai (77.Szabolcs Schön). Trainer: Marco Rossi (Italy).

19.06.2021   **HUNGARY - FRANCE**   **1-1(1-0)**   16th EC. Group Stage.

Puskás Aréna, Budapest; Referee: Michael Oliver (England); Attendance: 55,998
HUN: Péter Gulácsi, Endre Botka, Vilmos Tamás Orbán, Attila Árpád Szalai, Loïc Négo, László Kleinheisler (84.Gergő Lovrencsics), Ádám Nagy, András Schäfer (75.Tamás Cseri), Attila Fiola, Roland Sallai, Ádám Szalai (Cap) (26.Nemanja Nikolić). Trainer: Marco Rossi (Italy).
Goal: Attila Fiola (45+2).

23.06.2021   **GERMANY - HUNGARY**   **2-2(0-1)**   16th EC. Group Stage.

Football Arena (Allianz), München; Referee: Sergey Karasev (Russia); Attendance: 12,413
HUN: Péter Gulácsi, Endre Botka, Vilmos Tamás Orbán, Attila Árpád Szalai, Loïc Négo, László Kleinheisler (88.Gergő Lovrencsics), Ádám Nagy, András Schäfer, Attila Fiola (88.Nemanja Nikolić), Roland Sallai (75.Szabolcs Schön), Ádám Szalai (Cap) (82.Kevin Varga). Trainer: Marco Rossi (Italy).
Goals: Ádám Szalai (11), András Schäfer (68).

Name	DOB	Caps	Goals	2020/2021:	Club
Goalkeepers					
Ádám BOGDÁN	27.09.1987	21	0	2021:	Ferencvárosi TC
Dénes DIBUSZ	16.11.1990	15	0	2020/2021:	Ferencvárosi TC
Péter GULÁCSI	06.05.1990	42	0	2020/2021:	RasenBallsport Leipzig (GER)
Defenders					
Barnabás BESE	06.05.1994	20	0	2020:	Oud-Heverle Leuven (BEL)
Bendegúz BOLLA	22.11.1999	2	0	2021:	Fehérvár FC Székesfehérvár
Endre BOTKA	25.08.1994	13	0	2020/2021:	Ferencvárosi TC
Attila FIOLA	17.02.1990	38	2	2020/2021:	Fehérvár FC Székesfehérvár
Szilveszter HANGYA	02.01.1994	10	0	2020/2021:	Fehérvár FC Székesfehérvár
Ákos KECSKÉS	04.01.1996	2	0	2020/2021:	FC Lugano (SUI)
Ádám LANG	17.01.1993	39	1	2020/2021:	AC Omonia Nicosia (CYP)
Gergő LOVRENCSICS	01.09.1988	44	1	2020/2021:	Ferencvárosi TC
Loïc NÉGO	15.01.1991	14	2	2020/2021:	Fehérvár FC Székesfehérvár
Vilmos Tamás „Willi" ORBÁN	03.11.1992	25	5	2020/2021:	RasenBallsport Leipzig (GER)
Attila Árpád SZALAI	20.01.1998	16	0	2020:	Apollon Limassol FC (CYP)
				18.01.2021->	Fenerbahçe SK İstanbul (TUR)
Midfielders					
Tamás CSERI	15.01.1988	4	0	2020/2021:	Mezőkövesdi SE
Dániel GAZDAG	02.03.1996	6	1	2020/2021:	Budapest Honvéd FC
Zsolt KALMÁR	09.06.1995	27	2	2020/2021:	FC DAC 1904 Dunajská Streda (SVK)
László KLEINHEISLER	08.04.1994	37	3	2021:	NK Osijek (CRO)
Ádám NAGY	17.06.1995	51	1	2020/2021:	Bristol City FC (ENG)
András SCHÄFER	13.04.1999	9	2	2020/2021:	FC DAC 1904 Dunajská Streda (SVK)
Dávid Miklós SIGÉR	30.11.1990	14	1	2020/2021:	Ferencvárosi TC
Dominik SZOBOSZLAI	25.10.2000	12	3	2020:	FC Red Bull Salzburg (AUT)
Kevin VARGA	30.03.1996	10	1	2020/2021:	Kasımpaşa Spor Kulübü İstanbul (TUR)
Forwards					
Krisztián GÉRESI	14.06.1994	1	0	2021:	Puskás Ferenc Labdarugó Akadémia Felcsút
Ádám GYURCSÓ	06.03.1991	20	3	2020:	HNK Hajduk Split (CRO)
János Csaba HAHN	15.03.1995	2	0	2021:	Paksi FC
Filip HOLENDER	27.07.1994	15	1	2020:	FC Lugano (SUI)
				02.10.2020->	FK Partizan Beograd (SRB)
Norbert KÖNYVES	10.06.1989	5	1	2020:	Zalaegerszegi TE FC
Nemanja NIKOLIĆ	31.12.1987	40	8	2020/2021:	Fehérvár FC Székesfehérvár
Roland SALLAI	22.05.1997	25	4	2020/2021:	SC Freiburg (GER)
Szabolcs SCHÖN	27.09.2000	3	0	2021:	FC Dallas (USA)
Ádám Csaba SZALAI	09.12.1987	74	24	2020/2021:	1. FSV Mainz 05 (GER)
Roland VARGA	23.01.1990	23	3	2021:	MTK Budapest FC
Trainer					
Marco ROSSI (Italy) [from 19.06.2019]	09.09.1964			32 M; 15 W; 7 D; 10 L; 45-37	

ICELAND

The Country:
Ísland (Iceland)
Capital: Reykjavík
Surface: 102,775 km²
Inhabitants: 368,720 [2021]
Time: UTC

The FA:
Knattspyrnusamband Íslands
Laugardal 104, Reykjavík
Tel: +354 510 2900
Foundation date: 1947
Member of FIFA since: 1947
Member of UEFA since: 1954
Website: www.ksi.is

NATIONAL TEAM RECORDS

RECORDS
First international match:	17.07.1946, Reykjavík:	Iceland – Denmark 0-3
Most international caps:	Rúnar Kristinsson	- 104 caps (1987-2004)
Most international goals:	Eiður Smári Guðjohnsen	- 26 goals / 88 caps (1996-2016)
	Kolbeinn Sigþórsson	- 26 goals / 57 caps (2010-2021)

UEFA EUROPEAN CHAMPIONSHIP
1960	Did not enter
1964	Qualifiers
1968	Did not enter
1972	Did not enter
1976	Qualifiers
1980	Qualifiers
1984	Qualifiers
1988	Qualifiers
1992	Qualifiers
1996	Qualifiers
2000	Qualifiers
2004	Qualifiers
2008	Qualifiers
2012	Qualifiers
2016	Final Tournament (Quarter-Finals)
2020	Qualifiers

FIFA WORLD CUP
Year	Result
1930	-
1934	-
1938	-
1950	-
1954	*Entry not accepted by FIFA*
1958	Qualifiers
1962	Did not enter
1966	Did not enter
1970	Did not enter
1974	Qualifiers
1978	Qualifiers
1982	Qualifiers
1986	Qualifiers
1990	Qualifiers
1994	Qualifiers
1998	Qualifiers
2002	Qualifiers
2006	Qualifiers
2010	Qualifiers
2014	Qualifiers
2018	Final Tournament (Group Stage)

OLYMPIC TOURNAMENTS
Year	Result
1908	-
1912	-
1920	-
1924	-
1928	-
1936	-
1948	-
1952	-
1956	-
1960	Qualifiers
1964	Qualifiers
1968	Qualifiers
1972	Qualifiers
1976	Did not enter
1980	Did not enter
1984	Did not enter
1988	Qualifiers
1992	Qualifiers
1996	Qualifiers
2000	Qualifiers
2004	Qualifiers
2008	Qualifiers
2012	Qualifiers
2016	Qualifiers

UEFA NATIONS LEAGUE
2018/2019	League A
2020/2021	League A (relegated to League B)

FIFA CONFEDERATIONS CUP 1992-2017
None

ICELANDIAN CLUB HONOURS IN EUROPEAN CLUB COMPETITIONS:

European Champion Clubs' Cup (1956-1992) / UEFA Champions League (1993-2021)
None

Fairs Cup (1858-1971) / UEFA Cup (1972-2009) / UEFA Europa League (2010-2021)
None

UEFA Super Cup (1972-2020)
None

European Cup Winners' Cup 1961-1999 *
None

defunct competition

NATIONAL COMPETITIONS
TABLE OF HONOURS

	CHAMPIONS	CUP WINNERS	BEST GOALSCORERS	
1912	KR Reykjavík	-	-	
1913	Fram Reykjavík	-	-	
1914	Fram Reykjavík	-	-	
1915	Fram Reykjavík	-	-	
1916	Fram Reykjavík	-	-	
1917	Fram Reykjavík	-	-	
1918	Fram Reykjavík	-	-	
1919	KR Reykjavík	-	-	
1920	Víkingur Reykjavík	-	-	
1921	Fram Reykjavík	-	-	
1922	Fram Reykjavík	-	-	
1923	Fram Reykjavík	-	-	
1924	Víkingur Reykjavík	-	-	
1925	Fram Reykjavík	-	-	
1926	KR Reykjavík	-	-	
1927	KR Reykjavík	-	-	
1928	KR Reykjavík	-	-	
1929	KR Reykjavík	-	-	
1930	Valur Reykjavík	-	-	
1931	KR Reykjavík	-	-	
1932	KR Reykjavík	-	-	
1933	Valur Reykjavík	-	-	
1934	KR Reykjavík	-	-	
1935	Valur Reykjavík	-	-	
1936	Valur Reykjavík	-	-	
1937	Valur Reykjavík	-	-	
1938	Valur Reykjavík	-	-	
1939	Fram Reykjavík	-	-	
1940	Valur Reykjavík	-	-	
1941	KR Reykjavík	-	-	
1942	Valur Reykjavík	-	-	
1943	Valur Reykjavík	-	-	
1944	Valur Reykjavík	-	-	
1945	Valur Reykjavík	-	-	
1946	Fram Reykjavík	-	-	
1947	Fram Reykjavík	-	-	
1948	KR Reykjavík	-	-	
1949	KR Reykjavík	-	-	
1950	KR Reykjavík	-	-	
1951	ÍA Akranes	-	-	
1952	KR Reykjavík	-	-	
1953	ÍA Akranes	-	-	
1954	ÍA Akranes	-	-	
1955	KR Reykjavík	-	-	
1956	Valur Reykjavík	-	-	
1957	ÍA Akranes	-	-	
1958	ÍA Akranes	-	-	
1959	KR Reykjavík	-	-	
1960	ÍA Akranes	KR Reykjavík	-	
1961	KR Reykjavík	KR Reykjavík	-	
1962	Fram Reykjavík	KR Reykjavík	-	
1963	KR Reykjavík	KR Reykjavík	-	
1964	Keflavík ÍF	KR Reykjavík	-	
1965	KR Reykjavík	Valur Reykjavík	-	
1966	Valur Reykjavík	KR Reykjavík	-	
1967	Valur Reykjavík	KR Reykjavík	-	
1968	KR Reykjavík	ÍBV Vestmannaeyjar	-	
1969	Keflavík ÍF	KA Akureyrar	-	
1970	ÍA Akranes	Fram Reykjavík	-	
1971	Keflavík ÍF	Víkingur Reykjavík	-	
1972	Fram Reykjavík	ÍBV Vestmannaeyjar	-	
1973	Keflavík ÍF	Fram Reykjavík	-	
1974	ÍA Akranes	Valur Reykjavík	-	
1975	ÍA Akranes	Keflavík ÍF	-	
1976	Valur Reykjavík	Valur Reykjavík	-	
1977	ÍA Akranes	Valur Reykjavík	-	
1978	Valur Reykjavík	ÍA Akranes	-	
1979	ÍBV Vestmannaeyjar	Fram Reykjavík	-	
1980	Valur Reykjavík	Fram Reykjavík	Matthias Hallgrimsson (Valur Reykjavík)	15
1981	Víkingur Reykjavík	ÍBV Vestmannaeyjar	Sigurlás Þorleifsson (ÍBV Vestmannaeyjar) Larus Gudmundsson (Víkingur Reykjavík)	12

1982	Víkingur Reykjavík	ÍA Akranes	Sigurlás Þorleifsson (ÍBV Vestmannaeyjar)	
			Heimir Karlsson (Víkingur Reykjavík)	10
1983	ÍA Akranes	ÍA Akranes	Ingi Björn Albertsson (Valur Reykjavík)	14
1984	ÍA Akranes	ÍA Akranes	Guðmundur Steinsson (Fram Reykjavík)	10
1985	Valur Reykjavík	Fram Reykjavík	Ómar Torfason (Fram Reykjavík)	13
1986	Fram Reykjavík	ÍA Akranes	Gudmundur Torfason (Fram Reykjavík)	19
1987	Valur Reykjavík	Fram Reykjavík	Petur Ormslev (Fram Reykjavík)	12
1988	Fram Reykjavík	Valur Reykjavík	Sigurjón Kristjánsson (Valur Reykjavík)	13
1989	KA Akureyri	Fram Reykjavík	Hörður Magnússon (FH Hafnarfjörður)	12
1990	Fram Reykjavík	Valur Reykjavík	Hörður Magnússon (FH Hafnarfjörður)	13
1991	Víkingur Reykjavík	Valur Reykjavík	Hörður Magnússon (FH Hafnarfjörður)	
			Guðmundur Steinsson (Víkingur Reykjavík)	13
1992	ÍA Akranes	Valur Reykjavík	Arnar Gunnlaugsson (ÍA Akranes)	15
1993	ÍA Akranes	ÍA Akranes	Þórður Guðjónsson (ÍA Akranes)	19
1994	ÍA Akranes	KR Reykjavík	Mihajlo Biberčić (SRB, ÍA Akranes)	14
1995	ÍA Akranes	KR Reykjavík	Arnar Gunnlaugsson (ÍA Akranes)	15
1996	ÍA Akranes	ÍA Akranes	Ríkharður Daðason (KR Reykjavík)	14
1997	ÍBV Vestmannaeyjar	Keflavík ÍF	Tryggvi Guðmundsson (ÍBV Vestmannaeyjar)	19
1998	ÍBV Vestmannaeyjar	ÍBV Vestmannaeyjar	Steingrímur Jóhannesson (ÍBV Vestmannaeyjar)	16
1999	KR Reykjavík	KR Reykjavík	Steingrímur Jóhannesson (ÍBV Vestmannaeyjar)	12
2000	KR Reykjavík	ÍA Akranes	Guðmundur Steinarsson (Keflavík ÍF)	
			Andri Sigþórsson (KR Reykjavík)	14
2001	ÍA Akranes	Fylkir Reykjavík	Hjörtur Hjartarson (ÍA Akranes)	15
2002	KR Reykjavík	Fylkir Reykjavík	Grétar Hjartarson (UMF Grindavík)	13
2003	KR Reykjavík	ÍA Akranes	Björgólfur Takefusa (Þróttur Reykjavík)	10
2004	FH Hafnarfjörður	Keflavík ÍF	Gunnar Heiðar Þorvaldsson (ÍBV Vestmannaeyjar)	12
2005	FH Hafnarfjörður	Valur Reykjavík	Tryggvi Guðmundsson (FH Hafnarfjörður)	16
2006	FH Hafnarfjörður	Keflavík ÍF	Marel Baldvinsson (Breiðablik Kópavogur)	11
2007	Valur Reykjavík	FH Hafnarfjörður	Jónas Grani Garðarsson (Fram Reykjavík)	13
2008	FH Hafnarfjörður	KR Reykjavík	Guðmundur Steinarsson (Keflavík ÍF)	16
2009	FH Hafnarfjörður	Breiðablik Kópavogur	Björgólfur Takefusa (KR Reykjavík)	16
2010	Breiðablik Kópavogur	FH Hafnarfjörður	Gilles Mbang Ondo (GAB, UMF Grindavík)	14
2011	KR Reykjavík	KR Reykjavík	Garðar Jóhannsson (Stjarnan Garðabær)	15
2012	FH Hafnarfjörður	KR Reykjavík	Atli Guðnason (FH Hafnarfjörður)	12
2013	KR Reykjavík	Fram Reykjavík	Atli Viðar Björnsson (FH Hafnarfjörður)	
			Viðar Örn Kjartansson (Fylkir Reykjavík)	
			Gary Martin (ENG, KR Reykjavík)	13
2014	Stjarnan Garðabær	KR Reykjavík	Gary Martin (ENG, KR Reykjavík)	13
2015	FH Hafnarfjörður	Valur Reykjavík	Patrick Pedersen (DEN, Valur Reykjavík)	13
2016	FH Hafnarfjörður	Valur Reykjavík	Garðar Gunnlaugsson (ÍA Akranes)	14
2017	Valur Reykjavík	ÍBV Vestmannaeyjar	Andri Rúnar Bjarnason (UMF Grindavík)	19
2018	Valur Reykjavík	Stjarnan Garðabær	Patrick Pedersen (DEN, Valur Reykjavík)	17
2019	KR Reykjavík	Víkingur Reykjavík	Gary John Martin	
			(ENG, Valur Reykjavík / ÍBV Vestmannaeyjar)	14
2020	Valur Reykjavík	*Competition cancelled*	Steven Lennon (SCO, FH Hafnarfjörður)	17

NATIONAL CHAMPIONSHIP
Úrvalsdeild karla 2020
(13.06.2020 – 30.10.2020)

Results

Round 1 [13-15.06.2020]
Valur Reykjavík - KR Reykjavík 0-1(0-1)
ÍA Akranes - KA Akureyri 3-1(1-1)
Kópavogur - FH Hafnarfjörður 2-3(1-1)
Breiðablik - Grótta 3-0(1-0)
Víkingur - Fjölnir Reykjavík 1-1(1-0)
Stjarnan - Fylkir Reykjavík 2-1(1-1)

Round 2 [20-21.06.2020]
KA Akureyri - Víkingur 0-0
Grótta - Valur Reykjavík 0-3(0-2)
KR Reykjavík - Kópavogur 0-3(0-1)
Fjölnir Reykjavík - Stjarnan 1-4(1-1)
FH Hafnarfjörður - ÍA Akranes 2-1(0-0)
Fylkir Reykjavík - Breiðablik 0-1(0-0)

Round 3 [28-29.06.2020]
Kópavogur - Valur Reykjavík 0-4(0-3)
ÍA Akranes - KR Reykjavík 1-2(0-0)
Breiðablik - Fjölnir Reykjavík 3-1(1-0)
Fylkir Reykjavík - Grótta 2-0(0-0)
Víkingur - FH Hafnarfjörður 4-1(3-0)
Stjarnan - KA Akureyri 1-1(1-0) [26.08.]

Round 4 [03-05.07.2020]
Valur Reykjavík - ÍA Akranes 1-4(0-3)
Fjölnir Reykjavík - Fylkir Reykjavík 1-2(0-1)
Grótta - Kópavogur 4-4(2-1)
KR Reykjavík - Víkingur 2-0(0-0)
KA Akureyri - Breiðablik 2-2(0-1)
FH Hafnarfjörður - Stjarnan 1-2(0-0) [17.08.]

Round 5 [08-09.07.2020]
Víkingur - Valur Reykjavík 1-5(1-3)
Fjölnir Reykjavík - Grótta 0-3(0-0)
ÍA Akranes - Kópavogur 2-2(1-1)
Breiðablik - FH Hafnarfjörður 3-3(2-1)
Fylkir Reykjavík - KA Akureyri 4-1(1-0)
Stjarnan - KR Reykjavík *not played*

Round 6 [12-13.07.2020]
Grótta - ÍA Akranes 0-4(0-4)
Kópavogur - Víkingur 0-2(0-1)
KA Akureyri - Fjölnir Reykjavík 1-1(1-1)
Valur Reykjavík - Stjarnan 0-0
FH Hafnarfjörður - Fylkir Reykjavík 1-2(0-1)
KR Reykjavík - Breiðablik 3-1(2-1)

Round 7 [17-19.07.2020]
Stjarnan - Kópavogur 4-1(2-1)
KA Akureyri - Grótta 1-0(0-0)
Fjölnir Reykjavík - FH Hafnarfjörður 0-3(0-2)
Fylkir Reykjavík - KR Reykjavík 0-3(0-0)
Víkingur - ÍA Akranes 6-2(2-1)
Breiðablik - Valur Reykjavík 1-2(0-0)

Round 8 [22-23.07.2020]
FH Hafnarfjörður - KA Akureyri 0-0
KR Reykjavík - Fjölnir Reykjavík 2-2(1-1)
ÍA Akranes - Stjarnan 1-2(0-2)
Grótta - Víkingur 1-1(1-0)
Valur Reykjavík - Fylkir Reykjavík 3-0(2-0)
Kópavogur - Breiðablik 1-0(1-0)

Round 9 [26-27.07.2020]
KA Akureyri - KR Reykjavík 0-0
Breiðablik - ÍA Akranes 5-3(4-1)
Fylkir Reykjavík - Kópavogur 3-2(1-2)
FH Hafnarfjörður - Grótta 2-1(1-0)
Fjölnir Reykjavík - Valur Reykjavík 1-3(0-2)
Stjarnan - Víkingur 1-1(1-1)

Round 12 [14-16.08.2020]	Round 13 [20-22.08.2020]	Round 14 [25-26.08.2020]
KR Reykjavík - FH Hafnarfjörður 1-2(1-1)	Fjölnir Reykjavík - Víkingur 1-1(1-0)	Fylkir Reykjavík - Fjölnir Reykjavík 2-0(0-0)
Stjarnan - Grótta 1-1(1-0)	Grótta - Breiðablik 0-1(0-0)	Kópavogur - Grótta 3-0(1-0)
Valur Reykjavík - KA Akureyri 1-0(1-0)	Fylkir Reykjavík - Stjarnan 1-1(0-1)	Akranes - Valur Reykjavík 2-4(0-3) [17.09.]
ÍA Akranes - Fylkir Reykjavík 3-2(0-1)	KA Akureyri - ÍA Akranes 2-2(1-0)	Breiðablik - KA Akureyri 1-1(0-1) [01.10.]
Kópavogur - Fjölnir Reykjavík 3-1(0-0)	FH Hafnarfjörður - Kópavogur 4-0(2-0)	Víkingur - KR Reykjavík 0-2(0-1) [01.10.]
Víkingur - Breiðablik 2-4(1-3)	KR Reykjavík - Valur Reyk. 4-5(3-3) [26.08.]	Stjarnan - FH Hafnarfjörður 1-1(0-0) [01.10.]

Round 15 [30.08.2020]	Round 16 [13-14.09.2020]	Round 17 [19-21.09.2020]
KA Akureyri - Stjarnan 0-0	KR Reykjavík - Stjarnan 1-2(0-0)	Fjölnir Reykjavík - KA Akureyri 1-1(1-0)
KR Reykjavík - ÍA Akranes 4-1(2-0)	KA Akureyri - Fylkir Reykjavík 2-0(2-0)	ÍA Akranes - Grótta 3-0(1-0)
Grótta - Fylkir Reykjavík 0-2(0-2)	FH Hafnarfjörður - Breiðablik 3-1(1-1)	Stjarnan - Valur Reykjavík 1-5(0-5)
Valur Reykjavík - Kópavogur 1-0(0-0)	Kópavogur - ÍA Akranes 3-2(2-2)	Fylkir Reykjavík - FH Hafnarfjörður 1-4(0-0)
Fjölnir Reyk. - Breiðablik 1-4(0-2) [05.09.]	Valur Reykjavík - Víkingur 2-0(0-0)	Breiðablik - KR Reykjavík 0-2(0-1)
FH Hafnarfjörður - Víkingur 1-0(1-0) [17.09.]	Grótta - Fjölnir Reykjavík 2-2(0-1)	Víkingur - Kópavogur 1-1(0-0)

Round 10 [24.09.2020]	Round 18 [27.09.2020]	Round 11 [04.10.2020]
KA Akureyri - Kópavogur 1-1(0-1)	ÍA Akranes - Víkingur 2-2(0-0)	Víkingur - KA Akureyri 2-2(1-1)
FH Hafnarfjörður - Valur Reykjavík 1-4(1-2)	KR Reykjavík - Fylkir Reykjavík 1-2(0-1)	ÍA Akranes - FH Hafnarfjörður 0-4(0-1)
Fjölnir Reykjavík - ÍA Akranes 1-3(0-1)	FH Hafnarfjörður - Fjölnir Reykjavík 1-0(0-0)	Stjarnan - Fjölnir Reykjavík 1-0(0-0)
KR Reykjavík - Grótta 1-1(0-0)	Grótta - KA Akureyri 2-4(0-2)	Kópavogur - KR Reykjavík 1-1(0-1)
Fylkir Reykjavík - Víkingur 2-1(1-0)	Kópavogur - Stjarnan 2-3(0-2)	Valur Reykjavík - Grótta 6-0(3-0)
Breiðablik - Stjarnan 2-1(1-1)	Valur Reykjavík - Breiðablik 1-1(0-0)	Breiðablik - Fylkir Reykjavík 4-1(2-1)

Final Standings

							Total				Home				Away			
1.	**Valur Reykjavík**	(2.44)	18	14	2	2	50 - 17	44	5	2	2	15 - 6		9	0	0	35 - 11	
2.	FH Hafnarfjörður	(2.00)	18	11	3	4	37 - 23	36	6	1	3	16 - 11		5	2	1	21 - 12	
3.	Stjarnan Garðabær	(1.82)	17	8	7	2	27 - 20	31	3	4	1	12 - 11		5	3	1	15 - 9	
4.	Breiðablik Kópavogur	(1.72)	18	9	4	5	37 - 27	31	5	2	2	22 - 14		4	2	3	15 - 13	
5.	KR Reykjavík	(1.65)	17	8	4	5	30 - 21	28	3	2	5	19 - 19		5	2	0	11 - 2	
6.	Fylkir Reykjavík	(1.56)	18	9	1	8	27 - 30	28	5	1	3	15 - 13		4	0	5	12 - 17	
7.	KA Akureyri	(1.17)	18	3	12	3	20 - 21	21	2	7	0	9 - 6		1	5	3	11 - 15	
8.	ÍA Akranes	(1.17)	18	6	3	9	39 - 43	21	3	2	4	17 - 19		3	1	5	22 - 24	
9.	HK Kópavogur	(1.11)	18	5	5	8	29 - 36	20	4	1	4	15 - 16		1	4	4	14 - 20	
10.	Víkingur Reykjavík	(0.94)	18	3	8	7	25 - 30	17	2	3	3	17 - 18		1	5	4	8 - 12	
11.	IF Grótta Seltjarnarnes (Relegated)	(0.44)	18	1	5	12	15 - 43	8	0	3	5	9 - 21		1	2	7	6 - 22	
12.	Fjölnir Reykjavík (Relegated)	(0.33)	18	0	6	12	15 - 40	6	0	2	7	7 - 24		0	4	5	8 - 16	

Please note: the season was abandoned on 30.10.2020 due to COVID-19 pandemic. Standings were decided by a points by game average.

Top goalscorers:		
17	**Steven Lennon (SCO)**	*FH Hafnarfjörður*
15	Patrick Pedersen (DEN)	*Valur Reykjavík*
13	Thomas Mikkelsen (DEN)	*Breiðablik Kópavogur*
12	Tryggvi Hrafn Haraldsson	*ÍA Akranes*
9	Ottar Magnus Karlsson	*Víkingur Reykjavík*

NATIONAL CUP
Mjólkurbikarinn 2020

First Round [05-08.06.2020]			
ÍR Reykjavík - KA Akureyri	3-1	UMF Skallagrímur - Ýmir	0-2
UMF Selfoss - UMF Snæfell	5-0	Kría - Hamar	2-3
Smári FC - UMF Njarðvík	0-4	KF Garðabæjar - KB Breiðholt	7-1
KV Vesturbæjar – Kári Akranes	0-3 aet	Þróttur Reykjavík - Álafoss	1-0
Vængir Júpiters - KH Hlíðarendi	3-1	SR - IB Uppsveitir	2-0
Haukar Hafnarfjörður - Elliði	3-1	UMF Tindastóll - Kormákur/Hvöt	2-1
Hvíti riddarinn - KFS Vestmannaeyjar	2-1	Samherjar - Nökkvi	3-0
Álftanes - Fram Reykjavík	0-4	KFB - Víðir Garður	1-5
Vatnaliljur - Afturelding	0-12	Ísbjörninn - Björninn	4-5 aet
Þróttur Vogar - Ægir Þorlákshöfn	2-1	KFR Hvolsvöllur - GG Grindavík	0-2
Huginn/Höttur - Sindri Höfn	2-1 aet	Stokkseyri - Afríka	3-1
Dalvík/Reynir - KF Fjallabyggðar	1-2	Árborg - Augnablik	0-0 aet; 8-7 pen
Mídas - KM Reykjavík	4-1	Léttir - Reynir Sandgerði	1-9
Hörður Ísafjörður - IF Vestri	1-4	ÍH Hafnarfjörður - KF Berserkir	3-1

Second Round [12-14.06.2020]

ÍF Völsungur - Þór Akureyri	2-2 aet; 4-5 pen		Haukar Hafnarfjörður - Fram Reykjavík	1-2 aet
Leiknir Reykjavík - Kári	5-0		KF Garðabæjar - Afturelding	0-5
Ýmir - ÍR Reykjavík	1-4		Þróttur Reykjavík - IF Vestri	3-1
Keflavík ÍF - Björninn	5-0		Vængir Júpiters - Víðir Garður	2-1
Kórdrengir - Hamar	6-0		UMF Njarðvík - Árborg	1-1aet; 3-4 pen
Hvíti riddarinn - UMF Selfoss	0-1		Þróttur Vogar - Víkingur Ólafsvík	1-2
Mídas - Skautafélag Reykjavíkur	0-4		UMF Grindavík - ÍB Vestmannaeyja	1-5
ÍH Hafnarfjörður - GG Grindavík	3-0		UMF Tindastóll - Samherjar	2-1
Leiknir Fáskrúðsfirði - UMF Einherji	3-1		Huginn/Höttur - KF Fjarðabyggðar	2-1
Stokkseyri - Reynir Sandgerði	2-8		KF Fjallabyggðar - ÍF Magni	2-2 aet; 5-6 pen

Third Round [23-25.06.2020]

Fram Reykjavík - ÍR Reykjavík	3-1		Þór Akureyri - Reynir Sandgerði	2-1 aet
ÍBV Vestmannaeyjar - Samherjar	7-0		Þróttur Reykjavík - FH Hafnarfjörður	1-2
Skautafélag Reykjavíkur - Valur Reykjavík	0-3		Kórdrengir - ÍA Akranes	2-3 aet
Vængir Júpiters - KR Reykjavík	1-8		Fjölnir Reykjavík - UMF Selfoss	3-2
Afturelding - Árborg	3-0		ÍH Hafnarfjörður - Fylkir Reykjavík	0-8
IF Grótta Seltjarnarnes - Huginn/Höttur	3-0		Stjarnan Garðabær - Leiknir Fáskrúðsfirði	3-0
KA Akureyri - Leiknir Reykjavík	6-0		Víkingur Ólafsvík - Víkingur Reykjavík	1-1 aet; 4-5 pen
ÍF Magni - HK Kópavogur	1-2		Breiðablik Kópavogur - Keflavík	3-2

1/8-Finals [30.07./18.08.2020]

KA Akureyri - ÍBV Vestmannaeyjar	1-3 aet		Fram Reykjavík - Fylkir Reykjavík	1-1 aet; 4-3 pen
FH Hafnarfjörður - Þór Akureyri	3-1		HK Kópavogur - Afturelding	6-2
Breiðablik Kópavogur - IF Grótta Seltjarnarnes	3-0		Víkingur Reykjavík - Stjarnan Garðabær	1-2
KR Reykjavík - Fjölnir Reykjavík	2-0		Valur Reykjavík - ÍA Akranes	3-1

Quarter-Finals [25.08./10.09.2020]

ÍBV Vestmannaeyjar - Fram Reykjavík	2-1		Breiðablik Kópavogur - KR Reykjavík	2-4
FH Hafnarfjörður - Stjarnan Garðabær	3-0		Valur Reykjavík - HK Kópavogur	2-1 aet

Semi-Finals [04.11.2020]

Valur Reykjavík - KR Reykjavík	*not played*		ÍBV Vestmannaeyjar - FH Hafnarfjörður	*not played*

The competition was cancelled on 30.10.2020 due to COVID-19 pandemic.

THE CLUBS 2020

Breiðablik Kópavogur

Founded: 12.04.1950
Stadium: Kópavogsvöllur, Kópavogur (5,501)
Trainer: Óskar Hrafn Þorvaldsson   25.10.1973

Goalkeepers:	DOB	M	(s)	G
Anton Ari Einarsson	25.08.1994	18		
Defenders:	**DOB**	**M**	**(s)**	**G**
Elfar Helgason	27.07.1989	16		1
Davíð Ingvarsson	25.04.1999	12	(2)	
Viktor Örn Margeirsson	22.07.1994	9	(1)	
Damir Muminović (SRB)	13.05.1990	14	(1)	1
Róbert Þorkelsson	03.04.2002	9	(4)	1
Midfielders:	**DOB**	**M**	**(s)**	**G**
Atli Hrafn Andrason	04.01.1999		(5)	1
Viktor Einarsson	30.01.1997	13	(1)	5
Gísli Eyjólfsson	31.05.1994	13	(2)	2
Höskuldur Gunnlaugsson	26.09.1994	17	(1)	1
Hlynur Freyr Karlsson	06.04.2004		(1)	

	DOB	M	(s)	G
Anton Logi Lúðvíksson	13.03.2003		(1)	
Guðjón Lýðsson	28.12.1987	1	(2)	
Gunnar Heimir Ólafsson	26.01.2002		(1)	
Alexander Sigurðarson	08.04.1996	4	(8)	2
Oliver Sigurjónsson	03.03.1995	15	(2)	
Kristinn Steindórsson	29.04.1990	9	(2)	6
Benedikt Warén	03.10.2001		(2)	
Andri Yeoman	18.04.1992	14		
Forwards:	**DOB**	**M**	**(s)**	**G**
Thomas Mikkelsen (DEN)	19.01.1990	16		13
Kwame Quee (SLE)	07.09.1996	2	(8)	
Stefán Ingi Sigurðarson	27.01.2001	1	(3)	
Brynjólfur Willumsson	12.08.2000	15	(2)	4

Fimleikafélag Hafnarfjarðar

Founded: 15.10.1929
Stadium: Kaplakriki, Hafnarfjörður (6,738)
Trainer: Ólafur Helgi Kristjánsson   20.05.1968
(16.07.2020) Eiður Guðjohnsen   15.09.1978

Goalkeepers:	DOB	M	(s)	G
Daði Arnarsson	23.09.1998	1		
Gunnar Nielsen (FRO)	07.10.1986	17		
Defenders:	**DOB**	**M**	**(s)**	**G**
Hörður Ingi Gunnarsson	14.08.1998	17		
Guðmundur Kristjánsson	01.03.1989	17		
Logi Tómasson	13.09.2000	1	(6)	
Hjörtur Valgarðsson	27.09.1988	13	(1)	2
Pétur Viðarsson	25.11.1987	9	(3)	1
Þórður Þórðarson	22.02.1995		(1)	
Guðmann Þórisson	30.01.1987	14		
Midfielders:	**DOB**	**M**	**(s)**	**G**
Ólafur Karl Finsen	30.03.1992	7	(2)	1
Baldur Guðlaugsson	21.01.2002	1	(15)	

	DOB	M	(s)	G
Daníel Hafsteinsson	12.11.1999	10	(1)	3
Þórir Jóhann Helgason	28.09.2000	16	(2)	2
Eggert Gunnþór Jónsson	18.08.1988	9		
Logi Hrafn Róbertsson	22.07.2004	1	(6)	
Baldur Sigurðsson	24.04.1985	6	(7)	
Björn Sverrisson	29.05.1990	17		2
Forwards:	**DOB**	**M**	**(s)**	**G**
Morten Beck (DEN)	02.01.1988	6	(7)	1
Kristján Emilsson	26.04.1993		(2)	
Atli Guðnason	28.09.1984	3	(8)	2
Jónatan Jónsson	15.03.1999	15	(1)	4
Steven Lennon (SCO)	20.01.1988	18		17
Óskar Atli Magnússon	24.06.1905		(1)	

Ungmennafélagið Fjölnir Reykjavík

Founded: 1988
Stadium: Fjölnisvöllur, Grafarvogur, Reykjavík (1,030)
Trainer: Ásmundur Arnarsson — 14.03.1972

Goalkeepers:	DOB	M	(s)	G
Atli Gunnar Guðmundsson	08.10.1993	17		
Sigurjón Daði Harðarson	24.02.2001	1		
Defenders:	**DOB**	**M**	**(s)**	**G**
Arnór Breki Ásþórsson	08.02.1998	18		1
Hans Viktor Guðmundsson	09.09.1996	18		
Torfi Gunnarsson	31.01.1999	4	(2)	
Vilhjálmur Hjálmarsson	12.02.2002	3	(2)	
Valdimar Ingi Jónsson	12.03.1998	2	(7)	
Péter Zachán (HUN)	12.12.1997	14	(1)	
Midfielders:	**DOB**	**M**	**(s)**	**G**
Guðmundur Guðmundsson	30.03.1991	14	(2)	1
Grétar Snær Gunnarsson	08.01.1997	17		1
Jóhann Árni Gunnarsson	06.04.2001	15	(3)	4

	DOB	M	(s)	G
Nicklas Halse (DEN)	03.05.1997	5		
Sigurpáll Melberg Pálsson	13.09.1996	16		1
Jeffrey Monakana (ENG)	05.11.1993	4		
Orri Þórhallsson	14.11.2001	13	(4)	2
Forwards:	**DOB**	**M**	**(s)**	**G**
Örvar Eggertsson	28.02.1999	13	(2)	
Viktor Hafþórsson	16.08.2001	6	(9)	1
Lúkas Heimisson	04.04.2003		(6)	
Kristófer Óskar Óskarsson	22.06.2000	1	(12)	
Hallvarður Sigurðarson	13.01.1999	4	(3)	1
Ingibergur Kort Sigurðsson	27.04.1998	7	(5)	1
Christian Justesen Sivebæk (DEN)	19.02.1988	3	(1)	
Jón Gísli Ström	26.02.1993	3	(8)	2

Íþróttafélagið Fylkir Reykjavík

Founded: 28.05.1967
Stadium: Floridana völlurinn, Reykjavík (5,000)
Trainer: Atli Sveinn Þórarinsson & — 24.01.1980
Ólafur Ingi Stígsson — 16.12.1975

Goalkeepers:	DOB	M	(s)	G
Aron Snær Friðriksson	29.01.1997	17		
Arnar Pétursson	16.03.1991	1		
Defenders:	**DOB**	**M**	**(s)**	**G**
Ásgeir Eyþórsson	29.04.1993	18		3
Arnar Sveinn Geirsson	30.08.1991	9	(1)	
Axel Máni Guðbjörnsson	05.07.2002	1		
Andrés Jóhannesson	21.12.1988		(3)	
Arnór Jónsson	31.05.2002	5	(2)	
Michael Kedman (ENG)	16.12.1996	3	(5)	
Daníel Steinar Kjartansson	21.03.1998	1	(3)	
Daði Ólafsson	05.01.1994	16		1
Orri Sveinn Stefánsson	20.02.1996	16		3
Midfielders:	**DOB**	**M**	**(s)**	**G**
Helgi Daníelsson	13.07.1981	3		

	DOB	M	(s)	G
Birkir Eyþórsson	07.05.2000	3	(4)	
Nikulás Gunnarsson	17.01.2000	12	(2)	
Sam Hewson (ENG)	28.11.1988	7	(4)	1
Orri Hrafn Kjartansson	05.02.2002	3	(2)	1
Kári Sigfússon	22.06.2002		(1)	
Ólafur Skúlason	01.04.1983	9	(3)	
Forwards:	**DOB**	**M**	**(s)**	**G**
Arnór Guðjohnsen	16.09.2000	7	(10)	2
Þórður Hafþórsson	10.08.2001	7	(10)	1
Valdimar Þór Ingimundarson	28.04.1999	14		8
Hákon Ingi Jónsson	10.11.1995	9	(8)	2
Djair Parfitt-Williams (BER)	01.10.1996	18		2
Arnór Gauti Ragnarsson	04.02.1997	11	(3)	3
Ragnar Sveinsson	18.12.1994	8	(2)	

Íþróttafélagið Grótta Seltjarnarnes

Founded: 24.04.1967
Stadium: Vivaldivöllurinn, Seltjarnarnes (1,050)
Trainer: Ágúst Þór Gylfason — 01.08.1971

Goalkeepers:	DOB	M	(s)	G
Hákon Valdimarsson	13.10.2001	18		
Defenders:	**DOB**	**M**	**(s)**	**G**
Halldór Baldursson	16.07.1994	9	(3)	1
Dagur Guðjónsson	10.03.1997		(1)	
Karl Gunnarsson	06.07.2001	12	(4)	6
Arnar Helgason	09.07.1996	16		
Bjarki Leósson	05.07.1998	8	(2)	
Kristófer Melsted	08.06.1999	13	(3)	
Patrik Pétursson	17.12.2000	7	(1)	
Ástbjörn Þórðarson	26.07.1999	12	(2)	1
Midfielders:	**DOB**	**M**	**(s)**	**G**
Ólafur Karel Eiríksson	27.07.2001	3	(2)	
Gabríel Eyjólfsson	12.09.1999	1	(6)	

	DOB	M	(s)	G
Grímur Jakobsson	26.06.2003		(4)	
Óskar Jónsson	28.01.1997	9	(5)	
Valtýr Már Michaelsson	21.08.1998	6	(3)	
Sigurvin Reynisson	10.11.1995	14	(2)	
Tobias Sommer (DEN)	27.11.2001	4	(1)	1
Óliver Dagur Thorlacius	19.03.1999	10	(6)	
Forwards:	**DOB**	**M**	**(s)**	**G**
Pétur Theódór Árnason	04.06.1995	17	(1)	3
Kjartan Halldórsson	02.07.2003		(6)	
Ágúst Freyr Hallsson	04.06.1994		(4)	
Axel Freyr Harðarson	22.10.1999	10	(7)	
Kieran Hugh Dolan McGrath (SCO)	28.03.2001	1	(11)	1
Kristófer Pétursson	10.07.1998	16	(2)	
Axel Sigurðarson	18.04.1998	12	(2)	

Knattspyrnufélag Akureyrar

Founded: 1928
Stadium: Akureyrarvöllur, Akureyri (1,770)
Trainer: Óli Stefán Flóventsson — 07.12.1975
(15.07.2020) Arnar Grétarsson — 20.02.1972

Goalkeepers:	DOB	M	(s)	G
Aron Dagur Birnuson	03.07.1999	5		
Kristijan Jajalo (BIH)	04.03.1993	13		
Defenders:	**DOB**	**M**	**(s)**	**G**
Brynjar Ingi Bjarnason	06.12.1999	18		2
Ýmir Már Geirsson	11.11.1997	1	(2)	
Adam Örn Guðmundsson	11.01.2001		(2)	
Haukur Hauksson	01.09.1991		(1)	
Hallgrímur Jónasson	04.05.1986	2		
Mikkel Mena Qvist (DEN)	22.04.1993	15		
Hrannar Steingrímsson	19.06.1992	15	(2)	
Midfielders:	**DOB**	**M**	**(s)**	**G**
Bjarni Aðalsteinsson	01.09.1999	13	(5)	
Ívar Örn Árnason	12.04.1996	13	(3)	

	DOB	M	(s)	G
Almarr Ormarsson	25.02.1988	17	(1)	1
Rodri (ESP)	09.02.1989	14	(1)	
Andri Stefánsson	22.04.1991	12	(6)	
Þorri Mar Þórisson	13.08.1999		(4)	
Forwards:	**DOB**	**M**	**(s)**	**G**
Jibrill Abubakar Antala (DEN)	06.01.2000		(3)	
Guðmundur Hafsteinsson	14.06.1989	13	(4)	6
Sveinn Hauksson	02.11.2001	9	(7)	1
Ásgeir Sigurgeirsson	11.12.1996	15	(3)	2
Gunnar Stefánsson	13.02.1994	1	(5)	
Hallgrímur Steingrímsson	02.10.1990	16	(2)	4
Nökkvi Þórisson	13.08.1999	3	(6)	1
Steinþór Þorsteinsson	29.07.1985	3	(12)	3

Knattspyrnufélag Reykjavíkur

Founded: 16.02.1899
Stadium: Alvogenvöllurinn, Reykjavík (3,333)
Trainer: Rúnar Kristinsson 05.09.1969

Goalkeepers:	DOB	M	(s)	G
Beitir Ólafsson	02.07.1986	16		
Guðjón Sigurjónsson	01.12.1992	1	(1)	
Defenders:	DOB	M	(s)	G
Arnór Aðalsteinsson	26.01.1986	13		
Kennie Chopart (DEN)	01.06.1990	16		1
Gunnar Gunnarsson	04.10.1985	1	(1)	
Kristinn Jónsson	04.08.1990	16		
Aron Jósepsson	21.11.1989	6	(3)	1
Finnur Tómas Pálmason	12.02.2001	11	(3)	
Hjalti Sigurðsson	19.09.2000	3	(2)	
Midfielders:	DOB	M	(s)	G
Jóhannes Bjarnason	27.06.1905		(1)	
Alex Freyr Hilmarsson	26.07.1993	1	(8)	
Ægir Jónasson	08.03.1998	6	(9)	2
Arnþór Ingi Kristinsson	15.03.1990	9	(1)	
Finnur Margeirsson	08.03.1991	8	(4)	
Pálmi Pálmason	09.11.1984	15	(2)	1
Pablo Oshan Battuto Punyed (SLV)	18.04.1990	14	(2)	7
Atli Sigurjónsson	01.07.1991	17		6
Forwards:	DOB	M	(s)	G
Kristján Finnbogason	12.01.1995	12	(2)	4
Stefán Árni Geirsson	06.11.2000	8	(5)	1
Óskar Hauksson	22.08.1984	12	(5)	5
Tobias Thomsen (DEN)	19.10.1992	2	(4)	1

Handknattleiksfélag Kópavogs

Founded: 26.01.1970
Stadium: Kórinn, Kopavogur (1,452)
Trainer: Brynjar Björn Gunnarsson 16.10.1975

Goalkeepers:	DOB	M	(s)	G
Sigurður Björnsson	26.12.1993	7	(1)	
Arnar Freyr Ólafsson	06.03.1993	11		
Defenders:	DOB	M	(s)	G
Hörður Árnason	19.05.1989	10	(1)	2
Martin Rauschenberg Brorsen (DEN)	15.01.1992	8		1
Birkir Valur Jónsson	02.11.1998	9		1
Ívar Örn Jónsson	02.02.1994	8	(3)	
Guðmundur Júlíusson	29.12.1993	9	(3)	1
Leifur Andri Leifsson	11.10.1989	15		
Alexander Sindrason	31.07.1993	4		
Þórður Þorsteinn Þórðarson	22.02.1995	7		
Midfielders:	DOB	M	(s)	G
Atli Arnarson	29.11.1993	12	(2)	3
Ásgeir Ásgeirsson	16.04.1987	17	(1)	
Arnþór Ari Atlason	12.10.1993	14	(1)	3
Ólafur Örn Eyjólfsson	14.10.1994	6	(8)	1
Ívar Orri Gissurarson	03.07.2003		(1)	
Bjarni Páll Linnet Runólfsson	10.09.1996		(2)	
Forwards:	DOB	M	(s)	G
Jón Arnar Barðdal	07.10.1995	12	(2)	2
Bjarni Gunnarsson	29.01.1993	6	(3)	1
Birnir Snær Ingason	04.12.1996	16	(2)	5
Stefan Ljubicic	05.10.1999	3	(9)	1
Ásgeir Marteinsson	07.07.1994	9	(5)	3
Ari Sigurpálsson	17.03.2003	2	(6)	1
Valgeir Valgeirsson	22.09.2002	13	(2)	4

Íþróttabandalag Akraness

Founded: 1946
Stadium: Norðurálsvöllurinn, Akranes (3,054)
Trainer: Jóhannes Karl Guðjónsson 25.05.1980

Goalkeepers:	DOB	M	(s)	G
Árni Ólafsson	16.08.1991	18		
Defenders:	DOB	M	(s)	G
Hallur Flosason	01.05.1993	9	(2)	
Jón Gíslason	25.02.2002	9	(7)	
Óttar Bjarni Guðmundsson	15.04.1990	17		1
Árni Salvar Heimisson	10.03.2003		(1)	
Marcus Johansson (SWE)	24.08.1993	10	(5)	1
Hlynur Sævar Jónsson	29.03.1999	7	(9)	2
Aron Kristófer Lárusson	17.09.1998	12	(2)	
Benjamín Mehic	05.02.2001	3	(1)	
Midfielders:	DOB	M	(s)	G
Sindri Snær Magnússon	18.02.1992	17		
Brynjar Pálsson	11.11.2001	15	(2)	2
Guðmundur Tyrfingsson	01.02.2003		(4)	
Ólafur Valdimarsson	13.12.1990	1	(9)	
Stefán Teitur Þórðarson	16.10.1998	17		8
Steinar Þorsteinsson	06.12.1997	13	(3)	3
Ísak Snær Þorvaldsson	01.05.2001	7		
Forwards:	DOB	M	(s)	G
Bjarki Steinn Bjarkason	11.05.2000	5		1
Tryggvi Hrafn Haraldsson	30.09.1996	17		12
Viktor Jónsson	23.06.1994	9		5
Ingi Sigurðsson	06.04.2004	1	(4)	
Marteinn Theodórsson	15.11.2001	1	(2)	
Gísli Unnarsson	28.02.2001	7	(10)	2
Sigurður Hrannar Þorsteinsson	19.04.2000	3	(11)	1

Ungmennafélagið Stjarnan Garðabær

Founded: 1960
Stadium: Samsung völlurinn, Garðabær (1,440)
Trainer: Rúnar Páll Sigmundsson 05.05.1974

Goalkeepers:	DOB	M	(s)	G
Haraldur Björnsson	11.01.1989	17		
Defenders:	DOB	M	(s)	G
Heiðar Ægisson	10.08.1995	17		
Elís Rafn Björnsson	13.10.1992	5	(5)	
Björn Bryde	08.07.1992	3	(1)	
Brynjar Guðjónsson	27.02.1992	16		
Jósef Kristinn Jósefsson	12.09.1989	11		1
Daníel Laxdal	22.09.1986	16		2
Jóhann Laxdal	27.01.1990	3	(4)	
Midfielders:	DOB	M	(s)	G
Alex Þór Hauksson	26.11.1999	16		2
Eyjólfur Héðinsson	01.01.1985	8	(2)	
Ævar Jóhannesson	31.01.1995		(1)	
Kristófer Konráðsson	31.03.1998	3	(3)	
Guðjón Pétur Lýðsson	28.12.1987	7	(6)	2
Kári Pétursson	01.10.1996		(1)	
Forwards:	DOB	M	(s)	G
Emil Atlason	22.07.1993	6	(7)	2
Guðjón Baldvinsson	15.02.1986	10	(4)	4
Adolf Daði Birgisson	03.06.2004		(1)	
Halldór Björnsson	02.03.1987	6	(8)	2
Sölvi Guðbjargarson	25.07.2001	11	(3)	2
Hilmar Árni Halldórsson	14.02.1992	17		7
Óli Ómarsson	09.01.2003		(7)	
Þorsteinn Már Ragnarsson	19.04.1990	15		1
Ísak Andri Sigurgeirsson	11.09.2003		(7)	1

Knattspyrnufélagið Valur Reykjavík

Founded: 11.05.1911
Stadium: Valsvöllur, Reykjavík (2,465)
Trainer: Heimir Guðjónsson   03.04.1969

Goalkeepers:	DOB	M	(s)	G
Hannes Þór Halldórsson	27.04.1984	18		
Defenders:	**DOB**	**M**	**(s)**	**G**
Rasmus Christiansen (DEN)	06.10.1989	18		
Magnus Egilsson (FRO)	19.03.1994	3	(3)	
Valgeir Lunddal Friðriksson	24.09.2001	13	(2)	3
Sebastian Hedlund (SWE)	05.04.1995	11		1
Birkir Már Sævarsson	11.11.1984	18		4
Eiður Sigurbjörnsson	26.02.1990	8	(4)	1
Midfielders:	**DOB**	**M**	**(s)**	**G**
Kristófer Cardoso	04.03.2002		(1)	
Sigurður Dagsson	07.08.2002		(1)	
Ólafur Finsen	30.03.1992		(1)	

	DOB	M	(s)	G
Birkir Heimisson	12.02.2000		(16)	1
Einar Karl Ingvarsson	08.10.1993	3	(11)	1
Orri Ómarsson	18.02.1995	4	(8)	
Lasse Petry (DEN)	19.09.1992	13	(4)	2
Haukur Sigurðsson	05.08.1987	17		1
Kristinn Sigurðsson	25.12.1991	13	(4)	5
Forwards:	**DOB**	**M**	**(s)**	**G**
Andri Adolphsson	01.12.1992		(1)	
Aron Bjarnason	14.10.1995	18		7
Kasper Waarts Høgh (DEN)	06.12.2000		(5)	
Kaj Leo í Bartalsstovu (FRO)	23.06.1991	10	(7)	2
Sigurður Lárusson	22.01.1992	15	(3)	6
Patrick Pedersen (DEN)	25.11.1991	16	(1)	15

Knattspyrnufélagið Víkingur Reykjavík

Founded: 21.04.1908
Stadium: Víkingsvöllur, Reykjavík (1,848)
Trainer: Arnar Gunnlaugsson   06.03.1973

Goalkeepers:	DOB	M	(s)	G
Þórður Ingason	30.03.1988	3	(1)	
Ingvar Jónsson	18.10.1989	15		
Defenders:	**DOB**	**M**	**(s)**	**G**
Kári Árnason	13.10.1982	12		
Davíð Atlason	18.08.1994	15		2
Atli Barkarson	19.03.2001	8	(6)	
Tómas Guðmundsson	10.02.1992	1		
Sölvi Ottesen	18.02.1984	11		1
Halldór Sigurðsson	04.10.1988	11	(1)	
Dofri Snorrason	21.07.1990	6	(3)	
Logi Tómasson	13.09.2000	1	(1)	
Midfielders:	**DOB**	**M**	**(s)**	**G**
Erlingur Agnarsson	05.03.1998	17		1

	DOB	M	(s)	G
Atli Hrafn Andrason	04.01.1999	5	(2)	1
Viktor Örlygur Andrason	05.02.2000	12	(4)	1
Sigurður Steinar Björnsson	2004		(2)	
Ágúst Hlynsson	28.03.2000	18		4
Kristall Máni Ingason	18.01.2002	9	(6)	1
Júlíus Magnússon	28.06.1998	16		
Adam Ægir Pálsson	30.11.1997	2	(6)	1
Kwame Quee (SLE)	07.09.1996	5	(1)	1
Bjarni Páll Runólfsson	10.09.1996		(2)	
Halldór Þórðarson	12.07.1996	6	(6)	1
Forwards:	**DOB**	**M**	**(s)**	**G**
Helgi Guðjónsson	04.08.1999	4	(8)	1
Nikolaj Hansen (DEN)	15.03.1993	7	(6)	1
Óttar Magnús Karlsson	21.02.1997	14		9

SECOND LEVEL
1. deild karla 2020

1.	Keflavík (*Promoted*)	19	13	4	2	57 - 27	43	(2.26)
2.	Leiknir Reykjavík (*Promoted*)	20	13	3	4	50 - 22	42	(2.10)
3.	Fram Reykjavík	20	12	6	2	41 - 24	42	(2.10)
4.	UMF Grindavík	19	8	8	3	40 - 31	32	(1.68)
5.	Þór Akureyri	20	9	4	7	37 - 35	31	(1.55)
6.	ÍBV Vestmannaeyjar	20	7	9	4	33 - 27	30	(1.50)
7.	Vestri Ísafjörður	20	8	5	7	29 - 28	29	(1.45)
8.	UMF Afturelding Mosfellsbær	20	7	4	9	37 - 33	25	(1.25)
9.	Víkingur Ólafsvík	20	5	4	11	26 - 44	19	(0.95)
10.	Þróttur Reykjavík	20	3	3	14	15 - 39	12	(0.60)
11.	IF Magni Grenivík (*Relegated*)	20	3	3	14	22 - 47	12	(0.60)
12.	Leiknir Fáskrúðsfjörður (*Relegated*)	20	3	3	14	19 - 49	12	(0.60)

Please note: the season was abandoned on 30.10.2020 due to COVID-19 pandemic. Standings were decided by a points by game average.

INTERNATIONAL MATCHES
(16.07.2020 – 15.07.2021)

05.09.2020	Reykjavík	Iceland - England	0-1(0-0)	(UNL)
08.09.2020	Bruxelles	Belgium - Iceland	5-1(2-1)	(UNL)
08.10.2020	Reykjavík	Iceland - Romania	2-1(2-0)	(ECQPO)
11.10.2020	Reykjavík	Iceland - Denmark	0-3(0-1)	(UNL)
14.10.2020	Reykjavík	Iceland - Belgium	1-2(1-2)	(UNL)
12.11.2020	Budapest	Hungary - Iceland	2-1(0-1)	(ECQPO)
15.11.2020	København	Denmark - Iceland	2-1(1-0)	(UNL)
18.11.2020	London	England - Iceland	4-0(2-0)	(UNL)
25.03.2021	Duisburg	Germany - Iceland	3-0(2-0)	(WCQ)
28.03.2021	Yerevan	Armenia - Iceland	2-0(0-0)	(WCQ)
31.03.2021	Vaduz	Liechtenstein - Iceland	1-4(0-2)	(WCQ)
29.05.2021	Arlington	Mexico - Iceland	2-1(0-1)	(F)
04.06.2021	Tórshavn	Faroe Islands - Iceland	0-1(0-0)	(F)
08.06.2021	Poznań	Poland - Iceland	2-2(1-1)	(F)

05.09.2020   **ICELAND - ENGLAND**   **0-1(0-0)**   2nd UEFA Nations League A, Group 2
Laugardalsvöllur, Reykjavík; Referee: Srđan Jovanović (Serbia); Attendance: 0
ISL: Hannes Þór Halldórsson, Kári Árnason (Cap), Hörður Björgvin Magnússon, Sverrir Ingi Ingason [*sent off 89*], Hjörtur Hermannsson, Birkir Bjarnason, Guðlaugur Victor Pálsson, Arnór Ingvi Traustason (76.Emil Hallfreðsson), Jón Thorsteinsson (66.Arnór Sigurðsson), Jón Daði Böðvarsson (90+1.Hólmbert Aron Briem Friðjónsson), Albert Guðmundsson. Trainer: Erik Anders Hamrén (Sweden).

08.09.2020   **BELGIUM - ICELAND**   **5-1(2-1)**   2nd UEFA Nations League A, Group 2
Stade "Roi Baudouin", Bruxelles; Referee: Paweł Raczkowski (Poland); Attendance: 0
ISL: Ögmundur Kristinsson, Jón Guðni Fjóluson, Ari Freyr Skúlason (Cap), Hólmar Örn Eyjólfsson, Hjörtur Hermannsson, Birkir Bjarnason, Guðlaugur Victor Pálsson, Arnór Sigurðsson (72.Mikael Neville Anderson), Andri Fannar Baldursson (53.Emil Hallfreðsson), Hólmbert Aron Briem Friðjónsson (70.Jón Daði Böðvarsson), Albert Guðmundsson. Trainer: Erik Anders Hamrén (Sweden).
Goal: Hólmbert Aron Fridjonsson (11).

08.10.2020   **ICELAND - ROMANIA**   **2-1(2-0)**   16th EC. Qualifiers Play-offs, Semi-Finals
Laugardalsvöllur, Reykjavík; Referee: Damir Skomina (Slovenia); Attendance: 59
ISL: Hannes Þór Halldórsson, Ragnar Sigurðsson, Kári Árnason (86.Sverrir Ingi Ingason), Hörður Björgvin Magnússon, Birkir Bjarnason, Aron Einar Malmquist Gunnarsson (Cap), Jóhann Berg Guðmundsson (83.Rúnar Már Sigurlaugarson Sigurjónsson), Gylfi Þór Sigurðsson, Guðlaugur Victor Pálsson, Arnór Ingvi Traustason, Alfreð Finnbogason (75.Kolbeinn Sigþórsson). Trainer: Erik Anders Hamrén (Sweden).
Goals: Gylfi Þór Sigurðsson (16, 35).

11.10.2020   **ICELAND - DENMARK**   **0-3(0-1)**   2nd UEFA Nations League A, Group 2
Laugardalsvöllur, Reykjavík; Referee: Bojan Pandžić (Sweden); Attendance: 60
ISL: Hannes Þór Halldórsson, Ragnar Sigurðsson, Hörður Björgvin Magnússon, Sverrir Ingi Ingason, Birkir Bjarnason, Gylfi Þór Sigurðsson, Aron Einar Malmquist Gunnarsson (Cap) (46.Mikael Neville Anderson), Rúnar Már Sigurlaugarson Sigurjónsson (73.Hólmar Örn Eyjólfsson), Guðlaugur Victor Pálsson, Arnór Ingvi Traustason (68.Albert Guðmundsson), Alfreð Finnbogason (12.Jón Daði Böðvarsson). Trainer: Erik Anders Hamrén (Sweden).

14.10.2020   **ICELAND - BELGIUM**   **1-2(1-2)**   2nd UEFA Nations League A, Group 2
Laugardalsvöllur, Reykjavík; Referee: Andris Treimanis (Latvia); Attendance: 59
ISL: Rúnar Alex Rúnarsson, Birkir Már Sævarsson, Ari Freyr Skúlason, Hólmar Örn Eyjólfsson, Hörður Björgvin Magnússon (86.Arnór Ingvi Traustason), Sverrir Ingi Ingason, Birkir Bjarnason (Cap), Rúnar Már Sigurlaugarson Sigurjónsson (69.Jón Thorsteinsson), Guðlaugur Victor Pálsson (82.Hjörtur Hermannsson), Jón Daði Böðvarsson (69.Viðar Örn Kjartansson), Albert Guðmundsson (82.Kolbeinn Sigþórsson). Trainer: Erik Anders Hamrén (Sweden).
Goal: Birkir Már Sævarsson (17).

12.11.2020   **HUNGARY - ICELAND**   **2-1(0-1)**   16th EC. Qualifiers Play-offs, Finals
Puskás Aréna, Budapest; Referee: Björn Kuipers (Netherlands); Attendance: 0
ISL: Hannes Þór Halldórsson, Ragnar Sigurðsson, Kári Árnason, Hörður Björgvin Magnússon, Birkir Bjarnason, Aron Einar Malmquist Gunnarsson (Cap) (83.Ari Freyr Skúlason), Jóhann Berg Guðmundsson (72.Jón Daði Böðvarsson), Rúnar Már Sigurlaugarson Sigurjónsson (87.Sverrir Ingi Ingason), Gylfi Þór Sigurðsson, Guðlaugur Victor Pálsson, Alfreð Finnbogason (73.Albert Guðmundsson). Trainer: Erik Anders Hamrén (Sweden).
Goal: Gylfi Þór Sigurðsson (11).

15.11.2020   **DENMARK - ICELAND**   **2-1(1-0)**   2nd UEFA Nations League A, Group 2
Parken Stadium, København; Referee: Halil Umut Meler (Turkey); Attendance: 141
ISL: Rúnar Alex Rúnarsson, Birkir Már Sævarsson, Ari Freyr Skúlason, Hólmar Örn Eyjólfsson, Hörður Björgvin Magnússon, Sverrir Ingi Ingason, Birkir Bjarnason (46.Guðlaugur Victor Pálsson), Gylfi Þór Sigurðsson (Cap), Arnór Sigurðsson (70.Aron Einar Malmquist Gunnarsson), Jón Daði Böðvarsson (70.Viðar Örn Kjartansson), Albert Guðmundsson (74.Alfreð Finnbogason). Trainer: Erik Anders Hamrén (Sweden).
Goal: Viðar Örn Kjartansson (85).

18.11.2020   **ENGLAND - ICELAND**   **4-0(2-0)**   2nd UEFA Nations League A, Group 2
Wembley Stadium, London; Referee: Fábio José Costa Veríssimo (Portugal); Attendance: 0
ISL: Ögmundur Kristinsson (46.Hannes Þór Halldórsson), Birkir Már Sævarsson [*sent off 54*], Ari Freyr Skúlason, Kári Árnason (Cap), Sverrir Ingi Ingason, Hjörtur Hermannsson, Birkir Bjarnason (88.Ísak Bergmann Jóhannesson), Rúnar Már Sigurlaugarson Sigurjónsson (62.Hólmar Örn Eyjólfsson), Guðlaugur Victor Pálsson, Jón Daði Böðvarsson (73.Kolbeinn Sigþórsson), Albert Guðmundsson (73.Jón Thorsteinsson). Trainer: Erik Anders Hamrén (Sweden).

25.03.2021   **GERMANY - ICELAND**   **3-0(2-0)**   22nd FIFA WC.Qualifiers
MSV-Arena, Duisburg; Referee: Srđan Jovanović (Serbia); Attendance: 0
ISL: Hannes Þór Halldórsson, Kári Árnason, Hörður Björgvin Magnússon, Sverrir Ingi Ingason, Alfons Sampsted, Birkir Bjarnason, Aron Einar Malmquist Gunnarsson (Cap), Rúnar Már Sigurlaugarson Sigurjónsson (40.Albert Guðmundsson), Arnór Ingvi Traustason (71.Arnór Sigurðsson), Jón Daði Böðvarsson (89.Kolbeinn Sigþórsson), Guðlaugur Victor Pálsson (89.Ari Freyr Skúlason). Trainer: Arnar Viðarsson.

28.03.2021   **ARMENIA - ICELAND**   **2-0(0-0)**   22nd FIFA WC.Qualifiers
„Vazgen Sargsyan" Hanrapetakan Stadium, Yerevan; Referee: Enea Jorgji (Albania); Attendance: 4,300
ISL: Hannes Þór Halldórsson, Kári Árnason, Birkir Már Sævarsson, Ari Freyr Skúlason, Sverrir Ingi Ingason, Birkir Bjarnason (84.Guðlaugur Victor Pálsson), Aron Einar Malmquist Gunnarsson (Cap), Jóhann Berg Guðmundsson (77.Arnór Ingvi Traustason), Arnór Sigurðsson (55.Kolbeinn Sigþórsson), Jón Daði Böðvarsson (77.Hólmbert Aron Briem Friðjónsson), Albert Guðmundsson. Trainer: Arnar Viðarsson.

31.03.2021   **LIECHTENSTEIN - ICELAND**   **1-4(0-2)**   22nd FIFA WC.Qualifiers
Rheinpark Stadion, Vaduz; Referee: Mohammed Al Hakim (Sweden); Attendance: 0
ISL: Rúnar Alex Rúnarsson, Birkir Már Sævarsson, Hörður Björgvin Magnússon, Sverrir Ingi Ingason, Hjörtur Hermannsson, Birkir Bjarnason (72.Jón Dagur Þorsteinsson), Aron Einar Malmquist Gunnarsson (Cap) (46.Rúnar Már Sigurlaugarson Sigurjónsson), Jóhann Berg Guðmundsson (63.Arnór Sigurðsson), Guðlaugur Victor Pálsson, Sveinn Aron Guðjohnsen (63.Hólmbert Aron Briem Friðjónsson), Arnór Ingvi Traustason (81.Ísak Bergmann Jóhannesson). Trainer: Arnar Viðarsson.
Goals: Birkir Már Sævarsson (12), Birkir Bjarnason (45+1), Guðlaugur Victor Pálsson (77), Rúnar Már Sigurlaugarson Sigurjónsson (90+4 penalty).

29.05.2021   **MEXICO - ICELAND**   **2-1(0-1)**   Friendly International
AT&T Stadium, Arlington (United States); Referee: Ted Unkel (United States); Attendance: 44,892
ISL: Rúnar Alex Rúnarsson, Birkir Már Sævarsson (74.Rúnar Þór Sigurgeirsson), Hjörtur Hermannsson, Hörður Ingi Gunnarsson, Brynjar Ingi Bjarnason (80.Ísak Óli Ólafsson), Birkir Bjarnason (80.Aron Elís Þrándarson), Aron Einar Malmquist Gunnarsson (Cap) (60.Andri Fannar Baldursson), Þórir Jóhann Helgason, Ísak Bergmann Jóhannesson, Kolbeinn Sigþórsson (74.Gísli Eyjólfsson), Jón Daði Böðvarsson (74.Sveinn Aron Guðjohnsen). Trainer: Arnar Viðarsson.
Goal: Edson Omar Álvarez Velázquez (14 own goal).

04.06.2021   **FAROE ISLANDS - ICELAND**   **0-1(0-0)**   Friendly International
Tórsvøllur, Tórshavn; Referee: Kristo Tohver (Estonia); Attendance: 0
ISL: Ögmundur Kristinsson, Hjörtur Hermannsson, Alfons Sampsted, Brynjar Ingi Bjarnason, Valgeir Lunddal Friðriksson (78.Guðmundur Þórarinsson), Birkir Bjarnason (78.Sveinn Aron Guðjohnsen), Aron Einar Malmquist Gunnarsson (Cap) (78.Andri Fannar Baldursson), Jón Dagur Þorsteinsson, Ísak Bergmann Jóhannesson (62.Stefán Teitur Þórðarson), Kolbeinn Sigþórsson (46.Albert Guðmundsson), Jón Daði Böðvarsson (62.Mikael Neville Anderson). Trainer: Arnar Viðarsson.
Goal: Mikael Neville Anderson (70).

08.06.2021   **POLAND - ICELAND**   **2-2(1-1)**   Friendly International
Stadion Miejski, Poznań; Referee: Balázs Berke (Hungary); Attendance: 19,614
ISL: Rúnar Alex Rúnarsson (46.Ögmundur Kristinsson), Guðmundur Þórarinsson, Hjörtur Hermannsson, Alfons Sampsted, Brynjar Ingi Bjarnason, Birkir Bjarnason, Aron Einar Malmquist Gunnarsson (Cap) (87.Kolbeinn Þórðarson), Albert Guðmundsson (90+1.Jón Dagur Þorsteinsson), Mikael Neville Anderson (74.Gísli Eyjólfsson), Andri Fannar Baldursson (78.Stefán Teitur Þórðarson), Jón Daði Böðvarsson (84.Sveinn Aron Guðjohnsen). Trainer: Arnar Viðarsson.
Goals: Albert Guðmundsson (24), Brynjar Ingi Bjarnason (47).

NATIONAL TEAM PLAYERS
(16.07.2020 – 15.07.2021)

Name	DOB	Caps	Goals	2020/2021:	Club
Goalkeepers					
Hannes Þór HALLDÓRSSON	27.04.1984	76	0	2020/2021:	*Valur Reykjavík*
Ögmundur KRISTINSSON	19.06.1989	19	0	2020/2021:	*Olympiacos SFP Peiraiás (GRE)*
Rúnar Alex RÚNARSSON	18.02.1995	10	0	2020/2021:	*Arsenal FC London (ENG)*
Defenders					
Kári ÁRNASON	13.10.1982	89	6	2020/2021:	*Víkingur Reykjavík*
Brynjar Ingi BJARNASON	06.12.1999	3	1	2021:	*KA Akureyri*
Hólmar Örn EYJÓLFSSON	06.08.1990	19	2	2020: 19.09.2020->	*PFC Levski Sofia (BUL) Rosenborg BK Trondheim (NOR)*
Jón Guðni FJÓLUSON	10.04.1989	17	1	2020:	*FK Krasnodar (RUS)*
Valgeir Lunddal FRIÐRIKSSON	24.09.2001	1	0	2021:	*BK Häcken Göteborg (SWE)*
Hörður Ingi GUNNARSSON	14.08.1998	1	0	2021:	*FH Hafnarfjörður*
Hjörtur HERMANNSSON	08.02.1995	22	1	2020/2021:	*Brøndby IF (DEN)*
Sverrir Ingi INGASON	05.05.1993	39	3	2020/2021:	*PAOK Thessaloníki (GRE)*
Hörður Björgvin MAGNÚSSON	11.02.1993	36	2	2020/2021:	*FK CSKA Moskva (RUS)*
Ísak Óli ÓLAFSSON	30.06.2000	1	0	2021:	*Keflavík*
Alfons SAMPSTED	06.04.1998	5	0	2021:	*FK Bodø/Glimt (NOR)*
Rúnar Þór SIGURGEIRSSON	28.12.1999	1	0	2021:	*Keflavík*
Ragnar SIGURÐSSON	19.06.1986	97	5	2020:	*FC København (DEN)*
Ari Freyr SKÚLASON	14.05.1987	79	0	2020/2021:	*KV Oostende (BEL)*
Birkir Már SÆVARSSON	11.11.1984	98	3	2020/2021:	*Valur Reykjavík*
Guðmundur ÞÓRARINSSON	15.04.1992	7	0	2021:	*New York City FC (USA)*
Kolbeinn ÞÓRÐARSON	12.03.2000	1	0	2021:	*Lommel SK (BEL)*
Midfielders					
Mikael Neville ANDERSON	01.07.1998	9	1	2020/2021:	*FC Midtjylland Herning (DEN)*
Andri Fannar BALDURSSON	10.01.2002	4	0	2020/2021:	*Bologna FC 1909 (ITA)*
Birkir BJARNASON	27.05.1988	98	14	2020/2021:	*Brescia Calcio (ITA)*
Gísli EYJÓLFSSON	31.05.1994	2	0	2021:	*Breiðablik Kópavogur*
Aron Einar Malmquist GUNNARSSON	22.04.1989	97	2	2020/2021:	*Al-Arabi SC Doha (QAT)*
Jóhann Berg GUÐMUNDSSON	27.10.1990	79	7	2020/2021:	*Burnley FC (ENG)*
Emil HALLFREÐSSON	29.06.1984	73	1	2020/2021:	*Unattached*
Þórir Jóhann HELGASON	28.09.2000	1	0	2021:	*FH Hafnarfjörður*
Ísak Bergmann JÓHANNESSON	23.03.2003	4	0	2020/2021:	*IFK Norrköping (SWE)*
Guðlaugur Victor PÁLSSON	30.04.1991	26	1	2020/2021:	*SV Darmstadt 98 (GER)*
Rúnar Már Sigurlaugarson SIGURJÓNSSON	18.06.1990	32	2	2020: 08.02.2021->	*Astana FC Nur-Sultan (KAZ) FC CFR 1907 Cluj-Napoca (ROU)*
Arnór SIGURÐSSON	15.05.1999	14	1	2020/2021:	*FK CSKA Moskva (RUS)*
Gylfi Þór SIGURÐSSON	08.09.1989	78	25	2020:	*Everton FC Liverpool (ENG)*
Arnór Ingvi TRAUSTASON	30.04.1993	40	5	2020: 16.03.2021->	*Malmö FF (SWE) New England Revolution Boston (USA)*
Jón Dagur ÞORSTEINSSON	26.11.1998	9	1	2020/2021:	*AGF Aarhus (DEN)*
Aron Elís ÞRÁNDARSON	10.11.1994	6	0	2021:	*Odense BK (DEN)*
Forwards					
Jón Daði BÖÐVARSSON	25.05.1992	60	3	2020/2021:	*Millwall FC London (ENG)*
Alfreð FINNBOGASON	01.02.1989	61	15	2020/2021:	*FC Augsburg (GER)*
Hólmbert Aron Briem FRIÐJÓNSSON	19.04.1993	6	2	2020: 05.10.2020->	*Aalesunds FK (NOR) Brescia Calcio (ITA)*
Sveinn Aron GUÐJOHNSEN	12.05.1998	4	0	2020/2021:	*OB Odense (DEN)*
Albert GUÐMUNDSSON	15.06.1997	22	4	2020/2021:	*AZ Alkmaar (NED)*
Viðar Örn KJARTANSSON	11.03.1990	28	4	2020/2021:	*FK Rostov (RUS)*
Kolbeinn SIGÞÓRSSON	14.03.1990	64	26	2020:	*AIK Stockholm (SWE)*
Stefán Teitur ÞÓRÐARSON	16.10.1998	2	0	2020/2021:	*Silkeborg IF (DEN)*

Trainer		
Erik Anders HAMRÉN (Sweden) [08.08.2018 – 19.11.2020]	27.06.1957	28 M; 9 W; 5 D; 14 L; 29-50
Arnar VIÐARSSON [from 22.12.2020]	15.03.1978	7 M; 2 W; 1 D; 4 L; 8-12

ISRAEL

The Country:
יִשְׂרָאֵל מְדִינַת (State of Israel)
Capital: Jerusalem
Surface: 20,770–22,072 km²
Inhabitants: 9,398,200 [2021]
Time: UTC+2

The FA:
Israel Football Association
Ramat Gan Stadium, 299 Aba Hilell Street, P.O. Box 3591, 52134 Ramat Gan, Tel Aviv
Tel: +972 3 617 1500
Foundation date: 18.07.1928
Member of FIFA since: 1929
Member of UEFA since: 1994
Website: www.football.org.il

NATIONAL TEAM RECORDS

RECORDS

First international match:	16.03.1934, Cairo: Egypt – Palestina 7-1	
Most international caps:	Yosef Shay Benayoun	- 102 caps (1998-2017)
Most international goals:	Mordechai Spiegler	- 32 goals / 83 caps (1963-1977)

UEFA EUROPEAN CHAMPIONSHIP	
1960	-
1964	-
1968	-
1972	-
1976	-
1980	-
1984	-
1988	-
1992	-
1996	Qualifiers
2000	Qualifiers
2004	Qualifiers
2008	Qualifiers
2012	Qualifiers
2016	Qualifiers
2020	Qualifiers

FIFA WORLD CUP	
1930	Did not enter
1934	Qualifiers
1938	Qualifiers
1950	Qualifiers
1954	Qualifiers
1958	Qualifiers
1962	Qualifiers
1966	Qualifiers
1970	Final Tournament (Group Stage)
1974	Qualifiers
1978	Qualifiers
1982	Qualifiers
1986	Qualifiers
1990	Qualifiers
1994	Qualifiers
1998	Qualifiers
2002	Qualifiers
2006	Qualifiers
2010	Qualifiers
2014	Qualifiers
2018	Qualifiers

OLYMPIC TOURNAMENTS	
1908	-
1912	-
1920	-
1924	-
1928	-
1936	-
1948	-
1952	Qualifiers
1956	Qualifiers
1960	Qualifiers
1964	Qualifiers
1968	FT/Quarter-Finals
1972	Qualifiers
1976	FT/Quarter-Finals
1980	*Withdrew*
1984	Qualifiers
1988	Qualifiers
1992	Qualifiers
1996	Qualifiers
2000	Qualifiers
2004	Qualifiers
2008	Qualifiers
2012	Qualifiers
2016	Qualifiers

UEFA NATIONS LEAGUE

2018/2019	League C
2020/2021	League B

FIFA CONFEDERATIONS CUP 1992-2017

None

ISRAELI CLUB HONOURS IN EUROPEAN CLUB COMPETITIONS:

European Champion Clubs' Cup (1956-1992) / UEFA Champions League (1993-2021)
None

Fairs Cup (1858-1971) / UEFA Cup (1972-2009) / UEFA Europa League (2010-2021)
None

UEFA Super Cup (1972-2020)
None

*European Cup Winners' Cup 1961-1999**
None

defunct competition

NATIONAL COMPETITIONS
TABLE OF HONOURS

	CHAMPIONS	CUP WINNERS	BEST GOALSCORERS	
1927/1928	–	Hapoel Tel Aviv FC Maccabi Hasmonean Jerusalem FC (shared)		
1928/1929	–	Maccabi Tel Aviv FC	–	
1929/1930	–	Maccabi Tel Aviv FC	–	
1930/1931	–	No competition	–	
1931/1932	United Kingdom British Police	United Kingdom British Police	–	
1932/1933	No Championship	Maccabi Tel Aviv FC	–	
1933/1934	Hapoel Tel Aviv FC	Hapoel Tel Aviv FC	–	
1934/1935	Hapoel Tel Aviv FC	Maccabi Petah Tikva FC	–	
1935/1936	Maccabi Tel Aviv FC	No competition	–	
1936/1937	Maccabi Tel Aviv FC	Hapoel Tel Aviv FC	–	
1937/1938	Hapoel Tel Aviv FC	Hapoel Tel Aviv FC	–	
1938/1939	No Championship	Hapoel Tel Aviv FC	–	
1939/1940	Hapoel Tel Aviv FC	Beitar Tel Aviv FC	–	
1940/1941	No Championship	Maccabi Tel Aviv FC	–	
1941/1942	Maccabi Tel Aviv FC	Beitar Tel Aviv FC	–	
1942/1943	Championship not finished	No competition	–	
1943/1944	Hapoel Tel Aviv FC	No competition	–	
1944/1945	Hapoel Tel Aviv FC Beitar Tel Aviv FC (shared)	No competition	–	
1945/1946	No Championship	Maccabi Tel Aviv FC	–	
1946/1947	Maccabi Tel Aviv FC	Maccabi Tel Aviv FC	–	
1947/1948	Championship not finished	No competition	–	
1948	Championship not finished	No competition	–	
1949/1950	Maccabi Tel Aviv FC	No competition	Yosef Merimovich (Maccabi Tel Aviv FC)	25
1950/1951	No Championship	No competition	–	–
1951/1952	Maccabi Tel Aviv FC	Maccabi Petah Tikva FC	Yehoshua Glazer (Maccabi Tel Aviv FC)	24
1952/1953	No Championship	No competition	–	–
1953/1954	Maccabi Tel Aviv FC	Maccabi Tel Aviv FC	Eliezer Spiegel (Maccabi Petah Tikva FC)	16
1954/1955	Hapoel Petah Tikva FC	Maccabi Tel Aviv FC	Nisim Elmaliah (Beitar Tel Aviv FC)	30
1955/1956	Maccabi Tel Aviv FC	No competition	Avraham Levi (Beitar Tel Aviv FC) Michael Michaelov (Beitar Tel Aviv FC)	16
1956/1957	Hapoel Tel Aviv FC	Hapoel Petah Tikva FC	Avraham Ginzburg (Hapoel Haifa FC)	16
1957/1958	Maccabi Tel Aviv FC	Maccabi Tel Aviv FC	Rafi Levi (Maccabi Tel Aviv FC)	14
1958/1959	Hapoel Petah Tikva FC	Maccabi Tel Aviv FC	Aharon Amar (Maccabi Haifa FC)	17
1959/1960	Hapoel Petah Tikva FC	No competition	Rafi Levi (Maccabi Tel Aviv FC)	19
1960/1961	Hapoel Petah Tikva FC	Hapoel Tel Aviv FC	Shlomo Levi (Hapoel Haifa FC) Zharia Ratzabi (Hapoel Petah Tikva FC)	15
1961/1962	Hapoel Petah Tikva FC	Maccabi Haifa FC	Shlomo Levi (Maccabi Haifa FC) Itzhak Nizri (Hapoel Tiberias)	16
1962/1963	Hapoel Petah Tikva FC	Hapoel Haifa FC	Zharia Ratzabi (Hapoel Petah Tikva FC)	12
1963/1964	Hapoel Haifa FC	Maccabi Tel Aviv FC	Israel Ashkenazi (Maccabi Jaffa FC)	21
1964/1965	Hakoah Ramat Gan FC	Maccabi Tel Aviv FC	Israel Ashkenazi (Maccabi Jaffa FC) Itzhak Mizrahi (Bnei Yehuda Tel Aviv FC)	18
1965/1966	Hapoel Tel Aviv FC	Hapoel Haifa FC	Moshe Romano (Shimshon Tel Aviv FC) Mordechai Spiegler (Maccabi Netanya FC)	17
1966/1967	-	Maccabi Tel Aviv FC		
1967/1968	Maccabi Tel Aviv FC [1966-1968]	Bnei Yehuda Tel Aviv FC	Mordechai Spiegler (Maccabi Netanya FC)	38
1968/1969	Hapoel Tel Aviv FC	Hakoah Ramat Gan FC	Mordechai Spiegler (Maccabi Netanya FC)	25
1969/1970	Maccabi Tel Aviv FC	Maccabi Tel Aviv FC	Moshe Romano (Shimshon Tel Aviv FC)	15
1970/1971	Maccabi Netanya FC	Hakoah Ramat Gan FC	Eli Ben Rimoz (Hapoel Jerusalem FC)	20
1971/1972	Maccabi Tel Aviv FC	Hapoel Tel Aviv FC	Yehouda Shaharabani (Hakoah Ramat Gan FC)	21
1972/1973	Hakoah Ramat Gan FC	Hapoel Jerusalem FC	Moshe Romano (Beitar Tel Aviv FC)	18
1973/1974	Maccabi Netanya FC	Hapoel Haifa FC	Benny Alon (Hapoel Haifa FC)	15
1974/1975	Hapoel Be'er Sheva FC	Hapoel Kfar Saba FC	Moshe Romano (Shimshon Tel Aviv FC)	17
1975/1976	Hapoel Be'er Sheva FC	Beitar Jerusalem FC	Oded Machnes (Maccabi Netanya FC)	21
1976/1977	Maccabi Tel Aviv FC	Maccabi Tel Aviv FC	Vicky Peretz (Maccabi Tel Aviv FC)	17
1977/1978	Maccabi Netanya FC	Maccabi Netanya FC	David Lavi (Maccabi Netanya FC)	16
1978/1979	Maccabi Tel Aviv FC	Beitar Jerusalem FC	Oded Machnes (Maccabi Netanya FC) Eli Miali (Beitar Jerusalem FC)	18
1979/1980	Maccabi Netanya FC	Hapoel Kfar Saba FC	David Lavi (Maccabi Netanya FC)	18
1980/1981	Hapoel Tel Aviv FC	Bnei Yehuda Tel Aviv FC	Hertzel Fitusi (Maccabi Petah Tikva FC)	22
1981/1982	Hapoel Kfar Saba FC	Hapoel Yehud	Oded Machnes (Maccabi Netanya FC)	26
1982/1983	Maccabi Netanya FC	Hapoel Tel Aviv FC	Oded Machnes (Maccabi Netanya FC)	22
1983/1984	Maccabi Haifa FC	Hapoel Lod	David Lavi (Maccabi Netanya FC)	16
1984/1985	Maccabi Haifa FC	Beitar Jerusalem FC	David Lavi (Maccabi Netanya FC)	18
1985/1986	Hapoel Tel Aviv FC	Beitar Jerusalem FC	Uri Malmilian (Beitar Jerusalem FC) Doron Rabinzon (Maccabi Petah Tikva FC)	14
1986/1987	Beitar Jerusalem FC	Maccabi Tel Aviv FC	Eli Yani (Hapoel Kfar Saba FC)	16
1987/1988	Hapoel Tel Aviv FC	Maccabi Tel Aviv FC	Zahi Armeli (Maccabi Haifa FC)	25
1988/1989	Maccabi Haifa FC	Beitar Jerusalem FC	Benny Tabak (Maccabi Tel Aviv FC)	18

1989/1990	Bnei Yehuda Tel Aviv FC	Hapoel Kfar Saba FC	Uri Malmilian (Maccabi Tel Aviv FC)	16
1990/1991	Maccabi Haifa FC	Maccabi Haifa FC	Nir Levine (Hapoel Petah Tikva FC)	20
1991/1992	Maccabi Tel Aviv FC	Hapoel Petah Tikva FC	Alon Mizrahi (Bnei Yehuda Tel Aviv FC)	20
1992/1993	Beitar Jerusalem FC	Maccabi Haifa FC	Alon Mizrahi (Bnei Yehuda Tel Aviv FC)	26
1993/1994	Maccabi Haifa FC	Maccabi Tel Aviv FC	Alon Mizrahi (Maccabi Haifa FC)	28
1994/1995	Maccabi Tel Aviv FC	Maccabi Haifa FC	Haim Revivo (Maccabi Haifa FC) Amir Turgeman (Maccabi Ironi Ashdod FC FC)	17
1995/1996	Maccabi Tel Aviv FC	Maccabi Tel Aviv FC	Haim Revivo (Maccabi Haifa FC)	26
1996/1997	Beitar Jerusalem FC	Hapoel Be'er Sheva FC	Motti Kakoun (Hapoel Petah Tikva FC)	21
1997/1998	Beitar Jerusalem FC	Maccabi Haifa FC	Alon Mizrahi (Maccabi Haifa FC)	18
1998/1999	Hapoel Haifa FC	Hapoel Tel Aviv FC	Andrzej Kubica (Maccabi Tel Aviv FC)	21
1999/2000	Hapoel Tel Aviv FC	Hapoel Tel Aviv FC	Assi Tubi (Maccabi Petah Tikva FC)	27
2000/2001	Maccabi Haifa FC	Maccabi Tel Aviv FC	Avi Nimni (Maccabi Tel Aviv FC)	25
2001/2002	Maccabi Haifa FC	Maccabi Tel Aviv FC	Kobi Refua (Maccabi Petah Tikva FC)	18
2002/2003	Maccabi Tel Aviv FC	Hapoel Haifa FC	Yaniv Abargil (Hapoel Kfar Saba FC) Shay Holtzman (Ironi Rishon LeZion FC / FC Ashdod)	18
2003/2004	Maccabi Haifa FC	Bnei Sakhnin FC	Ofir Haim (Hapoel Be'er Sheva FC) Shay Holtzman (FC Ashdod)	16
2004/2005	Maccabi Haifa FC	Maccabi Tel Aviv FC	Roberto Colautti (Maccabi Haifa FC)	19
2005/2006	Maccabi Haifa FC	Hapoel Tel Aviv FC	Shay Holtzman (FC Ashdod)	18
2006/2007	Beitar Jerusalem FC	Hapoel Tel Aviv FC	Yaniv Azran (FC Ashdod)	15
2007/2008	Beitar Jerusalem FC	Beitar Jerusalem FC	Samuel Yeboah (Hapoel Kfar Saba FC)	15
2008/2009	Maccabi Haifa FC	Beitar Jerusalem FC	Barak Yitzhaki (Beitar Jerusalem FC) Shimon Abuhatzira (Hapoel Petah Tikva FC) Eliran Atar (Bnei Yehuda Tel Aviv FC)	14
2009/2010	Hapoel Tel Aviv FC	Hapoel Tel Aviv FC	Shlomi Arbeitman (Maccabi Haifa FC)	28
2010/2011	Maccabi Haifa FC	Hapoel Tel Aviv FC	Toto Tamuz (Hapoel Tel Aviv FC)	21
2011/2012	Ironi Kiryat	Hapoel Tel Aviv FC	Achmad Saba'a (Maccabi Netanya FC)	20
2012/2013	Maccabi Tel Aviv FC	Hapoel Haifa FC	Eliran Atar (Maccabi Tel Aviv FC)	22
2013/2014	Maccabi Tel Aviv FC	Hapoel Ironi Kiryat Shmona FC	Eran Zahavi (Maccabi Tel Aviv FC)	29
2014/2015	Maccabi Tel Aviv FC	Maccabi Tel Aviv FC	Eran Zahavi (Maccabi Tel Aviv FC)	27
2015/2016	Hapoel Be'er Sheva FC	Maccabi Haifa FC	Eran Zahavi (Maccabi Tel Aviv FC)	35
2016/2017	Hapoel Be'er Sheva FC	Bnei Yehuda Tel Aviv FC	Viðar Örn Kjartansson (ISL, Maccabi Tel Aviv FC)	19
2017/2018	Hapoel Be'er Sheva FC	Hapoel Haifa FC	Dia Saba (Maccabi Netanya FC)	24
2018/2019	Maccabi Tel Aviv FC	Bnei Yehuda Tel Aviv FC	Ben Sahar (Hapoel Be'er Sheva FC)	15
2019/2020	Maccabi Tel Aviv FC	Hapoel Be'er Sheva FC	Nikita Rukavytsya (AUS, Maccabi Haifa FC)	22
2020/2021	Maccabi Haifa FC	Maccabi Tel Aviv FC	Nikita Rukavytsya (AUS, Maccabi Haifa FC)	19

NATIONAL CHAMPIONSHIP
Israeli Premier League (Ligat Winner) 2020/2021
(29.08.2020 – 30.05.2021)

Regular Season - Results

Round 1 [29-30.08.2020]
FC Ashdod - Hapoel Ironi K.S. 0-2(0-0)
Bnei Sachnin - Bnei Yehuda 0-3(0-1)
Hapoel Kfar Saba - Hapoel Tel Aviv 2-1(1-0)
Hapoel Be'er Sheva-Maccabi Netanya 3-2(1-0)
Hapoel Haifa - Beitar Jerusalem 0-1(0-0)
Hapoel Hadera - Maccabi Haifa 1-2(1-2)
Maccabi Tel Aviv - Petach-Tikva 1-2(0-0)

Round 2 [12-14.09.2020]
Hapoel Ironi K.S. - Hapoel Haifa 1-1(1-0)
Petach-Tikva - Hapoel Kfar Saba 2-0(1-0)
Bnei Yehuda - Maccabi Tel Aviv 2-2(1-0)
Hapoel Tel Aviv - FC Ashdod 0-2(0-1)
Maccabi Haifa - Hapoel Be'er Sheva 3-1(1-0)
Maccabi Netanya - Bnei Sachnin 7-0(4-0)
Beitar Jer. - Hapoel Hadera 4-0(0-0) [04.11.]

Round 3 [21.09.2020]
FC Ashdod - Maccabi Petach-Tikva 1-0(1-0)
Hapoel Kfar Saba - Bnei Yehuda 3-1(0-1)
Bnei Sachnin-Maccabi Haifa 0-3(0-1) [08.12.]
Hapoel Haifa - Hapoel T. A. 2-0(0-0) [09.12.]
Hapoel Hadera - Be'er Sheva 2-2(1-1) [16.12.]
Maccabi T.A. - M. Netanya 2-2(0-1) [16.12.]
Beitar Jer.- Hapoel Ironi K.S. 1-0(1-0) [17.12.]

Round 4 [31.10.-02.11.2020]
Maccabi Petach-Tikva - Hapoel Haifa 2-0(2-0)
Maccabi Netanya - Hapoel Kfar Saba 3-0(3-0)
Hapoel Ironi K.S. - Hapoel Hadera 1-1(0-0)
Hapoel Tel Aviv - Beitar Jerusalem 1-1(1-0)
Bnei Yehuda - FC Ashdod 1-0(0-0)
Hapoel Be'er Sheva - Bnei Sachnin 2-2(1-2)
Maccabi Haifa - Maccabi Tel Aviv 2-2(2-1)

Round 5 [24-25.11.2020]
Maccabi Tel Aviv - Hapoel Be'er Sheva 0-0
Hapoel Haifa - Bnei Yehuda 2-1(0-0) [25.10.]
Hapoel Ironi K.S. - Hapoel Tel Aviv 1-0(0-0)
Hapoel Kfar Saba - Maccabi Haifa 3-2(0-1)
Hapoel Hadera - Bnei Sachnin 4-0(1-0)
FC Ashdod - Maccabi Netanya 4-0(0-0)
Beitar Jerusalem - Petach-Tikva 1-2(1-2)

Round 6 [07-09.11.2020]
Maccabi Netanya - Hapoel Haifa 2-1(0-0)
Maccabi Haifa - FC Ashdod 2-1(1-0)
Bnei Yehuda - Beitar Jerusalem 1-0(1-0)
Petach-Tikva - Hapoel Ironi K.S. 0-1(0-0)
Bnei Sachnin - Maccabi Tel Aviv 1-2(0-1)
Hapoel Be'er Sheva - Hapoel Kfar Saba 0-0
Hapoel Tel Aviv - Hapoel Hadera 1-0(0-0)

Round 7 [21-22.11.2020]
Hapoel Tel Aviv - Maccabi Petach-Tikva 0-0
Hapoel Ironi K.S. - Bnei Yehuda 2-0(2-0)
FC Ashdod - Hapoel Be'er Sheva 2-0(2-0)
Hapoel Kfar Saba - Bnei Sachnin 0-1(0-1)
Hapoel Haifa - Maccabi Haifa 2-1(0-0)
Hapoel Hadera - Maccabi Tel Aviv 0-1(0-1)
Beitar Jerusalem - Maccabi Netanya 1-1(1-1)

Round 8 [28-30.11.2020]
Petach-Tikva - Hapoel Hadera 1-0(0-0)
Bnei Sachnin - FC Ashdod 1-0(0-0)
Bnei Yehuda - Hapoel Tel Aviv 1-0(0-0)
Maccabi Netanya - Hapoel Ironi K.S. 0-0
Maccabi Tel Aviv - Kfar Saba 3-0(2-0)
Hapoel Be'er Sheva - Hapoel Haifa 2-2(2-1)
Maccabi Haifa - Beitar Jerusalem 2-0(2-0)

Round 9 [05-07.12.2020]
Hapoel Ironi K.S. - Maccabi Haifa 0-3(0-0)
Maccabi Petach-Tikva - Bnei Yehuda 1-0(0-0)
Hapoel Haifa - Bnei Sachnin 0-2(0-0)
Hapoel Tel Aviv - Maccabi Netanya 0-0
Hapoel Hadera - Hapoel Kfar Saba 1-1(1-0)
FC Ashdod - Maccabi Tel Aviv 3-2(1-0)
Beitar Jerusalem - Hap. Be'er Sheva 1-2(1-0)

Round 10 [12-14.12.2020]
Hapoel Kfar Saba - FC Ashdod 0-1(0-1)
Bnei Yehuda - Hapoel Hadera 0-3(0-3)
Maccabi Netanya - Petach-Tikva 3-2(2-0)
Be'er Sheva - Hapoel Ironi K.S. 2-1(2-0)
Maccabi Tel Aviv - Hapoel Haifa 4-3(1-2)
Maccabi Haifa - Hapoel Tel Aviv 1-0(1-0)
Bnei Sachnin-Beitar Jerusalem 0-0 [18.02.21]

Round 11 [19-21.12.2020]
Hapoel Haifa - Hapoel Kfar Saba 2-1(0-1)
Hapoel Hadera - FC Ashdod 1-1(0-0)
Bnei Yehuda - Maccabi Netanya 1-1(1-0)
Petach-Tikva - Maccabi Haifa 1-2(1-1)
Hapoel Ironi K.S. - Bnei Sachnin 0-1(0-0)
Hapoel Tel Aviv - Be'er Sheva 0-3(0-1)
Beitar Jerusalem - Maccabi Tel Aviv 0-0

Round 12 [22-24.12.2020]
FC Ashdod - Hapoel Haifa 0-1(0-0)
Hapoel Hadera - Maccabi Netanya 2-1(1-1)
Maccabi Haifa - Bnei Yehuda 3-0(1-0)
Bnei Sachnin - Hapoel Tel Aviv 0-1(0-1)
Hapoel Be'er Sheva - Petach-Tikva 1-2(0-0)
Maccabi Tel Aviv - Hapoel Ironi K.S. 1-0(0-0)
Hapoel Kfar Saba - Beitar Jerusalem 1-1(1-1)

Round 13 [26-28.12.2020]
Hapoel Haifa - Hapoel Hadera 0-0
Maccabi Netanya - Maccabi Haifa 0-2(0-2)
Maccabi Petach-Tikva - Bnei Sachnin 0-0
Hapoel Ironi K.S. - Hapoel Kfar Saba 1-0(1-0)
Bnei Yehuda - Hapoel Be'er Sheva 0-2(0-0)
Beitar Jerusalem - FC Ashdod 1-2(1-1)
Hapoel Tel Aviv - Maccabi Tel Aviv 0-4(0-0)

Round 14 [02-04.01.2021]
Hapoel Tel Aviv - Hapoel Kfar Saba 1-1(1-1)
Maccabi Haifa - Hapoel Hadera 1-0(0-0)
Maccabi Netanya - Be'er Sheva 0-1(0-1)
Beitar Jerusalem - Hapoel Haifa 3-3(0-1)
Bnei Yehuda - Bnei Sachnin 1-1(0-1)
Petach-Tikva - Maccabi Tel Aviv 0-1(0-0)
Hapoel Ironi K.S. - Ashdod 2-1(0-0) [18.02.]

Round 15 [05-07.01.2021]
Hapoel Haifa - Hapoel Ironi K.S. 0-2(0-1)
Hapoel Be'er Sheva - Maccabi Haifa 1-1(1-0)
Bnei Sachnin - Maccabi Netanya 0-1(0-1)
Hapoel Hadera - Beitar Jerusalem 0-4(0-3)
Hapoel Kfar Saba - Petach-Tikva 2-0(0-0)
FC Ashdod - Hapoel Tel Aviv 2-1(2-1)
Maccabi Tel Aviv - Bnei Yehuda 0-0

Round 16 [23-25.01.2021]
Hapoel Tel Aviv - Hapoel Haifa 2-2(2-1)
Maccabi Petach-Tikva - FC Ashdod 2-1(1-1)
Hapoel Ironi K.S. - Beitar Jerusalem 0-2(0-1)
Maccabi Haifa - Bnei Sachnin 3-0(1-0)
Maccabi Netanya - Maccabi Tel Aviv 1-3(0-2)
Bnei Yehuda - Hapoel Kfar Saba 1-3(1-2)
Hapoel Be'er Sheva - Hapoel Hadera 1-0(0-0)

Round 17 [26-28.01.2021]
Hapoel Haifa - Maccabi Petach-Tikva 1-2(1-0)
Beitar Jerusalem - Hapoel Tel Aviv 0-1(0-1)
FC Ashdod - Bnei Yehuda 4-0(1-0)
Hapoel Kfar Saba - Maccabi Netanya 0-1(0-1)
Maccabi Tel Aviv - Maccabi Haifa 2-1(1-1)
Hapoel Hadera - Hapoel Ironi K.S. 0-1(0-1)
Bnei Sachnin - Hapoel Be'er Sheva 1-0(0-0)

Round 18 [30.01.-01.02.2021]
Maccabi Netanya - FC Ashdod 3-0(2-0)
Hapoel Tel Aviv - Hapoel Ironi K.S. 1-1(0-0)
Maccabi Haifa - Hapoel Kfar Saba 3-0(1-0)
Bnei Yehuda - Hapoel Haifa 0-2(0-1)
Bnei Sachnin - Hapoel Hadera 0-2(0-1)
Hap. Be'er Sheva - Maccabi Tel Aviv 0-1(0-1)
Petach-Tikva - Beitar Jerus. 0-1(0-1) [24.02.]

Round 19 [06-07.02.2021]
Hapoel Haifa - Maccabi Netanya 0-0
Hapoel Kfar Saba - Hap. Be'er Sheva 0-1(0-1)
Maccabi Tel Aviv - Bnei Sachnin 1-0(0-0)
FC Ashdod - Maccabi Haifa 1-0(0-0)
Hapoel Hadera - Hapoel Tel Aviv 1-1(0-0)
Ironi K.S. - Petach-Tikva 2-1(1-0) [10.03.]
Beitar Jerus. - Bnei Yehuda 1-1(0-0) [11.03.]

Round 20 [09-11.02.2021]
Bnei Sachnin - Hapoel Kfar Saba 0-1(0-0)
Hapoel Be'er Sheva - FC Ashdod 0-3(0-1)
Petach-Tikva - Hapoel Tel Aviv 0-2(0-1)
Maccabi Tel Aviv - Hapoel Hadera 3-1(2-1)
Maccabi Haifa - Hapoel Haifa 2-0(0-0)
Maccabi Netanya - Beitar Jerusalem 1-2(0-1)
Bnei Yehuda - Ironi K.S. 1-0(1-0) [24.02.]

Round 21 [13-15.02.2021]
Hapoel Haifa - Hapoel Be'er Sheva 2-2(0-2)
FC Ashdod - Bnei Sachnin 0-0
Kfar Saba - Maccabi Tel Aviv 0-1(0-1)
Hapoel Hadera - Petach-Tikva 1-0(1-0)
Hapoel Ironi K.S. - Maccabi Netanya 1-4(1-2)
Hapoel Tel Aviv - Bnei Yehuda 0-0
Beitar Jerusalem - Maccabi Haifa 0-3(0-1)

Round 22 [27.02.-01.03.2021]
Bnei Sachnin - Hapoel Haifa 0-1(0-0)
Hapoel Kfar Saba - Hapoel Hadera 0-1(0-0)
Bnei Yehuda - Maccabi Petach-Tikva 0-1(0-1)
Maccabi Netanya - Hapoel Tel Aviv 0-1(0-1)
Maccabi Haifa - Hapoel Ironi K.S. 4-2(2-1)
Hapoel Be'er Sheva-Beitar Jerusalem 1-1(0-0)
Maccabi Tel Aviv - FC Ashdod 3-1(1-0)

Round 23 [02-04.03.2021]
Hapoel Hadera - Bnei Yehuda 0-0
Petach-Tikva - Maccabi Netanya 1-1(0-1)
Hapoel Ironi K.S. - Be'er Sheva 2-2(1-1)
Hapoel Tel Aviv - Maccabi Haifa 1-2(1-2)
FC Ashdod - Hapoel Kfar Saba 2-0(2-0)
Beitar Jerusalem - Bnei Sachnin 2-3(0-2)
Hapoel Haifa - Maccabi Tel Aviv 0-2(0-0)

Round 24 [06-08.03.2021]
Maccabi Netanya - Bnei Yehuda 1-0(0-0)
Maccabi Haifa - Petach-Tikva 0-2(0-0)
Bnei Sachnin - Hapoel Ironi K.S. 0-2(0-0)
Hapoel Kfar Saba - Hapoel Haifa 0-0
Be'er Sheva - Hapoel Tel Aviv 0-1(0-1)
FC Ashdod - Hapoel Hadera 1-1(0-1)
Maccabi Tel Aviv - Beitar Jerusalem 4-1(1-0)

Round 25 [13-14.03.2021]
Hapoel Tel Aviv - Bnei Sachnin 0-1(0-1)
Maccabi Netanya - Hapoel Hadera 0-1(0-1)
Hapoel Haifa - FC Ashdod 2-2(1-2)
Hapoel Ironi K.S. - Maccabi Tel Aviv 0-2(0-1)
Petach-Tikva - Hapoel Be'er Sheva 0-0
Beitar Jerusalem - Hapoel Kfar Saba 2-1(1-1)
Bnei Yehuda - Maccabi Haifa 0-2(0-0)

Round 26 [20-22.03.2021]
Bnei Sachnin - Maccabi Petach-Tikva 1-0(0-0)
FC Ashdod - Beitar Jerusalem 2-0(2-0)
Hapoel Be'er Sheva - Bnei Yehuda 2-0(1-0)
Hapoel Kfar Saba - Hapoel Ironi K.S. 0-1(0-1)
Maccabi Haifa - Maccabi Netanya 2-0(1-0)
Maccabi Tel Aviv - Hapoel Tel Aviv 1-1(0-1)
Hapoel Hadera - Hapoel Haifa 3-1(2-0)

Final Standings

1.	Maccabi Haifa FC	26	19	2	5	52	-	20	59
2.	Maccabi Tel Aviv FC	26	17	7	2	48	-	21	58
3.	FC Ashdod	26	13	4	9	37	-	25	43
4.	Hapoel Ironi Kiryat Shmona FC	26	11	5	10	26	-	28	38
5.	Hapoel Be'er Sheva FC	26	9	10	7	31	-	29	37
6.	Maccabi Petah Tikva FC	26	11	4	11	24	-	23	37
7.	Maccabi Netanya FC	26	9	7	10	35	-	30	34
8.	Beitar Jerusalem FC	26	8	8	10	31	-	32	32
9.	Hapoel Hadera–Giv'at Olga "Shulem Schwarz"	26	8	8	10	26	-	28	32
10.	Hapoel Haifa FC	26	7	9	10	30	-	37	30
11.	Bnei Sakhnin FC	26	8	5	13	15	-	36	29
12.	Hapoel Tel Aviv FC	26	6	9	11	17	-	28	27
13.	Hapoel Kfar Saba FC	26	6	5	15	19	-	33	23
14.	Bnei Yehuda Tel Aviv FC	26	5	7	14	15	-	36	22

Teams ranked 1-6 were qualified for the Championship Round, while teams ranked 7-14 were qualified for the Relegation Round.

Relegation Round

Round 27 [03-05.04.2021]
Hapoel Hadera - Hapoel Tel Aviv 0-1(0-0)
Maccabi Netanya - Bnei Sachnin 0-0
Hapoel Haifa - Bnei Yehuda 1-3(1-2)
Beitar Jerusalem - Hapoel Kfar Saba 3-1(0-1)

Round 28 [10-11.04.2021]
Hapoel Tel Aviv - Hapoel Haifa 0-2(0-1)
Bnei Sachnin - Bnei Yehuda 1-1(1-0)
Maccabi Netanya - Beitar Jerusalem 1-0(1-0)
Hapoel Kfar Saba - Hapoel Hadera 1-2(0-1)

Round 29 [17-19.04.2021]
Bnei Sachnin - Hapoel Kfar Saba 3-0(1-0)
Maccabi Netanya - Hapoel Tel Aviv 0-1(0-0)
Hapoel Hadera - Hapoel Haifa 3-0(1-0)
Beitar Jerusalem - Bnei Yehuda 2-2(0-2)

Round 30 [24-25.04.2021]
Hapoel Haifa - Bnei Sachnin 1-0(1-0)
Hapoel Kfar Saba - Maccabi Netanya 0-1(0-1)
Hapoel Tel Aviv - Beitar Jerusalem 0-0
Bnei Yehuda - Hapoel Hadera 2-3(0-1)

Round 31 [01-03.05.2021]
Bnei Yehuda - Maccabi Netanya 1-2(1-0)
Hapoel Hadera - Bnei Sachnin 1-0(1-0)
Hapoel Tel Aviv - Hapoel Kfar Saba 2-2(2-1)
Hapoel Haifa - Beitar Jerusalem 3-1(1-1)

Round 32 [08-09.05.2021]
Bnei Yehuda - Hapoel Tel Aviv 1-0(0-0)
Hapoel Haifa - Hapoel Kfar Saba 3-2(3-0)
Beitar Jerusalem - Bnei Sachnin 3-1(2-0)
Hapoel Hadera - Maccabi Netanya 2-2(1-1)

Round 33 [19-20.05.2021]
Beitar Jerusalem - Hapoel Hadera 0-3(0-1)
Maccabi Netanya - Hapoel Haifa 2-0(0-0)
Hapoel Kfar Saba - Bnei Yehuda 1-2(0-1)
Bnei Sachnin - Hapoel T.A. 2-3(1-2) [24.05.]

Final Standings

					Total			Home					Away				
7. Maccabi Netanya FC	33	13	9	11	43	-	34	48	8	2	7	24 - 14	5	7	4	19 - 20
8. Hapoel Hadera–Giv'at Olga "Shulem Schwarz"	33	13	9	11	40	-	34	48	6	6	5	22 - 18	7	3	6	18 - 16
9. Hapoel Haifa FC	33	11	9	13	40	-	48	42	7	4	6	21 - 22	4	5	7	19 - 26
10. Beitar Jerusalem FC	33	10	10	13	40	-	43	40	5	5	7	25 - 26	5	5	6	15 - 17
11. Hapoel Tel Aviv FC	33	9	11	13	24	-	35	38	1	9	6	9 - 21	8	2	7	15 - 14
12. Bnei Sakhnin FC	33	9	7	17	22	-	45	34	4	2	10	10 - 20	5	5	7	12 - 25
13. Bnei Yehuda Tel Aviv FC (*Relegated*)	33	8	9	16	27	-	46	33	5	3	8	13 - 22	3	6	8	14 - 24
14. Hapoel Kfar Saba FC (*Relegated*)	33	6	6	21	26	-	49	24	4	2	10	13 - 17	2	4	11	13 - 32

Championship Round

Results

Round 27 [03.04.2021]
FC Ashdod - Hapoel Ironi K.S. 1-1(0-1)
Maccabi Haifa - Petach-Tikva 1-1(1-0)
Maccabi Tel Aviv - Be'er Sheva 2-1(1-0)

Round 28 [06.04.2021]
Petach-Tikva - Hapoel Ironi K.S. 2-0(2-0)
Hapoel Be'er Sheva - FC Ashdod 1-2(0-2)
Maccabi Haifa - Maccabi Tel Aviv 1-1(1-0)

Round 29 [10-12.04.2021]
Hapoel Ironi K.S. - Be'er Sheva 1-1(1-0)
Maccabi Tel Aviv - Petach-Tikva 3-1(1-0)
FC Ashdod - Maccabi Haifa 0-3(0-1)

Round 30 [17-18.04.2021]
Petach-Tikva - Hapoel Be'er Sheva 0-0
Maccabi Haifa - Hapoel Ironi K.S. 4-0(2-0)
Maccabi Tel Aviv - FC Ashdod 1-1(0-0)

Round 31 [25-26.04.2021]
FC Ashdod - Maccabi Petach-Tikva 0-0
Hapoel Ironi K.S. - Maccabi Tel Aviv 2-0(1-0)
Hapoel Be'er Sheva - Maccabi Haifa 1-1(1-0)

Round 32 [01-03.05.2021]
Hapoel Ironi K.S. - FC Ashdod 1-1(1-0)
Petach-Tikva - Maccabi Haifa 1-2(0-1)
Be'er Sheva - Maccabi Tel Aviv 1-1(0-1)

Round 33 [08-09.05.2021]
Hapoel Ironi K.S. - Petach-Tikva 1-2(0-2)
Maccabi Tel Aviv - Maccabi Haifa 2-2(2-2)
FC Ashdod - Be'er Sheva 2-2(1-1) [20.05.]

Round 34 [23.05.2021]
Petach-Tikva - Maccabi Tel Aviv 0-3(0-0)
Maccabi Haifa - FC Ashdod 2-0(1-0)
Be'er Sheva - Hapoel Ironi K.S. 3-2(1-1)

Round 35 [26.05.2021]
Be'er Sheva - Maccabi Petach-Tikva 2-0(0-0)
Hapoel Ironi K.S. - Maccabi Haifa 1-1(0-0)
FC Ashdod - Maccabi Tel Aviv 1-2(0-0)

Round 36 [30.05.2021]
Maccabi Petach-Tikva - FC Ashdod 1-3(0-0)
Maccabi Tel Aviv - Hapoel Ironi K.S. 2-2(2-0)
Maccabi Haifa - Hapoel Be'er Sheva 3-2(3-0)

Final Standings

					Total			Home					Away				
1. **Maccabi Haifa FC**	36	24	7	5	72	-	29	79	14	3	1	39 - 12	10	4	4	33 - 17
2. Maccabi Tel Aviv FC	36	21	12	3	65	-	33	75	10	7	1	35 - 19	11	5	2	30 - 14
3. FC Ashdod	36	15	9	12	48	-	39	54	9	5	4	26 - 15	6	4	8	22 - 24
4. Hapoel Be'er Sheva FC	36	11	15	10	45	-	43	48	6	7	5	23 - 22	5	8	5	22 - 21
5. Maccabi Petah Tikva FC	36	13	7	16	32	-	38	46	6	4	8	14 - 17	7	3	8	18 - 21
6. Hapoel Ironi Kiryat Shmona FC	36	12	10	14	37	-	45	46	6	6	6	19 - 23	6	4	8	18 - 22

Top goalscorers:

19	**Nikita Rukavytsya (AUS)**	*Maccabi Haifa FC*
12	Tjaronn Inteff Chefren Chery (SUR)	*Maccabi Haifa FC*
12	Liel Abada	*Maccabi Petah Tikva FC*
11	Eliran Atar	*Beitar Jerusalem FC*

NATIONAL CUP
Israel State Cup (Gvia HaMedina) 2020/2021

Eighth Round [19-22.02.2021]

Agudat Sport Nordia Jerusalem - FC Tira	10-9 pen	Maccabi Haifa FC - Hapoel Umm al-Fahm FC	2-1	
Maccabi Netanya FC - Hapoel Bik'at HaYarden	2-0	Beitar Tel Aviv Bat Yam - Ironi Kiryat Shmona FC	2-0	
Hapoel Ramat Gan FC- Hapoel Bnei Lod Rakevet FC	4-1 aet	Hapoel Kfar Shalem - Agudat Sport Ashdod FC	3-1	
FC Kafr Qasim - Hapoel Kfar Saba FC	0-2	Hapoel Acre FC - Beitar Jerusalem FC	0-2	
Hapoel Afula FC - Hapoel Nof HaGalil FC	5-3 pen	Hapoel Be'er Sheva FC - Maccabi Tel Aviv FC	0-1	
Hapoel Jerusalem FC - Hapoel Rishon LeZion FC	1-0 aet	Bnei Sakhnin FC - Hapoel Hadera–Giv'at Olga	3-0	
Sektzia Nes Tziona FC - Maccabi Petah Tikva FC	0-1 aet	FC Ashdod - Hapoel Ra'anana AFC	3-1	
Bnei Yehuda Tel Aviv FC - Hapoel Haifa FC	4-5 pen	Hapoel Tel Aviv FC - Hapoel Ashkelon FC	4-0	

1/8-Finals [15-17.03.2021]

Beitar Tel Aviv Bat Yam - Hapoel Ramat Gan FC	3-1	Hapoel Haifa FC - Maccabi Tel Aviv FC	2-3
Hapoel Kfar Shalem - Hapoel Jerusalem FC	1-0 aet	Beitar Jerusalem FC - FC Ashdod	1-2 aet
Maccabi Netanya FC - Hapoel Tel Aviv FC	1-3	Hapoel Kfar Saba FC - Hapoel Afula FC	0-3 aet
Bnei Sakhnin FC - Agudat Sport Nordia Jerusalem	1-0	Maccabi Haifa FC - Maccabi Petah Tikva FC	2-1

Quarter-Finals [20-22.04.2021]

Hapoel Kfar Shalem - Hapoel Tel Aviv FC	0-1	FC Ashdod - Maccabi Tel Aviv FC	0-1
Bnei Sakhnin FC - Beitar Tel Aviv Bat Yam FC	0-4	Maccabi Haifa FC - Hapoel Afula FC	4-1

Semi-Finals [19-20.05.2021]

Hapoel Tel Aviv FC - Beitar Tel Aviv Bat Yam FC	7-6 pen	Maccabi Haifa FC - Maccabi Tel Aviv FC	0-2

Final

02.06.2021, Bloomfield Stadium, Tel Aviv; Referee: Erez Papir; Attendance: 27,500
Maccabi Tel Aviv FC - Hapoel Tel Aviv FC   **2-1(0-1,1-1)**

Maccabi Tel Aviv: Daniel Miller Tenenbaum, André Geraldes de Barros, Matan Baltaxa, Luis Hernández Rodríguez, Enric Saborit Teixidor, Dan Glazer, Sheran Yeini (Cap) (70.Dan Biton), Dor Peretz, Eduardo Antonio Guerrero Locano, Itay Shechter (64.Yonatan Cohen), Tal Ben Haim (46.Matan Hozez). Trainer: Patrick van Leeuwen (Netherlands)

Hapoel Tel Aviv: Ernestas Šetkus, Ben Bitton, Edi Gotlieb, Iyad Abu Abaid, Danny Gruper, Dan Einbinder, Shay Elias (90+3.Shay Lee Izan [*sent off 120*]), Osher Davida (74.Raz Stain), Omri Altman (Cap) (106.Gil Itzhak), Lidor Cohen, Shlomi Azulay I (67.Emmanuel Boateng; 120+5.Raz Shlomo). Trainer: Nir Klinger.

Goals: 0-1 Omri Altman (31), 1-1 Yonatan Cohen (73), 2-1 Luis Hernández Rodríguez (96).

THE CLUBS 2020/2021

Please note: appearances and goals includes statistics of both regular season and play-offs (Championship Round and Relegation Round).

Beitar Jerusalem Football Club

Founded:	1936
Stadium:	Teddy Stadium, Jerusalem (31,733)
Trainer:	Slobodan Drapić 28.02.1965
[22.03.2021]	Yossi Mizrahi 04.04.1953

Goalkeepers:	DOB	M	(s)	G
Netanel Daloya	14.07.1998	3	(2)	
Itamar Nitzan	23.06.1987	30		
Defenders:	**DOB**	**M**	**(s)**	**G**
Tal Ben Haim	31.03.1982	10	(2)	
Oren Biton	16.06.1994	21	(4)	
Antoine Conte (FRA)	29.01.1994	10	(1)	
Orel Dgani	08.01.1989	24		
Diogo Sousa Verdasca (POR)	26.10.1996	1		
David Houja	27.04.2001		(1)	
Shay Konstantini	27.06.1996	16	(7)	1
Uri Magbo	12.09.1987	12	(11)	4
Santiago Ocampos Ibarra (PAR)	22.01.2002	14	(3)	
Or Zahavi	23.04.1996	17	(3)	
Midfielders:	**DOB**	**M**	**(s)**	**G**
Tamir Adi	02.05.1993	7	(5)	1
David Dego	09.05.2001		(5)	1
Shalom Edri	07.04.1994	6	(8)	1
Ofir Kriaf	17.03.1991	17	(6)	

	DOB	M	(s)	G
Hanan Maman	28.08.1989	1		
Matheus Leonardo Sales Cardoso Matheusinho (BRA)	11.02.1998	7	(6)	2
Ali Muhammad (NIG)	07.10.1995	30	(1)	2
Michael Ohana	04.10.1995	14	(10)	5
Nicolas Olsak	25.11.1991	3	(2)	
Miron Tal	2002		(1)	
Aviel Zargary	11.12.2002	22	(2)	
Forwards:	**DOB**	**M**	**(s)**	**G**
Eliran Atar	17.02.1987	19	(10)	11
Shlomi Azulay I	18.10.1989		(1)	
Roy Doga	23.07.2002		(2)	
Roy Fadida	31.03.2000	3	(10)	
Marko Janković (MNE)	09.07.1995	11	(1)	1
Uziel Pardo	16.06.1999	4	(14)	
Liran Rotman	07.06.1996	2	(12)	
Yarden Shua	16.06.1999	25	(6)	7
Idan Vered	25.05.1989	24	(6)	2
Gleofilo Sabrino Rudewald Hasselbaink Vlijter (SUR)	17.09.1999	10	(12)	1

Bnei Sakhnin Football Club

Founded: 1991
Stadium: Doha Stadium, Sakhnin (8,500)
Trainer: Eldad Shavit 09.07.1982
[18.10.2020] Nisso Avitan 29.09.1971
[01.03.2021] Sharon Mimer 06.09.1973

Goalkeepers:	DOB	M	(s)	G
Mohammed Abu Nil	03.05.2001		(1)	
Rami Hamadeh	24.03.1994	4	(2)	
Tomer Haran	26.10.1998	1		
Mahmoud Kannadil	11.08.1988	28		
Defenders:	**DOB**	**M**	**(s)**	**G**
Tanos Bana	18.05.2001		(2)	
Sari Falah	22.11.1991	2		
Maroun Gantus	15.06.1996	28	(3)	
Hagai Goldenberg	15.09.1990	28	(2)	1
Oswaldo José Henríquez Bocanegra (COL)	10.03.1989	6		
Hassan Hilo	25.11.1999	12	(7)	
Yazen Nassar	06.05.1997	18	(4)	
Ali Ottman	08.02.1987	17	(4)	
Muhammad Ottman	23.09.2000	9	(4)	
Ihab Shami	18.09.1993	13	(5)	
Lukas Spendlhofer (AUT)	02.06.1993	10	(1)	
Ikouwem Udo Utin (NGA)	11.11.1999	3	(6)	
Fadel Zbedat	11.12.2002		(1)	

Midfielders:	DOB	M	(s)	G
Mohamed Sayed Ahmed	14.07.1998	2	(9)	
Bashir Bahjat	03.08.1998		(2)	
Moti Barshazky	06.09.1996	23	(8)	3
Ihab Ganayem	11.06.1996	30	(1)	2
Ataa Jaber	03.10.1994	25	(5)	2
Beram Kayal	02.05.1988	20		3
Luanderson Johnala Marques da Silva (BRA)	07.06.1989		(1)	
Bashar Shaheen	27.04.2001		(1)	
Odai Shalata	15.07.1998		(3)	
Zen Aldin Shalata	28.07.2003		(1)	1
Daniel Twizer	21.06.1996	5	(8)	
Sebastián Velásquez (COL)	11.02.1991	12		2
Forwards:	**DOB**	**M**	**(s)**	**G**
Nigel Hasselbaink (SUR)	21.11.1990	19	(8)	
Dane Kelly (JAM)	09.02.1991	3	(12)	
Osama Khalaila	06.04.1998	29	(2)	7
Moti Malka	13.12.1990	3	(9)	
Ismaeel Rayan	24.04.1994	3	(8)	
Mufalah Shalata	03.07.2000	7	(8)	1
Emery Welshman (GUY)	09.11.1991	3	(7)	

Bnei Yehuda Tel Aviv Football Club

Founded: 1936
Stadium: Bloomfield Stadium, Tel Aviv (29,150)
Trainer: Elisha Levy 18.11.1957
[14.10.2020] Nir Berkovich 23.01.1983
[26.11.2020] Kfir Edri 12.10.1976
[03.01.2021] Tamir Ben Ami 28.02.1979
[31.01.2021] Yosef Abukasis 10.09.1970

Goalkeepers:	DOB	M	(s)	G
Shahar Amsalem	26.03.1999	3		
Barak Levi	07.01.1993	3		
Omer Niron	17.04.2001	27		
Defenders:	**DOB**	**M**	**(s)**	**G**
Allyson Aires dos Santos (BRA)	23.10.1990	16		1
Amit Cohen	21.11.1998	23	(5)	
Avishai Cohen	19.05.1995	29	(3)	
Amit Glazer	30.05.2000	10	(2)	
Obeida Khattab	14.07.1992	4	(1)	
Raz Nahmias	06.05.1996	7		
Michael Rangel dos Santos de Almeida (BRA)	27.05.1999	7	(2)	
Dan Mori	08.11.1988	27		
Fadi Najar	30.05.1998	8	(3)	
Amir Rustum	18.10.1998	6	(5)	2
Midfielders:	**DOB**	**M**	**(s)**	**G**
Stav Finish	26.03.1992	21	(9)	
George Fochive (USA)	24.03.1992	4	(3)	1

	DOB	M	(s)	G
Ariel Lazmi	17.04.1994	5	(11)	
Matija Ljujić (SRB)	28.10.1993	23	(1)	1
Shay Mazor	14.06.1993	26	(3)	1
Yusif Moussa (NIG)	04.09.1998	15	(1)	
Elian Rohana	06.11.1997	1	(4)	
Sagas Tambi	21.10.1994	23	(2)	
Forwards:	**DOB**	**M**	**(s)**	**G**
Fatos Bećiraj (MNE)	05.05.1988	8	(5)	2
Harel Ben Avi	06.02.2001		(1)	
Roei Ben Shimon	04.12.2000	16	(10)	2
Almog Buzaglo	08.12.1992	8	(9)	2
Pedro Pablo Campos Olavarría (CHI)	02.06.2000	7	(17)	
Mohammad Ghadir	21.01.1991	12	(10)	7
Dor Jan	16.12.1994	3		2
Ayi Silva Kangani	15.05.2003	1	(5)	
Shaked Navon	21.10.2002	1	(4)	
Amit Zenati	02.04.1997	10	(10)	4
Niv Zrihen	24.05.1994	9	(6)	2

Football Club Ashdod

Founded: 1999
Stadium: Yud-Alef Stadium, Ashdod (7,800)
Trainer: Ran Ben Shimon 28.11.1970

Goalkeepers:	DOB	M	(s)	G
Yoav Gerafi	29.08.1993	26		
Roi Mishpati	23.11.1992	10		
Defenders:	**DOB**	**M**	**(s)**	**G**
Timothy Dennis Awany (UGA)	06.08.1996	20		
Nir Bardea	25.01.1996	5	(1)	
Omri Ben Harush	07.03.1990	12	(4)	
Tom Ben Zaken	29.10.1994	26		
Gil Cohen	08.11.2000	12	(9)	
Nenad Cvetković (SRB)	06.01.1996	32	(1)	2
Montari Kamaheni (GHA)	01.02.2000	33	(2)	1
Zohar Zasano	21.11.2001	11	(13)	
Midfielders:	**DOB**	**M**	**(s)**	**G**
Fares Abu Akel	08.02.1997	22	(7)	
Samuel Alabi Borquaye (GHA)	06.05.2000	1		
Shlomi Azulay II	30.03.1990	19	(9)	4
Moussa Bagayoko (MLI)	18.12.1998	21	(6)	2

	DOB	M	(s)	G
Oz Bilu	16.01.2001	3	(16)	1
Roei Gordana	06.07.1990	30	(2)	4
Shalev Harush	08.05.2002	4	(3)	
Nir Hasson	19.12.2001		(4)	
Forwards:	**DOB**	**M**	**(s)**	**G**
Hayford Adjei (GHA)	24.04.1999	3	(10)	
Fahad Bayo (UGA)	10.05.1998	17	(6)	6
Yaakov Brihon	06.07.1993	7	(22)	4
Idan Dahan	07.03.2001	3	(13)	1
Dean David	14.03.1996	27	(4)	9
Mohamad Kna'an	14.01.2000	27	(4)	2
Hamza Mowasi	09.02.2001	2	(4)	1
Benzion Moshel	31.07.1993		(6)	
Zakaria Mugeese (GHA)	27.12.2001		(5)	2
Ramzi Safuri	21.10.1995	10	(3)	3
Stav Turiel	14.01.2001	2	(11)	1
Sagiv Yehezkel	21.03.1995	11	(4)	5

Hapoel Be'er Sheva Football Club

Founded:	01.05.1949		
Stadium:	Turner Stadium, Be'er Sheva (16,126)		
Trainer:	Yosef Abukasis		10.09.1970
[31.01.2021]	Elyaniv Barda		15.12.1981
[18.02.2021]	Ronny Levy		14.11.1966

Goalkeepers:	DOB	M	(s)	G
Ohad Levita	17.02.1986	36		
Defenders:	**DOB**	**M**	**(s)**	**G**
Amit Biton	24.07.1996	1	(3)	
Or Dadia	12.07.1997	26	(2)	
Hatem Abd Elhamed	18.03.1991	8	(1)	
Shon Goldberg	13.06.1995	25		
Miguel Ângelo Leonardo Vítor (POR)	30.06.1989	25	(1)	
Eitan Ratzon	01.04.1998	4	(2)	
Loai Taha	26.11.1989	22	(4)	
Dudu Twitto	06.02.1994	11	(5)	
Shir Tzedek	22.08.1989	6	(3)	
Midfielders:	**DOB**	**M**	**(s)**	**G**
Lucas Mariano Bareiro (ARG)	08.05.1995	27	(1)	2
Josué Filipe Soares Pesqueira (POR)	17.09.1990	25		9
Marwan Kabha	23.02.1991	17	(3)	1

	DOB	M	(s)	G
David Keltjens	11.06.1995	18	(8)	2
Ilay Madmon	23.02.1993	4	(14)	
César Marcelo Meli (ARG)	20.06.1992	25	(6)	1
Naor Sabag	23.05.1993		(1)	
Tomer Yosefi	02.02.1999	17	(11)	5
Forwards:	**DOB**	**M**	**(s)**	**G**
Elton Acolatse (NED)	25.07.1995	22	(6)	1
Jhonatan Alexander Agudelo Velásquez (COL)	17.12.1992	7	(16)	
Rom Alyagon	24.12.2002		(3)	
Farley Vieira Rosa (BRA)	14.01.1994	5	(6)	2
Rotem Hatuel	12.04.1998	8	(16)	4
Ramzi Safuri	21.10.1995	5	(7)	1
Sintayehu Sallalich	20.06.1991	19	(8)	3
Itamar Shviro	17.06.1998	8	(16)	3
Gaëtan Antony Varenne	24.06.1990	13	(17)	7
Sagiv Yehezkel	21.03.1995	12		3

Hapoel Hadera–Giv'at Olga "Shulem Schwarz" Football Club

Founded:	1936		
Stadium:	Netanya Stadium, Netanya (13,610)		
Trainer:	Sharon Mimer		06.09.1973
[29.01.2021]	Menahem Koretski		04.04.1974

Goalkeepers:	DOB	M	(s)	G
Rubi Levkovich	31.08.1988	30		
Adi Tabachnik	16.11.1998	3		
Defenders:	**DOB**	**M**	**(s)**	**G**
Jonathan Cissé (CIV)	18.05.1997	31		2
Noam Cohen	06.01.1999	13	(13)	
Maksim Grechkin	04.03.1996	8	(2)	
Abdallah Jaber (PLE)	17.02.1993	23	(4)	
Tal Kahila	26.06.1992	7	(8)	1
Obeida Khattab	14.07.1992	11		1
Dia Lababidi	26.07.1992	22	(3)	
Ido Levy	31.07.1990	15		
Aviv Lin	30.06.2001		(1)	
Raz Nahmias	06.05.1996	1	(1)	
Wessam Rabah	13.03.1994	3		
Ron Unger	05.09.2001		(1)	
Midfielders:	**DOB**	**M**	**(s)**	**G**
Gilad Avramov	30.03.2000	11	(12)	3
Raz Buhbut	24.07.2000		(3)	

	DOB	M	(s)	G
Sekou Doumbia (CIV)	13.06.1994	2	(4)	
Shalom Edri	07.04.1994	3	(4)	
Tamir Glazer	30.05.2000	22	(5)	
Omer Lakao	07.02.1998	5	(4)	
Reef Messika	15.06.1989	9	(6)	
Yaya Meledje Omnibes (CIV)	25.09.1997	6	(1)	
Maxim Plakushchenko	04.01.1996	21	(3)	5
Mohamad Rabia	17.04.2002		(1)	
Mohammed Usman (NGA)	02.03.1994	8	(5)	
Menashe Zalka	01.07.1990	17	(10)	
Forwards:	**DOB**	**M**	**(s)**	**G**
Yahav Afriat	25.01.1997	1	(4)	
Karem Arshid	24.01.1995		(9)	
Louis Marie Rodrigue Bongongui Assougou (CMR)	07.02.1993	12	(6)	
Shoval Gozlan	25.04.1994	17	(11)	6
Assi Guma	07.10.1989		(17)	1
Gustavo Marmentini dos Santos (ARG)	08.03.1994	31	(1)	7
Odah Marshal (NGA)	14.04.1992	20	(9)	8
Liran Rotman	07.06.1996	11	(4)	5

Hapoel Haifa Football Club

Founded:	24.04.1924		
Stadium:	„Sammy Ofer" Stadium, Haifa (30,780)		
Trainer:	Haim Silvas		21.11.1975
[05.04.2021]	Elisha Levy		18.11.1957

Goalkeepers:	DOB	M	(s)	G
Jasmin Burić (BIH)	18.02.1987	6		
Ran Kadosh	04.10.1985	25		
Amit Suiri	20.04.2001	2	(1)	
Defenders:	**DOB**	**M**	**(s)**	**G**
Yahav Gurfinkel	27.06.1998	30		
Nisso Kapiloto	10.01.1989	21		3
Ido Levy	31.07.1990	2		
Dor Malul	30.04.1989	29		
Guy Mishpati	21.06.1990	11	(6)	
Raz Nahmias	06.05.1996	3		
Michael Siroshten	25.04.1989	16	(3)	
Ben Vahaba	27.03.1992	18	(2)	
Midfielders:	**DOB**	**M**	**(s)**	**G**
Tomer Altman	08.02.1998	12	(13)	
Gal Arel	09.07.1989	23	(7)	3
Roslan Barsky	03.01.1992	24	(2)	2

	DOB	M	(s)	G
Bar Cohen	10.03.2001		(3)	
Yarin Gabari	23.05.2002		(1)	
Mohamad Jaradat	2002		(1)	
Hanan Maman	28.08.1989	26	(1)	8
Liran Sardal	02.07.1994	28		4
Ido Shahar	20.08.2001	9	(12)	
Forwards:	**DOB**	**M**	**(s)**	**G**
William Agada (NGA)	17.09.1999	20	(5)	6
Eden Ben Basat	08.09.1986	3	(12)	2
Itay Buganim	29.05.2001		(9)	1
Almog Buzaglo	08.12.1992	2	(8)	
Ahmad Darawshe	14.05.1998		(9)	
Saar Fadida	04.01.1997	13	(18)	1
Qays Ghanem	31.12.1997	11	(3)	2
Raz Stain	23.02.1994	5	(10)	2
Alon Turgeman	09.06.1991	11	(2)	2
Ness Zamir	31.10.1990	13	(4)	4

Hapoel Ironi Kiryat Shmona Football Club

Founded:	2000		
Stadium:	Kiryat Shmona Municipal Stadium, Kiryat Shmona (5,300)		
Trainer:	Kobi Refua		03.09.1974

Goalkeepers:	DOB	M	(s)	G
Dziugas Bartkus (LTU)	07.11.1989	35		
Nadav Zamir	07.06.2001	1	(1)	
Defenders:	**DOB**	**M**	**(s)**	**G**
Amir Ben Shimon	14.12.1993	8	(15)	
Ori Dahan	07.12.1999	33	(2)	
Nir David Drori	25.12.2001		(2)	
Dor Elo	26.09.1993	32		
Yuval Levin	13.02.2000	4	(3)	
Ziv Morgan	19.01.2000	32	(2)	
Idan Nachmias	17.03.1997	35		1
Midfielders:	**DOB**	**M**	**(s)**	**G**
Mike Amanga (NGA)	01.09.2002	1	(7)	1
Samuel Bar-On	03.03.1998	28		

Yoav Hofmayster	25.12.2000	28	(1)	
Roi Kehat	12.05.1992	34	(2)	6
Yadin Lugasi	04.04.1999	3		
Adrian Rochet	26.05.1987	2	(26)	
Ariel Sheratzky	24.09.2001		(1)	
Saikou Touray (GAM)	06.06.2000	24	(4)	
Forwards:	**DOB**	**M**	**(s)**	**G**
Eugene Ansah (GHA)	16.12.1994	33		10
Guy Ben Lulu	19.05.2000	3	(13)	1
Abdallah Khalaihal	11.01.2001	4	(19)	4
Lucielmo Palhano Soares „Lucio Maranhão" (BRA)	28.09.1988	32	(1)	8
Ofir Mizrahi	04.12.1993	4	(14)	1
Mohammed Shakar	14.11.1996	20	(9)	4

Hapoel Kfar Saba Football Club

Founded:	1928		
Stadium:	HaMoshava Stadium, Petah Tikva (11,500)		
Trainer:	Amir Turgeman		05.10.1972
[28.12.2020]	Elisha Levy		18.11.1957
[22.03.2021]	Idan Shum		26.03.1976

Goalkeepers:	DOB	M	(s)	G
Matan Galanti	11.02.2001	2		
Itamar Israeli	22.03.1992	18		
Matan Zalmanovich	13.08.1994	13		
Defenders:	**DOB**	**M**	**(s)**	**G**
Sodiq Atanda (NGA)	26.08.1993	28	(1)	
Omer Danino	17.02.1995	18	(5)	
Maor Gerassi	03.10.1994	1	(2)	
Ben Hayun	08.11.2000	4	(9)	
Tal Machluf	31.08.1991	18	(1)	1
Tom Shelach	10.07.1996	17	(3)	
Aviv Solomon	10.01.1995	29		2
Itay Shor	18.02.2001	12	(4)	
Yehoshua Shtrimling	19.03.2003	3	(1)	
Midfielders:	**DOB**	**M**	**(s)**	**G**
Omer Barami	13.05.2000		(1)	
Raz Cohen	11.11.1994	18	(9)	
Or Dasa	20.09.1998	13	(15)	2
George Fochive (USA)	24.03.1992	16	(1)	

Triko Gateon	01.01.1995	10	(7)	
Jamie Ryan Hopcutt (ENG)	23.06.1992	5	(5)	
Omer Lakao	07.02.1998	11	(2)	
Michael Omoh (NGA)	29.08.1991	7	(8)	1
Omer Peretz	01.04.2002	1	(1)	
Ben Reichert	04.03.1994	22	(3)	
Alon Sabag	12.04.2001		(2)	
Domantas Šimkus (LTU)	10.02.1996	10	(2)	
Yoni Stoyanov	22.05.2001	5	(9)	
Forwards:	**DOB**	**M**	**(s)**	**G**
Yahav Afriat	25.01.1997	4	(7)	
Roy Becker	04.04.2003	1	(3)	
Kerfala Cissoko (GUI)	16.08.1999	1	(3)	
Sagi Dror	07.08.1995	2	(6)	
Omer Fadida	17.07.1994	13	(7)	8
Florent Hasani (KVX)	30.03.1997	8	(2)	
Luwagga William Kizito (UGA)	20.12.1993	29	(2)	7
Timothy Muzie	24.08.2001	8	(6)	3
Amadou Soukouna (FRA)	21.06.1992	16	(12)	1

Hapoel Tel Aviv Football Club

Founded:	1923		
Stadium:	Bloomfield Stadium, Tel Aviv (29,150)		
Trainer:	Nir Klinger		25.05.1966

Goalkeepers:	DOB	M	(s)	G
Roy Baranes	07.12.2001		(1)	
Yigal Becker	09.09.1999	4		
Ernestas Šetkus (LTU)	25.05.1985	29		
Defenders:	**DOB**	**M**	**(s)**	**G**
Iyad Abu Abaid	31.12.1994	29		1
Ben Bitton	03.01.1991	15		1
Ofek Shimon Balas	08.08.1999	1	(2)	
Edi Gotlieb	16.08.1992	10	(2)	
Danny Gruper	16.03.1999	29		
Doron Leidner	26.04.2002	5	(12)	
Mor Na'aman	26.01.1998	1		
Niv Sardal	12.03.1993	9	(7)	
Raz Shlomo	13.08.1999	9	(9)	1
Siyanda Xulu (RSA)	30.12.1991	30	(1)	
Midfielders:	**DOB**	**M**	**(s)**	**G**
Dan Azaria	29.08.1995	5	(11)	
Ofek Biton	27.09.1999	3	(8)	1
Emmanuel Boateng (GHA)	17.06.1997	17	(7)	1
Omar Ezequiel Browne Zúñiga (PAN)	03.05.1994		(1)	
Armando Enrique Cooper Whitaker (PAN)	26.11.1987	2	(4)	

Dan Einbinder	16.02.1989	17		1
Shay Elias	25.02.1999	22	(6)	1
Shay Lee Izan	27.08.2000	13	(6)	
El Yam Kancepolsky	22.12.2003	1		
Guy Sivilia	26.02.2002		(1)	
Ilay Tamam	07.05.2001	1		
Forwards:	**DOB**	**M**	**(s)**	**G**
Omri Altman	23.03.1994	28	(2)	7
Shlomi Azulay I	18.10.1989	11	(5)	2
Lidor Cohen	16.12.1992	14	(4)	1
Osher Davida	18.02.2001	26	(4)	3
Eden Hershkovitz	23.08.1997	2	(4)	
Shahar Hirsh	13.02.1993	3	(4)	1
Gil Itzhak	29.06.1993	10	(12)	2
Levan Kutalia (GEO)	19.07.1989	3	(5)	
Shavit Mazal	29.11.2001		(1)	
Ofek Ovadia	30.01.2001	1	(3)	
Omer Senior	23.02.2003		(1)	
Raz Stain	23.02.1994	5	(10)	
Roei Zikri	13.10.1992	8	(8)	

Maccabi Haifa Football Club

Founded: 1913
Stadium: "Sammy Ofer" Stadium, Haifa (30,780)
Trainer: Barak Bakhar   21.09.1979

Goalkeepers:	DOB	M	(s)	G
Joshua Cohen (USA)	18.08.1992	32		
Omri Glazer	11.03.1996	4		
Defenders:	**DOB**	**M**	**(s)**	**G**
Ofri Arad	11.09.1998	30	(2)	1
Rami Gershon	12.08.1988	4	(7)	
Ayid Habashi	10.05.1995	8	(2)	
Ernest Mabouka (CMR)	16.06.1988	15	(3)	
Raz Meir	30.11.1996	21	(6)	1
Sun Menahem	07.09.1993	31	(3)	4
Bogdan Planić (SRB)	19.01.1992	31		4
Taleb Tawatha	21.06.1992	5	(10)	
Midfielders:	**DOB**	**M**	**(s)**	**G**
Mohammed Abu Fani	27.04.1998	31	(3)	2
Yuval Ashkenazi	13.02.1992	4	(18)	1
Tjaronn Inteff Chefren Chery (SUR)	04.06.1988	30	(4)	12
José Rodríguez Martínez (ESP)	16.12.1994	26	(3)	1
Neta Lavi	25.08.1996	34		2
Maor Levi	18.06.2000		(22)	
Saikou Touray	06.06.2000		(2)	
Forwards:	**DOB**	**M**	**(s)**	**G**
Ihab Abu Alshikh	06.03.2000	1	(11)	
Omer Atzili	27.07.1993	18	(3)	4
Mohamad Awad	09.06.1997	1	(9)	
Godsway Donyoh (GHA)	14.10.1994	9	(19)	8
Dolev Haziza	05.07.1995	31	(1)	8
Nehorai Ifrah	07.05.2003		(2)	
Timothy Muzie	24.08.2001		(5)	
Stav Nachmani	06.10.2002		(8)	
Nikita Rukavytsya (AUS)	22.06.1987	25	(3)	19
Yarden Shua	16.06.1999		(2)	
Yanic Wildschut (NED)	01.11.1991	5	(17)	1

Maccabi Netanya Football Club

Founded: 1934
Stadium: Netanya Stadium, Netanya (13,610)
Trainer: Raymond Atteveld (NED)   08.09.1966

Goalkeepers:	DOB	M	(s)	G
Dani Amos	02.02.1987	23		
Raz Karmi	27.01.1996	10		
Defenders:	**DOB**	**M**	**(s)**	**G**
Akinsola Akinyemi (NOR)	12.07.1993	9		
Dolev Azulay	09.10.1997	3	(10)	1
Karem Jaber	31.10.2000	21	(2)	1
Rotem Keller	09.11.2002	8	(10)	
Zlatko Šehović (SRB)	08.08.2000	19		
Shir Tzedek	22.08.1989	10	(1)	
Ido Vaier	10.10.1996	15	(9)	
Kellian van der Kaap (NED)	08.11.1998	23	(3)	1
Midfielders:	**DOB**	**M**	**(s)**	**G**
Aviv Avraham	30.03.1996	24	(7)	1
Almog Cohen	01.09.1988	24		
Omri Gandelman	16.05.2000	23	(9)	1
Aviv Kanarik	16.04.2003		(1)	
Gavriel Kanichowsky	24.08.1997	32		9
Yuval Sade	10.05.2000	15	(13)	2
Elad Shahaf	13.01.1998	4	(13)	1
Yarin Sharabi	26.01.1999		(5)	
Eilon Yerushalmi	10.03.1997	5	(5)	
Forwards:	**DOB**	**M**	**(s)**	**G**
Ron Ashkenazi	20.08.1998		(1)	1
Ben Azubel	19.09.1993	6	(11)	1
Lameck Banda (ZAM)	29.01.2001	17	(7)	2
Aboubacar Doumbia (CIV)	12.11.1999	10	(5)	2
Hen Ezra	19.01.1989	24	(4)	5
Kevaughn Frater (JAM)	14.12.1994	19	(12)	5
Fernand Gouré (CIV)	12.04.2002	6	(7)	2
Roy Korine	10.09.2002	2	(13)	
Yonas Malede	14.11.1999	11	(3)	7

Maccabi Petah Tikva Football Club

Founded: 1912
Stadium: HaMoshava Stadium, Petah Tikva (11,500)
Trainer: Guy Luzon   07.08.1975

Goalkeepers:	DOB	M	(s)	G
Dor Hevron	28.06.2001	1		
Arik Yanko	21.12.1991	35		
Defenders:	**DOB**	**M**	**(s)**	**G**
Or Blorian	07.03.2000	34	(2)	1
Yarden Cohen	26.03.1997	20	(9)	
Yinon Eliyahu	01.11.1993	26	(6)	1
Daniel Felczer	26.07.1997	22	(8)	
Mohammed Hindi	29.10.1995	18	(4)	1
Tomer Levi	25.05.1993	9	(5)	
Marcus Plínio Diniz Paixão (BRA)	01.08.1987	21	(3)	
Midfielders:	**DOB**	**M**	**(s)**	**G**
Arad Bar	29.01.2000	26	(4)	1
Ethane Azoulay	26.05.2002	14	(5)	
Armando Enrique Cooper Whitaker (PAN)	26.11.1987	11	(6)	1
Guy Hadida	23.07.1995	12	(9)	2
Amit Meir	07.01.2001	9	(14)	
Naor Sabag	23.05.1993	21	(6)	1
Elvis Sakyi (GHA)	24.11.1996	14	(3)	
Muhamad Sarsur	26.04.1999	2	(3)	
Forwards:	**DOB**	**M**	**(s)**	**G**
Liel Abada	03.10.2001	34	(2)	12
Ihab Abu Alshikh	06.03.2000	2		
Yoel Abuhatzira	12.07.1996	3	(3)	
Abdiel Arroyo Molinar (PAN)	13.12.1993	14	(9)	
Tai Baribo	15.01.1998	9	(19)	6
Morgan Ferrier (ENG)	15.11.1994	9	(5)	1
Eyal Inbrum	03.09.2001		(3)	
Or Inbrum	12.01.1996	17	(14)	2
Daniel Joulani (UKR)	19.03.2003		(9)	
Joaquim Manuel Welo "Jucie" Lupeta (POR)	24.03.1993	4	(6)	
Elior Mishali	05.07.1995		(2)	
Roy Ronen	17.01.1998		(2)	
Amir Suljić (BIH)	11.09.1991	9	(5)	

Maccabi Tel Aviv Football Club

Founded: 1906 (*as HaRishon LeZion-Yaffo*)
Stadium: Bloomfield Stadium, Tel Aviv (29,150)
Trainer: Giorgos Donis (GRE)
[24.12.2020]   Patrick van Leeuwen (NED)   08.08.1969

Goalkeepers:	DOB	M	(s)	G
Daniel Miller Tenenbaum (BRA)	19.04.1995	36		
Defenders:	**DOB**	**M**	**(s)**	**G**
André Geraldes de Barros (POR)	02.05.1991	13	(3)	
Matan Baltaxa	20.09.1995	6	(2)	
Ben Bitton	03.01.1991	3		
Ofir Davidzada	05.05.1991	8	(9)	
Maor Kandil	27.11.1993	12	(6)	1
Luis Hernández Rodríguez (ESP)	14.04.1989	31		1
Shahar Piven-Bachtiar	21.09.1995	8	(8)	
Enric Saborit Teixidor (ESP)	27.04.1992	29		2
Eitan Tibi	16.11.1987	25	(1)	1
Sheran Yeini	08.12.1986	23	(7)	
Midfielders:	**DOB**	**M**	**(s)**	**G**
Dan Biton	20.07.1995	17	(11)	4
Dan Glazer	20.09.1996	19	(4)	
Eyal Golasa	07.10.1991	20	(4)	2
Eden Karzev	11.04.2000	8	(6)	1
Dor Peretz	17.05.1995	32	(2)	7
Avi Rikan	10.09.1988	11	(15)	4
Forwards:	**DOB**	**M**	**(s)**	**G**
Eylon Almog	08.01.1999	9	(18)	2
Nick Blackman (BRB)	11.11.1989	7	(10)	3
Tal Ben Haim	05.08.1989	17	(11)	2
Yonatan Cohen	29.06.1996	16	(5)	10
Eduardo Antonio Guerrero Locano (PAN)	21.02.2000	8	(9)	7
Matan Hozez	12.08.1996	9	(13)	2
Aleksandar Pešić (SRB)	21.05.1992	19	(4)	10
Or Roizman	22.03.2002		(1)	
Itay Shechter	22.02.1987	10	(19)	4
Dor Turgeman	24.10.2003		(1)	

SECOND LEVEL
Liga Leumit 2020/2021

Regular Season

1.	Hapoel Nof HaGalil FC	30	16	9	5	39	-	20	57	
2.	Hapoel Jerusalem FC	30	14	12	4	37	-	16	54	
3.	Sektzia Nes Tziona FC	30	12	10	8	28	-	30	46	
4.	Beitar Tel Aviv Bat Yam FC	30	12	8	10	44	-	36	44	
5.	Hapoel Nir Ramat HaSharon FC	30	11	10	9	27	-	23	43	
6.	Hapoel Iksal FC	30	11	10	9	42	-	42	43	
7.	Hapoel Rishon LeZion FC	30	9	15	6	32	-	27	42	
8.	Hapoel Ramat Gan Givatayim FC	30	9	13	8	33	-	28	40	
9.	Hapoel Afula FC	30	10	9	11	32	-	28	39	
10.	Maccabi Ahi Nazareth FC	30	10	9	11	32	-	31	39	
11.	Hapoel Ra'anana AFC	30	8	11	11	30	-	31	35	
12.	FC Kafr Qasim	30	7	14	9	25	-	31	35	
13.	Hapoel Umm al-Fahm FC	30	7	11	12	21	-	33	32	
14.	Hapoel Acre FC	30	5	16	9	22	-	35	31	
15.	Hapoel Petah Tikva FC	30	6	9	15	17	-	30	27	
16.	Hapoel Kfar Shaslem FC	30	6	8	16	32	-	52	26	

Promotion Play-offs

1.	Hapoel Nof HaGalil FC (*Promoted*)	37	20	12	5	57	-	26	72	
2.	Hapoel Jerusalem FC (*Promoted*)	37	19	14	4	52	-	20	71	
3.	Sektzia Nes Tziona FC	37	16	11	10	37	-	38	59	
4.	Hapoel Rishon LeZion FC	37	12	17	8	41	-	35	53	
5.	Beitar Tel Aviv Bat Yam FC	37	13	12	12	55	-	48	51	
6.	Hapoel Ramat Gan Givatayim FC	37	11	15	11	44	-	38	48	
7.	Hapoel Nir Ramat HaSharon FC	37	12	11	14	32	-	30	47	
8.	Hapoel Iksal FC* (*Relegated*)	37	11	11	15	44	-	67	44	

relegated to third level due to financial reasons.

Relegation Play-offs

9.	Hapoel Afula FC	37	13	10	14	50	-	39	49	
10.	Hapoel Ra'anana AFC	37	12	12	13	47	-	42	48	
11.	Maccabi Ahi Nazareth FC	37	12	9	16	37	-	47	45	
12.	FC Kafr Qasim	37	9	15	13	32	-	40	42	
13.	Hapoel Acre FC	37	8	18	11	34	-	43	42	
14.	Hapoel Umm al-Fahm FC (*Relegation Play-off*)	37	10	12	15	30	-	41	42	
15.	Hapoel Petah Tikva FC	37	10	11	16	22	-	33	41	
16.	Hapoel Kfar Shaslem FC (*Relegated*)	37	8	10	19	37	-	64	34	

Relegation Play-off: Hapoel Umm al-Fahm FC – Maccabi Jaffa FC   1-0(1-0)

Hapoel Umm al-Fahm FC remains at Second Level.

NATIONAL TEAM

INTERNATIONAL MATCHES
(16.07.2020 – 15.07.2021)

04.09.2020	Glasgow	Scotland - Israel	1-1(1-0)	(UNL)
07.09.2020	Netanya	Israel - Slovakia	1-1(0-1)	(UNL)
08.10.2020	Glasgow	Scotland - Israel	0-0; 5-3 on penalties	(ECQPO)
11.10.2020	Haifa	Israel - Czech Republic	1-2(1-1)	(UNL)
14.10.2020	Trnava	Slovakia - Israel	2-3(2-0)	(UNL)
15.11.2020	Plzeň	Czech Republic - Israel	1-0(1-0)	(UNL)
18.11.2020	Netanya	Israel - Scotland	1-0(1-0)	(UNL)
25.03.2021	Tel Aviv	Israel - Denmark	0-2(0-1)	(WCQ)
28.03.2021	Tel Aviv	Israel - Scotland	1-1(1-0)	(WCQ)
31.03.2021	Chişinău	Moldova - Israel	1-4(1-1)	(WCQ)
05.06.2021	Podgorica	Montenegro - Israel	1-3(0-0)	(F)
09.06.2021	Lisboa	Portugal - Israel	4-0(2-0)	(F)

04.09.2020   SCOTLAND - ISRAEL   1-1(1-0)   2nd UEFA Nations League B, Group 2
Hampden Park, Glasgow; Referee: Slavko Vinčić (Slovenia); Attendance: 295
ISR: Ofir Meir Marciano, Taleb Tawatha, Eytan Tibi, Hatem Abd Elhamed, Elazar Dasa, Bibras Natkho (Cap), Nir Biton, Dor Peretz (72.Yonatan Cohen), Eran Zahavi, Moanes Dabour (79.Shon Weissman), Manor Solomon (90.Dan Leon Glazer). Trainer: Willibald Ruttensteiner (Austria).
Goal: Eran Zahavi (73).

07.09.2020   ISRAEL - SLOVAKIA   **1-1(0-1)**   2nd UEFA Nations League B, Group 2
Netanya Stadium, Netanya; Referee: Nikola Dabanović (Montenegro); Attendance: 0
ISR: Ofir Meir Marciano, Taleb Tawatha (71.Ilay Eliyau Elmkies), Eytan Tibi, Hatem Abd Elhamed, Elazar Dasa, Bibras Natkho (Cap) (46.Yonatan Cohen), Nir Biton, Dor Peretz, Manor Solomon, Eran Zahavi, Moanes Dabour (57.Shon Weissman). Trainer: Willibald Ruttensteiner (Austria).
Goal: Ilay Eliyau Elmkies (90+1).

08.10.2020   SCOTLAND - ISRAEL   **0-0; 5-3 on penalties**   16th EC. Qualifiers Play-offs, Semi-Finals
Hampden Park, Glasgow; Referee: Ovidiu Alin Haţegan (Romania); Attendance: 0
ISR: Ofir Meir Marciano, Shiran Yeini, Eytan Tibi, Hatem Abd Elhamed, Elazar Dasa, Bibras Natkho (Cap) (69.Mohammad Abu Fani), Manor Solomon, Nir Biton, Eyal Golasa (100.Ilay Eliyau Elmkies), Eran Zahavi, Moanes Dabour (83.Shon Weissman). Trainer: Willibald Ruttensteiner (Austria).
Penalties: Eran Zahavi (saved), Nir Biton, Shon Weissman, Mohammad Abu Fani.

11.10.2020   ISRAEL - CZECH REPUBLIC   **1-2(1-1)**   2nd UEFA Nations League B, Group 2
"Sammy Ofer" Stadium, Haifa; Referee: Tiago Bruno Lopes Martins (Portugal); Attendance: 0
ISR: Ofir Meir Marciano, Shiran Yeini, Eytan Tibi, Elazar Dasa (75.Moanes Dabour), Hatem Abd Elhamed, Joel Abu Hanna (46.Sun Menahem), Bibras Natkho (Cap) (75.Eyal Golasa), Manor Solomon, Mohammad Abu Fani (88.Eden Karzev), Eran Zahavi, Shon Weissman (66.Dia Saba). Trainer: Willibald Ruttensteiner (Austria).
Goal: Eran Zahavi (56).

14.10.2020   SLOVAKIA - ISRAEL   **2-3(2-0)**   2nd UEFA Nations League B, Group 2
Štadión "Antona Malatinského", Trnava; Referee: Alejandro José Hernández Hernández (Spain); Attendance: 0
ISR: Ofir Meir Marciano, Orel Dgani (90+3.Idan Nachmias), Shiran Yeini (46.Ofri Arad), Eytan Tibi, Elazar Dasa, Maor Kandil (69.Shon Weissman), Bibras Natkho (Cap) (58.Neta Lavi), Eyal Golasa, Manor Solomon, Eran Zahavi, Moanes Dabour. Trainer: Willibald Ruttensteiner (Austria).
Goals: Eran Zahavi (68, 76, 89).

15.11.2020   CZECH REPUBLIC - ISRAEL   **1-0(1-0)**   2nd UEFA Nations League B, Group 2
Doosan Arena, Plzeň; Referee: Srđan Jovanović (Serbia); Attendance: 0
ISR: Ofir Meir Marciano, Taleb Tawatha (46.Sun Menahem), Eytan Tibi, Hatem Abd Elhamed [*sent off 81*], Elazar Dasa, Nir Biton, Bibras Natkho (Cap) (46.Neta Lavi), Eyal Golasa (86.Mohammad Abu Fani), Dor Peretz (73.Shon Weissman), Manor Solomon, Eran Zahavi. Trainer: Willibald Ruttensteiner (Austria).

18.11.2020   ISRAEL - SCOTLAND   **1-0(1-0)**   2nd UEFA Nations League B, Group 2
Netanya Stadium, Netanya: Referee: Paweł Raczkowski (Poland); Attendance: 0
ISR: Ofir Meir Marciano, Shiran Yeini (78.Orel Dgani), Eytan Tibi, Elazar Dasa, Sun Menahem, Bibras Natkho (Cap) (62.Eyal Golasa), Nir Biton, Manor Solomon (84.Yonatan Cohen), Eran Zahavi, Shon Weissman, Neta Lavi (78.Mohammad Abu Fani). Trainer: Willibald Ruttensteiner (Austria).
Goal: Manor Solomon (44).

25.03.2021   ISRAEL - DENMARK   **0-2(0-1)**   22nd FIFA WC. Qualifiers
Bloomfield Stadium, Tel Aviv; Referee: Craig Pawson (England); Attendance: 5,000
ISR: Ofir Meir Marciano, Eytan Tibi, Hatem Abd Elhamed, Elazar Dasa (85.Maor Kandil), Joel Abu Hanna (46.Neta Lavi), Bibras Natkho (Cap) (68.Eyal Golasa), Dor Peretz, Manor Solomon, Sun Menahem (85.Dolev Haziza), Moanes Dabour (60.Shon Weissman), Eran Zahavi. Trainer: Willibald Ruttensteiner (Austria).

28.03.2021   ISRAEL - SCOTLAND   **1-1(1-0)**   22nd FIFA WC. Qualifiers
Bloomfield Stadium, Tel Aviv; Referee: Deniz Aytekin (Germany); Attendance: 5,000
ISR: Ofir Meir Marciano, Eytan Tibi, Hatem Abd Elhamed, Elazar Dasa, Sun Menahem (79.Beram Kayal), Ofri Arad, Bibras Natkho (Cap) (63.Neta Lavi), Dor Peretz, Manor Solomon, Eran Zahavi, Shon Weissman (74.Moanes Dabour). Trainer: Willibald Ruttensteiner (Austria).
Goal: Dor Peretz (44).

31.03.2021   MOLDOVA - ISRAEL   **1-4(1-1)**   22nd FIFA WC. Qualifiers
Stadionul Zimbru, Chişinău; Referee: Bojan Pandžić (Sweden); Attendance: 0
ISR: Ofir Meir Marciano, Eytan Tibi (70.Joel Abu Hanna), Loai Taha (58.Mohammad Abu Fani), Sun Menahem (46.Neta Lavi), Ofri Arad, Bibras Natkho (Cap), Elazar Dasa (70.Dolev Haziza), Manor Solomon, Dor Peretz, Eran Zahavi (79.Shon Weissman), Moanes Dabour. Trainer: Willibald Ruttensteiner (Austria).
Goal: Eran Zahavi (45+2), Manor Solomon (57), Moanes Dabour (64), Bibras Natkho (66).

05.06.2021   MONTENEGRO - ISRAEL   **1-3(0-0)**   Friendly International
Stadion pod Goricom, Podgorica; Referee: Irfan Peljto (Bosnia and Herzegovina); Attendance: 860
ISR: Itamar Nizan, Orel Dgani, Eytan Tibi, Ofri Arad (73.Ofir Davidzada), Joel Abu Hanna, Neta Lavi, Elazar Dasa, Manor Solomon (73.Gadi Kinda), Bibras Natkho (Cap) (61.Mohammad Abu Fani), Eran Zahavi (90+2.Aviel Yosef Zargary), Yonas Malede (61.Liel Abada). Trainer: Willibald Ruttensteiner (Austria).
Goals: Eran Zahavi (67), Manor Solomon (69), Gadi Kinda (90+1).

09.06.2021   PORTUGAL - ISRAEL   **4-0(2-0)**   Friendly International
Estádio "José Alvalade", Lisboa; Referee: Jérémie Pignard (France); Attendance: 0
ISR: Ofir Meir Marciano, Eytan Tibi, Orel Dgani (72.Matan Baltaxa), Elazar Dasa (88.Yonas Malede), Sun Menahem (46.Joel Abu Hanna), Ofri Arad, Bibras Natkho (Cap) (61.Mohammad Abu Fani), Gadi Kinda (61.Osama Khalaila), Neta Lavi (88.Aviel Yosef Zargary), Eran Zahavi, Manor Solomon. Trainer: Willibald Ruttensteiner (Austria).

NATIONAL TEAM PLAYERS
(16.07.2020 – 15.07.2021)

Name	DOB	Caps	Goals	2020/2021:	Club
Goalkeepers					
Ofir Meir MARCIANO	07.10.1989	27	0	2020/2021:	*Hibernian FC Edinburgh (SCO)*
Itamar NIZAN	23.06.1987	1	0	2021:	*Beitar Jerusalem FC*
Defenders					
Joel ABU HANNA	22.01.1998	5	0	2020/2021:	*FK Zorya Luhansk (UKR)*
Ofri ARAD	11.09.1998	5	0	2020/2021:	*Maccabi Haifa FC*
Matan BALTAXA	20.09.1995	1	0	2021:	*Maccabi Tel Aviv FC*
Elazar DASA	03.12.1992	37	0	2020/2021:	*SBV Vitesse Arnhem (NED)*
Ofir DAVIDZADA	05.05.1991	12	0	2021:	*Maccabi Tel Aviv FC*
Orel DGANI	08.01.1989	16	0	2020/2021:	*Beitar Jerusalem FC*
Hatem Abd ELHAMED	18.03.1991	12	0	2020: 10.02.2021->	*Celtic FC Glasgow (SCO)* *Hapoel Be'er Sheva FC*
Maor KANDIL	27.11.1993	2	0	2020/2021:	*Maccabi Tel Aviv FC*
Sun MENAHEM	07.09.1993	10	0	2020/2021:	*Maccabi Haifa FC*
Idan NACHMIAS	17.03.1997	1	0	2020:	*Hapoel Ironi Kiryat Shmona FC*
Loai TAHA	26.11.1989	13	0	2021:	*Hapoel Be'er Sheva FC*
Eytan TIBI	16.11.1987	53	1	2020/2021:	*Maccabi Tel Aviv FC*
Taleb TAWATHA	21.06.1992	21	1	2020: 16.10.2020->	*PFC Ludogorets Razgrad (BUL)* *Maccabi Haifa FC*
Shiran YEINI	08.12.1986	32	0	2020:	*Maccabi Tel Aviv FC*
Midfielders					
Mohammad ABU FANI	27.04.1998	7	0	2020/2021:	*Maccabi Haifa FC*
Nir BITON	30.10.1991	32	2	2020:	*Celtic FC Glasgow (SCO)*
Yonatan COHEN	29.06.1996	7	0	2020:	*Maccabi Tel Aviv FC*
Ilay Eliyau ELMKIES	10.03.2000	5	0	2020: 18.09.2020->	*TSG 1899 Hoffenheim (GER)* *ADO Den Haag (NED)*
Dan Leon GLAZER	20.09.1996	8	0	2020:	*Maccabi Tel Aviv FC*
Eyal GOLASA	07.10.1991	17	0	2020/2021:	*Maccabi Tel Aviv FC*
Dolev HAZIZA	05.07.1995	4	0	2021:	*Maccabi Haifa FC*
Eden KARZEV	11.04.2000	1	0	2020:	*Maccabi Tel Aviv FC*
Beram KAYAL	02.05.1988	47	2	2021:	*Bnei Sakhnin FC*
Gadi KINDA	23.03.1994	2	1	2021:	*Sporting Kansas City (USA)*
Neta LAVI	25.08.1996	9	0	2020/2021:	*Maccabi Haifa FC*
Bibras NATKHO	18.02.1988	78	3	2020/2021:	*FK Partizan Beograd (SRB)*
Dor PERETZ	17.05.1995	20	2	2020/2021:	*Maccabi Tel Aviv FC*
Aviel Yosef ZARGARY	11.12.2002	2	0	2021:	*Beitar Jerusalem FC*
Forwards					
Liel ABADA	03.10.2001	1	0	2021:	*Maccabi Petah Tikva FC*
Moanes DABOUR	14.05.1992	29	8	2020/2021:	*TSG 1899 Hoffenheim (GER)*
Osama KHALAILA	06.04.1998	1	0	2021:	*Bnei Sakhnin FC*
Yonas MALEDE	14.11.1999	2	0	2021:	*KAA Gent (BEL)*
Dia SABA	18.11.1992	11	3	2020:	*Al-Nassr FC Riyadh (KSA)*
Manor SOLOMON	24.07.1999	19	3	2020/2021:	*FK Shakhtar Donetsk (UKR)*
Shon WEISSMAN	14.02.1996	14	0	2020/2021:	*Real Valladolid CF (ESP)*
Eran ZAHAVI	25.07.1987	64	26	2020: 20.09.2020->	*Guangzhou R&F FC (CHN)* *PSV Eindhoven (NED)*
Trainer					
Willibald RUTTENSTEINER (Austria) [from 22.07.2020]	12.11.1962	12 M; 4 W; 4 D; 4 L; 15-16			

ITALY

The Country:
Repubblica Italiana (Italian Republic)
Capital: Roma
Surface: 301,338 km²
Inhabitants: 60,317,116 [2020]
Time: UTC+1

The FA:
Federazione Italiana Giuoco Calcio
Via Gregorio Allegri 14, CP 2450 00198, Roma
Tel: +39 06 84 912 553
Foundation date: 1898
Member of FIFA since: 1905
Member of UEFA since: 1954
Website: www.figc.it

NATIONAL TEAM RECORDS

RECORDS
First international match:	15.05.1910, Milano:	Italy – France 6-2
Most international caps:	Gianluigi Buffon	- 176 caps (1997-2018)
Most international goals:	Luigi Riva	- 35 goals / 42 caps (1965-1974)

UEFA EUROPEAN CHAMPIONSHIP	
1960	Did not enter
1964	Qualifiers
1968	**Final Tournament (Winners)**
1972	Qualifiers
1976	Qualifiers
1980	Final Tournament (4th Place)
1984	Qualifiers
1988	Final Tournament (Semi-Finals)
1992	Qualifiers
1996	Final Tournament (Group Stage)
2000	Final Tournament (Runners-up)
2004	Final Tournament (Group Stage)
2008	Final Tournament (Quarter-Finals)
2012	Final Tournament (Runners-up)
2016	Final Tournament (Quarter-Finals)
2020	**Final Tournament (Winners)**

FIFA WORLD CUP	
1930	Did not enter
1934	**Final Tournament (Winners)**
1938	**Final Tournament (Winners)**
1950	Final Tournament (Group Stage)
1954	Final Tournament (Group Stage)
1958	Qualifiers
1962	Final Tournament (Group Stage)
1966	Final Tournament (Group Stage)
1970	Final Tournament (Runners-up)
1974	Final Tournament (Group Stage)
1978	Final Tournament (4th Place)
1982	**Final Tournament (Winners)**
1986	Final Tournament (Second Round of 16)
1990	Final Tournament (3rd Place)
1994	Final Tournament (Runners-up)
1998	Final Tournament (Quarter-Finals)
2002	Final Tournament (Second Round of 16)
2006	**Final Tournament (Winners)**
2010	Final Tournament (Group Stage)
2014	Final Tournament (Group Stage)
2018	Qualifiers

OLYMPIC TOURNAMENTS	
1908	-
1912	Round 1
1920	Quarter-Finals
1924	Quarter-Finals
1928	3rd Place
1936	**Winners**
1948	Quarter-Finals
1952	Round 1
1956	Did not enter
1960	4th Place
1964	Qualifiers
1968	*Withdrew*
1972	Qualifiers
1976	Did not enter
1980	Group Stage
1984	4th Place
1988	4th Place
1992	Quarter-Finals
1996	Group Stage
2000	Quarter-Finals
2004	3rd Place
2008	Quarter-Finals
2012	Qualifiers
2016	Qualifiers

UEFA NATIONS LEAGUE
2018/2019	League A
2020/2021	League A (Qualified for the Final Tournament)

FIFA CONFEDERATIONS CUP 1992-2017
2009 (Group Stage), 2013 (3rd Place)

ITALIAN CLUB HONOURS IN EUROPEAN CLUB COMPETITIONS:

European Champion Clubs' Cup (1956-1992) / UEFA Champions League (1993-2021)		
AC Milan	7	1962/1963, 1968/1969, 1988/1989, 1989/1990, 1993/1994, 2002/2003, 2006/2007
FC Internazionale Milano	3	1963/1964, 1964/1965, 2009/2010
Juventus FC Torino	2	1984/1985, 1995/1996
Fairs Cup (1858-1971) / UEFA Cup (1972-2009) / UEFA Europa League (2010-2021)		
Juventus FC Torino	3	1976/1977, 1989/1990, 1992/1993
FC Internazionale Milano	3	1990/1991, 1993/1994, 1997/1998
AC Parma	2	1994/1995, 1998/1999
AS Roma	1	1960/1961
SSC Napoli	1	1988/1989
UEFA Super Cup (1972-2020)		
AC Milan	5	1989, 1990, 1994, 2003, 2007

Juventus FC Torino	2	1984, 1996	
AC Parma	1	1993	
SS Lazio Roma	1	1999	
European Cup Winners' Cup 1961-1999*			
AC Milan	2	1967/1968, 1972/1973	
AC Fiorentina	1	1960/1961	
Juventus FC Torino	1	1983/1984	
UC Sampdoria Genova	1	1989/1990	
AC Parma	1	1992/1993	

*defunct competition

NATIONAL COMPETITIONS
TABLE OF HONOURS

	CHAMPIONS	CUP WINNERS	BEST GOALSCORERS	
1898	Genoa CFC	-	-	
1899	Genoa CFC	-	-	
1900	Genoa CFC	-	-	
1901	AC Milan	-	-	
1902	Genoa CFC	-	-	
1903	Genoa CFC	-	-	
1904	Genoa CFC	-	-	
1905	Juventus FC Torino	-	-	
1906	AC Milan	-	-	
1907	AC Milan	-	-	
1908	FC Pro Vercelli	-	-	
1909	FC Pro Vercelli	-	-	
1909/1910	FC Internazionale Milano	-	-	
1910/1911	FC Pro Vercelli	-	-	
1911/1912	FC Pro Vercelli	-	-	
1912/1913	FC Pro Vercelli	-	-	
1913/1914	Casale FBC	-	-	
1914/1915	Genoa CFC	-	-	
1915/1916	*No competition*	-	-	
1916/1917	*No competition*	-	-	
1917/1918	*No competition*	-	-	
1918/1919	*No competition*	-	-	
1919/1920	FC Internazionale Milano	-	-	
1920/1921	FC Pro Vercelli	-	-	
1921/1922	USD Novese Novi Ligure (FIGC) FC Pro Vercelli (CCI)	FC Vado	-	
1922/1923	Genoa CFC	*No competition*	-	
1923/1924	Genoa CFC	*No competition*	Heinrich Schönfeld (AUT, FBC Torino)	22
1924/1925	Bologna SC	*No competition*	Mario Magnozzi (AS Livorno Calcio)	19
1925/1926	Juventus FC Torino	*No competition*	Ferenc Hirzer (HUN, Juventus FC Torino)	35
1926/1927	*Not awarded*	*No competition*	Anton Powolny (FC Internazionale Milano)	22
1927/1928	FBC Torino	*No competition*	Julio Libonatti (ARG, FBC Torino)	35
1928/1929	Bologna SC	*No competition*	Gino Rossetti (FBC Torino)	36
1929/1930	Ambrosiana-Inter Milano	*No competition*	Giuseppe Meazza (Ambrosiana-Inter Milano)	31
1930/1931	Juventus FC Torino	*No competition*	Rodolfo Volk (AS Roma)	29
1931/1932	Juventus FC Torino	*No competition*	Pedro Petrone Schiavione (URU, ACF Fiorentina) Angelo Schiavio (Bologna SC)	25
1932/1933	Juventus FC Torino	*No competition*	Felice Placido Borel (Juventus FC Torino)	29
1933/1934	Juventus FC Torino	*No competition*	Felice Placido Borel (Juventus FC Torino)	31
1934/1935	Juventus FC Torino	*No competition*	Enrico Guaita (ARG, AS Roma)	31
1935/1936	Bologna AGC	FBC Torino	Giuseppe Meazza (Ambrosiana-Inter Milano)	25
1936/1937	Bologna AGC	Genoa CFC	Silvio Piola (SS Lazio Roma)	21
1937/1938	Ambrosiana-Inter Milano	Juventus FC Torino	Giuseppe Meazza (Ambrosiana-Inter Milano)	20
1938/1939	Bologna AGC	FC Internazionale Milano	Aldo Boffi (AC Milan) Héctor Puricelli (URU, Bologna AGC)	19
1939/1940	Ambrosiana-Inter Milano	ACF Fiorentina	Aldo Boffi (AC Milan)	24
1940/1941	Bologna AGC	Venezia FBC	Héctor Puricelli (URU, Bologna AGC)	22
1941/1942	AS Roma	Juventus FC Torino	Aldo Boffi (AC Milan)	22
1942/1943	AC Torino	AC Torino	Silvio Piola (SS Lazio Roma)	21
1944	AC Spezia (*honorific title awarded in 2002*)	*No competition*	-	
1944/1945	*No competition*	*No competition*	-	
1945/1946	AC Torino	*No competition*	Guglielmo Gabetto (AC Torino)	22
1946/1947	AC Torino	*No competition*	Valentino Mazzola (AC Torino)	29
1947/1948	AC Torino	*No competition*	Giampiero Boniperti (Juventus FC Torino)	27
1948/1949	AC Torino	*No competition*	István Nyers (HUN, FC Internazionale Milano)	26
1949/1950	Juventus FC Torino	*No competition*	Gunnar Nordahl (SWE, AC Milan)	35
1950/1951	AC Milan	*No competition*	Gunnar Nordahl (SWE, AC Milan)	34
1951/1952	Juventus FC Torino	*No competition*	John Hansen (DEN, Juventus FC Torino)	30

1952/1953	FC Internazionale Milano	*No competition*	Gunnar Nordahl (SWE, AC Milan)	26
1953/1954	FC Internazionale Milano	*No competition*	Gunnar Nordahl (SWE, AC Milan)	23
1954/1955	AC Milan	*No competition*	Gunnar Nordahl (SWE, AC Milan)	26
1955/1956	ACF Fiorentina	*No competition*	Gino Pivatelli (Bologna FC)	29
1956/1957	AC Milan	*No competition*	Dino da Costa (BRA, AS Roma)	22
1957/1958	Juventus FC Torino	SS Lazio Roma	William John Charles (WAL, Juventus FC Torino)	28
1958/1959	AC Milan	Juventus FC Torino	Antonio Valentin Angelillo (ARG, FC Internazionale Milano)	33
1959/1960	Juventus FC Torino	Juventus FC Torino	Enrique Omar Sivori (ARG, Juventus FC Torino)	28
1960/1961	Juventus FC Torino	ACF Fiorentina	Sergio Brighenti (Sampdoria UC Genova)	27
1961/1962	AC Milan	SSC Napoli	José João Altafini "Mazzola" (BRA, AC Milan) Aurelio Milani (ACF Fiorentina)	22
1962/1963	FC Internazionale Milano	Atalanta Bergamasca Calcio	Harald Nielsen (DEN, Bologna FC) Pedro Waldemar Manfredini (ARG, AS Roma)	19
1963/1964	Bologna FC	AS Roma	Harald Nielsen (DEN, Bologna FC)	21
1964/1965	FC Internazionale Milano	Juventus FC Torino	Alessandro Mazzola (FC Internazionale Milano) Alberto Orlando (ACF Fiorentina)	17
1965/1966	FC Internazionale Milano	ACF Fiorentina	Luis Vinicio (Lanerossi Vicenza)	25
1966/1967	Juventus FC Torino	AC Milan	Luigi Riva (US Cagliari)	18
1967/1968	AC Milan	AC Torino	Pierino Prati (AC Milan)	15
1968/1969	ACF Fiorentina	AS Roma	Luigi Riva (US Cagliari)	21
1969/1970	US Cagliari	Bologna FC	Luigi Riva (US Cagliari)	21
1970/1971	FC Internazionale Milano	AC Torino	Roberto Boninsegna (FC Internazionale Milano)	24
1971/1972	Juventus FC Torino	AC Milan	Roberto Boninsegna (FC Internazionale Milano)	22
1972/1973	Juventus FC Torino	AC Milan	Giuseppe Savoldi (Bologna FC) Paolino Pulici (AC Torino) Gianni Rivera (AC Milan)	17
1973/1974	SS Lazio Roma	Bologna FC	Giorgio Chinaglia (SS Lazio Roma)	24
1974/1975	Juventus FC Torino	ACF Fiorentina	Paolino Pulici (AC Torino)	18
1975/1976	AC Torino	SSC Napoli	Paolino Pulici (AC Torino)	21
1976/1977	Juventus FC Torino	AC Milan	Francesco Graziani (AC Torino)	21
1977/1978	Juventus FC Torino	FC Internazionale Milano	Paolo Rossi (Lanerossi Vicenza)	24
1978/1979	AC Milan	Juventus FC Torino	Bruno Giordano (SS Lazio Roma)	19
1979/1980	FC Internazionale Milano	AS Roma	Roberto Bettega (Juventus FC Torino)	16
1980/1981	Juventus FC Torino	AS Roma	Roberto Pruzzo (AS Roma)	18
1981/1982	Juventus FC Torino	FC Internazionale Milano	Roberto Pruzzo (AS Roma)	15
1982/1983	AS Roma	Juventus FC Torino	Michel Platini (FRA, Juventus FC Torino)	16
1983/1984	Juventus FC Torino	AS Roma	Michel Platini (FRA, Juventus FC Torino)	20
1984/1985	AC Hellas Verona	Sampdoria UC Genova	Michel Platini (FRA, Juventus FC Torino)	18
1985/1986	Juventus FC Torino	AS Roma	Roberto Pruzzo (AS Roma)	19
1986/1987	SSC Napoli	SSC Napoli	Pietro Paolo Virdis (AC Milan)	17
1987/1988	AC Milan	Sampdoria UC Genova	Diego Armando Maradona (ARG, SSC Napoli)	15
1988/1989	FC Internazionale Milano	Sampdoria UC Genova	Aldo Serena (FC Internazionale Milano)	22
1989/1990	SSC Napoli	Juventus FC Torino	Marcel van Basten (NED, AC Milan)	19
1990/1991	Sampdoria UC Genova	AS Roma	Gianluca Vialli (Sampdoria UC Genova)	19
1991/1992	AC Milan	AC Parma	Marcel van Basten (NED, AC Milan)	25
1992/1993	AC Milan	Torino Calcio	Giuseppe Signori (SS Lazio Roma)	26
1993/1994	AC Milan	Sampdoria UC Genova	Giuseppe Signori (SS Lazio Roma)	23
1994/1995	Juventus FC Torino	Juventus FC Torino	Gabriel Omar Batistuta (ARG, ACF Fiorentina)	26
1995/1996	AC Milan	ACF Fiorentina	Igor Protti (AS Bari) Giuseppe Signori (SS Lazio Roma)	24
1996/1997	Juventus FC Torino	Vicenza Calcio	Filippo Inzaghi (Atalanta Bergamasca Calcio)	24
1997/1998	Juventus FC Torino	SS Lazio Roma	Oliver Bierhoff (GER, Udinese Calcio)	27
1998/1999	AC Milan	AC Parma	Márcio Amoroso dos Santos (BRA, Udinese Calcio)	22
1999/2000	SS Lazio Roma	SS Lazio Roma	Andriy Shevchenko (UKR, AC Milan)	24
2000/2001	AS Roma	ACF Fiorentina	Hernán Jorge Crespo (ARG, SS Lazio Roma)	26
2001/2002	Juventus FC Torino	AC Parma	David Sergio Trezeguet (FRA, Juventus FC Torino) Dario Hübner (Piacenza Calcio)	24
2002/2003	Juventus FC Torino	AC Milan	Christian Vieri (FC Internazionale Milano)	24
2003/2004	AC Milan	SS Lazio Roma	Andriy Shevchenko (UKR, AC Milan)	24
2004/2005	*Not awarded*	FC Internazionale Milano	Cristiano Lucarelli (AS Livorno Calcio)	24
2005/2006	FC Internazionale Milano	FC Internazionale Milano	Luca Toni (ACF Fiorentina)	31
2006/2007	FC Internazionale Milano	AS Roma	Francesco Totti (AS Roma)	26
2007/2008	FC Internazionale Milano	AS Roma	Alessandro Del Piero (Juventus FC Torino)	21
2008/2009	FC Internazionale Milano	SS Lazio Roma	Zlatan Ibrahimović (SWE, FC Internazionale Milano)	25
2009/2010	FC Internazionale Milano	FC Internazionale Milano	Antonio Di Natale (Udinese Calcio)	29
2010/2011	AC Milan	FC Internazionale Milano	Antonio Di Natale (Udinese Calcio)	28
2011/2012	Juventus FC Torino	SSC Napoli	Zlatan Ibrahimović (SWE, AC Milan)	28
2012/2013	Juventus FC Torino	SS Lazio Roma	Edinson Roberto Cavani Gómez (URU, SSC Napoli)	29
2013/2014	Juventus FC Torino	SSC Napoli	Ciro Immobile (Torino FC)	22
2014/2015	Juventus FC Torino	Juventus FC Torino	Mauro Emanuel Icardi (ARG, FC Internazionale Milano) Luca Toni (Hellas Verona FC)	22
2015/2016	Juventus FC Torino	Juventus FC Torino	Gonzalo Gerardo Higuaín (ARG, SSC Napoli)	36
2016/2017	Juventus FC Torino	Juventus FC Torino	Edin Džeko (BIH, AS Roma)	29
2017/2018	Juventus FC Torino	Juventus FC Torino	Mauro Emanuel Icardi (ARG, FC Internazionale Milano) Ciro Immobile (SS Lazio Roma)	29
2018/2019	Juventus FC Torino	SS Lazio Roma	Fabio Quagliarella (Sampdoria UC Genova)	26
2019/2020	Juventus FC Torino	SSC Napoli	Ciro Immobile (SS Lazio Roma)	36

NATIONAL CHAMPIONSHIP
Serie A 2020/2021
(19.09.2020 – 23.05.2021)

Results

Round 1 [19-21.09.2020]
Fiorentina - Torino FC 1-0(0-0)
Hellas Verona - AS Roma 3-0 *awarded*
Parma - SSC Napoli 0-2(0-0)
Genoa CFC - FC Crotone 4-1(3-1)
US Sassuolo - Cagliari 1-1(0-0)
Juventus - Sampdoria 3-0(1-0)
AC Milan - Bologna FC 2-0(1-0)
Benevento - Internazionale 2-5(1-4) [30.09.]
Udinese - Spezia 0-2(0-1) [30.09.]
Lazio Roma - Atalanta 1-4(0-3) [30.09.]

Round 2 [26-28.09.2020]
Torino FC - Atalanta 2-4(2-3)
Cagliari - Lazio Roma 0-2(0-1)
Sampdoria - Benevento 2-3(2-1)
Internazionale - Fiorentina 4-3(1-1)
Spezia - US Sassuolo 1-4(1-1)
Hellas Verona - Udinese 1-0(0-0)
FC Crotone - AC Milan 0-2(0-1)
SSC Napoli - Genoa CFC 6-0(1-0)
AS Roma - Juventus 2-2(2-1)
Bologna FC - Parma 4-1(2-0)

Round 3 [02-04.10.2020]
Fiorentina - Sampdoria 1-2(0-1)
US Sassuolo - FC Crotone 4-1(1-0)
Udinese - AS Roma 0-1(0-0)
Atalanta - Cagliari 5-2(4-1)
Benevento - Bologna FC 1-0(0-0)
Lazio Roma - Internazionale 1-1(0-1)
Parma - Hellas Verona 1-0(1-0)
AC Milan - Spezia 3-0(0-0)
Genoa CFC - Torino FC 1-2(0-2) [04.11.]
Juventus - SSC Napoli 2-1(1-0) [07.04.2021]

Round 4 [17-19.10.2020]
SSC Napoli - Atalanta 4-1(4-0)
Internazionale - AC Milan 1-2(1-2)
Sampdoria - Lazio Roma 3-0(2-0)
FC Crotone - Juventus 1-1(1-1)
Bologna FC - US Sassuolo 3-4(2-1)
Spezia - Fiorentina 2-2(1-2)
Torino FC - Cagliari 2-3(1-2)
Udinese - Parma 3-2(1-1)
AS Roma - Benevento 5-2(2-1)
Hellas Verona - Genoa CFC 0-0

Round 5 [23-26.10.2020]
US Sassuolo - Torino FC 3-3(0-1)
Atalanta - Sampdoria 1-3(0-1)
Genoa CFC - Internazionale 0-2(0-0)
Lazio Roma - Bologna FC 2-1(0-0)
Cagliari - FC Crotone 4-2(3-2)
Benevento - SSC Napoli 1-2(1-0)
Parma - Spezia 2-2(1-2)
Fiorentina - Udinese 3-2(2-1)
Juventus - Hellas Verona 1-1(0-0)
AC Milan - AS Roma 3-3(1-1)

Round 6 [31.10.-02.11.2020]
FC Crotone - Atalanta 1-2(1-2)
Internazionale - Parma 2-2(0-0)
Bologna FC - Cagliari 3-2(1-1)
Udinese - AC Milan 1-2(0-1)
Spezia - Juventus 1-4(1-1)
Torino FC - Lazio Roma 3-4(2-1)
SSC Napoli - US Sassuolo 0-2(0-0)
AS Roma - Fiorentina 2-0(1-0)
Sampdoria - Genoa CFC 1-1(1-1)
Hellas Verona - Benevento 3-1(1-0)

Round 7 [06-08.11.2020]
US Sassuolo - Udinese 0-0
Cagliari - Sampdoria 2-0(0-0)
Benevento - Spezia 0-3(0-1)
Parma - Fiorentina 0-0
Lazio Roma - Juventus 1-1(0-1)
Atalanta - Internazionale 1-1(0-0)
Genoa CFC - AS Roma 1-3(0-1)
Torino FC - FC Crotone 0-0
Bologna FC - SSC Napoli 0-1(0-1)
AC Milan - Hellas Verona 2-2(1-2)

Round 8 [21-22.11.2020]
FC Crotone - Lazio Roma 0-2(0-1)
Spezia - Atalanta 0-0
Juventus - Cagliari 2-0(2-0)
Fiorentina - Benevento 0-1(0-0)
Internazionale - Torino FC 4-2(0-1)
AS Roma - Parma 3-0(3-0)
Sampdoria - Bologna FC 1-2(1-1)
Hellas Verona - US Sassuolo 0-2(0-1)
Udinese - Genoa CFC 1-0(1-0)
SSC Napoli - AC Milan 1-3(0-1)

Round 9 [28-30.11.2020]
US Sassuolo - Internazionale 0-3(0-2)
Benevento - Juventus 1-1(1-1)
Atalanta - Hellas Verona 0-2(0-0)
Lazio Roma - Udinese 1-3(0-2)
Bologna FC - FC Crotone 1-0(1-0)
AC Milan - Fiorentina 2-0(2-0)
Cagliari - Spezia 2-2(0-1)
SSC Napoli - AS Roma 4-0(1-0)
Torino FC - Sampdoria 2-2(1-0)
Genoa CFC - Parma 1-2(0-1)

Round 10 [05-07.12.2020]
Spezia - Lazio Roma 1-2(0-2)
Juventus - Torino FC 2-1(0-1)
Internazionale - Bologna FC 3-1(2-0)
Hellas Verona - Cagliari 1-1(1-0)
Parma - Benevento 0-0
AS Roma - US Sassuolo 0-0
FC Crotone - SSC Napoli 0-4(0-1)
Sampdoria - AC Milan 1-2(0-1)
Fiorentina - Genoa CFC 1-1(0-0)
Udinese - Atalanta 1-1(1-1) [20.01.2021]

Round 11 [11-13.12.2020]
US Sassuolo - Benevento 1-0(1-0)
FC Crotone - Spezia 4-1(1-1)
Torino FC - Udinese 2-3(0-1)
Lazio Roma - Hellas Verona 1-2(0-1)
Cagliari - Internazionale 1-3(1-0)
Atalanta - Fiorentina 3-0(1-0)
Bologna FC - AS Roma 1-5(1-5)
SSC Napoli - Sampdoria 2-1(0-1)
Genoa CFC - Juventus 1-3(0-0)
AC Milan - Parma 2-2(0-1)

Round 12 [15-17.12.2020]
Udinese - FC Crotone 0-0
Benevento - Lazio Roma 1-1(1-1)
Juventus - Atalanta 1-1(1-0)
Fiorentina - US Sassuolo 1-1(1-1)
Genoa CFC - AC Milan 2-2(0-0)
Internazionale - SSC Napoli 1-0(0-0)
Parma - Cagliari 0-0
Spezia - Bologna FC 2-2(1-0)
Hellas Verona - Sampdoria 1-2(0-1)
AS Roma - Torino FC 3-1(2-0)

Round 13 [19-20.12.2020]
Fiorentina - Hellas Verona 1-1(1-1)
Sampdoria - FC Crotone 3-1(2-1)
Parma - Juventus 0-4(0-2)
Torino FC - Bologna FC 1-1(0-0)
Benevento - Genoa CFC 2-0(0-0)
Cagliari - Udinese 1-1(1-0)
Internazionale - Spezia 2-1(0-0)
US Sassuolo - AC Milan 1-2(0-2)
Atalanta - AS Roma 4-1(0-1)
Lazio Roma - SSC Napoli 2-0(1-0)

Round 14 [22-23.12.2020]
FC Crotone - Parma 2-1(2-0)
Juventus - Fiorentina 0-3(0-1)
Hellas Verona - Internazionale 1-2(0-0)
Bologna FC - Atalanta 2-2(0-2)
AC Milan - Lazio Roma 3-2(2-1)
SSC Napoli - Torino FC 1-1(0-0)
AS Roma - Cagliari 3-2(1-0)
Sampdoria - US Sassuolo 2-3(0-1)
Spezia - Genoa CFC 1-2(1-1)
Udinese - Benevento 0-2(0-1)

Round 15 [03.01.2021]
Internazionale - FC Crotone 6-2(2-2)
Atalanta - US Sassuolo 5-1(2-0)
Cagliari - SSC Napoli 1-4(0-1)
Fiorentina - Bologna FC 0-0
Genoa CFC - Lazio Roma 1-1(0-1)
Parma - Torino FC 0-3(0-1)
AS Roma - Sampdoria 1-0(0-0)
Spezia - Hellas Verona 0-1(0-0)
Benevento - AC Milan 0-2(0-1)
Juventus - Udinese 4-1(1-0)

Round 16 [06.01.2021]
Cagliari - Benevento 1-2(1-2)
Atalanta - Parma 3-0(1-0)
Bologna FC - Udinese 2-2(2-1)
FC Crotone - AS Roma 1-3(0-3)
Lazio Roma - Fiorentina 2-1(1-0)
Sampdoria - Internazionale 2-1(2-0)
US Sassuolo - Genoa CFC 2-1(0-0)
Torino FC - Hellas Verona 1-1(0-0)
SSC Napoli - Spezia 1-2(0-0)
AC Milan - Juventus 1-3(1-1)

Round 17 [09-11.01.2021]
Benevento - Atalanta 1-4(0-1)
Genoa CFC - Bologna FC 2-0(1-0)
AC Milan - Torino FC 2-0(2-0)
AS Roma - Internazionale 2-2(1-0)
Parma - Lazio Roma 0-2(0-0)
Udinese - SSC Napoli 1-2(1-1)
Hellas Verona - FC Crotone 2-1(2-0)
Fiorentina - Cagliari 1-0(0-0)
Juventus - US Sassuolo 3-1(0-0)
Spezia - Sampdoria 2-1(1-1)

Round 18 [15-18.01.2021]
Lazio Roma - AS Roma 3-0(2-0)
Bologna FC - Hellas Verona 1-0(1-0)
Torino FC - Spezia 0-0
Sampdoria - Udinese 2-1(0-0)
SSC Napoli - Fiorentina 6-0(4-0)
FC Crotone - Benevento 4-1(2-0)
US Sassuolo - Parma 1-1(0-1)
Atalanta - Genoa CFC 0-0
Internazionale - Juventus 2-0(1-0)
Cagliari - AC Milan 0-2(0-1)

Round 19 [22-24.01.2021]
Benevento - Torino FC 2-2(1-0)
AS Roma - Spezia 4-3(1-1)
AC Milan - Atalanta 0-3(0-1)
Udinese - Internazionale 0-0
Fiorentina - FC Crotone 2-1(2-0)
Juventus - Bologna FC 2-0(1-0)
Genoa CFC - Cagliari 1-0(1-0)
Hellas Verona - SSC Napoli 3-1(1-1)
Lazio Roma - US Sassuolo 2-1(1-1)
Parma - Sampdoria 0-2(0-2)

Round 20 [29-31.01.2021]
Torino FC - Fiorentina 1-1(0-0)
Bologna FC - AC Milan 1-2(0-1)
Sampdoria - Juventus 0-2(0-1)
Internazionale - Benevento 4-0(1-0)
Spezia - Udinese 0-1(0-0)
FC Crotone - Genoa CFC 0-3(0-2)
Atalanta - Lazio Roma 1-3(0-1)
Cagliari - US Sassuolo 1-1(0-0)
SSC Napoli - Parma 2-0(1-0)
AS Roma - Hellas Verona 3-1(3-0)

Round 21 [05-07.02.2021]
Fiorentina - Internazionale 0-2(0-1)
US Sassuolo - Spezia 1-2(1-1)
Atalanta - Torino FC 3-3(3-2)
Juventus - AS Roma 2-0(1-0)
Genoa CFC - SSC Napoli 2-1(2-0)
Benevento - Sampdoria 1-1(0-0)
AC Milan - FC Crotone 4-0(1-0)
Udinese - Hellas Verona 2-0(0-0)
Parma - Bologna FC 0-3(0-2)
Lazio Roma - Cagliari 1-0(0-0)

Round 22 [12-15.02.2021]
Bologna FC - Benevento 1-1(1-0)
Torino FC - Genoa CFC 0-0
SSC Napoli - Juventus 1-0(1-0)
Spezia - AC Milan 2-0(0-0)
AS Roma - Udinese 3-0(2-0)
Cagliari - Atalanta 0-1(0-0)
Sampdoria - Fiorentina 2-1(1-1)
FC Crotone - US Sassuolo 1-2(1-1)
Internazionale - Lazio Roma 3-1(2-0)
Hellas Verona - Parma 2-1(1-1)

Round 23 [19-22.02.2021]
Fiorentina - Spezia 3-0(0-0)
Cagliari - Torino FC 0-1(0-0)
Lazio Roma - Sampdoria 1-0(1-0)
Genoa CFC - Hellas Verona 2-2(0-1)
US Sassuolo - Bologna FC 1-1(0-1)
Parma - Udinese 2-2(2-0)
AC Milan - Internazionale 0-3(0-1)
Atalanta - SSC Napoli 4-2(0-0)
Benevento - AS Roma 0-0
Juventus - FC Crotone 3-0(2-0)

Round 24 [27-28.02.2021]
Spezia - Parma 2-2(0-2)
Bologna FC - Lazio Roma 2-0(1-0)
Hellas Verona - Juventus 1-1(0-0)
Sampdoria - Atalanta 0-2(0-1)
FC Crotone - Cagliari 0-2(0-0)
Udinese - Fiorentina 1-0(0-0)
Internazionale - Genoa CFC 3-0(1-0)
SSC Napoli - Benevento 2-0(1-0)
AS Roma - AC Milan 1-2(0-1)
Torino FC - US Sassuolo 3-2(0-2) [17.03.]

Round 25 [02-04.03.2021]
Juventus - Spezia 3-0(0-0)
US Sassuolo - SSC Napoli 3-3(2-1)
Cagliari - Bologna FC 1-0(1-0)
Atalanta - FC Crotone 5-1(1-1)
Fiorentina - AS Roma 1-2(0-0)
AC Milan - Udinese 1-1(0-0)
Benevento - Hellas Verona 0-3(0-2)
Genoa CFC - Sampdoria 1-1(0-0)
Parma - Internazionale 1-2(0-0)
Lazio Roma - Torino FC 0-0 [18.05.]

Round 26 [06-08.03.2021]
Spezia - Benevento 1-1(0-1)
Udinese - US Sassuolo 2-0(1-0)
Juventus - Lazio Roma 3-1(1-1)
AS Roma - Genoa CFC 1-0(1-0)
Hellas Verona - AC Milan 0-2(0-1)
Fiorentina - Parma 3-3(2-1)
FC Crotone - Torino FC 4-2(1-1)
Sampdoria - Cagliari 2-2(0-1)
SSC Napoli - Bologna FC 3-1(1-0)
Internazionale - Atalanta 1-0(0-0)

Round 27 [12-14.03.2021]
Lazio Roma - FC Crotone 3-2(2-1)
Atalanta - Spezia 3-1(0-0)
US Sassuolo - Hellas Verona 3-2(1-1)
Benevento - Fiorentina 1-4(0-3)
Genoa CFC - Udinese 1-1(1-1)
Bologna FC - Sampdoria 3-1(2-1)
Torino FC - Internazionale 1-2(0-0)
Parma - AS Roma 2-0(1-0)
Cagliari - Juventus 1-3(0-3)
AC Milan - SSC Napoli 0-1(0-0)

Round 28 [19-21.03.2021]
Parma - Genoa CFC 1-2(1-0)
FC Crotone - Bologna FC 2-3(2-0)
Spezia - Cagliari 2-1(0-0)
Hellas Verona - Atalanta 0-2(0-2)
Juventus - Benevento 0-1(0-0)
Udinese - Lazio Roma 0-1(0-1)
Sampdoria - Torino FC 1-0(1-0)
Fiorentina - AC Milan 2-3(1-1)
AS Roma - SSC Napoli 0-2(0-2)
Internazionale - US Sassuolo 2-1(1-0) [07.04.]

Round 29 [03.04.2021]
AC Milan - Sampdoria 1-1(0-0)
SSC Napoli - FC Crotone 4-3(3-1)
Genoa CFC - Fiorentina 1-1(1-1)
Benevento - Parma 2-2(1-0)
US Sassuolo - AS Roma 2-2(0-1)
Lazio Roma - Spezia 2-1(0-0)
Atalanta - Udinese 3-2(2-1)
Cagliari - Hellas Verona 0-2(0-0)
Torino FC - Juventus 2-2(1-1)
Bologna FC - Internazionale 0-1(0-1)

Round 30 [10-12.04.2021]
Spezia - FC Crotone 3-2(0-1)
Parma - AC Milan 1-3(0-2)
Udinese - Torino FC 0-0
Internazionale - Cagliari 1-0(0-0)
Juventus - Genoa CFC 3-1(2-0)
Hellas Verona - Lazio Roma 0-1(0-0)
Sampdoria - SSC Napoli 0-2(0-1)
AS Roma - Bologna FC 1-0(1-0)
Fiorentina - Atalanta 2-3(0-2)
Benevento - US Sassuolo 0-1(0-1)

Round 31 [17-18.04.2021]
FC Crotone - Udinese 1-2(0-1)
Sampdoria - Hellas Verona 3-1(0-1)
US Sassuolo - Fiorentina 3-1(0-1)
Cagliari - Parma 4-3(1-2)
AC Milan - Genoa CFC 2-1(1-1)
Lazio Roma - Benevento 5-3(3-1)
Atalanta - Juventus 1-0(0-0)
Bologna FC - Spezia 4-1(2-1)
Torino FC - AS Roma 3-1(0-1)
SSC Napoli - Internazionale 1-1(1-0)

Round 32 [20-22.04.2021]
Hellas Verona - Fiorentina 1-2(0-1)
AC Milan - US Sassuolo 1-2(1-0)
Genoa CFC - Benevento 2-2(2-2)
Udinese - Cagliari 0-1(0-0)
Spezia - Internazionale 1-1(1-1)
Juventus - Parma 3-1(1-1)
FC Crotone - Sampdoria 0-1(0-0)
Bologna FC - Torino FC 1-1(1-0)
AS Roma - Atalanta 1-1(1-0)
SSC Napoli - Lazio Roma 5-2(2-0)

Round 33 [24-26.04.2021]
Genoa CFC - Spezia 2-0(0-0)
Parma - FC Crotone 3-4(1-3)
US Sassuolo - Sampdoria 1-0(0-0)
Benevento - Udinese 2-4(1-2)
Fiorentina - Juventus 1-1(1-0)
Internazionale - Hellas Verona 1-0(0-0)
Cagliari - AS Roma 3-2(1-1)
Atalanta - Bologna FC 5-0(2-0)
Torino FC - SSC Napoli 0-2(0-2)
Lazio Roma - AC Milan 3-0(1-0)

Round 34 [01-03.05.2021]
Hellas Verona - Spezia 1-1(0-0)
FC Crotone - Internazionale 0-2(0-0)
AC Milan - Benevento 2-0(1-0)
Lazio Roma - Genoa CFC 4-3(2-0)
US Sassuolo - Atalanta 1-1(0-1)
SSC Napoli - Cagliari 1-1(1-0)
Bologna FC - Fiorentina 3-3(1-1)
Udinese - Juventus 1-2(1-0)
Sampdoria - AS Roma 2-0(1-0)
Torino FC - Parma 1-0(0-0)

Round 35 [08-09.05.2021]
Udinese - Bologna FC 1-1(1-0)
Spezia - SSC Napoli 1-4(0-3)
Internazionale - Sampdoria 5-1(3-1)
Fiorentina - Lazio Roma 2-0(1-0)
Genoa CFC - US Sassuolo 1-2(0-1)
Parma - Atalanta 2-5(0-1)
Benevento - Cagliari 1-3(1-1)
Hellas Verona - Torino FC 1-1(0-0)
AS Roma - FC Crotone 5-0(0-0)
Juventus - AC Milan 0-3(0-1)

Round 36 [11-13.05.2021]
SSC Napoli - Udinese 5-1(2-1)
Cagliari - Fiorentina 0-0
Atalanta - Benevento 2-0(1-0)
Bologna FC - Genoa CFC 0-2(0-1)
US Sassuolo - Juventus 1-3(0-2)
Torino FC - AC Milan 0-7(0-2)
Lazio Roma - Parma 1-0(0-0)
Internazionale - AS Roma 3-1(2-1)
Sampdoria - Spezia 2-2(1-1)
FC Crotone - Hellas Verona 2-1(1-0)

Round 37 [15-17.05.2021]
Genoa CFC - Atalanta 3-4(0-3)
Spezia - Torino FC 4-1(2-0)
Juventus - Internazionale 3-2(2-1)
AS Roma - Lazio Roma 2-0(1-0)
Fiorentina - SSC Napoli 0-2(0-0)
Benevento - FC Crotone 1-1(1-0)
Udinese - Sampdoria 0-1(0-0)
Parma - US Sassuolo 1-3(1-1)
AC Milan - Cagliari 0-0
Hellas Verona - Bologna FC 2-2(1-1)

Round 38 [22-23.05.2021]
FC Crotone - Fiorentina 0-0
Cagliari - Genoa CFC 0-1(0-1)
Sampdoria - Parma 3-0(2-0)
Internazionale - Udinese 5-1(2-0)
Torino FC - Benevento 1-1(1-0)
Bologna FC - Juventus 1-4(0-3)
US Sassuolo - Lazio Roma 2-0(1-0)
Atalanta - AC Milan 0-2(0-1)
Spezia - AS Roma 2-2(2-0)
SSC Napoli - Hellas Verona 1-1(0-0)

Final Standings

								Total			Home					Away			
1.	FC Internazionale Milano	38	28	7	3	89	-	35	91	17	1	1	53 - 18	11	6	2	36 - 17
2.	AC Milan	38	24	7	7	74	-	41	79	8	6	5	31 - 24	16	1	2	43 - 17
3.	Atalanta Bergamasca Calcio	38	23	9	6	90	-	47	78	12	3	4	49 - 24	11	6	2	41 - 23
4.	Juventus FC Torino	38	23	9	6	77	-	38	78	14	2	3	40 - 18	9	7	3	37 - 20
5.	SSC Napoli	38	24	5	9	86	-	41	77	12	4	3	50 - 20	12	1	6	36 - 21
6.	SS Lazio Roma	38	21	5	12	61	-	55	68	13	3	3	36 - 23	8	2	9	25 - 32
7.	AS Roma	38	18	8	12	68	-	58	62	13	4	2	42 - 18	5	4	10	26 - 40
8.	US Sassuolo Calcio	38	17	11	10	64	-	56	62	7	8	4	31 - 27	10	3	6	33 - 29
9.	Sampdoria UC Genova	38	15	7	16	52	-	54	52	9	3	7	32 - 26	6	4	9	20 - 28
10.	Hellas Verona FC	38	11	12	15	46	-	48	45	6	6	7	23 - 23	5	6	8	23 - 25
11.	Genoa C&FC	38	10	12	16	47	-	58	42	5	7	7	29 - 30	5	5	9	18 - 28
12.	Bologna FC 1909	38	10	11	17	51	-	65	41	7	5	7	33 - 33	3	6	10	18 - 32
13.	ACF Fiorentina	38	9	13	16	47	-	59	40	6	6	7	25 - 25	3	7	9	22 - 34
14.	Udinese Calcio	38	10	10	18	42	-	58	40	5	4	10	14 - 19	5	6	8	28 - 39
15.	Spezia Calcio La Spezia	38	9	12	17	52	-	72	39	5	7	7	28 - 33	4	5	10	24 - 39
16.	Cagliari Calcio	38	9	10	19	43	-	59	37	5	4	10	22 - 32	4	6	9	21 - 27
17.	Torino FC	38	7	16	15	50	-	69	37	3	9	7	25 - 36	4	7	8	25 - 33
18.	Benevento Calcio (*Relegated*)	38	7	12	19	40	-	75	33	2	7	10	19 - 39	5	5	9	21 - 36
19.	FC Crotone (*Relegated*)	38	6	5	27	45	-	92	23	5	2	12	23 - 35	1	3	15	22 - 57
20.	Parma Calcio 1913 (*Relegated*)	38	3	11	24	39	-	83	20	2	5	12	16 - 39	1	6	12	23 - 44

Top goalscorers:

29	**Cristiano Ronaldo dos Santos Aveiro (POR)**	*Juventus FC Torino*
24	Romelu Menama Lukaku Bolingoli (BEL)	*FC Internazionale Milano*
22	Luis Fernando Muriel Fruito (COL)	*Atalanta Bergamasca Calcio*
21	Dušan Vlahović (SRB)	*ACF Fiorentina*
20	Ciro Immobile	*SS Lazio Roma*
20	Simeon Tochukwu Nwankwo (NGA)	*FC Crotone*
19	Lorenzo Insigne	*SSC Napoli*
17	Domenico Berardi	*US Sassuolo Calcio*

NATIONAL CUP
Coppa Italia 2020/2021

First Round [22-23.09.2020]

FC Südtirol Bolzano – SSD Sassari Calcio L. Dolce	2-1(2-0)		US Catanzaro 1929 - Virtus Francavilla Calcio	2-1(2-1)
Ternana Calcio - UC AlbinoLeffe	1-2(0-2)		SSC Bari - ASD Trastevere Calcio	4-0(3-0)
Piacenza Calcio 1919 - SS Teramo Calcio	1-2(1-2)		AC Renate - US Avellino 1912	2-1(1-0)
Carpi FC 1909 - SSD Casarano Calcio	1-3(0-1,1-1)		SS Juve Stabia - Tritium Calcio 1908	2-1(1-0)
US Alessandria Calcio 1912 - SS Sambenedettese	3-2(2-1)		Feralpisalò - ASD Pineto Calcio	1-0(1-0)
Novara Calcio - ASD Gelbison Cilento	3-1(2-1)		Potenza Calcio - US Triestina Calcio 1918	0-2(0-2)
US Città di Pontedera - SS Arezzo	1-2(0-0)		Calcio Padova - US Breno	2-0(1-0)
Carrarese Calcio 1908 - GSD Ambrosiana	4-0(3-0)		SS Monopoli 1966 - Modena FC 2018	1-0(0-0)
AS Livorno Calcio - Aurora Pro Patria 1919	1-2(0-1)		Calcio Catania – SSD San Nicolò Calcio	1-2(1-0,1-1)

Second Round [29-30.09.2020]

AC Monza - US Triestina Calcio 1918	3-0(1-0)		Ascoli Calcio 1898 FC - AC Perugia Calcio	1-4(0-3)
Reggina 1914 - SS Teramo Calcio	1-0(1-0)		LR Vicenza - Aurora Pro Patria 1919	3-2(1-1,1-1)
US Cremonese - SS Arezzo	4-0(0-0)		Venezia FC - Carrarese Calcio 1908	2-0(0-0)
Cosenza Calcio - US Alessandria Calcio 1912	0-0 aet; 3-1 pen		AC Reggiana 1919 - SS Monopoli 1966	0-3 awarded
AS Cittadella - Novara Calcio	3-1(1-0)		US Lecce - Feralpisalò	2-0(0-0)
Frosinone Calcio - Calcio Padova	1-3(1-3)		Pordenone Calcio - SSD Casarano Calcio	3-0(2-0)
AC Pisa 1909 - SS Juve Stabia	2-0(1-0)		US Salernitana 1919 - FC Südtirol Bolzano	3-0(0-0)
Delfino Pescara 1936 - SSD San Nicolò Calcio	1-1 aet; 8-7 pen		AC Chievo Verona - US Catanzaro 1929	1-1 aet; 6-7 pen
Virtus Entella - UC AlbinoLeffe	2-1(2-0)		Brescia Calcio - Trapani Calcio	3-0 awarded
Empoli FC - AC Renate	2-1(1-0)		SPAL Ferrara - SSC Bari	0-0 aet; 4-2 pen

Third Round [27-28.10.2020]

UC Sampdoria Genova - US Salernitana 1919	1-0(0-0)		Benevento Calcio - Empoli FC	2-4(0-0)
Bologna FC - Reggina 1914	2-0(1-0)		Brescia Calcio - AC Perugia Calcio	3-0(2-0)
Virtus Entella - AC Pisa 1909	3-1(1-0)		Hellas Verona FC - Venezia FC	3-3 aet; 3-1 pen
Pordenone Calcio - AC Monza	0-0 aet; 1-4 pen		FC Crotone - SPAL Ferrara	1-1 aet; 3-4 pen
Torino FC - US Lecce	3-1(1-1,1-1)		Genoa C&FC - US Catanzaro 1929	2-1(1-0)
Cagliari Calcio - US Cremonese	1-0(0-0)		ACF Fiorentina - Calcio Padova	2-1(2-0)
Cosenza Calcio - SS Monopoli 1966	2-1(1-0)		Parma Calcio 1913 - Delfino Pescara 1936	3-1(2-0)
AS Cittadella - Spezia Calcio	0-2(0-0)		Udinese Calcio - LR Vicenza	3-1(1-0)

Fourth Round [24-26.11.2020]

SPAL Ferrara - AC Monza	2-0(0-0)		Bologna FC 1909 - Spezia Calcio	2-4(2-1,2-2)
Empoli FC - Brescia Calcio	3-0 awarded		Udinese Calcio - ACF Fiorentina	0-1(0-0,0-0)
Parma Calcio 1913 - Cosenza Calcio	2-1(2-1)		Torino FC - Virtus Entella	2-0(2-0)
Cagliari Calcio - Hellas Verona FC	2-1(1-0)		UC Sampdoria Genova - Genoa C&FC	1-3(1-0)

1/8-Finals [12-14/19/21.01.2021]

AC Milan - Torino FC	0-0 aet; 5-4 pen		Sassuolo Calcio - SPAL Ferrara	0-2(0-0)
ACF Fiorentina – FC Internazionale Milano	1-2(0-1,1-1)		Atalanta Bergamasca Calcio - Cagliari Calcio	3-1(1-0)
SSC Napoli - Empoli FC	3-2(2-1)		AS Roma - Spezia Calcio La Spezia	0-3 awarded
Juventus FC Torino - Genoa C&FC	3-2(2-1,2-2)		SS Lazio Roma - Parma Calcio 1913	2-1(1-0)

Quarter-Finals [26-28.01.2021]

FC Internazionale Milano - AC Milan	2-1(0-1)		Juventus FC Torino - SPAL Ferrara	4-0(2-0)
Atalanta Bergamasca Calcio - SS Lazio Roma	3-2(2-2)		SSC Napoli - Spezia Calcio La Spezia	4-2(4-0)

Semi-Finals 02-03.02./09-10.02.2021 [ ]

First Leg			Second Leg	
FC Internazionale Milano - Juventus FC Torino	1-2(1-2)		Juventus FC Torino - FC Internazionale Milano	0-0
SSC Napoli - Atalanta Bergamasca Calcio	0-0		Atalanta Bergamasca Calcio - SSC Napoli	3-1(2-0)

Final

19.05.2021; Mappei Stadium – Città del Tricolore, Reggio Emilia; Referee: Davide Massa; Attendance: 4,300

Juventus FC Torino - Atalanta Bergamasca Calcio　　　　　　　　　　　**2-1(1-1)**

Juventus: Gianluigi Buffon, Juan Guillermo Cuadrado Bello, Matthijs de Ligt, Giorgio Chiellini (Cap), Danilo Luiz da Silva, Weston James Earl McKennie, Rodrigo Bentancur Colmán, Adrien Rabiot-Provost, Federico Chiesa (74.Paulo Bruno Exequiel Dybala), Dejan Kulusevski (83.Leonardo Bonucci), Cristiano Ronaldo dos Santos Aveiro. Trainer: Andrea Pirlo.

Atalanta: Pierluigi Gollini, Rafael Tolói (Cap) [sent off 88], Cristian Gabriel Romero, José Luis Palomino, Hans Hateboer (76.Josip Iličič), Remo Freuler, Marten Elco de Roon, Robin Gosens (83.Aleksey Miranchuk), Ruslan Malinovskiy (68.Mario Pašalić), Matteo Pessina (68.Luis Fernando Muriel Fruito), Duván Esteban Zapata Banguero. Trainer: Gian Piero Gasperini.

Goals: 1-0 Dejan Kulusevski (31), 1-1 Ruslan Malinovskiy (41), 2-1 Federico Chiesa (73).

Atalanta Bergamasca Calcio

Founded: 17.10.1907
Stadium: Gewiss Stadium, Bergamo (21,300)
Trainer: Gian Piero Gasperini   26.01.1958

Goalkeepers:	DOB	M	(s)	G
Pierluigi Gollini	18.03.1995	25		
Marco Sportiello	10.05.1992	13	(2)	
Defenders:	**DOB**	**M**	**(s)**	**G**
Mattia Caldara	05.05.1994	1	(5)	
Fabio Depaoli	24.04.1997	3	(2)	
Berat Djimsiti (ALB)	19.02.1993	28	(5)	
Davide Ghislandi	16.06.2001		(1)	
Robin Gosens (GER)	05.07.1994	30	(2)	11
Hans Hateboer (NED)	09.01.1994	20	(2)	2
Joakim Mæhle Pedersen (DEN)	20.05.1997	12	(8)	
Johan Andrés Mojica Palacio (COL)	21.08.1992	3	(8)	
José Luis Palomino (ARG)	05.01.1990	25	(11)	1
Cristiano Piccini	26.09.1992		(1)	
Cristian Gabriel Romero (ARG)	27.04.1998	29	(2)	2
Matteo Ruggeri	11.07.2002	3	(3)	
Boško Šutalo (CRO)	01.01.2000	3	(4)	
Rafael Tolói	10.10.1990	29	(2)	2
Midfielders:	**DOB**	**M**	**(s)**	**G**
Marten Elco de Roon (NED)	29.03.1991	33	(2)	1
Remo Freuler (SUI)	15.04.1992	32	(2)	2
Emmanuel Gyabuaa	21.09.2001		(1)	
Viktor Kovalenko (UKR)	14.02.1996		(1)	
Ruslan Malinovskiy (UKR)	04.05.1993	22	(14)	8
Aleksey Miranchuk (RUS)	17.10.1995	4	(21)	4
Mario Pašalić (CRO)	09.02.1995	10	(15)	6
Matteo Pessina	21.04.1997	21	(7)	2
Forwards:	**DOB**	**M**	**(s)**	**G**
Amad Diallo (CIV)	11.07.2002		(1)	
Alejandro Darío Gómez (ARG)	15.02.1988	9	(1)	4
Josip Iličić (SVN)	29.01.1988	17	(11)	6
Sam Lammers (NED)	30.04.1997	1	(14)	2
Luis Fernando Muriel Fruito (COL)	16.04.1991	16	(20)	22
Duván Esteban Zapata Banguero (COL)	01.04.1991	29	(8)	15

Benevento Calcio

Founded: 1929
Stadium: Stadio „Ciro Vigorito", Benevento (16,867)
Trainer: Filippo Inzaghi   09.08.1973

Goalkeepers:	DOB	M	(s)	G
Nicoló Manfredini	01.05.1988	1		
Lorenzo Montipò	20.02.1996	37		
Defenders:	**DOB**	**M**	**(s)**	**G**
Federico Barba	01.09.1993	31	(1)	
Luca Caldirola	01.02.1991	17	(8)	2
Fabio Depaoli	24.04.1997	14	(1)	
Daam Foulon (BEL)	23.03.1999	11	(12)	
Kamil Glik (POL)	03.02.1988	36		2
Gaetano Letizia	29.06.1990	18	(6)	3
Christian Maggio	11.02.1982	2	(6)	
Christian Pastina	15.02.2001		(3)	
Alessandro Tuia	08.06.1990	19	(8)	1
Midfielders:	**DOB**	**M**	**(s)**	**G**
Bryan Dabo (BFA)	18.02.1992	12	(13)	
Lorenzo Del Pinto	17.06.1990		(1)	
Amadou Diambo (GHA)	12.02.2001		(1)	
Përparim Hetemaj (FIN)	12.12.1986	27	(4)	
Artur Ioniță (MDA)	17.08.1990	34	(2)	2
Siriki Sanogo (CIV)	21.12.2001		(1)	
Pasquale Schiattarella	30.05.1987	26	(3)	1
Andrés Felipe Tello Muñoz (COL)	06.09.1996	2	(15)	1
Nicolas Viola	12.10.1989	12	(5)	5
Forwards:	**DOB**	**M**	**(s)**	**G**
Gianluca Caprari	30.07.1993	23	(7)	5
Giuseppe Di Serio	20.07.2001	1	(15)	
Adolfo Julián Gaich (ARG)	26.02.1999	9	(6)	2
Iago Falqué Silva (ESP)	04.01.1990	4	(7)	1
Riccardo Improta	19.12.1993	23	(11)	1
Roberto Insigne	11.05.1994	17	(13)	2
Gianluca Lapadula (PER)	07.02.1990	29	(8)	8
Gabriele Moncini	26.04.1996	4	(6)	
Marco Sau	03.11.1987	9	(15)	4

Bologna Football Club 1909

Founded: 03.10.1909
Stadium: Stadio "Renato Dall'Ara", Bologna (36,462)
Trainer: Siniša Mihajlović (SRB)   20.02.1969

Goalkeepers:	DOB	M	(s)	G
Angelo Esmael da Costa Júnior (BRA)	12.11.1983	6		
Federico Ravaglia	11.11.1999	4		
Łukasz Skorupski (POL)	05.05.1991	28		
Defenders:	**DOB**	**M**	**(s)**	**G**
Wisdom Amey	11.08.2005		(1)	
Valentin Antov (BUL)	09.11.2000	2	(3)	
Arturo Calabresi	17.03.1996		(1)	
Danilo Larangeira (BRA)	10.05.1984	34	(1)	
Stefano Denswil (NED)	07.05.1993	1	(4)	
Lorenzo De Silvestri	23.05.1988	25	(4)	2
Mitchell Dijks (NED)	09.02.1993	18	(2)	
Paolo Faragò	12.02.1993		(1)	
Aaron Hickey (SCO)	10.06.2002	10	(1)	
Omar Khailoti	05.09.2001		(1)	
Ibrahima M'Baye (SEN)	19.11.1994	5	(3)	1
Nehuén Mario Paz (ARG)	28.04.1993	3	(3)	1
Adama Soumaoro (FRA)	18.06.1992	19	(1)	1
Takehiro Tomiyasu (JPN)	05.11.1998	31		2
Midfielders:	**DOB**	**M**	**(s)**	**G**
Andri Fannar Baldursson (ISL)	10.01.2002	1	(7)	
Nicolás Martín Domínguez (ARG)	28.06.1998	15	(13)	1
Gary Alexis Medel Soto (CHI)	03.08.1987	6	(5)	
Andrea Poli	29.09.1989	4	(14)	1
Jerdy Schouten (NED)	12.01.1997	28	(6)	1
Roberto Soriano	08.02.1991	37		9
Mattias Svanberg (SWE)	05.01.1999	24	(10)	5
Kacper Urbański (POL)	07.09.2004		(1)	
Forwards:	**DOB**	**M**	**(s)**	**G**
Musa Barrow (GAM)	14.11.1998	34	(4)	8
Musa Juwara (GAM)	26.12.2001		(5)	
Riccardo Orsolini	24.01.1997	21	(13)	7
Mattia Pagliuca	25.04.2002		(1)	
Rodrigo Sebastián Palacio Alcalde (ARG)	05.02.1982	28	(8)	5
Simone Rabbi	30.10.2001		(4)	
Antonio Raimondo	18.03.2004		(1)	
Nicola Sansone	10.09.1991	11	(15)	2
Federico Javier Santander Mereles (PAR)	04.06.1991		(4)	
Andreas Skov Olsen (DEN)	29.12.1999	12	(14)	2
Edoardo Vergani	06.02.2001		(1)	
Emanuel Vignato	24.08.2000	11	(20)	1

Cagliari Calcio

Founded: 30.05.1920
Stadium: Sardegna Arena, Cagliari (16,416)
Trainer: Eusebio Di Francesco — 08.09.1969
[22.02.2021] Leonardo Semplici — 18.07.1967

Goalkeepers:	DOB	M	(s)	G
Alessio Cragno	28.06.1994	34		
Guglielmo Vicario	07.10.1996	4		
Defenders:	**DOB**	**M**	**(s)**	**G**
Arturo Calabresi	17.03.1996		(2)	
Andrea Carboni	04.02.2001	12	(3)	
Luca Ceppitelli	11.08.1989	16	(3)	
Paolo Faragò	12.02.1993	4	(4)	
Diego Roberto Godín Leal (URU)	16.02.1986	28		1
Ragnar Klavan (EST)	30.10.1985	9	(6)	
Charalampos Lykogiannis (GRE)	22.10.1993	29	(2)	4
Fabio Pisacane	28.01.1986	2	(3)	
Daniele Rugani	29.07.1994	12	(4)	1
Alessandro Tripaldelli	09.02.1999	3	(7)	
Sebastian Wiktor Walukiewicz (POL)	05.04.2000	18	(1)	
Gabriele Zappa	22.12.1999	27	(7)	
Midfielders:	**DOB**	**M**	**(s)**	**G**
Kwadwo Asamoah (GHA)	09.12.1988	1	(8)	
Fabrizio Caligara	12.04.2000	2	(8)	
Alessandro Deiola	01.08.1995	7	(5)	
Alfred Duncan (GHA)	10.03.1993	12	(7)	
Răzvan Gabriel Marin (ROU)	23.05.1996	35	(2)	3
Radja Nainggolan (BEL)	04.05.1988	22		1
Nahitan Michel Nández Acosta (URU)	28.12.1995	31	(1)	2
Christian Gabriel Oliva Giménez (URU)	01.06.1996	3	(7)	
Gastón Rodrigo Pereiro López (URU)	11.06.1995	2	(13)	2
Marko Rog (CRO)	19.07.1995	14		
Forwards:	**DOB**	**M**	**(s)**	**G**
Alberto Cerri	16.04.1996	3	(21)	1
Kiril Despodov (BUL)	11.11.1996		(1)	
João Pedro Geraldino dos Santos Galvão(BRA)	09.03.1992	37		16
Adam Ounas (ALG)	11.11.1996	3	(4)	
Leonardo Pavoletti	26.11.1988	17	(16)	4
Giovanni Simeone (ARG)	05.07.1995	19	(14)	6
Riccardo Sottil	03.06.1999	12	(9)	2
Mattéo Tramoni (FRA)	20.01.2000		(6)	

Football Club Crotone

Founded: 1910
Stadium: Stadio „Ezio Scida", Crotone (16,640)
Trainer: Giovanni Stroppa — 24.01.1968
[01.03.2021] Serse Cosmi — 05.05.1958

Goalkeepers:	DOB	M	(s)	G
Alex Cordaz	01.01.1983	36		
Gian Marco Crespi	28.06.2001	1		
Marco Festa	06.06.1992	1		
Defenders:	**DOB**	**M**	**(s)**	**G**
Giuseppe Cuomo	02.02.1998	8	(5)	
Koffi Djidji (CIV)	30.11.1992	16	(4)	1
Vladimir Golemić (SRB)	28.06.1991	26	(4)	2
Sebastiano Luperto	06.09.1996	22	(1)	
Lisandro Magallán Orueta (ARG)	27.09.1993	25	(3)	1
Luca Marrone	28.03.1990	18	(3)	
Midfielders:	**DOB**	**M**	**(s)**	**G**
Ahmad Fahim Benali (LBY)	07.02.1992	15	(3)	
Luca Cigarini	20.06.1986	13	(1)	
Giovanni Crociata	11.08.1997		(2)	
Eduardo Henrique da Silva (BRA)	17.05.1995	8	(10)	1
Tomislav Gomelt (CRO)	07.01.1995		(2)	
Antonio Mazzotta	02.08.1989	1	(1)	
Salvatore Molina	01.01.1992	28	(1)	1
Pedro Miguel Almeida Lopes Pereira (POR)	22.01.1998	29	(6)	
Jacopo Petriccione	22.02.1995	11	(9)	
Arkadiusz Reca (POL)	17.06.1995	28	(2)	2
Andrea Rispoli	29.09.1988	5	(14)	
Luis José Esteban Rojas Zamora (CHI)	06.03.2002		(7)	
Miloš Vulić (SRB)	19.08.1996	13	(12)	1
Niccolò Zanellato	24.06.1998	18	(9)	1
Forwards:	**DOB**	**M**	**(s)**	**G**
Samuel Di Carmine	29.09.1988	6	(5)	
Denis Mihai Drăguş (ROU)	06.07.1999	1	(8)	
Augustus Kargbo (SLE)	24.08.1999		(1)	
Junior Walter Messias (BRA)	13.05.1991	36		9
Simeon Tochukwu Nwankwo (NGA)	07.05.1992	31	(7)	20
Adam Ounas (ALG)	11.11.1996	15		4
Emmanuel Rivière (MTQ)	03.03.1990	7	(14)	1
Luca Siligardi	26.01.1988		(4)	

Associazione Calcio Fiorentina Firenze

Founded: 29.08.1926 (re-founded 01.08.2002)
Stadium: Stadio "Artemio Franchi", Firenze (43,147)
Trainer: Giuseppe Iachini — 07.05.1964
[09.11.2020] Claudio Cesare Prandelli — 19.08.1957
[24.03.2021] Giuseppe Iachini — 07.05.1964

Goalkeepers:	DOB	M	(s)	G
Bartłomiej Drągowski (POL)	19.08.1997	36		
Pietro Terracciano	08.03.1990	2	(2)	
Defenders:	**DOB**	**M**	**(s)**	**G**
Antonio Barreca	18.03.1995	1	(2)	
Cristiano Biraghi	01.09.1992	31	(4)	1
José Martín Cáceres Silva (URU)	07.04.1987	26	(3)	2
Federico Ceccherini	11.05.1992	3		
Igor Julio dos Santos de Paulo (BRA)	07.02.1998	13	(8)	
Kévin Malcuit (FRA)	31.07.1991	2	(3)	
Lucas Martínez Quarta (ARG)	10.05.1996	15	(6)	1
Nikola Milenković (SRB)	12.10.1997	34		3
Maximiliano Martín Olivera de Andrea (URU)	05.03.1992	1	(1)	
Germán Alejo Pezzella (ARG)	27.06.1991	32		1
Pol Mikel Lirola Kosok (ESP)	13.08.1997	4	(8)	
Lorenzo Venuti	12.04.1995	21	(7)	
Midfielders:	**DOB**	**M**	**(s)**	**G**
Sofyan Amrabat (MAR)	21.08.1996	28	(3)	
Giacomo Bonaventura	22.08.1989	27	(7)	3
Borja Valero Iglesias (ESP)	12.01.1985	4	(16)	
Gaetano Castrovilli	17.02.1997	29	(5)	5
Alfred Joseph Duncan (GHA)	10.03.1993	2	(2)	
Valentin Eysseric (FRA)	25.03.1992	6	(10)	2
Erick Antonio Pulgar Farfán (CHI)	15.01.1994	21	(10)	1
Riccardo Saponara	21.12.1991		(2)	
Cristóbal Montiel Rodríguez „Tòfol Montiel" (ESP)	11.04.2000		(2)	
Forwards:	**DOB**	**M**	**(s)**	**G**
Federico Chiesa	25.10.1997	3		1
Patrick Cutrone	03.01.1998		(11)	
José María Callejón Bueno (ESP)	11.02.1987	6	(14)	
Aleksandr Kokorin (RUS)	19.03.1991		(4)	
Christian Kouamé (CIV)	06.12.1997	9	(24)	1
Franck Bilal Ribéry (FRA)	07.04.1983	28	(1)	2
Dušan Vlahović (SRB)	28.01.2000	34	(3)	21

Genoa Cricket and Football Club

Founded: 07.09.1893
Stadium: Stadio „Luigi Ferraris", Genova (36,685)
Trainer: Rolando Maran   14.07.1963
[21.12.2020]   Davide Ballardini   06.01.1964

Goalkeepers:	DOB	M	(s)	G
Federico Marchetti	07.02.1983	4		
Alberto Paleari	29.08.1992	2	(1)	
Mattia Perin	10.11.1992	32		
Defenders:	**DOB**	**M**	**(s)**	**G**
Mattia Bani	10.12.1993	10	(1)	
Davide Biraschi	02.07.1994	11	(2)	
Domenico Criscito	30.12.1986	20	(3)	1
Edoardo Goldaniga	02.11.1993	19	(6)	
Andrea Masiello	05.02.1986	30		
Jérôme Junior Onguéné (CMR)	22.12.1997	1	(3)	
Luca Pellegrini	07.03.1999	7	(4)	
Cristián Eduardo Zapata Valencia (COL)	30.09.1986	12		
Midfielders:	**DOB**	**M**	**(s)**	**G**
Milan Badelj (CRO)	25.02.1989	29	(1)	1
Valon Behrami (SUI)	19.04.1985	8	(18)	
Francesco Cassata	16.07.1997	2	(6)	
Lennart Czyborra (GER)	03.05.1999	15	(2)	1
Steeve-Mike Eboa Ebongue (FRA)	20.02.2001		(3)	

	DOB	M	(s)	G
Paolo Ghiglione	02.02.1997	14	(9)	
Lukas Lerager (DEN)	12.07.1993	13	(3)	
Filippo Melegoni	18.02.1999	3	(11)	
Manolo Portanova	02.06.2000		(3)	
Ivan Radovanović (SRB)	29.08.1988	24	(9)	
Nicolò Rovella	04.12.2001	12	(8)	
Kevin Strootman (NED)	13.02.1990	18		
Stefano Sturaro	09.03.1993	6		1
Miha Zajc (SVN)	01.07.1994	22	(9)	1
Davide Zappacosta	11.06.1992	23	(2)	4
Forwards:	**DOB**	**M**	**(s)**	**G**
Giuseppe Caso	09.12.1998		(2)	
Mattia Destro	20.03.1991	22	(7)	11
Yayah Kallon (SLE)	30.06.2001		(1)	
Goran Pandev (MKD)	27.07.1983	15	(14)	7
Vittorio Parigini	25.03.1996		(4)	
Marko Pjaca (CRO)	06.05.1995	15	(20)	3
Gianluca Scamacca	01.01.1999	13	(13)	8
Eldor Shomurodov (UZB)	29.06.1995	16	(15)	8

Hellas Verona Football Club

Founded: 1903 (*as AC Hellas Verona*; re-founded 1995)
Stadium: Stadio „Marc'Antonio Bentegodi", Verona (39,371)
Trainer: Ivan Jurić (CRO)   25.08.1975

Goalkeepers:	DOB	M	(s)	G
Alessandro Berardi	16.01.1991		(1)	
Ivor Pandur (CRO)	25.03.2000	4		
Marco Silvestri	02.03.1991	34		
Defenders:	**DOB**	**M**	**(s)**	**G**
Alan Pereira Empereur (BRA)	10.03.1994	4		
Federico Ceccherini	11.05.1992	23	(2)	
Yıldırım Mert Çetin (TUR)	01.01.1997	4	(2)	
Paweł Dawidowicz (POL)	20.05.1995	22	(8)	
Federico Dimarco	10.11.1997	29	(6)	5
Koray Günter (GER)	16.08.1994	21	(6)	
Matteo Lovato	14.02.2000	14	(10)	
Giangiacomo Magnani	04.10.1995	15	(10)	
Kevin Rüegg (SUI)	05.08.1998	1	(6)	
Destiny Udogie	28.11.2002		(6)	
Midfielders:	**DOB**	**M**	**(s)**	**G**
Antonín Barák (CZE)	03.12.1994	32	(2)	7
Daniel Bessa	14.01.1993	4	(14)	

	DOB	M	(s)	G
Andrea Danzi	25.02.1999	1	(1)	
Davide Faraoni	25.10.1991	33	(1)	4
Ivan Ilić (SRB)	17.03.2001	19	(10)	2
Darko Lazović (SRB)	15.09.1990	27	(5)	3
Miguel Luís Pinto Veloso (POR)	11.05.1986	15	(6)	2
Stefano Sturaro	09.03.1993	4	(6)	
Adrien Tamèze (FRA)	04.02.1994	28	(5)	1
Ronaldo Vieira (ENG)	19.07.1998	2	(2)	
Mattia Zaccagni	16.06.1995	33	(3)	5
Forwards:	**DOB**	**M**	**(s)**	**G**
Ebrima Colley (GAM)	01.02.2000	4	(19)	1
Samuel Di Carmine	29.09.1988	6	(5)	
Andrea Favilli	17.05.1997	2	(9)	2
Nikola Kalinić (CRO)	05.01.1988	15	(4)	2
Kevin Lasagna	10.08.1992	14	(5)	2
Eddie Salcedo	01.10.2001	7	(14)	2
Ľubomír Tupta (SVK)	27.03.1998	1	(1)	
Philip Yeboah (GHA)	27.09.2002		(1)	

Football Club Internazionale Milano

Founded: 09.03.1908
Stadium: Stadio "Giuseppe Meazza", Milano (75,923)
Trainer: Antonio Conte   31.07.1969

Goalkeepers:	DOB	M	(s)	G
Samir Handanovič (SVN)	14.07.1984	37		
Daniele Padelli	25.10.1985		(1)	
Ionuţ Andrei Radu (ROU)	28.05.1997	1	(1)	
Defenders:	**DOB**	**M**	**(s)**	**G**
Alessandro Bastoni	13.04.1999	33		
Danilo D'Ambrosio	09.09.1988	7	(12)	3
Matteo Darmian	02.12.1989	14	(12)	3
Stefan de Vrij (NED)	05.02.1992	30	(2)	1
Achraf Hakimi (MAR)	04.11.1998	29	(8)	7
Aleksandar Kolarov (SRB)	10.11.1985	4	(3)	
Andrea Ranocchia	16.02.1988	8		
Milan Škriniar (SVK)	11.02.1995	31	(1)	3
Ashley Simon Young (ENG)	09.07.1985	16	(10)	1

Midfielders:	DOB	M	(s)	G
Nicolò Barella	07.02.1997	32	(4)	3
Marcelo Brozović (CRO)	16.11.1992	29	(4)	2
Christian Dannemann Eriksen (DEN)	14.02.1992	17	(9)	3
Roberto Gagliardini	07.04.1994	14	(14)	3
Radja Nainggolan (BEL)	04.05.1988		(4)	
Stefano Sensi	05.08.1995	4	(14)	
Matías Vecino Falero (URU)	24.08.1991	3	(5)	1
Arturo Erasmo Vidal Pardo (CHI)	22.05.1987	14	(9)	1
Forwards:	**DOB**	**M**	**(s)**	**G**
Romelu Menama Lukaku Bolingoli (BEL)	13.05.1993	32	(4)	24
Lautaro Javier Martínez (ARG)	22.08.1997	30	(8)	17
Ivan Perišić (CRO)	02.02.1989	20	(12)	4
Andrea Pinamonti	19.05.1999	1	(7)	1
Alexis Alejandro Sánchez Sánchez (CHI)	19.12.1988	12	(18)	7

Juventus Football Club Torino

Founded: 01.11.1897
Stadium: Allianz Stadium, Torino (41,507)
Trainer: Andrea Pirlo   19.05.1979

Goalkeepers:	DOB	M	(s)	G
Gianluigi Buffon	28.01.1978	8		
Carlo Pinsoglio	16.03.1990		(1)	
Wojciech Szczęsny (POL)	18.04.1990	30		
Defenders:	**DOB**	**M**	**(s)**	**G**
Alex Sandro Lobo Silva (BRA)	26.01.1991	20	(6)	2
Leonardo Bonucci	01.05.1987	23	(3)	2
Giorgio Chiellini	14.08.1984	16	(1)	
Juan Guillermo Cuadrado Bello (COL)	26.05.1988	26	(4)	2
Danilo Luiz da Silva (BRA)	15.07.1991	32	(2)	1
Mattia De Sciglio	20.10.1992		(1)	
Matthijs de Ligt (NED)	12.08.1999	25	(2)	1
Merih Demiral (TUR)	05.03.1998	10	(5)	
Radu Matei Drăgușin (ROU)	03.02.2002		(1)	
Gianluca Frabotta	24.06.1999	8	(7)	
Midfielders:	**DOB**	**M**	**(s)**	**G**
Arthur Henrique Ramos de Oliveira Melo (BRA)	12.08.1996	13	(9)	1
Rodrigo Bentancur Colmán (URU)	05.06.1997	27	(6)	
Alessandro Di Pardo	18.07.1999		(4)	
Nicolò Fagioli	12.02.2001		(1)	
Weston James Earl McKennie (USA)	28.08.1998	18	(16)	5
Manolo Portanova	02.06.2000	1	(1)	
Adrien Rabiot-Provost (FRA)	03.04.1995	25	(9)	4
Aaron James Ramsey (WAL)	26.12.1990	13	(9)	2
Forwards:	**DOB**	**M**	**(s)**	**G**
Federico Bernardeschi	16.02.1994	8	(19)	
Federico Chiesa	25.10.1997	28	(2)	8
Cristiano Ronaldo dos Santos Aveiro (POR)	05.02.1985	31	(2)	29
Douglas Costa de Souza (BRA)	14.09.1990		(2)	
Paulo Bruno Exequiel Dybala (ARG)	15.11.1993	14	(6)	4
Félix Alexandre Andrade Sanches Correia (POR)	22.01.2001		(1)	
Dejan Kulusevski (SWE)	25.04.2000	19	(16)	4
Álvaro Borja Morata Martín (ESP)	23.10.1992	23	(9)	11
Giacomo Vrioni (ALB)	15.10.1998		(1)	

Società Sportiva Lazio Roma

Founded: 09.01.1900
Stadium: Stadio Olimpico, Roma (70,634)
Trainer: Simone Inzaghi   05.04.1976

Goalkeepers:	DOB	M	(s)	G
José Manuel Reina Páez (ESP)	31.08.1982	29		
Thomas Strakosha (ALB)	19.03.1995	9		
Defenders:	**DOB**	**M**	**(s)**	**G**
Francesco Acerbi	10.02.1988	32		
Nicolò Armini	07.03.2001		(1)	
Bartolomeu Jacinto Quissanga „Bastos" (ANG)	23.11.1991		(2)	
Wesley Hoedt (NED)	06.03.1994	10	(7)	
Luiz Felipe Ramos Marchi (BRA)	22.03.1997	10	(4)	
Mateo Pablo Musacchio (ARG)	26.08.1990	2	(3)	
Patricio Gabarrón Gil „Patric" (ESP)	17.04.1993	18	(7)	
Ştefan Daniel Radu (ROU)	22.10.1986	30	(1)	
Denis Vavro (SVK)	10.04.1996		(1)	
Midfielders:	**DOB**	**M**	**(s)**	**G**
Jean-Daniel Akpa-Akpro (CIV)	11.10.1992	6	(26)	
Djavan Anderson (NED)	21.04.1995	1	(2)	
Andreas Hugo Hoelgebaum Pereira (BRA)	01.01.1996	3	(23)	1
Marco Bertini	07.08.2002		(1)	
Danilo Cataldi	06.08.1994	4	(15)	
Gonzalo Escalante (ARG)	27.03.1993	4	(20)	
Mohamed Fares (ALG)	15.02.1996	12	(9)	
Manuel Lazzari	29.11.1993	30	(2)	2
Lucas Pezzini Leiva (BRA)	09.01.1987	30	(2)	
Luis Alberto Romero Alconchel (ESP)	28.11.1992	33	(1)	9
Senad Lulić (BIH)	18.01.1986	8	(8)	
Adam Marušić (MNE)	17.10.1992	33	(3)	2
Sergej Milinković-Savić (SRB)	27.02.1995	32		8
Marco Parolo	25.01.1985	7	(11)	
Forwards:	**DOB**	**M**	**(s)**	**G**
Felipe Salvador Caicedo Corozo (ECU)	05.09.1988	9	(16)	8
Carlos Joaquín Correa (ARG)	13.08.1994	25	(3)	8
Ciro Immobile	20.02.1990	34	(1)	20
Vedat Muriqi (KVX)	24.04.1994	7	(20)	1
Raúl Moro Prescoli (ESP)	05.12.2002		(1)	

Associazione Calcio Milan

Founded: 16.12.1899
Stadium: Stadio "Giuseppe Meazza", Milano (75,923)
Trainer: Stefano Pioli   20.10.1965

Goalkeepers:	DOB	M	(s)	G
Gianluigi Donnarumma	25.02.1999	37		
Ciprian Anton Tătărușanu (ROU)	09.02.1986	1		
Defenders:	**DOB**	**M**	**(s)**	**G**
Davide Calabria	06.12.1996	30	(2)	2
Andrea Conti	02.03.1994		(3)	
José Diogo Dalot Teixeira (POR)	18.03.1999	10	(11)	1
Leonardo Campos „Léo" Duarte Da Silva (BRA)	17.07.1996		(1)	
Matteo Gabbia	21.10.1999	7	(1)	
Theo Bernard François Hernández (FRA)	06.10.1997	33		7
Pierre Kalulu Kyatengwa (FRA)	05.06.2000	7	(6)	1
Simon Thorup Kjær (DEN)	26.03.1989	28		
Mateo Pablo Musacchio (ARG)	26.08.1990		(1)	
Alessio Romagnoli	12.01.1995	21	(1)	1
Oluwafikayomi Oluwadamilola Tomori (ENG)	19.12.1997	16	(1)	1
Midfielders:	**DOB**	**M**	**(s)**	**G**
Ismaël Bennacer (ALG)	01.12.1997	17	(4)	
Brahim Abdelkader Díaz (ESP)	03.08.1999	15	(12)	4
Hakan Çalhanoğlu (TUR)	08.02.1994	30	(3)	4
Franck Yannick Kessié (CIV)	19.12.1996	36	(1)	13
Rade Krunić (BIH)	07.10.1993	5	(20)	1
Daniel Maldini	11.10.2001		(5)	
Soualiho Meïté (FRA)	17.03.1994	4	(12)	
Sandro Tonali	08.05.2000	17	(8)	
Forwards:	**DOB**	**M**	**(s)**	**G**
Lorenzo Colombo	08.03.2002	1	(3)	
Jens Petter Hauge (NOR)	12.10.1999	3	(15)	2
Zlatan Ibrahimović (SWE)	03.10.1981	18	(1)	15
Mario Mandžukić (CRO)	21.05.1986	1	(9)	
Rafael Alexandre da Conceição Leão (POR)	10.06.1999	22	(8)	6
Ante Rebić (CRO)	21.09.1993	20	(7)	11
Alexis Saelemaekers (BEL)	27.06.1999	27	(5)	2
Samuel Castillejo Azuaga (ESP)	18.01.1995	12	(16)	1

Società Sportiva Calcio Napoli

Founded: 01.08.1926 (*as Associazione Calcio Napoli*)
Stadium: Stadio "Diego Armando Maradona", Napoli (54,726)
Trainer: Gennaro Gattuso   09.01.1978

Goalkeepers:	DOB	M	(s)	G
Alex Meret	22.03.1997	22		
David Ospina (COL)	31.08.1988	16		
Defenders:	**DOB**	**M**	**(s)**	**G**
Giovanni Di Lorenzo	04.08.1993	36		3
Faouzi Ghoulam (ALG)	01.02.1991	3	(8)	
Elseid Hysaj (ALB)	02.02.1994	20	(4)	
Kalidou Koulibaly (SEN)	20.06.1991	25	(1)	
Nikola Maksimović (SRB)	25.11.1991	12	(5)	
Kévin Malcuit (FRA)	31.07.1991		(2)	
Konstantinos Manolas (GRE)	14.06.1991	27	(3)	
Mário Rui Silva Duarte (POR)	27.05.1991	17	(10)	
Amir Rrahmani (KVX)	24.02.1994	12	(4)	1
Midfielders:	**DOB**	**M**	**(s)**	**G**
Tiemoué Bakayoko (FRA)	17.08.1994	23	(9)	2
Diego Demme (GER)	21.11.1991	20	(4)	2
Eljif Elmas (MKD)	24.09.1999	3	(30)	2
Fabián Ruiz Peña (ESP)	03.04.1996	29	(4)	3
Stanislav Lobotka (SVK)	25.11.1994		(15)	
Piotr Zieliński (POL)	20.05.1994	32	(4)	8
Forwards:	**DOB**	**M**	**(s)**	**G**
Antonio Cioffi	19.12.2002		(1)	
Lorenzo Insigne	04.06.1991	33	(2)	19
Fernando Llorente Torrès (ESP)	26.02.1985		(3)	
Hirving Rodrigo Lozano Bahena (MEX)	30.07.1995	23	(9)	11
Dries Mertens (BEL)	06.05.1987	18	(11)	9
Victor James Osimhen (NGA)	29.12.1998	16	(8)	10
Andrea Petagna	30.06.1995	9	(17)	4
Matteo Politano	03.08.1993	22	(15)	9

Parma Calcio 1913

Founded: 16.12.1913 (*as Parma Foot Ball Club*)
Stadium: Stadio „Ennio Tardini", Parma (27,906)
Trainer: Fabio Liverani — 29.04.1976
[07.01.2021] Roberto D'Aversa — 12.08.1975

Goalkeepers:	DOB	M	(s)	G
Simone Colombi	01.07.1991	2		
Luigi Sepe	08.05.1991	36		
Defenders:	**DOB**	**M**	**(s)**	**G**
Botond Balogh (HUN)	06.06.2002	1	(2)	
Mattia Bani	10.12.1993	14	(1)	
Bruno Eduardo Regufe Alves (POR)	27.11.1981	18	(1)	1
Maxime Busi (BEL)	14.10.1999	11	(13)	
Andrea Conti	02.03.1994	9	(2)	
Matteo Darmian	02.12.1989	2	(1)	
Kastriot Dermaku (KVX)	15.01.1992	1	(1)	
Daan Dierckx (BEL)	24.02.2003	6	(1)	
Riccardo Gagliolo (SWE)	28.04.1990	22	(6)	2
Simone Iacoponi	30.04.1987	13	(3)	
Vincent Alain Laurini (FRA)	10.06.1989	10	(4)	
Yordan Hernando Osorio Paredes (VEN)	10.05.1994	21	(2)	
Giuseppe Pezzella	29.11.1997	21	(3)	1
Giacomo Ricci	02.09.1996		(3)	
Lautaro Rodrigo Valenti (ARG)	14.01.1999	6	(5)	
Vasilios Zagaritis (GRE)	04.05.2001		(2)	
Midfielders:	**DOB**	**M**	**(s)**	**G**
Gastón Brugman Duarte (URU)	07.09.1992	21	(5)	1
Juan Francisco Brunetta (ARG)	12.05.1997	4	(8)	1
Drissa Camara (CIV)	18.02.2002		(1)	
Wylan Cyprien (FRA)	28.01.1995	2	(11)	
Jacopo Dezi	10.02.1992	1	(1)	
Alberto Grassi	07.03.1995	13	(10)	
Hernani Azevedo Junior (BRA)	27.03.1994	27	(6)	7
Márk Kosznovszky (HUN)	17.04.2002	1		
Juraj Kucka (SVK)	26.02.1987	28		7
Jasmin Kurtić (SVN)	10.01.1989	31	(3)	4
Matteo Scozzarella	05.06.1988	3		
Simon Sohm (SUI)	11.04.2001	8	(10)	1
Forwards:	**DOB**	**M**	**(s)**	**G**
Andrea Adorante	05.02.2000		(1)	
Andreas Cornelius (DEN)	16.03.1993	21	(8)	1
Gervais Lombe Yao Kouassi „Gervinho" (CIV)	27.05.1987	25	(2)	5
Roberto Inglese	12.11.1991	6	(8)	
Yann Karamoh (FRA)	08.07.1998	16	(8)	2
Dennis Man (ROU)	26.08.1998	8	(6)	2
Valentin Mihai Mihăilă (ROU)	02.02.2000	4	(12)	3
Graziano Pellè	15.07.1985	6	(7)	1
Luca Siligardi	26.01.1988		(2)	
Mattia Sprocati	28.04.1993		(1)	
Chaka Traorè (CIV)	23.12.2004		(3)	
Joshua Orobosa Zirkzee (NED)	22.05.2001		(4)	

Associazione Sportiva Roma

Founded: 07.06.1927
Stadium: Stadio Olimpico, Roma (70,634)
Trainer: Paulo Alexandre Rodrigues Fonseca (POR) — 05.03.1973

Goalkeepers:	DOB	M	(s)	G
Daniel Cerantola Fuzato (BRA)	04.07.1997	5		
Antonio Mirante	08.07.1983	13		
Pau López Sabata (ESP)	13.12.1994	20	(1)	
Defenders:	**DOB**	**M**	**(s)**	**G**
Bruno da Silva Peres (BRA)	01.03.1990	14	(16)	1
Riccardo Calafiori	19.05.2002	1	(2)	
Federico Julián Fazio (ARG)	17.03.1987	5	(1)	1
Roger Ibanez da Silva „Ibañez" (BRA)	23.11.1998	28	(2)	
Juan Guilherme Nunes Jesus (BRA)	10.06.1991		(5)	
Rick Karsdorp (NED)	11.02.1995	28	(6)	1
Marash Kumbulla (ALB)	08.02.2000	14	(7)	1
Gianluca Mancini	17.04.1996	33		4
Bryan Keith Reynolds Jr. (USA)	28.06.2001	3	(2)	
Davide Santon	02.01.1991	7	(3)	
Christopher Lloyd Smalling (ENG)	22.11.1989	13	(3)	
Leonardo Spinazzola	25.03.1993	25	(2)	2
Midfielders:	**DOB**	**M**	**(s)**	**G**
Edoardo Bove	16.05.2002		(1)	
Bryan Cristante	03.03.1995	22	(12)	1
Ebrima Darboe (GAM)	01.06.2001	4	(1)	
Amadou Diawara (GUI)	17.07.1997	7	(11)	1
Gonzalo Villar del Fraile (ESP)	23.03.1998	21	(12)	
Henrikh Mkhitaryan (ARM)	21.01.1989	30	(4)	13
Javier Matías Pastore (ARG)	20.06.1989		(5)	
Lorenzo Pellegrini	19.06.1996	30	(4)	7
Jordan Veretout (FRA)	01.03.1993	25	(4)	10
Nicola Zalewski	23.01.2002		(1)	
Forwards:	**DOB**	**M**	**(s)**	**G**
Borja Mayoral Moya (ESP)	05.04.1997	18	(13)	10
Carles Pérez Sayol (ESP)	16.02.1998	6	(15)	2
Edin Džeko (BIH)	17.03.1986	20	(7)	7
Stephan Kareem El Shaarawy	27.10.1992	6	(4)	1
Justin Kluivert (NED)	05.05.1999		(2)	
Pedro Eliezer Rodríguez Ledesma (ESP)	28.07.1987	20	(7)	5

Unione Calcio Sampdoria Genova

Founded: 12.08.1946
Stadium: Stadio "Luigi Ferraris", Genova (36,599)
Trainer: Eusebio Di Francesco — 08.09.1969
[12.10.2019] Claudio Ranieri — 20.10.1951

Goalkeepers:	DOB	M	(s)	G
Emil Audero	18.01.1997	37		
Karlo Letica (CRO)	11.02.1997	1		
Defenders:	**DOB**	**M**	**(s)**	**G**
Tommaso Augello	30.08.1994	37		1
Bartosz Bereszyński (POL)	12.07.1992	29	(2)	1
Omar Colley (GAM)	24.10.1992	28	(1)	2
Fabio Depaoli	24.04.1997	1	(1)	
Alex Ferrari	01.07.1994	11	(1)	
Vasco Regini	09.09.1990	1	(2)	
Lorenzo Tonelli	17.01.1990	21	(2)	1
Maya Yoshida (JPN)	24.08.1988	25	(7)	1
Midfielders:	**DOB**	**M**	**(s)**	**G**
Adrien Sebastian Perruchet Silva (POR)	15.03.1989	18	(6)	1
Kristoffer Askildsen (NOR)	09.01.2001		(6)	
Antonio Candreva	28.02.1987	28	(7)	5
Albin Ekdal (SWE)	28.07.1989	26	(6)	2
Jakub Jankto (CZE)	19.01.1996	29	(6)	6
Mehdi Léris (FRA)	23.05.1998	3	(17)	
Antonio Palumbo	06.08.1996		(1)	
Gastón Exequiel Ramírez Pereyra (URU)	02.12.1990	10	(15)	
Morten Thorsby (NOR)	05.05.1996	29	(4)	3
Valerio Verre	11.01.1994	12	(15)	3
Forwards:	**DOB**	**M**	**(s)**	**G**
Keita Baldé (SEN)	08.03.1995	12	(13)	7
Federico Bonazzoli	21.05.1997	2		
Mikkel Krogh Damsgaard (DEN)	03.07.2000	18	(17)	2
Manolo Gabbiadini	26.11.1991	10	(6)	3
Antonino La Gumina	06.03.1996	4	(5)	
Fabio Quagliarella	31.01.1983	25	(8)	13
Ernesto Torregrossa	28.06.1992	1	(5)	1

Unione Sportiva Sassuolo Calcio

Founded: 17.07.1920
Stadium: Mapei Stadium – Città del Tricolore, Reggio Emilia (23,717)
Trainer: Roberto De Zerbi   06.06.1979

Goalkeepers:	DOB	M	(s)	G
Andrea Consigli	27.01.1987	37		
Gianluca Pegolo	25.03.1981	1		
Defenders:	**DOB**	**M**	**(s)**	**G**
Kaan Ayhan (TUR)	10.11.1994	7	(12)	
Vlad Iulian Chircheş (ROU)	14.11.1989	22	(2)	2
Gianmarco Ferrari	15.02.1992	33	(1)	
Giorgos Kyriakopoulos (GRE)	05.02.1996	16	(7)	1
Marlon Santos da Silva Barbosa (BRA)	07.09.1995	19	(5)	
Mert Müldür (TUR)	03.04.1999	18	(10)	
Federico Peluso	20.01.1984	2	(5)	
Rogério Oliveira da Silva (BRA)	13.01.1998	21	(7)	
Jeremy Toljan (GER)	08.08.1994	18	(8)	
Midfielders:	**DOB**	**M**	**(s)**	**G**
Mehdi Bourabia (FRA)	07.08.1991	4	(11)	1
Filip Đuričić (SRB)	30.01.1992	27	(5)	5

	DOB	M	(s)	G
Manuel Locatelli	08.01.1998	32	(2)	4
Maxime López (FRA)	04.12.1997	22	(7)	2
Francesco Magnanelli	12.11.1984	7	(3)	
Pedro Obiang (EQG)	27.03.1992	16	(17)	
Hamed Junior Traorè (CIV)	16.02.2000	20	(15)	5
Forwards:	**DOB**	**M**	**(s)**	**G**
Domenico Berardi	01.08.1994	28	(2)	17
Jérémie Boga (CIV)	03.01.1997	20	(7)	4
Francesco Caputo	06.08.1987	19	(6)	11
Grégoire Defrel (MTQ)	17.06.1991	14	(14)	3
Lukáš Haraslín (SVK)	26.05.1996	2	(12)	
Isaac Karamoko (FRA)	26.05.2002		(1)	
Brian Oddei	18.09.2002		(5)	
Giacomo Raspadori	18.02.2000	13	(14)	6
Federico Ricci	27.05.1994		(1)	
Nicolás Javier Schiappacasse Oliva (URU)	12.01.1999		(1)	

Spezia Calcio La Spezia

Founded: 10.10.1906
Stadium: Stadio „Alberto Picco", La Spezia (10,336)
Trainer: Vincenzo Italiano   10.12.1977

Goalkeepers:	DOB	M	(s)	G
Ivan Provedel	17.03.1994	29		
Rafael De Andrade Bittencourt Pinheiro (BRA)	03.03.1982	2	(1)	
Jeroen Zoet (NED)	06.01.1991	7		
Defenders:	**DOB**	**M**	**(s)**	**G**
Simone Bastoni	05.11.1996	19	(3)	1
Elio Capradossi	11.03.1996	1		
Julian Chabot (GER)	12.02.1998	19	(6)	1
Cristian Dell'Orco	10.02.1994	2	(6)	
Martin Erlić (CRO)	24.01.1998	19	(8)	3
Ardian Ismajli (ALB)	30.09.1996	14	(3)	1
Riccardo Marchizza	26.03.1998	17	(7)	
Federico Mattiello	14.07.1995		(1)	
Juan Manuel Ramos (URU)	11.12.1996	2	(4)	
Jacopo Sala	05.12.1991	4	(2)	
Salvador „Salva" Ferrer Canals (ESP)	21.01.1998	14	(4)	
Claudio Terzi	19.06.1984	22	(3)	1
Luca Vignali	11.01.1996	19	(2)	
Midfielders:	**DOB**	**M**	**(s)**	**G**
Gennaro Acampora	29.03.1994	2	(12)	

	DOB	M	(s)	G
Lucien Agoumé (FRA)	09.02.2002	9	(3)	
Paolo Bartolomei	22.08.1989	3	(3)	
Alessandro Deiola	01.08.1995	4	(8)	
Nahuel Estévez (ARG)	14.11.1995	19	(8)	
Leonardo de Souza Sena „Léo Sena" (BRA)	31.12.1995	8	(8)	
Giulio Maggiore	12.03.1998	26	(7)	3
Luca Mora	10.05.1988	1	(3)	
Tommaso Pobega	15.07.1999	17	(3)	6
Matteo Ricci	27.05.1994	26	(3)	
Riccardo Saponara	21.12.1991	5	(4)	2
Forwards:	**DOB**	**M**	**(s)**	**G**
Kevin Andrés Agudelo Ardila (COL)	14.11.1998	14	(15)	1
Diego Farias da Silva (BRA)	10.05.1990	17	(12)	4
Andrey Galabinov (BUL)	13.11.1988	4	(8)	3
Emmanuel Gyasi (GHA)	11.01.1994	32	(5)	4
Giuseppe Mastinu	09.10.1991		(3)	
M'bala Nzola (FRA)	18.08.1996	21	(4)	11
Roberto Piccoli	27.01.2001	8	(12)	5
Daniele Verde	20.06.1996	12	(9)	6

Torino Football Club

Founded: 03.12.1906
Stadium: Stadio Olimpico Grande Torino, Torino (27,958)
Trainer: Marco Giampaolo   02.08.1967
[19.01.2021] Davide Nicola   05.03.1973

Goalkeepers:	DOB	M	(s)	G
Vanja Milinković-Savić (SRB)	20.02.1997	5		
Salvatore Sirigu	12.01.1987	32		
Samir Ujkani (KVX)	05.07.1988	1		
Defenders:	**DOB**	**M**	**(s)**	**G**
Cristian Daniel Ansaldi (ARG)	20.09.1986	20	(11)	1
Gleison Bremer Silva Nascimento (BRA)	18.03.1997	33		5
Alessandro Buongiorno	06.06.1999	9	(3)	
Armando Izzo	02.03.1992	24	(1)	2
Lyanco Evangelista Silveira Neves Vojnović(SRB)	01.02.1997	21	(2)	
Nicola Murru	16.12.1994	7	(7)	
Nicolas Alexis Julio Nkoulou Ndoubena (CMR)	27.03.1990	16	(2)	1
Ricardo Ivan Rodríguez Araya (SUI)	25.08.1992	15	(1)	
Wilfried Singo (CIV)	25.12.2000	20	(8)	1
Mërgim Vojvoda (KVX)	01.02.1995	17	(7)	2
Midfielders:	**DOB**	**M**	**(s)**	**G**
Daniele Baselli	12.03.1992	3	(12)	

	DOB	M	(s)	G
Amer Gojak (BIH)	13.02.1997	6	(9)	1
Karol Linetty (POL)	02.02.1995	20	(7)	1
Saša Lukić (SRB)	13.08.1996	24	(8)	3
Rolando Mandragora	29.06.1997	17		3
Soualiho Meïté	17.03.1994	11	(3)	1
Tomás Eduardo Rincón Hernández (VEN)	13.01.1988	33	(3)	1
Jacopo Segre	17.02.1997	1	(8)	
Simone Verdi	12.07.1992	17	(16)	1
Forwards:	**DOB**	**M**	**(s)**	**G**
Alejandro Berenguer Remiro „Álex" (ESP)	04.07.1995	2		
Andrea Belotti	20.12.1993	33	(2)	13
Federico Bonazzoli	21.05.1997	4	(16)	2
Simone Edera	09.01.1997		(2)	
Vincenzo Millico	12.08.2000		(3)	
Arnaldo Antonio Sanabria Ayala (PAR)	04.03.1996	12	(2)	5
Simone Zaza	25.06.1991	15	(14)	6

Udinese Calcio				

Founded:	1896		
Stadium:	Stadio Friuli, Udine (25,144)		
Trainer:	Luca Gotti		13.09.1967

Goalkeepers:	DOB	M	(s)	G
Manuel Gasparini	19.05.2002		(1)	
Juan Agustín Musso (ARG)	06.05.1994	35		
Nícolas David Andrade (BRA)	12.04.1988	2		
Simone Scuffet	31.05.1996	1		
Defenders:	**DOB**	**M**	**(s)**	**G**
Kevin Bonifazi	19.05.1996	28	(2)	
Sebastien De Maio (FRA)	05.03.1987	9	(6)	
Nahuel Molina Lucero (ARG)	02.12.1997	18	(11)	2
Bram Nuytinck (NED)	04.05.1990	19	(1)	1
Thomas Ouwejan (NED)	30.09.1996	3	(12)	
Rodrigo Nascimento Franca „Rodrigo Becão" (BRA)	19.01.1996	32	(3)	1
Samir Caetano de Souza Santos (BRA)	05.12.1994	24	(6)	1
Jens Stryger Larsen (DEN)	21.02.1991	30	(3)	2
Hidde ter Avest (NED)	20.05.1997	4	(2)	
Marvin Zeegelaar (NED)	12.08.1990	23	(1)	1
Midfielders:	**DOB**	**M**	**(s)**	**G**
Tolgay Arslan (GER)	16.08.1990	25	(5)	3
Mamadou Coulibaly (SEN)	03.02.1999	2	(1)	

	DOB	M	(s)	G
Rodrigo Javier de Paul (ARG)	24.05.1994	36		9
Mato Jajalo (BIH)	24.05.1988		(1)	
Jean-Victor Makengo (FRA)	12.06.1998	5	(12)	
Rolando Mandragora	29.06.1997	3	(7)	
Petar Mićin (SRB)	29.09.1998		(1)	
Martin Palumbo (NOR)	05.03.2002	1	(2)	
Roberto Maximiliano Pereyra (ARG)	07.01.1991	34		5
Walace Souza Silva (BRA)	04.04.1995	23	(7)	
Forwards:	**DOB**	**M**	**(s)**	**G**
Jayden Jezairo Braaf (NED)	31.08.2002	1	(3)	1
Fernando Forestieri	16.01.1990	3	(16)	1
Gerard Deulofeu Lázaro (ESP)	13.03.1994	7	(6)	1
Kevin Lasagna	10.08.1992	12	(5)	2
Fernando Llorente Torres (ESP)	26.02.1985	8	(6)	1
Ilija Nestorovski (MKD)	12.03.1990	4	(18)	2
Stefano Okaka Chuka	09.08.1989	17	(5)	4
Ignacio Pussetto (ARG)	21.12.1995	9	(2)	3
Ryder Matos Santos Pinto (ARG)	27.02.1993		(1)	

SECOND LEVEL
Serie B 2020/2021

1.	Empoli FC (*Promoted*)	38	19	16	3	68 - 35	73
2.	US Salernitana 1919 (*Promoted*)	38	19	12	7	46 - 34	69
3.	AC Monza	38	17	13	8	51 - 33	64
4.	US Lecce	38	16	14	8	68 - 47	62
5.	Venezia FC	38	15	14	9	53 - 39	59
6.	AS Cittadella	38	15	12	11	48 - 35	57
7.	Brescia Calcio	38	15	11	12	61 - 53	56
8.	AC Chievo Verona	38	14	14	10	50 - 37	56
9.	SPAL Ferrara	38	14	14	10	44 - 42	56
10.	Frosinone Calcio	38	12	14	12	38 - 42	50
11.	Reggina 1914	38	12	14	12	42 - 45	50
12.	LR Vicenza	38	11	15	12	48 - 53	48
13.	US Cremonese	38	12	12	14	46 - 44	48
14.	AC Pisa 1909	38	11	15	12	54 - 59	48
15.	Pordenone Calcio	38	10	15	13	40 - 39	45
16.	Ascoli Calcio 1898 FC	38	11	11	16	37 - 48	44
17.	Cosenza Calcio (*Relegated*)	38	6	17	15	29 - 47	35
18.	AC Reggiana 1919 (*Relegated*)	38	9	7	22	31 - 57	34
19.	Delfino Pescara 1936 (*Relegated*)	38	7	11	20	29 - 60	32
20.	Virtus Entella Chiavari (*Relegated*)	38	4	11	23	30 - 64	23

Teams ranked 3-8 were qualified for the Promotion Play-offs.

Promotion Play-offs [1-20.08.2020]			

Preliminary Round [13.05.2021]	AS Cittadella - Brescia Calcio	1-0(1-0)	
	Venezia FC - AC Chievo Verona	3-2(0-1,1-1)	

Semi-Finals [17-20.05.2021]	AS Cittadella - AC Monza	3-0(2-0)	0-2(0-0)
	Venezia FC - US Lecce	1-0(0-0)	1-1(1-0)

Finals [23-27.05.2021]	AS Cittadella - Venezia FC	0-1(0-0)	1-1(1-0)

Venezia FC promoted to 2021/2022 Serie A.

INTERNATIONAL MATCHES
(16.07.2020 – 15.07.2021)

Date	City	Match	Score	Type
04.09.2020	Firenze	Italy - Bosnia and Herzegovina	1-1(0-0)	(UNL)
07.09.2020	Amsterdam	Netherlands - Italy	0-1(0-1)	(UNL)
07.10.2020	Firenze	Italy - Moldova	6-0(5-0)	(F)
11.10.2020	Gdańsk	Poland - Italy	0-0	(UNL)
14.10.2020	Bergamo	Italy - Netherlands	1-1(1-1)	(UNL)
11.11.2020	Firenze	Italy - Estonia	4-0(2-0)	(F)
15.11.2020	Reggio Emilia	Italy - Poland	2-0(1-0)	(UNL)
18.11.2020	Sarajevo	Bosnia and Herzegovina - Italy	0-2(0-1)	(UNL)
25.03.2021	Parma	Italy - Northern Ireland	2-0(2-0)	(WCQ)
28.03.2021	Sofia	Bulgaria - Italy	0-2(0-1)	(WCQ)
31.03.2021	Vilnius	Lithuania - Italy	0-2(0-0)	(WCQ)
28.05.2021	Cagliari	Italy - San Marino	7-0(2-0)	(F)
04.06.2021	Bologna	Italy - Czech Republic	4-0(2-0)	(F)
11.06.2021	Roma	Turkey - Italy	0-3(0-0)	(EC)
16.06.2021	Roma	Italy - Switzerland	3-0(1-0)	(EC)
20.06.2021	Roma	Italy - Wales	1-0(1-0)	(EC)
26.06.2021	London	Italy - Austria	2-1(0-0,0-0)	(EC)
02.07.2021	München	Belgium - Italy	1-2(1-2)	(EC)
06.07.2021	London	Italy - Spain	1-1(0-0,1-1,1-1); 4-2 on penalties	(EC)
11.07.2021	London	Italy - England	1-1(0-1,1-1,1-1); 3-2 on penalties	(EC)

04.09.2020 ITALY - BOSNIA AND HERZEGOVINA 1-1(0-0) 2nd UEFA Nations League A, Group 1
Stadio "Artemio Franchi", Firenze; Referee: Anastasios Sidiropoulos (Greece); Attendance: 0
ITA: Gianluigi Donnarumma, Leonardo Bonucci (Cap), Francesco Acerbi, Cristiano Biraghi, Alessandro Florenzi, Stefano Sensi, Nicolò Barella, Lorenzo Pellegrini (86.Moise Bioty Kean), Lorenzo Insigne, Andrea Belotti (73.Ciro Immobile), Federico Chiesa (72.Nicolò Zaniolo). Trainer: Roberto Mancini.
Goal: Stefano Sensi (67).

07.09.2020 NETHERLANDS - ITALY 0-1(0-1) 2nd UEFA Nations League A, Group 1
"Johan Cruyff" Arena, Amsterdam; Referee: Dr. Felix Brych (Germany); Attendance: 0
ITA: Gianluigi Donnarumma, Leonardo Bonucci, Giorgio Chiellini (Cap), Danilo D'Ambrosio, Leonardo Spinazzola, Jorginho, Nicolò Barella, Manuel Locatelli (81.Bryan Cristante), Nicolò Zaniolo (42.Moise Bioty Kean), Ciro Immobile, Lorenzo Insigne (90.Federico Chiesa). Trainer: Roberto Mancini.
Goal: Nicolò Barella (45+1).

07.10.2020 ITALY - MOLDOVA 6-0(5-0) Friendly International
Stadio "Artemio Franchi", Firenze; Referee: Daniel Siebert (Germany); Attendance: 0
ITA: Salvatore Sirigu (67.Alessio Cragno), Francesco Acerbi, Cristiano Biraghi (66.Emerson), Gianluca Mancini, Giacomo Bonaventura (68.Stefano Sensi), Bryan Cristante, Manuel Lazzari, Manuel Locatelli, Francesco Caputo (75.Kevin Lasagna), Domenico Berardi (75.Moise Bioty Kean), Stephan Kareem El Shaarawy (Cap) (67.Vincenzo Grifo). Trainer: Roberto Mancini.
Goals: Bryan Cristante (19), Francesco Caputo (23), Stephan Kareem El Shaarawy (30), Veaceslav Posmac (38 own goal), Stephan Kareem El Shaarawy (45+1), Domenico Berardi (72).

11.10.2020 POLAND - ITALY 0-0 2nd UEFA Nations League A, Group 1
Stadion Energa, Gdańsk; Referee: José María Sánchez Martínez (Spain); Attendance: 9,200
ITA: Gianluigi Donnarumma, Alessandro Florenzi, Leonardo Bonucci (Cap), Francesco Acerbi, Emerson, Marco Verratti, Jorginho, Nicolò Barella (78.Manuel Locatelli), Lorenzo Pellegrini (83.Domenico Berardi), Andrea Belotti (83.Francesco Caputo), Federico Chiesa (70.Moise Bioty Kean). Trainer: Roberto Mancini.

14.10.2020 ITALY - NETHERLANDS 1-1(1-1) 2nd UEFA Nations League A, Group 1
Stadio Atleti Azzurri d'Italia, Bergamo; Referee: Anthony Taylor (England); Attendance: 623
ITA: Gianluigi Donnarumma, Leonardo Bonucci, Giorgio Chiellini (Cap), Danilo D'Ambrosio, Leonardo Spinazzola, Marco Verratti (56.Manuel Locatelli), Jorginho, Nicolò Barella, Lorenzo Pellegrini (72.Alessandro Florenzi), Ciro Immobile, Federico Chiesa (55.Moise Bioty Kean). Trainer: Roberto Mancini.
Goal: Lorenzo Pellegrini (16).

11.11.2020 ITALY - ESTONIA 4-0(2-0) Friendly International
Stadio "Artemio Franchi", Firenze; Referee: Rade Obrenovič (Slovenia); Attendance: 0
ITA: Salvatore Sirigu (Cap), Giovanni Di Lorenzo, Danilo D'Ambrosio (80.Davide Calabria), Emerson (71.Luca Pellegrini), Alessandro Bastoni, Roberto Soriano, Vincenzo Grifo (80.Stephan Kareem El Shaarawy), Roberto Gagliardini, Sandro Tonali (46.Matteo Pessina), Federico Bernardeschi (71.Riccardo Orsolini), Kevin Lasagna (71.Pietro Pellegri). Trainer: Roberto Mancini.
Goals: Vincenzo Grifo (14), Federico Bernardeschi (27), Vincenzo Grifo (75 penalty), Riccardo Orsolini (86 penalty).

15.11.2020 ITALY - POLAND 2-0(1-0) 2nd UEFA Nations League A, Group 1
Stadio Città del Tricolore, Reggio Emilia; Referee: Clément Turpin (France); Attendance: 0
ITA: Gianluigi Donnarumma, Alessandro Florenzi (Cap) (89.Giovanni Di Lorenzo), Alessandro Bastoni, Francesco Acerbi, Emerson, Jorginho, Nicolò Barella, Manuel Locatelli, Lorenzo Insigne (89.Stephan Kareem El Shaarawy), Andrea Belotti (79.Stefano Okaka Chuka), Federico Bernardeschi (64.Domenico Berardi). Trainer: Roberto Mancini.
Goals: Jorge Luiz Frello Filho „Jorginho" (27 penalty), Domenico Berardi (84).

18.11.2020 BOSNIA AND HERZEGOVINA - ITALY 0-2(0-1) 2nd UEFA Nations League A, Group 1
Stadion Grbavica, Sarajevo; Referee: Artur Manuel Ribeiro Soares Dias (Portugal); Attendance: 0
ITA: Gianluigi Donnarumma, Alessandro Florenzi (Cap) (46.Giovanni Di Lorenzo), Francesco Acerbi, Alessandro Bastoni, Emerson, Jorginho, Nicolò Barella, Manuel Locatelli, Lorenzo Insigne (90+3.Davide Calabria), Andrea Belotti (82.Kevin Lasagna), Domenico Berardi (82.Federico Bernardeschi). Trainer: Roberto Mancini.
Goals: Andrea Belotti (22), Domenico Berardi (68).

25.03.2021   ITALY - NORTHERN IRELAND   2-0(2-0)   22nd FIFA WC. Qualifiers

Stadio "Ennio Tardini", Parma; Referee: Ali Palabıyık (Turkey); Attendance: 0
ITA: Gianluigi Donnarumma, Alessandro Florenzi, Leonardo Bonucci, Giorgio Chiellini (Cap), Emerson (75.Leonardo Spinazzola), Marco Verratti, Manuel Locatelli (84.Matteo Pessina), Lorenzo Pellegrini (63.Nicolò Barella), Ciro Immobile, Lorenzo Insigne (84.Vincenzo Grifo), Domenico Berardi (75.Federico Chiesa). Trainer: Roberto Mancini.
Goals: Domenico Berardi (14), Ciro Immobile (39).

28.03.2021   BULGARIA - ITALY   0-2(0-1)   22nd FIFA WC. Qualifiers

Nationalen Stadion "Vasil Levski", Sofia; Referee: Slavko Vinčić (Slovenia); Attendance: 0
ITA: Gianluigi Donnarumma, Alessandro Florenzi (68.Giovanni Di Lorenzo), Leonardo Bonucci (Cap), Francesco Acerbi, Leonardo Spinazzola, Marco Verratti (88.Matteo Pessina), Stefano Sensi (68.Manuel Locatelli), Nicolò Barella, Lorenzo Insigne, Andrea Belotti (75.Ciro Immobile, Federico Chiesa (76.Federico Bernardeschi). Trainer: Roberto Mancini.
Goals: Andrea Belotti (43 penalty), Manuel Locatelli (83).

31.03.2021   LITHUANIA - ITALY   0-2(0-0)   22nd FIFA WC. Qualifiers

LFF stadionas, Vilnius; Referee: Referee: Paweł Raczkowski (Poland); Attendance: 0
ITA: Gianluigi Donnarumma, Rafael Tolói, Emerson (56.Leonardo Spinazzola), Gianluca Mancini, Alessandro Bastoni (89.Francesco Acerbi), Matteo Pessina (63.Nicolò Barella), Manuel Locatelli, Lorenzo Pellegrini (46.Stefano Sensi), Stephan Kareem El Shaarawy (46.Federico Chiesa), Ciro Immobile (Cap), Federico Bernardeschi. Trainer: Roberto Mancini.
Goals: Stefano Sensi (48), Ciro Immobile (90+4 penalty).

28.05.2021   ITALY - SAN MARINO   7-0(2-0)   Friendly International

Sardegna Arena, Cagliari; Referee: Trustin Farrugia Cann (Malta); Attendance: 0
ITA: Alessio Cragno (63.Alex Meret), Rafael Tolói, Cristiano Biraghi (73.Alessandro Bastoni), Gian Marco Ferrari, Gianluca Mancini (63.Giovanni Di Lorenzo), Bryan Cristante, Vincenzo Grifo (63.Andrea Belotti), Matteo Pessina (87.Nicolò Barella), Gaetano Castrovilli, Federico Bernardeschi (Cap), Moise Bioty Kean (46.Matteo Politano). Trainer: Roberto Mancini.
Goals: Federico Bernardeschi (32), Gian Marco Ferrari (34), Matteo Politano (49), Andrea Belotti (67), Matteo Pessina (75), Matteo Politano (77), Matteo Pessina (87).

04.06.2021   ITALY - CZECH REPUBLIC   4-0(2-0)   Friendly International

Stadio "Renato Dall'Ara", Bologna; Referee: Lionel Tschudi (Switzerland); Attendance: 0
ITA: Gianluigi Donnarumma, Alessandro Florenzi (86.Rafael Tolói), Leonardo Bonucci, Giorgio Chiellini (Cap) (64.Francesco Acerbi), Leonardo Spinazzola (63.Emerson), Jorginho (63.Bryan Cristante), Nicolò Barella, Manuel Locatelli, Ciro Immobile (78.Giacomo Raspadori), Lorenzo Insigne, Domenico Berardi (77.Federico Chiesa). Trainer: Roberto Mancini.
Goals: Ciro Immobile (23), Nicolò Barella (42), Lorenzo Insigne (66), Domenico Berardi (73).

11.06.2021   TURKEY - ITALY   0-3(0-0)   16th EC. Group Stage.

Stadio Olimpico, Roma; Referee: Danny Desmond Makkelie (Netherlands); Attendance: 12,916
ITA: Gianluigi Donnarumma, Alessandro Florenzi (46.Giovanni Di Lorenzo), Leonardo Bonucci, Giorgio Chiellini (Cap), Leonardo Spinazzola, Jorginho, Nicolò Barella, Manuel Locatelli (74.Bryan Cristante), Ciro Immobile (81.Andrea Belotti), Domenico Berardi (85.Federico Bernardeschi), Lorenzo Insigne (81.Federico Chiesa). Trainer: Roberto Mancini.
Goals: Merih Demiral (53 own goal), Ciro Immobile (66), Lorenzo Insigne (79).

16.06.2021   ITALY - SWITZERLAND   3-0(1-0)   16th EC. Group Stage.

Stadio Olimpico, Roma; Referee: Sergey Karasev (Russia); Attendance: 12,445
ITA: Gianluigi Donnarumma, Giovanni Di Lorenzo, Leonardo Bonucci, Giorgio Chiellini (Cap) (24.Francesco Acerbi), Leonardo Spinazzola, Jorginho, Nicolò Barella (87.Bryan Cristante), Manuel Locatelli (86.Matteo Pessina), Ciro Immobile, Domenico Berardi (70.Rafael Tolói), Lorenzo Insigne (69.Federico Chiesa). Trainer: Roberto Mancini.
Goals: Manuel Locatelli (26, 52), Ciro Immobile (89).

20.06.2021   ITALY - WALES   1-0(1-0)   16th EC. Group Stage.

Stadio Olimpico, Roma; Referee: Ovidiu Alin Haţegan (Romania); Attendance: 11,541
ITA: Gianluigi Donnarumma (89.Salvatore Sirigu), Rafael Tolói, Leonardo Bonucci (Cap) (46.Francesco Acerbi), Alessandro Bastoni, Emerson, Marco Verratti, Jorginho (75.Bryan Cristante), Matteo Pessina (87.Gaetano Castrovilli), Federico Chiesa, Andrea Belotti, Federico Bernardeschi (75.Giacomo Raspadori). Trainer: Roberto Mancini.
Goal: Matteo Pessina (39).

26.06.2021   ITALY - AUSTRIA   2-1(0-0,0-0)   16th EC. 2nd Round of 16.

Wembley Stadium, London (England); Referee: Anthony Taylor (England); Attendance: 18,910
ITA: Gianluigi Donnarumma, Giovanni Di Lorenzo, Leonardo Bonucci (Cap), Francesco Acerbi, Leonardo Spinazzola, Marco Verratti (67.Manuel Locatelli), Jorginho, Nicolò Barella (67.Matteo Pessina), Domenico Berardi (84.Federico Chiesa), Ciro Immobile (84.Andrea Belotti), Lorenzo Insigne (108.Bryan Cristante). Trainer: Roberto Mancini.
Goals: Federico Chiesa (95), Matteo Pessina (105).

02.07.2021   BELGIUM - ITALY   1-2(1-2)   16th EC. Quarter-Finals.

Football Arena (Allianz), München (Germany); Referee: Slavko Vinčić (Slovenia); Attendance: 12,984
ITA: Gianluigi Donnarumma, Giovanni Di Lorenzo, Leonardo Bonucci, Giorgio Chiellini (Cap), Leonardo Spinazzola (79.Emerson), Marco Verratti (74.Bryan Cristante), Jorginho, Nicolò Barella, Federico Chiesa (90+1.Rafael Tolói), Ciro Immobile (74.Andrea Belotti), Lorenzo Insigne (79.Domenico Berardi). Trainer: Roberto Mancini.
Goals: Nicolò Barella (31), Lorenzo Insigne (44).

06.07.2021   ITALY - SPAIN   1-1(0-0,1-1,1-1); 4-2 on penalties   16th EC. Semi-Finals.

Wembley Stadium, London (England); Referee: Dr. Felix Brych (Germany); Attendance: 57,811
ITA: Gianluigi Donnarumma, Giovanni Di Lorenzo, Leonardo Bonucci, Giorgio Chiellini (Cap), Emerson (74.Rafael Tolói), Marco Verratti (74.Matteo Pessina), Jorginho, Nicolò Barella (85.Manuel Locatelli), Federico Chiesa (107.Federico Bernardeschi), Ciro Immobile (61.Domenico Berardi), Lorenzo Insigne (85.Andrea Belotti). Trainer: Roberto Mancini.
Goal: Federico Chiesa (60).
Penalties: Manuel Locatelli (saved), Andrea Belotti, Leonardo Bonucci, Federico Bernardeschi, Jorginho.

11.07.2021   ITALY - ENGLAND   1-1(0-1,1-1,1-1); 3-2 on penalties   16th EC. Final.

Wembley Stadium, London; Referee: Björn Kuipers (Netherlands); Attendance: 67,173

ITA: Gianluigi Donnarumma, Giovanni Di Lorenzo, Leonardo Bonucci, Giorgio Chiellini (Cap), Emerson (118.Alessandro Florenzi), Marco Verratti (96.Manuel Locatelli), Jorginho, Nicolò Barella (54.Bryan Cristante), Federico Chiesa (86.Federico Bernardeschi), Ciro Immobile (55.Domenico Berardi), Lorenzo Insigne (91.Andrea Belotti). Trainer: Roberto Mancini.

Goal: Leonardo Bonucci (67).

Penalties: Domenico Berardi, Andrea Belotti (saved), Leonardo Bonucci, Federico Bernardeschi, Jorginho (saved).

NATIONAL TEAM PLAYERS
(16.07.2020 – 15.07.2021)

Name	DOB	Caps	Goals	2020/2021:	Club
Goalkeepers					
Alessio CRAGNO	28.06.1994	2	0	2020/2021:	Cagliari Calcio
Gianluigi DONNARUMMA	25.02.1999	33	0	2020/2021:	AC Milan
Alex MERET	22.03.1997	2	0	2021:	SSC Napoli
Salvatore SIRIGU	12.01.1987	27	0	2020/2021:	Torino FC
Defenders					
Francesco ACERBI	10.08.1988	17	1	2020/2021:	SS Lazio Roma
Alessandro BASTONI	13.04.1999	6	0	2020/2021:	FC Internazionale Milano
Cristiano BIRAGHI	01.09.1992	10	1	2020/2021:	ACF Fiorentina
Leonardo BONUCCI	01.05.1987	109	8	2020/2021:	Juventus FC Torino
Davide CALABRIA	06.12.1996	2	0	2020:	AC Milan
Giorgio CHIELLINI	14.08.1984	112	8	2020/2021:	Juventus FC Torino
Danilo D'AMBROSIO	09.09.1988	6	0	2020:	FC Internazionale Milano
Giovanni DI LORENZO	04.08.1993	13	0	2020/2021:	SSC Napoli
EMERSON Palmieri dos Santos	03.08.1994	19	0	2020/2021:	Chelsea FC London (ENG)
Gian Marco FERRARI	15.05.1992	1	1	2021:	US Sassuolo Calcio
Alessandro FLORENZI	11.03.1991	45	2	2020:	AS Roma
				11.09.2020->	Paris Saint-Germain FC (FRA)
Manuel LAZZARI	29.11.1993	2	0	2020:	SS Lazio Roma
Gianluca MANCINI	17.04.1996	6	0	2020/2021:	AS Roma
Luca PELLEGRINI	07.03.1999	1	0	2020:	Genoa C&FC
Leonardo SPINAZZOLA	25.03.1993	18	0	2020/2021:	AS Roma
Rafael TOLÓI	10.10.1990	7	0	2021:	Atalanta Bergamasca Calcio
Midfielders					
Nicolò BARELLA	07.02.1997	29	6	2020/2021:	FC Internazionale Milano
Giacomo BONAVENTURA	22.08.1989	15	0	2020:	ACF Fiorentina
Gaetano CASTROVILLI	17.02.1997	3	0	2021:	ACF Fiorentina
Bryan CRISTANTE	03.03.1995	17	1	2020/2021:	AS Roma
Roberto GAGLIARDINI	07.04.1994	7	0	2020:	FC Internazionale Milano
Jorge Luiz Frello Filho "JORGINHO"	20.12.1991	35	5	2020/2021:	Chelsea FC London (ENG)
Manuel LOCATELLI	08.01.1998	15	3	2020/2021:	US Sassuolo Calcio
Lorenzo PELLEGRINI	19.06.1996	17	2	2020/2021:	AS Roma
Matteo PESSINA	21.04.1997	9	4	2020/2021:	Atalanta Bergamasca Calcio
Stefano SENSI	05.08.1995	8	3	2020/2021:	FC Internazionale Milano
Roberto SORIANO	08.02.1991	9	0	2020:	Bologna FC 1909
Sandro TONALI	08.05.2000	4	0	2020:	AC Milan
Marco VERRATTI	05.11.1992	45	3	2020/2021:	Paris Saint-Germain FC (FRA)
Nicolò ZANIOLO	02.07.1999	7	2	2020:	AS Roma

				Forwards	
Andrea BELOTTI	20.12.1993	39	12	2020/2021:	*Torino FC*
Domenico BERARDI	01.08.1994	17	5	2020/2021:	*US Sassuolo Calcio*
Federico BERNARDESCHI	16.02.1994	34	6	2020/2021:	*Juventus FC Torino*
Francesco CAPUTO	06.08.1987	2	1	2020:	*US Sassuolo Calcio*
Federico CHIESA	25.10.1997	32	3	2020: 05.10.2020->	*ACF Fiorentina* *Juventus FC Torino*
Stephan Kareem EL SHAARAWY	27.10.1992	29	6	2020: 30.01.2021->	*Shanghai Greenland Shenhua FC (CHN)* *AS Roma*
Vincenzo GRIFO	07.04.1993	6	2	2020/2021:	*SC Freiburg (GER)*
Ciro IMMOBILE	20.02.1990	52	15	2020/2021:	*SS Lazio Roma*
Lorenzo INSIGNE	04.06.1991	47	10	2020/2021:	*SSC Napoli*
Moise Bioty KEAN	28.02.2000	9	2	2020: 04.10.2020->	*Everton FC Liverpool (ENG)* *Paris Saint-Germain FC (FRA)*
Kevin LASAGNA	10.08.1992	7	0	2020:	*Udinese Calcio*
Stefano OKAKA Chuka	09.08.1989	5	1	2020:	*Udinese Calcio*
Riccardo ORSOLINI	24.01.1997	2	0	2020:	*Bologna FC 1909*
Pietro PELLEGRI	17.03.2001	1	0	2020:	*AS Monaco FC (FRA)*
Matteo POLITANO	03.08.1993	4	3	2021:	*SSC Napoli*
Giacomo RASPADORI	18.02.2000	2	0	2021:	*US Sassuolo Calcio*

	National team coach	
Roberto MANCINI [from 14.05.2018]	27.11.1964	39 M; 28 W; 9 D; 2 L; 92-18

KAZAKHSTAN

The Country:
Қазақстан Республикасы (Republic of Kazakhstan)
Capital: Nur-Sultan
Surface: 2,724,900 km²
Inhabitants: 18,711,560 [2020]
Time: UTC+5/+6

The FA:
Қазақстанның Футбол Федерациясы (Football Federation of Kazakhstan)
5a, Momyshuly Avenue, 010000 Nur-Sultan
Tel: +7 7172 790780
Foundation date: 1914
Member of FIFA since: 1994
Member of UEFA since: 2002
Website: www.kff.kz

NATIONAL TEAM RECORDS

RECORDS

First international match:	01.06.1992, Almaty:	Kazakhstan – Turkmenistan 1-0
Most international caps:	Samat Smakov	- 76 caps (2000-2016)
Most international goals:	Ruslan Baltiyev	- 13 goals / 73 caps (1997-2009)

UEFA EUROPEAN CHAMPIONSHIP		FIFA WORLD CUP		OLYMPIC TOURNAMENTS	
1960	-*	1930	-*	1908	-*
1964	-	1934	-	1912	-
1968	-	1938	-	1920	-
1972	-	1950	-	1924	-
1976	-	1954	-	1928	-
1980	-	1958	-	1936	-
1984	-	1962	-	1948	-
1988	-	1966	-	1952	-
1992	-	1970	-	1956	-
1996	-	1974	-	1960	-
2000	-	1978	-	1964	-
2004	-	1982	-	1968	-
2008	Qualifiers	1986	-	1972	-
2012	Qualifiers	1990	-	1976	-
2016	Qualifiers	1994	Did not enter	1980	-
2020	Qualifiers	1998	Qualifiers	1984	-
		2002	Qualifiers	1988	-
		2006	Qualifiers	1992	-
		2010	Qualifiers	1996	Qualifiers
		2014	Qualifiers	2000	Qualifiers
		2018	Qualifiers	2004	Did not enter
				2008	Qualifiers
				2012	Qualifiers
				2016	Qualifiers

*was part of Soviet Union until 1990

UEFA NATIONS LEAGUE

2018/2019	League D (promoted to League C)
2020/2021	League C

FIFA CONFEDERATIONS CUP 1992-2017

None

KAZAKH CLUB HONOURS IN EUROPEAN CLUB COMPETITIONS:

European Champion Clubs' Cup (1956-1992) / UEFA Champions League (1993-2021)
None

Fairs Cup (1858-1971) / UEFA Cup (1972-2009) / UEFA Europa League (2010-2021)
None

UEFA Super Cup (1972-2020)
None

*European Cup Winners' Cup 1961-1999**
None

*defunct competition

NATIONAL COMPETITIONS
TABLE OF HONOURS

KAZAKH SSR (SOVIET ERA) CHAMPIONS

1936	Sbornaya Alma-Aty	1960	Yenbek Guryev	1977	Khimik Stepnogorsk
1937	Dinamo Alma-Ata	1961	Avangard Petropavlovsk	1978	Trud Shevchenko
1938	Dinamo Alma-Ata	1962	ADK Alma-Ata	1979	Khimik Stepnogorsk
1939/1945	*No Championship*	1963	Tselinnik Semipalatinsk	1980	Meliorator Chimkent
1946	Dinamo Alma-Ata	1964	ADK Alma-Ata	1981	Burevestnik Kustanay
1947	Lokomotiv Jambul	1965	ADK Alma-Ata	1980	Traktor Pavlodar
1948	Trudovye Rezervy Alma-Ata	1966	Aktyubinets Aktyubinsk	1981	Aktyubinets Aktyubinsk
1949	Dinamo Karaganda	1967	Torpedo Kokchetav	1982	Shakhtyor Karaganda
1950	Sbornaya Alma-Aty	1968	Gornyak Jezkangan	1983	Shakhtyor Karaganda
1951	Meliorator Chimkent	1969	Shakhtyor Saran'	1984	Tselinnik Tselinograd
1952	Meliorator Chimkent	1970	Stroitel Temir-Tau	1985	Meliorator Chimkent
1953	Meliorator Chimkent	1971	Yenbek Jezkangan	1986	Meliorator Chimkent
1954	Dinamo Alma-Ata	1972	Traktor Pavlodar	1987	Meliorator Chimkent
1955	Dinamo Alma-Ata	1973	Yenbek Jezkangan	1988	Traktor Pavlodar
1956	Sbornaya Alma-Aty	1974	Gornyak Nikol'sky	1989	Traktor Pavlodar
1957	Stroitel Alma-Ata	1975	Meliorator Chimkent	1990	Vostok Ust'-Kamenogorsk
1958	Spartak Alma-Ata	1976	Khimik Stepnogorsk	1991	Aktyubinets Aktyubinsk
1959	Spartak Alma-Ata				

	CHAMPIONS	CUP WINNERS	BEST GOALSCORERS	
1992	FC Kairat Almaty	FC Kairat Almaty	Sergey Kogai (FC Kaysar Kyzylorda)	21
1993	FC Irtysh Pavlodar	FC Dostyk Almaty	Aleksandr Shmarikov (FC Taraz)	28
1994	FC Spartak Semey	FC Vostok Oskemen	Oleg Litvinenko (FC Taraz)	20
1995	FC Spartak Semey	FC Spartak Semey	Andrei Miroshnichenko (FC Spartak Semey)	23
1996	FC Taraz	-	Viktor Antonov (FC Irtysh Pavlodar)	21
1997	FC Irtysh Pavlodar	FC Kairat Almaty (1996/97)	Nurken Mazbaev (FC Taraz)	16
1998	FC Spartak Semey	FC Irtysh Pavlodar (1997/98)	Oleg Litvinenko (FC Spartak Semey)	14
1999	FC Irtysh Pavlodar	FC Kaysar Kyzylorda (1998/99)	Rejepmyrat Agabaýew (TKM, FC Kairat Almaty)	24
2000	FC Astana-64	FC Kairat Almaty (1999/2000)	Nilton Pereira Mendes (BRA, FC Irtysh Pavlodar)	21
#	-	FC Astana-64 (2000/2001)		
2001	FC Astana-64	FC Kairat Almaty	Arsen Tlekhugov (FC Astana-64)	30
2002	FC Irtysh Pavlodar	FC Astana-64	Evgeniy Lunev (FC Shakhter Karagandy)	16
2003	FC Irtysh Pavlodar	FC Kairat Almaty	Andrei Finonchenko (FC Shakhter Karagandy)	18
2004	FC Kairat Almaty	FC Taraz	Ulugbek Bakaev (UZB, FC Tobol Kostanay) Arsen Tlekhugov (FC Kairat Almaty)	22
2005	FC Aktobe	FC Astana-64	Murat Tleshev (FC Irtysh Pavlodar)	20
2006	FC Astana-64	FC Alma-Ata	Jafar Irismetov (UZB, FC Alma-Ata)	17
2007	FC Aktobe	FC Tobol Kostanay	Jafar Irismetov (UZB, FC Alma-Ata)	17
2008	FC Aktobe	FC Aktobe	Murat Tleshev (FC Irtysh Pavlodar)	13
2009	FC Aktobe	FC Atyrau	Murat Tleshev (FC Aktobe) Wladimir Baýramow (TKM, FC Tobol Kostanay)	20
2010	FC Tobol Kostanay	FC Lokomotiv Astana	Ulugbek Bakaev (UZB, FC Tobol Kostanay)	16
2011	FC Shakhter Karagandy	FC Ordabasy	Ulugbek Bakaev (UZB, FC Zhetysu Taldykorgan)	18
2012	FC Shakhter Karagandy	Astana FC	Ulugbek Bakaev (UZB, FC Irtysh Pavlodar)	14
2013	FC Aktobe	FC Shakhter Karagandy	Ihar Zenkovich (BLR, FC Shakhter Karagandy)	15
2014	Astana FC	FC Kairat Almaty	Foxi Kéthévoama (CTA, Astana FC)	16
2015	Astana FC	FC Kairat Almaty	Gerard Bi Goua Gohou (CIV, FC Kairat Almaty)	22
2016	Astana FC	Astana FC	Gerard Bi Goua Gohou (CIV, FC Kairat Almaty)	22
2017	Astana FC	FC Kairat Almaty	Gerard Bi Goua Gohou (CIV, FC Kairat Almaty)	24
2018	Astana FC	FC Kairat Almaty	Marcos Pinheiro Pizzelli (FC Aktobe)	18
2019	Astana FC Nur-Sultan	FC Kaysar Kyzylorda	Marin Tomasov (CRO, Astana FC Nur-Sultan) Aderinsola Habib Eseola (UKR, FC Kairat Almaty)	19
2020	FC Kairat Almaty	*Competition cancelled*	João Paulo da Silva Araújo (BRA, FC Ordabasy Shymkent)	12

Please note: FC Lokomotiv Astana changed its name to Astana FC in 2011.

NATIONAL CHAMPIONSHIP
Kazakhstan Premier League 2020
(07.03.2020 – 30.11.2020)

<u>Please note</u>: FC Irtysh Pavlodar withdrawn from the league after Round 2 due to financial issues, all their matches being excluded from the league results.

Results

Round 1 [07-08.03.2020]
Astana FC - FC Kyzylzhar 4-0(0-0)
FC Kairat - FC Taraz 2-1(1-1)
FC Ordabasy - FC Okzhetpes 1-0(0-0)
Tobol Kostanay - Shakhter Karag. 3-1(1-0)
Kaysar Kyzylorda - Irtysh Pavlodar *annulled*
FC Kaspiy - FC Zhetysu 0-2(0-0)

Round 2 [14-15.03.2020]
Irtysh Pavlodar - FC Kyzylzhar *annulled*
FC Zhetysu - Tobol Kostanay 0-0
FC Okzhetpes - Kaysar Kyzylorda 0-1(0-1)
FC Taraz - FC Ordabasy 3-2(2-0)
FC Kaspiy - Astana FC 2-3(0-3)
Shakhter Karagandy - FC Kairat 1-0(1-0)

Round 3 [01.07.2020]
Astana FC - Irtysh Pavlodar *not played*
FC Kairat - FC Zhetysu 3-0(1-0)
FC Kyzylzhar - FC Okzhetpes 3-1(1-1)
Tobol Kostanay - FC Kaspiy 2-0(0-0)
Kaysar Kyzylorda - FC Taraz 1-1(1-0)
FC Ordabasy - Shakhter Karagandy 0-1(0-0)

Round 4 [18-19.08.2020]
FC Okzhetpes - Irtysh Pavlodar *not played*
FC Kaspiy - FC Kairat 0-3(0-1)
FC Zhetysu - FC Ordabasy 2-3(2-1)
FC Taraz - FC Kyzylzhar 0-0
Shakhter Karag. - Kaysar Kyzylorda 0-1(0-0)
Tobol Kostanay - Astana FC 2-0(1-0) [25.08.]

Round 5 [21-22.08.2020]
Irtysh Pavlodar - FC Taraz *not played*
FC Ordabasy - FC Kaspiy 1-0(1-0)
FC Kairat - Tobol Kostanay 3-1(2-0)
Astana FC - FC Okzhetpes 2-0(1-0)
Kaysar Kyzylorda - FC Zhetysu 1-0(0-0)
FC Kyzylzhar - Shakhter Karagandy 1-3(0-1)

Round 6 [26-27.08.2020]
Shakhter Karag. - Irtysh Pavlodar *not played*
FC Taraz - FC Okzhetpes 2-3(1-0)
FC Kaspiy - Kaysar Kyzylorda 1-0(0-0)
FC Zhetysu - FC Kyzylzhar 3-0(2-0)
Tobol Kostanay - Ordabasy 0-4(0-1) [16.09.]
FC Kairat - Astana FC 3-0(1-0) [04.10.]

Round 7 [29-30.08.2020]
Irtysh Pavlodar - FC Zhetysu *not played*
Kaysar Kyzylorda - Tobol Kostanay 2-1(1-0)
FC Okzhetpes - Shakhter Karagandy 1-1(0-1)
FC Ordabasy - FC Kairat 1-3(1-3)
Astana FC - FC Taraz 1-1(1-0)
FC Kyzylzhar - FC Kaspiy 1-0(1-0)

Round 8 [11-12.09.2020]
FC Zhetysu - FC Okzhetpes 1-0(1-0)
Shakhter Karagandy - FC Taraz 1-1(0-0)
FC Kaspiy - Irtysh Pavlodar *not played*
FC Ordabasy - Astana FC 1-2(0-0)
Tobol Kostanay - FC Kyzylzhar 2-0(1-0)
FC Kairat - Kaysar Kyzylorda 2-1(0-1)

Round 9 [18-21.09.2020]
Irtysh Pavlodar - Tobol Kostanay *not played*
FC Okzhetpes - FC Kaspiy 2-2(1-1)
FC Taraz - FC Zhetysu 0-2(0-2)
Astana FC - Shakhter Karagandy 1-1(0-0)
Kaysar Kyzylorda - FC Ordabasy 1-1(0-1)
FC Kyzylzhar - FC Kairat 0-1(0-1)

Round 10 [22-24.09.2020]
Tobol Kostanay - FC Okzhetpes 1-0(0-0)
FC Kaspiy - FC Taraz 0-2(0-1)
FC Kairat - Irtysh Pavlodar *not played*
FC Zhetysu - Shakhter Karagandy 3-2(0-1)
FC Ordabasy - FC Kyzylzhar 1-0(0-0)
Kaysar Kyzylorda - Astana FC 0-1(0-0)

Round 11 [26-28.09.2020]
FC Taraz - Tobol Kostanay 0-0
Irtysh Pavlodar - FC Ordabasy *not played*
FC Okzhetpes - FC Kairat 3-3(2-2)
Astana FC - FC Zhetysu 3-0(1-0)
FC Kyzylzhar - Kaysar Kyzylorda 0-0
Shakhter Karagandy - FC Kaspiy 2-1(1-0)

Round 12 [01-02.10.2020]
FC Kyzylzhar - Irtysh Pavlodar *not played*
Astana FC - FC Kaspiy 1-2(1-0)
FC Kairat - Shakhter Karagandy 1-1(0-0)
Kaysar Kyzylorda - FC Okzhetpes 0-0
FC Ordabasy - FC Taraz 1-1(0-0)
Tobol Kostanay - FC Zhetysu 2-0(0-0)

Round 13 [17-18.10.2020]
Irtysh Pavlodar - Astana FC *not played*
FC Okzhetpes - FC Kyzylzhar 2-1(0-1)
FC Taraz - Kaysar Kyzylorda 2-2(2-0)
Shakhter Karagandy - FC Ordabasy 0-1(0-0)
FC Zhetysu - FC Kairat 2-4(2-1)
FC Kaspiy - Tobol Kostanay 0-1(0-0)

Round 14 [21-22.10.2020]
Irtysh Pavlodar - FC Okzhetpes *not played*
FC Kyzylzhar - FC Taraz 1-0(0-0)
Kaysar Kyzylorda - Shakhter Karag. 2-0(1-0)
FC Ordabasy - FC Zhetysu 3-1(2-0)
Astana FC - Tobol Kostanay 1-0(0-0)
FC Kairat - FC Kaspiy 3-1(2-1)

Round 15 [26-27.10.2020]
FC Taraz - Irtysh Pavlodar *not played*
FC Zhetysu - Kaysar Kyzylorda 3-1(1-0)
Tobol Kostanay - FC Kairat 0-4(0-3)
FC Kaspiy - FC Ordabasy 1-2(1-0)
FC Okzhetpes - Astana FC 1-5(0-3)
Shakhter Karagandy - FC Kyzylzhar 0-0

Round 16 [30-31.10.2020]
Irtysh Pavlodar - Shakhter Karag. *not played*
FC Ordabasy - Tobol Kostanay 0-3(0-0)
Astana FC - FC Kairat 0-1(0-1)
Kaysar Kyzylorda - FC Kaspiy 0-1(0-0)
FC Okzhetpes - FC Taraz 0-0
FC Kyzylzhar - FC Zhetysu 2-1(2-0)

Round 17 [03-04.11.2020]
FC Zhetysu - Irtysh Pavlodar *not played*
FC Kairat - FC Ordabasy 3-1(2-0)
Tobol Kostanay - Kaysar Kyzylorda 3-0(0-0)
Shakhter Karagandy - FC Okzhetpes 2-1(0-1)
FC Kaspiy - FC Kyzylzhar 1-1(0-1)
FC Taraz - Astana FC 1-0(1-0)

Round 18 [07-08.11.2020]
Astana FC - FC Ordabasy 1-1(0-1) [11.03.]
Irtysh Pavlodar - FC Kaspiy *not played*
Kaysar Kyzylorda - FC Kairat 2-2(0-1)
FC Kyzylzhar - Tobol Kostanay 0-1(0-0)
FC Taraz - Shakhter Karagandy 2-4
FC Okzhetpes - FC Zhetysu 0-1(0-1)

Round 19 [21.11.2020]
Tobol Kostanay - Irtysh Pavlodar *not played*
Shakhter Karagandy - Astana FC 3-1(2-0)
FC Ordabasy - Kaysar Kyzylorda 0-3(0-0)
FC Zhetysu - FC Taraz 0-1(0-1)
FC Kairat - FC Kyzylzhar 2-3(2-2)
FC Kaspiy - FC Okzhetpes 2-1(1-0)

Round 20 [24.11.2020]
Irtysh Pavlodar - FC Kairat *not played*
Astana FC - Kaysar Kyzylorda 3-1(1-1)
FC Kyzylzhar - FC Ordabasy 0-0
FC Taraz - FC Kaspiy 0-1(0-1)
FC Okzhetpes - Tobol Kostanay 0-2(0-1)
Shakhter Karagandy - FC Zhetysu 1-2(0-1)

Round 21 [27.11.2020]
FC Kairat - FC Okzhetpes 5-0(2-0) [11.03.]
FC Ordabasy - Irtysh Pavlodar *not played*
FC Zhetysu - Astana FC 1-2(1-0)
Kaysar Kyzylorda - FC Kyzylzhar 1-2(1-1)
FC Kaspiy - Shakhter Karagandy 0-4(0-3)
Tobol Kostanay - FC Taraz 2-0(1-0)

Round 22 [30.11.2020]
Irtysh Pavlodar - Kaysar Kyzylorda *not played*
FC Kyzylzhar - Astana FC 0-1(0-1)
FC Okzhetpes - FC Ordabasy 1-3(1-1)
Shakhter Karag. - Tobol Kostanay 1-0(0-0)
FC Taraz - FC Kairat 1-0(0-0)
FC Zhetysu - FC Kaspiy 3-0(2-0)

Final Standings

		Total						Home					Away			
1. **FC Kairat Almaty**	20	14	3	3	48 - 19	45	8	1	1	27 - 9		6	2	2	21 - 10
2. FC Tobol Kostanay	20	12	2	6	26 - 16	38	8	0	2	17 - 9		4	2	4	9 - 7
3. Astana FC Nur-Sultan	20	11	3	6	32 - 21	36	5	3	2	17 - 7		6	0	4	15 - 14
4. FC Shakhter Karagandy	20	9	5	6	29 - 22	32	5	2	3	11 - 8		4	3	3	18 - 14
5. FC Ordabasy Shymkent	20	9	4	7	27 - 26	31	4	1	5	9 - 14		5	3	2	18 - 12
6. FC Zhetysu Taldiqorghan	20	9	1	10	27 - 28	28	5	1	4	18 - 13		4	0	6	9 - 15
7. FC Kaysar Kyzylorda	20	6	6	8	20 - 23	24	3	4	3	10 - 9		3	2	5	10 - 14
8. FC Taraz	20	5	8	7	19 - 23	23	3	3	4	11 - 14		2	5	3	8 - 9
9. FC Kyzylzhar SK Petropavl	20	6	5	9	15 - 24	23	4	2	4	8 - 8		2	3	5	7 - 16
10. FC Caspiy Aqtau (*Relegation Play-offs*)	20	5	2	13	15 - 34	17	2	1	7	7 - 19		3	1	6	8 - 15
11. FC Okzhetpes Kokshetau (*Relegated*)	20	2	5	13	16 - 38	11	1	4	5	10 - 19		1	1	8	6 - 19
12. FC Irtysh Pavlodar (*Relegated*)	(*withdrawn*)														

Top goalscorers:

12	**João Paulo da Silva Araújo (BRA)**	*FC Ordabasy Shymkent*
10	Abat Aymbetov	*FC Kairat Almaty*
7	Elguja Lobjanidze (GEO)	*FC Kaysar Kyzylorda*
7	Vágner Silva de Souza "Vágner Love" (BRA)	*FC Kairat Almaty*

NATIONAL CUP
Kazakhstan Kubok 2020

The competition was cancelled due to COVID-19 pandemic.

THE CLUBS 2020

Astana Football Club

Founded:	2009 (*as FC Lokomotiv Astana*)		
Stadium:	Astana Arena, Nur-Sultan (30,000)		
Trainer:	Michal Bílek (CZE)		13.04.1965
(26.08.2020)	Paul Ashworth (ENG)		29.09.1969
(16.10.2020)	Andrey Tikhonov (RUS)		16.10.1979

Goalkeepers:	DOB	M	(s)	G
Nenad Erić	26.05.1982	15		
Dmitriy Nepogodov	17.02.1988	5		
Defenders:	**DOB**	**M**	**(s)**	**G**
Abzal Beysebekov	30.11.1992	15	(2)	1
Sergey Maliy	05.06.1990	3		
Evgeni Postnikov	16.04.1986	11	(2)	
Uroš Radaković (SRB)	31.03.1994	12		
Antonio Rukavina (SRB)	26.01.1984	10	(1)	
Dmitry Shomko	19.03.1990	16		
Luka Šimunović (CRO)	24.05.1997	7	(1)	
Žarko Tomašević (MNE)	22.02.1990	10	(1)	3
Midfielders:	**DOB**	**M**	**(s)**	**G**
Maks Ebong (BLR)	26.08.1999	18		
Yuri Logvinenko	22.07.1988	8	(6)	1

	DOB	M	(s)	G
Ivan Maevskiy (BLR)	05.05.1988	14	(1)	1
Yuri Pertsukh	13.05.1996	5	(4)	
Sultan Sagnaev	14.01.2000		(2)	
Rúnar Már Sigurjónsson (ISL)	18.06.1990	12	(3)	6
Madi Zhakipbaev	21.03.2000		(4)	
Didar Zhalmukan	22.05.1996	1	(12)	2
Forwards:	**DOB**	**M**	**(s)**	**G**
Tigran Barseghyan (ARM)	22.09.1993	17	(2)	3
Stanislav Basmanov	24.06.2001		(1)	
Ramazan Karimov	05.07.1999		(3)	
Dorin Rotariu (ROU)	29.07.1995	6	(7)	1
Aleksey Shchetkin	21.05.1991	7	(8)	4
Pieros Sotiriou (CYP)	13.01.1993	11	(4)	6
Marin Tomasov (CRO)	31.08.1987	17		4

Football Club Caspiy Aktau

Founded:	1962	
Stadium:	Zhastar Stadium, Aktau (5,000)	
Trainer:	Srđan Blagojević (SRB)	06.06.1973

Goalkeepers:	DOB	M	(s)	G
Nurlybek Ayazbaev	24.01.1991		(1)	
Denis Kavlinov (RUS)	10.01.1995	1		
Marko Milošević (SRB)	07.02.1991	19		
Defenders:	**DOB**	**M**	**(s)**	**G**
Lionel Adams (RUS)	09.08.1994	14	(1)	
Rafkat Aslan	02.02.1994	4	(6)	
Taras Bondarenko (UKR)	23.09.1992	3		
Mikhail Gabyshev	02.01.1990	14	(1)	1
Erlan Kadyrbaev	05.10.1991	1	(1)	
Bojan Kovačević (SRB)	28.04.1996	1		
Timur Redzhepov	06.07.2002		(1)	
Maksat Taykenov	14.08.1997	17		
Ilya Vorotnikov	01.02.1986	12		
Midfielders:	**DOB**	**M**	**(s)**	**G**
Stefan Bukorac (SRB)	15.02.1991	17	(1)	1
Bekzat Kabylan	03.03.1996	3	(4)	1
Bakdaulet Konlimkos	05.12.2000		(1)	
Amandyk Nabikhanov	09.11.1997	11	(7)	1
Erkebulan Nurgaliev	12.09.1993	9	(2)	

	DOB	M	(s)	G
Arman Nusip	22.01.1994	10	(5)	1
Rakhimzhan Rozybakiev	02.01.1991	5	(5)	
Sultan Sagnaev	14.01.2000	1	(1)	
Ruslan Sakhalbaev	27.06.1984	14	(3)	2
Billal Sebaihi (FRA)	31.05.1992	16	(2)	4
Marat Shakhmetov	06.02.1989	12	(4)	1
Kirill Shestakov	19.06.1985	1		
Erkin Tapalov	03.09.1993	2		
Ruslan Zhanysbaev	04.11.1995	2	(9)	
Forwards:	**DOB**	**M**	**(s)**	**G**
Almas Armenov	27.01.1992	1	(9)	
Branko Čubrilo (CRO)	20.05.1988	6	(9)	
Ramazan Karimov	05.07.1999	1	(1)	
Maksym Marusych (UKR)	17.07.1993	9		1
Kuandyk Nursultanov	24.04.1999		(1)	
Serge Nyuiadzi (TOG)	17.09.1991	2		
Vladislav Sirotov (RUS)	27.10.1991	8	(2)	
Aleksandar Stanisavljević (SRB)	11.06.1989	1		1
Aydos Tattibayev	26.04.1990	3		

Football Club Irtysh Pavlodar

Founded:	1965	
Stadium:	Pavlodar Central Stadium, Pavlodar (15,000)	
Trainer:	Samvel Babayan	19.05.1971

Football Club Kairat Almaty

Founded: 1954 (*as Lokomotiv Alma-Ata*)
Stadium: Almaty Central Stadium, Almaty (25,057)
Trainer: Aleksey Shpilevski   17.02.1988

Goalkeepers:	DOB	M	(s)	G
Temirlan Anarbekov	14.10.2003		(1)	
Stas Pokatilov	08.12.1992	12	(1)	
Danil Ustimenko	08.08.2000	7	(1)	
Dinmukhammed Zhomart	06.12.2000	1		
Defenders:	**DOB**	**M**	**(s)**	**G**
Nuraly Alip	22.12.1999	13	(1)	4
Nurlan Dairov	26.06.1995	1	(1)	
Rade Dugalić (SRB)	05.11.1992	16		1
Ravil Ibragimov	25.12.2000	1		
Sergey Keyler	08.11.1994	4	(2)	1
Dino Mikanović (CRO)	07.05.1994	19		
Denis Polyakov (BLR)	17.04.1991	7	(2)	1
Aleksandr Shirobokov	02.01.2003	1	(1)	
Gafurzhan Suyumbaev	19.08.1990	15	(1)	1
Midfielders:	**DOB**	**M**	**(s)**	**G**
Aybol Abiken	01.06.1996	12	(4)	3
Adam Adakhadzhiev	23.11.1998	3	(4)	
Arsen Buranchiev	12.09.2001		(2)	
Jacek Góralski (POL)	21.09.1992	16		
Kamo Hovhannisyan (ARM)	05.10.1992	5	(9)	1
Nebojša Kosović (MNE)	24.02.1995	16		4
Andrey Ulshin	18.04.2000	1	(1)	1
Daniyar Usenov	18.02.2001	4	(4)	2
Forwards:	**DOB**	**M**	**(s)**	**G**
Aybar Abdulla	22.01.2002		(2)	
Gulzhigit Alykulov (KGZ)	25.11.2000	14	(4)	1
Sultanbek Astanov	23.03.1999	2	(9)	
Abat Aymbetov	07.08.1995	19	(1)	10
Aderinsola Habib Eseola (UKR)	28.06.1991	3	(14)	2
Glymzhan Kenzhebek	12.02.2003	1		
Artur Shushenachev	07.04.1998	4	(10)	3
Erkebulan Tungyshbaev	14.01.1995	3	(7)	
Vágner Silva de Souza "Vágner Love" (BRA)	11.06.1984	11	(2)	7
Konrad Wrzesiński (POL)	10.09.1993	9	(2)	3

Football Club Kaysar Kyzylorda

Founded: 1968
Stadium: "Gany Muratbayev" Stadium, Kyzylorda (7,500)
Trainer: Stoicho Mladenov (BUL)   12.04.1957
(19.11.2020)   Kanat Sherimbetov   25.10.1982

Goalkeepers:	DOB	M	(s)	G
Marsel Islamkulov	18.04.1994	2		
Nurimzhan Salaydin	27.10.1995	1		
Aleksandr Zarutskiy	26.08.1993	17		
Defenders:	**DOB**	**M**	**(s)**	**G**
Eldos Akhmetov	01.06.1990		(3)	
Olzhas Altaev	15.07.1989	2	(6)	
Ilyas Amirseitov	22.10.1989	18		
Ivan Graf (CRO)	17.06.1987	17		2
Bagdat Kairov	27.04.1993	19		
Kuanysh Kalmuratov	27.08.1996	2		
Dinmukhammed Kashken	04.01.2000	2	(5)	
Aleksandr Marochkin	14.07.1990	18		1
Elzhas Sarbay	24.07.1998		(1)	
Aleksey Shumskikh (RUS)	01.07.1990		(1)	
Abylaykhan Tolegenov	13.07.1992		(1)	
Midfielders:	**DOB**	**M**	**(s)**	**G**
Clarence Junior Bitang (CMR)	02.09.1992	14	(3)	
Ruslan Duysenbayev	22.04.1993		(1)	
Mark Gurman	09.02.1989	10	(7)	
Ayman Kulmaganbetov	11.11.2000		(4)	
Duman Narzildaev	06.09.1993	17		1
Magomed Paragulgov	26.03.1994	1		
Askhat Tagybergen	09.08.1990	13		4
Forwards:	**DOB**	**M**	**(s)**	**G**
Shokan Abzalov	11.09.1993	1	(5)	
Elzhas Altynbekov	22.11.1993	2	(2)	1
Reginaldo Artur Faife (MOZ)	04.06.1990	12	(3)	2
Maksim Fedin	08.06.1996	13	(2)	1
Alvin Fortes (CPV)	25.05.1994	7	(7)	1
Aleksandar Kolev (BUL)	08.12.1992	7	(4)	
Elguja Lobjanidze (GEO)	17.09.1992	12		7
Orken Makhan	27.01.1998		(1)	
Ivan Pešić (CRO)	06.04.1992	1		
Aleksandar Stanisavljević (SRB)	11.06.1989	12	(5)	

Football Club Kyzylzhar Petropavl

Founded: 1968
Stadium: Karasai Stadium, Petropavl (11,000)
Trainer: Veaceslav Rusnac (MDA)   27.08.1975

Goalkeepers:	DOB	M	(s)	G
Miroslav Lobantsev (RUS)	27.05.1995	18		
Vadim Petrov	11.06.2000	2		
Defenders:	**DOB**	**M**	**(s)**	**G**
Ildar Aitov	02.03.1990	8	(2)	
Vytautas Andriuškevičius (LTU)	08.10.1990	10		
Artem Baranovskiy (UKR)	17.03.1990	8	(3)	
Gabriel Enache (ROU)	18.08.1990	2	(3)	2
Igor Gubanov (RUS)	04.02.1992	6	(4)	
Viktor Gunchenko	25.08.1994	11	(3)	
Alibek Kasym	27.05.1998	12	(1)	1
Berik Shaykhov	20.02.1994	12	(2)	
Aleksandr Sokolenko	23.11.1996	7	(2)	1
Midfielders:	**DOB**	**M**	**(s)**	**G**
Artem Cheredinov	17.07.1998	2	(4)	
Uroš Delić (MNE)	10.08.1987	16	(1)	
Maksym Drachenko (UKR)	28.01.1990	18		3
Shota Grigalashvili (GEO)	21.06.1986	14	(3)	3
Moussa Koné (CIV)	12.02.1990	15		
Mihail Plătică (MDA)	15.03.1990	13	(5)	
Pablo Joaquin Podio (ARG)	07.08.1989	8	(3)	
Tamaz Tsekskhladze (GEO)	08.12.1996	1	(2)	
Forwards:	**DOB**	**M**	**(s)**	**G**
Nikita Bezlikhotnov	19.08.1990	2	(1)	
Momodou Ceesay (GAM)	24.12.1988	10	(4)	1
Ruslan Koryan (ARM)	15.06.1988	3	(5)	
Ivan Markelov (RUS)	17.04.1988	11	(6)	
Timur Muldinov	19.09.1993	7	(9)	3
Maksim Skorykh	20.04.2000	3	(3)	1
Igor Zenkovich	17.09.1987	1	(1)	

Football Club Okzhetpes Kokshetau

Founded: 1957
Stadium: „Alisher Sagynbayev" Stadium, Kokshetau (4,158)
Trainer: Andrey Karpovich   18.01.1981

Goalkeepers:	DOB	M	(s)	G
Ruslan Abzhanov	28.04.1990	7		
Yaroslav Baginskiy	03.10.1987	8		
Aleksandr Sheplyakov (RUS)	13.08.1996	5		
Defenders:	**DOB**	**M**	**(s)**	**G**
Aliyu Abubakar (NGA)	15.06.1996	11		
Taras Bondarenko (UKR)	23.09.1992	16		2
Daniil Chertov (RUS)	15.11.1990	3	(4)	
Plamen Dimov (BUL)	29.10.1990	17	(1)	1
Azat Ersalimov	19.07.1988	7	(2)	
Aleksey Gavrilovich (BLR)	05.01.1990	14	(2)	
Niyaz Idrisov	21.07.1999		(1)	
Talgat Kusyapov	14.02.1999	1	(3)	
Andriy Mishchenko (UKR)	07.04.1991	3		
Dmitry Schmidt	17.11.1993	11		
Timur Zhakupov	06.09.1995	4	(9)	
Midfielders:	**DOB**	**M**	**(s)**	**G**
Artjom Dmitrijev (EST)	14.11.1988	13	(4)	5
Gian dos Santos Martins (BRA)	02.04.1993	19		1
Ilya Kalinin	03.02.1992	3		
Vsevolod Nihaev (MDA)	04.05.1999	2	(4)	
Altynbek Saparov	26.04.1995	3	(6)	
Milan Stojanović (SRB)	10.05.1988	13	(4)	1
Miras Tuliev	30.08.1994	8	(3)	
Forwards:	**DOB**	**M**	**(s)**	**G**
Islamnur Abdulavov (RUS)	07.03.1994	4	(6)	
Magomed-Emi Dzhabrailov (RUS)	24.03.1993	3	(3)	
Zhasulan Moldakaraev	07.05.1987	14	(3)	1
Marko Obradović (SRB)	30.06.1991	7	(3)	2
Arman Tolegenov	18.04.2000	2	(1)	
Sanat Zhumakhanov	30.01.1988	12	(5)	1
Darko Zorić (MNE)	12.09.1993	10	(1)	2

Football Club Ordabasy Shymkent

Founded: 2000
Stadium: "Kazhymukan Munaitpasov" Stadium, Shymkent (20,000)
Trainer: Kakhaber Tskhadadze — 07.09.1968

Goalkeepers:	DOB	M	(s)	G
Vladimir Plotnikov	03.04.1986	12		
Bekkhan Shayzada	28.02.1998	8		
Defenders:	DOB	M	(s)	G
Marat Bystrov	19.06.1992	4		
Damir Dautov	03.03.1990	9		
Viktor Dmitrenko	04.04.1991	10	(2)	1
Pablo Ezequiel Fontanello (ARG)	26.09.1984	17		1
Aleksandr Kleshchenko (RUS)	02.11.1995	14	(1)	
Andrey Shabaev	15.02.1987	1	(1)	
Aleksandar Simčević (SRB)	15.02.1987	10	(1)	1
Midfielders:	DOB	M	(s)	G
Timur Dosmagambetov	01.05.1989	18		
Abdoulaye Diakhaté (SEN)	16.01.1988	18		3
Asludin Khadzhiev	24.10.2000	6	(5)	
May Sphiwe Mahlangu (RSA)	01.05.1989	14	(5)	
Rúben Luís Maurício Brígido (POR)	23.06.1991	15	(5)	3
Mirzad Mehanović (BIH)	05.01.1993	7	(6)	
Ular Zhaksybaev	20.10.1994		(7)	
Forwards:	DOB	M	(s)	G
Elkhan Astanov	21.05.2000	3	(8)	
Ziguy Badibanga (BEL)	26.11.1991	16	(2)	2
João Paulo da Silva Araújo (BRA)	02.06.1988	19	(1)	12
Sergey Khizhnichenko	17.07.1991	12	(7)	3
Samat Shamshi	05.02.1996		(3)	
Mardan Tolebek	18.12.1990	4	(2)	
Maksim Vaganov	08.08.2000		(1)	
Toktar Zhangylyshbay	25.05.1993	3	(12)	1

Football Club Shakhter Karagandy

Founded: 1958
Stadium: Shakhter Stadium, Karaganda (20,000)
Trainer: Vyacheslav Hroznyi (UKR) — 12.07.1956
(15.06.2020) Konstantin Gorovenka — 10.01.1977

Goalkeepers:	DOB	M	(s)	G
Egor Tsuprikov	27.05.1997	7		
David Yurchenko (ARM)	27.03.1986	7		
Timurbek Zakirov	01.03.1996	6		
Defenders:	DOB	M	(s)	G
Aliyu Abubakar (NGA)	15.06.1996		(1)	
Gideon Baah (GHA)	01.10.1991	19		2
Andrey Buyvolov	12.01.1987	19		2
Aleksandr Kislitsyn	08.03.1986	1		
Abdel Lamanje (FRA)	27.07.1990	17		2
Soslan Takulov	28.04.1995	14	(2)	
Evhen Tkachuk (UKR)	27.06.1991	10	(1)	1
Dmitry Yatchenko (RUS)	25.08.1986	11	(5)	
Midfielders:	DOB	M	(s)	G
Egor Ališauskas	18.12.1997		(1)	
Mikhail Bakaev (RUS)	05.08.1987	11	(6)	
Jérémy Manzorro (FRA)	11.11.1991	3		1
Gevorg Nadzharyan	06.01.1998	7	(4)	
Yerkebulan Nurgaliev	12.09.1993		(2)	
Tair Nurseitov	11.07.2000		(1)	
Erkin Tapalov	03.09.1993	9	(3)	1
Mohammed Usman Edu (NGA)	02.03.1994	18		1
Forwards:	DOB	M	(s)	G
Aslanbek Kakimov	02.10.1993	1	(4)	
Arsen Khubulov (RUS)	13.12.1990	15	(4)	5
Cédric Khaleb Kouadio (CIV)	25.07.1997		(1)	
Pavel Kriventsev	16.01.1996	11	(8)	
Ruslan Mingazov (TKM)	23.11.1991	9	(4)	2
Zhan-Ali Payruz	12.08.1999		(11)	1
Aydos Tattybaev	26.04.1990	6	(11)	5
Bauyrzhan Turysbek	15.10.1991	3		1
Sergei Zenjov (EST)	20.04.1989	16	(1)	3

Football Club Taraz

Founded: 1960
Stadium: „Yerkebulan Babayev" Stadium, Taraz (11,525)
Trainer: Vladimir Nikitenko — 08.01.1957

Goalkeepers:	DOB	M	(s)	G
Dzhurakhon Babakhanov	31.10.1991	9		
Almaz Khamytbekov	29.09.1991	1		
Mukhamedzhan Seysen	14.02.1999	10		
Defenders:	DOB	M	(s)	G
Berik Aytbaev	26.06.1991	13	(3)	
Dmitry Evstigneev	21.11.1986	3	(2)	
Valeriy Karshakevich (BLR)	15.02.1988	20		1
Mikhail Mishchenko (RUS)	27.06.1989	3	(2)	
Madiyar Nuraly	20.01.1995	1		
Bekzat Shadmanov	12.08.1997	13	(3)	
Midfielders:	DOB	M	(s)	G
Maksat Amirkhanov	10.02.1992	18		
Ayub Batsuev (RUS)	09.02.1997	1	(6)	1
Bauyrzhan Baytana	06.05.1992	4	(3)	
Dejan Boljević (MNE)	30.05.1990	14	(4)	1
Goran Brkić (SRB)	28.04.1991	17	(1)	1
Jovan Čađenović (MNE)	13.01.1995	20		1
Sheykhislam Kulakhmetov	15.01.1996		(1)	
Alisher Suley	01.11.1995	16	(2)	
Ovidijus Verbickas (LTU)	04.07.1993	11	(3)	
Forwards:	DOB	M	(s)	G
Dinmukhamed Karaman	26.06.2000		(1)	
Serge Komla Nyuiadzi (TOG)	17.09.1991	12	(1)	2
Bratislav Punoševac (SRB)	09.07.1987	2	(10)	
Abzal Taubay	18.02.1995	7	(6)	1
Toni Brito Silva Sá (GNB)	15.09.1993	13	(4)	4
Bauyrzhan Turysbek	15.10.1991	10	(4)	3
Nils Zatl (AUT)	03.04.1992	2		1
Abylaykhan Zhumabek	19.10.2001		(5)	1

Football Club Tobol Kostanay

Founded: 1967
Stadium: „Bauyrzhan Sagintayev" Stadium, Kostanay (10,500)
Trainer: Grigori Babayan — 02.04.1980

Goalkeepers:	DOB	M	(s)	G
Sultan Busurmanov	10.05.1996	1		
Aleksandr Mokin	19.06.1981	13		
Igor Shatskiy	11.05.1989	6		
Defenders:	DOB	M	(s)	G
Sultan Abilgazy	22.02.1997	6	(6)	1
Aleksa Amanović (MKD)	24.10.1996	18		
Roman Asrankulov	30.07.1999	4	(1)	
Temirlan Erlanov	09.07.1993	17		1
Arman Hovhannisyan (ARM)	07.07.1993	1	(2)	
Sergey Maliy	05.06.1990	11		2
Dmitry Miroshnichenko	26.02.1992	12	(4)	1
Sagadat Tursynbay	26.03.1999	2		
Midfielders:	DOB	M	(s)	G
Petros Avetisyan (ARM)	07.01.1996	2	(9)	1
Jaba Kankava (GEO)	18.03.1986	19		1
Nika Kvekveskiri (GEO)	29.05.1992	10	(6)	
Jérémy Manzorro (FRA)	11.11.1991	14	(1)	4
Serikzhan Muzhikov	17.06.1989	14	(4)	1
Daniyar Semchenkov	12.02.1997	1		
Ruslan Valiullin	09.09.1994	12	(1)	1
Samat Zharynbetov	04.01.1994	6	(4)	1
Forwards:	DOB	M	(s)	G
Carlos Manuel Costa Fernandes Fonseca (POR)	23.08.1987	9	(3)	
Roman Murtazayev	10.09.1993	10	(7)	2
Azat Nurgaliev	30.06.1986	14	(5)	5
Oralkhan Omirtaev	16.07.1998	2	(11)	1
Senin Sebai (CIV)	18.12.1993	13	(1)	2
Luka Zarandia (GEO)	17.02.1996	2		1
Zhaslan Zhumashev	27.09.2001	1		

Football Club Zhetysu Taldykorgan

Founded:	1981
Stadium:	„Samat Suyumbayev" Stadium, Taldykorgan (4,000)
Trainer:	Dmitriy Ogai 14.05.1960

Goalkeepers:	DOB	M	(s)	G
Almat Bekbaev	14.07.1984	9	(1)	
Andrey Shabanov	17.11.1986	11		
Defenders:	**DOB**	**M**	**(s)**	**G**
Olzhas Kerimzhanov	16.05.1989	13		1
Madi Khaseyn	17.12.2000		(1)	
Eskendir Kybyray	14.08.1997	5	(3)	
Andrey Lebedev (BLR)	01.02.1991	3	(2)	
David Gordon Mawutor (GHA)	12.04.1992	16	(2)	1
Nikita Naumov (BLR)	15.11.1989	17		
Ruan Orynbassar	01.03.1998	1		
Miram Sapanov	12.03.1986	10	(3)	
Andrey Zaleskiy (BLR)	20.01.1991	12	(2)	1
Stefan Živković (SRB)	01.06.1990	16	(1)	

Midfielders:	DOB	M	(s)	G
Nenad Adamović (SRB)	12.01.1989	16	(4)	1
Aslan Darabaev	21.01.1989	12	(5)	1
Ermek Kuantaev	13.10.1990	4	(8)	
Almir Mukhutdinov	09.06.1985	1	(1)	
Donjet Shkodra (BEL)	30.04.1989	17		2
Artūras Žulpa (LTU)	10.06.1990	10	(4)	1
Forwards:	**DOB**	**M**	**(s)**	**G**
Dias Kalybayev	25.08.1999		(1)	
Pedro Miguel Pina Eugénio (POR)	26.06.1990	16	(2)	5
Vadim Pobudey (BLR)	17.12.1994	7	(7)	1
Erkebulan Seydakhmet	04.02.2000	2	(4)	
Martin Toshev (BUL)	17.04.1990	12	(3)	4
Aybar Zhaksylykov	24.07.1997	5	(11)	6
Egor Zubovich (BLR)	01.06.1989	5	(14)	1

SECOND LEVEL
Kazakhstan First Division / Pervaia Liga 2020

Conference 1								
1. FC Aktobe (*Promoted*)	12	9	2	1	23	-	4	29
2. FC Arys (*Promoted*)	12	6	3	3	19	-	16	21
3. FC Kyran Shimkent	12	6	2	4	15	-	10	20
4. FC Maqtaaral Jetisay	12	5	2	5	15	-	16	17
5. FC Ekibastuz	12	3	3	6	14	-	16	12
6. FC Baykonur Kyzylorda	12	3	1	8	14	-	30	10
7. FC Altay Semey	12	2	3	7	10	-	18	9

Conference 2								
1. FC Atyrau (*Promoted*)	12	8	3	1	21	-	11	27
2. FC Zhetisu II Taldiqorghan	12	7	2	3	21	-	11	23
3. FC Akzhayik Oral (*Promoted*)	12	7	2	3	17	-	12	23
4. FK SDYuShOR-8 Nur-Sultan	12	6	2	4	25	-	20	20
5. FK Akademiya Ontustik	12	5	1	6	15	-	18	16
6. Sport Academy Kayrat Almaty	12	2	2	8	12	-	21	8
7. FC Shakhtar-Bulat Temirtau	12	0	2	10	9	-	27	2

NATIONAL TEAM

INTERNATIONAL MATCHES
(16.07.2020 – 15.07.2021)

04.09.2020	Vilnius	Lithuania - Kazakhstan	0-2(0-1)	(UNL)
07.09.2020	Almaty	Kazakhstan - Belarus	1-2(0-0)	(UNL)
11.10.2020	Almaty	Kazakhstan - Albania	0-0	(UNL)
14.10.2020	Minsk	Belarus - Kazakhstan	2-0(1-0)	(UNL)
11.11.2020	Podgorica	Montenegro - Kazakhstan	0-0	(F)
15.11.2020	Tiranë	Albania - Kazakhstan	3-1(2-1)	(UNL)
18.11.2020	Almaty	Kazakhstan - Lithuania	1-2(1-1)	(UNL)
28.03.2021	Nur-Sultan	Kazakhstan - France	0-2(0-2)	(WCQ)
31.03.2021	Kyiv	Ukraine - Kazakhstan	1-1(1-0)	(WCQ)
04.06.2021	Skopje	North Macedonia - Kazakhstan	4-0(1-0)	(F)

04.09.2020   LITHUANIA - KAZAKHSTAN   0-2(0-1)   2nd UEFA Nations League C, Group 4
LFF stadionas, Vilnius; Referee: Rade Obrenovič (Slovenia); Attendance: 0
KAZ: Stas Pokatilov, Sergey Malyi, Gafurzhan Suyumbayev, Marat Bystrov, Aleksandr Marochkin, Nuraly Alip, Bauyrzhan Islamkhan (Cap) (70.Abat Aymbetov), Yan Vorogovskiy, Baktiyar Zainutdinov (30.Maxim Fedin), Yuriy Pertsukh (82.Islambek Kuat), Aybol Abiken. Trainer: Michal Bílek (Czech Republic).
Goals: Baktiyor Zainutdinov (4), Islambek Kuat (86).

07.09.2020   KAZAKHSTAN - BELARUS   1-2(0-0)   2nd UEFA Nations League C, Group 4
Central Stadium, Almaty; Referee: Giorgi Kruashvili (Georgia); Attendance: 0
KAZ: Stas Pokatilov, Sergey Malyi, Abzal Beysebekov, Gafurzhan Suyumbayev, Aleksandr Marochkin, Nuraly Alip, Bauyrzhan Islamkhan (Cap) (81.Yuriy Pertsukh), Yan Vorogovskiy, Aybol Abiken, Abat Aymbetov (72.Sergey Khizhnichenko), Maxim Fedin (64.Islambek Kuat). Trainer: Michal Bílek (Czech Republic).
Goal: Abat Aymbetov (62).

11.10.2020   KAZAKHSTAN - ALBANIA   0-0   2nd UEFA Nations League C, Group 4
Central Stadium, Almaty; Referee: Dumitru Muntean (Moldova); Attendance: 0
KAZ: Stas Pokatilov, Olzhas Kerymzhanov, Gafurzhan Suyumbayev (Cap), Temirlan Yerlanov, Marat Bystrov, Aleksandr Marochkin (46.Abzal Beysebekov), Islambek Kuat (69.Yuriy Pertsukh), Askhat Tagybergen, Baktiyar Zainutdinov (86.Aybar Zhaksylykov), Aybol Abiken, Abat Aymbetov (69.Maxim Fedin). Trainer: Michal Bílek (Czech Republic).

14.10.2020   **BELARUS - KAZAKHSTAN**   **2-0(1-0)**   2nd UEFA Nations League C, Group 4
Stadion Dynama, Minsk; Referee: Chris Kavanagh (England); Attendance: 1,985
KAZ: Stas Pokatilov, Sergey Malyi (Cap), Olzhas Kerymzhanov, Timur Dosmagambetov, Temirlan Yerlanov, Marat Bystrov (78.Abzal Beysebekov), Askhat Tagybergen, Baktiyar Zainutdinov, Aybol Abiken (57.Islambek Kuat), Abat Aymbetov (57.Aybar Zhaksylykov), Vladislav Vasiljev (78.Duman Narzildayev). Trainer: Michal Bílek (Czech Republic).

11.11.2020   **MONTENEGRO - KAZAKHSTAN**   **0-0**   Friendly International
Stadion pod Goricom, Podgorica; Referee: Dimitar Meckarovski (North Macedonia); Attendance: 0
KAZ: Dmytro Nepohodov, Yuriy Logvinenko (74.Aleksandr Marochkin), Abzal Beysebekov (46.Nuraly Alip), Olzhas Kerymzhanov, Timur Dosmagambetov, Marat Bystrov (61.Yan Vorogovskiy), Aslan Darabayev (61.Yuriy Pertsukh), Islambek Kuat (Cap), Toktar Zhangylyshbay (61.Aleksey Shchetkin), Sergey Khizhnichenko (85.Aybol Abiken), Maxim Fedin. Trainer: Michal Bílek (Czech Republic).

15.11.2020   **ALBANIA - KAZAKHSTAN**   **3-1(2-1)**   2nd UEFA Nations League C, Group 4
Arena Kombëtare, Tiranë; Referee: Xavier Estrada Fernández (Spain); Attendance: 0
KAZ: Stas Pokatilov, Abzal Beysebekov (Cap), Olzhas Kerymzhanov (46.Maxim Fedin), Gafurzhan Suyumbayev (71.Marat Bystrov), Aleksandr Marochkin, Nuraly Alip, Islambek Kuat (88.Aslan Darabayev), Yan Vorogovskiy, Aybol Abiken (46.Askhat Tagybergen), Aleksey Shchetkin, Abat Aymbetov (71.Sergey Khizhnichenko). Trainer: Michal Bílek (Czech Republic).
Goal: Aybol Abiken (25).

18.11.2020   **KAZAKHSTAN - LITHUANIA**   **1-2(1-1)**   2nd UEFA Nations League C, Group 4
Central Stadium, Almaty; Referee: Hüseyin Göçek (Turkey); Attendance: 0
KAZ: Stas Pokatilov, Yuriy Logvinenko, Timur Dosmagambetov (69.Dmitriy Miroshnichenko), Aleksandr Marochkin, Nuraly Alip (87.Sergey Khizhnichenko), Islambek Kuat (Cap) [*sent off 50*], Askhat Tagybergen, Yan Vorogovskiy, Aybol Abiken, Aleksey Shchetkin, Abat Aymbetov (69.Toktar Zhangylyshbay). Trainer: Michal Bílek (Czech Republic).
Goal: Abat Aymbetov (38).

28.03.2021   **KAZAKHSTAN - FRANCE**   **0-2(0-2)**   22nd FIFA WC.Qualifiers
Astana Arena, Nur-Sultan; Referee: Aleksei Kulbakov (Belarus); Attendance: 0
KAZ: Aleksandr Mokin, Sergey Malyi, Temirlan Yerlanov, Marat Bystrov, Nuraly Alip, Azat Nurgaliyev (Cap) (83.Ramazan Karimov), Serikzhan Muzhikov (65.Yan Vorogovskiy), Askhat Tagybergen, Maxim Fedin (65.Yerkebulan Tungyshbayev), Ruslan Valiullin (83.Maksim Samorodov), Vladislav Vasiljev (88.Elkhan Astanov). Trainer: Talgat Baysufinov.

31.03.2021   **UKRAINE - KAZAKHSTAN**   **1-1(1-0)**   22nd FIFA WC.Qualifiers
NSC Olimpiyskiy Stadium, Kyiv; Referee: Matej Jug (Slovenia); Attendance: 0
KAZ: Stas Pokatilov, Sergey Malyi, Timur Dosmagambetov (46.Marat Bystrov), Aleksandr Marochkin, Nuraly Alip, Azat Nurgaliyev (Cap) (87.Yerkebulan Tungyshbayev), Serikzhan Muzhikov, Askhat Tagybergen (46.Ramazan Orazov), Ruslan Valiullin, Aybol Abiken (46.Yan Vorogovskiy), Abat Aymbetov (60.Ramazan Karimov). Trainer: Talgat Baysufinov.
Goal: Serikzhan Muzhikov (59).

01.06.2021   **NORTH MACEDONIA - KAZAKHSTAN**   **4-0(1-0)**   Friendly International
Nacionalna Arena "Toše Proeski", Skopje; Referee: Milovan Milačić (Montenegro); Attendance: 3,094
KAZ: Stas Pokatilov (46.Mukhammedzhan Seysen), Ruslan Valiullin (46.Gafurzhan Suyumbayev), Abzal Beysebekov (73.Alibek Kasym), Aleksandr Marochkin, Sergey Malyi, Yerkin Tapalov (83.Mikhail Gabyshev), Islambek Kuat, Askhat Tagybergen, Serikzhan Muzhikov [*sent off 45+2*], Aleksey Shchetkin (46.Roman Murtazayev), Azat Nurgaliyev (Cap) (72.Bauyrzhan Baytana). Trainer: Talgat Baysufinov.

NATIONAL TEAM PLAYERS (16.07.2020 – 15.07.2021)					
Name	**DOB**	**Caps**	**Goals**	**2020/2021:**	***Club***
Goalkeepers					
Aleksandr MOKIN	19.06.1981	**22**	**0**	2021:	*FC Tobol Kostanay*
Dmytro NEPOHODOV	17.02.1988	**13**	**0**	2020:	*Astana FC Nur-Sultan*
Stas POKATILOV	08.12.1992	**23**	**0**	2020/2021:	*FC Kairat Almaty*
Mukhammedzhan SEYSEN	14.02.1999	**1**	**0**	2021:	*FC Taraz*
Defenders					
Nuraly ALIP	22.12.1999	**8**	**0**	2020/2021:	*FC Kairat Almaty*
Abzal BEYSEBEKOV	30.11.1992	**34**	**0**	2020/2021:	*Astana FC Nur-Sultan*
Marat BYSTROV	19.06.1992	**8**	**0**	2020/2021:	*RFK Akhmat Grozny (RUS)*
Mikhail GABYSHEV	02.01.1990	**1**	**0**	2021:	*FC Shakhter Karagandy*
Alibek KASYM	27.05.1998	**1**	**0**	2021:	*FC Kyzylzhar SK Petropavl*
Olzhas KERYMZHANOV	16.05.1989	**5**	**0**	2020:	*FC Zhetisu Taldiqorghan*
Yuriy LOGVINENKO	22.07.1988	**53**	**5**	2020:	*Astana FC Nur-Sultan*
Sergey MALYI	05.06.1990	**47**	**0**	2020/2021:	*FC Tobol Kostanay*
Aleksandr MAROCHKIN	14.07.1990	**15**	**0**	2020:	*FC Kaysar Kyzylorda*
				31.12.2020->	*FC Tobol Kostanay*
Dmitriy MIROSHNICHENKO	26.02.1992	**11**	**0**	2020/2021:	*FC Tobol Kostanay*
Gafurzhan SUYUMBAYEV	19.08.1990	**39**	**4**	2020/2021:	*FC Kairat Almaty*
Ruslan VALIULLIN	09.09.1994	**3**	**0**	2021:	*FC Tobol Kostanay*
Temirlan YERLANOV	09.07.1993	**10**	**1**	2020:	*FC Tobol Kostanay*
				28.02.2021->	*FC Ordabasy Shymkent*

Midfielders

Name	DOB	M	G	Years	Club
Aybol ABIKEN	01.06.1996	12	1	2020/2021:	FC Kairat Almaty
Elkhan ASTANOV	21.05.2000	1	0	2021:	FC Ordabasy Shymkent
Bauyrzhan BAYTANA	06.06.1992	2	0	2021:	FC Taraz
Aslan DARABAYEV	21.01.1989	8	0	2020:	FC Zhetysu Taldiqorghan
Timur DOSMAGAMBETOV	01.05.1989	9	0	2020/2021:	FC Ordabasy Shymkent
Bauyrzhan ISLAMKHAN	23.02.1993	46	3	2020:	Al Ain FC (UAE)
Islambek KUAT	12.01.1993	39	5	2020:	Unattached; 11.09.2020-> FK Khimki (RUS)
				16.03.2021->	Astana FC Nur-Sultan
Serikzhan MUZHIKOV	17.06.1989	26	2	2021:	FC Tobol Kostanay
Duman NARZILDAYEV	06.09.1993	1	0	2020:	FC Kaysar Kyzylorda
Azat NURGALIYEV	30.06.1986	43	3	2021:	FC Tobol Kostanay
Ramazan ORAZOV	30.01.1998	1	0	2021:	FK Chayka Peschanokopskoye (RUS)
Askat TAGYBERGEN	09.08.1990	30	0	2020:	FC Kaysar Kyzylorda
				18.02.2021->	FC Tobol Kostanay
Yerkin TAPALOV	03.09.1993	2	0	2021:	FC Akzhayik Oral
Yerkebulan TUNGYSHBAYEV	14.01.1995	12	1	2021:	FC Ordabasy Shymkent
Vladislav VASILJEV	10.04.1997	2	0	2020:	FC Rukh Brest (BLR); 31.12.Dinamo Brest(BLR)
				05.03.2021->	FC Energetik-BGU Minsk (BLR, on loan)
Yan VOROGOVSKIY	07.08.1996	18	1	2020/2021:	K Beerschot VA (BEL)
Baktiyor ZAYNUTDINOV	02.04.1998	16	7	2020/2021:	FK CSKA Moskva (RUS)

Forwards

Name	DOB	M	G	Years	Club
Abat AYMBETOV	07.08.1995	13	2	2020:	FC Kairat Almaty
				20.02.2021->	PFK Krylia Sovetov Samara (RUS)
Maxim FEDIN	08.06.1996	13	1	2020:	FC Kaysar Kyzylorda (on loan from FC Tobol)
				27.02.2021->	FC Aktobe
Ramazan KARIMOV	05.07.1999	2	0	2021:	FC Caspiy Aqtau
Sergey KHIZHNICHENKO	17.07.1991	52	8	2020:	FC Ordabasy Shymkent
Roman MURTAZAYEV	10.09.1993	23	3	2021:	Astana FC Nur-Sultan
Yuriy PERTSUKH	13.05.1996	17	1	2020:	Astana FC Nur-Sultan
Maksim SAMORODOV	29.06.2002	1	0	2021:	FC Aktobe
Aleksey SHCHETKIN	21.05.1991	35	3	2021:	Astana FC Nur-Sultan
				13.01.2021->	FK Rotor Volgograd (RUS)
Aybar ZHAKSYLYKOV	24.07.1997	2	0	2020:	FC Zhetysu Taldiqorghan

Trainer

Michal BÍLEK (Czech Republic) [18.01.2019 – 19.11.2020]	13.04.1965	18 M; 5 W; 3 D; 10 L; 19-26
Talgat BAYSUFINOV [from 14.12.2020]	04.09.1968	3 M; 0 W; 1 D; 2 L; 1-7
		Complete record as trainer of Kazakhstan:
		11 M; 2 W; 4 D; 5 L; 7-21
		(26.03.2016 – 11.11.2016) & (from 14.12.2020)

KOSOVO

The Country:
Republika e Kosovës (Republic of Kosovo)
Capital: Prishtina
Surface: 10,908 km²
Inhabitants: 1,935,259 [2021]
Time: UTC+1

The FA:
Federata e Futbollit e Kosovës
Rruga "28 Nëntori", nr. 171, Prishtina / Kosovë 10000
Tel: +383 38 600 220
Foundation date: 1946
Member of FIFA since: 13.05.2016
Member of UEFA since: 03.05.2016
Website: www.ffk-kosova.com

NATIONAL TEAM RECORDS

RECORDS		
First international match:	05.03.2014, Mitrovicë:	Kosovo – Haiti 0-0
Most international caps:	Amir Kadri Rrahmani	- 38 caps (since 2014)
Most international goals:	Vedat Muriqi	- 15 goals / 30 caps (since 2016)

UEFA EUROPEAN CHAMPIONSHIP	
1960	-
1964	-
1968	-
1972	-
1976	-
1980	-
1984	-
1988	-
1992	-
1996	-
2000	-
2004	-
2008	-
2012	-
2016	-
2020	Qualifiers

FIFA WORLD CUP	
1930	-
1934	-
1938	-
1950	-
1954	-
1958	-
1962	-
1966	-
1970	-
1974	-
1978	-
1982	-
1986	-
1990	-
1994	-
1998	-
2002	-
2006	-
2010	-
2014	-
2018	Qualifiers

OLYMPIC TOURNAMENTS	
1908	-
1912	-
1920	-
1924	-
1928	-
1936	-
1948	-
1952	-
1956	-
1960	-
1964	-
1968	-
1972	-
1976	-
1980	-
1984	-
1988	-
1992	-
1996	-
2000	-
2004	-
2008	-
2012	-
2016	-

Please note: was part of Yugoslavia / Serbia and Montenegro / Serbia until 17.02.2008

UEFA NATIONS LEAGUE

2018/2019	League D (promoted to League C)
2020/2021	League C

FIFA CONFEDERATIONS CUP 1992-2017

None

KOSOVO CLUB HONOURS IN EUROPEAN CLUB COMPETITIONS:

European Champion Clubs' Cup (1956-1992) / UEFA Champions League (1993-2021)
None

Fairs Cup (1858-1971) / UEFA Cup (1972-2009) / UEFA Europa League (2010-2021)
None

UEFA Super Cup (1972-2020)
None

*European Cup Winners' Cup 1961-1999**
None

*defunct competition

NATIONAL COMPETITIONS
TABLE OF HONOURS

Kosovo Province League (within F.R. Yugoslavia)

	CHAMPIONS	CUP WINNERS
1945	Jedinstvo Prishtina	-
1946	Jedinstvo Prishtina	-
1947	KF Trepça Mitrovicë	-
1947/1948	Proleteri Prishtina	-
1948/1949	KF Trepça Mitrovicë	-
1950	KF Trepça Mitrovicë	-
1951	Kosova Prishtina	-
1952	KF Trepça Mitrovicë	-
1953/1954	Kosova Prishtina	-
1954/1955	KF Trepça Mitrovicë	-
1955/1956	Rudari Stantërg	-
1956/1957	Rudniku Hajvali	-
1957/1958	Rudari Stantërg	-
1958/1959	FC Prishtina	-
1959/1960	Rudari Stantërg	-
1960/1961	FC Prishtina	-
1961/1962	Buduqnosti Pejë	-
1962/1963	Crvena zvezda Gjilani	-
1963/1964	Slloga Lipyan	-
1964/1965	Slloga Lipyan	-
1965/1966	Buduqnosti Pejë	-
1966/1967	Obiliqi Kastriot	-
1967/1968	FC Vëllaznimi Gjakovë	-
1968/1969	FC Vëllaznimi Gjakovë	-
1969/1970	FC Vëllaznimi Gjakovë	-
1970/1971	FC Vëllaznimi Gjakovë	-
1971/1972	FC Obiliqi	-
1972/1973	KF Fushë Kosova	-
1973/1974	FC Vëllaznimi Gjakovë	-
1974/1975	KF Liria Prizreni	-
1975/1976	RHMK Obilić	-
1976/1977	FC Prishtina	-
1977/1978	Buduqnosti Pejë	-
1978/1979	FC Prishtina	-
1979/1980	FC Vëllaznimi Gjakovë	-
1980/1981	KF Liria Prizreni	-
1981/1982	FC Vëllaznimi Gjakovë	-
1982/1983	KNI Ramiz Sadiku	-
1983/1984	KF Liria Prizreni	-
1984/1985	Crvena zvezda Gjilani	FC Vëllaznimi Gjakovë
1985/1986	FC Vëllaznimi Gjakovë	FC Vëllaznimi Gjakovë
1986/1987	KF Liria Prizreni	FC Vëllaznimi Gjakovë
1987/1988	Crvena zvezda Gjilani	*No competition*
1988/1989	Buduqnosti Pejë	*No competition*
1989/1990	FC Vëllaznimi Gjakovë	*No competition*

Independent League of Kosovo

	CHAMPIONS	CUP WINNERS
1990/1991	KF Fushë-Kosova	*No competition*
1991/1992	FC Prishtina	KF Trepça Mitrovicë
1992/1993	KF Trepça Mitrovicë	KF Flamurtari Prishtina
1993/1994	KF Dukagjini Klinë	FC Prishtina
1994/1995	KF Liria Prizreni	KF Liria Prizreni
1995/1996	FC Prishtina	KF Flamurtari Prishtina
1996/1997	FC Prishtina	*Final not played*
1997/1998	*Tournament abandoned*	*No competition*
1998/1999	*No competition*	*No competition*

Establishment as top-league after UNMIK* take-over of Kosovo

	CHAMPIONS	CUP WINNERS
1999/2000	FC Prishtina	SC Gjilani
2000/2001	FC Prishtina	FC Drita Gjilani
2001/2002	KF Besiana Podujevë	KF Besiana Podujevo
2002/2003	FC Drita Gjilani	KF KEK-u Obilić
2003/2004	FC Prishtina	KF Kosova Prishtina
2004/2005	KF Besa Pejë Peć	KF Besa Pejë Peć
2005/2006	KF Besa Pejë Peć	FC Prishtina
2006/2007	KF Besa Pejë Peć	KF Liria Prizreni
2007/2008	FC Prishtina	FC Vëllaznimi Gjakovë

After proclamation of independence

	CHAMPIONS	CUP WINNERS
2008/2009	FC Prishtina	KF Hysi Podujevo
2009/2010	KF Trepça Mitrovicë	KF Liria Prizreni
2010/2011	KF Hysi Milloshevë	FC Prishtina
2011/2012	FC Prishtina	KF Trepça'89 Mitrovicë
2012/2013	FC Prishtina	FC Prishtina
2013/2014	KF Vushtria	KF Hajvalia
2014/2015	KF Feronikeli Glogovac	KV Feronikeli Glogovac
2015/2016	KF Feronikeli Glogovac	FC Prishtina

United Nations Mission in Kosovo

<u>Please note</u>: Jedinstvo Prishtina changed its name to Proleteri Prishtina, Kosova Prishtina and finally to FC Prishtina.
Buduqnosti Pejë became KF Besa Pejë Peć; FC Obiliqi changed its name to RHMK Obilić and later KF KEK-u Obilić

After membership in UEFA and FIFA

	CHAMPIONS	CUP WINNERS	BEST GOALSCORERS	
2016/2017	KF Trepça'89 Mitrovicë	KF Llapi Podujevë	John Otto John (NGA, KF Trepça'89 Mitrovicë)	24
2017/2018	KF Drita Gjilan	FC Vëllaznimi Gjakovë	John Otto John (NGA, KF Trepça'89 Mitrovicë) Mirlind Daku (KF Llapi Podujevë)	17
2018/2019	KF Feronikeli Glogovac	KF Feronikeli Glogovac	Kastriot Rexha (KF Feronikeli Glogovac)	21
2019/2020	KF Drita Gjilan	KF Prishtina	Blendi Baftiu (KF Ballkani Suva Reka) Arb Manaj (KF Trepça'89 Mitrovicë)	19
2020/2021	KF Prishtina	KF Llapi Podujevë	Mirlind Daku (KF Ballkani Suva Reka)	31

NATIONAL CHAMPIONSHIP
Football Superleague of Kosovo 2020/2021
(18.09.2020 – 16.05.2021)

Results

Round 1 [18-20.09.2020]
KF Trepça'89 - KF Arbëria 0-2
FC Prishtina - KF Drenica 3-0
KF Besa Pejë - KF Ballkani 1-4
KF Feronikeli - KF Gjilani 4-0
KF Drita Gjilan - KF Llapi 1-0 [03.12.]

Round 2 [22-23.09.2020]
KF Arbëria - FC Prishtina 1-1
KF Drenica - KF Besa Pejë 2-1
KF Ballkani - KF Feronikeli 3-2
KF Llapi - KF Gjilani 0-1
KF Drita Gjilan - KF Trepça'89 1-0 [14.10.]

Round 3 [25-27.09.2020]
KF Besa Pejë - KF Arbëria 0-3
KF Trepça'89 - KF Llapi 1-0
KF Feronikeli - KF Drenica 2-2
KF Gjilani - KF Ballkani 0-0
FC Prishtina - KF Drita Gjilan 1-1 [20.12.]

Round 4 [29.09.-01.10.2020]
KF Arbëria - KF Feronikeli 0-0
KF Llapi - KF Ballkani 1-3
KF Trepça'89 - FC Prishtina 1-0
KF Drita Gjilan - KF Besa Pejë 3-1
KF Drenica - KF Gjilani 0-0

Round 5 [03-05.10.2020]
KF Besa Pejë - KF Trepça'89 2-1
KF Feronikeli - KF Drita Gjilan 1-2
FC Prishtina - KF Llapi 0-0
KF Ballkani - KF Drenica 5-0
KF Gjilani - KF Arbëria 3-1

Round 6 [16-18.10.2020]
KF Arbëria - KF Ballkani 2-4
FC Prishtina - KF Besa Pejë 4-0
KF Llapi - KF Drenica 0-1
KF Drita Gjilan - KF Gjilani 0-0
KF Trepça'89 - KF Feronikeli 0-0

Round 7 [20-21.10.2020]
KF Besa Pejë - KF Llapi 2-2
KF Drenica - KF Arbëria 0-1
KF Feronikeli - FC Prishtina 1-2
KF Ballkani - KF Drita Gjilan 2-0
KF Gjilani - KF Trepça'89 0-0

Round 8 [24-25.10.2020]
KF Besa Pejë - KF Feronikeli 1-1
KF Drita Gjilan - KF Drenica 4-1
KF Llapi - KF Arbëria 2-0
FC Prishtina - KF Gjilani 0-2
KF Trepça'89 - KF Ballkani 4-3

Round 9 [27-28.10.2020]
KF Arbëria - KF Drita Gjilan 0-1
KF Feronikeli - KF Llapi 1-0
KF Drenica - KF Trepça'89 2-1
KF Gjilani - KF Besa Pejë 1-0
KF Ballkani - FC Prishtina 2-1

Round 10 [31.10.-01.11.2020]
KF Arbëria - KF Trepça'89 1-2
KF Ballkani - KF Besa Pejë 4-1
KF Gjilani - KF Feronikeli 0-0
KF Drenica - FC Prishtina 1-0
KF Llapi - KF Drita Gjilan 1-2

Round 11 [04-05.11.2020]
KF Besa Pejë - KF Drenica 0-0
FC Prishtina - KF Arbëria 1-0
KF Trepça'89 - KF Drita Gjilan 0-1
KF Feronikeli - KF Ballkani 1-1
KF Gjilani - KF Llapi 2-0

Round 12 [10-11.11.2020]
KF Drita Gjilan - FC Prishtina 0-0
KF Llapi - KF Trepça'89 5-0
KF Drenica - KF Feronikeli 1-0
KF Arbëria - KF Besa Pejë 1-0
KF Ballkani - KF Gjilani 0-4 [19.12.]

Round 13 [21-22.11.2020]
KF Feronikeli - KF Arbëria 1-0
KF Besa Pejë - KF Drita Gjilan 1-4
KF Gjilani - KF Drenica 1-0
FC Prishtina - KF Trepça'89 4-2
KF Ballkani - KF Llapi 4-2

Round 14 [24-26.11.2020]
KF Drita Gjilan - KF Feronikeli 1-1
KF Arbëria - KF Gjilani 1-0
KF Trepça'89 - KF Besa Pejë 4-2
KF Llapi - FC Prishtina 0-2
KF Drenica - KF Ballkani 1-2

Round 15 [28-30.11.2020]
KF Besa Pejë - FC Prishtina 0-2
KF Feronikeli - KF Trepça'89 2-0
KF Gjilani - KF Drita Gjilan 2-3
KF Ballkani - KF Arbëria 2-1
KF Drenica - KF Llapi 0-1

Round 16 [04-06.12.2020]
FC Prishtina - KF Feronikeli 0-0
KF Arbëria - KF Drenica 1-0
KF Trepça'89 - KF Gjilani 3-0
KF Llapi - KF Besa Pejë 2-0
KF Drita Gjilan - KF Ballkani 2-1

Round 17 [09-10.12.2020]
KF Drenica - KF Drita Gjilan 0-3
KF Feronikeli - KF Besa Pejë 3-0
KF Gjilani - FC Prishtina 0-3
KF Arbëria - KF Llapi 1-2
KF Ballkani - KF Trepça'89 2-0

Round 18 [12-14.12.2020]
KF Besa Pejë - KF Gjilani 1-2
KF Llapi - KF Feronikeli 3-2
FC Prishtina - KF Ballkani 2-1
KF Drita Gjilan - KF Arbëria 1-1
KF Trepça'89 - KF Drenica 0-0

Round 19 [13-15.02.2021]
KF Besa Pejë - KF Ballkani 0-3
FC Prishtina - KF Drenica 3-1
KF Drita Gjilan - KF Llapi 1-0
KF Trepça'89 - KF Arbëria 1-1
KF Feronikeli - KF Gjilani 1-1

Round 20 [19-21.02.2021]
KF Arbëria - FC Prishtina 0-4
KF Drenica - KF Besa Pejë 0-0
KF Drita Gjilan - KF Trepça'89 1-2
KF Llapi - KF Gjilani 3-1
KF Ballkani - KF Feronikeli 1-0

Round 21 [24-25.02.2021]
FC Prishtina - KF Drita Gjilan 2-0
KF Trepça'89 - KF Llapi 1-0
KF Gjilani - KF Ballkani 1-1
KF Feronikeli - KF Drenica 1-3
KF Besa Pejë - KF Arbëria 0-3

Round 22 [27.02.-01.03.2021]
KF Trepça'89 - FC Prishtina 1-2
KF Drita Gjilan - KF Besa Pejë 3-1
KF Llapi - KF Ballkani 1-0
KF Arbëria - KF Feronikeli 0-3
KF Drenica - KF Gjilani 0-0

Round 23 [05-07.03.2021]
KF Besa Pejë - KF Trepça'89 1-2
KF Ballkani - KF Drenica 2-1
KF Gjilani - KF Arbëria 1-1
FC Prishtina - KF Llapi 2-0
KF Feronikeli - KF Drita Gjilan 0-1

Round 24 [10-11.03.2021]
FC Prishtina - KF Besa Pejë 5-1
KF Trepça'89 - KF Feronikeli 0-0
KF Llapi - KF Drenica 3-3
KF Drita Gjilan - KF Gjilani 2-0
KF Arbëria - KF Ballkani 2-6

Round 25 [13-14.03.2021]
KF Feronikeli - FC Prishtina 2-0
KF Besa Pejë - KF Llapi 1-4
KF Drenica - KF Arbëria 1-1
KF Gjilani - KF Trepça'89 2-1
KF Ballkani - KF Drita Gjilan 0-0

Round 26 [20-21.03.2021]
KF Drita Gjilan - KF Drenica 1-1
KF Besa Pejë - KF Feronikeli 2-1
KF Llapi - KF Arbëria 4-3
KF Trepça'89 - KF Ballkani 0-2
FC Prishtina - KF Gjilani 0-0 [30.03.]

Round 27 [03-05.04.2021]
KF Arbëria - KF Drita Gjilan 1-3
KF Drenica - KF Trepça'89 2-0
KF Feronikeli - KF Llapi 4-0
KF Ballkani - FC Prishtina 0-1
KF Gjilani - KF Besa Pejë 5-1

Round 28 [09-11.04.2021]
KF Arbëria - KF Trepça'89 0-1
KF Gjilani - KF Feronikeli 1-0
KF Ballkani - KF Besa Pejë 4-1
KF Llapi - KF Drita Gjilan 2-4
KF Drenica - FC Prishtina 0-1

Round 29 [16-18.04.2021]
KF Besa Pejë - KF Drenica 1-2
KF Gjilani - KF Llapi 0-2
FC Prishtina - KF Arbëria 2-0
KF Trepça'89 - KF Drita Gjilan 0-1
KF Feronikeli - KF Ballkani 0-2

Round 30 [24-25.04.2021]
KF Drenica - KF Feronikeli 1-1
KF Arbëria - KF Besa Pejë 2-1
KF Llapi - KF Trepça'89 2-1
KF Ballkani - KF Gjilani 1-0
KF Drita Gjilan - FC Prishtina 1-2

Round 31 [27-28.04.2021]	Round 32 [01-02.05.2021]	Round 33 [05-06.05.2021]
KF Feronikeli - KF Arbëria 0-1	KF Drita Gjilan - KF Feronikeli 3-1	KF Besa Pejë - FC Prishtina 0-3
KF Besa Pejë - KF Drita Gjilan 1-1	KF Arbëria - KF Gjilani 3-4	KF Feronikeli - KF Trepça'89 3-0
KF Gjilani - KF Drenica 0-0	KF Trepça'89 - KF Besa Pejë 1-1	KF Gjilani - KF Drita Gjilan 1-1
KF Ballkani - KF Llapi 1-0	KF Llapi - FC Prishtina 1-3	KF Drenica - KF Llapi 4-2
FC Prishtina - KF Trepça'89 3-1	KF Drenica - KF Ballkani 2-1	KF Ballkani - KF Arbëria 2-3

Round 34 [09.05.2021]	Round 35 [16.05.2021]	Round 36 [23.05.2021]
FC Prishtina - KF Feronikeli 2-1	KF Drenica - KF Drita Gjilan 0-3	KF Besa Pejë - KF Gjilani 1-0
KF Arbëria - KF Drenica 1-1	KF Gjilani - FC Prishtina 1-2	KF Llapi - KF Feronikeli 1-1
KF Trepça'89 - KF Gjilani 2-1	KF Feronikeli - KF Besa Pejë 3-1	FC Prishtina - KF Ballkani 2-5
KF Llapi - KF Besa Pejë 1-0	KF Arbëria - KF Llapi 3-2	KF Drita Gjilan - KF Arbëria 2-0
KF Drita Gjilan - KF Ballkani 1-1	KF Ballkani - KF Trepça'89 4-3	KF Trepça'89 - KF Drenica 2-1

Final Standings

									Total				Home				Away		
1.	**KF Prishtina**	36	24	6	6	65	-	27	78	12	4	2	36 - 15	12	2	4	29 - 12
2.	KF Drita Gjilan	36	22	10	4	59	-	28	76	10	6	2	28 - 13	12	4	2	31 - 15
3.	KF Ballkani Suva Reka	36	23	5	8	79	-	43	74	14	1	3	39 - 20	9	4	5	40 - 23
4.	SC Gjilani	36	12	12	12	37	-	38	48	7	7	4	21 - 16	5	5	8	16 - 22
5.	KF Llapi Podujevë	36	13	4	19	49	-	56	43	9	2	7	32 - 27	4	2	12	17 - 29
6.	KF Drenica Skenderaj	36	10	12	14	34	-	48	42	7	5	6	17 - 18	3	7	8	17 - 30
7.	KF Feronikeli Glogovac	36	10	12	14	44	-	36	42	9	3	6	30 - 16	1	9	8	14 - 20
8.	KF Trepça'89 Mitrovicë	36	12	6	18	38	-	54	42	8	5	5	21 - 17	4	1	13	17 - 37
	(*Relegation Play-offs*)																
9.	KF Arbëria Lipljan (*Relegated*)	36	11	7	18	42	-	58	40	5	3	10	20 - 35	6	4	8	22 - 23
10.	KF Besa Pejë (*Relegated*)	36	3	6	27	27	-	86	15	3	4	11	15 - 38	0	2	16	12 - 48

Top goalscorers:	
31 Mirlind Daku	***KF Ballkani Suva Reka***
12 Marko Simonovski (MKD)	*KF Feronikeli Glogovac*
10 Marclei Cesar Chaves Santos (BRA)	*KF Arbëria Lipljan*
10 John Otto John (NGA)	*KF Prishtina*

Relegation Play-offs [28.05.2021]

KF Trepça'89 Mitrovicë - KF Dukagjini Klinë   1-1(1-0,1-1,1-1); 3-4 on penalties

KF Dukagjini Klinë promoted for the Football Superleague of Kosovo 2021/2022

NATIONAL CUP
Kosovo Cup / Kupa e Kosovës 2020/2021

Round 0f 32 [12-17.12.2020]			
KF Vitia - KF Ferizaj	2-3	KF Onix Banjë - KF Llapi Podujevë	2-4
KF Vllaznia Pozheran - KF Dukagjini Klinë	1-4	KF Kosova VR Prishtinë - KF Prishtina	2-6
KF UV Malisheva - KF 2 Korriku Prishtina	2-3 aet	KF Dardana Kamenicë - KF Ballkani Suva Reka	0-1
KF Ulpiana Lipljan - KF Liria Prizren	2-0	KF Prizreni - KF Feronikeli Glogovac	0-4
SC Gjilani - KF KEK-u Obilić	5-0	KF Vëllaznimi Gjakovë - KF Trepça'89 Mitrovicë	1-3
KF Flamurtari Prishtina - KF Drenasi	2-1 aet	KF Drita Gjilan - KF Trepça Mitrovicë	2-1
KF A&N Prizren - KF Kika Hogosht	5-1	KF Vushtrria - KF Drenica Skenderaj	0-1
KF Besa Pejë - KF Istogu	0-2	KF Ramiz Sadiku Prishtina - KF Arbëria Lipljan	1-2

1/8-Finals [09-11.02.2021]			
KF Llapi Podujevë - KF Ballkani Suva Reka	0-0; 4-3 pen	KF Trepça'89 Mitrovicë - KF Ferizaj	4-0
KF Prishtina - KF Drita Gjilan	1-0 aet	KF Istogu - SC Gjilani	2-0
KF Drenica Skenderaj - KF Ulpiana Lipljan	4-0	KF Arbëria Lipljan - KF Feronikeli Glogovac	0-1
KF A&N Prizren - KF Flamurtari Prishtina	1-0	KF Dukagjini Klinë - KF 2 Korriku Prishtina	3-1

Quarter-Finals [17-18.03.2021]			
KF Feronikeli Glogovac - KF Prishtina	0-0; 2-4 pen	KF Trepça'89 Mitrovicë - KF Llapi Podujevë	1-2
KF Dukagjini Klinë - KF Drenica Skenderaj	1-0	KF Istogu - KF A&N Prizren	1-1; 7-6 pen

Semi-Finals [ ]			
First Leg		**Second Leg**	
KF Istogu - KF Dukagjini Klinë	0-3 (awarded)	KF Dukagjini Klinë - KF Istogu	*not played*
KF Prishtina - KF Llapi Podujevë	2-3	KF Llapi Podujevë - KF Prishtina	2-2

12.05.2021; Stadiumi „Fadil Vokrri", Prishtina; Referee: Genc Nuza; Attendance: 0
KF Dukagjini Klinë - KF Llapi Podujevë   **1-1(0-0,0-0,1-1); 3-4 on penalties**

KF Dukagjini: Altik Muhaxhiri, Donat Hasanaj, Ilir Syla, Elton Basriu, Rinor Kuqi, Labinot Jashanica (66.Vildan Kerim), Met Millaku (73.Mhill Grabanica), Fatlum Gashi, Erblind Mulaj (90.Leorant Marmullaku), Labinot Osmani (73.Abu Kamara), Altin Merlaku. Trainer: Armend Dallku.

KF Llapi: Marijan Ćorić, Benjamin Emini, Bujar Idrizi, Elvis Prençi, Ardit Peposhi (114.Muhamet Hyseni), Arbnor Ramadani, Kushtrim Shabani, Kastriot Selmani (64.Valmir Veliu), Engjell Hoti (106.Sava Gardašević), Edon Sadriu, Ahmed Januzi. Trainer: Tahir Batatina.

Goals: 1-0 Altin Merlaku (113), 1-1 Elvis Prençi (120).

Penalties: Vildan Kerim 1-0; Arbnor Ramadani 1-1; Elton Basriu 2-1; Sava Gardašević 2-2; Fatlum Gashi 3-2; Bujar Idrizi 3-3; Ilir Syla (saved); Ahmed Januzi (saved); Altin Merlaku (saved); Muhamet Hyseni 3-4.

THE CLUBS 2020/2021

Klubi Futbollistik Arbëria Dobrajë e Madhe

Founded:	1977 (*as KF Përparimi*); re-founded 30.05.2016.		
Stadium:	Stadiumi "Agron Rama", Obilić (5,000)		
Trainer:	Arbnor Morina		02.06.1963

Goalkeepers:	DOB	M	(s)	G
Donat Kaçiu	20.09.1993	24	(1)	
Armend Miftari	28.04.1995	2		
Andi Thaqi	13.04.1996	10		
Defenders:	**DOB**	**M**	**(s)**	**G**
Qlirim Avdulli	06.06.1999	34		
Leutrim Beqiri	05.04.1990	10	(4)	
Ergon Hyseni	18.01.1994	15	(6)	
Labinot Ibrahimi	25.06.1986	27		1
Elmir Lekaj	18.01.2000	8	(3)	
Destin Prince-Loïc Mambouana (FRA)	10.09.1990	1		
Arbër Pira	09.02.1995	31		
Midfielders:	**DOB**	**M**	**(s)**	**G**
Aldin Adžović (MNE)	18.04.1994	5	(6)	
Bruno Arrabal Passamani (BRA)	22.02.1992	27		
Fidan Bahtiri	05.11.1995	1	(1)	1
Kreshnik Bahtiri	29.07.1992	32		6

Agron Bruqi	27.01.1993	31	(1)	
Aladin Djakovac (SRB)	22.05.1991		(1)	
Korab Hasanaj	01.03.1991	1	(4)	
Qlirim Koshtanjeva	04.02.1999	11	(10)	2
Agon Llugiqi	31.07.1991	10	(11)	3
Gëzim Rusi	29.11.1994	4	(4)	
Andi Seferi	14.08.2001	1	(5)	
Filonit Shaqiri	29.05.1993	3	(2)	
Dior Zabërgja	18.04.1995	29	(6)	5
Forwards:	**DOB**	**M**	**(s)**	**G**
Lutfi Bilali	14.04.1992	10	(3)	2
Hysen Bytyqi	30.09.1995	2	(14)	2
Sunaj Hasan	03.08.1996	8	(2)	1
Anes Hot	20.06.1995	3	(2)	1
Almir Kryeziu	14.12.1998	32		5
Griseld Lika	02.11.1997	10	(4)	
Marclei Cesar Chaves Santos (BRA)	18.06.1989	14	(1)	9

Klubi Futbollistik Ballkani Suva Reka

Founded:	1947		
Stadium:	Stadiumi i Qytetit të Suharekës, Suva Reka (1,500)		
Trainer:	Ismet Munishi		03.10.1974
[04.01.2021]	Bledi Shkëmbi (ALB)		13.08.1979

Goalkeepers:	DOB	M	(s)	G
Kenan Haxhihamza	28.12.1996	7		
Damir Ljuljanović (MNE)	23.05.1992	16		
Armend Rugji	30.12.1985	13		
Defenders:	**DOB**	**M**	**(s)**	**G**
Visar Berisha	07.12.1986	16	(5)	
Ramiz Bytyqi	10.01.1999	3	(10)	
Bajram Jashanica	25.09.1990	22	(1)	1
Albin Kapra	07.06.2000	1	(4)	
Arber Potoku	19.04.1994	32		
Arbër Prekazi	11.10.1989	21		2
Arbër Shala	23.12.1991	3	(1)	1
Egzon Sinani	07.06.1994	18	(4)	1
Armend Thaqi	10.10.1992	32		3

Midfielders:	DOB	M	(s)	G
Blend Baftiu	17.02.1998	26	(2)	6
Liridon Fetahaj	21.09.1991		(1)	
Kushtrim Gashi	05.11.1992	19	(2)	
Roni Gashi	04.06.1998	1	(3)	
Nazmi Gripshi (ALB)	05.07.1997	28	(3)	6
Meriton Korenica	15.12.1996	25	(5)	3
Edvin Kuc (MNE)	27.10.1993	32		2
Diar Miftaraj	20.10.1990	1		
Bleon Sekiraqa	17.10.2000		(1)	
Forwards:	**DOB**	**M**	**(s)**	**G**
Mirlind Daku	01.01.1998	33	(1)	31
Arbër Hoxha	06.10.1998	12	(5)	8
Ermal Krasniqi	07.09.1998	27	(3)	8
Edi Maksutaj	04.10.2000		(2)	
Mevlan Zeka	28.05.1994	8	(14)	6

Klubi Futbollistik Besa Pejë

Founded: 1923
Stadium: Stadiumi „Tahir Vokshi", Bresovik (1,500)
Trainer: Leotrim Krasniqi

Goalkeepers:	DOB	M	(s)	G
Visar Haxhijaj	14.08.1989	12		
Agron Kolaj	19.03.2001	23		
Kreshnik Ndreca	31.10.1999	1		
Defenders:	**DOB**	**M**	**(s)**	**G**
Ardi Ajdini	04.11.2002			
Guri Hana	27.08.2001			
Diar Halili	02.07.2003			
Valton Ibrahimi	22.02.2003			
Fisnik Papuqi	01.07.1983			
Blažo Rajović (MNE)	26.03.1986			
Filip Šćekić (MNE)	28.12.1999			
Agon Xhaka	09.06.1997			
Midfielders:	**DOB**	**M**	**(s)**	**G**
Diellor Beseni (ALB)	31.05.2002			
Etnik Brruti	04.03.2004			
Festim Haxhiu	18.06.2003			
Dren Idrizi	04.09.2000			
Norik Krasniqi	31.05.2000			

	DOB
Ethmane M'Heimar (MTN)	05.02.2002
Bekim Maliqi	26.07.2001
Arber Maznikolli	03.02.2001
Erjon Morina	16.07.2002
Florent Qorraj	14.01.1995
Ardi Qorri	15.02.2001
Ron Raqi	18.09.2002
Gentrit Salihu	25.06.2003
Lucas Sebastian Marques da Silva (BRA)	03.10.1998
Donart Sheqerolli	29.01.1995
Forwards:	**DOB**
Breno Barbosa Matos (BRA)	28.10.1999
Rinor Jahmutaraj	
Ahmed Salem M'Bracek (MTN)	06.03.2002
Matheus Henrique de Paula (BRA)	06.04.1995
Redon Syla	09.02.2003
Bilal Taghiyoullah	09.06.2002
Ardit Tahiri	06.10.2002
Dhurim Zhuri	20.09.2002

Please note: the transmitted data were incomplete because several line-ups from various match days were not available or not complete. Therefore, these statistical data (with the exception of goalkeepers) have not been entered.

Klubi Futbollistik Drenica Skenderaj

Founded: 1958
Stadium: Stadiumi"Bajram Aliu", Skenderaj (3,000)
Trainer: Bledar Devolli · 15.01.1978
[17.03.2021] Johanes Tafaj · 13.03.1991
[24.03.2021] Sami Sermaxhaj

Goalkeepers:	DOB	M	(s)	G
Gentrit Hasi	24.04.1997	3		
Arion Ymeri	30.03.1995	33		
Defenders:	**DOB**	**M**	**(s)**	**G**
Azem Bejta	03.08.1990	33	(1)	1
Gentrit Dumani	13.07.1993	27	(1)	1
Erlis Frashëri	13.05.1988	13		
Eglentin Gjoni	02.12.1992	14	(1)	2
Shkelzen Lushtaku	22.06.1990	19	(4)	1
Harallamb Qaqi	17.09.1993	7		
Donald Rapo	04.10.1990	13		2
Valdo Zeqaj	24.08.1995	14		
Midfielders:	**DOB**	**M**	**(s)**	**G**
José Denisson Silva dos Santos (BRA)	29.11.1997	10		2
Besfort Dervishaj	24.09.1998	11	(1)	
Lulzim Doshlaku	28.01.1991	4	(4)	
Jeton Dushi	06.03.1996	12	(1)	
Qemail Elshani	28.06.1991	18	(4)	2
Genc Hamiti	21.09.1993	12		
Hasan Hyseni	14.04.1997	1		

	DOB	M	(s)	G
Granit Jashari	20.08.1998	8	(2)	
Diar Miftaraj	20.10.1990	12	(1)	
Albutrint Morina	20.02.1993	9	(3)	
Argjent Mustafa	30.08.1992	10	(1)	
Gentrit Olluri	11.05.2001	3	(3)	
Behar Ramadani	06.04.1990	14		
Arbios Thaçi	13.10.1993	9	(1)	
Ermal Veliqi	25.07.2001	1	(4)	1
Forwards:	**DOB**	**M**	**(s)**	**G**
Dionis Cikani (GRE)	10.03.1999	3	(2)	
Egzon Fazliu	30.05.2003	3	(8)	1
Kreshnik Lushtaku	20.07.1994	1	(1)	
Osman Mëziu	05.09.1999	6	(6)	2
Almedin Murati (ALB)	19.02.1995	11	(2)	2
Vildan Kerim (MKD)	04.08.1994	4	(1)	
Dardan Rogova	09.08.1990	9		1
Klevis Shaqe	17.11.1999	2	(1)	
Hysen Tahiri	28.09.1992	10	(5)	1
Kreshnik Uka	07.01.1995	14		6
Baton Zabergja	18.04.2001	23		4

Klubi Futbollistik Drita Gjilan

Founded: 1947
Stadium: Stadiumi i Qytetit, Gjilan (15,000)
Trainer: Ardijan Nuhiji (MKD) · 07.12.1978

Goalkeepers:	DOB	M	(s)	G
Faton Maloku	14.06.1991	26		
Leutrim Rexhepi	16.04.1994	10		
Defenders:	**DOB**	**M**	**(s)**	**G**
Jamal Arago (GHA)	28.08.1993	24	(3)	
Ilir Blakçori	01.02.1993	29		
Vladica Brdarovski (MKD)	07.02.1990	16	(2)	
Enhar Cakolli	26.05.2000		(2)	
Ardian Cuc-uli (MKD)	19.07.1987	25		
Fidan Gërbeshi	19.05.1985	13	(6)	2
Ardian Limani	18.11.1993	32	(1)	4
Midfielders:	**DOB**	**M**	**(s)**	**G**
Ergyn Ahmeti	21.12.1995	6	(19)	
Astrit Fazliu	28.10.1987	31	(3)	6

	DOB	M	(s)	G
Drilon Islami	18.07.2000		(14)	
Albin Krasniqi	03.06.2001	1	(8)	
Hamdi Namani	16.10.1994	25	(3)	4
Henry Austine Onoka (NGA)	08.08.1998	3	(1)	
Bujar Shabani	11.10.1990	25	(9)	4
Erjon Vucaj (ALB)	25.12.1990	25	(4)	
Forwards:	**DOB**	**M**	**(s)**	**G**
Almir Ajzeraj	05.10.1997	18	(7)	3
Festim Alidema	05.10.1997	15	(13)	7
Betim Haxhimusa	14.04.1992	18	(16)	9
Esosa Priestley	25.06.1996	1	(12)	3
Kastriot Rexha	27.09.1988	19	(2)	8
Xhevdet Shabani	10.10.1986	34	(1)	8

Klubi Futbollistik Feronikeli Glogovac

Founded: 1974
Stadium: Stadiumi "Rexhep Rexhepi", Glogovac (2,000)
Trainer: Afrim Tovërlani   17.01.1967
[01.05.2021] Faruk Elshani   20.07.1973

Goalkeepers:	DOB	M	(s)	G
Ilir Avdyli	20.05.1990	22		
Florjan Smakiqi	10.08.1998	14		
Defenders:	DOB	M	(s)	G
Prince Balde (LBR)	23.03.1998	19	(3)	
Perparim Islami	01.05.1993	5	(3)	
Ozbej Kuhar	21.04.1997	1		
Viktor Kuka	25.06.1990	5		
Lapidar Lladrovci	15.12.1990	20	(2)	1
Simon Loshi (NED)	16.02.2000	8	(3)	
Bujar Pllana	29.10.2001	13	(6)	
Alban Pnishi	20.10.1990	4		
Lorent Shala	20.08.2000	1	(1)	
Astrit Thaqi	20.04.1993	25	(3)	
Yll Hoxha	26.12.1987	32		1
Midfielders:	DOB	M	(s)	G
Argjend Bardhi	28.04.1993		(4)	
Besmir Bojku (MKD)	03.01.1995	27	(4)	1
Albert Dabiqaj	10.07.1996	34		5
Dorent Hajdari	28.01.2001		(1)	
Jean Agostinho da Silva "Jean Carioca" (BRA)	01.06.1988	19	(3)	1
Damir Kojašević (MNE)	03.06.1987	5	(1)	1
Argjend Malaj	16.10.1993	32		2
Marko Miličković (MNE)	31.03.1998	20	(6)	5
Ardi Qorri	15.02.2001	1		
Forwards:	DOB	M	(s)	G
Bedri Greca	23.10.1990	9	(1)	3
Mendurim Hoti	23.02.1996	26	(3)	4
Rizon Hoti		1		
Sokol Kiqina			(5)	
Adem Maliqi	17.07.1997	30	(3)	4
Marclei César Chaves Santos (BRA)	18.06.1989	3	(3)	3
Pajazit Rexhepi			(1)	
Marko Simonovski	02.01.1992	20		12

Soccer Club Gjilani

Founded: 1945
Stadium: Stadiumi i Qytetit, Gjilan (15,000)
Trainer: Gentian Mezani (ALB)   13.10.1975
[13.12.2000] Bylbyl Sokoli   19.12.1958
[12.03.2021] Ismet Munishi   03.10.1974

Goalkeepers:	DOB	M	(s)	G
Enea Koliçi	13.02.1986	33		
Shkëlzen Ruçi (ALB)	01.07.1992	2		
Petrit Terziu	03.12.2001	1		
Defenders:	DOB	M	(s)	G
Ardin Dallku	01.11.1994	6	(1)	
Erlis Frashëri (ALB)	13.05.1988	13		
Ivan Fustar (CRO)	18.08.1989	20		1
Drin Govori	17.05.1999	1		
Armend Halili	22.06.1997	12	(9)	
Jackson Ferreira Silvério (BRA)	12.04.1991	17		
Ylber Kastrati	09.04.1987	14	(1)	
Oltion Rapa (ALB)	30.09.1989	24	(3)	
Tomislav Šorša (CRO)	11.05.1989	7	(3)	
Franc Veliu (ALB)	11.11.1988	20	(1)	
Midfielders:	DOB	M	(s)	G
Arbër Çyrbja	18.09.1993	14	(7)	2
Qendrim Dautaj	07.01.1991	2	(4)	
Ardit Hila (ALB)	06.01.1993	29	(1)	5
Edison Kqiku	16.01.1999	13	(6)	1
Gramoz Kurtaj	30.04.1991	4	(5)	1
Keita Lanzeni Aziz (CIV)	28.12.1996	19	(3)	
Besar Musolli	28.02.1989	28	(2)	1
Muhamed Useini (MKD)	21.11.1988	26	(2)	1
Forwards:	DOB	M	(s)	G
Tomislav Bušić (CRO)	02.02.1986	3	(4)	
Muhamed Dubova	14.06.2001		(3)	
Fiton Hajdari	19.09.1991	25	(5)	3
Shend Kelmendi	21.09.1994	5	(9)	2
Darko Nikač (MNE)	15.09.1990	22	(3)	7
Gerhard Progni (ALB)	06.11.1986	31	(1)	9
Keita Alassane Razak (CIV)	28.09.1996	5	(2)	1

Klubi Futbollistik Llapi Podujevë

Founded: 1932
Stadium: Stadiumi „Zahir Pajaziti", Podujevë (10,000)
Trainer: Tahir Batatina   12.07.1977

Goalkeepers:	DOB	M	(s)	G
Drilon Ajeti (ENG)	26.06.2000	3	(1)	
Marijan Ćorić (CRO)	06.02.1995	11	(1)	
Steven Hoffman (RSA)	31.01.1994	10		
Giacomo Nava (ITA)	27.01.1997	9		
Arlis Shala	26.07.2000	3		
Defenders:	DOB	M	(s)	G
Benjamin Emini	20.07.1992	27	(1)	
Eglentin Gjoni (ALB)	02.12.1992	1		
Ahmet Haliti	01.10.1988	9	(3)	
Amir Hossari (LIB)	19.09.1993	3	(1)	1
Bujar Idrizi	11.12.1991	26	(1)	1
Liridon Leci	11.02.1985		(2)	
Anthony Monin (FRA)	03.05.1996	5		
Granit Musa	22.02.2002	3	(1)	
Ardit Peposhi (ALB)	14.09.1993	30	(2)	1
Elvis Prençi (ALB)	26.06.1993	31		5
Midfielders:	DOB	M	(s)	G
Gentrit Begolli	21.02.1992	2	(6)	
Lis Behrami	27.08.2002		(2)	
Engjell Hoti (GER)	26.02.1997	22	(5)	4
Taulant Kicmari	23.02.2002		(2)	
Almedin Klinaku	16.12.2002		(3)	
Ilir Krasniqi	02.04.2000	6	(6)	
Bekim Maliqi	26.07.2001	4	(2)	
Alban Ramadani (SUI)	10.09.1994	11	(9)	
Arbnor Ramadani	03.06.1994	28		6
Edon Sadriu	25.05.1997	14	(18)	7
Kushtrim Shabani	08.02.1997	26	(3)	1
Kastriot Selmani	08.07.1999	23	(7)	3
Enis Stublla	09.07.1999		(2)	
Diar Vokrri	27.06.2004		(2)	
Ersil Ymeri (ALB)	06.07.1994	1		
Edon Zeqiri	04.06.1990	8	(6)	
Mentor Zhdrella	06.10.1990	16	(2)	2
Forwards:	DOB	M	(s)	G
Adonis Aliu	01.03.2001	4	(10)	2
Sava Gardašević (MNE)	27.01.1993	6	(12)	2
Muhamet Hyseni	06.02.2001	7	(14)	3
Ahmed Januzi (ALB)	08.07.1988	24	(3)	5
Premtim Jakupi (MKD)	01.04.2000		(2)	
Valmir Veliu	04.06.2000	23	(8)	4

<table>
<tr><td colspan="2">Klubi Futbollistik Prishtina</td></tr>
</table>

Founded:	1922		
Stadium:	Stadiumi "Fadil Vokrri", Prishtina (13,500)		
Trainer:	Armend Dallku (ALB)		16.06.1983
[09.09.2019]	Zekirija Ramadani (MKD)		21.01.1978

Goalkeepers:	DOB	M	(s)	G
Eglant Haxho (ALB)	11.11.1988	22		
Ivan Jelić (CRO)	19.11.1997	1		
Ardit Nika	12.01.1998	13		
Defenders:	**DOB**	**M**	**(s)**	**G**
Tun Bardhoku	12.09.1993	7	(16)	1
Leotrim Bekteshi	21.04.1992	35		3
Lumbardh Dellova	01.01.1999	27		1
Erdin Dushi	07.10.2002		(1)	
Besnik Krasniqi	01.02.1990	34		10
Gledi Mici (ALB)	06.02.1991	33		1
Gentian Muça (ALB)	13.05.1987	7	(3)	2
Ahmed Raddaoui (TUN)	17.06.1997		(2)	
Midfielders:	**DOB**	**M**	**(s)**	**G**
Lorik Boshnjaku	07.07.1995	28	(3)	
Donat Hasanaj	18.09.1998		(1)	

	DOB	M	(s)	G
Endrit Krasniqi	26.10.1994	35		7
Sabien Lilaj (ALB)	18.02.1989	22	(3)	2
Behar Maliqi	22.09.1986	2	(9)	
Mergim Pefqeli	25.11.1993	4	(12)	1
Qëndrim Zyba	03.01.2001	24	(8)	1
Forwards:	**DOB**	**M**	**(s)**	**G**
Leonit Abazi (ALB)	05.07.1993	31	(1)	6
Samuel Mone Andoh (GHA)	24.07.2002		(2)	
Enis Gavazaj (ALB)	21.03.1995	4	(6)	1
John Otto John (NGA)	25.01.1998	13	(6)	10
Leotrim Kryeziu	25.01.1999	25	(4)	9
Gauthier Mankenda (CGO)	20.07.1997	19	(13)	4
Albin Prapashtica	08.09.2001		(15)	1
Alban Shillova	13.08.1992	9	(6)	2
Kreshnik Uka	07.01.1995	1	(2)	

<table>
<tr><td colspan="2">Klubi Futbollistik Trepça'89 Mitrovicë</td></tr>
</table>

Founded:	1992		
Stadium:	Stadiumi "Riza Lushta", Mitrovicë (12,000)		
Trainer:	Shpëtim Idrizi		12.11.1981

Goalkeepers:	DOB	M	(s)	G
Marly Prince Heritier (CGO)	10.04.1999	16	(1)	
Ardit Hyseni	28.12.1999	8		
Darko Tofiloski (MKD)	13.01.1986	12		
Defenders:	**DOB**	**M**	**(s)**	**G**
Leuart Avdyli	14.04.2002	2		
Sedat Berisha (MKD)	03.09.1989	33		3
Gustavo Carbonieri Santa Rosa (BRA)	04.03.1992	7		
Albert Kaçiku	21.01.1995	6		
Happy Takalani Mashau (RSA)	24.03.1993	28		
Ardian Muja	09.12.1997	30	(1)	2
Albion Pllana	20.08.2000	18	(2)	
Midfielders:	**DOB**	**M**	**(s)**	**G**
Zeki Ademi	23.01.2001	6	(2)	1
Milot Avdyli	28.07.2002	7	(5)	
Mohamed Darwish (PLE)	20.02.1997	26		3
Valon Dedia	31.08.2000	17	(5)	

	DOB	M	(s)	G
Muharrem Jashari	21.02.1998	33		3
Ervin Kačar (SRB)	25.10.1991	13		
Nikson Memaj	13.02.2000	4	(5)	1
Kreshnik Nebihi	18.06.1997	3		
Mphakamiseni Nene (RSA)	01.01.1992	8		
Rilind Nimani	11.01.1999	31	(1)	3
Joseph Okonkwo (NGA)	05.04.2000	6	(2)	
Lulzim Peci	27.02.2002		(1)	
Robert Rrahmani	28.01.2001	6	(9)	1
Beshir Sheremeti	12.07.2000		(1)	
Forwards:	**DOB**	**M**	**(s)**	**G**
Bismark Charles Kwarena Sie (GHA)	26.05.2001	14	(3)	6
Ranga Piniel Chivaviro (RSA)	21.11.1992	5		
Arb Manaj	23.07.1998	3		
Arbnor Muja	29.11.1998	29	(2)	8
Adenis Shala	23.10.1998	25	(1)	5

SECOND LEVEL
First Football of Kosovo - Liga e Parë 2020/2021

Group A

1. KF UV Malisheva (*Promoted*)	27	19	3	5	56 - 20	60
2. KF Dukagjini Klinë (*Promotion Play-offs*)	27	17	7	3	52 - 24	58
3. KF Istogu	27	13	8	6	34 - 18	47
4. FK A&N Prizren	27	11	4	12	41 - 36	37
5. KF Liria Prizren	27	8	10	9	34 - 25	34
6. KF Trepça Mitrovicë	27	9	6	12	36 - 49	33
7. KF Vëllaznimi Gjakovë	27	8	5	14	22 - 36	29
8. KF Onix Banjë	27	7	7	13	26 - 45	28
9. KF Drenasi	27	5	10	12	26 - 40	25
10. KF Vushtrria* (*Relegated*)	27	4	8	15	17 - 51	20

Group B

1. KF Ulpiana Lipljan (*Promoted*)	27	15	8	4	40 - 19	53
2. KF Flamurtari Prishtina (*Promotion Play-offs*)	27	14	10	3	43 - 20	52
3. KF 2 Korriku Prishtina	27	13	3	11	43 - 30	42
4. KF Vitia	27	9	8	10	33 - 36	35
5. KF Kika Hogosht	27	10	4	13	33 - 42	34
6. KF Ramiz Sadiku Prishtina	27	8	8	11	24 - 30	32
7. KF Dardana Kamenicë	27	8	8	11	25 - 35	32
8. KF Vllaznia Požaranje	27	8	7	12	24 - 42	31
9. KF Ferizaj	27	7	9	11	31 - 38	30
10. KF KEK-u Obilić (*Relegated*)	27	7	7	13	24 - 32	28

*Please <u>note</u>: KF Vushtrria were not relegated after merging with KF Dardana Kamenicë.

Promotion Play-offs [21.05.2021]

Semi-Final	KF Dukagjini Klinë - KF Flamurtari Prishtina	2-1(1-0)

KF Dukagjini Klinë were qualified for the Final against KF Trepça'89 Mitrovicë.

INTERNATIONAL MATCHES
(16.07.2020 – 15.07.2021)

03.09.2020	Parma	Moldova - Kosovo	1-1(1-0)	(UNL)
06.09.2020	Prishtina	Kosovo - Greece	1-2(0-1)	(UNL)
08.10.2020	Skopje	North Macedonia - Kosovo	2-1(2-1)	(ECQPO)
11.10.2020	Prishtina	Kosovo - Slovenia	0-1(0-1)	(UNL)
14.10.2020	Athína	Greece - Kosovo	0-0	(UNL)
11.11.2020	Elbasan	Albania - Kosovo	2-1(1-0)	(F)
15.11.2020	Ljubljana	Slovenia - Kosovo	2-1(0-0)	(UNL)
18.11.2020	Prishtina	Kosovo - Moldova	1-0(1-0)	(UNL)
24.03.2021	Prishtina	Kosovo - Lithuania	4-0(1-0)	(F)
28.03.2021	Prishtina	Kosovo - Sweden	0-3(0-2)	(WCQ)
31.03.2021	Sevilla	Spain - Kosovo	3-1(2-0)	(WCQ)
01.06.2021	Prishtina	Kosovo - San Marino	4-1(2-0)	(F)
04.06.2021	Klagenfurt	Malta - Kosovo	1-2(1-1)	(F)
08.06.2021	Manavgat	Kosovo - Guinea	1-2(0-0)	(F)
11.06.2021	Manavgat	Kosovo - Gambia	1-0(0-0)	(F)

03.09.2020 MOLDOVA - KOSOVO   **1-1(1-0)**   2nd UEFA Nations League C, Group 3
Stadio "Ennio Tardini", Parma (Italy); Referee: Kai Erik Steen (Norway); Attendance: 0
KVX: Arijanet Anan Muriqi, Fidan Aliti, Leart Paqarada, Amir Rrahmani (Cap), Mërgim Vojvoda (60.Florent Hadergjonaj), Herolind Shala (60.Bersant Celina), Valon Berisha, Hekuran Kryeziu, Benjamin Kololli, Milot Nexhmedin Rashica (75.Elbasan Rashani), Arbër Zeneli. Trainer: Bernard Challandes (Switzerland).
Goal: Benjamin Kololli (71).

06.09.2020 KOSOVO - GREECE   **1-2(0-1)**   2nd UEFA Nations League C, Group 3
Stadiumi „Fadil Vokrri", Prishtina; Referee: Pavel Královec (Czech Republic); Attendance: 0
KVX: Samir Ujkani (Cap), Fidan Aliti, Amir Rrahmani, Florent Hadergjonaj, Mërgim Vojvoda (58.Anel Rashkaj), Ibrahim Dreshaj, Valon Berisha, Besar Halimi (55.Florent Hasani), Bersant Celina, Atdhe Nuhiu, Arbër Zeneli (54.Bernard Berisha). Trainer: Bernard Challandes (Switzerland).
Goal: Bernard Berisha (82).

08.10.2020 NORTH MACEDONIA - KOSOVO   **2-1(2-1)**   16th EC. Qualifiers Play-offs, Semi-Finals
"Toše Proeski" Arena, Skopje; Referee: Danny Desmond Makkelie (Netherlands); Attendance: 0
KVX: Arijanet Anan Muriqi, Fidan Aliti, Florent Hadergjonaj, Mërgim Vojvoda (64.Edon Zhegrova), Ibrahim Dreshaj, Herolind Shala (87.Leart Paqarada), Valon Berisha (Cap), Bersant Celina (75.Lirim M. Kastrati), Benjamin Kololli, Atdhe Nuhiu (46.Elbasan Rashani), Arbër Zeneli. Trainer: Bernard Challandes (Switzerland).
Goal: Florent Hadergjonaj (33).

11.10.2020 KOSOVO - SLOVENIA   **0-1(0-1)**   2nd UEFA Nations League C, Group 3
Stadiumi „Fadil Vokrri", Prishtina; Referee: Andrew Madley (England); Attendance: 0
KVX: Arijanet Anan Muriqi, Fidan Aliti, Leart Paqarada, Florent Hadergjonaj, Ibrahim Dreshaj, Herolind Shala (84.Florent Muslija), Valon Berisha (Cap), Bersant Celina, Edon Zhegrova (89.Florent Hasani), Arbër Zeneli (78.Lirim M. Kastrati), Benjamin Kololli (83.Elbasan Rashani). Trainer: Bernard Challandes (Switzerland).

14.10.2020 GREECE - KOSOVO   **0-0**   2nd UEFA Nations League C, Group 3
Stádio Olympiako „Spiros Louis", Athína; Referee: Roi Reinshreiber (Israel); Attendance: 0
KVX: Arijanet Anan Muriqi, Fidan Aliti, Leart Paqarada, Florent Hadergjonaj, Mërgim Vojvoda, Ibrahim Dreshaj, Herolind Shala (Cap), Bersant Celina (63.Florent Hasani), Benjamin Kololli (80.Elbasan Rashani), Florian Loshaj (34.Anel Rashkaj), Lirim M. Kastrati. Trainer: Bernard Challandes (Switzerland).

11.11.2020 ALBANIA - KOSOVO   **2-1(1-0)**   Friendly International
Elbasan Arena, Elbasan; Referee: Hüseyin Göçek (Turkey); Attendance: 0
KVX: Arijanet Anan Muriqi, Fidan Aliti (84.Mërgim Vojvoda), Amir Rrahmani (Cap), Florent Hadergjonaj (84.Mirlind Daku), Herolind Shala, Hekuran Kryeziu (46.Anel Rashkaj), Bersant Celina (46.Florent Hasani), Bernard Berisha (46.Elbasan Rashani), Betim Fazlija, Vedat Muriqi, Lirim M. Kastrati (46.Edon Zhegrova). Trainer: Bernard Challandes (Switzerland).
Goal: Vedat Muriqi (85 penalty).

15.11.2020 SLOVENIA - KOSOVO   **2-1(0-0)**   2nd UEFA Nations League C, Group 3
Stadion Stožice, Ljubljana; Referee: Bartosz Frankowski (Poland); Attendance: 0
KVX: Arijanet Anan Muriqi, Fidan Aliti, Amir Rrahmani (Cap), Florent Hadergjonaj, Mërgim Vojvoda, Anel Rashkaj, Valon Berisha, Hekuran Kryeziu (71.Lirim M. Kastrati), Bernard Berisha (84.Elbasan Rashani), Edon Zhegrova (90+1.Florent Hasani), Vedat Muriqi. Trainer: Bernard Challandes (Switzerland).
Goal: Vedat Muriqi (58).

18.11.2020 KOSOVO - MOLDOVA   **1-0(1-0)**   2nd UEFA Nations League C, Group 3
Stadiumi „Fadil Vokrri", Prishtina; Referee: Roomer Tarajev (Estonia); Attendance: 0
KVX: Samir Ujkani (Cap), Amir Rrahmani (20.Fidan Aliti), Florent Hadergjonaj, Mërgim Vojvoda, Ibrahim Dreshaj [*sent off 84*], Herolind Shala, Valon Berisha, Bersant Celina (90.Armend Qazim Thaqi), Edon Zhegrova (83.Hekuran Kryeziu), Vedat Muriqi, Lirim M. Kastrati. Trainer: Bernard Challandes (Switzerland).
Goal: Lirim M. Kastrati (31).

24.03.2021   **KOSOVO - LITHUANIA**   **4-0(1-0)**   Friendly International
Stadiumi „Fadil Vokrri", Prishtina; Referee: Enea Jorgji (Albania); Attendance: 0
KVX: Samir Ujkani (Cap), Florent Hadergjonaj, Mërgim Vojvoda, Ibrahim Dreshaj, Fidan Aliti (46.Leart Paqarada), Hekuran Kryeziu, Valon Berisha (46.Idriz Naser Voca), Bersant Celina (46.Besar Halimi), Arbër Zeneli (76.Bernard Berisha), Milot Nexhmedin Rashica (67.Lirim M. Kastrati), Vedat Muriqi (66.Benjamin Kololli). Trainer: Bernard Challandes (Switzerland).
Goals: Arbër Zeneli (27), Vedat Muriqi (63), Arbër Zeneli (71), Besar Halimi (79).

28.03.2021   **KOSOVO - SWEDEN**   **0-3(0-2)**   22nd FIFA WC. Qualifiers
Stadiumi "Fadil Vokrri", Prishtina; Referee: Tamás Bognár (Hungary); Attendance: 0
KVX: Samir Ujkani (Cap), Fidan Aliti, Florent Hadergjonaj, Mërgim Vojvoda, Hekuran Kryeziu, Arbër Zeneli (83.Bernard Berisha [sent off 90+2]), Besar Halimi (75.Idriz Naser Voca), Bersant Celina, Benjamin Kololli, Milot Nexhmedin Rashica (71.Lirim M. Kastrati), Vedat Muriqi. Trainer: Bernard Challandes (Switzerland).

31.03.2021   **SPAIN - KOSOVO**   **3-1(2-0)**   22nd FIFA WC. Qualifiers
Estadio La Cartuja, Sevilla; Referee: Jakob Kehlet (Denmark); Attendance: 0
KVX: Samir Ujkani (Cap), Fidan Aliti, Florent Hadergjonaj, Mërgim Vojvoda, Ibrahim Dreshaj, Hekuran Kryeziu, Besar Halimi (82.Idriz Naser Voca), Bersant Celina, Benjamin Kololli (57.Arbër Zeneli), Milot Nexhmedin Rashica (55.Lirim M. Kastrati), Vedat Muriqi. Trainer: Bernard Challandes (Switzerland).
Goal: Besar Halimi (70).

01.06.2021   **KOSOVO - SAN MARINO**   **4-1(2-0)**   Friendly International
Stadiumi "Fadil Vokrri", Prishtina; Referee: Yaşar Kemal Uğurlu (Turkey); Attendance: 0
KVX: Samir Ujkani (Cap), Amir Rrahmani, Mërgim Vojvoda, Destan Bajselmani, Hekuran Kryeziu (70.Idriz Naser Voca), Arbër Zeneli (70.Zymer Bytyqi), Besar Halimi (71.Lorik Emini), Blendi Idrizi (82.Valmir Sulejmani), Betim Fazlija, Vedat Muriqi (82.Mirlind Daku), Lirim M. Kastrati. Trainer: Bernard Challandes (Switzerland).
Goals: Vedat Muriqi (28, 45+1, 46, 76 penalty).

04.06.2021   **MALTA - KOSOVO**   **1-2(1-1)**   Friendly International
Wörthersee Stadion, Klagenfurt (Austria); Referee: Christopher Jäger (Austria); Attendance: 0
KVX: Visar Bekaj, Fidan Aliti (88.Destan Bajselmani), Amir Rrahmani (Cap), Mërgim Vojvoda, Herolind Shala (61.Besar Halimi), Hekuran Kryeziu (72.Idriz Naser Voca), Arbër Zeneli, Milot Nexhmedin Rashica (88.Mirlind Daku), Blendi Idrizi, Betim Fazlija, Lirim M. Kastrati (61.Zymer Bytyqi). Trainer: Bernard Challandes (Switzerland).
Goals: Milot Nexhmedin Rashica (19, 84).

08.06.2021   **KOSOVO - GUINEA**   **1-2(0-0)**   Friendly International
Arslan Zeki Demirci Spor Kompleksi, Manavgat (Austria); Referee: Sarper Barış Saka (Turkey); Attendance: 0
KVX: Visar Bekaj (Cap), Bajram Jashanica (46.Lavdrim Hajrullahu), Armend Qazim Thaqi, David Nue Domgjoni, Destan Bajselmani, Rron Broja (76.Muharrem Jashari), Florian Loshaj, Donat Rrudhani (85.Blendi Baftiu), Arbër Hoxha (46.Liridon Balaj), Mirlind Daku (46.Arb Manaj), Jetmir Topalli (62.Mersim Asllani). Trainer: Bernard Challandes (Switzerland).
Goal: Arb Manaj (90+3).

11.06.2021   **KOSOVO - GAMBIA**   **1-0(0-0)**   Friendly International
Arslan Zeki Demirci Spor Kompleksi, Manavgat (Austria); Referee: Arda Kardeşler (Turkey); Attendance: 0
KVX: Betim Halimi, Armend Qazim Thaqi (59.Mersim Asllani), David Nue Domgjoni, Lavdrim Hajrullahu, Destan Bajselmani, Eroll Zejnullahu (59.Rron Broja), Florian Loshaj (Cap), Liridon Balaj (69.Arbër Hoxha), Donat Rrudhani, Mirlind Daku (69.Arb Manaj), Jetmir Topalli. Trainer: Bernard Challandes (Switzerland).
Goal: Arbër Hoxha (80).

	NATIONAL TEAM PLAYERS (16.07.2020 – 15.07.2021)				
Name	**DOB**	**Caps**	**Goals**	**2020/2021:**	*Club*
	Goalkeepers				
Visar BEKAJ	24.05.1997	4	0	2021:	*KF Tiranë (ALB)*
Betim HALIMI	28.02.1996	1	0	2021:	*FK Olimpik Donetsk (UKR)*
Arijanet Anan MURIQI	07.11.1998	16	0	2020: 18.09.2020->	*Manchester City FC FC (ENG) Girona FC (ESP)*
Samir UJKANI	05.07.1988	32	0	2020/2021:	*Torino FC (ITA)*

Defenders

Name	DOB			Season	Club
Fidan ALITI	03.10.1993	33	0	2020: 02.10.2020->	*Kalmar FF (SWE)* *FC Zürich (SUI)*
Destan BAJSELMANI	13.05.1999	4	0	2021:	*PEC Zwolle (NED)*
David Nue DOMGJONI	21.05.1997	2	0	2021:	*Menemenspor Kulübü İzmir (TUR)*
Ibrahim DRESHAJ	24.01.1997	9	0	2020/2021:	*SC Heerenveen (NED)*
Betim FAZLIJA	25.04.1999	3	0	2020/2021:	*FC St. Gallen (SUI)*
Florent HADERGJONAJ	31.07.1994	18	1	2020: 25.09.2020->	*Huddersfield Town FC (ENG)* *Kasımpaşa Spor Kulübü İstanbul (TUR)*
Lavdrim HAJRULLAHU	07.03.1998	2	0	2021:	*FC Stade Lausanne Ouchy (SUI)*
Bajram JASHANICA	25.09.1990	8	0	2021:	*KF Ballkani Suva Reka*
Leart PAQARADA	10.08.1994	24	1	2020/2021:	*FC St. Pauli Hamburg (GER)*
Amir Kadri RRAHMANI	24.02.1994	36	5	2020/2021:	*SSC Napoli (ITA)*
Armend Qazim THAQI	10.10.1992	5	0	2020/2021:	*KF Ballkani Suva Reka*
Mërgim VOJVODA	01.02.1995	36	1	2020/2021:	*Torino FC (ITA)*

Midfielders

Name	DOB			Season	Club
Mersim ASLLANI	07.06.1999	2	0	2021:	*FC Stade Lausanne Ouchy (SUI)*
Blendi BAFTIU	17.02.1998	2	0	2021:	*KF Ballkani Suva Reka*
Liridon BALAJ	15.08.1999	2	0	2021:	*FC Aarau (SUI)*
Bernard BERISHA	21.10.1991	20	1	2020/2021:	*RFK Akhmat Grozny (RUS)*
Valon BERISHA	07.02.1993	27	3	2020/2021:	*Stade de Reims (FRA)*
Rron BROJA	09.04.1996	3	0	2021:	*FK Partizani Tiranë (ALB)*
Zymer BYTYQI	11.09.1996	4	0	2021:	*Konyaspor Kulübü (TUR)*
Bersant CELINA	09.09.1996	30	2	2020: 09.09.2020->	*Swansea City AFC (WAL)* *Dijon FCO (FRA)*
Lorik EMINI	29.08.1999	1	0	2021:	*FC Luzern (SUI)*
Besar HALIMI	12.12.1994	29	3	2020/2021:	*SV Sandhausen (GER)*
Florent HASANI	30.03.1997	8	1	2020:	*Diósgyőri VTK (HUN)*
Blendi IDRIZI	02.05.1998	2	0	2021:	*FC Schalke 04 Gelsenkirchen (GER)*
Muharrem JASHARI	21.02.1998	1	0	2021:	*KF Trepça'89 Mitrovicë*
Benjamin KOLOLLI	15.05.1992	23	4	2020/2021:	*FC Zürich (SUI)*
Hekuran KRYEZIU	12.02.1993	28	0	2020/2021:	*FC Zürich (SUI)*
Florian LOSHAJ	13.08.1996	4	0	2020/2021:	*KS Cracovia Kraków (POL)*
Florent MUSLIJA	06.07.1998	4	0	2020:	*SV Hannover 96 (GER)*
Milot Nexhmedin RASHICA	28.06.1996	32	6	2020/2021:	*SV Werder Bremen (GER)*
Anel RASHKAJ	19.08.1989	14	0	2020:	*SJK Seinäjoki (FIN)*
Donat RRUDHANI	02.05.1999	2	0	2021:	*FC Aarau (SUI)*
Herolind SHALA	02.01.1992	24	0	2020: 05.03.2021->	*Vålerenga Fotball Oslo (NOR)* *Stabæk Fotball Bærum (NOR)*
Idriz Naser VOCA	15.05.1997	15	0	2020/2021:	*MKE Ankaragücü (TUR)*
Eroll ZEJNULLAHU	19.10.1994	4	0	2021:	*FC Nitra (SVK)*
Arbër ZENELI	25.02.1995	27	9	2020/2021:	*Stade de Reims (FRA)*
Edon ZHEGROVA	31.03.1999	22	2	2020:	*FC Basel (SUI)*

Forwards

Name	DOB			Season	Club
Mirlind DAKU	01.01.1998	5	0	2020/2021:	*KF Ballkani Suva Reka*
Arbër HOXHA	06.10.1998	3	1	2021:	*KF Ballkani Suva Reka*
Lirim M. KASTRATI	16.01.1999	14	1	2020/2021:	*GNK Dinamo Zagreb (CRO)*
Arb MANAJ	01.01.1997	3	0	2021:	*Balıkesirspor Kulübü Derneği (TUR)*
Vedat MURIQI	24.04.1994	30	15	2020/2021:	*SS Lazio Roma (ITA)*
Atdhe NUHIU	29.07.1989	19	3	2020:	*APOEL FC Nicosia (CYP)*
Elbasan RASHANI	09.05.1993	18	4	2020:	*Odds BK Skien (NOR)*
Valmir SULEJMANI	01.02.1996	4	0	2021:	*SV Hannover 96 (GER)*
Jetmir TOPALLI	07.02.1998	3	0	2021:	*Yeni Malatya Spor Kulübü (TUR)*

Trainer

Name	DOB	Record
Bernard CHALLANDES (Switzerland) [from 02.03.2018]	26.07.1951	35 M; 16 W; 7 D; 12 L; 56-41

LATVIA

The Country:
Latvijas Republika (Republic of Latvia)
Capital: Rīga
Surface: 64,589 km²
Inhabitants: 1,907,675 [2020]
Time: UTC+2

The FA:
Latvijas Futbola federācija
Olympic Sports Centre, Grostonas Street 6b, 1013 Rīga
Tel: +371 6729 2988
Foundation date: 19.06.1921
Member of FIFA since: 1922
Member of UEFA since: 1992
Website: www.lff.lv

NATIONAL TEAM RECORDS

RECORDS
First international match:	24.09.1922, Rīga:	Latvia – Estonia 1-1
Most international caps:	Vitālijs Astafjevs	- 167 caps (1992-2010)
Most international goals:	Māris Verpakovskis	- 29 goals / 104 caps (1999-2014)

UEFA EUROPEAN CHAMPIONSHIP		FIFA WORLD CUP		OLYMPIC TOURNAMENTS	
1960	-	1930	Did not enter	1908	-
1964	-	1934	Did not enter	1912	-
1968	-	1938	*Entry not accepted by FIFA*	1920	-
1972	-	1950	-	1924	-
1976	-	1954	-	1928	1/8 - Finals
1980	-	1958	-	1936	Did not enter
1984	-	1962	-	1948	-
1988	-	1966	-	1952	-
1992	-	1970	-	1956	-
1996	Qualifiers	1974	-	1960	-
2000	Qualifiers	1978	-	1964	-
2004	Final Tournament (Group Stage)	1982	-	1968	-
2008	Qualifiers	1986	-	1972	-
2012	Qualifiers	1990	-	1976	-
2016	Qualifiers	1994	Qualifiers	1980	-
2020	Qualifiers	1998	Qualifiers	1984	-
		2002	Qualifiers	1988	-
		2006	Qualifiers	1992	-
		2010	Qualifiers	1996	Qualifiers
		2014	Qualifiers	2000	Qualifiers
		2018	Qualifiers	2004	Qualifiers
				2008	Qualifiers
				2012	Qualifiers
				2016	Qualifiers

UEFA NATIONS LEAGUE
2018/2019	League D
2020/2021	League D

FIFA CONFEDERATIONS CUP 1992-2017
None

LATVIAN CLUB HONOURS IN EUROPEAN CLUB COMPETITIONS:

European Champion Clubs' Cup (1956-1992) / UEFA Champions League (1993-2021)
None

Fairs Cup (1858-1971) / UEFA Cup (1972-2009) / UEFA Europa League (2010-2021)
None

UEFA Super Cup (1972-2020)
None

*European Cup Winners' Cup 1961-1999**
None

*defunct competition

NATIONAL COMPETITIONS
TABLE OF HONOURS

LATVIAN SSR (SOVIET ERA) CHAMPIONS

Year	Champion	Year	Champion	Year	Champion
1941	*Championship Cancelled*	1959	RER Rīga	1975	VEF Rīga
1942/1944	*Championship Interrupted*	1960	ASK Rīga	1976	Enerģija Rīga
1945	FK Dinamo Rīga	1961	ASK Rīga	1977	Enerģija Rīga
1946	Daugava Liepāja	1962	ASK Rīga	1978	Ķīmiķis Daugavpils
1947	Daugava Liepāja	1963	ASK Rīga	1979	Elektrons Rīga
1948	Žmiļova Komanda	1964	ASK Rīga	1980	Ķīmiķis Daugavpils
1949	Sarkanais Metalurgs Liepāja	1965	ASK Rīga	1981	Elektrons Rīga
1950	AVN Rīga	1966	ESR Rīga	1982	Elektrons Rīga
1951	Sarkanais Metalurgs Liepāja	1967	ESR Rīga	1983	VEF Rīga
1952	AVN Rīga	1968	Starts Brocēni	1984	Torpedo Rīga
1953	Sarkanais Metalurgs Liepāja	1969	FK Venta Ventspils	1985	FK Alfa
1954	Sarkanais Metalurgs Liepāja	1970	VEF Rīga	1986	Torpedo Rīga
1955	Darba Rezerves Rīga	1971	VEF Rīga	1987	Torpedo Rīga
1956	Sarkanais Metalurgs Liepāja	1972	FK Jūrnieks	1988	RAF Jelgava
1957	Sarkanais Metalurgs Liepāja	1973	VEF Rīga	1989	RAF Jelgava
1958	Sarkanais Metalurgs Liepāja	1974	VEF Rīga	1990	Gauja Valmiera

Year	CHAMPIONS*	CUP WINNERS	BEST GOALSCORERS	
1910	RV Union Rīga	-	-	
1911	Britannia FC Rīga	-	-	
1912	RV Union Rīga	-	-	
1913	SV Kaiserwald Rīga	-	-	
1914	Britannia FC Rīga	-	-	
1915	Britannia FC Rīga	-	-	
	------------	------------	------------	
1922	Kaiserwald Rīga	-	-	
1923	Kaiserwald Rīga	-	-	
1924	RFK Rīga	-	-	
1925	RFK Rīga	-	-	
1926	RFK Rīga	-	-	
1927	Olimpia Liepaja	-	-	
1928	Olimpia Liepaja	-	-	
1929	Olimpia Liepaja	-	-	
1930	RFK Rīga	-	-	
1931	RFK Rīga	-	-	
1932	ASK Rīga	-	-	
1933	Olimpia Liepaja	-	-	
1934	RFK Rīga	-	-	
1935	RFK Rīga	-	-	
1936	Olimpia Liepaja	-	-	
1937	*No competition*	RFK Rīga	-	
1938	Olimpia Liepaja	Rīgas Vilki	-	
1939	Olimpia Liepaja	RFK Rīga	-	
1940	RFK Rīga	*No competition*	-	
	------------	------------	------------	
1991	Skonto FC Rīga	Celtnieks Daugavpils	Vjačeslavs Ževnerovičs (Celtnieks Daugavpils)	27
1992	Skonto FC Rīga	Skonto FC Rīga	Vjačeslavs Ževnerovičs (VEF Riga)	19
1993	Skonto FC Rīga	RAF Jelgava	Aleksandrs Jeļisejevs (Skonto FC Rīga)	20
1994	Skonto FC Rīga	Olimpija Rīga	Vladimirs Babičevs (Skonto FC Rīga)	14
1995	Skonto FC Rīga	Skonto FC Rīga	Vitālijs Astafjevs (Skonto FC Rīga)	19
1996	Skonto FC Rīga	RAF Jelgava	Mihails Miholaps (FK Daugava Rīga)	33
1997	Skonto FC Rīga	Skonto FC Rīga	David Chaladze (GEO, Skonto FC Rīga)	25
1998	Skonto FC Rīga	Skonto FC Rīga	Viktors Dobrecovs (FK Liepājas Metalurgs)	23
1999	Skonto FC Rīga	FK Rīga	Viktors Dobrecovs (FK Liepājas Metalurgs)	22
2000	Skonto FC Rīga	Skonto FC Rīga	Vladimirs Koļesņičenko (Skonto FC Rīga)	17
2001	Skonto FC Rīga	Skonto FC Rīga	Mihails Miholaps (Skonto FC Rīga)	24
2002	Skonto FC Rīga	Skonto FC Rīga	Mihails Miholaps (Skonto FC Rīga)	23
2003	Skonto FC Rīga	FK Ventspils	Viktors Dobrecovs (FK Liepājas Metalurgs)	36
2004	Skonto FC Rīga	FK Ventspils	Aleksandr Katasonov (RUS, FK Liepājas Metalurgs)	21
2005	FK Liepājas Metalurgs	FK Ventspils	Viktors Dobrecovs (FK Liepājas Metalurgs) Igors Sļesarčuks (FK Venta/FK Ventspils)	18
2006	FK Ventspils	FK Liepājas Metalurgs	Mihails Miholaps (Skonto FC Rīga)	15
2007	FK Ventspils	FK Ventspils	Vits Rimkus (FK Ventspils)	20
2008	FK Ventspils	FK Daugava Daugavpils	Vits Rimkus (FK Ventspils)	14
2009	FK Liepājas Metalurgs	*No competition*	Kristaps Grebis (FK Liepājas Metalurgs)	30
2010	Skonto FC Rīga	FK Jelgava	Deniss Rakeļs (FK Liepājas Metalurgs) Nathan Júnior Soares de Carvalho (BRA, Skonto FC Rīga)	18
2011	FK Ventspils	FK Ventspils	Nathan Júnior Soares de Carvalho (BRA, Skonto FC Rīga)	22

2012	FC Daugava Daugavpils	Skonto FC Rīga	Mamuka Ghonghadze (GEO, FC Daugava Daugavpils)	18
2013	FK Ventspils	FK Ventspils	Artūrs Karašausks (Skonto FC Rīga) Andrejs Kovaļovs (FC Daugava Daugavpils)	16
2014	FK Ventspils	FK Jelgava	Vladislavs Gutkovskis (Skonto FC Rīga)	28
2015	FK Liepāja	FK Jelgava	Dāvis Ikaunieks (FK Liepaja)	15
2016	JPFS/FK Spartaks Jūrmala	FK Jelgava FK Ventspils (2016/2017)	Ģirts Karlsons (FK Ventspils)	17
2017	JPFS/FK Spartaks Jūrmala	FK Liepāja	Yevgeniy Kozlov (RUS, JPFS/FK Spartaks Jūrmala) Artūrs Karašausks (FK Liepāja)	12
2018	Rīga FC	Rīga FC	Darko Lemajić (SRB, Rīga FC)	15
2019	Rīga FC	FK Rīgas Futbola Skola	Darko Lemajić (SRB, Rīga FC / FK Rīgas Futbola Skola)	15
2020	Rīga FC	FK Liepāja	Luiz Paulo Hilario „Dodô" (BRA, FK Liepāja)	18

*Please note: Champions of the Riga Football League (1910-1915) and Latvian Championship (1922–1940 and since 1991); RAF Jelgava was called later FK Jelgava.

NATIONAL CHAMPIONSHIP
Virsliga 2020
(15.06.2020 – 29.11.2020)

Results

Round 1 [15-16.06.2020]
BFC Daugavpils - FK Liepāja 0-2(0-2)
FK Rīgas F. S. - FK Ventspils 1-0(1-0)
Rīga FC - Valmiera FC 2-0(1-0)
FS Metta/LU - Spartaks Jūrmala 1-2(0-0)
FK Tukums - FK Jelgava 1-2(1-0)

Round 2 [20-21.06.2020]
FK Ventspils - FK Tukums 3-0(1-0)
FK Jelgava - BFC Daugavpils 1-0(0-0)
Valmiera FC - FK Rīgas F. S. 0-4(0-2)
Spartaks Jūrmala - Rīga FC 2-1(1-0)
FK Liepāja - FS Metta/LU 3-0(1-0)

Round 3 [25-26.06.2020]
FK Tukums - BFC Daugavpils 0-6(0-1)
FK Ventspils - Valmiera FC 2-2(0-1)
FS Metta/LU - FK Jelgava 1-0(1-0)
FK Rīgas F. S. - Spartaks Jūrmala 4-1(4-1)
Rīga FC - FK Liepāja 2-0(1-0)

Round 4 [29-30.06.2020]
BFC Daugavpils - FS Metta/LU 4-2(3-1)
Spartaks Jūrmala - FK Ventspils 1-3(0-1)
Valmiera FC - FK Tukums 2-0(0-0)
FK Jelgava - Rīga FC 0-3(0-1)
FK Liepāja - FK Rīgas F. S. 2-5(2-3)

Round 5 [03-04.07.2020]
FK Tukums - FS Metta/LU 1-3(0-3)
Valmiera FC - Spartaks Jūrmala 2-2(0-1)
FK Ventspils - FK Liepāja 2-1(1-0)
Rīga FC - BFC Daugavpils 3-1(0-0)
FK Rīgas F. S. - FK Jelgava 1-0(0-0)

Round 6 [07-09.07.2020]
Spartaks Jūrmala - FK Tukums 1-1(0-1)
BFC Daugavpils - FK Rīgas F. S. 2-3(2-0)
Rīga FC - FS Metta/LU 2-0(1-0)
FK Liepāja - Valmiera FC 0-1(0-1)
FK Jelgava - FK Ventspils 1-0(1-0)

Round 7 [12-13.07.2020]
FK Tukums - Rīga FC 1-5(0-2)
FS Metta/LU - FK Rīgas F. S. 0-1(0-1)
BFC Daugavpils - FK Ventspils 3-1(1-1)
FK Jelgava - Valmiera FC 1-2(1-1)
FK Liepāja - Spartaks Jūrm. 3-2(2-0) [16.09.]

Round 8 [16-18.07.2020]
FK Liepāja - FK Tukums 2-2(1-0)
FK Ventspils - FS Metta/LU 0-0
FK Rīgas F. S. - Rīga FC 1-2(0-0)
Valmiera FC - BFC Daugavpils 3-0(2-0)
Spartaks Jūrmala - FK Jelgava 4-1(2-1)

Round 9 [21-22.07.2020]
FK Tukums - FK Rīgas F. S. 0-3(0-1)
FS Metta/LU - Valmiera FC 2-2(0-1)
Rīga FC - FK Ventspils 1-0(0-0)
BFC Daugavpils - Spartaks Jūrmala 0-2(0-0)
FK Jelgava - FK Liepāja 1-5(0-3)

Round 10 [25-26.07.2020]
FK Ventspils - FK Rīgas F. S. 3-2(3-0)
Valmiera FC - Rīga FC 0-1(0-0)
FK Jelgava - FK Tukums 2-1(0-0)
Spartaks Jūrmala - FS Metta/LU 2-0(1-0)
FK Liepāja - BFC Daugavpils 1-1(0-1)

Round 11 [29-30.07.2020]
FK Rīgas F. S. - Valmiera FC 5-2(2-1)
FK Tukums - FK Ventspils 0-0
BFC Daugavpils - FK Jelgava 0-0
FS Metta/LU - FK Liepāja 2-1(0-0)
Rīga FC - Spartaks Jūrmala 4-2(1-2)

Round 12 [03.08.2020]
FK Jelgava - FS Metta/LU 2-2(1-1)
BFC Daugavpils - FK Tukums 1-1(0-0)
Spartaks Jūrmala - FK Rīgas F. S. 1-1(1-0)
Valmiera FC - FK Ventspils 3-0(1-0)
FK Liepāja - Rīga FC 1-4(1-2)

Round 13 [07-08.08.2020]
FS Metta/LU - BFC Daugavpils 1-4(0-1)
FK Tukums - Valmiera FC 2-3(1-1)
Rīga FC - FK Jelgava 3-0(2-0)
FK Ventspils - Spartaks Jūrmala 1-1(0-0)
FK Rīgas F. S. - FK Liepāja 3-0(1-0)

Round 14 [11-12.08.2020]
FS Metta/LU - FK Tukums 2-0(0-0)
BFC Daugavpils - Rīga FC 0-1(0-1)
Spartaks Jūrmala - Valmiera FC 2-3(2-2)
FK Jelgava - FK Rīgas F. S. 0-4(0-3)
FK Liepāja - FK Ventspils 1-1(0-0)

Round 15 [16-17.08.2020]
FK Ventspils - FK Jelgava 5-0(3-0)
Valmiera FC - FK Liepāja 1-1(1-0)
FK Rīgas F. S. - BFC Daugavpils 2-1(1-0)
FK Tukums - Spartaks Jūrmala 0-2(0-2)
FS Metta/LU - Rīga FC 0-3(0-0) [26.08.]

Round 16 [21-23.08.2020]
FK Rīgas F. S. - FS Metta/LU 5-1(2-0)
Spartaks Jūrmala - FK Liepāja 2-2(0-0)
Rīga FC - FK Tukums 5-2(3-0)
FK Ventspils - BFC Daugavpils 2-0(1-0)
Valmiera FC - FK Jelgava 2-0(0-0)

Round 17 [29-30.08.2020]
FK Tukums - FK Liepāja 0-5(0-3)
FK Jelgava - Spartaks Jūrmala 2-3(1-1)
FS Metta/LU - FK Ventspils 1-2(0-0)
BFC Daugavpils - Valmiera FC 0-2(0-1)
FK Rīgas F. S. - Rīga FC 2-0(0-0)

Round 18 [12-13.09.2020]
Spartaks Jūrmala - BFC Daugavpils 3-3(2-2)
FK Ventspils - Rīga FC 0-2(0-1)
FK Liepāja - FK Jelgava 3-1(1-0)
Valmiera FC - FS Metta/LU 1-0(0-0)
FK Rīgas F. S. - FK Tukums 3-0(2-0)

Round 19 [20.09.2020]
FS Metta/LU - Spartaks Jūrmala 1-1(1-0)
BFC Daugavpils - FK Liepāja 0-4(0-1)
FK Tukums - FK Jelgava 0-0
FK Rīgas F. S. - FK Ventspils 1-1(1-0)
Rīga FC - Valmiera FC 1-0(1-0)

Round 20 [27-28.09.2020]
FK Jelgava - BFC Daugavpils 2-0(0-0)
FK Ventspils - FK Tukums 2-0(0-0)
Spartaks Jūrmala - Rīga FC 1-2(0-0)
Valmiera FC - FK Rīgas F. S. 2-2(1-0)
FK Liepāja - FS Metta/LU 3-0(0-0)

Round 21 [03-04.10.2020]
FK Ventspils - Valmiera FC 1-1(0-0)
FK Rīgas F. S. - Spartaks Jūrmala 2-1(1-1)
FK Tukums - BFC Daugavpils 2-1(1-1)
FK Jelgava - FS Metta/LU 1-0(0-0)
Rīga FC - FK Liepāja 2-1(2-1)

Round 22 [17.10.2020]
FK Jelgava - Rīga FC 0-2(0-1)
BFC Daugavpils - FS Metta/LU 1-0(0-0)
Spartaks Jūrmala - FK Ventspils 1-2(1-1)
Valmiera FC - FK Tukums 5-0(3-0)
FK Liepāja - FK Rīgas F. S. 1-0(0-0) [20.11.]

Round 23 [25.10.2020]
FK Tukums - FS Metta/LU 3-1(0-1)
FK Ventspils - FK Liepāja 0-2(0-0)
Valmiera FC - Spartaks Jūrmala 0-1(0-0)
Rīga FC - BFC Daugavpils 2-0(1-0)
FK Rīgas F. S. - FK Jelgava 1-0(1-0)

Round 24 [01.11.2020]
Spartaks Jūrmala - FK Tukums 2-4(1-0)
FK Jelgava - FK Ventspils 0-5(0-2)
BFC Daugavpils - FK Rīgas F. S. 1-2(1-2)
FS Metta/LU - Rīga FC 1-5(0-1)
FK Liepāja - Valmiera FC 1-1(1-1) [23.11.]

Round 25 [04-07.11.2020]	Round 26 [26.11.2020]	Round 27 [29.11.2020]
BFC Daugavpils - FK Ventspils 0-0	Spartaks Jūrmala - FK Jelgava 7-0(2-0)	Rīga FC - FK Ventspils 0-3 *awarded*
FK Liepāja - Spartaks Jūrmala 0-1(0-0)	FK Liepāja - FK Tukums 5-0(2-0)	BFC Daugavpils - Spartaks Jūrmala 1-3(1-1)
FK Tukums - Rīga FC 0-2(0-2)	FK Ventspils - FS Metta/LU 1-0(1-0)	FK Tukums - FK Rīgas F. S. 0-2(0-1)
FS Metta/LU - FK Rīgas F. S. 0-3(0-0)	Valmiera FC - BFC Daugavpils 3-0 *awarded*	FS Metta/LU - Valmiera FC 1-2(1-1)
FK Jelgava - Valmiera FC 2-2(1-0) [20.11.]	FK Rīgas F. S. - Rīga FC 3-0(0-0)	FK Jelgava - FK Liepāja 0-7(0-3)

Final Standings

								Total						Home						Away		
1.	**Rīga FC**	27	23	0	4	60	-	21	69	12	0	2	32	-	12	11	0	2	28	-	9
2.	FK Rīgas Futbola Skola	27	21	3	3	66	-	21	66	11	1	1	32	-	9	10	2	2	34	-	12
3.	Valmiera FC	27	13	8	6	47	-	33	47	7	3	3	24	-	11	6	5	3	23	-	22
4.	FK Ventspils	27	12	8	7	40	-	25	44	7	4	2	22	-	11	5	4	5	18	-	14
5.	FK Liepāja	27	12	6	9	57	-	34	42	6	4	4	26	-	19	6	2	5	31	-	15
6.	JPFS/FK Spartaks Jūrmala	27	11	7	9	53	-	44	40	4	4	5	29	-	23	7	3	4	24	-	21
7.	FK Jelgava	27	6	4	17	19	-	64	22	4	2	8	14	-	36	2	2	9	5	-	28
8.	BFC Daugavpils	27	5	5	17	30	-	48	20	3	3	8	13	-	23	2	2	9	17	-	25
9.	FS Metta/Latvijas Universitāte Rīga	27	4	4	19	22	-	55	16	3	2	8	12	-	22	1	2	11	10	-	33
10.	FK Tukums 2000 (*Relegated*)	27	3	5	19	21	-	70	14	2	2	10	10	-	35	1	3	9	11	-	35

Top goalscorers:

18	Luiz Paulo Hilario „Dodô" (BRA)	*FK Liepāja*
15	Toluwalase Emmanuel Arokodare (NGA)	*Valmiera FC*
15	Nemanja Belaković (SRB)	*JPFS/FK Spartaks Jūrmala*
12	Richard Kule Mbombo (COD)	*Rīga FC*
11	Evgeny Kozlov (RUS)	*FK Ventspils*
11	Raimonds Krollis	*FS Metta/Latvijas Universitāte Rīga*

NATIONAL CUP
Latvijas Kauss 2020

1/8-Finals [23-24.09./30.09.-01.10.2020]

FK Dinamo Rīga - Valmiera FC	1-5		FK Liepāja - BFC Daugavpils	1-0
FC Lokomotīve Daugavpils - FK Ventspils	0-4		JFC Kauguri Jūrmala - FK Jelgava	0-9
Grobiņas SC - JPFS/FK Spartaks Jūrmala	2-5 aet		FK Auda Rīga - FK Rīgas Futbola Skola	0-8
Rēzeknes FA/BJSS - FK Tukums 2000	1-3		Rīga FC - FS Metta/Latvijas Universitāte Rīga	4-0

Quarter-Finals [21.10.2020]

FK Jelgava - FK Ventspils	3-4 pen		Valmiera FC - FK Tukums 2000	1-0
JPFS/FK Spartaks Jūrmala - FK Liepāja	1-3		FK Rīgas Futbola Skola - Rīga FC	3-2

Semi-Finals [28.10.2020]

FK Ventspils - FK Rīgas Futbola Skola	1-0		FK Liepāja - Valmiera FC	2-0

Final

08.11.2020; Ventspils Stadions, Ventspils; Referee: Mareks Kere; Attendance: 0

FK Liepāja - FK Ventspils   **1-0(0-0,0-0)**

FK Liepāja: Oleksandr Rybka, Milan Joksimović, Seydina Aboubakr Lamine Keita, Marko Simić, Seidu Yahaya, Eduards Tīdenbergs, Raivis Andris Jurkovskis, Mārtiņš Ķigurs (120.Vadims Žuļevs), Artūrs Karašausks (107.Evgeniy Berezkin), Valery Gorbachik (75.Ingars Stuglis), Luiz Paulo Hilario „Dodô". Trainer: Dzmitry Molosh.

FK Ventspils: Konstantin Machnovskiy [*sent off 98*], Andriy Sakhnevych (108.Giorgi Mchedlishvili), Dmitrijs Litvinskis, Abdoul Gafar Mamah (99.Dele Sunday Alampasu), Giorgi Rekhviashvili, Beka Varshanidze, Daniils Ulimbaševs, Lucas Villela Rezende, Chris Marlon Ondong Mba, Evgeny Kozlov (96.Dumte Pyagbara), Kaspars Svārups (96.Kaspars Kokins). Trainer: Viorel Frunză (Moldova).

Goal: 1-0 Luiz Paulo Hilario „Dodô" (93).

Bērnu Futbola Centrs Daugavpils

Founded: 11.12.2009 (*as BFC Daugava*)
Stadium: Celtnieks stadions, Daugavpils (4,070)
Trainer: Aleksandr Gorshkov (RUS)   08.02.1970

Goalkeepers:	DOB	M	(s)	G
Ivans Dubodelovs	08.02.2001	22		
Ņikita Šaraņins	04.01.2003	4		
Defenders:	**DOB**	**M**	**(s)**	**G**
Daniel Adjetey (DEN)	15.03.2000	8	(4)	
Joshua Akpudje (NGA)	23.07.1998	23		
Nnamdi Chinonso Offor (NGA)	27.05.2000	8		4
David Idowu (NGA)	23.06.2000	24		2
Aleksejs Kudeļkins	08.05.2002	1	(2)	
Viktors Litvinskis	07.02.1996	11		
Anton Miterev (RUS)	03.05.1996	1	(2)	
Stanislav Nechyporenko (UKR)	22.01.1997	13	(3)	1
Salvis Petriks	06.01.2002	1	(4)	
Leonīds Truskovskis	06.02.2001		(1)	
Midfielders:	**DOB**	**M**	**(s)**	**G**
Valerijs Afanasjevs	20.09.1982	16	(3)	2
Dāvis Cucurs	19.03.2000	13	(7)	
Kirils Iļjins	03.05.2001	19		

	DOB	M	(s)	G
Edgars Ivanovs	07.10.2001	16	(9)	1
Andrejs Kovaļjovs	23.03.1989	22	(2)	3
Raivis Ķiršs	15.01.2000	17	(8)	3
Ryuya Maeda (JPN)	14.09.2000		(2)	
Tatsuro Nagamatsu (JPN)	23.04.1995	18	(3)	1
Ryonosuke Ohori (JPN)	10.01.2001		(3)	
Ramazan Orazov (KAZ)	30.01.1998	2	(1)	
Oļģerts Raščevskis	18.02.2003	1	(11)	
Vladislavs Timofejevs	25.05.2002	1	(2)	
Ričards Žaldovskis	05.06.1999		(5)	
Forwards:	**DOB**	**M**	**(s)**	**G**
Vüqar Əsgərov (AZE)	14.05.1985	2	(3)	1
Valerijs Lizunovs	24.02.2004		(2)	
Kirill Makeev (RUS)	18.05.1998	18	(5)	4
Jevgenijs Miņins	17.03.2002		(3)	
Marko Regža	20.01.1999	15		7
Maksims Toņiševs	12.05.2000	10	(3)	1

Please note: Valmiera FC - BFC Daugavpils 3-0 awarded (Round 26) not counted

Futbola klubs Jelgava

Founded: 2004
Stadium: Zemgales Olimpiskā centra, Jelgava (1,560)
Trainer: Oleg Kubarev (BLR)   08.02.1966
(24.08.2020)   Davis Caune   06.10.1977

Goalkeepers:	DOB	M	(s)	G
Edgars Andrejevs	21.10.1992	1		
Dmitrijs Grigorjevs	13.05.1992	6		
Vladislavs Kurakins	09.07.1996	20		
Defenders:	**DOB**	**M**	**(s)**	**G**
Daniels Balodis	10.06.1998	5	(2)	
Kevins Cēsnieks	06.03.2005		(4)	
Vladislavs Gabovs	13.07.1987	3	(1)	
Ingus Valters Grinbergs	01.02.2002	5	(2)	
Raivis Hščanovičs	15.02.1987		(1)	
Volodymyr Kirychuk (UKR)	28.02.1996	1	(2)	
Weslie John Leskon (TRI)	29.07.1991	9		
Ivo Minkevičs	28.06.1999	24	(1)	2
Mareks Plonis	19.10.1999	1		
Dmytro Semenov (UKR)	04.11.1999	17	(1)	
Ingus Šlampe	31.01.1989	20	(3)	
Jēkabs Šteinburgs	08.09.1999	4		
Gatis Štrauss	21.07.1997	2		
Midfielders:	**DOB**	**M**	**(s)**	**G**
Emeka Michael Basil (NGA)	22.01.2001		(4)	
Boriss Bogdaškins	21.02.1990	6	(1)	1
Aleksandrs Cauņa	19.01.1988		(1)	
Jānis Grīnbergs	28.02.1999	8	(1)	
Aleksejs Grjaznovs	01.10.1997	4	(2)	2
Dāvis Indrāns	06.06.1995	4	(11)	
Jevgēņijs Kazačoks	12.08.1995	18	(2)	

	DOB	M	(s)	G
Igors Kozlovs	26.03.1987	12	(3)	
Markuss Kruglaužs	28.01.2002	2	(4)	
Andris Krušatins	01.09.1996	20	(1)	2
Raivo Mincevičs	28.03.2002	1		
Olabanjo Alexander Ogunji (NGA)	20.01.2001		(3)	
Kristers Pantelejevs	05.04.2002		(1)	
Rihards Pauniņš	10.09.2002		(2)	
Mārtiņš Pivarovičs	15.02.1999	3	(5)	
Bogdans Samoilovs	13.03.2000	2	(1)	
Alans Siņeļņikovs	14.05.1990	1	(3)	
Vladislavs Soloveičiks	25.05.1999	5	(2)	
Youssouf Sow (GUI)	13.05.1993	6	(2)	
Aldis Trukšāns	19.07.1990	1	(1)	
Forwards:	**DOB**	**M**	**(s)**	**G**
Yentl De Baets (BEL)	11.08.2000		(2)	
Yuriy Golubka (UKR)	31.05.1996	5	(3)	1
Daņiils Hvoiņickis	08.04.1998	23	(1)	
Ņikita Ivanovs	25.03.1996	10		2
Ričards Jirgensons	04.07.1995	1	(1)	
Ričards Korzāns	03.05.1997	10	(12)	2
Marks Kurtišs	26.01.1998	15	(3)	
Artem Radchenko (UKR)	02.01.1995	8	(1)	
Mareks Rudakovs	06.03.1999		(1)	
Germans Saveļjevs	20.05.1999	1	(7)	
Yuri Zakharkiv (UKR)	21.03.1996	13	(3)	5

Futbola klubs Liepāja

Founded: 2014
Stadium: Daugava stadions, Liepāja (5,008)
Trainer: Andrejs Kalinins   26.05.1981
(06.06.2020)   Dzmitry Molosh (BLR)   10.12.1981

Goalkeepers:	DOB	M	(s)	G
Valentīns Raļkevičs	08.03.1991	6		
Oleksandr Rybka (UKR)	10.04.1987	9		
Krišjānis Zviedris	25.01.1997	12		
Defenders:	**DOB**	**M**	**(s)**	**G**
Rami Bedoui (TUN)	19.01.1990	6		
Vladislavs Gabovs	13.07.1987	5	(6)	
Deniss Ivanovs	11.01.1984	1	(2)	
Seydina Aboubakr Lamine Keita (SEN)	28.12.1992	18	(1)	
Marko Simic (MNE)	16.06.1987	10	(1)	
Vadims Žuļevs	01.03.1988	8	(5)	
Midfielders:	**DOB**	**M**	**(s)**	**G**
Abdullahi Alfa (NGA)	29.07.1996	1	(2)	
Evgeniy Berezkin (BLR)	05.07.1991	9		2
Kristers Čudars	03.09.1999	8	(3)	
Hogan Ukpa Effiong (NGA)	28.09.2001	7	(6)	1
Maksims Fjodorovs	24.09.2003		(1)	
Richard Friday (NGA)	16.02.2000	11	(10)	6
Dele Ola Israel (NGA)	27.10.2001	4	(5)	

	DOB	M	(s)	G
Milan Joksimović (SRB)	09.02.1990	13		
Raivis Andris Jurkovskis	09.12.1996	25	(1)	2
Mārtiņš Ķigurs	31.03.1997	22	(5)	3
Ingars Sarmis Stuglis	12.02.1996	8	(4)	
Leandro Nicolás Teijo (ARG)	27.07.1991	9		1
Eduards Tīdenbergs	18.12.1994	14	(1)	5
Cristián Damián Torres	18.06.1985	5	(13)	1
Edgars Vardanjans	09.05.1993		(1)	
Seidu Yahaya (GHA)	31.12.1989	23		1
Roberts Zelmanis	18.04.2001	8	(4)	
Viktors Ziemelis	27.01.2000		(1)	
Forwards:	**DOB**	**M**	**(s)**	**G**
Amâncio José Pinto Fortes (ANG)	18.04.1990	6	(3)	2
Luiz Paulo Hilario „Dodô" (BRA)	16.10.1987	17	(7)	18
Valery Gorbachik (BLR)	19.01.1995	6	(3)	3
Filipp Ivanov (BLR)	21.07.1990	5	(3)	1
Artūrs Karašausks	29.01.1992	19	(1)	9
Dmytro Semeniv (UKR)	24.06.1998	2	(3)	

Futbola klubs Metta / Latvijas Universitāte Rīga

Goalkeepers:	DOB	M	(s)	G
Jānis Beks	01.11.2002	2		
Helmuts Saulītis	18.05.1998	25		
Defenders:	**DOB**	**M**	**(s)**	**G**
Emīls Birka	25.04.2000	23	(1)	2
Daniels Fedorovičs	07.10.2001	3		
Krists Gulbis	15.01.1997	16	(2)	1
Roberts Ķipsts	21.10.1999	15	(4)	
Gabriels Kirkils	25.05.2001	7	(5)	
Jegors Novikovs	09.02.2003		(2)	
Rendijs Šibass	01.05.1997	20	(2)	1
Normunds Uldriķis	29.01.2001	13	(7)	1
Lukman Halilu Zakari (NGA)	23.12.1998	9		
Midfielders:	**DOB**	**M**	**(s)**	**G**
Benson Fazili (CAN)	12.01.2000	14		
Franklin Joseph Tochukwu Onwudiwe (BRA)	23.02.1999	24		1

Founded: 02.05.2006
Stadium: Hanzas vidusskolas laukums, Rīga (2,000)
Trainer: Andris Riherts   31.05.1981

	DOB	M	(s)	G
Renārs Guliaks	13.05.2001	1	(6)	
Alban Kadriu (NOR)	23.12.2000	7		
Sylvin Kayembe (SWE)	06.06.2001	11	(7)	
Iļja Korotkovs	24.05.2000	6	(4)	
Aleksejs Krjukovičs	05.01.2001		(3)	
Bruno Melnis	21.01.2004		(3)	
Rihards Ozoliņš	31.05.2001	25	(2)	3
Danilo Perassolli (BRA)	07.04.1999	9	(1)	
Lūkass Vapne	31.08.2003	7	(10)	
Oskars Vientiess	08.10.2002	7	(7)	
Forwards:	**DOB**	**M**	**(s)**	**G**
Raimonds Krollis	28.10.2001	23	(1)	11
Kgotso Masangane (RSA)	27.05.1998	19	(2)	1
Artjoms Puzirevskis	11.01.2003	3	(6)	
Ričards Žaldovskis	05.06.1999	4	(3)	1
Matīss Zēģele	24.09.2000	4	(11)	

Rīga Football Club

Goalkeepers:	DOB	M	(s)	G
Ilja Isajevs	05.12.2000		(1)	
Roberts Ozols	10.09.1995	23		
Nils Puriņš*	01.08.1998	4		
Defenders:	**DOB**	**M**	**(s)**	**G**
Federico Bravo (ARG)	05.10.1993	1	(1)	
Antonijs Černomordijs	26.09.1996	16		1
João Carlos Araújo Fonseca Silva (POR)	30.08.1989	2		
Antons Kurakins	01.01.1990	9	(3)	
Herdi Prenga (ALB)	31.08.1994	17		4
Elvis Stuglis	04.07.1993	17	(2)	3
Midfielders:	**DOB**	**M**	**(s)**	**G**
Brayan Edinson Angulo Mosquera (COL)	19.07.1993	2	(1)	
Marko Đurišić (SRB)	17.07.1997	14	(5)	
Felipe Bezerra Brisola (BRA)	06.06.1990	18	(6)	4
Jakub Hora (CZE)	23.02.1991	16	(8)	3
Vladimir Kamešs	28.10.1988	6	(10)	
Oļegs Laizāns	28.03.1987	2	(11)	2

Please note: Rīga FC - FK Ventspils 0-3 awarded (Round 27) not counted

Founded: 2014 (*as merger of FC Caramba Riga and Dinamo Rīga*)
Stadium: Skonto stadions, Rīga (8,207)
Trainer: Oleg Kononov (RUS)   23.03.1966
(01.09.2020) Mihails Koņevs

	DOB	M	(s)	G
Stefan Panić (SRB)	20.09.1992	21	(1)	5
Pedro Filipe Barbosa Moreira „Pedrinho" (POR)	20.12.1992	5	(5)	2
Armands Pētersons	05.12.1990	10	(6)	1
Roger Junio Rodrigues Ferreira (BRA)	01.03.1996	13	(7)	5
Ritvars Rugins	17.10.1989	15	(2)	
Vyacheslav Sharpar (UKR)	02.06.1987	13	(2)	
Nikita Silakovs	07.06.2002	1		
Danila Yanov (RUS)	27.01.2000		(2)	
Forwards:	**DOB**	**M**	**(s)**	**G**
Dário Frederico da Silva (BRA)	11.09.1991	3	(5)	
Roman Debelko (UKR)	08.08.1993	8	(8)	4
Vladislavs Fjodorovs	27.09.1996	17	(6)	2
Stefan Milošević (MNE)	23.06.1996	4	(4)	5
Richard Kule Mbombo (COD)	10.05.1996	11	(10)	12
Michaël Jordan N'Kololo (COD)	09.11.1992	10	(8)	3
Stênio Marcos da Fonseca Salazar Júnior (BRA)	10.06.1991	7	(4)	2
Wesley Natã Wachholz (BRA)	18.04.1995	1	(2)	1

*played as midfielder in Round 26

Futbola klubs Rīgas Futbola Skola

Goalkeepers:	DOB	M	(s)	G
Kaspars Ikstens	05.06.1988	8		
Danylo Kucher (UKR)	25.01.1997	19		
Sergejs Vilkovs	03.09.2002		(1)	
Defenders:	**DOB**	**M**	**(s)**	**G**
Nnamdi Chinonso Offor (NGA)	27.05.2000	7	(6)	6
Adama Doumbia (CIV)	01.01.2000	6	(2)	
Vjačeslavs Isajevs	27.08.1993	11	(5)	1
Vitālijs Jagodinskis	28.02.1992	17		2
Žiga Lipušček (SVN)	05.01.1997	21	(1)	5
Niks Sliede	08.03.2004		(1)	
Luka Smoljo (CRO)	28.01.1996		(2)	
Aleksandrs Solovjovs	25.02.1988	21	(1)	1
Vladislavs Sorokins	10.05.1997	13	(12)	
Midfielders:	**DOB**	**M**	**(s)**	**G**
Mikhail Babichev (BLR)	02.02.1995	7	(8)	

Founded: 2011
Stadium: Stadions Arkādija, Rīga (1,000)
Trainer: Viktors Morozs   30.07.1980

	DOB	M	(s)	G
Emerson Santana Deocleciano (BRA)	27.07.1999	21	(3)	10
Jānis Ikaunieks	16.02.1995	10	(4)	7
Jēkabs Lagūns	16.01.2002	2	(4)	
Tomislav Šarić (SVN)	24.06.1990	26		5
Roberts Savaļnieks	04.02.1993	17	(7)	1
Tomáš Šimkovič (AUT)	16.04.1987	22	(2)	8
Leonel Strumia (ARG)	29.09.1992	22		
Artūrs Zjuzins	18.06.1991	13	(9)	4
Forwards:	**DOB**	**M**	**(s)**	**G**
Bonfils-Caleb Bimenyimana (BDI)	21.11.1997		(4)	1
Alain Cedric Herve Kouadio (CIV)	19.05.1996	16	(8)	7
Darko Lemajić (SRB)	20.08.1993	13	(4)	5
Ivan Lukjanovs	24.01.1987	2	(7)	
Anastasijs Mordatenko	24.08.1996		(1)	
Maksims Toņiševs	12.05.2000		(3)	
Renārs Varslavāns	23.08.2001	3	(10)	1

Jūrmalas Futbola un Peldēšanas skola/ Futbola klubs Spartaks Jūrmala

Goalkeepers:	DOB	M	(s)	G
Jevģēnijs Nerugals	26.02.1989	9		
Dāvis Ošs	03.12.1994	18		
Defenders:	**DOB**	**M**	**(s)**	**G**
Abdulrahim Abdulrahman (UAE)	24.10.1994	8		
Ņikita Bērenfelds	07.06.1995	18		
Nauris Bulvītis	15.03.1987	21		2
Badra Ali Camara (CIV)	23.01.2002	15	(3)	
Klāvs Kramēns	07.07.2000	6	(5)	
Anatolie Prepeliță (MDA)	06.08.1997	1	(2)	
Edgaras Žarskis (LTU)	04.05.1994	7	(5)	1
Midfielders:	**DOB**	**M**	**(s)**	**G**
Samiru Kwari Abdullahi (NGA)	03.01.2001	24	(1)	2
Aliyu Yau Adam (NGA)	07.05.2000	9	(6)	2
Didine Djouhary (FRA)	08.02.1999	12	(4)	1
Cristian Dros (MDA)	15.04.1998	14	(4)	
Kyrylo Dryshliuk (UKR)	16.09.1999	15	(8)	1

Founded: 2007
Stadium: Slokas stadions, Jūrmala (2,800)
Trainer: Alexey Eremenko Sr. (RUS)   17.01.1974

	DOB	M	(s)	G
Sergey Eremenko (RUS)	06.01.1999	11	(5)	
Jānis Krautmanis	22.04.1997	1	(1)	
Romāns Mickevičs	29.03.1993	7	(6)	1
Chikezie Miracle Nwaorisa (NGA)	12.11.2000	10	(12)	6
Lucky Onyebuchi Opara (NGA)	09.12.1999	18	(2)	3
Pam Dalyop Samuel (NGA)	16.12.2000	2	(2)	
Raivis Skrebels	26.09.1999	6	(15)	
Forwards:	**DOB**	**M**	**(s)**	**G**
Markuss Maksimuss Alpēns	24.01.2004	1	(2)	
Kwadwo Asamoah (GHA)	15.07.2002	6	(11)	3
Nemanja Belaković (SRB)	08.01.1997	25	(1)	15
Ariagner Steven Smith Medina (NCA)	13.12.1998	18	(7)	7
Eduards Višņakovs	10.05.1990	1	(7)	
Newton Aubrey Williams Richards (PAN)	02.01.2001	5	(6)	1
Samat Sarsenov (RUS)	19.08.1996	4	(2)	1
Leon Šipoš (CRO)	28.02.2000	5	(6)	2

Futbola klubs Tukums 2000

Founded: 2000
Stadium: Tukuma pilsētas stadions, Tukums (1,000)
Trainer: Marek Dariusz Zub (POL) 24.08.1964
(04.06.2020) Jurģis Kalns 05.10.1982

Goalkeepers:	DOB	M	(s)	G
Ivans Baturins	25.06.1997	22		
Vladislav Kapustins	21.02.2002	1		
Maksim Kuchinskiy (UKR)	28.06.1988	4		
Defenders:	**DOB**	**M**	**(s)**	**G**
Toms Aizgrāvis	30.04.1989	13	(5)	
Reinis Bečers	14.11.2002		(5)	
Kristaps Gailis	26.02.1998	3	(5)	1
Roberts Jaunarājs-Janvāris	23.03.2000	19	(1)	
Daniels Pelcis	01.11.1999	7	(2)	
Rūdolfs Reingolcs	01.07.2002	5	(5)	
Dāvis Strods	24.02.1996	22		
Edgaras Žarskis (LTU)	04.05.1994	7		1
Midfielders:	**DOB**	**M**	**(s)**	**G**
Kaspars Anmanis	22.01.2002	6	(7)	1
Emeka Michael Basil (NGA)	22.01.2001	16	(1)	4
Einars Blumers	02.11.1999	7	(10)	
Boriss Bogdaškins	21.02.1990	16		
Rūdolfs Fogelis	31.07.1999	2	(3)	

	DOB	M	(s)	G
Jānis Krautmanis	22.04.1997	17		2
Kristaps Kārlis Krieviņš	06.04.2004		(2)	
Krists Krumins	21.08.1998	1	(4)	
Gatis Lūks	18.11.2000	14	(4)	1
Romāns Mickevičs	29.03.1993	7		
Daniels Mīļais	14.11.2003		(3)	
Olabanjo Alexander Ogunji (NGA)	20.01.2001	12	(2)	4
Kristers Penkevics	28.01.2003	13	(10)	
Pāvels Pilāts	04.02.1997	10	(6)	
Alekss Regža	16.07.1994	5	(6)	1
Pam Dalyop Samuel (NGA)	16.12.2000	16	(1)	2
Jonas Skinderis (LTU)	04.04.1997	14	(1)	
Forwards:	**DOB**	**M**	**(s)**	**G**
Mateusz Cetnarski (POL)	06.07.1988	10		
Ronalds Leja	13.11.2002	1	(2)	
Atis Ozols	16.03.2000	6	(6)	
Maksims Sidorovs	17.09.2001	11	(1)	
Kristers Svans	30.05.1999	5	(7)	
Raivis Vītolnieks	29.07.1995	5	(5)	2

Valmieras Football Club

Founded: 1996
Stadium: „Jānis Daliņš" stadions, Valmiera (2,000)
Trainer: Tamaz Pertia (GEO) 23.12.1974

Goalkeepers:	DOB	M	(s)	G
Vlad Eleferenko (RUS)	20.06.2000	8		
Andriy Kozhukhar (UKR)	20.07.1999	3		
Vladislavs Lazarevs	25.11.1997	6		
Rūdolfs Soloha	16.03.2000	8		
Kristaps Zommers	07.01.1997	1		
Defenders:	**DOB**	**M**	**(s)**	**G**
Olaide Muhammed Badmus (NGA)	12.04.1999	15	(4)	
Daniels Balodis	10.06.1998	9	(7)	
Artūrs Bērziņš	01.12.2003		(2)	
Julien Celestine (FRA)	24.07.1997	25		1
Joyskim Dawa Tchakonte (CMR)	09.04.1996	3		
Pape Yaré Fall (SEN)	09.09.2000	9	(1)	
Luka Gadrani (GEO)	12.04.1997	6	(1)	
Vitālijs Jagodinskis	28.02.1992	4		
Joshua Kudu (FRA)	13.05.1996	2	(1)	
Midfielders:	**DOB**	**M**	**(s)**	**G**
Māris Barkovskis	12.02.2002		(1)	
Victor Diagne (SEN)	13.10.2000	21	(1)	
Aleksejs Grjaznovs	01.10.1997		(1)	

	DOB	M	(s)	G
Dāvis Indrāns	06.06.1995	1		
Alvis Jaunzems	16.06.1999	24	(2)	
Kriss Kārkliņš	31.01.1996	23		4
Kristaps Liepa	14.03.1998	4	(12)	1
Mykola Musolitin (UKR)	21.01.1999	16	(1)	
Luka Silagadze (GEO)	21.04.1999	14	(8)	4
Daniils Skopenko	23.03.2000	3	(11)	1
Mootez Zaddem (TUN)	05.01.2001	12	(5)	
Rūdolfs Zeņģis	21.03.2002	1	(1)	
Kārlis Zvirbulis	16.03.2001			
Forwards:	**DOB**	**M**	**(s)**	**G**
Toluwalase Emmanuel Arokodare (NGA)	23.11.2000	16		15
Djibril Gueyé (SEN)	19.11.1996	8	(2)	4
Jorge Duarte Rodrigues Mendes Teixeira (POR)	08.03.1999	14	(4)	4
Kristers Lūsiņš	09.05.2000	1	(6)	
Alioune Ndoye (SEN)	05.10.2001	7		2
Ingars Pūlis	24.01.2001	1		1
Ēriks Punculs	18.01.1994	12	(11)	7
Samat Sarsenov (RUS)	19.08.1996	7	(2)	
Vladimirs Stepanovs	06.02.2000	1	(3)	

Please note: Valmiera FC - BFC Daugavpils 3-0 awarded (Round 26) not counted

Futbola klubs Ventspils

Founded: 1997
Stadium: Ventspils Olimpiskais stadions, Ventspils (3,044)
Trainer: Viorel Frunză (MDA) 06.12.1979

Goalkeepers:	DOB	M	(s)	G
Dele Alampasu (NGA)	24.12.1996	6		
Konstantin Machnovskiy (UKR)	01.01.1989	20		
Defenders:	**DOB**	**M**	**(s)**	**G**
Dmitrijs Litvinskis	17.08.1999	16		
Artūrs Ļotčikovs	26.01.2000	5	(3)	
Abdoul Gafar Mamah (TOG)	24.08.1985	21		
Giorgi Mchedlishvili (GEO)	18.01.1992	18	(4)	1
Giorgi Rekhviashvili (GEO)	01.02.1988	18	(2)	
Andriy Sakhnevych (UKR)	17.04.1989	22		
Midfielders:	**DOB**	**M**	**(s)**	**G**
Mariss Bite	08.11.1999	1	(8)	
Niks Dusalijevs	17.07.2001	3	(3)	
Giorgi Eristavi (GEO)	04.02.1994	10	(8)	2
Fabio Alexander Freitas de Almeida (BRA)	07.07.1996	3		
Abdulla Genaev (RUS)	18.01.2001	5	(4)	

	DOB	M	(s)	G
Robins Kokarītis	21.10.1999		(2)	
Kristers Neilands	09.09.2000		(2)	
Guga Palavandishvili (GEO)	14.08.1993	6	(2)	
Dumte Christian Pyagbara (NGA)	13.03.1996	9	(10)	2
Ingars Stuglis	12.02.1996	12	(1)	
Raens Tālbergs	14.09.2000	1	(9)	
Eduards Tīdenbergs	18.12.1994	9	(1)	
Daniils Ulimbaševs	12.03.1992	16	(4)	2
Beka Varshanidze (GEO)	01.11.1993	8		
Forwards:	**DOB**	**M**	**(s)**	**G**
Kazeem Ojo Aderounmu (NGA)	10.01.2000	2	(10)	
Kaspars Kokins	26.04.2000	5	(14)	
Evgeny Kozlov (RUS)	04.02.1995	18	(8)	11
Lucas Villela Rezende (BRA)	24.03.1994	23	(1)	4
Chris Marlon Ondong Mba (FRA)	07.08.1993	12	(6)	1
Kaspars Svārups	28.01.1994	17	(6)	8

Please note: Rīga FC - FK Ventspils 0-3 awarded (Round 27) not counted

1. FC Lokomotīve Daugavpils (*Promoted*)	12	10	1	1	39	-	10	31	(2.583)
2. FK Auda Rīga	13	9	1	3	32	-	15	28	(2.154)
3. Grobiņas SC	12	5	3	4	23	-	14	18	(1.500)
4. JDFS Alberts Rīga	12	5	3	4	11	-	16	18	(1.500)
5. FK Staiceles Bebri	12	5	1	6	20	-	12	16	(1.333)
6. SK Super Nova Olaine	13	4	4	5	20	-	20	16	(1.230)
7. Rēzeknes FA/BJSS	13	4	2	7	14	-	32	14	(1.077)
8. FK Smiltene/BJSS	14	3	3	8	18	-	40	12	(0.857)
9. JFK Saldus (*Relegated*)	11	0	4	7	8	-	26	4	(0.363)

Please note: the season was cancelled on 06.11.2020 due to COVID-19 pandemic. Standings were decided by a points by game average.

NATIONAL TEAM

INTERNATIONAL MATCHES
(16.07.2020 – 15.07.2021)

03.09.2020	Rīga	Latvia - Andorra	0-0	(UNL)
06.09.2020	Attard	Malta - Latvia	1-1(1-1)	(UNL)
07.10.2020	Podgorica	Montenegro - Latvia	1-1(0-1)	(F)
10.10.2020	Tórshavn	Faroe Islands - Latvia	1-1(1-1)	(UNL)
13.10.2020	Rīga	Latvia - Malta	0-1(0-0)	(UNL)
11.11.2020	Serravalle	San Marino - Latvia	0-3(0-1)	(F)
14.11.2020	Rīga	Latvia - Faroe Islands	1-1(0-0)	(UNL)
17.11.2020	Andorra la Vella	Andorra - Latvia	0-5(0-1)	(UNL)
24.03.2021	Rīga	Latvia - Montenegro	1-2(1-1)	(WCQ)
27.03.2021	Amsterdam	Netherlands - Latvia	2-0(1-0)	(WCQ)
30.03.2021	İstanbul	Turkey - Latvia	3-3(2-1)	(WCQ)
04.06.2021	Rīga	Latvia - Lithuania	3-1(1-0)	(BC)
07.06.2021	Düsseldorf	Germany - Latvia	7-1(5-0)	(F)
10.06.2021	Tallinn	Estonia - Latvia	2-1(2-0)	(BC)

03.09.2020   LATVIA - ANDORRA   0-0   2nd UEFA Nations League D, Group 1
Daugava stadions, Rīga; Referee: Timotheos Christofi (Cyprus); Attendance: 0
LVA: Pāvels Šteinbors (Cap), Kaspars Dubra, Antonijs Černomordijs, Raivis Andris Jurkovskis, Artūrs Zjuzins (81.Alvis Jaunzems), Roberts Savaļnieks, Jānis Ikaunieks, Andrejs Cigaņiks (81.Mārtiņš Ķigurs), Eduards Emsis, Vladislavs Fjodorovs (46.Roberts Uldriķis), Vladislavs Gutkovskis [*sent off 71*]. Trainer: Dainis Kazakevičs.

06.09.2020   MALTA - LATVIA   1-1(1-1)   2nd UEFA Nations League D, Group 1
Ta'Qali National Stadium, Attard; Referee: Stéphanie Frappart (France); Attendance: 0
LVA: Pāvels Šteinbors (Cap), Kaspars Dubra, Antonijs Černomordijs, Raivis Andris Jurkovskis, Artūrs Zjuzins (86.Kriss Kārkliņš), Roberts Savaļnieks (67.Ritvars Rugins), Jānis Ikaunieks, Andrejs Cigaņiks, Eduards Emsis, Alvis Jaunzems, Raimonds Krollis (62.Dāvis Ikaunieks). Trainer: Dainis Kazakevičs.
Goals: Matthew Guillaumier (25 own goal).

07.10.2020   MONTENEGRO - LATVIA   1-1(0-1)   Friendly International
Stadion pod Goricom, Podgorica; Referee: Admir Šehović (Bosnia and Herzegovina); Attendance: 0
LVA: Roberts Ozols, Igors Tarasovs, Mārcis Ošs (Cap) (46.Elvis Stuglis), Raivis Andris Jurkovskis, Kristers Tobers (46.Eduards Emsis), Dāvis Ikaunieks (84.Raimonds Krollis), Kriss Kārkliņš (75.Artūrs Zjuzins), Andrejs Cigaņiks (46.Eduards Tīdenbergs), Vladislavs Fjodorovs, Mārtiņš Ķigurs (79.Roberts Uldriķis), Vladislavs Gutkovskis. Trainer: Dainis Kazakevičs.
Goal: Igors Tarasovs (26).

10.10.2020   FAROE ISLANDS - LATVIA   1-1(1-1)   2nd UEFA Nations League D, Group 1
Tórsvøllur, Tórshavn; Referee: Ivaylo Stoyanov (Bulgaria); Attendance: 447
LVA: Pāvels Šteinbors (Cap), Elvis Stuglis, Mārcis Ošs, Kristers Tobers (68.Kriss Kārkliņš), Ritvars Rugins, Artūrs Zjuzins (82.Eduards Emsis), Roberts Savaļnieks, Jānis Ikaunieks, Andrejs Cigaņiks, Alvis Jaunzems (67.Mārtiņš Ķigurs), Roberts Uldriķis (82.Raimonds Krollis). Trainer: Dainis Kazakevičs.
Goal: Jānis Ikaunieks (25).

13.10.2020   LATVIA - MALTA   0-1(0-0)   2nd UEFA Nations League D, Group 1
Daugava stadions, Rīga; Referee: Iwan Arwel Griffith (Wales); Attendance: 953
LVA: Pāvels Šteinbors (Cap), Igors Tarasovs, Mārcis Ošs, Raivis Andris Jurkovskis, Kristers Tobers (63.Eduards Emsis), Artūrs Zjuzins (54.Kriss Kārkliņš), Roberts Savaļnieks, Dāvis Ikaunieks (64.Mārtiņš Ķigurs), Jānis Ikaunieks, Vladislavs Gutkovskis (64.Roberts Uldriķis), Andrejs Cigaņiks (84.Alvis Jaunzems). Trainer: Dainis Kazakevičs.

11.11.2020   SAN MARINO - LATVIA   0-3(0-1)   Friendly International
San Marino Stadium, Serravalle; Referee: Fabio Maresca (Italy); Attendance: 0
LVA: Roberts Ozols, Elvis Stuglis, Mārcis Ošs (Cap) (67.Kaspars Dubra), Vladislavs Sorokins, Vladimirs Kamešs (46.Dāvis Ikaunieks), Jānis Ikaunieks (61.Alvis Jaunzems), Kriss Kārkliņš (61.Ritvars Rugins), Vladislavs Fjodorovs, Aleksejs Saveljevs, Daniels Ontužāns (61.Andrejs Cigaņiks), Roberts Uldriķis (72.Vladislavs Gutkovskis). Trainer: Dainis Kazakevičs.
Goals: Cristian Brolli (32 own goal), Kaspars Dubra (71), Vladislavs Gutkovskis (78 penalty).

14.11.2020　　**LATVIA - FAROE ISLANDS**　　　　　　　**1-1(0-0)**　　　　　2nd UEFA Nations League D, Group 1
Daugava stadions, Rīga; Referee: Nikola Dabanović (Montenegro); Attendance: 0
LVA: Roberts Ozols, Kaspars Dubra, Antonijs Černomordijs (Cap), Raivis Andris Jurkovskis, Vladimirs Kamešs (61.Daniels Ontužāns), Ritvars Rugins (61.Aleksejs Saveljevs), Roberts Savaļnieks, Jānis Ikaunieks (90+1.Alvis Jaunzems), Krišs Kārkliņš, Andrejs Cigaņiks (71.Mārtiņš Ķigurs), Vladislavs Gutkovskis). Trainer: Dainis Kazakevičs.
Goal: Vladimirs Kamešs (59).

17.11.2020　　**ANDORRA - LATVIA**　　　　　　　　　**0-5(0-1)**　　　　　2nd UEFA Nations League D, Group 1
Estadi Nacional, Andorra la Vella; Referee: Dimitar Meckarovski (North Macedonia); Attendance: 0
LVA: Roberts Ozols, Kaspars Dubra, Antonijs Černomordijs (Cap), Raivis Andris Jurkovskis, Vladimirs Kamešs (74.Daniels Ontužāns), Artūrs Zjuzins (55.Aleksejs Saveljevs), Roberts Savaļnieks, Jānis Ikaunieks (75.Mārtiņš Ķigurs), Krišs Kārkliņš, Vladislavs Gutkovskis (75.Raimonds Krollis), Andrejs Cigaņiks (82.Dāvis Ikaunieks). Trainer: Dainis Kazakevičs.
Goals: Antonijs Černomordijs (6), Jānis Ikaunieks (57, 60), Vladislavs Gutkovskis (70 penalty), Raimonds Krollis (90 penalty).

24.03.2021　　**LATVIA - MONTENEGRO**　　　　　　　**1-2(1-1)**　　　　　22nd FIFA WC.Qualifiers
Skonto stadions, Rīga; Referee: Alain Durieux (Luxembourg); Attendance: 0
LVA: Pāvels Šteinbors, Mārcis Ošs, Antonijs Černomordijs (Cap), Raivis Andris Jurkovskis, Kristers Tobers, Vladimirs Kamešs (71.Alvis Jaunzems), Artūrs Zjuzins (71.Krišs Kārkliņš), Roberts Savaļnieks, Jānis Ikaunieks, Andrejs Cigaņiks (81.Dāvis Ikaunieks), Roberts Uldriķis (81.Raimonds Krollis). Trainer: Dainis Kazakevičs.
Goal: Jānis Ikaunieks (40).

27.03.2021　　**NETHERLANDS - LATVIA**　　　　　　　**2-0(1-0)**　　　　　22nd FIFA WC.Qualifiers
"Johan Cruyff" Arena, Amsterdam; Referee: Stéphanie Frappart (France); Attendance: 5,000
LVA: Roberts Ozols, Igors Tarasovs, Antonijs Černomordijs (Cap), Raivis Andris Jurkovskis, Kristers Tobers, Vladimirs Kamešs (79.Roberts Savaļnieks), Artūrs Zjuzins (46.Krišs Kārkliņš), Jānis Ikaunieks (87.Raimonds Krollis), Andrejs Cigaņiks (85.Aleksandrs Solovjovs), Vladislavs Fjodorovs, Roberts Uldriķis (46.Vladislavs Gutkovskis). Trainer: Dainis Kazakevičs.

30.03.2021　　**TURKEY - LATVIA**　　　　　　　　　**3-3(2-1)**　　　　　22nd FIFA WC.Qualifiers
Atatürk Olimpiyat Stadı, İstanbul; Referee: Daniel Stefański (Poland); Attendance: 223
LVA: Pāvels Šteinbors, Mārcis Ošs, Antonijs Černomordijs (Cap), Raivis Andris Jurkovskis, Kristers Tobers, Roberts Savaļnieks (90+4.Alvis Jaunzems), Jānis Ikaunieks (65.Dāvis Ikaunieks), Andrejs Cigaņiks (46.Vladimirs Kamešs), Eduards Emsis, Vladislavs Fjodorovs, Roberts Uldriķis (73.Raimonds Krollis). Trainer: Dainis Kazakevičs.
Goals: Roberts Savaļnieks (35), Roberts Uldriķis (58), Jānis Ikaunieks (79).

04.06.2021　　**LATVIA - LITHUANIA**　　　　　　　　**3-1(1-0)**　　　　　19th Baltic Cup
Daugava stadions, Rīga; Referee: Juri Frischer (Estonia); Attendance: 0
LVA: Roberts Ozols, Mārcis Ošs, Antonijs Černomordijs (Cap), Raivis Andris Jurkovskis (61.Vitālijs Maksimenko), Artūrs Zjuzins (62.Vladislavs Fjodorovs), Roberts Savaļnieks, Krišs Kārkliņš (73.Aleksejs Saveljevs), Andrejs Cigaņiks (62.62.Raimonds Krollis), Eduards Emsis, Alvis Jaunzems (37.Dāvis Ikaunieks), Roberts Uldriķis. Trainer: Dainis Kazakevičs.
Goals: Markas Beneta (37 own goal), Eduards Emsis (69), Roberts Uldriķis (85).

07.06.2021　　**GERMANY - LATVIA**　　　　　　　　　**7-1(5-0)**　　　　　Friendly International
Merkur Spiel-Arena, Düsseldorf; Referee: Nikola Dabanović (Montenegro); Attendance: 1,000
LVA: Roberts Ozols, Mārcis Ošs (46.Igors Tarasovs), Antonijs Černomordijs (Cap), Raivis Andris Jurkovskis, Artūrs Zjuzins (68.Aleksejs Saveljevs), Dāvis Ikaunieks (46.Vitālijs Maksimenko), Krišs Kārkliņš (61.Raimonds Krollis), Andrejs Cigaņiks (68.Alvis Jaunzems), Eduards Emsis, Vladislavs Fjodorovs, Roberts Uldriķis (80.Renārs Varslavāns). Trainer: Dainis Kazakevičs.
Goal: Aleksejs Saveljevs (75).

10.06.2021　　**ESTONIA - LATVIA**　　　　　　　　　**2-1(2-0)**　　　　　19th Baltic Cup
A. Le Coq Arena, Tallinn; Referee: Robertas Valikonis (Lithuania); Attendance: 740
LVA: Roberts Ozols, Kaspars Dubra (Cap), Mārcis Ošs, Raivis Andris Jurkovskis (61.Vladislavs Sorokins), Artūrs Zjuzins (46.Raimonds Krollis), Roberts Savaļnieks (86.Elvis Stuglis), Andrejs Cigaņiks (77.Dāvis Ikaunieks), Eduards Emsis, Vladislavs Fjodorovs (61.Alvis Jaunzems), Aleksejs Saveljevs (46.Krišs Kārkliņš), Roberts Uldriķis. Trainer: Dainis Kazakevičs.
Goal: Jānis Ikaunieks (84 penalty).

NATIONAL TEAM PLAYERS
(16.07.2020 – 15.07.2021)

Name	DOB	Caps	Goals	2020/2021:	Club
Goalkeepers					
Roberts OZOLS	10.09.1995	8	0	2020/2021:	Rīga FC
Pāvels ŠTEINBORS	21.09.1985	18	0	2020/2021:	Jagiellonia Białystok (POL)
Defenders					
Antonijs ČERNOMORDIJS	26.09.1996	13	1	2020/2021:	Rīga FC
Kaspars DUBRA	20.12.1990	43	3	2020/2021:	FK Oleksandriya (UKR)
Raivis Andris JURKOVSKIS	09.12.1996	19	0	2020: 08.01.2021->	FK Liepāja Dundalk FC (IRL)
Krišs KĀRKLIŅŠ	31.01.1996	12	0	2020: 19.01.2021->	Valmiera FC FK Liepāja
Vitālijs MAKSIMENKO	08.12.1990	53	1	2020/2021:	NK Olimpija Ljubljana (SVN)
Mārcis OŠS	25.07.1991	20	1	2020/2021:	FC Lugano (SUI)
Aleksandrs SOLOVJOVS	25.02.1988	11	0	2021:	FK Rīgas Futbola Skola
Vladislavs SOROKINS	10.05.1997	2	0	2020/2021:	FK Rīgas Futbola Skola
Elvis STUGLIS	04.07.1993	4	0	2020: 01.01.2021->	Rīga FC FK Rīgas Futbola Skola
Igors TARASOVS	16.10.1988	38	2	2020: 07.01.2021->	Kuopion Palloseura (FIN) Ethnikos Achna FC (CYP)
Midfielders					
Andrejs CIGAŅIKS	12.04.1997	22	0	2020/2021:	FK Zorya Luhansk (UKR)
Eduards EMSIS	23.02.1996	10	1	2020/2021:	FC Noah Yerevan (ARM)
Jānis IKAUNIEKS	16.02.1995	36	7	2020: 22.02.2021->	FK Rīgas Futbola Skola Kuopion Palloseura (FIN)
Alvis JAUNZEMS	16.06.1999	11	0	2020/2021:	Valmiera FC
Vladimirs KAMEŠS	28.10.1988	30	3	2020/2021:	Rīga FC
Mārtiņš ĶIGURS	31.03.1997	9	0	2020:	FK Liepāja
Daniels ONTUŽĀNS	07.03.2000	5	0	2020:	FC Bayern München II (GER)
Ritvars RUGINS	17.10.1989	39	0	2020:	Rīga FC
Roberts SAVAĻNIEKS	04.02.1993	31	1	2020/2021:	FK Rīgas Futbola Skola
Aleksejs SAVELJEVS	30.01.1999	6	1	2020/2021:	Mantova 1911 SRL (ITA)
Kristers TOBERS	13.12.2000	12	0	2020/2021:	KS Lechia Gdańsk (POL)
Eduards TĪDENBERGS	18.12.1994	1	0	2020:	FK Liepāja
Renārs VARSLAVĀNS	23.08.2001	1	0	2021:	FK Rīgas Futbola Skola
Artūrs ZJUZINS	18.06.1991	47	7	2020/2021:	FK Rīgas Futbola Skola
Forwards					
Vladislavs FJODOROVS	27.09.1996	13	1	2020/2021:	Rīga FC
Vladislavs GUTKOVSKIS	02.04.1995	25	2	2020/2021:	RKS Raków Częstochowa (POL)
Dāvis IKAUNIEKS	07.01.1994	33	6	2020: 25.01.2021->	FK Mladá Boleslav FK Liepāja (on loan from FK Jablonec (CZE))
Raimonds KROLLIS	28.10.2001	10	1	2020: 28.01.2021->	FS Metta/Latvijas Universitāte Rīga Valmiera FC
Roberts ULDRIĶIS	03.04.1998	25	3	2020/2021:	FC Sion (SUI)
Trainer					
Dainis KAZAKEVIČS [from 20.01.2020]	30.03.1981			14 M; 3 W; 6 D; 5 L; 21-22	

LIECHTENSTEIN

The Country:
Fürstentum Liechtenstein (Principality of Liechtenstein)
Capital: Vaduz
Surface: 160 km²
Inhabitants: 38,896 [2020]
Time: UTC+1

The FA:
Liechtensteiner Fussballverband
Landstrasse 149, 9494 Schaan
+423 238 24 00
Foundation date: 1934
Member of FIFA since: 1974
Member of UEFA since: 1974
Website: www.lfv.li

NATIONAL TEAM RECORDS

RECORDS
First international match:	09.03.1982, Balzers:	Liechtenstein – Switzerland 0-1
Most international caps:	Peter Karl Jehle	- 132 caps (1998-2018)
Most international goals:	Mario Frick	- 16 goals / 125 caps (1993-2015)

UEFA EUROPEAN CHAMPIONSHIP		FIFA WORLD CUP		OLYMPIC TOURNAMENTS	
1960	-	1930	-	1908	-
1964	-	1934	-	1912	-
1968	-	1938	-	1920	-
1972	-	1950	-	1924	-
1976	Did not enter	1954	-	1928	-
1980	Did not enter	1958	-	1936	-
1984	Did not enter	1962	-	1948	-
1988	Did not enter	1966	-	1952	-
1992	Did not enter	1970	-	1956	-
1996	Qualifiers	1974	-	1960	-
2000	Qualifiers	1978	Did not enter	1964	-
2004	Qualifiers	1982	Did not enter	1968	-
2008	Qualifiers	1986	Did not enter	1972	-
2012	Qualifiers	1990	Did not enter	1976	Did not enter
2016	Qualifiers	1994	Did not enter	1980	Did not enter
2020	Qualifiers	1998	Qualifiers	1984	Did not enter
		2002	Qualifiers	1988	Qualifiers
		2006	Qualifiers	1992	Did not enter
		2010	Qualifiers	1996	Did not enter
		2014	Qualifiers	2000	Did not enter
		2018	Qualifiers	2004	Did not enter
				2008	Qualifiers
				2012	Qualifiers
				2016	Qualifiers

UEFA NATIONS LEAGUE
2018/2019	League D
2020/2021	League D

FIFA CONFEDERATIONS CUP 1992-2017
None

LIECHTENSTEIN CLUB HONOURS IN EUROPEAN CLUB COMPETITIONS:

European Champion Clubs' Cup (1956-1992) / UEFA Champions League (1993-2021)
None

Fairs Cup (1858-1971) / UEFA Cup (1972-2009) / UEFA Europa League (2010-2021)
None

UEFA Super Cup (1972-2020)
None

*European Cup Winners' Cup 1961-1999**
None

defunct competition

NATIONAL COMPETITIONS
TABLE OF HONOURS

	CHAMPIONS
1932	FC Vaduz (*unofficial*)
1934	FC Triesen
1935	FC Triesen
1936	FC Vaduz
1937	FC Triesen

CUP WINNERS

Season	Winner	Season	Winner	Season	Winner
1945/1946	FC Triesen	1971/1972	FC Triesen	1996/1997	FC Balzers
1946/1947	FC Triesen	1972/1973	FC Balzers	1997/1998	FC Vaduz
1947/1948	FC Triesen	1973/1974	FC Vaduz	1998/1999	FC Vaduz
1948/1949	FC Vaduz	1974/1975	FC Triesen	1999/2000	FC Vaduz
1949/1950	FC Triesen	1975/1976	USV Eschen/Mauren	2000/2001	FC Vaduz
1950/1951	FC Triesen	1976/1977	USV Eschen/Mauren	2001/2002	FC Vaduz
1951/1952	FC Vaduz	1977/1978	USV Eschen/Mauren	2002/2003	FC Vaduz
1952/1953	FC Vaduz	1978/1979	FC Balzers	2003/2004	FC Vaduz
1953/1954	FC Vaduz	1979/1980	FC Vaduz	2004/2005	FC Vaduz
1954/1955	FC Schaan	1980/1981	FC Balzers	2005/2006	FC Vaduz
1955/1956	FC Vaduz	1981/1982	FC Balzers	2006/2007	FC Vaduz
1956/1957	FC Vaduz	1982/1983	FC Balzers	2007/2008	FC Vaduz
1957/1958	FC Vaduz	1983/1984	FC Balzers	2008/2009	FC Vaduz
1958/1959	FC Vaduz	1984/1985	FC Vaduz	2009/2010	FC Vaduz
1959/1960	FC Vaduz	1985/1986	FC Vaduz	2010/2011	FC Vaduz
1960/1961	FC Vaduz	1986/1987	USV Eschen/Mauren	2011/2012	USV Eschen/Mauren
1961/1962	FC Vaduz	1987/1988	FC Vaduz	2012/2013	FC Vaduz
1962/1963	FC Schaan	1988/1989	FC Balzers	2013/2014	FC Vaduz
1963/1964	FC Balzers	1989/1990	FC Vaduz	2014/2015	FC Vaduz
1964/1965	FC Triesen	1990/1991	FC Balzers	2015/2016	FC Vaduz
1965/1966	FC Vaduz	1991/1992	FC Vaduz	2016/2017	FC Vaduz
1966/1967	FC Vaduz	1992/1993	FC Balzers	2017/2018	FC Vaduz
1967/1968	FC Vaduz	1993/1994	FC Schaan	2018/2019	FC Vaduz
1968/1969	FC Vaduz	1994/1995	FC Vaduz	2019/2020	*Competition abandoned*
1969/1970	FC Vaduz	1995/1996	FC Vaduz	2020/2021	*Competition abandoned*
1970/1971	FC Vaduz				

NATIONAL CUP
Liechtensteiner Cup 2020/2021

First Round [27-28.08.2019]	
FC Schaan - USV Eschen/Mauren III	4-4 aet; 5-4 pen
FC Schaan II - FC Triesenberg	0-6
FC Balzers II - USV Eschen/Mauren II	4-1

Secoond Round [17-18.09.2019]	
FC Rugell II - FC Triesen	2-2 aet; 3-4 pen
FC Schaan - FC Triesen II	6-1
FC Triesenberg II - FC Balzers II	0-6
FC Vaduz III - FC Triesenberg	1-11

Quarter-Finals [23/29/30.10.2019]			
FC Schaan - FC Vaduz	*Cancelled*	FC Triesenberg - USV Eschen/Mauren	*Cancelled*
FC Triesen - FC Balzers	*Cancelled*	FC Balzers II - FC Rugell	*Cancelled*

The competition was abandoned due to the COVID-19 pandemic.
The Liechtenstein Football Association selected FC Vaduz (with the highest UEFA club coefficient), to play in the 2021/2022 UEFA Europa Conference League.

LIECHTENSTEIN NATIONAL TEAM

INTERNATIONAL MATCHES
(16.07.2020 – 15.07.2021)

08.09.2020	Rimini	San Marino - Liechtenstein	0-2(0-2)	(UNL)
07.10.2020	Lëtzebuerg	Luxembourg - Liechtenstein	1-2(1-1)	(F)
10.10.2020	Vaduz	Liechtenstein - Gibraltar	0-1(0-1)	(UNL)
13.10.2020	Vaduz	Liechtenstein - San Marino	0-0	(UNL)
11.11.2020	Attard	Malta - Liechtenstein	3-0(2-0)	(F)
17.11.2020	Gibraltar	Gibraltar - Liechtenstein	1-1(1-1)	(UNL)
25.03.2021	Vaduz	Liechtenstein - Armenia	0-1(0-0)	(WCQ)
28.03.2021	Skopje	North Macedonia - Liechtenstein	5-0(1-0)	(WCQ)
31.03.2021	Vaduz	Liechtenstein - Iceland	1-4(0-2)	(WCQ)
01.06.2021	St. Gallen	Switzerland - Liechtenstein	7-0(1-0)	(F)
01.06.2021	Tórshavn	Faroe Islands - Liechtenstein	5-1(3-1)	(F)

08.09.2020   SAN MARINO - LIECHTENSTEIN   0-2(0-2)   2nd UEFA Nations League D, Group 2
Stadio Romeo Neri, Rimini (Italy); Referee: Enea Jorgji (Albania); Attendance: 50
LIE: Benjamin Büchel, Daniel Kaufmann, Nicolas Hasler (Cap), Seyhan Yildiz, Maximilian Göppel, Andreas Malin, Marcel Büchel, Dennis Salanović (90+3.Philipp Ospelt), Aron Sele, Yanik Frick (87.Sandro Wolfinger), Noah Zinedine Frick (77.Noah Frommelt). Trainer: Helgi Kolviðsson (Iceland).
Goals: Nicolas Hasler (3 penalty), Yanik Frick (14).

07.10.2020   LUXEMBOURG - LIECHTENSTEIN   1-2(1-1)   Friendly International
Stade "Josy Barthel", Lëtzebuerg; Referee: Alexandre Boucaut (Belgium); Attendance: 0
LIE: Justin Ospelt, Sandro Wolfinger (73.Philipp Ospelt), Maximilian Göppel, Andreas Malin, Jens Hofer (58.Seyhan Yildiz), Martin Büchel (Cap) (46.Noah Frommelt), Nicolas Hasler, Aron Sele (86.Nicola Kollmann), Fabio Wolfinger (58.Daniel Matthias Brändle), Dennis Salanović, Yanik Frick (51.Simon Kühne). Trainer: Helgi Kolviðsson (Iceland).
Goals: Fabio Wolfinger (23), Nicolas Hasler (62 penalty).

10.10.2020   LIECHTENSTEIN - GIBRALTAR   0-1(0-1)   2nd UEFA Nations League D, Group 2
Rheinpark Stadion, Vaduz; Referee: Kirill Levnikov (Russia); Attendance: 178
LIE: Benjamin Büchel, Nicolas Hasler, Maximilian Göppel, Sandro Wolfinger (59.Daniel Matthias Brändle), Jens Hofer, Martin Büchel (Cap), Andreas Malin, Aron Sele (46.Noah Frommelt), Fabio Wolfinger (46.Seyhan Yildiz), Dennis Salanović, Simon Kühne (86.Philipp Ospelt). Trainer: Helgi Kolviðsson (Iceland).

13.10.2020   LIECHTENSTEIN - SAN MARINO   0-0   2nd UEFA Nations League D, Group 2
Rheinpark Stadion, Vaduz; Referee: Jørgen Daugbjerg Burchardt (Denmark); Attendance: 178
LIE: Benjamin Büchel, Daniel Kaufmann, Nicolas Hasler, Seyhan Yildiz, Maximilian Göppel (46.Sandro Wolfinger), Andreas Malin, Jens Hofer (46.Philipp Ospelt), Martin Büchel (Cap) (8.Livio Meier), Aron Sele, Dennis Salanović, Daniel Matthias Brändle (75.Fabio Wolfinger). Trainer: Helgi Kolviðsson (Iceland).

11.11.2020   MALTA - LIECHTENSTEIN   3-0(2-0)   Friendly International
Ta`Qali National Stadium, Attard; Referee: Manfredas Lukjančukas (Lithuania); Attendance: 0
LIE: Thomas Hobi, Seyhan Yildiz, Sandro Wolfinger (78.Andrin Netzer), Maximilian Göppel, Andreas Malin, Martin Büchel (Cap) (86.Alexander Marxer), Nicolas Hasler, Daniel Matthias Brändle, Aron Sele (69.Philipp Ospelt), Ridvan Kardesoglu, Fabio Wolfinger (70.Noah Graber). Trainer: Helgi Kolviðsson (Iceland).

17.11.2020   GIBRALTAR - LIECHTENSTEIN   1-1(1-1)   2nd UEFA Nations League D, Group 2
Victoria Stadium, Gibraltar; Referee: Trustin Farrugia Cann (Malta); Attendance: 0
LIE: Thomas Hobi, Nicolas Hasler, Maximilian Göppel, Andreas Malin, Jens Hofer, Martin Büchel (Cap) (72.Ridvan Kardesoglu), Daniel Matthias Brändle (56.Seyhan Yildiz), Noah Frommelt, Simon Kühne (72.Fabio Wolfinger), Yanik Frick, Noah Zinedine Frick (79.Philipp Ospelt). Trainer: Helgi Kolviðsson (Iceland).
Goal: Noah Zinedine Frick (44).

25.03.2021   LIECHTENSTEIN - ARMENIA   0-1(0-0)   22nd FIFA WC. Qualifiers
Rheinpark Stadion, Vaduz; Referee: Julian Weinberger (Austria); Attendance: 0
LIE: Benjamin Büchel, Daniel Kaufmann, Nicolas Hasler (Cap), Seyhan Yildiz (65.Daniel Matthias Brändle), Maximilian Göppel, Andreas Malin (46.Rafael Grünenfelder), Jens Hofer, Aron Sele, Livio Meier (65.Noah Frommelt), Yanik Frick, Noah Zinedine Frick (76.Niklas Beck). Trainer: Martin Stocklasa.

28.03.2021   NORTH MACEDONIA - LIECHTENSTEIN   5-0(1-0)   22nd FIFA WC. Qualifiers
"Toše Proeski" National Arena, Skopje; Referee: Mykola Balakin (Ukraine); Attendance: 0
LIE: Benjamin Büchel, Nicolas Hasler (Cap) (41.Aron Sele), Maximilian Göppel (78.Martin Marxer), Jens Hofer, Andreas Malin, Daniel Matthias Brändle, Sandro Wolfinger, Fabio Wolfinger (66.Alexander Marxer), Livio Meier (46.Philipp Ospelt), Noah Frommelt (67.Benjamin Vogt), Yanik Frick. Trainer: Martin Stocklasa.

31.03.2021   LIECHTENSTEIN - ICELAND   1-4(0-2)   22nd FIFA WC. Qualifiers
Rheinpark Stadion, Vaduz; Referee: Mohammed Al Hakim (Sweden); Attendance: 0
LIE: Justin Ospelt, Daniel Kaufmann, Seyhan Yildiz (46.Daniel Matthias Brändle), Maximilian Göppel, Jens Hofer (78.Alexander Marxer), Martin Büchel (Cap) (69.Noah Frommelt), Sandro Wolfinger, Aron Sele (69.Fabio Wolfinger), Livio Meier, Yanik Frick, Noah Zinedine Frick (84.Philipp Ospelt). Trainer: Martin Stocklasa.
Goal: Yanik Frick (79).

03.06.2021   SWITZERLAND - LIECHTENSTEIN   7-0(1-0)   Friendly International
Kybunpark, St. Gallen; Referee: Nejc Kajtazović (Slovenia); Attendance: 0
LIE: Benjamin Büchel (Cap), Maximilian Göppel (89.Sandro Wolfinger), Rafael Grünenfelder, Jens Hofer, Daniel Matthias Brändle (46.Seyhan Yildiz), Fabio Wolfinger (46.Roman Spirig), Dennis Salanović, Livio Meier (67.Aron Sele), Noah Frommelt, Yanik Frick (83.Philipp Ospelt), Noah Zinedine Frick (83.Nicola Kollmann). Trainer: Martin Stocklasa.

07.06.2021 **FAROE ISLANDS - LIECHTENSTEIN** **5-1(3-1)** Friendly International

Tórsvøllur, Tórshavn; Referee: Ívar Orri Kristjánsson (Iceland); Attendance: 0

LIE: Thomas Hobi, Sandro Wolfinger (84.Seyhan Yildiz), Maximilian Göppel, Rafael Grünenfelder, Jens Hofer (Cap), Daniel Matthias Brändle (62.Simon Lüchinger), Aron Sele, Livio Meier (62.Philipp Ospelt), Noah Frommelt, Yanik Frick, Noah Zinedine Frick (53.Fabio Wolfinger). Trainer: Martin Stocklasa.

Goal: Maximilian Göppel (19).

NATIONAL TEAM PLAYERS
(16.07.2020 – 15.07.2021)

Name	DOB	Caps	Goals	2020/2021:	Club
Goalkeepers					
Benjamin BÜCHEL	04.07.1989	35	0	2020/2021:	FC Vaduz
Thomas HOBI	20.06.1993	5	0	2020/2021:	FC Balzers
Justin OSPELT	07.09.1999	2	0	2020/2021:	FC Vaduz
Defenders					
Daniel Matthias BRÄNDLE	23.01.1992	37	0	2020/2021:	SV Pullach (GER)
Maximilian GÖPPEL	31.08.1997	41	1	2020/2021:	FC Vaduz
Rafael GRÜNENFELDER	20.03.1999	3	0	2021:	FC Balzers
Jens HOFER	01.10.1997	15	0	2020/2021:	FC Biel-Bienne (SUI)
Daniel KAUFMANN	22.12.1990	61	1	2020/2021:	USV Eschen/Mauren
Andreas MALIN	31.01.1994	27	0	2020/2021:	FC Dornbirn (AUT)
Alexander MARXER	04.04.1994	3	0	2020: 01.01.2021->	FC Ruggell USV Eschen/Mauren
Martin MARXER	04.10.1999	1	0	2021:	FC Ostermundigen (SUI)
Roman SPIRIG	07.01.1998	1	0	2021:	FC Balzers
Seyhan YILDIZ	30.04.1989	46	1	2020/2021:	FC Balzers
Midfielders					
Niklas BECK	25.03.2001	1	0	2021:	FC Rugell
Marcel BÜCHEL	18.03.1991	18	1	2020:	Unattached
Martin BÜCHEL	19.02.1987	88	2	2020: 25.01.2021->	FC Red Star Zürich (SUI) FC Rugell
Noah FROMMELT	18.12.2000	10	0	2020/2021:	USV Eschen/Mauren
Noah GRABER	03.05.2001	1	0	2020:	USV Eschen/Mauren
Nicolas HASLER	04.05.1991	75	3	2020: 09.2020->	Unattached FC Thun (SUI)
Ridvan KARDESOGLU	12.10.1996	3	0	2020:	FC Balzers
Nicola KOLLMANN	23.11.1994	2	0	2020/2021:	FC Rugell
Simon LÜCHINGER	28.11.2002	1	0	2021:	FC Vaduz
Livio MEIER	10.01.1998	18	0	2020/2021:	USV Eschen/Mauren
Andrin NETZER	11.01.2002	1	0	2020:	FC Vaduz
Philipp OSPELT	07.10.1992	14	0	2020/2021:	USV Eschen/Mauren
Aron SELE	02.09.1996	29	0	2020/2021:	FC Chur 97 (SUI)
Fabio WOLFINGER	11.05.1996	10	0	2020/2021:	USV Eschen/Mauren
Sandro WOLFINGER	24.08.1991	42	2	2020/2021:	USV Eschen/Mauren
Forwards					
Noah Zinedine FRICK	26.10.2001	8	1	2020: 24.09.2020->	Unattached Neuchâtel Xamax FCS (SUI)
Yanik FRICK	27.05.1998	19	3	2020: 06.10.2020->	Unattached FC Energie Cottbus (GER)
Simon KÜHNE	30.04.1994	25	0	2020:	USV Eschen/Mauren
Dennis SALANOVIĆ	26.02.1996	46	4	2020/2021:	FC Thun (SUI)
Benjamin VOGT	28.06.1999	1	0	2021:	FC Balzers
Trainer					
Helgi KOLVIÐSSON (Iceland) [01.01.2019 – 31.12.2020]	13.09.1971			16 M; 2 W; 4 D; 10 L; 7-37	
Martin STOCKLASA [from 01.01.2021]	29.05.1979			5 M; 0 W; 0 D; 5 L; 2-22	

LITHUANIA

The Country:
Lietuvos Respublika (Republic of Lithuania)
Capital: Vilnius
Surface: 65,300 km²
Inhabitants: 2,784,279 [2021]
Time: UTC+2

The FA:
Lietuvos futbolo federacija
Stadiono g. 2, 02106 Vilnius
Tel: +370 5263 8741
Foundation date: 1922
Member of FIFA since: 1923
Member of UEFA since: 1992
Website: www.lff.lt

NATIONAL TEAM RECORDS

First international match:	24.06.1923, Kaunas:	Lithuania – Estonia 0-5
Most international caps:	Saulius Mikoliūnas	- 96 caps (2004-2021)
Most international goals:	Tomas Danilevičius	- 19 goals / 71 caps (1998-2014)

UEFA EUROPEAN CHAMPIONSHIP

1960	-
1964	-
1968	-
1972	-
1976	-
1980	-
1984	-
1988	-
1992	-
1996	Qualifiers
2000	Qualifiers
2004	Qualifiers
2008	Qualifiers
2012	Qualifiers
2016	Qualifiers
2020	Qualifiers

FIFA WORLD CUP

1930	Did Not Enter
1934	Qualifiers
1938	Qualifiers
1950	-
1954	-
1958	-
1962	-
1966	-
1970	-
1974	-
1978	-
1982	-
1986	-
1990	-
1994	Qualifiers
1998	Qualifiers
2002	Qualifiers
2006	Qualifiers
2010	Qualifiers
2014	Qualifiers
2018	Qualifiers

OLYMPIC TOURNAMENTS

1908	-
1912	-
1920	-
1924	FT/Preliminary Round
1928	-
1936	-
1948	-
1952	-
1956	-
1960	-
1964	-
1968	-
1972	-
1976	-
1980	-
1984	-
1988	-
1992	-
1996	Qualifiers
2000	Qualifiers
2004	Qualifiers
2008	Qualifiers
2012	Qualifiers
2016	Qualifiers

<u>Please note</u>: *was part of Soviet Union from 1944 to 1990.*

UEFA NATIONS LEAGUE

2018/2019	League C
2020/2021	League C

FIFA CONFEDERATIONS CUP 1992-2017

None

LITHUANIAN CLUB HONOURS IN EUROPEAN CLUB COMPETITIONS:

European Champion Clubs' Cup (1956-1992) / UEFA Champions League (1993-2021)
None

Fairs Cup (1858-1971) / UEFA Cup (1972-2009) / UEFA Europa League (2010-2021)
None

UEFA Super Cup (1972-2020)
None

European Cup Winners' Cup 1961-1999
None

*defunct competition

NATIONAL COMPETITIONS
TABLE OF HONOURS

LITHUANIAN SSR (SOVIET ERA) CHAMPIONS

1945	Spartakas Kaunas	1959/1960	Elnias Šiauliai	1975	Dainava Alytus
1946	Dinamo Kaunas	1960/1961	Elnias Šiauliai	1976	Atmosfera Mažeikiai
1947	Lokomotyvas Kaunas	1961/1962	FK Atletas Kaunas	1977	Statybininkas Šiauliai
1948	Elnias Šiauliai	1962/1963	Statyba Panevėžys	1978	Atlantas Klaipėda
1949	Elnias Šiauliai	1964	Inkaras Kaunas	1979	Atmosfera Mažeikiai
1950	Inkaras Kaunas	1965	Inkaras Kaunas	1980	Atlantas Klaipėda
1951	Inkaras Kaunas	1966	Nevėžis Kėdainiai	1981	Atlantas Klaipėda
1952	Karininkų Namai Vilnius	1967	Saliutas Vilnius	1982	Pažanga Vilnius
1953	Elnias Šiauliai	1968	Statyba Panevėžys	1983	Pažanga Vilnius
1954	Inkaras Kaunas	1969	Statybininkas Šiauliai	1984	Atlantas Klaipėda
1955	Lima Kaunas	1970	FK Atletas Kaunas	1985	Ekranas Panevėžys
1956	Linų Audiniai Plungė	1971	Pažanga Vilnius	1986	Banga Kaunas
1957	Elnias Šiauliai	1972	Nevėžis Kėdainiai	1987	Tauras Tauragė
1958	Elnias Šiauliai	1973	Nevėžis Kėdainiai	1988	SRT Vilnius
1958/1959	Raudonoji Žvaigždė Vilnius	1974	Tauras Šiauliai	1989	Banga Kaunas

	CHAMPIONS	CUP WINNERS	BEST GOALSCORERS	
1922	LFLS Kaunas	-	-	
1923	LFLS Kaunas	-	-	
1924	Kovas Kaunas	-	-	
1925	Kovas Kaunas	-	-	
1926	Kovas Kaunas	-	-	
1927	LFLS Kaunas	-	-	
1928	KSS Klaipėda	-	-	
1929	KSS Klaipėda	-	-	
1930	KSS Klaipėda	-	-	
1931	KSS Klaipėda	-	-	
1932	LFLS Kaunas	-	-	
1933	Kovas Kaunas	-	-	
1934	MSK Kaunas	-	-	
1935	Kovas Kaunas	-	-	
1936	Kovas Kaunas	-	-	
1937	KSS Klaipėda	-	-	
1937/1938	KSS Klaipėda	-	-	
1938/1939	LGSF Kaunas	-	-	
1939/1940	*Competition abandoned*	-	-	
1941	*Competition not finished*	-	-	
1942	LFLS Kaunas	-	-	
1942/1943	Tauras Kaunas	-	-	
1943/1944	*Competition not finished*	-	-	
----------	----------	----------	----------	
1990	FK Sirijus Klaipėda	FK Sirijus Klaipėda	Dalius Bajorūnas (FK Tauras Šiauliai)	22
1991	FK Žalgiris Vilnius	FK Žalgiris Vilnius	Egidijus Meidus (Vilija Kaunas)	13
1991/1992	FK Žalgiris Vilnius	FK Makabi Vilnius	Remigijus Pocius (FK Granitas Klaipėda / FK Sakalas Šiauliai) Vaidotas Šlekys (FK Ekranas Panevėžys)	14
1992/1993	FK Ekranas Panevėžys	FK Žalgiris Vilnius	Vaidotas Šlekys (FK Ekranas Panevėžys)	16
1993/1994	ROMAR Mažeikiai	FK Žalgiris Vilnius	Vaidotas Šlekys (FK Ekranas Panevėžys) Robertas Žalys (FBK Kaunas)	16
1994/1995	FK Inkaras-Grifas Kaunas	FK Inkaras-Grifas Kaunas	Eimantas Poderis (FK Žalgiris Vilnius / FK Inkaras-Grifas Kaunas)	24
1995/1996	FK Inkaras-Grifas Kaunas	FK Kareda-Sakalas Šiauliai	Edgaras Jankauskas (FK Žalgiris Vilnius)	25
1996/1997	FK Kareda Šiauliai	FK Žalgiris Vilnius	Remigijus Pocius (FK Kareda Šiauliai)	14
1997/1998	FK Kareda Šiauliai	FK Ekranas Panevėžys	Vidas Dančenka (FK Kareda Šiauliai)	26
1998/1999	FK Žalgiris Vilnius	FK Kareda Šiauliai	Artūras Fomenka (FK Kareda Šiauliai)	14
1999	FBK Kaunas	*No competition*	Nerijus Vasiliauskas (FK Žalgiris Vilnius)	10
2000	FBK Kaunas	FK Ekranas Panevėžys (1999/2000)	Andrius Velička (FBK Kaunas)	26
2001	FBK Kaunas	FK Atlantas Klaipėda (2000/01)	Remigijus Pocius (FBK Kaunas)	22
2002	FBK Kaunas	FBK Kaunas (2001/02)	Audrius Šlekys (FBK Kaunas)	19
2003	FBK Kaunas	FK Sūduva Marijampolė (2002/03) FK Žalgiris Vilnius (2003)	Ričardas Beniušis (FK Atlantas Klaipėda / FBK Kaunas)	16
2004	FBK Kaunas	FBK Kaunas	Povilas Lukšys (FK Ekranas Panevėžys)	19
2005	FK Ekranas Panevėžys	FBK Kaunas	Mantas Savėnas (FK Ekranas Panevėžys)	27
2006	FBK Kaunas	FK Sūduva Marijampolė	Serhiy Kuznetsov (UKR, FK Vėtra Vilnius)	18
2007	FBK Kaunas	*No competition*	Povilas Lukšys (FK Ekranas Panevėžys)	26
2008	FK Ekranas Panevėžys	FBK Kaunas (2007/08)	Rafael Pompeo Rodrigues Ledesma (BRA, FBK Kaunas)	14
2009	FK Ekranas Panevėžys	FK Sūduva Marijampolė (2008/09)	Valdas Trakys (FK Ekranas Panevėžys)	20
2010	FK Ekranas Panevėžys	FK Ekranas Panevėžys (2009/10)	Povilas Lukšys (FK Sūduva Marijampolė)	16

2011	FK Ekranas Panevėžys	FK Ekranas Panevėžys (2010/11)	Deivydas Matulevičius (FK Žalgiris Vilnius)	19
2012	FK Ekranas Panevėžys	FK Žalgiris Vilnius (2011/12)	Artūras Rimkevičius (FK Šiauliai)	35
2013	FK Žalgiris Vilnius	FK Žalgiris Vilnius (2012/13)	Nerijus Valskis (FK Sūduva Marijampolė)	27
2014	FK Žalgiris Vilnius	FK Žalgiris Vilnius (2013/14)	Niko Tokić (CRO, FK Šiauliai)	19
2015	FK Žalgiris Vilnius	FK Žalgiris Vilnius (2014/15)	Tomas Radzinevičius (FK Sūduva Marijampolė)	28
2016	FK Žalgiris Vilnius	FK Žalgiris Vilnius (2015/16) FK Žalgiris Vilnius (2016)	Andrija Kaluđerović (SRB, FK Žalgiris Vilnius)	20
2017	FK Sūduva Marijampolė	FC Stumbras Kaunas	Darvydas Šernas (FK Žalgiris Vilnius)	18
2018	FK Sūduva Marijampolė	FK Žalgiris Vilnius	Liviu Ion Antal (ROU, FK Žalgiris Vilnius)	23
2019	FK Sūduva Marijampolė	FK Sūduva Marijampolė	Tomislav Kiš (CRO, FK Žalgiris Vilnius)	27
2020	FK Žalgiris Vilnius	FK Panevėžys	Hugo Robin Vidémont (FRA, FK Žalgiris Vilnius)	13

NATIONAL CHAMPIONSHIP
A Lyga 2020
(06.03.2020 – 14.11.2020)

Please note: FC Džiugas Telšiai failed to meet A Lyga licensing criteria, while FK Atlantas Klaipėda were disqualified.

Results

Round 1 [06-08.03.2020]
FK Žalgiris - FK Panevėžys 4-0(2-0)
FK Sūduva - FK Banga Gargždai 1-0(0-0)
FK Riteriai - FK Kauno Žalgiris 0-3(0-1)

Round 2 [30.05.-01.06.2020]
FK Žalgiris - FK Riteriai 0-1(0-1)
FK Banga Gargždai - FK Panevėžys 2-0(2-0)
FK Sūduva - FK Kauno Žalgiris 1-0(0-0)

Round 3 [06-07.06.2020]
FK Kauno Žalgiris - FK Žalgiris 0-1(0-1)
FK Panevėžys - FK Sūduva 1-3(0-2)
FK Riteriai - FK Banga Gargždai 0-1(0-0)

Round 4 [13-14.06.2020]
FK Kauno Žalgiris - FK Panevėžys 2-0(1-0)
FK Banga Gargždai - FK Žalgiris 0-1(0-0)
FK Riteriai - FK Sūduva 1-3(0-0)

Round 5 [19-20.06.2020]
FK Riteriai - FK Panevėžys 1-1(1-0)
Banga Gargždai - FK Kauno Žalgiris 1-1(0-0)
FK Sūduva - FK Žalgiris 1-1(0-1)

Round 6 [24.06.2020]
FK Sūduva - FK Panevėžys 3-0(3-0)
FK Žalgiris - FK Kauno Žalgiris 2-3(0-2)
FK Banga Gargždai - FK Riteriai 1-1(0-1)

Round 7 [28.06.2020]
FK Kauno Žalgiris - FK Sūduva 0-1(0-0)
FK Riteriai - FK Žalgiris 0-7(0-4)
FK Panevėžys - FK Banga Gargždai 2-1(1-0)

Round 8 [03-04.07.2020]
FK Žalgiris - FK Banga Gargždai 0-0
FK Panevėžys - FK Kauno Žalgiris 0-2(0-0)
FK Sūduva - FK Riteriai 1-0(0-0)

Round 9 [11-12.07.2020]
FK Kauno Žalgiris - Banga Gargždai 2-0(1-0)
FK Panevėžys - FK Riteriai 2-1(1-0)
FK Žalgiris - FK Sūduva 4-0(1-0)

Round 10 [18-19.07.2020]
FK Kauno Žalgiris - FK Riteriai 2-1(2-1)
FK Panevėžys - FK Žalgiris 1-2(0-1)
FK Banga Gargždai - FK Sūduva 0-2(0-2)

Round 11 [23.07.2020]
FK Kauno Žalgiris - FK Panevėžys 3-2(1-0)
FK Sūduva - FK Banga Gargždai 0-0
FK Žalgiris - FK Riteriai 1-0(1-0)

Round 12 [28.07.2020]
FK Kauno Žalgiris - Banga Gargždai 2-3(0-2)
FK Panevėžys - FK Žalgiris 1-2(0-0)
FK Riteriai - FK Sūduva 1-2(1-1)

Round 13 [01-02.08.2020]
FK Banga Gargždai - FK Riteriai 1-1(1-1)
FK Sūduva - FK Panevėžys 1-0(1-0)
FK Žalgiris - FK Kauno Žalgiris 3-1(1-0)

Round 14 [07-08.08.2020]
FK Žalgiris - FK Banga Gargždai 1-0(1-0)
FK Kauno Žalgiris - FK Sūduva 3-0(0-0)
FK Panevėžys - FK Riteriai 1-1(0-0)

Round 15 [12-16.08.2020]
FK Sūduva - FK Žalgiris 2-0(0-0)
FK Riteriai - FK Kauno Žalgiris 0-1(0-1)
FK Banga Gargždai - FK Panevėžys 3-3(1-0)

Round 16 [20.08.2020]
FK Panevėžys - FK Kauno Žalgiris 0-1(0-0)
FK Riteriai - FK Žalgiris 2-2(1-1)
Banga Gargždai - FK Sūduva 1-2(1-1) [10.10.]

Round 17 [27.09.2020]
Banga Gargždai - FK Kauno Žalgiris 1-2(0-1)
FK Žalgiris - FK Panevėžys 3-2(3-0)
FK Sūduva - FK Riteriai 7-1(4-1)

Round 18 [02-03.10.2020]
FK Riteriai - FK Banga Gargždai 4-0(2-0)
FK Kauno Žalgiris - FK Žalgiris 0-1(0-1)
FK Panevėžys - FK Sūduva 1-1(1-0)

Round 19 [20-28.10.2020]
FK Banga Gargždai - FK Žalgiris 0-4(0-1)
FK Sūduva - FK Kauno Žalgiris 1-1(1-1)
FK Riteriai - FK Panevėžys 1-1(0-0)

Round 20 [31.10.-14.11.2020]
FK Panevėžys - FK Banga Gargždai 1-1(1-1)
FK Kauno Žalgiris - FK Riteriai 1-0(0-0)
FK Žalgiris - FK Sūduva 3-0(2-0)

Final Standings

					Total		Home					Away					
1.	**FK Žalgiris Vilnius**	20	14	3	3	42 - 14	7	1	2	21 - 7	7	2	1	21 - 7
2.	FK Sūduva Marijampolė	20	13	4	3	32 - 18	7	3	0	18 - 3	6	1	3	14 - 15
3.	FK Kauno Žalgiris Kaunas	20	12	6	2	30 - 18	6	0	4	15 - 9	6	2	2	15 - 9
4.	FK Banga Gargždai	20	3	7	10	16 - 30	1	4	5	10 - 17	2	3	5	6 - 13
5.	FK Panevėžys	20	2	6	12	19 - 38	2	3	5	10 - 15	0	3	7	9 - 23
6.	FK Riteriai Vilnius	20	2	6	12	17 - 38	1	3	6	10 - 21	1	3	6	7 - 17

Top goalscorers:
13	**Hugo Robin Vidémont (FRA)**	*FK Žalgiris Vilnius*
11	Josip Tadić (CRO)	*FK Sūduva Marijampolė*
8	Linas Pilibaitis	*FK Kauno Žalgiris Kaunas*

NATIONAL CUP
Lietuvos futbolo taurė 2020

Second Round [24-30.06.2020]				
FK Viltis Vilnius - SANED Joniškis	11-0	FK Utenis - FK Sveikata Kybartai	0-2	
DFK Dainava - FK Atmosfera Mažeikiai	3-0	ŠŠPC Radviliškis - FK Jonava	1-5	
FK Vidzgiris Alytus - FK Minija Kretinga	2-6	FK Babrungas Plungė - FK Tauras Tauragė	2-1	
FK Šilas Kazlų Rūda - Baltijos Futbolo Akademija	2-3	FC Vilniaus Vytis - FC Džiugas Telšiai	1-0	

1/8-Finals [07/14-15.07.2020]				
FK Babrungas Plungė - FC Hegelmann Litauen	1-4	FK Riteriai Vilnius - FK Banga Gargždai	2-0	
FA Šiauliai - FK Žalgiris Vilnius	0-2	FK Viltis Vilnius - FC Vilniaus Vytis	0-4	
FK Jonava - FK Panevėžys	0-3	FK Minija Kretinga - FK Sūduva	0-3	
FK Sveikata Kybartai - FK Kauno Žalgiris Kaunas	0-4	Baltijos Futbolo Akademija Vilnius - DFK Dainava	1-2	

Quarter-Finals [11.08./11-12-.09.2020]				
FC Hegelmann Litauen Kaunas - FK Panevėžys	0-3	FC Vilniaus Vytis - FK Sūduva	0-3	
DFK Dainava - FK Riteriai Vilnius	0-2	FK Žalgiris Vilnius - FK Kauno Žalgiris Kaunas	2-1	

Semi-Finals [17-20.10.2020]				
FK Kauno Žalgiris Kaunas - FK Sūduva	1-2 aet	FK Panevėžys - FK Riteriai Vilnius	4-0	

Final

19.10.2020; Aukštaitija stadionas, Panevėžys; Referee: Robertas Valikonis; Attendance: 1,000
FK Panevėžys - FK Sūduva Marijampolė   **1-1(1-1,1-1,1-1); 5-4 on penalties**

FK Panevėžys: Rafael Broetto Henrique, Vytas Gašpuitis (105.Justinas Januševskis), Lukas Čerkauskas, Rafael da Silva Floro, Matheus Bissi da Silva, Ernestas Veliulis, Tautvydas Eliošius (114.Edenilson Bergonsi), Hrysovalantis Kozoronis, Elivelto Ribeiro Dantas, Jorge Elias Dos Santos (64.Sebastián Vásquez Gamboa), Ignas Kružikas (89.Kotaro Amemiya). Trainer: Alexandru Curteian (Moldova).

FK Sūduva: Ivan Kardum, Semir Kerla, Aleksandar Živanović, Algis Jankauskas, Nicolás Martín Gorobsov [*sent off 114*], Renan Henrique Oliveira Vieira (57.Thomas Salamon), Andro Švrljuga (33.Evgen Efremov), Giedrius Matulevičius (89.Povilas Leimonas), Vaidas Slavickas (101.Ivan Hladík), Domagoj Pušić, Josip Tadić. Trainer: Saulius Širmelis.

Goals: 1-0 Ernestas Veliulis (23), 1-1 Renan Henrique Oliveira Vieira (26 penalty).

Penalties: Domagoj Pušić 0-1; Elivelto Ribeiro Dantas 1-1; Algis Jankauskas 1-2; Hrysovalantis Kozoronis 2-2; Thomas Salamon 2-3; Rafael da Silva Floro 3-3; Evgen Efremov 3-4; Justinas Januševskis 4-4; Aleksandar Živanović (missed); Sebastián Vásquez Gamboa 5-4.

THE CLUBS 2020

Futbolo klubas Banga Gargždai

Founded:	1966	
Stadium:	Gargždai stadionas, Gargždai (2,323)	
Trainer:	Tomas Tamošauskas	22.05.1983

Goalkeepers:	DOB	M	(s)	G
Ignas Driomovas	27.04.1997	20		
Defenders:	**DOB**	**M**	**(s)**	**G**
Olexandr Aksionov (UKR)	07.01.1994	19		
Valdas Antužis	19.06.2000	13	(1)	
Edvinas Bračkus	11.09.1990	2	(3)	
Paulius Lotužys	15.01.1998	1	(14)	1
Deividas Padaigis	02.02.1986	19		1
Yuri Pavlik (UKR)	15.02.1994	20		
Armandas Šveistrys	08.07.2002		(1)	
Karolis Urbaitis	12.12.1990	19		3
Midfielders:	**DOB**	**M**	**(s)**	**G**
Jonas Bičkus	14.02.2000		(16)	
Dovydas Norvilas	05.04.1993	19		
Mantas Petrikas	15.01.2001		(1)	
Skirmantas Rakauskas	07.01.1996	11	(4)	2
Pijus Srebalius	24.07.2002		(1)	
Shogo Yoshikawa (JPN)	08.04.1995	19	(1)	1
Forwards:	**DOB**	**M**	**(s)**	**G**
Julius Kasparavičius	03.04.1995	11	(3)	2
Sergey Kundik (POR)	10.07.1995	1	(4)	
Deividas Lukošius	24.01.1991	7	(8)	1
Renato Matos da Silva (BRA)	03.05.1996	18		3
Ignas Venckus	17.07.2001	1	(10)	
Robertas Vėževičius	05.01.1986	18		2
Darius Zubauskas	11.04.2000	2	(7)	

Futbolo klubas Kauno Žalgiris Kaunas

Founded:	2004	
Stadium:	SM Tauras stadionas, Kaunas (500)	
Trainer:	Rokas Garastas	17.08.1988

Goalkeepers:	DOB	M	(s)	G
Airidas Mickevičius	07.07.1999	1		
Deividas Mikelionis	08.05.1995	17		
Armantas Vitkauskas	23.03.1989	2		
Defenders:	**DOB**	**M**	**(s)**	**G**
Martynas Dapkus	16.02.1993	19		
Rudinilson Gomes Brito Silva „Rudi" (GNB)	20.08.1994	13		
Rimvydas Sadauskas	21.07.1996	12	(3)	
Karolis Šilkaitis	02.06.1996	19		3
Pijus Širvys	01.04.1998	1	(11)	
Steven Thicot (FRA)	14.02.1987	17		
Egidijus Vaitkūnas	08.08.1988	18	(1)	1
Midfielders:	**DOB**	**M**	**(s)**	**G**
Benas Anisas	29.02.2000	10	(9)	
Yuriy Bushman (UKR)	14.05.1990	16	(3)	4
Lukas Odincovas	20.09.2000		(1)	
Simonas Paulius	12.05.1991	2	(9)	1
Linas Pilibaitis	05.04.1985	19	(1)	8
Domantas Putrius	08.08.1999	1	(3)	
Gratas Sirgėdas	17.12.1994	13	(2)	2
Deitonas Vinckus	17.04.2002		(1)	
Domantas Vitkus	12.05.1999	1	(5)	1
Forwards:	**DOB**	**M**	**(s)**	**G**
Emmanuel David (NGA)	07.07.2001	12	(3)	4
Philip Porwei Otele (NGA)	15.04.1999	11	(7)	3
Deividas Šešplaukis	02.02.1998	6	(6)	
Simonas Urbys	07.11.1995	10	(9)	2

Futbolo Klubas Panevėžys

Founded: 2015
Stadium: Aukštaitija stadionas, Panevėžys (6,600)
Trainer: Alexandru Curtianu (MDA) 11.02.1974
(15.06.2020) Dainius Gleveckas 05.03.1977
(04.07.2020) João Luís Gouveia Martins (POR) 24.04.1967

Goalkeepers:	DOB	M	(s)	G
Šarūnas Jurevičius	05.03.1989	2	(1)	
Rafael Broetto Henrique (BRA)	18.08.1990	18		
Defenders:	**DOB**	**M**	**(s)**	**G**
Lukas Čerkauskas	12.03.1994	20		
Bruno Fandhinho Franzo (BRA)	10.06.1989	7	(3)	
Vytas Gašpuitis	04.03.1994	18	(1)	
Hugo Figueiredo Pereira (BRA)	18.05.1992	10	(2)	
Justinas Januševskis	26.03.1994	17		1
Midfielders:	**DOB**	**M**	**(s)**	**G**
Kotaro Amemiya (JPN)	16.04.1994	3	(9)	1
Žygimantas Baguška	04.02.2002		(3)	
Edenilson Bergonsi (BRA)	13.09.1987	6	(10)	1
Elivelto Ribeiro Dantas (BRA)	02.01.1992	3		1

	DOB	M	(s)	G
Tautvydas Eliošius	03.11.1991	17	(1)	1
Paulius Janušauskas	28.02.1989	14		1
Hrysovalantis Kozoronis (GRE)	03.08.1992	4	(1)	1
Matheus Bissi da Silva (BRA)	19.03.1991	16	(1)	
Rafael da Silva Floro (POR)	19.01.1994	13	(4)	1
Faustas Steponavičius	08.06.2004		(1)	
Domantas Vaičekauskas	27.09.2003		(2)	
Ernestas Veliulis	22.08.1992	18	(1)	3
Sanjin Vrebac (AUT)	25.02.2000	2	(3)	
Forwards:	**DOB**	**M**	**(s)**	**G**
Eimantas Abramavicius	13.02.2002		(6)	
Jorge Elias Dos Santos (BRA)	06.06.1991	7	(6)	5
Ignas Kružikas	14.12.1998	12	(7)	2
Sebastián Vásquez Gamboa (COL)	24.05.1996	13	(3)	1

Futbolo Klubas Riteriai Vilnius

Founded: 2005
Stadium: LFF stadionas, Vilnius (5,067)
Trainer: Mindaugas Cepas 06.08.1978
(29.06.2020) Vaidas Sabaliauskas 21.02.1992
(11.08.2020) Tommi Pikkarainen (FIN) 06.12.1969

Goalkeepers:	DOB	M	(s)	G
Lukas Paukštė	25.09.1998	3		
Tadas Simaitis	29.12.1990	17		
Defenders:	**DOB**	**M**	**(s)**	**G**
Dominykas Barauskas	18.04.1997	20		2
Valdemars Borovskis	05.02.1984	19		2
Akseli Kalermo (FIN)	17.03.1997	6	(2)	
Deividas Malžinskas	01.05.1999	6	(2)	
Rokas Masenzovas	02.08.1994	8		
Ernestas Stočkūnas	11.05.1998	1	(4)	
Ricardas Šveikauskas	09.04.1997	10	(3)	
Midfielders:	**DOB**	**M**	**(s)**	**G**
Tomas Dombrauskis	24.09.1996	16	(1)	
Rokas Filipavicius	22.12.1999	2	(4)	1
Mindaugas Grigaravičius	15.07.1992	10	(4)	1
Valentin Jeriomenko	19.02.1989	9	(3)	

	DOB	M	(s)	G
Donatas Kazlauskas	31.03.1994	16		2
Aleksandr Levšinas	14.08.1999	12		
Ángel Ronniel Lezama Arteaga (VEN)	25.09.1997	7	(1)	3
Juozas Lubas	22.05.2002	2	(2)	
Justinas Marazas	23.02.2000	5	(6)	1
Valdas Paulauskas	04.02.2001		(2)	
Matas Ramanauskas	28.06.2000	14	(1)	
Lajo Traoré (CIV)	20.12.1993	11	(1)	1
Dovydas Virkšas	01.07.1997	4	(11)	
Forwards:	**DOB**	**M**	**(s)**	**G**
Bright Osuoha Godwin (NGA)	05.12.2001		(1)	
Dominyk Kodz	25.04.2000	2	(13)	1
Michael Thuíque Dias Santos (BRA)	21.03.1993	7	(9)	1
Gytis Paulauskas	27.09.1999	12	(4)	2
Cyrille Tchayi Tchamba (CAM)	25.02.1998	1	(1)	

Futbolo Klubas Sūduva Marijampolė

Founded: 1921
Stadium: Marijampolė Football Arena, Marijampolė (6,250)
Trainer: Heimo Pfeifenberger (AUT) 29.12.1966
(22.05.2020) Saulius Širmelis 31.05.1956

Goalkeepers:	DOB	M	(s)	G
Ivan Kardum (CRO)	18.07.1987	20		
Defenders:	**DOB**	**M**	**(s)**	**G**
Evgen Efremov (UKR)	17.01.1994	5	(1)	
Ivan Hladík (SVK)	30.01.1993	10	(1)	
Algis Jankauskas	27.09.1982	8	(2)	
Semir Kerla (BIH)	26.09.1987	15		3
Linas Klimavičius	10.04.1989	4		
Hamdi Nagguez (TUN)	28.10.1992	1		
Aleksandar Živanović (SRB)	08.04.1987	20		
Midfielders:	**DOB**	**M**	**(s)**	**G**
Renatas Banevičius	18.10.2000		(1)	
Nicolás Martín Gorobsov (ARG)	25.11.1989	5		2
Glebs Kļuškins (LVA)	01.10.1992	8	(7)	

	DOB	M	(s)	G
Povilas Leimonas	16.11.1987	7	(4)	1
Giedrius Matulevičius	05.03.1997	12	(4)	
Daniel Offenbacher (AUT)	18.02.1992	8	(2)	1
Domagoj Pušić (CRO)	24.10.1991	14	(4)	
Renan Henrique Oliveira Vieira (BRA)	29.12.1989	4	(7)	
Thomas Salamon (AUT)	18.01.1989	16	(2)	2
Vaidas Slavickas	26.02.1986	9	(6)	
Andro Švrljuga (CRO)	24.10.1985	14	(1)	1
Forwards:	**DOB**	**M**	**(s)**	**G**
Eligijus Jankauskas	22.06.1998	4	(13)	2
Valērijs Šabala (LVA)	12.10.1994	4	(9)	4
Josip Tadić (CRO)	22.08.1987	17	(2)	11
Mihret Topčagić (AUT)	21.06.1988	15	(2)	5

Futbolo klubas Žalgiris Vilnius

Founded: 1947
Stadium: LFF stadionas, Vilnius (5,067)
Trainer: Aleksei Baga (BLR) 04.02.1981

Goalkeepers:	DOB	M	(s)	G
Martin Berkovec (CZE)	12.02.1989	14		
Edvinas Gertmonas	01.06.1996	6		
Defenders:	**DOB**	**M**	**(s)**	**G**
Klemen Bolha (SVN)	19.03.1993	2	(3)	
Marko Karamarko (CRO)	27.03.1993	11	(7)	2
Nemanja Ljubisavljević (SRB)	26.11.1996	19		
Saulius Mikoliūnas	02.05.1984	19		1
Donovan Carlos Saverio Slijngard (SUR)	28.08.1987	16		
Ivan Tatomirović (SRB)	11.01.1989	18		3
Midfielders:	**DOB**	**M**	**(s)**	**G**
Higor Felipe Vidal (BRA)	26.09.1996	1	(2)	
Karlo Kamenar (CRO)	15.03.1994	2	(3)	1
Mantas Kuklys	10.06.1987	14	(3)	1

	DOB	M	(s)	G
Francis Kyeremeh (GHA)	23.06.1997	10	(2)	2
Domantas Šimkus	10.02.1996	17	(3)	1
Karolis Uzéla	11.03.2000	4	(7)	
Modestas Vorobjovas	30.12.1995	15	(1)	1
Forwards:	**DOB**	**M**	**(s)**	**G**
Liviu Ion Antal (ROU)	02.06.1989	14	(3)	6
Motiejus Burba	10.08.2003		(6)	
Richlord Ennin (CAN)	17.09.1998	10	(1)	4
Gustas Jarusevičius	23.05.2003	1	(6)	
Andrija Kaluđerović (SRB)	05.07.1987	5	(4)	4
David N'Gog (FRA)	01.04.1989	2		1
Matas Vareika	27.01.2000	2	(6)	
Hugo Robin Vidémont (FRA)	19.02.1993	18	(2)	13

League Table

1.	FK Jonava	13	9	4	0	28	-	11	31
2.	FK Nevėžis Kėdainiai	13	10	1	2	34	-	9	31
3.	FC Džiugas Telšiai	13	9	3	1	28	-	11	30
4.	FC Hegelmann Litauen Kaunas	13	8	4	1	24	-	6	28
5.	FC Vilniaus Vytis	13	8	3	2	26	-	17	27
6.	DFK Dainava Alytus	13	7	1	5	20	-	12	22
7.	FA Šiauliai	13	7	1	5	30	-	18	22
8.	FK Panevėžys „B"	13	5	2	6	25	-	25	17
9.	FK Žalgiris Vilnius "B"	13	5	2	6	24	-	25	17
10.	FK Minija Kretinga	13	3	2	8	19	-	30	11
11.	FK Atmosfera Mažeikiai	13	3	1	9	10	-	26	10
12.	FK Kauno Žalgiris Kaunas „B"	13	2	0	11	13	-	36	6
13.	Baltijos Futbolo Akademija Vilnius	13	2	0	11	11	-	40	6
14.	FK Riteriai Vilnius „B"	13	0	2	11	9	-	35	2

Top-8 teams were qualified for the Promotion Round, while teams ranked 9-14 were qualified for the Relegation Round.

Promotion Round

1.	FK Nevėžis Kėdainiai (*Promoted*)	20	15	3	2	46	-	12	48
2.	FC Hegelmann Litauen Kaunas (*Promoted*)	20	14	4	2	39	-	12	46
3.	FK Jonava (*Promoted*)	20	12	5	3	38	-	19	41
4.	FC Džiugas Telšiai (*Promoted*)	20	11	5	4	34	-	19	38
5.	FA Šiauliai	20	10	2	8	42	-	27	32
6.	DFK Dainava Alytus	20	10	2	8	28	-	19	32
7.	FC Vilniaus Vytis	20	9	3	8	35	-	38	30
8.	FK Panevėžys „B"	20	6	3	11	34	-	44	21

Relegation Round

1.	FK Žalgiris Vilnius "B"	18	7	3	8	33	-	32	24
2.	FK Minija Kretinga	18	6	3	9	33	-	38	21
3.	FK Kauno Žalgiris Kaunas „B"	18	5	1	12	21	-	41	16
4.	FK Atmosfera Mažeikiai	18	4	3	11	20	-	38	15
5.	Baltijos Futbolo Akademija Vilnius	18	4	2	12	20	-	48	14
6.	FK Riteriai Vilnius „B"	18	0	3	15	14	-	50	3

NATIONAL TEAM

INTERNATIONAL MATCHES
(16.07.2020 – 15.07.2021)

04.09.2020	Vilnius	Lithuania - Kazakhstan	0-2(0-1)	(UNL)
07.09.2020	Tiranë	Albania - Lithuania	0-1(0-0)	(UNL)
07.10.2020	Tallinn	Estonia - Lithuania	1-3(0-2)	(F)
11.10.2020	Vilnius	Lithuania - Belarus	2-2(1-0)	(UNL)
14.10.2020	Vilnius	Lithuania - Albania	0-0	(UNL)
11.11.2020	Vilnius	Lithuania - Faroe Islands	2-1(2-0)	(F)
15.11.2020	Minsk	Belarus - Lithuania	2-0(2-0)	(UNL)
18.11.2020	Almaty	Kazakhstan - Lithuania	1-2(1-1)	(UNL)
24.03.2021	Prishtina	Kosovo - Lithuania	4-0(1-0)	(F)
28.03.2021	St. Gallen	Switzerland - Lithuania	1-0(1-0)	(WCQ)
31.03.2021	Vilnius	Lithuania - Italy	0-2(0-0)	(WCQ)
01.06.2021	Vilnius	Lithuania - Estonia	0-1(0-0)	(BC)
04.06.2021	Rīga	Latvia - Lithuania	3-1(1-0)	(BC)
08.06.2021	Leganés	Spain - Lithuania	4-0(2-0)	(F)

04.09.2020   LITHUANIA - KAZAKHSTAN   **0-2(0-1)**   2nd UEFA Nations League C, Group 4
LFF stadionas, Vilnius; Referee: Rade Obrenovič (Slovenia); Attendance: 0
LTU: Džiugas Bartkus, Saulius Mikoliūnas, Markus Palionis, Edvinas Girdvainis, Rolandas Baravykas (82.Ovidijus Verbickas), Domantas Šimkus, Modestas Vorobjovas, Gratas Sirgedas (89.Martynas Dapkus), Justas Lasickas, Fedor Černych (Cap) (46.Karolis Laukžemis), Donatas Kazlauskas. Trainer: Valdas Urbonas.

07.09.2020   ALBANIA - LITHUANIA   **0-1(0-0)**   2nd UEFA Nations League C, Group 4
Air Albania Stadium, Tiranë; Referee: Serhiy Boyko (Ukraine); Attendance: 0
LTU: Tomas Švedkauskas, Saulius Mikoliūnas (Cap), Markus Palionis, Egidijus Vaitkūnas, Edvinas Girdvainis, Martynas Dapkus, Domantas Šimkus, Modestas Vorobjovas, Justas Lasickas (61.Gratas Sirgedas), Donatas Kazlauskas (74.Ovidijus Verbickas), Karolis Laukžemis (78.Daniel Romanovskij). Trainer: Valdas Urbonas.
Goal: Donatas Kazlauskas (51).

07.10.2020 **ESTONIA - LITHUANIA** 1-3(0-2) Friendly International
A. Le Coq Arena, Tallinn; Referee: Antti Munukka (Finland); Attendance: 718
LTU: Tomas Švedkauskas, Saulius Mikoliūnas (Cap) (55.Ovidijus Verbickas), Markus Palionis, Egidijus Vaitkūnas, Edvinas Girdvainis, Arvydas Novikovas (55.Fedor Černych), Domantas Šimkus (88.Martynas Dapkus), Modestas Vorobjovas, Gratas Sirgedas (68.Paulius Golubickas), Justas Lasickas (68.Markas Beneta), Donatas Kazlauskas (68.Gytis Paulauskas). Trainer: Valdas Urbonas.
Goals: Arvydas Novikovas (14), Gratas Sirgedas (32), Arvydas Novikovas (46).

11.10.2020 **LITHUANIA - BELARUS** 2-2(1-0) 2nd UEFA Nations League C, Group 4
LFF stadionas, Vilnius; Referee: Julian Weinberger (Austria); Attendance: 963
LTU: Tomas Švedkauskas, Saulius Mikoliūnas (Cap), Markus Palionis, Egidijus Vaitkūnas (64.Markas Beneta), Edvinas Girdvainis, Arvydas Novikovas (72.Fedor Černych), Domantas Šimkus (72.Martynas Dapkus), Modestas Vorobjovas, Gratas Sirgedas (72.Paulius Golubickas), Justas Lasickas, Donatas Kazlauskas (60.Karolis Laukžemis). Trainer: Valdas Urbonas.
Goals: Arvydas Novikovas (7), Karolis Laukžemis (75).

14.10.2020 **LITHUANIA - ALBANIA** 0-0 2nd UEFA Nations League C, Group 4
LFF stadionas, Vilnius; Referee: Karim Abed (France); Attendance: 696
LTU: Tomas Švedkauskas, Saulius Mikoliūnas (Cap) (69.Egidijus Vaitkūnas), Markus Palionis, Edvinas Girdvainis, Markas Beneta, Arvydas Novikovas, Martynas Dapkus, Domantas Šimkus, Justas Lasickas (90+1.Ovidijus Verbickas), Paulius Golubickas (46.Gratas Sirgedas), Karolis Laukžemis (87.Fedor Černych). Trainer: Valdas Urbonas.

11.11.2020 **LITHUANIA - FAROE ISLANDS** 2-1(2-0) Friendly International
LFF stadionas, Vilnius; Referee: Aleksandrs Anufrijevs (Latvia); Attendance: 0
LTU: Tomas Švedkauskas (Cap), Egidijus Vaitkūnas, Edvinas Girdvainis, Vytas Gašpuitis, Markas Beneta, Vykintas Slivka (75.Tautvydas Eliošius), Gratas Sirgedas (53.Daniel Romanovskij), Linas Mėgelaitis (68.Edgaras Utkus), Justas Lasickas (53.Ovidijus Verbickas), Donatas Kazlauskas (68.Arvydas Novikovas), Karolis Laukžemis (68.Deimantas Petravičius). Trainer: Valdas Urbonas.
Goals: Gratas Sirgedas (42, 45+1).

15.11.2020 **BELARUS - LITHUANIA** 2-0(2-0) 2nd UEFA Nations League C, Group 4
Stadion Dynama, Minsk; Referee: Chris Kavanagh (England); Attendance: 1,985
LTU: Tomas Švedkauskas (Cap), Egidijus Vaitkūnas, Edvinas Girdvainis, Vytas Gašpuitis, Markas Beneta, Arvydas Novikovas (82.Deimantas Petravičius), Tautvydas Eliošius (55.Gratas Sirgedas), Vykintas Slivka, Justas Lasickas (46.Karolis Laukžemis), Edgaras Utkus (75.Daniel Romanovskij), Donatas Kazlauskas (55.Ernestas Veliulis). Trainer: Valdas Urbonas.

18.11.2020 **KAZAKHSTAN - LITHUANIA** 1-2(1-1) 2nd UEFA Nations League C, Group 4
Central Stadium, Almaty; Referee: Hüseyin Göçek (Turkey); Attendance: 0
LTU: Tomas Švedkauskas, Saulius Mikoliūnas (Cap), Egidijus Vaitkūnas (46.Vytas Gašpuitis), Edvinas Girdvainis, Markas Beneta, Arvydas Novikovas, Vykintas Slivka (76.Donatas Kazlauskas), Domantas Šimkus, Modestas Vorobjovas, Gratas Sirgedas (66.Tautvydas Eliošius), Karolis Laukžemis (84.Deimantas Petravičius). Trainer: Valdas Urbonas.
Goals: Modestas Vorobjovas (40), Arvydas Novikovas (90+4).

24.03.2021 **KOSOVO - LITHUANIA** 4-0(1-0) Friendly International
Stadiumi „Fadil Vokrri", Prishtina; Referee: Enea Jorgji (Albania); Attendance: 0
LTU: Tomas Švedkauskas, Egidijus Vaitkūnas, Markas Beneta, Vytas Gašpuitis, Saulius Mikoliūnas (Cap) (46.Domantas Šimkus), Vykintas Slivka (60.Daniel Romanovskij), Martynas Dapkus, Justas Lasickas (72.Deimantas Petravičius, Arvydas Novikovas (60.Nerijus Valskis), Gratas Sirgedas (46.Tautvydas Eliošius), Fedor Černych (72.Karolis Laukžemis). Trainer: Valdas Urbonas.

28.03.2021 **SWITZERLAND - LITHUANIA** 1-0(1-0) 22nd FIFA WC.Qualifiers
Kybunpark, St. Gallen; Referee: Mattias Gestranius (Finland); Attendance: 0
LTU: Tomas Švedkauskas, Saulius Mikoliūnas (Cap), Egidijus Vaitkūnas, Vytas Gašpuitis, Markas Beneta, Arvydas Novikovas, Martynas Dapkus, Vykintas Slivka (75.Tautvydas Eliošius), Domantas Šimkus, Justas Lasickas (58.Karolis Laukžemis), Fedor Černych (81.Deimantas Petravičius). Trainer: Valdas Urbonas.

31.03.2021 **LITHUANIA - ITALY** 0-2(0-0) 22nd FIFA WC.Qualifiers
LFF stadionas, Vilnius; Referee: Referee: Paweł Raczkowski (Poland); Attendance: 0
LTU: Tomas Švedkauskas, Saulius Mikoliūnas (Cap) (74.Vytas Gašpuitis), Egidijus Vaitkūnas, Edvinas Girdvainis, Markas Beneta, Arvydas Novikovas, Martynas Dapkus, Vykintas Slivka, Domantas Šimkus (83.Deimantas Petravičius), Gratas Sirgedas (58.Tautvydas Eliošius), Fedor Černych (74.Donatas Kazlauskas). Trainer: Valdas Urbonas.

01.06.2021 **LITHUANIA - ESTONIA** 0-1(0-0) 19th Baltic Cup
LFF stadionas, Vilnius; Referee: Aleksandrs Anufrijevs (Latvia); Attendance: 0
LTU: Tomas Švedkauskas, Saulius Mikoliūnas (Cap), Egidijus Vaitkūnas, Edvinas Girdvainis, Markas Beneta, Arvydas Novikovas, Tautvydas Eliošius (46.Donatas Kazlauskas), Martynas Dapkus (69.Ovidijus Verbickas), Domantas Šimkus, Justas Lasickas (59.Fedor Černych), Karolis Laukžemis (69.Deimantas Petravičius). Trainer: Valdas Urbonas.

04.06.2021 **LATVIA - LITHUANIA** 3-1(1-0) 19th Baltic Cup
Daugava stadions, Rīga; Referee: Juri Frischer (Estonia); Attendance: 0
LTU: Tomas Švedkauskas, Saulius Mikoliūnas (Cap) (56.Linas Mėgelaitis), Egidijus Vaitkūnas, Edvinas Girdvainis, Markas Beneta, Arvydas Novikovas (76.Karolis Laukžemis), Martynas Dapkus (56.Vytas Gašpuitis), Ovidijus Verbickas, Domantas Šimkus (65.Donatas Kazlauskas), Justas Lasickas (46.Paulius Golubickas), Fedor Černych (56.Deimantas Petravičius). Trainer: Valdas Urbonas.
Goal: Paulius Golubickas (67).

08.06.2021 **SPAIN - LITHUANIA** 4-0(2-0) Friendly International
Estadio Municipal de Butarque, Leganés; Referee: Willy Delajod (France); Attendance: 903
LTU: Tomas Švedkauskas, Saulius Mikoliūnas (Cap) (62.Vytas Gašpuitis), Egidijus Vaitkūnas, Edvinas Girdvainis, Markas Beneta, Arvydas Novikovas (75.Edgaras Dubickas), Ovidijus Verbickas (61.Martynas Dapkus), Domantas Šimkus (71.Justas Lasickas), Linas Mėgelaitis, Paulius Golubickas (71.Tautvydas Eliošius), Fedor Černych (46.Deimantas Petravičius). Trainer: Valdas Urbonas.

NATIONAL TEAM PLAYERS
(16.07.2020 – 15.07.2021)

Name	DOB	Caps	Goals	2020/2021:	Club
Goalkeepers					
Džiugas BARTKUS	07.11.1989	6	0	2020:	*Hapoel Ironi Kiryat Shmona FC (ISR)*
Tomas ŠVEDKAUSKAS	22.06.1994	14	0	2020/2021:	*Lommel SK (BEL)*
Defenders					
Rolandas BARAVYKAS	23.08.1995	20	1	2020:	*Nea Salamis Famagusta FC (CYP)*
Markas BENETA	08.07.1993	13	0	2020/2021:	*FK Sūduva Marijampolė*
Vytas GAŠPUITIS	04.03.1994	8	0	2020/2021:	*FK Panevėžys*
Edvinas GIRDVAINIS	17.01.1993	34	0	2020/2021:	*KFC Uerdingen 05 (GER)*
Saulius MIKOLIŪNAS	02.05.1984	96	5	2020/2021:	*FK Žalgiris Vilnius*
Markus PALIONIS	12.05.1987	14	0	2020:	*SSV Jahn Regensburg (GER)*
Vaidas SLAVICKAS	26.02.1986	19	0	2021:	*FK Sūduva Marijampolė*
Egidijus VAITKŪNAS	08.08.1988	57	0	2020/2021:	*FK Kauno Žalgiris Kaunas*
Midfielders					
Martynas DAPKUS	16.02.1993	13	0	2020/2021:	*FK Kauno Žalgiris Kaunas*
Tautvydas ELIOŠIUS	03.11.1991	10	0	2020/2021:	*FK Panevėžys*
Paulius GOLUBICKAS	19.08.1999	12	1	2020:	*HNK Gorica (CRO)*
				11.03.2021->	*DFK Dainava Alytus*
Donatas KAZLAUSKAS	31.03.1994	24	2	2020/2021:	*FK Lviv (UKR)*
Justas LASICKAS	06.10.1997	23	0	2020/2021:	*FK Voždovac Beograd (SRB)*
Linas MĖGELAITIS	09.09.1998	3	0	2020/2021:	*AS Gubbio 1910 (ITA)*
Arvydas NOVIKOVAS	18.12.1990	70	12	2020/2021:	*Büyükşehir Belediye Erzurumspor (TUR)*
Deimantas PETRAVIČIUS	02.09.1995	24	1	2020/2021:	*Águilas FC (ESP)*
Daniel ROMANOVSKIJ	19.06.1996	6	0	2020/2021:	*FK Olimpik Donetsk (UKR)*
Gratas SIRGEDAS	17.12.1994	17	3	2020/2021:	*FK Kauno Žalgiris Kaunas*
Vykintas SLIVKA	29.04.1995	45	2	2020/2021:	*GS Apollon Smyrna (GRE)*
Domantas ŠIMKUS	10.02.1996	21	0	2020/2021:	*FK Žalgiris Vilnius*
Edgaras UTKUS	22.06.2000	2	0	2020:	*AS Monaco FC (FRA)*
Ernestas VELIULIS	22.08.1992	3	0	2020:	*FK Panevėžys*
Ovidijus VERBICKAS	04.07.1993	24	1	2020:	*FC Taraz (KAZ)*
				22.01.2021->	*FK Žalgiris Vilnius*
Modestas VOROBJOVAS	30.12.1995	22	1	2020/2021:	*FK Žalgiris Vilnius*
Forwards					
Fedor ČERNYCH	21.05.1991	65	9	2020:	*FK Dinamo Moskva (RUS)*
				17.09.2020->	*Jagiellonia Białystok (POL)*
Edgaras DUBICKAS	09.07.1998	1	0	2021:	*AS Livorno (ITA)*
Karolis LAUKŽEMIS	11.03.1992	23	2	2020:	*NK Istra 1961 Pula (CRO)*
				24.10.2020->	*Hibernians FC Paola (MLT)*
				09.02.2021->	*FC Kaysar Kyzylorda (KAZ)*
Gytis PAULAUSKAS	27.09.1999	1	0	2020:	*FK Riteriai Vilnius*
National team coach					
Valdas URBONAS [from 02.02.2019]	29.11.1967	24 M; 5 W; 4 D; 15 L; 17-49			

LUXEMBOURG

The Country:
Groussherzogtum Lëtzebuerg (Grand Duchy of Luxembourg)
Capital: Lëtzebuerg
Surface: 2,586.4 km²
Inhabitants: 633,622 [2021]
Time: UTC+1

The FA:
Fédération Luxembourgeoise de Football / Lëtzebuerger Foussballfederatioun
BP 5, Rue de Limpach, 3901 Mondercange
Tel: +352 488 665 1
Foundation date: 1908
Member of FIFA since: 1910
Member of UEFA since: 1954
Website: www.flf.lu

NATIONAL TEAM RECORDS

RECORDS

First international match:	29.10.1911, Lëtzebuerg:	Luxembourg – France 1-4
Most international caps:	Mario Mutsch	- 102 caps (2005-2019)
Most international goals:	Léon Mart	- 16 goals / 24 caps (1933-1946)

UEFA EUROPEAN CHAMPIONSHIP

1960	Did not enter
1964	Qualifiers
1968	Qualifiers
1972	Qualifiers
1976	Qualifiers
1980	Qualifiers
1984	Qualifiers
1988	Qualifiers
1992	Qualifiers
1996	Qualifiers
2000	Qualifiers
2004	Qualifiers
2008	Qualifiers
2012	Qualifiers
2016	Qualifiers
2020	Qualifiers

FIFA WORLD CUP

1930	Did not enter
1934	Qualifiers
1938	Qualifiers
1950	Qualifiers
1954	Qualifiers
1958	Qualifiers
1962	Qualifiers
1966	Qualifiers
1970	Qualifiers
1974	Qualifiers
1978	Qualifiers
1982	Qualifiers
1986	Qualifiers
1990	Qualifiers
1994	Qualifiers
1998	Qualifiers
2002	Qualifiers
2006	Qualifiers
2010	Qualifiers
2014	Qualifiers
2018	Qualifiers

OLYMPIC TOURNAMENTS

1908	-
1912	-
1920	Round 1
1924	1/8 - Finals
1928	1/8 - Finals
1936	1/8 - Finals
1948	1/8 - Finals
1952	Round 1
1956	-
1960	Qualifiers
1964	Did not enter
1968	Did not enter
1972	Qualifiers
1976	Qualifiers
1980	Did not enter
1984	Did not enter
1988	Did not enter
1992	Qualifiers
1996	Qualifiers
2000	Qualifiers
2004	Qualifiers
2008	Qualifiers
2012	Qualifiers
2016	Qualifiers

UEFA NATIONS LEAGUE

2018/2019	League D (promoted to League C)
2020/2021	League C

FIFA CONFEDERATIONS CUP 1992-2017

None

LUXEMBOURGIAN CLUB HONOURS IN EUROPEAN CLUB COMPETITIONS:

European Champion Clubs.Cup (1956-1992) / UEFA Champions League (1993-2021)
None

Fairs Cup (1858-1971) / UEFA Cup (1972-2009) / UEFA Europa League (2010-2021)
None

UEFA Super Cup (1972-2020)
None

*European Cup Winners.Cup 1961-1999**
None

*defunct competition

NATIONAL COMPETITIONS
TABLE OF HONOURS

	CHAMPIONS	CUP WINNERS	BEST GOALSCORERS
1909/1910	Racing Club Lëtzebuerg	-	-
1910/1911	Sporting Club Lëtzebuerg	-	-
1911/1912	US Hollerich Bonnevoie	-	-
1912/1913	*No competition*	-	-
1913/1914	US Hollerich Bonnevoie	-	-
1914/1915	US Hollerich Bonnevoie	-	-
1915/1916	US Hollerich Bonnevoie	-	-
1916/1917	US Hollerich Bonnevoie	-	-
1917/1918	CS Fola Esch	-	-
1918/1919	Sporting Club Lëtzebuerg	-	-
1919/1920	CS Fola Esch	-	-
1920/1921	AS la Jeunesse d'Esch/Alzette	-	-
1921/1922	CS Fola Esch	Racing Club Lëtzebuerg	-
1922/1923	FA Red Boys Differdange	CS Fola Esch	-
1923/1924	CS Fola Esch	CS Fola Esch	-
1924/1925	CA Spora Lëtzebuerg	FA Red Boys Differdange	-
1925/1926	FA Red Boys Differdange	FA Red Boys Differdange	-
1926/1927	Union Sportive Lëtzebuerg	FA Red Boys Differdange	-
1927/1928	CA Spora Lëtzebuerg	CA Spora Lëtzebuerg	-
1928/1929	CA Spora Lëtzebuerg	FA Red Boys Differdange	-
1929/1930	CS Fola Esch	FA Red Boys Differdange	-
1930/1931	FA Red Boys Differdange	FA Red Boys Differdange	-
1931/1932	FA Red Boys Differdange	CA Spora Lëtzebuerg	-
1932/1933	FA Red Boys Differdange	FC Progrès Niederkorn	-
1933/1934	CA Spora Lëtzebuerg	FA Red Boys Differdange	-
1934/1935	CA Spora Lëtzebuerg	AS la Jeunesse d'Esch/Alzette	-
1935/1936	CA Spora Lëtzebuerg	FA Red Boys Differdange	-
1936/1937	AS la Jeunesse d'Esch/Alzette	AS la Jeunesse d'Esch/Alzette	-
1937/1938	CA Spora Lëtzebuerg	Stade Dudelange	-
1938/1939	Stade Dudelange	Union Sportive Dudelange	-
1939/1940	Stade Dudelange	CA Spora Lëtzebuerg	-
1940-1944	*No competition*	*No competition*	-
1944/1945	Stade Dudelange	FC Progrès Niederkorn	-
1945/1946	Stade Dudelange	AS la Jeunesse d'Esch/Alzette	-
1946/1947	Stade Dudelange	Union Sportive Lëtzebuerg	-
1947/1948	Stade Dudelange	Stade Dudelange	-
1948/1949	CA Spora Lëtzebuerg	Stade Dudelange	-
1949/1950	Stade Dudelange	CA Spora Lëtzebuerg	-
1950/1951	AS la Jeunesse d'Esch/Alzette	SC Tétange	-
1951/1952	National Schifflange	FA Red Boys Differdange	-
1952/1953	FC Progrès Niederkorn	FA Red Boys Differdange	-
1953/1954	AS la Jeunesse d'Esch/Alzette	AS la Jeunesse d'Esch/Alzette	-
1954/1955	Stade Dudelange	CS Fola Esch	-
1955/1956	CA Spora Lëtzebuerg	Stade Dudelange	-
1956/1957	Stade Dudelange	CA Spora Lëtzebuerg	-
1957/1958	AS la Jeunesse d'Esch/Alzette	FA Red Boys Differdange	-
1958/1959	AS la Jeunesse d'Esch/Alzette	Union Sportive Lëtzebuerg	-
1959/1960	AS la Jeunesse d'Esch/Alzette	National Schifflange	-
1960/1961	CA Spora Lëtzebuerg	Alliance Dudelange	-
1961/1962	Union Sportive Lëtzebuerg	Alliance Dudelange	-
1962/1963	AS la Jeunesse d'Esch/Alzette	Union Sportive Lëtzebuerg	-
1963/1964	FC Aris Bonnevoie	Union Sportive Lëtzebuerg	-
1964/1965	Stade Dudelange	CA Spora Lëtzebuerg	-
1965/1966	FC Aris Bonnevoie	CA Spora Lëtzebuerg	-
1966/1967	AS la Jeunesse d'Esch/Alzette	FC Aris Bonnevoie	-
1967/1968	AS la Jeunesse d'Esch/Alzette	Union Sportive Rumelange	-
1968/1969	FC Avenir Beggen	Union Sportive Lëtzebuerg	-
1969/1970	AS la Jeunesse d'Esch/Alzette	Union Sportive Lëtzebuerg	-
1970/1971	Union Sportive Lëtzebuerg	Jeunesse Hautcharage	-
1971/1972	FC Aris Bonnevoie	FA Red Boys Differdange	-
1972/1973	AS la Jeunesse d'Esch/Alzette	AS la Jeunesse d'Esch/Alzette	-
1973/1974	AS la Jeunesse d'Esch/Alzette	AS la Jeunesse d'Esch/Alzette	-
1974/1975	AS la Jeunesse d'Esch/Alzette	Union Sportive Rumelange	-
1975/1976	AS la Jeunesse d'Esch/Alzette	AS la Jeunesse d'Esch/Alzette	-
1976/1977	AS la Jeunesse d'Esch/Alzette	FC Progrès Niederkorn	-
1977/1978	FC Progrès Niederkorn	FC Progrès Niederkorn	-
1978/1979	FA Red Boys Differdange	FA Red Boys Differdange	-
1979/1980	AS la Jeunesse d'Esch/Alzette	CA Spora Lëtzebuerg	-
1980/1981	FC Progrès Niederkorn	AS la Jeunesse d'Esch/Alzette	-
1981/1982	FC Avenir Beggen	FA Red Boys Differdange	-
1982/1983	AS la Jeunesse d'Esch/Alzette	FC Avenir Beggen	-

1983/1984	FC Avenir Beggen	FC Avenir Beggen	-	
1984/1985	AS la Jeunesse d'Esch/Alzette	FA Red Boys Differdange	-	
1985/1986	FC Avenir Beggen	Union Sportive Lëtzebuerg	-	
1986/1987	AS la Jeunesse d'Esch/Alzette	FC Avenir Beggen	-	
1987/1988	AS la Jeunesse d'Esch/Alzette	AS la Jeunesse d'Esch/Alzette	Patrick Morocutti (Union Sportive Lëtzebuerg)	26
1988/1989	CA Spora Lëtzebuerg	Union Sportive Lëtzebuerg	Theo Scholten (AS la Jeunesse d'Esch/Alzette) Markus Krahen (GER, FC Avenir Beggen) Armin Krings (FC Avenir Beggen)	21
1989/1990	Union Sportive Lëtzebuerg	FC Swift Hesperange	Markus Krahen (GER, FC Avenir Beggen)	30
1990/1991	Union Sportive Lëtzebuerg	Union Sportive Lëtzebuerg	Patrick Morocutti (Union Sportive Lëtzebuerg)	23
1991/1992	Union Sportive Lëtzebuerg	FC Avenir Beggen	Markus Krahen (GER, FC Avenir Beggen)	19
1992/1993	FC Avenir Beggen	FC Avenir Beggen	Armin Krings (FC Avenir Beggen)	23
1993/1994	FC Avenir Beggen	FC Avenir Beggen	Stefano Fanelli (F91 Dudelange)	19
1994/1995	AS la Jeunesse d'Esch/Alzette	CS Grevenmacher	Yves Heinen (FC Differdange 03)	22
1995/1996	AS la Jeunesse d'Esch/Alzette	Union Sportive Lëtzebuerg	Mikhail Zaritski (FC Avenir Beggen)	18
1996/1997	AS la Jeunesse d'Esch/Alzette	AS la Jeunesse d'Esch/Alzette	Mikhail Zaritski (FC Sporting Mertzig) Franco Iovino (FC Wiltz 71)	19
1997/1998	AS la Jeunesse d'Esch/Alzette	CS Grevenmacher	Mikhail Zaritski (FC Sporting Mertzig)	29
1998/1999	AS la Jeunesse d'Esch/Alzette	AS la Jeunesse d'Esch/Alzette	Frédéric Cicchirillo (FRA, (FC Sporting Mertzig)	25
1999/2000	F91 Dudelange	AS la Jeunesse d'Esch/Alzette	Marcel Christophe (FC Mondercange)	26
2000/2001	F91 Dudelange	FC Etzella Ettelbruck	Mikhail Zaritski (FC Sporting Mertzig)	23
2001/2002	F91 Dudelange	FC Avenir Beggen	Frédéric Cicchirillo (FRA, F91 Dudelange)	24
2002/2003	CS Grevenmacher	CS Grevenmacher	Daniel Huss (CS Grevenmacher)	22
2003/2004	AS la Jeunesse d'Esch/Alzette	F91 Dudelange	José Manuel Gomes de Andrade (POR, CA Spora Lëtzebuerg)	24
2004/2005	F91 Dudelange	CS Pétange	Sergio Pupovac (CS Alliance 01 Lëtzebuerg)	24
2005/2006	F91 Dudelange	F91 Dudelange	Fatih Sözen (TUR, CS Grevenmacher)	23
2006/2007	F91 Dudelange	F91 Dudelange	Daniel da Mota Alves (FC Etzella Ettelbruck)	24
2007/2008	F91 Dudelange	CS Grevenmacher	Emmanuel Coquelet (FRA, F91 Dudelange)	20
2008/2009	F91 Dudelange	F91 Dudelange	Pierre Piskor (FRA, FC Differdange 03)	30
2009/2010	AS la Jeunesse d'Esch/Alzette	FC Differdange 03	Daniel Huss (CS Grevenmacher)	22
2010/2011	F91 Dudelange	FC Differdange 03	Sanel Ibrahimović (BIH, FC Wiltz 71)	18
2011/2012	F91 Dudelange	F91 Dudelange	Omar Er Rafik (MAR, FC Differdange 03)	23
2012/2013	CS Fola Esch	AS la Jeunesse d'Esch/Alzette	Edis Osmanović (BIH, FC Wiltz 71)	21
2013/2014	F91 Dudelange	FC Differdange 03	Sanel Ibrahimović (BIH, AS la Jeunesse d'Esch/Alzette)	22
2014/2015	CS Fola Esch	FC Differdange 03	Sanel Ibrahimović (BIH, AS la Jeunesse d'Esch/Alzette)	21
2015/2016	F91 Dudelange	F91 Dudelange	Julien Jahier (FRA, RFCU Lëtzebuerg)	18
2016/2017	F91 Dudelange	F91 Dudelange	Omar Er Rafik (MAR, FC Differdange 03)	26
2017/2018	F91 Dudelange	Racing FC	David Turpel (F91 Dudelange)	33
2018/2019	F91 Dudelange	F91 Dudelange	Samir Ali Hadji (FRA, CS Fola Esch)	23
2019/2020	*Championship abandoned*	*Competition abandoned*	-	
2020/2021	CS Fola Esch	*Competition abandoned*	Zachary Hadji (FRA, CS Fola Esch)	33

NATIONAL CHAMPIONSHIP
Division Nationale BGL Ligue 2020/2021
(22.08.2020 – 30.05.2021)

Results

Round 1 [22-23.08.2020]
FC Wiltz 71 - Etzella Ettelbruck 2-1
UT Pétange - UNA Strassen 2-0
Swift Hesperange - FC Differdange 03 3-1
Fola Esch - Jeunesse d'Esch 1-1
US Mondorf - US Hostert 1-1
Victoria Rosport - FC Rodange 91 3-1
RM Hamm - F91 Dudelange 1-2 [17.02.2021]
Progrès Nied. - Racing FCU 2-0 [31.03.2021]

Round 2 [29-30.08.2020]
Racing FCU - Fola Esch 1-3
F91 Dudelange - UT Pétange 3-0
US Hostert - Etzella Ettelbruck 3-0
FC Rodange 91 - US Mondorf 0-0
FC Wiltz 71 - RM Hamm Benfica 5-3
FC Differdange 03 - Victoria Rosport 2-3
Jeunesse d'Esch - Swift Hesperange 1-3
UNA Strassen - Progrès Niedercorn 0-4

Round 3 [12-13.09.2020]
Fola Esch - UNA Strassen 4-1
Progrès Niedercorn - F91 Dudelange 1-2
Etzella Ettelbruck - FC Rodange 91 1-1
Swift Hesperange - Racing FCU 1-2
US Hostert - FC Wiltz 71 1-2
US Mondorf - FC Differdange 03 1-3
UT Pétange - RM Hamm Benfica 0-0
Victoria Rosport - Jeunesse d'Esch 2-3

Round 4 [18-20.09.2020]
Jeunesse d'Esch - US Mondorf 2-1
Racing FCU - Victoria Rosport 0-3
UNA Strassen - Swift Hesperange 2-2
FC Differdange 03 - Etzella Ettelbruck 3-0
FC Rodange 91 - US Hostert 1-1
FC Wiltz 71 - UT Pétange 2-1
F91 Dudelange - Fola Esch 2-0
RM Hamm Benfica - Progrès Niedercorn 0-0

Round 5 [23.09.2020]
Fola Esch - RM Hamm Benfica 4-0
Etzella Ettelbruck - Jeunesse d'Esch 1-1
Progrès Niedercorn - UT Pétange 3-2
Swift Hesperange - F91 Dudelange 1-2
US Hostert - FC Differdange 03 4-5
US Mondorf - Racing FCU 3-2
FC Rodange 91 - FC Wiltz 71 1-0
Victoria Rosport - UNA Strassen 2-0

Round 6 [27-28.09.2020]
F91 Dudelange - Victoria Rosport 2-0
FC Differdange 03 - FC Rodange 91 1-0
RM Hamm Benfica - Swift Hesperange 1-1
Jeunesse d'Esch - US Hostert 1-0
Racing FCU - Etzella Ettelbruck 3-1
UNA Strassen - US Mondorf 3-0
FC Wiltz 71 - Progrès Niedercorn 3-0
UT Pétange - Fola Esch 1-2

Round 7 [03-04.10.2020]
Fola Esch - Progrès Niedercorn 4-3
Swift Hesperange - UT Pétange 1-0
US Mondorf - F91 Dudelange 0-3
FC Differdange 03 - FC Wiltz 71 1-1
Etzella Ettelbruck - UNA Strassen 2-4
US Hostert - Racing FCU 0-5
FC Rodange 91 - Jeunesse d'Esch 2-1
Victoria Rosport - RM Hamm Benfica 2-2

Round 8 [21.10.2020]
F91 Dudelange - Etzella Ettelbruck 3-0
RM Hamm Benfica - US Mondorf 0-2
Jeunesse d'Esch - FC Differdange 03 1-4
Racing FCU - FC Rodange 91 0-0
UNA Strassen - US Hostert 3-2
UT Pétange - Victoria Rosport 2-0
FC Wiltz 71 - Fola Esch 1-2
Progrès N. - Swift Hesperange 2-5 [17.02.21]

Round 9 [22.11.2020]
Etzella Ettelbruck - RM Hamm Benfica 2-1
FC Differdange 03 - Racing FCU 2-1
Swift Hesperange - Fola Esch 2-2
US Hostert - F91 Dudelange 2-1
Jeunesse d'Esch - FC Wiltz 71 1-1
US Mondorf - UT Pétange 0-1
FC Rodange 91 - UNA Strassen 1-1
Victoria Rosport - Progrès Niedercorn 1-0

Round 10 [03.03.2021]
Fola Esch - Victoria Rosport 2-0
F91 Dudelange - FC Rodange 91 5-1
Progrès Niedercorn - US Mondorf 1-0
RM Hamm Benfica - US Hostert 0-1
Racing FCU - Jeunesse d'Esch 1-0
UNA Strassen - FC Differdange 03 1-1
UT Pétange - Etzella Ettelbruck 0-0
FC Wiltz 71 - Swift Hesperange 0-2

Round 11 [10.03.2021]
Etzella Ettelbruck - Progrès Niedercorn 0-1
FC Differdange 03 - F91 Dudelange 1-0
US Hostert - UT Pétange 2-0
Jeunesse d'Esch - UNA Strassen 3-0
US Mondorf - Fola Esch 1-2
Racing FCU - FC Wiltz 71 1-0
FC Rodange 91 - RM Hamm Benfica 1-2
Victoria Rosport - Swift Hesperange 0-4

Round 12 [19-21.02.2021]
FC Rodange 91 - UT Pétange 1-0
UNA Strassen - Racing FCU 2-1
F91 Dudelange - Jeunesse d'Esch 0-0
Swift Hesperange - US Mondorf 2-1
FC Wiltz 71 - Victoria Rosport 2-0
Fola Esch - Etzella Ettelbruck 3-0
Progrès Niedercorn - US Hostert 0-0
RM Hamm Benfica - FC Differdange 03 1-1

Round 13 [24.02.2021]
Etzella Ettelbruck - Swift Hesperange 0-0
FC Differdange 03 - UT Pétange 2-2
US Hostert - Fola Esch 3-3
Jeunesse d'Esch - RM Hamm Benfica 1-0
US Mondorf - Victoria Rosport 2-2
Racing FCU - F91 Dudelange 1-2
FC Rodange 91 - Progrès Niedercorn 0-2
UNA Strassen - FC Wiltz 71 2-0

Round 14 [27-28.02.2021]
Swift Hesperange - US Hostert 2-0
Fola Esch - FC Rodange 91 4-1
F91 Dudelange - UNA Strassen 1-1
Progrès Niedercorn - FC Differdange 03 1-1
RM Hamm Benfica - Racing FCU 0-1
UT Pétange - Jeunesse d'Esch 1-2
Victoria Rosport - Etzella Ettelbruck 0-3
FC Wiltz 71 - US Mondorf 5-0

Round 15 [06-07.03.2021]
F91 Dudelange - FC Wiltz 71 3-3
Jeunesse d'Esch - Progrès Niedercorn 2-2
FC Rodange 91 - Swift Hesperange 1-2
Etzella Ettelbruck - US Mondorf 0-1
FC Differdange 03 - Fola Esch 1-4
US Hostert - Victoria Rosport 3-1
Racing FCU - UT Pétange 1-0
UNA Strassen - RM Hamm Benfica 1-1

Round 16 [14.03.2021]
Fola Esch - Racing FCU 3-2
Etzella Ettelbruck - US Hostert 2-2
Progrès Niedercorn - UNA Strassen 2-1
RM Hamm Benfica - FC Wiltz 71 1-1
Swift Hesperange - Jeunesse d'Esch 5-1
US Mondorf - FC Rodange 91 0-0
UT Pétange - F91 Dudelange 0-3
Victoria Rosport - FC Differdange 03 3-2

Round 17 [20-21.03.2021]
Jeunesse d'Esch - Victoria Rosport 1-0
F91 Dudelange - Progrès Niedercorn 1-0
FC Rodange 91 - Etzella Ettelbruck 1-0
Racing FCU - Swift Hesperange 0-1
FC Differdange 03 - US Mondorf 1-2
RM Hamm Benfica - UT Pétange 1-1
UNA Strassen - Fola Esch 1-4
FC Wiltz 71 - US Hostert 1-2 [31.03.]

Round 18 [27-28.03.2021]
Victoria Rosport - Racing FCU 1-2
Progrès Niedercorn - RM Hamm Benfica 4-1
Etzella Ettelbruck - FC Differdange 03 0-3
US Hostert - FC Rodange 91 3-3
Fola Esch - F91 Dudelange 5-0 [14.04.]
Swift Hesperange - UNA Strassen 7-0 [14.04.]
US Mondorf - Jeunesse d'Esch 2-3 [14.04.]
UT Pétange - FC Wiltz 71 5-1 [05.05.]

Round 19 [03-05.04.2021]
UNA Strassen - Victoria Rosport 1-3
RM Hamm Benfica - Fola Esch 0-2
FC Differdange 03 - US Hostert 0-1
Jeunesse d'Esch - Etzella Ettelbruck 1-1
Racing FCU - US Mondorf 1-0
UT Pétange - Progrès Niedercorn 1-0
FC Wiltz 71 - FC Rodange 91 2-0
F91 Dudelange - Swift Hesperange 2-3

Round 20 [10-11.04.2021]
Victoria Rosport - F91 Dudelange 0-4
Etzella Ettelbruck - Racing FCU 0-2
Fola Esch - UT Pétange 4-0
Swift Hesperange - RM Hamm Benfica 1-1
Progrès Niedercorn - FC Wiltz 71 2-0
US Hostert - Jeunesse d'Esch 1-1
US Mondorf - UNA Strassen 1-4
FC Rodange 91 - FC Differdange 03 1-3

Round 21 [17-18.04.2021]
RM Hamm Benfica - Victoria Rosport 5-0
Racing FCU - US Hostert 0-2
Jeunesse d'Esch - FC Rodange 91 2-1
F91 Dudelange - US Mondorf 3-0
Progrès Niedercorn - Fola Esch 1-1
UNA Strassen - Etzella Ettelbruck 1-1
UT Pétange - Swift Hesperange 0-1
FC Wiltz 71 - FC Differdange 03 0-2 [19.05.]

Round 22 [21.04.2021]
Etzella Ettelbruck - F91 Dudelange 0-3
FC Differdange 03 - Jeunesse d'Esch 1-2
Swift Hesperange - Progrès Niedercorn 1-1
US Hostert - UNA Strassen 2-4
FC Rodange 91 - Racing FCU 0-4
Victoria Rosport - UT Pétange 3-0
US Mondorf - RM Hamm Benfica 0-0 [05.05.]
Fola Esch - FC Wiltz 71 5-0 [26.05.]

Round 23 [24-25.04.2021]
FC Wiltz 71 - Jeunesse d'Esch 1-0
Fola Esch - Swift Hesperange 2-2
F91 Dudelange - US Hostert 1-1
Progrès Niedercorn - Victoria Rosport 3-2
Racing FCU - FC Differdange 03 3-0
UNA Strassen - FC Rodange 91 1-1
UT Pétange - US Mondorf 0-1
RM Hamm - Etzella Ettelbruck 1-1 [19.05.]

Round 24 [28.04.2021]
Etzella Ettelbruck - UT Pétange 2-2
FC Differdange 03 - UNA Strassen 1-1
Swift Hesperange - FC Wiltz 71 4-2
US Hostert - RM Hamm Benfica 0-3
Jeunesse d'Esch - Racing FCU 0-1
US Mondorf - Progrès Niedercorn 0-1
FC Rodange 91 - F91 Dudelange 0-3
Victoria Rosport - Fola Esch 1-5

Round 25 [02.05.2021]
Fola Esch - US Mondorf 2-3
F91 Dudelange - FC Differdange 03 3-1
Progrès Niedercorn - Etzella Ettelbruck 3-1
RM Hamm Benfica - FC Rodange 91 3-2
Swift Hesperange - Victoria Rosport 1-0
UNA Strassen - Jeunesse d'Esch 0-5
UT Pétange - US Hostert 1-1
FC Wiltz 71 - Racing FCU 0-1

Round 26 [08-09.05.2021]
US Hostert - Progrès Niedercorn 0-3
Victoria Rosport - FC Wiltz 71 0-2
Racing FCU - UNA Strassen 2-1
Etzella Ettelbruck - Fola Esch 3-2
Jeunesse d'Esch - F91 Dudelange 1-5
FC Differdange 03 - RM Hamm Benfica 3-0
US Mondorf - Swift Hesperange 1-1
UT Pétange - FC Rodange 91 0-1

Round 27 [12.05.2021]
Fola Esch - US Hostert 5-2
F91 Dudelange - Racing FCU 1-1
Progrès Niedercorn - FC Rodange 91 1-1
RM Hamm Benfica - Jeunesse d'Esch 1-0
Swift Hesperange - Etzella Ettelbruck 5-2
UT Pétange - FC Differdange 03 0-2
Victoria Rosport - US Mondorf 3-4
FC Wiltz 71 - UNA Strassen 2-0

Round 28 [16.05.2021]
Etzella Ettelbruck - Victoria Rosport 4-0
FC Differdange 03 - Progrès Niedercorn 0-3
US Hostert - Swift Hesperange 0-3
US Mondorf - FC Wiltz 71 0-3
Racing FCU - RM Hamm Benfica 3-0
FC Rodange 91 - Fola Esch 2-1
UNA Strassen - F91 Dudelange 2-6
Jeunesse d'Esch - UT Pétange 4-0

Round 29 [22.05.2021]
Fola Esch - FC Differdange 03 5-0
Progrès Niedercorn - Jeunesse d'Esch 2-0
RM Hamm Benfica - UNA Strassen 1-2
Swift Hesperange - FC Rodange 91 4-0
US Mondorf - Etzella Ettelbruck 2-3
UT Pétange - Racing FCU 0-5
Victoria Rosport - US Hostert 0-3
FC Wiltz 71 - F91 Dudelange 0-0

Round 30 [30.05.2021]
Etzella Ettelbruck - FC Wiltz 71 1-3
F91 Dudelange - RM Hamm Benfica 4-3
FC Differdange 03 - Swift Hesperange 3-1
US Hostert - US Mondorf 4-4
Jeunesse d'Esch - Fola Esch 0-3
Racing FCU - Progrès Niedercorn 0-0
FC Rodange 91 - Victoria Rosport 2-2
UNA Strassen - UT Pétange 4-1

Final Standings

											Home					Away			
			Total																	
1. **CS Fola Esch**	30	21	5	4	89	-	35	68	12	2	1	53	-	15	9	3	3	36	-	20
2. F91 Dudelange	30	20	6	4	70	-	29	66	9	5	1	34	-	14	11	1	3	36	-	15
3. FC Swift Hesperange	30	19	8	3	72	-	30	65	10	3	2	40	-	15	9	5	1	32	-	15
4. Racing FC Union Lëtzebuerg	30	17	3	10	47	-	29	54	8	2	5	17	-	14	9	1	5	30	-	15
5. FC Progrès Niederkorn	30	15	8	7	48	-	30	53	9	4	2	28	-	17	6	4	5	20	-	13
6. FC Differdange 03	30	13	6	11	51	-	48	45	6	3	6	22	-	21	7	3	5	29	-	27
7. FC Wiltz 71	30	13	5	12	45	-	42	44	9	1	5	26	-	14	4	4	7	19	-	28
8. AS La Jeunesse d'Esch/Alzette	30	12	7	11	41	-	43	43	7	3	5	21	-	22	5	4	6	20	-	21
9. US Hostert	30	9	10	11	47	-	56	37	4	4	7	28	-	38	5	6	4	19	-	18
10. FC UNA Strassen	30	9	8	13	44	-	65	35	5	5	5	24	-	32	4	3	8	20	-	33
11. US Mondorf-les-Bains	30	7	7	16	33	-	56	28	1	5	9	14	-	29	6	2	7	19	-	27
12. FC Rodange 91	30	6	10	14	27	-	52	28	5	4	6	14	-	22	1	6	8	13	-	30
13. FC Victoria Rosport	30	8	3	19	37	-	67	27	5	1	9	21	-	35	3	2	10	16	-	32
14. FC RM Hamm Benfica	30	5	11	14	33	-	48	26	3	6	6	16	-	17	2	5	8	17	-	31
15. FC Etzella Ettelbrück	30	5	9	16	32	-	57	24	3	5	7	18	-	26	2	4	9	14	-	31
16. Union Titus Pétange	30	5	6	19	23	-	52	21	4	3	8	13	-	19	1	3	11	10	-	33

Please note: no teams were relegated or promoted for 2021/2022.

Top goalscorers:

33	**Zachary Hadji (FRA)**	*CS Fola Esch*
23	Hakim Abdallah (MAD)	*FC Swift Hesperange*
17	Adel Bettaieb (FRA)	*F91 Dudelange*
17	Dominik Stolz (GER)	*FC Swift Hesperange*
16	Dejvid Sinani	*CS Fola Esch*
16	Ryad Habbas (FRA)	*FC Progrès Niederkorn*

NATIONAL CUP
Coupe du Luxembourg 2020/2021

First Round [09.09.2020]

Etoile Sportive Clemency - Jeunesse Schieren	1-3	FC Ehlerange - FC Kopstal 33	3-0
US Moutfort-Medingen - Red Black Egalité	1-4	FC 47 Bastendorf - FC Stengefort	3-4
AS Colmarberg - Sporting Mertzig	1-5	Les Ardoisiers Perlé - FC Schengen	1-4
Red Boys Aspelt - FC Käerch	0-1	Kischpelt Wilwerwiltz - Minière Lasauvage	4-2
FC Minerva Lintgen - Blo Weiss Itzig	1-2	Jeunesse Gilsdorf - Résidence Walferdange	3-2
FC Green Boys 77 - US Berdorf Consdorf	2-1	Syra Mensdorf - US Boevange-Attert	8-0
Tricolore Gasperich - US Feulen	1-2	Luna Oberkorn - Union 05 Kayl-Tétange	0-2
Rupensia Lusitanos Larochette - Alliance Äischdall	1-0	FC Avenir Beggen - Jeunesse Useldange	2-2 aet; 5-4 pen
CS Grevenmacher - Union Remich-Bous	6-2	SC Ell - FC Lorentzweiler	1-5
The Belval Belvaux - FF Norden 02	2-3	FC Brouch - FC Pratzerthal-Redange	2-3
AS Luxemburg Porto - Koeppchen Wormeldange	4-3	Les Aiglons Dalheim - FC Erpeldange 72	1-3
Claravallis Clervaux - FC Noertzange	2-3	Racing Troisvierges - Sporting Bertrange	2-1
CS Bourscheid - FC Munsbach	1-2	US Folschette - CS Oberkorn	0-2
Olympia Christnach-Waldbillig - AS Wincrange	0-5	FC Kehlen - AS Hosingen	1-0
US Reisdorf - FC CeBra Grund 2001	0-5	US Rambrouch - FCM Young Boys Diekirch	0-5
ES Schouweiler - CS Sanem	2-3	US Sandweiler - Daring Echternach	0-0 aet; 4-5 pen

Second Round [16-18.10.2020]

FC Käerch - Atert Bissen	2-4	Union 05 Kayl-Tétange - Yellow Boys Weiler	3-4
FC Green Boys 77 - FC Wiltz 71	0-8	FCM Young Boys Diekirch - US Mondorf-les-Bains	0-6
FC Pratzerthal-Redange - CS Fola Esch	0-4	FC Munsbach - Alisontia Steinsel	2-4
CS Oberkorn - US Esch/Alzette	1-1 aet; 5-3 pen	FC Lorentzweiler - FC Marisca Mersch	2-0
AS Wincrange - FC Rodange 91	0-2	Racing Troisvierges - Racing FC Union Lëtzebuerg	0-11
FF Norden 02 - FC RM Hamm Benfica	1-2	FC Kehlen - FC Progrès Niederkorn	0-2
FC Avenir Beggen - FC Mondercange	3-2 aet	AS Luxemburg Porto - FC Victoria Rosport	2-5
Kischpelt Wilwerwiltz - US Rumelange	0-10	FC Stengefort - FC Jeunesse Junglinster	1-3
Sporting Mertzig - F91 Dudelange	0-5	FC Erpeldange 72 - FC Schifflange 95	1-3
FC Schengen - FC Differdange 03	1-5	FC Swift Hesperange - Blo Weiss Itzig	4-0
US Feulen - US Hostert	0-1	Rupensia Lusitanos Larochette - FC Jeunesse Canach	0-4
FC Noertzange - AS La Jeunesse d'Esch/Alzette	0-6	FC CeBra Grund 2001- FC UNA Strassen	2-3
Jeunesse Gilsdorf - FC Etzella Ettelbrück	1-2	CS Grevenmacher - UN Käerjéng 97	2-3
Jeunesse Schieren - Union Titus Pétange	1-2	Daring Echternach - Union Mertert/Wasserbillig	1-3
CS Sanem - SC Bettembourg	1-0	Syra Mensdorf - FC Mamer 32	1-0
FC Ehlerange - FC Berdenia Berbourg	4-3	Red Black Egalité - FC Blô-Weiss Medernach	*not played*

The competition was cancelled due to COVID-19 pandemic. No title was awarded.

Foussballclub Déifferdeng 03

Founded:	2003 (*as merger of FA Red Boys Differdange and AS Differdange*)	
Stadium:	Stade Municipal, Differdange (3,000)	
Trainer:	Paolo Amodio	28.05.1973
[25.03.2021]	Jean-Philippe Caillet (FRA)	24.06.1977

Goalkeepers:	DOB	M	(s)	G
Andrea Amodio	13.07.1997	27		
Kevin Straus	28.03.1990	3		
Defenders:	**DOB**	**M**	**(s)**	**G**
Théo Brusco	20.11.1999	23	(1)	2
Maxime De Taddeo	11.07.1994	21	(1)	5
Geoffrey Franzoni	18.02.1991	27		1
Dylan Lempereur (FRA)	24.10.1998	27		3
Edin Osmanovic	30.08.2001	17	(2)	
Midfielders:	**DOB**	**M**	**(s)**	**G**
Mamadou Sanoussy Baldé (USA)	28.04.1995	16	(3)	
Yabnnick Cervellera	04.04.2001		(6)	
Kevin d´Anzico	14.08.2000	16	(4)	1
William Ferreira da Cruz	07.12.2000	4	(14)	3
Shean Garlito y Romo (BEL)	19.02.1994	17	(5)	
Kilian Gulluni (FRA)	20.04.1999	14	(7)	1
Hugo Komano (FRA)	14.04.2000	12	(4)	2
Quentin Emile Ange Leite Pereira (FRA)	21.01.1992	15	(3)	1
Joel Lopes	04.05.2002	1	(4)	
Gianni Medina da Mata	22.12.2001	9	(5)	1
Lucas Prudhomme	31.05.1999	11	(1)	2
Moïse Sakava Sangola (CMR)	26.12.2000	9	(3)	1
Forwards:	**DOB**	**M**	**(s)**	**G**
Arlindo Agostinho Barbosa da Silva (POR)	27.05.2004	2	(1)	
Gonçalo Jorge Almeida da Silva	26.11.1990	16	(2)	1
Andreas Buch (GER)	25.04.1993	23	(5)	14
Fadel Gobitaka (BEL)	16.01.1998	6	(5)	1
Aurélien Joachim	10.08.1986	14	(4)	9
Ryan Lohei	11.04.2001		(2)	
Valentino Vujinović (CRO)	20.02.1999		(1)	

F91 Dudelange

Founded:	1991	
Stadium:	Stade „Jos Nosbaum", Dudelange (2,558)	
Trainer:	Carlos Manuel Fangueiro Soares (POR)	19.12.1976

Goalkeepers:	DOB	M	(s)	G
Enzo Esposito	06.10.1998	2		
Tim Kips	01.11.2000	23		
Miguel Ângelo Torres Palha (POR)	26.02.1995	5		
Defenders:	**DOB**	**M**	**(s)**	**G**
Kobe Cools (BEL)	25.07.2000	27		2
Ricardo Aleixo Delgado	22.02.1994	24	(1)	2
Jules Diouf (FRA)	05.03.1992	21		2
Mehdi Kirch	27.01.1990	24		6
Delvin Skenderović	23.01.1994	18	(1)	1
Chris Stumpf	28.08.1994	4	(10)	1
Dylan Martins Teixeira	27.01.2001	1		
Kevin Van Den Kerkhof (FRA)	14.03.1996	30		9
Midfielders:	**DOB**	**M**	**(s)**	**G**
Filip Bojić (CRO)	05.10.1992	17	(3)	3
Charles Morren (BEL)	28.02.1992	22		
Mario Pokar (GER)	18.01.1990	17		2
Tiago Rodrigues da Costa	21.01.2003		(6)	
Ian Fialho Santos	17.09.2002	1		
Nelito Carlos da Cruz „Vova"	29.12.1985	18		
Forwards:	**DOB**	**M**	**(s)**	**G**
Edis Agović	12.07.1993	3	(3)	
Adel Bettaieb (FRA)	28.01.1997	20	(4)	17
Magnus Hansen	26.03.2001	2	(6)	
Mohcine Hassan (MAR)	30.09.1994	13	(12)	8
Ryan Klapp	10.01.1993		(1)	
Edvin Muratović	15.02.1997	18	(3)	7
Yannick Schaus	11.03.2000	3	(22)	5
Bertino João Cabral Barbosa "Tino" (POR)	06.05.1992	11	(10)	3
Jordann Yéyé	02.11.1988	6	(6)	1

Foussballclub Etzella Ettelbruck

Founded:	21.05.1917	
Stadium:	Stade Am Deich, Ettelbruck (2,020)	
Trainer:	Neil Pattison	13.03.1979

Goalkeepers:	DOB	M	(s)	G
Heathcliff Collin (BEL)	06.11.1997	1		
Michel Witte (GER)	22.03.1999	29		1
Defenders:	**DOB**	**M**	**(s)**	**G**
Lucas Figueiredo	14.05.2003	4	(8)	
Losseni Keita (GUI)	01.04.1984	7	(3)	
Godmer Mabouba (FRA)	23.09.1990	22		
Joël Magalhaes de Oliveira	22.04.1991	6	(3)	
Yanis N'Gbin	22.10.1999	18	(2)	
Lex Nicolay	27.03.1997	9		1
Pol Schlesser	12.06.1996	10	(1)	
Rick Schwitz	18.12.2003	1	(6)	
Jader Soares	19.08.1996	27		
Antero Diogo da Silva Ferreira „Vila" (POR)	07.02.1990	23	(1)	
Midfielders:	**DOB**	**M**	**(s)**	**G**
Adriel Guimaraes Santos (POR)	29.04.1998	9	(6)	2
Ernest Agović	09.02.1997		(1)	
Ilhan Agović	21.09.2003	2	(2)	
Georgy Bella Abega	27.10.2001		(2)	
Raphael de Sousa	05.03.1993	21	(1)	
Miguel Teixeira Fernandes	17.06.2001		(2)	
Dwain Glineur Brito	07.09.2001	9	(14)	1
Gustavo Alexandre Henkemaier (BRA)	19.06.1997	28		7
Mefail Kadrija (GER)	22.09.1991	24	(3)	5
Len Kneip	26.12.2001	1	(6)	
Nicola Schreiner	01.09.1995	21	(5)	1
Forwards:	**DOB**	**M**	**(s)**	**G**
Julian Bidon (GER)	22.10.1990	19	(7)	2
Edgar Antonio da Silva	14.02.1998	8		
Ken Decker	16.09.1994	1	(6)	
Téo Herr (FRA)	12.02.2001	5	(1)	2
Kevin N'Cho (FRA)	19.05.1991	2		
Patrick Stumpf (GER)	11.04.1988	23	(4)	10

Cercle sportif Fola Esch

Founded:	1906	
Stadium:	Stade „Émile Mayrisch", Esch-sur-Alzette (3,826)	
Trainer:	Sébastien Grandjean (BEL)	16.06.1970

Goalkeepers:	DOB	M	(s)	G
Emmanuel Tomas Cabral (POR)	02.08.1996	13		
Thomas Hym (FRA)	29.08.1987	17		
Defenders:	**DOB**	**M**	**(s)**	**G**
Lenny Almada Correia	19.09.2002	8	(5)	
Billy Bernard	29.04.1991	5	(1)	
Fabio Cerqueira Martins	08.01.2003	2	(2)	
Gilson Delgado	19.10.1992	19	(5)	
Hugo Domingos	28.04.2002		(1)	
Julien Klein (FRA)	07.04.1988	28	(1)	
Guillaume Mura (FRA)	09.01.1986	6		
Sylvio Ouassiero (MAD)	07.05.1994	21	(2)	1
Cédric Sacras	28.09.1996	24	(2)	
Midfielders:	**DOB**	**M**	**(s)**	**G**
Lucas Correia	18.04.2002	17	(5)	3
Rodrigue Dikaba (COD)	28.10.1985	16	(5)	2
Bruno Adelino Freire Fernandes (POR)	27.03.1999	23	(3)	2
Veldin Muharemović (BIH)	06.12.1984	6	(3)	
Diogo Pimentel	16.07.1997	24		3
Taigo Semedo Monteiro	03.08.2001	3	(4)	
Bob Simon	17.01.1996	5	(1)	
Dejvid Sinani	02.04.1993	16	(6)	16
Forwards:	**DOB**	**M**	**(s)**	**G**
Stefano Bensi	11.08.1988	12	(9)	7
Idrir Boutrif (ALG)	06.02.2000	6	(5)	4
Gauthier Caron (FRA)	27.12.1989	4	(13)	1
Rui Jorge Costa de Sousa	26.12.2002	1		
Jules Diallo (FRA)	08.03.1993	20	(4)	13
Achraf Drif (FRA)	22.03.1992	11	(7)	2
Zachary Hadji (FRA)	08.10.1996	23	(4)	33

Football Club Union Sportive Hostert

Founded:	1946		
Stadium:	Stade „Jos Becker", Hostert (1,500)		
Trainer:	Henri Bossi		20.02.1958

Goalkeepers:	DOB	M	(s)	G
Michal Augustyn (POL)	13.04.1991	5		
Geordan Dupire	28.09.1993	16		
Lucas Rodrigues Antunes	14.02.2003		(1)	
Valentin Roulez	12.12.1996	9		
Defenders:	DOB	M	(s)	G
Beno Adrović	17.11.1996	12	(7)	
Papa Aye Dione (SEN)	08.03.1986	4		
Amar Duracak (CRO)	17.06.1992	7	(1)	1
Benôit Eixler	06.02.2003		(3)	
Demir Koljenović (BIH)	09.05.1990	14		
Alexandre Sacras	14.12.2000	28	(2)	
Léon Schmit	28.09.2001	21	(4)	3
Cedric Steinmetz	27.09.1999	23	(4)	
Quentin Zilli	16.02.1999	25	(2)	2
Midfielders:	DOB	M	(s)	G
Grégory Adler (FRA)	27.04.1989	11		2
Rasheed Eichhorn (GER)	19.09.1997	13		
Adriano de Sousa Ferraz	20.04.2001		(2)	
Max Mangen	08.02.1996		(6)	
Yacer Mogni (FRA)	22.05.1997		(3)	
Tarek Nouidra (FRA)	09.05.1987	27		
Yannick Olm	29.05.2004	2	(1)	
Jordan Steiner (FRA)	10.03.1990	19	(2)	4
Guillaume Trani (FRA)	17.12.1997	21		5
Juncai Wang	05.04.1990	1	(7)	
Forwards:	DOB	M	(s)	G
Khaled Ayari (TUN)	17.01.1990	6	(8)	5
Yann Ferreira	16.01.2004		(1)	
Kevin Hoffmann	03.10.1997		(1)	
Bigen Yala Lusala (BEL)	20.10.1992	22	(3)	9
William Junior Delgado Rodrigues	27.01.2000	7	(19)	2
Théo Sully (FRA)	13.02.1996	18	(5)	7
Jean-Désiré Tibor (BEL)	02.09.1993	19	(4)	6

Association Sportive la Jeunesse d'Esch/Alzette

Founded:	1907		
Stadium:	Stade de la Frontière, Esch-sur-Alzette (5,400)		
Trainer:	Marcus Weiss (GER)		15.10.1986
[13.10.2020]	Georgios Petrakis (GRE)		08.02.1988

Goalkeepers:	DOB	M	(s)	G
Lucas Fox	02.10.2000	30		
Defenders:	DOB	M	(s)	G
Dennis Besch	02.04.1999	17	(5)	2
Abdoulaye Diallo (SEN)	21.10.1992	4	(1)	
Alessandro Fiorani	19.02.1989	7	(5)	
Dylan Meireles	24.12.1997		(1)	
David Mendes Merces	08.11.2000	12	(6)	
Clayton de Sousa Moreira	24.02.1998	15	(1)	
Rick Brito Oliveira	25.11.2000	3	(2)	
Xavier Tomas (FRA)	04.01.1986	26	(1)	
Midfielders:	DOB	M	(s)	G
Alexis Boury (FRA)	31.10.2001	5	(13)	
Steven Crolet (FRA)	05.01.1996	7	(1)	
Aldin Dervišević	19.08.1989	7	(2)	
Dany de Sousa Xavier	08.11.2000		(2)	
Markus Einsiedler (GER)	27.01.1989	12	(7)	
Mégan Laurent (BEL)	24.03.1992	14	(3)	4
David Soares de Sousa	15.07.1995	6	(3)	
Stélvio Rosa da Cruz (ANG)	24.01.1989	20		1
Miloš Todorović	18.08.1995	24	(5)	2
Georgios Xenitidis (GRE)	04.09.1999	27	(1)	2
Forwards:	DOB	M	(s)	G
Gary Bernard	24.10.2000	24	(4)	8
Andrea Deidda	15.12.1993	9	(6)	1
Almir Klica (MNE)	10.11.1998	18	(5)	1
Frederick Kyereh (GER)	18.10.1993	1	(4)	
Moussa Maâzou (NIG)	25.08.1988	19	(1)	9
Cedric Soares	19.10.1995	1		1
Aexandros Voilis (GRE)	26.05.2000	22	(7)	6

Union sportive de Mondorf-les-Bains

Founded:	1915		
Stadium:	Stade "John Grün", Mondorf-les-Bains (3,600)		
Trainer:	Serge Wolf (FRA)		11.10.1969

Goalkeepers:	DOB	M	(s)	G
Luca Bernardini	18.12.1997		(1)	
Max de Cillia	14.03.2003	1		
João Ricardo Silva Machado	09.04.1999	17		
Koray Ozcan (FRA)	01.02.1995	12		
Defenders:	DOB	M	(s)	G
Tim Bartholomey	01.10.2000	7	(2)	1
Ahmed Benhemine (FRA)	15.01.1987	22	(1)	
Julien Cétout (FRA)	02.01.1988	14		
Fatih Eren (TUR)	17.01.1995	28		1
Pit Fehlen	04.02.1996	2		1
André Miguel da Silva Ferreira	16.05.1996	1		
William Kevin Rocha Josefa	29.05.1997	4	(1)	
Yohan Merlet (FRA)	26.11.1991	9		
Amine Nabli (FRA)	27.05.1985	9		1
Bosson Romaric (CIV)	12.04.1988	4		
Midfielders:	DOB	M	(s)	G
Cleidir Paulo Neves Luis (POR)	16.10.1993	12	(11)	2
Alexis Heintz (FRA)	24.06.1999	6	(7)	1
João Carlos Amaral Marques Coimbra (POR)	24.05.1986	6	(3)	
Yassine Mohammed (FRA)	07.01.1991	21		7
Michael Monteiro	11.12.1991	26	(1)	
Rinel Pieume Mafossi	29.01.1997	6	(2)	
Ricardo Couto Pinto	14.01.1996	8	(6)	1
Oliver Schermuly	12.01.2000	1	(1)	
David Mendes da Silva (CPV)	10.11.1986	21	(4)	2
Admir Škrijelj	03.06.1992	13	(5)	
Ali Škrijelj	22.06.2000	3		
Faraji Taarimte (FRA)	17.08.1994	17	(4)	2
Forwards:	DOB	M	(s)	G
Aleksandar Biedermann (GER)	03.01.1995	4	(3)	
André Oliveira Barros da Silva (FRA)	26.01.1997	5	(12)	1
Brian Dauphin (FRA)	03.09.1991	10	(3)	
Gent Dinaj (KVX)	30.03.1998	4	(4)	
Marianel Faladé (FRA)	17.10.1992	3	(7)	1
Marvin Géran (FRA)	01.01.1996	11	(4)	1
Alessandro Scanzano	14.03.1996	23	(3)	9

Football Club Progrès Niederkorn

Founded:	1919		
Stadium:	Stade „Jos Haupert", Niederkorn (2,800)		
Trainer:	Roland Vrabec (GER)		06.03.1974
[23.11.2020]	Stéphane Leoni (FRA)		05.03.1976

Goalkeepers:	DOB	M	(s)	G
Sebastien Flauss (FRA)	19.08.1989	24		
Kévin Sommer (FRA)	08.11.1989	6		
Defenders:	DOB	M	(s)	G
Lamine Ba (FRA)	24.08.1997	22	(4)	1
Yannick Bastos	30.05.1993	18	(2)	
Adrien Ferino (FRA)	16.06.1992	19	(5)	
Mathias Jänisch	27.08.1990	18	(5)	
Metin Karayer (FRA)	18.05.1992	14	(2)	1
Tom Laterza	09.05.1992	12		
Yann Matias Marques	12.11.1996	1	(2)	
Aldin Skenderović	28.06.1997	26		
Midfielders:	DOB	M	(s)	G
Yannis Dublin	19.03.1998	11	(7)	
Kevin Holtz	06.03.1993	9		
Irvin Latić	24.05.2002	18	(4)	1
Belmin Muratović (MNE)	27.03.1998	2	(3)	
Christian Silaj (GER)	07.04.1992	15	(7)	1
Kempes Waldemar Tekiela (GER)	15.10.1997	24	(3)	6
Sébastien Thill	29.12.1993	1		
Ben Vogel	22.12.1994	15	(5)	1
Forwards:	DOB	M	(s)	G
Issa Bah (POR)	05.07.2002	16	(6)	5
Ryad Habbas (FRA)	16.07.1997	19	(4)	16
Bilal Hend	18.01.2000	17	(3)	3
Ryan Klapp	10.01.1993	6	(3)	
Antonio Luisi	07.10.1994	10	(10)	7
Florik Shala	19.07.1997	7	(12)	6

Racing Football Club Union Lëtzebuerg

Founded: 12.05.2005 (*as merger of Spora, Union and CS Alliance 01 Lëtzebuerg*)
Stadium: Stade "Achille Hammerel", Lëtzebuerg (5,814)
Trainer: Régis Brouard (FRA) 17.01.1967

Goalkeepers:	DOB	M	(s)	G
Romain Ruffier (FRA)	04.10.1989	30		
Defenders:	**DOB**	**M**	**(s)**	**G**
Thomas Birk (GER)	05.07.1988	10		
Judicaël Crillon (FRA)	21.11.1988	22		
Jonathan Hennetier (FRA)	06.11.1991	12		
Julien Humbert (FRA)	23.06.1984	6	(3)	
Amdy Konnte (SEN)	13.07.1997	7	(1)	
Gérard Mersch	08.09.1996	4	(3)	
Benoit Nyssen (BEL)	12.09.1997	16	(2)	
Pit Simon	17.02.1998	25	(2)	2
Midfielders:	**DOB**	**M**	**(s)**	**G**
Hadi Bentebbal (FRA)	06.07.2001	1	(3)	
Yan Bouché	19.03.1999	10	(17)	3
Dwayn Holter	15.05.1995	24	(3)	1
Farid Ikene	15.12.2000	23	(2)	2
Dylan Kuete Nsidjine	12.07.2000	1	(7)	
Kevin Nakache (FRA)	05.04.1989	16	(7)	3
Abdelhakim Omrani (FRA)	18.02.1991	26		
Jérôme Simon (FRA)	12.09.1993	21	(3)	5
Yannis Tafer (ALG)	11.02.1991	8	(2)	
Loris Tinelli	02.02.1999	9	(19)	2
Forwards:	**DOB**	**M**	**(s)**	**G**
Mana Dembélé (MLI)	29.11.1988	27		14
Alain Logrillo (FRA)	30.12.2001		(6)	
Yann Mabella (CGO)	22.02.1996	29		13
Jacky Mmaee (BEL)	16.11.1994	3	(1)	1

Football Club Rapid Mansfeldia Hamm Benfica

Founded: 26.03.2004
Stadium: Terrain de Football Cents, Lëtzebuerg (2,800)
Trainer: Pedro Miguel Resende dos Reis Morais (POR) 19.04.1977

Goalkeepers:	DOB	M	(s)	G
Dany Rodrigues da Silva (POR)	10.02.1004	21		
Yannick Lopes	22.02.2000	9		
Defenders:	**DOB**	**M**	**(s)**	**G**
Samuel Correia (POR)	29.09.1997	14	(4)	
Pedro Miguel Neves da Costa „Costinha" (POR)	11.03.1994	19		
Gianluca Bei	17.05.1995	30		2
Bruno Da Rocha	13.02.1998	3	(2)	
Bilal Hadraoui (FRA)	28.05.1999	16	(2)	3
Jasmin Hodžić (SRB)	28.06.1988	6		1
Filipe Jonni Correia Santos (POR)	06.05.1996	21	(1)	2
Hugo Lopes	09.12.2002	1		1
Tripy Makonda (FRA)	24.01.1990	12	(3)	
Cristiano Mendes	06.10.1998	18	(2)	1
Ivo Silva	21.10.2001	7	(7)	
Midfielders:	**DOB**	**M**	**(s)**	**G**
Fábio Santos Cardoso (POR)	16.01.1992	23		1
Gonçalo de Oliveira Geral (POR)	12.02.1999	3		
Amel Hodžić	27.07.2000	2	(2)	
Jan Ostrowski	14.04.1999	16		
Bruno Correia Mendes (POR)	10.12.1994	21	(2)	1
Forwards:	**DOB**	**M**	**(s)**	**G**
Mário Filipe Curito Santos Ferreira (FRA)	20.04.2000	1		
Maxime Deruffe (FRA)	13.05.1988	25	(2)	13
Clément Huet (FRA)	31.07.1998	14	(6)	
Bakary Kaboré (FRA)	19.11.2000	5	(8)	1
Alexio Alexandre dos Santos „Lelé Mendes" (POR)	08.10.1993	3	(1)	
Leandro Paulo Roberto Souza (BRA)	23.02.1987	18	(6)	5
Bryan Ntambani (FRA)	16.01.1999	1		
Tshomba Oliveira (FRA)	09.08.1995	4	(5)	
Igor Tele Santos	27.04.2000	14	(10)	1
Elvis Lima Sousa	23.03.1997	3	(11)	

Football Club Rodange 91

Founded: 1991
Stadium: Stade „Joseph Phillippart", Rodange (3,400)
Trainer: Nedžib Selimović (BIH) 10.04.1964

Goalkeepers:	DOB	M	(s)	G
Erkan Agović	24.08.2000	4		
Eldin Latik	22.12.2002	2		
Anthony Mfa Mezui (GAB)	07.03.1991	24		
Defenders:	**DOB**	**M**	**(s)**	**G**
Noah Dédenon	08.01.2001	11	(3)	
Samuel Dog (FRA)	13.02.1985	1		
Leonel Monteiro Domingos	30.08.1999		(1)	
Ervin Latik	21.02.2002	6	(5)	
Joshua Nadeau (FRA)	12.09.1994	29		
Irwin Ramdedović	24.09.1999	4	(5)	
Henid Ramdedović	20.07.1987	12	(1)	
Marco António Freitas Semedo (POR)	08.10.1987	25		1
David Marques Soares	20.02.1991	20		1
Midfielders:	**DOB**	**M**	**(s)**	**G**
Luca Alverdi	17.10.1999	3	(1)	
Sam Alverdi	23.08.1997	3	(4)	
Mohamed Anas Ammar (MAR)	24.10.1992	11	(3)	1
Marco De Sousa	17.08.1986		(3)	
David Fleurival (GLP)	19.02.1984	23		
Julian Ganser	10.07.2002	1	(9)	
Alexis Larriere (FRA)	20.03.1997	28		6
Alexis Lopes	17.08.2002	5	(2)	
Jean-Paul Makasso (CMR)	05.11.1993	27		
Luka Rakić	09.07.2002		(3)	
Dzenid Ramdedović	25.02.1992	2	(3)	
Forwards:	**DOB**	**M**	**(s)**	**G**
Kilian Amehi	14.11.1997	16	(4)	2
Valerio Barbaro	16.02.1998	12	(11)	1
Moussa Diallo (BEL)	20.11.1990	3	(4)	3
Semsudin Džanić (BIH)	12.07.1992	19	(1)	
Rafael Ferreira Baros	04.05.2001		(1)	
Deniz Muric (FRA)	06.03.1995	10	(4)	1
Momar N`Diaye (SEN)	13.07.1987	22	(1)	7
Arthur Njo-Léa (SUI)	30.11.1995	7	(4)	1

Football Club Swift Hesperange

Founded: 1916
Stadium: Stade „Alphonse Theis", Hesperange (3,058)
Trainer: Jeff Strasser 05.10.1974
[15.10.2020] Pascal Carzaniga (FRA) 04.05.1971

Goalkeepers:	DOB	M	(s)	G
Jonathan Joubert	12.09.1979	30		
Defenders:	**DOB**	**M**	**(s)**	**G**
Loris Bernardy	22.01.2001	4	(2)	
Lamine Fall (FRA)	22.02.1994	1	(1)	
Elysée Lecomte (BEL)	12.10.1999	1	(1)	
Kevin Malget	15.01.1991	15	(4)	
Bryan Mélisse (FRA)	25.03.1989	28		2
Hakim Menaï (FRA)	27.03.1986	17		
Roman Pierrard (FRA)	11.09.1997	17		
Jerry Prempeh (GHA)	29.12.1988	15	(1)	
Tom Schnell	08.10.1985	22	(2)	4
Midfielders:	**DOB**	**M**	**(s)**	**G**
Grégory Adler (FRA)	27.04.1989	1		
Kenan Avdušinović	03.03.1998	3	(17)	1
Hugo Colella (FRA)	16.09.1999	12	(3)	2
Aydine Correia	05.03.1992		(2)	
Joël de Almeida Pedro	10.04.1992	5	(10)	1
Mickaël Garos (FRA)	10.05.1988	28		1
Mohamed Loua (BEL)	20.04.2000	13		
Olivier Marques	21.03.1992	15	(8)	1
Dominik Stolz (GER)	04.05.1990	28	(1)	17
Forwards:	**DOB**	**M**	**(s)**	**G**
Hakim Abdallah (MAD)	09.01.1998	24	(6)	23
Brian Babit (FRA)	21.03.1993	5	(3)	
Marwane Benamra (ALG)	09.04.1995	1		
Ken Corral	08.05.1992	9	(3)	3
Emmanuel Françoise (FRA)	08.06.1987	19	(3)	4
Lenny Leonil (FRA)	30.03.1998	4	(4)	3
Nicolas Perez (FRA)	26.10.1990	13	(12)	9
Fabrice Yao (NIG)	29.12.1995		(1)	

Football Club UNA Strassen

	Founded:	1922		
	Stadium:	Complexe Sportif „Jean Wirtz", Strassen (2,000)		
	Trainer:	Manuel Correia (POR)		28.03.1976

Goalkeepers:	DOB	M	(s)	G
Youn Czekanowicz	08.08.2000	23		
Hugo Filipe Nascimento Magalhães (POR)	29.04.1985	2		
Aaditya Pattabiraman	21.05.2003	5	(1)	
Defenders:	**DOB**	**M**	**(s)**	**G**
Alen Agović	28.11.1997	13	(6)	
Denis Agović	13.07.1993	23		
Gauthier Bernardelli (FRA)	21.08.1992	15	(3)	5
Tony Mastrangelo	01.09.1994	7	(5)	
Tom Siebenaler	28.09.1990	20		2
Alan Stulin (POL)	05.06.1990	23	(1)	
Midfielders:	**DOB**	**M**	**(s)**	**G**
Cédric Baiverlin	12.03.2003	7	(2)	
Rafael Delgado	16.06.1995	1	(2)	

	DOB	M	(s)	G
Ryunosuke Hayasaka (JPN)	07.06.1994	25	(1)	3
Khalid Lahyani (GER)	24.02.1993	20	(4)	
Kevin Lourenço Joaquim	12.05.1992	23	(3)	3
Ben Payal	08.09.1988	11	(8)	
Benjamin Schmit (BEL)	24.01.1997	29	(1)	4
Florian Weirich (GER)	23.09.1990	5	(13)	1
Forwards:	**DOB**	**M**	**(s)**	**G**
Frederick Kyereh (GER)	18.10.1993	4	(9)	2
Omar Natami	15.12.1998	22	(2)	3
Stefan Rocha Lopes	24.09.1998	12	(11)	1
Benjamin Runser (FRA)	04.09.1991	23	(1)	13
Manfredas Ruzgis (LTU)	05.01.1997	3	(1)	1
Sebastian Szimayer (GER)	15.05.1990	14	(10)	4

Union Titus Pétange

	Founded:	2015	
	Stadium:	Stade Municipal de Pétange, Pétange (2,400)	
	Trainer:	Ismaël Bouzid (ALG)	21.07.1983
	[01.10.2020]	Nicolas Huysman (FRA)	09.02.1968
	[23.03.2021]	Nicolas-Charles Grezault (FRA)	19.04.1982

Goalkeepers:	DOB	M	(s)	G
André Barrela	22.01.2001	10		
Boris Bassene (SEN)	16.09.1993	1		
Tom Otellé	20.01.1998	19	(1)	
Defenders:	**DOB**	**M**	**(s)**	**G**
Syphax Bouaraba (FRA)	15.02.1994		(2)	
Yannick Dias da Graça	13.07.1996	12	(5)	
Mounir Hamzaoui (TUN)	09.12.1987	25		1
Allan Hauguel (FRA)	01.05.1999	25		
Kenan Korac	18.05.2000	3		
Anthony Labata	26.08.2003	1		
Alexandre Laurienté (FRA)	19.11.1989	24	(1)	1
Nathanaël Saintini (FRA)	30.05.2000	18		
Mike Schneider	01.02.1995	10	(7)	
Sonhy Sefil (MTQ)	16.06.1994	12		
Anthony Vacheron (FRA)	05.03.1998	3		
Midfielders:	**DOB**	**M**	**(s)**	**G**
Emir Bijelić (BIH)	16.01.1998	16	(3)	1
Hugo dos Santos de Castro	05.03.2003	1	(2)	
Fodé Dramé	31.03.1997		(1)	

	DOB	M	(s)	G
Bilel El Hamzaoui (FRA)	01.04.1992	23	(2)	4
Abdoul Aziz Kaboré (BFA)	01.01.1994	14	(1)	
Yannick Kakoko (GER)	26.01.1990	11	(5)	
Kevin Kerger	17.11.1994	10	(4)	1
Nestor Kodjia (CIV)	11.06.1989	6	(2)	
Joel Rodrigues da Cruz	18.02.2001	3	(11)	4
Jonathan Salvado Fernandes	21.02.2003	1	(2)	
Denis Stumpf	09.09.1997	6	(3)	
Forwards:	**DOB**	**M**	**(s)**	**G**
Artur Abreu Pereira	11.08.1994	7	(2)	1
Mamadou Baldé	12.12.2002		(1)	
Bi Youan Sylvère Boueti (FRA)	19.07.1996	3	(5)	1
Luca Duriatti	11.02.1998	9	(1)	
Eliot Gashi	15.04.1995	11	(8)	3
Emanuel Robert Maah (FRA)	25.03.1985	7	(2)	4
Eddire Mokrani (ALG)	23.01.1991	17	(6)	1
Jonathan Nanizayamo (FRA)	21.02.1992	2	(1)	
Patrik Teixeira Pinto	10.05.1996	15	(5)	1
Leandro Zorbo (BEL)	01.06.1993	5	(2)	

Football Club Victoria Rosport

	Founded:	01.10.1928	
	Stadium:	VictoriArena, Rosport (1,000)	
	Trainer:	Marc Thomé	04.11.1963

Goalkeepers:	DOB	M	(s)	G
Niklas Bürger (GER)	07.10.1992	8		
Tim Stemper (GER)	22.03.2001	17		
Daniel Ternes (GER)	22.07.1992	5		
Defenders:	**DOB**	**M**	**(s)**	**G**
Eric Brandenburger	08.09.1998	28		1
Gilles Feltes	06.12.1995	15	(4)	3
Gonçalo Rodrigues Fernandes (POR)	05.10.2002	7	(17)	
Noah Rossler	10.04.2003	22	(6)	5
David Soladio (BEL)	18.02.1997	1		1
Dāvis Sprūds (LVA)	28.12.1998	17	(1)	2
Johannes Steinbach (GER)	02.07.1992	21		
Julius von Kymmel	27.10.2002	2	(2)	
Noa Windal	18.04.2002	1	(3)	
Midfielders:	**DOB**	**M**	**(s)**	**G**
Daniel Bartsch (GER)	07.05.1987	25	(3)	2
Michel Bechtold	01.07.1995	9	(8)	

	DOB	M	(s)	G
Gabriel Gaspar Pereira	20.07.1990	23	(3)	
Timo Heinz (GER)	06.03.1991	24	(6)	2
Marc Inhestern (GER)	18.09.1994		(1)	
Mathieu Leroux (FRA)	26.03.1996	29	(1)	9
Kevin Marques	16.01.1998	24	(2)	1
Ramiro Soares Valente	26.01.1989	20	(10)	2
Nelson Rodrigues Afonso	28.05.2002	1		
Hamdoo Rujović			(1)	
Dans Sprūds (LVA)	24.08.2004	3		1
Mike Tchantchou	21.08.1998	5	(4)	
Daito Terauchi (JPN)	14.06.1995	6		1
Forwards:	**DOB**	**M**	**(s)**	**G**
Raul Ferreira	18.11.2002		(4)	
Jeff Lascak	13.02.1994	5	(3)	2
Joé Neves Araujo	06.12.2004	5	(9)	
Jordy Soladio (BEL)	12.02.1998	7		6

Football Club Wiltz 71

Founded: 12.03.1971
Stadium: Stade Géitz, Wiltz (2,000)
Trainer: Dan Huet   18.07.1986

Goalkeepers:	DOB	M	(s)	G
Jules Ismaël Djoujou (CMR)	22.12.1990	6		
Olivier Mabille	01.03.1988		(1)	
Ralph Schon	20.01.1990	24		
Defenders:	**DOB**	**M**	**(s)**	**G**
Miguel Dachelet (BEL)	16.01.1988	29		3
Randy Giargiana (BEL)	22.11.1995	29		2
Isidro Mendes Tavares (POR)	25.02.2001		(4)	
Eric Antoine Kaba Ntangu (COD)	21.01.2001	7	(3)	
Wesley Orville (BEL)	08.08.2001	2	(1)	
Mattis Poitoux (BEL)	05.12.2003	1	(5)	
Alexandre Semedo	22.08.1989	12	(10)	
David Vandenbroeck (BEL)	12.07.1985	26	(1)	3
Midfielders:	**DOB**	**M**	**(s)**	**G**
Emir Burkić (SVN)	27.07.1993	27		1
Dany Fernandes	09.05.1994	3	(2)	

	DOB	M	(s)	G
Rodrigue Kouayep (CMR)	07.12.1986	1	(5)	
Beno Kovačević	17.04.2002		(1)	
Dino Mahmutović	11.01.2001	13	(8)	
Edis Osmanović (BIH)	30.06.1988	18	(2)	7
Chris Philipps	08.03.1994	17	(2)	4
Pita Schimei (BEL)	28.07.1998	15	(7)	3
Christophe Schroeder	24.05.2000	5	(10)	
Luigi Vaccaro (BEL)	26.03.1991	19	(1)	5
Forwards:	**DOB**	**M**	**(s)**	**G**
Ben Biver	31.10.1997	26	(3)	1
Rabbi-Daudet Djongambo Dihumba (BEL)	01.03.1999	1	(3)	
Bryan Gonçalves Dos Santos	14.09.2002	1	(6)	
Denis Dragolovcanin	17.12.1990		(4)	
Sanel Ibrahimović (BIH)	24.11.1987	29		10
David Timmermans (BEL)	10.04.1993	19	(4)	6

SECOND LEVEL
Éierepromotioun / Promotion d'Honneur 2020/2021

1.	US Rumelange	7	6	0	1	23	-	8	18
2.	US Esch/Alzette	7	5	2	0	18	-	7	17
3.	FC Mondercange	7	5	0	2	14	-	8	15
4.	FC Jeunesse Canach	6	4	1	1	18	-	9	13
5.	FC Marisca Mersch	7	4	0	3	12	-	9	12
6.	FC Yellow Boys Weiler-la-Tour	7	3	2	2	14	-	9	11
7.	FC Alisontia Steinsel	6	3	2	1	11	-	6	11
8.	FC Jeunesse Junglinster	7	3	1	3	10	-	12	10
9.	FC Blô-Weiss Medernach	6	2	2	2	12	-	13	8
10.	SC Bettembourg	7	2	1	4	12	-	17	7
11.	FC Atert Bissen	7	2	1	4	13	-	21	7
12.	FC Mamer 32	7	1	2	4	12	-	14	5
13.	FC Schifflange 95	7	1	2	4	10	-	15	5
14.	Union Mertert/Wasserbillig	6	1	2	3	5	-	15	5
15.	FC Berdenia Berbourg	7	1	2	4	9	-	20	5
16.	UN Kaerjeng 97	7	1	0	6	9	-	19	3

The championship was suspended after 7 Rounds due to COVID-19 pandemic.

NATIONAL TEAM

INTERNATIONAL MATCHES
(16.07.2020 – 15.07.2021)

05.09.2020	Bakı	Azerbaijan - Luxembourg	1-2(1-0)	(UNL)
08.09.2020	Lëtzebuerg	Luxembourg - Montenegro	0-1(0-0)	(UNL)
07.10.2020	Lëtzebuerg	Luxembourg - Liechtenstein	1-2(0-1)	(F)
10.10.2020	Lëtzebuerg	Luxembourg - Cyprus	2-0(2-0)	(UNL)
13.10.2020	Podgorica	Montenegro - Luxembourg	1-2(1-1)	(UNL)
11.11.2020	Lëtzebuerg	Luxembourg - Austria	0-3(0-0)	(F)
14.11.2020	Nicosia	Cyprus - Luxembourg	2-1(1-1)	(UNL)
17.11.2020	Lëtzebuerg	Luxembourg - Azerbaijan	0-0	(UNL)
24.03.2021	Debrecen	Qatar - Luxembourg	1-0(1-0)	(F)
27.03.2021	Dublin	Republic of Ireland - Luxembourg	0-1(0-0)	(WCQ)
30.03.2021	Lëtzebuerg	Luxembourg - Portugal	1-3(1-1)	(WCQ)
02.06.2021	Málaga	Norway - Luxembourg	1-0(0-0)	(F)
06.06.2021	Lëtzebuerg	Luxembourg - Scotland	0-1(0-1)	(F)

05.09.2020   AZERBAIJAN - LUXEMBOURG   1-2(1-0)   2nd UEFA Nations League C, Group 1
Bakı Olimpiya Stadionu, Bakı; Referee: Chris Kavanagh (England); Attendance: 0
LUX: Anthony Moris, Lars Christian Krogh Gerson, Laurent Jans (Cap), Dirk Carlson, Vahid Selimović, Christopher Martins Pereira, Olivier Thill (58.Danel Sinani), Vincent Thill (90+1.Aldin Skenderović), Maurice John Deville (52.Stefano Bensi), Gerson Rodrigues Correia Leal, Leandro Barreiro Martins. Trainer: Luc Holtz.
Goals: Anton Krivotsyuk (48 own goal), Gerson Rodrigues Correia Leal (72 penalty).

08.09.2020   LUXEMBOURG - MONTENEGRO   0-1(0-0)   2nd UEFA Nations League C, Group 1
Stade "Josy Barthel", Lëtzebuerg; Referee: Lawrence Visser (Belgium); Attendance: 0
LUX: Anthony Moris, Lars Christian Krogh Gerson, Laurent Jans (Cap), Dirk Carlson, Vahid Selimović, Christopher Martins Pereira [sent off 84], Olivier Thill, Danel Sinani, Vincent Thill, Leandro Barreiro Martins, Gerson Rodrigues Correia Leal. Trainer: Luc Holtz.

07.10.2020   **LUXEMBOURG - LIECHTENSTEIN**   **1-2(0-1)**   Friendly International
Stade "Josy Barthel", Lëtzebuerg; Referee: Alexandre Boucaut (Belgium); Attendance: 0
LUX: Ralph Schon, Kevin Malget, Laurent Jans (Cap) (46.Marvin Martins Santos da Graça), Michael Gonçalves Pinto (46.Leandro Barreiro Martins), Tim Hall, Dirk Carlson (46.Edvin Muratović), Florian Bohnert, Aldin Skenderović, Olivier Thill (46.Timothé Rupil), Stefano Bensi (64.Danel Sinani), Maurice John Deville (64.Gerson Rodrigues Correia Leal). Trainer: Luc Holtz.
Goal: Gerson Rodrigues Correia Leal (72 penalty).

10.10.2020   **LUXEMBOURG - CYPRUS**   **2-0(2-0)**   2nd UEFA Nations League C, Group 1
Stade "Josy Barthel", Lëtzebuerg; Referee: Donald Robertson (Scotland); Attendance: 1,334
LUX: Anthony Moris, Lars Christian Krogh Gerson, Laurent Jans (Cap), Michael Gonçalves Pinto (68.Stefano Bensi), Dirk Carlson, Vahid Selimović (69.Marvin Martins Santos da Graça), Olivier Thill, Vincent Thill, Leandro Barreiro Martins, Gerson Rodrigues Correia Leal, Danel Sinani (79.Aldin Skenderović). Trainer: Luc Holtz.
Goals: Danel Sinani (12, 26).

13.10.2020   **MONTENEGRO - LUXEMBOURG**   **1-2(1-1)**   2nd UEFA Nations League C, Group 1
Stadion pod Goricom, Podgorica; Referee: Sascha Stegemann (Germany); Attendance: 0
LUX: Anthony Moris, Lars Christian Krogh Gerson, Laurent Jans (Cap), Michael Gonçalves Pinto, Aldin Skenderović, Dirk Carlson, Vincent Thill (58.Maurice John Deville), Leandro Barreiro Martins, Gerson Rodrigues Correia Leal, Edvin Muratović (89.Marvin Martins Santos da Graça), Danel Sinani (90+3.Olivier Thill [sent off 90+6]). Trainer: Luc Holtz.
Goals: Edvin Muratović (42), Danel Sinani (86).

11.11.2020   **LUXEMBOURG - AUSTRIA**   **0-3(0-0)**   Friendly International
Stade "Josy Barthel", Lëtzebuerg; Referee: Amaury Delerue (France); Attendance: 0
LUX: Anthony Moris, Lars Christian Krogh Gerson (Cap) (46.Florian Bohnert), Marvin Martins Santos da Graça, Enes Mahmutović, Dirk Carlson (46.Danel Sinani), Aldin Skenderović (46.Seid Korac), Leandro Barreiro Martins (46.Laurent Jans), Stefano Bensi, Maurice John Deville, Edvin Muratović (67.Gerson Rodrigues Correia Leal), Vincent Thill (46.Vahid Selimović). Trainer: Luc Holtz.

14.11.2020   **CYPRUS - LUXEMBOURG**   **2-1(1-1)**   2nd UEFA Nations League C, Group 1
Stádio GSP, Nicosia; Referee: Referee: Mattias Gestranius (Finland); Attendance: 0
LUX: Anthony Moris, Lars Christian Krogh Gerson, Laurent Jans (Cap), Michael Gonçalves Pinto, Dirk Carlson, Vahid Selimović [sent off 33], Vincent Thill (70.Maurice John Deville), Leandro Barreiro Martins, Gerson Rodrigues Correia Leal, Edvin Muratović (55.Aldin Skenderović), Danel Sinani. Trainer: Luc Holtz.
Goals: Ioannis Kousoulos (5 own goal).

17.11.2020   **LUXEMBOURG - AZERBAIJAN**   **0-0**   2nd UEFA Nations League C, Group 1
Stade "Josy Barthel", Lëtzebuerg; Referee: Felix Zwayer (Germany); Attendance: 100
LUX: Ralph Schon, Lars Christian Krogh Gerson, Laurent Jans (Cap), Michael Gonçalves Pinto, Aldin Skenderović (90+1.Florian Bohnert), Enes Mahmutović, Vincent Thill (80.Sébastien Thill), Leandro Barreiro Martins, Maurice John Deville (67.Stefano Bensi), Edvin Muratović (90+1.Marvin Martins Santos da Graça), Danel Sinani. Trainer: Luc Holtz.

24.03.2021   **QATAR - LUXEMBOURG**   **1-0(1-0)**   Friendly International
Nagyerdei Stadion, Debrecen (Hungary); Referee: Miloš Đorđić (Serbia); Attendance: 0
LUX: Anthony Moris, Lars Christian Krogh Gerson (46.Enes Mahmutović), Maxime Chanot, Laurent Jans (Cap) (71.Eldin Dzogović), Michael Gonçalves Pinto (10.Marvin Martins Santos da Graça), Sébastien Thill, Christopher Martins Pereira (60.Aldin Skenderović [sent off 88]), Florian Bohnert, Maurice John Deville (70.Gerson Rodrigues Correia Leal), Edvin Muratović, Danel Sinani (59.Olivier Thill). Trainer: Luc Holtz.

27.03.2021   **REPUBLIC OF IRELAND - LUXEMBOURG**   **0-1(0-0)**   22nd FIFA WC. Qualifiers
Aviva Stadium, Dublin; Referee: Fran Jović (Croatia); Attendance: 0
LUX: Anthony Moris, Maxime Chanot, Laurent Jans (Cap), Marvin Martins Santos da Graça, Enes Mahmutović, Christopher Martins Pereira, Olivier Thill, Vincent Thill (79.Maurice John Deville), Danel Sinani (90+2.Lars Christian Krogh Gerson), Leandro Barreiro Martins, Gerson Rodrigues Correia Leal. Trainer: Luc Holtz.
Goal: Gerson Rodrigues Correia Leal (85).

30.03.2021   **LUXEMBOURG - PORTUGAL**   **1-3(1-1)**   22nd FIFA WC. Qualifiers
Stade "Josy Barthel", Lëtzebuerg; Referee: Sergey Ivanov (Russia); Attendance: 0
LUX: Anthony Moris, Lars Christian Krogh Gerson, Maxime Chanot [sent off 87], Laurent Jans (Cap), Michael Gonçalves Pinto (66.Marvin Martins Santos da Graça), Christopher Martins Pereira (87.Aldin Skenderović), Olivier Thill (58.Sébastien Thill), Vincent Thill (58.Maurice John Deville), Leandro Barreiro Martins, Gerson Rodrigues Correia Leal, Danel Sinani (87.Edvin Muratović). Trainer: Luc Holtz.
Goal: Gerson Rodrigues Correia Leal (30).

02.06.2021   **NORWAY - LUXEMBOURG**   **1-0(0-0)**   Friendly International
Estadio La Rosaleda, Málaga (Spain); Referee: Kristoffer Karlsson (Sweden); Attendance: 0
LUX: Anthony Moris, Laurent Jans (Cap), Michael Gonçalves Pinto (81.Eric Veiga), Marvin Martins Santos da Graça (60.Florian Bohnert), Enes Mahmutović, Dirk Carlson, Christopher Martins Pereira (69.Sébastien Thill), Olivier Thill (59.Vahid Selimović), Maurice John Deville (81.Daniel da Mota Alves), Gerson Rodrigues Correia Leal, Danel Sinani. Trainer: Luc Holtz.

06.06.2021   **LUXEMBOURG - SCOTLAND**   **0-1(0-1)**   Friendly International
Stade "Josy Barthel", Lëtzebuerg; Referee: Eldorjan Hamiti (Albania); Attendance: 1,000
LUX: Anthony Moris, Laurent Jans (Cap), Michael Gonçalves Pinto, Enes Mahmutović, Dirk Carlson, Vahid Selimović [sent off 35], Sébastien Thill (84.Marvin Martins Santos da Graça), Aldin Skenderović (84.Daniel da Mota Alves), Maurice John Deville (64.Florian Bohnert), Gerson Rodrigues Correia Leal, Danel Sinani (71.Olivier Thill). Trainer: Luc Holtz.

NATIONAL TEAM PLAYERS
(16.07.2020 – 15.07.2021)

Name	DOB	Caps	Goals	2020/2021:	Club
Goalkeepers					
Anthony MORIS	29.04.1990	39	0	2020/2021:	*Royale Union Saint-Gilloise (BEL)*
Ralph SCHON	20.01.1990	13	0	2020:	*FC Wiltz 71*
Defenders					
Dirk CARLSON	01.04.1998	32	0	2020/2021:	*Karlsruher SC (GER)*
Maxime CHANOT	21.11.1989	42	3	2020/2021:	*New York City FC (USA)*
Eldin DZOGOVIĆ	08.06.2003	1	0	2021:	*1.FC Magdeburg (GER)*
Tim HALL	15.04.1997	4	0	2020:	*Gil Vicente FC Barcelos (POR)*
Seid KORAC	20.10.2001	1	0	2020:	*1.FC Nürnberg (GER)*
Enes MAHMUTOVIĆ	22.05.1997	17	0	2020/2021:	*FK Lviv (UKR)*
Kevin MALGET	15.01.1991	35	2	2020:	*FC Swift Hesperange*
Marvin MARTINS Santos da Graça	17.02.1995	17	1	2020/2021:	*Casa Pia Atlético Clube Lisboa (POR)*
Michael "Mica" Gonçalves PINTO	04.06.1993	9	0	2020/2021:	*Sparta Rotterdam (NED)*
Vahid SELIMOVIĆ	03.04.1997	9	1	2020/2021:	*OFI Heraklion (GRE)*
Eric VEIGA	18.02.1997	3	0	2021:	*UD Vilafranquense Vila Franca de Xira (POR)*
Midfielders					
Leandro BARREIRO Martins	03.01.2000	26	1	2020/2021:	*1.FSV Mainz 05 (GER)*
Lars Christian Krogh GERSON	05.02.1990	85	4	2020:	*IFK Norrköping (SWE)*
				08.02.2021:	*Racing Santander (ESP)*
Laurent JANS	05.08.1992	77	1	2020:	*FC Metz (FRA)*
				05.10.2020->	*R Standard Liège (DEN)*
Christopher MARTINS Pereira	19.02.1997	44	1	2020/2021:	*BSC Young Boys Bern (SUI)*
Gerson RODRIGUES Correia Leal	20.06.1995	36	7	2020/2021:	*FK Dinamo Kyiv (UKR)*
Timothé RUPIL	12.06.2003	1	0	2020:	*1. FSV Mainz 05 (GER)*
Danel SINANI	05.04.1997	34	3	2020/2021:	*KVRS Waasland-Beveren (BEL)*
Aldin SKENDEROVIĆ	28.06.1997	23	0	2020/2021:	*FC Progrès Niederkorn*
Olivier THILL	17.12.1997	32	2	2020:	*FK Ufa (RUS) until 17.10.2020 -> Unattached*
				01.01.2021->	*FK Vorskla Poltava (UKR)*
Sébastien THILL	01.02.1994	14	1	2020:	*FK Tambov (RUS)*
				18.01.2021->	*FC Sheriff Tiraspol (MDA)*
Vincent THILL	04.02.2000	38	3	2020:	*FC Metz (FRA)*
				10.09.2020->	*CS Nacional Funchal (POR)*
Forwards					
Stefano BENSI	11.08.1988	55	5	2020/2021:	*CS Fola Esch*
Florian BOHNERT	09.11.1997	22	1	2020/2021:	*1.FSV Mainz 05 (GER)*
Daniel DA MOTA Alves	11.09.1985	101	7	2020/2021:	*AC Desenzano Calvina Caravaggio (ITA)*
Maurice John DEVILLE	31.07.1992	52	3	2020/2021:	*1.FC Saarbrücken (GER)*
Edvin MURATOVIĆ	15.02.1997	7	1	2020/2021:	*F91 Dudelange*
Trainer					
Luc HOLTZ [from 03.08.2010]		14.06.1969		102 M; 20 W; 18 D; 64 L; 78-202	

MALTA

The Country:
Republic of Malta (Repubblika ta' Malta)
Capital: Valletta
Surface: 316 km²
Inhabitants: 514,564 [2019]
Time: UTC+1

The FA:
Assoċjazzjoni tal-Futbol ta' Malta
Millennium Stand, Floor 2 National Stadium, Ta'Qali, ATD4000 Malta
Tel: +356 23 386 000
Foundation date: 1900
Member of FIFA since: 1959
Member of UEFA since: 1960
Website: www.mfa.com.mt

NATIONAL TEAM RECORDS

RECORDS		
First international match:	24.02.1957, Gzira:	Malta – Austria 2-3
Most international caps:	Michael Mifsud	- 143 caps (2000-2020)
Most international goals:	Michael Mifsud	- 42 goals / 143 caps (2000-2020)

UEFA EUROPEAN CHAMPIONSHIP	
1960	Did not enter
1964	Qualifiers
1968	Did not enter
1972	Qualifiers
1976	Qualifiers
1980	Qualifiers
1984	Qualifiers
1988	Qualifiers
1992	Qualifiers
1996	Qualifiers
2000	Qualifiers
2004	Qualifiers
2008	Qualifiers
2012	Qualifiers
2016	Qualifiers
2020	Qualifiers

FIFA WORLD CUP	
1930	Did not enter
1934	Did not enter
1938	Did not enter
1950	Did not enter
1954	Did not enter
1958	Did not enter
1962	Did not enter
1966	Did not enter
1970	Did not enter
1974	Qualifiers
1978	Qualifiers
1982	Qualifiers
1986	Qualifiers
1990	Qualifiers
1994	Qualifiers
1998	Qualifiers
2002	Qualifiers
2006	Qualifiers
2010	Qualifiers
2014	Qualifiers
2018	Qualifiers

OLYMPIC TOURNAMENTS	
1908	-
1912	-
1920	-
1924	-
1928	-
1936	-
1948	-
1952	-
1956	-
1960	Did not enter
1964	Did not enter
1968	Did not enter
1972	Withdrew
1976	Did not enter
1980	Did not enter
1984	Did not enter
1988	Did not enter
1992	Qualifiers
1996	Qualifiers
2000	Qualifiers
2004	Qualifiers
2008	Qualifiers
2012	Qualifiers
2016	Qualifiers

UEFA NATIONS LEAGUE	
2018/2019	League D
2020/2021	League D

FIFA CONFEDERATIONS CUP 1992-2017
None

MALTESE CLUB HONOURS IN EUROPEAN CLUB COMPETITIONS:

European Champion Clubs' Cup (1956-1992) / UEFA Champions League (1993-2021)
None

Fairs Cup (1858-1971) / UEFA Cup (1972-2009) / UEFA Europa League (2010-2021)
None

UEFA Super Cup (1972-2020)
None

European Cup Winners' Cup 1961-1999*
None

*defunct competition

	CHAMPIONS	CUP WINNERS	BEST GOALSCORERS	
1909/1910	Floriana FC	-	Salvu Samuele (Floriana FC)	4
1910/1911	*No championship*	-	-	
1911/1912	Floriana FC	-	*not known*	
1912/1913	Floriana FC	-	*not known*	
1913/1914	Hamrun Spartans FC	-	*not known*	
1914/1915	Valletta United FC	-	*not known*	
1915/1916	*No championship*	-	-	
1916/1917	St. George's FC	-	*not known*	
1917/1918	Hamrun Spartans FC	-	*not known*	
1918/1919	The King's Own Malta Regiment	-	*not known*	
1919/1920	Sliema Wanderers FC	-	*not known*	
1920/1921	Floriana FC	-	*not known*	
1921/1922	Floriana FC	-	*not known*	
1922/1923	Sliema Wanderers FC	-	*not known*	
1923/1924	Sliema Wanderers FC	-	*not known*	
1924/1925	Floriana FC	-	*not known*	
1925/1926	Sliema Wanderers FC	-	*not known*	
1926/1927	Floriana FC	-	*not known*	
1927/1928	Floriana FC	-	*not known*	
1928/1929	Floriana FC	-	P. Friggieri (Floriana FC)	4
1929/1930	Sliema Wanderers FC	-	*not known*	
1930/1931	Floriana FC	-	C. Cauchi (Floriana FC)	4
1931/1932	Valletta United FC	-	not known	
1932/1933	Sliema Wanderers FC	-	not known	
1933/1934	Sliema Wanderers FC	-	A. Brincat (Sliema Wanderers FC)	2
1934/1935	Floriana FC	Sliema Wanderers FC	Tony Nicholl (Sliema Wanderers FC)	11
1935/1936	Sliema Wanderers FC	Sliema Wanderers FC	Anton Mayerhoffer (AUT, Floriana FC)	3
1936/1937	Floriana FC	Sliema Wanderers FC	George Albert Bond (ENG, Floriana FC)	4
1937/1938	Sliema Wanderers FC	Floriana FC	Tony Nicholl (Sliema Wanderers FC) C. Cauchi (Floriana FC)	5
1938/1939	Sliema Wanderers FC	Melita FC St. Julian's	Tony Nicholl (Sliema Wanderers FC)	8
1939/1940	Sliema Wanderers FC	Sliema Wanderers FC	Tony Nicholl (Sliema Wanderers FC)	18
1940-1944	*No championship*	-	-	
1944/1945	Valletta FC	Floriana FC	Tony Nicholl (Sliema Athletics FC)	6
1945/1946	Valletta FC	Sliema Wanderers FC	*not known*	
1946/1947	Hamrun Spartans FC	Floriana FC	Maurice Decesare (Melita FC St. Julian's) C. Galea (Floriana FC)	11
1947/1948	Valletta FC	Sliema Wanderers FC	Freddie Landolina (Hamrun Spartans FC)	16
1948/1949	Sliema Wanderers FC	Floriana FC	Salvinu Schembri (Valletta FC) Tony Nicholl (Sliema Wanderers FC)	11
1949/1950	Floriana FC	Floriana FC	Pace (Valletta FC)	16
1950/1951	Floriana FC	Sliema Wanderers FC	Pullu Demanuele (Valletta FC)	14
1951/1952	Floriana FC	Sliema Wanderers FC	Lolly Borg (Floriana FC)	17
1952/1953	Floriana FC	Floriana FC	Pace (Valletta FC)	9
1953/1954	Sliema Wanderers FC	Floriana FC	Tony Nicholl (Sliema Wanderers FC)	12
1954/1955	Floriana FC	Floriana FC	Lolly Borg (Floriana FC) Tony Cauchi (Floriana FC)	13
1955/1956	Sliema Wanderers FC	Sliema Wanderers FC	Sammy Nicholl (Sliema Wanderers FC)	15
1956/1957	Sliema Wanderers FC	Floriana FC	Sammy Nicholl (Sliema Wanderers FC)	14
1957/1958	Floriana FC	Floriana FC	Pullu Demanuele (Floriana FC)	14
1958/1959	Valletta FC	Sliema Wanderers FC	A. Cassar (Hamrun Spartans FC)	11
1959/1960	Valletta FC	Valletta FC	F. Zammit (Valletta FC) M. Azzopardi (Valletta FC)	12
1960/1961	Hibernians FC Paola	Floriana FC	Tony Cauchi (Floriana FC)	12
1961/1962	Floriana FC	Hibernians FC Paola	Tony Cauchi (Floriana FC)	17
1962/1963	Valletta FC	Sliema Wanderers FC	M. Azzopardi (Valletta FC)	20
1963/1964	Sliema Wanderers FC	Valletta FC	A. Borg (Valletta FC)	11
1964/1965	Sliema Wanderers FC	Sliema Wanderers FC	Joseph Cini (Sliema Wanderers FC)	12
1965/1966	Sliema Wanderers FC	Floriana FC	John Bonnett (Sliema Wanderers FC) Ronald Cocks (Sliema Wanderers FC)	6
1966/1967	Hibernians FC Paola	Floriana FC	A. Delia (Hibernians FC Paola)	8
1967/1968	Floriana FC	Sliema Wanderers FC	Joseph Cini (Sliema Wanderers FC)	10
1968/1969	Hibernians FC Paola	Sliema Wanderers FC	C. Cassar (Hibernians FC Paola)	9
1969/1970	Floriana FC	Hibernians FC Paola	Joseph Cini (Sliema Wanderers FC) Ronald Cocks (Sliema Wanderers FC)	7
1970/1971	Sliema Wanderers FC	Hibernians FC Paola	Raymond Xuereb (Floriana FC)	5
1971/1972	Sliema Wanderers FC	Floriana FC	Tony Giglio (Valletta FC)	9
1972/1973	Floriana FC	Gżira United FC	C. Borg (Hamrun Spartans FC)	10
1973/1974	Valletta FC	Sliema Wanderers FC	T. Camilleri (Sliema Wanderers FC)	9
1974/1975	Floriana FC	Valletta FC	Raymond Xuereb (Floriana FC)	17

1975/1976	Sliema Wanderers FC	Floriana FC	Richard Aquilina (Sliema Wanderers FC)	9
1976/1977	Floriana FC	Valletta FC	Raymond Xuereb (Floriana FC)	16
1977/1978	Valletta FC	Valletta FC	Leonard Farrugia (Valletta FC)	16
1978/1979	Hibernians FC Paola	Sliema Wanderers FC	C. Brincat (Marsa FC)	11
1979/1980	Valletta FC	Hibernians FC Paola	Emanuel Fabri (Sliema Wanderers FC) Leonard Farrugia (Valletta FC) F. Cristiano (Valletta FC)	15
1980/1981	Hibernians FC Paola	Floriana FC	Ernest Spiteri-Gonzi (Hibernians FC Paola)	13
1981/1982	Hibernians FC Paola	Hibernians FC Paola	Ernest Spiteri-Gonzi (Hibernians FC Paola)	12
1982/1983	Hamrun Spartans FC	Hamrun Spartans FC	Leo Refalo (Hamrun Spartans FC)	7
1983/1984	Valletta FC	Hamrun Spartans FC	Georgi Ivanov (BUL, Hamrun Spartans FC) Charles Muscat (Żurrieq FC)	7
1984/1985	Rabat Ajax FC	Żurrieq FC	Leonard Farrugia (Valletta FC)	9
1985/1986	Rabat Ajax FC	Rabat Ajax FC	Gianluca De Ponti (ITA, Żurrieq FC)	8
1986/1987	Hamrun Spartans FC	Hamrun Spartans FC	Carmel Busuttil (Rabat Ajax FC)	10
1987/1988	Hamrun Spartans FC	Hamrun Spartans FC	Barry Gallagher (ENG, Hamrun Spartans FC)	7
1988/1989	Sliema Wanderers FC	Hamrun Spartans FC	Joseph Zarb (Valletta FC)	11
1989/1990	Valletta FC	Sliema Wanderers FC	Joseph Zarb (Valletta FC)	17
1990/1991	Hamrun Spartans FC	Valletta FC	Joseph Zarb (Valletta FC)	12
1991/1992	Valletta FC	Hamrun Spartans FC	Stefan Sultana (Hamrun Spartans FC)	22
1992/1993	Floriana FC	Floriana FC	Carl Zachhau (DEN, Hibernians FC Paola)	22
1993/1994	Hibernians FC Paola	Floriana FC	Carl Zachhau (DEN, Hibernians FC Paola) Joseph Zarb (Valletta FC)	17
1994/1995	Hibernians FC Paola	Valletta FC	Carl Saunders (ENG, Sliema Wanderers FC)	18
1995/1996	Sliema Wanderers FC	Valletta FC	Aldrin Muscat (Sliema Wanderers FC)	18
1996/1997	Valletta FC	Valletta FC	Danilo Dončić (SRB, Valletta FC)	32
1997/1998	Valletta FC	Hibernians FC Paola	Joseph Brincat (Birkirkara FC/Floriana FC)	19
1998/1999	Valletta FC	Valletta FC	Gilbert Agius (Valletta FC)	20
1999/2000	Birkirkara FC	Sliema Wanderers FC	Michael Mifsud (Sliema Wanderers FC)	21
2000/2001	Valletta FC	Valletta FC	Michael Mifsud (Sliema Wanderers FC)	30
2001/2002	Hibernians FC Paola	Birkirkara FC	Danilo Dončić (SRB, Sliema Wanderers FC)	32
2002/2003	Sliema Wanderers FC	Birkirkara FC	Adrian Mifsud (Hibernians FC Paola) Danilo Dončić (SRB, Sliema Wanderers FC) Michael Galea (Birkirkara FC)	18
2003/2004	Sliema Wanderers FC	Sliema Wanderers FC	Danilo Dončić (SRB, Sliema Wanderers FC)	19
2004/2005	Sliema Wanderers FC	Birkirkara FC	Andrew Cohen (Hibernians FC Paola)	21
2005/2006	Birkirkara FC	Hibernians FC Paola	Michael Galea (Birkirkara FC)	19
2006/2007	Marsaxlokk FC	Hibernians FC Paola	Daniel Bogdanović (Marsaxlokk FC)	31
2007/2008	Valletta FC	Birkirkara FC	Omar Sebastián Monesterolo (ARG, Valletta FC)	19
2008/2009	Hibernians FC Paola	Sliema Wanderers FC	Terence Scerri (Hibernians FC Paola)	26
2009/2010	Birkirkara FC	Valletta FC	Camilo Sanvezzo (BRA, Qormi FC)	24
2010/2011	Valletta FC	Floriana FC	Alfred Effiong (NGA, Marsaxlokk FC)	17
2011/2012	Valletta FC	Hibernians FC Paola	Obinna Obiefule (NGA, Marsaxlokk FC/Mosta FC)	34
2012/2013	Birkirkara FC	Hibernians FC Paola	José Luis Negrín (ESP, Melita FC St. Julian's/Rabat Ajax FC)	22
2013/2014	Valletta FC	Valletta FC	Jhonnattann Benites da Conceiçao (BRA, Birkirkara FC) Edison Luiz dos Santos "Tarabai" (BRA, Hibernians FC Paola)	21
2014/2015	Hibernians FC Paola	Birkirkara FC	Jorginho (BRA, Hibernians FC Paola) Edison Luiz dos Santos "Tarabai" (BRA, Hibernians FC Paola)	25
2015/2016	Valletta FC	Sliema Wanderers FC	Mario Fontanella (ITA, Floriana FC)	20
2016/2017	Hibernians FC Paola	Floriana FC	Bojan Kaljević (MNE, Balzan FC)	23
2017/2018	Valletta FC	Valletta FC	Amadou Samb (SEN, Gżira United FC)	21
2018/2019	Valletta FC	Balzan FC	Taylon Nicolas Correa Marcolino (BRA, Hibernians FC Paola)	19
2019/2020	Floriana FC	*Competition abandoned*	Kristian Keqi (ALB, Floriana FC)	14
2020/2021	Hamrun Spartans FC	*Competition abandoned*	Kevin Duvan Ante Rosero (COL, Santa Luċija FC)	17

NATIONAL CHAMPIONSHIP
Maltese Premier League 2020/2021
(19.09.2020 – 07.03.2021)

Results

Round 1 [19-21.09.2020]
Żejtun Corinthians - St. Luċija FC 2-2(0-1)
Mosta FC - Gudja United 2-2(1-0)
Lija Athletic - Senglea Athletic 4-0(2-0)
Tarxien Rainbows - Balzan FC 0-1(0-0)
Sliema Wanderers - Hibernians FC 3-1(1-1)
Floriana FC - Gżira United 2-1(1-1)
Ħamrun Spartans - Sirens FC 5-1(4-1)
Valletta FC - Birkirkara FC 4-2(2-1)

Round 2 [25-27.09.2020]
Senglea Athletic - Żejtun Corinthians 1-1(1-0)
Sirens FC - Sliema Wanderers 0-0
Birkirkara FC - Mosta FC 0-3(0-0)
Gudja United - Lija Athletic 2-0(1-0)
Balzan FC - Valletta FC 0-1(0-1)
Gżira United - Tarxien Rainbows 1-1(0-0)
St. Luċija FC - Ħamrun Spartans 1-4(0-4)
Hibernians FC - Floriana FC 3-1(1-0)

Round 3 [30.09.-01.10.2020]
Tarxien Rainbows - Hibernians FC 0-1(0-0)
Lija Athletic - Birkirkara FC 0-0
Ħamrun Spartans - Senglea Athletic 3-0(2-0)
Valletta FC - Gżira United 1-3(1-1)
Mosta FC - Balzan FC 3-3(0-2)
Floriana FC - Sirens FC 3-2(1-1)
Żejtun Corinthians - Gudja United 0-1(0-0)
Sliema Wanderers - St. Luċija FC 3-1(2-0)

Round 4 [16-18.10.2020]
Gżira United - Mosta FC 6-1(4-1)
St. Luċija FC - Floriana FC 2-1(0-1)
Balzan FC - Lija Athletic 1-0(1-0)
Gudja United - Ħamrun Spartans 0-1(0-0)
Birkirkara FC - Żejtun Corinthians 2-3(2-2)
Hibernians FC - Valletta FC 1-1(0-1)
Senglea Athletic - Sliema Wanderers 0-2(0-1)
Sirens FC - Tarxien Rainb. 2-2(2-1) [07.11.]

Round 5 [20-21.10.2020]
Lija Athletic - Gżira United 0-3(0-1)
Tarxien Rainbows - St. Luċija FC 0-2(0-1)
Ħamrun Spartans - Birkirkara FC 0-2(0-1)
Żejtun Corinthians - Balzan FC 0-0
Floriana FC - Senglea Athletic 1-0(1-0)
Mosta FC - Hibernians FC 2-3(2-2)
Sliema Wanderers - Gudja United 1-2(1-1)
Valletta FC - Sirens FC 1-1(0-0) [24.11.]

Round 6 [24-26.10.2020]
Senglea Athletic - Tarxien Rainbows 0-5(0-1)
Gżira United - Żejtun Corinthians 2-1(0-1)
St. Luċija FC - Valletta FC 1-1(0-1)
Hibernians FC - Lija Athletic 8-1(3-1)
Gudja United - Floriana FC 1-2(0-2)
Balzan FC - Ħamrun Spartans 2-2(1-1)
Birkirkara FC - Sliema Wanderers 1-2(1-0)
Sirens FC - Mosta FC 2-2(1-2) [22.12.]

Round 7 [30.10.-01.11.2020]
Mosta FC - St. Luċija FC 1-0(1-0)
Żejtun Corinthians - Hibernians FC 2-3(2-2)
Tarxien Rainbows - Gudja United 0-5(0-2)
Ħamrun Spartans - Gżira United 2-2(2-2)
Sliema Wanderers - Balzan FC 3-1(2-0)
Valletta FC - Senglea Athletic 2-1(1-1)
Lija Athletic - Sirens FC 0-2(0-0) [15.11.]
Floriana FC - Birkirkara FC 2-5(1-2) [22.12.]

Round 8 [20-22.11.2020]
St. Luċija FC - Lija Athletic 3-2(0-2)
Sirens FC - Żejtun Corinthians 0-4(0-3)
Gudja United - Valletta FC 0-0
Gżira United - Sliema Wanderers 3-2(1-0)
Hibernians FC - Ħamrun Spartans 2-2(1-2)
Balzan FC - Floriana FC 0-0
Senglea Athletic - Mosta FC 1-3(0-0)
Birkirkara FC - Tarxien Ra. 3-0(1-0) [02.12.]

Round 9 [28-29.11.2020]
Hibernians FC - Sirens FC 1-2(0-1)
Birkirkara FC - Gudja United 3-0(3-0)
Sliema Wanderers - Lija Athletic 4-1(1-1)
Gżira United - St. Luċija FC 2-2(1-2)
Balzan FC - Senglea Athletic 1-1(0-0)
Ħamrun Spartans - Żejtun Corinth. 4-0(1-0)
Tarxien Rainbows - Valletta FC 3-1(1-0)
Floriana FC - Mosta FC 0-2(0-1)

Round 10 [04-06.12.2020]
Lija Athletic - Ħamrun Spartans 2-2(1-1)
Gudja United - Balzan FC 3-2(2-1)
Mosta FC - Tarxien Rainbows 1-0(1-0)
St. Luċija FC - Hibernians FC 0-3(0-1)
Sirens FC - Gżira United 1-0(1-0)
Żejtun Corinth. - Sliema Wanderers 2-4(1-2)
Valletta FC - Floriana FC 0-3(0-1)
Senglea Athletic - Birkirkara FC 1-2(0-1)

Round 11 [08-09.12.2020]
Sirens FC - St. Luċija FC 0-2(0-0)
Sliema Wanderers - Ħamrun Spartans 0-2(0-1)
Gżira United - Hibernians FC 0-1(0-1)
Żejtun Corinthians - Lija Athletic 2-0(0-0)
Birkirkara FC - Balzan FC 2-2(0-2)
Senglea Athletic - Gudja United 0-2(0-0)
Mosta FC - Valletta FC 2-2(2-2)
Tarxien R.- Floriana FC 2-2(1-2) [13.01.2021]

Round 12 [12-14.12.2020]
Balzan FC - Gżira United 0-2(0-1)
Gudja United - Sirens FC 1-3(0-2)
Lija Athletic - Mosta FC 1-1(0-0)
Hibernians FC - Birkirkara FC 0-1(0-1)
Floriana FC - Sliema Wanderers 0-1(0-0)
Valletta FC - Żejtun Corinthians 2-1(0-0)
St. Luċija FC - Senglea Athletic 4-1(0-1)
Ħamrun Spartans - Tarxien R.5-0(2-0) [23.12.]

Round 13 [18-20.12.2020]
Lija Athletic - Valletta FC 1-2(1-1)
Tarxien Rainb. - Sliema Wanderers 1-2(1-0)
Ħamrun Spartans - Floriana FC 3-1(2-1)
Birkirkara FC - Gżira United 1-1(0-0)
Mosta FC - Żejtun Corinthians 3-0(1-0)
Hibernians FC - Balzan FC 2-1(0-0)
St. Luċija FC - Gudja United 3-2(2-1)
Senglea Ath.- Sirens FC 0-1(0-0) [12.01.2021]

Round 14 [05-07.01.2021]
Sirens FC - Birkirkara FC 2-4(2-2)
Balzan FC - St. Luċija FC 1-1(1-1)
Gżira United - Senglea Athletic 4-0(3-0)
Sliema Wanderers - Mosta FC 1-3(0-0)
Żejtun Corinth. - Tarxien Rainbows 3-1(1-0)
Gudja Unit. - Hibernians FC 1-4(0-0) [27.01.]
Valletta FC - Hamrun Spart. 0-3(0-1) [27.01.]
Floriana FC - Lija Athletic 1-2(0-2) [27.01.]

Round 15 [09-10.01.2021]
Hibernians FC - Senglea Athletic 3-0(1-0)
Balzan FC - Sirens FC 1-0(0-0)
Floriana FC - Żejtun Corinthians 0-0
St. Luċija FC - Birkirkara FC 0-0
Ħamrun Spartans - Mosta FC 3-1(1-1)
Gudja United - Gżira United 0-3 *awarded*
Valletta FC - Sliema Wanderers 0-0 [03.02.]
Lija Athletic - Tarxien Rainb.2-0(1-0) [03.02.]

Round 16 [15-17.01.2021]
Sirens FC - Ħamrun Spartans 0-1(0-0)
Gżira United - Floriana FC 4-1(2-0)
Hibernians FC - Sliema Wanderers 1-0(0-0)
Balzan FC - Tarxien Rainbows 0-1(0-1)
St. Luċija FC - Żejtun Corinthians 1-1(0-1)
Senglea Athl. - Lija Athletic 1-3(1-1) [17.02.]
Birkirkara FC - Valletta FC 2-0(1-0) [17.02.]
Gudja United - Mosta FC 0-1(0-0) [17.02.]

Round 17 [22-24.01.2021]
Tarxien Rainbows - Gżira United 0-2(0-0)
Valletta FC - Balzan FC 1-0(1-0)
Floriana FC - Hibernians FC 1-1(0-1)
Lija Athletic - Gudja United 0-1(0-0)
Żejtun Corinthians - Senglea Athletic 3-1(2-0)
Sliema Wanderers - Sirens FC 1-3(0-2)
Mosta FC - Birkirkara FC 0-1(0-0)
Ħamrun Spartans - St. Luċija FC 2-2(0-1)

Round 18 [29-31.01.2021]
Balzan FC - Mosta FC 4-1(2-1)
St. Luċija FC - Sliema Wanderers 0-1(0-0)
Sirens FC - Floriana FC 2-1(0-1)
Hibernians FC - Tarxien Rainbows 2-0(0-0)
Senglea Athletic - Ħamrun Spartans 0-1(0-1)
Gudja United - Żejtun Corinthians 0-1(0-1)
Gżira United - Valletta FC 2-0(1-0)
Birkirkara FC - Lija Athletic 4-1(2-0)

Round 19 [05-07.02.2021]
Żejtun Corinthians - Birkirkara FC 0-3(0-1)
Floriana FC - St. Luċija FC 1-1(1-0)
Lija Athletic - Balzan FC 1-1(1-1)
Tarxien Rainbows - Sirens FC 3-1(0-0)
Mosta FC - Gżira United 1-2(0-2)
Sliema Wanderers - Senglea Athletic 3-1(1-1)
Valletta FC - Hibernians FC 1-4(1-1)
Ħamrun Spartans - Gudja United 3-1(1-0)

Round 20 [13-14.02.2021]
Birkirkara FC - Ħamrun Spartans 0-2(0-1)
Hibernians FC - Mosta FC 2-0(0-0)
St. Luċija FC - Tarxien Rainbows 7-0(2-0)
Senglea Athletic - Floriana FC 0-2(0-1)
Gżira United - Lija Athletic 1-0(0-0)
Sirens FC - Valletta FC 0-1(0-0)
Gudja United - Sliema Wanderers 1-1(0-0)
Balzan FC - Żejtun Corinth. 3-1(3-1) [10.03.]

Round 21 [20-21.02.2021]
Tarxien Rainbows - Senglea Athletic 4-2(2-0)
Sliema Wanderers - Birkirkara FC 2-2(1-1)
Żejtun Corinthians - Gżira United 0-4(0-2)
Floriana FC - Gudja United 1-0(1-0)
Valletta FC - St. Luċija FC 1-0(0-0)
Lija Athletic - Hibernians FC 0-5(0-2)
Mosta FC - Sirens FC 0-0
Ħamrun Spartans - Balzan FC 3-2(2-0)

Round 22 [26-28.02.2021]		Round 23 [06-07.03.2021]	
Gudja United - Tarxien Rainbows	0-2(0-0)	Hamrun Spartans - Hibernians FC	1-0(0-0)
Sirens FC - Lija Athletic	1-1(0-1)	Floriana FC - Balzan FC	0-0
St. Luċija FC - Mosta FC	2-3(0-1)	Tarxien Rainbows - Birkirkara FC	0-3(0-0)
Birkirkara FC - Floriana FC	2-0(0-0)	Lija Athletic - St. Luċija FC	3-1(0-0)
Hibernians FC - Żejtun Corinthians	2-0(1-0)	Sliema Wanderers - Gżira United	2-0(2-0)
Gżira United - Hamrun Spartans	1-2(0-1)	Mosta FC - Senglea Athletic	5-1(1-1)
Balzan FC - Sliema Wanderers	5-1(3-1)	Żejtun Corinthians - Sirens FC	1-1(0-0)
Senglea Athletic - Valletta FC	1-3(0-2)	Valletta FC - Gudja United	2-4(1-0)

Please note: the league was suspended on 10.03.2021 due to COVID-19 pandemic. On 09.04.2021, the MFA Executive Committee decided to terminate the league competition. Hamrun Spartans FC, topping the league at time of suspension, were declared champions.

Final Standings

								Total					Home					Away		
1.	**Hamrun Spartans FC**	23	17	5	1	56	-	20	56	9	2	1	34	-	12	8	3	0	22	- 8
2.	Hibernians FC Paola	23	16	3	4	53	-	20	51	8	2	2	27	-	9	8	1	2	26	- 11
3.	Gżira United FC	23	14	4	5	49	-	21	46	7	2	2	26	-	11	7	2	3	23	- 10
4.	Birkirkara FC	23	13	5	5	45	-	25	44	5	2	4	20	-	14	8	3	1	25	- 11
5.	Sliema Wanderers FC	23	12	4	7	39	-	31	40	6	1	4	23	-	17	6	3	3	16	- 14
6.	Mosta FC	23	10	6	7	41	-	36	36	4	4	3	20	-	14	6	2	4	21	- 22
7.	Valletta FC	23	9	6	8	27	-	35	33	5	2	5	15	-	22	4	4	3	12	- 13
8.	Santa Luċija FC	23	7	8	8	38	-	35	29	5	3	4	24	-	19	2	5	4	14	- 16
9.	Sirens FC San Pawl il-Baħar	23	7	7	9	27	-	35	28	2	4	5	10	-	18	5	3	4	17	- 17
10.	Balzan FC	23	6	9	8	31	-	29	27	5	4	3	18	-	11	1	5	5	13	- 18
11.	Gudja United FC	23	8	3	12	29	-	35	27	2	2	8	9	-	20	6	1	4	20	- 15
12.	Floriana FC	23	7	6	10	26	-	34	27	4	4	4	12	-	15	3	2	6	14	- 19
13.	Żejtun Corinthians FC *(Relegated)*	23	6	6	11	28	-	40	24	3	3	5	15	-	20	3	3	6	13	- 20
14.	Tarxien Rainbows FC *(Relegated)*	23	6	3	14	25	-	48	21	3	1	7	13	-	22	3	2	7	12	- 26
15.	Lija Athletic FC *(Relegated)*	23	5	5	13	25	-	46	20	3	4	5	14	-	18	2	1	8	11	- 28
16.	Senglea Athletic FC *(Relegated)*	23	0	2	21	13	-	62	2	0	1	10	5	-	25	0	1	11	8	- 37

Top goalscorers:	
17 Kevin Duvan Ante Rosero (COL)	*Santa Luċija FC*
14 Bojan Kaljević (MNE)	*Mosta FC*
13 Ailton Jorge dos Santos Soares "Dodô" (CPV)	*Hamrun Spartans FC*
13 Luke Montebello	*Birkirkara FC*
13 Franklin Olanitori Sasere (NGA)	*Hamrun Spartans FC*

NATIONAL CUP
Maltese FA Trophy 2020/2021

Preliminary Round [15-27.12.2020]			
St. George's FC - Pembroke Athleta FC	1-3	Xewkija Tigers FC - Fgura United FC	0-3
Mqabba FC - San Ġwann FC	5-3 aet	Birżebbuġa St. Peter's FC - Siġġiewi FC	2-1 aet
St. Andrews FC - Żurrieq FC	1-0	Kerċem Ajax FC - Marsa FC	0-3
Naxxar Lions FC - Qrendi FC	2-0	Victoria Hotspurs FC - Vittoriosa Stars FC Birgu	1-0
Nadur Youngsters FC - Msida Saint Joseph FC	3-1	Marsaxlokk FC - SK Victoria Wanderers FC	3-0
Għajnsielem FC - Pietà Hotspurs FC	3-1	Oratory Youths FC Victoria - Żebbuġ Rangers FC	1-8

First Round [02-24.02.2021]			
Sirens FC San Pawl il-Baħar - Fgura United FC	5-0	Qormi FC - Tarxien Rainbows FC	0-3
Nadur Youngsters FC - Senglea Athletic FC	2-3	Sannat Lions FC - Hamrun Spartans FC	1-3
Pembroke Athleta FC - Marsaxlokk FC	4-2	Birżebbuġa St. Peter's FC - Xagħra United FC	1-4
Għajnsielem FC - Victoria Hotspurs FC	2-0	Balzan FC - Mosta FC	1-3
Birkirkara FC - Lija Athletic FC	6-0	St. Andrews FC - Sliema Wanderers FC	1-0
Floriana FC - Santa Luċija FC	1-3	Naxxar Lions FC - Swieqi United FC	6-1
Valletta FC - Gudja United FC	2-1	Gżira United FC - Mqabba FC	8-0
Żebbuġ Rangers FC - Marsa FC	0-1	Hibernians FC Paola - Żejtun Corinthians FC	3-0

Second Round [02-04.03.2021]			
Gżira United FC - Tarxien Rainbows FC	4-2 aet	Santa Luċija FC - Mosta FC	0-2
Għajnsielem FC - Birkirkara FC	1-4	Xagħra United FC - Hamrun Spartans FC	0-6
Naxxar Lions FC - St. Andrews FC	0-0 aet; 2-4 pen	Senglea Athletic FC - Valletta FC	0-1
Pembroke Athleta FC - Hibernians FC Paola	0-1	Marsa FC - Sirens FC San Pawl il-Baħar	0-1

The competition was cancelled on 09.04.2021 due to COVID-19 pandemic.

THE CLUBS 2020/2021

Balzan Football Club

Founded: 1937
Stadium: St. Aloysius Sports and Recreational Complex, Birkirkara (100)
Trainer: Mark Miller (ENG) 22.09.1962

Goalkeepers:	DOB	M	(s)	G
Sean Mintoff	13.10.1985	7		
Vukašin Vranješ (SRB)	22.07.1997	16	(1)	
Defenders:	**DOB**	**M**	**(s)**	**G**
Samir Arab	25.03.1994	21	(1)	
Steven Bezzina	05.01.1987	11	(4)	1
Gary Camilleri	05.08.1999	1	(11)	
Zak Grech	21.07.1999		(2)	
Michael Johnson	11.05.1994	18	(2)	4
Moussa Kamara (GAM)	03.04.1999	13	(1)	1
Augustine Loof (NED)	01.01.1996	23		2
Midfielders:	**DOB**	**M**	**(s)**	**G**
Adam Bradshaw	31.10.2001		(5)	
Sean Cipriott	10.09.1997	10	(7)	
William Rupert James Donkin (TPE)	26.12.2000		(3)	
Milan Đurić (SRB)	03.10.1987	8		3

	DOB	M	(s)	G
Paul Fenech	20.12.1986	21		
Neil Frendo	04.01.1999		(5)	
Marcus Grima	22.07.2000	5	(9)	
Markos Moustakis (CYP)	25.10.1999	2		
Stephan Pisani	07.08.1992	16		
Forwards:	**DOB**	**M**	**(s)**	**G**
Aleksa Andrejić (SRB)	24.01.1993	8	(1)	5
Stefan Dimić (SRB)	01.05.1993	14		1
Alfred Effiong	29.11.1984	3	(20)	2
Suleiman Jalu (NED)	20.03.2000	6	(1)	2
Uroš Ljubomirac (SRB)	12.04.1990	21		5
Eric McWoods	21.10.1995	10	(4)	1
Pedro Augusto Mota de Lima (BRA)	13.06.2000	2	(4)	
Moussa Sanoh (NED)	20.07.1995	5	(1)	2
Wéverton Gomes Souza (BRA)	08.03.1992	12	(2)	1

Birkirkara Football Club

Founded: 1950
Stadium: Mġarr Ground, Imgarr (300)
Trainer: Andréas Gerardus Maria Paus (NED) 09.10.1965

Goalkeepers:	DOB	M	(s)	G
Alessandro Guarnone (ITA)	27.03.1999	19		
Andrew James Hogg	02.03.1985	3		
Amary Sylla	16.09.2001	1		
Defenders:	**DOB**	**M**	**(s)**	**G**
Cain Attard	10.09.1994	21		2
Óscar Matías Carniello (URU)	18.09.1988	19		1
Neil Friggieri	14.03.2001		(2)	
Isaac Ntow (GHA)	26.05.1994	4	(4)	
Enrico Pepe	12.11.1989	16		
Francesco Verde (ITA)	18.03.2000	7	(5)	
Kurt Zammit	26.02.1996	16	(4)	1

Midfielders:	**DOB**	**M**	**(s)**	**G**
Claudio Bonanni (ITA)	05.03.1997	18	(5)	2
Roderick Briffa	24.08.1981	14	(3)	
Glending Farrugia	27.03.2003		(6)	
Matthew Guillaumier	09.04.1998	2		
Réginald Mbu Alidor (FRA)	19.05.1993	10	(3)	
Yannick Yankam	12.12.1997	21	(1)	3
Forwards:	**DOB**	**M**	**(s)**	**G**
Caio Henrique Rocha De Almeida Prado(BRA)	11.01.1995	15	(5)	4
Federico Matías Falcone (ARG)	21.02.1990	20	(2)	8
Alex da Paixão Alves „Lecão" (BRA)	17.01.1993	14	(2)	6
Paul Mbong	02.09.2001	17	(4)	3
Luke Montebello	13.08.1995	16	(4)	13

Floriana Football Club

Founded: 1894
Stadium: Independence Arena, Floriana (3,000)
Trainer: Vincenzo Potenza (ITA) 03.05.1970
[25.12.2020] John Buttigieg 05.10.1963
[15.02.2021] Vincenzo Potenza (ITA) 03.05.1970

Goalkeepers:	DOB	M	(s)	G
Ini Etim Akpan (NGA)	03.08.1984	15		
Andrea Cassar	19.12.1992	5		
Justin Spiteri	27.07.1985	3		
Defenders:	**DOB**	**M**	**(s)**	**G**
Moustapha Beye (SEN)	06.08.1995	7	(1)	
Alex Cini	28.10.1991	11	(6)	
Alejandro Garzia	21.03.2002		(1)	
Marcelo Mariano Dias (BRA)	29.09.1985	15	(1)	
Jurgen Pisani	03.09.1992	19	(1)	2
Enzo Adrián Ruiz (ARG)	20.06.1989	20		2
Midfielders:	**DOB**	**M**	**(s)**	**G**
Ulises Jesús Arias (ARG)	05.08.1996	15		1
Ayrton Azzopardi	12.09.1993		(3)	

	DOB	M	(s)	G
Jan Busuttil	06.03.1999	11	(9)	2
Ryan Camenzuli	08.09.1994	20	(2)	1
Francisco Diego Venancio da Silva (BRA)	27.06.1993	15	(2)	
Matías Nicolás García (ARG)	22.07.1996	17		1
Kristian Keqi (ALB)	28.07.1996	21	(1)	6
Nicola Leone (ITA)	26.08.1992	14	(1)	
Brandon Diego Paiber	05.06.1995	14	(6)	2
Forwards:	**DOB**	**M**	**(s)**	**G**
Adriano Louzada e Silva (BRA)	16.02.1994	3		1
Daniel Agius	15.11.1996	1	(11)	
Siraj Arab	25.03.1994	1	(16)	1
Flávio dos Santos da Silva Cheveresan (BRA)	11.12.1988	12	(1)	3
Jeroen Lumu (NED)	27.05.1995	2	(1)	
Tiago Adan Fonseca (BRA)	14.03.1988	12		1

Gudja United Football Club

Founded: 1945
Stadium: „Louis Azzopardi" Stadium, Gudja (1,000)
Trainer: Jesmond Zammit 11.02.1965

Goalkeepers:	DOB	M	(s)	G
Glenn Zammit	05.08.1987	23		
Defenders:	**DOB**	**M**	**(s)**	**G**
Goran Adamović (SRB)	24.04.1987	10		
Juan Andrés Bolaños Ramírez (COL)	22.07.1991	20		1
Jurgen Farrugia	14.08.1991	9	(5)	
Imanol González Benac (ARG)	06.01.1998	21		1
Justin Grioli	20.09.1987	16	(1)	
Neil Anthony Micallef	23.11.1998	11	(7)	
Thomas Veronese (ITA)	02.11.1986	5		
Midfielders:	**DOB**	**M**	**(s)**	**G**
Dale Camilleri	17.10.1992	10	(3)	
Tensior Gusman	24.01.1997	2	(11)	2
Patrick Silva Mota (BRA)	07.08.1992	17		1

	DOB	M	(s)	G
Filip Pankarićan (SRB)	28.03.1993	7		
Lee Pisani	03.07.1999		(3)	
Hubert Vella	07.02.1994	10	(2)	
Forwards:	**DOB**	**M**	**(s)**	**G**
James Brincat	03.12.1996	2	(18)	1
Augusto René Cáseres (ARG)	21.11.1997	5	(4)	
Llywelyn Cremona	07.05.1995	18	(3)	
Élton Alexandre da Silva (BRA)	20.09.1985	6	(4)	1
Aidan Friggieri	28.04.1998	20	(2)	3
Gabriel Mensah (GHA)	05.10.1995	19	(2)	6
Sérgio Pereira Cruz (BRA)	22.08.1988		(1)	
Vanger Conceição da Silva (BRA)	27.01.1987	5	(2)	
Terence Vella	20.04.1990	3	(10)	1
Yuri de Jesus Messias (BRA)	11.09.1991	14		13

Gżira United Football Club

Founded: 1947
Stadium: Gżira Football Ground, Gżira (n/a)
Trainer: Darren Abdilla   10.07.1979

Goalkeepers:	DOB	M	(s)	G
Anthony Curmi	20.11.1982	9		
Justin Haber	09.06.1981	14		
Defenders:	**DOB**	**M**	**(s)**	**G**
Sacha Borg	26.04.1993	20	(1)	
Steve Borg	15.05.1988	22		2
Camilo Del Castillo Escobar (COL)	09.05.1995	4	(1)	
Gabriel Bohrer Mentz (BRA)	11.08.1998	21		
Karl Pulo	30.07.1989		(4)	
Alexander Scicluna	15.07.1999		(1)	
Dexter Xuereb	21.09.1997	8	(7)	
Midfielders:	**DOB**	**M**	**(s)**	**G**
Bahrudin Atajić (BIH)	16.11.1993	5	(2)	1
Clyde Borg	20.03.1992	4	(11)	
Andrew Cohen	13.05.1981	1	(9)	1
Ricardo Calixto Correa Duarte (URU)	20.07.1994	22		8

	DOB	M	(s)	G
Martin George Edward Davis (JAM)	11.10.1996	19		9
Ben Hamed Koné (CIV)	02.11.1987	6	(3)	1
Nicky Muscat	13.07.1996	22		3
Stephen Pisani	07.08.1992	3	(3)	
Zachary Scerri	08.03.1996	1		
Jackson David Usuga Mendonza (COL)	20.04.1998	17		
Forwards:	**DOB**	**M**	**(s)**	**G**
Omar Elouni	16.03.1999		(10)	
Jefferson Mateus de Assis Estácio (BRA)	21.10.1994	18	(4)	4
Rafael Alain Kooh Sohna (CMR)	22.04.1990	6		3
Filype Pinheiro Mendonça „Lipão" (BRA)	11.12.1996	1	(2)	
Máxuell Maia da Silva (BRA)	30.09.1991	9		7
Nevin Portelli	16.09.1999	12	(6)	1
Amadou Samb (SEN)	22.04.1988	8	(2)	5
Abdeen Temitope Abdul	30.04.1995	1		

Ħamrun Spartans Football Club

Founded: 1907
Stadium: "Victor Tedesco" Stadium, Ħamrun (6,000)
Trainer: Mark Buttigieg

Goalkeepers:	DOB	M	(s)	G
Manuel Bartolo	26.08.1983	16		
Jonathan Debono	17.07.1985	5		
Matthias Debono	11.02.2002		(2)	
Pablo Guillermo Sánchez Niño (ENG)	20.10.1995	2		
Defenders:	**DOB**	**M**	**(s)**	**G**
Claude Dielna (FRA)	14.12.1987	2		1
Darko Gojković (SRB)	26.09.1988	20		
Arthur Henrique Ricciardi Oyama (BRA)	14.01.1987	3	(1)	
Michele Laraspata (ITA)	02.06.2001		(1)	
Karl Micallef	08.09.1996	17	(4)	
Nikolai Micallef	17.08.2003		(3)	
Xylon Portelli	19.12.2002		(3)	
Elkin Orlando Serrano Valero (COL)	17.03.1984	21		1
Midfielders:	**DOB**	**M**	**(s)**	**G**
Conor Borg	13.05.1997		(3)	
Darren Borg	18.06.1999	3	(9)	

	DOB	M	(s)	G
Andreas Blas Cittadini (ARG)	15.02.1997	1	(3)	
Juan Carlos Corbalan	03.03.1997	21		
Predrag Djordjević (SRB)	23.08.1989	20		8
Emerson Marcelina (BRA)	24.02.1991	19		
Christopher Galea	04.04.2001		(3)	
Matthew Guillaumier	09.04.1998	19		1
Kieran Higgans	13.08.2001		(2)	
Miguel Tabone	08.01.2002		(1)	
Forwards:	**DOB**	**M**	**(s)**	**G**
Ige Abdullahi Adeshina (NGA)	01.08.1986	11	(12)	3
Ailton Jorge dos Santos Soares "Dodô" (CPV)	06.12.1990	20	(1)	13
Seydou Doumbia (CIV)	31.12.1987	2	(3)	3
Imanol Iriberri (ARG)	04.03.1987	1	(4)	
Soufiane Lagzir (MAR)	25.10.1994	1	(2)	
Marcelo Barbosa Junior (BRA)	10.08.1991	8	(3)	5
Joseph Essien Mbong	15.07.1997	22		7
Franklin Olanitori Sasere (NGA)	27.06.1998	19	(3)	14

Hibernians Football Club Paola

Founded: 1922
Stadium: Hibernians Ground, Paola (2,968)
Trainer: Stefano Sanderra (ITA)   21.06.1967

Goalkeepers:	DOB	M	(s)	G
Rudi Briffa	21.08.1996		(1)	
Matthew Calleja Cremona	14.09.1994	23		
Defenders:	**DOB**	**M**	**(s)**	**G**
Andrei Agius	12.08.1986	21	(1)	2
Leandro Almeida da Silva (BRA)	14.03.1987	22		
Ferdinando Apap	29.07.1992	21		3
Timothy Tabone Desira	15.07.1995		(1)	
Matthew Ellul	23.05.2002		(7)	
Gabriel Izquier Artiles „Gabri Izquier" (ESP)	29.04.1993	21		1
Zachary Grech	25.08.2000	7	(9)	
Sergio Raphael dos Anjos (BRA)	23.10.1992	6	(1)	
Connor Zammit	26.09.1988		(3)	
Midfielders:	**DOB**	**M**	**(s)**	**G**
Jeffries Rudy Cassar	24.01.2001		(1)	
Matthew Farrugia	26.02.2001		(1)	
Gilmar da Silva Ribeiro (BRA)	26.03.1990	5		3

	DOB	M	(s)	G
Jake Grech	18.11.1997	20	(3)	12
Brite Anayochi Ihoumah (NGA)	17.02.2003		(1)	
Bjorn Kristensen	05.04.1993	19		2
Edafe Uzeh (NGA)	22.03.1988	2	(7)	
Dunstan Vella	27.04.1996	16	(4)	4
David Xuereb	30.03.1998		(1)	
Forwards:	**DOB**	**M**	**(s)**	**G**
Tiago Adan Fonseca (BRA)	14.03.1988	4	(3)	2
Ayrton Attard	05.11.2000	10	(11)	1
Kane Bonello	28.11.2000		(1)	
Jurgen Degabriele	10.10.1996	20	(3)	11
Imanol Iriberri (ARG)	04.03.1987	4	(5)	1
Karolis Laukzemis (LTU)	11.03.1992	5	(1)	4
Shola Shodiya (NGA)	17.06.1991	11	(6)	3
José Wilkson Teixeira Rocha (BRA)	22.03.1992	13	(8)	2
Rundell Winchester (TRI)	16.12.1993	3	(8)	2

Lija Athletic Football Club

Founded: 1949
Stadium: Lija Athletic Complex, Lija (500)
Trainer: Joseph Galea

Goalkeepers:	DOB	M	(s)	G
Luke Bonnici	02.09.1986	23		
Dylan Galea	16.02.1996		(1)	
Defenders:	**DOB**	**M**	**(s)**	**G**
Ismael Borg	06.06.2002	12		
Juan Cruz Gill (ARG)	18.07.1983	20		
Clayton Giordimaina	27.10.1987	14	(3)	
Clinch McAllister	23.08.1994	1	(3)	
Pedro Luiz Soares Gusso (BRA)	08.01.1994	8	(1)	1
Valdo Gonçalves Alhinho (POR)	17.12.1988	11	(2)	
Jordan Wells	15.05.2000	1		
Andre White	01.01.1991	5	(3)	
Midfielders:	**DOB**	**M**	**(s)**	**G**
Beppe Antignolo	14.01.1985		(3)	
Antoine Borg	04.04.1994	1		
Gianluca Falzan	12.12.2003		(2)	
Carlos Manuel Flores (MEX)	17.03.1998	13		2

	DOB	M	(s)	G
Neil Micallef	12.01.1999	7	(9)	
Andrea Mizzi	12.09.2001		(1)	
Leon Muscat	17.08.1995	14	(1)	
Daniel Scerri	21.11.1983	13	(9)	
Walter Omar Serrano (ARG)	02.07.1986	10		
Gonzalo Nicolás Virano (ARG)	22.07.1999	11	(1)	
Harry Wood	03.02.2000	11	(3)	
Forwards:	**DOB**	**M**	**(s)**	**G**
Erjon Beu (ALB)	13.07.1991	14		9
Fernando Daniel Brandán (ARG)	27.03.1990	21		7
Carl Cassar	27.03.1997	16		1
Ryan Dalli	18.03.1993	1	(5)	
Ryan Darmanin	12.12.1985	3	(6)	
Alessio Galea	18.05.2000		(1)	
Chevaughn Nicolas Mclaren (JAM)	04.05.1994	3		
Miguel Antonio Pérez Jiménez (COL)	22.09.1992	20		4
Gianluca Zammit	19.08.1999		(4)	

Mosta Football Club

Founded: 1935
Stadium: "Charles Abela" Memorial Stadium, Mosta (600)
Trainer: Davor Filipović (CRO)   13.07.1970

Goalkeepers:	DOB	M	(s)	G
Yves Stéphane Bitseki Moto (GAB)	23.04.1983	5		
Luca Camilleri	30.11.2004		(1)	
Dylan Ciappara	12.07.2002		(1)	
Christoffer Henri Mafoumbi (CGO)	03.03.1994	17		
Andre Spiteri	14.04.2001	1		
Defenders:	**DOB**	**M**	**(s)**	**G**
Miguel Aquilina	18.01.2000		(1)	
Matthew Attard	04.09.2000	1	(6)	
Duane Bonnici	10.10.1995	9	(5)	
Dejan Debono	20.11.2000	9	(6)	
Jonas Rodriguez Ekani (CMR)	13.10.1992	12		
Tyron Farrugia	22.02.1989	20		
Jeferson De Sousa Ferreira (BRA)	24.11.1995	4		
Rafael Morisco da Silva (BRA)	04.08.1986	22		2
Owen Sammut	17.09.2003		(5)	
Laurens Vella	30.09.2001		(2)	
Matteo Vella	26.02.2002		(1)	
Midfielders:	**DOB**	**M**	**(s)**	**G**
Nathan Agius	16.11.2003		(7)	
Johan Bezzina	30.05.1994	15	(2)	1
Nikola Braunović (MNE)	21.07.1997	2	(1)	
William Rupert James Donkin (TPE)	26.12.2000	3	(2)	1
Clayton Failla	08.01.1986	16	(1)	2
Luke Formosa	18.01.2002	1		
Watson Hounkpe (BEN)	31.07.2001	1	(1)	
Santiago Martínez Perlaza (COL)	27.02.1998	2	(1)	
Matías Roberto Muchardi (ARG)	09.02.1988	17		
Divine Naah (GHA)	20.04.1996	6		3
Liam Portelli	21.11.2000	2	(11)	
Kenny Anthony Romero Alvarado (VEN)	03.06.1995	1		
Gianluca Sciberras	02.08.2002	12	(7)	1
Kevin Tulimieri (ITA)	15.03.1992	17	(2)	3
Forwards:	**DOB**	**M**	**(s)**	**G**
Zachary Brincat	24.06.1998	10	(6)	3
Evo Christ Ememe (NGA)	30.04.2001	19		7
Bojan Kaljević (MNE)	25.01.1986	20		14
Michael Mifsud	17.04.1981	5	(3)	2
Nixon Darlanio Reis Cardoso (BRA)	20.07.1992	1	(1)	
Andrei Spiteri	18.04.2000	1	(3)	
Takanori Yokochi (JPN)	27.08.1994	2	(2)	1

Santa Luċija Football Club

Founded: 1974
Stadium: Grawnd Santa Luċija, Santa Luċija (1,000)
Trainer: Oliver Spiteri   04.07.1970

Goalkeepers:	DOB	M	(s)	G
Chrsitopher Farrugia	13.07.2001	10	(2)	
Miguel Montfort	26.06.1986	6		
Andreas Vella I	14.10.1998	7	(1)	
Defenders:	**DOB**	**M**	**(s)**	**G**
Brady Agius	05.09.2002		(1)	
André Fausto Prates Rodrigues (BRA)	02.05.1994	23		1
Romario Camilleri	13.05.2000		(5)	
Kevin Pinheiro Correia (BRA)	16.07.1996	23		3
Liam Mckay	22.05.2001		(5)	
Adam Magri Overend	03.05.2000	16	(1)	1
Nicolas Pulis	29.01.1998	4	(1)	1
Timothy Tabone Desira	15.07.1995	20	(2)	1
Victor Luiz Prestes Filho (BRA)	05.12.1997	19		
Midfielders:	**DOB**	**M**	**(s)**	**G**
Jeremy Delmar	27.07.2001		(4)	
Izaías Junio Duarte da Silva (BRA)	20.08.1999	4		
Leandro Wallace Motta dos Santos (BRA)	14.01.1992	8	(5)	
Rei Tachikawa (JPN)	18.01.1998	16	(1)	3
Edafe Uzeh (NGA)	22.03.1988	4		
Andreas Vella II	27.01.2001	1	(6)	
Jacques Vella Critien	14.03.2000	1	(3)	
Kieran Xuereb	22.07.1998	12	(8)	
Jamie Zerafa	02.03.1998	20		1
Forwards:	**DOB**	**M**	**(s)**	**G**
Alan da Silva Souza (BRA)	09.12.1987	20		6
Michael Camilleri	23.03.1993	7	(12)	1
Augusto René Cáseres (ARG)	21.11.1997	7	(1)	1
Gláucio José de Araújo Silva (BRA)	03.02.1994	3	(4)	3
Kevin Duvan Ante Rosero (COL)	03.12.1998	22		17

Senglea Athletic Football Club

Founded: 22.03.1943
Stadium: Corradino C Stadium, Dingli (100)
Trainer: Ryan Newell   27.09.1984
[26.10.2020] Clive Mizzi   01.05.1973

Goalkeepers:	DOB	M	(s)	G
Dorian Bugeja	24.01.1998	1	(2)	
Matthew Farrugia	17.03.1985	21		
Jonathan Martinelli	19.10.1994	1		
Andrew Zammit	30.11.1995		(1)	
Defenders:	**DOB**	**M**	**(s)**	**G**
Alan Abela	01.11.1992	21	(2)	
Joseph Attard	14.10.2002		(6)	
Samuel Buhagiar	14.11.1995	5	(1)	
Charlo Buttigieg	13.06.1998		(2)	
Zachary Cassar	02.11.1991	21	(1)	
Dion Fava	29.01.1995	8	(2)	
Lee Galea	14.02.1988	1	(1)	
Dejan Kukić (SRB)	04.08.1995	18		
Uroš Parežanin (SVN)	22.07.1998	4		
Andre Scicluna	22.09.1988	12	(1)	
Nikola Terzin (SRB)	25.01.1996	7	(2)	
Sergio Osagho Uyi (NGA)	22.06.1993	9		
Midfielders:	**DOB**	**M**	**(s)**	**G**
Firaz Aboulezz	25.07.1985	4	(6)	
Clyde Borg	20.03.1992	1		
Ricardo Adrian Martin (JAM)	04.06.1988	2	(3)	
Igor Mišan (SRB)	05.05.1990	17	(2)	
Luis Carlos Riascos Torres (COL)	17.09.2001	13		
David Xuereb	30.03.1998	10	(8)	2
Forwards:	**DOB**	**M**	**(s)**	**G**
Daneel Abela	08.01.1999	5	(9)	
Kevaughn St. Michael Atkinson (JAM)	11.11.1995	11	(1)	2
Wilkerson Junnior de Souza Gomes „Batata" (BRA)	09.08.1991	13	(3)	1
Luca Brincat	04.07.1997	1	(6)	
Dibola Diwoto Júnior (CMR)	06.01.1994	19		5
Freud Codjo Gnindokponou (FRA)	01.02.1994	10		1
Zwivhuya Chris Matombo (RSA)	26.09.1993	4		
Ronny Song	04.12.1995	2	(6)	1
Jan Tanti	10.04.1998	12	(4)	1

Sirens Football Club San Pawl il-Baħar

Founded: 1968
Stadium: Sirens Stadium, San Pawl il-Baħar (600)
Trainer: Steve D'Amato
[14.12.2020] Giovanni Tedesco (ITA)   13.05.1972

Goalkeepers:	DOB	M	(s)	G
David Cassar	24.11.1987	15		
Entonjo Elezaj (ALB)	14.07.1996	2		
Miguel Montfort	26.06.1986	6		
Defenders:	**DOB**	**M**	**(s)**	**G**
Adrian Borg	20.05.1989	16	(3)	
Manuel Ángel Bustos (ARG)	27.06.1995	12	(5)	3
Emiliano Callegari Torre (ARG)	22.06.1996	9		
Luke Grech	06.01.1994		(6)	
Jonathan Pearson	13.01.1987	9	(2)	
Romeu Péricles Romão (BRA)	10.04.1990	5	(2)	
Sean Schembri	27.02.2002		(1)	
Sergio Raphael dos Anjos (BRA)	23.10.1992	14		
Thiago Espíndola de Paula „Thiaguinho"(BRA)	14.05.1993	18		
Jacob Walker	31.07.1997	17	(4)	

Midfielders:	DOB	M	(s)	G
Terence Agius	15.01.1994	19	(4)	1
Sharlton Briffa	03.03.2001		(1)	
Ryan Grech	03.04.1985	10	(8)	
Tamsir Jammeh (GAB)	30.12.1996	7		
Ben Hamed Koné (CIV)	02.11.1987	6	(2)	1
Ryan Scicluna	30.07.1993	16	(2)	
Forwards:	**DOB**	**M**	**(s)**	**G**
Lamin Bittaye (GAM)	22.07.1995	7		2
Ryan Darmanin	12.12.1985		(5)	
Wilfried Domoraud (FRA)	18.08.1988	22	(1)	8
Máxuell Maia da Silva (BRA)	30.09.1991	10	(1)	4
Michael Mifsud	17.04.1981	2	(7)	1
Romário Lucas Menezes de Araújo (BRA)	05.07.1994	2	(3)	
Samba Tounkara (MLI)	23.05.1990	19	(1)	3
Wellington Oliveira Vieira „Wellington Petinha" (BRA)	20.01.1993	10		3

Sliema Wanderers Football Club

Founded: 1909
Stadium: Tigne Sports Complex, Sliema (1,000)
Trainer: Andrea Pisanu (ITA)   07.01.1982

Goalkeepers:	DOB	M	(s)	G
Jake Galea	15.04.1996	23		
Defenders:	**DOB**	**M**	**(s)**	**G**
Myles Beerman	13.03.1999	21	(2)	
Arthur Cunha da Rocha (BRA)	10.01.1990	4		
Sebastian Grech	02.04.2001		(1)	
Óscar Antonio Linton Bethancourt (PAN)	29.01.1993	13		1
Nuno Jorge Nobre Barbosa Malheiro (POR)	01.02.1994	1	(3)	
Kurt Shaw	01.04.1999	20	(1)	1
Dejan Vuković	04.01.1993	14	(8)	
Midfielders:	**DOB**	**M**	**(s)**	**G**
Edmond Agius	23.02.1987	8	(11)	
Gabriel Aquilina	07.12.1995	17	(5)	
Jean Borg	30.05.2001		(1)	
Denílson Pereira Neves (BRA)	16.02.1988	10	(4)	

	DOB	M	(s)	G
Gilmar da Silva Ribeiro (BRA)	26.03.1990	10	(4)	4
Danny Holla (NED)	31.12.1987	8	(4)	4
Riki Kakinuma (JPN)	11.12.1999	9	(8)	2
Alessandro Milesi Germoni (PER)	21.12.1999	12	(4)	2
John Mintoff	23.08.1988	11	(6)	
Michele Sansone	02.07.1998	4	(6)	
Mark Scerri	16.01.1990	4	(1)	
Forwards:	**DOB**	**M**	**(s)**	**G**
Juri Cisotti (ITA)	05.05.1993	23		5
Sylvano Comvalius (NED)	10.08.1987	4	(6)	2
Jake Engerer	06.07.2002		(3)	
Jean Paul Farrugia	21.03.1992	14	(3)	12
Ruslan Kisil (UKR)	23.10.1991	11	(4)	
Alexander Satariano	25.10.2001	12	(4)	6

Tarxien Rainbows Football Club

Founded: 1934 (*as Rainbows Tarxien*)
Stadium: "Tony Cassar" Sports Ground, Tarxien (1,000)
Trainer: Winston Muscat   29.08.1969
[18.02.2021] Steve D'Amato

Goalkeepers:	DOB	M	(s)	G
Jurgen Borg	08.08.1994	7		
Daniel Márcio Fernandes (POR)	25.09.1983	16		
Defenders:	**DOB**	**M**	**(s)**	**G**
Anderson do Nascimento Carneiro (BRA)	04.03.1993	9	(1)	
Keith Attard	01.05.2001		(11)	
Carlos da Silva Conceição Filho „Chabá" (BRA)	17.11.1994	10		1
Camilo Del Castillo Escobar (COL)	09.05.1995	6		1
Eduardo Rosado Souza (BRA)	03.02.1999	21		
Kyle Gatt	12.06.1996	10	(2)	1
Karl Pulo	30.07.1989	5	(4)	
Matthew Tabone	29.04.1992	15		
Cedric Zahra	20.10.1999		(7)	
Daniel Zerafa	08.04.1994	7	(1)	
Midfielders:	**DOB**	**M**	**(s)**	**G**
Édison David Bilbao Zárate (CHI)	06.03.1987	12	(1)	
Miguel Ciantar	17.10.1990	1	(3)	
Brandon Debono	30.07.1994	1		
Jurgen Debono	13.12.1995	17	(2)	

	DOB	M	(s)	G
Daren Falzon	08.05.1992	15	(6)	3
Shunsuke Kanayama (JPN)	16.09.2000		(1)	
Lincoln de Oliveira Santos (BRA)	30.09.1992	1	(1)	
Misael Miranda Gómez (MEX)	23.04.1996	6	(1)	
Brandon Muscat	03.11.1994	14		
Yuki Omuro (JPN)	28.08.2000		(1)	
Matthew Spiteri	06.10.1998	11	(3)	1
Forwards:	**DOB**	**M**	**(s)**	**G**
Kyle Gatt	18.04.1999	8	(1)	
Rafael Alain Kooh Sohna (CMR)	22.04.1990	7		2
Leonardo Henrique Ferreira „Leozinho" (BRA)	11.02.1993	4	(2)	2
Iván Edgardo Paz (ARG)	25.01.1996	10		
Vito Plut (SVN)	08.07.1988	22		9
Ricardo Pires Santos Júnior (BRA)	22.09.1987		(2)	
Luke Sciberras	15.09.1989	3	(7)	
Erisa Ssekisambu (UGA)	28.08.1995	3		
Dale Tabone	09.05.2001		(3)	
Vanger Conceição da Silva (BRA)	27.01.1987	12		3

Valletta Football Club

Founded:	1943		
Stadium:	Sirens Stadium, San Pawl il-Baħar (600)		
Trainer:	Jesmond Zerafa		03.08.1965
[01.12.2020]	Gilbert Agius		21.02.1974
[28.12.2020]	António José Cardoso Mendes (POR)		12.03.1979

Goalkeepers:	DOB	M	(s)	G
Henry Bonello	13.10.1988	16		
Yenez Cini	04.01.1994	7	(1)	
Defenders:	**DOB**	**M**	**(s)**	**G**
Leandro Damián Aguirre (ARG)	08.02.1989	16	(3)	2
Jean Borg	08.01.1998	3		
Ryan Camilleri	22.05.1988	9	(7)	
Jonathan Caruana	24.07.1986	11	(1)	1
Mihailo Jovanović (SRB)	15.02.1989	7		
Ivan Marić (SRB)	03.08.1994	4		
Nicolas Pulis	29.01.1998	2	(3)	
Joseph Zerafa	31.05.1988	14		
Midfielders:	**DOB**	**M**	**(s)**	**G**
Tristan Caruana	15.09.1991	18	(4)	
Shaun Dimech	08.08.2001	10	(12)	2
Ryan Fenech	20.04.1986	7	(9)	1
Sheldon MacKay	20.09.2003		(1)	

	DOB	M	(s)	G
Taisei Marukawa (JPN)	30.01.1997	4	(4)	2
Rowen Muscat	05.06.1991	15	(1)	1
Enmy Manuel Peña Beltré (DOM)	17.09.1992	14	(1)	1
Jonathan Iván Requena (ARG)	11.06.1996	2	(1)	
Eslit Sala (ALB)	09.05.2000	18	(2)	2
Kenley Scerri	07.11.2001		(1)	
Ryan Tonna	27.04.2001		(8)	
Forwards:	**DOB**	**M**	**(s)**	**G**
Miguel Ángel Alba (ARG)	14.08.1988	9	(4)	3
Lucas da Silva Ribeiro Campos (BRA)	30.10.1997	4		
Mario Fontanella (ITA)	28.06.1989	17	(1)	4
Santiago Malano (ARG)	29.01.1987	20	(2)	2
Isaiah Micallef	28.04.2004		(3)	
Kyrian Nwoko	04.07.1997	6	(8)	2
Matteo Piciollo (ITA)	15.10.1992	13	(3)	3
Taylon Nicolas Correa Marcolino (BRA)	16.03.1995	4	(1)	
Wellington Oliveira Vieira „Wellington Petinha" (BRA)	20.01.1993	3		

Żejtun Corinthians Football Club

Founded:	1944	
Stadium:	Żejtun Ground, Żejtun (1,000)	
Trainer:	Orosco Anonam (NGA)	15.06.1979

Goalkeepers:	DOB	M	(s)	G
Christian Cassar	22.03.1992	20	(1)	
Ibrahim Koné (GUI)	05.12.1989	3		
Defenders:	**DOB**	**M**	**(s)**	**G**
Diego Albanese	14.06.1996	13		
Gianluca Bugeja	05.09.1999	4	(11)	
Lucas Gama Moreira "Lucão" (BRA)	10.07.1993	22		
Christian Grech	20.02.1993	16	(4)	
Edward Herrera	14.07.1986	13	(5)	
Henrique Marcelino Motta (BRA)	10.01.1991	6		
Midfielders:	**DOB**	**M**	**(s)**	**G**
Dylan Agius	26.12.1996	3	(9)	
Gilmore Azzopardi	09.11.1996	6	(6)	
Alessio Cassar	27.02.1992		(1)	
Anderson Francisco de Barros „Dê" (BRA)	09.04.1986	17	(1)	

	DOB	M	(s)	G
Rafael Júnior de Fex Marriaga (VEN)	11.05.1990	4	(1)	2
Mattia Del Negro	07.09.1992		(1)	
Fernando José Gomes Júnior „Fernandinho"(BRA)	15.09.1994	10		5
Marcelo Muniz (BRA)	14.01.1991	11		
Kemar David Reid (JAM)	15.08.1994	19		8
Neil Tabone	01.10.1997	18	(1)	
Thiago Bonfim dos Santos (BRA)	12.07.1992	11		1
Vitor da Silva Vieira (BRA)	29.10.1997	13	(1)	6
Douglas Washington Cataneo (BRA)	24.08.1988	5		
Forwards:	**DOB**	**M**	**(s)**	**G**
Sérgio Barboza da Silva Júnior (BRA)	30.05.1993	9		1
Adrian Carabott	04.01.1991	6	(9)	2
Ricardo da Silva Faria „Ricardinho" (BRA)	09.02.1992	7		1
Robério do Nascimento Santos (BRA)	16.09.1994	4	(3)	1
Jurgen Suda	24.09.1996	13	(5)	1

SECOND LEVEL
Maltese Challenge League 2020/2021

1.	Marsa FC (*Promoted*)	22	15	5	2	54	-	21	50
2.	Pembroke Athleta FC (*Promoted*)	22	13	8	1	41	-	18	47
3.	San Ġwann FC	22	9	9	4	43	-	32	36
4.	Żebbuġ Rangers FC	22	10	4	8	45	-	30	34
5.	Swieqi United FC	22	10	4	8	41	-	30	34
6.	Naxxar Lions FC	20	9	3	8	28	-	25	30
7.	Qrendi FC	21	8	5	8	28	-	39	29
8.	Pietà Hotspurs FC	21	8	3	10	35	-	35	27
9.	St. Andrews FC	22	8	3	11	29	-	33	27
10.	Vittoriosa Stars FC Birgu	21	6	9	6	20	-	25	27
11.	Marsaxlokk FC (*Relegated*)	19	6	8	5	25	-	13	26
12.	Fgura United FC (*Relegated*)	21	7	5	9	26	-	35	26
13.	Mqabba FC (*Relegated*)	21	6	6	9	19	-	29	24
14.	FC St. George's Cospicua (*Relegated*)	20	3	4	13	16	-	40	13
15.	Qormi FC* (*Relegated*)	22	1	4	17	15	-	60	2

*5 points deducted for breaching the Challenge League's Payment Regulations.
Please note: the league was abandoned on 11.04.2021 due to COVID-19 pandemic..

INTERNATIONAL MATCHES
(16.07.2020 – 15.07.2021)

03.09.2020	Tórshavn	Faroe Islands - Malta	3-2(1-1)	(UNL)
06.09.2020	Attard	Malta - Latvia	1-1(1-1)	(UNL)
07.10.2020	Attard	Malta - Gibraltar	2-0(1-0)	(F)
10.10.2020	Andorra la Vella	Andorra - Malta	0-0	(UNL)
13.10.2020	Rīga	Latvia - Malta	0-1(0-0)	(UNL)
11.11.2020	Attard	Malta - Liechtenstein	3-0(2-0)	(F)
14.11.2020	Attard	Malta - Andorra	3-1(0-1)	(UNL)
17.11.2020	Attard	Malta - Faroe Islands	1-1(0-0)	(UNL)
24.03.2021	Attard	Malta - Russia	1-3(0-2)	(WCQ)
27.03.2021	Trnava	Slovakia - Malta	2-2(0-2)	(WCQ)
30.03.2021	Rijeka	Croatia - Malta	3-0(0-0)	(WCQ)
30.05.2021	Klagenfurt	Malta - Northern Ireland	0-3(0-1)	(F)
04.06.2021	Klagenfurt	Malta - Kosovo	1-2(1-1)	(F)

03.09.2020   FAROE ISLANDS - MALTA   3-2(1-1)   2nd UEFA Nations League D, Group 1
Tórsvøllur, Tórshavn; Referee: Ádám Farkas (Hungary); Attendance: 0
MLT: Henry Bonello, Andrei Agius (Cap), Steve Borg, Zach Muscat, Ryan Camenzuli, Luke Gambin, Kyrian Nwoko, Matthew Guillaumier (79.Teddy Teuma), Joseph Essien Mbong, Stephen Pisani (85.Rowen Muscat), Jurgen Degabriele (71.Paul Mbong). Trainer: Devis Mangia (Italy).
Goals: Jurgen Degabriele (37), Andrei Agius (73).

06.09.2020   MALTA - LATVIA   1-1(1-1)   2nd UEFA Nations League D, Group 1
Ta`Qali National Stadium, Attard; Referee: Stéphanie Frappart (France); Attendance: 0
MLT: Henry Bonello, Steve Borg (Cap) (84.Andrei Agius), Enrico Pepe, Zach Muscat, Ryan Camenzuli, Teddy Teuma, Luke Gambin, Kyrian Nwoko, Matthew Guillaumier (89.Stephen Pisani), Joseph Essien Mbong, Jurgen Degabriele (60.Jake Grech). Trainer: Devis Mangia (Italy).
Goal: Kyrian Nwoko (15).

07.10.2020   MALTA - GIBRALTAR   2-0(1-0)   Friendly International
Ta`Qali National Stadium, Attard; Referee: Nikola Popov (Bulgaria); Attendance: 0
MLT: Jake Galea, Andrei Agius (Cap) (46.Steve Borg), Samir Arab (46.Triston Caruana), Joseph Muscatt (87.Cain Attard), Rowen Muscat, Ryan Camenzuli (59.Paul Mbong), Kyrian Nwoko (40.Luke Montebello), Matthew Guillaumier, Jake Grech, Kurt Shaw, Shaun Dimech (60.Myles Beerman). Trainer: Devis Mangia (Italy).
Goals: Kyrian Nwoko (8), Triston Caruana (90).

10.10.2020   ANDORRA - MALTA   0-0   2nd UEFA Nations League D, Group 1
Estadi Nacional, Andorra la Vella; Referee: Referee: Alain Durieux (Luxembourg); Attendance: 0
MLT: Henry Bonello, Andrei Agius (Cap), Steve Borg, Zach Muscat, Ryan Camenzuli, Teddy Teuma, Luke Gambin, Joseph Essien Mbong, Stephen Pisani (79.Bjorn Kristensen), Jurgen Degabriele (61.Luke Montebello), Paul Mbong (79.Jake Grech). Trainer: Devis Mangia (Italy).

13.10.2020   LATVIA - MALTA   0-1(0-0)   2nd UEFA Nations League D, Group 1
Daugavas Stadions, Rīga; Referee: Iwan Arwel Griffith (Wales); Attendance: 0
MLT: Henry Bonello, Andrei AgiusCaptain, Steve Borg, Ryan Camenzuli, Teddy Teuma (75.Stephen Pisani), Luke Gambin (89.Jake Grech), Matthew Guillaumier, Joseph Essien Mbong, Kurt Shaw, Luke Montebello, Paul Mbong (69.Jurgen Degabriele). Trainer: Devis Mangia (Italy).
Goal: Steve Borg (90+7).

11.11.2020   MALTA - LIECHTENSTEIN   3-0(2-0)   Friendly International
Ta`Qali National Stadium, Attard; Referee: Manfredas Lukjančukas (Lithuania); Attendance: 0
MLT: Jake Galea, Steve Borg (77.Kurt Shaw), Jean Borg (28.Karl Micallef), Triston Caruana, Bjorn Kristensen, Juan Carlos Corbalan, Neil Tabone, Jake Grech (77.Jan Busuttil), Shaun Dimech (78.Jean Paul Farrugia), Michael Mifsud(Cap) (60.Alexander Satariano), Stephen Pisani (60.Rowen Muscat). Trainer: Devis Mangia (Italy).
Goals: Michael Mifsud (5), Steve Borg (20), Jean Paul Farrugia (84 penalty).

14.11.2020   MALTA - ANDORRA   3-1(0-1)   2nd UEFA Nations League D, Group 1
Ta`Qali National Stadium, Attard; Referee: Peter Kralović (Slovakia); Attendance: 0
MLT: Henry Bonello, Andrei Agius (Cap), Karl Micallef, Ryan Camenzuli, Teddy Teuma, Luke Gambin (89.Shaun Dimech), Matthew Guillaumier (84.Stephen Pisani), Joseph Essien Mbong, Kurt Shaw, Luke Montebello (75.Alexander Satariano), Jurgen Degabriele (89.Jake Grech). Trainer: Devis Mangia (Italy).
Goals: Emili Josep García Miramontes (56 own goal), Jurgen Degabriele (59), Shaun Dimech (90+3).

17.11.2020   MALTA - FAROE ISLANDS   1-1(0-0)   2nd UEFA Nations League D, Group 1
Ta`Qali National Stadium, Attard; Referee: Kristo Tohver (Estonia); Attendance: 0
MLT: Henry Bonello, Andrei Agius (Cap) (84.Shaun Dimech), Steve Borg, Ryan Camenzuli, Teddy Teuma (78.Stephen Pisani), Luke Gambin, Matthew Guillaumier, Joseph Essien Mbong, Kurt Shaw, Luke Montebello (75.Kyrian Nwoko), Jurgen Degabriele (84.Alexander Satariano). Trainer: Devis Mangia (Italy).
Goal: Matthew Guillaumier (54).

24.03.2021   MALTA - RUSSIA   1-3(0-2)   22nd FIFA WC.Qualifiers
Ta`Qali National Stadium, Attard; Referee: Peter Kjaesgaard (Denmark); Attendance: 0
MLT: Henry Bonello, Andrei Agius (Cap) (88.Kyrian Nwoko), Steve Borg, Bjorn Kristensen (74.Stephen Pisani), Ryan Camenzuli (86.Juan Carlos Corbalan), Teddy Teuma, Matthew Guillaumier, Joseph Essien Mbong, Kurt Shaw, Luke Montebello (46.Alexander Satariano), Jurgen Degabriele (46.Paul Mbong). Trainer: Devis Mangia (Italy).
Goal: Joseph Essien Mbong (56).

27.03.2021　　**SLOVAKIA - MALTA**　　　　　　　　**2-2(0-2)**　　　　　　　　22nd FIFA WC.Qualifiers

Štadión "Antona Malatinského", Trnava; Referee: Harald Lechner (Austria); Attendance: 0

MLT: Henry Bonello, Steve Borg (Cap), Enrico Pepe, Ryan Camenzuli, Teddy Teuma (90+1.Bjorn Kristensen), Luke Gambin (68.Jake Grech), Matthew Guillaumier, Joseph Essien Mbong, Kurt Shaw, Alexander Satariano (79.Stephen Pisani), Paul Mbong (68.Kyrian Nwoko). Trainer: Devis Mangia (Italy).

Goals: Luke David Gambin (16), Alexander Satariano (20).

30.03.2021　　**CROATIA - MALTA**　　　　　　　　**3-0(0-0)**　　　　　　　　22nd FIFA WC.Qualifiers

Stadion Rujevica, Rijeka; Referee: Lionel Tschudi (Switzerland); Attendance: 0

MLT: Henry Bonello, Steve Borg (Cap) (67.Zach Muscat), Enrico Pepe, Bjorn Kristensen (81.Luke Gambin), Ryan Camenzuli, Teddy Teuma, Matthew Guillaumier, Joseph Essien Mbong (67.Juan Carlos Corbalan), Kurt Shaw, Stephen Pisani (62.Jake Grech), Alexander Satariano (46.Kyrian Nwoko). Trainer: Devis Mangia (Italy).

30.05.2021　　**MALTA - NORTHERN IRELAND**　　　　　　　　**0-3(0-1)**　　　　　　　　Friendly International

Wörthersee Stadion, Klagenfurt (Austria); Referee: Sebastian Gishamer (Austria); Attendance: 0

MLT: Henry Bonello, Andrei Agius (Cap), Ferdinando Apap (70.Jean Borg), Bjorn Kristensen (82.Rowen Muscat), Ryan Camenzuli, Teddy Teuma (61.Dunstan Vella), Joseph Essien Mbong (70.Dexter Xuereb), Shaun Dimech, Kurt Shaw, Luke Montebello (61.Jurgen Degabriele), Alexander Satariano (82.Jean Paul Farrugia). Trainer: Devis Mangia (Italy).

04.06.2021　　**MALTA - KOSOVO**　　　　　　　　**1-2(1-1)**　　　　　　　　Friendly International

Wörthersee Stadion, Klagenfurt (Austria); Referee: Christopher Jäger (Austria); Attendance: 0

MLT: Henry Bonello, Andrei Agius (Cap) (88.Triston Caruana), Rowen Muscat (64.Nikolai Muscat), Ryan Camenzuli (88.Bjorn Kristensen), Teddy Teuma, Juan Carlos Corbalan (65.Jean Borg), Joseph Essien Mbong, Kurt Shaw, Shaun Dimech (64.Jurgen Degabriele), Luke Montebello, Alexander Satariano (46.Cain Attard). Trainer: Devis Mangia (Italy).

Goal: Shaun Dimech (45+2).

NATIONAL TEAM PLAYERS
(16.07.2020 – 15.07.2021)

Name	DOB	Caps	Goals	2020/2021:	Club
Goalkeepers					
Henry BONELLO	13.10.1988	28	0	2020/2021:	*Valletta FC*
Jake GALEA	15.04.1996	2	0	2020:	*Sliema Wanderers FC*
Defenders					
Andrei AGIUS	12.08.1986	100	6	2020/2021:	*Hibernians FC Paola*
Ferdinando APAP	29.07.1992	7	0	2021:	*Hibernians FC Paola*
Jean BORG	08.01.1998	5	0	2020/2021:	*Valletta FC*
Steve BORG	15.05.1988	59	3	2020/2021:	*Gżira United FC*
Karl MICALLEF	08.09.1996	4	0	2020:	*Ħamrun Spartans FC*
Zach MUSCAT	22.08.1993	44	1	2020: 05.09.2020->	*without club; Casa Pia AC Lisboa (POR)*
Joseph MUSCATT	15.12.1997	1	0	2020:	*SC Paderborn 07 (GER)*
Enrico PEPE	12.11.1989	3	0	2020/2021:	*Birkirkara FC*
Kurt SHAW	01.04.1999	11	0	2020/2021:	*Sliema Wanderers FC*
Dexter XUEREB	21.09.1997	1	0	2021:	*Gżira United FC*
Midfielders					
Samir ARAB	25.03.1994	1	0	2020:	*Balzan FC*
Cain ATTARD	10.09.1994	7	0	2020/2021:	*Birkirkara FC*
Myles BEERMAN	13.03.1999	6	0	2020:	*Sliema Wanderers FC*
Ryan CAMENZULI	08.09.1994	16	0	2020/2021:	*Floriana FC*
Triston CARUANA	15.09.1991	5	1	2020/2021:	*Valletta FC*
Juan Carlos CORBALAN	13.03.1997	15	1	2020/2021:	*Ħamrun Spartans FC*
Jake GRECH	18.11.1997	17	0	2020/2021:	*Hibernians FC Paola*
Matthew GUILLAUMIER	09.04.1998	11	1	2020: 28.09.2020->	*Birkirkara FC Ħamrun Spartans FC*
Bjorn KRISTENSEN	05.04.1993	30	0	2020/2021:	*Hibernians FC Paola*
Nikolai MUSCAT	13.07.1996	2	0	2021:	*Gżira United FC*
Rowen MUSCAT	05.06.1991	52	1	2020:	*Valletta FC*
Stephen PISANI	07.08.1992	28	0	2020: 31.01.2021->	*Balzan FC Gżira United FC*
Neil TABONE	01.10.1997	1	0	2020:	*Żejtun Corinthians FC*
Teddy TEUMA	30.09.1993	11	0	2020/2021:	*Royale Union Saint-Gilloise (BEL)*
Dunstan VELLA	27.04.1996	8	0	2021:	*Hibernians FC Paola*
Forwards					
Jan BUSUTTIL	06.03.1999	1	0	2020:	*Floriana FC*
Jurgen DEGABRIELE	10.10.1996	11	2	2020/2021:	*Hibernians FC Paola*
Shaun DIMECH	08.08.2001	6	2	2020/2021:	*Valletta FC*
Jean Paul FARRUGIA	21.03.1992	18	2	2020/2021:	*Sliema Wanderers FC*
Luke David GAMBIN	16.03.1993	30	1	2020/2021:	*Newport County AFC (WAL)*
Joseph Essien MBONG	15.07.1997	29	1	2020/2021:	*Ħamrun Spartans FC*
Paul MBONG	02.09.2001	6	0	2020/2021:	*Birkirkara FC*
Michael MIFSUD	17.04.1981	143	42	2020:	*Sirens FC San Pawl il-Baħar*
Luke MONTEBELLO	13.08.1995	11	0	2020/2021:	*Birkirkara FC*
Kyrian NWOKO	04.07.1997	20	3	2020/2021:	*Valletta FC*
Alexander SATARIANO	25.10.2001	8	1	2020/2021:	*Sliema Wanderers FC*
Trainer					
Devis MANGIA (Italy) [from 30.12.2019]	06.06.1974		13 M; 4 W; 4 D; 5 L; 17-19		

MOLDOVA

The Country:
Republica Moldova (Republic of Moldova)
Capital: Chişinău
Surface: 33,846 km²
Inhabitants: 2,640,438 [2020]
Time: UTC+2

The FA:
Federaţia Moldovenească de Fotbal
Strada Tricolorului 39, 2012 Chişinău
Tel: +373 22 210 413
Foundation date: 1990
Member of FIFA since: 1994
Member of UEFA since: 1993
Website: www.fmf.md

NATIONAL TEAM RECORDS

RECORDS		
First international match:	02.07.1991, Chişinău:	Moldova – Georgia 2-4
Most international caps:	Alexandru Ion Epureanu	- 100 caps (2006-2021)
Most international goals:	Serghei Cleşcenco	- 11 goals / 69 caps (1991-2006)

UEFA EUROPEAN CHAMPIONSHIP		FIFA WORLD CUP		OLYMPIC TOURNAMENTS	
1960	-	1930	-	1908	-
1964	-	1934	-	1912	-
1968	-	1938	-	1920	-
1972	-	1950	-	1924	-
1976	-	1954	-	1928	-
1980	-	1958	-	1936	-
1984	-	1962	-	1948	-
1988	-	1966	-	1952	-
1992	-	1970	-	1956	-
1996	Qualifiers	1974	-	1960	-
2000	Qualifiers	1978	-	1964	-
2004	Qualifiers	1982	-	1968	-
2008	Qualifiers	1986	-	1972	-
2012	Qualifiers	1990	-	1976	-
2016	Qualifiers	1994	Did Not Enter	1980	-
2020	Qualifiers	1998	Qualifiers	1984	-
		2002	Qualifiers	1988	-
		2006	Qualifiers	1992	Did Not Enter
		2010	Qualifiers	1996	Qualifiers
		2014	Qualifiers	2000	Qualifiers
		2018	Qualifiers	2004	Qualifiers
				2008	Qualifiers
				2012	Qualifiers
				2016	Qualifiers

UEFA NATIONS LEAGUE	
2018/2019	League D (promoted to League C)
2020/2021	League C (*qualified to relegation play-outs*)

FIFA CONFEDERATIONS CUP 1992-2017
None

MOLDOVAN CLUB HONOURS IN EUROPEAN CLUB COMPETITIONS:

European Champion Clubs' Cup (1956-1992) / UEFA Champions League (1993-2021)
None

Fairs Cup (1858-1971) / UEFA Cup (1972-2009) / UEFA Europa League (2010-2021)
None

UEFA Super Cup (1972-2020)
None

*European Cup Winners' Cup 1961-1999**
None

*defunct competition

NATIONAL COMPETITIONS
TABLE OF HONOURS

MOLDOVAN SSR (SOVIET ERA) CHAMPIONS

Year	Champion	Year	Champion	Year	Champion
1945	Dinamo Chişinău	1961	KSKhI Chişinău	1977	Stroitel Tiraspol
1946	Dinamo Chişinău	1962	Universitet Chişinău	1978	Nistru Tiraspol
1947	Dinamo Chişinău	1963	Temp Tiraspol	1979	Nistru Ciobruciu
1948	Dinamo Chişinău	1964	Temp Tiraspol'	1980	Nistru Ciobruciu
1949	Burevestnik Bender	1965	Energhia Tiraspol	1981	Grănicerul Glodeni
1950	Krasnoe Znamia Chişinău	1966	Stroindustria Bălţi	1982	Grănicerul Glodeni
1951	Krasnoe Znamia Chişinău	1967	Nistrul Bender	1983	Grănicerul Glodeni
1952	Dinamo Chişinău	1968	Temp Tiraspol	1984	Grănicerul Glodeni
1953	Dinamo Chişinău	1969	Politehnik Chişinău	1985	Iskra-Stal
1954	KSKhI Chişinău	1970	Politehnik Chişinău	1986	Avangard Lazovsk
1955	Burevestnik Bender	1971	Pişcevik Bender	1987	Tekstilshchik Tiraspol
1956	Spartak Tiraspol	1972	Kolhoz im. Lenina Edineţ	1988	Tighina Bender
1957	KSKhI Chişinău	1973	Pişcevik Bender	1989	Tekstilshchik Tiraspol
1958	Moldavkabel' Bender	1974	Dinamo Chişinău	1990	Moldovgidromaş Chişinău
1959	NIISVIV Chişinău	1975	Dinamo Chişinău	1991	Speranţa Nisporeni
1960	Tiraspol	1976	Stroitel Tiraspol		

	CHAMPIONS	CUP WINNERS	BEST GOALSCORERS	
1992	FC Zimbru Chişinău	FC Bugeac Comrat	Serghei Alexandrov (FC Bugeac Comrat) Oleg Flentea (FC Constructorul Chişinău)	13
1992/1993	FC Zimbru Chişinău	FC Tiligul-Tiras Tiraspol	Vladimir Kosse (FC Tiligul-Tiras Tiraspol)	30
1993/1994	FC Zimbru Chişinău	FC Tiligul-Tiras Tiraspol	Vladimir Kosse (FC Tiligul-Tiras Tiraspol)	24
1994/1995	FC Zimbru Chişinău	FC Tiligul-Tiras Tiraspol	Vladislav Gavriliuc (FC Nistru Otaci / FC Zimbru Chişinău)	20
1995/1996	FC Zimbru Chişinău	FC Constructorul Chişinău	Vladislav Gavriliuc (FC Zimbru Chişinău)	34
1996/1997	FC Constructorul Chişinău	FC Zimbru Chişinău	Serghei Rogaciov (FC Constructorul Chişinău / FC Olimpia Bălţi)	35
1997/1998	FC Zimbru Chişinău	FC Zimbru Chişinău	Serghei Clescenco (FC Zimbru Chişinău)	25
1998/1999	FC Zimbru Chişinău	FC Sheriff Tiraspol	Serghei Rogaciov (FC Sheriff Tiraspol)	21
1999/2000	FC Zimbru Chişinău	FC Constructorul Chişinău	Serghei Rogaciov (FC Sheriff Tiraspol)	20
2000/2001	FC Sheriff Tiraspol	FC Sheriff Tiraspol	Ruslan Barburoş (Haiducul Sporting Hânceşti / FC Agro Chişinău / FC Sheriff Tiraspol) David Mujiri (GEO, FC Sheriff Tiraspol)	17
2001/2002	FC Sheriff Tiraspol	FC Sheriff Tiraspol	Ruslan Barburoş (FC Sheriff Tiraspol)	17
2002/2003	FC Sheriff Tiraspol	FC Zimbru Chişinău	Serghei Dadu (FC Tiraspol / FC Sheriff Tiraspol)	19
2003/2004	FC Sheriff Tiraspol	FC Zimbru Chişinău	Vladimir Shishelov (UZB, FC Zimbru Chişinău)	15
2004/2005	FC Sheriff Tiraspol	FC Nistru Otaci	Cătălin Sergiu Lichioiu (ROU, FC Nistru Otaci)	16
2005/2006	FC Sheriff Tiraspol	FC Sheriff Tiraspol	Aliaksei Kuchuk (BLR, FC Sheriff Tiraspol)	13
2006/2007	FC Sheriff Tiraspol	FC Zimbru Chişinău	Aliaksei Kuchuk (BLR, FC Sheriff Tiraspol)	17
2007/2008	FC Sheriff Tiraspol	FC Sheriff Tiraspol	Igor Picuşceac (FC Tiraspol / FC Sheriff Tiraspol)	14
2008/2009	FC Sheriff Tiraspol	FC Sheriff Tiraspol	Oleg Andronic (FC Zimbru Chişinău)	16
2009/2010	FC Sheriff Tiraspol	FC Sheriff Tiraspol	Alexandru Maximov (FC Viitorul Orhei) Jymmy Dougllas França (BRA, FC Sheriff Tiraspol)	13
2010/2011	FC Dacia Chişinău	FC Iskra-Stal Rîbniţa	Gheorghe Boghiu (FC Mîlsami Orhei)	26
2011/2012	FC Sheriff Tiraspol	FC Milsami Orhei	Wilfried Bendjamin Balima (BFA, FC Sheriff Tiraspol)	18
2012/2013	FC Sheriff Tiraspol	FC Tiraspol	Gheorghe Boghiu (FC Milsami Orhei)	16
2013/2014	FC Sheriff Tiraspol	FC Zimbru Chişinău	Luvannor Henrique de Sousa Silva (BRA, FC Sheriff Tiraspol)	26
2014/2015	FC Milsami Orhei	FC Sheriff Tiraspol	Ricardo Cavalcante Mendes "Ricardinho" (BRA, FC Sheriff Tiraspol)	19
2015/2016	FC Sheriff Tiraspol	FC Zaria Bălţi	Danijel Subotić (SUI, FC Sheriff Tiraspol)	12
2016/2017	FC Sheriff Tiraspol	FC Sheriff Tiraspol	Ricardo Cavalcante Mendes "Ricardinho" (BRA, FC Sheriff Tiraspol)	15
2017	FC Sheriff Tiraspol	FC Milsami Orhei (2017/18)	Vitalie Damaşcan (FC Sheriff Tiraspol)	13
2018	FC Sheriff Tiraspol	FC Sheriff Tiraspol (2018/19)	Vladimir Ambros (CS Petrocub Hînceşti)	12
2019	FC Sheriff Tiraspol	CS Petrocub Hînceşti (2019/20)	Yuri Kendysh (BLR, FC Sheriff Tiraspol)	13
2020/2021	FC Sheriff Tiraspol	FC Sfântul Gheorghe Suruceni	Frank Andersson Castañeda Vélez (COL, FC Sheriff Tiraspol)	28

NATIONAL CHAMPIONSHIP
Divizia Naţională 2020/2021
(03.07.2020 – 26.05.2021)

Results

Round 1 [03-05.07.2020]
Dinamo-Auto - FC Floreşti 3-1(2-0)
FC Sheriff - Speranţa Nisporeni 2-0(1-0)
FC Sfântul Gheorghe - Codru Lozova 5-1(2-0)
Milsami Orhei - Petrocub Hînceşti 0-0
FC Zimbru - Dacia Buiucani 0-1(0-0)

Round 2 [07-09.07.2020]
Codru Lozova - FC Floreşti 0-1(0-0)
FC Sfântul Gheorghe - FC Sheriff 0-1(0-0)
Petrocub Hînceşti - Dinamo-Auto 3-1(2-1)
Dacia Buiucani - Milsami Orhei 0-0
Speranţa Nisporeni - FC Zimbru 2-2(0-1)

Round 3 [11-13.07.2020]
FC Floreşti - Petrocub Hînceşti 0-4(0-2)
FC Sheriff - Codru Lozova 6-0(5-0)
Dinamo-Auto - Dacia Buiucani 1-0(0-0)
FC Zimbru - FC Sfântul Gheorghe 1-3(1-1)
Milsami Orhei - Speranţa Nisporeni 3-0(3-0)

Round 4 [17-19.07.2020]
Codru Lozova - Petrocub Hînceşti 0-7(0-4)
FC Sheriff - FC Zimbru 2-0(0-0)
Dacia Buiucani - FC Floreşti 2-0(0-0)
Speranţa Nisporeni - Dinamo-Auto 1-2(1-1)
FC Sfântul Gheorghe - Milsami Orhei 3-1(2-1)

Round 5 [21-23.07.2020]
FC Zimbru - Codru Lozova 3-1(0-1)
FC Floreşti - Speranţa Nisporeni 1-1(0-1)
Petrocub Hînceşti - Dacia Buiucani 2-0(1-0)
Dinamo-Auto - FC Sfântul Gheorghe 0-1(0-1)
Milsami Orhei - FC Sheriff 0-1(0-1)

Round 6 [25-27.07.2020]
Dacia Buiucani - Codru Lozova 4-0(2-0)
Speranţa Nisporeni-Petrocub Hînceşti 1-4(1-2)
FC Sheriff - Dinamo-Auto 6-0(2-0)
FC Sfântul Gheorghe - FC Floreşti 2-0(2-0)
FC Zimbru - Milsami Orhei 0-1(0-1)

Round 7 [31.07.-02.08.2020]
Dacia Buiucani - Speranţa Nisporeni 0-3(0-0)
Milsami Orhei - Codru Lozova 3-1(1-0)
FC Floreşti - FC Sheriff 0-1(0-0)
Petrocub Hînceşti - Sfântul Gheorghe 1-0(1-0)
Dinamo-Auto - FC Zimbru 1-1(1-0)

Round 8 [04-06.08.2020]
Codru Lozova - Speranţa Nisporeni 0-1(0-1)
Milsami Orhei - Dinamo-Auto 1-0(0-0)
FC Sheriff - Petrocub Hînceşti 4-1(2-0)
Sfântul Gheorghe - Dacia Buiucani 2-1(2-0)
FC Zimbru - FC Floreşti 0-2(0-0)

Round 9 [10-13.09.2020]
Speranţa Nisporeni-Sfântul Gheorghe 0-2(0-2)
Dinamo-Auto - Codru Lozova 7-0(5-0)
Dacia Buiucani - FC Sheriff 0-3(0-1)
Petrocub Hînceşti - FC Zimbru 2-0(0-0)
FC Floreşti - Milsami Orhei 0-4(0-2)

Round 10 [18-20.09.2020]
FC Floreşti - Dinamo-Auto 0-5(0-1)
Speranţa Nisporeni - FC Sheriff 1-2(0-1)
Dacia Buiucani - FC Zimbru 2-1(1-1)
Petrocub Hînceşti - Milsami Orhei 1-2(0-1)
Codru Lozova - FC Sfântul Gheorghe 2-2(0-1)

Round 11 [22-24.09.2020]
Dinamo-Auto - Petrocub Hînceşti 1-1(0-1)
Milsami Orhei - Dacia Buiucani 2-0(0-0)
FC Zimbru - Speranţa Nisporeni 0-2(0-1)
Codru Lozova - FC Floreşti 1-1(0-0)
Sheriff - Sfântul Gheorghe 4-1(1-0) [20.02.21]

Round 12 [26-28.09.2020]
Dacia Buiucani - Dinamo-Auto 4-0(2-0)
Speranţa Nisporeni - Milsami Orhei 0-1(0-0)
FC Sfântul Gheorghe - FC Zimbru 2-0(1-0)
FC Sheriff - Codru Lozova 6-0(2-0)
Petrocub Hînceşti - FC Floreşti 4-0(1-0)

Round 13 [02-04.10.2020]
Codru Lozova - Petrocub Hînceşti 1-4(0-2)
Milsami Orhei - FC Sfântul Gheorghe 1-1(0-1)
FC Floreşti - Dacia Buiucani 1-0(1-0)
FC Zimbru - FC Sheriff 0-4(0-1)
Dinamo-Auto - Speranţa Nisporeni 3-3(1-1)

Round 14 [16-18.10.2020]
Speranţa Nisporeni - FC Floreşti 0-0
Codru Lozova - FC Zimbru 0-2(0-0)
FC Sfântul Gheorghe - Dinamo-Auto 1-1(1-1)
FC Sheriff - Milsami Orhei 1-0(0-0)
Dacia Buiucani - Petrocub Hînceşti 0-0

Round 15 [20-21.10.2020]
Dinamo-Auto - FC Sheriff 1-2(0-0)
FC Floreşti - FC Sfântul Gheorghe 1-4(0-2)
Milsami Orhei - FC Zimbru 2-0(1-0)
Codru Lozova - Dacia Buiucani 0-1(0-0)
Petrocub Hînceşti-Speranţa Nisporeni 2-0(2-0)

Round 16 [24-25.10.2020]
Codru Lozova - Milsami Orhei 1-4(1-1)
FC Sheriff - FC Floreşti 5-0(1-0)
Sfântul Gheorghe - Petrocub Hînceşti 0-4(0-2)
FC Zimbru - Dinamo-Auto 0-0
Speranţa Nisporeni - Dacia Buiucani 0-0

Round 17 [31.10.-02.11.2020]
Dinamo-Auto - Milsami Orhei 1-1(0-1)
Speranţa Nisporeni - Codru Lozova 3-0(2-0)
Dacia Buiucani - Sfântul Gheorghe 0-4(0-3)
Petrocub Hînceşti - FC Sheriff 1-0(0-0)
FC Floreşti - FC Zimbru 1-0(1-0)

Round 18 [06-08.11.2020]
FC Zimbru - Petrocub Hînceşti 0-1(0-1)
Sfântul Gheorghe-Speranţa Nisporeni 1-0(0-0)
Milsami Orhei - FC Floreşti 3-0(2-0)
FC Sheriff - Dacia Buiucani 0-0
Codru Lozova - Dinamo-Auto 1-4(0-2)

Round 19 [20-22.11.2020]
Dinamo-Auto - FC Floreşti 2-1(1-1)
FC Zimbru - Dacia Buiucani 1-3(1-2)
Codru Lozova - FC Sfântul Gheorghe 0-0
FC Sheriff - Speranţa Nisporeni 3-0(1-0)
Milsami Orhei - Petrocub Hînceşti 1-3(0-1)

Round 20 [24-26.11.2020]
Codru Lozova - FC Floreşti 2-1(2-1)
FC Sfântul Gheorghe - FC Sheriff 0-2(0-0)
Speranţa Nisporeni - FC Zimbru 2-2(1-0)
Dacia Buiucani - Milsami Orhei 0-0
Petrocub Hînceşti - Dinamo-Auto 1-1(0-0)

Round 21 [28-29.11.2020]
Codru Lozova - FC Sheriff 1-2(1-1)
Dinamo-Auto - Dacia Buiucani 1-1(0-0)
FC Floreşti - Petrocub Hînceşti 0-1(0-1)
FC Zimbru - FC Sfântul Gheorghe 2-3(1-2)
Milsami - Speranţa Nisp. 3-0(3-0) [20.02.21]

Round 22 [23-25.02.2021]
Codru Lozova - Petrocub Hînceşti 1-9(0-6)
Dacia Buiucani - FC Floreşti 2-2(1-1)
Speranţa Nisporeni - Dinamo-Auto 0-4(0-0)
FC Zimbru - FC Sheriff 0-4(0-1)
FC Sfântul Gheorghe - Milsami Orhei 1-3(0-1)

Round 23 [27.02.-01.03.2021]
Petrocub Hînceşti - Dacia Buiucani 4-1(2-0)
FC Floreşti - Speranţa Nisporeni 4-4(2-2)
FC Zimbru - Codru Lozova 2-1(2-1)
Dinamo-Auto - FC Sfântul Gheorghe 0-2(0-1)
Milsami Orhei - FC Sheriff 0-1(0-0)

Round 24 [06-08.03.2021]
Codru Lozova - Dacia Buiucani 1-5(0-2)
FC Sheriff - Dinamo-Auto 7-0(3-0)
Speranţa Nisporeni-Petrocub Hînceşti 1-3(0-1)
FC Zimbru - Milsami Orhei 1-2(0-1)
FC Sfântul Gheorghe - FC Floreşti 3-2(1-0)

Round 25 [12-14.03.2021]
Milsami Orhei - Codru Lozova 7-2(4-2)
Dinamo-Auto - FC Zimbru 3-0(1-0)
FC Floreşti - FC Sheriff 0-6(0-2)
Petrocub Hînceşti - Sfântul Gheorghe 2-0(1-0)
Dacia Buiucani - Speranţa Nisporeni 4-1(1-0)

Round 26 [19.03.2021]
Milsami Orhei - Dinamo-Auto 2-2(2-1)
Sfântul Gheorghe - Dacia Buiucani 2-0(0-0)
FC Sheriff - Petrocub Hînceşti 0-0
Codru Lozova - Speranţa N. 1-2(1-0) [26.04.]
FC Zimbru - FC Floreşti 3-0(1-0) [27.04.]

Round 27 [11-12.04.2021]
Dinamo-Auto - Codru Lozova 1-0(0-0)
Speranţa Nisporeni-Sfântul Gheorghe 0-3(0-1)
Dacia Buiucani - FC Sheriff 0-4(0-1)
FC Floreşti - Milsami Orhei 2-5(1-3)
Petrocub Hînceşti - FC Zimbru 3-0(0-0)

Round 28 [15-16.04.2021]
FC Floreşti - Dinamo-Auto 4-1(1-1)
Codru Lozova - FC Sfântul Gheorghe 1-2(1-0)
Dacia Buiucani - FC Zimbru 1-1(0-0)
Speranţa Nisporeni - FC Sheriff 0-10(0-5)
Petrocub Hînceşti - Milsami Orhei 1-1(0-0)

Round 29 [23-24.04.2021]
Dinamo-Auto - Petrocub Hînceşti 0-0
FC Floreşti - Codru Lozova 2-1(2-0)
FC Zimbru - Speranţa Nisporeni 6-0(2-0)
Milsami Orhei - Dacia Buiucani 3-0(2-0)
FC Sheriff - FC Sfântul Gheorghe 2-0(1-0)

Round 30 [29-30.04.2021]
Dacia Buiucani - Dinamo-Auto 2-1(1-0)
Codru Lozova - FC Sheriff 0-6(0-3)
FC Sfântul Gheorghe - FC Zimbru 4-3(3-1)
Speranţa Nisporeni - Milsami Orhei 0-4(0-1)
Petrocub Hînceşti - FC Floreşti 4-0(0-0)

Round 31 [07-08.05.2021]	
Dinamo-Auto - Speranţa Nisporeni	0-0
FC Floreşti - Dacia Buiucani	2-0(1-0)
Petrocub Hînceşti - Codru Lozova	1-0(0-0)
FC Zimbru - FC Sheriff	0-1(0-0)
Milsami Orhei - FC Sfântul Gheorghe	2-1(0-1)

Round 32 [11-12.05.2021]	
Dacia Buiucani - Petrocub Hînceşti	1-2(0-1)
Speranţa Nisporeni - FC Floreşti	1-3(1-0)
Codru Lozova - FC Zimbru	1-5(0-2)
FC Sfântul Gheorghe - Dinamo-Auto	3-1(1-0)
FC Sheriff - Milsami Orhei	6-0(4-0)

Round 33 [15-16.05.2021]	
Dinamo-Auto - FC Sheriff	0-7(0-2)
Dacia Buiucani - Codru Lozova	4-0(1-0)
Milsami Orhei - FC Zimbru	2-1(2-1)
Petrocub Hînceşti - Speranţa N.	3-0 *awarded*
FC Floreşti - FC Sfântul Gheorghe	0-4(0-2)

Round 34 [18-19.05.2021]	
FC Zimbru - Dinamo-Auto	1-1(0-1)
Codru Lozova - Milsami Orhei	2-4(0-2)
Sfântul Gheorghe - Petrocub Hînceşti	0-3(0-0)
FC Sheriff - FC Floreşti	3-0(0-0)
Speranţa Nisp. - Dacia Buiucani	0-3 *awarded*

Round 35 [22-23.05.2021]	
Speranţa Nisp. - Codru Lozova	0-3 *awarded*
Dinamo-Auto - Milsami Orhei	2-0(2-0)
Petrocub Hînceşti - FC Sheriff	0-1(0-0)
Dacia Buiucani - Sfântul Gheorghe	1-0(0-0)
FC Floreşti - FC Zimbru	3-1(1-0)

Round 36 [26.05.2021]	
Codru Lozova - Dinamo-Auto	0-2(0-1)
Milsami Orhei - FC Floreşti	3-2(3-0)
Sfântul Gheorghe - Speranţa N.	3-0 *awarded*
FC Sheriff - Dacia Buiucani	1-1(0-0)
FC Zimbru - Petrocub Hînceşti	0-0

Final Standings

						Total			Home				Away		
1. **FC Sheriff Tiraspol**	36	32	3	1	116 - 7	99	15	3	0	65 - 3	17	0	1	51 - 4
2. CS Petrocub Hînceşti	36	25	8	3	82 - 18	83	14	2	2	42 - 7	11	6	1	40 - 11
3. FC Milsami Orhei	36	22	7	7	71 - 37	73	12	3	3	38 - 15	10	4	4	33 - 22
4. FC Sfântul Gheorghe Suruceni	36	21	4	11	65 - 43	67	11	2	5	34 - 25	10	2	6	31 - 18
5. FC Dacia Buiucani Chişinău (*Relegated*)*	36	13	9	14	44 - 45	48	8	5	5	28 - 23	5	4	9	16 - 22
6. FC Dinamo-Auto Tiraspol	36	12	12	12	53 - 58	48	7	7	4	27 - 21	5	5	8	26 - 37
7. FC Floreşti	36	9	5	22	37 - 85	32	7	2	9	22 - 39	2	3	13	15 - 46
8. FC Zimbru Chişinău	36	6	7	23	39 - 63	25	4	3	11	20 - 26	2	4	12	19 - 37
9. CSF Speranţa Nisporeni (*Expelled*)**	36	5	8	23	29 - 87	23	1	4	13	12 - 48	4	4	10	17 - 39
10. FC Codru Lozova (*Relegated*)	36	2	3	31	26 - 119	9	1	2	15	13 - 54	1	1	16	13 - 65

Please note: *FC Dacia Buiucani Chişinău was relegated due to financial reasons.
**CSF Speranţa Nisporeni failed to arrive to their matches from Round 33 and 34 and subsequently were expelled from the competition, all remaining fixtures being awarded 0-3 against them.

Top goalscorers:		
28	**Frank Andersson Castañeda Vélez (COL)**	*FC Sheriff Tiraspol*
16	Vladimir Ambros	*CS Petrocub Hînceşti*
15	Alexandru Antoniuc	*FC Milsami Orhei*
12	Maxim Mihailov	*FC Dinamo-Auto Tiraspol*
12	Roman Volkov (BLR)	*FC Sfântul Gheorghe Suruceni*

NATIONAL CUP
Cupa Moldovei 2020/2021

Second Round [28-29.08.2020]			
FC Iskra Rîbniţa - FC Sireţi	4-0	FC Făleşti - FC Victoria Bardar	1-5
FC Bălţi - FC Floreşti	0-2	FC Sokol Copceac - CSF Spartanii Selemet	2-0
FC Tighina Bender - FC Dacia Buiucani Chişinău	0-4	ARF Ialoveni Mileştii Mici - FC Cahul-2005	0-5
CS Moldova-03 Ungheni - FC Sîngerei	3-2	FC Sporting Trestieni - FC Sucleia	3-1

1/8-Finals [27-28.10.2020]			
FC Milsami Orhei - FC Victoria Bardar	7-1	FC Dinamo-Auto Tiraspol - FC Sokol Copceac	13-0
FC Codru Lozova - FC Cahul-2005	1-0	FC Sporting Trestieni - FC Sfântul Gheorghe	0-4
FC Zimbru Chişinău - FC Floreşti	0-1	CSF Speranţa Nisporeni - FC Dacia Buiucani Chiş.	2-1 aet
CS Petrocub Hînceşti - CS Moldova-03 Ungheni	4-1	FC Sheriff Tiraspol - FC Iskra Rîbniţa	2-1

Quarter-Finals [19-20.04.2021]			
FC Floreşti - CS Petrocub Hînceşti	1-2 aet	FC Sfântul Gheorghe - CSF Speranţa Nisporeni	5-1 aet
FC Dinamo-Auto Tiraspol - FC Codru Lozova	2-1 aet	FC Sheriff Tiraspol - FC Milsami Orhei	4-1

Semi-Finals [04.05.2021]			
FC Dinamo-Auto Tiraspol - FC Sfântul Gheorghe	1-2 aet	FC Sheriff Tiraspol - CS Petrocub Hînceşti	3-1

Final

30.05.2021; Stadionul Zimbru, Chişinău; Referee: Gabriel Tupicica; Attendance: 2,737
FC Sheriff Tiraspol - FC Sfântul Gheorghe Suruceni   0-0; 2-3 on penalties

Sheriff Tiraspol: Dušan Marković, Stjepan Radeljić, Fernando Peixoto Costanza (120+1.Alexandr Belousov), Cristiano da Silva Leite, Gustavo Alfonso Dulanto Sanguinetti, Dimitrios Kolovos, Moussa Kyabou, Rifet Kapič (91.Sébastien Thill), Adama Traoré I, Frank Andersson Castañeda Vélez (Cap), Lovro Bizjak (77.Nadrey Dago). Trainer: Yuriy Vernydub (Ukraine).

FC Sfântul Gheorghe: Nicolae Calancea, Petru Ojog, Mihail Ştefan, Serghei Svinarenco (120.Dan Taras), Sidy Sagna, Artur Crăciun, Vitalie Plămădeală (Cap) (65.Aliyu Yau Adam), Mihail Ghecev (114.Alexandru Osipov), Teodor Lungu (100.Eugeniu Slivca), Victor Stînă (106.Alexandru Suvorov), Nicolai Solodovnicov [sent off 120+5 on the bench] (65.Roman Volkov). Trainer: Serghei Cebotari.

Penalties: Frank Andersson Castañeda Vélez (missed); Eugeniu Slivca 0-1; Adama Traoré I (saved); Dan Taras (saved); Sébastien Thill 1-1; Artur Crăciun 1-2; Dimitrios Kolovos 2-2; Alexandru Suvorov 2-3; Alexandr Belousov (saved).

Fotbal Club Codru Lozova

Founded:	2008		
Stadium:	Stadionul „Nicolae Simatoc", Lozova (1,100)		
Trainer:	Denis Calincov (7 matches)		15.09.1985
	Sergiu Chirilov (14 matches)		05.06.1973
[18.01.2021]	Alexei Savinov		19.04.1979

Goalkeepers:	DOB	M	(s)	G
Vladislav Butuc	21.07.1999	16	(2)	
Mikhail Kizeev	17.03.1997	11		
Igor Mostovei	25.09.1999	8		
Defenders:	**DOB**	**M**	**(s)**	**G**
Dušan Babić (SRB)	07.01.1994	17	(1)	
Valentin Chişca	14.08.1999	17	(2)	
Anatolie Ciuntu	02.05.2001	6	(3)	1
Vasile Cojocari	02.09.2001	16	(3)	1
Andrei Conohov	12.01.2000	10	(1)	
Eugeniu Dragomeretchii	15.07.2001		(1)	
Itsuki Kurata (JPN)	10.11.1999	8	(7)	
Nicolae Munteanu	22.05.2001	4		
Bogdan Mytsyk (UKR)	08.03.1998	17	(1)	1
Aleksey Nestratov (RUS)	09.08.1996	10	(1)	
Ion Sandu	09.03.1993	28	(1)	
Vadim Sontovoi	17.04.2002	1	(1)	
Dumitru Tofilat	13.07.2000	4	(5)	
Eduard Zaplitnîi	30.04.1998	15	(5)	
Midfielders:	**DOB**	**M**	**(s)**	**G**
Ilya Azyavin (RUS)	24.07.2000	7		1
Maxim Calincov	04.05.2000	14	(4)	1
Aleksandros Dhamo (ALB)	14.08.1998	12		2
Dan Doroftei	11.05.2001		(3)	
Hamed Fondikou (CMR)	14.10.2002	7	(1)	1
Dumitru Garşinschi	25.05.1999	1		
Maximilian Ihekuna (NGA)	15.09.2001	10		
Ion Lăcustă	24.02.1995	15	(4)	2
Andrei Mincev	30.09.1998	1		
Peter Oluka (NGA)	02.09.2000	8	(1)	
Ion Oprea	19.11.2002	6	(7)	
Artem Pestryakov (RUS)	30.07.1999	13	(9)	3
Marian Puiu	21.09.1997	19	(3)	
Dumitru Reniţă	02.12.1999	5	(3)	
Abubakar Salifu (GHA)	22.01.1998	10		
Forwards:	**DOB**	**M**	**(s)**	**G**
Emmanuel Alaribe (NGA)	24.08.2000	8		
Oleg Creţul	30.05.2000	3	(6)	2
Rostislav Garganciuc		2	(3)	1
Ion Ibrean	21.03.1998	7		1
Rinat Jalbă	02.02.1997	5		
Nichita Malţev	11.11.2000	3	(6)	1
Ion Mamaliga	28.04.1999	16		
Marius Manole	27.03.2002	11	(3)	3
Chidiebere Ogbodo (NGA)	28.04.2002	2	(8)	
Dumitru Prodan	02.02.2004	2	(8)	
Nikolay Vdovichenko	21.04.1989	10		1

Fotbal Club Dacia Buiucani Chişinău

Founded:	25.09.1997	
Stadium:	Stadionul Zimbru-2, Chişinău (2,000)	
Trainer:	Andrei Martin	27.06.1974

Goalkeepers:	DOB	M	(s)	G
Dumitru Coval	06.11.2000	35		
Artiom Cubani	14.01.2002		(2)	
Defenders:	**DOB**	**M**	**(s)**	**G**
Vasile Bitlan	31.01.2004	5	(5)	
Vicu Bulmaga	05.07.2003	23	(5)	
Doru Calestru	15.11.2002	28	(4)	
Adrian Ciobanu	17.07.2001		(4)	
Vadim Cravcescu	07.03.1985	27		1
Denis Furtună	13.10.1999	11	(1)	1
Sandu Mateescu	20.12.1998	9	(5)	
Ghenadie Ochincă	01.03.1984		(1)	
Ioan-Călin Revenco	26.06.2000	32		3
Gheorghe Suciu	06.06.1999	11	(4)	
Mihai Ţipac	20.11.2000	18	(2)	
Midfielders:	**DOB**	**M**	**(s)**	**G**
Ilie Botnari	25.07.2003		(4)	
Corneliu Cotogoi	23.06.2001	33		6
Dumitru Demian	08.02.1999	29	(1)	6
Ion Gurulea	19.07.2001	3	(16)	
Alexandru Gutium	15.07.2003		(6)	
Teodor Lungu	12.06.1995	19		
Andrei Rusnac	22.09.1996	9	(1)	
Gheorghe Spînu	25.07.2001		(2)	
Forwards:	**DOB**	**M**	**(s)**	**G**
Dumitru Bivol	03.10.2001	7	(20)	3
Marin Căruntu	28.11.1997	24	(6)	5
Vadim Crîcimari	22.08.1988	27	(8)	10
Valeriu Gurgurov	29.01.2002		(8)	
Marius Iosipoi	28.04.2000	18	(1)	1
Ion Mamaliga	28.04.1999	6	(4)	
Oleg Martin	21.10.1999		(12)	
Nicu Namolovan	28.01.2002	3	(19)	2
Nicolae Nemerenco	26.10.1992	8	(14)	2

Football Club Dinamo-Auto Tiraspol

Founded:	24.07.2009	
Stadium:	Stadionul Dinamo-Auto, Tiraspol (1,300)	
Trainer:	Igor Dobrovolski (RUS)	27.08.1967

Goalkeepers:	DOB	M	(s)	G
Cristian Apostolachi	13.09.2000	3		
Maxim Bardîş	16.07.1997	14		
Victor Străistari	21.06.1999	19		
Defenders:	**DOB**	**M**	**(s)**	**G**
Alexandr Belousov	14.05.1998	9	(7)	1
Vladislav Boico	26.05.1999	8	(2)	
Octavian Bulat	23.08.2000	2	(7)	1
Igor Chiperi	04.08.1999	21	(1)	1
Andrei Conohov	12.01.2000		(2)	
Vadim Dijinari	01.04.1999	30		1
Sergiu Gafina	10.11.1984	17	(1)	
Artiom Litviakov	23.10.1996	19	(4)	4
Oleksandr Masalov (UKR)	22.01.1997	23	(2)	
Dmitri Nagiyev (AZE)	27.11.1995	21		1
Evgheni Pleşco	25.02.2001	3	(1)	
Radu Rogac	07.06.1995	4	(1)	
Midfielders:	**DOB**	**M**	**(s)**	**G**
Artiom Bilinschii	19.11.1996	18	(5)	
Alexandr Cuzmenco	26.03.2000	2	(2)	
Abdulla Genaev (RUS)	18.01.2001	6	(1)	
Denis Macalici	07.04.2000	3	(6)	
Maxim Mihaliov	22.08.1986	34		12
Maksym Pyrogov	30.12.1996	19		2
Orkhan Qurbanly (AZE)	12.07.1995	6	(3)	
Serghei Schitenco	27.05.1997	6	(2)	
Vasile Smîntînă	23.12.2001	1	(3)	
Forwards:	**DOB**	**M**	**(s)**	**G**
Vadim Cemîrtan	21.07.1987	5	(6)	1
Andrei Cobeţ	03.01.1997		(6)	
Artem Fedorov (UKR)	18.09.1998	21	(3)	5
Yehor Kondratiuk (UKR)	02.08.2000	27	(7)	3
Petru Leucă	19.07.1990		(5)	1
Vadim Paireli	08.11.1995	14	(7)	7
Andrii Panych (UKR)	27.06.1997	1	(6)	
Dan Puşcaş	01.06.2001	12	(11)	1
Dumitru Rogac	07.11.1998	4	(15)	3
Shakhrom Samiev (TJK)	08.02.2001	17	(2)	7
Nicolai Solodovnicov	18.04.2000	6	(3)	1
Vladimir Titievschii	18.06.1998	1		

Fotbal Club Floreşti

Founded: 2017
Stadium: Stadionul Dinamo, Bender (5,000)
Trainer: Iurie Groşev   16.05.1976

Goalkeepers:	DOB	M	(s)	G
Stanislav Ivanov	22.04.1996	4		
Vladislav Liharev	25.09.2000	19		
Denis Macogonenco	20.02.1996	13		
Defenders:	DOB	M	(s)	G
Fiodor Andriuhin	18.02.1997	13		
Ion Arabadji	31.07.1984	15		
Igor Bondarenco	28.06.1995	27		3
Vladimir Covcenco	19.06.2000	21	(10)	3
Serghei Diulgher	21.03.1991	12	(2)	
Vladimir Ghinaitis	30.03.1995	26	(5)	3
Artyom Khachaturov	18.06.1992	15	(1)	
Sandu Mateescu	20.12.1998	12	(2)	
Alexei Solomin	05.06.1993		(6)	
Ivan Voropai	21.04.1998	17	(2)	
Midfielders:	DOB	M	(s)	G
Anatoli Cheptine	20.05.1990	12	(3)	1
Grigore Coşcodan	26.01.2000	3	(12)	1

Aleksei Dizov	20.03.1988	9	(4)	
Denis Janu	18.05.1995	12	(2)	
Daniel Lisu	02.04.2002	8	(7)	
Constantin Mandricenco	19.02.1991	9	(2)	
Aleksandr Paşcenco	28.05.1989	2	(1)	
Dmitri Semirov	27.12.1995	31	(2)	3
Gheorghe Spînu	25.07.2001		(10)	
Artiom Zeleniuc	16.11.1997	17	(6)	1
Forwards:	DOB	M	(s)	G
Serghei Bobrov	07.09.1991	14	(14)	2
Igor Bugaev	26.06.1984	13	(6)	1
Andrei Calac	14.03.1999	14	(4)	
Andrei Cobeţ	03.01.1997	23	(3)	11
Viktor Gulvas (UKR)	13.10.1997		(3)	
Dumitru Maneacov	06.03.1992	14	(3)	4
Alexandru Osipov	30.07.2000	9	(2)	
Eugeniu Rebenja	05.03.1995	8	(1)	3
Vasili Stefu	26.07.2000	4	(13)	1

Football Club Milsami Orhei

Founded: 2005
Stadium: Complexul Sportiv Raional, Orhei (2,539)
Trainer: Serghei Dubrovin   04.01.1952

Goalkeepers:	DOB	M	(s)	G
Victor Buga	29.06.1994	2	(1)	
Oleg Malac	22.11.2001	2	(1)	
Emil Tîmbur	21.07.1997	32		
Defenders:	DOB	M	(s)	G
Fiodor Andriuhin	18.02.1997	9	(3)	
Igor Arhirii	17.02.1997	31		
Constantin Bogdan	29.12.1993	19	(5)	3
Vadim Bolohan	15.08.1986	33		1
Omar Gaye (GAM)	18.09.1998	23	(5)	1
Ion Ghimp	11.09.1996	16	(9)	
Midfielders:	DOB	M	(s)	G
Vitus Amougui (CMR)	15.01.1991	17	(2)	3
Amit Guluzade (AZE)	20.11.1992	3	(5)	
Vasile Jardan	20.07.1993	28	(1)	5

Igor Lambarskiy (RUS)	26.11.1992	13	(2)	1
Daniel Pîslă	14.06.1986	13	(2)	3
Dumitru Reniţă	02.12.1999		(7)	
Andrei Rusnac	22.09.1996	3	(4)	
Eugen Zasaviţchi	24.11.1992	15	(2)	1
Forwards:	DOB	M	(s)	G
Alexandru Antoniuc	23.05.1989	36		15
Maxim Antoniuc	15.01.1991	5	(17)	3
Alexandru Dedov	26.07.1989	24	(3)	7
Ion Drăgan	14.06.1996	30	(3)	7
Nichita Iuraşco	17.05.1999	5	(14)	1
Oleg Martin	21.10.1999	2	(5)	1
Sergiu Nazar	02.07.1997	17	(13)	8
Artiom Puntus	31.05.1995	16	(8)	10
Veaceslav Zagaevschii	04.04.1996	2		

Club Sportiv Petrocub Hînceşti

Founded: 1994
Stadium: Stadionul Municipal, Hînceşti (1,500)
Trainer: Lilian Popescu   15.11.1973

Goalkeepers:	DOB	M	(s)	G
Cristian Avram	27.07.1994	26	(2)	
Denis Guţul	15.08.1999	2		
Mickaël Meira (POR)	25.01.1994	7		
Defenders:	DOB	M	(s)	G
Gheorghe Brînzaniuc	06.05.2001		(1)	
Donalio Melachio Douanla (CMR)	24.09.1997	22	(5)	1
Ştefan Efros	08.05.1990	27	(2)	1
Ion Jardan	10.01.1990	35		7
Nicolae Munteanu	22.05.2001		(1)	
Jacques Onana Ndzomo (CMR)	23.08.1993	21	(9)	2
Maxim Potîrniche	13.06.1989	20	(3)	1
Petru Racu	17.07.1987	24	(3)	3
Artiom Rozgoniuc	01.10.1995	8	(4)	
Arcadie Rusu	28.06.1993		(2)	
Alexandru Vacarciuc	16.04.2001		(3)	

Midfielders:	DOB	M	(s)	G
Alexandru Bejan	07.05.1996	19	(12)	3
Victor Bogaciuc	17.10.1999	15	(16)	
Andrei Cojocari	21.01.1987	24	(6)	2
Alexandru Onica	25.07.1984	9	(25)	5
Mihai Plătică	15.03.1990	11	(2)	4
Dan Taras	13.02.1994	10	(7)	3
Iaser Ţurcan	07.01.1998	31	(4)	9
Alexandru Vlas	24.08.2003		(2)	
Forwards:	DOB	M	(s)	G
Vladimir Ambros	30.12.1993	30	(2)	16
Oleg Creţul	30.05.2000		(2)	
Ilie Damaşcan	12.10.1995	1	(7)	2
Vadim Gulceac	06.08.1998	10	(19)	7
Miracle Chinaza Nwautobo (NGA)	25.10.2011		(6)	
Sergiu Plătică	05.06.1991	33	(1)	11
Eugeniu Rebenja	05.03.1995		(2)	
Constantin Sandu	15.09.1993		(7)	

Fotbal Club Sfântul Gheorghe Suruceni

Founded: 2003
Stadium: Stadionul Suruceni, Suruceni (1,500)
Trainer: Serghei Cebotari 21.02.1981

Goalkeepers:	DOB	M	(s)	G
Nicolae Calancea	29.08.1986	21		
Nicolae Cebotari	24.05.1997	7		
Maxim Railean	27.03.2000	7		
Defenders:	**DOB**	**M**	**(s)**	**G**
Igor Bondarenco	28.06.1995	1	(2)	
Ion Borș	25.07.2002	7	(2)	
Cassius Vinicius Coelho (ESP)	15.09.1995	3	(1)	
Artur Crăciun	29.06.1998	7	(1)	
Maxim Focșa	21.04.1992	22	(1)	
Andrey Novicov	24.04.1986	24	(3)	
Petru Ojog	17.07.1990	24	(4)	3
Yevhen Smirnov (UKR)	16.04.1993	17	(1)	2
Valeri Stepanenko (UKR)	19.10.1998	5	(3)	
Serghei Svinarenco	18.09.1996	17	(3)	1
Mihail Ștefan	07.08.2001	3	(2)	
Midfielders:	**DOB**	**M**	**(s)**	**G**
Aliyu Yau Adam (NGA)	07.05.2000	13	(8)	2
Mihail Ghecev	05.11.1997	15	(5)	6
Teodor Lungu	12.06.1995	11	(2)	1
Dimitrii Mandrîcenco	13.05.1997	10	(9)	5
Rienat Mochulyak (UKR)	15.02.1998	7	(8)	2
Vitalie Plămădeală	21.01.1985	15	(11)	2
Sidy Sagna (SEN)	04.02.1990	19	(7)	
Eugeniu Slivca	13.07.1989	17	(10)	4
Victor Stînă	20.03.1998	23	(9)	8
Alexandru Suvorov	02.02.1987	18	(10)	6
Dan Taras	13.04.1994	4	(6)	1
Daniel Vădrariu (ROU)	25.06.1990	4	(1)	
Alexandru Vremea	03.11.1991	3	(3)	
Forwards:	**DOB**	**M**	**(s)**	**G**
Artiom Carastoian	10.10.1999	10	(6)	1
Sergiu Istrati	07.08.1988	12	(7)	
Maxim Iurcu	01.02.1993	4	(4)	1
Alexandru Osipov	30.07.2000	6	(6)	
Nicolai Solodovnicov	27.12.2014	4	(9)	4
Roman Volkov (BLR)	08.01.1987	25	(4)	12

Fotbal Club Sheriff Tiraspol

Founded: 04.04.1997
Stadium: Stadionul Sheriff, Tiraspol (12,726)
Trainer: Zoran Zekić (CRO) 29.04.1974
[21.10.2020] Victor Mihailov 18.12.1981
[14.01.2021] Yuriy Vernydub (UKR) 22.01.1966

Goalkeepers:	DOB	M	(s)	G
Dumitru Celeadnic	23.04.1992	11		
Dušan Marković (SRB)	03.04.1998	11		
Zvonimir Mikulić (CRO)	05.02.1990	14		
Defenders:	**DOB**	**M**	**(s)**	**G**
Danilo Arboleda Hurtado (COL)	16.05.1995	11	(1)	
Alexandr Belousov	14.05.1998	7	(3)	
Cristiano da Silva Leite (BRA)	29.08.1993	25	(3)	1
Gustavo Alfonso Dulanto Sanguinetti (PER)	05.09.1995	9	(2)	2
Fernando Peixoto Costanza (BRA)	29.11.1998	10	(4)	
Valeriu Gaiu	06.02.2001	12	(5)	
Adrian Hatman	05.01.2003		(1)	
Keston Anthony Julien (TRI)	26.10.1998	9	(7)	1
Andrej Lukić (CRO)	02.04.1994	8	(7)	1
Alec Takunda Mudimu (ZIM)	08.04.1995	6		1
Ousmane N'Diaye (SEN)	19.08.1991	9		1
Faith Friday Obilor (NGA)	05.03.1991	15	(2)	
Ionuț Andrei Peteleu	20.08.1992	4	(4)	
Veaceslav Posmac	07.11.1990	15	(6)	1
Stjepan Radeljić (BIH)	05.09.1997	10	(2)	
Midfielders:	**DOB**	**M**	**(s)**	**G**
Maxim Cojocaru	13.01.1998	1	(2)	
Sebastian Dahlström (FIN)	05.11.1996	6	(10)	1
Eugeniu Gliga	30.01.2001	1	(4)	
Rifet Kapič (BIH)	03.07.1995	17	(6)	3
Moussa Kyabou (MLI)	18.04.1998	7	(1)	
Benedik Mioč (CRO)	06.10.1994	9	(2)	
William Parra Sinisterra (COL)	01.03.1995	18		2
Charles Petro (MWI)	08.02.2001	13	(9)	1
Sébastien Thill (LUX)	29.12.1993	10	(4)	4
Max Veloso (SUI)	27.03.1992	2	(4)	2
Forwards:	**DOB**	**M**	**(s)**	**G**
Anatole Bertrand Abang (CMR)	06.07.1996	6	(2)	5
Peter Banda (MWI)	22.09.2000	2	(12)	5
Lovro Bizjak (SVN)	12.11.1993	16		9
Andriy Blyznychenko (UKR)	24.07.1994	9	(7)	8
Gabrijel Boban (CRO)	23.07.1989	7	(1)	3
Frank Andersson Castañeda Vélez (COL)	17.07.1994	31	(4)	28
Nadrey Dago (CIV)	07.05.1997	5	(9)	5
Dabney dos Santos (NED)	31.07.1996		(6)	
Richard Gadze (GHA)	23.08.1994	10	(8)	5
Dimitrios Kolovos (GRE)	27.04.1993	20	(2)	10
Adama Traoré I (MLI)	05.06.1995	13	(2)	9
Peter Wilson (SWE)	09.10.1996	7	(10)	7

Clubul Sportiv de Fotbal Speranța Nisporeni

Founded: 1991
Stadium: Complexul Sportiv Raional, Orhei (2,539)
Trainer: Iurie Osipenco 06.07.1974
[24.02.2021] Volodymyr Prokopynenko (UKR) 08.11.1962

Goalkeepers:	DOB	M	(s)	G
Orest Budyuk (UKR)	23.08.1995	20	(1)	
Anatolii Chirinciuc	04.02.1989	12		
Defenders:	**DOB**	**M**	**(s)**	**G**
Mihail Bolun	16.05.1989	13	(7)	
Ștefan Burghiu	28.03.1991	2		
Matvey Guyganov (RUS)	28.07.1994	15		
Oleksandr Nasonov (UKR)	28.04.1992	16	(1)	1
Eugeniu Podirca	14.09.2000	5	(6)	
Arcadie Rusu	28.06.1993	16	(5)	3
Alexandru Stariș	04.01.1995	24	(1)	
Ichaka Tiehi (CIV)	01.01.1996	10	(2)	
Vadym Voronchenko (UKR)	11.01.1989	17	(4)	1
Midfielders:	**DOB**	**M**	**(s)**	**G**
Gheorghe Andronic	25.09.1991	4		1
Andrei Bursuc	23.05.1997	20	(8)	2
Vadim Călugher	07.09.1995	9	(7)	
Ruslan Chelari	27.02.1999	25	(4)	
Andrei Cojocari	21.01.1987	2		
Ion Gavrilița	24.07.2001	3	(2)	
Daniel Guștiuc	05.03.1997	14	(1)	1
Iulian Orbu	11.03.2004	1		
Vladyslav Pavlenko (UKR)	05.04.1994	22	(1)	1
Artur Pătraș	01.10.1988	1		
Daniel Pîslă	14.06.1986	9	(7)	3
Ion Sclifos	10.02.2000	2	(3)	
Forwards:	**DOB**	**M**	**(s)**	**G**
Dmytro Kozban (UKR)	27.04.1989	19	(2)	3
Constantin Sandu	15.09.1993	7	(1)	1
Serghei Trofan	08.11.1997	15	(9)	5
Andriy Yakovlev (UKR)	20.02.1989	27	(3)	3
Oleksandr Yermachenko (UKR)	29.01.1993	22	(5)	4

<table>
<tr><td colspan="4">Fotbal Club Zimbru Chişinău</td></tr>
</table>

Founded:	1947	
Stadium:	Stadionul Zimbru, Chişinău (10,400)	
Trainer:	Vlad Goian	14.11.1970
[16.10.2020]	Simeon Bulgaru	26.05.1985
[14.01.2021]	Vlad Goian	14.11.1970

Goalkeepers:	DOB	M	(s)	G
Maksimilian Kovalov (UKR)	11.07.2000	19		
Silviu Şmalena	09.12.2002	17		
Defenders:	**DOB**	**M**	**(s)**	**G**
Gheorghe Brînzaniuc	06.05.2001	15	(3)	1
Ştefan Burghiu	28.03.1991	31		2
Valentin Chişca	14.08.1999	11	(1)	
Alexei Ciopa	27.10.1998	32	(2)	3
Okezie Prince Ebenezer (NGA)	28.02.2001	22	(2)	2
Denis Furtună	13.10.1999	15	(2)	
Tudor Iapără	16.05.2000	1	(1)	
Danil Kuznetsov (KAZ)	11.12.1999	1	(2)	
Tudor Pavalachi	05.02.2004	1		
Alexandru Vacarciuc	16.04.2001	14	(1)	
Vladislav Zavalişcă	30.01.2003	8	(5)	
Midfielders:	**DOB**	**M**	**(s)**	**G**
Iulian Bejan	04.03.2004		(13)	
Marius Curos	30.10.2003		(3)	
Alexandru Gău	27.01.2004	10	(5)	
Alexandru Graur	11.02.2001	20	(12)	
Bruno Carlos Moura Gomes (POR)	29.09.1993	4		
Artur Pătraş	01.10.1988	31		10

	DOB	M	(s)	G
Vlad Răileanu	09.01.2003	14		
Alexandru Vremea	03.11.1991	10		
Forwards:	**DOB**	**M**	**(s)**	**G**
Artur Barabaş	25.09.2000	1	(3)	
Pascal Chidi Bolu (NGA)	23.11.2000	2	(3)	
Andrei Calac	14.03.1999	3		
Ian-Simon Carabageac	18.03.2004		(2)	
Vadim Cemîrtan	21.07.1987	7	(3)	3
Daniel Ciobanu	11.07.1998	1		
Cristian Dani	09.03.2003	19	(7)	4
Jhonata Pereira dos Santos (BRA)	23.03.1999	5	(2)	1
Alvaro Lucio Lirio Lopes Junior (BRA)	31.03.1998	4	(1)	
Igor Lavrenciuc	08.02.2003		(1)	
Daniel Muntean	03.11.2003		(5)	1
Petru Neagu	13.08.1999	26	(5)	3
Ion Postica	10.01.1999	16	(2)	1
Marius-Adrian Scutaru	11.12.2004		(1)	
Vasili Stefu	26.07.2000	8	(5)	2
Maxim Şoimu	17.07.1990	4	(1)	
Boubacar Traoré (MLI)	24.05.1998	5		
Ibrahim Saleh Yahaya (NGA)	17.06.1999	19	(7)	4

SECOND LEVEL
Divizia A 2020/2021

1.	FC Bălţi (*Promoted*)	26	23	0	3	85	-	17	69
2.	FC Cahul-2005	26	18	3	5	70	-	23	57
3.	FC Sheriff-2 Tiraspol	26	17	3	6	46	-	24	54
4.	CSF Spartanii Selemet	26	14	4	8	57	-	42	46
5.	FC Sucleia	26	14	4	8	64	-	38	46
6.	FC Speranţa Drochia	26	12	6	8	49	-	41	42
7.	FC Olimp Comrat	26	11	5	10	51	-	44	38
8.	FC Iskra Rîbniţa	26	9	8	9	53	-	49	35
9.	FC Tighina Bender	26	9	3	14	42	-	61	30
10.	FC Real Succes Chişinău	26	7	7	12	44	-	35	28
11.	FC Victoria Bardar	26	7	5	14	61	-	65	26
12.	FC Grănicerul Glodeni	26	7	1	18	25	-	61	22
13.	FC Făleşti (*Relegated*)	26	6	0	20	40	-	92	18
14.	FC Sireţi (*Relegated*)	26	2	3	21	26	-	121	9

<u>Please note</u>: FC Cahul-2005 were also promoted, but the club did not apply for the First Level licence.

NATIONAL TEAM

INTERNATIONAL MATCHES
(16.07.2020 – 15.07.2021)

03.09.2020	Parma	Moldova - Kosovo	1-1(1-0)	(UNL)
06.09.2020	Ljubljana	Slovenia - Moldova	1-0(1-0)	(UNL)
07.10.2020	Firenze	Italy - Moldova	6-0(5-0)	(F)
11.10.2020	Athína	Greece - Moldova	2-0(1-0)	(UNL)
14.10.2020	Chişinău	Moldova - Slovenia	0-4(0-3)	(UNL)
12.11.2020	Chişinău	Moldova - Russia	0-0	(F)
15.11.2020	Chişinău	Moldova - Greece	0-2(0-2)	(UNL)
18.11.2020	Prishtina	Kosovo - Moldova	1-0(1-0)	(UNL)
25.03.2021	Chişinău	Moldova - Faroe Islands	1-1(1-0)	(WCQ)
28.03.2021	Herning	Denmark - Moldova	8-0(5-0)	(WCQ)
31.03.2021	Chişinău	Moldova - Israel	1-4(1-1)	(WCQ)
03.06.2021	Paderborn	Turkey - Moldova	2-0(0-0)	(F)
06.06.2021	Chişinău	Moldova - Azerbaijan	1-0(1-0)	(F)

03.09.2020   MOLDOVA - KOSOVO   1-1(1-0)   2nd UEFA Nations League C, Group 3

Stadio "Ennio Tardini", Parma (Italy); Referee: Kai Erik Steen (Norway); Attendance: 0
MDA: Alexei Coşelev, Igor Armaş (Cap), Veaceslav Posmac, Victor Mudrac, Artur Ioniţă, Oleg Reabciuk, Vadim Raţă (81.Denis Marandici), Cătălin Carp (71.Alexandru Epureanu), Mihail Caimacov (56.Eugeniu Cociuc), Sergiu Plătică, Ion Nicolăescu. Trainer: Engin Fırat (Turkey).
Goal: Ion Nicolăescu (20).

06.09.2020   SLOVENIA - MOLDOVA   1-0(1-0)   2nd UEFA Nations League C, Group 3

Stadion Stožice, Ljubljana; Referee: Jérôme Brisard (France); Attendance: 0
MDA: Alexei Coşelev, Igor Armaş (Cap), Veaceslav Posmac, Victor Mudrac, Oleg Reabciuk, Artur Ioniţă, Vadim Raţă (69.Alexandru Suvorov), Cătălin Carp, Mihail Caimacov (46.Alexandru Epureanu), Sergiu Plătică, Vitalie Damaşcan (60.Nicolae Milinceanu). Trainer: Engin Fırat (Turkey).

07.10.2020   **ITALY - MOLDOVA**   **6-0(5-0)**   Friendly International
Stadio "Artemio Franchi", Firenze; Referee: Daniel Siebert (Germany); Attendance: 0
MDA: Alexei Coşelev (46.Stanislav Namaşco), Igor Armaş, Artur Crăciun (46.Victor Mudrac), Denis Marandici (46.Oleg Reabciuk), Alexandru Suvorov (46.Eugeniu Cociuc), Artur Ioniţă (Cap), Veaceslav Posmac, Vadim Raţă, Cătălin Carp (28.Alexandru Epureanu), Sergiu Plătică, Ion Nicolăescu (79.Nicolae Milinceanu). Trainer: Engin Fırat (Turkey).

11.10.2020   **GREECE - MOLDOVA**   **2-0(1-0)**   2nd UEFA Nations League C, Group 3
Stádio Olympiako „Spiros Louis", Athína; Referee: Dennis Higler (Netherlands); Attendance: 0
MDA: Stanislav Namaşco, Igor Armaş (Cap), Veaceslav Posmac [*sent off 45+1*], Victor Mudrac, Oleg Reabciuk, Artur Ioniţă (76.Petru Racu), Vadim Raţă (66.Denis Marandici), Eugeniu Cociuc, Mihail Caimacov (46.Alexandru Epureanu), Sergiu Plătică, Ion Nicolăescu (58.Nicolae Milinceanu). Trainer: Engin Fırat (Turkey).

14.10.2020   **MOLDOVA - SLOVENIA**   **0-4(0-3)**   2nd UEFA Nations League C, Group 3
Stadionul Zimbru, Chişinău; Referee: João Pedro da Silva Pinheiro (Portugal); Attendance: 0
MDA: Stanislav Namaşco, Petru Racu, Igor Armaş (Cap), Victor Mudrac (46.Artur Crăciun), Oleg Reabciuk, Artur Ioniţă (74.Dan Taras), Vadim Raţă, Cătălin Carp (46.Mihail Caimacov), Eugeniu Cociuc, Sergiu Plătică (59.Nicolae Milinceanu), Ion Nicolăescu (79.Danu Spătaru). Trainer: Engin Fırat (Turkey).

12.11.2020   **MOLDOVA - RUSSIA**   **0-0**   Friendly International
Stadionul Zimbru, Chişinău; Referee: Radu Marian Petrescu (Romania); Attendance: 0
MDA: Stanislav Namaşco, Alexandru Epureanu (Cap), Igor Armaş, Ion Jardan, Oleg Reabciuk, Eugeniu Cebotaru (83.Danu Spătaru), Artur Ioniţă, Vadim Raţă, Mihail Caimacov (64.Eugeniu Cociuc), Sergiu Plătică (90+1.Cristian Dros), Ion Nicolăescu (64.Vitalie Damaşcan). Trainer: Engin Fırat (Turkey).

15.11.2020   **MOLDOVA - GREECE**   **0-2(0-2)**   2nd UEFA Nations League C, Group 3
Stadionul Zimbru, Chişinău; Referee: Fran Jović (Croatia); Attendance: 0
MDA: Stanislav Namaşco, Igor Armaş (Cap), Ion Jardan, Veaceslav Posmac, Oleg Reabciuk, Eugeniu Cebotaru (46.Alexandru Epureanu), Artur Ioniţă (83.Alexandru Boiciuc), Eugeniu Cociuc (46.Mihail Caimacov), Danu Spătaru, Vadim Raţă (62.Iaser Ţurcan), Vitalie Damaşcan (71.Cristian Dros). Trainer: Engin Fırat (Turkey).

18.11.2020   **KOSOVO - MOLDOVA**   **1-0(1-0)**   2nd UEFA Nations League C, Group 3
Stadiumi „Fadil Vokrri", Prishtina; Referee: Roomer Tarajev (Estonia); Attendance: 0
MDA: Stanislav Namaşco, Igor Armaş (Cap), Ion Jardan, Iaser Ţurcan, Ştefan Efros, Oleg Reabciuk, Eugeniu Cebotaru, Artur Ioniţă (59.Mihail Caimacov), Danu Spătaru (85.Alexandr Belousov), Sergiu Plătică (38.Vadim Raţă), Ion Nicolăescu. Trainer: Engin Fırat (Turkey).

25.03.2021   **MOLDOVA - FAROE ISLANDS**   **1-1(1-0)**   22nd FIFA WC. Qualifiers
Stadionul Zimbru, Chişinău; Referee: Iwan Arwel Griffith (Wales); Attendance: 0
MDA: Stanislav Namaşco, Alexandru Epureanu (Cap), Igor Armaş, Ion Jardan, Veaceslav Posmac, Oleg Reabciuk, Artur Ioniţă, Vadim Raţă (86.Andrei Cojocari), Cătălin Carp (72.Mihail Caimacov), Vitalie Damaşcan (73.Virgiliu Postolachi), Ion Nicolăescu. Trainer: Roberto Bordin (Italy).
Goal: Ion Nicolăescu (9).

28.03.2021   **DENMARK - MOLDOVA**   **8-0(5-0)**   22nd FIFA WC. Qualifiers
MCH Arena, Herning; Referee: Əliyar Ağayev (Azerbaijan); Attendance: 0
MDA: Stanislav Namaşco, Alexandru Epureanu (Cap), Igor Armaş, Igor Arhirii (46.Vadim Bolohan), Oleg Reabciuk, Artur Ioniţă, Alexandru Antoniuc (46.Ion Jardan), Vadim Raţă, Cătălin Carp (54.Andrei Cojocari), Sergiu Plătică (54.Marius Iosipoi), Ion Nicolăescu (75.Vitalie Damaşcan). Trainer: Roberto Bordin (Italy).

31.03.2021   **MOLDOVA - ISRAEL**   **1-4(1-1)**   22nd FIFA WC. Qualifiers
Stadionul Zimbru, Chişinău; Referee: Bojan Pandžić (Sweden); Attendance: 0
MDA: Alexei Coşelev, Alexandru Epureanu (Cap), Igor Armaş, Vadim Bolohan (80.Daniel Dumbrăvanu), Ion Jardan, Oleg Reabciuk, Andrei Cojocari (72.Corneliu Cotogoi), Vadim Raţă (79.Marius Iosipoi), Cătălin Carp (62.Ion Drăgan), Sergiu Plătică, Ion Nicolăescu [*sent off 50*]. Trainer: Roberto Bordin (Italy).
Goal: Cătălin Carp (29).

03.06.2021   **TURKEY - MOLDOVA**   **2-0(0-0)**   Friendly International
Benteler-Arena, Paderborn (Germany); Referee: Sascha Stegemann (Germany); Attendance: 0
MDA: Dumitru Celeadnic, Maxim Potîrniche, Ion Jardan, Veaceslav Posmac (Cap), Igor Arhirii, Alexandru Antoniuc (67.Igor Costrov), Vadim Raţă, Gheorghe Anton (56.Cristian Dros), Danu Spătaru (87.Nicky Serghei Cleşcenco), Sergiu Plătică, Vitalie Damaşcan (67.Ion Nicolăescu). Trainer: Roberto Bordin (Italy).

06.06.2021   **MOLDOVA - AZERBAIJAN**   **1-0(1-0)**   Friendly International
Stadionul Zimbru, Chişinău; Referee: Marian Alexandru Barbu (Romania); Attendance: 2,130
MDA: Cristian Avram, Igor Armaş (Cap), Vadim Bolohan (64.Maxim Potîrniche), Ion Jardan, Veaceslav Posmac, Igor Costrov (46.Gheorghe Anton), Vadim Raţă (59.Danu Spătaru), Cristian Dros, Alexandr Belousov, Sergiu Plătică (90+1.Daniel Dumbrăvanu), Vitalie Damaşcan (58.Ion Nicolăescu). Trainer: Roberto Bordin (Italy).
Goal: Vitalie Damaşcan (8).

NATIONAL TEAM PLAYERS (16.07.2020 – 15.07.2021)					

Name	DOB	Caps	Goals	2020/2021:	Club
Goalkeepers					
Cristian AVRAM	27.07.1994	1	0	2021:	*CS Petrocub Hînceşti*
Dumitru CELEADNIC	23.04.1992	2	0	2021:	*FC Sheriff Tiraspol*
Alexei COŞELEV	19.11.1993	25	0	2020:	*Fortuna Sittard (NED)*
				01.03.2021->	*Júbilo Iwata (JPN)*
Stanislav NAMAŞCO	10.11.1986	53	0	2020/2021:	*Keşlə FK Bakı (AZE)*

Defenders

Igor ARHIRII	17.02.1997	2	0	2021:	FC Milsami Orhei
Igor ARMAŞ	14.07.1987	70	5	2020/2021:	FC Voluntari (ROU)
Alexandr BELOUSOV	14.05.1998	2	0	2020:	FC Dinamo-Auto Tiraspol
				31.12.2020->	FC Sheriff Tiraspol
Vadim BOLOHAN	15.08.1986	25	0	2021:	FC Milsami Orhei
Artur CRĂCIUN	29.06.1998	4	0	2020:	Budapest Honvéd FC (HUN)
Daniel DUMBRĂVANU	22.07.2001	2	0	2021:	Genoa C&FC (ITA)
Ştefan EFROS	08.05.1990	4	0	2020/2021:	CS Petrocub Hînceşti
Alexandru EPUREANU	27.09.1986	100	7	2020/2021:	İstanbul Başakşehir FK (TUR)
Ion JARDAN	10.01.1990	38	0	2020/2021:	CS Petrocub Hînceşti
Denis MARANDICI	18.09.1996	3	0	2020:	NK Celje (SVN)
Victor MUDRAC	03.03.1994	8	0	2020:	SK Slavia Praha (CZE)
Veaceslav POSMAC	07.11.1990	45	2	2020/2021:	FC Sheriff Tiraspol
Maxim POTÎRNICHE	13.06.1989	9	0	2021:	CS Petrocub Hînceşti
Petru RACU	17.07.1987	50	0	2020:	CS Petrocub Hînceşti
Oleg REABCIUK	16.01.1998	27	0	2020:	FC Paços de Ferreira (POR)
				01.01.2021->	Olympiacos SFP Peiraiás (GRE)

Midfielders

Gheorghe ANTON	27.01.1993	10	0	2020/2021:	SCM Gloria Buzău (ROU)
Mihail CAIMACOV	22.07.1998	8	0	2020:	NK Olimpija Ljubljana (SVN)
				31.01.2021->	NK Osijek (CRO)
				01.02.2021->	FC Koper (SVN)
Cătălin CARP	20.10.1993	36	2	2020:	FK Ufa (RUS)
				24.02.2021->	FK Tambov (RUS)
Eugeniu CEBOTARU	16.10.1984	68	1	2020/2021:	FC Academica Clinceni (ROU)
Eugeniu COCIUC	11.05.1993	25	0	2020/2021:	Sabah FC Bakı (AZE)
Andrei COJOCARI	21.01.1987	43	2	2021:	CS Petrocub Hînceşti
Igor COSTROV	03.08.1987	2	0	2021:	FC Gomel (BLR)
Corneliu COTOGOI	23.06.2001	1	0	2021:	FC Dacia Buiucani Chişinău
Ion DRĂGAN	14.07.1996	1	0	2021:	FC Milsami Orhei
Cristian DROS	15.04.1998	5	0	2020/2021:	JPFS/FK Spartaks Jūrmala (LVA)
Artur IONIȚĂ	17.08.1990	55	3	2020/2021:	Benevento Calcio (ITA)
Sergiu PLĂTICĂ	09.06.1991	25	0	2020/2021:	CS Petrocub Hînceşti
Vadim RAȚĂ	05.03.1993	20	1	2020/2021:	AFC Chindia Târgovişte (ROU)
Alexandru SUVOROV	02.02.1987	59	5	2020:	FC Sfântul Gheorghe Suruceni
Dan TARAS	13.02.1994	5	0	2020:	CS Petrocub Hînceşti
Iaser ȚURCAN	07.01.1998	6	0	2020:	CS Petrocub Hînceşti

Forwards

Alexandru ANTONIUC	23.05.1989	46	3	2021:	FC Milsami Orhei
Alexandru BOICIUC	21.08.1997	10	0	2020/2021:	FRC Academica Clinceni (ROU)
Nicky Serghei CLEŞCENCO	23.07.2001	1	0	2021:	FC Sion (SUI)
Vitalie DAMAŞCAN	24.01.1999	13	1	2020:	Torino FC (ITA)
				15.09.2020->	RKC Waalwijk (NED)
Marius IOSIPOI	28.04.2000	2	0	2021:	FK Veles Moskva (RUS)
Nicolae MILINCEANU	01.08.1992	14	1	2020:	FC Vaduz (LIE)
Ion NICOLĂESCU	07.09.1998	18	2	2020:	FC Vitebsk (BLR)
				15.09.2020->	FC Shakhtyor Solihorsk (BLR)
				16.09.2020->	FK DAC Dunajská Streda (SVK)
Virgiliu POSTOLACHI	17.03.2000	1	0	2021:	Vendsyssel FF Hjørring (DEN)
Dan SPĂTARU	24.05.1994	15	0	2020:	FC Noah Yerevan (ARM)
				01.01.2021->	FC Ararat-Armenia Yerevan (ARM)

Trainer

Engin FIRAT (Turkey) [28.10.2019 – 31.12.2020]	11.06.1970	11 M; 0 W; 2 D; 9 L; 3-22
Roberto BORDIN (Italy) [from 12.02.2021]	10.01.1965	5 M; 1 W; 1 D; 3 L; 3-15

MONTENEGRO

The Country:
Crna Gora (Montenegro)
Capital: Podgorica
Surface: 13,812 km²
Inhabitants: 621,873 [2020]
Time: UTC+1

The FA:
Fudbalski savez Crne Gore
Bulevar Veljka Vlahovica bb ME, 81000 Podgorica
Tel: +382 20 445 600
Foundation date: 1931
Member of FIFA since: 2007
Member of UEFA since: 2007
Website: www.fscg.me

NATIONAL TEAM RECORDS

RECORDS		
First international match:	24.03.2007, Podgorica:	Montenegro – Hungary 2-1
Most international caps:	Fatos Bećiraj	- 80 caps (since 2009)
Most international goals:	Stevan Jovetić	- 31 goals / 61 caps (since 2007)

UEFA EUROPEAN CHAMPIONSHIP	
1960	-
1964	-
1968	-
1972	-
1976	-
1980	-
1984	-
1988	-
1992	-
1996	-
2000	-
2004	-
2008	-
2012	Qualifiers
2016	Qualifiers
2020	Qualifiers

was part of Yugoslavia/Serbia until 2006

FIFA WORLD CUP	
1930	-
1934	-
1938	-
1950	-
1954	-
1958	-
1962	-
1966	-
1970	-
1974	-
1978	-
1982	-
1986	-
1990	-
1994	-
1998	-
2002	-
2006	-
2010	Qualifiers
2014	Qualifiers
2018	Qualifiers

OLYMPIC TOURNAMENTS	
1908	-
1912	-
1920	-
1924	-
1928	-
1936	-
1948	-
1952	-
1956	-
1960	-
1964	-
1968	-
1972	-
1976	-
1980	-
1984	-
1988	-
1992	-
1996	-
2000	-
2004	-
2008	-
2012	Qualifiers
2016	Qualifiers

UEFA NATIONS LEAGUE	
2018/2019	League C
2020/2021	League C (promoted to League B)

FIFA CONFEDERATIONS CUP 1992-2017
None

MONTENEGRIN CLUB HONOURS IN EUROPEAN CLUB COMPETITIONS:

European Champion Clubs.Cup (1956-1992) / UEFA Champions League (1993-2021)
None
Fairs Cup (1858-1971) / UEFA Cup (1972-2009) / UEFA Europa League (2010-2021)
None
UEFA Super Cup (1972-2020)
None
*European Cup Winners.Cup 1961-1999**
None

defunct competition

NATIONAL COMPETITIONS
TABLE OF HONOURS

	CHAMPIONS	CUP WINNERS	BEST GOALSCORERS	
2006/2007	FK Zeta Golubovci	FK Rudar Pljevlja	Damir Čakar (FK Rudar Pljevlja)	
			Žarko Korać (FK Zeta Golubovci)	16
2007/2008	FK Budućnost Podgorica	FK Mogren Budva	Ivan Jablan (FK Lovćen Cetinje)	13
2008/2009	FK Mogren Budva	OFK Petrovac	Fatos Bećiraj (FK Budućnost Podgorica)	18
2009/2010	FK Rudar Pljevlja	FK Rudar Pljevlja	Ivan Bošković (OFK Grbalj)	28
2010/2011	FK Mogren Budva	FK Rudar Pljevlja	Ivan Vuković (FK Budućnost Podgorica)	20
2011/2012	FK Budućnost Podgorica	FK Čelik Nikšić	Admir Adrović (FK Budućnost Podgorica)	22
2012/2013	FK Sutjeska Nikšić	FK Budućnost Podgorica	Admir Adrović (FK Budućnost Podgorica)	
			Žarko Korać (FK Zeta Golubovci)	15
2013/2014	FK Sutjeska Nikšić	FK Lovćen Cetinje	Stefan Mugoša (OFK Titograd Podgorica)	15
2014/2015	FK Rudar Pljevlja	FK Mladost Podgorica	Goran Vujović (FK Sutjeska Nikšić)	21
2015/2016	FK Mladost Podgorica	FK Rudar Pljevlja	Marko Šćepanović (FK Mladost Podgorica)	19
2016/2017	FK Budućnost Podgorica	FK Sutjeska Nikšić	Zoran Petrović (OFK Titograd Podgorica)	14
2017/2018	FK Sutjeska Nikšić	FK Mladost Podgorica	Igor Ivanović (FK Sutjeska Nikšić)	14
2018/2019	FK Sutjeska Nikšić	FK Budućnost Podgorica	Nikola Krstović (FK Zeta Golubovci)	17
2019/2020	FK Budućnost Podgorica	*Competition cancelled*	Marko Ćetković (FK Sutjeska Nikšić)	10
2020/2021	FK Budućnost Podgorica	FK Budućnost Podgorica	Božo Marković (FK Sutjeska Nikšić)	16

NATIONAL CHAMPIONSHIP
Prva Crnogorska Fudbal Liga 2020/2021
(14.08.2020 – 25.05.2021)

Results

Round 1 [14-15.08.2020]
FK Dečić - FK Budućnost 2-0(1-0)
FK Jezero - Rudar Pljevlja 1-0(1-0)
FK Podgorica - OFK Titograd 2-0(0-0)
Sutjeska Nikšić - OFK Petrovac 3-3(0-2)
FK Zeta - Iskra Danilovgrad 0-1(0-0)

Round 2 [22-23.08.2020]
FK Jezero - FK Zeta 1-1(0-1)
FK Budućnost - Sutjeska Nikšić 1-0(0-0)
Iskra Danilovgrad - FK Dečić 0-0
OFK Petrovac - FK Podgorica 0-1(0-0)
Rudar Pljevlja - OFK Titograd 3-1(1-1)

Round 3 [29.08.2020]
FK Dečić - FK Jezero 0-0
FK Podgorica - FK Budućnost 4-0(3-0)
OFK Titograd - OFK Petrovac 2-2(1-1)
Sutjeska Nikšić - Iskra Danil. 3-2(1-1) [16.09.]
FK Zeta - Rudar Pljevlja 2-1(2-1) [16.09.]

Round 4 [12.09.2020]
FK Jezero - Sutjeska Nikšić 0-2(0-1)
Iskra Danilovgrad - FK Podgorica 1-1(1-1)
Rudar Pljevlja - OFK Petrovac 1-0(0-0)
FK Budućnost - OFK Titograd 3-1(0-1)
FK Zeta - FK Dečić 0-2(0-1)

Round 5 [20.09.2020]
Sutjeska Nikšić - FK Zeta 0-2(0-0)
FK Podgorica - FK Jezero 1-0(0-0)
FK Dečić - Rudar Pljevlja 4-1(3-0)
OFK Titograd - Iskra Danilovgrad 1-1(1-0)
OFK Petrovac - Budućnost 0-1(0-0) [17.12.]

Round 6 [26-27.09.2020]
FK Jezero - OFK Titograd 1-0(0-0)
Rudar Pljevlja - FK Budućnost 1-2(1-2)
FK Dečić - Sutjeska Nikšić 1-1(1-0)
Iskra Danilovgrad - OFK Petrovac 1-0(0-0)
FK Zeta - FK Podgorica 1-1(0-0)

Round 7 [30.09.2020]
OFK Petrovac - FK Jezero 0-1(0-1)
Sutjeska Nikšić - Rudar Pljevlja 2-0(0-0)
OFK Titograd - FK Zeta 1-0(0-0)
FK Podgorica - FK Dečić 1-1(0-0)
FK Budućnost - Iskra Danilovgrad 1-0(0-0)

Round 8 [04.10.2020]
FK Jezero - FK Budućnost 0-2(0-1)
Sutjeska Nikšić - FK Podgorica 3-0(2-0)
Rudar Pljevlja - Iskra Danilovgrad 4-0(2-0)
FK Zeta - OFK Petrovac 1-0(0-0)
FK Dečić - OFK Titograd 3-0(0-0)

Round 9 [17.10.2020]
FK Budućnost - FK Zeta 3-0 *awarded*
OFK Petrovac - FK Dečić 1-1(1-0)
FK Podgorica - Rudar Pljevlja 2-0(1-0)
Iskra Danilovgrad - FK Jezero 2-1(0-0)
OFK Titograd - Sutjeska Nikšić 0-0

Round 10 [25.10.2020]
OFK Petrovac - Sutjeska Nikšić 1-1(1-0)
Rudar Pljevlja - FK Jezero 0-1(0-1)
OFK Titograd - FK Podgorica 1-0(0-0)
Iskra Danilovgrad - FK Zeta 0-0
FK Budućnost - FK Dečić 2-2(2-1)

Round 11 [31.10.2020]
FK Podgorica - OFK Petrovac 1-3(1-1)
Sutjeska Nikšić - FK Budućnost 0-1(0-1)
FK Zeta - FK Jezero 1-0(1-0)
OFK Titograd - Rudar Pljevlja 0-2(0-0)
FK Dečić - Iskra Danilovgrad 2-0(1-0)

Round 12 [04.11.2020]
FK Jezero - FK Dečić 0-0
Rudar Pljevlja - FK Zeta 0-3(0-1)
OFK Petrovac - OFK Titograd 1-3(1-1)
FK Budućnost - FK Podgorica 1-0(0-0)
Iskra Danilovgrad - Sutjeska Nikšić 3-0(1-0)

Round 13 [08.11.2020]
Sutjeska Nikšić - FK Jezero 0-1(0-1)
OFK Petrovac - Rudar Pljevlja 1-1(1-1)
OFK Titograd - FK Budućnost 0-4(0-2)
FK Podgorica - Iskra Danilovgrad 1-1(0-0)
FK Dečić - FK Zeta 0-0

Round 14 [21.11.2020]
Rudar Pljevlja - FK Dečić 0-3(0-0)
FK Jezero - FK Podgorica 0-0
FK Zeta - Sutjeska Nikšić 0-1(0-1)
Iskra Danilovgrad - OFK Titograd 1-1(1-0)
FK Budućnost - OFK Petrovac 2-1(0-1)

Round 15 [29.11.2020]
FK Budućnost - Rudar Pljevlja 4-2(3-1)
Sutjeska Nikšić - FK Dečić 1-1(0-1)
OFK Titograd - FK Jezero 1-0(0-0)
FK Podgorica - FK Zeta 0-1(0-0)
OFK Petrovac - Iskra Danilovgrad 1-0(0-0)

Round 16 [02.12.2020]
FK Jezero - OFK Petrovac 2-0(1-0)
Rudar Pljevlja - Sutjeska Nikšić 0-4(0-3)
Iskra Danilovgrad - FK Budućnost 0-2(0-1)
FK Zeta - OFK Titograd 1-0(0-0)
FK Dečić - FK Podgorica 0-3(0-1)

Round 17 [06.12.2020]
FK Budućnost - FK Jezero 2-1(2-0)
Iskra Danilovgrad - Rudar Pljevlja 0-1(0-0)
FK Podgorica - Sutjeska Nikšić 1-1(0-1)
OFK Petrovac - FK Zeta 1-1(1-0)
OFK Titograd - FK Dečić 1-1(0-0)

Round 18 [09.12.2020]
FK Jezero - Iskra Danilovgrad 0-2(0-0)
Rudar Pljevlja - FK Podgorica 1-0(0-0)
FK Dečić - OFK Petrovac 1-0(0-0)
Sutjeska Nikšić - OFK Titograd 3-0(1-0)
FK Zeta - FK Budućnost 0-2(0-0)

Round 19 [13.12.2020]
FK Jezero - Rudar Pljevlja 1-2(0-1)
Sutjeska Nikšić - OFK Petrovac 2-1(2-0)
FK Dečić - FK Budućnost 0-4(0-2)
FK Zeta - Iskra Danilovgrad 0-2(0-0)
FK Podgorica - OFK Titograd 2-1(1-1)

Round 20 [19.02.2021]
Rudar Pljevlja - OFK Titograd 4-2(4-1)
FK Jezero - FK Zeta 0-1(0-0)
OFK Petrovac - FK Podgorica 2-1(1-1)
Iskra Danilovgrad - FK Dečić 2-1(2-1)
FK Budućnost - Sutjeska Nikšić 1-1(1-1)

Round 21 [23.02.2021]
FK Zeta - Rudar Pljevlja 0-1(0-1)
FK Dečić - FK Jezero 0-0
Sutjeska Nikšić - Iskra Danilovgrad 2-2(1-0)
FK Podgorica - FK Budućnost 0-1(0-0)
OFK Titograd - OFK Petrovac 1-0(0-0)

Round 22 [28.02.2021]
FK Budućnost - OFK Titograd 1-0(0-0)
FK Zeta - FK Dečić 1-2(0-1)
Iskra Danilovgrad - FK Podgorica 1-0(0-0)
FK Jezero - Sutjeska Nikšić 0-2(0-1)
Rudar Pljevlja - OFK Petrovac 2-0(1-0)

Round 23 [06.03.2021]
Sutjeska Nikšić - FK Zeta 4-3(2-3)
FK Dečić - Rudar Pljevlja 0-1(0-0)
FK Podgorica - FK Jezero 2-1(1-0)
OFK Titograd - Iskra Danilovgrad 0-0
OFK Petrovac - FK Budućnost 1-4(1-0)

Round 24 [10.03.2021]
Rudar Pljevlja - FK Budućnost 1-1(0-1)
Iskra Danilovgrad - OFK Petrovac 0-0
FK Dečić - Sutjeska Nikšić 2-1(0-1)
FK Zeta - FK Podgorica 1-3(0-1)
FK Jezero - OFK Titograd 0-0 [21.04.]

Round 25 [14.03.2021]
FK Budućnost - Iskra Danilovgrad 1-0(1-0)
OFK Petrovac - FK Jezero 0-2(0-1)
Sutjeska Nikšić - Rudar Pljevlja 1-1(1-0)
OFK Titograd - FK Zeta 0-2(0-1)
FK Podgorica - FK Dečić 0-3(0-2)

Round 26 [20.03.2021]
FK Zeta - OFK Petrovac 1-1(1-0)
FK Jezero - FK Budućnost 1-2(0-2)
Rudar Pljevlja - Iskra Danilovgrad 0-0
Sutjeska Nikšić - FK Podgorica 1-1(0-1)
FK Dečić - OFK Titograd 1-0(0-0)

Round 27 [03.04.2021]
FK Podgorica - Rudar Pljevlja 2-1(2-1)
OFK Petrovac - FK Dečić 0-0
OFK Titograd - Sutjeska Nikšić 0-4(0-2)
Iskra Danilovgrad - FK Jezero 1-1(1-0)
FK Budućnost - FK Zeta 0-1(0-0)

Round 28 [07.04.2021]
OFK Petrovac - Sutjeska Nikšić 1-3(0-2)
Rudar Pljevlja - FK Jezero 4-2(1-1)
OFK Titograd - FK Podgorica 0-1(0-1)
FK Budućnost - FK Dečić 2-0(1-0)
Iskra Danilovgrad - FK Zeta 1-1(0-1)

Round 29 [11.04.2021]
FK Dečić - Iskra Danilovgrad 0-0
FK Podgorica - OFK Petrovac 0-1(0-1)
Sutjeska Nikšić - FK Budućnost 0-1(0-0)
FK Zeta - FK Jezero 0-1(0-0)
OFK Titograd - Rudar Pljevlja 0-0

Round 30 [17.04.2021]
Iskra Danilovgrad - Sutjeska Nikšić 0-0
FK Jezero - FK Dečić 1-0(1-0)
OFK Petrovac - OFK Titograd 0-0
Rudar Pljevlja - FK Zeta 0-1(0-0)
FK Budućnost - FK Podgorica 1-2(0-1)

Round 31 [25.04.2021]
OFK Petrovac - Rudar Pljevlja 3-1(2-1)
Sutjeska Nikšić - FK Jezero 0-0
FK Dečić - FK Zeta 3-1(2-0)
FK Podgorica - Iskra Danilovgrad 1-0(1-0)
OFK Titograd - FK Budućnost 0-2(0-2)

Round 32 [01.05.2021]
Iskra Danilovgrad - OFK Titograd 1-1(1-0)
FK Jezero - FK Podgorica 3-2(3-0)
Rudar Pljevlja - FK Dečić 0-0
FK Zeta - Sutjeska Nikšić 0-2(0-1)
FK Budućnost - OFK Petrovac 0-2(0-0)

Round 33 [09.05.2021]
FK Budućnost - Rudar Pljevlja 3-1(0-0)
FK Podgorica - FK Zeta 2-1(2-0)
Sutjeska Nikšić - FK Dečić 1-2(0-0)
OFK Petrovac - Iskra Danilovgrad 1-0(1-0)
OFK Titograd - FK Jezero 1-2(0-1)

Round 34 [14.05.2021]
FK Dečić - FK Podgorica 0-1(0-0)
FK Zeta - OFK Titograd 2-1(0-0)
Iskra Danilovgrad - FK Budućnost 1-1(1-1)
FK Jezero - OFK Petrovac 1-0(0-0)
Rudar Pljevlja - Sutjeska Nikšić 0-2(0-1)

Round 35 [19.05.2021]
FK Budućnost - FK Jezero 3-2(3-2)
FK Podgorica - Sutjeska Nikšić 0-4(0-2)
Iskra Danilovgrad - Rudar Pljevlja 2-0(1-0)
OFK Petrovac - FK Zeta 0-2(0-1)
OFK Titograd - FK Dečić 1-0(0-0)

Round 36 [25.05.2021]
FK Dečić - OFK Petrovac 1-1(1-0)
Sutjeska Nikšić - OFK Titograd 1-2(1-2)
FK Zeta - FK Budućnost 2-4(0-0)
FK Jezero - Iskra Danilovgrad 0-0
Rudar Pljevlja - FK Podgorica 1-0(0-0)

Final Standings

					Total			Home					Away				
1.	**FK Budućnost Podgorica**	36	27	4	5	65 - 29	85	13	2	3	31 - 16	14	2	2	34 - 13
2.	FK Sutjeska Nikšić	36	15	12	9	56 - 34	57	6	6	6	27 - 23	9	6	3	29 - 11
3.	FK Dečić Tuzi	36	13	15	8	39 - 28	54	8	6	4	20 - 14	5	9	4	19 - 14
4.	FK Podgorica	36	15	7	14	39 - 38	52	9	3	6	22 - 20	6	4	8	17 - 18
5.	FK Jezero Plav	36	12	9	15	28 - 34	45	6	5	7	12 - 16	6	4	8	16 - 18
6.	FK Zeta Golubovci*	36	13	7	16	34 - 41	45	5	2	11	13 - 25	8	5	5	21 - 16
7.	FK Rudar Pljevlja	36	13	6	17	38 - 50	45	8	3	7	22 - 22	5	3	10	16 - 28
8.	FK Iskra Danilovgrad (*Relegation Play-offs*)	36	9	17	10	28 - 29	44	6	10	2	17 - 11	3	7	8	11 - 18
9.	OFK Petrovac (*Relegation Play-offs*)	36	7	11	18	29 - 45	32	4	6	8	14 - 23	3	5	10	15 - 22
10.	OFK Titograd Podgorica (*Relegated*)	36	7	10	19	23 - 51	31	5	6	7	10 - 21	2	4	12	13 - 30

2 points deducted, for leaving the pitch in Round 9, later reduced to 1 point.

Top goalscorers:

16	Božo Marković	*FK Sutjeska Nikšić*
15	Draško Božović	*FK Budućnost Podgorica*
13	Milutin Osmajić	*FK Sutjeska Nikšić*
12	Vuk Striković	*FK Rudar Pljevlja*

Promotion / Relegation Play-offs [01-06.06.2021]

FK Iskra Danilovgrad – FK Igalo	2-1(0-0)	1-0(1-0)
OFK Petrovac - FK Arsenal Tivat	2-1(1-1)	1-2 aet; 6-5 pen

Both FK Iskra Danilovgrad and OFK Petrovac keeped their places at first level for 2021/2022.

NATIONAL CUP
Kup Crne Gore 2020/2021

1/8-Finals [21.10.2020]

OFK Grbalj Radanovići - FK Arsenal Tivat	0-4		FK Sutjeska Nikšić - FK Jedinstvo Bijelo Polje	3-0
FK Bokelj Kotor - FK KOM Podgorica	3-0		FK Zeta Golubovci - FK Ibar Rožaje	8-0
OFK Petrovac - FK Dečić Tuzi	1-5		FK Podgorica - FK Jezero Plav	2-0
FK Budućnost Podgorica - FK Rudar Pljevlja	3-1		FK Iskra Danilovgrad - OFK Titograd	3-0

Quarter-Finals [25.11.2020]

FK Bokelj Kotor - FK Budućnost Podgorica	0-6		FK Podgorica - FK Zeta Golubovci	2-3
FK Arsenal Tivat - FK Iskra Danilovgrad	0-1		FK Dečić Tuzi - FK Sutjeska Nikšić	1-0

Semi-Finals [21.04./05.05.2021]

First Leg			Second Leg	
FK Zeta Golubovci - FK Budućnost Podgorica	2-1		FK Budućnost Podgorica - FK Zeta Golubovci	3-0
FK Iskra Danilovgrad - FK Dečić Tuzi	0-0		FK Dečić Tuzi - FK Iskra Danilovgrad	1-0

Final

30.05.2021; Stadion pod Goricom, Podgorica; Referee: Mileta Šćepanović; Attendance: 1,200
FK Budućnost Podgorica - FK Dečić Tuzi   **3-1(2-1)**

FK Budućnost: Miloš Dragojević, Andrija Ražnatović, Anto Babić, Marko Vučić, Vladan Adžić, Draško Božović, Petar Grbić, Miloš Raičković (90.Miomir Đuričković), Vasilije Terzić, Igor Ivanović (90.Viktor Đukanović), Lazar Mijović (86.Marko Mrvaljević). Trainer: Mladen Milinković (Serbia).

FK Dečić Tuzi: Stefan Popović, Adrijan Rudović, Matija Božanović (58.Jovan Nikolić), Jonathan Drešaj, Marko Tući, Kristijan Vulaj, Danilo Marković (80.Andjelo Rudović), Pjeter Ljuljđuraj, Ilir Camaj (65.Admir Adrović), Mario Gjolaj, Danilo Pešukić. Trainer: Edis Mulalić (Bosnia and Herzegovina).

Goals: 1-0 Marko Vučić (3), 2-0 Lazar Mijović (28), 2-1 Danilo Pešukić (38), 3-1 Igor Ivanović (90).

THE CLUBS 2020/2021

Fudbalski Klub Budućnost Podgorica

Founded:	1925
Stadium:	Stadion pod Goricom, Podgorica (15,230)
Trainer:	Mladen Milinković (SRB) 14.05.1968

Goalkeepers:	DOB	M	(s)	G
Miloš Dragojević	03.02.1989	33		
Đorđije Pavličić	03.12.1996	3		
Defenders:	**DOB**	**M**	**(s)**	**G**
Vladan Adžić	05.07.1987	19	(1)	
Anto Babić	25.01.2000	25	(3)	1
Igor Ćuković	06.06.1993	23	(1)	1
Bogdan Milić	12.09.2001	22	(4)	1
Andrija Ražnatović	24.12.2000	8	(3)	
Nemanja Sekulić	29.03.1994	5		
Velimir Vlahović	20.01.2000	4	(3)	
Marko Vučić	30.12.1996	22	(2)	
Midfielders:	**DOB**	**M**	**(s)**	**G**
Ivan Bojović	20.02.2001	9	(2)	1
Draško Božović	30.06.1988	26	(4)	15
Aleksa Ćetković	13.02.2004	7	(3)	
Damjan Dakić	28.04.2004		(1)	
Jovan Dašić	29.03.2003		(1)	
Miomir Đuričković	26.07.1997	14	(11)	2

	DOB	M	(s)	G
Petar Grbić	07.08.1988	17	(6)	4
Velizar Janketić	15.11.1996		(13)	
Sava Milić	23.01.2003	1	(1)	
Luka Mirković	01.11.1990	22	(2)	
Vladimir Perišić	26.08.2004		(2)	
Miloš Raičković	02.12.1993	28		6
Vasilije Terzić	12.05.1999	24	(8)	3
Petar Vukčević	02.03.2001	3		
Milan Vukotić	05.10.2002	1		
Forwards:	**DOB**	**M**	**(s)**	**G**
Balša Ćetković	20.12.2003	1	(2)	
Viktor Đukanović	29.01.2004	8	(12)	2
Igor Ivanović	09.09.1990	29	(1)	9
Lazar Mijović	12.03.2003	9	(11)	6
Panagiotis Moraitis (GRE)	01.02.1997	10	(5)	1
Marko Mrvaljević	05.06.2001	6	(6)	1
Aleksandar Vujačić	19.03.1990		(20)	2
Dejan Zarubica	11.04.1993	17	(10)	8

Fudbalski klub Dečić Tuzi

Founded:	1926
Stadium:	Stadion „Tuško Polje", Tuzi (2,000)
Trainer:	Edis Mulalić (BIH) 23.10.1975

Goalkeepers:	DOB	M	(s)	G
Damir Ljuljanović	23.05.1992	4	(1)	
Stefan Popović	11.01.1993	12	(1)	
Pavle Velimirović	11.04.1990	20	(1)	
Defenders:	**DOB**	**M**	**(s)**	**G**
Balša Banović	26.01.1998	3	(4)	
Matija Božanović	13.04.1994	32		1
Jonathan Drešaj	15.03.2000	35		
Robert Gjelaj	23.09.2002		(3)	
Martin Prenkočević	17.02.1999	12	(5)	
Adrijan Rudović	10.06.1995	33		1
Marko Tući	04.12.1998	32		1
Mladen Zeljković (SRB)	18.11.1987	5	(4)	
Midfielders:	**DOB**	**M**	**(s)**	**G**
Adil Adžović	21.04.2002	5	(6)	
Mario Gjolaj	06.04.2002	20	(6)	1
Abedin Hakšabanović	11.02.2001	2	(2)	

	DOB	M	(s)	G
Demir Krkanović	19.08.1996	1	(1)	
Pjeter Ljuljđuraj	29.06.1992	25	(4)	
Elvir Maloku (ALB)	14.05.1996	1	(7)	
Danilo Marković	15.07.1998	26	(6)	1
Ivan Mijušković	17.02.1988		(7)	
Jovan Nikolić	21.07.1991	10	(4)	
Rijad Pepić	12.07.1991	1	(9)	
Andjelo Rudović	03.05.1996	23	(6)	5
Leon Ujkaj	03.03.1997	1	(8)	
Kristijan Vulaj	25.06.1998	34		11
Forwards:	**DOB**	**M**	**(s)**	**G**
Admir Adrović	08.05.1988	9	(6)	1
Ilir Camaj	24.06.1996	25	(6)	10
Danilo Pešukić	20.09.2000	21	(11)	3
Ognjen Rolović	25.08.1993	4	(16)	3
Ibrahima Touré (BEL)	23.12.1999		(2)	

Fudbalski klub Iskra Danilovgrad

Founded: 1919
Stadium: Stadion „Braće Velašević", Danilovgrad (2,000)
Trainer: Aleksandar Nedović   05.09.1978
[15.05.2021] Srđan Nikić   28.05.1978

Goalkeepers:	DOB	M	(s)	G
Srđan Blažić	26.11.1982	2		
Marko Kordić	22.02.1995	34		
Defenders:	DOB	M	(s)	G
Miloš Bakrač	25.02.1992	16		1
Miloš Drinčić	14.02.1999	32		3
Milan Đurišić	11.04.1987	13	(11)	1
Nikola Kumburović	13.11.1999	11		
Miloš Lakić	21.12.1985	2	(1)	
Luka Malešević	01.08.1998	29	(2)	
Vuk Orlandić	05.01.1997	4	(2)	
Nemanja Popović	27.03.2002	2	(4)	
Midfielders:	DOB	M	(s)	G
Aldin Adžović	18.04.1994	8	(6)	
Balša Boričić	07.01.1997	18	(7)	1
Ivan Đorić (SRB)	07.07.1995	10	(1)	
Miroje Jovanović	10.03.1987	11	(5)	
Kōhei Katō (JPN)	14.06.1989	14	(1)	
Stevan Luković (SRB)	16.03.1993	9	(5)	

	DOB	M	(s)	G
Blagota Marković	09.01.2002	3	(6)	
Bogdan Obradović	02.05.2002	6	(1)	
Ognjen Obradović	15.03.2000	22	(2)	1
Jovan Perišić	25.08.2003		(3)	
Matija Račić	01.09.2001	9	(6)	
Vladislav Rogošić	21.09.1994	5	(18)	3
Pavle Stojanović (SRB)	20.08.2001		(5)	
Irfan Šahman	05.10.1993	27	(3)	
Petar Tadić	04.08.2002	2	(3)	
Borko Tomašević	05.01.2002		(2)	
Forwards:	DOB	M	(s)	G
Andrija Kolundzić	23.09.2002		(1)	
Alija Krnić	02.01.1998	9	(3)	1
Bogdan Mandić (MKD)	01.09.1998	1	(9)	
Bogdan Milić	24.11.1987	12	(22)	5
Zoran Petrović	14.07.1997	18	(6)	4
Đorđe Šaletić	06.01.2002	23	(5)	
Ivan Vuković	09.02.1987	30	(3)	6
Sho Yamamoto (JPN)	12.11.1996	14	(8)	1

Fudbalski klub Jezero Plav

Founded: 1934
Stadium: Stadion pod Racinom, Plav (2,500)
Trainer: Milija Savović   08.02.1979

Goalkeepers:	DOB	M	(s)	G
Igor Asanović	20.04.1992	28		
Stefan Kastratović	04.01.1994	8		
Defenders:	DOB	M	(s)	G
Radoš Dedić	17.05.1993	26		
Meldin Drešković	26.03.1998	32		
Kujtim Dinosha	22.11.1999	12	(3)	
Nikola Jovićević	04.01.1996	13	(7)	2
Aleksandar Raković	21.02.1994	1		
Nikola Tmušić	29.01.1994	1	(1)	
Petar Vuković	27.02.2002	17		
Midfielders:	DOB	M	(s)	G
Denis Agustín Brizuela (ARG)	12.05.1997	7	(8)	1
Nikola Đurković	03.01.1994	31		
Ernes Isljami	22.09.1993	22	(3)	2
Davor Kontić	30.10.1999	8	(15)	
Nikola Lekić	25.11.2001		(4)	

	DOB	M	(s)	G
Mendy Mamadou (SEN)	04.10.1998	13	(4)	3
Marko Matanović	17.07.2000	31	(3)	1
Fatih Muković	07.09.2001	10	(11)	
Vojin Pavlović	09.11.1993	30	(1)	4
Saša Radenović	26.04.1991	3	(17)	1
Ilija Radunović	01.08.1993	34		
Nemanja Tmušić	20.05.1996	3	(11)	
Petar Vučković	15.08.1987	12	(1)	1
Danilo Vukićević	14.12.1998	3	(4)	
Forwards:	DOB	M	(s)	G
Egzon Dinosha	18.01.2001	2	(2)	
Anil Julević	01.11.2002		(2)	
Ndue Mujeci (ALB)	24.02.1993	26	(1)	7
Božo Osmajlić	01.02.1994	10	(7)	3
Edis Redžepagić	27.07.1997	4	(10)	3
Lazar Vučićević	05.01.1998	9	(5)	

Omladinski fudbalski klub Petrovac

Founded: 1969
Stadium: Stadion pod Malim brdom, Petrovac (1,630)
Trainer: Nenad Vukčević   25.11.1974

Goalkeepers:	DOB	M	(s)	G
Ljubomir Đurović (SRB)	19.06.1989	14	(1)	
Sava Mugoša	10.07.1993	1		
Vidoje Popović	28.06.1997	21	(1)	
Defenders:	DOB	M	(s)	G
Danilo Bracanović	09.04.2000	6	(3)	
Drago Bumbar	10.11.1997	9		
Luka Medigović	03.04.1995	21	(2)	
Zoran Mikijelj	13.12.1991	32		4
Jovan Mugoša	27.10.1998	3	(1)	
Andrija Ražnatović	24.12.2000	14		2
Nikola Savović	30.09.1994	28	(1)	1
Ryoya Tachibana (JPN)	04.04.1996	28	(5)	3
Mihailo Vojvodić		13	(5)	
Nenad Vujović	02.01.1989	1	(2)	
Midfielders:	DOB	M	(s)	G
Adnan Bašić (BIH)	13.12.1996	4	(4)	1
Zaim Divanović	09.12.2000	30	(5)	5

	DOB	M	(s)	G
Mirza Đurđević (BIH)	06.09.2000	16	(8)	3
Nikola Ivanović	20.03.1996	11	(7)	
Petar Mališić	04.09.2001		(5)	
Marko Marković	05.09.1987	31	(1)	3
Andrew Marveggio (AUS)	22.04.1992	6	(5)	
Ivan Mijušković	17.02.1988	10	(2)	
Misaki Sato (JPN)	12.06.1998	1	(1)	
Stefan Savić	09.01.1995	8	(2)	
Pavle Savković	15.08.1999	2	(4)	
Nikola Stojanović	17.02.1995	10	(5)	
Forwards:	DOB	M	(s)	G
Milovan Ilić	03.12.1997	9	(5)	2
Luka Merdović	14.03.1989	25	(7)	2
Balša Rogošić	17.09.1996	4	(5)	
Valentin Rudović	25.06.1997	11	(14)	
Ivan Vasović	11.11.1996	1	(2)	
Igor Vukčević	07.11.1999	18	(8)	1
Nikola Zvrko	07.03.1995	8	(9)	2

Fudbalski klub Podgorica

Founded: 1970
Stadium: DG Arena, Podgorica (4,300)
Trainer: Milorad Peković   05.08.1977

Goalkeepers:	DOB	M	(s)	G
Nikola Ivezić	01.04.2003	35		
Igor Nikić		1		
Defenders:	**DOB**	**M**	**(s)**	**G**
Nemanja Božović	26.04.2003	1		
Marko Čavor	05.07.1999	4	(9)	
Nikola Čelebić	04.07.1989	30	(2)	4
Darko Đajić (BIH)	30.08.1992	15	(9)	
Stefan Marjanović (SRB)	25.07.1994	16	(4)	
Nikola Ukšanović	30.08.2001	4	(5)	
Marko Vukčević	07.06.1993	33	(1)	1
Midfielders:	**DOB**	**M**	**(s)**	**G**
Andrej Bajović	06.06.2003	3	(7)	
Anđelko Jovanović	18.11.1999	25	(3)	5
Andrija Kaluđerović	29.10.1993	33		
Kōhei Katō (JPN)	14.06.1989	13	(2)	1
Andrija Krivokapić	23.06.2001		(2)	
Jovan Nikolić	21.07.1991	16	(3)	
Arihiro Sentoku (JPN)	09.12.1998	31	(4)	5
Keita Suzuki (JPN)	20.12.1997	26	(3)	
Nikola Tripković	26.10.2000		(9)	1
Jovan Vujović (BIH)	20.01.1996	11	(14)	4
Petar Vukčević	02.03.2001	8	(5)	
Dušan Vuković	27.07.2003	3	(9)	1
Radule Živković (SRB)	20.10.1990	18	(4)	1
Forwards:	**DOB**	**M**	**(s)**	**G**
Vuk Dapčević	15.04.2002	1		
Šaleta Kordić	19.04.1993	20	(4)	10
Matija Krivokapić	19.03.2003	9	(3)	3
Luka Maraš	24.05.1996	23	(11)	
Halil Muharemović	06.11.1997	13	(16)	1
Petar Prelević	10.10.2001	1	(1)	
Balša Sekulić	10.06.1998	3	(21)	2

Fudbalski klub Rudar Pljevlja

Founded: 1920
Stadium: Stadion pod Golubinjom, Pljevlja (10,000)
Trainer: Vuko Bogavac   23.02.1971

Goalkeepers:	DOB	M	(s)	G
Lazar Baltić	27.03.2002	17		
Ervin Helić	22.07.2002	19		
Defenders:	**DOB**	**M**	**(s)**	**G**
Milija Golubović	25.04.1996	25	(5)	
Nemanja Kartal	17.07.1994	32		3
Predrag Kašćelan	30.06.1990	30	(1)	1
Marko Merdović	17.11.1998	33		3
Matija Pejović	04.10.2000	15	(7)	
Željko Tomašević	05.04.1988	13	(1)	
Nikola Vukotić	09.01.2003	13		
Midfielders:	**DOB**	**M**	**(s)**	**G**
Aleksa Golubović	19.11.2002		(3)	
Janko Gogić	22.02.2000		(7)	
Orhan Hajrović	16.05.1996	5	(5)	
Dejan Kotorac	31.05.1996	17	(9)	1
Brajan Matanović			(1)	
Hikaru Matsui (JPN)	02.12.1998	27	(3)	
Berin Tahirović	19.11.1999	10	(11)	2
Miljan Vlaisavljević	16.04.1991	17		2
Miloš Zečević	28.01.1999	24	(3)	5
Dušan Zivković (SRB)	31.07.1996	15	(2)	1
Forwards:	**DOB**	**M**	**(s)**	**G**
Jakša Bajčetić	09.07.2002	1	(1)	
Kristijan Ernec	19.01.2003	2	(8)	
Ljubomir Kovačević	23.02.2000		(15)	2
Marko Mujović	03.05.2000		(16)	
Vuk Striković	10.06.2002	32	(1)	12
Zakaria Suraka (GHA)	17.01.1996	16		3
Danin Talović	08.03.1995	28	(5)	3
Ilija Vujović	15.02.2001	5	(16)	

Fudbalski klub Sutjeska Nikšić

Founded: 1927
Stadium: Stadion kraj Bistrice, Nikšić (5,214)
Trainer: Dragan Radojičić   03.06.1970
[15.11.2020]   Miljan Radović   18.10.1975

Goalkeepers:	DOB	M	(s)	G
Vladan Giljen	07.12.1989	28		
Suad Ličina	08.02.1995	8	(1)	
Defenders:	**DOB**	**M**	**(s)**	**G**
Darko Bulatović	05.09.1989	29	(1)	
Stefan Cicmil	16.08.1990	16	(4)	1
Dragan Grivić	12.02.1996	31	(2)	3
Nikola Janjić	14.07.2002	22	(3)	5
Filip Mitrović	17.11.1993	4	(2)	
Igor Pajović	01.06.2001	13	(13)	4
Nikola Stijepović	02.11.1993	17	(5)	
Aleksandar Šofranac	21.10.1990	26	(1)	
Aleksandar Vlahović	10.03.2000	11	(5)	
Midfielders:	**DOB**	**M**	**(s)**	**G**
Vladan Bubanja	21.02.1999	9	(4)	1
Marko Ćetković	10.07.1986	25	(5)	3
Caique Augusto Correia Chagas (BRA)	26.04.1994	16		
Balša Dubljević	02.12.2001	17	(3)	
Novica Eraković	12.11.1999	18	(9)	
Branislav Janković	08.02.1992	7	(4)	
Damir Kojašević	03.06.1987	5	(2)	1
Rene Mihelič (SVN)	05.07.1988	13		2
Dušan Vuković	06.08.2002		(2)	
Forwards:	**DOB**	**M**	**(s)**	**G**
Admir Adrović	08.05.1988	6	(10)	1
Marko Bojović	15.06.2002	3	(9)	
Božo Marković	26.10.1989	24	(5)	16
Aleksa Marušić	08.06.1999	5	(17)	2
Milutin Osmajić	25.07.1999	32	(2)	13
Milivoje Raičević	21.07.1993	7	(6)	3
Marko Vuković	20.03.1996	4	(16)	1

Omladinski fudbalski klub Titograd Podgorica

Founded:	1951	
Stadium:	Stadion FK Mladost, Podgorica (1,250)	
Trainer:	Zoran Govedarica (SRB)	14.04.1968
[07.09.2020]	Nikola Rakojević	15.01.1958
[09.04.2021]	Vladimir Janković (SRB)	01.08.1970

Goalkeepers:	DOB	M	(s)	G
Sergej Joksimović	16.08.2002	17		
Stefan Spasojević	23.08.1993	19		
Defenders:	**DOB**	**M**	**(s)**	**G**
Ermin Alić	23.02.1992	14	(1)	
Igor Bašić (SRB)	11.10.1996	12		
Luka Boričić	24.06.1905	17	(2)	
Amir Muzurović	17.10.2001	28		
Ivan Novović	26.04.1989	33		2
Abdel Osmanović	12.01.2001	4	(1)	
Ljubomir Pejović	26.05.2003	4	(1)	
Bojan Roganović	28.09.2000	31		
Marko Roganović	21.06.1996	32		3
Midfielders:	**DOB**	**M**	**(s)**	**G**
Ivan Bojović	20.02.2001	16		2
Miloš Brnović	26.04.2000	27	(2)	3
Miloš Kalezić	09.08.1993	12	(5)	1

	DOB	M	(s)	G
Mendy Mamadou (SEN)	04.10.1998	3	(8)	
Luka Mihaljević	24.02.2003	1	(1)	
Ognjen Peličić	05.02.1999	12	(4)	
Žarko Popović	11.10.1999	28	(1)	2
Pavle Savković	15.08.1999	2	(1)	
Masato Shimokawa (JPN)	11.06.1996	14	(1)	
Vedad Turusković	26.06.1905		(2)	
Marko Vujačić	18.03.2003		(4)	
Petar Vukčević	15.08.1987	13	(6)	1
Forwards:	**DOB**	**M**	**(s)**	**G**
Ognjen Gašević	02.04.2002	12	(4)	
Đorđe Magdelinić	06.05.2003	4	(3)	
Bogdan Mandić (MKD)	01.09.1998	11	(3)	1
Marko Mrvaljević	05.06.2001	15	(1)	5
Bojan Pavićević	02.07.2004	1	(3)	
Alden Škrijelj	18.10.2000	14	(12)	2
Balša Tošković	2003		(15)	

Fudbalski klub Zeta Golubovci

Founded:	1927	
Stadium:	Stadion Trešnjica, Golubovci (4,000)	
Trainer:	Dejan Roganović	28.10.1972
[10.01.2021]	Ratko Dostanić (SRB)	25.10.1959

Goalkeepers:	DOB	M	(s)	G
Zoran Aković	26.12.1985	24		
Igor Mrvaljević	02.05.1998	1	(1)	
Petar Radulović	10.11.2001	11	(2)	
Defenders:	**DOB**	**M**	**(s)**	**G**
Zvonko Ceklić	11.04.1999	29	(2)	1
Ognjen Đinović	12.09.2003	13	(11)	
Nemanja Đurović	18.12.2000	8	(8)	
Aleksandar Milić	24.08.1998	32		
Vaso Peličić	05.11.2002		(1)	
Andrej Pupović	09.06.2001		(3)	
Janko Simović	02.04.1987	22		1
Amel Tuzović	31.03.1995	23	(3)	
Midfielders:	**DOB**	**M**	**(s)**	**G**
Vuk Ajković	10.10.1998		(2)	
Marko Burzanović	13.01.1998	18	(11)	5
Jovan Đukić			(1)	
Balša Goranović	06.02.1998	1	(2)	

	DOB	M	(s)	G
Srdjan Krstović	05.08.2000	26	(6)	1
Lazar Lambulić	12.03.2000	18	(16)	
Matija Lambulić	12.03.2000	6	(21)	1
Mijat Lambulić	14.11.2001	27	(4)	3
Goran Milojko	05.01.1994	33		6
Elom Nya-Vedji (TOG)	24.11.1997	11	(5)	4
Simo Popović		1	(4)	
Hrvoje Rizvanović	26.09.1997	1		
Alphonse Denis Soppo (CMR)	15.05.1985	23	(2)	
Vojislav Šišević	28.11.1997	1	(4)	
Ilija Tripunović	12.01.2001		(1)	
Alex Yamoah (GHA)	10.01.1995	9	(4)	1
Forwards:	**DOB**	**M**	**(s)**	**G**
Vasko Kalezić	14.03.1994	34		6
Petar Orlandić	06.08.1990	5	(5)	1
Ivan Vukčević	04.12.2001	19	(6)	4
Nikola Vukčević			(2)	

SECOND LEVEL
Druga Liga 2020/2021

1.	FK Mornar Bar (*Promoted*)	36	22	9	5	70	-	22	75
2.	FK Arsenal Tivat (*Promotion Play-offs*)	36	20	7	9	47	-	39	67
3.	FK Igalo (*Promotion Play-offs*)	36	15	12	9	53	-	34	57
4.	FK Kom Zlatica	36	15	7	14	45	-	45	52
5.	FK Bokelj Kotor	36	11	15	10	42	-	36	48
6.	FK Jedinstvo Bijelo Polje	36	11	11	14	49	-	42	44
7.	FK Berane	36	12	9	15	43	-	51	44
8.	OFK Grbalj Radanovići	36	12	6	18	36	-	45	42
9.	FK Ibar Rožaje (*Relegated*)	36	12	5	19	33	-	57	41
10.	FK Drezga (*Relegated*)	36	7	5	24	30	-	77	25

05.09.2020	Nicosia	Cyprus - Montenegro	0-2(0-0)	(UNL)
08.09.2020	Lëtzebuerg	Luxembourg - Montenegro	0-1(0-0)	(UNL)
07.10.2020	Podgorica	Montenegro - Latvia	1-1(0-1)	(F)
10.10.2020	Podgorica	Montenegro - Azerbaijan	2-0(1-0)	(UNL)
13.10.2020	Podgorica	Montenegro - Luxembourg	1-2(1-1)	(UNL)
11.11.2020	Podgorica	Montenegro - Kazakhstan	0-0	(F)
14.11.2020	Zaprešić	Azerbaijan - Montenegro	0-0	(UNL)
17.11.2020	Podgorica	Montenegro - Cyprus	4-0(3-0)	(UNL)
24.03.2021	Rīga	Latvia - Montenegro	1-2(1-1)	(WCQ)
27.03.2021	Podgorica	Montenegro - Gibraltar	4-1(2-1)	(WCQ)
30.03.2021	Podgorica	Montenegro - Norway	0-1(0-1)	(WCQ)
02.06.2021	Sarajevo	Bosnia and Herzegovina - Montenegro	0-0	(F)
05.06.2021	Podgorica	Montenegro - Israel	1-3(0-0)	(F)

05.09.2020   CYPRUS - MONTENEGRO   0-2(0-0)   2nd UEFA Nations League C, Group 1
Stádio GSP, Nicosia; Referee: Harm Osmers (Germany); Attendance: 0
MNE: Milan Mijatović, Momčilo Raspopović, Igor Vujačić, Stefan Savić (Cap), Adam Marušić, Nikola Vukčević (75.Aleksandar Šćekić), Nebojša Kosović (57.Dino Islamović), Sead Hakšabanović, Marko Bakić, Aleksandar Boljević, Fatos Bećiraj (46.Stevan Jovetić). Trainer: Faruk Hadžibegić.
Goals: Stevan Jovetić (60, 73).

08.09.2020   LUXEMBOURG - MONTENEGRO   0-1(0-0)   2nd UEFA Nations League C, Group 1
Stade "Josy Barthel", Lëtzebuerg; Referee: Lawrence Visser (Belgium); Attendance: 0
MNE: Milan Mijatović, Stefan Savić, Momčilo Raspopović, Igor Vujačić, Adam Marušić, Nebojša Kosović, Nikola Vukčević, Aleksandar Boljević (71.Marko Janković), Sead Hakšabanović, Stevan Jovetić (Cap) (62.Marko Bakić), Dino Islamović (75.Fatos Bećiraj). Trainer: Faruk Hadžibegić.
Goal: Fatos Bećiraj (90+3 penalty).

07.10.2020   MONTENEGRO - LATVIA   1-1(0-1)   Friendly International
Stadion pod Goricom, Podgorica; Referee: Admir Šehović (Bosnia and Herzegovina); Attendance: 0
MNE: Danijel Petković (Cap), Darko Bulatović, Vladan Adžić, Aleksandar Šofranac, Aleksandar Šćekić, Marko Vukčević, Deni Hočko (57.Branislav Janković), Igor Ivanović, Marko Janković (72.Miloš Raičković), Šaleta Kordić (72.Fatos Bećiraj), Nikola Vujnović (57.Vasko Kalezić). Trainer: Faruk Hadžibegić.
Goal: Igor Ivanović (26).

10.10.2020   MONTENEGRO - AZERBAIJAN   2-0(1-0)   2nd UEFA Nations League C, Group 1
Stadion pod Goricom, Podgorica; Referee: Ricardo de Burgos Bengoetxea (Spain); Attendance: 0
MNE: Milan Mijatović, Risto Radunović, Marko Simić, Momčilo Raspopović, Igor Vujačić, Aleksandar Boljević (71.Igor Ivanović), Sead Hakšabanović, Stevan Jovetić (Cap) (81.Branislav Janković), Dino Islamović (71.Fatos Bećiraj), Marko Bakić (63.Nebojša Kosović). Trainer: Faruk Hadžibegić.
Goals: Stevan Jovetić (9), Igor Ivanović (71).

13.10.2020   MONTENEGRO - LUXEMBOURG   1-2(1-1)   2nd UEFA Nations League C, Group 1
Stadion pod Goricom, Podgorica; Referee: Sascha Stegemann (Germany); Attendance: 0
MNE: Milan Mijatović, Stefan Savić, Risto Radunović, Marko Simić [*sent off 90+6*], Sead Hakšabanović, Nebojša Kosović (78.Aleksandar Šćekić), Nikola Vukčević, Momčilo Raspopović (79.Marko Vukčević), Stevan Jovetić (Cap), Igor Ivanović (86.Marko Janković [*sent off 90+5*]), Dino Islamović (66.Fatos Bećiraj). Trainer: Faruk Hadžibegić.
Goal: Igor Ivanović (34).

11.11.2020   MONTENEGRO - KAZAKHSTAN   0-0   Friendly International
Stadion pod Goricom, Podgorica; Referee: Dimitar Meckarovski (North Macedonia); Attendance: 0
MNE: Danijel Petković, Saša Balić, Luka Mirković (76.Branislav Janković), Aleksandar Šofranac, Momčilo Raspopović, Miloš Milović (22.Marko Simić), Miloš Raičković, Vladimir Jovović (57.Milutin Osmajić), Fatos Bećiraj (Cap) (56.Dino Islamović), Aleksandar Boljević (77.Anđelko Jovanović), Nikola Vujnović (56.Stevan Jovetić). Trainer: Faruk Hadžibegić.

14.11.2020   AZERBAIJAN - MONTENEGRO   0-0   2nd UEFA Nations League C, Group 1
Stadion "Ivan Laljak-Ivić", Zaprešić (Croatia); Referee: Sergei Ivanov (Russia); Attendance: 0
MNE: Milan Mijatović, Risto Radunović, Aleksandar Šofranac, Igor Vujačić, Adam Marušić, Aleksandar Šćekić (81.Vukan Savićević), Marko Bakić, Sead Hakšabanović, Stevan Jovetić (Cap) (90+3.Dino Islamović), Stefan Mugoša (58.Aleksandar Boljević), Igor Ivanović [*sent off 45+2*]. Trainer: Faruk Hadžibegić.

17.11.2020   MONTENEGRO - CYPRUS   4-0(3-0)   2nd UEFA Nations League C, Group 1
Stadion pod Goricom, Gorica; Referee: Eitan Shemeulevitch (Israel); Attendance: 0
MNE: Milan Mijatović, Marko Simić, Igor Vujačić, Adam Marušić, Aleksandar Šćekić (72.Risto Radunović), Marko Vukčević, Marko Bakić (61.Nebojša Kosović), Aleksandar Boljević (71.Vladimir Jovović), Sead Hakšabanović, Stevan Jovetić (Cap) (61.Vukan Savićević), Stefan Mugoša (71.Dino Islamović). Trainer: Faruk Hadžibegić.
Goals: Stevan Jovetić (14), Aleksandar Boljević (25, 28), Stefan Mugoša (60).

24.03.2021   LATVIA - MONTENEGRO   1-2(1-1)   22nd FIFA WC. Qualifiers
Skonto stadions, Rīga; Referee: Alain Durieux (Luxembourg); Attendance: 0
MNE: Milan Mijatović, Stefan Savić, Risto Radunović, Igor Vujačić, Adam Marušić, Aleksandar Šćekić, Nebojša Kosović, Sead Hakšabanović (90+1.Aleksandar Boljević), Stevan Jovetić (Cap) (87.Fatos Bećiraj), Igor Ivanović (75.Vladimir Jovović), Uroš Đurđević. Trainer: Miodrag Radulović.
Goals: Stevan Jovetić (41, 83).

27.03.2021   **MONTENEGRO - GIBRALTAR**   **4-1(2-1)**   22nd FIFA WC. Qualifiers

Stadion pod Goricom, Podgorica; Referee: Manuel Schüttengruber (Austria); Attendance: 0

MNE: Milan Mijatović, Žarko Tomašević, Risto Radunović, Marko Simić, Marko Vukčević, Nebojša Kosović (60.Dušan Lagator), Marko Bakić (25.Kristijan Vulaj), Vladimir Jovović, Sead Hakšabanović (60.Aleksandar Boljević), Fatos Bećiraj (Cap) (46.Stevan Jovetić), Uroš Đurđević (77.Ilija Martinović). Trainer: Miodrag Radulović.

Goals: Fatos Bećiraj (26), Marko Simić (43), Žarko Tomašević (53), Stevan Jovetić (80).

30.03.2021   **MONTENEGRO - NORWAY**   **0-1(0-1)**   22nd FIFA WC. Qualifiers

Stadion pod Goricom, Podgorica; Referee: Anthony Taylor (England); Attendance: 0

MNE: Milan Mijatović, Žarko Tomašević, Stefan Savić, Adam Marušić (88.Fatos Bećiraj), Igor Vujačić, Nebojša Kosović (80.Igor Ivanović), Aleksandar Šćekić, Dušan Lagator (63.Vladimir Jovović), Sead Hakšabanović (81.Aleksandar Boljević), Stevan Jovetić (Cap), Uroš Đurđević (63.Dino Islamović). Trainer: Miodrag Radulović.

02.06.2021   **BOSNIA AND HERZEGOVINA - MONTENEGRO**   **0-0**   Friendly International

Stadion Grbavica, Sarajevo; Referee: Novak Simović (Serbia); Attendance: 0

MNE: Miloš Dragojević, Marko Vešović (76.Marko Vučić), Žarko Tomašević, Marko Simić, Ilija Martinović, Marko Vukčević, Nebojša Kosović (75.Miloš Raičković), Vladimir Jovović (63.Milutin Osmajić), Vukan Savićević (63.Marko Janković), Sead Hakšabanović (81.Igor Ivanović), Fatos Bećiraj (Cap) (46.Stefan Milošević). Trainer: Miodrag Radulović.

05.06.2021   **MONTENEGRO - ISRAEL**   **1-3(0-0)**   Friendly International

Stadion pod Goricom, Podgorica; Referee: Irfan Peljto (Bosnia and Herzegovina); Attendance: 860

MNE: Miloš Dragojević, Marko Vešović (82.Marko Vučić), Žarko Tomašević (36.Ilija Martinović), Marko Simić (Cap), Igor Vujačić, Dragan Grivić, Nebojša Kosović (60.Vukan Savićević), Vladimir Jovović (60.Miloš Raičković), Milutin Osmajić (60.Fatos Bećiraj), Marko Janković, Stefan Milošević (46.Igor Ivanović). Trainer: Miodrag Radulović.

Goal: Fatos Bećiraj (81 penalty).

NATIONAL TEAM PLAYERS
(16.07.2020 – 15.07.2021)

Name	DOB	Caps	Goals	2020/2021:	*Club*
Goalkeepers					
Miloš DRAGOJEVIĆ	03.02.1989	2	0	2021:	*FK Budućnost Podgorica*
Milan MIJATOVIĆ	26.07.1987	18	0	2020/2021:	*MTK Budapest FC (HUN)*
Danijel PETKOVIĆ	25.05.1993	23	0	2020:	*Angers SCO (FRA)*
Defenders					
Vladan ADŽIĆ	05.07.1987	1	0	2020:	*FK Budućnost Podgorica*
Saša BALIĆ	29.01.1990	13	0	2020:	*Zagłębie Lubin (POL)*
Darko BULATOVIĆ	05.09.1989	3	0	2020:	*FK Sutjeska Nikšić*
Dragan GRIVIĆ	12.02.1996	1	0	2021:	*FK Sutjeska Nikšić*
Ilija MARTINOVIĆ	31.01.1994	3	0	2021:	*NK Maribor (SVN)*
Adam MARUŠIĆ	17.10.1992	39	0	2020/2021:	*SS Lazio Roma (ITA)*
Miloš MILOVIĆ	22.12.1995	1	0	2020:	*FK Voždovac (SRB)*
Risto RADUNOVIĆ	04.05.1992	11	0	2020:	*AFC Astra Giurgiu (ROU)*
				01.01.2021->	*SC FCSB Bucurfeşti (ROU)*
Momčilo RASPOPOVIĆ	18.03.1994	7	0	2020:	*HNK Rijeka (CRO)*
Stefan SAVIĆ	08.01.1991	57	5	2020/2021:	*Club Atlético de Madrid (ESP)*
Marko SIMIĆ	16.06.1987	48	2	2020/2021:	*FK Liepāja (LVA)*
Aleksandar ŠOFRANAC	21.10.1990	8	0	2020/2021:	*FK Sutjeska Nikšić*
Žarko TOMAŠEVIĆ	22.02.1990	42	5	2021:	*Astana FC (KAZ)*
Marko VUČIĆ	30.12.1996	2	0	2021:	*FK Budućnost Podgorica*
Igor VUJAČIĆ	08.08.1994	11	0	2020/2021:	*FK Partizan Beograd (SRB)*

Midfielders					
Marko BAKIĆ	01.11.1993	21	0	2020/2021:	Royal Excel Mouscron (BEL)
Aleksandar BOLJEVIĆ	12.12.1995	26	2	2020:	R Standard Liège (BEL)
				29.01.2021->	KAS Eupen (BEL)
Sead HAKŠABANOVIĆ	04.05.1999	18	1	2020/2021:	IFK Norrköping (SWE)
Deni HOČKO	22.04.1994	6	0	2020/2021:	Royal Excel Mouscron (BEL)
Igor IVANOVIĆ	09.09.1990	8	3	2020/2021:	FK Budućnost Podgorica
Branislav JANKOVIĆ	13.06.1992	8	0	2020/2021:	FK Sutjeska Nikšić
Marko JANKOVIĆ	09.07.1995	26	1	2020:	SPAL Ferrara (ITA)
				03.02.2021->	Beitar Jerusalem FC (ISR)
Anđelko JOVANOVIĆ	18.11.1999	1	0	2020:	FK Podgorica
Vladimir JOVOVIĆ	26.10.1994	39	0	2020/2021:	FK Jablonec (CZE)
Vasko KALEZIĆ	14.03.1994	1	0	2020:	FK Zeta Golubovci
Nebojša KOSOVIĆ	24.02.1995	28	1	2020/2021:	FC Kairat Almaty (KAZ)
Dušan LAGATOR	29.03.1994	8	0	2021:	Wisła Płock (POL)
Luka MIRKOVIĆ	01.11.1990	4	0	2020/2021:	FK Budućnost Podgorica
Milutin OSMAJIĆ	25.07.1999	3	0	2020/2021:	FK Sutjeska Nikšić
Miloš RAIČKOVIĆ	02.12.1993	5	0	2020/2021:	FK Budućnost Podgorica
Vukan SAVIĆEVIĆ	29.01.1994	8	0	2020/2021:	Samsunspor (TUR)
Marko VEŠOVIĆ	28.08.1991	32	2	2020/2021:	Legia Warszawa (POL)
Marko VUKČEVIĆ	07.06.1993	6	0	2020/2021:	FK Podgorica
Nikola VUKČEVIĆ	13.12.1991	44	1	2020:	Levante UD Valencia (ESP)
Kristijan VULAJ	25.06.1998	1	0	2021:	FK Dečić Tuzi

Forwards					
Fatos BEĆIRAJ	22.05.1988	80	12	2020:	Wisła Kraków (POL)
				11.02.2021->	Bnei Yehuda Tel Aviv FC (ISR)
Uroš ĐURĐEVIĆ	02.03.1994	3	0	2021:	Real Sporting de Gijón (ESP)
Dino ISLAMOVIĆ	17.01.1994	8	0	2020/2021:	Rosenborg BK Trondheim (NOR)
Stevan JOVETIĆ	02.11.1989	61	31	2020/2021:	AS Monaco FC (FRA)
Šaleta KORDIĆ	19.04.1993	1	0	2020:	FK Podgorica
Stefan MILOŠEVIĆ	23.06.1996	2	0	2021:	Rīga FC (LVA)
Stefan MUGOŠA	23.02.1992	37	11	2020:	Incheon United FC (KOR)
Aleksandar ŠĆEKIĆ	12.12.1991	24	0	2020/2021:	FK Partizan Beograd (SRB)
Nikola VUJNOVIĆ	11.01.1997	2	0	2020:	FK Voždovac (SRB)

Trainer			
Faruk HADŽIBEGIĆ [25.07.2019 – 28.12.2020]	07.10.1957	14 M; 6 W; 4 D; 4 L; 15-16	
Miodrag RADULOVIĆ [from 29.12.2020]	23.10.1967	5 M; 2 W; 1 D; 2 L; 7-6	

NETHERLANDS

The Country:
Nederland (Netherlands)
Capital: Amsterdam
Surface: 41,543 km²
Inhabitants: 17,641,100 [2021]
Time: UTC+1

The FA:
Koninklijke Nederlandse Voetbalbond
Woudenbergseweg 56-58 Postbus 515 3700, Am Zeist
Tel: +31 343 499 201
Foundation date: 1889
Member of FIFA since: 1904
Member of UEFA since: 1954
Website: www.knvb.nl

NATIONAL TEAM RECORDS

RECORDS

First international match:	30.04.1905, Antwerpen: Belgium – Netherlands 1-4
Most international caps:	Wesley Benjamin Sneijder — 134 caps (2003-2018)
Most international goals:	Robin van Persie — 50 goals / 102 caps (2005-2017)

UEFA EUROPEAN CHAMPIONSHIP

1960	Did not enter
1964	Qualifiers
1968	Qualifiers
1972	Qualifiers
1976	Final Tournament (3rd Place)
1980	Final Tournament (Group Stage)
1984	Qualifiers
1988	**Final Tournament (Winners)**
1992	Final Tournament (Semi-Finals)
1996	Final Tournament (Quarter-Finals)
2000	Final Tournament (Semi-Finals)
2004	Final Tournament (Semi-Finals)
2008	Final Tournament (Quarter-Finals)
2012	Final Tournament (Group Stage)
2016	Qualifiers
2020	Final Tournament (2nd Round of 16)

FIFA WORLD CUP

1930	Did not enter
1934	Final Tournament (1st Round)
1938	Final Tournament (1st Round)
1950	Did not enter
1954	Did not enter
1958	Qualifiers
1962	Qualifiers
1966	Qualifiers
1970	Qualifiers
1974	Final Tournament (Runners-up)
1978	Final Tournament (Runners-up)
1982	Qualifiers
1986	Qualifiers
1990	Final Tournament (2nd Round of 16)
1994	Final Tournament (Quarter-Finals)
1998	Final Tournament (4th Place)
2002	Qualifiers
2006	Final Tournament (2nd Round of 16)
2010	Final Tournament (Runners-up)
2014	Final Tournament (3rd Place)
2018	Qualifiers

OLYMPIC TOURNAMENTS

1908	3rd Place
1912	3rd Place
1920	3rd Place
1924	4th Place
1928	1/8 - Finals
1936	Did not enter
1948	1/8 - Finals
1952	Qualifiers
1956	Did not enter
1960	Qualifiers
1964	Qualifiers
1968	Qualifiers
1972	Qualifiers
1976	Qualifiers
1980	Qualifiers
1984	Qualifiers
1988	Qualifiers
1992	Qualifiers
1996	Qualifiers
2000	Qualifiers
2004	Qualifiers
2008	Quarter-Finals
2012	Qualifiers
2016	Qualifiers

UEFA NATIONS LEAGUE

2018/2019	League A; Final Tournament – 4th Place
2020/2021	League A

FIFA CONFEDERATIONS CUP 1992-2017

None

NETHERLANDIAN CLUB HONOURS IN EUROPEAN CLUB COMPETITIONS:

European Champion Clubs' Cup (1956-1992) / UEFA Champions League (1993-2021)		
AFC Ajax Amsterdam	4	1970/1971, 1971/1972, 1972/1973, 1994/1995
Feyenoord Rotterdam	1	1969/1970
PSV Eindhoven	1	1987/1988
Fairs Cup (1858-1971) / UEFA Cup (1972-2009) / UEFA Europa League (2010-2021)		
Feyenoord Rotterdam	2	1973/1974, 2001/2002
PSV Eindhoven	1	1977/1978
AFC Ajax Amsterdam	1	1991/1992
UEFA Super Cup (1972-2020)		
AFC Ajax Amsterdam	2	1973, 1995
European Cup Winners' Cup 1961-1999*		
AFC Ajax Amsterdam	1	1986/1987

defunct competition

NATIONAL COMPETITIONS
TABLE OF HONOURS

	CHAMPIONS*	CUP WINNERS	BEST GOALSCORERS	
1888/1889	VV Concordia Rotterdam	-	-	
1889/1890	HFC Haarlem	-	-	
1890/1891	HVV Den Haag	-	-	
1891/1892	RAP Amsterdam	-	-	
1892/1893	HFC Haarlem	-	-	
1893/1894	RAP Amsterdam	-	-	
1894/1895	HFC Haarlem	-	-	
1895/1896	HVV Den Haag	-	-	
1896/1897	RAP Amsterdam	-	-	
1897/1898	RAP Amsterdam	-	-	
1898/1899	RAP Amsterdam	RAP Amsterdam	-	
1899/1900	HVV Den Haag	Velocitas Breda	-	
1900/1901	HVV Den Haag	HBS Craeyenhout	-	
1901/1902	HVV Den Haag	Haarlem	-	
1902/1903	HVV Den Haag	HVV Den Haag	-	
1903/1904	HBS Craeyenhout	HFC Haarlem	-	
1904/1905	HVV Den Haag	VOC Rotterdam	-	
1905/1906	HBS Craeyenhout	VV Concordia Rotterdam	-	
1906/1907	HVV Den Haag	VOC Rotterdam	-	
1907/1908	Quick Den Haag	HBS Craeyenhout 2	-	
1908/1909	Sparta Rotterdam	Quick Den Haag 2	-	
1909/1910	HVV Den Haag	Quick Den Haag 2	-	
1910/1911	Sparta Rotterdam	Quick Den Haag	-	
1911/1912	Sparta Rotterdam	HFC Haarlem	-	
1912/1913	Sparta Rotterdam	Koninklijke HFC Haarlem	-	
1913/1914	HVV Den Haag	Dordrechtsche FC	-	
1914/1915	Sparta Rotterdam	Koninklijke HFC Haarlem	-	
1915/1916	Willem II Tilburg	Quick Den Haag	-	
1916/1917	Go Ahead Eagles Deventer	AFC Ajax Amsterdam	-	
1917/1918	AFC Ajax Amsterdam	Racing Club Heemstede	-	
1918/1919	AFC Ajax Amsterdam	*No competition*	-	
1919/1920	Be Quick 1887 Groningen	CVV Rotterdam	-	
1920/1921	NAC Breda	Schoten Harlem	-	
1921/1922	Go Ahead Eagles Deventer	*No competition*	-	
1922/1923	Racing Club Heemstede	*No competition*	-	
1923/1924	SC Feijenoord Rotterdam	*No competition*	-	
1924/1925	HBS Craeyenhout	Zaanlandsche FC	-	
1925/1926	SC Enschede	LONGA Lichtenvoorde	-	
1926/1927	Heracles Almelo	VUC Den Haag	-	
1927/1928	SC Feijenoord Rotterdam	Racing Club Heemstede	-	
1928/1929	PSV Eindhoven	*No competition*	-	
1929/1930	Go Ahead Eagles Deventer	SC Feijenoord Rotterdam	-	
1930/1931	AFC Ajax Amsterdam	*No competition*	-	
1931/1932	AFC Ajax Amsterdam	DFC	-	
1932/1933	Go Ahead Eagles Deventer	*No competition*	-	
1933/1934	AFC Ajax Amsterdam	Velocitas Groningen	-	
1934/1935	PSV Eindhoven	SC Feijenoord Rotterdam	-	
1935/1936	SC Feijenoord Rotterdam	Roermond FC	-	
1936/1937	AFC Ajax Amsterdam	FC Eindhoven	-	
1937/1938	SC Feijenoord Rotterdam	VSV Velsen	-	
1938/1939	AFC Ajax Amsterdam	FC Wageningen	-	
1939/1940	SC Feijenoord Rotterdam	*No competition*	-	
1940/1941	Heracles Almelo	*No competition*	-	
1941/1942	ADO Den Haag	*No competition*	-	
1942/1943	ADO Den Haag	AFC Ajax Amsterdam	-	
1943/1944	AVV De Volewijckers Amsterdam	Willem II Tilburg	-	
1944/1945	*No competition*	*No competition*	-	
1945/1946	HFC Haarlem	*No competition*	-	
1946/1947	AFC Ajax Amsterdam	*No competition*	-	
1947/1948	BVV Den Bosch	FC Wageningen	-	
1948/1949	Schiedamse VV	Quick 1888 Nijmegen	-	
1949/1950	SV Limburgia Brunssum	PSV Eindhoven	-	
1950/1951	PSV Eindhoven	*No competition*	-	
1951/1952	Willem II Tilburg	*No competition*	-	
1952/1953	Racing Club Heemstede	*No competition*	-	
1953/1954	FC Eindhoven	*No competition*	-	
1954/1955	Willem II Tilburg	*No competition*	-	
1955/1956	Rapid JC Kerkrade	*No competition*	-	
1956/1957	AFC Ajax Amsterdam	Fortuna '54 Geleen	Coenraad Henrik Dillen (PSV Eindhoven)	43
1957/1958	VV DOS Utrecht	Sparta Rotterdam	Leonard Canjels (NAC Breda)	32
1958/1959	Sparta Rotterdam	VVV	Leonard Canjels (NAC Breda)	34
1959/1960	AFC Ajax Amsterdam	*No competition*	Hendrik Groot (AFC Ajax Amsterdam)	38

1960/1961	SC Feijenoord Rotterdam	AFC Ajax Amsterdam	Hendrik Groot (AFC Ajax Amsterdam)	41
1961/1962	SC Feijenoord Rotterdam	Sparta Rotterdam	Dick Tol (FC Volendam)	27
1962/1963	PSV Eindhoven	Willem II Tilburg	Pierre Kerkhofs (PSV Eindhoven)	22
1963/1964	DWS Amsterdam	Fortuna '54 Geleen	Frans Geurtsen (DWS Amsterdam)	28
1964/1965	SC Feijenoord Rotterdam	SC Feijenoord Rotterdam	Frans Geurtsen (DWS Amsterdam)	23
1965/1966	AFC Ajax Amsterdam	Sparta Rotterdam	Wilhelmus Martinus Leonardus Johannes van der Kuijlen (PSV Eindhoven) Piet Kruiver (SC Feijenoord Rotterdam)	23
1966/1967	AFC Ajax Amsterdam	AFC Ajax Amsterdam	Hendrik Johannes Cruijff (AFC Ajax Amsterdam)	33
1967/1968	AFC Ajax Amsterdam	ADO Den Haag	Ove Kindvall (SWE, SC Feijenoord Rotterdam)	28
1968/1969	SC Feijenoord Rotterdam	SC Feijenoord Rotterdam	Dirk Wouter Johannes van Dijk (FC Twente Enschede) Bengt Ove Kindvall (SWE, SC Feijenoord Rotterdam)	30
1969/1970	AFC Ajax Amsterdam	AFC Ajax Amsterdam	Wilhelmus Martinus Leonardus Johannes van der Kuijlen (PSV Eindhoven)	26
1970/1971	SC Feijenoord Rotterdam	AFC Ajax Amsterdam	Bengt Ove Kindvall (SWE, SC Feijenoord Rotterdam)	24
1971/1972	AFC Ajax Amsterdam	AFC Ajax Amsterdam	Hendrik Johannes Cruijff (AFC Ajax Amsterdam)	25
1972/1973	AFC Ajax Amsterdam	NAC Breda	Franciscus Janssens (NEC Nijmegen) Willy Brokamp (MVV Maastricht)	18
1973/1974	SC Feyenoord Rotterdam	PSV Eindhoven	Wilhelmus Martinus Leonardus Johannes van der Kuijlen (PSV Eindhoven)	27
1974/1975	PSV Eindhoven	FC Den Haag	Geertruida Maria Geels (AFC Ajax Amsterdam)	30
1975/1976	PSV Eindhoven	PSV Eindhoven	Geertruida Maria Geels (AFC Ajax Amsterdam)	29
1976/1977	AFC Ajax Amsterdam	FC Twente Enschede	Geertruida Maria Geels (AFC Ajax Amsterdam)	34
1977/1978	PSV Eindhoven	AZ'67 Alkmaar	Geertruida Maria Geels (AFC Ajax Amsterdam)	30
1978/1979	AFC Ajax Amsterdam	AFC Ajax Amsterdam	Cornelis Kist (AZ'67 Alkmaar)	34
1979/1980	AFC Ajax Amsterdam	SC Feyenoord Rotterdam	Cornelis Kist (AZ'67 Alkmaar)	27
1980/1981	AZ'67 Alkmaar '67	AZ'67 Alkmaar	Geertruida Maria Geels (Sparta Rotterdam)	22
1981/1982	AFC Ajax Amsterdam	AZ'67 Alkmaar	Willem Cornelis Nicolaas Kieft (AFC Ajax Amsterdam)	32
1982/1983	AFC Ajax Amsterdam	AFC Ajax Amsterdam	Peter Houtman (SC Feyenoord Rotterdam)	30
1983/1984	SC Feyenoord Rotterdam	SC Feyenoord Rotterdam	Marcel van Basten (AFC Ajax Amsterdam)	28
1984/1985	AFC Ajax Amsterdam	FC Utrecht	Marcel van Basten (AFC Ajax Amsterdam)	22
1985/1986	PSV Eindhoven	AFC Ajax Amsterdam	Marcel van Basten (AFC Ajax Amsterdam)	37
1986/1987	PSV Eindhoven	AFC Ajax Amsterdam	Marcel van Basten (AFC Ajax Amsterdam)	31
1987/1988	PSV Eindhoven	PSV Eindhoven	Willem Cornelis Nicolaas Kieft (PSV Eindhoven)	29
1988/1989	PSV Eindhoven	PSV Eindhoven	Romário de Souza Faria (BRA, PSV Eindhoven)	19
1989/1990	AFC Ajax Amsterdam	PSV Eindhoven	Romário de Souza Faria (BRA, PSV Eindhoven)	23
1990/1991	PSV Eindhoven	SC Feyenoord Rotterdam	Romário de Souza Faria (BRA, PSV Eindhoven) Dennis Nicolaas Maria Bergkamp (AFC Ajax Amsterdam)	25
1991/1992	PSV Eindhoven	SC Feyenoord Rotterdam	Dennis Nicolaas Maria Bergkamp (AFC Ajax Amsterdam)	24
1992/1993	SC Feyenoord Rotterdam	AFC Ajax Amsterdam	Dennis Nicolaas Maria Bergkamp (AFC Ajax Amsterdam)	26
1993/1994	AFC Ajax Amsterdam	SC Feyenoord Rotterdam	Jari Olavi Litmanen (FIN, AFC Ajax Amsterdam)	26
1994/1995	AFC Ajax Amsterdam	SC Feyenoord Rotterdam	Ronaldo Luís Nazário de Lima (BRA, PSV Eindhoven)	30
1995/1996	AFC Ajax Amsterdam	PSV Eindhoven	Luc Gilbert Cyrille Nilis (BEL, PSV Eindhoven)	21
1996/1997	PSV Eindhoven	Roda JC Kerkrade	Luc Gilbert Cyrille Nilis (BEL, PSV Eindhoven)	21
1997/1998	AFC Ajax Amsterdam	AFC Ajax Amsterdam	Nikolaos Machlas (GRE, SBV Vitesse Arnhem)	34
1998/1999	SC Feyenoord Rotterdam	AFC Ajax Amsterdam	Rutgerus Johannes Martinus van Nistelrooy (PSV Eindhoven)	31
1999/2000	PSV Eindhoven	Roda JC Kerkrade	Rutgerus Johannes Martinus van Nistelrooy (PSV Eindhoven)	29
2000/2001	PSV Eindhoven	FC Twente Enschede	Mateja Kežman (SRB, PSV Eindhoven)	24
2001/2002	AFC Ajax Amsterdam	AFC Ajax Amsterdam	Petrus Ferdinandus Johannes van Hooijdonk (SC Feyenoord Rotterdam)	24
2002/2003	PSV Eindhoven	FC Utrecht	Mateja Kežman (SRB, PSV Eindhoven)	35
2003/2004	AFC Ajax Amsterdam	FC Utrecht	Mateja Kežman (SRB, PSV Eindhoven)	31
2004/2005	PSV Eindhoven	PSV Eindhoven	Dirk Kuyt (SC Feyenoord Rotterdam)	29
2005/2006	PSV Eindhoven	AFC Ajax Amsterdam	Dirk Jan Klaas Huntelaar (SC Heerenveen/AFC Ajax Amsterdam)	33
2006/2007	PSV Eindhoven	AFC Ajax Amsterdam	Afonso Alves Martins Júnior (BRA, SC Heerenveen)	34
2007/2008	PSV Eindhoven	SC Feyenoord Rotterdam	Dirk Jan Klaas Huntelaar (AFC Ajax Amsterdam)	33
2008/2009	AZ Alkmaar	SC Heerenveen	Mounir El Hamdaoui (MAR, AZ Alkmaar)	23
2009/2010	FC Twente Enschede	AFC Ajax Amsterdam	Luis Alberto Suárez Díaz (URU, AFC Ajax Amsterdam)	35
2010/2011	AFC Ajax Amsterdam	FC Twente Enschede	Björn Vleminckx (BEL, NEC Nijmegen)	23
2011/2012	AFC Ajax Amsterdam	PSV Eindhoven	Bas Dost (SC Heerenveen)	32
2012/2013	AFC Ajax Amsterdam	AZ Alkmaar	Wilfried Guemiand Bony (CIV, SBV Vitesse Arnhem)	31
2013/2014	AFC Ajax Amsterdam	PEC Zwolle	Alfreð Finnbogason (ISL, SC Heerenveen)	29
2014/2015	PSV Eindhoven	FC Groningen	Memphis Depay (PSV Eindhoven)	22
2015/2016	PSV Eindhoven	Feyenoord Rotterdam	Vincent Janssen (AZ Alkmaar)	27
2016/2017	Feyenoord Rotterdam	SBV Vitesse Arnhem	Nicolai Mick Jørgensen (DEN, Feyenoord Rotterdam)	21
2017/2018	PSV Eindhoven	Feyenoord Rotterdam	Alireza Jahanbakhsh (IRN, AZ Alkmaar)	21
2018/2019	AFC Ajax Amsterdam	AFC Ajax Amsterdam	Luuk de Jong (PSV Eindhoven) Dušan Tadić (SRB, AFC Ajax Amsterdam)	28

2019/2020	*Championship cancelled*	*Competition cancelled*	-	
2020/2021	AFC Ajax Amsterdam	AFC Ajax Amsterdam	Georgios Giakoumakis (GRE, VVV-Venlo)	26

*National Champions (1888–1956), Eredivisie (since 1956)

NATIONAL CHAMPIONSHIP
Eredivisie 2020/2021
(12.09.2020 – 16.05.2021)

Results

Round 1 [12-13.09.2020]
SC Heerenveen - Willem II 2-0(1-0)
PEC Zwolle - Feyenoord 0-2(0-1)
FC Twente - Fortuna Sittard 2-0(1-0)
FC Emmen - VVV-Venlo 3-5(1-0)
Heracles Almelo - ADO Den Haag 2-0(0-0)
Sparta Rotterdam - AFC Ajax 0-1(0-1)
FC Groningen - PSV Eindhoven 1-3(0-1)
RKC Waalwijk - Vitesse 0-1(0-1)
FC Utrecht - AZ Alkmaar 2-2(1-0) [27.12.]

Round 2 [18-20.09.2020]
VVV-Venlo - FC Utrecht 1-1(1-0)
AZ Alkmaar - PEC Zwolle 1-1(0-1)
Vitesse - Sparta Rotterdam 2-0(1-0)
PSV Eindhoven - FC Emmen 2-1(1-0)
Fortuna Sittard - SC Heerenveen 1-3(0-3)
ADO Den Haag - FC Groningen 0-1(0-1)
Feyenoord - FC Twente 1-1(1-1)
Willem II - Heracles Almelo 4-0(0-0)
AFC Ajax - RKC Waalwijk 3-0(2-0)

Round 3 [25-27.09.2020]
FC Twente - FC Groningen 3-1(2-0)
PEC Zwolle - Sparta Rotterdam 4-0(1-0)
Fortuna Sittard - AZ Alkmaar 3-3(1-1)
SC Heerenveen - VVV-Venlo 1-0(1-0)
AFC Ajax - Vitesse 2-1(1-0)
Feyenoord - ADO Den Haag 4-2(1-1)
FC Utrecht - RKC Waalwijk 3-1(1-0)
Heracles Almelo - PSV Eindhoven 1-1(1-0)
FC Emmen - Willem II 1-1(1-1)

Round 4 [02-04.10.2020]
FC Utrecht - SC Heerenveen 1-1(1-1)
Vitesse - Heracles Almelo 3-0(2-0)
VVV-Venlo - ADO Den Haag 1-2(1-1)
FC Twente - FC Emmen 1-1(0-0)
FC Groningen - AFC Ajax 1-0(0-0)
Sparta Rotterdam - AZ Alkmaar 4-4(0-4)
Willem II - Feyenoord 1-4(1-1)
PSV Eindhoven - Fortuna Sittard 2-0(1-0)
RKC Waalwijk - PEC Zwolle 1-1(0-0)[21.10.]

Round 5 [17-18.10.2020]
Heracles Almelo - RKC Waalwijk 0-1(0-1)
AZ Alkmaar - VVV-Venlo 2-2(2-0)
Willem II - FC Twente 0-3(0-1)
Feyenoord - Sparta Rotterdam 1-1(1-0)
AFC Ajax - SC Heerenveen 5-1(3-0)
ADO Den Haag - Vitesse 0-2(0-1)
FC Groningen - FC Utrecht 0-0
PEC Zwolle - PSV Eindhoven 0-3(0-3)
FC Emmen - Fortuna Sittard 2-2(0-2)

Round 6 [24-25.10.2020]
VVV-Venlo - AFC Ajax 0-13(0-4)
FC Utrecht - FC Twente 2-1(1-1)
PEC Zwolle - Willem II 0-0
SC Heerenveen - FC Emmen 4-0(2-0)
Fortuna Sittard - FC Groningen 1-3(0-2)
Vitesse - PSV Eindhoven 2-1(1-0)
Sparta Rotterdam - Heracles Almelo 1-1(0-0)
RKC Waalwijk - Feyenoord 2-2(0-0)
ADO Den Haag - AZ Alkmaar 2-2(0-1)

Round 7 [31.10.-01.11.2020]
FC Twente - PEC Zwolle 5-1(3-0)
AFC Ajax - Fortuna Sittard 5-2(2-1)
FC Groningen - VVV-Venlo 2-1(1-0)
Willem II - Vitesse 1-3(1-0)
Heracles Almelo - FC Utrecht 4-1(2-0)
Sparta Rotterdam - SC Heerenveen 1-4(0-3)
FC Emmen - Feyenoord 2-3(2-2)
PSV Eindhoven - ADO Den Haag 4-0(1-0)
AZ Alkmaar - RKC Waalwijk 3-0(1-0)

Round 8 [06-08.11.2020]
Fortuna Sittard - PEC Zwolle 2-2(2-1)
ADO Den Haag - FC Twente 2-4(0-1)
VVV-Venlo - Heracles Almelo 3-2(0-1)
RKC Waalwijk - Sparta Rotterdam 0-2(0-0)
FC Utrecht - AFC Ajax 0-3(0-0)
Vitesse - FC Emmen 3-1(3-0)
Feyenoord - FC Groningen 2-0(0-0)
SC Heerenveen - AZ Alkmaar 0-3(0-2)
PSV Eindhoven - Willem II 3-0(2-0)

Round 9 [21-22.11.2020]
Willem II - VVV-Venlo 2-1(2-1)
FC Groningen - Vitesse 1-1(1-1)
PEC Zwolle - FC Utrecht 1-1(1-0)
AFC Ajax - Heracles Almelo 5-0(3-0)
Sparta Rotterdam - ADO Den Haag 6-0(1-0)
Fortuna Sittard - Feyenoord 1-3(1-2)
FC Twente - PSV Eindhoven 1-1(0-1)
RKC Waalwijk - SC Heerenveen 1-1(0-1)
AZ Alkmaar - FC Emmen 1-0(1-0)

Round 10 [27-29.11.2020]
FC Twente - RKC Waalwijk 0-2(0-2)
FC Emmen - AFC Ajax 0-5(0-3)
ADO Den Haag - SC Heerenveen 1-1(1-1)
VVV-Venlo - PEC Zwolle 2-2(1-1)
Vitesse - Fortuna Sittard 2-0(0-0)
FC Groningen - Willem II 1-0(0-0)
Feyenoord - FC Utrecht 1-1(0-0)
Heracles Almelo - AZ Alkmaar 1-2(0-2)
PSV Eindhoven - Sparta Rotterdam 1-0(0-0)

Round 11 [04-06.12.2020]
Sparta Rotterdam - FC Emmen 2-1(1-0)
RKC Waalwijk - VVV-Venlo 3-2(1-1)
Fortuna Sittard - Willem II 3-2(3-0)
AFC Ajax - FC Twente 1-2(0-1)
PEC Zwolle - Vitesse 2-1(0-1)
Feyenoord - Heracles Almelo 0-0
AZ Alkmaar - FC Groningen 1-2(1-0)
FC Utrecht - ADO Den Haag 1-1(0-0)
SC Heerenveen - PSV Eindhoven 2-2(0-1)

Round 12 [11-13.12.2020]
Heracles Almelo - Fortuna Sittard 1-2(0-1)
FC Groningen - RKC Waalwijk 2-0(0-0)
FC Emmen - ADO Den Haag 1-1(0-1)
AFC Ajax - PEC Zwolle 4-0(3-0)
Vitesse - SC Heerenveen 1-1(1-0)
VVV-Venlo - Feyenoord 0-3(0-0)
Willem II - Sparta Rotterdam 1-3(0-2)
PSV Eindhoven - FC Utrecht 2-1(2-0)
FC Twente - AZ Alkmaar 1-3(0-2)

Round 13 [18-20.12.2020]
PEC Zwolle - FC Emmen 0-0
Sparta Rotterdam - FC Groningen 2-3(1-1)
VVV-Venlo - FC Twente 1-2(0-1)
RKC Waalwijk - PSV Eindhoven 1-4(0-2)
FC Utrecht - Fortuna Sittard 1-1(0-0)
Vitesse - Feyenoord 1-0(1-0)
ADO Den Haag - AFC Ajax 2-4(0-4)
SC Heerenveen - Heracles Almelo 1-2(0-1)
AZ Alkmaar - Willem II 5-3(2-2)

Round 14 [22-23.12.2020]
Fortuna Sittard - RKC Waalwijk 2-1(1-1)
FC Emmen - FC Utrecht 2-3(2-1)
PSV Eindhoven - VVV-Venlo 4-1(1-1)
FC Twente - Sparta Rotterdam 0-2(0-1)
AZ Alkmaar - Vitesse 3-1(2-0)
Willem II - AFC Ajax 1-1(0-1)
FC Groningen - Heracles Almelo 0-1(0-0)
ADO Den Haag - PEC Zwolle 0-2(0-0)
Feyenoord - SC Heerenveen 3-0(0-0)

Round 15 [09-10.01.2021]
RKC Waalwijk - ADO Den Haag 0-1(0-1)
FC Emmen - FC Twente 1-4(0-3)
Heracles Almelo - Vitesse 0-2(0-1)
PEC Zwolle - AZ Alkmaar 1-1(1-0)
FC Utrecht - FC Groningen 2-2(1-2)
Sparta Rotterdam - Feyenoord 0-2(0-1)
SC Heerenveen - Fortuna Sittard 1-3(0-3)
VVV-Venlo - Willem II 2-1(0-1)
AFC Ajax - PSV Eindhoven 2-2(1-2)

Round 16 [12-14.01.2021]
Vitesse - FC Utrecht 1-0(1-0)
Heracles Almelo - FC Emmen 4-0(2-0)
PSV Eindhoven - AZ Alkmaar 1-3(0-2)
Fortuna Sittard - Sparta Rotterdam 0-1(0-0)
ADO Den Haag - VVV-Venlo 1-4(0-1)
Feyenoord - PEC Zwolle 1-0(0-0)
SC Heerenveen - RKC Waalwijk 1-1(1-0)
FC Twente - AFC Ajax 1-3(0-1)
Willem II - FC Groningen 2-3(0-0)

Round 17 [16-17.01.2021]
FC Emmen - Vitesse 1-4(0-2)
Sparta Rotterdam - PSV Eindhoven 3-5(1-1)
FC Utrecht - Heracles Almelo 2-0(1-0)
PEC Zwolle - Fortuna Sittard 0-2(0-0)
AZ Alkmaar - ADO Den Haag 2-1(0-0)
RKC Waalwijk - Willem II 1-1(1-0)
FC Groningen - FC Twente 2-2(0-2)
VVV-Venlo - SC Heerenveen 1-1(0-0)
AFC Ajax - Feyenoord 1-0(1-0)

Round 18 [22-24.01.2021]
Willem II - PEC Zwolle 1-3(1-0)
ADO Den Haag - FC Emmen 0-0
Vitesse - FC Groningen 1-0(1-0)
PSV Eindhoven - RKC Waalwijk 2-0(1-0)
Heracles Almelo - SC Heerenveen 1-0(0-0)
Fortuna Sittard - AFC Ajax 1-2(0-1)
FC Twente - VVV-Venlo 1-0(1-0)
FC Utrecht - Sparta Rotterdam 1-0(0-0)
Feyenoord - AZ Alkmaar 2-3(1-1)

Round 19 [26-28.01.2021]
PEC Zwolle - Heracles Almelo 2-2(0-2)
FC Emmen - PSV Eindhoven 0-2(0-0)
FC Groningen - ADO Den Haag 3-0(2-0)
AZ Alkmaar - FC Utrecht 0-1(0-0)
RKC Waalwijk - Fortuna Sittard 1-2(0-0)
VVV-Venlo - Vitesse 4-1(3-0)
SC Heerenveen - Feyenoord 3-0(2-0)
Sparta Rotterdam - FC Twente 0-0
AFC Ajax - Willem II 3-1(0-0)

Round 20 [30-31.01.2021]
Heracles Almelo - FC Groningen 1-0(1-0)
FC Utrecht - PEC Zwolle 3-3(1-2)
Fortuna Sittard - VVV-Venlo 3-2(1-0)
Vitesse - RKC Waalwijk 1-1(0-0)
FC Twente - SC Heerenveen 0-0
Feyenoord - PSV Eindhoven 3-1(3-0)
Willem II - FC Emmen 2-0(1-0)
AZ Alkmaar - AFC Ajax 0-3(0-1)
ADO Den Haag - Sparta Rotterdam 1-1(1-0)

Round 21 [05-06.02.2021]
Fortuna Sittard - Heracles Almelo 0-1(0-1)
PEC Zwolle - RKC Waalwijk 1-1(0-1)
FC Emmen - AZ Alkmaar 0-1(0-0)
PSV Eindhoven - FC Twente 3-0(2-0)
SC Heerenveen - Vitesse 1-0(0-0)
Willem II - ADO Den Haag 1-1(0-0) [24.02.]
FC Groningen - Feyenoord 0-0 [24.02.]
VVV-Venlo - Sparta Rotterd. 0-1(0-0) [09.03.]
AFC Ajax - FC Utrecht 1-1(0-1) [22.04.]

Round 22 [12-14.02.2021]
RKC Waalwijk - FC Emmen 1-0(0-0)
FC Groningen - PEC Zwolle 1-0(1-0)
Sparta Rotterdam - Fortuna Sittard 1-2(1-1)
ADO Den Haag - PSV Eindhoven 2-2(1-0)
Heracles Almelo - AFC Ajax 0-2(0-1)
AZ Alkmaar - SC Heerenveen 3-1(1-0)
FC Utrecht - VVV-Venlo 3-1(0-0)
Feyenoord - Willem II 5-0(1-0)
Vitesse - FC Twente 0-2(0-1)

Round 23 [19-21.02.2021]
Willem II - FC Utrecht 0-6(0-3)
FC Emmen - PEC Zwolle 3-2(2-1)
VVV-Venlo - AZ Alkmaar 1-4(1-1)
Fortuna Sittard - ADO Den Haag 2-0(1-0)
FC Twente - Feyenoord 2-2(2-1)
RKC Waalwijk - Heracles Almelo 3-0(2-0)
SC Heerenveen - FC Groningen 1-1(1-0)
PSV Eindhoven - Vitesse 3-1(0-1)
AFC Ajax - Sparta Rotterdam 4-2(3-0)

Round 24 [26-28.02.2021]
PEC Zwolle - SC Heerenveen 4-1(0-1)
FC Utrecht - FC Emmen 0-1(0-1)
ADO Den Haag - RKC Waalwijk 0-0
Vitesse - VVV-Venlo 4-1(1-0)
Heracles Almelo - FC Twente 2-2(1-1)
Sparta Rotterdam - Willem II 0-2(0-0)
FC Groningen - Fortuna Sittard 1-0(0-0)
PSV Eindhoven - AFC Ajax 1-1(1-0)
AZ Alkmaar - Feyenoord 4-2(2-2)

Round 25 [05-07.03.2021]
FC Emmen - Sparta Rotterdam 1-1(0-1)
Feyenoord - VVV-Venlo 6-0(3-0)
FC Twente - Willem II 1-1(0-0)
SC Heerenveen - ADO Den Haag 3-0(1-0)
RKC Waalwijk - FC Utrecht 1-2(0-1)
AFC Ajax - FC Groningen 3-1(1-0)
Fortuna Sittard - PSV Eindhoven 1-3(0-2)
Heracles Almelo - PEC Zwolle 2-1(0-0)
Vitesse - AZ Alkmaar 2-1(1-0)

Round 26 [13-14.03.2021]
Willem II - SC Heerenveen 3-1(1-0)
ADO Den Haag - Heracles Almelo 1-2(0-0)
AZ Alkmaar - FC Twente 4-1(3-1)
FC Groningen - FC Emmen 1-1(0-1)
Sparta Rotterdam - RKC Waalwijk 2-0(0-0)
VVV-Venlo - Fortuna Sittard 1-3(0-1)
FC Utrecht - Vitesse 1-3(1-1)
PSV Eindhoven - Feyenoord 1-1(1-1)
PEC Zwolle - AFC Ajax 0-2(0-2)

Round 27 [19-21.03.2021]
SC Heerenveen - FC Twente 0-0
Fortuna Sittard - FC Utrecht 1-0(1-0)
Feyenoord - FC Emmen 1-1(1-0)
RKC Waalwijk - FC Groningen 3-1(2-1)
PEC Zwolle - VVV-Venlo 2-1(0-0)
AZ Alkmaar - PSV Eindhoven 2-0(1-0)
Vitesse - Willem II 0-0
Heracles Almelo - Sparta Rotterdam 1-1(0-0)
AFC Ajax - ADO Den Haag 5-0(4-0)

Round 28 [03-04.04.2021]
VVV-Venlo - FC Groningen 0-1(0-0)
FC Twente - Vitesse 1-2(1-1)
Willem II - AZ Alkmaar 0-1(0-0)
Sparta Rotterdam - PEC Zwolle 3-2(1-0)
Feyenoord - Fortuna Sittard 2-0(0-0)
ADO Den Haag - FC Utrecht 1-4(0-3)
PSV Eindhoven - Heracles Almelo 3-0(2-0)
FC Emmen - RKC Waalwijk 3-1(3-0)
SC Heerenveen - AFC Ajax 1-2(1-1)

Round 29 [09-11.04.2021]
Vitesse - ADO Den Haag 0-0
Heracles Almelo - Willem II 4-0(2-0)
AZ Alkmaar - Sparta Rotterdam 2-0(1-0)
Fortuna Sittard - FC Emmen 1-3(0-0)
PEC Zwolle - FC Twente 1-0(1-0)
FC Utrecht - Feyenoord 1-2(1-1)
FC Groningen - SC Heerenveen 0-2(0-0)
VVV-Venlo - PSV Eindhoven 0-2(0-1)
RKC Waalwijk - AFC Ajax 0-1(0-1)

Round 30 [23-25.04.2021]
Willem II - RKC Waalwijk 1-0(0-0)
SC Heerenveen - PEC Zwolle 0-2(0-1)
PSV Eindhoven - FC Groningen 1-0(0-0)
Sparta Rotterdam - VVV-Venlo 2-0(1-0)
FC Emmen - Heracles Almelo 3-0(0-0)
ADO Den Haag - Fortuna Sittard 0-3(0-1)
AFC Ajax - AZ Alkmaar 2-0(0-0)
FC Twente - FC Utrecht 1-2(1-0)
Feyenoord - Vitesse 0-0

Round 31 [01-02.05.2021]
Heracles Almelo - VVV-Venlo 4-0(2-0)
Fortuna Sittard - FC Twente 3-0(1-0)
RKC Waalwijk - AZ Alkmaar 1-3(1-1)
Vitesse - PEC Zwolle 2-1(1-0)
FC Utrecht - Willem II 3-2(2-0)
ADO Den Haag - Feyenoord 3-2(2-1)
AFC Ajax - FC Emmen 4-0(1-0)
FC Groningen - Sparta Rotterdam 1-2(0-1)
PSV Eindhoven - SC Heerenveen 2-2(0-1)

Round 32 [07-09.05.2021]
Sparta Rotterdam - Vitesse 3-0(1-0)
FC Twente - Heracles Almelo 1-1(0-0)
SC Heerenveen - FC Utrecht 0-0
AZ Alkmaar - Fortuna Sittard 1-0(1-0)
VVV-Venlo - RKC Waalwijk 3-3(2-2)
FC Emmen - FC Groningen 0-4(0-1)
Feyenoord - AFC Ajax 0-3(0-1)
PEC Zwolle - ADO Den Haag 0-1(0-1)
Willem II - PSV Eindhoven 0-2(0-1)

Round 33 [13.05.2021]
ADO Den Haag - Willem II 1-4(0-3)
AFC Ajax - VVV-Venlo 3-1(1-0)
FC Emmen - SC Heerenveen 3-1(1-0)
FC Groningen - AZ Alkmaar 0-0
Fortuna Sittard - Vitesse 3-3(2-2)
Heracles Almelo - Feyenoord 1-1(0-0)
PSV Eindhoven - PEC Zwolle 4-2(3-0)
RKC Waalwijk - FC Twente 2-1(0-0)
Sparta Rotterdam - FC Utrecht 0-0

Round 34 [16.05.2021]
AZ Alkmaar - Heracles Almelo 5-0(1-0)
FC Twente - ADO Den Haag 3-2(2-2)
FC Utrecht - PSV Eindhoven 1-1(1-0)
Feyenoord - RKC Waalwijk 3-0(2-0)
PEC Zwolle - FC Groningen 1-0(0-0)
SC Heerenveen - Sparta Rotterdam 1-2(0-2)
Vitesse - AFC Ajax 1-3(1-2)
VVV-Venlo - FC Emmen 0-4(0-1)
Willem II - Fortuna Sittard 2-1(1-0)

Final Standings

					Total			Home					Away				
1. **AFC Ajax Amsterdam**	34	28	4	2	102 - 23	88	14	2	1	53 - 14	14	2	1	49 - 9
2. PSV Eindhoven	34	21	9	4	74 - 35	72	13	3	1	39 - 13	8	6	3	35 - 22
3. AZ Alkmaar	34	21	8	5	75 - 41	71	12	2	3	39 - 18	9	6	2	36 - 23
4. SBV Vitesse Arnhem	34	18	7	9	52 - 38	61	11	4	2	26 - 12	7	3	7	26 - 26
5. Feyenoord Rotterdam	34	16	11	7	64 - 36	59	9	6	2	35 - 13	7	5	5	29 - 23
6. FC Utrecht	34	13	14	7	52 - 41	53	6	7	4	27 - 25	7	7	3	25 - 16
7. FC Groningen	34	14	8	12	40 - 37	50	7	6	4	17 - 13	7	2	8	23 - 24
8. Sparta Rotterdam	34	13	8	13	49 - 48	47	6	4	7	30 - 27	7	4	6	19 - 21
9. Heracles Almelo	34	12	8	14	42 - 53	44	8	4	5	29 - 16	4	4	9	13 - 37
10. FC Twente Enschede	34	10	11	13	48 - 50	41	4	6	7	23 - 25	6	5	6	25 - 25
11. Fortuna Sittard	34	12	5	17	50 - 58	41	5	3	9	27 - 33	7	2	8	23 - 25
12. SC Heerenveen	34	9	12	13	43 - 49	39	6	5	6	22 - 18	3	7	7	21 - 31
13. PEC Zwolle	34	9	11	14	44 - 53	38	6	6	5	19 - 18	3	5	9	25 - 35
14. Willem II Tilburg	34	8	7	19	40 - 68	31	6	2	9	22 - 33	2	5	10	18 - 35
15. RKC Waalwijk	34	7	9	18	33 - 55	30	5	4	8	21 - 25	2	5	10	12 - 30
16. FC Emmen (*Relegation Play-offs*)	34	7	9	18	40 - 68	30	4	4	9	26 - 41	3	5	9	14 - 27
17. VVV-Venlo (*Relegated*)	34	6	5	23	43 - 91	23	3	4	10	20 - 46	3	1	13	23 - 45
18. ADO Den Haag (*Relegated*)	34	4	10	20	29 - 76	22	1	6	10	17 - 38	3	4	10	12 - 38

<u>Please note</u>: teams ranked 5-8 were qualified for the European competition Play-offs.

Top goalscorers:

26	**Georgios Giakoumakis (GRE)**	*VVV-Venlo*
19	Donyell Malen	*PSV Eindhoven*
18	Steven Berghuis	*Feyenoord Rotterdam*
17	Danilo Pereira Da Silva (BRA)	*FC Twente Enschede*
16	Rai Vloet	*Heracles Almelo*

European competition Play-offs

Semi-Finals [19.05.2021]	FC Utrecht - FC Groningen	1-0(0-0)
	Feyenoord Rotterdam - Sparta Rotterdam	2-0(2-0)

Final [23.05.2021]	**Feyenoord Rotterdam** - FC Utrecht	2-0(1-0)

Promotion / Relegation Play-offs (1st / 2nd Level)

First Round [15.05.2021]	NAC Breda - FC Volendam	4-1(1-0)
	VBV De Graafschap Doetinchem - SV Roda JC Kerkrade	2-3(2-1)
	Almere City FC - NEC Nijmegen	0-4(0-2)

Semi-Finals [20.05.2021]	NEC Nijmegen - SV Roda JC Kerkrade	3-0(2-0)
	FC Emmen - NAC Breda	1-1(0-1,1-1,1-1); 3-4 on penalties

Final [23.05.2021]	NAC Breda - NEC Nijmegen	1-2(0-1)

NEC Nijmegen promoted to 2021/2022 Eredivisie.

NATIONAL CUP
KNVB 2020/2021

First Round [26-28.10./01-02.12.2020]

SBV Excelsior Rotterdam - Helmond Sport	4-0(2-0)	OFC Oostzaan - MVV Maastricht	*not played*
Go Ahead Eagles Deventer - NAC Breda	6-0(5-0)	HSV ODIN '59 Heemskerk - FC Volendam	*not played*
FC Twente Enschede - VBV De Graafschap Doetin.	1-3(0-2)	DTS'35 Ede - Quick Boys Katwijk aan Zee	*not played*
VVV-Venlo - FC Den Bosch	4-2(0-1)	VV Staphorst - PEC Zwolle	*not played*
SC Heerenveen - Tot Ons Plezier Oss	3-1(3-1)	VV Sliedrecht - IJsselmeervogels	*not played*
FC Dordrecht - FC Utrecht	2-4(1-3)	HV & CV Quick Den Haag - NEC Nijmegen	*not played*
ADO Den Haag - Sparta Rotterdam	1-1 aet; 5-3 pen	VV Capelle - Amsterdamsche FC	*not played*
FC Emmen - FC Eindhoven	2-0(0-0)	DVS'33 Ermelo - Willem II Tilburg	*not played*
Heracles Almelo - SC Telstar Velsen	3-0(1-0)	Kozakken Boys Werkendam - Harkemase Boys	*not played*
RKC Waalwijk - SC Cambuur Leeuwarden	2-2 aet; 3-5 pen	HHC Hardenberg - SBV Vitesse Arnhem	*not played*
Roda JC Kerkrade - Fortuna Sittard	0-2(0-2)	SV OSS '20 - VV Katwijk	*not played*
SVV Scheveningen - Almere City FC	*not played*	RKVV Westlandia - VV SteDoCo	*not played*
Rijnsburgse Boys - VV Excelsior Maassluis	*not played*	VV UNA Zeelst - RKSV Groene Ster Heerlerheide	*not played*
BVV Barendrecht - Achilles Veen	*not played*	SV TEC Tiel - FC Groningen	*not played*

Second Round [15-17.12.2020]

SBV Excelsior Rotterdam - PEC Zwolle	2-0(0-0)	AFC Ajax Amsterdam - FC Utrecht	5-4(2-1)
FC Emmen - FC Groningen	2-1(0-1)	SC Cambuur Leeuwarden - Go Ahead Eagles Devent.	1-2(1-1)
Almere City FC - VVV-Venlo	1-4(1-2)	Willem II Tilburg - SBV Vitesse Arnhem	0-2(0-1)
VBV De Graafschap Doetinchem - PSV Eindhoven	1-2(0-0)		

1/8-Finals [19-21.01.2021]		
MVV Maastricht - SBV Excelsior Rotterdam	2-2 aet; 4-5 pen	
SBV Vitesse Arnhem - ADO Den Haag	2-1(1-0)	
FC Volendam - PSV Eindhoven	0-2(0-0)	
FC Emmen - SC Heerenveen	1-2(1-0)	
Feyenoord - Heracles Almelo	3-2(1-1)	
AZ Alkmaar - AFC Ajax Amsterdam	0-1(0-1)	
NEC Nijmegen - Fortuna Sittard	3-2(0-0,1-1)	
VVV-Venlo - Go Ahead Eagles Deventer	1-0(1-0)	

Quarter-Finals [09-10/17..02.2021]		
SBV Excelsior Rotterdam - SBV Vitesse Arnhem	0-1(0-0)	
AFC Ajax Amsterdam - PSV Eindhoven	2-1(2-0)	
NEC Nijmegen - VVV-Venlo	1-2(0-1,1-1)	
SC Heerenveen - Feyenoord	4-3(1-0)	

Semi-Finals [02-03.03.2021]		
SBV Vitesse Arnhem - VVV-Venlo	2-0(0-0)	
SC Heerenveen - AFC Ajax Amsterdam	0-3(0-1)	

Final

18.04.2021; Stadion Feijenoord, Rotterdam; Referee: Björn Kuipers; Attendance: 0
AFC Ajax Amsterdam - SBV Vitesse Arnhem   **2-1(1-1)**

Ajax Amsterdam: Maarten Stekelenburg, Devyne Rensch (75.Perr Schuurs), Jurriën David Norman Timber, Nicolás Alejandro Tagliafico, Edson Omar Álvarez Velázquez, Davy Klaassen (87.Jurgen Ekkelenkamp), Ryan Jiro Gravenberch, Antony Matheus dos Santos (87.David Neres Campos), Sébastien Haller, Dušan Tadić (Cap). Trainer: Erik ten Hag.

Vitesse Arnhem: Remko Pasveer (Cap), Eli Dasa (46.Alois Dominik Oroz), Danilho Doekhi, Riechedly Bazoer, Jacob Rasmussen [*sent off 86*], Maximilian Wittek (89.Tomáš Hajek), Sondre Tronstad, Oussama Tannane (89.Oussama Darfalou), Matúš Bero, Loïs Openda (65.Idrissa Touré), Armando Broja. Trainer: Thomas Letsch (Germany).

Goals: 1-0 Ryan Jiro Gravenberch (23), 1-1 Loïs Openda (30), 2-1 David Neres Campos (90).

THE CLUBS 2020/2021

Alles Door Oefening Den Haag

Founded:	01.02.1905
Stadium:	Stadion "Cars Jeans", Den Haag (15,000)
Trainer:	Aleksandar Ranković (SRB) 31.08.1978
[10.11.2020]	Ruud Brood 19.10.1962

Goalkeepers:	DOB	M	(s)	G
Martin Fraisl (AUT)	10.05.1993	15		
Luuk Koopmans	18.11.1993	19		
Defenders:	**DOB**	**M**	**(s)**	**G**
Jamal Amofa	25.11.1998	5	(1)	
Peet Bijen	28.01.1995	6		
Dario Del Fabro (ITA)	24.03.1995	15	(4)	
Silvinho Esajas	08.07.2002		(2)	
Juan Carlos Familia-Castillo	13.01.2000	9	(7)	
Lassana Faye	15.06.1998	12		
Daryl Janmaat	22.07.1989	3	(1)	
Boy Kemper	21.06.1999	24	(2)	1
Jonathan Mulder	02.01.2002		(1)	
Shaquille Pinas (SUR)	19.03.1998	24	(3)	3
Andrei Florin Rațiu (ROU)	20.06.1998	7	(3)	
Cain Seedorf	19.01.2000	2	(1)	
Milan van Ewijk	08.09.2000	33		1
Gianni Zuiverloon	30.12.1986	7	(1)	
Midfielders:	**DOB**	**M**	**(s)**	**G**
Samy Bourard (BEL)	10.07.1996	10	(7)	3
Kees de Boer	13.05.2000	16	(4)	

	DOB	M	(s)	G
Nasser el Khayati	07.02.1989	11		2
Ilay Elmkies (ISR)	10.03.2000	4	(5)	
Tomislav Gomelt (CRO)	07.01.1995	6	(4)	1
John Goossens	25.07.1988	18	(6)	2
Ravel Ryan Morrison (JAM)	02.02.1993	1	(3)	
José Pascual Alba Seva „Pascu" (ESP)	02.04.2000	6	(7)	
Dante Rigo (BEL)	11.12.1998	9	(2)	
Marko Vejinović	03.02.1990	14	(3)	
Forwards:	**DOB**	**M**	**(s)**	**G**
Bobby Adekanye	14.02.1999	11	(3)	2
Jonas Arweiler (GER)	10.04.1997	11	(14)	3
Vicente Besuijen	10.04.2001	23	(7)	1
Amar Ćatić (BIH)	21.01.1999	4	(10)	
Nikolaos Karelis (GRE)	24.02.1992	2	(7)	
Ricardo Kishna	04.01.1995	13	(3)	
Michiel Kramer	03.12.1988	21	(8)	6
Youness Mokhtar (MAR)	29.08.1991	5	(5)	
Bilal Ould-Chikh (MAR)	28.07.1997	3	(11)	
David Philipp (GER)	10.04.2000	4	(11)	2
Xander Severina	12.04.2001	1	(1)	

Amsterdamsche Football Club Ajax

Founded:	18.03.1900
Stadium:	"Johann Cruijff ArenA", Amsterdam (55,500)
Trainer:	Erik ten Hag 02.02.1970

Goalkeepers:	DOB	M	(s)	G
André Onana (CMR)	02.04.1996	20		
Kjell Scherpen	23.01.2000	2		
Maarten Stekelenburg	22.09.1982	12		
Defenders:	**DOB**	**M**	**(s)**	**G**
Daley Blind	09.03.1990	23		1
Sergiño Dest (USA)	03.11.2000		(3)	
Sean Klaiber (SUR)	13.07.1994	6	(9)	
Lisandro Martínez (ARG)	18.01.1998	17	(9)	3
Noussair Mazraoui (MAR)	14.11.1997	16	(3)	
Devyne Rensch	18.01.2003	12	(6)	3
Perr Schuurs	26.11.1999	20	(7)	1
Nicolás Alejandro Tagliafico (ARG)	31.08.1992	25		1
Jurriën David Norman Timber	17.06.2001	16	(4)	1
Midfielders:	**DOB**	**M**	**(s)**	**G**
Edson Omar Álvarez Velázquez (MEX)	24.10.1997	18	(6)	2
Jurgen Ekkelenkamp	05.04.2000	4	(11)	3

	DOB	M	(s)	G
Ryan Jiro Gravenberch	15.06.2002	31	(1)	3
Victor Christoffer Jensen (DEN)	08.02.2000		(1)	
Davy Klaassen	21.02.1993	27	(2)	12
Mohammed Kudus (GHA)	02.08.2000	8	(9)	4
Zakaria Labyad (MAR)	09.03.1993	12	(10)	5
Kenneth Taylor	16.05.2002		(3)	
Forwards:	**DOB**	**M**	**(s)**	**G**
Antony Matheus dos Santos (BRA)	24.02.2000	24	(8)	9
Brian Brobbey	01.02.2002	1	(11)	3
David Neres Campos (BRA)	03.03.1997	10	(15)	3
Sébastien Haller (CIV)	22.06.1994	18	(1)	11
Dirk Jan Klaas Huntelaar	12.08.1983	3	(8)	7
Oussama Idrissi (MAR)	26.02.1996	1	(6)	
Noa Lang	17.06.1999		(1)	
Quincy Anton Promes	04.01.1992	10	(9)	6
Dušan Tadić (SRB)	20.11.1988	31	(3)	14
Lassina Traoré (BFA)	12.01.2001	7	(5)	7

Alkmaar Zaanstreek Alkmaar

Founded: 10.05.1967
Stadium: Stadion AFAS, Alkmaar (17,023)
Trainer: Arnold Martijn Slot   17.09.1978
[05.12.2020]   Pascal Jansen   02.05.1973

Goalkeepers:	DOB	M	(s)	G
Marco Bizot	10.03.1991	33		
Hobie Verhulst	02.04.1993	1	(1)	
Defenders:	**DOB**	**M**	**(s)**	**G**
Jorn Berkhout	18.03.2002		(1)	
Juan Carlos Familia-Castillo	13.01.2000		(1)	
Pantelis Hatzidiakos (GRE)	18.01.1997	22	(1)	
Ramon Leeuwin (SUR)	01.09.1987	1	(6)	
Timo Letschert	25.05.1993	16	(4)	
Bruno Martins Indi	08.02.1992	27		1
Yukinari Sugawara (JPN)	28.06.2000	17	(8)	2
Jonas Svensson (NOR)	06.03.1993	17	(1)	
Owen Wijndal	28.11.1999	34		1
Midfielders:	**DOB**	**M**	**(s)**	**G**
Jordy Clasie	27.06.1991	4	(4)	1
Dani de Wit	28.01.1998	12	(8)	4
Kenzo Goudmijn	18.12.2001		(3)	
Teun Koopmeiners	28.02.1998	31		15
Fredrik Midtsjø (NOR)	11.08.1993	31		2
Tijjani Reijnders	29.07.1998	6	(16)	
Forwards:	**DOB**	**M**	**(s)**	**G**
Zakaria Aboukhlal (MAR)	18.02.2000	6	(18)	4
Myron Boadu	14.01.2001	28	(3)	15
Jelle Duin	27.01.1999		(4)	
Ferdy Druijf	12.02.1998		(9)	1
Håkon Evjen (NOR)	14.02.2000	2	(7)	1
Albert Guðmundsson (ISL)	15.06.1997	25	(1)	7
Jesper Karlsson (SWE)	25.07.1998	31	(1)	11
Calvin Stengs	18.12.1998	30		7

Football Club Emmen

Founded: 21.08.1925
Stadium: De Oude Meerdijk, Emmen (8,600)
Trainer: Dick Lukkien   28.03.1972

Goalkeepers:	DOB	M	(s)	G
Dennis Telgenkamp	09.05.1987	14		
Michael Verrips	03.12.1996	14		
Felix Wiedwald (GER)	15.03.1990	6		
Defenders:	**DOB**	**M**	**(s)**	**G**
Miguel Gianpierre Araujo Blanco (PER)	24.10.1994	33		4
Nick Bakker	21.07.1992	24	(4)	1
Glenn Bijl	13.07.1995	30		2
Caner Çavlan	05.02.1992	32		
Denis Granečný (CZE)	07.09.1998		(2)	
Desevio Payne (USA)	30.11.1995		(2)	
Jean-Pierre Rhyner Pebe (PER)	15.03.1996	1	(1)	
Ricardo van Rhijn	13.06.1991	14	(1)	
Keziah Veendorp	17.02.1997	14	(11)	
Midfielders:	**DOB**	**M**	**(s)**	**G**
Hilal Ben Moussa	22.05.1992	14	(9)	
Lucas Bernadou (FRA)	24.09.2000	14	(5)	1
Michael Steven Chacón Ibarguen	11.04.1994	8	(3)	
Robbert de Vos	26.05.1996	3	(10)	1
Sergio Peña (PER)	28.09.1995	32		6
Ben Scholte	10.08.2001		(1)	
Simon Tibbling (SWE)	07.09.1994	12	(3)	
Jari Vlak	15.08.1998	15	(2)	1
Forwards:	**DOB**	**M**	**(s)**	**G**
Luka Adžić (SRB)	17.09.1998	12		3
Donis Avdijaj (KVX)	25.08.1996	1	(7)	
Lentini Caciano (CUW)	15.08.2001	1	(3)	
Luciano Carty	02.10.2001		(2)	
Michael de Leeuw	07.10.1986	29		13
Kerim Frei (TUR)	19.11.1993	17		
Paul Gladon	18.03.1992	3	(10)	2
Anco Jansen	09.03.1989	8	(9)	1
Marko Kolar (CRO)	31.05.1995	9	(5)	1
Didier Jeanpier La Torre Arana (PER)	21.03.2002		(3)	
Nikolai Laursen (DEN)	19.02.1998	14	(15)	3
Sékou Sidibé (BEL)	05.05.2001		(3)	

Feyenoord Rotterdam

Founded: 19.07.1908
Stadium: Stadion Feijenoord, Rotterdam (51,177)
Trainer: Dirk Nicolaas Advocaat   27.09.1947

Goalkeepers:	DOB	M	(s)	G
Justin Bijlow	22.01.1998	14		
Nick Marsman	01.10.1990	20	(1)	
Defenders:	**DOB**	**M**	**(s)**	**G**
Eric Fernando Botteghin (BRA)	31.08.1987	18	(5)	1
Lutsharel Geertruida	18.07.2000	25	(5)	5
Ridgeciano Haps (SUR)	12.06.1993	13	(8)	3
George Johnston (SCO)	01.09.1998	1	(3)	
Tyrell Malacia	17.08.1999	24	(2)	
Bart Nieuwkoop	07.03.1996	12	(3)	
Marcos Nicolás Senesi Barón (ARG)	10.05.1997	32		3
Uroš Spajić (SRB)	13.02.1993	19		
Midfielders:	**DOB**	**M**	**(s)**	**G**
Wouter Burger	16.02.2001		(1)	
Mark Diemers	11.10.1993	23	(6)	3
Achraf el Bouchataoui	12.01.2000	1	(2)	
Leroy Fer	05.01.1990	22	(3)	
João Carlos Vilaça Teixeira (POR)	18.01.1993	8	(10)	
Orkun Kökçü (TUR)	29.12.2000	20	(2)	3
Jens Toornstra	04.04.1989	30	(1)	8
Jordy Wehrmann	25.03.1999	1	(6)	
Forwards:	**DOB**	**M**	**(s)**	**G**
Marouan Azarkan	08.12.2001		(1)	
Aliou Balde (SEN)	12.12.2002		(3)	
Naoufal Bannis	11.03.2002		(6)	1
Steven Berghuis	19.12.1991	30	(1)	18
Róbert Boženík (SVK)	18.11.1999	4	(11)	1
Christian Conteh (GER)	27.08.1999		(2)	
Nicolai Jørgensen (DEN)	15.01.1991	12	(11)	5
Bryan Linssen	08.10.1990	27	(2)	8
Luciano Narsingh	13.09.1990	3	(6)	1
Lucas David Pratto (ARG)	04.06.1988	2	(5)	
Luis Fernando Sinisterra Lucumí (COL)	17.06.1999	13	(7)	3
Dylan Vente	09.05.1999		(1)	

Fortuna Sittard

Founded: 01.07.1968
Stadium: Fortuna Sittard Stadion, Sittard (10,300)
Trainer: Kevin Hofland 07.06.1979
[11.11.2020] Sjors Ultee 23.05.1987

Goalkeepers:	DOB	M	(s)	G
Alexei Koşelev (MDA)	19.11.1993	6	(2)	
Yanick van Osch	24.03.1997	26		
Piet Velthuizen	03.11.1986	2		
Defenders:	**DOB**	**M**	**(s)**	**G**
Grégoire Amiot (FRA)	10.05.1995		(1)	
Martin Angha (SUI)	22.01.1994	31	(1)	
George Cox (ENG)	14.01.1998	32	(1)	5
Clint Essers	21.01.1997	1	(3)	
Jarosław Przemysław Jach (POL)	17.02.1994	2	(1)	
Roel Janssen	16.06.1990	30		
Branislav Niňaj (SVK)	17.05.1994	4	(4)	
Lazaros Rota (GRE)	23.08.1997	20	(4)	
Mike van Beijnen	07.03.1999		(4)	
Dario Van Den Buijs (BEL)	12.09.1995	1	(8)	
Midfielders:	**DOB**	**M**	**(s)**	**G**
Nassim el Ablak	07.01.2000		(3)	
Zian Flemming	01.08.1998	33		12
Samuel Moutoussamy (COD)	12.08.1996	1	(13)	
Ben Rienstra	05.06.1990	30		3
Mats Seuntjens	17.04.1992	28	(3)	6
Jorrit Smeets	25.03.1995	10	(5)	
Tesfaldet Tekie (SWE)	04.06.1997	31	(2)	1
Mickaël Tirpan (TUR)	23.10.1993	11	(1)	1
Forwards:	**DOB**	**M**	**(s)**	**G**
Djibril Dianessy (FRA)	29.03.1996		(5)	
Dimitrios Emmanouilidis (GRE)	24.10.2000		(6)	1
Leroy George	21.04.1987		(3)	
Emil Hansson (SWE)	15.06.1998	17	(15)	2
Arian Kastrati (KVX)	15.07.2001		(7)	
Lisandro Pedro Varela Semedo (CPV)	12.03.1996	26	(8)	9
Sebastian Polter (GER)	01.04.1991	31	(1)	9
Bassala Sambou (ENG)	15.10.1997		(3)	
Thibaud Verlinden (BEL)	09.07.1999	1	(4)	

Football Club Groningen

Founded: 16.06.1971
Stadium: Stadion Hitachi Capital Mobility, Groningen (22,550)
Trainer: Danny Buijs 21.06.1982

Goalkeepers:	DOB	M	(s)	G
Sergio Padt	06.06.1990	34		
Defenders:	**DOB**	**M**	**(s)**	**G**
Wessel Dammers	01.03.1995	16	(11)	1
Damil Dankerlui (SUR)	24.08.1996	21	(7)	
Gabriel Gudmundsson (SWE)	29.04.1999	20	(3)	
Ko Itakura (JPN)	27.01.1997	34		1
Bjorn Meijer	18.03.2003		(1)	
Leonel Miguel	24.03.2001	1		
Miguel Ángel Leal Díaz (ESP)	01.02.1997	3	(7)	
Thomas Poll	28.08.2001		(4)	
Mike te Wierik	08.06.1992	14	(1)	
Bart van Hintum	16.01.1987	29	(2)	2
Joël van Kaam	08.03.2002	3	(3)	
Midfielders:	**DOB**	**M**	**(s)**	**G**
Ahmed El Messaoudi (MAR)	03.08.1995	25	(3)	8
Ajdin Hrustić (AUS)	05.07.1996	1		
Ramon Pascal Lundqvist (SWE)	10.05.1997	15	(10)	2
Azor Matusiwa	28.04.1998	21	(1)	
Sam Schreck (GER)	29.01.1999	2	(11)	
Tomáš Suslov (SVK)	07.06.2002	17	(11)	2
Daniël van Kaam	23.06.2000	29	(3)	1
Forwards:	**DOB**	**M**	**(s)**	**G**
Paulos Abraham (SWE)	16.07.2002	2	(11)	2
Remco Balk	02.03.2001	3	(8)	1
Alessio Da Cruz	18.01.1997	18	(4)	4
Thijs Dallinga	03.08.2000		(6)	
Mohammed El Hankouri (MAR)	01.07.1997	22	(11)	3
Patrick Joosten	14.04.1996	14	(11)	3
Romano Postema	07.02.2002		(3)	
Arjen Robben	23.01.1984	2	(4)	
Kian Slor	23.03.2002		(5)	
Jørgen Strand Larsen (NOR)	06.02.2000	28	(2)	9

Sportclub Heerenveen

Founded: 20.07.1920
Stadium: Stadion "Abe Lenstra", Heerenveen (27,224)
Trainer: Johnny Jansen 02.03.1975

Goalkeepers:	DOB	M	(s)	G
Erwin Mulder	03.03.1989	34		
Defenders:	**DOB**	**M**	**(s)**	**G**
Hamdi Akujobi	20.01.2000	3	(3)	
Paweł Bochniewicz (POL)	30.01.1996	30	(1)	2
Ibrahim Drešević (KVX)	24.01.1997	20	(10)	
Sherel Floranus	23.08.1998	26	(3)	1
Rami Kaib (SWE)	08.05.1997	12	(3)	
Jan Paul van Hecke	08.06.2000	26	(2)	1
Sijb van Ottele	02.02.2002	2	(1)	
Lucas Woudenberg	25.04.1994	23	(6)	1
Midfielders:	**DOB**	**M**	**(s)**	**G**
Rami Al Hajj (SWE)	17.09.2001	2	(21)	
Siem de Jong	28.01.1989	17	(2)	4
Sieben Dewaele (BEL)	02.02.1999	2	(5)	
Tibor Halilović (CRO)	18.03.1995	19		2
Rodney Kongolo	09.01.1998	23	(8)	1
Lasse Schöne (DEN)	27.05.1986	12		1
Joey Veerman	19.11.1998	30	(1)	7
Forwards:	**DOB**	**M**	**(s)**	**G**
Oliver Batista-Meier (GER)	16.02.2001	10	(5)	1
Couhaib Driouech	17.04.2002	1	(4)	
Ulysses Llanez (USA)	02.04.2001		(5)	
Benjamin Nygren (SWE)	08.07.2001	15	(13)	4
Rein Smit	05.01.2001		(5)	
Mitchell van Bergen	27.08.1999	32		4
Arjen van der Heide	19.11.2001	6	(8)	
Henk Veerman	26.02.1991	29	(2)	14

Heracles Almelo

Founded: 1903
Stadium: Stadion Polman, Almelo (12,080)
Trainer: Frank Wormuth (GER) 13.09.1960

Goalkeepers:	DOB	M	(s)	G
Janis Blaswich (GER)	02.05.1991	26		
Michael Brouwer	21.01.1993	6	(1)	
Koen Bucker	18.06.1996	2		
Defenders:	**DOB**	**M**	**(s)**	**G**
Tim Breukers	04.11.1987	21	(5)	
Noah Fadiga (BEL)	03.12.1999	12	(3)	
Jeff Hardeveld	27.02.1995	10	(4)	
Mats Knoester	19.11.1998	22	(5)	2
Mateo Leš (CRO)	25.03.2000	1	(2)	
Robin Pröpper	23.09.1993	30		1
Giacomo Quagliata (ITA)	19.02.2000	24	(1)	
Marco Rente (GER)	25.02.1997	20	(5)	
Midfielders:	**DOB**	**M**	**(s)**	**G**
Rohat Ağca	03.09.2001		(4)	
Teun Bijleveld	27.05.1998	11	(9)	
Luca de la Torre (USA)	23.05.1998	26	(6)	1
Melih İbrahimoğlu (TUR)	17.07.2000		(2)	
Orestis Kiomourtzoglou (GER)	07.05.1998	17	(10)	
Lucas Schoofs (BEL)	03.01.1997	27	(3)	2
Elias Sierra (BEL)	25.08.2001	1	(4)	
Rai Vloet	08.05.1995	33		16
Forwards:	**DOB**	**M**	**(s)**	**G**
Mohamed Amissi (BDI)	03.08.2000		(2)	
Ismail Azzaoui (BEL)	06.01.1998	11	(7)	1
Sinan Bakış (TUR)	22.04.1994	20	(7)	10
Delano Burgzorg	07.11.1998	24	(8)	5
Jeremy Cijntje (CUW)	08.01.1998		(7)	
Ahmed Kutucu (TUR)	01.03.2000	3	(12)	
Kasper Lunding (DEN)	17.07.1999	6	(13)	
Adrian Szőke (HUN)	01.07.1998	7	(12)	1
Silvester van der Water	30.09.1995	14	(4)	3

Prins Hendrik Ende Desespereert Nimmer Combinatie Zwolle

Founded: 12.06.1910
Stadium: Stadion MAC³PARK, Zwolle (14,000)
Trainer: John Stegeman — 27.08.1976
[20.02.2021] Lee-Roy Echteld — 30.06.1968
[01.03.2021] Bert Konterman — 14.01.1971

Goalkeepers:	DOB	M	(s)	G
Xavier Mous	04.08.1995	15		
Michael Zetterer (GER)	12.07.1995	19		
Defenders:	**DOB**	**M**	**(s)**	**G**
Destan Bajselmani (KVX)	13.05.1999	4	(2)	
Marc-Olivier Doué (FRA)	11.10.2000	1	(5)	
Sam Kersten	30.01.1998	28		
Thomas Lam (FIN)	18.12.1993	23	(3)	3
Yuta Nakayama (JPN)	16.02.1997	25	(7)	2
Kenneth Paal	24.06.1997	25	(2)	
Rav van den Berg	07.07.2004	1		
Bram van Polen	11.10.1985	22	(3)	4
Sai van Wermeskerken (JPN)	28.06.1994	22		
Midfielders:	**DOB**	**M**	**(s)**	**G**
Pelle Clement	19.05.1996	13	(10)	2
Jesper Drost	11.01.1993	13	(11)	2
Dean Huiberts	16.05.2000	25	(4)	
Samir Lagsir	20.05.2003		(4)	1
Clint Leemans	15.09.1995	7	(9)	3
Immanuël Pherai	25.04.2001	15	(12)	2
Mustafa Saymak	11.02.1993	18	(6)	2
Rico Strieder (GER)	06.07.1992	17	(7)	
Thomas van den Belt	18.06.2001	4	(5)	
Forwards:	**DOB**	**M**	**(s)**	**G**
Thomas Buitink	14.01.2000	9		2
Reza Ghoochannejhad (IRN)	20.09.1987	7	(14)	6
Benson Manuel (BEL)	28.03.1997	9	(4)	
Virgil Misidjan	24.07.1993	13	(2)	4
Eliano Reijnders	23.10.2000	17	(12)	3
Slobodan Tedić (SRB)	13.04.2000	10	(5)	2
Mike van Duinen	06.11.1991	12	(11)	3

Philips Sport Vereniging Eindhoven

Founded: 31.08.1913
Stadium: Stadion Philips, Eindhoven (36,500)
Trainer: Roger Schmidt (GER) — 13.03.1967

Goalkeepers:	DOB	M	(s)	G
Yvon Mvogo (SUI)	06.06.1994	33		
Lars Unnerstall (GER)	20.07.1990	1		
Defenders:	**DOB**	**M**	**(s)**	**G**
Timo Baumgartl (GER)	04.03.1996	6	(2)	
Olivier Boscagli (FRA)	18.11.1997	29	(1)	2
Luis Felipe Hungria Martins (BRA)	17.05.2001		(1)	
Philipp Max (GER)	30.09.1993	29	(2)	5
Armando Obispo	05.03.1999	1	(4)	
Fredrik Oppegård (NOR)	07.08.2002		(1)	
Shurandy Sambo	19.08.2001		(1)	
Jordan Teze	30.09.1999	31	(2)	
Nick Viergever	03.08.1989	13	(4)	
Midfielders:	**DOB**	**M**	**(s)**	**G**
Denzel Justus Morris Dumfries	18.04.1996	27	(3)	2
Adrian Fein (GER)	18.03.1999	4	(9)	1
Mario Götze (GER)	03.06.1992	17	(1)	5
Érick Gabriel Gutiérrez Galaviz (MEX)	15.06.1995	1	(7)	
Jorrit Hendrix	06.02.1995	3	(6)	
Mohamed Ihattaren	12.02.2002	13	(9)	3
Ismael Saibari (MAR)	28.01.2001		(1)	
Mathias Kjølø (NOR)	27.06.2001		(1)	
Richard Ledezma (USA)	06.09.2000	1	(2)	
Mauro Jaqueson Júnior Ferreira Dos Santos (BRA)	06.05.1999	12	(7)	2
Pablo Rosario	07.01.1997	26	(3)	1
Michal Sadílek (CZE)	31.05.1999	1	(1)	
Ibrahim Sangaré (CIV)	02.12.1997	25	(4)	1
Ryan Thomas (NZL)	20.12.1994	11	(5)	1
Marco van Ginkel	01.12.1992	3	(8)	1
Forwards:	**DOB**	**M**	**(s)**	**G**
Jeremy Antonisse (CUW)	29.03.2002		(1)	
Armindo Tué Na Bangna „Bruma" (POR)	24.10.1994	1	(2)	
Cody Mathès Gakpo	07.05.1999	22	(1)	7
Sam Lammers	30.04.1997	1		
Noni Madueke (ENG)	10.03.2002	7	(17)	7
Donyell Malen	19.01.1999	26	(6)	19
Joël Piroe	02.08.1999		(11)	1
Maximiliano Samuel Romero (ARG)	09.01.1999		(1)	1
Yorbe Vertessen (BEL)	08.01.2001	6	(9)	2
Eran Zahavi (ISR)	25.07.1987	24	(1)	11

Rooms Katholieke Combinatie Waalwijk

Founded: 26.08.1940
Stadium: Mandemakers Stadion, Waalwijk (7,500)
Trainer: Johann Georg Friedrich "Fred" Grim — 17.08.1965

Goalkeepers:	DOB	M	(s)	G
Kostas Lamprou (GRE)	18.09.1991	34		
Defenders:	**DOB**	**M**	**(s)**	**G**
Shawn Adewoye (BEL)	29.06.2000	1	(2)	
Saïd Bakari (COM)	22.09.1994	29	(1)	1
Juriën Gaari (CUW)	23.12.1993	5	(4)	
Thierry Lutonda (BEL)	27.10.2000	5	(16)	
Melle Meulensteen	04.07.1999	33		
Lars Nieuwpoort	29.10.1994	2	(1)	
Paul Quasten	13.03.1985	20	(2)	
Ahmed Touba (ALG)	13.03.1998	32		3
Luuk Wouters	08.06.1999	9	(2)	
Midfielders:	**DOB**	**M**	**(s)**	**G**
Vurnon Anita (CUW)	04.04.1989	29		
Sebbe Augustijns (BEL)	03.09.1999		(8)	
Ayman Azhil (GER)	10.04.2001	8	(14)	
Hans Mulder	27.04.1987		(12)	
Nicolás Olsak (ISR)	25.11.1991	6	(2)	
Thijs Oosting	02.05.2000	15	(2)	4
Anas Tahiri (BEL)	15.05.1995	33		1
Richard van der Venne	16.05.1992	25	(4)	4
Forwards:	**DOB**	**M**	**(s)**	**G**
Vitalie Damaşcan (MDA)	24.01.1999	5	(14)	2
Lennerd Daneels (BEL)	10.04.1998	20	(13)	2
James Efmorfidis (GRE)	18.01.1996	5	(2)	
Morad El Haddouti	09.05.1998		(6)	
Ola John	19.05.1992	16	(7)	2
David Min	23.06.1999		(5)	1
Cyril Ngonge (BEL)	26.05.2000	15	(5)	5
Sylla Sow	08.08.1996	11	(17)	3
Finn Stokkers	18.04.1996	16	(14)	5

Sparta Rotterdam

	Founded:	01.04.1888
Stadium:	Stadion Sparta, Rotterdam (11,000)
Trainer:	Hendrikus "Henk" Fraser	07.07.1966

Goalkeepers:	DOB	M	(s)	G
Maduka Okoye (NGA)	28.08.1999	28		
Benjamin van Leer	09.04.1992	6		
Defenders:	**DOB**	**M**	**(s)**	**G**
Dirk Abels	13.06.1997	28	(3)	1
Tom Beugelsdijk	07.08.1990	22	(7)	2
Jeffry Fortes (CPV)	22.03.1989	9	(9)	
Michaël Heylen (BEL)	03.01.1994	26	(2)	
Aaron Meijers	28.10.1987	12	(12)	
Michael „Mica" Gonçalves Pinto (POR)	04.06.1993	23	(2)	1
Jeremy van Mullem	18.03.1999		(1)	
Bart Vriends	09.05.1991	23		
Midfielders:	**DOB**	**M**	**(s)**	**G**
Adil Auassar	06.10.1986	29	(1)	
Wouter Burger	16.02.2001	9	(9)	2
Deroy Duarte	04.07.1999	19	(10)	4
Laros Duarte	28.02.1997	10	(7)	2
Abdou Harroui	13.01.1998	32		6
Sven Mijnans	09.03.2000	20	(11)	2
Mohamed Rayhi	01.07.1994	3		
Bryan Smeets	22.11.1992	21	(5)	4
Forwards:	**DOB**	**M**	**(s)**	**G**
Emanuel Emegha	03.02.2003	1	(15)	1
Mario Engels (GER)	22.10.1993	16	(11)	3
Danzell Gravenberch	13.02.1994	3	(17)	4
Reda Kharchouch	27.08.1995		(19)	2
Lennart Thy (GER)	25.02.1992	34		14

Football Club Twente Enschede

	Founded:	01.07.1965
Stadium:	Stadion De Groisch Veste, Enschede (30,205)
Trainer:	Ron Jans	29.09.1958

Goalkeepers:	DOB	M	(s)	G
Joël Drommel	16.11.1996	34		
Defenders:	**DOB**	**M**	**(s)**	**G**
Dario Dumić (BIH)	30.01.1992	17	(7)	2
Tyronne Ebuehi (NGA)	16.12.1995	33		1
Mees Hilgers	13.05.2001		(3)	
Julio José Pleguezuelo Selva (ESP)	26.01.1997	18	(1)	1
Nathan Markelo	07.01.1999	3	(10)	
Jayden Oosterwolde	26.04.2001	24	(2)	1
Kik Pierie	20.07.2000	24		
Xandro Schenk	28.04.1993	3		
Gijs Smal	31.08.1997	13	(9)	
Midfielders:	**DOB**	**M**	**(s)**	**G**
Jesse Bosch	01.02.2000	26	(6)	2
Wout Brama	21.08.1986	17	(3)	1
Max Bruns	06.11.2002		(1)	
Luka Ilić (SRB)	02.07.1999	14	(10)	2
Godfried Roemeratoe	19.08.1999	25	(5)	
Lindon Selahi (ALB)	26.02.1999		(5)	
Casper Staring	01.02.2001	1	(5)	
Ramiz Zerrouki (ALG)	26.05.1998	23	(8)	
Forwards:	**DOB**	**M**	**(s)**	**G**
Issah Abass (GHA)	26.09.1998		(8)	
Vaclav Černý (CZE)	17.10.1997	16		6
Danilo Pereira Da Silva (BRA)	07.04.1999	31	(2)	17
İbrahim Halil Dervişoğlu (TUR)	08.12.1999	2	(7)	
Alexander Thomas Jeremejeff (SWE)	12.10.1993		(9)	1
Lazaros Lamprou (GRE)	19.12.1997		(7)	
Queensy Menig	19.08.1995	31	(1)	8
Luciano Narsingh	13.09.1990	13	(4)	1
Daan Rots	25.07.2001	1	(10)	1
Thijs van Leeuwen	15.07.2001	5	(16)	3

Football Club Utrecht

	Founded:	01.07.1970
Stadium:	Stadion Galgenwaard, Utrecht (23,750)
Trainer:	John van den Brom	04.10.1966
[07.11.2020]	René Hake	18.12.1971

Goalkeepers:	DOB	M	(s)	G
Thijmen Nijhuis	25.07.1998	3		
Eric Oelschlägel (GER)	20.09.1995	23		
Maarten Paes	14.05.1998	8		
Defenders:	**DOB**	**M**	**(s)**	**G**
Benaissa Benamar (MAR)	08.04.1997	2	(1)	
Emil Bergström (SWE)	19.05.1993	4	(5)	
Leon Guwara (GER)	28.06.1996		(1)	
Justin Hoogma	11.06.1998	14	(5)	1
Willem Janssen	04.07.1986	20	(2)	
Sean Klaiber	13.07.1994	2		1
Sylian Mokono	22.03.1999		(2)	
Tommy St. Jago	03.01.2000	23	(1)	
Hidde ter Avest	20.05.1997	18		2
Giovanni Troupée	20.03.1998	1	(5)	
Mark van der Maarel	12.08.1989	19	(6)	2
Django Warmerdam	02.09.1995	33		
Midfielders:	**DOB**	**M**	**(s)**	**G**
Othmane Boussaid (BEL)	07.03.2000	16	(10)	2
Urby Emanuelson	16.06.1986	1	(12)	
Simon Gustafson (SWE)	11.01.1995	17	(3)	2
Adam Maher	20.07.1993	25		2
Bart Ramselaar	29.06.1996	23	(4)	4
Sander van de Streek	24.03.1993	27	(5)	11
Joris van Overeem	01.06.1994	29	(1)	2
Odysseus Velanas	05.06.1998		(1)	
Forwards:	**DOB**	**M**	**(s)**	**G**
Daniel Arzani (AUS)	04.01.1999		(4)	
Remco Balk	02.03.2001		(2)	
Adrián Dalmau Vaquer (ESP)	27.03.1994	5	(14)	4
Eljero George Rinaldo Elia	13.02.1987	10	(10)	2
Jeredy Hilterman	20.06.1998		(3)	
Gyrano Kerk	02.12.1995	33	(1)	8
Mimoun Mahi (MAR)	13.03.1994	14	(8)	7
Moussa Sylla (FRA)	25.11.1999	4	(17)	

Stichting Betaald Voetbal Vitesse Arnhem

	Founded:	14.05.1892
Stadium:	GelreDome, Arnhem (21,248)
Trainer:	Thomas Letsch (GER)	26.08.1968

Goalkeepers:	DOB	M	(s)	G
Jeroen Houwen	18.02.1996	1		
Remko Pasveer	08.11.1983	33		
Defenders:	**DOB**	**M**	**(s)**	**G**
Riechedly Bazoer	12.10.1996	29		5
Enzo Cornelisse	01.01.2003	4	(2)	
Eli Dasa (ISR)	03.12.1992	30		
Danilho Doekhi	30.06.1998	32		1
Tomáš Hajek (CZE)	01.12.1991	8	(6)	
Million Manhoef	03.01.2002	3	(8)	
Alois Dominik Oroz (CRO)	29.10.2000	3	(4)	
Jacob Rasmussen (DEN)	28.05.1997	28		2
Maximilian Wittek (GER)	21.08.1995	32		1
Midfielders:	**DOB**	**M**	**(s)**	**G**
Matúš Bero (SVK)	06.09.1995	26	(1)	2
Thomas Bruns	07.01.1992	14	(7)	
Daan Huisman	26.07.2002	4	(16)	
Oussama Tannane (MAR)	23.03.1994	29		7
Idrissa Touré (GER)	29.04.1998	4	(16)	1
Sondre Tronstad (NOR)	26.08.1995	22	(1)	2
Patrick Vroegh	29.11.1999	3	(13)	2
Forwards:	**DOB**	**M**	**(s)**	**G**
Armando Broja (ALB)	10.09.2001	21	(9)	10
Thomas Buitink	14.01.2000	1	(13)	1
Oussama Darfalou (ALG)	29.09.1993	15	(17)	8
Filip Møller Delaveris (NOR)	10.12.2000		(1)	
Hilary Chukwah Gong (NGA)	10.10.1998	1	(6)	
Enrico Erick Dueñas Hernández (SLV)	23.02.2001	1	(1)	
Noah Chidiebere Junior Anyanwu Ohio	16.01.2003		(4)	
Loïs Openda (BEL)	16.02.2000	30	(3)	10

Venlose Voetbal Vereniging Venlo

Founded: 07.02.1903
Stadium: Stadion Covebo – De Koel, Venlo (8,000)
Trainer: Hans de Koning   05.04.1960
[17.03.2021]   Jos Luhukay   13.06.1963

Goalkeepers:	DOB	M	(s)	G
Thorsten Kirschbaum (GER)	20.04.1987	29		
Delano van Crooij	05.06.1991	5	(1)	
Defenders:	**DOB**	**M**	**(s)**	**G**
Kristopher Da Graca (SWE)	16.01.1998	19	(1)	
Tristan Dekker	27.03.1998	13	(2)	
Roy Gelmi (SUI)	01.03.1995	21	(3)	1
Leon Guwara (GER)	28.06.1996	16		
Christian Kum	13.09.1985	15	(9)	
Tobias Pachonik (GER)	04.01.1995	28	(1)	
Steffen Schäfer (GER)	01.05.1994	11	(2)	
Lukas Schmitz (GER)	13.10.1988	9	(3)	
Arjan Swinkels	15.10.1984	12	(8)	
Stan van Dijck	07.10.2000		(7)	
Midfielders:	**DOB**	**M**	**(s)**	**G**
Ante Ćorić (CRO)	14.04.1997		(1)	
Christos Donis (GRE)	09.10.1994	8	(1)	1
Wassim Essanoussi	28.10.2003	1	(4)	
Simon Janssen	25.09.2000	10	(9)	
Evert Linthorst	03.03.2000	15	(1)	2
Zinédine Machach (MAR)	05.01.1996	18	(6)	
Danny Post	07.04.1989	30		
Meritan Shabani (GER)	15.03.1999	4	(1)	
Forwards:	**DOB**	**M**	**(s)**	**G**
Jafar Arias (CUW)	16.06.1995	11	(18)	4
Aaron Bastiaans	04.04.2002		(1)	
Anastasios Donis (GRE)	29.08.1996	1	(4)	
Georgios Giakoumakis (GRE)	09.12.1994	30		26
Torino Hunte	14.12.1990	12	(9)	2
Guus Hupperts	25.04.1992	5	(6)	1
Joshua John (ARU)	01.10.1988	15	(10)	2
Yahcuroo Roemer	22.07.2001	6	(9)	
Vito van Crooij	29.01.1996	30	(1)	3

Willem II Tilburg

Founded: 12.08.1896
Stadium: Stadion „Koning Willem II", Tilburg (14,500)
Trainer: Adrianus Cornelis Koster   18.11.1954
[29.01.2021]   Željko Petrović (MNE)   13.11.1965

Goalkeepers:	DOB	M	(s)	G
Jorn Brondeel (BEL)	07.09.1993	10	(1)	
Aro Murić (KVX)	07.11.1998	14		
Robbin Ruiter	25.03.1987	10		
Defenders:	**DOB**	**M**	**(s)**	**G**
Freek Heerkens	13.09.1989	11	(3)	
Sebastian Holmén (SWE)	29.04.1992	29	(1)	3
Derrick Köhn (GER)	04.02.1999	30	(1)	
Paddy Miquel Nelom (SUR)	22.09.1990	5	(2)	
Leeroy Owusu	13.08.1996	29		
Jordens Peters	03.05.1987	13	(5)	
Vincent Schippers	04.03.2001	1	(3)	
Ian Smeulers	12.01.2000		(3)	
Sven van Beek	28.07.1994	13	(1)	
Victor van den Bogert	12.08.1999	1	(4)	
Jop van der Avert	11.05.2000	1	(2)	
Jan-Arie van der Heijden	03.03.1988	11	(3)	2
Midfielders:	**DOB**	**M**	**(s)**	**G**
Pol Llonch Puyaltó (ESP)	07.10.1992	26	(1)	
Driess Saddiki (MAR)	09.08.1996	12	(2)	
Görkem Sağlam (GER)	11.04.1998	14	(7)	2
Lindon Selahi (ALB)	26.02.1999	3	(13)	
Wesley Spieringhs	16.01.2002	13	(8)	
Mike Trésor (BEL)	28.05.1999	28	(6)	4
Rick Zuijderwijk	13.04.2001		(2)	
Forwards:	**DOB**	**M**	**(s)**	**G**
Jasper Dahlhaus	27.11.2001		(2)	
Paul Gladon	18.03.1992	1	(3)	
Mats Köhlert (GER)	02.05.1998	15	(17)	
Ché Nunnely	04.02.1999	28	(4)	7
Vangelis Pavlidis (GRE)	21.11.1998	33	(1)	12
Ole Romeny	20.06.2000	2	(9)	
Kwasi Wriedt (GHA)	10.07.1994	20	(4)	8
John Yeboah Zamora (GER)	23.06.2000	1	(8)	1

SECOND LEVEL
Eerste Divisie 2020/2021

1.	SC Cambuur Leeuwarden (*Promoted*)	38	29	5	4	109 - 36	92
2.	Go Ahead Eagles Deventer (*Promoted*)	38	23	8	7	62 - 25	77
3.	VBV De Graafschap Doetinchem	38	23	8	7	67 - 47	77
4.	Almere City FC	38	22	9	7	75 - 48	75
5.	NAC Breda	38	22	7	9	75 - 41	73
6.	FC Volendam	38	19	9	10	79 - 52	66
7.	NEC Nijmegen	38	20	6	12	68 - 45	66
8.	SV Roda JC Kerkrade	38	15	12	11	67 - 61	57
9.	SBV Excelsior Rotterdam	38	14	6	18	65 - 66	48
10.	Tot Ons Plezier Oss	38	13	8	17	40 - 57	47
11.	MVV Maastricht	38	13	7	18	50 - 72	46
12.	Helmond Sport	38	11	12	15	51 - 68	45
13.	SC Telstar Velsen	38	10	11	17	57 - 61	41
14.	Jong PSV Eindhoven*	38	10	10	18	54 - 65	40
15.	FC Eindhoven	38	10	10	18	50 - 62	40
16.	Jong Ajax Amsterdam*	38	10	10	18	55 - 71	40
17.	Jong AZ Alkmaar*	38	11	5	22	56 - 92	38
18.	Jong FC Utrecht*	38	11	2	25	53 - 77	35
19.	FC Den Bosch	38	8	8	22	59 - 85	32
20.	FC Dordrecht	38	8	3	27	36 - 97	27

Teams ranked 3-8 were qualified for the Promotion Play-offs.
*Reserve teams are not eligible to be promoted.

INTERNATIONAL MATCHES
(16.07.2020 – 15.07.2021)

04.09.2020	Amsterdam	Netherlands - Poland	1-0(0-0)	(UNL)
07.09.2020	Amsterdam	Netherlands - Italy	0-1(0-1)	(UNL)
07.10.2020	Amsterdam	Netherlands - Mexico	0-1(0-0)	(F)
11.10.2020	Zenica	Bosnia and Herzegovina - Netherlands	0-0	(UNL)
14.10.2020	Bergamo	Italy - Netherlands	1-1(1-1)	(UNL)
11.11.2020	Amsterdam	Netherlands - Spain	1-1(0-1)	(F)
15.11.2020	Amsterdam	Netherlands - Bosnia and Herzegovina	3-1(2-0)	(UNL)
18.11.2020	Chorzów	Poland - Netherlands	1-2(1-0)	(UNL)
24.03.2021	İstanbul	Turkey - Netherlands	4-2(2-0)	(WCQ)
27.03.2021	Amsterdam	Netherlands - Latvia	2-0(1-0)	(WCQ)
30.03.2021	Gibraltar	Gibraltar - Netherlands	0-7(0-1)	(WCQ)
02.06.2021	Faro/Loulé	Netherlands - Scotland	2-2(1-1)	(F)
06.06.2021	Enschede	Netherlands - Georgia	3-0(1-0)	(F)
13.06.2021	Amsterdam	Netherlands - Ukraine	3-2(0-0)	(EC)
17.06.2021	Amsterdam	Netherlands - Austria	2-0(1-0)	(EC)
21.06.2021	Amsterdam	North Macedonia - Netherlands	0-3(0-1)	(EC)
27.06.2021	Budapest	Netherlands - Czech Republic	0-2(0-0)	(EC)

04.09.2020   **NETHERLANDS - POLAND**   **1-0(0-0)**   2nd UEFA Nations League A, Group 1
"Johan Cruyff" Arena, Amsterdam; Referee: Georgi Kabakov (Bulgaria); Attendance: 0
NED: Jacobus Antonius Peter Cillessen, Joël Ivo Veltman, Nathan Benjamin Aké, Virgil van Dijk (Cap), Hans Hateboer, Georginio Gregion Emile Wijnaldum, Marten Elco de Roon, Frenkie de Jong, Memphis Depay, Quincy Anton Promes (90+2.Luuk de Jong), Steven Charles Bergwijn (74.Donny van de Beek). Trainer: Dwight Bernard Lodeweges.
Goal: Steven Charles Bergwijn (61).

07.09.2020   **NETHERLANDS - ITALY**   **0-1(0-1)**   2nd UEFA Nations League A, Group 1
"Johan Cruyff" Arena, Amsterdam; Referee: Dr. Felix Brych (Germany); Attendance: 0
NED: Jacobus Antonius Peter Cillessen, Joël Ivo Veltman, Nathan Benjamin Aké (81.Luuk de Jong), Virgil van Dijk (Cap), Hans Hateboer (70.Denzel Justus Morris Dumfries), Georginio Gregion Emile Wijnaldum, Marten Elco de Roon, Donny van de Beek (57.Steven Charles Bergwijn), Frenkie de Jong, Memphis Depay, Quincy Anton Promes. Trainer: Dwight Bernard Lodeweges.

07.10.2020   **NETHERLANDS - MEXICO**   **0-1(0-0)**   Friendly International
"Johan Cruyff" Arena, Amsterdam; Referee: Srđan Jovanović (Serbia); Attendance: 0
NED: Timothy Michael Krul, Stefan de Vrij (46.Joël Ivo Veltman), Virgil van Dijk (Cap) (46.Nathan Benjamin Aké), Hans Hateboer, Owen Wijndal (84.Quincy Anton Promes), Teun Koopmeiners, Georginio Gregion Emile Wijnaldum (63.Marten Elco de Roon), Donny van de Beek, Ryan Miguel Guno Babel (63.Luuk de Jong), Steven Berghuis (63.Calvin Stengs), Memphis Depay. Trainer: Franciscus de Boer.

11.10.2020   **BOSNIA AND HERZEGOVINA - NETHERLANDS**   **0-0**   2nd UEFA Nations League A, Group 1
Stadion Bilino Polje, Zenica; Referee: István Kovács (Romania); Attendance: 1,600
NED: Jacobus Antonius Peter Cillessen, Daley Blind (86.Nathan Benjamin Aké), Stefan de Vrij, Virgil van Dijk (Cap), Denzel Justus Morris Dumfries (70.Hans Hateboer), Georginio Gregion Emile Wijnaldum, Marten Elco de Roon, Frenkie de Jong, Luuk de Jong, Quincy Anton Promes (86.Ryan Miguel Guno Babel), Donyell Malen (69.Steven Berghuis). Trainer: Franciscus de Boer.

14.10.2020   **ITALY - NETHERLANDS**   **1-1(1-1)**   2nd UEFA Nations League A, Group 1
Stadio Atleti Azzurri d'Italia, Bergamo; Referee: Anthony Taylor (England); Attendance: 623
NED: Jacobus Antonius Peter Cillessen, Stefan de Vrij, Nathan Benjamin Aké, Virgil van Dijk (Cap), Daley Blind (77.Joël Ivo Veltman), Hans Hateboer, Georginio Gregion Emile Wijnaldum, Donny van de Beek, Frenkie de Jong, Luuk de Jong, Memphis Depay (90+2.Ryan Miguel Guno Babel). Trainer: Franciscus de Boer.
Goal: Donny van de Beek (25).

11.11.2020   **NETHERLANDS - SPAIN**   **1-1(0-1)**   Friendly International
"Johan Cruyff" Arena, Amsterdam, City; Referee: Davide Massa (Italy); Attendance: 0
NED: Marco Bizot, Joël Ivo Veltman, Hans Hateboer (46.Denzel Justus Morris Dumfries), Nathan Benjamin Aké (6.Daley Blind), Owen Wijndal, Georginio Gregion Emile Wijnaldum (Cap) (46.Davy Klaassen), Donny van de Beek, Frenkie de Jong (46.Stefan de Vrij), Memphis Depay (79.Ryan Miguel Guno Babel), Steven Berghuis (46.Calvin Stengs), Luuk de Jong. Trainer: Franciscus de Boer.
Goal: Donny van de Beek (47).

15.11.2020   **NETHERLANDS - BOSNIA AND HERZEGOVINA**   **3-1(2-0)**   2nd UEFA Nations League A, Group 1
"Johan Cruyff" Arena, Amsterdam; Referee: François Letexier (France); Attendance: 0
NED: Timothy Michael Krul, Denzel Justus Morris Dumfries (64.Hans Hateboer), Stefan de Vrij, Owen Wijndal (79.Patrick John Miguel van Aanholt), Daley Blind, Georginio Gregion Emile Wijnaldum (Cap) (64.Donny van de Beek), Davy Klaassen, Frenkie de Jong, Memphis Depay (78.Quincy Anton Promes), Luuk de Jong, Steven Berghuis (89.Calvin Stengs). Trainer: Franciscus de Boer.
Goals: Georginio Gregion Emile Wijnaldum (6, 14), Memphis Depay (55).

18.11.2020   **POLAND - NETHERLANDS**   **1-2(1-0)**   2nd UEFA Nations League A, Group 1
Stadion Śląski, Chorzów; Referee: Orel Grinfeld (Israel); Attendance: 0
NED: Timothy Michael Krul, Patrick John Miguel van Aanholt (70.Owen Wijndal), Stefan de Vrij, Hans Hateboer (57.Denzel Justus Morris Dumfries), Daley Blind (84.Luuk de Jong), Georginio Gregion Emile Wijnaldum (Cap), Davy Klaassen (70.Donny van de Beek), Frenkie de Jong, Memphis Depay, Donyell Malen, Calvin Stengs (70.Steven Berghuis). Trainer: Franciscus de Boer.
Goals: Memphis Depay (77 penalty), Georginio Gregion Emile Wijnaldum (84).

24.03.2021   **TURKEY - NETHERLANDS**   **4-2(2-0)**   22nd FIFA WC. Qualifiers
Atatürk Olimpiyat Stadı, İstanbul; Referee: Michael Oliver (England); Attendance: 0
NED: Timothy Michael Krul, Kenny Joelle Tete (69.Denzel Justus Morris Dumfries), Matthijs de Ligt, Owen Wijndal (82.Patrick John Miguel van Aanholt), Daley Blind (82.Ryan Jiro Gravenberch), Georginio Gregion Emile Wijnaldum (Cap), Marten Elco de Roon (62.Luuk de Jong), Frenkie de Jong, Memphis Depay, Donyell Malen (69.Davy Klaassen), Steven Berghuis. Trainer: Franciscus de Boer.
Goals: Davy Klaassen (75), Luuk de Jong (77).

27.03.2021   **NETHERLANDS - LATVIA**   **2-0(1-0)**   22nd FIFA WC. Qualifiers
"Johan Cruyff" Arena, Amsterdam; Referee: Stéphanie Frappart (France); Attendance: 5,000
NED: Timothy Michael Krul, Denzel Justus Morris Dumfries, Matthijs de Ligt, Owen Wijndal, Daley Blind, Georginio Gregion Emile Wijnaldum (Cap) (79.Donny van de Beek), Davy Klaassen (79.Ryan Jiro Gravenberch), Frenkie de Jong, Memphis Depay (90.Steven Charles Bergwijn), Luuk de Jong (79.Ryan Miguel Guno Babel), Steven Berghuis (84.Calvin Stengs). Trainer: Franciscus de Boer.
Goals: Steven Berghuis (32), Luuk de Jong (69).

30.03.2021   **GIBRALTAR - NETHERLANDS**   **0-7(0-1)**   22nd FIFA WC. Qualifiers
Victoria Stadium, Gibraltar; Referee: João Pedro da Silva Pinheiro (Portugal); Attendance: 335
NED: Timothy Michael Krul, Daley Blind (54.Donyell Malen), Denzel Justus Morris Dumfries (46.Ryan Jiro Gravenberch), Matthijs de Ligt, Owen Wijndal, Georginio Gregion Emile Wijnaldum (Cap), Davy Klaassen (77.Donny van de Beek), Frenkie de Jong, Memphis Depay, Luuk de Jong (81.Ryan Miguel Guno Babel), Steven Berghuis (81.Calvin Stengs). Trainer: Franciscus de Boer.
Goals: Steven Berghuis (42), Luuk de Jong (55), Memphis Depay (61), Georginio Gregion Emile Wijnaldum (62), Donyell Malen (64), Donny van de Beek (85), Memphis Depay (88).

02.06.2021   **NETHERLANDS - SCOTLAND**   **2-2(1-1)**   Friendly International
Estádio Algarve, Faro/Loulé (Portugal); Referee: Vítor Jorge Fernandes Ferreira (Portugal); Attendance: 0
NED: Timothy Michael Krul, Denzel Justus Morris Dumfries, Stefan de Vrij (85.Luuk de Jong), Matthijs de Ligt, Jurriën David Norman Timber (69.Steven Berghuis), Owen Wijndal (69.Patrick John Miguel van Aanholt), Georginio Gregion Emile Wijnaldum (Cap) (31.Ryan Jiro Gravenberch), Marten Elco de Roon, Frenkie de Jong (31.Davy Klaassen), Memphis Depay, Wout Weghorst (69.Quincy Anton Promes). Trainer: Franciscus de Boer.
Goals: Memphis Depay (17, 89).

06.06.2021   **NETHERLANDS - GEORGIA**   **3-0(1-0)**   Friendly International
De Grolsch Veste, Enschede; Referee: Erik Lambrechts (Belgium); Attendance: 7,600
NED: Maarten Stekelenburg, Denzel Justus Morris Dumfries, Stefan de Vrij, Owen Wijndal (73.Patrick John Miguel van Aanholt), Daley Blind (46.Nathan Benjamin Aké), Jurriën David Norman Timber (77.Steven Berghuis), Georginio Gregion Emile Wijnaldum (Cap) (66.Davy Klaassen), Marten Elco de Roon, Frenkie de Jong (66.Ryan Jiro Gravenberch), Memphis Depay, Wout Weghorst (66.Donyell Malen). Trainer: Franciscus de Boer.
Goals: Memphis Depay (10 penalty), Wout Weghorst (55), Ryan Jiro Gravenberch (76).

13.06.2021   **NETHERLANDS - UKRAINE**   **3-2(0-0)**   16th EC. Group Stage.
"Johan Cruyff" Arena, Amsterdam; Referee: Dr. Felix Brych (Germany); Attendance: 15,837
NED: Maarten Stekelenburg, Denzel Justus Morris Dumfries, Patrick John Miguel van Aanholt (64.Owen Wijndal), Stefan de Vrij, Daley Blind (64.Nathan Benjamin Aké), Jurriën David Norman Timber (88.Joël Ivo Veltman), Georginio Gregion Emile Wijnaldum (Cap), Marten Elco de Roon, Frenkie de Jong, Memphis Depay (90+1.Donyell Malen), Wout Weghorst (88.Luuk de Jong). Trainer: Franciscus de Boer.
Goals: Georginio Gregion Emile Wijnaldum (52), Wout Weghorst (58), Denzel Justus Morris Dumfries (85).

17.06.2021   **NETHERLANDS - AUSTRIA**   **2-0(1-0)**   16th EC. Group Stage.
"Johan Cruyff" Arena, Amsterdam; Referee: Orel Grinfeld (Israel); Attendance: 15,243
NED: Maarten Stekelenburg, Denzel Justus Morris Dumfries, Patrick John Miguel van Aanholt (65.Owen Wijndal), Stefan de Vrij, Daley Blind (64.Nathan Benjamin Aké), Matthijs de Ligt, Georginio Gregion Emile Wijnaldum (Cap), Marten Elco de Roon (74.Ryan Jiro Gravenberch), Frenkie de Jong, Memphis Depay (82.Luuk de Jong), Wout Weghorst (64.Donyell Malen). Trainer: Franciscus de Boer.
Goals: Memphis Depay (11 penalty), Denzel Justus Morris Dumfries (67).

21.06.2021   **NORTH MACEDONIA - NETHERLANDS**   **0-3(0-1)**   16th EC. Group Stage.
"Johan Cruyff" Arena, Amsterdam; Referee: István Kovács (Romania); Attendance: 15,227
NED: Maarten Stekelenburg, Denzel Justus Morris Dumfries (46.Steven Berghuis), Patrick John Miguel van Aanholt, Stefan de Vrij (46.Jurriën David Norman Timber), Daley Blind, Matthijs de Ligt, Georginio Gregion Emile Wijnaldum (Cap), Frenkie de Jong (79.Cody Mathès Gakpo), Ryan Jiro Gravenberch, Memphis Depay (66.Wout Weghorst), Donyell Malen (66.Quincy Anton Promes). Trainer: Franciscus de Boer.
Goals: Memphis Depay (24), Georginio Gregion Emile Wijnaldum (51, 58).

27.06.2021   **NETHERLANDS - CZECH REPUBLIC**   **0-2(0-0)**   16th EC. 2nd Round of 16.
Puskás Aréna, Budapest (Hungary); Referee: Sergei Karasev (Russia); Attendance: 52,834
NED: Maarten Stekelenburg, Denzel Justus Morris Dumfries, Patrick John Miguel van Aanholt (81.Steven Berghuis), Stefan de Vrij, Daley Blind (81.Jurriën David Norman Timber), Matthijs de Ligt [*sent off* 55], Georginio Gregion Emile Wijnaldum (Cap), Marten Elco de Roon (73.Wout Weghorst), Frenkie de Jong, Memphis Depay, Donyell Malen (57.Quincy Anton Promes). Trainer: Franciscus de Boer.

NATIONAL TEAM PLAYERS
(16.07.2020 – 15.07.2021)

Name	DOB	Caps	Goals	2020/2021:	Club
Goalkeepers					
Marco BIZOT	10.03.1991	1	0	2020:	*AZ Alkmaar*
Jacobus Antonius Peter CILLESSEN	22.04.1989	60	0	2020/2021:	*Valencia CF (ESP)*
Timothy Michael KRUL	03.04.1988	15	0	2020/2021:	*Norwich City FC (ENG)*
Maarten STEKELENBURG	22.09.1982	63	0	2021:	*AFC Ajax Amsterdam*
Defenders					
Nathan Benjamin AKÉ	18.02.1995	22	2	2020/2021:	*Manchester City FC (ENG)*
Daley BLIND	09.03.1990	82	2	2020/2021:	*AFC Ajax Amsterdam*
Matthijs DE LIGT	12.08.1999	30	2	2021:	*Juventus FC Torino (ITA)*
Stefan DE VRIJ	05.02.1992	49	3	2020/2021:	*FC Internazionale Milano (ITA)*
Denzel Justus Morris DUMFRIES	18.04.1996	23	2	2020/2021:	*PSV Eindhoven*
Hans HATEBOER	09.01.1994	11	0	2020:	*Atalanta Bergamasca Calcio (ITA)*
Kenny Joelle TETE	09.10.1995	14	0	2021:	*Fulham FC London (ENG)*
Jurriën David Norman TIMBER	17.06.2001	5	0	2021:	*AFC Ajax Amsterdam*
Patrick John Miguel VAN AANHOLT	29.08.1990	19	0	2020/2021:	*Crystal Palace FC London (ENG)*
Virgil VAN DIJK	08.07.1991	38	4	2020:	*Liverpool FC (ENG)*
Joël Ivo VELTMAN	15.01.1992	28	2	2020/2021:	*Brighton & Hove Albion FC (ENG)*
Owen WIJNDAL	28.11.1999	11	0	2020/2021:	*AZ Alkmaar*
Midfielders					
Frenkie DE JONG	12.05.1997	31	1	2020/2021:	*FC Barcelona (ESP)*
Marten Elco DE ROON	29.03.1991	26	0	2020/2021:	*Atalanta Bergamasca Calcio (ITA)*
Ryan Jiro GRAVENBERCH	16.05.2002	7	1	2021:	*AFC Ajax Amsterdam*
Davy KLAASSEN	21.02.1993	24	5	2020/2021:	*AFC Ajax Amsterdam*
Teun KOOPMEINERS	28.02.1998	1	0	2020:	*AZ Alkmaar*
Donny VAN DE BEEK	18.04.1997	19	3	2020/2021:	*Manchester United FC (ENG)*
Georginio Gregion Emile WIJNALDUM	11.11.1990	79	25	2020/2021:	*Liverpool FC (ENG)*
Forwards					
Ryan Miguel Guno BABEL	19.12.1986	69	10	2020/2021:	*Galatasaray SK İstanbul (TUR)*
Steven BERGHUIS	19.12.1991	28	2	2020/2021:	*Feyenoord Rotterdam*
Steven Charles BERGWIJN	08.10.1997	12	1	2020/2021:	*Tottenham Hotspur FC London (ENG)*
Luuk DE JONG	27.08.1990	38	8	2020/2021:	*Sevilla FC (ESP)*
Memphis Depay	13.02.1994	68	28	2020/2021:	*Olympique Lyonnais (FRA)*
Cody Mathès GAKPO	07.05.1999	1	0	2021:	*PSV Eindhoven*
Donyell MALEN	19.01.1999	13	2	2020/2021:	*PSV Eindhoven*
Quincy Anton PROMES	04.01.1992	50	7	2020: 24.02.2021->	*AFC Ajax Amsterdam* *FK Spartak Moskva (RUS)*
Calvin STENGS	18.12.1998	7	0	2020/2021:	*AZ Alkmaar*
Wout WEGHORST	07.08.1992	10	2	2021:	*VfL Wolfsburg (GER)*

Trainer		
Dwight Bernard LODEWEGES [19.08. – 23.09.2020;Caretaker]	26.10.1957	2 M; 1 W; 0 D; 1 L; 1-1
Franciscus DE BOER [23.09.2020 – 29.06.2021]	15.05.1970	15 M; 8 W; 4 D; 3 L; 31-15

NORTH MACEDONIA

The Country:
Република Северна Македонија (Republic of North Macedonia)
Capital: Skopje
Surface: 25,713 km²
Inhabitants: 2,077,132 [2019]
Time: UTC+1

The FA:
Fudbalska Federacija na Severna Makedonija
bul. Asnom br.21, 1000 Skopje
Tel: +389 2 3204 470
Foundation date: 1926
Member of FIFA since: 1926/1994
Member of UEFA since: 1954/1994
Website: www.ffm.com.mk

NATIONAL TEAM RECORDS

RECORDS		
First international match:	13.10.1993, Kranj:	Slovenia – Macedonia 1-4
Most international caps:	Goran Pandev	- 122 caps (since 2001)
Most international goals:	Goran Pandev	- 38 goals / 122 caps (since 2001)

UEFA EUROPEAN CHAMPIONSHIP	
1960	-
1964	-
1968	-
1972	-
1976	-
1980	-
1984	-
1988	-
1992	-
1996	Qualifiers
2000	Qualifiers
2004	Qualifiers
2008	Qualifiers
2012	Qualifiers
2016	Qualifiers
2020	Final Tournament (Group Stage)

FIFA WORLD CUP	
1930	-
1934	-
1938	-
1950	-
1954	-
1958	-
1962	-
1966	-
1970	-
1974	-
1978	-
1982	-
1986	-
1990	-
1994	Did not enter
1998	Qualifiers
2002	Qualifiers
2006	Qualifiers
2010	Qualifiers
2014	Qualifiers
2018	Qualifiers

OLYMPIC TOURNAMENTS	
1908	-
1912	-
1920	-
1924	-
1928	-
1936	-
1948	-
1952	-
1956	-
1960	-
1964	-
1968	-
1972	-
1976	-
1980	-
1984	-
1988	-
1992	Did not enter
1996	Qualifiers
2000	Qualifiers
2004	Qualifiers
2008	Qualifiers
2012	Qualifiers
2016	Qualifiers

was part of Yugoslavia until 08.09.1991

UEFA NATIONS LEAGUE

2018/2019	League D (promoted to League C)
2020/2021	League C

FIFA CONFEDERATIONS CUP 1992-2017

None

MACEDONIAN CLUB HONOURS IN EUROPEAN CLUB COMPETITIONS:

European Champion Clubs' Cup (1956-1992) / UEFA Champions League (1993-2021)
None
Fairs Cup (1858-1971) / UEFA Cup (1972-2009) / UEFA Europa League (2010-2021)
None
UEFA Super Cup (1972-2020)
None
*European Cup Winners' Cup 1961-1999**
None

defunct competition

NATIONAL COMPETITIONS
TABLE OF HONOURS

Royal League
(territory of Vardarska Banovina belonging to the Kingdom of Yugoslavia)

	CHAMPIONS
1929	Pobeda Skopje
1930	Jug Skopje, SSK Skopje, Sparta Skopje*
1931	*Championship not finished*
1932	SSK Skopje
1933	SSK Skopje
1934	SSK Skopje
1935	*Championship not finished*
1936	Gragjanski Skopje
1937	*Championship not finished*
1938	Gragjanski Skopje
1939	Gragjanski Skopje
1940	SSK Skopje
1941	SSK Skopje

All 3 teams finished with equal number of points

As part of Bulgaria

	CHAMPIONS
1942	Makedonija Skopje
1943	ZhSK Skopje
1944	ZhSK Skopje

Republic League (within F.R. Yugoslavia)

1944/1945	Makedonija Skopje	1960/1961	Pelister Bitola	1976/1977	Rabotnichki Skopje
1945/1946	Pobeda Skopje	1961/1962	Pobeda Prilep	1977/1978	Tikvesh Kavadarci
1946/1947	Makedonija Skopje	1962/1963	Pobeda Prilep	1978/1979	Pobeda Prilep
1947/1948	Dinamo Skopje	1963/1964	Bregalnica Shtip	1979/1980	Rabotnichki Skopje
1948/1949	11 Oktomvri Kumanovo	1964/1965	Teteks Tetovo	1980/1981	Pobeda Prilep
1949/1950	Rabotnik Bitola	1965/1966	Rabotnichki Skopje	1981/1982	Pelister Bitola
1950/1951	Rabotnik Bitola	1966/1967	Bregalnica Shtip	1982/1983	Belasica Strumica
1951/1952	Rabotnichki Skopje	1967/1968	Rabotnichki Skopje	1983/1984	Bregalnica Shtip
1952/1953	Pobeda Prilep	1968/1969	Teteks Tetovo	1984/1985	Teteks Tetovo
1953/1954	Rabotnichki Skopje	1969/1970	MIK Skopje	1985/1986	Pobeda Prilep
1954/1955	Rabotnichki Skopje	1970/1971	Kumanovo	1986/1987	Metalurg Skopje
1955/1956	Vardar Skopje	1971/1972	Tikvesh Kavadarci	1987/1988	Belasica Strumica
1956/1957	Rabotnichki Skopje	1972/1973	Rabotnichki Skopje	1988/1989	Borec-Titov Veles
1957/1958	Rabotnichki Skopje	1973/1974	Teteks Tetovo	1989/1990	Balkan Skopje
1958/1959	Pobeda Prilep	1974/1975	Pelister Bitola	1990/1991	Makedonija Skopje
1959/1960	Pelister Bitola	1975/1976	Bregalnica Shtip	1991/1992	Sasa Makedonska Kamenica

After proclamation of independence - Macedonian First League

	CHAMPIONS	CUP WINNERS	BEST GOALSCORERS	
1992/1993	FK Vardar Skopje	FK Vardar Skopje	Saša Ćirić (FK Vardar Skopje)	36
1993/1994	FK Vardar Skopje	FK Sileks Kratovo	Zoran Boshkovski (FK Sileks Kratovo)	21
1994/1995	FK Vardar Skopje	FK Vardar Skopje	Saša Ćirić (FK Vardar Skopje)	35
1995/1996	FK Sileks Kratovo	FK Sloga Jugomagnat Skopje	Zoran Boshkovski (FK Sileks Kratovo)	20
1996/1997	FK Sileks Kratovo	FK Sileks Kratovo	Vancho Micevski (FK Sileks Kratovo) Miroslav Gjokić (FK Sileks Kratovo)	16
1997/1998	FK Sileks Kratovo	FK Vardar Skopje	Vancho Atanasov (FK Belasica Stremica)	12
1998/1999	FK Sloga Jugomagnat Skopje	FK Vardar Skopje	Rogério Oliveira da Costa (FK Pobeda Prilep)	22
1999/2000	FK Sloga Jugomagnat Skopje	FK Sloga Jugomagnat Skopje	Argjend Beqiri (FK Sloga Jugomagnat Skopje)	19
2000/2001	FK Sloga Jugomagnat Skopje	FK Pelister Bitola	Argjend Beqiri (FK Sloga Jugomagnat Skopje)	27
2001/2002	FK Vardar Skopje	FK Pobeda Prilep	Miroslav Gjokić (FK Pobeda Prilep)	22
2002/2003	FK Vardar Skopje	FK Cementarnica 55 Skopje	Ljubiša Savić (FK Bregalnica Štip / FK Sloga Jugomagnat Skopje)	25
2003/2004	FK Pobeda Prilep	FK Sloga Jugomagnat Skopje	Dragan Dimitrovski (FK Pobeda Prilep)	25
2004/2005	FK Rabotnički Skopje	KF Bashkimi Kumanovo	Aleksandar Stojanovski (FK Belasica Stremica) Stevica Ristić (FK Sileks Kratovo)	26
2005/2006	FK Rabotnički Skopje	FK Makedonija Gjorče Petrov	Stevica Ristić (FK Sileks Kratovo)	27
2006/2007	FK Pobeda Prilep	FK Vardar Skopje	Boban Janchevski (KF Bashkimi Kumanovo / KF Renova Džepčište)	26
2007/2008	FK Rabotnički Skopje	FK Rabotnički Skopje	Ivica Gligorovski (FK Milano Kumanovo)	15
2008/2009	FK Makedonija Gjorče Petrov	FK Rabotnički Skopje	Ivica Gligorovski (FK Milano Kumanovo)	14
2009/2010	KF Renova Džepčište	FK Teteks Tetovo	Bobi Bozhinovski (FK Rabotnički Skopje)	15
2010/2011	KF Shkëndija Tetovo	FK Metalurg Skopje	Hristijan Kirovski (FK Skopje)	20
2011/2012	FK Vardar Skopje	KF Renova Džepčište	Filip Ivanovski (FK Vardar Skopje)	24
2012/2013	FK Vardar Skopje	FK Teteks Tetovo	Jovan Kostovski (FK Vardar Skopje)	22
2013/2014	FK Rabotnički Skopje	FK Rabotnički Skopje	Dejan Blazhevski (FK Horizont Turnovo)	19
2014/2015	FK Vardar Skopje	FK Rabotnički Skopje	Izair Emini (KF Renova Džepčište)	20
2015/2016	FK Vardar Skopje	KF Shkëndija Tetovo	Besart Ibraimi (KF Shkëndija Tetovo)	26
2016/2017	FK Vardar Skopje	FK Pelister Bitola	Besart Ibraimi (KF Shkëndija Tetovo)	20
2017/2018	KF Shkëndija Tetovo	KF Shkëndija Tetovo	Ferhan Hasani (KF Shkëndija Tetovo)	

			Besart Ibraimi (KF Shkëndija Tetovo)	22
2018/2019	KF Shkëndija Tetovo	Fudb. Akademija Pandev Strumica	Vlatko Stojanovski (KF Renova Džepčište)	18
2019/2020	FK Vardar Skopje	*Competition cancelled*	Daniel Avramovski (FK Vardar Skopje)	11
2020/2021	KF Shkëndija Tetovo	FK Sileks Kratovo	Besart Ibraimi (KF Shkëndija Tetovo)	24

NATIONAL CHAMPIONSHIP
Macedonian First Football League – Prva Liga 2020/2021
(08.08.2020 – 16.05.2021)

Results

Round 1 [08-09.08.2020]
Vardar Skopje - FK Borec 0-1(0-1)
FK Belasica - Sileks Kratovo 0-6(0-0)
FK Pelister - Akademija Pandev 1-0(1-0)
KF Shkupi - KF Shkëndija 2-2(2-0)
FK Makedonija - FK Rabotnički 2-1(1-0)
KF Renova - FC Struga 0-0

Round 2 [14-16.08.2020]
Sileks Kratovo - FK Pelister 2-2(1-1)
FK Rabotnički - FK Belasica 2-0(1-0)
Akademija Pandev - Vardar Skopje 0-1(0-0)
FK Borec - KF Renova 1-1(1-0)
KF Shkupi - FK Makedonija 3-1(1-0)
KF Shkëndija - FC Struga 2-0(1-0)

Round 3 [21-23.08.2020]
FK Belasica - KF Shkupi 0-2(0-0)
FK Makedonija - KF Shkëndija 0-1(0-0)
KF Renova - Akademija Pandev 2-0(1-0)
FK Pelister - FK Rabotnički 0-0
FC Struga - FK Borec 1-0(0-0)
Vardar Skopje - Sileks Kratovo 0-4(0-1)

Round 4 [29-31.08.2020]
Akademija Pandev - FC Struga 1-0(0-0)
FK Rabotnički - Vardar Skopje 1-1(0-0)
FK Makedonija - FK Belasica 2-1(2-1)
KF Shkupi - FK Pelister 1-0(0-0)
KF Shkëndija - FK Borec 1-1(1-1)
Sileks Kratovo - KF Renova 3-1(2-1)

Round 5 [12-13.09.2020]
FK Belasica - KF Shkëndija 0-3(0-0)
FC Struga - Sileks Kratovo 2-0(0-0)
FK Borec - Akademija Pandev 2-0(0-0)
FK Pelister - FK Makedonija 0-0
KF Renova - FK Rabotnički 0-1(0-0)
Vardar Skopje - KF Shkupi 1-0(0-0)

Round 6 [19-20.09.2020]
FK Rabotnički - FC Struga 1-1(0-0)
FK Makedonija - Vardar Skopje 2-1(2-1)
FK Belasica - FK Pelister 0-2(0-1)
KF Shkupi - KF Renova 4-3(2-2)
KF Shkëndija - Akademija Pandev 2-1(1-0)
Sileks Kratovo - FK Borec 1-2(1-0)

Round 7 [26-27.09.2020]
FK Borec - FK Rabotnički 0-0
Akademija Pandev - Sileks Kratovo 1-0(0-0)
FK Pelister - KF Shkëndija 1-3(1-1)
KF Renova - FK Makedonija 1-3(0-2)
FC Struga - KF Shkupi 2-0(1-0)
Vardar Skopje - FK Belasica 3-1(2-0)

Round 8 [03-04.10.2020]
FK Belasica - KF Renova 1-1(1-0)
FK Rabotnički - Akademija Pandev 0-0
KF Shkupi - FK Borec 3-0(0-0)
KF Shkëndija - Sileks Kratovo 1-1(1-1)
FK Makedonija - FC Struga 2-0(0-0)
FK Pelister - Vardar Skopje 1-1(0-1)

Round 9 [17-18.10.2020]
Vardar Skopje - KF Shkëndija 1-5(1-2)
Akademija Pandev - KF Shkupi 0-1(0-0)
FK Borec - FK Makedonija 2-1(0-0)
KF Renova - FK Pelister 0-0
Sileks Kratovo - FK Rabotnički 4-3(1-0)
FC Struga - FK Belasica 3-0(2-0)

Round 10 [24-25.10.2020]
KF Shkupi - Sileks Kratovo 1-0(0-0)
FK Belasica - FK Borec 2-2(1-0)
FK Pelister - FC Struga 1-1(0-0)
KF Shkëndija - FK Rabotnički 1-1(1-0)
FK Makedonija - Akademija Pandev 3-1(1-1)
Vardar Skopje - KF Renova 3-3(3-2)

Round 11 [07-08.11.2020]
Akademija Pandev - FK Belasica 1-2(1-1)
FK Borec - FK Pelister 3-0(1-0)
FK Rabotnički - KF Shkupi 2-2(1-1)
KF Renova - KF Shkëndija 1-3(0-2)
FC Struga - Vardar Skopje 2-2(2-1)
Sileks Kratovo - FK Makedonija 0-3(0-0)

Round 12 [21-22.11.2020]
FK Borec - Vardar Skopje 0-2(0-0)
Akademija Pandev - FK Pelister 3-2(2-1)
FK Rabotnički - FK Makedonija 1-3(1-2)
KF Shkëndija - KF Shkupi 1-1(1-0)
Sileks Kratovo - FK Belasica 0-1(0-0)
FC Struga - KF Renova 1-0(1-0)

Round 13 [28-29.11.2020]
Vardar Skopje - Akademija Pandev 2-0(0-0)
FK Belasica - FK Rabotnički 2-2(1-2)
FK Pelister - Sileks Kratovo 1-2(0-2)
FK Makedonija - KF Shkupi 0-0
KF Renova - FK Borec 1-0(0-0)
FC Struga - KF Shkëndija 1-1(1-0)

Round 14 [02.12.2020]
Akademija Pandev - KF Renova 0-1(0-0)
FK Borec - FC Struga 2-1(0-0)
FK Rabotnički - FK Pelister 1-0(1-0)
KF Shkupi - FK Belasica 3-1(2-0)
KF Shkëndija - FK Makedonija 5-0(3-0)
Sileks Kratovo - Vardar Skopje 1-0(0-0)

Round 15 [05-06.12.2020]
FK Borec - KF Shkëndija 0-2(0-1)
FK Belasica - FK Makedonija 1-3(1-1)
FK Pelister - KF Shkupi 1-3(1-2)
KF Renova - Sileks Kratovo 0-0
FC Struga - Akademija Pandev 1-1(0-0)
Vardar Skopje - FK Rabotnički 0-0

Round 16 [09.12.2020]
Akademija Pandev - FK Borec 2-1(0-1)
FK Rabotnički - KF Renova 3-1(1-0)
KF Shkupi - Vardar Skopje 1-1(0-0)
KF Shkëndija - FK Belasica 2-0(1-0)
FK Makedonija - FK Pelister 2-1(1-1)
Sileks Kratovo - FC Struga 0-0

Round 17 [12-13.12.2020]
KF Renova - KF Shkupi 0-0
Akademija Pandev - KF Shkëndija 0-1(0-0)
FK Borec - Sileks Kratovo 2-0(2-0)
FK Pelister - FK Belasica 1-0(0-0)
FC Struga - FK Rabotnički 2-1(1-1)
Vardar Skopje - FK Makedonija 2-2(1-0)

Round 18 [16.12.2020]
FK Belasica - Vardar Skopje 0-3(0-1)
FK Rabotnički - FK Borec 2-1(1-1)
KF Shkupi - FC Struga 1-2(0-0)
KF Shkëndija - FK Pelister 0-1(0-0)
FK Makedonija - KF Renova 2-3(0-1)
Sileks Kratovo - Akademija Pandev 1-2(0-1)

Round 19 [21.02.2021]
Akademija P.-FK Rabotnički 0-1(0-0) [13.02.]
FK Borec - KF Shkupi 0-1(0-0)
KF Renova - FK Belasica 2-4(0-1)
Sileks Kratovo - KF Shkëndija 1-2(1-1)
FC Struga - FK Makedonija 1-1(0-0)
Vardar Skopje - FK Pelister 2-2(1-1)

Round 20 [27-28.02.2021]
FK Rabotnički - Sileks Kratovo 1-1(0-0)
FK Belasica - FC Struga 1-2(0-1)
FK Pelister - KF Renova 3-1(2-1)
KF Shkupi - Akademija Pandev 0-0
KF Shkëndija - Vardar Skopje 2-1(1-1)
FK Makedonija - FK Borec 0-0

Round 21 [03.03.2021]
Akademija Pandev - FK Makedonija 2-1(1-0)
FK Borec - FK Belasica 2-1(2-1)
FK Rabotnički - KF Shkëndija 0-0
KF Renova - Vardar Skopje 3-0(2-0)
Sileks Kratovo - KF Shkupi 0-1(0-0)
FC Struga - FK Pelister 0-1(0-0)

Round 22 [06-07.03.2021]
FK Makedonija - Sileks Kratovo 1-0(1-0)
FK Belasica - Akademija Pandev 0-0
FK Pelister - FK Borec 1-0(1-0)
KF Shkupi - FK Rabotnički 0-2(0-2)
KF Shkëndija - KF Renova 0-0
Vardar Skopje - FC Struga 1-1(0-1)

Round 23 [13-14.03.2021]
FK Rabotnički - Akademija Pandev 0-2(0-1)
FK Borec - FK Belasica 1-0(0-0)
KF Shkupi - Vardar Skopje 2-0(1-0)
KF Shkëndija - FK Pelister 1-0(0-0)
FK Makedonija - Sileks Kratovo 0-3(0-1)
FC Struga - KF Renova 0-0

Round 24 [20-21.03.2021]
Akademija Pandev - FC Struga 1-0(1-0)
FK Belasica - FK Rabotnički 1-1(1-0)
KF Renova - FK Makedonija 1-2(1-1)
Sileks Kratovo - KF Shkupi 1-3(1-1)
Vardar Skopje - KF Shkëndija 1-6(1-2)
FK Borec - FK Pelister 0-0

Round 25 [03-04.04.2021]
FK Makedonija - Akademija Pandev 1-2(0-2)
FK Pelister - Vardar Skopje 2-0(1-0)
FK Rabotnički - FK Borec 2-1(0-0)
KF Shkupi - KF Renova 1-2(0-1)
KF Shkëndija - Sileks Kratovo 2-1(0-0)
FC Struga - FK Belasica 3-1(2-0)

Round 26 [10-11.04.2021]
FK Rabotnički - FK Pelister 3-1(2-0)
Akademija Pandev - KF Shkupi 0-1(0-0)
FK Belasica - FK Makedonija 0-2(0-1)
FK Borec - FC Struga 0-1(0-0)
KF Renova - KF Shkëndija 0-3(0-0)
Sileks Kratovo - Vardar Skopje 6-0(2-0)

Round 27 [14.04.2021]
FK Pelister - Sileks Kratovo 3-2(2-2)
KF Shkupi - FK Belasica 0-1(0-1)
KF Shkëndija - Akademija Pandev 1-0(0-0)
FK Makedonija - FK Borec 2-1(1-0)
FC Struga - FK Rabotnički 1-1(1-0)
Vardar Skopje - KF Renova 1-1(1-1)

Round 28 [17-18.04.2021]
KF Renova - Sileks Kratovo 2-1(2-0)
Akademija Pandev - Vardar Skopje 3-0(3-0)
FK Belasica - KF Shkëndija 0-3(0-2)
FK Borec - KF Shkupi 0-1(0-0)
FK Rabotnički - FK Makedonija 2-2(2-2)
FC Struga - FK Pelister 3-0(0-0)

Round 29 [24-25.04.2021]
Sileks Kratovo - Akademija Pandev 3-2(2-0)
FK Pelister - KF Renova 1-0(1-0)
KF Shkupi - FK Rabotnički 2-0(0-0)
KF Shkëndija - FK Borec 3-1(0-1)
FK Makedonija - FC Struga 2-3(1-0)
Vardar Skopje - FK Belasica 1-0(1-0)

Round 30 [28.04.2021]
Akademija Pandev - KF Renova 1-1(1-0)
FK Belasica - Sileks Kratovo 1-3(1-1)
FK Borec - Vardar Skopje 2-0(1-0)
FK Rabotnički - KF Shkëndija 3-5(1-2)
FK Makedonija - FK Pelister 3-0(1-0)
FC Struga - KF Shkupi 0-0

Round 31 [01.05.2021]
FK Pelister - Akademija Pandev 3-1(1-1)
KF Shkupi - FK Makedonija 0-0
KF Shkëndija - FC Struga 0-2(0-2)
KF Renova - FK Belasica 3-1(2-0)
Sileks Kratovo - FK Borec 1-1(1-0)
Vardar Skopje - FK Rabotnički 1-3(0-2)

Round 32 [09.05.2021]
FK Belasica - Akademija Pandev 0-2(0-2)
FK Borec - KF Renova 2-0(1-0)
FK Rabotnički - Sileks Kratovo 3-1(1-1)
KF Shkupi - FK Pelister 0-0
FK Makedonija - KF Shkëndija 3-4(2-2)
FC Struga - Vardar Skopje 1-0(0-0)

Round 33 [16.05.2021]
Akademija Pandev - FK Borec 3-1(2-1)
FK Pelister - FK Belasica 2-0(1-0)
KF Shkëndija - KF Shkupi 1-1(1-0)
KF Renova - FK Rabotnički 1-1(1-0)
Sileks Kratovo - FC Struga 0-1(0-0)
Vardar Skopje - FK Makedonija 0-2(0-0)

Final Standings

							Total						Home						Away		
1.	**KF Shkëndija Tetovo**	33	22	9	2	69	-	26	75	9	6	2	25	-	12	13	3	0	44	-	14
2.	KF Shkupi Čair	33	16	11	6	41	-	24	59	8	5	4	24	-	15	8	6	2	17	-	9
3.	FC Struga Trim-Lum	33	15	12	6	39	-	24	57	9	7	1	24	-	9	6	5	5	15	-	15
4.	FK Makedonija Gjorče Petrov Skopje	33	16	7	10	53	-	43	55	9	2	6	27	-	22	7	5	4	26	-	21
5.	FK Rabotnički Skopje	33	11	15	7	45	-	39	48	7	7	3	27	-	22	4	8	4	18	-	17
6.	FK Pelister Bitola	33	12	9	12	34	-	38	45	9	4	3	22	-	14	3	5	9	12	-	24
7.	Fudbalska Akademija Pandev Strumica	33	12	5	16	32	-	36	41	8	1	7	18	-	14	4	4	9	14	-	22
8.	FK Borec Veles	33	11	7	15	32	-	36	40	9	3	5	19	-	11	2	4	10	13	-	25
9.	FK Sileks Kratovo (*Relegation Play-offs*)	33	10	6	17	49	-	45	36	5	3	8	24	-	24	5	3	9	25	-	21
10.	KF Renova Džepčište (*Relegation Play-offs*)	33	8	12	13	36	-	46	36	5	5	6	17	-	19	3	7	7	19	-	27
11.	FK Vardar Skopje (*Relegated*)	33	7	10	16	32	-	60	31	4	6	6	19	-	31	3	4	10	13	-	29
12.	FK Belasica Strumica (*Relegated*)	33	4	5	24	23	-	68	17	0	5	11	9	-	37	4	0	13	14	-	31

Top goalscorers:

24	**Besart Ibraimi**	*KF Shkëndija Tetovo*
16	Dembo Darboe (GAM)	*KF Shkupi Čair*
13	Pepi Georgiev	*FK Sileks Kratovo*
12	Fahrudin Đurđević	*FK Rabotnički Skopje*

Relegation Play-offs [25.05.2021]

KF Renova Džepčište - GFK Ohrid   2-2(1-1,2-2,2-2); 3-2 on penalties
GFK Tikveš 1930 Kavadarci - FK Sileks Kratovo   1-0(0-0)

Both KF Renova Džepčište and GFK Tikveš 1930 Kavadarci will play next year's season at first level.

NATIONAL CUP
Kup na Makedonija 2020/2021

First Round [22-23.09.2020]

KF Vardari Forinë - FK Vardar Skopje	2-2 aet; 6-7 pen		GFK Ohrid - KF Renova Džepčište	0-4
FK Makedonija G. P. Skopje - FK Pobeda AD Prilep	0-0 aet; 5-4 pen		FK Sileks Kratovo - FK Labuništa	3-0
FK Ljuboten Tetovo - FK Pelister Bitola	0-4		FK Sasa Makedonska Kamenica - FK Borec Veles	2-2 aet; 3-1 pen
FK Sloga 1934 Vinica - KF Shkupi Čair	1-2		KF Gostivari - GFK Tikveš 1930 Kavadarci	5-0
KF Veleshtë - FK Kožuf Gevgelija	1-2		KF Vëllazërimi 77 Kičevo - FK Rabotnički Skopje	0-0 aet; 3-4 pen
FK Rosoman 83 - FK Belasica Strumica	1-5		FK Kit-Go Pehčevo - FK Skopje	2-1

1/8-Finals [21.10.2020]

Fud. Akademija Pandev Strumica - FK Vardar Skopje	1-0		FK Kožuf Gevgelija - FK Sileks Kratovo	1-3
FK Makedonija G. P. Skopje - FK Sasa Makedonska	6-0		FC Struga Trim-Lum - FK Rabotnički Skopje	0-0 aet; 4-3 pen
KF Shkëndija Tetovo - KF Gostivari	1-0		FK Bregalnica Štip - FK Belasica Strumica	0-1
KF Shkupi Čair - FK Kit-Go Pehčevo	5-0		KF Renova Džepčište - FK Pelister Bitola	2-2 aet; 6-5 pen

Quarter-Finals [25.11.2020]

Fud. Akademija Pandev Strumica - KF Shkupi Čair	2-1(1-0)		FK Sileks Kratovo - KF Shkëndija Tetovo	0-0 aet; 4-2 pen
FK Belasica Strumica - FK Makedonija G. P. Skopje	1-4(1-1)		FC Struga Trim-Lum - KF Renova Džepčište	1-0(0-0)

Semi-Finals [06-07.04.2021]

FK Makedonija G. P. Skopje - F. Akademija Pandev	1-3(1-1)		FC Struga Trim-Lum - FK Sileks Kratovo	0-1(0-0)

Final

19.05.2021; Nacionalna Arena "Toše Proeski", Skopje; Referee: Aleksandar Stavrev; Attendance: 0
Fudbalska Akademija Pandev Strumica - FK Sileks Kratovo　　　　　　　　　**0-0; 3-4 on penalties**

Akademija Pandev: Marko Jovanovski, Vane Jovanov (99.Nikolce Sarkoski), Kosta Manev, Tomislav Iliev, Nikola Serafimov, Marko Martinaga, Georgi Stoilov, Goran Tomovski (72.Bojan Dimoski), Daniel Milovanovikj (72.Kristijan Velinovski), Marjan Radeski, Mario Krstovski (87.Kire Markoski). Trainer: Aleksandar Vasoski.

Sileks Kratovo: Daniel Božinovski, Srđan Drasković, Riste Karakamisev, Angelce Timovski, Daniel Karceski, David Manasievski (46.Filip Duranski), Viktor Serafimovski, Denis Ristov (96.Svilen Shterev), Ivan Ivanovski, Pepi Georgiev, Dejan Tanturovski (113.Krsta Đorđević). Trainer: Goran Simov (Serbia).

Penalties: Ivan Ivanovski 0-1; Georgi Stoilov 1-1; Svilen Shterev 1-2; Tomislav Iliev 2-2; Angelce Timovski 2-3; Kire Markoski 3-3; Pepi Georgiev (saved); Bojan Dimoski (saved); Daniel Karceski 3-4; Kristijan Velinovski (missed).

THE CLUBS 2020/2021

Fudbalska Akademija Pandev Strumica

Founded:	2010	
Stadium:	Stadion „Blagoj Istatov", Strumica (9,200)	
Trainer:	Aleksandar Tanevski	24.07.1983
[15.09.2020]	Jugoslav Trencovski	29.11.1976
[25.12.2020]	Aleksandar Vasoski	21.11.1979

Goalkeepers:	DOB	M	(s)	G
Marko Alchevski	16.04.2002	16		
Marko Jovanovski	24.07.1988	15		
Filip Kupanov	09.09.2002	2	(1)	
Defenders:	**DOB**	**M**	**(s)**	**G**
Dime Dimov	25.07.1994	18		
Tomislav Iliev	02.12.1993	28	(2)	
Vane Jovanov	28.12.1998	18	(8)	
Kosta Manev (FIN)	07.04.1993	11		1
Marko Martinaga (CRO)	27.05.1998	15		
Mario Maslać (SRB)	09.09.1990	10	(2)	1
Igor Panoski	18.03.1999	4		1
Nikola Serafimov	11.08.1999	24	(1)	
Spase Terziev	22.01.2002	2	(2)	
Midfielders:	**DOB**	**M**	**(s)**	**G**
Bojan Dimoski	23.11.2001	21	(9)	1
Besnik Ferati	19.04.2000	10	(3)	

	DOB	M	(s)	G
Vane Krstevski	28.04.2003		(3)	
Ivan Nikolov	17.02.2002	15	(4)	
Georgi Stoilov	25.08.1995	24	(2)	3
Andrej Stojčevski	26.05.2003	2	(8)	
Martin Talakov	09.03.2003	1	(6)	
Milan Tomić (SRB)	11.02.2000	4	(4)	
Goran Tomovski	21.07.1998	16	(6)	
Forwards:	**DOB**	**M**	**(s)**	**G**
Mario Krstovski	03.04.1998	22	(9)	7
Kire Markoski	20.02.1995	5	(7)	2
Daniel Milovanovikj	10.08.1998	17	(10)	4
Saško Pandev	01.05.1987	5	(19)	1
Marjan Radeski	10.02.1995	29	(2)	7
Nikolce Sarkoski	08.03.1994	3	(5)	
Emir Skenderi	01.04.2000	1	(2)	
Kristijan Trapanovski	14.08.1999	6	(9)	1
Kristijan Velinovski	31.05.1999	19	(11)	2

Fudbalski klub Belasica Strumica

Founded: 22.04.1922
Stadium: Stadion „Blagoj Istatov", Strumica (9,200)
Trainer: Vane Milkov — 11.07.1990
[25.09.2020] Sefki Arifovski — 25.09.2020
[08.01.2021] Gjorgji Jovanovski — 29.03.1956
[06.03.2021] Andrey Chernyshov (RUS) — 07.01.1968

Goalkeepers:	DOB	M	(s)	G
Dimitar Gjorgiev	23.01.1997	8		
Mitko Mircovski	25.05.2003		(1)	
Dejan Siljanovski	10.03.1994	10		
Aleksandar Vulić (SRB)	08.06.2001	15		
Defenders:	**DOB**	**M**	**(s)**	**G**
Medin Bajrami	27.02.1998	17	(2)	
Hristijan Chukarski	18.04.2002	3	(4)	
Zoran Ivanovski	07.05.2000	23	(4)	1
Aleksandar Milusev	05.04.1988	30		1
Zoran Mitevski	03.02.1995	22	(1)	2
Igor Panoski	18.03.1999	8		
Jordan Serafimovski	13.05.1991	15	(1)	
Nikola Spasov	27.02.2000	2	(2)	
David Stojkov	09.10.2001	12	(1)	
Strahinja Ševo (SRB)	07.05.2002	11		
Arben Tafe	06.04.1992	2		
Midfielders:	**DOB**	**M**	**(s)**	**G**
Damir Avramović (SRB)	07.02.2001	8	(2)	
Panče Bozinov	11.03.2004		(1)	
David Kalpacki	01.06.2000	23	(6)	1
Aleksandar Kocev	27.04.2003	10	(10)	1

	DOB	M	(s)	G
Vasko Kocev	23.03.2001		(6)	
Filip Mihailov	10.07.1998	16	(10)	
Martin Mircevski	11.02.1997	3		
Slavce Mitovski	08.05.2003	1	(1)	
Oliver Peev	08.06.1987	7	(2)	
Robson da Silva (BRA)	14.07.1995	17		1
Stefan Sulev	24.08.1989	19	(9)	2
Damjan Trajanovski	04.03.2002	4	(7)	
Forwards:	**DOB**	**M**	**(s)**	**G**
Anderson Pinto Ferreira Barbosa (BRA)	17.03.1999	1	(5)	
Benjamin Demir	16.05.1996	12	(1)	2
Besart Gudjufi	29.05.2004	6	(4)	2
Blagoj Istatov	14.10.1999	1	(9)	
Boris Jakjimovski	08.02.2001	3	(2)	
Antonio Kalanoski	25.04.1994	26		8
Ivan Kostov	06.02.2004		(1)	
Milenko Mijatović (SRB)	10.02.2003	3	(10)	
Robert Mitev	13.04.1994	4	(2)	
Daniel Radojchikj	16.10.1997	6	(8)	
Darko Razmoski	19.10.1999	15	(3)	1
Filip Zilamov	06.12.2002		(2)	

Fudbalski klub Borec Veles

Founded: 1919
Stadium: Stadion „Zoran Paunov", Veles (2,000)
Trainer: Gorazd Mihajlov — 21.08.1974
[03.02.2021] Borce Hristov — 02.10.1970

Goalkeepers:	DOB	M	(s)	G
Andreja Efremov	02.09.1992	6		
Mikica Gjorgievski	17.05.1994	14		
Burhan Mustafa	22.07.1990	13		
Defenders:	**DOB**	**M**	**(s)**	**G**
Kristijan Eftimov	01.09.1999	27	(1)	
Nikola Gavrić (CRO)	17.03.1995	3	(2)	
Daniel Ivanov	24.05.2000		(2)	
Filip Manasievski	22.05.2001	1	(2)	
Teodor Mircevski	25.02.2001		(2)	
Filip Misevski	01.11.1991	13		
Nikola Risteski	20.12.1996	17		
Filip Ristovski	03.01.1995	31	(1)	
Marjan Ristovski	25.07.1996	14	(4)	5
Oliver Stoimenovski	26.03.1999	27	(2)	1
Stojan Stojčevski	30.10.1992	18		
Vanče Šikov	19.07.1985	4		
Filip Trajanovski	21.03.1999	6		
Midfielders:	**DOB**	**M**	**(s)**	**G**
Milan Chichevski	11.06.1995	5	(10)	
Fernando Silva dos Santos (BRA)	18.05.1991	20	(5)	1

	DOB	M	(s)	G
Robert Kocev	14.06.1994	32		
Mihailo Mitrov	05.03.1995		(4)	
Anes Osmanoski	14.06.2000	9	(6)	
Lazar Peev	19.06.1997		(1)	
Oliver Peev	08.06.1987	9	(7)	1
Ilija Ristevski	04.08.2001		(1)	
Martin Talakov	09.03.2003	6	(5)	
Trajce Trajkov	29.11.1993	11	(9)	1
Forwards:	**DOB**	**M**	**(s)**	**G**
Murat Adili	22.09.1992	4	(10)	3
Edi Baša (CRO)	29.06.1993	9	(2)	3
Dario Desnikj	13.05.1994	1	(13)	1
Gjorgi Gjorgiev	18.06.1996	10	(14)	3
Dzemal Ibrahimovikj	25.03.2001	1	(10)	
Aleksandar Mishov	21.07.1998	6	(3)	4
Azer Omeragikj	14.07.2002	4	(2)	
Nikola Prelčec (CRO)	12.11.1989	18		5
Nikola Radović (SRB)	10.07.1992	10	(5)	2
Mario Stankovski	06.09.1999	6	(5)	1
Luka Trajkoski	08.02.2000	8	(3)	

Fudbalski klub Makedonija Gjorče Petrov Skopje

Founded: 1932
Stadium: Stadion „Gjorče Petrov", Skopje (3,000)
Trainer: Zikica Tasevski — 15.02.1978
[26.04.2021] Aleksandar Tanevski — 24.07.1983

Goalkeepers:	DOB	M	(s)	G
Damjan Serafimov	20.06.2000	7		
Hristijan Stevkovski	27.02.1999	24		
Stefan Tasev	08.07.2004	2		
Defenders:	**DOB**	**M**	**(s)**	**G**
David Atanasovski	21.10.1996	22		
Charleston Silva dos Santos (BRA)	23.09.1996	15		2
Fernando Augusto Rodrigues de Araujo (BRA)	25.07.1993	24	(7)	6
Tome Kitanovski	21.05.1992	30		
Martin Kovachev (BUL)	12.03.1982	11	(2)	
Esmin Licina	20.03.1998	29	(2)	1
Filip Misevski	01.11.1991	10	(5)	1
Nikola Pavlevski	11.04.2004		(1)	
Denis Stosik (GER)	27.02.1999		(5)	
Stojan Stojčevski	30.10.1992	7	(2)	
Midfielders:	**DOB**	**M**	**(s)**	**G**
Ermadin Adem	07.07.1990	20	(4)	4
Bobi Božinovski	24.02.1981	33		8
Sefer Emini	15.07.2000	8		4

	DOB	M	(s)	G
Kristijan Filipovski	02.10.1996	20	(10)	1
Stefan Kuzevski	12.07.2002		(1)	
Mario Nastevski	10.04.1995	5	(19)	
Robson da Silva (BRA)	14.07.1995	13	(1)	5
Andrej Stojanov	09.11.2002		(1)	
Leonid Stojanovski	20.06.2002		(1)	
Alban Sulejmani	14.04.1998		(4)	
Forwards:	**DOB**	**M**	**(s)**	**G**
Izet Ajrullahu	08.05.1998	6	(8)	
Filip Aleksovski	25.03.2000	5	(8)	2
Anderson Pinto Ferreira Barbosa (BRA)	17.03.1999	1	(9)	
Abdul Khalid Basit (GHA)	10.08.1996	14		8
Benjamin Demir	16.05.1996	8	(3)	
Samir Fazli	22.04.1991	8	(2)	4
Atdhe Kadriu	20.03.2004		(1)	
Kodjo Mavunio Ludvig Amla (CAN)	13.11.2000	5	(5)	1
Damjan Peshovski	13.06.2002		(1)	
Filip Petrov	23.02.1989	14	(16)	4
Arbin Vosha	04.08.2001	22	(6)	2

Fudbalski Klub Pelister Bitola

Founded: 1945
Stadium: Stadion Tumbe Kafe, Bitola (9,100)
Trainer: Zoran Sterjovski 26.08.1975
[01.12.2020] Dimitar Kapinkovski 27.05.1975

Goalkeepers:	DOB	M	(s)	G
Davor Taleski	19.05.1995	29		
Filip Trajčevski	08.09.1998	4		
Defenders:	DOB	M	(s)	G
Filip Boskovski	28.10.2000	16	(12)	
Alexander Borja Córdoba (COL)	25.10.1998	11		
Hristijan Dragarski	16.04.1992	31		3
Darko Ilieski	14.10.1995	31		
Bojan Ilievski	01.09.1999	29	(2)	1
Riste Ilijovski	27.09.1994	8	(1)	2
Ysni Ismaili (ALB)	13.03.2002		(8)	
Mihail Milevski	20.11.2002		(1)	
Bojan Stefanovski	26.03.2002		(1)	
Filip Stojanovski	01.12.1996	6	(3)	
Midfielders:	DOB	M	(s)	G
Valentin Kočoski	01.03.1997	21	(4)	3

	DOB	M	(s)	G
Nikola Naumoski	02.06.2002		(2)	
Kristijan Nikolovski	20.07.1997	19	(9)	
Aleksandar Popovski	20.03.2001	2	(10)	
Blagoja Spirkoski	13.07.1996	24		
Gjorgji Tanušev	07.01.1991	14	(5)	2
Forwards:	DOB	M	(s)	G
Aldair Sapalo Amaro Neto (POR)	22.07.1994	22	(8)	2
Prince Amponsah (GHA)	16.12.1996	2	(10)	
Martin Andonovski	15.12.2003		(1)	
Lavdrim Fazliu	06.10.1999	22	(10)	2
Oumar Goudiaby (SEN)	01.01.1995	13	(1)	4
Anes Hot (SRB)	20.06.1995	11	(3)	2
Borče Manevski	05.07.1985	15	(13)	7
Ivan Pejaković (MNE)	22.08.1992	21	(7)	3
Darko Razmoski	19.10.1999	7	(5)	1
Mihail Talevski	09.02.2004	5	(4)	1

Fudbalski klub Rabotnički Skopje

Founded: 04.10.1937
Stadium: Nacionalna Arena "Toše Proeski", Skopje (36,460)
Trainer: Ratko Dostanić (SRB) 25.10.1959
[01.01.2021] Aleksandar Vlaho 18.01.1976

Goalkeepers:	DOB	M	(s)	G
Risto Jankov	05.09.1998	29		
Filip Lazarevski	13.04.1997	2		
Burhan Mustafa	22.07.1990	2		
Defenders:	DOB	M	(s)	G
Yannick Dao (BFA)	04.12.1998		(5)	
Draško Đorđević (SRB)	01.08.1993	32		1
Hristijan Grozdanoski	05.06.1993	12		
Andrej Kirovski	11.02.1999	8		
Borjan Panovski	26.07.2000	1		
Hristijan Pecov	30.04.1994	14	(6)	
Nikola Risteski	20.12.1996	8	(2)	
Marjan Ristovski	25.07.1996	14		
Goran Siljanovski	01.07.1990	28		1
Branislav Trajković	29.08.1989	18		
Fisnik Zuka	03.09.1995	12	(6)	
Midfielders:	DOB	M	(s)	G
Matej Angelov	11.07.2004		(3)	

	DOB	M	(s)	G
Stefan Jevtoski	02.09.1997	21	(6)	4
Andrej Lazarov	08.09.1999	1	(6)	
Jordan Lomba Mpiandi (BEL)	29.12.1997		(1)	
Muarem Muarem	22.10.1988	4	(9)	
Luka Stankovski	02.09.2002	25	(4)	8
Dragan Stojkov	23.02.1988	19	(3)	
Kristijan Stojkovski	17.09.1991	13	(11)	2
Dimitar Todorovski	07.03.2002	26	(7)	
Miloš Tošeski	24.02.1998	5	(12)	1
Forwards:	DOB	M	(s)	G
Luka Čumić (SRB)	25.05.2001	4	(8)	1
Fahrudin Đurđević	17.02.1992	19	(7)	12
Bujar Hajdari	23.08.2002		(1)	
Metodi Maksimov	20.08.2002	12	(13)	
Petar Petkovski	03.01.1997	9	(9)	2
Nikola Prelčec (CRO)	12.11.1989	8	(5)	2
Nikolce Sarkoski	08.03.1994	8	(6)	3
Mario Stankovski	06.09.1999	9	(5)	5

Klubi Futbollit Renova Džepčište

Founded: 2003
Stadium: Ecolog Arena, Tetovo (15,000)
Trainer: Bujar Islami 29.11.1978
[27.11.2020] Qatip Osmani 29.06.1969

Goalkeepers:	DOB	M	(s)	G
Hadis Velii	20.05.1990	33		
Defenders:	DOB	M	(s)	G
Xhelil Abdulla	25.09.1991	31		
Arlind Aliti	24.11.1999	8	(2)	1
Souleymane Coulibaly (FRA)	26.01.1998	2	(2)	
Saimir Fetai	04.04.1989	17	(8)	
Nenad Miškovski	26.12.1986	31		1
Nehar Sadiki	16.03.1998		(1)	
Altin Sefo	27.08.2000	3		
Arbër Shala (KVX)	23.12.1991	13		1
Arben Tafe	06.04.1992	3	(6)	
Bashkim Velija	01.08.1993	32		1
Midfielders:	DOB	M	(s)	G
Marko Gajić (SVN)	10.04.1997		(1)	
Alush Gavazaj (KVX)	24.03.1995	30	(2)	1

	DOB	M	(s)	G
Burim Sadiki	05.08.1989	30	(1)	
Jasir Selmani	21.01.1991	1	(6)	
Filip Stojčevski	04.02.1999	5	(20)	1
Forwards:	DOB	M	(s)	G
Festim Ebibi	18.12.2001	4	(1)	
Amar Emurli	04.01.2003		(1)	
Argjent Gafuri	30.03.1988	8	(1)	
Alen Jasaroski	06.11.1991	12	(20)	8
Fatjon Jusufi	17.12.1995	13	(1)	2
Jhon Edy Mena Pérez (COL)	06.06.1997	1	(10)	
Suhejlj Muharem	25.08.2001	19	(5)	1
Emran Ramadani	29.01.1992	17	(14)	1
Remzi Selmani	05.05.1997	22	(5)	8
Shefit Shefiti (ALB)	19.02.1998	24	(7)	8
Artan Veliu	09.12.1997	4	(11)	1

Klubi Futbollistik Shkëndija Tetovo

Founded: 27.08.1979
Stadium: Ecolog Arena, Tetovo (15,000)
Trainer: Ernest Gjoka (ALB) 25.01.1970

Goalkeepers:	DOB	M	(s)	G
Ferat Ramani	28.10.1994	2		
Bekim Redjepi	27.10.1996	1		
Kostadin Zahov	08.11.1987	30		
Defenders:	**DOB**	**M**	**(s)**	**G**
Arlind Aliti	24.11.1999	2		
Egzon Bejtulai	07.01.1994	28		1
Ján Krivák (SVK)	10.11.1993	22		1
Zija Merdjani	22.10.1995	3	(5)	
Mevlan Murati	05.03.1994	27	(2)	2
Medzit Neziri	02.09.1990	19	(5)	
Antonio Pavić (CRO)	18.11.1994	29	(1)	
Leard Sadriu (KVX)	22.04.2001	1	(1)	
Midfielders:	**DOB**	**M**	**(s)**	**G**
Valon Ahmedi (ALB)	07.10.1994	12	(1)	4
Armend Alimi	11.12.1987	27	(3)	3
Bruno Dita (ALB)	18.02.1993	21	(7)	1
Kamer Qaka (ALB)	11.04.1995	8	(6)	1
Oktaj Rakipi	30.07.2003	1		
Florent Ramadani	27.08.2000	15	(7)	2
Ennur Totre	29.10.1996	14	(3)	4
Arbin Zejnullai (ALB)	15.02.1999	10	(18)	
Forwards:	**DOB**	**M**	**(s)**	**G**
Ljupco Doriev	13.09.1995	25	(6)	7
Dashmir Elezi	21.11.2004	14	(6)	6
Abou Baker Es Sahhal (FRA)	29.01.2001		(12)	
Rubin Hebaj (ALB)	30.07.1998	3	(12)	4
Besart Ibraimi	17.12.1986	30	(2)	24
Igor Wanderson da Silva (BRA)	04.05.1996	5	(10)	2
Omar Imeri (ALB)	13.12.1999	1	(2)	
Ensar Ljuma	17.06.2000	1	(3)	1
Valmir Nafiu	23.04.1994	12	(20)	5

Klubi Futbollistik Shkupi Čair

Founded: 1927
Stadium: Stadion Čair, Skopje (6,000)
Trainer: Muharem Bajrami 29.11.1985
[01.10.2020] Ümit Karan (TUR) 01.10.1976
[05.01.2021] Hasan Özer (TUR) 01.10.1974
[16.04.2021] Goce Sedloski 10.04.1974

Goalkeepers:	DOB	M	(s)	G
Artan Iljazi	24.02.1999	6		
Kristijan Naumovski	17.09.1988	27		
Defenders:	**DOB**	**M**	**(s)**	**G**
Bianor das Graças Lima da Silva (BRA)	28.06.1994	28	(1)	3
Filip Gligorov	31.07.1993	23	(5)	1
Darko Glisić	23.09.1991	12	(2)	
Ardit Iljazi	16.06.2000	13	(4)	
Fatih Ismaili	29.08.1997	1	(5)	
Besart Krivanjeva	28.02.1996	32		
Abdul Rwatubyaye (RWA)	23.10.1996	13		1
Faustin Senghor (SEN)	02.01.1994	9	(4)	
Elvin Yunuszada (AZE)	22.08.1992	2		
Midfielders:	**DOB**	**M**	**(s)**	**G**
Ali Adem	01.06.2000	7	(3)	1
Ramin Alii	18.05.2001	5	(1)	
Freddy Antonio Álvarez Rodríguez (CRC)	26.04.1995	29	(3)	2
Sabit Bilalli	15.08.1997	16	(15)	
Lamine Diack (SEN)	15.11.2000	27	(3)	4
Salim Farsak (TUR)	10.06.1998		(4)	
Firat Güllü (TUR)	18.03.2001		(4)	
Besar Iseni	18.01.1997	25	(7)	2
Forwards:	**DOB**	**M**	**(s)**	**G**
Rejjan Abazi	21.07.2002		(3)	
Ilirid Ademi	04.03.1995	20	(11)	4
Mamadouba Bangoura (GUI)	20.03.2000		(7)	
Jakup Berisha	20.02.2000	8	(17)	1
Matej Cvetanoski	18.08.1997	11	(3)	2
Dembo Darboe (GAM)	17.08.1998	18		16
Oumar Goudiaby (SEN)	01.01.1995	8	(8)	
Fatjon Jusufi	17.12.1995	3	(13)	2
Reginaldo Artur Faife (MOZ)	14.06.1990	12	(2)	2
Kristijan Trapanovski	14.08.1999	8	(5)	

Fudbalski klub Sileks Kratovo

Founded: 1965
Stadium: Stadion Sileks, Kratovo (4,800)
Trainer: Goran Simov (SRB) 31.03.1975

Goalkeepers:	DOB	M	(s)	G
Daniel Božinovski	08.07.1989	22		
Goran Trajkovski	20.05.1997	11	(1)	
Defenders:	**DOB**	**M**	**(s)**	**G**
Dejan Blagojević (SRB)	18.01.1990	9	(6)	
Kristijan Dodevski	27.07.2000	6	(9)	
Srdan Drasković (SRB)	08.01.1991	28		2
Hristijan Grozdanoski	05.06.1993	17		
Riste Karakamisev	16.06.1995	10	(2)	1
Daniel Karceski	07.03.1992	28	(1)	
Andrej Kirovski	11.02.1999	2	(1)	
Jordan Serafimovski	13.05.1991	5	(4)	
Darko Spirovski	20.07.2001		(1)	
Angelce Timovski	13.11.1994	28	(1)	
Midfielders:	**DOB**	**M**	**(s)**	**G**
Filip Duranski	17.07.1991	3	(5)	
David Manasievski	25.09.2001	12	(2)	2
Burhan Mustafov	02.03.1994	23	(8)	3
Denis Ristov (SRB)	24.06.1990	24	(5)	9
Viktor Serafimovski	24.10.1995	24	(4)	
Svilen Shterev (BUL)	14.12.1992	4	(6)	2
Bojan Spirkoski	22.04.1995		(5)	1
Miloš Žeravica (SRB)	22.07.1988	2	(8)	
Forwards:	**DOB**	**M**	**(s)**	**G**
Krsta Đorđević (SRB)	24.09.1993	1	(4)	
Stefan Đurić (SRB)	22.05.1995	8	(10)	3
Ivan Galevski	15.11.1996	6	(5)	2
Pepi Georgiev	04.10.1994	16	(5)	13
Ivan Ivanovski	27.06.1995	17	(4)	8
Filip Kostovski	23.10.2002	3	(10)	
Kristijan Kostovski	15.12.1995	7	(7)	1
Nenad Nesovski	27.06.1999	19	(9)	
Dejan Tanturovski	12.08.1992	28	(3)	3

Football Club Struga Trim-Lum

	Founded:	2015	
	Stadium:	Stadion Gradska Plaža, Struga (2,500)	
	Trainer:	Srgjan Zaharievski	12.09.1973

Goalkeepers:	DOB	M	(s)	G
Uroš Đurić (SRB)	01.12.1993	27		
Raif Mirseloski	29.11.1984	6		
Defenders:	**DOB**	**M**	**(s)**	**G**
Klisman Cake (ALB)	02.05.1999	31		4
Agon Hani	06.04.1998	1	(11)	
Besir Iseni	02.05.2000	5	(2)	
Jasmin Mecinović	22.10.1990	26	(4)	1
Filip Milenkovski	07.01.1990	15	(14)	3
Besir Ramadani (ALB)	09.06.2000	13		
Aleksandar Ristevski	11.05.1992	26		5
Blerton Sheji	21.10.2000	26	(6)	
Midfielders:	**DOB**	**M**	**(s)**	**G**
Malsor Ajeti (KVX)	27.04.2000	1	(2)	
Nemanja Bosančić (SRB)	01.03.1995	14	(1)	2

	DOB	M	(s)	G
Ard Kasami	03.01.1998	17		
Nijaz Lena	25.06.1986	13	(6)	6
Arlind Shabani (KVX)	16.10.2001	13	(10)	
Bunjamin Shabani	30.01.1991	27	(1)	
Ardit Saqiri	04.05.1985		(2)	
Flamur Tairi	24.11.1990	18	(11)	1
Arijeton Ziba	08.04.1988	2	(1)	
Forwards:	**DOB**	**M**	**(s)**	**G**
Marijan Altiparmakovski	18.07.1991	22	(7)	7
Dejan Cvetanoski	15.05.1990	8	(9)	2
Abdulhadi Jahja	03.06.1999	23	(6)	3
Atdhe Mazari (ALB)	02.06.2001		(7)	
Florent Osmani	28.05.1988	12	(6)	2
Pajazit Saliu	27.04.1994	9	(7)	
Emir Skenderi	01.04.2000	8	(14)	1

Fudbalski Klub Vardar Skopje

	Founded:	22.07.1947	
	Stadium:	Nacionalna Arena "Toše Proeski", Skopje (36,460)	
	Trainer:	Aleksandar Vasoski	21.11.1979
	[01.02.2021]	Nikola Ilievski	16.12.1954

Goalkeepers:	DOB	M	(s)	G
Aleksandar Igeski	12.05.1992	1		
Filip Ilikj	26.01.1997	31		
Luka Stojkovski	09.06.2003	1		
Defenders:	**DOB**	**M**	**(s)**	**G**
Charleston Silva dos Santos (BRA)	23.09.1996	8		
Gregori Davkov	18.03.2003		(4)	
Aleksandar Gjurkovski	11.02.2002	17	(2)	
Dario Jovanovski	15.01.2003	1	(2)	
Viktor Krstevski	04.04.2002	20	(1)	1
Marko Martinaga (CRO)	27.05.1998	8	(5)	
Ivan Micevski	16.07.2002	4	(3)	
Filip Najdovski	13.09.1992	1		
Stefan Naumceski	07.08.2000	3		
Anatolij Petejchuk	22.10.2002	2	(9)	1
Jovan Popzlatanov	06.07.1996	16		2
Martin Radulovikj-Veličkovikj	07.02.2002	22	(3)	
David Velkovski	15.12.2000	12	(8)	
Viktor Velkoski	14.11.1995	33		

Midfielders:	DOB	M	(s)	G
Leo Andreski	27.03.2003		(1)	
Petar Davidoski	01.03.2003	6	(3)	
Petar Guguljanov	23.02.2002	6	(6)	
Abdulah Hasani	09.02.2003		(1)	
Stefan Lazarevikj	18.02.1997	29	(2)	1
Darko Micevski	12.04.1992	12	(3)	3
Martin Mircevski	11.02.1997	22	(5)	8
Bojan Najdenov	27.08.1991	25	(5)	
Eren Partalko	04.07.2002	1	(4)	
Milovan Petrovikj	23.01.1990	14		1
Fitor Redjepi	20.03.2000	7	(9)	
Andrej Stojčevski	26.05.2003	4	(1)	1
Forwards:	**DOB**	**M**	**(s)**	**G**
Dejan Blaževski	06.12.1985	13	(14)	2
Matej Cvetanoski	18.08.1997	14	(2)	6
Besart Gudjufi	29.05.2004		(2)	
Bojan Kolevski	20.06.2000	5	(2)	
Antonio Mirkov	12.03.2003		(6)	
Filip Petkovski	24.05.1990	22	(10)	5
Georg Stojanovski	12.01.2004	3	(12)	

SECOND LEVEL
Vtora Liga 2020/2021

2. MFL Istok (Group East)								
1. FK Bregalnica 2008 Štip (Promoted)	27	23	4	0	73	-	18	73
2. GFK Tikveš 1930 Kavadarci	27	18	7	2	59	-	23	61
(Promotion Play-offs)								
3. FK Kit-Go Pehčevo	27	12	6	9	41	-	33	42
4. FK Sloga 1934 Vinica	27	9	9	9	33	-	34	36
5. FK Kožuf Gevgelija	27	9	9	9	29	-	35	36
6. FK Sasa Makedonska Kamenica	27	9	8	10	35	-	32	35
7. GFK Osogovo Kočani	27	7	8	12	32	-	43	29
8. FK Pobeda AD Prilep	27	6	9	12	30	-	35	27
9. FK Plačkovica Radoviš (Relegated)	27	5	7	15	20	-	42	22
10. FK Rosoman 83 (Relegated)	27	2	3	22	26	-	83	9

2. MFL Zapad (Group West)								
1. FK Skopje (Promoted)	26	18	6	2	50	-	20	60
2. GFK Ohrid (Promotion Play-offs)	26	13	7	6	26	-	13	46
3. KF Veleshtë	26	13	7	6	32	-	23	46
4. KF Gostivari	26	12	7	7	33	-	30	43
5. KF Korabi Debar	26	10	6	10	28	-	27	36
6. FK Kadino	26	7	7	12	24	-	24	28
7. FK Teteks Tetovo	26	8	3	15	19	-	34	27
8. KF Vëllazërimi 77 Kičevo (Relegated)	26	7	6	13	26	-	34	27
9. KF Drita Bogovinë (Relegated)	26	4	9	13	28	-	41	21
10. KF Vardari Forinë* (Relegated)	18	3	4	11	15	-	35	10

*3 points deducted

INTERNATIONAL MATCHES
(16.07.2020 – 15.07.2021)

05.09.2020	Skopje	North Macedonia - Armenia	2-1(2-0)	(UNL)
08.09.2020	Tbilisi	Georgia - North Macedonia	1-1(1-1)	(UNL)
08.10.2020	Skopje	North Macedonia - Kosovo	2-1(2-1)	(ECQPO)
11.10.2020	Tallinn	Estonia - North Macedonia	3-3(1-1)	(UNL)
14.10.2020	Skopje	North Macedonia - Georgia	1-1(0-0)	(UNL)
12.11.2020	Tbilisi	Georgia - North Macedonia	0-1(0-0)	(ECQPO)
15.11.2020	Skopje	North Macedonia - Estonia	2-1(1-0)	(UNL)
18.11.2020	Nicosia	Armenia - North Macedonia	1-0(0-0)	(UNL)
25.03.2021	Bucureşti	Romania - North Macedonia	3-2(1-0)	(WCQ)
28.03.2021	Skopje	North Macedonia - Liechtenstein	5-0(1-0)	(WCQ)
31.03.2021	Duisburg	Germany - North Macedonia	1-2(0-1)	(WCQ)
01.06.2021	Skopje	North Macedonia - Slovenia	1-1(0-0)	(F)
04.06.2021	Skopje	North Macedonia - Kazakhstan	4-0(1-0)	(F)
13.06.2021	Bucureşti	Austria - North Macedonia	3-1(1-1)	(EC)
17.06.2021	Bucureşti	Ukraine - North Macedonia	2-1(2-0)	(EC)
21.06.2021	Amsterdam	North Macedonia - Netherlands	0-3(0-1)	(EC)

05.09.2020 NORTH MACEDONIA - ARMENIA 2-1(2-0) 2nd UEFA Nations League C, Group 2
Nacionalna Arena "Toše Proeski", Skopje; Referee: Irfan Peljto (Bosnia and Herzegovina); Attendance: 0
MKD: Damjan Šiškovski, Stefan Ristovski (Cap), Kire Ristevski (71.Stefan Spirovski), Visar Musliu, Darko Velkovski, Arijan Ademi, Boban Nikolov (75.Aleksandar Trajkovski), Enis Bardi, Eljif Elmas, Ilija Nestorovski (61.Goran Pandev), Ezgjan Alioski. Trainer: Igor Angelovski.
Goals: Ezgjan Alioski (5 penalty), Ilija Nestorovski (38 penalty).

08.09.2020 GEORGIA - NORTH MACEDONIA 1-1(1-1) 2nd UEFA Nations League C, Group 2
„Boris Paichadze" Dinamo Arena, Tbilisi; Referee: Peter Kjærsgaard-Andersen (Denmark); Attendance: 0
MKD: Damjan Šiškovski, Stefan Ristovski, Visar Musliu [*sent off 64*], Darko Velkovski, Arijan Ademi (59.Boban Nikolov), Stefan Spirovski, Enis Bardi, Eljif Elmas, Goran Pandev (Cap) (78.Egzon Bejtulai), Aleksandar Trajkovski (59.Ilija Nestorovski), Ezgjan Alioski. Trainer: Igor Angelovski.
Goal: Stefan Ristovski (33).

08.10.2020 NORTH MACEDONIA - KOSOVO 2-1(2-1) 16th EC. Qualifiers Play-offs, Semi-Finals
Nacionalna Arena "Toše Proeski", Skopje; Referee: Danny Desmond Makkelie (Netherlands); Attendance: 0
MKD: Stole Dimitrievski, Stefan Ristovski (88.Tihomir Kostadinov), Visar Musliu, Darko Velkovski, Egzon Bejtulai (51.Kire Ristevski), Arijan Ademi (80.Stefan Spirovski), Boban Nikolov, Enis Bardi, Goran Pandev (Cap) (80.Ivan Tričkovski), Ilija Nestorovski (88.Aleksandar Trajkovski), Ezgjan Alioski. Trainer: Igor Angelovski.
Goals: Benjamin Kololli (16 own goal), Darko Velkovski (33).

11.10.2020 ESTONIA - NORTH MACEDONIA 3-3(1-1) 2nd UEFA Nations League C, Group 2
A. Le Coq Arena, Tallinn; Referee: Mohammed Al Hakim (Sweden); Attendance: 908
MKD: Damjan Šiškovski, Stefan Ristovski, Kire Ristevski, Gjoko Zajkov, Stefan Spirovski, Ivan Tričkovski (Cap) (64.Ilija Nestorovski), Ferhan Hasani (46.Enis Bardi), Boban Nikolov (64.Goran Pandev), Aleksandar Trajkovski (79.Krste Velkoski), Tihomir Kostadinov (78.Vlatko Stojanovski), Ezgjan Alioski. Trainer: Igor Angelovski.
Goals: Märten Kuusk (3 own goal), Goran Pandev (80), Gjoko Zajkov (88).

14.10.2020 NORTH MACEDONIA - GEORGIA 1-1(0-0) 2nd UEFA Nations League C, Group 2
Nacionalna Arena "Toše Proeski", Skopje; Referee: Bartosz Frankowski (Poland); Attendance: 0
MKD: Stole Dimitrievski [*sent off 68*], Stefan Ristovski, Kire Ristevski (80.Vlatko Stojanovski), Gjoko Zajkov, Darko Velkovski, Ivan Tričkovski (80.Krste Velkoski), Boban Nikolov (88.Enur Totre), Goran Pandev (Cap), Ilija Nestorovski (71.Damjan Šiškovski), Ezgjan Alioski, Tihomir Kostadinov (89.Darko Micevski). Trainer: Igor Angelovski.
Goal: Ezgjan Alioski (90+3).

12.11.2020 GEORGIA - NORTH MACEDONIA 0-1(0-0) 16th EC. Qualifiers Play-offs, Finals
„Boris Paichadze" Dinamo Arena, Tbilisi; Referee: Anthony Taylor (England); Attendance: 0
MKD: Stole Dimitrievski, Stefan Ristovski (89.Gjoko Zajkov), Visar Musliu, Darko Velkovski, Egzon Bejtulai, Arijan Ademi (67.Stefan Spirovski), Boban Nikolov (84.Tihomir Kostadinov), Eljif Elmas, Goran Pandev (Cap), Ilija Nestorovski (89.Ivan Tričkovski), Ezgjan Alioski. Trainer: Igor Angelovski.
Goal: Goran Pandev (56).

15.11.2020 NORTH MACEDONIA - ESTONIA 2-1(1-0) 2nd UEFA Nations League C, Group 2
Nacionalna Arena "Toše Proeski", Skopje; Referee: Ionuţ Marius Avram (Romania); Attendance: 0
MKD: Damjan Šiškovski, Stefan Ristovski, Visar Musliu, Darko Velkovski, Egzon Bejtulai, Stefan Spirovski (59.Tihomir Kostadinov), Ivan Tričkovski (Cap), Boban Nikolov, Ilija Nestorovski (78.Ljupche Doriev), Aleksandar Trajkovski (59.Vlatko Stojanovski), Eljif Elmas (85.Gjoko Zajkov). Trainer: Igor Angelovski.
Goals: Ivan Tričkovski (29), Vlatko Stojanovski (68).

18.11.2020 ARMENIA - NORTH MACEDONIA 1-0(0-0) 2nd UEFA Nations League C, Group 2
Stádio GSP, Nicosia (Cyprus); Referee: Robert Adam Madden (Scotland); Attendance: 0
MKD: Damjan Šiškovski, Visar Musliu (70.Tome Kitanovski), Gjoko Zajkov, Darko Velkovski, Egzon Bejtulai, Stefan Ristovski (70.Ljupche Doriev), Ivan Tričkovski (Cap), Tihomir Kostadinov (62.Darko Micevski), Aleksandar Trajkovski, Vlatko Stojanovski (62.Ilija Nestorovski), Enur Totre (84.Duško Trajčevski). Trainer: Igor Angelovski.

25.03.2021 **ROMANIA - NORTH MACEDONIA** 3-2(1-0) 22nd FIFA WC. Qualifiers

Arena Naţională, Bucureşti; Referee: Fábio José Costa Veríssimo (Portugal); Attendance: 0
MKD: Stole Dimitrievski, Stefan Ristovski, Kire Ristevski (88.Agim Ibraimi), Visar Musliu, Egzon Bejtulai, Boban Nikolov (54.Arijan Ademi), Enis Bardi, Eljif Elmas, Goran Pandev (Cap) (78.Aleksandar Trajkovski), Ilija Nestorovski (54.Vlatko Stojanovski), Ezgjan Alioski. Trainer: Igor Angelovski.
Goals: Arijan Ademi (82), Aleksandar Trajkovski (83).

28.03.2021 **NORTH MACEDONIA - LIECHTENSTEIN** 5-0(1-0) 22nd FIFA WC. Qualifiers

Nacionalna Arena "Toše Proeski", Skopje; Referee: Mykola Balakin (Ukraine); Attendance: 0
MKD: Stole Dimitrievski, Stefan Ristovski (58.Egzon Bejtulai), Kire Ristevski, Visar Musliu, Stefan Spirovski, Enis Bardi (58.Boban Nikolov), Eljif Elmas, Goran Pandev (Cap) (58.Ilija Nestorovski), Ezgjan Alioski (66.Stefan Aškovski), Marjan Radeski, Aleksandar Trajkovski (66.Ferhan Hasani). Trainer: Igor Angelovski.
Goals: Enis Bardi (7), Aleksandar Trajkovski (51, 54), Eljif Elmas (62), Ilija Nestorovski (82 penalty).

31.03.2021 **GERMANY - NORTH MACEDONIA** 1-2(0-1) 22nd FIFA WC. Qualifiers

MSV-Arena, Duisburg; Referee: Sergei Karasev (Russia); Attendance: 0
MKD: Stole Dimitrievski, Stefan Ristovski, Visar Musliu, Darko Velkovski, Arijan Ademi, Boban Nikolov (59.Egzon Bejtulai), Enis Bardi, Eljif Elmas, Goran Pandev (Cap) (90.Vlatko Stojanovski), Aleksandar Trajkovski (72.Stefan Spirovski), Ezgjan Alioski (90.Kire Ristevski). Trainer: Igor Angelovski.
Goals: Goran Pandev (45+2), Eljif Elmas (85).

01.06.2021 **NORTH MACEDONIA - SLOVENIA** 1-1(0-0) Friendly International

Nacionalna Arena "Toše Proeski", Skopje; Referee: Besfort Kasumi (Kosovo); Attendance: 10,000
MKD: Stole Dimitrievski, Stefan Ristovski, Visar Musliu, Darko Velkovski, Egzon Bejtulai (70.Kire Ristevski), Arijan Ademi (82.Darko Churlinov), Boban Nikolov (58.Tihomir Kostadinov), Eljif Elmas (82.Ferhan Hasani), Aleksandar Trajkovski (58.Ivan Tričkovski), Goran Pandev (Cap) (70.Daniel Avramovski), Ezgjan Alioski. Trainer: Igor Angelovski.
Goal: Eljif Elmas (55).

04.06.2021 **NORTH MACEDONIA - KAZAKHSTAN** 4-0(1-0) Friendly International

Nacionalna Arena "Toše Proeski", Skopje; Referee: Milovan Milačić (Montenegro); Attendance: 3,094
MKD: Stole Dimitrievski, Stefan Ristovski (81.Egzon Bejtulai), Visar Musliu, Kire Ristevski, Stefan Spirovski, Boban Nikolov (81.Krste Velkoski), Tihomir Kostadinov (73.Darko Churlinov), Eljif Elmas (73.Aleksandar Trajkovski), Ivan Tričkovski (62.Milan Ristovski), Goran Pandev (Cap) (62.Daniel Avramovski), Ezgjan Alioski. Trainer: Igor Angelovski.
Goals: Ezgjan Alioski (35 penalty), Ivan Tričkovski (57), Milan Ristovski (74), Darko Churlinov (76).

13.06.2021 **AUSTRIA - NORTH MACEDONIA** 3-1(1-1) 16th EC. Group Stage.

Arena Naţională, Bucureşti (Romania); Referee: Andreas Ekberg (Sweden); Attendance: 9,082
MKD: Stole Dimitrievski, Stefan Ristovski, Visar Musliu (86.Milan Ristovski), Darko Velkovski, Arijan Ademi, Boban Nikolov (63.Egzon Bejtulai), Enis Bardi (82.Ivan Tričkovski), Eljif Elmas, Aleksandar Trajkovski (63.Tihomir Kostadinov), Goran Pandev (Cap), Ezgjan Alioski. Trainer: Igor Angelovski.
Goal: Goran Pandev (28).

17.06.2021 **UKRAINE - NORTH MACEDONIA** 2-1(2-0) 16th EC. Group Stage.

Arena Naţională, Bucureşti (Romania); Referee: Fernando Andrés Rapallini (Argentina); Attendance: 10,001
MKD: Stole Dimitrievski, Stefan Ristovski, Visar Musliu, Arijan Ademi (85.Kire Ristevski), Darko Velkovski (85.Ivan Tričkovski), Stefan Spirovski (46.Darko Churlinov), Ezgjan Alioski, Boban Nikolov (46.Aleksandar Trajkovski), Eljif Elmas, Goran Pandev (Cap), Enis Bardi (77.Daniel Avramovski). Trainer: Igor Angelovski.
Goal: Ezgjan Alioski (57).

21.06.2021 **NORTH MACEDONIA - NETHERLANDS** 0-3(0-1) 16th EC. Group Stage.

"Johan Cruyff" Arena, Amsterdam; Referee: István Kovács (Romania); Attendance: 15,227
MKD: Stole Dimitrievski, Stefan Ristovski, Visar Musliu, Darko Velkovski, Arijan Ademi (78.Boban Nikolov), Ezgjan Alioski, Enis Bardi (78.Vlatko Stojanovski), Eljif Elmas, Goran Pandev (Cap) (69.Tihomir Kostadinov), Ivan Tričkovski (56.Darko Churlinov), Aleksandar Trajkovski (68.Ferhan Hasani). Trainer: Igor Angelovski.

NATIONAL TEAM PLAYERS
(16.07.2020 – 15.07.2021)

Name	DOB	Caps	Goals	2020/2021:	Club
Goalkeepers					
Stole DIMITRIEVSKI	25.12.1993	45	0	2020/2021:	*Rayo Vallecano de Madrid (ESP)*
Damjan ŠIŠKOVSKI	18.03.1995	6	0	2020:	*Doxa Katokopias FC (CYP)*
Defenders					
Stefan AŠKOVSKI	24.02.1992	4	0	2021:	*FC Botoşani (ROU)*
Egzon BEJTULAI	07.01.1994	22	0	2020/2021:	*KF Shkëndija Tetovo*
Tome KITANOVSKI	21.05.1992	2	0	2020:	*FK Makedonija Gjorče Petrov Skopje*
Visar MUSLIU	13.11.1994	34	1	2020/2021:	*Fehérvár FC Székesfehérvár (HUN)*
Kire RISTEVSKI	22.10.1990	48	0	2020/2021:	*Újpest FC (HUN)*
Stefan RISTOVSKI	12.02.1992	68	2	2020: 02.02.2021->	*Sporting Clube de Portugal Lisboa (POR)* *GNK Dinamo Zagreb (CRO)*
Darko VELKOVSKI	21.06.1995	31	1	2020/2021:	*HNK Rijeka (CRO)*
Gjoko ZAJKOV	10.02.1995	17	1	2020:	*SC Charleroi (BEL)*
Midfielders					
Arijan ADEMI	29.05.1991	24	4	2020/2021:	*GNK Dinamo Zagreb (CRO)*
Ezgjan ALIOSKI	12.02.1992	47	9	2020/2021:	*Leeds United FC (ENG)*
Daniel AVRAMOVSKI	20.02.1995	7	0	2020/2021:	*Kayserispor Kulübü (TUR)*
Enis BARDI	02.07.1995	37	6	2020/2021:	*Levante UD Valencia (ESP)*
Darko CHURLINOV	11.07.2000	5	1	2021:	*VfB Stuttgart (GER)*
Ljupche DORIEV	13.09.1995	3	0	2020:	*KF Shkëndija Tetovo*
Eljif ELMAS	27.09.1999	30	7	2020/2021:	*SSC Napoli (ITA)*
Ferhan HASANI	18.06.1990	42	2	2020: 26.01.2021->	*HJK Helsinki (FIN)* *FK Partizani Tiranë (ALB)*
Agim IBRAIMI	29.08.1988	40	7	2021:	*FK Kukësi (ALB)*
Tihomir KOSTADINOV	04.03.1996	12	0	2020/2021:	*MFK Ružomberok (SVK)*
Darko MICEVSKI	12.04.1992	2	0	2020:	*FK Vardar Skopje*
Boban NIKOLOV	28.07.1994	37	2	2020: 19.01.2021->	*Fehérvár FC Székesfehérvár (HUN)* *US Lecce (ITA)*
Marjan RADESKI	10.02.1995	17	1	2021:	*Fudbalska Akademija Pandev Strumica*
Stefan SPIROVSKI	23.08.1990	41	1	2020/2021:	*AEK Larnaca FC (CYP)*
Enur TOTRE	29.10.1996	2	0	2020:	*KF Shkëndija Tetovo*
Duško TRAJČEVSKI	01.11.1990	6	0	2020:	*Doxa Katokopias FC (CYP)*
Forwards					
Ilija NESTOROVSKI	12.03.1990	46	10	2020/2021:	*Udinese Calcio (ITA)*
Goran PANDEV	27.07.1983	122	38	2020/2021:	*Genoa C&FC (ITA)*
Milan RISTOVSKI	08.04.1998	2	1	2021:	*FC Spartak Trnava (SVK)*
Vlatko STOJANOVSKI	23.04.1997	9	2	2020/2021:	*FC Chambly Oise (FRA)*
Aleksandar TRAJKOVSKI	05.09.1992	68	18	2020/2021:	*RCD Mallorca (ESP)*
Ivan TRIČKOVSKI	18.04.1987	67	7	2020/2021:	*AEK Larnaca FC (CYP)*
Krste VELKOSKI	20.02.1988	15	0	2020/2021:	*FK Sarajevo (BIH)*

Trainer

Igor ANGELOVSKI [16.10.2015 – 31.07.2021]	02.06.1976	53 M; 23 W; 11 D; 19 L; 83-65	

NORTHERN IRELAND

The Country:
Tuaisceart Éireann (Northern Ireland)
Capital: Belfast
Surface: 14,130 km²
Inhabitants: 1,900,000 [2019]
Time: UTC

The FA:
Irish Football Association
National Football Stadium Donegal Avenue BT12 6LW, Belfast
Tel: +44 28 9066 9458
Foundation date: 1880
Member of FIFA since: 1911
Member of UEFA since: 1954
Website: www.irishfa.com

NATIONAL TEAM RECORDS

RECORDS
First international match:	18.02.1882, Belfast:	Ireland – England 0-13
Most international caps:	Steven Davis	- 126 caps (since 2005)
Most international goals:	David Jonathan Healy	- 36 goals / 95 caps (2000-2013)

UEFA EUROPEAN CHAMPIONSHIP		FIFA WORLD CUP		OLYMPIC TOURNAMENTS	
1960	Did not enter	1930	Did not enter	1908	-
1964	Qualifiers	1934	Did not enter	1912	-
1968	Qualifiers	1938	Did not enter	1920	-
1972	Qualifiers	1950	Qualifiers	1924	-
1976	Qualifiers	1954	Qualifiers	1928	-
1980	Qualifiers	1958	Final Tournament (Quarter-Finals)	1936	-
1984	Qualifiers	1962	Qualifiers	1948	-
1988	Qualifiers	1966	Qualifiers	1952	-
1992	Qualifiers	1970	Qualifiers	1956	-
1996	Qualifiers	1974	Qualifiers	1960	-
2000	Qualifiers	1978	Qualifiers	1964	-
2004	Qualifiers	1982	Final Tournament (2nd Round)	1968	-
2008	Qualifiers	1986	Final Tournament (Group Stage)	1972	-
2012	Qualifiers	1990	Qualifiers	1976	-
2016	Final Tournament (2nd Round of 16)	1994	Qualifiers	1980	-
2020	Qualifiers	1998	Qualifiers	1984	-
		2002	Qualifiers	1988	-
		2006	Qualifiers	1992	-
		2010	Qualifiers	1996	-
		2014	Qualifiers	2000	-
		2018	Qualifiers	2004	-
				2008	-
				2012	-
				2016	-

UEFA NATIONS LEAGUE
2018/2019	League B
2020/2021	League B (relegation to League C)

FIFA CONFEDERATIONS CUP 1992-2017
None

NORTHERN IRISH CLUB HONOURS IN EUROPEAN CLUB COMPETITIONS:

European Champion Clubs.Cup (1956-1992) / UEFA Champions League (1993-2021)
None

Fairs Cup (1858-1971) / UEFA Cup (1972-2009) / UEFA Europa League (2010-2021)
None

UEFA Super Cup (1972-2020)
None

*European Cup Winners.Cup 1961-1999**
None

*defunct competition

NATIONAL COMPETITIONS
TABLE OF HONOURS

	CHAMPIONS	CUP WINNERS	BEST GOALSCORERS	
1880/1881	-	Moyola Park AFC	-	
1881/1882	-	Queen's Island FC Belfast	-	
1882/1883	-	Cliftonville FAC	-	
1883/1884	-	Distillery FC Ballyskeagh	-	
1884/1885	-	Distillery FC Ballyskeagh	-	
1885/1886	-	Distillery FC Ballyskeagh	-	
1886/1887	-	Ulster FC Ballynafeigh	-	
1887/1888	-	Cliftonville FAC	-	
1888/1889	-	Distillery FC Ballyskeagh	-	
1889/1890	-	Gordon Highlanders	-	
1890/1891	Linfield FC Belfast	Linfield FC Belfast	Robert Hill (Linfield FC Belfast)	20
1891/1892	Linfield FC Belfast	Linfield FC Belfast	Tim Morrison (Linfield FC Belfast)	21
1892/1893	Linfield FC Belfast	Linfield FC Belfast	Robert Hill (Linfield FC Belfast) James Percy (Cliftonville FAC)	9
1893/1894	Glentoran FC Belfast	Distillery FC Ballyskeagh	Michael McErlean (Linfield FC Belfast)	9
1894/1895	Linfield FC Belfast	Linfield FC Belfast	George Gaukrodger (Linfield FC Belfast) Joe McAllen (Linfield FC Belfast)	4
1895/1896	Distillery FC Ballyskeagh	Distillery FC Ballyskeagh	-	
1896/1897	Glentoran FC Belfast	Cliftonville FAC	Johnny Darling (Linfield FC Belfast) Richard Peden (Linfield FC Belfast)	6
1897/1898	Linfield FC Belfast	Linfield FC Belfast	-	
1898/1899	Distillery FC Ballyskeagh	Linfield FC Belfast	-	
1899/1900	Belfast Celtic FC	Cliftonville FAC	-	
1900/1901	Distillery FC Ballyskeagh	Cliftonville FAC	-	
1901/1902	Linfield FC Belfast	Linfield FC Belfast	-	
1902/1903	Distillery FC Ballyskeagh	Distillery FC Ballyskeagh	-	
1903/1904	Linfield FC Belfast	Linfield FC Belfast	-	
1904/1905	Glentoran FC Belfast	Distillery FC Ballyskeagh	-	
1905/1906	Cliftonville FAC Distillery FC Ballyskeagh (shared)	Shelbourne FC Dublin	-	
1906/1907	Linfield FC Belfast	Cliftonville FAC	-	
1907/1908	Linfield FC Belfast	Bohemians FC Dublin	-	
1908/1909	Linfield FC Belfast	Cliftonville FAC	-	
1909/1910	Cliftonville FAC	Distillery FC Ballyskeagh	-	
1910/1911	Linfield FC Belfast	Shelbourne FC Dublin	-	
1911/1912	Glentoran FC Belfast	Linfield FC Belfast	-	
1912/1913	Glentoran FC Belfast	Linfield FC Belfast	-	
1913/1914	Linfield FC Belfast	Glentoran FC Belfast	-	
1914/1915	Belfast Celtic FC	Linfield FC Belfast	-	
1915/1916	*No competition*	Linfield FC Belfast	-	
1916/1917	*No competition*	Glentoran FC Belfast	-	
1917/1918	*No competition*	Belfast Celtic FC	-	
1918/1919	*No competition*	Linfield FC Belfast	-	
1919/1920	Belfast Celtic FC	Shelbourne FC Dublin	-	
1920/1921	Glentoran FC Belfast	Glentoran FC Belfast	-	
1921/1922	Linfield FC Belfast	Linfield FC Belfast	-	
1922/1923	Linfield FC Belfast	Linfield FC Belfast	-	
1923/1924	Queen's Island FC Belfast	Queen's Island FC Belfast	-	
1924/1925	Glentoran FC Belfast	Distillery FC Ballyskeagh	-	
1925/1926	Belfast Celtic FC	Belfast Celtic FC	-	
1926/1927	Belfast Celtic FC	Ards FC Newtownards	Joseph Gardiner Absolom Bambrick (Glentoran FC Belfast)	28
1927/1928	Belfast Celtic FC	Willowfield FC	-	
1928/1929	Belfast Celtic FC	Ballymena FC	Joseph Gardiner Absolom Bambrick (Linfield FC Belfast)	43
1929/1930	Linfield FC Belfast	Linfield FC Belfast	Joseph Gardiner Absolom Bambrick (Linfield FC Belfast)	50
1930/1931	Glentoran FC Belfast	Linfield FC Belfast	Fred Roberts (Glentoran FC Belfast)	55
1931/1932	Linfield FC Belfast	Glentoran FC Belfast	-	
1932/1933	Belfast Celtic FC	Glentoran FC Belfast	Joseph Gardiner Absolom Bambrick (Linfield FC Belfast)	40
1933/1934	Linfield FC Belfast	Linfield FC Belfast	-	
1934/1935	Linfield FC Belfast	Glentoran FC Belfast	-	
1935/1936	Belfast Celtic FC	Linfield FC Belfast	-	
1936/1937	Belfast Celtic FC	Belfast Celtic FC	-	
1937/1938	Belfast Celtic FC	Belfast Celtic FC	-	
1938/1939	Belfast Celtic FC	Linfield FC Belfast	-	
1939/1940	Belfast Celtic FC	Ballymena United FC	-	
1940/1941	*No competition*	Belfast Celtic FC	-	
1941/1942	*No competition*	Linfield FC Belfast	-	
1942/1943	*No competition*	Belfast Celtic FC	-	

1943/1944	*No competition*	Belfast Celtic FC	-
1944/1945	*No competition*	Linfield FC Belfast	-
1945/1946	*No competition*	Linfield FC Belfast	-
1946/1947	*No competition*	Belfast Celtic FC	-
1947/1948	Belfast Celtic FC	Linfield FC Belfast	James Jones (Belfast Celtic FC)	28
1948/1949	Linfield FC Belfast	Derry City FC	William Simpson (Linfield FC Belfast)	19
1949/1950	Linfield FC Belfast	Linfield FC Belfast	Sammy Hughes (Glentoran FC Belfast)	23
1950/1951	Glentoran FC Belfast	Glentoran FC Belfast	Sammy Hughes (Glentoran FC Belfast) Walter Allen (Portadown FC)	23
1951/1952	Glenavon FC Lurgan	Ards FC Newtownards	James Jones (Glenavon FC Lurgan)	27
1952/1953	Glentoran FC Belfast	Linfield FC Belfast	Sammy Hughes (Glentoran FC Belfast)	28
1953/1954	Linfield FC Belfast	Derry City FC	James Jones (Glenavon FC Lurgan)	32
1954/1955	Linfield FC Belfast	Dundela FC Belfast	Francis Coyle (Coleraine FC)	20
1955/1956	Linfield FC Belfast	Distillery FC Ballyskeagh	James Jones (Glenavon FC Lurgan)	26
1956/1957	Glenavon FC Lurgan	Glenavon FC Lurgan	James Jones (Glenavon FC Lurgan)	33
1957/1958	Ards FC Newtownards	Ballymena United FC	John Edward Thompson Milburn (Linfield FC Belfast)	29
1958/1959	Linfield FC Belfast	Glenavon FC Lurgan	John Edward Thompson Milburn (Linfield FC Belfast)	26
1959/1960	Glenavon FC Lurgan	Linfield FC Belfast	James Jones (Glenavon FC Lurgan)	29
1960/1961	Linfield FC Belfast	Glenavon FC Lurgan	Trevor Thompson (Glentoran FC Belfast)	22
1961/1962	Linfield FC Belfast	Linfield FC Belfast	Mick Lynch (Ards FC Newtownards)	20
1962/1963	Distillery FC Ballyskeagh	Linfield FC Belfast	Joe Meldrum (Distillery FC Ballyskeagh)	27
1963/1964	Glentoran FC Belfast	Derry City FC	Trevor Thompson (Linfield FC Belfast)	21
1964/1965	Derry City FC	Coleraine FC	Kenny Halliday (Coleraine FC) Dennis Guy (Glenavon FC Lurgan)	19
1965/1966	Linfield FC Belfast	Glentoran FC Belfast	Sammy Pavis (Linfield FC Belfast)	28
1966/1967	Glentoran FC Belfast	Crusaders FC Belfast	Sammy Pavis (Linfield FC Belfast)	25
1967/1968	Glentoran FC Belfast	Crusaders FC Belfast	Sammy Pavis (Linfield FC Belfast)	30
1968/1969	Linfield FC Belfast	Ards FC Newtownards	Danny Hale (Derry City FC)	21
1969/1970	Glentoran FC Belfast	Linfield FC Belfast	Des Dickson (Coleraine FC)	21
1970/1971	Linfield FC Belfast	Distillery FC Ballyskeagh	Bryan Hamilton (Linfield FC Belfast)	18
1971/1972	Glentoran FC Belfast	Coleraine FC	Peter Watson (Distillery FC Ballyskeagh) Des Dickson (Coleraine FC)	15
1972/1973	Crusaders FC Belfast	Glentoran FC Belfast	Des Dickson (Coleraine FC)	23
1973/1974	Coleraine FC	Ards FC Newtownards	Des Dickson (Coleraine FC)	24
1974/1975	Linfield FC Belfast	Coleraine FC	Martin Malone (Portadown FC)	15
1975/1976	Crusaders FC Belfast	Carrick Rangers FC	Des Dickson (Coleraine FC)	23
1976/1977	Glentoran FC Belfast	Coleraine FC	Ronnie McAteer (Crusaders FC Belfast)	20
1977/1978	Linfield FC Belfast	Linfield FC Belfast	Warren Feeney (Glentoran FC Belfast)	17
1978/1979	Linfield FC Belfast	Cliftonville FAC	Tommy Armstrong (Ards FC Newtownards)	21
1979/1980	Linfield FC Belfast	Linfield FC Belfast	James Martin (Glentoran FC Belfast)	17
1980/1981	Glentoran FC Belfast	Ballymena United FC	Des Dickson (Coleraine FC) Paul Malone (Ballymena United FC)	18
1981/1982	Linfield FC Belfast	Linfield FC Belfast	Gary Blackledge (Glentoran FC Belfast)	18
1982/1983	Linfield FC Belfast	Glentoran FC Belfast	James Campbell (Ards FC Newtownards)	15
1983/1984	Linfield FC Belfast	Ballymena United FC	Martin McGaughey (Linfield FC Belfast) Trevor Anderson (Linfield FC Belfast)	15
1984/1985	Linfield FC Belfast	Glentoran FC Belfast	Martin McGaughey (Linfield FC Belfast)	34
1985/1986	Linfield FC Belfast	Glentoran FC Belfast	Trevor Anderson (Linfield FC Belfast)	14
1986/1987	Linfield FC Belfast	Glentoran FC Belfast	Ray McCoy (Coleraine FC) Gary Macartney (Glentoran FC Belfast)	14
1987/1988	Glentoran FC Belfast	Glentoran FC Belfast	Martin McGaughey (Linfield FC Belfast)	18
1988/1989	Linfield FC Belfast	Ballymena United FC	Stephen Baxter (Linfield FC Belfast)	17
1989/1990	Portadown FC	Glentoran FC Belfast	Martin McGaughey (Linfield FC Belfast)	19
1990/1991	Portadown FC	Portadown FC	Stephen Derek McBride (Glenavon FC Lurgan)	22
1991/1992	Glentoran FC Belfast	Glenavon FC Lurgan	Harry McCourt (Omagh Town FAC) Stephen Derek McBride (Glenavon FC Lurgan)	18
1992/1993	Linfield FC Belfast	Bangor FC	Steve Cowan (Portadown FC)	23
1993/1994	Linfield FC Belfast	Linfield FC Belfast	Darren Erskine (Ards FC Newtownards) Stephen Derek McBride (Glenavon FC Lurgan)	22
1994/1995	Crusaders FC Belfast	Linfield FC Belfast	Glenn Ferguson (Glenavon FC Lurgan)	27
1995/1996	Portadown FC	Glentoran FC Belfast	Garry Andrew Haylock (Portadown FC)	19
1996/1997	Crusaders FC Belfast	Glenavon FC Lurgan	Garry Andrew Haylock (Portadown FC)	16
1997/1998	Cliftonville FAC	Glentoran FC Belfast	Vincent Thomas Arkins (Portadown FC)	22
1998/1999	Glentoran FC Belfast	Portadown FC	Vincent Thomas Arkins (Portadown FC)	19
1999/2000	Linfield FC Belfast	Glentoran FC Belfast	Vincent Thomas Arkins (Portadown FC)	29
2000/2001	Linfield FC Belfast	Glentoran FC Belfast	David James Larmour (Linfield FC Belfast)	17
2001/2002	Portadown FC	Linfield FC Belfast	Vincent Thomas Arkins (Portadown FC)	30
2002/2003	Glentoran FC Belfast	Coleraine FC	Vincent Thomas Arkins (Portadown FC)	29
2003/2004	Linfield FC Belfast	Glentoran FC Belfast	Glenn Ferguson (Linfield FC Belfast)	25
2004/2005	Glentoran FC Belfast	Portadown FC	Christopher Morgan (Glentoran FC Belfast)	19
2005/2006	Linfield FC Belfast	Linfield FC Belfast	Peter Thompson (Linfield FC Belfast)	25
2006/2007	Linfield FC Belfast	Linfield FC Belfast	Gary Hamilton (Glentoran FC Belfast)	27
2007/2008	Linfield FC Belfast	Linfield FC Belfast	Peter Thompson (Linfield FC Belfast)	29
2008/2009	Glentoran FC Belfast	Crusaders FC Belfast	Curtis Allen (Lisburn Distillery FC Ballyskeagh)	19
2009/2010	Linfield FC Belfast	Linfield FC Belfast	Rory Christopher Patterson (Coleraine FC)	30
2010/2011	Linfield FC Belfast	Linfield FC Belfast	Peter Thompson (Linfield FC Belfast)	23

2011/2012	Linfield FC Belfast	Linfield FC Belfast	Gary Kyle McCutcheon (Ballymena United FC)	27
2012/2013	Cliftonville FAC	Glentoran FC Belfast	Liam Boyce (Cliftonville FAC)	29
2013/2014	Cliftonville FAC	Glenavon FC Lurgan	Joseph Anthony Gormley (Cliftonville FAC)	27
2014/2015	Crusaders FC Belfast	Glentoran FC Belfast	Joseph Anthony Gormley (Cliftonville FAC)	31
2015/2016	Crusaders FC Belfast	Glenavon FC Lurgan	Paul Heatley (Crusaders FC Belfast) Andrew Waterworth (Linfield FC Belfast)	22
2016/2017	Linfield FC Belfast	Linfield FC Belfast	Andrew Mitchell (Dungannon Swifts)	25
2017/2018	Crusaders FC Belfast	Coleraine FC	Joseph Anthony Gormley (Cliftonville FAC)	22
2018/2019	Linfield FC Belfast	Crusaders FC Belfast	Joseph Anthony Gormley (Cliftonville FAC)	20
2019/2020	Linfield FC Belfast	Glentoran FC Belfast	Joseph Anthony Gormley (Cliftonville FAC)	18
2020/2021	Linfield FC Belfast	Linfield FC Belfast	Shayne Francis Lavery (Linfield FC Belfast)	23

NATIONAL CHAMPIONSHIP
NIFL Premiership 2020/2021
(16.10.2020 – 29.05.2021)

Regular Season - Results

Round 1 [16-17.10.2020]
Coleraine FC - Ballymena United 0-1(0-1)
Cliftonville FAC - Glentoran FC 1-0(0-0)
Larne FC - Dungannon Swifts 3-0(2-0)
Linfield FC - Carrick Rangers 5-1(2-1)
Warrenpoint Town - Crusaders FC 0-1(0-1)
Glenavon FC - Portadown FC 2-4(0-2)

Round 2 [23-24.10.2020]
Crusaders FC - Cliftonville FAC 1-0(0-0)
Carrick Rangers - Larne FC 1-2(0-1)
Dungannon Swifts - Warrenpoint T. 0-2(0-0)
Glentoran FC - Glenavon FC 1-1(0-0)
Portadown FC - Coleraine FC 0-3(0-1)
Ballymena United - Linfield FC 2-3(1-2)

Round 3 [30-31.10.2020]
Linfield FC - Crusaders FC 2-1(1-0)
Cliftonville FAC - Carrick Rangers 3-0(0-0)
Coleraine FC - Glentoran FC 2-1(2-0)
Glenavon FC - Dungannon Swifts 0-0
Larne FC - Ballymena United 2-0(0-0)
Warrenpoint Town - Portadown FC 1-1(0-1)

Round 4 [07.11.2020]
Ballymena United - Crusaders FC 1-4(1-0)
Carrick Rangers - Dungannon Swifts 0-0
Cliftonville FAC - Warrenpoint T. 3-0(1-0)
Glenavon FC - Coleraine FC 4-4(2-3)
Portadown FC - Linfield FC 1-2(0-1)
Glentoran FC - Larne FC 0-0

Round 5 [10.11.2020]
Ballymena United - Glenavon FC 0-2(0-1)
Carrick Rangers - Portadown FC 4-1(2-1)
Crusaders FC - Coleraine FC 1-0(0-0)
Dungannon Swifts - Cliftonville FAC 2-1(1-0)
Warrenpoint Town - Larne FC 1-1(0-0)
Linfield FC - Glentoran FC 3-3(1-0) [24.11.]

Round 6 [14.11.2020]
Coleraine FC - Linfield FC 0-2(0-1)
Larne FC - Crusaders FC 2-1(0-0)
Cliftonville - Ballymena 0-4(0-1) [24.11.20]
Dungannon - Portadown 0-3(0-1) [08.12.20]
Glentoran FC - Warrenpoint T. 0-0 [15.12.20]
Glenavon FC - Carrick R. 1-1(1-0) [16.02.21]

Round 7 [21.11.2020]
Ballymena United - Warrenpoint T. 2-0(2-0)
Crusaders FC - Dungannon Swifts 3-1(1-1)
Larne FC - Cliftonville FAC 1-0(0-0)
Linfield FC - Glenavon FC 2-0(1-0)
Portadown - Glentoran 1-3(0-2) [16.02.2021]
Carrick R. - Coleraine 0-2(0-0) [23.02.2021]

Round 8 [28.11.2020]
Cliftonville FAC - Portadown FC 5-0(2-0)
Coleraine FC - Larne FC 0-2(0-2)
Glenavon FC - Crusaders FC 3-1(0-1)
Glentoran FC - Dungannon Swifts 5-1(4-1)
Warrenpoint Town - Linfield FC 2-1(1-1)
Ballymena Unit. - Carrick R. 2-0(1-0) [01.12.]

Round 9 [04-05.12.2020]
Dungannon Swifts - Coleraine FC 2-0(1-0)
Carrick Rangers - Warrenpoint Town 1-3(0-2)
Crusaders FC - Glentoran FC 2-0(0-0)
Larne FC - Glenavon FC 2-1(0-1)
Portadown FC - Ballymena United 0-0
Linfield FC - Cliftonville FAC 2-0(0-0)

Round 10 [11-14.12.2020]
Larne FC - Linfield FC 3-1(0-1)
Coleraine FC - Warrenpoint Town 2-1(1-0)
Crusaders FC - Portadown FC 5-0(3-0)
Dungannon Swifts - Ballymena Unit. 1-5(1-0)
Glentoran FC - Carrick Rangers 6-0(3-0)
Glenavon FC - Cliftonville FAC 1-1(0-0)

Round 11 [19.12.2020]
Ballymena United - Glentoran FC 1-1(0-0)
Linfield FC - Dungannon Swifts 4-0(0-0)
Warrenpoint Town - Glenavon FC 1-2(1-1)
Cliftonville FAC - Coleraine FC 0-2(0-0)
Carrick R. - Crusaders FC 1-3(1-1) [09.03.21]
Portadown FC - Larne FC 2-1(1-0) [20.04.21]

Round 12
Cliftonville - Crusaders 2-2(1-1) [09.01.21]
Ballymena - Coleraine FC 0-1(0-0) [16.02.21]
Warrenpoint - Dungannon 1-1(0-0) [16.02.21]
Linfield - Glentoran FC 0-1(0-0) [23.02.21]
Portadown - Glenavon FC 1-2(0-1) [09.03.21]
Carrick R. - Larne FC 1-3(1-2) [16.03.21]

Round 13 [06.02.2021]
Coleraine FC - Portadown FC 1-1(0-0)
Dungannon Swifts - Carrick Rangers 0-2(0-1)
Glenavon FC - Ballymena United 2-1(2-0)
Glentoran FC - Cliftonville FAC 1-0(0-0)
Larne FC - Warrenpoint Town 1-1(1-0)
Crusaders FC - Linfield FC 1-2(0-0)

Round 14 [02.01.2021]
Coleraine FC - Carrick Rangers 3-0(0-0)
Crusaders FC - Warrenpoint Town 4-0(1-0)
Dungannon Swifts - Cliftonville FAC 1-2(1-0)
Glenavon FC - Linfield FC 1-2(1-0)
Larne FC - Ballymena United 0-1(0-0)
Glentoran FC - Portadown FC 2-1(2-0)

Round 15 [20.02.2021]
Carrick Rangers - Glenavon FC 3-4(1-2)
Cliftonville FAC - Larne FC 1-0(1-0)
Crusaders FC - Ballymena United 2-1(1-1)
Linfield FC - Coleraine FC 0-0
Warrenpoint - Glentoran FC 1-2(0-0) [23.03.]
Portadown - Dungannon Sw. 1-0(0-0) [13.04.]

Round 16 [23.01.2021]
Crusaders FC - Larne FC 3-3(1-2)
Coleraine FC - Dungannon Swifts 2-0(1-0)
Linfield FC - Warrenpoint Town 6-0(0-0)
Cliftonville - Ballymena Un. 2-1(1-1) [23.02.]
Glenavon FC - Glentoran FC 2-1(0-1) [16.03.]
Carrick Rangers - Portadown 5-3(3-2) [23.03.]

Round 17 [26.01.2021]
Cliftonville FAC - Linfield FC 4-3(1-1)
Glentoran FC - Carrick Rangers 2-0(1-0)
Larne FC - Coleraine FC 1-2(0-2)
Portadown FC - Crusaders FC 2-2(1-1)
Dungannon Sw. - Glenavon 1-2(0-2) [23.02.]
Warrenpoint - Ballymena U. 1-1(1-1) [16.03.]

Round 18 [29-30.01.2021]
Larne FC - Glentoran FC 1-1(1-0)
Cliftonville FAC - Glenavon FC 1-1(0-0)
Coleraine FC - Crusaders FC 2-1(1-1)
Portadown FC - Warrenpoint Town 0-2(0-0)
Carrick Rangers - Ballymena United 0-2(0-1)
Linfield FC - Dungannon S. 2-0(1-0) [16.03.]

Round 19 [02.02.2021]
Glenavon FC - Larne FC 1-4(1-1)
Ballymena Unit. - Dungannon Swifts 0-1(0-0)
Coleraine FC - Cliftonville FAC 2-2(2-1)
Crusaders FC - Glentoran FC 1-0(1-0)
Linfield FC - Portadown FC 3-0(2-0)
Warrenpoint T. - Carrick Rangers 0-0 [13.04.]

Round 20 [09.02.2021]
Carrick Rangers - Linfield FC 1-1(0-1)
Cliftonville FAC - Warrenpoint T. 3-0(1-0)
Larne FC - Portadown FC 2-2(2-1)
Glentoran - Ballymena U. 0-2(0-1) [09.03.]
Dungannon Sw. - Crusaders 2-1(1-0) [23.03.]
Glenavon FC - Coleraine FC 1-1(0-0) [23.03.]

Round 21 [13.02.2021]
Crusaders FC - Carrick Rangers 1-3(0-1)
Portadown FC - Cliftonville FAC 1-1(0-0)
Larne FC - Dungannon Swifts 3-0(1-0)
Ballymena U. - Linfield FC 2-1(0-0) [23.03.]
Glentoran FC - Coleraine FC 2-2(1-1) [13.04.]
Warrenpoint - Glenavon FC 3-4(1-4) [20.04.]

Round 22 [26-27.02.2021]
Linfield FC - Larne FC 2-1(1-0)
Carrick Rangers - Cliftonville FAC 0-1(0-1)
Coleraine FC - Warrenpoint Town 2-1(2-1)
Crusaders FC - Glenavon FC 0-1(0-0)
Portadown FC - Ballymena United 1-2(1-1)
Dungannon Swifts - Glentoran FC 0-1(0-1)

Round 23 [02.03.2021]
Glentoran FC - Linfield FC 3-1(2-1)
Ballymena United - Cliftonville FAC 1-1(0-0)
Coleraine FC - Portadown FC 2-0(1-0)
Glenavon FC - Carrick Rangers 1-1(0-1)
Larne FC - Crusaders FC 0-3(0-0)
Warrenpoint T. - Dungannon Swifts 4-1(2-1)

Round 24 [05-06.03.2021]
Carrick Rangers - Glentoran FC 0-5(0-5)
Crusaders FC - Warrenpoint Town 0-2(0-2)
Dungannon Swifts - Coleraine FC 2-3(1-1)
Linfield FC - Cliftonville FAC 2-0(0-0)
Portadown FC - Glenavon FC 4-1(2-0)
Ballymena United - Larne FC 1-1(1-0)

Round 25 [19-20.03.2021]
Crusaders FC - Linfield FC 1-2(1-0)
Coleraine FC - Carrick Rangers 1-0(0-0)
Dungannon Swifts - Portadown FC 0-1(0-1)
Glentoran FC - Glenavon FC 3-1(2-1)
Larne FC - Cliftonville FAC 0-0
Warrenpoint T. - Ballymena United 2-2(1-0)

Round 26 [27.03.2021]
Ballymena Unit. - Dungannon Swifts 5-1(4-0)
Carrick Rangers - Warrenpoint Town 1-1(1-0)
Cliftonville FAC - Coleraine FC 2-1(1-0)
Glenavon FC - Larne FC 2-2(1-2)
Glentoran FC - Crusaders FC 1-0(0-0)
Portadown FC - Linfield FC 0-1(0-1)

Round 27 [30.03.2021]
Linfield FC - Warrenpoint T. 5-0(3-0) [09.03.]
Coleraine FC - Larne FC 2-0(1-0)
Ballymena United - Carrick Rangers 2-0(1-0)
Dungannon Swifts - Glenavon FC 0-4(0-3)
Portadown FC - Crusaders FC 1-2(0-0)
Cliftonville - Glentoran FC 0-2(0-0) [20.04.]

Round 28 [02-03.04.2021]
Ballymena United - Crusaders FC 0-1(0-0)
Coleraine FC - Glenavon FC 0-0
Glentoran FC - Portadown FC 4-0(1-0)
Larne FC - Carrick Rangers 3-0(3-0)
Warrenpoint Town - Cliftonville 0-5(0-3)
Dungannon Swifts - Linfield FC 0-2(0-1)

Round 29 [06-07.04.2021]
Ballymena United - Glentoran FC 2-2(0-1)
Carrick Rangers - Crusaders FC 1-1(0-1)
Cliftonville FAC - Dungannon Swifts 3-0(1-0)
Glenavon FC - Warrenpoint Town 1-0(1-0)
Portadown FC - Larne FC 1-2(1-1)
Linfield FC - Coleraine FC 2-1(2-0)

Round 30 [10.04.2021]
Crusaders FC - Cliftonville FAC 2-2(1-0)
Glenavon FC - Ballymena United 3-2(2-0)
Glentoran FC - Dungannon Swifts 2-0(2-0)
Larne FC - Linfield FC 1-1(1-0)
Portadown FC - Carrick Rangers 2-0(1-0)
Warrenpoint Town - Coleraine FC 1-2(0-0)

Round 31 [12-13.03.2021]
Coleraine FC - Crusaders FC 2-0(1-0)
Ballymena United - Portadown FC 2-1(1-1)
Cliftonville FAC - Glenavon FC 2-1(2-0)
Dungannon Swifts - Larne FC 0-2(0-1)
Linfield FC - Carrick Rangers 7-0(4-0)
Warrenpoint Town - Glentoran FC 0-2(0-0)

Round 32 [16-17.04.2021]
Coleraine FC - Glentoran FC 1-1(0-1)
Carrick Rangers - Dungannon Swifts 1-1(0-1)
Crusaders FC - Glenavon FC 6-1(2-1)
Larne FC - Warrenpoint Town 5-0(2-0)
Linfield FC - Ballymena United 2-1(1-1)
Portadown FC - Cliftonville FAC 1-2(1-2)

Round 33 [23-24.04.2021]
Glentoran FC - Larne FC 3-2(1-2)
Ballymena United - Coleraine FC 1-2(0-1)
Cliftonville FAC - Carrick Rangers 5-0(4-0)
Dungannon Swifts - Crusaders FC 0-2(0-1)
Warrenpoint Town - Portadown FC 1-3(1-1)
Glenavon FC - Linfield FC 3-2(2-1)

Final Standings

1.	Linfield FC Belfast	33	22	4	7	76 - 34	70
2.	Glentoran FC Belfast	33	18	9	6	61 - 29	63
3.	Coleraine FC	33	18	8	7	50 - 32	62
4.	Cliftonville FAC	33	16	8	9	55 - 35	56
5.	Larne FC	33	15	10	8	56 - 35	55
6.	Crusaders FC Belfast	33	16	5	12	59 - 40	53
7.	Glenavon FC Lurgan	33	14	10	9	56 - 57	52
8.	Ballymena United FC	33	13	7	13	50 - 40	46
9.	Portadown FC	33	8	6	19	40 - 65	30
10.	Warrenpoint Town FC	33	6	9	18	32 - 65	27
11.	Carrick Rangers FC	33	4	8	21	28 - 77	20
12.	Dungannon Swifts FC	33	4	4	25	18 - 72	16

Teams ranked 1-6 were qualified for the Championship Round, while teams ranked 7-12 were qualified for the Relegation Round.

Relegation Round

Results

Round 34 [30.04.-01.05.2021]
Dungannon Swifts - Carrick Rangers 0-2(0-2)
Ballymena United - Glenavon FC 3-1(0-0)
Portadown FC - Warrenpoint Town 1-2(1-1)

Round 35 [04.05.2021]
Carrick Rangers - Ballymena United 0-4(0-1)
Dungannon Swifts - Warrenpoint T. 0-1(0-0)
Glenavon FC - Portadown FC 4-1(1-1)

Round 36 [14-15.05.2021]
Glenavon FC - Warrenpoint Town 4-0(2-0)
Dungannon Swifts - Ballymena Unit. 1-3(0-1)
Portadown FC - Carrick Rangers 2-1(1-0)

Round 37 [25.05.2021]
Ballymena United - Warrenpoint T. 3-0(2-0)
Carrick Rangers - Glenavon FC 3-6(1-0)
Portadown FC - Dungannon Swifts 4-2(1-0)

Round 38 [29.05.2021]
Ballymena United - Portadown FC 4-2(2-2)
Glenavon FC - Dungannon Swifts 1-1(1-1)
Warrenpoint Town - Carrick Rangers 3-1(2-1)

Championship Round

Results

Round 34 [01.05.2021]
Coleraine FC - Cliftonville FAC 2-0(1-0)
Glentoran FC - Linfield FC 0-0
Crusaders FC - Larne FC 1-3(1-0)

Round 35 [04.05.2021]
Cliftonville FAC - Larne FC 1-2(0-1)
Glentoran FC - Coleraine FC 1-1(0-0)
Linfield FC - Crusaders FC 3-1(1-0)

Round 36 [15.05.2021]
Crusaders FC - Coleraine FC 0-1(0-0)
Glentoran FC - Cliftonville FAC 0-2(0-0)
Linfield FC - Larne FC 1-2(0-0)

Round 37 [25.05.2021]
Larne FC - Glentoran FC 0-1(0-0)
Cliftonville FAC - Crusaders FC 1-1(1-0)
Coleraine FC - Linfield FC 1-1(1-1)

Round 38 [29.05.2021]
Cliftonville FAC - Linfield FC 0-2(0-1)
Glentoran FC - Crusaders FC 2-0(0-0)
Larne FC - Coleraine FC 1-2(1-0)

Final Standings

					Total				**Home**					**Away**			
1.	**Linfield FC Belfast**	38	24	6	8	83 - 38	78	15	2	2	53 - 12	9	4	6	30 - 26
2.	Coleraine FC	38	21	10	7	57 - 35	73	11	5	3	27 - 14	10	5	4	30 - 21
3.	Glentoran FC Belfast	38	20	11	7	65 - 32	71	12	6	2	38 - 14	8	5	5	27 - 18
4.	Larne FC	38	18	10	10	64 - 41	64	9	5	5	31 - 17	9	5	5	33 - 24
5.	Cliftonville FAC	38	17	9	12	59 - 42	60	12	3	5	39 - 22	5	6	7	20 - 20
6.	Crusaders FC Belfast	38	16	6	16	62 - 50	54	9	2	7	34 - 22	7	4	9	28 - 28
7.	Glenavon FC Lurgan	38	17	11	10	72 - 65	62	8	8	3	37 - 29	9	3	7	35 - 36
8.	Ballymena United FC	38	18	7	13	67 - 44	61	9	4	7	34 - 25	9	3	6	33 - 19
9.	Portadown FC	38	10	6	22	50 - 78	36	6	3	11	26 - 31	4	3	11	24 - 47
10.	Warrenpoint Town FC	38	9	9	20	38 - 74	36	3	6	8	22 - 30	6	3	12	16 - 44
11.	Carrick Rangers FC	38	5	8	25	35 - 92	23	2	5	11	23 - 43	3	3	14	12 - 49
12.	Dungannon Swifts FC	38	4	5	29	22 - 83	17	3	0	16	12 - 39	1	5	13	10 - 44

No teams were relegated.

Top goalscorers:

23	**Shayne Francis Lavery**	*Linfield FC Belfast*
18	Seamus Vincent McCartan	*Ballymena United FC*
17	Jay Donnelly	*Glentoran FC Belfast*
15	Andrew Waterworth	*Linfield FC Belfast*

UEFA Europa Conference League Play-offs

Semi-Finals [01.06.2021]	Larne FC - Glenavon FC Lurgan	2-1(1-1)
	Cliftonville FAC - Crusaders FC Belfast	0-0 aet; 5-4 on penalties
Final [05.06.2021]	**Larne FC** - Cliftonville FAC	3-1(1-0)

NATIONAL CUP
Irish Cup 2020/2021

Fifth Round [27.04./01.05.2021]

Ards FC - Dollingstown FC	*not played*	Cliftonville FAC - Portstewart FC	5-1
Glentoran FC Belfast - Dundela FC	*not played*	Coleraine FC - Crusaders FC Belfast	0-1
Harland & Wolff Welders FC - St. James' Swifts	*not played*	Glenavon FC Lurgan - Dungannon Swifts FC	1-2
Institute FC Derry - Police Service of N. Ireland FC	*not played*	Linfield FC Belfast - Annagh United FC	2-0
Larne FC - Newry City AFC	*not played*	Warrenpoint Town FC - Ballyclare Comrades FC	2-1
Queen's University AFC Belfast - Bangor FC	*not played*	Knockbreda FC Belfast - Newington FC	2-1
Ballymena United FC - Portadown FC	4-1	Ballinamallard United FC - Dergview FC	2-2 aet; 8-9 pen
Carrick Rangers FC - Belfast Celtic FC	3-0	Loughgall FC - Banbridge Town FC	1-1 aet; 3-2 pen

1/8-Finals [08.05.2021]

Ballymena Unit. FC - Police Service of N. Ireland FC	5-0	Larne FC - Dollingstown FC	8-1
Carrick Rangers FC - Bangor FC	2-2 aet; 3-1 pen	Linfield FC Belfast - Dungannon Swifts FC	5-2
Dergview FC - St. James' Swifts	2-0	Loughgall FC - Warrenpoint Town FC	1-0
Knockbreda FC Belfast - Crusaders FC Belfast	0-5	Glentoran FC Belfast - Cliftonville FAC	1-0

Quarter-Finals [11.05.2021]

Ballymena United FC - Dergview FC	5-0	Loughgall FC - Linfield FC Belfast	1-3
Larne FC - Carrick Rangers FC	2-1	Glentoran FC Belfast - Crusaders FC Belfast	0-1

Semi-Finals [18.05.2021]

Larne FC - Crusaders FC Belfast	1-1 aet; 6-5 pen	Ballymena United FC - Linfield FC Belfast	0-3

Final

21.05.2021; Mournevuew Park, Lurgan; Referee: Andrew Davey; Attendance: 1,000

Linfield FC Belfast – Larne FC   **2-1(2-0)**

Linfield FC: Christopher Johns, Mark Haughey, Jimmy Callacher, Matthew Clarke, Niall Quinn, Jamie Mulgrew, Conor Pepper, Cammy Palmer, Joel Cooper, Kirk Millar, Shayne Francis Lavery (74.Christy Manzinga). Trainer: David Jonathan Healy.

Larne FC: Conor Mitchell, Albert Watson, Joshua Robinson, Tomas Cosgrove, Dean Jarvis, John Herron, Fuad Sule, Martin Donnelly (46.David McDaid), Lee Lynch (53.Mark Randall), Jeff Hughes, Ronan Hale (67.Jonathan McMurray). Trainer: Tiernan Lynch.

Goals: 1-0 Shayne Francis Lavery (5), 2-0 Joel Cooper (32), 2-1 Jeff Hughes (90+2).

Please note: appearances and goals are including statistics of both regular season and play-offs (Championship and Relegation Round).

Ballymena United Football Club

Founded: 07.04.1928
Stadium: The Showgrounds, Ballymena (3,600)
Trainer: David Jeffrey   28.10.1962

Goalkeepers:	DOB	M	(s)	G
Ross Glendinning	18.05.1993	14		
Dylan Graham	31.10.2004	3		
Jordan Williamson	23.05.1995	21		
Defenders:	**DOB**	**M**	**(s)**	**G**
Jonathan Addis	27.09.1992	18	(3)	1
Kofi Balmer	19.09.2000	16		4
Jim Ervin	05.06.1985	19	(1)	
Sean Graham	20.11.2000	11	(5)	
Trai Hume	18.03.2002	34		5
Anthony Kane (IRL)	29.08.1987	9	(6)	2
Conor Keeley	12.12.1997	16	(1)	4
Ciaran Kelly (IRL)	04.07.1998	12		1
Steven McCullough	30.08.1994	2		
Ross Redman	23.11.1989	36	(2)	3

Midfielders:	DOB	M	(s)	G
Spencer Beatti	16.01.2002		(2)	
Ryan Harpur (IRL)	01.12.1988	5	(9)	1
Joshua Kelly	08.03.1999	33	(2)	2
James Knowles	06.04.1993	4	(4)	
Andy McGrory	15.12.1991	8	(3)	
Owen McKeown	07.06.1997	7	(5)	
Leroy Millar	01.09.1995	17	(1)	4
Jude Winchester	13.04.1993	15	(5)	2
Ben Wylie	29.06.2002	13	(4)	
Forwards:	**DOB**	**M**	**(s)**	**G**
Cathair Friel	25.05.1993	3		1
Kenneth Kane	13.08.1999		(5)	
Seamus Vincent McCartan	18.05.1994	34	(2)	18
Joe McCready	24.07.1990	10	(11)	3
Paul McElroy	07.07.1994	35	(3)	12
Ryan Waide	12.02.2000	23	(11)	1

Carrick Rangers Football Club

Founded: 1939
Stadium: Loughshore Hotel Arena, Carrickfergus (2,500)
Trainer: Niall Currie   12.09.1972
[17.05.2021] Scott Irvine   01.10.1984

Goalkeepers:	DOB	M	(s)	G
Aaron Hogg	14.01.1988	37		
Geoff McKinty	29.02.1996	1		
Defenders:	**DOB**	**M**	**(s)**	**G**
Lee Chapman	09.11.1994	34	(1)	2
Lee Colligan	11.02.1989	1		
James Ferrin	23.09.1989	3		
Kurtis Forsythe	28.09.2002	8	(8)	
Reece Glendinning	09.06.1995	12	(10)	
Caolan Loughran	09.01.1995	27	(3)	10
Matthew Mulholland	04.03.2001	1		
Reece Neale	14.05.1998	22	(4)	
Chris Ramsey	24.05.1990	19	(1)	
Chris Rodgers	03.01.1991	28	(2)	
Mark Surgenor	19.12.1985	14		1
Midfielders:	**DOB**	**M**	**(s)**	**G**
Lloyd Anderson	09.03.1998	30	(6)	3
Kyle Cherry	13.05.1993	25	(4)	2

	DOB	M	(s)	G
Jordan Gibson	23.06.1995	32	(5)	2
Steven Gordon	27.07.1993	16	(3)	
Ronan Kalla	08.03.2003		(2)	
Daniel Kelly	06.01.1993	30		4
Ross McGimpsey	28.09.2001		(1)	
Liam McKenna	02.04.1999		(3)	
Corey McMullan	03.05.1996	4	(8)	1
Gerard Storey	05.02.2002	2	(11)	
Forwards:	**DOB**	**M**	**(s)**	**G**
David Fearon	09.08.1996		(4)	
Jonathan Frazer	30.05.1996	9	(3)	2
Cathair Friel	25.05.1993	18	(1)	4
Alex Gawne	22.05.2001	4	(3)	1
Jordan Jenkins	28.02.2000	11	(9)	
Josh McGreevy	19.05.2001	1		
Jack Millar	04.11.2000	1	(4)	
Michael Smith	01.07.1992	27	(6)	3
Joseph Tully	23.05.1998	1	(5)	

Cliftonville Football & Athletic Club

Founded: 1879
Stadium: Solitude Stadium, Belfast (2,530)
Trainer: Paddy McLaughlin   10.10.1979

Goalkeepers:	DOB	M	(s)	G
Declan Breen	24.09.2002		(1)	
Richard Brush (ENG)	26.11.1984	12		
Declan Dunne	31.03.2000	2	(1)	
Aaron McCarey (IRL)	14.01.1992	24		
Defenders:	**DOB**	**M**	**(s)**	**G**
Garry Breen (IRL)	17.03.1989	24	(1)	2
Aaron Donnelly	22.03.2000	33	(1)	1
Seanan Foster	29.01.1997	6	(7)	
Jamie Harney	04.03.1996	20	(2)	1
Levi Ives	28.07.1997	4		
Conor McDermott	18.09.1997	13		
Stephen McGuinness	17.07.2003	1	(1)	
Ryan O'Reilly (IRL)	07.07.1995	26	(1)	1
Midfielders:	**DOB**	**M**	**(s)**	**G**
Liam Bagnall	17.05.1992	32		
Odhran Casey	09.04.2002	1	(4)	

	DOB	M	(s)	G
Barry Coffey (IRL)	27.03.2001	9	(6)	2
Chris Curran	05.01.1991	31	(3)	2
Ronan Doherty	10.01.1996	19	(10)	1
Rory Hale (IRL)	27.11.1996	25	(1)	4
Daniel Kearns (IRL)	26.08.1991	9	(5)	
Kris Lowe	06.01.1996	22	(2)	
Mark McKee	01.12.1998	1		
Daire O'Connor (IRL)	15.04.1997	15	(20)	5
Forwards:	**DOB**	**M**	**(s)**	**G**
Ryan Curran	13.10.1993	33	(4)	14
Joe Gormley	26.11.1989	8	(5)	2
Thomas Maguire	09.09.1999	5	(5)	2
Michael McCrudden	31.07.1991	18	(8)	14
Conor McMenamin	24.08.1995	13	(2)	3
Lee O'Brien	07.05.2001		(1)	
Paul O'Neill	07.01.2000	12	(6)	4
Eoin Teggart	06.02.2002		(2)	

Coleraine Football Club

Founded: 1927
Stadium: The Showgrounds, Coleraine (3,500)
Trainer: Oran Kearney   29.07.1978

Goalkeepers:	DOB	M	(s)	G
Gareth Deane	14.06.1994	27		
Martin Gallagher	26.10.1990	11	(1)	
Defenders:	**DOB**	**M**	**(s)**	**G**
Howard Beverland	30.03.1990	2	(1)	
Aaron Canning	07.03.1992	25	(1)	1
Steven Douglas	27.09.1977	3	(2)	
Lyndon Kane	15.02.1997	36		1
Gareth McConaghie	05.04.1988	16	(1)	
Adam Mullan	24.10.1995	2	(1)	
Stephen O'Donnell	01.09.1992	29		3
Aaron Traynor	24.07.1990	22		2
Midfielders:	**DOB**	**M**	**(s)**	**G**
Ben Doherty	24.03.1997	24	(3)	14
Jamie Glackin	16.02.1995	33	(3)	2
Aaron Jarvis	10.05.1997	16	(5)	2
Stephen Lowry	14.10.1986	37	(1)	5
Ian Parkhill	07.04.1990	12	(13)	
Evan Tweed (IRL)	01.03.1999	17	(3)	
Ronan Wilson	01.09.1998	5	(9)	
Forwards:	**DOB**	**M**	**(s)**	**G**
Curtis Allen	22.02.1988	17	(10)	9
Eoin Bradley	31.12.1983	14	(13)	2
Caiolan Brennan	23.11.2001		(1)	
Josh Carson	03.06.1993	31	(3)	
James McLaughlin	06.03.1990	13	(12)	8
Stewart Nixon	08.05.1997	15	(10)	4
Matthew Shevlin	07.12.1998	11	(8)	4

Crusaders Football Club Belfast

Founded: 1898
Stadium: Seaview Stadium, Belfast (3,383)
Trainer: Stephen Baxter   01.10.1965

Goalkeepers:	DOB	M	(s)	G
Gerard Doherty (IRL)	24.08.1981	7		
Sean O'Neill	11.04.1988	16		
Neil Shields	17.01.1997	2		
Jonny Tuffey	20.01.1987	13		
Defenders:	**DOB**	**M**	**(s)**	**G**
Brandon Bradshaw	01.12.2003	2		
Rodney Brown	13.08.1995	16	(3)	
Billy Joe Burns	28.04.1989	25		
Chris Hegarty	13.08.1992	23	(2)	2
Daniel Larmour	03.09.1998	6	(2)	
Ben McKeown	10.04.2001	1		
Sam Morrow	09.10.2002		(1)	
Jarlath O'Rourke	13.02.1995	22	(1)	
Michael Ruddy	05.08.1993	11	(3)	1
Aidan Wilson (SCO)	02.01.1999	23	(2)	2
Midfielders:	**DOB**	**M**	**(s)**	**G**
Thomas Burns	29.11.2002	1	(2)	
Declan Caddell	13.04.1988	26	(8)	3
Andrew Clarke	12.12.2002	3	(1)	
Rory Hale (IRL)	27.11.1996	2	(2)	
Thomas Logan	12.08.2001	1		
Philip Lowry	15.07.1989	33		7
Reece McGinley	01.03.2000	2	(1)	
James Owens	24.08.2002	1		
Jack Patterson	16.10.2005	1	(2)	
Conor Rafferty	23.12.2002	1		
Gary Thompson	26.05.1990	13	(3)	
Joel Thompson	25.07.2005		(1)	
Robbie Weir	09.12.1988	13	(3)	
Forwards:	**DOB**	**M**	**(s)**	**G**
Lewis Barr	20.04.2003	1		
Jay Boyd	09.01.2003		(1)	
Ross Clarke	17.05.1993	16	(5)	5
David Cushley	22.07.1989	3	(11)	1
Jordan Forsythe	11.02.1991	33		3
Paul Heatley	30.06.1987	25	(3)	10
James Holland	20.11.2002	1		
Ben Kennedy	12.01.1997	14	(9)	5
Adam Lecky	03.05.1991	22	(10)	6
Jamie McGonigle	05.03.1996	24	(10)	10
Jordan Owens	09.07.1989	15	(16)	7

Dungannon Swifts Football Club

Founded: 1949
Stadium: Stangmore Park, Dungannon (2,000)
Trainer: Kris Lindsay   05.02.1984
[18.02.2021] Dixie Robinson   26.09.1963
[14.03.2021] Dean Shiels   01.02.1985

Goalkeepers:	DOB	M	(s)	G
Conner Byrne	27.03.2003	1	(1)	
Roy Carroll	30.09.1977	20		
Samuel Johnston	26.03.1996	17		
Defenders:	**DOB**	**M**	**(s)**	**G**
Callum Byers	28.07.1997	27	(1)	1
Caolin Coyle	23.04.2000	24	(2)	
Adam Glenny	30.05.2002	21	(2)	
Dylan King	27.08.1998	11		
Ethan McGee	23.08.2002	15	(4)	
Cahal McGinty	29.09.2000	7		1
Matthew Smyth	08.05.1998	21	(2)	
Midfielders:	**DOB**	**M**	**(s)**	**G**
Francis Brennan	11.08.1991	2		
Rhyss Campbell	30.11.1998	31	(3)	5
Shea Conway	30.09.2002	3		
Terry Devlin	06.11.2003	8	(3)	
Lorcan Forde	07.11.1999	10	(6)	
Ben Gallagher	30.03.2002	11	(10)	3
Kris Lowe	06.01.1996	11	(1)	
Ryan Mayse	07.12.1993	10	(10)	
Shane McGinty (IRL)	14.04.1994	16	(5)	
Corey McMullan	03.05.1996	3	(1)	
Dylan O'Kane	14.01.1998	6	(2)	
Mark Patton	08.07.1990	11	(6)	
Darren Robinson	29.12.2004		(1)	
Oisin Smyth	05.05.2000	31	(2)	2
Alan Teggart	24.11.1986	14	(3)	
Douglas Wilson	03.03.1994	14		4
Forwards:	**DOB**	**M**	**(s)**	**G**
Michael Carvill	03.04.1988	30	(3)	2
James Convie	01.07.2002	12	(11)	1
Nathaniel Ferris	03.12.1998		(1)	
Zach Ferson	02.08.2002	1	(1)	
Daniel Hughes	03.05.1992	7	(8)	
Caolan McAleer	19.08.1993	8	(4)	
Rory Patterson	16.07.1984	12	(7)	2
James Teelan	17.10.2002	3	(5)	

Glenavon Football Club Lurgan

Founded: 1889
Stadium: Mourneview Park, Lurgan (4,160)
Trainer: Gary Hamilton   06.10.1980

Goalkeepers:	DOB	M	(s)	G
Craig Hyland (IRL)	08.09.1990	27		
James Taylor	12.05.1984	2		
Jonny Tuffey	20.01.1987	9		
Defenders:	**DOB**	**M**	**(s)**	**G**
Calum Birney	19.04.1993	4		1
Colin Coates	26.10.1985	20		3
Calvin Douglas	19.09.1997	8	(4)	1
Andrew Doyle	28.10.1990	25	(3)	1
Aaron Harmon	05.11.1989	9	(5)	
Daniel Larmour	03.09.1998	8	(2)	
Lee McNulty	01.01.1995	5	(2)	
James Singleton	22.08.1995	35		2
Owen Taylor	03.10.2002		(1)	
Sean Ward	12.01.1984	34		1
Midfielders:	**DOB**	**M**	**(s)**	**G**
Conan Byrne (IRL)	10.07.1985	5	(11)	1
Sammy Clingan	13.01.1984	1	(1)	
Jamie Doran	11.02.2004		(1)	
Robert Garrett	05.05.1988	33		2
Andrew Hall	19.09.1989	13	(5)	8
Robbie Norton	16.04.1998	1	(6)	
Michael O'Connor	06.10.1987	16	(5)	6
Jack O'Mahony	26.01.2000	5	(11)	1
Matthew Snoddy	02.06.1993	27	(1)	
Forwards:	**DOB**	**M**	**(s)**	**G**
Peter Campbell	16.09.1997	32		6
Josh Doyle (IRL)	19.06.2002	2	(8)	
Matthew Fitzpatrick	02.09.1994	31	(4)	13
Gary Hamilton	06.10.1980		(1)	
Jordan Jenkins	28.02.2000	2	(4)	
Gareth McCaffrey (IRL)	26.01.1996	4	(13)	1
Conor McCloskey	29.01.1992	20	(3)	6
Gregory Moorhouse (IRL)	10.07.1994	8	(11)	3
Daniel Purkis	10.06.1995	32	(3)	13

Glentoran Football Club Belfast

Founded: 1882
Stadium: The Oval, Belfast (6,054)
Trainer: Michael McDermott   07.02.1974

Goalkeepers:	DOB	M	(s)	G
Rory Brown (IRL)	25.05.2000	17	(1)	
Dayle Coleing (GIB)	23.10.1996	20		
Elliott Morris	04.05.1981	1		
Defenders:	**DOB**	**M**	**(s)**	**G**
Robert Burns	07.10.1999	3		
Keith Cowan (IRL)	23.08.1985	3		
Joe Crowe	20.04.1998	5	(2)	
Marcus Kane	08.12.1991	32		1
Caolan Marron	04.07.1998	31		
Rhys Marshall	16.01.1995	26		2
James McCarthy	19.10.2000		(1)	
Patrick McClean	22.11.1996	34	(1)	2
Luke McCullough	15.02.1994	35		
Malachy Smith	08.04.2001	1	(1)	
Midfielders:	**DOB**	**M**	**(s)**	**G**
Gaël Bigirimana (BDI)	22.10.1993	24	(6)	
Seanan Clucas	08.11.1992	11	(6)	2
Chris Gallagher	30.03.1999	21	(5)	
Dale Gorman	28.06.1996	14	(10)	1
Ciarán O'Connor (IRL)	04.07.1996	8	(15)	1
Hrvoje Plum (CRO)	28.05.1994	16	(6)	2
Aaron Wightman	23.02.2004		(1)	
Forwards:	**DOB**	**M**	**(s)**	**G**
Ben Cushnie	07.08.2001	1		1
Jay Donnelly	10.04.1995	29	(4)	17
Rory Donnelly	18.02.1992	21	(8)	10
Robbie McDaid	23.10.1996	28	(2)	12
Jamie McDonagh	08.05.1996	5	(16)	1
Conor McMenamin	24.08.1995	14		6
Andrew Mitchell	25.01.1994	7	(8)	2
Paul O'Neill	07.01.2000	9	(4)	2
Cameron Stewart	11.03.1997	2	(6)	

Larne Football Club

Founded: 1889
Stadium: Inver Park, Larne (2,000)
Trainer: Tiernan Lynch   27.03.1980

Goalkeepers:	DOB	M	(s)	G
Conor Devlin	23.09.1991	32		
Conor Mitchell	09.05.1996	6	(1)	
Defenders:	**DOB**	**M**	**(s)**	**G**
Tomas Cosgrove	11.12.1992	37		2
Ryley D'Sena (AUS)	31.01.2003	1		
Max Greer	15.04.2004	1		
Dean Jarvis	01.06.1992	26	(2)	
Graham Kelly (IRL)	16.10.1997	16	(3)	1
Joshua Robinson	30.06.1993	31	(1)	5
Albert Watson	08.09.1985	34		1
Elliot Wood	08.02.2004		(1)	
Midfielders:	**DOB**	**M**	**(s)**	**G**
Harry Adair	22.01.2002		(1)	
Martin Donnelly	28.08.1988	25	(5)	6
John Herron (SCO)	01.02.1994	29	(3)	1
Jeff Hughes	29.05.1985	26	(4)	3
Lee Lynch (IRL)	27.11.1991	16	(9)	3
Andrew Mitchell	06.04.1992	6	(1)	2
Andy Mitchell (SCO)	21.04.1973	13	(4)	4
Dylan Mottley-Henry (ENG)	02.08.1997	6	(5)	2
Mark Randall (ENG)	28.09.1989	20	(7)	3
Andrew Scott	19.06.2000	1	(5)	
Dylan Sloan	15.04.2004		(1)	
Fuad Sule (IRL)	20.01.1997	27	(1)	
Luke Wade-Slater (IRL)	02.03.1998	7	(6)	
Forwards:	**DOB**	**M**	**(s)**	**G**
Ronan Hale (IRL)	08.09.1998	22	(9)	12
Matthew Lusty	14.07.2003	1		1
David McDaid	03.12.1990	25	(10)	12
Conor McKendry	21.10.1998	3	(10)	1
Jonathan McMurray	19.09.1994	7	(15)	4

Linfield Football Club Belfast

Founded: 1886
Stadium: Windsor Park, Belfast (18,614)
Trainer: David Jonathan Healy   05.08.1979

Goalkeepers:	DOB	M	(s)	G
Christopher Johns	13.05.1995	35		
David Walsh	05.07.2002	3		
Defenders:	**DOB**	**M**	**(s)**	**G**
Jimmy Callacher	11.06.1991	37		6
Matthew Clarke	03.03.1994	20	(4)	
Mark Haughey	23.01.1991	31	(4)	2
Ross Larkin	10.06.1999	9	(2)	
Ryan McGivern	08.01.1990		(4)	1
Michael Newberry	30.12.1997	6		1
Niall Quinn	02.08.1993	30	(2)	4
Mark Stafford	20.08.1987	12	(2)	1
Midfielders:	**DOB**	**M**	**(s)**	**G**
Joel Cooper	29.02.1996	18	(2)	3
Stephen Fallon	03.03.1997	15	(7)	2
Bastien Héry (FRA)	23.03.1992	1	(5)	
Daniel Kearns (IRL)	26.08.1991	1	(3)	
Kyle McClean	03.10.1998	20	(1)	
Kirk Millar	07.08.1992	35	(2)	6
Jamie Mulgrew	05.06.1986	27	(3)	1
Cammy Palmer	15.05.2000	12	(4)	1
Conor Pepper (IRL)	04.05.1994	17		
Jordan Stewart	31.03.1995	33	(3)	11
Forwards:	**DOB**	**M**	**(s)**	**G**
Brandon Doyle	20.08.1998		(1)	
Shayne Francis Lavery	08.12.1998	26	(5)	23
Christy Manzinga (FRA)	31.01.1995	2	(13)	2
Navid Nasseri (IRN)	26.07.1996	15	(11)	2
Matthew Shevlin	07.12.1998		(2)	
Andrew Waterworth	11.04.1986	13	(20)	15

Portadown Football Club

Founded: 1887
Stadium: Shamrock Park, Portadown (3,940)
Trainer: Matthew Tipton   29.06.1980

Goalkeepers:	DOB	M	(s)	G
Gareth Buchanan	11.10.1991	2		
Jacob Carney (ENG)	21.04.2001	26		
Scott Pengelly	31.10.2001	1		
Ben Pierce (ENG)	20.09.1998	9		
Defenders:	**DOB**	**M**	**(s)**	**G**
Christopher Crane	10.02.1999	3	(1)	
Paul Finnegan (IRL)	18.06.1996	34		
Greg Hall	11.09.1989	30	(2)	
Kevin Healy (IRL)	03.07.2000	10		
Reece Jordan	06.03.2005	1	(1)	
Nathan Kerr	20.01.1998	23	(3)	
Adam McCallum	18.07.1997	28	(2)	4
Barney McKeown	29.06.2001	17	(7)	1
Patrick McNally	20.08.1994	7		
Eamon Scannell	10.01.1999	10	(2)	
Tommy Smyth	31.07.2004		(1)	
Ben Tilney (ENG)	28.02.1997	23	(1)	3

Midfielders:	DOB	M	(s)	G
Zach Cowan	20.09.2005		(1)	
Ben Tyler Guy (ENG)	02.11.2000	18	(3)	3
Cónnall McGrandless	12.01.1994		(1)	
Stephen Teggart	19.01.1998	17	(8)	2
George Tipton	03.11.2002	19	(8)	
Sam Warde (IRL)	13.03.1998	18	(3)	3
Luke Wilson	15.02.2000	19		1
Forwards:	**DOB**	**M**	**(s)**	**G**
Lee Bonis	03.08.1999	32	(3)	14
Aaron Burns	29.05.1992	3	(1)	1
Oisin Conaty	17.02.2003	14	(12)	
Ruairi Croskery	20.12.1996	8	(7)	1
Samuel Glenfield	10.05.2005		(3)	
Chris Lavery	20.01.1991	15	(9)	3
Stephen Murray	29.12.1988	13	(9)	3
Adam Salley	07.02.1997	18	(10)	11

Warrenpoint Town Football Club

Founded: 1987
Stadium: Milltown Stadium, Warrenpoint (1,280)
Trainer: Barry Gray   11.04.1980

Goalkeepers:	DOB	M	(s)	G
Andrew Coleman	13.06.1985	18	(1)	
Gabriel Sava (ITA)	15.10.1986	20		
Defenders:	**DOB**	**M**	**(s)**	**G**
Steven Ball (IRL)	17.09.1997	35		
Daniel Byrne (IRL)	07.05.1993	19		2
Mark Carson	09.11.1992	1		
Kris Cowan	14.01.2002	1	(3)	
Colm Deasy (IRL)	04.01.1997	30	(3)	
Luke Gallagher (IRL)	29.07.1994	25	(3)	
Ben Mullen (IRL)	22.06.2001	8	(3)	
Gavin Peers (IRL)	10.11.1985	7		
Daniel Wallace	21.10.1994	31	(2)	
Midfielders:	**DOB**	**M**	**(s)**	**G**
Kealan Dillon (IRL)	21.02.1994	36	(2)	4

	DOB	M	(s)	G
Adam Evans (IRL)	03.05.1994	11	(3)	1
Stuart Hutchinson	10.05.1991	32	(1)	1
Francis McCaffrey	22.04.1993	29	(4)	4
Dermot McVeigh	24.07.1990	18	(7)	
Jake O'Connor (IRL)	28.10.1998	8	(7)	
Dylan Quinn (IRL)	07.05.2003		(2)	
Forwards:	**DOB**	**M**	**(s)**	**G**
Colm Carney (IRL)	30.07.1993		(2)	
Adam Carroll	02.09.2001	11	(15)	4
Brandon Doyle	20.08.1998	18	(6)	4
David Forsythe	09.04.2002		(1)	
Matthew Knox (SCO)	22.12.1999	6	(4)	1
Thomas Maguire	09.09.1999		(2)	1
Alan O'Sullivan (IRL)	24.03.1995	21	(10)	8
Ryan Swan (IRL)	13.05.1996	33	(4)	8

SECOND LEVEL
NIFL Championship 2020/2021

The season was cancelled due to COVID-19 pandemic.

NATIONAL TEAM

INTERNATIONAL MATCHES
(16.07.2020 – 15.07.2021)

04.09.2020	Bucureşti	Romania - Northern Ireland	1-1(1-0)	(UNL)
07.09.2020	Belfast	Northern Ireland - Norway	1-5(1-3)	(UNL)
08.10.2020	Sarajevo	Bosnia and Herzegovina - Northern Ireland	1-1(1-0,1-1,1-1); 3-4 on penalties	(ECQPO)
11.10.2020	Belfast	Northern Ireland - Austria	0-1(0-1)	(UNL)
14.10.2020	Oslo	Norway - Northern Ireland	1-0(0-0)	(UNL)
12.11.2020	Belfast	Northern Ireland - Slovakia	1-2(0-1,1-1)	(ECQPO)
15.11.2020	Wien	Austria - Northern Ireland	2-1(0-0)	(UNL)
18.11.2020	Belfast	Northern Ireland - Romania	1-1(0-0)	(UNL)
25.03.2021	Parma	Italy - Northern Ireland	2-0(2-0)	(WCQ)
28.03.2021	Belfast	Northern Ireland - United States	1-2(0-1)	(F)
31.03.2021	Belfast	Northern Ireland - Bulgaria	0-0	(WCQ)
30.05.2021	Klagenfurt	Malta - Northern Ireland	0-3(0-1)	(F)
03.06.2021	Dnipro	Ukraine - Northern Ireland	1-0(1-0)	(F)

04.09.2020 ROMANIA - NORTHERN IRELAND 1-1(1-0) 2nd UEFA Nations League B, Group 1
Arena Naţională, Bucureşti; Referee: François Letexier (France); Attendance: 0
NIR: Bailey Peacock-Farrell, Craig George Cathcart, Stuart Alan Dallas, Jamal Piaras Lewis, Daniel George Ballard (90+1.Michael Smith), Steven Davis (Cap), Patrick James Coleman McNair, Corry John Evans (76.Kyle Joseph George Lafferty), George Alan Saville, Joshua Brendan David Magennis [*sent off 39*], Conor James Washington (65.Gavin Whyte). Trainer: Ian Robert Baraclough (England).
Goal: Gavin Whyte (86).

07.09.2020 NORTHERN IRELAND - NORWAY 1-5(1-3) 2nd UEFA Nations League B, Group 1
Windsor Park, Belfast; Referee: Bartosz Frankowski (Poland); Attendance: 0
NIR: Bailey Peacock-Farrell, Craig George Cathcart, Michael Smith, Shane Kevin Ferguson, Stuart Alan Dallas, Daniel George Ballard (46.Liam Boyce), Steven Davis (Cap), Patrick James Coleman McNair, George Alan Saville (71.Corry John Evans), Jordan Andrew Thompson, Conor James Washington (77.Shayne Francis Lavery). Trainer: Ian Robert Baraclough (England).
Goal: Patrick James Coleman McNair (6).

08.10.2020 BOSNIA AND HERZEGOVINA - NORTHERN IRELAND 1-1 aet; 3-4 pen. 16th EC. Qualifiers Play-offs, Semi-Finals
Stadion Grbavica, Sarajevo; Referee: Antonio Miguel Mateu Lahoz (Spain); Attendance: 1,800
NIR: Bailey Peacock-Farrell, Jonathan Grant Evans, Craig George Cathcart, Stuart Alan Dallas, Jamal Piaras Lewis, Steven Davis (Cap), Niall McGinn (82.Jordan Lewis Jones; 120+1.Conor James Washington), Patrick James Coleman McNair (90+3.Jordan Andrew Thompson; 120+1.Liam Boyce), George Alan Saville, Corry John Evans (73.Gavin Whyte), Joshua Brendan David Magennis (90+3.Kyle Joseph George Lafferty). Trainer: Ian Robert Baraclough (England).
Goal: Niall McGinn (53).
Penalties: Stuart Alan Dallas, Kyle Joseph George Lafferty, George Alan Saville (missed), Conor James Washington, Liam Boyce.

11.10.2020 NORTHERN IRELAND - AUSTRIA 0-1(0-1) 2nd UEFA Nations League B, Group 1
Windsor Park, Belfast; Referee: Petr Ardeleánu (Czech Republic); Attendance: 600
NIR: Michael McGovern, Jonathan Grant Evans, Craig George Cathcart, Conor Gerard McLaughlin, Stuart Alan Dallas (73.Jordan Andrew Thompson), Jamal Piaras Lewis, Steven Davis (Cap) (73.Corry John Evans), Patrick James Coleman McNair (83.Joshua Brendan David Magennis), Kyle Joseph George Lafferty (61.Conor James Washington), Jordan Lewis Jones, Gavin Whyte (83.Liam Boyce). Trainer: Ian Robert Baraclough (England).

14.10.2020 NORWAY - NORTHERN IRELAND 1-0(0-0) 2nd UEFA Nations League B, Group 1
Ullevaal Stadion, Oslo; Referee: Kristo Tohver (Estonia); Attendance: 200
NIR: Trevor Carson, Jonathan Grant Evans (Cap) (46.Conor Gerard McLaughlin), Michael Smith (60.Stuart Alan Dallas), Shane Kevin Ferguson, Thomas Michael Flanagan, Daniel George Ballard, Corry John Evans, George Alan Saville (60.Patrick James Coleman McNair), Jordan Andrew Thompson (85.Steven Davis), Joshua Brendan David Magennis, Conor James Washington (75.Gavin Whyte). Trainer: Ian Robert Baraclough (England).

12.11.2020 NORTHERN IRELAND - SLOVAKIA 1-2(0-1,1-1) 16th EC. Qualifiers Play-offs, Finals
Windsor Park, Belfast; Referee: Dr. Felix Brych (Germany); Attendance: 1,060
NIR: Bailey Peacock-Farrell, Craig George Cathcart (99.Thomas Michael Flanagan), Stuart Alan Dallas, Jonathan Grant Evans, Steven Davis (Cap), Niall McGinn (77.Kyle Joseph George Lafferty), George Alan Saville (65.Jordan Andrew Thompson), Jamal Piaras Lewis, Conor James Washington (66.Gavin Whyte), Joshua Brendan David Magennis (77.Liam Boyce), Patrick James Coleman McNair (104.Shane Kevin Ferguson). Trainer: Ian Robert Baraclough (England).
Goal: Milan Škriniar (88 own goal).

15.11.2020 AUSTRIA - NORTHERN IRELAND 2-1(0-0) 2nd UEFA Nations League B, Group 1
"Ernst Happel Stadion", Wien; Referee: Maurizio Mariani (Italy); Attendance: 0
NIR: Michael McGovern, Michael Smith, Thomas Michael Flanagan, Shane Kevin Ferguson (36.Jamal Piaras Lewis), Conor Gerard McLaughlin, Stuart Alan Dallas (Cap), Daniel George Ballard (83.Craig George Cathcart), Patrick James Coleman McNair, Alistair Edward McCann (83.Steven Davis), Liam Boyce (62.Gavin Whyte), Conor James Washington (62.Joshua Brendan David Magennis). Trainer: Ian Robert Baraclough (England).
Goal: Joshua Brendan David Magennis (75).

18.11.2020 NORTHERN IRELAND - ROMANIA 1-1(0-0) 2nd UEFA Nations League B, Group 1
Windsor Park, Belfast; Referee: Sandro Schärer (Switzerland); Attendance: 1,060
NIR: Bailey Peacock-Farrell, Jonathan Grant Evans (Cap), Craig George Cathcart, Michael Smith (79.Ethan Stuart William Galbraith), Stuart Alan Dallas, Daniel George Ballard, Matthew Kennedy (66.Jamal Piaras Lewis), Patrick James Coleman McNair, Alistair Edward McCann, Liam Boyce (66.Conor James Washington), Joshua Brendan David Magennis (79.Conor Gerard McLaughlin). Trainer: Ian Robert Baraclough (England).
Goal: Liam Boyce (56).

25.03.2021   **ITALY - NORTHERN IRELAND**   2-0(2-0)   22nd FIFA WC. Qualifiers
Stadio "Ennio Tardini", Parma; Referee: Ali Palabıyık (Turkey); Attendance: 0
NIR: Bailey Peacock-Farrell, Jonathan Grant Evans, Craig George Cathcart, Michael Smith, Stuart Alan Dallas, Steven Davis (Cap), Corry John Evans (46.George Alan Saville), Patrick James Coleman McNair, Gavin Whyte (63.Shayne Francis Lavery), Alistair Edward McCann (78.Jordan Andrew Thompson), Joshua Brendan David Magennis (78.Kyle Joseph George Lafferty). Trainer: Ian Robert Baraclough (England).

28.03.2021   **NORTHERN IRELAND - UNITED STATES**   1-2(0-1)   Friendly International
Windsor Park, Belfast; Referee: Robert Jenkins (Wales); Attendance: 0
NIR: Conor William Hazard, Shane Kevin Ferguson (60.Jamal Piaras Lewis), Conor Gerard McLaughlin, Ciaron Maurice Brown, Daniel George Ballard (78.Michael Smith), Corry John Evans (60.Patrick James Coleman McNair), Matthew Kennedy (67.Niall McGinn), George Alan Saville (60.Alistair Edward McCann), Jordan Andrew Thompson, Kyle Joseph George Lafferty (Cap), Shayne Francis Lavery (60.Dion Charles). Trainer: Ian Robert Baraclough (England).
Goal: Niall McGinn (88).

31.03.2021   **NORTHERN IRELAND - BULGARIA**   0-0   22nd FIFA WC. Qualifiers
Windsor Park, Belfast; Referee: Yigal Frid (Israel); Attendance: 0
NIR: Bailey Peacock-Farrell, Jonathan Grant Evans, Craig George Cathcart, Stuart Alan Dallas, Jamal Piaras Lewis, Daniel George Ballard (74.Michael Smith), Steven Davis (Cap), Patrick James Coleman McNair, George Alan Saville (74.Matthew Kennedy), Gavin Whyte (64.Niall McGinn), Joshua Brendan David Magennis (82.Kyle Joseph George Lafferty). Trainer: Ian Robert Baraclough (England).

30.05.2021   **MALTA - NORTHERN IRELAND**   0-3(0-1)   Friendly International
Wörthersee Stadion, Klagenfurt (Austria); Referee: Sebastian Gishamer (Austria); Attendance: 0
NIR: Bailey Peacock-Farrell, Craig George Cathcart, Stuart Alan Dallas (Cap) (85.Conor Bradley), Ciaron Maurice Brown, Niall McGinn (61.George Alan Saville), Patrick James Coleman McNair, Jordan Andrew Thompson (85.Alfie John McCalmont), Gavin Whyte (73.Shane Kevin Ferguson), Alistair Edward McCann, Joshua Brendan David Magennis (62.Dion Charles), Jordan Lewis Jones (73.Liam Boyce). Trainer: Ian Robert Baraclough (England).
Goals: Jordan Lewis Jones (2), Gavin Whyte (53), Alistair Edward McCann (55).

03.06.2021   **UKRAINE - NORTHERN IRELAND**   1-0(1-0)   Friendly International
Dnipro Arena, Dnipro; Referee: Szymon Marciniak (Poland); Attendance: 15,000
NIR: Bailey Peacock-Farrell, Craig George Cathcart, Shane Kevin Ferguson (68.Paul Smyth), Stuart Alan Dallas (Cap) (89.Dion Charles), Ciaron Maurice Brown (89.Sam McClelland), Daniel George Ballard, Niall McGinn (46.Jordan Andrew Thompson), Patrick James Coleman McNair, George Alan Saville, Alistair Edward McCann (81.Gavin Whyte), Joshua Brendan David Magennis (61.Kyle Joseph George Lafferty). Trainer: Ian Robert Baraclough (England).

NATIONAL TEAM PLAYERS
(16.07.2020 – 15.07.2021)

Name	DOB	Caps	Goals	2020/2021:	Club
Goalkeepers					
Trevor CARSON	05.03.1988	6	0	2020:	*Motherwell FC (SCO)*
Conor William HAZARD	05.03.1998	2	0	2021:	*Celtic FC Glasgow (SCO)*
Michael McGOVERN	12.07.1984	33	0	2020:	*Norwich City FC (ENG)*
Bailey PEACOCK-FARRELL	29.10.1996	23	0	2020/2021:	*Burnley FC (ENG)*
Defenders					
Daniel George BALLARD	22.09.1999	8	0	2020:	*Arsenal FC London (ENG)*
				05.10.2020->	*Blackpool FC (ENG)*
				31.05.2021->	*Arsenal FC London (ENG)*
Conor BRADLEY	09.07.2003	1	0	2021:	*Liverpool FC (ENG)*
Ciaron Maurice BROWN	14.01.1998	4	0	2020/2021:	*Cardiff City FC (WAL)*
Craig George CATHCART	06.02.1989	61	2	2020/2021:	*Watford FC (ENG)*
Jonathan Grant EVANS	03.01.1988	91	4	2020/2021:	*Leicester City FC (ENG)*
Thomas Michael FLANAGAN	21.10.1991	8	0	2020:	*Sunderland AFC (ENG)*
Jamal Piaras LEWIS	25.01.1998	20	0	2020:	*Norwich City FC*
				08.09.2020->	*Newcastle United FC (ENG)*
Sam McCLELLAND	04.01.2002	1	0	2021:	*Chelsea FC London (ENG)*
Conor Gerard McLAUGHLIN	26.07.1991	43	1	2020/2021:	*Sunderland AFC (ENG)*
Patrick James Coleman McNAIR	27.04.1995	47	4	2020/2021:	*Middlesbrough FC (ENG)*
Michael SMITH	04.09.1988	17	1	2020/2021:	*Heart of Midlothian FC Edinburgh (SCO)*
Midfielders					
Stuart Alan DALLAS	19.04.1991	56	3	2020/2021:	*Leeds United FC (ENG)*
Steven DAVIS	01.01.1985	126	12	2020/2021:	*Rangers FC Glasgow (SCO)*
Corry John EVANS	17.07.1990	66	2	2020/2021:	*Blackburn Rovers FC (ENG)*
Shane Kevin FERGUSON	12.07.1991	49	1	2020/2021:	*Millwall FC London (ENG)*
Ethan Stuart William GALBRAITH	11.05.2001	2	0	2020/2021:	*Manchester United FC (ENG)*
Jordan Lewis JONES	24.10.1994	12	1	2020:	*Rangers FC Glasgow (SCO)*
				29.01.2021->	*Sunderland AFC (ENG)*
Matthew KENNEDY	01.11.1994	3	0	2020/2021:	*Aberdeen FC (SCO)*
Alfie John McCALMONT	25.03.2000	2	0	2021:	*Oldham Athletic AFC (ENG)*
Alistair Edward McCANN	04.12.1999	6	1	2020/2021:	*St. Johnstone FC Perth (SCO)*
Niall McGINN	20.07.1987	66	6	2020/2021:	*Aberdeen FC (SCO)*
George Alan SAVILLE	01.06.1993	31	0	2020/2021:	*Middlesbrough FC (ENG)*
Jordan Andrew THOMPSON	03.01.1997	16	0	2020/2021:	*Stoke City FC (ENG)*
Gavin WHYTE	31.01.1996	19	3	2020/2021:	*Cardiff City FC (WAL)*
Forwards					
Liam BOYCE	08.04.1991	28	2	2020/2021:	*Heart of Midlothian FC Edinburgh (SCO)*
Dion CHARLES	07.10.1995	3	0	2021:	*Accrington Stanley FC (ENG)*
Kyle Joseph George LAFFERTY	16.09.1987	83	20	2020:	*Reggina 1914 Reggio Calabria (ITA)*
				12.02.2021->	*Kilmarnock FC (SCO)*
Shayne Francis LAVERY	08.12.1998	7	0	2020/2021:	*Linfield FC Belfast*
Joshua Brendan David MAGENNIS	15.05.1990	61	8	2020/2021:	*Hull City AFC (ENG)*
Conor James WASHINGTON	18.05.1992	29	4	2020/2021:	*Charlton Athletic FC London (ENG)*
Trainer					
Ian Robert BARACLOUGH (England) [from 27.06.2020]	04.12.1970	13 M; 1 W; 4 D; 8 L; 10-19			

NORWAY

The Country:
Kongeriket Norge (Kingdom of Norway)
Capital: Oslo
Surface: 385,203 km²
Inhabitants: 5,391,369 [2021]
Time: UTC+1

The FA:
Norges Fotballforbund
Serviceboks 1 Ulleval Stadium, 0840 Oslo
Tel: +47 2102 9300
Founded: 1902
Member of FIFA since: 1908
Member of UEFA since: 1954
Website: www.fotball.no

NATIONAL TEAM RECORDS

RECORDS
First international match:	12.07.1908, Göteborg:	Sweden – Norway 11-3
Most international caps:	John Arne Semundseth Riise	- 110 caps (2000-2013)
Most international goals:	Jørgen Juve	- 33 goals / 45 caps (1928-1937)

UEFA EUROPEAN CHAMPIONSHIP
1960	Qualifiers
1964	Qualifiers
1968	Qualifiers
1972	Qualifiers
1976	Qualifiers
1980	Qualifiers
1984	Qualifiers
1988	Qualifiers
1992	Qualifiers
1996	Qualifiers
2000	Final Tournament (Group Stage)
2004	Qualifiers
2008	Qualifiers
2012	Qualifiers
2016	Qualifiers
2020	Qualifiers

FIFA WORLD CUP
1930	Did not enter
1934	Did not enter
1938	Final Tournament (1st Round)
1950	Did not enter
1954	Qualifiers
1958	Qualifiers
1962	Qualifiers
1966	Qualifiers
1970	Qualifiers
1974	Qualifiers
1978	Qualifiers
1982	Qualifiers
1986	Qualifiers
1990	Qualifiers
1994	Final Tournament (Group Stage)
1998	Final Tournament (2nd Round of 16)
2002	Qualifiers
2006	Qualifiers
2010	Qualifiers
2014	Qualifiers
2018	Qualifiers

OLYMPIC TOURNAMENTS
1908	-
1912	Final Tournament (Quarter-Finals)
1920	Final Tournament (Quarter-Finals)
1924	Did not enter
1928	Did not enter
1936	Final Tournament (3rd Place)
1948	Did not enter
1952	Final Tournament (Round 1)
1956	Did not enter
1960	Qualifiers
1964	Did not enter
1968	Did not enter
1972	Did not enter
1976	Qualifiers
1980	Qualifiers
1984	Final Tournament (Group Stage)
1988	Qualifiers
1992	Qualifiers
1996	Qualifiers
2000	Qualifiers
2004	Qualifiers
2008	Qualifiers
2012	Qualifiers
2016	Qualifiers

UEFA NATIONS LEAGUE
2018/2019	League C (promoted to League B)
2020/2021	League B

FIFA CONFEDERATIONS CUP 1992-2017
None

NORWEGIAN CLUB HONOURS IN EUROPEAN CLUB COMPETITIONS:

European Champion Clubs.Cup (1956-1992) / UEFA Champions League (1993-2021)
None

Fairs Cup (1858-1971) / UEFA Cup (1972-2009) / UEFA Europa League (2010-2021)
None

UEFA Super Cup (1972-2020)
None

*European Cup Winners.Cup 1961-1999**
None

defunct competition

NATIONAL COMPETITIONS
TABLE OF HONOURS

	CHAMPIONS	CUP WINNERS	BEST GOALSCORERS	
1902	-	Sportsklubben Grane	-	
1903	-	Odds BK Skien	-	
1904	-	Odds BK Skien	-	
1905	-	Odds BK Skien	-	
1906	-	Odds BK Skien	-	
1907	-	Mercantile FK	-	
1908	-	Lyn 1896 FK Oslo	-	
1909	-	Lyn 1896 FK Oslo	-	
1910	-	Lyn 1896 FK Oslo	-	
1911	-	Lyn 1896 FK Oslo	-	
1912	-	Mercantile FK	-	
1913	-	Odds BK Skien	-	
1914	-	Frigg Oslo FK	-	
1915	-	Odds BK Skien	-	
1916	-	Frigg Oslo FK	-	
1917	-	Sarpsborg FK	-	
1918	-	Kvik FK Fredrikshald	-	
1919	-	Odds BK Skien	-	
1920	-	FK Ørn-Horten	-	
1921	-	Frigg Oslo FK Oslo	-	
1922	-	Odds BK Skien	-	
1923	-	SK Brann Bergen	-	
1924	-	Odds BK Skien	-	
1925	-	SK Brann Bergen	-	
1926	-	Odds BK Skien	-	
1927	-	FK Ørn-Horten	-	
1928	-	FK Ørn-Horten	-	
1929	-	Sarpsborg FK	-	
1930	-	FK Ørn-Horten	-	
1931	-	Odds BK Skien	-	
1932	-	Fredrikstad FK	-	
1933	-	Mjøndalen IF	-	
1934	-	Mjøndalen IF	-	
1935	-	Fredrikstad FK	-	
1936	-	Fredrikstad FK	-	
1937	-	Mjøndalen IF	-	
1937/1938	Fredrikstad FK	Fredrikstad FK	-	
1938/1939	Fredrikstad FK	Sarpsborg FK	-	
1939/1940	*Championship abandoned*	Fredrikstad FK	-	
1940/1941	*No competition*	*No competition*	-	
1941/1942	*No competition*	*No competition*	-	
1942/1943	*No competition*	*No competition*	-	
1943/1944	*No competition*	*No competition*	-	
1944/1945	*No competition*	Lyn 1896 FK Oslo	-	
1945/1946	*No competition*	Lyn 1896 FK Oslo	-	
1946/1947	*No competition*	Skeid Fotball Oslo	-	
1947/1948	SK Freidig Trondheim	Sarpsborg FK	-	
1948/1949	Fredrikstad FK	Sarpsborg FK	Arvid Havnås (Sandefjord BK)	12
1949/1950	IF Fram Larvik	Fredrikstad FK	Reidar Dørum (FK Ørn-Horten)	13
1950/1951	Fredrikstad FK	Sarpsborg FK	John Sveinsson (Lyn 1896 FK Oslo)	19
1951/1952	Fredrikstad FK	IL Sparta Sparsborg	Jan Tangen (Strømmen IF)	15
1952/1953	Larvik Turn & Idrettsforening	Viking FK Stavanger	Gunnar Thoresen (Larvik Turn & Idrettsforening) Per Jacobsen (Odds BK Skien)	15
1953/1954	Fredrikstad FK	Skeid Fotball Oslo	Gunnar Thoresen (Larvik Turn & Idrettsforening)	15
1954/1955	Larvik Turn & Idrettsforening	Skeid Fotball Oslo	Harald Hennum (Skeid Fotball Oslo)	13
1955/1956	Larvik Turn & Idrettsforening	Skeid Fotball Oslo	Willy Fossli (Asker Fotball)	17
1956/1957	Fredrikstad FK	Fredrikstad FK	Per Kristoffersen (Fredrikstad FK)	15
1957/1958	Viking FK Stavanger	Skeid Fotball Oslo	Harald Hennum (Skeid Fotball Oslo)	17
1958/1959	Lillestrøm SK	Viking FK Stavanger	Reidar Sundby (Larvik Turn & Idrettsforening)	13
1959/1960	Fredrikstad FK	Rosenborg BK Trondheim	Per Kristoffersen (Fredrikstad FK)	13
1960/1961	Fredrikstad FK	Fredrikstad FK	Per Kristoffersen (Fredrikstad FK)	15
1961/1962	SK Brann Bergen	SK Gjøvik-Lyn	Rolf Birger Pedersen (SK Brann Bergen)	26
1963	SK Brann Bergen	Skeid Fotball Oslo	Leif Eriksen (Vålerenga Fotball Oslo)	16
1964	Lyn 1896 FK Oslo	Rosenborg BK Trondheim	Ole Stavrum (Lyn 1896 FK Oslo)	18
1965	Vålerenga Fotball Oslo	Skeid Fotball Oslo	Harald Berg (Lyn 1896 FK Oslo)	19
1966	Skeid Fotball Oslo	Fredrikstad FK	Per Kristoffersen (Fredrikstad FK)	20
1967	Rosenborg BK Trondheim	Lyn 1896 FK Oslo	Odd Iversen (Rosenborg BK Trondheim)	17
1968	Lyn 1896 FK Oslo	Lyn 1896 FK Oslo	Odd Iversen (Rosenborg BK Trondheim)	30
1969	Rosenborg BK Trondheim	Strømsgodset IF Drammen	Odd Iversen (Rosenborg BK Trondheim)	26
1970	Strømsgodset IF Drammen	Strømsgodset IF Drammen	Steinar Pettersen (Strømsgodset IF Drammen)	16
1971	Rosenborg BK Trondheim	Rosenborg BK Trondheim	Jan Fuglset (Fredrikstad FK)	17
1972	Viking FK Stavanger	SK Brann Bergen	Egil Solberg (Mjøndalen IF)	

			Johannes Vold (Viking FK Stavanger)	16
1973	Viking FK Stavanger	Strømsgodset IF Drammen	Stein Karlsen (Hamarkameratene)	17
1974	Viking FK Stavanger	Skeid Fotball Oslo	Odd Berg (Molde FK)	13
1975	Viking FK Stavanger	FK Bodø/Glimt	Arne Dokken (Lillestrøm SK)	18
1976	Lillestrøm SK	SK Brann Bergen	Jan Fuglset (Molde FK)	17
1977	Lillestrøm SK	Lillestrøm SK	Trygve Johannessen (Viking FK Stavanger)	17
1978	IK Start Kristiansand	Lillestrøm SK	Tom Lund (Lillestrøm SK)	17
1979	Viking FK Stavanger	Viking FK Stavanger	Odd Iversen (Vålerenga Fotball Oslo)	16
1980	IK Start Kristiansand	Vålerenga Fotball Oslo	Arne Dokken (Lillestrøm SK)	14
1981	Vålerenga Fotball Oslo	Lillestrøm SK	Pål Jacobsen (Vålerenga Fotball Oslo)	16
1982	Viking FK Stavanger	SK Brann Bergen	Tor Arne Granerud (Hamarkameratene) Trygve Johannessen (Viking FK Stavanger)	11
1983	Vålerenga Fotball Oslo	Moss FK	Olav Nysæter (Kongsvinger IL)	14
1984	Vålerenga Fotball Oslo	Fredrikstad FK	Sverre Brandhaug (Rosenborg BK Trondheim)	13
1985	Rosenborg BK Trondheim	Lillestrøm SK	Jørn Andersen (Vålerenga Fotball Oslo)	23
1986	Lillestrøm SK	Tromsø IL	Arve Seland (IK Start Kristiansand)	12
1987	Moss FK	Bryne FK	Jan Kristian Fjærestad (Moss FK)	18
1988	Rosenborg BK Trondheim	Rosenborg BK Trondheim	Jan Åge Fjørtoft (Lillestrøm SK)	14
1989	Lillestrøm SK	Viking FK Stavanger	Jahn Ivar Jakobsen (Rosenborg BK Trondheim)	18
1990	Rosenborg BK Trondheim	Rosenborg BK Trondheim	Tore André Dahlum (IK Start Kristiansand)	20
1991	Viking FK Stavanger	Strømsgodset IF Drammen	Karl Petter Løken (Rosenborg BK Trondheim)	12
1992	Rosenborg BK Trondheim	Rosenborg BK Trondheim	Kjell Roar Kaasa (Kongsvinger IL)	17
1993	Rosenborg BK Trondheim	FK Bodø/Glimt	Mons Ivar Mjelde (Lillestrøm SK)	19
1994	Rosenborg BK Trondheim	Molde FK	Harald Martin Brattbakk (Rosenborg BK Trondheim)	17
1995	Rosenborg BK Trondheim	Rosenborg BK Trondheim	Harald Martin Brattbakk (Rosenborg BK Trondheim)	26
1996	Rosenborg BK Trondheim	Tromsø IL	Harald Martin Brattbakk (Rosenborg BK Trondheim)	28
1997	Rosenborg BK Trondheim	Vålerenga Fotball Oslo	Sigurd Rushfeldt (Rosenborg BK Trondheim)	27
1998	Rosenborg BK Trondheim	Stabæk Fotball Bærum	Sigurd Rushfeldt (Rosenborg BK Trondheim)	25
1999	Rosenborg BK Trondheim	Rosenborg BK Trondheim	Rune Lange (Tromsø IL)	23
2000	Rosenborg BK Trondheim	Odd Grenland Skien	Thorstein Helstad (SK Brann Bergen)	18
2001	Rosenborg BK Trondheim	Viking FK Stavanger	Frode Johnsen (Rosenborg BK Trondheim) Thorstein Helstad (SK Brann Bergen) Clayton Zane (AUS, Lillestrøm SK)	17
2002	Rosenborg BK Trondheim	Vålerenga Fotball Oslo	Harald Martin Brattbakk (Rosenborg BK Trondheim)	17
2003	Rosenborg BK Trondheim	Rosenborg BK Trondheim	Harald Martin Brattbakk (Rosenborg BK Trondheim)	17
2004	Rosenborg BK Trondheim	SK Brann Bergen	Frode Johnsen (Rosenborg BK Trondheim)	19
2005	Vålerenga Fotball Oslo	Molde FK	Ole Martin Årst (Tromsø IL)	16
2006	Rosenborg BK Trondheim	Fredrikstad FK	Daniel Nannskog (SWE, Stabæk Fotball Bærum)	19
2007	SK Brann Bergen	Lillestrøm SK	Thorstein Helstad (SK Brann Bergen)	22
2008	Stabæk Fotball Bærum	Vålerenga Fotball Oslo	Daniel Nannskog (SWE, Stabæk Fotball Bærum)	16
2009	Rosenborg BK Trondheim	Aalesunds FK	Rade Prica (SWE, Rosenborg BK Trondheim)	17
2010	Rosenborg BK Trondheim	Strømsgodset IF Drammen	Baye Djiby Fall (SEN, Molde FK)	16
2011	Molde FK	Aalesunds FK	Mustafa Abdellaoue (Tromsø IL)	17
2012	Molde FK	IL Hødd Ulsteinvik	Péter Kovács (HUN, Strømsgodset IF Drammen) Zdeněk Ondrášek (CZE, Tromsø IL)	14
2013	Strømsgodset IF Drammen	Molde FK	Frode Johnsen (Odds BK Skien)	16
2014	Molde FK	Molde FK	Viðar Örn Kjartansson (ISL, Vålerenga Fotball Oslo)	25
2015	Rosenborg BK Trondheim	Rosenborg BK Trondheim	Alexander Toft Søderlund (Rosenborg BK Trondheim)	22
2016	Rosenborg BK Trondheim	Rosenborg BK Trondheim	Christian Gytkjær (DEN, Rosenborg BK Trondheim)	19
2017	Rosenborg BK Trondheim	Lillestrøm SK	Nicklas Bendtner (DEN, Rosenborg BK Trondheim)	19
2018	Rosenborg BK Trondheim	Rosenborg BK Trondheim	Bi Sylvestre Franck Fortune Boli (CIV, Stabæk Fotball Bærum)	17
2019	Molde FK	Viking FK Stavanger	Torgeir Børven (Odds BK Skien)	21
2020	FK Bodø/Glimt	*Competition cancelled*	Kasper Junker (DEN, FK Bodø/Glimt)	27

Please note: the Norwegian Championship was called Norgesserien (1937–1948), Hovedserien (1948–1962), 1. divisjon (1963–1989), Tippeligaen (1990–2016) and Eliteserien (since 2017).

NATIONAL CHAMPIONSHIP
Eliteserien 2020
(16.06.2020 – 22.12.2020)

Results

Round 1 [16-17.06.2020]
Rosenborg BK - Kristiansund BK 0-0
Viking - FK Bodø/Glimt 2-4(2-1)
Odds BK - Sandefjord 1-2(0-0)
Stabæk - Mjøndalen 0-0
Aalesunds FK - Molde FK 1-4(1-2)
Sarpsborg 08 - Vålerenga 0-1(0-1)
IK Start - Strømsgodset 2-2(0-1)
FK Haugesund - SK Brann 1-2(0-0)

Round 2 [20-21.06.2020]
Mjøndalen - Sarpsborg 08 1-0(1-0)
Molde FK - Rosenborg BK 1-0(0-0)
Kristiansund BK - Aalesunds FK 7-2(3-2)
Vålerenga - Stabæk 2-2(1-2)
FK Bodø/Glimt - FK Haugesund 6-1(3-0)
Strømsgodset - Odds BK 1-0(1-0)
Sandefjord - IK Start 2-2(1-2)
SK Brann - Viking 3-0(0-0)

Round 3 [24-25.06.2020]
Aalesunds FK - SK Brann 2-2(1-0)
Viking - Mjøndalen 1-1(1-1)
FK Haugesund - Kristiansund BK 2-2(0-1)
Stabæk - Sandefjord 2-0(1-0)
IK Start - Molde FK 2-3(1-2)
Odds BK - Vålerenga 4-1(1-1)
Sarpsborg 08 - Strømsgodset 2-3(0-2)
Rosenborg BK - FK Bodø/Glimt 2-3(0-1)

Round 4 [27-28.06.2020]
IK Start - Odds BK 0-5(0-2)
Vålerenga - Viking 2-1(1-0)
Molde FK - Stabæk 4-1(1-0)
Mjøndalen - Kristiansund BK 1-2(0-0)
Sandefjord - FK Haugesund 0-1(0-1)
Strømsgodset - Aalesunds FK 1-1(0-1)
FK Bodø/Glimt - Sarpsborg 08 2-1(1-0)
SK Brann - Rosenborg BK 1-2(1-1)

Round 5 [01-02.07.2020]
Odds BK - FK Bodø/Glimt 0-4(0-2)
Viking - Sandefjord 2-0(0-0)
FK Haugesund - IK Start 1-0(0-0)
Aalesunds FK - Mjøndalen 1-3(0-2)
Stabæk - Strømsgodset 2-0(2-0)
Rosenborg BK - Vålerenga 1-1(1-0)
Kristiansund BK - Molde FK 2-2(0-0)
Sarpsborg 08 - SK Brann 0-1(0-1)

Round 6 [04-05.07.2020]
IK Start - Viking 1-1(0-0)
Vålerenga - Aalesunds FK 2-2(0-1)
Molde FK - Mjøndalen 2-1(2-0)
FK Bodø/Glimt - SK Brann 5-0(4-0)
Strømsgodset - Kristiansund BK 2-2(0-2)
Sandefjord - Sarpsborg 08 0-3(0-2)
Odds BK - FK Haugesund 0-0
Stabæk - Rosenborg BK 0-3(0-0)

Round 7 [11-12.07.2020]
FK Haugesund - Molde FK 0-3(0-2)
Rosenborg BK - Strømsgodset 3-0(0-0)
Viking - Odds BK 1-2(0-1)
Kristiansund BK - Stabæk 1-2(1-1)
Sarpsborg 08 - IK Start 1-0(1-0)
Aalesunds FK - FK Bodø/Glimt 1-6(1-3)
Mjøndalen - Vålerenga 0-1(0-1)
SK Brann - Sandefjord 3-1(3-1)

Round 8 [15-16.07.2020]
FK Bodø/Glimt - Kristiansund BK 2-1(0-1)
Molde FK - Viking 5-0(2-0)
Sandefjord - Aalesunds FK 1-0(1-0)
Strømsgodset - Mjøndalen 2-1(0-0)
Vålerenga - FK Haugesund 1-0(0-0)
Odds BK - SK Brann 1-0(0-0)
Stabæk - Sarpsborg 08 1-1(1-0)
IK Start - Rosenborg BK 0-0

Round 9 [18-19.07.2020]
Mjøndalen - FK Bodø/Glimt 2-3(0-2)
FK Haugesund - Viking 1-0(2-0)
Aalesunds FK - Stabæk 1-3(1-1)
Kristiansund BK - Vålerenga 0-0
Rosenborg BK - Sandefjord 2-1(1-0)
Sarpsborg 08 - Odds BK 2-0(0-0)
Strømsgodset - Molde FK 0-4(0-1)
SK Brann - IK Start 1-1(1-1)

Round 10 [25-26.07.2020]
Odds BK - Aalesunds FK 3-2(2-2)
SK Brann - Kristiansund BK 1-1(0-0)
FK Bodø/Glimt - Molde FK 3-1(1-1)
Sandefjord - Mjøndalen 1-0(0-0)
IK Start - Stabæk 0-0
Viking - Sarpsborg 08 3-0(2-0)
Vålerenga - Strømsgodset 2-0(2-0)
FK Haugesund - Rosenborg BK 1-0(1-0)

Round 11 [29-30.07.2020]
Aalesunds FK - IK Start 3-2(1-2)
Kristiansund BK - Sandefjord 3-1(0-1)
Mjøndalen - Odds BK 0-2(0-1)
Sarpsborg 08 - FK Haugesund 0-0
Strømsgodset - SK Brann 3-1(1-0)
Molde FK - Vålerenga 4-1(1-0)
Stabæk - FK Bodø/Glimt 2-2(1-2)
Rosenborg BK - Viking 3-0(1-0)

Round 12 [01-02.08.2020]
Sandefjord - Molde FK 2-1(1-1)
SK Brann - Vålerenga 1-2(1-1)
FK Bodø/Glimt - Strømsgodset 3-2(2-1)
FK Haugesund - Stabæk 3-1(2-0)
Sarpsborg 08 - Aalesunds FK 4-0(0-0)
IK Start - Mjøndalen 3-0(1-0)
Viking - Kristiansund BK 1-2(1-0)
Odds BK - Rosenborg BK 2-1(1-0)

Round 13 [08-10.08.2020]
Vålerenga - FK Bodø/Glimt 2-2(1-2)
Aalesunds FK - Viking 2-2(1-2)
Kristiansund BK - IK Start 3-2(1-0)
Mjøndalen - FK Haugesund 1-0(1-0)
Stabæk - Odds BK 0-1(0-0)
Strømsgodset - Sandefjord 3-4(1-2)
Rosenborg BK - Sarpsborg 08 5-1(1-1)
Molde FK - SK Brann 1-2(1-1)

Round 14 [15-17.08.2020]
Sarpsborg 08 - Molde FK 2-1(1-0)
SK Brann - Mjøndalen 0-1(0-0)
FK Haugesund - Strømsgodset 2-3(0-1)
Odds BK - Kristiansund BK 2-1(2-1)
Sandefjord - FK Bodø/Glimt 1-2(0-1)
Viking - Stabæk 3-3(1-2)
Rosenborg BK - Aalesunds FK 3-2(3-1)
IK Start - Vålerenga 2-1(1-0)

Round 15 [22-24.08.2020]
Molde FK - Odds BK 2-0(0-0)
Aalesunds FK - FK Haugesund 1-3(1-2)
FK Bodø/Glimt - IK Start 6-0(2-0)
Kristiansund BK - Sarpsborg 08 4-1(0-0)
Strømsgodset - Viking 0-2(0-0)
Vålerenga - Sandefjord 2-1(0-1)
Mjøndalen - Rosenborg BK 0-2(0-2)
Stabæk - SK Brann 0-2(0-0)

Round 16 [29-30.08.2020]
FK Haugesund - Vålerenga 2-1(2-0)
SK Brann - Strømsgodset 1-1(1-1)
Odds BK - Mjøndalen 6-1(4-1)
Rosenborg BK - Stabæk 2-2(1-0)
Sarpsborg 08 - FK Bodø/Glimt 0-3(0-1)
IK Start - Aalesunds FK 1-0(1-0)
Sandefjord - Kristiansund BK 0-2(0-1)
Viking - Molde FK 3-2(0-0)

Round 17 [12-13.09.2020]
Molde FK - IK Start 5-0(1-0) [05.08.]
Kristiansund BK - Viking 3-5(1-1)
Stabæk - FK Haugesund 2-1(1-1)
Aalesunds FK - Sarpsborg 08 0-1(0-0)
FK Bodø/Glimt - Odds BK 6-1(4-1)
Mjøndalen - Sandefjord 0-2(0-1)
Strømsgodset - Rosenborg BK 3-3(2-1)
Vålerenga - SK Brann 5-1(5-1)

Round 18 [19-20.09.2020]
Vålerenga - Molde FK 2-1(1-0)
Sarpsborg 08 - Mjøndalen 2-0(2-0)
SK Brann - FK Bodø/Glimt 1-3(0-0)
Rosenborg BK - FK Haugesund 2-1(0-1)
Sandefjord - Strømsgodset 0-0
IK Start - Kristiansund BK 1-2(0-2)
Viking - Aalesunds FK 5-2(1-1)
Odds BK - Stabæk 2-0(1-0)

Round 19 [26-27.09.2020]
Molde FK - Sandefjord 0-1(0-1)
Strømsgodset - Sarpsborg 08 0-0
Aalesunds FK - Rosenborg BK 1-2(0-1)
FK Haugesund - Odds BK 4-4(1-2)
Kristiansund BK - SK Brann 1-1(0-0)
Mjøndalen - Viking 1-2(1-1)
Stabæk - IK Start 2-0(0-0)
FK Bodø/Glimt - Vålerenga 2-0(2-0)

Round 20 [03-04.10.2020]
Sarpsborg 08 - Stabæk 4-0(4-0)
Vålerenga - Mjøndalen 4-1(1-0)
Aalesunds FK - Kristiansund BK 1-2(1-0)
FK Bodø/Glimt - Sandefjord 2-1(2-1)
SK Brann - Molde FK 1-2(1-1)
IK Start - FK Haugesund 5-1(3-0)
Viking - Strømsgodset 2-2(0-0)
Rosenborg BK - Odds BK 4-1(1-0)

Round 21 [17-18.10.2020]
Mjøndalen - SK Brann 2-0(2-0)
Molde FK - FK Bodø/Glimt 4-2(2-1)
FK Haugesund - Sarpsborg 08 2-0(1-0)
Kristiansund BK - Rosenborg BK 0-0
Stabæk - Aalesunds FK 4-0(1-0)
Strømsgodset - IK Start 1-1(0-1)
Sandefjord - Vålerenga 0-3(0-1)
Odds BK - Viking 3-0(1-0) [04.11.]

Round 22 [24-27.10.2020]
IK Start - Sandefjord 0-1(0-0)
SK Brann - Stabæk 1-1(0-0)
Molde FK - Strømsgodset 2-1(0-0)
Sarpsborg 08 - Rosenborg BK 1-2(0-2)
Vålerenga - Kristiansund BK 1-1(0-0)
Aalesunds FK - Odds BK 0-3(0-1)
FK Bodø/Glimt - Mjøndalen 2-0(1-0)
Viking - FK Haugesund 0-1(0-1)

Round 23 [31.10.-01.11.2020]
Odds BK - Sarpsborg 08 1-1(0-0)
FK Haugesund - Aalesunds FK 0-1(0-0)
Mjøndalen - Molde FK 1-3(1-0)
Kristiansund BK - FK Bodø/Glimt 2-3(1-2)
Rosenborg BK - IK Start 1-0(0-0)
Sandefjord - SK Brann 3-3(1-0)
Stabæk - Viking 1-1(1-1)
Strømsgodset - Vålerenga 0-2(0-1)

Round 24 [07-08.11.2020]
Mjøndalen - Strømsgodset 3-0(1-0)
SK Brann - FK Haugesund 1-2(0-0)
FK Bodø/Glimt - Aalesunds FK 7-0(2-0)
Molde FK - Kristiansund BK 2-2(1-2)
Sandefjord - Stabæk 0-0
IK Start - Sarpsborg 08 3-2(1-2)
Viking - Rosenborg BK 3-0(3-0)
Vålerenga - Odds BK 2-0(1-0)

Round 25 [21-24.11.2020]
Stabæk - Molde FK 0-3(0-1)
Aalesunds FK - Vålerenga 1-1(1-0)
FK Haugesund - Sandefjord 3-2(2-1)
Kristiansund BK - Mjøndalen 1-0(1-0)
Odds BK - IK Start 1-2(0-0)
Sarpsborg 08 - Viking 1-2(0-0)
Strømsgodset - FK Bodø/Glimt 1-2(0-2)
Rosenborg BK - SK Brann 2-3(0-2)

Round 26 [28-29.11.2020]
Viking - IK Start 4-1(1-0)
SK Brann - Aalesunds FK 3-1(2-1)
FK Bodø/Glimt - Rosenborg BK 5-1(2-0)
Kristiansund BK - Strømsgodset 2-1(0-1)
Mjøndalen - Stabæk 0-1(0-1)
Molde FK - FK Haugesund 3-1(2-1)
Vålerenga - Sarpsborg 08 1-1(0-1)
Sandefjord - Odds BK 1-1(0-0) [13.12.]

Round 27 [02.12.2020]
Aalesunds FK - Sandefjord 0-1(0-1)
FK Haugesund - Mjøndalen 1-1(0-0)
Sarpsborg 08 - Kristiansund BK 1-1(0-1)
IK Start - FK Bodø/Glimt 1-1(1-1)
Viking - SK Brann 2-0(1-0)
Stabæk - Vålerenga 1-1(0-1)
Rosenborg BK - Molde FK 3-1(1-1) [13.12.]
Odds BK - Strømsgodset 1-3(1-1) [19.12.]

Round 28 [06-07.12.2020]
FK Bodø/Glimt - Stabæk 5-2(3-0)
SK Brann - Sarpsborg 08 1-1(0-0)
Mjøndalen - IK Start 1-0(0-0)
Sandefjord - Viking 2-2(1-0)
Strømsgodset - FK Haugesund 2-2(1-0)
Molde FK - Aalesunds FK 2-1(1-0)
Vålerenga - Rosenborg BK 1-0(0-0)
Kristiansund BK - Odds BK 4-3(1-1) [09.12.]

Round 29 [09-16.12.2020]
Aalesunds FK - Strømsgodset 1-4(0-1)
FK Haugesund - FK Bodø/Glimt 0-4(0-2)
Sarpsborg 08 - Sandefjord 0-0
IK Start - SK Brann 1-0(0-0)
Rosenborg BK - Mjøndalen 1-0(0-0)
Viking - Vålerenga 2-2(0-1)
Stabæk - Kristiansund BK 2-2(0-0)
Odds BK - Molde FK 1-4(1-0)

Round 30 [19-22.12.2020]
Molde FK - Sarpsborg 08 5-0(3-0)
FK Bodø/Glimt - Viking 3-0(2-0)
SK Brann - Odds BK 2-1(1-0)
Kristiansund BK - FK Haugesund 1-3(1-0)
Mjøndalen - Aalesunds FK 3-0(3-0)
Sandefjord - Rosenborg BK 0-0
Strømsgodset - Stabæk 0-4(0-1)
Vålerenga - IK Start 4-0(3-0)

Final Standings

						Total					Home					Away		
1.	**FK Bodø/Glimt**	30	26	3	1	103 - 32	81	15	0	0	59 - 11	11	3	1	44 - 21
2.	Molde FK	30	20	2	8	77 - 36	62	12	1	2	42 - 13	8	1	6	35 - 23
3.	Vålerenga Fotball Oslo	30	15	10	5	51 - 33	55	10	5	0	33 - 13	5	5	5	18 - 20
4.	Rosenborg BK Trondheim	30	15	7	8	50 - 35	52	10	3	2	34 - 16	5	4	6	16 - 19
5.	Kristiansund BK	30	12	12	6	57 - 45	48	7	4	4	34 - 26	5	8	2	23 - 19
6.	Viking FK Stavanger	30	12	8	10	54 - 52	44	7	4	4	34 - 22	5	4	6	20 - 30
7.	Odds BK Skien	30	13	4	13	52 - 51	43	8	2	5	28 - 22	5	2	8	24 - 29
8.	Stabæk Fotball Bærum	30	9	12	9	41 - 45	39	5	6	4	19 - 17	4	6	5	22 - 28
9.	FK Haugesund	30	11	6	13	39 - 51	39	6	3	6	22 - 26	5	3	7	17 - 25
10.	SK Brann Bergen	30	9	9	12	40 - 49	36	4	5	6	21 - 20	5	4	6	19 - 29
11.	Sandefjord Fotball	30	9	8	13	31 - 43	35	3	7	5	13 - 20	6	1	8	18 - 23
12.	Sarpsborg 08 FF	30	8	8	14	33 - 43	32	6	3	6	20 - 14	2	5	8	13 - 29
13.	Strømsgodset IF Drammen	30	7	10	13	41 - 57	31	3	6	6	19 - 29	4	4	7	22 - 28
14.	Mjøndalen IF (*Relegation Play-offs*)	30	8	3	19	26 - 45	27	6	0	9	16 - 18	2	3	10	10 - 27
15.	IK Start Kristiansand (*Relegated*)	30	6	9	15	33 - 56	27	5	6	4	22 - 20	1	3	11	11 - 36
16.	Aalesunds FK (*Relegated*)	30	2	5	23	30 - 85	11	1	3	11	16 - 39	1	2	12	14 - 46

Top goalscorers:

27	**Kasper Junker (DEN)**	*FK Bodø/Glimt*
25	Amahl Willilam D'vaz Pellegrino	*Kristiansund BK*
19	Philip Aksel Frigast Zinckernagel (DEN)	*FK Bodø/Glimt*
16	Veton Berisha	*Viking FK Stavanger*
15	Mushagalusa Bakenga Joar Bahati Namugunga	*Odds BK Skien*
14	Jens Petter Hauge	*FK Bodø/Glimt*

Relegation Play-offs [28.12.2020]

Mjøndalen IF - Sogndal Fotball   3-2(

Mjøndalen IF remains at first level for 2021.

NATIONAL CUP
Norgesmesterskapet 2020

Firstly postponed due to COVID-19 pandemic, the competition was later cancelled.

Aalesunds Fotballklubb

	Founded:	25.06.1914	
	Stadium:	Color Line Stadion, Ålesund (10,778)	
	Trainer:	Lars Bohinen	08.09.1969
	(25.08.2020)	Lars Arne Nilsen	06.04.1964

Goalkeepers:	DOB	M	(s)	G
Gudmund Kongshavn	23.01.1991	14		
Andreas Lie	31.08.1987	15	(1)	
Enock Mawete Mwimba	07.02.2000	1	(1)	
Defenders:	**DOB**	**M**	**(s)**	**G**
Håvard Mork Breivik	24.01.2001		(1)	
Daniel Leó Grétarsson (ISL)	02.10.1995	13	(1)	
Jonas Grønner	11.04.1994	22	(4)	
Jørgen Hatlehol	18.06.1997	9	(5)	
Kasper Jørgensen	07.11.1999	10		
Ben Karamoko (CIV)	17.05.1995	11		
Daan Klinkenberg (NED)	12.01.1996	19	(8)	
Oddbjørn Lie	31.08.1987	9	(4)	
Davíð Kristján Ólafsson (ISL)	15.05.1995	24	(3)	
Ståle Sæthre	02.04.1993	11	(7)	
Shaquill Sno (NED)	05.01.1996	11	(12)	
Sigurd Vidhammer Tafjord	30.01.1997		(4)	

Midfielders:	DOB	M	(s)	G
Parfait Bizoza (BDI)	03.03.1999	18	(5)	2
Fredrik Carlsen	01.12.1989	12	(2)	
Markus Karlsbakk	07.05.2000	4	(15)	2
Peter Orry Larsen	25.02.1989	13	(9)	1
Isak Dybvik Määttä	19.09.2001	10	(2)	
Jordon Mutch (ENG)	02.12.1991		(1)	
Erikson Spinola Lima „Nenass" (CPV)	05.07.1995	12	(2)	
Kristoffer Strand Ødven	10.02.2002		(2)	
Izunna Arnest Uzochukwu (NGA)	11.04.1990	6	(18)	
Forwards:	**DOB**	**M**	**(s)**	**G**
Niklas Fernando Nygård Castro (CHI)	08.01.1996	23	(1)	4
Mamadou Diaw (SEN)	02.01.2001		(4)	
Vetle Fiskerstrand	14.03.2000	4	(4)	1
Hólmbert Aron Friðjónsson (ISL)	19.04.1993	13	(2)	11
Sigurd Haugen	17.07.1997	20	(5)	4
Simen Bolkan Nordli	25.12.1999	26	(2)	4

Fotballklubben Bodø/Glimt

	Founded:	19.09.2016	
	Stadium:	Aspmyra Stadion, Bodø (7,354)	
	Trainer:	Kjetil Knutsen	02.10.1968

Goalkeepers:	DOB	M	(s)	G
Nikita Haikin (RUS)	11.07.1995	20		
Joshua Smits (NED)	06.11.1992	10		
Defenders:	**DOB**	**M**	**(s)**	**G**
Isak Helstad Amundsen	14.10.1999	3	(7)	
Fredrik André Bjørkan	21.08.1998	30		1
Aleksander Foosnæs	05.06.1994		(8)	
Marius Høibråten	23.01.1995	18	(11)	1
Marius Lode	11.03.1993	26		1
Brede Moe	15.12.1991	13		
Alfons Sampsted (ISL)	06.04.1998	29		
Midfielders:	**DOB**	**M**	**(s)**	**G**
Patrick Berg	24.11.1997	28		4
Sondre Fet	17.01.1997	23	(3)	5
Elias Kristoffersen Hagen	20.01.2000	1	(7)	
Runar Hauge	01.09.2001		(8)	

Morten Konradsen	03.05.1996	4	(6)	1
Vegard Moberg	23.01.1991	3	(4)	3
Ulrik Saltnes	10.11.1992	30		12
Sammy Skytte (DEN)	20.02.1997		(11)	2
Ole Amund Sveen	05.01.1990		(8)	
Ask Tjærandsen-Skau	14.01.2001		(1)	
Hugo Vetlesen	29.02.2000	2	(6)	1
Forwards:	**DOB**	**M**	**(s)**	**G**
Victor Okoh Boniface (NGA)	23.12.2000	7	(17)	6
Jens Petter Hauge	12.10.1999	18		14
Adan Abadala Hussein	13.10.2002		(1)	
Kasper Junker (DEN)	05.03.1994	24	(1)	27
Ola Solbakken	07.09.1998	11	(11)	3
Sebastian Tounekti	13.07.2002	2	(7)	1
Philip Aksel Frigast Zinckernagel (DEN)	16.12.1994	28		19

Sportsklubben Brann Bergen

	Founded:	26.09.1908	
	Stadium:	Brann Stadion, Bergen (17,686)	
	Trainer:	Lars Arne Nilsen	06.04.1964
	(08.08.2020)	Kare Ingebrigtsen	11.11.1965

Goalkeepers:	DOB	M	(s)	G
Ali Nadhoim Ahamada (COM)	19.08.1991	10		
Håkon Opdal	11.06.1982	17		
Markus Pettersen	12.02.1999	3		
Defenders:	**DOB**	**M**	**(s)**	**G**
Bismar Gilberto Acosta Evans (CRC)	19.12.1986	4	(6)	
Ole Didrik Blomberg	12.06.2000	7	(1)	
Jón Gudni Fjóluson (ISL)	10.04.1989	11		
Vegard Forren	16.02.1988	25		
Thomas Grøgaard	08.02.1994	19	(5)	1
Ole Martin Kolskogen	20.01.2001	19	(2)	
Ruben Kristiansen	20.02.1988	18	(3)	
Mathias Rasmussen	25.11.1997	6	(2)	
Christian Eggen Rismark	01.08.1991	1	(7)	
Taijo Teniste (EST)	31.01.1988	7	(3)	
Jon-Helge Tveita	22.10.1992	12	(8)	2

Midfielders:	DOB	M	(s)	G
Kristoffer Barmen	19.08.1993	21	(5)	3
Fredrik Haugen	13.06.1992	12	(9)	1
Amer Ordagić (BIH)	05.05.1993	11		
Daniel Pedersen (DEN)	27.07.1992	19		2
Petter Strand	24.08.1994	27	(3)	4
Robert Taylor (FIN)	21.10.1994	24	(6)	6
Forwards:	**DOB**	**M**	**(s)**	**G**
Daouda Karamoko Bamba (CIV)	05.03.1995	30		10
Sondre Eide	07.04.2002		(1)	
Erlend Hustad	03.01.1997		(19)	1
Gilbert Koomson (GHA)	09.09.1994	17		8
Mikael Berg Kvinge	24.06.2003	1	(1)	
Marcus Johansen Mehnert	28.10.1997		(7)	
Gilli Rólantsson (FRO)	11.08.1992	1	(12)	
Sander Svendsen	06.08.1997	8	(2)	1

Fotballklubben Haugesund

	Founded:	28.10.1993	
	Stadium:	Haugesund Stadion, Haugesund (8,754)	
	Trainer:	Jostein Grindhaug	20.02.1973

Goalkeepers:	DOB	M	(s)	G
Helge Sandvik	05.02.1990	28		
Frank Stople	12.02.2002	2		
Defenders:	**DOB**	**M**	**(s)**	**G**
Mikkel Desler (DEN)	19.02.1995	28		
Ulrik Fredriksen	17.06.1999	19	(3)	1
Ben Karamoko (CIV)	17.05.1995	1	(2)	
Fredrik Knudsen	30.08.1996	14	(2)	1
Thore Baardsen Pedersen	11.08.1996	29	(1)	
Alexander Stølås	30.04.1989	19	(4)	
Benjamin Tiedemann Hansen (DEN)	07.02.1994	29		1
Midfielders:	**DOB**	**M**	**(s)**	**G**
Bruno Miguel Santos Leite (POR)	26.03.1995	22	(1)	
Christian Grindheim	17.07.1983	12	(13)	

Kristoffer Gunnarshaug	05.11.1999		(10)	
Kevin Martin Krygård	17.05.2000	17	(11)	
Joakim Vage Nilsen	24.04.1991	7	(8)	
Niklas Sandberg	18.05.1995	23	(1)	7
Mads Sande	22.03.1998	2	(7)	
Peter Therkildsen	13.06.1998	6	(2)	2
Forwards:	**DOB**	**M**	**(s)**	**G**
Alexander Ammitzbøll (DEN)	17.02.1999	14	(13)	4
Andreas Endresen	21.01.2003		(2)	
Benjamin Källman (FIN)	17.06.1998	9	(1)	
Oliver Klitten	01.05.2000	1	(4)	
Ibrahima Koné (MLI)	16.06.1999	2	(8)	2
Kristoffer Velde	09.09.1999	27	(1)	8
Ibrahima Wadji (SEN)	05.05.1995	19	(1)	7

Kristiansund Ballklubb

Founded: 02.09.2003
Stadium: Kristiansund Stadion, Kristiansund (4,444)
Trainer: Christian Michelsen   14.03.1976

Goalkeepers:	DOB	M	(s)	G
Eirik Johansen	12.07.1992	6	(2)	
Mor Mbaye (SEN)	03.01.1996	12		
Sean McDermott (IRL)	30.05.1993	12		
Defenders:	**DOB**	**M**	**(s)**	**G**
Christoffer Aasbak	22.07.1993	21	(2)	1
Amin Soleiman Askar	01.10.1985	11	(17)	2
Aliou Coly (SEN)	10.12.1992	18	(5)	1
Ivar Furu	07.05.1994	7	(3)	
Christophe Charles Steven René Psyché (FRA)	28.07.1988	15	(7)	2
Erlend Sivertsen	28.01.1991	5	(6)	
Bent Sørmo	22.09.1996	28	(2)	1
Dan Peter Ulvestad	04.04.1989	22		3
Max Williamsen	24.07.2003		(2)	

Midfielders:	DOB	M	(s)	G
Ousseynou Diagne (SEN)	05.06.1999	1	(6)	
Amidou Diop	27.02.1992	14	(4)	
Andreas Hopmark	06.07.1991	27	(3)	1
Liridon Kalludra (SWE)	05.11.1991	19	(7)	4
Olaus Skarsem	02.07.1998	22	(4)	3
Noah Solskjær	08.06.2000		(2)	
Pål Erik Ulvestad	08.09.1990	8	(13)	
Forwards:	**DOB**	**M**	**(s)**	**G**
Bendik Bye	09.03.1990	9	(15)	6
Flamur Kastrati	14.11.1991	17	(6)	
Faris Pemi Moumbagna (CMR)	01.07.2000	10	(14)	4
Amahl Willaim D'vaz Pellegrino	18.06.1990	27	(2)	25
Oskar Sivertsen	15.02.2004		(2)	1
Sondre Sørli	30.10.1995	19	(8)	3

Mjøndalen Idrettsforening Football

Founded: 22.08.1910
Stadium: Consto Arena, Mjøndalen (4,200)
Trainer: Vegard Hansen   08.08.1969

Goalkeepers:	DOB	M	(s)	G
Jorge Miguel Soares Vieira (POR)	08.01.1991	2	(1)	
Sousha Makani (IRN)	18.11.1986	28		
Defenders:	**DOB**	**M**	**(s)**	**G**
Vetle Dragsnes	06.02.1994	30		2
Syver Skaar Eriksen	29.04.2001	11	(1)	
Alexander Hansen	01.11.1996	12	(6)	
Quint Jansen (NED)	10.09.1990	4	(12)	1
Sondre Johansen	07.07.1995	29	(1)	
Markus Nakkim	21.07.1996	30		2
William Sell	20.12.1998	5	(9)	
Joackim Solberg	11.04.1989	13	(13)	
Midfielders:	**DOB**	**M**	**(s)**	**G**
Stian Aasmundsen	02.11.1989	24	(3)	1
Tonny Brochmann (DEN)	11.08.1989	16	(5)	2
Christian Gauseth	26.06.1984	12	(6)	1

	DOB	M	(s)	G
Lars Olden Larsen	17.09.1998	18	(10)	
Martin Ovenstad	18.04.1994	13	(12)	1
Erik Stavås Skistad	12.06.2001		(2)	
Ole Amund Sveen	05.01.1990	9		1
Isaac Twum	14.02.1998	9	(2)	1
Dagur Dan Þórhallsson (ISL)	02.05.2000	1	(11)	
Forwards:	**DOB**	**M**	**(s)**	**G**
Frank Bamenye Bizoza	23.10.2001		(4)	
Fredrik Brustad	22.06.1989	22	(8)	2
Mathias Fredriksen	28.04.1994		(1)	
Gustav Sving Helling	16.08.2001		(3)	
Andreas Hellum	19.11.1997	1	(15)	1
Shuaibu Lalle Ibrahim (NGA)	19.12.1996	20	(7)	6
Sondre Liseth	30.09.1997	21	(6)	4
Alfred Scriven	26.01.1998		(1)	

Molde Fotballklubb

Founded: 19.06.1911
Stadium: Aker Stadion, Molde (11,249)
Trainer: Erling Moe   22.07.1970

Goalkeepers:	DOB	M	(s)	G
Álex Craninx (BEL)	21.10.1995	3		
Andreas Linde (SWE)	24.07.1993	27		
Defenders:	**DOB**	**M**	**(s)**	**G**
Martin Bjørnbak	22.03.1992	19	(1)	
Stian Rode Gregersen	17.05.1995	10	(2)	2
Kristoffer Haugen	21.02.1994	12	(3)	1
John Kitolano	18.10.1999	10		1
Marcus Holmgren Pedersen	16.07.2000	18	(3)	2
Birk Risa	13.02.1998	7		
Sheriff Sinyan (GAM)	19.07.1996	14	(5)	
Henry Wingo (USA)	04.10.1995	12	(8)	2
Midfielders:	**DOB**	**M**	**(s)**	**G**
Fredrik Aursnes	10.12.1995	26	(1)	3
Tobias Christensen	11.05.2000	11	(9)	1

	DOB	M	(s)	G
Magnus Wolff Eikrem	08.08.1990	20	(7)	7
Martin Ellingsen	04.05.1995	21	(6)	5
Etzaz Hussain	27.01.1993	27	(1)	8
Fredrik Sjølstad	29.03.1994	4	(2)	
Forwards:	**DOB**	**M**	**(s)**	**G**
Eirik Andersen	21.09.1992	7	(10)	4
Mathis Bolly (CIV)	14.11.1990	2	(12)	1
Ola Brynhildsen	27.04.1999	18	(12)	5
Eirik Hestad	26.06.1995	14	(9)	4
Leke Samson James (NGA)	01.11.1992	16	(6)	13
Erling Knudtzon	15.12.1988	12	(15)	2
Mattias Moström (SWE)	25.02.1983	3	(6)	1
Ohi Omoijuanfo	10.01.1994	17	(10)	12
Ole Sebastian Sundgot	12.01.2001		(1)	

Odds Ballklubb Skien

Founded: 31.03.1894
Stadium: Skagerak Arena, Skien (11,767)
Trainer: Jan Frode Nornes   08.01.1973

Goalkeepers:	DOB	M	(s)	G
Sondre Rossbach	07.02.1996	29		
Egil Selvik	30.07.1997	1		
Defenders:	**DOB**	**M**	**(s)**	**G**
Odin Luras Bjørtuft	19.12.1998	30		1
Kevin Egell-Johnsen	13.05.2000	3	(2)	1
Eirik Asante Gayi	23.01.2001		(2)	
Steffen Hagen	08.03.1986	24		
John Kitolano	18.10.1999	8		
Bjørn Mæland	24.02.2001		(5)	
Birk Risa	13.02.1998	20		1
Espen Ruud	26.02.1984	27		6
Midfielders:	**DOB**	**M**	**(s)**	**G**
Vebjørn Hoff	13.02.1996	27		2
Filip Rönningen Jørgensen	27.05.2002	17	(6)	

	DOB	M	(s)	G
Markus André Kaasa	15.07.1997	28	(1)	2
Joshua Kitolano	03.08.2001	27		4
Kasper Lunding	17.07.1999	9	(6)	4
Fredrik Nordkvelle	13.09.1985	5	(19)	
Vladimir Rodić (MNE)	07.09.1993	9	(1)	
Elias Skogvoll	05.05.1996		(3)	
Forwards:	**DOB**	**M**	**(s)**	**G**
Mushagalusa Bakenga Joar Bahati Namugunga	08.08.1992	19	(7)	15
Torgeir Børven	03.12.1991	4		6
Marius Bustgaard Larsen	14.05.2000		(3)	
Tobias Lauritsen	30.08.1997	8	(12)	3
Bilal Njie	13.06.1998	2	(8)	
Elbasan Rashani (KVX)	09.05.1993	22	(2)	3
Robin Simović (SWE)	29.05.1991	6	(7)	2
Onyekachi Hope Ugwuadu (NGA)	05.05.1997	5	(17)	

Rosenborg Ballklub Trondheim

Founded: 19.05.1917
Stadium: Lerkendal Stadion, Trondheim (21,421)
Trainer: Eirik Horneland   14.03.1975
(27.06.2020) Trond Henriksen   28.04.1964
(01.09.2020) Åge Fridtjof Hareide   23.09.1953

Goalkeepers:	DOB	M	(s)	G
André Hansen	17.12.1989	19		
Julian Lund	20.05.1999	11	(1)	
Defenders:	DOB	M	(s)	G
Hólmar Örn Eyjólfsson (ISL)	06.08.1990	9	(1)	1
Vegar Eggen Hedenstad	26.06.1991	17	(2)	1
Even Hovland	14.02.1989	17	(1)	2
Pa Konaté (GUI)	25.04.1994	11		1
Birger Solberg Meling	17.12.1994	2	(1)	
Tore Reginiussen	10.04.1986	26		1
Erlend Dahl Reitan	11.09.1997	19	(3)	1
Gustav Valsvik	26.05.1993	8	(3)	1
Midfielders:	DOB	M	(s)	G
Gjermund Åsen	22.05.1991	13	(9)	2
Markus Henriksen	25.07.1992	9		
Anders Konradsen	18.07.1990	9	(2)	
Marius Lundemo	11.04.1994	7	(1)	1
Per Ciran Skjelbred	16.06.1987	14	(1)	1
Edvard Tagseth	23.01.2001	11	(15)	
Anders Trondsen	30.03.1995	12	(1)	1
Kristoffer Zachariassen	27.01.1994	29		12
Forwards:	DOB	M	(s)	G
Samuel Adeniyi Adegbenro (NGA)	03.12.1995	5	(7)	
Erik Botheim	10.01.2000		(3)	
Torgeir Børven	03.12.1991	11	(3)	4
Filip Brattbakk	24.04.2000		(6)	
Emil Konradsen Ceide	03.09.2001	19	(9)	
Pål André Helland	04.01.1990	13	(6)	2
Carl Holse (DEN)	02.06.1999	17	(13)	5
Dino Islamović (MNE)	17.01.1994	21	(6)	12
Rasmus Wiedesheim-Paul	08.02.1999	1	(3)	

Sandefjord Fotball

Founded: 10.09.1998
Stadium: Sandefjord Arena, Sandefjord (6,582)
Trainer: Martí Cifuentes Corvillo (ESP)   07.07.1982

Goalkeepers:	DOB	M	(s)	G
Jacob Storevik	29.07.1996	30		
Defenders:	DOB	M	(s)	G
Sander Moen Foss	31.12.1998	13	(7)	1
Lars Grorud	02.07.1983	18	(4)	1
Mats Haakenstad	14.11.1993	5	(4)	
Viðar Ari Jónsson (ISL)	10.03.1994	20	(7)	2
Anton Kralj (SWE)	12.03.1998	18	(4)	
Martin Kreuzriegler (AUT)	10.01.1994	22	(2)	1
Lars Markmanrud	01.03.2001	16	(6)	1
Marc Vales González (AND)	04.04.1990	19	(5)	3
Brice Wembangomo	18.12.1996	18		
Midfielders:	DOB	M	(s)	G
Erik Brenden	07.01.1994	10	(15)	1
Henrik Falchener	08.05.2003		(1)	
Peder Meen Johansen	27.08.2003	3	(3)	
William Kurtović (SWE)	22.06.1996	16	(3)	
Sander Risan Mørk	06.12.2000	5	(7)	
Emil Pálsson (ISL)	10.06.1993	18	(6)	
Harmeet Singh		6	(3)	2
Enric Vallès (NED)	01.03.1990	13	(1)	
José Eduardo de Araújo „Zé Eduardo" (BRA)	16.08.1991	1	(3)	1
Forwards:	DOB	M	(s)	G
Marcos Celorrio Yecora (ESP)	19.02.1997	4	(9)	1
George Nuah Gibson	29.08.2000	4	(12)	
Sivert Gussiås	11.08.1999	23	(7)	7
Kristoffer Normann Hansen	12.08.1994	15	(10)	2
Stefan Mladenović	03.04.1994		(2)	
Rubén Herráiz Alcaraz „Rufo" (ESP)	13.01.1993	21	(6)	7
Deyver Antonio Vega Álvarez (CRC)	19.09.1992	12	(2)	

Sarpsborg 08 Fotballforening

Founded: 15.01.2008
Stadium: Sarpsborg Stadion, Sarpsborg (8,022)
Trainer: Mikael Stahre   05.07.1975

Goalkeepers:	DOB	M	(s)	G
Aslak Falch	25.05.1992	3		
David Nilsson (MKD)	12.01.1991	26		
Simon Thomas	12.04.1990	1		
Defenders:	DOB	M	(s)	G
Sulayman Bojang	03.09.1997	11	(13)	
Mikael Dyrestam (GUI)	10.12.1991	13	(1)	2
Jørgen Horn	07.06.1987	8	(2)	
Nicolai Næss	18.01.1993	29		
Magnar Ødegaard	11.05.1993	28	(1)	
Joachim Thomassen	04.05.1988	24		
Bjørn Inge Utvik	28.02.1996	27	(1)	2
Midfielders:	DOB	M	(s)	G
Jordan Adéoti (BEN)	12.03.1989	4	(9)	
Ismaila Coulibaly (MLI)	25.12.2000	11	(3)	4
Emir Derviškadić (BIH)	07.06.2004		(1)	
Sebastian Jarl	11.01.2000	3	(10)	1
Jonathan Lindseth	25.02.1996	23	(3)	3
Anton Salétros (SWE)	12.04.1996	17	(2)	1
Joachim Soltvedt	09.09.1995	12	(12)	3
Gaute Høberg Vetti	02.09.1998	10	(5)	1
Forwards:	DOB	M	(s)	G
Anwar Elyounoussi	29.03.1999		(2)	
Ole Halvorsen	02.10.1987	25	(2)	5
Tobias Heintz	13.07.1998	14		2
Alexander Jakobsen (EGY)	18.03.1994	1	(9)	
Aboubacar Konté (MLI)	02.03.2001	1	(6)	
Mustafa Abdellaoue „Mos"	01.08.1988	8	(9)	6
Mohamed Ofkir	04.08.1996	10	(15)	
Jørgen Strand Larsen	06.02.2000	15	(1)	2
Guillermo Federico Molins Palmeiro (SWE)	26.09.1988	4	(1)	
Alexander Ruud Tveter	07.03.1991	2	(10)	

Stabæk Fotball Bærum

Founded: 16.03.1912
Stadium: Nadderud Stadion, Bærum (4,938)
Trainer: Jan Jönsson (SWE)   24.05.1960

Goalkeepers:	DOB	M	(s)	G
Marcus Sandberg (SWE)	07.11.1990	30		
Defenders:	DOB	M	(s)	G
Yaw Ihle Amankwah	07.07.1988	17	(3)	
Andreas Schjølberg Hanche-Olsen	17.01.1997	18		3
Nicolas Pignatel Jenssen	12.01.2002	3	(5)	
Emil Jonassen	17.02.1993	13	(7)	
Sturla Ottesen	25.05.2001	9		
Jørgen Øveraas	03.12.1989	14	(5)	1
Mats Solheim	03.12.1987	29		2
Gustav Valsvik	26.05.1993	10		1
Peder Vogt	11.02.2000	7	(5)	
Midfielders:	DOB	M	(s)	G
Emil Bohinen	12.03.1999	24		5
Kornelius Hansen	06.05.2001	15	(12)	6
Jesper Isaksen	13.10.1999		(9)	
Luc Kassi (CIV)	20.08.1994	8	(7)	3
Kaloyan Kostadinov	18.07.2002	11	(1)	
Tortol Lumanza-Lembi (BEL)	13.04.1994	19	(4)	
Magnus Lundal	06.04.2000	5	(9)	1
Sammy Solitaire Siddharta Skytte (DEN)	20.02.1997	14		
Kristian Bernt Torgersen	16.05.2003		(1)	
Filip Valenčič (SVN)	07.01.1992		(6)	
Hugo Vetlesen	29.02.2000	18	(1)	4
Forwards:	DOB	M	(s)	G
Marcus Antonsson (SWE)	08.05.1991	10		1
Erik Botheim	10.01.2000	8	(7)	
Oliver Valaker Edvardsen	19.03.1999	28	(2)	6
Romain Gall (USA)	31.01.1995	4	(6)	
Kosuke Kinoshita (JPN)	03.10.1994	7	(15)	5
Darren Maatsen (NED)	30.01.1991	9	(9)	3

Idrettsklubben Start Kristiansand

Founded: 19.09.1905
Stadium: Sør Arena, Kristiansand (14,448)
Trainer: Jóhannes Þór Harðarson (ISL) 28.07.1976

Goalkeepers:	DOB	M	(s)	G
Jonas Deumeland (GER)	09.02.1988	19		
Amund Wichne	12.05.1997	11	(1)	
Defenders:	DOB	M	(s)	G
Vegard Bergan	20.02.1995	23	(4)	
Jesper Daland	06.01.2000	30		1
Joackim Jørgensen	20.09.1988	17	(5)	
Henrik Robstad	12.05.1991	7	(13)	
Kristoffer Tønnesen	01.10.1997	28	(1)	1
Eirik Wichne	12.05.1997	27	(2)	
Midfielders:	DOB	M	(s)	G
Afeez Aremu (NGA)	03.10.1999	4		
Espen Børufsen	04.03.1988	5	(13)	
Mohamed El Makrini (NED)	06.07.1987	10		1
Adnan Hadžić	08.03.1999		(1)	
Kevin Kabran (SWE)	22.11.1993	27	(2)	3
Eirik Schulze	07.01.1993	28	(1)	10
Erlend Segberg	12.04.1997	9	(9)	2
Sander Sjøkvist	09.03.1999		(3)	
Kasper Skaanes	19.03.1995	9	(15)	2
Isaac Twum (GHA)	14.02.1998	8	(2)	1
Mikael Ugland	24.01.2000	5	(8)	1
Forwards:	DOB	M	(s)	G
Adeleke Akinyemi (NGA)	11.08.1998		(3)	
Christian Bolaños Navarro (CRC)	17.05.1984	12		2
Mathias Bringaker	30.01.1997	12	(8)	4
Eman Marković	08.05.1999	20	(8)	1
Martin Ramsland	02.04.1993	9	(8)	
Steffen Skålevik	31.01.1993	10	(11)	1

Strømsgodset Toppfotball Drammen

Founded: 10.02.1907
Stadium: Marienlyst Stadion, Drammen (8,935)
Trainer: Henrik Pedersen 02.01.1978

Goalkeepers:	DOB	M	(s)	G
Viljar Myhra	21.07.1996	30		
Defenders:	DOB	M	(s)	G
Niklas Gunnarsson	27.04.1991	26		
Sondre Fosnaess Hanssen	25.05.2001	18	(1)	
Ari Leifsson (ISL)	19.04.1998	8	(6)	
Nicholas Mickelson	24.07.1999	21	(1)	
Andreas Rosendahl Nyhagen	04.11.1998	1	(4)	
Jonathan Parr	21.10.1988	3	(1)	
Duplexe Tchamba Bangou (CMR)	10.07.1998	11	(1)	1
Lars-Christopher Vilsvik	18.10.1988	24	(1)	1
Midfielders:	DOB	M	(s)	G
Tobias Fjeld Gulliksen	09.07.2003	1	(6)	
Johan Hove	07.09.2000	29	(1)	10
Jānis Ikaunieks (LVA)	16.02.1995	2	(4)	
Jack Ipalibo (NGA)	06.04.1998	22		
Kreshnik Krasniqi	22.12.2000		(5)	
Mikkel Maigaard (DEN)	20.09.1995	28		5
Sebastian Pop	24.05.2002		(2)	
Halldor Stenevik	02.02.2000	9	(13)	
Herman Stengel	26.08.1995	10	(5)	1
Aleksander Stenseth	23.07.2000		(6)	
Forwards:	DOB	M	(s)	G
Simen Hammershaug	02.08.2000		(2)	
Valdimar Þór Ingimundarson (ISL)	28.04.1999	8	(3)	2
Moses Mawa	04.08.1996	27	(3)	6
Marcus Mølvadgaard (DEN)	03.08.1999		(18)	1
Lars-Jørgen Salvesen	19.02.1996	30		10
Kristoffer Tokstad	05.07.1991	22	(6)	2

Viking Fotballklubb Stavanger

Founded: 10.08.1899
Stadium: Viking Stadion, Stavanger (15,900)
Trainer: Bjarne Berntsen 21.12.1956

Goalkeepers:	DOB	M	(s)	G
Iven Austbø	22.02.1985	17		
Michael Crowe (WAL)	13.11.1995		(1)	
Arild Østbø	19.04.1991	13		
Defenders:	DOB	M	(s)	G
Axel Óskar Andrésson (ISL)	27.01.1998	15	(2)	
Sondre Bjørshol	30.04.1994	10		
Henrik Heggheim	22.04.2001	26		
Runar Hove	08.08.1995	3		
Kristoffer Paulsen	31.01.2004		(1)	
Adrian Nilsen Pereira	31.08.1999	13	(2)	2
Fredrik Torsteinbø	13.03.1991	28	(2)	4
Viljar Vevatne	07.12.1994	27		3
Rolf Daniel Vikstøl	22.02.1989	11	(7)	1
Midfielders:	DOB	M	(s)	G
Sondre Auklend	10.06.2003	2	(14)	
Joe Bell (NZL)	27.04.1999	21	(8)	2
Samúel Kári Friðjónsson (ISL)	22.02.1996	3	(4)	1
Johnny Furdal	04.05.1986	10	(1)	
Kristoffer Løkberg	22.01.1992	23	(1)	2
Sebastian Søraas Sebulonsen	27.01.2000	4	(16)	1
Harald Tangen	03.01.2001	1	(4)	
Forwards:	DOB	M	(s)	G
Veton Berisha	13.04.1994	27	(1)	16
Zymer Bytyqi	11.09.1996	24	(5)	10
Yann-Erik de Lanlay	14.05.1992	14	(5)	2
Jefferson De Souza	27.09.1995	3	(3)	
Tommy Høiland	11.04.1989	2	(24)	1
Ylldren Ibrahimaj	24.12.1995	27	(2)	7
Even Østensen	02.06.1993	6	(11)	1

Vålerenga Fotball Oslo

Founded: 29.07.1913
Stadium: Intility Arena, Oslo (16,555)
Trainer: Dag-Eilev Fagermo 28.01.1967

Goalkeepers:	DOB	M	(s)	G
Kjetil Haug	12.06.1998	1	(1)	
Kristoffer Klaesson	27.11.2000	29		
Defenders:	DOB	M	(s)	G
Sam Adekugbe (CAN)	16.01.1995	25	(1)	
Johan Bjørdal	05.05.1986	8	(4)	
Christian Dale Borchgrevink	11.05.1999	29		1
Ivan Näsberg	22.04.1996	29		2
Amin Nouri	10.01.1990		(1)	
Oskar Aron Opsahl	25.08.2001		(1)	
Brage Skaret	28.04.2002		(1)	
Jonatan Tollås	01.07.1990	23		
Midfielders:	DOB	M	(s)	G
Aron Leonard Dønnum	20.04.1998	27		8
Odin Holm	18.01.2003	1	(15)	1
Fredrik Jensen	18.05.1993	20	(1)	1
Magnus Lekven	13.01.1988	27	(1)	
Felix Horn Myhre	04.03.1999	6	(18)	
Herolind Shala (KVX)	01.02.1992	21	(6)	2
Forwards:	DOB	M	(s)	G
Henrik Bjørdal	04.02.1997	14		3
Ousmane Camara (GUI)	28.12.1998		(4)	
Bård Finne	13.02.1995	13	(13)	8
Viðar Örn Kjartansson (ISL)	11.03.1990	13	(1)	9
Osame Sahraoui	11.06.2001	21	(7)	5
Benjamin Stokke	20.08.1990	5	(10)	3
Deyver Antonio Vega Álvarez (CRC)	19.09.1992		(6)	1
Matthías Vilhjálmsson (ISL)	30.01.1987	18	(11)	6

SECOND LEVEL
OBOS-ligaen 2020

1.	Tromsø IL (*Promoted*)	30	19	6	5	60	-	29	63
2.	Lillestrøm SK (*Promoted*)	30	16	9	5	49	-	26	57
3.	Sogndal Fotball (*Promotion Play-offs*)	30	15	6	9	57	-	36	51
4.	Ranheim IL Trondheim (*Promotion Play-offs*)	30	13	8	9	61	-	41	47
5.	Åsane Fotball (*Promotion Play-offs*)	30	12	9	9	60	-	48	45
6.	Raufoss IL (*Promotion Play-offs*)	30	11	10	9	53	-	44	42
7.	Sandnes Ulf	30	11	8	11	46	-	55	41
8.	KFUM-Kameratene Oslo	30	10	9	11	44	-	44	39
9.	Hamarkameratene	30	10	9	11	49	-	52	39
10.	Strømmen IF	30	10	8	12	47	-	51	35
11.	FK Jerv Grimstad	30	9	8	13	41	-	57	35
12.	Ullensaker/Kisa IL	30	10	5	15	45	-	63	35
13.	Grorud IL Oslo	30	9	7	14	45	-	56	34
14.	IL Stjørdals-Blink (*Relegation Play-offs*)	30	8	9	13	52	-	59	33
15.	Kongsvinger IL (*Relegated*)	30	6	10	14	35	-	53	28
16.	Øygarden FK (*Relegated*)	30	6	9	15	37	-	67	27

<u>Please note</u>: Nest-Sotra Fotball was renamed Øygarden FK (as a cooperation with Nordre Fjell, Sund SK, Skogsvåg IL, Telavåg IL and Skjergard IL).

Promotion Play-offs

First Round [16.12.2020]	Åsane Fotball - Raufoss IL	3-1(2-1)
Second Round [19.12.2020]	Ranheim IL Trondheim - Åsane Fotball	4-1(2-0)
Third Round [22.12.2020]	Sogndal Fotball - Ranheim IL Trondheim	3-1(2-1)

Sogndal Fotball qualified for the First Level Relegation/Promotion Play-offs .

Relegation Play-offs (2nd / 3rd Level)

IL Stjørdals-Blink - Asker Fotball	3-0(1-0)	3-1(1-1)

NATIONAL TEAM

INTERNATIONAL MATCHES
(16.07.2020 – 15.07.2021)

04.09.2020	Oslo	Norway - Austria	1-2(0-1)	(UNL)
07.09.2020	Belfast	Northern Ireland - Norway	1-5(1-3)	(UNL)
08.10.2020	Oslo	Norway - Serbia	1-2(0-0,1-1)	(ECQPO)
11.10.2020	Oslo	Norway - Romania	4-0(2-0)	(UNL)
14.10.2020	Oslo	Norway - Northern Ireland	1-0(0-0)	(UNL)
15.11.2020	Bucureşti	Romania - Norway	3-0 (*awarded*)	(UNL)
18.11.2020	Wien	Austria - Norway	1-1(0-0)	(UNL)
24.03.2021	Gibraltar	Gibraltar - Norway	0-3(0-2)	(WCQ)
27.03.2021	Málaga	Norway - Turkey	0-3(0-2)	(WCQ)
30.03.2021	Podgorica	Montenegro - Norway	0-1(0-1)	(WCQ)
02.06.2021	Málaga	Norway - Luxembourg	1-0(0-0)	(F)
06.06.2021	Málaga	Norway - Greece	1-2(0-2)	(F)

04.09.2020 NORWAY - AUSTRIA 1-2(0-1) 2nd UEFA Nations League B, Group 1
Ullevaal Stadion, Oslo; Referee: Mattias Gestranius (Finland); Attendance: 0
NOR: Rune Almenning Jarstein, Tore Reginiussen, Omar Elabdellaoui, Haitam Aleesami, Kristoffer Vassbakk Ajer, Stefan Marius Johansen (Cap) (68.Markus Henriksen), Mathias Antonsen Normann, Morten Thorsby (60.Martin Linnes), Sander Gard Bolin Berge, Joshua Christian Kojo King (64.Alexander Sørloth), Erling Braut Håland. Trainer: Lars Edvin Lagerbäck (Sweden).
Goal: Erling Braut Håland (66).

07.09.2020 NORTHERN IRELAND - NORWAY 1-5(1-3) 2nd UEFA Nations League B, Group 1
Windsor Park, Belfast; Referee: Bartosz Frankowski (Poland); Attendance: 0
NOR: Rune Almenning Jarstein, Even Hovland, Omar Elabdellaoui (80.Jonas Svensson), Haitam Aleesami (77.Birger Solberg Meling), Kristoffer Vassbakk Ajer, Stefan Marius Johansen (Cap) (71.Joshua Christian Kojo King), Markus Henriksen, Mohamed Amine Elyounoussi, Mathias Antonsen Normann, Alexander Sørloth, Erling Braut Håland. Trainer: Lars Edvin Lagerbäck (Sweden).
Goals: Mohamed Amine Elyounoussi (2), Erling Braut Håland (7), Alexander Sørloth (19, 47), Erling Braut Håland (58).

08.10.2020 NORWAY - SERBIA 1-2(0-0,1-1) 16th EC. Qualifiers Play-offs, Semi-Finals
Ullevaal Stadion, Oslo; Referee: Daniele Orsato (Italy); Attendance: 200
NOR: Rune Almenning Jarstein, Tore Reginiussen (91.Ken Remi Stefan Strandberg), Omar Elabdellaoui (116.Morten Thorsby), Haitam Aleesami (106.Martin Linnes), Kristoffer Vassbakk Ajer, Stefan Marius Johansen (Cap) (66.Joshua Christian Kojo King), Markus Henriksen (46.Mathias Antonsen Normann), Martin Ødegaard (111.Mohamed Amine Elyounoussi), Sander Gard Bolin Berge, Alexander Sørloth, Erling Braut Håland. Trainer: Lars Edvin Lagerbäck (Sweden).
Goal: Mathias Antonsen Normann (88).

11.10.2020   **NORWAY - ROMANIA**   4-0(2-0)   2nd UEFA Nations League B, Group 1
Ullevaal Stadion, Oslo; Referee: Ivan Kružliak (Slovakia); Attendance: 200
NOR: Rune Almenning Jarstein, Ken Remi Stefan Strandberg, Omar Elabdellaoui (Cap) (78.Jonas Svensson), Birger Solberg Meling, Kristoffer Vassbakk Ajer, Mohamed Amine Elyounoussi (85.Jens Hauge), Mathias Antonsen Normann (70.Fredrik Midtsjø), Martin Ødegaard (70.Martin Linnes), Sander Gard Bolin Berge, Alexander Sørloth, Erling Braut Håland (78.Joshua Christian Kojo King). Trainer: Lars Edvin Lagerbäck (Sweden).
Goals: Erling Braut Håland (13), Alexander Sørloth (39), Erling Braut Håland (64, 74).

14.10.2020   **NORWAY - NORTHERN IRELAND**   1-0(0-0)   2nd UEFA Nations League B, Group 1
Ullevaal Stadion, Oslo; Referee: Kristo Tohver (Estonia); Attendance: 200
NOR: André Hansen, Ken Remi Stefan Strandberg, Omar Elabdellaoui (Cap), Birger Solberg Meling, Kristoffer Vassbakk Ajer, Mohamed Amine Elyounoussi, Mathias Antonsen Normann (65.Fredrik Midtsjø), Martin Ødegaard (78.Martin Linnes), Sander Gard Bolin Berge, Joshua Christian Kojo King (65.Alexander Sørloth), Erling Braut Håland (87.Markus Henriksen). Trainer: Lars Edvin Lagerbäck (Sweden).
Goal: Stuart Dallas (68 own goal).

15.11.2020   **ROMANIA - NORWAY**   3-0 (*awarded*)   2nd UEFA Nations League B, Group 1
Arena Naţională, Bucureşti; Referee: Ali Palabıyık (Turkey); Attendance: 0
Please note: the match was cancelled and awarded as a 3–0 win to Romania after the Norway national team were prohibited from travelling to Romania by the Norwegian government due to a positive COVID-19 test in the squad.

18.11.2020   **AUSTRIA - NORWAY**   1-1(0-0)   2nd UEFA Nations League B, Group 1
"Ernst Happel Stadion", Wien; Referee: Benoît Bastien (France); Attendance: 0
NOR: Per Kristian Bråtveit, Lunan Ruben Gabrielsen, Jørgen Skjelvik, Andreas Schjølberg Hanche-Olsen, Julian Ryerson (81.Daniel Granli), Fredrik Stensøe Ulvestad, Mats Møller Dæhli (Cap) (67.Kristian Thorstvedt), Sondre Bjorvand Tronstad, Ghayas Zahid (81.Kristoffer Askildsen), Veton Berisha (86.Andreas Aalen Vindheim), Jørgen Strand Larsen (86.Håkon Evjen). Trainer: Lars Edvin Lagerbäck (Sweden) [in quarantine and replaced by Leif Gunnar Smerud].
Goal: Ghayas Zahid (61).

24.03.2021   **GIBRALTAR - NORWAY**   0-3(0-2)   22nd FIFA WC.Qualifiers
Victoria Stadium, Gibraltar; Referee: Duje Strukan (Croatia); Attendance: 0
NOR: Rune Almenning Jarstein, Ken Remi Stefan Strandberg, Jonas Svensson (62.Martin Linnes), Marius Lode, Birger Solberg Meling, Fredrik Midtsjø (62.Tokmac Chol Nguen), Mohamed Amine Elyounoussi (46.Jens Petter Hauge), Martin Ødegaard (Cap) (46.Patrick Berg), Kristian Thorstvedt, Alexander Sørloth, Erling Braut Håland (62.Joshua Christian Kojo King). Trainer: Ståle Solbakken.
Goals: Alexander Sørloth (43), Kristian Thorstvedt (45), Jonas Svensson (57).

27.03.2021   **NORWAY - TURKEY**   0-3(0-2)   22nd FIFA WC.Qualifiers
Estadio La Rosaleda, Málaga; Referee: Alejandro José Hernández Hernández (Spain); Attendance: 0
NOR: Rune Almenning Jarstein (46.André Hansen), Stian Rode Gregersen, Birger Solberg Meling, Kristoffer Vassbakk Ajer, Julian Ryerson (67.Jonas Svensson), Mohamed Amine Elyounoussi (67.Joshua Christian Kojo King), Patrick Berg, Martin Ødegaard (Cap), Alexander Sørloth, Fredrik Midtsjø (67.Kristian Thorstvedt), Erling Braut Håland (83.Morten Thorsby). Trainer: Ståle Solbakken.

30.03.2021   **MONTENEGRO - NORWAY**   0-1(0-1)   22nd FIFA WC.Qualifiers
Stadion pod Goricom, Podgorica; Referee: Anthony Taylor (England); Attendance: 0
NOR: Rune Almenning Jarstein, Jonas Svensson (66.Julian Ryerson), Stian Rode Gregersen, Birger Solberg Meling, Kristoffer Vassbakk Ajer, Mohamed Amine Elyounoussi (90.Ken Remi Stefan Strandberg), Morten Thorsby, Patrick Berg (66.Fredrik Midtsjø), Martin Ødegaard (Cap) (81.Martin Linnes), Alexander Sørloth, Erling Braut Håland (80.Joshua Christian Kojo King). Trainer: Ståle Solbakken.
Goal: Alexander Sørloth (35).

02.06.2021   **NORWAY - LUXEMBOURG**   1-0(0-0)   Friendly International
Estadio La Rosaleda, Málaga (Spain); Referee: Kristoffer Karlsson (Sweden); Attendance: 0
NOR: André Hansen, Ken Remi Stefan Strandberg, Jonas Svensson (65.Julian Ryerson), Birger Solberg Meling, Kristoffer Vassbakk Ajer (72.Andreas Schjølberg Hanche-Olsen), Mohamed Amine Elyounoussi, Morten Thorsby (65.Fredrik Midtsjø), Martin Ødegaard (Cap), Jens Petter Hauge (64.Aron Leonard Dønnum), Alexander Sørloth (85.Kristian Thorstvedt), Erling Braut Håland. Trainer: Ståle Solbakken.
Goal: Erling Braut Håland (90+2).

06.06.2021   **NORWAY - GREECE**   1-2(0-2)   Friendly International
Estadio La Rosaleda, Málaga (Spain); Referee: Jakob Kehlet (Denmark); Attendance: 0
NOR: André Hansen, Kristoffer Vassbakk Ajer (88.Andreas Schjølberg Hanche-Olsen), Stian Rode Gregersen, Birger Solberg Meling (69.Fredrik André Bjørkan), Ken Remi Stefan Strandberg, Fredrik Midtsjø (46.Alexander Sørloth), Morten Thorsby (46.Kristian Thorstvedt), Kristoffer Zachariassen (46.Julian Ryerson), Martin Ødegaard (Cap), Erling Braut Håland, Patrick Berg (69.Fredrik Aursnes). Trainer: Ståle Solbakken.
Goal: Ken Remi Stefan Strandberg (64).

NATIONAL TEAM PLAYERS (16.07.2020 – 15.07.2021)					
Name	**DOB**	**Caps**	**Goals**	**2020/2021:**	***Club***
Goalkeepers					
Per Kristian BRÅTVEIT	15.02.1996	**1**	**0**	2020:	*Djurgårdens IF Stockholm (SWE)*
André HANSEN	17.12.1989	**8**	**0**	2020/2021:	*Rosenborg BK Trondheim*
Rune Almenning JARSTEIN	29.09.1984	**72**	**0**	2020/2021:	*Hertha BSC Berlin (GER)*

Defenders

Kristoffer Vassbakk AJER	17.04.1998	23	0	2020/2021:	Celtic FC Glasgow (SCO)
Haitam ALEESAMI	31.07.1991	31	0	2020:	Unattached
Fredrik André BJØRKAN	21.08.1998	1	0	2021:	FK Bodø/Glimt
Omar ELABDELLAOUI	05.12.1991	49	0	2020/2021:	Galatasaray SK İstanbul (TUR)
Lunan Ruben GABRIELSEN	10.03.1992	1	0	2020:	Toulouse FC (FRA)
Daniel Fredrik GRANLI	01.05.1994	1	0	2020:	Aalborg BK (DEN)
Stian Rode GREGERSEN	17.05.1995	3	0	2021:	Molde FK
Andreas Schjølberg HANCHE-OLSEN	17.01.1997	3	0	2020/2021:	KAA Gent (BEL)
Even HOVLAND	14.02.1989	29	0	2020:	Rosenborg BK Trondheim
Martin LINNES	20.09.1991	29	1	2020/2021:	Galatasaray SK İstanbul (TUR)
Marius LODE	11.03.1993	1	0	2021:	FK Bodø/Glimt
Birger Solberg MELING	17.12.1994	19	0	2020/2021:	Nîmes Olympique (FRA)
Tore REGINIUSSEN	10.04.1986	31	4	2020/2021:	Rosenborg BK Trondheim
Julian RYERSON	17.11.1997	5	0	2020/2021:	1.FC Union Berlin (GER)
Jørgen SKJELVIK	05.07.1991	8	0	2020:	Odense Boldklub (DEN)
Ken Remi Stefan STRANDBERG	25.07.1990	17	1	2020/2021:	FK Ural Yekaterinburg (RUS)
Jonas SVENSSON	06.03.1993	23	1	2020/2021:	AZ Alkmaar (NED)
Andreas Aalen VINDHEIM	04.08.1995	1	0	2020:	AC Sparta Praha (CZE)

Midfielders

Fredrik AURSNES	10.12.1995	1	0	2021:	Molde FK
Kristoffer ASKILDSEN	09.01.2001	1	0	2020:	UC Sampdoria Genova (ITA)
Patrick BERG	24.11.1997	4	0	2021:	FK Bodø/Glimt
Sander Gard Bolin BERGE	14.02.1998	24	1	2020/2021:	Sheffield United FC (ENG)
Aron Leonard DØNNUM	20.04.1998	1	0	2021:	Vålerenga Fotball Oslo
Mohamed Amine ELYOUNOUSSI	04.08.1994	32	6	2020/2021:	Celtic FC Glasgow (SCO)
Håkon EVJEN	14.02.2000	1	0	2020:	AZ Alkmaar (NED)
Jens Petter HAUGE	12.10.1999	3	0	2020/2021:	AC Milan (ITA)
Markus HENRIKSEN	25.07.1992	58	3	2020:	Unattached
				07.09.2020->	Rosenborg BK Trondheim
Stefan Marius JOHANSEN	08.01.1991	55	6	2020/2021:	Fulham FC London (ENG)
Fredrik MIDTSJØ	11.08.1993	11	0	2020/2021:	AZ Alkmaar (NED)
Mats MØLLER Dæhli	02.03.1995	24	1	2020:	KAA Gent (BEL)
Mathias Antonsen NORMANN	28.05.1996	7	1	2020:	FK Rostov-na-Donu (RUS)
Morten THORSBY	05.05.1996	7	0	2020/2021:	UC Sampdoria Genova (ITA)
Sondre Bjorvand TRONSTAD	26.08.1995	1	0	2020:	SBV Vitesse Arnhem (NED)
Fredrik Stensøe ULVESTAD	17.06.1992	4	0	2020/2021:	Djurgårdens IF Stockholm (SWE)
Kristoffer ZACHARIASSEN	27.01.1994	1	0	2021:	Rosenborg BK Trondheim
Ghayas ZAHID	08.09.1994	2	1	2020:	APOEL FC Nicosia (CYP)
Martin ØDEGAARD	17.12.1998	30	1	2020:	Real Madrid CF (ESP)
				27.01.2021->	Arsenal FC London (ENG, on loan)

Forwards

Veton BERISHA	13.04.1994	5	1	2020:	Viking FK Stavanger
Erling Braut HÅLAND	21.07.2000	12	7	2020/2021:	BV Borussia Dortmund (GER)
Joshua Christian Kojo KING	15.01.1992	54	17	2020:	AFC Bournemouth (ENG)
				01.02.2021->	Everton FC Liverpool (ENG)
Tokmac Chol NGUEN	20.10.1993	1	0	2021:	Ferencvárosi FC (HUN)
Jørgen Strand LARSEN	06.02.2000	1	0	2020:	FC Groningen (NED)
Alexander SØRLOTH	05.12.1995	32	11	2020:	Trabzonspor Kulübü (TUR, on loan)
				22.09.2020->	RasenBallsport Leipzig (GER, on loan)
Kristian THORSTVEDT	13.03.1999	5	1	2020/2021:	KRC Genk (BEL)

Trainer

Lars Edvin LAGERBÄCK (Sweden) [01.02.2017 – 06.12.2020]	16.07.1948	35 M; 18 W; 9 D; 8 L; 61-35
Ståle SOLBAKKEN [from 07.12.2020]	27.02.1968	5 M; 3 W; 0 D; 2 L; 6-5

POLAND

PZPN

The Country:
Rzeczpospolita Polska (Republic of Poland)
Capital: Warszawa
Surface: 312,679 km²
Inhabitants: 38,268,000 [2020]
Time: UTC+1

The FA:
Polski Związek Piłki Nożnej
Bitwy Warszawskiej 1920 r. 7-366, Warszawa
Tel: +48 22 551 2300
Founded: 1919
Member of FIFA since: 1923
Member of UEFA since: 1954
Website: www.pzpn.pl

NATIONAL TEAM RECORDS

RECORDS		
First international match:	18.12.1921, Budapest:	Hungary – Poland 1-0
Most international caps:	Robert Lewandowski	- 122 caps (since 2008)
Most international goals:	Robert Lewandowski	- 69 goals / 122 caps (since 2008)

UEFA EUROPEAN CHAMPIONSHIP	
1960	Qualifiers
1964	Qualifiers
1968	Qualifiers
1972	Qualifiers
1976	Qualifiers
1980	Qualifiers
1984	Qualifiers
1988	Qualifiers
1992	Qualifiers
1996	Qualifiers
2000	Qualifiers
2004	Qualifiers
2008	Final Tournament (Group Stage)
2012	Final Tournament (Group Stage)
2016	Final Tournament (Quarter-Finals)
2020	Final Tournament (Group Stage)

FIFA WORLD CUP	
1930	Did not enter
1934	Qualifiers
1938	Final Tournament (1st Round)
1950	Did not enter
1954	*Withdrew*
1958	Qualifiers
1962	Qualifiers
1966	Qualifiers
1970	Qualifiers
1974	Final Tournament (3rd Place)
1978	Final Tournament (Round 2)
1982	Final Tournament (3rd Place)
1986	Final Tournament (2nd Round of 16)
1990	Qualifiers
1994	Qualifiers
1998	Qualifiers
2002	Final Tournament (Group Stage)
2006	Final Tournament (Group Stage)
2010	Qualifiers
2014	Qualifiers
2018	Final Tournament (Group Stage)

OLYMPIC TOURNAMENTS	
1908	-
1912	-
1920	-
1924	Preliminary Round
1928	Did not enter
1936	4th Place
1948	Did not enter
1952	Round 1
1956	Did not enter
1960	Group Stage
1964	Qualifiers
1968	Qualifiers
1972	**Winners**
1976	Runners-up
1980	Qualifiers
1984	Qualifiers
1988	Qualifiers
1992	Runners-up
1996	Qualifiers
2000	Qualifiers
2004	Qualifiers
2008	Qualifiers
2012	Qualifiers
2016	Qualifiers

UEFA NATIONS LEAGUE	
2018/2019	League A
2020/2021	League A

FIFA CONFEDERATIONS CUP 1992-2017
None

POLISH CLUB HONOURS IN EUROPEAN CLUB COMPETITIONS:

European Champion Clubs' Cup (1956-1992) / UEFA Champions League (1993-2021)
None

Fairs Cup (1858-1971) / UEFA Cup (1972-2009) / UEFA Europa League (2010-2021)
None

UEFA Super Cup (1972-2020)
None

European Cup Winners' Cup 1961-1999*
None

*defunct competition

NATIONAL COMPETITIONS
TABLE OF HONOURS

	CHAMPIONS	CUP WINNERS	BEST GOALSCORERS	
1920	*Championship abandoned*	-	-	
1921	KS Cracovia Kraków	-	-	
1922	LKS Pogoń Lwów	-	-	
1923	LKS Pogoń Lwów	-	-	
1924	*No competition*	-	-	
1925	LKS Pogoń Lwów	-	-	
1926	LKS Pogoń Lwów	Wisła Kraków	-	
1927	Wisła Kraków	-	Henryk Reyman (Wisła Kraków)	37
1928	Wisła Kraków	-	Ludwik Gintel (KS Cracovia Kraków)	28
1929	KS Warta Poznań	-	Rochus Nastula (Czarni Lwów)	25
1930	KS Cracovia Kraków	-	Karol Kossok (KS Cracovia Kraków)	24
1931	RKS Garbarnia Kraków	-	Walerian Kisieliński (Wisła Kraków)	24
1932	KS Cracovia Kraków	-	Kajetan Kryszkiewicz (KS Warta Poznań)	16
1933	KS Ruch Wielkie Hajduki Chorzów	-	Artur Woźniak (Wisła Kraków)	19
1934	KS Ruch Wielkie Hajduki Chorzów	-	Ernst Wilimowski (KS Ruch Wielkie Hajduki Chorzów)	33
1935	KS Ruch Wielkie Hajduki Chorzów	-	Michał Matyas (LKS Pogoń Lwów)	22
1936	KS Ruch Wielkie Hajduki Chorzów	-	Teodor Peterek (KS Ruch Wielkie Hajduki Chorzów) Ernst Wilimowski (KS Ruch Wielkie Hajduki Chorzów)	18
1937	KS Cracovia Kraków	-	Artur Woźniak (Wisła Kraków)	12
1938	KS Ruch Wielkie Hajduki Chorzów	-	Teodor Peterek (KS Ruch Wielkie Hajduki Chorzów)	21
1939	*Championship abandoned*	-	Ernst Wilimowski (KS Ruch Wielkie Hajduki Chorzów)	12
1940	*No competition*	-	-	
1941	*No competition*	-	-	
1942	*No competition*	-	-	
1943	*No competition*	-	-	
1944	*No competition*	-	-	
1945	*No competition*	-	-	
1946	Polonia Warszawa	-	-	
1947	KS Warta Poznań	-	-	
1948	KS Cracovia Kraków	-	Józef Kohut (Wisła Kraków)	31
1949	Wisła Kraków	-	Teodor Anioła (KKS Lech Poznań)	20
1950	Wisła Kraków	-	Teodor Anioła (KKS Lech Poznań)	21
1951	Unia Chorzów	Unia Chorzów	Teodor Anioła (KKS Lech Poznań)	20
1952	Unia Chorzów	Kolejarz Warszawa	Gerard Cieślik (Unia Chorzów)	11
1953	Unia Chorzów	WKS Gwardia Warszawa (1953/54)	Gerard Cieślik (Unia Chorzów)	24
1954	KS Polonia Bytom	WKS Gwardia Warszawa	Henryk Kempny (KS Polonia Bytom) Ernst Pohl (Legia Warszawa)	13
1955	CWKS Warszawa	CWKS Warszawa	Stanisław Hachorek (WKS Gwardia Warszawa)	16
1956	CWKS Warszawa	CWKS Warszawa	Henryk Kempny (Legia Warszawa)	21
1957	KS Górnik Zabrze	ŁKS Łódź	Lucjan Brychczy (Legia Warszawa)	19
1958	ŁKS Łódź	*No competition*	Władysław Soporek (ŁKS Łódź)	19
1959	KS Górnik Zabrze	*No competition*	Jan Liberda (KS Polonia Bytom) Ernst Pohl (KS Górnik Zabrze)	21
1960	Ruch Chorzów	*No competition*	Marian Norkowski (Polonia Bydgoszcz)	17
1961	KS Górnik Zabrze	*No competition*	Ernst Pohl (KS Górnik Zabrze)	24
1962	KS Polonia Bytom	Zagłębie Sosnowiec	Jan Liberda (KS Polonia Bytom)	16
1962/1963	KS Górnik Zabrze	Zagłębie Sosnowiec	Marian Kielec (MKS Pogoń Szczecin)	18
1963/1964	KS Górnik Zabrze	CWKS Warszawa	Lucjan Brychczy (Legia Warszawa) Józef Gałeczka (Zagłębie Sosnowiec) Jerzy Wilim (TS Szombierki Bytom)	18
1964/1965	KS Górnik Zabrze	KS Górnik Zabrze	Lucjan Brychczy (Legia Warszawa)	18
1965/1966	KS Górnik Zabrze	CWKS Warszawa	Włodzimierz Lubański (KS Górnik Zabrze)	23
1966/1967	KS Górnik Zabrze	Wisła Kraków	Włodzimierz Lubański (KS Górnik Zabrze)	18
1967/1968	Ruch Chorzów	KS Górnik Zabrze	Włodzimierz Lubański (KS Górnik Zabrze)	24
1968/1969	CWKS Legia Warszawa	KS Górnik Zabrze	Włodzimierz Lubański (KS Górnik Zabrze)	22
1969/1970	CWKS Legia Warszawa	KS Górnik Zabrze	Andrzej Jarosik (Zagłębie Sosnowiec)	18
1970/1971	KS Górnik Zabrze	KS Górnik Zabrze	Andrzej Jarosik (Zagłębie Sosnowiec)	13
1971/1972	KS Górnik Zabrze	KS Górnik Zabrze	Ryszard Szymczak (WKS Gwardia Warszawa)	16
1972/1973	FKS Stal Mielec	CWKS Legia Warszawa	Grzegorz Lato (FKS Stal Mielec)	13
1973/1974	Ruch Chorzów	Ruch Chorzów	Zdzisław Kapka (Wisła Kraków)	15
1974/1975	Ruch Chorzów	Stal Rzeszów	Grzegorz Lato (FKS Stal Mielec)	19
1975/1976	FKS Stal Mielec	KS Śląsk Wrocław	Kazimierz Kmiecik (Wisła Kraków)	20
1976/1977	KS Śląsk Wrocław	Zagłębie Sosnowiec	Włodzimierz Mazur (Zagłębie Sosnowiec)	17
1977/1978	Wisła Kraków	Zagłębie Sosnowiec	Kazimierz Kmiecik (Wisła Kraków)	15
1978/1979	Ruch Chorzów	MZKS Arka Gdynia	Kazimierz Kmiecik (Wisła Kraków)	17
1979/1980	TS Szombierki Bytom	CWKS Legia Warszawa	Kazimierz Kmiecik (Wisła Kraków)	24
1980/1981	RTS Widzew Łódź	CWKS Legia Warszawa	Krzysztof Adamczyk (Legia Warszawa)	18
1981/1982	RTS Widzew Łódź	KKS Lech Poznań	Grzegorz Kapica (TS Szombierki Bytom)	15

1982/1983	KKS Lech Poznań	KS Lechia Gdańsk	Mirosław Okoński (KKS Lech Poznań) Mirosław Tłokiński (RTS Widzew Łódź)	15
1983/1984	KKS Lech Poznań	KKS Lech Poznań	Włodzimierz Ciołek (Górnik Wałbrzych)	14
1984/1985	KS Górnik Zabrze	RTS Widzew Łódź	Leszek Iwanicki (LKP Motor Lublin)	14
1985/1986	KS Górnik Zabrze	GKS Katowice	Andrzej Zgutczyński (KS Górnik Zabrze)	20
1986/1987	KS Górnik Zabrze	KS Śląsk Wrocław	Marek Leśniak (MKS Pogoń Szczecin)	24
1987/1988	KS Górnik Zabrze	KKS Lech Poznań	Dariusz Dziekanowski (Legia Warszawa)	20
1988/1989	Ruch Chorzów	CWKS Legia Warszawa	Krzysztof Warzycha (Ruch Chorzów)	24
1989/1990	KKS Lech Poznań	CWKS Legia Warszawa	Andrzej Juskowiak (KKS Lech Poznań)	18
1990/1991	Zagłębie Lubin	GKS Katowice	Tomasz Dziubiński (Wisła Kraków)	21
1991/1992	KKS Lech Poznań	MKS Miedź Legnica	Jerzy Podbrożny (KKS Lech Poznań) Mirosław Waligóra (KS Hutnik Kraków)	20
1992/1993	KKS Lech Poznań	GKS Katowice	Jerzy Podbrożny (KKS Lech Poznań)	25
1993/1994	Legia Warszawa	Legia Warszawa	Zenon Burzawa (Sokół Pniewy)	21
1994/1995	Legia Warszawa	Legia Warszawa	Bogusław Cygan (FKS Stal Mielec)	16
1995/1996	RTS Widzew Łódź	Ruch Chorzów	Marek Koniarek (RTS Widzew Łódź)	29
1996/1997	RTS Widzew Łódź	Legia Warszawa	Mirosław Trzeciak (ŁKS Łódź)	18
1997/1998	ŁKS Łódź	KS Amica Wronki	Arkadiusz Bąk (Polonia Warszawa) Sylwester Czereszewski (Legia Warszawa) Mariusz Śrutwa (Ruch Chorzów)	14
1998/1999	Wisła Kraków	KS Amica Wronki	Tomasz Frankowski (Wisła Kraków)	21
1999/2000	Polonia Warszawa	KS Amica Wronki	Adam Kompała (KS Górnik Zabrze)	19
2000/2001	Wisła Kraków	Polonia Warszawa	Tomasz Frankowski (Wisła Kraków)	18
2001/2002	Legia Warszawa	Wisła Kraków	Maciej Żurawski (Wisła Kraków)	21
2002/2003	Wisła Kraków	Wisła Kraków	Stanko Svitlica (SRB, Legia Warszawa)	24
2003/2004	Wisła Kraków	KKS Lech Poznań	Maciej Żurawski (Wisła Kraków)	20
2004/2005	Wisła Kraków	KS Dyskobolia Grodzisk Wielkopolski	Tomasz Frankowski (Wisła Kraków)	25
2005/2006	Legia Warszawa	Wisła Płock	Grzegorz Piechna (Korona Kielce)	21
2006/2007	Zagłębie Lubin	KS Dyskobolia Grodzisk Wielkopolski	Piotr Reiss (KKS Lech Poznań)	15
2007/2008	Wisła Kraków	Legia Warszawa	Paweł Brożek (Wisła Kraków)	23
2008/2009	Wisła Kraków	KKS Lech Poznań	Paweł Brożek (Wisła Kraków) Takesure Chinyama (ZIM, Legia Warszawa)	19
2009/2010	KKS Lech Poznań	Jagiellonia Białystok	Robert Lewandowski (KKS Lech Poznań)	18
2010/2011	Wisła Kraków	Legia Warszawa	Tomasz Frankowski (Jagiellonia Białystok)	14
2011/2012	KS Śląsk Wrocław	Legia Warszawa	Artjoms Rudņevs (LVA, KKS Lech Poznań)	22
2012/2013	Legia Warszawa	Legia Warszawa	Róbert Demjan (SVK, TS Podbeskidzie Bielsko-Biała)	14
2013/2014	Legia Warszawa	SP Zawisza Bydgoszcz	Marcin Robak (GKS Piast Gliwice / MKS Pogoń Szczecin)	22
2014/2015	KKS Lech Poznań	Legia Warszawa	Kamil Wilczek (GKS Piast Gliwice)	20
2015/2016	Legia Warszawa	Legia Warszawa	Nemanja Nikolić (HUN, Legia Warszawa)	28
2016/2017	Legia Warszawa	MZKS Arka Gdynia	Marco Filipe Lopes Paixão (POR, KS Lechia Gdańsk) Marcin Robak (KKS Lech Poznań)	18
2017/2018	Legia Warszawa	Legia Warszawa	Carlos Daniel López Huesca "Carlitos" (ESP, Wisła Kraków)	24
2018/2019	GKS Piast Gliwice	KS Lechia Gdańsk	Igor Angulo Alboniga (ESP, KS Górnik Zabrze)	24
2019/2020	Legia Warszawa	KS Cracovia Kraków	Christian Lund Gytkjær (DEN, KKS Lech Poznań)	24
2020/2021	Legia Warszawa	RKS Raków Częstochowa	Tomáš Pekhart (CZE, Legia Warszawa)	22

Ruch Chorzów = KS Ruch Wielkie Hajduki Chorzów (1927-1939), Unia Chorzów (1949-1954), Unia-Ruch Chorzów (1955).
Legia Warszawa = CWKS Warszawa (1950-1967), CWKS Legia Warszawa (1967-1990).

NATIONAL CHAMPIONSHIP
Ekstraklasa 2020/2021
(21.08.2020 – 16.05.2021)

Results

Round 1 [21-24.08.2020]
Zagłębie Lubin - Lech Poznań 2-1(0-1)
Cracovia Kraków - Pogoń Szczecin 2-1(0-0)
Śląsk Wrocław - Piast Gliwice 2-0(1-0)
Raków Częstoch. - Legia Warszawa 1-2(0-1)
Wisła Płock - Stal Mielec 1-1(0-0)
Warta Poznań - Lechia Gdańsk 0-1(0-0)
Górnik Zabrze - TS Podbeskidzie 4-2(3-0)
Jagiellonia Białystok - Wisła Kraków 1-1(1-1)

Round 2 [28-30.08.2020]
Zagłębie Lubin - Warta Poznań 1-0(0-0)
Stal Mielec - Górnik Zabrze 0-2(0-1)
Lechia Gdańsk - Raków Częstoch. 1-3(1-0)
Wisła Kraków - Śląsk Wrocław 1-3(1-1)
Legia Warszawa - Jagiellonia B. 1-2(0-2)
Piast Gliwice - Pogoń Szczecin 0-1(0-0)
TS Podbeskidzie - Cracovia Kraków 2-2(1-1)
Lech Poznań - Wisła Płock 2-2(0-1)

Round 3 [11-14.09.2020]
Jagiellonia B. - TS Podbeskidzie 2-2(0-2)
Wisła Płock - Legia Warszawa 0-1(0-1)
Cracovia Kraków - Stal Mielec 1-1(0-0)
Warta Poznań - Piast Gliwice 0-0
Śląsk Wrocław - Lech Poznań 3-3(2-3)
Pogoń Szczecin - Wisła Kraków 2-2(1-1)
Górnik Zabrze - Lechia Gdańsk 3-0(1-0)
Raków Częstoch. - Zagłębie Lubin 2-1(1-0)

Round 4 [18-21.09.2020]
TS Podbeskidzie - Raków Częstoch. 1-4(1-4)
Wisła Kraków - Wisła Płock 0-3(0-2)
Lechia Gdańsk - Stal Mielec 4-2(2-2)
Pogoń Szczecin - Śląsk Wrocław 1-0(0-0)
Legia Warszawa - Górnik Zabrze 1-3(0-2)
Zagłębie Lubin - Cracovia Kraków 1-1(0-0)
Lech Poznań - Warta Poznań 1-0(0-0)
Piast Gliwice - Jagiellonia Białystok 0-1(0-0)

Round 5 [25-28.09.2020]
Wisła Płock - Warta Poznań 1-3(0-1)
Górnik Zabrze - Wisła Kraków 0-0
Cracovia Kraków - Raków Częstoch. 2-2(1-2)
Lechia Gdańsk - TS Podbeskidzie 4-0(3-0)
Jagiellonia B. - Zagłębie Lubin 0-1(0-1)
Stal Mielec - Piast Gliwice 3-2(1-0)
Legia W. - Śląsk Wrocław 2-1(0-0) [21.10.]
Lech Poznań - Pogoń Szcz. 0-4(0-3) [16.12.]

Round 6 [02-04.10.2020]
Raków Częstochowa - Wisła Płock 3-0(1-0)
Śląsk Wrocław - Cracovia Kraków 3-1(2-0)
TS Podbeskidzie - Stal Mielec 1-0(1-0)
Zagłębie Lubin - Górnik Zabrze 2-0(2-0)
Piast Gliwice - Lech Poznań 1-4(0-2)
Wisła Krak. - Lechia Gdańsk 1-3(1-1) [28.10.]
Pogoń Szcz. - Jagiellonia B. 3-0(1-0) [30.10.]
Warta Poznań - Legia Warsz. 0-3(0-3) [02.11.]

Round 7 [17-19.10.2020]
Cracovia Kraków - Piast Gliwice 1-0(1-0)
Górnik Zabrze - Raków Częstochowa 1-3(1-2)
Jagiellonia Białystok - Lech Poznań 2-1(1-0)
Wisła Płock - Śląsk Wrocław 1-0(0-0)
Stal Mielec - Wisła Kraków 0-6(0-3)
Legia Warszawa - Zagłębie Lubin 2-1(1-1)
TS Podbeskidzie - Warta Poznań 1-2(0-0)
Lechia Gdańsk - Pogoń Szczecin 0-1(0-1)

Round 8 [23-26.10.2020]
Piast Gliwice - Wisła Płock 2-2(0-0)
Zagłębie Lubin - Lechia Gdańsk 1-1(1-0)
Wisła Kraków - TS Podbeskidzie 3-0(1-0)
Śląsk Wrocław - Jagiellonia B. 1-0(0-0)
Pogoń Szczecin - Legia Warszawa 0-0
Raków Częstochowa - Stal Mielec 2-1(1-0)
Lech Poznań - Cracovia Kraków 1-1(0-1)
Warta Poznań - Górnik Zabrze 0-1(0-0)

Round 9 [07-08.11.2020]
Stal Mielec - Warta Poznań 0-1(0-0)
Cracovia Kraków - Jagiellonia B. 3-1(1-1)
Legia Warszawa - Lech Poznań 2-1(0-1)
Raków Częstochowa - Wisła Kraków 0-0
Lechia Gd. - Śląsk Wrocław 3-2(0-1) [20.11.]
Górnik Zabr. - Piast Gliwice 1-2(0-1) [20.11.]
TS Podbeskidzie-Zagłębie L. 2-1(1-0) [24.11.]
Wisła Płock - Pogoń Szczecin 0-0 [02.12.]

Round 10 [21-23.11.2020]
Śląsk Wrocław - Górnik Zabrze 0-0 [07.11.]
Pogoń Sz. - TS Podbeskidzie 1-1(0-1) [09.11.]
Zagłębie Lubin - Stal Mielec 2-2(2-1)
Warta Poznań - Wisła Kraków 2-1(0-1)
Lech Poznań - Raków Częstochowa 3-3(1-2)
Cracovia Kraków - Legia Warszawa 0-1(0-0)
Piast Gliwice - Lechia Gdańsk 2-0(2-0)
Jagiellonia Białystok - Wisła Płock 5-2(2-0)

Round 11 [27-30.11.2020]
Wisła Płock - Cracovia Kraków 0-1(0-1)
Górnik Zabrze - Pogoń Szczecin 2-1(1-1)
Stal Mielec - Jagiellonia Białystok 3-1(1-1)
TS Podbeskidzie - Śląsk Wrocław 0-2(0-1)
Wisła Kraków - Zagłębie Lubin 1-2(0-0)
Raków Częstochowa - Warta Poznań 1-0(0-0)
Legia Warszawa - Piast Gliwice 2-2(1-1)
Lechia Gdańsk - Lech Poznań 0-1(0-0)

Round 12 [04-07.12.2020]
Cracovia Kraków - Wisła Kraków 1-0(0-0)
Jagiellonia Białystok - Warta Poznań 4-3(2-3)
Śląsk Wrocław - Raków Częstoch. 1-0(0-0)
Legia Warszawa - Lechia Gdańsk 2-0(0-0)
Piast Gliwice - Zagłębie Lubin 1-1(1-1)
Lech Poznań - TS Podbeskidzie 4-0(2-0)
Pogoń Szczecin - Stal Mielec 2-0(1-0)
Wisła Płock - Górnik Zabrze 0-1(0-0)

Round 13 [11-14.12.2020]
TS Podbeskidzie - Piast Gliwice 0-5(0-2)
Zagłębie Lubin - Śląsk Wrocław 2-1(0-1)
Warta Poznań - Pogoń Szczecin 1-2(0-2)
Górnik Zabrze - Cracovia Kraków 0-2(0-1)
Wisła Kraków - Legia Warszawa 1-2(1-0)
Stal Mielec - Lech Poznań 1-1(1-0)
Raków Częstochowa - Jagiellonia B. 3-2(1-0)
Lechia Gdańsk - Wisła Płock 0-1(0-0)

Round 14 [17-20.12.2020]
Śląsk Wrocław - Warta Poznań 2-1(1-0)
Wisła Płock - TS Podbeskidzie 4-1(3-0)
Legia Warszawa - Stal Mielec 2-3(2-2)
Pogoń Szczecin - Zagłębie Lubin 1-0(0-0)
Cracovia Kraków - Lechia Gdańsk 0-3(0-1)
Lech Poznań - Wisła Kraków 0-1(0-0)
Piast Gliwice - Raków Częstochowa 0-0
Jagiellonia Białystok - Górnik Zabrze 1-0(0-0)

Round 15 [29.01.-01.02.2021]
Zagłębie Lubin - Wisła Płock 0-2(0-2)
Raków Częstoch. - Pogoń Szczecin 0-1(0-0)
Warta Poznań - Cracovia Kraków 1-0(0-0)
Lechia Gdańsk - Jagiellonia B. 0-2(0-1)
Górnik Zabrze - Lech Poznań 1-1(1-0)
Wisła Kraków - Piast Gliwice 3-4(3-2)
TS Podbeskidzie - Legia Warszawa 1-0(0-0)
Stal Mielec - Śląsk Wrocław 0-0

Round 16 [05-07.02.2021]
Lechia Gdańsk - Warta Poznań 1-1(1-0)
Lech Poznań - Zagłębie Lubin 0-0
Piast Gliwice - Śląsk Wrocław 2-0(1-0)
Pogoń Szczecin - Cracovia Kraków 1-0(1-0)
Legia Warszawa - Raków Częstoch. 2-0(1-0)
TS Podbeskidzie - Górnik Zabrze 2-1(0-1)
Wisła Kraków - Jagiellonia Białystok 2-0(0-0)
Stal Mielec - Wisła Płock 2-2(0-1) [04.03.]

Round 17 [12-15.02.2021]
Śląsk Wrocław - Wisła Płock 1-1(1-1)
Cracovia Kraków - TS Podbeskidzie 1-1(1-1)
Pogoń Szczecin - Piast Gliwice 0-0
Raków Częstoch. - Lechia Gdańsk 0-1(0-0)
Wisła Płock - Lech Poznań 1-0(0-0)
Jagiellonia B. - Legia Warszawa 1-1(1-1)
Warta Poznań - Zagłębie Lubin 1-0(0-0)
Górnik Zabrze - Stal Mielec 2-1(0-1)

Round 18 [19-22.02.2021]
Stal Mielec - Cracovia Kraków 0-0
Wisła Kraków - Pogoń Szczecin 2-1(2-0)
Legia Warszawa - Wisła Płock 5-2(3-2)
TS Podbeskidzie - Jagiellonia B. 1-1(1-0)
Lechia Gdańsk - Górnik Zabrze 2-0(2-0)
Zagłębie Lubin - Raków Częstoch. 1-2(1-1)
Lech Poznań - Śląsk Wrocław 1-0(0-0)
Piast Gliwice - Warta Poznań 0-1(0-0)

Round 19 [26-28.02.2021]
Raków Częstoch. - TS Podbeskidzie 1-0(0-0)
Warta Poznań - Lech Poznań 1-2(0-0)
Stal Mielec - Lechia Gdańsk 0-1(0-1)
Jagiellonia Białystok - Piast Gliwice 0-1(0-0)
Górnik Zabrze - Legia Warszawa 1-2(1-1)
Wisła Płock - Wisła Kraków 1-3(0-0)
Cracovia Kraków - Zagłębie Lubin 2-4(1-2)
Śląsk Wrocław - Pogoń Szczecin 2-1(2-1)

Round 20 [05-08.03.2021]
Wisła Kraków - Górnik Zabrze 0-0
TS Podbeskidzie - Lechia Gdańsk 2-2(1-1)
Zagłębie Lubin - Jagiellonia B. 3-0(0-0)
Raków Częstochowa - Cracovia Kraków 0-0
Piast Gliwice - Stal Mielec 2-1(0-1)
Pogoń Szczecin - Lech Poznań 0-1(0-1)
Śląsk Wrocław - Legia Warszawa 0-1(0-0)
Warta Poznań - Wisła Płock 2-0(1-0)

Round 21 [12-15.03.2021]
Cracovia Kraków - Śląsk Wrocław 1-1(0-0)
Jagiellonia B. - Pogoń Szczecin 0-1(0-0)
Wisła Płock - Raków Częstochowa 2-2(0-0)
Lechia Gdańsk - Wisła Kraków 2-0(0-0)
Legia Warszawa - Warta Poznań 3-2(2-1)
Górnik Zabrze - Zagłębie Lubin 2-0(1-0)
Lech Poznań - Piast Gliwice 0-0
Stal Mielec - TS Podbeskidzie 2-1(0-1)

Round 22 [19-21.03.2021]
Piast Gliwice - Cracovia Kraków 2-0(1-0)
Pogoń Szczecin - Lechia Gdańsk 1-0(0-0)
Śląsk Wrocław - Wisła Płock 0-0
Raków Częstochowa - Górnik Zabrze 0-0
Lech Poznań - Jagiellonia Białystok 2-3(2-1)
Warta Poznań - TS Podbeskidzie 2-0(0-0)
Wisła Kraków - Stal Mielec 3-1(0-0)
Zagłębie Lubin - Legia Warszawa 0-4(0-3)

Round 23 [03-05.04.2021]
Wisła Płock - Piast Gliwice 0-1(0-0)
Legia Warszawa - Pogoń Szczecin 4-2(4-1)
Cracovia Kraków - Lech Poznań 2-1(1-1)
Górnik Zabrze - Warta Poznań 1-2(0-1)
TS Podbeskidzie - Wisła Kraków 2-0(1-0)
Jagiellonia B. - Śląsk Wrocław 0-1(0-1)
Lechia Gdańsk - Zagłębie Lubin 3-1(2-1)
Stal Mielec - Raków Częst. 0-1(0-0) [05.05.]

Round 24 [09-12.04.2021]
Jagiellonia B. - Cracovia Kraków 2-1(2-1)
Wisła Kraków - Raków Częstochowa 1-2(1-1)
Pogoń Szczecin - Wisła Płock 2-0(1-0)
Warta Poznań - Stal Mielec 0-0
Śląsk Wrocław - Lechia Gdańsk 1-1(1-1)
Zagłębie Lubin - TS Podbeskidzie 2-1(0-1)
Lech Poznań - Legia Warszawa 0-0
Piast Gliwice - Górnik Zabrze 2-0(1-0)

Round 25 [16-18.04.2021]
TS Podbeskidzie - Pogoń Szczecin 0-2(0-1)
Górnik Zabrze - Śląsk Wrocław 1-1(1-0)
Lechia Gdańsk - Piast Gliwice 2-2(0-1)
Raków Częstochowa - Lech Poznań 3-1(2-0)
Wisła Kraków - Warta Poznań 0-1(0-0)
Stal Mielec - Zagłębie Lubin 0-2(0-1)
Wisła Płock - Jagiellonia Białystok 2-2(0-1)
Legia Warszawa - Cracovia Kraków 0-0

Round 26 [20-21.04.2021]
Pogoń Szczecin - Górnik Zabrze 1-0(1-0)
Warta Poznań - Raków Częstochowa 0-2(0-1)
Lech Poznań - Lechia Gdańsk 3-0(0-0)
Śląsk Wrocław - TS Podbeskidzie 4-3(1-1)
Jagiellonia Białystok - Stal Mielec 3-3(2-1)
Zagłębie Lubin - Wisła Kraków 4-1(1-1)
Cracovia Kraków - Wisła Płock 1-0(1-0)
Piast Gliwice - Legia Warszawa 0-1(0-0)

Round 27 [23-25.04.2021]
Raków Częstoch. - Śląsk Wrocław 2-0(0-0)
TS Podbeskidzie - Lech Poznań 1-0(0-0)
Górnik Zabrze - Wisła Płock 0-2(0-0)
Zagłębie Lubin - Piast Gliwice 2-2(2-1)
Wisła Kraków - Cracovia Kraków 0-0
Warta Poznań - Jagiellonia Białystok 2-0(1-0)
Stal Mielec - Pogoń Szczecin 1-0(1-0)
Lechia Gdańsk - Legia Warszawa 0-1(0-0)

Round 28 [28.04.-03.05.2021]
Jagiellonia B. - Raków Częstochowa 0-0
Wisła Płock - Lechia Gdańsk 1-3(0-1)
Śląsk Wrocław - Zagłębie Lubin 0-0
Legia Warszawa - Wisła Kraków 2-3(1-2)
Pogoń Szczecin - Warta Poznań 1-1(0-0)
Lech Poznań - Stal Mielec 1-2(0-0)
Piast Gliwice - TS Podbeskidzie 2-0(1-0)
Cracovia Kraków - Górnik Zabrze 1-0(1-0)

Round 29 [07-10.05.2021]
Górnik Zabrze - Jagiellonia Białystok 3-1(1-1)
Zagłębie Lubin - Pogoń Szczecin 1-1(0-1)
TS Podbeskidzie - Wisła Płock 1-1(1-1)
Lechia Gdańsk - Cracovia Kraków 1-1(0-1)
Wisła Kraków - Lech Poznań 1-2(0-1)
Warta Poznań - Śląsk Wrocław 2-3(1-0)
Stal Mielec - Legia Warszawa 0-0
Raków Częstochowa - Piast Gliwice 1-0(1-0)

Round 30 [16.05.2021]
Jagiellonia B. - Lechia Gdańsk 2-1(1-0)
Lech Poznań - Górnik Zabrze 1-1(1-0)
Legia Warszawa - TS Podbeskidzie 1-0(1-0)
Piast Gliwice - Wisła Kraków 2-3(1-2)
Pogoń Szczecin - Raków Częstoch. 1-3(0-1)
Śląsk Wrocław - Stal Mielec 1-1(1-0)
Wisła Płock - Zagłębie Lubin 4-0(2-0)
Cracovia Kraków - Warta Poznań 0-1(0-0)

Final Standings

						Total			Home					Away			
1.	**Legia Warszawa**	30	19	7	4	48 - 24	64	9	3	3	29 - 19	10	4	1	19 - 5
2.	RKS Raków Częstochowa	30	17	8	5	46 - 25	59	9	3	3	19 - 9	8	5	2	27 - 16
3.	MKS Pogoń Szczecin	30	15	7	8	36 - 23	52	8	5	2	17 - 8	7	2	6	19 - 15
4.	WKS Śląsk Wrocław	30	11	10	9	36 - 32	43	7	7	1	21 - 13	4	3	8	15 - 19
5.	KS Warta Poznań	30	13	4	13	33 - 32	43	6	2	7	14 - 15	7	2	6	19 - 17
6.	GKS Piast Gliwice	30	11	9	10	39 - 32	42	6	3	6	18 - 15	5	6	4	21 - 17
7.	KS Lechia Gdańsk	30	12	6	12	40 - 37	42	6	3	6	23 - 18	6	3	6	17 - 19
8.	Zagłębie Lubin	30	11	8	11	38 - 40	41	7	5	3	24 - 19	4	3	8	14 - 21
9.	Jagiellonia Białystok	30	10	7	13	39 - 48	37	6	5	4	23 - 19	4	2	9	16 - 29
10.	KS Górnik Zabrze	30	10	7	13	31 - 33	37	6	3	6	22 - 20	4	4	7	9 - 13
11.	KKS Lech Poznań	30	9	10	11	39 - 38	37	4	7	4	19 - 17	5	3	7	20 - 21
12.	Wisła Płock	30	8	9	13	37 - 44	33	4	4	7	18 - 19	4	5	6	19 - 25
13.	Wisła Kraków	30	8	9	13	39 - 42	33	4	2	9	19 - 24	4	7	4	20 - 18
14.	KS Cracovia Kraków	30	8	13	9	28 - 32	32	6	5	4	18 - 18	2	8	5	10 - 14
15.	FKS Stal Mielec	30	6	11	13	31 - 47	29	4	5	6	12 - 20	2	6	7	19 - 27
16.	TS Podbeskidzie Bielsko-Biała (Relegated)	30	6	7	17	29 - 60	25	6	4	5	17 - 23	0	3	12	12 - 37

Top goalscorers:

22	**Tomáš Pekhart (CZE)**	*Legia Warszawa*
15	Jakub Świerczok	*GKS Piast Gliwice*
12	Mikael Ishak (SWE)	*KKS Lech Poznań*
12	Jesús Jiménez Núñez (ESP)	*KS Górnik Zabrze*
12	Flávio Emanuel Lopes Paixão (POR)	*KS Lechia Gdańsk*

NATIONAL CUP
Puchar Polski 2020/2021

First Round [13-16.08./19.08./21-23.08./25.08./02.09.2020]

Ślęza Wrocław - Wigry Suwałki	2-1(1-0)		OKS Odra Opole - KKS Lech Poznań	1-3(0-1)
Świt Nowy Dwór - Zagłębie Lubin	1-3(0-1)		Błękitni Stargard Szczeciński - KS Warta Poznań	3-3 aet; 4-5 pen
Lechia Zielona Gora - Świt Skolwin	1-4(0-0)		Chrobry Głogów - KS Cracovia Kraków	1-2(0-0,1-1)
KS Górnik Zabrze - Jagiellonia Białystok	3-1(1-1)		ŁKS Łódź - WKS Śląsk Wrocław	2-2 aet; 4-1 pen
Ruch Wysokie Mazowieckie - MKS Znicz Pruszkow	0-2(0-1)		Stal Stalowa Wola - KS Lechia Gdańsk	0-4(0-2)
Jaguar Gdańsk - MKS Puszcza Niepołomice	1-4(0-3)		Chojniczanka Chojnice - Concordia Elbląg	1-0(1-0)
GKS Bełchatów - Legia Warszawa	1-6(1-3)		Garbarnia Krakow - GKS Katowice	1-0(0-0)
Pniowek Pawlowice Slaskie - Sokół Ostróda	2-3(0-1)		RKS Radomiak Radom - Miedź Legnica	4-0(2-0)
Stal Rzeszow - TS Podbeskidzie Bielsko-Biała	0-1(0-1)		Olimpia Grudziądz - KKS Lech Poznań II	2-0(1-0)
KS Unia Skierniewice - RTS Widzew Łódź	0-4(0-3)		OKS Stomil Olsztyn - GKS Jastrzębie	2-3(1-1)
KKS 1925 Kalisz - Korona Kielce	0-3 awarded		KS Polkowice - MZKS Arka Gdynia	0-5(0-0)
Unia Janikowo - Zagłębie Sosnowiec	1-0(1-0)		Bytovia Bytów - Bruk-Bet Termalica Nieciecza KS	0-4(0-3)
KKS Karpaty Krosno - FKS Stal Mielec	0-2(0-0)		Sandecja Nowy Sącz - RKS Raków Częstochowa	0-3(0-2)
CWKS Resovia Rzeszów - GKS Piast Gliwice	0-4(0-2)		NKP Podhale - MKS Pogoń Szczecin	0-5(0-3)
GKS Tychy - Wisła Płock	1-2(0-1)		Polonia Nysa - GKS Górnik Łęczna	1-3(1-0)
KSZO Ostrowiec Świętokrzyski - Wisła Kraków	2-1(0-0)		Orlęta Radzyń Podlaski - MKP Pogoń Siedlce	0-2(0-1)

Second Round [30-31.10./02-04.11./14.11./17.11./20.11./25.11./01-02.12.2020]

Garbarnia Krakow - Chojniczanka Chojnice	1-3(0-0,1-1)		GKS Jastrzębie - MKS Puszcza Niepołomice	0-2(0-1)
KSZO Ostrowiec Świętokrzyski - KS Górnik Zabrze	2-3(1-1)		MZKS Arka Gdynia - Korona Kielce	2-0(1-0)
Bruk-Bet Termalica Nieciecza - RKS Raków Częst.	0-2(0-1)		Świt Skolwin - KS Cracovia Kraków	0-1(0-0)
Sokół Ostróda - KS Warta Poznań	1-3(0-0,0-0)		Olimpia Grudziądz - KS Lechia Gdańsk	0-1(0-0)
Unia Janikowo - ŁKS Łódź	0-2(0-2)		Wisła Płock - MKS Pogoń Szczecin	1-1 aet; 3-4 pen
MKP Pogoń Siedlce - RKS Radomiak Radom	0-1(0-0)		RTS Widzew Łódź - Legia Warszawa	0-1(0-1)
MKS Znicz Pruszkow - KKS Lech Poznań	2-3(1-1)		TS Podbeskidzie Bielsko-Biała - Zagłębie Lubin	2-4(0-0,1-1)
Ślęza Wrocław - GKS Górnik Łęczna	0-2(0-0)		FKS Stal Mielec - GKS Piast Gliwice	1-1 aet; 3-4 pen

1/8-Finals [09-11.02./16.02.2021]

MKS Puszcza Niepołomice - KS Lechia Gdańsk	3-1(1-1)		RKS Raków Częstochowa - KS Górnik Zabrze	4-2(2-0)
KS Warta Poznań - KS Cracovia Kraków	0-1(0-1)		Zagłębie Lubin - Chojniczanka Chojnice	0-0 aet; 5-6 pen
ŁKS Łódź - Legia Warszawa	2-3(1-1)		RKS Radomiak Radom - KKS Lech Poznań	1-1 aet; 3-4 pen
MKS Pogoń Szczecin - GKS Piast Gliwice	1-2(0-1)		MZKS Arka Gdynia - GKS Górnik Łęczna	2-1(1-1)

Quarter-Finals [02-03.03.2021]

MKS Puszcza Niepołomice - MZKS Arka Gdynia	2-5(1-1)		Chojniczanka Chojnice - KS Cracovia Kraków	0-3(0-1)
KKS Lech Poznań - RKS Raków Częstochowa	0-2(0-0)		Legia Warszawa - GKS Piast Gliwice	1-2(0-1)

Semi-Finals [07.04./14.04.2021]

MZKS Arka Gdynia - GKS Piast Gliwice	0-0 aet; 4-3 pen		KS Cracovia Kraków - RKS Raków Częstochowa	1-2(0-1)

Final

02.05.2021; Arena Lublin, Lublin; Referee: Paweł Gil; Attendance: 0
RKS Raków Częstochowa – MZKS Arka Gdynia   **2-1(0-0)**

Raków Częstochowa: Dominik Holec, Kamil Piątkowski, Andrzej Niewulis, Zoran Arsenić (80.Petr Schwarz), Fran Tudor, Igor Sapała (46.Marko Poletanović), Ben Lederman (85.Daniel Szelągowski), Patryk Kun, Marcin Cebula (80.David Tijanić), Iván López Álvarez „Ivi", Vladislavs Gutkovskis (68. Jakub Arak). Trainer: Marek Papszun.

Arka Gdynia: Kacper Krzepisz, Arkadiusz Kasperkiewicz, Michał Marcjanik, Haris Memic, Adam Danch, Adam Deja, Juliusz Letniowski (46.Marcus Vinicius da Silva de Oliveira), Fabian Hiszpanski (59.Kacper Skóra), Luis Valcarce Vidal (59.Artur Siemaszko), Mateusz Żebrowski (80.Paweł Sasin), Maciej Rosołek. Trainer: Dariusz Marzec.

Goals: 0-1 Mateusz Żebrowski (57), 1-1 Iván López Álvarez „Ivi" (81), 2-1 David Tijanić (89).

Miejski Klub Sportowy Cracovia Kraków

Founded: 13.06.1906
Stadium: Stadion "Marszałek Józef Piłsudski", Kraków (15,016)
Trainer: Michał Probierz   24.09.1972

Goalkeepers:	DOB	M	(s)	G
Lukáš Hrošśo (SVK)	19.04.1987	4		
Karol Niemczycki	05.07.1999	26	(1)	
Defenders:	**DOB**	**M**	**(s)**	**G**
Diego Gustavo Ferraresso Scheda (BRA)	21.05.1992	5	(3)	
Michael Gardawski (GER)	25.09.1990	4	(1)	
Michał Sławomir Helik	09.09.1995	1		
Iván Márquez Álvarez (ESP)	09.06.1994	15	(2)	
David Jablonský (CZE)	08.10.1991	2		1
Luís Augusto Martins Rocha (POR)	27.06.1993	10		
Kamil Pestka	22.08.1998	1		
Cornel Emilian Râpă (ROU)	16.01.1990	29	(1)	1
Matej Rodin (CRO)	13.02.1996	23		
Michal Sipľak (SVK)	02.02.1996	10	(3)	2
Dawid Szymonowicz	07.07.1995	20	(4)	1
Midfielders:	**DOB**	**M**	**(s)**	**G**
Marcin Budziński	06.07.1990	1	(1)	
Milan Dimun (SVK)	19.09.1996	14	(9)	
Ivan Fiolić (CRO)	29.04.1996	15	(4)	1
Florian Loshaj (KVX)	13.08.1996	14	(9)	2
Sylwester Łusiusz	18.09.1999	6		
Damir Sadiković (BIH)	07.04.1995	17	(3)	
Thiago Rodrigues de Souza (BRA)	18.03.1997	9	(16)	2
Pelle van Amersfoort (NED)	01.04.1996	28		6
Forwards:	**DOB**	**M**	**(s)**	**G**
Marcos Raphael Álvarez Giráldez (GER)	30.09.1991	16	(5)	2
Jakub Gut	13.05.2003		(1)	
Sergiu Cătălin Hanca (ROU)	04.04.1992	21		4
Przemysław Kapek	07.05.2003		(2)	
Jakub Kosecki	29.08.1990	2	(6)	
Jakub Myszor	07.06.2002		(1)	
Daniel Pik	20.07.2000	4	(5)	
Filip Piszczek	26.05.1995	4	(18)	2
Rivaldo Vítor Borba Ferreira Jr. „Rivaldinho" (BRA)	29.04.1995	18	(6)	1
Sebastian Strózik	15.05.1999		(6)	
Tomáš Vestenický (SVK)	06.04.1996	3	(8)	2
Mateusz Wdowiak	28.08.1996	2	(1)	
Patryk Zaucha	19.04.2000	6	(1)	

Klub Sportowy Górnik Zabrze

Founded: 14.12.1948
Stadium: Stadion „Ernest Pohl", Zabrze (24,413)
Trainer: Marcin Brosz   11.04.1973

Goalkeepers:	DOB	M	(s)	G
Martin Chudý (SVK)	23.04.1989	30		
Defenders:	**DOB**	**M**	**(s)**	**G**
Paweł Bochniewicz	30.01.1996	2		1
Stefanos Evangelou (GRE)	12.05.1998	6	(3)	
Adrian Gryszkiewicz	13.12.1999	27		
Erik Janža (SVN)	21.06.1993	26	(2)	
Michał Koj	28.07.1993	11	(3)	1
Giannis Masouras (GRE)	24.08.1996	20	(3)	
Kacper Michalski	03.01.2000		(3)	
Aleksander Paluszek	09.04.2001	12	(1)	
Dariusz Pawłowski	25.02.1999	9	(1)	
Przemysław Wiśniewski	27.07.1998	28	(1)	1
Midfielders:	**DOB**	**M**	**(s)**	**G**
Filip Bainović (SRB)	23.06.1996		(7)	
Wojciech Hajda	23.05.2000		(4)	
Krzysztof Kubica	25.05.2000	14	(8)	
Alasana Manneh (GAM)	08.04.1998	21	(6)	3
Bartosz Nowak	25.08.1993	25	(4)	5
Roman Procházka (SVK)	14.03.1989	19	(9)	
Michal Rostkowski	10.08.2000	5	(6)	
Daniel Ściślak	13.03.2000	4	(16)	1
Norbert Wojtuszek	05.10.2001	7	(7)	
Forwards:	**DOB**	**M**	**(s)**	**G**
Richmond Boakye (GHA)	28.01.1993	7	(6)	
Jesús Jiménez Núñez (ESP)	05.11.1993	28	(1)	12
Piotr Krawczyk	29.12.1994	8	(18)	4
Adam Ryczkowski	30.04.1997		(5)	
Alex Sobczyk (AUT)	20.05.1997	21	(5)	3
Łukasz Wolsztyński	08.12.1994		(2)	

Jagiellonia Białystok Sportowa Spółka Akcyjna

Founded: 30.05.1920
Stadium: Stadion Miejski, Białystok (22,432)
Trainer: Bogdan Zając   16.11.1972
[17.03.2021]   Rafał Grzyb   16.01.1983

Goalkeepers:	DOB	M	(s)	G
Xavier Dziekonski	06.10.2003	15	(1)	
Pāvels Šteinbors (LVA)	21.09.1985	10		
Damian Węglarz	21.03.1996	5		
Defenders:	**DOB**	**M**	**(s)**	**G**
Zoran Arsenić (CRO)	02.06.1994	1		
Błażej Augustyn	26.01.1988	21	(3)	
Böðvar Böðvarsson (ISL)	09.04.1995	9	(4)	
Andrej Kadlec (SVK)	02.02.1996		(3)	
Bartosz Kwiecień	07.05.1994	7	(5)	
Myroslav Mazur (UKR)	11.08.1998	2	(1)	
Bojan Nastić (BIH)	06.07.1994	9		1
Paweł Olszewski	07.06.1999	17		
Szymon Pankiewicz	09.02.2001	2		
Ivan Runje (CRO)	09.10.1990	14	(1)	
Godfrey Bitok Stephen (NGA)	22.08.2000	2	(1)	
Bogdan Ionuț Țîru (ROU)	15.03.1994	23	(2)	2
Bartłomiej Wdowik	25.09.2000	17	(4)	2
Midfielders:	**DOB**	**M**	**(s)**	**G**
Ariel Borysiuk	29.07.1991	5	(10)	
Fernán Ferreiroa López (ESP)	10.02.1995	6	(5)	
Jesús Imaz Ballesté (ESP)	26.09.1990	25	(2)	11
Milosz Matysik	26.04.2004		(1)	
Przemysław Mystkowski	25.04.1998	10	(8)	1
Jakub Orpik	26.10.2003	1		
Martin Pospíšil (CZE)	26.06.1991	26	(3)	1
Taras Romanczuk (UKR)	14.11.1991	23	(2)	2
Forwards:	**DOB**	**M**	**(s)**	**G**
Bartosz Bida	21.02.2001	7	(10)	2
Maciej Bortniczuk	06.09.2001	1	(10)	
Fiodor Černych (LTU)	21.05.1991	9	(7)	1
Juan del Carmen Cámara Mesa (ESP)	13.02.1994	1	(1)	
Maciej Makuszewski	29.09.1989	17	(6)	3
Tomáš Přikryl (CZE)	04.07.1992	13	(5)	2
Jakov Puljić (CRO)	04.08.1993	21	(4)	11
Szymon Sobczak	07.12.1992		(1)	
Krzysztof Toporkiewicz	21.04.2002		(1)	
Kristopher David Twardek (CAN)	08.03.1997	8	(7)	
Maciej Twarowski	13.03.2001		(1)	
Mateusz Wyjadłowski	04.01.2000		(3)	
Kamil Wojtkowski	26.02.1998	1	(6)	
Konrad Wrzesiński	10.09.1993	2	(5)	

Kolejowy Klub Sportowy Lech Poznań

Founded:	19.03.1922		
Stadium:	Stadion Miejski, Poznań (43,269)		
Trainer:	Dariusz Zuraw	14.11.1972	
[06.04.2021]	Janusz Góra	08.07.1963	
[12.04.2021]	Maciej Skorza	10.01.1972	

Goalkeepers:	DOB	M	(s)	G
Filip Bednarek	26.09.1992	15		
Mickey van der Hart (NED)	13.06.1994	15		
Defenders:	**DOB**	**M**	**(s)**	**G**
Bogdan Butko (UKR)	13.01.1991	1	(2)	
Đorđe Crnomarković (SRB)	10.09.1993	7	(1)	
Alan Czerwiński	02.02.1993	22	(3)	
Tomasz Dejewski	22.04.1995	3	(2)	
Robert Gumny	04.06.1998	1		
Vasyl Kravets (UKR)	20.08.1997	10	(8)	
Antonio Milić (CRO)	10.03.1994	8	(1)	
Krystian Palacz	19.07.2003		(3)	
Tymoteusz Puchacz	23.01.1999	22	(5)	1
Thomas Rogne (NOR)	29.06.1990	18		2
Bartosz Salamon	01.05.1991	12	(1)	1
Ľubomír Šatka (SVK)	02.12.1995	17		
Midfielders:	**DOB**	**M**	**(s)**	**G**
Daniel „Dani" Ramírez Fernández (ESP)	18.06.1992	27	(3)	6
Kamil Jóźwiak	22.04.1998	2		
Jesper Karlström (SWE)	21.06.1995	15	(1)	
Antoni Kozubal	18.08.2004		(1)	
Nika Kvekveskiri (GEO)	29.05.1992	6	(6)	
Filip Marchwiński	10.01.2002	5	(16)	1
Jakub Piotr Moder	07.04.1999	14		4
Karlo Muhar (CRO)	17.01.1996	2	(4)	
Pedro Miguel Amorim Pereira Silva „Pedro Tiba" (POR)	31.08.1988	25	(3)	4
Forwards:	**DOB**	**M**	**(s)**	**G**
Mohammad Awwad (ISR)	09.06.1997	1	(8)	
Mikael Ishak (SWE)	31.03.1993	21	(1)	12
Aron Jóhannsson (USA)	10.11.1990	5	(4)	2
Nika Kacharava (GEO)	13.01.1994	1	(6)	1
Jakub Kamiński	05.06.2002	25	(3)	1
Norbert Pacławski	19.02.2004		(2)	
Michał Skóraś	15.02.2000	14	(12)	2
Hubert Sobol	25.06.2000		(3)	
Jan Sýkora (CZE)	29.12.1993	14	(8)	
Filip Szymczak	06.05.2002	2	(9)	

Klub Sportowy Lechia Gdańsk Spółka Akcyjna

Founded:	07.08.1945	
Stadium:	Stadion Energa, Gdańsk (43,615)	
Trainer:	Piotr Stokowiec	25.05.1972

Goalkeepers:	DOB	M	(s)	G
Zlatan Alomerović (GER)	15.06.1991	2		
Dušan Kuciak (SVK)	21.05.1985	28		
Defenders:	**DOB**	**M**	**(s)**	**G**
Conrado Buchanelli Holz (BRA)	03.04.1997	20	(7)	3
Karol Fila	13.06.1998	19	(7)	1
Rafał Kobryń	05.12.1999	1		
Bartosz Kopacz	21.05.1992	27	(2)	2
Mario Maloča (CRO)	04.05.1989	13	(2)	1
Michał Nalepa	22.01.1993	15	(1)	3
Rafał Pietrzak	30.01.1992	24	(2)	1
Midfielders:	**DOB**	**M**	**(s)**	**G**
Jan Biegański	04.12.2002	12	(1)	
Joseph Ceesay (SWE)	03.06.1998	7	(4)	1
Maciej Gajos	19.03.1991	20	(8)	2
Jakub Kałuziński	31.10.2002	6	(5)	
Filip Koperski	24.02.2004		(1)	
Egzon Kryeziu (SVN)	25.04.2000	1	(1)	
Jarosław Kubicki	07.08.1995	27	(1)	1
Tomasz Makowski	19.07.1999	14	(5)	1
Jaroslav Mihalík (SVK)	27.07.1994	3	(6)	1
Mykola Musolitin (UKR)	21.01.1999		(3)	
Kenny Saief (USA)	17.12.1993	16	(6)	
Mateusz Sopoćko	26.06.1999	1	(3)	
Kristers Tobers (LVA)	13.12.2000	15	(2)	
Žarko Udovičić (SRB)	31.08.1987	5	(9)	2
Kacper Urbański	07.09.2004		(1)	
Egy Vikri (IDN)	07.07.2000		(7)	
Forwards:	**DOB**	**M**	**(s)**	**G**
Jakub Arak	02.04.1995		(4)	
Flávio Emanuel Lopes Paixão (POR)	19.09.1984	28	(2)	12
Omran Haydary (AFG)	13.01.1998	12	(6)	1
Mateusz Żukowski	23.11.2001	1	(15)	
Łukasz Zwoliński	24.02.1993	13	(9)	6

Legia Warszawa

Founded:	1916	
Stadium:	Stadion "Marszałek Józef Piłsudski", Warszawa (31,800)	
Trainer:	Czesław Michniewicz	12.02.1970

Goalkeepers:	DOB	M	(s)	G
Artur Boruc	20.02.1980	25		
Radosław Cierzniak	24.04.1983		(1)	
Cezary Miszta	30.10.2001	5	(1)	
Defenders:	**DOB**	**M**	**(s)**	**G**
Mateusz Hołownia	06.05.1998	8	(1)	
Artur Jędrzejczyk	04.11.1987	27		
Josip Juranović (CRO)	16.08.1995	25	(1)	1
Michał Karbownik	13.03.2001	7	(1)	
Igor Lewczuk	30.05.1985	10	(1)	
Luís Augusto Martins Rocha (POR)	27.06.1993	2		
Filip Mladenović (SRB)	15.08.1991	27	(2)	7
William Rémy (FRA)	04.04.1991	3		
Artem Shabanov (UKR)	07.03.1992	6	(1)	
Paweł Stolarski	28.01.1996	2	(2)	
Marko Vešović (MNE)	28.08.1991		(1)	
Mateusz Wieteska	11.02.1997	17	(1)	1
Midfielders:	**DOB**	**M**	**(s)**	**G**
André Renato Soares Martins (POR)	21.01.1990	22	(3)	
Domagoj Antolić (CRO)	30.06.1990	3	(5)	
Valeriane Gvilia (GEO)	24.05.1994	10	(8)	
José Kanté Martínez (GUI)	27.09.1990	3	(1)	
Bartosz Kapustka	23.12.1996	22	(3)	3
Jakub Kisiel	05.02.2003		(3)	
Bartosz Slisz	29.03.1999	25	(2)	2
Forwards:	**DOB**	**M**	**(s)**	**G**
Mateusz Cholewiak	05.02.1990		(4)	
Kacper Kostorz	21.08.1999		(6)	1
Lucas Lima Linhares „Luquinhas" (BRA)	28.09.1996	21	(4)	3
Ernest Muçi (ALB)	19.03.2001	2	(4)	
Tomáš Pekhart (CZE)	26.05.1989	23	(2)	22
Rafael Guimarães Lopes (POR)	28.07.1991	8	(12)	4
Maciej Rosołek	02.09.2001	2	(6)	
Kacper Skibicki	11.10.2001	2	(4)	1
César Joel Valencia Castillo (ECU)	16.11.1994	4	(4)	
Szymon Włodarczyk	05.01.2003	1	(1)	
Paweł Wszołek	30.04.1992	18	(6)	3
Jasurbek Yakhshiboev (UZB)	24.06.1997		(2)	

Gliwicki Klub Sportowy Piast Gliwice

Founded: 18.06.1945
Stadium: Stadion Miejski im. Piotra Wieczorka, Gliwice (10,037)
Trainer: Waldemar Fornalik   11.04.1963

Goalkeepers:	DOB	M	(s)	G
František Plach (SVK)	08.03.1992	30		
Defenders:	**DOB**	**M**	**(s)**	**G**
Jakub Czerwiński	06.08.1991	26		1
Jakub Holúbek (SVK)	12.01.1991	22	(1)	
Tomáš Huk (SVK)	22.12.1994	23	(1)	
Mikkel Kirkeskov (DEN)	05.09.1991	7		
Martin Konczkowski	14.09.1993	21	(4)	
Piotr Malarczyk	01.08.1991	14		2
Tomasz Mokwa	10.02.1993	2	(2)	
Bartosz Rymaniak	13.11.1989	10	(3)	
Midfielders:	**DOB**	**M**	**(s)**	**G**
Michał Chrapek	03.04.1992	21	(2)	1
Javier Hyjek	12.01.2001		(1)	
Tomasz Jodłowiec	08.09.1985	14	(13)	
Patryk Lipski	12.06.1994	12	(13)	1
Sebastian Milewski	30.04.1998	10	(8)	2
Michał Rakowiecki	18.02.2001		(1)	
Patryk Sokołowski	25.09.1994	28	(1)	2
Forwards:	**DOB**	**M**	**(s)**	**G**
Gerard Badía Cortés (ESP)	18.10.1989	15	(7)	
Piotr Parzyszek	08.09.1993	3	(1)	
Arkadiusz Pyrka	20.09.2002	8	(15)	
Dominik Steczyk	04.05.1999	22	(4)	4
Jakub Świerczok	28.12.1992	20	(3)	15
Tiago Alexandre Mendes Alves (POR)	19.06.1996	4	(17)	5
Krisztófer Vida (HUN)	23.06.1995	10	(9)	1
Mateusz Winciersz	05.10.2000		(2)	
Michał Żyro	20.09.1992	8	(18)	4

Towarzystwo Sportowe Podbeskidzie Bielsko-Biała

Founded: 11.07.1997
Stadium: Stadion Miejski, Bielsko-Biała (15,076)
Trainer: Krzysztof Brede   08.02.1981
[15.12.2020] Hubert Kosciukiewicz   24.10.1978
[22.12.2020] Robert Kasperczyk   22.01.1967

Goalkeepers:	DOB	M	(s)	G
Rafał Leszczyński	26.04.1992	3		
Michal Peškovič (SVK)	08.02.1982	22		
Martin Polaček (SVK)	02.04.1990	5		
Defenders:	**DOB**	**M**	**(s)**	**G**
Dmytro Bashlay (UKR)	25.04.1990	14	(1)	
Kacper Gach	11.07.1998	12		
Rafał Janicki	05.07.1992	13		3
Bartosz Jaroch	25.01.1995	3	(2)	
Aleksander Komor	24.06.1994	11	(1)	1
Petar Mamić (CRO)	06.03.1996	12		
Marco Tulio De Paula Medeiros (BRA)	31.05.1998	3	(7)	
Filip Modelski	28.09.1992	22	(1)	
Szymon Mroczko	18.01.2001	2	(2)	
David Niepsuj (GER)	16.08.1995	7	(2)	1
Kornel Osyra	07.02.1993	2		
Milan Rundić (SRB)	29.03.1992	20	(1)	1
Midfielders:	**DOB**	**M**	**(s)**	**G**
Jakub Bieroński	18.04.2003	11	(4)	
Rafał Figiel	08.05.1991	6	(2)	
Dominik Frelek	11.10.2001	1	(8)	
Konrad Gutowski	22.03.1999	1	(3)	
Jakub Hora (CZE)	23.02.1991	13	(3)	2
Gergő Kocsis (HUN)	07.03.1994	13	(6)	
Filip Laskowski	04.05.2001	2	(5)	
Mateusz Marzec	13.08.1994	7	(9)	1
Tomasz Nowak	30.10.1985	8	(3)	1
Michał Rzuchowski	27.12.1993	22	(4)	1
Maksymilian Sitek	04.12.2000	12	(6)	1
Desley Ubbink (NED)	15.06.1993	8	(2)	
Forwards:	**DOB**	**M**	**(s)**	**G**
Kamil Biliński	23.01.1988	23	(3)	11
Karol Danielak	29.09.1991	17	(9)	1
Iván Martín Gómez (ESP)	04.03.1995		(4)	
Bartłomiej Kręcichwost	13.08.1999	1	(1)	
Sergiy Myakushko (UKR)	15.04.1993	2	(13)	
Marko Roginić (CRO)	05.09.1995	16	(6)	2
Łukasz Sierpina	27.03.1988	12	(10)	
Peter Wilson (SWE)	09.10.1996	4	(9)	

Morski Klub Sportowy Pogoń Szczecin

Founded: 21.04.1948
Stadium: Stadion „Florian Krygier", Szczecin (18,027)
Trainer: Kosta Runjaić (GER)   04.06.1971

Goalkeepers:	DOB	M	(s)	G
Dante Stipica (CRO)	30.05.1991	30		
Defenders:	**DOB**	**M**	**(s)**	**G**
Jakub Bartkowski	07.11.1991	18	(3)	1
Luís Mata (POR)	06.07.1997	15	(3)	
Igor Łasicki	26.06.1995		(1)	
Mariusz Malec	04.04.1995	17	(3)	
Hubert Matynia	04.11.1995	13	(1)	
Bartłomiej Mruk	21.08.2001		(1)	
David Steć (AUT)	10.05.1994	9	(1)	
Paweł Stolarski	28.01.1996	3	(2)	
Konstantinos Triantafyllopoulos (GRE)	03.04.1993	17		1
Benedikt Zech (AUT)	03.11.1990	26	(1)	
Midfielders:	**DOB**	**M**	**(s)**	**G**
Damian Dąbrowski	27.08.1992	25	(1)	
Kamil Drygas	07.09.1991	16	(11)	3
Mariusz Fornalczyk	15.01.2003		(6)	
Kacper Kozłowski	16.10.2003	14	(6)	1
Kapcer Smoliński	02.07.2001	8	(19)	1
Tomás Podstawski (POR)	30.01.1995	4	(15)	1
Maciej Żurawski	22.12.2000	4	(3)	1
Forwards:	**DOB**	**M**	**(s)**	**G**
Adrian Benedyczak	24.11.2000	10	(15)	3
Paweł Cibicki (SWE)	09.01.1994	1	(3)	
Adam Frączczak	07.08.1987	4	(11)	3
Alexander Gorgon (AUT)	28.10.1988	20	(4)	5
Santeri Hostikka (FIN)	30.09.1997	3	(9)	
Sebastian Kowalczyk	22.08.1998	26	(3)	3
Michał Kucharczyk	20.03.1991	26	(4)	6
Rafał Kurzawa	29.01.1993	6	(4)	2
Hubert Turski	31.01.2003		(1)	
Luka Zahović (SVN)	15.11.1995	15	(10)	2

Robotniczy Klub Sportowy Raków Częstochowa

Founded: 1921
Stadium: GIEKSA Arena, Belchatów (5,264)
Trainer: Marek Papszun   08.08.1974

Goalkeepers:	DOB	M	(s)	G
Dominik Holec (SVK)	28.07.1994	16		
Branislav Pindroch (SVK)	30.10.1991	2		
Jakub Szumski	06.03.1992	12		
Defenders:	**DOB**	**M**	**(s)**	**G**
Zoran Arsenić (CRO)	02.06.1994	9		1
Jarosław Jach	17.02.1994	9	(1)	
Daniel Mikołajewski	25.08.1999	2	(1)	
Andrzej Niewulis	21.04.1989	19	(4)	2
Tomáš Petrášek (CZE)	02.03.1992	8		2
Kamil Piątkowski	21.06.2000	27		2
Fran Tudor (CRO)	27.09.1995	26	(3)	1
Maciej Wilusz	25.09.1988	10		
Midfielders:	**DOB**	**M**	**(s)**	**G**
Daniel Bartl (CZE)	05.07.1989	4	(7)	
Marcin Cebula	06.12.1995	17	(7)	6
Felicio Brown Forbes (CRC)	28.08.1991		(1)	
Iwo Kaczmarski	16.04.2004	2		
Patryk Kun	20.04.1995	26	(3)	1
Ben Lederman (USA)	08.05.2000	4	(9)	
Piotr Malinowski	25.03.1984		(15)	
Marko Poletanović (SRB)	20.07.1993	18	(3)	
Igor Sapała	11.10.1995	23	(1)	
Petr Schwarz (CZE)	12.11.1991	15	(12)	4
Daniel Szelągowski	02.09.2002	2	(14)	1
David Tijanič (SVN)	16.07.1997	24	(4)	6
Forwards:	**DOB**	**M**	**(s)**	**G**
Jakub Arak	02.04.1995	3	(9)	1
Wiktor Długosz	01.07.2000	3	(3)	
Vladislavs Gutkovskis (LVA)	02.04.1995	24	(5)	7
Iván López Álvarez „Ivi" (ESP)	29.06.1994	17	(9)	9
Sebastian Musiolik	19.05.1996		(4)	
Giannis Papanikolaou (GRE)	18.11.1998	1	(6)	
Mateusz Wdowiak	28.08.1996	4	(5)	
Oskar Zawada	01.02.1996	3	(4)	1

Fabryczny Klub Sportowy Stal Mielec

Founded: 10.04.1939
Stadium: Stadion Miejski, Mielec (6,864)
Trainer: Dariusz Skrzypczak   13.11.1967
[11.11.2020] Leszek Ojrzyński   31.05.1972
[12.04.2021] Włodzimierz Gąsior   17.08.1948

Goalkeepers:	DOB	M	(s)	G
Michał Gliwa	08.04.1988	5		
Damian Primel	16.04.1992		(1)	
Rafał Strączek	12.02.1999	25		
Defenders:	**DOB**	**M**	**(s)**	**G**
Wojciech Błyszko	05.10.1999	2	(1)	
Bozhidar Chorbadzhiyski (BUL)	08.08.1995	19	(1)	
Marcin Flis	10.02.1994	25	(3)	3
Krystian Getinger	29.08.1988	28	(1)	2
Albin Granlund (FIN)	01.09.1989	11	(1)	
Jonathan de Amo Pérez (ESP)	13.01.1990	11	(1)	2
Kamil Kościelny	04.08.1991	14		
Wojciech Lisowski	10.02.1992	1	(2)	
Łukasz Seweryn	29.03.2002		(1)	
Szymon Stasik	04.02.1999	2	(2)	
Martin Sus (CZE)	15.03.1990		(6)	
Mateusz Żyro	28.10.1998	15	(5)	
Midfielders:	**DOB**	**M**	**(s)**	**G**
Maciej Domański	05.09.1990	28	(2)	6
Petteri Forsell (FIN)	16.10.1990	15	(11)	1
Przemyslaw Maj	06.04.2003		(1)	
Mateusz Matras	23.01.1991	25	(2)	1
Damian Pawłowski	27.01.1999	2	(5)	
Grzegorz Tomasiewicz	05.05.1996	28	(1)	3
Maciej Urbańczyk	02.04.1995	9	(2)	
Forwards:	**DOB**	**M**	**(s)**	**G**
Robert Dadok	24.12.1996	8	(16)	
Maciej Jankowski	04.01.1990	6	(5)	2
Aleksandar Kolev (BUL)	08.12.1992	11	(4)	2
Mateusz Mak	14.11.1991	12	(13)	4
Andreja Prokić (SRB)	09.04.1989	15	(14)	2
Kacper Sadłocha	01.12.2002		(2)	
Paweł Tomczyk	04.05.1998	1	(10)	1
Jakub Wróbel	30.07.1993	2	(6)	
Łukasz Zjawiński	11.07.2001	10	(14)	1

Wrocławski Klub Sportowy Śląsk Wrocław Spółka Akcyjna

Founded: 18.03.1946
Stadium: Stadion Wrocław, Wrocław (42,771)
Trainer: Vitezslav Lavicka (CZE)   30.04.1963
[22.03.2021] Jacek Magiera   01.01.1977

Goalkeepers:	DOB	M	(s)	G
Matúš Putnocký (SVK)	01.11.1984	19		
Michał Szromnik	04.03.1993	11		
Defenders:	**DOB**	**M**	**(s)**	**G**
Łukasz Bejger	11.01.2002	10	(1)	
Piotr Celeban	25.06.1985	13	(1)	2
Guillermo Gastón Cotugno Lima (URU)	17.03.1995	6	(3)	
Wojciech Golla	12.01.1992	8		1
Israel Puerto Pineda (ESP)	15.06.1993	17		1
Patryk Janasik	25.08.1997	14	(3)	
Mariusz Pawelec	14.04.1986	8	(2)	
Konrad Poprawa	04.06.1998	5	(1)	1
Dino Štiglec (CRO)	03.10.1990	24	(1)	
Márk Tamás (HUN)	28.10.1993	22	(2)	
Midfielders:	**DOB**	**M**	**(s)**	**G**
Przemysław Bargiel	26.03.2000		(3)	
Szymon Lewkot	18.02.1999	4	(3)	
Jakub Łabojko	03.10.1997	3		
Adrian Łyszczarz	22.08.1999		(2)	
Krzysztof Mączyński	23.05.1987	18		2
Rafał Makowski	05.08.1996	3	(8)	
Maciej Pałaszewski	07.04.1998	7	(6)	
Mateusz Praszelik	26.09.2000	21	(5)	1
Waldemar Sobota	19.05.1987	17	(11)	1
Marcin Szpakowski	26.09.2001		(2)	
Marcel Żyła	14.01.2000	7	(13)	1
Forwards:	**DOB**	**M**	**(s)**	**G**
Sebastian Bergier	20.12.1999		(2)	
Erik Alexander Expósito Hernández (ESP)	23.06.1996	22	(5)	9
Lubambo Musonda (ZAM)	01.03.1995	14	(3)	
Bartłomiej Pawłowski	13.11.1992	13	(9)	3
Fabian Piasecki	04.05.1995	6	(20)	4
Róbert Pich (SVK)	12.11.1988	27	(3)	7
Piotr Samiec-Talar	02.11.2001	1	(7)	
Mathieu Scalet (FRA)	01.04.1997	10	(4)	2

Klub Sportowy Warta Poznań

Founded: 15.06.1912
Stadium: Stadion Miejski, Grodzisk Wielkopolski (5,383)
Trainer: Piotr Tworek   10.03.1975

Goalkeepers:	DOB	M	(s)	G
Daniel Bielica	30.04.1999	5		
Adrian Lis	28.05.1992	25		
Defenders:	**DOB**	**M**	**(s)**	**G**
Jan Grzesik	21.10.1994	26	(1)	4
Robert Ivanov (FIN)	19.09.1994	21	(1)	
Bartosz Kieliba	01.08.1990	14		1
Jakub Kiełb	15.07.1993	21	(2)	1
Jakub Kuzdra	08.12.1997	21	(2)	1
Aleks Ławniczak	05.05.1999	22	(1)	1
Maik Nawrocki	07.02.2001	2	(1)	1
Mateusz Spychała	28.01.1998	4	(3)	
Midfielders:	**DOB**	**M**	**(s)**	**G**
Bartłomiej Burman	01.05.2001	1	(3)	
Mateusz Czyżycki	08.02.1998	12	(10)	
Konrad Handzlik	13.02.1998		(2)	
Robert Janicki	07.06.1997	7	(12)	1
Michał Kopczyński	15.06.1992	5	(2)	
Mateusz Kupczak	20.02.1992	20	(5)	3
Adrian Laskowski	16.03.1992	7	(2)	
Mateusz Sopoćko	26.06.1999		(2)	
Łukasz Trałka	11.05.1984	28	(1)	3
Maciej Żurawski	22.12.2000	12	(3)	
Forwards:	**DOB**	**M**	**(s)**	**G**
Makana Baku (GER)	08.04.1998	12	(1)	6
Michał Jakóbowski	08.09.1992	20	(3)	2
Gracjan Jaroch	15.04.1998	2	(12)	
Mateusz Kuzimski	26.06.1991	24	(5)	7
Mario Rodríguez Ruiz (ESP)	03.03.1997	5	(7)	1
Mariusz Rybicki	13.03.1993	8	(5)	1
Kajetan Szmyt	29.05.2002	1	(4)	
Adam Zreľák (SVK)	05.05.1994	5	(3)	

Wisła Kraków Spółka Akcyjna

Founded: 1906
Stadium: Stadion „Henryk Reyman", Kraków (33,326)
Trainer: Artur Skowronek   22.05.1982
[02.12.2020] Peter Hyballa (GER)   05.12.1975
[14.05.2020] Kazimierz Kmiecik   19.09.1951

Goalkeepers:	DOB	M	(s)	G
Michał Buchalik	03.02.1989	3		
Mateusz Lis	27.02.1997	27		
Defenders:	**DOB**	**M**	**(s)**	**G**
Dawid Abramowicz	16.05.1991	8	(4)	
Łukasz Burliga	10.05.1988	18	(4)	1
Michal Frydrych (CZE)	27.02.1990	24		3
Konrad Gruszkowski	27.01.2001	4	(3)	1
Daniel Hoyo-Kowalski	12.07.2003		(1)	
Rafał Janicki	05.07.1992	4		
Łukasz Klemenz	24.09.1995	3	(1)	
Souleymane Koné (CIV)	01.05.1996	5	(2)	
Adi Mehremić (BIH)	26.04.1992	11		1
David Niepsuj (GER)	16.08.1995	1	(1)	
Uroš Radaković (SRB)	31.03.1994	5	(1)	1
Maciej Sadlok	29.06.1989	24	(1)	2
Dawid Szot	29.04.2001	15	(5)	
Serafin Szota	04.03.1999	3	(5)	
Krystian Wachowiak	19.10.2001		(1)	
Midfielders:	**DOB**	**M**	**(s)**	**G**
Vullnet Basha (ALB)	11.07.1990	5	(4)	
Rafał Boguski	09.06.1984	1	(10)	2
Víctor Moya Martínez „Chuca" (ESP)	10.06.1997	10	(3)	3
Nikola Kuveljić (SRB)	06.04.1997	8	(4)	
David Mawutor (GHA)	12.04.1992	3	(4)	
Patryk Plewka	02.01.2000	17		1
Stefan Savić (AUT)	09.01.1994	23	(4)	2
Piotr Starzyński	22.01.2000	10	(5)	1
Georgiy Zhukov (KAZ)	19.11.1994	21	(4)	
Forwards:	**DOB**	**M**	**(s)**	**G**
Fatos Bećiraj (MNE)	05.05.1988	1	(9)	
Jakub Błaszczykowski	14.12.1985	3	(13)	4
Felicio Brown Forbes (CRC)	28.08.1991	22		7
Aleksander Buksa	15.01.2003	1	(12)	
Jean Carlos Silva Rocha (BRA)	10.05.1996	18	(4)	3
Michał Mak	14.11.1991	1	(3)	
Žan Medved (SVN)	14.06.1999	5	(8)	
Yaw Yeboah (GHA)	28.03.1997	26	(2)	4

Wisła Płock Spółka Akcyjna

Founded: 1947
Stadium: Stadion „Kazimierza Górski", Płock (12,800)
Trainer: Radosław Sobolewski   13.12.1976
[13.04.2021] Maciej Bartoszek   12.04.1977

Goalkeepers:	DOB	M	(s)	G
Bartłomiej Gradecki	26.12.1999	1		
Krzysztof Kamiński	26.11.1990	29		
Defenders:	**DOB**	**M**	**(s)**	**G**
Ángel García Cabezali (ESP)	03.02.1993	27	(1)	
Julio César Rodríguez López (ESP)	07.12.1995	1		
Damian Michalski	17.05.1998	10	(3)	2
Milan Obradović (SRB)	27.12.1999	6	(2)	
Jakub Rzeźniczak	26.10.1986	21		1
Bartłomiej Sielewski	09.08.1984		(1)	
Piotr Tomasik	31.10.1987	12	(2)	
Alan Uryga	19.02.1994	27		5
Kristián Vallo (SVK)	02.06.1998	7	(1)	
Damian Zbozień	25.04.1989	17	(1)	
Paweł Żuk	29.01.2001	2	(1)	
Midfielders:	**DOB**	**M**	**(s)**	**G**
Hubert Adamczyk	23.02.1998	5	(5)	
Maciej Ambrosiewicz	24.05.1998		(2)	
Dušan Lagator (MNE)	29.03.1994	21	(5)	3
Filip Lesniak (SVK)	14.05.1996	24	(2)	1
Aleksander Pawlak	14.11.2001		(2)	
Damian Rasak	08.02.1996	23	(3)	3
Kacper Rogoziński	20.04.2001	1	(1)	
Wojciech Szumilas	07.11.1996	1	(2)	
Mateusz Szwoch	19.03.1993	27	(3)	7
Rafał Wolski	10.11.1992	3	(4)	2
Bartosz Zynek	14.03.2002		(1)	
Forwards:	**DOB**	**M**	**(s)**	**G**
Airam López Cabrera (ESP)	21.10.1987	1	(4)	
Torgil Øwre Gjertsen (NOR)	12.03.1992	7	(12)	1
Dawid Kocyła	23.07.2002	21	(6)	3
Mateusz Lewandowski	04.03.1999	6	(10)	1
Giorgi Merebashvili (GEO)	15.08.1986	3	(7)	
Piotr Pyrdoł	27.04.1999	2	(13)	
Cillian Sheridan (IRL)	23.02.1989	7	(8)	
Luka Šušnjara (SVN)	04.04.1997	1	(3)	1
Patryk Tuszyński	13.12.1989	17	(8)	6

Zagłębie Lubin Spółka Akcyjna

Founded: 10.09.1945
Stadium: Stadion Zagłębia, Lubin (16,068)
Trainer: Martin Ševela (SVK)   20.11.1975

Goalkeepers:	DOB	M	(s)	G
Dominik Hładun	17.09.1995	30		
Defenders:	**DOB**	**M**	**(s)**	**G**
Saša Balić (MNE)	29.01.1990	25		2
Mateusz Bartolewski	12.01.1998	4	(6)	
Jakub Bednarczyk	02.01.1999	3	(5)	
Kacper Chodyna	24.05.1999	22	(2)	2
Đorđe Crnomarković (SRB)	10.09.1993	9		
Lubomír Guldan (SVK)	30.01.1983	14		2
Dominik Jończy	17.05.1997	8	(3)	
Kamil Kruk	13.03.2000	8	(4)	2
Damian Oko	22.01.1997	7	(1)	1
Milan Posmyk	02.02.2002		(1)	
Lorenco Šimić (CRO)	15.07.1996	14	(3)	4
Jakub Wójcicki	09.07.1988	8	(3)	
Midfielders:	**DOB**	**M**	**(s)**	**G**
Evgeniy Bashkirov (RUS)	06.07.1991	20	(5)	1

	DOB	M	(s)	G
Łukasz Łakomy	18.01.2001		(8)	
Dawid Pakulski	23.07.1998		(1)	
Łukasz Poręba	13.03.2000	18	(6)	
Filip Starzyński	27.05.1991	25	(1)	7
Jakub Sypek	07.04.2001		(1)	
Jakub Żubrowski	21.03.1992	22	(5)	
Forwards:	**DOB**	**M**	**(s)**	**G**
Damjan Bohar (SVN)	18.10.1991	4		1
Dejan Drazič (SRB)	26.09.1995	19	(3)	1
Samuel Mráz (SVK)	13.05.1997	13	(14)	2
Karol Podliński	06.11.1997	12		2
Adam Ratajczyk	12.06.2002	1	(13)	
Rok Sirk (SVN)	10.09.1993	3	(13)	2
Miroslav Stoch (SVK)	19.10.1989	6	(2)	
Patryk Szysz	01.04.1998	27	(3)	8
Saša Živec (SVN)	02.04.1991	8	(3)	1

SECOND LEVEL
I liga 2020/2021

1.	RKS Radomiak Radom (*Promoted*)	34	20	8	6	49 - 20	68
2.	Bruk-Bet Termalica Nieciecza KS (*Promoted*)	34	18	11	5	56 - 28	65
3.	GKS Tychy (*Promotion Play-offs*)	34	18	9	7	49 - 27	63
4.	MZKS Arka Gdynia (*Promotion Play-offs*)	34	17	9	8	51 - 32	60
5.	ŁKS Łódź (*Promotion Play-offs*)	34	17	7	10	59 - 41	58
6.	GKS Górnik Łęczna (*Promotion Play-offs*)	34	15	11	8	47 - 30	56
7.	MKS Miedź Legnica	34	13	12	9	49 - 36	51
8.	OKS Odra Opole	34	13	10	11	35 - 41	49
9.	RTS Widzew Łódź	34	11	13	10	30 - 36	46
10.	MKS Sandecja Nowy Sącz	34	12	9	13	42 - 50	45
11.	MKS Chrobry Głogów	34	12	8	14	34 - 45	44
12.	Korona Kielce	34	11	8	15	31 - 46	41
13.	MKS Puszcza Niepołomice	34	10	7	17	32 - 46	37
14.	GKS Jastrzębie-Zdrój	34	10	5	19	32 - 48	35
15.	OKS Stomil Olsztyn	34	9	8	17	31 - 48	35
16.	CWKS Resovia Rzeszów	34	8	8	18	27 - 45	32
17.	Zagłębie Sosnowiec	34	8	6	20	35 - 43	30
18.	PGE GKS Bełchatów* (*Relegated*)	34	6	7	21	24 - 51	23

2 points deducted for licensing process violating.

Promotion Play-offs (1st / 2nd Level)

Play-offs Semi-Finals (16.06.2021)	GKS Tychy - GKS Górnik Łęczna	1-1(1-0,1-1,1-1); 2-4 on penalties
	MZKS Arka Gdynia - ŁKS Łódź	0-1(0-0)
Play-offs Final (20.06.2021)	ŁKS Łódź - GKS Górnik Łęczna	0-1(0-1)

GKS Górnik Łęczna were promoted to the 2021/2022 Ekstraklasa.

INTERNATIONAL MATCHES
(16.07.2020 – 15.07.2021)

04.09.2020	Amsterdam	Netherlands - Poland	1-0(0-0)	(UNL)
07.09.2020	Zenica	Bosnia and Herzegovina - Poland	1-2(1-1)	(UNL)
07.10.2020	Gdańsk	Poland - Finland	5-1(3-0)	(F)
11.10.2020	Gdańsk	Poland - Italy	0-0	(UNL)
14.10.2020	Wrocław	Poland - Bosnia and Herzegovina	3-0(2-0)	(UNL)
11.11.2020	Chorzów	Poland - Ukraine	2-0(1-0)	(F)
15.11.2020	Reggio Emilia	Italy - Poland	2-0(1-0)	(UNL)
18.11.2020	Chorzów	Poland - Netherlands	1-2(1-0)	(UNL)
25.03.2021	Budapest	Hungary - Poland	3-3(1-0)	(WCQ)
28.03.2021	Warszawa	Poland - Andorra	3-0(1-0)	(WCQ)
31.03.2021	London	England - Poland	2-1(1-0)	(WCQ)
01.06.2021	Wrocław	Poland - Russia	1-1(1-1)	(F)
08.06.2021	Poznań	Poland - Iceland	2-2(1-1)	(F)
14.06.2021	Saint Petersburg	Poland - Slovakia	1-2(0-1)	(EC)
19.06.2021	Sevilla	Spain - Poland	1-1(1-0)	(EC)
23.06.2021	Saint Petersburg	Sweden - Poland	3-2(1-0)	(EC)

04.09.2020   NETHERLANDS - POLAND   1-0(0-0)   2nd UEFA Nations League A, Group 1
"Johan Cruyff" Arena, Amsterdam; Referee: Georgi Kabakov (Bulgaria); Attendance: 0
POL: Wojciech Tomasz Szczęsny, Tomasz Karol Kędziora, Kamil Jacek Glik (Cap), Jan Kacper Bednarek, Bartosz Bereszyński, Sebastian Szymański, Grzegorz Krychowiak, Mateusz Andrzej Klich, Piotr Sebastian Zieliński (77.Jakub Piotr Moder), Kamil Jóźwiak (71.Kamil Grosicki), Krzysztof Piątek (63.Arkadiusz Krystian Milik). Trainer: Jerzy Józef Brzęczek.

07.09.2020   BOSNIA AND HERZEGOVINA - POLAND   1-2(1-1)   2nd UEFA Nations League A, Group 1
Stadion Bilino Polje, Zenica; Referee: Cüneyt Çakır (Turkey); Attendance: 0
POL: Łukasz Marek Fabiański, Tomasz Karol Kędziora, Maciej Rybus, Kamil Jacek Glik (Cap), Jan Kacper Bednarek, Kamil Grosicki (80.Sebastian Szymański), Grzegorz Krychowiak (68.Mateusz Andrzej Klich), Piotr Sebastian Zieliński (85.Karol Linetty), Kamil Jóźwiak, Jacek Góralski, Arkadiusz Krystian Milik. Trainer: Jerzy Józef Brzęczek.
Goals: Kamil Jacek Glik (45), Kamil Grosicki (67).

07.10.2020   POLAND - FINLAND   5-1(3-0)   Friendly International
Stadion Energa, Gdańsk; Referee: Michal Očenáš (Slovakia); Attendance: 3,000
POL: Bartłomiej Drągowski, Bartosz Bereszyński (62.Alan Czerwiński), Jan Kacper Bednarek, Sebastian Wiktor Walukiewicz (46.Paweł Bochniewicz), Michał Karbownik, Kamil Grosicki (Cap) (62.Rafał Pietrzak), Karol Linetty, Jakub Piotr Moder (61.Grzegorz Krychowiak), Arkadiusz Krystian Milik, Damian Kądzior (83. Kamil Jóźwiak), Krzysztof Piątek (71.Mateusz Andrzej Klich). Trainer: Jerzy Józef Brzęczek.
Goals: Kamil Grosicki (9, 18, 28), Krzysztof Piątek (53), Arkadiusz Krystian Milik (87).

11.10.2020   POLAND - ITALY   0-0   2nd UEFA Nations League A, Group 1
Stadion Energa, Gdańsk; Referee: José María Sánchez Martínez (Spain); Attendance: 9,200
POL: Łukasz Marek Fabiański, Tomasz Karol Kędziora, Kamil Jacek Glik, Bartosz Bereszyński, Sebastian Wiktor Walukiewicz, Mateusz Andrzej Klich (70.Arkadiusz Krystian Milik), Grzegorz Krychowiak, Kamil Jóźwiak (82.Michał Karbownik), Jakub Piotr Moder, Sebastian Szymański (59.Kamil Grosicki), Robert Lewandowski (Cap) (82.Karol Linetty). Trainer: Jerzy Józef Brzęczek.

14.10.2020   POLAND - BOSNIA AND HERZEGOVINA   3-0(2-0)   2nd UEFA Nations League A, Group 1
Stadion Wrocław, Wrocław; Referee: Craig Pawson (England); Attendance: 8,152
POL: Wojciech Tomasz Szczęsny, Tomasz Karol Kędziora (72.Bartosz Bereszyński), Kamil Jacek Glik, Jan Kacper Bednarek, Kamil Grosicki (64.Damian Kądzior), Mateusz Andrzej Klich (64.Krzysztof Piątek), Jacek Góralski, Karol Linetty, Arkadiusz Reca, Kamil Jóźwiak (72.Michał Karbownik), Robert Lewandowski (Cap) (58.Arkadiusz Krystian Milik). Trainer: Jerzy Józef Brzęczek.
Goals: Robert Lewandowski (40), Karol Linetty (45+1), Robert Lewandowski (52).

11.11.2020   POLAND - UKRAINE   2-0(1-0)   Friendly International
Stadion Śląski, Chorzów; Referee: Manuel Schüttengruber (Austria); Attendance: 0
POL: Łukasz Skorupski, Maciej Rybus (79.Arkadiusz Reca), Paweł Bochniewicz, Robert Gumny (78.Bartosz Bereszyński), Sebastian Wiktor Walukiewicz, Mateusz Andrzej Klich, Piotr Sebastian Zieliński (46. Kamil Jóźwiak), Jacek Góralski (62.Karol Linetty), Przemysław Płacheta (83.Sebastian Szymański), Arkadiusz Krystian Milik (Cap) (62.Jakub Piotr Moder), Krzysztof Piątek. Trainer: Jerzy Józef Brzęczek.
Goals: Krzysztof Piątek (40), Jakub Piotr Molder (63).

15.11.2020   ITALY - POLAND   2-0(1-0)   2nd UEFA Nations League A, Group 1
Stadio Città del Tricolore, Reggio Emilia; Referee: Clément Turpin (France); Attendance: 0
POL: Wojciech Tomasz Szczęsny, Bartosz Bereszyński, Kamil Jacek Glik, Jan Kacper Bednarek, Grzegorz Krychowiak, Karol Linetty (74.Arkadiusz Krystian Milik), Arkadiusz Reca, Kamil Jóźwiak (46.Kamil Grosicki), Jakub Piotr Moder (46.Jacek Góralski [sent off 77]), Sebastian Szymański (46.Piotr Sebastian Zieliński), Robert Lewandowski (Cap). Trainer: Jerzy Józef Brzęczek.

18.11.2020   POLAND - NETHERLANDS   1-2(1-0)   2nd UEFA Nations League A, Group 1
Stadion Śląski, Chorzów; Referee: Orel Grinfeld (Israel); Attendance: 0
POL: Łukasz Marek Fabiański, Kamil Jacek Glik, Tomasz Karol Kędziora, Jan Kacper Bednarek, Mateusz Andrzej Klich, Arkadiusz Reca (81.Maciej Rybus), Grzegorz Krychowiak (71.Karol Linetty), Piotr Sebastian Zieliński (71.Jakub Piotr Moder), Kamil Jóźwiak, Przemysław Płacheta (76.Kamil Grosicki), Robert Lewandowski (Cap) (46.Krzysztof Piątek). Trainer: Jerzy Józef Brzęczek.
Goal: Kamil Jóźwiak (6).

25.03.2021 HUNGARY - POLAND   **3-3(1-0)**   22nd FIFA WC. Qualifiers
Puskás Aréna, Budapest; Referee: Dr. Felix Brych (Germany); Attendance: 0
POL: Wojciech Tomasz Szczęsny, Bartosz Bereszyński, Jan Kacper Bednarek, Michał Sławomir Helik (58.Kamil Jacek Glik), Grzegorz Krychowiak, Piotr Sebastian Zieliński, Arkadiusz Reca (79.Maciej Rybus), Jakub Piotr Moder (59.Krzysztof Piątek), Sebastian Szymański (59. Kamil Jóźwiak), Arkadiusz Krystian Milik (84.Kamil Grosicki), Robert Lewandowski (Cap). Trainer: Paulo Manuel Carvalho Sousa (Portugal).
Goals: Krzysztof Piątek (60), Kamil Jóźwiak (61), Robert Lewandowski (83).

28.03.2021 POLAND - ANDORRA   **3-0(1-0)**   22nd FIFA WC. Qualifiers
Stadion Wojska Polskiego, Warszawa; Referee: Erik Lambrechts (Belgium); Attendance: 0
POL: Wojciech Tomasz Szczęsny, Bartosz Bereszyński (60.Paweł Marek Dawidowicz), Maciej Rybus (60.Kamil Grosicki), Kamil Jacek Glik, Kamil Piątkowski, Grzegorz Krychowiak, Piotr Sebastian Zieliński (73.Kacper Kozłowski), Kamil Jóźwiak, Arkadiusz Krystian Milik (60.Przemysław Płacheta), Robert Lewandowski (Cap) (63.Karol Świderski), Krzysztof Piątek. Trainer: Paulo Manuel Carvalho Sousa (Portugal).
Goals: Robert Lewandowski (30, 55), Karol Świderski (88).

31.03.2021 ENGLAND - POLAND   **2-1(1-0)**   22nd FIFA WC. Qualifiers
Wembley Stadium, London; Referee: Björn Kuipers (Netherlands); Attendance: 0
POL: Wojciech Tomasz Szczęsny, Bartosz Bereszyński, Maciej Rybus (86.Arkadiusz Reca), Kamil Jacek Glik (Cap), Michał Sławomir Helik (54. Kamil Jóźwiak), Grzegorz Krychowiak, Piotr Sebastian Zieliński (86.Kamil Grosicki), Jan Kacper Bednarek, Jakub Piotr Moder, Krzysztof Piątek (76.Rafał Augustyniak), Karol Świderski (46.Arkadiusz Krystian Milik). Trainer: Paulo Manuel Carvalho Sousa (Portugal).
Goal: Jakub Piotr Molder (58).

01.06.2021 POLAND - RUSSIA   **1-1(1-1)**   Friendly International
Stadion Wrocław, Wrocław; Referee: Marco Guida (Italy); Attendance: 19,297
POL: Łukasz Marek Fabiański, Tomasz Karol Kędziora (56.Bartosz Bereszyński), Michał Sławomir Helik, Tymoteusz Puchacz, Kamil Piątkowski (56.Jan Kacper Bednarek), Mateusz Andrzej Klich (70.Kacper Kozłowski), Grzegorz Krychowiak (Cap), Przemysław Frankowski (80.Karol Linetty), Jakub Świerczok, Dawid Igor Kownacki (56. Kamil Jóźwiak), Karol Świderski (67.Jakub Piotr Moder). Trainer: Paulo Manuel Carvalho Sousa (Portugal).
Goal: Jakub Świerczok (4).

08.06.2021 POLAND - ICELAND   **2-2(1-1)**   Friendly International
Stadion Miejski, Poznań; Referee: Balázs Berke (Hungary); Attendance: 19,614
POL: Wojciech Tomasz Szczęsny, Kamil Jacek Glik, Tomasz Karol Kędziora, Paweł Marek Dawidowicz, Tymoteusz Puchacz (80.Maciej Rybus), Grzegorz Krychowiak (64.Karol Linetty), Piotr Sebastian Zieliński (46.Kacper Kozłowski), Przemysław Frankowski (64.Przemysław Płacheta), Jakub Piotr Moder, Robert Lewandowski (Cap) (81.Karol Świderski), Jakub Świerczok (58. Kamil Jóźwiak). Trainer: Paulo Manuel Carvalho Sousa (Portugal).
Goals: Piotr Sebastian Zieliński (34), Karol Świdersk (88).

14.06.2021 POLAND - SLOVAKIA   **1-2(0-1)**   16th EC. Group Stage.
Krestovsky Stadium, Saint Petersburg (Russia); Referee: Ovidiu Alin Haţegan (Romania); Attendance: 12,862
POL: Wojciech Tomasz Szczęsny, Maciej Rybus (74.Tymoteusz Puchacz), Kamil Jacek Glik, Bartosz Bereszyński, Jan Kacper Bednarek, Mateusz Andrzej Klich (85.Jakub Piotr Moder), Grzegorz Krychowiak [sent off 62], Piotr Sebastian Zieliński (85.Karol Świderski), Karol Linetty (74.Przemysław Frankowski), Kamil Jóźwiak, Robert Lewandowski (Cap). Trainer: Paulo Manuel Carvalho Sousa (Portugal).
Goal: Karol Linetty (46).

19.06.2021 SPAIN - POLAND   **1-1(1-0)**   16th EC. Group Stage.
Estadio La Cartuja, Sevilla; Referee: Daniele Orsato (Italy); Attendance: 11,732
POL: Wojciech Tomasz Szczęsny, Kamil Jacek Glik, Bartosz Bereszyński, Jan Kacper Bednarek (85.Paweł Marek Dawidowicz), Tymoteusz Puchacz, Mateusz Andrzej Klich (55.Kacper Kozłowski), Piotr Sebastian Zieliński, Kamil Jóźwiak, Jakub Piotr Moder (85.Karol Linetty), Robert Lewandowski (Cap), Karol Świderski (68.Przemysław Frankowski). Trainer: Paulo Manuel Carvalho Sousa (Portugal).
Goal: Robert Lewandowski (54).

23.06.2021 SWEDEN - POLAND   **3-2(1-0)**   16th EC. Group Stage.
Krestovsky Stadium, Saint Petersburg (Russia); Referee: Michael Oliver (England); Attendance: 14,252
POL: Wojciech Tomasz Szczęsny, Kamil Jacek Glik, Bartosz Bereszyński, Jan Kacper Bednarek, Tymoteusz Puchacz (46.Przemysław Frankowski), Mateusz Andrzej Klich (73.Kacper Kozłowski), Grzegorz Krychowiak (78.Przemysław Płacheta), Piotr Sebastian Zieliński, Kamil Jóźwiak (61.Jakub Świerczok), Robert Lewandowski (Cap), Karol Świderski. Trainer: Paulo Manuel Carvalho Sousa (Portugal).
Goals: Robert Lewandowski (61, 84).

NATIONAL TEAM PLAYERS
(16.07.2020 – 15.07.2021)

Name	DOB	Caps	Goals	2020/2021:	Club
Goalkeepers					
Bartłomiej DRĄGOWSKI	19.08.1997	1	0	2020:	ACF Fiorentina (ITA)
Łukasz Marek FABIAŃSKI	18.04.1985	56	0	2020/2021:	West Ham United FC London (ENG)
Łukasz SKORUPSKI	05.05.1991	4	0	2020:	Bologna FC 1909 (ITA)
Wojciech Tomasz SZCZĘSNY	18.04.1990	56	0	2020/2021:	Juventus FC Torino (ITA)
Defenders					
Jan Kacper BEDNAREK	12.04.1996	33	1	2020/2021:	Southampton FC (ENG)
Bartosz BERESZYŃSKI	12.07.1992	35	0	2020/2021:	UC Sampdoria Genova (ITA)
Paweł BOCHNIEWICZ	30.01.1996	2	0	2020:	SC Heerenveen (NED)
Alan CZERWIŃSKI	02.02.1993	1	0	2020:	KKS Lech Poznań
Paweł Marek DAWIDOWICZ	20.05.1995	4	0	2021:	Hellas Verona FC (ITA)
Kamil Jacek GLIK	03.02.1988	86	6	2020/2021:	Benevento Calcio (ITA)
Robert GUMNY	04.06.1998	1	0	2020:	FC Augsburg (GER)
Michał Sławomir HELIK	09.09.1995	3	0	2021:	Barnsley FC (ENG)
Tomasz Karol KĘDZIORA	11.06.1994	23	0	2020/2021:	FK Dynamo Kyiv (UKR)
Kamil PIĄTKOWSKI	21.06.2000	2	0	2021:	RKS Raków Częstochowa
Rafał PIETRZAK	30.01.1992	3	0	2020:	KS Lechia Gdańsk
Tymoteusz PUCHACZ	23.01.1999	5	0	2021:	KKS Lech Poznań
Arkadiusz RECA	17.06.1995	14	0	2020/2021:	FC Crotone (ITA)
Maciej RYBUS	19.08.1989	63	2	2020/2021:	FK Lokomotiv Moscow (RUS)
Sebastian Wiktor WALUKIEWICZ	05.04.2000	3	0	2020:	Cagliari Calcio (ITA)
Midfielders					
Rafał AUGUSTYNIAK	14.10.1993	1	0	2021:	FK Ural Yekaterinburg (RUS)
Przemysław FRANKOWSKI	12.04.1995	15	1	2020/2021:	Chicago Fire SC (USA)
Jacek GÓRALSKI	21.09.1992	17	1	2020:	FC Kairat Almaty (KAZ)
Kamil GROSICKI	08.06.1988	83	17	2020/2021:	West Bromwich Albion FC (ENG)
Kamil JÓŹWIAK	22.04.1998	17	2	2020: 16.09.2020->	KKS Lech Poznań Derby County FC (ENG)
Michał KARBOWNIK	13.03.2001	3	0	2020:	Legia Warszawa
Mateusz Andrzej KLICH	13.06.1990	34	2	2020/2021:	Leeds United FC (ENG)
Kacper KOZŁOWSKI	16.10.2003	5	0	2021:	MKS Pogoń Szczecin
Grzegorz KRYCHOWIAK	29.01.1990	82	4	2020/2021:	FK Lokomotiv Moskva (RUS)
Damian KĄDZIOR	16.06.1992	6	1	2020:	SD Eibar (ESP)
Karol LINETTY	02.02.1995	34	3	2020/2021:	Torino FC (ITA)
Jakub Piotr MODER	07.04.1999	12	2	2020: 31.12.2020->	KKS Lech Poznań Brighton & Hove Albion FC (ENG)
Przemysław PŁACHETA	23.03.1998	5	0	2020/2021:	Norwich City FC (ENG)
Sebastian SZYMAŃSKI	10.05.1999	11	1	2020/2021:	FK Dinamo Moskva (RUS)
Piotr Sebastian ZIELIŃSKI	20.05.1994	63	7	2020/2021:	SSC Napoli (ITA)
Forwards					
Dawid Igor KOWNACKI	14.03.1997	7	1	2021:	TSV Fortuna Düsseldorf (GER)
Robert LEWANDOWSKI	21.08.1988	122	69	2020/2021:	FC Bayern München (GER)
Arkadiusz Krystian MILIK	28.02.1994	59	15	2020: 21.01.2021->	SSC Napoli (ITA) Olympique de Marseille (FRA)
Krzysztof PIĄTEK	01.07.1995	18	8	2020/2021:	Hertha BSC Berlin (GER)
Karol ŚWIDERSKI	23.01.1997	7	2	2021:	PAOK Thessaloníki (GRE)
Jakub ŚWIERCZOK	28.12.1992	6	1	2021:	GKS Piast Gliwice
Trainer					
Jerzy Józef BRZĘCZEK [from 12.07.2019 – 18.01.2021]	18.03.1971			24 M; 12 W; 5 D; 7 L; 36-20	
PAULO Manuel Carvalho SOUSA (Portugal) [from 21.01.2021]	30.08.1970			8 M; 1 W; 4 D; 3 L; 14-14	

PORTUGAL

The Country:
República Portuguesa (Portuguese Republic)
Capital: Lisboa
Surface: 92,212 km²
Inhabitants: 10,347,892 [2021]
Time: UTC

The FA:
Federação Portuguesa de Futebol
Avenida das Seleções 1495-433, Cruz Quebrada - Dafundo
Tel: +351 21 325 2700
Founded: 31.03.1914
Member of FIFA since: 1923
Member of UEFA since: 1954
Website: www.fpf.pt

NATIONAL TEAM RECORDS

RECORDS

First international match:	18.12.1921, Madrid:	Spain – Portugal 3-1(2-0)
Most international caps:	Cristiano Ronaldo dos Santos Aveiro	- 179 caps (since 2003)
Most international goals:	Cristiano Ronaldo dos Santos Aveiro	- 109 goals / 179 caps (since 2003)

UEFA EUROPEAN CHAMPIONSHIP

1960	Qualifiers
1964	Qualifiers
1968	Qualifiers
1972	Qualifiers
1976	Qualifiers
1980	Qualifiers
1984	Final Tournament (Semi-Finals)
1988	Qualifiers
1992	Qualifiers
1996	Final Tournament (Quarter-Finals)
2000	Final Tournament (Semi-Finals)
2004	Final Tournament (Runners-up)
2008	Final Tournament (Quarter-Finals)
2012	Final Tournament (Semi-Finals)
2016	**Final Tournament (Winners)**
2020	Final Tournament (2nd Round of 16)

FIFA WORLD CUP

1930	Did not enter
1934	Qualifiers
1938	Qualifiers
1950	Qualifiers
1954	Qualifiers
1958	Qualifiers
1962	Qualifiers
1966	Final Tournament (3rd Place)
1970	Qualifiers
1974	Qualifiers
1978	Qualifiers
1982	Qualifiers
1986	Final Tournament (Group Stage)
1990	Qualifiers
1994	Qualifiers
1998	Qualifiers
2002	Final Tournament (Group Stage)
2006	Final Tournament (4th Place)
2010	Final Tournament (2nd Round of 16)
2014	Final Tournament (Group Stage)
2018	Final Tournament (2nd Round of 16)

OLYMPIC TOURNAMENTS

Year	Result
1908	-
1912	-
1920	-
1924	-
1928	Quarter-Finals
1936	Did not enter
1948	Did not enter
1952	Did not enter
1956	Did not enter
1960	Did not enter
1964	Did not enter
1968	Did not enter
1972	Did not enter
1976	Did not enter
1980	Did not enter
1984	Qualifiers
1988	Qualifiers
1992	Qualifiers
1996	4th Place
2000	Qualifiers
2004	Group Stage
2008	Qualifiers
2012	Qualifiers
2016	Quarter-Finals

UEFA NATIONS LEAGUE

2018/2019	League A; Final Tournament – **Winners**
2020/2021	League A

FIFA CONFEDERATIONS CUP 1992-2017

2017 (3rd Place)

PORTUGUESE CLUB HONOURS IN EUROPEAN CLUB COMPETITIONS:

European Champion Clubs.Cup (1956-1992) / UEFA Champions League (1993-2021)		
Sport Lisboa e Benfica	2	1960/1961, 1961/1962
FC do Porto	2	1986/1987, 2003/2004
Fairs Cup (1858-1971) / UEFA Cup (1972-2009) / UEFA Europa League (2010-2021)		
FC do Porto	2	2002/2003, 2010/2011
UEFA Super Cup (1972-2020)		
FC do Porto	1	1987
*European Cup Winners.Cup 1961-1999**		
Sporting Clube de Portugal Lisboa	1	1963/1964

*defunct competition

NATIONAL COMPETITIONS
TABLE OF HONOURS

Campeonato de Portugal (1922–1938)*

*created in 1922 and played in cup system, with all the clubs participating in elimination rounds, the winners were named Champions of Portugal. The league sytem started in 1934.

	CHAMPIONS
1922	FC do Porto
1922/1923	Sporting Clube de Portugal Lisboa
1923/1924	SC Olhanense
1924/1925	FC do Porto
1925/1926	CS Marítimo Funchal
1926/1927	CF Os Belenenses Lisboa
1927/1928	Carcavelinhos FC
1928/1929	CF Os Belenenses Lisboa
1929/1930	Sport Lisboa e Benfica
1930/1931	Sport Lisboa e Benfica
1931/1932	FC do Porto
1932/1933	CF Os Belenenses Lisboa
1933/1934	Sporting Clube de Portugal Lisboa
1934/1935	Sport Lisboa e Benfica
1935/1936	Sporting Clube de Portugal Lisboa
1936/1937	FC do Porto
1937/1938	Sporting Clube de Portugal Lisboa

	CHAMPIONS*	CUP WINNERS	BEST GOALSCORERS	
1934/1935	FC do Porto	-	Manuel Esteves Soeiro Vasques (Sporting Clube de Portugal Lisboa)	14
1935/1936	Sport Lisboa e Benfica	-	Artur de Sousa "Pinga" (FC do Porto)	21
1936/1937	Sport Lisboa e Benfica	-	Manuel Esteves Soeiro Vasques (Sporting Clube de Portugal Lisboa)	24
1937/1938	Sport Lisboa e Benfica	-	Fernando Baptista de Seixas Peyroteo de Vasconcelos (Sporting Clube de Portugal Lisboa)	34
1938/1939	FC do Porto	Associação Académica de Coimbra	José Monteiro "Costuras" (FC do Porto)	18
1939/1940	FC do Porto	Sport Lisboa e Benfica	Fernando Baptista de Seixas Peyroteo de Vasconcelos (Sporting Clube de Portugal Lisboa) Slavko Kodrnja (CRO, FC do Porto)	29
1940/1941	Sporting Clube de Portugal Lisboa	Sporting Clube de Portugal Lisboa	Fernando Baptista de Seixas Peyroteo de Vasconcelos (Sporting Clube de Portugal Lisboa)	29
1941/1942	Sport Lisboa e Benfica	CF Os Belenenses Lisboa	Manuel BeloCorreia Dias (FC do Porto)	36
1942/1943	Sport Lisboa e Benfica	Sport Lisboa e Benfica	Júlio Correia da Silva "Julinho" (Sport Lisboa e Benfica)	24
1943/1944	Sporting Clube de Portugal Lisboa	Sport Lisboa e Benfica	Francisco Rodrigues (Vitória FC Setúbal)	28
1944/1945	Sport Lisboa e Benfica	Sporting Clube de Portugal Lisboa	Francisco Rodrigues (Vitória FC Setúbal)	21
1945/1946	CF Os Belenenses Lisboa	Sporting Clube de Portugal Lisboa	Fernando Baptista de Seixas Peyroteo de Vasconcelos (Sporting Clube de Portugal Lisboa)	37
1946/1947	Sporting Clube de Portugal Lisboa	*No competition*	Fernando Baptista de Seixas Peyroteo de Vasconcelos (Sporting Clube de Portugal Lisboa)	43
1947/1948	Sporting Clube de Portugal Lisboa	Sporting Clube de Portugal Lisboa	António Araújo (FC do Porto)	36
1948/1949	Sporting Clube de Portugal Lisboa	Sport Lisboa e Benfica	Fernando Baptista de Seixas Peyroteo de Vasconcelos (Sporting Clube de Portugal Lisboa)	40
1949/1950	Sport Lisboa e Benfica	*No competition*	Júlio Correia da Silva "Julinho" (Sport Lisboa e Benfica)	29
1950/1951	Sporting Clube de Portugal Lisboa	Sport Lisboa e Benfica	Manuel Soeiro Vasques (Sporting Clube de Portugal Lisboa)	29
1951/1952	Sporting Clube de Portugal Lisboa	Sport Lisboa e Benfica	José Pinto de Carvalho Santos Águas (Sport Lisboa e Benfica)	28
1952/1953	Sporting Clube de Portugal Lisboa	Sport Lisboa e Benfica	Sebastião Lucas da Fonseca „Matateu" (CF Os Belenenses Lisboa)	29
1953/1954	Sporting Clube de Portugal Lisboa	Sporting Clube de Portugal Lisboa	João Baptista Martins (Sporting Clube de Portugal Lisboa)	31
1954/1955	Sport Lisboa e Benfica	Sport Lisboa e Benfica	Sebastião Lucas da Fonseca „Matateu" (CF Os Belenenses Lisboa)	32
1955/1956	FC do Porto	FC do Porto	José Pinto de Carvalho Santos Águas (Sport Lisboa e Benfica)	28
1956/1957	Sport Lisboa e Benfica	Sport Lisboa e Benfica	José Pinto de Carvalho Santos Águas (Sport Lisboa e Benfica)	30
1957/1958	Sporting Clube de Portugal Lisboa	FC do Porto	Arsénio Trindade Duarte (GD CUF do Barreiro)	23
1958/1959	FC do Porto	Sport Lisboa e Benfica	José Pinto de Carvalho Santos Águas (Sport Lisboa e Benfica)	26
1959/1960	Sport Lisboa e Benfica	CF Os Belenenses Lisboa	Edmur Pinto Ribeiro (Vitória SC Guimarães)	25
1960/1961	Sport Lisboa e Benfica	Leixões SC Porto	José Pinto de Carvalho Santos Águas (Sport Lisboa e Benfica)	27
1961/1962	Sporting Clube de Portugal Lisboa	Sport Lisboa e Benfica	Azumir Luis Casimiro Veríssimo	23

			(BRA, FC do Porto)	
1962/1963	Sport Lisboa e Benfica	Sporting Clube de Portugal Lisboa	José Augusto Costa Sénica Torres (Sport Lisboa e Benfica)	26
1963/1964	Sport Lisboa e Benfica	Sport Lisboa e Benfica	Eusébio da Silva Ferreira (Sport Lisboa e Benfica)	28
1964/1965	Sport Lisboa e Benfica	Vitória FC Setúbal	Eusébio da Silva Ferreira (Sport Lisboa e Benfica)	28
1965/1966	Sporting Clube de Portugal Lisboa	Sporting Clube de Braga	Eusébio da Silva Ferreira (Sport Lisboa e Benfica) Ernesto de Figueiredo (Sporting Clube de Portugal Lisboa)	25
1966/1967	Sport Lisboa e Benfica	Vitória FC Setúbal	Eusébio da Silva Ferreira (Sport Lisboa e Benfica)	31
1967/1968	Sport Lisboa e Benfica	FC do Porto	Eusébio da Silva Ferreira (Sport Lisboa e Benfica)	43
1968/1969	Sport Lisboa e Benfica	Sport Lisboa e Benfica	Manuel António Leitão da Silva (Associação Académica de Coimbra)	19
1969/1970	Sporting Clube de Portugal Lisboa	Sport Lisboa e Benfica	Eusébio da Silva Ferreira (Sport Lisboa e Benfica)	20
1970/1971	Sport Lisboa e Benfica	Sporting Clube de Portugal Lisboa	Artur Jorge Braga Melo Teixeira (Sport Lisboa e Benfica)	23
1971/1972	Sport Lisboa e Benfica	Sport Lisboa e Benfica	Artur Jorge Braga Melo Teixeira (Sport Lisboa e Benfica)	27
1972/1973	Sport Lisboa e Benfica	Sporting Clube de Portugal Lisboa	Eusébio da Silva Ferreira (Sport Lisboa e Benfica)	40
1973/1974	Sporting Clube de Portugal Lisboa	Sporting Clube de Portugal Lisboa	Héctor Casimiro Yazalde (ARG, Sporting Clube de Portugal Lisboa)	46
1974/1975	Sport Lisboa e Benfica	Boavista FC do Porto	Héctor Casimiro Yazalde (ARG, Sporting Clube de Portugal Lisboa)	30
1975/1976	Sport Lisboa e Benfica	Boavista FC do Porto	Rui Manuel Trindade Jordão (Sport Lisboa e Benfica)	30
1976/1977	Sport Lisboa e Benfica	FC do Porto	Fernando Mendes Soares Gomes (FC do Porto)	26
1977/1978	FC do Porto	Sporting Clube de Portugal Lisboa	Fernando Mendes Soares Gomes (FC do Porto)	25
1978/1979	FC do Porto	Boavista FC do Porto	Fernando Mendes Soares Gomes (FC do Porto)	27
1979/1980	Sporting Clube de Portugal Lisboa	Sport Lisboa e Benfica	Rui Manuel Trindade Jordão (Sporting Clube de Portugal Lisboa)	31
1980/1981	Sport Lisboa e Benfica	Sport Lisboa e Benfica	Tamagnini Manuel Gomes Batista "Nené" (Sport Lisboa e Benfica)	20
1981/1982	Sporting Clube de Portugal Lisboa	Sporting Clube de Portugal Lisboa	Jacques Pereira (FC do Porto)	27
1982/1983	Sport Lisboa e Benfica	Sport Lisboa e Benfica	Fernando Mendes Soares Gomes (FC do Porto)	36
1983/1984	Sport Lisboa e Benfica	FC do Porto	Fernando Mendes Soares Gomes (FC do Porto) Tamagnini Manuel Gomes Batista "Nené" (Sport Lisboa e Benfica)	21
1984/1985	FC do Porto	Sport Lisboa e Benfica	Fernando Mendes Soares Gomes (FC do Porto)	39
1985/1986	FC do Porto	Sport Lisboa e Benfica	Manuel José Tavares Fernandes (Sporting Clube de Portugal Lisboa)	30
1986/1987	Sport Lisboa e Benfica	Sport Lisboa e Benfica	Paulo Roberto Bacinello "Paulinho Cascavel" (BRA, Vitória SC Guimarães)	22
1987/1988	FC do Porto	FC do Porto	Paulo Roberto Bacinello "Paulinho Cascavel" (BRA, Sporting Clube de Portugal Lisboa)	23
1988/1989	Sport Lisboa e Benfica	CF Os Belenenses Lisboa	Vata Matanu Garcia (ANG, Sport Lisboa e Benfica)	16
1989/1990	FC do Porto	CF Estrela da Amadora	Mats Magnusson (SWE, Sport Lisboa e Benfica)	33
1990/1991	Sport Lisboa e Benfica	FC do Porto	José Rui Lopes Águas (Sport Lisboa e Benfica)	25
1991/1992	FC do Porto	Boavista FC do Porto	Richard Daddy Owubokiri (NGA, Boavista FC do Porto)	30
1992/1993	FC do Porto	Sport Lisboa e Benfica	Jorge Paulo Cadete Santos Reis (Sporting Clube de Portugal Lisboa)	18
1993/1994	Sport Lisboa e Benfica	FC do Porto	Rashidi Yekini (NGA, Vitória FC Setúbal)	21
1994/1995	FC do Porto	Sporting Clube de Portugal Lisboa	Hassan Nader (MAR, SC Farense)	21
1995/1996	FC do Porto	Sport Lisboa e Benfica	Domingos José Paciência Oliveira (FC do Porto)	25
1996/1997	FC do Porto	Boavista FC do Porto	Mário Jardel de Almeida Ribeiro (BRA, FC do Porto)	30
1997/1998	FC do Porto	FC do Porto	Mário Jardel de Almeida Ribeiro (BRA, FC do Porto)	26
1998/1999	FC do Porto	SC Beira-Mar Aveiro	Mário Jardel de Almeida Ribeiro (BRA, FC do Porto)	36
1999/2000	Sporting Clube de Portugal Lisboa	FC do Porto	Mário Jardel de Almeida Ribeiro (BRA, FC do Porto)	37
2000/2001	Boavista FC do Porto	FC do Porto	Renivaldo Pereira de Jesus "Pena" (BRA, FC do Porto)	22
2001/2002	Sporting Clube de Portugal Lisboa	Sporting Clube de Portugal Lisboa	Mário Jardel de Almeida Ribeiro (BRA, Sporting Clube de Portugal Lisboa)	42
2002/2003	FC do Porto	FC do Porto	Fary Faye (SEN, SC Beira-Mar Aveiro)	18
2003/2004	FC do Porto	Sport Lisboa e Benfica	Benedict Saul McCarthy (RSA, FC do Porto)	20
2004/2005	Sport Lisboa e Benfica	Vitória FC Setúbal	Liédson da Silva Muniz (BRA, Sporting Clube de Portugal Lisboa)	25
2005/2006	FC do Porto	FC do Porto	Albert Meyong Zé (CMR, CF Os Belenenses Lisboa)	17
2006/2007	FC do Porto	Sporting Clube de Portugal Lisboa	Liédson da Silva Muniz (BRA, Sporting Clube de Portugal Lisboa)	15
2007/2008	FC do Porto	Sporting Clube de Portugal Lisboa	Lisandro López (ARG, FC do Porto)	24
2008/2009	FC do Porto	FC do Porto	Ânderson Miguel da Silva "Nenê" (BRA, CD Nacional Funchal)	20
2009/2010	Sport Lisboa e Benfica	FC do Porto	Óscar René Cardozo Marín (PAR, Sport Lisboa e Benfica)	26
2010/2011	FC do Porto	FC do Porto	Givanildo Vieira de Sousa "Hulk" (BRA, FC do Porto)	23

2011/2012	FC do Porto	Associação Académica de Coimbra	Óscar René Cardozo Marín (PAR, Sport Lisboa e Benfica)	20
2012/2013	FC do Porto	Vitória SC Guimarães	Jackson Arley Martínez Valencia (COL, FC do Porto)	26
2013/2014	Sport Lisboa e Benfica	Sport Lisboa e Benfica	Jackson Arley Martínez Valencia (COL, FC do Porto)	20
2014/2015	Sport Lisboa e Benfica	Sporting Clube de Portugal Lisboa	Jackson Arley Martínez Valencia (COL, FC do Porto)	21
2015/2016	Sport Lisboa e Benfica	Sporting Clube de Braga	Jonas Gonçalves Oliveira (BRA, Sport Lisboa e Benfica)	32
2016/2017	Sport Lisboa e Benfica	Sport Lisboa e Benfica	Bas Dost (NED, Sporting Clube de Portugal Lisboa)	34
2017/2018	FC do Porto	Desportivo das Aves	Jonas Gonçalves Oliveira (BRA, Sport Lisboa e Benfica)	34
2018/2019	Sport Lisboa e Benfica	Sporting Clube de Portugal Lisboa	Haris Seferović (SUI, Sport Lisboa e Benfica)	23
2019/2020	FC do Porto	FC do Porto	Carlos Vinícius Alves Morais (BRA, Sport Lisboa e Benfica) Luis Miguel Afonso Fernandes "Pizzi" (Sport Lisboa e Benfica) Mehdi Taremi (IRN, Rio Ave FC Vila do Conde)	18
2020/2021	Sporting Clube de Portugal Lisboa	Sporting Clube de Braga	Pedro António Pereira Gonçalves (Sporting Clube de Portugal Lisboa)	23

*Please note: Campeonato da Liga da Primeira Divisão (1934-1938), Campeonato Nacional da Primeira Divisão (1938-1999), Primeira Liga (since 1999).

NATIONAL CHAMPIONSHIP
Primeira Liga 2020/2021
(18.09.2020 – 19.05.2021)

Results

Round 1 [18-21.09.2020]
Famalicão - Benfica 1-5(0-3)
Vitória Guimarães - Belenenses 0-1(0-0)
Nacional - Boavista 3-3(2-2)
FC Porto - Sporting Braga 3-1(2-1)
Santa Clara - Marítimo 2-0(0-0)
Moreirense FC - SC Farense 2-0(1-0)
CD Tondela - Rio Ave 1-1(1-0)
Portimonense - Paços de Ferreira 1-1(0-1)
Sporting - Gil Vicente 3-1(0-0) [28.10.]

Round 2 [25-28.09.2020]
Sporting Braga - Santa Clara 0-1(0-1)
Marítimo - CD Tondela 2-1(2-1)
Benfica - Moreirense FC 2-0(1-0)
Boavista - FC Porto 0-5(0-0)
SC Farense - Nacional 0-1(0-0)
Gil Vicente - Portimonense 1-0(0-0)
Paços de Ferreira - Sporting 0-2(0-1)
Rio Ave - Vitória Guimarães 0-0
Belenenses - Famalicão 1-2(1-0)

Round 3 [02-04.10.2020]
Moreirense FC - Boavista 1-1(0-1)
Vitória Guimarães - Paços de Ferreira 1-0(0-0)
Santa Clara - Gil Vicente 0-0
FC Porto - Marítimo 2-3(1-1)
CD Tondela - Sporting Braga 0-4(0-4)
Nacional - Belenenses 0-0
Benfica - SC Farense 3-2(1-0)
Famalicão - Rio Ave 1-1(1-0)
Portimonense - Sporting 0-2(0-2)

Round 4 [17-19.10.2020]
Gil Vicente - CD Tondela 1-1(1-0)
Marítimo - Portimonense 1-2(0-0)
Sporting Braga - Nacional 2-1(2-0)
Sporting - FC Porto 2-2(1-2)
Belenenses - Moreirense FC 0-0
Paços de Ferreira - Santa Clara 2-1(1-0)
SC Farense - Famalicão 3-3(2-0)
Rio Ave - Benfica 0-3(0-2)
Boavista - Vitória Guimarães 0-1(0-1)

Round 5 [23-26.10.2020]
CD Tondela - Portimonense 1-0(1-0)
Nacional - Paços de Ferreira 1-1(0-0)
Santa Clara - Sporting 1-2(1-1)
FC Porto - Gil Vicente 1-0(1-0)
SC Farense - Rio Ave 0-1(0-1)
Moreirense FC - Marítimo 1-2(0-0)
Famalicão - Boavista 2-2(0-0)
Vitória Guimarães - Sporting Braga 0-1(0-1)
Benfica - Belenenses 2-0(1-0)

Round 6 [30.10.-02.11.2020]
Paços de Ferreira - FC Porto 3-2(2-1)
Belenenses - SC Farense 1-1(0-0)
Rio Ave - Moreirense FC 2-0(1-0)
Marítimo - Nacional 0-0
Portimonense - Santa Clara 1-2(0-1)
Gil Vicente - Vitória Guimarães 1-2(0-1)
Sporting - CD Tondela 4-0(1-0)
Sporting Braga - Famalicão 1-0(0-0)
Boavista - Benfica 3-0(2-0)

Round 7 [06-08.11.2020]
Belenenses - Rio Ave 0-0
CD Tondela - Santa Clara 2-0(1-0)
Famalicão - Marítimo 2-1(2-1)
Vitória Guimarães - Sporting 0-4(0-2)
SC Farense - Boavista 3-1(1-1)
Nacional - Gil Vicente 2-1(0-1)
FC Porto - Portimonense 3-1(1-1)
Benfica - Sporting Braga 2-3(0-1)
Moreirense-Paços de Ferreira 0-1(0-1) [01.12.]

Round 8 [27-30.11.2020]
Paços de Ferreira - Famalicão 2-0(1-0)
CD Tondela - Vitória Guimarães 0-2(0-0)
Santa Clara - FC Porto 0-1(0-1)
Sporting - Moreirense FC 2-1(1-1)
Gil Vicente - Rio Ave 2-0(1-0)
Portimonense - Nacional 1-0(0-0)
Boavista - Belenenses 0-0
Sporting Braga - SC Farense 1-0(0-0)
Marítimo - Benfica 1-2(1-1)

Round 9 [05-07.12.2020]
Moreirense FC - Gil Vicente 1-1(0-0)
Vitória Guimarães - Portimonense 1-0(1-0)
Famalicão - Sporting 2-2(1-2)
FC Porto - CD Tondela 4-3(2-2)
Nacional - Santa Clara 1-3(1-2)
Rio Ave - Boavista 0-0
Benfica - Paços de Ferreira 2-1(0-1)
Belenenses - Sporting Braga 2-1(2-0)
SC Farense - Marítimo 2-1(1-0)

Round 10 [18-22.12.2020]
Portimonense - Famalicão 0-0
Marítimo - Belenenses 1-0(0-0)
CD Tondela - Moreirense FC 0-0
Sporting - SC Farense 1-0(0-0)
Paços de Ferreira - Boavista 1-1(0-0)
Gil Vicente - Benfica 0-2(0-0)
FC Porto - Nacional 2-0(2-0)
Santa Clara - Vitória Guimarães 0-4(0-3)
Sporting Braga - Rio Ave 3-0(1-0)

Round 11 [27-29.12.2020]
Famalicão - Gil Vicente 0-1(0-1)
Nacional - CD Tondela 2-0(1-0)
SC Farense - Paços de Ferreira 1-1(0-0)
Belenenses - Sporting 1-2(1-2)
Rio Ave - Marítimo 1-3(1-0)
Boavista - Sporting Braga 1-4(0-3)
Benfica - Portimonense 2-1(2-0)
Moreirense FC - Santa Clara 1-0(0-0)
Vitória Guimarães - FC Porto 2-3(1-1)

Round 12 [02-04.01.2021]
Sporting - Sporting Braga 2-0(0-0)
CD Tondela - Famalicão 1-0(0-0)
Marítimo - Boavista 0-0
Paços de Ferreira - Rio Ave 2-0(1-0)
FC Porto - Moreirense FC 3-0(1-0)
Santa Clara - Benfica 1-1(0-1)
Gil Vicente - Belenenses 0-0
Portimonense - SC Farense 2-0(0-0)
Vit. Guimarães - Nacional 3-1(1-1) [21.01.]

Round 13 [07-10.01.2021]
Sporting Braga - Marítimo 2-1(1-0)
Nacional - Sporting 0-2(0-1)
Benfica - CD Tondela 2-0(0-0)
Rio Ave - Portimonense 3-0(0-0)
Famalicão - FC Porto 1-4(1-2)
Moreirense FC - Vitória Guimarães 2-2(1-1)
Boavista - Santa Clara 1-1(1-1)
SC Farense - Gil Vicente 3-1(2-1)
Belenenses - Paços de Ferreira 0-2(0-1)

Round 14 [15-18.01.2021]
Sporting - Rio Ave 1-1(1-1)
FC Porto - Benfica 1-1(1-1)
Paços de Ferreira - Sporting Braga 2-0(0-0)
CD Tondela - Boavista 3-1(1-0)
Nacional - Moreirense FC 0-1(0-0)
Santa Clara - Famalicão 1-2(0-0)
Gil Vicente - Marítimo 1-0(0-0)
Portimonense - Belenenses 1-0(1-0)
Vit. Guimarães - SC Farense 2-2(2-1) [17.02.]

Round 15 [24-26.01.2021]
Marítimo - Paços de Ferreira 0-3(0-1)
Moreirense FC - Portimonense 2-2(2-1)
Famalicão - Vitória Guimarães 0-1(0-1)
Belenenses - CD Tondela 2-0(2-0)
Rio Ave - Santa Clara 1-2(1-1)
Benfica - Nacional 1-1(1-0)
SC Farense - FC Porto 0-1(0-1)
Sporting Braga - Gil Vicente 1-0(0-0)
Boavista - Sporting 0-2(0-1)

Round 16 [30.01.-02.02.2021]
Nacional - Famalicão 2-1(0-1)
CD Tondela - SC Farense 2-0(0-0)
Portimonense - Boavista 1-2(1-1)
Vitória Guimarães - Marítimo 1-0(0-0)
Santa Clara - Belenenses 2-0(1-0)
FC Porto - Rio Ave 2-0(1-0)
Moreirense FC - Sporting Braga 0-4(0-3)
Sporting - Benfica 1-0(0-0)
Gil Vicente - Paços de Ferreira 1-2(0-2)

Round 17 [04-05.02.2021]
SC Farense - Santa Clara 1-1(1-0)
Belenenses - FC Porto 0-0
Sporting Braga - Portimonense 2-1(0-1)
Famalicão - Moreirense FC 0-2(0-2)
Rio Ave - Nacional 0-0
Benfica - Vitória Guimarães 0-0
Marítimo - Sporting 0-2(0-1)
Boavista - Gil Vicente 1-2(1-1)
Paços de Ferreira - CD Tondela 2-1(1-0)

Round 18 [07-09.02.2021]
Sporting Braga - FC Porto 2-2(0-1)
SC Farense - Moreirense FC 1-2(0-1)
Benfica - Famalicão 2-0(2-0)
Marítimo - Santa Clara 1-2(0-0)
Belenenses - Vitória Guimarães 1-1(1-1)
Paços de Ferreira - Portimonense 0-0
Rio Ave - CD Tondela 2-1(0-1)
Boavista - Nacional 0-1(0-1)
Gil Vicente - Sporting 1-2(1-0)

Round 19 [12-16.02.2021]
Famalicão - Belenenses 0-0
Nacional - SC Farense 2-3(0-0)
Vitória Guimarães - Rio Ave 1-3(0-2)
FC Porto - Boavista 2-2(0-2)
Portimonense - Gil Vicente 4-1(2-1)
Santa Clara - Sporting Braga 0-1(0-1)
Moreirense FC - Benfica 1-1(1-1)
Sporting - Paços de Ferreira 2-0(1-0)
CD Tondela - Marítimo 2-1(1-1)

Round 20 [19-22.02.2021]
Boavista - Moreirense FC 1-0(0-0)
Belenenses - Nacional 2-1(1-1)
Gil Vicente - Santa Clara 1-0(0-0)
Sporting - Portimonense 2-0(2-0)
Rio Ave - Famalicão 0-1(0-1)
Paços de Ferreira - Vitória Guimarães 2-1(1-1)
Sporting Braga - CD Tondela 4-2(3-0)
SC Farense - Benfica 0-0
Marítimo - FC Porto 1-2(1-1)

Round 21 [26.02.-01.03.2021]
Vitória Guimarães - Boavista 2-1(1-1)
Famalicão - SC Farense 0-0
Santa Clara - Paços de Ferreira 3-0(2-0)
FC Porto - Sporting 0-0
Portimonense - Marítimo 0-0
CD Tondela - Gil Vicente 1-0(1-0)
Nacional - Sporting Braga 1-2(0-2)
Benfica - Rio Ave 2-0(0-0)
Moreirense FC - Belenenses 2-2(2-1)

Round 22 [05-09.03.2021]
Paços de Ferreira - Nacional 2-1(2-0)
Sporting - Santa Clara 2-1(1-0)
Portimonense - CD Tondela 3-0(2-0)
Gil Vicente - FC Porto 0-2(0-1)
Boavista - Famalicão 3-0(1-0)
Marítimo - Moreirense FC 0-2(0-1)
Rio Ave - SC Farense 2-0(1-0)
Belenenses - Benfica 0-3(0-0)
Sporting Braga - Vitória Guimarães 3-0(2-0)

Round 23 [12-15.03.2021]
Nacional - Marítimo 1-2(1-0)
SC Farense - Belenenses 0-1(0-0)
Benfica - Boavista 2-0(1-0)
Santa Clara - Portimonense 2-0(1-0)
CD Tondela - Sporting 0-1(0-0)
Moreirense FC - Rio Ave 1-1(0-1)
Vitória Guimarães - Gil Vicente 2-4(1-3)
FC Porto - Paços de Ferreira 2-0(0-0)
Famalicão - Sporting Braga 2-2(1-2)

Round 24 [19-21.03.2021]
Gil Vicente - Nacional 2-0(0-0)
Santa Clara - CD Tondela 1-1(0-1)
Paços de Ferreira - Moreirense FC 3-0(3-0)
Portimonense - FC Porto 1-2(0-1)
Sporting - Vitória Guimarães 1-0(1-0)
Rio Ave - Belenenses 0-0
Boavista - SC Farense 0-1(0-1)
Marítimo - Famalicão 0-4(0-2)
Sporting Braga - Benfica 0-2(0-1)

Round 25 [02-05.04.2021]
Nacional - Portimonense 1-5(0-2)
Rio Ave - Gil Vicente 0-2(0-0)
FC Porto - Santa Clara 2-1(0-0)
Belenenses - Boavista 0-2(0-1)
Vitória Guimarães - CD Tondela 1-2(1-1)
Famalicão - Paços de Ferreira 2-0(1-0)
SC Farense - Sporting Braga 1-2(1-1)
Benfica - Marítimo 1-0(1-0)
Moreirense FC - Sporting 1-1(0-1)

Round 26 [09-11.04.2021]
Portimonense - Vitória Guimarães 3-0(1-0)
Marítimo - SC Farense 1-0(1-0)
Boavista - Rio Ave 3-3(2-1)
CD Tondela - FC Porto 0-2(0-1)
Paços de Ferreira - Benfica 0-5(0-3)
Gil Vicente - Moreirense FC 1-2(0-1)
Santa Clara - Nacional 5-1(2-0)
Sporting Braga - Belenenses 1-1(1-1)
Sporting - Famalicão 1-1(1-1)

Round 27 [16-18.04.2021]
Boavista - Paços de Ferreira 2-0(2-0)
SC Farense - Sporting 0-1(0-1)
Moreirense FC - CD Tondela 2-3(2-3)
Vitória Guimarães - Santa Clara 1-0(1-0)
Benfica - Gil Vicente 1-2(0-1)
Belenenses - Marítimo 2-0(1-0)
Rio Ave - Sporting Braga 0-0
Famalicão - Portimonense 0-1(0-1)
Nacional - FC Porto 0-1(0-1)

Round 28 [20-22.04.2021]
Paços de Ferreira - SC Farense 0-2(0-0)
Santa Clara - Moreirense FC 0-0
Marítimo - Rio Ave 1-0(1-0)
Sporting Braga - Boavista 2-1(1-1)
Sporting - Belenenses 2-0(1-0)
CD Tondela - Nacional 2-1(1-1)
Gil Vicente - Famalicão 0-3(0-0)
Portimonense - Benfica 1-5(1-1)
FC Porto - Vitória Guimarães 1-0(0-0)

Round 29 [25-27.04.2021]
Boavista - Marítimo 0-1(0-0)
Rio Ave - Paços de Ferreira 1-1(0-1)
Sporting Braga - Sporting 0-1(0-0)
Belenenses - Gil Vicente 2-1(0-1)
Benfica - Santa Clara 2-0(1-0)
Famalicão - CD Tondela 2-2(2-2)
Nacional - Vitória Guimarães 1-0(1-0)
Moreirense FC - FC Porto 1-1(1-0)
SC Farense - Portimonense 1-1(1-0)

Round 30 [29.04.-01.05.2021]
Marítimo - Sporting Braga 1-0(0-0)
Paços de Ferreira - Belenenses 1-0(0-0)
Vitória Guimarães - Moreirense FC 2-0(2-0)
CD Tondela - Benfica 0-2(0-2)
FC Porto - Famalicão 3-2(1-1)
Gil Vicente - SC Farense 0-0
Santa Clara - Boavista 3-3(1-1)
Portimonense - Rio Ave 0-0
Sporting - Nacional 2-0(0-0)

Round 31 [05-07.05.2021]
Marítimo - Gil Vicente 0-1(0-1)
Sporting Braga - Paços de Ferreira 1-1(0-1)
Rio Ave - Sporting 0-2(0-1)
Moreirense FC - Nacional 2-2(0-1)
Belenenses - Portimonense 1-0(1-0)
Benfica - FC Porto 1-1(1-0)
SC Farense - Vitória Guimarães 2-2(2-1)
Famalicão - Santa Clara 1-0(0-0)
Boavista - CD Tondela 1-1(0-0)

Round 32 [09-12.05.2021]
Paços de Ferreira - Marítimo 1-1(1-1)
Gil Vicente - Sporting Braga 1-1(1-1)
Portimonense - Moreirense FC 1-2(1-1)
FC Porto - SC Farense 5-1(3-0)
Santa Clara - Rio Ave 1-0(0-0)
CD Tondela - Belenenses 1-3(1-2)
Nacional - Benfica 1-3(1-0)
Sporting - Boavista 1-0(1-0)
Vitória Guimarães - Famalicão 1-2(1-1)

Round 33 [14-16.05.2021]
Paços de Ferreira - Gil Vicente 0-2(0-1)
Sporting Braga - Moreirense FC 2-1(1-0)
Boavista - Portimonense 1-0(0-0)
SC Farense - CD Tondela 1-0(0-0)
Benfica - Sporting 4-3(3-1)
Rio Ave - FC Porto 0-3(0-0)
Famalicão - Nacional 3-0(1-0)
Belenenses - Santa Clara 0-2(0-1)
Marítimo - Vitória Guimarães 0-0

Round 34 [18-19.05.2021]

CD Tondela - Paços de Ferreira 2-3(2-2)
FC Porto - Belenenses 4-0(2-0)
Santa Clara - SC Farense 4-0(2-0)
Moreirense FC - Famalicão 3-0(2-0)
Gil Vicente - Boavista 1-2(1-0)
Nacional - Rio Ave 1-2(1-0)
Portimonense - Sporting Braga 0-0
Vitória Guimarães - Benfica 1-3(0-0)
Sporting - Marítimo 5-1(3-0)

Final Standings

										Home					Away			
1.	**Sporting Clube de Portugal Lisboa**	34	26	7	1	65	-	20	85	13	4	0	34 - 10	13	3	1	31 - 10
2.	FC do Porto	34	24	8	2	74	-	29	80	13	3	1	40 - 15	11	5	1	34 - 14
3.	Sport Lisboa e Benfica	34	23	7	4	69	-	27	76	12	3	2	31 - 15	11	4	2	38 - 12
4.	Sporting Clube de Braga	34	19	7	8	53	-	33	64	11	3	3	27 - 15	8	4	5	26 - 18
5.	FC Paços de Ferreira	34	15	8	11	40	-	41	53	10	3	4	23 - 19	5	5	7	17 - 22
6.	CD Santa Clara Açores	34	13	7	14	44	-	36	46	7	5	5	26 - 16	6	2	9	18 - 20
7.	Vitória SC Guimarães	34	12	7	15	37	-	44	43	7	1	9	21 - 27	5	6	6	16 - 17
8.	Moreirense FC Moreira de Cónegos	34	10	13	11	37	-	43	43	4	10	3	24 - 23	6	3	8	13 - 20
9.	FC Famalicão	34	10	10	14	40	-	48	40	4	7	6	19 - 24	6	3	8	21 - 24
10.	Belenenses SAD Lisboa	34	9	13	12	25	-	35	40	6	5	6	15 - 18	3	8	6	10 - 17
11.	Gil Vicente FC Barcelos	34	11	6	17	33	-	42	39	4	4	9	13 - 20	7	2	8	20 - 22
12.	CD Tondela	34	10	6	18	36	-	57	36	8	2	7	18 - 21	2	4	11	18 - 36
13.	Boavista FC Porto	34	8	12	14	39	-	49	36	5	4	8	17 - 22	3	8	6	22 - 27
14.	Portimonense SC Portimão	34	9	8	17	34	-	41	35	6	5	6	20 - 17	3	3	11	14 - 24
15.	CS Marítimo Funchal	34	10	5	19	27	-	47	35	5	3	9	10 - 21	5	2	10	17 - 26
16.	Rio Ave FC Vila do Conde *(Relegation Play-offs)*	34	7	13	14	25	-	40	34	4	6	7	12 - 18	3	7	7	13 - 22
17.	SC Farense Faro *(Relegated)*	34	7	10	17	31	-	48	31	4	6	7	19 - 20	3	4	10	12 - 28
18.	CD Nacional Funchal *(Relegated)*	34	6	7	21	30	-	59	25	4	3	10	19 - 30	2	4	11	11 - 29

Top goalscorers:

23	**Pedro António Pereira Gonçalves**	*Sporting Clube de Portugal Lisboa*
22	Haris Seferović (SUI)	*Sport Lisboa e Benfica*
16	Mehdi Taremi (IRN)	*FC do Porto*
15	Mario González Gutiérrez (ESP)	*CD Tondela*
14	Carlos Alberto Carvalho da Silva Júnior (BRA)	*CD Santa Clara Açores*

Relegation Play-offs [26-30.05.2021]

FC de Arouca - Rio Ave FC Vila do Conde   3-0(1-0)   2-0(1-0)

FC de Arouca were promoted to 2021/2022 Primeira Liga.

NATIONAL CUP
Taça de Portugal 2020/2021

Third Round [20-23./2511./03.12./09.12.2020]

ARC Oleiros - Gil Vicente FC Barcelos	0-0 aet; 2-4 pen		SC União Torreense - FC de Alverca	2-0(0-0)
CD Feirense Santa Maria da Feira - Amora FC	0-1(0-1)		Lank FC Vilaverdense - Clube Olímpico de Montijo	2-3(0-0)
UD de Leiria - Portimonense SC Portimão	1-0(0-0)		SC Beira-Mar - CD Santa Clara Açores	1-3(0-0)
Oriental Dragon FC - Leixões SC Porto	0-0 aet; 3-4 pen		Desportivo de Monção - Rio Ave FC Vila do Conde	1-2(0-1)
Clube Oriental de Lisboa - FC Famalicão	0-3(0-0)		Merelinense FC - Moreirense FC Moreira de Cóneg.	0-1(0-0)
CDC Montalegre - Académico de Viseu FC	2-3(0-2)		UD Oliveirense - FC Paços de Ferreira	0-4(0-1)
GD Fabril do Barreiro - FC do Porto	0-2(0-1)		FC de Vizela - Boavista FC Porto	0-1(0-0,0-0)
AC Marinhense - CD Cova da Piedade	1-1 aet; 3-5 pen		SC Salgueiros Porto - Sporting da Covilhã	2-1(2-1)
FC de Arouca - Vitória SC Guimarães	0-0 aet; 6-7 pen		FC de Penafiel - CS Marítimo Funchal	2-3(1-1,2-2)
CD Trofense - Sporting Clube de Braga	1-2(0-1)		Real SC Queluz - Belenenses SAD Lisboa	0-2(0-1)
USC Paredes - Sport Lisboa e Benfica	0-1(0-1)		Associação Académica de Coimbra - Varzim SC	1-0(0-0)
AD Fafe - GD Vilar de Perdizes	5-1(4-1)		SG Sacavenense - Sporting Clube de Portugal Lisboa	1-7(0-3)
AD Os Limianos Ponte de Lima - GD Fontinhas	1-2(0-1)		Casa Pia Atlét. Clube Lisboa - CD Nacional Funchal	2-3(0-1,1-1)
Anadia FC - CD Pinhalnovense	2-1(0-0)		CF Estrela da Amadora - SC Farense Faro	2-0(1-0)
FC Felgueiras 1932 - CD Tondela	0-1(0-0)		GD Estoril Praia - Lusitano GC Évora	5-0(2-0)
SC Espinho - Gondomar SC	2-1(1-1)		UD Vilafranquense - AD Sanjoanense	2-1(2-1)

Fourth Round [11-14/23.12.2020]				
Académico de Viseu FC - As.Académica de Coimbra	3-0(2-0)	Sport Lisboa e Benfica - UD Vilafranquense	5-0(4-0)
Sporting Clube de Portugal L. - FC Paços de Ferreira	3-0(2-0)	SC União Torreense - Amora FC	1-0(1-0)
GD Fontinhas - AD Fafe	1-1 aet; 3-4 pen	Anadia FC - Estrela Amadora	0-1(0-0)
Rio Ave FC Vila do Conde - FC Famalicão	2-1(1-0)	Clube Olímpico de Montijo - Sport. Clube de Braga	0-7(0-2)
GD Estoril Praia - Boavista FC Porto	2-1(0-0)	CS Marítimo Funchal - SC Salgueiros Porto	2-1(0-1,1-1)
CD Cova da Piedade - Moreirense FC	2-3(1-1,1-1)	UD de Leiria - Gil Vicente FC Barcelos	0-3(0-2)
Vitória SC Guimarães - CD Santa Clara Açores	0-1(0-1)	Belenenses SAD Lisboa - SC Espinho	3-0(0-0,0-0)
FC do Porto - CD Tondela	2-1(2-1)	CD Nacional Funchal - Leixões SC Porto	3-1(1-1)

1/8-Finals [11-14.01.2021]				
CS Marítimo Funchal - Sporting Clube de Portugal	2-0(0-0)	Estrela Amadora - Sport Lisboa e Benfica	0-4(0-1)
Rio Ave FC Vila do Conde - GD Estoril Praia	1-2(0-2)	Sporting Clube de Braga - SC União Torreense	5-0(2-0)
Moreirense FC - CD Santa Clara Açores	1-2(0-1)	AD Fafe - Belenenses SAD Lisboa	2-3(2-0,2-2)
CD Nacional Funchal - FC do Porto	2-4(1-1,2-2)	Gil Vicente FC Barcelos - Académico de Viseu FC	3-2(1-1,2-2)

Quarter-Finals [27-29.01.2021]				
CS Marítimo Funchal - GD Estoril Praia	1-3(1-0,1-1)	Sporting Clube de Braga - CD Santa Clara Açores	2-1(2-0)
Sport Lisboa e Benfica - Belenenses SAD Lisboa	3-0(2-0)	Gil Vicente FC Barcelos - FC do Porto	0-2(0-1)

Semi-Finals [10-11.02./03-04.03.2021]				
First Leg		**Second Leg**	
Sporting Clube de Braga - FC do Porto	1-1(0-1)	FC do Porto - Sporting Clube de Braga	2-3(1-3)
GD Estoril Praia - Sport Lisboa e Benfica	1-3(1-1)	Sport Lisboa e Benfica - GD Estoril Praia	2-0(1-0)

Final

23.05.2021; Estádio Cidade de Coimbra, Coimbra; Referee: Nuno Miguel Serrano Almeida; Attendance: 0
Sporting Clube de Braga - Sport Lisboa e Benfica   2-0(1-0)

SC Braga: Matheus Magalhães, Ricardo Esgaio (Cap), Raúl Silva, Nuno Sequeira, Vítor Tormena, Ricardo Horta, Almoatasembellah Ali Mohamed Al Musrati (75.André Horta), André Castro (70.João Novais), Galeno, Abel Ruiz (87.Andraž Šporar), Lucas Piazón [*sent off 90+4*]. Trainer: Carlos Augusto Soares da Costa Faria Carvalhal.

Benfica: Helton Leite [*sent off 16*], Jan Vertonghen, Nicolás Hernán Otamendi, Morato (81.Chiquinho), Diogo Gonçalves (57.Nuno Tavares), Julian Weigl, Adel Taarabt [*sent off 90+3*], Álex Grimaldo, Pizzi (Cap) (21.Odisseas Vlachodimos), Haris Seferović (57.Darwin Gabriel Núñez Ribeiro), Éverton (57.Rafa Silva). Trainer: Jorge Fernando Pinheiro de Jesus.

Goals: 1-0 Lucas Piazón (45+3), 2-0 Ricardo Horta (85).

THE CLUBS 2020/2021

Belenenses Sociedade Anónima Desportiva Lisboa

Founded: 30.06.2018
Stadium: Complexo Desportivo do Estádio Nacional, Oeiras (37,593)
Trainer: Armando Gonçalves Teixeira Petit   25.09.1976

Goalkeepers:	DOB	M	(s)	G
André Moreira	02.12.1995	7	(1)	
Guilherme Oliveira	12.04.1995		(1)	
Stanislav Kritsyuk (RUS)	01.12.1990	27		
Defenders:	DOB	M	(s)	G
Chima Akas (NGA)	03.05.1994		(2)	
Danny Henriques (NED)	29.07.1997	6	(2)	
Diogo Calila	10.10.1998	9	(11)	
Gonçalo Silva	04.06.1991	18		1
Henrique (BRA)	14.10.1986	25		
Nilton Varela	25.05.2001		(4)	
Thibang Phete (RSA)	04.04.1994	24	(2)	1
Rúben Lima	03.10.1989	32	(1)	
Tiago Esgaio	01.08.1995	32		1
Tomás Ribeiro	30.04.1999	32		1
Midfielders:	DOB	M	(s)	G
Afonso Sousa	03.05.2000	20	(12)	2

	DOB	M	(s)	G
Afonso Taira	17.06.1992	19	(12)	
Bruno Ramires (BRA)	18.03.1994	9	(23)	1
Cauê (BRA)	24.05.1989	6	(6)	
César Sousa	20.05.2000		(1)	
Chico Teixeira	26.04.1998	2	(22)	2
Richard Rodrigues (BRA)	11.10.1999	2	(8)	
Sphephelo S'Miso Sithole (RSA)	03.03.1999	21	(4)	
Jordan van der Gaag (NED)	03.01.1999		(2)	
Forwards:	DOB	M	(s)	G
Zander Mateo Cassierra Cabezas (COL)	13.04.1997	23	(9)	10
Dieguinho (BRA)	07.06.1992		(3)	
Edgar Pacheco	23.06.2000		(1)	
Edi Semedo	01.06.1999	1	(10)	
Miguel Cardoso	19.06.1994	30		6
Robinho	31.07.1997		(4)	
Varela	02.02.1985	29	(1)	

Sport Lisboa e Benfica

Founded: 28.02.1904
Stadium: Estádio da Luz, Lisboa (64,642)
Trainer: Jorge Fernando Pinheiro de Jesus   24.07.1954

Goalkeepers:	DOB	M	(s)	G
Helton Leite (BRA)	02.11.1990	15		
Mile Svilar (BEL)	27.08.1999	1		
Odisseas Vlachodimos (GRE)	26.04.1994	18		
Defenders:	**DOB**	**M**	**(s)**	**G**
Álex Grimaldo (ESP)	20.09.1995	27	(4)	2
André Almeida	10.09.1990	4		
Diogo Gonçalves	06.02.1997	12	(9)	1
Ferro	26.03.1997	2	(2)	
Gilberto (BRA)	07.03.1993	17	(8)	
Jardel (BRA)	29.03.1986	5	(3)	
João Ferreira	22.03.2001	1		
Lucas Veríssimo (BRA)	02.07.1995	14		2
Morato (BRA)	30.06.2001	1	(1)	
Nuno Tavares	26.01.2000	7	(7)	
Nicolás Hernán Otamendi (ARG)	12.02.1988	27		1
Rúben Dias	14.05.1997	2		1
Jan Vertonghen (BEL)	24.04.1987	26	(2)	

Midfielders:	DOB	M	(s)	G
Chiquinho	19.07.1995	2	(16)	2
Gabriel (BRA)	18.09.1993	10	(10)	1
Andreas Samaris (GRE)	13.06.1989	1	(5)	
Adel Taarabt (MAR)	24.05.1989	19	(7)	
Julian Weigl (GER)	08.09.1995	23	(5)	
Forwards:	**DOB**	**M**	**(s)**	**G**
Carlos Vinícius (BRA)	25.03.1995		(1)	
Franco Cervi (ARG)	26.05.1994	5	(9)	
Éverton (BRA)	22.03.1996	24	(8)	7
Facundo Ferreyra (ARG)	14.03.1991		(1)	
Gonçalo Ramos	20.06.2001		(4)	2
Darwin Gabriel Núñez Ribeiro (URU)	24.06.1999	19	(10)	6
Pedrinho (BRA)	13.04.1998	4	(15)	
Pizzi	06.10.1989	19	(13)	6
Rafa Silva	17.05.1993	27	(2)	5
Haris Seferović (SUI)	22.02.1992	24	(7)	22
Gian-Luca Waldschmidt (GER)	19.05.1996	18	(9)	7

Boavista Futebol Clube Porto

Founded: 01.08.1903
Stadium: Estádio do Bessa, Porto (27,363)
Trainer: Vasco César Freire de Seabra   15.09.1983
[09.12.2020]   Daniel Rosendo Alves Gonçalves   30.12.1982
[13.12.2020]   Manuel Jesualdo Ferreira   24.05.1946

Goalkeepers:	DOB	M	(s)	G
Léo Jardim (BRA)	20.03.1995	34		
Defenders:	**DOB**	**M**	**(s)**	**G**
Chidozie Awaziem (NGA)	01.01.1997	27		
Reggie Cannon (USA)	11.06.1998	30	(1)	
Cristian Castro Devenish (COL)	25.01.2001	24	(3)	1
Jesús Alejandro Gómez Molina (MEX)	31.01.2002	3	(4)	
Yanis Hamache (FRA)	13.07.1999	13	(11)	2
Nathan (BRA)	05.09.2001	1	(13)	
Jackson Gabriel Porozo Vernaza (ECU)	04.08.2000	7	(4)	2
Adil Rami (FRA)	27.12.1985	22		
Ricardo Mangas	19.03.1998	21	(7)	3
Midfielders:	**DOB**	**M**	**(s)**	**G**
Angel Gomes (ENG)	31.08.2000	29	(1)	6
Javi García (ESP)	08.02.1987	19	(2)	1

	DOB	M	(s)	G
Nuno Santos	02.03.1999	20	(9)	1
Paulinho	08.01.1997	30	(1)	2
Sebastián Pérez Cardona (COL)	29.03.1993	8	(8)	2
Reisinho	09.04.1999	2	(4)	
Manuel Luis da Silva Cafumana „Show" (ANG)	06.03.1999	13	(18)	
Forwards:	**DOB**	**M**	**(s)**	**G**
Jorge Renán Benguché Ramírez (HON)	21.05.1996	4	(10)	
Jeriel Nicolás De Santis Córdova (VEN)	18.06.2002		(3)	
Alberth Josué Elis Martínez (HON)	12.02.1996	28	(3)	8
Kuku Fidelis (NGA)	10.03.1999		(6)	
Gustavo Sauer (BRA)	30.04.1993	28	(4)	2
Musa Juwara (GAM)	26.12.2001		(3)	
Yusupha Njie (GAM)	03.01.1994	11	(10)	5
Tiago Morais	03.09.2003		(4)	

Sporting Clube de Braga

Founded: 19.01.1921
Stadium: Estádio Municipal de Braga, Braga (30,287)
Trainer: Carlos Augusto Soares da Costa Faria Carvalhal   04.12.1965

Goalkeepers:	DOB	M	(s)	G
Matheus Magalhães (BRA)	19.07.1992	32		
Tiago Sá	11.01.1995	2		
Defenders:	**DOB**	**M**	**(s)**	**G**
Cristian Alexis Borja González (COL)	18.02.1993	8	(5)	1
Bruno Rodrigues	08.06.2001	8	(2)	
Bruno Viana (BRA)	05.02.1995	13		2
Caju (BRA)	17.07.1995		(1)	
David Carmo	19.07.1999	11	(1)	
Francisco Moura	16.08.1999	2	(3)	2
Guilherme Soares	08.02.2001	1		
Nuno Sequeira	19.08.1990	24	(2)	
Raúl Silva (BRA)	04.11.1989	13	(2)	1
Ricardo Esgaio	16.05.1993	32		1
Rolando	31.08.1985	6	(4)	
Vítor Tormena (BRA)	04.01.1996	20	(5)	
Zé Carlos	31.07.1998	2	(2)	
Midfielders:	**DOB**	**M**	**(s)**	**G**
Almoatasembellah Ali Mohamed Al Musrati (LBY)	06.04.1996	23	(5)	3

	DOB	M	(s)	G
Galeno (BRA)	22.10.1997	29	(4)	3
André Horta	07.11.1996	3	(18)	1
André Castro	02.04.1988	20	(1)	2
Fransérgio (BRA)	18.10.1990	25	(5)	6
Osvaldo Nicolás Fabián Gaitán (ARG)	23.02.1988	5	(13)	2
João Novais	10.07.1993	9	(17)	2
Forwards:	**DOB**	**M**	**(s)**	**G**
Abel Ruiz (ESP)	28.01.2000	16	(9)	3
Guilherme Schettine (BRA)	10.10.1995	1	(9)	
Hernâni Infande (GNB)	03.04.2001		(1)	
Iuri Medeiros	10.07.1994	11	(4)	5
Lucas Piazón (BRA)	20.01.1994	11	(9)	4
Paulinho	09.11.1992	12		3
Ricardo Horta	15.09.1994	30	(2)	9
Rodrigo Gomes	07.07.2003		(4)	
Rui Fonte	23.04.1990	1	(4)	
Andraž Šporar (SVN)	27.02.1994	4	(12)	3
Vítor Oliveira	15.03.2000		(1)	

Futebol Clube de Famalicão

Founded: 21.08.1931
Stadium: Estádio Municipal 22 de Junho, Vila Nova de Famalicão (5,307)
Trainer: João Pedro Ramos Borges de Sousa (ANG) — 04.08.1971
[01.02.2021] Jorge Manuel Rebelo Fernandes "Silas" — 01.09.1976
[08.03.2021] Ivo Ricardo Abreu Vieira — 10.01.1976

Goalkeepers:	DOB	M	(s)	G
Luiz Junior (BRA)	14.01.2001	23		
Vaná (BRA)	25.04.1991	6		
Ivan Zlobin (RUS)	07.03.1997	5		
Defenders:	**DOB**	**M**	**(s)**	**G**
Srđan Babić (SRB)	22.04.1996	27		1
Dani Morer (ESP)	05.02.1998	3	(4)	
Diogo Figueiras	01.07.1991	15	(4)	
Diogo Queirós	05.01.1999	16	(4)	
Gil Dias	28.09.1996	26	(5)	
Henrique Trevisan (BRA)	20.01.1997		(4)	
Edwin Alberto Herrera Hernández (COL)	02.09.1998	8	(4)	
Abdul Ibrahim (GHA)	13.01.1999		(1)	
Patrick Willian (BRA)	03.06.1997	16	(4)	
Riccieli (BRA)	17.09.1998	22	(4)	1
Rúben Vinagre	09.04.1999	20		
Calvin Verdonk (NED)	26.04.1997	6	(6)	
Midfielders:	**DOB**	**M**	**(s)**	**G**
Bruno Jordão	12.10.1998	7	(2)	1
Guga	18.07.1997	3	(3)	
Gustavo Assunção (BRA)	30.03.2000	23	(3)	1
Iván Jaime (ESP)	26.09.2000	14	(8)	4
Jorge Pereira	10.03.1998	1		
Bozhidar Kraev (BUL)	23.06.1997	5	(9)	1
Andrija Luković (SRB)	24.10.1994	6	(8)	1
Matheus Clemente	10.06.1998		(1)	
Pêpê	20.05.1997	17	(1)	
Joaquin Nicolás Pereyra (ARG)	01.12.1998	10	(5)	
Manuel Ugarte Ribeiro (URU)	11.04.2001	18	(2)	1
Forwards:	**DOB**	**M**	**(s)**	**G**
Alexandre Guedes	11.02.1994	8	(6)	
Anderson Silva (BRA)	21.11.1997	12	(10)	7
Leonardo Campana Romero (ECU)	24.07.2000	3	(6)	2
Rubén del Campo (SUI)	22.02.2000	3	(2)	
Dyego Sousa	14.09.1989	3	(2)	
Ivo Rodrigues	30.03.1995	12	(2)	6
Jhonata Robert (BRA)	26.10.1999	5	(15)	4
João Neto (BRA)	21.05.2003	1	(5)	
Rúben Lameiras	22.12.1994	11		4
Heriberto Tavares	19.02.1997	8	(9)	2
Antonio Martínez López „Toni Martínez" (ESP)	30.06.1997	1		
Marcello Trotta (ITA)	29.09.1992	2	(4)	
Carlos Valenzuela (ARG)	22.04.1997	8	(16)	3
Walterson (BRA)	28.12.1994		(2)	

Sporting Clube Farense

Founded: 01.04.1910
Stadium: Estádio de São Luís, Faro (7,000)
Trainer: Sérgio Agostinho de Oliveira Vieira — 15.01.1983
[04.02.2021] Jorge Paulo Costa Almeida — 14.10.1971

Goalkeepers:	DOB	M	(s)	G
Beto	01.05.1982	11		
Hugo Marques (ANG)	15.01.1986	4	(2)	
Rafael Defendi (BRA)	22.12.1983	19		
Defenders:	**DOB**	**M**	**(s)**	**G**
Abner Felipe (BRA)	30.05.1996	14		
Alex Pinto	08.07.1998	13	(2)	
André Pinto	05.10.1989	10	(2)	1
Cássio Scheid (BRA)	03.01.1994	8	(3)	
César Martins (BRA)	28.12.1992	16		1
Eduardo Mancha (BRA)	24.11.1995	21	(1)	2
Miguel Bandarra	17.01.1996		(6)	
Ricardo Ferreira	25.11.1992		(1)	
Tomás Tavares	07.03.2001	18		
Midfielders:	**DOB**	**M**	**(s)**	**G**
Jorge Braima Nogueira „Bura" (GNB)	22.12.1995	7	(8)	
Claudio Falcão (BRA)	03.07.1994	14	(7)	
Fábio Nunes	24.07.1992	20	(2)	
Fabrício Isidoro (BRA)	28.01.1992	17	(8)	2
Filipe Melo	03.11.1989	5	(4)	
Ryan Gauld (SCO)	16.12.1995	33		9
Jonatan Lucca (BRA)	02.06.1994	21	(4)	1
Amine Oudrhiri (MAR)	04.11.1992	31	(1)	
Forwards:	**DOB**	**M**	**(s)**	**G**
Alvarinho	03.09.1990		(4)	
Bilel Aouacheria (FRA)	02.04.1994	13	(5)	1
Djalma Braume Manuel Abel Campos (ANG)	30.05.1987		(7)	
Hugo Seco	17.06.1988	6	(11)	
Licá	08.09.1988	19	(4)	3
Brian Ezequiel Mansilla (ARG)	16.04.1997	13	(13)	1
Fábio Patrick dos Reis dos Santos Fernandes(CPV)	13.12.1993	3	(8)	1
Pedro Henrique (BRA)	08.11.1996	16	(10)	5
Madi Queta	21.10.1998	8	(13)	
Nikola Stojiljković (SRB)	17.08.1992	14	(7)	3

Gil Vicente Futebol Clube Barcelos

Founded: 1924
Stadium: Estádio Cidade de Barcelos, Barcelos (12,504)
Trainer: Rui Miguel Garcia Lopes de Almeida — 29.09.1969
[13.11.2020] José Ricardo Soares Ribeiro — 11.11.1974

Goalkeepers:	DOB	M	(s)	G
Quentin Beunardeau (FRA)	27.02.1994	1		
Brian	29.04.2000	1		
Dênis (BRA)	14.04.1987	32		
Defenders:	**DOB**	**M**	**(s)**	**G**
Diogo Silva (BRA)	11.01.1995		(3)	
Tim Hall (LUX)	15.04.1997		(1)	
Henrique Gomes	30.11.1995	6	(4)	
João Talocha	30.08.1989	28	(3)	2
Joel Pereira	28.09.1996	28	(4)	
Paulinho	13.07.1991	6	(3)	
Rodrigão (BRA)	11.09.1995	23	(7)	1
Rúben Fernandes	06.05.1986	32		1
Ygor Nogueira (BRA)	27.03.1995	21	(3)	
Midfielders:	**DOB**	**M**	**(s)**	**G**
Claude Gonçalves	09.04.1994	26	(7)	2
Kanya Fujimoto (JPN)	01.07.1999	12	(15)	1
Ahmed Isaiah (NGA)	10.10.1995		(3)	
João Afonso (BRA)	09.02.1995	14	(6)	
Leandrinho (BRA)	21.09.1996	2	(3)	
Lucas Mineiro (BRA)	24.02.1996	27	(6)	2
Pedrinho	20.12.1992	15	(4)	1
Vitor Carvalho (BRA)	27.05.1997	12	(10)	
Forwards:	**DOB**	**M**	**(s)**	**G**
Alaa Abbas Abdulnabi Al Fartoosi (IRQ)	27.07.1997	1	(3)	1
Yves Baraye (SEN)	22.06.1992	5	(15)	1
Boubacar Hanne	26.02.1999	1	(5)	
Antoine Leautey (FRA)	14.04.1996	16	(9)	1
Lourency (BRA)	02.01.1996	27	(7)	5
Miullen (BRA)	19.05.1998	3	(5)	
Pedro Marques	25.04.1998	11	(4)	5
Renan (BRA)	08.05.1997	3	(7)	
Samuel Lino (BRA)	23.12.1999	21	(12)	9

Club Sport Marítimo Funchal

Founded: 20.09.1910
Stadium: Estádio do Marítimo, Funchal (10,932)
Trainer: José Carlos Fernandes Vidigal "Lito"(ANG) 11.07.1969
[05.12.2020] Milton Mendes (BRA) 25.04.1965
[11.03.2021] Julio Velázquez Santiago (ESP) 05.10.1981

Goalkeepers:	DOB	M	(s)	G
Amir Abedzadeh (IRN)	26.04.1993	29		
Caio Secco (BRA)	22.12.1990	2		
Charles (BRA)	04.02.1994	3		
Defenders:	**DOB**	**M**	**(s)**	**G**
Cláudio Winck (BRA)	15.04.1994	28	(1)	
Fábio China	07.07.1992	11	(4)	
Andreas Karo (CYP)	09.09.1996	6	(3)	
Dejan Kerkez (SRB)	20.01.1996	1	(1)	
Léo Andrade (BRA)	18.04.1998	21		1
Lucas Áfrico (BRA)	05.02.1995	15	(2)	1
Marcelo Hermes (BRA)	02.01.1995	22	(5)	1
Eulânio Ângelo Chipela Gomes „Nanú" (GNB)	17.05.1994	3		1
Renê (BRA)	21.04.1992	23	(4)	
Tim Söderström (SWE)	04.01.1994	3	(3)	
Zainadine Abdula Mulungo Chavango Júnior (MOZ)	24.06.1988	28		1
Midfielders:	**DOB**	**M**	**(s)**	**G**
Franck Bambock (FRA)	07.04.1995	18	(8)	
Stefano Beltrame (ITA)	08.02.1993	1	(2)	1

Jean Cleber (BRA)	29.04.1990	2	(4)	
Rafik Guitane (FRA)	26.05.1999	18	(8)	
Jean (BRA)	26.09.1994	24	(3)	
Pedro Pelágio	21.04.2000	18	(5)	
Forwards:	**DOB**	**M**	**(s)**	**G**
Ali Alipour (IRN)	11.11.1995	11	(15)	2
Jorge Iván Correa (ARG)	04.04.1993	15	(15)	
Edgar Costa	14.04.1987	15	(7)	
François-Xavier Fumu Tamuzo (FRA)	03.04.1995	1	(11)	
Getterson (BRA)	16.05.1991	2		
Jefferson (BRA)	13.03.2000	1	(3)	
José Marcelo	31.08.1998		(1)	
Marcelinho (BRA)	17.07.1996		(1)	
Felicio Mendes Joao Milson (ANG)	12.10.1999	5	(16)	1
Rodrigo Pinho (BRA)	30.05.1991	13	(5)	9
Rúben Macedo	09.03.1996	7	(11)	
Sassá (BRA)	11.01.1994	1	(6)	
Diederrick Joel Tagueu Tadjo (CMR)	06.12.1993	27	(5)	9

Moreirense Futebol Clube Moreira de Cónegos

Founded: 01.11.1938
Stadium: Parque de Jogos "Comendador Joaquim de Almeida Freitas", Moreira de Cónegos (6,152)
Trainer: José Ricardo Soares Ribeiro 11.11.1974
[10.11.2020] Paulo César Silva Peixoto 12.05.1980
[02.01.2021] Leandro Sousa Mendes 14.09.1982
[06.01.2021] Vasco César Freire de Seabra 15.09.1983

Goalkeepers:	DOB	M	(s)	G
Kewin (BRA)	25.01.1995	2		
Mateus Pasinato (BRA)	28.06.1992	30		
Miguel Oliveira	25.05.1994	2		
Defenders:	**DOB**	**M**	**(s)**	**G**
Abdu Conté	24.03.1998	21	(1)	
Afonso Figueiredo	06.01.1993	9	(2)	
Abdoulaye Ba (SEN)	01.01.1991	11	(1)	
Anthony D'Alberto (BEL)	13.10.1994	21	(3)	
Nahuel Adolfo Ferraresi Hernández (VEN)	19.11.1998	20	(4)	3
Matheus Silva (BRA)	03.10.1997	7	(5)	
Pedro Amador	18.12.1998	4		
Reynaldo (BRA)	03.01.1997		(1)	
Lazar Rosić (SRB)	29.06.1993	32	(1)	
Steven Vitória (CAN)	11.01.1987	16	(3)	3
Midfielders:	**DOB**	**M**	**(s)**	**G**
Alex Soares	01.03.1991	22	(5)	1
Ibrahima Camará (GUI)	25.01.1999	4	(12)	

David Simão	15.05.1990	6	(10)	
David Tavares	18.03.1999	1	(10)	
Fábio Pacheco	26.05.1988	30		
Filipe Soares	20.05.1999	27	(4)	2
Gonçalo Franco	17.11.2000	10	(16)	1
Manconi Soriano Mané „Sori Mané" (GNB)	03.04.1996		(2)	
Forwards:	**DOB**	**M**	**(s)**	**G**
André Luis (BRA)	09.03.1994	6	(8)	1
Derik (BRA)	27.09.1999	3	(10)	
Fábio Abreu	29.01.1993	3		2
Felipe Pires (BRA)	18.04.1995	18	(7)	4
Galego (BRA)	04.04.1997		(15)	
Lucas Silva (BRA)	27.08.1999	5	(9)	
Pedro Nuno	13.01.1995	6		2
Rafael Martins (BRA)	17.03.1989	13	(6)	7
Walterson (BRA)	28.12.1994	27	(5)	2
Yan Santos (BRA)	04.09.1998	18	(10)	4

Clube Desportivo Nacional Funchal

Founded: 08.12.1910
Stadium: Estádio da Madeira, Funchal (5,132)
Trainer: Luís Carlos Batalha Freire 03.11.1985
[22.03.3021] Manuel António Marques Machado 04.12.1955

Goalkeepers:	DOB	M	(s)	G
Antonio Filipe	14.04.1985	9		
Daniel (BRA)	18.04.1987	14		
Riccardo Piscitelli (ITA)	10.10.1993	11		
Defenders:	**DOB**	**M**	**(s)**	**G**
João Vigário	20.11.1995	18	(3)	1
Júlio César (BRA)	21.03.1995	13	(3)	
Kalindi (BRA)	29.08.1993	14		
Lucas Kal (BRA)	16.03.1996	23	(1)	
Pedrão (BRA)	03.05.1997	30		1
Rúben Freitas	02.01.1993	18	(3)	
Rui Correia	23.08.1990	13		1
Midfielders:	**DOB**	**M**	**(s)**	**G**
Ibrahim Alhassan (NGA)	03.11.1996	12	(9)	
Larry Azouni (TUN)	23.03.1994	21	(6)	
Chico Ramos	10.04.1995	12	(4)	1
Vladan Danilović (BIH)	27.07.1999	3	(5)	

Éber Bessa (BRA)	21.03.1992	6	(8)	
Vincent Koziello (FRA)	28.10.1995	8	(6)	
Nuno Miguel Oliveira Borges (CPV)	31.03.1988	20	(5)	1
Mabrouk Rouai (FRA)	01.11.2000	2	(4)	
Rúben Micael	19.08.1986	17	(13)	1
Vincent Thill (LUX)	04.02.2000	13	(4)	
Forwards:	**DOB**	**M**	**(s)**	**G**
Gergely Bobál (HUN)	31.08.1995		(2)	
Dudu (BRA)	10.08.1994	1	(1)	1
João Camacho	23.06.1994	20	(8)	3
João Victor (BRA)	25.02.1999	3	(8)	1
Kenji Gorré (CUW)	29.09.1994	15	(14)	4
Marco Matias	10.05.1989	3	(6)	
Pedro Mendes	01.08.1990	7	(5)	2
José Brayan Riascos Valencia (COL)	10.10.1994	25	(5)	5
Bryan Giovanni Róchez Mejía (HON)	01.01.1995	12	(21)	6
Witness Chimoio João Quembo „Witi" (MOZ)	26.08.1996	11	(8)	

Futebol Clube Paços de Ferreira

Founded: 05.04.1950
Stadium: Estádio Capital do Móvel, Paços de Ferreira (9,076)
Trainer: Pedro Miguel Marques da Costa Filipe "Pêpa"   14.12.1980

Goalkeepers:	DOB	M	(s)	G
Jordi (BRA)	03.09.1993	32		
José Oliveira	06.04.2002		(1)	
Michael (BRA)	08.04.1995	2		
Defenders:	**DOB**	**M**	**(s)**	**G**
Fernando Fonseca	14.03.1997	30	(2)	
Jorge Silva	22.03.1996	2		
Maracás (BRA)	27.04.1994	23		
Marcelo (BRA)	27.07.1989	26	(2)	
Marco Baixinho	11.07.1989	19	(4)	
Pedro Marques	18.03.1998		(1)	
Pedro Rebocho	23.01.1995	16	(4)	
Oleg Reabciuk (MDA)	16.01.1998	11		2
Midfielders:	**DOB**	**M**	**(s)**	**G**
Adriano Castanheira	07.04.1993	1	(17)	
Bruno Costa	19.04.1997	30	(1)	4
João Amaral	07.09.1991	11	(18)	1
Mohamed Diaby (FRA)	03.09.1996	3	(13)	1
Stephen Eustáquio (CAN)	21.12.1996	32		2
Abbas Ibrahim (NGA)	02.01.1998	3	(7)	
Luíz Carlos (BRA)	05.02.1985	31	(3)	3
Martín Manuel Calderón Gómez (ESP)	01.03.1999	1	(7)	
Matchoi Djaló	10.04.2003	1	(2)	
Forwards:	**DOB**	**M**	**(s)**	**G**
Douglas Tanque (BRA)	27.10.1993	29	(2)	9
Hélder Ferreira	05.04.1997	25	(8)	4
Dor Jan (ISR)	16.12.1994	2	(8)	1
João Pedro	13.11.1996	3	(23)	5
Lucas Silva (BRA)	30.01.1998	1	(5)	
Luther Singh (RSA)	05.08.1997	24	(5)	5
Uilton (BRA)	25.07.1992	16	(17)	2

Portimonense Sporting Clube Portimão

Founded: 14.08.1914
Stadium: Estádio Municipal, Portimão (6,204)
Trainer: Paulo Sérgio Bento Brito   19.02.1968

Goalkeepers:	DOB	M	(s)	G
Ricardo Ferreira	03.12.1989	5		
Samuel (BRA)	29.03.1994	29	(1)	
Defenders:	**DOB**	**M**	**(s)**	**G**
Koki Anzai (JPN)	31.05.1995	29	(2)	
Casagrande (BRA)	12.05.1999		(1)	
Fali Candé (GNB)	24.01.1998	15	(7)	2
Henrique Gelain (BRA)	05.01.1995	2	(17)	
Lucas Possignolo (BRA)	11.05.1994	28		2
Lucas Tagliapietra (BRA)	05.11.1990	2	(3)	
Maurício Antônio (BRA)	06.02.1992	33		1
Fahd Moufi (MAR)	05.05.1996	25	(1)	
Willyan Rocha (BRA)	27.01.1995	29	(3)	
Midfielders:	**DOB**	**M**	**(s)**	**G**
Anderson Oliveira (BRA)	16.07.1998	15	(14)	1
Dener Clemente (BRA)	13.03.1992	32		4
Ewerton Pereira (BRA)	01.12.1992	13	(5)	1
Fernando Medeiros (BRA)	10.02.1996		(7)	
Lucas Fernandes (BRA)	20.09.1997	7		
Luquinha (BRA)	03.10.2000	11	(9)	1
Pedro Sá	01.12.1993	11	(5)	
Denis Will Poha (FRA)	28.05.1997	4	(8)	
Forwards:	**DOB**	**M**	**(s)**	**G**
Aylton Boa Morte	23.09.1993	29	(5)	5
Beto	31.01.1998	21	(9)	11
Bruno Moreira	06.09.1987	4	(12)	
Fabrício (BRA)	28.03.1990	21	(7)	4
Júlio César (BRA)	12.08.1994	3	(4)	
Lee Seung-woo (KOR)	06.01.1998		(4)	
Ricardo Vaz Tê	01.10.1986		(9)	
Jafar Salmani (IRN)	12.01.1997	2	(9)	1
Welinton	08.06.1993	4	(6)	

Futebol Clube do Porto

Founded: 28.09.1893
Stadium: Estádio do Dragão, Porto (50,034)
Trainer: Sérgio Paulo Merceiro Da Conceição   15.11.1974

Goalkeepers:	DOB	M	(s)	G
Diogo Costa	19.09.1999	1		
Agustín Federico Marchesín (ARG)	16.03.1988	33		
Defenders:	**DOB**	**M**	**(s)**	**G**
Alex Telles (BRA)	15.12.1992	3		2
Carraça	01.03.1993		(2)	
Diogo Leite	23.01.1999	12	(7)	1
João Mário	03.01.2000	4	(10)	2
Iván Marcano Sierra (ESP)	23.06.1987		(1)	
Chancel Mbemba (COD)	08.08.1994	27		1
Eulânio Ângelo Chipela Gomes „Nanú" (GNB)	17.05.1994	8	(4)	
Pepe	26.02.1983	26	(1)	2
Zaidu Sanusi (NGA)	13.06.1997	19	(6)	1
Malang Sarr (FRA)	23.01.1999	5	(3)	
Wilson Manafá	23.07.1994	31		
Midfielders:	**DOB**	**M**	**(s)**	**G**
Jesús Manuel Corona Ruiz (MEX)	06.01.1993	27	(3)	2
Danilo Pereira	09.09.1991	3		
Luis Fernando Díaz Marulanda (COL)	13.01.1997	16	(14)	6
Fábio Vieira	30.05.2000	3	(16)	
Francisco Conceição	14.12.2002	1	(13)	
Marko Grujić (SRB)	13.04.1996	9	(14)	2
Mamadou Loum (SEN)	30.12.1996		(3)	
Shoya Nakajima (JPN)	23.08.1994	1	(3)	
Otávio (BRA)	09.02.1995	24	(2)	3
Romário Baró	25.01.2000	1	(9)	
Sérgio Oliveira	02.06.1992	28	(4)	13
Andrés Mateus Uribe Villa (COL)	21.03.1991	30	(1)	4
Forwards:	**DOB**	**M**	**(s)**	**G**
Evanilson (BRA)	06.10.1999	4	(11)	3
Felipe Anderson (BRA)	15.04.1993	1	(4)	
Moussa Marega (MLI)	14.04.1991	25	(5)	7
Mehdi Taremi (IRN)	18.07.1992	26	(8)	16
Antonio „Toni" Martínez López (ESP)	30.06.1997	6	(12)	7
José Luís Mendes Andrade „Zé Luís" (CPV)	24.01.1991		(1)	

Rio Ave Futebol Clube Vila do Conde

Founded: 10.05.1939
Stadium: Estádio dos Arcos, Vila do Conde (9,065)
Trainer: Mário Fernando Magalhães da Silva — 24.04.1977
[30.12.2020] Pedro Filipe Fernandes da Silva Cunha — 15.11.1966
[29.01.2021] José Miguel Azevedo Cardoso — 28.05.1972

Goalkeepers:	DOB	M	(s)	G
Paweł Kieszek (POL)	16.04.1984	34		
Defenders:	**DOB**	**M**	**(s)**	**G**
Aderllan Santos (BRA)	09.04.1989	32		2
Toni Borevković (CRO)	18.06.1997	31	(1)	
Costinha	26.03.2000	6	(3)	
Fábio Coentrão	11.03.1988	11	(2)	2
Ivo Pinto	07.01.1990	26		
Nélson Monte	30.07.1995	10	(6)	
Pedro Amaral	25.08.1997	18	(11)	
Sávio (BRA)	26.05.1995	7	(3)	
Midfielders:	**DOB**	**M**	**(s)**	**G**
Chico Geraldes	18.04.1995	23	(9)	
Diego Lopes (BRA)	03.05.1994	9	(2)	1
Diogo Teixeira	20.01.1999		(1)	
Filipe Augusto (BRA)	12.08.1993	23	(2)	
Gabrielzinho (BRA)	29.09.1996	3	(15)	
Guga	18.07.1997	12	(8)	
Nikola Jambor (CRO)	25.09.1995	3	(3)	
Judilson Mamadú Tuncará Gomes „Pelé" (GNB)	29.09.1991	21	(4)	2
Tarantini	07.10.1983	17	(9)	
Forwards:	**DOB**	**M**	**(s)**	**G**
Anderson Emanuel Castelo Branco de Cruz (ANG)	09.04.1996		(8)	
André Pereira	05.05.1995	5	(5)	
Bruno Moreira	06.09.1987	2	(6)	
Carlos Mané	11.03.1994	27	(5)	6
Jacinto Muondo Dala „Gelson Dala" (ANG)	13.07.1996	28	(3)	3
Júnior Brandão (BRA)	07.01.1995	3	(7)	
Leandro Silva (BRA)	16.01.1999		(1)	
Lucas Piazón (BRA)	20.01.1994	6	(2)	2
Manuel Namora	12.02.1998		(2)	
Ryotaro Meshino (JPN)	18.06.1998	4	(15)	3
Rafael Camacho	22.05.2000	9	(2)	3
Ronan (BRA)	22.04.1995	4	(9)	

Clube Desportivo Santa Clara Ponta Delgada

Founded: 31.01.1921
Stadium: Estádio de São Miguel, Ponta Delgada (13,277)
Trainer: Daniel António Lopes Ramos — 25.12.1970

Goalkeepers:	DOB	M	(s)	G
André Ferreira	29.05.1996	1		
Marco Pereira	01.12.1987	33		
Defenders:	**DOB**	**M**	**(s)**	**G**
Fábio Cardoso	19.04.1994	28		3
Cristian Marcelo González Tassano (URU)	23.07.1996	1	(1)	
João Afonso	28.05.1990	14	(11)	
João Lucas	15.01.1996	5	(3)	
Mansur (BRA)	17.04.1993	26		
Rafael Ramos	09.01.1995	29	(1)	
Pierre Sagna (SEN)	21.08.1990	5	(9)	
Mikel Villanueva Álvarez (VEN)	14.04.1993	29		1
Midfielders:	**DOB**	**M**	**(s)**	**G**
Anderson Carvalho (BRA)	20.05.1990	24	(5)	1
Costinha	25.08.1992	7	(17)	
Júlio Romão (BRA)	29.03.1998	2	(3)	
Lincoln (BRA)	07.11.1998	25	(5)	1
Lucas Marques (BRA)	24.05.1995		(2)	
Hidemasa Morita (JPN)	10.05.1995	20		2
Nené	10.06.1995	11	(14)	
Osama Rashid (IRQ)	17.01.1992	10	(4)	1
Rúben Oliveira	14.12.1994		(3)	
Forwards:	**DOB**	**M**	**(s)**	**G**
Allano (BRA)	24.04.1995	14	(4)	2
Carlos Júnior (BRA)	15.08.1995	31	(1)	14
Crysan (BRA)	07.07.1996	15	(9)	4
Diogo Salomão	14.09.1988	10	(7)	
Jean Patric (BRA)	14.05.1997	5	(15)	
Shahriar Moghanlou (IRN)	21.12.1994	4	(7)	
Rui Costa	20.02.1996	6	(10)	4
Thiago Santana (BRA)	04.02.1993	9		7
Ukra	16.03.1988	10	(17)	1
Gustavo Daniel Viera Moreira (URU)	21.10.2000		(1)	

Sporting Clube de Portugal Lisboa

Founded: 01.07.1906
Stadium: Estádio "José Alvalade", Lisboa (50,095)
Trainer: Rúben Filipe Marques Amorim — 27.01.1985

Goalkeepers:	DOB	M	(s)	G
André Paulo	18.12.1996		(1)	
Antonio Adán (ESP)	13.05.1987	32		
Luís Maximiano	05.01.1999	2		
Defenders:	**DOB**	**M**	**(s)**	**G**
Antunes	01.04.1987	4	(4)	
Cristian Alexis Borja González (COL)	18.02.1993	1	(1)	
Sebastián Coates Nion (URU)	07.10.1990	33		5
Eduardo Quaresma	02.03.2002	1	(1)	
Zouhair Feddal (MAR)	23.12.1989	28		2
Gonçalo Inácio	25.08.2001	15	(5)	1
João Pereira	25.02.1984	3	(2)	
Luís Neto	26.05.1988	20	(2)	
Matheus Reis (BRA)	18.02.1995	4	(11)	
Nuno Mendes	19.06.2002	29		1
Pedro Antonio Porro Sauceda (ESP)	13.09.1999	30		3
Midfielders:	**DOB**	**M**	**(s)**	**G**
Daniel Bragança	27.05.1999	6	(15)	
Dário Essugo	14.03.2005		(1)	
João Mário	19.01.1993	24	(4)	2
João Palhinha	09.07.1995	28	(4)	1
Matheus Nunes (BRA)	27.08.1998	12	(19)	3
Tómas Silva	15.10.1999		(1)	
Wendel (BRA)	28.08.1997	1		
Forwards:	**DOB**	**M**	**(s)**	**G**
Jovane Eduardo Borges Cabral (CPV)	14.06.1998	6	(18)	5
Nuno Santos	13.02.1995	23	(8)	7
Paulinho	09.11.1992	13	(1)	3
Pedro Gonçalves	28.06.1998	32		23
Gonzalo Jordy Plata Jimeénez (ECU)	01.11.2000	1	(8)	1
Andraž Šporar (SVN)	27.02.1994	6	(7)	3
Tabata (BRA)	30.03.1997	2	(14)	
Tiago Tomás	16.06.2002	16	(14)	3
Luciano Darío Vietto (ARG)	05.12.1993	2	(1)	1

Clube Desportivo de Tondela

Founded:	06.06.1933
Stadium:	Estádio "João Cardoso", Tondela (5,000)
Trainer:	Francisco Martín "Pako" Ayestarán Barandiarán (ESP) 05.02.1963

Goalkeepers:	DOB	M	(s)	G
Joel Sousa	17.03.2000	1		
Babacar Niasse (SEN)	20.12.1996	17		
Pedro Trigueira	04.01.1988	16	(1)	
Defenders:	**DOB**	**M**	**(s)**	**G**
Bebeto (BRA)	01.01.1990	18	(7)	
Filipe Ferreira	27.09.1990	31	(1)	1
Jota Gonçalves	17.06.2000	1	(3)	
Naoufel Khacef (ALG)	27.10.1997	7	(10)	
Enzo Gabriel Martínez Suárez (URU)	29.04.1998	21	(8)	
Abdel Medioub (ALG)	28.08.1997	12	(4)	
Ricardo Alves	09.05.1991	14	(5)	2
Tiago Almeida	28.08.2001	12	(10)	
Yohan Tavares	02.03.1988	28		

Midfielders:	DOB	M	(s)	G
Jaume Grau Ciscar (ESP)	05.05.1997	24	(6)	
João Lamine Jaquité (GNB)	22.02.1996	7	(9)	1
João Mendes	21.10.1994	1	(5)	
João Pedro	03.04.1993	31		5
Pedro Augusto (BRA)	03.03.1997	20	(7)	1
Rafael Barbosa	29.03.1996	17	(13)	3
Roberto Olabe del Arco (ESP)	05.05.1996	13	(4)	
Telmo Emanuel Gomes Arcanjo (CPV)	21.06.2001	2	(12)	
Forwards:	**DOB**	**M**	**(s)**	**G**
Souleymane Anne (MTN)	05.12.1997		(17)	1
Mario González Gutiérrez (ESP)	25.02.1996	25	(2)	15
Jhon Eduard Murillo Romaña (VEN)	21.11.1995	22	(4)	4
Rúben Fonseca	24.02.2000	1	(2)	
Salvador Agra	11.11.1991	26	(5)	3
Tomislav Štrkalj (CRO)	02.08.1996	7	(10)	

Vitória Sport Clube de Guimarães

Founded:	22.09.1922
Stadium:	Estádio "D. Afonso Henriques", Guimarães (30,007)
Trainer:	Tiago Cardoso Mendes 02.05.1981
[31.10.1972]	João Alexandre Oliveira Nunes Henriques 31.10.1972
[05.04.2021]	Manuel Albino Morim Maçães "Bino" 19.12.1972
[13.05.2021]	João Miguel da Cunha Teixeira 19.08.1981

Goalkeepers:	DOB	M	(s)	G
Bruno Varela	04.11.1994	31		
Matouš Trmal (CZE)	02.10.1998	3		
Defenders:	**DOB**	**M**	**(s)**	**G**
André Amaro	13.08.2002	10	(2)	1
Jonas Carls (GER)	25.03.1997	1		
Hélder Sá	10.11.2002	1	(1)	
Jorge Fernandes	02.04.1997	30		1
Gideon Mensah (GHA)	18.07.1998	22		
Abdul Mumin (GHA)	06.06.1998	24	(1)	
Zié Ouattara (CIV)	09.01.2000	6	(4)	
Falaye Sacko (MLI)	01.05.1995	28		
Sílvio	28.09.1987	10		
Easah Suliman (ENG)	26.01.1998	9	(3)	
Midfielders:	**DOB**	**M**	**(s)**	**G**
Mikel Agu (NGA)	27.05.1993	8	(6)	
André Almeida	30.05.2000	21	(9)	2

	DOB	M	(s)	G
André André	26.08.1989	32		6
Nicolas Janvier (FRA)	11.08.1998	2	(14)	
Jacob Maddox (ENG)	03.11.1998	1	(2)	
Miguel Luís	27.02.1999	2	(16)	
José Luis García Vayá „Pepelu" (ESP)	11.08.1998	26	(4)	1
Denis Will Poha (FRA)	28.05.1997	3	(2)	
Alhassan Wakaso (GHA)	07.01.1992	3	(4)	
Forwards:	**DOB**	**M**	**(s)**	**G**
Bruno Duarte (BRA)	24.03.1996	10	(15)	3
Marcus Edwards (ENG)	03.12.1998	21	(12)	3
Oscar Eduardo Estupiñán Vallesilla (COL)	29.12.1996	21	(2)	8
Lyle Foster (RSA)	03.09.2000	1	(4)	
Noah Holm (NOR)	23.05.2001	1	(15)	
Abou Ouattara (BFA)	26.12.1999		(1)	
Ricardo Quaresma	26.09.1983	17	(11)	4
Rochinha	03.05.1995	23	(10)	6
Rúben Lameiras	22.12.1994	7	(13)	1

SECOND LEVEL
LigaPro 2020/2021

1.	GD Estoril Praia (*Promoted*)	34	20	10	4	55	-	26	70
2.	FC de Vizela (*Promoted*)	34	18	12	4	59	-	35	66
3.	FC de Arouca (*Promotion Play-offs*)	34	19	8	7	45	-	25	65
4.	Associação Académica de Coimbra	34	17	11	6	46	-	30	62
5.	CD Feirense Santa Maria da Feira	34	17	7	10	48	-	33	58
6.	GD Chaves	34	16	9	9	46	-	36	57
7.	FC de Penafiel	34	12	10	12	42	-	42	46
8.	Sport Lisboa e Benfica "B"	34	12	8	14	52	-	43	44
9.	Casa Pia Atlético Clube Lisboa	34	10	13	11	41	-	46	43
10.	Leixões SC Porto	34	10	10	14	35	-	43	40
11.	CD Cova da Piedade (*Relegated*)	34	8	13	13	39	-	48	37
12.	CD Mafra	34	9	10	15	35	-	48	37
13.	Sporting da Covilhã	34	8	13	13	36	-	42	37
14.	Académico de Viseu FC	34	9	9	16	32	-	45	36
15.	Varzim SC	34	9	6	19	26	-	44	33
16.	FC do Porto "B"	34	7	11	16	45	-	52	32
17.	UD Vilafranquense	34	5	16	13	34	-	54	31
18.	UD Oliveirense (*Relegated*)	34	7	10	17	25	-	49	31

<u>Please note</u>: CD Cova da Piedade were relegated after failing to produce valid licensing documentation for the next season. A a result, UD Vilafranquense remains at second level for 2021/2022.

INTERNATIONAL MATCHES
(16.07.2020 – 15.07.2021)

Date	City	Match	Score	Comp
05.09.2020	Porto	Portugal - Croatia	4-1(1-0)	(UNL)
08.09.2020	Stockholm	Sweden - Portugal	0-2(0-1)	(UNL)
07.10.2020	Lisboa	Portugal - Spain	0-0	(F)
11.10.2020	Paris	France - Portugal	0-0	(UNL)
14.10.2020	Lisboa	Portugal - Sweden	3-0(2-0)	(UNL)
11.11.2020	Lisboa	Portugal - Andorra	7-0(2-0)	(F)
14.11.2020	Lisboa	Portugal - France	0-1(0-0)	(UNL)
17.11.2020	Split	Croatia - Portugal	2-3(1-0)	(UNL)
24.03.2021	Torino	Portugal - Azerbaijan	1-0(0-0)	(WCQ)
27.03.2021	Beograd	Serbia - Portugal	2-2(0-2)	(WCQ)
30.03.2021	Lëtzebuerg	Luxembourg - Portugal	1-3(1-1)	(WCQ)
04.06.2021	Madrid	Spain - Portugal	0-0	(F)
09.06.2021	Lisboa	Portugal - Israel	4-0(2-0)	(F)
15.06.2021	Budapest	Hungary - Portugal	0-3(0-0)	(EC)
19.06.2021	München	Portugal - Germany	2-4(1-2)	(EC)
23.06.2021	Budapest	Portugal - France	2-2(1-1)	(EC)
27.06.2021	Sevilla	Belgium - Portugal	1-0(1-0)	(EC)

05.09.2020 PORTUGAL - CROATIA **4-1(1-0)** 2nd UEFA Nations League A, Group 3
Estádio do Dragão, Porto; Referee: Davide Massa (Italy); Attendance: 0
POR: Anthony Lopes, João Cancelo, Rúben Dias, Pepe, Raphaël Guerreiro, Danilo Pereira, João Moutinho (Cap) (81.Sérgio Oliveira), Bruno Fernandes, Bernardo Silva (78.Francisco Trincão), Diogo Jota, João Félix (88.André Silva). Trainer: Fernando Manuel Fernandes da Costa Santos.
Goals: João Cancelo (41), Diogo Jota (58), João Félix (70), André Silva (90+4).

08.09.2020 SWEDEN - PORTUGAL **0-2(0-1)** 2nd UEFA Nations League A, Group 3
Friends Arena, Stockholm; Referee: Danny Desmond Makkelie (Netherlands); Attendance: 0
POR: Anthony Lopes, João Cancelo, Rúben Dias, Pepe, Raphaël Guerreiro, Danilo Pereira, João Moutinho (73.Rúben Neves), Bruno Fernandes, Bernardo Silva (22.Gonçalo Guedes), Cristiano Ronaldo (Cap) (81.Diogo Jota), João Félix. Trainer: Fernando Manuel Fernandes da Costa Santos.
Goals: Cristiano Ronaldo (45+1, 72).

07.10.2020 PORTUGAL - SPAIN **0-0** Friendly International
Estádio "José Alvalade", Lisboa; Referee: Paolo Valeri (Italy); Attendance: 2,500
POR: Rui Patrício, João Cancelo, Pepe (46.Rúben Dias), Rúben Semedo, Raphaël Guerreiro (68.Nélson Semedo), Rúben Neves, Renato Sanches, João Moutinho (46.William Carvalho), André Silva (46.Bernardo Silva), Cristiano Ronaldo (Cap) (72.João Félix), Francisco Trincão (79.Diogo Jota). Trainer: Fernando Manuel Fernandes da Costa Santos.

11.10.2020 FRANCE - PORTUGAL **0-0** 2nd UEFA Nations League A, Group 3
Stade de France, Saint-Denis, Paris; Referee: Carlos del Cerro Grande (Spain); Attendance: 1,000
POR: Rui Patrício, Nélson Semedo, Rúben Dias, Pepe, Raphaël Guerreiro (89.João Cancelo), Danilo Pereira, Bruno Fernandes (80.Renato Sanches), William Carvalho (88.João Moutinho), Bernardo Silva (61.Diogo Jota), Cristiano Ronaldo (Cap), João Félix (89.Francisco Trincão). Trainer: Fernando Manuel Fernandes da Costa Santos.

14.10.2020 PORTUGAL - SWEDEN **3-0(2-0)** 2nd UEFA Nations League A, Group 3
Estádio "José Alvalade", Lisboa; Referee: Srđan Jovanović (Serbia); Attendance: 5,000
POR: Rui Patrício, João Cancelo, Rúben Dias, Pepe (Cap), Raphaël Guerreiro, Danilo Pereira, William Carvalho (80.João Moutinho), Bernardo Silva (75.André Silva), Bruno Fernandes (88.Renato Sanches), João Félix (75.Daniel Podence), Diogo Jota (88.Rafa Silva). Trainer: Fernando Manuel Fernandes da Costa Santos.
Goals: Bernardo Silva (21), Diogo Jota (44, 72).

11.11.2020 PORTUGAL - ANDORRA **7-0(2-0)** Friendly International
Estádio da Luz, Lisboa; Referee: Alain Bieri (Switzerland); Attendance: 0
POR: Anthony Lopes, Mário Rui, Rúben Semedo, Nélson Semedo, Domingos Duarte, João Moutinho (Cap) (74.Danilo Pereira), Sérgio Oliveira (46.Bernardo Silva), Renato Sanches (63.William Carvalho), Paulinho (63.João Félix), Pedro Neto (46.Cristiano Ronaldo), Francisco Trincão (74.Diogo Jota). Trainer: Fernando Manuel Fernandes da Costa Santos.
Goals: Pedro Neto (8), Paulinho (29), Renato Sanches (56), Paulinho (61), Emili Josep García Miramontes (76 own goal), Cristiano Ronaldo (85), João Félix (88).

14.11.2020 PORTUGAL - FRANCE **0-1(0-0)** 2nd UEFA Nations League A, Group 3
Estádio da Luz, Lisboa; Referee: Tobias Stieler (Germany); Attendance: 0
POR: Rui Patrício, João Cancelo, José Fonte, Rúben Dias, Raphaël Guerreiro, Danilo Pereira (84.Sérgio Oliveira), William Carvalho (56.Diogo Jota), Bruno Fernandes (72.João Moutinho), Bernardo Silva (71.Francisco Trincão), Cristiano Ronaldo (Cap), João Félix (84.Paulinho). Trainer: Fernando Manuel Fernandes da Costa Santos.

17.11.2020 CROATIA - PORTUGAL **2-3(1-0)** 2nd UEFA Nations League A, Group 3
Stadion Poljud, Split; Referee: Michael Oliver (England); Attendance: 0
POR: Rui Patrício, Mário Rui (71.João Cancelo), Rúben Semedo, Nélson Semedo, Rúben Dias, João Moutinho, Danilo Pereira (77.Sérgio Oliveira), Bruno Fernandes (46.Francisco Trincão), Cristiano Ronaldo (Cap), Diogo Jota (77.Paulinho), João Félix (71.Bernardo Silva). Trainer: Fernando Manuel Fernandes da Costa Santos.
Goals: Rúben Dias (52), João Félix (60), Rúben Dias (90).

24.03.2021 **PORTUGAL - AZERBAIJAN** 1-0(0-0) 22nd FIFA WC. Qualifiers
Juventus Stadium, Turin (Italy); Referee: Daniel Siebert (Germany); Attendance: 0
POR: Anthony Lopes, João Cancelo, Rúben Dias, Domingos Duarte, Nuno Mendes, João Moutinho (46.Bruno Fernandes), Rúben Neves (88.João Palhinha), André Silva (75.João Félix), Pedro Neto (63.Rafa Silva), Bernardo Silva (88.Sérgio Oliveira), Cristiano Ronaldo (Cap). Trainer: Fernando Manuel Fernandes da Costa Santos.
Goal: Maksim Medvedev (37 own goal).

27.03.2021 **SERBIA - PORTUGAL** 2-2(0-2) 22nd FIFA WC. Qualifiers
Stadion "Rajko Mitić", Beograd; Referee: Danny Desmond Makkelie (Netherlands); Attendance: 0
POR: Anthony Lopes, Cédric Soares, José Fonte, João Cancelo (72.Nuno Mendes), Rúben Dias, Sérgio Oliveira (72.Renato Sanches), Danilo Pereira, Bruno Fernandes (90+1.João Palhinha), Bernardo Silva, Cristiano Ronaldo (Cap), Diogo Jota (85.João Félix). Trainer: Fernando Manuel Fernandes da Costa Santos.
Goals: Diogo Jota (11, 36).

30.03.2021 **LUXEMBOURG - PORTUGAL** 1-3(1-1) 22nd FIFA WC. Qualifiers
Stade "Josy Barthel", Lëtzebuerg; Referee: Sergey Ivanov (Russia); Attendance: 0
POR: Anthony Lopes, José Fonte, João Cancelo, Rúben Dias, Nuno Mendes, Rúben Neves (89.Sérgio Oliveira), Renato Sanches, Bernardo Silva (68.João Palhinha), Cristiano Ronaldo (Cap), João Félix (41.Pedro Neto), Diogo Jota (68.Rafa Silva). Trainer: Fernando Manuel Fernandes da Costa Santos.
Goals: Diogo Jota (45+2), Cristiano Ronaldo (51), João Palhinha (80).

04.06.2021 **SPAIN - PORTUGAL** 0-0 Friendly International
Estadio Wanda Metropolitano, Madrid; Referee: Craig Pawson (England); Attendance: 14,743
POR: Rui Patrício, Nélson Semedo, José Fonte, Pepe (59.William Carvalho), Raphaël Guerreiro (81.Nuno Mendes), Sérgio Oliveira (59.Bruno Fernandes), Danilo Pereira, Renato Sanches (69.Rafa Silva), Cristiano Ronaldo (Cap), João Félix (46.Pedro Gonçalves), Diogo Jota (70.João Palhinha). Trainer: Fernando Manuel Fernandes da Costa Santos.

09.06.2021 **PORTUGAL - ISRAEL** 4-0(2-0) Friendly International
Estádio "José Alvalade", Lisboa; Referee: Jérémie Pignard (France); Attendance: 0
POR: Rui Silva, João Cancelo, Pepe, Rúben Dias (62.Danilo Pereira), Nuno Mendes, William Carvalho (71.Renato Sanches), Rúben Neves (62.João Moutinho), Bruno Fernandes, Bernardo Silva (71.Pedro Gonçalves), Diogo Jota (46.André Silva), Cristiano Ronaldo (Cap) (71.Gonçalo Guedes). Trainer: Fernando Manuel Fernandes da Costa Santos.
Goals: Bruno Fernandes (42), Cristiano Ronaldo (44), João Cancelo (86), Bruno Fernandes (90+1).

15.06.2021 **HUNGARY - PORTUGAL** 0-3(0-0) 16th EC. Group Stage.
Puskás Aréna, Budapest; Referee: Cüneyt Çakir (Turkey); Attendance: 55,662
POR: Rui Patrício, Nélson Semedo, Rúben Dias, Pepe, Raphaël Guerreiro, Danilo Pereira, William Carvalho (81.Renato Sanches), Bernardo Silva (71.Rafa Silva), Bruno Fernandes (89.João Moutinho), Cristiano Ronaldo (Cap), Diogo Jota (81.André Silva). Trainer: Fernando Manuel Fernandes da Costa Santos.
Goals: Raphaël Guerreiro (84), Cristiano Ronaldo (87 penalty, 90+2).

19.06.2021 **PORTUGAL - GERMANY** 2-4(1-2) 16th EC. Group Stage.
Football Arena (Allianz), München; Referee: Anthony Taylor (England); Attendance: 12,926
POR: Rui Patrício, Nélson Semedo, Rúben Dias, Pepe, Raphaël Guerreiro, Danilo Pereira, William Carvalho (58.Rafa Silva), Bruno Fernandes (64.João Moutinho), Bernardo Silva (46.Renato Sanches), Cristiano Ronaldo (Cap), Diogo Jota (83.André Silva). Trainer: Fernando Manuel Fernandes da Costa Santos.
Goals: Cristiano Ronaldo (15), Diogo Jota (67).

23.06.2021 **PORTUGAL - FRANCE** 2-2(1-1) 16th EC. Group Stage.
Puskás Aréna, Budapest (Hungary); Referee: Antonio Miguel Mateu Lahoz (Spain); Attendance: 54,886
POR: Rui Patrício, Nélson Semedo (79.Diogo Dalot), Rúben Dias, Pepe, Raphaël Guerreiro, Danilo Pereira (46.João Palhinha), João Moutinho (72.Rúben Neves), Bernardo Silva (72.Bruno Fernandes), Renato Sanches (88.Sérgio Oliveira), Cristiano Ronaldo (Cap), Diogo Jota. Trainer: Fernando Manuel Fernandes da Costa Santos.
Goals: Cristiano Ronaldo (31 penalty, 60 penalty).

27.06.2021 **BELGIUM - PORTUGAL** 1-0(1-0) 16th EC. 2nd Round of 16.
Estadio La Cartuja, Sevilla (Spain); Referee: Dr. Felix Brych (Germany); Attendance: 11,504
POR: Rui Patrício, Diogo Dalot, Rúben Dias, Pepe, Raphaël Guerreiro, Renato Sanches (78.Sérgio Oliveira), João Moutinho (55.João Félix), João Palhinha (78.Danilo Pereira), Bernardo Silva (55.Bruno Fernandes), Cristiano Ronaldo (Cap), Diogo Jota (70.André Silva). Trainer: Fernando Manuel Fernandes da Costa Santos.

NATIONAL TEAM PLAYERS
(16.07.2020 – 15.07.2021)

Name	DOB	Caps	Goals	2020/2021:	Club
Goalkeepers					
ANTHONY LOPES	01.10.1990	13	0	2020/2021:	Olympique Lyonnais (FRA)
RUI Pedro dos Santos PATRÍCIO	15.02.1988	97	0	2020/2021:	Wolverhampton Wanderers FC (ENG)
RUI Tiago Dantas da SILVA	07.02.1994	1	0	2021:	Granada CF (ESP)
Defenders					
CÉDRIC Ricardo Alves SOARES	31.08.1991	34	1	2021:	Arsenal FC London (ENG)
José DIOGO DALOT Teixeira	18.03.1999	2	0	2021:	Manchester United FC (ENG)
DOMINGOS Sousa Coutinho Meneses DUARTE	10.03.1995	2	0	2020/2021:	Granada CF (ESP)
JOÃO Pedro Cavaco CANCELO	27.05.1994	27	5	2020/2021:	Manchester City FC (ENG)
JOSÉ Miguel da Rocha FONTE	22.12.1983	46	0	2020/2021:	Lille OSC (FRA)
MÁRIO RUI Silva Duarte	27.05.1991	11	0	2020:	SSC Napoli (ITA)
NÉLSON Cabral SEMEDO "Nelsinho"	16.11.1993	21	0	2020/2021:	Wolverhampton Wanderers FC (ENG)
Nuno Alexandre Tavares MENDES	19.06.2002	5	0	2021:	Sporting Clube de Portugal Lisboa
Képler Laveran Lima Ferreira "PEPE"	26.02.1983	119	7	2020/2021:	FC do Porto
RAPHAËL Adelino José GUERREIRO	22.12.1993	50	3	2020/2021:	BV Borussia Dortmund (GER)
RÚBEN Santos Gato Alves DIAS	14.05.1997	32	2	2020: 29.09.2020->	Sport Lisboa e Benfica Manchester City FC (ENG)
RÚBEN Afonso Borges SEMEDO	04.04.1994	3	0	2020:	Olympiacos SFP Peiraiás (GRE)
Midfielders					
BRUNO Miguel Borges FERNANDES	08.09.1994	33	4	2020/2021:	Manchester United FC (ENG)
DANIEL Castelo PODENCE	21.10.1995	1	0	2020:	Wolverhampton Wanderers FC (ENG)
DANILO Luís Hélio PEREIRA	09.09.1991	51	2	2020: 05.10.2020->	FC do Porto Paris Saint-Germain FC (FRA)
JOÃO Filipe Iria Santos MOUTINHO	08.09.1986	135	7	2020/2021:	Wolverhampton Wanderers FC (ENG)
JOÃO Maria Lobo Alves PALHINHA Gonçalves	09.07.1995	6	1	2021:	Sporting Clube de Portugal Lisboa
PEDRO António Pereira GONÇALVES	28.06.1998	2	0	2021:	Sporting Clube de Portugal Lisboa
Rafael Alexandre "RAFA" Fernandes Ferreira da SILVA	17.05.1993	23	0	2020/2021:	Sport Lisboa e Benfica
RENATO Júnior Luz SANCHES	18.08.1997	30	2	2020/2021:	Lille OSC (FRA)
RÚBEN Diogo da Silva NEVES	13.03.1997	22	0	2020/2021:	Wolverhampton Wanderers FC (ENG)
SÉRGIO Miguel Relvas de OLIVEIRA	02.06.1992	13	0	2020/2021:	FC do Porto
WILLIAM Silva de CARVALHO	07.04.1992	68	4	2020/2021:	Real Betis Balompié Sevilla (ESP)
Forwards					
ANDRÉ Miguel Valente SILVA	06.11.1995	42	16	2020/2021:	Eintracht Frankfurt (GER)
BERNARDO Mota Veiga de Carvalho e SILVA	10.08.1994	59	7	2020/2021:	Manchester City FC (ENG)
CRISTIANO RONALDO dos Santos Aveiro	05.02.1985	179	109	2020/2021:	Juventus FC Torino (ITA)
Diogo José Teixeira da Silva "DIOGO JOTA"	04.12.1996	18	7	2020/2021:	Liverpool FC (ENG)
FRANCISCO António Machado Mota Castro TRINCÃO	29.12.1999	6	0	2020:	Wolverhampton Wanderers FC (ENG)
GONÇALO Manuel Ganchinho GUEDES	29.11.1996	23	6	2020/2021:	Valencia CF (ESP)
JOÃO FÉLIX Sequeira	10.11.1999	18	3	2020/2021:	Club Atlético de Madrid (ESP)
João Paulo Dias Fernandes "PAULINHO"	09.11.1992	3	2	2020:	Sporting Clube de Braga
PEDRO Lomba NETO	09.03.2000	3	1	2020/2021:	Wolverhampton Wanderers FC (ENG)

Trainer

FERNANDO Manuel Fernandes da Costa SANTOS
[from 23.09.2014]
10.10.1954   88 M; 53 W; 21 D; 14 L; 178-67

REPUBLIC OF IRELAND

The Country:
Éire (Republic of Ireland)
Capital: Dublin
Surface: 70,273 km²
Inhabitants: 5,011,500 [2021]
Time: UTC

The FA:
Football Association of Ireland
National Sports Campus Abbotstown, Dublin 15
Tel: +353 1 8999 500
Founded: 1921
Member of FIFA since: 1923
Member of UEFA since: 1954
Website: www.fai.ie

NATIONAL TEAM RECORDS

RECORDS		
First international match:	21.03.1926, Torino:	Italy – Republic of Ireland 3-0
Most international caps:	Robert David Keane	- 146 caps (1998-2016)
Most international goals:	Robert David Keane	- 68 goals / 146 caps (1998-2016)

UEFA EUROPEAN CHAMPIONSHIP
1960	Qualifiers
1964	Qualifiers
1968	Qualifiers
1972	Qualifiers
1976	Qualifiers
1980	Qualifiers
1984	Qualifiers
1988	Final Tournament (Group Stage)
1992	Qualifiers
1996	Qualifiers
2000	Qualifiers
2004	Qualifiers
2008	Qualifiers
2012	Final Tournament (Group Stage)
2016	Final Tournament (2nd Round of 16)
2020	Qualifiers

FIFA WORLD CUP
1930	Did not enter
1934	Qualifiers
1938	Qualifiers
1950	Qualifiers
1954	Qualifiers
1958	Qualifiers
1962	Qualifiers
1966	Qualifiers
1970	Qualifiers
1974	Qualifiers
1978	Qualifiers
1982	Qualifiers
1986	Qualifiers
1990	Final Tournament (Quarter-Finals)
1994	Final Tournament (2nd Round of 16)
1998	Qualifiers
2002	Final Tournament (2nd Round of 16)
2006	Qualifiers
2010	Qualifiers
2014	Qualifiers
2018	Qualifiers

OLYMPIC TOURNAMENTS
1908	-
1912	-
1920	-
1924	Quarter-Finals
1928	-
1936	-
1948	Preliminary Round
1952	Did not enter
1956	Did not enter
1960	Qualifiers
1964	Did not enter
1968	Did not enter
1972	Qualifiers
1976	Qualifiers
1980	Qualifiers
1984	Did not enter
1988	Qualifiers
1992	Qualifiers
1996	Qualifiers
2000	Qualifiers
2004	Qualifiers
2008	Qualifiers
2012	Qualifiers
2016	Qualifiers

UEFA NATIONS LEAGUE

2018/2019	League B
2020/2021	League B

FIFA CONFEDERATIONS CUP 1992-2017

None

IRISH CLUB HONOURS IN EUROPEAN CLUB COMPETITIONS:

European Champion Clubs.Cup (1956-1992) / UEFA Champions League (1993-2021)
None

Fairs Cup (1858-1971) / UEFA Cup (1972-2009) / UEFA Europa League (2010-2021)
None

UEFA Super Cup (1972-2020)
None

European Cup Winners.Cup 1961-1999*
None

*defunct competition

NATIONAL COMPETITIONS
TABLE OF HONOURS

	CHAMPIONS	CUP WINNERS	BEST GOALSCORERS	
1921/1922	St. James' Gate	St. James' Gate FC Dublin	Jack Kelly (St. James' Gate FC Dublin)	11
1922/1923	Shamrock Rovers FC Dublin	Alton United	Bob Fullam (Shamrock Rovers FC Dublin)	27
1923/1924	Bohemian FC Dublin	Athlone Town FC	Dave Roberts (Bohemian FC Dublin)	20
1924/1925	Shamrock Rovers FC Dublin	Shamrock Rovers FC Dublin	Billy Farrell (Shamrock Rovers FC Dublin)	25
1925/1926	Shelbourne FC Dublin	Fordsons FC Cork	Billy Farrell (Shamrock Rovers FC Dublin)	24
1926/1927	Shamrock Rovers FC Dublin	Drumcondra	David Byrne (Shamrock Rovers FC Dublin) John McMillan (Shelbourne FC Dublin)	17
1927/1928	Bohemian FC Dublin	Bohemian FC Dublin	Charlie Heinemann (Fordsons FC Cork)	24
1928/1929	Shelbourne FC Dublin	Shamrock Rovers FC Dublin	Eddie Carroll (Dundalk FC)	17
1929/1930	Bohemian FC Dublin	Shamrock Rovers FC Dublin	Johnny Ledwidge (Shelbourne FC Dublin)	16
1930/1931	Shelbourne FC Dublin	Shamrock Rovers FC Dublin	Alec Hair (Shelbourne FC Dublin)	29
1931/1932	Shamrock Rovers FC Dublin	Shamrock Rovers FC Dublin	Pearson Ferguson (Cork FC) Jack Forster (Waterford FC)	21
1932/1933	Dundalk FC	Shamrock Rovers FC Dublin	George Ebbs (St. James' Gate FC Dublin)	20
1933/1934	Bohemian FC Dublin	Cork FC	Alf Rigby (St. James' Gate FC Dublin)	13
1934/1935	Dolphin	Bohemian FC Dublin	Alf Rigby (St. James' Gate FC Dublin)	17
1935/1936	Bohemian FC Dublin	Shamrock Rovers FC Dublin	Jimmy Turnbull (Cork FC)	37
1936/1937	Sligo Rovers FC	Waterford FC	Bob Slater (Shelbourne FC Dublin, Waterford FC)	20
1937/1938	Shamrock Rovers FC Dublin	St. James' Gate FC Dublin	Willie Byrne (St. James' Gate FC Dublin)	25
1938/1939	Shamrock Rovers FC Dublin	Shelbourne FC Dublin	Paddy Bradshaw (St. James' Gate FC Dublin)	22
1939/1940	St. James' Gate	Shamrock Rovers FC Dublin	Paddy Bradshaw (St. James' Gate FC Dublin)	29
1940/1941	Cork United FC	Cork United FC	Mick O'Flanagan (Bohemian FC Dublin)	19
1941/1942	Cork United FC	Dundalk FC	Tommy Byrne (Limerick FC)	20
1942/1943	Cork United FC	Drumcondra	Sean McCarthy (Cork United FC)	16
1943/1944	Shelbourne FC Dublin	Shamrock Rovers FC Dublin	Sean McCarthy (Cork United FC)	16
1944/1945	Cork United FC	Shamrock Rovers FC Dublin	Sean McCarthy (Cork United FC)	26
1945/1946	Cork United FC	Drumcondra FC Dublin	Paddy O'Leary (Cork United FC)	15
1946/1947	Shelbourne FC Dublin	Cork United FC	Paddy Coad (Shamrock Rovers FC Dublin) Alf Hanson (Shelbourne FC Dublin)	11
1947/1948	Drumcondra FC Dublin	Shamrock Rovers FC Dublin	Sean McCarthy (Cork United FC)	13
1948/1949	Drumcondra FC Dublin	Dundalk FC	Bernard Lester (Transport FC Dublin) Eugene Noonan (Waterford FC) Paddy O'Leary (Cork Athletic FC)	12
1949/1950	Cork Athletic FC	Transport FC Dublin	Dave McCulloch (Waterford FC)	19
1950/1951	Cork Athletic FC	Cork Athletic FC	Dessie Glynn (Drumcondra FC Dublin)	20
1951/1952	St. Patrick's Athletic FC Dublin	Dundalk FC	Shay Gibbons (St. Patrick's Athletic FC Dublin)	26
1952/1953	Shelbourne FC Dublin	Cork Athletic FC	Shay Gibbons (St. Patrick's Athletic FC Dublin)	22
1953/1954	Shamrock Rovers FC Dublin	Drumcondra FC Dublin	Danny Jordan (Bohemian FC Dublin)	14
1954/1955	St. Patrick's Athletic FC Dublin	Shamrock Rovers FC Dublin	Jimmy Gauld (Waterford FC)	30
1955/1956	St. Patrick's Athletic FC Dublin	Shamrock Rovers FC Dublin	Shay Gibbons (St. Patrick's Athletic FC Dublin)	21
1956/1957	Shamrock Rovers FC Dublin	Drumcondra FC Dublin	Tommy Hamilton (Shamrock Rovers FC Dublin) Donal Leahy (Evergreen United FC Cork)	15
1957/1958	Drumcondra FC Dublin	Dundalk FC	Donal Leahy (Evergreen United FC Cork)	16
1958/1959	Shamrock Rovers FC Dublin	St. Patrick's Athletic FC Dublin	Donal Leahy (Evergreen United FC Cork)	22
1959/1960	Limerick FC	Shelbourne FC Dublin	Austin Noonan (Cork Celtic FC)	27
1960/1961	Drumcondra FC Dublin	St. Patrick's Athletic FC Dublin	Dan McCaffrey (Drumcondra FC Dublin)	29
1961/1962	Shelbourne FC Dublin	Shamrock Rovers FC Dublin	Eddie Bailham (Shamrock Rovers FC Dublin)	21
1962/1963	Dundalk FC	Shelbourne FC Dublin	Mick Lynch (Waterford FC)	12
1963/1964	Shamrock Rovers FC Dublin	Shamrock Rovers FC Dublin	Eddie Bailham (Shamrock Rovers FC Dublin) Jimmy Hasty (Dundalk FC) Johnny Kingston (Cork Hibernians FC)	18
1964/1965	Drumcondra FC Dublin	Shamrock Rovers FC Dublin	Jackie Mooney (Shamrock Rovers FC Dublin)	16
1965/1966	Waterford FC	Shamrock Rovers FC Dublin	Mick Lynch (Waterford FC)	17
1966/1967	Dundalk FC	Shamrock Rovers FC Dublin	Johnny Brooks (Sligo Rovers FC) Danny Hale (Dundalk FC)	15
1967/1968	Waterford FC	Shamrock Rovers FC Dublin	Carl Davenport (Cork Celtic FC) Ben Hannigan (Dundalk FC)	15
1968/1969	Waterford FC	Shamrock Rovers FC Dublin	Mick Leech (Shamrock Rovers FC Dublin)	19
1969/1970	Waterford FC	Bohemian FC Dublin	Brendan Bradley (Finn Harps FC Ballybofey)	18
1970/1971	Cork Hibernians FC	Limerick FC	Brendan Bradley (Finn Harps FC Ballybofey)	20
1971/1972	Waterford FC	Cork Hibernians FC	Alfie Hale (Waterford FC) Tony Marsden (Cork Hibernians FC)	22
1972/1973	Waterford FC	Cork Hibernians FC	Alfie Hale (Waterford FC) Terry Harkin (Finn Harps FC Ballybofey)	20
1973/1974	Cork Celtic FC	Finn Harps FC Ballybofey	Terry Flanagan (Bohemian FC Dublin) Turlough O'Connor (Bohemian FC Dublin)	18
1974/1975	Bohemian FC Dublin	Home Farm FC Dublin	Brendan Bradley (Finn Harps FC Ballybofey)	21
1975/1976	Dundalk FC	Bohemian FC Dublin	Brendan Bradley (Finn Harps FC Ballybofey)	29
1976/1977	Sligo Rovers FC	Dundalk FC	Syd Wallace (Waterford FC)	16
1977/1978	Bohemian FC Dublin	Shamrock Rovers FC Dublin	Turlough O'Connor (Bohemian FC Dublin)	24
1978/1979	Dundalk FC	Dundalk FC	John Delamere (Sligo Rovers FC, Shelbourne FC Dublin)	17

1979/1980	Limerick United FC	Waterford FC	Alan Campbell (Shamrock Rovers FC Dublin)	22
1980/1981	Athlone Town FC	Dundalk FC	Eugene Davis (Athlone Town FC)	23
1981/1982	Dundalk FC	Limerick United FC	Michael O'Connor (Athlone Town FC)	22
1982/1983	Athlone Town FC	Sligo Rovers FC	Noel Larkin (Athlone Town FC)	18
1983/1984	Shamrock Rovers FC Dublin	UCD	Alan Campbell (Shamrock Rovers FC Dublin)	24
1984/1985	Shamrock Rovers FC Dublin	Shamrock Rovers FC Dublin	Thomas Gaynor (Limerick City FC) Michael O'Connor (Athlone Town FC)	17
1985/1986	Shamrock Rovers FC Dublin	Shamrock Rovers FC Dublin	Tommy Gaynor (Limerick City FC)	15
1986/1987	Shamrock Rovers FC Dublin	Shamrock Rovers FC Dublin	Michael Byrne (Shamrock Rovers FC Dublin)	12
1987/1988	Dundalk FC	Dundalk FC	Jonathan Speak (Derry City FC)	24
1988/1989	Derry City FC	Derry City FC	William Robert Hamilton (NIR, Limerick City FC)	21
1989/1990	St. Patrick's Athletic FC Dublin	Bray Wanderers FC	Mark Ennis (St. Patrick's Athletic FC Dublin)	19
1990/1991	Dundalk FC	Galway United FC	Peter Hanrahan (Dundalk FC)	18
1991/1992	Shelbourne FC Dublin	Bohemian FC Dublin	John Caulfield (Cork City FC)	16
1992/1993	Cork City FC	Shelbourne FC Dublin	Pat Morley (Cork City FC)	20
1993/1994	Shamrock Rovers FC Dublin	Sligo Rovers FC	Stephen Geoghegan (Shamrock Rovers FC Dublin)	23
1994/1995	Dundalk FC	Derry City FC	John Caulfield (Cork City FC)	16
1995/1996	St. Patrick's Athletic FC Dublin	Shelbourne FC Dublin	Stephen Geoghegan (Shelbourne FC Dublin)	19
1996/1997	Derry City FC	Shelbourne FC Dublin	Anthony Cousins (Shamrock Rovers FC Dublin) Stephen Geoghegan (Shelbourne FC Dublin)	16
1997/1998	St. Patrick's Athletic FC Dublin	Cork City FC	Stephen Geoghegan (Shelbourne FC Dublin)	17
1998/1999	St. Patrick's Athletic FC Dublin	Bray Wanderers FC	Trevor Molloy (St. Patrick's Athletic FC Dublin)	15
1999/2000	Shelbourne FC Dublin	Shelbourne FC Dublin	Patrick Morley (Cork City FC)	20
2000/2001	Bohemian FC Dublin	Bohemian FC Dublin	Glen Crowe (Bohemian FC Dublin)	25
2001/2002	Shelbourne FC Dublin	Dundalk FC	Glen Crowe (Bohemian FC Dublin)	21
2002/2003	Bohemian FC Dublin	Derry City FC (2000)	Glen Crowe (Bohemian FC Dublin)	18
2003	Shelbourne FC Dublin	Longford Town FC	Jason Byrne (Shelbourne FC Dublin)	21
2004	Shelbourne FC Dublin	Longford Town FC	Jason Byrne (Shelbourne FC Dublin)	25
2005	Cork City FC	Drogheda United FC	Jason Byrne (Shelbourne FC Dublin)	22
2006	Shelbourne FC Dublin	Derry City FC	Jason Byrne (Shelbourne FC Dublin)	15
2007	Drogheda United FC	Cork City FC	Dave Mooney (Longford Town FC)	19
2008	Bohemian FC Dublin	Bohemian FC Dublin	Dave Mooney (Cork City FC) Mark Quigley (St. Patrick's Athletic FC Dublin) Mark Farren (Derry City FC)	15
2009	Bohemian FC Dublin	Sporting Fingal	Gary Michael Nolan Twigg (SCO, Shamrock Rovers FC Dublin)	24
2010	Shamrock Rovers FC Dublin	Sligo Rovers FC	Gary Michael Nolan Twigg (SCO, Shamrock Rovers FC Dublin)	20
2011	Shamrock Rovers FC Dublin	Sligo Rovers FC	Eamon Zayed (LBY, Derry City FC)	22
2012	Sligo Rovers FC	Derry City FC	Gary Michael Nolan Twigg (SCO, Shamrock Rovers FC Dublin)	22
2013	St. Patrick's Athletic FC Dublin	Sligo Rovers FC	Rory Christopher Patterson (NIR, Derry City FC)	18
2014	Dundalk FC	St. Patrick's Athletic FC Dublin	Patrick James Hoban (Dundalk FC) Christopher Joseph Fagan (St. Patrick's Athletic FC Dublin)	20
2015	Dundalk FC	Dundalk FC	Richard Patrick Towell (Dundalk FC)	25
2016	Dundalk FC	Cork City FC	Seán Patrick Maguire (Cork City FC)	18
2017	Cork City FC	Cork City FC	Seán Patrick Maguire (Cork City FC)	20
2018	Dundalk FC	Dundalk FC	Patrick James Hoban (Dundalk FC)	29
2019	Dundalk FC	Shamrock Rovers FC	Joseph Ogedi Junior Chukwuemka Ogedi-Uzokwe (ENG, Derry City FC)	14
2020	Shamrock Rovers FC Dublin		Patrick James Hoban (Dundalk FC)	10

Results

Round 1 [14-15.02.2020]
Cork City - Shelbourne FC 0-1(0-0)
Dundalk FC - Derry City 1-0(0-0)
St. Patrick's Athletic - Waterford FC 0-1(0-0)
Finn Harps - Sligo Rovers 1-0(0-0)
Bohemian FC - Shamrock Rovers 0-1(0-0)

Round 2 [21.02.2020]
Derry City - Finn Harps 1-1(0-1)
Shelbourne FC - Dundalk FC 1-2(0-2)
Sligo Rovers - St. Patrick's Athletic 0-2(0-2)
Waterford FC - Bohemian FC 0-2(0-2)
Shamrock Rovers - Cork City 6-0(2-0)

Round 3 [24.02.2020]
Waterford FC - Shamrock Rovers 0-2(0-2)
Bohemian FC - Sligo Rovers 2-0(1-0)
Dundalk FC - Cork City 3-0(1-0)
St. Patrick's Ath. - Derry City 0-2(0-0)[03.08.]
Finn Harps - Shelbourne FC 0-1(0-1) [04.08.]

Round 4 [28.02.2020]
Cork City - Finn Harps 1-0(0-0)
Derry City - Bohemian FC 2-0(0-0)
Shelbourne FC - St. Patrick's Athletic 1-0(1-0)
Shamrock Rovers - Dundalk FC 3-2(1-1)
Sligo Rovers - Waterford FC 2-1(0-1) [18.08.]

Round 5 [06-07.03.2020]
St. Patrick's Athletic - Cork City 1-0(0-0)
Waterford FC - Derry City 2-1(1-1)
Bohemian FC - Shelbourne FC 2-0(0-0)
Finn Harps - Dundalk FC 0-4(0-2)
Sligo Rovers - Shamrock Rovers 2-3(1-1)

Round 6 [31.07.-02.08.2020]
Derry City - Sligo Rovers 0-2(0-1)
Dundalk FC - St. Patrick's Athletic 1-1(1-1)
Shelbourne FC - Waterford FC 0-1(0-1)
Shamrock Rovers - Finn Harps 3-1(3-1)
Cork City - Bohemian FC 0-1(0-1)

Round 7 [07-09.08.2020]
Bohemian FC - Dundalk FC 2-1(2-1)
St. Patrick's Athletic - Finn Harps 2-0(2-0)
Waterford FC - Cork City 0-0
Sligo Rovers - Shelbourne FC 2-1(1-0)
Derry City - Shamrock Rovers 1-2(1-0)

Round 8 [14-16.08.2020]
Dundalk FC - Waterford FC 2-2(0-1)
Cork City - Sligo Rovers 3-0(1-0)
Finn Harps - Bohemian FC 0-1(0-1)
Shelbourne FC - Derry City 1-1(0-1)
St. Patrick's Athletic - Shamrock Rovers 0-0

Round 9 [21-23.08.2020]
Derry City - Cork City 3-1(0-1)
Shamrock Rovers - Shelbourne FC 0-0
Bohemian FC - St. Patrick's Athletic 2-0(2-0)
Sligo Rovers - Dundalk FC 3-1(1-0)
Waterford FC - Finn Harps 2-3(1-0)

Round 10 [04-07.09.2020]
Waterford FC - St. Patrick's Athletic 3-0(2-0)
Shamrock Rovers - Bohemian FC 1-0(1-0)
Shelbourne FC - Cork City 1-1(1-0)
Sligo Rovers - Finn Harps 3-1(1-0)
Derry City - Dundalk FC 1-2(1-2) [19.10.]

Round 11 [11-13.09.2020]
Bohemian FC - Waterford FC 0-2(0-2)
Dundalk FC - Shelbourne FC 3-2(2-2)
Cork City - Shamrock Rovers 0-3(0-2)
St. Patrick's Athletic - Sligo Rovers 0-0
Finn Harps - Derry City 0-0

Round 12 [18-21.09.2020]
Derry City - St. Patrick's Athletic 0-0
Sligo Rovers - Bohemian FC 0-1(0-0)
Shelbourne FC - Finn Harps 1-1(1-0)
Shamrock Rovers - Waterford FC 6-1(3-0)
Cork City - Dundalk FC 0-2(0-0) [13.10.]

Round 13 [25-27.09.2020]
Bohemian FC - Derry City 2-1(0-1)
Waterford FC - Sligo Rovers 1-0(1-0)
St. Patrick's Athletic - Shelbourne FC 2-0(1-0)
Finn Harps - Cork City 1-1(0-0)
Dundalk FC - Shamrock Rovers 0-4(0-3)

Round 14 [02-04.10.2020]
Derry City - Waterford FC 2-0(1-0)
Shamrock Rovers - Sligo Rovers 4-0(2-0)
Cork City - St. Patrick's Athletic 1-2(1-2)
Shelbourne FC - Bohemian FC 1-3(0-1)
Dundalk FC - Finn Harps 0-0

Round 15 [09-10.10.2020]
Sligo Rovers - Derry City 1-0(0-0) [29.09.]
Bohemian FC - Cork City 3-0(2-0)
Waterford FC - Shelbourne FC 0-1(0-0)
St. Patrick's Ath. - Dundalk 1-1(0-1) [01.11.]
Finn Harps - Shamrock Rov. 0-2(0-1) [01.11.]

Round 16 [16-18.10.2020]
Dundalk FC - Bohemian FC 0-0
Cork City - Waterford FC 0-0
Shelbourne FC - Sligo Rovers 1-0(1-0)
Finn Harps - St. Patrick's A. 3-2(2-1) [28.10.]
Shamrock Rov. - Derry City 2-0(0-0) [07.11.]

Round 17 [23-25.10.2020]
Derry City - Shelbourne FC 2-0(1-0)
Sligo Rovers - Cork City 2-1(1-0)
Bohemian FC - Finn Harps 0-2(0-1)
Waterford FC - Dundalk FC 1-0(0-0)
Shamrock Rov. - St. Patrick's Ath 0-0 [04.11.]

Round 18 [09.11.2020]
Cork City - Derry City 1-1(0-0)
Dundalk FC - Sligo Rovers 0-2(0-1)
St. Patrick's Athletic - Bohemian FC 1-2(1-1)
Shelbourne FC - Shamrock Rovers 0-2(0-1)
Finn Harps - Waterford FC 1-0(1-0)

Final Standings

			Total						**Home**						**Away**			
1. **Shamrock Rovers FC**	18	15	3	0	44	-	7	48	7	2	0	25	-	4	8	1	0	19	-	3
2. Bohemian FC Dublin	18	12	1	5	23	-	12	37	6	0	3	13	-	7	6	1	2	10	-	5
3. Dundalk FC	18	7	5	6	25	-	23	26	3	4	2	10	-	11	4	1	4	15	-	12
4. Sligo Rovers FC	18	8	1	9	19	-	23	25	6	0	3	15	-	11	2	1	6	4	-	12
5. Waterford FC	18	7	3	8	17	-	22	24	4	1	4	9	-	9	3	2	4	8	-	13
6. St. Patrick's Athletic FC Dublin	18	5	6	7	14	-	17	21	3	3	3	7	-	6	2	3	4	7	-	11
7. Derry City FC	18	5	5	8	18	-	18	20	4	2	3	12	-	8	1	3	5	6	-	10
8. Finn Harps FC Ballybofey	18	5	5	8	15	-	24	20	3	2	4	6	-	11	2	3	4	9	-	13
9. Shelbourne FC Dublin (*Relegation Play-offs*)	18	5	4	9	13	-	22	19	2	3	4	7	-	11	3	1	5	6	-	11
10. Cork City FC (*Relegated*)	18	2	5	11	10	-	30	11	2	2	5	6	-	10	0	3	6	4	-	20

Top goalscorers:

10	**Patrick James Hoban**	*Dundalk FC*
9	Jack Byrne	*Shamrock Rovers FC*
8	Graham Burke	*Shamrock Rovers FC*
8	Andre Antonio Wright	*Bohemian FC Dublin*

Relegation Play-offs [15.11.2020]

Shelbourne FC Dublin - Longford Town FC   0-1(0-0)

Longford Town FC promoted for the Premier Division 2021.

NATIONAL CUP
FAI Cup 2020

First Round [10-11.08.2020]					
Finn Harps FC Ballybofey - St. Patrick's Athletic FC	1-0(1-0)		Dundalk FC - Waterford FC		1-0(1-0)
Cork City FC - Longford Town FC	1-0 aet				

1/8-Finals [28-31.08.2020]				
Athlone Town FC - Wexford FC Crossabeg	5-3 aet	Cobh Ramblers FC - Dundalk FC	0-2
Galway United - Shelbourne FC Dublin	2-5	University College Dublin AFC - Sligo Rovers FC	1-3
Drogheda United FC - Derry City FC	0-2	Shamrock Rovers FC - Cork City FC	2-1
Bray Wanderers FC - Finn Harps FC Ballybofey	0-2	Bohemian FC Dublin - Cabinteely FC	2-0

Quarter-Finals [31.10./20.11./25.11.2020]				
Athlone Town FC - Shelbourne FC Dublin	4-1(2-1)	Bohemian FC Dublin - Dundalk FC	1-4(1-3)
Finn Harps FC Ballybofey - Shamrock Rovers FC	2-3(2-0)	Sligo Rovers FC - Derry City FC	0-0 aet; 3-1 pen

Semi-Finals [29.11.2020]				
Shamrock Rovers FC - Sligo Rovers FC	2-0(2-0)	Athlone Town FC - Dundalk FC	0-11(0-6)

Final

06.12.2020; Aviva Stadium, Dublin; Referee: Robert Harvey; Attendance: 0
Shamrock Rovers FC - Dundalk FC   **2-4(0-0,2-2)**

Shamrock Rovers: Alan Mannus, Roberto Lopes, Sean Kavanagh (84.Danny Lafferty), Liam Scales, Joey O'Brien (46.Lee Grace), Dylan Watts (83.Rhys Marshall), Ronan Finn (83.Greg Bolger), Aaron McEneff, Jack Byrne, Aaron Greene (106.Dean Williams), Graham Burke. Trainer: Stephen Bradley.

Dundalk FC: Gary Rogers, Sean Gannon (95.Darragh Leahy), Brian Gartland (106.Sean Hoare), Daniel Cleary, Cameron Dummigan, Andy Boyle, Chris Shields, Gregory Sloggett (87.Jordan Flores), Michael Duffy (111.Daniel Kelly), Patrick McEleney (95.John Mountney), David McMillan. Trainer: Filippo Giovagnoli (Italy).

Goals: 1-0 (49), 1-1 David McMillan (69), 1-2 David McMillan (72 penalty), 2-2 (74), 2-3 Sean Hoare (111), David McMillan (117).

THE CLUBS 2020

Bohemian Football Club Dublin

Founded:	06.09.1890	
Stadium:	Dalymount Park, Dublin (7,955)	
Trainer:	Keith Long	14.11.1973

Goalkeepers:	DOB	M	(s)	G
Stephen McGuinness	10.03.1995	10		
James Talbot	24.04.1997	8		
Defenders:	**DOB**	**M**	**(s)**	**G**
Michael Barker	16.08.1993	6	(2)	
Anto Breslin	13.02.1997	15		1
Dan Casey	29.10.1997	15		
Robert Cornwall	16.10.1994	14		
James Finnerty	01.02.1999	3	(1)	
Ciaran Kelly	04.07.1998	1	(1)	
Patrick Kirk	02.06.1998	4		
Andy Lyons	02.08.2000	14		
Luke Wade-Slater	02.03.1998	2	(1)	
Midfielders:	**DOB**	**M**	**(s)**	**G**
Keith Buckley	17.06.1992	17		1

Conor Levingston	21.01.1998	8	(2)	
Jonathan Lunney	02.02.1998	10	(3)	
Daniel Mandriou	20.10.1998	5	(4)	3
Jack Moylan	01.09.2001		(2)	
Kris Twardek (CAN)	08.03.1997	13		1
Keith Ward	12.10.1990	9	(6)	1
Forwards:	**DOB**	**M**	**(s)**	**G**
Dinny Corcoran	13.02.1989	1	(5)	
Dawson Devoy	20.11.2001	5	(5)	
Evan Ferguson	19.10.2004	1	(1)	
Daniel Grant	23.10.2000	14	(3)	7
Glen McAuley	24.02.2000	3	(2)	
Promise Omochere (NGA)	18.10.2000	5	(1)	
Ross Tierney	06.03.2001	1	(7)	
Andre Antonio Wright (ENG)	07.12.1996	14	(2)	8

Cork City Football Club

Founded:	1984	
Stadium:	Turners Cross, Cork (7,485)	
Trainer:	Neale Michael Charles Fenn (ENG)	18.01.1977
(09.10.2020)	Colin Healy	14.03.1980

Goalkeepers:	DOB	M	(s)	G
Liam Bossin	15.07.1996	7		
Mark McNulty	13.10.1980	11	(1)	
Defenders:	**DOB**	**M**	**(s)**	**G**
Alan Bennett	04.10.1981	8		
Charlie Fleming	09.04.1998	2	(2)	
Ronan Hurley	11.09.1999	7	(4)	
Uniss Kargbo	07.01.2002	6		
Jake O'Brien	15.05.2001	6	(2)	
Kevin O'Connor	07.05.1995	13		
Joseph Olowu (ENG)	27.11.1999	15		1
Joe Redmond	23.01.2000	5		
Rob Slevin	14.07.1998	5	(1)	
Kyron Stabana (ENG)	27.08.1998	4		
Midfielders:	**DOB**	**M**	**(s)**	**G**
Alec Byrne	21.06.1999	9	(2)	1
Cian Coleman	01.01.1997	14		

Deshane Dalling (ENG)	13.08.1998	12	(1)	2
Cory Galvin	10.01.1996	3	(4)	
Dale Holland	07.01.2000	3	(2)	
Sean Kennedy	23.07.2002		(1)	
Gearóid Morrissey	17.11.1991	13	(1)	1
Henry Ochieng (ENG)	11.11.1998	15	(2)	
Forwards:	**DOB**	**M**	**(s)**	**G**
Cian Bargary	22.11.2000	2	(4)	
Reyon Dillon (ENG)	03.11.1997	1	(2)	
Ricardo Dinanga	06.12.2001	1	(5)	1
Kit Elliott (ENG)	22.03.2002	4	(1)	1
Scott James Fenwick (ENG)	09.04.1990	3	(3)	
Dylan McGlade	22.04.1995	13	(4)	2
Cian Murphy	08.06.2000	2	(6)	
Daire O'Connor	15.04.1997	8	(1)	
Connor Mark Simpson (ENG)	24.01.2000	2	(3)	
Beineon Whitmarsh	11.01.2000	4	(2)	1

Derry City Football Club

Founded: 1928
Stadium: "Ryan McBride" Brandywell Stadium, Derry (3,700)
Trainer: Declan Devine (NIR)   15.09.1973

Goalkeepers:	DOB	M	(s)	G
Peter Cherrie (SCO)	01.10.1983	18		
Defenders:	**DOB**	**M**	**(s)**	**G**
Ronan Boyce	12.05.2001		(1)	
Darren Cole (SCO)	03.01.1992	8	(1)	1
Ciarán Coll	19.08.1991	16		
Ally Gilchrist (SCO)	03.03.1995	6		
Colm Horgan	02.07.1994	8	(3)	
Danny Lupano (BEL)	23.08.2000	4		
Mark McChrystal (NIR)	26.06.1984	1	(2)	
Jamie McDonagh (NIR)	08.05.1996	4		
Cameron McJannett (ENG)	06.09.1998	9		
Eoin Toal (NIR)	15.02.1999	18		
Midfielders:	**DOB**	**M**	**(s)**	**G**
Gerardo Alfredo Bruna Blanco (ARG)	29.01.1991	4	(3)	
Connor Clifford	01.10.1991	9	(2)	2
Jake Dunwoody (NIR)	28.09.1998	3	(3)	
Ciaron Harkin (NIR)	15.01.1996	9	(9)	
Stephen Mallon	07.02.1999	7	(7)	2
Jack Malone	05.04.2000	11	(7)	
Conor McCormack	18.05.1990	16	(1)	1
Joseph Thomson (SCO)	14.01.1997	8	(1)	1
Forwards:	**DOB**	**M**	**(s)**	**G**
James Oluwaseun Ewerogba Akintunde (ENG)	29.03.1996	7	(3)	4
Patrick Ferry	13.12.2002		(2)	
Walter Figueira (ENG)	17.03.1995	16	(2)	4
Adam Hammill (ENG)	25.01.1988	7	(4)	1
Adam Liddle (ENG)	26.10.1999		(4)	1
Ibrahim Meité (ENG)	26.08.1996	5	(3)	1
Tim Nilsen (NOR)	07.10.1992	4		

Dundalk Football Club

Founded: 1903
Stadium: Oriel Park, Dundalk (4,500)
Trainer: Vinny Perth   02.08.1976
(25.08.2020)   Filippo Giovagnoli (ITA)   01.12.1970

Goalkeepers:	DOB	M	(s)	G
Aaron McCarey	14.01.1992	5		
Gary Rogers	25.09.1981	13		
Defenders:	**DOB**	**M**	**(s)**	**G**
Andy Boyle	07.03.1991	11	(1)	1
Daniel Cleary	09.03.1996	12		1
Cameron Dummigan (NIR)	02.06.1996	6	(2)	
Sean Gannon	11.07.1991	12	(3)	
Brian Gartland	04.11.1986	7	(1)	1
Sean Hoare	15.03.1994	9	(1)	
Darragh Leahy	15.04.1998	5	(3)	
Dane Massey	17.04.1988	7	(1)	1
Andrew Quinn	24.01.2002	1		
Jamie Wynne	30.07.2001		(1)	
Midfielders:	**DOB**	**M**	**(s)**	**G**
Jordan Flores (ENG)	04.10.1995	10	(3)	3
John Mountney	22.02.1993	4	(7)	
Sean Murray	11.10.1993	5	(3)	1
William Patching (ENG)	18.10.1993	2	(5)	
Chris Shields	27.12.1990	16	(1)	
Gregory Sloggett	03.07.1996	10	(4)	2
Forwards:	**DOB**	**M**	**(s)**	**G**
Valentin Adedokun	14.02.2003		(1)	
Stefan Čolović (SRB)	16.04.1994	8	(6)	1
Michael Duffy (NIR)	28.07.1994	15	(1)	4
Joshua Gatt	29.08.1991	1	(1)	
Patrick Hoban	28.07.1991	13	(2)	10
Daniel Kelly	21.05.1996	8	(5)	
Georgie Kelly (NIR)	12.11.1996		(2)	
Lido Lotefa (CGO)	18.04.2000		(1)	
Patrick McEleney (NIR)	26.09.1992	4	(5)	
David McMillan	14.12.1988	5	(6)	
Nathan Oduwa (ENG)	05.03.1996	4	(6)	
Cameron Smith (SCO)	24.08.1995	5		

Finn Harps Football Club Ballybofey

Founded: 1954
Stadium: Finn Park, Ballybofey (6,000)
Trainer: Oliver Horgan   17.02.1968

Goalkeepers:	DOB	M	(s)	G
Mark McGinley	26.03.1990	18		
Defenders:	**DOB**	**M**	**(s)**	**G**
Jamie Browne (NIR)	10.09.2000		(1)	
Adrian Delap	30.11.1998	1	(8)	1
Stephen Folan	14.01.1992	12		1
Shane McEleney (NIR)	31.01.1991	16	(1)	
Mark Russell (SCO)	22.03.1996	15	(2)	3
Kosovar Sadiki (CAN)	27.08.1998	16		
Sam Todd (NIR)	28.04.1998	13	(3)	
David Webster	07.04.1990	16		1
Midfielders:	**DOB**	**M**	**(s)**	**G**
Ryan Connolly	13.01.1992	15	(3)	2
Mark Coyle	13.02.1997	8	(6)	
Rafael Cretaro	15.10.1981	3	(9)	1
Leo Donnellan	07.07.1998	10	(1)	
Adam Foley	11.12.1989	3	(6)	2
Gareth Harkin (NIR)	19.12.1987	6	(7)	
Ruairí Harkin (NIR)	11.10.1989	4	(4)	
Barry McNamee (NIR)	17.02.1992	13	(1)	1
Tony McNamee	16.08.1993	5	(7)	
Karl O'Sullivan	31.10.1999	13	(1)	2
Forwards:	**DOB**	**M**	**(s)**	**G**
Stephen Doherty	22.06.2000		(3)	
Alexander Kogler (AUT)	01.02.1998	11	(3)	1
Cameron Saul (ENG)	28.06.1995		(1)	
Jack Serrant-Green (ENG)	02.02.1994		(2)	

Shamrock Rovers Football Club Dublin

Founded: 1899
Stadium: Tallaght Stadium, Dublin (6,000)
Trainer: Stephen Bradley   19.11.1984

Goalkeepers:	DOB	M	(s)	G
Alan Mannus (NIR)	19.05.1982	18		
Defenders:	**DOB**	**M**	**(s)**	**G**
Lee Grace	01.12.1992	17		1
Sean Kavanagh	20.01.1994	3	(4)	
Danny Lafferty (NIR)	18.05.1989	6	(5)	1
Roberto Lopes (CPV)	17.06.1992	13	(2)	3
Rhys Marshall (NIR)	16.01.1995	4	(9)	1
Max Murphy	02.06.2001		(2)	1
Joey O'Brien	17.02.1986	13	(1)	1
Liam Scales	08.08.1998	11	(5)	1
Midfielders:	**DOB**	**M**	**(s)**	**G**
Greg Bolger	09.09.1988	3		
Jack Byrne	24.04.1996	16	(1)	9
Ronan Finn	21.12.1987	16	(1)	1
Brandon Kavanagh	21.09.2000		(2)	
Aaron McEneff	09.07.1995	17		3
Darragh Nugent	01.03.2001		(2)	
Gary O'Neill	27.01.1995	10	(2)	
Dylan Watts	11.04.1997	9	(9)	3
Forwards:	**DOB**	**M**	**(s)**	**G**
Graham Burke	21.09.1993	12	(2)	8
Neil Farrugia	19.05.1999	9	(5)	1
Rory Gaffney	23.10.1989	1	(5)	
Aaron Greene	02.01.1990	17	(1)	7
Thomas Oluwa	08.02.2001		(4)	
Dean Williams	09.02.2000	3	(9)	1

Shelbourne Football Club Dublin

Founded: 1895
Stadium: Tolka Park, Dublin (3,600)
Trainer: Ian Morris   27.02.1987

Goalkeepers:	DOB	M	(s)	G
Jack Brady	17.12.1996	8		
Colin McCabe	06.01.1997	10		
Defenders:	**DOB**	**M**	**(s)**	**G**
Daniel Byrne	07.05.1993	11	(2)	1
Luke Byrne	08.07.1993	12		
Lorcan Fitzgerald	03.01.1989	2		
Aidan Friel (NIR)	15.01.1991	8		
Daniel O'Reilly	11.04.1995	6	(3)	
Midfielders:	**DOB**	**M**	**(s)**	**G**
Oscar Brennan	17.03.1996	7	(3)	
Ryan Brennan	11.11.1991	12	(4)	3
Mark Byrne	09.11.1988	5	(5)	
Gary Deegan	28.09.1987	18		3

	DOB	M	(s)	G
Denzil Fernandes	21.02.1998	8	(2)	
Brian McManus	29.11.2001	1	(1)	
Alex O'Hanlon	24.04.1996	16	(1)	
Georgie Poynton	28.08.1997	10	(4)	2
Sean Quinn	05.02.1999	12	(4)	
Dayle Rooney	24.02.1998	14	(3)	1
Forwards:	**DOB**	**M**	**(s)**	**G**
Alex Cetiner	20.07.2001	1	(2)	
Aaron Dobbs	06.01.1999	6	(11)	
Shane Farrell	26.06.2000	4	(7)	
Jaze Kabia	08.07.2000	4	(7)	1
Ciarán Kilduff	29.09.1988	14	(3)	2
Karl Sheppard	14.02.1991	9	(2)	

Sligo Rovers Football Club

Founded: 1928
Stadium: The Showgrounds, Sligo (5,500)
Trainer: Liam Buckley   14.04.1960

Goalkeepers:	DOB	M	(s)	G
Edward McGinty	05.08.1999	18		
Defenders:	**DOB**	**M**	**(s)**	**G**
Lewis Banks (ENG)	14.04.1997	9	(3)	
Kyle Callan-McFadden	20.04.1995	13		1
Regan Donelon	17.04.1996	12		1
John Dunleavy	03.07.1991	1		
Danny Kane	23.04.1997	4		
Scott Lynch	21.04.2000		(1)	
John Mahon	26.11.1999	3		
Niall Morahan	30.05.2000	17		1
Sigitas Olberkis (LTU)	19.04.1997	2	(1)	
Teemu Penninkangas (FIN)	24.07.1992	12	(1)	

Midfielders:	DOB	M	(s)	G
Garry Buckley	19.08.1993	11	(1)	
Mark Byrne	12.08.2000		(2)	
David Cawley	17.09.1991	15	(1)	1
Alex Cooper (SCO)	04.11.1991	3	(9)	1
Darragh Noone	28.04.1997	9	(7)	
John Russell	18.05.1985		(2)	
Will Seymore (USA)	29.02.1992	11	(2)	
Forwards:	**DOB**	**M**	**(s)**	**G**
Darren Collins	29.09.2000		(1)	
Ronan Coughlan	02.10.1995	18		6
Ryan De Vries (NZL)	14.09.1991	12	(2)	3
Jesse Devers	11.01.1997	15	(3)	2
Ronan Murray	12.09.1991	2	(6)	1
Joseph Chukwuemka Ogedi-Uzokwe (ENG)	03.03.1994	11	(1)	2

St. Patrick's Athletic Football Club Dublin

Founded: 1929
Stadium: Richmond Park, Dublin (2,800)
Trainer: Stephen O'Donnell   15.01.1986

Goalkeepers:	DOB	M	(s)	G
Brendan Clarke	17.09.1985	18		
Defenders:	**DOB**	**M**	**(s)**	**G**
Ian Bermingham	08.01.1989	8	(3)	
Lee Desmond	22.01.1995	17	(1)	
Rory Feely	03.01.1997	17		1
Shane Griffin	08.09.1994	14		
Jason McClelland	03.05.1997	7	(8)	
Luke McNally	20.09.1999	18		1
Deivids Titovs (LVA)	05.01.2000	4		
Oliver Younger (ENG)	14.11.1999	2		
Midfielders:	**DOB**	**M**	**(s)**	**G**
Darragh Burns (NIR)	08.06.2002		(6)	
James Doona	15.01.1998	1	(6)	

	DOB	M	(s)	G
Chris Forrester	17.12.1992	15	(2)	2
Jordan Lewis Gibson (ENG)	28.02.1998	12	(2)	2
Jamie Lennon	09.05.1998	14	(2)	
Darragh Markey	23.05.1997	2	(8)	
Ben McCormack	04.04.2003		(2)	
Dan Ward (ENG)	30.09.1997	4	(2)	
Forwards:	**DOB**	**M**	**(s)**	**G**
Robbie Benson	07.05.1992	16		2
Dean Clarke	29.03.1993	3	(1)	
Ronan Hale	08.09.1998	2	(1)	1
Georgie Kelly (NIR)	12.11.1996	12		3
Billy King (SCO)	12.05.1994	10	(4)	1
Martin Rennie (SCO)	09.05.1994	2	(8)	
Jake Walker	19.08.2000		(1)	

Waterford Football Club Dublin

Founded: 1930
Stadium: Waterford Regional Sports Centre, Waterford (5,500)
Trainer: Alan Reynolds   12.06.1974
(08.07.2020) John Joseph Sheridan   01.10.1964
(12.09.2020) Fran Rockett   02.09.1983

Goalkeepers:	DOB	M	(s)	G
Brian Murphy	07.05.1983	16		
Tadhg Ryan	01.03.1997	2	(1)	
Defenders:	**DOB**	**M**	**(s)**	**G**
Sam Bone (ENG)	06.02.1998	8		1
Andre Maurice Keith Burley (SKN)	10.09.1999	3		
Jake Davidson (SCO)	06.10.2000	12		
Kevin O'Connor	07.05.1995	5		1
Niall O'Keeffe	01.01.2000	6	(4)	
Akinwale Odimayo (ENG)	28.11.1999	4		
Darragh Power	29.12.2000	3	(4)	
Tunmise Sobowale	19.03.1999	11	(2)	
Tyreke Wilson	02.12.1998	18		1
Midfielders:	**DOB**	**M**	**(s)**	**G**
Scott Allardice (SCO)	31.03.1998	2	(1)	

	DOB	M	(s)	G
Ali Coote (SCO)	11.06.1998	17		3
William Fitzgerald	19.05.1999	5	(6)	
Shane Griffin	31.12.1999	5	(5)	1
John Martin	05.01.1999	9	(2)	4
Robert McCourt	06.04.1998	17		
Alex Phelan	25.10.1991		(1)	
Robert James Weir (NIR)	09.12.1988	14		
Forwards:	**DOB**	**M**	**(s)**	**G**
Kurtis Byrne	09.04.1990	9	(4)	1
Graham Cummins	29.12.1987	1	(1)	
Will Longbottom (ENG)	12.12.1998	1	(9)	
Daryl Murphy	15.03.1983	2	(2)	
Michael O'Connor	31.07.1998	10		3
Matty Smith (SCO)	13.03.1997	18		2
Dean Walsh	28.04.1997		(6)	

SECOND LEVEL
League of Ireland First Division 2020

1.	Drogheda United FC (*Promoted*)	18	12	3	3	39	-	17	39
2.	Bray Wanderers FC (*Promotion Play-offs*)	18	12	2	4	30	-	13	38
3.	University College Dublin AFC (*Promotion Play-offs*)	18	9	3	6	44	-	29	30
4.	Longford Town FC (*Promotion Play-offs*)	18	9	2	7	26	-	23	29
5.	Galway United FC (*Promotion Play-offs*)	18	7	6	5	26	-	19	27
6.	Cobh Ramblers FC	18	8	3	7	22	-	20	27
7.	Cabinteely FC	18	8	2	8	22	-	33	26
8.	Shamrock Rovers FC Dublin II	18	4	3	11	22	-	28	15
9.	Athlone Town FC	18	4	3	11	23	-	40	15
10.	Wexford FC Crossabeg	18	2	2	14	10	-	45	8

Promotion Play-offs (1st / 2nd Level)

Semi-Finals [31.10.2020]	Bray Wanderers FC - Galway United FC	0-1(0-0)
	University College Dublin AFC - Longford Town FC	2-3(1-0,1-1)

Finals [06.11.2020]	Galway United FC - **Longford Town FC**	1-2(0-1)

NATIONAL TEAM

INTERNATIONAL MATCHES
(16.07.2020 – 15.07.2021)

03.09.2020	Sofia	Bulgaria - Republic of Ireland	1-1(0-0)	(UNL)
06.09.2020	Dublin	Republic of Ireland - Finland	0-1(0-0)	(UNL)
08.10.2020	Bratislava	Slovakia - Republic of Ireland	0-0; 4-2 on penalties	(ECQPO)
11.10.2020	Dublin	Republic of Ireland - Wales	0-0	(UNL)
14.10.2020	Helsinki	Finland - Republic of Ireland	1-0(0-0)	(UNL)
12.11.2020	London	England - Republic of Ireland	3-0(2-0)	(F)
15.11.2020	Cardiff	Wales - Republic of Ireland	1-0(0-0)	(UNL)
18.11.2020	Dublin	Republic of Ireland - Bulgaria	0-0	(UNL)
24.03.2021	Beograd	Serbia - Republic of Ireland	3-2(1-1)	(WCQ)
27.03.2021	Dublin	Republic of Ireland - Luxembourg	0-1(0-0)	(WCQ)
30.03.2021	Debrecen	Qatar - Republic of Ireland	1-1(0-1)	(F)
03.06.2021	Andorra la Vella	Andorra - Republic of Ireland	1-4(0-0)	(F)
08.06.2021	Budapest	Hungary - Republic of Ireland	0-0	(F)

03.09.2020 BULGARIA - REPUBLIC OF IRELAND 1-1(0-0) 2nd UEFA Nations League B, Group 4
Nationalen Stadion "Vasil Levski", Sofia; Referee: Manuel Schüttengruber (Austria); Attendance: 0
IRL: Darren Edward Andrew Randolph, Enda John Stevens, Shane Patrick Michael Duffy (Cap), John Egan, Matthew James Doherty, James Patrick McCarthy (70.Robert Brady), Conor Hourihane, Jeffrey Patrick Hendrick, Callum Joshua Ryan O'Dowda (74.Callum Jack Robinson), Aaron Anthony Connolly, Adam Uche Idah (77.Shane Patrick Long). Trainer: Stephen Kenny.
Goal: Shane Patrick Michael Duffy (90+3).

06.09.2020 REPUBLIC OF IRELAND - FINLAND 0-1(0-0) 2nd UEFA Nations League B, Group 4
Aviva Stadium, Dublin; Referee: Fabio Maresca (Italy); Attendance: 0
IRL: Darren Edward Andrew Randolph, Enda John Stevens, Shane Patrick Michael Duffy (Cap), John Egan, Matthew James Doherty, Harry Nicholas Arter, Robert Brady, Callum Joshua Ryan O'Dowda (59.Callum Jack Robinson), Jayson Patrick Molumby, Aaron Anthony Connolly (77.James Joseph McClean), Adam Uche Idah (66.David James McGoldrick). Trainer: Stephen Kenny.

08.10.2020 SLOVAKIA - REPUBLIC OF IRELAND 0-0; 4-2 on penalties 16th EC. Qualifiers Play-offs, Semi-Finals
Štadión Tehelné pole, Bratislava; Referee: Clément Turpin (France); Attendance: 0
IRL: Darren Edward Andrew Randolph, Enda John Stevens, Shane Patrick Michael Duffy (Cap), John Egan, Matthew James Doherty, James Patrick McCarthy (61.Alan James Browne), Conor Hourihane, James Joseph McClean (60.Robert Brady), Jeffrey Patrick Hendrick, David James McGoldrick (112.Shane Patrick Long), Callum Jack Robinson (99.Callum Joshua Ryan O'Dowda). Trainer: Stephen Kenny.
Penalties: Conor Hourihane, Robert Brady, Alan James Browne (saved), Matthew James Doherty (missed).

11.10.2020 REPUBLIC OF IRELAND - WALES 0-0 2nd UEFA Nations League B, Group 4
Aviva Stadium, Dublin; Referee: Anastasios Sidiropoulos (Greece); Attendance: 0
IRL: Darren Edward Andrew Randolph, Enda John Stevens, Kevin Long (25.Cyrus Sylvester Frederick Christie), Shane Patrick Michael Duffy (Cap), Matthew James Doherty, Conor Hourihane, James Joseph McClean [*sent off 84*], Robert Brady (73.Daryl Jeremiah Horgan), Jeffrey Patrick Hendrick, Jayson Patrick Molumby (90.Joshua Jon Cullen), Shane Patrick Long (74.Seán Patrick Maguire). Trainer: Stephen Kenny.

14.10.2020 FINLAND - REPUBLIC OF IRELAND 1-0(0-0) 2nd UEFA Nations League B, Group 4
Olympiastadion, Helsinki; Referee: Lionel Tschudi (Switzerland); Attendance: 7,900
IRL: Darren Edward Andrew Randolph, Enda John Stevens, Shane Patrick Michael Duffy (Cap), Matthew James Doherty, Dara Joseph O'Shea, Daryl Jeremiah Horgan (75.Ronan Curtis), Conor Hourihane, Jeffrey Patrick Hendrick (75.Adam Uche Idah), Seán Patrick Maguire (53.Robert Brady), Aaron Anthony Connolly, Jayson Patrick Molumby (83.Jason Paul Knight). Trainer: Stephen Kenny.

12.11.2020   **ENGLAND - REPUBLIC OF IRELAND**   3-0(2-0)   Friendly International
Wembley Stadium, London; Referee: Carlos del Cerro Grande (Spain); Attendance: 0
IRL: Darren Edward Andrew Randolph, Shane Patrick Michael Duffy (Cap), John Egan (14.Dara Joseph O'Shea), Cyrus Sylvester Frederick Christie (61.Kevin Long), Matthew James Doherty, Daryl Jeremiah Horgan (61.Robert Brady), Jeffrey Patrick Hendrick, Callum Joshua Ryan O'Dowda (61.James Joseph McClean), Alan James Browne, Adam Uche Idah (71.Ronan Curtis), Conor Hourihane 71.71.Jayson Patrick Molumby). Trainer: Stephen Kenny.

15.11.2020   **WALES - REPUBLIC OF IRELAND**   1-0(0-0)   2nd UEFA Nations League B, Group 4
Cardiff City Stadium, Cardiff; Referee: Petr Ardeleánu (Czech Republic); Attendance: 0
IRL: Darren Edward Andrew Randolph, Kevin Long, Shane Patrick Michael Duffy (Cap) , Matthew James Doherty, Dara Joseph O'Shea (81.Callum Joshua Ryan O'Dowda), James Joseph McClean, Daryl Jeremiah Horgan (59.Jason Paul Knight), Robert Brady (82.Jack Byrne), Jeffrey Patrick Hendrick [*sent off 90+4*], Jayson Patrick Molumby (76.Conor Hourihane), Adam Uche Idah (76.James Steven Collins). Trainer: Stephen Kenny.

18.11.2020   **REPUBLIC OF IRELAND - BULGARIA**   0-0   2nd UEFA Nations League B, Group 4
Aviva Stadium, Dublin; Referee: Lawrence Visser (Belgium); Attendance: 0
IRL: Darren Edward Andrew Randolph, Kevin Long, Shane Patrick Michael Duffy (Cap), Dara Joseph O'Shea, Conor Hourihane, Robert Brady (80.Jack Byrne), Ryan Phelim Manning (87.Cyrus Sylvester Frederick Christie), Daryl Jeremiah Horgan (67.Joshua Jon Cullen), Ronan Curtis (87.Troy Daniel Parrott), James Steven Collins (87.Seán Patrick Maguire), Jason Paul Knight. Trainer: Stephen Kenny.

24.03.2021   **SERBIA - REPUBLIC OF IRELAND**   3-2(1-1)   22nd FIFA WC.Qualifiers
Stadion „Rajko Mitić", Belgrade; Referee: Davide Massa (Italy); Attendance: 0
IRL: Mark Travers, Séamus Coleman (Cap), Enda John Stevens, Ciaran Clark (79.Robert Brady), Matthew James Doherty, Dara Joseph O'Shea, Alan James Browne (79.James Steven Collins), Joshua Jon Cullen, Jayson Patrick Molumby (61.Jeffrey Patrick Hendrick), Callum Jack Robinson (79.James Joseph McClean), Aaron Anthony Connolly (67.Shane Patrick Long). Trainer: Stephen Kenny.
Goals: Alan James Browne (18), James Steven Collins (86).

27.03.2021   **REPUBLIC OF IRELAND - LUXEMBOURG**   0-1(0-0)   22nd FIFA WC.Qualifiers
Aviva Stadium, Dublin; Referee: Fran Jović (Croatia); Attendance: 0
IRL: Gavin Okeroghene Bazunu, Séamus Coleman (Cap), Enda John Stevens, Ciaran Clark (61.James Joseph McClean), Matthew James Doherty (46.Robert Brady), Dara Joseph O'Shea, Alan James Browne, Joshua Jon Cullen (88.Jayson Patrick Molumby), Jason Paul Knight, Callum Jack Robinson (73.Shane Patrick Long), James Steven Collins (88.Troy Daniel Parrott). Trainer: Stephen Kenny.

30.03.2021   **QATAR - REPUBLIC OF IRELAND**   1-1(0-1)   Friendly International
Nagyerdei Stadion, Debrecen (Hungary); Referee: Balázs Berke (Hungary); Attendance: 0
IRL: Gavin Okeroghene Bazunu, Séamus Coleman (Cap), James Joseph McClean (84.Ryan Phelim Manning), Shane Patrick Michael Duffy, Cyrus Sylvester Frederick Christie, Dara Joseph O'Shea, Robert Brady (22.Troy Daniel Parrott), Jeffrey Patrick Hendrick (84.Alan James Browne), Jayson Patrick Molumby (84.Joshua Jon Cullen), Shane Patrick Long (57.Callum Jack Robinson), Daryl Jeremiah Horgan (57.Jason Paul Knight). Trainer: Stephen Kenny.
Goal: James Joseph McClean (4).

03.06.2021   **ANDORRA - REPUBLIC OF IRELAND**   1-4(0-0)   Friendly International
Estadi Nacional, Andorra la Vella; Referee: Xavier Estrada Fernández (Spain); Attendance: 320
IRL: Gavin Okeroghene Bazunu, James Joseph McClean (86.Ryan Phelim Manning), John Egan (Cap), Matthew James Doherty, Dara Joseph O'Shea (86.Shane Patrick Michael Duffy), Conor Hourihane (87.Harry Nicholas Arter), Joshua Jon Cullen, Jason Paul Knight, James Steven Collins (66.Adam Uche Idah), Ronan Curtis (66.Daryl Jeremiah Horgan), Troy Daniel Parrott (82.Jamie McGrath). Trainer: Stephen Kenny.
Goals: Troy Daniel Parrott (58, 61), Jason Paul Knight (84), Daryl Jeremiah Horgan (89).

08.06.2021   **HUNGARY - REPUBLIC OF IRELAND**   0-0   Friendly International
"Szusza Ferenc" Stadion, Budapest; Referee: Daniel Stefański (Poland); Attendance: 7,396
IRL: Gavin Okeroghene Bazunu (46.Caoimhín Odhrán Kelleher), James Joseph McClean (85.Ryan Phelim Manning), Shane Patrick Michael Duffy, John Egan (Cap), Matthew James Doherty, Dara Joseph O'Shea, Conor Hourihane (56.Jayson Patrick Molumby), Joshua Jon Cullen, Jason Paul Knight (89.Chiedozie Ogbene), Adam Uche Idah (89.James Steven Collins), Troy Daniel Parrott (56.Daryl Jeremiah Horgan). Trainer: Stephen Kenny.

NATIONAL TEAM PLAYERS
(16.07.2020 – 15.07.2021)

Name	DOB	Caps	Goals	2020/2021:	Club
Goalkeepers					
Gavin Okeroghene BAZUNU	20.02.2002	4	0	2021: 31.05.2021->	*Rochdale AFC (ENG)* *Manchester City FC (ENG)*
Caoimhín Odhrán KELLEHER	23.11.1998	1	0	2021:	*Liverpool FC (ENG)*
Darren Edward Andrew RANDOLPH	12.05.1987	50	0	2020:	*West Ham United FC London (ENG)*
Mark TRAVERS	18.05.1999	3	0	2021:	*AFC Bournemouth (ENG)*
Defenders					
Cyrus Sylvester Frederick CHRISTIE	30.09.1992	28	2	2020/2021:	*Nottingham Forest FC (ENG)*
Ciaran CLARK	26.09.1989	36	2	2021:	*Newcastle United FC (ENG)*
Séamus COLEMAN	11.10.1988	59	1	2020/2021:	*Everton FC Liverpool (ENG)*
Matthew James DOHERTY	16.01.1992	20	1	2020/2021:	*Wolverhampton Wanderers FC (ENG)*
Shane Patrick Michael DUFFY	01.01.1992	44	4	2020/2021: 07.05.2021->	*Celtic Glasgow FC (SCO)* *Brighton & Hove Albion FC (ENG)*
John EGAN	20.10.1992	14	0	2020/2021:	*Sheffield United FC (ENG)*
Kevin Finbarr LONG	18.08.1990	17	1	2020:	*Burnley FC (ENG)*
Ryan Phelim MANNING	14.06.1986	4	0	2020/2021:	*Swansea City AFC (WAL)*
Dara Joseph O'SHEA	04.03.1999	9	0	2020/2021:	*West Bromwich Albion FC (ENG)*
Midfielders					
Harry Nicholas ARTER	28.12.1989	18	0	2020: 22.09.2020->	*AFC Bournemouth (ENG)* *Nottingham Forest FC (ENG)*
Robert BRADY	14.01.1992	57	8	2020/2021:	*Burnley FC (ENG)*
Alan James BROWNE	15.04.1995	14	1	2020/2021:	*Preston North End FC (ENG)*
Jack BYRNE	24.04.1996	4	0	2020:	*Shamrock Rovers FC Dublin*
Ronan CURTIS	29.03.1996	7	0	2020/2021:	*Portsmouth FC (ENG)*
Jeffrey Patrick HENDRICK	31.01.1992	62	2	2020/2021:	*Burnley FC (ENG)*
Daryl Jeremiah HORGAN	10.08.1992	14	1	2020/2021:	*Wycombe Wanderers FC (ENG)*
Conor HOURIHANE	02.02.1991	26	1	2020/2021:	*Aston Villa FC Birmingham (ENG)*
Jason Paul KNIGHT	13.02.2001	7	1	2020/2021:	*Derby County FC (ENG)*
James Patrick McCARTHY	12.11.1990	43	0	2020:	*Crystal Palace FC London (ENG)*
James Joseph McCLEAN	22.04.1989	82	11	2020/2021:	*Stoke City FC (ENG)*
Jamie McGRATH	30.09.1996	1	0	2021:	*St. Mirren FC Paisley (SCO)*
Jayson Patrick MOLUMBY	06.08.1999	9	0	2020: 05.01.2021-> 31.05.2021->	*Brighton & Hove Albion FC (ENG)* *Preston North End FC (ENG)* *Brighton & Hove Albion FC (ENG)*
Callum Joshua Ryan O'DOWDA	23.04.1995	23	0	2020:	*Bristol City FC (ENG)*
Chiedozie OGBENE	01.05.1997	1	0	2021:	*Rotherham United FC (ENG)*
Enda John STEVENS	09.07.1990	21	0	2020/2021:	*Sheffield United FC (ENG)*
Forwards					
James Steven COLLINS	01.12.1990	10	2	2020/2021:	*Luton Town FC (ENG)*
Aaron Anthony CONNOLLY	28.01.2000	6	0	2020/2021:	*Brighton & Hove Albion FC (ENG)*
Joshua Jon CULLEN	07.04.1996	9	0	2020/2021:	*RSC Anderlecht Bruxelles (BEL)*
Adam Uche IDAH	11.02.2001	7	0	2020/2021:	*Norwich City FC (ENG)*
Shane Patrick LONG	22.01.1987	88	17	2020: 01.02.2021->	*Southampton FC (ENG)* *AFC Bournemouth (ENG)*
Seán Patrick MAGUIRE	01.05.1994	11	1	2020:	*Preston North End FC (ENG)*
David James McGOLDRICK	29.11.1987	14	1	2020:	*Sheffield United FC (ENG)*
Troy Daniel PARROTT	04.02.2002	6	2	2020/2021: 01.02.2021-> 31.05.2021->	*Millwall FC London (ENG)* *Ipswich Town FC (ENG)* *Tottenham Hotspur FC London (ENG)*
Callum Jack ROBINSON	02.02.1995	18	1	2020: 09.09.2020->	*Sheffield United FC (ENG)* *West Bromwich Albion FC (ENG)*
Trainer					
Stephen KENNY [from 04.04.2020]		30.10.1971		13 M; 1 W; 6 D; 6 L; 8-13	

ROMANIA

The Country:
România (Romania)
Capital: Bucureşti
Surface: 238,397 km²
Inhabitants: 19,186,201 [2021]
Time: UTC+2

The FA:
Federaţia Română de Fotbal
Casa Fotbalului, Str. Serg. Şerbanică Vasile 12, 22186 Bucureşti
Tel: +40 21 302 9150
Founded: 00.00.1909
Member of FIFA since: 1923
Member of UEFA since: 1954
Website: www.frf.ro

NATIONAL TEAM RECORDS

RECORDS
First international match:	08.06.1922, Beograd:	Yugoslavia – Romania 1-2
Most international caps:	Dorinel Ionel Munteanu	- 134 caps (1991-2007)
Most international goals:	Gheorghe Hagi	- 35 goals / 125 caps (1983-2000)
	Adrian Mutu	- 35 goals / 77 caps (2000-2013)

UEFA EUROPEAN CHAMPIONSHIP		FIFA WORLD CUP		OLYMPIC TOURNAMENTS	
1960	Qualifiers	1930	Final Tournament (Group Stage)	1908	-
1964	Qualifiers	1934	Final Tournament (1st Round)	1912	-
1968	Qualifiers	1938	Final Tournament (1st Round)	1920	-
1972	Qualifiers	1950	Did not enter	1924	-
1976	Qualifiers	1954	Qualifiers	1928	1/8 - Finals
1980	Qualifiers	1958	Qualifiers	1936	Did not enter
1984	Final Tournament (Group Stage)	1962	*Withdrew*	1948	Did not enter
1988	Qualifiers	1966	Qualifiers	1952	Preliminary Round
1992	Qualifiers	1970	Final Tournament (Group Stage)	1956	Did not enter
1996	Final Tournament (Group Stage)	1974	Qualifiers	1960	Qualifiers
2000	Final Tournament (Quarter-Finals)	1978	Qualifiers	1964	Quarter-Finals
2004	Qualifiers	1982	Qualifiers	1968	Qualifiers
2008	Final Tournament (Group Stage)	1986	Qualifiers	1972	Qualifiers
2012	Qualifiers	1990	Final Tournament (2nd Round of 16)	1976	Qualifiers
2016	Final Tournament (Group Stage)	1994	Final Tournament (Quarter-Finals)	1980	Qualifiers
2020	Qualifiers	1998	Final Tournament (2nd Round of 16)	1984	Qualifiers
		2002	Qualifiers	1988	Qualifiers
		2006	Qualifiers	1992	Qualifiers
		2010	Qualifiers	1996	Qualifiers
		2014	Qualifiers	2000	Qualifiers
		2018	Qualifiers	2004	Qualifiers
				2008	Qualifiers
				2012	Qualifiers
				2016	Qualifiers

UEFA NATIONS LEAGUE
2018/2019	League C (promoted to League B)
2020/2021	League B

FIFA CONFEDERATIONS CUP 1992-2017
None

ROMANIAN CLUB HONOURS IN EUROPEAN CLUB COMPETITIONS:

European Champion Clubs.Cup (1956-1992) / UEFA Champions League (1993-2021)		
FC Steaua Bucureşti	1	1985/1986
Fairs Cup (1858-1971) / UEFA Cup (1972-2009) / UEFA Europa League (2010-2021)		
None		
UEFA Super Cup (1972-2020)		
FC Steaua Bucureşti	1	1986
European Cup Winners.Cup 1961-1999		
None		

*defunct competition

NATIONAL COMPETITIONS
TABLE OF HONOURS

	CHAMPIONS*	CUP WINNERS	BEST GOALSCORERS	
1909/1910	Olympia Bucureşti	-	-	
1910/1911	Olympia Bucureşti	-	-	
1911/1912	United Ploieşti	-	-	
1912/1913	Colentina AC Bucureşti	-	-	
1913/1914	Colentina AC Bucureşti	-	-	
1914/1915	Româno-Americană Bucureşti	-	-	
1915/1916	Prahova Ploieşti	-	-	
1916/1917	*No competition*	-	-	
1917/1918	*No competition*	-	-	
1918/1919	*No competition*	-	-	
1919/1920	AS Venus Bucureşti	-	-	
1920/1921	AS Venus Bucureşti	-	-	
1921/1922	Chinezul Timişoara	-	-	
1922/1923	Chinezul Timişoara	-	-	
1923/1924	Chinezul Timişoara	-	-	
1924/1925	Chinezul Timişoara	-	-	
1925/1926	Chinezul Timişoara	-	-	
1926/1927	Chinezul Timişoara	-	-	
1927/1928	CS Colţea Braşov	-	-	
1928/1929	AS Venus Bucureşti	-	-	
1929/1930	FC Juventus Bucureşti	-	-	
1930/1931	UD Reşiţa	-	-	
1931/1932	AS Venus Bucureşti	-	-	
1932/1933	FC Ripensia Timişoara	-	-	
1933/1934	AS Venus Bucureşti	FC Ripensia Timişoara	Ştefan Dobay (FC Ripensia Timişoara)	25
1934/1935	FC Ripensia Timişoara	ACS CFR Bucureşti	Ştefan Dobay (FC Ripensia Timişoara)	24
1935/1936	FC Ripensia Timişoara	FC Ripensia Timişoara	Ştefan Barbu (ACS CFR Bucureşti)	23
1936/1937	AS Venus Bucureşti	FC Rapid Bucureşti	Ştefan Dobay (FC Ripensia Timişoara) Traian Iordache (Unirea Tricolor Bucureşti)	21
1937/1938	FC Ripensia Timişoara	FC Rapid Bucureşti	Árpád Thierjung (Chinezul Timişoara)	22
1938/1939	AS Venus Bucureşti	FC Rapid Bucureşti	Adalbert Marksteiner [Béla Marosvári] (FC Ripensia Timişoara)	21
1939/1940	AS Venus Bucureşti	FC Rapid Bucureşti	Ştefan Auer II [István Avar] (FC Rapid Bucureşti)	21
1940/1941	Unirea Tricolor Bucureşti	FC Rapid Bucureşti	Ion Bogdan (FC Rapid Bucureşti) Valeriu Niculescu (Unirea Tricolor Bucureşti)	21
1941/1942	*No competition*	FC Rapid Bucureşti	-	
1942/1943	*No competition*	CFR Turnu Severin	-	
1943/1944	*No competition*	*No competition*	-	
1944/1945	*No competition*	*No competition*	-	
1945/1946	*No competition*	*No competition*	-	
1946/1947	IT Arad	*No competition*	Ladislau Bonyhádi (IT Arad)	26
1947/1948	IT Arad	IT Arad	Ladislau Bonyhádi (IT Arad)	49
1948/1949	IC Oradea	CSCA Bucureşti	Gheorghe Váczi (IC Oradea)	24
1950	Flamura Roşie Arad	CCA Bucureşti	Andrei Rădulescu (Locomotiva Bucureşti)	18
1951	CCA Bucureşti	CCA Bucureşti	Gheorghe Váczi (Progresul Oradea)	23
1952	CCA Bucureşti	CCA Bucureşti	Titus Ozon (CS Dinamo Bucureşti)	17
1953	CCA Bucureşti	Flamura Roşie Arad	Titus Ozon (CS Dinamo Bucureşti)	12
1954	Flamura Roşie Arad	Metalul Reşiţa	Alexandru Ene I (CS Dinamo Bucureşti)	20
1955	CS Dinamo Bucureşti	CCA Bucureşti	Ion Ciosescu (Ştiinţa Timişoara)	18
1956	CCA Bucureşti	Progresul Oradea	Ion Alecsandrescu (CCA Bucureşti)	18
1957/1958	FC Petrolul Ploieşti	CS Ştiinţa Timişoara	Ion Ciosescu (CS Ştiinţa Timişoara)	21
1958/1959	FC Petrolul Ploieşti	CS Dinamo Bucureşti	Gheorghe Ene (CS Rapid Bucureşti)	17
1959/1960	CCA Bucureşti	Progresul Bucureşti	Gheorghe Constantin (CCA Bucureşti)	20
1960/1961	CCA Bucureşti	Arieşul Turda	Gheorghe Constantin (CCA Bucureşti)	22
1961/1962	CS Dinamo Bucureşti	CSA Steaua Bucureşti	Gheorghe Constantin (CSA Steaua Bucureşti)	24
1962/1963	CS Dinamo Bucureşti	FC Petrolul Ploieşti	Ion Gheorghe Ionescu (CS Rapid Bucureşti)	20
1963/1964	CS Dinamo Bucureşti	CS Dinamo Bucureşti	Constantin Frăţilă (CS Dinamo Bucureşti) Cornel Pavlovici (CSA Steaua Bucureşti)	19
1964/1965	CS Dinamo Bucureşti	Ştiinţa Cluj	Mihai Adam (Ştiinţa Cluj)	18
1965/1966	FC Petrolul Ploieşti	CSA Steaua Bucureşti	Ion Gheorghe Ionescu (CS Rapid Bucureşti)	24
1966/1967	CS Rapid Bucureşti	CSA Steaua Bucureşti	Ion Oblemenco (Universitatea Craiova)	17
1967/1968	CSA Steaua Bucureşti	CS Dinamo Bucureşti	Mihai Adam (CS Universitatea Cluj)	15
1968/1969	UT Arad	CSA Steaua Bucureşti	Florea Dumitrache (CS Dinamo Bucureşti)	22
1969/1970	UT Arad	CSA Steaua Bucureşti	Ion Oblemenco (CS Universitatea Craiova)	19
1970/1971	CS Dinamo Bucureşti	CSA Steaua Bucureşti	Constantin Moldoveanu (Politehnica Iaşi) Florea Dumitrache (CS Dinamo Bucureşti) Gheorghe Tătaru (CSA Steaua Bucureşti)	15
1971/1972	FC Argeş Piteşti	CS Rapid Bucureşti	Ion Oblemenco (CS Universitatea Craiova)	20
1972/1973	CS Dinamo Bucureşti	CS Chimia Râmnicu Vâlcea	Ion Oblemenco (CS Universitatea Craiova)	21
1973/1974	CS Universitatea Craiova	CSM Jiul Petroşani	Mihai Adam (CFR Cluj-Napoca)	23
1974/1975	CS Dinamo Bucureşti	CS Rapid Bucureşti	Dudu Georgescu (CS Dinamo Bucureşti)	33

Season	Champion	Runner-up	Top scorer	Goals
1975/1976	CSA Steaua Bucureşti	CSA Steaua Bucureşti	Dudu Georgescu (CS Dinamo Bucureşti)	31
1976/1977	CS Dinamo Bucureşti	CS Universitatea Craiova	Dudu Georgescu (CS Dinamo Bucureşti)	47
1977/1978	CSA Steaua Bucureşti	CS Universitatea Craiova	Dudu Georgescu (CS Dinamo Bucureşti)	24
1978/1979	FC Argeş Piteşti	CSA Steaua Bucureşti	Marin Radu II (FC Argeş Piteşti)	22
1979/1980	CS Universitatea Craiova	CS Politehnica Timişoara	Septimiu Câmpeanu II (CS Universitatea Cluj)	24
1980/1981	CS Universitatea Craiova	CS Universitatea Craiova	Marin Radu II (FC Argeş Piteşti)	28
1981/1982	CS Dinamo Bucureşti	CS Dinamo Bucureşti	Anghel Iordănescu (CSA Steaua Bucureşti)	20
1982/1983	CS Dinamo Bucureşti	CS Universitatea Craiova	Petre Grosu (FC Bihor Oradea)	20
1983/1984	CS Dinamo Bucureşti	CS Dinamo Bucureşti	Marcel Coraş (CF Sportul Studenţesc Bucureşti)	20
1984/1985	CSA Steaua Bucureşti	CSA Steaua Bucureşti	Gheorghe Hagi (CF Sportul Studenţesc Bucureşti)	20
1985/1986	CSA Steaua Bucureşti	CS Dinamo Bucureşti	Gheorghe Hagi (CF Sportul Studenţesc Bucureşti)	31
1986/1987	CSA Steaua Bucureşti	CSA Steaua Bucureşti	Rodion Gorun Cămătaru (CS Dinamo Bucureşti)	44
1987/1988	CSA Steaua Bucureşti	CSA Steaua Bucureşti	Victor Piţurcă (CSA Steaua Bucureşti)	34
1988/1989	CSA Steaua Bucureşti	CSA Steaua Bucureşti	Dorin Mateuţ (CS Dinamo Bucureşti)	43
1989/1990	CS Dinamo Bucureşti	CS Dinamo Bucureşti	Gavril Balint (CSA Steaua Bucureşti)	19
1990/1991	CS Universitatea Craiova	CS Universitatea Craiova	Ovidiu Cornel Hanganu (FC Corvinul Hunedoara)	24
1991/1992	CS Dinamo Bucureşti	CSA Steaua Bucureşti	Gábor Gerstenmájer (CS Dinamo Bucureşti)	21
1992/1993	CSA Steaua Bucureşti	FC Universitatea Craiova	Ilie Dumitrescu (CSA Steaua Bucureşti)	24
1993/1994	CSA Steaua Bucureşti	ACF Gloria Bistriţa	Gheorghe Craioveanu (FC Universitatea Craiova)	21
1994/1995	CSA Steaua Bucureşti	FC Petrolul Ploieşti	Gheorghe Craioveanu (FC Universitatea Craiova)	27
1995/1996	CSA Steaua Bucureşti	CSA Steaua Bucureşti	Ion Vlădoiu (CSA Steaua Bucureşti)	25
1996/1997	CSA Steaua Bucureşti	CSA Steaua Bucureşti	Sabin Ilie (CSA Steaua Bucureşti)	31
1997/1998	CSA Steaua Bucureşti	UFC Rapid Bucureşti	Constantin Barbu (FC Argeş Piteşti) Ion Vasile Oană (ACF Gloria Bistriţa)	22
1998/1999	UFC Rapid Bucureşti	FC Steaua Bucureşti	Ioan Viorel Ganea (ACF Gloria Bistriţa)	28
1999/2000	FC Dinamo Bucureşti	FC Dinamo Bucureşti	Marian Savu (FC Naţional Bucureşti)	20
2000/2001	FC Steaua Bucureşti	FC Dinamo Bucureşti	Marius Constantin Niculae (FC Dinamo Bucureşti)	20
2001/2002	FC Dinamo Bucureşti	UFC Rapid Bucureşti	Cătălin Cursaru (FCM Bacău)	17
2002/2003	UFC Rapid Bucureşti	FC Dinamo Bucureşti	Claudiu Nicu Răducanu (FC Steaua Bucureşti)	21
2003/2004	FC Dinamo Bucureşti	FC Dinamo Bucureşti	Ionel Daniel Dănciulescu (FC Dinamo Bucureşti)	21
2004/2005	FC Steaua Bucureşti	FC Dinamo Bucureşti	Gheorghe Bucur (CF Sportul Studenţesc Bucureşti) Claudiu Iulian Niculescu (FC Dinamo Bucureşti)	21
2005/2006	FC Steaua Bucureşti	UFC Rapid Bucureşti	Ionuţ Costinel Mazilu (CF Sportul Studenţesc Bucureşti)	22
2006/2007	FC Dinamo Bucureşti	UFC Rapid Bucureşti	Claudiu Iulian Niculescu (FC Dinamo Bucureşti)	18
2007/2008	FC CFR 1907 Cluj-Napoca	FC CFR 1907 Cluj-Napoca	Ionel Daniel Dănciulescu (FC Dinamo Bucureşti)	21
2008/2009	FC Unirea Urziceni	FC CFR 1907 Cluj-Napoca	Gheorghe Bucur (FC Timişoara) Florin Constantin Costea (FC Universitatea Craiova)	17
2009/2010	FC CFR 1907 Cluj-Napoca	FC CFR 1907 Cluj-Napoca	Andrei Cristea (FC Dinamo Bucureşti)	16
2010/2011	ASC Oţelul Galaţi	FC Steaua Bucureşti	Ianis Alin Zicu (FC Timişoara)	18
2011/2012	FC CFR 1907 Cluj-Napoca	FC Dinamo Bucureşti	Wesley Lopes da Silva (BRA, FC Vaslui)	27
2012/2013	FC Steaua Bucureşti	FC Petrolul Ploieşti	Raul Andrei Rusescu (FC Steaua Bucureşti)	21
2013/2014	FC Steaua Bucureşti	AFC Astra Giurgiu	Liviu Ion Antal (FC Vaslui)	14
2014/2015	FC Steaua Bucureşti	FC Steaua Bucureşti	Grégory Tadé (FRA, FC CFR 1907 Cluj-Napoca)	18
2015/2016	AFC Astra Giurgiu	FC CFR 1907 Cluj-Napoca	Adrian Ioan Hora (CS Pandurii Târgu Jiu)	19
2016/2017	FC Viitorul Constanţa	FC Voluntari	Azdren Llullaku (ALB, CS Gaz Metan Mediaş)	16
2017/2018	FC CFR 1907 Cluj-Napoca	CS Universitatea Craiova	Marius George Ţucudean (FC Viitorul Constanţa, FC CFR 1907 Cluj-Napoca) Harlem-Eddy Gnohéré (FRA, FCSB Bucureşti)	15
2018/2019	FC CFR 1907 Cluj-Napoca	FC Viitorul Constanţa	Marius George Ţucudean (FC CFR 1907 Cluj-Napoca)	18
2019/2020	FC CFR 1907 Cluj-Napoca	SC FCSB Bucureşti	Gabriel Cristian Iancu (FC Viitorul Constanţa)	18
2020/2021	FC CFR 1907 Cluj-Napoca	CS Universitatea Craiova	Florin Lucian Tănase (SC FCSB Bucureşti)	24

* Romanian Football Championship (1909–1921), Divizia A (1921–2006), Liga I (since 2006).

Club name changements:

FC Rapid Bucureşti = ACS CFR Bucureşti (1923-1936), FC Rapid Bucureşti (1936-1945), CFR Bucureşti (1945-1949), Locomotiva Bucureşti (1949-1958), CS Rapid Bucureşti (1958-1992), UFC Rapid Bucureşti (1992-2016), Academia Rapid Bucureşti (2017), FC Rapid Bucureşti (since 2018).

UT Arad = IT Arad (1945–1949), Flamura Roşie Arad (1950–1957), UT Arad (1958–2014), UTA Bătrâna Doamnă Arad (2014–2017), UT Arad (since 2017).

ACS CAO Oradea = CA Oradea (1919-1940), Nagyváradi AC (1940-1944), Libertatea Oradea (1945-1948), IC Oradea (1948-1951), Progresul Oradea (1951-1958), CS Oradea (1958-1961), Crişana Oradea (1961-1963).

FCSB Bucureşti = ASA Bucureşti (1947-1948), CSCA Bucureşti (1948-1950), CCA Bucureşti (1950-1961), CSA Steaua Bucureşti (1961-1998), FC Steaua Bucureşti (1998-2017), FCSB Bucureşti (since 2017).

FC Dinamo Bucureşti = CS Dinamo Bucureşti (1945-1992), FC Dinamo Bucureşti (since 1992).

ACS Poli Timişoara = SS Politehnica Timişoara (1921-1948), CSU Timişoara (1948-1950), CS Ştiinţa Timişoara (1950-1966), CS Politehnica Timişoara (1966-1969), FC Ripensia Timişoata (1969), CS Politehnica Timişoara (1969-1992), FC Politehnica Timişoara (1992-2012), ACS Poli Timişoara (since 2012).

FC Universitatea Cluj-Napoca = Universitatea Cluj (1919-1948), CSU Cluj (1948-1949), Ştiinţa Cluj (1949-1966), CS Universitatea Cluj (1966-1974), CS Universitatea Cluj-Napoca (1974-1992), FC Universitatea Cluj-Napoca (since 1992).

CS Universitatea Craiova = CSU Craiova (1948-1950), Ştiinţa Craiova (1950-1966), CS Universitatea Craiova (1966-1992), FC Universitatea Craiova (1992-2011), CS Universitatea Craiova (since 2013).

NATIONAL CHAMPIONSHIP
Liga I 2020/2021
(21.08.2020 – 27.05.2021)

Regular Season - Results

Round 1 [21-24.08.2020]
FC Argeş - FC Botoşani 2-3(0-1)
Astra Giurgiu - FCSB Bucureşti 0-3(0-2)
Viitorul Constanţa - UTA Arad 1-1(1-1)
Sepsi OSK - U Craiova 0-1(0-0)
Politehnica Iaşi - Chindia Târgovişte 1-0(1-0)
FC Academica - CFR Cluj 1-2(0-1)
FC Voluntari - Gaz Metan 2-1(1-0)
Dinamo Bucureşti - Hermannstadt 1-1(0-1)

Round 2 [28-31.08.2020]
Gaz Metan - FC Argeş 2-0(1-0)
UTA Arad - FC Voluntari 0-0
Hermannstadt - FC Academica 2-2(1-0)
CFR Cluj - Sepsi OSK 0-0
FC Botoşani - Politehnica Iaşi 4-0(0-0)
U Craiova - Astra Giurgiu 2-0(2-0)
FCSB Bucureşti - Viitorul Constanţa 3-0(1-0)
Chindia Târgovişte - Dinamo Bucur. 1-0(1-0)

Round 3 [11-14.09.2020]
FC Argeş - UTA Arad 1-1(0-1)
Dinamo Bucureşti - FC Botoşani 1-1(0-1)
FC Academica - Chindia Târgovişte 0-0
Politehnica Iaşi - Gaz Metan 1-4(1-2)
FC Voluntari - FCSB Bucureşti 2-1(1-0)
Astra Giurgiu - Sepsi OSK 2-2(1-1)
CFR Cluj - Hermannstadt 1-0(0-0)
Viitorul Constanţa - U Craiova 1-4(1-1)

Round 4 [18-21.09.2020]
Chindia Târgovişte - Hermannstadt 1-3(1-2)
Astra Giurgiu - CFR Cluj 0-2(0-1)
Sepsi OSK - Viitorul Constanţa 1-1(0-1)
U Craiova - FC Voluntari 2-1(1-0)
FC Botoşani - FC Academica 0-0
UTA Arad - Politehnica Iaşi 2-3(1-1)
FCSB Bucureşti - FC Argeş 3-0(2-0)
Gaz Metan - Dinamo Bucureşti 1-3(0-0)

Round 5 [25-28.09.2020]
FC Voluntari - Sepsi OSK 1-2(1-0)
FC Argeş - U Craiova 1-2(0-2)
FC Academica - Gaz Metan 2-0(0-0)
Viitorul Constanţa - Astra Giurgiu 4-1(3-0)
CFR Cluj - Chindia Târgovişte 0-0
Politehnica Iaşi - FCSB Bucureşti 5-2(3-1)
Hermannstadt - FC Botoşani 2-1(1-1)
Dinamo Bucureşti - UTA Arad 0-1(0-1)

Round 6 [02-05.10.2020]
U Craiova - Politehnica Iaşi 1-0(0-0)
Sepsi OSK - FC Argeş 1-0(0-0)
Astra Giurgiu - FC Voluntari 2-3(0-1)
FCSB Bucureşti - Dinamo Bucureşti 3-2(2-2)
FC Botoşani - Chindia Târgovişte 0-2(0-0)
Gaz Metan - Hermannstadt 1-1(1-0)
Viitorul Constanţa - CFR Cluj 1-1(1-0)
UTA Arad - FC Academica 0-0

Round 7 [16-19.10.2020]
FC Argeş - Astra Giurgiu 1-0(0-0)
Chindia Târgovişte - Gaz Metan 1-0(0-0)
Politehnica Iaşi - Sepsi OSK 1-4(0-3)
CFR Cluj - FC Botoşani 2-1(1-1)
Hermannstadt - UTA Arad 1-1(1-0)
Dinamo Bucureşti - U Craiova 0-1(0-1)
FC Voluntari - Viitorul Constanţa 0-2(0-0)
FC Academica - FCSB Bucureşti 0-2(0-0)

Round 8 [23-26.10.2020]
Gaz Metan - FC Botoşani 1-2(0-1)
U Craiova - FC Academica 0-1(0-0)
UTA Arad - Chindia Târgovişte 1-0(0-0)
Astra Giurgiu - Politehnica Iaşi 4-0(0-0)
Sepsi OSK - Dinamo Bucureşti 2-0(1-0)
Viitorul Constanţa - FC Argeş 2-2(0-1)
FC Voluntari - CFR Cluj 0-1(0-0)
FCSB Bucureşti - Hermannstadt 5-0(4-0)

Round 9 [30.10.-02.11.2020]
FC Argeş - FC Voluntari 2-1(1-0)
FC Academica - Sepsi OSK 2-0(2-0)
FC Botoşani - UTA Arad 2-3(2-1)
Hermannstadt - U Craiova 0-1(0-1)
Politehnica Iaşi - Viitorul Const. 0-3 *awarded*
CFR Cluj - Gaz Metan 1-2(0-1)
Chindia Târgovişte - FCSB Bucureşti 0-2(0-1)
Dinamo Buc. - Astra Giurgiu 1-1(0-0) [14.11.]

Round 10 [06-09.11.2020]
Astra Giurgiu - FC Academica 0-2(0-0)
U Craiova - Chindia Târgovişte 0-1(0-1)
FC Voluntari - Politehnica Iaşi 4-0(2-0)
Sepsi OSK - Hermannstadt 1-1(0-0)
FCSB Bucureşti - FC Botoşani 4-1(1-1)
FC Argeş - CFR Cluj 0-2(0-2)
Viitorul Constanţa - Dinamo Bucur. 2-1(0-0)
UTA Arad - Gaz Metan 1-3(1-2)

Round 11 [20-23.11.2020]
Politehnica Iaşi - FC Argeş 1-1(1-0)
Dinamo Bucureşti - FC Voluntari 3-0(0-0)
FC Academica - Viitorul Constanţa 1-0(1-0)
FC Botoşani - U Craiova 0-0
Hermannstadt - Astra Giurgiu 0-1(0-0)
CFR Cluj - UTA Arad 0-1(0-0)
Chindia Târgovişte - Sepsi OSK 1-2(1-0)
Gaz Metan - FCSB Bucureşti 2-3(1-2)

Round 12 [04-07.12.2020]
FC Voluntari - FC Academica 3-3(2-2)
FC Argeş - Dinamo Bucureşti 0-1(0-1)
Sepsi OSK - FC Botoşani 2-2(0-1)
FCSB Bucureşti - UTA Arad 3-0(0-0)
Politehnica Iaşi - CFR Cluj 0-2(0-1)
Astra Giurgiu - Chindia Târgovişte 0-0
U Craiova - Gaz Metan 3-1(2-0)
Viitorul C. - Hermannstadt 2-1(1-1) [10.01.21]

Round 13 [11-14.12.2020]
FC Botoşani - Astra Giurgiu 1-1(0-0)
Dinamo Bucureşti - Politehnica Iaşi 4-1(1-1)
Gaz Metan - Sepsi OSK 0-3(0-2)
Chindia Târgovişte - Viitorul Const. 1-1(0-1)
FC Academica - FC Argeş 1-0(0-0)
Hermannstadt - FC Voluntari 3-2(1-2)
CFR Cluj - FCSB Bucureşti 2-0(1-0)
UTA Arad - U Craiova 1-2(1-2)

Round 14 [15-18.12.2020]
Astra Giurgiu - Gaz Metan 3-0(3-0)
Viitorul Constanţa - FC Botoşani 1-2(0-1)
Politehnica Iaşi - FC Academica 0-0
FC Argeş - Hermannstadt 2-2(0-1)
FC Voluntari - Chindia Târgovişte 0-2(0-0)
Sepsi OSK - UTA Arad 3-0(1-0)
Dinamo Bucureşti - CFR Cluj 0-2(0-2)
U Craiova - FCSB Bucureşti 0-2(0-1)

Round 15 [19-22.12.2020]
Chindia Târgovişte - FC Argeş 2-2(2-1)
Gaz Metan - Viitorul Constanţa 1-0(0-0)
Hermannstadt - Politehnica Iaşi 0-1(0-0)
FC Botoşani - FC Voluntari 1-1(0-0)
FC Academica - Dinamo Bucureşti 1-1(0-0)
UTA Arad - Astra Giurgiu 0-6(0-2)
FCSB Bucureşti - Sepsi OSK 1-1(1-1)
CFR Cluj - U Craiova 0-0

Round 16 [12-15.01.2021]
Gaz Metan - FC Voluntari 2-0(0-0)
U Craiova - Sepsi OSK 0-0
Chindia Târgovişte - Politehnica Iaşi 1-1(1-0)
Hermannstadt - Dinamo Bucureşti 0-2(0-2)
FC Botoşani - FC Argeş 0-1(0-0)
CFR Cluj - FC Academica 3-1(1-0)
UTA Arad - Viitorul Constanţa 0-0
FCSB Bucureşti - Astra Giurgiu 3-0(0-0)

Round 17 [16-19.01.2021]
Dinamo Buc. - Chindia Târgovişte 0-1(0-0)
FC Argeş - Gaz Metan 1-1(1-0)
Sepsi OSK - CFR Cluj 0-1(0-0)
FC Academica - Hermannstadt 0-0
Politehnica Iaşi - FC Botoşani 0-1(0-0)
Astra Giurgiu - U Craiova 1-1(1-1)
FC Voluntari - UTA Arad 0-1(0-0)
Viitorul Constanţa - FCSB Bucureşti 2-2(1-0)

Round 18 [22-25.01.2021]
Chindia Târgovişte - FC Academica 2-1(2-0)
FCSB Bucureşti - FC Voluntari 2-1(1-0)
Sepsi OSK - Astra Giurgiu 4-1(3-0)
UTA Arad - FC Argeş 1-2(0-0)
U Craiova - Viitorul Constanţa 1-1(1-0)
Gaz Metan - Politehnica Iaşi 2-1(2-0)
FC Botoşani - Dinamo Bucureşti 4-0(3-0)
Hermannstadt - CFR Cluj 1-3(1-1)

Round 19 [26-28.01.2021]
Viitorul Constanţa - Sepsi OSK 3-3(2-1)
FC Voluntari - U Craiova 1-1(1-1)
FC Argeş - FCSB Bucureşti 0-0
FC Academica - FC Botoşani 2-1(1-1)
Politehnica Iaşi - UTA Arad 1-2(1-0)
Dinamo Bucureşti - Gaz Metan 2-1(2-1)
Hermannstadt - Chindia Târgovişte 1-1(1-0)
CFR Cluj - Astra Giurgiu 1-1(0-1)

Round 20 [29.01.-01.02.2021]
U Craiova - FC Argeş 1-1(0-0)
Gaz Metan - FC Academica 1-1(0-0)
Sepsi OSK - FC Voluntari 2-2(2-0)
FCSB Bucureşti - Politehnica Iaşi 3-1(1-0)
FC Botoşani - Hermannstadt 1-0(1-0)
Astra Giurgiu - Viitorul Constanţa 1-1(0-1)
UTA Arad - Dinamo Bucureşti 0-1(0-1)
Chindia Târgovişte - CFR Cluj 0-1(0-0)

Round 21 [02-04.02.2021]
Politehnica Iaşi - U Craiova 0-3(0-2)
Hermannstadt - Gaz Metan 1-1(0-0)
FC Voluntari - Astra Giurgiu 1-3(0-2)
Dinamo Bucureşti - FCSB Bucureşti 0-1(0-1)
FC Academica - UTA Arad 0-3(0-1)
Chindia Târgovişte - FC Botoşani 2-3(2-2)
CFR Cluj - Viitorul Constanţa 2-1(1-0)
FC Argeş - Sepsi OSK 1-1(0-1) [16.02.2021]

Round 22 [05-08.02.2021]
Sepsi OSK - Politehnica Iași 3-3(3-1)
Astra Giurgiu - FC Argeș 0-2(0-0)
U Craiova - Dinamo București 1-0(1-0)
UTA Arad - Hermannstadt 1-1(0-0)
Gaz Metan - Chindia Târgoviște 1-0(1-0)
FCSB București - FC Academica 0-1(0-0)
Viitorul Constanța - FC Voluntari 0-1(0-1)
FC Botoșani - CFR Cluj 2-1(2-1)

Round 23 [12-15.02.2021]
FC Argeș - Viitorul Constanța 1-0(0-0)
Chindia Târgoviște - UTA Arad 1-1(1-0)
Dinamo București - Sepsi OSK 0-0
Politehnica Iași - Astra Giurgiu 2-3(1-3)
FC Academica - U Craiova 0-0
Hermannstadt - FCSB București 1-0(1-0)
FC Botoșani - Gaz Metan 2-1(0-0)
CFR Cluj - FC Voluntari 0-0

Round 24 [19-22.02.2021]
FC Voluntari - FC Argeș 0-1(0-1)
U Craiova - Hermannstadt 1-0(1-0)
Sepsi OSK - FC Academica 0-0
FCSB București - Chindia Târgoviște 1-0(1-0)
Gaz Metan - CFR Cluj 0-1(0-0)
Astra Giurgiu - Dinamo București 2-0(2-0)
UTA Arad - FC Botoșani 0-0
Viitorul C. - Politehnica Iași 1-2(0-0) [08.04.]

Round 25 [26.02.-01.03.2021]
Dinamo București - Viitorul Const. 0-5(0-3)
Gaz Metan - UTA Arad 1-2(0-1)
FC Academica - Astra Giurgiu 1-1(1-0)
Chindia Târgoviște - U Craiova 1-0(0-0)
Hermannstadt - Sepsi OSK 1-2(1-1)
FC Botoșani - FCSB București 0-2(0-0)
Politehnica Iași - FC Voluntari 0-2(0-1)
CFR Cluj - FC Argeș 5-0(2-0)

Round 26 [05-08.03.2021]
Sepsi OSK - Chindia Târgoviște 0-1(0-0)
Viitorul Constanța - FC Academica 1-1(0-1)
U Craiova - FC Botoșani 1-0(1-0)
UTA Arad - CFR Cluj 0-1(0-0)
Astra Giurgiu - Hermannstadt 2-1(1-1)
FCSB București - Gaz Metan 1-0(0-0)
FC Argeș - Politehnica Iași 2-1(1-0)
FC Voluntari - Dinamo București 1-1(0-1)

Round 27 [12-15.03.2021]
Gaz Metan - U Craiova 0-2(0-0)
FC Academica - FC Voluntari 0-1(0-1)
Hermannstadt - Viitorul Constanța 0-0
UTA Arad - FCSB București 0-1(0-1)
Chindia Târgoviște - Astra Giurgiu 0-1(0-0)
CFR Cluj - Politehnica Iași 4-0(2-0)
FC Botoșani - Sepsi OSK 1-2(0-1)
Dinamo București - FC Argeș 1-2(0-1)

Round 28 [16-21.03.2021]
U Craiova - UTA Arad 2-0(0-0)
Viitorul Constanța - Chindia Târgoviște 0-0
Astra Giurgiu - FC Botoșani 1-1(0-1)
FC Voluntari - Hermannstadt 0-0(0-0)
FCSB București - CFR Cluj 3-0(0-0)
FC Argeș - FC Academica 1-1(0-0)
Politehnica Iași - Dinamo București 1-0(0-0)
Sepsi OSK - Gaz Metan 1-1(1-0)

Round 29 [02-05.04.2021]
FC Academica - Politehnica Iași 2-1(0-1)
Gaz Metan - Astra Giurgiu 0-0
Hermannstadt - FC Argeș 4-1(1-1)
FC Botoșani - Viitorul Constanța 1-0(0-0)
UTA Arad - Sepsi OSK 2-0(1-0)
FCSB București - U Craiova 0-0
Chindia Târgoviște - FC Voluntari 1-0(1-0)
CFR Cluj - Dinamo București 1-0(0-0)

Round 30 [09-12.04.2021]
Astra Giurgiu - UTA Arad 0-0
Dinamo București - FC Academica 1-3(0-3)
FC Argeș - Chindia Târgoviște 3-1(0-1)
FC Voluntari - FC Botoșani 1-1(0-1)
Sepsi OSK - FCSB București 1-1(0-1)
U Craiova - CFR Cluj 0-0
Politehnica Iași - Hermannstadt 1-0(1-0)
Viitorul Constanța - Gaz Metan 0-2(0-2)

Final Standings

								Home				Away			
					Total										
1.	SC FCSB București	30	20	5	5	57 - 22	65	12	2	1	35 - 7	8	3	4	22 - 15
2.	FC CFR 1907 Cluj-Napoca	30	19	7	4	42 - 15	64	8	5	2	22 - 7	11	2	2	20 - 8
3.	CS Universitatea Craiova	30	16	10	4	33 - 14	58	8	4	3	15 - 8	8	6	1	18 - 6
4.	ACS Sepsi OSK Sfântu Gheorghe	30	10	15	5	43 - 31	45	4	8	3	21 - 15	6	7	2	22 - 16
5.	FC Academica Clinceni	30	10	14	6	30 - 26	44	6	5	4	13 - 12	4	9	2	17 - 14
6.	FC Botoșani	30	11	9	10	39 - 36	42	6	4	5	19 - 14	5	5	5	20 - 22
7.	FC Argeș Pitești	30	10	10	10	33 - 41	40	5	6	4	18 - 17	5	4	6	15 - 24
8.	AFC Chindia Târgoviște	30	10	9	11	24 - 26	39	5	4	6	15 - 18	5	5	5	9 - 8
9.	AFC Astra Giurgiu	30	9	11	10	38 - 39	38	4	6	5	18 - 18	5	5	5	20 - 21
10.	FC UT Arad	30	9	10	11	26 - 36	37	2	5	8	9 - 20	7	5	3	17 - 16
11.	CS Gaz Metan Mediaș	30	9	6	15	33 - 41	33	5	3	7	15 - 19	4	3	8	18 - 22
12.	FC Voluntari	30	8	8	14	32 - 40	32	4	4	7	17 - 20	4	4	7	15 - 20
13.	FC Viitorul Constanța	30	6	13	11	36 - 37	31	3	7	5	21 - 24	3	6	6	15 - 13
14.	FC Dinamo București	30	7	6	17	26 - 41	27	3	4	8	14 - 21	4	2	9	12 - 20
15.	AFC Hermannstadt Sibiu	30	5	11	14	28 - 40	31	4	5	6	17 - 19	1	6	8	11 - 21
16.	FC Politehnica Iași	30	7	4	19	29 - 64	27	4	2	9	14 - 27	3	2	10	15 - 37

Teams ranked 1-6 were qualified for the Championship Round, while teams ranked 7-16 were qualified for the Relegation Round.
In both rounds, points from Regular Season were halved and rounded upwards.

Relegation Round

Results

Round 1 [16-18.04.2021]
UTA Arad - Viitorul Constanța 1-0(0-0)
Astra Giurgiu - Dinamo București 0-0
Chindia Târgoviște - Hermannstadt 2-0(1-0)
Gaz Metan - FC Voluntari 1-1(1-1)
FC Argeș - Politehnica Iași 0-0

Round 2 [20-22.04.2021]
Hermannstadt - Astra Giurgiu 1-3(0-0)
Viitorul Constanța - Gaz Metan 1-0(0-0)
Dinamo București - UTA Arad 0-1(0-1)
FC Argeș - Chindia Târgoviște 0-1(0-0)
Politehnica Iași - FC Voluntari 0-1(0-1)

Round 3 [23-26.04.2021]
UTA Arad - Hermannstadt 0-1(0-0)
Gaz Metan - Dinamo București 4-1(3-1)
Astra Giurgiu - FC Argeș 0-1(0-0)
Chindia Târgoviște - Politehnica Iași 2-0(1-0)
FC Voluntari - Viitorul Constanța 1-0(1-0)

Round 4 [27-29.04.2021]
Hermannstadt - Gaz Metan 1-2(1-2)
FC Argeș - UTA Arad 4-1(2-1)
Chindia Târgoviște - Astra Giurgiu 0-0
Politehnica Iași - Viitorul Constanța 0-3(0-2)
Dinamo București - FC Voluntari 2-0(0-0)

Round 5 [30.04.-02.05.2021]
Gaz Metan - FC Argeș 1-1(1-0)
UTA Arad - Chindia Târgoviște 0-1(0-0)
Astra Giurgiu - Politehnica Iași 1-2(0-2)
FC Voluntari - Hermannstadt 0-1(0-1)
Viitorul Constanța - Dinamo Bucur. 1-2(0-0)

Round 6 [04-06.05.2021]
Chindia Târgoviște - Gaz Metan 1-1(0-0)
Astra Giurgiu - UTA Arad 1-2(0-1)
Hermannstadt - Viitorul Constanța 0-0
Politehnica Iași - Dinamo București 1-2(1-1)
FC Argeș - FC Voluntari 3-0(1-0)

Round 7 [08-10.05.2021]
Gaz Metan - Astra Giurgiu 2-1(0-0)
Dinamo București - Hermannstadt 2-0(1-0)
UTA Arad - Politehnica Iași 1-2(0-2)
Viitorul Constanța - FC Argeș 1-0(0-0)
FC Voluntari - Chindia Târgoviște 0-0

Round 8 [14-16.05.2021]
Chindia Târgoviște - Viitorul Const. 0-2(0-0)
Politehnica Iași - Hermannstadt 0-1(0-0)
Astra Giurgiu - FC Voluntari 0-3(0-1)
UTA Arad - Gaz Metan 1-0(0-0)
FC Argeș - Dinamo București 1-2(0-1)

Round 9 [19.05.2021]
Hermannstadt - FC Argeș 1-0(0-0)
Dinamo București - Chindia Târgoviște 0-0
Viitorul Constanța - Astra Giurgiu 1-0(0-0)
FC Voluntari - UTA Arad 0-0
Gaz Metan - Politehnica Iași 4-2(3-0)

Final Standings

	Total						Home					Away			
7. AFC Chindia Târgovişte	9	4	4	1	7 - 3	36	2	2	1	5 - 3		2	2	0	2 - 0
8. FC UT Arad	9	4	1	4	7 - 9	32	2	0	3	3 - 4		2	1	1	4 - 5
9. CS Gaz Metan Mediaş	9	4	3	2	15 - 10	32	3	2	0	12 - 6		1	1	2	3 - 4
10. FC Viitorul Constanţa	9	5	1	3	9 - 4	32	3	0	1	4 - 2		2	1	2	5 - 2
11. FC Argeş Piteşti	9	3	2	4	10 - 7	31	2	1	2	8 - 4		1	1	2	2 - 3
12. FC Dinamo Bucureşti	9	5	2	2	11 - 8	31	2	1	1	4 - 1		3	1	1	7 - 7
13. FC Voluntari (Relegation Play-offs)	9	3	3	3	6 - 7	28	1	2	1	1 - 1		2	1	2	5 - 6
14. AFC Hermannstadt Sibiu (Relegation Play-offs)	9	4	1	4	6 - 9	26	1	1	2	3 - 5		3	0	2	3 - 4
15. AFC Astra Giurgiu (Relegated)	9	1	2	6	6 - 12	24	0	1	4	2 - 8		1	1	2	4 - 4
16. FC Politehnica Iaşi (Relegated)	9	2	1	6	7 - 15	20	0	0	4	1 - 7		2	1	2	6 - 8

AFC Chindia Târgovişte and FC Viitorul Constanţa were qualified for the European competiton play-offs Semi-Final (FC UT Arad and CS Gaz Metan Mediaş failed to obtain a UEFA licence!).

Championship Round

Results

Round 1 [17-18.04.2021]
U Craiova - Sepsi OSK 0-0
CFR Cluj - FC Academica 3-0(0-0)
FCSB Bucureşti - FC Botoşani 2-1(0-1)

Round 2 [21-22.04.2021]
FC Botoşani - U Craiova 1-1(1-0)
Sepsi OSK - CFR Cluj 0-1(0-1)
FC Academica - FCSB Bucureşti 0-2(0-1)

Round 3 [24-25.04.2021]
CFR Cluj - U Craiova 1-2(0-1)
FC Botoşani - FC Academica 2-1(1-0)
FCSB Bucureşti - Sepsi OSK 1-2(0-1)

Round 4 [28-29.04.2021]
Sepsi OSK - FC Academica 1-0(1-0)
CFR Cluj - FC Botoşani 2-0(2-0)
U Craiova - FCSB Bucureşti 2-0(1-0)

Round 5 [01-03.05.2021]
FC Botoşani - Sepsi OSK 2-1(1-0)
FC Academica - U Craiova 1-0(0-0)
FCSB Bucureşti - CFR Cluj 1-1(1-0)

Round 6 [05-06.05.2021]
Sepsi OSK - U Craiova 2-0(1-0)
FC Academica - CFR Cluj 0-1(0-1)
FC Botoşani - FCSB Bucureşti 1-3(1-2)

Round 7 [09-10.05.2021]
U Craiova - FC Botoşani 2-3(1-2)
CFR Cluj - Sepsi OSK 0-1(0-1)
FCSB Bucureşti - FC Academica 2-2(1-2)

Round 8 [14-16.05.2021]
FC Academica - FC Botoşani 4-3(1-3)
U Craiova - CFR Cluj 1-3(1-1)
Sepsi OSK - FCSB Bucureşti 2-2(0-0)

Round 9 [18-20.05.2021]
FC Botoşani - CFR Cluj 0-1(0-0)
FCSB Bucureşti - U Craiova 0-1(0-0)
FC Academica - Sepsi OSK 2-1(1-1)

Round 10 [25-27.05.2021]
CFR Cluj - FCSB Bucureşti 2-0(1-0)
U Craiova - FC Academica 0-0
Sepsi OSK - FC Botoşani 1-0(0-0)

Final Standings

	Total						Home					Away			
1. **FC CFR 1907 Cluj-Napoca**	10	7	1	2	15 - 5	54	3	0	2	8 - 3		4	1	0	7 - 2
2. SC FCSB Bucureşti	10	3	3	4	13 - 14	45	1	2	2	6 - 7		2	1	2	7 - 7
3. CS Universitatea Craiova	10	3	3	4	9 - 11	41	1	2	2	5 - 6		2	1	2	4 - 5
4. ACS Sepsi OSK Sfântu Gheorghe	10	5	2	3	11 - 8	40	3	1	1	6 - 3		2	1	2	5 - 5
5. FC Academica Clinceni	10	3	2	5	10 - 15	33	3	0	2	7 - 7		0	2	3	3 - 8
6. FC Botoşani	10	3	1	6	13 - 18	31	2	1	2	6 - 7		1	0	4	7 - 11

ACS Sepsi OSK Sfântu Gheorghe were qualified for the European competiton play-offs Final.

Top goalscorers:	
24 **Florinel Teodor Coman**	*SC FCSB Bucureşti*
18 Cephas Malele (ANG)	*FC Argeş Piteşti*
14 Dennis Man	*SC FCSB Bucureşti*
14 Hamidou Keyta (FRA)	*FC Botoşani*
13 Ciprian Ioan Deac	*FC CFR 1907 Cluj-Napoca*

European competition Play-offs

Semi-Final [27.05.2021] | AFC Chindia Târgovişte - FC Viitorul Constanţa | 2-3(1-1)

Final [30.05.2021] | **ACS Sepsi OSK Sfântu Gheorghe** - FC Viitorul Constanţa | 1-0(1-0)

Relegation Play-offs [29.05.-02/03.06.]

CS Mioveni - AFC Hermannstadt Sibiu   0-0   2-1(0-0)
AFC Dunărea 2005 Călăraşi - FC Voluntari   1-2(1-1)   0-4(0-2)
CS Mioveni and FC Voluntari will play at first level in 2021/2022.

NATIONAL CUP
Cupa României 2020/2021

Fifth Round [27-30.11.2020]

AFC Chindia Târgovişte - AFC Hermannstadt Sibiu	1-1 aet; 4-2 pen		CSM Ceahlăul Piatra Neamt - FC Petrolul Ploieşti	1-2(1-0)
AFC Progresul Spartac B. - CS Universitatea Craiova	0-5(0-3)		FC Dinamo Bucureşti - Viitorul Constanţa	3-0(2-0)
AFC Turris-Oltul Turnu Măgurele - ACS Sepsi OSK	1-0(0-0)		FC Ripensia Timisoara - AFC Astra Giurgiu	1-5(1-1)
CSC Sânmartin - FC Dunărea Călăraşi	0-1(0-0)		ACS Huşana Huşi - FC Universitatea Cluj	2-8(1-5)
FC Universitatea Craiova - SSU Poli Timişoara	1-3(1-1)		FC Voluntari - CS Gaz Metan Mediaş	0-6(0-1)
FC Farul Constanţa 1920- FC Academica Clinceni	2-1(1-0)		FC Politehnica Iaşi - FC CFR 1907 Cluj-Napoca	1-0(0-0)
CS Concordia Chiajna - FC Botoşani	0-2(0-0)		FK Miercurea Ciuc - FC UT Arad	0-2(0-2)
ACS Viitorul Pandurii Târgu Jiu - FC Argeş Piteşti	1-0(0-0)		SCM Gloria Buzău - SC FCSB Bucureşti	0-3 *awarded*

1/8-Finals [09-11.02.2021]

FC Dunărea Călăraşi - AFC Turris-Oltul Tr.Măgurele	3-0 *awarded*		FC Dinamo Bucureşti - SC FCSB Bucureşti	1-0(0-0)
FC Petrolul Ploieşti - FC Politehnica Iaşi	3-0(2-0)		ACS Viitorul Pandurii T.Jiu - CS Gaz Metan Mediaş	1-0(1-0)
FC Farul Constanţa 1920- AFC Chindia Târgovişte	0-3(0-1)		SSU Poli Timişoara - AFC Astra Giurgiu	1-2(1-0)
FC Universitatea Cluj - FC UT Arad	2-1(1-0)		FC Botoşani - CS Universitatea Craiova	0-1(0-1)

Quarter-Finals [02-04.03.2021]

AFC Chindia Târgovişte - CS Universitatea Craiova	0-1(0-1)		FC Petrolul Ploieşti - AFC Astra Giurgiu	0-3(0-0)
FC Universitatea Cluj - ACS Viitorul Pandurii Tg. Jiu	1-3(1-0)		FC Dunărea Călăraşi - FC Dinamo Bucureşti	1-3(0-2)

Semi-Finals [13-14.04./11-12.05.2021]

First Leg			Second Leg	
AFC Astra Giurgiu - FC Dinamo Bucureşti	1-0(1-0)		FC Dinamo Bucureşti - AFC Astra Giurgiu	1-0 aet; 4-5 pen
CS Univ. Craiova - ACS Viitorul Pandurii Târgu Jiu	3-0(1-0)		ACS Viitorul Pandurii Târgu Jiu - CS Univ. Craiova	2-2(2-2)

Final

22.05.2021; Stadionul "Ilie Oană", Ploieşti; Referee: Horaţiu Feşnic; Attendance: 1,500
AFC Astra Giurgiu - CS Universitatea Craiova   **2-3(1-1,1-1)**

Astra Giurgiu: Mihai Popa, Igor Jovanović, Abdel Lamanje, Valerică Găman, Hugo Filipe Gonçalves Martins de Sousa (68.Robert Riza), Yann Boé-Kane, Dario Čanađija (118.Abdul Fatai Adeshina), Ljuban Crepulja, Valentin Gheorghe (118.Dragoş Gheorghe), Albert Stahl (67.Silviu Balaure), Sulejman Krpić. Trainer: Ionuţ Badea.

Universitatea Craiova: Mirko Pigliacelli, Marius Constantin (74.Stephane Acka), Bogdan Vătăjelu, Nicuşor Silviu Bancu, Mihai Alexandru Bălaşa, Alexandru Mateiu (74.Alexandru Tudorie), Dan Nicolae Nistor, Alexandru Cicâldău, George Cîmpanu (66.Juan del Carmen Cámara Mesa; 109.Matteo Fedele), Andrei Virgil Ivan, Ştefan Baiaram (74.Vladimir Screciu). Trainer: Marinos Ouzounidis (Greece).

Goals: 0-1 Andrei Virgil Ivan (14), 1-1 Valerică Găman (17 penalty), 2-1 Yann Boé-Kane (93), 2-2 Dan Nicolae Nistor (100), 2-3 Vladimir Screciu (113).

THE CLUBS 2020/2021

Please <u>note</u>: appearances and goals are including statistics of both regular season and play-offs (Championship or Relegation).

Football Club Academica Clinceni

Founded:	2005 (*as CS Buftea*)
Stadium:	Stadionul Clinceni, Clinceni (4,500)
Trainer:	Ilie Poenaru 11.11.1976

Goalkeepers:	DOB	M	(s)	G
Aurelian Păun	05.05.2001	2		
Andrei Ureche	27.07.1998	6		
Octavian Vâlceanu	13.10.1996	32		
Defenders:	**DOB**	**M**	**(s)**	**G**
Florin Achim	16.07.1991	18	(12)	
Amir Bilali (ALB)	15.05.1994	13	(2)	1
Mihai Dobrescu	12.09.1992	30	(2)	
Florin Gardoş	29.10.1988	24	(2)	
Mladen Jutrić (AUT)	19.04.1996	19	(2)	1
Georgi Pashov (BUL)	04.03.1990	27	(5)	1
Răzvan Patrichi	29.04.1986	27	(2)	2
Paul Pîrvulescu	11.08.1988	10	(9)	
Midfielders:	**DOB**	**M**	**(s)**	**G**
Răzvan Andronic	07.01.2000	8	(14)	2
Juan Bautista Cascini (ARG)	04.06.1997	23	(5)	2
Eugeniu Cebotaru (MDA)	16.10.1984	26	(3)	3
Asen Chandarov (BUL)	13.11.1998	9	(15)	2
Lucian Dumitriu	21.09.1992	9	(14)	
Ciprian Gliga	17.04.1997		(3)	

	DOB	M	(s)	G
Thibault Moulin (FRA)	13.01.1990	13	(4)	1
Ionuţ Petrişor Petrescu	29.06.1993	4	(6)	1
Florinel Sandu	23.01.2001	3		
Marian Şerban	07.07.2000	1	(3)	1
Iulian Ştefan	01.06.2001		(1)	
Cristian Tănase	18.02.1987	12	(14)	1
Denis Ventúra (SVK)	01.08.1995	10	(11)	
Forwards:	**DOB**	**M**	**(s)**	**G**
Alexandru Boiciuc (MDA)	21.08.1997	6	(7)	
Tsvetelin Chunchukov (BUL)	26.12.1994	23	(6)	5
Andrei Cordea	24.06.1999	31	(2)	3
Cristian Cosmin Dumitru	13.12.2001	5		
Robert Jerdea	28.09.2003	1		
Aleksandru Longher	08.06.2000	14	(2)	
Jovan Marković	23.03.2001	2	(11)	4
David Morar	27.07.2004	7		
Adrian Dumitru Popa	24.07.1988	10	(9)	2
Raul Andrei Rusescu	09.07.1988	15	(14)	6
Martin Toshev	17.04.1990		(1)	

Asociația Sport Club Campionii Fotbal Club Argeș Pitești

Founded:	06.08.1953 (*as Dinamo Pitești*)		
Stadium:	Stadionul „Nicolae Dobrin", Pitești (15,000)		
Trainer:	Ionuț Badea		14.10.1975
[05.10.2020]	Ionuț Moșteanu		10.08.1975
[30.11.2020]	Adrian Dulcea		25.11.1978
[02.12.2020]	Augustin Eduard		01.08.1962
[30.12.2020]	Mihăiță Ianovschi		19.04.1975

Goalkeepers:	DOB	M	(s)	G
Flavius Croitoru	13.07.1992	5		
Alexandru Greab	26.05.1992	28		
George Micle	08.11.2001	6		
Defenders:	**DOB**	**M**	**(s)**	**G**
Deian Boldor	03.02.1995	5	(4)	
Jimmy De Jonghe (BEL)	13.02.1992	4	(5)	
Sylvain Deslandes (FRA)	25.04.1997	14	(6)	2
Mihai Leca	14.04.1992	15	(2)	
Luka Marić (CRO)	25.04.1987	23		1
Gabriel Matei	26.02.1990	7	(1)	
Nicolae Mușat	04.12.1986	35	(1)	
Daniel Șerbănică	25.06.1996	2	(4)	
Costinel Tofan	02.08.1996	31		
Grigore Turda	30.07.1997	22	(5)	1
Midfielders:	**DOB**	**M**	**(s)**	**G**
Angelo Cocian	25.07.2000	1		
Andre José Cozma	30.11.2002	2		
Pablo de Lucas Torres (ESP)	20.09.1986	1	(3)	
Gabriel Deac	26.04.1995	1	(4)	1
Georgian Honciu	24.04.1989	8	(16)	1
Alexander Maes (BEL)	26.03.1992	5	(8)	1
Sérgio Marakis (RSA)	11.11.1991	1	(3)	
Derlis David Meza Colli (PAR)	15.08.1988	38		1
Andrei Mirică	13.03.2001	4	(3)	
Mario Mitoi	13.08.2004	1		
Antun Palić (CRO)	25.06.1988	18	(6)	2
Mihai Andrei Panait	16.05.1989		(1)	
Alin Popa	01.01.1991		(2)	
Nini Adrian Popescu	26.04.1994	1		
Andrei Prepeliță	08.12.1985	10		
Ionuț Șerban	09.03.1992	33	(1)	3
Forwards:	**DOB**	**M**	**(s)**	**G**
Cătălin Barbu	05.08.1999	3	(4)	
Andrei Blejdea	22.06.1996	4	(7)	
Vasile Buhăescu	02.02.1988	1	(1)	
Stephan Drăghici	30.01.1998	18	(8)	2
Cristián Dumitru	13.12.2001	23	(1)	3
Robert Grecu	02.06.1998	20	(13)	4
Cephas Malele (ANG)	08.01.1994	26	(4)	18
Răzvan Matiș	25.01.2001	2		
Ionuț Năstăsie	07.01.1992		(20)	2
Mediop Ndiaye (SEN)	02.06.1991	10	(14)	1
Ruan Ribeiro Teles (BRA)	23.10.1997	1	(5)	

Asociația Fotbal Club Astra Giurgiu

Founded:	18.09.1921 (*as Clubul Sportiv Astra-Română Giurgiu*)		
Stadium:	Stadionul "Marin Anastasovici", Giurgiu (8,500)		
Trainer:	Bogdan Andone		07.01.1975
[01.10.2020]	Alexandru Radu		09.08.1978
[11.11.2020]	Eugen Neagoe		22.08.1967
[09.05.2021]	Ionuț Badea		14.10.1975

Goalkeepers:	DOB	M	(s)	G
David Beniamin Lazar	08.08.1991	28		
Mihai Popa	12.10.2000	11	(2)	
Defenders:	**DOB**	**M**	**(s)**	**G**
Alexandru Dandea	23.01.1988	3	(2)	
David Carneiro Dias Resende Bruno (POR)	14.02.1992	29	(2)	
Constantin Dima	21.07.1999	8	(1)	
Valerică Găman	25.02.1989	21	(4)	1
Daniel Graovac (BIH)	08.08.1993	38		1
Dinu Graur (MDA)	27.12.1994	1	(1)	
Hugo Filipe Gonçalves Martins de Sousa(POR)	04.06.1992	20	(1)	1
Igor Jovanović (CRO)	03.05.1989	4	(6)	
Abdel Lamanje (FRA)	27.07.1990	8		
Marius Pahonțu	22.08.1999	6	(1)	
Risto Radunović (MNE)	04.05.1992	13		2
Momčilo Raspopović (MNE)	18.03.1994	9	(4)	1
Robert Riza	09.06.1999	4	(1)	1
Midfielders:	**DOB**	**M**	**(s)**	**G**
Paulian Banu	21.10.2000	1		
Yann Boé-Kane (FRA)	05.04.1991	15	(4)	
Constantin Valentin Budescu	19.02.1989	17	(1)	8
Dario Čanađija (CRO)	17.04.1994	24	(6)	1
Ljuban Crepulja (CRO)	02.09.1993	30	(9)	
Dragoș Gheorghe	10.01.1999	3	(3)	
Romario Moise	21.09.1996	4	(9)	
Gabriel Șerban	11.02.2000	6	(2)	
Takayuki Seto (JPN)	05.02.1986	2	(2)	
Sébastien Wüthrich (SUI)	29.05.1990	10	(13)	3
Forwards:	**DOB**	**M**	**(s)**	**G**
Denis Alibec	05.01.1991	5		1
Shlomi Azulay (ISR)	18.10.1989	3	(3)	2
Raoul Baicu	05.04.2000		(2)	
Silviu Balaure	06.02.1996	2	(23)	
Kehinde Fatai (NGA)	19.02.1990	1	(3)	
Valentin Gheorghe	14.02.1997	25	(9)	8
Alexandru Ioniță	14.12.1994		(2)	
Sulejman Krpić (BIH)	01.01.1991	8	(9)	2
George Merloi	15.10.1999	16	(10)	2
Mattia Montini (ITA)	28.02.1992	12	(16)	5
Mihai Răduț	18.03.1990	17	(6)	1
Albert Stahl	11.01.1999	24	(9)	3
Ionuț Zaharia	19.07.2003	1		

Fotbal Club Botoșani

Founded:	2001		
Stadium:	Stadionul Municipal, Botoșani (7,782)		
Trainer:	Marius Croitoru		02.10.1980

Goalkeepers:	DOB	M	(s)	G
Hidajet Hankič (AUT)	29.06.1994	23		
Eduard Pap	01.07.1994	17		
Defenders:	**DOB**	**M**	**(s)**	**G**
Christopher Braun (GER)	15.07.1991	20	(4)	
Andrei Chindriș	12.01.1999	35	(1)	3
Denis Hăruț	25.02.1999	17		1
Marcel Holzmann (AUT)	03.09.1990	12	(4)	
Ulrich Meleke (CIV)	24.05.1999	8	(4)	
Adrian Moescu	31.05.2001	1	(1)	
Andrei Patache	29.10.1987	17	(10)	
Florin Plămadă	30.04.1992	1	(4)	
Bogdan Racovițan (FRA)	06.06.2000	1	(1)	
Alin Șeroni	26.03.1987	25	(5)	
Alexandru Țigănașu	12.06.1990	29	(4)	
Midfielders:	**DOB**	**M**	**(s)**	**G**
David Babunski (MKD)	01.03.1994	3	(4)	
Juan Bautista Cascini (ARG)	04.06.1997	1	(1)	
George Cimpanu	08.10.2000	3		1
David Marian Croitoru	09.08.2003	14		
Eduard Florescu	27.06.1997	21	(9)	2
Enriko Papa (ALB)	12.03.1993	22	(4)	4
Jonathan Yoni Emanuel Rodríguez (ARG)	07.06.1990	34		
Marian Târșă	16.04.1998		(3)	
Andrei Tîrcoveanu	22.05.1997	11	(14)	1
Forwards:	**DOB**	**M**	**(s)**	**G**
Mahmoud Al Mawas (SYR)	01.01.1993	21	(3)	4
Stefan Aškovski (MKD)	24.02.1992	11	(10)	2
Alexandru Caia	10.04.2003	11		
Sekou Camara (GUI)	20.07.1997	1	(12)	1
Minas Chalkiadakis (GRE)	05.02.1995	1	(3)	
Marko Dugandžić (CRO)	07.04.1994	5		2
Realdo Fili (ALB)	14.05.1996	8	(17)	7
Hamidou Keyta (FRA)	17.12.1994	22	(7)	14
Bogdan Melinte	11.09.1998	1		
Reagy Ofosu (GER)	20.09.1991	5	(1)	1
Hervin Ongenda (FRA)	24.06.1995	29	(2)	4
Mihai Roman I	16.10.1984	8	(21)	2
Youssef Toutouh (DEN)	06.10.1992	2	(12)	
Víctor Fernández Satué (ESP)	02.05.1998		(2)	

Fotbal Club Căile Ferate Române 1907 Cluj-Napoca

Founded: 1907 (*as Kolozsvári Vasutas Sport Club*)
Stadium: Stadionul "Dr. Constantin Rădulescu", Cluj-Napoca (23,500)
Trainer: Dan Vasile Petrescu 22.12.1967
[01.12.2020] Valeriu Bordeanu 02.02.1977
[04.12.2020] Edward Iordănescu 16.06.1978

Goalkeepers:	DOB	M	(s)	G
Giedrius Arlauskis (LTU)	01.12.1987	6		
Cristian Bălgrădean	21.03.1988	25	(1)	
Rareş Murariu	05.04.1999		(1)	
Grzegorz Sandomierski (POL)	05.09.1989	9	(2)	
Defenders:	**DOB**	**M**	**(s)**	**G**
Syam Ben Youssef (TUN)	31.03.1989	7		
Kévin Boli (CIV)	21.06.1991	1		
Andrei Andonie Burcă	15.04.1993	33	(2)	1
Mihai Butean	14.09.1996	1		
Mário Jorge Melico Paulino "Camora" (POR)	21.09.1986	35		
Mike Botuli Cestor (COD)	30.04.1992	6		
Denis Ciobotariu	10.06.1998	10	(1)	1
Iasmin Latovlevici	11.05.1986	2	(5)	
Cristian Marian Manea	09.08.1997	21	(5)	
Paulo Vinícius de Souza Nascimento (BRA)	12.08.1984	24	(1)	3
Mateo Sušić (BIH)	18.11.1990	20	(6)	
Ivica Žunić (BIH)	11.09.1988		(1)	
Midfielders:	**DOB**	**M**	**(s)**	**G**
Mihai Bordeianu	18.11.1991	15	(1)	
Alexandru Chipciu	18.05.1989	11	(19)	2
Damjan Đoković (CRO)	18.04.1990	9	(7)	
Adrian Gîdea	13.03.2000	19	(2)	1
Ovidiu Hoban	27.12.1982	12	(16)	1
Cătălin Itu	26.10.1999	18	(6)	3
Luís Miguel Coimbra Aurélio (POR)	17.08.1988	4	(7)	
Rúnar Már Sigurjónsson (ISL)	18.06.1990	7	(5)	3
William Soares da Silva (BRA)	30.12.1988	10	(6)	
Forwards:	**DOB**	**M**	**(s)**	**G**
Nicolae Cârnaţ	08.04.1998	3	(7)	
Valentin Costache	02.08.1998	26	(9)	4
Ciprian Ioan Deac	16.02.1986	33	(1)	13
Gabriel Debeljuh (CRO)	28.09.1996	22	(10)	8
Cătălin Golofca	21.04.1990		(1)	
Gheorghe Gondiu (MDA)	05.05.2002		(1)	
Andrei Joca	22.06.2000	5		
Billel Omrani (FRA)	02.06.1993	4	(12)	3
Adrian Păun	01.04.1995	16	(23)	5
Mickaël Pereira (FRA)	08.12.1987	10	(11)	
Claudiu Petrila	07.11.2000		(6)	1
Mário Júnior Rondón Fernández (VEN)	26.03.1986	14	(15)	5
Jakub Vojtuš (SVK)	22.10.1993	2	(5)	

Asociaţia Fotbal Club Chindia Târgovişte

Founded: 11.08.2010
Stadium: Stadionul Municipal, Buzău (12,000)
Trainer: Emil Săndoi 01.03.1965

Goalkeepers:	DOB	M	(s)	G
Mihai Aioani	07.11.1999	32		
Dinu Moldovan	03.05.1990	7	(1)	
Defenders:	**DOB**	**M**	**(s)**	**G**
Tiberiu Ionuţ Căpuşă	06.04.1998	32	(1)	1
Daniel Celea	06.07.1995	13		
Laurenţiu Corbu	10.05.1994		(1)	
Cornel Dinu	09.06.1989	30	(4)	
Bourama Fomba (MLI)	10.07.1999	10	(5)	
Paul Iacob	21.06.1996	32		2
Adrian Ioniţă	11.03.2000	5		
Milan Kocič (SVN)	16.02.1990	3	(7)	
Marius Martac	05.07.1991	8	(4)	
Florinel Mitrea	06.07.1993		(5)	
Alex Negrea	01.10.1998		(1)	
Andrei Piţian	16.11.1995	33	(1)	
Midfielders:	**DOB**	**M**	**(s)**	**G**
Cosmin Atanase	03.01.2001	1	(3)	
Cristian Cherchez	01.02.1991	1	(6)	
Marco Dulca	11.05.1999	31		2
Denis Dumitraşcu	27.04.1995	32	(3)	4
Liviu Mihai	12.03.1988		(1)	
Vadim Raţă (MDA)	05.05.1993	33	(3)	1
Andrei Şerban	31.10.2000	2	(3)	
Forwards:	**DOB**	**M**	**(s)**	**G**
Cătălin Barbu	05.08.1999		(2)	
Valmir Berisha (SWE)	06.06.1996	6	(23)	2
Mihai Costea	29.05.1988	2	(11)	
Tomás Díaz Grassano (ARG)	24.04.1997	8	(6)	
Daniel Florea	17.04.1988	33	(4)	8
Cristian Neguţ	09.12.1995	32	(2)	2
Mihai Neicutescu	29.09.1998	2	(10)	
Daniel Popa	14.07.1994	31	(3)	7
Blaise Yaméogo (BFA)	28.12.1993	10	(16)	

Fotbal Club Dinamo Bucureşti

Founded: 14.05.1948
Stadium: Stadionul Dinamo, Bucureşti (15,032)
Trainer: Gheorghe Mulţescu 13.11.1951
[26.08.2020] Cosmin Marius Contra 15.12.1975
[03.12.2020] Ionel Tersinio Gane 12.10.1971
[16.03.2021] Gheorghe Mulţescu 13.11.1951
[14.04.2021] Dušan Uhrin Jr. (CZE) 11.10.1967

Goalkeepers:	DOB	M	(s)	G
Mihai Eşanu	25.07.1998	19	(1)	
Gudmund Kongshavn (NOR)	23.01.1991	5		
Tomás Mejías Osorio (ESP)	30.01.1989	10		
René Román Hinojo (ESP)	15.12.1983	2		
Cătălin George Straton	09.10.1989	3		
Defenders:	**DOB**	**M**	**(s)**	**G**
Abdoulaye Ba (SEN)	01.01.1991	2	(1)	
Florin Bejan	28.03.1991	20	(2)	1
Marco Ehmann (GER)	03.08.2000	15	(2)	
Steliano Filip	15.05.1994	17		1
Alexander David González Sibulo (VEN)	13.09.1992	5	(2)	1
Ricardo Grigore	07.04.1999	17	(3)	1
Ismael López Blanco „Isma López" (ESP)	29.01.1990	8		
Ante Puljić (CRO)	05.11.1987	30	(3)	1
Andrei Radu	21.06.1996	12	(4)	
Raúl Albentosa Redal (ESP)	07.09.1988	10		1
Andrei Sin	26.10.1991	2		
Midfielders:	**DOB**	**M**	**(s)**	**G**
Vlad Achim	07.04.1989	16	(12)	1
Aleix García Serrano (ESP)	28.06.1997	4	(3)	
Paul Anton	10.05.1991	29	(1)	5
Andrei Bani	22.08.2002	6	(7)	
Ioan Borcea	06.07.2002	6	(3)	
Antonio Borduşanu	10.08.2004		(2)	
Geani Creţu	12.01.2000	11	(3)	
Diego Fabbrini (ITA)	31.07.1990	20	(15)	1
Janusz Gol (POL)	11.11.1985	19	(5)	
Alexandru Răuţă	17.06.1992	23	(2)	
Ionuţ Şerban	07.08.1995		(2)	
Forwards:	**DOB**	**M**	**(s)**	**G**
Joseph Akpala (NGA)	24.08.1986		(1)	
Andrei Blejdea	22.06.1996	2	(8)	
Borja Valle Balonga (ESP)	09.07.1992	4	(5)	5
Magaye Gueye (SEN)	06.07.1990	10	(7)	2
Juan del Carmen Cámara Mesa (ESP)	13.02.1994	10	(2)	2
Cătălin Măgureanu	05.06.2000	5	(6)	
Andreas Mihaiu	19.08.1998	10	(7)	1
Robert Moldoveanu	08.03.1999	2	(8)	
Jonathan Morsay (SWE)	05.10.1997	5	(8)	2
Mihai Neicuţescu	29.09.1998	1	(1)	
Adam Nemec (SVK)	02.09.1985	28	(2)	4
Gevaro Giomar Magno Nepomuceno (CUW)	10.11.1992	4	(6)	
Daniel Popa	14.07.1994	1	(1)	
Deian Cristian Sorescu	29.08.1997	36	(1)	7
Giani Stere	14.06.1999		(4)	

Sport Club Fotbal Club FCSB Bucureşti

Founded: 07.06.1947 (*as AS Armata Bucureşti*)
Stadium: Arena Naţională, Bucureşti (55,634)
Trainer: Anton Petrea   09.03.1975

Goalkeepers:	DOB	M	(s)	G
Cătălin George Straton	09.10.1989	4	(1)	
Ştefan Târnovanu	09.05.2000	2		
Andrei Vlad	15.04.1999	34		
Defenders:	**DOB**	**M**	**(s)**	**G**
Marius Briceag	06.04.1992	4	(3)	
Ştefan Cană	07.08.2000	2		
Valentin Iulian Creţu	02.01.1989	24	(5)	
Iulian Lucian Cristea	17.07.1994	32	(3)	4
Denis Hăruţ	25.02.1999	10		
George Miron	28.05.1994	29	(3)	
Dragoş Nedelcu	16.02.1997	5	(2)	
Alexandru Pantea	11.09.2003	2	(1)	
Ionuţ Panţîru	22.03.1996	13	(9)	1
Risto Radunović (MNE)	04.05.1992	20	(2)	
Aristides Soiledis (GRE)	08.02.1991	1		
Sorin Şerban	17.03.2000	2		
Midfielders:	**DOB**	**M**	**(s)**	**G**
Laurenţiu Ardelean	08.02.2001		(2)	
Aurelian Ciuciulete	04.04.2003		(1)	
Gabriel Enache	18.08.1990	1		
Lucian Filip	25.09.1990	1	(1)	
Cătălin Gogor	27.05.2001		(1)	
Ovidiu Horşia	30.10.2000		(1)	

	DOB	M	(s)	G
Robert Ion	05.09.2000	1	(1)	
Olimpiu Moruţan	25.04.1999	30	(3)	8
Răzvan Oaidă	02.03.1998	9	(16)	
Darius Olaru	03.03.1998	25	(5)	7
Ovidiu Perianu	16.04.2002	8	(15)	
Ovidiu Marian Popescu	27.02.1994	29	(6)	
Gabriel Simion	22.05.1998	10	(9)	
Adrian Şut	30.04.1999	18	(6)	
Florin Lucian Tănase	30.12.1994	33	(1)	24
Ionuţ Vînă	20.02.1995	10	(15)	1
Forwards:	**DOB**	**M**	**(s)**	**G**
Sergiu Florin Buş	02.11.1992	7	(3)	2
Alexandru Buziuc	15.03.1994	3	(19)	1
Florinel Teodor Coman	10.04.1998	17	(2)	1
Cristián Dumitru	13.12.2001		(1)	
Gabriel Fulga	28.02.2004	1	(1)	
Andrei Istrate	15.03.2002	2	(6)	1
Dennis Man	26.08.1998	18		14
Alexandru Musi	17.04.2004	2		
Adrian Niţă	08.03.2003	3	(2)	
Adrian Petre	11.02.1998	2		
Octavian Popescu	27.12.2002	26	(6)	4
Ante Vukušic (CRO)	04.06.1991		(5)	

Clubul Sportiv Gaz Metan Mediaş

Founded: 1945 (*as Karres Mediaş*)
Stadium: Stadionul Gaz Metan, Mediaş (7,814)
Trainer: Dušan Uhrin Jr. (CZE)   11.10.1967
[30.09.2020] Jorge Paulo Costa Almeida (POR) 14.10.1971
[02.02.2021] Mihai Teja   22.09.1978

Goalkeepers:	DOB	M	(s)	G
Alexandru Buzbuchi	31.10.1993	16		
Răzvan Pleşca	25.11.1982	23		
Defenders:	**DOB**	**M**	**(s)**	**G**
Ondřej Bačo (CZE)	25.03.1996	30	(2)	2
Mihai Butean	14.09.1996	33	(2)	1
Gabriel Rodrigues de Moura (BRA)	18.06.1988	16	(2)	
Răzvan Horj	17.12.1995	7		
Bogdan Jica	03.07.2000	1		
Fernander Paul Christian Kassaï (CTA)	01.07.1987		(1)	
Ionuţ Larie	16.01.1987	23	(3)	1
Răzvan Popa	04.01.1997	3		
Roberto Romeo (ITA)	27.04.1990	9	(12)	1
Răzvan Trif	09.10.1997	19	(5)	
Mihai Velisar	30.08.1998	25	(3)	
Jefferson Yuri de Sousa Matias (BRA)	10.02.1995	26	(1)	2
Midfielders:	**DOB**	**M**	**(s)**	**G**
Bryan Alceus (HAI)	01.02.1996	22	(6)	
Sergiu Ciocan	22.09.1998	12	(7)	2
Paul Costea	02.03.1999	9	(8)	

	DOB	M	(s)	G
Ronaldo Deaconu	13.05.1997	32	(5)	9
Lukáš Droppa (CZE)	22.04.1989	6		
Francisco Santos Silva Júnior (POR)	18.01.1992	17	(7)	
Ovidiu Horşia	30.10.2000	14	(9)	1
Yves Simon Pambou Loembet (CGO)	27.11.1995	7	(15)	
Gabriel Plumbuitu	14.02.2004	4		
Forwards:	**DOB**	**M**	**(s)**	**G**
Nasser Chamed (COM)	04.10.1993	15	(17)	2
Rareş Dogaru	11.12.2003	2		
Nicolao Dumitru (ITA)	12.10.1991	10	(2)	7
Dragoş Iancu	29.09.2002	1		
Mihai Mateş	11.12.2000	1	(1)	
Vlad Morar	01.08.1993	7	(6)	3
Luis Emanuel Niţu	30.05.2001	9	(5)	1
Ricardo Jorge Oliveira Valente (POR)	03.04.1991	18	(13)	10
Idrisa Sidi Sambú (POR)	27.03.1998		(12)	1
Moussa Sanoh (NED)	20.07.1995	2	(3)	
Adama Sarr (FRA)	15.03.1991	3	(6)	
Tomáš Smola (CZE)	19.01.1989	1	(2)	
José Manuel Silva Oliveira „Zé Manuel"(POR)	23.10.1990	6	(21)	3

Asociaţia Fotbal Club Hermannstadt Sibiu

Founded: 29.07.2015
Stadium: Stadionul Gaz Metan, Mediaş (7,814)
        [Stadionul Municipal, Sibiu (5,000) under renovation]
Trainer: Rubén Albés Yáñez (ESP) 24.02.1985
[15.01.2021] Liviu Ciobotariu 26.03.1971
[23.03.2021] Eugen Beza 01.07.1978

Goalkeepers:	DOB	M	(s)	G
Cristiano Pereira Figueiredo (POR)	29.11.1990	37		
Ionuţ Pop	01.08.1997	2		
Defenders:	**DOB**	**M**	**(s)**	**G**
Ángel Bastos Teijeira (ESP)	03.05.1992		(6)	
Claudiu Belu-Iordache	07.11.1993	16	(8)	1
Sorin Buşu	08.07.1989	1	(1)	
Luca Alexandru Florică	06.10.2002	1		
Saeed Issah (GHA)	11.01.2000	1	(1)	
Alexandru Măţel	17.10.1989	16	(6)	1
Patricio Martín Matricardi (ARG)	07.01.1994	12	(2)	1
Raul Opruţ	04.01.1998	37		1
Adrian Scarlatache	05.12.1986	19	(3)	1
Ionuţ Stoica	06.01.1988	31	(2)	
Ousmane Viera (CIV)	21.12.1986	25	(1)	
Midfielders:	**DOB**	**M**	**(s)**	**G**
Bright Addae (GHA)	19.12.1992	22	(7)	2
Baba Alhassan (GHA)	03.01.2000	8	(13)	1
Lucian Buzan	09.03.1999	10	(4)	
David Caiado Dias (POR)	02.05.1987	4	(2)	
Răzvan Dâlbea	08.10.1981	26	(5)	2

	DOB	M	(s)	G
Lucian Dumitru	21.09.1992		(1)	
Soni Mustivar (HAI)	12.02.1990	5	(4)	
Alexandru Oroian	27.01.2001	2		
Aias Osman (SYR)	21.10.1994	11	(2)	1
Petrişor Petrescu	29.06.1993	13	(13)	2
Călin Popescu	15.11.2001	1		
Romário Santos Pires (BRA)	16.01.1989	23	(7)	4
Billal Sebaihi (FRA)	31.05.1992	4	(6)	
Alexandru Vodă	22.07.1998	11	(5)	
Forwards:	**DOB**	**M**	**(s)**	**G**
Ante Aralica (CRO)	23.07.1996	1	(14)	
Dražen Bagarić (CRO)	12.11.1992	9	(8)	2
Adrian Bălan	14.03.1990	3		1
David Mayoral Lastras (ESP)	05.04.1997	22	(5)	5
Stanley Elbers (NED)	14.05.1992		(6)	
Fábio Fortes Moreira (POR)	06.03.1992	7	(5)	1
Joálisson „Jô" Santos Oliveira (BRA)	31.03.1991	16	(2)	2
Goran Karanović (SUI)	13.10.1987	4	(11)	1
Andrei Sîntean	16.06.1999	20	(8)	2
Adrian Ster	19.04.1998	1	(3)	
Yazalde Gomes Pinto (GNB)	21.09.1988	8	(4)	2

Asociația Fotbal Club Sportiv Municipal [Fotbal Club] Politehnica Iași

Founded: 16.08.2010 (*as ACSMU Politehnica Iași*)
Stadium: Stadionul "Emil Alexandrescu", Iași (11,390)
Trainer: Daniel Gabriel Pancu   17.08.1977
[30.01.2021] Adrian Kerezsy   05.05.1961
[01.02.2021] Andrei Cristea   15.05.1984
[12.03.2021] Nicolò Napoli (ITA)   07.02.1962

Goalkeepers:	DOB	M	(s)	G
Teodor Axinte	02.02.2000	8		
Levente Bősz (HUN)	06.05.1994	5		
Laurențiu Brănescu	30.03.1994	18		
Ianoş Brînză (MDA)	12.09.1998	8	(2)	
Defenders:	**DOB**	**M**	**(s)**	**G**
Manuel Charly Angiulli (BEL)	26.06.1995	1	(1)	
Nikos Baxevanos (GRE)	16.07.1999	34	(1)	
Sorin Bușu	08.07.1989	33	(1)	
Ştefan Cană	07.08.2000	5	(2)	
Daniel Ciobanu	01.11.1993	1		
Cosmin Frăsinescu	10.02.1985	15	(1)	
Rodny Lopes Cabral (NED)	28.01.1995	5	(2)	
Ovidiu Marius Mihalache	14.12.1984	14	(2)	
Razvan Onea	19.05.1998	38		2
Răzvan Popa	04.01.1997	17		
Cosmin Saizu	08.03.2003	1		
Dan Talmaciu	22.04.2002	1		
Midfielders:	**DOB**	**M**	**(s)**	**G**
Donaldo Açka (ALB)	17.09.1997	1	(7)	
Nicandro Breeveld (SUR)	07.10.1986	7	(2)	
Rafael Eduardo Acosta Cammarota (VEN)	13.02.1989	3	(4)	
Francisc Cristea	15.01.2001	8	(9)	1
Manuel Ignacio De Iriondo (ARG)	06.05.1993	22	(7)	1
Dylan Armando Flores Knowles (CRC)	30.05.1993	6	(5)	1
Pablo Leonel Gaitán (ARG)	09.05.1992	6	(6)	1
Andrei Ionuţ Moisa	07.02.2002	3	(1)	
Juan Pablo Passaglia (ARG)	24.05.1989	32		4
Doru Popadiuc	18.02.1995	13	(18)	4
Antonio Stan	03.10.2000	17		
Floriano Vanzo (BEL)	28.04.1994	25	(8)	
Alexandru Cristian Zaharia	01.07.1999		(1)	
Forwards:	**DOB**	**M**	**(s)**	**G**
Gai Assulin (ISR)	09.04.1991	1	(1)	
Andreiaş Calcan	09.04.1994	14	(8)	4
Lucas Nicolás Chacana (ARG)	16.06.1993	1	(4)	
Andrei Cristea	15.05.1984	11	(6)	7
Uroš Đuranović (MNE)	01.02.1994	14	(1)	4
Joseph Mensah (GHA)	29.09.1994	5	(9)	
Luís Carlos Almada Soares „Platini" (CPV)	16.04.1986	20	(3)	3
Deyver Antonio Vega Álvarez (CRC)	19.09.1992	5	(9)	1
Alexandru Iulian Zaharia	09.09.2000	1	(4)	1
Dženan Zajmović (BIH)	11.11.1994	10	(9)	3

Asociația Club Sportiv Sepsi Oltul Sport Klub Sfântu Gheorghe

Founded: 2011
Stadium: Stadionul Municipal, Sfântu Gheorghe (5,200)
Trainer: Leontin Florian Grozavu   19.08.1967

Goalkeepers:	DOB	M	(s)	G
Csongor Béla Fejér	11.10.1995	2		
Jesús Fernández Collado (ESP)	11.06.1988	8		
Roland Niczuly	21.09.1995	30		
Defenders:	**DOB**	**M**	**(s)**	**G**
Rachid Bouhenna (ALG)	29.06.1991	30		3
Balázs Csiszér	03.03.1999	11	(1)	
Panagiotis Deligiannidis (GRE)	29.08.1996	10	(5)	
Radoslav Dimitrov (BUL)	12.08.1988	23	(2)	1
Andres Dumitrescu	11.03.2001	4	(5)	
Bogdan Mitrea	29.09.1987	37		5
Branislav Niňaj (SVK)	17.05.1994	12	(4)	
Florin Ştefan	09.05.1996	18	(2)	
Marius Ştefănescu	14.08.1998	23	(8)	
Răzvan Tincu	15.07.1987	8	(5)	
Midfielders:	**DOB**	**M**	**(s)**	**G**
Anass Achahbar (NED)	13.01.1994	10	(17)	2
Adnan Aganović (CRO)	03.10.1987	17	(15)	3
Eder González Tortella (ESP)	07.01.1997	15	(7)	2
Boubacar Fofana (GUI)	06.11.1989	22	(5)	2
István Fülöp	18.05.1990	5	(2)	2
Lóránd Fülöp	24.07.1997	9	(13)	2
Peter Gál-Andrezly (SVK)	03.05.1990	1	(2)	
Lóránt Kovács	06.06.1993	4	(9)	1
Aleksa Marković (AUT)	13.04.2001		(2)	
Vlad Nicolae Mitrea	23.01.2001	3	(2)	
Nicolae Păun	19.01.1990	7	(1)	
Florin Purece	06.11.1991	8	(12)	1
Gabriel Vaşvari	13.11.1986	27	(3)	6
Forwards:	**DOB**	**M**	**(s)**	**G**
Admir Bajrović (SWE)	06.08.1995	5	(8)	2
Nicolae Cârnaţ	08.04.1998	4		
George Dragomir	06.08.2003	7		
Andrei Ioan Dumiter	10.04.1999	6	(2)	1
Cătălin Golofca	21.04.1990	16	(15)	3
Bryan Nouvier (FRA)	21.06.1995	8	(12)	1
Claudiu Petrila	07.11.2000	16	(10)	5
Simone Rapp (SUI)	01.10.1992		(2)	
Pavol Šafranko (SVK)	16.11.1994	28	(5)	9
Nándor Tamás	24.10.2000	6	(4)	1

Universitatea Craiova 1948 Club Sportiv

Founded: 1948; re-founded 2013
Stadium: Stadionul "Ion Oblemenco", Craiova (30,929)
Trainer: Cristiano Bergodi (ITA)   14.10.1964
[10.11.2020] Corneliu Papură   05.09.1973
[30.01.2021] Dragoş Bon   13.06.1980
[07.02.2021] Marinos Ouzounidis (GRE)   10.10.1968

Goalkeepers:	DOB	M	(s)	G
Mirko Pigliacelli (ITA)	30.06.1993	40		
Defenders:	**DOB**	**M**	**(s)**	**G**
Stephane Acka (CIV)	11.10.1990	10	(1)	
Mihai Alexandru Bălaşa	14.01.1995	24	(3)	
Nicuşor Silviu Bancu	18.09.1992	35		2
Marius Constantin	25.10.1984	33	(2)	
Ionuţ Mitran	09.03.2002	9		
Alexandru Olteanu	05.04.2000	1		
Paul Papp	11.11.1989	14	(4)	1
Bogdan Vătăjelu	24.04.1993	16	(12)	
Ştefan Vlădoiu	28.12.1998	21	(6)	
Midfielders:	**DOB**	**M**	**(s)**	**G**
Ovidiu Bic	23.02.1994	15	(7)	
Mihai Căpăţînă	16.12.1995	6	(18)	
Alexandru Cicâldău	08.07.1997	36	(2)	11
George Cîmpanu	08.10.2000	16	(5)	1
Vasile Constantin	18.01.1998	1	(4)	
Matteo Fedele (SUI)	20.07.1992	1	(9)	
Alexandru Mateiu	10.12.1989	21	(5)	
Dan Nicolae Nistor	06.05.1988	38		4
Vladimir Screciu	13.01.2000	6	(10)	
Atanas Trică	09.07.2004		(1)	
Forwards:	**DOB**	**M**	**(s)**	**G**
Ştefan Baiaram	31.12.2002	22	(9)	2
Cristi Bărbuţ	22.04.1995	7	(14)	2
Andrei Virgil Ivan	04.01.1997	26	(8)	8
Juan del Carmen Cámara Mesa (ESP)	13.02.1994	3	(9)	
Elvir Koljič (BIH)	08.07.1995	6	(2)	6
Ivan Mamut (CRO)	30.04.1997	13	(10)	1
Valentin Mihai Mihăilă	02.02.2000	4	(1)	
Reagy Ofosu (GER)	20.09.1991	13	(5)	2
Alexandru Tudorie	19.03.1996	3	(14)	2

Fotbal Club Uzina Textilă Arad

Founded: 18.04.1945
Stadium: Stadionul „Francisc von Neuman", Arad (12,700)
Trainer: László Bálint — 29.03.1979

Goalkeepers:	DOB	M	(s)	G
Dragoş Balauru	11.11.1989	6	(1)	
Florin Iacob	16.08.1993	29		
Horaţiu Moldovan	20.01.1998	4		
Defenders:	**DOB**	**M**	**(s)**	**G**
Alexandru Benga	15.06.1989	22		
Sorin Buştea	22.12.1994	11	(9)	1
Erico Constantino da Silva (BRA)	20.07.1989	30	(4)	5
Florin Ilie	18.06.1992	19	(1)	
Cristian Melinte	09.05.1988	4	(11)	
Andrei Peteleu	20.08.1992	8	(3)	
Marian Pleaşcă	06.02.1990	1	(1)	
Simon Rrumbullaku (ALB)	30.12.1991	21	(6)	
Evgeniy Shlyakov (RUS)	30.08.1991	17	(2)	1
Marius Tomozei	09.09.1990	19	(5)	1
Midfielders:	**DOB**	**M**	**(s)**	**G**
Cristian Alexandru Albu	17.08.1993	32	(4)	2
Damian Isac	31.01.2001	12	(1)	
Mihovil-Jeronim Klapan (CRO)	27.03.1995		(2)	

Alexandru Oroian	27.01.2001	5	(4)	
Călin Popescu	15.11.2001		(3)	
Roger Junio Rodrigues Ferreira (BRA)	01.03.1996	23		2
Neluţ Roşu	05.07.1993	14	(11)	
Modestas Vorobjovas (LTU)	30.12.1995	22	(1)	
Forwards:	**DOB**	**M**	**(s)**	**G**
Liviu Antal	02.06.1989	10	(11)	3
Valentin Buhăcianu	28.10.1993	14	(16)	2
Adrian Ioan Hora	21.08.1988	24	(7)	6
Alexandru Ioniţă	05.08.1989	2	(7)	
David Miculescu	02.05.2001	17	(11)	2
Vlad Morar	01.08.1993	7	(5)	3
Claudiu Negoescu	23.03.2003		(1)	
Adrian Petre	11.02.1998	8	(6)	
Ciprian Rus	01.03.1991	9	(17)	2
Denis Rusu	21.03.2001	29	(6)	2
Dragoş Tescan	15.09.1999	7	(4)	
Octavian Ursu	15.11.1994	2	(9)	1
Albert Voinea	06.12.1992	1	(6)	

Fotbal Club Viitorul Constanţa

Founded: 2009
Stadium: Stadionul Viitorul, Constanţa (4,554)
Trainer: Rubén de la Barrera Fernández (ESP) — 18.01.1985
[01.12.2020] Mircea Rednic — 09.04.1962
[09.04.2021] Cătălin Anghel — 04.10.1974

Goalkeepers:	DOB	M	(s)	G
Cătălin Căbuz	18.06.1996	7	(2)	
Valentin Cojocaru	01.10.1995	30		
Árpád Tordai	11.03.1997	2		
Defenders:	**DOB**	**M**	**(s)**	**G**
Ángel Martínez Ortega (ESP)	15.05.1991	4		
Romario Benzar	26.03.1992	17	(6)	
Radu Boboc	24.04.1999	30	(2)	
Gabriel Buta	29.01.2002		(2)	
Bradley de Nooijer (NED)	07.11.1997	10	(2)	
Alin Dobrosavlevici	24.10.1994	28		3
Damien Dussaut (FRA)	08.11.1994	17	(7)	
Alexandru Georgescu	10.07.2001		(1)	
Virgil Ghiţă	04.06.1998	14		
Marcos Garbellotto Pedroso „Marquinhos" (BRA)	04.10.1993	3	(6)	
Sebastian Mladen	11.12.1991	33	(2)	
Midfielders:	**DOB**	**M**	**(s)**	**G**
Andrei Artean	14.08.1993	25	(4)	2
David Babunski (MKD)	01.03.1994	5	(8)	
Stefan Bodişteanu	01.02.2003	1	(3)	
Carlos Casap	29.12.1998	4	(5)	1
Andrei Ciobanu	18.01.1998	32	(3)	9

Ion Gaztañaga Arrospide (ESP)	28.06.1991	10	(8)	1
Răzvan Grădinaru	23.08.1995	10	(8)	
Constantin Grameni	23.10.2002	6	(5)	
José "Josemi" Miguel Castañeda Macho (ESP)	26.02.1998		(4)	
Cosmin Matei	30.09.1991	30	(3)	1
Alexandru Irinel Măţan	29.08.1999	18	(4)	1
Forwards:	**DOB**	**M**	**(s)**	**G**
Luca Andronache	26.07.2003	1	(10)	
Aurelian Chiţu	25.03.1991	5	(3)	2
Ely Ernesto Lopes Fernandes (CPV)	04.11.1990	9	(9)	1
George Ganea	26.05.1999	19	(10)	2
Florian Haită	29.10.2000	2	(4)	
Gabriel Cristian Iancu	15.04.1994	9		4
Joálisson "Jô" Santos Oliveira (BRA)	31.03.1991	11	(4)	4
Kevin Luckassen (NED)	27.07.1993	18		9
Răzvan Matiş	25.01.2001		(1)	
Louis Munteanu	16.06.2002	1	(1)	
Alexi Pitu	05.06.2002	2	(15)	
Adrian Stoian	11.02.1991	1	(3)	
Valērijs Šabala (LVA)	12.10.1994	1	(4)	
Hama Juvhel Fred Tsoumou (CGO)	27.12.1990	12	(4)	3
Víctor Fernández Satué (ESP)	02.05.1998	2	(4)	

Fotbal Club Voluntari

Founded: 2010 (*as Inter Voluntari*)
Stadium: Stadionul „Anghel Iordănescu", Voluntari (4,600)
Trainer: Mihai Teja — 22.09.1978
[30.12.2020] Bogdan Andone — 07.01.1975
[07.05.2021] Liviu Ciobotariu — 26.03.1971

Goalkeepers:	DOB	M	(s)	G
Mihai Cotolan	18.01.1999	1		
Marcos Lavín Rodríguez (ESP)	02.09.1996	7		
Victor Rîmniceanu	11.04.1990	31	(1)	
Defenders:	**DOB**	**M**	**(s)**	**G**
Cosmin Achim	19.09.1995	13	(5)	3
Igor Armaş (MDA)	14.07.1987	33	(1)	1
Ionuţ Balaur	06.06.1989	29	(3)	
Marius Briceag	06.04.1992	15	(1)	
Cristian Costin	17.06.1998	28	(5)	1
Milan Kocič (SVN)	16.02.1990	3	(3)	
Ionuţ Oktay Ozkara	11.08.2000		(1)	
Grégoire Puel (FRA)	20.02.1992		(2)	
Ricardo José Veiga Varzim „Ricardinho" (POR)	24.03.1994	18	(11)	1
Mourad Satli (ALG)	29.01.1990	5		
Gabriel Tamaş	09.11.1983	15	(1)	
Alexandru Vlad	06.12.1989	19	(8)	
Midfielders:	**DOB**	**M**	**(s)**	**G**
Claudiu Borţoneanu	04.10.1999	8	(12)	
George Buliga	26.04.1998	1	(1)	
Mihai Căpăţînă	16.12.1995	6		2
Pablo de Lucas Torres (ESP)	20.09.1986	11	(1)	

Adrian Dorobanţu	19.06.1999	1	(1)	
Lukáš Droppa (CZE)	22.04.1989	20		2
Eric de Oliveira Pereira (BRA)	05.12.1985	6	(1)	
Ion Gheorghe	08.10.1999	35	(3)	5
Răzvan Grădinaru	23.08.1995	12	(3)	1
Hélder Luís Lopes Vieira Tavares (CPV)	26.12.1989	9	(5)	
Alexandru Ilie	19.01.2000	10	(7)	
Antoni Ivanov (BUL)	11.09.1995	15	(2)	3
Vasile Mihai	29.11.1995		(4)	
Martin Remacle (BEL)	16.05.1997	2	(4)	
Robert Tangulea	20.10.2001		(1)	
Forwards:	**DOB**	**M**	**(s)**	**G**
John Anderson Souza Fonseca (BRA)	03.05.1997	2	(8)	
Viktor Angelov (MKD)	27.03.1994	7	(11)	1
Jefté Betancor Sánchez (ESP)	06.07.1993	23	(6)	7
Haruna Garba (NGA)	17.01.1994	1	(3)	
Sebastian Mailat	12.12.1997	14	(7)	4
Marcelo André Veiga Lopes (POR)	21.04.1994	8	(16)	2
Ivan Pešić (CRO)	06.04.1992	9	(9)	1
Adrian Dumitru Popa	24.07.1988	7		2
Alexandru Ionuţ Stoica	23.01.2000	5	(9)	1
Adelin Voinescu	01.04.1998		(3)	

Regular Season

1.	FC Universitatea Craiova 1948	19	9	8	2	30	-	15	35
2.	AFC Dunărea 2005 Călăraşi	19	10	4	5	25	-	22	34
3.	CS Mioveni	19	9	6	4	23	-	11	33
4.	FC Rapid 1923 Bucureşti	19	10	3	6	33	-	28	33
5.	FK Miercurea Ciuc	19	9	5	5	23	-	15	32
6.	SSU Politehnica Timişoara	19	8	8	3	18	-	14	32
7.	FC Farul Constanţa 1920	19	9	5	5	24	-	18	32
8.	ACS Viitorul Pandurii Târgu Jiu	19	10	2	7	32	-	27	32
9.	FC Petrolul Ploieşti	19	9	4	6	30	-	16	31
10.	FC Metaloglobus Bucureşti	19	9	3	7	25	-	15	30
11.	FC Universitatea Cluj	19	9	2	8	20	-	19	29
12.	FC Buzău	19	6	8	5	21	-	20	26
13.	CS Concordia Chiajna	19	6	6	7	21	-	18	24
14.	ACS Fotbal Maramureş Comuna Recea	19	6	5	8	29	-	29	23
15.	FC Ripensia Timişoara	19	6	4	9	15	-	30	22
16.	AFC Unirea 04 Slobozia	19	5	4	10	15	-	26	19
17.	CSM Reşiţa	19	5	4	10	10	-	26	19
18.	CSM Slatina	19	4	3	12	17	-	25	15
19.	CS Pandurii Lignitul Târgu Jiu	19	3	4	12	18	-	37	13
20.	CS Aerostar Bacău	19	2	4	13	19	-	37	10
21.	AFC Turris-Oltul Turnu Măgurele (excluded)	0	0	0	0	0	-	0	0

Team ranked 1-6 were qualified for the Promotion Play-off Round, while teams ranked 7-20 were qualified for the Play-out Round.
Please note: AFC Turris-Oltul Turnu Măgurele withdrew after 14 Rounds, all its results being cancelled.

Promotion Play-off

1.	FC Universitatea Craiova 1948 (Promoted)	10	5	4	1	13	-	7	54
2.	FC Rapid 1923 Bucureşti (Promoted)	10	5	1	4	14	-	11	49
3.	CS Mioveni (Promotion Play-offs)	10	3	6	1	18	-	11	48
4.	AFC Dunărea 2005 Călăraşi (Promotion Play-offs)	10	2	4	4	10	-	18	44
5.	FK Miercurea Ciuc	10	2	4	4	9	-	11	42
6.	SSU Politehnica Timişoara	10	2	3	5	9	-	15	41

Play-out Round – Group A

1.	FC Farul Constanţa 1920*	6	3	1	2	10	-	8	42
2.	FC Universitatea Cluj	6	3	1	2	13	-	9	39
3.	FC Metaloglobus Bucureşti	6	3	0	3	6	-	7	39
4.	FC Ripensia Timişoara	6	4	2	0	9	-	3	36
5.	ACS Fotbal Maramureş Comuna Recea (Liga II Play-out)	6	4	0	2	18	-	10	35
6.	CSM Slatina (Relegated)	6	1	1	4	8	-	15	19
7.	CS Pandurii Lignitul Târgu Jiu (Relegated)	6	0	1	5	5	-	17	14

*Please note: FC Farul Constanţa 1920 merged with FC Viitorul Constanţa and were promoted to Liga I.

Play-out Round – Group B

1.	FC Petrolul Ploieşti	6	3	2	1	8	-	4	42
2.	ACS Viitorul Pandurii Târgu Jiu	6	3	0	3	15	-	14	41
3.	FC Buzău	6	2	3	1	9	-	7	35
4.	CS Concordia Chiajna	6	3	1	2	8	-	6	34
5.	AFC Unirea 04 Slobozia (Liga II Play-out)	6	2	4	0	8	-	5	29
6.	CSM Reşiţa (Relegated)	6	2	1	3	8	-	7	26
7.	CS Aerostar Bacău (Relegated)	6	0	1	5	4		17	11

Liga II – Play-out [15-22.05.2021]

ACS Fotbal Maramureş Comuna Recea - AFC Unirea 04 Slobozia	2-0(0-0)	0-3(0-0)

ACS Fotbal Maramureş Comuna Recea were relegated.

INTERNATIONAL MATCHES
(16.07.2020 – 15.07.2021)

04.09.2020	Bucureşti	Romania - Northern Ireland	1-1(1-0)	(UNL)
07.09.2020	Klagenfurt	Austria - Romania	2-3(1-1)	(UNL)
08.10.2020	Reykjavík	Iceland - Romania	2-1(2-0)	(ECQPO)
11.10.2020	Oslo	Norway - Romania	4-0(2-0)	(UNL)
14.10.2020	Ploieşti	Romania - Austria	0-1(0-0)	(UNL)
11.11.2020	Ploieşti	Romania - Belarus	5-3(4-0)	(F)
15.11.2020	Bucureşti	Romania - Norway	3-0 (awarded)	(UNL)
18.11.2020	Belfast	Northern Ireland - Romania	1-1(0-0)	(UNL)
25.03.2021	Bucureşti	Romania - North Macedonia	3-2(1-0)	(WCQ)
28.03.2021	Bucureşti	Romania - Germany	0-1(0-1)	(WCQ)
31.03.2021	Yerevan	Armenia- Romania	3-2(0-0)	(WCQ)
02.06.2021	Ploieşti	Romania - Georgia	1-2(0-0)	(F)
06.06.2021	Middlesbrough	England - Romania	1-0(0-0)	(F)

04.09.2020   ROMANIA - NORTHERN IRELAND   1-1(1-0)   2nd UEFA Nations League B, Group 1

2nd UEFA Nations League B, Group 1

Arena Naţională, Bucureşti; Referee: François Letexier (France); Attendance: 0
ROU: Anton Ciprian Tătăruşanu, Alin Dorinel Toşca, Vlad Iulian Chircheş (Cap), Sergiu Cătălin Hanca (86.Ionuţ Nedelceanu), Nicuşor Silviu Bancu, Ianis Hagi (55.Alexandru Creţu), Nicolae Claudiu Stanciu, Alexandru Cicâldău (73.Dan Nicolae Nistor), Alexandru Iulian Maxim, Denis Alibec, George Alexandru Puşcaş. Trainer: Mirel Matei Rădoi.
Goal: George Alexandru Puşcaş (25).

07.09.2020   AUSTRIA - ROMANIA   2-3(1-1) 2nd UEFA Nations League B, Group 1

Wörthersee Stadion, Klagenfurt; Referee: Glenn Nyberg (Sweden); Attendance: 0
ROU: Anton Ciprian Tătăruşanu, Andrei Andonie Burcă, Dragoş Grigore, Vlad Iulian Chircheş (Cap) (74.Ionuţ Nedelceanu), Nicuşor Silviu Bancu, Alexandru Creţu, Ciprian Ioan Deac (40.Gabriel Cristian Iancu), Nicolae Claudiu Stanciu, Alexandru Iulian Maxim, Denis Alibec (68.George Alexandru Puşcaş), Florinel Teodor Coman. Trainer: Mirel Matei Rădoi.
Goals: Denis Alibec (3), Dragoş Grigore (51), Alexandru Iulian Maxim (70).

08.10.2020   ICELAND - ROMANIA   2-1(2-0)   16th EC. Qualifiers Play-offs, Semi-Finals

Laugardalsvöllur, Reykjavík; Referee: Damir Skomina (Slovenia); Attendance: 59
ROU: Anton Ciprian Tătăruşanu (Cap), Cristian Marian Manea, Mihai Alexandru Bălaşa, Andrei Andonie Burcă, Mário Jorge Malico Paulino "Camora", Alexandru Creţu, Ciprian Ioan Deac (46.Gabriel Cristian Iancu), Nicolae Claudiu Stanciu (87.Alexandru Cicâldău), Alexandru Iulian Maxim (80.Claudiu Andrei Keşerü), Denis Alibec (46.George Alexandru Puşcaş), Alexandru Ionuţ Mitriţă (46.Ianis Hagi). Trainer: Mirel Matei Rădoi.
Goal: Alexandru Iulian Maxim (63 penalty).

11.10.2020   NORWAY - ROMANIA   4-0(2-0) 2nd UEFA Nations League B, Group 1

Ullevaal Stadion, Oslo; Referee: Ivan Kružliak (Slovakia); Attendance: 200
ROU: Anton Ciprian Tătăruşanu (Cap), Cristian Marian Manea, Alin Dorinel Toşca, Nicuşor Silviu Bancu, Andrei Andonie Burcă, Alexandru Creţu (75.Alexandru Iulian Maxim), Răzvan Gabriel Marin, Alexandru Cicâldău (75.Nicolae Claudiu Stanciu), Ianis Hagi (63.Alexandru Ionuţ Mitriţă), George Alexandru Puşcaş (64.Claudiu Andrei Keşerü), Gabriel Cristian Iancu (90+1.Denis Alibec). Trainer: Mirel Matei Rădoi.

14.10.2020   ROMANIA - AUSTRIA   0-1(0-0) 2nd UEFA Nations League B, Group 1

Stadionul "Ilie Oană", Ploieşti; Referee: Daniel Stefański (Poland); Attendance: 0
ROU: Anton Ciprian Tătăruşanu (Cap), Alin Dorinel Toşca, Nicuşor Silviu Bancu, Mihai Alexandru Bălaşa, Andrei Andonie Burcă, Ciprian Ioan Deac (83.George Alexandru Puşcaş), Răzvan Gabriel Marin, Nicolae Claudiu Stanciu (83.Gabriel Cristian Iancu), Alexandru Iulian Maxim (62.Alexandru Cicâldău), Denis Alibec (62.Claudiu Andrei Keşerü), Alexandru Ionuţ Mitriţă (76.Ianis Hagi). Trainer: Mirel Matei Rădoi.

11.11.2020   ROMANIA - BELARUS   5-3(4-0)   Friendly International

Stadionul "Ilie Oană", Ploieşti; Referee: Georgi Kabakov (Bulgaria); Attendance: 0
ROU: David Beniamin Lazar, Alin Dorinel Toşca (46.Iulian Lucian Cristea), Bogdan Alexandru Mitrea, Ionuţ Nedelceanu, Cristian George Ganea, Vasile Mogoş (69.Valentin Iulian Creţu), Dan Nicolae Nistor, Răzvan Gabriel Marin (Cap) (70.Eric Cosmin Bicfalvi), Dennis Man (57.Alexandru Mihai Băluţă), Florin Lucian Tănase (57.Alexandru Iulian Maxim), George Alexandru Puşcaş (58.Denis Alibec). Trainer: Mirel Matei Rădoi.
Goals: Bogdan Alexandru Mitrea (11), Răzvan Gabriel Marin (20 penalty), Ionuţ Nedelceanu (31), George Alexandru Puşcaş (44), Ionuţ Nedelceanu (55).

15.11.2020   ROMANIA - NORWAY   3-0 (awarded) 2nd UEFA Nations League B, Group 1

Arena Naţională, Bucureşti; Referee: Ali Palabıyık (Turkey); Attendance: 0
Please note: the match was cancelled and awarded as a 3–0 win to Romania after the Norway national team were prohibited from travelling to Romania by the Norwegian government due to a positive COVID-19 test in the squad.

18.11.2020   NORTHERN IRELAND - ROMANIA   1-1(0-0) 2nd UEFA Nations League B, Group 1

Windsor Park, Belfast; Referee: Sandro Schärer (Switzerland); Attendance: 1,060
ROU: Anton Ciprian Tătăruşanu (Cap), Alin Dorinel Toşca (74.Eric Cosmin Bicfalvi), Valentin Iulian Creţu (64.Vasile Mogoş), Ionuţ Nedelceanu, Mário Jorge Malico Paulino "Camora", Iulian Lucian Cristea, Dan Nicolae Nistor, Răzvan Gabriel Marin, Dennis Man (64.Alexandru Iulian Maxim), Florin Lucian Tănase (87.Cristian George Ganea), Denis Alibec (87.Alexandru Mihai Băluţă). Trainer: Mirel Matei Rădoi.
Goal: Eric Cosmin Bicfalvi (81).

25.03.2021   ROMANIA - NORTH MACEDONIA   3-2(1-0)   22nd FIFA WC. Qualifiers

Arena Naţională, Bucureşti; Referee: Fábio José Costa Veríssimo (Portugal); Attendance: 0
ROU: Florin Constantin Niţă, Nicuşor Silviu Bancu, Vlad Iulian Chircheş (Cap), Andrei Andonie Burcă, Nicolae Claudiu Stanciu (76.Eric Cosmin Bicfalvi), Răzvan Gabriel Marin, Ovidiu Marian Popescu, Florin Lucian Tănase (76.Ianis Hagi), Florinel Teodor Coman (14.Valentin Mihai Mihăilă), Dennis Man (76.Alexandru Iulian Maxim), Claudiu Andrei Keşerü (63.George Alexandru Puşcaş). Trainer: Mirel Matei Rădoi.
Goals: Florin Lucian Tănase (28), Valentin Mihai Mihăilă (50), Ianis Hagi (86).

28.03.2021 **ROMANIA - GERMANY** 0-1(0-1) 22nd FIFA WC. Qualifiers
Arena Naţională, Bucureşti; Referee: Clément Turpin (France); Attendance: 0
ROU: Florin Constantin Niţă, Alin Dorinel Toşca, Vlad Iulian Chircheş (Cap), Mário Jorge Malico Paulino "Camora" (46.Andrei Andonie Burcă), Nicolae Claudiu Stanciu, Răzvan Gabriel Marin, Ovidiu Marian Popescu, Ianis Hagi (83.Alexandru Iulian Maxim), Valentin Mihai Mihăilă (66.Dennis Man), Florin Lucian Tănase (83.Alexandru Cicâldău), Claudiu Andrei Keşerü (65.George Alexandru Puşcaş). Trainer: Mirel Matei Rădoi.

31.03.2021 **ARMENIA- ROMANIA** 3-2(0-0) 22nd FIFA WC. Qualifiers
„Vazgen Sargsyan" Hanrapetakan Stadium, Yerevan; Referee: Andris Treimanis (Latvia); Attendance: 4,300
ROU: Florin Constantin Niţă, Alin Dorinel Toşca, Vlad Iulian Chircheş (Cap), Nicuşor Silviu Bancu, Vasile Mogoş, Nicolae Claudiu Stanciu (74.Florin Lucian Tănase), Alexandru Iulian Maxim (74.Claudiu Andrei Keşerü), Răzvan Gabriel Marin, Alexandru Cicâldău (81.Alexandru Creţu), Dennis Man (81.Valentin Mihai Mihăilă), George Alexandru Puşcaş [*sent off 78*]. Trainer: Mirel Matei Rădoi.
Goals: Alexandru Cicâldău (62, 72).

02.06.2021 **ROMANIA - GEORGIA** 1-2(0-0) Friendly International
Stadionul "Ilie Oană", Ploieşti; Referee: Anastasios Sidiropoulos (Greece); Attendance: 1,000
ROU: Andrei Daniel Vlad, Ionuţ Nedelcearu, Răzvan Gabriel Marin (77.Nicolae Claudiu Stanciu), Vlad Iulian Chircheş (Cap), Cristian George Ganea, Darius Dumitru Olaru (57.Alexandru Cicâldău), Deian Cristian Sorescu, Alexandru Iulian Maxim (58.Constantin Valentin Budescu), Florin Lucian Tănase [*sent off 42*], Ianis Hagi (77.Claudiu Andrei Keşerü), Denis Alibec (58.Andrei Virgil Ivan). Trainer: Mirel Matei Rădoi.
Goal: Andrei Virgil Ivan (78).

06.06.2021 **ENGLAND - ROMANIA** 1-0(0-0) Friendly International
Riverside Stadium, Middlesbrough; Referee: Tiago Bruno Lopes Martins (Portugal); Attendance: 6,952
ROU: Florin Constantin Niţă, Vlad Iulian Chircheş (Cap), Ionuţ Nedelcearu (84.Adrián Rus), Mário Jorge Malico Paulino "Camora", Nicolae Claudiu Stanciu, Adrian Constantin Alexandru Păun (80.Alexandru Mihai Băluţă), Deian Cristian Sorescu (66.Tiberiu Ionuţ Căpuşă), Răzvan Gabriel Marin, Alexandru Cicâldău (80.Constantin Valentin Budescu), Denis Alibec (66.Ianis Hagi), Andrei Virgil Ivan. Trainer: Mirel Matei Rădoi.

NATIONAL TEAM PLAYERS
(16.07.2020 – 15.07.2021)

Name	DOB	Caps	Goals	2020/2021:	Club
Goalkeepers					
David Beniamin LAZAR	08.08.1991	1	0	2020:	*AFC Astra Giurgiu*
Florin Constantin NIŢĂ	03.07.1987	6	0	2021:	*AC Sparta Praha (CZE)*
Anton Ciprian TĂTĂRUŞAN	09.02.1986	74	0	2020: 11.09.2020->	*Olympique Lyonnais (FRA) AC Milan (ITA)*
Andrei Daniel VLAD	14.04.1999	1	0	2021:	*SC FCSB Bucureşti*
Defenders					
Nicuşor Silviu BANCU	18.09.1992	19	0	2020/2021:	*CS Universitatea Craiova*
Andrei Andonie BURCĂ	15.04.1993	6	0	2020/2021:	*FC CFR 1907 Cluj-Napoca*
Mihai Alexandru BĂLAŞA	14.01.1995	8	0	2020:	*SC FCSB Bucureşti*
Mário Jorge Malico Paulino "CAMORA"	10.11.1986	4	0	2020/2021:	*FC CFR 1907 Cluj-Napoca*
Tiberiu Ionuţ CĂPUŞĂ	06.04.1998	1	0	2021:	*AFC Chindia Târgovişte*
Vlad Iulian CHIRICHEŞ	14.11.1989	65	0	2020/2021:	*US Sassuolo Calcio (ITA)*
Iulian Lucian CRISTEA	17.07.1994	3	0	2020:	*SC FCSB Bucureşti*
Cristian George GANEA	24.05.1992	8	0	2020/2021:	*Aris Thessaloníki (GRE)*
Dragoş GRIGORE	07.09.1986	38	1	2020/2021:	*PFC Ludogorets Razgrad (BUL)*
Sergiu Cătălin HANCA	04.04.1992	5	0	2020:	*KS Cracovia Kraków (POL)*
Cristian Marian MANEA	09.08.1997	10	1	2020:	*FC CFR 1907 Cluj-Napoca*
Bogdan Alexandru MITREA	29.09.1987	1	1	2020:	*ACS Sepsi OSK Sfântu Gheorghe*
Vasile MOGOŞ	31.10.1992	4	0	2020/2021:	*AC Chievo Verona (ITA)*
Ionuţ NEDELCEARU	25.04.1996	15	0	2020: 05.10.2020->	*FK Ufa (RUS) AEK Athína (GRE)*
Ovidiu Marian POPESCU	27.02.1994	2	0	2021:	*SC FCSB Bucureşti*
Adrián RUS	18.03.1996	6	0	2021:	*Fehérvár FC Székesfehérvár (HUN)*
Alin Dorinel TOŞCA	14.03.1992	25	0	2020/2021:	*Gaziantep FK (TUR)*

Midfielders					
Eric Cosmin BICFALVI	05.02.1988	9	1	2020/2021:	FK Ural Yekaterinburg (RUS)
Constantin Valentin BUDESCU	19.02.1989	14	5	2021:	Damac FC Khamis Mushait (KSA)
Alexandru Mihai BĂLUȚĂ	13.09.1993	8	1	2020/2021:	Puskás Ferenc Labdarugó Akadémia (HUN)
Alexandru CICÂLDĂU	08.07.1997	14	0	2020/2021:	CS Universitatea Craiova
Alexandru CREȚU	24.04.1992	5	0	2020/2021:	NK Maribor (SVN)
Valentin Iulian CREȚU	02.01.1989	2	0	2020:	SC FCSB București
Ciprian Ioan DEAC	16.02.1986	26	4	2020:	FC CFR 1907 Cluj-Napoca
Ianis HAGI	22.10.1998	18	1	2020/2021:	Rangers FC Glasgow (SCO)
Dennis MAN	26.08.1998	9	1	2020:	SC FCSB București
				29.01.2021->	Parma Calcio 1913 (ITA)
Răzvan Gabriel MARIN	23.05.1996	30	2	2020/2021:	Cagliari Calcio (ITA)
Alexandru Iulian MAXIM	08.07.1990	49	7	2020/2021:	Gaziantep FK (TUR)
Valentin Mihai MIHĂILĂ	02.02.2000	3	1	2021:	Parma Calcio 1913 (ITA)
Alexandru Ionuț MITRIȚĂ	08.02.1995	14	2	2020:	Al Ahly SC Jeddah (KSA)
Dan Nicolae NISTOR	06.05.1988	7	0	2020:	CS Universitatea Craiova
Darius Dumitru OLARU	03.03.1998	1	0	2021:	SC FCSB București
Adrian Constantin Alexandru PĂUN	01.04.1995	1	0	2021:	FC CFR 1907 Cluj-Napoca
Deian Cristian SORESCU	29.08.1997	2	0	2021:	FC Dinamo București
Nicolae Claudiu STANCIU	07.05.1993	47	10	2020/2021:	SK Slavia Praha (CZE)
Florin Lucian TĂNASE	30.12.1994	9	1	2020/2021:	SC FCSB București

Forwards					
Denis ALIBEC	05.01.1991	19	2	2020:	AFC Astra Giurgiu
				02.10.2020->	Kayserispor Kulübü (TUR)
Florinel Teodor COMAN	10.04.1998	5	0	2020/2021:	SC FCSB București
Gabriel Cristian IANCU	15.04.1994	4	0	2020:	FC Viitorul Constanța
Andrei Virgil IVAN	04.01.1997	9	1	2021:	CS Universitatea Craiova
Claudiu Andrei KEȘERÜ	02.12.1986	44	13	2020/2021:	PFC Ludogorets Razgrad (BUL)
George Alexandru PUȘCAȘ	08.04.1996	23	8	2020/2021:	Reading FC (ENG)

Trainer			
Mirel Matei RĂDOI [from 26.11.2019]	22.03.1981	12 M; 3 W; 2 D; 7 L; 17-23	

RUSSIA

The Country:
Российская Федерация (Russian Federation)
Capital: Moskva
Surface: 17,098,246 km²
Inhabitants: 146,171,015 [2021]
Time: UTC+2 to +12

The FA:
Российский Футбольный Союз (Russian Football Union)
Ulitsa Narodnaya 7, 115 172 Moskva
Tel: +7 495 926 1300
Founded: 19.01.1912
Member of FIFA since: 1912-1917 and since 1992
Member of UEFA since: 1954
Website: www.rfs.ru

NATIONAL TEAM RECORDS

RECORDS

First international match:	30.06.1912, Stockholm:	Finland – Russia 2-1
Most international caps:	Sergey Ignashevich	- 127 caps (2002-2018)
Most international goals:	Aleksandr Kerzhakov	- 30 goals / 91 caps (2002-2016)
	Artyom Dzyuba	- 30 goals / 55 caps (since 2011)

UEFA EUROPEAN CHAMPIONSHIP

1960	-*
1964	-
1968	-
1972	-
1976	-
1980	-
1984	-
1988	-
1992	-
1996	Final Tournament (Group Stage)
2000	Qualifiers
2004	Final Tournament (Group Stage)
2008	Final Tournament (Semi-Finals)
2012	Final Tournament (Group Stage)
2016	Final Tournament (Group Stage)
2020	Final Tournament (Group Stage)

from 1960 to 1992 as Soviet Union/C.I.S.

FIFA WORLD CUP

1930	-**
1934	-
1938	-
1950	-
1954	-
1958	-
1962	-
1966	-
1970	-
1974	-
1978	-
1982	-
1986	-
1990	-
1994	Final Tournament (Group Stage)
1998	Qualifiers
2002	Final Tournament (Group Stage)
2006	Qualifiers
2010	Qualifiers
2014	Final Tournament (Group Stage)
2018	Final Tournament (Quarter-Finals)

from 1930 to 1990 as Soviet Union

OLYMPIC TOURNAMENTS

1908	-
1912	Quarter-Finals
1920	-
1924	-
1928	-
1936	-
1948	-
1952	-
1956	-
1960	-
1964	-
1968	-
1972	-
1976	-
1980	-
1984	-
1988	-
1992	-
1996	Qualifiers
2000	Qualifiers
2004	Qualifiers
2008	Qualifiers
2012	Qualifiers
2016	Qualifiers

UEFA NATIONS LEAGUE

2018/2019	League B
2020/2021	League B

FIFA CONFEDERATIONS CUP 1992-2017

2017 (Group Stage)

RUSSIAN CLUB HONOURS IN EUROPEAN CLUB COMPETITIONS:

European Champion Clubs.Cup (1956-1992) / UEFA Champions League (1993-2021)		
None		
Fairs Cup (1858-1971) / UEFA Cup (1972-2009) / UEFA Europa League (2010-2021)		
FK CSKA Moskva	1	2004/2005
FK Zenit Saint Petersburg	1	2007/2008
UEFA Super Cup (1972-2020)		
FK Zenit Saint Petersburg	1	2008
*European Cup Winners.Cup 1961-1999**		
None		

defunct competition

NATIONAL COMPETITIONS
TABLE OF HONOURS

Football championship of Russian Empire	
1912	Saint Petersburg
1913	Odessa
1914	*Championship cancelled*

Football championship of Russian SFSR among city teams	
1920	Moskva
1921	*No competition*
1922	Moskva
1923	*No competition*
1924	Leningrad
1925	*No competition*
1926	*No competition*
1927	Moskva
1928	Moskva
1929	*No competition*
1930	*No competition*
1931	Moskva
1932	Leningrad
1933	*No competition*
1934	Voronezh
1935	*No competition*

Soviet League (1936–1991)

	CHAMPIONS	CUP WINNERS	BEST GOALSCORERS	
1936 (spring)	Dinamo Moskva	-	Mikhail Semichastny (Dinamo Moskva)	6
1936 (autumn)	Spartak Moskva	Lokomotiv Moskva	Georgy Glazkov (Spartak Moskva)	7
1937	Dinamo Moskva	Dinamo Moskva	Boris Paichadze (Dinamo Tbilisi) Leonid Rumyantsev (Spartak Moskva) Vasily Smirnov (Dinamo Moskva)	8
1938	Spartak Moskva	Spartak Moskva	Makar Goncharenko (Dinamo Kiev)	19
1939	Spartak Moskva	Spartak Moskva	Grigory Fedotov (CDKA Moskva)	21
1940	Dinamo Moskva	*No competition*	Grigory Fedotov (CDKA Moskva) Sergey Solovyov (Dinamo Moskva)	21
1941	*No competition*	*No competition*	-	
1942	*No competition*	*No competition*	-	
1943	*No competition*	*No competition*	-	
1944	*No competition*	Zenit Leningrad	-	
1945	Dinamo Moskva	CDKA Moskva	Vsevolod Bobrov (CDKA Moskva)	24
1946	CDKA Moskva	Spartak Moskva	Aleksandr Ponomaryov (Torpedo Moskva)	18
1947	CDKA Moskva	Spartak Moskva	Vsevolod Bobrov (CDKA Moskva) Valentin Nikolayev (CDKA Moskva) Sergey Solovyov (Dinamo Moskva)	14
1948	CDKA Moskva	CDKA Moskva	Sergey Solovyov (Dinamo Moskva)	25
1949	Dinamo Moskva	Torpedo Moskva	Nikita Simonyan (Spartak Moskva)	26
1950	CDKA Moskva	Spartak Moskva	Nikita Simonyan (Spartak Moskva)	34
1951	CDSA Moskva	CDSA Moskva	Avtandil Gogoberidze (Dinamo Tbilisi)	16
1952	Spartak Moskva	Torpedo Moskva	Andrey Zazroyev (Dinamo Kiev)	11
1953	Spartak Moskva	Dinamo Moskva	Nikita Simonyan (Spartak Moskva)	14
1954	Dinamo Moskva	Dynamo Kiev	Anatoli Ilyin (Spartak Moskva) Vladimir Ilyin (Dinamo Moskva) Antonin Sochnev (Trudovye Reservy Leningrad)	11
1955	Dinamo Moskva	CDSA Moskva	Eduard Streltsov (Torpedo Moskva)	15
1956	Spartak Moskva	*No competition*	Vasily Buzunov (ODO Sverdlovsk)	17
1957	Dinamo Moskva	Lokomotiv Moskva	Vasily Buzunov (CSK MO Moskva)	16
1958	Spartak Moskva	Spartak Moskva	Anatoli Ilyin (Spartak Moskva)	19
1959	Dinamo Moskva	-	Zaur Kaloyev (Dinamo Tbilisi)	16
1960	Torpedo Moskva	Torpedo Moskva (1959/60)	Zaur Kaloyev (Dinamo Tbilisi) Gennady Gusarov (Torpedo Moskva)	20
1961	Dinamo Kiev	Shakhtyor Stalino	Gennady Gusarov (Torpedo Moskva)	22
1962	Spartak Moskva	Shakhtyor Stalino	Mikhail Mustygin (Belarus Minsk)	17
1963	Dinamo Moskva	Spartak Moskva	Oleg Kopaev (SKA Rostov-na-Donu)	27
1964	Dinamo Tbilisi	Dynamo Kiev	Vladimir Fedotov (CSKA Moskva)	16
1965	Torpedo Moskva	Spartak Moskva	Oleg Kopaev (SKA Rostov-na-Donu)	18
1966	Dinamo Kiev	Dynamo Kiev (1965/66)	Ilya Datunashvili (Dinamo Tbilisi)	20
1967	Dinamo Kiev	Dinamo Moskva (1966/67)	Mikhail Mustygin (Dinamo Minsk)	19
1968	Dinamo Kiev	Torpedo Moskva (1967/68)	Georgi Gavasheli (Dinamo Tbilisi) Berador Abduraimov (Pakhtakor Tashkent)	22
1969	Spartak Moskva	Karpaty Lviv	Nikolai Osyanin (Spartak Moskva) Vladimir Proskurin (SKA Rostov-na-Donu) Dzhemal Kherhadze (Torpedo Kutaisi)	16
1970	CSKA Moskva	Dinamo Moskva	Givi Nodia (Dinamo Tbilisi)	17

1971	Dinamo Kiev	Spartak Moskva	Eduard Malofeev (Dinamo Minsk)	16
1972	Zarya Voroshilovgrad	Torpedo Moskva	Oleg Blokhin (Dinamo Kiev)	14
1973	Ararat Yerevan	Ararat Yerevan	Oleg Blokhin (Dinamo Kiev)	18
1974	Dinamo Kiev	Dynamo Kiev	Oleg Blokhin (Dinamo Kiev)	20
1975	Dinamo Kiev	Ararat Yerevan	Oleg Blokhin (Dinamo Kiev)	18
1976 (spring)	Dinamo Moskva	-	Arkady Andreasian (Ararat Yerevan)	8
1976 (autumn)	Torpedo Moskva	Dinamo Tbilisi	Aleksandr Markin (Zenit Leningrad)	13
1977	Dinamo Kiev	Dinamo Moskva	Oleg Blokhin (Dinamo Kiev)	17
1978	Dinamo Tbilisi	Dynamo Kiev	Georgi Yartsev (Spartak Moskva)	19
1979	Spartak Moskva	Dinamo Tbilisi	Vitali Starukhin (Shakhtar Donetsk)	26
1980	Dinamo Kiev	Shakhtar Donetsk	Sergey Andreev (SKA Rostov-na-Donu)	20
1981	Dinamo Kiev	SKA Rostov-on-Don	Ramaz Shengelia (Dinamo Tbilisi)	23
1982	Dinamo Minsk	Dynamo Kiev	Andrei Yakubik (Pakhtakor Tashkent)	23
1983	Dnipro Dnipropetrovsk	Shakhtar Donetsk	Yuriy Gavrilov (Spartak Moskva)	18
1984	Zenit Leningrad	Dinamo Moskva	Sergey Andreev (SKA Rostov-na-Donu)	20
1985	Dinamo Kiev	Dynamo Kiev	Oleg Protasov (Dnipro Dnipropetrovsk)	35
1986	Dinamo Kiev	Torpedo Moskva	Aleksandr Borodyuk (Dinamo Moskva)	21
1987	Spartak Moskva	Dynamo Kiev	Oleg Protasov (Dnipro Dnipropetrovsk)	18
1988	Dnipro Dnipropetrovsk	Metalist Kharkiv	Yevhen Shakhov (Dnipro Dnipropetrovsk) Aleksandr Borodyuk (Dinamo Moskva)	16
1989	Spartak Moskva	Dnipro Dnipropetrovsk	Sergey Rodionov (Spartak Moskva)	16
1990	Dinamo Kiev	Dynamo Kiev	Oleg Protasov (Dinamo Kiev) Valery Shmarov (Spartak Moskva)	12
1991	CSKA Moskva	CSKA Moskva	Igor Kolyvanov (Dinamo Moskva)	18

Russian League (1992–present)

	CHAMPIONS	CUP WINNERS	BEST GOALSCORERS	
1992	FK Spartak Moskva	FK Spartak Moskva	Vali Gasimov (AZE, FK Dinamo Moskva)	16
1993	FK Spartak Moskva	FK Torpedo Moskva	Viktor Panchenko (FK KamAZ Naberezhnye Chelny)	21
1994	FK Spartak Moskva	FK Spartak Moskva	Igor Simutenkov (FK Dinamo Moskva)	21
1995	FK Alania Vladikavkaz	FK Dinamo Moskva	Oleg Veretennikov (Rotor Volgograd)	25
1996	FK Spartak Moskva	FK Lokomotiv Moskva	Aleksandr Maslov (FK Rostselmash Rostov-na-Donu)	23
1997	FK Spartak Moskva	FK Lokomotiv Moskva	Oleg Veretennikov (FK Rotor Volgograd)	22
1998	FK Spartak Moskva	FK Spartak Moskva	Oleg Veretennikov (FK Rotor Volgograd)	22
1999	FK Spartak Moskva	FK Zenit Saint Petersburg	Georgi Demetradze (GEO, FK Alania Vladikavkaz)	21
2000	FK Spartak Moskva	FK Lokomotiv Moskva	Dmitriy Loskov (FK Lokomotiv Moskva)	18
2001	FK Spartak Moskva	FK Lokomotiv Moskva	Dmitriy Vyazmikin (FK Torpedo Moskva)	18
2002	FK Lokomotiv Moskva	FK CSKA Moskva	Rolan Gusev (FK CSKA Moskva) Dmitriy Kirichenko (FK CSKA Moskva)	15
2003	FK CSKA Moskva	FK Spartak Moskva	Dmitriy Loskov (FK Lokomotiv Moskva)	14
2004	FK Lokomotiv Moskva	FK Terek Grozny	Aleksandr Kerzhakov (FK Zenit Saint Petersburg)	18
2005	FK CSKA Moskva	FK CSKA Moskva	Dmitriy Kirichenko (FK Moskva)	14
2006	FK CSKA Moskva	FK CSKA Moskva	Roman Pavlyuchenko (FK Spartak Moskva)	18
2007	FK Zenit Saint Petersburg	FK Lokomotiv Moskva	Roman Pavlyuchenko (FK Spartak Moskva) Roman Adamov (FK Moskva)	14
2008	FK Rubin Kazan	FK CSKA Moskva	Vágner Silva de Souza "Vágner Love" (BRA, FK CSKA Moskva)	20
2009	FK Rubin Kazan	FK CSKA Moskva	Welliton Soares de Morais (BRA, FK Spartak Moskva)	21
2010	FK Zenit Saint Petersburg	FK Zenit Saint Petersburg	Welliton Soares de Morais (BRA, FK Spartak Moskva)	19
2010/2011	-	FK CSKA Moskva	-	
2011/2012	FK Zenit Saint Petersburg	FK Rubin Kazan	Seydou Doumbia (CIV, FK CSKA Moskva)	28
2012/2013	FK CSKA Moskva	FK CSKA Moskva	Yura Movsisyan (ARM, FK Spartak Moskva) Francisco Wánderson do Carmo Carneiro (BRA, FK Krasnodar)	13
2013/2014	FK CSKA Moskva	FK Rostov	Seydou Doumbia (CIV, FK CSKA Moskva)	18
2014/2015	FK Zenit Saint Petersburg	FK Lokomotiv Moskva	Givanildo Vieira de Sousa "Hulk" (BRA, FK Zenit Saint Petersburg)	15
2015/2016	FK CSKA Moskva	FK Zenit Saint Petersburg	Fyodor Smolov (FK Krasnodar)	20
2016/2017	FK Spartak Moskva	FK Lokomotiv Moskva	Fyodor Smolov (FK Krasnodar)	18
2017/2018	FK Lokomotiv Moskva	FK Tosno	Quincy Anton Promes (NED, FK Spartak Moskva)	15
2018/2019	FK Zenit Saint Petersburg	FK Lokomotiv Moskva	Fedor Chalov (FK CSKA Moskva)	15
2019/2020	FK Zenit Saint Petersburg	FK Zenit Saint Petersburg	Sardar Azmoun (IRN, FK Zenit Saint Petersburg) Artyom Dzyuba (FK Zenit Saint Petersburg)	17
2020/2021	FK Zenit Saint Petersburg	FK Lokomotiv Moskva	Artyom Dzyuba (FK Zenit Saint Petersburg)	20

Club name changements: **FK CSKA Moskva** = OPPW Moskva (1924-1928), CDKA Moskva (1928-1951), CDSA Moskva (1951-1953), WWS Moskva (1953-1957), CSKMO Moskva (1957-1960), CSKA Moskva (1960-1988), FK CSKA Moskva (since 1988).

NATIONAL CHAMPIONSHIP
Premier League 2020/2021
(08.08.2020 – 16.05.2021)

Results

Round 1 [08-11.08.2020]
FK Khimki - CSKA Moskva 0-2(0-2)
FK Tambov - FK Rostov 0-1(0-1)
FK Ufa - FK Krasnodar 0-3(0-0)
Arsenal Tula - Akhmat Grozny 0-0
Spartak Moskva - PFK Sochi 2-2(2-1)
FK Ural - Dinamo Moskva 0-2(0-1)
Rotor Volgograd - FK Zenit 0-2(0-1)
Rubin Kazan - Lokomotiv Moskva 0-2(0-2)

Round 2 [14-15.08.2020]
Arsenal Tula - FK Ufa 2-3(1-1)
PFK Sochi - FK Khimki 1-1(0-1)
Spartak Moskva - Akhmat Grozny 2-0(0-0)
Dinamo Moskva - Rotor Volgograd 0-0
Rubin Kazan - FK Ural 1-1(1-1)
CSKA Moskva - FK Tambov 2-1(1-1)
Lokomotiv Moskva - FK Krasnodar 1-0(1-0)
FK Rostov - FK Zenit 0-2(0-1)

Round 3 [18-19.08.2020]
PFK Sochi - Rubin Kazan 3-2(1-0)
FK Tambov - FK Khimki 1-0(1-0)
FK Krasnodar - Arsenal Tula 2-0(1-0)
FK Ufa - Spartak Moskva 1-1(1-1)
FK Ural - Lokomotiv Moskva 1-1(0-0)
Akhmat Grozny - Rotor Volgograd 3-1(0-0)
Dinamo Moskva - FK Rostov 2-0(2-0)
FK Zenit - CSKA Moskva 2-1(1-1)

Round 4 [22-23.08.2020]
FK Ural - FK Krasnodar 1-0(1-0)
FK Khimki - Akhmat Grozny 1-2(1-0)
Arsenal Tula - Dinamo Moskva 2-0(1-0)
FK Zenit - FK Tambov 4-1(1-0)
Rotor Volgograd - PFK Sochi 1-2(0-1)
CSKA Moskva - Rubin Kazan 1-2(1-1)
FK Ufa - FK Rostov 0-1(0-0)
Spartak Moskva-Lokomotiv Moskva 2-1(0-1)

Round 5 [25-26.08.2020]
FK Tambov - PFK Sochi 0-1(0-0)
Arsenal Tula - FK Khimki 1-1(0-1)
Lokomotiv Moskva - Akhmat Grozny 2-3(0-2)
Rotor Volgograd - Spartak Moskva 0-1(0-0)
Rubin Kazan - FK Ufa 3-0(0-0)
FK Krasnodar - CSKA Moskva 1-1(0-1)
FK Rostov - FK Ural 1-0(0-0)
Dinamo Moskva - FK Zenit 1-0(1-0)

Round 6 [29-30.08.2020]
Spartak Moskva - Arsenal Tula 2-1(2-1)
FK Khimki - Rotor Volgograd 1-0(0-0)
FK Ufa - Dinamo Moskva 1-1(0-1)
Lokomotiv Moskva - FK Zenit 0-0
Akhmat Grozny - CSKA Moskva 0-3(0-1)
Rubin Kazan - FK Tambov 2-2(1-1)
FK Krasnodar - FK Rostov 1-1(0-0)
PFK Sochi - FK Ural 0-0

Round 7 [12-14.09.2020]
FK Tambov - FK Ufa 2-0(1-0)
FK Ural - FK Khimki 3-1(2-0)
Akhmat Grozny - PFK Sochi 0-1(0-1)
Rotor Volgograd - FK Krasnodar 0-3 *awarded*
Dinamo Moskva - Rubin Kazan 0-1(0-1)
CSKA Moskva - Spartak Moskva 3-1(2-1)
FK Zenit - Arsenal Tula 3-1(2-0)
FK Rostov - Lokomotiv Moskva 0-0

Round 8 [18-21.09.2020]
FK Krasnodar - FK Khimki 7-2(3-2)
FK Rostov - Rotor Volgograd 3-0 *awarded*
FK Ural - FK Zenit 1-1(0-1)
Arsenal Tula - PFK Sochi 3-2(2-1)
FK Ufa - CSKA Moskva 0-1(0-0)
Rubin Kazan - Spartak Moskva 0-2(0-2)
Lokomotiv Moskva - FK Tambov 1-0(1-0)
Dinamo Moskva - Akhmat Grozny 1-0(0-0)

Round 9 [26-28.09.2020]
FK Tambov - Spartak Moskva 0-2(0-0)
FK Zenit - FK Ufa 6-0(2-0)
PFK Sochi - FK Krasnodar 1-1(1-0)
Arsenal Tula - FK Rostov 2-3(1-3)
Akhmat Grozny - FK Ural 2-0(1-0)
Rotor Volgograd - Rubin Kazan 1-3(0-1)
CSKA Moskva - Lokomotiv Moskva 0-1(0-1)
FK Khimki - Dinamo Moskva 1-0(1-0)

Round 10 [03-04.10.2020]
FK Ufa - Rotor Volgograd 0-0
FK Tambov - Arsenal Tula 1-1(0-1)
FK Ural - CSKA Moskva 0-2(0-0)
Spartak Moskva - FK Zenit 1-1(0-0)
Lokomotiv Moskva - FK Khimki 2-1(1-0)
Rubin Kazan - Akhmat Grozny 1-1(0-0)
PFK Sochi - FK Rostov 4-2(1-0)
Dinamo Moskva - FK Krasnodar 2-0(1-0)

Round 11 [17-18.10.2020]
FK Zenit - PFK Sochi 3-1(2-0)
FK Krasnodar - Rubin Kazan 3-1(1-0)
Lokomotiv Moskva - FK Ufa 1-0(0-0)
FK Khimki - Spartak Moskva 2-3(0-0)
Arsenal Tula - FK Ural 1-0(1-0)
Rotor Volgograd - FK Tambov 0-2(0-0)
CSKA Moskva - Dinamo Moskva 3-1(0-0)
FK Rostov - Akhmat Grozny 3-0(1-0)

Round 12 [24-26.10.2020]
Dinamo Moskva - PFK Sochi 3-1(2-1)
FK Zenit - Rubin Kazan 1-2(1-1)
FK Krasnodar - Spartak Moskva 1-3(0-2)
Lokomotiv Moskva-Rotor Volgograd 1-2(1-1)
FK Ural - FK Tambov 0-0
FK Rostov - FK Khimki 0-2(0-0)
Akhmat Grozny - FK Ufa 3-1(1-0)
CSKA Moskva - Arsenal Tula 5-1(1-0)

Round 13 [31.10.-01.11.2020]
Rubin Kazan - Arsenal Tula 3-1(2-0)
Akhmat Grozny - FK Krasnodar 2-0(0-0)
Spartak Moskva - FK Rostov 0-1(0-1)
PFK Sochi - Lokomotiv Moskva 2-1(2-0)
FK Ufa - FK Ural 1-2(0-2)
FK Khimki - FK Zenit 0-2(0-1)
Rotor Volgograd - CSKA Moskva 0-1(0-1)
FK Tambov - Dinamo Moskva 1-2(0-1)

Round 14 [06-08.11.2020]
PFK Sochi - FK Ufa 1-1(0-0)
FK Ural - Spartak Moskva 2-2(1-2)
Arsenal Tula - Rotor Volgograd 1-1(1-0)
FK Tambov - Akhmat Grozny 0-1(0-0)
FK Khimki - Rubin Kazan 2-0(0-0)
CSKA Moskva - FK Rostov 2-0(1-0)
Dinamo Moskva-Lokomotiv Moskva 5-1(2-1)
FK Zenit - FK Krasnodar 3-1(0-1)

Round 15 21-23.11.2020 [ ]
FK Krasnodar - FK Tambov 1-0(1-0)
Akhmat Grozny - FK Zenit 2-2(1-1)
Lokomotiv Moskva - Arsenal Tula 1-0(0-0)
Spartak Moskva - Dinamo Moskva 1-1(0-0)
CSKA Moskva - PFK Sochi 1-1(1-1)
Rotor Volgograd - FK Ural 0-0
Rubin Kazan - FK Rostov 0-2(0-0)
FK Ufa - FK Khimki 1-2(0-2)

Round 16 [28-29.11.2020]
Arsenal Tula - FK Zenit 0-0
FK Khimki - FK Krasnodar 1-0(0-0)
Akhmat Grozny - Lokomotiv Moskva 0-0
FK Rostov - Dinamo Moskva 4-1(1-0)
FK Ural - PFK Sochi 1-0(0-0)
FK Ufa - FK Tambov 4-0(2-0)
Rubin Kazan - CSKA Moskva 1-0(0-0)
Spartak Moskva - Rotor Volgograd 2-0(1-0)

Round 17 [05-07.12.2020]
Lokomotiv Moskva - Rubin Kazan 3-1(1-1)
Spartak Moskva - FK Tambov 5-1(1-0)
FK Krasnodar - Rotor Volgograd 5-0(3-0)
FK Zenit - FK Ural 5-1(4-0)
FK Rostov - FK Ufa 0-1(0-0)
Dinamo Moskva - Arsenal Tula 1-0(1-0)
CSKA Moskva - FK Khimki 2-2(1-0)
PFK Sochi - Akhmat Grozny 2-0(2-0)

Round 18 [11-13.12.2020]
FK Khimki - Arsenal Tula 1-0(1-0)
Rotor Volgograd - FK Ufa 1-0(0-0)
PFK Sochi - Spartak Moskva 1-0(0-0)
FK Zenit - Dinamo Moskva 3-1(2-0)
FK Tambov - Rubin Kazan 0-1(0-1)
FK Krasnodar - Lokomotiv Moskva 5-0(2-0)
Akhmat Grozny - FK Rostov 0-1(0-0)
CSKA Moskva - FK Ural 2-2(1-1)

Round 19 [16-18.12.2020]
Rotor Volgograd - Arsenal Tula 1-0(0-0)
PFK Sochi - Dinamo Moskva 2-0(0-0)
FK Zenit - Spartak Moskva 3-1(1-1)
FK Krasnodar - FK Ufa 1-0(1-0)
FK Khimki - Lokomotiv Moskva 3-2(1-2)
Akhmat Grozny - Rubin Kazan 0-0
FK Rostov - CSKA Moskva 1-3(0-1)
FK Tambov - FK Ural 1-1(1-1)

Round 20 [26-28.02.2021]
FK Tambov - Rotor Volgograd 1-3(1-0)
FK Khimki - FK Ufa 2-1(0-0)
FK Zenit - FK Rostov 2-2(0-1)
Lokomotiv Moskva - CSKA Moskva 2-0(2-0)
PFK Sochi - Arsenal Tula 4-0(0-0)
Spartak Moskva - Rubin Kazan 0-2(0-0)
Akhmat Grozny - Dinamo Moskva 1-2(0-2)
FK Krasnodar - FK Ural 2-2(1-0)

Round 21 [06-08.03.2021]
CSKA Moskva - Akhmat Grozny 2-0(1-0)
Rotor Volgograd - FK Khimki 0-0
FK Rostov - PFK Sochi 0-0
FK Ural - FK Ufa 0-0
Dinamo Moskva - FK Tambov 2-0(1-0)
Spartak Moskva - FK Krasnodar 6-1(2-0)
Arsenal Tula - Lokomotiv Moskva 0-3(0-0)
Rubin Kazan - FK Zenit 2-1(1-0)

Round 22 [12-14.03.2021]
FK Khimki - FK Rostov 1-0(0-0)
FK Ural - Rotor Volgograd 1-0(0-0)
Arsenal Tula - CSKA Moskva 2-1(2-0)
FK Zenit - Akhmat Grozny 4-0(0-0)
Dinamo Moskva - Spartak Moskva 1-2(1-1)
FK Ufa - Rubin Kazan 0-3(0-2)
FK Tambov - FK Krasnodar 0-4(0-1)
Lokomotiv Moskva - PFK Sochi 3-1(1-0)

Round 23 [17-19.03.2021]
Rotor Volgograd - FK Rostov 0-4(0-1)
Akhmat Grozny - Arsenal Tula 2-0(1-0)
CSKA Moskva - FK Zenit 2-3(1-1)
FK Ufa - Lokomotiv Moskva 0-1(0-0)
FK Krasnodar - Dinamo Moskva 2-3(1-0)
Spartak Moskva - FK Ural 5-1(3-0)
Rubin Kazan - FK Khimki 1-3(1-2)
PFK Sochi - FK Tambov 5-0(1-0)

Round 24 [03-05.04.2021]
Rotor Volgograd-Lokomotiv Moskva 0-2(0-1)
FK Krasnodar - Akhmat Grozny 0-5(0-1)
Rubin Kazan - PFK Sochi 1-0(0-0)
Dinamo Moskva - FK Ufa 4-0(2-0)
FK Ural - Arsenal Tula 2-0(1-0)
FK Tambov - CSKA Moskva 1-2(1-1)
FK Rostov - Spartak Moskva 2-3(2-2)
FK Zenit - FK Khimki 2-0(1-0)

Round 25 [10-12.04.2021]
FK Khimki - FK Tambov 1-0(0-0)
FK Ufa - Akhmat Grozny 3-0(2-0)
FK Rostov - Rubin Kazan 0-1(0-0)
Arsenal Tula - FK Krasnodar 1-0(0-0)
Dinamo Moskva - FK Ural 2-2(0-1)
PFK Sochi - FK Zenit 1-2(0-0)
Lokomotiv Moskva-Spartak Moskva 2-0(2-0)
CSKA Moskva - Rotor Volgograd 2-0(1-0)

Round 26 [17-18.04.2021]
Akhmat Grozny - FK Khimki 3-1(2-0)
Lokomotiv Moskva - FK Rostov 4-1(2-1)
Rotor Volgograd - Dinamo Moskva 0-3(0-0)
FK Krasnodar - FK Zenit 2-2(1-0)
FK Ural - Rubin Kazan 0-1(0-1)
Arsenal Tula - FK Tambov 4-0(2-0)
PFK Sochi - CSKA Moskva 2-1(1-0)
Spartak Moskva - FK Ufa 0-3(0-1)

Round 27 [24-25.04.2021]
FK Ural - Akhmat Grozny 1-1(0-1)
FK Zenit - Rotor Volgograd 6-0(1-0)
Dinamo Moskva - FK Khimki 0-1(0-0)
FK Tambov - Lokomotiv Moskva 2-5(1-1)
FK Ufa - PFK Sochi 2-3(1-2)
FK Rostov - Arsenal Tula 1-0(0-0)
Spartak Moskva - CSKA Moskva 1-0(0-0)
Rubin Kazan - FK Krasnodar 0-1(0-1)

Round 28 [01-03.05.2021]
Rotor Volgograd - Akhmat Grozny 1-0(1-0)
Rubin Kazan - Dinamo Moskva 2-0(1-0)
CSKA Moskva - FK Ufa 1-1(0-0)
FK Krasnodar - PFK Sochi 1-3(0-1)
FK Khimki - FK Ural 1-0(1-0)
FK Rostov - FK Tambov 2-0(0-0)
FK Zenit - Lokomotiv Moskva 6-1(3-0)
Arsenal Tula - Spartak Moskva 1-2(1-1)

Round 29 [07-10.05.2021]
Akhmat Grozny - FK Tambov 3-1(2-0)
PFK Sochi - Rotor Volgograd 2-1(1-1)
FK Ufa - FK Zenit 0-0
Arsenal Tula - Rubin Kazan 2-4(2-0)
Lokomotiv Moskva - Dinamo Moskva 0-0
CSKA Moskva - FK Krasnodar 3-1(1-1)
FK Ural - FK Rostov 1-0(1-0)
Spartak Moskva - FK Khimki 2-1(0-1)

Round 30 [16.05.2021]
Akhmat Grozny - Spartak Moskva 2-2(2-0)
Dinamo Moskva - CSKA Moskva 3-2(0-1)
FK Rostov - FK Krasnodar 1-3(0-1)
FK Tambov - FK Zenit 1-5(1-1)
FK Khimki - PFK Sochi 0-0
Lokomotiv Moskva - FK Ural 1-0(0-0)
Rubin Kazan - Rotor Volgograd 1-1(0-0)
FK Ufa - Arsenal Tula 2-1(2-1)

Please note: both matches FK Rotor Volgograd - FK Krasnodar (Round 8) and FK Rostov - FK Rotor Volgograd (Round 9), were nt played as FK Rotor Volgograd players and club staff had more than 7 positive COVID-19 test! Both matches were counted as 3-0 victories for FK Krasnodar and FK Rostov respectively.

								Total				Home					Away				
1.	**FK Zenit Saint Petersburg**	30	19	8	3	76	-	26	65	13	1	1	53	-	13	6	7	2	23	-	13
2.	FK Spartak Moskva	30	17	6	7	56	-	37	57	9	3	3	31	-	16	8	3	4	25	-	21
3.	FK Lokomotiv Moskva	30	17	5	8	45	-	35	56	11	2	2	24	-	9	6	3	6	21	-	26
4.	FK Rubin Kazan	30	16	5	9	42	-	33	53	6	4	5	18	-	17	10	1	4	24	-	16
5.	PFK Sochi	30	15	8	7	49	-	33	53	10	4	1	31	-	12	5	4	6	18	-	21
6.	FK CSKA Moskva	30	15	5	10	51	-	33	50	8	4	3	31	-	17	7	1	7	20	-	16
7.	FK Dinamo Moskva	30	15	5	10	44	-	33	50	10	2	3	27	-	10	5	3	7	17	-	23
8.	FK Khimki	30	13	6	11	35	-	39	45	9	2	4	17	-	13	4	4	7	18	-	26
9.	FK Rostov	30	13	4	13	37	-	35	43	6	2	7	18	-	16	7	2	6	19	-	19
10.	FK Krasnodar	30	12	5	13	52	-	45	41	7	4	4	34	-	23	5	1	9	18	-	22
11.	RFK Akhmat Grozny	30	11	7	12	36	-	38	40	7	4	4	23	-	15	4	3	8	13	-	23
12.	FK Ural Yekaterinburg	30	7	13	10	26	-	36	34	6	6	3	14	-	11	1	7	7	12	-	25
13.	FK Ufa	30	6	7	17	26	-	46	25	3	4	8	15	-	19	3	3	9	11	-	27
14.	FK Arsenal Tula	30	6	5	19	28	-	51	23	6	4	5	22	-	20	0	1	14	6	-	31
15.	FK Rotor Volgograd (*Relegated*)	30	5	7	18	15	-	52	22	3	2	10	5	-	23	2	5	8	10	-	29
16.	FK Tambov (*Dissolved*)	30	3	4	23	19	-	65	13	2	2	11	11	-	29	1	2	12	8	-	36

Please note: FK Tambov were dissolved after the end of the season.

Top goalscorers:	
20 **Artyom Dzyuba**	*FK Zenit St Petersburg*
19 Sardar Azmoun (IRN)	*FK Zenit St Petersburg*
15 Carl Henrik Jordan Larsson (SWE)	*FK Spartak Moskva*
14 Đorđe Despotović (SRB)	*FK Rubin Kazan*
14 Aleksandr Sobolev	*FK Spartak Moskva*

NATIONAL CUP
Kubok Rossii (Кубок России) 2020/2021

Fourth Round [26.08./02.09.2020]

FK SKA-Khabarovsk - FK Fakel Voronezh	0-0 aet; 8-7 pen		FK Zenit Irkutsk - FK Novosibirsk	1-1 aet; 4-3 pen
FK Tom Tomsk - FK Nizhny Novgorod	0-1(0-1)		FK Leningradets L. Oblast - FK Olimp-Dolgoprudny	2-1(0-1)
FK Akron Tolyatti - FK Chertanovo Moskva	0-1(0-1)		FK Mashuk-KMV Pyatigorsk - FK Legion-Dinamo	2-1(1-0)
FK Yenisey Krasnoyarsk - FK Volgar Astrakhan	2-1(0-1)		FK Znamya Noginsk - FK Sokol Saratov	0-0 aet; 6-5 pen
FK Orenburg - FK Alania Vladikavkaz	2-1(2-0)		FK Zvezda Perm - FK Chelyabinsk	3-1(1-0)
PFK Krylia Sovetov Samara - FK Irtysh Omsk	5-0(3-0)		FK Kolomna - FK Rodina Moskva	2-3
FK Neftekhimik Nizhnekamsk - FK Dinamo Bryansk	0-1(0-0)		FK Volga Ulyanovsk - FK Kamaz	2-0
FK Veles Moskva - FK Baltika Kaliningrad	4-1(1-1)		FK Kuban-H. Pavlovskaya - PFK Dinamo Stavropol	3-4
FK Chayka Peschanok. - FK Tekstilshchik Ivanovo	0-2(0-1)		FK Kaluga - FK Salyut Belgorod	0-0 aet; 6-7 pen
FK Torpedo Moskva - FK Shinnik Yaroslavl	1-2(0-2)		FK Chernomorets Novor. - FK Biolog Novokubansk	4-0(0-0)

Elite Group Stage [16.09.-04.11.2020]

Group 1	
FK Volga Ulyanovsk - FK Ural Yekaterinburg	0-3(0-2)
FK Volga Ulyanovsk - FK Veles Moskva	2-4(0-3)
FK Veles Moskva - FK Ural Yekaterinburg	1-3(0-0)
Qualified: FK Ural Yekaterinburg	

Group 2	
FK Rodina Moskva - FK Spartak Moskva	1-5(0-1)
FK Rodina Moskva - FK Yenisey Krasnoyarsk	3-0(1-0)
FK Yenisey Krasnoyarsk - FK Spartak Moskva	1-0(0-0)
Qualified: FK Spartak Moskva	

Group 3	
FK Salyut Belgorod - FK Arsenal Tula	1-1 aet; 3-4 pen
FK Salyut Belgorod - FK Tekstilshchik Ivanovo	0-3(0-3)
FK Tekstilshchik Ivanovo - FK Arsenal Tula	0-0 aet; 3-4 pen
Qualified: FK Arsenal Tula	

Group 4	
FK Leningradets Leningrad Oblast - FK Ufa	0-1(0-0)
FK Leningradets L. Oblast - FK Chertanovo Moskva	0-0 aet; 6-5 pen
FK Chertanovo Moskva - FK Ufa	0-4(0-1)
Qualified: FK Ufa	

Group 5	
FK Zenit Irkutsk - FK Khimki	0-1(0-0)
FK Zenit Irkutsk - FK Nizhny Novgorod	0-0 aet; 3-4 pen
FK Nizhny Novgorod - FK Khimki	1-1 aet;9-10pen
Qualified: FK Khimki	

Group 6	
FK Znamya Noginsk - RFK Akhmat Grozny	0-3(0-2)
FK Znamya Noginsk - FK Shinnik Yaroslavl	3-0 *awarded*
FK Shinnik Yaroslavl - RFK Akhmat Grozny	1-1 aet; 3-4 pen
Qualified: RFK Akhmat Grozny	

Group 7	
PFK Dinamo Stavropol - FK Rotor Volgograd	3-0 *awarded*
PFK Dinamo Stavropol - PFK Krylia Sovetov Samara	1-4(0-1)
PFK Krylia Sovetov Samara - FK Rotor Volgograd	3-0(2-0)
Qualified: PFK Krylia Sovetov Samara	

Group 8	
FK Zvezda Perm - PFK Krylia Sovetov Samara	0-1(0-1)
FK Zvezda Perm - FK Orenburg	0-3 *awarded*
FK Orenburg - PFK Sochi	1-1 aet; 2-4 pen
Qualified: PFK Sochi	

Group 9	
FK Chernomorets Novorossisk - FK Rubin Kazan	2-4(1-1)
FK Chernomorets Novorossisk - FK SKA-Khabarovsk	1-3(0-3)
FK SKA-Khabarovsk - FK Rubin Kazan	1-0(0-0)
Qualified: FK SKA-Khabarovsk	

Group 10	
FK Mashuk-KMV Pyatigorsk - FK Tambov	1-2(0-1)
FK Mashuk-KMV Pyatigorsk - FK Dinamo Bryansk	1-0(0-0)
FK Dinamo Bryansk - FK Tambov	0-2(0-1)
Qualified: FK Tambov	

1/8-Finals [20-22.02./03.03.2021]

FK Zenit Saint Petersburg - FK Arsenal Tula	1-2(1-2)		FK Krasnodar - PFK Sochi	1-2(0-0)
FK Dinamo Moskva - FK Spartak Moskva	2-0(1-0)		FK Rostov - RFK Akhmat Grozny	0-1(0-1)
FK CSKA Moskva - FK SKA-Khabarovsk	2-0(1-0)		FK Khimki - PFK Krylia Sovetov Samara	0-4(0-1)
FK Lokomotiv Moskva - FK Tambov	3-0(1-0)		FK Ufa - FK Ural Yekaterinburg	3-0(0-0)

Quarter-Finals [07-08.04.2021]

RFK Akhmat Grozny - FK Ufa	1-0(0-0)		PFK Krylia Sovetov Samara - FK Dinamo Moskva	2-0(1-0)
PFK Sochi - FK Lokomotiv Moskva	1-3(0-1)		FK Arsenal Tula - FK CSKA Moskva	1-2(1-0)

Semi-Finals [21.04.2021]

RFK Akhmat Grozny - PFK Krylia Sovetov Samara	0-0 aet; 1-4 pen		FK Lokomotiv Moskva - FK CSKA Moskva	3-0(1-0)

Final

12.05.2021; Nizhny Novgorod Stadium, Nizhny Novgorod; Referee: Sergey Ivanov; Attendance: 20,808
FK Lokomotiv Moskva - PFK Krylia Sovetov Samara　　　　　　　**3-1(1-1)**

Lokomotiv Moskva: Guilherme Alvin Marinato, Pablo Nascimento Castro, Vedran Ćorluka (75.Murilo Cerqueira Paim), Maciej Rybus, Dmitry Barinov (46.Daniil Kulikov), Grzegorz Krychowiak, Maksim Mukhin (67.Stanislav Magkeev), Dmitry Rybchinsky, Fedor Smolov (87.Éderzito António Macedo Lopes „Éder"),Rifat Zhemaletdinov (75.Anton Miranchuk), François Kamano. Trainer: Marko Nikolić (Serbia).

Krylia Sovetov: Ivan Lomaev, Aleksandr Soldatenkov, Yuri Gorshkov, Mehdi Zeffane (79.Dmitry Kabutov), Sergey Bozhin (90.Nikita Chernov), Denis Yakuba (44.Maksim Vityugov), Ricardo Alves Coelho da Silva, Vladislav Sarveli (80.Egor Golenkov), Roman Ezhov (90.Dmitriy Efremov), Anton Zinkovskiy, Ivan Sergeev. Trainer: Igor Osinkin.

Goals: 1-0 François Kamano (14), 1-1 Vladislav Sarveli (22), 2-1 Fedor Smolov (47 penalty), 3-1 Murilo Cerqueira Paim (84).

Respublikanskiy Fudbolnij Klub Akhmat Grozny

Founded: 1958
Stadium: Akhmat-Arena, Grozny (30,597)
Trainer: Andrei Talalayev   05.10.1972

Goalkeepers:	DOB	M	(s)	G
Vitaliy Gudiev	22.04.1995	14		
Georgi Sheliya (GEO)	11.12.1988	16		
Defenders:	DOB	M	(s)	G
Arsen Adamov	20.10.1999		(3)	
Wilker José Ángel Romero (VEN)	18.03.1993	11	(5)	1
Miroslav Bogosavac (SRB)	14.10.1996	28	(1)	
Marat Bystrov (KAZ)	19.06.1992	15	(7)	
Nikita Karmaev	17.07.2000		(5)	
Maksim Nenakhov	13.12.1998	26	(1)	
Zoran Nižić (CRO)	11.10.1989	23	(1)	
Aleksandr Putsko	24.02.1993	13	(4)	
Andrei Semyonov	24.03.1989	18		2
Rizvan Utsiev	07.02.1988		(1)	
Midfielders:	DOB	M	(s)	G
Alvi Adilkhanov	09.03.2003		(1)	
Amir Adouyev (FRA)	11.05.1999		(8)	
Ismael Silva Lima (BRA)	01.12.1994	21	(5)	1
Oleg Ivanov	04.08.1986	3	(10)	
Evgeny Kharin	11.06.1995	22	(7)	3
Artem Polyarus (UKR)	05.07.1992	8	(4)	1
Odise Roshi (ALB)	22.05.1991	1	(5)	2
Lechi Sadulaev	08.01.2000	2	(16)	1
Anton Shvets	26.04.1993	14	(7)	1
Artiom Timofeev	12.01.1994	25	(1)	3
Forwards:	DOB	M	(s)	G
Ladislav Almási (SVK)	06.03.1999	1	(7)	
Islam Alsultanov	18.08.2001		(8)	
Bernard Berisha (KVX)	24.10.1991	23	(4)	8
Gabriel Cristian Iancu (ROU)	15.04.1994	2	(5)	
Vladimir Ilyin	20.05.1992	25	(3)	9
Abubakar Kadyrov	26.08.1996		(1)	
Khalid Kadyrov	19.04.1994		(5)	
Georgi Melkadze	04.04.1997	12	(7)	3
Andrés Fabián Ponce Núñez (VEN)	11.11.1996	5	(4)	
Idris Umaev	15.01.1999	2	(2)	

Fudbolnij Klub Arsenal Tula

Founded: 1946
Stadium: Arsenal Stadium, Tula (20,048)
Trainer: Sergey Podpaly   13.09.1963
[02.11.2020] Dmytro Parfenov (UKR)   11.09.1974

Goalkeepers:	DOB	M	(s)	G
Mikhail Levashov	04.10.1991	3		
Artur Nigmatullin	17.05.1991	9		
Egor Shamov	02.06.1994	18	(1)	
Defenders:	DOB	M	(s)	G
Robert Bauer (GER)	09.04.1995	22		1
Maksim Belyaev	30.09.1991	15	(1)	
Taras Burlak	22.02.1990	13	(2)	
Aleksandr Dovbnya	14.02.1996	11	(2)	
Gia Grigalava (GEO)	05.08.1989	18		
Anri Khagush	23.09.1986	1	(3)	
Kirill Kombarov	22.01.1987	3	(1)	
Nikolai Rasskazov	04.01.1998	15	(1)	
Artem Sokol	11.06.1997	10	(5)	
Nikolai Zlobin	14.05.1996		(1)	
Midfielders:	DOB	M	(s)	G
Lameck Banda (ZAM)	29.01.2001		(2)	
Goran Čaušić (SRB)	05.05.1992	21	(1)	1
Aleksandr Denisov	23.02.1989	1	(1)	
Igor Gorbatenko	13.02.1989	4	(10)	
Valeriy Gromyko (BLR)	23.01.1997	4	(12)	
Mohammed Kadiri (GHA)	07.03.1996	9	(2)	2
Kings Kangwa (ZAM)	04.06.1999	14	(7)	1
Daniil Khlusevich	26.02.2001	13	(12)	3
Igor Konovalov	08.07.1996	3	(6)	
Georgi Kostadinov (BUL)	07.09.1990	17	(3)	
Yuriy Kovalev (BLR)	27.01.1993	8	(3)	1
Vladislav Panteleev	15.08.1996	11	(8)	1
Sergey Tkachev	19.05.1989	11	(10)	3
Forwards:	DOB	M	(s)	G
Guram Adzhoev	27.02.1995		(5)	
Luka Đorđević (MNE)	09.07.1994	10	(4)	2
Evans Kangwa (ZAM)	21.06.1992	19	(6)	4
Daniil Lesovoy	12.01.1998	6		2
Aleksandr Lomovitskiy	27.01.1998	17	(1)	2
Evgeniy Lutsenko	25.02.1987	14	(5)	2
Roman Minaev	24.12.1997		(4)	
Kirill Panchenko	16.10.1989	10	(6)	2

Profesionalniy Fudbolnij Klub CSKA [Central Sport Club of the Army] Moskva

Founded: 27.08.1911
Stadium: VEB Arena, Moskva (30,000)
Trainer: Viktor Goncharenko   10.09.1977
[23.03.3021] Ivica Olić (CRO)   14.09.1979

Goalkeepers:	DOB	M	(s)	G
Igor Akinfeev	08.04.1986	28		
Ilya Pomazun	16.08.1996	2		
Defenders:	DOB	M	(s)	G
Bruno da Lara Fuchs (BRA)	01.04.1999		(1)	
Igor Diveev	27.09.1999	23		2
Vadim Karpov	14.07.2002	10	(2)	
Hörður Magnússon (ISL)	11.02.1993	21	(1)	1
Mário Figueira Fernandes	19.09.1990	23		1
Kirill Nababkin	08.09.1986	3		
Georgiy Shchennikov	27.04.1991	20	(2)	
Viktor Vasin	06.10.1988	10	(3)	
Midfielders:	DOB	M	(s)	G
Ilzat Akhmetov	31.12.1997	8	(6)	
Jaka Bijol (SVN)	05.02.1999		(5)	
Kristijan Bistrović (CRO)	09.04.1998	1	(13)	2
Emil Bohinen (NOR)	12.03.1999	2	(2)	
Alan Dzagoev	17.06.1990	11	(4)	2
Konstantin Kuchaev	18.03.1998	18	(3)	6
Konstantin Maradishvili	07.02.2000	24	(2)	1
Ivan Oblyakov	05.07.1998	23	(4)	1
Arnór Sigurðsson (ISL)	15.05.1999	10	(13)	2
Nayair Tiknizyan	12.05.1999	8	(20)	2
Nikola Vlašić (CRO)	04.10.1997	26		11
Baktiyor Zaynutdinov (KAZ)	02.04.1998	14	(4)	1
Forwards:	DOB	M	(s)	G
Fedor Chalov	10.04.1998	13	(14)	7
Chidera Ejuke (NGA)	02.01.1998	18	(7)	5
Adolfo Julián Gaich (ARG)	26.02.1999	2	(11)	
José Salomón Rondón Giménez (VEN)	16.09.1989	9	(1)	4
Ilya Shkurin (BLR)	17.08.1999	3	(6)	3
Vladislav Yakovlev	14.02.2002		(2)	

Fudbolnij Klub Dinamo Moskva

Founded: 18.04.1923
Stadium: VTB Arena, Moskva (26,319)
Trainer: Kirill Novikov — 14.01.1981
[29.09.2020] Alyaksandr Kulchy (BLR) — 01.11.1973
[14.10.2020] Sandro Schwarz (GER) — 17.10.1978

Goalkeepers:	DOB	M	(s)	G
Igor Leshchuk	20.02.1996	3		
Anton Shunin	27.01.1987	27		
Defenders:	DOB	M	(s)	G
Roman Evgenyev	23.02.1999	27		1
Grigori Morozov	06.06.1994		(3)	
Ivan Ordets (UKR)	08.07.1992	27		3
Sergey Parshivlyuk	18.03.1989	21	(1)	
Zaurbek Pliev	27.09.1991	1	(6)	
Konstantin Rausch	15.03.1990		(4)	1
Dmitriy Skopintsev	02.03.1997	22	(2)	1
Sergey Slepov	19.05.1999	2	(2)	
Toni Šunjić (BIH)	15.12.1988	2		1
Guillermo Varela Olivera (URU)	24.03.1993	15	(2)	
Midfielders:	DOB	M	(s)	G
Daniil Fomin	02.03.1997	29		6
Charles Kaboré (BFA)	09.02.1988	9	(10)	
Danil Lipovoy	22.09.1999		(2)	
Nikola Moro (CRO)	12.03.1998	18	(6)	3
Vladimir Moskvichev	02.03.2000		(2)	
Roman Neustädter	18.02.1988	10	(6)	1
Maximilian Philipp (GER)	01.03.1994	4	(3)	1
Igor Shkolik	09.01.2001		(4)	
Sebastian Szymański (POL)	10.05.1999	28		1
Arsen Zakharyan	26.05.2003	10	(3)	3
Forwards:	DOB	M	(s)	G
Vyacheslav Grulev	23.03.1999	15	(10)	4
Sylvester Emeka Igboun (NGA)	08.09.1990	5	(12)	1
Vladislav Karapuzov	06.01.2000		(5)	
Nikolay Komlichenko	29.06.1995	11	(14)	4
Daniil Lesovoy	12.01.1998	21	(1)	5
Clinton Mua N'Jie (CMR)	15.08.1993	15	(8)	4
Anton Terekhov	30.01.1998	2	(5)	
Konstantin Tyukavin	22.06.2002	6	(9)	3

Fudbolnij Klub Khimki

Founded: 1997
Stadium: Arena Khimki, Khimki (18,636)
Trainer: Dmitriy Gunko — 01.03.1976
[25.09.2020] Igor Cherevchenko (TJK) — 21.08.1974

Goalkeepers:	DOB	M	(s)	G
Ilya Lantratov	11.11.1995	30		
Defenders:	DOB	M	(s)	G
Per Filip Dagerstål (SWE)	01.02.1997	10		
Egor Danilkin	01.08.1995	28	(1)	
Oleksandr Filin (UKR)	25.06.1996	16		
Evgeniy Gapon	20.04.1991	5	(1)	
Brian Oladapo Idowu (NGA)	18.05.1992	28		3
Arseniy Logashov	20.08.1991	5	(2)	
Dmitry Tikhiy	29.10.1992	28		
Midfielders:	DOB	M	(s)	G
Denis Glushakov	27.01.1987	14	(1)	3
Ilya Kamyshev	13.07.1997	3	(4)	
Danil Kazantsev	05.01.2001	2	(1)	
Islambek Kuat (KAZ)	12.01.1993	5	(1)	
Danil Lipovoy	22.09.1999	1	(7)	
Maksim Martusevich	07.03.1995	4	(2)	
Pavel Mogilevets	25.01.1993	7	(6)	1
Andrey Murnin	11.05.1985	2	(2)	
Artyom Polyarus (UKR)	05.07.1992	7	(1)	
Mikhail Tikhonov	17.07.1998	2	(3)	
Alexander Troshechkin	23.04.1996	22	(2)	2
Gela Zaseev	20.01.1993		(1)	
Forwards:	DOB	M	(s)	G
Kamran Aliev	15.10.1998	4	(7)	1
Kirill Bozhenov	07.12.2000	26		1
Aleksandr Dolgov	24.09.1998	2	(4)	1
Vladimir Dyadyun	12.07.1988	12	(3)	
Maksim Glushenkov	28.07.1999	2	(4)	2
Mohamed Konaté (CIV)	12.12.1997	15	(11)	3
Arshak Koryan	17.06.1995	9	(5)	4
Ilya Kukharchuk	02.08.1990	16	(5)	5
Aleksandr Lomovitskiy	27.01.1998	6	(2)	2
Reziuan Mirzov	22.06.1993	14	(3)	6
Senin Sebai (CIV)	18.12.1993	5	(3)	
Nikolay Signevich (BLR)	20.02.1992		(2)	
Ilya Vorobyov	11.07.1999		(3)	

Fudbolnij Klub Krasnodar

Founded: 22.02.2008
Stadium: Krasnodar Stadium, Krasnodar (34,291)
Trainer: Murad Musayev — 10.11.1983
[06.04.2021] Viktor Goncharenko — 10.09.1977

Goalkeepers:	DOB	M	(s)	G
Stanislav Agkatsev	09.01.2002	2		
Egor Baburin	09.08.1993	2		
Evgeniy Gorodov	13.12.1985	4		
Matvey Safonov	25.02.1999	21		
Defenders:	DOB	M	(s)	G
Evgeniy Chernov	23.10.1992	14	(4)	
Kaio Pantaleão (BRA)	08.09.1995	22	(2)	1
Vyacheslav Litvinov	01.04.2001	1	(1)	
Aleksandr Martinovich (BLR)	26.08.1987	23	(1)	
Ambroise Oyongo Bitolo (NGA)	22.06.1991		(1)	
Sergey Petrov	02.01.1991	9	(1)	2
Cristian Leonel Ramírez Zambrano (ECU)	12.08.1994	12	(4)	
Igor Smolnikov	08.08.1988	17	(6)	
Egor Sorokin	04.11.1995	13	(2)	
Dmitriy Stotskiy	01.12.1989	3	(3)	1
Midfielders:	DOB	M	(s)	G
Rémy Cabella (FRA)	08.03.1990	19	(5)	8
Aleksandr Chernikov	01.02.2000		(1)	
Yuriy Gazinskiy	20.07.1989	25	(1)	3
Ruslan Kambolov	01.01.1990	1	(9)	
Aleks Matsukatov	11.01.1999		(6)	
Mats Kristoffer Olsson (SWE)	30.06.1995	18	(8)	3
Eduard Spertsyan	07.06.2000	2	(3)	
Daniil Utkin	12.10.1999	9	(11)	1
Tonny Vilhena (NED)	03.01.1995	17	(7)	2
Forwards:	DOB	M	(s)	G
Ariclenes da Silva Ferreira „Ari"	11.12.1985	3	(6)	2
Bengt Erik Marcus Berg (SWE)	17.08.1986	19	(2)	9
Viktor Johan Anton Claesson (SWE)	02.01.1992	20	(4)	6
Aleksey Ionov	18.02.1989	16	(3)	4
Maksim Kutovoi	01.07.2001	1	(6)	
Evgeniy Markov	07.07.1994	2	(5)	
Leon Sabua	01.09.2000		(2)	1
Magomed Suleymanov	16.12.1999	8	(19)	4
Wanderson Maciel Sousa Campos (BRA)	07.10.1994	16	(5)	2

Fudbolnij Klub Lokomotiv Moskva

Founded: 23.07.1922
Stadium: RZD Arena, Moskva (27,320)
Trainer: Marko Nikolić (SRB) 20.07.1979

Goalkeepers:	DOB	M	(s)	G
Guilherme Alvin Marinato	12.12.1985	25		
Anton Kochenkov	02.04.1987	5	(1)	
Defenders:	**DOB**	**M**	**(s)**	**G**
Vedran Ćorluka (CRO)	05.02.1986	22		
Vladislav Ignatiev	20.01.1987	11	(5)	3
Mikhail Lysov	29.01.1998	1		
Vitaliy Lystsov	11.07.1995	2	(3)	
Murilo Cerqueira Paim (BRA)	27.03.1997	22		4
Pablo Nascimento Castro (BRA)	21.06.1991	10		
Slobodan Rajković (SRB)	03.02.1989	4	(1)	
Maciej Rybus (POL)	19.08.1989	26		1
Aleksandr Silyanov	17.02.2001	2		
Dmitriy Zhivoglyadov	29.05.1994	19	(5)	
Midfielders:	**DOB**	**M**	**(s)**	**G**
Dmitry Barinov	11.09.1996	8	(5)	1
Nikita Iosifov	11.04.2001		(4)	
Grzegorz Krychowiak (POL)	29.01.1990	25	(1)	9
Daniil Kulikov	24.06.1998	18	(7)	
Stanislav Magkeev	27.03.1999	12	(12)	
Aleksey Miranchuk	17.10.1995	4		2
Anton Miranchuk	17.10.1995	13	(10)	4
Maksim Mukhin	04.11.2001	8	(2)	
Dmitry Rybchinsky	19.08.1998	18	(8)	2
Nikolai Titkov	18.08.2000		(4)	
Forwards:	**DOB**	**M**	**(s)**	**G**
Mikhail Ageev	22.04.2000		(1)	
Éderzito António Macedo Lopes „Éder" (POR)	22.12.1987	12	(8)	1
François Kamano (GUI)	02.05.1996	19	(6)	5
Vitaliy Lisakovich (BLR)	08.02.1998	8	(18)	2
Fedor Smolov	09.02.1990	16	(5)	7
José Luís Mendes Andrade „Zé Luís" (CPV)	24.01.1991	3	(5)	1
Rifat Zhemaletdinov	20.09.1996	17	(5)	3

Fudbolnij Klub Rostov

Founded: 1930
Stadium: Rostov Arena, Rostov-na-Donu (45,000)
Trainer: Valeriy Karpin 02.02.1969

Goalkeepers:	DOB	M	(s)	G
Egor Baburin	09.08.1993	4		
Sergey Pesyakov	16.12.1988	24		
Maksim Rudakov	22.01.1996	1		
Defenders:	**DOB**	**M**	**(s)**	**G**
Haitam Aleesami (NOR)	31.07.1991	8	(5)	
Evgeniy Chernov	23.10.1992	8	(1)	1
Dmitriy Chistyakov	13.01.1994	1	(1)	
Aleksandr Gapechkin	16.06.2002		(1)	
Dennis Hadžikadunić (BIH)	09.07.1998	25		1
Aleksey Ionov	18.02.1989	9		1
Konstantin Kovalev	14.01.2000		(1)	
Aleksey Kozlov	25.12.1986	20	(4)	1
Arseniy Logashov	20.08.1991		(4)	
Maksim Osipenko	16.05.1994	28		
Aleksandr Pavlovets (BLR)	13.08.1996	2	(3)	
Nikolay Poyarkov	16.10.1999	12	(5)	
Aleksandr Smirnov	12.04.1996		(1)	
Denis Terentyev	13.08.1992	12	(3)	
Midfielders:	**DOB**	**M**	**(s)**	**G**
Khoren Bairamyan (ARM)	07.01.1992	14	(9)	3
Roman Eremenko (FIN)	19.03.1987	13	(3)	1
Kirill Folmer	25.02.2000	1	(5)	
Armin Gigović (SWE)	06.04.2002	9	(8)	1
Danil Glebov	03.11.1999	21	(5)	1
Kento Hashimoto (JPN)	16.08.1993	14	(5)	6
Georgi Makhatadze	26.03.1998	8	(2)	1
Pavel Mamaev	17.09.1988	7	(6)	2
Mathias Normann (NOR)	28.05.1996	15		1
Ivelin Popov (BUL)	26.10.1987	2		
Aleksandr Saplinov	12.08.1997		(3)	1
Danila Sukhomlinov	31.08.2002		(3)	
Baktiyor Zaynutdinov (KAZ)	02.04.1998	4		
Forwards:	**DOB**	**M**	**(s)**	**G**
Pontus Skule Erik Almqvist (SWE)	10.07.1999	11	(8)	1
Aleksandr Dolgov	24.09.1998		(5)	
Vladimir Obukhov	08.02.1992	2	(8)	
Dmitriy Poloz	12.07.1991	18	(8)	6
Eldor Shomurodov (UZB)	29.06.1995	8		
Artur Sokhiev	27.09.2002		(3)	
Ali Sowe (GAM)	14.06.1994	11		3
David Tosevski (MKD)	16.07.2001		(6)	
Roman Tugarev	22.07.1998	7	(9)	1
Maksim Turishchev	05.03.2002		(1)	

Sports Club Rotor Volgograd

Founded: 1929
Stadium: Volgograd Arena, Volgograd (45,568)
Trainer: Alyaksandr Khatskevich (BLR) 19.10.1973
[20.03.2021] Yuriy Baturenko (TJK) 29.12.1964

Goalkeepers:	DOB	M	(s)	G
Josip Čondrić (CRO)	27.08.1993	22		
Aleksandr Dovbnya	14.04.1987	6		
Defenders:	**DOB**	**M**	**(s)**	**G**
Azat Bayryev	17.02.1989	12	(4)	
Kirill Dontsov	21.12.2001		(1)	
Cèdric Gogoua (CIV)	10.07.1994	22		
Oleg Kozhemyakin	30.05.1995	16	(3)	
Solomon Kverkvelia (GEO)	06.02.1992	18	(1)	
Armen Manucharyan (ARM)	03.02.1995	4	(3)	
Patricio Martín Matricardi (ARG)	07.01.1994	2		
Anton Piskunov	13.02.1989	4		
Dmitriy Shomko (KAZ)	19.03.1990	4		
Danil Stepanov	25.01.2000	21	(1)	1
Dmitriy Vershkov	27.05.2002		(1)	
Midfielders:	**DOB**	**M**	**(s)**	**G**
Oleg Aleynik	08.02.1989	20	(3)	
Zuriko Davitashvili (GEO)	15.02.2001	19	(1)	
Ivan Maevski (BLR)	05.05.1988	4	(1)	
Sergey Makarov	03.10.1996	26		
Vladimir Medved (BLR)	04.10.1999		(3)	
Evgeniy Pesegov	21.02.1989	15	(9)	
Aleksandr Saplinov	12.08.1997		(1)	
Mukhammad Sultonov	22.12.1992	3	(2)	
Ilya Zhigulev	01.02.1996	23	(3)	
Forwards:	**DOB**	**M**	**(s)**	**G**
Giorgi Arabidze (GEO)	04.03.1998		(4)	
Flamarion Jovino Filho (BRA)	30.07.1996	18	(2)	4
Nikolai Kipiani	25.01.1997	10	(4)	1
Kirill Kolesnichenko	31.01.2000	1	(1)	
Beka Mikeltadze (GEO)	26.11.1997	1	(11)	
Kamil Mullin	05.01.1994	16	(9)	3
Oleg Nikolaev	21.05.1998	1	(3)	
Andrés Fabián Ponce Núñez (VEN)	11.11.1996	11	(3)	2
Sergey Serchenkov	01.01.1997	4	(12)	1
Aleksey Shchetkin (KAZ)	21.05.1991	5		2

Fudbolnij Klub Rubin Kazan

Founded: 20.04.1958
Stadium: Ak Bars Arena, Kazan (45,093)
Trainer: Leonid Slutski   04.05.1971

Goalkeepers:	DOB	M	(s)	G
Yury Dyupin	17.03.1988	26		
Nikita Medvedev	17.12.1994	4		
Defenders:	**DOB**	**M**	**(s)**	**G**
Silvije Begić (CRO)	03.06.1993	15	(3)	
Mikhail Merkulov	26.01.1994	8	(1)	
Ilya Samoshnikov	14.11.1997	21	(3)	2
Carl Anders Theodor Starfelt (SWE)	01.06.1995	29		3
Filip Uremović (CRO)	11.02.1997	22	(2)	
Georgii Zotov	12.01.1990	15	(2)	
Aleksandr Zuev	26.06.1996	13	(10)	
Midfielders:	**DOB**	**M**	**(s)**	**G**
Oliver Abildgaard (DEN)	10.06.1996	28		
Zuriko Davitashvili (GEO)	15.02.2001	1	(1)	
Hwang In-beom (KOR)	20.09.1996	13	(5)	3
Darko Jevtić (SUI)	08.02.1993	22	(3)	3
Igor Konovalov	08.07.1996	2	(4)	
Denis Makarov	18.02.1998	20	(8)	7
Pavel Mogilevets	25.01.1993		(1)	
Leon Musaev	25.01.1999	5	(5)	
Oleg Shatov	29.07.1990	17	(4)	1
Dmitriy Tarasov	18.03.1987	1	(6)	
Forwards:	**DOB**	**M**	**(s)**	**G**
Soltmurad Bakaev	05.08.1999	16	(12)	2
Đorđe Despotović (SRB)	04.03.1992	21	(5)	14
Ivan Ignatyev	06.01.1999	8	(9)	2
Kirill Klimov	30.01.2001		(3)	
Kirill Kosarev	01.08.2001		(3)	
Mikhail Kostyukov	09.08.1991	3	(5)	1
Khvicha Kvaratskhelia (GEO)	12.02.2001	20	(3)	4

Professionalnij Fudbolnij Klub Sochi

Founded: 06.06.2018
Stadium: Fisht Olympic Stadium, Sochi (47,659)
Trainer: Vladimir Fedotov   12.08.1966

Goalkeepers:	DOB	M	(s)	G
Soslan Dzhanaev	13.03.1987	21		
Nikolay Zabolotniy	16.04.1990	9		
Defenders:	**DOB**	**M**	**(s)**	**G**
Nikita Kalugin	12.03.1998		(1)	
Emanuel Hernán Mammana (ARG)	10.02.1996	14	(4)	
Timofey Margasov	12.06.1992	22	(1)	
Miha Mevlja (SVN)	12.06.1990	29		3
Ivan Miladinović (SRB)	14.08.1994	18	(6)	1
Elmir Nabiullin	08.03.1995	7	(9)	
Ivan Novoseltsev	25.08.1991	11	(4)	
Danila Prokhin	24.05.2001	6	(1)	1
Sergey Terekhov	27.06.1990	27		3
Kirill Zaika	07.10.1992	16	(7)	1
Midfielders:	**DOB**	**M**	**(s)**	**G**
Akmal Bakhtiyarov (KAZ)	02.06.1998		(1)	
Andrey Bokovoy	04.03.2000		(2)	
Anatoliy Nemchenko	22.08.2000		(2)	
Christian Fernando Noboa Tello (ECU)	09.04.1985	25		12
Ivelin Popov (BUL)	26.10.1987		(1)	
Danil Prutsev	25.03.2000	3	(12)	
Egor Prutsev	23.12.2002	1	(5)	
Ibrahim Tsallagov	12.12.1990	24	(2)	
Erik Vardanyan (ARM)	07.06.1998		(1)	
Artur Yusupov	01.09.1989	22	(1)	7
Forwards:	**DOB**	**M**	**(s)**	**G**
Maksim Barsov	29.04.1993		(4)	1
Nikita Burmistrov	06.07.1989	19	(2)	6
Marko Dugandžić (CRO)	07.04.1994	4	(10)	1
João Natailton Ramos dos Santos „Joãozinho" (BRA)	25.12.1988	21	(2)	1
Dmitriy Poloz	12.07.1991	3		1
Aleksandr Rudenko	15.03.1999	7	(13)	2
Anton Zabolotny	13.06.1991	21	(6)	9

Fudbolnij Klub Spartak Moskva

Founded: 18.04.1922
Stadium: Otkrytiye Arena, Moskva (44,307)
Trainer: Domenico Tedesco (GER)   12.09.1985

Goalkeepers:	DOB	M	(s)	G
Aleksandr Maksimenko	19.03.1998	29		
Aleksandr Selikhov	07.04.1994	1		
Defenders:	**DOB**	**M**	**(s)**	**G**
Ayrton Lucas Dantas de Medeiros (BRA)	19.06.1997	27		2
Georgi Dzhikiya	21.11.1993	27	(1)	
Andrey Eshchenko	09.02.1984		(15)	
Ilya Gaponov	25.10.1997	3	(8)	
Samuel Gigot (FRA)	12.10.1993	26		3
Ilya Kutepov	29.07.1993	10	(6)	
Pavel Maslov	14.04.2000	24	(1)	
Midfielders:	**DOB**	**M**	**(s)**	**G**
Zelimkhan Bakayev	01.07.1996	13	(10)	1
Jorrit Hendrix (NED)	06.02.1995	1	(9)	
Mikhail Ignatov	04.05.2000		(2)	
Alex Král (CZE)	19.05.1998	28	(1)	
Ruslan Litvinov	18.08.2001		(6)	
Dmitry Markitesov	22.03.2001		(6)	
Victor Moses (NGA)	12.12.1990	18	(1)	4
Stepan Oganesyan	28.09.2001		(1)	
Guus Til (NED)	22.12.1997		(3)	
Nail Umyarov	27.06.2000	16	(10)	
Oston Urunov (UZB)	19.12.2000	1	(7)	
Roman Zobnin	11.02.1994	28		1
Forwards:	**DOB**	**M**	**(s)**	**G**
Maksim Glushenkov	28.07.1999	1	(4)	
Carl Henrik Jordan Larsson (SWE)	20.06.1997	29		15
Aleksandr Kokorin	19.03.1991	4	(4)	2
Ezequiel Ponce Martínez (ARG)	29.03.1997	18	(7)	9
Reziuan Mirzov	22.06.1993		(1)	
Quincy Anton Promes (NED)	04.01.1992	10	(1)	3
Aleksandr Sobolev	07.03.1997	16	(6)	14

Fudbolnij Klub Tambov

Founded: 2013
Stadium: Mordovia Arena, Tambov (44,442)
Trainer: Sergey Pervushin   19.03.1970

Goalkeepers:	DOB	M	(s)	G
Nikita Chagrov	24.04.1995	1		
Sergey Ryzhikov	19.09.1980	20		
Rodion Syamuk (BLR)	11.03.1989	5		
Vitali Sychev	02.03.2000	4		
Defenders:	**DOB**	**M**	**(s)**	**G**
Nikita Chicherin	18.08.1990	8	(2)	
Aleksandr Denisov	23.02.1989	10		
Zurab Gigashvili	20.11.2001	5	(3)	
Aleksandr Golovnya	27.10.1998		(1)	
Aleksey Gritsaenko	25.05.1995	10		1
Varazdat Haroyan	24.08.1992	8		
Oleksandr Kaplienko (UKR)	07.03.1996	14	(2)	
Denis Kaykov	12.08.1997	9		1
Ilya Martynov	25.01.2000	5	(1)	
Moris Nusuev	28.06.1997		(2)	
Adessoye Oyewole	18.09.1982	10	(2)	
Aleksey Rybin	26.01.1988	13		
Vitaliy Shakov	09.01.1991	9	(3)	
Evgeniy Shlyakov	30.08.1991	11	(5)	
Soslan Takazov	28.02.1993	6	(1)	
Farkhod Vasiev (TJK)	14.04.1990	7	(2)	
Maksim Volodko (BLR)	10.11.1992	4		
Midfielders:	**DOB**	**M**	**(s)**	**G**
Azer Aliev	12.05.1994	8	(2)	1
Tigran Avanesyan	13.04.2002		(3)	
Yuriy Bavin	05.02.1994	10		

	DOB	M	(s)	G
Cătălin Carp (MDA)	20.10.1993	8	(1)	
Valeriu Ciupercă (MDA)	12.06.1992	16		2
Nikita Drozdov	21.04.1992	2	(7)	
Dmitriy German (BLR)	12.06.1988	3	(3)	
Vladimir Kabakhidze	09.09.1999	10	(6)	
Pavel Karasev	10.07.1992	15	(4)	1
Anton Kilin	14.11.1990	7	(6)	
Lawrence Anwan Nicholas (NGA)	17.05.2001	1	(1)	
Kirill Panchenko	16.10.1989	6	(4)	1
Mohammed Rabiu (GHA)	31.12.1989	1	(1)	
Guram Tetrashvili	02.08.1988	10	(2)	
Sébastien Thill (LUX)	29.12.1993	2	(5)	
Forwards:	**DOB**	**M**	**(s)**	**G**
Said-Ali Akhmaev	30.05.1996		(4)	
Artem Arkhipov	15.12.1996	10	(1)	3
Vitaliy Balashov (UKR)	15.01.1991	2	(4)	
Evgeni Chabanov	08.08.1997		(3)	
Alexander Karapetyan (ARM)	23.12.1987	12	(4)	3
Vladsilav Karapuzov	06.01.2000	10		
Kirill Klimov	30.01.2001	5	(6)	1
Mikhail Kostyukov	09.08.1991	11	(5)	1
Dmitriy Merenchukov	03.03.1999	2		
Roman Minaev	24.12.1997	2	(4)	
Vladimir Obubev	08.02.1992	6	(3)	
German Onugkha	06.07.1996	7	(4)	4
Anton Terekhov	30.01.1998	5	(6)	
Aleksandr Yerkin	01.09.1989		(2)	

Fudbolnij Klub Ufa

Founded: 2009
Stadium: Neftyanik Stadium, Ufa (15,132)
Trainer: Vadim Evseyev   08.01.1976
[07.10.2020] Arslan Khalimbekov   21.08.1967
[11.10.2020] Rashid Rakhimov (TJK)   18.03.1965
[03.04.2021] Nikolai Safronidi   10.09.1983
[09.04.2021] Aleksey Stufalov   24.11.1983

Goalkeepers:	DOB	M	(s)	G
Aleksandr Belenov	13.09.1986	29		
Aleksey Chernov	03.06.1998	1		
Defenders:	**DOB**	**M**	**(s)**	**G**
Pavel Alikin	06.03.1984	7	(3)	1
Moritz Bauer (AUT)	25.01.1992	7		
Parfait Bizoza (BDI)	03.03.1999	3	(4)	
Sergey Borodin	30.01.1999		(1)	
Oleg Danchenko (UKR)	01.08.1994	11	(4)	
Bojan Jokić (SVN)	17.05.1986	23	(1)	1
Nemanja Miletić (SRB)	26.07.1991	8	(1)	1
Grigori Morozov	06.06.1994	9	(4)	
Ionuț Nedelcearu (ROU)	25.04.1996	9		
Aleksey Nikitin	27.01.1992	22	(1)	
Konstantin Pliev	26.10.1996	17		
Aleksandr Sukhov	03.01.1986	12	(2)	
Jemal Tabidze (GEO)	18.03.1996	22		
Midfielders:	**DOB**	**M**	**(s)**	**G**
Akhmed Alibekov (UKR)	29.05.1998	2		
Azer Aliev	12.05.1994	11	(3)	1

	DOB	M	(s)	G
Nikita Belousov	26.02.2002		(2)	
Igor Bezdenezhnykh	08.08.1996	4	(4)	
Cătălin Carp (MDA)	20.10.1993	9	(3)	
Danila Emelyanov	23.01.2000	1	(2)	
Kirill Folmer	25.02.2000	6	(7)	
Artem Golubev	21.01.1999	13	(13)	1
Oleg Ivanov	04.08.1986	8	(1)	1
Vladislav Kamilov	29.08.1995	17	(1)	4
Filip Mrzljak (CRO)	16.04.1993	13	(2)	4
Oliver Thill (LUX)	17.12.1996	1	(5)	
Oston Urunov (UZB)	19.12.2000	4	(4)	
Forwards:	**DOB**	**M**	**(s)**	**G**
Gamid Agalarov	16.07.2000	1	(4)	
Komnen Andrić (SRB)	01.07.1995	15	(1)	3
Lovro Bizjak (SVN)	12.11.1993	3	(4)	1
Nikolay Giorgobiani	16.07.1997		(4)	
Vyacheslav Krotov	14.02.1993	18	(5)	2
Dmitry Sysuyev	13.01.1988	3	(19)	
Andrés Vombergar (SVN)	20.11.1994	1	(2)	
Timur Zhamaletdinov	21.05.1997	20	(8)	4

Fudbolnij Klub Ural Yekaterinburg

Founded: 1930
Stadium: Central Stadium, Yekaterinburg (35,696)
Trainer: Yuriy Matveyev   08.06.1977

Goalkeepers:	DOB	M	(s)	G
Yaroslav Godzyur (UKR)	06.03.1985	12		
Ivan Konovalov	18.08.1994	1		
Ilya Pomazun	16.08.1996	17		
Defenders:	**DOB**	**M**	**(s)**	**G**
Arsen Adamov	20.10.1999	7	(1)	
Aleksei Gerasimov	15.04.1993	16	(3)	
Varazdat Haroyan (ARM)	24.08.1992	1		
Igor Kalinin	11.11.1995	22		1
Denis Kulakov (UKR)	01.05.1986	24	(1)	
Ivan Kuzmichev	20.10.2000		(1)	
Vladimir Rykov	13.11.1987	20	(1)	
Stefan Strandberg (NOR)	25.07.1990	17		1
Nikolai Zolotov (BLR)	11.11.1994	7	(1)	
Midfielders:	**DOB**	**M**	**(s)**	**G**
Marco Aratore (SUI)	04.06.1991	2		
Rafał Augustyniak (POL)	14.10.1993	22	(3)	4
Yuriy Bavin	05.02.1994	3	(4)	
Eric Cosmin Bicfalvi (ROU)	05.02.1988	22		7

	DOB	M	(s)	G
Dmitriy Efremov	01.04.1995	5	(5)	
Andrey Egorychev	14.02.1993	26		2
Othman El Kabir (NED)	17.07.1991	13	(1)	1
Roman Emelyanov	08.05.1992	4	(7)	
Aleksey Evseev	30.03.1994	2	(16)	1
Branko Jovićić (SRB)	18.03.1993	19		
Chingiz Magomadov	01.08.1998		(2)	
Danijel Miškić (CRO)	11.10.1993	21	(5)	
Vyacheslav Podberezkin	21.06.1992	12	(7)	1
Artyom Shabolin	19.07.2000		(9)	1
Forwards:	**DOB**	**M**	**(s)**	**G**
Ramazan Gadzhimuradov	09.01.1998	6	(5)	2
Ylldren Ibrahimaj (KVX)	24.12.1995	3	(3)	
David Karaev	10.03.1995	1	(5)	
Artem Maksimenko	27.05.1998	1	(2)	
Andrey Panyukov	25.09.1994	8	(8)	1
Pavel Pogrebnyak	08.11.1983	16	(2)	4
Evgeniy Tatarinov	06.02.1999		(3)	

Fudbolnij Klub Zenit Saint Petersburg

Founded: 25.05.1925
Stadium: Gazprom Arena, Saint Petersburg (67,800)
Trainer: Sergei Semak   27.02.1976

Goalkeepers:	DOB	M	(s)	G
Mikhail Kerzhakov	28.01.1987	18		
Andrey Lunev	13.11.1991	11	(1)	
Daniil Odoevskiy	22.01.2003	1		
Defenders:	**DOB**	**M**	**(s)**	**G**
Sergey Chibisov	01.03.2000		(1)	
Dmitriy Chistyakov	13.01.1994	9	(5)	
Douglas dos Santos Justino de Melo (BRA)	22.03.1994	28		3
Vyacheslav Karavayev	20.05.1995	25		3
Danila Khotulev	01.10.2002	1	(3)	
Danil Krugovoy	28.05.1998	5	(14)	
Dejan Lovren (CRO)	05.07.1989	21		2
Danila Prokhin	24.05.2001	1	(4)	
Yaroslav Rakitskiy (UKR)	03.08.1989	24		1
Saba Sazonov	01.02.2002		(1)	
Denis Terentyev	13.08.1992		(1)	
Yuriy Zhirkov	20.08.1983	7	(8)	

Midfielders:	DOB	M	(s)	G
Wilmar Enrique Barrios Teherán (COL)	17.10.1993	26		
Aleksandr Erokhin	13.10.1989	9	(16)	7
Kirill Kravtsov	14.06.2002		(4)	
Daler Kuzyaev	15.01.1993	14	(4)	3
Leon Musaev	25.01.1999		(3)	
Magomed Ozdoev	05.11.1992	21	(7)	
Daniil Shamkin	22.06.2002		(3)	
Marcus Wendel Valle da Silva (BRA)	28.08.1997	13	(2)	2
Forwards:	**DOB**	**M**	**(s)**	**G**
Sardar Azmoun (IRN)	01.01.1995	21	(3)	19
Sebastián Driussi (ARG)	09.02.1996	11	(5)	1
Artyom Dzyuba	22.08.1988	26	(1)	20
Stanislav Krapukhin	28.03.1998		(3)	
Malcom Filipe Silva de Oliveira (BRA)	26.02.1997	20	(1)	3
Andrey Mostovoy	05.11.1997	8	(18)	6
Emiliano Ariel Rigoni (ARG)	04.02.1993	1	(6)	
Aleksey Sutormin	10.01.1994	9	(17)	3

SECOND LEVEL
Russian National Football League 2020/2021

1.	PFK Krylia Sovetov Samara (*Promoted*)	42	32	5	5	100 - 26	101
2.	FK Orenburg*	42	28	10	4	78 - 33	94
3.	FK Nizhny Novgorod (*Promoted*)	42	27	7	8	67 - 28	88
4.	FK Alania Vladikavkaz*	42	22	11	9	74 - 40	77
5.	FK Baltika Kaliningrad	42	22	7	13	49 - 35	73
6.	FK Torpedo Moskva	42	21	9	12	65 - 41	72
7.	FK Neftekhimik Nizhnekamsk	42	20	10	12	64 - 44	70
8.	FK Veles Moskva	42	18	12	12	54 - 46	66
9.	FK Fakel Voronezh	42	17	13	12	57 - 43	64
10.	FK Yenisey Krasnoyarsk	42	19	6	17	52 - 54	63
11.	FK SKA-Khabarovsk	42	17	9	16	52 - 47	60
12.	FK Chayka Peschanokopskoye	42	15	11	16	44 - 53	56
13.	FK Volgar Astrakhan	42	14	12	16	47 - 45	54
14.	FK Spartak-2 Moskva	42	14	7	21	53 - 77	49
15.	FK Tekstilshchik Ivanovo	42	12	11	19	32 - 51	47
16.	FK Krasnodar-2	42	11	12	19	46 - 68	45
17.	FK Akron Tolyatti**	42	10	12	20	35 - 54	42
18.	FK Tom Tomsk (*Relegated*)	42	10	11	21	32 - 50	41
19.	FK Irtysh Omsk (*Relegated*)	42	9	8	25	33 - 61	35
20.	FK Dinamo Bryansk (*Relegated*)	42	10	5	27	24 - 66	32
21.	FK Chertanovo Moskva (*Relegated*)	42	7	6	29	35 - 80	27
22.	FK Shinnik Yaroslavl (*Relegated*)	42	5	10	27	39 - 90	25

*both not promoted after failing to receive a Premier League licensing due to stadium deficiencies! As result, the promotion play-off was not held, two teams being promoted directly.

**not relegated, because FK Tambov (last placed in Premier League) was dissolved and did not participate in next year's Russian National Football League.

NATIONAL TEAM

INTERNATIONAL MATCHES
(16.07.2020 – 15.07.2021)

03.09.2020	Moskva	Russia - Serbia	3-1(0-0)	(UNL)
06.09.2020	Budapest	Hungary - Russia	2-3(0-2)	(UNL)
08.10.2020	Moskva	Russia - Sweden	1-2(0-1)	(F)
11.10.2020	Moskva	Russia - Turkey	1-1(1-0)	(UNL)
14.10.2020	Moskva	Russia - Hungary	0-0	(UNL)
12.11.2020	Chişinău	Moldova - Russia	0-0	(F)
15.11.2020	İstanbul	Turkey - Russia	3-2(2-1)	(UNL)
18.11.2020	Beograd	Serbia - Russia	5-0(4-0)	(UNL)
24.03.2021	Attard	Malta - Russia	1-3(0-2)	(WCQ)
27.03.2021	Sochi	Russia - Slovenia	2-1(2-1)	(WCQ)
30.03.2021	Trnava	Slovakia - Russia	2-1(1-0)	(WCQ)
01.06.2021	Wrocław	Poland - Russia	1-1(1-1)	(F)
05.06.2021	Moskva	Russia - Bulgaria	1-0(0-0)	(F)
12.06.2021	Saint Petersburg	Belgium - Russia	3-0(2-0)	(EC)
16.06.2021	Saint Petersburg	Finland - Russia	0-1(0-1)	(EC)
21.06.2021	København	Russia - Denmark	1-4(0-1)	(EC)

03.09.2020   RUSSIA - SERBIA   3-1(0-0)   2nd UEFA Nations League B, Group 3
VTB Arena, Moskva; Referee: William Collum (Scotland); Attendance: 0
RUS: Anton Shunin, Mário Figueira Fernandes, Andrey Semyonov (77.Roman Neustädter), Georgiy Dzhikiya, Vyacheslav Karavayev, Yuriy Zhirkov (80.Daler Kuzyayev), Aleksey Ionov, Magomed Ozdoyev, Roman Zobnin, Zelimkhan Bakayev (68.Anton Miranchuk), Artyom Dzyuba (Cap). Trainer: Stanislav Cherchesov.
Goals: Artyom Dzyuba (48 penalty), Vyacheslav Karavayev (69), Artyom Dzyuba (81).

06.09.2020   HUNGARY - RUSSIA   2-3(0-2)   2nd UEFA Nations League B, Group 3
Puskás Aréna, Budapest; Referee: Maurizio Mariani (Italy); Attendance: 0
RUS: Anton Shunin, Mário Figueira Fernandes, Fyodor Kudryashov, Andrey Semyonov, Georgiy Dzhikiya, Aleksey Ionov (75.Vyacheslav Karavayev), Magomed Ozdoyev, Roman Zobnin, Daler Kuzyayev (57.Yuriy Zhirkov), Anton Miranchuk (67.Yuriy Gazinskiy), Artyom Dzyuba (Cap). Trainer: Stanislav Cherchesov.
Goals: Aleksey Miranchuk (15), Magomed Ozdoyev (34), Mário Figueira Fernandes (46).

08.10.2020   RUSSIA - SWEDEN   1-2(0-1)   Friendly International
VEB Arena, Moskva; Referee: Halis Özkahya (Turkey); Attendance: 5,000
RUS: Soslan Dzhanayev, Mário Figueira Fernandes (61.Denis Cheryshev), Fyodor Kudryashov, Ilya Kutepov, Vyacheslav Karavayev, Yuriy Zhirkov, Yuriy Gazinskiy (73.Daler Kuzyayev), Magomed Ozdoyev (46.Roman Zobnin), Anton Miranchuk (74.Zelimkhan Bakayev), Andrey Mostovoy (61.Aleksey Ionov), Artyom Dzyuba (Cap) (46.Aleksandr Sobolev). Trainer: Stanislav Cherchesov.
Goal: Aleksandr Sobolev (90+1).

11.10.2020   RUSSIA - TURKEY   1-1(1-0)   2nd UEFA Nations League B, Group 3
VTB Arena, Moskva; Referee: Matej Jug (Slovenia); Attendance: 5,019
RUS: Anton Shunin, Fyodor Kudryashov, Andrey Semyonov, Vyacheslav Karavayev, Yuriy Zhirkov, Aleksey Ionov (70.Andrey Mostovoy; 90.Daniil Fomin), Magomed Ozdoyev, Roman Zobnin, Daler Kuzyayev (59.Denis Cheryshev), Anton Miranchuk (70.Yuriy Gazinskiy), Artyom Dzyuba (Cap). Trainer: Stanislav Cherchesov.
Goal: Aleksey Miranchuk (28).

14.10.2020   RUSSIA - HUNGARY   0-0   2nd UEFA Nations League B, Group 3
VTB Arena, Moskva; Referee: Michael Oliver (England); Attendance: 0
RUS: Anton Shunin, Fyodor Kudryashov, Igor Smolnikov, Andrey Semyonov, Yuriy Zhirkov (67.Vyacheslav Karavayev), Aleksey Ionov (67.Yuriy Gazinskiy), Magomed Ozdoyev (81.Aleksandr Sobolev), Roman Zobnin, Daler Kuzyayev (55.Andrey Mostovoy), Anton Miranchuk (55.Zelimkhan Bakayev), Artyom Dzyuba (Cap). Trainer: Stanislav Cherchesov.

12.11.2020   MOLDOVA - RUSSIA   0-0   Friendly International
Stadionul Zimbru, Chişinău; Referee: Radu Petrescu (Romania); Attendance: 0
RUS: Guilherme Alvim Marinato, Georgiy Dzhikiya(Cap), Vyacheslav Karavayev, Igor Diveyev, Yuriy Zhirkov (68.Fyodor Kudryashov), Aleksey Ionov (46.Konstantin Kuchayev), Denis Cheryshev (66.Andrey Mostovoy), Daler Kuzyayev (53.Ivan Oblyakov), Aleksey Miranchuk (68.Anton Miranchuk), Daniil Fomin, Fyodor Chalov (64.Aleksandr Sobolev). Trainer: Stanislav Cherchesov.

15.11.2020   TURKEY - RUSSIA   3-2(2-1)   2nd UEFA Nations League B, Group 3
„Şükrü Saracoğlu" Stadyumu, İstanbul; Referee: Szymon Marciniak (Poland); Attendance: 0
RUS: Guilherme Alvim Marinato, Fyodor Kudryashov, Andrey Semyonov [*sent off 24*], Georgiy Dzhikiya (Cap), Yuriy Zhirkov, Magomed Ozdoyev, Denis Cheryshev (37.Vyacheslav Karavayev), Roman Zobnin (79.Daniil Fomin), Daler Kuzyayev (70.Anton Miranchuk), Aleksey Miranchuk (79.Aleksey Ionov), Anton Zabolotniy (70.Aleksandr Yerokhin). Trainer: Stanislav Cherchesov.
Goals: Denis Cheryshev (11), Daler Kuzyayev (57).

18.11.2020   SERBIA - RUSSIA   5-0(4-0)   2nd UEFA Nations League B, Group 3
Stadion "Rajko Mitić", Beograd; Referee: Anthony Taylor (England); Attendance: 0
RUS: Guilherme Alvim Marinato (46.Soslan Dzhanayev), Georgiy Dzhikiya (Cap), Vyacheslav Karavayev, Igor Diveyev (46.Roman Yevgenyev), Yuriy Zhirkov, Aleksandr Yerokhin, Magomed Ozdoyev, Daler Kuzyayev, Aleksey Miranchuk (46.Andrey Mostovoy), Anton Miranchuk (46.Ivan Oblyakov), Anton Zabolotniy (72.Denis Cheryshev). Trainer: Stanislav Cherchesov.

24.03.2021   MALTA - RUSSIA   1-3(0-2)   22nd FIFA WC. Qualifiers

Ta`Qali National Stadium, Attard; Referee: Peter Kjaesgaard (Denmark); Attendance: 0
RUS: Anton Shunin, Mário Figueira Fernandes, Andrey Semyonov, Georgiy Dzhikiya, Vyacheslav Karavayev, Aleksey Ionov (57.Rifat Zhemaletdinov), Daler Kuzyayev (78.Andrey Mostovoy), Aleksandr Golovin, Ilzat Akhmetov, Daniil Fomin (57.Aleksey Miranchuk), Artyom Dzyuba (Cap) (83.Aleksandr Sobolev). Trainer: Stanislav Cherchesov.
Goals: Artyom Dzyuba (23), Mário Figueira Fernandes (35), Aleksandr Sobolev (90).

27.03.2021   RUSSIA - SLOVENIA   2-1(2-1)   22nd FIFA WC. Qualifiers

Fisht Olympic Stadium, Sochi; Referee: Marco Di Bello (Italy); Attendance: 13,008
RUS: Anton Shunin, Mário Figueira Fernandes, Fyodor Kudryashov, Andrey Semyonov, Georgiy Dzhikiya, Yuriy Zhirkov (68.Vyacheslav Karavayev), Magomed Ozdoyev, Daler Kuzyayev, Aleksandr Golovin (49.Aleksey Miranchuk), Artyom Dzyuba (Cap) (86.Anton Zabolotniy), Rifat Zhemaletdinov (86.Maksim Mukhin). Trainer: Stanislav Cherchesov.
Goals: Artyom Dzyuba (26, 35).

30.03.2021   SLOVAKIA - RUSSIA   2-1(1-0)   22nd FIFA WC. Qualifiers

Štadión "Antona Malatinského", Trnava; Referee: Carlos del Cerro Grande (Spain); Attendance: 0
RUS: Anton Shunin, Mário Figueira Fernandes, Fyodor Kudryashov, Andrey Semyonov, Georgiy Dzhikiya, Yuriy Zhirkov (46.Andrey Mostovoy; 65.Aleksandr Sobolev), Magomed Ozdoyev, Daler Kuzyayev, Aleksandr Golovin, Artyom Dzyuba (Cap), Rifat Zhemaletdinov (58.Aleksey Miranchuk). Trainer: Stanislav Cherchesov.
Goal: Mário Figueira Fernandes (71).

01.06.2021   POLAND - RUSSIA   1-1(1-1)   Friendly International

Stadion Wrocław, Wrocław; Referee: Marco Guida (Italy); Attendance: 19,297
RUS: Anton Shunin (63.Matvei Safonov), Fyodor Kudryashov, Andrey Semyonov (46.Igor Diveyev), Georgiy Dzhikiya, Vyacheslav Karavayev, Magomed Ozdoyev (57.Maksim Mukhin), Roman Zobnin, Daler Kuzyayev (67.Yuriy Zhirkov), Aleksandr Golovin, Aleksey Miranchuk (63.Rifat Zhemaletdinov), Artyom Dzyuba (Cap) (67.Anton Zabolotniy). Trainer: Stanislav Cherchesov.
Goal: Vyacheslav Karavayev (21).

05.06.2021   RUSSIA - BULGARIA   1-0(0-0)   Friendly International

VTB Arena, Moskva; Referee: Aleksei Kulbakov (Belarus); Attendance: 11,100
RUS: Anton Shunin, Andrey Semyonov, Georgiy Dzhikiya, Yuriy Zhirkov (78.Aleksey Miranchuk), Vyacheslav Karavayev (72.Mário Figueira Fernandes), Aleksey Ionov (46.Daler Kuzyayev), Magomed Ozdoyev, Roman Zobnin, Dmitriy Barinov (50.Igor Diveyev), Aleksandr Golovin (62.Andrey Mostovoy), Artyom Dzyuba (Cap) (58.Aleksandr Sobolev). Trainer: Stanislav Cherchesov.
Goal: Aleksandr Sobolev (84 penalty)

12.06.2021   BELGIUM - RUSSIA   3-0(2-0)   16th EC. Group Stage.

Krestovsky Stadium, Saint Petersburg; Referee: Antonio Miguel Mateu Lahoz (Spain); Attendance: 26,264
RUS: Anton Shunin, Mário Figueira Fernandes, Andrey Semyonov, Georgiy Dzhikiya, Yuriy Zhirkov (43.Vyacheslav Karavayev), Magomed Ozdoyev, Roman Zobnin (63.Maksim Mukhin), Daler Kuzyayev (30.Denis Cheryshev, 63.Aleksey Miranchuk), Aleksandr Golovin, Dmitriy Barinov (46.Igor Diveyev), Artyom Dzyuba (Cap). Trainer: Stanislav Cherchesov.

16.06.2021   FINLAND - RUSSIA   0-1(0-1)   16th EC. Group Stage.

Krestovsky Stadium, Saint Petersburg; Referee: Danny Desmond Makkelie (Netherlands); Attendance: 24,540
RUS: Matvei Safonov, Mário Figueira Fernandes (26.Vyacheslav Karavayev), Georgiy Dzhikiya, Igor Diveyev, Magomed Ozdoyev (61.Rifat Zhemaletdinov), Roman Zobnin, Daler Kuzyayev, Dmitriy Barinov, Aleksandr Golovin, Aleksey Miranchuk (85.Maksim Mukhin), Artyom Dzyuba (Cap) (85.Aleksandr Sobolev). Trainer: Stanislav Cherchesov.
Goal: Aleksey Miranchuk (45+2).

21.06.2021   RUSSIA - DENMARK   1-4(0-1)   16th EC. Group Stage.

Parken Stadium, København; Referee: Clément Turpin (France); Attendance: 23,644
RUS: Matvei Safonov, Mário Figueira Fernandes, Fyodor Kudryashov (67.Vyacheslav Karavayev), Georgiy Dzhikiya, Igor Diveyev, Magomed Ozdoyev (61.Rifat Zhemaletdinov), Roman Zobnin, Daler Kuzyayev (67.Maksim Mukhin), Aleksandr Golovin, Aleksey Miranchuk (61.Aleksandr Sobolev), Artyom Dzyuba (Cap). Trainer: Stanislav Cherchesov.
Goal: Artyom Dzyuba (70 penalty).

NATIONAL TEAM PLAYERS
(16.07.2020 – 15.07.2021)

Name	DOB	Caps	Goals	2020/2021:	Club
Goalkeepers					
Soslan DZHANAYEV	13.03.1987	3	0	2020:	PFK Sochi
GUILHERME Alvim Marinato	12.12.1985	16	0	2020:	FK Lokomotiv Moskva
Matvei SAFONOV	25.02.1999	3	0	2021:	FK Krasnodar
Anton SHUNIN	27.01.1987	13	0	2020/2021:	FK Dinamo Moskva
Defenders					
Igor DIVEYEV	27.09.1999	7	0	2020/2021:	FK CSKA Moskva
Georgiy DZHIKIYA	21.11.1993	36	1	2020/2021:	FK Spartak Moskva
Mário Figueira FERNANDES	19.09.1990	32	5	2020/2021:	FK CSKA Moskva
Vyacheslav KARAVAYEV	20.05.1995	16	2	2020/2021:	FK Zenit Saint Petersburg
Fyodor KUDRYASHOV	05.04.1987	45	1	2020/2021:	Antalyaspor Kulübü (TUR)
Ilya KUTEPOV	29.07.1993	13	0	2020:	FK Spartak Moskva
Roman NEUSTÄDTER	18.02.1988	13	1	2020:	Unattached
Andrey SEMYONOV	24.03.1989	27	0	2020/2021:	RFK Akhmat Grozny
Igor SMOLNIKOV	08.08.1988	30	0	2020:	FK Krasnodar
Roman YEVGENYEV	23.02.1999	1	0	2020:	FK Dinamo Moskva
Midfielders					
Ilzat AKHMETOV	31.12.1997	8	0	2021:	FK CSKA Moskva
Zelimkhan BAKAYEV	01.07.1996	6	0	2020:	FK Spartak Moskva
Dmitriy BARINOV	11.09.1996	7	0	2021:	FK Lokomotiv Moskva
Denis CHERYSHEV	26.12.1990	31	12	2020/2021:	Valencia CF (ESP)
Daniil FOMIN	02.03.1997	4	0	2020/2021:	FK Dinamo Moskva
Yuriy GAZINSKIY	20.07.1989	21	1	2020:	FK Krasnodar
Aleksandr GOLOVIN	30.05.1996	41	5	2020/2021:	AS Monaco FC (FRA)
Aleksey IONOV	18.02.1989	35	4	2020:	FK Rostov
				15.10.2020->	FK Krasnodar
Konstantin KUCHAYEV	18.03.1998	1	0	2020:	FK CSKA Moskva
Daler KUZYAYEV	15.01.1993	37	2	2020/2021:	FK Zenit Saint Petersburg
Aleksey MIRANCHUK	17.10.1995	36	6	2020/2021:	Atalanta Bergamasca Calcio (ITA)
Anton MIRANCHUK	17.10. 1995	19	3	2020:	FK Lokomotiv Moskva
Andrey MOSTOVOY	05.11.1997	8	0	2020/2021:	FK Zenit Saint Petersburg
Maksim MUKHIN	04.11.2001	5	0	2021:	FK Lokomotiv Moskva
Ivan OBLYAKOV	05.07.1998	2	0	2020:	FK CSKA Moskva
Magomed OZDOYEV	05.11.1992	35	4	2020/2021:	FK Zenit Saint Petersburg
Aleksandr YEROKHIN	13.10.1989	26	1	2020:	FK Zenit Saint Petersburg
Rifat ZHEMALETDINOV	20.09.1996	6	0	2021:	FK Lokomotiv Moskva
Yuriy ZHIRKOV	20.08.1983	105	2	2020/2021:	FK Zenit Saint Petersburg
Roman ZOBNIN	11.02.1994	38	0	2020/2021:	FK Spartak Moskva
Forwards					
Fyodor CHALOV	10.04.1998	3	0	2020:	FK CSKA Moskva
Artyom DZYUBA	22.08.1988	55	30	2020/2021:	FK Zenit Saint Petersburg
Aleksandr SOBOLEV	07.03.1997	8	3	2020/2021:	FK Spartak Moskva
Anton ZABOLOTNIY	13.06.1991	13	1	2020/2021:	PFK Sochi

Trainer

Stanislav CHERCHESOV [11.08.2016 - 08.07.2021]   02.09.1963   57 M; 24 W; 13 D; 20 L; 99-78

SAN MARINO

The Country:
Repubblica di San Marino (Republic of San Marino)
Capital: San Marino
Surface: 61,2 km²
Inhabitants: 33,600 [2021]
Time: UTC+1

The FA:
Federazione Sammarinese Giuoco Calcio
Strada di Montecchio 17, 47890 San Marino
Tel: +378 054 999 0515
Founded: 1931
Member of FIFA since: 1988
Member of UEFA since: 1988
Website: www.fsgc.sm

NATIONAL TEAM RECORDS

RECORDS		
First international match:	23.08.1986, Serravalle:	San Marino – Canada Olympic Team 0-1
Most international caps:	Andy Selva	- 73 caps (1998-2016)
Most international goals:	Andy Selva	- 8 goals / 73 caps (1998-2016)

UEFA EUROPEAN CHAMPIONSHIP	
1960	Did not enter
1964	Did not enter
1968	Did not enter
1972	Did not enter
1976	Did not enter
1980	Did not enter
1984	Did not enter
1988	Did not enter
1992	Qualifiers
1996	Qualifiers
2000	Qualifiers
2004	Qualifiers
2008	Qualifiers
2012	Qualifiers
2016	Qualifiers
2020	Qualifiers

FIFA WORLD CUP	
1930	Did not enter
1934	Did not enter
1938	Did not enter
1950	Did not enter
1954	Did not enter
1958	Did not enter
1962	Did not enter
1966	Did not enter
1970	Did not enter
1974	Did not enter
1978	Did not enter
1982	Did not enter
1986	Did not enter
1990	Did not enter
1994	Qualifiers
1998	Qualifiers
2002	Qualifiers
2006	Qualifiers
2010	Qualifiers
2014	Qualifiers
2018	Qualifiers

OLYMPIC TOURNAMENTS	
1908	-
1912	-
1920	-
1924	-
1928	-
1936	Did not enter
1948	Did not enter
1952	Did not enter
1956	Did not enter
1960	Did not enter
1964	Did not enter
1968	Did not enter
1972	Did not enter
1976	Did not enter
1980	Did not enter
1984	Did not enter
1988	Did not enter
1992	Did not enter
1996	Qualifiers
2000	Did not enter
2004	Qualifiers
2008	Qualifiers
2012	Qualifiers
2016	Qualifiers

UEFA NATIONS LEAGUE	
2018/2019	League D
2020/2021	League D

FIFA CONFEDERATIONS CUP 1992-2017
None

SAN MARINESE CLUB HONOURS IN EUROPEAN CLUB COMPETITIONS:

European Champion Clubs' Cup (1956-1992) / UEFA Champions League (1993-2021)
None
Fairs Cup (1858-1971) / UEFA Cup (1972-2009) / UEFA Europa League (2010-2021)
None
UEFA Super Cup (1972-2020)
None
*European Cup Winners' Cup 1961-1999**
None

*defunct competition

<u>Please note</u>: until the introduction of a regular championship in 1985/86, the Coppa Titano was the only annual tournament for San Marinese clubs.

CUP WINNERS 1937-1985

Year	Winner	Year	Winner
1937	AC Libertas Borgo Maggiore	1970	SP Tre Penne Città di San Marino
1938-1949	*No competition*	1971	SP Tre Fiori Fiorentino
1950	AC Libertas Borgo Maggiore	1972	FC Domagnano
1951-1953	*No competition*	1973	*Competition abandoned*
1954	AC Libertas Borgo Maggiore	1974	SP Tre Fiori Fiorentino
1955-1957	*No competition*	1975	SP Tre Fiori Fiorentino
1958	AC Libertas Borgo Maggiore	1976	SS Juvenes Serravalle
1959	AC Libertas Borgo Maggiore	1977	SS Juvenes Serravalle
1960	*No competition*	1978	SS Juvenes Serravalle
1961	AC Libertas Borgo Maggiore	1979	SS Juvenes Serravalle
1962-1964	*No competition*	1980	SS Cosmos Serravalle
1965	SS Juvenes Serravalle	1981	SS Cosmos Serravalle
1966	SP Tre Fiori Fiorentino	1982	SP Tre Penne Città di San Marino
1967	SP Tre Penne Città di San Marino	1983	SP Tre Penne Città di San Marino
1968	SS Juvenes Serravalle	1984	SS Juvenes Serravalle
1969	*Competition abandoned*	1985	SP Tre Fiori Fiorentino

	CHAMPIONS	CUP WINNERS	BEST GOALSCORERS	
1985/1986	SC Faetano	SP La Fiorita Montegiardino	-	
1986/1987	SP La Fiorita Montegiardino	AC Libertas Borgo Maggiore	-	
1987/1988	SP Tre Fiori Fiorentino	FC Domagnano	-	
1988/1989	FC Domagnano	AC Libertas Borgo Maggiore	-	
1989/1990	SP La Fiorita Montegiardino	FC Domagnano	-	
1990/1991	SC Faetano	AC Libertas Borgo Maggiore	-	
1991/1992	SS Montevito Fiorentino	FC Domagnano	-	
1992/1993	SP Tre Fiori Fiorentino	SC Faetano	-	
1993/1994	SP Tre Fiori Fiorentino	SC Faetano	-	
1994/1995	SP Tre Fiori Fiorentino	SS Cosmos Serravalle	-	
1995/1996	AC Libertas Borgo Maggiore	FC Domagnano	-	
1996/1997	SS Folgore/Falciano Serravalle	SS Murata	-	
1997/1998	SS Folgore/Falciano Serravalle	SC Faetano	Damiano Vannucci (SS Virtus Acquaviva)	21
1998/1999	SC Faetano	SS Cosmos Serravalle	-	
1999/2000	SS Folgore/Falciano Serravalle	SP Tre Penne Città di San Marino	-	
2000/2001	SS Cosmos Serravalle	FC Domagnano	-	
2001/2002	FC Domagnano	FC Domagnano	-	
2002/2003	FC Domagnano	FC Domagnano	-	
2003/2004	SS Pennarossa Chiesanuova	SS Pennarossa Chiesanuova	Damiano Vannucci (SS Virtus Acquaviva)	15
2004/2005	FC Domagnano	SS Pennarossa Chiesanuova	Matteo Pazzaglia (SS Montevito Fiorentino)	19
2005/2006	SS Murata	AC Libertas Borgo Maggiore	-	
2006/2007	SS Murata	SS Murata	-	
2007/2008	SS Murata	SS Murata	-	
2008/2009	SP Tre Fiori Fiorentino	AC Juvenes/Dogana	-	
2009/2010	SP Tre Fiori Fiorentino	SP Tre Fiori Fiorentino	Simon Parma (SS Virtus Acquaviva)	13
2010/2011	SP Tre Fiori Fiorentino	AC Juvenes/Dogana	Jose Hirsch (SS Virtus Acquaviva) Marco Fantini (AC Juvenes/Dogana) Roberto Gatti (ITA, SS Murata) Alessandro Giunta (ITA, SP Tre Fiori Fiorentino) Francesco Viroli (ITA, SC Faetano)	13
2011/2012	SP Tre Penne Città di San Marino	SP La Fiorita Montegiardino	Cristian Rubén Menin (SS SS Cosmos Serravalle) Simon Parma (SP La Fiorita Montegiardino)	11
2012/2013	SP Tre Penne Città di San Marino	SP La Fiorita Montegiardino	Alberto Cannini (SP Tre Fiori Fiorentino) Denis Iencinella (FC Fiorentino)	17
2013/2014	SP La Fiorita Montegiardino	AC Libertas Borgo Maggiore	Valentin Grigore (ROU, SS Cosmos Serravalle) Giacomo Gualtieri (SP La Fiorita Montegiardino)	18
2014/2015	SS Folgore/Falciano Serravalle	SS Folgore/Falciano Serravalle	Daniele Friguglietti (ITA, San Giovanni)	16
2015/2016	SP Tre Penne Città di San Marino	SP La Fiorita Montegiardino	Marco Martini (ITA, SP La Fiorita Montegiardino)	20
2016/2017	SP La Fiorita Montegiardino	SP Tre Penne Città di San Marino	Marco Martini (ITA, SP La Fiorita Montegiardino)	27
2017/2018	SP La Fiorita Montegiardino	SP La Fiorita Montegiardino	Imre Badalassi (ITA, SP Tre Fiori Fiorentino)	18
2018/2019	SP Tre Penne Città di San Marino	SP Tre Fiori Fiorentino	Andrea Compagno (ITA, SP Tre Fiori Fiorentino)	22
2019/2020	SP Tre Fiori Fiorentino	*Competition cancelled*	Eric Fedeli (ITA, SS Murata Città di San Marino)	16
2020/2021	SS Folgore Falciano Calcio	SP La Fiorita Montegiardino	Imre Badalassi (ITA, SS Folgore Falciano Calcio)	13

NATIONAL CHAMPIONSHIP
Campionato Sammarinese di Calcio 2020/2021
(12.09.2020 – 22.05.2021)

First Phase - Results

Please note: the championship was interrupted due to the COVID-19 pandemic from 25.10.2020 to 24.02.2021. Teams played each other once instead of twice in order to finish the league on 22 May 2021.

Round 1 [12-13.09.2020]
FC Domagnano - SS Virtus 0-0
SS Pennarossa - SS Folgore/Falciano 2-0
AC Juvenes/Dogana - SS Murata 1-1
SP La Fiorita - AC Libertas 1-0
FC Fiorentino - SP Cailungo 1-1
SC Faetano - SP Tre Penne 2-4
SS San Giovanni - SS Cosmos 1-0

Round 2 [19-22.09.2020]
SS Murata - FC Domagnano 1-2
AC Libertas - SS Pennarossa 2-0
SP Tre Penne - FC Fiorentino 4-0
SP Cailungo - SS San Giovanni 0-1
SS Folgore/Falciano - SP La Fiorita 0-1
SS Virtus - SC Faetano 2-2
SS Cosmos - SP Tre Fiori 1-6

Round 3 [26-27.09.2020]
SC Faetano - SS Cosmos 1-2
SS Pennarossa - SP Tre Penne 1-3
AC Juvenes/Dogana - SS Virtus 0-2
SP La Fiorita - SP Cailungo 7-2
AC Libertas - SS Folgore/Falciano 2-1
SP Tre Fiori - FC Domagnano 0-0
SS San Giovanni - SS Murata 0-4

Round 4 [03-04.10.2020]
SP Tre Penne - SP Cailungo 3-2
SS Cosmos - AC Libertas 0-2
FC Domagnano - AC Juvenes/Dogana 0-2
SS Virtus - FC Fiorentino 3-1
SS San Giovanni - SS Pennarossa 1-0
SS Murata - SS Folgore/Falciano 0-0
SP Tre Fiori - SC Faetano 3-0

Round 5 [16-18.10.2020]
FC Domagnano - SS San Giovanni 3-1
SP Cailungo - AC Libertas 2-3
SS Murata - SS Virtus 1-1
SS Folgore/Falciano - SP Tre Fiori 1-0
SS Pennarossa - SP La Fiorita 0-1
AC Juvenes/Dogana - SP Tre Penne 2-1
SC Faetano - FC Fiorentino 0-1

Round 6 [24-25.10.2020]
SP Tre Fiori - SS Murata 0-0
SP Cailungo - SS Folgore/Falciano 0-1
SP La Fiorita - SC Faetano 3-0
FC Fiorentino - SS Pennarossa 0-1
AC Libertas - AC Juvenes/Dogana 1-0
SS Virtus - SS San Giovanni 1-1
SS Cosmos - FC Domagnano 1-1 [24.02.2021]

Round 7 [27-28.02.2021]
SC Faetano - AC Libertas 1-2
SS Cosmos - SP La Fiorita 0-3
AC Juvenes/Dogana - FC Fiorentino 2-3
SS Murata - SS Pennarossa 0-1
FC Domagnano - SP Cailungo 2-3
SS San Giovanni - SP Tre Fiori 1-1
SS Folgore/Falciano - SP Tre Penne 1-0

Round 8 [06-07.03.2021]
AC Libertas - SP Tre Penne 0-3
AC Juvenes/Dogana - SS San Giovanni 2-1
SP La Fiorita - FC Domagnano 3-0
FC Fiorentino - SS Cosmos 5-2
SP Cailungo - SS Murata 1-2
SS Virtus - SP Tre Fiori 0-1
SS Folgore/Falciano - SC Faetano 2-0

Round 9 [13-14.03.2021]
SS Murata - AC Libertas 0-1
SP Tre Penne - SP La Fiorita 0-1
SP Tre Fiori - AC Juvenes/Dogana 4-0
SS Cosmos - SS Virtus 0-1
SS San Giovanni - FC Fiorentino 4-1
SC Faetano - SP Cailungo 1-0
FC Domagnano - SS Pennarossa 2-2

Round 10 [20-21.03.2021]
FC Fiorentino - SP Tre Fiori 2-2
SP Cailungo - SS Cosmos 3-0
SP La Fiorita - SS San Giovanni 2-1
SS Pennarossa - AC Juvenes/Dogana 2-1
SP Tre Penne - SS Murata 2-1
SC Faetano - FC Domagnano 2-2
SS Folgore/Falciano - SS Virtus 1-0

Round 11 [06-07.04.2021]
SP Tre Fiori - AC Libertas 3-2
FC Domagnano - FC Fiorentino 1-2
AC Juvenes/Dogana - SC Faetano 3-2
SS Murata - SP La Fiorita 1-0
SS Cosmos - SS Folgore/Falciano 0-5
SS San Giovanni - SP Tre Penne 4-2
SS Virtus - SS Pennarossa 0-1

Round 12 [10-11.04.2021]
SP La Fiorita - AC Juvenes/Dogana 6-0
FC Fiorentino - SS Murata 0-0
AC Libertas - FC Domagnano 3-0
SS Folgore/Falciano - SS San Giovanni 3-0
SP Tre Penne - SS Cosmos 2-1
SP Cailungo - SS Virtus 1-2
SS Pennarossa - SP Tre Fiori 1-1

Round 13 [13-14.04.2021]
SS San Giovanni - AC Libertas 0-0
SS Murata - SC Faetano 0-0
AC Juvenes/Dogana - SS Folgore/Falciano 1-6
FC Fiorentino - SP La Fiorita 0-4
SS Cosmos - SS Pennarossa 1-2
SP Tre Fiori - SP Cailungo 3-1
SS Virtus - SP Tre Penne 0-1

Round 14 [17-18.04.2021]
SP Cailungo - SS Pennarossa 1-1
SS Folgore/Falciano - FC Fiorentino 2-1
SP Tre Penne - FC Domagnano 4-3
SS Cosmos - AC Juvenes/Dogana 2-5
SC Faetano - SS San Giovanni 1-1
AC Libertas - SS Virtus 1-0
SP La Fiorita - SP Tre Fiori 1-0

Round 15 [24-25.04.2021]
SP Tre Fiori - SP Tre Penne 2-1
FC Domagnano - SS Folgore/Falciano 2-2
SS Pennarossa - SC Faetano 1-2
SS Murata - SS Cosmos 3-0
AC Juvenes/Dogana - SP Cailungo 4-0
FC Fiorentino - AC Libertas 0-0
SS Virtus - SP La Fiorita 1-1

Final Standings

					Total			Home				Away			
1. SP La Fiorita Montegiardino	14	12	1	1	34 - 5	37	7	0	0	23 - 3	5	1	1	11 - 2
2. AC Libertas Borgo Maggiore	14	9	2	3	21 - 11	29	5	0	1	11 - 4	4	2	2	10 - 7
3. SS Folgore Falciano Calcio Serravalle	14	8	3	3	25 - 10	27	5	1	1	10 - 3	3	2	2	15 - 7
4. SP Tre Penne Città di San Marino	14	9	0	5	30 - 20	27	5	0	1	15 - 8	4	0	4	15 - 12
5. SP Tre Fiori Fiorentino	14	7	5	2	26 - 11	26	5	2	0	15 - 4	2	3	2	11 - 7
6. SS Pennarossa Chiesanuova	14	6	3	5	15 - 15	21	2	1	3	7 - 8	4	2	2	8 - 7
7. SS San Giovanni Borgo Maggiore	14	5	4	5	17 - 20	19	4	2	1	11 - 8	1	2	4	6 - 12
8. AC Juvenes/Dogana Serravalle	14	6	1	7	23 - 34	19	4	1	3	15 - 17	2	0	4	8 - 17
9. SS Murata Città di San Marino	14	4	6	4	14 - 9	18	2	3	3	6 - 5	2	3	1	8 - 4
10. SS Virtus Acquaviva	14	4	6	4	14 - 12	18	1	3	3	7 - 8	3	3	1	7 - 4
11. FC Fiorentino	14	4	4	6	18 - 26	16	1	4	2	8 - 10	3	0	4	10 - 16
12. FC Domagnano	14	2	6	6	16 - 26	12	1	3	3	8 - 12	1	3	3	8 - 14
13. SC Faetano	14	2	4	8	14 - 26	10	1	2	4	8 - 12	1	2	4	6 - 14
14. SP Cailungo Borgo Maggiore	14	2	2	10	17 - 29	8	1	1	5	8 - 10	1	1	5	9 - 19
15. SS Cosmos Serravalle	14	1	1	12	10 - 40	4	0	1	7	5 - 25	1	0	5	5 - 15

Teams ranked 1-4 were qualified for the Second Phase Quarter-Finals, while teams ranked 5-12 were qualified for the Second Phase Play-offs.

Please note: When a match ends in a draw, team with better regular season position will advance in the next Round..

Play-offs [01-02.05.2021]	SS Pennarossa Chiesanuova - FC Fiorentino	0-0
	AC Juvenes/Dogana Serravalle - SS Virtus Acquaviva	0-3
	SP Tre Fiori Fiorentino - FC Domagnano	0-2
	SS San Giovanni Borgo Maggiore - SS Murata Città di San Marino	0-3

Winners were qualified for the Quarter-Finals.

Quarter-Finals [05-06.05.2021]	SS Pennarossa Chiesanuova - SP Tre Penne Città di San Marino	1-2
	SS Virtus Acquaviva - AC Libertas Borgo Maggiore	2-3
	SS Folgore Falciano Calcio Serravalle - SS Murata Città di San Marino	1-1
	SP La Fiorita Montegiardino - FC Domagnano	0-0

| **Semi-Finals** [10-11.05.2021] | SP La Fiorita Montegiardino - SP Tre Penne Città di San Marino | 1-0 |
| | SS Folgore Falciano Calcio Serravalle - AC Libertas Borgo Maggiore | 3-1 |

| **Third Place Play-off** [21.05.2021] | SP Tre Penne Città di San Marino - AC Libertas Borgo Maggiore | 1-0 |

Championship Final

22.05.2021; San Marino Stadium, Serravalle; Referee: Andrea Mei; Attendance: 0
SS Folgore Falciano Calcio Serravalle - SP La Fiorita Montegiardino   **1-0(0-0,0-0)**

SS Folgore: Davide Bicchiarelli, Cristian Brolli, Roberto Rosini, Daniel Piscaglia, Fabio Sottile, Marco Domeniconi (87.Matteo Giardi), Mirco Spighi, Matteo Serafini (116.Riccardo Aluigi), Lorenzo Dormi, Imre Badalassi (115.Marco Bernardi), Manuele Pasolini (72.Andrea Nucci [*sent off 120*]). Trainer: Omar Lepri (Italy).

La Fiorita: Gianluca Vivan, Andrea Brighi, Roberto Di Maio, Marco Gasperoni (97.Manuel Miori), Andrea Grandoni (117.Samuel Pancotti), Danilo Rinaldi, Simone Loiodice (97.Fabrizio Castellazzi), Armando Amati [*sent off 118*], Marcello Mularoni (88.Tommaso Guidi), Simone Errico (46.Lucio Peluso), Michele Pieri (46.Tommaso Zafferani). Trainer: Nicola Berardi.

Goals: 1-0 Fabio Sottile (93).

Top goalscorer: Imre Badalassi (ITA, SS Folgore Falciano Calcio) – 13 goals

NATIONAL CUP
Coppa Titano Final 2020/2021

1/8-Finals [29.09.-01.10./20-21.10.2020]

SS Cosmos Serravalle - SP Cailungo Borgo Maggiore	3-0	1-2
SC Faetano - FC Fiorentino	1-1	1-3
SS Pennarossa Chiesanuova - SP Tre Fiori Fiorentino	2-1	0-2
AC Juvenes/Dogana Serravalle - FC Domagnano	1-3	2-0 aet; 4-5 pen
SS Folgore Falciano Calcio Serravalle - SS Virtus Acquaviva	2-0	2-0
AC Libertas Borgo Maggiore - SP La Fiorita Montegiardino	0-4	1-1
SS Murata Città di San Marino - SS San Giovanni Borgo Maggiore	1-1	1-0

Quarter-Finals [10.03.2021]

SS Cosmos Serravalle - SP Tre Fiori Fiorentino	0-1	SS Murata Città di San Marino - SP La Fiorita Montegiardino	3-4
SS Folgore Falciano Calcio Serravalle - FC Fiorentino	4-1	SP Tre Penne Città di San Marino - FC Domagnano	2-0

Semi-Finals [28-29.04.2021]

SP Tre Penne Città di San Marino - SP Tre Fiori Fiorentino	0-2	SS Folgore Falciano Calcio - SP La Fiorita Montegiardino	1-2

Final

15.05.2021; San Marino Stadium, Serravalle; Referee: Luca Barbeno; Attendance: 0
SP Tre Fiori Fiorentino - SP La Fiorita Montegiardino   **0-0; 9-10 on penalties**

Tre Fiori: Aldo Simoncini, Simone Rea, Alessandro D'Addario, Giuseppe Gargiulo, Paolo Vandi, Francesco Lunardini, Giacomo Pracucci (80.Nicola Della Valle), Tommaso Domini, Lounseny Kalissa, Nicholas Santoni, Joel Apezteguía Hijuelos (77.Patrik Bordon). Trainer: Matteo Cecchetti (Italy).

SP La Fiorita: Gianluca Vivan, Andrea Brighi, Roberto Di Maio, Marco Gasperoni, Andrea Grandoni (98.Manuel Miori), Danilo Rinaldi, Simone Loiodice, Armando Amati (74.Simone Errico), Tommaso Zafferani, Marcello Mularoni (85.Michele Pieri), Fabrizio Castellazzi (57.Thomas Sapori; 91.Tommaso Guidi). Trainer: Nicola Berardi.

Penalties: Francesco Lunardini 1-0; Simone Errico 1-1; Patrik Bordon 2-1; Tommaso Guidi 2-2; Giuseppe Gargiulo 3-2; Michele Pieri 3-3; Nicholas Santoni 4-3; Simone Loiodice 4-4; Tommaso Domini (saved); Danilo Rinaldi (missed); Lounseny Kalissa 5-4; Marco Gasperoni 5-5; Paolo Vandi 6-5; Manuel Miori 6-6; Alessandro D'Addario (saved); Roberto Di Maio (saved); Nicola Della Valle 7-6; Andrea Brighi 7-7; Simone Rea 8-7; Tommaso Zafferani 8-8; Aldo Simoncini 9-8; Gianluca Vivan 9-9; Francesco Lunardini (saved); Simone Errico 9-10.

Please note: appearances and goals are including statistics of both first and second stage.

Società Polisportiva Cailungo Borgo Maggiore

Founded:	1974	
Stadium:	Stadio Fonte Dell'Ovo, Città di San Marino (500)	
Trainer:	Antonio Bianchi	08.03.1959
[02.10.2020]	Giuliano Bianchi	

Goalkeepers:	DOB	M	(s)	G
Alberto Gallinetta (ITA)	16.04.1992	10		
Massimiliano La Monaca	26.04.1995	4	(1)	
Defenders:	**DOB**	**M**	**(s)**	**G**
Luca Carnesecchi	31.05.1995	10	(1)	
Andrea Genghini (ITA)	03.10.1992	12	(2)	
Manuel Iuzzolino (ITA)	05.05.1990	8	(2)	1
Matteo Lepri (ITA)	19.04.1989	8		
Luca Ricci	25.03.1993	5		
Enea Righetti (ITA)	08.10.1986	4	(1)	
Michele Rossi	26.01.1995	5	(2)	
Enrico Stacchini	21.07.1999	1	(1)	
Alberto Tomassini	19.02.2002	8		
Mattia Vitali (ITA)	26.05.2000	8	(6)	1

Midfielders:	DOB	M	(s)	G
Mariano Gastón Alvarez	05.02.1996		(2)	
Luca Baravelli (ITA)	26.03.2000	3	(2)	
Luca Cecchetti	03.07.2000	5	(2)	2
Marco Cecchetti	03.02.1997	8		
Aziz Diallo (SEN)	11.05.1997	4	(1)	
Simone Matteoni	26.04.1992	2	(5)	
Alessandro Rossi (ITA)	27.03.1989	11	(3)	2
Denis Veronesi	17.07.1988		(3)	
Samuele Zannoni	29.04.2002	5	(2)	2
Forwards:	**DOB**	**M**	**(s)**	**G**
Daniele Santoni (ITA)	13.10.1992	7	(1)	
Oleksander Tadzhybayev (UKR)	10.04.1994	5	(5)	1
Raul Ura (ITA)	10.09.1998	9	(4)	
Mattia Urbinati (ITA)	17.12.1995	12	(1)	7
Valeriano Viespoli (ITA)	12.11.1994		(3)	

Società Sportiva Cosmos Serravalle

Founded:	1979	
Stadium:	San Marino Stadium, Serravalle (7,000)	
Trainer:	Cristian Protti	17.04.1973

Goalkeepers:	DOB	M	(s)	G
Lorenzo Batori (ITA)	07.11.1993	3		
Andrea Gregori	30.12.1987	11		
Defenders:	**DOB**	**M**	**(s)**	**G**
Francesco Baschetti	08.01.1986	2	(1)	
Matteo Camillini (ITA)	10.01.1984	8	(2)	
Michele Camillini (ITA)	10.01.1984	12	(1)	
Thomas Cavalli (ITA)	17.01.1988		(2)	
Fabiano Grassi (ITA)	06.05.1988	1	(3)	
Daniele Lusini (ITA)	10.03.1982	11		
Francesco Matteucci (ITA)	30.08.1995	8		2
Daniele Rocchi (ITA)	23.06.1982	2		
Stefano Sartini	02.05.2000	4	(4)	
Amedeo Valentini (ITA)	06.05.1994	7	(2)	
Nicola Zafferani	06.11.1991	10	(1)	1

Midfielders:	DOB	M	(s)	G
Michele Cervellini	14.04.1988	6	(6)	
Gabriele Della Croce (ITA)	20.06.2000	1	(3)	
Fabio Giovagnoli (ITA)	10.06.1992	2	(2)	1
Stefano Pari	13.12.1993	1	(2)	
Riccardo Santini	13.10.1986	4	(2)	
Armando Senja (ALB)	26.07.1997	6	(7)	1
Giacomo Valentini	26.06.2001	8	(2)	
Guido Zaghini (ITA)	06.12.1988	10	(1)	
Kevin Zonzini	11.08.1997	11		
Forwards:	**DOB**	**M**	**(s)**	**G**
Riccardo Bonfigli (ITA)	13.12.1997	3		
Filippo Burioni	20.05.1998	2		
Federico Cornia (ITA)	04.03.1999	1	(4)	1
Achille Della Valle	31.01.1989	5	(5)	
Marseljan Mema (ALB)	13.02.1997	12	(2)	3
Simone Rossi (ITA)	13.06.1987	3	(1)	1

Football Club Domagnano

Founded:	1966	
Stadium:	Campo sportivo, Domagnano (500)	
Trainer:	Paolo Cangini	26.07.1967

Goalkeepers:	DOB	M	(s)	G
Davide Colonna	10.11.2000	4		
Gabriele Giulianelli	09.09.1998	1		
Nicolas Leardini (ITA)	20.03.1996	11		
Defenders:	**DOB**	**M**	**(s)**	**G**
Samuel Averhoff	19.11.1999	3	(1)	
Juri Biordi	01.01.1995	3	(1)	
Giovanni Bonini	05.09.1986	9		1
Dario De Luigi (ITA)	19.03.1990	11		
Angelo Faetanini	17.01.1993	5	(7)	
Guido Ghetti (ITA)	25.06.1978	14		
Michael Parma	28.03.1998	10	(2)	
Giovanni Rossi (ITA)	15.02.1989	12		
Midfielders:	**DOB**	**M**	**(s)**	**G**
Nicolò Bacchiocchi	26.02.1991	10		

	DOB	M	(s)	G
Thomas Brighi (ITA)	09.01.1996	1	(4)	
Alessio Cangini (ITA)	05.01.1991	16		3
Mattia Ceccaroli	03.02.1999	8	(3)	
Andrea Venerucci	21.11.1989	4	(6)	
Davide Venerucci	08.06.1997		(7)	
Forwards:	**DOB**	**M**	**(s)**	**G**
Alessio Ambrogetti (ITA)	14.01.1989	11	(4)	6
Nicolò Angelini	15.03.1992	5	(9)	
Alessandro Bianchini (ITA)	26.04.1994		(4)	
Enea Jaupi	06.10.1993		(3)	
Alessandro Rossi	22.08.1983	11		6
Christopher Santucci (ITA)	06.03.1991	7	(1)	1
Pietro Semprini	27.01.1993	12	(2)	2
Luca Simoncelli (ITA)	07.07.1997	8	(4)	1

Società Calcio Faetano

Founded:	1962		
Stadium:	San Marino Stadium, Serravalle (7,000)		
Trainer:	Alessandro Fabbri		01.07.1978
[09.10.2020]	Fulvio Fabiani		
[14.03.2021]	Alessandro Fabbri		01.07.1978

Goalkeepers:	DOB	M	(s)	G
Gennaro Del Prete (ITA)	03.08.2000	4		
Manuel Ermeti (ITA)	11.08.1981	6		
Simone Guidi	14.06.2000	4		
Marco Spadazzi (ITA)	18.07.1970		(1)	
Defenders:	**DOB**	**M**	**(s)**	**G**
Marco Ballarini (ITA)	19.03.1985	5		
Alex Cavalli	26.02.1992	10	(1)	
Alex Della Valle	13.06.1990	10	(1)	
Túlio Medici Macedo Carvalho (BRA)	31.07.1995	7		
Bujar Musabelliu (ALB)	03.11.1996	11		
Thomas Rosti	03.05.2001	4		
Antonio Solazzo (ITA)	14.10.2000	1		
Francesco Zaghini (ITA)	18.10.1999	9		
Midfielders:	**DOB**	**M**	**(s)**	**G**
Matias Leandro Barbuio	17.09.1990	5	(2)	1
Matteo Bonavitacola (ITA)	02.05.1989	9	(1)	
German Dominella	20.07.2000	4	(2)	

Assane Fall (SEN)	26.02.1994	12	(1)	1
Alessandro Grilli	04.06.1989	2	(5)	1
Denys Klyvchuk (UKR)	24.05.1999	5	(2)	
Jacopo Muggeo (ITA)	19.08.1990	5	(1)	
Andrea Pasini (ITA)	04.01.1997	6		
Luca Tomassoni (ITA)	21.11.1994	1	(5)	
Forwards:	**DOB**	**M**	**(s)**	**G**
Paolo Basile (ITA)	08.06.1992	1	(2)	
Elia Giacobbi (ITA)	04.05.1994	8		
Francesco Gori (ITA)	25.10.1989	1	(4)	2
Emanuele Gregori	12.07.1995	3	(1)	1
Adil Mezgour (MAR)	11.03.1983	6	(2)	3
Massimo Moroni	17.02.1990	1	(3)	
Roberto Neri (ITA)	06.08.1983	7	(3)	2
Alex Ortolani	02.11.2000	2	(1)	
Francisco Palladino (ITA)	25.01.1999		(2)	
Manuele Pasolini (ITA)	26.12.1989	5		3

Football Club Fiorentino

Founded:	1974	
Stadium:	Campo Sportivo, Fiorentino (700)	
Trainer:	Enrico Malandri (ITA)	30.05.1983

Goalkeepers:	DOB	M	(s)	G
Michele Berardi	30.11.1991	2		
Luca Bianchi (ITA)	07.01.1990	13		
Defenders:	**DOB**	**M**	**(s)**	**G**
Mattia Anastasi	19.03.1997	7	(1)	
Andrea Ceccoli	22.09.1993	1	(5)	
Andrea Contadini	18.02.2002	10		
Luca Filippi (ITA)	27.09.1988	5	(1)	
Nicola Generali (ITA)	28.05.1999	8	(3)	
Andrea La Serra	02.11.1999	5		
Mirko Paglialonga (ITA)	19.09.1983	13		
Samuele Paoloni	18.01.1997	5	(3)	
Alberto Rossini	21.08.1998	4		
Piero Tamagnini (ITA)	03.10.1999	9	(1)	4
Alessandro Terenzi	23.05.2000		(1)	

Midfielders:	DOB	M	(s)	G
Maximiliano Baizan	23.03.1993	4	(6)	
Leonardo Balestra	17.05.1998	3	(2)	
Pietro Calzolari	28.10.1991	8	(2)	
Enrico Candoli (ITA)	20.09.2000	2	(5)	2
Nicola Casoli (ITA)	10.01.1994	9	(1)	1
Henrik Cekirri (ALB)	18.12.1994	2	(5)	
Riccardo Colonna	10.04.1999		(1)	
Fabio Dall'Ara	18.06.1984	9		
Alessandro Molinari	14.05.1989	12	(1)	
Giovanni Pacchioni (ITA)	28.07.1998	14		8
Eros Tommasi (ITA)	15.08.1992	2	(6)	
Forwards:	**DOB**	**M**	**(s)**	**G**
Roberto Cevoli (ITA)	23.11.1994	3	(8)	
Paco Piscaglia	22.08.2002	5	(3)	
Sorin Rădoi (ROU)	16.02.1990	10		3

Società Sportiva Folgore Falciano Calcio Serravalle

Founded:	1972	
Stadium:	San Marino Stadium, Serravalle (7,000)	
Trainer:	Omar Lepri (ITA)	10.05.1977

Goalkeepers:	DOB	M	(s)	G
Davide Bicchiarelli (ITA)	19.05.1985	15		
Emanuele Semprini (ITA)	25.12.1988	2		
Defenders:	**DOB**	**M**	**(s)**	**G**
Cristian Brolli	28.02.1992	17		
Giacomo Francioni	25.10.2000		(2)	
Luca Nanni	30.01.1995	6	(5)	
Daniel Piscaglia (ITA)	06.12.1992	13	(1)	2
Roberto Rosini (ITA)	27.09.1991	16		
Fabio Sottile (ITA)	05.02.1993	15	(1)	1
Midfielders:	**DOB**	**M**	**(s)**	**G**
Riccardo Aluigi	29.03.1994	3	(7)	1
Luca Bezzi (ITA)	05.06.1989	1	(4)	

Marco Domeniconi	29.01.1984	16		
Mattia Giardi	15.12.1991	9	(5)	
Davide Lisi (ITA)	16.07.2001		(2)	
Andrea Nucci (ITA)	06.09.1986	6	(3)	
Matteo Serafini	13.02.1994	10		
Mirco Spighi (ITA)	27.08.1990	16		1
Forwards:	**DOB**	**M**	**(s)**	**G**
Imre Badalassi (ITA)	08.02.1995	17		13
Marco Bernardi	02.01.1994	2	(10)	1
Lorenzo Dormi (ITA)	11.02.1995	16	(1)	6
William Edoardo Garcia (ITA)	13.05.2002	2	(2)	
Matteo Giardi	14.04.1997	2	(6)	
Manuele Pasolini (ITA)	26.12.1989	3	(7)	5

Associazione Calcio Juvenes/Dogana Serravalle

Founded:	2000 (*as merger of SS Juvenes Serravalle and GS Dogana*)	
Stadium:	San Marino Stadium, Serravalle (7,000)	
Trainer:	Manuel Amati (ITA)	01.01.1980

Goalkeepers:	DOB	M	(s)	G
Eros Gobbi	16.10.1989	2	(1)	
Mattia Manzaroli	03.10.1991	13		
Alex Parrotta	21.12.2000		(1)	
Defenders:	**DOB**	**M**	**(s)**	**G**
Maicol Acquarelli (ITA)	21.09.1993	12	(2)	
Francesco Benedetti (ITA)	18.11.1979	1	(2)	
Michele Cevoli	22.07.1998	9	(1)	
Simone Franciosi	03.09.2001	7	(1)	
Paolo Gori (ITA)	28.06.1994	11	(2)	
Manuel Muccini (ITA)	24.11.1989	4	(1)	
Filippo Quaranta	11.09.1998	3	(4)	
Thomas Raschi	11.07.1996	6	(4)	
Luca Rossi	14.04.1993	5	(3)	
Riccardo Tonti (ITA)	22.06.1994	5	(3)	

Midfielders:	DOB	M	(s)	G
Mattia Ancora (ITA)	11.03.1999	2	(3)	
Alberto Baldazzi	08.11.2001	1	(9)	
Francesco Boldrini (ITA)	09.01.1995	13		3
Cristian Gatti	06.05.1990	14		1
Mattia Michelotti	07.05.1999		(6)	
Eugenio Zucchi	26.02.1999	2	(4)	
Forwards:	**DOB**	**M**	**(s)**	**G**
Matteo Baldini (ITA)	02.10.1998	15		12
Lorenzo Cevoli	05.07.1997		(1)	
Davide Merli (ITA)	08.02.2000	14	(1)	3
Pietro Protino (ITA)	26.05.1999	9	(4)	3
Jacopo Raschi	28.04.1998	6	(5)	
Francesco Stella (ITA)	25.05.1995	9	(1)	1
Federico Tumidei	30.09.2001	2	(1)	

Società Polisportiva La Fiorita Montegiardino

Founded: 1967
Stadium: Stadio "Igor Crescentini", Montegiardino (700)
Trainer: Nicola Berardi   05.08.1969

Goalkeepers:	DOB	M	(s)	G
Federico Andreani (ITA)	01.09.1994	1		
Simone Venturini (ITA)	27.05.1998	4		
Gianluca Vivan (ITA)	27.12.1983	12		
Defenders:	**DOB**	**M**	**(s)**	**G**
Andrea Brighi (ITA)	29.07.1992	14	(2)	2
Roberto Di Maio (ITA)	21.09.1982	15	(1)	2
Marco Gasperoni (ITA)	18.02.1992	12	(2)	
Andrea Grandoni	23.03.1997	14	(3)	2
Manuel Miori (ITA)	28.04.2000	2	(7)	1
Filippo Santi	23.01.2001	4	(3)	2
Michele Zanotti	25.11.1988	1		
Midfielders:	**DOB**	**M**	**(s)**	**G**
Armando Amati (ITA)	15.01.1995	9	(5)	2

	DOB	M	(s)	G
Simone Errico (ITA)	30.04.1992	12	(4)	3
Matteo Gasperoni (ITA)	11.09.1998	2	(2)	2
Simone Loiodice (ITA)	16.03.1989	14	(1)	
Riccardo Michelotti	13.09.1999	2	(3)	
Marcello Mularoni	08.09.1998	8	(3)	1
Danilo Rinaldi	18.04.1986	12	(2)	2
Thomas Sapori (ITA)	18.08.2001	2	(6)	
Tommaso Zafferani	19.02.1996	7	(10)	1
Forwards:	**DOB**	**M**	**(s)**	**G**
Fabrizio Castellazzi (ITA)	29.07.1984	5	(6)	3
Tommaso Guidi	21.10.1990	11	(3)	2
Samuel Pancotti	31.10.2000	6	(6)	3
Lucio Peluso (ITA)	27.11.1990	8	(3)	3
Michele Pieri (ITA)	16.06.1992	10	(4)	4

Associazione Calcio Libertas Borgo Maggiore

Founded: 1928
Stadium: Campo sportivo, Borgo Maggiore (1,000)
Trainer: Mirco Papini (ITA)   27.08.1960

Goalkeepers:	DOB	M	(s)	G
Fabio Gentilini (ITA)	09.09.1984	13	(1)	
Matteo Zavoli	06.07.1996	4		
Defenders:	**DOB**	**M**	**(s)**	**G**
Marco Ballarini (ITA)	19.03.1985	7	(2)	1
Tommaso Bertoni (ITA)	03.10.1990	1		
David Mirzoyan (ARM)	15.03.1999	1	(1)	
Diego Moretti	07.02.2000	15		1
Samuele Olivi (ITA)	01.08.1980	4	(3)	
Federico Pesaresi (ITA)	09.08.1996	15		
Francesco Sartori (ITA)	07.03.1993	14	(1)	1
Riccardo Tisselli (ITA)	29.07.1997	6		
Midfielders:	**DOB**	**M**	**(s)**	**G**
Mariano Alvarez	05.02.1996		(2)	
Maicol Berretti	01.05.1989	4	(5)	1
Matteo Gaiani (ITA)	02.01.1995	4	(3)	

	DOB	M	(s)	G
Enrico Golinucci	16.07.1991	12	(2)	3
Andrea Grassi (ITA)	30.09.1993	5		
Marcello Luzzi (ITA)	30.06.1997	5		
Marco Narducci (ITA)	16.09.1989	15	(1)	1
Luca Righini (ITA)	25.12.1990	12	(1)	3
Dario Spadaro (ITA)	03.11.1995	6		2
Francesco Stacchini	18.01.1997		(1)	
Andrea Ulizio (ITA)	06.03.1994	2	(5)	
Forwards:	**DOB**	**M**	**(s)**	**G**
Armando Aruci	10.07.1989	2	(1)	
Marco Bernacci (ITA)	15.12.1983	15	(2)	9
Gian Luca Morelli (ITA)	13.02.1985	10	(5)	1
Michael Noschese (ITA)	29.01.1998	2	(3)	
Peniel Obeng (GHA)	18.10.2000	2	(5)	1
Antonio Salomone (ITA)	07.10.1986		(5)	
Pietro Sopranzi	29.01.1998	11		1

Società Sportiva Murata Città di San Marino

Founded: 1966
Stadium: Campo sportivo, Montegiardino (1,000)
Trainer: Achille Fabbri (ITA)   24.02.1966

Goalkeepers:	DOB	M	(s)	G
Simone Benedettini	21.01.1997	12		
Denis Broccoli (ITA)	10.08.1988	4	(1)	
Defenders:	**DOB**	**M**	**(s)**	**G**
Nicholas Arrigoni (ITA)	09.01.1995	15		
Christian Babbini (ITA)	01.02.1986	5	(2)	
Diego Campidelli (ITA)	20.07.1994	13		
Hervé Diedhiou (SEN)	05.01.1994	10		
Giovanni Dominici (ITA)	22.05.1994	4		
Filippo Fabbri (ITA)	09.06.1995	6	(2)	5
Luca Ortibaldi (ITA)	29.04.1988	2	(2)	
Raffaello Rinaldi (ITA)	28.06.1991	7	(3)	
Giacomo Salvatori (ITA)	28.08.1999	11	(2)	

Midfielders:	DOB	M	(s)	G
Michele Bozzetto (ITA)	08.05.1996	13		
Patrik Giulianelli (ITA)	18.04.1998	9	(5)	3
Matteo Nanni	07.03.1993	3	(5)	
Stefano Sacco (ITA)	10.02.1991	6	(4)	
Ivan Tani (ITA)	19.05.1993	14		1
Alex Toccaceli (ITA)	16.01.2002	2	(3)	
David Tomassini	14.03.2000	14		
Forwards:	**DOB**	**M**	**(s)**	**G**
Daniele Babboni (ITA)	09.01.2000	2	(4)	
Gianmarco Baschetti	29.04.1991	3	(11)	1
Marco Casadei	20.09.1985	1	(8)	
Eric Fedeli (ITA)	13.01.1992	8	(1)	3
Simone Pippi (ITA)	30.07.1999	12		4

Società Sportiva Pennarossa Chiesanuova

Founded: 1968
Stadium: Campo sportivo, Chiesanuova (300)
Trainer: Andy Selva   23.05.1976

Goalkeepers:	DOB	M	(s)	G
Eugenio Marconi	22.10.1998	1	(1)	
Alessandro Semprini (ITA)	29.01.1994	13		
Federico Valentini	22.01.1982	2	(1)	
Defenders:	**DOB**	**M**	**(s)**	**G**
Mattia Alberighi (ITA)	08.01.1998	7		
Marco Baldani	05.12.1997	3		
Antonio Barretta (ITA)	19.09.1995	7		
Gustavo Nahuel Beresiarte Ledesma (ARG)	26.02.1996	2	(2)	
Bruno Calabrese (ITA)	21.03.2001	3	(2)	
Claudio Cola (ITA)	24.04.1986	11	(1)	
Daniele Conti (ITA)	06.06.1990	1	(2)	
Manuel De Biagi	07.03.2002	3	(3)	
Kevin Martin (ITA)	24.03.1995	13	(1)	
Gabriele Raffaelli (ITA)	28.05.1994	10	(1)	
Luca Righi	01.04.1995	5	(2)	

Midfielders:	DOB	M	(s)	G
Adam Adami Martins (BRA)	24.06.1992	15		2
Matias Colagiovanni (ARG)	16.01.1993	6	(7)	
Alessandro Conti (ITA)	07.01.1998	9	(1)	
Marco Evaristi (ITA)	20.01.2000	8	(2)	2
Stefano Fabbri (ITA)	27.09.1982		(2)	
Matteo Sebastiani (ITA)	12.12.1990	10	(3)	
Fabio Ramón Tomassini	05.02.1996	3	(2)	
Danilo Vittozzi (ITA)	07.06.1998	4	(2)	
Forwards:	**DOB**	**M**	**(s)**	**G**
Nicola Ciacci	07.07.1982	2	(5)	
Francesko Halilaj (ITA)	09.05.1992	6	(3)	2
Adolfo José Hirsch	31.01.1986	8	(3)	2
Francesco Ottaviani (ITA)	17.09.2000	1		1
Moussa Souare (GUI)	01.07.1998	12	(3)	3
Mattia Stefanelli	12.03.1993	8	(1)	4
Matteo Vitaioli	27.10.1989	3		

Società Sportiva San Giovanni Borgo Maggiore

Founded: 1948
Stadium: Stadio Borgo Maggiore, Borgo Maggiore (1,000)
Trainer: Paolo Baffoni (ITA) 05.01.1964

Goalkeepers:	DOB	M	(s)	G
Santino Arena (ITA)	11.02.1987	4	(2)	
Federico D'Ercoli (ITA)	09.06.1997	1		
Andrea Manzaroli (ITA)	12.02.1995	10		
Defenders:	**DOB**	**M**	**(s)**	**G**
Nicola Conti (ITA)	04.01.1997	3		
Giacomo Conti	21.07.1999	7		
Alex de Biagi	02.01.2000	1	(2)	
Cristian Grieco (ITA)	27.10.1998	4		
Luca Olivieri (ITA)	23.12.1995	12		
Alberto Righini (ITA)	12.05.1998		(3)	
Enea Senja (ALB)	10.01.1999	13		1
Nicolo Tamagnini	07.02.1988	9	(1)	
Michele Tasini (ITA)	01.11.1995	5	(2)	
Federico Urbinati (ITA)	16.01.1997	6	(2)	1

Midfielders:	DOB	M	(s)	G
Federico Berardi (ITA)	17.09.1997	9	(5)	2
Andrea Borgagni	21.10.1996	2	(3)	
Edoardo Cecchetti	14.07.1993		(1)	
Lorenzo Enchisi (ITA)	18.07.1997	9		1
Alessandro Gobbi (ITA)	26.06.1998	8	(4)	1
Lorenzo Lunadei	12.07.1997	7		1
Leonardo Magnani (ITA)	08.10.1998	10	(2)	1
Daniele Savini (ITA)	20.10.1992		(2)	
Forwards:	**DOB**	**M**	**(s)**	**G**
Andrea Comuniello (ITA)	27.04.1995	11	(2)	2
Nicolò Fancellu (ITA)	03.10.1999	7	(4)	2
Lorenzo Fortunato (ITA)	13.12.1998	1	(4)	1
Andrea Moroni	10.10.1985	4	(1)	
Mamadou Ndiaye (SEN)	20.10.1998	8		
Marco Rosti	21.10.1988	1	(3)	
Marco Ugolini (ITA)	23.12.1986	13		1

Società Polisportiva Tre Fiori Fiorentino

Founded: 1949
Stadium: Stadio di Fiorentino, Fiorentino (1,000)
Trainer: Matteo Cecchetti (ITA)

Goalkeepers:	DOB	M	(s)	G
Mirco De Angelis	03.03.2000	5		
Aldo Simoncini	30.08.1986	10		
Defenders:	**DOB**	**M**	**(s)**	**G**
Luca Angelini (ITA)	17.09.1989	6	(3)	1
Durel Bilendo Duma (FRA)	18.04.1999	2	(1)	
Giovanni Bonini	05.09.1986	3		
Alessandro D'Addario	09.09.1997	12	(2)	
Nicola Della Valle	19.05.1997	6	(8)	1
Giuseppe Gargiulo (ITA)	11.07.1997	8	(1)	
Giacomo Matteoni	11.04.2002	3	(3)	
Simone Rea (ITA)	27.04.1993	6		
Davide Simoncini	30.08.1986	12	(1)	
Antonio Stelitano (ITA)	22.10.1987	3	(1)	
Paolo Vandi (ITA)	23.09.1994	9	(4)	

Midfielders:	DOB	M	(s)	G
Federico Dolcini	22.03.2000	5	(3)	1
Tommaso Domini (ITA)	18.08.1989	5	(1)	1
Pier Francesco Figone (ITA)	28.06.1996	4	(3)	
Lounseny Kalissa (GUI)	07.02.1999	12	(3)	1
Francesco Lunardini (ITA)	03.11.1984	9	(1)	
Giacomo Pracucci (ITA)	21.01.1997	4	(10)	1
Nicholas Santoni (ITA)	11.10.1997	12		5
Andrea Tamagnini	27.09.1997		(3)	
Forwards:	**DOB**	**M**	**(s)**	**G**
Joel Apezteguía Hijuelos (CUB)	17.12.1983	6	(4)	5
Patrik Bordon (SVN)	06.04.1988	8		4
Stefano Del Sante (ITA)	13.01.1987	2	(2)	1
Bojan Gjurchinoski (CRO)	13.04.1994	4	(1)	2
Matteo Sartori (ITA)	28.06.1991	9		3

Società Polisportiva Tre Penne Città di San Marino

Founded: 1956
Stadium: Stadio Fonte Dell'Ovo, Città di San Marino (500)
Trainer: Stefano Ceci 16.10.1969

Goalkeepers:	DOB	M	(s)	G
Mauro Lanzoni (ITA)	20.09.1987	3		
Mattia Migani (ITA)	10.03.1992	14		
Defenders:	**DOB**	**M**	**(s)**	**G**
Enrico Casadei	18.02.1996	2		1
Davide Cesarini	16.02.1995	8	(4)	
Lorenzo Costa	01.03.1992	9		
Christofer Genestreti (ITA)	30.05.1984	16		
Nicolas Lombardi (ITA)	21.05.1995	16		1
Riccardo Mezzadri (ITA)	14.04.1986	6	(2)	
Simone Nanni	03.08.2000	2	(1)	
Midfielders:	**DOB**	**M**	**(s)**	**G**
Michael Battistini	08.10.1996	14	(2)	
Nicola Chiaruzzi	25.12.1987	3	(6)	

	DOB	M	(s)	G
Enrico Cibelli	14.07.1987	5	(9)	3
Nicola Gai (ITA)	06.12.1987	14		6
Alex Gasperoni	30.06.1984	12		
Lorenzo Liverani	13.05.1993	1	(1)	
Luca Patregnani (ITA)	08.04.1985	11	(2)	
Francesco Perrotta (ITA)	27.08.1981	2	(5)	
Matteo Semprini (ITA)	30.03.1995	7	(10)	
Andrea Zanotti	05.05.1992		(1)	
Forwards:	**DOB**	**M**	**(s)**	**G**
Luca Ceccaroli	05.07.1995	10	(2)	
Alessandro Chiurato (ITA)	16.01.1983	8	(3)	4
Tommaso Costantini (ITA)	23.06.1996	4	(7)	2
Riccardo Pieri (ITA)	27.10.1994	10		9
Luca Sorrentino (ITA)	08.05.1994	10	(2)	7

Società Sportiva Virtus Acquaviva

Founded: 1964
Stadium: Stadio di Acquaviva, Acquaviva (2,000)
Trainer: Luigi Bizzotto (ITA) 08.03.1960

Goalkeepers:	DOB	M	(s)	G
Thomas Paolini	21.06.2002	3		
Alex Stimac	22.06.1996	13		
Defenders:	**DOB**	**M**	**(s)**	**G**
Manuel Battistini	22.07.1994	14	(2)	2
Patrik D'Altri (ITA)	25.12.1992	14		1
Aron Giacomoni	22.08.1987	14		
Nicolò Maini (ITA)	07.04.1997	4	(3)	
Mirko Mantovani	14.11.1986	2	(2)	
Giacomo Massari	30.09.1999	12		1
Giammaria Rigoni	11.12.1998	9	(5)	
Simone Rizzato	21.09.1981	3		
Midfielders:	**DOB**	**M**	**(s)**	**G**
Roberto Baiardi (ITA)	18.09.1987	15		2

	DOB	M	(s)	G
Elia Ciacci	13.11.2001	3	(12)	
Alessandro Golinucci	10.10.1994	3	(2)	
Lut Alijahej (ALB)	28.01.1995	11	(5)	2
Youssef Limouni (MAR)	12.07.1996	1	(8)	
Alessandro Liverani	12.10.2000		(2)	
Filippo Magri (ITA)	27.12.1990	7	(1)	1
Kevin Marigliano (ITA)	10.05.1993	3	(6)	
Giacomo Santucci (ITA)	06.11.2000	11	(4)	1
Forwards:	**DOB**	**M**	**(s)**	**G**
Nicola Angeli (ITA)	28.05.1989	14	(2)	7
Simone Brigliadori (ITA)	28.04.1995	3	(10)	
Riccardo Innocenti (ITA)	15.10.1974	10		1
Ramiro Lago (ARG)	14.10.1987	7	(2)	1

INTERNATIONAL MATCHES
(16.07.2020 – 15.07.2021)

05.09.2020	Gibraltar	Gibraltar - San Marino	1-0(1-0)	(UNL)
08.09.2020	Rimini	San Marino - Liechtenstein	0-2(0-2)	(UNL)
07.10.2020	Ljubljana	Slovenia - San Marino	4-0(3-0)	(F)
13.10.2020	Vaduz	Liechtenstein - San Marino	0-0	(UNL)
11.11.2020	Serravalle	San Marino - Latvia	0-3(0-1)	(F)
14.11.2020	Serravalle	San Marino - Gibraltar	0-0	(UNL)
25.03.2021	London	England - San Marino	5-0(3-0)	(WCQ)
28.03.2021	Serravalle	San Marino - Hungary	0-3(0-1)	(WCQ)
31.03.2021	Serravalle	San Marino - Albania	0-2(0-0)	(WCQ)
28.05.2021	Cagliari	Italy - San Marino	7-0(2-0)	(F)
01.06.2021	Prishtina	Kosovo - San Marino	4-1(2-0)	(F)

05.09.2020   **GIBRALTAR - SAN MARINO**   1-0(1-0)   2nd UEFA Nations League D, Group 2
Victoria Stadium, Gibraltar; Referee: Aleksandrs Anufrijevs (Latvia); Attendance: 0
SMR: Elia Benedettini, Davide Simoncini (Cap), Mirko Palazzi, Cristian Brolli, Manuel Battistini (46.Alessandro D'Addario), Dante Carlos Rossi (78.Adolfo José Hirsch), Enrico Golinucci, Marcello Mularoni, Filippo Berardi, Kevin Zonzini (65.Luca Ceccaroli), Nicola Nanni. Trainer: Franco Varrella (Italy).

08.09.2020   **SAN MARINO - LIECHTENSTEIN**   0-2(0-2)   2nd UEFA Nations League D, Group 2
Stadio Romeo Neri, Rimini (Italy); Referee: Enea Jorgji (Albania); Attendance: 50
SMR: Elia Benedettini, Davide Simoncini (Cap), Manuel Battistini, Andrea Grandoni, Dante Carlos Rossi, Enrico Golinucci, Luca Ceccaroli (67.Fabio Ramón Tomassini), Filippo Berardi, Luca Tosi (46.Alessandro Golinucci), Lorenzo Lunadei (46.Adolfo José Hirsch), Matteo Giampaolo Vitaioli. Trainer: Franco Varrella (Italy).

07.10.2020   **SLOVENIA - SAN MARINO**   4-0(3-0)   Friendly International
Stadion Stožice, Ljubljana; Referee: Sebastian Gishamer (Austria); Attendance: 500
SMR: Simone Benedettini, Manuel Battistini, Cristian Brolli, Enrico Golinucci (83.Giacomo Conti), Alessandro D'Addario (77.Kevin Zonzini), Dante Carlos Rossi, Adolfo José Hirsch (63.Giovanni Bonini), Alessandro Golinucci (64.Mattia Giardi), Michael Battistini (46.Luca Ceccaroli), Matteo Giampaolo Vitaioli (Cap), Fabio Ramón Tomassini (78.Andrea Grandoni). Trainer: Franco Varrella (Italy).

13.10.2020   **LIECHTENSTEIN - SAN MARINO**   0-0   2nd UEFA Nations League D, Group 2
Rheinpark Stadion, Vaduz; Referee: Jørgen Daugbjerg Burchardt (Denmark); Attendance: 178
SMR: Simone Benedettini, Mirko Palazzi (Cap), Cristian Brolli, Manuel Battistini, Dante Carlos Rossi, Enrico Golinucci, Adolfo José Hirsch, Filippo Berardi, Lorenzo Lunadei (86.Marcello Mularoni), Fabio Ramón Tomassini, Nicola Nanni. Trainer: Franco Varrella (Italy).

11.11.2020   **SAN MARINO - LATVIA**   0-3(0-1)   Friendly International
San Marino Stadium, Serravalle; Referee: Fabio Maresca (Italy); Attendance: 0
SMR: Simone Benedettini, Davide Simoncini (Cap), Cristian Brolli, Andrea Grandoni, Alessandro D'Addario, Adolfo José Hirsch (74.Tommaso Zafferani), Alessandro Golinucci (46.Enrico Golinucci), Luca Ceccaroli (74.Michael Battistini), Lorenzo Lunadei (74.Kevin Zonzini), Matteo Giampaolo Vitaioli (87.Mattia Giardi), Fabio Ramón Tomassini (46.Marcello Mularoni). Trainer: Franco Varrella (Italy).

14.11.2020   **SAN MARINO - GIBRALTAR**   0-0   2nd UEFA Nations League D, Group 2
San Marino Stadium, Serravalle; Referee: Kateryna Monzul (Ukraine); Attendance: 0
SMR: Elia Benedettini, Davide Simoncini (Cap) [*sent off 49*], Mirko Palazzi, Cristian Brolli, Dante Carlos Rossi, Adolfo José Hirsch (57.Marcello Mularoni), Alessandro Golinucci, Filippo Berardi (67.Matteo Giampaolo Vitaioli), Lorenzo Lunadei, Fabio Ramón Tomassini (57.Manuel Battistini), Nicola Nanni. Trainer: Franco Varrella (Italy).

25.03.2021   **ENGLAND - SAN MARINO**   5-0(3-0)   22nd FIFA WC. Qualifiers
Wembley Stadium, London; Referee: Kirill Levnikov (Russia); Attendance: 0
SMR: Elia Benedettini, Mirko Palazzi (Cap), Cristian Brolli, Manuel Battistini, Andrea Grandoni (55.Luca Ceccaroli), Dante Carlos Rossi, Enrico Golinucci (71.Michael Battistini), Adolfo José Hirsch (55.Marcello Mularoni), Filippo Berardi (79.Alessandro D'Addario), Lorenzo Lunadei (79.Mattia Giardi), Nicola Nanni. Trainer: Franco Varrella (Italy).

28.03.2021   **SAN MARINO - HUNGARY**   0-3(0-1)   22nd FIFA WC. Qualifiers
San Marino Stadium, Serravalle; Referee: Nicholas Walsh (Scotland); Attendance: 0
SMR: Elia Benedettini, Cristian Brolli, Mirko Palazzi (Cap), Manuel Battistini, Filippo Fabbri, Dante Carlos Rossi, Enrico Golinucci, Marcello Mularoni, Filippo Berardi (80.Marco Bernardi), Lorenzo Lunadei (53.Kevin Zonzini), Nicola Nanni (80.Adolfo José Hirsch). Trainer: Franco Varrella (Italy).

31.03.2021   **SAN MARINO - ALBANIA**   0-2(0-0)   22nd FIFA WC. Qualifiers
San Marino Stadium, Serravalle; Referee: Kai Erik Steen (Norway); Attendance: 0
SMR: Elia Benedettini, Filippo Fabbri, Davide Simoncini (Cap), Mirko Palazzi (80.Luca Ceccaroli), Manuel Battistini (80.Alessandro D'Addario), Dante Carlos Rossi (55.Cristian Brolli), Enrico Golinucci (64.Andrea Grandoni), Marcello Mularoni, Filippo Berardi, Nicola Nanni, David Tomassini (55.Lorenzo Lunadei). Trainer: Franco Varrella (Italy).

28.05.2021   **ITALY - SAN MARINO**   7-0(2-0)   Friendly International
Sardegna Arena, Cagliari; Referee: Trustin Farrugia Cann (Malta); Attendance: 0
SMR: Elia Benedettini, Mirko Palazzi (Cap) (73.Alessandro D'Addario), Manuel Battistini, Andrea Grandoni (52.Matteo Giampaolo Vitaioli), Filippo Fabbri, Dante Carlos Rossi, Enrico Golinucci, Adolfo José Hirsch (51.Lorenzo Lunadei), Fabio Ramón Tomassini (51.Cristian Brolli), Marcello Mularoni (87.Alessandro Golinucci), Nicola Nanni (87.David Tomassini). Trainer: Franco Varrella (Italy).

01.06.2021   **KOSOVO - SAN MARINO**   **4-1(2-0)**   Friendly International

Stadiumi "Fadil Vokrri", Prishtina; Referee: Yaşar Kemal Uğurlu (Turkey); Attendance: 0
SMR: Simone Benedettini, Mirko Palazzi, Alessandro D'Addario, Filippo Fabbri (58.Giacomo Conti), Dante Carlos Rossi (46.Michele Cevoli), Alessandro Golinucci (70.Enrico Golinucci), Marcello Mularoni, Lorenzo Lunadei, Matteo Giampaolo Vitaioli (Cap) (58.Adolfo José Hirsch), Fabio Ramón Tomassini (70.Kevin Zonzini), Nicola Nanni (82.David Tomassini). Trainer: Franco Varrella (Italy).
Goal: David Tomassini (85).

NATIONAL TEAM PLAYERS
(16.07.2020 – 15.07.2021)

Name	DOB	Caps	Goals	2020/2021:	*Club*
Goalkeepers					
Elia BENEDETTINI	22.06.1995	24	0	2020:	*Novara Calcio (ITA)-> Unattached (05.10.2020)*
				14.01.2021->	*Cesena FC (ITA)*
Simone BENEDETTINI	21.01.1997	8	0	2020/2021:	*SS Murata Città di San Marino*
Defenders					
Manuel BATTISTINI	11.07.1994	38	0	2020:	*AC Juvenes/Dogana Serravalle*
				15.01.2021->	*SS Virtus Acquaviva*
Cristian BROLLI	28.02.1992	38	0	2020/2021:	*SS Folgore Falciano Calcio Serravalle*
Michele CEVOLI	22.07.1998	8	0	2021:	*AC Cattolica Calcio (ITA)*
Giacomo CONTI	21.07.1999	2	0	2020:	*ASD Tropical Coriano (ITA)*
				12.02.2021->	*SS San Giovanni Borgo Maggiore*
Alessandro D'ADDARIO	09.09.1997	11	0	2020/2021:	*SP Tre Fiori Fiorentino*
Filippo FABBRI	07.01.2002	4	0	2021:	*Cesena FC (ITA)*
Andrea GRANDONI	23.03.1997	22	0	2020/2021:	*SP La Fiorita Montegiardino*
Mirko PALAZZI	21.03.1987	50	1	2020:	*SP Tre Penne Città di San Marino*
				09.2020->	*SSDRL Marignanese Calcio (ITA)*
Dante Carlos ROSSI	12.07.1987	10	0	2020:	*SS Pennarossa Chiesanuova*
				20.02.2020->	*APC Chions (ITA)*
Davide SIMONCINI	30.08.1986	67	0	2020/2021:	*SP Tre Fiori Fiorentino*
Midfielders					
Michael BATTISTINI	08.10.1996	7	0	2020/2021:	*SP Tre Penne Città di San Marino*
Giovanni BONINI	05.09.1986	29	0	2020:	*SP Tre Fiori Fiorentino*
Luca CECCAROLI	05.07.1995	8	0	2020/2021:	*SP Tre Penne Città di San Marino*
Mattia GIARDI	15.12.1991	13	0	2020/2021:	*SS Folgore Falciano Calcio Serravalle*
Alessandro GOLINUCCI	10.10.1994	24	0	2020:	*ASD Tropical Coriano (ITA)*
				13.02.2021->	*SS Virtus Acquaviva*
Enrico GOLINUCCI	16.07.1991	28	0	2020/2021:	*AC Libertas Borgo Maggiore*
Lorenzo LUNADEI	12.07.1997	22	0	2020/2021:	*SSD Fya Riccione (ITA)*
Marcello MULARONI	08.09.1998	20	0	2020/2021:	*SP La Fiorita Montegiardino*
Luca TOSI	04.11.1992	19	0	2020:	*SS Virtus Acquaviva*
Tommaso ZAFFERANI	19.02.1996	9	0	2020:	*SP La Fiorita Montegiardino*
Kevin ZONZINI	11.08.1997	5	0	2020/2021:	*SS Cosmos Serravalle*
Forwards					
Filippo BERARDI	18.05.1997	21	1	2020/2021:	*US Vibonese Calcio (ITA)*
Marco BERNARDI	02.01.1994	8	0	2021:	*SS Folgore Falciano Calcio Serravalle*
Adolfo José HIRSCH	31.01.1986	43	0	2020/2021:	*SS Pennarossa Chiesanuova*
Nicola NANNI	02.05.2000	18	0	2020/2021:	*Cesena FC (ITA)*
David TOMASSINI	14.03.2000	3	0	2021:	*SS Murata Città di San Marino*
Fabio Ramón TOMASSINI	05.02.1996	22	0	2020:	*US Pietracuta San Leo (ITA)*
				16.02.2021->	*SS Pennarossa Chiesanuova*
Matteo Giampaolo VITAIOLI	27.10.1989	65	1	2020:	*ASD Tropical Coriano (ITA)*
				16.02.2021->	*SS Pennarossa Chiesanuova*
Trainer					
Franco VARRELLA (Italy) [from 15.01.2018]		25.01.1953	27 M; 0 W; 2 D; 25 L; 2-98		

SCOTLAND

The Country:
Scotland
Capital: Edinburgh
Surface: 77,933 km²
Inhabitants: 5,463,300 [2019]
Time: UTC

The FA:
Scottish Football Association
Hampden Park G42, 9AY Glasgow
Tel: +44 141 616 6000
Founded: 1873
Member of FIFA since: 1910
Member of UEFA since: 1954
Website: www.scottishfa.co.uk

NATIONAL TEAM RECORDS

RECORDS

First international match:	30.11.1872, Glasgow: Scotland – England 0-0
Most international caps:	Kenneth Mathieson Dalglish - 102 caps (1971-1986)
Most international goals:	Denis Law - 30 goals / 55 caps (1958-1974)
	Kenneth Mathieson Dalglish - 30 goals / 102 caps (1971-1986)

UEFA EUROPEAN CHAMPIONSHIP

1960	Did not enter
1964	Did not enter
1968	Qualifiers
1972	Qualifiers
1976	Qualifiers
1980	Qualifiers
1984	Qualifiers
1988	Qualifiers
1992	Final Tournament (Group Stage)
1996	Final Tournament (Group Stage)
2000	Qualifiers
2004	Qualifiers
2008	Qualifiers
2012	Qualifiers
2016	Qualifiers
2020	Final Tournament (Group Stage)

FIFA WORLD CUP

1930	Did not enter
1934	Did not enter
1938	Did not enter
1950	*Withdrew after being qualified*
1954	Final Tournament (Group Stage)
1958	Final Tournament (Group Stage)
1962	Qualifiers
1966	Qualifiers
1970	Qualifiers
1974	Final Tournament (Group Stage)
1978	Final Tournament (Group Stage)
1982	Final Tournament (Group Stage)
1986	Final Tournament (Group Stage)
1990	Final Tournament (Group Stage)
1994	Qualifiers
1998	Final Tournament (Group Stage)
2002	Qualifiers
2006	Qualifiers
2010	Qualifiers
2014	Qualifiers
2018	Qualifiers

OLYMPIC TOURNAMENTS

1908	-
1912	-
1920	-
1924	-
1928	-
1936	-
1948	-
1952	-
1956	-
1960	-
1964	-
1968	-
1972	-
1976	-
1980	-
1984	-
1988	-
1992	-
1996	-
2000	-
2004	-
2008	-
2012	-
2016	-

UEFA NATIONS LEAGUE

2018/2019	League C (promoted to League B)
2020/2021	League B

FIFA CONFEDERATIONS CUP 1992-2017

None

SCOTTISH CLUB HONOURS IN EUROPEAN CLUB COMPETITIONS:

European Champion Clubs.Cup (1956-1992) / UEFA Champions League (1993-2021)

Celtic FC Glasgow	1	1966/1967

Fairs Cup (1858-1971) / UEFA Cup (1972-2009) / UEFA Europa League (2010-2021)

None

UEFA Super Cup (1972-2020)

Aberdeen FC	1	1983

*European Cup Winners.Cup 1961-1999**

Rangers FC Glasgow	1	1971/1972
Aberdeen FC	1	1982/1983

*defunct competition

NATIONAL COMPETITIONS
TABLE OF HONOURS

	CHAMPIONS	CUP WINNERS	BEST GOALSCORERS	
1873/1874	-	Queen's Park FC Glasgow	-	
1874/1875	-	Queen's Park FC Glasgow	-	
1875/1876	-	Queen's Park FC Glasgow	-	
1876/1877	-	Vale of Leven FC Alexandria	-	
1877/1878	-	Vale of Leven FC Alexandria	-	
1878/1879	-	Vale of Leven FC Alexandria	-	
1879/1880	-	Queen's Park FC Glasgow	-	
1880/1881	-	Queen's Park FC Glasgow	-	
1881/1882	-	Queen's Park FC Glasgow	-	
1882/1883	-	Dumbarton FC	-	
1883/1884	-	Queen's Park FC Glasgow	-	
1884/1885	-	Renton FC	-	
1885/1886	-	Queen's Park FC Glasgow	-	
1886/1887	-	Hibernian FC Edinburgh	-	
1887/1888	-	Renton FC	-	
1888/1889	-	Third Lanark AC Glasgow	-	
1889/1890	-	Queen's Park FC Glasgow	-	
1890/1891	Dumbarton FC Rangers FC Glasgow [joint winners]	Heart of Midlothian FC Edinburgh	Jack Bell (Dumbarton FC)	20
1891/1892	Dumbarton FC	Celtic FC Glasgow	Jack Bell (Dumbarton FC)	23
1892/1893	Celtic FC Glasgow	Queen's Park FC Glasgow	Sandy McMahon (Celtic FC Glasgow) John Campbell (Celtic FC Glasgow)	11
1893/1894	Celtic FC Glasgow	Rangers FC Glasgow	Sandy McMahon (Celtic FC Glasgow)	16
1894/1895	Heart of Midlothian FC Edinburgh	St. Bernard's FC Edinburgh	James Miller (Clyde FC Cumbernauld)	12
1895/1896	Celtic FC Glasgow	Heart of Midlothian FC Edinburgh	Allan Martin (Celtic FC Glasgow)	19
1896/1897	Heart of Midlothian FC Edinburgh	Rangers FC Glasgow	Willie Taylor (Heart of Midlothian FC Edinburgh)	12
1897/1898	Celtic FC Glasgow	Rangers FC Glasgow	Robert Hamilton (Rangers FC Glasgow)	18
1898/1899	Rangers FC Glasgow	Celtic FC Glasgow	Robert Hamilton (Rangers FC Glasgow)	25
1899/1900	Rangers FC Glasgow	Celtic FC Glasgow	Robert Hamilton (Rangers FC Glasgow) William Michael (Heart of Midlothian FC Edinburgh)	15
1900/1901	Rangers FC Glasgow	Heart of Midlothian FC Edinburgh	Robert Hamilton (Rangers FC Glasgow)	20
1901/1902	Rangers FC Glasgow	Hibernian FC Edinburgh	William Maxwell (Third Lanark AC Glasgow)	10
1902/1903	Hibernian FC Edinburgh	Rangers FC Glasgow	David Reid (Hibernian FC Edinburgh)	14
1903/1904	Third Lanark AC Glasgow	Celtic FC Glasgow	Robert Hamilton (Rangers FC Glasgow)	28
1904/1905	Celtic FC Glasgow	Third Lanark AC Glasgow	Robert Hamilton (Rangers FC Glasgow) James Quinn (Celtic FC Glasgow)	19
1905/1906	Celtic FC Glasgow	Heart of Midlothian FC Edinburgh	James Quinn (Celtic FC Glasgow)	20
1906/1907	Celtic FC Glasgow	Celtic FC Glasgow	James Quinn (Celtic FC Glasgow)	29
1907/1908	Celtic FC Glasgow	Celtic FC Glasgow	Jock Simpson (Falkirk FC)	32
1908/1909	Celtic FC Glasgow	*No competition*	John Hunter (Dundee FC)	29
1909/1910	Celtic FC Glasgow	Dundee FC	James Quinn (Celtic FC Glasgow) Jock Simpson (Falkirk FC)	24
1910/1911	Rangers FC Glasgow	Celtic FC Glasgow	William Reid (Rangers FC Glasgow)	38
1911/1912	Rangers FC Glasgow	Celtic FC Glasgow	William Reid (Rangers FC Glasgow)	33
1912/1913	Rangers FC Glasgow	Falkirk FC	James Reid (Airdrieonians FC)	30
1913/1914	Celtic FC Glasgow	Celtic FC Glasgow	James Reid (Airdrieonians FC)	27
1914/1915	Celtic FC Glasgow	*No competition*	Tom Gracie (Heart of Midlothian FC Edinburgh) James Richardson (Ayr United FC)	29
1915/1916	Celtic FC Glasgow	*No competition*	James McColl (Celtic FC Glasgow)	34
1916/1917	Celtic FC Glasgow	*No competition*	Herbert George Yarnall (ENG, Airdrieonians FC)	39
1917/1918	Rangers FC Glasgow	*No competition*	Hugh Ferguson (Motherwell FC)	35
1918/1919	Celtic FC Glasgow	*No competition*	David McLean (Rangers FC Glasgow)	29
1919/1920	Rangers FC Glasgow	Kilmarnock FC	Hugh Ferguson (Motherwell FC)	33
1920/1921	Rangers FC Glasgow	Partick Thistle FC Glasgow	Hugh Ferguson (Motherwell FC)	43
1921/1922	Celtic FC Glasgow	Greenock Morton FC	Duncan Walker (St. Mirren FC Paisley)	45
1922/1923	Rangers FC Glasgow	Celtic FC Glasgow	John White (Heart of Midlothian FC Edinburgh)	30
1923/1924	Rangers FC Glasgow	Airdrieonians FC	David Halliday (Dundee FC)	38
1924/1925	Rangers FC Glasgow	Celtic FC Glasgow	William Alexander Devlin (Cowdenbeath FC)	33
1925/1926	Celtic FC Glasgow	St. Mirren FC Paisley	William Alexander Devlin (Cowdenbeath FC)	40
1926/1927	Rangers FC Glasgow	Celtic FC Glasgow	James Edward McGrory (Celtic FC Glasgow)	49
1927/1928	Rangers FC Glasgow	Rangers FC Glasgow	James Edward McGrory (Celtic FC Glasgow)	47
1928/1929	Rangers FC Glasgow	Kilmarnock FC	Evelyn Morrison (Falkirk FC)	43
1929/1930	Rangers FC Glasgow	Rangers FC Glasgow	Benjamin Collard Yorston (Aberdeen FC)	38
1930/1931	Rangers FC Glasgow	Celtic FC Glasgow	Bernard Joseph Battles Jr. (Heart of Midlothian FC Edinburgh)	44
1931/1932	Motherwell FC	Rangers FC Glasgow	William MacFadyen (Motherwell FC)	52
1932/1933	Rangers FC Glasgow	Celtic FC Glasgow	William MacFadyen (Motherwell FC)	45
1933/1934	Rangers FC Glasgow	Rangers FC Glasgow	James Smith (Rangers FC Glasgow)	41
1934/1935	Rangers FC Glasgow	Rangers FC Glasgow	James Smith (Rangers FC Glasgow)	36
1935/1936	Celtic FC Glasgow	Rangers FC Glasgow	James Edward McGrory (Celtic FC Glasgow)	50

1936/1937	Rangers FC Glasgow	Celtic FC Glasgow	David Wilson (Hamilton Academical)	34
1937/1938	Celtic FC Glasgow	East Fife FC Methil	Andrew Black (Heart of Midlothian FC Edinburgh)	40
1938/1939	Rangers FC Glasgow	Clyde FC Cumbernauld	Alexander Venters (Rangers FC Glasgow)	35
1939/1940	*No competition*	*No competition*	-	
1940/1941	*No competition*	*No competition*	-	
1941/1942	*No competition*	*No competition*	-	
1942/1943	*No competition*	*No competition*	-	
1943/1944	*No competition*	*No competition*	-	
1944/1945	*No competition*	*No competition*	-	
1945/1946	*No competition*	*No competition*	-	
1946/1947	Rangers FC Glasgow	Aberdeen FC	Robert Carmichael Mitchell (Third Lanark AC Glasgow)	22
1947/1948	Hibernian FC Edinburgh	Rangers FC Glasgow	Archie Aikman (Falkirk FC)	20
1948/1949	Rangers FC Glasgow	Rangers FC Glasgow	Alexander Gair Stott (Dundee FC)	30
1949/1950	Rangers FC Glasgow	Rangers FC Glasgow	Willie Bauld (Heart of Midlothian FC Edinburgh)	30
1950/1951	Hibernian FC Edinburgh	Celtic FC Glasgow	Lawrance Reilly (Hibernian FC Edinburgh)	22
1951/1952	Hibernian FC Edinburgh	Motherwell FC	Lawrance Reilly (Hibernian FC Edinburgh)	27
1952/1953	Rangers FC Glasgow	Rangers FC Glasgow	Lawrance Reilly (Hibernian FC Edinburgh) Charlie Fleming (East Fife FC Methil)	30
1953/1954	Celtic FC Glasgow	Celtic FC Glasgow	James Wardhaugh (Heart of Midlothian FC Edinburgh)	27
1954/1955	Aberdeen FC	Clyde FC Cumbernauld	Willie Bauld (Heart of Midlothian FC Edinburgh)	21
1955/1956	Rangers FC Glasgow	Heart of Midlothian FC Edinburgh	James Wardhaugh (Heart of Midlothian FC Edinburgh)	28
1956/1957	Rangers FC Glasgow	Falkirk FC	Hugh Baird (Airdrieonians FC)	33
1957/1958	Heart of Midlothian FC Edinburgh	Clyde FC Cumbernauld	James Wardhaugh (Heart of Midlothian FC Edinburgh) James Murray (Heart of Midlothian FC Edinburgh)	28
1958/1959	Rangers FC Glasgow	St. Mirren FC Paisley	Joseph Henry Baker (Hibernian FC Edinburgh)	25
1959/1960	Heart of Midlothian FC Edinburgh	Rangers FC Glasgow	Joseph Henry Baker (Hibernian FC Edinburgh)	42
1960/1961	Rangers FC Glasgow	Dunfermline Athletic FC	Alexander Harley (Third Lanark AC Glasgow)	42
1961/1962	Dundee FC	Rangers FC Glasgow	Alan John Gilzean (Dundee FC)	24
1962/1963	Rangers FC Glasgow	Rangers FC Glasgow	James Millar (Rangers FC Glasgow)	27
1963/1964	Rangers FC Glasgow	Rangers FC Glasgow	Alan John Gilzean (Dundee FC)	32
1964/1965	Kilmarnock FC	Celtic FC Glasgow	Jim Forrest (Rangers FC Glasgow)	30
1965/1966	Celtic FC Glasgow	Rangers FC Glasgow	James McBride (Celtic FC Glasgow) Alexander Chapman Ferguson (Dunfermline Athletic FC)	31
1966/1967	Celtic FC Glasgow	Celtic FC Glasgow	Thomas Stephen Chalmers (Celtic FC Glasgow)	21
1967/1968	Celtic FC Glasgow	Dunfermline Athletic FC	Robert Lennox (Celtic FC Glasgow)	32
1968/1969	Celtic FC Glasgow	Celtic FC Glasgow	Kenneth Cameron (Dundee United FC)	26
1969/1970	Celtic FC Glasgow	Aberdeen FC	Colin Anderson Stein (Rangers FC Glasgow)	24
1970/1971	Celtic FC Glasgow	Celtic FC Glasgow	Henry Anthony Hood (Celtic FC Glasgow)	22
1971/1972	Celtic FC Glasgow	Celtic FC Glasgow	Joseph Montgomery Harper (Aberdeen FC)	33
1972/1973	Celtic FC Glasgow	Rangers FC Glasgow	Alan Fordyce Gordon (Hibernian FC Edinburgh)	27
1973/1974	Celtic FC Glasgow	Celtic FC Glasgow	John Kelly Deans (Celtic FC Glasgow)	26
1974/1975	Rangers FC Glasgow	Celtic FC Glasgow	Andrew Mullen Gray (Dundee United FC) William Pettigrew (Motherwell FC)	20
1975/1976	Rangers FC Glasgow	Rangers FC Glasgow	Kenneth Mathieson Dalglish (Celtic FC Glasgow)	24
1976/1977	Celtic FC Glasgow	Celtic FC Glasgow	William Pettigrew (Motherwell FC)	21
1977/1978	Rangers FC Glasgow	Rangers FC Glasgow	Derek Joseph Johnstone (Rangers FC Glasgow)	25
1978/1979	Celtic FC Glasgow	Rangers FC Glasgow	Andrew Ritchie (Greenock Morton FC)	22
1979/1980	Aberdeen FC	Celtic FC Glasgow	Douglas McKenzie Somner (St. Mirren FC Paisley)	25
1980/1981	Celtic FC Glasgow	Rangers FC Glasgow	Francis Peter McGarvey (Celtic FC Glasgow)	23
1981/1982	Celtic FC Glasgow	Aberdeen FC	George McKinley Cassidy McCluskey (Celtic FC Glasgow)	21
1982/1983	Dundee United FC	Aberdeen FC	Charles Nicholas (Celtic FC Glasgow)	29
1983/1984	Aberdeen FC	Aberdeen FC	Brian John McClair (Celtic FC Glasgow)	23
1984/1985	Aberdeen FC	Celtic FC Glasgow	Douglas Francis McDougall (Aberdeen FC)	22
1985/1986	Celtic FC Glasgow	Aberdeen FC	Alistair Murdoch McCoist (Rangers FC Glasgow)	24
1986/1987	Rangers FC Glasgow	St. Mirren FC Paisley	Brian John McClair (Celtic FC Glasgow)	35
1987/1988	Celtic FC Glasgow	Celtic FC Glasgow	Tommy Coyne (Dundee FC)	33
1988/1989	Rangers FC Glasgow	Celtic FC Glasgow	Mark Edward McGhee (Celtic FC Glasgow) Charles Nicholas (Aberdeen FC)	16
1989/1990	Rangers FC Glasgow	Aberdeen FC	John Grant Robertson (Heart of Midlothian FC Edinburgh)	17
1990/1991	Rangers FC Glasgow	Motherwell FC	Tommy Coyne (Celtic FC Glasgow)	18
1991/1992	Rangers FC Glasgow	Rangers FC Glasgow	Alistair Murdoch McCoist (Rangers FC Glasgow)	34
1992/1993	Rangers FC Glasgow	Rangers FC Glasgow	Alistair Murdoch McCoist (Rangers FC Glasgow)	34
1993/1994	Rangers FC Glasgow	Dundee United FC	Mark Wayne Hateley (ENG, Rangers FC Glasgow)	22
1994/1995	Rangers FC Glasgow	Celtic FC Glasgow	Tommy Coyne (Motherwell FC)	16
1995/1996	Rangers FC Glasgow	Rangers FC Glasgow	Petrus Ferdinandus Johannes van Hooijdonk (NED, Celtic FC Glasgow)	26
1996/1997	Rangers FC Glasgow	Kilmarnock FC	Jorge Paulo Cadete Santos Reis (POR, Celtic FC Glasgow)	25
1997/1998	Celtic FC Glasgow	Heart of Midlothian FC Edinburgh	Marco Negri (ITA, Rangers FC Glasgow)	32
1998/1999	Rangers FC Glasgow	Rangers FC Glasgow	Henrik Edward Larsson (SWE, Celtic FC Glasgow)	29

1999/2000	Rangers FC Glasgow	Rangers FC Glasgow	Mark Anthony Viduka (AUS, Celtic FC Glasgow)	25
2000/2001	Celtic FC Glasgow	Celtic FC Glasgow	Henrik Edward Larsson (SWE, Celtic FC Glasgow)	35
2001/2002	Celtic FC Glasgow	Rangers FC Glasgow	Henrik Edward Larsson (SWE, Celtic FC Glasgow)	29
2002/2003	Rangers FC Glasgow	Rangers FC Glasgow	Henrik Edward Larsson (SWE, Celtic FC Glasgow)	28
2003/2004	Celtic FC Glasgow	Celtic FC Glasgow	Henrik Edward Larsson (SWE, Celtic FC Glasgow)	30
2004/2005	Rangers FC Glasgow	Celtic FC Glasgow	John Hartson (WAL, Celtic FC Glasgow)	25
2005/2006	Celtic FC Glasgow	Heart of Midlothian FC Edinburgh	Kris Boyd (Kilmarnock FC / Rangers FC Glasgow)	32
2006/2007	Celtic FC Glasgow	Celtic FC Glasgow	Kris Boyd (Rangers FC Glasgow)	20
2007/2008	Celtic FC Glasgow	Rangers FC Glasgow	Scott Douglas McDonald (AUS, Celtic FC Glasgow)	25
2008/2009	Rangers FC Glasgow	Rangers FC Glasgow	Kris Boyd (Rangers FC Glasgow)	27
2009/2010	Rangers FC Glasgow	Dundee United FC	Kris Boyd (Rangers FC Glasgow)	23
2010/2011	Rangers FC Glasgow	Celtic FC Glasgow	Kenneth Miller (Rangers FC Glasgow)	21
2011/2012	Celtic FC Glasgow	Heart of Midlothian FC Edinburgh	Gary Hooper (ENG, Celtic FC Glasgow)	24
2012/2013	Celtic FC Glasgow	Celtic FC Glasgow	Michael Higdon (ENG, Motherwell FC)	26
2013/2014	Celtic FC Glasgow	St. Johnstone FC Perth	Kristian Arran Commons (Celtic FC Glasgow)	27
2014/2015	Celtic FC Glasgow	Inverness Caledonian Thistle FC	Adam Christopher Rooney (IRL, Aberdeen FC)	18
2015/2016	Celtic FC Glasgow	Hibernian FC Edinburgh	Leigh Griffiths (Celtic FC Glasgow)	31
2016/2017	Celtic FC Glasgow	Celtic FC Glasgow	Liam Boyce (NIR, Ross County FC Dingwall)	23
2017/2018	Celtic FC Glasgow	Celtic FC Glasgow	Kris Boyd (Kilmarnock FC)	18
2018/2019	Celtic FC Glasgow	Celtic FC Glasgow	Alfredo José Morelos Aviléz (COL, Rangers FC Glasgow)	18
2019/2020	Celtic FC Glasgow	Celtic FC Glasgow	Odsonne Édouard (FRA, Celtic FC Glasgow)	22
2020/2021	Rangers FC Glasgow	St. Johnstone FC Perth	Odsonne Édouard (FRA, Celtic FC Glasgow)	18

NATIONAL CHAMPIONSHIP
Scottish Premiership 2020/2021
(01.08.2020 – 16.05.2021)

Results

Round 1 [01-03.08.2020]
Aberdeen FC - Rangers FC 0-1(0-1)
Dundee United - St. Johnstone FC 1-1(1-0)
Hibernian FC - Kilmarnock FC 2-1(2-1)
St. Mirren FC - Livingston FC 1-0(1-0)
Celtic FC - Hamilton 5-1(2-1)
Ross County FC - Motherwell FC 1-0(1-0)

Round 2 [08-09.08.2020]
Hamilton - Ross County FC 0-1(0-0)
Livingston FC - Hibernian FC 1-4(0-3)
Motherwell FC - Dundee United 0-1(0-0)
Rangers FC - St. Mirren FC 3-0(1-0)
Kilmarnock FC - Celtic FC 1-1(1-1)
St. Johnstone FC - Aberdeen 0-1(0-0) [20.08.]

Round 3 [11-12.08.2020]
Dundee United - Hibernian FC 0-1(0-0)
Motherwell FC - Livingston FC 2-2(2-1)
Rangers FC - St. Johnstone FC 3-0(2-0)
Ross County FC - Kilmarnock FC 2-2(1-0)
St. Mirren FC - Celtic FC 1-2(1-2) [16.09.]
Aberdeen FC - Hamilton 4-2(4-1) [20.10.]

Round 4 [15-16.08.2020]
Hamilton - St. Mirren FC 0-1(0-1)
Kilmarnock FC - St. Johnstone FC 1-2(0-0)
Ross County FC - Dundee United 1-2(1-1)
Hibernian FC - Motherwell FC 0-0
Livingston FC - Rangers FC 0-0
Celtic FC - Aberdeen 1-0(1-0) [17.02.2021]

Round 5 [22-23.08.2020]
Motherwell FC - Hamilton 0-1(0-0)
Rangers FC - Kilmarnock FC 2-0(0-0)
St. Mirren FC - Ross County FC 1-1(1-0)
Dundee United - Celtic FC 0-1(0-0)
Aberdeen FC - Livingston FC 2-1(0-0)
St. Johnstone FC - Hibernian FC 0-1(0-0)

Round 6 [29-30.08.2020]
Kilmarnock FC - Dundee United 4-0(2-0)
Livingston FC - Ross County FC 1-0(0-0)
St. Johnstone FC - St. Mirren FC 1-0(0-0)
Hamilton - Rangers FC 0-2(0-2)
Celtic FC - Motherwell FC 3-0(1-0)
Hibernian FC - Aberdeen FC 0-1(0-1)

Round 7 [12.09.2020]
Aberdeen FC - Kilmarnock FC 1-0(1-0)
Livingston FC - Hamilton 1-2(1-0)
Motherwell FC - St. Johnstone FC 1-0(1-0)
Rangers FC - Dundee United 4-0(2-0)
Ross County FC - Celtic FC 0-5(0-2)
St. Mirren FC - Hibernian FC 0-3(0-2)

Round 8 [19-20.09.2020]
Celtic FC - Livingston FC 3-2(2-1)
Dundee United - St. Mirren FC 2-1(1-0)
Kilmarnock FC - Hamilton 2-1(1-1)
St. Johnstone FC - Ross County FC 0-1(0-1)
Hibernian FC - Rangers FC 2-2(1-1)
Aberdeen FC - Motherwell FC 0-3(0-3)

Round 9 [26-27.09.2020]
Hamilton - Dundee United 1-1(0-1)
Livingston FC - St. Johnstone FC 2-0(2-0)
St. Mirren FC - Kilmarnock FC 0-1(0-1)
Motherwell FC - Rangers FC 1-5(0-3)
Celtic FC - Hibernian FC 3-0(2-0)
Ross County FC - Aberdeen FC 0-3(0-1)

Round 10 [02-04.10.2020]
Aberdeen FC - St. Mirren FC 2-1(0-0)
Dundee United - Livingston FC 1-2(1-0)
Hibernian FC - Hamilton 3-2(2-0)
St. Johnstone FC - Celtic FC 0-2(0-0)
Rangers FC - Ross County FC 2-0(1-0)
Kilmarnock-Motherwell 0-1(0-0) [10.02.2021]

Round 11 [17.10.2020]
Celtic FC - Rangers FC 0-2(0-1)
Dundee United - Aberdeen FC 0-0
Hamilton - St. Johnstone FC 3-5(2-3)
Livingston FC - Kilmarnock FC 1-3(1-2)
Ross County FC - Hibernian FC 0-0
St. Mirren FC - Motherwell 0-0 [24.02.2021]

Round 12 [24-25.10.2020]
Kilmarnock FC - Hibernian FC 0-1(0-1)
Motherwell FC - Ross County FC 4-0(1-0)
St. Johnstone FC - Dundee United 0-0
Aberdeen FC - Celtic FC 3-3(1-0)
Rangers FC - Livingston FC 2-0(2-0)
St. Mirren - Hamilton 1-1(0-0) [17.02.2021]

Round 13 [31.10.-01.11.2020]
Dundee United - Ross County FC 2-1(1-0)
Livingston FC - Motherwell FC 0-2(0-2)
Kilmarnock FC - Rangers FC 0-1(0-1)
Hibernian FC - St. Johnstone 2-2(1-1) [24.11.]
Hamilton - Aberdeen FC 1-1(0-1) [25.11.]
Celtic FC - St. Mirren 1-2(1-2) 30.01.2021]

Round 14 [06-08.11.2020]
Aberdeen FC - Hibernian FC 2-0(2-0)
Ross County FC - Livingston FC 1-1(1-0)
St. Johnstone FC - Kilmarnock FC 1-0(0-0)
St. Mirren FC - Dundee United 0-0
Motherwell FC - Celtic FC 1-4(0-2)
Rangers FC - Hamilton 8-0(4-0)

Round 15 [21-22.11.2020]
Dundee United - Hamilton 2-1(0-0)
Hibernian FC - Celtic FC 2-2(0-0)
Kilmarnock FC - Ross County FC 3-1(1-1)
Livingston FC - St. Mirren FC 0-1(0-0)
St. Johnstone FC - Motherwell FC 1-1(1-1)
Rangers FC - Aberdeen FC 4-0(2-0)

Round 16 [05-06.12.2020]
Hamilton - Kilmarnock FC 1-0(0-0)
Livingston FC - Dundee United 2-0(0-0)
Motherwell FC - Hibernian FC 0-3(0-0)
St. Mirren FC - Aberdeen FC 1-1(1-1)
Ross County FC - Rangers FC 0-4(0-1)
Celtic FC - St. Johnstone FC 1-1(0-0)

Round 17 [12-13.12.2020]
Aberdeen FC - Ross County FC 2-0(1-0)
Hamilton - Hibernian FC 0-4(0-2)
Motherwell FC - St. Mirren FC 0-1(0-1)
St. Johnstone FC - Livingston FC 1-2(0-0)
Dundee United - Rangers FC 1-2(1-2)
Celtic FC - Kilmarnock FC 2-0(0-0)

Round 18 [19-20.12.2020]
Hibernian FC - Dundee United 1-1(1-0)
Rangers FC - Motherwell FC 3-1(0-1)
Ross County FC - Hamilton 0-2(0-1)
St. Mirren FC - St. Johnstone FC 3-2(1-2)
Kilmarnock FC - Aberdeen FC 0-2(0-0)
Livingston FC - Celtic 2-2(1-2) [20.01.2021]

Round 19 [23.12.2020]
Celtic FC - Ross County FC 2-0(1-0)
Hamilton - Livingston FC 0-2(0-0)
Hibernian FC - St. Mirren FC 1-0(1-0)
St. Johnstone FC - Rangers FC 0-3(0-2)
Motherwell FC - Aberdeen FC 0-0
Dundee United - Kilmarnock FC 2-0(2-0)

Round 20 [26.12.2020]
Rangers FC - Hibernian FC 1-0(1-0)
Aberdeen FC - St. Johnstone FC 2-1(1-1)
Dundee United - Motherwell FC 1-1(0-1)
Hamilton - Celtic FC 0-3(0-0)
Kilmarnock FC - Livingston FC 1-2(0-0)
Ross County FC - St. Mirren FC 0-2(0-0)

Round 21 [30.12.2020]
Celtic FC - Dundee United 3-0(2-0)
St. Johnstone FC - Hamilton 0-0
St. Mirren FC - Rangers FC 0-2(0-2)
Hibernian FC - Ross County FC 0-2(0-1)
Motherwell FC - Kilmarnock FC 0-2(0-1)
Livingston FC - Aberdeen FC 0-0 [30.01.2021]

Round 22 [02.01.2021]
Rangers FC - Celtic FC 1-0(0-0)
Aberdeen FC - Dundee United 0-0
Hamilton - Motherwell FC 3-0(1-0)
Hibernian FC - Livingston FC 0-3(0-2)
Kilmarnock FC - St. Mirren FC 1-1(1-0)
Ross County FC - St. Johnstone FC 1-1(1-1)

Round 23 [09-12.01.2021]
Kilmarnock FC - Hamilton 2-0(1-0)
St. Mirren FC - Motherwell FC 1-1(0-1)
Aberdeen FC - Rangers FC 1-2(0-1)
Livingston FC - Ross County FC 3-1(1-1)
Celtic FC - Hibernian FC 1-1(0-0)
Dundee United - St. Johnstone FC 2-2(1-2)

Round 24 [16-17.01.2021]
Celtic FC - Livingston FC 0-0
Hamilton - Dundee United 0-0
Hibernian FC - Kilmarnock FC 2-0(0-0)
Ross County FC - Aberdeen FC 4-1(2-1)
St. Johnstone FC - St. Mirren FC 1-0(0-0)
Motherwell FC - Rangers FC 1-1(1-0)

Round 25 [23.01.2021]
Aberdeen FC - Motherwell FC 2-0(1-0)
Rangers FC - Ross County FC 5-0(3-0)
Dundee United - Hibernian 0-2(0-1) [30.01.]
Kilmarnock - St. Johnstone 2-3(2-0) [30.01.]
St. Mirren FC - Celtic FC 0-4(0-1) [10.02.]
Livingston FC - Hamilton 2-1(2-1) [13.03.]

Round 26 [27.01.2021]
Dundee United - St. Mirren FC 1-5(0-3)
Ross County FC - Motherwell FC 1-2(1-0)
St. Johnstone FC - Aberdeen FC 0-0
Celtic FC - Hamilton 2-0(1-0)
Hibernian FC - Rangers FC 0-1(0-0)
Livingston FC - Kilmarnock FC 2-0(0-0)

Round 27 [02-03.02.2021]
Aberdeen FC - Livingston FC 0-2(0-2)
St. Mirren FC - Hibernian FC 1-2(0-0)
Kilmarnock FC - Celtic FC 0-4(0-1)
Hamilton - Ross County FC 1-2(1-0)
Motherwell FC - Dundee United 2-1(2-0)
Rangers FC - St. Johnstone FC 1-0(0-0)

Round 28 [06-07.02.2021]
Celtic FC - Motherwell FC 2-1(1-0)
Hibernian FC - Aberdeen FC 2-0(1-0)
Livingston FC - St. Johnstone FC 1-2(0-1)
Ross County FC - Dundee United 0-2(0-0)
St. Mirren FC - Kilmarnock FC 2-0(1-0)
Hamilton - Rangers FC 1-1(0-0)

Round 29 [13-14.02.2021]
Aberdeen FC - St. Mirren FC 0-0
Dundee United - Livingston FC 3-0(2-0)
Motherwell FC - Hamilton 1-4(0-3)
Rangers FC - Kilmarnock FC 1-0(1-0)
St. Johnstone FC - Celtic FC 1-2(0-0)
Ross County FC - Hibernian FC 1-2(0-0)

Round 30 [27.02.2021]
Celtic FC - Aberdeen FC 1-0(1-0)
Hibernian FC - Motherwell FC 0-2(0-1)
Kilmarnock FC - Dundee United 1-1(0-1)
St. Mirren FC - Ross County FC 1-0(0-0)
Hamilton - St. Johnstone FC 1-1(1-0) [03.03.]
Livingston FC - Rangers FC 0-1(0-0) [03.03.]

Round 31 [06-07.03.2021]
Aberdeen FC - Hamilton 0-0
Motherwell FC - Livingston FC 3-1(1-0)
Rangers FC - St. Mirren FC 3-0(2-0)
Ross County FC - Kilmarnock FC 3-2(1-1)
St. Johnstone FC - Hibernian FC 1-0(1-0)
Dundee United - Celtic FC 0-0

Round 32 [20-21.03.2021]
Kilmarnock FC - Motherwell FC 4-1(1-1)
Dundee United - Aberdeen FC 0-0(0-0)
Hamilton - St. Mirren FC 1-1(0-1)
Livingston FC - Hibernian FC 1-1(1-1)
St. Johnstone FC - Ross County FC 1-0(0-0)
Celtic FC - Rangers FC 1-1(1-1)

Round 33 [20-21.02.2021]
Aberdeen FC - Kilmarnock FC 1-0(1-0)
Hibernian FC - Hamilton 2-0(1-0)
Motherwell FC - St. Johnstone FC 0-3(0-2)
St. Mirren FC - Livingston FC 1-1(1-1)
Rangers FC - Dundee United 4-1(2-0)
Ross County FC - Celtic FC 1-0(0-0)

Final Standings

			Total					Home					Away			
1. Rangers FC Glasgow	33	28	5	0	78	-	10	89	16	0	0	47	-	2	12	5	0	31 - 8
2. Celtic FC Glasgow	33	20	9	4	66	-	24	69	11	4	2	31	-	11	9	5	2	35 - 13
3. Hibernian FC Edinburgh	33	16	8	9	44	-	31	56	6	5	5	19	-	19	10	3	4	25 - 12
4. Aberdeen FC	33	13	10	10	32	-	31	49	9	4	4	22	-	16	4	6	6	10 - 15
5. Livingston FC	33	12	8	13	40	-	41	44	6	4	7	19	-	20	6	4	6	21 - 21
6. St. Johnstone FC Perth	33	10	10	13	34	-	40	40	5	4	7	8	-	13	5	6	6	26 - 27
7. St. Mirren FC Paisley	33	10	10	13	30	-	38	40	4	7	6	14	-	21	6	3	7	16 - 17
8. Dundee United FC	33	9	12	12	29	-	43	39	6	5	6	19	-	20	3	7	6	10 - 23
9. Motherwell FC	33	9	8	16	32	-	51	35	4	3	9	16	-	29	5	5	7	16 - 22
10. Ross County FC Dingwall	33	8	5	20	26	-	59	29	4	4	9	16	-	31	4	1	11	10 - 28
11. Kilmarnock FC	33	8	4	21	33	-	47	28	5	3	8	22	-	22	3	1	13	11 - 25
12. Hamilton Academical FC	33	6	9	18	31	-	60	27	2	6	8	13	-	25	4	3	10	18 - 35

Teams ranked 1-6 were qualified for the Championship Round, while teams ranked 7-12 were qualified for the Relegation Round.

Relegation Round

Round 34 [10.04.2021]
Hamilton - Dundee United 0-1(0-1)
Kilmarnock FC - Ross County FC 2-2(2-1)
Motherwell FC - St. Mirren FC 1-0(0-0)

Round 35 [21.04.2021]
Hamilton - Motherwell FC 0-1(0-1)
Kilmarnock FC - Dundee United 3-0(3-0)
Ross County FC - St. Mirren FC 1-3(1-0)

Round 36 [01.05.2021]
Dundee United - Ross County FC 0-2(0-2)
Motherwell FC - Kilmarnock FC 2-0(0-0)
St. Mirren FC - Hamilton 1-2(0-1)

Round 37 [12.05.2021]
Dundee United - Motherwell FC 2-2(2-0)
Kilmarnock FC - St. Mirren FC 3-3(1-0)
Ross County FC - Hamilton 2-1(1-1)

Round 38 [16.05.2021]
Hamilton - Kilmarnock FC 0-2(0-2)
Motherwell FC - Ross County FC 1-2(1-0)
St. Mirren FC - Dundee United 0-0

Final Standings

		Total							Home						Away		
7. St. Mirren FC Paisley	38	11	12	15	37	-	45	45	4	8	7	15 - 23	7	4	8	22 - 22
8. Motherwell FC	38	12	9	17	39	-	55	45	6	3	10	20 - 31	6	6	7	19 - 24
9. Dundee United FC	38	10	14	14	32	-	50	44	6	6	7	21 - 24	4	8	7	11 - 26
10. Ross County FC Dingwall	38	11	6	21	35	-	66	39	5	4	10	19 - 35	6	2	11	16 - 31
11. Kilmarnock FC (*Relegation Play-offs*)	38	10	6	22	43	-	54	36	6	5	8	30 - 27	4	1	14	13 - 27
12. Hamilton Academical FC (*Relegated*)	38	7	9	22	34	-	67	30	2	6	11	13 - 29	5	3	11	21 - 38

Championship Round

Results

Round 34 [10-11.04.2021]
Celtic FC - Livingston FC 6-0(2-0)
St. Johnstone FC - Aberdeen FC 0-1(0-0)
Rangers FC - Hibernian FC 2-1(1-0)

Round 35 [21.04.2021]
Hibernian FC - Livingston FC 2-1(2-0)
St. Johnstone FC - Rangers FC 1-1(0-0)
Aberdeen FC - Celtic FC 1-1(1-0)

Round 36 [01-02.05.2021]
Hibernian FC - St. Johnstone FC 0-1(0-1)
Livingston FC - Aberdeen FC 1-2(0-0)
Rangers FC - Celtic FC 4-1(2-1)

Round 37 [12.05.2021]
Livingston FC - Rangers FC 0-3(0-1)
Celtic FC - St. Johnstone FC 4-0(2-0)
Aberdeen FC - Hibernian FC 0-1(0-1)

Round 38 [15.05.2021]
Hibernian FC - Celtic FC 0-0
Rangers FC - Aberdeen FC 4-0(2-0)
St. Johnstone FC - Livingston FC 0-0

Final Standings

		Total							Home						Away		
1. **Rangers FC Glasgow**	38	32	6	0	92	-	13	102	19	0	0	57 - 4	13	6	0	35 - 9
2. Celtic FC Glasgow	38	22	11	5	78	-	29	77	13	4	2	41 - 11	9	7	3	37 - 18
3. Hibernian FC Edinburgh	38	18	9	11	48	-	35	63	7	6	6	21 - 21	11	3	5	27 - 14
4. Aberdeen FC	38	15	11	12	36	-	38	56	9	5	5	23 - 18	6	6	7	13 - 20
5. St. Johnstone FC Perth	38	11	12	15	36	-	46	45	5	6	8	9 - 15	6	6	7	27 - 31
6. Livingston FC	38	12	9	17	42	-	54	45	6	4	9	20 - 25	6	5	8	22 - 29

Top goalscorers:	
22 **Odsonne Édouard (FRA)**	*Celtic FC Glasgow*
14 Kevin Michael Nisbet	*Hibernian FC Edinburgh*
14 Kemar Roofe (JAM)	*Rangers FC Glasgow*
12 Martin Collie Boyle	*Hibernian FC Edinburgh*
12 Alfredo José Morelos Aviléz (COL)	*Rangers FC Glasgow*
12 James Henry Tavernier	*Celtic FC Glasgow*

Relegation Play-offs [20-24.05.2021]

Dundee FC – Kilmarnock FC   2-1(1-0)   2-1(2-0)

Dundee FC will play at first level in the 2021/2022 season.

NATIONAL CUP
Scottish Cup 2019/2020

The competition was suspended on 13.03.2020 due to Covid-19 pandemic. The Semi-Finals and Final were postponed (the competition was continued in autumn 2020). Missing results are presented in this year's yearbook.

Semi-Finals [31.10.-01.11.2020]			
Heart of Midlothian FC - Hibernian FC Edinburgh	2-1 aet	Celtic FC Glasgow - Aberdeen FC	2-0(2-0)

Final

20.12.2020; Hampden Park, Glasgow; Referee: John William Beaton; Attendance: 0
Celtic FC Glasgow – Heart of Midlothian FC Edinburgh   **3-3(2-0,3-3,3-3); 4-3 on penalties**

Celtic FC: Conor William Hazard, Kristoffer Vassbakk Ajer, Christopher Jullien, Shane Patrick Michael Duffy (90.Michael Andrew Johnston), Greg John Taylor (83.Jeremie Agyekum Frimpong), Scott Brown (105.Ismaila Wafougossani Soro), Callum William McGregor, Ryan Christie, David Turnbull (68.Tomas Petar Rogić), Mohamed Amine Elyounoussi (83.Diego Sebastián Laxalt Suárez), Odsonne Édouard (97.Leigh Griffiths). Trainer: Neil Francis Lennon (Northern Ireland).

Heart of Midlothian: Craig Sinclair Gordon, Michael Smith, Craig Halkett, Christophe Didier Berra, Stephen Kingsley, Andrew Irving (109.Elliott Thomas Frear), Andrew William Halliday (90.Peter Haring), Jamie Walker (57.Joshua Lloyd Ginnelly), Steven John Naismith, Aidan Peter White (82.Oliver Robert Lee), Liam Boyce (70.Craig Ross Wighton). Trainer: Robert Neilson.

Goals: 1-0 Ryan Christie (19), 2-0 Odsonne Édouard (29 penalty), 2-1 Liam Boyce (48), 2-2 Stephen Kingsley (67), 3-2 (105), 3-3 Joshua Lloyd Ginnelly (111).

Penalties: Steven John Naismith 0-1; Leigh Griffiths 1-1; Michael Smith 1-2; Callum William McGregor 2-2; Oliver Robert Lee 2-3; Ryan Christie (saved); Stephen Kingsley (saved); Michael Andrew Johnston 3-3; Craig Ross Wighton (saved); Kristoffer Vassbakk Ajer 4-3.

NATIONAL CUP
Scottish Cup 2020/2021

First Round [26.12./28.12.2020/01.01./06.01.11.01.2021]			
Albion Rovers FC Coatbridge - Buckie Thistle FC	0-3(0-2)	Lothian Thistle Hutchison Vale - Banks O' Dee FC	0-3(0-0)
Berwick Rangers FC Glasgow - Stirling Albion FC	0-3(0-2)	Nairn County FC - Broxburn Athletic FC	0-0 aet; 4-3 pen
Brechin City FC - Linlithgow Rose FC	2-3(1-1)	Rothes FC - Fraserburgh FC	1-3(1-2)
Cowdenbeath FC - Wick Academy FC	2-0(1-0)	Stenhousemuir FC - Preston Athletic FC	4-1(2-0)
Edinburgh City FC - Caledonian Braves FC	3-1(1-1)	Stranraer FC – The Spartans FC Edinburgh	5-0(3-0)
Elgin City FC - Civil Service Strollers FC Edinburgh	4-0(1-0)	Tranent Juniors FC - East Stirlingshire FC Falkirk	4-1(4-0)
Gala Fairydean Rovers FC - Annan Athletic FC	1-2(0-1)	Dundonald Bluebell FC - Queen's Park FC Glasgow	1-3(0-0,1-1)
Haddington Athletic FC - Formartine United FC	1-2(0-0)	Bonnyrigg Rose Athletic FC - Bo'ness United FC	5-2(0-1)
Keith FC - Hill of Beath Hawthorn FC	4-2(1-2,2-2)	Huntly FC - Cumbernauld Colts FC	3-1(1-1)
Kelty Hearts FC - Jeanfield Swifts FC Perth	2-1(1-0)	Camelon Juniors FC - Brora Rangers FC Glasgow	1-2(1-0)

Second Round [08-10.01./23.01.2021]			
Queen's Park FC Glasgow - Queen Of The South FC	0-3(0-1)	Arbroath FC - Falkirk FC	1-2(1-1)
Forfar Athletic FC - Linlithgow Rose FC	4-1(1-1,1-1)	Dumbarton FC - Huntly FC	4-0(2-0)
East Fife FC Methil - Tranent Juniors FC	5-1(2-1)	Stirling Albion FC - Raith Rovers FC Kirkcaldy	0-2(0-1)
Alloa Athletic FC - Cove Rangers FC Glasgow	2-3(2-1)	Brora Rangers FC Glasgow - Heart of Midlothian FC	2-1(1-0)
Fraserburgh FC - Banks O' Dee FC Aberdeen	2-1(0-0)	Formartine United FC - Annan Athletic FC	1-1 aet; 3-1 pen
Kelty Hearts FC - Stranraer FC	2-3(2-0)	Elgin City FC - Ayr United FC	0-4(0-4)
Dundee FC - Bonnyrigg Rose Athletic FC	3-2(0-1,1-1)	Peterhead FC - Stenhousemuir FC	0-1(0-1)
Airdrieonians FC - Edinburgh City FC	0-1(0-0)	Greenock Morton FC - Dunfermline Athletic FC	0-0 aet; 6-5 pen
Nairn County FC - Montrose FC	1-7(0-4)	Partick Thistle FC Glasgow - Cowdenbeath FC	3-0(1-0)
Keith FC - Clyde FC Cumbernauld	0-2(0-2)	Buckie Thistle FC - Inverness Caledonian Thistle FC	2-3(1-2)

Third Round [02-05.04.2021]			
Ross County FC - Inverness Caledonian Thistle FC	1-3(1-1)	Hamilton Academical FC - St. Mirren FC	0-3(0-1)
Dumbarton FC - Aberdeen FC	0-1(0-0)	Dundee FC - St. Johnstone FC Perth	0-1(0-1)
Forfar Athletic FC - Edinburgh City FC	2-2 aet; 5-3 pen	Ayr United FC - Clyde FC Cumbernauld	0-1(0-1)
Dundee United FC - Partick Thistle FC Glasgow	2-1(0-1)	Formartine United FC Pitmedden - Motherwell FC	0-5(0-2)
Livingston FC - Raith Rovers FC Kirkcaldy	2-1(0-1,1-1)	Fraserburgh FC - Montrose FC	2-4(2-2)
Brora Rangers FC Glasgow - Stranraer FC	1-3(1-0,1-1)	Celtic FC Glasgow - Falkirk FC	3-0(0-0)
Stenhousemuir FC - Kilmarnock FC	0-4(0-2)	Rangers FC Glasgow - Cove Rangers FC Glasgow	4-0(4-0)
East Fife FC Methil - Greenock Morton FC	1-2(0-0,1-1)	Queen Of The South FC - Hibernian FC Edinburgh	1-3(0-1)

1/8-Finals [16-18.04.2021]			
St. Mirren FC - Inverness Caledonian Thistle FC	2-1(0-0)	St. Johnstone FC Perth - Clyde FC Cumbernauld	2-0(2-0)
Motherwell FC - Greenock Morton FC	1-1 aet; 5-3 pen	Aberdeen FC - Livingston FC	2-2 aet; 5-3 pen
Forfar Athletic FC - Dundee United FC	0-1(0-0)	Stranraer FC - Hibernian FC Edinburgh	0-4(0-1)
Kilmarnock FC - Montrose FC	3-1(2-0)	Rangers FC Glasgow - Celtic FC Glasgow	2-0(2-0)

Quarter-Finals [24-26.04.2021]				
Hibernian FC Edinburgh - Motherwell FC	2-2 aet; 4-2 pen		Rangers FC Glasgow - St. Johnstone FC Perth	1-1 aet; 2-4 pen
Aberdeen FC - Dundee United FC	0-3(0-2)		Kilmarnock FC - St. Mirren FC	3-3 aet; 4-5 pen

Semi-Finals [08-09.05.2021]				
Dundee United FC - Hibernian FC Edinburgh	0-2(0-1)		St. Mirren FC - St. Johnstone FC Perth	1-2(0-0)

Final

22.05.2021; Hampden Park, Glasgow; Referee: Nicholas Walsh; Attendance: 0
Hibernian FC Edinburgh - St. Johnstone FC Perth   0-1(0-1)

Hibernian FC: Matthew Ryan Macey, Paul McGinn, Ryan Porteous, Paul Thomas Hanlon (Cap), Josh Doig (76.Lewis Stevenson), Martin Callie Boyle, Alexandros Gogić (56.James Murphy), Joseph Peter Newell (72.Melker Hallberg), Jackson Alexander Irvine, Christian Rhys Doidge, Kevin Michael Nisbet. Trainer: John James Ross.

St. Johnstone FC: Zander Clark, Jason Kerr (Cap), Liam Craig Gordon, Jamie Daniel McCart, Shaun Anthony Rooney (79.James Dominic Brown), Alistair Edward McCann, Craig James Bryson (64.Murray Davidson), Callum Booth, Glenn Middleton (82.Michael Francis O'Halloran), David Wotherspoon, Christopher Kane. Trainer: Callum Iain Davidson.

Goal: 0-1 Shaun Anthony Rooney (32).

THE CLUBS 2020/2021

Please note: appearances and goals are including statistics of both regular season and play-offs (Championship and Relegation Round).

Aberdeen Football Club

Founded:	14.04.1903
Stadium:	Pittodrie Stadium, Aberdeen (20,866)
Trainer:	Derek-John McInnes 05.07.1971
[08.03.2021]	Paul Sheerin 28.08.1974
[23.03.2021]	Stephen Glass 23.05.1976

Goalkeepers:	DOB	M	(s)	G
Joseph Peter Lewis (ENG)	06.10.1987	35		
Gary Woods (ENG)	01.10.1990	3		
Defenders:	**DOB**	**M**	**(s)**	**G**
Andrew Considine	01.04.1987	36		1
Michael James Devlin	03.10.1993		(1)	
Ronald José Hernández Pimentel (VEN)	04.10.1997	2	(2)	
Thomas Michael Hoban (IRL)	24.01.1994	35	(2)	2
Gregory Alex Leigh (JAM)	30.09.1994	6	(2)	
Shaleum Narval Logan (ENG)	29.01.1988	2	(10)	
Jack MacKenzie	04.07.2000	5	(1)	
Scott Fraser McKenna	12.11.1996	4		
Kieran Ngwenya	25.09.2002		(2)	
Calvin Ramsay	31.07.2003		(4)	
Ashton John Taylor (WAL)	02.09.1990	30	(1)	1
Midfielders:	**DOB**	**M**	**(s)**	**G**
Craig James Bryson	06.11.1986	1	(1)	
Dean Graeme Campbell	19.03.2001	12	(8)	
Ryan Duncan	18.01.2004		(1)	
Lewis Ferguson	24.08.1999	35		9
Johnathan Hayes (IRL)	09.07.1987	34		2

Ross McCrorie	18.03.1998	28	(1)	1
Dylan McGeouch	15.01.1993	7	(8)	
Funso Ojo (BEL)	28.08.1991	6	(5)	
Ethan Ross	15.08.2001		(2)	
Miko Virtanen (FIN)	29.01.1999		(2)	
Forwards:	**DOB**	**M**	**(s)**	**G**
Bruce Anderson	23.09.1998	1	(5)	
Sam Benjamin Cosgrove (ENG)	02.12.1996	9	(5)	3
Ryan David Edmondson (ENG)	20.05.2001	3	(11)	2
Ryan Peter Hedges (WAL)	08.07.1995	25	(3)	5
Callum David Hendry	08.12.1997	5	(7)	2
Fraser David Ingham Hornby	13.09.1999	5	(5)	
Florian Kamberi (ALB)	08.03.1995	11		
Matthew Kennedy (NIR)	01.11.1994	22	(9)	1
Curtis Lee Main (ENG)	20.06.1992	8	(6)	2
Niall McGinn (NIR)	20.07.1987	12	(13)	
Connor McLennan	05.10.1999	13	(14)	
Michael Ruth	08.01.2002		(1)	
Marley Joseph Watkins (WAL)	17.10.1990	9		2
Scott Wright	08.08.1997	14	(3)	2

Celtic Football Club Glasgow

Founded:	06.11.1887
Stadium:	Celtic Park, Glasgow (60,411)
Trainer:	Neil Francis Lennon (NIR) 25.06.1971
[24.02.2021]	John Kennedy 18.08.1983

Goalkeepers:	DOB	M	(s)	G
Scott Bain	22.11.1991	18		
Vassilis Barkas (GRE)	30.05.1994	15		
Conor William Hazard (NIR)	05.03.1998	5		
Defenders:	**DOB**	**M**	**(s)**	**G**
Hatem Abd Elhamed (ISR)	18.03.1991	4	(4)	
Kristoffer Vassbakk Ajer (NOR)	17.04.1998	34	(1)	2
Boli Bolingoli-Mbombo (BEL)	01.07.1995		(1)	
Shane Patrick Michael Duffy (IRL)	01.01.1992	14	(4)	3
Jeremie Agyekum Frimpong (NED)	10.12.2000	19	(3)	1
Christopher Jullien (FRA)	22.03.1993	9		1
Jonjoe Kenny (ENG)	15.03.1997	14		
Diego Sebastián Laxalt Suárez (URU)	07.02.1993	13	(4)	1
Tony Ralston	16.11.1998	1		
Greg John Taylor	05.11.1997	23	(3)	
Stephen Welsh	19.01.2000	15	(1)	1
Midfielders:	**DOB**	**M**	**(s)**	**G**
Nir Bitton (ISR)	30.10.1991	12	(2)	1
Scott Brown	25.06.1985	25	(6)	1

Ryan Christie	22.02.1995	26	(8)	5
James Forrest	07.07.1991	8	(5)	3
Ewan Henderson	27.03.2000		(2)	
Callum William McGregor	14.06.1993	37		3
Jules Olivier Ntcham (FRA)	09.02.1996	7	(7)	1
Tomas Petar Rogić (AUS)	16.12.1992	10	(13)	1
Ismaila Wafougossani Soro (CIV)	07.05.1998	11	(8)	1
David Turnbull	10.07.1999	25	(6)	8
Forwards:	**DOB**	**M**	**(s)**	**G**
Albian Ajeti (SUI)	26.02.1997	10	(10)	6
Karamoko Dembélé (ENG)	22.02.2003		(5)	1
Odsonne Édouard (FRA)	16.01.1998	28	(3)	18
Mohamed Amine Elyounoussi (NOR)	04.08.1994	21	(13)	10
Leigh Griffiths	20.08.1990	7	(15)	6
Cameron Harper (USA)	19.11.2001	1		
Michael Andrew Johnston	19.04.1999	2	(8)	
Patryk Klimala (POL)	05.08.1998	3	(14)	3
Adam Montgomery	18.07.2002	1	(1)	
Armstrong Oko-Flex (IRL)	02.03.2002		(2)	

Dundee United Football Club

Founded: 24.05.1909
Stadium: Tannadice Park, Dundee (14,223)
Trainer: Michael Joseph Mellon   18.03.1972

Goalkeepers:	DOB	M	(s)	G
Ross Doohan	29.03.1998	2		
Deniz Mehmet (TUR)	19.09.1992	4		
Benjamin Siegrist (SUI)	31.01.1992	32		
Defenders:	**DOB**	**M**	**(s)**	**G**
Mark Gerard Connolly (IRL)	16.12.1991	23	(2)	
Ryan Christopher Edwards (ENG)	07.10.1993	24		2
Kieran Freeman	30.03.2000	1	(2)	
Lewis Neilson	15.05.2003	7	(2)	
Mark Reynolds	07.05.1987	33	(1)	1
Jamie David Robson	19.12.1997	34	(2)	
Kerr David Smith	12.12.2004	3	(2)	
Liam Smith	10.04.1996	28	(2)	1
Adrián Marcelo Spörle (ARG)	13.07.1995	15	(9)	4
Midfielders:	**DOB**	**M**	**(s)**	**G**
Luke Philip Bolton (ENG)	07.10.1999	18	(6)	1
Calum James Butcher (ENG)	26.02.1991	27	(1)	
Jeando Pourrat Fuchs (CMR)	11.10.1997	19	(1)	
Declan David Glass	07.06.2000		(1)	
Ian Andrew Harkes (USA)	30.03.1995	30	(5)	1
Florent Hoti (KVX)	11.12.2000	1	(3)	
Paul James McMullan	25.02.1996	3	(5)	
Archie Alexander Meekison	04.05.2002	2	(1)	1
Peter Ian Pawlett	03.02.1991	15	(11)	1
Dillon Thomas Powers (USA)	14.02.1991	6	(8)	
Forwards:	**DOB**	**M**	**(s)**	**G**
Louis George Appéré	26.03.1999	11	(11)	1
Logan Chalmers	24.03.2000	9	(6)	
Nicholas Alexander McCormack Clark	03.06.1991	24	(7)	8
Kai Fotheringham	18.04.2003		(1)	
Marc Graeme McNulty	14.09.1992	17	(8)	3
Lawrence Shankland	10.08.1995	30	(2)	8
Cameron Smith	24.08.1995		(4)	
Darren Watson	10.08.2003		(1)	

Hamilton Academical Football Club

Founded: 1874
Stadium: New Douglas Park, Hamilton (6,018)
Trainer: Brian Rice   11.10.1963

Goalkeepers:	DOB	M	(s)	G
Ryan Fulton	23.05.1996	28		
Kyle Gourlay	24.09.1998	9	(1)	
Jamie Smith	08.05.2002	1		
Defenders:	**DOB**	**M**	**(s)**	**G**
Brian Neil Easton	05.03.1988	24		
Markus Fjørtoft (NOR)	12.01.1994	1	(1)	
Jamie Hamilton	01.03.2002	21	(6)	
Lee James Stephen Hodson (NIR)	02.10.1991	33		1
Aaron Martin (ENG)	29.09.1989	24		
Ciaran McKenna	25.03.1998		(1)	
Scott McMann	09.07.1996	36		1
Hakeem Odoffin (ENG)	13.04.1998	37		3
George William Stanger (NZL)	15.08.2000	1	(4)	
Ben Stirling	16.08.1998	16	(4)	
Shaun Want	09.02.1997	11		
Midfielders:	**DOB**	**M**	**(s)**	**G**
Ross Callachan	04.09.1993	32	(1)	10
Will Collar (ENG)	03.02.1997	5	(1)	
Ronan Hughes	15.12.1998	7	(9)	2
Scott Anthony Martin	01.04.1997	21	(3)	2
Reegan Mimnaugh	18.12.2001	8	(9)	
Marley Redfern	13.12.2002		(1)	
Lewis Smith	16.03.2000	4	(5)	
Charlie Trafford (CAN)	24.05.1992	9	(7)	
Forwards:	**DOB**	**M**	**(s)**	**G**
Bruce Anderson	23.09.1998	13		2
Justin Johnson (NED)	27.08.1996	1	(4)	
David Philani Moyo (ZIM)	17.12.1994	23	(10)	3
Kyle Munro	29.11.2001	9	(7)	2
Marios Ogboe (GRE)	10.10.1994	15	(5)	3
Tunde Owolabi (NGA)	26.07.1996	1	(6)	
Callum Smith	13.11.1999	8	(15)	2
David Cooper Templeton	07.01.1989	7	(1)	1
Nathan Thomas (ENG)	27.09.1994	3	(7)	
Andrew Winter	10.03.2002	10	(12)	

Hibernian Football Club Edinburgh

Founded: 06.08.1875
Stadium: Easter Road Stadium, Edinburgh (20,421)
Trainer: John James Ross   05.06.1976

Goalkeepers:	DOB	M	(s)	G
Dillon Barnes (JAM)	08.04.1996	3	(1)	
Matthew Ryan Macey (ENG)	09.09.1994	3		
Ofir Marciano (ISR)	07.10.1989	32		
Defenders:	**DOB**	**M**	**(s)**	**G**
Josh Doig	18.05.2002	25	(3)	1
Alexandros Gogić (CYP)	13.04.1994	30	(4)	1
David Peter Gray	04.05.1988	1	(1)	
Paul Thomas Hanlon	20.01.1990	36	(1)	1
Sean Mackie	04.11.1998	2		
Paul McGinn	22.10.1990	37	(1)	3
Darren McGregor	07.08.1985	8	(2)	1
Ryan Porteous	25.03.1999	32	(2)	1
Lewis Stevenson	05.01.1988	11	(11)	
Midfielders:	**DOB**	**M**	**(s)**	**G**
Scott Allan	28.11.1991	3	(5)	
Christopher Cadden	19.09.1996	8	(2)	
Jamie Gullan	02.07.1999		(14)	
Melker Hallberg (SWE)	20.10.1995	12	(13)	
Daryl Jeremiah Horgan (IRL)	10.08.1992	4	(1)	
Jackson Alexander Irvine (AUS)	07.03.1993	14	(1)	
Kyle Magennis	26.08.1998	4	(10)	1
Stephen Patrick Mallan	25.03.1996	4	(10)	1
Stephen McGinn	02.12.1988		(5)	1
Joseph Peter Newell (ENG)	15.03.1993	32		1
Drey Jermaine Wright (ENG)	30.04.1995	11	(9)	1
Forwards:	**DOB**	**M**	**(s)**	**G**
Martin Callie Boyle (AUS)	25.04.1993	35	(1)	12
Steven Bradley	16.03.2002		(1)	
Christian Rhys Doidge (WAL)	25.08.1992	29	(7)	7
Steven Elder	16.03.2002		(1)	
James Murphy	28.08.1989	14	(5)	1
Kevin Michael Nisbet	08.03.1997	28	(5)	14
Ryan Shanley	16.01.2001		(1)	

Kilmarnock Football Club

Founded:	05.01.1869		
Stadium:	Rugby Park, Kilmarnock (17,889)		
Trainer:	Alexander Constantine Dyer (ENG)	14.11.1965	
[30.01.2021]	James Fowler	26.10.1980	
[08.02.2021]	Thomas James Wright (NIR)	29.08.1963	

Goalkeepers:	DOB	M	(s)	G
Colin Anthony Doyle (IRL)	12.06.1985	11		
Jake Eastwood (ENG)	03.10.1996	1		
Daniel Rogers (IRL)	23.03.1994	26	(1)	
Defenders:	**DOB**	**M**	**(s)**	**G**
Kirk John Broadfoot	08.08.1984	31		
Clevid Florian Dikamona (CGO)	23.06.1990	10	(2)	
Stuart John Findlay	14.09.1995	21	(1)	
Brandon Neil Haunstrup (ENG)	26.10.1996	21	(6)	
Zeno Ibsen Rossi (ENG)	28.10.2000	11	(3)	
Aaron Joseph McGowan (ENG)	24.07.1996	15	(3)	
Zecheriah Joshua Henry Medley (ENG)	09.07.2000	7	(1)	1
Ross Millen	28.09.1994	18	(1)	
Calum Waters	10.03.1996	18		
Midfielders:	**DOB**	**M**	**(s)**	**G**
Tomas Brindley	13.10.2001		(1)	

	DOB	M	(s)	G
Eamonn Brophy	10.03.1996	8	(7)	2
Christopher Robert Burke	02.12.1983	28	(9)	9
Diaguely Dabo (FRA)	26.08.1992	1	(5)	
Gary Richard Perry Dicker (IRL)	31.07.1986	26		
Pierrick Brandon Leroy Keutcha (ENG)	10.12.2001	1	(2)	
Youssouf Chafiq Mulumbu Ngangu (COD)	25.01.1987	6	(11)	
Alan Thomas Daniel Power (IRL)	23.01.1988	32		1
Aaron Tshibola (ENG)	02.01.1995	26	(5)	3
Forwards:	**DOB**	**M**	**(s)**	**G**
Nicke Kabamba (COD)	01.02.1994	21	(12)	5
Greg Kiltie	18.01.1997	23	(6)	6
Kyle Joseph George Lafferty (NIR)	16.09.1987	8	(1)	8
Rory McKenzie	07.10.1993	23	(6)	2
George Oakley (ENG)	18.11.1995	3	(3)	
Mitchell Bernard Pinnock (ENG)	12.12.1994	17	(13)	4
Danny Whitehall (ENG)	08.10.1995	5	(12)	2

Livingston Football Club

Founded:	1943		
Stadium:	Almondvale Stadium, Livingston (9,512)		
Trainer:	Gary Holt	09.03.1973	
[21.12.2020]	David Paul Martindale	13.07.1974	

Goalkeepers:	DOB	M	(s)	G
Robbie McCrorie	18.03.1998	16		
Max Stryjek (POL)	18.07.1996	22		
Defenders:	**DOB**	**M**	**(s)**	**G**
Efe Eric Ambrose Emoubo (NGA)	18.10.1988	17	(5)	
Ciaron Maurice Brown (ENG)	14.01.1998	13	(3)	1
Nicholas Devlin	17.10.1993	35	(1)	2
Jack Joseph Fitzwater (ENG)	23.09.1997	20		1
Jonathan Neill Guthrie (ENG)	29.07.1992	36		5
Alan Lithgow	12.03.1988	1	(1)	
Jackson Longridge	12.04.1995	7	(1)	
Jack McMillan	18.12.1997	4	(4)	
Carlo Pignatiello	16.10.2000		(1)	
Julien Serrano (FRA)	13.02.1998	19	(5)	1
Aaron Taylor-Sinclair	08.04.1991	5	(1)	
Midfielders:	**DOB**	**M**	**(s)**	**G**
Marvin Clement Bartley (ENG)	04.07.1986	32	(1)	1
Robbie Crawford	22.06.1994		(1)	
Djibril Diani (FRA)	11.02.1998	2	(2)	

	DOB	M	(s)	G
Alan Forrest	09.09.1996	21	(9)	4
Jason Derek Holt	19.02.1993	27	(3)	1
Tevi Steve Lawson (TOG)	08.08.1994	7	(8)	
Joshua Mullin	23.09.1992	16	(6)	2
Scott Robinson	11.03.1992	16	(10)	4
Forwards:	**DOB**	**M**	**(s)**	**G**
Lyndon John Dykes	07.10.1995	3		2
Jay Aston Emmanuel-Thomas (ENG)	27.12.1990	14	(10)	5
Raffaele De Vita (ITA)	23.09.1987	2		
Jack Hamilton	30.06.2000	2	(3)	1
Jaze Kabia (IRL)	08.07.2000	1	(7)	1
Salim Kouider-Aïssa	22.03.1996		(4)	
Lars Lokotsch (GER)	17.05.1996	2	(2)	
Scott Pittman	09.07.1992	37	(1)	7
Matej Poplatnik (SVN)	15.07.1992	5	(14)	
Gavin Christopher Reilly	10.05.1993	3	(2)	
Craig Sibbald	18.05.1995	29	(3)	1
Aymen Souda (FRA)	28.02.1993		(2)	
Scott Tiffoney	26.08.1998	4	(8)	1

Motherwell Football Club

Founded:	17.05.1886		
Stadium:	Fir Park, Motherwell (13,677)		
Trainer:	Stephen Robinson (NIR)	10.12.1974	
[31.12.2020]	Keith Lasley	21.09.1979	
[07.01.2021]	Graham Alexander	10.10.1971	

Goalkeepers:	DOB	M	(s)	G
Jordan Archer	12.04.1993	4		
Trevor Carson (NIR)	05.03.1988	12		
Aaron Jems Chapman (ENG)	29.05.1990	4	(2)	
Liam Patrick Kelly	23.01.1996	18		
Defenders:	**DOB**	**M**	**(s)**	**G**
Jake Carroll (IRL)	11.08.1991	14	(1)	
Declan Patrick Gallagher	13.02.1991	27	(2)	1
Liam David Grimshaw (ENG)	02.02.1995	12	(2)	
Max Johnston	24.12.2003	1	(1)	
Ricki Lamie	20.06.1993	27	(4)	
Tyler Magloire (ENG)	21.12.1998	8	(2)	
Nathan McGinley (ENG)	15.09.1996	12	(7)	
Bevis Kristofer Kizito Mugabi (UGA)	01.05.1995	21	(2)	2
Stephen Gerard O'Donnell	11.05.1992	34		1
Midfielders:	**DOB**	**M**	**(s)**	**G**
Allan Campbell	04.07.1998	34		4
Dean Cornelius	11.04.2001		(1)	
Robbie Crawford	22.06.1994	19	(3)	
Liam Francis Peadar Donnelly (NIR)	07.03.1996	1		

	DOB	M	(s)	G
Samuel Robert Foley (IRL)	17.10.1986	3	(1)	1
Steven Lawless	12.04.1991	3	(4)	
Barry Maguire	27.04.1998	14	(10)	1
Mark O'Hara	12.12.1995	23	(4)	5
Liam Polworth	12.10.1994	18	(3)	
Jordan Stephen Roberts (ENG)	05.01.1994	5	(2)	1
David Turnbull	10.07.1999	5		1
Forwards:	**DOB**	**M**	**(s)**	**G**
Devante Lavon Andrew Cole (ENG)	10.05.1995	24	(3)	11
Jake Hastie	18.03.1998	7	(7)	
Jermaine Samuel Hylton (ENG)	28.06.1993		(5)	
Callum Joseph Lang (ENG)	08.09.1998	12	(5)	3
Christopher Michael Long (ENG)	25.02.1995	19	(10)	4
Ross MacIver	28.02.1999		(1)	
Harry David Robinson (NIR)	26.09.2000		(1)	
Sherwin Dandery Seedorf (NED)	17.03.1998	6	(4)	
Harry Smith (ENG)	18.05.1995		(5)	
Anthony Paul Watt	29.12.1993	28	(7)	3
Jordan Neill White	04.02.1992	3	(15)	

Rangers Football Club Glasgow

Founded:	1872		
Stadium:	Ibrox Park Stadium, Glasgow (50,817)		
Trainer:	Steven George Gerrard (ENG)		30.05.1980

Goalkeepers:	DOB	M	(s)	G
Allan James McGregor	31.01.1982	27		
Jonathan Peter McLaughlin	09.09.1987	11		
Defenders:	**DOB**	**M**	**(s)**	**G**
Leon-Aderemi Balogun (NGA)	28.06.1988	15	(4)	
Borna Barišić (CRO)	10.11.1992	33		1
Calvin Bassey (ENG)	31.12.1999	3	(5)	
George Edmundson (ENG)	31.08.1997		(1)	
Connor Lambert Goldson (ENG)	18.12.1992	38		4
Filip Viktor Helander (SWE)	22.04.1993	21	(1)	1
Leon Thomson King	14.01.2004		(1)	
Nathan Kenneth Patterson	16.10.2001	3	(4)	
Jack Benjamin Simpson (ENG)	18.12.1996	4	(1)	
James Henry Tavernier (ENG)	31.10.1991	33		12
Midfielders:	**DOB**	**M**	**(s)**	**G**
Scott Nathaniel Arfield (CAN)	01.11.1988	11	(17)	4
Joseph Oluwaseyi Temitope Ayodele-Aribo(NGA)	21.07.1996	27	(4)	7
Steven Davis (NIR)	01.01.1985	29	(6)	
Ianis Hagi (ROU)	22.10.1998	23	(10)	7
Ryan Jack	27.02.1992	16	(3)	2
Jordan Jones (NIR)	24.10.1994	2	(1)	1
Glen Adjei Kamara (FIN)	28.10.1995	28	(5)	1
Bongani Zungu (RSA)	09.10.1992	1	(13)	
Forwards:	**DOB**	**M**	**(s)**	**G**
Brandon Barker (ENG)	04.10.1996	4	(6)	2
Jermain Colin Defoe (ENG)	07.10.1982	3	(12)	4
Cedric Itten (SUI)	27.12.1996	5	(22)	4
Ryan Kent (ENG)	11.11.1996	36	(1)	10
Alfredo José Morelos Aviléz (COL)	21.06.1996	26	(3)	12
Kemar Roofe (JAM)	06.01.1993	18	(6)	14
Greg Alexander James Stewart	17.03.1990		(5)	
Scott Wright	08.08.1997	1	(8)	1

Ross County Football Club Dingwall

Founded:	1929		
Stadium:	Victoria Park, Dingwall (6,541)		
Trainer:	Stuart Kettlewell		04.06.1984
[21.12.2020]	John Hughes		09.09.1964

Goalkeepers:	DOB	M	(s)	G
Ross Doohan	29.03.1998	5		
Ross Laidlaw	12.07.1992	33		
Defenders:	**DOB**	**M**	**(s)**	**G**
Coll Donaldson	09.04.1995	26	(2)	1
Tom Grivosti (ENG)	15.06.1999	3	(2)	1
Leo Fuhr Hjelde (NOR)	26.08.2003	10	(1)	1
Alexander Iacovitti	02.09.1997	34	(2)	2
Callum Morris (NIR)	03.02.1990	12		
Joshua Mullin	23.09.1992	1	(4)	
Jason Naismith	25.06.1994	17		
Connor Steven Randall (ENG)	21.10.1995	13	(2)	
Josh Reid	03.05.2002	17	(3)	
Carl Philip Tremarco (ENG)	11.10.1985	8	(4)	
Keith Watson	14.11.1989	17	(6)	
Midfielders:	**DOB**	**M**	**(s)**	**G**
Anthony Andreu (FRA)	22.05.1988	4	(2)	
Ross James Draper (ENG)	20.10.1988	13	(8)	2
Stephen Kelly	13.04.2000	16	(9)	
Charlie Lakin (ENG)	08.05.1999	14	(5)	3
Harrison Theodore Paton (CAN)	23.05.1998	25	(10)	1
Blair Spittal	19.12.1995	7	(2)	1
Jordan Roy Tillson (ENG)	05.03.1993	20	(12)	
Iain Angus Vigurs	07.05.1988	28	(2)	2
Forwards:	**DOB**	**M**	**(s)**	**G**
Regan Evans Charles-Cook (ENG)	14.02.1997	9	(17)	
Lee Harry Erwin	19.03.1994	2	(2)	
Michael Gardyne	23.01.1986	21	(10)	2
Jermaine Samuel Hylton (ENG)	28.06.1993	7	(11)	1
William Robert McKay (NIR)	22.10.1988	14	(14)	5
Oliver Shaw	12.09.1998	12	(13)	6
Ross Cameron Stewart	01.09.1996	19		2
Jordan Neill White	04.02.1992	11	(1)	4
Matthew Wright	16.10.2002		(2)	

St. Johnstone Football Club Perth

Founded:	1884		
Stadium:	McDiarmid Park, Perth (10,696)		
Trainer:	Callum Iain Davidson		25.06.1976

Goalkeepers:	DOB	M	(s)	G
Zander Clark	26.06.1992	27		
Elliot Charles Parish (ENG)	20.05.1990	9		
Zdeněk Zlámal	05.11.1985	2		
Defenders:	**DOB**	**M**	**(s)**	**G**
Callum Booth	30.05.1991	15	(3)	
James Dominic Brown (ENG)	12.01.1998	4	(1)	
Liam Craig Gordon	26.01.1996	35	(1)	1
Jason Kerr	06.02.1997	31		1
Jamie Daniel McCart	20.06.1997	37		
Danny John McNamara (IRL)	27.12.1998	22		1
Shaun Anthony Rooney	26.07.1996	20	(7)	2
Scott Tanser (ENG)	23.10.1994	23	(7)	2
Midfielders:	**DOB**	**M**	**(s)**	**G**
Craig James Bryson	06.11.1986	12	(8)	
Liam Craig	27.12.1986	18	(5)	3
Murray Davidson	07.03.1988	14	(7)	1
Alexander Ferguson	10.09.2003		(1)	
Charlie Ian Gilmour	11.02.1999	1	(1)	
Alistair Edward McCann (NIR)	04.12.1999	32	(2)	2
David Wotherspoon (CAN)	16.01.1990	28	(9)	3
Forwards:	**DOB**	**M**	**(s)**	**G**
Craig Ian Conway	02.05.1985	19	(9)	3
Callum David Hendry	08.12.1997	8	(8)	
Christopher Kane	05.09.1994	17	(11)	4
Steven May	03.11.1992	17	(16)	5
Guy Melamed (ISR)	21.12.1992	11	(7)	5
Glenn Middleton	01.01.2000	3	(6)	2
Michael Francis O'Halloran	06.01.1991	13	(12)	1
Isaac Tanitoluwaloba Olaofe (ENG)	21.11.1999		(2)	
John Robertson	26.08.2001		(5)	

St. Mirren Football Club Paisley

Founded:	1877		
Stadium:	St. Mirren Park, St. Mirren (7,937)		
Trainer:	James Michael Goodwin (IRL)		20.11.1981

Goalkeepers:	DOB	M	(s)	G
Jak Alnwick (ENG)	17.06.1993	34		
Dean James Lyness (ENG)	20.07.1991	1	(1)	
Zdeněk Zlámal	05.11.1985	3		
Defenders:	**DOB**	**M**	**(s)**	**G**
Danny Finlayson (NIR)	19.01.2001	2	(1)	
Marcus Fraser	23.06.1994	37		1
Brandon Alexander Mason (ENG)	30.09.1997	5	(2)	
Conor McCarthy (IRL)	11.04.1998	37		
Joseph Thomas Gordan Shaughnessy (IRL)	06.07.1992	33		1
Richard Neil Peter Tait	02.12.1989	31	(2)	1
Midfielders:	**DOB**	**M**	**(s)**	**G**
Dylan Edward Connolly (IRL)	02.05.1995	18	(11)	2
Jake Billy Doyle-Hayes (IRL)	30.12.1998	21	(1)	1
İlkay Durmuş (TUR)	01.05.1994	23	(8)	3
Ethan Erhahon	09.05.2001	28	(3)	2
Ryan Flynn	04.09.1988	8	(6)	
Samuel Robert Foley (IRL)	17.10.1986	10	(1)	
Jay Henderson	07.03.2002	4	(1)	
Cameron MacPherson	29.12.1998	14	(18)	2
Jamie McGrath (IRL)	30.09.1996	34	(1)	10
Dylan Reid	01.03.2005		(1)	
Nathan Sheron (ENG)	04.10.1997	6	(1)	
İsak Snær Þorvaldsson (ISL)	01.05.2001		(2)	
Forwards:	**DOB**	**M**	**(s)**	**G**
Eamonn Brophy	10.03.1996	4	(2)	
Kristian Dennis (ENG)	12.03.1990	6	(11)	3
Lee Harry Erwin	19.03.1994	17	(10)	3
Lewis Jamieson	17.04.2002		(2)	
Kyle McAllister	21.01.1999	12	(23)	1
Junior Augustus Morias (ENG)	04.07.1995	7	(7)	
Jonathan Chiedozie Obika (ENG)	12.09.1990	21	(13)	5
Collin Quaner (GER)	18.06.1991	2	(4)	1

SECOND LEVEL
Scottish Championship 2020/2021

1. Heart of Midlothian FC Edinburgh (*Promoted*)	27	17	6	4	63	-	24	57
2. Dundee FC	27	12	9	6	49	-	40	45
3. Raith Rovers FC Kirkcaldy	27	12	7	8	45	-	36	43
4. Dunfermline Athletic FC	27	10	9	8	38	-	34	39
5. Inverness Caledonian Thistle FC	27	8	12	7	36	-	31	36
6. Queen of the South FC Dumfries	27	9	5	13	38	-	51	32
7. Arbroath FC	27	7	9	11	28	-	34	30
8. Ayr United FC	27	6	11	10	31	-	37	29
9. Greenock Morton FC (*Relegation Play-offs*)	27	6	11	10	22	-	33	29
10. Alloa Athletic FC (*Relegated*)	27	5	7	15	30	-	60	22

Please note: runners-up were qualified for the Premiership Play-offs Semi-Finals, while teams ranked 3-4 were qualified for the Premiership Play-offs Quarter-Finals.

Premiership Play-offs

Quarter-Finals [04-08.05.2021]	Dunfermline Athletic FC - Raith Rovers FC Kirkcaldy	0-0	0-2(0-0)
Semi-Finals [12-15.05.2021]	Raith Rovers FC Kirkcaldy - Dundee FC	0-3(0-1)	1-0(1-0)

Dundee FC were qualified for the Promotion Play-offs.

Relegation Play-offs (2nd / 3rd Level)

Semi-Finals [08-11.05.2021]	Montrose FC - Greenock Morton FC	2-1(0-1)	1-3(1-2,1-2)
	Cove Rangers FC - Airdrieonians FC	1-1(0-0)	2-3(1-1,2-2)
Final [18-21.05.2021]	Airdrieonians FC - Greenock Morton FC	0-1(0-0)	0-3(0-2)

Greenock Morton FC remains at second level.

NATIONAL TEAM

INTERNATIONAL MATCHES
(16.07.2020 – 15.07.2021)

04.09.2020	Glasgow	Scotland - Israel	1-1(1-0)	(UNL)
07.09.2020	Olomouc	Czech Republic - Scotland	1-2(1-1)	(UNL)
08.10.2020	Glasgow	Scotland - Israel	0-0; 5-3 on penalties	(ECQPO)
11.10.2020	Glasgow	Scotland - Slovakia	1-0(0-0)	(UNL)
14.10.2020	Glasgow	Scotland - Czech Republic	1-0(1-0)	(UNL)
12.11.2020	Beograd	Serbia - Scotland	1-1(0-0,1-1,1-1); 4-5 on penalties	(ECQPO)
15.11.2020	Trnava	Slovakia - Scotland	1-0(1-0)	(UNL)
18.11.2020	Netanya	Israel - Scotland	1-0(1-0)	(UNL)
25.03.2021	Glasgow	Scotland - Austria	2-2(0-0)	(WCQ)
28.03.2021	Tel Aviv	Israel - Scotland	1-1(1-0)	(WCQ)
31.03.2021	Glasgow	Scotland - Faroe Islands	4-0(1-0)	(WCQ)
02.06.2021	Faro/Loulé	Netherlands - Scotland	2-2(1-1)	(F)
06.06.2021	Lëtzebuerg	Luxembourg - Scotland	0-1(0-1)	(F)
14.06.2021	Glasgow	Scotland - Czech Republic	0-2(0-1)	(EC)
18.06.2021	London	England - Scotland	0-0	(EC)
22.06.2021	Glasgow	Croatia - Scotland	3-1(1-1)	(EC)

04.09.2020   SCOTLAND - ISRAEL   1-1(1-0)   2nd UEFA Nations League B, Group 2
Hampden Park, Glasgow; Referee: Slavko Vinčić (Slovenia); Attendance: 295
SCO: David James Marshall, Andrew Henry Robertson (Cap), Scott Fraser McKenna, Kieran Tierney, Ryan Jack, James Forrest, Callum William McGregor, John McGinn (79.Stuart Armstrong), Ryan Christie, Scott Francis McTominay, Lyndon Dykes (74.Oliver Jasen Burke). Trainer: Stephen Clarke.
Goal: Ryan Christie (45 penalty).

07.09.2020   CZECH REPUBLIC - SCOTLAND   1-2(1-1)   2nd UEFA Nations League B, Group 2
Andrův stadion, Olomouc; Referee: Serdar Gözübüyük (Netherlands); Attendance: 0
SCO: David James Marshall, Liam David Ian Cooper, Andrew Henry Robertson (Cap), Scott Fraser McKenna, John Alexander Fleck (71.John McGinn), Kenneth McLean, Liam Jordan Palmer, Stuart Armstrong (80.Callum William McGregor), Ryan Christie, Scott Francis McTominay, Lyndon Dykes (67.Callum Thomas Owen Paterson). Trainer: Stephen Clarke.
Goals: Lyndon Dykes (27), Ryan Christie (45 penalty).

08.10.2020   SCOTLAND - ISRAEL   0-0; 5-3 on penalties   16th EC. Qualifiers Play-offs, Semi-Finals
Hampden Park, Glasgow; Referee: Ovidiu Alin Haţegan (Romania); Attendance: 0
SCO: David James Marshall, Liam David Ian Cooper, Declan Patrick Gallagher, Stephen Gerard O'Donnell (113.Kenneth McLean), Andrew Henry Robertson (Cap), Ryan Jack (83.Ryan Fraser), Callum William McGregor, John McGinn, Scott Francis McTominay, Oliver Robert McBurnie (73.Lawrence Shankland), Lyndon Dykes (91.Callum Thomas Owen Paterson). Trainer: Stephen Clarke.
Penalties: John McGinn, Callum William McGregor, Scott Francis McTominay, Lawrence Shankland, Kenneth McLean.

11.10.2020   **SCOTLAND - SLOVAKIA**   1-0(0-0)   2nd UEFA Nations League B, Group 2

Hampden Park, Glasgow; Referee: Davide Massa (Italy); Attendance: 93
SCO: David James Marshall, Andrew Maclaren Considine, Declan Patrick Gallagher, Stephen Gerard O'Donnell, Andrew Henry Robertson (Cap), John Alexander Fleck (72.Callum William McGregor), Kenneth McLean, Ryan Fraser (85.Callum Thomas Owen Paterson), John McGinn (89.Ryan Jack), Scott Francis McTominay, Lyndon Dykes (72.Oliver Robert McBurnie). Trainer: Stephen Clarke.
Goal: Lyndon Dykes (54).

14.10.2020   **SCOTLAND - CZECH REPUBLIC**   1-0(1-0)   2nd UEFA Nations League B, Group 2

Hampden Park, Glasgow; Referee: Felix Zwayer (Germany); Attendance: 299
SCO: David James Marshall, Andrew Maclaren Considine, Declan Patrick Gallagher, Stephen Gerard O'Donnell, Greg John Taylor (79.Paul Thomas Hanlon), Ryan Jack, Callum William McGregor, Ryan Fraser (70.Kenneth McLean), John McGinn (Cap) (79.Callum Thomas Owen Paterson), Scott Francis McTominay, Lyndon Dykes (65.Oliver Robert McBurnie). Trainer: Stephen Clarke.
Goal: Ryan Fraser (6).

12.11.2020   **SERBIA - SCOTLAND**   1-1(0-0,1-1,1-1); 4-5 on penalties   16th EC. Qualifiers Play-offs, Finals

Stadion "Rajko Mitić", Beograd; Referee: Antonio Miguel Mateu Lahoz (Spain); Attendance: 0
SCO: David James Marshall, Declan Patrick Gallagher, Stephen Gerard O'Donnell (118.Leigh Griffiths), Andrew Henry Robertson (Cap), Kieran Tierney, Ryan Jack, Callum William McGregor, John McGinn (83.Kenneth McLean), Ryan Christie (87.Callum Thomas Owen Paterson), Scott Francis McTominay, Lyndon Dykes (82.Oliver Robert McBurnie). Trainer: Stephen Clarke.
Goal: Ryan Christie (52).
Penalties: Leigh Griffiths, Callum William McGregor, Scott Francis McTominay, Oliver Robert McBurnie, Kenneth McLean.

15.11.2020   **SLOVAKIA - SCOTLAND**   1-0(1-0)   2nd UEFA Nations League B, Group 2

Štadión "Antona Malatinského", Trnava; Referee: István Kovács (Romania); Attendance: 0
SCO: Craig Sinclair Gordon, Andrew Maclaren Considine (68.Leigh Griffiths), Liam David Ian Cooper, Scott Fraser McKenna, Kieran Tierney, Kenneth McLean, Liam Jordan Palmer, Stuart Armstrong (87.Lawrence Shankland), John McGinn (Cap), Ryan Christie, Oliver Robert McBurnie. Trainer: Stephen Clarke.

18.11.2020   **ISRAEL - SCOTLAND**   1-0(1-0)   2nd UEFA Nations League B, Group 2

Netanya Stadium, Netanya: Referee: Paweł Raczkowski (Poland); Attendance: 0
SCO: David James Marshall, Declan Patrick Gallagher (73.Scott Fraser McKenna), Stephen Gerard O'Donnell (73.Oliver Jasen Burke), Andrew Henry Robertson (Cap), Kieran Tierney, Ryan Jack, Callum William McGregor (82.Kenneth McLean), John McGinn (61.Leigh Griffiths), Ryan Christie, Scott Francis McTominay, Lyndon Dykes (61.Oliver Robert McBurnie). Trainer: Stephen Clarke.

25.03.2021   **SCOTLAND - AUSTRIA**   2-2(0-0)   22nd FIFA WC. Qualifiers

Hampden Park, Glasgow; Referee: Carlos del Cerro Grande (Spain); Attendance: 0
SCO: David James Marshall, Grant Campbell Hanley, Stephen Gerard O'Donnell, Andrew Henry Robertson (Cap), Kieran Tierney, Jack William Hendry, Stuart Armstrong (66.Ché Zach Everton Fred Adams), John McGinn, Ryan Christie (88.Kenneth McLean), Scott Francis McTominay, Lyndon Dykes (78.Callum William McGregor). Trainer: Stephen Clarke.
Goals: Grant Campbell Hanley (71), John McGinn (85).

28.03.2021   **ISRAEL - SCOTLAND**   1-1(1-0)   22nd FIFA WC. Qualifiers

Bloomfield Stadium, Tel Aviv; Referee: Deniz Aytekin (Germany); Attendance: 5,000
SCO: David James Marshall, Grant Campbell Hanley, Stephen Gerard O'Donnell, Andrew Henry Robertson (Cap), Kieran Tierney, Jack William Hendry (46.Ryan Christie), Callum William McGregor, Ryan Fraser (86.Stuart Armstrong), John McGinn (74.Kenneth McLean), Scott Francis McTominay, Ché Zach Everton Fred Adams (75.Lyndon Dykes). Trainer: Stephen Clarke.
Goal: Ryan Fraser (56).

31.03.2021   **SCOTLAND - FAROE ISLANDS**   4-0(1-0)   22nd FIFA WC. Qualifiers

Hampden Park, Glasgow; Referee: Trustin Farrugia Cann (Malta); Attendance: 0
SCO: Craig Sinclair Gordon, Grant Campbell Hanley, Andrew Henry Robertson (Cap), Kieran Tierney (79.Scott Fraser McKenna), Kenneth McLean, Callum William McGregor (73.John Alexander Fleck), Ryan Fraser (79.Liam Jordan Palmer), John McGinn, Scott Francis McTominay, Ché Zach Everton Fred Adams (73.Oliver Robert McBurnie), Lyndon Dykes (68.Kevin Michael Nisbet). Trainer: Stephen Clarke.
Goals: John McGinn (7, 53), Ché Zach Everton Fred Adams (60), Ryan Fraser (70).

02.06.2021   **NETHERLANDS - SCOTLAND**   2-2(1-1)   Friendly International

Estádio Algarve, Faro/Loulé (Portugal); Referee: Vítor Jorge Fernandes Ferreira (Portugal); Attendance: 0
SCO: Craig Sinclair Gordon, Liam David Ian Cooper (62.Declan Patrick Gallagher), Andrew Henry Robertson (Cap) (69.Greg John Taylor), Kieran Tierney (69.Scott Fraser McKenna), Jack William Hendry, James Forrest (61.Ryan Fraser), Stuart Armstrong, Callum William McGregor, Ryan Christie, David Turnbull (81.Billy Clifford Gilmour), Lyndon Dykes (61.Kevin Michael Nisbet). Trainer: Stephen Clarke.
Goals: Jack William Hendry (11), Kevin Michael Nisbet (64).

06.06.2021   **LUXEMBOURG - SCOTLAND**   0-1(0-1)   Friendly International

Stade "Josy Barthel", Lëtzebuerg; Referee: Eldorjan Hamiti (Albania); Attendance: 1,000
SCO: David James Marshall, Grant Campbell Hanley, Declan Patrick Gallagher (46.Scott Fraser McKenna), Stephen Gerard O'Donnell (64.Nathan Kenneth Patterson), Andrew Henry Robertson (Cap) 64.64.Ryan Fraser), Kieran Tierney, Callum William McGregor (46.Billy Clifford Gilmour; 76.James Forrest), John McGinn, Scott Francis McTominay, Ché Zach Everton Fred Adams, Lyndon Dykes (82.Kevin Michael Nisbet). Trainer: Stephen Clarke.
Goal: Ché Zach Everton Fred Adams (27).

14.06.2021   **SCOTLAND - CZECH REPUBLIC**   0-2(0-1)   16th EC. Group Stage.

Hampden Park, Glasgow; Referee: Daniel Siebert (Germany); Attendance: 9,847
SCO: David James Marshall, Liam David Ian Cooper, Grant Campbell Hanley, Stephen Gerard O'Donnell (79.James Forrest), Andrew Henry Robertson (Cap), Jack William Hendry (67.Callum William McGregor), Stuart Armstrong (67.Ryan Fraser), John McGinn, Ryan Christie (46.Ché Zach Everton Fred Adams), Scott Francis McTominay, Lyndon Dykes (79.Kevin Michael Nisbet). Trainer: Stephen Clarke.

18.06.2021   **ENGLAND - SCOTLAND**   0-0   16th EC. Group Stage.

Wembley Stadium, London; Referee: Antonio Miguel Mateu Lahoz (Spain); Attendance: 20,306
SCO: David James Marshall, Grant Campbell Hanley, Stephen Gerard O'Donnell, Andrew Henry Robertson (Cap), Kieran Tierney, Callum William McGregor, John McGinn, Scott Francis McTominay, Billy Clifford Gilmour (76.Stuart Armstrong), Ché Zach Everton Fred Adams (86.Kevin Michael Nisbet), Lyndon Dykes. Trainer: Stephen Clarke.

22.06.2021   **CROATIA - SCOTLAND**   **3-1(1-1)**   16th EC. Group Stage.

Hampden Park, Glasgow; Referee: Fernando Andrés Rapallini (Argentina); Attendance: 9,896

SCO: David James Marshall, Grant Campbell Hanley (33.Scott Fraser McKenna), Kieran Tierney, Andrew Henry Robertson (Cap), Callum William McGregor, Stuart Armstrong (70.Ryan Fraser), Stephen Gerard O'Donnell (84.Nathan Kenneth Patterson), John McGinn, Scott Francis McTominay, Ché Zach Everton Fred Adams (84.Kevin Michael Nisbet), Lyndon Dykes. Trainer: Stephen Clarke.

Goal: Callum William McGregor (42).

NATIONAL TEAM PLAYERS
(16.07.2020 – 15.07.2021)

Name	DOB	Caps	Goals	2020/2021:	Club
Goalkeepers					
Craig Sinclair GORDON	31.12.1982	57	0	2020/2021:	*Heart of Midlothian FC Edinburgh*
David James MARSHALL	05.03.1985	47	0	2020/2021:	*Derby County FC (ENG)*
Defenders					
Andrew Maclaren CONSIDINE	01.04.1987	3	0	2020:	*Aberdeen FC*
Liam David Ian COOPER	30.08.1991	7	0	2020/2021:	*Leeds United FC (ENG)*
Declan Patrick GALLAGHER	13.02.1991	9	0	2020/2021:	*Motherwell FC*
Grant Campbell HANLEY	20.11.1991	36	2	2021:	*Norwich City FC (ENG)*
Paul Thomas HANLON	20.01.1990	1	0	2020:	*Hibernian FC Edinburgh*
Jack William HENDRY	07.05.1995	7	1	2021:	*KV Oostende (BEL)*
Scott Fraser McKENNA	12.11.1996	22	0	2020:	*Aberdeen FC*
				23.09.2020->	*Nottingham Forest FC (ENG)*
Stephen Gerard O'DONNELL	11.05.1992	22	0	2020/2021:	*Motherwell FC*
Liam Jordan PALMER	19.09.1991	8	0	2020/2021:	*Sheffield Wednesday FC (ENG)*
Nathan Kenneth PATTERSON	16.10.2001	2	0	2021:	*Rangers FC Glasgow (SCO)*
Andrew Henry ROBERTSON	11.03.1994	48	3	2020/2021:	*Liverpool FC (ENG)*
Greg John TAYLOR	05.11.1997	5	0	2020/2021:	*Celtic FC Glasgow*
Kieran TIERNEY	05.06.1997	23	0	2020/2021:	*Arsenal FC London (ENG)*
Midfielders					
Stuart ARMSTRONG	30.03.1992	28	2	2020/2021:	*Southampton FC (ENG)*
John Alexander FLECK	24.08.1991	5	0	2020/2021:	*Sheffield United FC (ENG)*
James FORREST	07.07.1991	38	5	2020/2021:	*Celtic FC Glasgow*
Billy Clifford GILMOUR	11.06.2001	3	0	2021:	*Chelsea FC London (ENG)*
Ryan JACK	27.02.1992	10	0	2020:	*Rangers FC Glasgow*
John McGINN	18.10.1994	36	10	2020/2021:	*Aston Villa FC Birmingham (ENG)*
Callum William McGREGOR	14.06.1993	34	1	2020/2021:	*Celtic FC Glasgow*
Kenneth McLEAN	08.01.1992	20	1	2020/2021:	*Norwich City FC (ENG)*
Scott Francis McTOMINAY	08.12.1996	26	0	2020/2021:	*Manchester United FC (ENG)*
David TURNBULL	10.07.1999	1	0	2021:	*Celtic FC Glasgow*
Forwards					
Ché Zach Everton Fred ADAMS	13.07.1996	7	2	2021:	*Southampton FC (ENG)*
Oliver Jasen BURKE	07.04.1997	13	1	2020:	*West Bromwich Albion FC (ENG)*
				09.09.2020->	*Sheffield United FC (ENG)*
Ryan CHRISTIE	22.02.1995	20	4	2020/2021:	*Celtic FC Glasgow*
Lyndon DYKES	07.10.1995	15	2	2020/2021:	*Queens Park Rangers FC London (ENG)*
Ryan FRASER	24.02.1994	20	4	2020/2021:	*Newcastle United FC (ENG)*
Leigh GRIFFITHS	20.08.1990	22	4	2020:	*Celtic FC Glasgow*
Oliver Robert McBURNIE	04.06.1996	16	0	2020/2021:	*Sheffield United FC (ENG)*
Kevin Michael NISBET	08.03.1997	6	1	2021:	*Hibernian FC Edinburgh*
Callum Thomas Owen PATERSON	13.10.1994	17	0	2020:	*Cardiff City FC (WAL)*
				30.09.2020->	*Sheffield Wednesday FC (ENG)*
Lawrence SHANKLAND	10.08.1995	4	1	2020/2021:	*Dundee United FC*
Trainer					
Stephen "Steve" CLARKE [from 20.05.2019]	29.08.1963	24 M; 9 W; 7 D; 8 L; 31-31			

SERBIA

The Country:
Република Србија (Republic of Serbia)
Capital: Beograd
Surface: 77,474 km²
Inhabitants: 6,871,547 [2021]
Time: UTC+1

The FA:
Fudbalski savez Srbije
Terazije 35, CP 263, 11000 Beograd
Tel: +381 11 323 4253
Founded: 1919
Member of FIFA since: 1921
Member of UEFA since: 1954
Website: www.fss.rs

NATIONAL TEAM RECORDS

RECORDS

First international match:	28.08.1920, Antwerpen:	Czechoslovakia – Yugoslavia 7-0
Most international caps:	Branislav Ivanović	- 105 caps (2005-2018)
Most international goals:	Aleksandar Mitrović	- 41 goals / 64 caps (since 2013)

UEFA EUROPEAN CHAMPIONSHIP*

1960	Final Tournament (Runners-up)
1964	Qualifiers
1968	Final Tournament (Runners-up)
1972	Qualifiers
1976	Final Tournament (4th Place)
1980	Qualifiers
1984	Final Tournament (Group Stage)
1988	Qualifiers
1992	*Qualified / Suspended*
1996	*Suspended*
2000	Final Tournament (Quarter-Finals)
2004	Qualifiers
2008	Qualifiers
2012	Qualifiers
2016	Qualifiers
2020	Qualifiers

FIFA WORLD CUP*

1930	Final Tournament (4th Place)
1934	Qualifiers
1938	Qualifiers
1950	Final Tournament (Group Stage)
1954	Final Tournament (Quarter-Finals)
1958	Final Tournament (Quarter-Finals)
1962	Final Tournament (4th Place)
1966	Qualifiers
1970	Qualifiers
1974	Final Tournament (2nd Round)
1978	Qualifiers
1982	Final Tournament (Group Stage)
1986	Qualifiers
1990	Final Tournament (Quarter-Finals)
1994	*Suspended*
1998	Final Tournament (2nd Round of 16)
2002	Qualifiers
2006	Final Tournament (Group Stage)
2010	Final Tournament (Group Stage)
2014	Qualifiers
2018	Final Tournament (Group Stage)

OLYMPIC TOURNAMENTS*

1908	-
1912	-
1920	Round 1
1924	Qualifiers
1928	1/8 - Finals
1936	Did not enter
1948	Runners-up
1952	Runners-up
1956	Runners-up
1960	**Winners**
1964	Quarter-Finals
1968	Did not enter
1972	Qualifiers
1976	Qualifiers
1980	4th Place
1984	3rd Place
1988	Group Stage
1992	Qualifiers
1996	*Suspended*
2000	Qualifiers
2004	Group Stage
2008	Group Stage
2012	Qualifiers
2016	Qualifiers

as Yugoslavia (1930-2002), Serbia and Montenegro (2002-2006).

UEFA NATIONS LEAGUE

2018/2019	League C (promoted to League B)
2020/2021	League B

FIFA CONFEDERATIONS CUP 1992-2017

None

SERBIAN CLUB HONOURS IN EUROPEAN CLUB COMPETITIONS:

European Champion Clubs.Cup (1956-1992) / UEFA Champions League (1993-2021)		
FK Crvena Zvezda Beograd	1	1990/1991
Fairs Cup (1858-1971) / UEFA Cup (1972-2009) / UEFA Europa League (2010-2021)		
None		
UEFA Super Cup (1972-2020)		
None		
European Cup Winners.Cup 1961-1999		
None		

defunct competition

NATIONAL COMPETITIONS
TABLE OF HONOURS

Kingdom of Yugoslavia (1923–1940)

	CHAMPIONS	CUP WINNERS	BEST GOALSCORERS	
1923	HŠK Građanski Zagreb	HAŠK Zagreb	Dragan Jovanović (SK Jugoslavija Beograd)	4
1924	SK Jugoslavija Beograd	Zagreb XI	Dragan Jovanović (SK Jugoslavija Beograd)	6
1925	SK Jugoslavija Beograd	Zagreb XI	Dragan Jovanović (SK Jugoslavija Beograd)	4
1926	HŠK Građanski Zagreb	Zagreb XI	Dušan Petković (SK Jugoslavija Beograd)	4
1927	NK Hajduk Split	Beograd XI	Kuzman Sotirović (BSK Beograd)	6
1928	HŠK Građanski Zagreb	*No competition*	Ljubo Benčić (NK Hajduk Split)	8
1929	NK Hajduk Split	*No competition*	Đorđe Vujadinović (BSK Beograd)	10
1930	HŠK Concordia Zagreb	*No competition*	Blagoje Marjanović (BSK Beograd)	10
1930/1931	BSK Beograd	*No competition*	Đorđe Vujadinović (BSK Beograd)	12
1931/1932	HŠK Concordia Zagreb	*No competition*	Svetislav Valjarević (HŠK Concordia Zagreb)	10
1932/1933	BSK Beograd	*No competition*	Vladimir Kragić (NK Hajduk Split)	21
1933/1934	*No competition*	BSK Beograd	-	
1934/1935	BSK Beograd	*No competition*	Leo Lemešić (NK Hajduk Split)	18
1935/1936	BSK Beograd	SK Jugoslavija	Blagoje Marjanović (BSK Beograd)	5
1936/1937	HŠK Građanski Zagreb	*No competition*	Blagoje Marjanović (BSK Beograd)	21
1937/1938	HAŠK Zagreb	*No competition*	August Lešnik (HŠK Građanski Zagreb)	17
1938/1939	BSK Beograd	*No competition*	August Lešnik (HŠK Građanski Zagreb)	22
1939/1940	HŠK Građanski Zagreb	HŠK Građanski Zagreb	Svetislav Glišović (BSK Beograd)	10

SFR Yugoslavia (1945–1992)

	CHAMPIONS	CUP WINNERS	BEST GOALSCORERS	
1945	S.R. Serbia	*No competition*	Stjepan Bobek (JNA)	8
1946/1947	FK Partizan Beograd	FK Partizan Beograd	Franjo Wölfl (NK Dinamo Zagreb)	28
1947/1948	NK Dinamo Zagreb	FK Crvena Zvezda Beograd	Franjo Wölfl (NK Dinamo Zagreb)	22
1948/1949	FK Partizan Beograd	FK Crvena Zvezda Beograd	Frane Matošić (NK Hajduk Split)	17
1950	NK Hajduk Split	FK Crvena Zvezda Beograd	Marko Valok (FK Partizan Beograd)	17
1951	FK Crvena Zvezda Beograd	NK Dinamo Zagreb	Kosta Tomašević (FK Crvena Zvezda Beograd)	16
1952	NK Hajduk Split	FK Partizan Beograd	Stanoje Jocić (BSK Beograd)	13
1952/1953	FK Crvena Zvezda Beograd	BSK Beograd	Todor Živanović (FK Crvena Zvezda Beograd)	17
1953/1954	NK Dinamo Zagreb	FK Partizan Beograd	Stjepan Bobek (FK Partizan Beograd)	21
1954/1955	NK Hajduk Split	BSK Beograd	Predrag Marković (BSK Beograd) Kosta Tomašević (FK Spartak Subotica) Bernard Vukas (NK Hajduk Split)	20
1955/1956	FK Crvena Zvezda Beograd	*No competition*	Muhamed Mujić (FK Velež Mostar) Tihomir Ognjanov (FK Spartak Subotica) Todor Veselinović (FK Vojvodina Novi Sad)	21
1956/1957	FK Crvena Zvezda Beograd	FK Partizan Beograd	Todor Veselinović (FK Vojvodina Novi Sad)	28
1957/1958	NK Dinamo Zagreb	FK Crvena Zvezda Beograd	Todor Veselinović (FK Vojvodina Novi Sad)	19
1958/1959	FK Crvena Zvezda Beograd	FK Crvena Zvezda Beograd	Bora Kostić (FK Crvena Zvezda Beograd)	25
1959/1960	FK Crvena Zvezda Beograd	NK Dinamo Zagreb	Bora Kostić (FK Crvena Zvezda Beograd)	19
1960/1961	FK Partizan Beograd	FK Vardar Skoplje	Zoran Prljinčević (FK Radnički Beograd) Todor Veselinović (FK Vojvodina Novi Sad)	16
1961/1962	FK Partizan Beograd	OFK Beograd	Dražan Jerković (NK Dinamo Zagreb)	16
1962/1963	FK Partizan Beograd	NK Dinamo Zagreb	Mišo Smajlović (FK Željezničar Sarajevo)	18
1963/1964	FK Crvena Zvezda Beograd	FK Crvena Zvezda Beograd	Asim Ferhatović (FK Sarajevo)	19
1964/1965	FK Partizan Beograd	NK Dinamo Zagreb	Zlatko Dračić (NK Zagreb)	23
1965/1966	FK Vojvodina Novi Sad	OFK Beograd	Petar Nadoveza (NK Hajduk Split)	21
1966/1967	FK Sarajevo	NK Hajduk Split	Mustafa Hasanagić (FK Partizan Beograd)	18
1967/1968	FK Crvena Zvezda Beograd	FK Crvena Zvezda Beograd	Slobodan Santrač (OFK Beograd)	22
1968/1969	FK Crvena Zvezda Beograd	NK Dinamo Zagreb	Vojin Lazarević (FK Crvena Zvezda Beograd)	22
1969/1970	FK Crvena Zvezda Beograd	FK Crvena Zvezda Beograd	Slobodan Santrač (OFK Beograd) Dušan Bajević (FK Velež Mostar)	20
1970/1971	NK Hajduk Split	FK Crvena Zvezda Beograd	Petar Nadoveza (NK Hajduk Split) Božo Janković (FK Željezničar Sarajevo)	20
1971/1972	FK Željezničar Sarajevo	NK Hajduk Split	Slobodan Santrač (OFK Beograd)	33
1972/1973	FK Crvena Zvezda Beograd	NK Hajduk Split	Slobodan Santrač (OFK Beograd) Vojin Lazarević (FK Crvena Zvezda Beograd)	25
1973/1974	NK Hajduk Split	NK Hajduk Split	Danilo Popivoda (Olimpija Ljubljana)	17
1974/1975	NK Hajduk Split	NK Hajduk Split	Dušan Savić (FK Crvena Zvezda Beograd) Boško Đorđević (FK Partizan Beograd)	20
1975/1976	FK Partizan Beograd	NK Hajduk Split	Nenad Bjeković (FK Partizan Beograd)	24
1976/1977	FK Crvena Zvezda Beograd	NK Rijeka	Zoran Filipović (FK Crvena Zvezda Beograd)	21
1977/1978	FK Partizan Beograd	NK Rijeka	Radomir Savić (FK Sarajevo)	21
1978/1979	NK Hajduk Split	NK Dinamo Zagreb	Dušan Savić (FK Crvena Zvezda Beograd)	24
1979/1980	FK Crvena Zvezda Beograd	FK Crvena Zvezda Beograd	Safet Sušić (FK Sarajevo) Dragoljub Kostić (FK Napredak Kruševac)	17
1980/1981	FK Crvena Zvezda Beograd	FK Velež Mostar	Milan Radović (NK Rijeka)	26
1981/1982	NK Dinamo Zagreb	FK Crvena Zvezda Beograd	Snješko Cerin (NK Dinamo Zagreb)	19

1982/1983	FK Partizan Beograd	NK Dinamo Zagreb	Sulejman Halilović (NK Dinamo Vinkovci)	18
1983/1984	FK Crvena Zvezda Beograd	NK Hajduk Split	Darko Pančev (FK Vardar Skoplje)	19
1984/1985	FK Sarajevo	FK Crvena Zvezda Beograd	Zlatko Vujović (NK Hajduk Split)	25
1985/1986	FK Partizan Beograd	FK Velež Mostar	Davor Čop (NK Dinamo Vinkovci)	20
1986/1987	FK Vardar Skoplje	NK Hajduk Split	Radmilo Mihajlović (FK Željezničar Sarajevo)	23
1987/1988	FK Crvena Zvezda Beograd	FK Borac Banja Luka	Duško Milinković (FK Rad Beograd)	16
1988/1989	FK Vojvodina Novi Sad	FK Partizan Beograd	Davor Šuker (NK Osijek)	18
1989/1990	FK Crvena Zvezda Beograd	FK Crvena Zvezda Beograd	Darko Pančev (FK Crvena Zvezda Beograd)	25
1990/1991	FK Crvena Zvezda Beograd	NK Hajduk Split	Darko Pančev (FK Crvena Zvezda Beograd)	34
1991/1992	FK Crvena Zvezda Beograd	*No competition*	Darko Pančev (FK Crvena Zvezda Beograd)	25

First League of Serbia and Montenegro (1992–2006)

	CHAMPIONS	CUP WINNERS	BEST GOALSCORERS	
1992/1993	FK Partizan Beograd	FK Crvena Zvezda Beograd	Anto Drobnjak (FK Crvena Zvezda Beograd) Vesko Mihajlović (FK Vojvodina Novi Sad)	22
1993/1994	FK Partizan Beograd	FK Partizan Beograd	Savo Milošević (FK Partizan Beograd)	21
1994/1995	FK Crvena Zvezda Beograd	FK Crvena Zvezda Beograd	Savo Milošević (FK Partizan Beograd)	30
1995/1996	FK Partizan Beograd	FK Crvena Zvezda Beograd	Vojislav Budimirović (FK Čukarički)	23
1996/1997	FK Partizan Beograd	FK Crvena Zvezda Beograd	Zoran Jovičić (FK Crvena Zvezda Beograd)	21
1997/1998	FK Obilić Beograd	FK Partizan Beograd	Saša Marković (FK Železnik Beograd/ FK Crvena Zvezda Beograd)	27
1998/1999	FK Partizan Beograd	FK Crvena Zvezda Beograd	Dejan Osmanović (FK Hajduk Kula)	16
1999/2000	FK Crvena Zvezda Beograd	FK Crvena Zvezda Beograd	Mateja Kežman (FK Partizan Beograd)	27
2000/2001	FK Crvena Zvezda Beograd	FK Partizan Beograd	Petar Divić (OFK Beograd)	27
2001/2002	FK Partizan Beograd	FK Crvena Zvezda Beograd	Zoran Đurašković (FK Mladost Lučani)	27
2002/2003	FK Partizan Beograd	FK Sartid Smederevo	Zvonimir Vukić (FK Partizan Beograd)	22
2003/2004	FK Crvena Zvezda Beograd	FK Crvena Zvezda Beograd	Nikola Žigić (FK Crvena Zvezda Beograd)	19
2004/2005	FK Partizan Beograd	FK Železnik Beograd	Marko Pantelić (FK Crvena Zvezda Beograd)	21
2005/2006	FK Crvena Zvezda Beograd	FK Crvena Zvezda Beograd	Srđan Radonjić (FK Partizan Beograd)	20

Serbian Superliga (since 2006)

	CHAMPIONS	CUP WINNERS	BEST GOALSCORERS	
2006/2007	FK Crvena Zvezda Beograd	FK Crvena Zvezda Beograd	Srđan Baljak (FK Banat Zrenjanin)	18
2007/2008	FK Partizan Beograd	FK Partizan Beograd	Nenad Jestrović (FK Crvena Zvezda Beograd)	13
2008/2009	FK Partizan Beograd	FK Partizan Beograd	Lamine Diarra (SEN, FK Partizan Beograd)	19
2009/2010	FK Partizan Beograd	FK Crvena Zvezda Beograd	Dragan Mrđa (FK Vojvodina Novi Sad)	22
2010/2011	FK Partizan Beograd	FK Partizan Beograd	Ivica Iliev (FK Partizan Beograd) Andrija Kaluđerović (FK Crvena Zvezda Beograd)	13
2011/2012	FK Partizan Beograd	FK Crvena Zvezda Beograd	Darko Spalević (FK Radnički Kragujevac)	19
2012/2013	FK Partizan Beograd	FK Jagodina	Miloš Stojanović (FK Jagodina)	19
2013/2014	FK Crvena Zvezda Beograd	FK Vojvodina Novi Sad	Dragan Mrđa (FK Crvena Zvezda Beograd)	19
2014/2015	FK Partizan Beograd	FK Čukarički	Patrick Friday Eze (NGA, FK Mladost Lučani)	15
2015/2016	FK Crvena Zvezda Beograd	FK Partizan Beograd	Aleksandar Katai (FK Crvena Zvezda Beograd)	21
2016/2017	FK Partizan Beograd	FK Partizan Beograd	Uroš Đurđević (FK Partizan Beograd) Leonardo da Silva Souza (BRA, FK Partizan Beograd)	24
2017/2018	FK Crvena Zvezda Beograd	FK Partizan Beograd	Aleksandar Pešić (FK Crvena Zvezda Beograd)	25
2018/2019	FK Crvena Zvezda Beograd	FK Partizan Beograd	Nermin Haskić (BIH, FK Radnički Niš)	24
2019/2020	FK Crvena Zvezda Beograd	FK Vojvodina Novi Sad	Nenad Lukić (TSC Bačka Topola) Vladimir Silađi (TSC Bačka Topola) Nikola Petković (FK Javor Ivanjica)	16
2020/2021	FK Crvena Zvezda Beograd	FK Crvena Zvezda Beograd	Milan Makarić (FK Radnik Surdulica)	25

NATIONAL CHAMPIONSHIP
Serbian SuperLiga 2020/2021
(31.07.2020 – 19.05.2021)

Results

Round 1 [31.07.-01.08.2020]
Spartak Subotica - FK Zlatibor 3-0(2-0)
Bačka Topola - Vojvodina 2-2(1-1)
Mladost Lučani - FK Javor 2-1(2-0)
FK Napredak - Partizan 1-3(1-0)
FK Čukarički - FK Inđija 3-0(2-0)
FK Mačva - OFK Bačka 1-0(0-0)
FK Voždovac - Radnik Surdulica 1-3(0-1)
Proleter Novi Sad - Rad Beograd 2-0(2-0)
Radnički Niš - FK Metalac 3-0(2-0)
Crvena Zvezda - FK Novi Pazar 3-0(2-0)

Round 2 [05.08.2020]
FK Inđija - FK Voždovac 0-1(0-1)
FK Novi Pazar - Partizan 3-2(1-0)
OFK Bačka - Spartak Subotica 1-3(1-2)
FK Javor - FK Napredak 3-0(1-0)
FK Metalac - FK Mačva 2-1(2-1)
Rad Beograd - Bačka Topola 1-3(1-2)
Radnik Surdulica - Mladost Lučani 2-3(1-1)
Crvena Zvezda - Radnički Niš 3-0(2-0)
FK Zlatibor - Proleter Novi Sad 0-2(0-2)
Vojvodina - FK Čukarički 2-2(0-1)

Round 3 [09.08.2020]
FK Mačva - Crvena Zvezda 0-3(0-1)
Mladost Lučani - FK Inđija 2-0(2-0)
FK Napredak - Radnik Surdulica 2-1(0-0)
Radnički Niš - FK Novi Pazar 2-1(2-0)
Spartak Subotica - FK Metalac 4-1(0-1)
Bačka Topola - FK Zlatibor 5-1(2-0)
FK Čukarički - Rad Beograd 3-0(3-0)
FK Voždovac - Vojvodina 1-3(0-3)
Partizan - FK Javor 4-0(3-0)
Proleter Novi Sad - OFK Bačka 1-1(0-0)

Round 4 [14-16.08.2020]
Crvena Zvezda - Spartak Subotica 3-2(1-1)
FK Inđija - FK Napredak 1-0(1-0)
FK Novi Pazar - FK Javor 2-3(2-2)
Radnički Niš - FK Mačva 1-0(1-0)
Radnik Surdulica - Partizan 0-2(0-0)
FK Zlatibor - FK Čukarički 1-5(1-2)
OFK Bačka - Bačka Topola 1-1(0-1)
FK Metalac - Proleter Novi Sad 1-1(0-1)
Rad Beograd - FK Voždovac 1-3(1-0)
Vojvodina - Mladost Lučani 3-0(0-0)

Round 5 [21-23.08.2020]
Proleter Novi Sad - Crvena Zvezda 0-1(0-0)
Bačka Topola - FK Metalac 2-3(0-1)
FK Čukarički - OFK Bačka 1-0(0-0)
FK Javor - Radnik Surdulica 2-1(2-1)
Spartak Subotica - Radnički Niš 2-0(2-0)
Partizan - FK Inđija 5-0(1-0)
FK Napredak - Vojvodina 0-1(0-0)
FK Mačva - FK Novi Pazar 1-1(1-0)
Mladost Lučani - Rad Beograd 1-0(0-0)
FK Voždovac - FK Zlatibor 1-1(0-0)

Round 6 [28-30.08.2020]
FK Inđija - FK Javor 3-2(1-0)
FK Metalac - FK Čukarički 0-0
Rad Beograd - FK Napredak 3-1(1-1)
OFK Bačka - FK Voždovac 2-1(2-0)
FK Novi Pazar - Radnik Surdulica 0-0
Radnički Niš - Proleter Novi Sad 3-0 *awarded*
FK Zlatibor - Mladost Lučani 1-0(0-0)
Vojvodina - Partizan 3-2(0-1)
FK Mačva - Spartak Subotica 0-4(0-3)
Crvena Zvezda - Bačka Topola 5-0(3-0)

Round 7 [11-13.09.2020]
FK Čukarički - Crvena Zvezda 1-3(0-1)
FK Voždovac - FK Metalac 4-0(3-0)
Radnik Surdulica - FK Inđija 0-2(0-2)
Spartak Subotica - FK Novi Pazar 1-1(0-0)
Bačka Topola - Radnički Niš 1-3(0-1)
Partizan - Rad Beograd 3-0(1-0)
FK Javor - Vojvodina 2-1(1-0)
Mladost Lučani - OFK Bačka 2-1(1-1)
FK Napredak - FK Zlatibor 1-1(0-0)
Proleter Novi Sad - FK Mačva 0-0

Round 8 [18-21.09.2020]
Vojvodina - Radnik Surdulica 2-0(0-0)
OFK Bačka - FK Napredak 0-0
FK Metalac - Mladost Lučani 1-1(1-0)
Radnički Niš - FK Čukarički 0-0
Rad Beograd - FK Javor 1-0(0-0)
FK Novi Pazar - FK Inđija 1-0(1-0)
Spartak Subotica - Proleter Novi Sad 1-2(1-1)
FK Zlatibor - Partizan 0-1(0-0)
Crvena Zvezda - FK Voždovac 6-0(3-0)
FK Mačva - Bačka Topola 1-4(0-3)

Round 9 [25-28.09.2020]
FK Voždovac - Radnički Niš 5-0(3-0)
FK Čukarički - FK Mačva 4-0(1-0)
FK Javor - FK Zlatibor 1-1(1-1)
Radnik Surdulica - Rad Beograd 4-2(1-1)
Bačka Topola - Spartak Subotica 3-0(2-0)
Mladost Lučani - Crvena Zvezda 0-4(0-1)
FK Napredak - FK Metalac 1-2(0-1)
Proleter Novi Sad - FK Novi Pazar 1-0(1-0)
FK Inđija - Vojvodina 0-2(0-0)
Partizan - OFK Bačka 2-1(0-0)

Round 10 [02-04.10.2020]
Radnički Niš - Mladost Lučani 1-1(0-0)
OFK Bačka - FK Javor 2-2(0-2)
FK Mačva - FK Voždovac 0-2(0-0)
FK Novi Pazar - Vojvodina 3-1(3-0)
Spartak Subotica - FK Čukarički 4-2(2-2)
FK Metalac - Partizan 1-1(0-0)
Rad Beograd - FK Inđija 2-1(1-1)
Proleter Novi Sad - Bačka Topola 1-0(1-0)
FK Zlatibor - Radnik Surdulica 1-4(1-1)
Crvena Zvezda - FK Napredak 3-0(2-0)

Round 11 [16-18.10.2020]
FK Čukarički - Proleter Novi Sad 1-2(0-1)
Vojvodina - Rad Beograd 4-1(1-0)
Radnik Surdulica - OFK Bačka 1-0(1-0)
Bačka Topola - FK Novi Pazar 7-0(4-0)
FK Inđija - FK Zlatibor 1-0(1-0)
FK Javor - FK Metalac 1-3(1-2)
Mladost Lučani - FK Mačva 2-1(0-1)
FK Napredak - Radnički Niš 0-0
FK Voždovac - Spartak Subotica 2-1(2-1)
Partizan - Crvena Zvezda 1-1(1-0)

Round 12 [25-26.10.2020]
OFK Bačka - FK Inđija 1-2(1-1)
FK Novi Pazar - Rad Beograd 2-1(2-1)
FK Zlatibor - Vojvodina 0-2(0-0)
FK Mačva - FK Napredak 1-2(0-2)
Proleter Novi Sad - FK Voždovac 1-1(1-0)
Crvena Zvezda - FK Javor 0-0
FK Metalac - Radnik Surdulica 1-1(0-1)
Radnički Niš - Partizan 1-0(0-0)
Spartak Subotica - Mladost Lučani 1-0(0-0)
Bačka Topola - FK Čukarički 0-0

Round 13 [30.10.-01.11.2020]
Vojvodina - OFK Bačka 3-1(2-0)
FK Inđija - FK Metalac 0-1(0-0)
FK Čukarički - FK Novi Pazar 4-0(1-0)
Rad Beograd - FK Zlatibor 0-2(0-1)
FK Voždovac - Bačka Topola 2-0(1-0)
Partizan - FK Mačva 2-0(0-0)
FK Javor - Radnički Niš 1-0(0-0)
Mladost Lučani - Proleter Novi Sad 0-0
FK Napredak - Spartak Subotica 1-1(1-0)
Radnik Surdulica - Crvena Zvezda 1-4(0-2)

Round 14 [06-08.11.2020]
FK Metalac - Vojvodina 3-3(1-1)
OFK Bačka - Rad Beograd 0-1(0-1)
FK Novi Pazar - FK Zlatibor 1-2(1-1)
Proleter Novi Sad - FK Napredak 1-0(0-0)
FK Čukarički - FK Voždovac 3-2(1-1)
FK Mačva - FK Javor 1-0(0-0)
Radnički Niš - Radnik Surdulica 0-1(0-1)
Bačka Topola - Mladost Lučani 5-0(3-0)
Spartak Subotica - Partizan 1-2(0-1)
Crvena Zvezda - FK Inđija 3-2(1-1)

Round 15 [20-22.11.2020]
FK Javor - Spartak Subotica 1-3(1-3)
Mladost Lučani - FK Čukarički 1-1(0-0)
Radnik Surdulica - FK Mačva 3-0(2-0)
FK Inđija - Radnički Niš 1-0(0-0)
FK Napredak - Bačka Topola 2-1(2-1)
FK Voždovac - FK Novi Pazar 1-1(1-0)
Partizan - Proleter Novi Sad 1-0(0-0)
FK Zlatibor - OFK Bačka 1-0(0-0)
Vojvodina - Crvena Zvezda 0-2(0-1)
Rad Beograd - FK Metalac 1-1(0-1) [03.12.]

Round 16 [28-30.11.2020]
FK Mačva - FK Inđija 3-0(2-0)
FK Čukarički - FK Napredak 3-0(0-0)
FK Metalac - FK Zlatibor 2-0(1-0)
FK Voždovac - Mladost Lučani 3-2(2-1)
FK Novi Pazar - OFK Bačka 0-0
Bačka Topola - Partizan 0-4(0-1)
Crvena Zvezda - Rad Beograd 3-0(2-0)
Proleter Novi Sad - FK Javor 2-1(1-0)
Radnički Niš - Vojvodina 0-1(0-1)
Spartak Subotica - Radnik Surdulica 0-0

Round 17 [04-07.12.2020]
FK Napredak - FK Voždovac 3-1(1-1)
Vojvodina - FK Mačva 1-0(1-0)
Partizan - FK Čukarički 1-0(0-0)
FK Inđija - Spartak Subotica 3-4(3-3)
Mladost Lučani - FK Novi Pazar 3-2(2-1)
Radnik Surdulica - Proleter Novi Sad 2-0(0-0)
FK Zlatibor - Crvena Zvezda 0-1(0-1)
OFK Bačka - FK Metalac 3-1(1-1)
Rad Beograd - Radnički Niš 0-1(0-0)
FK Javor - Bačka Topola 1-2(0-0) [20.12.]

Round 18 [11-13.12.2020]
Mladost Lučani - FK Napredak 0-0
Proleter Novi Sad - FK Inđija 1-0(0-0)
Bačka Topola - Radnik Surdulica 1-3(1-0)
FK Čukarički - FK Javor 3-0(1-0)
FK Mačva - Rad Beograd 0-1(0-0)
FK Novi Pazar - FK Metalac 1-0(0-0)
Radnički Niš - FK Zlatibor 2-1(1-0)
Spartak Subotica - Vojvodina 0-1(0-0)
FK Voždovac - Partizan 0-2(0-0)
Crvena Zvezda - OFK Bačka 2-0(0-0)

Round 19 [16-17.12.2020]
OFK Bačka - Radnički Niš 1-2(0-1)
Rad Beograd - Spartak Subotica 0-1(0-1)
Partizan - Mladost Lučani 4-0(2-0)
FK Zlatibor - FK Mačva 0-1(0-0)
FK Javor - FK Voždovac 3-1(2-1)
FK Metalac - Crvena Zvezda 0-1(0-1)
FK Napredak - FK Novi Pazar 0-0
Radnik Surdulica - FK Čukarički 0-1(0-1)
FK Inđija - Bačka Topola 0-3(0-2)
Vojvodina - Proleter Novi Sad 2-0(0-0)

Round 20 [05-07.02.2021]
Vojvodina - Bačka Topola 0-1(0-1)
FK Inđija - FK Čukarički 0-1(0-1)
FK Metalac - Radnički Niš 1-1(0-0)
Radnik Surdulica - FK Voždovac 1-1(1-0)
FK Zlatibor - Spartak Subotica 1-1(0-1)
Partizan - FK Napredak 3-0(2-0)
FK Novi Pazar - Crvena Zvezda 1-3(0-1)
OFK Bačka - FK Mačva 2-0(1-0)
FK Javor - Mladost Lučani 4-1(3-0)
Rad Beograd - Proleter Novi Sad 1-0(0-0)

Round 21 [12-13.02.2021]
FK Napredak - FK Javor 1-1(1-1)
Proleter Novi Sad - FK Zlatibor 2-2(2-2)
Spartak Subotica - OFK Bačka 1-0(1-0)
Bačka Topola - Rad Beograd 0-0
Partizan - FK Novi Pazar 4-1(0-0)
FK Čukarički - Vojvodina 3-3(2-0)
FK Mačva - FK Metalac 2-1(0-0)
Mladost Lučani - Radnik Surdulica 2-2(1-1)
FK Voždovac - FK Inđija 1-1(1-1)
Radnički Niš - Crvena Zvezda 0-1(0-1)

Round 22 [16-17.02.2021]
FK Zlatibor - Bačka Topola 0-1(0-0)
Rad Beograd - FK Čukarički 0-2(0-1)
FK Inđija - Mladost Lučani 1-0(0-0)
FK Javor - Partizan 0-1(0-1)
OFK Bačka - Proleter Novi Sad 0-2(0-1)
Vojvodina - FK Voždovac 2-0(0-0)
FK Novi Pazar - Radnički Niš 3-1(1-1)
Radnik Surdulica - FK Napredak 2-1(2-1)
FK Metalac - Spartak Subotica 3-0(1-0)
Crvena Zvezda - FK Mačva 4-0(2-0) [11.03.]

Round 23 [20-22.02.2021]
FK Čukarički - FK Zlatibor 2-0(0-0)
Mladost Lučani - Vojvodina 1-1(0-1)
FK Napredak - FK Inđija 1-0(0-0)
Partizan - Radnik Surdulica 3-0(1-0)
Proleter Novi Sad - FK Metalac 1-2(1-1)
Spartak Subotica - Crvena Zvezda 1-2(1-0)
FK Javor - FK Novi Pazar 1-0(0-0)
FK Mačva - Radnički Niš 0-2(0-1)
FK Voždovac - Rad Beograd 0-1(0-1)
Bačka Topola - OFK Bačka 3-0(3-0)

Round 24 [26-28.02.2021]
FK Inđija - Partizan 0-6(0-3)
Vojvodina - FK Napredak 1-0(0-0)
OFK Bačka - FK Čukarički 1-2(0-0)
FK Novi Pazar - FK Mačva 4-0(3-0)
Radnički Niš - Spartak Subotica 0-1(0-0)
Radnik Surdulica - FK Javor 2-0(0-0)
FK Metalac - Bačka Topola 0-0
Rad Beograd - Mladost Lučani 0-1(0-0)
FK Zlatibor - FK Voždovac 0-0
Crvena Zvezda - Proleter Novi Sad 4-0(2-0)

Round 25 [02-03.03.2021]
Partizan - Vojvodina 2-0(1-0)
FK Čukarički - FK Metalac 2-0(1-0)
Mladost Lučani - FK Zlatibor 0-2(0-2)
FK Napredak - Rad Beograd 0-2(0-1)
FK Voždovac - OFK Bačka 2-1(0-1)
Radnik Surdulica - FK Novi Pazar 4-1(1-1)
FK Javor - FK Inđija 1-1(1-0)
Proleter Novi Sad - Radnički Niš 2-1(1-0)
Spartak Subotica - FK Mačva 3-2(1-1)
Bačka Topola - Crvena Zvezda 1-3(0-0)

Round 26 [07-08.03.2021]
FK Inđija - Radnik Surdulica 0-1(0-0)
FK Mačva - Proleter Novi Sad 3-1(2-1)
FK Metalac - FK Voždovac 2-1(0-0)
Vojvodina - FK Javor 2-0(2-0)
FK Novi Pazar - Spartak Subotica 2-1(1-1)
Radnički Niš - Bačka Topola 2-0(1-0)
Rad Beograd - Partizan 0-5(0-2)
Crvena Zvezda - FK Čukarički 2-0(0-0)
OFK Bačka - Mladost Lučani 1-1(1-0)
FK Zlatibor - FK Napredak 1-2(1-1)

Round 27 [13-15.03.2021]
FK Čukarički - Radnički Niš 0-0
FK Inđija - FK Novi Pazar 1-0(0-0)
FK Javor - Rad Beograd 1-1(0-1)
Mladost Lučani - FK Metalac 1-1(1-1)
FK Napredak - OFK Bačka 2-1(1-0)
Proleter Novi Sad - Spartak Subotica 2-0(0-0)
Radnik Surdulica - Vojvodina 2-2(2-1)
Bačka Topola - FK Mačva 3-0(2-0)
FK Voždovac - Crvena Zvezda 1-4(1-2)
Partizan - FK Zlatibor 5-1(3-0)

Round 28 [19-21.03.2021]
FK Metalac - FK Napredak 2-2(1-1)
OFK Bačka - Partizan 0-4(0-1)
Radnički Niš - FK Voždovac 0-1(0-0)
Spartak Subotica - Bačka Topola 2-2(1-0)
FK Zlatibor - FK Javor 0-2(0-1)
Crvena Zvezda - Mladost Lučani 4-1(3-1)
FK Mačva - FK Čukarički 1-2(1-1)
Rad Beograd - Radnik Surdulica 2-0(1-0)
Vojvodina - FK Inđija 2-1(2-0)
FK Novi Pazar - Proleter Novi Sad 5-0(3-0)

Round 29 [02-03.04.2021]
Mladost Lučani - Radnički Niš 4-1(0-0)
Vojvodina - FK Novi Pazar 1-0(0-0)
FK Voždovac - FK Mačva 0-0
Bačka Topola - Proleter Novi Sad 2-0(1-0)
FK Čukarički - Spartak Subotica 5-1(2-1)
FK Inđija - Rad Beograd 1-0(0-0)
FK Javor - OFK Bačka 1-1(0-1)
Radnik Surdulica - FK Zlatibor 2-1(0-0)
FK Napredak - Crvena Zvezda 1-4(0-2)
Partizan - FK Metalac 3-0(1-0)

Round 30 [06-08.04.2021]
FK Mačva - Mladost Lučani 0-2(0-1)
FK Novi Pazar - Bačka Topola 2-1(1-0)
Proleter Novi Sad - FK Čukarički 0-1(0-0)
Spartak Subotica - FK Voždovac 3-0(1-0)
OFK Bačka - Radnik Surdulica 0-2(0-1)
Rad Beograd - Vojvodina 2-0(0-0)
Radnički Niš - FK Napredak 1-2(0-1)
Crvena Zvezda - Partizan 1-0(0-0)
FK Metalac - FK Javor 1-2(0-2)
FK Zlatibor - FK Inđija 2-2(1-2)

Round 31 [10-12.04.2021]
FK Čukarički - Bačka Topola 0-0
Mladost Lučani - Spartak Subotica 1-0(0-0)
FK Voždovac - Proleter Novi Sad 1-1(1-0)
FK Javor - Crvena Zvezda 1-5(1-2)
Partizan - Radnički Niš 2-0(1-0)
FK Inđija - OFK Bačka 1-0(1-0)
FK Napredak - FK Mačva 2-0(1-0)
Rad Beograd - FK Novi Pazar 3-2(1-1)
Vojvodina - FK Zlatibor 2-1(1-0)
Radnik Surdulica - FK Metalac 1-2(1-1)

Round 32 [16-18.04.2021]
OFK Bačka - Vojvodina 1-2(0-2)
FK Mačva - Partizan 1-2(1-1)
Crvena Zvezda - Radnik Surdulica 2-1(0-1)
FK Metalac - FK Inđija 0-0
FK Novi Pazar - FK Čukarički 1-3(1-1)
FK Zlatibor - Rad Beograd 1-2(0-0)
Proleter Novi Sad - Mladost Lučani 0-1(0-0)
Radnički Niš - FK Javor 0-0
Spartak Subotica - FK Napredak 0-2(0-1)
Bačka Topola - FK Voždovac 4-1(1-0)

Round 33 [23-25.04.2021]
FK Zlatibor - FK Novi Pazar 0-1(0-0)
FK Javor - FK Mačva 2-0(2-0)
Mladost Lučani - Bačka Topola 2-1(0-1)
FK Napredak - Proleter Novi Sad 5-0(1-0)
Rad Beograd - OFK Bačka 3-0(1-0)
FK Voždovac - FK Čukarički 2-1(1-1)
Vojvodina - FK Metalac 1-2(0-0)
Radnik Surdulica - Radnički Niš 0-0
FK Inđija - Crvena Zvezda 1-5(0-4)
Partizan - Spartak Subotica 2-1(1-0)

Round 34 [28-29.04.2021]
OFK Bačka - FK Zlatibor 0-1(0-1)
FK Čukarički - Mladost Lučani 4-2(1-0)
FK Novi Pazar - FK Voždovac 0-2(0-2)
FK Mačva - Radnik Surdulica 0-5(0-4)
FK Metalac - Rad Beograd 3-0(2-0)
Radnički Niš - FK Inđija 2-0(1-0)
Spartak Subotica - FK Javor 0-2(0-0)
Bačka Topola - FK Napredak 1-3(0-1)
Proleter Novi Sad - Partizan 1-3(0-1)
Crvena Zvezda - Vojvodina 1-0(1-0)

Round 35 [04-05.05.2021]
OFK Bačka - FK Novi Pazar 0-1(0-1)
FK Javor - Proleter Novi Sad 1-1(1-0)
Mladost Lučani - FK Voždovac 1-0(1-0)
FK Napredak - FK Čukarički 1-0(0-0)
Radnik Surdulica - Spartak Subotica 2-0(0-0)
FK Inđija - FK Mačva 2-2(1-0)
Vojvodina - Radnički Niš 0-0
Partizan - Bačka Topola 3-1(0-0)
FK Zlatibor - FK Metalac 1-0(1-0)
Rad Beograd - Crvena Zvezda 2-2(1-2)

Round 36 [08-09.05.2021]
FK Voždovac - FK Napredak 4-2(3-0)
FK Novi Pazar - Mladost Lučani 4-1(3-1)
Proleter Novi Sad - Radnik Surdulica 3-0(0-0)
FK Mačva - Vojvodina 2-5(1-3)
FK Metalac - OFK Bačka 3-0(2-0)
Radnički Niš - Rad Beograd 2-2(1-1)
Spartak Subotica - FK Inđija 1-0(0-0)
Bačka Topola - FK Javor 2-1(2-1)
FK Čukarički - Partizan 0-2(0-1)
Crvena Zvezda - FK Zlatibor 6-1(0-1)

Round 37 [14-15.05.2021]	
Vojvodina - Spartak Subotica	1-1(0-1)
Radnik Surdulica - Bačka Topola	0-3(0-0)
OFK Bačka - Crvena Zvezda	0-5(0-4)
FK Inđija - Proleter Novi Sad	0-5(0-3)
FK Javor - FK Čukarički	1-2(0-0)
FK Metalac - FK Novi Pazar	1-1(1-0)
FK Napredak - Mladost Lučani	2-0(1-0)
Rad Beograd - FK Mačva	7-1(4-0)
FK Zlatibor - Radnički Niš	0-0
Partizan - FK Voždovac	3-0(1-0)

Round 38 [18-19.05.2021]	
FK Čukarički - Radnik Surdulica	2-1(2-0)
FK Mačva - FK Zlatibor	1-0(0-0)
Bačka Topola - FK Inđija	2-1(1-1)
Mladost Lučani - Partizan	1-0(1-0)
Crvena Zvezda - FK Metalac	5-1(3-0)
FK Voždovac - FK Javor	0-0
FK Novi Pazar - FK Napredak	2-1(1-0)
Proleter Novi Sad - Vojvodina	2-0(0-0)
Radnički Niš - OFK Bačka	5-1(4-1)
Spartak Subotica - Rad Beograd	1-1(1-1)

Final Standings

							Total		Home					Away				
1.	**FK Crvena Zvezda Beograd**	38	35	3	0	114 - 20	108	18	1	0	60 - 8	17	2	0	54 - 12
2.	FK Partizan Beograd	38	31	2	5	95 - 20	95	18	1	0	53 - 6	13	1	5	42 - 14
3.	FK Čukarički Beograd	38	22	8	8	69 - 34	74	13	3	3	44 - 16	9	5	5	25 - 18
4.	FK Vojvodina Novi Sad	38	21	8	9	62 - 41	71	13	3	3	32 - 14	8	5	6	30 - 27
5.	FK TSC Bačka Topola	38	17	7	14	68 - 50	58	10	3	6	44 - 25	7	4	8	24 - 25
6.	FK Radnik Surdulica	38	16	7	15	55 - 49	55	9	3	7	29 - 25	7	4	8	26 - 24
7.	FK Mladost Lučani	38	15	9	14	43 - 59	54	11	6	2	26 - 18	4	3	12	17 - 41
8.	FK Proleter Novi Sad	38	15	8	15	40 - 47	53	10	4	5	23 - 14	5	4	10	17 - 33
9.	FK Metalac Gornji Milanovac	38	13	13	12	48 - 53	52	6	11	2	27 - 16	7	2	10	21 - 37
10.	FK Spartak Subotica	38	15	7	16	54 - 53	52	9	4	6	29 - 20	6	3	10	25 - 33
11.	FK Napredak Kruševac	38	14	8	16	44 - 51	50	9	5	5	26 - 19	5	3	11	18 - 32
12.	FK Novi Pazar	38	14	7	17	50 - 60	49	12	2	5	37 - 22	2	5	12	13 - 38
13.	FK Radnički Niš	38	13	10	15	37 - 39	49	9	4	6	25 - 13	4	6	9	12 - 26
14.	FK Voždovac Beograd	38	13	9	16	49 - 59	48	8	6	5	31 - 24	5	3	11	18 - 35
15.	FK Rad Beograd (*Relegated*)	38	14	6	18	44 - 57	48	9	2	8	29 - 26	5	4	10	15 - 31
16.	FK Javor Ivanjica (*Relegated*)	38	12	10	16	45 - 53	46	8	5	6	28 - 25	4	5	10	17 - 28
17.	FK Inđija (*Relegated*)	38	10	5	23	29 - 66	35	8	1	10	16 - 33	2	4	13	13 - 33
18.	FK Zlatibor Čajetina (*Relegated*)	38	7	8	23	28 - 64	29	3	4	12	10 - 27	4	4	11	18 - 37
19.	FK Mačva Šabac (*Relegated*)	38	7	4	27	26 - 81	25	6	1	12	18 - 37	1	3	15	8 - 44
20.	OFK Bačka Bačka Palanka (*Relegated*)	38	3	7	28	24 - 68	16	3	4	12	16 - 33	0	3	16	8 - 35

Top goalscorers:

25	**Milan Makarić**	***FK Radnik Surdulica***
18	Takumi Asano (JPN)	*FK Partizan Beograd*
18	Milan Bojović	*FK Mladost Lučani*
18	Nenad Lukić	*FK TSC Bačka Topola*

NATIONAL CUP
Kup Srbije 2020/2021

First Round [20-21.10./16.11.2020]

FK Napredak Kruševac - OFK Žarkovo	2-1(0-1)		FK Mladost Lučani - FK Dinamo Vranje	3-0(2-0)
FK Mačva Šabac - FK Metalac Gornji Milanovac	1-2(0-0)		FK IMT Beograd - FK Inđija	2-1(1-1)
FK Voždovac Beograd - FK Grafičar Beograd	2-2 aet; 4-2 pen		FK Rad Beograd - FK Kolubara Lazarevac	0-0 aet; 5-3 pen
FK Smederevo 1924 - FK Radnički Niš	1-2(0-2)		FK Kabel Novi Sad - FK Radnik Surdulica	3-4(3-1)
FK Jedinstvo Rumenka - FK Vojvodina Novi Sad	0-2(0-0)		FK Radnički Pirot - FK Proleter Novi Sad	0-2(0-0)
FK Sušica Kragujevac - FK Spartak Subotica	0-2(0-0)		FK Partizan Beograd - OFK Bačka Bačka Palanka	2-0(1-0)
FK Novi Pazar - FK Čukarički Beograd	1-3(1-1)		FK Javor Ivanjica - FK Radnički 1923 Kragujevac	2-1(2-0)
FK Trayal Kruševac - FK TSC Bačka Topola	0-2(0-0)		FK Crvena Zvezda Beograd - FK Zlatibor Čajetina	4-2(0-1)

1/8-Finals [25-26.11./18.12.2020]

FK IMT Beograd - FK Radnički Niš	2-1(1-0)		FK TSC Bačka Topola - FK Napredak Kruševac	2-0(1-0)
FK Javor Ivanjica - FK Voždovac Beograd	1-1 aet; 0-3 pen		FK Metalac Gornji Milanovac - FK Partizan Beograd	0-1(0-1)
FK Spartak Subotica - FK Mladost Lučani	1-1 aet; 4-2 pen		FK Proleter Novi Sad - FK Vojvodina Novi Sad	0-2(0-1)
FK Radnik Surdulica - FK Čukarički Beograd	2-2 aet; 4-2 pen		FK Rad Beograd - FK Crvena Zvezda Beograd	1-2(1-1)

Quarter-Finals [11/30.03.2021]

FK TSC Bačka Topola - FK Radnik Surdulica	1-1 aet; 3-4 pen		FK Partizan Beograd - FK Voždovac Beograd	4-0(2-0)
FK Spartak Subotica - FK Vojvodina Novi Sad	1-2(0-0)		FK Crvena Zvezda Beograd - FK IMT Beograd	3-0(3-0)

Semi-Finals [21.04.2021]

FK Crvena Zvezda Beograd - FK Radnik Surdulica	2-1(2-0)	FK Vojvodina Novi Sad - FK Partizan Beograd	0-1(0-1)

25.05.2021; Stadion „Rajko Mitić", Beograd; Referee: Srđan Jovanović; Attendance: 0
FK Crvena Zvezda Beograd - FK Partizan Beograd   **0-0; 4-3 on penalties**

Crvena Zvezda: Milan Borjan, Milan Gajić (72.Marko Gobeljić), Radovan Pankov, Nemanja Milunović, Milan Rodić, Mirko Ivanić (91.Miloš Degenek), Guélor Kanga (66.Veljko Nikolić), Sékou Sanogo, Aleksandar Katai (72.Slavoljub Srnić), Diego Falcinelli (91.Aleksa Vukanović), El Fardou Ben (101.Nikola Krstović). Trainer: Dejan Stanković.

Partizan Beograd: Vladimir Stojković, Svetozar Marković (46.Bojan Ostojić), Igor Vujačić, Aleksandar Miljković, Slobodan Urošević (111.Marko Živković), Saša Zdjelar (106.Filip Stevanović), Aleksandar Šćekić, Miloš Jojić, Filip Holender (88.Nikola Štulić), Lazar Marković (73.Bibras Natcho), Nemanja Jović (73.Aleksandar Lutovac). Trainer: Aleksandar Stanojević.

Penalties: Bibras Natcho 0-1; Milan Rodić 1-1; Marko Živković 1-2; Radovan Pankov 2-2; Filip Stevanović 2-3; Nikola Krstović 3-3; Miloš Jojić (saved); Veljko Nikolić 4-3; Nikola Štulić (saved).

THE CLUBS 2020/2021

Omladinski fudbalski klub Bačka Bačka Palanka

Founded:	1945		
Stadium:	Stadion „Slavko Maletin Vava", Bačka Palanka (4,000)		
Trainer:	Dejan Radjenović		08.05.1975
[02.11.2020]	Goran Milojević		06.12.1964
[04.01.2021]	Nenad Vanić		30.08.1970
[28.02.2021]	Milan Kuljić		24.12.1975

Goalkeepers:	DOB	M	(s)	G
Aleksa Milojević	08.01.2000	36		
Vukašin Pilipović	03.12.1999	2		
Defenders:	DOB	M	(s)	G
Danilo Aleksić	25.11.1992	1	(2)	
Stefan Jovanović	07.04.1994	18	(2)	
Marko Klisura	15.10.1992	8		
Nemanja Lakić-Pešić	22.09.1991	5		
Slađan Mijatović	23.05.1994	26	(5)	
Filip Mitrović (MNE)	17.11.1993	4	(3)	
Dejan Parađina	05.02.1999	24	(4)	1
Strahinja Proković	15.10.2002		(3)	
Danilo Rađen (USA)	21.06.1994	17	(3)	
Dimitrije Tomović	29.04.1996	3	(4)	
Mladen Veselinović	15.03.1992	1	(1)	
Nemanja Zdravković	24.02.1993	26		
Dušan Živić	14.07.1996	7	(1)	
Midfielders:	DOB	M	(s)	G
Nikola Eskić	19.12.1997	29	(4)	
Nebojša Gavrić	27.08.1991	5	(5)	
Jevgēnijs Kazačoks (LVA)	12.08.1995	3	(4)	
Nikola Krčmarević	18.12.1991	6	(6)	2
Mladen Lukić	14.02.1995	1	(2)	
Lazar Mihailović	09.07.2001	3	(5)	

	DOB	M	(s)	G
Nikola Nedeljković	04.03.1990	16	(2)	
Rista Pajkanović	22.04.2003		(1)	
Marko Pantić	18.06.1998	27	(5)	2
Marko Stojanović	02.08.1998	12	(5)	
Milenko Škorić	22.04.1992	15	(3)	
Nemanja Trifunović	05.02.2003		(2)	
Nikola Zindović	26.06.1905		(2)	
Nikola Žakula	18.08.1992	22	(8)	6
Forwards:	DOB	M	(s)	G
Nikola Ašćerić	19.04.1991	4	(4)	2
Krsta Đorđević	24.09.1993	11	(4)	1
Stefan Ilić	07.04.1995		(3)	
Nebojša Ivančević	01.09.1994	1	(6)	
Andreja Lazović	04.08.1994		(2)	
Shabat Logua (RUS)	22.03.1995	2	(1)	
Miljan Marinković	01.01.2003		(1)	
Ryohei Miyazaki (JPN)	20.09.1995		(2)	
Nikola Njamculović	24.05.2002	8	(8)	
Luka Pisačić (CRO)	29.08.1997	3	(11)	1
Luka Ratković	09.04.1997	21	(8)	4
Slaviša Stojanović	27.01.1989	8	(5)	
Kaspars Svārups (LVA)	28.01.1994	4	(4)	
Dobrivoje Velemir	14.03.1997	11	(6)	1
Miloš Zličić	29.12.1999	28	(6)	4

Fudbalski Klub Crvena Zvezda Beograd

Founded:	04.03.1945		
Stadium:	Stadion „Rajko Mitić", Beograd (51,755)		
Trainer:	Dejan Stanković		11.09.1978

Goalkeepers:	DOB	M	(s)	G
Milan Borjan (CAN)	23.10.1987	32		
Zoran Popović	28.05.1988	6	(1)	
Defenders:	DOB	M	(s)	G
Axel Bakayoko (FRA)	06.01.1998		(2)	
Miloš Degenek (AUS)	28.04.1994	25	(5)	
Strahinja Eraković	22.01.2001	9	(4)	
Milan Gajić	28.01.1996	28	(7)	2
Marko Gobeljić	13.09.1992	13	(13)	
Nemanja Milunović	31.05.1989	19	(3)	4
Radovan Pankov	05.08.1995	28	(4)	1
Milan Rodić	02.04.1991	26	(2)	1
Midfielders:	DOB	M	(s)	G
Mirko Ivanić (MNE)	13.09.1993	28	(5)	16
Branko Jovičić	18.03.1993		(2)	
Guélor Kanga (GAB)	01.09.1990	13	(13)	6
Veljko Nikolić	29.08.1999	30	(5)	7
Richard Odada (KEN)	25.11.2000		(2)	
Njegoš Petrović	18.07.1999	26	(9)	1

	DOB	M	(s)	G
Sékou Sanogo (CIV)	05.05.1989	18	(5)	2
Slavoljub Srnić	12.01.1992	3	(14)	
Miloš Vulić	19.08.1996	1	(3)	2
Forwards:	DOB	M	(s)	G
El Fardou Ben (COM)	10.06.1989	21	(8)	12
Richmond Boakye (GHA)	28.01.1993	5	(3)	2
Diego Falcinelli (ITA)	26.06.1991	15	(8)	9
Filippo Falco (ITA)	11.02.1992	4	(3)	3
Željko Gavrić	05.12.2000	21	(6)	3
Aleksandar Katai	06.02.1991	19	(4)	14
Nikola Krstović (MNE)	05.04.2000	2	(9)	1
Marko Lazetić	22.01.2004		(1)	
Milan Pavkov	09.02.1994	11	(14)	14
Andrija Radulović	03.07.2002	2	(4)	
Veljko Simić	17.02.1995		(1)	
Srđan Spiridonović (AUT)	13.10.1993	8	(8)	3
António Manuel Fernandes Mendes „Tomané" (POR)	23.10.1992	2	(2)	1
Aleksa Vukanović	18.06.1992	3	(18)	3

Fudbalski Klub Čukarički Beograd

Founded: 04.07.1926 (*as Čukarički SK*)
Stadium: Stadion Čukarički, Beograd (4,070)
Trainer: Aleksandar Veselinović   23.05.1970
[21.09.2020]   Dušan Đorđević   23.04.1970

Goalkeepers:	DOB	M	(s)	G
Nemanja Belić	24.04.1987	2		
Novak Mićović	25.10.2001	2		
Đorđe Petrović	08.10.1999	34		
Defenders:	**DOB**	**M**	**(s)**	**G**
Nikola Ćirković	04.12.1991	19	(7)	1
Dimitrije Kamenović	16.07.2000	30		2
Miloš Ostojić	03.08.1991	17	(5)	2
Darko Puškarić	13.07.1985	8	(5)	
Viktor Rogan	12.12.2002		(1)	
Miladin Stevanović	11.02.1996	21	(2)	
Stefan Šapić	26.02.1997	35		4
Strahinja Tanasijević	12.06.1997	11	(1)	1
Nemanja Tošić	23.01.1997	8	(11)	
Stefan Veličković	17.01.1999		(1)	
Midfielders:	**DOB**	**M**	**(s)**	**G**
Marko Docić	21.04.1993	24		4
Uros Drezgić	04.10.2002	5	(1)	
Aleksandar Đorđević	20.12.1999		(3)	
Mitar Ergelaš	05.08.2002	4	(8)	1

	DOB	M	(s)	G
Dario Grgić	16.03.2003		(1)	
Asmir Kajević (MNE)	15.02.1990	21	(5)	6
Stefan Kovač	14.01.1999	25	(5)	3
Jovan Lukić	20.01.2002	8	(13)	1
Srđan Mijailović	10.11.1993	22	(1)	1
Bojica Nikčević (MNE)	04.02.2000	1	(1)	
Danilo Pantić	26.10.1996	18	(10)	1
Nikola Petković	23.02.2003		(1)	
Forwards:	**DOB**	**M**	**(s)**	**G**
Mihajlo Baić	21.11.2002		(5)	1
Veljko Birmančević	05.03.1998	22		9
Stefan Čolović	16.04.1994	9	(8)	2
Đorđe Jovanović	15.02.1999	16	(1)	9
Ibrahima N'Diaye (SEN)	01.02.1994	12	(3)	6
Eze Vincent Okeuhie (NGA)	06.06.1993	12	(5)	5
Marko Rakonjac (MNE)	25.04.2000	4	(27)	1
Milan Savić (BIH)	19.05.2000	20	(8)	4
Mihajlo Spasojević	15.02.2004	1		
Marko Šarić	28.11.1998	3	(4)	1
Milutin Vidosavljević	21.02.2001	4	(22)	3

Fudbalski klub Inđija

Founded: 1933
Stadium: Stadion Inđija, Inđija (4,500)
Trainer: Bratislav Živković   28.11.1970
[05.10.2020]   Dejan Čelar   30.05.1975
[27.03.2021]   Goran Milojević   06.12.1964

Goalkeepers:	DOB	M	(s)	G
Marko Jovičić	02.02.1995	28		
Radomir Novaković	24.01.2000	5		
Miloje Preković	07.06.1991	5		
Defenders:	**DOB**	**M**	**(s)**	**G**
Nikola Anđelković	18.12.1992		(1)	
Vasilije Bakić	24.05.2000	22	(3)	1
Daniil Chalov (RUS)	17.06.1994	3	(1)	
Luka Cucin	24.11.1998	30	(1)	
Luka Čermelj	29.07.1995	5	(2)	
Nikola Dimitrijević	10.05.1991	4	(6)	
Srđan Dimitrov	28.07.1992	6	(2)	1
Nikola Đurić	06.11.1989	1	(3)	
David Hrubik	19.06.1997	2	(3)	
Miljan Ilić	23.05.1993	8	(7)	2
Mihailo Jovanović	15.02.1989	2		
Daniel Kamy (CMR)	08.03.1996	8	(1)	
Marko Konatar	25.03.2000	1		
Jovan Krneta	04.05.1992	22	(1)	
Miloš Mihajlov	15.12.1982	12	(3)	
Igor Nedeljković	26.05.2001		(2)	
Radoš Protić	31.01.1987	32		
Stefan Veličković	17.01.1999	1	(2)	

Midfielders:	DOB	M	(s)	G
Kosta Aleksić	09.03.1998	21	(17)	1
Aleksandar Đorđević	20.12.1999	24	(5)	1
Vasilije Đurić	18.07.1998	13	(6)	1
Aleksa Jovanović	27.05.1999	12	(18)	
Nikola Mrđa	10.01.2003		(1)	
Milisav Perošević (MNE)	05.04.2002		(2)	
Stefan Purtić	06.08.1998	5	(6)	1
Stefan Radić	11.11.2002		(3)	
Milán Rádin	25.06.1991	9		
Branko Riznić	04.10.1999	1	(10)	
Milenko Škorić	22.04.1992	16		
Mile Vujasin	10.10.1993		(2)	
Forwards:	**DOB**	**M**	**(s)**	**G**
Nebojša Bastajić	20.08.1990	34	(3)	9
Željko Dimitrov	19.02.1994	16	(3)	4
Eliomar Correia Silva (BRA)	16.03.1988	7	(6)	1
Brana Ilić	16.02.1985	11	(12)	
Modou Jobe (GAM)	13.06.2000		(10)	
Ivan Marković	23.12.1991		(3)	
Miroslav Marković	04.11.1989	1	(2)	
Mihajlo Nešković	09.02.2000	33	(2)	4
Nemanja Obradović	29.05.1989	9		2
Đorđe Pantelić	29.11.1999	9	(9)	
Nikola Tripković	28.01.1998		(7)	

Fudbalski klub Javor Ivanjica

Founded: 1912
Stadium: Stadion Ivanjica, Ivanjica (3,000)
Trainer: Igor Bondžulić   05.10.1980

Goalkeepers:	DOB	M	(s)	G
Đorđe Lazović	16.11.1992	37		
Boris Velimirović	08.09.2001	1		
Defenders:	**DOB**	**M**	**(s)**	**G**
Boubacari Doucouré (FRA)	19.03.1999	18		
Marko Jevremović	23.02.1996	34	(2)	1
Marko Jevtić	17.02.1996	20	(10)	1
Miroslav Maričić	21.01.1998	35	(2)	3
Bojan Mijailović	28.08.1995		(1)	
Ivan Ostojić	26.06.1989	19		
Vladimir Otašević	08.06.1986	8	(3)	1
Filip Pavišić	15.01.1994	35		2
Nenad Sević	25.04.1996	1	(12)	
Nikola Tričković	15.11.1999	10	(3)	
Stefan Vico (MNE)	28.02.1995	5	(6)	
Midfielders:	**DOB**	**M**	**(s)**	**G**
Milorad Balabanović	18.01.1990	8	(10)	1

	DOB	M	(s)	G
Nikola Dimitrijević	10.05.1991	7		
Nedeljko Piščević	20.04.1995	19		4
Luka Radivojević	09.11.1999	10	(9)	1
Mateja Stojanović	17.01.2001		(3)	
Srđan Šćepanović	23.10.1998	21	(7)	
Vanja Zvekanov	25.05.2000	14	(16)	1
Forwards:	**DOB**	**M**	**(s)**	**G**
Andrej Ilić	03.04.2000	26	(1)	9
Bojan Jelić	28.04.2001		(2)	
Vladimir Jovanović	06.03.2001		(2)	
Alija Krnić (MNE)	02.01.1998		(6)	
Luka Luković	11.10.1996	36	(1)	16
Nemanja Mladenović	03.03.1993	9	(6)	
Lazar Nikolić	01.08.1999	27	(7)	2
Anes Rušević	02.12.1996	4	(26)	1
Ibrahim Tanko (GHA)	30.04.1999	14	(14)	1

Fudbalski Klub Mačva Šabac

Founded:	1919	
Stadium:	Stadion Gradski, Šabac (5,494)	
Trainer:	Dragan Aničić	04.11.1970
[14.12.2020]	Slavko Jeličić	
[02.01.2021]	Slaviša Jelić	23.04.1973

Goalkeepers:	DOB	M	(s)	G
Miloš Gordić	05.03.2000	31		
Nikola Perić	04.02.1992	5		
Filip Samurović	23.09.2002	2		
Defenders:	**DOB**	**M**	**(s)**	**G**
Stefan Dabić	09.03.1997	26	(1)	
Nikola Dukić	10.01.1998	5	(5)	
Vladimir Jovanović	24.07.2002	2	(1)	
Milan Kremenović (GER)	08.03.2002	6	(1)	
Marko Mijailović	14.08.1997	34		1
Mario Nikolić (CRO)	24.01.2001	7	(1)	
Filip Pejović	26.06.1982	23	(4)	
Miroljub Pešić	23.10.1993	15	(3)	
Igor Ristivojević	08.08.1988	14		
Slobodan Sladojević	02.10.2002	4	(3)	
Nikola Subotić	28.08.2002	10	(2)	
Midfielders:	**DOB**	**M**	**(s)**	**G**
Miloš Adamović	19.06.1988	25	(1)	4
Filip Božić (BIH)	09.03.1999	11	(3)	1
Lazar Ivić	24.10.1992	18		
Branislav Knežević	21.07.2002	26	(5)	6
Omar Kočar (SVN)	06.06.2001	7	(2)	
Ognjen Mijailović	30.01.2003	13	(6)	
Nikola Milinković	18.02.1991		(5)	
Ivan Obrovac	08.12.1986	21	(11)	1
Nemanja Panić	29.06.2003	2	(7)	
Ognjen Ristanović	13.01.2002		(2)	
Stefan Tripković	19.09.1994	15	(12)	1
Nikša Vujčić	25.09.1998		(2)	
Forwards:	**DOB**	**M**	**(s)**	**G**
Aleksandar Ćirković	21.09.2001	15		1
Aleksandar Đoković	16.12.1991	7	(9)	1
Branislav Marković	12.10.1998	23		1
Luka Marković	19.02.2000	1	(5)	
Stefan Mihajlović	01.02.1999	6	(8)	
Dilan Andrés Ortíz Aragón (COL)	15.03.2000	23	(5)	7
Vanja Panić (SVN)	27.01.2002	3	(7)	
Đorđe Šušnjar	18.02.1992		(10)	
Stefan Trimanović	23.01.2001	7	(11)	1
Miloš Zukanović	08.02.1996	11	(5)	1

Fudbalski Klub Metalac Gornji Milanovac

Founded:	12.06.1961	
Stadium:	Stadion Metalac, Gornji Milanovac (4,400)	
Trainer:	Žarko Lazetić	22.02.1982

Goalkeepers:	DOB	M	(s)	G
Mateja Premović	28.01.2004		(1)	
Dušan Puletić	05.01.1989	30		
Strahinja Savić	06.08.1999	8		
Defenders:	**DOB**	**M**	**(s)**	**G**
Nemanja Anđelković	26.04.1997	2		
Filip Antonijević	24.07.2000	15	(2)	3
Veljko Mijailović	29.12.2000	1	(1)	
Ilija Miličević	20.06.2001	7	(10)	
Bojan Mlađović	16.10.1995	16		
Ljubiša Pecelj	29.09.1993	19	(8)	2
Ivan Rogač	18.06.1992	33	(1)	
Aleksandar Vasiljević	29.08.2001	35	(1)	2
Jovan Vlalukin	21.05.1999	32		
Miloš Vranjanin	11.06.1996	15		1
Midfielders:	**DOB**	**M**	**(s)**	**G**
Aleksandar Desančić	20.02.1996	7	(1)	
Stefan Fićović	31.05.1998	2	(8)	
Nikola Grbović	18.02.1998	7	(21)	1
Bojan Gočanin	11.10.1997	1	(5)	
Milan Jokić	21.03.1995	19	(10)	3
Damjan Krajišnik (BIH)	24.04.1997	17		2
Igor Maksimović	31.07.1999	33	(4)	8
Miloš Milisavljević	26.10.1992	5	(4)	1
Marko Zoćević	19.05.1993	27	(6)	
Forwards:	**DOB**	**M**	**(s)**	**G**
Savo Arambašić	27.01.2001		(19)	2
Stefan Cvetković	12.01.1998	15	(3)	8
Stefan Đurić	22.08.1997	2	(4)	
Aleksandar Katanić	15.08.1995	25	(6)	8
Jovan Kokir	25.04.2000	6	(18)	
Ognjen Luković	26.06.1905		(5)	
Prestige Mboungou (CGO)	10.07.2000	32	(1)	7
Luka Pavlović	03.02.2004		(2)	
Nikola Popović	31.05.1994	7	(6)	

Fudbalski Klub Mladost Lučani

Founded:	1952	
Stadium:	Stadion Mladost, Lučani (5,944)	
Trainer:	Goran Stanić (MKD)	18.09.1972
[21.09.2020]	Nenad Milovanović	15.08.1969
[02.03.2021]	Darko Rakočević	13.09.1981

Goalkeepers:	DOB	M	(s)	G
Damjan Knežević	08.01.2000	4		
Maksim Milović (MNE)	23.04.1999	17		
Željko Samčović	12.09.2002	1		
Zlatko Zečević	10.08.1983	16		
Defenders:	**DOB**	**M**	**(s)**	**G**
Miloš Cvetković	06.01.1990	27	(3)	
Petar Jovanović	12.07.1982	25	(6)	
Nikola Leković	19.12.1989	14	(1)	
Stefan Maksimović	13.04.2002	1	(1)	
Nemanja Mićević	28.01.1999	24	(3)	1
Bogdan Milošević	17.02.1989	8		
Ivan Milošević	03.11.1984	19	(1)	1
Nenad Perović	20.06.2002	2	(4)	
Miloš Šatara (BIH)	28.10.1995	34	(1)	4
Mihailo Vesnić	05.01.2001		(1)	
Nemanja Žunić	09.09.2003	1		
Midfielders:	**DOB**	**M**	**(s)**	**G**
Regis Baha (CMR)	21.10.1996	26	(1)	
Đorđe Gordić	05.11.2004	1		
Aleksandar Ješić	13.09.1994	32		3
Saša Jovanović	15.12.1991	19		3
Damjan Krajišnik (BIH)	24.04.1997	17		1
Vukasin Marković	13.06.2001	6	(1)	1
Regan Obeng (GHA)	15.08.1994	3	(6)	
Miloš Ožegović	11.05.1992	4	(8)	
Vladimir Radivojević	04.02.1986	23	(13)	
Lazar Selenić	21.08.1999	2	(3)	
Marko Stanić	04.06.2001	1		
Filip Stanisavljević	20.05.1987	1	(9)	
Filip Žunić	16.05.2002	2	(2)	
Forwards:	**DOB**	**M**	**(s)**	**G**
Đorđe Babić	04.08.2000	19	(7)	1
Milan Bojović	13.04.1987	24	(5)	18
Filip Đorđević	24.10.1994	1	(1)	
Lazar Jovanović	13.07.1993	21	(11)	6
Nemanja Kos	30.11.2002	10	(5)	2
Ognjen Milanović	04.10.2001	3	(1)	
Obiora Odita (NGA)	14.05.1983	10	(25)	2
Stefan Tešić	18.06.1998		(1)	

Fudbalski Klub Napredak Kruševac

Founded: 08.12.1946
Stadium: Stadion Mladost, Kruševac (10,331)
Trainer: Dragan Ivanović — 02.12.1969
[28.09.2020] Ivan Babić — 02.01.1981
[05.10.2020] Goran Stevanović — 27.11.1966
[08.01.2021] Milan Đuričić — 31.10.1961

Goalkeepers:	DOB	M	(s)	G
Aleksa Jordanov	10.04.2002	10	(1)	
Miloš Ostojić	21.04.1996	26		
Mladen Živković	26.08.1989	2		
Defenders:	**DOB**	**M**	**(s)**	**G**
Mitar Ćuković (MNE)	06.04.1995	9	(14)	1
Nemanja Đeković	09.05.2003		(4)	
Uroš Gajić	19.06.2000		(1)	
Nikola Leković	19.12.1989	17	(1)	
Slavko Lukić	14.03.1989		(2)	
Jovan Marinković	12.09.1996	32	(2)	2
Miloš Milovanović	09.12.1987	21	(1)	
Ognjen Mršić	13.02.1999	29	(2)	
Milan Obradović	27.12.1999	1		
Milan Spremo	27.04.1995	35	(1)	1
Dušan Stević	25.07.1995	12	(1)	1
Stefan Todorović	26.08.1997	2	(1)	
Marko Tomić	28.10.1991	12	(4)	
Aleksandar Trajković	05.11.1999		(1)	
Stanislav Zeljajić	16.01.2001		(3)	
Mladen Zeljković	18.11.1987	4	(1)	
Igor Zonjić (MNE)	16.10.1991	7	(3)	
Midfielders:	**DOB**	**M**	**(s)**	**G**
Nenad Ivanić	11.03.2000	4	(1)	1
Miroljub Kostić	05.06.1988	34	(1)	1
Luka Laban	07.04.2004	1	(3)	
Saša Marjanović	13.11.1987	19		3
Jovan Markoski	23.06.1980	4		
Miloš Mijić	22.11.1989	12	(4)	1
Nemanja Milovanović	12.06.1991	11	(15)	
Luka Milunović	21.12.1992	18	(7)	5
Aboubakar Oumarou (CMR)	04.01.1987	3		
Uroš Rasković	02.09.2000	5	(4)	
Dino Šarac	06.09.1990	5	(6)	
Marko Živanović	16.01.1997	1	(4)	
Forwards:	**DOB**	**M**	**(s)**	**G**
Marko Bačanin	09.07.1998	4	(12)	7
Bojan Čečarić	10.10.1993	16		1
Srđan Kočić	16.02.1999	31	(1)	3
Nikola Marinković	10.07.2003		(1)	
Srđan Matić	15.09.1994	1	(2)	
Alen Melunović (BIH)	26.01.1990	20	(3)	14
Lazar Milošev	20.06.1996	4	(21)	1
Marko Mrkić	20.08.1996	5	(4)	1
Marko Pavićević	03.09.1986	1	(2)	
Igor Vučićević	20.08.1999		(2)	
Mateja Zuvić	13.02.2000		(1)	

Fudbalski Klub Novi Pazar

Founded: 1928
Stadium: Gradski stadion, Novi Pazar (13,000)
Trainer: Kenan Kolasinac — 28.03.1969
[11.11.2020] Radoslav Batak (MNE) — 15.08.1977
[26.02.2021] Davor Berber — 22.05.1977

Goalkeepers:	DOB	M	(s)	G
Marko Drobnjak	17.05.1995	36		
Miloš Rnić	10.06.1993	2		
Defenders:	**DOB**	**M**	**(s)**	**G**
Semir Alić	27.03.2004		(1)	
Uroš Blagojević	21.03.2002	4	(1)	1
Jovo Kojić (BIH)	08.04.1988	18		1
Numan Kurdić (BIH)	01.07.1999	11	(5)	
Marko Marinković	06.01.1994	14	(8)	
Periša Pešukić (MNE)	07.12.1997	10	(6)	1
Luka Šarac	07.02.1995	3		
Jasmin Trtovac	27.12.1986	25	(1)	
Nikola Vlajković	13.09.1995	29	(4)	1
Nikola Vukajlović	13.05.1996	9	(5)	
Vahid Zimonjić	14.07.2000	5	(1)	
Dušan Živić	14.07.1996	9	(5)	
Midfielders:	**DOB**	**M**	**(s)**	**G**
Abdoulayé Cissé (GUI)	13.02.1996	30		6
Mirza Delimeđac	24.10.1999	22	(8)	2
Andrija Fratrović	20.01.2001	1		
Semir Hadžibulić	16.08.1986	7	(19)	2
Sead Islamović	24.09.1999	12	(4)	
Danko Kiković	21.09.1994	7	(7)	1
Nikola Kovačević	14.04.1994	14	(5)	
Luka Marković	19.02.2000	8	(2)	3
Miloš Mijić	22.11.1989	13	(3)	2
Stefan Milosavljević	09.05.1992	1	(6)	
Nikola Nedeljković	04.03.1990	8	(4)	2
Lazar Pajović	26.08.1991	1	(3)	
Ševkija Resić (BIH)	04.12.1999	11	(4)	1
Forwards:	**DOB**	**M**	**(s)**	**G**
Almir Aganspahić (BIH)	12.09.1996	25	(9)	11
Luka Čumić	25.05.2001		(2)	
Semir Dacić (BIH)	10.04.1999	1	(3)	
Nemanja Dragutinović (BIH)	09.04.1999	13	(10)	2
Petar Gigić	07.03.1997	5	(8)	2
Miloš Gordić	10.12.1992		(3)	1
Admir Kecap	25.11.1987	3	(5)	
Ervin Kurti	29.03.1995		(7)	1
Luka Mićić	28.02.1995	1	(7)	
Bojica Nikčević (MNE)	04.02.2000	13	(4)	2
Nemanja Perić	16.10.1997	4	(15)	1
Dušan Stoiljković	05.09.1994	13	(5)	2
Branislav Tomić	12.02.1995	30	(2)	4

Fudbalski Klub Partizan Beograd

Founded: 04.10.1945
Stadium: Stadion Partizan, Beograd (29,775)
Trainer: Savo Milošević — 01.09.1973
[01.09.2020] Aleksandar Stanojević — 28.10.1973

Goalkeepers:	DOB	M	(s)	G
Aleksandar Popović	27.09.1999	21		
Nemanja Stevanović	08.05.1992	2		
Vladimir Stojković	28.07.1983	15		
Defenders:	**DOB**	**M**	**(s)**	**G**
Macky Bagnack (CMR)	07.06.1995	16		
Rajko Brežančić	21.08.1989	2	(2)	
Svetozar Marković	23.03.2000	24		1
Nemanja Miletić	16.01.1991	4		
Aleksandar Miljković	26.02.1990	25		
Ivan Obradović	25.07.1988	15	(2)	1
Bojan Ostojić	12.02.1984	7	(2)	
Slobodan Urošević	15.04.1994	21	(4)	2
Uroš Vitas	06.07.1992	10	(1)	
Igor Vujačić (MNE)	08.08.1994	22		4
Marko Živković	17.05.1994	4	(1)	
Midfielders:	**DOB**	**M**	**(s)**	**G**
Miloš Jojić	19.03.1992	18	(7)	4
Bibras Natcho (ISR)	18.02.1988	26	(7)	12
Lazar Pavlović	02.11.2001	5	(14)	1
Milan Smiljanić	19.11.1986	1	(5)	
Seydouba Soumah (GUI)	11.06.1991	13	(12)	5
Aleksandar Šćekić (MNE)	12.12.1991	26	(7)	4
Saša Zdjelar	20.03.1995	28	(3)	1
Forwards:	**DOB**	**M**	**(s)**	**G**
Takuma Asano (JPN)	10.11.1994	31	(2)	18
Jean-Christophe Bahebeck (FRA)	01.05.1993	1	(6)	1
Samed Baždar	31.01.2004		(1)	
Nikola Čolić	17.08.2002		(7)	1
Filip Holender (HUN)	27.07.1994	22	(4)	9
Đorđe Ivanović	20.11.1995		(5)	
Nemanja Jović (BIH)	08.08.2002	12	(8)	5
Aleksandar Lutovac	28.06.1997	4	(14)	
Lazar Marković	02.03.1994	12	(15)	11
Bojan Matić	22.12.1991	1	(7)	
Umar Sadiq (NGA)	02.02.1997	9	(1)	6
Filip Stevanović	25.09.2002	16	(11)	4
Dennis Stojković	03.08.2002	2	(5)	
Nikola Štulić	08.09.2001	3	(16)	1
Nikola Terzić	28.09.2000		(1)	

Fudbalski Klub Proleter Novi Sad

Founded: 1951
Stadium: Stadion Karađorđe, Novi Sad (14,458)
Trainer: Branko Žigić — 30.12.1981

Goalkeepers:	DOB	M	(s)	G
Mihajlo Dragićević	03.05.2000	1		
Vladan Elesin	12.12.1995	2		
Nikola Vasiljević	24.06.1996	16		
Nikola Petrić	11.05.1991	17		
Kristijan Župić	30.06.2000	2		
Defenders:	**DOB**	**M**	**(s)**	**G**
Aleksandar Andrejević	28.03.1992	15	(1)	
Đorđe Bašanović	31.07.1996	11	(6)	1
Stefan Golubović	08.03.1999	4		
Marko Janković	29.08.2000	7	(4)	
Dušan Joković	04.07.1999	13	(1)	
Bojan Kovačević	28.04.1996	32		1
Leandro Pinto (BRA)	24.01.1994	28	(1)	3
Nikola Marjanović	21.05.2001	13	(1)	
Branislav Milošević	13.05.1988	25	(2)	
Ognjen Mitrović	30.06.1999	26	(7)	2

Midfielders:	DOB	M	(s)	G
Siniša Babić	13.02.1991	12	(1)	5
Danilo Bacanović	12.08.2000	7	(16)	
Jovan Ilić	30.01.2000	19	(13)	1
Branislav Jovanović	21.09.1985	19	(4)	
Lazar Kojić	11.12.1999	16	(12)	
Aleksa Pejić	09.07.1999	27	(6)	1
Stefan Tomović	14.10.2001	14	(4)	3
Forwards:	**DOB**	**M**	**(s)**	**G**
Mladen Galić	09.10.1987	1	(14)	
Nikola Gluščević (MNE)	11.06.2001	3	(7)	
Nemanja Ivanović	14.05.1997	6	(5)	
Filip Knežević	08.11.1991	18	(15)	6
Danilo Milenković	31.08.1994	4	(6)	
Milan Mirosavljev	24.04.1995	29	(7)	8
Boško Papović	22.12.1996		(1)	
Uroš Vesić	28.06.1998	4	(15)	
Viktor Živojinović	15.03.1999	27	(9)	8

Fudbalski Klub Rad Beograd

Founded: 10.03.1958
Stadium: Stadion „Kralj Petar Prvi", Beograd (3,919)
Trainer: Branko Mirjačić — 14.03.1983
[02.09.2020] Zoran Njeguš — 25.06.1973
[06.10.2020] Milan Milanović — 10.01.1963

Goalkeepers:	DOB	M	(s)	G
Damir Kahriman	19.11.1984	28		
Stojan Leković	07.08.2001		(1)	
Dušan Marković	03.04.1998	9		
Danijel Mićanović	30.01.1999	1		
Defenders:	**DOB**	**M**	**(s)**	**G**
Đorđe Bašanović	31.07.1996	4	(1)	
Bojan Ciger	18.06.1994	27	(1)	
Marko Dobrijević	19.03.2002	3	(1)	
Nikola Đorić	03.03.2000	21	(1)	
Milan Lazarević	10.01.1997	31	(1)	2
Miloš Miličković	30.08.1996	2		
Mihailo Milutinović	14.02.1995	5	(1)	
Miloš Radivojević	05.04.1990	22	(1)	1
Petar Stojanović	23.03.2001	2	(3)	
Lazar Stojsavljević	05.05.1998	17	(4)	1
Miloš Tanović	19.05.1996	1	(4)	
Ilija Tučević (MNE)	18.10.1995	5	(12)	1
Midfielders:	**DOB**	**M**	**(s)**	**G**
Nenad Adžibaba	15.01.2001		(1)	
Marko Blažić	02.08.1985	22	(2)	
Aleksandar Busnić	04.12.1997	28	(9)	1

	DOB	M	(s)	G
Uroš Damnjanović	08.02.1995	11	(18)	2
Milan Đurić	03.10.1987	10	(2)	1
Savo Gazivoda (MNE)	18.07.1994	2	(9)	
Luka Gojković	28.11.1999	7	(1)	2
Nikola Grubišić	26.06.2001	3	(2)	
Martin Novaković	05.01.2001	24	(2)	4
Branko Riznić	04.10.1999	1	(1)	
Filip Stanisavljević	20.05.1987	8	(7)	
Aleksandar Trninić	27.03.1987	16	(10)	2
Dušan Zivković	31.07.1996	13	(2)	1
Forwards:	**DOB**	**M**	**(s)**	**G**
Marko Dedijer	08.05.2001		(3)	
Saša Jovanović	30.08.1993	16	(21)	3
Vanja Ilić	03.01.1999	2	(4)	
Andrija Kaluđerović	05.07.1987	18	(1)	9
Petar Karaklajić	01.02.2000	14	(1)	1
Ljubomir Kovacević (MNE)	23.02.2000	8	(5)	1
Nemanja Mladenović	03.03.1993	12	(6)	3
Pavle Radunović	26.05.1996	3	(6)	1
Marko Šarić	28.11.1996	14	(4)	5
Veljko Trifunović	04.08.1998	5	(11)	
Jovan Zogović	11.02.2001	3	(5)	

Fudbalski Klub Radnički Niš

Founded: 24.04.1923
Stadium: Stadion Čair, Niš (18,151)
Trainer: Radoslav Batak (MNE) — 15.08.1977
[06.10.2020] Milan Đuričić — 31.10.1961
[27.11.2020] Vladimir Gaćinović — 03.01.1966
[12.04.2021] Aleksandar Stanković — 07.03.1981

Goalkeepers:	DOB	M	(s)	G
Milorad Kojić	03.02.1999	10		
Borivoje Ristić	19.09.1983	28		
Defenders:	**DOB**	**M**	**(s)**	**G**
Nikola Aksentijević	09.03.1993	35	(1)	
Petar Ćirković	19.11.1999	28	(6)	
Darko Lazić	19.07.1994	2	(1)	
Bojan Letić (BIH)	21.12.1992	1		
Žarko Marković	28.01.1987	20	(1)	4
Marko Momčilović	11.06.1987	7	(4)	
Nikola Stanković	18.12.1993	11	(4)	
Nikola Stevanović	13.09.1998	31	(2)	1
Midfielders:	**DOB**	**M**	**(s)**	**G**
Ognjen Bjeličić	29.07.1997	22	(6)	
Danilo Dašić (MNE)	28.10.2000		(4)	
Petar Đuričković	20.06.1991	26	(1)	2
Aleksandar Kovačević	09.01.1992	18	(2)	1
Stefan Mitrović	15.08.2002	11	(2)	2
Dušan Pantelić	15.04.1993	30	(1)	1
Aleksandr Pejović	28.12.1990	3		1

	DOB	M	(s)	G
Todor Petrović	18.08.1994	20	(13)	
Nemanja Subotić	23.01.1992	5	(4)	
Nenad Šljivić	08.06.1985	5	(3)	
Forwards:	**DOB**	**M**	**(s)**	**G**
Stefan Đurić	22.08.1997		(4)	
Uroš Đuranović (MNE)	01.02.1994	6	(6)	2
Ognjen Đuričin	03.09.1995	5	(10)	1
Nenad Gavrić	12.12.1991	23	(8)	9
Filip Kasalica (MNE)	17.12.1988	8	(20)	2
Nemanja Kojić	03.02.1990	11	(5)	3
Mladen Kovačević	30.12.1994	4	(2)	
Filip Marković	03.03.1992	6	(4)	
Uroš Milovanović	18.10.2000	1	(2)	
Danijel Randelov	29.03.2003		(2)	
Petar Ristić	29.03.2000	11	(3)	
Dušan Stoiljkovič	05.09.1994	11	(7)	4
Ilija Spasić	31.07.2003		(6)	
Veljko Trifunović	04.08.1998	3	(9)	2
Kristijan Živković	21.02.1999	16	(4)	

Fudbalski Klub Radnik Surdulica

	Founded:	1926		
	Stadium:	Stadion Surdulica, Surdulica (3,312)		
	Trainer:	Simo Krunić (BIH)		13.01.1967
	[26.08.2020]	Dejan Đuričić		15.12.1973
	[01.09.2020]	Slavoljub Đorđević		15.02.1981

Goalkeepers:	DOB	M	(s)	G
Ivan Kostić	24.10.1995	31		
Stefan Ranđelović	27.01.1999	7	(1)	
Defenders:	**DOB**	**M**	**(s)**	**G**
Dušan Brković	20.01.1989	1	(1)	
Predrag Đorđević	30.06.1990	27		
Ranko Jokić	22.04.1999	16	(5)	1
Ivan Kričak	19.07.1996	25		1
Nikola Radmanovac	30.01.1997	15	(4)	
Dušan Stevanović	22.06.1996	30		
Uroš Stojanović	23.08.1995	27	(6)	
Midfielders:	**DOB**	**M**	**(s)**	**G**
Filip Bainović	23.06.1996	12	(4)	
Edin Biber (BIH)	06.01.1999	7	(4)	
Ognjen Dimitrić	04.06.1998	1	(6)	1
Filip Jović	06.08.1997	21	(2)	
Viktor Lukić	06.10.2000	30	(1)	1
Vuk Mitošević	12.02.1991	18		4
Mihailo Oreščanin	07.09.1997	12	(12)	
Bratislav Pejčić	17.01.1983		(3)	
Nemanja Subotić	23.01.1992	12	(14)	4
Witan Sulaeman (IDN)	08.10.2001		(3)	
Forwards:	**DOB**	**M**	**(s)**	**G**
Nikola Bogdanovski (MKD)	25.01.1999	33	(3)	2
Bojan Bojić	03.03.2000		(2)	
Zoran Danoski (MKD)	20.10.1990	22	(11)	2
Sead Islamović	24.09.1999	3	(1)	
Milan Makarić	04.10.1995	36	(2)	25
Uroš Milovanović	18.10.2000	4	(15)	2
Evgeniy Pavlov (UKR)	12.03.1991	1	(16)	5
Miloš Spasić	29.07.1997	20	(18)	3
Bogdan Stamenković	19.01.1998	7	(16)	1

Fudbalski Klub Spartak Subotica

	Founded:	21.04.1945		
	Stadium:	Stadion Subotica, Subotica (13,000)		
	Trainer:	Vladimir Gaćinović (BIH)		03.01.1966
	[25.11.2020]	Vladimir Buač		26.12.1984

Goalkeepers:	DOB	M	(s)	G
Mišo Dubljanić (MNE)	20.12.1999	3		
Filip Dujmović (BIH)	12.03.1999	33		
Đorđe Vukanić	09.12.2000	2		
Defenders:	**DOB**	**M**	**(s)**	**G**
Nemanja Branković	18.06.1997	6	(12)	
David Dunđerski	28.10.1999	30	(1)	
Mihajlo Ivančević	07.04.1999	27		
Filip Jović	27.02.2000	5	(3)	
Ognjen Mažić	22.06.2002	1	(1)	
Stefan Milošević	07.04.1995	21		2
Nemanja Tekijaški	02.03.1997	34		1
Aleksa Urošević	09.05.2000		(1)	
Aleksandar Vidović	12.05.2001	17	(9)	
Midfielders:	**DOB**	**M**	**(s)**	**G**
Aleksa Đurasović	23.12.2002	8	(15)	
Jakša Jevremović	21.10.2003		(1)	
Branimir Jočić	10.07.1994	5	(5)	
Milan Marčić	14.03.1996	31	(1)	7
Andrija Rajović (DEN)	07.06.2001		(9)	
Noboru Shimura (JPN)	11.03.1993	33	(1)	5
Lazar Tufegdžić	22.02.1997	36		16
Vladan Vidaković	14.03.1999	15	(17)	3
Forwards:	**DOB**	**M**	**(s)**	**G**
Mihajlo Baić	21.11.2002		(12)	
Luka Bijelović	11.04.2001	18	(13)	
Stefan Denković (MNE)	16.06.1991	13	(1)	3
Nikola Furtula	11.09.1997	13	(3)	3
Srđan Hrstić	18.07.2003		(4)	
Strahinja Jovanović	01.06.1999	7	(9)	
Nemanja Nikolić	19.10.1992	9	(1)	7
Mile Savković	11.03.1992	22	(12)	3
Nikola Srećković	26.04.1996	27	(5)	4
Stefan Šormaz	10.08.1999	2	(8)	
Nikša Vujanović (MNE)	03.03.2001		(8)	

Fudbalski Klub Topolyai Sport Club Bačka Topola

	Founded:	1913 (as Topolyai Sport Club)		
	Stadium:	Stadion Senta, Senta (5,000)		
	Trainer:	Zoltán Sabo [†15.12.2020]		26.05.1972
	[16.12.2020]	Mirko Jovanović		14.03.1971
	[04.01.2021]	Mladen Krstajić		04.03.1974

Goalkeepers:	DOB	M	(s)	G
Nenad Filipović	24.04.1987	36		
Nemanja Jorgić	07.04.1988	2	(1)	
Defenders:	**DOB**	**M**	**(s)**	**G**
Goran Antonić	03.11.1990	22	(7)	1
Filip Babić	27.05.1995	22	(3)	2
Bojan Balaž	05.01.2001	13		
Slavko Damjanović	02.11.1992	11		1
Vasilije Đurić	10.07.1998	2	(11)	1
Srđan Grabež	02.04.1991	5	(1)	
Marko Petković	03.09.1992	21	(3)	3
Nemanja Petrović	17.04.1992	24	(5)	
Dajan Ponjević	10.02.1989	6	(4)	
Nebojša Skopljak	12.05.1987	7	(3)	1
Boris Varga	14.08.1993	16	(5)	
Midfielders:	**DOB**	**M**	**(s)**	**G**
Mihajlo Banjac	10.11.1999	31	(7)	7
Ifet Đakovac	05.12.1997	5	(12)	
Nemanja Krsmanović	09.05.2003		(1)	
Dejan Milićević	10.03.1992	26	(7)	4
Stefan Santrač (BIH)	24.01.2000	9	(8)	1
Saša Tomanović	20.09.1989	34	(1)	4
Janko Tumbasević	14.01.1985	13	(16)	1
Forwards:	**DOB**	**M**	**(s)**	**G**
Damjan Dostanić	03.12.2001	1	(5)	1
Borko Duronjić	24.09.1997	6	(29)	2
Milan Đokić	12.09.1997		(2)	
Nenad Lukić	02.09.1992	37	(1)	18
Petar Ratkov	18.08.2003		(9)	
Vladimir Silađi	23.04.1993	9	(7)	4
Jug Stanojev	29.07.1999	26	(3)	5
Nemanja Tomašević	09.08.1999	4	(4)	
Đuro Zec	06.03.1990	30	(5)	11

Fudbalski Klub Vojvodina Novi Sad

Founded: 06.03.1914
Stadium: Stadion Karađorđe, Novi Sad (14,458)
Trainer: Nenad Lalatović 22.12.1977

Goalkeepers:	DOB	M	(s)	G
Nikola Simić	21.12.1996	17	(1)	
Nemanja Toroman	26.12.2000	1	(1)	
Goran Vukliš (BIH)	24.09.1987	20		
Defenders:	**DOB**	**M**	**(s)**	**G**
Nikola Andrić	23.05.1992	26	(5)	1
Marko Bjeković	21.09.2000	10	(2)	
Slavko Bralić (CRO)	15.12.1992	30		1
Mladen Devetak	12.03.1999	29	(1)	
Stefan Đorđević	13.03.1991	23	(10)	1
Đorđe Đurić	10.08.1991	4	(5)	
Vladimir Kovačević	11.11.1992	5	(4)	
Siniša Saničanin (BIH)	24.04.1995	18	(2)	3
Aranđel Stojković	02.03.1995	19	(17)	2
Midfielders:	**DOB**	**M**	**(s)**	**G**
Petar Bojić	04.09.1991	19	(9)	9
Nikola Drinčić (MNE)	07.09.1984	33		2

	DOB	M	(s)	G
Dragan Kokanović	01.05.2002		(1)	
Novica Maksimović	04.04.1988	12	(6)	
Vladimir Miletić	05.03.2003	1	(2)	
Bogdan Mladenović	04.04.1996	2	(11)	1
Vladan Novevski (MKD)	13.05.2002	2	(10)	
Mirko Topić	05.02.2001	13	(2)	
Dejan Zukić	07.05.2001	26	(10)	4
Forwards:	**DOB**	**M**	**(s)**	**G**
Nemanja Čović	18.06.1991	24	(6)	9
Ognjen Đuričin	03.09.1995		(9)	2
Miodrag Gemović	25.12.1994	18	(17)	5
Uroš Kabić	01.01.2004		(6)	
Matvey Martinkevich (RUS)	02.11.2002		(1)	
Momčilo Mrkaić (BIH)	21.09.1990	27	(11)	6
Đorđe Pantelić	29.11.1999		(1)	
Veljko Simić	17.02.1995	15	(4)	3
Miljan Vukadinović	27.12.1992	24	(7)	11

Fudbalski Klub Voždovac Beograd

Founded: 1912
Stadium: Stadion Shopping Center, Beograd (5,175)
Trainer: Jovan Damjanović 04.10.1982
[14.04.2021] Predrag Rogan 02.08.1974

Goalkeepers:	DOB	M	(s)	G
Marko Ilić	03.02.1998	5		
Miloš Krunić	22.11.1996	7		
Miloje Preković	07.06.1991	25		
Marko Trkulja	21.06.1990	1		
Defenders:	**DOB**	**M**	**(s)**	**G**
Aleksandar Bogdanović	05.03.1999	15	(2)	1
Vuk Bogdanović	03.04.2002		(1)	
Nikola Dukić	10.01.1998	2	(4)	
Marko Gajić	10.03.1992	34		2
Stefan Hajdin	15.04.1994	17		1
Luka Jakovljević	18.04.2000	1	(1)	
Justas Lasickas (LTU)	06.10.1997	26	(5)	2
Vasilije Mijailović	01.11.2001	1	(2)	
Miloš Milović (MNE)	22.12.1995	21	(1)	
Rashid Obuobi (GHA)	18.12.1994	3		
Nemanja Pejčinović	04.11.1987	2		
Nikola Stanković	18.12.1993	10	(1)	
Nemanja Vučić	11.06.1996		(3)	
Marko Živković	17.05.1994	19		2

Midfielders:	DOB	M	(s)	G
Edin Ajdinović	07.06.2001	21	(9)	2
Lazar Arsić	24.09.1991	7	(5)	2
Ivan Đorić	07.07.1995		(13)	
Marko Ivezić	02.12.2001	3	(2)	
Nemanja Milojević (GRE)	23.02.1998	11	(12)	1
Ivan Milosavljević	19.03.2000	27	(6)	3
Jovan Nišić	03.03.1998	23	(6)	5
Stefan Purtić	06.08.1998	16	(1)	3
Marko Putinčanin	16.12.1987	19		5
Miloš Stojčev (MNE)	19.01.1987	27	(6)	5
Forwards:	**DOB**	**M**	**(s)**	**G**
Filip Avrić	14.06.2001	3	(3)	
Luka Cvetićanin	11.02.2003	16	(13)	1
Marko Gjorgjievski (MKD)	18.04.2000		(1)	
Aleksa Janković	12.04.2000	8	(13)	1
Miloš Pantović	24.08.2002	11	(5)	3
Aleksandar Stanisavljević	11.06.1989	12	(5)	1
Dragan Stoisavljević	25.11.2003	10	(24)	4
Nikola Vujnović (MNE)	11.01.1997	15	(6)	5

Fudbalski Klub Zlatibor Čajetina

Founded: 1945
Stadium: Gradski stadion, Užice (15,000)
Trainer: Predrag Ristanović 29.09.1972
[06.10.2020] Zoran Njeguš 25.06.1973
[15.02.2021] Ljubomir Ristovski 29.11.1969
[17.03.2021] Predrag Ristanović 29.09.1972

Goalkeepers:	DOB	M	(s)	G
Dušan Čubraković	21.07.1995	16		
Miloš Čupić	24.04.1999	18		
Luka Savić	17.06.2001	3		
Marko Stailković	07.06.1997	1		
Defenders:	**DOB**	**M**	**(s)**	**G**
Nemanja Anđelković	26.04.1997	14		
Rade Glišović	09.02.1995	10	(3)	
Adnan Islamović	06.04.1997	8	(2)	1
Milan Jezdimirović	05.09.1996	33	(1)	
Zarija Lambulić	25.05.1998	11		
Bojan Mijailović	28.08.1995	6	(2)	
Bogdan Miličić	06.01.1989	11	(4)	
Marko Momčilović	11.06.1987	15		2
Miloš Nikolić	03.10.1994	5	(3)	
Matej Nikolov (MKD)	26.01.2001		(3)	
Stefan Radmanovac	08.11.2001	3		
Jovan Radović	31.10.2000	2	(2)	
Nenad Sević	25.04.1996	17		2
Filip Stamenković	15.09.1998	22		
Stefan Todorović	26.08.1997	2	(1)	
Aleksa Vidić	29.09.1994	1	(3)	
Midfielders:	**DOB**	**M**	**(s)**	**G**
Nikola Bjeloš (BIH)	03.08.1998	3	(5)	
Milisav Ćirović	12.10.2003		(1)	
Danilo Dašić (MNE)	28.10.2000	13		
Stefan Denić	09.11.1999	5	(2)	
Ifet Đakovac	05.12.1997	19		3

	DOB	M	(s)	G
Mustapha Ibrahim (GHA)	18.06.2000		(5)	
Ismar Hairlahović (BIH)	04.03.1996	4	(8)	
Adama Jarju (GAM)	12.12.1997			
Nemanja Krstić	05.08.1994	26	(5)	1
Uroš Miloradović	14.10.2000	21	(1)	
Mladen Mirković	23.03.2003		(1)	
Seid Mulamuratović	24.07.2001	1	(1)	
Aleksandar Njeguš	24.06.2001		(1)	
Dimitrije Petronijević	21.06.2001	13	(7)	1
Miloš Plavšić	04.04.1990		(5)	
Daniel Sudar (AUT)	28.01.1998	9	(1)	
Nemanja Stojić	15.01.1998	4		
Marko Živanović	16.01.1997	9	(17)	
Forwards:	**DOB**	**M**	**(s)**	**G**
Andrej Bogicević	03.01.2002	7	(4)	
Milan Đokić	12.09.1997	8	(7)	3
Lazar Đurović	19.02.1997		(1)	
Eliomar Correia Silva (BRA)	16.03.1988	6	(2)	
Nemanja Ivanović	14.05.1997	1	(5)	
Vasilije Janjić	25.01.1995	31	(1)	5
Shabat Logua (RUS)	22.03.1995		(3)	
Marko Maletić (BIH)	25.10.1993		(1)	
Ivan Marković	23.12.1991	1		
Danilo Milenković	31.08.1994	2	(6)	
Igor Poček (MNE)	23.12.1994	4	(10)	1
Uroš Stamenić	14.10.1996	1	(1)	
Predrag Vladić	04.02.1999	6	(1)	
Stefan Vukić	29.06.1995	26	(4)	9

1.	FK Radnički 1923 Kragujevac (*Promoted*)	34	20	9	5	52	-	26	69
2.	FK Kolubara Lazarevac (*Promoted*)	34	21	6	7	53	-	31	69
3.	FK Kabel Novi Sad	34	18	11	5	41	-	18	65
4.	FK IMT Beograd	34	18	6	10	57	-	35	60
5.	FK Loznica	34	15	9	10	57	-	42	54
6.	OFK Žarkovo	34	16	5	13	35	-	34	53
7.	FK Grafičar Beograd	34	13	12	9	46	-	34	51
8.	FK Budućnost Dobanovci	34	14	8	12	39	-	37	50
9.	FK Radnički Sremska Mitrovica	34	14	5	15	39	-	30	47
10.	FK Železničar Pančevo	34	13	5	16	38	-	43	44
11.	FK Radnički Pirot (*Relegated*)	34	10	9	15	32	-	46	39
12.	FK Dubočica Leskovac (*Relegated*)	34	9	12	13	30	-	43	39
13.	FK Dinamo Vranje (*Relegated*)	34	11	5	18	39	-	53	38
14.	FK Borac 1926 Čačak* (*Relegated*)	34	11	9	14	38	-	37	36
15.	FK Trayal Kruševac (*Relegated*)	34	9	8	17	31	-	44	35
16.	FK Jagodina* (*Relegated*)	34	7	14	13	30	-	48	29
17.	FK Zemun Beograd (*Relegated*)	34	7	6	21	24	-	51	27
18.	FK Sloga Kraljevo (*Relegated*)	34	5	11	18	24	-	53	26

6 points deducted for match fixing.

NATIONAL TEAM

INTERNATIONAL MATCHES
(16.07.2020 – 15.07.2021)

03.09.2020	Moskva	Russia - Serbia	3-1(0-0)	(UNL)
06.09.2020	Beograd	Serbia - Turkey	0-0	(UNL)
08.10.2020	Oslo	Norway - Serbia	1-2(0-0,1-1)	(ECQPO)
11.10.2020	Beograd	Serbia - Hungary	0-1(0-1)	(UNL)
14.10.2020	Istanbul	Turkey - Serbia	2-2(0-1)	(UNL)
12.11.2020	Beograd	Serbia - Scotland	1-1(0-0,1-1,1-1); 4-5 on penalties	(ECQPO)
15.11.2020	Budapest	Hungary - Serbia	1-1(1-1)	(UNL)
18.11.2020	Beograd	Serbia - Russia	5-0(4-0)	(UNL)
25.01.2021	Santo Domingo	Dominican Republic - Serbia	0-0	(F)
28.01.2021	Ciudad de Panamá	Panama - Serbia	0-0	(F)
24.03.2021	Beograd	Serbia - Republic of Ireland	3-2(1-1)	(WCQ)
27.03.2021	Beograd	Serbia - Portugal	2-2(0-2)	(WCQ)
30.03.2021	Bakı	Azerbaijan - Serbia	1-2(0-1)	(WCQ)
07.06.2021	Miki	Serbia - Jamaica	1-1(0-1)	(F)
11.06.2021	Kobe	Japan - Serbia	1-0(0-0)	(F)

03.09.2020 RUSSIA - SERBIA   **3-1(0-0)**   2nd UEFA Nations League B, Group 3
VTB Arena, Moskva; Referee: William Collum (Scotland); Attendance: 0
SRB: Marko Dmitrović, Nikola Maksimović, Nikola Milenković, Strahinja Pavlović (64.Aleksandar Kolarov), Darko Lazović, Nemanja Gudelj, Filip Kostić, Sergej Milinković-Savić (65.Filip Đuričić), Nemanja Maksimović (85.Adem Ljajić), Dušan Tadić (Cap), Aleksandar Mitrović. Trainer: Ljubiša Tumbaković.
Goal: Aleksandar Mitrović (78).

06.09.2020 SERBIA - TURKEY   **0-0**   2nd UEFA Nations League B, Group 3
Stadion "Rajko Mitić", Beograd; Referee: Aleksei Kulbakov (Belarus); Attendance: 0
SRB: Predrag Rajković, Nikola Milenković, Strahinja Pavlović, Aleksandar Kolarov (Cap) [*sent off 49*], Darko Lazović (27.Mijat Gaćinović), Nemanja Gudelj, Filip Kostić, Nemanja Radonjić (87.Filip Đuričić), Dušan Tadić, Nemanja Maksimović (61.Stefan Mitrović), Aleksandar Mitrović. Trainer: Ljubiša Tumbaković.

08.10.2020 NORWAY - SERBIA   **1-2(0-0,1-1)**   16th EC. Qualifiers Play-offs, Semi-Finals
Ullevaal Stadion, Oslo; Referee: Daniele Orsato (Italy); Attendance: 200
SRB: Predrag Rajković, Stefan Mitrović, Nikola Milenković, Aleksandar Kolarov (Cap), Darko Lazović (106.Mijat Gaćinović), Nemanja Gudelj, Filip Đuričić (80.Sergej Milinković-Savić), Nemanja Maksimović (80.Luka Milivojević), Mihailo Ristić, Dušan Tadić (119.Saša Lukić), Aleksandar Mitrović. Trainer: Ljubiša Tumbaković.
Goals: Sergej Milinković-Savić (82, 102).

11.10.2020 SERBIA - HUNGARY   **0-1(0-1)**   2nd UEFA Nations League B, Group 3
Stadion "Rajko Mitić", Beograd; Referee: Sandro Schärer (Switzerland); Attendance: 0
SRB: Predrag Rajković, Stefan Mitrović, Filip Mladenović, Nikola Milenković, Strahinja Pavlović, Adem Ljajić (46.Nemanja Radonjić), Nemanja Gudelj, Luka Milivojević (46.Saša Lukić), Mijat Gaćinović (66.Dušan Vlahović), Dušan Tadić (Cap), Luka Jović. Trainer: Ljubiša Tumbaković.

14.10.2020 TURKEY - SERBIA   **2-2(0-1)**   2nd UEFA Nations League B, Group 3
Türk Telekom Stadyumu, İstanbul; Referee: Georgi Kabakov (Bulgaria); Attendance: 519
SRB: Marko Dmitrović, Stefan Mitrović (75.Nemanja Gudelj), Nikola Milenković, Aleksandar Kolarov (Cap), Darko Lazović, Filip Đuričić (75.Dušan Vlahović), Saša Lukić, Sergej Milinković-Savić, Nemanja Maksimović, Mihailo Ristić (46.Filip Mladenović), Aleksandar Mitrović. Trainer: Ljubiša Tumbaković.
Goals: (22), Aleksandar Mitrović (49 penalty).

12.11.2020   **SERBIA - SCOTLAND**   **1-1(0-0,1-1,1-1); 4-5 on penalties**   16th EC. Qualifiers Play-offs, Finals
Stadion "Rajko Mitić", Beograd; Referee: Antonio Miguel Mateu Lahoz (Spain); Attendance: 0
SRB: Predrag Rajković, Stefan Mitrović (108.Uroš Spajić), Nikola Milenković, Darko Lazović, Nemanja Gudelj, Filip Kostić (59.Filip Mladenović), Saša Lukić, Sergej Milinković-Savić (70.Aleksandar Katai), Nemanja Maksimović (70.Luka Jović), Dušan Tadić (Cap), Aleksandar Mitrović. Trainer: Ljubiša Tumbaković.
Goals: Luka Jović (90).
Penalties: Dušan Tadić, Luka Jović, Nemanja Gudelj, Aleksandar Katai, Aleksandar Mitrović (saved).

15.11.2020   **HUNGARY - SERBIA**   **1-1(1-1)**   2nd UEFA Nations League B, Group 3
Puskás Aréna, Budapest; Referee: Glenn Nyberg (Sweden); Attendance: 0
SRB: Marko Dmitrović, Uroš Spajić, Nikola Milenković, Darko Lazović (57.Mijat Gaćinović), Nemanja Gudelj, Saša Lukić, Luka Jović, Nemanja Maksimović (62.Marko Grujić), Mihailo Ristić (62.Filip Mladenović), Dušan Tadić (Cap) (79.Sergej Milinković-Savić), Nemanja Radonjić (79.Dušan Vlahović). Trainer: Ljubiša Tumbaković.
Goal: Nemanja Radonjić (17).

18.11.2020   **SERBIA - RUSSIA**   **5-0(4-0)**   2nd UEFA Nations League B, Group 3
Stadion "Rajko Mitić", Beograd; Referee: Anthony Taylor (England); Attendance: 0
SRB: Predrag Rajković, Stefan Mitrović (90.Strahinja Pavlović), Filip Mladenović (90.Lazar Ranđelović), Uroš Spajić, Nikola Milenković, Nemanja Gudelj (90.Saša Zdjelar), Nemanja Radonjić (31.Dušan Vlahović), Nemanja Maksimović (46.Mijat Gaćinović), Mihailo Ristić, Aleksandar Mitrović (Cap), Luka Jović. Trainer: Ljubiša Tumbaković.
Goals: Nemanja Radonjić (10), Luka Jović (25), Dušan Vlahović (41), Luka Jović (45+1), Filip Mladenović (64).

25.01.2021   **DOMINICAN REPUBLIC - SERBIA**   **0-0**   Friendly International
Estadio Olímpico "Félix Sánchez", Santo Domingo; Referee: William Anderson (Puerto Rico); Attendance: 0
SRB: Đorđe Petrović, Slobodan Urošević (Cap), Jovan Vlalukin (46.Nikola Aksentijević), Ranko Veselinović, Nemanja Mićević (46.Nikola Stevanović), Miljan Vukadinović (70.Kosta Aleksić), Lazar Tufegdžić (46.Nemanja Čović), Jovan Nišić (84.Aleksandar Busnić), Veljko Birmančević, Aleksa Pejić, Nenad Lukić (46.Milan Makarić). Trainer: Ilija Stolica.

28.01.2021   **PANAMA - SERBIA**   **0-0**   Friendly International
Estadio Olímpico "Rommel Fernández Gutiérrez", Ciudad de Panamá; Referee: Ameth Ariel Sánchez Pinzón (Panama); Attendance: 0
SRB: Aleksandar Popović (84.Miloš Gordić), Aleksandar Andrejević, Marko Gajić, Slobodan Urošević (Cap) (61.Marko Jevremović), Aranđel Stojković, Milan Radin (61.Jovan Vlalukin), Miljan Vukadinović, Lazar Tufegdžić (46.Nemanja Čović), Jovan Nišić (61.Aleksa Pejić), Veljko Birmančević, Nenad Lukić (72.Kosta Aleksić). Trainer: Ilija Stolica.

24.03.2021   **SERBIA - REPUBLIC OF IRELAND**   **3-2(1-1)**   22nd FIFA WC. Qualifiers
Stadion „Rajko Mitić", Belgrade; Referee: Davide Massa (Italy); Attendance: 0
SRB: Marko Dmitrović, Stefan Mitrović, Filip Mladenović (46.Filip Kostić), Milan Gajić, Nikola Milenković, Strahinja Pavlović, Filip Đuričić (63.Aleksandar Mitrović), Saša Lukić, Uroš Račić (63.Nemanja Maksimović), Dušan Tadić (Cap) (77.Nemanja Gudelj), Dušan Vlahović (82.Luka Jović). Trainer: Dragan Stojković.
Goals: Dušan Vlahović (40), Aleksandar Mitrović (69, 76).

27.03.2021   **SERBIA - PORTUGAL**   **2-2(0-2)**   22nd FIFA WC. Qualifiers
Stadion "Rajko Mitić", Beograd; Referee: Danny Desmond Makkelie (Netherlands); Attendance: 0
SRB: Marko Dmitrović, Stefan Mitrović, Nikola Milenković [*sent off 90+2*], Strahinja Pavlović, Darko Lazović (46.Nemanja Maksimović), Nemanja Gudelj, Filip Kostić (71.Mihailo Ristić), Sergej Milinković-Savić, Dušan Tadić (Cap) (81.Filip Đuričić), Dušan Vlahović (46.Nemanja Radonjić), Aleksandar Mitrović (87.Luka Jović). Trainer: Dragan Stojković.
Goals: Aleksandar Mitrović (46), Filip Kostić (60).

30.03.2021   **AZERBAIJAN - SERBIA**   **1-2(0-1)**   22nd FIFA WC. Qualifiers
Bakı Olimpiya Stadionu, Bakı; Referee: Roi Reinshreiber (Israel); Attendance: 0
SRB: Predrag Rajković, Stefan Mitrović, Uroš Spajić, Strahinja Pavlović, Nemanja Gudelj, Filip Kostić (64.Andrija Živković), Nemanja Radonjić (86.Mihailo Ristić), Sergej Milinković-Savić, Nemanja Maksimović (64.Marko Grujić), Dušan Tadić (Cap) (75.Luka Jović), Aleksandar Mitrović (86.Dušan Vlahović). Trainer: Dragan Stojković.
Goals: Aleksandar Mitrović (16, 81).

07.06.2021   **SERBIA - JAMAICA**   **1-1(0-1)**   Friendly International
Miki Athletic Stadium, Miki (Japan); Referee: Yudai Yamamoto (Japan); Attendance: 0
SRB: Đorđe Nikolić (46.Marko Ilić), Stefan Mitrović (Cap), Marko Petković (74.Miloš Vulić), Aleksa Terzić, Sava-Arangel Čestić (46.Strahinja Pavlović), Nemanja Gudelj, Marko Grujić (64.Nemanja Maksimović), Ivan Ilić (46.Uroš Spajić), Željko Gavrić (46.Milan Makarić), Dejan Joveljić, Nemanja Jović. Trainer: Dragan Stojković.
Goal: Strahinja Pavlović (61).

11.06.2021   **JAPAN - SERBIA**   **1-0(0-0)**   Friendly International [Kirin Challenge Cup]
Noevir Stadium, Kobe; Referee: Ahmed Eisa Mohamed (United Arab Emirates); Attendance: 0
SRB: Predrag Rajković, Stefan Mitrović (Cap) (72.Sava-Arangel Čestić), Uroš Spajić, Aleksa Terzić, Strahinja Pavlović, Nemanja Gudelj, Marko Grujić (46.Marko Petković), Nemanja Maksimović (78.Ivan Ilić), Milan Makarić (46.Miloš Vulić), Dejan Joveljić, Nemanja Jović (58.Željko Gavrić). Trainer: Dragan Stojković.

NATIONAL TEAM PLAYERS
(16.07.2020 – 15.07.2021)

Name	DOB	Caps	Goals	2020/2021:	Club
Goalkeepers					
Marko DMITROVIĆ	24.01.1992	18	0	2020/2021:	SD Eibar (ESP)
Miloš GORDIĆ	05.03.2000	1	0	2021:	FK Mačva Šabac
Marko ILIĆ	03.02.1998	1	0	2021:	KV Kortrijk (BEL)
Đorđe NIKOLIĆ	13.04.1997	1	0	2021:	FC Basel (SUI)
Đorđe PETROVIĆ	08.10.1999	1	0	2021:	FK Čukarički Beograd
Aleksandar POPOVIĆ	29.09.1999	1	0	2021:	FK Partizan Beograd
Predrag RAJKOVIĆ	31.10.1995	20	0	2020/2021:	Stade de Reims (FRA)
Defenders					
Nikola AKSENTIJEVIĆ	09.03.1993	2	0	2021:	FK Radnički Niš
Aleksandar ANDREJEVIĆ	28.03.1992	1	0	2021:	FK Proleter Novi Sad
Sava-Arangel ČESTIĆ	19.02.2001	2	0	2021:	1.FC Köln (GER)
Marko GAJIĆ	10.03.1992	1	0	2021:	FK Voždovac Beograd
Milan GAJIĆ	28.01.1996	1	0	2021:	FK Crvena Zvezda Beograd
Marko JEVREMOVIĆ	23.02.1996	1	0	2021:	FK Javor Ivanjica
Aleksandar KOLAROV	10.11.1985	94	11	2020:	AS Roma (ITA)
				08.09.2020->	FC Internazionale Milano (ITA)
Nikola MAKSIMOVIĆ	25.11.1991	25	0	2020:	SSC Napoli (ITA)
Nikola MILENKOVIĆ	12.10.1997	29	1	2020/2021:	ACF Fiorentina (ITA)
Stefan MITROVIĆ	22.05.1990	26	0	2020/2021:	Racing Club Strasbourg (FRA)
Nemanja MIĆEVIĆ	28.01.1999	1	0	2021:	FK Mladost Lučani
Filip MLADENOVIĆ	15.08.1991	16	1	2020/2021:	Legia Warszawa (POL)
Strahinja PAVLOVIĆ	24.05.2001	9	1	2020:	AS Monaco FC (FRA)
				21.01.2021->	Cercle Brugge KSV (BEL)
Marko PETKOVIĆ	03.09.1992	4	0	2021:	FK TSC Bačka Topola
Mihailo RISTIĆ	31.10.1995	7	0	2020/2021:	Montpellier Hérault SC (FRA)
Uroš SPAJIĆ	13.02.1993	17	0	2020/2021:	Feyenoord Rotterdam (NED)
Nikola STEVANOVIĆ	13.09.1998	1	0	2021:	FK Radnički Niš
Aranđel STOJKOVIĆ	02.03.1995	1	0	2021:	FK Vojvodina Novi Sad
Aleksa TERZIĆ	17.08.1999	2	0	2021:	Empoli FC (ITA)
Slobodan UROŠEVIĆ	15.04.1994	3	0	2021:	FK Partizan Beograd
Ranko VESELINOVIĆ	24.03.1999	1	0	2021:	Vancouver Whitecaps FC (CAN)
Jovan VLALUKIN	21.05.1999	2	0	2021:	FK Metalac Gornji Milanovac
Midfielders					
Kosta ALEKSIĆ	09.03.1998	2	0	2021:	FK Inđija
Veljko BIRMANČEVIĆ	05.03.1998	2	0	2021:	FK Čukarički Beograd
Aleksandar BUSNIĆ	04.12.1997	1	0	2021:	FK Rad Beograd
Filip ĐURIČIĆ	30.01.1992	31	4	2020/2021:	US Sassuolo Calcio (ITA)
Mijat GAĆINOVIĆ	08.02.1995	23	2	2020/2021:	TSG 1899 Hoffenheim (GER)
Željko GAVRIĆ	05.12.2000	2	0	2021:	FK Crvena Zvezda Beograd
Marko GRUJIĆ	13.04.1996	12	0	2020/2021:	FC do Porto (POR)
Nemanja GUDELJ	16.11.1991	38	1	2020/2021:	Sevilla FC (ESP)
Ivan ILIĆ	17.03.2001	2	0	2021:	Hellas Verona FC (ITA)
Aleksandar KATAI	06.02.1991	10	0	2020:	FK Crvena Zvezda Beograd
Filip KOSTIĆ	01.11.1992	38	3	2020/2021:	Eintracht Frankfurt (GER)
Darko LAZOVIĆ	15.09.1990	16	0	2020/2021:	Hellas Verona FC (ITA)
Adem LJAJIĆ	29.09.1991	47	9	2020:	Beşiktaş JK İstanbul (TUR)
Saša LUKIĆ	13.08.1996	18	0	2020/2021:	Torino FC (ITA)
Nemanja MAKSIMOVIĆ	26.01.1995	31	0	2020/2021:	Getafe CF (ESP)
Sergej MILINKOVIĆ-SAVIĆ	27.02.1995	22	3	2020/2021:	SS Lazio Roma (ITA)
Luka MILIVOJEVIĆ	07.04.1991	38	1	2020:	Crystal Palace FC London (ENG)
Jovan NIŠIĆ	03.03.1998	2	0	2021:	FK Voždovac Beograd
Aleksa PEJIĆ	09.07.1999	2	0	2021:	FK Proleter Novi Sad
Milan RADIN	25.06.1991	1	0	2021:	FC Dinamo Tbilisi (GEO)
Nemanja RADONJIĆ	15.02.1996	22	4	2020:	Olympique de Marseille (ITA)
				02.01.2021->	Hertha BSC Berlin (GER)
Uroš RAČIĆ	17.03.1998	1	0	2021:	Valencia CF (ESP)
Lazar RANĐELOVIĆ	05.08.1997	1	0	2020:	Olympiacos SFP Peiraiás (GRE)
Dušan TADIĆ	20.11.1988	76	16	2020/2021:	AFC Ajax Amsterdam (NED)

Lazar TUFEGDŽIĆ	22.02.1997	2	0	2021:	*FK Spartak Subotica*
Miloš VULIĆ	19.08.1996	2	0	2021:	*FC Crotone (ITA)*
Saša ZDJELAR	20.03.1995	3	0	2020:	*FK Partizan Beograd*
Andrija ŽIVKOVIĆ	11.07.1996	18	0	2021:	*PAOK Thessaloníki)GRE)*

Forwards

Nemanja ČOVIĆ	18.06.1991	2	0	2021:	*FK Vojvodina Novi Sad*
Dejan JOVELJIĆ	07.08.1999	2	0	2021:	*Wolfsberger AC (AUT)*
Luka JOVIĆ	23.12.1997	14	5	2020:	*Real Madrid CF (ESP)*
				14.01.2021->	*Eintracht Frankfurt (GER)*
Nemanja JOVIĆ	08.08.2002	2	0	2021:	*FK Partizan Beograd*
Nenad LUKIĆ	02.09.1992	2	0	2021:	*FK TSC Bačka Topola*
Milan MAKARIĆ	04.10.1995	3	0	2021:	*FK Radnik Surdulica*
Aleksandar MITROVIĆ	16.09.1994	64	41	2020/2021:	*Fulham FC London (ENG)*
Dušan VLAHOVIĆ	28.01.2000	7	2	2020/2021:	*ACF Fiorentina (ITA)*
Miljan VUKADINOVIĆ	27.12.1992	2	0	2021:	*FK Vojvodina Novi Sad*

National team coach

Ljubiša TUMBAKOVIĆ [01.07.2019 – 14.12.2020]	02.09.1952	14 M; 6 W; 5 D; 3 L; 25-19
Ilija STOLICA [Caretaker]	07.07.1978	2 M; 0 W; 2 D; 0 L; 0-0
Dragan STOJKOVIĆ [from 03.03.2021]	03.03.1965	5 M; 2 W; 2 D; 1 L; 8-7

SLOVAKIA

The Country:
Slovenská republika (Slovak Republic)
Capital: Bratislava
Surface: 49,035 km²
Inhabitants: 5,457,926 [2020]
Time: UTC+1

The FA:
Slovenský futbalový zväz
Tomášikova 30C, 821 01 Bratislava
Tel: +421 2 4820 6000
Founded: 04.11.1938
Member of FIFA since: 1994
Member of UEFA since: 1993
Website: www.futbalsfz.sk

NATIONAL TEAM RECORDS

RECORDS

First international match:	27.08.1939, Bratislava:	Slovakia – Germany 2-0
Most international caps:	Marek Hamšik	- 129 caps (since 2007)
Most international goals:	Marek Hamšik	- 26 goals / 129 caps (since 2007)

UEFA EUROPEAN CHAMPIONSHIP

1960	-
1964	-
1968	-
1972	-
1976	-
1980	-
1984	-
1988	-
1992	-
1996	Qualifiers
2000	Qualifiers
2004	Qualifiers
2008	Qualifiers
2012	Qualifiers
2016	Final Tournament (2nd Round of 16)
2020	Final Tournament (Group Stage)

FIFA WORLD CUP

1930	-
1934	-
1938	-
1950	-
1954	-
1958	-
1962	-
1966	-
1970	-
1974	-
1978	-
1982	-
1986	-
1990	-
1994	-
1998	Qualifiers
2002	Qualifiers
2006	Qualifiers
2010	Final Tournament (2nd Round of 16)
2014	Qualifiers
2018	Qualifiers

OLYMPIC TOURNAMENTS

1908	-
1912	-
1920	-
1924	-
1928	-
1936	-
1948	-
1952	-
1956	-
1960	-
1964	-
1968	-
1972	-
1976	-
1980	-
1984	-
1988	-
1992	-
1996	Qualifiers
2000	Group Stage
2004	Qualifiers
2008	Qualifiers
2012	Qualifiers
2016	Qualifiers

Please note: was part of Czechoslovakia 1918-1939 and 1945-1992.

UEFA NATIONS LEAGUE

2018/2019	League B
2020/2021	League B (Relegated to League C)

FIFA CONFEDERATIONS CUP 1992-2017

None

SLOVAK CLUB HONOURS IN EUROPEAN CLUB COMPETITIONS:

European Champion Clubs.Cup (1956-1992) / UEFA Champions League (1993-2021)		
None		

Fairs Cup (1858-1971) / UEFA Cup (1972-2009) / UEFA Europa League (2010-2021)		
None		

UEFA Super Cup (1972-2020)		
None		

*European Cup Winners.Cup 1961-1999**		
ŠK Slovan Bratislava*	1	1968/1969
represented Czechoslovakia		

defunct competition

NATIONAL COMPETITIONS
TABLE OF HONOURS

Please note: Slovakia was part of Czechoslovakia (1918–1993). The first Slovak championship [Zväzové Majstrovstvá Slovenska] was played between Slovak teams (1925–1933).

Zväzové Majstrovstvá Slovenska (1925-1933)

	CHAMPIONS
1925	1. ČsŠK Bratislava
1925/1926	1. ČsŠK Bratislava
1926/1927	1. ČsŠK Bratislava
1927/1928	SK Žilina
1928/1929	SK Žilina
1929/1930	1. ČsŠK Bratislava
1930/1931	Ligeti SC Bratislava
1931/1932	1. ČsŠK Bratislava
1932/1933	SC Rusj Uzhorod

Slovenská liga (1939–1945)

	CHAMPIONS
1938/1939	Sparta Považská Bystrica
1939/1940	ŠK Bratislava
1940/1941	ŠK Bratislava
1941/1942	ŠK Bratislava
1942/1943	OAP Bratislava
1943/1944	ŠK Bratislava

	CHAMPIONS	CUP WINNERS	BEST GOALSCORERS	
1993/1994	ŠK Slovan Bratislava	ŠK Slovan Bratislava	Pavol Diňa (DAC Dunajska Streda)	19
1994/1995	ŠK Slovan Bratislava	FK Inter Bratislava	Robert Semenik (MFK Dukla Banská Bystrica)	18
1995/1996	ŠK Slovan Bratislava	FC Chemlon Humenné	Robert Semenik (1. FC Košice)	29
1996/1997	1. FC Košice	ŠK Slovan Bratislava	Jozef Kožlej (1. FC Košice)	22
1997/1998	1. FC Košice	FC Spartak Trnava	Ľubomír Luhový (FC Spartak Trnava)	17
1998/1999	ŠK Slovan Bratislava	ŠK Slovan Bratislava	Martin Fabuš (TJ Ozeta Dukla Trenčín)	19
1999/2000	FK Inter Bratislava	FK Inter Bratislava	Szilárd Németh (FK Inter Bratislava)	16
2000/2001	FK Inter Bratislava	FK Inter Bratislava	Szilárd Németh (FK Inter Bratislava)	23
2001/2002	MŠK Žilina	FK VTJ Koba Senec	Marek Mintál (MŠK Žilina)	21
2002/2003	MŠK Žilina	FK Matador Púchov	Marek Mintál (MŠK Žilina) Martin Fabuš (Laugaricio Trenčín / MŠK Žilina)	20
2003/2004	MŠK Žilina	FC Artmedia Petržalka	Roland Števko (MFK Ružomberok)	17
2004/2005	Artmedia Bratislava	MFK Dukla Banská Bystrica	Filip Šebo (FC Artmedia Petržalka)	22
2005/2006	MFK Ružomberok	MFK Ružomberok	Róbert Rák (FC Nitra) Erik Jendrišek (MFK Ružomberok)	21
2006/2007	MŠK Žilina	FC ViOn Zlaté Moravce	Tomáš Oravec (FC Artmedia Petržalka)	16
2007/2008	FC Artmedia Petržalka	FC Artmedia Petržalka	Ján Novák (MFK Košice)	17
2008/2009	ŠK Slovan Bratislava	MFK Košice	Pavol Masaryk (ŠK Slovan Bratislava)	15
2009/2010	MŠK Žilina	ŠK Slovan Bratislava	Róbert Rák (FC Nitra)	18
2010/2011	ŠK Slovan Bratislava	ŠK Slovan Bratislava	Filip Šebo (ŠK Slovan Bratislava)	22
2011/2012	MŠK Žilina	MŠK Žilina	Pavol Masaryk (MFK Ružomberok)	18
2012/2013	ŠK Slovan Bratislava	ŠK Slovan Bratislava	David Depetris (AS Trenčín)	16
2013/2014	ŠK Slovan Bratislava	MFK Košice	Tomáš Malec (AS Trenčín)	14
2014/2015	AS Trenčín	AS Trenčín	Matej Jelić (CRO, MŠK Žilina) Jan Kalabiška (CZE, FK Senica)	19
2015/2016	AS Trenčín	AS Trenčín	Gino Ronald van Kessel (CUW, AS Trenčín)	17
2016/2017	MŠK Žilina	ŠK Slovan Bratislava	Filip Hlohovský (MŠK Žilina) Seydouba Soumah (GUI, ŠK Slovan Bratislava)	20
2017/2018	FC Spartak Trnava	ŠK Slovan Bratislava	Samuel Mráz (MŠK Žilina)	21
2018/2019	ŠK Slovan Bratislava	FC Spartak Trnava	Andraž Šporar (SVN, ŠK Slovan Bratislava)	29
2019/2020	ŠK Slovan Bratislava	ŠK Slovan Bratislava	Andraž Šporar (SVN, ŠK Slovan Bratislava)	12
2020/2021	ŠK Slovan Bratislava	ŠK Slovan Bratislava	Dawid Kuminowski (POL, MŠK Žilina)	19

NATIONAL CHAMPIONSHIP
Slovak Fortuna Liga 2020/2021
(08.08.2020 – 22.05.2021)

Regular Season - Results

Round 1 [08-09.08.2020]
FC Nitra - Slovan Bratislava 0-5(0-4)
Zlaté Moravce - FK Pohronie 2-2(2-0)
MFK Ružomberok - AS Trenčín 2-2(0-2)
MFK Zemplín - Spartak Trnava 0-2(0-2)
FK Senica - MŠK Žilina 0-4(0-0)
Dunajská Streda - ŠKF Sereď 6-0(3-0)

Round 2 [11-12.08.2020]
Spartak Trnava - MFK Ružomberok 3-1(1-0)
MŠK Žilina - FC Nitra 1-2(1-0)
Slovan Bratislava - MFK Zemplín 5-0(1-0)
AS Trenčín - Zlaté Moravce 1-1(0-0)
FK Pohronie - Dunajská Streda 1-2(0-0)
ŠKF Sereď - FK Senica 4-0(2-0)

Round 3 [15.08.2020]
AS Trenčín - MŠK Žilina 2-4(1-1)
Dunajská Streda - FC Nitra 6-0(2-0)
Zlaté Moravce - Slovan Bratislava 2-1(1-1)
MFK Ružomberok - ŠKF Sereď 0-0
FK Senica - MFK Zemplín 3-0(1-0)
Spartak Trnava - FK Pohronie 1-1(1-0)

Round 4 [22-25.08.2020]
Dunajská Streda - Spartak Trnava 2-1(1-1)
FC Nitra - MFK Ružomberok 1-1(0-0)
FK Pohronie - MŠK Žilina 2-1(1-0)
MFK Zemplín - Zlaté Moravce 1-0(1-0)
ŠKF Sereď - AS Trenčín 1-1(0-1) [22.09.]
Slovan Bratislava-FK Senica 2-0(1-0) [30.09.]

Round 5 [29-31.08.2020]
FK Senica - FC Nitra 0-0
Spartak Trnava - ŠKF Sereď 0-2(0-1)
Zlaté Moravce - Dunajská Streda 1-2(1-1)
MFK Ružomberok - FK Pohronie 0-0
MŠK Žilina - MFK Zemplín 6-2(2-0)
AS Trenčín - Slovan Bratislava 1-2(1-1)

Round 6 [11-12.09.2020]
Zlaté Moravce - FK Senica 2-2(1-2)
Slovan Bratislava - Spartak Trnava 2-0(2-0)
Dunajská Streda - MFK Ružomberok 3-2(0-1)
MFK Zemplín - AS Trenčín 1-1(0-1)
FC Nitra - FK Pohronie 3-1(1-0)
ŠKF Sereď - MŠK Žilina 3-2(2-0)

Round 7 [19-20.09.2020]
AS Trenčín - FC Nitra 3-2(2-1)
FK Pohronie - ŠKF Sereď 2-2(2-2)
Spartak Trnava - Zlaté Moravce 1-0(0-0)
MFK Ružomberok - MFK Zemplín 4-0(2-0)
MŠK Žilina - Slovan Bratislava 2-2(2-2)
FK Senica - Dunajská Streda 2-4(1-1)

Round 8 [26-27.09.2020]
FK Senica - Spartak Trnava 0-2(0-1)
Zlaté Moravce - MŠK Žilina 4-0(3-0)
MFK Zemplín - FK Pohronie 2-0(1-0)
FC Nitra - ŠKF Sereď 3-0(2-0)
Slovan Bratislava-MFK Ružomberok 5-0(2-0)
Dunajská Streda - AS Trenčín 3-1(2-1)

Round 9 [03-04.10.2020]
MŠK Žilina - Dunajská Streda 4-1(3-1)
MFK Ružomberok - Zlaté Moravce 2-1(1-0)
ŠKF Sereď - MFK Zemplín 1-1(0-1)
Spartak Trnava - FC Nitra 0-2(0-1)
FK Pohronie - Slovan Bratislava 1-2(1-1)
AS Trenčín - FK Senica 0-1(0-0)

Round 10 [17-18.10.2020]
AS Trenčín - FK Pohronie 1-1(1-0)
Zlaté Moravce - FC Nitra 3-1(1-1)
MFK Zemplín - Dunajská Streda 2-4(0-1)
FK Senica - MFK Ružomberok 1-2(0-0)
Slovan Bratislava - ŠKF Sereď 3-0(3-0)
MŠK Žilina - Spartak Trnava 2-1(1-0)

Round 11 [24-25.10.2020]
FK Pohronie - FK Senica 1-2(1-0)
MFK Ružomberok - MŠK Žilina 2-1(0-1)
FC Nitra - MFK Zemplín 1-1(1-1)
ŠKF Sereď - Zlaté Moravce 1-2(1-1)
Spartak Trnava - AS Trenčín 2-0(0-0)
Dunajská Streda - Slovan Bratislava 1-1(1-1)

Round 12 [31.10.-01.11.2020]
FK Pohronie - Zlaté Moravce 2-2(1-1)
MŠK Žilina - FK Senica 3-1(2-1)
Spartak Trnava - MFK Zemplín 1-2(0-0)
AS Trenčín - MFK Ružomberok 3-1(1-0)
Slovan Bratislava - FC Nitra 0-1(0-0)
ŠKF Sereď - Dunajská Streda 1-0(0-0)[02.12.]

Round 13 [07-08.11.2020]
Dunajská Streda - FK Pohronie 0-0
Zlaté Moravce - AS Trenčín 5-0(2-0)
MFK Ružomberok - Spartak Trnava 0-1(0-0)
MFK Zemplín - Slovan Bratislava 0-2(0-1)
FC Nitra - MŠK Žilina 0-3(0-0)
FK Senica - ŠKF Sereď 2-2(1-0) [17.11.]

Round 14 [21-22.11.2020]
FK Pohronie - Spartak Trnava 3-3(1-0)
MFK Zemplín - FK Senica 0-1(0-1)
ŠKF Sereď - MFK Ružomberok 0-0
MŠK Žilina - AS Trenčín 2-0(1-0)
FC Nitra - Dunajská Streda 0-1(0-0)
Slovan Bratislava - Zlaté Moravce 2-1(1-0)

Round 15 [28-29.11.2020]
Zlaté Moravce - MFK Zemplín 0-0
MFK Ružomberok - FC Nitra 3-0(3-0)
MŠK Žilina - FK Pohronie 2-1(1-0)
Spartak Trnava - Dunajská Streda 0-2(0-0)
AS Trenčín - ŠKF Sereď 1-0(1-0)
FK Senica - Slovan Bratislava 0-3(0-1)

Round 16 [05-06.12.2020]
FK Pohronie - MFK Ružomberok 2-2(1-1)
MFK Zemplín - MŠK Žilina 1-1(0-0)
FC Nitra - FK Senica 1-1(0-1)
ŠKF Sereď - Spartak Trnava 2-6(0-4)
Slovan Bratislava - AS Trenčín 2-0(1-0)
Dunajská Streda - Zlaté Moravce 1-3(1-2)

Round 17 [12-13.12.2020]
MŠK Žilina - ŠKF Sereď 0-0
FK Senica - Zlaté Moravce 1-1(0-1)
MFK Ružomberok - Dunajská Streda 1-1(0-0)
AS Trenčín - MFK Zemplín 2-2(0-2)
Spartak Trnava - Slovan Bratislava 0-3(0-2)
FK Pohronie - FC Nitra 3-1(1-1) [06.02.2021]

Round 18 [15-16.12.2020]
Dunajská Streda - FK Senica 2-0(0-0)
MFK Zemplín - MFK Ružomberok 4-3(2-3)
FC Nitra - AS Trenčín 1-2(0-0)
Slovan Bratislava - MŠK Žilina 3-2(0-1)
Zlaté Moravce-Sp. Trnava 2-4(2-3) [06.02.21]
Sereď - FK Pohronie 0-2(0-0) [09.02.2021]

Round 19 [13-14.02.2021]
MŠK Žilina - Zlaté Moravce 4-1(1-0)
Spartak Trnava - FK Senica 1-0(0-0)
MFK Ružomberok - Slovan Bratislava 0-0
FK Pohronie - MFK Zemplín 1-1(1-1)
AS Trenčín - Dunajská Streda 3-3(2-0)
ŠKF Sereď - FC Nitra 1-2(1-1) [23.02.]

Round 20 [20-21.02.2021]
Zlaté Moravce - MFK Ružomberok 3-1(2-0)
MFK Zemplín - ŠKF Sereď 0-2(0-0)
FK Senica - AS Trenčín 2-3(1-1)
Slovan Bratislava - FK Pohronie 1-0(0-0)
FC Nitra - Spartak Trnava 0-1(0-0)
Dunajská Streda - MŠK Žilina 1-1(1-0)

Round 21 [27-28.02.2021]
Dunajská Streda - MFK Zemplín 2-1(1-0)
FK Pohronie - AS Trenčín 0-1(0-0)
MFK Ružomberok - FK Senica 2-3(1-2)
FC Nitra - Zlaté Moravce 0-1(0-1)
Spartak Trnava - MŠK Žilina 2-1(2-1)
ŠKF Sereď - Slovan Bratislava 0-5(0-2)

Round 22 [06.03.2021]
AS Trenčín - Spartak Trnava 2-0(1-0)
Zlaté Moravce - ŠKF Sereď 1-0(1-0)
MFK Zemplín - FC Nitra 1-0(0-0)
MŠK Žilina - MFK Ružomberok 3-2(3-1)
FK Senica - FK Pohronie 1-1(0-1)
Slovan Bratislava - Dunajská Streda 3-1(2-1)

Final Standings

1.	ŠK Slovan Bratislava	22	17	3	2	54	-	12	54
2.	FK DAC Dunajská Streda	22	13	5	4	48	-	28	44
3.	MŠK Žilina	22	11	4	7	49	-	33	37
4.	FC Spartak Trnava	22	11	2	9	32	-	29	35
5.	FC ViOn Zlaté Moravce	22	9	6	7	38	-	29	33
6.	AS Trenčín	22	7	7	8	30	-	38	28
7.	MFK Ružomberok	22	5	8	9	31	-	37	23
8.	FC Nitra	22	6	4	12	21	-	38	22
9.	MFK Zemplín Michalovce	22	5	7	10	22	-	42	22
10.	ŠKF Sereď	22	5	7	10	22	-	39	22
11.	FK Senica	22	5	6	11	23	-	40	21
12.	FK Pohronie Žiar nad Hronom	22	3	11	8	27	-	32	20

Teams ranked 1-6 were qualified for the Championship Round, while teams ranked 7-12 were qualified for the Relegation Round.

Round 23 [13.03.2021]
MFK Zemplín - FC Nitra 1-1(0-0)
ŠKF Sereď - MFK Ružomberok 1-0(0-0)
FK Pohronie - FK Senica 3-0(0-0)

Round 24 [20.03.2021]
MFK Ružomberok - MFK Zemplín 2-0(0-0)
FC Nitra - FK Pohronie 2-3(1-1)
FK Senica - ŠKF Sereď 1-0(0-0)

Round 25 [03.04.2021]
FK Pohronie - ŠKF Sereď 1-2(0-1)
MFK Zemplín - FK Senica 1-0(0-0)
FC Nitra - MFK Ružomberok 1-0(0-0)

Round 26 [10.04.2021]
FK Senica - MFK Ružomberok 0-1(0-1)
ŠKF Sereď - FC Nitra 2-1(0-1)
MFK Zemplín - FK Pohronie 1-2(0-0)

Round 27 [17.04.2021]
MFK Ružomberok - FK Pohronie 1-0(0-0)
ŠKF Sereď - MFK Zemplín 2-0(1-0)
FC Nitra - FK Senica 0-3(0-3)

Round 28 [24.04.2021]
MFK Ružomberok - ŠKF Sereď 2-1(0-0)
FK Senica - MFK Zemplín 1-1(1-1)
FK Pohronie - FC Nitra 0-0

Round 29 [01.05.2021]
FK Senica - FC Nitra 1-0(0-0)
MFK Zemplín - MFK Ružomberok 2-1(1-1)
ŠKF Sereď - FK Pohronie 0-1(0-0)

Round 30 [08-09.05.2021]
MFK Ružomberok - FK Senica 1-1(1-1)
FK Pohronie - MFK Zemplín 0-0
FC Nitra - ŠKF Sereď 0-1(0-1)

Round 31 [15.05.2021]
MFK Ružomberok - FC Nitra 2-0(0-0)
MFK Zemplín - ŠKF Sereď 2-2(1-1)
FK Senica - FK Pohronie 0-0

Round 32 [22.05.2021]
ŠKF Sereď - FK Senica 4-1(2-0)
FK Pohronie - MFK Ružomberok 1-0(0-0)
FC Nitra - MFK Zemplín 0-4(0-2)

Final Standings

					Total				Home					Away		
7. ŠKF Sereď	32	11	8	13	37 - 48	71	7	3	6	23 - 24		4	5	7	14 - 24
8. MFK Ružomberok	32	10	9	13	41 - 44	65	8	6	2	24 - 11		2	3	11	17 - 33
9. FK Pohronie Žiar nad Hronom	32	8	14	10	38 - 38	55	4	7	5	23 - 21		4	7	5	15 - 17
10. MFK Zemplín Michalovce	32	8	11	13	34 - 53	52	6	4	6	19 - 22		2	7	7	15 - 31
11. FK Senica (*Relegation Play-offs*)	32	8	9	15	31 - 51	40	3	6	7	15 - 24		5	3	8	16 - 27
12. FC Nitra (*Relegated*)	32	7	6	19	26 - 55	32	3	3	10	13 - 28		4	3	9	13 - 27

Please note: AS Trenčín were qualified for the Europa League play-offs.

Championship Round

Round 23 [13-14.03.2021]
Dunajská Streda - Zlaté Moravce 2-0(0-0)
MŠK Žilina - Spartak Trnava 2-1(0-0)
AS Trenčín - Slovan Bratislava 2-6(2-2)

Round 24 [20-21.03.2021]
Zlaté Moravce - AS Trenčín 1-0(0-0)
Slovan Bratislava - MŠK Žilina 2-2(0-1)
Spartak Trnava - Dunajská Streda 3-2(0-1)

Round 25 [03-04.04.2021]
Slovan Bratislava - Zlaté Moravce 4-1(0-1)
AS Trenčín - Spartak Trnava 0-1(0-0)
MŠK Žilina - Dunajská Streda 3-3(3-3)

Round 26 [10-11.04.2021]
AS Trenčín - MŠK Žilina 2-3(1-2)
Spartak Trnava - Zlaté Moravce 3-0(1-0)
Dunajská Streda - Slovan Bratislava 2-2(0-1)

Round 27 [17-18.04.2021]
Slovan Bratislava - Spartak Trnava 1-2(0-1)
Dunajská Streda - AS Trenčín 2-0(2-0)
Zlaté Moravce - MŠK Žilina 1-0(0-0)

Round 28 [24-25.04.2021]
Zlaté Moravce - Dunajská Streda 0-1(0-0)
Spartak Trnava - AS Trenčín 2-0(2-0)
MŠK Žilina - Slovan Bratislava 2-3(1-2)

Round 29 [01-02.05.2021]
Dunajská Streda - MŠK Žilina 2-1(1-1)
AS Trenčín - Zlaté Moravce 3-0(1-0)
Spartak Trnava - Slovan Bratislava 3-0(1-0)

Round 30 [08-09.05.2021]
Zlaté Moravce - Spartak Trnava 0-0
MŠK Žilina - AS Trenčín 5-3(1-1)
Slovan Bratislava - Dunajská Streda 0-1(0-0)

Round 31 [15-16.05.2021]
Zlaté Moravce - Slovan Bratislava 0-4(0-2)
AS Trenčín - Dunajská Streda 1-1(0-0)
Spartak Trnava - MŠK Žilina 1-1(1-0)

Round 32 [22.05.2021]
Dunajská Streda - Spartak Trnava 2-0(1-0)
MŠK Žilina - Zlaté Moravce 5-1(3-0)
Slovan Bratislava - AS Trenčín 2-1(2-0)

Final Standings

					Total				Home					Away		
1. **ŠK Slovan Bratislava**	32	22	5	5	78 - 28	68	12	1	3	37 - 12		10	4	2	41 - 16
2. FK DAC Dunajská Streda	32	19	8	5	66 - 38	51	11	4	1	37 - 13		8	4	4	29 - 25
3. FC Spartak Trnava	32	17	4	11	48 - 37	50	9	2	5	23 - 17		8	2	6	25 - 20
4. MŠK Žilina	32	15	7	10	73 - 52	35	11	3	2	46 - 24		4	4	8	27 - 28
5. FC ViOn Zlaté Moravce	32	11	7	14	42 - 51	32	8	4	4	27 - 18		3	3	10	15 - 33
6. AS Trenčín	32	8	8	16	42 - 61	32	5	5	6	27 - 28		3	3	10	15 - 33

Please note: teams ranked 4-6 were qualified for the Europa Conference League play-offs.

Top goalscorers:		
19 **Dawid Kuminowski (POL)**		**MŠK Žilina**
16 Eric Kleybel Ramírez Matheus (VEN)		*FK DAC Dunajská Streda*
14 Filip Balaj		*FC ViOn Zlaté Moravce*
14 Rafael Rogério da Silva „Rafael Ratão" (BRA)		*ŠK Slovan Bratislava*
13 Zsolt Kalmár (HUN)		*FK DAC Dunajská Streda*

Europa Conference League Play-offs [25-28.05.2021]

Semi-Finals	MŠK Žilina - ŠKF Sereď	4-2(3-0)
	FC ViOn Zlaté Moravce - AS Trenčín	2-0(0-0)
Final	**MŠK Žilina - FC ViOn Zlaté Moravce**	3-2(2-2,2-2)

Relegation Play-offs [25-28.06.2021]

MFK Dukla Banská Bystrica - FK Senica	1-2(0-1)	1-1(0-1)

FK Senica remains at first level.

NATIONAL CUP
Slovenský Pohár 2020/2021

1/8-Finals [06-07.04.2021]

FC Spartak Trnava - AS Trenčín	0-1(0-0)	FC ViOn Zlaté Moravce - MFK Skalica	3-1(1-0)
FC Košice - ŠKF Sereď	0-0 aet; 4-2 pen	Slovan Bratislava - MFK Tatran Liptovský Mikuláš	1-0(0-0)
MFK Dukla Banská Bystrica - KFC Komárno	0-0 aet; 5-4 pen	MFK Ružomberok - FK DAC Dunajská Streda	1-3(0-2)
FK Pohronie Žiar nad Hr. - FC Petržalka Bratislava	1-2(1-1)	MŠK Žilina - FK Železiarne Podbrezová	1-1 aet; 6-5 pen

Quarter-Finals [13-14.04.2021]

FC Košice - AS Trenčín	3-0(1-0)	MFK Dukla Banská Bystrica - DAC Dunajská Streda	3-2(1-1)
FC ViOn Zlaté Moravce - MŠK Žilina	0-2(0-1)	ŠK Slovan Bratislava - FC Petržalka Bratislava	5-1(3-0)

Semi-Finals [28-29.04./04-05.05.2021]

First Leg		Second Leg	
FC Košice - MŠK Žilina	2-4(0-2)	MŠK Žilina - FC Košice	4-1(3-1)
ŠK Slovan Bratislava - MFK Dukla Banská Bystrica	3-0(1-0)	MFK Dukla Banská Bystrica - ŠK Slovan Bratislava	1-3(1-2)

Final

19.05.2021; Stadion Tehelné pole, Bratislava; Referee: Peter Kráľovič; Attendance: 0
MŠK Žilina - ŠK Slovan Bratislava　　　　　　　　　　　　　　**1-2(1-0,1-1)**

MŠK Žilina: Ľubomír Belko, Dominik Javorček (105.Branislav Sluka), Jakub Kiwior, Jan Minarik [*sent off 26*], Benson Anang, Miroslav Gono (78.Patrik Myslovič), Jakub Paur (64.Dawid Kurminowski), Enis Fazlagić, Dávid Ďuriš (105.Vahan Bichakhchyan), Ján Bernát (40.Adam Kopas), Matúš Rusnák (78.Adrián Kaprálik). Trainer: Pavol Staňo.

Slovan Bratislava: Michal Šulla, Myenty Abena, Jurij Medveděv, Vasil Bozhikov (105.Kenan Bajrič), Vernon De Marco (78.Lukáš Pauschek), Joeri de Kamps (71.José Antonio Delgado Villar „Nono"),Dávid Holman (46.Dávid Strelec), Ibrahim Rabiu, Ezekiel Henty, Rafael Rogério da Silva „Rafael Ratão" (46.Vladimír Weiss Jr.), Aleksandar Čavrić (78.Erik Daniel). Trainer: Vladimír Weiss.

Goals: 1-0 Jakub Kiwior (30), 1-1 Ezekiel Henty (61), 1-2 Vladimír Weiss Jr. (105 penalty).

THE CLUBS 2020/2021

Please note: appearances and goals includes statistics of both regular season and play-offs (Championship or Relegation Round).

Futbalový klub DAC 1904 Dunajská Streda

Founded:	1904 (*as Dunaszerdahelyi Atlétikai Club*)	
Stadium:	MOL Aréna, Dunajská Streda (12,700)	
Trainer:	Bernd Storck (GER)	25.01.1963
[22.04.2021]	Antal Németh (HUN)	01.03.1974

Goalkeepers:	DOB	M	(s)	G
Martin Jedlička (CZE)	24.01.1998	31		
Benjamín Szaráz	09.03.1998	1		
Defenders:	**DOB**	**M**	**(s)**	**G**
Danilo Beskorovaynyi (UKR)	07.02.1999	16	(2)	1
César Rodolfo Blackman Camarena (PAN)	02.04.1998	26	(1)	
Éric Javier Davis Grajales (PAN)	31.03.1991	23	(2)	4
Dominik Kružliak	10.07.1996	30		1
Matúš Malý	11.07.2001	2	(6)	
Jannik Müller (GER)	18.01.1994	24	(3)	
Niklas Sommer (GER)	02.04.1998	8	(4)	
Luciano Fabián Vera (ARG)	09.02.2002		(1)	
Midfielders:	**DOB**	**M**	**(s)**	**G**
Andrija Balić (CRO)	11.08.1997	29	(1)	7
Martin Bednár	22.04.1999		(4)	1
Isaac Christie-Davies (WAL)	18.10.1997	8	(1)	

	DOB	M	(s)	G
Andrej Fábry	01.03.1997	6	(6)	1
Sidney Deon Bruce Friede (GER)	12.04.1998	7	(3)	3
Zsolt Kalmár (HUN)	09.06.1995	23		13
Sebastián Nebyla	25.01.2002	9	(3)	
Sainey Njie (GAM)	30.08.2001	7	(11)	
András Schäfer (HUN)	13.04.1999	25	(2)	
Máté Vida (HUN)	08.03.1996		(1)	
Forwards:	**DOB**	**M**	**(s)**	**G**
Yhoan Andzouana (CGO)	13.12.1996	9	(14)	1
Marko Divković (CRO)	11.06.1999	29	(3)	12
Jorge Antonio Méndez Castillo (PAN)	06.04.2001	1	(4)	
Brahim Moumou (GER)	06.05.2001		(6)	
Ion Nicolăescu (MDA)	07.09.1998	5	(17)	4
Eric Kleybel Ramírez Matheus (VEN)	20.11.1998	29	(2)	16
Abdulrahman Taiwo (NGA)	05.08.1998	4	(7)	2
Sharani Zuberu (GHA)	07.01.2000		(5)	

Football Club Nitra

Founded:	1909 (*as as Nyitrai ÖTTSO*)	
Stadium:	Štadión pod Zoborom, Nitra (7,480)	
Trainer:	Gergely Geri	19.01.1977
[01.12.2020]	Ivan Galád	10.04.1963
[04.01.2021]	Michal Ščasný (CZE)	19.08.1978
[22.01.2021]	Peter Lérant	30.01.1977
[28.03.2021]	Michal Ščasný (CZE)	19.08.1978

Goalkeepers:	DOB	M	(s)	G
Ariel Harush (ISR)	25.05.1988	3		
Dávid Šipoš	14.08.1998	26		
Michal Trnovský	10.08.2001	3		
Defenders:	**DOB**	**M**	**(s)**	**G**
Tidiane Djiby Ba (SEN)	21.03.1993	10		
Michal Cehula	19.09.2001	1		
Peter Chríbik	02.02.1999	4	(4)	
Ekin Çelebi (GER)	06.06.2000	12	(1)	
Lukáš Fabiš	05.05.1998	18	(7)	
Kristián Kolčák	30.01.1990	28		2
Matúš Kuník	14.05.1997	16		
Daniel Magda	25.11.1997	11	(3)	
Oliver Podhorín	06.07.1992	17		1
Patrik Rédeky	05.02.2002	1		
Yanni Regäsel (GER)	14.01.1996	9	(4)	
Erik Sula	30.05.1995	4	(1)	
Wallace Bonilha Felix (BRA)	26.01.1996		(2)	
Timotej Zahumenský	17.07.1995	13	(1)	
Midfielders:	**DOB**	**M**	**(s)**	**G**
Martin Adamec	14.08.1998	12	(4)	2
Daniel Junio de Jesus Nascimento (BRA)	22.05.1998	1	(1)	

	DOB	M	(s)	G
Gabriel Demian	04.12.2004		(1)	
Michal Faško	24.08.1994	17		8
Nikola Gatarić (CRO)	09.03.1992	8	(5)	1
Ole Käuper (GER)	09.01.1997	1	(6)	
Alen Mustafić (BIH)	05.07.1999	30	(1)	2
Andrej Pekar	16.03.2002		(1)	
Ondrej Vrábel	23.04.1999	9	(7)	
Eroll Zejnullahu (KVX)	19.10.1994	6	(2)	
Forwards:	**DOB**	**M**	**(s)**	**G**
Marián Chobot	31.08.1999	18	(5)	1
Patrik Danek	02.10.2001	2	(9)	1
Matej Franko	14.02.2001	13	(13)	1
Armen Hovhannisyan (ARM)	07.03.2000	1	(4)	
Erik Jendrišek	26.10.1986	12	(1)	2
Benjamin Kindsvater (GER)	08.02.1993	8	(5)	
Sinan Kurt (GER)	23.07.1996	7	(6)	
Ádam Mészáros	20.04.1993	3	(4)	
Matteo Olivero (ITA)	29.07.2000	1		
Kilian Pagliuca (SUI)	02.09.1996	2	(2)	1
Branislav Spáčil	20.09.2003	1	(3)	
Samuel Šefčík	04.11.1996	17	(6)	1
Jakub Tancík	04.01.2000	7	(8)	2

Futbalový klub Pohronie Žiar nad Hronom Dolná Ždaňa

Founded:	2012	
Stadium:	Štadión Mestský, Žiar nad Hronom (2,309)	
Trainer:	Mikuláš Radványi	22.11.1968
[12.10.2020]	Jan Kameník (CZE)	25.01.1982

Goalkeepers:	DOB	M	(s)	G
Samuel Dovec	15.12.2001	1		
Libor Hrdlička	02.01.1986	14		
Tomáš Jenčo	29.09.1988	15	(1)	
Martin Repiský	04.11.2000	2		
Defenders:	**DOB**	**M**	**(s)**	**G**
Willie Britto (CIV)	15.12.1996	1		
Peter Chríbik	02.02.1999	9	(5)	
Thomas Heurtaux (FRA)	03.07.1988	15	(1)	
Patrik Jacko	26.09.1992	7	(2)	
Petr Pavlík (CZE)	22.07.1987	26	(1)	1
Bernard Petrak	15.12.1999	22	(4)	1
Dominik Špiriak	22.03.1999	15	(5)	1
Andrej Štrba	28.02.1998	15	(1)	1
Richard Župa	27.04.1998	14	(6)	1
Midfielders:	**DOB**	**M**	**(s)**	**G**
Martin Adamec	14.08.1998	9	(5)	
Ivan Audino (SUI)	13.07.1991	3	(3)	

	DOB	M	(s)	G
Cédric Badolo (BFA)	04.11.1998	17	(8)	
David Bangala (FRA)	14.06.1997	7	(2)	
Patrick Blahut	07.10.1997	28	(4)	4
Elie N'Zeyi (FRA)	17.10.1997	3	(7)	
Michal Obročník	04.06.1991	6	(2)	
Lukáš Pelegríni	10.05.1988		(3)	
James Michael Weir (ENG)	04.08.1995	30	(1)	6
Forwards:	**DOB**	**M**	**(s)**	**G**
Patrik Abrahám	10.12.1991	1	(6)	
Bonfils-Caleb Bimenyimana (BDI)	21.11.1997	12	(2)	4
Adler da Silva (SUI)	28.12.1998	11		6
Ondřej Chvěja (CZE)	17.07.1998	14	(1)	5
Alieu Fadera (GAM)	03.11.2001	26	(5)	5
Petr Galuška (CZE)	08.07.1996	4	(10)	
Ladji Mallé (MLI)	12.12.2001	1	(12)	
Kojo Matić (SRB)	07.11.1995	1	(12)	
Peter Mazán	13.05.1990	23	(3)	2
Viktor Vondryska	12.03.2001		(1)	

Mestský futbalový klub Ružomberok

Founded:	1906 (*as Rózsahegyi Sport Club*)	
Stadium:	Štadión pod Čebraťom, Ružomberok (4,817)	
Trainer:	Ján Haspra	29.05.1969

Goalkeepers:	DOB	M	(s)	G
Jakub Červeň	08.04.2001	1		
Ivan Krajčírik	15.06.2000	14		
Matúš Macík	19.05.1993	17		
Defenders:	**DOB**	**M**	**(s)**	**G**
Matej Čurma	27.03.1996	25	(2)	
Alex Holub	15.03.2000		(1)	
Lukáš Kojnok	30.05.1997	9	(7)	
Jakub Luka	18.08.2003	2		
Matej Madlenak	07.02.1999	19	(2)	1
Ján Maslo	05.02.1986	29	(1)	4
Alexander Mojžiš	02.01.1999	24	(1)	1
Mário Mrva	16.02.1999	25	(2)	
Midfielders:	**DOB**	**M**	**(s)**	**G**
Adam Brenkus	08.01.1999	16	(7)	1
Michal Dopater	26.02.2001		(2)	
David Filinsky	18.01.1999	2	(11)	

	DOB	M	(s)	G
Matúš Kmeť	27.06.2000	11	(6)	2
Matej Kochan	21.11.1992	19	(6)	1
Tihomir Kostadinov (MKD)	04.03.1996	19	(5)	2
Tomáš Kubík	22.01.2002	1	(7)	1
Oliver Luteran	06.09.2001	1	(2)	
Timotej Múdry	04.04.2000	14	(14)	
Dalibor Takáč	11.10.1997	13	(7)	1
Marek Zsigmund	20.04.1997	20	(3)	2
Forwards:	**DOB**	**M**	**(s)**	**G**
Ladislav Almási	06.03.1999	10	(4)	6
Tomáš Bočček	08.09.2001	1	(4)	
Martin Boda	02.02.1997	1	(16)	1
Peter Ďungel	06.09.1993	12	(10)	2
Štefan Gerec	10.11.1992	21	(8)	2
Rastislav Kružliak	11.07.1999	7	(5)	1
Martin Regáli	12.10.1993	19	(6)	11

Futbalový klub Senica

Founded: 1921
Stadium: OMS Arena, Senica (5,070)
Trainer: Anton Šoltis   05.02.1976
[22.02.2021] Karol Praženica   15.11.1970

Goalkeepers:	DOB	M	(s)	G
Tomáš Fryšták (CZE)	18.08.1987	23		
Olivier Vliegen (BEL)	07.02.1999	9		
Defenders:	**DOB**	**M**	**(s)**	**G**
Antonio Asanović (CRO)	09.08.1991	19		1
José Carrillo Mancilla (ESP)	04.03.1995	23		
Joss Didiba Moudoumbou (CMR)	07.11.1997	4		
Miloš Kopečný (CZE)	26.12.1993	18	(1)	
Vladimír Majdan	07.04.1999	4	(6)	
Matúš Malý	11.07.2001		(1)	
Jakub Nemec	11.01.1992	16	(4)	
Noí Snæhólm Ólafsson (ISL)	03.07.1994	5		
Tomáš Šalata	08.02.1997	3	(3)	
Milan Šimčák	23.08.1995	28	(2)	1
Midfielders:	**DOB**	**M**	**(s)**	**G**
Edmund Addo (GHA)	17.05.2000	26	(2)	2
Dominik Duda (CZE)	03.03.1995	10	(17)	
Peter Eneji Moses (NGA)	08.04.1999	5	(5)	

	DOB	M	(s)	G
Dávid Gallovič	23.04.1996	13	(12)	
Martin Gamboš	23.01.1998	12	(1)	
Marin Ljubičić (CRO)	15.07.1988	6	(1)	1
Daniel Mašulovič	30.01.1998		(6)	
Juraj Piroška	27.02.1987	30	(1)	5
Marko Totka	12.09.2000	13	(10)	
Forwards:	**DOB**	**M**	**(s)**	**G**
Jurica Bajić (CRO)	29.02.2000		(1)	
Vladimír Barbora	02.01.2001		(1)	
Ardian Berisha (SWE)	07.05.1998	1	(5)	
Oskar Fotr (CZE)	09.01.1996	4	(5)	2
Dávid Guba	29.06.1991	7	(2)	1
Martin Košťál	23.02.1996	23	(2)	6
Tomáš Malec	05.01.1993	31		8
Damien Clément Marie (FRA)	19.06.1994	1	(4)	
Ioannis Niarchos (GRE)	26.06.2002	1	(6)	
Boris Turčák	21.02.1993	5	(8)	1
Tenton Yenne (NGA)	07.07.2000	12	(5)	2

Športový Klub Futbalu Sereď

Founded: 28.06.1914 (*as Sereďský športový klub*)
Stadium: Štadión FC ViOn, Zlaté Moravce (4,000)
Trainer: Peter Lérant   30.01.1977
[01.01.2021] František Šturma (CZE)   07.08.1972
[16.02.2021] Ján Blaháč   03.11.1971
[08.03.2021] Gergely Geri   19.11.1977

Goalkeepers:	DOB	M	(s)	G
Ezekiel Ikuepamitan (NGA)	14.12.1996	2		
Adnan Kanurić (BIH)	08.08.2000	1		
Mathew Yakubu (NGA)	03.09.1999	29		
Defenders:	**DOB**	**M**	**(s)**	**G**
Tidiane Djiby Ba (SEN)	21.03.1993	15		1
Jasmin Čeliković (BIH)	07.01.1999	5	(3)	
Tomáš Hučko	03.10.1985	25	(1)	1
Matúš Kuník	14.05.1997	2	(1)	
Martin Mečiar	23.07.1993	11	(7)	
Ľubomír Michalík	13.08.1983	24	(2)	
Tilen Mlakar (SVN)	26.04.1995	5	(2)	
Adam Morong	16.06.1993	30		2
Álvaro Daniel Pereira Barragán (URU)	28.11.1985		(1)	
Iman Salimi (IRN)	01.06.1996	4	(2)	
Martin Slaninka	26.03.1996	14	(11)	1
Alexander Tóth	04.08.2001		(1)	
Midfielders:	**DOB**	**M**	**(s)**	**G**
Banjole Olawale Adekuoroye (NGA)	16.02.1996	5		
Bae Beom-geun (KOR)	04.03.1993		(4)	
Daniel „Dani" Espinar Vallejo (ESP)	17.04.1995	1	(2)	
Stanislav Danko	17.03.1994	4	(2)	

	DOB	M	(s)	G
Iván Santiago Díaz (ARG)	23.01.1993	8	(2)	
Filip Duranski (MKD)	17.07.1991	11	(2)	
Peter Moses Eneji (NGA)	08.04.1999	6	(1)	1
Andrej Fábry	01.03.1997	14		3
Alex Iván	11.10.1997	25	(3)	5
Ondřej Machuča (CZE)	13.04.1996	9	(1)	
Alen Mehić (BIH)	23.02.2001		(2)	
Filip Pankarićan (SRB)	28.03.1993	9	(5)	4
Denis Potoma	15.02.2000	15	(11)	
Nicolas Šumský (CZE)	13.11.1993	13	(10)	1
Filip Tatranský	06.01.2001	4	(6)	
Forwards:	**DOB**	**M**	**(s)**	**G**
Denis Bušnja (CRO)	14.04.2000	19	(7)	3
Carlos Alberto Ibarguen Hinosjosa (COL)	07.10.1995		(1)	
Senad Jarović (GER)	20.01.1998	3	(12)	1
Roko Jureš* (CRO)	29.09.2000	10	(20)	2
Mario Kvesić (CRO)	02.08.2002		(3)	
Miloš Lačný	08.03.1988	19		7
András Mészáros	29.03.1996	1	(2)	
Samuel Prachar	16.05.2003		(1)	
Dino Špehar (CRO)	08.02.1994	9		4

Športový klub Slovan Bratislava

Founded: 03.05.1919 (*as 1. ČsŠK Bratislava*)
Stadium: Štadión Tehelné pole, Bratislava (22,500)
Trainer: Ján Kozák   22.04.1980
[07.09.2020] Darko Milanič (SVN)   18.12.1967
[11.05.2021] Vladimír Weiss   22.09.1964

Goalkeepers:	DOB	M	(s)	G
Dominik Greif	06.04.1997	26		
Matúš Ružinský	15.01.1992	2		
Michal Šulla	15.07.1991	4		
Defenders:	**DOB**	**M**	**(s)**	**G**
Myenty Abena (SUR)	12.12.1994	18	(2)	
Mitch Apau (NED)	27.04.1990	1		
Kenan Bajrič (SVN)	20.12.1994	25	(1)	2
Vasil Bozhikov (BUL)	02.06.1988	20	(3)	
Vernon De Marco	18.11.1992	24	(2)	5
Adam Laczkó	02.04.1997		(1)	
Lucas Lovat (BRA)	15.01.1997	4	(9)	
Jurij Medveděv (CZE)	18.06.1996	13	(3)	1
Lukáš Pauschek	09.12.1992	24	(1)	
Midfielders:	**DOB**	**M**	**(s)**	**G**
Joeri de Kamps (NED)	10.02.1992	26	(2)	
Dávid Holman (HUN)	17.03.1993	20	(4)	10
Martin Hubert	20.04.1996		(1)	

	DOB	M	(s)	G
Martin Kušnír	03.06.2003		(1)	
Filip Lichý	25.01.2001	1		1
José Antonio Delgado Villar „Nono" (ESP)	30.03.1993	24	(2)	2
Ondřej Petrák (CZE)	11.03.1992	1	(2)	
Ibrahim Rabiu (NGA)	15.03.1991	8	(14)	3
Forwards:	**DOB**	**M**	**(s)**	**G**
Boris Cmiljanić (MNE)	17.03.1996		(1)	
Aleksandar Čavrić (SRB)	18.05.1994	19	(11)	3
Erik Daniel (CZE)	04.02.1992	13	(15)	4
Dejan Drazič (SRB)	26.09.1995		(1)	
Ezekiel Henty (NGA)	13.05.1993	5	(10)	3
Mohammed Rharsalla Khadfi (MAR)	15.09.1993	12	(3)	6
Žan Medved (SVN)	14.06.1999	9	(9)	4
Alen Ožbolt (SVN)	24.06.1996	7	(14)	6
Rafael Rogério da Silva „Rafael Ratão" (BRA)	30.11.1995	19	(10)	14
Dávid Strelec	04.04.2001	17	(8)	9
Vladimír Weiss	30.11.1989	10	(7)	3

Football Club Spartak Trnava

Founded: 30.05.1923 (*as TŠS Trnava*)
Stadium: Štadión "Antona Malatinského", Trnava (19,200)
Trainer: Marián Šarmír — 01.05.1976
[14.09.2020] Norbert Hrnčár — 09.06.1970
[01.01.2021] Michal Gašparík — 19.12.1981

Goalkeepers:	DOB	M	(s)	G
Ľuboš Kamenár	17.06.1987	2	(1)	
Dobrivoj Rusov	13.01.1993	23		
Dominik Takáč	12.01.1999	7		
Defenders:	**DOB**	**M**	**(s)**	**G**
Izuchukwu Jude Anthony (NGA)	03.11.1997	17	(1)	
Lukas Jendrek	29.11.2002		(1)	
Birkir Valur Jónsson (ISL)	02.11.1998	2	(1)	
Dimitrios Konstantinidis (GRE)	02.06.1994		(1)	
Sebastián Kóša	13.09.2003	8	(10)	1
Kristián Koštrna	15.12.1993	14		
Mario Mihal	27.02.2001	3	(2)	
Martin Mikovič	12.09.1990	27		2
Dejan Trajkovski (SVN)	14.04.1992	1	(4)	
Marios Tsaousis (GRE)	11.05.2000	8	(4)	
Gergely Tumma	10.02.2000	11	(7)	1
Matúš Turňa	11.05.1986	13	(5)	
Filip Twardzik (CZE)	10.02.1993	13		1
Marek Ujlaky	03.12.2003		(1)	
Marek Václav	26.07.1996	2	(1)	

Midfielders:	DOB	M	(s)	G
Samuel Benovič	03.01.2001	2	(11)	
Martin Bukata	02.10.1993	19	(3)	3
Daniel „Dani" Iglesias Gago (ESP)	17.07.1995	4	(7)	
Jakub Grič	05.07.1996	31		1
Matej Jakúbek	19.01.1995	3		
Patrik Karhan	19.06.2003		(1)	
Peter Kolesár	09.07.1998	6	(12)	
Kristián Mihálek	10.03.2000		(2)	
Kyriakos Savvidis (GRE)	20.06.1995	23	(2)	3
Ján Vlasko	11.01.1990	17	(7)	5
Forwards:	**DOB**	**M**	**(s)**	**G**
Allecks Godinho Alves (BRA)	11.03.2001		(1)	
Yusuf Isa Bamidele (NGA)	22.02.2001	26	(3)	9
Nsumoh Johnson Kalu (NGA)	14.06.2001		(9)	
Stanislav Olejnik	31.03.2002	5	(8)	
Erik Pačinda	09.05.1989	8	(4)	5
Milan Ristovski (MKD)	08.04.1998	11	(1)	5
Saymon De Barros Cabral (BRA)	09.07.2001	30	(2)	6
Yann Michael Yao (CIV)	20.06.1997	16	(5)	2

Asociácia športov Trenčín

Founded: 1992 (*as TJ Ozeta Dukla Trenčín*)
Stadium: Štadión Sihoť, Trenčín (10,000)
Trainer: Stijn Vreven (BEL) — 18.07.1983
[28.04.2021] Juraj Ančic — 12.07.1981

Goalkeepers:	DOB	M	(s)	G
Menno Bergsen (NED)	26.08.1999	4		
Michal Kukučka	12.04.2002	11		
Igor Šemrinec	22.11.1987	17		
Defenders:	**DOB**	**M**	**(s)**	**G**
Steve Kapuadi (FRA)	30.04.1998	14		
Richard Križan	23.09.1997	22	(1)	1
Ruben Ligeon (NED)	24.05.1992	12	(3)	1
Kingsley Madu (NGA)	12.12.1995	3	(1)	
Urban Mazanovský	17.12.2003	2	(2)	
Kelvin Spencer Pires (CPV)	05.06.2000		(2)	
Juha Pirinen (FIN)	22.10.1991	24		1
Rámon Rodríguez da Silva (BRA)	22.08.1990	4	(1)	
Adrián Slávik	12.04.1999	10	(2)	
Martin Šulek	15.01.1998	25	(1)	
Reuben Yem (NGA)	29.10.1997	12	(4)	
Midfielders:	**DOB**	**M**	**(s)**	**G**
Aschraf El Mahdioui (NED)	24.05.1996	29		1
Artur Gajdoš	20.01.2004	1	(7)	

Jakub Kadák	14.12.2000	23	(6)	2
Matúš Kmeť	27.06.2000	5		
Samuel Lavrinčík	10.07.2001	4	(5)	
Ante Roguljić (CRO)	11.03.1996	15	(1)	2
Abdul Zubairu (NGA)	03.10.1998	17	(8)	1
Forwards:	**DOB**	**M**	**(s)**	**G**
Philip Azango (NGA)	21.05.1997	3	(1)	
Osman Bukari (GHA)	13.12.1998	2	(2)	1
Ivenzo Comvalius (SUR)	24.06.1997		(6)	
Milan Corryn (BEL)	04.04.1999	17	(9)	4
Hamza Ćataković (BIH)	15.01.1997	18	(9)	12
Lucas Demitra	09.04.2003	5		2
David Alberto Depetris (ARG)	11.11.1988	3	(6)	
Adam Gaži	01.03.2003	7	(8)	
Abubakar Ghali (NGA)	23.06.2000	23	(5)	4
Eduvie Ikoba (USA)	26.10.1997	12	(13)	5
Lukáš Letenay	19.04.2001	2	(4)	
Adam Tučný	21.05.2002	6	(10)	1

Mestský Futbalový klub Zemplín Michalovce

Founded: 1912 (*as NAC Michalovce*)
Stadium: Mestský futbalový štadión, Michalovce (4,440)
Trainer: Jozef Majoroš — 21.03.1978
[13.04.2021] Anton Šoltís — 05.02.1976

Goalkeepers:	DOB	M	(s)	G
Rostyslav Degtyar (UKR)	30.03.1999	2		
Tomáš Dráb	01.06.1999	5		
Matej Marković (CRO)	22.07.1996	25		
Defenders:	**DOB**	**M**	**(s)**	**G**
Martin Kolesár	10.12.1997	12	(2)	
Daniel Magda	25.11.1997	13	(1)	
Alejandro Méndez García (ESP)	28.07.2001	10	(4)	
Dimitrios Siopis (GRE)	06.09.1995	8	(3)	
Ían Pino Soler (ESP)	23.01.1996	28		1
Filip Vaško	11.08.1999	21		2
Matúš Vojtko	05.10.2000	22	(1)	
Artem Vovkun (UKR)	07.09.2001	6	(2)	
Midfielders:	**DOB**	**M**	**(s)**	**G**
Banjole Olawale Adekuoroye (NGA)	16.02.1996	7	(3)	
Martin Bednár	22.04.1999	17	(1)	1
Matúš Begala	07.04.2001	14	(6)	1
Vasilios Dotis (GRE)	08.02.2002		(4)	
Sergey Ivanov (RUS)	07.01.1997	9	(4)	

Lukas Lukco	27.07.2001	1	(1)	
Giorgos Neofytidis (GRE)	28.07.2000	19	(6)	
Takuto Oshima (JPN)	01.06.1998	12	(1)	2
Danilo Spoljarić (CYP)	14.07.1999	12	(2)	
Michal Toth	25.02.2003		(2)	
Igor Žofčák	10.04.1983	20	(7)	6
Forwards:	**DOB**	**M**	**(s)**	**G**
Cheick Alan Diarra (FRA)	23.06.1993	3	(5)	
Adam Gríger	16.03.2004		(5)	
Maksym Hirnyi (UKR)	06.04.2001		(5)	
Christos Kountouriotis (GRE)	02.01.1998	2	(4)	
Ricardo Antonio Phillips Hinds (PAN)	06.05.2001	18	(3)	2
Dimitrios Popovits (GRE)	11.02.1995	16	(12)	3
Kamil Rečičar	26.02.2002		(1)	
Modibo Issa Sidibé (NIG)	05.12.1985	3		
Abdulrahman Taiwo	05.08.1998	6	(2)	6
Ismar Tandir (BIH)	19.08.1995	13	(8)	3
Matej Trusa	29.11.2000	22	(7)	5
Sharani Zuberu (GHA)	07.01.2000	6	(5)	2

Football Club Viliam Ondrejka Zlaté Moravce

	Founded:	1995	
	Stadium:	Štadión FC ViOn, Zlaté Moravce (4,000)	
	Trainer:	Ľuboš Benkovský	22.02.1989

Goalkeepers:	DOB	M	(s)	G
Adrián Chovan	08.10.1995	31		
Žan Pelko (SVN)	28.09.1990	1		
Defenders:	**DOB**	**M**	**(s)**	**G**
Martin Chren	02.01.1984	17	(4)	
Peter Čögley	11.08.1988	31		1
Matúš Čonka	15.10.1990	18	(1)	1
David Haspra	06.11.2000	1	(8)	
Jozef Menich	15.09.1994	27		1
Matej Moško	26.02.1999	22	(2)	
Michal Pintér	04.02.1994	7	(2)	
Martin Tóth	13.10.1986	23		
Marko Vujić (SRB)	25.07.2000	1	(3)	

Midfielders:	DOB	M	(s)	G
Tomáš Ďubek	22.01.1987	24	(5)	4
Denis Duga	05.09.1994	24		2
Tomce Grozdanovski (MKD)	14.03.2000	21	(4)	
Alexandros Kyziridis (GRE)	16.09.2000	17	(10)	5
Adam Mihálik	24.07.2000	1	(5)	
Peter Orávik	18.12.1988	4	(12)	
Anton Sloboda	10.07.1987	8	(1)	
Marián Šmatlák	23.05.2003	3	(6)	
Forwards:	**DOB**	**M**	**(s)**	**G**
Filip Balaj	02.08.1997	26		14
Dávid Hrnčár	10.12.1997	30		6
Martin Kovaľ	10.02.1999	14	(9)	4
Marek Švec	31.12.2003	1	(2)	1
Vladimír Tkáč	09.01.1998		(6)	

Mestský Športový klub Žilina

	Founded:	20.06.1908 (as Zsolnai Testgyakorlók Köre)	
	Stadium:	Štadión pod Dubňom, Žilina (11,253)	
	Trainer:	Pavol Staňo	29.09.1977

Goalkeepers:	DOB	M	(s)	G
Samuel Petráš	10.04.1999	32		
Defenders:	**DOB**	**M**	**(s)**	**G**
Benson Anang (GHA)	01.05.2000	13	(2)	
Dominik Javorček	02.11.2002	11	(3)	1
Jakub Kiwior (POL)	15.02.2000	27	(1)	2
Adam Kopas	16.08.1999	16	(3)	
Patrik Leitner	07.02.2002		(1)	
Jan Minarik	25.07.1997	22	(1)	1
Tomáš Nemčík	19.04.2001	2	(1)	
Branislav Sluka	23.01.1999	19	(1)	
Samuel Šuľa	12.04.2000	1		
Kristián Vallo	02.06.1998	14		1
Midfielders:	**DOB**	**M**	**(s)**	**G**
Ján Bernát	10.01.2001	20	(10)	5
Vahan Bichakhchyan (ARM)	09.07.1999	14	(13)	9
Enis Fazlagić (MKD)	27.03.2000	20	(2)	1

	DOB	M	(s)	G
Martin Gamboš	23.01.1998	3	(2)	1
Miroslav Gono	01.11.2000	28	(3)	
Filip Mráz	19.05.2001		(1)	
Patrik Myslovič	28.05.2001	10	(12)	2
Jakub Paur	04.07.1992	10	(8)	4
Matúš Rusnák	14.07.1999	17	(15)	1
Mário Sauer	15.05.2004		(1)	
Tibor Slebodnik	21.09.2000	2	(7)	1
Vladimir Trabalik	02.11.2002		(1)	
Forwards:	**DOB**	**M**	**(s)**	**G**
Dávid Ďuriš	22.03.1999	25	(5)	8
Adam Goljan	15.04.2001		(5)	1
Patrik Iľko	16.02.2001	10	(6)	4
Timotej Jambor	04.04.2003		(4)	1
Taofiq Jibril (NGA)	23.04.1998	5	(9)	3
Adrián Kaprálik	10.06.2002	7	(22)	2
Dawid Kurminowski (POL)	24.02.1999	24	(8)	19

SECOND LEVEL
2. Liga 2020/2021

1.	MFK Tatran Liptovský Mikuláš (*Promoted*)	28	18	6	4	55	-	26	60
2.	MFK Dukla Banská Bystrica (*Promotion Play-offs*)	28	17	5	6	70	-	38	56
3.	MFK Skalica	28	16	7	5	55	-	32	55
4.	FK Železiarne Podbrezová	28	16	6	6	57	-	25	54
5.	FC Košice	28	15	4	9	40	-	27	49
6.	FC ŠTK 1914 Šamorín	28	12	5	11	41	-	34	41
7.	MŠK Púchov	28	11	5	12	40	-	45	38
8.	KFC Komárno	28	11	5	12	31	-	42	38
9.	FC Petržalka Bratislava	28	10	7	11	37	-	41	37
10.	FK Slavoj Trebišov	28	9	8	11	47	-	48	35
11.	FK Dubnica nad Váhom	28	8	9	11	28	-	37	33
12.	MŠK Žilina „B"	28	9	6	13	56	-	47	33
13.	ŠK Partizán Bardejov	28	6	10	12	27	-	41	28
14.	ŠK Slovan Bratislava "U21"	28	7	0	21	32	-	70	21
15.	FK Poprad* (*Relegated*)	28	3	1	24	25	-	88	4

*6 points deducted.

INTERNATIONAL MATCHES
(16.07.2020 – 15.07.2021)

04.09.2020	Bratislava	Slovakia - Czech Republic	1-3(0-0)	(UNL)
07.09.2020	Netanya	Israel - Slovakia	1-1(0-1)	(UNL)
08.10.2020	Bratislava	Slovakia - Republic of Ireland	0-0; 4-2 on penalties	(ECQPO)
11.10.2020	Glasgow	Scotland - Slovakia	1-0(1-0)	(UNL)
14.10.2020	Trnava	Slovakia - Israel	2-3(2-0)	(UNL)
12.11.2020	Belfast	Northern Ireland - Slovakia	1-2(0-1,1-1)	(ECQPO)
15.11.2020	Trnava	Slovakia - Scotland	1-0(1-0)	(UNL)
18.11.2020	Plzeň	Czech Republic - Slovakia	2-0(1-0)	(UNL)
24.03.2021	Nicosia	Cyprus- Slovakia	0-0	(WCQ)
27.03.2021	Trnava	Slovakia - Malta	2-2(0-2)	(WCQ)
30.03.2021	Trnava	Slovakia - Russia	2-1(1-0)	(WCQ)
01.06.2021	Ried im Innkreis	Slovakia - Bulgaria	1-1(1-1)	(F)
06.06.2021	Wien	Austria - Slovakia	0-0	(F)
14.06.2021	Saint Petersburg	Poland - Slovakia	1-2(0-1)	(EC)
18.06.2021	Saint Petersburg	Sweden - Slovakia	1-0(0-0)	(EC)
23.06.2021	Sevilla	Slovakia - Spain	0-5(0-2)	(EC)

04.09.2020   SLOVAKIA - CZECH REPUBLIC   1-3(0-0)   2nd UEFA Nations League B, Group 2
Štadión Tehelné pole, Bratislava; Referee: Andris Treimanis (Latvia); Attendance: 0
SVK: Dominik Greif, Peter Pekarík, Lukáš Štetina (32.Martin Valjent), Norbert Gyömbér, Milan Škriniar, Juraj Kucka (Cap), Stanislav Lobotka, Patrik Hrošovský, Ondrej Duda (17.Adam Zreľák), Lukáš Haraslín, Róbert Boženík (65.Ivan Schranz). Trainer: Pavel Hapal (Czech Republic).
Goal: Ivan Schranz (88).

07.09.2020   ISRAEL - SLOVAKIA   1-1(0-1)   2nd UEFA Nations League B, Group 2
Netanya Stadium, Netanya; Referee: Nikola Dabanović (Montenegro); Attendance: 0
SVK: Marek Rodák, Norbert Gyömbér, Milan Škriniar, Martin Valjent, Juraj Kucka (Cap), Erik Sabo (67.Ivan Schranz), Jaroslav Mihalík (87.Lukáš Haraslín), Stanislav Lobotka, Martin Koscelník, Matúš Bero, Michal Ďuriš (78.Róbert Boženík). Trainer: Pavel Hapal (Czech Republic).
Goal: Michal Ďuriš (14).

08.10.2020   SLOVAKIA - REPUBLIC OF IRELAND   0-0; 4-2 on penalties   16th EC. Qualifiers Play-offs, Semi-Finals
Štadión Tehelné pole, Bratislava; Referee: Clément Turpin (France); Attendance: 0
SVK: Marek Rodák, Peter Pekarík, Róbert Mazáň, Denis Vavro (112.Norbert Gyömbér), Martin Valjent, Marek Hamšík (Cap), Jaroslav Mihalík (73.Lukáš Haraslín), Albert Rusnák (86.Róbert Mak), Patrik Hrošovský, Juraj Kucka (86.Ján Greguš), Ondrej Duda (107.Róbert Boženík). Trainer: Pavel Hapal (Czech Republic).
Penalties: Marek Hamšík, Patrik Hrošovský, Lukáš Haraslín, Ján Greguš.

11.10.2020   SCOTLAND - SLOVAKIA   1-0(1-0)   2nd UEFA Nations League B, Group 2
Hampden Park, Glasgow; Referee: Davide Massa (Italy); Attendance: 93
SVK: Dušan Kuciak, Jakub Holúbek, Branislav Niňaj, Martin Valjent, Martin Koscelník, Ján Greguš, Marek Hamšík (Cap) (62.Juraj Kucka), Matúš Bero (22.Ondrej Duda), Ivan Schranz (62.Róbert Mak), Lukáš Haraslín (76.Albert Rusnák), Róbert Boženík 76.76.Pavol Šafranko). Trainer: Pavel Hapal (Czech Republic).

14.10.2020   SLOVAKIA - ISRAEL   2-3(2-0)   2nd UEFA Nations League B, Group 2
Štadión "Antona Malatinského", Trnava; Referee: Alejandro José Hernández Hernández (Spain); Attendance: 0
SVK: Dominik Greif, Peter Pekarík, Róbert Mazáň, Denis Vavro, Martin Valjent, Marek Hamšík (Cap), Róbert Mak (56.Lukáš Haraslín), Albert Rusnák, Patrik Hrošovský, Ondrej Duda (71.Ján Greguš), Róbert Boženík (71.Pavol Šafranko). Trainer: Pavel Hapal (Czech Republic).
Goals: Marek Hamšík (16), Róbert Mak (38).

12.11.2020   NORTHERN IRELAND - SLOVAKIA   1-2(0-1,1-1)   16th EC. Qualifiers Play-offs, Finals
Windsor Park, Belfast; Referee: Dr. Felix Brych (Germany); Attendance: 1,060
SVK: Marek Rodák, Tomáš Hubočan, Peter Pekarík, Ľubomír Šatka, Milan Škriniar, Marek Hamšík (Cap) (107.Ján Greguš), Juraj Kucka, Róbert Mak (65.Michal Ďuriš), Albert Rusnák (118.Norbert Gyömbér), Stanislav Lobotka (65.Patrik Hrošovský), Ondrej Duda (85.Samuel Mráz). Trainer: Štefan Tarkovič.
Goals: Juraj Kucka (17), Michal Ďuriš (110).

15.11.2020   SLOVAKIA - SCOTLAND   1-0(1-0)   2nd UEFA Nations League B, Group 2
Štadión "Antona Malatinského", Trnava; Referee: István Kovács (Romania); Attendance: 0
SVK: Marek Rodák, Peter Pekarík, Róbert Mazáň, Ľubomír Šatka, Milan Škriniar, Marek Hamšík (Cap) (68.Albert Rusnák), Juraj Kucka (61.Stanislav Lobotka), Ján Greguš, Patrik Hrošovský, Ondrej Duda, Michal Ďuriš (90+3.Pavol Šafranko). Trainer: Štefan Tarkovič.
Goal: Ján Greguš (31).

18.11.2020   CZECH REPUBLIC - SLOVAKIA   2-0(1-0)   2nd UEFA Nations League B, Group 2
Doosan Arena, Plzeň; Referee: Cüneyt Çakır (Turkey); Attendance: 0
SVK: Marek Rodák, Tomáš Hubočan, Peter Pekarík, Norbert Gyömbér, Milan Škriniar, Marek Hamšík (Cap), Juraj Kucka (67.Ján Greguš), Albert Rusnák (62.Tomáš Suslov), Stanislav Lobotka (62.Patrik Hrošovský), Róbert Mak (62.Pavol Šafranko), Michal Ďuriš (81.Ivan Schranz). Trainer: Štefan Tarkovič.

24.03.2021   CYPRUS- SLOVAKIA   0-0   22nd FIFA WC. Qualifiers
Stádio GSP, Nicosia; Referee: Aleksandar Stavrev (North Macedonia); Attendance: 0
SVK: Martin Dúbravka, Tomáš Hubočan, Peter Pekarík, Milan Škriniar, Dávid Hancko, Juraj Kucka (Cap), Albert Rusnák (60.Ján Greguš), Matúš Bero (78.Ivan Schranz), Ondrej Duda (84.Dávid Strelec), Róbert Boženík (60.Michal Ďuriš), Patrik Hrošovský. Trainer: Štefan Tarkovič.

27.03.2021 SLOVAKIA - MALTA   2-2(0-2)   22nd FIFA WC. Qualifiers
Štadión "Antona Malatinského", Trnava; Referee: Harald Lechner (Austria); Attendance: 0
SVK: Dušan Kuciak, Milan Škriniar, Martin Valjent, Martin Koscelník, Dávid Hancko (39.Jakub Holúbek), Juraj Kucka (Cap) (46.Dávid Strelec), Ján Greguš, Róbert Mak, Patrik Hrošovský (82.Ivan Schranz), Michal Ďuriš (46.Róbert Boženík), Tomáš Suslov (72.Albert Rusnák). Trainer: Štefan Tarkovič.
Goals: Dávid Strelec (49), Milan Škriniar (53).

30.03.2021 SLOVAKIA - RUSSIA   2-1(1-0)   22nd FIFA WC. Qualifiers
Štadión "Antona Malatinského", Trnava; Referee: Carlos del Cerro Grande (Spain); Attendance: 0
SVK: Dušan Kuciak, Tomáš Hubočan, Peter Pekarík (90+2.Lukáš Pauschek), Ľubomír Šatka, Milan Škriniar, Martin Koscelník, Juraj Kucka (Cap), Róbert Mak (76.Michal Ďuriš), Ondrej Duda, Jakub Hromada (61.Patrik Hrošovský), Ivan Schranz (90+2.Dávid Strelec). Trainer: Štefan Tarkovič.
Goals: Milan Škriniar (38), Róbert Mak (74).

01.06.2021 SLOVAKIA - BULGARIA   1-1(1-1)   Friendly International
Keine Sorgen Stadion, Ried im Innkreis (Austria); Referee: Walter Altmann (Austria); Attendance: 0
SVK: Dušan Kuciak (46.Marek Rodák), Peter Pekarík (Cap), Jakub Holúbek, Ľubomír Šatka, Denis Vavro, Vladimír Weiss (56.Erik Jirka), Matúš Bero (72.Patrik Hrošovský), Stanislav Lobotka (81.Michal Ďuriš), Lukáš Haraslín (56.Tomáš Suslov), Róbert Boženík (46.Dávid Strelec), László Bénes. Trainer: Štefan Tarkovič.
Goal: László Bénes (27).

06.06.2021 AUSTRIA - SLOVAKIA   0-0   Friendly International
"Ernst Happel Stadion", Wien; Referee: Urs Schnyder (Switzerland); Attendance: 3,000
SVK: Martin Dúbravka, Milan Škriniar, Ľubomír Šatka, Tomáš Hubočan, Peter Pekarík, Róbert Mak (63.Vladimír Weiss), Ondrej Duda (76.László Bénes), Juraj Kucka (Cap) (63.Patrik Hrošovský), Jakub Hromada (63.Ján Greguš), Ivan Schranz (7.Michal Ďuriš), Lukáš Haraslín (76.Martin Koscelník). Trainer: Štefan Tarkovič.

14.06.2021 POLAND - SLOVAKIA   1-2(0-1)   16th EC. Group Stage.
Krestovsky Stadium, Saint Petersburg (Russia); Referee: Ovidiu Alin Haţegan (Romania); Attendance: 12,862
SVK: Martin Dúbravka, Tomáš Hubočan, Peter Pekarík (79.Martin Koscelník), Ľubomír Šatka, Milan Škriniar, Marek Hamšík (Cap), Juraj Kucka, Róbert Mak (87.Tomáš Suslov), Ondrej Duda (90+2.Ján Greguš), Lukáš Haraslín (87.Michal Ďuriš), Jakub Hromada (79.Patrik Hrošovský). Trainer: Štefan Tarkovič.
Goals: Wojciech Tomasz Szczęsny (18 own goal), Michal Ďuriš (69).

18.06.2021 SWEDEN - SLOVAKIA   1-0(0-0)   16th EC. Group Stage.
Krestovsky Stadium, Saint Petersburg (Russia); Referee: Daniel Siebert (Germany): Attendance: 11,525
SVK: Martin Dúbravka, Tomáš Hubočan (84.Dávid Hancko), Peter Pekarík (65.Lukáš Haraslín), Ľubomír Šatka, Milan Škriniar, Martin Koscelník, Marek Hamšík (Cap) (77.László Bénes), Juraj Kucka, Róbert Mak (77.Vladimír Weiss), Ondrej Duda, Patrik Hrošovský (84.Michal Ďuriš). Trainer: Štefan Tarkovič.

23.06.2021 SLOVAKIA - SPAIN   0-5(0-2)   16th EC. Group Stage.
Estadio La Cartuja, Sevilla; Referee: Björn Kuipers (Netherlands); Attendance: 11,204
SVK: Martin Dúbravka, Tomáš Hubočan, Peter Pekarík, Ľubomír Šatka, Milan Škriniar, Juraj Kucka, Marek Hamšík (Cap) (90.László Bénes), Róbert Mak (69.Vladimír Weiss), Ondrej Duda (46.Michal Ďuriš), Jakub Hromada (46.Stanislav Lobotka), Lukáš Haraslín (69.Tomáš Suslov). Trainer: Štefan Tarkovič.

NATIONAL TEAM PLAYERS (16.07.2020 – 15.07.2021)					
Name	**DOB**	**Caps**	**Goals**	**2020/2021:**	*Club*
Goalkeepers					
Martin DÚBRAVKA	15.01.1989	28	0	2021:	*Newcastle United FC (ENG)*
Dominik GREIF	06.04.1997	4	0	2020:	*ŠK Slovan Bratislava*
Dušan KUCIAK	21.05.1985	14	0	2020/2021:	*KS Lechia Gdańsk (POL)*
Marek RODÁK	13.12.1996	7	0	2020/2021:	*Fulham FC London (ENG)*
Defenders					
Norbert GYÖMBÉR	03.07.1992	28	0	2020: 12.09.2020->	*AC Perugia Calcio (ITA) US Salernitana 1919 (ITA)*
Dávid HANCKO	13.12.1997	15	1	2021:	*AC Sparta Praha (CZE)*
Jakub HOLÚBEK	12.01.1991	6	0	2020/2021:	*GKS Piast Gliwice (POL)*
Tomáš HUBOČAN	17.09.1985	73	0	2020/2021:	*AC Omonia Nicosia (CYP)*
Martin KOSCELNÍK	02.03.1995	7	0	2020/2021:	*FC Slovan Liberec (CZE)*
Róbert MAZÁŇ	09.02.1994	11	0	2020:	*FK Mladá Boleslav (CZE)*
Branislav NIŇAJ	17.05.1994	3	0	2020:	*Fortuna Sittard (NED)*
Lukáš PAUSCHEK	09.12.1992	6	0	2021:	*ŠK Slovan Bratislava*
Peter PEKARÍK	30.10.1986	104	2	2020/2021:	*Hertha BSC Berlin (GER)*
Ľubomír ŠATKA	02.12.1995	17	0	2020/2021:	*KKS Lech Poznań (POL)*
Milan ŠKRINIAR	11.02.1995	43	3	2020/2021:	*FC Internazionale Milano (ITA)*
Lukáš ŠTETINA	28.07.1991	4	1	2020:	*AC Sparta Praha (CZE)*
Martin VALJENT	11.12.1995	9	0	2020/2021:	*RCD Mallorca (ESP)*
Denis VAVRO	10.04.1996	10	0	2020: 01.02.2021->	*SS Lazio Roma (ITA) SD Huesca (ESP)*

		Midfielders			
Matúš BERO	06.09.1995	15	0	2020/2021:	SBV Vitesse Arnhem (NED)
László BÉNES	09.09.1997	7	1	2020/2021:	FC Augsburg (GER)
Ondrej DUDA	05.12.1994	48	5	2020:	Hertha BSC Berlin (GER)
				16.09.2020->	1.FC Köln (GER)
Ján GREGUŠ	29.01.1991	36	4	2020/2021:	Minnesota United FC (USA)
Marek HAMŠÍK	27.07.1987	129	26	2020:	Dalian Yifamg / Dalian Professional FC(CHN)
				08.03.2021->	IFK Göteborg (SWE)
Lukáš HARASLÍN	26.05.1996	18	1	2020/2021:	US Sassuolo Calcio (ITA)
Jakub HROMADA	25.05.1996	4	0	2021:	SK Slavia Praha (CZE)
Patrik HROŠOVSKÝ	22.04.1992	38	0	2020/2021:	KRC Genk (BEL)
Erik JIRKA	19.09.1997	1	0	2021:	CD Mirandés (ESP)
Juraj KUCKA	26.02.1987	86	10	2020/2021:	Parma Calcio 1913 (ITA)
Stanislav LOBOTKA	25.11.1994	29	3	2020/2021:	SSC Napoli (ITA)
Jaroslav MIHALÍK	27.07.1994	8	1	2020:	KS Lechia Gdańsk (POL)
Albert RUSNÁK	07.07.1994	32	5	2020/2021:	Real Salt Lake (USA)
Erik SABO	22.11.1991	18	0	2020:	Fatih Karagümrük SK (TUR)
Tomáš SUSLOV	07.06.2002	5	0	2020/2021:	FC Groningen (NED)
Vladimír WEISS	30.11.1989	71	7	2021:	ŠK Slovan Bratislava

		Forwards			
Róbert BOŽENÍK	18.11.1999	16	4	2020/2021:	Feyenoord Rotterdam (NED)
Michal ĎURIŠ	01.06.1988	59	7	2020/2021:	AC Omonia Nicosia (CYP)
Róbert MAK	08.03.1991	69	14	2020/2021:	Ferencvárosi TC (HUN)
Samuel MRÁZ	13.05.1997	4	1	2020:	Zagłębie Lubin (POL)
Ivan SCHRANZ	13.09.1993	8	1	2020/2021:	FK Jablonec (CZE)
Dávid STRELEC	04.04.2001	4	1	2021:	ŠK Slovan Bratislava
Pavol ŠAFRANKO	16.11.1994	8	0	2020:	ACS Sepsi OSK Sfântu Gheorghe (ROU)
Adam ZREĽÁK	05.05.1994	5	2	2020:	1.FC Nürnberg (GER)

		National team coach	
Pavel HAPAL (Czech Republic) [22.10.2018 – 16.10.2020]	27.07.1969	17 M; 6 W; 4 D; 7 L; 27-23	
Štefan TARKOVIČ [from 20.10.2020]	18.02.1973	11 M; 4 W; 4 D; 3 L; 10-14	
		Complete record as trainer of Slovakia:	
		12 M; 4 W; 5 D; 3 L; 9-13	
		(16.10.2018) & (from 20.10.2020)	

SLOVENIA

The Country:
Republika Slovenija (Republic of Slovenia)
Capital: Ljubljana
Surface: 20,273 km²
Inhabitants: 2,095,861 [2020]
Time: UTC+1

The FA:
Nogometna zveza Slovenije
Predoslje 40 a, p.p. 130, 4000 Kranj
Tel: +386 4 27 59 400
Founded: 23.04.1920
Member of FIFA since: 1992
Member of UEFA since: 1992
Website: www.nzs.si

NATIONAL TEAM RECORDS

RECORDS		
First international match:	03.06.1992, Tallinn:	Estonia – Slovenia 1-1
Most international caps:	Boštjan Cesar	- 101 caps (2003-2018)
Most international goals:	Zlatko Zahovič	- 35 goals / 80 caps (1992-2004)

UEFA EUROPEAN CHAMPIONSHIP	
1960	-
1964	-
1968	-
1972	-
1976	-
1980	-
1984	-
1988	-
1992	-
1996	Qualifiers
2000	Final Tournament (Group Stage)
2004	Qualifiers
2008	Qualifiers
2012	Qualifiers
2016	Qualifiers
2020	Qualifiers

FIFA WORLD CUP	
1930	-
1934	-
1938	-
1950	-
1954	-
1958	-
1962	-
1966	-
1970	-
1974	-
1978	-
1982	-
1986	-
1990	-
1994	Did not enter
1998	Qualifiers
2002	Final Tournament (Group Stage)
2006	Qualifiers
2010	Final Tournament (Group Stage)
2014	Qualifiers
2018	Qualifiers

OLYMPIC TOURNAMENTS	
1908	-
1912	-
1920	-
1924	-
1928	-
1936	-
1948	-
1952	-
1956	-
1960	-
1964	-
1968	-
1972	-
1976	-
1980	-
1984	-
1988	-
1992	-
1996	Qualifiers
2000	Qualifiers
2004	Qualifiers
2008	Qualifiers
2012	Qualifiers
2016	Qualifiers

Please note: was part of Yugoslavia between 1930-1990.

UEFA NATIONS LEAGUE

2018/2019	League C
2020/2021	League C (promoted to League B)

FIFA CONFEDERATIONS CUP 1992-2017

None

SLOVENIAN CLUB HONOURS IN EUROPEAN CLUB COMPETITIONS:

European Champion Clubs.Cup (1956-1992) / UEFA Champions League (1993-2021)
None

Fairs Cup (1858-1971) / UEFA Cup (1972-2009) / UEFA Europa League (2010-2021)
None

UEFA Super Cup (1972-2020)
None

European Cup Winners.Cup 1961-1999*
None

*defunct competition

	CHAMPIONS	CUP WINNERS	BEST GOALSCORERS	
1991/1992	NK Olimpija Ljubljana	NK Maribor	Zoran Ubavič (NK Olimpija Ljubljana)	29
1992/1993	NK Olimpija Ljubljana	NK Olimpija Ljubljana	Sašo Udovič (ND Slovan Ljubljana)	25
1993/1994	NK Olimpija Ljubljana	NK Maribor	Štefan Škaper (NK Beltinci)	23
1994/1995	NK Olimpija Ljubljana	NK Mura Murska Sobota	Štefan Škaper (NK Beltinci)	25
1995/1996	ND Gorica	NK Olimpija Ljubljana	Ermin Šiljak (NK Olimpija Ljubljana)	28
1996/1997	NK Maribor	NK Maribor	Faik Kamberović (BIH, NK Celje)	21
1997/1998	NK Maribor	NK Rudar Velenje	Ismet Ekmečić (NK Olimpija Ljubljana)	21
1998/1999	NK Maribor	NK Maribor	Novica Nikčević (SRB, ND Gorica)	17
1999/2000	NK Maribor	NK Olimpija Ljubljana	Kliton Bozgo (ALB, NK Maribor)	24
2000/2001	NK Maribor	ND Gorica	Damir Pekič (NK Celje)	23
2001/2002	NK Maribor	ND Gorica	Romano Obilinović (CRO, NK Primorje Ajdovščina)	16
2002/2003	NK Maribor	NK Olimpija Ljubljana	Marko Kmetec (NK Ljubljana / NK Olimpija Ljubljana)	21
2003/2004	ND Gorica	NK Maribor	Dražen Žeželj (NK Ljubljana / NK Primorje Ajdovščina)	19
2004/2005	ND Gorica	NK Celje	Kliton Bozgo (ALB, NK Maribor)	18
2005/2006	ND Gorica	FC Koper	Miran Burgič (ND Gorica)	24
2006/2007	NK Domžale	FC Koper	Nikola Nikezić (MNE, NK Domžale / ND Gorica)	22
2007/2008	NK Domžale	NK Interblock Ljubljana	Dario Zahora (CRO, NK Domžale)	22
2008/2009	NK Maribor	NK Interblock Ljubljana	Etien Velikonja (ND Gorica)	17
2009/2010	FC Koper	NK Maribor	Milan Osterc (FC Koper)	23
2010/2011	NK Maribor	NK Domžale	Marcos Magno Morales Tavares (BRA, NK Maribor)	16
2011/2012	NK Maribor	NK Maribor	Dare Vršič (NK Olimpija Ljubljana)	22
2012/2013	NK Maribor	NK Maribor	Marcos Magno Morales Tavares (BRA, NK Maribor)	17
2013/2014	NK Maribor	ND Gorica	Mate Eterović (CRO, NK Rudar Velenje)	19
2014/2015	NK Maribor	FC Koper	Marcos Magno Morales Tavares (BRA, NK Maribor)	17
2015/2016	NK Olimpija Ljubljana	NK Maribor	Rok Kronaveter (NK Olimpija Ljubljana) Jean-Philippe Mendy (FRA, NK Maribor) Andraž Šporar (NK Olimpija Ljubljana)	17
2016/2017	NK Maribor	NK Domžale	John Mary Honi Uzuegbunam (CMR, NK Rudar Velenje)	17
2017/2018	NK Olimpija Ljubljana	NK Olimpija Ljubljana	Luka Zahović (NK Maribor)	18
2018/2019	NK Maribor	NK Olimpija Ljubljana	Luka Zahović (NK Maribor)	18
2019/2020	NK Celje	NŠ Mura Murska Sobota	Ante Vukušic (CRO, NK Olimpija Ljubljana)	26
2020/2021	NŠ Mura Murska Sobota	NK Olimpija Ljubljana	Jan Mlakar (NK Maribor) Nardin Mulahusejnović (BIH, FC Koper)	14

NATIONAL CHAMPIONSHIP
Prva liga Slovenije 2020/2021
(22.08.2020 – 22.05.2021)

Results

Round 1 [22-23.08.2020]
NK Tabor - FC Koper 1-0(1-0)
NK Domžale - NK Bravo 1-2(1-1)
NK Celje - NŠ Mura 0-2(0-1)
NK Maribor - NK Aluminij 3-0 *awarded*
Olimpija Ljublj. - ND Gorica 1-0(1-0) [30.09.]

Round 2 [29-30.08.2020]
NK Bravo - ND Gorica 4-1(1-0)
NK Aluminij - NK Celje 0-0
NŠ Mura - NK Tabor 3-0(1-0)
FC Koper - Olimpija Ljubljana 1-1(1-1)
NK Domžale - NK Maribor 1-1(0-1)

Round 3 [12-13.09.2020]
NK Maribor - NK Bravo 4-1(3-0)
NK Celje - NK Domžale 1-2(0-2)
NK Tabor - NK Aluminij 3-1(1-0)
ND Gorica - FC Koper 2-4(1-1)
Olimpija Ljubljana - NŠ Mura 0-0

Round 4 [19-20.09.2020]
NK Bravo - FC Koper 0-0
NK Maribor - NK Celje 2-2(0-1)
NK Domžale - NK Tabor 3-1(1-1)
NK Aluminij - Olimpija Ljubljana 1-0(0-0)
NŠ Mura - ND Gorica 1-0(0-0)

Round 5 [26-27.09.2020]
NK Tabor - NK Maribor 3-1(1-0)
ND Gorica - NK Aluminij 2-0(1-0)
NK Celje - NK Bravo 2-0(1-0)
FC Koper - NŠ Mura 1-3(0-2)
Olimpija Ljubljana - NK Domžale 3-2(3-1)

Round 6 [03-04.10.2020]
NK Domžale - ND Gorica 1-1(0-0)
NK Bravo - NŠ Mura 2-1(1-1)
NK Celje - NK Tabor 2-1(1-1)
NK Maribor - Olimpija Ljubljana 1-1(1-0)
NK Aluminij - FC Koper 1-1(0-1) [13.10.]

Round 7 [17-18.10.2020]
FC Koper - NK Domžale 2-0(1-0)
ND Gorica - NK Maribor 0-4(0-1)
NK Tabor - NK Bravo 2-0(1-0)
Olimpija Ljubljana - NK Celje 1-0(0-0)
NŠ Mura - NK Aluminij 1-2(1-2)

Round 8 [24-25.10.2020]
NK Celje - ND Gorica 1-1(0-1)
NK Maribor - FC Koper 1-1(1-1)
NK Bravo - NK Aluminij 1-1(1-0)
NK Tabor - Olimpija Ljubljana 2-1(1-1)
NK Domžale - NŠ Mura 1-1(0-0)

Round 9 [28-29.10.2020]
ND Gorica - NK Tabor 2-1(2-0)
FC Koper - NK Celje 3-0(2-0)
Olimpija Ljubljana - NK Bravo 2-0(0-0)
NŠ Mura - NK Maribor 2-0(1-0)
NK Aluminij - NK Domžale 1-2(1-0) [14.11.]

Round 10 [02-03.11.2020]
NŠ Mura - NK Celje 0-0
NK Aluminij - NK Maribor 1-3(0-2)
FC Koper - NK Tabor 2-1(1-0)
ND Gorica - Olimpija Ljubljana 0-2(0-1)
NK Bravo - NK Domžale 1-0(1-0) [09.12.]

Round 11 [06-07.11.2020]
NK Celje - NK Aluminij 4-0(1-0)
NK Tabor - NŠ Mura 0-0
Olimpija Ljubljana - FC Koper 1-2(0-0)
NK Maribor - NK Domžale 4-3(0-1)
ND Gorica - NK Bravo 0-0

Round 12 [21-22.11.2020]
NK Bravo - NK Maribor 1-2(1-2)
NŠ Mura - Olimpija Ljubljana 0-1(0-1)
FC Koper - ND Gorica 1-1(0-1)
NK Aluminij - NK Tabor 0-0
NK Domžale - NK Celje 0-1(0-0)

Round 13 [24-26.11.2020]
FC Koper - NK Bravo 2-1(1-0)
ND Gorica - NŠ Mura 0-1(0-1)
NK Tabor - NK Domžale 1-1(1-1)
NK Celje - NK Maribor 0-2(0-1)
Olimpija Ljubljana - NK Aluminij 3-0(2-0)

Round 14 [28-29.11.2020]
NŠ Mura - FC Koper 2-1(0-0)
NK Maribor - NK Tabor 1-0(0-0)
NK Bravo - NK Celje 2-1(1-1)
NK Aluminij - ND Gorica 2-1(1-1)
NK Domžale - Olimpija Ljubljana 3-1(2-0)

Round 15 [02-03.12.2020]
ND Gorica - NK Domžale 0-2(0-0)
NŠ Mura - NK Bravo 0-0
FC Koper - NK Aluminij 1-0(1-0)
Olimpija Ljubljana - NK Maribor 2-0(1-0)
NK Tabor - NK Celje 1-0(0-0) [09.12.]

Round 16 [05-06.12.2020]
NK Domžale - FC Koper 1-1(1-0)
NK Aluminij - NŠ Mura 1-2(1-0)
NK Celje - Olimpija Ljubljana 1-1(0-1)
NK Maribor - ND Gorica 3-1(1-1)
NK Bravo - NK Tabor 3-1(0-0) [06.02.2021]

Round 17 [12-13.12.2020]
ND Gorica - NK Celje 0-2(0-1)
NK Aluminij - NK Bravo 1-1(0-0)
Olimpija Ljubljana - NK Tabor 2-1(1-0)
FC Koper - NK Maribor 1-2(0-1)
NŠ Mura - NK Domžale 1-1(1-0)

Round 18 [15-17.12.2020]
NK Bravo - Olimpija Ljubljana 0-0
NK Tabor - ND Gorica 1-0(0-0)
NK Celje - FC Koper 2-0(0-0)
NK Domžale - NK Aluminij 2-1(1-1)
NK Maribor - NŠ Mura 2-1(0-0)

Round 19 [19-20.12.2020]
NK Tabor - FC Koper 3-4(1-4)
Olimpija Ljubljana - ND Gorica 2-0(0-0)
NK Domžale - NK Bravo 0-0
NK Celje - NŠ Mura 1-3(0-1)
NK Maribor - NK Aluminij 2-2(2-2)

Round 20 [10-11.02.2021]
NK Bravo - ND Gorica 0-0
NK Domžale - NK Maribor 3-3(3-1)
FC Koper - Olimpija Ljubljana 1-2(0-1)
NŠ Mura - NK Tabor 0-0
NK Aluminij - NK Celje 1-0(0-0) [17.02.]

Round 21 [13-14.02.2021]
ND Gorica - FC Koper 2-1(1-0)
NK Maribor - NK Bravo 1-1(0-1)
NK Tabor - NK Aluminij 1-1(0-1)
NK Celje - NK Domžale 0-2(0-1)
Olimpija Ljubljana - NŠ Mura 2-0(0-0)

Round 22 [20-21.02.2021]
NK Bravo - FC Koper 3-0(1-0)
NK Maribor - NK Celje 0-1(0-0)
NŠ Mura - ND Gorica 3-1(1-1)
NK Domžale - NK Tabor 2-1(0-1)
NK Aluminij - Olimpija Ljubljana 0-0

Round 23 [24-25.02.2021]
NK Tabor - NK Maribor 0-4(0-1)
Olimpija Ljubljana - NK Domžale 0-0
NK Celje - NK Bravo 2-3(0-1)
ND Gorica - NK Aluminij 0-0
FC Koper - NŠ Mura 1-0(1-0)

Round 24 [27.02.-01.03.2021]
NK Celje - NK Tabor 0-3(0-1)
NK Maribor - Olimpija Ljubljana 1-1(1-1)
NK Bravo - NŠ Mura 0-1(0-0)
NK Domžale - ND Gorica 1-0(0-0)
NK Aluminij - FC Koper 0-1(0-1)

Round 25 [06-07.03.2021]
NŠ Mura - NK Aluminij 2-0(1-0)
ND Gorica - NK Maribor 1-1(1-1)
FC Koper - NK Domžale 0-2(0-2)
NK Tabor - NK Bravo 0-0
Olimpija Ljubljana - NK Celje 1-0(1-0)

Round 26 [10-11.03.2021]
NK Bravo - NK Aluminij 0-1(0-1)
NK Domžale - NŠ Mura 1-1(0-1)
NK Tabor - Olimpija Ljubljana 0-3(0-1)
NK Celje - ND Gorica 0-1(0-1)
NK Maribor - FC Koper 4-2(1-1)

Round 27 [13-15.03.2021]
NK Aluminij - NK Domžale 1-0(1-0)
NŠ Mura - NK Maribor 0-0
FC Koper - NK Celje 1-1(1-0)
ND Gorica - NK Tabor 0-3(0-0)
Olimpija Ljublj. - NK Bravo 1-1(1-1) [13.04.]

Round 28 [16-17.04.2021]
NK Aluminij - NK Maribor 0-0
NŠ Mura - NK Celje 0-0
NK Bravo - NK Domžale 2-2(1-0)
ND Gorica - Olimpija Ljubljana 0-1(0-0)
FC Koper - NK Tabor 1-0(0-0)

Round 29 [20-21.04.2021]
NK Celje - NK Aluminij 0-1(0-0)
NK Maribor - NK Domžale 1-3(0-3)
NK Tabor - NŠ Mura 3-1(1-1)
Olimpija Ljubljana - FC Koper 6-2(3-1)
ND Gorica - NK Bravo 3-2(1-1)

Round 30 [24-25.04.2021]
NK Bravo - NK Maribor 0-1(0-0)
NK Domžale - NK Celje 3-1(1-1)
FC Koper - ND Gorica 0-0
NK Aluminij - NK Tabor 0-2(0-2)
NŠ Mura - Olimpija Ljubljana 3-0(0-0)

Round 31 [30.04.-02.05.2021]
ND Gorica - NŠ Mura 1-5(1-2)
NK Tabor - NK Domžale 0-0
NK Celje - NK Maribor 2-1(1-0)
FC Koper - NK Bravo 0-0
Olimpija Ljubljana - NK Aluminij 2-2(0-1)

Round 32 [04-06.05.2021]
NK Bravo - NK Celje 2-0(0-0)
NK Maribor - NK Tabor 2-1(0-1)
NŠ Mura - FC Koper 2-1(0-0)
NK Domžale - Olimpija Ljubljana 2-0(2-0)
NK Aluminij - ND Gorica 2-0(2-0)

Round 33 [08-09.05.2021]
NK Tabor - NK Celje 0-1(0-1)
NŠ Mura - NK Bravo 2-2(2-0)
ND Gorica - NK Domžale 2-1(2-0)
Olimpija Ljubljana - NK Maribor 0-0
FC Koper - NK Aluminij 0-3(0-2)

Round 34 [15-16.05.2021]
NK Bravo - NK Tabor 1-1(1-1)
NK Maribor - ND Gorica 3-0(2-0)
NK Aluminij - NŠ Mura 0-0
NK Celje - Olimpija Ljubljana 4-0(2-0)
NK Domžale - FC Koper 3-1(1-0)

Round 35 [18-19.05.2021]
NK Aluminij - NK Bravo 3-0(2-0)
NŠ Mura - NK Domžale 3-0(1-0)
FC Koper - NK Maribor 0-3(0-1)
ND Gorica - NK Celje 0-2(0-1)
Olimpija Ljubljana - NK Tabor 1-2(1-0)

Round 36 [22.05.2021]
NK Bravo - Olimpija Ljubljana 3-0(0-0)
NK Celje - FC Koper 2-1(1-1)
NK Domžale - NK Aluminij 1-1(0-0)
NK Tabor - ND Gorica 0-1(0-0)
NK Maribor - NŠ Mura 1-3(1-1)

Final Standings

									Total						Home						Away		
1.	**NŠ Mura Murska Sobota**	36	17	12	7	50	-	26	63	9	7	2	25	-	9	8	5	5	25	-	17
2.	NK Maribor	36	17	12	7	64	-	41	63	9	6	3	36	-	24	8	6	4	28	-	17
3.	NK Olimpija Ljubljana	36	16	11	9	45	-	35	59	11	5	2	30	-	12	5	6	7	15	-	23
4.	NK Domžale	36	14	13	9	52	-	41	55	8	8	2	29	-	18	6	5	7	23	-	23
5.	NK Bravo Ljubljana	36	10	15	11	39	-	39	45	8	6	4	25	-	13	2	9	7	14	-	26
6.	NK Tabor Sežana	36	12	8	16	40	-	44	44	8	5	5	21	-	19	4	3	11	19	-	25
7.	NK Aluminij Kidričevo	36	12	7	17	36	-	41	43	7	2	9	24	-	24	5	5	8	12	-	17
8.	NK Celje	36	10	13	13	31	-	41	43	6	7	5	15	-	13	4	6	8	16	-	28
9.	FC Koper (*Relegation Play-offs*)	36	11	9	16	41	-	56	42	7	5	6	18	-	20	4	4	10	23	-	36
10.	ND Gorica (*Relegated*)	36	7	8	21	24	-	58	29	5	3	10	15	-	32	2	5	11	9	-	26

Top goalscorers:

14	**Jan Mlakar**	*NK Maribor*
14	**Nardin Mulahusejnović (BIH)**	*FC Koper*
12	Dario Kolobarić	*NK Domžale*
11	Luka Bobičanec (CRO)	*NŠ Mura Murska Sobota*
11	Đorđe Ivanović (SRB)	*NK Olimpija Ljubljana*
11	Andrés Vombergar	*NK Olimpija Ljubljana*

NK Krka Novo Mesto - FC Koper   0-2(0-0)   3-2(2-0)

FC Koper remains at first level for 2021/2022.

NATIONAL CUP
Pokal Nogometne zveze Slovenije 2020/2021

First Round [02/16/23.09.2020]

NK Bohinj - FC Koper	0-10	NK Virs Bistrica - NK Tabor Sežana	1-2
NK Adria Miren - NK Aluminij Kidričevo	0-2	NK Fužinar Ravne na Koroškem - NK Brda Dobrovo	3-1
ŠD Šenčur - NK Nafta Lendava 1903	0-7	NK Odranci - NK Triglav Kranj	0-1 aet
NK Čarda Martjanci - NK Rudar Velenje	1-5	NK Brežice 1919 - NK Jadran Dekani	4-0
NK Mons Claudius Rogatec - NK Radomlje	0-8	ND Ilirija 1911 Ljubljana - NK Domžale	0-6
NK Koroška Dravograd - NK Drava Ptuj	0-6	ND Beltinci - NK Bravo Ljubljana	2-0

1/8-Finals [20-22.10.2020/17-18.03.2021]

NK Rudar Velenje - NK Maribor	0-3	NK Drava Ptuj - NŠ Mura Murska Sobota	2-0
NK Radomlje - NK Tabor Sežana	3-2	NK Nafta Lendava 1903 - NK Fužinar R. Koroškem	3-2
NK Brežice 1919 - NK Olimpija Ljubljana	3-3 aet; 0-2 pen	ND Beltinci - NK Domžale	0-3
FC Koper - NK Aluminij Kidričevo	3-1 aet	NK Triglav Kranj - NK Celje	1-2

Quarter-Finals [27-28.04.2021]

NK Celje - NK Radomlje	2-0(0-0)	NK Drava Ptuj - FC Koper	0-2(0-1)
NK Domžale - NK Maribor	2-1(2-0)	NK Nafta Lendava 1903 - NK Olimpija Ljubljana	0-1(0-0,0-0)

Semi-Finals [12-13.05.2021]

NK Domžale - NK Olimpija Ljubljana	0-1(0-0)	NK Celje - FC Koper	1-0(1-0)

Final

25.05.2021; Stadion Bonifika, Koper; Referee: Dragoslav Perić; Attendance: 1,201

NK Celje - NK Olimpija Ljubljana   **1-2(0-1)**

Celje: Matjaž Rozman, Dušan Stojinović, Žan Zaletel, Advan Kadušić, Jon Šporn (74.Jakob Novak), Matic Vrbanec, Žan Benedičič, Ester Sokler (56.Filip Dangubić), Luka Kerin (80.Stjepan Vego), Mićo Kuzmanović (80.Jure Matjašič), Ivan Božić. Trainer: Agron Šalja.

Olimpija Ljubljana: Nejc Vidmar, Vitālijs Maksimenko (89.Michael Pavlović), Eric Boakye, Antonio Delamea Mlinar, Uroš Korun, Timi Elšnik, Nik Kapun (78.Nino Pungaršek), Enrik Ostrc, Andrés Vombergar, Radivoj Bosić (84.Gal Kurež), Đorđe Ivanović (89.Mihailo Perović). Trainer: Goran Stanković.

Goals: 0-1 Đorđe Ivanović (32), 1-1 Ivan Božić (46), 1-2 Nik Kapun (53).

THE CLUBS 2020/2021

Please note: NK Aluminij Kidričevo forfeited the match against NK Maribor (Round 1). Both played 35 matches.

Nogometni klub Aluminij Kidričevo

Founded:	1946	
Stadium:	Aluminij Sports Park, Kidričevo (532)	
Trainer:	Slobodan Grubor (AUT)	09.09.1968
[07.12.2020]	Oskar Drobne	06.02.1975

Goalkeepers:	DOB	M	(s)	G
Luka Janžeković	14.03.1997	35		
Defenders:	**DOB**	**M**	**(s)**	**G**
Emir Azemović (MNE)	06.01.1997	33		1
Aljaž Džankić (CRO)	19.03.2002	1	(1)	
Nemanja Jakšić (SRB)	11.07.1995	26	(5)	3
Alen Krajnc	01.07.1995	10	(11)	3
Aljaž Krefl	20.02.1994	14	(7)	2
Renato Pantalon (CRO)	27.10.1997	15	(8)	
Gašper Pečnik	18.05.2003	11	(6)	1
Luka Petek	13.10.1997	24		2
Aljaž Ploj	30.08.1998	19	(4)	
Midfielders:	**DOB**	**M**	**(s)**	**G**
Klemen Bolha	19.03.1993	13	(3)	
Marcel Čermák (CZE)	25.11.1998	25	(7)	
Armin Đerlek (SRB)	15.07.2000	10	(1)	1
Lovro Grajfoner	25.01.2000	10	(4)	

Lucas Mario Horvat	13.10.1985	14		1
Kim Do-hyun (KOR)	09.04.1994	12	(9)	
Jan Majcen	25.07.2002		(2)	
Nik Marinšek	16.02.1999	6	(7)	
Roko Prša (CRO)	16.02.1996	19	(6)	3
Juš Štusej	20.04.2000	1	(4)	
Forwards:	**DOB**	**M**	**(s)**	**G**
David Flakus Bosilj	01.02.2002	28	(5)	5
Filip Jauk	25.07.2000	2	(6)	
Haris Kadrić	16.03.2000	11	(1)	2
Mihael Klepač (CRO)	19.09.1997	8	(5)	
Filip Kukuličić (MNE)	13.02.1996		(4)	1
Marko Maletić (BIH)	25.10.1993	1	(13)	
Jure Matjašič	31.05.1992	12	(6)	2
Tonći Mujan (CRO)	19.07.1995	7	(4)	2
Tilen Pečnik	16.05.1998	18	(11)	2

Nogometni klub Bravo Ljubljana

Founded: 2006
Stadium: Ljubljana Sports Park, Ljubljana (2,308)
Trainer: Dejan Grabić   21.09.1980

Goalkeepers:	DOB	M	(s)	G
Matija Orbanić (CRO)	29.05.2000	2		
Igor Vekič	06.05.1998	34		
Defenders:	**DOB**	**M**	**(s)**	**G**
David Brekalo	03.12.1998	29	(2)	3
Vanja Drkušič	30.10.1999	35		1
Marko Klemenčič	09.03.1997	3	(2)	
Almin Kurtović	16.03.2000	24	(5)	
Matevž Matko	09.10.2001	4	(4)	
Mark Španring	13.06.2001	26	(2)	
Žan Trontelj	21.01.2000	21	(2)	1
Midfielders:	**DOB**	**M**	**(s)**	**G**
Ovbokha Agboyi (NGA)	14.12.1994	13	(2)	
Miha Kancilija	04.04.2001	8	(15)	2
Kim Chan-woo (KOR)	11.06.1999	1	(2)	

	DOB	M	(s)	G
Andraž Kirm	06.09.1984	11	(9)	
Martin Kramarič	14.11.1997	26	(2)	3
Rok Maher	20.07.2001	12	(10)	1
Sandi Ogrinec	05.06.1998	25	(4)	1
Gal Puconja	21.04.2004		(1)	
Luka Žinko	23.03.1983	32	(1)	2
Forwards:	**DOB**	**M**	**(s)**	**G**
Rok Kidrič	27.04.1995	10	(9)	2
Mitja Križan	05.06.1997	10	(4)	1
Loren Maružin (CRO)	04.12.1997	8	(6)	2
Ibrahim Mensah (GHA)	11.01.1995		(3)	
Mustafa Nukić	03.12.1990	30		7
Michele Šego (CRO)	05.08.2000	10	(3)	1
Milan Tučić	15.08.1996	17	(1)	10
Nino Žugelj	23.05.2000	5	(13)	

Nogometni klub Celje

Founded: 28.12.1919 (*as SK Celje*)
Stadium: Stadion Z'dežele, Celje (13,059)
Trainer: Dušan Kosič   23.04.1971
[25.12.2020] Jiří Jarošík (CZE)   27.10.1977
[26.04.2021] Agron Šalja   20.08.1972

Goalkeepers:	DOB	M	(s)	G
Metod Jurhar	07.12.1997	5		
Matjaž Rozman	03.01.1987	31		
Defenders:	**DOB**	**M**	**(s)**	**G**
Amadej Brecl	06.04.1997	27	(2)	
Josip Čalušić (CRO)	11.10.1993	14	(6)	1
Advan Kadušić (BIH)	14.10.1997	26	(4)	
Denis Marandici (MDA)	18.09.1996	5		
Bradley Martis (CUW)	13.07.1998	5	(4)	
Dušan Stojinović	26.08.2000	26	(1)	
Deni Štraus	20.04.1996		(1)	
Stjepan Vego (CRO)	09.07.1997	1	(2)	
Žan Zaletel	16.09.1999	34	(1)	2
Midfielders:	**DOB**	**M**	**(s)**	**G**
Žan Benedičič	03.10.1995	22	(6)	1
Mitja Lotrič	03.09.1994	3	(1)	1
Jakob Novak	04.03.1998	15	(16)	1
Nino Pungaršek	01.11.1995	8	(9)	1

	DOB	M	(s)	G
Maj Rorić	07.02.2000	12	(9)	
Jon Šporn	22.05.1997	14	(6)	
Rok Štraus	03.03.1987		(2)	
Lan Štravs	03.03.2000	4	(3)	
Matic Vrbanec	28.10.1996	31	(3)	2
Forwards:	**DOB**	**M**	**(s)**	**G**
Roman Bezjak	21.02.1989	6	(4)	
Ivan Božić (CRO)	08.06.1997	23	(6)	6
Filip Dangubić (CRO)	05.05.1995	23	(11)	10
Anel Hajrič (BIH)	04.03.1996		(5)	
Luka Kerin	23.03.1999	22	(7)	
Tom Kljun	29.01.2004	2	(9)	
Gašper Koritnik	06.01.2001		(7)	
Mićo Kuzmanović (BIH)	18.03.1996	24	(9)	6
Jure Matjašič	31.05.1992	4	(3)	
Ester Sokler	04.06.1999	8	(6)	3
Dario Vizinger (CRO)	06.06.1998	1		

Nogometni klub Domžale

Founded: 07.11.1920 (*as SK Disk Domžale*)
Stadium: Športni park Domžale (3,100)
Trainer: Dejan Djuranović   05.05.1968

Goalkeepers:	DOB	M	(s)	G
Klemen Mihelak	31.12.2001	1		
Ajdin Mulalič	13.09.1994	16		
Grega Sorčan	05.03.1996	19		
Defenders:	**DOB**	**M**	**(s)**	**G**
Gaber Dobrovoljc	27.01.1993	7		
Tibor Gorenc Stanković	29.12.1999		(2)	
Mitja Ilenič	26.12.2004	1		
Sven Šoštarič Karič	07.03.1998	30		3
Tilen Klemenčič	21.08.1995	10	(3)	1
Ivan Makovec	27.03.2001	3		
Gregor Sikošek	13.02.1994	27	(1)	2
Jošt Urbančič	12.04.2001	5	(4)	
Damjan Vukliševič	28.06.1995	29	(2)	6
Andraž Žinič	12.02.1999	28	(2)	
Midfielders:	**DOB**	**M**	**(s)**	**G**
Denis Adamov (AUT)	16.05.1999	3	(3)	
Gašper Černe	24.02.2004	1	(3)	
Zeni Husmani (MKD)	28.11.1990	24	(2)	

	DOB	M	(s)	G
Senijad Ibričić (BIH)	26.09.1985	34		6
Mattias Käit (EST)	29.06.1998	10	(12)	
Kim Do-hyun (KOR)	09.04.1994		(2)	
Benjamin Markuš	30.01.2001	8	(7)	
Marko Martinović (CRO)	08.08.2000	1	(7)	
Til Mavretič	19.11.1997		(4)	
Janez Pišek	04.05.1998	29	(4)	1
Jošt Pišek	10.03.2002		(1)	
Matej Podlogar	23.02.1991	14	(20)	3
Tamar Svetlin	30.07.2001	30	(2)	3
Forwards:	**DOB**	**M**	**(s)**	**G**
Arnel Jakupović (AUT)	29.05.1998	23	(4)	7
Dario Kolobarić	06.02.2000	30	(5)	12
Tonći Mujan (CRO)	19.07.1995	3	(5)	1
Nick Perc	27.05.2003		(2)	
Emir Saitoski (MKD)	08.05.2003	1	(2)	
Predrag Sikimić (SRB)	29.08.1982	4	(7)	
Slobodan Vuk	15.09.1989	5	(11)	3

Nogometno društvo Gorica

Founded: 1947
Stadium: Novo Gorica Sports Park, Nova Gorica (3,100)
Trainer: Borivoje Lučić (BIH)   15.01.1961
[18.09.2020] Gordan Petrić (SRB)   30.07.1969
[14.12.2020] Aleksandar Jović (SRB)   13.04.1972

Goalkeepers:	DOB	M	(s)	G
Uroš Likar	01.10.1999	22		
Darko Marjanović	11.10.1993	11		
Gregor Sorčan	05.03.1996	3		
Defenders:	DOB	M	(s)	G
Diego Bardanca Flores (PHI)	20.03.1993	3	(4)	
Aleksandar Bjelica (SRB)	07.01.1994	11		1
Adis Hodžič	16.01.1999	20	(10)	1
Matija Kavčič	11.07.1997	27	(2)	1
Tine Kavčič	16.02.1994	28		
Rok Ljutić	20.07.2003	1		1
Nejc Mevlja	12.06.1990	22		1
Matic Paljk	02.10.1997	11	(4)	1
Matija Širok	31.05.1991	20	(2)	
Matteo Tomiček (CRO)	24.01.1997	20	(7)	
Matko Zirdum (CRO)	21.07.1998	5		
Midfielders:	DOB	M	(s)	G
Luka Baruca	09.01.2003		(4)	
Tjaš Begić	30.06.2003	15	(13)	3
Goran Cvijanović	09.09.1986	25	(6)	1
Abdou Diakhate (SEN)	31.12.1998		(1)	
Rok Grudina	24.12.1994	25		
Mateo Itrak (CRO)	15.05.2000		(2)	
Nik Jermol	17.08.1999		(4)	
Aaron Kacinari	18.08.2001	5	(6)	
Til Mavretič	19.11.1997	15		
Mihael Mlinarić (CRO)	16.06.2000	1	(5)	
Chinwendu Johan Nkama (NGA)	07.01.1998	26	(2)	
Luka Volarič	13.01.1991	5	(1)	1
Forwards:	DOB	M	(s)	G
Lamin Colley (GAM)	05.07.1993	12	(5)	3
Matic Črnic	12.06.1992		(2)	
Leon Marinič	21.11.1997	3	(7)	
Mathias Oyewusi (NGA)	02.02.1999	16	(12)	3
Semir Smajlagić (BIH)	18.09.1998	16	(2)	2
Edin Šehić (BIH)	03.02.1995	6	(4)	
Etien Velikonja	26.12.1988	18	(14)	3
Victor Aliaga Verdú (ESP)	24.09.1997		(1)	
Žan Vipotnik	18.03.2002	5	(12)	1

Football Club Koper

Founded: 1920
Stadium: Stadion Bonifika, Koper (4,047)
Trainer: Miran Srebrnič   08.01.1970
[17.02.2021] Rodolfo Vanoli (ITA)   11.01.1963

Goalkeepers:	DOB	M	(s)	G
David Adam	15.11.1993	7		
Ivan Vargić (CRO)	15.03.1987	29		
Defenders:	DOB	M	(s)	G
Luka Badžim	20.10.1997		(3)	
Denis Cerovec (CRO)	04.04.1991	15	(1)	
Ivan Jelić (CRO)	17.09.1992	16	(8)	1
Goran Jozinović (CRO)	27.08.1990	17	(3)	
Darko Mišić (CRO)	27.06.1991	20	(10)	1
Maj Mittendorfer	11.05.2000	6	(1)	
Tilen Mlakar	26.04.1995	3	(2)	
Matej Palčič	21.06.1993	25	(2)	3
Aleksander Rajčevič	17.11.1986	25		1
Mitja Viler	01.09.1986	6	(6)	
Žan Žužek	26.01.1997	35		5
Midfielders:	DOB	M	(s)	G
Mihail Caimacov (MDA)	22.07.1998	9	(4)	
Timotej Dodlek	23.11.1989	28	(5)	
Ivica Guberac	05.07.1988	13	(3)	
Bojan Knežević (CRO)	28.01.1997	13	(9)	
Marko Pejić (CRO)	24.02.1995	22	(6)	
Nildo Victor Juffo (BRA)	24.02.1993	1		
Adam Vošnjak	26.07.2000	1	(4)	
Forwards:	DOB	M	(s)	G
Maks Barišič	06.03.1995	21	(4)	2
Zan Besir	17.10.2000	1	(6)	
Lovre Čirjak (CRO)	02.11.1991	3	(6)	
Nikola Krajinović (CRO)	09.11.1999	8	(13)	2
Nardin Mulahusejnović (BIH)	09.02.1998	34	(1)	14
Claudio Paul Spinelli (ARG)	21.01.1997	4	(23)	3
Stefan Stevanović (SRB)	23.11.1990	13	(16)	2
Luka Vekič	10.04.1995		(17)	
Dare Vršič	26.09.1984	21	(10)	7

Nogometni klub Maribor

Founded: 12.12.1960
Stadium: Stadion Ljudski vrt, Maribor (12,702)
Trainer: Sergej Jakirović (BIH)   23.12.1976
[29.08.2020] Saša Gajser   11.02.1974
[03.09.2020] Mauro Germán Camoranesi Serra (ITA)   04.10.1976
[20.03.2021] Simon Rožman   06.04.1983

Goalkeepers:	DOB	M	(s)	G
Ažbe Jug	03.03.1992	35		
Defenders:	DOB	M	(s)	G
Alexandru Crețu (ROU)	24.04.1992	14	(6)	2
Ignacio Guerrico (ARG)	09.07.1998	3		
Denis Klinar	21.02.1992	23	(2)	1
Luka Koblar	08.08.1999	4		
Vid Koderman	18.04.2003	7		
Žan Kolmanič	03.03.2000	20		
Ilija Martinović (MNE)	31.01.1994	21	(1)	1
Martin Milec	20.09.1991	10		
Nemanja Mitrović	15.10.1992	10		3
Žiga Obreht	25.07.2002	1	(1)	
Špiro Peričić (CRO)	08.10.1993	21	(2)	1
Luka Uskoković (MNE)	10.04.1996	11	(4)	
Mitja Viler	01.09.1986	1	(2)	
Midfielders:	DOB	M	(s)	G
Amir Dervišević	04.07.1992	7	(8)	
Gal Gorenak	24.10.2003	7	(1)	
Andrej Kotnik	04.08.1995	6	(14)	1
Martin Kramarič	14.11.1997		(1)	
Rok Kronaveter	07.12.1986	17	(12)	7
Rene Mihelič	05.07.1988	2	(3)	
Aleks Pihler	15.01.1994	22	(3)	2
Jan Repas	19.03.1997	24	(7)	6
Blaž Vrhovec	20.02.1992	24	(4)	1
Forwards:	DOB	M	(s)	G
Gregor Bajde	29.04.1994	2	(7)	1
Felipe Silva Correa dos Santos (BRA)	03.01.1997	10	(9)	1
Marcos Magno Morales Tavares (BRA)	30.03.1984	3	(22)	2
Aljoša Matko	29.03.2000	21	(8)	7
Jasmin Mešanović (BIH)	06.01.1992	10	(7)	3
Jan Mlakar	23.10.1998	24	(8)	14
Rudi Vancaš	15.03.1994	24	(5)	7
Luka Zahovič	15.11.1995	1		

Nogometna šola Mura Murska Sobota

Founded: 14.05.2012
Stadium: Mestni stadion Fazanerija, Murska Sobota (3,782)
Trainer: Ante Šimundža   28.09.1971

Goalkeepers:	DOB	M	(s)	G
Matko Obradović (CRO)	11.05.1991	30		
Marko Zalokar	18.06.1990	6		
Defenders:	**DOB**	**M**	**(s)**	**G**
Jan Gorenc	26.07.1999	26	(2)	3
Žan Karničnik	18.09.1994	32	(2)	3
Filip Kosi	20.09.2002		(2)	
Dragan Lovrić (CRO)	03.01.1996	19	(2)	
Matic Maruško	30.11.1990	20	(2)	
Klemen Pučko	27.01.1996	12	(3)	
Klemen Šturm	27.06.1994	23	(4)	1
Jure Travner	28.09.1985	8	(4)	
Midfielders:	**DOB**	**M**	**(s)**	**G**
Aljaž Antolin	02.08.2002	2	(1)	
Luka Bobičanec (CRO)	23.05.1993	30	(3)	11
Marko Brkić (BIH)	11.04.2000	4	(3)	

	DOB	M	(s)	G
Tio Cipot	20.04.2003		(4)	
David Đurak (CRO)	09.03.2000		(5)	
Tomi Horvat	24.03.1999	26	(7)	2
Žiga Kous	27.10.1992	25	(3)	1
Nino Kouter	19.12.1993	32	(3)	6
Alen Kozar	07.04.1995	8	(6)	1
Samsondin Ouro (GER)	02.03.2000	9	(4)	
Forwards:	**DOB**	**M**	**(s)**	**G**
Kai Cipot	28.04.2001	14	(18)	3
Andrija Filipović (CRO)	18.04.1997	15	(8)	4
Mihael Klepač (CRO)	19.09.1997	6	(7)	1
Staniša Mandić (MNE)	27.01.1995	4	(2)	3
Luka Marič	13.06.2001	4	(6)	
Amadej Maroša	07.02.1994	23	(9)	5
Vito Štrakl	31.01.2002	2	(10)	1
Kevin Žižek	21.06.1998	16	(16)	3

Nogometni klub Olimpija Ljubljana

Founded: 02.03.2005 (*as NK Bežigrad Ljubljana*)
Stadium: Stadion Stožice, Ljubljana (16,038)
Trainer: Dino Skender (CRO)   10.12.1983
[11.01.2021]   Goran Stanković   03.11.1979

Goalkeepers:	DOB	M	(s)	G
Žiga Frelih	06.02.1998	36		
Defenders:	**DOB**	**M**	**(s)**	**G**
Jan Andrejašič	16.09.1995	16	(10)	
Eric Boakye (GHA)	19.11.1999	15	(10)	
Antonio Delamea Mlinar	10.06.1991	13		2
Matic Fink	27.02.1990	13	(8)	
Maj Fogec	01.07.2002	1		
Uroš Korun	25.05.1987	28	(1)	
Angel Lyaskov (BUL)	16.03.1998	3	(1)	
Vitālijs Maksimenko (LVA)	08.12.1990	6	(3)	
Luka Marin	16.03.1998	10	(2)	1
Goran Milović (CRO)	29.01.1989	8		1
Michael Pavlović	12.06.2001	24	(2)	1
Marko Perković (CRO)	30.08.1991	9	(4)	
Miral Samardžič	17.02.1987	11	(1)	2
Vujadin Savić (SRB)	01.07.1990	10		2
Denis Šme	22.03.1994	2	(5)	
Midfielders:	**DOB**	**M**	**(s)**	**G**
Ognjen Bakić (MNE)	06.01.2003		(1)	
Žan Baskera	27.02.2003	2	(3)	
Jakov Blagaić (CRO)	08.02.2000		(5)	

	DOB	M	(s)	G
Mihail Caimacov (MDA)	22.07.1998	17	(1)	
Endri Çekiçi (ALB)	23.11.1996	3		1
Ante Ćorić (CRO)	14.04.1997	4	(2)	
Timi Elšnik	29.04.1998	31		3
Nik Kapun	09.01.1994	10	(7)	1
Mario Kvesić (BIH)	12.01.1992	8		1
Ivan Močinić (CRO)	30.04.1993	4	(2)	
Enrik Ostrc	21.06.2002	7	(17)	
Nino Pungaršek	01.11.1995	9	(4)	1
Svit Seslar	09.01.2002	1	(3)	
Vitja Valenčič	12.03.1999	3	(1)	
Adrian Zeljković	19.08.2002	2	(2)	
Forwards:	**DOB**	**M**	**(s)**	**G**
Dražen Bagarić (CRO)	12.11.1992	2	(4)	
Radivoj Bosić (SRB)	01.12.2000	11	(10)	3
Đorđe Ivanović (SRB)	20.11.1995	33	(1)	11
Joaquim Manuel Welo Lupeta „Jucie" (POR)	24.03.1993		(1)	
Haris Kadrić	16.03.2000		(2)	
Gal Kurež	27.04.2001	6	(17)	1
Mihailo Perović (MNE)	23.01.1997	8	(6)	2
Andrés Vombergar	20.11.1994	28	(5)	11
Ante Vukušić (CRO)	04.06.1991	2	(5)	

Nogometni klub Tabor Sežana

Founded: 1923
Stadium: Stadion „Rajko Štolfa", Sežana (1,200)
Trainer: Mauro Germán Camoranesi Serra (ITA)   04.10.1976
[08.09.2020]   Goran Stanković   03.11.1979
[14.01.2020]   Igor Božič   06.02.1977
[13.04.2021]   Sabit Šljivo (BIH)   05.06.1969

Goalkeepers:	DOB	M	(s)	G
Jan Koprivec	15.07.1988	31		
Arian Rener	06.03.1999	5		
Defenders:	**DOB**	**M**	**(s)**	**G**
Toni Aliaj (CRO)	06.01.1999	2	(4)	
Antonio Azinović (CRO)	17.01.1992	12		1
Mihael Briški (CRO)	02.01.1999	28	(2)	3
Denis Kouao (CIV)	23.11.1996	22		1
Klemen Nemanič	07.11.1996	33	(1)	
Marko Ristić (SRB)	09.03.1987	31		
Erik Salkič	14.10.1987	21	(7)	
Midfielders:	**DOB**	**M**	**(s)**	**G**
Mario Babić (CRO)	03.07.1992	16	(2)	2
Kevin Doukouré (CIV)	30.03.1999	27	(3)	
Miha Hlad	13.01.2002	3	(2)	
Marko Krivičič	01.02.1996	15	(7)	2
Antoine Makoumbou (CGO)	18.07.1998	19	(4)	

	DOB	M	(s)	G
Dominik Mihaljević (CRO)	27.08.1994	25	(1)	
Žiga Ovsenek	21.01.1998	1	(4)	
Leon Sever	09.04.1998	17	(16)	3
Mattia Specogna (ITA)	19.03.2002		(2)	
Jakoslav Stanković	10.04.2001		(10)	1
Tom Alen Tolić (CRO)	09.04.1999	7	(10)	
Marko Vukelić	19.01.1992		(1)	
Mario Zebić (CRO)	17.12.1995	11	(1)	
Forwards:	**DOB**	**M**	**(s)**	**G**
Andrew Agnoletti (ITA)	17.06.2002		(2)	
Aldair Adulai Djaló Baldé (GNB)	31.01.1992	28	(5)	6
Fahd Ndzengue (GAB)	07.07.2000	10	(7)	2
Mathias Pogba (GUI)	19.08.1990		(1)	
Christos Rovas (GRE)	02.09.1994	17	(11)	9
Dino Stančič	25.01.1992	13	(19)	5
Marsel Stare	28.08.2000	2	(11)	2

Regular Stage

1.	NK Radomlje	15	12	2	1	39	-	11	38
2.	NK Dob	15	11	1	3	38	-	20	34
3.	NK Krka Novo Mesto	15	10	4	1	38	-	15	34
4.	NK Brežice 1919	15	8	4	3	22	-	19	28
5.	NK Nafta Lendava 1903	15	8	4	3	47	-	20	28
6.	NK Vitanest Bilje	15	8	2	5	28	-	23	26
7.	NK Triglav Kranj	15	7	2	6	18	-	17	23
8.	NK Rudar Velenje	15	6	4	5	18	-	18	22
9.	NK Krško	15	5	3	7	15	-	25	18
10.	NK Fužinar Ravne na Koroškem	15	4	5	6	31	-	23	17
11.	ND Beltinci	15	5	1	9	22	-	28	16
12.	NK Jadran Dekani	15	4	3	8	16	-	24	15
13.	NK Drava Ptuj	15	4	1	10	22	-	33	10
14.	NK Brda Dobrovo	15	3	0	12	9	-	39	9
15.	ND Primorje Ajdovščina	15	2	3	10	10	-	27	9
16.	NK Šmartno 1928	15	2	3	10	12	-	43	9

Team ranked 1-8 were qualified for the Promotion Play-offs, while teams ranked 9-16 were qualified for the Relegation Play-offs.

Promotion Play-offs / Liga za prvaka

1.	NK Radomlje (*Promoted*)	22	16	2	4	51	-	17	50
2.	NK Krka Novo Mesto (*Promotion Play-offs*)	22	13	6	3	50	-	25	45
3.	NK Nafta Lendava 1903	22	13	5	4	60	-	26	44
4.	NK Dob	22	12	4	6	48	-	38	40
5.	NK Brežice 1919	22	11	6	5	35	-	27	39
6.	NK Vitanest Bilje	22	10	4	8	43	-	40	34
7.	NK Triglav Kranj	22	9	5	8	25	-	24	32
8.	NK Rudar Velenje	22	7	5	10	24	-	34	26

Relegation Play-offs / Liga za obstanek

9.	NK Jadran Dekani	22	7	6	9	26	-	35	27
10.	NK Krško	22	7	5	10	24	-	38	26
11.	NK Fužinar Ravne na Koroškem	22	6	7	9	44	-	33	25
12.	ND Primorje Ajdovščina	22	6	5	11	24	-	32	23
13.	NK Drava Ptuj	22	7	4	11	32	-	40	22
14.	ND Beltinci	22	6	4	12	32	-	41	22
15.	NK Šmartno 1928 (*Relegated*)	22	5	4	13	20	-	51	19
16.	NK Brda Dobrovo (*Relegated*)	22	4	2	16	18	-	55	14

NATIONAL TEAM

INTERNATIONAL MATCHES
(16.07.2020 – 15.07.2021)

03.09.2020	Ljubljana	Slovenia - Greece	0-0	(UNL)
06.09.2020	Ljubljana	Slovenia - Moldova	1-0(1-0)	(UNL)
07.10.2020	Ljubljana	Slovenia - San Marino	4-0(3-0)	(F)
11.10.2020	Prishtina	Kosovo - Slovenia	0-1(0-1)	(UNL)
14.10.2020	Chişinău	Moldova - Slovenia	0-4(0-3)	(UNL)
11.11.2020	Ljubljana	Slovenia - Azerbaijan	0-0	(F)
15.11.2020	Ljubljana	Slovenia - Kosovo	2-1(0-0)	(UNL)
18.11.2020	Athína	Greece - Slovenia	0-0	(UNL)
24.03.2021	Ljubljana	Slovenia - Croatia	1-0(1-0)	(WCQ)
27.03.2021	Sochi	Russia - Slovenia	2-1(2-1)	(WCQ)
30.03.2021	Nicosia	Cyprus - Slovenia	1-0(1-0)	(WCQ)
01.06.2021	Skopje	North Macedonia - Slovenia	1-1(0-0)	(F)
04.06.2021	Koper	Slovenia - Gibraltar	6-0(4-0)	(F)

03.09.2020   **SLOVENIA - GREECE**   **0-0**   2nd UEFA Nations League C, Group 3

03.09.2020   **SLOVENIA - GREECE**   **0-0**   2nd UEFA Nations League C, Group 3
Stadion Stožice, Ljubljana; Referee: Robert Adam Madden (Scotland); Attendance: 0
SVN: Jan Oblak (Cap), Miha Mevlja, Miha Blažič, Jure Balkovec, Petar Stojanović, Amedej Vetrih, Haris Vučkič (61.Miha Zajc), Damjan Bohar, Rajko Rep (52.Saša Živec), Andraž Šporar, Jaka Bijol (78.Nino Kouter). Trainer: Matjaž Kek.

06.09.2020   **SLOVENIA - MOLDOVA**   **1-0(1-0)**   2nd UEFA Nations League C, Group 3
Stadion Stožice, Ljubljana; Referee: Jérôme Brisard (France); Attendance: 0
SVN: Jan Oblak (Cap), Miha Mevlja, Miha Blažič, Jure Balkovec, Petar Stojanović, Haris Vučkič (68.Amedej Vetrih), Jasmin Kurtič, Damjan Bohar, Nino Kouter, Miha Zajc (57.Saša Živec), Andraž Šporar (85.Blaž Kramer). Trainer: Matjaž Kek.
Goal: Damjan Bohar (28).

07.10.2020   **SLOVENIA - SAN MARINO**   4-0(3-0)   Friendly International
Stadion Stožice, Ljubljana; Referee: Sebastian Gishamer (Austria); Attendance: 500
SVN: Vid Belec, Nejc Skubic (71.Petar Stojanović), Nemanja Mitrovič, Mario Jurčevič, Jasmin Kurtič (Cap) (59.Amedej Vetrih), Damjan Bohar (46.Rajko Rep), Jon Gorenc Stankovič, David Tijanič, Sandi Lovrić (59.Benjamin Verbič), Jaka Bijol (46.Dejan Petrovič), Haris Vučkič (46.Blaž Kramer). Trainer: Matjaž Kek.
Goals: Nemanja Mitrovič (17), Haris Vučkič (25 penalty), Nemanja Mitrovič (42), Rajko Rep (48).

11.10.2020   **KOSOVO - SLOVENIA**   0-1(0-1)   2nd UEFA Nations League C, Group 3
Stadiumi „Fadil Vokrri", Prishtina; Referee: Andrew Madley (England); Attendance: 0
SVN: Jan Oblak (Cap), Miha Mevlja, Miha Blažič, Jure Balkovec, Petar Stojanović, Haris Vučkič (85.Blaž Kramer), Jasmin Kurtič, Benjamin Verbič (75.Nejc Skubic), Sandi Lovrić (85.Amedej Vetrih), Rajko Rep (55.Damjan Bohar), Jaka Bijol. Trainer: Matjaž Kek.
Goal: Haris Vučkič (22).

14.10.2020   **MOLDOVA - SLOVENIA**   0-4(0-3)   2nd UEFA Nations League C, Group 3
Stadionul Zimbru, Chişinău; Referee: João Pedro da Silva Pinheiro (Portugal); Attendance: 0
SVN: Jan Oblak (Cap), Nejc Skubic, Miha Mevlja, Miha Blažič (74.Nemanja Mitrovič), Jure Balkovec, Haris Vučkič (77.Lovro Bizjak), Jasmin Kurtič, Damjan Bohar (74.Rajko Rep), Benjamin Verbič, Sandi Lovrić (78.Amedej Vetrih), Jaka Bijol (83.Dejan Petrovič). Trainer: Matjaž Kek.
Goals: Sandi Lovrić (8), Haris Vučkič (37 penalty, 42, 55 penalty).

11.11.2020   **SLOVENIA - AZERBAIJAN**   0-0   Friendly International
Stadion Stožice, Ljubljana; Referee: Ferenc Karakó (Hungary); Attendance: 0
SVN: Vid Belec, Nejc Skubic, Miha Mevlja, Kenan Bajrič, Mario Jurčevič, Josip Iličić (Cap) (66.Amedej Vetrih), Jasmin Kurtič (83.Jaka Bijol), Miha Zajc (66.Damjan Bohar), Sandi Lovrić (46.Benjamin Verbič), Adam Gnezda Čerin (46.Nino Kouter), Tim Matavž (46.Andraž Šporar). Trainer: Matjaž Kek.

15.11.2020   **SLOVENIA - KOSOVO**   2-1(0-0)   2nd UEFA Nations League C, Group 3
Stadion Stožice, Ljubljana; Referee: Bartosz Frankowski (Poland); Attendance: 0
SVN: Vid Belec, Miha Mevlja, Miha Blažič, Jure Balkovec, Petar Stojanović, Josip Iličić (Cap) (90+6.Nino Kouter), Amedej Vetrih, Haris Vučkič (68.Andraž Šporar), Jasmin Kurtič, Damjan Bohar, Sandi Lovrić (87.Domen Črnigoj). Trainer: Matjaž Kek.
Goals: Jasmin Kurtič (63), Josip Iličić (90+4).

18.11.2020   **GREECE - SLOVENIA**   0-0   2nd UEFA Nations League C, Group 3
Stádio "Georgios Kamaras", Athína; Referee: Carlos del Cerro Grande (Spain); Attendance: 0
SVN: Jan Oblak (Cap), Miha Mevlja, Miha Blažič, Jure Balkovec, Petar Stojanović, Josip Iličić (90+2.Kenan Bajrič), Haris Vučkič (76.Andraž Šporar), Jasmin Kurtič, Damjan Bohar (67.Benjamin Verbič), Jaka Bijol (77.Amedej Vetrih), Sandi Lovrić (90+2.Nejc Skubic). Trainer: Matjaž Kek.

24.03.2021   **SLOVENIA - CROATIA**   1-0(1-0)   22nd FIFA WC. Qualifiers
Stadion Stožice, Ljubljana; Referee: Antonio Miguel Mateu Lahoz (Spain); Attendance: 0
SVN: Jan Oblak (Cap), Miha Mevlja, Miha Blažič, Jure Balkovec, Petar Stojanović, Josip Iličić (87.Nejc Skubic), Jasmin Kurtič, Damjan Bohar (64.Domen Črnigoj), Jaka Bijol (69.Amedej Vetrih), Andraž Šporar (69.Blaž Kramer), Sandi Lovrić (87.Kenan Bajrič). Trainer: Matjaž Kek.
Goal: Sandi Lovrić (15).

27.03.2021   **RUSSIA - SLOVENIA**   2-1(2-1)   22nd FIFA WC. Qualifiers
Fisht Olympic Stadium, Sochi; Referee: Marco Di Bello (Italy); Attendance: 13,008
SVN: Jan Oblak (Cap), Miha Mevlja, Miha Blažič, Jure Balkovec, Petar Stojanović (61.Nejc Skubic), Josip Iličić, Jasmin Kurtič, Miha Zajc (75.Damjan Bohar), Jaka Bijol (62.Amedej Vetrih), Andraž Šporar (75.Haris Vučkič), Sandi Lovrić (86.Luka Zahovič). Trainer: Matjaž Kek.
Goal: Josip Iličić (36).

30.03.2021   **CYPRUS - SLOVENIA**   1-0(1-0)   22nd FIFA WC. Qualifiers
Stádio GSP, Nicosia; Referee: Andreas Ekberg (Sweden); Attendance: 0
SVN: Jan Oblak (Cap), Miha Blažič, Jure Balkovec (81.Nino Kouter), Petar Stojanović, Kenan Bajrič, Josip Iličić, Jasmin Kurtič, Miha Zajc (46.Damjan Bohar), Jaka Bijol (58.Domen Črnigoj), Blaž Kramer (58.Haris Vučkič), Sandi Lovrić (81.Luka Zahovič). Trainer: Matjaž Kek.

01.06.2021   **NORTH MACEDONIA - SLOVENIA**   1-1(0-0)   Friendly International
Nacionalna Arena "Toše Proeski", Skopje; Referee: Besfort Kasumi (Kosovo); Attendance: 10,000
SVN: Jan Oblak (Cap) (46.Vid Belec), Miha Mevlja, Jure Balkovec (4.Mario Jurčevič), Petar Stojanović, Josip Iličić (61.Domen Črnigoj), Jasmin Kurtič, Leo Štulac, Jon Gorenc Stankovič, Sandi Lovrić (62.Jaka Bijol), Andraž Šporar (61.Benjamin Šeško), Jan Mlakar (79.Damjan Bohar). Trainer: Matjaž Kek.
Goal: Domen Črnigoj (90+7).

04.06.2021   **SLOVENIA - GIBRALTAR**   6-0(4-0)   Friendly International
Stadion Bonifika, Koper; Referee: Haris Kaljanac (Bosnia and Herzegovina); Attendance: 1,035
SVN: Vid Belec, Miha Mevlja, Petar Stojanović (46.Žan Rogelj), Sven Šoštarič Karič, Josip Iličić (Cap), Nino Kouter (46.Sandi Lovrić), Leo Štulac (62.Jaka Bijol), Jon Gorenc Stankovič, Andraž Šporar (46.Benjamin Šeško), Luka Zahovič (62.Miha Zajc), Jan Mlakar (62.Domen Črnigoj). Trainer: Matjaž Kek.
Goals: Andraž Šporar (11), Josip Iličić (17), Andraž Šporar (34), Jan Mlakar (38), Josip Iličić (57), Jon Gorenc Stankovič (61).

NATIONAL TEAM PLAYERS
(16.07.2020 – 15.07.2021)

Name	DOB	Caps	Goals	2020/2021:	Club
Goalkeepers					
Vid BELEC	06.06.1990	**18**	**0**	2020/2021:	*US Salernitana 1919 (ITA)*
Jan OBLAK	07.01.1993	**37**	**0**	2019:	*Club Atlético de Madrid (ESP)*
Defenders					
Kenan BAJRIČ	20.12.1994	**4**	**0**	2020/2021:	*ŠK Slovan Bratislava (SVK)*
Jure BALKOVEC	09.09.1994	**16**	**0**	2020:	*Hellas Verona FC (ITA)*
				14.09.2020->	*Fatih Karagümrük SK (TUR)*
Miha BLAŽIČ	08.05.1993	**14**	**0**	2020/2021:	*Ferencvárosi TC (HUN)*
Mario JURČEVIČ	01.06.1995	**3**	**0**	2020/2021:	*NK Osijek (CRO)*
Sven Šoštarič KARIČ	07.03.1998	**1**	**0**	2021:	*NK Domžale*
Miha MEVLJA	12.06.1990	**38**	**1**	2020/2021:	*PFK Sochi (RUS)*
Nemanja MITROVIČ	15.10.1992	**5**	**2**	2020:	*NK Maribor*
Žan ROGELJ	25.11.1999	**1**	**0**	2021:	*WSG Swarovski Tirol Wattens (AUT)*
Nejc SKUBIC	13.06.1989	**22**	**1**	2020/2021:	*Konyaspor Kulübü (TUR)*
Petar STOJANOVIĆ	07.10.1995	**27**	**0**	2020/2021:	*GNK Dinamo Zagreb (CRO)*
Midfielders					
Jaka BIJOL	05.02.1999	**8**	**0**	2020:	*FK CSKA Moskva (RUS)*
				18.09.2020->	*SV Hannover 96 (GER)*
Damjan BOHAR	18.10.1991	**15**	**1**	2020:	*Zagłębie Lubin (POL)*
				23.09.2020->	*NK Osijek (CRO)*
Adam Gnezda ČERIN	16.07.1999	**1**	**0**	2020:	*HNK Rijeka (CRO)*
Domen ČRNIGOJ	18.11.1995	**17**	**3**	2020/2021:	*Venezia FC (ITA)*
Josip ILIČIĆ	29.01.1988	**73**	**13**	2020/2021:	*Atalanta Bergamasca Calcio (ITA)*
Nino KOUTER	19.12.1993	**6**	**0**	2020/2021:	*NŠ Mura Murska Sobota*
Jasmin KURTIĆ	10.01.1989	**69**	**2**	2020/2021:	*Parma Calcio 1913 (ITA)*
Sandi LOVRIĆ	28.03.1998	**11**	**2**	2020/2021:	*FC Lugano (SUI)*
Dejan PETROVIČ	12.01.1998	**2**	**0**	2020:	*SK Rapid Wien (AUT)*
Jon Gorenc STANKOVIČ	14.01.1996	**3**	**0**	2020/2021:	*SK Sturm Graz (AUT)*
Leo ŠTULAC	26.09.1994	**5**	**0**	2021:	*Empoli FC (ITA)*
Benjamin VERBIČ	27.11.1993	**34**	**5**	2020:	*FK Dinamo Kyiv (UKR)*
Amedej VETRIH	16.09.1990	**13**	**0**	2020:	*Çaykur Rizespor Kulübü (TUR)*
				05.10.2020->	*Gaziantep FK (TUR)*
Haris VUČKIČ	21.08.1992	**12**	**5**	2020/2021:	*Real Zaragoza (ESP)*
Miha ZAJC	01.07.1994	**19**	**5**	2020:	*Fenerbahçe SK İstanbul (TUR)*
				13.09.2020->	*Genoa C&FC (ITA)*
Saša ŽIVEC	02.04.1991	**2**	**0**	2020:	*Zagłębie Lubin (POL)*
Forwards					
Lovro BIZJAK	12.11.1993	**1**	**0**	2020:	*FK Ufa (RUS)*
Blaž KRAMER	01.06.1996	**5**	**0**	2020/2021:	*FC Zürich (SUI)*
Tim MATAVŽ	13.01.1989	**39**	**11**	2020/2021:	*Al Wahda FC Abu Dhabi (UAE)*
Jan MLAKAR	23.10.1998	**2**	**1**	2021:	*NK Maribor*
Rajko REP	20.06.1990	**5**	**1**	2020:	*TSV Hartberg (AUT)*
Benjamin ŠEŠKO	31.05.2003	**2**	**0**	2021:	*FC Red Bull Salzburg (AUT)*
Andraž ŠPORAR	27.02.1994	**28**	**4**	2020:	*Sporting Clube de Portugal Lisboa (POR)*
				01.02.2021->	*Sporting Clube de Braga (POR)*
David TIJANIČ	16.07.1997	**1**	**0**	2020:	*RKS Raków Częstochowa (POL)*
Luka ZAHOVIČ	15.11.1995	**6**	**0**	2021:	*MKS Pogoń Szczecin (POL)*

National team coach		
Matjaž KEK [from 27.11.2019]	09.09.1961	23 M; 11 W; 6 D; 6 L; 37-16
		Complete record as trainer of Slovenia:
		72 M; 32 W; 14 D; 26 L; 98-57
		(07.02.2007 – 11.10.2011) & (from 27.11.2019)

SPAIN

The Country:
Reino de España (Kingdom of Spain)
Capital: Madrid
Surface: 505,990 km²
Inhabitants: 47,450,795 [2020]
Time: UTC

The FA:
Real Federación Española de Fútbol
Ramón y Cajal, s/n Apartado postal 385, 28230 Las Rozas (Madrid)
Tel: +34 91 495 9800
Founded: 14.10.1909
Member of FIFA since: 1913
Member of UEFA since: 1954
Website: www.rfef.es

NATIONAL TEAM RECORDS

RECORDS
First international match:	28.08.1920, Bruxelles:	Spain – Denmark 1-0
Most international caps:	Sergio Ramos García	- 180 caps (since 2005)
Most international goals:	David Villa Sánchez	- 59 goals / 98 caps (2005-2017)

UEFA EUROPEAN CHAMPIONSHIP
1960	Qualifiers
1964	**Final Tournament (Winners)**
1968	Qualifiers
1972	Qualifiers
1976	Qualifiers
1980	Final Tournament (Group Stage)
1984	Final Tournament (Runners-up)
1988	Final Tournament (Group Stage)
1992	Qualifiers
1996	Final Tournament (Quarter-Finals)
2000	Final Tournament (Quarter-Finals)
2004	Final Tournament (Group Stage)
2008	**Final Tournament (Winners)**
2012	**Final Tournament (Winners)**
2016	Final Tournament (2nd Round of 16)
2020	Final Tournament (Semi-Finals)

FIFA WORLD CUP
1930	Did not enter
1934	Final Tournament (Quarter-Finals)
1938	*Withdrew*
1950	Final Tournament (4th Place)
1954	Qualifiers
1958	Qualifiers
1962	Final Tournament (Group Stage)
1966	Final Tournament (Group Stage)
1970	Qualifiers
1974	Qualifiers
1978	Final Tournament (Group Stage)
1982	Final Tournament (2nd Round)
1986	Final Tournament (Quarter-Finals)
1990	Final Tournament (2nd Round of 16)
1994	Final Tournament (Quarter-Finals)
1998	Final Tournament (Group Stage)
2002	Final Tournament (Quarter-Finals)
2006	Final Tournament (2nd Round of 16)
2010	**Final Tournament (Winners)**
2014	Final Tournament (Group Stage)
2018	Final Tournament (2nd Round of 16)

OLYMPIC TOURNAMENTS
1908	-
1912	-
1920	Quarter-Finals
1924	Preliminary Round
1928	Quarter-Finals
1936	Did not enter
1948	Did not enter
1952	Did not enter
1956	Did not enter
1960	Did not enter
1964	Qualifiers
1968	Quarter-Finals
1972	Qualifiers
1976	Group Stage
1980	Group Stage
1984	Qualifiers
1988	Qualifiers
1992	**Winners**
1996	Quarter-Finals
2000	Runners-up
2004	Qualifiers
2008	Qualifiers
2012	Group Stage
2016	Qualifiers

UEFA NATIONS LEAGUE
2018/2019	League A
2020/2021	League A (Qualified for the Final Tournament)

FIFA CONFEDERATIONS CUP 1992-2017
2009 (3rd Place), 2013 (Runners-up)

SPANISH CLUB HONOURS IN EUROPEAN CLUB COMPETITIONS:

European Champion Clubs.Cup (1956-1992) / UEFA Champions League (1993-2021)
Real Madrid CF	13	1955/1956, 1956/1957, 1957/1958, 1958/1959, 1959/1960, 1965/1966, 1997/1998, 1999/2000, 2001/2002, 2013/2014, 2015/2016, 2016/2017, 2017/2018
FC Barcelona	5	1991/1992, 2005/2006, 2008/2009, 2010/2011, 2014/2015

Fairs Cup (1858-1971) / UEFA Cup (1972-2009) / UEFA Europa League (2010-2021)
Sevilla FC	6	2005/2006, 2006/2007, 2013/2014, 2014/2015, 2015/2016, 2019-2020
FC Barcelona	3	1955-1958, 1958-1960, 1965/1966
Club Atlético de Madrid	3	2009/2010, 2011/2012, 2017/2018
Valencia CF	3	1961/1962, 1962/1963, 2003/2004

Real Madrid CF		2	1984/1985, 1985/1986	
Real Zaragoza		1	1963/1964	
Villarreal CF		1	2020/2021	
UEFA Super Cup (1972-2020)				
FC Barcelona		5	1992, 1997, 2009, 2011, 2015	
Real Madrid CF		4	2002, 2014, 2016, 2017	
Club Atlético de Madrid		3	2010, 2012, 2018	
Valencia CF		2	1980, 2004	
Sevilla FC		1	2006	
European Cup Winners.Cup 1961-1999*				
FC Barcelona		4	1978/1979, 1981/1982, 1988/1989, 1996/1997	
Club Atlético de Madrid		1	1961/1962	
Valencia CF		1	1979/1980	
Real Zaragoza		1	1994/1995	

defunct competition

NATIONAL COMPETITIONS
TABLE OF HONOURS

	CHAMPIONS	CUP WINNERS	BEST GOALSCORERS	
1903	-	Athletic Club Bilbao	-	
1904	-	Athletic Club Bilbao	-	
1905	-	Madrid FC	-	
1906	-	Madrid FC	-	
1907	-	Madrid FC	-	
1908	-	Madrid FC	-	
1909	-	Real Sociedad de Fútbol San Sebastián	-	
1910	-	FC Barcelona (FEF)* Athletic Club Bilbao (UECF)**	-	
1911	-	Athletic Club Bilbao	-	
1912	-	FC Barcelona	-	
1913	-	Racing Club de Irún (FEF) FC Barcelona (UECF)	-	
1914	-	Athletic Club Bilbao	-	
1915	-	Athletic Club Bilbao	-	
1916	-	Athletic Club Bilbao	-	
1917	-	Madrid FC	-	
1918	-	Real Unión Club de Irún	-	
1919	-	Arenas Club de Getxo	-	
1920	-	FC Barcelona	-	
1921	-	Athletic Club Bilbao	-	
1922	-	FC Barcelona	-	
1923	-	Athletic Club Bilbao	-	
1924	-	Real Unión Club de Irún	-	
1925	-	FC Barcelona	-	
1926	-	FC Barcelona	-	
1927	-	Real Unión Club de Irún	-	
1928	-	FC Barcelona	-	
1929	FC Barcelona	RCD Español Barcelona	Francisco "Paco" Bienzobas Ocáriz (Real Sociedad de Fútbol San Sebastián)	14
1929/1930	Athletic Club Bilbao	Athletic Club Bilbao	Guillermo Gorostiza Paredes (Athletic Club Bilbao)	19
1930/1931	Athletic Club Bilbao	Athletic Club Bilbao	Agustín Sauto Arana "Bata" (Athletic Club Bilbao)	27
1931/1932	Real Madrid FC	Athletic Club Bilbao	Guillermo Gorostiza Paredes (Athletic Club Bilbao)	12
1932/1933	Real Madrid FC	Athletic Club Bilbao	Manuel Olivares Lapeña (Real Madrid FC)	16
1933/1934	Athletic Club Bilbao	Real Madrid FC	Isidro Lángara Galarraga (Real Oviedo CF)	27
1934/1935	Real Betis Balompié Sevilla	Sevilla FC	Isidro Lángara Galarraga (Real Oviedo CF)	26
1935/1936	Athletic Club Bilbao	Real Madrid FC	Isidro Lángara Galarraga (Real Oviedo CF)	27
1936/1937	*League Cancelled*	*No competition*	-	
1937/1938	*League Cancelled*	*No competition*	-	
1938/1939	*League Cancelled*	Sevilla FC	-	
1939/1940	Atlético Aviación Madrid	RCD Español Barcelona	Víctor Unamuno Ibarzabal (Athletic Club Bilbao)	22
1940/1941	Atlético Aviación Madrid	Valencia CF	Prudencio Sánchez Fernández "Pruden" (Atlético Aviación Madrid)	30
1941/1942	Valencia CF	CF Barcelona	Edmundo Suárez Trabanco "Mundo" (Valencia CF)	27
1942/1943	Atlético Club de Bilbao	Atlético Club de Bilbao	Mariano Martín Alonso (CF Barcelona)	32
1943/1944	Valencia CF	Atlético Club de Bilbao	Edmundo Suárez Trabanco "Mundo" (Valencia CF)	27
1944/1945	CF Barcelona	Atlético Club de Bilbao	Pedro Telmo Zarraonandía Montoya (Atlético Club de Bilbao)	19
1945/1946	Sevilla FC	Real Madrid CF	Pedro Telmo Zarraonandía Montoya (Atlético Club de Bilbao)	24
1946/1947	Valencia CF	Real Madrid CF	Pedro Telmo Zarraonandía Montoya (Atlético Club de Bilbao)	34
1947/1948	CF Barcelona	Sevilla FC	Manuel Fernández Fernández "Pahiño" (RC Celta de Vigo)	23
1948/1949	CF Barcelona	Valencia CF	César Rodríguez Álvarez (CF Barcelona)	28

1949/1950	Club Atlético de Madrid	Atlético Club de Bilbao	Pedro Telmo Zarraonandía Montoya (Atlético Club de Bilbao) 25
1950/1951	Club Atlético de Madrid	CF Barcelona	Pedro Telmo Zarraonandía Montoya (Atlético Club de Bilbao) 38
1951/1952	CF Barcelona	CF Barcelona	Manuel Fernández Fernández "Pahiño" (Real Madrid CF) 28
1952/1953	CF Barcelona	CF Barcelona	Pedro Telmo Zarraonandía Montoya (Atlético Club de Bilbao) 24
1953/1954	Real Madrid CF	Valencia CF	Alfredo Stéfano Di Stéfano Laulhé (Real Madrid CF) 27
1954/1955	Real Madrid CF	Atlético Club de Bilbao	Juan Arza Iñigo (Sevilla FC) 28
1955/1956	Atlético Club de Bilbao	Atlético Club de Bilbao	Alfredo Stéfano Di Stéfano Laulhé (Real Madrid CF) 24
1956/1957	Real Madrid CF	CF Barcelona	Alfredo Stéfano Di Stéfano Laulhé (Real Madrid CF) 31
1957/1958	Real Madrid CF	Atlético Club de Bilbao	Manuel Badenes Calduch (Real Valladolid CF) Alfredo Stéfano Di Stéfano Laulhé (Real Madrid CF) Ricardo de la Virgen (Valencia CF) 19
1958/1959	CF Barcelona	CF Barcelona	Alfredo Stéfano Di Stéfano Laulhé (Real Madrid CF 23
1959/1960	CF Barcelona	Club Atlético de Madrid	Ferenc Puskás (HUN, Real Madrid CF) 26
1960/1961	Real Madrid CF	Club Atlético de Madrid	Ferenc Puskás (HUN, Real Madrid CF) 27
1961/1962	Real Madrid CF	Real Madrid CF	Juan Roberto Seminario Rodríguez (PER, Real Zaragoza) 25
1962/1963	Real Madrid CF	CF Barcelona	Ferenc Puskás (HUN, Real Madrid CF) 26
1963/1964	Real Madrid CF	Real Zaragoza	Ferenc Puskás (HUN, Real Madrid CF) 20
1964/1965	Real Madrid CF	Club Atlético de Madrid	Cayetano Ré Ramírez (PAR, CF Barcelona) 25
1965/1966	Club Atlético de Madrid	Real Zaragoza	Luciano Sánchez Rodríguez "Vavá" (Elche CF) 19
1966/1967	Real Madrid CF	Valencia CF	Waldo Machado da Silva (BRA, Valencia CF) 24
1967/1968	Real Madrid CF	CF Barcelona	Fidel Uriarte Macho (Atlético Club de Bilbao) 22
1968/1969	Real Madrid CF	Atlético Club de Bilbao	Amancio Amaro Varela (Club Atlético de Madrid) José Eulogio Gárate Ormaechea (Real Madrid CF) 14
1969/1970	Club Atlético de Madrid	Real Madrid CF	Amancio Amaro Varela (Real Madrid CF) José Luis Aragonés Suárez (Club Atlético de Madrid) José Eulogio Gárate Ormaechea (Club Atlético de Madrid) 16
1970/1971	Valencia CF	CF Barcelona	José Eulogio Gárate Ormaechea (Club Atlético de Madrid) Carles Rexach i Cerdà (CF Barcelona) 17
1971/1972	Real Madrid CF	Club Atlético de Madrid	Enrique Porta Guíu (Granada CF) 20
1972/1973	Club Atlético de Madrid	Athletic Club Bilbao	Mariano Arias Chamorro "Marianín" (Real Oviedo CF) 19
1973/1974	CF Barcelona	Real Madrid CF	Enrique Castro González "Quini" (Real Sporting de Gijón) 20
1974/1975	Real Madrid CF	Real Madrid CF	Carlos Ruiz Herrero (Athletic Club Bilbao) 19
1975/1976	Real Madrid CF	Club Atlético de Madrid	Enrique Castro González "Quini" (Real Sporting de Gijón) 21
1976/1977	Club Atlético de Madrid	Real Betis Balompié Sevilla	Mario Alberto Kempes Chiodi (ARG, Valencia CF) 24
1977/1978	Real Madrid CF	FC Barcelona	Mario Alberto Kempes Chiodi (ARG, Valencia CF) 28
1978/1979	Real Madrid CF	Valencia CF	Johann Krankl (AUT, FC Barcelona) 29
1979/1980	Real Madrid CF	Real Madrid CF	Enrique Castro González "Quini" (Real Sporting de Gijón) 24
1980/1981	Real Sociedad de Fútbol San Sebastián	FC Barcelona	Enrique Castro González "Quini" (FC Barcelona) 20
1981/1982	Real Sociedad de Fútbol San Sebastián	Real Madrid CF	Enrique Castro González "Quini" (FC Barcelona) 26
1982/1983	Athletic Club Bilbao	FC Barcelona	Hipólito Rincón Povedano (Real Betis Balompié Sevilla) 20
1983/1984	Athletic Club Bilbao	Athletic Club Bilbao	Jorge Orosmán da Silva Echeverrito (URU, Real Valladolid CF) Juan Gómez González "Juanito" (Real Madrid CF) 17
1984/1985	FC Barcelona	Club Atlético de Madrid	Hugo Sánchez Márquez (MEX, Club Atlético de Madrid) 19
1985/1986	Real Madrid CF	Real Zaragoza	Hugo Sánchez Márquez (MEX, Real Madrid CF) 22
1986/1987	Real Madrid CF	Real Sociedad de Fútbol San Sebastián	Hugo Sánchez Márquez (MEX, Real Madrid CF) 34
1987/1988	Real Madrid CF	FC Barcelona	Hugo Sánchez Márquez (MEX, Real Madrid CF) 29
1988/1989	Real Madrid CF	Real Madrid CF	Baltazar Maria de Morais Júnior (BRA, Club Atlético de Madrid) 35
1989/1990	Real Madrid CF	FC Barcelona	Hugo Sánchez Márquez (MEX, Real Madrid CF) 38
1990/1991	FC Barcelona	Club Atlético de Madrid	Emilio Butragueño Santos (Real Madrid CF) 19
1991/1992	FC Barcelona	Club Atlético de Madrid	Manuel Sánchez Delgado "Manolo" (Club Atlético de Madrid) 27
1992/1993	FC Barcelona	Real Madrid CF	José Roberto Gama de Oliveira "Bebeto" (RC Deportivo La Coruña) 29
1993/1994	FC Barcelona	Real Zaragoza	Romário de Souza Faria (BRA, FC Barcelona) 30
1994/1995	Real Madrid CF	RC Deportivo La Coruña	Iván Luis Zamorano Zamora (CHI, Real Madrid CF) 28
1995/1996	Club Atlético de Madrid	Club Atlético de Madrid	Juan Antonio Pizzi Torroja (CD Tenerife) 31
1996/1997	Real Madrid CF	FC Barcelona	Ronaldo Luís Nazário de Lima (BRA, FC Barcelona) 34
1997/1998	FC Barcelona	FC Barcelona	Christian Vieri (Club Atlético de Madrid) 24
1998/1999	FC Barcelona	Valencia CF	Raúl González Blanco (Real Madrid CF) 25
1999/2000	RC Deportivo La Coruña	RCD Espanyol Barcelona	Salvador Ballesta Vialcho "Salva" (Real Racing Club de Santander) 27
2000/2001	Real Madrid CF	Real Zaragoza	Raúl González Blanco (Real Madrid CF) 24
2001/2002	Valencia CF	RC Deportivo La Coruña	Diego Tristán Herrera (RC Deportivo La Coruña) 21
2002/2003	Real Madrid CF	RCD Mallorca	Rudolphus Antonius "Roy" Makaay (NED, RC Deportivo La Coruña) 29

2003/2004	Valencia CF	Real Zaragoza	Ronaldo Luís Nazário de Lima (BRA, Real Madrid CF)	25
2004/2005	FC Barcelona	Real Betis Balompié Sevilla	Diego Forlán Corazzo (URU, Villarreal CF)	25
2005/2006	FC Barcelona	RCD Espanyol Barcelona	Samuel Eto'o Fils (CMR, FC Barcelona)	26
2006/2007	Real Madrid CF	Sevilla FC	Rutgerus Johannes Martinus "Ruud" van Nistelrooy (NED, Real Madrid CF)	25
2007/2008	Real Madrid CF	Valencia CF	Daniel González Güiza (RCD Mallorca)	27
2008/2009	FC Barcelona	FC Barcelona	Diego Forlán Corazzo (URU, Club Atlético de Madrid)	32
2009/2010	FC Barcelona	Sevilla FC	Lionel Andrés Messi Cuccittini (ARG, FC Barcelona)	34
2010/2011	FC Barcelona	Real Madrid CF	Cristiano Ronaldo dos Santos Aveiro (POR, Real Madrid CF)	40
2011/2012	Real Madrid CF	FC Barcelona	Lionel Andrés Messi Cuccittini (ARG, FC Barcelona)	50
2012/2013	FC Barcelona	Club Atlético de Madrid	Lionel Andrés Messi Cuccittini (ARG, FC Barcelona)	46
2013/2014	Club Atlético de Madrid	Real Madrid CF	Cristiano Ronaldo dos Santos Aveiro (POR, Real Madrid CF)	31
2014/2015	FC Barcelona	FC Barcelona	Cristiano Ronaldo dos Santos Aveiro (POR, Real Madrid CF)	48
2015/2016	FC Barcelona	FC Barcelona	Luis Alberto Suárez Díaz (URU, FC Barcelona)	40
2016/2017	Real Madrid CF	FC Barcelona	Lionel Andrés Messi Cuccittini (ARG, FC Barcelona)	37
2017/2018	FC Barcelona	FC Barcelona	Lionel Andrés Messi Cuccittini (ARG, FC Barcelona)	34
2018/2019	FC Barcelona	Valencia CF	Lionel Andrés Messi Cuccittini (ARG, FC Barcelona)	36
2019/2020	Real Madrid CF	Real Sociedad de Fútbol San Sebastián	Lionel Andrés Messi Cuccittini (ARG, FC Barcelona)	25
2020/2021	Club Atlético de Madrid	FC Barcelona	Lionel Andrés Messi Cuccittini (ARG, FC Barcelona)	30

*FEF = Federación Española de Fútbol
**UECF = Unión Española de Clubes de Fútbol
Name changements:
Real Madrid CF = Madrid FC (1902-1920); Real Madrid FC (1920-1938), Real Madrid CF (since 1938).
Athletic Club Bilbao = Atlético Club de Bilbao (1940-1972)
FC FC Barcelona = CF FC Barcelona (1941-1974)
Real Unión Club de Irún = Racing Club de Irún (1901-1915)
RCD Espayol Barcelona = RCD Español Barcelona Barcelona (1910-1995)
Sevilla FC = Sevilla CF (1938-1986)
Club Atlético de Madrid = Athletic Club Madrid (1903-1926); Club Club Atlético de Madrid (1926-1939); Atlético Aviación Madrid (1939-1947); Club Atlético de Madrid (since 1947)
Valencia CF = Valencia FC (1919-1940)

NATIONAL CHAMPIONSHIP
La Liga 2020/2021
(12.09.2020 – 23.05.2021)

Results

Round 1 [12-13.09.2020]
Eibar - Celta Vigo 0-0
Granada - Athletic Bilbao 2-0(0-0)
Cádiz - Osasuna 0-2(0-1)
Alavés - Real Betis 0-1(0-0)
Real Valladolid - Real Sociedad 1-1(1-0)
Villarreal - Huesca 1-1(0-1)
Valencia - Levante 4-2(2-2)
Atlét. Madrid - Sevilla 2-0(1-0) [12.01.2021]
Real Madrid - Getafe 2-0(0-0) [09.02.2021]
FC Barcelona - Elche 3-0(0-0) [24.02.2021]

Round 2 [19-20.09.2020]
Villarreal - Eibar 2-1(0-0)
Getafe - Osasuna 1-0(0-0)
Celta Vigo - Valencia 2-1(1-0)
Huesca - Cádiz 0-2(0-1)
Real Betis - Real Valladolid 2-0(2-0)
Granada - Alavés 2-1(1-1)
Real Sociedad - Real Madrid 0-0
Athl. Bilbao - Barcelona 2-3(1-2) [06.01.2021]
Levante - Atlét. Madrid 1-1(1-1) [17.02.2021]
Sevilla FC - Elche 2-0(1-0) [17.03.2021]

Round 3 [26-27.09.2020]
Alavés - Getafe 0-0
Valencia - Huesca 1-1(1-0)
Elche - Real Sociedad 0-3(0-0)
Real Betis - Real Madrid 2-3(2-1)
Osasuna - Levante 1-3(1-1)
Eibar - Athletic Bilbao 1-2(0-1)
Atlético Madrid - Granada 6-1(1-0)
Cádiz - Sevilla FC 1-3(0-0)
Real Valladolid - Celta Vigo 1-1(0-1)
FC Barcelona - Villarreal 4-0(4-0)

Round 4 [29.09.-01.10.2020]
Real Sociedad - Valencia 0-1(0-0)
Getafe - Real Betis 3-0(3-0)
Huesca - Atlético Madrid 0-0
Villarreal - Alavés 3-1(2-1)
Eibar - Elche 0-1(0-1)
Real Madrid - Real Valladolid 1-0(0-0)
Athletic Bilbao - Cádiz 0-1(0-0)
Sevilla FC - Levante 1-0(0-0)
Celta Vigo - FC Barcelona 0-3(0-1)
Granada - Osasuna 2-0(2-0) [12.01.2021]

Round 5 [03-04.10.2020]
Real Valladolid - Eibar 1-2(1-1)
Atlético Madrid - Villarreal 0-0
Real Sociedad - Getafe 3-0(1-0)
Elche - Huesca 0-0
Valencia - Real Betis 0-2(0-1)
Osasuna - Celta Vigo 2-0(1-0)
Alavés - Athletic Bilbao 1-0(0-0)
Levante - Real Madrid 0-2(0-1)
Cádiz - Granada 1-1(0-1)
FC Barcelona - Sevilla FC 1-1(1-1)

Round 6 [17-18.10.2020]
Granada - Sevilla FC 1-0(0-0)
Celta Vigo - Atlético Madrid 0-2(0-1)
Real Madrid - Cádiz 0-1(0-1)
Getafe - FC Barcelona 1-0(0-0)
Eibar - Osasuna 0-0
Athletic Bilbao - Levante 2-0(0-0)
Villarreal - Valencia 2-1(1-1)
Alavés - Elche 0-2(0-1)
Huesca - Real Valladolid 2-2(0-1)
Real Betis - Real Sociedad 0-3(0-1)

Round 7 [23-26.10.2020]
Elche - Valencia 2-1(2-0)
FC Barcelona - Real Madrid 1-3(1-1)
Osasuna - Athletic Bilbao 1-0(0-0)
Sevilla FC - Eibar 0-1(0-1)
Atlético Madrid - Real Betis 2-0(0-0)
Real Valladolid - Alavés 0-2(0-0)
Cádiz - Villarreal 0-0
Getafe - Granada 0-1(0-1)
Real Sociedad - Huesca 4-1(1-0)
Levante - Celta Vigo 1-1(0-0)

Round 8 [30.10.-02.11.2020]
Eibar - Cádiz 0-2(0-2)
Real Madrid - Huesca 4-1(2-0)
Athletic Bilbao - Sevilla FC 2-1(0-1)
Osasuna - Atlético Madrid 1-3(0-1)
Alavés - FC Barcelona 1-1(1-0)
Real Betis - Elche 3-1(2-0)
Celta Vigo - Real Sociedad 1-4(0-2)
Granada - Levante 1-1(1-1)
Valencia - Getafe 2-2(1-0)
Villarreal - Real Valladolid 2-0(2-0)

Round 9 [06-08.11.2020]
Elche - Celta Vigo 1-1(1-1)
Huesca - Eibar 1-1(0-1)
FC Barcelona - Real Betis 5-2(1-1)
Sevilla FC - Osasuna 1-0(0-0)
Atlético Madrid - Cádiz 4-0(2-0)
Getafe - Villarreal 1-3(1-2)
Real Sociedad - Granada 2-0(2-0)
Levante - Alavés 1-1(0-1)
Real Valladolid - Athletic Bilbao 2-1(1-0)
Valencia - Real Madrid 4-1(2-1)

Round 10 [20-23.11.2020]
Osasuna - Huesca 1-1(0-1)
Levante - Elche 1-1(1-0)
Villarreal - Real Madrid 1-1(0-1)
Sevilla FC - Celta Vigo 4-2(2-2)
Atlético Madrid - FC Barcelona 1-0(1-0)
Eibar - Getafe 0-0
Cádiz - Real Sociedad 0-1(0-0)
Granada - Real Valladolid 1-3(0-1)
Alavés - Valencia 2-2(2-0)
Athletic Bilbao - Real Betis 4-0(2-0)

Round 11 [27-30.11.2020]
Real Valladolid - Levante 1-1(0-0)
Elche - Cádiz 1-1(1-0)
Valencia - Atlético Madrid 0-1(0-0)
Huesca - Sevilla FC 0-1(0-0)
Real Madrid - Alavés 1-2(0-1)
FC Barcelona - Osasuna 4-0(2-0)
Getafe - Athletic Bilbao 1-0(0-1)
Celta Vigo - Granada 3-1(1-1)
Real Sociedad - Villarreal 1-1(1-1)
Real Betis - Eibar 0-2(0-0)

Round 12 [04-07.12.2020]
Athletic Bilbao - Celta Vigo 0-2(0-0)
Levante - Getafe 3-0(2-0)
Sevilla FC - Real Madrid 0-1(0-0)
Atlético Madrid - Real Valladolid 2-0(0-0)
Cádiz - FC Barcelona 2-1(1-0)
Granada - Huesca 3-3(1-1)
Osasuna - Real Betis 2-0(0-0)
Villarreal - Elche 0-0
Alavés - Real Sociedad 0-0
Eibar - Valencia 0-0

Round 13 [11-14.12.2020]
Real Valladolid - Osasuna 3-2(1-2)
Valencia - Athletic Bilbao 2-2(1-0)
Getafe - Sevilla FC 0-1(0-0)
Huesca - Alavés 1-0(0-0)
Real Madrid - Atlético Madrid 2-0(1-0)
Real Sociedad - Eibar 1-1(1-0)
Real Betis - Villarreal 1-1(0-1)
Elche - Granada 0-1(0-1)
FC Barcelona - Levante 1-0(0-0)
Celta Vigo - Cádiz 4-0(4-0)

Round 14 [18-20.12.2020]
Athletic Bilbao - Huesca 2-0(0-0)
Atlético Madrid - Elche 3-1(1-0)
FC Barcelona - Valencia 2-2(1-1)
Levante - Real Sociedad 2-1(1-1)
Osasuna - Villarreal 1-3(0-2)
Sevilla FC - Real Valladolid 1-1(1-0)
Celta Vigo - Alavés 2-0(1-0)
Granada - Real Betis 2-0(2-0)
Cádiz - Getafe 0-2(0-1)
Eibar - Real Madrid 1-3(1-2)

Round 15 [22-23.12.2020]
Valencia - Sevilla FC 0-1(0-0)
Elche - Osasuna 2-2(0-1)
Huesca - Levante 1-1(1-0)
Real Sociedad - Atlético Madrid 0-2(0-0)
Real Valladolid - FC Barcelona 0-3(0-2)
Villarreal - Athletic Bilbao 1-1(0-1)
Getafe - Celta Vigo 1-1(1-1)
Real Madrid - Granada 2-0(0-0)
Alavés - Eibar 2-1(2-1)
Real Betis - Cádiz 1-0(0-0)

Round 16 [29-31.12.2020]
Sevilla FC - Villarreal 2-0(1-0)
FC Barcelona - Eibar 1-1(0-0)
Cádiz - Real Valladolid 0-0
Levante - Real Betis 4-3(3-1)
Granada - Valencia 2-1(1-1)
Atlético Madrid - Getafe 1-0(1-0)
Celta Vigo - Huesca 2-1(1-0)
Elche - Real Madrid 1-1(0-1)
Athletic Bilbao - Real Sociedad 0-1(0-1)
Osasuna - Alavés 1-1(0-0)

Round 17 [02-04.01.2021]
Villarreal - Levante 2-1(1-0)
Real Betis - Sevilla FC 1-1(0-0)
Getafe - Real Valladolid 0-1(0-1)
Real Madrid - Celta Vigo 2-0(1-0)
Athletic Bilbao - Elche 1-0(1-0)
Alavés - Atlético Madrid 1-2(0-1)
Eibar - Granada 2-0(0-0)
Real Sociedad - Osasuna 1-1(0-1)
Huesca - FC Barcelona 0-1(0-1)
Valencia - Cádiz 1-1(0-0)

Round 18 [08-11.01.2021]
Celta Vigo - Villarreal 0-4(0-4)
Sevilla FC - Real Sociedad 3-2(2-2)
Granada - FC Barcelona 0-4(0-3)
Osasuna - Real Madrid 0-0
Levante - Eibar 2-1(0-0)
Cádiz - Alavés 3-1(1-1)
Real Valladolid - Valencia 0-1(0-0)
Elche - Getafe 1-3(1-1)
Huesca - Real Betis 0-2(0-0)
Atl. Madrid - At. Bilbao 2-1(1-1) [10.03.2021]

Round 19 [19-21.01.2021]
Real Madrid - At. Bilbao 3-1(1-0)[15.12.2020]
Barcelona – R.Sociedad 2-1(2-1) [16.12.2020]
Cádiz - Levante 2-2(2-2)
Real Valladolid - Elche 2-2(0-2)
Alavés - Sevilla FC 1-2(1-2)
Getafe - Huesca 1-0(0-0)
Real Betis - Celta Vigo 2-1(2-1)
Villarreal - Granada 2-2(1-1)
Valencia - Osasuna 1-1(0-1)
Eibar - Atlético Madrid 1-2(1-1)

Round 20 [22-25.01.2021]
Levante - Real Valladolid 2-2(0-0)
Huesca - Villarreal 0-0
Sevilla FC - Cádiz 3-0(2-0)
Real Sociedad - Real Betis 2-2(0-0)
Alavés - Real Madrid 1-4(0-3)
Osasuna - Granada 3-1(2-0)
Elche - FC Barcelona 0-2(0-1)
Celta Vigo - Eibar 1-1(1-0)
Atlético Madrid - Valencia 3-1(1-1)
Athletic Bilbao - Getafe 5-1(1-1)

Round 21 [29.01.-01.02.2021]
Real Valladolid - Huesca 1-3(0-1)
Eibar - Sevilla FC 0-2(0-1)
Real Madrid - Levante 1-2(1-1)
Valencia - Elche 1-0(1-0)
Villarreal - Real Sociedad 1-1(1-0)
Getafe - Alavés 0-0
Cádiz - Atlético Madrid 2-4(1-2)
Granada - Celta Vigo 0-0
FC Barcelona - Athletic Bilbao 2-1(1-0)
Real Betis - Osasuna 1-0(0-0)

Round 22 [05-08.02.2021]
Alavés - Real Valladolid 1-0(0-0)
Levante - Granada 2-2(1-1)
Huesca - Real Madrid 1-2(0-0)
Elche - Villarreal 2-2(0-2)
Sevilla FC - Getafe 3-0(0-0)
Real Sociedad - Cádiz 4-1(2-0)
Athletic Bilbao - Valencia 1-1(1-0)
Osasuna - Eibar 2-1(1-1)
Real Betis - FC Barcelona 2-3(1-0)
Atlético Madrid - Celta Vigo 2-2(1-1)

Round 23 [12-15.02.2021]
Celta Vigo - Elche 3-1(2-0)
Granada - Atlético Madrid 1-2(0-0)
Sevilla FC - Huesca 1-0(1-0)
Eibar - Real Valladolid 1-1(1-1)
FC Barcelona - Alavés 5-1(2-0)
Getafe - Real Sociedad 0-1(0-1)
Real Madrid - Valencia 2-0(2-0)
Levante - Osasuna 0-1(0-0)
Villarreal - Real Betis 1-2(0-1)
Cádiz - Athletic Bilbao 0-4(0-3)

Round 24 [19-22.02.2021]
Real Betis - Getafe 1-0(0-0)
Elche - Eibar 1-0(1-0)
Atlético Madrid - Levante 0-2(0-1)
Valencia - Celta Vigo 2-0(0-0)
Real Valladolid - Real Madrid 0-1(0-0)
FC Barcelona - Cádiz 1-1(1-0)
Real Sociedad - Alavés 4-0(1-0)
Huesca - Granada 3-2(3-1)
Athletic Bilbao - Villarreal 1-1(1-1)
Osasuna - Sevilla FC 0-2(0-1)

Round 25 [26.02.-01.03.2021]
Levante - Athletic Bilbao 1-1(1-0)
Eibar - Huesca 1-1(0-0)
Sevilla FC - FC Barcelona 0-2(0-1)
Alavés - Osasuna 0-1(0-0)
Getafe - Valencia 3-0(1-0)
Celta Vigo - Real Valladolid 1-1(0-0)
Cádiz - Real Betis 0-1(0-0)
Granada - Elche 2-1(1-1)
Villarreal - Atlético Madrid 0-2(0-1)
Real Madrid - Real Sociedad 1-1(0-0)

Round 26 [05-08.03.2021]
Valencia - Villarreal 2-1(0-1)
Real Valladolid - Getafe 2-1(2-1)
Elche - Sevilla FC 2-1(0-0)
Cádiz - Eibar 1-0(1-0)
Osasuna - FC Barcelona 0-2(0-1)
Huesca - Celta Vigo 3-4(2-2)
Atlético Madrid - Real Madrid 1-1(1-0)
Real Sociedad - Levante 1-0(1-0)
Athletic Bilbao - Granada 2-1(1-0)
Real Betis - Alavés 3-2(0-2)

Round 27 [12-15.03.2021]
Levante - Valencia 1-0(1-0)
Alavés - Cádiz 1-1(1-0)
Real Madrid - Elche 2-1(0-0)
Osasuna - Real Valladolid 0-0
Getafe - Atlético Madrid 0-0
Celta Vigo - Athletic Bilbao 0-0
Granada - Real Sociedad 1-0(0-0)
Eibar - Villarreal 1-3(0-2)
Sevilla FC - Real Betis 1-0(1-0)
FC Barcelona - Huesca 4-1(2-1)

Round 28 [19-21.03.2021]
Real Betis - Levante 2-0(0-0)
Athletic Bilbao - Eibar 1-1(1-1)
Celta Vigo - Real Madrid 1-3(1-2)
Huesca - Osasuna 0-0
Real Valladolid - Sevilla FC 1-1(1-0)
Getafe - Elche 1-1(0-1)
Valencia - Granada 2-1(1-0)
Villarreal - Cádiz 2-1(1-0)
Atlético Madrid - Alavés 1-0(0-0)
Real Sociedad - FC Barcelona 1-6(0-2)

Round 29 [02-05.04.2021]
Levante - Huesca 0-2(0-1)
Granada - Villarreal 0-3(0-2)
Real Madrid - Eibar 2-0(1-0)
Osasuna - Getafe 0-0
Alavés - Celta Vigo 1-3(0-3)
Elche - Real Betis 1-1(1-1)
Cádiz - Valencia 2-1(1-1)
Sevilla FC - Atlético Madrid 1-0(0-0)
FC Barcelona - Real Valladolid 1-0(0-0)
Real Sociedad - Athl. Bilbao 1-1(0-0) [07.04.]

Round 30 [09-12.04.2021]
Huesca - Elche 3-1(2-1)
Getafe - Cádiz 0-1(0-0)
Athletic Bilbao - Alavés 0-0
Eibar - Levante 0-1(0-1)
Real Madrid - FC Barcelona 2-1(2-0)
Villarreal - Osasuna 1-2(0-0)
Valencia - Real Sociedad 2-2(0-2)
Real Valladolid - Granada 1-2(1-0)
Real Betis - Atlético Madrid 1-1(1-1)
Celta Vigo - Sevilla FC 3-4(3-2)

Round 31 [21-22.04.2021]
Levante - Sevilla FC 0-1(0-0)
Osasuna - Valencia 3-1(2-1)
Real Betis - Athletic Bilbao 0-0
Alavés - Villarreal 2-1(1-0)
Elche - Real Valladolid 1-1(1-0)
Cádiz - Real Madrid 0-3(0-3)
Atlético Madrid - Huesca 2-0(1-0)
Granada - Eibar 4-1(2-0)
Real Sociedad - Celta Vigo 2-1(2-1)
FC Barcelona - Getafe 5-2(3-1)

Round 32 [24-26.04.2021]
Elche - Levante 1-0(1-0)
Real Valladolid - Cádiz 1-1(1-0)
Valencia - Alavés 1-1(0-0)
Real Madrid - Real Betis 0-0
Huesca - Getafe 0-2(0-1)
Villarreal - FC Barcelona 1-2(1-2)
Celta Vigo - Osasuna 2-1(1-0)
Sevilla FC - Granada 2-1(1-0)
Athletic Bilbao - Atlético Madrid 2-1(1-0)
Eibar - Real Sociedad 0-1(0-1)

Round 33 [18.04.2021]
Osasuna - Elche 2-0(1-0)
Real Sociedad - Sevilla FC 1-2(1-2)
Alavés - Huesca 1-0(0-0)
Atlético Madrid - Eibar 5-0(2-0)
Real Betis - Valencia 2-2(2-1)
Cádiz - Celta Vigo 0-0
Getafe - Real Madrid 0-0
Levante - Villarreal 1-5(1-2)
Athletic Bilbao - Valladolid 2-2(1-0) [28.04.]
FC Barcelona - Granada 1-2(1-0) [29.04.]

Round 34 [30.04.-03.05.2021]
Celta Vigo - Levante 2-0(0-0)
Eibar - Alavés 3-0(1-0)
Elche - Atlético Madrid 0-1(0-1)
Huesca - Real Sociedad 1-0(0-0)
Real Madrid - Osasuna 2-0(0-0)
Real Valladolid - Real Betis 1-1(0-0)
Villarreal - Getafe 1-0(0-0)
Granada - Cádiz 0-1(0-1)
Valencia - FC Barcelona 2-3(0-0)
Sevilla FC - Athletic Bilbao 0-1(0-0)

Round 35 [07-10.05.2021]
Real Sociedad - Elche 2-0(0-0)
Alavés - Levante 2-2(1-2)
FC Barcelona - Atlético Madrid 0-0
Cádiz - Huesca 2-1(2-1)
Athletic Bilbao - Osasuna 2-2(1-1)
Getafe - Eibar 0-1(0-0)
Valencia - Real Valladolid 3-0(1-0)
Villarreal - Celta Vigo 2-4(1-3)
Real Madrid - Sevilla FC 2-2(0-1)
Real Betis - Granada 2-1(1-0)

Round 36 [11-13.05.2021]
Osasuna - Cádiz 3-2(1-0)
Elche - Alavés 0-2(0-1)
Levante - FC Barcelona 3-3(0-2)
Sevilla FC - Valencia 1-0(0-0)
Celta Vigo - Getafe 1-0(1-0)
Huesca - Athletic Bilbao 1-0(0-0)
Atlético Madrid - Real Sociedad 2-1(2-0)
Real Valladolid - Villarreal 0-2(0-0)
Eibar - Real Betis 1-1(0-1)
Granada - Real Madrid 1-4(0-2)

Round 37 [16.05.2021]
Alavés - Granada 4-2(2-1)
Athletic Bilbao - Real Madrid 0-1(0-0)
Atlético Madrid - Osasuna 2-1(0-0)
FC Barcelona - Celta Vigo 1-2(1-1)
Real Betis - Huesca 1-0(0-0)
Getafe - Levante 2-1(1-1)
Cádiz - Elche 1-3(1-0)
Real Sociedad - Real Valladolid 4-1(4-0)
Valencia - Eibar 4-1(3-1)
Villarreal - Sevilla FC 4-0(1-0)

Round 38 [21-23.05.2021]
Levante - Cádiz 2-2(1-2)
Celta Vigo - Real Betis 2-3(1-0)
Eibar - FC Barcelona 0-1(0-0)
Huesca - Valencia 0-0
Osasuna - Real Sociedad 0-1(0-0)
Real Madrid - Villarreal 2-1(0-1)
Real Valladolid - Atlético Madrid 1-2(1-0)
Elche - Athletic Bilbao 2-0(1-0)
Granada - Getafe 0-0
Sevilla FC - Alavés 1-0(0-0)

Final Standings

									Home						Away				
					Total															
1.	**Club Atlético de Madrid**	38	26	8	4	67	-	25	86	15	3	1	41	-	11	11	5	3	26	- 14
2.	Real Madrid CF	38	25	9	4	67	-	28	84	13	3	3	33	-	13	12	6	1	34	- 15
3.	FC Barcelona	38	24	7	7	85	-	38	79	11	5	3	44	-	20	13	2	4	41	- 18
4.	Sevilla FC	38	24	5	9	53	-	33	77	14	1	4	27	-	11	10	4	5	26	- 22
5.	Real Sociedad de Fútbol San Sebastián	38	17	11	10	59	-	38	62	9	6	4	34	-	21	8	5	6	25	- 17
6.	Real Betis Balompié Sevilla	38	17	10	11	50	-	50	61	10	5	4	27	-	21	7	5	7	23	- 29
7.	Villarreal CF	38	15	13	10	60	-	44	58	8	6	5	29	-	23	7	7	5	31	- 21
8.	RC Celta de Vigo	38	14	11	13	55	-	57	53	9	3	7	30	-	30	5	8	6	25	- 27
9.	Granada CF	38	13	7	18	47	-	65	46	9	4	6	25	-	25	4	3	12	22	- 40
10.	Athletic Club Bilbao	38	11	13	14	46	-	42	46	8	6	5	29	-	19	3	7	9	17	- 23
11.	CA Osasuna Pamplona	38	11	11	16	37	-	48	44	7	5	7	21	-	23	4	6	9	16	- 25
12.	Cádiz CF	38	11	11	16	36	-	58	44	5	5	9	17	-	30	6	6	7	19	- 28
13.	Valencia CF	38	10	13	15	50	-	53	43	8	7	4	34	-	23	2	6	11	16	- 30
14.	Levante UD Valencia	38	9	14	15	46	-	57	41	5	9	5	27	-	30	4	5	10	19	- 27
15.	Getafe CF	38	9	11	18	28	-	43	38	6	6	7	15	-	13	3	5	11	13	- 30
16.	Deportivo Alavés Vitoria-Gasteiz	38	9	11	18	36	-	57	38	6	6	7	21	-	25	3	5	11	15	- 32
17.	Elche CF	38	8	12	18	34	-	55	36	5	8	6	18	-	23	3	4	12	16	- 32
18.	SD Huesca *(Relegated)*	38	7	13	18	34	-	53	34	5	7	7	17	-	21	2	6	11	17	- 32
19.	Real Valladolid CF *(Relegated)*	38	5	16	17	34	-	57	31	3	7	9	19	-	30	2	9	8	15	- 27
20.	SD Eibar *(Relegated)*	38	6	12	20	29	-	52	30	2	7	10	12	-	21	4	5	10	17	- 31

Top goalscorers:		
30	**Lionel Andrés Messi Cuccittini (ARG)**	*FC Barcelona*
23	Karim Mostafa Benzema (FRA)	*Real Madrid CF*
23	Gerard Moreno Balagueró	*Villarreal CF*
21	Luis Alberto Suárez Díaz (URU)	*Club Atlético de Madrid*
18	Youssef En-Nesyri (MAR)	*Sevilla FC*
17	Alexander Isak (SWE)	*Real Sociedad de Fútbol San Sebastián*
14	Iago Aspas Juncal	*RC Celta de Vigo*

NATIONAL CUP
Copa del Rey 2019/2020

Final

The final between Athletic Club Bilbao and Real Sociedad de Fútbol San Sebastián was postponed due to COVID-19 pandemic.

03.04.2021; Estadio La Cartuja, Sevilla; Referee: Xavier Estrada Fernández; Attendance: 0
Athletic Club Bilbao - Real Sociedad de Fútbol San Sebastián   **0-1(0-0)**

Athletic Bilbao: Unai Simón Mendibil, Óscar de Marcos Arana, Yeray Álvarez López, Iñigo Martínez Berridi, Yuri Berchiche Izeta (90+3.Ander Capa Rodríguez), Alejandro „Álex" Berenguer Remiro (76.Mikel Vesga Arruti), Daniel „Dani" García Carrillo (76.Asier Villalibre Molina), Unai Vencedor París (68.Unai López Cabrera), Iker Muniain Goñi (Cap), Iñaki Williams Arthuer, Raúl García Escudero. Trainer: Marcelino García Toral.

Real Sociedad: Alejandro Remiro Gargallo, Andoni Gorosabel Espinosa (90+3.Aritz Elustondo Irribaría), Robin Le Normand, Ignacio „Nacho" Monreal Eraso, Igor Zubeldía Elorza, Martín Zubimendi Ibáñez, David Josué Jiménez Silva (85.Ander Guevara Lajo), Mikel Merino Zazón, Cristián Portugués Manzanera „Portu" (89.Carlos Fernández Luna), Alexander Isak (89.Ander Barrenetxea Muguruza), Mikel Oyarzabal Ugarte (Cap). Trainer: Imanol Alguacil Barrenetxea.

Goals: 0-1 Mikel Oyarzabal Ugarte (63 penalty).

NATIONAL CUP
Copa del Rey 2020/2021

First Round [15-17/23/30.12.2020]

CA Pulpileño - CD Lugo	1-2(0-0)	CF Rayo Majadahonda - Yeclano Deportivo	1-2(0-0)
CD Marchamalo - SD Huesca	2-3(0-1,1-1)	Marbella FC - Club Lleida Esportiu	1-0(0-0)
UD Tomares - CA Osasuna Pamplona	0-6(0-2)	CD Calahorra - CF La Nucía	0-1(0-0)
CD Cantolagua - Real Valladolid CF	0-5(0-2)	CD Buñol - Elche CF	1-2(1-0)
Sestao River Club - CD Tenerife	0-2(0-0,0-0)	CD Rincón - Deportivo Alavés Vitoria-Gasteiz	0-2(0-1)
Club Portugalete - SD Ponferradina	1-0(0-0)	SD Leioa - Villarreal CF	0-6(0-2)
CD Ciudad de Lucena - Sevilla FC	0-3(0-3)	CD Marino - UE Cornellà	0-1(0-0)
Ourense CF - CD Leganés	0-1(0-0,0-0)	RC Deportivo La Coruña - CD El Ejido 2012	1-0(1-0)
CD Coria - Real Oviedo	2-3(1-2)	CDA Navalcarnero - CD Badajoz	1-0(1-0)
Coruxo FC - Málaga CF	0-4(0-1)	CD Anaitasuna Azkoitia - Getafe CF	1-2(0-0)
CD Lealtad de Villaviciosa - AD Alcorcón	1-2(0-1)	CD Ribadumia - Cádiz CF	0-2(0-1)
Burgos CF - FC Andorra	2-0(0-0)	AD San Juan - Granada CF	0-2(0-2)
CD Quintanar del Rey - Real Sporting de Gijón	1-2(0-0)	Gimnástica Segoviana CF - Girona FC	0-2(0-1)
CE L'Hospitalet - UD Almería	1-4(0-2)	CD Teruel - Rayo Vallecano de Madrid	2-3(0-1,1-1)
San Fernando CD Isleño - CD Castellón	0-2(0-2)	UD Ibiza - SD Compostela	2-1(1-1,1-1)
Córdoba CF - Albacete Balompié	1-0(0-0)	CD Leonesa - CF Villanovense	1-0(1-0)
CD Numancia de Soria - CF Lorca Deportiva	4-1(2-0)	UD Mutilvera - Real Racing Club de Santander	1-0(0-0)
Racing Murcia City 1913 FC - Levante UD Valencia	0-5(0-2)	UCAM Murcia CF - Real Betis Balompié Sevilla	0-2(0-1)
CE Cardassar - Club Atlético de Madrid	0-3(0-2)	SCR Peña Deportiva - SD Tarazona	4-1(1-1)
Terrassa FC - Valencia CF	2-4(1-0,2-2)	CD Varea - UD Las Palmas	0-4(0-3)
Las Rozas CF - CD Mirandés	1-0(1-0)	Pontevedra CF - FC Cartagena	2-1(1-0)
RS Gimnástica Torrelavega - Real Zaragoza	0-2(0-0)	CD Alcoyano - CD Laredo	4-1(2-1)
UE Llagostera-Cos.Brava - RCD Espanyol Barcelona	0-1(0-0,0-0)	Extremadura UD Almendralejo - UD Socuéllamos	1-2(0-1)
CD Ibiza Islas Pitiusas - CE Sabadell FC	0-2(0-0)	Racing Rioja CF Logroño - SD Eibar	0-2(0-1)
CD Atlético Baleares - CF Fuenlabrada	0-1(0-0)	UD Llanera - Real Club Celta de Vigo	0-5(0-1)
SD Amorebieta - UD Logroñés	1-0(1-0)	Club Haro Deportivo - RB Linense	2-1(1-1)
DUX Internacional de Madrid - Linares Deportivo	0-3(0-1)	Zamora CF - SD Logroñés	2-1(1-0)
CD Guijuelo - RCD Mallorca	0-1(0-0)	UD Poblense - UE Olot	1-2(0-1)

Second Round [05-07.01.2021]

UD Ibiza - Real Club Celta de Vigo	5-2(3-0)	UE Cornellà - Club Atlético de Madrid	1-0(1-0)
Córdoba CF - Getafe CF	1-0(1-0)	UE Olot - CA Osasuna Pamplona	0-3(0-1)
Zamora CF - Villarreal CF	1-4(1-2)	Deportivo La Coruña - Deportivo Alavés Vit.-Gasteiz	0-1(0-0)
Linares Deportivo - Sevilla FC	0-2(0-1)	Burgos CF - RCD Espanyol Barcelona	0-2(0-0)
Marbella FC - Real Valladolid CF	2-3(0-0,2-2)	CD Castellón - CD Tenerife	0-2(0-2)
AD Alcorcón - Real Zaragoza	2-1(1-1)	CF Fuenlabrada - RCD Mallorca	2-2 aet; 7-6 pen
Club Portugalete - Levante UD Valencia	1-2(0-1)	Málaga CF - Real Oviedo	1-0(0-0,0-0)
CF La Nucía - Elche CF	0-1(0-0)	Yeclano Deportivo - Valencia CF	1-4(0-3)
CD Numancia de Soria - UD Almería	1-2(0-1)	Pontevedra CF - Cádiz CF	0-0 aet; 4-5 pen
UD Socuéllamos - CD Leganés	0-2(0-2)	SD Amorebieta - Real Sporting de Gijón	0-1(0-0)
UD Mutilvera - Real Betis Balompié Sevilla	1-3(1-2)	SCR Peña Deportiva - CE Sabadell	0-0 aet; 2-0 pen
CD Leonesa - Granada CF	1-2(1-1,1-1)	Girona FC - CD Lugo	2-1(0-0,0-0)
Club Haro Deportivo - Rayo Vallecano de Madrid	1-3(0-2)	Las Rozas CF - SD Eibar	3-4(0-2,3-3)
CDA Navalcarnero - UD Las Palmas	1-0(0-0)	CD Alcoyano - SD Huesca	2-1(1-1)

Third Round [16-17/20-21..01.2021]			
SCR Peña Deportiva - Real Valladolid CF	1-4(1-0,1-1)	CDA Navalcarnero - SD Eibar	3-1(1-1)
UD Almería - Deportivo Alavés Vitoria-Gasteiz	5-0(3-0)	Real Sporting de Gijón - Real Betis Balompié Sevilla	0-2(0-2)
Girona FC - Cádiz CF	2-0(0-0)	AD Alcorcón - Valencia CF	0-2(0-1)
Rayo Vallecano de Madrid - Elche CF	2-0(1-0)	CD Tenerife - Villarreal CF	0-1(0-0)
CF Fuenlabrada - Levante UD Valencia	1-1 aet; 2-4 pen	Córdoba CF - Real Sociedad de Fútbol San Sebastián	0-2(0-0)
CD Leganés - Sevilla FC	0-1(0-0,0-0)	CD Alcoyano - Real Madrid CF	2-1(0-1,1-1)
Málaga CF - Granada CF	1-2(0-2)	UD Ibiza - Athletic Club Bilbao	1-2(1-0)
RCD Espanyol Barcelona - CA Osasuna Pamplona	0-2(0-2)	UE Cornellà - FC Barcelona	0-2(0-0,0-0)

1/8-Finals [26-28.01.2021]			
Real Valladolid CF - Levante UD Valencia	2-4(1-2)	Rayo Vallecano de Madrid - FC Barcelona	1-2(0-0)
Girona FC - Villarreal CF	0-1(0-1)	UD Almería - CA Osasuna Pamplona	0-0 aet; 5-4 pen
Real Betis Bal. Sevilla - Real Sociedad San Sebastián	3-1(0-1,1-1)	CDA Navalcarnero - Granada CF	0-6(0-4)
Sevilla FC - Valencia CF	3-0(3-0)	CD Alcoyano - Athletic Club Bilbao	1-2(1-0)

Quarter-Finals [02-04.02.2021]			
UD Almería - Sevilla FC	0-1(0-0)	Granada CF - FC Barcelona	3-5(1-0,2-2)
Levante UD Valencia - Villarreal CF	1-0(0-0,0-0)	Real Betis Balompié Sevilla - Athletic Club Bilbao	1-1 aet; 1-4 pen

Semi-Finals [10-11.02./03-04.03.2021]			
First Leg		**Second Leg**	
Sevilla FC - FC Barcelona	2-0(1-0)	FC Barcelona - Sevilla FC	3-0(1-0,2-0)
Athletic Club Bilbao - Levante UD Valencia	1-1(0-1)	Levante UD Valencia - Athletic Club Bilbao	1-2(1-1,1-1)

Final

17.04.2021; Estadio La Cartuja, Sevilla; Referee: Juan Martínez Munuera; Attendance: 0
FC Barcelona - Athletic Club Bilbao   **4-0(0-0)**

FC Barcelona: Marc-André ter Stegen, Óscar Mingueza García (87.Martin Braithwaite Christensen), Gerard Piqué i Bernabéu (82.Ronald Federico Araújo da Silva), Clément Nicolas Laurent Lenglet, Sergio Busquets Burgos, Sergiño Gianni Dest (71.Sergi Roberto Carnicer), Frenkie de Jong, Pedro González López „Pedri" (81.Moriba Kourouma Kourouma „Ilaix"),Jordi Alba Ramos, Lionel Andrés Messi Cuccitini (Cap), Antoine Griezmann (88.Ousmane Dembélé). Trainer: Ronald Koeman (Netherlands).

Athletic Bilbao: Unai Simón Mendibil, Óscar de Marcos Arana, Yeray Álvarez López (67.Unai Núñez Gestoso), Iñigo Martínez Berridi, Mikel Balenziaga Oruesagasti, Alejandro „Álex" Berenguer (54.Mikel Vesga Arruti), Daniel „Dani" García Carrillo, Unai López Cabrera (67.Yuri Berchiche Izeta), Iker Muniain Goñi (Cap) (46.Iñigo Lekue Martínez), Iñaki Williams Arthuer (67.Asier Villalibre Molina), Raúl García Escudero. Trainer: Marcelino García Toral

Goals: 1-0 Antoine Griezmann (60), 2-0 Frenkie de Jong (63), 3-0 Lionel Andrés Messi Cuccitini (68), 4-0 Lionel Andrés Messi Cuccitini (72).

THE CLUBS 2020/2021

Deportivo Alavés Vitoria-Gasteiz

Founded:	23.01.1921	
Stadium:	Estadio Mendizorrotza, Vitoria-Gasteiz (19,840)	
Trainer:	Pablo Machín Díez	07.04.1975
[12.01.2021]	Abelardo Fernández Antuña	19.04.1970
[05.04.2021]	Javier Calleja Revilla	12.05.1978

Goalkeepers:	DOB	M	(s)	G
Antonio Sivera Salvá	11.08.1996	1		
Fernando Pacheco Flores	18.05.1992	37	(1)	
Defenders:	**DOB**	**M**	**(s)**	**G**
Adrián Marín Gómez	09.01.1997	1	(4)	
Rubén Duarte Sánchez	18.10.1995	29	(2)	1
Rodrigo Ely (ITA)	03.11.1993	6	(2)	1
Javier López Carballo	25.03.2002	1	(8)	
Stephane Paul Keller (CMR)	20.08.2001		(1)	
Victor Laguardia Cisneros	05.11.1989	30	(2)	
Florian Lejeune (FRA)	20.05.1991	34		1
Martín Aguirregabiria Padilla	10.05.1996	16	(10)	
Alberto Rodríguez Baro „Tachi"	10.09.1997	8	(4)	
Tomás Franco Tavares (POR)	07.03.2001		(3)	
Joaquín „Ximo" Navarro Jiménez	23.01.1990	28	(3)	1
Midfielders:	**DOB**	**M**	**(s)**	**G**
Rodrigo Andrés Battaglia (ARG)	12.07.1991	29	(3)	1

Mohamed Abdallahi Mahmoud (MTN)	04.05.2000	1	(1)	
Manuel „Manu„ Alejandro García Sánchez	26.04.1986	10	(15)	
Pere Pons Riera	20.02.1993	12	(10)	2
Tomás Pina Isla	14.10.1987	31	(2)	1
Sergi García Pérez	14.04.1999		(2)	
Forwards:	**DOB**	**M**	**(s)**	**G**
Borja Sainz Eguskiza	01.02.2001	2	(19)	1
Jorge Franco Alviz „Burgui"	29.10.1993		(1)	
Iñigo Córdoba Querejeta	13.03.1997	3	(4)	
Deyverson Brum Silva Acosta (BRA)	08.05.1991	11	(16)	1
Édgar Antonio Méndez Ortega	02.01.1990	26	(7)	5
John Alberto Guidetti (SWE)	15.04.1992	1	(9)	1
José Luis Mato Sanmartín „Joselu"	27.03.1990	34	(3)	11
José Ignacio Peleteiro Ramallo „Jota"	16.06.1991	18	(5)	
Lucas Pérez Martínez	10.09.1988	19	(9)	4
Luis Jesús Rioja González „Luisito"	16.10.1993	25	(10)	4
Facundo Pellistri Rebollo (URU)	20.12.2001	5	(7)	

Athletic Club Bilbao

Founded: 1898
Stadium: Estadio San Mamés, Bilbao (53,289)
Trainer: Gaizka Garitano Agirre 09.07.1975
[04.01.2021] Marcelino García Toral 14.08.1965

Goalkeepers:	DOB	M	(s)	G
Jokin Ezkieta Mendiburu	17.08.1996	1		
Unai Simón Mendibil	11.06.1997	37		
Defenders:	**DOB**	**M**	**(s)**	**G**
Mikel Balenziaga Oruesagasti	29.02.1988	17	(6)	
Ander Capa Rodríguez	08.02.1992	25	(3)	2
Óscar de Marcos Arana	14.04.1989	17	(8)	1
Iñigo Lekue Martínez	04.05.1993	5	(13)	
Iñigo Martínez Berridi	17.05.1991	28		1
Unai Núñez Gestoso	30.01.1997	23	(2)	1
Yeray Álvarez López	24.01.1995	22	(1)	1
Yuri Berchiche Izeta	10.02.1990	21	(2)	1
Midfielders:	**DOB**	**M**	**(s)**	**G**
Iñigo Córdoba Querejeta	13.03.1997	1	(2)	
Daniel „Dani" García Carrillo	24.05.1990	21	(6)	
Iker Muniain Goñi	19.12.1992	23	(5)	5
Oihan Sancet Tirapu	25.04.2000	11	(13)	2
Unai López Cabrera	30.10.1995	15	(11)	3
Unai Vencedor París	15.11.2000	19	(9)	
Mikel Vesga Arruti	08.04.1993	20	(10)	
Oier Zarraga Egaña	04.01.1999	1	(4)	
Forwards:	**DOB**	**M**	**(s)**	**G**
Alejandro „Álex" Berenguer Remiro	04.07.1995	27	(8)	8
Ibai Gómez Pérez	11.11.1989	4	(9)	
Iñigo Vicente Elorduy	06.01.1998		(3)	
Kenan Kodro (BIH)	19.08.1993		(3)	1
Jon Morcillo Conesa	15.09.1998	16	(14)	2
Nicholas „Nico" Williams Arthuer	12.07.2002		(2)	
Raúl García Escudero	11.07.1986	21	(13)	5
Asier Villalibre Molina	30.09.1997	16	(19)	4
Iñaki Williams Arthuer	15.06.1994	27	(11)	6

Club Atlético de Madrid

Founded: 26.04.1903 (*as Athletic Club de Madrid*)
Stadium: Estadio Metropolitano, Madrid (68,456)
Trainer: Diego Pablo Simeone (ARG) 28.04.1970

Goalkeepers:	DOB	M	(s)	G
Jan Oblak (SVN)	07.01.1993	38		
Defenders:	**DOB**	**M**	**(s)**	**G**
Felipe Augusto de Almeida Monteiro (BRA)	16.05.1989	23	(8)	
José María Giménez de Vargas (URU)	20.01.1995	20	(1)	
Manuel "Manu" Sánchez de la Peña	24.08.2000	1		
Mario Hermoso Canseco	18.06.1995	30	(1)	1
Renan Augusto Lodi dos Santos (BRA)	08.04.1998	11	(12)	1
Ricard Sánchez Sendra	22.02.2000		(1)	
Stefan Savić (MNE)	08.01.1991	33		1
Kieran John Trippier (ENG)	19.09.1990	28		
Šime Vrsaljko (CRO)	10.01.1992	6	(3)	
Midfielders:	**DOB**	**M**	**(s)**	**G**
Yannick Ferreira-Carrasco (BEL)	04.09.1993	25	(5)	6
Héctor Miguel Herrera López (MEX)	19.04.1990	8	(8)	
Jorge Resurrección Merodio „Koke"	08.01.1992	34	(3)	1
Geoffrey Edwin Kondogbia (CTA)	15.02.1993	4	(21)	
Thomas Benoît Lemar (FRA)	12.11.1995	19	(8)	1
Marcos Llorente Moreno	30.01.1995	33	(4)	12
Thomas Partey (GHA)	13.06.1993	2	(1)	
Saúl Ñíguez Esclapez	21.11.1994	22	(11)	2
Lucas Sebastián Torreira Di Pascua (URU)	11.02.1996	3	(16)	1
Forwards:	**DOB**	**M**	**(s)**	**G**
Ángel Martín Correa Martínez (ARG)	09.03.1995	29	(9)	9
Moussa Dembélé (FRA)	12.07.1996		(5)	
Diego da Silva Costa	07.10.1988	2	(5)	2
João Félix Sequeira (POR)	10.11.1999	14	(17)	7
Luis Alberto Suárez Díaz (URU)	24.01.1987	30	(2)	21
Víctor Machín Pérez „Vitolo"	02.11.1989	3	(7)	

Futbol Club Barcelona

Founded: 29.11.1899 (*as Foot-Ball Club Barcelona*)
Stadium: Estadio Camp Nou, Barcelona (99,354)
Trainer: Ronald Koeman (NED) 21.03.1963

Goalkeepers:	DOB	M	(s)	G
Norberto Murara Neto (BRA)	19.07.1989	7		
Marc-André ter Stegen (GER)	30.04.1992	31		
Defenders:	**DOB**	**M**	**(s)**	**G**
Ronald Federico Araújo da Silva (URU)	07.03.1999	16	(8)	2
Sergiño Gianni Dest (USA)	03.11.2000	23	(7)	2
Jordi Alba Ramos	21.03.1989	34	(1)	3
Héctor Junior Firpo Adamés	22.08.1996	3	(4)	1
Clément Nicolas Laurent Lenglet (FRA)	17.06.1995	29	(4)	1
Óscar Mingueza García	13.05.1999	23	(4)	2
Gerard Piqué i Bernabéu	02.02.1987	18		
Sergi Roberto Carnicer	07.02.1992	9	(6)	1
Samuel Yves Umtiti (FRA)	14.11.1993	6	(7)	
Midfielders:	**DOB**	**M**	**(s)**	**G**
Sergio Busquets Burgos	16.07.1988	32	(4)	
Carles Aleñá Castillo	05.01.1998		(2)	
Philippe Coutinho Correia (BRA)	12.06.1992	8	(4)	2
Frenkie de Jong (NED)	12.05.1997	35	(2)	3
Moriba Kourouma Kourouma „Ilaix"	19.01.2003	4	(10)	1
Pedro González López „Pedri"	25.11.2002	28	(9)	3
Miralem Pjanić (BIH)	02.04.1990	6	(13)	
Ricard "Riqui" Puig Martí	13.08.1999	2	(12)	1
Forwards:	**DOB**	**M**	**(s)**	**G**
Martin Braithwaite Christensen (DEN)	05.06.1991	11	(18)	2
Masour Ousmane Dembélé (FRA)	15.05.1997	19	(11)	6
Anssumane „Ansu" Fati	31.10.2002	6	(1)	4
Antoine Griezmann (FRA)	21.03.1991	32	(4)	13
Lionel Andrés Messi Cuccitini (ARG)	24.06.1987	33	(2)	30
Francisco António Machado Mota Castro „Trincão" (POR)	29.12.1999	3	(25)	3

Cádiz Club de Fútbol

Founded: 10.09.1910
Stadium: Estadio „Ramón de Carranza", Cádiz (20,724)
Trainer: Álvaro Cervera Díaz 20.09.1965

Goalkeepers:	DOB	M	(s)	G
Alberto Cifuentes Martínez	29.05.1979	2		
David Gil Mohedano	11.01.1994	4		
Jeremías Conán Ledesma (ARG)	13.04.1993	32		
Defenders:	**DOB**	**M**	**(s)**	**G**
José Alejandro „Álex" Martín Valeron	25.01.1998	1	(1)	
Juan Torres Ruiz „Cala"	26.11.1989	26	(2)	3
Carlos Akapo Martínez (EQG)	12.03.1993	10	(3)	1
Luis Alfonso Espino García (URU)	05.01.1992	31	(1)	
Rafael Jiménez Jarque „Fali"	12.08.1993	29	(5)	
Isaac Carcelén Valencia „Iza"	23.04.1993	31	(1)	
Marcos Mauro López Gutiérrez (ARG)	09.01.1991	22	(2)	2
Marc Baró Ortíz	23.08.1999	1		
Pedro Alcalá Guirado	19.03.1989	8	(5)	
Midfielders:	**DOB**	**M**	**(s)**	**G**
Alejandro Fernández Iglesias „Álex"	15.10.1992	21	(4)	4
Álvaro Bastida Moya	12.05.2004		(1)	
Augusto Matías Fernández (ARG)	10.04.1986	4	(8)	
Yann Yves Laurent Bodiger (FRA)	09.02.1995	2	(7)	
Jon Ander Garrido Moracia	09.10.1989	7	(16)	
Jairo Izquierdo González	22.10.1993	11	(19)	1
José María Martín Bejarano-Serrano „José Mari"	06.12.1987	18	(4)	1
Jens Jønsson (DEN)	10.01.1993	33	(2)	
Jorge Marcos Pombo Escobar	22.02.1994	5	(7)	1
Salvador Sánchez Ponce „Salvi"	30.03.1991	25	(3)	2
Sergio González Martínez	14.05.1997	1		
Forwards:	**DOB**	**M**	**(s)**	**G**
Habeeb Omobolaji Adekanye (NED)	14.02.1999		(3)	
Alberto Álvaro Perea Correoso	19.12.1990	16	(11)	2
Álvaro Giménez Candela	19.05.1991	3	(8)	2
Álvaro Negredo Sánchez	20.08.1985	29	(6)	8
Iván Alejo Peralta	10.02.1995	6	(16)	1
Anthony Rubén Lozano Colón (HON)	25.04.1993	18	(11)	3
Filip Malbašić (SRB)	18.11.1992	8	(20)	
Alexander Mesa Travieso „Nano Mesa"	05.02.1995		(1)	
Manuel Nieto Sánchez	29.03.1998		(2)	
Rubén Sobrino Pozuelo	01.06.1992	11	(5)	1
Ivan Šaponjić (SRB)	02.08.1997	3	(6)	1

Real Club Celta de Vigo

Founded: 23.08.1923
Stadium: Estadio Abanca-Balaídos, Vigo (29,000)
Trainer: Óscar García Junyent — 26.04.1973
[12.11.2020] Eduardo Germán Coudet (ARG) — 12.09.1974

Goalkeepers:	DOB	M	(s)	G
Iván Villar Martínez	09.07.1997	19	(2)	
Rubén Blanco Veiga	25.07.1995	19		
Defenders:	**DOB**	**M**	**(s)**	**G**
Aarón Martín Caricol	22.04.1997	17	(2)	
Joseph Aidoo (GHA)	29.09.1995	14	(11)	
Néstor Alejandro Araujo Razo (MEX)	29.08.1991	26	(7)	
Carlos Domínguez Cáceres	11.02.2001	4		
Hugo Mallo Novegil	22.06.1991	30	(1)	3
José Manuel Fontán Mondragón	11.02.2000	7	(7)	
Kevin Vázquez Comesaña	23.03.1993	5	(3)	
Jeison Fabián Murillo Cerón (COL)	27.05.1992	31		2
Lucas René Olaza Catrofe (URU)	21.07.1994	18		
Sergio Carreira Vilariño	13.10.2000	3		1
Midfielders:	**DOB**	**M**	**(s)**	**G**
Denis Suárez Fernández	06.01.1994	34	(1)	
Francisco José "Fran" Beltrán Peinado	03.02.1999	13	(19)	3
Gabriel „Gabri" Veiga Novas	27.05.2002	1	(5)	
Jordan William Holsgrove (SCO)	10.09.1999		(5)	
Hugo Sotelo Gómez	19.12.2003		(1)	
Miguel Baeza Pérez	27.03.2000	4	(18)	1
Okay Yokuşlu (TUR)	09.03.1994	3	(9)	
Renato Fabrizio Tapia Cortijo (PER)	28.07.1995	32		
Forwards:	**DOB**	**M**	**(s)**	**G**
Alfonso González Martínez „Alfon"	04.05.1999		(2)	
Brais Méndez Portela	07.01.1997	30	(4)	9
Lautaro De León Billar (URU)	09.02.2001		(1)	
Facundo Ferreyra (ARG)	14.03.1991	2	(11)	1
Iago Aspas Juncal	01.08.1987	33		14
Miguel Rodríguez Vidal	29.04.2003		(4)	
Emre Mor (TUR)	24.07.1997	6	(5)	
Manuel Agudo Durán „Nolito"	15.10.1986	35	(1)	7
Santiago „Santi" Mina Lorenzo	07.12.1995	29	(5)	12
Augusto Jorge Mateo Solari (ARG)	03.01.1992	3	(13)	2

Sociedad Deportiva Eibar

Founded: 30.11.1940
Stadium: Estadio Ipurua, Eibar (8,164)
Trainer: José Luis Mendilibar Etxebarria — 14.03.1961

Goalkeepers:	DOB	M	(s)	G
Marko Dmitrović (SRB)	24.01.1992	35		1
Yoel Rodríguez Oterino	28.08.1988	3	(1)	
Defenders:	**DOB**	**M**	**(s)**	**G**
Alejandro Pozo Pozo	22.02.1999	24	(6)	
Álvaro Tejero Sacristán	20.07.1996	1	(1)	
Anaitz Arbilla Zabala	15.05.1987	30	(4)	
Pedro Bigas Rigo	15.05.1990	19	(2)	
Esteban Rodrigo Burgos (ARG)	09.01.1992	12	(2)	3
José Ángel Valdés Díaz „Cote"	05.09.1989	11	(3)	
Paulo André Rodrigues de Oliveira (POR)	08.01.1992	29	(2)	
Luís Rafael Soares Alves „Rafa Soares" (POR)	09.05.1995	12	(7)	
Roberto „Rober" Antonio Correa Silva	20.09.1992	13	(2)	
Kévin Rodrigues (POR)	05.03.1994	11	(11)	1
Sergio Cubero Ezcurra	05.09.1999		(1)	
Unai Dufur Espelosín	21.02.1999	1		
Midfielders:	**DOB**	**M**	**(s)**	**G**
Aleix García Serrano	28.06.1997	5	(6)	
Miguel Ángel Atienza Villa	27.05.1999	9	(3)	
Pape Diop (SEN)	19.03.1986	28	(5)	1
Eduardo „Edu" Expósito Jaén	01.08.1996	27	(4)	
Takashi Inui (JPN)	02.06.1988	22	(6)	1
Pedro León Sánchez Gil	24.11.1986	10	(14)	1
José Luis García del Pozo „Recio"	11.01.1991	8	(9)	1
Sergio Álvarez Díaz	23.01.1992	17	(10)	
Forwards:	**DOB**	**M**	**(s)**	**G**
Bryan Gil Salvatierra	11.02.2001	26	(2)	4
Eñaut Mendiaren Berasategi	25.06.1999	1		
Damian Kądzior (POL)	16.06.1992	2	(4)	
Enrique García Martínez „Kike García"	25.11.1989	36	(1)	12
Yoshinori Mutō (JPN)	15.07.1992	13	(13)	1
Enrique González Casín „Quique"	16.05.1990		(12)	
Sergi Enrich Ametller	26.02.1990	13	(14)	3
Unai Arietaleanizbeaskoa Miota	16.06.1999		(4)	

Elche Club de Fútbol

Founded: 1923
Stadium: Estadio „Martínez Valero", Elche, (33,732)
Trainer: Jorge Francisco Almirón Quintana(ARG) — 19.06.1971
[14.02.2021] Francisco 'Fran' Escribá Segura — 03.05.1965

Goalkeepers:	DOB	M	(s)	G
Édgar Badía Guardiola	12.02.1992	30		
Paulo Dino Gazzaniga Farias (ARG)	02.01.1992	8		
Defenders:	**DOB**	**M**	**(s)**	**G**
Antonio Barragán Fernández	12.06.1987	26	(1)	
Daniel Pedro Calvo Sanromán „Dani Calvo"	01.04.1994	19	(4)	2
Diego González Polanco	28.01.1995	15	(4)	1
Gonzalo Cacicedo Verdú	21.10.1988	33		
José Manuel Sánchez Guillén „Josema"	06.06.1996	21	(8)	
Youssouf Koné (MLI)	05.07.1995	1	(2)	
Johan Andrés Mojica Palacio (COL)	21.08.1992	14	(3)	
Helibelton Palacios Zapata (COL)	09.06.1993	8	(3)	
Juan Manuel Sánchez Miño (ARG)	01.01.1990	5	(4)	
Midfielders:	**DOB**	**M**	**(s)**	**G**
John Chetauya Nwankwo Donald Okeh	30.08.2000	1	(1)	
Miguel Ángel Garrido Cifuentes	05.10.1990	4	(7)	
Jonathan Carmona Alamo „Jony Álamo"	25.09.2001	1		
Luis Miguel Sánchez Benítez „Luismi"	05.05.1992	2	(9)	
Iván José Marcone (ARG)	03.06.1990	30	(3)	
Oménuké Mfulu (COD)	20.03.1994	9	(11)	
Ramón Folch Frigola	04.10.1989		(1)	
José Raúl Gutiérrez Parejo „Raúl Guti"	30.12.1996	33	(3)	3
Víctor Rodríguez Romero	23.07.1989	2	(14)	
Forwards:	**DOB**	**M**	**(s)**	**G**
Lucas Ariel Boyé (ARG)	28.02.1996	32	(2)	7
Guido Marcelo Carrillo (ARG)	25.05.1991	11	(10)	3
Fidel Chaves De La Torre	27.10.1989	28	(2)	6
José Antonio Ferrández Pomares „Josan"	03.12.1989	24	(9)	4
Jeison Steven Lucumí Mina (COL)	08.04.1995	1	(1)	
Juan Francisco Martínez Modesto „Nino"	10.06.1980		(16)	
Pere Milla Peña	23.09.1992	22	(10)	4
Pablo Daniel Piatti (ARG)	31.03.1989	3	(6)	
Emiliano Ariel Rigoni (ARG)	04.02.1993	12	(11)	1
José Antonio „Tete" Morente Oliva	04.12.1996	23	(7)	2

Getafe Club de Fútbol

Founded: 08.07.1983
Stadium: Estadio Coliseum „Alfonso Pérez", Getafe (17,393)
Trainer: José „Pepe" Bordalás Jiménez   05.03.1964

Goalkeepers:	DOB	M	(s)	G
David Soria Solís	04.04.1993	28		
Orlando Rubén Yáñez Alabart	12.10.1993	10		
Defenders:	**DOB**	**M**	**(s)**	**G**
Emmanuel Amankwaa Akurugu (GHA)	20.11.2001		(1)	
Erick Cathriel Cabaco Almada (URU)	19.04.1995	15	(5)	
Sofian Chakla (MAR)	02.09.1993	9	(2)	
José Manuel Rodríguez Benito „Chema"	03.03.1992	7	(3)	
Dakonam Djené (TOG)	31.12.1991	34		
Xabier Etxeita Gorritxategi	31.10.1987	9	(2)	
Juan Antonio Iglesias Sánchez	03.07.1998	7	(3)	
Allan-Roméo Nyom (CMR)	10.05.1988	28	(3)	
Mathías Olivera Miramontes (URU)	31.10.1997	30	(1)	
Damián Nicolás Suárez Suárez (URU)	27.04.1988	28	(3)	1
Midfielders:	**DOB**	**M**	**(s)**	**G**
Sabit Abdulai (GHA)	11.05.1999		(3)	
Mauro Wilney Arambarri Rosa (URU)	30.09.1995	33	(1)	3
Carles Aleñá Castillo	05.01.1998	15	(7)	2
Marc Cucurella Saseta	22.07.1998	37		3
David Timor Copoví	17.10.1989	15	(15)	
José Antonio Miranda Boacho (EQG)	22.07.1998		(4)	
Nemanja Maksimović (SRB)	26.01.1995	34	(1)	1
Ante Palaversa (CRO)	06.04.2000		(2)	
Forwards:	**DOB**	**M**	**(s)**	**G**
Ángel Luís Rodríguez Díaz	26.04.1987	12	(21)	5
Darío Poveda Romera	13.03.1997		(1)	
Abdoulay Diaby (MLI)	21.05.1991		(1)	
Juan Camilo Hernández Suárez (COL)	20.04.1999	18	(5)	2
John Joe Patrick Finn Benoa (IRL)	24.10.2003		(6)	
Takefusa Kubo (JPN)	04.06.2001	8	(10)	1
Mamor Niang (SEN)	04.02.2002		(1)	
Jaime Mata Arnaiz	24.10.1988	23	(10)	5
Francisco Portillo Soler	13.06.1990	3	(13)	
Enes Ünal (TUR)	10.05.1997	15	(13)	4
Víctor Mollejo Carpintero	21.01.2001		(4)	

Granada Club de Fútbol

Founded: 14.04.1931 (*as Club Recreativo Granada*)
Stadium: Nuevo Estadio de los Cármenes, Granada (19,336)
Trainer: Diego Martínez Penas   16.12.1980

Goalkeepers:	DOB	M	(s)	G
Aarón Escandell Banacloche	27.09.1995	5		
Ángel Jiménez Gallego	22.06.2002	1		
Rui Tiago Dantas da Silva (POR)	07.02.1994	32		
Defenders:	**DOB**	**M**	**(s)**	**G**
Adrián Marín Gómez	09.01.1997	3	(6)	
Domingos Sousa Coutinho Meneses Duarte (POR)	10.03.1995	27	(2)	1
Kingsley Fobi (GHA)	20.09.1998		(1)	
Dimitri Foulquier (GPE)	23.03.1993	32		
Germán Sánchez Barahona	12.12.1986	29	(5)	3
Jesús Vallejo Lázaro	05.01.1997	15	(6)	
Carlos Neva Tey	12.06.1996	21	(1)	
José „Pepe" Sánchez Martínez	02.03.2000	3		
Patricio Nehuén Pérez (ARG)	24.06.2000	9	(5)	
Joaquín José Marín Ruiz „Quini"	24.09.1989	12	(7)	1
Sergio Barcia Larenxeira	31.12.2000	1		
Víctor David Díaz Miguel	12.06.1988	7	(10)	
Midfielders:	**DOB**	**M**	**(s)**	**G**
Álvaro Bravo Jiménez	04.02.1998		(1)	
Ramon Olamilekan Azeez (NGA)	12.12.1992	1	(1)	
Juan Brunet (ARG)	24.01.1998		(2)	
Domingos Quina (POR)	18.11.1999	5	(3)	2
Yan Brice Eteki (CMR)	26.08.1997	16	(9)	
Federico „Fede" Vico Villegas	04.07.1994	9	(11)	
Maxime Gonalons (FRA)	10.03.1989	18	(7)	
Yangel Clemente Herrera Ravelo (VEN)	07.01.1998	25	(7)	3
Ismael „Isma" Ruiz Sánchez	14.02.2001	1		
Luis Milla Manzanares	07.10.1994	14	(2)	1
Ángel Montoro Sánchez	25.06.1988	17	(5)	1
Forwards:	**DOB**	**M**	**(s)**	**G**
Alberto Soro Álvarez	09.03.1999	3	(12)	1
Daniel „Dani" Plomer Gordillo	30.11.1998		(1)	
Darwin Daniel Machís Marcano (VEN)	07.02.1993	21	(11)	4
Jorge Molina Vidal	22.04.1982	17	(16)	8
Robert Kenedy Nunes do Nascimento (BRA)	08.02.1996	18	(10)	4
José Antonio Rodríguez Díaz „Puertas"	21.02.1992	22	(13)	3
Roberto Soldado Rillo	27.05.1985	16	(13)	9
Luis Javier Suárez Charris (COL)	02.12.1997	18	(9)	5

Sociedad Deportiva Huesca

Founded: 29.03.1960
Stadium: Estadio El Alcoraz, Huesca (7,638)
Trainer: Miguel Ángel Sánchez Muñoz "Míchel"   30.10.1975
[12.01.2021]   José Rojo Martín "Pacheta"   23.03.1968

Goalkeepers:	DOB	M	(s)	G
Álvaro Fernández Llorente	13.04.1998	22		
Andrés Eduardo Fernández Moreno	17.12.1986	16		
Defenders:	**DOB**	**M**	**(s)**	**G**
Javier „Javi" Galán Gil	19.11.1994	34	(3)	1
Luis Carlos Correia Pinto „Luisinho" (POR)	05.05.1985	2	(3)	
Pablo Insua Blanco	09.09.1993	17	(3)	
Pablo Carmine Maffeo Becerra	12.07.1997	25		1
Pedro López Muñoz	01.11.1983	10	(12)	
Jorge Pulido Mayoral	08.04.1991	32	(1)	1
Gastón Alexis Silva Perdomo (URU)	05.03.1994	6	(6)	
Dimitrios Siovas (GRE)	16.09.1988	34	(2)	2
Denis Vavro (SVK)	10.04.1996	9	(2)	
Midfielders:	**DOB**	**M**	**(s)**	**G**
Borja García Freire	02.11.1990	13	(8)	1
Idrissa Doumbia (CIV)	14.04.1998	7	(16)	
Eugeni Valderrama Domènech	19.07.1994	1	(2)	
Juan Carlos Real Ruiz	15.03.1991	3	(12)	
Mikel Rico Moreno	04.11.1984	27	(5)	1
Pedro Mosquera Parada	21.04.1988	24	(3)	
Kelechi Nwakali (NGA)	05.06.1998	1	(4)	
Jaime Seoane Valenciano	22.01.1997	23	(6)	1
Sergio Gómez Martín	04.09.2000	4	(25)	
Forwards:	**DOB**	**M**	**(s)**	**G**
Daniel „Dani" Escriche Romero	24.03.1998	7	(16)	
David Ferreiro Quiroga	01.04.1988	29	(8)	2
Javier „Javi" Ontiveros Parra	09.09.1997	10	(10)	2
Joaquín Muñoz Benavides	10.03.1999		(3)	
Shinji Okazaki (JPN)	16.04.1986	14	(11)	1
Rafael „Rafa" Mir Vicente	18.06.1997	32	(6)	13
Sandro Ramírez Castillo	09.07.1995	16	(4)	5

Levante Unión Deportiva Valencia

Founded: 09.09.1909
Stadium: Estadio Ciutat de València, Valencia (26,354)
Trainer: Francisco José López Fernández   19.09.1967

Goalkeepers:	DOB	M	(s)	G
Aitor Fernández Abarisketa	03.05.1991	29		
Daniel „Dani" Cárdenas Lindez	28.03.1997	8		
Jorge Ruiz Ojeada „Koke Vegas"	27.09.1995	1		
Defenders:	**DOB**	**M**	**(s)**	**G**
Carlos Clerc Martínez	21.02.1992	30	(5)	
Jorge Andújar Moreno „Coke"	26.04.1987	11	(6)	
Óscar Esau Duarte Gaitan (CRC)	03.06.1989	23	(6)	1
Jorge Miramón Santagertrudis	02.06.1989	19	(7)	
Roberto Suárez Pier „Róber"	16.02.1995	16	(3)	
Rúben Miguel Nunes Vezo (POR)	25.04.1994	25	(7)	1
Sergio Postigo Redondo	04.11.1988	19	(3)	
Francisco Javier Hidalgo Gómez „Son"	30.03.1994	10	(18)	
Antonio García Aranda „Toño García"	07.11.1989	9	(3)	
Midfielders:	**DOB**	**M**	**(s)**	**G**
Alejandro „Álex" Blesa Pina	15.01.2002		(1)	
Enis Bardhi (MKD)	02.07.1995	19	(7)	1

	DOB	M	(s)	G
José Ángel Gómez Campaña	31.05.1993	8	(1)	1
Cheick Doukouré (CIV)	11.09.1992		(7)	
Giorgi Kochorashvili (GEO)	29.06.1999		(3)	
Mickaël Malsa (MTQ)	12.10.1995	25	(10)	1
Gonzalo Julián Melero Manzanares	02.01.1994	21	(8)	7
Nemanja Radoja (SRB)	06.02.1993	13	(8)	
Nikola Vukčević (MNE)	13.12.1991	11	(2)	
Forwards:	**DOB**	**M**	**(s)**	**G**
Alejandro Cantero Sánchez	08.06.2000	3	(1)	
Daniel „Dani" Gómez Alcón	30.07.1998	17	(17)	2
Jorge De Frutos Sebastián	20.02.1997	22	(15)	4
José Luis Morales Nogales	23.07.1987	30	(8)	13
Rubén Rochina Naixes	23.03.1991	17	(8)	
Roger Martí Salvador	03.01.1991	26	(7)	12
Sergio León Limones	06.01.1989	6	(22)	2
Edgar Sevikyan (RUS)	08.08.2001		(1)	

Club Atlético Osasuna Pamplona

Founded: 24.10.1920
Stadium: Estadio El Sadar, Pamplona (23,576)
Trainer: Jagoba Arrasate Elustondo   22.04.1978

Goalkeepers:	DOB	M	(s)	G
Sergio Herrera Pirón	05.06.1993	32	(1)	
Juan Manuel Pérez Ruiz	15.07.1996	3		
Rubén Iván Martínez Andrade	22.06.1984	3		
Defenders:	**DOB**	**M**	**(s)**	**G**
Aridane Hernández Umpiérrez	23.03.1989	24		
David García Zubiria	14.02.1994	35		1
Juan Cruz Álvaro Armada	28.07.1992	23	(3)	
Manuel "Manu" Sánchez de la Peña	24.08.2000	10	(6)	
Ignacio „Nacho" Vidal Miralles	24.01.1995	25	(9)	
Jonás Ramalho Chimeno	10.06.1993	3	(2)	
Raúl Rodríguez Navas	11.05.1988	2		
Facundo Sebastián Roncaglia (ARG)	10.02.1987	14	(3)	1
Unai García Lugea	03.09.1992	13	(4)	
Midfielders:	**DOB**	**M**	**(s)**	**G**
Darko Brašanac (SRB)	12.02.1992	9	(7)	2

	DOB	M	(s)	G
Iñigo Pérez Soto	18.01.1988	16	(6)	
Javier Martínez Calvo „Javi"	22.12.1999	6	(7)	1
Jonathan Rodríguez Menéndez „Jony"	09.07.1991	9	(13)	
Lucas Torró Marset	19.07.1994	17	(8)	
Jon Moncayola Tollar	13.05.1998	28	(8)	2
Oier Sanjurjo Maté	25.05.1986	24	(8)	
Roberto Torres Morales	07.03.1989	19	(16)	7
Forwards:	**DOB**	**M**	**(s)**	**G**
Adrián López Álvarez	08.01.1988	5	(12)	1
Luis Ezequiel Ávila (ARG)	06.02.1994	2	(6)	
Ante Budimir (CRO)	22.07.1991	18	(12)	11
Jonathan Calleri (ARG)	23.09.1993	20	(5)	5
Enric Gallego Puigsech	12.09.1986	8	(14)	
Enrique Barja Afonso „Kike Barja"	04.04.1997	17	(16)	2
Marc Cardona Rovira	08.07.1995		(3)	
Rubén García Santos	14.07.1993	33	(4)	3

Real Betis Balompié Sevilla

Founded: 12.09.1907
Stadium: Estadio "Benito Villamarín", Sevilla (60,721)
Trainer: Manuel Luis Pellegrini Ripamonti (CHI)   16.09.1953

Goalkeepers:	DOB	M	(s)	G
Claudio Andrés Bravo Muñoz (CHI)	13.04.1983	20		
Joel Robles Blázquez	17.06.1990	18		
Defenders:	**DOB**	**M**	**(s)**	**G**
Alexandre „Álex" Moreno Lopera	08.06.1993	20	(3)	
Marc Bartra Aragall	15.01.1991	19		
Emerson Aparecido Leite de Souza Junior (BRA)	14.01.1999	34		1
Juan Miranda González	19.01.2000	18	(4)	1
Aïssa Mandi (ALG)	22.10.1991	27	(1)	3
Martín Montoya Torralbo	14.04.1991	2	(3)	
Sidnei Rechel da Silva Júnior (BRA)	23.08.1989	7	(4)	
Víctor Ruiz Torre	25.01.1989	24	(3)	2
Midfielders:	**DOB**	**M**	**(s)**	**G**
Edgar Paul Akouokou (CIV)	20.12.1997	4	(6)	
Sergio Canales Madrazo	16.02.1991	28	(3)	8

	DOB	M	(s)	G
Nabil Fekir (FRA)	18.07.1993	33		5
José Andrés Guardado Hernández (MEX)	28.09.1986	17	(7)	1
Rodrigo Sánchez Rodríguez „Rodri"	16.02.2000	5	(10)	
Guido Rodríguez (ARG)	12.04.1994	34	(1)	1
William Silva de Carvalho (POR)	07.04.1992	12	(15)	2
Forwards:	**DOB**	**M**	**(s)**	**G**
Aitor Ruibal García	22.03.1996	21	(7)	2
Borja Iglesias Quintas	17.01.1993	15	(13)	11
Cristian Tello Herrera	11.08.1991	12	(17)	5
Joaquín Sánchez Rodríguez	21.07.1981	16	(11)	2
Juan Miguel Jiménez López „Juanmi"	20.05.1993	5	(11)	2
Diego Lainez Leyva (MEX)	09.06.2000	8	(13)	
Lorenzo Morón García „Loren"	30.12.1993	9	(17)	1
Arnaldo Antonio Sanabria Ayala (PAR)	04.03.1996	10	(6)	3

Real Madrid Club de Fútbol

Founded: 06.03.1902 (as Madrid Football Club)
Stadium: Estadio "Santiago Bernabéu" / "Alfredo Di Stéfano",
           Madrid (81,044 / 6,000)
Trainer: Zinédine Zidane (FRA)   23.06.1972

Goalkeepers:	DOB	M	(s)	G
Thibaut Courtois (BEL)	11.05.1992	38		
Defenders:	**DOB**	**M**	**(s)**	**G**
Víctor Chust García	05.03.2000	1	(1)	
Daniel „Dani" Carvajal Ramos	11.01.1992	11	(2)	
Eder Gabriel Militão (BRA)	18.01.1998	13	(1)	1
Marcelo Vieira da Silva Júnior (BRA)	12.05.1988	12	(4)	
Ferland Mendy (FRA)	08.06.1995	24	(2)	1
Miguel Gutiérrez Ortega	27.07.2001	3	(3)	
José Ignacio Fernández Iglesias „Nacho"	18.01.1990	22	(2)	1
Álvaro Odriozola Arzalluz	14.12.1995	9	(4)	2
Sergio Ramos García	30.03.1986	15		2
Raphaël Varane (FRA)	25.04.1993	31		2
Midfielders:	**DOB**	**M**	**(s)**	**G**
Antonio Blanco Conde	23.07.2000	2	(2)	
Carlos Henrique Casemiro (BRA)	23.02.1992	32	(2)	6
Francisco Román Alarcón Suárez „Isco"	21.04.1992	8	(17)	

	DOB	M	(s)	G
Toni Kroos (GER)	04.01.1990	24	(4)	3
Marvin Olawale Akinlabi Park	03.07.2000	2	(2)	
Luka Modrić (CRO)	09.09.1985	32	(3)	5
Martin Ødegaard (NOR)	17.12.1998	3	(4)	
Federico Santiago Valverde Dipetta (URU)	22.07.1998	15	(9)	3
Forwards:	**DOB**	**M**	**(s)**	**G**
Sergio Arribas Calvo	30.09.2001		(8)	
Karim Mostafa Benzema (FRA)	19.12.1987	33	(1)	23
Borja Mayoral Moya	05.04.1997		(2)	
Eden Michael Hazard (BEL)	07.01.1991	7	(7)	3
Hugo Duro Perales	10.11.1999		(2)	
Luka Jović (SRB)	23.12.1997	2	(2)	
Lucas Vázquez Iglesias	01.07.1991	21	(3)	2
Marco Asensio Willemsen	21.01.1996	21	(14)	5
Mariano Díaz Mejía (DOM)	01.08.1993	5	(11)	2
Rodrygo Silva de Goes (BRA)	09.01.2001	10	(12)	1
Vinícius José Paixão de Oliveira Júnior (BRA)	12.07.2000	22	(13)	3

Real Sociedad de Fútbol San Sebastián

Goalkeepers:	DOB	M	(s)	G
Alejandro Remiro Gargallo	24.03.1995	38		
Defenders:	DOB	M	(s)	G
Aihen Muñoz Capellán	16.08.1997	14	(2)	
Andoni Gorosabel Espinosa	04.08.1996	28	(4)	
Aritz Arambarri Murua	31.01.1998		(1)	
Aritz Elustondo Irribaría	28.03.1994	22	(1)	1
Jon Pacheco Dozagarat	08.01.2001		(1)	
Joseba Zaldúa Bengoetxea	24.06.1992	6	(6)	
Robin Le Normand (FRA)	11.11.1996	30	(3)	
Diego Javier Llorente Ríos	16.08.1993	1		
Ignacio „Nacho" Monreal Eraso	26.02.1986	23	(3)	1
Modibo Sagnan (MLI)	14.04.1999	7	(9)	
Urko González de Zarate Quirós	20.03.2001	1	(1)	
Midfielders:	DOB	M	(s)	G
David Josué Jiménez Silva	08.01.1986	17	(4)	2
Ander Guevara Lajo	07.07.1997	25	(6)	1

Founded: 07.09.1909
Stadium: Estadio Anoeta [Reale Arena], San Sebastián (39,500)
Trainer: Imanol Alguacil Barrenetxea 04.07.1971

	DOB	M	(s)	G
Asier Illarramendi Andonegu „Illarra"	08.03.1990	6		
Jon Guridi Aldalur	28.02.1995	8	(9)	
Martín Zubimendi Ibáñez	02.02.1999	17	(14)	
Mikel Merino Zazón	22.06.1996	25	(1)	2
Robert Navarro Muñoz	12.04.2002		(1)	
Roberto López Alcaide	24.04.2000	4	(13)	3
Igor Zubeldía Elorza	30.03.1997	21	(3)	1
Forwards:	DOB	M	(s)	G
Ander Barrenetxea Muguruza	27.12.2001	13	(18)	3
Carlos Fernández Luna	22.05.1996	4	(7)	1
Alexander Isak (SWE)	21.09.1999	30	(4)	17
Adnan Januzaj (BEL)	05.02.1995	12	(15)	4
Jon Bautista Orgilles	03.07.1995		(21)	
Martín Merquelanz Castellanos	12.06.1995	4	(9)	
Mikel Oyarzabal Ugarte	21.04.1997	30	(3)	11
Cristián Portugués Manzanera „Portu"	21.05.1992	24	(13)	8
Willian José da Silva (BRA)	23.11.1991	8	(5)	3

Sevilla Fútbol Club

Goalkeepers:	DOB	M	(s)	G
Yassine Bounou (MAR)	05.04.1991	33		1
Tomáš Vaclík (CZE)	29.03.1989	5		
Defenders:	DOB	M	(s)	G
Marcos Javier Acuña (ARG)	28.10.1991	26	(4)	1
Aleix Vidal Parreu	21.08.1989	5	(7)	
Diego Carlos Santos Silva (BRA)	15.03.1993	32	(1)	1
Sergio Escudero Palomo	02.09.1989	7	(2)	1
Jesús Navas González	21.11.1985	34		
Jules Koundé (FRA)	12.11.1998	33	(1)	2
Karim Rekik (NED)	02.12.1994	6	(5)	
Sergi Gómez Solà	28.03.1992	9		
Midfielders:	DOB	M	(s)	G
Fernando Francisco Reges (BRA)	25.07.1987	28	(3)	3
Nemanja Gudelj (SRB)	16.11.1991	10	(20)	

Founded: 25.01.1890
Stadium: Estadio "Ramón Sánchez Pizjuán", Sevilla (43,883)
Trainer: Julen Lopetegui Agote 28.09.1966

	DOB	M	(s)	G
Joan Jordán Moreno	06.07.1994	28	(7)	1
Óliver Torres Muñoz	10.11.1994	15	(18)	
Óscar Rodríguez Arnaiz	28.06.1998	4	(16)	
Ivan Rakitić (CRO)	10.03.1988	25	(12)	4
Franco Damián Vázquez (ARG)	22.02.1989	1	(14)	1
Forwards:	DOB	M	(s)	G
Bryan Gil Salvatierra	11.02.2001		(1)	
Carlos Fernández Luna	22.05.1996	2	(3)	
Luuk de Jong (NED)	27.08.1990	14	(20)	4
Youssef En-Nesyri (MAR)	01.06.1997	23	(15)	18
Alejandro Darío Gómez (ARG)	15.02.1988	11	(7)	3
Oussama Idrissi (MAR)	26.02.1996		(3)	
Munir El Haddadi Mohamed	01.09.1995	9	(15)	4
Lucas Ariel Ocampos (ARG)	11.07.1994	30	(4)	5
Jesús Joaquín Fernández Sáez de la Torre „Suso"	19.11.1993	28	(6)	3

Valencia Club de Fútbol

Goalkeepers:	DOB	M	(s)	G
Jacobus Antonius Peter Cillessen (NED)	22.04.1989	10		
Jaume Doménech Sánchez	05.11.1990	28		
Defenders:	DOB	M	(s)	G
Mouctar Diakhaby (FRA)	19.12.1996	24	(2)	1
Francisco Reis Ferreira „Ferro" (POR)	26.03.1997	2	(1)	
Gabriel Armando de Abreu „Gabriel Paulista" (BRA)	26.11.1990	31		4
José Luis Gayà Peña	25.05.1995	32	(1)	1
Guillem Molina Gutiérrez	03.05.2000	1	(1)	
Hugo Guillamón Sammartín	31.01.2000	21	(4)	1
Eliaquim Mangala (FRA)	13.02.1991	4	(3)	
Cristiano Piccini (ITA)	26.09.1992		(3)	
Thierry Rendall Correia (POR)	09.03.1999	25	(4)	1
Antonio Latorre Grueso „Toni Lato"	21.11.1997	8	(7)	1
Daniel Wass (DEN)	31.05.1989	35		4
Midfielders:	DOB	M	(s)	G
Carlos Soler Barragán	02.01.1997	31	(1)	11

Founded: 18.03.1909
Stadium: Estadio Mestalla, Valencia (55,000)
Trainer: Javier "Javi" Gracia Carlos 01.05.1970
[03.05.2021] Salvador González Marco „Voro" 09.10.1963

	DOB	M	(s)	G
Koba Lein Koindredi (FRA)	27.10.2001		(2)	
Geoffrey Edwin Kondogbia (CTA)	15.02.1993	5		
Lee Kang-in (KOR)	19.02.2001	15	(9)	
Christian Gabriel Oliva Giménez (URU)	01.06.1996	1	(8)	
Uroš Račić (SRB)	17.03.1998	25	(6)	1
Vicente Esquerdo Santas	02.01.1999	3	(1)	
Forwards:	DOB	M	(s)	G
Alejandro „Álex" Blanco Sánchez	16.12.1998	6	(7)	1
Denis Cheryshev (RUS)	26.12.1990	13	(8)	
Patrick Cutrone (ITA)	03.01.1998		(7)	
Kevin Dominique Gameiro (FRA)	09.05.1987	10	(17)	4
Maximiliano Gómez González (URU)	14.08.1996	31		7
Gonçalo Manuel Ganchinho Guedes (POR)	29.11.1996	27	(4)	5
David Remeseiro Salgueiro „Jason"	06.07.1994	4	(13)	
Manuel „Manu" Javier Vallejo Galván	14.02.1997	9	(21)	5
Yunus Dimoara Musah (USA)	29.11.2002	17	(15)	1
Rubén Sobrino Pozuelo	01.06.1992		(5)	

Real Valladolid Club de Fútbol

Goalkeepers:	DOB	M	(s)	G
Jordi Masip López	03.01.1989	25		
Roberto Jiménez Gago	10.02.1986	13		
Defenders:	DOB	M	(s)	G
Bruno González Cabrera	24.05.1990	25	(2)	1
Jawad El Yamiq (MAR)	29.02.1992	15	(4)	
Saidy Janko (SUI)	22.10.1995	14	(5)	
Javier „Javi" Moyano Lujano	23.02.1986	2		
Javier „Javi" Sánchez de Felipe	14.03.1997	11	(5)	
Joaquín Fernández Moreno	31.05.1996	24	(1)	1
Francisco José „Kiko" Olivas Alba	21.08.1988	1	(4)	
Luis Jesús Pérez Maqueda	04.02.1995	15	(7)	
Miguel Ángel Rubio Lestan	11.03.1998	1	(1)	
José Ignacio Martínez García „Nacho"	07.03.1989	21	(2)	
Lucas René Olaza Catrofe (URU)	21.07.1994	14		1
Raúl García Carnero	30.04.1989	5	(3)	1
Midfielders:	DOB	M	(s)	G
Rubén Alcaraz Jiménez	01.05.1991	25	(5)	1

Founded: 20.06.1928
Stadium: Estadio "José Zorrilla", Valladolid (28,012)
Trainer: Sergio González Soriano 10.11.1976

	DOB	M	(s)	G
Federico San Emeterio Díaz „Fede"	16.03.1997	17	(7)	
Enrique „Kike" Pérez Muñoz	14.02.1997	12	(12)	
Miguel Alfonso Herrero Javaloyas „Míchel"	29.07.1988	10	(12)	2
Oriol Rey Erenas	25.02.1998		(1)	
Roque Mesa Quevedo	07.06.1989	21	(4)	1
Forwards:	DOB	M	(s)	G
João Pedro Neves Filipe „Jota" (POR)	30.03.1999	7	(10)	1
Kenan Kodro (BIH)	19.08.1993	4	(10)	
José Luis Zalazar Martínez „Kuki"	05.05.1998		(2)	
Marcos André de Sousa Mendonça „Maranhão" (BRA)	20.10.1996	11	(12)	4
Fabián Ariel Orellana Valenzuela (CHI)	27.01.1986	27	(3)	6
Óscar Plano Pedreño	11.02.1991	30	(6)	5
Pablo Hervías Ruiz	08.03.1993	10	(17)	
Sergi Guardiola Navarro	29.05.1991	19	(10)	1
Sergio Benito Crujera	23.03.1999		(1)	
Laureano Antonio „Toni" Villa Suárez	07.01.1995	10	(11)	2
Waldo Rubio Marín	17.08.1995	5	(5)	1
Shon Weissman (ISR)	14.02.1996	24	(8)	6

Villarreal Club de Fútbol

Founded: 10.03.1923
Stadium: Estadio de la Cerámica, Villarreal (24,890)
Trainer: Unai Emery Etxegoien   03.11.1971

Goalkeepers:	DOB	M	(s)	G
Sergio Asenjo Andrés	28.06.1989	36		
Gerónimo Rulli (ARG)	20.05.1992	2		
Defenders:	**DOB**	**M**	**(s)**	**G**
Alberto Moreno Pérez	05.07.1992	2	(3)	
Sofian Chakla (MAR)	02.09.1993		(1)	
Pervis Josué Estupiñán Tenorio (ECU)	21.01.1998	12	(13)	
Juan Marcos Foyth (ARG)	12.01.1998	13	(3)	
Ramiro Funes Mori (ARG)	05.03.1991	8	(2)	
Jaume Vincent Costa Jordá	18.03.1988	3	(11)	
Mario Gaspar Pérez Martínez	24.11.1990	21	(3)	
Pau Francisco Torres	16.01.1997	33		2
Alfonso Pedraza Sag	09.04.1996	24	(5)	1
Raúl Albiol Tortajada	04.09.1985	35		
Rubén Peña Jiménez	18.07.1991	12	(7)	1
Midfielders:	**DOB**	**M**	**(s)**	**G**
Étienne Capoue (FRA)	11.07.1988	15	(1)	1

	DOB	M	(s)	G
Francis Coquelin (FRA)	13.05.1991	7	(15)	
Daniel „Dani" Parejo Muñoz	16.04.1989	36		3
Daniel Rabaseda Antolín „Dani Raba"	29.10.1995	1	(4)	
Vicente Iborra de la Fuente	16.01.1988	10	(3)	
Manuel Trigueros Muñoz	17.10.1991	30	(5)	1
Forwards:	**DOB**	**M**	**(s)**	**G**
Alejandro „Álex" Baena Rodríguez	20.07.2001	2	(4)	
Alejandro „Álex" Millán Iranzo	07.11.1999		(1)	
Carlos Arturo Bacca Ahumada (COL)	08.09.1986	9	(14)	5
Samuel Chukwueze (NGA)	22.05.1999	13	(15)	4
Fernando Niño Rodríguez „Fer Niño"	24.10.2000	8	(9)	3
Gerard Moreno Balagueró	07.04.1992	30	(3)	23
Takefusa Kubo (JPN)	04.06.2001	2	(11)	
Moisés „Moi" Gómez Bordonado	23.06.1994	29	(6)	4
Francisco Alcácer García „Paco Alcácer"	30.08.1993	19	(8)	6
Yeremi Jesús Pino Santos	20.10.2002	6	(18)	3

SECOND LEVEL
Segunda División 2020/2021

1.	RCD Espanyol Barcelona (*Promoted*)	42	24	10	8	71	-	28	82
2.	RCD Mallorca (*Promoted*)	42	24	10	8	54	-	28	82
3.	CD Leganés	42	21	10	11	51	-	31	73
4.	Unión Deportiva Almería	42	21	10	11	61	-	40	73
5.	Girona FC	42	20	11	11	47	-	36	71
6.	Rayo Vallecano de Madrid	42	19	10	13	52	-	40	67
7.	Real Sporting de Gijón	42	17	14	11	37	-	28	65
8.	SD Ponferradina	42	15	12	15	45	-	50	57
9.	UD Las Palmas	42	14	14	14	46	-	52	56
10.	CD Mirandés	42	14	12	16	38	-	41	54
11.	CF Fuenlabrada	42	12	18	12	45	-	46	54
12.	Málaga CF	42	14	11	17	37	-	47	53
13.	Real Oviedo CF	42	11	19	12	45	-	46	52
14.	CD Tenerife	42	13	13	16	36	-	36	52
15.	Real Zaragoza	42	13	11	18	37	-	43	50
16.	FC Cartagena	42	12	13	17	44	-	52	49
17.	Agrupación Deportiva Alcorcón	42	13	9	20	32	-	42	48
18.	CD Lugo	42	11	14	17	38	-	53	47
19.	Centre d'Esports Sabadell FC (*Relegated*)	42	11	13	18	40	-	48	46
20.	Unión Deportiva Logroñés (*Relegated*)	42	11	11	20	28	-	53	44
21.	CD Castellón (*Relegated*)	42	11	8	23	35	-	54	41
22.	Albacete Balompié (*Relegated*)	42	9	11	22	30	-	53	38

Teams ranked 3-6 were qualified for the Promotion Play-offs.

Promotion Play-offs [02]

Semi-Finals [02-06.06.2021]			
Girona FC - Unión Deportiva Almería	3-0(2-0)	0-0
Rayo Vallecano de Madrid - CD Leganés	3-0(0-0)	2-1(0-1)

Play-off Finals [13-20.06.2021]			
Rayo Vallecano de Madrid - Girona FC	1-2(1-1)	2-0(2-0)

Rayo Vallecano de Madrid promoted to La Liga 2021/2022.

NATIONAL TEAM

INTERNATIONAL MATCHES
(16.07.2020 – 15.07.2021)

03.09.2020	Stuttgart	Germany - Spain	1-1(0-0)	(UNL)
06.09.2020	Madrid	Spain - Ukraine	4-0(3-0)	(UNL)
07.10.2020	Lisboa	Portugal - Spain	0-0	(F)
10.10.2020	Madrid	Spain - Switzerland	1-0(1-0)	(UNL)
13.10.2020	Kyiv	Ukraine - Spain	1-0(0-0)	(UNL)
11.11.2020	Amsterdam	Netherlands - Spain	1-1(0-1)	(F)
14.11.2020	Basel	Switzerland - Spain	1-1(1-0)	(UNL)
17.11.2020	Sevilla	Spain - Germany	6-0(3-0)	(UNL)
25.03.2021	Granada	Spain - Greece	1-1(1-0)	(WCQ)
28.03.2021	Tbilisi	Georgia - Spain	1-2(1-0)	(WCQ)
31.03.2021	Sevilla	Spain - Kosovo	3-1(1-0)	(WCQ)
04.06.2021	Madrid	Spain - Portugal	0-0	(F)
08.06.2021	Leganés	Spain - Lithuania	4-0(2-0)	(F)
14.06.2021	Sevilla	Spain - Sweden	0-0	(EC)
19.06.2021	Sevilla	Spain - Poland	1-1(1-0)	(EC)
23.06.2021	Sevilla	Slovakia - Spain	0-5(0-2)	(EC)
28.06.2021	København	Croatia - Spain	3-5(1-1,3-3)	(EC)
02.07.2021	Saint Petersburg	Switzerland - Spain	1-1(0-1,1-1,1-1); 1-3 on penalties	(EC)
06.07.2021	London	Italy - Spain	1-1(0-0,1-1,1-1); 4-2 on penalties	(EC)

03.09.2020   GERMANY - SPAIN   **1-1(0-0)**   2nd UEFA Nations League A, Group 4
Mercedes-Benz Arena, Stuttgart; Referee: Daniele Orsato (Italy); Attendance: 0
ESP: David de Gea, Dani Carvajal, Sergio Ramos (Cap), Jesús Navas (46.Ansu Fati), José Gayá, Pau Torres, Sergio Busquets (57.Mikel Merino), Thiago Alcântara, Fabián Ruiz (80.Óscar Rodríguez), Rodrigo, Ferran Torres. Trainer: Luis Enrique Martínez García.
Goal: José Gayá (90+6).

06.09.2020   SPAIN - UKRAINE   **4-0(3-0)**   2nd UEFA Nations League A, Group 4
Estadio "Alfredo Di Stéfano", Madrid; Referee: Benoît Bastien (France); Attendance: 0
ESP: David de Gea, Sergio Reguilón, Sergio Ramos (Cap) (61.Eric García), Jesús Navas, Pau Torres, Rodri (69.Óscar Rodríguez), Thiago Alcântara, Mikel Merino, Daniel Olmo, Gerard Moreno (74.Ferran Torres), Ansu Fati. Trainer: Luis Enrique Martínez García.
Goals: Sergio Ramos (3 penalty, 29), Ansu Fati (32), Ferran Torres (84).

07.10.2020   PORTUGAL - SPAIN   **0-0**   Friendly International
Estádio "José Alvalade", Lisboa; Referee: Paolo Valeri (Italy); Attendance: 2,500
ESP: Kepa Arrizabalaga, Sergi Roberto, Diego Llorente, Sergio Reguilón (46.José Gayá), Eric García (81.Sergio Ramos), Sergio Busquets (Cap) (61.Rodri), Sergio Canales (79.Adama Traoré), Dani Ceballos (46.José Campaña), Daniel Olmo, Rodrigo (46.Mikel Merino), Gerard Moreno. Trainer: Luis Enrique Martínez García.

10.10.2020   SPAIN - SWITZERLAND   **1-0(1-0)**   2nd UEFA Nations League A, Group 4
Estadio "Alfredo Di Stéfano", Madrid; Referee: Ali Palabıyık (Turkey); Attendance: 0
ESP: David de Gea, Jesús Navas, Sergio Ramos (Cap), José Gayá, Pau Torres, Sergio Busquets, Mikel Merino, Daniel Olmo (57.Sergio Canales), Mikel Oyarzabal (73.Gerard Moreno), Ansu Fati (57.Adama Traoré), Ferran Torres (88.Rodri). Trainer: Luis Enrique Martínez García.
Goals: Mikel Oyarzabal (14).

13.10.2020   UKRAINE - SPAIN   **1-0(0-0)**   2nd UEFA Nations League A, Group 4
NSC Olimpiyskiy Stadium, Kyiv; Referee: Paweł Gil (Poland); Attendance: 10,495
ESP: David de Gea, Jesús Navas, Sergio Ramos (Cap), Sergio Reguilón, Pau Torres, Rodri, Sergio Canales (73.Daniel Olmo), Mikel Merino (46.Dani Ceballos), Rodrigo (58.Mikel Oyarzabal), Adama Traoré, Ansu Fati (58.Ferran Torres). Trainer: Luis Enrique Martínez García.

11.11.2020   NETHERLANDS - SPAIN   **1-1(0-1)**   Friendly International
"Johan Cruyff" Arena, Amsterdam, City; Referee: Davide Massa (Italy); Attendance: 0
ESP: Unai Simón, Iñigo Martínez (85.Sergio Ramos), Héctor Bellerín, José Gayá (29.Sergio Reguilón), Eric García, Sergio Canales (72.Marcos Llorente), Rodri, Koke (Cap), Álvaro Morata (62.Daniel Olmo), Gerard Moreno (61.Ferran Torres), Marco Asensio (62.Adama Traoré). Trainer: Luis Enrique Martínez García.
Goal: Sergio Canales (19).

14.11.2020   SWITZERLAND - SPAIN   **1-1(1-0)**   2nd UEFA Nations League A, Group 4
St. Jakob-Park, Basel; Referee: William Collum (Scotland); Attendance: 0
ESP: Unai Simón, Sergi Roberto, Sergio Ramos (Cap), Sergio Reguilón, Pau Torres, Sergio Busquets (73.Koke), Fabián Ruiz (56.Álvaro Morata), Daniel Olmo (73.Sergio Canales), Mikel Merino (80.Gerard Moreno), Mikel Oyarzabal (73.Adama Traoré), Ferran Torres. Trainer: Luis Enrique Martínez García.
Goal: Gerard (89).

17.11.2020   SPAIN - GERMANY   **6-0(3-0)**   2nd UEFA Nations League A, Group 4
Estadio La Cartuja, Sevilla; Referee: Andreas Ekberg (Sweden); Attendance: 0
ESP: Unai Simón, Sergi Roberto, Sergio Ramos (Cap) (43.Eric García), José Gayá, Pau Torres, Sergio Canales (12.Fabián Ruiz), Koke, Rodri, Daniel Olmo (73.Gerard Moreno), Álvaro Morata (73.Mikel Oyarzabal), Ferran Torres (73.Marco Asensio). Trainer: Luis Enrique Martínez García.
Goals: Álvaro Morata (17), Ferran Torres (33), Rodri (38), Ferran Torres (55, 71), Mikel Oyarzabal (89).

25.03.2021   SPAIN - GREECE   **1-1(1-0)**   22nd FIFA WC. Qualifiers
Nuevo Estadio Los Cármenes, Granada; Referee: Marco Guida (Italy); Attendance: 0
ESP: Unai Simón, Sergio Ramos (Cap) (46.Iñigo Martínez), José Gayá, Eric García, Sergio Canales (65.Bryan Gil), Koke (72.Thiago Alcântara), Rodri, Daniel Olmo (64.Pedri), Marcos Llorente, Álvaro Morata, Ferran Torres (72.Mikel Oyarzabal). Trainer: Luis Enrique Martínez García.
Goal: Álvaro Morata (33).

28.03.2021   **GEORGIA - SPAIN**   1-2(1-0)   22nd FIFA WC. Qualifiers

„Boris Paichadze" Dinamo Arena, Tbilisi; Referee: Radu Marian Petrescu (Romania); Attendance: 16,500
ESP: Unai Simón, Diego Llorente (46.Iñigo Martínez), Eric García, Jordi Alba, Pedro Porro (65.Marcos Llorente), Fabián Ruiz (54.Thiago Alcântara), Sergio Busquets (Cap) (73.Mikel Oyarzabal), Bryan Gil (46.Daniel Olmo), Álvaro Morata, Pedri, Ferran Torres. Trainer: Luis Enrique Martínez García.
Goals: Ferran Torres (56), Dani Olmo (90+2).

31.03.2021   **SPAIN - KOSOVO**   3-1(1-0)   22nd FIFA WC. Qualifiers

Estadio La Cartuja, Sevilla; Referee: Jakob Kehlet (Denmark); Attendance: 0
ESP: Unai Simón, Iñigo Martínez, Eric García (86.Sergio Ramos), Jordi Alba, Sergio Busquets (Cap) (82.Rodri), Koke, Marcos Llorente, Daniel Olmo (82.Sergio Canales), Álvaro Morata (68.Gerard Moreno), Pedri (68.Fabián Ruiz), Ferran Torres. Trainer: Luis Enrique Martínez García.
Goals: Dani Olmo (34), Ferran Torres (54), Javi Puado (73).

04.06.2021   **SPAIN - PORTUGAL**   0-0   Friendly International

Estadio Wanda Metropolitano, Madrid; Referee: Craig Pawson (England); Attendance: 14,743
ESP: Unai Simón, Pau Torres (63.Eric García), Aymeric Laporte (79.Diego Llorente), José Gayá, Sergio Busquets (Cap) (63.Rodri), Thiago Alcântara (63.Pedri), Marcos Llorente, Pablo Sarabia (75.Gerard Moreno), Fabián Ruiz (75.Koke), Álvaro Morata, Ferran Torres. Trainer: Luis Enrique Martínez García.

08.06.2021   **SPAIN - LITHUANIA**   4-0(2-0)   Friendly International

Estadio Municipal de Butarque, Leganés; Referee: Willy Delajod (France); Attendance: 903
ESP: Álvaro Fernández (68.Josep Martínez), Marc Cucurella (Cap) (46.Juan Miranda), Óscar Mingueza, Hugo Guillamón, Óscar Gil (46.Alejandro Pozo), Manu García (54.Antonio Blanco), Gonzalo Villar (74.Fran Beltrán), Martín Zubimendi (53.Javi Puado), Brahim Díaz, Abel Ruiz, Bryan Gil. Trainer: Luis Enrique Martínez García.
Goals: Hugo Guillamón (3), Brahim Díaz (24), Juan Miranda (54), Javi Puado (73).

14.06.2021   **SPAIN - SWEDEN**   0-0   16th EC. Group Stage.

Estadio La Cartuja, Sevilla; Referee: Slavko Vinčić (Slovenia); Attendance: 10,599
ESP: Unai Simón, Aymeric Laporte, Pau Torres, Jordi Alba (Cap), Koke (87.Fabián Ruiz), Marcos Llorente, Daniel Olmo (74.Gerard Moreno), Rodri (66.Thiago Alcântara), Pedri, Álvaro Morata (66.Pablo Sarabia), Ferran Torres (74.Mikel Oyarzabal). Trainer: Luis Enrique Martínez García.

19.06.2021   **SPAIN - POLAND**   1-1(1-0)   16th EC. Group Stage.

Estadio La Cartuja, Sevilla; Referee: Daniele Orsato (Italy); Attendance: 11,732
ESP: Unai Simón, Aymeric Laporte, Pau Torres, Jordi Alba (Cap), Koke (68.Pablo Sarabia), Marcos Llorente, Daniel Olmo (61.Ferran Torres), Rodri, Pedri, Álvaro Morata (87.Mikel Oyarzabal), Gerard Moreno (68.Fabián Ruiz). Trainer: Luis Enrique Martínez García.
Goal: Álvaro Morata (25).

23.06.2021   **SLOVAKIA - SPAIN**   0-5(0-2)   16th EC. Group Stage.

Estadio La Cartuja, Sevilla; Referee: Björn Kuipers (Netherlands); Attendance: 11,204
ESP: Unai Simón, César Azpilicueta (77.Mikel Oyarzabal), Aymeric Laporte, Eric García (71.Pau Torres), Jordi Alba, Sergio Busquets (Cap) (71.Thiago Alcântara), Pablo Sarabia, Koke, Pedri, Álvaro Morata (66.Ferran Torres), Gerard Moreno (77.Adama Traoré). Trainer: Luis Enrique Martínez García.
Goals: Martin Dúbravka (30 own goal), Aymeric Laporte (45+3), Pablo Sarabia (56), Ferran Torres (67), Juraj Kucka (71 own goal).

28.06.2021   **CROATIA - SPAIN**   3-5(1-1,3-3)   16th EC. 2nd Round of 16.

Parken Stadium, København (Denmark); Referee: Cüneyt Çakır (Turkey); Attendance: 22,771
ESP: Unai Simón, César Azpilicueta, Aymeric Laporte, Eric García (71.Pau Torres), José Gayá (77.Jordi Alba), Sergio Busquets (Cap) (101.Rodri), Pablo Sarabia (71.Daniel Olmo), Koke (77.Fabián Ruiz), Pedri, Álvaro Morata, Ferran Torres (88.Mikel Oyarzabal). Trainer: Luis Enrique Martínez García.
Goals: Pablo Sarabia (38), César Azpilicueta (57), Ferran Torres (77), Álvaro Morata (100), Mikel Oyarzabal (103).

02.07.2021   **SWITZERLAND - SPAIN**   1-1(0-1,1-1,1-1); 1-3 on penalties   16th EC. Quarter-Finals.

Krestovsky Stadium (Gazprom Arena), Saint Petersburg (Russia); Referee: Michael Oliver (England); Attendance: 24,764
ESP: Unai Simón, César Azpilicueta, Aymeric Laporte, Pau Torres (113.Thiago Alcântara), Jordi Alba, Sergio Busquets (Cap), Pablo Sarabia (46.Daniel Olmo), Koke (90+1.Marcos Llorente), Pedri (119.Rodri), Álvaro Morata (54.Gerard Moreno), Ferran Torres (91.Mikel Oyarzabal). Trainer: Luis Enrique Martínez García.
Goal: Denis Lemi Zakaria Lako Lado (8 own goal).
Penalties: Sergio Busquets (missed); Daniel Olmo, Rodri (saved); Gerard Moreno, Mikel Oyarzabal.

06.07.2021   **ITALY - SPAIN**   1-1(0-0,1-1,1-1); 4-2 on penalties   16th EC. Semi-Finals.

Wembley Stadium, London (England); Referee: Dr. Felix Brych (Germany); Attendance: 57,811
ESP: Unai Simón, César Azpilicueta (85.Marcos Llorente), Aymeric Laporte, Eric García (109.Pau Torres), Jordi Alba, Sergio Busquets (Cap) (106.Thiago Alcântara), Koke (70.Rodri), Daniel Olmo, Pedri, Mikel Oyarzabal (70.Gerard Moreno), Ferran Torres (61.Álvaro Morata). Trainer: Luis Enrique Martínez García.
Goal: Álvaro Morata (80).
Penalties: Daniel Olmo (missed); Gerard Moreno, Thiago Alcântara, Álvaro Morata (saved).

NATIONAL TEAM PLAYERS				
(16.07.2020 – 15.07.2021)				

Name	DOB	Caps	Goals	2020/2021: *Club*
Goalkeepers				
ÁLVARO FERNÁNDEZ Llorente	13.04.1998	1	0	2021: *SD Huesca*
DAVID DE GEA Quintana	07.11.1990	45	0	2020: *Manchester United FC (ENG)*
JOSEP MARTÍNEZ Riera	27.05.1998	1	0	2021: *RasenBallsport Leipzig (GER)*
KEPA Arrizabalaga Revuelta	03.10.1994	11	0	2020: *Chelsea FC London (ENG)*
UNAI SIMÓN Mendibil	11.06.1997	13	0	2020/2021: *Athletic Club Bilbao*

Defenders

ALEJANDRO POZO Pozo	22.02.1999	1	0	2021:	*Unión Deportiva Almería*
AYMERIC Jean Louis Gérard Alphonse LAPORTE	27.05.1994	7	1	2021:	*Manchester City FC (ENG)*
CÉSAR AZPILICUETA Tanco	28.08.1989	29	1	2021:	*Chelsea FC London (ENG)*
Daniel "DANI" CARVAJAL Ramos	11.01.1992	25	0	2020/2021:	*Real Madrid CF*
DIEGO Javier LLORENTE Ríos	16.08.1993	8	0	2020/2021:	*Leeds United FC (ENG)*
ERIC GARCÍA Martret	09.01.2001	11	0	2020/2021:	*Manchester City FC (ENG)*
HÉCTOR BELLERÍN Moruno	19.03.1995	4	0	2020:	*Arsenal FC London (ENG)*
HUGO GUILLAMÓN Sanmartín	31.01.2000	1	1	2021:	*Valencia CF*
IÑIGO MARTÍNEZ Berridi	17.05.1991	15	0	2020/2021:	*Athletic Club Bilbao*
JESÚS NAVAS González	21.11.1985	46	5	2020/2021:	*Sevilla FC*
JORDI ALBA Ramos	21.03.1989	78	8	2021:	*FC Barcelona*
JOSÉ Luis GAYÀ Peña	25.03.1995	15	2	2020/2021:	*Valencia CF*
JUAN MIRANDA González	19.01.2000	1	1	2021:	*Real Betis Balompié Sevilla*
MARC CUCURELLA Saseta	22.07.1998	1	0	2021:	*Getafe CF*
ÓSCAR GIL Regaño	26.04.1998	1	0	2021:	*RCD Espanyol Barcelona*
ÓSCAR MINGUEZA García	13.05.1999	1	0	2021:	*FC Barcelona*
PAU Francisco TORRES	16.01.1997	14	1	2020/2021:	*Villarreal CF*
PEDRO Antonio PORRO Sauceda	13.09.1999	1	0	2021:	*Sporting Clube de Portugal Lisboa (POR)*
SERGIO RAMOS García	30.03.1986	180	23	2020/2021:	*Real Madrid CF*
SERGIO REGUILÓN Rodríguez	16.12.1996	5	0	2020:	*Tottenham Hotspur FC London (ENG)*

Midfielders

ANTONIO BLANCO Conde	23.07.2000	1	0	2021:	*Real Madrid CF*
Daniel "DANI" CEBALLOS Fernández	07.08.1996	11	1	2020/2021:	*Arsenal FC London (ENG)*
DANIEL OLMO Carvajal	07.05.1998	16	3	2020/2021:	*RasenBallsport Leipzig (GER)*
FABIÁN RUIZ Peña	03.04.1996	15	1	2020/2021:	*SSC Napoli (ITA)*
Francisco José "FRAN" BELTRÁN Peinado	03.02.1999	1	0	2021:	*RC Celta de Vigo*
GONZALO VILLAR del Fraile	23.03.1998	1	0	2021:	*AS Roma (ITA)*
JOSÉ Ángel Gómez CAMPAÑA	31.05.1993	1	0	2020:	*Levante UD Valencia*
Joge Resurrección Merodio "KOKE"	08.01.1992	56	0	2020/2021:	*Club Atlético de Madrid*
Manuel "MANU" GARCÍA Alonso	02.01.1998	1	0	2021:	*Real Sporting de Gijón*
MARCO ASENSIO Willemsen	21.01.1996	26	1	2020:	*Real Madrid CF*
MARCOS LLORENTE Moreno	30.01.1995	9	0	2020/2021:	*Club Atlético de Madrid*
MARTÍN ZUBIMENDI Ibáñez	02.02.1999	1	0	2021:	*Real Sociedad de Fútbol San Sebastián*
MIKEL MERINO Zazón	22.06.1996	6	0	2020:	*Real Sociedad de Fútbol San Sebastián*
ÓSCAR RODRÍGUEZ Arnaiz	28.06.1998	2	0	2020:	*Sevilla FC*
PABLO SARABIA García	11.05.1992	9	3	2021:	*Paris Saint-Germain FC (FRA)*
Pedro González López "PEDRI"	25.11.2002	10	0	2021:	*FC Barcelona*
Rodrigo Hernández Cascante "RODRI"	22.06.1996	25	1	2020/2021:	*Manchester City FC (ENG)*
SERGI ROBERTO Carnicer	07.02.1992	10	1	2020/2021:	*FC Barcelona*
SERGIO BUSQUETS i Burgos	16.07.1988	127	2	2020/2021:	*FC Barcelona*
SERGIO CANALES Madrazo	16.02.1991	10	0	2020/2021:	*Real Betis Balompié Sevilla*
THIAGO ALCÂNTARA do Nascimento	11.04.1991	46	2	2020/2021:	*Liverpool FC (ENG)*

Forwards

ABEL RUIZ Ortega	28.01.2000	1	0	2021:	*Sporting Clube de Braga (POR)*
ÁLVARO Borja MORATA Martín	23.10.1992	46	22	2020/2021:	*Juventus FC Torino (ITA)*
Anssumane "ANSU" FATI Vieira	31.10.2002	4	1	2020:	*FC Barcelona*
BRAHIM Abdelkader DÍAZ	03.08.1999	1	0	2021:	*AC Milan*
BRYAN GIL Salvatierra	11.02.2001	3	0	2021:	*SD Eibar*
FERRAN TORRES García	29.02.2000	17	8	2020/2021:	*Manchester City FC (ENG)*
GERARD MORENO Balagueró	07.04.1992	16	5	2020/2021:	*Villarreal CF*
Javier "JAVI" PUADO Díaz	25.05.1998	1	1	2021:	*RCD Espanyol Barcelona*
MIKEL OYARZABAL Ugarte	21.04.1997	19	5	2020/2021:	*Real Sociedad de Fútbol San Sebastián*
RODRIGO Moreno Machado	06.03.1991	25	8	2020:	*Leeds United FC (ENG)*
Adama TRAORÉ Diarra	25.01.1996	6	0	2020/2021:	*Wolverhampton Wanderers FC (ENG)*

Trainer

LUIS ENRIQUE Martínez García [09.07.2018 – 10.03.2019] & [from 19.11.2019]	08.05.1970	29 M; 16 W; 10 D; 3 L; 65-23	

SWEDEN

The Country:
Konungariket Sverige (Kingdom of Sweden)
Capital: Stockholm
Surface: 450,295 km²
Inhabitants: 10,402,070 [2021]
Time: UTC+1

The FA:
Svenska Fotbollsförbundet
Evenemangsgatan 31A, PO Box 1216, 171 23 Solna
Tel: +46 8 735 0900
Founded: 1904
Member of FIFA since: 1904
Member of UEFA since: 1954
Website: www.svenskfotboll.se

NATIONAL TEAM RECORDS

RECORDS
First international match:	12.07.1908, Göteborg:	Sweden – Norway 11-3
Most international caps:	Anders Gunnar Svensson	- 148 caps (1999-2013)
Most international goals:	Zlatan Ibrahimović	- 62 goals / 118 caps (2001-2021)

UEFA EUROPEAN CHAMPIONSHIP
1960	Did not enter
1964	Qualifiers
1968	Qualifiers
1972	Qualifiers
1976	Qualifiers
1980	Qualifiers
1984	Qualifiers
1988	Qualifiers
1992	Final Tournament (Semi-Finals)
1996	Qualifiers
2000	Final Tournament (Group Stage)
2004	Final Tournament (Quarter-Finals)
2008	Final Tournament (Group Stage)
2012	Final Tournament (Group Stage)
2016	Final Tournament (Group Stage)
2020	Final Tournament (2nd Round of 16)

FIFA WORLD CUP
1930	Did not enter
1934	Final Tournament (Quarter-Finals)
1938	Final Tournament (4th Place)
1950	Final Tournament (3rd Place)
1954	Qualifiers
1958	Final Tournament (Runners-up)
1962	Qualifiers
1966	Qualifiers
1970	Final Tournament (Group Stage)
1974	Final Tournament (2nd Round)
1978	Final Tournament (Group Stage)
1982	Qualifiers
1986	Qualifiers
1990	Final Tournament (Group Stage)
1994	Final Tournament (3rd Place)
1998	Qualifiers
2002	Final Tournament (2nd Round of 16)
2006	Final Tournament (2nd Round of 16)
2010	Qualifiers
2014	Qualifiers
2018	Final Tournament (Quarter-Finals)

OLYMPIC TOURNAMENTS
1908	4th Place
1912	Round 1
1920	Quarter-Finals
1924	3rd Place
1928	Did not enter
1936	1/8 - Finals
1948	**Winners**
1952	3rd Place
1956	Did not enter
1960	Did not enter
1964	Qualifiers
1968	Did not enter
1972	Did not enter
1976	Did not enter
1980	Did not enter
1984	Did not enter
1988	Quarter-Finals
1992	Quarter-Finals
1996	Qualifiers
2000	Qualifiers
2004	Qualifiers
2008	Qualifiers
2012	Qualifiers
2016	Group Stage

UEFA NATIONS LEAGUE
2018/2019	League B (Promoted to League A)
2020/2021	League A (Relegated to League B)

FIFA CONFEDERATIONS CUP 1992-2017
None

SWEDISH CLUB HONOURS IN EUROPEAN CLUB COMPETITIONS:

European Champion Clubs.Cup (1956-1992) / UEFA Champions League (1993-2021)		
None		
Fairs Cup (1858-1971) / UEFA Cup (1972-2009) / UEFA Europa League (2010-2021)		
IFK Göteborg	2	10981/1982, 1986/1987
UEFA Super Cup (1972-2020)		
None		
*European Cup Winners.Cup 1961-1999**		
None		

*defunct competition

NATIONAL COMPETITIONS
TABLE OF HONOURS

	CHAMPIONS*	CUP WINNERS	BEST GOALSCORERS	
1896	Örgryte IS Göteborg	-	-	
1897	Örgryte IS Göteborg	-	-	
1898	Örgryte IS Göteborg	-	-	
1899	Örgryte IS Göteborg	-	-	
1900	AIK Stockholm	-	-	
1901	AIK Stockholm	-	-	
1902	Örgryte IS Göteborg	-	-	
1903	Göteborgs IF	-	-	
1904	Örgryte IS Göteborg	-	-	
1905	Örgryte IS Göteborg	-	-	
1906	Örgryte IS Göteborg	-	-	
1907	Örgryte IS Göteborg	-	-	
1908	IFK Göteborg	-	-	
1909	Örgryte IS Göteborg	-	-	
1910	IFK Göteborg	-	-	
1911	AIK Stockholm	-	-	
1912	Djurgårdens IF Stockholm	-	-	
1913	Örgryte IS Göteborg	-	-	
1914	AIK Stockholm	-	-	
1915	Djurgårdens IF Stockholm	-	-	
1916	AIK Stockholm	-	-	
1917	Djurgårdens IF Stockholm	-	-	
1918	IFK Göteborg	-	-	
1919	GAIS Göteborg	-	-	
1920	Djurgårdens IF Stockholm	-	-	
1921	IFK Eskilstuna	-	-	
1922	GAIS Göteborg	-	-	
1923	AIK Stockholm	-	-	
1924	Fässbergs IF Mölndal	-	-	
1925	Brynäs IF Gävle	-	-	
	--	--	--	
1930/1931	GAIS Göteborg	-	John Nilsson (GAIS Göteborg)	26
1931/1932	AIK Stockholm	-	Carl-Erik Holmberg (Örgryte IS Göteborg)	29
1932/1933	Helsingborgs IF	-	Torsten Bunke (Helsingborgs IF)	21
1933/1934	Helsingborgs IF	-	Sven Jonasson (IF Elfsborg Borås)	20
1934/1935	IFK Göteborg	-	Harry Andersson (IK Sleipner Norrköping)	23
1935/1936	IF Elfsborg Borås	-	Sven Jonasson (IF Elfsborg Borås)	24
1936/1937	AIK Stockholm	-	Olle Zethlerlund (AIK Stockholm)	23
1937/1938	IK Sleipner Norrköping	-	Curt Hjelm (IK Sleipner Norrköping)	13
1938/1939	IF Elfsborg Borås	-	Erik Persson (AIK Stockholm) Ove Andersson (Malmö FF) Yngve Lindgren (Örgryte IS Göteborg)	16
1939/1940	IF Elfsborg Borås	-	Anders Pålsson (Helsingborgs IF)	17
1940/1941	Helsingborgs IF	Helsingborgs IF	Stig Nyström (IK Brage Borlänge)	17
1941/1942	IFK Göteborg	GAIS Göteborg	Sven Jacobsson (GAIS Göteborg)	20
1942/1943	IFK Norrköping	IFK Norrköping	Gunnar Nordahl (Degerfors IF)	16
1943/1944	Malmö FF	Malmö FF	Leif Larsson (IFK Göteborg)	19
1944/1945	IFK Norrköping	IFK Norrköping	Gunnar Nordahl (IFK Norrköping)	27
1945/1946	IFK Norrköping	Malmö FF	Gunnar Nordahl (IFK Norrköping)	25
1946/1947	IFK Norrköping	Malmö FF	Gunnar Gren (IFK Göteborg)	18
1947/1948	IFK Norrköping	Råå IF	Gunnar Nordahl (IFK Norrköping)	18
1948/1949	Malmö FF	AIK Stockholm	Carl-Johan Franck (Helsingborgs IF)	19
1949/1950	Malmö FF	AIK Stockholm	Ingvar Rydell (Malmö FF)	22
1950/1951	Malmö FF	Malmö FF	Hasse Jeppson (Djurgårdens IF Stockholm)	17
1951/1952	IFK Norrköping	*No competition*	Karl-Alfred Jacobsson (GAIS Göteborg)	17
1952/1953	Malmö FF	Malmö FF	Karl-Alfred Jacobsson (GAIS Göteborg)	24
1953/1954	GAIS Göteborg	*No competition*	Karl-Alfred Jacobsson (GAIS Göteborg)	21
1954/1955	Djurgårdens IF Stockholm	*No competition*	Kurt Hamrin (AIK Stockholm)	22
1955/1956	IFK Norrköping	*No competition*	Sylve Bengtsson (Halmstads BK)	22
1956/1957	IFK Norrköping	*No competition*	Harry Bild (IFK Norrköping)	19
1957/1958	IFK Göteborg	*No competition*	Bertil Johansson (IFK Göteborg) Henry Källgren (IFK Norrköping)	27
1959	Djurgårdens IF Stockholm	*No competition*	Rune Börjesson (Örgryte IS Göteborg)	21
1960	IFK Norrköping	*No competition*	Rune Börjesson (Örgryte IS Göteborg)	24
1961	IF Elfsborg Borås	*No competition*	Bertil Johansson (IFK Göteborg)	20
1962	IFK Norrköping	*No competition*	Leif Skiöld (Djurgårdens IF Stockholm)	21
1963	IFK Norrköping	*No competition*	Lars Heinermann (Degerfors IF) Bo Larsson (Malmö FF)	17
1964	Djurgårdens IF Stockholm	*No competition*	Krister Granbom (Helsingborgs IF)	22
1965	Malmö FF	*No competition*	Bo Larsson (Malmö FF)	28
1966	Djurgårdens IF Stockholm	*No competition*	Ove Kindvall (IFK Norrköping)	20
1967	Malmö FF	Malmö FF	Dag Szepanski (Malmö FF)	22

1968	Östers IF Växjö	*No competition*	Ove Eklund (Åtvidabergs FF)	16
1969	IFK Göteborg	IFK Norrköping (1968/69)	Reine Almqvist (IFK Göteborg)	16
1970	Malmö FF	Åtvidabergs FF (1969/70)	Bo Larsson (Malmö FF)	16
1971	Malmö FF	Åtvidabergs FF (1970/71)	Roland Sandberg (Åtvidabergs FF)	17
1972	Åtvidabergs FF	Landskrona BoIS (1971/72)	Ralf Edström (Åtvidabergs FF) Roland Sandberg (Åtvidabergs FF)	16
1973	Åtvidabergs FF	Malmö FF (1972/73)	Jan Mattsson (Östers IF Växjö)	20
1974	Malmö FF	Malmö FF (1973/74)	Jan Mattsson (Östers IF Växjö)	22
1975	Malmö FF	Malmö FF (1974/75)	Jan Mattsson (Östers IF Växjö)	31
1976	Halmstads BK	AIK Stockholm (1975/76)	Rutger Backe (Halmstads BK)	21
1977	Malmö FF	Östers IF Växjö (1976/77)	Reine Almqvist (IFK Göteborg) Mats Aronsson (Landskrona BoIS)	15
1978	Östers IF Växjö	Malmö FF (1977/78)	Tommy Berggren (Djurgårdens IF Stockholm)	19
1979	Halmstads BK	IFK Göteborg (1978/79)	Mats Werner (Hammarby IF)	14
1980	Östers IF Växjö	Malmö FF (1979/80)	Billy Ohlsson (Hammarby IF)	19
1981	Östers IF Växjö	Kalmar FF (1980/81)	Torbjörn Nilsson (IFK Göteborg)	20
1982	IFK Göteborg	IFK Göteborg (1981/82)	Dan Corneliusson (IFK Göteborg)	12
1983	IFK Göteborg	IFK Göteborg (1982/83)	Thomas Ahlström (IF Elfsborg Borås)	16
1984	IFK Göteborg	Malmö FF (1983/84)	Billy Ohlsson (Hammarby IF)	14
1985	Örgryte IS Göteborg	AIK Stockholm (1984/85)	Sören Börjesson (Örgryte IS Göteborg) Peter Karlsson (Kalmar FF) William Lansdowne (ENG, Kalmar FF)	10
1986	Malmö FF	Malmö FF (1985/86)	Johnny Ekström (IFK Göteborg)	13
1987	IFK Göteborg	Kalmar FF (1986/87)	Lasse Larsson (Malmö FF)	19
1988	Malmö FF	IFK Norrköping (1987/88)	Dan Martin Nataniel Dahlin (Malmö FF)	17
1989	IFK Norrköping	Malmö FF (1988/89)	Jan Hellström (IFK Norrköping)	16
1990	IFK Göteborg	Djurgårdens IF Stockholm (1989/90)	Kaj Eskelinen (IFK Göteborg)	10
1991	IFK Göteborg	IFK Norrköping (1990/91) IFK Göteborg (1991)	Bernt Kennet Andersson (IFK Göteborg)	13
1992	AIK Stockholm	*No competition*	Hans Eklund (Östers IF Växjö)	16
1993	IFK Göteborg	Degerfors IF (1992/93)	Henrik Bertilsson (Halmstads BK) Mats Lilienberg (Trelleborgs FF)	18
1994	IFK Göteborg	IFK Norrköping (1993/94)	Niclas Kindvall (IFK Norrköping)	23
1995	IFK Göteborg	Halmstads BK (1994/95)	Niklas Skoog (Västra Frölunda IF)	17
1996	IFK Göteborg	AIK Stockholm (1995/96)	Andreas Andersson (IFK Göteborg)	19
1997	Halmstads BK	AIK Stockholm (1996/97)	Mats Lilienberg (Halmstads BK) Christer Mattiasson (IF Elfsborg Borås) Dan Sahlin (Örebro SK)	14
1998	AIK Stockholm	Helsingborgs IF (1997/98)	Arild Stavrum (Helsingborgs IF)	18
1999	Helsingborgs IF	AIK Stockholm (1998/99)	Marcus Allbäck (Örgryte IS Göteborg)	15
2000	Halmstads BK	Örgryte IS Göteborg (1999/2000)	Fredrik Berglund (IF Elfsborg Borås)	18
2001	Hammarby IF	IF Elfsborg Borås (2000/01)	Stefan Selaković (Halmstads BK)	15
2002	Djurgårdens IF Stockholm	Djurgårdens IF Stockholm	Peter Emeka Ijeh (NGA, Malmö FF)	24
2003	Djurgårdens IF Stockholm	IF Elfsborg Borås	Niklas Skoog (Malmö FF)	22
2004	Malmö FF	Djurgårdens IF Stockholm	Markus Rosenberg (Halmstads BK)	14
2005	Djurgårdens IF Stockholm	Djurgårdens IF Stockholm	Gunnar Heiðar Þorvaldsson (ISL, Halmstads BK)	16
2006	IF Elfsborg Borås	Helsingborgs IF	Ariclenes da Silva Ferreira "Ari" (BRA, Kalmar FF)	15
2007	IFK Göteborg	Kalmar FF	Bengt Eric Marcus Berg (IFK Göteborg) Razak Omotoyossi (BEN, Helsingborgs IF)	14
2008	Kalmar FF	IFK Göteborg	Patrik Ingelsten (Kalmar FF)	19
2009	AIK Stockholm	AIK Stockholm	Tobias Hysén (IFK Göteborg) Francisco Wánderson do Carmo Carneiro (BRA, GAIS Göteborg)	18
2010	Malmö FF	Helsingborgs IF	Alexander Gerndt (Gefle IF / Helsingborgs IF)	20
2011	Helsingborgs IF	Helsingborgs IF	Mathias Ranégie (BK Häcken Göteborg / Malmö FF)	21
2012	IF Elfsborg Borås	*No competition*	Abdul Majeed Waris (GHA, BK Häcken Göteborg)	23
2013	Malmö FF	IFK Göteborg (2012/13)	Imad Khalili (IFK Norrköping / Helsingborgs IF)	15
2014	Malmö FF	IF Elfsborg Borås (2013/14)	Lasse Vibe (IFK Göteborg)	23
2015	IFK Norrköping	IFK Göteborg (2014/15)	Emir Kujović (IFK Norrköping)	21
2016	Malmö FF	BK Häcken Göteborg (2015/16)	John Owoeri (NGA, BK Häcken Göteborg)	17
2017	Malmö FF	Östersunds FK (2016/17)	Karl Albin Elis Holmberg (IFK Norrköping) Magnus Eriksson (Djurgårdens IF Stockholm)	14
2018	AIK Stockholm	Djurgårdens IF Stockholm (2017/18)	Paulo José de Oliveira „Paulinho" (BRA, BK Häcken Göteborg)	20
2019	Djurgårdens IF Stockholm	BK Häcken Göteborg (2018/2019)	Mohamed Buya Turay (SLE, Djurgårdens IF Stockholm)	15
2020	Malmö FF	IFK Göteborg (2019/2020)	Christoffer Åke Sven Nyman (IFK Norrköping)	18

*Svenska Mästerskapet (1896–1925), Allsvenskan (1931–1981), Allsvenskan Play-offs (1982–1990), Mästerskapsserien (1991–1992), Allsvenskan (since 1993).

NATIONAL CHAMPIONSHIP
Allsvenskan 2020
(14.06.2020 – 06.12.2020)

Results

Round 1 [14-15.06.2020]
IK Sirius - Djurgårdens IF 0-2(0-1)
IFK Göteborg - IF Elfsborg 0-1(0-1)
IFK Norrköping - Kalmar FF 2-1(1-1)
Örebro SK - AIK Stockholm 0-2(0-0)
Hammarby IF - Östersunds FK 2-0(1-0)
Helsingborgs IF - Varbergs BoIS 0-3(0-1)
Falkenbergs FF - BK Häcken 1-1(1-1)
Malmö FF - Mjällby AIF 2-0(0-0)

Round 2 [17-18.06.2020]
IF Elfsborg - Hammarby IF 2-2(1-0)
AIK Stockholm - IFK Norrköping 1-4(0-4)
Djurgårdens IF - Örebro SK 1-1(1-1)
Mjällby AIF - Falkenbergs FF 0-1(0-1)
Östersunds FK - IK Sirius 0-2(0-0)
Kalmar FF - Helsingborgs IF 4-0(2-0)
Varbergs BoIS - IFK Göteborg 1-2(1-1)
BK Häcken - Malmö FF 1-1(0-1)

Round 3 [21-22.06.2020]
Falkenbergs FF - Kalmar FF 0-2(0-0)
Malmö FF - Varbergs BoIS 2-2(1-1)
IFK Norrköping - Djurgårdens IF 3-0(2-0)
Hammarby IF - AIK Stockholm 0-2(0-0)
Örebro SK - Östersunds FK 0-0
Helsingborgs IF - IF Elfsborg 0-0
IK Sirius - BK Häcken 2-2(1-2)
IFK Göteborg - Mjällby AIF 2-2(0-1)

Round 4 [27-29.06.2020]
Östersunds FK - IFK Norrköping 2-4(1-1)
IK Sirius - IFK Göteborg 2-2(1-1)
Djurgårdens IF - Kalmar FF 5-0(4-0)
Mjällby AIF - Hammarby IF 2-1(0-1)
IF Elfsborg - Örebro SK 1-1(0-1)
AIK Stockholm - Malmö FF 2-2(1-0)
BK Häcken - Helsingborgs IF 1-0(0-0)
Varbergs BoIS - Falkenbergs FF 3-1(2-0)

Round 5 [01-02.07.2020]
IFK Norrköping - IF Elfsborg 1-1(0-1)
Kalmar FF - Östersunds FK 1-2(1-0)
Malmö FF - Djurgårdens IF 1-0(1-0)
Hammarby IF - Varbergs BoIS 1-0(1-0)
IFK Göteborg - AIK Stockholm 1-0(0-0)
Falkenbergs FF - IK Sirius 1-2(1-0)
Örebro SK - BK Häcken 0-0
Helsingborgs IF - Mjällby AIF 0-1(0-0)

Round 6 [05-06.07.2020]
IF Elfsborg - Malmö FF 1-0(1-0)
AIK Stockholm - Falkenbergs FF 1-1(0-0)
IK Sirius - Örebro SK 2-1(0-1)
BK Häcken - Hammarby IF 3-0(1-0)
IFK Norrköping - IFK Göteborg 3-1(1-0)
Djurgårdens IF - Helsingborgs IF 2-2(2-1)
Östersunds FK - Mjällby AIF 0-1(0-0)
Varbergs BoIS - Kalmar FF 1-0(0-0)

Round 7 [11-13.07.2020]
Falkenbergs FF - Östersunds FK 0-1(0-0)
Hammarby IF - IK Sirius 0-0
Helsingborgs IF - AIK Stockholm 2-0(0-0)
Örebro SK - Varbergs BoIS 1-0(0-0)
IFK Göteborg - Djurgårdens IF 1-2(0-2)
Mjällby AIF - BK Häcken 3-1(1-0)
Kalmar FF - IF Elfsborg 1-2(1-0)
Malmö FF - IFK Norrköping 1-1(1-0)

Round 8 [15-16.07.2020]
IFK Göteborg - Helsingborgs IF 1-1(1-0)
AIK Stockholm - IK Sirius 1-0(0-0)
Djurgårdens IF - Falkenbergs FF 1-0(0-0)
BK Häcken - IF Elfsborg 6-0(2-0)
IFK Norrköping - Örebro SK 2-0(0-0)
Kalmar FF - Hammarby IF 1-2(1-1)
Östersunds FK - Malmö FF 1-2(0-1)
Varbergs BoIS - Mjällby AIF 1-0(0-0)

Round 9 [19-20.07.2020]
IK Sirius - IFK Norrköping 4-2(1-1)
Malmö FF - Kalmar FF 2-1(0-1)
Varbergs BoIS - AIK Stockholm 2-2(1-1)
Falkenbergs FF - Helsingborgs IF 2-2(1-0)
IF Elfsborg - Djurgårdens IF 1-0(0-0)
Östersunds FK - BK Häcken 2-2(0-0)
Hammarby IF - IFK Göteborg 1-1(0-0)
Örebro SK - Mjällby AIF 3-1(1-1)

Round 10 [22-23.07.2020]
BK Häcken - AIK Stockholm 4-0(2-0)
Djurgårdens IF - Östersunds FK 0-0
IFK Norrköping - Varbergs BoIS 2-0(1-0)
Helsingborgs IF - Örebro SK 1-1(0-1)
IFK Göteborg - Falkenbergs FF 2-2(1-0)
Kalmar FF - IK Sirius 1-1(0-0)
Malmö FF - Hammarby IF 3-0(2-0)
Mjällby AIF - IF Elfsborg 0-5(0-4)

Round 11 [26-27.07.2020]
BK Häcken - IFK Göteborg 0-0
Falkenbergs FF - IFK Norrköping 3-3(2-0)
IF Elfsborg - Varbergs BoIS 3-3(1-1)
AIK Stockholm - Djurgårdens IF 0-1(0-0)
IK Sirius - Malmö FF 2-5(1-0)
Hammarby IF - Örebro SK 3-0(1-0)
Mjällby AIF - Kalmar FF 2-2(1-0)
Östersunds FK - Helsingborgs IF 0-0

Round 12 [01-03.08.2020]
Djurgårdens IF - BK Häcken 3-1(2-1)
Örebro SK - Falkenbergs FF 1-2(0-0)
Helsingborgs IF - Hammarby IF 1-1(1-0)
IFK Göteborg - Malmö FF 0-3(0-2)
Varbergs BoIS - Östersunds FK 1-1(0-0)
Kalmar FF - AIK Stockholm 0-0
IF Elfsborg - IK Sirius 3-3(1-3)
IFK Norrköping - Mjällby AIF 1-1(0-0)

Round 13 [05-06.08.2020]
Hammarby IF - Falkenbergs FF 1-1(0-1)
Malmö FF - Helsingborgs IF 4-1(2-1)
Varbergs BoIS - Djurgårdens IF 1-2(0-2)
AIK Stockholm - IF Elfsborg 1-2(0-2)
BK Häcken - IFK Norrköping 2-1(1-0)
IFK Göteborg - Östersunds FK 2-2(1-2)
Kalmar FF - Örebro SK 0-3(0-1)
Mjällby AIF - IK Sirius 1-1(0-1)

Round 14 [09-10.08.2020]
BK Häcken - Kalmar FF 0-2(0-1)
Falkenbergs FF - Malmö FF 0-1(0-1)
Örebro SK - IFK Göteborg 1-1(0-0)
Djurgårdens IF - Hammarby IF 1-2(0-2)
Mjällby AIF - AIK Stockholm 3-1(2-1)
Östersunds FK - IF Elfsborg 0-1(0-0)
Helsingborgs IF - IFK Norrköping 3-2(2-1)
IK Sirius - Varbergs BoIS 3-3(2-1)

Round 15 [12-13.08.2020]
Djurgårdens IF - Mjällby AIF 2-1(0-1)
Malmö FF - Örebro SK 2-1(1-1)
AIK Stockholm - Östersunds FK 0-1(0-1)
IF Elfsborg - Falkenbergs FF 4-2(4-0)
IFK Norrköping - Hammarby IF 1-2(0-1)
IK Sirius - Helsingborgs IF 3-1(2-0)
Kalmar FF - IFK Göteborg 1-1(1-1)
Varbergs BoIS - BK Häcken 1-3(1-2)

Round 16 [15-17.08.2020]
Örebro SK - Djurgårdens IF 0-3(0-1)
Falkenbergs FF - AIK Stockholm 1-1(1-1)
Hammarby IF - IF Elfsborg 2-2(1-1)
Mjällby AIF - Malmö FF 2-2(1-0)
BK Häcken - Varbergs BoIS 2-1(1-0)
Helsingborgs IF - IK Sirius 1-2(1-1)
IFK Göteborg - IFK Norrköping 1-3(0-2)
Östersunds FK - Kalmar FF 2-0(1-0)

Round 17 [22-24.08.2020]
Djurgårdens IF - IFK Göteborg 2-2(0-1)
IK Sirius - Hammarby IF 3-1(0-1)
IF Elfsborg - Östersunds FK 0-1(0-0)
Malmö FF - Falkenbergs FF 2-1(1-0)
AIK Stockholm - Helsingborgs IF 2-0(1-0)
Varbergs BoIS - Örebro SK 2-1(0-1)
IFK Norrköping - BK Häcken 0-1(0-0)
Kalmar FF - Mjällby AIF 1-4(1-1)

Round 18 [29-30.08.2020]
Östersunds FK - Falkenbergs FF 2-1(2-0)
Varbergs BoIS - IK Sirius 2-0(0-0)
AIK Stockholm - BK Häcken 0-1(0-0)
Helsingborgs IF - Djurgårdens IF 3-1(0-0)
Mjällby AIF - IFK Göteborg 1-1(0-1)
Malmö FF - IF Elfsborg 1-1(1-1)
Örebro SK - IFK Norrköping 4-3(2-2)
Hammarby IF - Kalmar FF 3-3(1-2)

Round 19 [09-10.09.2020]
Helsingborgs IF - Kalmar FF 1-1(1-0)
IFK Göteborg - Hammarby IF 0-4(0-1)
IFK Norrköping - Östersunds FK 2-2(1-0)
Örebro SK - Malmö FF 3-2(2-1)
Falkenbergs FF - Varbergs 2-0(1-0) [17.09.]
IF Elfsborg - Mjällby AIF 2-2(1-1) [17.09.]
BK Häcken - Djurgårdens IF 0-2(0-1) [28.10.]
IK Sirius - AIK Stockholm 0-0 [29.10.]

Round 20 [12-14.09.2020]
Djurgårdens IF - IF Elfsborg 1-1(0-1)
Falkenbergs FF - IFK Göteborg 0-3(0-2)
Hammarby IF - Helsingborgs IF 2-2(1-0)
Malmö FF - AIK Stockholm 0-0
Mjällby AIF - Varbergs BoIS 2-3(0-2)
BK Häcken - IK Sirius 1-0(0-0)
Kalmar FF - IFK Norrköping 0-2(0-2)
Östersunds FK - Örebro SK 0-0

Round 21 [20-21.09.2020]
AIK Stockholm - Hammarby IF 3-0(2-0)
Östersunds FK - Djurgårdens IF 1-1(0-0)
IFK Göteborg - Kalmar FF 1-2(0-1)
IFK Norrköping - Malmö FF 1-1(0-0)
IF Elfsborg - BK Häcken 1-1(1-0)
IK Sirius - Falkenbergs FF 2-0(1-0)
Mjällby AIF - Örebro SK 1-0(0-0)
Varbergs BoIS - Helsingborgs IF 1-3(1-2)

Round 22 [26-28.09.2020]
Örebro SK - IK Sirius 2-1(1-0)
Falkenbergs FF - Hammarby IF 1-3(1-0)
Helsingborgs IF - Östersunds FK 0-1(0-0)
Malmö FF - BK Häcken 3-0(2-0)
Djurgårdens IF - IFK Norrköping 1-2(0-1)
IF Elfsborg - IFK Göteborg 0-0
AIK Stockholm - Mjällby AIF 1-0(0-0)
Kalmar FF - Varbergs BoIS 1-1(0-0)

Round 23 [03-04.10.2020]
BK Häcken - Falkenbergs FF 3-0(3-0)
Örebro SK - IF Elfsborg 3-2(2-2)
Hammarby IF - Djurgårdens IF 1-1(1-0)
Mjällby AIF - Helsingborgs IF 3-2(1-1)
Östersunds FK - AIK Stockholm 1-2(0-1)
IFK Göteborg - Varbergs BoIS 1-0(1-0)
Kalmar FF - Malmö FF 0-4(0-2)
IFK Norrköping - IK Sirius 1-2(1-1)

Round 24 [17-19.10.2020]
Falkenbergs FF - Örebro SK 2-1(0-0)
Hammarby IF - Mjällby AIF 4-2(3-1)
IF Elfsborg - Kalmar FF 3-1(2-0)
IK Sirius - Östersunds FK 2-3(0-1)
AIK Stockholm - IFK Göteborg 2-0(1-0)
Varbergs BoIS - IFK Norrköping 1-3(1-2)
Djurgårdens IF - Malmö FF 3-2(0-1)
Helsingborgs IF - BK Häcken 0-0

Round 25 [24-26.10.2020]
BK Häcken - Mjällby AIF 2-2(0-1)
Djurgårdens IF - IK Sirius 4-0(0-0)
Kalmar FF - Falkenbergs FF 0-0
Östersunds FK - Hammarby IF 1-3(0-0)
Malmö FF - IFK Göteborg 3-1(2-1)
Örebro SK - Helsingborgs IF 3-2(2-1)
IFK Norrköping - AIK Stockholm 2-2(0-1)
Varbergs BoIS - IF Elfsborg 0-0

Round 26 [01-02.11.2020]
IF Elfsborg - IFK Norrköping 2-1(1-1)
IK Sirius - Kalmar FF 2-2(2-1)
Mjällby AIF - Östersunds FK 3-0(3-0)
Falkenbergs FF - Djurgårdens IF 3-2(1-1)
Hammarby IF - BK Häcken 1-1(0-1)
IFK Göteborg - Örebro SK 0-1(0-1)
AIK Stockholm - Varbergs BoIS 1-0(0-0)
Helsingborgs IF - Malmö FF 0-1(0-1)

Round 27 [07-08.11.2020]
BK Häcken - Östersunds FK 2-1(1-0)
Falkenbergs FF - IF Elfsborg 1-3(0-2)
Mjällby AIF - IFK Norrköping 2-0(1-0)
Djurgårdens IF - AIK Stockholm 0-1(0-0)
Örebro SK - Kalmar FF 0-1(0-1)
Varbergs BoIS - Hammarby IF 5-2(2-1)
Helsingborgs IF - IFK Göteborg 0-1(0-1)
Malmö FF - IK Sirius 4-0(3-0)

Round 28 [22-23.11.2020]
AIK Stockholm - Örebro SK 0-2(0-1)
IF Elfsborg - Helsingborgs IF 2-1(0-0)
Kalmar FF - Djurgårdens IF 0-3(0-3)
Hammarby IF - Malmö FF 2-2(1-2)
Östersunds FK - Varbergs BoIS 0-4(0-2)
IFK Göteborg - BK Häcken 1-1(1-1)
IFK Norrköping - Falkenbergs FF 4-1(3-1)
IK Sirius - Mjällby AIF 0-1(0-1)

Round 29 [29-30.11.2020]
Helsingborgs IF - Falkenbergs FF 0-0
Östersunds FK - IFK Göteborg 0-4(0-2)
Varbergs BoIS - Malmö FF 3-2(1-0)
BK Häcken - Örebro SK 3-0(3-0)
IK Sirius - IF Elfsborg 1-1(1-0)
Mjällby AIF - Djurgårdens IF 2-1(1-0)
AIK Stockholm - Kalmar FF 0-1(0-0)
Hammarby IF - IFK Norrköping 0-1(0-1)

Round 30 [06.12.2020]
Djurgårdens IF - Varbergs BoIS 1-0(0-0)
Falkenbergs FF - Mjällby AIF 2-3(1-1)
IF Elfsborg - AIK Stockholm 2-2(2-0)
IFK Göteborg - IK Sirius 2-0(1-0)
IFK Norrköping - Helsingborgs IF 3-4(3-4)
Kalmar FF - BK Häcken 0-0
Malmö FF - Östersunds FK 4-0(4-0)
Örebro SK - Hammarby IF 2-1(1-0)

Final Standings

						Total				Home					Away	
1.	**Malmö FF**	30	17	9	4	64 - 30	60	11	4	0	34 - 9	6	5	4	30 - 21
2.	IF Elfsborg Borås	30	12	15	3	49 - 38	51	6	8	1	27 - 20	6	7	2	22 - 18
3.	BK Häcken Göteborg	30	12	13	5	45 - 29	49	9	4	2	30 - 11	3	9	3	15 - 18
4.	Djurgårdens IF Stockholm	30	14	6	10	48 - 33	48	7	4	4	27 - 16	7	2	6	21 - 17
5.	Mjällby AIF Hällevik	30	13	8	9	48 - 44	47	8	4	3	27 - 21	5	4	6	21 - 23
6.	IFK Norrköping	30	13	7	10	60 - 46	46	6	5	4	28 - 19	7	2	6	32 - 27
7.	Örebro SK	30	12	6	12	37 - 41	42	8	3	4	23 - 21	4	3	8	14 - 20
8.	Hammarby IF Stockholm	30	10	11	9	47 - 47	41	4	9	2	23 - 18	6	2	7	24 - 29
9.	AIK Stockholm	30	10	9	11	30 - 33	39	6	2	7	15 - 15	4	7	4	15 - 18
10.	IK Sirius Uppsala	30	9	11	10	43 - 51	38	5	6	4	28 - 27	4	5	6	15 - 24
11.	Varbergs BoIS	30	10	7	13	45 - 44	37	7	3	5	25 - 22	3	4	8	20 - 22
12.	IFK Göteborg	30	7	13	10	35 - 41	34	3	5	7	15 - 24	4	8	3	20 - 17
13.	Östersunds FK	30	8	9	13	27 - 46	33	2	4	9	12 - 27	6	5	4	15 - 19
14.	Kalmar FF (Relegation Play-offs)	30	6	10	14	30 - 49	28	1	6	8	11 - 25	5	4	6	19 - 24
15.	Helsingborgs IF (Relegated)	30	5	11	14	33 - 48	26	3	6	6	12 - 15	2	5	8	21 - 33
16.	Falkenbergs FF (Relegated)	30	5	9	16	33 - 54	24	3	4	8	19 - 28	2	5	8	14 - 26

Top goalscorers:

18	**Christoffer Åke Sven Nyman**	*IFK Norrköping*
15	Astrit Seljmani	*Varbergs BoIS*
14	Moses Owoicho Ogbu (NGA)	*Mjällby AIF Hällevik*
13	Anders Bleg Christiansen (DEN)	*Malmö FF*
13	Isaac Kiese Thelin	*Malmö FF*

Relegation Play-offs [09-13.12.2020]

Jönköpings Södra IF - Kalmar FF   1-3(1-2)   0-1(0-0)

Kalmar FF remains at First Level for the Allsvenskan 2021.

NATIONAL CUP
Svenska Cupen 2020/2021

Second Round [29.09.-01.10./06-08.10./15.10./18.10./21.10./11-12.11/19.11./02.12.2020 & 31.01.2021]

Vasalunds IF Stockholm - IK Brage Borlänge	0-5(0-1)		Asarums IF - Kalmar FF	1-4(0-3)
Bodens BK - Västerås SK Fotboll	0-3(0-2)		IF Karlstad Fotboll II - Dalkurd FF Uppsala	1-2(0-1)
BK Forward Örebro - Akropolis IF Spånga	0-3(0-0)		Karlslunds IF - AIK Stockholm	1-2(0-2)
IK Gauthiod Grästorp - Ljungskile SK	1-0(0-0)		Utsiktens BK Göteborg - Norrby IF Borås	1-0(0-0,0-0)
Angered BK - BK Häcken Göteborg	1-3(1-0)		Hässleholms IF - Halmstads BK	1-5(0-2)
BK Astrio Halmstad - Falkenbergs FF	0-9(0-2)		Hudiksvalls FF - GIF Sundsvall	0-3(0-1)
Sandvikens IF - Jönköpings Södra IF	2-0(0-0)		Gottne IF - IFK Norrköping	0-6(0-3)
FC Stockholm Internazionale - Degerfors IF	1-3(0-0,0-1)		IF Lödde - Örgryte IS Göteborg	2-1(0-1)
Täby FK - AFC Eskilstuna	0-2(0-0)		Nyköpings BIS - Östersunds FK	2-4(0-2)
Stenungsunds IF - IF Elfsborg Borås	0-3(0-1)		Ekedalens SK - GAIS Göteborg	0-2(0-1)
IS Halmia Halmstad - Helsingborgs IF	0-3(0-2)		IFK Haninge - Örebro SK	1-2(1-0)
Torns IF Stångby - Trelleborgs FF	2-3(0-1,1-1)		IF Brommapojkarna - IK Sirius Uppsala	1-3(0-2)
Assyriska BK Göteborg - Mjällby AIF Hällevik	0-5(0-2)		FC Gute Visby - Hammarby IF Stockholm	0-5(0-3)
Oskarshamns AIK - Varbergs BoIS	0-0 aet; 5-3 pen		Sollentuna FK - Djurgårdens IF Stockholm	0-4(0-2)
Husqvarna FF - IFK Göteborg	1-3(1-3)		Lunds BK - Malmö FF	0-3 awarded
Landskrona BoIS - Östers IF Växjö	1-0(0-0)		Newroz FC - Umeå FC	0-5(0-2)

Third Round [21.02.-07.03.2021]

Group 1
Malmö FF - Västerås SK Fotboll	1-2(0-1)
Halmstads BK - GAIS Göteborg	0-2(0-1)
Halmstads BK - Västerås SK Fotboll	0-0
GAIS Göteborg - Malmö FF	1-0(1-0)
Västerås SK Fotboll - GAIS Göteborg	3-0(1-0)
Malmö FF - Halmstads BK	4-1(1-1)
Qualified: Västerås SK Fotboll	

Group 2
IF Elfsborg Borås - Degerfors IF	0-1(0-0)
Utsiktens BK Göteborg - Falkenbergs FF	1-3(0-2)
Falkenbergs FF - Degerfors IF	1-3(1-2)
Utsiktens BK Göteborg - IF Elfsborg Borås	1-4(1-1)
Degerfors IF - Utsiktens BK Göteborg	2-0(1-0)
IF Elfsborg Borås - Falkenbergs FF	3-2(1-0)
Qualified: Degerfors IF	

Group 3
BK Häcken Göteborg - Dalkurd FF Uppsala	2-0(2-0)
IK Gauthiod Grästorp - Helsingborgs IF	1-1(1-0)
IK Gauthiod Grästorp - BK Häcken Göteborg	0-3(0-1)
Helsingborgs IF - Dalkurd FF Uppsala	1-2(0-2)
Dalkurd FF Uppsala - IK Gauthiod Grästorp	5-0(2-0)
BK Häcken Göteborg - Helsingborgs IF	1-1(0-0)
Qualified: BK Häcken Göteborg	

Group 4
Kalmar FF - Umeå FC	1-2(0-1)
Djurgårdens IF Stockholm - IK Brage Borlänge	1-0(1-0)
Kalmar FF - IK Brage Borlänge	1-0(0-0)
Djurgårdens IF Stockholm - Umeå FC	7-0(3-0)
Djurgårdens IF Stockholm - Kalmar FF	4-1(3-1)
IK Brage Borlänge - Umeå FC	1-0(0-0)
Qualified: Djurgårdens IF Stockholm	

Group 5
Mjällby AIF Hällevik - Akropolis IF Spånga	3-1(2-0)
Landskrona BoIS - Östersunds FK	0-3(0-1)
Landskrona BoIS - Mjällby AIF Hällevik	0-3(0-2)
Östersunds FK - Akropolis IF Spånga	1-1(0-0)
Akropolis IF Spånga - Landskrona BoIS	0-2(0-0)
Mjällby AIF Hällevik - Östersunds FK	0-1(0-0)
Qualified: Östersunds FK	

Group 6
IFK Norrköping - GIF Sundsvall	2-0(2-0)
Sandvikens IF - IFK Göteborg	3-4(1-1)
Sandvikens IF - IFK Norrköping	1-4(0-0)
IFK Göteborg - GIF Sundsvall	1-1(0-0)
GIF Sundsvall - Sandvikens IF	2-3(1-3)
IFK Norrköping - IFK Göteborg	1-1(1-1)
Qualified: IFK Norrköping	

Group 7
Örebro SK - Trelleborgs FF	0-1(0-1)
IF Lödde - IK Sirius Uppsala	0-1(0-0)
IF Lödde - Örebro SK	0-7(0-5)
IK Sirius Uppsala - Trelleborgs FF	1-1(0-0)
Trelleborgs FF - IF Lödde	3-1(2-1)
Örebro SK - IK Sirius Uppsala	2-2(0-1)
Qualified: Trelleborgs FF	

Group 8
Hammarby IF Stockholm - AFC Eskilstuna	4-1(2-0)
Oskarshamns AIK - AIK Stockholm	1-2(0-1)
AIK Stockholm - AFC Eskilstuna	4-0(3-0)
Oskarshamns AIK - Hammarby IF Stockholm	0-3(0-1)
AFC Eskilstuna - Oskarshamns AIK	4-1(4-1)
Hammarby IF Stockholm - AIK Stockholm	3-2(1-0)
Qualified: Hammarby IF Stockholm	

Quarter-Finals [13-14.03./01.04.2021]

IFK Norrköping - BK Häcken Göteborg	2-3(2-2)		Degerfors IF - Västerås SK Fotboll	3-4(1-0,2-2)
Djurgårdens IF Stockholm - Östersunds FK	3-0(1-0)		Hammarby IF Stockholm - Trelleborgs FF	3-2(1-0,1-1)

Semi-Finals [20.03./04.04.2021]

BK Häcken Göteborg - Västerås SK Fotboll	3-0(1-0)		Djurgårdens IF Stockh. - Hammarby IF Stockholm	0-1(0-1)

Final

30.05.2021; Tele2 Arena, Stockholm; Referee: Kaspar Sjöberg; Attendance: 0,000

Hammarby IF Stockholm - BK Häcken Göteborg **0-0; 5-4 on penalties**

Hammarby IF: David Ousted, Simon Sandberg (72.Aziz Ouattara), Mohanad Jeahze, Mads Fenger, Jón Fjóluson, Darijan Bojanić (73.Paulo José de Oliveira „Paulinho"), Jeppe Andersen [*sent off 120*], Vladimir Rodić (60.Akinkunmi Ayobami Amoo), Abdul Khalili (101.Aimar Sher), Gustav Ludwigson (110.David Accam), Astrit Selmani. Trainer: Stefan Billborn.

BK Häcken: Pontus Jacob Ragne Dahlberg, Johan Hammar, Joona Toivio, Elohor Godswill Ekpolo, Óskar Sverrisson (96.Valgeir Lunddal Friðriksson), Erik Friberg (83.Alexander Faltsetas), Tobias Heintz (55.Leo Bengtsson), Bénie Adama Traoré, Gustav Berggren, Patrik Walemark (55.Ali Youssef), Alexander Jeremejeff [*sent off 104*]. Trainer: Andreas Alm.

Penalties: Alexander Faltsetas 0-1; Paulo José de Oliveira „Paulinho" 1-1; Leo Bengtsson 1-2; David Accam 2-2; Joona Toivio 2-3; Mads Fenger 3-3; Bénie Adama Traoré (saved); Aimar Sher 4-3; Ali Youssef 4-4; Astrit Selmani 5-4.

THE CLUBS 2020

Allmänna Idrottsklubben Stockholm

Founded: 15.02.1891
Stadium: Friends Arena, Stockholm (50,000)
Trainer: Rikard Olof Norling — 04.06.1971
(01.08.2020) Bartosz Grzelak (POL) — 02.11.1978

Goalkeepers:	DOB	M	(s)	G
Jakob Haugaard (DEN)	01.05.1992	14		
Budimir Janošević (SRB)	21.10.1989	16		
Defenders:	**DOB**	**M**	**(s)**	**G**
Panajotis Dimitriadis	12.08.1986		(9)	
Eric Kahl	27.09.2001	23	(3)	
Per Karlsson	02.01.1986	23	(3)	1
Robert Lundström	01.11.1989	5	(9)	
Carl Mikael Lustig	13.12.1996	11	(2)	2
Karol Mets (EST)	16.05.1993	19	(1)	1
George Felix Michel Melki (LIB)	23.07.1994	5	(3)	
Erick Ouma Otieno (KEN)	27.09.1996	1	(3)	
Sotirios Papagiannopoulos	05.09.1990	12		
Robin Tihi (FIN)	16.03.2002	10	(3)	1
Midfielders:	**DOB**	**M**	**(s)**	**G**
Paulos Abraham	16.07.2002	22	(4)	3
Enoch Adu (GHA)	14.09.1990	16	(7)	1
Yasin Abbas Ayari	06.10.2003	1		
Nabil Bahoui	05.02.1991	10	(7)	4
Daniel Granli (NOR)	01.05.1994	11	(2)	
Bilal Hussein	22.04.2000	16	(9)	2
Sebastian Bengt Ulf Larsson	06.06.1985	27	(1)	5
Rasmus Lindkvist	16.05.1990	5	(5)	
Ebenezer Ofori (GHA)	01.07.1995	10	(6)	
Heradi Rashidi	24.07.1994	8	(3)	
Filip Roberto Rogić	14.06.1993	10	(1)	1
Tom Strannegaard	29.04.2002	8	(4)	
Saku Ylätupa (FIN)	04.08.1999	4	(3)	
Forwards:	**DOB**	**M**	**(s)**	**G**
Jasir Asani (ALB)	19.05.1995	2	(2)	1
Henok Goitom (ERI)	22.09.1984	26	(3)	8
Bojan Radulović (SRB)	29.12.1999	1	(2)	
Erik Ring	24.04.2002	7	(3)	
Kolbeinn Sigþórsson (ISL)	14.03.1990	5	(13)	
Stefan Silva	11.03.1990	2	(11)	

Djurgårdens Idrottsförening Stockholm

Founded: 12.03.1891
Stadium: Tele2 Arena, Stockholm (30,000)
Trainer: Thomas Lagerlöf & — 15.11.1971
Kim Bergstrand — 18.04.1968

Goalkeepers:	DOB	M	(s)	G
Per Kristian Bråtveit (NOR)	15.02.1996	18		
Tommi Vaiho	13.09.1988	12		
Defenders:	**DOB**	**M**	**(s)**	**G**
Jonathan Augustinsson	30.03.1996	26	(1)	2
Erik Berg	30.12.1988	16	(5)	3
Melker Jonsson	10.07.2002		(2)	
Elliot Käck	18.09.1989	18	(7)	
Jacob Larsson	08.04.1994	27		
Jesper Nyholm	10.09.1993	6	(5)	1
Aslak Witry (NOR)	10.03.1996	25	(1)	2
Midfielders:	**DOB**	**M**	**(s)**	**G**
Astrit Ajdarević (ALB)	17.04.1990	1	(3)	
Emmanuel Banda (ZAM)	29.09.1997	4	(4)	1
Curtis Edwards (ENG)	12.01.1994	18	(7)	3
Magnus Eriksson	08.04.1990	10	(3)	3
Jesper Karlström	21.06.1995	28		1
Mattias Mitku	20.07.2001		(3)	
Oscar Pettersson	01.02.2000		(6)	1
Haris Radetinac (SRB)	28.10.1985	24	(3)	1
Jonathan Ring	05.12.1991	17	(7)	
Fredrik Ulvestad (NOR)	17.06.1992	27		11
Kevin Walker	03.08.1989	5	(10)	1
Forwards:	**DOB**	**M**	**(s)**	**G**
Nicklas Bärkroth	19.01.1992	8	(7)	1
Edward Chilufya (ZAM)	17.09.1999	10	(6)	2
Karl Holmberg	03.03.1993	21	(9)	9
Emir Kujović	22.06.1988	9	(19)	5

Idrottsföreningen Elfsborg Borås

Founded: 26.06.1904 (as Borås Fotbollslag)
Stadium: Borås Arena, Borås (16,899)
Trainer: Bo Jimmy Thelin — 14.03.1978

Goalkeepers:	DOB	M	(s)	G
Mathias Dyngeland (NOR)	07.10.1995		(1)	
Tim Rönning	15.02.1999	30		
Defenders:	**DOB**	**M**	**(s)**	**G**
Gustav Henriksson	03.02.1998	10	(4)	2
Frederik Holst (DEN)	24.09.1994	21	(6)	2
Rami Kaib	08.05.1997	12	(4)	
Johan Larsson	05.05.1990	29		3
Christopher McVey	12.04.1997	2	(5)	
Joseph Stanley Okumu (KEN)	26.05.1997	24		
Simon Strand	25.05.1993	17	(7)	
Leo Väisänen (FIN)	23.07.1997	26		
Midfielders:	**DOB**	**M**	**(s)**	**G**
Rasmus Alm	17.08.1995	30		9
Robert Gojani	19.10.1992	17	(5)	
Samuel Holmén	28.06.1984	2	(22)	1
Issac Kouame	20.10.2000		(6)	
Sivert Heltne Nilsen (NOR)	02.10.1991	21	(2)	1
Simon Olsson	14.09.1997	29		4
Forwards:	**DOB**	**M**	**(s)**	**G**
Per Frick	14.04.1992	28		10
Deniz Hümmet	13.09.1996		(12)	
Karl Jesper Karlsson	25.07.1998	22		11
Marokhy Ndione	04.11.1999	2	(17)	
Jeppe Okkels (DEN)	27.07.1999	7	(4)	3
Jacob Ondrejka	02.09.2002	1	(20)	1

Falkenbergs Fotbollsförening

Founded: 03.01.1928
Stadium: Falcon Alkoholfri Arena, Falkenberg (5,565)
Trainer: Hans Eklund — 16.04.1979

Goalkeepers:	DOB	M	(s)	G
Johan Brattberg	28.12.1996	12	(1)	
Viktor Noring	03.02.1991	18	(1)	
Defenders:	**DOB**	**M**	**(s)**	**G**
Grégoire Amiot (FRA)	10.05.1995	12		
Jacob Ericsson	17.09.1993	17	(8)	
Rasmus Fridolf	21.09.1999		(1)	
Carl Johansson	23.05.1994	29		3
Gabriel Johansson	10.09.2000	1	(5)	
Tibor Joza	10.08.1986	12	(6)	
Tobias Karlsson	14.01.1989	14	(6)	1
Axel Norén	04.04.1999	10		1
Mahmut Özen	01.09.1988	2	(6)	
Sander van Looy (NED)	29.05.1997	16	(3)	
Midfielders:	**DOB**	**M**	**(s)**	**G**
Lorik Ademi	30.07.2001	2	(7)	
Mohammad Ahmadi	09.01.2000		(2)	
John Björkengren	09.12.1998	21		1
Christoffer Carlsson	15.01.1989	26	(3)	2
John Chibuike (NGA)	10.10.1988	15	(8)	2
Tobias Englund	06.02.1989	22	(2)	4
Marcus Mathisen (DEN)	27.02.1996	24	(1)	2
Melker Nilsson	26.04.2000	2	(5)	
Anton Wede	20.04.1990	17	(13)	3
Forwards:	**DOB**	**M**	**(s)**	**G**
Matthew Garbett (NZL)	13.04.2002	2	(11)	
Kwame Kizito (GHA)	21.07.1996	1		
Gustaf Nilsson	23.05.1997	6		
Nsima Peter (NGA)	28.12.1988	12	(9)	3
Karl Söderström	26.10.1985	21	(8)	3
Edi Sylisufaj	08.03.1999	16	(9)	7

Idrottsföreningen Kamraterna Göteborg

Founded: 04.10.1904
Stadium: Gamla Ullevi Stadion, Göteborg (18,600)
Trainer: Poya Asbaghi   17.07.1985
(04.09.2020) Ferran Sibila Pont (ESP)   13.07.1988
(11.09.2020) Roland Nilsson   27.11.1963

Goalkeepers:	DOB	M	(s)	G
Giannis Anestis (GRE)	09.03.1991	30		
Defenders:	**DOB**	**M**	**(s)**	**G**
Mattias Bjärsmyr	03.01.1986	17	(3)	4
André Calisir (ARM)	13.06.1990	15	(2)	
Kristopher Da Graca	16.01.1998	11	(7)	
Emil Holm	13.05.2000	7	(19)	2
Alexander Jallow	03.03.1998	24	(2)	
Yahya Kalley	20.03.2001	8	(1)	
Jesper Tolinsson	28.02.2003	5	(3)	
Victor Wernersson	06.07.1995	16	(2)	
Rasmus Wikström	18.03.2001		(1)	
Midfielders:	**DOB**	**M**	**(s)**	**G**
Sargon Abraham	07.02.1991	18	(9)	3
Amin Affane	21.01.1994		(5)	
Noah Alexandersson	30.09.2001	2	(6)	
Isak Dahlqvist	25.09.2001		(1)	
Sebastian Eriksson	31.01.1989	4	(1)	
August Erlingmark	22.04.1998	22	(3)	3
Alexander Farnerud	01.05.1984	9	(12)	4
Jakob Valdemar Olsson Johansson	21.06.1990	17	(1)	
Giorgi Kharaishvili (GEO)	29.07.1996	12	(3)	2
Tobias Sana	11.07.1989	26	(3)	5
Adil Titi	20.08.1999		(6)	
Nzuzi Bundebele Toko (COD)	20.11.1990	4		
Pontus Anders Mikael Wernbloom	25.06.1986	10	(3)	2
Alhassan Yusuf (NGA)	18.07.2000	28	(1)	
Forwards:	**DOB**	**M**	**(s)**	**G**
Hosam Aiesh	14.04.1995	14	(8)	3
Patrik Karlsson-Lagemyr	18.12.1996	24	(2)	5
Omil Christian Kouakou	20.04.1995	4	(3)	
Robin Söder	01.04.1991	3	(6)	
Oscar Vilhelmsson	02.10.2003		(3)	

Hammarby Idrottsförening Fotbollförening Stockholm

Founded: 07.03.1897
Stadium: Tele2 Arena, Stockholm (30,000)
Trainer: Stefan Billborn   15.11.1972

Goalkeepers:	DOB	M	(s)	G
Davor Blažević	07.02.1993	4		
Oliver Dovin	11.07.2002	1		
David Ousted (DEN)	01.02.1985	25		
Defenders:	**DOB**	**M**	**(s)**	**G**
Kalle Björklund	31.05.1999	6	(8)	1
David Fällman	02.04.1990	23	(2)	
Mads Fenger (DEN)	10.09.1990	26	(2)	1
Mohanad Jeahze	10.04.1997	8		
Jean Carlos de Brito (BRA)	09.06.1995		(2)	
Richard Göran Emil Magyar	03.05.1991	12	(2)	1
Simon Sandberg	25.03.1994	18	(2)	
Axel Sjöberg	12.04.2000		(1)	
Dennis Widgren	28.03.1994	12	(6)	
Midfielders:	**DOB**	**M**	**(s)**	**G**
Jeppe Andersen (DEN)	06.12.1992	25	(3)	
Darijan Bojanić	28.12.1994	17	(6)	
Alexander Kačaniklić	13.08.1991	19	(4)	4
Abdul Khalili	07.06.1992	26	(1)	2
Serge-Junior Martinsson Ngouali (GAB)	23.01.1992	9	(9)	
Vladimir Rodić (MNE)	07.09.1993	9	(8)	
Aimar Sher	20.12.2002	9	(11)	1
Forwards:	**DOB**	**M**	**(s)**	**G**
Akinkunmi Ayobami Amoo (NGA)	07.06.2002		(6)	
Aron Jóhannsson (USA)	10.11.1990	15	(7)	12
Imad Khalili (PLE)	03.04.1987	7	(15)	4
Gustav Ludwigson	20.10.1993	22	(7)	9
Paulo José de Oliveira „Paulinho" (BRA)	09.04.1986	10	(6)	3
Tim Söderström	04.01.1994	14	(10)	1
Muamer Tanković	22.02.1995	13	(1)	7

Bollklubben Häcken Göteborg

Founded: 02.08.1940
Stadium: Bravida Arena, Göteborg (6,500)
Trainer: Andreas Alm   19.06.1973

Goalkeepers:	DOB	M	(s)	G
Peter Abrahamsson	18.07.1988	12		
Pontus Jacob Ragne Dahlberg	21.01.1999	14		
Jonathan Rasheed	21.11.1991	4	(1)	
Defenders:	**DOB**	**M**	**(s)**	**G**
Tobias Carlsson	28.07.1995		(2)	
Elohor Godswill Ekpolo (NGA)	14.05.1995	29		
Johan Hammar	22.02.1991	5	(13)	2
Rasmus Lindgren	29.11.1984	27		1
Óskar Sverrisson	26.11.1992	1	(6)	
Joona Toivio (FIN)	10.03.1988	30		1
Leonardo Žuta (MKD)	09.08.1992	14	(2)	1
Midfielders:	**DOB**	**M**	**(s)**	**G**
Adam Andersson	11.11.1996	13	(11)	1
Leo Bengtsson	26.05.1998	24	(1)	8
Gustav Berggren	07.09.1997	24	(4)	3
Alexander Faltsetas	04.07.1987	6	(13)	1
Erik Friberg	10.02.1986	27	(1)	1
Nikola Gulan (SRB)	23.03.1989	3	(1)	
Daleho Irandust	04.06.1998	23		6
Adnan Marić	17.02.1997	1	(6)	
Kevin Yakob	10.10.2000		(2)	
Ahmed Yasin Ghani Mousa (IRQ)	22.04.1991	21	(7)	3
Ali Youssef	05.08.2000	4	(13)	2
Forwards:	**DOB**	**M**	**(s)**	**G**
Viktor Lundberg	04.03.1991	5	(18)	1
Gustaf Nilsson	23.05.1997	3	(5)	1
Leonardo Farah Shahin	10.08.2003		(1)	
Alexander Søderlund (NOR)	03.08.1987	22	(1)	8
Jasse Tuominen (FIN)	12.11.1995	5	(10)	1
Patrik Walemark	14.10.2001	13	(8)	3

Helsingborgs Idrottsförening

Founded: 04.06.1907
Stadium: Olympiastadion, Helsingborg (16,500)
Trainer: Olof Mellberg   03.09.1977

Goalkeepers:	DOB	M	(s)	G
Kalle Joelsson	21.03.1998	1		
Anders Lindegaard (DEN)	13.04.1984	11		1
Alexander Nilsson	22.08.1997	14	(1)	
Ian Pettersson	21.07.2002	4		
Defenders:	**DOB**	**M**	**(s)**	**G**
Kebba Ceesay	14.11.1987	11	(1)	
Adam Eriksson	13.07.1990	26	(1)	
Erik Figueroa	04.01.1991	6	(4)	
Andreas Granqvist	16.04.1985	1		
Marcus Jonas Munuhe Olsson	17.05.1988		(2)	
Martin Tony Waikwa Olsson	17.05.1988	24	(1)	
Anders Randrup (DEN)	16.07.1988	9	(3)	
Ravy Tsouka Dozi (FRA)	23.12.1994	12	(5)	
Casper Widell	05.05.2003	3	(4)	
Midfielders:	**DOB**	**M**	**(s)**	**G**
Mohammed Abubakari (GHA)	15.02.1986	15	(8)	
Ludvig Carlius	14.03.2001		(4)	
Joseph Ceesay	03.06.1998	18	(1)	
Mikkel Morgenstar Pålssønn Diskerud (USA)	02.10.1990	27	(1)	2
Armin Gigović	06.04.2002	18	(2)	1
Emil Hellman	20.04.2001	1	(2)	
Brandur Hendriksson Olsen (FRO)	19.12.1995	22	(2)	2
Andreas Landgren	17.03.1989	4	(5)	
Filip Sjöberg	12.04.2000		(6)	
Jakob Voelkerling-Persson	27.09.2000	11	(4)	
Forwards:	**DOB**	**M**	**(s)**	**G**
Assad Al Hamlawi	27.10.2000	3	(6)	1
Alex Timossi Andersson	19.01.2001	17	(11)	5
Salisu Abdullahi Gero (NGA)	10.10.1993	1	(16)	1
Rasmus Jönsson	27.01.1990	18	(6)	3
Shkodran Maholi	10.04.1993		(3)	
Noel Mbo (ENG)	14.03.1999	2	(10)	
Max Svensson	19.06.1998	25	(4)	6
Anthony van den Hurk (NED)	09.01.1993	26	(1)	11

Kalmar Fotbollsförening

Founded: 15.06.1910 (as IF Göta)
Stadium: Guldfågeln Arena, Kalmar (12,000)
Trainer: Kurt Arne René Bergstrand   28.04.1956

Goalkeepers:	DOB	M	(s)	G
Tobias Andersson	18.02.1994	2		
Lucas Johansson	11.07.1994	17		
Ole Söderberg	20.07.1990	11		
Defenders:	**DOB**	**M**	**(s)**	**G**
Fidan Aliti (KVX)	03.10.1993	20		2
Gbenga Arokoyo (NGA)	01.11.1992	4	(2)	
Jan Douglas Bergqvist	29.03.1993	18		
Henrik Löfkvist	05.05.1995	5	(1)	
Emin Nouri (AZE)	22.07.1985	15	(5)	
Sebastian Ring	18.04.1995	26	(2)	2
Johan Stenmark	26.02.1999	4	(1)	
Midfielders:	**DOB**	**M**	**(s)**	**G**
Johan Arvidsson	25.02.2000		(2)	
Viktor Elm	13.11.1985	16	(3)	1
Carl Gustafsson	18.03.2000	10	(7)	
Svante Ingelsson	14.06.1998	18		2
Erik Gustav Roger Israelsson	25.02.1989	19		3
Isak Jansson	31.01.2002	23	(6)	
Piotr Johansson	28.02.1995	21	(2)	4
Rafinha Gimenes da Silva (BRA)	05.08.1993	2	(2)	
Romario Pereira Sipião (BRA)	10.08.1985	27		2
Filip Sachpekidis	03.07.1997	17	(12)	
Forwards:	**DOB**	**M**	**(s)**	**G**
Edvin Crona	25.01.2000	8	(15)	2
Adrian Edqvist	20.05.1999	4	(2)	
Nils Fröling	20.04.2000	7	(3)	2
Mayron Antonio George Clayton (CRC)	23.10.1993	1	(2)	
Geir André Herrem (NOR)	28.01.1988	8	(6)	1
Alexander Holmström	04.04.1999	3	(9)	1
Isak Magnusson	16.06.1998	16	(10)	5
York Rafael	17.03.1999	8	(19)	

Malmö Fotbollförening

Founded: 24.02.1910
Stadium: Eleda Stadion, Malmö (22,500)
Trainer: Jon Dahl Tomasson (DEN)   29.08.1976

Goalkeepers:	DOB	M	(s)	G
Johan Dahlin	08.09.1986	14		
Marko Johansson	25.08.1998	16		
Lamin Sarr	11.03.2001		(1)	
Defenders:	**DOB**	**M**	**(s)**	**G**
Anel Ahmedhodžić (BIH)	26.03.1999	29		2
Felix Olof Allan Nelson Beijmo	31.01.1998		(3)	
Rasmus Bengtsson	26.06.1986		(1)	
Franz Brorsson	30.01.1996	12	(1)	2
Jonas Knudsen (DEN)	16.09.1992	24	(6)	
Eric Larsson	15.07.1991	29	(1)	3
Lasse Nielsen (DEN)	08.01.1988	14	(1)	1
Behrang Safari	09.02.1985	6	(7)	
Midfielders:	**DOB**	**M**	**(s)**	**G**
Samuel Adrian	02.03.1998		(1)	
Fouad Bachirou (COM)	15.04.1990	10	(2)	
Anders Bleg Christiansen (DEN)	08.06.1990	22	(1)	13
Bonke Innocent (NGA)	20.01.1996	8	(8)	
Oscar Lewicki	14.07.1992	18	(5)	
Adi Nalić	01.12.1997	5	(15)	2
Erdal Rakip	13.02.1996	18	(8)	1
Søren Rieks (DEN)	07.04.1987	18	(7)	5
Arnór Ingvi Traustason (ISL)	30.04.1993	11	(9)	1
Forwards:	**DOB**	**M**	**(s)**	**G**
Marcus Antonsson	08.05.1991	7	(1)	1
Jo Inge Berget (NOR)	11.09.1990	20	(3)	7
Isaac Kiese Thelin	24.06.1992	19	(6)	13
Guillermo Federico Molins Palmeiro	26.09.1988	4	(6)	1
Tim Prica	23.04.2002	2	(2)	
Amin Sarr	11.03.2001	6	(10)	1
Nils Ola Toivonen	03.07.1986	18	(3)	8

Mjällby Allmänna Idrottsförening Hällevik

Founded: 01.04.1939
Stadium: Strandvallen, Hällevik (6,750)
Trainer: Marcus Lantz   23.10.1975

Goalkeepers:	DOB	M	(s)	G
Carljohan Eriksson (FIN)	25.04.1995	22		
Marko Johansson	25.08.1998	8		
Defenders:	**DOB**	**M**	**(s)**	**G**
Viktor Agardius	23.10.1989	26		
Eric Björkander	11.06.1996	22	(1)	1
Amer Eriksson	06.10.1994		(1)	
Kadir Hodžić	05.08.1994	10	(1)	
Mohanad Jeahze	10.04.1997	12		
Jesper Löfgren	03.05.1997	26	(3)	1
Jonathan Tamimi-Syberg (JOR)	12.10.1994	16	(4)	
Max Watson	03.02.1996	18	(3)	2
Midfielders:	**DOB**	**M**	**(s)**	**G**
David Batanero Puigbó (ESP)	27.09.1988	14	(5)	1
Viktor Gustafsson	22.03.1995	7	(10)	1
Jesper Gustavsson	29.10.1994	20	(4)	1
David Löfqvist	06.08.1986	28		5
Joel Nilsson	11.07.1994	19	(5)	
Adam Petersson	25.08.2000	5	(9)	
Martin Spelmann (DEN)	21.03.1987	4	(2)	
Besard Šabović	05.01.1998	23	(4)	4
Forwards:	**DOB**	**M**	**(s)**	**G**
Jacob Bergström	26.04.1995	19	(9)	8
Mamudo Moro (GHA)	07.03.1995	12	(8)	5
Moses Owoicho Ogbu (NGA)	07.02.1991	19	(6)	14
Erik Pärsson	07.04.1994		(5)	
Taylor Silverholt	04.04.2001		(11)	1

Idrottsföreningen Kamraterna Norrköping

Founded: 29.05.1897
Stadium: Nya Parken, Norrköping (15,734)
Trainer: Jens Gustafsson 15.10.1978

Goalkeepers:	DOB	M	(s)	G
Isak Pettersson	06.06.1997	30		
Defenders:	**DOB**	**M**	**(s)**	**G**
Kevin Javier Álvarez Hernández (HON)	03.08.1996		(3)	
Egzon Binaku	27.08.1995	3	(5)	
Henrik Castegren	28.03.1996	22	(6)	2
Filip Dagerstål	01.02.1997	29		
Manasse Kusu	22.12.2001		(7)	
Rasmus Lauritsen (DEN)	27.02.1996	21	(1)	6
Theodore Rask	01.05.2000		(1)	
Linus Wahlqvist	11.11.1996	17		1
Midfielders:	**DOB**	**M**	**(s)**	**G**
Ishaq Abdulrazak	05.05.2002	3	(11)	2
Andreas Blomqvist	05.05.1992	6	(12)	
Alexander Fransson	02.04.1994	19	(6)	2
Lars Gerson (LUX)	05.02.1990	25	(1)	3
Sead Hakšabanović (MNE)	04.05.1999	25	(4)	7
Ísak Jóhannesson (ISL)	23.03.2003	25	(3)	3
Jonathan Levi	23.01.1996	18	(7)	9
Maic Ndongala Namputu Sema	02.12.1988	1	(9)	
Eric Smith	08.01.1997	27		
Christopher Rasmus Nilsson Telo	04.11.1989	2	(7)	
Simon Thern	18.09.1992	23	(1)	2
Forwards:	**DOB**	**M**	**(s)**	**G**
Pontus Almqvist	10.07.1999	5	(15)	5
Carl Björk	19.01.2000	1	(3)	
Linus Peter Hallenius	01.04.1989		(8)	
Christoffer Åke Sven Nyman	05.10.1992	28		18

Örebro Sportklubb

Founded: 28.10.1908
Stadium: Behrn Arena, Örebro (12,300)
Trainer: Axel Kjäll 01.06.1981

Goalkeepers:	DOB	M	(s)	G
Oscar Jansson	23.12.1990	30		
Defenders:	**DOB**	**M**	**(s)**	**G**
Hussein Ali	01.03.2002	12	(10)	
Michael Almebäck	04.04.1988	26		
Niclas Bergmark	07.01.2002		(2)	
Daniel Björkman	21.02.1993		(3)	
Daniel Björnkvist	08.01.1989		(3)	
Arvid Brorsson	08.05.1999	1	(1)	
Fabio De Sousa Silva (BRA)	13.01.1996		(2)	
Albin Granlund (FIN)	01.09.1989	20	(2)	
Andreas Skovgaard (DEN)	27.03.1997	25	(1)	1
Kevin Wright (ENG)	28.12.1995	22	(5)	
Midfielders:	**DOB**	**M**	**(s)**	**G**
Simon Amin	13.11.1997	7	(7)	
Nahir Besara	25.02.1991	26	(3)	12
Robin Book	05.04.1992	12	(4)	2
Martin Broberg	24.09.1990	1	(4)	
Dennis Collander	09.05.2002	6	(9)	
Romain Thierry Marie Gall (USA)	31.01.1995	7	(1)	
Nordin Gerzić	09.11.1983	23	(3)	
Benjamin Hjertstrand	22.01.1994	15	(10)	
Johan Mårtensson	16.02.1989	19	(3)	
David Seger	15.07.1999	18	(9)	3
Forwards:	**DOB**	**M**	**(s)**	**G**
Erik Björndahl	13.07.1990	7	(11)	3
Isaac Boye Edegware (NGA)	05.01.1997		(1)	
Deniz Hümmet	13.09.1996	12		5
Rasmus Karjalainen (FIN)	04.04.1996	5	(8)	4
Jack Lahne	24.10.2001	8	(2)	
Jake Larsson	09.01.1999	18	(4)	2
Agon Mehmeti (ALB)	20.11.1989	10	(8)	4

Östersunds Fotbollsklubb

Founded: 31.10.1996
Stadium: Jämtkraft Arena, Östersund (8,466)
Trainer: Ian Burchnall (ENG) 11.02.1983
(12.07.2020) Amir Azrafshan 17.08.1987

Goalkeepers:	DOB	M	(s)	G
Aly Keita	08.12.1986	29		
Andrew Mills (ENG)	15.07.1994	1		
Defenders:	**DOB**	**M**	**(s)**	**G**
Nikolaos Dosis	25.01.2001	3	(5)	
Eirik Haugan (NOR)	27.08.1997	25		
Thomas Isherwood	28.01.1998	26		2
Ronald Mukiibi	16.09.1991	9	(8)	
Kalpi Wilfried Ouattara (CIV)	29.12.1998	21	(5)	
Noah Sonko Sundberg	06.06.1996	25		2
Isak Ssewankambo	27.02.1996	27	(1)	1
Midfielders:	**DOB**	**M**	**(s)**	**G**
Rewan Amin (IRQ)	08.01.1996	14	(1)	1
Frank Arhin (GHA)	16.02.1999	2	(5)	
Henrik Bellman	24.03.1999	6	(11)	1
Charlie Colkett (ENG)	04.09.1996	18	(6)	
Ludvig Fritzson	25.08.1995	21	(3)	3
Felix Hörberg	19.05.1999	28		2
Simon Kroon	16.06.1993	7	(3)	1
Samuel Laryeal Mensah (GHA)	19.05.1989	10	(9)	
Alex Purver (ENG)	01.12.1995		(5)	
Jerell Sellars (ENG)	28.04.1995	1	(9)	1
Malcolm Stolt	30.12.2000		(5)	
Marco Weymans (BEL)	09.07.1997	5	(7)	
Forwards:	**DOB**	**M**	**(s)**	**G**
Ahmed Awad Mohammad (PLE)	01.06.1992		(6)	
Brian Martín Pagés (ESP)	09.04.1996		(4)	
Francis Jno-Baptiste (ENG)	08.11.1999	7	(8)	3
Jordan Attah Kadiri (NGA)	11.03.2000	11		2
Nebiyou Sundance Perry (USA)	02.10.1999	14	(12)	1
Blair Sebastian Turgott (ENG)	22.05.1994	20	(7)	7

Idrottsklubben Sirius Uppsala

Founded: 1907
Stadium: Studenternas IP, Uppsala (6,300)
Trainer: Henrik Rydström 16.02.1976

Goalkeepers:	DOB	M	(s)	G
Lukas Jonsson	21.10.1992	24		
Hannes Sveijer	28.04.2002	3		
Jon Viscosi (CAN)	18.03.1991	3		
Defenders:	**DOB**	**M**	**(s)**	**G**
Tim Björkström	08.01.1991	29		
Axel Björnström	10.09.1995	30		5
Kebba Ceesay	14.11.1987	3	(2)	
Hjalmar Ekdal	21.10.1998	22	(4)	
Noel Hansson	06.09.2003		(1)	
Daniel Jarl	13.04.1992	13	(5)	
Johan Karlsson	20.06.2001	6	(14)	
Erik Langwagen	10.08.2003		(2)	
Karl Larson	28.10.1991	21	(5)	1
Midfielders:	**DOB**	**M**	**(s)**	**G**
Elias Andersson	31.01.1996	28		6
Isak Bråholm	24.09.2000		(2)	
Simon Gefvert	28.03.1997	1	(5)	
Nahom Girmai Netabay	28.08.1994	20	(4)	4
Adam Hellborg	30.07.1998	24	(3)	
Jamie Roche	05.04.2001	11	(7)	
Mohammed Saeid	24.12.1990	28		7
Laorent Shabani (ALB)	19.08.1999	3	(23)	
Adam Ståhl	08.10.1994	7	(10)	
Niklas Thor	21.02.1986		(13)	
Samuel Wikman	22.01.2002		(1)	
Forwards:	**DOB**	**M**	**(s)**	**G**
Chibuike Kennedy Igboananike (NGA)	08.02.1989	1	(3)	
André Österholm	17.06.1996		(2)	
Joakim Persson	03.04.2002	8	(8)	
Yukiya Sugita (JPN)	07.04.1993	28		7
Stefano Holmquist Vecchia	23.01.1995	22	(4)	12

Varbergs Boll- och Idrottssällskap

Founded: 25.03.1925
Stadium: Påskbergsvallen, Varberg (4,500)
Trainer: Joakim Persson   03.04.1975

Goalkeepers:	DOB	M	(s)	G
Stojan Lukić	28.12.1979	19		
August Strömberg	28.02.1992	11		1
Defenders:	**DOB**	**M**	**(s)**	**G**
Jon Birkfeldt	03.06.1996	24	(1)	3
Anton Liljenbäck	21.02.1995	20	(7)	
Gideon Mensah (GHA)	09.10.2000	9	(5)	
Jesper Modig	06.09.1994	6	(7)	
Robin Tranberg	06.02.1993	14	(9)	2
Hampus Zackrisson	24.08.1994	22	(1)	1
Midfielders:	**DOB**	**M**	**(s)**	**G**
Keanin Ayer Boya (RSA)	21.04.2000	12	(11)	1
André Boman	15.11.2001		(2)	
Albert Ejupi	28.08.1992	19	(7)	1
Adama Fofana (CIV)	11.10.1999	22	(7)	1
Alexander Johansson	30.10.1995	7	(5)	2
Noah Johansson	21.09.2003		(1)	

	DOB	M	(s)	G
Daniel Krezić (MKD)	03.05.1996	7	(2)	2
Luke Gareth Le Roux (RSA)	10.03.2000	18	(3)	
Joakim Lindner	22.03.1991	20		
Liam Munther	14.02.2001		(1)	
Gustaf Norlin	09.01.1997	23	(5)	5
Erion Sadiku (KVX)	23.01.2002	9	(16)	2
Samuel Monday Ayinoko Abu (NGA)	12.11.1993	1	(5)	
Albin Winbo	27.10.1997	9	(16)	1
Forwards:	**DOB**	**M**	**(s)**	**G**
Alibek Aliev	16.08.1996	2	(7)	
Junes Barny	04.11.1989	14		3
Robin Book	05.04.1992	9	(2)	2
Rasmus Cronvall	20.03.2002	1	(5)	
Tashreeq Matthews (RSA)	12.09.2000	10	(8)	1
Sebastian Nanasi	16.05.2002		(6)	
Astrit Seljmani	13.05.1997	22	(2)	15

SECOND LEVEL
Superettan 2020

1.	Halmstads BK (*Promoted*)	30	21	5	4	61	-	18	68
2.	Degerfors IF (*Promoted*)	30	19	6	5	64	-	30	63
3.	Jönköpings Södra IF (*Promotion Play-offs*)	30	18	5	7	52	-	34	59
4.	Östers IF Växjö	30	15	6	9	41	-	36	51
5.	Akropolis IF Spånga	30	10	15	5	44	-	39	45
6.	GIF Sundsvall	30	12	7	11	53	-	48	43
7.	Västerås SK Fotboll	30	11	6	13	40	-	44	39
8.	IK Brage Borlänge	30	11	6	13	38	-	44	39
9.	AFC Eskilstuna	30	11	4	15	36	-	49	37
10.	GAIS Göteborg	30	9	9	12	30	-	41	36
11.	Norrby IF Borås	30	8	10	12	39	-	41	34
12.	Örgryte IS Göteborg	30	9	6	15	34	-	43	33
13.	Trelleborgs FF (*Relegation Play-offs*)	30	8	8	14	33	-	41	32
14.	Dalkurd FF Uppsala (*Relegation Play-offs*)	30	6	11	13	33	-	42	29
15.	Umeå FC (*Relegated*)	30	5	12	13	25	-	47	27
16.	Ljungskile SK (*Relegated*)	30	5	8	17	24	-	50	23

Relegation Play-offs (2nd / 3rd Level)

IF Brommapojkarna - Trelleborgs FF	1-1(0-0)
Landskrona BoIS - Dalkurd FF Uppsala	2-0(1-0)

INTERNATIONAL MATCHES
(16.07.2020 – 15.07.2021)

05.09.2020	Stockholm	Sweden - France	0-1(0-1)	(UNL)
08.09.2020	Stockholm	Sweden - Portugal	0-2(0-1)	(UNL)
08.10.2020	Moskva	Russia - Sweden	1-2(0-1)	(F)
11.10.2020	Zagreb	Croatia - Sweden	2-1(1-0)	(UNL)
14.10.2020	Lisboa	Portugal - Sweden	3-0(2-0)	(UNL)
11.11.2020	Brøndby	Denmark - Sweden	2-0(0-0)	(F)
14.11.2020	Stockholm	Sweden - Croatia	2-1(2-0)	(UNL)
17.11.2020	Paris	France - Sweden	4-2(2-1)	(UNL)
25.03.2021	Stockholm	Sweden - Georgia	1-0(1-0)	(WCQ)
28.03.2021	Prishtina	Kosovo - Sweden	0-3(0-2)	(WCQ)
31.03.2021	Stockholm	Sweden - Estonia	1-0(1-0)	(F)
29.05.2021	Stockholm	Sweden - Finland	2-0(1-0)	(F)
05.06.2021	Stockholm	Sweden - Armenia	3-1(2-0)	(F)
14.06.2021	Sevilla	Spain - Sweden	0-0	(EC)
18.06.2021	Saint Petersburg	Sweden - Slovakia	1-0(0-0)	(EC)
23.06.2021	Saint Petersburg	Sweden - Poland	3-2(1-0)	(EC)
29.06.2021	Glasgow	Sweden - Ukraine	1-2(1-1,1-1)	(EC)

05.09.2020   SWEDEN - FRANCE   0-1(0-1)   2nd UEFA Nations League A, Group 3
Friends Arena, Stockholm; Referee: Szymon Marciniak (Poland); Attendance: 0
SWE: Robin Patrick Olsen, Pierre Thomas Robin Bengtsson (88.Ken Nlata Sema), Carl Mikael Lustig, Pontus Sven Gustav Jansson, Victor Jörgen Nilsson Lindelöf, Bengt Ulf Sebastian Larsson (Cap) (70.Dejan Kuluševski), Albin Ekdal, Emil Peter Forsberg, Mats Kristoffer Olsson, Bengt Eric Marcus Berg, Robin Kwamina Quaison (77.John Olof Alberto Guidetti). Trainer: Jan Olof Andersson.

08.09.2020   SWEDEN - PORTUGAL   0-2(0-1)   2nd UEFA Nations League A, Group 3
Friends Arena, Stockholm; Referee: Danny Desmond Makkelie (Netherlands); Attendance: 0
SWE: Robin Patrick Olsen, Pontus Sven Gustav Jansson, Hans Carl Ludwig Augustinsson, Emil Henry Kristoffer Krafth, Mats Kristoffer Olsson, Filip Viktor Helander, Karl Gustav Johan Svensson [*sent off 44*], Emil Peter Forsberg (79.Mattias Olof Svanberg), Dejan Kuluševski (90.Albin Ekdal), Bengt Eric Marcus Berg (Cap), Alexander Isak (71.Robin Kwamina Quaison). Trainer: Jan Olof Andersson.

08.10.2020   RUSSIA - SWEDEN   1-2(0-1)   Friendly International
VEB Arena, Moskva; Referee: Halis Özkahya (Turkey); Attendance: 5,000
SWE: Karl-Johan Anton Johnsson, Pierre Thomas Robin Bengtsson (72.Martin Tony Waikwa Olsson), Emil Henry Kristoffer Krafth (46.Mattias Johansson), Rasmus Sebastian Holmén, Carl Anders Theodor Starfelt, Karl Gustav Johan Svensson, Bengt Ulf Sebastian Larsson (Cap) (46.Mats Kristoffer Olsson), Ken Nlata Sema (77.Viktor Johan Anton Claesson), Mattias Olof Svanberg, Carl Henrik Jordan Larsson, Alexander Isak (64.Robin Kwamina Quaison). Trainer: Jan Olof Andersson.
Goals: Alexander Isak (21), Mattias Johansson (73).

11.10.2020   CROATIA - SWEDEN   2-1(1-0)   2nd UEFA Nations League A, Group 3
Stadion Maksimir, City; Referee: John William Beaton (Scotland); Attendance: 2,020
SWE: Robin Patrick Olsen, Carl Mikael Lustig, Pontus Sven Gustav Jansson, Victor Jörgen Nilsson Lindelöf, Hans Carl Ludwig Augustinsson, Albin Ekdal (83.Bengt Ulf Sebastian Larsson), Mats Kristoffer Olsson, Dejan Kuluševski, Bengt Eric Marcus Berg (Cap), Emil Peter Forsberg, Alexander Isak (65.Viktor Johan Anton Claesson). Trainer: Jan Olof Andersson.
Goal: Bengt Eric Marcus Berg (66).

14.10.2020   PORTUGAL - SWEDEN   3-0(2-0)   2nd UEFA Nations League A, Group 3
Estádio "José Alvalade", Lisboa; Referee: Srđan Jovanović (Serbia); Attendance: 5,000
SWE: Robin Patrick Olsen, Pierre Thomas Robin Bengtsson, Carl Mikael Lustig (54.Mattias Johansson), Pontus Sven Gustav Jansson, Victor Jörgen Nilsson Lindelöf, Albin Ekdal, Viktor Johan Anton Claesson, Mats Kristoffer Olsson, Dejan Kuluševski (88.Bengt Ulf Sebastian Larsson), Robin Kwamina Quaison (62.Alexander Isak), Bengt Eric Marcus Berg (Cap) (88.Martin Tony Waikwa Olsson). Trainer: Jan Olof Andersson.

11.11.2020   DENMARK - SWEDEN   2-0(0-0)   Friendly International
Brøndby Stadium, Brøndby; Referee: Espen Eskås (Norway); Attendance: 141
SWE: Bo Kristoffer Nordfeldt, Martin Tony Waikwa Olsson, Mattias Johansson (64.Eric Joel Andersson), Marcus Andreas Danielsson, Carl Anders Theodor Starfelt (75.Rasmus Sebastian Holmén), Karl Gustav Johan Svensson (Cap) (75.Bengt Ulf Sebastian Larsson), Oscar Hiljemark (75.Dejan Kuluševski), Jens-Lys Michel Cajuste, Mattias Olof Svanberg, Robin Kwamina Quaison (64.Carl Henrik Jordan Larsson), Alexander Isak. Trainer: Jan Olof Andersson.

14.11.2020   SWEDEN - CROATIA   2-1(2-0)   2nd UEFA Nations League A, Group 3
Friends Arena, Stockholm; Referee: Daniel Siebert (Germany); Attendance: 0
SWE: Robin Patrick Olsen, Pierre Thomas Robin Bengtsson, Carl Mikael Lustig, Marcus Andreas Danielsson, Victor Jörgen Nilsson Lindelöf, Bengt Ulf Sebastian Larsson, Albin Ekdal, Emil Peter Forsberg, Mats Kristoffer Olsson, Dejan Kuluševski (74.Viktor Johan Anton Claesson), Bengt Eric Marcus Berg (Cap). Trainer: Jan Olof Andersson.
Goals: Dejan Kuluševski (36), Marcus Andreas Danielsson (45+2).

17.11.2020   FRANCE - SWEDEN   4-2(2-1)   2nd UEFA Nations League A, Group 3
Stade de France, Saint-Denis, Paris; Referee: Aleksei Kulbakov (Belarus); Attendance: 0
SWE: Robin Patrick Olsen, Pierre Thomas Robin Bengtsson, Carl Mikael Lustig (67.Emil Henry Kristoffer Krafth), Marcus Andreas Danielsson, Victor Jörgen Nilsson Lindelöf (66.Filip Viktor Helander), Viktor Johan Anton Claesson (66.Robin Kwamina Quaison), Mats Kristoffer Olsson, Dejan Kuluševski, Bengt Eric Marcus Berg (Cap) (86.Alexander Isak), Emil Peter Forsberg, Bengt Ulf Sebastian Larsson (87.Jens-Lys Michel Cajuste). Trainer: Jan Olof Andersson.
Goals: Viktor Johan Anton Claesson (4), Robin Kwamina Quaison (88).

25.03.2021   SWEDEN - GEORGIA   **1-0(1-0)**   22nd FIFA WC.Qualifiers

Friends Arena, Tockholm; Referee: Benoît Bastien (France); Attendance: 0
SWE: Bo Kristoffer Nordfeldt, Carl Mikael Lustig (84.Emil Henry Kristoffer Krafth), Victor Jörgen Nilsson Lindelöf, Hans Carl Ludwig Augustinsson, Filip Viktor Helander, Bengt Ulf Sebastian Larsson (Cap), Viktor Johan Anton Claesson (74.Emil Peter Forsberg), Mats Kristoffer Olsson (68.Albin Ekdal; 73.Mattias Olof Svanberg), Zlatan Ibrahimović (84.Robin Kwamina Quaison), Dejan Kuluševski, Alexander Isak. Trainer: Jan Olof Andersson.
Goal: Viktor Johan Anton Claesson (35).

28.03.2021   KOSOVO - SWEDEN   **0-3(0-2)**   22nd FIFA WC.Qualifiers

Stadiumi "Fadil Vokrri", Prishtina; Referee: Tamás Bognár (Hungary); Attendance: 0
SWE: Bo Kristoffer Nordfeldt, Carl Mikael Lustig, Victor Jörgen Nilsson Lindelöf, Hans Carl Ludwig Augustinsson (83.Pierre Thomas Robin Bengtsson), Filip Viktor Helander, Bengt Ulf Sebastian Larsson (Cap), Viktor Johan Anton Claesson (83.Dejan Kuluševski), Zlatan Ibrahimović (67.Bengt Eric Marcus Berg), Emil Peter Forsberg, Alexander Isak (68.Robin Kwamina Quaison), Mats Kristoffer Olsson (90.Mattias Olof Svanberg). Trainer: Jan Olof Andersson.
Goals: Hans Carl Ludwig Augustinsson (12), Alexander Isak (35), Bengt Ulf Sebastian Larsson (70 penalty).

31.03.2021   SWEDEN - ESTONIA   **1-0(1-0)**   Friendly International

Friends Arena, Stockholm; Referee: Marco Fritz (Germany); Attendance: 0
SWE: Karl-Johan Anton Johnsson, Pierre Thomas Robin Bengtsson, Emil Henry Kristoffer Krafth, Jörgen Joakim Nilsson, Carl Anders Theodor Starfelt, Ken Nlata Sema, Mattias Olof Svanberg, Jens-Lys Michel Cajuste, Karl Jesper Karlsson, Bengt Eric Marcus Berg (Cap) (63.Dejan Kuluševski), Robin Kwamina Quaison. Trainer: Jan Olof Andersson.
Goal: Bengt Eric Marcus Berg (4).

29.05.2021   SWEDEN - FINLAND   **2-0(1-0)**   Friendly International

Friends Arena, Stockholm; Referee: Jakob Kehlet (Denmark); Attendance: 0
SWE: Robin Patrick Olsen, Pierre Thomas Robin Bengtsson, Marcus Danielson, Emil Henry Kristoffer Krafth, Jörgen Joakim Nilsson, Bengt Ulf Sebastian Larsson (Cap) (66.Jens-Lys Michel Cajuste), Viktor Johan Anton Claesson (77.Dejan Kuluševski), Bengt Eric Marcus Berg (69.Carl Henrik Jordan Larsson), Emil Peter Forsberg (66.Ken Nlata Sema), Mattias Olof Svanberg (77.Karl Gustav Johan Svensson), Robin Kwamina Quaison (84.Alexander Isak). Trainer: Jan Olof Andersson.
Goals: Robin Kwamina Quaison (23), Bengt Ulf Sebastian Larsson (58 penalty).

05.06.2021   SWEDEN - ARMENIA   **3-1(2-0)**   Friendly International

Friends Arena, Stockholm; Referee: Mattias Gestranius (Finland); Attendance: 500
SWE: Robin Patrick Olsen, Pierre Thomas Robin Bengtsson, Carl Mikael Lustig (71.Emil Henry Kristoffer Krafth), Marcus Danielson, Victor Jörgen Nilsson Lindelöf, Bengt Ulf Sebastian Larsson (Cap) (46.Viktor Johan Anton Claesson), Albin Ekdal (70.Mattias Olof Svanberg), Mats Kristoffer Olsson, Emil Peter Forsberg (84.Ken Nlata Sema), Alexander Isak (71.Bengt Eric Marcus Berg), Dejan Kuluševski (70.Robin Kwamina Quaison). Trainer: Jan Olof Andersson.
Goals: Emil Peter Forsberg (16), Marcus Andreas Danielsson (34), Bengt Eric Marcus Berg (85).

14.06.2021   SPAIN - SWEDEN   **0-0**   16th EC. Group Stage.

Estadio La Cartuja, Sevilla; Referee: Slavko Vinčić (Slovenia); Attendance: 10,599
SWE: Robin Patrick Olsen, Carl Mikael Lustig (75.Emil Henry Kristoffer Krafth), Marcus Danielson, Victor Jörgen Nilsson Lindelöf, Hans Carl Ludwig Augustinsson, Bengt Ulf Sebastian Larsson (Cap), Albin Ekdal, Emil Peter Forsberg (84.Pierre Thomas Robin Bengtsson), Mats Kristoffer Olsson (84.Jens-Lys Michel Cajuste), Markus Berg (69.Robin Kwamina Quaison), Alexander Isak (69.Viktor Johan Anton Claesson). Trainer: Jan Olof Andersson.

18.06.2021   SWEDEN - SLOVAKIA   **1-0(0-0)**   16th EC. Group Stage.

Krestovsky Stadium, Saint Petersburg (Russia); Referee: Daniel Siebert (Germany): Attendance: 11,525
SWE: Robin Patrick Olsen, Carl Mikael Lustig, Marcus Danielson, Victor Jörgen Nilsson Lindelöf, Hans Carl Ludwig Augustinsson (88.Pierre Thomas Robin Bengtsson), Bengt Ulf Sebastian Larsson (Cap), Albin Ekdal (88.Karl Gustav Johan Svensson), Mats Kristoffer Olsson (64.Viktor Johan Anton Claesson), Emil Peter Forsberg (90+3.Emil Henry Kristoffer Krafth), Bengt Eric Marcus Berg (64.Robin Kwamina Quaison), Alexander Isak. Trainer: Jan Olof Andersson.
Goal: Emil Peter Forsberg (77 penalty).

23.06.2021   SWEDEN - POLAND   **3-2(1-0)**   16th EC. Group Stage.

Krestovsky Stadium, Saint Petersburg (Russia); Referee: Michael Oliver (England); Attendance: 14,252
SWE: Robin Patrick Olsen, Carl Mikael Lustig (68.Emil Henry Kristoffer Krafth), Marcus Danielson, Victor Jörgen Nilsson Lindelöf, Hans Carl Ludwig Augustinsson, Bengt Ulf Sebastian Larsson (Cap), Albin Ekdal, Emil Peter Forsberg (78.Viktor Johan Anton Claesson), Mats Kristoffer Olsson, Robin Kwamina Quaison (55.Dejan Kuluševski), Alexander Isak (68.Markus Berg). Trainer: Jan Olof Andersson.
Goals: Emil Peter Forsberg (2, 59), Viktor Johan Anton Claesson (90+4).

29.06.2021   SWEDEN - UKRAINE   **1-2(1-1,1-1)**   16th EC. 2nd Round of 16.

Hampden Park, Glasgow (Scotland); Referee: Daniele Orsato (Italy); Attendance: 9,221
SWE: Robin Patrick Olsen, Carl Mikael Lustig (83.Emil Henry Kristoffer Krafth), Marcus Danielson [*sent off 99*], Victor Jörgen Nilsson Lindelöf, Hans Carl Ludwig Augustinsson (83.Pierre Thomas Robin Bengtsson), Bengt Ulf Sebastian Larsson (Cap) (97.Viktor Johan Anton Claesson), Albin Ekdal, Emil Peter Forsberg, Mats Kristoffer Olsson (101.Filip Viktor Helander), Dejan Kuluševski (97.Robin Kwamina Quaison), Alexander Isak (97.Markus Berg). Trainer: Jan Olof Andersson.
Goal: Emil Peter Forsberg (43).

NATIONAL TEAM PLAYERS
(16.07.2020 – 15.07.2021)

Name	DOB	Caps	Goals	2020/2021:	Club

Goalkeepers

Name	DOB	Caps	Goals	2020/2021:	Club
Karl-Johan Anton JOHNSSON	28.01.1990	9	0	2020/2021:	FC København (DEN)
Bo Kristoffer NORDFELDT	23.06.1989	14	0	2020/2021:	Gençlerbirliği SK Ankara (TUR)
Robin Patrick OLSEN	08.01.1990	48	0	2020:	AS Roma (ITA)
				05.10.2020->	Everton FC Liverpool (ENG)

Defenders

Name	DOB	Caps	Goals	2020/2021:	Club
Eric Joel ANDERSSON	11.11.1996	6	0	2020:	FC Midtjylland Herning (DEN)
Hans Carl Ludwig AUGUSTINSSON	21.04.1994	36	2	2020/2021:	SV Werder Bremen (GER)
Pierre Thomas Robin BENGTSSON	12.04.1988	41	0	2020:	FC København (DEN)
				01.02.2021->	Vejle BK (DEN)
Marcus Andreas DANIELSSON	08.04.1989	13	3	2020/2021:	Dalian Professional FC (CHN)
Filip Viktor HELANDER	22.04.1993	16	0	2020/2021:	Rangers FC Glasgow (SCO)
Rasmus Sebastian HOLMÉN	29.04.1992	6	0	2020:	Willem II Tillburg (NED)
Pontus Sven Gustav JANSSON	13.02.1991	27	0	2020:	Brentford FC London (ENG)
Mattias JOHANSSON	16.02.1992	6	1	2020:	Gençlerbirliği SK Ankara (TUR)
Emil Henry Kristoffer KRAFTH	02.08.1994	32	0	2020/2021:	Newcastle United FC (ENG)
Victor Jörgen Nilsson LINDELÖF	17.07.1994	45	3	2020/2021:	Manchester United FC (ENG)
Carl Mikael LUSTIG	13.12.1986	94	6	2020/2021:	AIK Stockholm
Jörgen Joakim NILSSON	06.02.1994	6	0	2021:	DSC Arminia Bielefeld (GER)
Martin Tony Waikwa OLSSON	17.05.1988	51	5	2020:	Helsingborgs IF
Carl Anders Theodor STARFELT	01.06.1995	3	0	2020/2021:	FK Rubin Kazan (RUS)

Midfielders

Name	DOB	Caps	Goals	2020/2021:	Club
Jens-Lys Michel CAJUSTE	10.08.1999	5	0	2020/2021:	FC Midtjylland Herning (DEN)
Viktor Johan Anton CLAESSON	02.01.1992	50	10	2020/2021:	FK Krasnodar (RUS)
Albin EKDAL	28.07.1989	61	0	2020/2021:	UC Sampdoria Genova (ITA)
Emil Peter FORSBERG	23.10.1991	62	13	2020/2021:	RasenBallsport Leipzig (GER)
Oscar HILJEMARK	28.06.1992	28	2	2020:	Aalborg BK (DEN)
Karl Jesper KARLSSON	25.07.1998	3	0	2021:	AZ Alkmaar (NED)
Bengt Ulf Sebastian LARSSON	06.06.1985	133	10	2020/2021:	AIK Stockholm
Mats Kristoffer OLSSON	30.06.1995	29	0	2020/2021:	FK Krasnodar (RUS)
Mattias Olof SVANBERG	05.01.1999	9	1	2020/2021:	Bologna FC 1909 (ITA)
Ken Nlata SEMA	30.09.1993	12	0	2020/2021:	Warford FC (ENG)
Karl Gustav Johan SVENSSON	07.02.1987	27	0	2020:	Seattle Sounders (USA)
				09.04.2021->	Guangzhou City FC (CHN)

Forwards

Name	DOB	Caps	Goals	2020/2021:	Club
Bengt Eric Marcus BERG	17.08.1986	90	24	2020/2021:	FK Krasnodar (RUS)
John Olof Alberto GUIDETTI	15.04.1992	29	3	2020:	Deportivo Alavés Vitoria-Gasteiz (ESP)
Zlatan IBRAHIMOVIĆ	03.10.1981	118	62	2021:	AC Milan (ITA)
Alexander ISAK	21.09.1999	26	6	2020/2021:	Real Sociedad de Fútbol San Sebastián (ESP)
Dejan KULUŠEVSKI	25.04.2000	15	1	2020/2021:	Juventus FC Torino (ITA)
Carl Henrik Jordan LARSSON	20.06.1997	6	1	2020/2021:	FK Spartak Moskva (RUS)
Robin Kwamina QUAISON	09.10.1993	30	9	2020/2021:	1. FSV Mainz 05 (GER)

Trainer

Jan Olof "Janne" ANDERSSON [from 23.06.2016]	29.09.1962	65 M; 33 W; 13 D; 19 L; 104-61

SWITZERLAND

The Country:
Schweizerische Eidgenossenschaft (Swiss Confederation)
Capital: Bern
Surface: 41,285 km²
Inhabitants: 8,570,146 [2019]
Time: UTC+1

The FA:
Schweizerischer Fussballverband
Worbstrasse 48, Postfach 3000, Bern 15
Tel: +41 31 950 8111
Founded: 07.04.1895
Member of FIFA since: 1904
Member of UEFA since: 1954
Website: www.football.ch

NATIONAL TEAM RECORDS

RECORDS
First international match:	12.02.1905, Paris:	France – Switzerland 1-0
Most international caps:	Heinz Hermann	- 118 caps (1978-1991)
Most international goals:	Alexander Frei	- 42 goals / 84 caps (2001-2011)

UEFA EUROPEAN CHAMPIONSHIP
1960	Did not enter
1964	Qualifiers
1968	Qualifiers
1972	Qualifiers
1976	Qualifiers
1980	Qualifiers
1984	Qualifiers
1988	Qualifiers
1992	Qualifiers
1996	Final Tournament (Group Stage)
2000	Qualifiers
2004	Final Tournament (Group Stage)
2008	Final Tournament (Group Stage)
2012	Qualifiers
2016	Final Tournament (2nd Round of 16)
2020	Final Tournament (Quarter-Finals)

FIFA WORLD CUP
1930	Did not enter
1934	Final Tournament (Quarter-Finals)
1938	Final Tournament (Quarter-Finals)
1950	Final Tournament (Group Stage)
1954	Final Tournament (Quarter-Finals)
1958	Qualifiers
1962	Final Tournament (Group Stage)
1966	Final Tournament (Group Stage)
1970	Qualifiers
1974	Qualifiers
1978	Qualifiers
1982	Qualifiers
1986	Qualifiers
1990	Qualifiers
1994	Final Tournament (2nd Round of 16)
1998	Qualifiers
2002	Qualifiers
2006	Final Tournament (2nd Round of 16)
2010	Final Tournament (Group Stage)
2014	Final Tournament (2nd Round of 16)
2018	Final Tournament (2nd Round of 16)

OLYMPIC TOURNAMENTS
1908	-
1912	-
1920	-
1924	Runners-up
1928	1/8 - Finals
1936	Did not enter
1948	Did not enter
1952	Did not enter
1956	Did not enter
1960	Qualifiers
1964	Qualifiers
1968	Qualifiers
1972	Qualifiers
1976	Did not enter
1980	Did not enter
1984	Did not enter
1988	Qualifiers
1992	Qualifiers
1996	Qualifiers
2000	Qualifiers
2004	Qualifiers
2008	Qualifiers
2012	Group Stage
2016	Qualifiers

UEFA NATIONS LEAGUE
2018/2019	League A; Final Tournament: 4th Place
2020/2021	League A

FIFA CONFEDERATIONS CUP 1992-2017
None

SWISS CLUB HONOURS IN EUROPEAN CLUB COMPETITIONS:

European Champion Clubs' Cup (1956-1992) / UEFA Champions League (1993-2021)
None

Fairs Cup (1858-1971) / UEFA Cup (1972-2009) / UEFA Europa League (2010-2021)
None

UEFA Super Cup (1972-2020)
None

European Cup Winners' Cup 1961-1999*
None

*defunct competition

NATIONAL COMPETITIONS
TABLE OF HONOURS

	CHAMPIONS	CUP WINNERS	BEST GOALSCORERS	
1898/1899	Anglo-American Club FC Zürich	-	-	
1899/1900	Grasshopper Club Zürich	-	-	
1900/1901	Grasshopper Club Zürich	-	-	
1901/1902	FC Zürich	-	-	
1902/1903	BSC Young Boys Bern	-	-	
1903/1904	FC St. Gallen	-	-	
1904/1905	Grasshopper Club Zürich	-	-	
1905/1906	FC Winterthur	-	-	
1906/1907	Servette FC Genève	-	-	
1907/1908	FC Winterthur	-	-	
1908/1909	BSC Young Boys Bern	-	-	
1909/1910	BSC Young Boys Bern	-	-	
1910/1911	BSC Young Boys Bern	-	-	
1911/1912	FC Aarau	-	-	
1912/1913	Montriond Lausanne	-	-	
1913/1914	FC Aarau	-	-	
1914/1915	SC Brühl St. Gallen	-	-	
1915/1916	Cantonal Neuchâtel	-	-	
1916/1917	FC Winterthur	-	-	
1917/1918	Servette FC Genève	-	-	
1918/1919	Étoile La Chaux-de-Fonds	-	-	
1919/1920	BSC Young Boys Bern	-	-	
1920/1921	Grasshopper Club Zürich	-	-	
1921/1922	Servette FC Genève	-	-	
1922/1923	*Title not awarded*	-	-	
1923/1924	FC Zürich	-	-	
1924/1925	Servette FC Genève	-	-	
1925/1926	Servette FC Genève	Grasshopper Club Zürich	-	
1926/1927	Grasshopper Club Zürich	Grasshopper Club Zürich	-	
1927/1928	Grasshopper Club Zürich	Servette FC Genève FC	-	
1928/1929	BSC Young Boys Bern	Urania Genève Sport	-	
1929/1930	Servette FC Genève	BSC Young Boys Bern	-	
1930/1931	Grasshopper Club Zürich	FC Lugano	-	
1931/1932	FC Lausanne-Sport	Grasshopper Club Zürich	-	
1932/1933	Servette FC Genève	FC Basel	-	
1933/1934	Servette FC Genève	Grasshopper Club Zürich	Leopold Kielholz (Servette FC Genève)	40
1934/1935	FC Lausanne-Sport	FC Lausanne-Sport	Engelbert Bösch (AUT, FC Bern)	27
1935/1936	FC Lausanne-Sport	Young Fellows FC Zürich	Willy Jäggi (FC Lausanne-Sport)	27
1936/1937	Grasshopper Club Zürich	Grasshopper Club Zürich	Alessandro Frigerio Payán (Young Fellows FC Zürich)	23
1937/1938	FC Lugano	Grasshopper Club Zürich	Numa Monnard (FC Basel)	20
1938/1939	Grasshopper Club Zürich	FC Lausanne-Sport	Josef Artimovics (AUT, FC Grenchen)	15
1939/1940	Servette FC Genève	Grasshopper Club Zürich	Georges Aeby (Servette FC Genève)	22
1940/1941	FC Lugano	Grasshopper Club Zürich	Alessandro Frigerio Payán (FC Lugano)	26
1941/1942	Grasshopper Club Zürich	Grasshopper Club Zürich	Alessandro Frigerio Payán (FC Lugano)	23
1942/1943	Grasshopper Club Zürich	Grasshopper Club Zürich	Lauro Amadò (Grasshopper Club Zürich)	31
1943/1944	FC Lausanne-Sport	FC Lausanne-Sport	Erich Andres (Young Fellows FC Zürich)	23
1944/1945	Grasshopper Club Zürich	BSC Young Boys Bern	Hans-Peter Friedländer (Grasshopper Club Zürich)	26
1945/1946	Servette FC Genève	Grasshopper Club Zürich	Hans-Peter Friedländer (Grasshopper Club Zürich)	25
1946/1947	FC Biel-Bienne	FC Basel	Lauro Amadò (Grasshopper Club Zürich) Hans Blaser (BSC Young Boys Bern)	19
1947/1948	AC Bellinzona	FC La Chaux-de-Fonds	Josef Righetti (FC Grenchen)	26
1948/1949	FC Lugano	Servette FC Genève FC	Jacques Fatton (Servette FC Genève)	21
1949/1950	Servette FC Genève	FC Lausanne-Sport	Jacques Fatton (Servette FC Genève)	32
1950/1951	FC Lausanne-Sport	FC La Chaux-de-Fonds	Hans-Peter Friedländer (FC Lausanne-Sport)	23
1951/1952	Grasshopper Club Zürich	Grasshopper Club Zürich	Josef Hügi (FC Basel)	24
1952/1953	FC Basel	BSC Young Boys Bern	Josef Hügi (FC Basel) Eugen Meier (BSC Young Boys Bern)	32
1953/1954	FC La Chaux-de-Fonds	FC La Chaux-de-Fonds	Josef Hügi (FC Basel)	29
1954/1955	FC La Chaux-de-Fonds	FC La Chaux-de-Fonds	Marcel Mauron (FC La Chaux-de-Fonds)	30
1955/1956	Grasshopper Club Zürich	Grasshopper Club Zürich	Branislav Vukosavljević (YUG, Grasshopper Club Zürich)	33
1956/1957	BSC Young Boys Bern	FC La Chaux-de-Fonds	Adrien Kauer (FC La Chaux-de-Fonds)	29
1957/1958	BSC Young Boys Bern	BSC Young Boys Bern	Ernst Wechselberger (GER, BSC Young Boys Bern)	22
1958/1959	BSC Young Boys Bern	FC Grenchen	Eugen Meier (BSC Young Boys Bern)	24
1959/1960	BSC Young Boys Bern	FC Luzern	Willy Schneider (BSC Young Boys Bern)	25
1960/1961	Servette FC Genève	FC La Chaux-de-Fonds	Giuliano Robbiani (Grasshopper Club Zürich)	27
1961/1962	Servette FC Genève	FC Lausanne-Sport	Jacques Fatton (Servette FC Genève)	25
1962/1963	FC Zürich	FC Basel	Peter von Burg (FC Zürich)	24
1963/1964	FC La Chaux-de-Fonds	FC Lausanne-Sport	Michel Desbiolles (Servette FC Genève)	23

1964/1965	FC Lausanne-Sport	FC Sion	Rolf Blättler (Grasshopper Club Zürich)	
			Pierre Kerkhoffs (NED, FC Lausanne-Sport)	19
1965/1966	FC Zürich	FC Zürich	Rolf Blättler (Grasshopper Club Zürich)	28
1966/1967	FC Basel	FC Basel	Rolf Blättler (Grasshopper Club Zürich)	24
1967/1968	FC Zürich	FC Lugano	Friedrich Künzli (FC Zürich)	28
1968/1969	FC Basel	FC St. Gallen	Hans-Otto Peters (GER, FC Biel-Bienne)	24
1969/1970	FC Basel	FC Zürich	Friedrich Künzli (FC Zürich)	19
1970/1971	Grasshopper Club Zürich	Servette FC Genève FC	Walter Müller (BSC Young Boys Bern)	19
1971/1972	FC Basel	FC Zürich	Herbert Dimmeler (FC Winterthur)	
			Bernd Dörfel (GER, Servette FC Genève)	17
1972/1973	FC Basel	FC Zürich	Ottmar Hitzfeld (FC Basel)	
			Jan-Olof Grahn (FC Lausanne-Sport)	18
1973/1974	FC Zürich	FC Sion	Daniel Jeandupeux (FC Zürich)	22
1974/1975	FC Zürich	FC Basel	Ilija Katić (FC Zürich)	23
1975/1976	FC Zürich	FC Zürich	Peter Risi (FC Zürich)	33
1976/1977	FC Basel	BSC Young Boys Bern	Franco Cucinotta (ITA, FC Zürich)	28
1977/1978	Grasshopper Club Zürich	Servette FC Genève FC	Friedrich Künzli (FC Lausanne-Sport)	21
1978/1979	Servette FC Genève	Servette FC Genève FC	Peter Risi (FC Zürich)	16
1979/1980	FC Basel	FC Sion	Claudio Sulser (Grasshopper Club Zürich)	25
1980/1981	FC Zürich	FC Lausanne-Sport	Peter Risi (FC Luzern)	18
1981/1982	Grasshopper Club Zürich	FC Sion	Claudio Sulser (Grasshopper Club Zürich)	23
1982/1983	Grasshopper Club Zürich	Grasshopper Club Zürich	Jean-Paul Brigger (Servette FC Genève)	23
1983/1984	Grasshopper Club Zürich	Servette FC Genève FC	Georges Bregy (FC Sion)	21
1984/1985	Servette FC Genève	FC Aarau	Dominique Cina (FC Sion)	24
1985/1986	BSC Young Boys Bern	FC Sion	Steen Thychosen (DEN, FC Lausanne-Sport)	21
1986/1987	Neuchâtel Xamax FCS	BSC Young Boys Bern	John Hartmann Eriksen (DEN, Servette FC Genève)	28
1987/1988	Neuchâtel Xamax FCS	Grasshopper Club Zürich	John Hartmann Eriksen (DEN, Servette FC Genève)	36
1988/1989	FC Luzern	Grasshopper Club Zürich	Karl-Heinz Rummenigge	
			(GER, Servette FC Genève)	24
1989/1990	Grasshopper Club Zürich	Grasshopper Club Zürich	Iván Luis Zamorano Zamora (CHI, FC St. Gallen)	23
1990/1991	Grasshopper Club Zürich	FC Sion	Dario Zuffi (BSC Young Boys Bern)	17
1991/1992	FC Sion	FC Luzern	Miklos Jon Molnar (DEN, Servette FC Genève)	18
1992/1993	FC Aarau	FC Lugano	„Sonny" Anderson da Silva	
			(BRA, Servette FC Genève)	20
1993/1994	Servette FC Genève	Grasshopper Club Zürich	Élber de Souza (BRA, Grasshopper Club Zürich)	21
1994/1995	Grasshopper Club Zürich	FC Sion	Petar Aleksandrov (BUL, Neuchâtel Xamax FCS)	24
1995/1996	Grasshopper Club Zürich	FC Sion	Petar Aleksandrov (BUL, FC Luzern)	
			Viorel Dinu Moldovan	
			(ROU, Neuchâtel Xamax FCS)	19
1996/1997	FC Sion	FC Sion	Viorel Dinu Moldovan (ROU, Grasshopper Club Zürich)	27
1997/1998	Grasshopper Club Zürich	FC Lausanne-Sport	Shabani Christophe Nonda (COD, FC Zürich)	24
1998/1999	Servette FC Genève	FC Lausanne-Sport	Alexandre Rey (Servette FC Genève)	19
1999/2000	FC St. Gallen	FC Zürich	Charles Amoah (GHA, FC St. Gallen)	25
2000/2001	Grasshopper Club Zürich	Servette FC Genève FC	Stéphane Chapuisat (Grasshopper Club Zürich)	
			Christian Eduardo Giménez (ARG, FC Lugano)	21
2001/2002	FC Basel	FC Basel	Christian Eduardo Giménez (ARG, FC Lugano)	
			Richard Darío Núñez Pereyra	
			(URU, Grasshopper Club Zürich)	28
2002/2003	Grasshopper Club Zürich	FC Basel	Richard Darío Núñez Pereyra	
			(URU, Grasshopper Club Zürich)	27
2003/2004	FC Basel	FC Will 1900	Stéphane Chapuisat (BSC Young Boys Bern)	23
2004/2005	FC Basel	FC Zürich	Christian Eduardo Giménez (ARG, FC Basel)	27
2005/2006	FC Zürich	FC Sion	Alhassane Keita Otchico (GUI, FC Zürich)	20
2006/2007	FC Zürich	FC Basel	Mladen Petrić (CRO, FC Basel)	19
2007/2008	FC Basel	FC Basel	Hakan Yakin (BSC Young Boys Bern)	24
2008/2009	FC Zürich	FC Sion	Seydou Doumbia (CIV, BSC Young Boys Bern)	20
2009/2010	FC Basel	FC Basel	Seydou Doumbia (CIV, BSC Young Boys Bern)	30
2010/2011	FC Basel	FC Sion	Alexander Frei (FC Basel)	27
2011/2012	FC Basel	FC Basel	Alexander Frei (FC Basel)	24
2012/2013	FC Basel	Grasshopper Club Zürich	Ezequiel Óscar Scarione (ARG, FC St. Gallen)	21
2013/2014	FC Basel	FC Zürich	Shkëlzen Taib Gashi	
			(ALB, Grasshopper Club Zürich)	19
2014/2015	FC Basel	FC Sion	Shkëlzen Taib Gashi (ALB, FC Basel)	21
2015/2016	FC Basel	FC Zürich	Moanes Daobur (ISR, Grasshopper Club Zürich)	19
2016/2017	FC Basel	FC Basel	Seydou Doumbia (CIV, FC Basel)	20
2017/2018	BSC Young Boys Bern	FC Zürich	Albian Afrim Ajeti (FC Basel)	17
2018/2019	BSC Young Boys Bern	FC Basel	Guillaume Hoarau (FRA, BSC Young Boys Bern)	24
2019/2020	BSC Young Boys Bern	BSC Young Boys Bern	Jean-Pierre Nsamé (CMR, BSC Young Boys Bern)	32
2020/2021	BSC Young Boys Bern	FC Luzern	Jean-Pierre Nsamé (CMR, BSC Young Boys Bern)	19

Name changements of first level: Serie A (1898–1931), National League (1931–1944), National League A (1944–2003), Super League (since 2003).

NATIONAL CHAMPIONSHIP
Swiss Super League 2020/2021
(19.09.2020 – 21.05.2021)

Results

Round 1 [19-20.09.2020]
FC Lugano - FC Luzern 2-1(2-0)
Young Boys - FC Zürich 2-1(1-1)
FC Basel - FC Vaduz 2-2(2-1)
FC Lausanne-Sport - Servette Genève 2-1(1-0)
FC St. Gallen - FC Sion 1-0(1-0)

Round 2 [26-27.09.2020]
FC Sion - Young Boys 0-0
FC Zürich - FC Lugano 2-2(1-1)
FC Luzern - FC Lausanne-Sport 2-2(1-1)
FC Vaduz - FC St. Gallen 0-1(0-0)
Servette Genève - FC Basel 1-0(0-0)

Round 3 [03-04.10.2020]
FC Lausanne-Sport - FC Zürich 4-0(2-0)
FC Lugano - FC Sion 2-2(0-1)
FC Basel - FC Luzern 3-2(2-1)
FC St. Gallen - Servette Genève 1-0(1-0)
Young Boys - FC Vaduz 1-0(0-0)

Round 4 [17-18.10.2020]
FC Vaduz - FC Lugano 1-1(1-0)
Servette Genève - Young Boys 0-0
FC Luzern - FC St. Gallen 2-2(0-1)
FC Sion - FC Lausanne-Sport 0-0
FC Zürich - FC Basel 1-0(0-0) [04.11.]

Round 5 [24-25.10.2020]
FC Vaduz - FC Zürich 1-4(0-2)
FC Lugano - FC St. Gallen 1-0(1-0)
Young Boys - FC Luzern 2-1(0-1)
FC Basel - Lausanne-Sport 2-1(1-0) [25.11.]
FC Sion - Servette Genève 2-0(1-0) [25.11.]

Round 6 [01-02.11.2020]
FC St. Gallen - FC Basel 1-3(1-2)
FC Lausanne-Sport - FC Vaduz 3-0(0-0)
FC Luzern - FC Sion 2-0(0-0)
Servette Genève - FC Zürich 2-1(0-0)
Lugano - Young Boys 0-2(0-0) [20.01.2021]

Round 7 [07-08.11.2020]
FC Lausanne-Sport - FC Lugano 0-1(0-1)
FC Zürich - FC Luzern 2-0(2-0)
Young Boys - FC St. Gallen 0-0
FC Basel - FC Sion 4-2(3-1) [09.12.]
FC Vaduz - Servette Genève 0-2(0-1) [09.12.]

Round 8 [21-22.11.2020]
FC Luzern - FC Vaduz 1-1(1-0)
Young Boys - FC Basel 2-1(1-1)
FC Sion - FC Zürich 2-2(0-0)
FC St. Gallen - FC Lausanne-Sport 2-2(0-2)
Servette Genève - FC Lugano 1-1(1-0)

Round 9 [28-29.11.2020]
FC Vaduz - FC Sion 4-1(1-1)
Servette Genève - FC Luzern 1-3(0-1)
FC Lausanne-Sport - Young Boys 0-3(0-1)
FC Lugano - FC Basel 1-0(0-0)
FC Zürich - FC St. Gallen 1-2(1-2) [09.12.]

Round 10 [05-06.12.2020]
FC Basel - Servette Genève 1-0(0-0)
FC Luzern - Young Boys 2-3(0-3)
FC Zürich - FC Lausanne-Sport 4-0(2-0)
FC Sion - FC Lugano 1-1(0-0) [17.01.2021]
St. Gallen - FC Vaduz 2-0(0-0) [20.01.2021]

Round 11 [12-13.12.2020]
FC Sion - FC Luzern 1-2(0-0)
FC Vaduz - FC Basel 0-0
FC Lausanne-Sport - FC St. Gallen 0-1(0-0)
FC Lugano - FC Zürich 0-1(0-0)
Young Boys - Servette Genève 1-2(0-1)

Round 12 [16-17.12.2020]
FC Luzern - FC Zürich 0-0
FC Basel - Young Boys 0-2(0-2)
FC St. Gallen - FC Lugano 0-0
FC Vaduz - FC Lausanne-Sport 0-2(0-0)
Servette Genève - FC Sion 1-1(0-1)

Round 13 [19-20.12.2020]
Young Boys - FC Lugano 2-2(2-1)
FC Basel - FC St. Gallen 0-0
FC Lausanne-Sport - FC Luzern 2-1(0-1)
FC Sion - FC Vaduz 2-1(0-0)
FC Zürich - Servette Genève 0-1(0-0)

Round 14 [22-23.12.2020]
FC St. Gallen - Young Boys 1-2(0-0)
FC Luzern - FC Basel 1-2(0-2)
Servette Genève - FC Vaduz 1-1(0-0)
FC Lugano - FC Lausanne-Sport 0-0
FC Zürich - FC Sion 0-0

Round 15 [23-24.01.2021]
FC Lausanne-Sport - FC Sion 0-1(0-1)
FC Basel - FC Zürich 1-4(0-0)
FC Vaduz - Young Boys 0-0
FC Luzern - FC Lugano 1-1(0-1) [10.02.]
Servette Genève - St. Gallen 2-2(1-1) [10.02.]

Round 16 [27-28.01.2021]
FC Zürich - FC Vaduz 0-1(0-0)
FC Sion - FC Basel 2-3(0-2)
Young Boys-Lausanne-Sport 1-0(1-0) [10.02.]
FC Lugano-Servette Genève 1-1(1-0) [17.02.]
FC St. Gallen - FC Luzern 2-1(0-1) [17.02.]

Round 17 [30-31.01.2021]
FC St. Gallen - FC Zürich 2-3(2-3)
FC Basel - FC Lugano 2-2(0-1)
Servette Genève - FC Lausanne-Sport 1-1(0-1)
Young Boys - FC Sion 2-1(2-1)
FC Vaduz - FC Luzern 1-1(0-1) [24.02.]

Round 18 [03-04.02.2021]
FC Zürich - Young Boys 1-4(0-3)
FC Lugano - FC Vaduz 1-1(1-1)
FC Sion - FC St. Gallen 3-2(1-1)
FC Luzern - Servette Genève 3-0(1-0)
FC Lausanne-Sport - FC Basel 1-3(0-1)

Round 19 [06-07.02.2021]
FC St. Gallen - FC Lugano 0-1(0-0) [24.01.]
FC Vaduz - FC Zürich 3-2(0-1)
FC Basel - FC Sion 2-2(2-0)
Servette Genève - FC Luzern 4-2(2-1)
Young Boys - FC Lausanne-Sport 4-2(4-0)

Round 20 [13-14.02.2021]
FC Lausanne-Sport - Servette Genève 3-1(2-0)
FC Sion - FC St. Gallen 1-1(1-0)
FC Lugano - Young Boys 1-3(0-3)
FC Luzern - FC Vaduz 4-0(2-0)
FC Zürich - FC Basel 2-0(1-0)

Round 21 [20-21.02.2021]
FC Vaduz - FC St. Gallen 2-1(1-0)
FC Basel - FC Lausanne-Sport 0-0
FC Lugano - FC Luzern 2-3(1-1)
Young Boys - Servette Genève 2-0(2-0)
FC Zürich - FC Sion 1-1(1-1)

Round 22 [27-28.02.2021]
Servette Genève - FC Zürich 3-1(1-1)
FC St. Gallen - FC Basel 3-1(1-0)
FC Lausanne-Sport - FC Lugano 2-0(1-0)
FC Luzern - Young Boys 2-2(1-0)
FC Sion - FC Vaduz 0-2(0-0)

Round 23 [03-04.03.2021]
FC St. Gallen - Servette Genève 0-1(0-1)
FC Basel - Young Boys 1-1(1-1)
FC Vaduz - FC Lausanne-Sport 0-3(0-1)
FC Sion - FC Lugano 0-3(0-3)
FC Zürich - FC Luzern 1-2(0-2)

Round 24 [06-07.03.2021]
Young Boys - FC Vaduz 1-1(0-0)
Servette Genève - FC Basel 2-1(0-0)
FC Lausanne-Sport - FC Sion 1-3(1-1)
FC Lugano - FC Zürich 0-1(0-1)
FC Luzern - FC St. Gallen 4-2(1-2)

Round 25 [13-14.03.2021]
FC Zürich - FC Lausanne-Sport 1-1(1-0)
FC Basel - FC Luzern 4-1(1-0)
FC Sion - Servette Genève 1-2(0-2)
FC St. Gallen - Young Boys 2-2(1-0)
FC Vaduz - FC Lugano 0-3(0-2)

Round 26 [20-21.03.2021]
FC Lausanne-Sport - FC St. Gallen 4-3(3-1)
FC Lugano - FC Basel 2-1(0-1)
Young Boys - FC Zürich 4-0(1-0)
FC Luzern - FC Sion 1-1(0-0)
Servette Genève - FC Vaduz 1-2(0-1)

Round 27 [03-05.04.2021]
FC Lausanne-Sport - FC Luzern 2-1(2-0)
FC St. Gallen - FC Zürich 1-1(0-1)
Servette Genève - FC Lugano 1-1(0-0)
FC Sion - Young Boys 0-3(0-0)
FC Basel - FC Vaduz 1-2(0-1)

Round 28 [10-11.04.2021]
FC Lugano - FC Lausanne-Sport 1-0(1-0)
FC Luzern - FC Basel 3-4(1-3)
FC Vaduz - FC Sion 3-0(0-0)
Young Boys - FC St. Gallen 2-0(0-0)
FC Zürich - Servette Genève 1-2(0-0)

Round 29 [17-18.04.2021]
FC Sion - FC Zürich 2-2(1-1)
FC St. Gallen - FC Luzern 0-0
FC Basel - Servette Genève 5-0(3-0)
FC Lausanne-Sport - FC Vaduz 2-1(0-1)
Young Boys - FC Lugano 3-0(1-0)

Round 30 [21-22.04.2021]
FC Luzern - FC Lausanne-Sport 1-0(0-0)
FC Lugano - FC St. Gallen 2-0(1-0)
FC Vaduz - FC Basel 1-1(0-0)
Servette Genève - FC Sion 3-5(1-1)
FC Zürich - Young Boys 1-2(1-2)

Round 31 [24-25.04.2021]		Round 32 [01-02.05.2021]		Round 33 [08-09.05.2021]
FC St. Gallen - FC Vaduz 1-0(1-0)		FC Vaduz - FC Luzern 1-2(1-2)		FC Lugano - FC Vaduz 0-2(0-1)
FC Lausanne-Sport - FC Basel 3-3(2-1)		FC Basel - FC St. Gallen 1-0(0-0)		Young Boys - FC Basel 2-0(0-0)
FC Lugano - Servette Genève 0-1(0-1)		Servette Genève - Young Boys 2-1(0-0)		FC Lausanne-Sport - FC Zürich 2-2(0-2)
FC Luzern - FC Zürich 3-1(1-1)		FC Sion - FC Lausanne-Sport 1-1(0-0)		FC Luzern - Servette Genève 3-0(0-0)
Young Boys - FC Sion 2-1(1-1)		FC Zürich - FC Lugano 3-0(1-0)		FC St. Gallen - FC Sion 0-3(0-0)

Round 34 [11-12.05.2021]		Round 35 [15.05.2021]		Round 36 [21.05.2021]
FC Vaduz - Young Boys 0-2(0-1)		FC Basel - FC Zürich 4-0(2-0)		FC Lausanne-Sport - Young Boys 2-4(2-2)
FC Basel - FC Lugano 2-0(2-0)		FC Lugano - FC Sion 3-1(2-1)		FC Luzern - FC Lugano 1-2(0-1)
Servette Genève - FC Lausanne-Sport 1-4(1-3)		FC St. Gallen - FC Lausanne-Sport 5-0(3-0)		Servette Genève - FC St. Gallen 1-2(0-2)
FC Sion - FC Luzern 1-1(0-0)		FC Vaduz - Servette Genève 1-3(1-1)		FC Sion - FC Basel 4-0(3-0)
FC Zürich - FC St. Gallen 2-2(2-0)		Young Boys - FC Luzern 5-2(1-2)		FC Zürich - FC Vaduz 4-1(2-1)

Final Standings

					Total			Home					Away			
1.	**BSC Young Boys Bern**	36	25	9	2	74 - 29	84	14	3	1	38 - 14	11	6	1	36 - 15
2.	FC Basel	36	15	8	13	60 - 53	53	9	6	3	35 - 21	6	2	10	25 - 32
3.	Servette FC Genève	36	14	8	14	45 - 56	50	6	7	5	28 - 29	8	1	9	17 - 27
4.	FC Lugano	36	12	13	11	40 - 42	49	7	4	7	19 - 20	5	9	4	21 - 22
5.	FC Luzern	36	12	10	14	62 - 59	46	7	7	4	36 - 23	5	3	10	26 - 36
6.	FC Lausanne-Sport	36	12	10	14	52 - 55	46	9	2	7	33 - 29	3	8	7	19 - 26
7.	FC St. Gallen	36	11	11	14	45 - 48	44	7	5	6	24 - 20	4	6	8	21 - 28
8.	FC Zürich	36	11	10	15	53 - 57	43	6	5	7	27 - 21	5	5	8	26 - 36
9.	FC Sion (*Relegation Play-offs*)	36	8	14	14	48 - 58	38	4	8	6	23 - 26	4	6	8	25 - 32
10.	FC Vaduz (*Relegated*)	36	9	9	18	36 - 58	36	4	4	10	18 - 31	5	5	8	18 - 27

Top goalscorers:

19	**Jean-Pierre Nsamé (CMR)**	*BSC Young Boys Bern*
18	Arthur Mendonça Cabral (BRA)	*FC Basel*
13	Dejan Sorgić (SRB)	*FC Luzern*
13	Antonio Marchesano	*FC Zürich*
12	Pajtim Kasami	*FC Basel*
12	Grejohn Kyei (FRA)	*Servette FC Genève*
12	Theoson-Jordan Siebatcheu Pefok (USA)	*BSC Young Boys Bern*

Relegation Play-offs [27-30.05.2021]

FC Thun – FC Sion	1-4(0-2)	3-2(2-2)

FC Sion remains at first level for the Swiss Super League 2021/2022.

NATIONAL CUP
Schweizer Cup 2020/2021

First Round [29-31.08.2020]

SC Schöftland - FC Sierre	6-1(0-0)		FC Savièse - SC Balerna	0-2(0-0)
FC Monthey - FC Black Stars Basel	2-1(0-0)		FC Ajoie-Monterri - FC Tuggen	0-2(0-0)
AS Haute-Broye - FC Vevey United	1-4(0-2)		FC Zollbrück - FC Stade Nyonnais	0-7(0-5)
FC Laufen - FC Solothurn	0-6(0-2)		FC Dürrenast - FC Köniz	1-5(1-1)
FC Dübendorf - FC Schötz	1-2(0-0)			

Second Round [11-13/26.09.2020]

FC Schaffhausen - FC Lugano	1-2(1-1,1-1)		FC Vevey United - FC Köniz	3-0(0-0)
FC Tuggen - FC Winterthur	1-2(1-2)		SC Schöftland - FC Solothurn	1-5(0-2)
FC Schötz - FC Sion	0-3(0-0)		Neuchâtel Xamax FCS - SC Kriens	1-4(0-2)
FC Stade Nyonnais - FC Lausanne-Sport	1-3(0-0)		FC Chiasso - FC Zürich	3-2(2-1)
Stade Lausanne-Ouchy - Grasshopper Club Zürich	1-2(0-1)		FC Thun - FC Luzern	0-1(0-0)
FC Aarau - FC Wil 1900	0-0 aet; 4-3 pen		SC Balerna - FC Monthey	1-2(1-1)

1/8-Finals [10.02./17.02./24.02./10.03./07-08.04.2021]

FC Solothurn - SC Kriens	0-3 *awarded*		FC Chiasso - FC Luzern	1-2(0-0)
FC Aarau - FC Sion	4-2(1-0,2-2)		FC Vevey United - Servette FC Genève	2-4(1-0)
FC Winterthur - FC Basel	6-2(2-0)		FC Monthey - FC Lugano	0-3(0-2)
Grasshopper Club Zürich - FC Lausanne-Sport	2-0(0-0)		FC St. Gallen - BSC Young Boys Bern	4-1(1-0)

Quarter-Finals [06/13-14.04.2021]

FC Aarau - FC Winterthur	3-0(2-0)		SC Kriens - Servette FC Genève	2-3(1-0,2-2)
FC Lugano - FC Luzern	1-2(1-0,1-1)		Grasshopper Club Zürich - FC St. Gallen	1-2(0-2)

Semi-Finals [04-05.05.2021]

FC Aarau - FC Luzern	1-2(1-1)		Servette FC Genève - FC St. Gallen	0-1(0-0)

24.05.2021; Wankdorf Stadion, Bern; Referee: Lionel Tschudi; Attendance: 0
FC Luzern - FC St. Gallen   **3-1(2-1)**

FC Luzern: Marius Müller, Stefan Knežević, Christian Schwegler, Marco Burch, Jordy Wehrmann, Louis Schaub (87.Simon Grether), Pascal Schürpf, Martin Frýdek, Filip Ugrinić, Ibrahima N'Diaye (56.Varol Tasar), Dejan Sorgić. Trainer: Fabio Celestini.

FC St. Gallen: Lawrence Ati-Zigi (65.Lukas Watkowiak), Leonidas Stergiou (65.Euclides da Silva Cabral), Miro Muheim, Nicolas Lüchinger (46.Jérémy Guillemenot), Basil Stillhart, Jordi Quintillà Guasch, Lukas Görtler, Betim Fazliji, Chikwubuike Adamu (74.Kwadwo Duah), Víctor Ruiz Abril, Élie Youan (74.Boris Babic). Trainer: Peter Zeidler (Germany).

Goals: 1-0 Ibrahima N'Diaye (27), 2-0 Jordy Wehrmann (31), 2-1 Chikwubuike Adamu (42), 3-1 Pascal Schürpf (70).

THE CLUBS 2020/2021

Fussball Club Basel 1893

Founded:	15.11.1893		
Stadium:	St. Jakob-Park, Basel (37,994)		
Trainer:	Marcel Koller		11.11.1960
[01.09.2020]	Ciriaco Sforza		02.03.1970
[06.04.2021]	Patrick Rahmen		03.04.1969

Goalkeepers:	DOB	M	(s)	G
Heinz Lindner (AUT)	17.07.1990	31		
Đorđe Nikolić (SRB)	13.04.1997	5		
Defenders:	DOB	M	(s)	G
Omar Federico Alderete Fernández (PAR)	26.12.1996	3		
Eray Ervin Cömert	04.02.1998	30		1
Gonçalo Bento Soares Cardoso (POR)	21.10.2000	3	(2)	
Albian Hajdari	18.05.2003	5	(3)	
Jorge Marco de Oliveira Moraes (BRA)	28.03.1996	5		
Timm Klose	09.05.1988	28		2
Andrea Padula (ITA)	04.04.1996	9	(5)	
Raoul Petretta (ITA)	24.03.1997	23	(3)	3
Blas Miguel Riveros Galeano (PAR)	03.02.1998		(1)	
Jasper van der Werff	09.12.1998	12	(8)	1
Silvan Dominic Widmer	05.03.1993	22		
Midfielders:	DOB	M	(s)	G
Amir Abrashi (ALB)	27.03.1990	7	(3)	
Orges Bunjaku	05.07.2001	5	(2)	
Samuele Campo	06.07.1995	1	(5)	

Adrian Durrer	13.07.2001		(1)	1
Fabian Frei	08.01.1989	34		3
Pajtim Kasami	02.06.1992	31	(1)	12
Yannick Marchand	09.02.2000	4	(9)	1
Matías Damián Palacios (ARG)	10.05.2002	5	(4)	
Valentin Stocker	12.04.1989	23		6
Luca Zuffi	27.03.1990	14	(7)	
Forwards:	DOB	M	(s)	G
Arthur Mendonça Cabral (BRA)	25.04.1998	32	(1)	18
Carmine Chiappetta	09.03.2003		(4)	
Andrin Hunziker	21.02.2003		(4)	
Aldo Kalulu (FRA)	21.01.1996	7	(3)	
Darian Males	03.05.2001	12	(4)	2
Afimico Pululu (FRA)	23.03.1999	10	(15)	3
Kaly Sene (SEN)	28.05.2001	1	(4)	
Tician Tushi	02.04.2001		(4)	
Ricky van Wolfswinkel (NED)	27.01.1989	10	(15)	2
Julian von Moos	01.04.2001	3	(12)	
Edon Zhegrova (KVX)	31.03.1999	21	(9)	5

Football Club Lausanne-Sport

Founded:	1896	
Stadium:	Stade de la Tuilière / Stade Olympique de la Pontaise (12,544 / 12,500)	
Trainer:	Giorgio Contini	04.01.1974

Goalkeepers:	DOB	M	(s)	G
Thomas Castella	30.06.1993	2		
Mory Diaw (FRA)	22.06.1993	34		
Defenders:	DOB	M	(s)	G
Nikola Boranijašević (SRB)	19.05.1992	32	(1)	3
Stéphane Cueni	14.03.2001		(6)	
Per-Egil Flo (NOR)	18.01.1989	31		2
Nicolas Gétaz	11.06.1991		(2)	
Moritz Jenz (GER)	30.04.1999	26	(4)	1
Noah Loosli	23.01.1997	30	(2)	1
Elton Monteiro Almada (POR)	22.02.1994	15	(2)	
Mickaël Nanizayamo (FRA)	08.05.1998	13	(6)	
Marc Fred Tsoungui (CMR)	30.07.2002	4	(10)	1
Armel Zohouri (CIV)	05.04.2001	1	(4)	
Midfielders:	DOB	M	(s)	G
Gabriel Barès	29.08.2000	17	(17)	
Joël Geissmann	03.03.1993	5	(4)	1
Florian Hysenaj	20.07.2001		(1)	
Stjepan Kukuruzović (CRO)	07.06.1989	34		3

Brahima Ouattara (CIV)	23.11.2002		(6)	1
Pedro David Brazão Teixeira (POR)	30.12.2002	10	(10)	1
Cameron Puertas	18.08.1998	33		5
Christian Schneuwly	07.02.1988	6	(1)	1
Toichi Suzuki (JPN)	30.05.2000	13	(6)	2
Trazié Thomas (CIV)	01.07.1999	2	(11)	
Forwards:	DOB	M	(s)	G
Alvyn Antonio Sanches (POR)	12.02.2003		(2)	
Jonathan Bolingi (COD)	30.06.1994	10	(6)	5
Lucas Da Cunha (FRA)	09.06.2001	12	(15)	6
Evann Guessand (FRA)	01.07.2001	24	(10)	7
Josias Lukembila	09.09.1999		(5)	1
Hicham Mahou (FRA)	02.07.1999	17	(4)	2
Joël Almada Monteiro (POR)	05.08.1999	3	(1)	1
Isaac Schmidt	07.12.1999	1	(6)	
Aldin Turkes	22.04.1996	13		6
Rafik Zekhnini (NOR)	12.01.1998	7	(8)	2
Andi Zeqiri	22.06.1989	1		

Football Club Lugano

Founded: 1908; re-founded 2004 (*as AC Lugano*)
Stadium: Stadio Cornaredo, Lugano (6,390)
Trainer: Maurizio Jacobacci   11.01.1963

Goalkeepers:	DOB	M	(s)	G
Noam Baumann	10.04.1996	27		
Sebastian Osigwe (NGA)	26.03.1994	9		
Defenders:	**DOB**	**M**	**(s)**	**G**
Adriàn Guerrero Aguilar (ESP)	28.01.1998	28		
Fabio Daprelà	19.02.1991	24	(3)	2
Mickaël Facchinetti	15.02.1991	11	(13)	
Ákos Kecskés (HUN)	04.01.1996	29		
Numa Lavanchy	25.08.1993	34		3
Mijat Marić	30.04.1984	25		5
Mārcis Ošs (LVA)	25.07.1991	7	(6)	2
Reto Ziegler	16.01.1986	13	(2)	1
Midfielders:	**DOB**	**M**	**(s)**	**G**
Mattia Bottani	24.05.1991	23	(7)	6
Tommaso Centinaro (ITA)	01.10.2002		(1)	
Miroslav Čovilo (SRB)	06.05.1986	10	(21)	1
Olivier Custodio	10.02.1995	31	(1)	3
Stefano Guidotti (ITA)	16.06.1999	6	(12)	2
Sandi Lovrič (SVN)	28.03.1998	32	(1)	2
Christophe Lungoyi	04.07.2000	7	(19)	1
Roman Macek (CZE)	18.04.1997	5	(18)	
Lucky Onyebuchi Opara (NGA)	09.12.1999	2	(2)	1
Jonathan Maximiliano Sabbatini Perfecto (URU)	31.03.1988	27	(3)	
Forwards:	**DOB**	**M**	**(s)**	**G**
Asumah Abubakar-Ankra (POR)	10.05.1997	14	(6)	2
Joaquín Matías Ardaiz de los Santos (URU)	11.01.1999	9	(17)	3
Alexander Gerndt (SWE)	14.07.1986	18	(15)	5
Filip Holender (HUN)	27.07.1994		(2)	
Kévin Monzialo (FRA)	28.07.2000		(4)	
Nikolas Muci	08.02.2003		(1)	
Jens Odgaard (DEN)	31.03.1999	5	(1)	

Fussball-Club Luzern

Founded: 12.08.1901
Stadium: Swissporarena, Luzern (16,490)
Trainer: Fabio Celestini   31.10.1975

Goalkeepers:	DOB	M	(s)	G
Marius Müller (GER)	12.07.1993	34		
David Zibung	10.01.1984	2		
Defenders:	**DOB**	**M**	**(s)**	**G**
Ashvin Balaruban	08.08.2001		(6)	
Marco Burch	19.10.2000	17	(1)	1
Marco Bürki	10.07.1993	3	(2)	
Simon Grether	20.05.1992	8	(5)	1
Otar Kakabadze (GEO)	27.06.1995		(1)	
Stefan Knežević	30.10.1996	34		1
Lucas Alves de Araujo „Lucão"(BRA)	22.07.1992	19	(3)	1
Marvin Schulz (GER)	15.01.1995	22		7
Christian Schwegler	06.06.1984	10	(10)	
Silvan Sidler	07.07.1998	21	(5)	1
Midfielders:	**DOB**	**M**	**(s)**	**G**
Samuel Alabi (GHA)	06.05.2000	3	(4)	
Alejandro "Álex" Carbonell Vallés (ESP)	15.09.1997	7	(2)	
Lorik Emini	29.08.1999	13	(15)	
Martin Frýdek (CZE)	24.03.1992	29	(1)	
Tsiy William Ndenge (GER)	13.06.1997	6	(2)	
Louis Schaub (AUT)	29.12.1994	31	(1)	8
Pascal Schürpf	15.07.1989	23	(8)	6
Filip Ugrinić	05.01.1999	30	(3)	5
Idriz Voca (KVX)	15.05.1997	1		
Jordy Wehrmann (NED)	25.03.1999	16	(3)	
Forwards:	**DOB**	**M**	**(s)**	**G**
Yvan Gregory Alounga Avebe (CMR)	05.02.2002	4	(21)	1
Lino Lang	23.05.2000		(5)	
Mark Marleku (KVX)	27.04.2000	1		
Ibrahima N'Diaye (SEN)	06.07.1998	16	(19)	6
Dejan Sorgić (SRB)	15.09.1989	28	(3)	13
Varol Tasar (TUR)	04.10.1996	18	(12)	7

Servette Football Club Genève 1890

Founded: 20.03.1890
Stadium: Stade de Genève, Genève (30,084)
Trainer: Alain Geiger   05.11.1960

Goalkeepers:	DOB	M	(s)	G
Jérémy Frick	08.03.1993	33		
Joël Kiassumbua (COD)	06.04.1992	3		
Defenders:	**DOB**	**M**	**(s)**	**G**
Gaël Clichy (FRA)	26.07.1985	23		
Diogo Pinheiro Monteiro (POR)	28.01.2005		(1)	
Arial Mendy (SEN)	07.11.1994	10	(13)	
Steve Rouiller	10.07.1990	31	(2)	2
Vincent Sasso (FRA)	16.02.1991	20	(2)	
Anthony Sauthier	05.02.1991	28	(3)	
Yoan Severin (FRA)	24.01.1997	19	(7)	
Nicolas Vouilloz	11.05.2001	4	(6)	
Midfielders:	**DOB**	**M**	**(s)**	**G**
Alexis Antunes Gómez (ESP)	31.07.2000	5	(9)	
Ricardo Azevedo	02.12.2001		(9)	
Boris Cespedes	19.06.1995	16	(11)	1
Timothé Cognat (FRA)	25.01.1998	33	(1)	1
Moussa Diallo (FRA)	27.01.1997	9	(11)	
Boubacar Fofana (FRA)	07.09.1998	9	(14)	6
Mathis Holcbecher	21.01.2001		(3)	
Kastriot Imeri	27.06.2000	16	(13)	1
Alexis Martial (FRA)	15.06.2001		(2)	
Gaël Bella Ondoua (CMR)	04.11.1995	22	(2)	1
Nils Pédat	12.07.2001		(1)	
Miroslav Stevanović (BIH)	29.07.1990	27	(1)	5
Theo Valls (FRA)	18.12.1995	32	(1)	4
Forwards:	**DOB**	**M**	**(s)**	**G**
Alban Ajdini (ALB)	09.07.1999		(1)	
Koro Issa Ahmed Koné (CIV)	05.07.1989	5	(23)	1
Grejohn Kyei (FRA)	12.08.1995	29	(4)	12
Alex Schalk (NED)	07.08.1992	21	(10)	10
Varol Tasar (TUR)	04.10.1996	1		

Football Club de Sion

Founded: 1909
Stadium: Stade Tourbillon, Sion (14,283)
Trainer: Fabio Grosso (ITA) 28.11.1977
[05.03.2021] Christian Constantin 07.01.1957
[11.03.2021] Ugo Raczynski 30.11.1977
[16.03.2021] Marco Walker 02.05.1970

Goalkeepers:	DOB	M	(s)	G
Timothy Fayulu	24.07.1999	15		
Kevin Fickentscher	06.07.1988	21		
Defenders:	DOB	M	(s)	G
Ayoub Abdellaoui (ALG)	16.02.1993	22	(2)	2
Jan Bamert	09.03.1998	24	(2)	2
Dimitri Cavaré (FRA)	05.02.1995	7		1
Dennis Iapichino	27.07.1990	18	(5)	
Arian Kabashi (KVX)	26.09.1996	1		
Léo Lacroix	27.02.1992	6	(5)	
Noah Lovisa	21.06.2000	1	(1)	
Ivan Martić (CRO)	02.10.1990	10	(5)	
Jean Ruiz (FRA)	06.04.1998	9	(7)	
Wesley David de Oliveira Andrade (BRA)	13.03.2000	6		1
Midfielders:	DOB	M	(s)	G
José Aguilar Martínez (ESP)	05.02.2001	3		
Edgar André	28.06.1999	1	(6)	
Musa Araz	17.01.1994	18	(2)	1
Baltazar Costa Rodrigues de Oliveira (BRA)	06.05.2000	16	(5)	3

	DOB	M	(s)	G
Luca Clemenza (ITA)	09.07.1997	9	(5)	1
Serey Dié (CIV)	07.11.1984	17	(7)	1
Siyar Doldur	29.01.2000	4	(4)	
Anto Grgic	28.11.1996	28	(5)	9
Mauro Daniel Rodrigues Teixeira (POR)	15.04.2001		(2)	
Birama N'Doye (SEN)	27.03.1994	29	(1)	2
Sandro Theler	15.12.2000	18	(7)	
Matteo Tosetti	15.02.1992	24	(7)	2
Guy Christian Zock A Bep (CMR)	06.05.1994	12	(6)	1
Forwards:	DOB	M	(s)	G
Guillaume Hoarau (FRA)	05.03.1984	10	(12)	6
Cleilton Monteiro da Costa „Itaitinga" (BRA)	04.10.1998	5	(4)	
Gaëtan Karlen	07.06.1993	23	(9)	9
Jared Khasa (FRA)	04.11.1997	6	(20)	3
Patrick Luan dos Santos (BRA)	31.10.1998	6	(2)	
Ľubomír Tupta (SVK)	27.03.1998	9	(3)	
Roberts Uldriķis (LVA)	03.04.1998	12	(12)	3
Yamato Wakatsuki (JPN)	18.01.2002	6	(10)	1

Fussballclub St. Gallen 1879

Founded: 19.04.1879
Stadium: Kybunpark, St. Gallen (19,456)
Trainer: Peter Zeidler (GER) 08.08.1962

Goalkeepers:	DOB	M	(s)	G
Lawrence Ati-Zigi (GHA)	29.11.1996	35		
Lukas Watkowiak (GER)	06.03.1996	1		
Defenders:	DOB	M	(s)	G
Adonis Ajeti	26.02.1997		(1)	
Euclides da Silva Cabral (POR)	05.01.1999	10	(9)	
Michael Heule	27.04.2001		(1)	
David Jacovic	05.02.2001	1		
Yannis Letard (FRA)	18.08.1998	6	(2)	
Nicolas Lüchinger	16.10.1994	4	(2)	
Miro Muheim	24.03.1998	23	(1)	
Musah Nuhu (GHA)	17.01.1997	6	(5)	
Vincent Rüfli	22.01.1988	2	(6)	
Leonidas Stergiou	03.03.2002	31	(1)	
Midfielders:	DOB	M	(s)	G
Salifou Diarrassouba (BFA)	20.12.2001	1	(4)	1
Kwadwo Duah	24.02.1997	25	(7)	9
Betim Fazliji (KVX)	25.04.1999	31	(1)	1
Lukas Görtler (GER)	15.06.1994	32		2

	DOB	M	(s)	G
Jordi Quintillà Guasch (ESP)	25.10.1993	31		2
Alessandro Kräuchi	03.06.1998	18	(2)	1
Oliver Mayer	13.11.2000		(1)	
Nsana Simon (FRA)	11.03.2000	1	(1)	
Tim Staubli	16.04.2000	4	(26)	1
Basil Stillhart	24.03.1994	27	(5)	3
Forwards:	DOB	M	(s)	G
Chikwubuike Adamu (AUT)	06.06.2001	10	(4)	6
André David de Oliveira Ribeiro (POR)	09.06.1997	2	(8)	1
Boris Babic	10.11.1997	9	(20)	1
Alessio Besio	18.03.2004	1		1
Angelo Campos Oliveira (POR)	30.03.2000	1	(1)	
Lorenzo González	10.04.2000		(1)	
Jérémy Guillemenot	06.01.1998	23	(11)	3
Florian Kamberi (ALB)	08.03.1995	4	(4)	
Patrick Sutter	18.01.1999	1	(2)	
Boubacar Traorè (SEN)	26.07.1997	12	(10)	
Víctor Ruiz Abril (ESP)	02.11.1993	28	(4)	6
Élie Youan (FRA)	07.04.1999	16	(13)	5

Fussball Club Vaduz

Founded: 14.02.1932
Stadium: Rheinpark Stadion, Vaduz (Liechtenstein) (7,584)
Trainer: Mario Frick 07.09.1974

Goalkeepers:	DOB	M	(s)	G
Benjamin Büchel (LIE)	04.07.1989	35		
Justin Ospelt (BAH)	07.09.1999	1	(1)	
Defenders:	DOB	M	(s)	G
Gianni Antoniazzi	05.09.1998	1	(1)	
Pius Dorn (GER)	24.09.1996	34	(1)	2
Cédric Gasser	16.02.1998	22	(8)	
Nico Hug (GER)	26.10.1998	15	(10)	
Kevin Iodice	12.01.2001		(2)	
Linus Obexer	05.06.1997	18	(4)	
Fuad Rahimi (KVX)	11.04.1998	9	(7)	
Yannick Schmid	11.05.1995	35		3
Joël Schmied	23.09.1998	31	(1)	7
Denis Simani (ALB)	13.10.1991	32		

Midfielders:	DOB	M	(s)	G
Tunahan Çiçek	12.05.1992	20	(12)	4
Dejan Djokic (BIH)	26.09.2000	14	(14)	3
Milan Gajić (SRB)	17.11.1986	28	(7)	4
Yago Gomes	08.09.2001	2	(12)	
Gabriel Lüchinger	18.12.1992	30	(4)	4
Boris Prokopič (AUT)	29.03.1988	8	(13)	
Sebastian Santin (AUT)	15.06.1994	2	(6)	
Sandro Wieser (LIE)	03.02.1993	12	(4)	1
Forwards:	DOB	M	(s)	G
Mohamed Coulibaly (FRA)	07.08.1988	6	(10)	2
Matteo di Giusto	18.08.2000	20	(13)	4
Elvin Ibrisimovic (AUT)	19.04.1999	1	(5)	
Nicolae Milinceanu (MDA)	01.08.1992	3	(2)	1
Manuel Sutter (AUT)	08.03.1991	17	(14)	1

Berner Sport Club Young Boys

Founded:	14.03.1898		
Stadium:	Wankdorf Stadion, Bern (31,789)		
Trainer:	Gerardo Seoane		30.10.1978

Goalkeepers:	DOB	M	(s)	G
Guillaume Faivre	20.02.1987	5	(1)	
Joschua Neuenschwander	28.06.2000		(1)	
David von Ballmoos	30.12.1994	31		
Defenders:	**DOB**	**M**	**(s)**	**G**
Nicolas Bürgy	07.08.1995	1	(3)	
Mohamed Aly Camara (GUI)	28.08.1997	26	(3)	
Ulisses Garcia	11.01.1996	17	(8)	1
Silvan Hefti	25.10.1997	23	(7)	
Jordan Lefort (FRA)	09.08.1993	19	(9)	1
Quentin Maceiras	10.10.1995	16	(5)	1
Cédric Zesiger	24.06.1998	24	(4)	
Midfielders:	**DOB**	**M**	**(s)**	**G**
Michel Aebischer	06.01.1997	24	(3)	2
Gianluca Gaudino (GER)	11.11.1996	7	(17)	
Sandro Lauper	25.10.1996	12	(8)	4
Fabian Lustenberger	02.05.1988	21		
Nico Maier	02.07.2000	1	(1)	
Christopher Martins (LUX)	19.02.1997	9	(2)	2
Fabian Rieder	16.02.2002	10	(13)	
Vincent Sierro	08.10.1995	12	(5)	1
Marvin Spielmann	23.02.1996	5	(10)	3
Miralem Sulejmani (SRB)	05.12.1988	17	(11)	
Forwards:	**DOB**	**M**	**(s)**	**G**
Meschack Elia (COD)	06.08.1997	16	(9)	6
Christian Fassnacht	11.11.1993	27	(9)	10
Felix Mambimbi	18.01.2001	17	(14)	6
Nicolas Ngamaleu (CMR)	09.07.1994	18	(10)	3
Jean-Pierre Nsamé (CMR)	01.05.1993	24	(6)	19
Theoson-Jordan Siebatcheu Pefok (USA)	26.04.1996	14	(18)	12

Fussballclub Zürich

Founded:	01.08.1896		
Stadium:	Letzigrund Stadion, Zürich (26,104)		
Trainer:	Ludovic Magnin		20.04.1979
[05.10.2020]	Massimo Rizzo		14.03.1974

Goalkeepers:	DOB	M	(s)	G
Yanick Brecher	25.05.1993	36		
Defenders:	**DOB**	**M**	**(s)**	**G**
Fidan Aliti (KVX)	03.10.1993	32		1
Lindrit Kamberi	07.10.1999	3	(3)	
Mirlind Kryeziu	26.01.1997	1		
Nathan Raphael Pelae Cardoso (BRA)	13.05.1995	29	(3)	
Becir Omeragić	20.01.2002	28	(1)	
Tobias Schättin	05.06.1997	5	(1)	
Lasse Sobiech (GER)	18.01.1991	12		3
Silvan Wallner	15.01.2002	14	(5)	
Midfielders:	**DOB**	**M**	**(s)**	**G**
Toni Domgjoni (CRO)	04.09.1998	25	(7)	3
Ousmane Doumbia (CIV)	21.05.1992	29	(1)	
Blerim Džemaili	12.04.1986	10	(2)	
Salim Khelifi	26.01.1994	6	(4)	1
Benjamin Kololli (KVX)	15.05.1992	20	(1)	6
Hekuran Kryeziu (KVX)	12.02.1993	16	(11)	
Antonio Marchesano	18.01.1991	31	(3)	13
Nils Reichmuth	22.02.2002	1	(3)	
Fabian Rohner	17.08.1998	12	(10)	3
Marco Schönbächler	11.01.1990	15	(11)	3
Simon Sohm	11.04.2001	2		
Stephan Vinicius Seiler (BRA)	16.09.2000	3	(12)	1
Adrian Winter	08.07.1986	3	(14)	
Forwards:	**DOB**	**M**	**(s)**	**G**
Assan Ceesay (GAM)	17.03.1994	18	(14)	2
Wilfried Gnonto (ITA)	05.11.2003	3	(23)	2
Henri Koide	06.04.2001	1	(1)	
Blaž Kramer (SVN)	01.06.1996	19	(13)	6
Aiyegun Tosin (NGA)	26.06.1998	22	(2)	6

SECOND LEVEL
Swiss Challenge League 2020/2021

1.	Grasshopper Club Zürich (*Promoted*)	36	19	8	9	60 - 43	65
2.	FC Thun (*Promotion Play-offs*)	36	19	7	10	57 - 46	64
3.	FC Stade Lausanne Ouchy	36	15	13	8	57 - 39	58
4.	FC Schaffhausen	36	16	10	10	59 - 46	58
5.	FC Aarau	36	17	7	12	66 - 59	58
6.	FC Winterthur	36	11	10	15	50 - 52	43
7.	FC Wil 1900	36	10	9	17	43 - 52	39
8.	SC Kriens	36	9	11	16	40 - 48	38
9.	Neuchâtel Xamax FCS	36	10	6	20	36 - 58	36
10.	FC Chiasso (*Relegated*)	36	9	9	18	35 - 60	36

INTERNATIONAL MATCHES
(16.07.2020 – 15.07.2021)

03.09.2020	Lviv	Ukraine - Switzerland	2-1(1-1)	(UNL)
06.09.2020	Basel	Switzerland - Germany	1-1(0-1)	(UNL)
07.10.2020	St. Gallen	Switzerland - Croatia	1-2(1-1)	(F)
10.10.2020	Madrid	Spain - Switzerland	1-0(1-0)	(UNL)
13.10.2020	Köln	Germany - Switzerland	3-3(1-2)	(UNL)
11.11.2020	Leuven	Belgium - Switzerland	2-1(0-1)	(F)
14.11.2020	Basel	Switzerland - Spain	1-1(1-0)	(UNL)
17.11.2020	Luzern	Switzerland - Ukraine	3-0 (awarded)	(UNL)
25.03.2021	Sofia	Bulgaria - Switzerland	1-3(0-3)	(WCQ)
28.03.2021	St. Gallen	Switzerland - Lithuania	1-0(1-0)	(WCQ)
31.03.2021	St. Gallen	Switzerland - Finland	3-2(1-2)	(F)
30.05.2021	St. Gallen	Switzerland - United States	2-1(1-1)	(F)
03.06.2021	St. Gallen	Switzerland - Liechtenstein	7-0(1-0)	(F)
12.06.2021	Bakı	Wales - Switzerland	1-1(0-0)	(EC)
16.06.2021	Roma	Italy - Switzerland	3-0(1-0)	(EC)
20.06.2021	Bakı	Switzerland - Turkey	3-1(2-0)	(EC)
28.06.2021	Bucureşti	France - Switzerland	3-3(0-1,3-3,3-3); 4-5 on penalties	(EC)
02.07.2021	Saint Petersburg	Switzerland - Spain	1-1(0-1,1-1,1-1); 1-2 on penalties	(EC)

03.09.2020　UKRAINE - SWITZERLAND　　2-1(1-1)　　2nd UEFA Nations League A, Group 4
Arena Lviv, Lviv; Referee: Andreas Ekberg (Sweden); Attendance: 0
SUI: Yann Sommer, Melingo Kevin Mbabu, Nico Elvedi, Manuel Obafemi Akanji, Ricardo Iván Rodríguez Araya, Steven Zuber (46.Renato Steffen), Granit Xhaka (Cap), Mohameth Djibril Ibrahima Sow (82.Michel Aebischer), Rubén Estephan Vargas Martínez (73.Albian Afrim Ajeti), Haris Seferović, Breel Donald Embolo. Trainer: Vladimir Petković (Bosnia and Herzegovina).
Goal: Haris Seferović (41).

06.09.2020　SWITZERLAND - GERMANY　　1-1(0-1)　　2nd UEFA Nations League A, Group 4
St. Jakob-Park, Basel; Referee: Michael Oliver (England); Attendance: 0
SUI: Yann Sommer, Silvan Dominic Widmer, Loris Benito Souto, Nico Elvedi, Manuel Obafemi Akanji, Ricardo Iván Rodríguez Araya (64.Steven Zuber), Granit Xhaka (Cap), Renato Steffen, Mohameth Djibril Ibrahima Sow (80.Michel Aebischer), Haris Seferović, Breel Donald Embolo (72.Rubén Estephan Vargas Martínez). Trainer: Vladimir Petković (Bosnia and Herzegovina).
Goal: Silvan Dominic Widmer (58).

07.10.2020　SWITZERLAND - CROATIA　　1-2(1-1)　　Friendly International
Kybunpark, St. Gallen; Referee: Tiago Bruno Lopes Martins (Portugal); Attendance: 4,500
SUI: Jonas Omlin, Mvula Jordan Lotomba, Eray Ervin Cömert, Fabian Lukas Schär (76.Loris Benito Souto), Ricardo Iván Rodríguez Araya (46.Steven Zuber), Becir Omeragić, Admir Mehmedi (46.Rubén Estephan Vargas Martínez), Granit Xhaka (Cap) (46.Remo Marco Freuler), Mohameth Djibril Ibrahima Sow (64.Simon Sohm), Edimilson Fernandes Ribeiro (62.Cedric Jan Itten), Mario Gavranović. Trainer: Vladimir Petković (Bosnia and Herzegovina).
Goal: Mario Gavranović (31).

10.10.2020　SPAIN - SWITZERLAND　　1-0(1-0)　　2nd UEFA Nations League A, Group 4
Estadio "Alfredo di Stéfano", Madrid; Referee: Ali Palabıyık (Turkey); Attendance: 0
SUI: Yann Sommer, Silvan Dominic Widmer (86.Mario Gavranović), Fabian Lukas Schär, Nico Elvedi, Loris Benito Souto (81.Steven Zuber), Ricardo Iván Rodríguez Araya, Admir Mehmedi (60.Xherdan Shaqiri), Granit Xhaka (Cap), Remo Marco Freuler (86.Edimilson Fernandes Ribeiro), Mohameth Djibril Ibrahima Sow (60.Rubén Estephan Vargas Martínez), Haris Seferović. Trainer: Vladimir Petković (Bosnia and Herzegovina).

13.10.2020　GERMANY - SWITZERLAND　　3-3(1-2)　　2nd UEFA Nations League A, Group 4
RheinEnergie Stadion, Köln; Referee: Ruddy Buquet (France); Attendance: 0
SUI: Yann Sommer, Silvan Dominic Widmer, Fabian Lukas Schär [*sent off 90+4*], Nico Elvedi, Ricardo Iván Rodríguez Araya, Steven Zuber (66.Edimilson Fernandes Ribeiro), Granit Xhaka (Cap), Xherdan Shaqiri (66.Mohameth Djibril Ibrahima Sow), Remo Marco Freuler (85.Loris Benito Souto), Mario Gavranović (75.Admir Mehmedi), Haris Seferović (85.Cedric Jan Itten). Trainer: Vladimir Petković (Bosnia and Herzegovina).
Goals: Mario Gavranović (5), Remo Marco Freuler (26), Mario Gavranović (57).

11.11.2020　BELGIUM - SWITZERLAND　　2-1(0-1)　　Friendly International
King Power at Den Dreef Stadion, Leuven; Referee: Jérôme Brisard (France); Attendance: 0
SUI: Yvon Landry Mvogo Nganoma, Fabian Lukas Schär, Loris Benito Souto (75.Becir Omeragić), Eray Ervin Cömert, Steven Zuber (46.Rubén Estephan Vargas Martínez), Granit Xhaka (Cap) (46.Xherdan Shaqiri), Edimilson Fernandes Ribeiro, Mohameth Djibril Ibrahima Sow, Mario Gavranović (63.Haris Seferović), Admir Mehmedi (46.Renato Steffen), Breel Donald Embolo (46.Silvan Dominic Widmer). Trainer: Vladimir Petković (Bosnia and Herzegovina).
Goal: Admir Mehmedi (12).

14.11.2020　SWITZERLAND - SPAIN　　1-1(1-0)　　2nd UEFA Nations League A, Group 4
St. Jakob-Park, Basel; Referee: William Collum (Scotland); Attendance: 0
SUI: Yann Sommer, Ricardo Iván Rodríguez Araya, Nico Elvedi [*sent off 79*], Manuel Obafemi Akanji, Steven Zuber (73.Renato Steffen), Remo Marco Freuler, Granit Xhaka (Cap), Xherdan Shaqiri (73.Mohameth Djibril Ibrahima Sow), Edimilson Fernandes Ribeiro, Haris Seferović (84.Becir Omeragić), Breel Donald Embolo (90+1.Admir Mehmedi). Trainer: Vladimir Petković (Bosnia and Herzegovina).
Goal: Remo Marco Freuler (26).

17.11.2020　SWITZERLAND - UKRAINE　　3-0 (awarded)　　2nd UEFA Nations League A, Group 4
Swissporarena, Luzern; Referee: Anastasios Sidiropoulos (Greece); Attendance: 0
Please note: *the match was cancelled after the Ukraine national team was placed in quarantine due to several positive COVID-19 test in the squad, being awarded as a 3-0 win to Switzerland.*

25.03.2021 BULGARIA - SWITZERLAND   1-3(0-3)   22ⁿᵈ FIFA WC. Qualifiers

Nationalen Stadion "Vasil Levski", Sofia; Referee: Nikola Dabanović (Montenegro); Attendance: 0

SUI: Yann Sommer, Melingo Kevin Mbabu, Nico Elvedi, Manuel Obafemi Akanji, Ricardo Iván Rodríguez Araya, Steven Zuber (75.Denis Lemi Zakaria Lako Lado), Granit Xhaka (Cap), Xherdan Shaqiri (75.Rubén Estephan Vargas Martínez), Remo Marco Freuler (86.Mohameth Djibril Ibrahima Sow), Haris Seferović (86.Mario Gavranović), Breel Donald Embolo (90.Admir Mehmedi). Trainer: Vladimir Petković (Bosnia and Herzegovina).

Goals: Breel Donald Embolo (7), Haris Seferović (10), Steven Zuber (13).

28.03.2021 SWITZERLAND - LITHUANIA   1-0(1-0)   22ⁿᵈ FIFA WC. Qualifiers

Kybunpark, St. Gallen; Referee: Mattias Gestranius (Finland); Attendance: 0

SUI: Yann Sommer, Silvan Dominic Widmer (65.Edimilson Fernandes Ribeiro), Ricardo Iván Rodríguez Araya, Nico Elvedi, Manuel Obafemi Akanji, Remo Marco Freuler (66.Denis Lemi Zakaria Lako Lado), Granit Xhaka (Cap), Xherdan Shaqiri (80.Admir Mehmedi), Rubén Estephan Vargas Martínez (79.Steven Zuber), Haris Seferovic, Breel Donald Embolo (65.Mario Gavranović). Trainer: Vladimir Petković (Bosnia and Herzegovina).

Goal: Xherdan Shaqiri (2).

31.03.2021 SWITZERLAND - FINLAND   3-2(1-2)   22ⁿᵈ FIFA WC. Qualifiers

Kybunpark, St. Gallen; Referee: Manuel Schüttengruber (Austria); Attendance: 0

SUI: Jonas Omlin, Loris Benito Souto, Melingo Kevin Mbabu (46.Granit Xhaka), Nico Elvedi (46.Manuel Obafemi Akanji), Eray Ervin Cömert, Steven Zuber, Edimilson Fernandes Ribeiro, Xherdan Shaqiri (Cap) (46.Christian Fassnacht), Mohameth Djibril Ibrahima Sow (76.Silvan Dominic Widmer), Denis Lemi Zakaria Lako Lado (55.Rubén Estephan Vargas Martínez), Mario Gavranović (67.Haris Seferovic). Trainer: Vladimir Petković (Bosnia and Herzegovina).

Goals: Mario Gavranović (22), Rubén Estephan Vargas Martínez (57), Haris Seferović (86).

30.05.2021 SWITZERLAND - UNITED STATES   2-1(1-1)   Friendly International

Kybunpark, St. Gallen; Referee: Harm Osmers (Germany); Attendance: 0

SUI: Yann Sommer, Fabian Lukas Schär, Loris Benito Souto (46.Remo Marco Freuler), Silvan Dominic Widmer, Nico Elvedi (46.Manuel Obafemi Akanji), Ricardo Iván Rodríguez Araya (69.Eray Ervin Cömert), Denis Lemi Zakaria Lako Lado, Granit Xhaka (Cap), Xherdan Shaqiri (46.Steven Zuber), Haris Seferovic (84.Christian Fassnacht), Breel Donald Embolo (68.Admir Mehmedi). Trainer: Vladimir Petković (Bosnia and Herzegovina).

Goals: Ricardo Iván Rodríguez Araya (10), Steven Zuber (63).

03.06.2021 SWITZERLAND - LIECHTENSTEIN   7-0(1-0)   Friendly International

Kybunpark, St. Gallen; Referee: Nejc Kajtazović (Slovenia); Attendance: 0

SUI: Yvon Landry Mvogo Nganoma, Eray Ervin Cömert, Melingo Kevin Mbabu (68.Mvula Jordan Lotomba), Becir Omeragić, Fabian Lukas Schär (46.Ricardo Iván Rodríguez Araya), Remo Marco Freuler (46.Granit Xhaka), Mohameth Djibril Ibrahima Sow, Steven Zuber (67.Edimilson Fernandes Ribeiro), Xherdan Shaqiri (Cap) (46.Rubén Estephan Vargas Martínez), Mario Gavranović, Admir Mehmedi (46.Christian Fassnacht). Trainer: Vladimir Petković (Bosnia and Herzegovina).

Goals: Mario Gavranović (19), Christian Fassnacht (46), Noah Frick (57 own goal), Christian Fassnacht (70), Mario Gavranović (75, 79), Edimilson Fernandes Ribeiro (85).

12.06.2021 WALES - SWITZERLAND   1-1(0-0)   16ᵗʰ EC. Group Stage.

Bakı Olimpiya Stadionu, Bakı (Azerbaijan); Referee: Clément Turpin (France); Attendance: 8,782

SUI: Yann Sommer, Fabian Lukas Schär, Melingo Kevin Mbabu, Nico Elvedi, Ricardo Iván Rodríguez Araya, Manuel Obafemi Akanji, Remo Marco Freuler, Granit Xhaka (Cap), Xherdan Shaqiri (66.Denis Lemi Zakaria Lako Lado), Haris Seferovic (84.Mario Gavranović), Breel Donald Embolo. Trainer: Vladimir Petković (Bosnia and Herzegovina).

Goal: Breel Donald Embolo (49).

16.06.2021 ITALY - SWITZERLAND   3-0(1-0)   16ᵗʰ EC. Group Stage.

Stadio Olimpico, Roma; Referee: Sergey Karasev (Russia); Attendance: 12,445

SUI: Yann Sommer, Fabian Lukas Schär (58.Steven Zuber), Melingo Kevin Mbabu (58.Silvan Dominic Widmer), Nico Elvedi, Ricardo Iván Rodríguez Araya, Manuel Obafemi Akanji, Granit Xhaka (Cap), Remo Marco Freuler (84.Mohameth Djibril Ibrahima Sow), Xherdan Shaqiri (76.Rubén Estephan Vargas Martínez), Haris Seferovic (46.Mario Gavranović), Breel Donald Embolo. Trainer: Vladimir Petković (Bosnia and Herzegovina).

20.06.2021 SWITZERLAND - TURKEY   3-1(2-0)   16ᵗʰ EC. Group Stage.

Bakı Olimpiya Stadionu, Bakı (Azerbaijan); Referee: Slavko Vinčić (Slovenia); Attendance: 17,138

SUI: Yann Sommer, Silvan Dominic Widmer (90+2.Melingo Kevin Mbabu), Nico Elvedi, Manuel Obafemi Akanji, Ricardo Iván Rodríguez Araya, Steven Zuber (85.Loris Benito Souto), Granit Xhaka (Cap), Remo Marco Freuler, Xherdan Shaqiri (75.Rubén Estephan Vargas Martínez), Haris Seferovic (75.Mario Gavranović), Breel Donald Embolo (85.Admir Mehmedi). Trainer: Vladimir Petković (Bosnia and Herzegovina).

Goals: Haris Seferovic (6), Xherdan Shaqiri (26, 68).

28.06.2021 FRANCE - SWITZERLAND   3-3(0-1,3-3,3-3); 4-5 on penalties   16ᵗʰ EC. 2ⁿᵈ Round of 16.

Arena Naţională, Bucureşti (Romania); Referee: Fernando Andrés Rapallini (Argentina); Attendance: 22,642

SUI: Yann Sommer, Silvan Dominic Widmer (73.Melingo Kevin Mbabu), Nico Elvedi, Manuel Obafemi Akanji, Ricardo Iván Rodríguez Araya (87.Admir Mehmedi), Steven Zuber (79.Christian Fassnacht), Granit Xhaka (Cap), Remo Marco Freuler, Xherdan Shaqiri (73.Mario Gavranović), Haris Seferovic (97.Fabian Lukas Schär), Breel Donald Embolo (79.Rubén Estephan Vargas Martínez). Trainer: Vladimir Petković (Bosnia and Herzegovina).

Goals: Haris Seferovic (15, 81), Mario Gavranović (90).

Penalties: Mario Gavranović, Fabian Lukas Schär, Manuel Obafemi Akanji, Rubén Estephan Vargas Martínez, Admir Mehmedi.

02.07.2021 SWITZERLAND - SPAIN   1-1(0-1,1-1,1-1); 1-2 on penalties   16ᵗʰ EC. Quarter-Finals.

Krestovsky Stadium (Gazprom Arena), Saint Petersburg (Russia); Referee: Michael Oliver (England); Attendance: 24,764

SUI: Yann Sommer, Silvan Dominic Widmer (101.Melingo Kevin Mbabu), Nico Elvedi, Manuel Obafemi Akanji, Ricardo Iván Rodríguez Araya, Steven Zuber (90+2.Christian Fassnacht), Denis Lemi Zakaria Lako Lado (101.Fabian Lukas Schär), Xherdan Shaqiri (Cap) (81.Mohameth Djibril Ibrahima Sow), Remo Marco Freuler [sent off 77], Haris Seferovic (82.Mario Gavranović), Breel Donald Embolo (23.Rubén Estephan Vargas Martínez). Trainer: Vladimir Petković (Bosnia and Herzegovina).

Goal: Xherdan Shaqiri (68).

Penalties: Mario Gavranović, Fabian Lukas Schär (saved), Manuel Obafemi Akanji (saved), Rubén Estephan Vargas Martínez (missed).

NATIONAL TEAM PLAYERS
(16.07.2020 – 15.07.2021)

Name	DOB	Caps	Goals	2020/2021:	Club

Goalkeepers

Name	DOB	Caps	Goals	2020/2021:	Club
Yvon Landry MVOGO Nganoma	06.06.1994	4	0	2020/2021:	PSV Eindhoven (NED)
Jonas OMLIN	10.01.1994	2	0	2020/2021:	Montpellier Hérault SC (FRA)
Yann SOMMER	17.12.1988	66	0	2020/2021:	Borussia VfL Mönchengladbach (GER)

Defenders

Name	DOB	Caps	Goals	2020/2021:	Club
Manuel Obafemi AKANJI	19.07.1995	34	0	2020/2021:	BV Borussia 09 Dortmund (GER)
Loris BENITO Souto	07.01.1992	13	1	2020/2021:	FC Girondins de Bordeaux (FRA)
Eray Ervin CÖMERT	04.02.1998	6	0	2020/2021:	FC Basel
Nico ELVEDI	30.09.1996	31	1	2020/2021:	Borussia VfL Mönchengladbach (GER)
Mvula Jordan LOTOMBA	29.09.1998	2	0	2020/2021:	OGC Nice (FRA)
Melingo Kevin MBABU	19.04.1995	17	0	2020/2021:	VfL Wolfsburg (GER)
Becir OMERAGIĆ	20.01.2002	4	0	2020/2021:	FC Zürich (SUI)
Ricardo Iván RODRÍGUEZ Araya	25.08.1992	86	9	2020/2021:	Torino FC (ITA)
Fabian Lukas SCHÄR	20.12.1991	64	8	2020/2021:	Newcastle United FC (ENG)
Silvan Dominic WIDMER	05.03.1993	20	1	2020/2021:	FC Basel

Midfielders

Name	DOB	Caps	Goals	2020/2021:	Club
Michel AEBISCHER	06.01.1997	2	0	2020:	BSC Young Boys Bern
Christian FASSNACHT	11.11.1993	10	3	2020/2021:	BSC Young Boys Bern
Edimilson FERNANDES Ribeiro	15.04.1996	22	2	2020/2021:	1.FSV Mainz 05 (GER)
Remo Marco FREULER	15.04.1992	34	3	2020/2021:	Atalanta Bergamasca Calcio (ITA)
Xherdan SHAQIRI	10.10.1991	96	26	2020/2021:	Liverpool FC (ENG)
Simon SOHM	11.04.2001	1	0	2020:	Parma Calcio 1913 (ITA)
Mohameth Djibril Ibrahima SOW	06.02.1997	18	0	2020/2021:	Eintracht Frankfurt (GER)
Renato STEFFEN	03.11.1991	14	0	2020:	VfL Wolfsburg (GER)
Granit XHAKA	27.09.1992	98	12	2020/2021:	Arsenal FC London (ENG)
Denis Lemi ZAKARIA Lako Lado	20.11.1996	34	3	2020/2021:	Borussia VfL Mönchengladbach (GER)
Steven ZUBER	17.08.1991	41	8	2020/2021:	Eintracht Frankfurt (GER)

Forwards

Name	DOB	Caps	Goals	2020/2021:	Club
Albian Afrim AJETI	26.02.1997	11	1	2020/2021:	Celtic FC Glasgow (SCO)
Breel Donald EMBOLO	14.02.1997	48	6	2020/2021:	Borussia VfL Mönchengladbach (GER)
Mario GAVRANOVIĆ	24.11.1989	35	15	2020/2021:	GNK Dinamo Zagreb (CRO)
Cedric Jan ITTEN	27.12.1996	4	3	2020:	Rangers FC Glasgow (SCO)
Admir MEHMEDI	16.03.1991	76	10	2020/2021:	VfL Wolfsburg (GER)
Haris SEFEROVIĆ	22.02.1992	79	24	2020/2021:	Sport Lisboa e Benfica (POR)
Rubén Estephan VARGAS Martínez	05.08.1998	16	2	2020/2021:	FC Augsburg (GER)

Trainer

Vladimir PETKOVIĆ (Bosnia and Herzegovina) [01.08.2014 – 27.07.2021]	15.08.1963	77 M; 40 W; 18 D; 19 L; 146-77	

TURKEY

The Country:
Türkiye Cumhuriyeti (Republic of Turkey)
Capital: Ankara
Surface: 783,356 km²
Inhabitants: 83,614,362 [2020]
Time: UTC+3

The FA:
Türkiye Futbol Federasyonu
Hasan Dogan Milli Takimlar Kamp ve Egitim Tesisleri Riva Beykoz, İstanbul
Tel: +90 216 554 51 00
Founded: 1923
Member of FIFA since: 1923
Member of UEFA since: 1962
Website: www.tff.org

NATIONAL TEAM RECORDS

RECORDS		
First international match:	26.10.1923, İstanbul:	Turkey – Romania 2-2
Most international caps:	Rüştü Reçber	- 120 caps (1994-2012)
Most international goals:	Hakan Şükür	- 51 goals / 112 caps (1992-2007)

UEFA EUROPEAN CHAMPIONSHIP	
1960	Qualifiers
1964	Qualifiers
1968	Qualifiers
1972	Qualifiers
1976	Qualifiers
1980	Qualifiers
1984	Qualifiers
1988	Qualifiers
1992	Qualifiers
1996	Final Tournament (Group Stage)
2000	Final Tournament (Quarter-Finals)
2004	Qualifiers
2008	Final Tournament (Semi-Finals)
2012	Qualifiers
2016	Final Tournament (Group Stage)
2020	Final Tournament (Group Stage)

FIFA WORLD CUP	
1930	Did not enter
1934	*Withdrew*
1938	Did not enter
1950	*Qualified but withdrew*
1954	Final Tournament (Group Stage)
1958	*Withdrew*
1962	Qualifiers
1966	Qualifiers
1970	Qualifiers
1974	Qualifiers
1978	Qualifiers
1982	Qualifiers
1986	Qualifiers
1990	Qualifiers
1994	Qualifiers
1998	Qualifiers
2002	Final Tournament (3rd Place)
2006	Qualifiers
2010	Qualifiers
2014	Qualifiers
2018	Qualifiers

OLYMPIC TOURNAMENTS	
1908	-
1912	-
1920	-
1924	Preliminary Round
1928	1/8 - Finals
1936	1/8 - Finals
1948	Quarter-Finals
1952	Quarter-Finals
1956	*Withdrew*
1960	Group Stage
1964	Qualifiers
1968	Qualifiers
1972	Qualifiers
1976	Qualifiers
1980	Group Stage
1984	*Withdrew*
1988	Qualifiers
1992	Qualifiers
1996	Qualifiers
2000	Qualifiers
2004	Qualifiers
2008	Qualifiers
2012	Qualifiers
2016	Qualifiers

UEFA NATIONS LEAGUE

2018/2019	League B
2020/2021	League B (relegated to League C)

FIFA CONFEDERATIONS CUP 1992-2017

2003 (3rd Place)

TURKISH CLUB HONOURS IN EUROPEAN CLUB COMPETITIONS:

European Champion Clubs.Cup (1956-1992) / UEFA Champions League (1993-2021)		
None		
Fairs Cup (1858-1971) / UEFA Cup (1972-2009) / UEFA Europa League (2010-2021)		
Galatasaray SK İstanbul	1	1999/2000
UEFA Super Cup (1972-2020)		
Galatasaray SK İstanbul	1	2000
European Cup Winners.Cup 1961-1999*		
None		

*defunct competition

NATIONAL COMPETITIONS
TABLE OF HONOURS

Turkish Football Championship (1924–1951)*

	CHAMPIONS
1924	Harbiye Ankara
1925-1926	*No competition*
1927	Muhafızgücü SK Ankara
1928 - 1931	*No competition*
1932	İstanbulspor
1933	Fenerbahçe SK İstanbul
1934	Beşiktaş JK İstanbul
1935	Fenerbahçe SK İstanbul
1936 - 1939	*No competition*
1940	Eskişehir Demirspor
1941	Gençlerbirliği Ankara SK Ankara
1942	Harp Okulu SK Ankara
1943	*No competition*
1944	Fenerbahçe SK İstanbul
1945	Harp Okulu SK Ankara
1946	Gençlerbirliği Ankara SK Ankara
1947	Ankara Demirspor
1948	*No competition*
1949	MKE Ankaragücü
1950	Göztepe SK İzmir
1951	Beşiktaş JK İstanbul

*Not recognized by Turkish FA.

National Division (1937–1950)*

	CHAMPIONS
1937	Fenerbahçe SK İstanbul
1938	Güneş SK İstanbul
1939	Galatasaray SK İstanbul
1940	Fenerbahçe SK İstanbul
1941	Beşiktaş JK İstanbul
1942	*No competition*
1943	Fenerbahçe SK İstanbul
1944	Beşiktaş JK İstanbul
1945	Fenerbahçe SK İstanbul
1946	Fenerbahçe SK İstanbul
1947	Beşiktaş JK İstanbul
1948	*No competition*
1949	*No competition*
1950	Fenerbahçe SK İstanbul

	CHAMPIONS	CUP WINNERS	BEST GOALSCORERS	
1956/1957**	Beşiktaş JK İstanbul	-	Nazmi Bilge (Beşiktaş JK İstanbul)	8
1957/1958**	Beşiktaş JK İstanbul	-	Lefter Küçükandonyadis (Fenerbahçe SK İstanbul) Metin Oktay (Galatasaray SK İstanbul)	10
1958/1959	Fenerbahçe SK İstanbul	-	Metin Oktay (Galatasaray SK İstanbul)	11
1959/1960	Beşiktaş JK İstanbul	-	Metin Oktay (Galatasaray SK İstanbul)	33
1960/1961	Fenerbahçe SK İstanbul	-	Metin Oktay (Galatasaray SK İstanbul)	36
1961/1962	Galatasaray SK İstanbul	-	Fikri Elma (Ankara Demirspor)	21
1962/1963	Galatasaray SK İstanbul	Galatasaray SK İstanbul	Metin Oktay (Galatasaray SK İstanbul)	38
1963/1964	Fenerbahçe SK İstanbul	Galatasaray SK İstanbul	Güven Önüt (Beşiktaş JK İstanbul)	19
1964/1965	Fenerbahçe SK İstanbul	Galatasaray SK İstanbul	Metin Oktay (Galatasaray SK İstanbul)	17
1965/1966	Beşiktaş JK İstanbul	Galatasaray SK İstanbul	Ertan Adatepe (MKE Ankaragücü)	20
1966/1967	Beşiktaş JK İstanbul	Altay SK İzmir	Ertan Adatepe (MKE Ankaragücü)	18
1967/1968	Fenerbahçe SK İstanbul	Fenerbahçe SK İstanbul	Fevzi Zemzem (Göztepe SK İzmir)	19
1968/1969	Galatasaray SK İstanbul	Göztepe SK İzmir	Metin Oktay (Galatasaray SK İstanbul)	17
1969/1970	Fenerbahçe SK İstanbul	Göztepe SK İzmir	Fethi Heper (Eskişehirspor Kulübü)	13
1970/1971	Galatasaray SK İstanbul	Eskişehirspor Kulübü	Ogün Altıparmak (Fenerbahçe SK İstanbul)	16
1971/1972	Galatasaray SK İstanbul	MKE Ankaragücü	Fethi Heper (Eskişehirspor Kulübü)	20
1972/1973	Galatasaray SK İstanbul	Galatasaray SK İstanbul	Osman Arpacıoğlu (Fenerbahçe SK İstanbul)	16
1973/1974	Fenerbahçe SK İstanbul	Fenerbahçe SK İstanbul	Cemil Turan (Fenerbahçe SK İstanbul)	14
1974/1975	Fenerbahçe SK İstanbul	Beşiktaş JK İstanbul	Ömer Kaner (Eskişehirspor Kulübü)	14
1975/1976	Trabzonspor Kulübü	Galatasaray SK İstanbul	Cemil Turan (Fenerbahçe SK İstanbul) Ali Osman Renklibay (MKE Ankaragücü)	17
1976/1977	Trabzonspor Kulübü	Trabzonspor Kulübü	Necmi Perekli (Trabzonspor Kulübü)	18
1977/1978	Fenerbahçe SK İstanbul	Trabzonspor Kulübü	Cemil Turan (Fenerbahçe SK İstanbul)	17
1978/1979	Trabzonspor Kulübü	Fenerbahçe SK İstanbul	Özer Umdu (Adanaspor AŞ)	15
1979/1980	Trabzonspor Kulübü	Altay SK İzmir	Mustafa Denizli (Altay SK İzmir) Bahtiyar Yorulmaz (Bursaspor Kulübü)	12
1980/1981	Trabzonspor Kulübü	MKE Ankaragücü	Bora Öztürk (Adanaspor AŞ)	15
1981/1982	Beşiktaş JK İstanbul	Galatasaray SK İstanbul	Selçuk Yula (Fenerbahçe SK İstanbul)	16
1982/1983	Fenerbahçe SK İstanbul	Fenerbahçe SK İstanbul	Selçuk Yula (Fenerbahçe SK İstanbul)	19
1983/1984	Trabzonspor Kulübü	Trabzonspor Kulübü	Tarik Hodžić (YUG, Galatasaray SK İstanbul)	16
1984/1985	Fenerbahçe SK İstanbul	Galatasaray SK İstanbul	Aykut Yiğit (Sakaryaspor Kulübü)	20
1985/1986	Beşiktaş JK İstanbul	Bursaspor Kulübü	Tanju Çolak (Samsunspor Kulübü)	33
1986/1987	Galatasaray SK İstanbul	Gençlerbirliği Ankara	Tanju Çolak (Samsunspor Kulübü)	25
1987/1988	Galatasaray SK İstanbul	Sakaryaspor Kulübü	Tanju Çolak (Galatasaray SK İstanbul)	39
1988/1989	Fenerbahçe SK İstanbul	Beşiktaş JK İstanbul	Aykut Kocaman (Fenerbahçe SK İstanbul)	29
1989/1990	Beşiktaş JK İstanbul	Beşiktaş JK İstanbul	Feyyaz Uçar (Beşiktaş JK İstanbul)	28
1990/1991	Beşiktaş JK İstanbul	Galatasaray SK İstanbul	Tanju Çolak (Galatasaray SK İstanbul)	31
1991/1992	Beşiktaş JK İstanbul	Trabzonspor Kulübü	Aykut Kocaman (Fenerbahçe SK İstanbul)	25
1992/1993	Galatasaray SK İstanbul	Galatasaray SK İstanbul	Tanju Çolak (Fenerbahçe SK İstanbul)	27
1993/1994	Galatasaray SK İstanbul	Beşiktaş JK İstanbul	Bülent Uygun (Fenerbahçe SK İstanbul)	22
1994/1995	Beşiktaş JK İstanbul	Trabzonspor Kulübü	Aykut Kocaman (Fenerbahçe SK İstanbul)	27
1995/1996	Fenerbahçe SK İstanbul	Galatasaray SK İstanbul	Shota Arveladze (GEO, Trabzonspor Kulübü)	25
1996/1997	Galatasaray SK İstanbul	Kocaelispor Kulübü	Hakan Şükür (Galatasaray SK İstanbul)	38
1997/1998	Galatasaray SK İstanbul	Beşiktaş JK İstanbul	Hakan Şükür (Galatasaray SK İstanbul)	33

1998/1999	Galatasaray SK İstanbul	Galatasaray SK İstanbul	Hakan Şükür (Galatasaray SK İstanbul)	19
1999/2000	Galatasaray SK İstanbul	Galatasaray SK İstanbul	Serkan Aykut (Samsunspor Kulübü)	30
2000/2001	Fenerbahçe SK İstanbul	Gençlerbirliği Ankara	Okan Yılmaz (Bursaspor Kulübü)	23
2001/2002	Galatasaray SK İstanbul	Kocaelispor Kulübü	Arif Erdem (Galatasaray SK İstanbul) İlhan Mansız (Beşiktaş JK İstanbul)	21
2002/2003	Beşiktaş JK İstanbul	Trabzonspor Kulübü	Okan Yılmaz (Bursaspor Kulübü)	24
2003/2004	Fenerbahçe SK İstanbul	Trabzonspor Kulübü	Zafer Biryol (Atiker Konyaspor Kulübü)	25
2004/2005	Fenerbahçe SK İstanbul	Galatasaray SK İstanbul	Fatih Tekke (Trabzonspor Kulübü)	31
2005/2006	Galatasaray SK İstanbul	Beşiktaş JK İstanbul	Gökhan Ünal (Kayseri Erciyesspor Kulübü)	25
2006/2007	Fenerbahçe SK İstanbul	Beşiktaş JK İstanbul	Alexsandro de Souza "Alex" (BRA, Fenerbahçe SK İstanbul)	19
2007/2008	Galatasaray SK İstanbul	Kayseri Erciyesspor Kulübü	Semih Şentürk (Fenerbahçe SK İstanbul)	17
2008/2009	Beşiktaş JK İstanbul	Beşiktaş JK İstanbul	Milan Baroš (CZE, Galatasaray SK İstanbul)	20
2009/2010	Bursaspor Kulübü	Trabzonspor Kulübü	Ariza Makukula (POR, Kayseri Erciyesspor Kulübü)	21
2010/2011	Fenerbahçe SK İstanbul	Beşiktaş JK İstanbul	Alexsandro de Souza "Alex" (BRA, Fenerbahçe SK İstanbul)	28
2011/2012	Galatasaray SK İstanbul	Fenerbahçe SK İstanbul	Burak Yılmaz (Trabzonspor Kulübü)	33
2012/2013	Galatasaray SK İstanbul	Fenerbahçe SK İstanbul	Burak Yılmaz (Galatasaray SK İstanbul)	24
2013/2014	Fenerbahçe SK İstanbul	Galatasaray SK İstanbul	Aatif Chahechouhe (MAR, Sivasspor Kulübü)	17
2014/2015	Galatasaray SK İstanbul	Galatasaray SK İstanbul	José Fernando Viana de Santana "Fernandão" (BRA, Bursaspor Kulübü)	22
2015/2016	Beşiktaş JK İstanbul	Galatasaray SK İstanbul	Mario Gómez García (Beşiktaş JK İstanbul)	26
2016/2017	Beşiktaş JK İstanbul	Atiker Konyaspor Kulübü	Vágner Silva de Souza (BRA, Alanyaspor)	23
2017/2018	Galatasaray SK İstanbul	Akhisar Belediyespor Gençlik SK	Bafétimbi Gomis (FRA, Galatasaray SK İstanbul)	29
2018/2019	Galatasaray SK İstanbul	Galatasaray SK İstanbul	Mbaye Diagne (SEN, Kasımpaşa Spor Kulübü / Galatasaray SK İstanbul)	30
2019/2020	İstanbul Başakşehir FK	Trabzonspor Kulübü	Alexander Sørloth (NOR, Trabzonspor Kulübü)	24
2020/2021	Beşiktaş JK İstanbul	Beşiktaş JK İstanbul	Aaron Salem Boupendza Pozzi (GAB, Hatayspor Antakya)	22

**recognized by Turkish FA only since 2002.

NATIONAL CHAMPIONSHIP
Süper Lig 2020/2021
(11.09.2020 – 15.05.2021)

Results

Round 1 [11-14.09.2020]
Çaykur Rizespor - Fenerbahçe 1-2(0-0)
Fatih Karagümrük - Malatyaspor 3-0(1-0)
Sivasspor - Alanyaspor 0-2(0-1)
Galatasaray - Gaziantep 3-1(3-0)
Göztepe - Denizlispor 5-1(3-0)
Ankaragücü - Erzurumspor 1-2(0-0)
Kayserispor - Kasımpaşa 1-0(1-0)
Antalyaspor - Gençlerbirliği 2-0(1-0)
Trabzonspor - Beşiktaş 1-3(0-1)
Hatayspor - İstanbul Başakşehir 2-0(1-0)

Round 2 [18-21.09.2020]
Malatyaspor - Göztepe 1-1(1-1)
Gençlerbirliği - Konyaspor 0-0
Denizlispor - Trabzonspor 0-0
Alanyaspor - Kayserispor 2-0(1-0)
Beşiktaş - Antalyaspor 1-1(1-0)
Erzurumspor - Sivasspor 1-2(0-0)
Kasımpaşa - Çaykur Rizespor 2-0(1-0)
Gaziantep - Fatih Karagümrük 2-2(0-1)
İstanbul Başakşehir - Galatasaray 0-2(0-1)
Fenerbahçe - Hatayspor 0-0

Round 3 [25-28.09.2020]
Fatih Karagümrük – İst. Başakşehir 2-0(0-0)
Kayserispor - Erzurumspor 1-3(0-2)
Göztepe - Gaziantep 2-2(0-1)
Hatayspor - Kasımpaşa 1-0(0-0)
Trabzonspor - Malatyaspor 3-1(3-0)
Çaykur Rizespor - Alanyaspor 1-1(0-0)
Konyaspor - Beşiktaş 4-1(1-0)
Sivasspor - Ankaragücü 0-0
Galatasaray - Fenerbahçe 0-0
Antalyaspor - Denizlispor 1-0(0-0)

Round 4 [02-04.10.2020]
Ankaragücü - Kayserispor 0-1(0-1)
Gaziantep - Trabzonspor 1-1(0-0)
Malatyaspor - Antalyaspor 1-0(1-0)
Erzurumspor - Çaykur Rizespor 0-0
İstanbul Başakşehir - Göztepe 0-0
Fenerbahçe - Fatih Karagümrük 2-1(1-0)
Denizlispor - Konyaspor 0-0
Alanyaspor - Hatayspor 6-0(4-0)
Beşiktaş - Gençlerbirliği 0-1(0-1)
Kasımpaşa - Galatasaray 1-0(1-0)

Round 5 [17-19.10.2020]
Çaykur Rizespor - Ankaragücü 5-3(2-3)
Kayserispor - Sivasspor 1-3(0-1)
Konyaspor - Malatyaspor 1-1(0-0)
Trabzonspor - İstanbul Başakşehir 0-2(0-1)
Antalyaspor - Gaziantep 1-1(1-0)
Fatih Karagümrük - Kasımpaşa 1-1(1-0)
Göztepe - Fenerbahçe 2-3(1-2)
Galatasaray - Alanyaspor 1-2(1-1)
Gençlerbirliği - Denizlispor 1-2(0-2)
Hatayspor - Erzurumspor 3-0(1-0) [09.12.]

Round 6 [23-26.10.2020]
Kasımpaşa - Göztepe 0-0
Gaziantep - Konyaspor 1-0(0-0)
Erzurumspor - Galatasaray 1-2(1-1)
İstanbul Başakşehir - Antalyaspor 5-1(4-1)
Malatyaspor - Gençlerbirliği 2-1(1-1)
Alanyaspor - Fatih Karagümrük 2-0(1-0)
Fenerbahçe - Trabzonspor 3-1(0-1)
Denizlispor - Beşiktaş 2-3(0-2)
Sivasspor - Çaykur Rizespor 0-2(0-1)
Ankaragücü - Hatayspor 2-0(0-0) [15.12.]

Round 7 [30.10.-02.11.2020]
Fatih Karagümrük - Erzurumspor 5-1(3-0)
Trabzonspor - Kasımpaşa 3-4(3-2)
Gençlerbirliği - Gaziantep 1-1(0-1)
Galatasaray - Ankaragücü 1-0(1-0)
Çaykur Rizespor - Kayserispor 1-0(1-0)
Konyaspor - İstanbul Başakşehir 1-2(0-1)
Beşiktaş - Malatyaspor 1-0(0-0)
Antalyaspor - Fenerbahçe 1-2(0-0)
Hatayspor - Sivasspor 1-1(1-1)
Göztepe - Alanyaspor 1-0(0-0) [09.12.]

Round 8 [06-08.11.2020]
Gaziantep - Beşiktaş 3-1(1-0)
Kasımpaşa - Antalyaspor 2-2(1-0)
Alanyaspor - Trabzonspor 1-1(0-0)
Erzurumspor - Göztepe 1-1(0-1)
Fenerbahçe - Konyaspor 0-2(0-0)
Ankaragücü - Fatih Karagümrük 2-2(1-2)
Malatyaspor - Denizlispor 2-0(2-0)
İstanbul Başakşehir - Gençlerbirliği 2-1(0-1)
Kayserispor - Hatayspor 0-1(0-0)
Sivasspor - Galatasaray 1-2(0-1)

Round 9 [21-23.11.2020]
Fatih Karagümrük - Sivasspor 1-1(0-1)
Denizlispor - Gaziantep 0-1(0-1)
Gençlerbirliği - Fenerbahçe 1-5(1-2)
Beşiktaş - İstanbul Başakşehir 3-2(2-0)
Hatayspor - Çaykur Rizespor 2-2(1-1)
Göztepe - Ankaragücü 3-1(1-0)
Konyaspor - Kasımpaşa 2-1(0-1)
Antalyaspor - Alanyaspor 0-2(0-0)
Trabzonspor - Erzurumspor 1-0(1-0)
Galatasaray - Kayserispor 1-1(0-0)

Round 10 [27-30.11.2020]
Ankaragücü - Trabzonspor 0-1(0-1)
Gaziantep - Malatyaspor 2-2(1-0)
İstanbul Başakşehir - Denizlispor 3-3(2-0)
Çaykur Rizespor - Galatasaray 0-4(0-1)
Erzurumspor - Antalyaspor 2-2(1-0)
Alanyaspor - Konyaspor 1-0(1-0)
Kasımpaşa - Gençlerbirliği 2-0(2-0)
Fenerbahçe - Beşiktaş 3-4(1-2)
Kayserispor - Fatih Karagümrük 0-0
Sivasspor - Göztepe 0-1(0-0)

Round 11 [04-07.12.2020]
Beşiktaş - Kasımpaşa 3-0(1-0)
Gençlerbirliği - Alanyaspor 2-1(1-0)
Göztepe - Kayserispor 1-1(0-0)
Konyaspor - Erzurumspor 2-0(1-0)
Malatyaspor - İstanbul Başakşehir 1-1(0-1)
Galatasaray - Hatayspor 3-0(1-0)
Fatih Karagümrük - Çaykur Rizespor 2-1(2-1)
Antalyaspor - Ankaragücü 1-0(1-0)
Denizlispor - Fenerbahçe 0-2(0-2)
Trabzonspor - Sivasspor 1-1(1-0)

Round 12 [11-14.12.2020]
Kasımpaşa - Denizlispor 3-2(2-1)
Hatayspor - Fatih Karagümrük 3-1(1-0)
Çaykur Rizespor - Göztepe 3-2(1-0)
Kayserispor - Trabzonspor 0-0
Ankaragücü - Konyaspor 4-3(1-2)
Fenerbahçe - Malatyaspor 0-3(0-2)
Erzurumspor - Gençlerbirliği 0-1(0-0)
Alanyaspor - Beşiktaş 2-1(1-0)
İstanbul Başakşehir - Gaziantep 1-2(0-1)
Sivasspor - Antalyaspor 0-0

Round 13 [18-21.12.2020]
Fatih Karagümrük - Galatasaray 2-1(0-0)
Göztepe - Hatayspor 0-1(0-0)
Trabzonspor - Çaykur Rizespor 2-1(0-1)
Malatyaspor - Kasımpaşa 2-0(1-0)
Gaziantep - Fenerbahçe 3-1(2-1)
Gençlerbirliği - Ankaragücü 1-1(0-0)
Denizlispor - Alanyaspor 1-0(1-0)
Beşiktaş - Erzurumspor 4-0(0-0)
Antalyaspor - Kayserispor 2-0(2-0)
Konyaspor - Sivasspor 0-1(0-0)

Round 14 [22-24.12.2020]
Hatayspor - Trabzonspor 0-1(0-0)
Galatasaray - Göztepe 3-1(2-1)
Alanyaspor - Malatyaspor 1-1(1-0)
Erzurumspor - Denizlispor 1-2(0-1)
Fenerbahçe - İstanbul Başakşehir 4-1(1-1)
Kasımpaşa - Gaziantep 0-4(0-2)
Kayserispor - Konyaspor 1-2(1-0)
Sivasspor - Gençlerbirliği 3-1(1-0)
Ankaragücü - Beşiktaş 0-1(0-0)
Çaykur Rizespor - Antalyaspor 2-1(1-0)

Round 15 [26-29.12.2020]
Göztepe - Fatih Karagümrük 1-1(1-0)
Trabzonspor - Galatasaray 0-2(0-1)
Gaziantep - Alanyaspor 3-1(2-1)
Denizlispor - Ankaragücü 1-2(0-2)
Malatyaspor - Erzurumspor 1-3(0-1)
İstanbul Başakşehir - Kasımpaşa 2-2(1-1)
Gençlerbirliği - Kayserispor 3-2(1-1)
Konyaspor - Çaykur Rizespor 1-1(1-0)
Beşiktaş - Sivasspor 3-0(1-0)
Antalyaspor - Hatayspor 0-6(0-5)

Round 16 [02-04.01.2021]
Erzurumspor - Gaziantep 1-1(0-0)
Sivasspor - Denizlispor 2-2(2-1)
Alanyaspor - İstanbul Başakşehir 3-0(2-0)
Ankaragücü - Malatyaspor 3-1(2-0)
Galatasaray - Antalyaspor 0-0
Hatayspor - Konyaspor 2-1(1-1)
Çaykur Rizespor - Gençlerbirliği 1-1(1-0)
Fatih Karagümrük - Trabzonspor 1-2(0-0)
Kayserispor - Beşiktaş 0-2(0-0)
Kasımpaşa - Fenerbahçe 0-3(0-2)

Round 17 [05-07.01.2021]
Gaziantep - Ankaragücü 2-0(0-0)
Malatyaspor - Sivasspor 2-2(1-2)
Konyaspor - Galatasaray 4-3(1-1)
Denizlispor - Kayserispor 0-1(0-1)
Gençlerbirliği - Hatayspor 3-1(1-1)
İstanbul Başakşehir - Erzurumspor 1-0(1-0)
Trabzonspor - Göztepe 1-0(1-0)
Antalyaspor - Fatih Karagümrük 3-1(2-1)
Beşiktaş - Çaykur Rizespor 6-0(2-0)
Fenerbahçe - Alanyaspor 2-1(1-0)

Round 18 [09-11.01.2021]
Sivasspor - Gaziantep 2-1(1-1)
Göztepe - Antalyaspor 0-1(0-0)
Kayserispor - Malatyaspor 1-0(1-0)
Galatasaray - Gençlerbirliği 6-0(4-0)
Fatih Karagümrük - Konyaspor 2-1(0-0)
Ankaragücü - İstanbul Başakşehir 1-2(1-1)
Çaykur Rizespor - Denizlispor 1-1(0-1)
Hatayspor - Beşiktaş 2-2(2-2)
Erzurumspor - Fenerbahçe 0-3(0-1)
Alanyaspor - Kasımpaşa 1-2(1-2)

Round 19 [15-18.01.2021]
Gençlerbirliği - Fatih Karagümrük 1-3(0-2)
Konyaspor - Göztepe 2-3(0-2)
Gaziantep - Kayserispor 2-1(1-0)
İstanbul Başakşehir - Sivasspor 1-1(1-1)
Antalyaspor - Trabzonspor 1-1(1-0)
Denizlispor - Hatayspor 0-2(0-0)
Malatyaspor - Çaykur Rizespor 4-1(0-1)
Beşiktaş - Galatasaray 2-0(0-0)
Fenerbahçe - Ankaragücü 3-1(2-0)
Kasımpaşa - Erzurumspor 1-2(0-1)

Round 20 [19-21.01.2021]
Göztepe - Gençlerbirliği 4-0(3-0)
Kayserispor - İstanbul Başakşehir 2-0(1-0)
Trabzonspor - Konyaspor 3-1(1-0)
Çaykur Rizespor - Gaziantep 3-0(1-0)
Hatayspor - Malatyaspor 1-2(0-0)
Galatasaray - Denizlispor 6-1(3-0)
Erzurumspor - Alanyaspor 1-1(1-0)
Fatih Karagümrük - Beşiktaş 1-4(0-1)
Ankaragücü - Kasımpaşa 1-0(1-0)
Sivasspor - Fenerbahçe 1-1(1-1)

Round 21 [23-25.01.2021]
Gençlerbirliği - Trabzonspor 1-2(0-1)
İstanb. Başakşehir - Çaykur Rizespor 1-1(0-0)
Konyaspor - Antalyaspor 0-0
Denizlispor - Fatih Karagümrük 1-2(0-1)
Malatyaspor - Galatasaray 0-1(0-0)
Beşiktaş - Göztepe 2-1(0-1)
Gaziantep - Hatayspor 1-1(1-0)
Kasımpaşa - Sivasspor 2-0(2-0)
Alanyaspor - Ankaragücü 4-3(1-2)
Fenerbahçe - Kayserispor 3-0(1-0)

Round 22 [29-31.01.2021]
Malatyaspor - Fatih Karagümrük 0-0
Gaziantep - Galatasaray 1-2(0-0)
Kasımpaşa - Kayserispor 0-1(0-0)
İstanbul Başakşehir - Hatayspor 1-5(0-3)
Fenerbahçe - Çaykur Rizespor 1-0(1-0)
Erzurumspor - Ankaragücü 1-0(0-0)
Alanyaspor - Sivasspor 3-1(2-0)
Denizlispor - Göztepe 2-1(1-0)
Gençlerbirliği - Antalyaspor 0-1(0-0)
Beşiktaş - Trabzonspor 1-2(1-1)

Round 23 [02-04.02.2021]
Hatayspor - Fenerbahçe 1-2(0-1)
Çaykur Rizespor - Kasımpaşa 1-1(0-0)
Galatasaray - İstanbul Başakşehir 3-0(1-0)
Sivasspor - Erzurumspor 0-0
Fatih Karagümrük - Gaziantep 2-0(0-0)
Kayserispor - Alanyaspor 1-0(1-0)
Antalyaspor - Beşiktaş 1-1(1-0)
Konyaspor - Gençlerbirliği 0-0
Göztepe - Malatyaspor 2-2(1-1)
Trabzonspor - Denizlispor 1-0(0-0)

Round 24 [06-08.02.2021]
Kasımpaşa - Hatayspor 1-4(0-1)
Alanyaspor - Çaykur Rizespor 2-1(1-1)
İst. Başakşehir - Fatih Karagümrük 0-1(0-0)
Fenerbahçe - Galatasaray 0-1(0-0)
Erzurumspor - Kayserispor 1-1(1-0)
Ankaragücü - Sivasspor 1-4(0-1)
Denizlispor - Antalyaspor 1-1(1-0)
Beşiktaş - Konyaspor 1-0(1-0)
Gaziantep - Göztepe 2-0(0-0)
Malatyaspor - Trabzonspor 0-2(0-0)

Round 25 [12-15.02.2021]
Çaykur Rizespor - Erzurumspor 0-2(0-0)
Kayserispor - Ankaragücü 0-0
Trabzonspor - Gaziantep 1-0(0-0)
Fatih Karagümrük - Fenerbahçe 1-2(0-1)
Konyaspor - Denizlispor 2-0(0-0)
Galatasaray - Kasımpaşa 2-1(1-0)
Göztepe - İstanbul Başakşehir 2-1(1-0)
Hatayspor - Alanyaspor 0-0
Gençlerbirliği - Beşiktaş 0-3(0-1)
Antalyaspor - Malatyaspor 1-1(1-1)

Round 26 [19-22.02.2021]
İstanbul Başakşehir - Trabzonspor 0-1(0-0)
Kasımpaşa - Fatih Karagümrük 3-2(1-1)
Denizlispor - Gençlerbirliği 1-0(1-0)
Malatyaspor - Konyaspor 2-3(2-0)
Alanyaspor - Galatasaray 0-1(0-1)
Erzurumspor - Hatayspor 1-3(0-2)
Gaziantep - Antalyaspor 0-0
Sivasspor - Kayserispor 2-0(1-0)
Fenerbahçe - Göztepe 0-1(0-1)
Ankaragücü - Çaykur Rizespor 1-1(1-1)

Round 27 [26-28.02.2021]
Gençlerbirliği - Malatyaspor 1-1(0-1)
Konyaspor - Gaziantep 0-0
Beşiktaş - Denizlispor 3-0(3-0)
Hatayspor - Ankaragücü 4-1(1-1)
Fatih Karagümrük - Alanyaspor 2-0(0-0)
Antalyaspor - İstanbul Başakşehir 0-0
Çaykur Rizespor - Sivasspor 0-0
Galatasaray - Erzurumspor 2-0(2-0)
Göztepe - Kasımpaşa 1-0(1-0)
Trabzonspor - Fenerbahçe 0-1(0-0)

Round 28 [02-04.03.2021]
Gaziantep - Gençlerbirliği 2-1(0-1)
Malatyaspor - Beşiktaş 0-1(0-0)
Erzurumspor - Fatih Karagümrük 2-2(1-1)
İstanbul Başakşehir - Konyaspor 1-1(0-0)
Sivasspor - Hatayspor 1-1(0-0)
Ankaragücü - Galatasaray 2-1(1-0)
Kayserispor - Çaykur Rizespor 2-1(0-0)
Alanyaspor - Göztepe 1-1(0-1)
Kasımpaşa - Trabzonspor 1-2(1-1)
Fenerbahçe - Antalyaspor 1-1(0-1)

Round 29 [06-08.03.2021]
Denizlispor - Malatyaspor 3-2(2-1)
Beşiktaş - Gaziantep 2-1(1-0)
Fatih Karagümrük - Ankaragücü 0-1(0-0)
Gençlerbirliği - İstanbul Başakşehir 0-1(0-0)
Hatayspor - Kayserispor 1-3(0-2)
Galatasaray - Sivasspor 2-1(1-2)
Antalyaspor - Kasımpaşa 1-1(1-0)
Trabzonspor - Alanyaspor 1-3(0-0)
Göztepe - Erzurumspor 3-1(1-0)
Konyaspor - Fenerbahçe 0-3(0-2)

Round 30 [12-15.03.2021]
İstanbul Başakşehir - Beşiktaş 2-3(0-1)
Sivasspor - Fatih Karagümrük 1-0(1-0)
Alanyaspor - Antalyaspor 4-0(2-0)
Çaykur Rizespor - Hatayspor 1-0(0-0)
Kayserispor - Galatasaray 0-3(0-1)
Ankaragücü - Göztepe 3-0(1-0)
Erzurumspor - Trabzonspor 0-0
Gaziantep - Denizlispor 2-0(0-0)
Fenerbahçe - Gençlerbirliği 1-2(1-1)
Kasımpaşa - Konyaspor 1-1(0-0)

Round 31 [19-21.03.2021]
Fatih Karagümrük - Kayserispor 3-0(1-0)
Galatasaray - Çaykur Rizespor 3-4(2-2)
Gençlerbirliği - Kasımpaşa 2-1(0-0)
Göztepe - Sivasspor 3-5(0-4)
Malatyaspor - Gaziantep 2-2(1-1)
Trabzonspor - Ankaragücü 4-1(3-1)
Antalyaspor - Erzurumspor 3-1(0-1)
Konyaspor - Alanyaspor 1-0(1-0)
Denizlispor - İstanbul Başakşehir 0-0
Beşiktaş - Fenerbahçe 1-1(0-0)

Round 32 [03-05.04.2021]
Kayserispor - Göztepe 1-1(1-0)
Çaykur Rizespor - Fatih Karagümrük 0-0
Sivasspor - Trabzonspor 0-0
Hatayspor - Galatasaray 3-0(2-0)
Erzurumspor - Konyaspor 1-2(1-2)
Alanyaspor - Gençlerbirliği 1-2(1-1)
Ankaragücü - Antalyaspor 1-0(0-0)
İstanbul Başakşehir - Malatyaspor 3-1(1-0)
Kasımpaşa - Beşiktaş 1-0(1-0)
Fenerbahçe - Denizlispor 1-0(0-0)

Round 33 [06-08.04.2021]
Göztepe - Çaykur Rizespor 2-0(0-0)
Fatih Karagümrük - Hatayspor 1-0(0-0)
Trabzonspor - Kayserispor 1-1(1-1)
Gençlerbirliği - Erzurumspor 1-1(1-0)
Konyaspor - Ankaragücü 1-1(0-0)
Antalyaspor - Sivasspor 2-4(1-2)
Beşiktaş - Alanyaspor 3-0(1-0)
Denizlispor - Kasımpaşa 1-1(0-0)
Gaziantep - İstanbul Başakşehir 2-0(1-0)
Malatyaspor - Fenerbahçe 1-1(1-1)

Round 34 [10-12.04.2021]
Hatayspor - Göztepe 2-3(0-2)
Çaykur Rizespor - Trabzonspor 0-0
Galatasaray - Fatih Karagümrük 1-1(0-0)
Sivasspor - Konyaspor 3-1(1-0)
Ankaragücü - Gençlerbirliği 2-1(0-0)
Kayserispor - Antalyaspor 0-1(0-1)
Erzurumspor - Beşiktaş 2-4(2-2)
Kasımpaşa - Malatyaspor 0-0
Alanyaspor - Denizlispor 3-2(0-1)
Fenerbahçe - Gaziantep 3-1(0-0)

Round 35 [16-18.04.2021]
Gençlerbirliği - Sivasspor 2-3(2-0)
Konyaspor - Kayserispor 0-0
Antalyaspor - Çaykur Rizespor 2-3(1-2)
Beşiktaş - Ankaragücü 2-2(1-0)
Denizlispor - Erzurumspor 2-3(0-1)
Trabzonspor - Hatayspor 1-1(1-0)
Malatyaspor - Alanyaspor 1-0(0-0)
Göztepe - Galatasaray 1-3(1-2)
Gaziantep - Kasımpaşa 2-2(0-1)
İstanbul Başakşehir - Fenerbahçe 1-2(1-1)

Round 36 [20-22.04.2021]
Çaykur Rizespor - Konyaspor 5-3(2-2)
Fatih Karagümrük - Göztepe 1-1(1-0)
Kayserispor - Gençlerbirliği 2-2(1-0)
Hatayspor - Antalyaspor 3-2(1-0)
Sivasspor - Beşiktaş 0-0
Ankaragücü - Denizlispor 1-1(1-1)
Erzurumspor - Malatyaspor 1-0(0-0)
Galatasaray - Trabzonspor 1-1(0-0)
Alanyaspor - Gaziantep 3-2(2-2)
Kasımpaşa - İstanbul Başakşehir 0-1(0-1)

Round 37 [23-25.04.2021]
Gençlerbirliği - Çaykur Rizespor 2-1(1-0)
Konyaspor - Hatayspor 0-0
Trabzonspor - Fatih Karagümrük 2-0(1-0)
Antalyaspor - Galatasaray 0-1(0-0)
Beşiktaş - Kayserispor 3-1(2-1)
Denizlispor - Sivasspor 1-1(0-1)
Malatyaspor - Ankaragücü 2-1(0-0)
Gaziantep - Erzurumspor 2-3(0-0)
İstanbul Başakşehir - Alanyaspor 0-0
Fenerbahçe - Kasımpaşa 3-2(3-1)

Round 38 [27-29.04.2021]
Hatayspor - Gençlerbirliği 3-1(1-0)
Göztepe - Trabzonspor 1-1(1-0)
Fatih Karagümrük - Antalyaspor 2-2(2-1)
Kayserispor - Denizlispor 6-3(3-1)
Çaykur Rizespor - Beşiktaş 2-3(0-1)
Galatasaray - Konyaspor 1-0(0-0)
Erzurumspor - İstanbul Başakşehir 1-2(1-0)
Sivasspor - Malatyaspor 1-0(0-0)
Alanyaspor - Fenerbahçe 0-0
Ankaragücü - Gaziantep 0-1(0-0)

Round 39 [01-03.05.2021]
Beşiktaş - Hatayspor 7-0(5-0)
Antalyaspor - Göztepe 2-3(1-1)
Denizlispor - Çaykur Rizespor 0-1(0-0)
Konyaspor - Fatih Karagümrük 5-1(1-1)
Gençlerbirliği - Galatasaray 0-2(0-1)
İstanbul Başakşehir - Ankaragücü 2-1(0-1)
Kasımpaşa - Alanyaspor 3-0(2-0)
Malatyaspor - Kayserispor 1-1(0-1)
Fenerbahçe - Erzurumspor 3-1(3-0)
Gaziantep - Sivasspor 0-1(0-1)

Round 40 [08.05.2021]
Ankaragücü - Fenerbahçe 1-2(1-1)
Çaykur Rizespor - Malatyaspor 0-4(0-2)
Erzurumspor - Kasımpaşa 0-1(0-0)
Galatasaray - Beşiktaş 3-1(2-1)
Göztepe - Konyaspor 0-1(0-0)
Hatayspor - Denizlispor 0-0(0-0)
Fatih Karagümrük - Gençlerbirliği 5-1(2-0)
Kayserispor - Gaziantep 0-0
Sivasspor - İstanbul Başakşehir 0-0
Trabzonspor - Antalyaspor 2-1(1-0)

Round 41 [11.05.2021]
Konyaspor - Trabzonspor 1-1(0-0)
Alanyaspor - Erzurumspor 2-3(2-1)
Beşiktaş - Fatih Karagümrük 1-2(0-1)
Denizlispor - Galatasaray 1-4(0-2)
Fenerbahçe - Sivasspor 1-2(0-1)
Gaziantep - Çaykur Rizespor 4-5(0-3)
Gençlerbirliği - Göztepe 5-3(1-2)
İstanbul Başakşehir - Kayserispor 0-0
Kasımpaşa - Ankaragücü 3-1(2-0)
Malatyaspor - Hatayspor 1-0(0-1)

Round 42 [15.05.2021]
Ankaragücü - Alanyaspor 0-1(0-1)
Antalyaspor - Konyaspor 0-0
Çaykur Rizespor - İstanb. Başakşehir 0-2(0-2)
Hatayspor - Gaziantep 0-1(0-0)
Fatih Karagümrük - Denizlispor 5-1(2-1)
Sivasspor - Kasımpaşa 2-1(1-0)
Galatasaray - Malatyaspor 3-1(0-1)
Göztepe - Beşiktaş 1-2(1-1)
Kayserispor - Fenerbahçe 1-2(1-0)
Trabzonspor - Gençlerbirliği 2-1(1-0)

				Total						Home					Away		
1.	**Beşiktaş JK İstanbul**	40	26	6	8	89 - 44	84	14	3	3	49 - 14	12	3	5	40 - 30
2.	Galatasaray SK İstanbul	40	26	6	8	80 - 36	84	12	6	2	45 - 17	14	0	6	35 - 19
3.	Fenerbahçe SK İstanbul	40	25	7	8	72 - 41	82	11	2	7	34 - 25	14	5	1	38 - 16
4.	Trabzonspor Kulübü	40	19	14	7	50 - 37	71	11	3	6	30 - 24	8	11	1	20 - 13
5.	Sivasspor Kulübü	40	16	17	7	54 - 43	65	7	9	4	19 - 15	9	8	3	35 - 28
6.	Hatayspor Antakya	40	17	10	13	62 - 53	61	10	4	6	35 - 23	7	6	7	27 - 30
7.	Alanyaspor	40	17	9	14	58 - 45	60	12	4	4	42 - 21	5	5	10	16 - 24
8.	Fatih Karagümrük SK	40	16	12	12	64 - 52	60	12	4	4	42 - 20	4	8	8	22 - 32
9.	Gaziantep FK	40	15	13	12	59 - 51	58	10	6	4	37 - 24	5	7	8	22 - 27
10.	Göztepe SK İzmir	40	13	12	15	59 - 59	51	8	5	7	35 - 27	5	7	8	24 - 32
11.	Konyaspor Kulübü	40	12	14	14	49 - 48	50	7	9	4	27 - 19	5	5	10	22 - 29
12.	İstanbul Başakşehir FK	40	12	12	16	43 - 55	48	5	8	7	26 - 28	7	4	9	17 - 27
13.	Çaykur Rizespor Kulübü	40	12	12	16	53 - 69	48	7	7	6	27 - 30	5	5	10	26 - 39
14.	Kasımpaşa Spor Kulübü İstanbul	40	12	10	18	47 - 57	46	9	4	7	26 - 25	3	6	11	21 - 32
15.	Yeni Malatya Spor Kulübü	40	10	15	15	49 - 53	45	7	8	5	26 - 22	3	7	10	23 - 31
16.	Antalyaspor Kulübü	40	9	17	14	41 - 55	44	6	7	7	24 - 28	3	10	7	17 - 27
17.	Kayserispor Kulübü	40	9	14	17	35 - 52	41	5	7	8	20 - 25	4	7	9	15 - 27
18.	Büyükşehir Belediye Erzurumspor (*Relegated*)	40	10	10	20	44 - 68	40	2	8	10	18 - 30	8	2	10	26 - 38
19.	MKE Ankaragücü (*Relegated*)	40	10	8	22	46 - 65	38	8	3	9	26 - 25	2	5	13	20 - 40
20.	Gençlerbirliği SK Ankara (*Relegated*)	40	10	8	22	44 - 76	38	6	5	9	27 - 35	4	3	13	17 - 41
21.	Denizlispor Kulübü (*Relegated*)	40	6	10	24	38 - 77	28	4	6	10	17 - 27	2	4	14	21 - 50

Top goalscorers:	
22 Aaron Salem Boupendza Pozzi (GAB)	*Hatayspor Antakya*
19 Mame Biram Diouf (SEN)	*Hatayspor Antakya*
19 Cyle Christopher Larin (CAN)	*Beşiktaş JK İstanbul*
17 Adem Büyük	*Yeni Malatya Spor Kulübü*

NATIONAL CUP
Türkiye Kupasi 2020/2021

Fourth Round [24-26.11.2020]

Gençlerbirliği SK Ankara - Kırşehir Belediyespor	1-0(0-0)	Yeni Malatya SK - Etimesgut Belediyespor Ankara	2-0(0-0)
Ankaraspor Kulübü - Muğlaspor Kulübü	1-1 aet; 0-3 pen	Eskişehirspor Kulübü – Kastamonu SK	2-0(0-0)
Boluspor Kulübü – Kahramanmarasspor AŞ	2-1(0-0,1-1)	İstanbulspor - Tarsus İdman Yurdu	0-1(0-1)
Giresunspor Kulübü - Niğde Anadolu FK	1-1(0-0; 8-7 pen	Hatayspor Antakya - Karacabey Belediyespor	2-2 aet; 4-5 pen
Denizlispor Kulübü - Turgutluspor	1-2(0-1)	Gaziantep FK - Serik Belediyespor	3-0(1-0)
Fatih Karagümrük SK - Esenler Erokspor	0-3(0-2)	Adana Demirspor Kulübü - Afjet Afyonspor	4-1(2-1)
Adanaspor AŞ - Sakaryaspor Kulübü Derneği	2-2 aet; 4-3 pen	Antalyaspor Kulübü – Pendik SK İstanbul	2-0(1-0)
Bursaspor Kulübü - 1922 Konyaspor Kulübü	1-0(1-0)	Çaykur Rizespor Kulübü - Uşak Spor	6-0(3-0)
Fenerbahçe SK İstanbul - Sivas Belediye Spor	4-0(1-0)	Büyükş. Belediye Erzurumspor - Ankara Demirspor	3-2(1-1,2-2)
Altınordu FK – Çorum FK Anonim Şirketi	3-0 *awarded*	Kasımpaşa Spor Kulübü İstanbul - 24 Erzincanspor	3-0(0-0)
Ankara Keçiörengücü SK - Kocaelispor Kulübü İzmit	1-2(0-1,1-1)	Kayserispor Kulübü - Hekimoğlu Trabzon	3-3 aet; 3-4 pen
Bandırmaspor - Darıca Gençlerbirliği SK	0-1(0-1)	Konyaspor Kulübü - Manisa FK	7-0(4-0)
Tuzlaspor - Sultanbeyli Belediyespor	5-1(3-0)	Göztepe SK İzmir - Kırklarelispor	2-0(0-0)

Fifth Round [15-17.12.2020]

Kasımpaşa Spor Kulübü İstanbul - Muğlaspor Kulübü	5-0(3-0)	Trabzonspor Kulübü - Adana Demirspor Kulübü	2-2 aet; 3-4 pen
Çaykur Rizespor Kulübü - Eskişehirspor Kulübü	3-0(3-0)	Fenerbahçe SK İstanbul - Karacabey Belediyespor	1-0(1-0)
Yeni Malatya Spor Kulübü - Hekimoğlu Trabzon	5-0(2-0)	Konyaspor Kulübü - Altınordu FK	3-1(1-1)
Göztepe SK İzmir - Bursaspor Kulübü	4-5(1-1,3-3)	Gençlerbirliği SK Ankara - Tuzlaspor	0-2(0-2)
Galatasaray SK İstanbul - Darıca Gençlerbirliği SK	1-0(1-0)	Antalyaspor Kulübü - Boluspor Kulübü	1-0(0-0)
Büyükşehir Belediye Erzurumspor - Esenler Erokspor	5-1(3-1)	Sivasspor Kulübü - Giresunspor Kulübü	1-0(0-0)
Gaziantep FK - Kocaelispor Kulübü İzmit	3-2(1-1)	İstanbul Başakşehir FK - Turgutluspor	7-0(1-0)
Alanyaspor - Adanaspor AŞ	5-1(2-1)	Beşiktaş JK İstanbul - Tarsus İdman Yurdu	3-1(2-0)

1/8-Finals [12-14.01.2021]

Bursaspor Kulübü - Antalyaspor Kulübü	0-3(0-3)	Tuzlaspor - İstanbul Başakşehir FK	1-5(1-2)
Sivasspor Kulübü - Adana Demirspor Kulübü	2-1(1-1,1-1)	Beşiktaş JK İstanbul - Çaykur Rizespor Kulübü	1-0(0-0)
Yeni Malatya Spor Kulübü - Galatasaray SK İstanbul	1-1 aet; 6-7 pen	Alanyaspor - Büyükşehir Belediye Erzurumspor	4-1(2-1)
Konyaspor Kulübü - Gaziantep FK	2-1(2-0)	Fenerbahçe SK İstanbul - Kasımpaşa SK İstanbul	1-0(0-0)

Quarter-Finals [09-11.02.2021]

Fenerbahçe SK İstanbul - İstanbul Başakşehir FK	1-2(0-1,1-1)	Sivasspor Kulübü - Antalyaspor Kulübü	0-1(0-0)
Galatasaray SK İstanbul - Alanyaspor	2-3(0-2)	Konyaspor Kulübü - Beşiktaş JK İstanbul	1-1 aet; 2-3 pen

Semi-Finals [16-17.03.2021]

Beşiktaş JK İstanbul - İstanbul Başakşehir FK	3-2(2-0,2-2)	Antalyaspor Kulübü - Alanyaspor	2-0(1-0)

18.05.2021; "Gürsel Aksel" Stadyumu, İzmir; Referee: Ali Palabıyık; Attendance: 0
Beşiktaş JK İstanbul - Antalyaspor Kulübü   **2-0(2-0)**

Beşiktaş: Utku Yuvakuran, Valentin Rosier, Fabrice N'Sakala, Welinton Souza Silva, Domagoj Vida, Josef de Souza Dias, Atiba Hutchinson (78.Bernard Mensah), Necip Uysal (65.Dorukhan Toköz), Georges-Kévin N'Koudou (65.Gökhan Töre), Cyle Christopher Larin, Rachid Ghezzal (86.Rıdvan Yılmaz). Trainer: Sergen Yalçın.

Antalyaspor: Ruud Boffin, Edinaldo Gomes Pereira „Naldo",Fedor Kudryashov, Bünyamin Balcı (70.Sidney Sam), Veysel Sarı, Nuri Şahin (79.Ufuk Akyol), Alfredo Gomes Ribeiro „Fredy", Hakan Özmert (46.Mert Yılmaz), Lukas Josef Podolski, Amilton Minervino da Silva (79.Dever Akeem Orgill), Gökdeniz Bayrakdar. Trainer: Kazım Ersun Yanal.

Goals: 1-0 Josef de Souza Dias (3), 2-0 Valentin Rosier (30).

THE CLUBS 2020/2021

Alanyaspor

Founded: 1948
Stadium: Bahçeşehir Okulları Stadyumu, Alanya (10,130)
Trainer: Çağdaş Atan   29.02.1980

Goalkeepers:	DOB	M	(s)	G
José Carlos Coentrão Marafona (POR)	28.05.1987	37		
Serkan Kırıntılı	15.02.1985	3		
Defenders:	**DOB**	**M**	**(s)**	**G**
Ahmet Gülay	13.01.2003	2	(2)	
Alpay Çelebi	04.04.1999		(1)	
Steven Caulker (ENG)	29.12.1991	32		3
Fatih Aksoy	06.11.1997	18	(7)	1
José Carlos Coentrão Marafona „Juanfran" (ESP)	11.09.1988	33	(4)	
François Moubandje (SUI)	21.06.1990	35		3
Tayfur Bingöl	11.01.1993	10	(16)	1
Giorgos Tzavellas (GRE)	26.11.1987	34	(1)	2
Midfielders:	**DOB**	**M**	**(s)**	**G**
Berkan Kutlu	25.01.1998	26	(12)	3
Ceyhun Gülselam	25.12.1987	6	(15)	1
Efkan Bekiroglu	14.09.1995	7	(16)	2

	DOB	M	(s)	G
Hasan Acar	16.12.1994	1	(3)	
Damian Kądzior (POL)	16.06.1992	5	(12)	
Salih Uçan	06.01.1994	29	(6)	2
Manolis Siopis (GRE)	14.05.1994	30	(5)	
Umut Güneş	16.03.2000	5	(11)	
Yusuf Özdemir	10.01.2001		(1)	
Forwards:	**DOB**	**M**	**(s)**	**G**
Khouma Babacar (SEN)	17.03.1993	21	(4)	8
Anastasios Bakasetas (GRE)	28.06.1993	18	(1)	7
Adam Fernando Bareiro Gamarra (PAR)	26.07.1996	20	(17)	5
Davidson da Luz Pereira (BRA)	05.03.1991	33	(6)	11
Hasan Ayaroğlu	22.03.1995		(1)	
Efecan Karaca	16.11.1989	24	(5)	2
Mustafa Pektemek	11.08.1988	11	(24)	7
Muhammed Uzun	24.04.2005		(1)	

Makina ve Kimya Endüstrisi Ankaragücü

Founded: 31.08.1910
Stadium: Eryaman Stadyumu, Ankara (20,560)
Trainer: Fuat Çapa   15.08.1968
[26.11.2020] Mustafa Dalcı   01.07.1973
[10.02.2021] Hikmet Karaman   09.03.1960

Goalkeepers:	DOB	M	(s)	G
Korcan Çelikay	31.12.1987	16	(1)	
Mert Topuz	19.02.2001	1		
Ricardo Henrique Schuck Friedrich (BRA)	18.02.1993	23	(1)	
Defenders:	**DOB**	**M**	**(s)**	**G**
Alperen Babacan	18.07.1997		(1)	
Atila Turan	10.04.1992	20	(6)	
Cebrail Karayel	15.08.1994	1	(2)	
Erdi Dikmen	06.02.1997	15	(10)	
Stelios Kitsiou (GRE)	28.09.1993	29	(1)	1
Ante Kulušić (CRO)	06.06.1986	18	(1)	
Michał Pazdan (POL)	21.09.1987	14	(1)	
Zvonimir Šarlija (CRO)	29.08.1996	31	(1)	1
Tiago Miguel Baía Pinto (POR)	01.02.1988	25	(3)	
Midfielders:	**DOB**	**M**	**(s)**	**G**
Ali Güneren	08.04.2000	3	(1)	
Alper Potuk	08.04.1991	19	(5)	2
Atakan Ridvan Cankaya	25.06.1998	20	(4)	1
Berke Gürbüz	27.01.2003		(1)	
Assane Dioussé (SEN)	20.09.1997	9	(11)	

	DOB	M	(s)	G
Ender Aygören	16.06.2000	2	(1)	
Ibrahim Akdağ	21.07.1991	17	(1)	2
Daniel Łukasik (POL)	28.04.1991	17	(6)	2
Şahverdi Çetin (GER)	28.09.2000	1	(16)	
Idriz Voca (KVX)	15.05.1997	13	(13)	
Forwards:	**DOB**	**M**	**(s)**	**G**
Luka Adžić (SRB)	17.09.1998	4	(7)	
Aliou Badji (SEN)	10.10.1997	10	(3)	2
Jonathan Bolingi Mpangi Merikani (COD)	30.06.1994	12	(2)	1
Torgeir Børven (NOR)	03.12.1991	18	(11)	10
Embiya Ayyildiz	05.07.2000	1	(4)	
Endri Çekiçi (ALB)	23.11.1996	27	(4)	2
Emre Güral	05.04.1989	8	(18)	4
Paulo Bartolome Hermenegildo Da Costa „Geraldo" (ANG)	23.11.1991	7	(9)	
İlhan Parlak	18.01.1987	1		
Saba Lobzhanidze (GEO)	18.12.1994	32	(5)	3
Mücahit Can Akçay	13.04.1998		(2)	
Orkan Çınar	29.01.1996	2	(15)	
Joseph Paintsil (GHA)	01.02.1998	24	(9)	11

Antalyaspor Kulübü

Founded: 02.07.1966
Stadium: Antalya Stadyumu, Antalya (32,537)
Trainer: Tamer Tuna   01.07.1976
[11.11.2020] Kazım Ersun Yanal   17.12.1961

Goalkeepers:	DOB	M	(s)	G
Ruud Boffin (BEL)	05.11.1987	35		
Ferhat Kaplan	07.01.1989	5		
Defenders:	**DOB**	**M**	**(s)**	**G**
Ali Eren İyican	26.06.1999	3	(5)	
Bahadir Öztürk	10.01.1995	4		
Bünyamin Balcı	31.05.2001	34	(1)	2
Eren Albayrak	23.04.1991	23	(10)	1
Ersan Gülüm	17.05.1987	9	(5)	
Fedor Kudryashov (RUS)	05.04.1987	35	(2)	
Mert Yilmaz	08.03.1999	10	(1)	
Edinaldo Gomes Pereira „Naldo" (BRA)	25.08.1988	28	(1)	2
Nazim Sangaré	30.05.1994	1		
Veysel Sarı	25.07.1988	28	(2)	4
Midfielders:	**DOB**	**M**	**(s)**	**G**
Doğukan Sinik	21.01.1999	9	(12)	1

	DOB	M	(s)	G
Alfredo Gomes Ribeiro „Fredy" (ANG)	27.03.1990	31	(1)	8
Hakan Özmert	03.06.1985	23	(5)	3
Mevlut Ekelik	16.12.2004		(3)	
Nuri Şahin	05.09.1988	33	(3)	
Ufuk Akyol	27.08.1997	6	(9)	
Forwards:	**DOB**	**M**	**(s)**	**G**
Amilton Minervino da Silva (BRA)	12.08.1989	33	(2)	5
Gökdeniz Bayrakdar	23.11.2001	18	(13)	6
Jean Armel Drolé (CIV)	18.08.1997	1	(1)	
Omar Imeri (ALB)	13.12.1999	5	(11)	
Adis Jahović (MKD)	18.03.1987	11	(4)	1
Paul Omo Mukairu (NGA)	18.01.2000	2	(1)	
Dever Akeem Orgill (JAM)	08.03.1990	16	(16)	1
Lukas Josef Podolski (GER)	04.06.1985	20	(11)	4
Sidney Sam (GER)	31.01.1988	14	(11)	3
Serdar Gürler	14.09.1991	3	(12)	

Beşiktaş Jimnastik Kulübü İstanbul

Founded: 04.03.1903
Stadium: Vodafone Park, İstanbul (42,590)
Trainer: Sergen Yalçın 05.10.1972

Goalkeepers:	DOB	M	(s)	G
Ersin Destanoğlu	01.01.2001	35		
Utku Yuvakuran	02.11.1997	5	(1)	
Defenders:	**DOB**	**M**	**(s)**	**G**
Erdoğan Kaya	27.03.2001		(1)	
Francisco Javier Montero Rubio (ESP)	14.01.1999	9	(4)	
Fabrice N'Sakala (COD)	21.07.1990	26	(3)	1
Rıdvan Yılmaz	21.05.2001	13	(5)	1
Valentin Rosier (FRA)	19.08.1996	33		1
Domagoj Vida (CRO)	29.04.1989	34		5
Welinton Souza Silva (BRA)	10.04.1989	34	(1)	1
Midfielders:	**DOB**	**M**	**(s)**	**G**
Dorukhan Toköz	21.05.1996	13	(18)	
Atiba Hutchinson (CAN)	08.02.1983	35	(1)	4
Josef de Souza Dias (BRA)	11.02.1989	32	(1)	2
Kartal Yılmaz	04.11.2000		(1)	
Adem Ljajić (SRB)	29.09.1991	14	(8)	2
Bernard Mensah (GHA)	17.10.1994	13	(18)	4
Necip Uysal	24.01.1991	16	(13)	1
Oğuzhan Özyakup	23.09.1992	8	(11)	3
Forwards:	**DOB**	**M**	**(s)**	**G**
Vincent Pate Aboubakar (CMR)	22.01.1992	25	(1)	15
Tyler Boyd (NZL)	30.12.1994	4		1
Cenk Tosun	07.06.1991	2	(1)	3
Gökhan Töre	20.01.1992	5	(15)	3
Güven Yalçın	18.01.1999	3	(10)	1
Ajdin Hasić (BIH)	07.10.2001	2	(6)	2
Hüseyin Atakan Üner	16.06.1999	1	(2)	
Cyle Christopher Larin (CAN)	17.04.1995	33	(5)	19
Jeremain Marciano Lens (NED)	24.11.1987		(2)	1
Mehmet Nayir	28.06.1993		(2)	
Georges-Kévin N'Koudou (FRA)	13.02.1995	15	(17)	8
Rachid Ghezzal (ALG)	09.05.1992	30	(1)	8

Büyükşehir Belediye Erzurumspor

Founded: 2010
Stadium: „Kazım Karabekir" Stadyumu, Erzurum (21,374)
Trainer: Mehmet Özdilek 01.04.1966
[02.12.2020] Hüseyin Çimşir 26.05.1979
[25.12.2020] Mesut Bakkal 19.03.1964
[23.03.2021] İsmail Kartal 15.06.1961
[30.03.2021] Yılmaz Vural 01.01.1953

Goalkeepers:	DOB	M	(s)	G
Batuhan Ünsal	03.06.1997		(1)	
Fabien Ceddy Farnolle (BEN)	05.02.1985	13		
Mehmet Bakırbaş	01.06.1996	2	(1)	
Kayacan Erdoğan	21.03.1988	5	(1)	
Jakub Szumski (POL)	06.03.1992	20		
Defenders:	**DOB**	**M**	**(s)**	**G**
Zakarya Bergdich (MAR)	07.01.1989	5	(1)	
Buğra Çağıran	01.01.1995	2	(10)	1
Bogdan Butko (UKR)	13.01.1991	7	(3)	
Cenk Alkılıç	09.12.1987	27	(2)	3
Manuel Marouane Da Costa Trindade Senoussi (MAR)	06.05.1986	14		2
Gökhan Kardeş	15.05.1997	10	(3)	
Hasan Hatipoğlu	19.07.1989	21	(5)	1
Kaan Kanak	06.10.1990	12	(1)	1
Arturo Rafael Mina Meza (ECU)	08.10.1990	9		
Murat Uçar	01.08.1991	25	(5)	
Mücahid Albayrak	30.07.1991	2	(5)	
Léo Schwechlen (FRA)	05.06.1989	27		1
Ibrahim Sissoko (CIV)	29.11.1991	6	(7)	1
Adolphe Teikeu Kamgang (CMR)	23.06.1990	17	(1)	
Midfielders:	**DOB**	**M**	**(s)**	**G**
Yaw Ackah (GHA)	01.06.1999	1	(1)	
Mahamadou Ba (MLI)	21.09.1999		(1)	
Petrus Boumal Mayega (CMR)	20.04.1993	25	(6)	
Aatif Chahechouhe (MAR)	02.07.1986	15		4
Mitchell Glenn Donald (SUR)	10.12.1988	8	(8)	1
Ibrahim Akdağ	21.07.1961	11	(1)	
Gabriel Obertan (FRA)	26.02.1989	24	(4)	2
Johanna Omolo (KEN)	31.07.1989	19	(1)	
Osman Çelik	27.11.1991	14	(13)	1
Özgür Sert	11.01.2001		(3)	1
Forwards:	**DOB**	**M**	**(s)**	**G**
Emrah Başsan	17.04.1992	25	(13)	7
Brahim Darri (NED)	14.09.1994		(4)	
Mostafa El Kabir (MAR)	05.10.1988	7	(4)	
Jugurtha Hamroun (ALG)	27.01.1989	2	(5)	
Rashad Muhammed (FRA)	25.09.1993	8	(5)	1
Arvydas Novikovas (LTU)	18.12.1990	22	(9)	4
Oltan Karakullukçu	07.07.1991	2	(16)	4
Ömer Şişmanoğlu	01.08.1989	1	(11)	
Elbasan Rashani (KVX)	09.05.1993	4	(8)	3
Ricardo Jorge Pires Gomes (CPV)	18.12.1991	27	(4)	5
Armando Sadiku (ALB)	27.05.1991	1	(4)	

Çaykur Rizespor Kulübü

Founded: 19.05.1953
Stadium: "Yeni Rize Şehir" Stadı, Rize (15,332)
Trainer: Stjepan Tomas (CRO) 03.06.1976
[25.01.2021] Marius Ninel Şumudică (ROU) 04.03.1971
[07.03.2021] Bülent Uygun 01.08.1971

Goalkeepers:	DOB	M	(s)	G
Gökhan Akkan	01.01.1995	32		
Tarik Çetin	08.01.1997	6	(2)	
Zafer Görgen	21.06.2000	2		
Defenders:	**DOB**	**M**	**(s)**	**G**
Alberk Koç	15.02.1997	1	(7)	
Dimitrios Chatziisaias (GRE)	21.09.1992	1		
Emir Dilaver (AUT)	07.05.1991	20	(3)	
Ismail Köybaşı	10.07.1989	14	(6)	3
Dario Melnjak (CRO)	31.10.1992	24	(5)	
Yassine Meriah (TUN)	02.07.1993	26	(2)	1
Mikola Morozyuk (UKR)	17.01.1988	30	(3)	
Murat Sağlam	10.04.1998		(1)	
Selim Ay	31.07.1991	18	(1)	
Montassar Talbi (TUN)	26.05.1998	20	(1)	1
Midfielders:	**DOB**	**M**	**(s)**	**G**
Abdullah Durak	01.04.1987	19	(10)	
Doğan Erdoğan	22.08.1996	9	(10)	1
Godfred Donsah (GHA)	07.06.1996	18	(6)	1
Damjan Đoković (CRO)	18.04.1990	19		2
Fabricio Santos de Jesus „Fabricio Baiano" (BRA)	13.06.1992	24	(4)	1
Dušan Jovančić (SRB)	19.10.1990		(4)	
Mithat Pala	15.08.2000		(5)	
Onur Bulut	16.04.1994	9	(9)	
Yasin Pehlivan (AUT)	05.01.1989	8	(9)	1
Fernando Henrique Boldrin „Rick" (BRA)	23.02.1989	22	(2)	6
Erik Sabo (SVK)	22.11.1991	14	(4)	2
Amedej Vetrih (SVN)	16.09.1990	2		
Forwards:	**DOB**	**M**	**(s)**	**G**
Emir Dede	02.05.2001		(1)	
Fernando Andrade dos Santos (BRA)	08.01.1993	16	(13)	2
Kemal Rüzgar	20.06.1995		(8)	1
Konrad Michalak (POL)	19.09.1997	12	(19)	1
Nadir Çiftçi	12.02.1992		(1)	
Loïc Rémy (FRA)	02.01.1987	10	(9)	7
Braian Samudio (PAR)	23.12.1995	27	(10)	8
Milan Škoda (CZE)	16.01.1986	21	(8)	9
Alexander Søderlund (NOR)	03.08.1987	6	(6)	1
Tunay Torun	21.04.1990	10	(7)	2

Denizlispor Kulübü

Founded:	26.05.1966		
Stadium:	Denizli Atatürk Stadyumu, Denizli (18,745)		
Trainer:	Robert Prosinecki (CRO)		12.01.1969
[18.12.2020]	Yalçın Koşukavak		14.10.1972
[29.01.2021]	Hakan Kutlu		14.01.1972
[19.04.2021]	Ali Tandoğan		25.12.1977

Goalkeepers:	DOB	M	(s)	G
Abdülkadir Sünger	24.05.2000	7		
Cenk Gönen	21.02.1988	16		
Hüseyin Altıntaş	11.09.1994	2	(1)	
Costel Fane Pantilimon (ROU)	01.02.1987	15		
Defenders:	**DOB**	**M**	**(s)**	**G**
Ayman Ben Mohamed (TUN)	08.12.1994	4	(3)	
Emirhan Kascioglu	01.01.2001	1	(2)	
Emre Yıldırım	01.01.2002	1		
Fabiano Leismann (BRA)	18.11.1991	31	(2)	
Görkem Can	04.05.2000	1	(2)	
Muhammet Özkal	26.11.1999	10	(8)	
Mustafa Yumlu	25.09.1987	26	(1)	
Oğuz Yilmaz	01.01.1993	15	(3)	1
Özer Özdemir	05.02.1998	17	(8)	1
Özgür Çek	03.01.1991	1	(6)	
Sakıb Aytaç	24.11.1991	15	(2)	1
Neven Subotić (SRB)	10.12.1988	4	(1)	1
Tiago Jorge Oliveira Lopes (POR)	04.01.1989	23	(1)	
Midfielders:	**DOB**	**M**	**(s)**	**G**
Ismaïl Aissati (MAR)	16.08.1988	11	(2)	
Alaattin Öner	30.03.2004		(1)	
Marvin Bakalorz (GER)	13.09.1989	24	(7)	1
Zakarya Bergdich (MAR)	07.01.1989	13	(4)	
Mikkel Morgenstar Pålssønn Diskerud (USA)	02.10.1990	14	(4)	2
Ferhat Erdoğan	18.06.2001		(1)	
Hüseyin Uslu	06.09.2002		(1)	
Kubilay Aktaş	29.01.1995	9	(5)	
Mehmet Ulaman	03.04.2003		(1)	
Muhammed Kiryolcu	21.02.2003		(1)	
Radosław Murawski (POL)	22.04.1994	30	(2)	1
Recep Nıyaz	02.08.1995	21	(7)	5
Federico Nicolas Varela (ARG)	18.04.1997	3	(4)	
Ahmed Yasin Gheni (IRQ)	22.04.1991	3	(4)	
Forwards:	**DOB**	**M**	**(s)**	**G**
Ali Kol	29.01.2001	4	(4)	
Mathieu Dossevi (TOG)	12.02.1988	4	(14)	
Hasan Ayaroğlu	22.03.1995	6	(13)	
Hugo Rodallega Martínez (COL)	25.07.1985	37		14
Mert Sarıkuş	31.05.2001		(1)	
Muris Mešanović (BIH)	06.07.1990	19	(17)	6
Hadi Sacko (MLI)	24.03.1994	16	(11)	2
Ángelo Nicolás Sagal Tapia (CHI)	18.04.1993	33	(2)	1
Veton Tusha (KVX)	29.12.2002	4	(7)	2

Fatih Karagümrük Spor Kulübü İstanbul

Founded:	1926		
Stadium:	Atatürk Olimpiyat Stadı, İstanbul (75,145)		
Trainer:	Şenol Can (BUL)		03.04.1983
[22.03.2021]	Francesco Farioli (ITA)		10.04.1989

Goalkeepers:	DOB	M	(s)	G
Aykut Özer	01.01.1993	8	(1)	
Emiliano Viviano (ITA)	01.12.1985	32		
Yavuz Aygün	27.06.1996		(1)	
Defenders:	**DOB**	**M**	**(s)**	**G**
Alparslan Erdem	11.12.1988	6	(5)	
Jure Balkovec (SVN)	09.09.1994	33		2
Gastón Matías Campi (ARG)	06.04.1991	14	(1)	
Vegar Hedenstad (NOR)	26.06.1991	15	(3)	1
Fatih Kuruçuk	21.01.1998	14		
Koray Altınay	11.10.1991	16	(9)	
Eric Lichaj (USA)	17.11.1988	8	(2)	
Ramazan Civelek	22.01.1996	9	(7)	
Enzo Pablo Roco Roco (CHI)	16.08.1992	30	(1)	3
Ervin Zukanović (BIH)	11.02.1987	17		3
Midfielders:	**DOB**	**M**	**(s)**	**G**
Aksel Aktas	15.07.1999	4	(5)	
Andrea Bertolacci (ITA)	11.01.1991	19	(3)	2
Lucas Rodrigo Biglia (ARG)	30.01.1986	34	(1)	3
Bora Kadıoğlu	25.06.2001		(1)	
Lucas Nahuel Castro (ARG)	09.04.1989	12	(4)	3
Efe Tatli	29.07.2002	5	(1)	
Emre Çolak	20.05.1991		(9)	
Murat Sarıgül	24.02.2001	1	(2)	
Badou N'Diaye (SEN)	27.10.1990	14		3
Erik Sabo (SVK)	22.11.1991	11	(1)	5
Zeki Yildirim	15.01.1991		(5)	
Forwards:	**DOB**	**M**	**(s)**	**G**
Kemal Ademi (SUI)	23.01.1996	4	(2)	
Vato Arveladze (GEO)	04.03.1998	2	(14)	
Fabio Borini (ITA)	29.03.1991	19	(1)	9
Aatif Chachouhe (MAR)	02.07.1986	5	(9)	
Brahim Darri (NED)	14.09.1994	4	(2)	
Jakup Jimmy Durmaz (SWE)	22.03.1989	15	(14)	3
Jeremain Lens (NED)	24.11.1987	7	(9)	3
Mevlüt Erdinç	25.02.1987	9	(21)	3
Muhammed Pehlivan	11.01.2000	1	(7)	
Alassane Ndao (SEN)	20.12.1996	35	(3)	11
Yannis Salibur (FRA)	24.01.1991	8	(14)	
Serhat Ahmetoğlu	05.02.2002	5	(3)	
Artur Sobiech (POL)	12.06.1990	24	(10)	9

Fenerbahçe Spor Kulübü İstanbul

Founded:	03.05.1907 (as Fenerbahçe Futbol Kulübü)		
Stadium:	Ülker („Şükrü Saracoğlu") Stadyumu, İstanbul (47,834)		
Trainer:	Erol Bulut		31.01.1975
[25.03.2021]	Emre Belözoglu		07.09.1980

Goalkeepers:	DOB	M	(s)	G
Ahmet Özdoğan	16.06.1998	1		
Altay Bayındır	14.04.1998	33		
Harun Tekin	17.06.1989	6		
Defenders:	**DOB**	**M**	**(s)**	**G**
Caner Erkin	04.10.1988	30	(4)	
Deniz Türüç	29.01.1993	2	(1)	
Gökhan Gönül	04.01.1985	19	(2)	2
Mathias Jattah-Njie Jørgensen (DEN)	23.04.1990	2		
Paolo Mauricio Lemos Merladey (URU)	28.12.1995	6	(2)	
Filip Novák (CZE)	26.06.1990	9	(9)	1
Sadık Çiftpinar	01.01.1993	5	(1)	
Nazim Sangaré	30.05.1994	18	(1)	1
Serdar Aziz	23.10.1990	26	(1)	3
Attila Szalai (HUN)	20.01.1998	21		3
Marcel Tisserand (COD)	10.01.1993	22	(3)	1
Midfielders:	**DOB**	**M**	**(s)**	**G**
Fatih Şanlitürk	01.01.2003		(2)	
İrfan Can Kahveci	15.07.1995	8	(4)	
Ismail Yüksek	26.01.1999		(1)	
Luiz Gustavo Dias (BRA)	23.07.1987	25	(9)	1
Mert Hakan Yandaş	19.08.1994	19	(15)	4
Ozan Tufan	23.03.1995	32	(5)	6
Ömer Beyaz	29.08.2003		(1)	
Mesut Özil (GER)	15.10.1988	8	(2)	
Dimitrios Pelkas (GRE)	26.10.1993	30	(2)	7
José Ernesto Sosa (ARG)	19.06.1985	23	(11)	4
Tolga Ciğerci	23.03.1992	2	(2)	
Forwards:	**DOB**	**M**	**(s)**	**G**
Kemal Ademi (SUI)	23.01.1996	1	(6)	
Papiss Demba Cissé (SEN)	03.06.1985	5	(20)	5
Michael Frey (SUI)	19.07.1994	1		
Sinan Gümüş (GER)	15.01.1994	5	(13)	3
Ferdi Erenay Kadıoğlu (NED)	07.10.1999	6	(20)	1
Bright Osayi-Samuel (NGA)	31.12.1997	11	(7)	1
Diego Perotti (ARG)	26.07.1988	2	(2)	3
Mbwana Ally Samatta (TAN)	23.12.1992	14	(13)	5
Mame Thiam (SEN)	09.10.1992	19	(11)	6
Enner Remberto Valencia Lastra (ECU)	04.11.1989	29	(5)	12

Galatasaray Spor Kulübü İstanbul

Founded: 30.10.1905 (*as Galata-Serai Football Club*)
Stadium: Türk Telekom Stadyumu, İstanbul (52,650)
Trainer: Fatih Terim   04.09.1953

Goalkeepers:	DOB	M	(s)	G
Fatih Öztürk	22.12.1986	8		
Néstor Fernando Muslera Micol (URU)	16.06.1986	22		
Okan Koçuk	27.07.1995	10		
Defenders:	**DOB**	**M**	**(s)**	**G**
Ryan Henk Donk (SUR)	30.03.1986	24	(8)	2
Omar Elabdellaoui (NOR)	05.12.1991	9	(1)	
Emin Bayram	02.04.2003		(2)	
Emre Taşdemir	08.08.1995	5	(4)	
Martin Linnes (NOR)	20.09.1991	15	(7)	
Christian Luyindama Nekadio (COD)	08.01.1994	19	(5)	
Marcos do Nascimento Teixeira "Marcão" (BRA)	05.06.1996	37		
Valentine James Ozornwafor (NGA)	01.06.1999		(1)	
Marcelo Josemir Saracchi Pintos (URU)	23.04.1998	26	(1)	
Şener Özbayraklı	23.01.1990	8	(4)	
DeAndre Roselle Yedlin (USA)	09.07.1993	9	(2)	1
Midfielders:	**DOB**	**M**	**(s)**	**G**
Bartuğ Elmaz	19.02.2003		(1)	
Younès Belhanda (MAR)	25.02.1990	17	(5)	6
Emre Akbaba	04.10.1992	18	(9)	5

	DOB	M	(s)	G
Peter Etebo Oghenekaro (NGA)	09.11.1995	14	(10)	
Gedson Carvalho Fernandes (POR)	09.01.1999	17		
Ömer Bayram	27.07.1991	13	(19)	
Jesse Tamunobaraboye Sekidika (NGA)	14.07.1996		(6)	1
Taylan Antalyalı	08.01.1995	30	(4)	1
Forwards:	**DOB**	**M**	**(s)**	**G**
Ali Yavuz Kol	29.01.2001		(4)	
Arda Turan	30.01.1987	21	(11)	4
Ryan Guno Babel (NED)	19.12.1986	16	(16)	7
Mbaye Diagne (SEN)	28.10.1991	10	(5)	9
Jakup Jimmy Durmaz (SWE)	22.03.1989		(1)	
Emre Kılınç	23.08.1994	27	(8)	4
Radamel Falcao García Zárate (COL)	10.02.1986	9	(8)	9
Sofiane Féghouli (ALG)	26.12.1989	16	(6)	2
Halil İbrahi Dervişoğlu	08.12.1999	6	(6)	3
Kerem Aktürkoglu	21.10.1998	6	(21)	6
Mostafa Mohamed Ahmed Abdalla (EGY)	28.11.1997	10	(6)	8
Oğulcan Cağlayan	22.03.1996	10	(8)	4
Henry Chukwuemeka Onyekuru (NGA)	05.06.1997	8	(6)	5

Gaziantep Futbol Kulübü

Founded: 1988 (*as Sankospor*)
Stadium: Gaziantep Arena, Gaziantep (33,502)
Trainer: Marius Ninel Şumudică (ROU) 04.03.1971
[20.01.2021] Ricardo Manuel Andrade e Silva Sá Pinto (POR) 10.10.1972

Goalkeepers:	DOB	M	(s)	G
Çağlar Akbaba	17.03.1995	1		
Günay Güvenc	25.06.1991	38		
Mustafa Bozan	23.08.2000	1		
Defenders:	**DOB**	**M**	**(s)**	**G**
Papy Djilobodji (SEN)	01.12.1988	36		2
Ertuğrul Ersoy	13.02.1997	4	(2)	
Iraneuton Sousa Morais Junior (BRA)	22.07.1986	16	(6)	
Jean-Armel Kana-Biyik (CMR)	03.07.1989	17		2
Oğuz Ceylan	15.12.1990	24	(4)	
Paweł Olkowski (POL)	13.02.1990	28	(3)	
Roderick Jefferson Gonçalves Miranda (POR)	30.03.1991	12	(1)	
Alin Dorinel Toşca (ROU)	14.03.1992	32		
Ulas Zengin	25.06.1997	1	(1)	
Midfielders:	**DOB**	**M**	**(s)**	**G**
André Alexandre Carreira Sousa (POR)	09.07.1990	13	(11)	1
Furkan Soyalp	12.06.1995	2	(20)	1
Güray Vural	11.06.1988	25	(8)	

	DOB	M	(s)	G
Jefferson Nogueira Junior (BRA)	22.01.1994	15	(15)	4
Zvonimir Kožulj (BIH)	15.11.1993	3	(15)	
Kubilay Aktaş	29.01.1995	2	(3)	
Alexandru Iulian Maxim (ROU)	08.07.1990	38		15
Mehmet Uğurlu	09.07.1988		(1)	
Osama Jabar Shafia Rashid (IRQ)	13.01.1992	12	(2)	
Abdul-Aziz Tetteh (GHA)	25.05.1990		(1)	
Amedej Vetrih (SVN)	16.09.1990	20	(7)	1
Forwards:	**DOB**	**M**	**(s)**	**G**
André Felipe Ribeiro de Souza (BRA)	27.09.1990	4	(15)	2
Bilal Başaçıkoğlu	26.03.1995		(12)	
Cenk Şahin	22.09.1994	1	(25)	1
Nouha Dicko (MLI)	14.05.1992	23	(5)	4
Kenan Özer	16.08.1987	22	(16)	5
Kevin Antonio Joel Gislain Mirallas y Castillo (BEL)	05.10.1987	26	(2)	5
Mirza Cihan	26.10.2000		(4)	
Muhammed Demir	10.01.1992	24	(7)	15

Gençlerbirliği Spor Kulübü Ankara

Founded: 14.03.1923
Stadium: Eryaman Stadyumu, Ankara (20,071)
Trainer: Márcio Ferreira Nobre / Mert Nobre (BRA) 06.11.1980
[19.11.2020] Mustafa Kaplan 02.09.1967
[01.02.2021] Mehmet Altıparmak 01.05.1969
[12.03.2021] Özcan Bizati 31.05.1968

Goalkeepers:	DOB	M	(s)	G
Bo Kristoffer Nordfeldt (SWE)	23.06.1989	36		
Übeyd Adiyaman	02.10.1997	4		
Defenders:	**DOB**	**M**	**(s)**	**G**
Abdullah Şahindere	09.06.2003		(1)	
Arda Kızıldağ	15.10.1998	27	(4)	1
Diego Ângelo de Oliveira (BRA)	12.02.1986	21	(4)	3
Halil Pehlivan	21.08.1993	17	(6)	
Mattias Johansson (SWE)	16.02.1992	29		3
Metehan Mert	01.05.1999	4	(1)	
Mustafa Akbaş	30.05.1990	5	(1)	
Ömürcan Artan	27.07.1999	7	(3)	
Pierre-Yves Polomat (MTQ)	27.12.1993	27	(6)	
Zargo Touré (SEN)	11.11.1989	22	(1)	
Midfielders:	**DOB**	**M**	**(s)**	**G**
Berat Ayberk Özdemir	23.05.1998	12	(1)	3
Dominik Furman (POL)	06.07.1992	14	(7)	

	DOB	M	(s)	G
Lucas Andrés Mugni (ARG)	12.01.1992	2	(8)	
Murat Yıldırım	18.05.1987	16	(14)	1
Mustafa Seyhan	23.04.1996	1	(8)	
Robert Ayrton Piris da Motta (PAR)	26.07.1994	36		6
Rahmetullah Berişbek	22.03.1999	3	(13)	
Soner Dikmen	01.09.1994	28	(6)	1
Forwards:	**DOB**	**M**	**(s)**	**G**
Floyd Ama Nino Ayité (TOG)	15.12.1988	17	(13)	3
Daniel João Santos Candeias (POR)	25.02.1988	35		4
Gökhan Altiparmak	20.04.2001	1	(14)	
İlker Karakaş	11.01.1999	3	(17)	1
Mustafa Çeçenoğlu	12.01.1994	1	(5)	
Sandro César Cordovil de Lima (BRA)	28.10.1990	15	(1)	2
Sefa Yilmaz	14.02.1990	24	(11)	4
Giovanni Sio (CIV)	31.03.1989	15	(7)	2
Srđan Spiridonović (AUT)	13.10.1993		(6)	
Sorin Bogdan Stancu (ROU)	28.06.1987	18	(6)	7

Göztepe Spor Kulübü İzmir

Founded: 14.06.1925 (*as Göztepe Gençlik Kulübü*)
Stadium: „Gürsel Aksel" Stadyumu, İzmir (25,035)
Trainer: Ilhan Palut — 12.11.1976
[21.01.2021] Ünal Karaman — 29.06.1966

Goalkeepers:	DOB	M	(s)	G
Arda Özçimen	08.01.2002	3		
Irfan Eğribayat	30.06.1998	35		
Balázs Megyeri (HUN)	31.03.1990	2		
Defenders:	**DOB**	**M**	**(s)**	**G**
Alpaslan Öztürk	16.07.1993	19	(2)	3
Atınç Nukan	20.07.1993	26	(1)	2
Berkan Emir	06.02.1988	33		1
Dženan Bureković (BIH)	29.05.1995	8	(12)	
Lamine Gassama (SEN)	20.10.1989	15	(3)	
Kerim Alıcı	24.06.1997	4	(1)	
Marko Mihojević (BIH)	21.04.1996	18	(3)	2
Murat Paluli	09.08.1994	25	(9)	
Cristian Chagas Tarouco "Titi" (BRA)	12.03.1988	12	(8)	1
Midfielders:	**DOB**	**M**	**(s)**	**G**
Efe Binici	04.02.2001		(4)	
Anderson Esiti (NGA)	24.05.1994	7	(13)	1
Kubilay Sönmez	17.06.1994	6	(13)	
José Márcio da Costa „Márcio Mossoró"(BRA)	04.07.1983	7	(7)	1

	DOB	M	(s)	G
Obinna Emmanuel Nwobodo (NGA)	29.11.1996	25	(6)	
André Biyogo Poko (GAB)	07.03.1993	1	(1)	
Soner Aydoğdu	05.01.1991	38	(1)	4
Yalçın Kayan	30.01.1999	12	(6)	2
Peter Žulj (AUT)	09.06.1993	8	(8)	4
Forwards:	**DOB**	**M**	**(s)**	**G**
Beykan Şimşek	01.01.1995	1	(5)	1
Burak Süleyman	01.09.1994		(5)	
Fousséni Diabaté (MLI)	18.10.1995	13	(5)	2
Guilherme Costa Marques (BRA)	21.05.1991	8	(2)	2
Halil Akbunar	09.11.1993	39	(1)	9
Aide Brown Ideye (NGA)	10.10.1988	11	(18)	2
Adis Jahović (MKD)	18.03.1987	11	(8)	6
Batuhan Kırdaroğlu	10.09.2000		(1)	
Stefano Napoleoni (ITA)	26.06.1986	3	(12)	1
Cherif Ndiaye (SEN)	23.01.1996	31	(8)	10
Zlatko Tripić (NOR)	02.12.1992	19	(12)	3
Yılmaz Basravi	13.03.2000		(1)	

Hatayspor Antakya

Founded: 1967
Stadium: „Yeni Hatay" Stadyumu, Antakya (25,000)
Trainer: Ömer Erdoğan — 03.05.1977

Goalkeepers:	DOB	M	(s)	G
Akin Alkan	26.07.1989	3	(1)	
Munir Mohamedi (MAR)	10.05.1989	37		
Defenders:	**DOB**	**M**	**(s)**	**G**
Jean-Claude Billong (FRA)	28.12.1993	23	(3)	
Burak Çamoğlu	05.10.1996	7	(10)	
Alexandros Katranis (GRE)	04.05.1998	17	(5)	1
Youssouf Koné (MLI)	05.07.1995	1	(5)	
Mesut Çaytemel	24.04.1984	18	(5)	
Pablo Renan dos Santos (BRA)	18.03.1992	35	(1)	1
Strahil Popov (BUL)	31.08.1990	37		
Soner Örnek	28.02.1989		(4)	
Yusuf Abdioğlu	14.10.1989	19	(2)	
Midfielders:	**DOB**	**M**	**(s)**	**G**
Rayane Aabid (FRA)	19.01.1992	39		3

	DOB	M	(s)	G
Abdurrahman Canlı	04.05.1997	1	(11)	1
Joseph Akomadi (GHA)	23.09.1999		(2)	
Gökhan Karadeniz	02.05.1990	6	(3)	
Muhammed Mert (BEL)	09.02.1995	2	(16)	
Rúben Tiago Rodrigues Ribeiro (POR)	01.08.1987	32	(5)	1
Isaac Sackey (GHA)	04.04.1994	16	(12)	
Adama Traoré II (MLI)	28.06.1995	29	(6)	
Forwards:	**DOB**	**M**	**(s)**	**G**
David Babajide Akintola (NGA)	13.01.1996	34	(1)	6
Aaron Salem Boupendza Pozzi (GAB)	07.08.1996	25	(11)	22
Mame Biram Diouf (SEN)	16.12.1987	38		19
Hélder Jorge Leal Rodrigues Barbosa (POR)	25.05.1987	2	(7)	1
Selim Ilgaz (FRA)	22.06.1995	15	(12)	2
Mohammed Kamara (LBR)	31.10.1997	4	(17)	1
Mirkan Aydın	08.07.1987		(8)	1

İstanbul Başakşehir Futbol Kulübü

Founded: 1990 (*as İstanbul Büyükşehir Belediyespor*); re-founded 2004
Stadium: Başakşehir „Fatih Terim" Stadyumu, Istanbul (17,156)
Trainer: Okan Buruk — 19.10.1973
[01.02.2021] Aykut Kocaman — 05.04.1965

Goalkeepers:	DOB	M	(s)	G
Mert Günok	01.03.1989	21		
Volkan Babacan	11.08.1988	19		
Defenders:	**DOB**	**M**	**(s)**	**G**
Boli Bolingoli-Mbombo (BEL)	01.07.1995	10	(2)	
Cemali Sertel	06.01.2000	5	(7)	
Alexandru Epureanu (MDA)	27.09.1986	29	(1)	
Hasan-Ali Kaldırım	09.12.1989	21	(3)	
Uilson de Souza Paula Junior "Junior Caiçara" (BRA)	27.04.1989	5	(3)	
Leonardo Campos Duarte Da Silva „Léo" (BRA)	17.07.1996	15	(2)	
Muhammed Sarıkaya	03.01.2002	2	(2)	
Carlos dos Santos Rodrigues „Ponck" (CPV)	13.01.1995	20	(3)	
Rafael Pereira da Silva (BRA)	09.07.1990	18	(3)	
Martin Škrtel (SVK)	15.12.1984	10		
Ravil Tagir	06.05.2003	3	(4)	
Uğur Uçar	05.04.1987	4	(6)	
Midfielders:	**DOB**	**M**	**(s)**	**G**
Danijel Aleksić (SRB)	30.04.1991	21	(10)	6
Okechukwu Godson Azubuike (NGA)	19.04.1997	6	(5)	
Berkay Özcan	15.02.1998	17	(16)	

	DOB	M	(s)	G
Deniz Türüç	29.01.1993	26	(5)	2
Giuliano Victor de Paula (BRA)	31.05.1990	13	(10)	2
İrfan Can Kahveci	15.07.1995	18		2
Mahmut Tekdemir	20.01.1988	24	(7)	1
Mehmet Topal	03.03.1986	13	(12)	2
Metin Karaal	15.01.2003			
Youssouf Nyange Ndayishimiye (BDI)	27.10.1998	7	(7)	
Tolga Ciğerci	23.03.1992	10	(4)	1
Forwards:	**DOB**	**M**	**(s)**	**G**
Demba Ba (SEN)	25.05.1985	17	(9)	5
Nacer Chadli (BEL)	02.08.1989	12	(6)	3
Enzo Crivelli (FRA)	06.02.1995	21	(15)	2
Enes Karakus	03.01.2001		(2)	
Antenor Junior Fernandes da Silva Vitoria (CHI)	10.04.1988	3	(6)	1
Fredrik Gulbrandsen (NOR)	10.09.1992	11	(18)	7
Kerim Frei Koyunlu	19.11.1993	1	(6)	
Mete-Kaan Demir	13.05.1998	1	(3)	
Ömer Şahiner	02.01.1992	14	(2)	2
Edin Višća (BIH)	17.02.1990	23	(3)	5

Kasımpaşa Spor Kulübü İstanbul

Founded: 15.01.1921
Stadium: „Recep Tayyip Erdoğan" Stadyumu, Istanbul (14,234)
Trainer: Mehmet Altıparmak — 01.05.1969
[16.11.2020] İrfan Buz — 15.04.1967
[28.11.2020] Fuat Çapa — 15.08.1968
[24.03.2021] Şenol Can (BUL) — 03.04.1983

Goalkeepers:	DOB	M	(s)	G
Erdem Canpolat (GER)	13.04.2001	1		
Ertuğrul Taşkıran	05.11.1989	18		
Ramazan Köse	12.05.1988	21		
Defenders:	**DOB**	**M**	**(s)**	**G**
Ahmet Oğuz	16.01.1993	1	(5)	
Tomáš Břečka (CZE)	12.05.1994	28	(1)	
Evren Elmalı	07.07.2000	3	(1)	
Feyzi Yıldırım	23.01.1996	3	(7)	1
Oussema Haddadi (TUN)	28.01.1992	34	(1)	
Florent Hadergjonaj (KVX)	31.07.1994	36		2
Julian Jeanvier (FRA)	31.03.1992	4		
Derrick Luckassen (NED)	03.07.1995	16		
Duško Tošić (SRB)	19.01.1985	8	(2)	
Midfielders:	**DOB**	**M**	**(s)**	**G**
Aytaç Kara	23.03.1993	26		4
Berat Kalkan	02.03.2003		(1)	
Kristijan Bistrović (CRO)	09.04.1998	16	(4)	
Doğucan Haspolat	11.02.2000	2	(10)	
Danny Drinkwater (ENG)	05.03.1990	6	(5)	
Haris Hajradinović (BIH)	18.02.1994	35	(1)	5
Hasan Yesilyurt	18.08.2000		(3)	
David Pavelka (CZE)	18.05.1991	3	(1)	
Loret Sadiku (ALB)	28.07.1991	28	(3)	
Tarkan Serbest	02.05.1994	15	(5)	
Mickaël Sylvain Tirpan	23.10.1993	13	(3)	1
Forwards:	**DOB**	**M**	**(s)**	**G**
Alan Lima Cariús (BRA)	04.04.1997	8	(7)	1
Anıl Koç	29.01.1995	7	(18)	1
Furkan Kulekci	28.06.2001		(4)	
Gerard Gohou (CIV)	29.12.1988	1		
Armin Hodžić (BIH)	17.11.1994	17	(4)	5
Isaac Kiese Thelin (SWE)	24.06.1992	21		9
Bengali-Fodé Koita (FRA)	21.10.1990	6	(7)	3
Gilbert Koomson (GHA)	09.09.1994	16	(6)	
Kevin Varga (HUN)	30.03.1996	23	(14)	4
Yasin Dülger	25.10.1995		(11)	
Yusuf Erdoğan	07.08.1992	24	(5)	9

Kayseri Spor Kulübü

Founded: 1966
Stadium: „Kadir Has" Stadyumu, Kayseri (32,864)
Trainer: Bayram Bektaş — 10.02.1974
[16.11.2020] Samet Aybaba — 02.09.1955
[11.01.2021] Dan Vasile Petrescu (ROU) — 22.12.1967
[24.02.2021] Uğur Kulaksız — 15.06.1974
[26.03.2021] Hamza Hamzaoğlu — 01.07.1970
[27.04.2021] Yalçın Koşukavak — 14.10.1972

Goalkeepers:	DOB	M	(s)	G
Doğan Alemdar	29.10.2002	28		
İsmail Çipe	05.01.1995	4	(1)	
Silviu Lung jr. (ROU)	04.06.1989	8		
Defenders:	**DOB**	**M**	**(s)**	**G**
Adem Doğan	05.10.2001		(1)	
Aziz Eraltay Behich (AUS)	16.12.1990	33	(1)	
Karahan Subaşı	01.01.1996	7	(6)	
Dimitrios Kolovetsios (GRE)	16.10.1991	35		1
Hugo Miguel de Almeida Costa Lopes (POR)	19.12.1986	12	(2)	
Oğuzhan Çapar	08.10.1996	2	(1)	
Nehuén Mario Paz (ARG)	28.04.1993	8	(4)	1
Cristian Ionuţ Săpunaru (ROU)	05.04.1984	20	(5)	
Uğur Demirok	08.07.1988	12	(4)	2
Midfielders:	**DOB**	**M**	**(s)**	**G**
Yaw Ackah (GHA)	01.06.1999	6	(5)	
Joseph Attamah (GHA)	22.05.1994	25	(6)	
Daniel Avramovski (MKD)	20.02.1995	24		2
Emre Demir	15.01.2004	1	(13)	
Gustavo Campanharo (BRA)	04.04.1992	22	(2)	1
Hasan Acar	16.12.1994	8	(2)	
Manuel Henriques Tavares Fernandes (POR)	05.02.1986	7	(4)	
Melih Okutan	01.07.1996		(11)	1
Karlo Muhar (CRO)	17.01.1996	15	(1)	1
Besard Šabović (SWE)	05.01.1998	3	(8)	
Anthony Chigaemezu Uzodimma (NGA)	17.04.1999	2		
Forwards:	**DOB**	**M**	**(s)**	**G**
Denis Alibec (ROU)	05.01.1991	8	(7)	2
İlhan Depe	10.09.1992		(4)	
İlhan Parlak	18.01.1987	19	(18)	9
Wilfried Kanga (FRA)	21.02.1998	11	(3)	2
Zoran Kvržić (BIH)	07.08.1988	34	(2)	1
Aaron Lennon (ENG)	16.04.1987	33	(3)	
Kevin Luckassen (NED)	27.07.1993	4	(10)	
Anton Maglica (CRO)	11.11.1991	4	(4)	1
Harisson Manzala Tusumgama (COD)	06.03.1994	1	(3)	
Muğdat Çelik	03.01.1990	8	(6)	1
Nurettin Korkmaz	27.06.2002		(11)	
Pedro Henrique Konzen Medina da Silva (BRA)	16.06.1990	29	(4)	8
Ömer Uzun (GER)	23.02.2000	1	(1)	
Ramazan Civelek	22.01.1996	5	(13)	
Mario Šitum (CRO)	04.04.1992	1		

Konyaspor Kulübü

Founded: 22.06.1922
Stadium: Konya Büyükşehir Stadyumu, Konya (42,000)
Trainer: Bülent Korkmaz — 24.11.1968
[14.09.2020] İsmail Kartal — 15.06.1961
[10.02.2021] İlhan Palut — 12.11.1976

Goalkeepers:	DOB	M	(s)	G
Eray Birniçan	20.07.1988	9		
Erten Ersu	21.04.1994	1		
Ibrahim Šehić (BIH)	02.09.1988	30		
Defenders:	**DOB**	**M**	**(s)**	**G**
Abdülkerim Bardakçı	07.09.1994	37		2
Adil Demirbağ	10.12.1997	15	(8)	
Ahmet Çalık	26.02.1994	27	(2)	1
Alper Uludağ	11.12.1990	3	(3)	
Marin Aničić (BIH)	17.08.1989	2		
Barış Yardımcı	14.08.1992	4	(1)	
Guilherme Haubert Sityá (BRA)	01.04.1990	36		1
Nejc Skubić (SVN)	13.06.1989	38	(1)	2
Uğur Demirok	08.07.1988	6	(3)	4
Midfielders:	**DOB**	**M**	**(s)**	**G**
Zymer Bytyqi (KVX)	11.09.1996	9	(10)	2
Ismaël Diomandé (CIV)	28.08.1992	10	(5)	1
Amir Hadžiahmetović (BIH)	08.03.1997	29	(5)	4
İsmail Güven	16.04.1994		(2)	
Marko Jevtović (SRB)	24.07.1993	34	(1)	4
Farouk Miya (UGA)	26.11.1997	9	(7)	
Musa Çağıran	17.11.1992	3	(13)	1
Oğuz Güçtekin	06.04.1999	7	(12)	
Ömer Şahiner	02.01.1992	10	(2)	
Amar Rahmanović (BIH)	13.05.1994	9	(9)	
Volkan Fındıklı	13.10.1990		(2)	
Forwards:	**DOB**	**M**	**(s)**	**G**
Ahmet Karademir	02.04.2004		(2)	
Sokol Çikalleshi (ALB)	27.07.1990	29	(6)	8
Erdon Daci (MKD)	04.07.1998	6	(13)	2
Samuel Emem Eduok (NGA)	31.01.1994		(4)	
Doğan Gölpek (NED)	27.11.1994		(2)	
Cristopher Paolo César Hurtado Huertas (PER)	27.07.1990	2	(4)	
Artem Kravets (UKR)	03.06.1989	16	(13)	9
Deni Milošević (BIH)	09.03.1995	23	(7)	2
Jesse Tamunobaraboye Sekidika (NGA)	14.07.1996	18	(1)	1
Levan Shengelia (GEO)	27.10.1995	18	(15)	5
Rogerio Conceicão do Rosario „Thuram" (BRA)	01.02.1991		(1)	

Sivasspor Kulübü

	Founded:	09.05.1967		
	Stadium:	4 Eylül Stadyumu, Sivas (27,532)		
	Trainer:	Rıza Çalımbay		02.02.1963

Goalkeepers:	DOB	M	(s)	G
Ali Vural	10.07.1990	19	(1)	
Muammer Yıldırım	14.09.1990	4		
Mamadou Samassa (MLI)	16.02.1990	17	(1)	
Defenders:	**DOB**	**M**	**(s)**	**G**
Ahmet Oğuz	16.01.1993	18		
Aaron Appindangoyé (GAB)	20.02.1992	13		
Barış Yardımcı	14.08.1992	4	(1)	
Samba Camara (FRA)	14.11.1992	23	(5)	
Alaaddin Okumuş	23.08.1995	1	(3)	
Caner Osmanpaşa	15.01.1988	27	(1)	1
Uğur Çiftçi	04.05.1992	33	(2)	
Ziya Erdal	05.01.1988	8	(11)	1
Midfielders:	**DOB**	**M**	**(s)**	**G**
Claudemir Domingues de Souza (BRA)	27.03.1988	20	(10)	
Isaac Cofie (GHA)	20.09.1991	16	(9)	

Fayçal Fajr (MAR)	01.08.1988	36		4
Hakan Arslan	18.07.1988	35	(1)	7
Kerem Kesgin	05.11.2000		(3)	
Marcelo Augusto Ferreira Teixeira (BRA)	13.10.1987	9	(1)	
Robin Yalcin (GER)	25.01.1994	30	(4)	1
Yasin Öztekin	19.03.1987	4	(9)	
Forwards:	**DOB**	**M**	**(s)**	**G**
Tyler Dominic Boyd (USA)	30.12.1994	8	(6)	5
Erdoğan Yeşilyurt	06.11.1993	23	(6)	3
Max-Alain Gradel (CIV)	30.11.1987	39		11
Jorge Félix Muñoz García (ESP)	22.08.1991	1	(16)	2
Tobi Olarenwaju Ayobami Kayode (NGA)	08.05.1993	18	(15)	6
Arouna Koné (CIV)	11.11.1983	2	(31)	1
Casimir Ninga (CHA)	17.05.1993	5	(11)	
Mustapha Yatabaré (MLI)	26.01.1986	27	(5)	10

Trabzonspor Kulübü

	Founded:	02.08.1967		
	Stadium:	„Şenol Güneş" Stadyumu, Trabzon (40,782)		
	Trainer:	Edward Ikem Newton (ENG)		13.12.1971
[31.10.2020]		Ihsan Derelioglu		15.11.1961
[10.11.2020]		Abdullah Avcı		31.07.1963

Goalkeepers:	DOB	M	(s)	G
Erce Kardeşler	14.03.1994	1		
Kağan Moradaoğlu	10.01.2003	1		
Uğurcan Çakır	05.04.1996	38		
Defenders:	**DOB**	**M**	**(s)**	**G**
Abdurahim Dursun	01.12.1998	1	(1)	
Atakan Gündüz	01.01.2001		(1)	
Gastón Matías Campi (ARG)	06.04.1991	2	(1)	1
Edgar Miguel Ié (POR)	01.05.1994	37	(1)	2
Faruk Genç	16.02.2000	1		
Majid Hosseini (IRN)	20.06.1996	7	(11)	
Hüseyin Türkmen	01.01.1998	11		
Kâmil Çörekçi	01.02.1992	9	(9)	
Marlon Rodrigues Xavier (BRA)	20.05.1997	36		
Serkan Asan	28.04.1999	25	(3)	1
Vitor Hugo Franchescoli de Souza (BRA)	20.05.1991	30		2
Midfielders:	**DOB**	**M**	**(s)**	**G**
Abdülkadir Ömür	25.06.1999	18	(5)	2
Abdülkadir Parmak	28.12.1994	23	(3)	

Ahmet Canbaz	27.04.1998		(4)	
Lewis Renard Baker (ENG)	25.04.1995	29	(5)	2
Berat Özdemir	23.05.1998	12	(3)	
Flávio Medeiros da Silva (BRA)	10.02.1996	17	(14)	1
Guilherme Costa Marques (BRA)	21.05.1991	1	(1)	
João Pedro da Silva Pereira (POR)	25.02.1984	6	(2)	
Hakan Yeşil	01.01.2002		(1)	
Yunus Mallı	24.02.1992	5	(8)	
Forwards:	**DOB**	**M**	**(s)**	**G**
Benik Tunani Afobe (COD)	12.02.1993	10	(18)	5
Anastasios Bakasetas (GRE)	28.06.1993	18	(1)	6
Bilal Başaçıkoğlu	26.03.1995	2	(4)	
Fousséni Diabaté (MLI)	18.10.1995	2	(4)	
Jorge Djaniny Tavares Semedo (CPV)	21.03.1991	25	(5)	8
Caleb Ekuban (GHA)	23.03.1994	32		10
Anthony Nnaduzor Nwakaeme (NGA)	21.03.1989	34		7
Stiven Ricardo Plaza Castillo (ECU)	11.03.1999		(2)	
Safa Kınalı	23.04.1999	1	(7)	
Yusuf Sari	20.11.1998	5	(21)	1

Yeni Malatya Spor Kulübü

	Founded:	1986		
	Stadium:	Yeni Malatya Stadyumu, Malatya (27,044)		
	Trainer:	Hamza Hamzaoğlu		01.07.1970
[17.03.2021]		İrfan Buz		15.04.1967

Goalkeepers:	DOB	M	(s)	G
Abdulsamed Damlu	25.07.1999	13		
Ertaç Özbir	25.10.1989	24		
Guido Herrera (ARG)	29.02.1992	3		
Defenders:	**DOB**	**M**	**(s)**	**G**
Bülent Cevahir	13.02.1992	4	(6)	
Issam Chebake (MAR)	12.10.1989	33	(2)	
Erkan Kaş	10.09.1991	2	(1)	
Teenage Hadebe (ZIM)	17.09.1995	25	(4)	2
Karim Hafez (EGY)	12.03.1996	31	(2)	
Murat Akça	13.07.1990	3	(1)	
Eric Ndizeye (BDI)	22.08.1999		(2)	
Semih Kaya	24.02.1991	31	(1)	1
Wallace Fortuna dos Santos (BRA)	14.10.1994	28	(1)	
Zeki Yavru	05.09.1991	23	(9)	2
Midfielders:	**DOB**	**M**	**(s)**	**G**
Ahmed Ildız	29.11.1996	19	(16)	1
Afriyie Acquah (GHA)	05.01.1992	30	(3)	2

Christian Alberto Cueva Bravo (PER)	23.11.1991	7	(1)	
Stephen Mallan Junior (SCO)	25.03.1996	8	(9)	2
Youssouf Nyange Ndayishimiye (BDI)	27.10.1998	15	(4)	2
Fernando Zuqui (ARG)	27.11.1991	1	(10)	
Forwards:	**DOB**	**M**	**(s)**	**G**
Adem Büyük	30.08.1987	34		17
Berk Yıldız	09.01.1996		(2)	
Doğukan Emeksiz	05.01.2000		(1)	
Moryké Fofana (CIV)	23.11.1991	20	(11)	2
Kubilay Kanatsızkuş	28.03.1997	20	(9)	5
Jody Lukoki (COD)	15.11.1992	3	(7)	
Aly Mallé (MLI)	03.04.1998		(7)	
Mustafa Eskihellac	05.05.1997	11	(14)	2
Olcay Şahan	26.05.1987	4	(8)	
Benjamin Tetteh (GHA)	10.07.1997	27	(5)	5
Jetmir Topalli (KVX)	07.02.1998	1	(12)	1
Umut Bulut	15.03.1983	20	(11)	2

1. Adana Demirspor Kulübü (*Promoted*)	34	21	7	6	64	-	27	70
2. Giresunspor Kulübü (*Promoted*)	34	21	7	6	54	-	25	70
3. Samsunspor (*Promotion Play-offs*)	34	20	10	4	58	-	30	70
4. İstanbulspor (*Promotion Play-offs*)	34	19	7	8	62	-	34	64
5. Altay SK İzmir (*Promotion Play-offs*)	34	20	3	11	66	-	39	63
6. Altınordu FK İzmir (*Promotion Play-offs*)	34	17	9	8	58	-	45	60
7. Ankara Keçiörengücü SK	34	17	7	10	49	-	28	58
8. Ümraniyespor Kulübü	34	14	9	11	46	-	43	51
9. Tuzlaspor	34	14	5	15	46	-	53	47
10. Bursaspor Kulübü	34	14	4	16	56	-	57	46
11. Bandırmaspor	34	12	6	16	48	-	51	42
12. Boluspor Kulübü	34	12	6	16	38	-	41	42
13. Balıkesirspor Kulübü Derneği	34	9	8	17	35	-	53	35
14. Adanaspor AŞ	34	9	7	18	44	-	55	34
15. Menemenspor Kulübü İzmir	34	7	13	14	38	-	62	34
16. Ahkisar SK (*Relegated*)	34	8	6	20	36	-	59	30
17. Ankaraspor Kulübü (*Relegated*)	34	6	8	20	33	-	61	26
18. Eskişehirspor Kulübü[1] (*Relegated*)	34	1	8	25	23	-	91	8

[1] *3 points deducted*

Promotion Play-offs

Semi-Finals [17-22.05.2021]	Altay SK İzmir - İstanbulspor	3-2(3-1)	1-0(0-0)
	Altınordu FK İzmir - Samsunspor	1-0(0-0)	2-2(1-0)

Final [26.05.2021]	Altay SK İzmir - Altınordu FK İzmir	1-0(0-0)

Altay SK İzmir promoted to the 2021/2022 Süper Lig.

INTERNATIONAL MATCHES
(16.07.2020 – 15.07.2021)

03.09.2020	Sivas	Turkey - Hungary	0-1(0-0)	(UNL)
06.09.2020	Beograd	Serbia - Turkey	0-0	(UNL)
07.10.2020	Köln	Germany - Turkey	3-3(1-0)	(F)
11.10.2020	Moskva	Russia - Turkey	1-1(1-0)	(UNL)
14.10.2020	İstanbul	Turkey - Serbia	2-2(0-1)	(UNL)
11.11.2020	İstanbul	Turkey - Croatia	3-3(2-1)	(F)
15.11.2020	İstanbul	Turkey - Russia	3-2(2-1)	(UNL)
18.11.2020	Budapest	Hungary - Turkey	2-0(0-0)	(UNL)
24.03.2021	İstanbul	Turkey - Netherlands	4-2(2-0)	(WCQ)
27.03.2021	Malaga	Norway - Turkey	0-3(0-2)	(WCQ)
30.03.2021	İstanbul	Turkey - Latvia	3-3(2-1)	(WCQ)
27.05.2021	Alanya	Turkey - Azerbaijan	2-1(2-1)	(F)
31.05.2021	Antalya	Turkey - Guinea	0-0	(F)
03.06.2021	Paderborn	Turkey - Moldova	2-0(0-0)	(F)
11.06.2021	Roma	Turkey - Italy	0-3(0-0)	(EC)
16.06.2021	Bakı	Turkey - Wales	0-2(0-1)	(EC)
20.06.2021	Bakı	Switzerland - Turkey	3-1(2-0)	(EC)

03.09.2020   TURKEY - HUNGARY   **0-1(0-0)**   2nd UEFA Nations League B, Group 3
Yeni 4 Eylül Stadyumu, Sivas; Referee: Artur Manuel Soares Dias (Portugal); Attendance: 0
TUR: Uğurcan Çakır, Kaan Ayhan, Çağlar Söyüncü, Merih Demiral, Cengiz Umut Meraş, Mert Müldür, Hakan Çalhanoğlu, Emre Kılınç (76.Kenan Karaman), Mert Hakan Yandaş (58.İrfan Can Kahveci), Burak Yılmaz (Cap), Ahmed Kutucu (46.Yusuf Yazıcı). Trainer: Şenol Güneş.

06.09.2020   SERBIA - TURKEY   **0-0**   2nd UEFA Nations League B, Group 3
Stadion "Rajko Mitić", Beograd; Referee: Aleksei Kulbakov (Belarus); Attendance: 0
TUR: Fehmi Mert Günok, Hasan Ali Kaldırım, Mehmet Zeki Çelik (46.Nazim Sangaré), Çağlar Söyüncü, Ozan Muhammed Kabak, Mahmut Tekdemir, Ozan Tufan (Cap), Yusuf Yazıcı, Orkun Kökçü (60.Cengiz Ünder), Kenan Karaman, Enes Ünal (78.Burak Yılmaz). Trainer: Şenol Güneş.

07.10.2020   GERMANY - TURKEY   **3-3(1-0)**   Friendly International
RheinEnergie Stadion, Köln; Referee: Benoît Bastien (France); Attendance: 300
TUR: Fehmi Mert Günok, Hasan Ali Kaldırım, Kaan Ayhan (75.Ozan Muhammed Kabak), Nazim Sangaré, Merih Demiral, Efecan Karaca (70.Mahmut Tekdemir), Okay Yokuşlu (64.Kenan Karaman), Emre Kılınç (46.Cengiz Ünder), Ozan Tufan (Cap), Yusuf Yazıcı (46.Dorukhan Toköz), Enes Ünal (85.Abdülkadir Ömür). Trainer: Şenol Güneş.
Goals: Ozan Tufan (49), Efecan Karaca (67), Kenan Karaman (90+4).

11.10.2020   RUSSIA - TURKEY   **1-1(1-0)**   2nd UEFA Nations League B, Group 3
VTB Arena, Moskva; Referee: Matej Jug (Slovenia); Attendance: 5,019
TUR: Fehmi Mert Günok, Mehmet Zeki Çelik, Merih Demiral, Cengiz Umut Meraş, Ozan Muhammed Kabak, Mahmut Tekdemir (80.Okay Yokuşlu), Efecan Karaca (46.Cengiz Ünder), Hakan Çalhanoğlu (90+2.Yusuf Yazıcı), Ozan Tufan, Burak Yılmaz (Cap) (90+2.Enes Ünal), Kenan Karaman (81.Abdülkadir Ömür). Trainer: Şenol Güneş.
Goal: Kenan Karaman (62).

14.10.2020   TURKEY - SERBIA   **2-2(0-1)**   2nd UEFA Nations League B, Group 3
Türk Telekom Stadyumu, İstanbul; Referee: Georgi Kabakov (Bulgaria); Attendance: 519
TUR: Fehmi Mert Günok, Hasan Ali Kaldırım (27.Cengiz Umut Meraş), Mehmet Zeki Çelik, Merih Demiral, Mahmut Tekdemir (76.Yusuf Yazıcı), Okay Yokuşlu, Hakan Çalhanoğlu, Ozan Tufan, Cengiz Ünder (86.Abdülkadir Ömür), Burak Yılmaz (Cap) [*sent off 90+1*], Kenan Karaman. Trainer: Şenol Güneş.
Goals: Hakan Çalhanoğlu (57), Ozan Tufan (76).

11.11.2020   TURKEY - CROATIA   **3-3(2-1)**   Friendly International
Vodafone Park, İstanbul; Referee: Slavko Vinčić (Slovenia); Attendance: 0
TUR: Uğurcan Çakır, Caner Erkin (46.Ömer Bayram), Nazim Sangaré, Yıldırım Mert Çetin (46.Yusuf Yazıcı), Ozan Muhammed Kabak, Okay Yokuşlu, Deniz Türüç, Cengiz Ünder (77.Efecan Karaca), Dorukhan Toköz (54.Merih Demiral), Orkun Kökçü (34.Berkay Özcan), Cenk Tosun (Cap) (63.Enes Ünal). Trainer: Şenol Güneş.
Goals: Cenk Tosun (23 penalty), Deniz Türüç (41), Cengiz Ünder (58).

15.11.2020   TURKEY - RUSSIA   **3-2(2-1)**   2nd UEFA Nations League B, Group 3
„Şükrü Saracoğlu" Stadyumu, İstanbul; Referee: Szymon Marciniak (Poland); Attendance: 0
TUR: Fehmi Mert Günok, Caner Erkin, Kaan Ayhan, Mehmet Zeki Çelik (64.Ozan Muhammed Kabak), Merih Demiral, Okay Yokuşlu, Hakan Çalhanoğlu (86.Yusuf Yazıcı), Ozan Tufan (86.Mahmut Tekdemir), Cengiz Ünder (64.Deniz Türüç), Cenk Tosun (Cap) (80.İrfan Can Kahveci), Kenan Karaman. Trainer: Şenol Güneş.
Goals: Kenan Karaman (26), Cengiz Ünder (32), Cenk Tosun (52 penalty).

18.11.2020   HUNGARY - TURKEY   **2-0(0-0)**   2nd UEFA Nations League B, Group 3
Puskás Aréna, Budapest; Referee: Ivan Kružliak (Slovakia); Attendance: 0
TUR: Fehmi Mert Günok, Caner Erkin, Nazim Sangaré, Merih Demiral, Ozan Muhammed Kabak, Mahmut Tekdemir (88.Kaan Ayhan), Hakan Çalhanoğlu, İrfan Can Kahveci (55.Yusuf Yazıcı), Ozan Tufan (71.Berkay Özcan), Cenk Tosun (Cap) (71.Deniz Türüç), Kenan Karaman. Trainer: Şenol Güneş.

24.03.2021　TURKEY - NETHERLANDS　　　　4-2(2-0)　　　　22nd FIFA WC. Qualifiers
Atatürk Olimpiyat Stadı, İstanbul; Referee: Michael Oliver (England); Attendance: 0
TUR: Uğurcan Çakır, Mehmet Zeki Çelik, Çağlar Söyüncü, Cengiz Umut Meraş, Ozan Muhammed Kabak, Okay Yokuşlu, Hakan Çalhanoğlu (78.Enes Ünal), Ozan Tufan (64.Taylan Antalyalı), Yusuf Yazıcı (64.Caner Erkin), Burak Yılmaz (Cap) (90.Deniz Türüç), Kenan Karaman (78.Kaan Ayhan). Trainer: Şenol Güneş.
Goals: Burak Yılmaz (15, 34 penalty), Hakan Çalhanoğlu (46), Burak Yılmaz (81).

27.03.2021　NORWAY - TURKEY　　　　0-3(0-2)　　　　22nd FIFA WC. Qualifiers
Estadio La Rosaleda, Málaga; Referee: Alejandro José Hernández Hernández (Spain); Attendance: 0
TUR: Uğurcan Çakır, Kaan Ayhan, Çağlar Söyüncü, Cengiz Umut Meraş, Mert Müldür, Okay Yokuşlu, Hakan Çalhanoğlu (69.Taylan Antalyalı), Ozan Tufan (86.Ozan Muhammed Kabak), Yusuf Yazıcı (69.Caner Erkin), Burak Yılmaz (Cap) (86.Halil Akbunar), Kenan Karaman (72.Enes Ünal). Trainer: Şenol Güneş.
Goals: Ozan Tufan (4), Çağlar Söyüncü (28), Ozan Tufan (59).

30.03.2021　TURKEY - LATVIA　　　　3-3(2-1)　　　　22nd FIFA WC. Qualifiers
Atatürk Olimpiyat Stadı, İstanbul; Referee: Daniel Stefański (Poland); Attendance: 223
TUR: Uğurcan Çakır, Caner Erkin (83.Orkun Kökçü), Çağlar Söyüncü, Mert Müldür, Ozan Muhammed Kabak, Okay Yokuşlu, Hakan Çalhanoğlu (65.Cengiz Umut Meraş), Ozan Tufan (83.Deniz Türüç), Yusuf Yazıcı (66.Taylan Antalyalı), Burak Yılmaz (Cap), Kenan Karaman (73.Enes Ünal). Trainer: Şenol Güneş.
Goals: Kenan Karaman (2), Hakan Çalhanoğlu (33), Burak Yılmaz (52 penalty).

27.05.2021　TURKEY - AZERBAIJAN　　　　2-1(2-1)　　　　Friendly International
Bahçeşehir Okulları Stadyumu, Alanya; Referee: Genc Nuza (Kosovo); Attendance: 400
TUR: Altay Bayındır (73.Gökhan Akkan), Kaan Ayhan (Cap), Çağlar Söyüncü, Merih Demiral, Mert Müldür, Rıdvan Yılmaz (46.Efecan Karaca), Taylan Antalyalı, Halil Akbunar (84.Ozan Tufan), Cengiz Ünder (46.Kerem Aktürkoğlu), Orkun Kökçü (67.Abdülkadir Ömür), Halil İbrahi Dervişoğlu (67.Enes Ünal). Trainer: Şenol Güneş.
Goals: Halil İbrahi Dervişoğlu (34), Kaan Ayhan (45).

31.05.2021　TURKEY - GUINEA　　　　0-0　　　　Friendly International
Antalya Stadyumu, Antalya; Referee: Əliyar Ağayev (Azerbaijan); Attendance: 500
TUR: Fehmi Mert Günok, Kaan Ayhan (Cap), Mert Müldür, Ozan Muhammed Kabak (86.Efecan Karaca), Rıdvan Yılmaz, Mahmut Tekdemir (86.Taylan Antalyalı), İrfan Can Kahveci (46.Kenan Karaman), Cengiz Ünder, Dorukhan Toköz (65.Halil İbrahim Dervişoğlu), Abdülkadir Ömür (46.Orkun Kökçü), Enes Ünal (65.Okay Yokuşlu). Trainer: Şenol Güneş.

03.06.2021　TURKEY - MOLDOVA　　　　2-0(0-0)　　　　Friendly International
Benteler-Arena, Paderborn (Germany); Referee: Sascha Stegemann (Germany); Attendance: 0
TUR: Uğurcan Çakır, Mehmet Zeki Çelik, Çağlar Söyüncü (46.Kaan Ayhan), Merih Demiral, Cengiz Umut Meraş, Okay Yokuşlu (79.Taylan Antalyalı), Hakan Çalhanoğlu (69.Ozan Muhammed Kabak), Ozan Tufan (46.Cengiz Ünder), Yusuf Yazıcı (68.Orkun Kökçü), Burak Yılmaz (Cap) (84.Mert Müldür), Kenan Karaman. Trainer: Şenol Güneş.
Goals: Burak Yılmaz (58), Cengiz Ünder (77).

11.06.2021　TURKEY - ITALY　　　　0-3(0-0)　　　　16th EC. Group Stage.
Stadio Olimpico, Roma; Referee: Danny Desmond Makkelie (Netherlands); Attendance: 12,916
TUR: Uğurcan Çakır, Mehmet Zeki Çelik, Çağlar Söyüncü, Merih Demiral, Cengiz Umut Meraş, Okay Yokuşlu (65.İrfan Can Kahveci), Hakan Çalhanoğlu, Ozan Tufan (64.Kaan Ayhan), Yusuf Yazıcı (46.Cengiz Ünder), Burak Yılmaz (Cap), Kenan Karaman (76.Halil İbrahi Dervişoğlu). Trainer: Şenol Güneş.

16.06.2021　TURKEY - WALES　　　　0-2(0-1)　　　　16th EC. Group Stage.
Bakı Olimpiya Stadionu, Bakı (Azerbaijan); Referee: Artur Manuel Ribeiro Soares Dias (Wales); Attendance: 19,762
TUR: Uğurcan Çakır, Kaan Ayhan, Mehmet Zeki Çelik, Çağlar Söyüncü, Cengiz Umut Meraş (72.Mert Müldür), Okay Yokuşlu (46.Merih Demiral), Hakan Çalhanoğlu, Ozan Tufan (46.Yusuf Yazıcı), Burak Yılmaz (Cap), Kenan Karaman (75.Halil İbrahi Dervişoğlu), Cengiz Ünder (83.İrfan Can Kahveci). Trainer: Şenol Güneş.

20.06.2021　SWITZERLAND - TURKEY　　　　3-1(2-0)　　　　16th EC. Group Stage.
Bakı Olimpiya Stadionu, Bakı (Azerbaijan); Referee: Slavko Vinčić (Slovenia); Attendance: 17,138
TUR: Uğurcan Çakır, Kaan Ayhan (64.Okay Yokuşlu), Mehmet Zeki Çelik, Çağlar Söyüncü, Merih Demiral, Mert Müldür, Hakan Çalhanoğlu (86.Dorukhan Toköz), İrfan Can Kahveci (80.Orkun Kökçü), Ozan Tufan (64.Yusuf Yazıcı), Burak Yılmaz (Cap), Cengiz Ünder (80.Kenan Karaman). Trainer: Şenol Güneş.
Goal: İrfan Can Kahveci (62).

NATIONAL TEAM PLAYERS
(16.07.2020 – 15.07.2021)

Name	DOB	Caps	Goals	2020/2021:	Club
Goalkeepers					
ALTAY Bayındır	14.04.1998	1	0	2021:	Fenerbahçe SK İstanbul
FEHMI Mert Günok	01.03.1989	22	0	2020/2021:	İstanbul Başakşehir FK
GÖKHAN Akkan	01.01.1995	1	0	2021:	Çaykur Rizespor Kulübü
UĞURCAN Çakır	05.04.1996	11	0	2020/2021:	Trabzonspor Kulübü
Defenders					
CANER Erkin	04.10.1988	59	2	2020/2021:	Fenerbahçe SK İstanbul
ÇAĞLAR Söyüncü	23.05.1996	38	2	2020/2021:	Leicester City FC (ENG)
HASAN Ali Kaldırım	09.12.1989	35	1	2020:	İstanbul Başakşehir FK
KAAN Ayhan	10.11.1994	40	4	2020/2021:	US Sassuolo Calcio (ITA)
MERIH Demiral	05.03.1998	24	0	2020/2021:	Juventus FC Torino (ITA)
Yildırım MERT Çetin	01.01.1997	2	0	2020:	Hellas Verona FC (ITA)
MERT Müldür	03.04.1999	10	0	2020/2021: 23.09.2020->	US Sassuolo Calcio (ITA) Fenerbahçe SK İstanbul
OZAN Muhammed Kabak	25.03.2000	12	0	2020:	FC Schalke 04 Gelsenkirchen (GER)
ÖMER Bayram	27.07.1991	10	0	2020:	Galatasaray SK İstanbul
RIDVAN Yılmaz	21.05.2001	2	0	2021:	Beşiktaş JK İstanbul
Nazim SANGARÉ	30.05.1994	6	0	2020:	Antalyaspor Kulübü
Cengiz UMUT Meraş	20.12.1995	15	0	2020/2021:	Le Havre AC (FRA)
Mehmet ZEKI Çelik	17.02.1997	23	2	2020/2021:	Lille OSC (FRA)
Midfielders					
ABDÜLKADIR Ömür	25.06.1999	9	0	2020/2021:	Trabzonspor Kulübü
BERKAY Özcan	15.02.1998	6	0	2020:	İstanbul Başakşehir FK
DENIZ Türüç	29.01.1993	11	2	2020/2021:	İstanbul Başakşehir FK
DORUKHAN Toköz	21.05.1996	10	1	2020/2021:	Beşiktaş JK İstanbul
EFECAN Karaca	16.11.1989	7	1	2020/2021:	Alanyaspor
EMRE Kılınç	23.08.1994	4	0	2020/2021:	Galatasaray SK İstanbul
HAKAN Çalhanoğlu	08.02.1994	59	13	2020/2021:	AC Milan (ITA)
HALIL Akbunar	09.11.1993	2	0	2021:	Göztepe SK İzmir
İRFAN Can Kahveci	15.06.1995	21	1	2020: 31.01.2021->	İstanbul Başakşehir FK Fenerbahçe SK İstanbul
KENAN Karaman	05.03.1994	25	5	2020/2021:	TSV Fortuna Düsseldorf (GER)
KEREM Aktürkoğlu	21.10.1998	1	0	2021:	Galatasaray SK İstanbul
MAHMUT Tekdemir	20.01.1988	22	0	2020/2021:	İstanbul Başakşehir FK
MERT Hakan Yandaş	19.08.1994	1	0	2020:	Fenerbahçe SK İstanbul
OKAY Yokuşlu	09.03.1994	37	1	2021: 01.02.2021->	RC Celta de Vigo (ESP) West Bromwich Albion FC (ENG)
ORKUN Kökçü	29.12.2000	7	0	2020/2021:	Feyenoord Rotterdam (NED)
OZAN Tufan	23.03.1995	63	9	2020/2021:	Fenerbahçe SK İstanbul
TAYLAN Antalyalı	08.01.1995	6	0	2021:	Galatasaray SK İstanbul
YUSUF Yazıcı	29.01.1997	34	1	2020/2021:	Lille OSC (FRA)
Forwards					
AHMED Kutucu	01.03.2000	2	0	2020:	FC Schalke 04 Gelsenkirchen (GER)
BURAK Yılmaz	15.07.1985	70	29	2020/2021:	Lille OSC (FRA)
CENGIZ Ünder	14.07.1997	32	9	2020/2021:	Leicester City FC (ENG)
CENK Tosun	07.06.1991	45	18	2020:	Everton FC Liverpool (ENG)
ENES Ünal	10.05.1997	22	2	2020/2021:	Getafe CF (ESP)
HALIL İbrahi Dervişoğlu	08.12.1999	4	1	2021:	Galatasaray SK İstanbul

Trainer

ŞENOL Güneş [from 18.03.2019]	01.06.1952			29 M; 14 W; 9 D; 6 L; 49-32 Complete record as trainer of Turkey: 79 M; 37 W; 22 D; 20 L; 121-82 (16.08.2000 – 19.11.2003) & (from 18.03.2019)	

UKRAINE

UKRAINE

The Country:
Україна (Ukraine)
Capital: Kyiv
Surface: 603,628 km²
Inhabitants: 41,527,205 [2021]
Time: UTC+2

The FA:
Федерація Футболу України [Football Federation of Ukraine]
Provulok Laboratornyi, 7-A P.O. Box 55, 01133 Kyiv
Tel: +380 44 521 0521
Founded: 1991
Member of FIFA since: 1992
Member of UEFA since: 1992
Website: uaf.ua

NATIONAL TEAM RECORDS

RECORDS

First international match:	29.04.1992, Uzhgorod:	Ukraine – Hungary 1-3
Most international caps:	Anatoliy Tymoshchuk	- 144 caps (2000-2016)
Most international goals:	Andriy Shevchenko	- 48 goals / 111 caps (1995-2012)

UEFA EUROPEAN CHAMPIONSHIP		FIFA WORLD CUP		OLYMPIC TOURNAMENTS	
1960	-	1930	-	1908	-
1964	-	1934	-	1912	-
1968	-	1938	-	1920	-
1972	-	1950	-	1924	-
1976	-	1954	-	1928	-
1980	-	1958	-	1936	-
1984	-	1962	-	1948	-
1988	-	1966	-	1952	-
1992	-	1970	-	1956	-
1996	Qualifiers	1974	-	1960	-
2000	Qualifiers	1978	-	1964	-
2004	Qualifiers	1982	-	1968	-
2008	Qualifiers	1986	-	1972	-
2012	Final Tournament (Group Stage)	1990	-	1976	-
2016	Final Tournament (Group Stage)	1994	Did not enter	1980	-
2020	Final Tournament (Quarter-Finals)	1998	Qualifiers	1984	-
		2002	Qualifiers	1988	-
		2006	Final Tournament (Quarter-Finals)	1992	-
		2010	Qualifiers	1996	Qualifiers
		2014	Qualifiers	2000	Qualifiers
		2018	Qualifiers	2004	Qualifiers
				2008	Qualifiers
				2012	Qualifiers
				2016	Qualifiers

*was part of Soviet Union between 1930-1990

UEFA NATIONS LEAGUE

2018/2019	League B (promoted to League A)
2020/2021	League A (relegated to League B)

FIFA CONFEDERATIONS CUP 1992-2017

None

UKRAINIAN CLUB HONOURS IN EUROPEAN CLUB COMPETITIONS:

European Champion Clubs' Cup (1956-1992) / UEFA Champions League (1993-2021)		
None		
Fairs Cup (1858-1971) / UEFA Cup (1972-2009) / UEFA Europa League (2010-2021)		
FK Shakhtar Donetsk	1	2008/2009
UEFA Super Cup (1972-2020)		
FK Dinamo Kyiv*	1	1975
European Cup Winners' Cup 1961-1999*		
FK Dinamo Kyiv*	2	1974/1975, 1985/1986
*represented the Soviet Union		

*defunct competition

NATIONAL COMPETITIONS
TABLE OF HONOURS

Championship of cities

	CHAMPIONS
1921	Kharkiv
1922	Kharkiv
1923	Kharkiv
1924	Kharkiv
1925	*No competition*
1926	*No competition*
1927	Kharkiv
1928	Kharkiv
1929	*No competition*
1930	*No competition*
1931	Kyiv
1932	Kharkiv
1933	*No competition*
1934	Kharkiv
1935	Dnipropetrovsk

Championship of the Proletarian Sports Society Dinamo

	CHAMPIONS
1929	Dinamo Kharkiv
1931	Dinamo Kyiv
1932	Dinamo Kharkiv
1933	Dinamo Kyiv
1934	Dinamo Kharkiv
1935	Dinamo Kyiv

UKRAINIAN SSR (SOVIET ERA) CHAMPIONS

Year	Champion	Year	Champion	Year	Champion
1936	Zavod Ordzhonikidze Kramators'k	1958	Arsenal Kyiv	1975	Krivbas Kryvyi Rih
1937	Spartak Dnipropetrovs'k	1959	Avangard Zhovti Vody	1976	Krivbas Kryvyi Rih
1938	Dzerzhynec Voroshylovgrad	1960	Metalurg Zaporizhzhya	1977	SKA Odesa
1939	Lokomotyv Zaporizhzhya	1961	Chornomorets Odesa	1978	Metalist Kharkiv
1940	Lokomotyv Zaporizhzhya	1962	Trudovi Rezervy Voroshylovgrad	1979	Kolos Nikopil
1941-1945	*No competition*	1963	SKA Odesa	1980	SKA Kyiv
1946	Spartak Uzhgorod	1964	Lokomotyv Vinnytsa	1981	Krivbas Kryvyi Rih
1947	Bil'shovyk Mukacheve	1965	SKA L'viv	1982	Bukovyna Chernivtsi
1948	Torpedo Odesa	1966	Avangard Zhovti Vody	1983	SKA Kyiv
1949	Pishevik Odesa	1967	Avtomobilist Zhytomyr	1984	Nyva Vinnytsa
1950	Spartak Uzhgorod	1968	Avangard Ternopil	1985	Tavrya Simferopil
1951	Budinok ofitseriv Kyiv	1969	Spartak Ivano-Frankivs'k	1986	Zarya Voroshylovgrad
1952	Metalurg Zaporizhzhya	1970	Metalurg Zaporizhzhya	1987	Tavrya Simferopil
1953	Spartak Uzhgorod	1971	Krivbas Kryvyi Rih	1988	Bukovyna Chernivtsi
1954	Mashinobudivnik Kyiv	1972	Spartak Ivano-Frankivs'k	1989	Volyn Lutsk
1955	Spartak Stanislav	1973	Tavria Simferopil	1990	Bukovyna Chernivtsi
1956	Shakhtar Stakhanov	1974	Sudostroitel Nikolaev	1991	Karpaty Lviv
1957	SKVO Odesa				

	CHAMPIONS	CUP WINNERS	BEST GOALSCORERS	
1992	SC Tavriya Simferopol	FK Chornomorets Odesa	Yuriy Hudymenko (SC Tavriya Simferopol)	12
1992/1993	FK Dinamo Kyiv	FK Dinamo Kyiv	Serhiy Husyev (FK Chornomorets Odesa)	17
1993/1994	FK Dinamo Kyiv	FK Chornomorets Odesa	Tymerlan Huseinov (FK Chornomorets Odesa)	18
1994/1995	FK Dinamo Kyiv	FK Shakhtar Donetsk	Arsen Avakov (TJK, FK Metalurh Zaporizhya)	21
1995/1996	FK Dinamo Kyiv	FK Dinamo Kyiv	Tymerlan Huseinov (FK Chornomorets Odesa)	20
1996/1997	FK Dinamo Kyiv	FK Shakhtar Donetsk	Oleh Matveyev (FK Shakhtar Donetsk)	21
1997/1998	FK Dinamo Kyiv	FK Dinamo Kyiv	Serhiy Rebrov (FK Dinamo Kyiv)	22
1998/1999	FK Dinamo Kyiv	FK Dinamo Kyiv	Andriy Shevchenko (FK Dinamo Kyiv)	18
1999/2000	FK Dinamo Kyiv	FK Dinamo Kyiv	Maksim Shatskikh (UZB, FK Dinamo Kyiv)	20
2000/2001	FK Dinamo Kyiv	FK Shakhtar Donetsk	Andrij Vorobej (FK Shakhtar Donetsk)	21
2001/2002	FK Shakhtar Donetsk	FK Shakhtar Donetsk	Serhiy Shyshchenko (FK Metalurh Donetsk)	12
2002/2003	FK Dinamo Kyiv	FK Dinamo Kyiv	Maksim Shatskikh (UZB, FK Dinamo Kyiv)	22
2003/2004	FK Dinamo Kyiv	FK Shakhtar Donetsk	Giorgi Demetradze (GEO, FK Metalurh Donetsk)	18
2004/2005	FK Shakhtar Donetsk	FK Dinamo Kyiv	Olexandr Kosyrin (FK Chornomorets Odesa)	14
2005/2006	FK Shakhtar Donetsk	FK Dinamo Kyiv	Evaeverson Lemos da Silva "Brandão" (FK Shakhtar Donetsk) Emmanuel Osei Okoduwa (NGA, FK Arsenal Kyiv)	15
2006/2007	FK Dinamo Kyiv	FK Dinamo Kyiv	Oleksandr Hladkyi (FK Kharkhiv)	13
2007/2008	FK Shakhtar Donetsk	FK Shakhtar Donetsk	Marko Dević (FK Metalist Kharkhiv)	19
2008/2009	FK Dinamo Kyiv	FK Vorskla Poltava	Olexander Kowpak (SC Tavriya Simferopol)	17
2009/2010	FK Shakhtar Donetsk	SC Tavriya Simferopol	Artem Milevsky (FK Dinamo Kyiv)	17
2010/2011	FK Shakhtar Donetsk	FK Shakhtar Donetsk	Yevhen Seleznyov (FC Dnipro Dnipropetrovsk)	17
2011/2012	FK Shakhtar Donetsk	FK Shakhtar Donetsk	Yevhen Seleznyov (FK Shakhtar Donetsk) Maicon Pereira de Oliveira (VRA, FK Volyn Lutsk)	14
2012/2013	FK Shakhtar Donetsk	FK Shakhtar Donetsk	Henrikh Mkhitaryan (ARM, FK Shakhtar Donetsk)	25
2013/2014	FK Shakhtar Donetsk	FK Dinamo Kyiv	Luiz Adriano de Souza da Silva (FK Shakhtar Donetsk)	20
2014/2015	FK Dinamo Kyiv	FK Dinamo Kyiv	Alex Teixeira Santos (BRA, FK Shakhtar Donetsk) Eric Cosmin Bicfalvi (ROU, FK Volyn Lutsk)	17
2015/2016	FK Dinamo Kyiv	FK Shakhtar Donetsk	Alex Teixeira Santos (BRA, FK Shakhtar Donetsk)	22
2016/2017	FK Shakhtar Donetsk	FK Shakhtar Donetsk	Andriy Yarmolenko (FK Dinamo Kyiv)	15

2017/2018	FK Shakhtar Donetsk	FK Shakhtar Donetsk	Facundo Ferreyra (ARG, FK Shakhtar Donetsk)	21
2018/2019	FK Shakhtar Donetsk	FK Shakhtar Donetsk	Aluísio Chaves Ribeiro Moraes Júnior (FK Shakhtar Donetsk)	19
2019/2020	FK Shakhtar Donetsk	FK Dinamo Kyiv	Aluísio Chaves Ribeiro Moraes Júnior (FK Shakhtar Donetsk)	20
2020/2021	FK Dinamo Kyiv	FK Dinamo Kyiv	Vladyslav Kulach (FK Vorskla Poltava)	15

NATIONAL CHAMPIONSHIP
Ukrainian Premier League 2020/2021
(21.08.2020 – 09.05.2021)

Round 1 [21-23.08.2020]
Olimpik Donetsk - Dinamo Kyiv 1-4(1-2)
Shakhtar Donetsk - Kolos Kovalivka 3-1(0-0)
Desna Chernihiv - Zorya Luhansk 3-1(0-1)
FK Oleksandriya - FK Mariupol 4-1(1-0)
Inhulets Petrove - SC Dnipro-1 1-1(1-1)
Vorskla Poltava - Rukh Lviv 5-2(4-0)
FK Lviv - FK Mynai 1-0(1-0) [21.04.2021]

Round 2 [11-13.09.2020]
Dinamo Kyiv - Desna Chernihiv 0-0
SC Dnipro-1 - Olimpik Donetsk 1-3(0-1)
Kolos Kovalivka - FK Lviv 4-0(1-0)
FK Mynai - FK Oleksandriya 1-0(1-0)
Zorya Luhansk - FK Mariupol 0-1(0-0)
Vorskla Poltava - Inhulets Petrove 2-0(1-0)
Rukh Lviv - Shakhtar Don. 1-1(0-0) [23.09.]

Round 3 [18-20.09.2020]
SC Dnipro-1 - FK Mariupol 1-2(0-1)
FK Oleksandriya - Vorskla Poltava 0-2(0-1)
Inhulets Petrove - Desna Chernihiv 1-1(0-0)
Dinamo Kyiv - FK Lviv 3-1(0-0)
Olimpik Donetsk - FK Mynai 3-0(1-0)
Zorya Luhansk - Shakhtar Donetsk 2-2(2-1)
Rukh Lviv - Kolos Kovalivka 1-2(0-2)

Round 4 [26-27.09.2020]
FK Mynai - Dinamo Kyiv 0-4(0-2)
Vorskla Poltava - FK Mariupol 0-0
FK Oleksandriya - SC Dnipro-1 4-1(2-0)
FK Lviv - Zorya Luhansk 0-5(0-5)
Shakhtar Donetsk - Olimpik Donetsk 2-0(0-0)
Desna Chernihiv - Rukh Lviv 3-1(2-1)
Kolos Kovalivka - Inhulets Petrove 0-0

Round 5 [03-04.10.2020]
SC Dnipro-1 - Vorskla Poltava 2-2(1-1)
Rukh Lviv - FK Lviv 0-0
Inhulets Petrove - FK Mynai 1-1(1-1)
Olimpik Donetsk - FK Oleksandriya 3-2(3-0)
Desna Chernihiv - Shakhtar Donetsk 2-2(2-1)
Dinamo Kyiv - Zorya Luhansk 1-1(0-0)
Kolos Kovalivka - FK Mariupol 1-0(0-0)

Round 6 [17-18.10.2020]
FK Mynai - FK Mariupol 0-1(0-0)
Rukh Lviv - Dinamo Kyiv 0-2(0-1)
Shakhtar Donetsk - FK Lviv 5-1(4-1)
Zorya Luhansk - Kolos Kovalivka 1-1(1-0)
Olimpik Donetsk - Vorskla Poltava 0-1(0-0)
FK Oleksandriya - Inhulets Petrove 4-3(4-1)
SC Dnipro-1 - Desna Chernihiv 2-0(1-0)

Round 7 [24-25.10.2020]
Shakhtar Donetsk - Vorskla Poltava 1-1(1-1)
Olimpik Donetsk - Desna Chernihiv 0-2(0-2)
Dinamo Kyiv - FK Oleksandriya 1-0(1-0)
FK Lviv - SC Dnipro-1 1-3(1-2)
Inhulets Petrove - FK Mariupol 1-1(1-1)
Kolos Kovalivka - FK Mynai 2-2(1-1)
Zorya Luhansk - Rukh Lviv 4-0(0-0)

Round 8 [30.10.-01.11.2020]
Shakhtar Donetsk - FK Mariupol 4-1(2-0)
Kolos Kovalivka - Olimpik Donetsk 1-2(0-1)
FK Oleksandriya - Desna Chernihiv 2-2(0-1)
SC Dnipro-1 - Dinamo Kyiv 1-2(1-2)
FK Mynai - Rukh Lviv 0-0
FK Lviv - Vorskla Poltava 1-0(1-0)
Inhulets Petrove - Zorya Luhansk 1-1(0-0)

Round 9 [06-08.11.2020]
SC Dnipro-1 - Kolos Kovalivka 0-2(0-1)
Olimpik Donetsk - FK Mariupol 3-3(1-2)
FK Oleksandriya - FK Lviv 1-0(0-0)
Desna Chernihiv - FK Mynai 1-0(0-0)
Rukh Lviv - Inhulets Petrove 2-2(0-1)
Dinamo Kyiv - Shakhtar Donetsk 0-3(0-1)
Zorya Luhansk - Vorskla Poltava 0-0

Round 10 [20-22.11.2020]
Rukh Lviv - FK Mariupol 0-0
Inhulets Petrove - Dinamo Kyiv 0-2(0-1)
Shakhtar Donetsk - FK Oleksandriya 1-1(0-0)
FK Mynai - SC Dnipro-1 3-2(1-1)
Desna Chernihiv - FK Lviv 0-1(0-1)
Vorskla Poltava - Kolos Kovalivka 3-0(1-0)
Olimpik Don. - Zorya Luhan. 2-1(0-0) [28.04.]

Round 11 [27-29.11.2020]
FK Lviv - FK Mariupol 1-3(0-2)
FK Oleksandriya - Rukh Lviv 0-0
Dinamo Kyiv - Vorskla Poltava 2-0(2-0)
SC Dnipro-1 - Shakhtar Donetsk 0-1(0-0)
FK Mynai - Zorya Luhansk 0-3(0-0)
Kolos Kovalivka - Desna Chernihiv 1-1(1-1)
Inhulets Petrove - Olimpik Donetsk 2-1(1-0)

Round 12 [05-06.12.2020]
FK Lviv - Inhulets Petrove 1-1(1-1)
Shakhtar Donetsk - FK Mynai 5-1(3-1)
FK Mariupol - Dinamo Kyiv 2-0(1-0)
Olimpik Donetsk - Rukh Lviv 3-1(2-0)
Desna Chernihiv - Vorskla Poltava 1-0(0-0)
Zorya Luhansk - SC Dnipro-1 3-1(0-0)
Kolos Kovalivka - FK Oleksandriya 1-1(1-0)

Round 13 [11-13.12.2020]
Olimpik Donetsk - FK Lviv 1-1(0-0)
Vorskla Poltava - FK Mynai 1-1(0-1)
Dinamo Kyiv - Kolos Kovalivka 2-2(0-0)
Rukh Lviv - SC Dnipro-1 4-1(3-0)
Inhulets Petrove - Shakhtar Don. 0-3 *awarded*
Desna Chernihiv - FK Mariupol 2-0(0-0)
FK Oleksandriya - Zorya Luhansk 0-2(0-1)

Round 14 [13-14.02.2021]
FK Mynai - FK Lviv 1-2(0-2)
Zorya Luhansk - Desna Chernihiv 2-1(1-1)
Dinamo Kyiv - Olimpik Donetsk 3-1(1-1)
FK Mariupol - FK Oleksandriya 0-1(0-1)
Kolos Kovalivka - Shakhtar Donetsk 0-0
Rukh Lviv - Vorskla Poltava 1-1(1-0)
SC Dnipro-1 - Inhulets Petrove 2-0(2-0)

Round 15 [20-22.02.2021]
FK Mariupol - Zorya Luhansk 0-1(0-1)
FK Oleksandriya - FK Mynai 3-0(1-0)
FK Lviv - Kolos Kovalivka 0-2(0-1)
Inhulets Petrove - Vorskla Poltava 2-2(1-1)
Shakhtar Donetsk - Rukh Lviv 2-0(1-0)
Desna Chernihiv - Dinamo Kyiv 1-1(0-0)
Olimpik Donetsk - SC Dnipro-1 0-2(0-0)

Round 16 [26-28.02.2021]
Desna Chernihiv - Inhulets Petrove 3-0(1-0)
FK Mariupol - SC Dnipro-1 2-2(1-1)
Vorskla Poltava - FK Oleksandriya 3-1(1-0)
Kolos Kovalivka - Rukh Lviv 1-2(1-0)
FK Mynai - Olimpik Donetsk 2-1(2-1)
Shakhtar Donetsk - Zorya Luhansk 0-1(0-0)
FK Lviv - Dinamo Kyiv 1-4(0-2)

Round 17 [06-08.03.2021]
FK Mariupol - Vorskla Poltava 0-1(0-1)
Olimpik Donetsk - Shakhtar Donetsk 0-1(0-1)
Dinamo Kyiv - FK Mynai 3-0(0-0)
Zorya Luhansk - FK Lviv 4-0(4-0)
Inhulets Petrove - Kolos Kovalivka 0-0
SC Dnipro-1 - FK Oleksandriya 0-0
Rukh Lviv - Desna Chernihiv 0-4(0-2)

Round 18 [13-14.03.2021]
FK Mynai - Inhulets Petrove 0-1(0-1)
Vorskla Poltava - SC Dnipro-1 0-1(0-1)
FK Mariupol - Kolos Kovalivka 1-4(1-2)
Zorya Luhansk - Dinamo Kyiv 0-2(0-0)
Shakhtar Donetsk - Desna Chernihiv 4-0(1-0)
FK Oleksandriya - Olimpik Donetsk 2-0(1-0)
FK Lviv - Rukh Lviv 1-1(1-0) [28.04.]

Round 19 [20-21.03.2021]
FK Mariupol - FK Mynai 0-0
Desna Chernihiv - SC Dnipro-1 0-2(0-1)
Vorskla Poltava - Olimpik Donetsk 3-0(2-0)
Inhulets Petrove - FK Oleksandriya 1-0(1-0)
Dinamo Kyiv - Rukh Lviv 3-0(0-0)
FK Lviv - Shakhtar Donetsk 3-2(1-1)
Kolos Kovalivka - Zorya Luhansk 1-0(1-0)

Round 20 [02-04.04.2021]
SC Dnipro-1 - FK Lviv 5-1(1-0)
FK Mariupol - Inhulets Petrove 4-3(1-0)
Rukh Lviv - Zorya Luhansk 0-2(0-1)
Desna Chernihiv - Olimpik Donetsk 2-0(1-0)
FK Mynai - Kolos Kovalivka 0-0
Vorskla Poltava - Shakhtar Donetsk 0-2(0-1)
FK Oleksandriya - Dinamo Kyiv 1-2(1-1)

Round 21 [10-11.04.2021]
FK Mariupol - Shakhtar Donetsk 0-3(0-2)
Dinamo Kyiv - SC Dnipro-1 2-0(0-0)
Desna Chernihiv - FK Oleksandriya 4-1(1-1)
Vorskla Poltava - FK Lviv 2-1(0-0)
Zorya Luhansk - Inhulets Petrove 2-0(0-0)
Rukh Lviv - FK Mynai 2-0(0-0)
Olimpik Donetsk - Kolos Kovalivka 1-2(1-0)

Round 22 [16-18.04.2021]
FK Lviv - FK Oleksandriya 3-1(2-1)
FK Mynai - Desna Chernihiv 3-1(2-0)
Vorskla Poltava - Zorya Luhansk 4-2(3-0)
Shakhtar Donetsk - Dinamo Kyiv 0-1(0-1)
Inhulets Petrove - Rukh Lviv 0-0
FK Mariupol - Olimpik Donetsk 1-1(1-1)
Kolos Kovalivka - SC Dnipro-1 1-1(1-1)

Round 23 [23-25.04.2021]
FK Mariupol - Rukh Lviv 0-3(0-0)
SC Dnipro-1 - FK Mynai 3-0(3-0)
Kolos Kovalivka - Vorskla Poltava 3-0(0-0)
FK Lviv - Desna Chernihiv 1-0(1-0)
Zorya Luhansk - Olimpik Donetsk 2-1(1-0)
Dinamo Kyiv - Inhulets Petrove 5-0(2-0)
FK Oleksandriya - Shakhtar Donetsk 2-0(1-0)

Round 24 [01-02.05.2021]
Desna Chernihiv - Kolos Kovalivka 2-2(0-1)
Shakhtar Donetsk - SC Dnipro-1 2-1(2-0)
Vorskla Poltava - Dinamo Kyiv 1-5(1-3)
Rukh Lviv - FK Oleksandriya 2-1(0-1)
FK Mariupol - FK Lviv 1-2(1-1)
Zorya Luhansk - FK Mynai 1-0(0-0)
Olimpik Donetsk - Inhulets Petrove 0-3(0-1)

Round 25 [05-06.05.2021]		Round 26 [09.05.2021]	
Dinamo Kyiv - FK Mariupol	0-0	FK Mariupol - Desna Chernihiv	4-1(0-1)
FK Oleksandriya - Kolos Kovalivka	0-2(0-1)	Zorya Luhansk - FK Oleksandriya	2-1(0-0)
Vorskla Poltava - Desna Chernihiv	1-1(1-0)	Kolos Kovalivka - Dinamo Kyiv	0-3(0-1)
SC Dnipro-1 - Zorya Luhansk	0-1(0-0)	FK Mynai - Vorskla Poltava	1-2(1-2)
Inhulets Petrove - FK Lviv	1-0(1-0)	FK Lviv - Olimpik Donetsk	1-1(1-0)
Rukh Lviv - Olimpik Donetsk	3-0(3-0)	SC Dnipro-1 - Rukh Lviv	1-1(1-0)
FK Mynai - Shakhtar Donetsk	0-4(0-1)	Shakhtar Donetsk - Inhulets Petrove	1-0(1-0)

Please note: the match between FK Inhulets Petrove and FK Shakhtar Donetsk (Round 13) was not played, being awarded as a 3-0 win for FK Shakhtar Donetsk.

						Total			Home					Away			
1.	**FK Dinamo Kyiv**	26	20	5	1	59 - 15	65	8	4	1	25 - 8	12	1	0	34 - 7
2.	FK Shakhtar Donetsk	26	16	6	4	54 - 19	54	9	2	2	30 - 9	7	4	2	24 - 10
3.	FK Zorya Luhansk	26	15	5	6	44 - 22	50	8	3	2	23 - 10	7	2	4	21 - 12
4.	FK Kolos Kovalivka	26	10	11	5	36 - 26	41	4	6	3	16 - 12	6	5	2	20 - 14
5.	FK Vorskla Poltava	26	11	8	7	37 - 30	41	7	3	3	25 - 16	4	5	4	12 - 14
6.	FK Desna Chernihiv	26	10	8	8	38 - 32	38	8	3	2	24 - 11	2	5	6	14 - 21
7.	SC Dnipro-1	26	8	6	12	36 - 38	30	4	3	6	18 - 15	4	3	6	18 - 23
8.	FK Lviv	26	8	5	13	25 - 51	29	5	3	5	15 - 23	3	2	8	10 - 28
9.	FK Oleksandriya	26	8	5	13	33 - 37	29	7	2	4	23 - 15	1	3	9	10 - 22
10.	FK Rukh Lviv	26	6	10	10	27 - 39	28	4	5	4	16 - 16	2	5	6	11 - 23
11.	FK Mariupol	26	6	8	12	27 - 41	26	2	3	8	14 - 24	4	5	4	13 - 17
12.	FK Inhulets Petrove	26	5	11	10	24 - 39	26	3	8	2	11 - 13	2	3	8	13 - 26
13.	FK Olimpik Donetsk* (*Relegated*)	26	6	4	16	28 - 48	22	4	2	7	17 - 23	2	2	9	11 - 25
14.	FK Mynai Uzhgorod	26	4	6	16	16 - 47	18	4	2	7	11 - 21	0	4	9	5 - 26

Final Standings

*Please note: FK Olimpik Donetsk was relegated after its president and owner Vladyslav Helzin (sanctioned by Ukrainian FA) decided to withdraw the club from Ukrainian Premier League.

Top goalscorers:

15	Vladyslav Kulach	*FK Vorskla Poltava*
12	Viktor Tsyhankov	*FK Dinamo Kyiv*
10	Shahab Zahedi Tabar (IRN)	*FK Olimpik Donetsk / FK Zorya Luhansk*
10	Anatoliy Nuriyev (AZE)	*FK Mynai Uzhgorod*

NATIONAL CUP
Ukrainian Cup 2020/2021

Third Round [30.09./13.11.2020]

FK Hirnyk-Sport Horishni Plavni - SC Dnipro-1	3-5(2-3,3-3)	FK Desna Chernihiv - FK Rukh Lviv	2-1(0-0)
FK Polissya Zhytomyr - FK Mynai Uzhgorod	1-2(1-1)	FK Vorskla Poltava - FK Lviv	2-0(0-0)
NK Veres Rivne - MFK Mykolaiv	4-2(1-1,2-2)	FK Prykarpattia Iv.-Frankivsk - FK Kolos Kovalivka	0-1(0-0)
FK Viktoriya Mykolaivka - FK Mariupol	1-3(1-0)	FK Oleksandriya - FK Inhulets Petrove	4-1(0-0)
FK Kryvbas Kryvyi Rih - FK Nyva Vinnytsia	0-1(0-0)	FK VPK-Ahro Shevchenkivka - FK Olimpik Donetsk	1-0(0-0)
FK Epitsentr Dunaivtsi - FK Ahrobiznes Volochysk	1-2(1-1)		

Fourth Round [02./16.12.2020]

SC Dnipro-1 - FK VPK-Ahro Shevchenkivka	5-0(1-0)	FK Ahrobiznes Volochysk - FK Vorskla Poltava	1-0(1-0)
NK Veres Rivne - FK Mariupol	1-0(0-0)	FK Oleksandriya - FK Mynai Uzhgorod	3-0(1-0)
FK Nyva Vinnytsia - FK Kolos Kovalivka	0-4(0-1)	FK Desna Chernihiv - FK Zorya Luhansk	0-1(0-1)

Quarter-Finals [03.03.2021]

NK Veres Rivne - FK Zorya Luhansk	1-2(1-1)	SC Dnipro-1 - FK Oleksandriya	0-0 aet; 3-4 pen
FK Dinamo Kyiv - FK Kolos Kovalivka	0-0 aet; 4-3 pen	FK Ahrobiznes Volochysk - FK Shakhtar Donetsk	1-0(0-0,0-0)

Semi-Finals [21.04.2021]

FK Ahrobiznes Volochysk - FK Dinamo Kyiv	0-3(0-1)	FK Oleksandriya - FK Zorya Luhansk	1-1 aet; 3-4 pen

Final

13.05.2021; "Roman Sukhevych" City Stadium, Ternopil; Referee: Yuriy Ivanov; Attendance: 3,000

FK Dinamo Kyiv - FK Zorya Luhansk 1-0(0-0,0-0)

Dinamo Kyiv: Denis Boyko, Tomasz Kędziora, Denys Popov, Illya Zabarnyi, Vitaliy Mykolenko (11.Oleksandr Karavayev), Serhiy Sydorchuk (Cap), Mykola Shaparenko, Viktor Tsyhankov, Gerson Leal Rodrigues Gouveia (118.Carlos María de Pena Bonino), Vitaliy Buyalskiy (113.Denys Harmash), Artem Besyedin. Trainer: Mircea Lucescu (Romania).

Goal: 1-0 Viktor Tsyhankov (98).

Zorya Luhansk: Nikola Vasilj, Denis Favorov, Dmitriy Ivanisenya, Vitaliy Vernidub (Cap), Leovigildo Júnior Reis Rodrigues „Juninho", Yehor Nazaryna (63.Allahyar Sayyadmanesh), Dmytro Khomchenovsky, Vladyslav Kochergin, Vladlen Yurchenko (117.Lovro Cvek), Vladyslav Kabayev (82.Oleksandr Hladkiy), Artem Hromov (90+3.Shahab Zahedi Tabar). Trainer: Viktor Skrypnyk.

Futbolnij Klub Desna Chernihiv

Founded:	1960		
Stadium:	Chernihiv Stadium, Chernihiv (5,500)		
Trainer:	Oleksandr Ryabokon		21.02.1964

Goalkeepers:	DOB	M	(s)	G
Ihor Litovka	05.06.1988	5	(1)	
Evgen Past	16.03.1988	21		
Defenders:	**DOB**	**M**	**(s)**	**G**
Constantin Dima (ROU)	21.07.1999		(1)	
Andriy Gitchenko	02.10.1984	15	(5)	3
Maksym Imerekov	23.01.1991	15		2
Yukhym Konoplia	26.08.1999	20	(2)	1
Artem Sukhotskiy	06.12.1992	6	(4)	
Joonas Tamm (EST)	02.02.1992	20		1
Vitaliy Yermakov	07.06.1992	7	(9)	1
Artur Zapadnya	04.06.1990	1	(1)	
Midfielders:	**DOB**	**M**	**(s)**	**G**
Levan Arveladze	06.04.1993	8	(7)	
Bohdan Biloshevskyi	12.01.2000	2		
Evgen Chepurnenko	06.09.1989	4	(4)	1
Andriy Dombrovskyi	12.08.1995	12	(8)	
Vladislav Kalitvintsev	04.01.1993	19	(2)	1
Yehor Kartushov	05.01.1991	10	(13)	3
Andriy Mostoviy	24.01.1988	17	(3)	1
Mykhailo Mudryk	05.01.2001	8	(2)	
Vladislav Ohirya	03.04.1990	24		
Pavel Polegenko	06.01.1995	7	(3)	
Ilya Shevtsov	13.04.2000	2	(5)	1
Sergey Starenkiy	20.09.1984		(4)	
Andriy Totovytskyy	20.01.1993	16	(2)	9
Oleksandr Volkov	07.02.1989		(2)	
Forwards:	**DOB**	**M**	**(s)**	**G**
Denys Bezborodko	31.05.1994	5	(5)	1
Pylyp Budkovsky	10.03.1992	11	(5)	7
Maksym Degtyarev	30.05.1993	6	(13)	2
Denis Demyanenko	05.07.2000		(1)	
Oleksandr Filipov	23.10.1992	2		1
Oleksiy Gutsulyak	25.12.1997	19	(5)	2
Dmytro Khlyobas	09.05.1994	4	(2)	1

Sport Club Dnipro-1

Founded:	10.03.2017		
Stadium:	Dnipro Arena, Dnipro (31,003)		
Trainer:	Dmytro Mikhaylenko		13.07.1973
[22.09.2020]	Igor Jovičević (CRO)		30.11.1973

Goalkeepers:	DOB	M	(s)	G
Bogdan Sarnavskiy	29.01.1995	12	(1)	
Valeri Yurchuk	12.04.1990	14		
Defenders:	**DOB**	**M**	**(s)**	**G**
Volodymyr Adamyuk	17.07.1991	12	(4)	1
Kostiantyn Domaratskyi	27.06.2000		(2)	
Douglas Silva Bacelar (BRA)	04.04.1990	16	(1)	2
Vladyslav Dubinchak	01.07.1998	21	(1)	
Serhiy Loginov	24.08.1990	20		
Oleksandr Safronov	11.06.1999	3		
Oleksandr Svatok	27.09.1994	13	(3)	1
Andriy Tsurikov	05.10.1992	9	(10)	1
Serhiy Zaiets	03.10.2001		(1)	
Midfielders:	**DOB**	**M**	**(s)**	**G**
Arseniy Batagov	05.03.2002	5	(10)	
Serhiy Buletsa	16.02.1999	10	(9)	3
Danylo Ignatenko	13.03.1997	17		1
Ihor Kogut	07.03.1996	18	(2)	2
Serhiy Kravchenko	24.04.1983	6	(5)	
Lucas Taylor Maia Reis (BRA)	10.04.1995	22		
Oleksandr Nazarenko	01.02.2000	15	(4)	4
Oleksandr Pikhalonok	07.05.1997	14		
Vladyslav Shynkarenko	27.01.2001		(1)	
Yury Vakulko	10.11.1997	1	(3)	
Yehor Yarmolyuk	01.03.2004	3	(6)	
Forwards:	**DOB**	**M**	**(s)**	**G**
Fabricio Rodrigues da Silva Ferreira „Bill" (BRA)	07.05.1999		(5)	
Oleksiy Chichikov	30.09.1987		(9)	1
Mario Čuže (CRO)	24.04.1999	13		7
Francisco Di Franco (ARG)	28.01.1995	11	(9)	
Artem Dovbyk	21.06.1997	22	(2)	6
Oleksiy Khoblenko	04.04.1994	8	(10)	4
Kyrylo Khovaiko	17.06.2001		(1)	
Dmytro Korkishko	04.05.1990	1	(6)	1
Vagner Gonçalves Nogueira (FRA)	27.04.1996		(3)	1

Futbolnij Klub Dinamo Kyiv

Founded:	13.05.1927		
Stadium:	NSC Olimpiyskiy, Kyiv (70,050) /		
	"Lobanovsky" Dinamo Stadium, Kyiv (16,873)		
Trainer:	Mircea Lucescu (ROU)		29.07.1945

Goalkeepers:	DOB	M	(s)	G
Denis Boyko	29.01.1988	1		
Georgiy Bushchan	31.05.1994	22	(1)	
Ruslan Neshcheret	22.01.2002	3		
Defenders:	**DOB**	**M**	**(s)**	**G**
Tomasz Kędziora (POL)	11.06.1994	23	(2)	1
Vitaliy Mykolenko	29.05.1999	22		2
Denys Popov	17.02.1999	14	(1)	2
Sidcley Ferreira Pereira (BRA)	13.05.1993		(7)	2
Artem Shabanov	07.03.1992	1		
Oleksandr Syrota	11.06.2000	10		
Oleksandr Tymchyk	20.01.1997	4		
Illya Zabarnyi	01.09.2002	20	(1)	1
Midfielders:	**DOB**	**M**	**(s)**	**G**
Oleksandr Andrievsky	25.06.1994	9	(5)	1
Cristian Tudor Băluță (ROU)	27.03.1999		(1)	
Vitaliy Buyalskiy	06.01.1993	19	(1)	5
Mikkel Duelund (DEN)	29.06.1997	1	(3)	
Denys Harmash	19.04.1990	4	(8)	3
Oleksandr Karavayev	02.06.1992	16	(7)	2
Bohdan Liedniev	07.04.1998	1	(11)	1
Mykola Shaparenko	04.10.1998	19	(5)	4
Volodymyr Shepeliev	01.06.1997	9	(10)	
Serhiy Sydorchuk	02.05.1991	17	(4)	3
Viktor Tsyhankov	15.11.1997	15	(5)	12
Forwards:	**DOB**	**M**	**(s)**	**G**
Artem Besyedin	31.03.1996	12		5
Clayton da Silveira da Silva (BRA)	23.10.1995		(1)	
Carlos María de Pena Bonino (URU)	11.03.1992	17	(2)	3
Francisco Sol Ortíz (ESP)	13.03.1992		(2)	
Gerson Leal Rodrigues Gouveia (LUX)	20.06.1995	9	(13)	4
Artem Kravets	03.06.1989		(1)	
Nazariy Rusyn	25.10.1998		(1)	
Vladyslav Supryaga	15.02.2000	10	(7)	2
Heorhiy Tsitaishvili (UKR)	18.11.2000	2	(2)	
Vladyslav Vanat	04.01.2002		(1)	
Benjamin Verbič (SVN)	27.11.1993	6	(6)	3

Futbolnij Klub Inhulets Petrove

Founded:	2013		
Stadium:	Zirka Stadium, Kropyvnytskyi (14,628)		
Trainer:	Serhiy Lavrynenko		17.02.1975

Goalkeepers:	DOB	M	(s)	G
Vladimir Krynsky	14.01.1997	11		
Artem Malysh	15.07.2000	7		
Bogdan Shust	04.03.1986	7		
Defenders:	**DOB**	**M**	**(s)**	**G**
Hennos Asmelash (NED)	01.07.1999	2		
Denys Balan	18.08.1993	22		2
Maksim Kovalev	20.03.1989	14		
Oleksandr Kucherenko	01.10.1994	20	(1)	
Mykola Kvasnyi	04.01.1995	15	(3)	
Mohamed Salem (TUN)	06.01.1996	10		
Suleiman Seitkhalilov	14.02.2002		(1)	
Andriy Semenko	17.07.1993	11	(1)	
Mychailo Shyshka	05.07.1994	10	(3)	
Midfielders:	**DOB**	**M**	**(s)**	**G**
Vladimir Belotserkovets	22.01.2000		(6)	
Ihor Chaykovskiy	07.10.1991	1	(3)	
Dmytro Fateev	21.06.1994	2		

Andriy Korobenko	28.05.1997	3	(1)	
Ilya Kovalenko	20.03.1990	13	(9)	2
Oleksandr Kozak	25.07.1994	19	(3)	1
Bogdan Litvyak	05.05.1998		(2)	
Vladislav Lupashko	04.12.1986	8	(1)	
Vitaliy Pavlov	25.06.1988	12		
Artem Shchedry	09.11.1992	6	(10)	
Ilya Shevtsov	13.04.2000	1	(7)	2
Oleg Synohub	19.04.1989	8	(5)	
Yevhen Zaporozhets	20.09.1994	24		
Forwards:	**DOB**	**M**	**(s)**	**G**
Mladen Bartulović (CRO)	05.10.1986	16	(4)	7
Oleksandr Mishurenko	25.10.1988		(4)	
Yohana Mkomola (TAN)	18.04.2000	3	(9)	
Mykhaylo Plokhotnyuk	12.03.1999	4	(7)	1
Nikoloz Sitchinava (GEO)	17.07.1994	18	(4)	6
Denis Vasin	04.03.1989	3	(2)	
Denys Yanakov	01.01.1999	5	(7)	3

Futbolnij Klub Kolos Kovalivka

Founded:	2012		
Stadium:	Kolos Stadium, Kovalivka (5,000)		
Trainer:	Ruslan Kostyshyn		08.01.1977

Goalkeepers:	DOB	M	(s)	G
Vladyslav Kucheruk	14.02.1999	6		
Evgen Volinets	26.08.1993	20		
Defenders:	**DOB**	**M**	**(s)**	**G**
Oleksandr Chornomorets	05.04.1993	19	(1)	
Vladislav Emets	09.09.1997	6		
Maksym Maksymenko	28.05.1990	6		
Evgen Novak	01.02.1989	14	(2)	1
Kyrylo Petrov	22.06.1990	19	(1)	2
Matija Rom (SVN)	01.11.1998	1		
Nikolai Zolotov (BLR)	11.11.1994	7		
Oleksy Zozulya	15.04.1992	4	(1)	
Midfielders:	**DOB**	**M**	**(s)**	**G**
Andriy Bogdanov	21.01.1990	16	(3)	
Vitaly Gavrish	18.03.1986	18		1
Oleg Ilin	08.06.1997	8	(16)	
Mykyta Kravchenko	14.06.1997	19		
Vadim Milko	22.08.1986	13	(8)	3

Yevgeniy Morozko	15.02.1993	5	(3)	2
Thadee Alvaro Ngamba (CMR)	15.12.1998		(7)	
Pavel Orekhovskiy	13.05.1996	16	(5)	4
Yevheniy Smyrnyi	18.08.1998	10	(7)	2
Stanislav Sorokin	03.05.2000		(2)	
Evgeniy Zadoya	05.01.1991	11	(6)	
Forwards:	**DOB**	**M**	**(s)**	**G**
Denis Antyukh	30.07.1997	17	(5)	1
Oleksandr Bondarenko	28.07.1989	1		
Vyacheslav Churko	10.05.1993	11		3
Mamadou Danfa (SEN)	06.03.2001	2	(7)	1
Yevheniy Isaienko	07.08.2000	1	(14)	1
Dmytro Khlyobas	09.05.1994	2	(4)	
Denys Kostyshyn	31.08.1997	11	(8)	4
Vladimir Lisenko	20.04.1988	18	(5)	5
Anton Salabay	12.06.2002		(1)	
Yevhen Seleznyov	20.07.1985	5	(5)	5

Futbolnij Klub Lviv

Founded:	2006		
Stadium:	Ukraina Stadium / Arena Lviv, Lviv (28,051 / 34,915)		
Trainer:	Giorgi Tsetsadze (GEO)		03.09.1974
[29.10.2020]	Vitaliy Shumskiy		17.05.1972
[02.03.2021]	Anatoliy Bezsmertniy		21.01.1969

Goalkeepers:	DOB	M	(s)	G
Oleksandr Iliushchenkov	23.03.1990	7		
Orest Kostyk	16.04.1999	16		
Serhiy Litovchenko	04.10.1987	2		
German Penkov	26.05.1994	1		
Defenders:	**DOB**	**M**	**(s)**	**G**
Serhiy Borzenko	22.06.1986	4		
Maks Juraj Čelić (CRO)	08.03.1996	4		1
Oleksiy Dovgiy	02.11.1989	8	(4)	1
Yehor Klymenchuk	11.11.1997	7	(5)	
Maksym Komarets	23.05.2002	2	(1)	
Yury Kravchuk	06.04.1994	9	(2)	2
Ivan Lobay	21.05.1996	1	(4)	
Enes Mahmutović (LUX)	22.05.1997	20		1
Maroine Mihoubi (TUN)	26.07.1999	16	(1)	1
Oleksandr Romanchuk	16.12.1999	11	(8)	
Midfielders:	**DOB**	**M**	**(s)**	**G**
Mihkel Ainsalu (EST)	08.03.1996	10	(1)	
Ivan Brikner	30.06.1993	9	(2)	1
Andriy Busko	20.05.1997	8	(2)	

Frane Čirjak (CRO)	23.06.1995	12	(8)	
Donatas Kazlauskas (LTU)	31.03.1994	9	(4)	
Ihor Koshman	07.03.1995	6	(3)	
Borys Krushynskyi	10.05.2002		(3)	
Rafael Sabino dos Santos (BRA)	17.06.1996	10	(10)	1
Serhiy Topchiy	10.07.2001		(1)	
Welves Santos Damacena (BRA)	24.11.2000		(3)	
Volodymyr Yakimets	03.03.1998	15	(1)	
Forwards:	**DOB**	**M**	**(s)**	**G**
Alvaro Luis Tavares Vieira (BRA)	10.03.1995	13		4
Yaroslav Bogunov	04.09.1993	2	(2)	
Filipe Pachtmann (BRA)	11.04.2000	4	(3)	
Maksym Gryso	14.05.1996	19	(3)	1
Ernest Nyarko (GHA)	09.09.1995	11	(3)	2
Nazariy Nych	19.02.1999	18	(8)	4
Artur Remenyak	09.08.2000	7	(7)	
Renan Abner do Carmo de Oliveira (BRA)	08.05.1997	6	(3)	2
Dmytro Semeniv	24.06.1998	3	(11)	1
Rogerio Alves dos Santos „Shina" (BRA)	02.08.1996	13	(1)	2
Yuri Zakharkiv	21.03.1996	3	(5)	

Futbolnij Klub Mariupol

Founded: 1963
Stadium: "Volodymir Boiko" Stadium, Mariupol (12,680)
Trainer: Ostap Markevych   04.04.1978

Goalkeepers:	DOB	M	(s)	G
Evgen Galchuk	05.03.1992	15		
Pavlo Kravtsov	19.01.2000	1		
Oleh Kudryk	17.10.1996	10		
Defenders:	**DOB**	**M**	**(s)**	**G**
Oleksiy Bykov	29.03.1998	16	(2)	
Serhiy Chobotenko	16.01.1997	22	(1)	
Oleksandr Drambaev	21.04.2001	3	(7)	
Mykyta Fursenko	01.10.2002		(1)	
Ihor Kiryukhantsev	29.01.1996	13	(5)	
Mark Mampasi	12.03.2003	3	(3)	
Nazariy Muravskyi	03.02.2000	5	(1)	
Mikita Peterman	12.06.1999	4	(10)	
Danylo Sagutkin	19.04.1996	6	(3)	1
Pavlo Shushko	07.05.2000		(1)	
Petro Stasyuk	24.02.1995	22	(3)	1
Ihor Tishchenko	11.05.1989	2	(2)	
Illya Ukhan	01.06.2003	1		
Vyacheslav Velev	21.05.2000	2	(1)	
Midfielders:	**DOB**	**M**	**(s)**	**G**
Anton Baydal	08.02.2000		(1)	
Artem Bondarenko	21.08.2000	17	(4)	8
Maksym Chekh	03.01.1999	15	(7)	

	DOB	M	(s)	G
Danylo Dmytriyev	22.10.2002	1		
Yaroslav Dobrokhotov	01.11.2000	1	(2)	
Serhiy Gorbunov	14.03.1994	15	(4)	1
Danylo Ignatenko	13.03.1997	1	(2)	
Ivan Koshkosh	08.04.2001	1		
Oleksandr Kozhevnikov	17.04.2000		(1)	
Nikita Kozytsky	26.01.2002		(1)	
Eldar Kuliyev	24.03.2002	4	(3)	
Ivan Mamrosenko	27.03.2000	1		
Kyrylo Melichenko	07.06.1999	8	(2)	1
Dmytro Myshnov	26.01.1994	24		2
Oleh Ocheretko	25.05.2003	13	(4)	2
Vyacheslav Tankovski	16.08.1995	15		1
Dmytro Topalov	12.03.1998	16	(2)	3
Andriy Vyskrebentsevys	27.10.2000	1		
Forwards:	**DOB**	**M**	**(s)**	**G**
Stanislav Biblyk	17.08.2001		(3)	
Oleksiy Kashchuk	29.06.2000	5	(10)	
Andriy Kulakov	28.04.1999	9	(11)	3
Rodion Plaksa	22.01.2002	1	(2)	
Danylo Sikan	16.04.2001	12	(2)	4
Myroslav Trofymyuk	08.04.2001	1		

Futbolnij Klub Mynai

Founded: 2015
Stadium: Avanhard Stadium, Uzhhorod (12,000)
Trainer: Vasyl Kobin   24.05.1985
[26.03.2021] Mykola Tsymbal   07.09.1984

Goalkeepers:	DOB	M	(s)	G
Anton Kanibolotskiy	16.05.1988	6	(1)	
Andriy Popovich	04.04.1992	20		
Defenders:	**DOB**	**M**	**(s)**	**G**
Siaka Bagayoko (MLI)	04.07.1998	3	(2)	
Vladislav Chushenko	27.10.2000		(1)	
Oleg Dopilka	12.03.1986	1		
Danylo Karas	02.01.1997	4	(1)	
Oleksiy Kovtun	05.02.1995	4		
Maksim Lopyryonok	13.04.1995	19	(1)	
Repo Tercious Malepe (RSA)	18.02.1997	8	(6)	
Mislav Matić (CRO)	06.01.2000	22	(2)	
Oleksandr Matkobozhyk	03.01.1998	3	(4)	
Shemmy Mayembe (ZAM)	22.11.1997	16	(5)	
Dmytro Pavlish	30.09.1999	1	(3)	
Taras Sakiv	19.11.1997	19		
Midfielders:	**DOB**	**M**	**(s)**	**G**
Vitaliy Boyko	03.12.1997	4	(4)	
Oleg Golodyuk	02.01.1988	3	(6)	

	DOB	M	(s)	G
Artur Karnoza	02.08.1990		(1)	
Oleksiy Khakhlov	06.02.1999	6	(9)	1
Danylo Knysh	03.03.1996	9	(7)	
Kyrylo Melichenko	07.06.1999	11		
Anatoly Nuriyev	20.05.1996	22		10
Oleksandr Petrusenko	26.03.1998	7	(3)	
Oleksiy Shpak	15.08.1998	1	(6)	
Oleksandr Snyzhko	20.08.1996	13	(9)	
Andriy Tkachuk	18.11.1987	20	(3)	
Forwards:	**DOB**	**M**	**(s)**	**G**
Rustam Akhmedzade	25.12.2000	7	(13)	
Oleksandr Hlahola	19.07.1997	1		
Mikhaylo Kopolovets	29.01.1984		(1)	
Denis Kozhanov	13.06.1987	16	(4)	
Artem Milevskiy	12.01.1985	5	(5)	
Ugochukwu Ogbonnaya Oduenyi (NGA)	03.02.1996	2	(7)	
Vasyl Pynyashko	02.02.1992	16	(6)	2
Anton Shynder	13.06.1987	17	(3)	3

Futbolnij Klub Oleksandriya

Founded: 1948
Stadium: CSC Nika Stadium, Oleksandriya (7,000)
Trainer: Volodymyr Sharan   18.09.1971

Goalkeepers:	DOB	M	(s)	G
Oleg Bilyk	11.01.1998	7		
Vyacheslav Borisenko	24.03.2002	1		
Yuri Pankiv	03.11.1984	18		
Defenders:	**DOB**	**M**	**(s)**	**G**
Vladislav Baboglo	14.11.1998	15	(6)	1
Valeriy Bondarenko	03.02.1994	17	(1)	3
Glib Bukhal	12.11.1995	1		
Oleksiy Dovgiy	02.11.1989	2	(3)	
Kaspars Dubra (LVA)	20.12.1990	15	(1)	
Oleksandr Melnyk	10.02.2000	7	(2)	
Denis Miroshnichenko	11.10.1994	12	(3)	
Pavlo Pashaev (AZE)	04.01.1988	20		
Timur Stetskov	27.01.1998	4	(14)	1
Midfielders:	**DOB**	**M**	**(s)**	**G**
Yevhen Banada	29.02.1992	18	(2)	2
Kyrylo Dryshliuk	16.09.1999	3	(1)	
Mikita Dudka	18.12.2000	2		1
Andriy Globa	24.01.1999	1	(2)	

	DOB	M	(s)	G
Artem Gordienko	04.03.1991	4	(1)	1
Dmytro Grechyshkin	22.09.1991	22	(2)	2
Vasili Gritsuk	21.11.1987	3	(6)	1
Ivan Kalyuzhnyi	21.01.1998	1	(4)	
Kirilo Kovalets	02.07.1993	16	(2)	1
Valeri Luchkevych	11.01.1996	20	(1)	2
Emil Mustafaiev	24.09.2001		(1)	
Bogdan Myshenko	29.12.1994	6	(9)	1
Maksym Tretyakov	06.03.1996	16	(6)	3
Roman Vantukh	04.07.1998	16	(1)	2
Vadym Yanchak	07.02.1999		(1)	
Maksym Zaderaka	07.09.1994	1	(7)	
Forwards:	**DOB**	**M**	**(s)**	**G**
Denys Bezborodko	31.05.1994	3	(8)	2
Andriy Novikov	20.04.1999		(9)	
Dmytro Shastal	30.12.1995	11	(5)	3
Artem Sitalo	01.08.1989	17	(3)	4
Denys Ustymenko	12.04.1999	7	(13)	2

Futbolnij Klub Olimpik Donetsk

Founded:	2001			
Stadium:	"Lobanovsky" Dinamo Stadium, Kyiv (16,873)			
Trainer:	Ihor Klimovskiy			17.02.1972
[25.02.2021]	Yuriy Kalitvintsev			05.05.1968
[04.05.2021]	Roman Sanzhar			28.05.1979

Goalkeepers:	DOB	M	(s)	G
Andriy Chekotun	02.09.2002	2		
Betim Halimi (KVX)	28.02.1996	8		
Artem Kychak	16.05.1989	16	(1)	
Defenders:	**DOB**	**M**	**(s)**	**G**
Rizvan Ablitarov	18.04.1989		(2)	
Fabricio Oscar Alvarenga (ARG)	17.02.1996	9	(6)	1
Issiar Dramé (FRA)	16.02.1999	17	(1)	
Dmytro Grishko	02.12.1985	1	(1)	
Orest Lebedenko	23.09.1998	23		
Pavlo Lukyanchuk	19.05.1996		(1)	
Evgen Neplyakh	11.05.1992		(1)	
Ihor Snurnitsyn	07.03.2000	16	(2)	
Evgeniy Tsymbalyuk	19.06.1996	6	(3)	
Bogdan Veklyak	31.08.1999	4		
Ivan Zotko	09.07.1996	16		1
Midfielders:	**DOB**	**M**	**(s)**	**G**
Ruslan Babenko	08.07.1992	22		1
Geo Danny Ekra (CIV)	10.01.1999	2		
Vladislav Khamelyuk	05.04.1998	3	(1)	1
Andriy Kravchuk	26.02.1999	2	(2)	
Pavlo Ksonz	02.01.1987	4	(4)	
Evgeny Pasich	13.07.1993	22	(1)	
Serhiy Politylo	09.01.1989	25		3
Danielis Romanovskis (LTU)	19.06.1996	5	(8)	1
Talles Brener de Paula (BRA)	12.05.1998	9	(4)	
Taras Zaviyskiy	12.04.1995	11	(6)	
Forwards:	**DOB**	**M**	**(s)**	**G**
Denis Balanyuk	16.01.1997		(1)	
Temur Chogadze (GEO)	05.05.1998	4	(10)	
Maxime Do Couto Teixeira (FRA)	13.12.1996	18	(4)	3
Ibrahim Kargbo (BEL)	03.01.2000	8	(12)	3
Kirill Kirilenko (BLR)	08.10.2000		(2)	
Olabiran Blessing Muyiwa (NGA)	07.09.1998	14	(4)	3
Taddeus Nkeng Fomakwang (CMR)	26.02.2000	9	(1)	2
Shahab Zahedi Tabar (IRN)	18.08.1995	10	(1)	8

Futbolnij Klub Rukh Lviv

Founded:	2003		
Stadium:	Arena Lviv / Skif Stadium, Lviv (34,915 / 3,742)		
Trainer:	Ivan Fedyk		09.07.1987

Goalkeepers:	DOB	M	(s)	G
Aleksandr Bandura	30.05.1986	23		
Yuriy-Volodymyr Hereta	30.01.2004		(1)	
Roman Mysak	09.09.1991	3		
Defenders:	**DOB**	**M**	**(s)**	**G**
Maksym Bilyi	21.06.1990	17		
Bogdan Boychuk	30.05.1996	19	(4)	1
Ihor Boychuk	10.01.1994		(2)	1
Ihor Duts	11.04.1994	7	(1)	
Roman Gagun	16.07.1993	14	(1)	
Erik Gliha (SVN)	13.02.1997	8	(2)	
Vadym Paramonov	18.03.1991	9		
Taras Sakiv	19.11.1997	1		
Ragnar Sigurðsson (ISL)	19.06.1986	1		
Miloš Stamenković (SRB)	01.06.1990	15	(1)	
Volodymyr Zastavnyi	02.09.1990	1	(2)	
David Zec (SVN)	05.01.2000	7	(2)	
Midfielders:	**DOB**	**M**	**(s)**	**G**
Ivan Brikner	30.06.1993	4	(1)	
Valeriy Fedorchuk	05.10.1988	19	(3)	3
Ivan Kalyuzhnyi	21.01.1998	1	(2)	
Roman Karasyuk	27.03.1991	9	(2)	
Yuri Klimchuk	05.05.1997	21	(4)	5
Daniil Kondrakov	19.01.1998	12	(10)	6
Yuriy Kopyna	04.07.1996	9	(3)	
Andriy Kukharuk	13.12.1995	11	(9)	1
Ivan Lytvynenko	10.04.2001	1	(1)	
Marian Mysyk	02.10.1996	22	(2)	1
Ernest Nyarko (GHA)	09.09.1995	1	(2)	
Ostap Prytula	24.06.2000	7	(9)	2
Vasyl Runich	31.01.2000	1	(5)	1
Marko Sapuha	29.05.2003		(1)	
Oleksiy Sych	01.04.2001		(2)	
Oleg Synytsia	20.03.1996	1		
Ivan Varfolomeev	24.03.2004		(2)	
Forwards:	**DOB**	**M**	**(s)**	**G**
Andriy Boryachuk	23.04.1996	7	(3)	2
Yaroslav Karabin	19.11.2002		(2)	
Svyatoslav Kozlovsky	26.03.1994		(1)	
Mykola Kukharevych	01.07.2001	9	(8)	2
Rostyslav Liakh	12.10.2000		(2)	
Yaroslav Martinyuk	20.02.1989	19	(2)	
Bogdan Orynchak	10.09.1993		(1)	
Rostyslav Rusyn	26.10.1995	7	(7)	1

Futbolnij Klub Shakhtar Donetsk

Founded:	24.05.1936		
Stadium:	NSC Olimpiyskiy, Kyiv (70,050)		
Trainer:	Luís Manuel Ribeiro de Castro (POR)		03.09.1961

Goalkeepers:	DOB	M	(s)	G
Andriy Pyatov	28.06.1984	4		
Anatoliy Trubin	01.08.2001	21		
Defenders:	**DOB**	**M**	**(s)**	**G**
Valeriy Bondar	27.02.1999	10		
Domilson Cordeiro dos Santos „Dodô" (BRA)	17.11.1998	23		2
Ismaily Gonçalves dos Santos (BRA)	11.01.1990	3		
Davit Khotcholava (GEO)	08.02.1993	7		
Viktor Kornienko	14.02.1999	9	(2)	
Serhiy Krivtsov	15.03.1991	12		1
Mykola Matvienko	02.05.1996	19	(1)	1
Vitor Eduardo da Silva Matos „Vitão" (BRA)	02.02.2000	8	(2)	
Midfielders:	**DOB**	**M**	**(s)**	**G**
Alan Patrick Lourenço (BRA)	13.05.1991	17	(4)	4
Serhiy Bolbat	13.06.1993	3	(4)	
Yevhen Konoplyanka	29.09.1989	3	(5)	
Viktor Kovalenko	14.02.1996	3	(5)	4
Marcos Antônio Silva Santos (BRA)	13.06.2000	13	(10)	2
Marlos Romero Bonfim	07.06.1988	16	(3)	2
Maycon de Andrade Barberan(BRA)	15.07.1997	16	(3)	2
Mykhailo Mudryk	05.01.2001		(3)	
Taras Stepanenko	08.08.1989	13	(5)	2
Heorhiy Sudakov	01.09.2002	2	(8)	1
Forwards:	**DOB**	**M**	**(s)**	**G**
Bruno Ferreira Bonfim „Dentinho" (BRA)	19.01.1989	6	(8)	3
Fernando dos Santos Pedro (BRA)	01.03.1999	2	(15)	1
Aluísio Chaves Ribeiro Moraes Júnior	04.04.1987	16	(1)	6
Marcos Robson Cipriano (BRA)	27.02.1999	6	(2)	
Manor Solomon (ISR)	24.07.1999	14	(9)	9
Taison Barcellos Freda (BRA)	13.01.1988	11	(4)	2
Mateus Cardoso Lemos Martins „Tetê" (BRA)	15.02.2000	16	(8)	6
Vladislav Vakula	29.04.1999	1	(1)	
Bogdan V'Yunnik	21.05.2002	1	(3)	

Futbolnij Klub Vorskla Poltava

Founded: 1955
Stadium: Butovsky Vorskla Stadium, Poltava (24,795)
Trainer: Yuriy Maksimov   08.12.1968

Goalkeepers:	DOB	M	(s)	G
Dmytro Riznyk	30.01.1999	24		
Oleksandr Tkachenko	19.02.1993	2		
Defenders:	**DOB**	**M**	**(s)**	**G**
Volodimir Chesnakov	12.02.1988	23		
Bradley de Nooijer (NED)	07.11.1997		(3)	
Valeriy Dubko	22.03.2001		(2)	
Ibrahim Kané (MLI)	23.06.2000	22	(1)	4
Ilya Krupsky	02.10.2004		(1)	
Evgeniy Opanasenko	25.08.1990		(3)	
Ihor Perduta	15.11.1990	22		
Vadim Sapay	07.02.1986	7	(6)	
Daniil Semilet	07.03.2001	1	(1)	
Najeeb Yakubu (GHA)	01.05.2000	17	(2)	
Serhiy Yavorskiy	05.07.1995	24		1
Midfielders:	**DOB**	**M**	**(s)**	**G**
Artem Chelyadin	29.12.1999	3	(16)	
Ilya Gadzhuk	02.08.2002		(1)	
Daniil Khrypchuk	09.12.2003		(1)	
Oleksandr Kozhevnikov	17.04.2000		(1)	
Danilo Kravchuk	02.07.2001		(13)	1
Luiz Gustavo Novaes Palhares „Luizão"(BRA)	20.02.1998	4	(6)	
Pape-Alioune Ndiaye (FRA)	04.02.1998	19	(2)	
Ivan Nesterenko	23.07.2003		(1)	
David Puclin (CRO)	17.06.1992	24		2
Pavlo Rebenok	23.07.1985	6	(8)	
Aleksandr Sklyar	26.02.1991	20	(2)	2
Ruslan Stepanyuk	16.01.1992	24		7
Mykyta Tatarkov	04.01.1995		(1)	
Oliver Thill (LUX)	17.12.1996	13		2
Oleg Vlasov	25.10.2002		(1)	
Forwards:	**DOB**	**M**	**(s)**	**G**
Vladyslav Kulach	07.05.1993	21		15
Ivan Pešić (CRO)	06.04.1992		(8)	
Dmytro Shcherbak	08.12.1996	5	(8)	1
Heorhiy Tsitaishvili	18.11.2000	3	(1)	1
Denis Vasin	04.03.1989	2	(6)	

Futbolnij Klub Zorya Luhansk

Founded: 1923
Stadium: Slavutych-Arena, Zaporizhzhia (12,000)
Trainer: Viktor Skrypnyk   19.11.1969

Goalkeepers:	DOB	M	(s)	G
Dmytro Matsapura	10.03.2000	3		
Mykyta Shevchenko	26.01.1993	8	(1)	
Nikola Vasilj (BIH)	02.12.1995	15	(1)	
Defenders:	**DOB**	**M**	**(s)**	**G**
Joel Abu Hanna (GER)	22.01.1998	20		
Yuriy Dudnyk	12.09.2002		(1)	
Vladislav Emets	09.09.1997		(1)	
Denis Favorov	01.04.1991	19	(1)	2
Maksim Grechkin	04.03.1996	2	(1)	
Leovigildo Júnior Reis Rodrigues „Juninho" (BRA)	26.12.1995	10	(3)	1
Denys Nahnoinyi	03.02.2002		(1)	
Agron Rufati (MKD)	06.04.1999	4	(6)	
Vitaliy Vernidub	17.10.1987	19	(1)	
Midfielders:	**DOB**	**M**	**(s)**	**G**
Ihor Chaykovskiy	07.10.1991		(2)	
Andrejs Ciganiks (LVA)	12.04.1997	11	(6)	
Lovro Cvek (CRO)	06.07.1995	9	(5)	
Dmitriy Ivanisenya	11.01.1994	17	(4)	4
Vladyslav Kabayev	01.09.1995	19	(2)	
Maksym Kazakov	06.02.1996	1	(3)	
Dmytro Khomchenovsky	16.04.1990	15	(4)	
Vladyslav Kochergin	30.04.1996	23		6
Yehor Nazaryna	10.07.1997	16	(9)	
Dmytro Piddubnyi	15.01.2000		(2)	
Vladlen Yurchenko	22.01.1994	22	(1)	6
Forwards:	**DOB**	**M**	**(s)**	**G**
Danyil Alefirenko	19.04.2000		(3)	1
Serhiy Gryn	06.06.1994	1	(5)	
Oleksandr Hladkiy	24.08.1987	18	(4)	9
Artem Hromov	14.01.1990	14	(2)	6
Maksym Lunyov	22.05.1998	4	(7)	
Raymond Owusu (GHA)	20.04.2002		(1)	
Mihailo Perović (MNE)	23.01.1997		(9)	
Allahyar Sayyadmanesh (IRN)	29.06.2001	11	(8)	5
Shahab Zahedi Tabar (IRN)	18.08.1995	5	(7)	2
Denys Yanakov	01.01.1999		(2)	

SECOND LEVEL
Ukrainian First League 2020/2021

1.	NK Veres Rivne (*Promoted*)	30	21	5	4	56	-	21	68
2.	FK Chornomorets Odesa (*Promoted*)	30	18	7	5	45	-	23	61
3.	FC Metalist 1925 Kharkiv (*Promoted*)	30	16	8	6	36	-	22	56
4.	MFK Mykolaiv (*Relegated*)	30	15	8	7	49	-	23	53
5.	FK Ahrobiznes Volochysk	30	15	7	8	46	-	27	52
6.	FC Alians Lypova Dolyna	30	14	9	7	46	-	31	51
7.	FK Volyn Lutsk	30	13	7	10	39	-	28	46
8.	FK Obolon Kyiv	30	13	4	13	44	-	35	43
9.	FK Hirnyk-Sport Horishni Plavni	30	11	5	14	43	-	45	38
10.	FK VPK-Ahro Shevchenkivka	30	11	4	15	30	-	48	37
11.	FK Polissya Zhytomyr	30	9	8	13	32	-	37	35
12.	FK Avanhard Kramatorsk	30	9	5	16	32	-	51	32
13.	FK Nyva Ternopil	30	8	7	15	30	-	50	31
14.	FK Prykarpattia Ivano-Frankivsk	30	8	6	16	25	-	45	30
15.	MFK Kremin Kremenchuk	30	6	6	18	23	-	50	24
16.	FK Krystal Kherson (*Relegated*)	30	3	4	23	21	-	61	13

Please note: MFK Mykolaiv were relegated after they withdrew at end of the season.

INTERNATIONAL MATCHES
(16.07.2020 – 15.07.2021)

03.09.2020	Lviv	Ukraine - Switzerland	2-1(1-1)	(UNL)
06.09.2020	Madrid	Spain - Ukraine	4-0(3-0)	(UNL)
07.10.2020	Paris	France - Ukraine	7-1(4-0)	(F)
10.10.2020	Kyiv	Ukraine - Germany	1-2(0-1)	(UNL)
13.10.2020	Kyiv	Ukraine - Spain	1-0(0-0)	(UNL)
11.11.2020	Chorzów	Poland - Ukraine	2-0(1-0)	(F)
14.11.2020	Leipzig	Germany – Ukraine	3-1(2-1)	(UNL)
17.11.2020	Luzern	Switzerland - Ukraine	3-0 (awarded)	(UNL)
24.03.2021	Paris	France - Ukraine	1-1(1-0)	(WCQ)
28.03.2021	Kyiv	Ukraine - Finland	1-1(0-0)	(WCQ)
31.03.2021	Kyiv	Ukraine - Kazakhstan	1-1(1-0)	(WCQ)
23.05.2021	Kharkiv	Ukraine - Bahrain	1-1(0-0)	(F)
03.06.2021	Kharkiv	Ukraine - Northern Ireland	1-0(1-0)	(F)
07.06.2021	Kharkiv	Ukraine - Cyprus	4-0(2-0)	(F)
13.06.2021	Amsterdam	Netherlands - Ukraine	3-2(0-0)	(EC)
17.06.2021	Bucureşti	Ukraine - North Macedonia	2-1(2-0)	(EC)
21.06.2021	Bucureşti	Ukraine - Austria	0-1(0-1)	(EC)
29.06.2021	Glasgow	Sweden - Ukraine	1-2(1-1,1-1)	(EC)
03.07.2021	Roma	Ukraine - England	0-4(0-1)	(EC)

03.09.2020   UKRAINE - SWITZERLAND   **2-1(1-1)**   2nd UEFA Nations League A, Group 4
Arena Lviv, Lviv; Referee: Andreas Ekberg (Sweden); Attendance: 0
UKR: Andriy Pyatov (Cap), Serhiy Kryvtsov, Mykola Matviyenko, Oleksandr Tymchyk, Bohdan Mykhaylichenko, Taras Stepanenko, Yevhen Konoplyanka (54.Roman Yaremchuk), Ruslan Malinovskiy, Oleksandr Zinchenko, Aluísio Chaves Ribeiro Moraes Júnior, Andriy Yarmolenko. Trainer: Andriy Shevchenko.
Goals: Andriy Yarmolenko (14), Oleksandr Zinchenko (68).

06.09.2020   SPAIN - UKRAINE   **4-0(3-0)**   2nd UEFA Nations League A, Group 4
Estadio "Alfredo Di Stéfano", Madrid; Referee: Benoît Bastien (France); Attendance: 0
UKR: Andriy Pyatov (Cap), Serhiy Kryvtsov, Mykola Matviyenko, Oleksandr Tymchyk, Bohdan Mykhaylichenko, Marlos Romero Bonfim (55.Viktor Tsyhankov), Ihor Kharatin (63.Serhiy Sydorchuk), Ruslan Malinovskiy, Oleksandr Zinchenko, Andriy Yarmolenko (79.Viktor Kovalenko), Roman Yaremchuk. Trainer: Andriy Shevchenko.

07.10.2020   FRANCE - UKRAINE   **7-1(4-0)**   Friendly International
Stade de France, Saint-Denis, Paris; Referee: Andris Treimanis (Latvia); Attendance: 1,000
UKR: Heorhiy Bushchan, Bohdan Mykhaylichenko (46.Eduard Sobol), Vitaliy Mykolenko (46.Yevhen Cheberko), Yukhym Konoplya, Illya Zabarnyi, Yevhen Makarenko (62.Volodymyr Shepelev), Ihor Kharatin, Ruslan Malinovskiy (46.Viktor Tsyhankov), Mykola Shaparenko, Andriy Yarmolenko (Cap) (62.Roman Yaremchuk), Oleksandr Zubkov (71.Roman Bezus). Trainer: Andriy Shevchenko.
Goal: Viktor Tsyhankov (53).

10.10.2020   UKRAINE - GERMANY   **1-2(0-1)**   2nd UEFA Nations League A, Group 4
NSC Olimpiyskiy Stadium, Kyiv; Referee: Orel Grinfeld (Israel); Attendance: 17,573
UKR: Heorhiy Bushchan, Eduard Sobol, Oleksandr Karavaev, Vitaliy Mykolenko, Illya Zabarnyi, Serhiy Sydorchuk (84.Yevhen Makarenko), Ruslan Malinovskiy, Viktor Kovalenko (76.Mykola Shaparenko), Viktor Tsyhankov (69.Oleksandr Zubkov), Andriy Yarmolenko (Cap) (69.Marlos Romero Bonfim), Roman Yaremchuk. Trainer: Andriy Shevchenko.
Goal: Ruslan Malinovskiy (77 penalty).

13.10.2020   UKRAINE - SPAIN   **1-0(0-0)**   2nd UEFA Nations League A, Group 4
NSC Olimpiyskiy Stadium, Kyiv; Referee: Paweł Gil (Poland); Attendance: 10,495
UKR: Heorhiy Bushchan, Eduard Sobol, Oleksandr Karavaev, Vitaliy Mykolenko, Illya Zabarnyi, Serhiy Sydorchuk (60.Viktor Kovalenko), Yevhen Makarenko, Mykola Shaparenko, Andriy Yarmolenko (Cap), Roman Yaremchuk, Oleksandr Zubkov (65.Viktor Tsyhankov). Trainer: Andriy Shevchenko.
Goal: Viktor Tsyhankov (76).

11.11.2020   POLAND - UKRAINE   **2-0(1-0)**   Friendly International
Stadion Śląski, Chorzów; Referee: Manuel Schüttengruber (Austria); Attendance: 0
UKR: Andriy Lunin, Serhiy Kryvtsov, Mykola Matviyenko, Bohdan Mykhaylichenko, Yukhym Konoplya (63.Valeriy Bondar), Yevhen Makarenko, Viktor Kovalenko (76.Serhiy Sydorchuk), Oleksandr Zinchenko (56.Ihor Kharatin), Andriy Yarmolenko (Cap) (46.Marlos Romero Bonfim), Roman Yaremchuk (46.Aluísio Chaves Ribeiro Moraes Júnior), Oleksandr Zubkov (46.Viktor Tsyhankov). Trainer: Andriy Shevchenko.

14.11.2020   GERMANY – UKRAINE   **3-1(2-1)**   2nd UEFA Nations League A, Group 4
Red Bull Arena, Leipzig; Referee: Ovidiu Alin Haţegan (Romania); Attendance: 0
UKR: Andriy Pyatov (Cap), Eduard Sobol, Mykola Matviyenko, Yukhym Konoplya, Illya Zabarnyi, Marlos Romero Bonfim, Taras Stepanenko (69.Yevhen Makarenko), Ruslan Malinovskiy, Oleksandr Zinchenko (86.Ihor Kharatin), Roman Yaremchuk (75.Aluísio Chaves Ribeiro Moraes Júnior), Oleksandr Zubkov (75.Bohdan Mykhaylichenko). Trainer: Andriy Shevchenko.
Goal: Roman Yaremchuk (12).

17.11.2020   SWITZERLAND - UKRAINE   **3-0 (awarded)**   2nd UEFA Nations League A, Group 4
Swissporarena, Luzern; Referee: Anastasios Sidiropoulos (Greece); Attendance: 0
Please note: *the match was cancelled after the Ukraine national team was placed in quarantine due to several positive COVID-19 test in the squad, being awarded as a 3-0 win to Switzerland.*

24.03.2021   FRANCE - UKRAINE   1-1(1-0)   22nd FIFA WC. Qualifiers
Stade de France, Saint-Denis, Paris; Referee: Tobias Stieler (Germany); Attendance: 0
UKR: Heorhiy Bushchan, Serhiy Kryvtsov, Oleksandr Karavaev, Mykola Matviyenko, Vitaliy Mykolenko, Illya Zabarnyi, Serhiy Sydorchuk (79.Viktor Kovalenko), Ruslan Malinovskiy, Oleksandr Zinchenko (Cap), Mykola Shaparenko (86.Oleksandr Zubkov), Roman Yaremchuk (72.Aluísio Chaves Ribeiro Moraes Júnior). Trainer: Andriy Shevchenko.
Goal: Serhiy Sydorchuk (57).

28.03.2021   UKRAINE - FINLAND   1-1(0-0)   22nd FIFA WC. Qualifiers
NSC Olimpiyskiy Stadium, Kyiv; Referee: István Kovács (Romania); Attendance: 0
UKR: Heorhiy Bushchan, Eduard Sobol, Oleksandr Karavaev, Mykola Matviyenko, Vitaliy Mykolenko [*sent off 88*], Illya Zabarnyi, Yevhen Makarenko (78.Viktor Kovalenko), Ruslan Malinovskiy, Oleksandr Zinchenko (Cap), Roman Yaremchuk (67.Aluísio Chaves Ribeiro Moraes Júnior), Oleksandr Zubkov (58.Marlos Romero Bonfim). Trainer: Andriy Shevchenko.
Goal: Aluísio Chaves Ribeiro Moraes Júnior (80).

31.03.2021   UKRAINE - KAZAKHSTAN   1-1(1-0)   22nd FIFA WC. Qualifiers
NSC Olimpiyskiy Stadium, Kyiv; Referee: Matej Jug (Slovenia); Attendance: 0
UKR: Anatoliy Trubin, Serhiy Kryvtsov, Oleksandr Karavaev (87.Oleksandr Tymchyk), Mykola Matviyenko, Bohdan Mykhaylichenko, Serhiy Sydorchuk (67.Marlos Romero Bonfim), Ruslan Malinovskiy, Oleksandr Zinchenko (Cap), Mykola Shaparenko (81.Artem Dovbyk), Aluísio Chaves Ribeiro Moraes Júnior (67.Oleksandr Zubkov), Roman Yaremchuk. Trainer: Andriy Shevchenko.
Goal: Roman Yaremchuk (20).

23.05.2021   UKRAINE - BAHRAIN   1-1(0-0)   Friendly International
Regional Sport Complex Metalist, Kharkiv; Referee: Pavel Orel (Czech Republic); Attendance: 19,000
UKR: Anatoliy Trubin, Serhiy Kryvtsov (63.Denys Popov), Mykola Matviyenko, Oleksandr Tymchyk (78.Oleksandr Karavaev), Vitaliy Mykolenko, Marlos Romero Bonfim, Taras Stepanenko (Cap) (46.Heorhiy Sudakov), Yevhen Makarenko (63.Serhiy Sydorchuk), Oleksandr Zubkov (46.Viktor Tsyhankov), Mykola Shaparenko, Artem Besyedin (46.Artem Dovbyk). Trainer: Andriy Shevchenko.
Goal: Viktor Tsyhankov (90+1).

03.06.2021   UKRAINE - NORTHERN IRELAND   1-0(1-0)   Friendly International
Dnipro Arena, Dnipro; Referee: Szymon Marciniak (Poland); Attendance: 15,000
UKR: Heorhiy Bushchan, Oleksandr Karavaev, Mykola Matviyenko, Vitaliy Mykolenko, Illya Zabarnyi, Serhiy Sydorchuk (76.Taras Stepanenko), Andriy Yarmolenko (Cap), Ruslan Malinovskiy, Oleksandr Zubkov (46.Marlos Romero Bonfim), Mykola Shaparenko (72.Heorhiy Sudakov), Roman Yaremchuk (46.Artem Besyedin). Trainer: Andriy Shevchenko.
Goal: Oleksandr Zubkov (10).

07.06.2021   UKRAINE - CYPRUS   4-0(2-0)   Friendly International
Regional Sport Complex Metalist, Kharkiv; Referee: Vitālijs Spasjoņņikovs (Latvia); Attendance: 18,000
UKR: Andriy Pyatov (Cap), Serhiy Kryvtsov, Eduard Sobol, Mykola Matviyenko (60.Oleksandr Karavaev), Illya Zabarnyi, Yevhen Makarenko (46.Taras Stepanenko), Andriy Yarmolenko (70.Mykola Shaparenko), Ruslan Malinovskiy (67.Heorhiy Sudakov), Oleksandr Zinchenko, Oleksandr Zubkov (46.Marlos Romero Bonfim), Roman Yaremchuk (67.Artem Besyedin). Trainer: Andriy Shevchenko.
Goals: Andriy Yarmolenko (37 penalty), Oleksandr Zinchenko (45+2), Roman Yaremchuk (59), Andriy Yarmolenko (65).

13.06.2021   NETHERLANDS - UKRAINE   3-2(0-0)   16th EC. Group Stage.
"Johan Cruyff" Arena, Amsterdam; Referee: Dr. Felix Brych (Germany); Attendance: 15,837
UKR: Heorhiy Bushchan, Oleksandr Karavaev, Mykola Matviyenko, Vitaliy Mykolenko, Illya Zabarnyi, Serhiy Sydorchuk, Ruslan Malinovskiy, Andriy Yarmolenko (Cap), Oleksandr Zinchenko, Oleksandr Zubkov (13.Marlos Romero Bonfim; 64.Mykola Shaparenko), Roman Yaremchuk. Trainer: Andriy Shevchenko.
Goals: Andriy Yarmolenko (75), Roman Yaremchuk (79).

17.06.2021   UKRAINE - NORTH MACEDONIA   2-1(2-0)   16th EC. Group Stage.
Arena Națională, București (Romania); Referee: Fernando Andrés Rapallini (Argentina); Attendance: 10,001
UKR: Heorhiy Bushchan, Oleksandr Karavaev, Mykola Matviyenko, Vitaliy Mykolenko, Illya Zabarnyi, Taras Stepanenko, Ruslan Malinovskiy (90+2.Eduard Sobol), Mykola Shaparenko (78.Serhiy Sydorchuk), Oleksandr Zinchenko, Andriy Yarmolenko (Cap) (70.Viktor Tsyhankov), Roman Yaremchuk (70.Artem Besyedin). Trainer: Andriy Shevchenko.
Goals: Andriy Yarmolenko (29), Roman Yaremchuk (34).

21.06.2021   UKRAINE - AUSTRIA   0-1(0-1)   16th EC. Group Stage.
Arena Națională, București (Romania); Referee: Cüneyt Çakır (Turkey); Attendance: 10,472
UKR: Heorhiy Bushchan, Oleksandr Karavaev, Mykola Matviyenko, Vitaliy Mykolenko (85.Artem Besyedin), Illya Zabarnyi, Serhiy Sydorchuk, Ruslan Malinovskiy (46.Viktor Tsyhankov), Andriy Yarmolenko (Cap), Oleksandr Zinchenko, Mykola Shaparenko (68.Marlos Romero Bonfim), Roman Yaremchuk. Trainer: Andriy Shevchenko.

29.06.2021   SWEDEN - UKRAINE   1-2(1-1,1-1)   16th EC. 2nd Round of 16.
Hampden Park, Glasgow (Scotland); Referee: Daniele Orsato (Italy); Attendance: 9,221
UKR: Heorhiy Bushchan, Serhiy Kryvtsov, Oleksandr Karavaev, Mykola Matviyenko, Illya Zabarnyi, Taras Stepanenko (94.Yevhen Makarenko), Serhiy Sydorchuk (118.Roman Bezus), Roman Yaremchuk (91.Artem Besyedin; 101.Viktor Tsyhankov), Oleksandr Zinchenko, Mykola Shaparenko (61.Ruslan Malinovskiy), Andriy Yarmolenko (Cap) (106.Artem Dovbyk). Trainer: Andriy Shevchenko.
Goals: Oleksandr Zinchenko (27), Artem Dovbyk (120+1).

03.07.2021   UKRAINE - ENGLAND   0-4(0-1)   16th EC. Quarter-Finals.
Stadio Olimpico, Rome (Italy); Referee: Dr. Felix Brych (Germany); Attendance: 11,880
UKR: Heorhiy Bushchan, Serhiy Kryvtsov (35.Viktor Tsyhankov), Oleksandr Karavaev, Mykola Matviyenko, Vitaliy Mykolenko, Illya Zabarnyi, Serhiy Sydorchuk (64.Yevhen Makarenko), Andriy Yarmolenko (Cap), Oleksandr Zinchenko, Mykola Shaparenko, Roman Yaremchuk. Trainer: Andriy Shevchenko.

NATIONAL TEAM PLAYERS
(16.07.2020 – 15.07.2021)

Name	DOB	Caps	Goals	2020/2021:	Club
Goalkeepers					
Heorhiy BUSHCHAN	31.05.1994	11	0	2020/2021:	*FK Dinamo Kyiv*
Andriy LUNIN	11.02.1999	6	0	2020/2021:	*Real Madrid CF (ESP)*
Andriy PYATOV	28.06.1984	97	0	2020/2021:	*FK Shakhtar Donetsk*
Anatoliy TRUBIN	01.08.2001	2	0	2021:	*FK Shakhtar Donetsk*
Defenders					
Valeriy BONDAR	27.02.1999	1	0	2020:	*FK Shakhtar Donetsk*
Yevhen CHEBERKO	23.01.1998	1	0	2020:	*Linzer ASK (AUT)*
Oleksandr KARAVAYEV	02.06.1992	38	1	2020/2021:	*FK Dinamo Kyiv*
Yukhym KONOPLYA	26.08.1999	3	0	2020:	*FK Desna Chernihiv*
Serhiy KRYVTSOV	15.03.1991	25	0	2020/2021:	*FK Shakhtar Donetsk*
Mykola MATVIYENKO	02.05.1996	41	0	2020/2021:	*FK Shakhtar Donetsk*
Bohdan MYKHAYLICHENKO	21.03.1997	6	0	2020/2021:	*RSC Anderlecht Bruxelles (BEL)*
Vitaliy MYKOLENKO	29.05.1999	19	0	2020/2021:	*FK Dinamo Kyiv*
Denys POPOV	17.02.1999	1	0	2021:	*FK Dinamo Kyiv*
Eduard SOBOL	20.04.1995	21	0	2020/2021:	*Club Brugge KV (BEL)*
Oleksandr TYMCHYK	20.01.1997	4	0	2020/2021:	*FK Dinamo Kyiv*
Illya ZABARNYI	01.09.2002	13	0	2020/2021:	*FK Dinamo Kyiv*
Midfielders					
Roman BEZUS	26.09.1990	24	5	2020/2021:	*KAA Gent (BEL)*
Ihor KHARATIN	02.02.1995	4	0	2020:	*Ferencváros TC (HUN)*
Yevhen KONOPLYANKA	29.09.1989	86	21	2020/2021:	*FK Shakhtar Donetsk*
Viktor KOVALENKO	14.02.1996	32	0	2020:	*FK Shakhtar Donetsk*
				01.02.2021->	*Atalanta Bergamasca Calcio (ITA)*
Yevhen MAKARENKO	21.05.1991	14	0	2020/2021:	*KV Kortrijk (BEL)*
Ruslan MALINOVSKIY	04.05.1993	41	6	2020/2021:	*Atalanta Bergamasca Calcio (ITA)*
MARLOS Romero Bonfim	07.06.1988	27	1	2020/2021:	*FK Shakhtar Donetsk*
Mykola SHAPARENKO	04.10.1998	17	0	2020/2021:	*FK Dinamo Kyiv*
Volodymyr SHEPELEV	01.06.1997	7	0	2020:	*FK Dinamo Kyiv*
Taras STEPANENKO	08.08.1989	64	3	2020/2021:	*FK Shakhtar Donetsk*
Heorhiy SUDAKOV	01.09.2002	3	0	2021:	*FK Shakhtar Donetsk*
Serhiy SYDORCHUK	02.05.1991	41	2	2020/2021:	*FK Dinamo Kyiv*
Viktor TSYHANKOV	15.11.1997	30	6	2020/2021:	*FK Dinamo Kyiv*
Oleksandr ZINCHENKO	15.12.1996	44	7	2020/2021:	*Manchester City FC (ENG)*
Oleksandr ZUBKOV	03.08.1996	12	1	2020/2021:	*Ferencváros TC (HUN)*
Forwards					
Artem BESYEDIN	31.03.1996	19	2	2020/2021:	*FK Dinamo Kyiv*
Artem DOVBYK	21.06.1997	3	1	2021:	*SC Dnipro-1*
Aluísio Chaves Ribeiro MORAES Júnior	04.04.1987	11	1	2020/2021:	*FK Shakhtar Donetsk*
Roman YAREMCHUK	27.11.1995	29	10	2020/2021:	*KAA Gent (BEL)*
Andriy YARMOLENKO	23.10.1989	99	42	2020/2021:	*West Ham United FC London (ENG)*

National team coach

Andriy SHEVCHENKO [15.07.2016 – 01.08.2021]	29.09.1976	51 M; 25 W; 13 D; 13 L; 71-59	

WALES

The Country:
Cymru (Wales)
Capital: Cardiff
Surface: 20,779 km²
Inhabitants: 3,153,000 [2019]
Time: UTC

The FA:
Football Association of Wales
Hensol, Vanguard Way 72, 8JY Glamorgan
Tel: +44 29 2043 5830
Founded: 1876
Member of FIFA: 1910-1920; 1924-1928; since 1946
Member of UEFA since: 1954
Website: www.faw.cymru

NATIONAL TEAM RECORDS

RECORDS
First international match:	25.03.1876, Glasgow:	Scotland – Wales 4-0
Most international caps:	Christopher Ross Gunter	- 102 caps (since 2007)
Most international goals:	Gareth Frank Bale	- 33 goals / 96 caps (since 2006)

UEFA EUROPEAN CHAMPIONSHIP		FIFA WORLD CUP		OLYMPIC TOURNAMENTS	
1960	Did not enter	1930	*Not a FIFA member*	1908	-
1964	Qualifiers	1934	*Not a FIFA member*	1912	-
1968	Qualifiers	1938	*Not a FIFA member*	1920	-
1972	Qualifiers	1950	Qualifiers	1924	-
1976	Qualifiers	1954	Qualifiers	1928	-
1980	Qualifiers	1958	Final Tournament (Quarter-Finals)	1936	-
1984	Qualifiers	1962	Qualifiers	1948	-
1988	Qualifiers	1966	Qualifiers	1952	-
1992	Qualifiers	1970	Qualifiers	1956	-
1996	Qualifiers	1974	Qualifiers	1960	-
2000	Qualifiers	1978	Qualifiers	1964	-
2004	Qualifiers	1982	Qualifiers	1968	-
2008	Qualifiers	1986	Qualifiers	1972	-
2012	Qualifiers	1990	Qualifiers	1976	-
2016	Final Tournament (Semi-Finals)	1994	Qualifiers	1980	-
2020	Final Tournament (2nd Round of 16)	1998	Qualifiers	1984	-
		2002	Qualifiers	1988	-
		2006	Qualifiers	1992	-
		2010	Qualifiers	1996	-
		2014	Qualifiers	2000	-
		2018	Qualifiers	2004	-
				2008	-
				2012	-
				2016	-

UEFA NATIONS LEAGUE
2018/2019	League B
2020/2021	League B (Promoted to League A)

FIFA CONFEDERATIONS CUP 1992-2017
None

WELSH CLUB HONOURS IN EUROPEAN CLUB COMPETITIONS:

European Champion Clubs.Cup (1956-1992) / UEFA Champions League (1993-2021)
None

Fairs Cup (1858-1971) / UEFA Cup (1972-2009) / UEFA Europa League (2010-2021)
None

UEFA Super Cup (1972-2020)
None

*European Cup Winners.Cup 1961-1999**
None

*defunct competition

NATIONAL COMPETITIONS
TABLE OF HONOURS

CUP WINNERS 1878-1992

Year	Winner	Year	Winner	Year	Winner
1877/1878	Wrexham AFC	1916/1917	*No competition*	1954/1955	Barry Town United FC
1878/1879	Newtown White Stars FC	1917/1918	*No competition*	1955/1956	Cardiff City FC
1879/1880	Ruabon Druids FC	1918/1919	*No competition*	1956/1957	Wrexham AFC
1880/1881	Ruabon Druids FC	1919/1920	Cardiff City FC	1957/1958	Wrexham AFC
1881/1882	Ruabon Druids FC	1920/1921	Wrexham AFC	1958/1959	Cardiff City FC
1882/1883	Wrexham AFC	1921/1922	Cardiff City FC	1959/1960	Wrexham AFC
1883/1884	Oswestry Town FC Shropshire(ENG)	1922/1923	Cardiff City FC	1960/1961	Swansea Town AFC
1884/1885	Ruabon Druids FC	1923/1924	Wrexham AFC	1961/1962	Bangor City FC
1885/1886	Ruabon Druids FC	1924/1925	Wrexham AFC	1962/1963	Borough United FC
1886/1887	Chirk AAA FC	1925/1926	Ebbw Vale FC	1963/1964	Cardiff City FC
1887/1888	Chirk AAA FC	1926/1927	Cardiff City FC	1964/1965	Cardiff City FC
1888/1889	Bangor City FC	1927/1928	Cardiff City FC	1965/1966	Swansea Town AFC
1889/1890	Chirk AAA FC	1928/1929	Connah's Quay & Shotton FC	1966/1967	Cardiff City FC
1890/1891	Shrewsbury Town FC (ENG)	1929/1930	Cardiff City FC	1967/1968	Cardiff City FC
1891/1892	Chirk AAA FC	1930/1931	Wrexham AFC	1968/1969	Cardiff City FC
1892/1893	Wrexham AFC	1931/1932	Swansea Town AFC	1969/1970	Cardiff City FC
1893/1894	Chirk AAA FC	1932/1933	Chester City FC (ENG)	1970/1971	Cardiff City FC
1894/1895	Newtown AFC	1933/1934	Bristol City FC (ENG)	1971/1972	Wrexham AFC
1895/1896	Bangor City FC	1934/1935	Tranmere Rovers FC (ENG)	1972/1973	Cardiff City FC
1896/1897	Wrexham AFC	1935/1936	Crewe Alexandra FC (ENG)	1973/1974	Cardiff City FC
1897/1898	Ruabon Druids FC	1936/1937	Crewe Alexandra FC (ENG)	1974/1975	Wrexham AFC
1898/1899	Ruabon Druids FC	1937/1938	Shrewsbury Town FC (ENG)	1975/1976	Cardiff City FC
1899/1900	Aberystwyth Town FC	1938/1939	South Liverpool FC (ENG)	1976/1977	Shrewsbury Town FC (ENG)
1900/1901	Oswestry Town FC (ENG)	1939/1940	Wellington Town FC (ENG)	1977/1978	Wrexham AFC
1901/1902	Wellington Town FC (ENG)	1940/1941	*No competition*	1978/1979	Shrewsbury Town FC (ENG)
1902/1903	Wrexham AFC	1941/1942	*No competition*	1979/1980	Newport County AFC
1903/1904	Ruabon Druids FC	1942/1943	*No competition*	1980/1981	Swansea City FC
1904/1905	Wrexham AFC	1943/1944	*No competition*	1981/1982	Swansea City FC
1905/1906	Wellington Town FC (ENG)	1944/1945	*No competition*	1982/1983	Swansea City FC
1906/1907	Oswestry Town FC (ENG)	1945/1946	*No competition*	1983/1984	Shrewsbury Town FC (ENG)
1907/1908	Chester City FC (ENG)	1946/1947	Chester City FC (ENG)	1984/1985	Shrewsbury Town FC (ENG)
1908/1909	Wrexham AFC	1947/1948	Lovell's Athletic FC	1985/1986	Wrexham AFC
1909/1910	Wrexham AFC	1948/1949	Merthyr Tydfil FC	1986/1987	Merthyr Tydfil FC
1910/1911	Wrexham AFC	1949/1950	Swansea Town AFC	1987/1988	Cardiff City FC
1911/1912	Cardiff City	1950/1951	Merthyr Tydfil FC	1988/1989	Swansea City FC
1912/1913	Swansea Town AFC	1951/1952	Rhyl FC	1989/1990	Hereford United FC (ENG)
1913/1914	Wrexham AFC	1952/1953	Rhyl FC	1990/1991	Swansea City FC
1914/1915	Wrexham AFC	1953/1954	Flint Town United FC	1991/1992	Cardiff City FC
1915/1916	*No competition*				

	CHAMPIONS*	CUP WINNERS	BEST GOALSCORERS	
1992/1993	Cwmbrân Town AFC	Cardiff City FC	Steve Woods (Ebbw Vale FC)	29
1993/1994	Bangor City FC	Barry Town United FC	Dave Taylor (Porthmadog FC)	43
1994/1995	Bangor City FC	Wrexham AFC	Frank Mottram (Bangor City FC)	31
1995/1996	Barry Town United FC	Llansantffraid FC	Ken McKenna (Conwy United FC)	38
1996/1997	Barry Town United FC	Barry Town United FC	Anthony Bird (Barry Town United FC)	42
1997/1998	Barry Town United FC	Bangor City FC	Eifion Wyn Williams (Barry Town United FC)	40
1998/1999	Barry Town United FC	Inter CableTel Cardiff	Eifion Wyn Williams (Barry Town United FC)	28
1999/2000	Total Network Solutions	Bangor City FC	Chris Summers (Cwmbrân Town AFC)	28
2000/2001	Barry Town United FC	Barry Town United FC	Graham Evans (Caersws FC)	25
2001/2002	Barry Town United FC	Barry Town United FC	Marc Lloyd-Williams (Bangor City FC)	47
2002/2003	Barry Town United FC	Barry Town United FC	Graham Evans (Caersws FC)	24
2003/2004	Rhyl FC	Rhyl FC	Graham Evans (Caersws FC)	24
2004/2005	Total Network Solutions	Total Network Solutions	Marc Lloyd-Williams (Total Network Solutions)	31
2005/2006	Total Network Solutions	Rhyl FC	Rhys Griffiths (Port Talbot Town FC)	28
2006/2007	The New Saints FC	Carmarthen Town FC	Rhys Griffiths (Llanelli Town AFC)	30
2007/2008	Llanelli Town AFC	Bangor City FC	Rhys Griffiths (Llanelli Town AFC)	40
2008/2009	Rhyl FC	Bangor City FC	Rhys Griffiths (Llanelli Town AFC)	31
2009/2010	The New Saints FC	Bangor City FC	Rhys Griffiths (Llanelli Town AFC)	30
2010/2011	Bangor City FC	Llanelli Town AFC	Rhys Griffiths (Llanelli Town AFC)	25
2011/2012	The New Saints FC	The New Saints FC	Rhys Griffiths (Llanelli Town AFC)	24
2012/2013	The New Saints FC	Prestatyn Town FC	Michael Wilde (The New Saints FC)	25
2013/2014	The New Saints FC	The New Saints FC	Chris Venables (Aberystwyth Town FC)	20
2014/2015	The New Saints FC	The New Saints FC	Chris Venables (Aberystwyth Town FC)	28
2015/2016	The New Saints FC	The New Saints FC	Chris Venables (Bala Town FC)	20
2016/2017	The New Saints FC	Bala Town FC	Jason Oswell (ENG, Newtown AFC)	22
2017/2018	The New Saints FC	Connah's Quay Nomads FC	Gregory Alexander Draper (NZL, The New Saints FC)	11
2018/2019	The New Saints FC	The New Saints FC	Steven Anthony Tames (ENG, Bala Town FC)	17

| 2019/2020 | Connah's Quay Nomads FC | *Competition postponed* | Chris Venables (Bala Town FC) | 22 |
| 2020/2021 | Connah's Quay Nomads FC | *No competition* | Chris Venables (Bala Town FC) | 24 |

Please note: Championship called League of Wales (1992–2002) and Welsh Premier League (since 2002).

NATIONAL CHAMPIONSHIP
Cymru Premier League 2020/2021
(12.09.2020 – 15.05.2021)

Regular Season - Results

Round 1 [12.09.2020]
Aberystwyth Town - Metropolitan 2-3(1-0)
Barry Town - The New Saints 0-3(0-0)
Caernarfon Town - Penybont FC 1-1(0-0)
Flint Town - Newtown AFC 1-0(1-0)
Connah's Quay - Bala Town 1-1(0-1)
Haverfordwest - Cefn Druids 1-1(0-0) [05.12.]

Round 2 [15.09.2020]
Metropolitan - Haverfordwest 0-0
Newtown AFC - Caernarfon Town 2-3(1-1)
Penybont FC - Aberystwyth Town 1-1(1-0)
Cefn Druids - Flint Town 1-2(0-1) [23.09.]
The New Saints-Connah's Q. 1-0(1-0) [13.10.]
Bala Town - Barry Town 4-0(3-0) [14.10.]

Round 3 [18-20.09.2020]
Aberystwyth Town - Flint Town 3-1(1-1)
Barry Town - Caernarfon Town 3-1(1-0)
Haverfordwest - Newtown AFC 2-2(0-1)
Bala Town - Cefn Druids 2-1(1-0)
Connah's Quay - Penybont FC 1-0(1-0)
The New Saints - Metropolitan 2-0(1-0)

Round 4 [25-27.09.2020]
Newtown AFC - Aberystwyth Town 1-1(0-1)
Cefn Druids - Metropolitan 1-1(1-0)
Penybont FC - Bala Town 1-5(1-0)
Flint Town - Barry Town 0-1(0-0)
Caernarfon Town - The New Saints 0-4(0-0)
Haverfordwest - Connah's Quay 1-4(1-1)

Round 5 [29-30.09.2020]
Newtown AFC - Cefn Druids 4-1(1-1)
Barry Town - Haverfordwest 2-1(1-0)
Caernarfon Town - Flint Town 2-1(0-0)
Metropolitan - Penybont FC 0-1(0-0)
Connah's Quay - Aberystwyth Town 2-0(2-0)
Bala Town - The New Saints 1-1(0-0) [07.11.]

Round 6 [03.10.2020]
Aberystwyth Town - Barry Town 1-2(0-0)
Bala Town - Haverfordwest 1-2(1-1)
Cefn Druids - Connah's Quay 0-5(0-1)
Penybont FC - Newtown AFC 2-1(0-1)
The New Saints - Flint Town 10-0(3-0)
Metropolitan - Caernarfon Town 0-3(0-1)

Round 7 [06.10.2020]
Barry Town - Metropolitan 1-0(0-0)
Connah's Quay - Caernarfon Town 3-1(0-1)
Cefn Druids - Aberystwyth Town 0-4(0-2)
Haverfordwest - Penybont FC 0-4(0-2)
The New Saints - Newtown AFC 2-0(0-0)
Flint Town - Bala Town 1-2(1-1) [20.10.]

Round 8 [09-10.10.2020]
Caernarfon Town - Cefn Druids 1-2(0-2)
Metropolitan - Connah's Quay 1-2(1-0)
Flint Town - Haverfordwest 0-2(0-0)
Newtown AFC - Barry Town 1-1(1-0)
Penybont FC - The New Saints 0-4(0-2)
Bala Town - Aberystwyth Town 5-2(2-1)

Round 9 [16-17.10.2020]
Aberystwyth Town - The New Saints 2-2(0-1)
Metropolitan - Flint Town 2-1(0-0)
Cefn Druids - Penybont FC 0-2(0-1)
Haverfordwest - Caernarfon Town 1-1(0-0)
Newtown AFC - Bala Town 0-2(0-1)
Barry Town - Connah's Quay 0-0

Round 10 [24.10.2020]
The New Saints - Haverfordwest 3-2(1-1)
Bala Town - Metropolitan 4-1(3-0) [12.12.20]
Caernarfon - Aberystwyth 2-2(0-1) [06.03.21]
Connah's Q. - Newtown 2-1(1-1) [06.03.21]
Cefn Druids - Barry Town 0-1(0-1) [06.03.21]
Penybont FC - Flint Town 1-2(0-2) [20.03.21]

Round 11
Connah's Q. - New Saints 2-0(0-0) [12.12.20]
Flint Town - Caernarfon 0-2(0-0) [13.03.21]
Metropolitan - Cefn Druids 0-0 [20.03.2021]
Aberystwyth - Penybont 1-1(1-0) [27.03.21]
Barry Town - Bala Town 6-2(2-1) [27.03.21]
Newtown - Haverfordwest 0-3(0-1) [27.03.21]

Round 12
Caernarfon - Barry Town 2-0(0-0) [12.12.20]
Haverfordw.-Metropolitan 1-0(1-0) [06.03.21]
Cefn Druids - Bala Town 1-3(1-1) [13.03.21]
Penybont FC - Connah's Quay 0-0 [13.03.21]
Aberystwyth - Newtown 1-0(0-0) [20.03.21]
Flint Town - New Saints 0-6(0-5) [27.03.21]

Round 13 [13-14.11.2020]
Caernarfon Town - Connah's Quay 1-2(0-0)
Metropolitan - Aberystwyth Town 1-1(0-0)
Bala Town - Penybont FC 4-1(3-1)
Newtown AFC - Flint Town 3-2(1-1)
The New Saints - Barry Town 2-1(1-0)
Cefn Druids - Haverfordwest 4-1(1-0) [12.12.]

Round 14 [20-21.11.2020]
Connah's Quay - Cefn Druids 2-1(2-0)
Barry Town - Newtown AFC 0-0
Metropolitan - The New Saints 0-1(0-0)
Haverfordwest - Flint Town 0-3(0-1)
Penybont - Caernarfon Town 6-0(2-0) [05.12.]
Aberystwyth - Bala Town 1-2(1-2) [09.12.]

Round 15 [27-29.11.2020]
Bala Town - Newtown AFC 3-1(2-0)
Connah's Quay - Barry Town 3-1(2-1)
Caernarfon Town - Haverfordwest 1-4(1-2)
Flint Town - Metropolitan 0-1(0-0)
The New Saints - Aberystwyth Town 4-1(1-1)
Penybont FC - Cefn Druids 1-1(0-0)

Round 16 [04-08.12.2020]
Aberystwyth Town - Connah's Quay 1-3(0-1)
Barry Town - Flint Town 6-3(3-1)
Metropolitan - Bala Town 1-1(0-0)
Cefn Druids - Caernarfon Town 1-2(0-2)
Newtown - Penybont FC 2-0(1-0) [02.03.21]
Haverfordw. - New Saints 2-1(1-0) [13.03.21]

Round 17 [18-19.12.2020]
Haverfordwest - Bala Town 1-1(0-0) [31.10.]
Caernarfon Town - Newtown AFC 1-1(1-0)
Barry Town - Cefn Druids 4-1(2-0)
Connah's Quay - Metropolitan 3-1(1-1)
The New Saints - Penybont FC 2-1(2-1)
Flint Town - Aberystwyth Town 3-0(1-0)

Round 18
Aberystwyth - Haverfordw. 2-1(0-0)[09.03.21]
Flint Town - Connah's Q. 0-1(0-0) [09.03.21]
Newtown - Metropolitan 4-1(2-1) [13.03.21]
Penybont - Barry Town 1-0(0-0) [16.03.21]
New Saints - Cefn Druids 5-0(3-0) [16.03.21]
Bala Town - Caernarfon 1-2(1-0) [20.03.21]

Round 19 [01-02.12.2020]
Caernarfon Town - Bala Town 1-1(1-1)
Metropolitan - Newtown AFC 2-1(2-1)
Connah's Quay - Flint Town 2-0(1-0)
Haverfordwest - Aberystwyth Town 2-0(2-0)
Cefn Druids - The New Saints 0-4(0-3)
Barry Town - Penybont 0-1(0-0) [09.03.21]

Round 20 [15-16.12.2020]
Aberystwyth - Caernarfon Town 1-2(0-2)
Flint Town - Cefn Druids 1-2(1-0)
Newtown AFC - The New Saints 0-4(0-2)
Penybont FC - Metropolitan 1-0(1-0)
Haverfordwest - Barry Town 2-1(0-0)
Bala Town - Connah's Q. 1-3(1-1) [16.03.21]

Round 21 [06-09.03.2021]
Flint Town - Penybont FC 0-1(0-1)
The New Saints - Bala Town 0-0
Cefn Druids - Newtown AFC 2-4(2-4)
Barry Town - Aberystwyth 1-0(0-0) [13.03.]
Connah's Q. - Haverfordwest 2-0(1-0) [20.03.]
Caernarfon - Metropolitan 3-2(1-0) [27.03.]

Round 22 [02.04.2021]
Aberystwyth Town - Cefn Druids 3-1(3-0)
Bala Town - Flint Town 5-0(1-0)
Metropolitan - Barry Town 1-2(0-0)
Newtown AFC - Connah's Quay 1-5(1-1)
Penybont FC - Haverfordwest 2-0(1-0)
The New Saints - Caernarfon Town 4-1(1-0)

1.	Connah's Quay Nomads FC	22	18	3	1	48	-	13	57
2.	The New Saints FC	22	17	3	2	65	-	13	54
3.	Bala Town FC	22	12	6	4	51	-	28	42
4.	Barry Town United FC	22	11	3	8	33	-	29	36
5.	Penybont FC Bridgend	22	10	5	7	29	-	25	35
6.	Caernarfon Town FC	22	9	5	8	33	-	42	32
7.	Haverfordwest County AFC	22	8	5	9	29	-	35	29
8.	Aberystwyth Town FC	22	5	6	11	30	-	40	21
9.	Newtown AFC	22	5	5	12	29	-	41	20
10.	Cardiff Metropolitan University FC	22	4	5	13	18	-	35	17
11.	Flint Town United FC	22	5	0	17	21	-	53	15
12.	Cefn Druids AFC	22	3	4	15	21	-	53	13

Teams ranked 1-6 were qualified for the Championship Round, while teams ranked 7-12 were qualified for the Relegation Round.

Relegation Round

Round 23 [09-10.04.2021]
Aberystwyth Town - Newtown AFC 1-2(1-0)
Flint Town - Metropolitan 2-0(1-0)
Cefn Druids - Haverfordwest 2-1(1-0)

Round 24 [13.04.2021]
Metropolitan - Newtown AFC 2-2(1-2)
Haverfordwest - Aberystwyth Town 1-0(0-0)
Flint Town - Cefn Druids 5-0(2-0)

Round 25 [16-17.04.2021]
Aberystwyth Town - Flint Town 0-1(0-0)
Cefn Druids - Metropolitan 1-2(1-1)
Newtown AFC - Haverfordwest 5-1(3-0)

Round 26 [20.04.2021]
Metropolitan - Haverfordwest 6-1(6-0)
Flint Town - Newtown AFC 0-2(0-1)
Cefn Druids - Aberystwyth Town 0-3(0-2)

Round 27 [23-24.04.2021]
Aberystwyth Town - Metropolitan 1-1(0-0)
Newtown AFC - Cefn Druids 5-0(2-0)
Haverfordwest - Flint Town 0-0

Round 28 [27.04.2021]
Haverfordwest - Metropolitan 0-2(0-0)
Newtown AFC - Flint Town 1-0(0-0)
Aberystwyth Town - Cefn Druids 5-1(2-0)

Round 29 [30.04.-01.05.2021]
Metropolitan - Aberystwyth Town 5-1(2-0)
Cefn Druids - Newtown AFC 0-7(0-1)
Flint Town - Haverfordwest 2-0(1-0)

Round 30 [04.05.2021]
Aberystwyth Town - Haverfordwest 2-2(2-2)
Cefn Druids - Flint Town 0-6(0-1)
Newtown AFC - Metropolitan 2-3(1-1)

Round 31 [08.05.2021]
Metropolitan - Cefn Druids 6-0(5-0)
Flint Town - Aberystwyth Town 0-0
Haverfordwest - Newtown AFC 1-2(1-2)

Round 32 [15.05.2021]
Metropolitan - Flint Town 2-1(1-0)
Haverfordwest - Cefn Druids 2-0(1-0)
Newtown AFC - Aberystwyth Town 0-4(0-1)

Championship Round

Round 23 [10.04.2021]
Caernarfon Town - Barry Town 0-1(0-0)
Connah's Quay - Penybont FC 0-2(0-1)
Bala Town - The New Saints 0-1(0-1)

Round 24 [13.04.2021]
Barry Town - The New Saints 0-6(0-3)
Penybont FC - Bala Town 2-3(0-1)
Caernarfon Town - Connah's Quay 1-6(1-2)

Round 25 [17.04.2021]
Connah's Quay - Barry Town 1-0(1-0)
Bala Town - Caernarfon Town 5-2(1-2)
The New Saints - Penybont FC 1-0(0-0)

Round 26 [20.04.2021]
Barry Town - Penybont FC 3-3(3-1)
Caernarfon Town - The New Saints 0-2(0-0)
Connah's Quay - Bala Town 2-0(0-0)

Round 27 [24.04.2021]
Bala Town - Barry Town 1-0(0-0)
Penybont FC - Caernarfon Town 2-0(1-0)
The New Saints - Connah's Quay 1-4(1-3)

Round 28 [27-28.04.2021]
Penybont FC - Barry Town 2-0(1-0)
The New Saints - Caernarfon Town 0-0
Bala Town - Connah's Quay 2-1(1-0)

Round 29 [01.05.2021]
Barry Town - Bala Town 1-4(1-2)
Caernarfon Town - Penybont FC 2-2(1-1)
Connah's Quay - The New Saints 0-0

Round 30 [04.05.2021]
Barry Town - Connah's Quay 1-2(0-0)
Caernarfon Town - Bala Town 3-0(2-0)
Penybont FC - The New Saints 0-3(0-0)

Round 31 [08.05.2021]
The New Saints - Barry Town 3-0(0-0)
Bala Town - Penybont FC 1-0(0-0)
Connah's Quay - Caernarfon Town 4-0(1-0)

Round 32 [15.05.2021]
Barry Town - Caernarfon Town 3-2(0-1)
Penybont FC - Connah's Quay 0-2(0-1)
The New Saints - Bala Town 2-0(1-0)

Final Standings

								Total					Home					Away		
1.	**Connah's Quay Nomads FC**	32	25	4	3	70	-	20	79	13	2	1	30	-	8	12	2	2	40	- 12
2.	The New Saints FC	32	24	5	3	84	-	17	77	13	2	1	42	-	10	11	3	2	42	- 7
3.	Bala Town FC	32	18	6	8	67	-	42	60	11	1	4	40	-	18	7	5	4	27	- 24
4.	Penybont FC Bridgend	32	13	7	12	42	-	40	46	7	3	6	22	-	22	6	4	6	20	- 18
5.	Barry Town United FC	32	13	4	15	42	-	53	43	8	3	5	31	-	29	5	1	10	11	- 24
6.	Caernarfon Town FC	32	10	7	15	43	-	67	37	4	5	7	21	-	31	6	2	8	22	- 36
7.	Newtown AFC	32	12	6	14	57	-	53	42	7	2	7	31	-	31	5	4	7	26	- 22
8.	Cardiff Metropolitan University FC	32	11	7	14	47	-	46	40	6	5	5	29	-	18	5	2	9	18	- 28
9.	Haverfordwest County AFC	32	10	7	15	38	-	56	37	6	5	5	17	-	22	4	2	10	21	- 34
10.	Aberystwyth Town FC	32	8	9	15	47	-	53	33	5	4	7	27	-	25	3	5	8	20	- 28
11.	Flint Town United FC	32	10	2	20	38	-	58	32	5	1	10	15	-	20	5	1	10	23	- 38
12.	Cefn Druids AFC	32	4	4	24	25	-	95	16	2	1	13	13	-	48	2	3	11	12	- 47

No teams were relegated.
Teams ranked 4-7 were qualified for the Europa Conference League Play-offs.

Top goalscorers:

24	**Chris Venables**	*Bala Town FC*
18	Michael Wilde	*Connah's Quay Nomads FC*
14	Gregory Alexander Draper (NZL)	*The New Saints FC*

UEFA Europa Conference League Play-offs

Semi-Finals [22-23.05.2021]	Barry Town United FC - Caernarfon Town FC	1-3(1-1)
	Penybont FC Bridgend - Newtown AFC	0-1(0-0)
Final [29.05.2021]	Caernarfon Town FC - **Newtown AFC**	3-5(1-2)

NATIONAL CUP
Welsh Cup 2020/2021

The competition was not contested in the 2020/2021 season.

THE CLUBS 2020/2021

Please note: appearances and goals includes statistics of both regular season and play-offs (Championship and Relegation).

Aberystwyth Town Football Club

Founded: 1884
Stadium: Park Avenue, Aberystwyth (5,000)
Trainer: Gavin Allen   17.06.1976

Goalkeepers:	DOB	M	(s)	G
Dylan Evans*	30.05.1995		(3)	
Alexander Anthony Pennock	07.02.2001	6	(1)	
Connor Roberts	08.12.1992	26		
Defenders:	**DOB**	**M**	**(s)**	**G**
Samuel Barnes	16.10.1991	1		
Louis Bradford	21.02.2002	25	(1)	2
Rhys Davies	03.05.2001	15	(4)	2
Jonathan Foligno	26.06.1981	6	(2)	1
Lee Jenkins	28.06.1979	28		2
Miles John	19.01.1995	3		
Ian Kearney	15.06.1987	4	(1)	
Jack Rimmer	29.03.1999	20	(5)	
Midfielders:	**DOB**	**M**	**(s)**	**G**
Juan Matias Etchegoyen (ARG)	24.02.1995	3		
Jonathan Evans	10.03.1993	17	(8)	4
Harry Franklin	02.12.1999	15		4
Louis Gerrard	04.09.1992	1	(2)	
Steven Hewitt	05.12.1993	15	(4)	3
Ilan Hughes	22.04.1993	1	(1)	

	DOB	M	(s)	G
Gavin Jones	22.10.1999	1	(1)	
Matthew Jones	14.07.1999	25	(1)	4
Geoff Kellaway (ENG)	07.04.1986		(5)	
Gwion Owen	28.06.1995	13	(2)	
Richard Ricketts	24.09.2002		(5)	
Harri Rowe	17.11.2000	4	(2)	
Joseph Saunders			(1)	
Jack Thorn	22.03.2001	21	(2)	1
Jamie Veale	28.11.1996	28	(1)	2
Forwards:	**DOB**	**M**	**(s)**	**G**
Shama Bako	16.08.2000		(1)	
Dan Cockerline	15.11.1996	1	(2)	
Adam Davies	19.11.1993	1	(6)	
Steff Davies	14.07.1989	14	(1)	3
George Harry	07.06.1999		(2)	
Owain Jones	01.10.1996	13	(10)	5
John Owen	18.08.1992	9	(6)	3
James Reed	13.08.1987	9	(4)	5
Marc Williams	27.07.1988	27	(3)	6

*Please note: goalkeeper Dylan Evans was used as a field player.

Bala Town Football Club

Founded: 1880
Stadium: Maes Tegid Stadium, Bala (3,000)
Trainer: Colin Caton   22.08.1970

Goalkeepers:	DOB	M	(s)	G
Harri Lloyd	30.04.1997	2		
Alex Ramsay	15.07.1993	28		
Jon Rushton	17.05.1990	2		
Defenders:	**DOB**	**M**	**(s)**	**G**
Andrew Burns (IRL)	02.07.1993	5	(2)	
Shaun Kelly (ENG)	11.12.1988	2		
Nathan Peate	02.05.1991	24	(2)	4
Ryan Pryce	30.06.1997	13	(5)	
Sean Smith (ENG)	12.12.1994	31		1
Jonny Spittle (ENG)	13.08.1994	20	(3)	1
Anthony Stephens (ENG)	21.01.1994	22	(1)	
Midfielders:	**DOB**	**M**	**(s)**	**G**
Liam Davies (ENG)	02.07.1996	4	(12)	
William Albert Evans	01.07.1997	31		13
Danny Gosset	30.09.1994	2	(6)	
Henry Jones	18.09.1993	12	(15)	2
Antony Kay	21.10.1982	27	(1)	5
Steven Leslie (SCO)	05.11.1987	14	(11)	4
Lassana Nalatche Mendes (GNB)	26.12.1996	19	(5)	3
Oliver Shannon (ENG)	12.09.1995	23		2
Kieran Smith (ENG)	03.06.1992	12	(6)	2
Forwards:	**DOB**	**M**	**(s)**	**G**
Raúl Correia (ANG)	28.08.1994	18	(5)	2
Jack Mackreth	13.04.1992	8	(3)	
Llyr Morris	18.05.1996		(5)	
Gary Roberts	18.03.1984	2	(2)	1
Chris Venables	23.07.1985	31		24

Barry Town United Football Club

Founded: 1912 (*as Barry AFC*)
Stadium: Jenner Park, Barry (3,500)
Trainer: Gavin Chesterfield   18.08.1979

Goalkeepers:	DOB	M	(s)	G
Joshua Gould (ENG)	27.03.1997	3	(1)	
Lee Idzi	08.02.1988	2	(1)	
Mike Lewis	04.04.1989	27		
Defenders:	**DOB**	**M**	**(s)**	**G**
Rhys Abbruzzese	23.03.1998	9	(7)	
Luke Cooper	02.04.1993	28		1
Luke Cummings	25.10.1991	20	(2)	
Chris Hugh	22.01.1992	23		1
Curtis McDonald	24.03.1988	24		1
Paul Morgan	28.06.1994		(1)	
Kyle Patten	21.07.1994	7	(6)	
Midfielders:	**DOB**	**M**	**(s)**	**G**
Samuel Bowen	14.01.2001	6	(1)	2
Jordan Cotterill	20.10.1988	25		5
Michael George	12.06.1999	10	(13)	
Clayton Green	27.02.1994	21		
Robbie Patten	29.11.1996	9	(4)	
Evan Press	26.06.2000	27	(5)	3
Callum Sainty	12.05.1996	4	(7)	
Theo Wharton (SKN)	15.11.1994	16	(4)	1
Forwards:	**DOB**	**M**	**(s)**	**G**
Jamie Bird	30.12.1997	7	(5)	1
David Cotterill	04.12.1987	19	(6)	5
Joshua Graham	03.04.1994		(6)	1
Nathaniel Jarvis (ATG)	20.10.1991	25	(1)	6
Curtis Jemmett-Hutson (BRB)	14.08.1994	13	(16)	2
Rhys Kavanagh	29.09.1998	8	(6)	1
Kayne McLaggon	21.09.1990	19		11

Caernarfon Town Football Club

Founded: 1937
Stadium: The Oval, Caernarfon (3,000)
Trainer: Huw Griffiths   09.02.1977

Goalkeepers:	DOB	M	(s)	G
Lewis Brass (ENG)	26.08.1996	5		
Tyler French	14.10.1996	4	(2)	
Harry Rees		1		
Josh Tibbetts (ENG)	05.07.1998	22		
Defenders:	**DOB**	**M**	**(s)**	**G**
Jonathan Anderson (ITA)	19.10.2001	4		
Max Cleworth	09.08.2002	12	(2)	2
Gareth Edwards	20.07.1983	19	(2)	2
Jack Fleming	10.01.1999	1	(1)	
Gruffydd John	22.06.1994	14	(4)	
Daniel Jones			(1)	
Cai Owen	12.07.1998		(1)	
Iddon Price	18.01.1991	1	(1)	
Telor Williams	03.07.2001	12	(5)	
Joe Williams	17.02.1989	23	(1)	
Midfielders:	**DOB**	**M**	**(s)**	**G**
Sion Bradley	20.02.1998	29	(2)	7
Jamie Crowther	10.02.1992	7	(1)	
Noah Edwards	30.05.1996	25		2
Gareth Evans	29.04.1987	1		
Louis Malandjou (FRA)		10	(3)	
Arnaldo Paulo Fernandes Mendes (POR)	08.07.1993	31		6
Mike Parker	31.10.1987	16		
Ryan Williams	10.05.1998	22	(3)	
Forwards:	**DOB**	**M**	**(s)**	**G**
Jake Bickerstaff	11.09.2001	9	(5)	5
Danny Brookwell	09.03.1993	4	(5)	
Mohammed El-Arab			(2)	
Cian Evans	01.06.2003		(5)	
Asa Hamilton	21.01.1992	1	(4)	
Mike Hayes	21.11.1987	27	(1)	8
Sam Jones	09.11.1992	2	(9)	1
Cai Jones	03.10.1992	13	(13)	4
Jack Kenny (ENG)	14.10.1991	16	(4)	3
Darren Thomas	20.01.1987	21	(5)	4
Cory Williams	26.09.1995		(1)	

Cardiff Metropolitan University Football Club

Founded: 2000 (*as UWIC Inter Cardiff*)
Stadium: Cyncoed Campus, Cardiff (1,620)
Trainer: Christian Edwards   25.11.1975

Goalkeepers:	DOB	M	(s)	G
Will Fuller	07.07.1993	9	(1)	
Alex Lang	10.10.1999	23	(1)	
Defenders:	**DOB**	**M**	**(s)**	**G**
Liam Black	02.07.1994	12	(1)	
Matthew Blake	14.11.1999	4	(1)	
Matthew Chubb	31.08.1998	13	(7)	1
Joe Evans	26.11.1997	14	(5)	
Harri Horwood	24.04.2000		(2)	
Emlyn Lewis	14.06.1996	19		3
Kyle McCarthy	12.04.1993	29		
Rhydian Morgan	19.06.1999	19	(5)	
Dylan Rees	17.09.1996	20	(1)	2
Brandon Roberts	26.08.2003		(1)	
Guto Williams	10.05.2000	3	(1)	
Bradley Woolridge	16.12.1992	26		2
Tom Wright	04.09.2002		(2)	

Midfielders:	DOB	M	(s)	G
Chris Baker	29.11.1993	16	(2)	2
Charlie Corsby (ENG)	14.10.1991	28	(1)	
Jac Tomos Davies	28.02.2001	5	(3)	
Matthew Jones	03.04.2001	1	(3)	
Sam Pashen (ENG)	27.03.1998		(3)	
Tom Price	26.11.1999	12	(2)	1
Forwards:	**DOB**	**M**	**(s)**	**G**
Ashton Ajibola-Gleed (ENG)			(1)	1
Craig Davies	18.10.2000	3	(8)	1
Eliot Evans	26.11.1991	30		12
Oliver Hulbert (ENG)	25.02.2003	21	(2)	13
Harry Owen (ENG)	15.02.1996	6	(8)	1
Keiron Proctor	10.02.2000		(2)	
Lewis Rees	01.07.2002	11	(2)	
Joshua Thomas	24.09.2002	1	(3)	
Liam Warman	01.05.1999	20	(9)	4
Harry Warwick (ENG)	09.05.2000	7	(2)	

Cefn Druids Association Football Club Cefn Mawr

Founded:	1872	
Stadium:	The Rock Stadium, Wrexham (3,000)	
Trainer:	Bruno Alexandre Carvalho Lopes (POR)	11.04.1984
[10.03.2021]	Jayson Starkey	02.12.1986

Goalkeepers:	DOB	M	(s)	G
Benjamin Edwards		2		
Michael Jones (ENG)	03.12.1987	24		
Dawid Szczepaniak (POL)	13.04.2000	6		
Defenders:	**DOB**	**M**	**(s)**	**G**
Naim Arsan	14.12.1993	21	(2)	1
Ben Barratt	26.10.1999	8	(2)	
Josh Green	11.01.1995	22		
Phil Mooney (ENG)	19.01.1991	17		
Max Pritchard	16.08.2001	3	(2)	
Aaron Simpson	19.10.1995	23	(2)	1
Jacob Wise	09.09.1993	18	(8)	1
Midfielders:	**DOB**	**M**	**(s)**	**G**
Harry Brazel (ENG)	09.09.1991	10	(7)	
Ethan Cartwright (ENG)	14.08.2001	12	(1)	
Iwan Cartwright	09.08.1996	21	(3)	3
Charley Edge	14.05.1997	14	(8)	2
Steffan Edwards	10.10.1989	19	(3)	1
Joseph Faux (AUS)	08.07.1999	17	(2)	2
Niall Flint	15.08.1997	27	(2)	5
Joshua Hughes			(1)	
Ryan Kershaw	21.09.1995	12	(2)	1
Harry Killick			(1)	
Matthew Marshall	14.11.2002		(2)	
Tom Reilly (ENG)	07.02.2000	4	(4)	
Kieran Smith		7	(8)	
Jack Weston			(1)	
Mitchell Williams		2	(3)	
Forwards:	**DOB**	**M**	**(s)**	**G**
Christoph Aziamale (GER)	18.12.1997	5	(4)	
Alex Darlington	26.12.1988	21	(4)	4
Harry Fuller	11.10.2002	3	(9)	
Brad Knight (ENG)		4	(3)	
Sam Phillips	24.02.1999	17	(3)	
Jamie Reed	13.08.1987	9	(4)	2
Cody Ruberto (ITA)	29.10.1990	2	(1)	1
Jonathan Taylor	12.05.1989	2	(5)	

Connah's Quay Nomads Football Club

Founded:	1946	
Stadium:	Deeside Stadium, Connah's Quay (1,500)	
Trainer:	Andrew Morrison (SCO)	30.07.1970

Goalkeepers:	DOB	M	(s)	G
Lewis Brass	26.08.1996	10		
Oliver Byrne	31.12.1997	22		
Defenders:	**DOB**	**M**	**(s)**	**G**
Danny Davies	28.06.1995	29	(1)	4
John Disney	15.05.1992	30		1
Priestley Farquharson	15.03.1997	14	(1)	3
Danny Holmes	06.01.1989	15	(1)	
George Horan (ENG)	18.02.1982	20	(2)	7
Johnny Hunt	23.08.1990	3	(7)	
Tom Moore	16.04.1999		(2)	
Kris Owens	07.12.1998	17	(3)	1
Callum Roberts	16.10.1998	4	(3)	
Doug Tharme	17.08.1999		(4)	
Midfielders:	**DOB**	**M**	**(s)**	**G**
Neill Danns (GUY)	23.11.1982	9	(7)	1
Sameron Dool	07.06.1999	11	(4)	2
Aeron Edwards	16.02.1988	21	(3)	5
Danny Harrison (ENG)	04.11.1982	18	(3)	
Jamie Insall (ENG)	01.03.1992	7	(6)	3
Callum Morris (ENG)	01.09.1992	29	(1)	10
Jay Owen	14.01.1991	8	(2)	
Declan Poole (ENG)	05.09.1995	26	(2)	4
Forwards:	**DOB**	**M**	**(s)**	**G**
Craig Curran (ENG)	23.08.1989	19	(9)	6
Brayden Shaw (ENG)	25.02.1997	1	(4)	
Michael Wilde	27.08.1983	26	(1)	18
Aron Williams	08.11.1995	13	(14)	2

Flint Town United Football Club

Founded:	1886	
Stadium:	Cae-y-Castell Stadium, Flint (1,000)	
Trainer:	Niall McGuiness	14.05.1991
[07.12.2020]	Neil Gibson	11.10.1979

Goalkeepers:	DOB	M	(s)	G
John Danby	20.09.1981	11		
Aaron Jones	02.07.1999	5	(1)	
Jon Rushton	17.05.1990	14		
Ryan Woods	21.10.1990	2		
Defenders:	**DOB**	**M**	**(s)**	**G**
Wes Baynes	12.10.1988	12		
Ben Burrows	06.10.1998	2	(3)	
Eddie Clarke (ENG)	29.12.1998	11	(2)	
Kai Edwards	29.01.1991	19	(1)	
Dominic Elsey-McHugh	27.11.1999		(1)	
Evan Gumbs (ENG)	21.07.1997	11	(3)	
Sam Hart (ENG)	29.11.1991	22	(2)	2
Tom Kemp	30.12.1994	8	(4)	
Ben Lockley	20.01.2002	1	(1)	
Ben Nash	23.07.1998	27	(2)	
Dan Roberts	26.05.2000	2	(2)	
Matthew Russell	19.07.1990	1	(2)	
Darren Thornton	03.11.1987	6		
Midfielders:	**DOB**	**M**	**(s)**	**G**
Mason Blackwell-Jones	05.01.2002		(5)	
Brandon Burrows	04.01.2000	4	(1)	
Nathan Craig	25.10.1991	10		1
Mitch Duggan (ENG)	20.03.1997	1		
Richie Foulkes	21.12.1985	23	(3)	4
Connor Harwood (ENG)	02.02.2000	18	(8)	5
Robert Hughes	22.04.1992	11	(2)	2
Alex Jones	04.08.1984	18		4
Ben Maher	28.09.1995	24		2
Joe Palmer	13.08.1999	4		
Kyle Smyth	01.01.1999	2	(2)	
Kai Wallis	21.03.2000		(1)	
Ross Weaver	31.07.1996	8	(4)	
Forwards:	**DOB**	**M**	**(s)**	**G**
Josh Amis (ENG)	24.10.1994	13	(1)	6
Callum Bratley (ENG)	12.03.1995	29	(2)	3
Aandy Brown	25.01.1995	1	(3)	
Nathan Brown	11.10.1998	2		
Jordan Buckley (ENG)	01.05.1996	5	(6)	1
Mark Cadwallader	08.07.1988	14	(12)	6
Les Davies	29.10.1984	2	(4)	
Liam Ellis			(1)	
Jake Hampson	18.01.2003	3	(4)	
Ben Steer	23.11.1995		(7)	1
Alex Titchiner	13.06.1991	4		
Thomas Weir	21.02.2001	2	(7)	

Haverfordwest County Association Football Club

Founded: 1899
Stadium: Bridge Meadow Stadium, Haverfordwest (2,100)
Trainer: Wayne Jones   26.07.1979

Goalkeepers:	DOB	M	(s)	G
Wojciech Gajda (USA)	21.10.1998	17	(2)	
Steven Hall	11.04.1985	6		
Joshua Legrice	07.01.2004		(1)	
Matthew Turner	27.03.2002	9		
Defenders:	**DOB**	**M**	**(s)**	**G**
Trystan Jones	07.10.2000	8	(9)	
Alaric Jones	09.02.2001	23	(1)	
Cameron Keetch	20.08.1999	19	(8)	2
Sean Pemberton	15.12.1985	18	(9)	1
Jazz Richards	12.04.1991	4	(1)	
Cory Saunders (ENG)	19.10.1995		(1)	
Daniel Summerfield (ENG)	10.06.1995	26	(1)	
Scott Tancock	29.12.1993	25	(3)	1
Ricky Watts	07.11.1991	28	(1)	

Midfielders:	DOB	M	(s)	G
Jack Britton	06.10.1994	1	(8)	
Kieran Lewis	26.06.1993	21	(1)	2
Nicky Palmer	11.06.1981	1	(3)	
Kurtis Rees	14.02.1999	22	(4)	
Elliot Scotcher	03.03.1994	21	(1)	1
Corey Shephard	28.12.1997	25	(3)	2
Forwards:	**DOB**	**M**	**(s)**	**G**
Ben Fawcett	07.09.2000	24	(7)	7
Marcus Griffiths	06.10.1989	8	(20)	2
Daniel James	30.11.2004		(4)	
Mark Jones	01.05.1989	4	(3)	
Daniel Williams	18.02.2000	28	(2)	10
Jack Wilson	12.04.2001	14	(7)	9

Newtown Association Football Club

Founded: 1875
Stadium: Latham Park, Newtown (5,000)
Trainer: Chris Hughes (SCO)   12.09.1979

Goalkeepers:	DOB	M	(s)	G
David Jones	03.02.1990	31		
Khamran Steventon	15.09.2001	1		
Defenders:	**DOB**	**M**	**(s)**	**G**
Tom Davies	11.12.2001	2		
Alfie Jones	20.06.2003		(3)	
Jack Kelly (ENG)	01.01.1996	16	(3)	1
Kieran Mills-Evans	11.10.1992	31		2
James O'Neill (ENG)	17.02.1995	15	(7)	
Jake Phillips	31.01.1997	15	(8)	
Callum Roberts	16.10.1998	11		
Shane Sutton (ENG)	31.01.1989	15		3
Craig T. Williams	21.12.1987	22	(2)	
Midfielders:	**DOB**	**M**	**(s)**	**G**
Dylan Downs	07.01.2002		(2)	

	DOB	M	(s)	G
Ryan Edwards	25.05.1994	16	(7)	1
Jordan Evans	23.09.1995	19	(11)	10
Alex Fletcher (ENG)	17.11.1996	15	(1)	3
Rhys Hesden (ENG)	20.10.2002		(1)	
George Hughes (ENG)	23.03.1999	25	(1)	
Sean McAllister (ENG)	15.08.1987	18	(7)	
Forwards:	**DOB**	**M**	**(s)**	**G**
Jamie Breese	10.01.1992	12	(18)	1
James Davies	02.10.1993	19	(7)	9
Jonathan Letford (ENG)	19.03.1994	1	(3)	
Neil Mitchell (ENG)	01.04.1988	16		2
Lifumpa Mwandwe (ENG)	29.12.2000	11	(4)	4
Tyrone Ofori (ENG)	26.07.2000	16	(10)	9
Nicky Rushton	03.02.1992	24	(5)	9
Matthew Williams	05.11.1982	1	(6)	1

Penybont Football Club Bridgend

Founded: 2013 (as *merger of Bridgend Town AFC and Bryntirion Athletic FC*)
Stadium: Bryntirion Park, Bridgend (3,000)
Trainer: Rhys Griffiths   01.03.1980

Goalkeepers:	DOB	M	(s)	G
Ashley Morris	31.07.1984	32		
Defenders:	**DOB**	**M**	**(s)**	**G**
Lewis Baldwin	26.09.1998	1		
Billy Borge	22.05.1998	15	(9)	
Oliver Dalton	12.05.1990	19	(4)	1
Connor Davies	07.05.2002	16	(8)	
Mael Davies	10.10.1998	28	(1)	5
Matthew Greenwood	10.11.2002		(1)	
Dan Jefferies	30.01.1999	29	(1)	1
Kane Owen	22.10.1994	28	(1)	4
Liam Walsh	26.07.1996	2	(5)	
Ismail Yakubu (ENG)	08.04.1985	17	(3)	

Midfielders:	DOB	M	(s)	G
Lewis Clutton	31.08.2001	8	(13)	1
Ioan Emanuel	28.12.1996	2	(4)	
Ashley Evans	18.07.1989	22	(3)	
Lewis Harling	11.06.1992	27	(1)	6
Matthew Harris (ENG)	16.01.1994	18	(2)	1
Rhys Stevens			(3)	
Forwards:	**DOB**	**M**	**(s)**	**G**
Ben Ahmun	02.02.1992	23	(4)	6
Kostya Georgievsky (ENG)	28.06.1996	25	(6)	6
Mason Jones-Thomas	05.12.2000	1	(5)	
Sam Snaith	05.05.2000	11	(18)	3
Ian Traylor	26.04.1989	1	(5)	1
Nathan Daniel Wood	23.04.1997	27	(3)	4

The New Saints of Oswestry Town & Llansantffraid Football Club

Founded: 1959
Stadium: Park Hall Stadium, Oswestry (2,034)
Trainer: Scott Ruscoe (ENG)   15.12.1977
[07.03.2021] Christian Seargeant (ENG)   13.09.1986
[02.04.2021] Anthony Limbrick (AUS)   09.04.1983

Goalkeepers:	DOB	M	(s)	G
Paul Harrison (ENG)	18.12.1984	32		
Defenders:	**DOB**	**M**	**(s)**	**G**
Ryan Astles (ENG)	01.07.1994	31		3
Joshua Bailey (ENG)	10.12.2001	1	(4)	
Kwame Boateng (ENG)	21.11.1998	6	(4)	1
Keston Davies	02.10.1996	6	(4)	
Ryan Harrington	03.10.1998	20	(3)	2
Blaine Hudson (ENG)	28.10.1991	20	(2)	6
Chris Marriott (ENG)	24.09.1989	24		
Simon Spender	15.11.1985	12	(1)	
Midfielders:	**DOB**	**M**	**(s)**	**G**
Ryan Brobbel (NIR)	05.03.1993	11	(3)	12
Jack Canavan (ENG)	17.12.2003		(2)	

	DOB	M	(s)	G
Ben Clark	14.10.2000	19	(9)	8
Beau Cornish	05.11.2001		(2)	
Tom Holland (IRL)	22.04.1997	11	(7)	
Daniel Redmond (ENG)	02.03.1991	22	(1)	
Jon Routledge (ENG)	23.11.1989	29	(1)	3
Leo Smith	15.05.1998	20	(9)	2
Forwards:	**DOB**	**M**	**(s)**	**G**
Adrian Cieslewicz (POL)	16.11.1990	28	(2)	8
Gregory Alexander Draper (NZL)	13.08.1989	11	(19)	14
Dean Ebbe (IRL)	16.07.1994	10	(4)	5
Jamie Mullan (ENG)	10.02.1988	11	(13)	
Lewis Rees	01.07.2002		(6)	
Louis Robles (ENG)	11.09.1996	23	(2)	12
Adam Roscrow	17.02.1995	5	(6)	2

SECOND LEVEL
2020/2021

The season was cancelled by Football Association of Wales as a result of COVID-19 pandemic restrictions.

INTERNATIONAL MATCHES
(16.07.2020 – 15.07.2021)

03.09.2020	Helsinki	Finland - Wales	0-1(0-0)	(UNL)
06.09.2020	Cardiff	Wales - Bulgaria	1-0(0-0)	(UNL)
08.10.2020	London	England - Wales	3-0(1-0)	(F)
11.10.2020	Dublin	Republic of Ireland - Wales	0-0	(UNL)
14.10.2020	Sofia	Bulgaria - Wales	0-1(0-0)	(UNL)
12.11.2020	Swansea	Wales - United States	0-0	(F)
15.11.2020	Cardiff	Wales - Republic of Ireland	1-0(0-0)	(UNL)
18.11.2020	Cardiff	Wales - Finland	3-1(1-0)	(UNL)
24.03.2021	Leuven	Belgium - Wales	3-1(2-1)	(WCQ)
27.03.2021	Cardiff	Wales - Mexico	1-0(1-0)	(F)
30.03.2021	Cardiff	Wales - Czech Republic	1-0(0-0)	(WCQ)
02.06.2021	Nice	France - Wales	3-0(1-0)	(F)
05.06.2021	Cardiff	Wales - Albania	0-0	(F)
12.06.2021	Bakı	Wales - Switzerland	1-1(0-0)	(EC)
16.06.2021	Bakı	Turkey - Wales	0-2(0-1)	(EC)
20.06.2021	Roma	Italy - Wales	1-0(1-0)	(EC)
26.06.2021	Amsterdam	Wales - Denmark	0-4(0-1)	(EC)

03.09.2020 FINLAND - WALES   **0-1(0-0)**   2nd UEFA Nations League B, Group 4
Olympiastadion, Helsinki; Referee: Daniel Siebert (Germany); Attendance: 0
WAL: Wayne Robert Hennessey, Benjamin Thomas Davies, Thomas Alun Lockyer, Connor Richard John Roberts, Jonathan Peter Williams (60.Neco Shay Williams), Joseff John Morrell, Ethan Kwame Colm Raymond Ampadu, Dylan James Christopher Levitt, Gareth Frank Bale (Cap) (46.Harry Wilson), Kieffer Roberto Francisco Moore, Daniel Owen James (90+2.Benjamin Cabango). Trainer: Ryan Joseph Giggs.
Goal: Kieffer Roberto Francisco Moore (80).

06.09.2020 WALES - BULGARIA   **1-0(0-0)**   2nd UEFA Nations League B, Group 4
Cardiff City Stadium, Cardiff; Referee: Fábio José Costa Veríssimo (Portugal); Attendance: 0
WAL: Wayne Robert Hennessey, Benjamin Thomas Davies, Thomas Alun Lockyer, Connor Richard John Roberts (65.Neco Shay Williams), Joseff John Morrell, Ethan Kwame Colm Raymond Ampadu, David Robert Brooks (76.Jonathan Peter Williams), Matthew Robert Smith, Gareth Frank Bale (Cap), Kieffer Roberto Francisco Moore (61.Thomas Henry Alex Robson-Kanu), Daniel Owen James. Trainer: Ryan Joseph Giggs.
Goal: Neco Shay Williams (90+4).

08.10.2020 ENGLAND - WALES   **3-0(1-0)**   Friendly International
Wembley Stadium, London; Referee: Robert Adam Madden (Scotland); Attendance: 0
WAL: Wayne Robert Hennessey, Benjamin Thomas Davies (Cap), Connor Richard John Roberts (73.Christopher Ross Gunter), Joseph Peter Rodon (46.Benjamin Cabango), Christopher James Mepham, Jonathan Peter Williams (73.Matthew Robert Smith), Joseff John Morrell (46.Dylan James Christopher Levitt), Ethan Kwame Colm Raymond Ampadu (62.William Robert Vaulks), Kieffer Roberto Francisco Moore (40.Neco Shay Williams), Tyler D'Whyte Roberts, Rabbi Matondo. Trainer: Ryan Joseph Giggs.

11.10.2020 REPUBLIC OF IRELAND - WALES   **0-0**   2nd UEFA Nations League B, Group 4
Aviva Stadium, Dublin; Referee: Anastasios Sidiropoulos (Greece); Attendance: 0
WAL: Wayne Robert Hennessey, Benjamin Thomas Davies, Connor Richard John Roberts, Joseph Peter Rodon, Aaron James Ramsey (Cap), Joseff John Morrell, Ethan Kwame Colm Raymond Ampadu, Harry Wilson (67.Neco Shay Williams), Matthew Robert Smith (67.Dylan James Christopher Levitt), Kieffer Roberto Francisco Moore, Daniel Owen James (77.David Robert Brooks). Trainer: Ryan Joseph Giggs.

14.10.2020 BULGARIA - WALES   **0-1(0-0)**   2nd UEFA Nations League B, Group 4
Nationalen Stadion "Vasil Levski", Sofia; Referee: Əliyar Ağayev (Azerbaijan); Attendance: 478
WAL: Wayne Robert Hennessey (79.Adam Rhys Davies), Benjamin Thomas Davies (Cap), Joseph Peter Rodon, Ethan Kwame Colm Raymond Ampadu, Neco Shay Williams, Christopher James Mepham, Rhys Llewelyn Norrington-Davies, Matthew Robert Smith (72.Dylan James Christopher Levitt), Tyler D'Whyte Roberts, Harry Wilson (72.Jonathan Peter Williams), Daniel Owen James (54.Rabbi Matondo). Trainer: Ryan Joseph Giggs.
Goal: Jonathan Peter Williams (85).

12.11.2020 WALES - UNITED STATES   **0-0**   Friendly International
Liberty Stadium, Swansea; Referee: Nicholas Walsh (Scotland); Attendance: 0
WAL: Daniel Ward, Christopher Ross Gunter (Cap), James Alexander Lawrence (69.Joseph Peter Rodon), Thomas Alun Lockyer, Connor Richard John Roberts, Thomas Morris Lawrence, Harry Wilson, Matthew Robert Smith (46.Joshua Luke Sheehan), Dylan James Christopher Levitt (80.Joseff John Morrell), Kieffer Roberto Francisco Moore (62.Brennan Price Johnson), Rabbi Matondo (62.Daniel Owen James). Trainer: Robert John Page.

15.11.2020 WALES - REPUBLIC OF IRELAND   **1-0(0-0)**   2nd UEFA Nations League B, Group 4
Cardiff City Stadium, Cardiff; Referee: Petr Ardeleánu (Czech Republic); Attendance: 0
WAL: Daniel Ward, Benjamin Thomas Davies, Joseph Peter Rodon, Neco Shay Williams, Christopher James Mepham, Rhys Llewelyn Norrington-Davies (62.Kieffer Roberto Francisco Moore), Joseff John Morrell, Ethan Kwame Colm Raymond Ampadu, David Robert Brooks (88.Tyler D'Whyte Roberts), Daniel Owen James, Gareth Frank Bale (Cap). Trainer: Robert John Page.
Goal: David Robert Brooks (67).

18.11.2020 WALES - FINLAND   **3-1(1-0)**   2nd UEFA Nations League B, Group 4
Cardiff City Stadium, Cardiff; Referee: Jesús Gil Manzano (Spain); Attendance: 0
WAL: Daniel Ward, James Alexander Lawrence (46.Kieffer Roberto Francisco Moore), Connor Richard John Roberts, Joseph Peter Rodon, Ethan Kwame Colm Raymond Ampadu, Christopher James Mepham, Rhys Llewelyn Norrington-Davies (90+3.Christopher Ross Gunter), Joseff John Morrell, Harry Wilson (89.Tyler D'Whyte Roberts), Gareth Frank Bale (Cap) (61.Thomas Morris Lawrence), Daniel Owen James (89.David Robert Brooks). Trainer: Robert John Page.
Goals: Harry Wilson (29), Daniel Owen James (46), Kieffer Roberto Francisco Moore (84).

24.03.2021   BELGIUM - WALES   **3-1(2-1)**   22nd FIFA WC. Qualifiers
Den Dreef Stadion, Leuven; Referee: Cüneyt Çakır (Turkey); Attendance: 0
WAL: Daniel Ward, James Alexander Lawrence, Connor Richard John Roberts, Joseph Peter Rodon, Ethan Kwame Colm Raymond Ampadu, Neco Shay Williams, Christopher James Mepham, Joseph Michael Allen (8.Joseff John Morrell), Daniel Owen James, Harry Wilson (66.Tyler D'Whyte Roberts), Gareth Frank Bale (Cap) (84.Kieffer Roberto Francisco Moore). Trainer: Robert John Page.
Goal: Harry Wilson (10).

27.03.2021   WALES - MEXICO   **1-0(1-0)**   Friendly International
Cardiff City Stadium, Cardiff; Referee: Ian McNabb (Northern Ireland); Attendance: 0
WAL: Wayne Robert Hennessey, Christopher Ross Gunter (Cap), Benjamin Cabango, Rhys Llewelyn Norrington-Davies, Jonathan Peter Williams (86.Connor Richard John Roberts), Thomas Morris Lawrence (65.Neco Shay Williams), Matthew Robert Smith, Dylan James Christopher Levitt (46.Joshua Luke Sheehan), Kieffer Roberto Francisco Moore (46.Thomas Henry Alex Robson-Kanu), Tyler D'Whyte Roberts (65.Brennan Price Johnson), Rabbi Matondo (81.Gareth Frank Bale). Trainer: Robert John Page.
Goal: Kieffer Roberto Francisco Moore (11).

30.03.2021   WALES - CZECH REPUBLIC   **1-0(0-0)**   22nd FIFA WC. Qualifiers
Cardiff City Stadium, Cardiff; Referee: Ovidiu Alin Haţegan (Romania); Attendance: 0
WAL: Daniel Ward, James Alexander Lawrence, Connor Richard John Roberts [*sent off 77*], Joseph Peter Rodon, Ethan Kwame Colm Raymond Ampadu, Neco Shay Williams, Christopher James Mepham (57.Kieffer Roberto Francisco Moore), Daniel Owen James, Joseff John Morrell, Harry Wilson (76.Jonathan Peter Williams), Gareth Frank Bale (Cap). Trainer: Robert John Page.
Goal: Daniel Owen James (82).

02.06.2021   FRANCE - WALES   **3-0(1-0)**   Friendly International
Allianz Riviera, Nice; Referee: Luis Miguel Branco Godinho (Portugal); Attendance: 0
WAL: Daniel Ward, Connor Richard John Roberts, Christopher James Mepham (60.Benjamin Thomas Davies), Joseph Peter Rodon, Christopher Ross Gunter, Joseff John Morrell (83.Rubin James Colwill), Neco Shay Williams [*sent off 26*], Joseph Michael Allen (59.Dylan James Christopher Levitt), Harry Wilson (60.Aaron James Ramsey), Gareth Frank Bale (Cap) (59.Kieffer Roberto Francisco Moore), Daniel Owen James (72.David Robert Brooks). Trainer: Robert John Page.

05.06.2021   WALES - ALBANIA   **0-0**   Friendly International
Cardiff City Stadium, Cardiff; Referee: Neil Anthony Doyle (Republic of Ireland); Attendance: 6,500
WAL: Wayne Robert Hennessey, Benjamin Thomas Davies (Cap) (61.Joseph Peter Rodon), Neco Shay Williams, Christopher James Mepham, Rhys Llewelyn Norrington-Davies, Joseph Michael Allen (61.Matthew Robert Smith), Aaron James Ramsey (61.Harry Wilson), David Robert Brooks (76.Jonathan Peter Williams), Ethan Kwame Colm Raymond Ampadu (46.Kieffer Roberto Francisco Moore), Dylan James Christopher Levitt, Tyler D'Whyte Roberts (71.Gareth Frank Bale). Trainer: Robert John Page.

12.06.2021   WALES - SWITZERLAND   **1-1(0-0)**   16th EC. Group Stage.
Bakı Olimpiya Stadionu, Bakı (Azerbaijan); Referee: Clément Turpin (France); Attendance: 8,782
WAL: Daniel Ward, Benjamin Thomas Davies, Connor Richard John Roberts, Joseph Peter Rodon, Christopher James Mepham, Joseph Michael Allen, Aaron James Ramsey (90+3.Ethan Kwame Colm Raymond Ampadu), Joseff John Morrell, Gareth Frank Bale (Cap), Kieffer Roberto Francisco Moore, Daniel Owen James (75.David Robert Brooks). Trainer: Robert John Page.
Goal: Kieffer Roberto Francisco Moore (74).

16.06.2021   TURKEY - WALES   **0-2(0-1)**   16th EC. Group Stage.
Bakı Olimpiya Stadionu, Bakı (Azerbaijan); Referee: Artur Manuel Ribeiro Soares Dias (Wales); Attendance: 19,762
WAL: Daniel Ward, Benjamin Thomas Davies, Connor Richard John Roberts, Joseph Peter Rodon, Christopher James Mepham, Joseph Michael Allen (73.Ethan Kwame Colm Raymond Ampadu), Aaron James Ramsey (85.Harry Wilson), Joseff John Morrell, Gareth Frank Bale (Cap), Kieffer Roberto Francisco Moore, Daniel Owen James (90+4.Neco Shay Williams). Trainer: Robert John Page.
Goals: Aaron James Ramsey (42), Connor Richard John Roberts (90+5).

20.06.2021   ITALY - WALES   **1-0(1-0)**   16th EC. Group Stage.
Stadio Olimpico, Roma; Referee: Ovidiu Alin Haţegan (Romania); Attendance: 11,541
WAL: Daniel Ward, Christopher Ross Gunter, Connor Richard John Roberts, Aaron James Ramsey, Joseph Peter Rodon, Neco Shay Williams (86.Benjamin Thomas Davies), Joseph Michael Allen (86.Dylan James Christopher Levitt), Joseff John Morrell (60.Kieffer Roberto Francisco Moore), Ethan Kwame Colm Raymond Ampadu [*sent off 55*], Gareth Frank Bale (Cap) (86.David Robert Brooks), Daniel Owen James (74.Harry Wilson). Trainer: Robert John Page.

26.06.2021   WALES - DENMARK   **0-4(0-1)**   16th EC. 2nd Round of 16.
"Johan Cruyff" Arena, Amsterdam (Netherlands); Referee: Daniel Siebert (Germany); Attendance: 14,645
WAL: Daniel Ward, Benjamin Thomas Davies, Connor Richard John Roberts (40.Neco Shay Williams), Joseph Peter Rodon, Christopher James Mepham, Joseph Michael Allen, Aaron James Ramsey, Joseff John Morrell (60.Harry Wilson [*sent off 90*]), Gareth Frank Bale (Cap), Kieffer Roberto Francisco Moore (78.Tyler D'Whyte Roberts), Daniel Owen James (78.David Robert Brooks). Trainer: Robert John Page.

Name	DOB	Caps	Goals	2020/2021:	Club
Goalkeepers					
Adam Rhys DAVIES	17.07.1992	2	0	2020:	*Stoke City FC (ENG)*
Wayne Robert HENNESSEY	24.01.1987	96	0	2020/2021:	*Crystal Palace FC London (ENG)*
Daniel WARD	22.06.1993	17	0	2020/2021:	*Leicester City FC (ENG)*
Defenders					
Benjamin CABANGO	30.05.2000	3	0	2020/2021:	*Swansea City AFC*
Benjamin Thomas DAVIES	24.04.1993	64	0	2020/2021:	*Tottenham Hotspur FC London (ENG)*
Christopher Ross GUNTER	21.07.1989	102	0	2020/2021:	*Charlton Athletic FC (ENG)*
James Alexander LAWRENCE	22.08.1992	9	0	2020/2021:	*FC St. Pauli Hamburg (GER)*
Thomas Alun LOCKYER	03.12.1994	13	0	2020:	*Luton Town FC (ENG)*
Christopher James MEPHAM	05.10.1997	21	0	2020/2021:	*AFC Bournemouth (ENG)*
Rhys Llewelyn NORRINGTON-DAVIES	22.04.1999	5	0	2020: 12.01.2021->	*Luton Town FC (ENG)* *Stoke City FC (ENG)*
Connor Richard John ROBERTS	23.09.1995	30	2	2020/2021:	*Swansea City AFC*
Joseph Peter RODON	22.10.1997	18	0	2020/2021:	*Tottenham Hotspur FC London (ENG)*
Neco Shay WILLIAMS	13.04.2001	14	1	2020/2021:	*Liverpool FC (ENG)*
Midfielders					
Joseph Michael ALLEN	14.03.1990	63	2	2020/2021:	*Stoke City FC (ENG)*
Ethan Kwame Colm Raymond AMPADU	14.09.2000	26	0	2020/2021:	*RasenBallsport Leipzig (GER)*
David Robert BROOKS	08.07.1997	21	2	2020/2021:	*AFC Bournemouth (ENG)*
Rubin James COLWILL	27.04.2002	1	0	2021:	*Cardiff City FC*
Dylan James Christopher LEVITT	17.11.2000	9	0	2020/2021: 15.02.2021->	*Charlton Athletic FC (ENG)* *NK Istra 1961 Pula (CRO)*
Joseff John MORRELL	03.01.1997	19	0	2020: 15.10.2020->	*Bristol City FC (ENG)* *Luton Town FC (ENG)*
Aaron James RAMSEY	26.12.1990	67	17	2020/2021:	*Juventus FC Torino (ITA)*
Joshua Luke SHEEHAN	30.03.1995	2	0	2020/2021:	*Newport County AFC*
Matthew Robert SMITH	22.11.1999	14	0	2020/2021:	*Doncaster Rovers FC (ENG)*
William Robert VAULKS	13.09.1993	6	0	2020/2021:	*Cardiff City FC*
Jonathan Peter WILLIAMS	09.10.1993	28	0	2020: 01.02.2021->	*Charlton Athletic FC London (ENG)* *Cardiff City FC*
Harry WILSON	22.03.1997	29	5	2020: 16.10.2020-> 31.05.2021->	*Liverpool FC (ENG)* *Cardiff City FC* *Liverpool FC (ENG)*
Forwards					
Gareth Frank BALE	16.07.1989	96	33	2020: 19.09.2020->	*Real Madrid CF (ESP)* *Tottenham Hotspur FC London (ENG)*
Daniel Owen JAMES	10.11.1997	24	4	2020/2021:	*Manchester United FC (ENG)*
Brennan Price JOHNSON	23.05.2001	2	0	2020/2021:	*Lincoln City FC (ENG)*
Thomas Morris LAWRENCE	13.01.1994	23	3	2020/2021:	*Derby County FC (ENG)*
Rabbi MATONDO	09.09.2000	8	0	2020: 07.01.2021->	*FC Schalke 04 Gelsenkirchen (GER)* *Stoke City FC (ENG)*
Kieffer Roberto Francisco MOORE	08.08.1992	21	6	2020/2021:	*Cardiff City FC*
Tyler D'Whyte ROBERTS	12.01.1999	15	0	2020/2021:	*Leeds United FC (ENG)*
Thomas Henry Alex ROBSON-KANU	21.05.1989	46	5	2020/2021:	*West Bromwich Albion FC (ENG)*
Trainer					
Ryan Joseph GIGGS [from 15.01.2018]	29.11.1973	24 M; 5 W; 2 D; 6 L; 18-13			
Robert John PAGE [caretaker from 03.11.2020*]	03.09.1974	12 M; 5 W; 3 D; 4 L; 10-13			

Please note: Robert Page has acted as manager since 03.11.2020, after Ryan Giggs was arrested and subsequently charged with assault. Ryan Giggs remains the official manager.